BESTSELLING BILINGUAL DICTIONARIES

William Collins' dream of knowledge for all began with the publication of his first book in 1819. A self-educated mill worker, he not only enriched millions of lives, but also founded a flourishing publishing house. Today, staying true to this spirit, Collins books are packed with inspiration, innovation, and practical expertise. They place you at the centre of a world of possibility and give you exactly what you need to explore it.

Language is the key to this exploration, and at the heart of Collins Dictionaries is language as it is really used. New words, phrases, and meanings spring up every day, and all of them are captured and analysed by the Collins Word Web. Constantly updated, and with over 2.5 billion entries, this living language resource is unique to our dictionaries.

Words are tools for life. And a Collins Dictionary makes them work for you.

Collins. Do more.

Collins
French
Dictionary

BESTSELLING BILINGUAL DICTIONARIES

Published by Collins
An imprint of HarperCollins Publishers
Westerhill Road
Bishopbriggs
Glasgow G64 2QT
www.harpercollins.co.uk

This Edition 2014

10 9 8 7 6 5 4 3

© HarperCollins Publishers 2011, 2014

ISBN 978-0-00-789781-0

Collins® is a registered trademark of
HarperCollins Publishers Limited

www.collinsdictionary.com
www.collins.co.uk

Dictionary and grammar typeset by
Thomas Callan

Printed in Great Britain by Clays Ltd,
St Ives plc

A catalogue record for this book is
available from the British Library.

If you would like to comment on any
aspect of this book, please contact us at
the above address or online.
E-mail: dictionaries@harpercollins.co.uk

Acknowledgements
We would like to thank those authors and
publishers who kindly gave permission for
copyright material to be used in the
Collins Corpus. We would also like to
thank Times Newspapers Ltd for providing
valuable data.

Table des matières

Contents

Introduction

You may be starting French for the first time, or you may wish to extend your knowledge of the language. Perhaps you want to read and study French books, newspapers and magazines, or perhaps simply have a conversation with French speakers. Whatever the reason, whether you're a student, a tourist or want to use French for business, this is the ideal book to help you understand and communicate. This modern, user-friendly dictionary gives priority to everyday vocabulary and the language of current affairs, business, computing and tourism, and, as in all Collins dictionaries, the emphasis is firmly placed on contemporary language and expressions.

How to use the dictionary
Below you will find an outline of how information is presented in your dictionary. Our aim is to give you the maximum amount of detail in the clearest and most helpful way.

Entries
A typical entry in your dictionary will be made up of the following elements:

Phonetic transcription
Phonetics appear in square brackets immediately after the headword. They are shown using the International Phonetic Alphabet (IPA), and a complete list of the symbols used in this system can be found on pages xii and xiii.

Grammatical information
All words belong to one of the following parts of speech: noun, verb, adjective, adverb, pronoun, article, conjunction, preposition.

Nouns can be singular or plural and, in French, masculine or feminine. Verbs can be transitive, intransitive, reflexive or impersonal. Parts of speech appear in *italics* immediately after the phonetic spelling of the headword. The gender of the translation appears in *italics* immediately following the key element of the translation.

Often a word can have more than one part of speech. Just as the English word **chemical** can be an adjective or a noun, the French word **rose** can be an adjective ("pink") or a feminine noun ("rose"). In the same way the verb **to walk** is sometimes transitive, ie it takes an object ("to walk the dog") and sometimes intransitive, ie it doesn't take an object ("to walk to school"). To help you find the meaning you are looking for quickly and for clarity of presentation, the different part of speech categories are separated by a right facing triangle ▷.

Meaning divisions

Most words have more than one meaning. Take, for example, **punch** which can be, amongst other things, a blow with the fist or an object used for making holes. Other words are translated differently depending on the context in which they are used. The transitive verb **to roll up**, for example, can be translated by "rouler" or "retrousser" depending on what it is you are rolling up. To help you select the most appropriate translation in every context, entries are divided according to meaning. Different meanings are introduced by an "indicator" in *italics* and in brackets. Thus, the examples given above will be shown as follows:

> **punch** *n* (*blow*) coup *m* de poing; (*tool*) poinçon *m*
> **roll up** *vt* (*carpet, cloth, map*) rouler; (*sleeves*) retrousser

Likewise, some words can have a different meaning when used to talk about a specific subject area or field. For example, **bishop**, which we generally use to mean a high-ranking clergyman, is also the name of a chess piece. To show English speakers which translation to use, we have added "subject field labels" in *italics*, starting with a capital letter, and in brackets, in this case (*Chess*):

> **bishop** *n* évêque *m*; (*Chess*) fou *m*

Field labels are often shortened to save space. You will find a complete list of abbreviations used in the dictionary on pages x and xi.

Translations

Most English words have a direct translation in French and vice versa, as shown in the examples given above. Sometimes, however, no exact equivalent exists in the target language. In such cases we have given an approximate equivalent, indicated by the sign ≈. An example is **National Insurance**, the French equivalent of which is "Sécurité Sociale". There is no exact equivalent since the systems of the two countries are quite different:

> **National Insurance** *n* (*Brit*) ≈ Sécurité Sociale

On occasion it is impossible to find even an approximate equivalent. This may be the case, for example, with the names of types of food:

> **mince pie** *n* *sorte de tarte aux fruits secs*

Here the translation (which doesn't exist) is replaced by an explanation. For increased clarity the explanation, or "gloss", is shown in *italics*.

It is often the case that a word, or a particular meaning of a word, cannot be translated in isolation. The translation of **Dutch**, for example, is "hollandais(e), neérlandais(e)". However, the phrase **to go Dutch** is rendered by "partager les frais".

Even an expression as simple as **washing powder** needs a separate translation since it translates as "lessive (en poudre)", not "poudre à laver". This is where your dictionary will prove to be particularly informative and useful since it contains an abundance of compounds, phrases and idiomatic expressions.

Levels of formality and familiarity
In English you instinctively know when to say "I don't have any money" and when to say "I'm broke" or "I'm a bit short of cash". When you are trying to understand someone who is speaking French, however, or when you yourself try to speak French, it is important to know what is polite and what is less so, and what you can say in a relaxed situation but not in a formal context. To help you with this, on the French–English side we have added the label (*inf*) to show that a French meaning or expression is colloquial, while those meanings or expressions which are vulgar are given an exclamation mark (*inf!*), warning you they can cause serious offence. Note also that on the English–French side, translations which are vulgar are followed by an exclamation mark in brackets.

Keywords
Words labelled in the text as KEYWORDS, such as **be** and **do** or their French equivalents **être** and **faire**, have been given special treatment because they form the basic elements of the language. This extra help will ensure that you know how to use these complex words with confidence.

Cultural information
Entries which appear distinguished in the text by a column of dots explain aspects of culture in French and English-speaking countries. Subject areas covered include politics, education, media and national festivals, for example **Assemblée nationale**, **baccalauréat**, **BBC** and **Hallowe'en**.

Abréviations   Abbreviations

abréviation	*ab(b)r*	abbreviation
adjectif, locution adjectivale	*adj*	adjective, adjectival phrase
administration	*Admin*	administration
adverbe, locution adverbiale	*adv*	adverb, adverbial phrase
agriculture	*Agr*	agriculture
anatomie	*Anat*	anatomy
architecture	*Archit*	architecture
article défini	*art déf*	definite article
article indéfini	*art indéf*	indefinite article
automobile	*Aut(o)*	the motor car and motoring
aviation, voyages aériens	*Aviat*	flying, air travel
biologie	*Bio(l)*	biology
botanique	*Bot*	botany
anglais britannique	*Brit*	British English
chimie	*Chem*	chemistry
cinéma	*Ciné, Cine*	cinema
commerce, finance, banque	*Comm*	commerce, finance, banking
informatique	*Comput*	computing
conjonction	*conj*	conjunction
construction	*Constr*	building
nom utilisé comme adjectif	*cpd*	compound element
cuisine	*Culin*	cookery
article défini	*def art*	definite article
déterminant: article; adjectif	*dét*	determiner: article,
démonstratif *ou* indéfini etc		demonstrative etc
économie	*Écon, Econ*	economics
électricité, électronique	*Élec, Elec*	electricity, electronics
en particulier	*esp*	especially
exclamation, interjection	*excl*	exclamation, interjection
féminin	*f*	feminine
langue familière	*fam(!)*	colloquial usage
(! emploi vulgaire)		(! particularly offensive)
emploi figuré	*fig*	figurative use
(verbe anglais) dont la	*fus*	(phrasal verb) where the
particule est inséparable		particle is inseparable
généralement	*gén, gen*	generally
géographie, géologie	*Géo, Geo*	geography, geology
géométrie	*Géom, Geom*	geometry
langue familière	*inf(!)*	colloquial usage
(! emploi vulgaire)		(! particularly offensive)
infinitif	*infin*	infinitive
informatique	*Inform*	computing
invariable	*inv*	invariable
irrégulier	*irrég, irreg*	irregular
domaine juridique	*Jur*	law

Abréviations

Abbreviations

grammaire, linguistique	*Ling*	grammar, linguistics
masculin	*m*	masculine
mathématiques, algèbre	*Math*	mathematics, calculus
médecine	*Méd, Med*	medical term, medicine
masculin *ou* féminin	*m/f*	masculine *or* feminine
domaine militaire, armée	*Mil*	military matters
musique	*Mus*	music
nom	*n*	noun
navigation, nautisme	*Navig, Naut*	sailing, navigation
nom *ou* adjectif numéral	*num*	numeral noun *or* adjective
	o.s.	oneself
péjoratif	*péj, pej*	derogatory, pejorative
photographie	*Phot(o)*	photography
physiologie	*Physiol*	physiology
pluriel	*pl*	plural
politique	*Pol*	politics
participe passé	*pp*	past participle
préposition	*prép, prep*	preposition
pronom	*pron*	pronoun
psychologie, psychiatrie	*Psych*	psychology, psychiatry
temps du passé	*pt*	past tense
quelque chose	*qch*	
quelqu'un	*qn*	
religion, domaine ecclésiastique	*Rel*	religion
	sb	somebody
enseignement, système scolaire et universitaire	*Scol*	schooling, schools and universities
singulier	*sg*	singular
	sth	something
subjonctif	*sub*	subjunctive
sujet (grammatical)	*su(b)j*	(grammatical) subject
superlatif	*superl*	superlative
techniques, technologie	*Tech*	technical term, technology
télécommunications	*Tél, Tel*	telecommunications
télévision	TV	television
typographie	*Typ(o)*	typography, printing
anglais des USA	*US*	American English
verbe (auxiliare)	*vb (aux)*	(auxiliary) verb
verbe intransitif	*vi*	intransitive verb
verbe transitif	*vt*	transitive verb
zoologie	*Zool*	zoology
marque déposée	®	registered trademark
indique une équivalence culturelle	≈	introduces a cultural equivalent

Transcription phonétique

Consonnes		Consonants
poupée	p	puppy
bombe	b	baby
tente thermal	t	tent
dinde	d	daddy
coq qui képi	k	cork kiss chord
gag bague	g	gag guess
sale ce nation	s	so rice kiss
zéro rose	z	cousin buzz
tache chat	ʃ	sheep sugar
gilet juge	ʒ	pleasure beige
	tʃ	church
	dʒ	judge general
fer phare	f	farm raffle
valve	v	very rev
	θ	thin maths
	ð	that other
lent salle	l	little ball
rare rentrer	ʀ	
	r	rat rare
maman femme	m	mummy comb
non nonne	n	no ran
agneau vigne	ɲ	
	ŋ	singing bank
hop!	h	hat reheat
yeux paille pied	j	yet
nouer oui	w	wall bewail
huile lui	ɥ	
	x	loch

Divers		Miscellaneous
pour l'anglais: le "r" final se prononce en liaison devant une voyelle	ʳ	in English transcription: final "r" can be pronounced before a vowel
pour l'anglais: précède la syllabe accentuée	'	in French wordlist: no liaison before aspirate "h"

NB: p, b, t, d, k, g sont suivis d'une aspiration en anglais.
p, b, t, d, k, g are not aspirated in French.

En règle générale, la prononciation est donnée entre crochets après chaque entrée. Toutefois, du côté anglais-français et dans le cas des expressions composées de deux ou plusieurs mots non réunis par un trait d'union et faisant l'objet d'une entrée séparée, la prononciation doit être cherchée sous chacun des mots constitutifs de l'expression en question.

Phonetic transcription

Voyelles

ici vie lyrique	i iː	
	ɪ	
jouer été	e	
lait jouet merci	ɛ	
plat amour	a æ	
bas pâte	ɑ ɑː	
	ʌ	
le premier	ə	
beurre peur	œ	
peu deux	ø əː	
or homme	ɔ	
mot eau gauche	o ɔː	
genou roue	u	
	uː	
rue urne	y	

Vowels

i iː	heel bead
ɪ	hit pity
e	
ɛ	set tent
a æ	bat apple
ɑ ɑː	after car calm
ʌ	fun cousin
ə	over above
œ	
ø əː	urgent fern work
ɔ	wash pot
o ɔː	born cork
u	full hook
uː	boom shoe
y	

Diphtongues

Diphthongs

ɪə	beer tier
ɛə	tear fair there
eɪ	date plaice day
aɪ	life buy cry
au	owl foul now
əu	low no
ɔɪ	boil boy oily
uə	poor tour

Nasales

matin plein	ɛ̃
brun	œ̃
sang an dans	ɑ̃
non pont	ɔ̃

Nasal vowels

NB: La mise en équivalence de certains sons n'indique qu'une ressemblance approximative.

The pairing of some vowel sounds only indicates approximate equivalence.

In general, we give the pronunciation of each entry in square brackets after the word in question. However, on the English-French side, where the entry is composed of two or more unhyphenated words, each of which is given elsewhere in this dictionary, you will find the pronunciation of each word in its alphabetical position.

French verb forms

1 Present participle 2 Past participle 3 Present 4 Imperfect 5 Future 6 Conditional
7 Present subjunctive 8 Impératif

acquérir 1 acquérant 2 acquis 3 acquiers,
acquérons, acquièrent 4 acquérais
5 acquerrai 7 acquière

ALLER 1 allant 2 allé 3 vais, vas, va, allons,
allez, vont 4 allais 5 irai 6 irais 7 aille

asseoir 1 asseyant 2 assis 3 assieds,
asseyons, asseyez, asseyent 4 asseyais
5 assiérai 7 asseye

atteindre 1 atteignant 2 atteint 3 atteins,
atteignons 4 atteignais 7 atteigne

AVOIR 1 ayant 2 eu 3 ai, as, a, avons, avez,
ont 4 avais 5 aurai 6 aurais 7 aie, aies, ait,
ayons, ayez, aient

battre 1 battant 2 battu 3 bats, bat, battons
4 battais 7 batte

boire 1 buvant 2 bu 3 bois, buvons, boivent
4 buvais 7 boive

bouillir 1 bouillant 2 bouilli 3 bous,
bouillons 4 bouillais 7 bouille

conclure 1 concluant 2 conclu 3 conclus,
concluons 4 concluais 7 conclue

conduire 1 conduisant 2 conduit 3 conduis,
conduisons 4 conduisais 7 conduise

connaître 1 connaissant 2 connu 3 connais,
connaît, connaissons 4 connaissais
7 connaisse

coudre 1 cousant 2 cousu 3 couds, cousons,
cousez, cousent 4 cousais 7 couse

courir 1 courant 2 couru 3 cours, courons
4 courais 5 courrai 7 coure

couvrir 1 couvrant 2 couvert 3 couvre,
couvrons 4 couvrais 7 couvre

craindre 1 craignant 2 craint 3 crains,
craignons 4 craignais 7 craigne

croire 1 croyant 2 cru 3 crois, croyons,
croient 4 croyais 7 croie

croître 1 croissant 2 crû, crue, crus, crues
3 croîs, croissons 4 croissais 7 croisse

cueillir 1 cueillant 2 cueilli 3 cueille,
cueillons 4 cueillais 5 cueillerai 7 cueille

devoir 1 devant 2 dû, due, dus, dues 3 dois,
devons, doivent 4 devais 5 devrai 7 doive

dire 1 disant 2 dit 3 dis, disons, dites,
disent 4 disais 7 dise

dormir 1 dormant 2 dormi 3 dors, dormons
4 dormais 7 dorme

écrire 1 écrivant 2 écrit 3 écris, écrivons
4 écrivais 7 écrive

ÊTRE 1 étant 2 été 3 suis, es, est, sommes,
êtes, sont 4 étais 5 serai 6 serais 7 sois,
sois, soit, soyons, soyez, soient

FAIRE 1 faisant 2 fait 3 fais, fais, fait,
faisons, faites, font 4 faisais 5 ferai
6 ferais 7 fasse

falloir 2 fallu 3 faut 4 fallait 5 faudra
7 faille

FINIR 1 finissant 2 fini 3 finis, finis, finit,
finissons, finissez, finissent 4 finissais
5 finirai 6 finirais 7 finisse

fuir 1 fuyant 2 fui 3 fuis, fuyons, fuient
4 fuyais 7 fuie

joindre 1 joignant 2 joint 3 joins, joignons
4 joignais 7 joigne

lire 1 lisant 2 lu 3 lis, lisons 4 lisais 7 lise

luire 1 luisant 2 lui 3 luis, luisons 4 luisais
7 luise

maudire 1 maudissant 2 maudit
3 maudis, maudissons 4 maudissait
7 maudisse

mentir 1 mentant 2 menti 3 mens,
mentons 4 mentais 7 mente

mettre 1 mettant 2 mis 3 mets, mettons
4 mettais 7 mette

mourir 1 mourant 2 mort 3 meurs,
mourons, meurent 4 mourais 5 mourrai
7 meure

naître 1 naissant 2 né 3 nais, naît,
naissons 4 naissais 7 naisse

offrir 1 offrant 2 offert 3 offre, offrons
4 offrais 7 offre

PARLER 1 parlant 2 parlé 3 parle, parles,
parle, parlons, parlez, parlent 4 parlais,
parlais, parlait, parlions, parliez, parlaient
5 parlerai, parleras, parlera, parlerons,

parlerez, parleront **6** parlerais, parlerais, parlerait, parlerions, parleriez, parleraient **7** parle, parles, parle, parlions, parliez, parlent **8** parle! parlons! parlez!

partir **1** partant **2** parti **3** pars, partons **4** partais **7** parte

plaire **1** plaisant **2** plu **3** plais, plaît, plaisons **4** plaisais **7** plaise

pleuvoir **1** pleuvant **2** plu **3** pleut, pleuvent **4** pleuvait **5** pleuvra **7** pleuve

pourvoir **1** pourvoyant **2** pourvu **3** pourvois, pourvoyons, pourvoient **4** pourvoyais **7** pourvoie

pouvoir **1** pouvant **2** pu **3** peux, peut, pouvons, peuvent **4** pouvais **5** pourrai **7** puisse

prendre **1** prenant **2** pris **3** prends, prenons, prennent **4** prenais **7** prenne

prévoir _like_ **voir** **5** prévoirai

RECEVOIR **1** recevant **2** reçu **3** reçois, reçois, reçoit, recevons, recevez, rerçoivent **4** recevais **5** recevrai **6** recevrais **7** reçoive

RENDRE **1** rendant **2** rendu **3** rends, rends, rend, rendons, rendez, rendent **4** rendais **5** rendrai **6** rendrais **7** rende

résoudre **1** résolvant **2** résolu **3** résous, résout, résolvons **4** résolvais **7** résolve

rire **1** riant **2** ri **3** ris, rions **4** riais **7** rie

savoir **1** sachant **2** su **3** sais, savons, savent **4** savais **5** saurai **7** sache **8** sache! sachons! sachez!

servir **1** servant **2** servi **3** sers, servons **4** servais **7** serve

sortir **1** sortant **2** sorti **3** sors, sortons **4** sortais **7** sorte

souffrir **1** souffrant **2** souffert **3** souffre, souffrons **4** souffrais **7** souffre

suffire **1** suffisant **2** suffi **3** suffis, suffisons **4** suffisais **7** suffise

suivre **1** suivant **2** suivi **3** suis, suivons **4** suivais **7** suive

taire **1** taisant **2** tu **3** tais, taisons **4** taisais **7** taise

tenir **1** tenant **2** tenu **3** tiens, tenons, tiennent **4** tenais **5** tiendrai **7** tienne

vaincre **1** vainquant **2** vaincu **3** vaincs, vainc, vainquons **4** vainquais **7** vainque

valoir **1** valant **2** valu **3** vaux, vaut, valons **4** valais **5** vaudrai **7** vaille

venir **1** venant **2** venu **3** viens, venons, viennent **4** venais **5** viendrai **7** vienne

vivre **1** vivant **2** vécu **3** vis, vivons **4** vivais **7** vive

voir **1** voyant **2** vu **3** vois, voyons, voient **4** voyais **5** verrai **7** voie

vouloir **1** voulant **2** voulu **3** veux, veut, voulons, veulent **4** voulais **5** voudrai **7** veuille **8** veuillez!

For additional information on French verb formation see pages 6-131 of Grammar section.

Les nombres

Numbers

un (une)	1	one
deux	2	two
trois	3	three
quatre	4	four
cinq	5	five
six	6	six
sept	7	seven
huit	8	eight
neuf	9	nine
dix	10	ten
onze	11	eleven
douze	12	twelve
treize	13	thirteen
quatorze	14	fourteen
quinze	15	fifteen
seize	16	sixteen
dix-sept	17	seventeen
dix-huit	18	eighteen
dix-neuf	19	nineteen
vingt	20	twenty
vingt et un (une)	21	twenty-one
vingt-deux	22	twenty-two
trente	30	thirty
quarante	40	forty
cinquante	50	fifty
soixante	60	sixty
soixante-dix	70	seventy
soixante-et-onze	71	seventy-one
soixante-douze	72	seventy-two
quatre-vingts	80	eighty
quatre-vingt-un (-une)	81	eighty-one
quatre-vingt-dix	90	ninety
cent	100	a hundred, one hundred
cent un (une)	101	a hundred and one
deux cents	200	two hundred
deux cent un (une)	201	two hundred and one
quatre cents	400	four hundred
mille	1000	a thousand
cinq mille	5000	five thousand
un million	1000000	a million

Les nombres

Numbers

premier (première), 1er (1ère)	first, 1st
deuxième, 2e or 2ème	second, 2nd
troisième, 3e or 3ème	third, 3rd
quatrième, 4e or 4ème	fourth, 4th
cinquième, 5e or 5ème	fifth, 5th
sixième, 6e or 6ème	sixth, 6th
septième	seventh
huitième	eighth
neuvième	ninth
dixième	tenth
onzième	eleventh
douzième	twelfth
treizième	thirteenth
quartorzième	fourteenth
quinzième	fifteenth
seizième	sixteenth
dix-septième	seventeenth
dix-huitième	eighteenth
dix-neuvième	nineteenth
vingtième	twentieth
vingt-et-unième	twenty-first
vingt-deuxième	twenty-second
trentième	thirtieth
centième	hundredth
cent-unième	hundred-and-first
millième	thousandth

L'heure

quelle heure est-il?
   il est ...

minuit

une heure (du matin)

une heure cinq

une heure dix

une heure et quart

une heure vingt-cinq

une heure et demie,
   une heure trente

deux heures moins vingt-cinq,
   une heure trente-cinq

deux heures moins vingt,
   une heure quarante

deux heures moins le quart,
   une heure quarante-cinq

deux heures moins dix,
   une heure cinquante

midi

deux heures (de l'après-midi),
   quatorze heures

sept heures (du soir),
   dix-sept heures

à quelle heure?

à minuit

à sept heures

dans vingt minutes

il y a un quart d'heure

The time

what time is it?
   it's ...

midnight, twelve p.m.

one o'clock (in the morning), one (a.m.)

five past one

ten past one

a quarter past one, one fifteen

twenty-five past one, one twenty-five

half-past one,
   one thirty

twenty-five to two,
   one thirty-five

twenty to two,
   one forty

a quarter to two,
   one forty-five

ten to two,
   one fifty

twelve o'clock, midday, noon

two o'clock (in the afternoon),
   two (p.m.)

seven o'clock (in the evening),
   seven (p.m.)

(at) what time?

at midnight

at seven o'clock

in twenty minutes

fifteen minutes ago

La date

aujourd'hui	today
demain	tomorrow
après-demain	the day after tomorrow
hier	yesterday
avant-hier	the day before yesterday
la veille	the day before, the previous day
le lendemain	the next or following day
le matin	morning
le soir	evening
ce matin	this morning
ce soir	this evening
cet après-midi	this afternoon
hier matin	yesterday morning
hier soir	yesterday evening
demain matin	tomorrow morning
demain soir	tomorrow evening
dans la nuit du samedi au dimanche	during Saturday night, during the night of Saturday to Sunday
il viendra samedi	he's coming on Saturday
le samedi	on Saturdays
tous les samedis	every Saturday
samedi passé ou dernier	last Saturday
samedi prochain	next Saturday
samedi en huit	a week on Saturday
samedi en quinze	a fortnight or two weeks on Saturday
du lundi au samedi	from Monday to Saturday
tous les jours	every day
une fois par semaine	once a week
une fois par mois	once a month
deux fois par semaine	twice a week
il y a une semaine ou huit jours	a week ago
il y a quinze jours	a fortnight or two weeks ago
l'année passée ou dernière	last year
dans deux jours	in two days
dans huit jours ou une semaine	in a week
dans quinze jours	in a fortnight or two weeks
le mois prochain	next month
l'année prochaine	next year
quel jour sommes-nous?	*what day is it?*
le 1er/24 octobre 2007	the 1st/24th of October 2007, October 1st/24th 2007
en 2007	in 2007
mille neuf cent quatre-vingt seize	nineteen ninety-six
44 av. J.-C.	44 BC
14 apr. J.-C.	14 AD
au XIXe (siècle)	in the nineteenth century
dans les années trente	in the thirties
il était une fois ...	once upon a time ...

Aa

A, a [ɑ] *nm inv* A, a ▷ *abr* = **anticyclone**; **are**; (*ampère*) amp; (*autoroute*) ≈ M (*Brit*); **A comme Anatole** A for Andrew (*Brit*) *ou* Able (*US*); **de a à z** from a to z; **prouver qch par a + b** to prove sth conclusively

a [a] *vb voir* **avoir**

○ **MOT-CLÉ**

à [a] (*à+le* = **au**, *à+les* = **aux**) *prép* **1** (*endroit, situation*) at, in; **être à Paris/au Portugal** to be in Paris/Portugal; **être à la maison/à l'école** to be at home/at school; **à la campagne** in the country; **c'est à 10 m/km/à 20 minutes (d'ici)** it's 10 m/km/20 minutes away
2 (*direction*) to; **aller à Paris/au Portugal** to go to Paris/Portugal; **aller à la maison/à l'école** to go home/to school; **à la campagne** to the country
3 (*temps*): **à 3 heures/minuit** at 3 o'clock/midnight; **au printemps** in the spring; **au mois de juin** in June; **au départ** at the start, at the outset; **à demain/la semaine prochaine!** see you tomorrow/next week!; **visites de 5 heures à 6 heures** visiting from 5 to *ou* till 6 o'clock
4 (*attribution, appartenance*) to; **le livre est à Paul/à lui/à nous** this book is Paul's/his/ours; **donner qch à qn** to give sth to sb; **un ami à moi** a friend of mine; **c'est à moi de le faire** it's up to me to do it
5 (*moyen*) with; **se chauffer au gaz** to have gas heating; **à bicyclette** on a *ou* by bicycle; **à la main/machine** by hand/machine; **à la télévision/la radio** on television/the radio
6 (*provenance*) from; **boire à la bouteille** to drink from the bottle
7 (*caractérisation, manière*): **l'homme aux yeux bleus** the man with the blue eyes; **à la russe** the Russian way; **glace à la framboise** raspberry ice cream
8 (*but, destination*): **tasse à café** coffee cup; **maison à vendre** house for sale; **problème à régler** problem to sort out
9 (*rapport, évaluation, distribution*): **100 km/unités à l'heure** 100 km/units per *ou* an hour; **payé à l'heure** paid by the hour; **cinq à six** five to six 10 (*conséquence, résultat*): **à ce qu'il prétend** according to him; **à leur grande surprise** much to their surprise; **à nous trois nous n'avons pas su le faire** we couldn't do it even between the three of us; **ils sont arrivés à quatre** four of them arrived (together)

Å *abr* (= Ångstrom) Å *ou* A
AB *abr* = **assez bien**
abaissement [abɛsmɑ̃] *nm* lowering; pulling down
abaisser [abese] *vt* to lower, bring down; (*manette*) to pull down; (*fig*) to debase; to humiliate; **s'abaisser** *vi* to go down; (*fig*) to demean o.s.; **s'~ à faire/à qch** to stoop *ou* descend to doing/to sth
abandon [abɑ̃dɔ̃] *nm* abandoning; deserting; giving up; withdrawal; surrender, relinquishing; (*fig*) lack of constraint; relaxed pose *ou* mood; **être à l'~** to be in a state of neglect; **laisser à l'~** to abandon
abandonné, e [abɑ̃dɔne] *adj* (*solitaire*) deserted; (*route, usine*) disused; (*jardin*) abandoned
abandonner [abɑ̃dɔne] *vt* to leave, abandon, desert; (*projet, activité*) to abandon, give up; (*Sport*) to retire *ou* withdraw from; (*Inform*) to abort; (*céder*) to surrender, relinquish; **s'abandonner** *vi* to let o.s. go; **s'~ à** (*paresse, plaisirs*) to give o.s. up to; **~ qch à qn** to give sth up to sb
abasourdir [abazuʀdiʀ] *vt* to stun, stagger
abat *etc* [aba] *vb voir* **abattre**
abat-jour [abaʒuʀ] *nm inv* lampshade
abats [aba] *vb voir* **abattre** ▷ *nmpl* (*de bœuf, porc*) offal *sg* (*Brit*), entrails (*US*); (*de volaille*) giblets
abattage [abataʒ] *nm* cutting down, felling
abattant [abatɑ̃] *vb voir* **abattre** ▷ *nm* leaf, flap
abattement [abatmɑ̃] *nm* (*physique*) enfeeblement; (*moral*) dejection, despondency; (*déduction*) reduction; **~ fiscal** ≈ tax allowance
abattis [abati] *vb voir* **abattre** ▷ *nmpl* giblets
abattoir [abatwaʀ] *nm* abattoir (*Brit*), slaughterhouse
abattre [abatʀ(ə)] *vt* (*arbre*) to cut down, fell; (*mur, maison*) to pull down; (*avion, personne*) to

shoot down; (*animal*) to shoot, kill; (*fig: physiquement*) to wear out, tire out; (*: moralement*) to demoralize; **s'abattre** *vi* to crash down; **s'~ sur** (*pluie*) to beat down on; (*: coups, injures*) to rain down on; **~ ses cartes** (*aussi fig*) to lay one's cards on the table; **~ du travail** *ou* **de la besogne** to get through a lot of work

abattu, e [abaty] *pp de* **abattre** ▷ *adj* (*déprimé*) downcast

abbatiale [abasjal] *nf* abbey (*church*)

abbaye [abei] *nf* abbey

abbé [abe] *nm* priest; (*d'une abbaye*) abbot; **M l'~** Father

abbesse [abɛs] *nf* abbess

abc, ABC [abese] *nm* alphabet primer; (*fig*) rudiments *pl*

abcès [apsɛ] *nm* abscess

abdication [abdikasjɔ̃] *nf* abdication

abdiquer [abdike] *vi* to abdicate ▷ *vt* to renounce, give up

abdomen [abdɔmɛn] *nm* abdomen

abdominal, e, -aux [abdɔminal, -o] *adj* abdominal ▷ *nmpl*: **faire des abdominaux** to do exercises for the stomach muscles

abécédaire [abesedɛʀ] *nm* alphabet primer

abeille [abɛj] *nf* bee

aberrant, e [abɛʀɑ̃, -ɑ̃t] *adj* absurd

aberration [abɛʀasjɔ̃] *nf* aberration

abêtir [abetiʀ] *vt* to make morons (*ou* a moron) of

abêtissant, e [abetisɑ̃, -ɑ̃t] *adj* stultifying

abhorrer [abɔʀe] *vt* to abhor, loathe

abîme [abim] *nm* abyss, gulf

abîmer [abime] *vt* to spoil, damage; **s'abîmer** *vi* to get spoilt *ou* damaged; (*fruits*) to spoil; (*tomber*) to sink, founder; **s'~ les yeux** to ruin one's eyes *ou* eyesight

abject, e [abʒɛkt] *adj* abject, despicable

abjurer [abʒyʀe] *vt* to abjure, renounce

ablatif [ablatif] *nm* ablative

ablation [ablasjɔ̃] *nf* removal

ablutions [ablysjɔ̃] *nfpl*: **faire ses ~** to perform one's ablutions

abnégation [abnegasjɔ̃] *nf* (self-)abnegation

aboie *etc* [abwa] *vb voir* **aboyer**

aboiement [abwamɑ̃] *nm* bark, barking *no pl*

aboierai *etc* [abwajəʀe] *vb voir* **aboyer**

abois [abwa] *nmpl*: **aux ~** at bay

abolir [abɔliʀ] *vt* to abolish

abolition [abɔlisjɔ̃] *nf* abolition

abolitionniste [abɔlisjɔnist(ə)] *adj, nm/f* abolitionist

abominable [abɔminabl(ə)] *adj* abominable

abomination [abɔminasjɔ̃] *nf* abomination

abondamment [abɔ̃damɑ̃] *adv* abundantly

abondance [abɔ̃dɑ̃s] *nf* abundance; (*richesse*) affluence; **en ~** in abundance

abondant, e [abɔ̃dɑ̃, -ɑ̃t] *adj* plentiful, abundant, copious

abonder [abɔ̃de] *vi* to abound, be plentiful; **~ en** to be full of, abound in; **~ dans le sens de qn** to concur with sb

abonné, e [abɔne] *nm/f* subscriber; season ticket holder ▷ *adj*: **être ~ à un journal** to subscribe to *ou* have a subscription to a periodical; **être ~ au téléphone** to be on the (tele)phone

abonnement [abɔnmɑ̃] *nm* subscription; (*pour transports en commun, concerts*) season ticket

abonner [abɔne] *vt*: **s'abonner à** to subscribe to, take out a subscription to

abord [abɔʀ] *nm*: **être d'un ~ facile** to be approachable; **être d'un ~ difficile** (*personne*) to be unapproachable; (*lieu*) to be hard to reach *ou* difficult to get to; **de prime ~, au premier ~** at first sight; **d'~** *adv* first; **tout d'~** first of all

abordable [abɔʀdabl(ə)] *adj* (*personne*) approachable; (*marchandise*) reasonably priced; (*prix*) affordable, reasonable

abordage [abɔʀdaʒ] *nm* boarding

aborder [abɔʀde] *vi* to land ▷ *vt* (*sujet, difficulté*) to tackle; (*personne*) to approach; (*rivage etc*) to reach; (*Navig: attaquer*) to board; (*: heurter*) to collide with

abords [abɔʀ] *nmpl* surroundings

aborigène [abɔʀiʒɛn] *nm* aborigine, native

Abou Dhabî, Abu Dhabî [abudabi] *nm* Abu Dhabi

aboulique [abulik] *adj* totally lacking in willpower

aboutir [abutiʀ] *vi* (*négociations etc*) to succeed; (*abcès*) to come to a head; **~ à/dans/sur** to end up at/in/on

aboutissants [abutisɑ̃] *nmpl voir* **tenants**

aboutissement [abutismɑ̃] *nm* success; (*de concept, projet*) successful realization; (*d'années de travail*) successful conclusion

aboyer [abwaje] *vi* to bark

abracadabrant, e [abʀakadabʀɑ̃, -ɑ̃t] *adj* incredible, preposterous

abrasif, -ive [abʀazif, -iv] *adj, nm* abrasive

abrégé [abʀeʒe] *nm* summary; **en ~** in a shortened *ou* abbreviated form

abréger [abʀeʒe] *vt* (*texte*) to shorten, abridge; (*mot*) to shorten, abbreviate; (*réunion, voyage*) to cut short, shorten

abreuver [abʀœve] *vt* to water; (*fig*): **~ qn de** to shower *ou* swamp sb with; (*injures etc*) to shower sb with; **s'abreuver** *vi* to drink

abreuvoir [abʀœvwaʀ] *nm* watering place

abréviation [abʀevjasjɔ̃] *nf* abbreviation

abri [abʀi] *nm* shelter; **à l'~** under cover; **être/ se mettre à l'~** to be/get under cover *ou* shelter; **à l'~ de** sheltered from; (*fig*) safe from

Abribus® [abʀibys] *nm* bus shelter

abricot [abʀiko] *nm* apricot

abricotier [abʀikɔtje] *nm* apricot tree

abrité, e [abʀite] *adj* sheltered

abriter [abʀite] *vt* to shelter; (*loger*) to accommodate; **s'abriter** *vi* to shelter, take cover

abrogation [abʀɔgasjɔ̃] *nf* (*Jur*) repeal, abrogation

abroger [abʀɔʒe] *vt* to repeal, abrogate

abrupt, e [abʀypt] *adj* sheer, steep; *(ton)* abrupt
abruti, e [abʀyti] *nm/f (fam)* idiot, moron
abrutir [abʀytiʀ] *vt* to daze; *(fatiguer)* to exhaust; *(abêtir)* to stupefy
abrutissant, e [abʀytisɑ̃, -ɑ̃t] *adj (bruit, travail)* stupefying
abscisse [apsis] *nf* X axis, abscissa
absence [apsɑ̃s] *nf* absence; *(Méd)* blackout; *(distraction)* mental blank; **en l'~ de** in the absence of
absent, e [apsɑ̃, -ɑ̃t] *adj* absent; *(chose)* missing, lacking; *(distrait: air)* vacant, faraway ▷ *nm/f* absentee
absentéisme [apsɑ̃teism(ə)] *nm* absenteeism
absenter [apsɑ̃te]: **s'absenter** *vi* to take time off work; *(sortir)* to leave, go out
abside [apsid] *nf (Archit)* apse
absinthe [apsɛ̃t] *nf (boisson)* absinth(e); *(Bot)* wormwood, absinth(e)
absolu, e [apsɔly] *adj* absolute; *(caractère)* rigid, uncompromising ▷ *nm (Philosophie)*: **l'~** the Absolute; **dans l'~** in the absolute, in a vacuum
absolument [apsɔlymɑ̃] *adv* absolutely
absolution [apsɔlysjɔ̃] *nf* absolution; *(Jur)* dismissal *(of case)*
absolutisme [apsɔlytism(ə)] *nm* absolutism
absolvais *etc* [apsɔlvɛ] *vb voir* **absoudre**
absorbant, e [apsɔʀbɑ̃, -ɑ̃t] *adj* absorbent; *(tâche)* absorbing, engrossing
absorbé, e [apsɔʀbe] *adj* absorbed, engrossed
absorber [apsɔʀbe] *vt* to absorb; *(gén Méd: manger, boire)* to take; *(Écon: firme)* to take over, absorb
absorption [apsɔʀpsjɔ̃] *nf* absorption
absoudre [apsudʀ(ə)] *vt* to absolve; *(Jur)* to dismiss
absous, -oute [apsu, -ut] *pp de* **absoudre**
abstenir [apstəniʀ]: **s'abstenir** *vi (Pol)* to abstain; **s'~ de qch/de faire** to refrain from sth/from doing
abstention [apstɑ̃sjɔ̃] *nf* abstention
abstentionnisme [apstɑ̃sjɔnism(ə)] *nm* abstaining
abstentionniste [apstɑ̃sjɔnist(ə)] *nm* abstentionist
abstenu, e [apstəny] *pp de* **abstenir**
abstiendrai [apstjɛ̃dʀe], **abstiens** *etc* [apstjɛ̃] *vb voir* **abstenir**
abstinence [apstinɑ̃s] *nf* abstinence; **faire ~** to abstain *(from meat on Fridays)*
abstint *etc* [apstɛ̃] *vb voir* **abstenir**
abstraction [apstʀaksjɔ̃] *nf* abstraction; **faire ~ de** to set *ou* leave aside; **~ faite de ...** leaving aside ...
abstraire [apstʀɛʀ] *vt* to abstract; **s'abstraire** *vi*: **s'~ (de)** *(s'isoler)* to cut o.s. off (from)
abstrait, e [apstʀɛ, -ɛt] *pp de* **abstraire** ▷ *adj* abstract ▷ *nm*: **dans l'~** in the abstract
abstraitement [apstʀɛtmɑ̃] *adv* abstractly
abstrayais *etc* [apstʀɛjɛ] *vb voir* **abstraire**
absurde [apsyʀd(ə)] *adj* absurd ▷ *nm* absurdity; *(Philosophie)*: **l'~** absurd; **par l'~** ad absurdio

absurdité [apsyʀdite] *nf* absurdity
abus [aby] *nm (excès)* abuse, misuse; *(injustice)* abuse; **~ de confiance** breach of trust; *(détournement de fonds)* embezzlement
abuser [abyze] *vi* to go too far, overstep the mark ▷ *vt* to deceive, mislead; **s'abuser** *vi (se méprendre)* to be mistaken; **~ de** *vt (force, droit)* to misuse; *(alcool)* to take to excess; *(violer, duper)* to take advantage of
abusif, -ive [abyzif, -iv] *adj* exorbitant; *(punition)* excessive; *(pratique)* improper
abusivement [abyzivmɑ̃] *adv* exorbitantly; excessively; improperly
AC *sigle f* = **appellation contrôlée**
acabit [akabi] *nm*: **du même ~** of the same type
acacia [akasja] *nm (Bot)* acacia
académicien, ne [akademisjɛ̃, -ɛn] *nm/f* academician
académie [akademi] *nf (société)* learned society; *(école: d'art, de danse)* academy; *(Art: nu)* nude; *(Scol: circonscription)* ≈ regional education authority; **l'A~ (française)** the French Academy; *see note*

⬤ **ACADÉMIE FRANÇAISE**
⬤
⬤ The *Académie française* was founded by
⬤ Cardinal Richelieu in 1635, during the reign
⬤ of Louis XIII. It is made up of forty elected
⬤ scholars and writers who are known as "les
⬤ Quarante" or "les Immortels". One of the
⬤ *Académie's* functions is to keep an eye on the
⬤ development of the French language, and
⬤ its recommendations are frequently the
⬤ subject of lively public debate. It has
⬤ produced several editions of its famous
⬤ dictionary and also awards various literary
⬤ prizes.

académique [akademik] *adj* academic
Acadie [akadi] *nf*: **l'~** the Maritime Provinces
acadien, ne [akadjɛ̃, -ɛn] *adj* Acadian, of *ou* from the Maritime Provinces
acajou [akaʒu] *nm* mahogany
acariâtre [akaʀjɑtʀ(ə)] *adj* sour(-tempered) *(Brit)*, cantankerous
accablant, e [akablɑ̃, -ɑ̃t] *adj (témoignage, preuve)* overwhelming
accablement [akabləmɑ̃] *nm* deep despondency
accabler [akable] *vt* to overwhelm, overcome; *(témoignage)* to condemn, damn; **~ qn d'injures** to heap *ou* shower abuse on sb; **~ qn de travail** to overburden sb with work; **accablé de dettes/soucis** weighed down with debts/cares
accalmie [akalmi] *nf* lull
accaparant, e [akapaʀɑ̃, -ɑ̃t] *adj* that takes up all one's time *ou* attention
accaparer [akapaʀe] *vt* to monopolize; *(travail etc)* to take up (all) the time *ou* attention of
accéder [aksede]: **~ à** *vt (lieu)* to reach; *(fig: pouvoir)* to accede to; *(: poste)* to attain; *(accorder:*

requête) to grant, accede to

accélérateur [akseleʀatœʀ] *nm* accelerator

accélération [akseleʀɑsjɔ̃] *nf* speeding up; acceleration

accéléré [akseleʀe] *nm*: **en ~** (*Ciné*) speeded up

accélérer [akseleʀe] *vt* (*mouvement, travaux*) to speed up ▷ *vi* (*Auto*) to accelerate

accent [aksɑ̃] *nm* accent; (*inflexions expressives*) tone (of voice); (*Phonétique, fig*) stress; **aux ~s de** (*musique*) to the strains of; **mettre l'~ sur** (*fig*) to stress; **~ aigu/grave/circonflexe** acute/grave/circumflex accent

accentuation [aksɑ̃tɥɑsjɔ̃] *nf* accenting; stressing

accentué, e [aksɑ̃tɥe] *adj* marked, pronounced

accentuer [aksɑ̃tɥe] *vt* (*Ling: orthographe*) to accent; (: *phonétique*) to stress, accent; (*fig*) to accentuate, emphasize; (: *effort, pression*) to increase; **s'accentuer** *vi* to become more marked *ou* pronounced

acceptable [aksɛptabl(ə)] *adj* satisfactory, acceptable

acceptation [aksɛptɑsjɔ̃] *nf* acceptance

accepter [aksɛpte] *vt* to accept; (*tolérer*): **~ que qn fasse** to agree to sb doing; **~ de faire** to agree to do

acception [aksɛpsjɔ̃] *nf* meaning, sense; **dans toute l'~ du terme** in the full sense *ou* meaning of the word

accès [aksɛ] *nm* (*à un lieu, Inform*) access; (*Méd*) attack; (: *de toux*) fit, bout ▷ *nmpl* (*routes etc*) means of access, approaches; **d'~ facile/ malaisé** easily/not easily accessible; **donner ~ à** (*lieu*) to give access to; (*carrière*) to open the door to; **avoir ~ auprès de qn** to have access to sb; **l'~ aux quais est interdit aux personnes non munies d'un billet** ticket-holders only on platforms, no access to platforms without a ticket; **~ de colère** fit of anger; **~ de joie** burst of joy

accessible [aksesibl(ə)] *adj* accessible; (*personne*) approachable; (*livre, sujet*): **~ à qn** within the reach of sb; (*sensible*): **~ à la pitié/l'amour** open to pity/love

accession [aksesjɔ̃] *nf*: **~ à** accession to; (*à un poste*) attainment of; **~ à la propriété** home-ownership

accessit [aksesit] *nm* (*Scol*) ≈ certificate of merit

accessoire [akseswaʀ] *adj* secondary, of secondary importance; (*frais*) incidental ▷ *nm* accessory; (*Théât*) prop

accessoirement [akseswaʀmɑ̃] *adv* secondarily; incidentally

accessoiriste [akseswaʀist(ə)] *nm/f* (*TV, Ciné*) property man/woman

accident [aksidɑ̃] *nm* accident; **par ~** by chance; **~ de parcours** mishap; **~ de la route** road accident; **~ du travail** accident at work; industrial injury *ou* accident; **~s de terrain** unevenness of the ground

accidenté, e [aksidɑ̃te] *adj* damaged *ou* injured (in an accident); (*relief, terrain*) uneven; hilly

accidentel, le [aksidɑ̃tɛl] *adj* accidental

accidentellement [aksidɑ̃tɛlmɑ̃] *adv* (*par hasard*) accidentally; (*mourir*) in an accident

accise [aksiz] *nf*: **droit d'~(s)** excise duty

acclamation [aklamɑsjɔ̃] *nf*: **par ~** (*vote*) by acclamation; **acclamations** *nfpl* cheers, cheering *sg*

acclamer [aklame] *vt* to cheer, acclaim

acclimatation [aklimatɑsjɔ̃] *nf* acclimatization

acclimater [aklimate] *vt* to acclimatize; **s'acclimater** *vi* to become acclimatized

accointances [akwɛ̃tɑ̃s] *nfpl*: **avoir des ~ avec** to have contacts with

accolade [akɔlad] *nf* (*amicale*) embrace; (*signe*) brace; **donner l'~ à qn** to embrace sb

accoler [akɔle] *vt* to place side by side

accommodant, e [akɔmɔdɑ̃, -ɑ̃t] *adj* accommodating, easy-going

accommodement [akɔmɔdmɑ̃] *nm* compromise

accommoder [akɔmɔde] *vt* (*Culin*) to prepare; (*points de vue*) to reconcile; **~ qch à** (*adapter*) to adapt sth to; **s'accommoder de** to put up with; (*se contenter de*) to make do with; **s'~ à** (*s'adapter*) to adapt to

accompagnateur, -trice [akɔ̃paɲatœʀ, -tʀis] *nm/f* (*Mus*) accompanist; (*de voyage*) guide; (*de voyage organisé*) courier; (*d'enfants*) accompanying adult

accompagnement [akɔ̃paɲmɑ̃] *nm* (*Mus*) accompaniment; (*Mil*) support

accompagner [akɔ̃paɲe] *vt* to accompany, be *ou* go *ou* come with; (*Mus*) to accompany; **s'accompagner de** to bring, be accompanied by

accompli, e [akɔ̃pli] *adj* accomplished

accomplir [akɔ̃pliʀ] *vt* (*tâche, projet*) to carry out; (*souhait*) to fulfil; **s'accomplir** *vi* to be fulfilled

accomplissement [akɔ̃plismɑ̃] *nm* carrying out; fulfilment (*Brit*), fulfillment (*US*)

accord [akɔʀ] *nm* (*entente, convention, Ling*) agreement; (*entre des styles, tons etc*) harmony; (*consentement*) agreement, consent; (*Mus*) chord; **donner son ~** to give one's agreement; **mettre deux personnes d'~** to make two people come to an agreement, reconcile two people; **se mettre d'~** to come to an agreement (with each other); **être d'~** to agree; **être d'~ avec qn** to agree with sb; **d'~!** OK!, right!; **d'un commun ~** of one accord; **~ parfait** (*Mus*) tonic chord

accord-cadre [akɔʀkɑdʀ(ə)] (*pl* **accords-cadres**) *nm* framework *ou* outline agreement

accordéon [akɔʀdeɔ̃] *nm* (*Mus*) accordion

accordéoniste [akɔʀdeɔnist(ə)] *nm/f* accordionist

accorder [akɔʀde] *vt* (*faveur, délai*) to grant; (*attribuer*): **~ de l'importance/de la valeur à qch** to attach importance/value to sth; (*harmoniser*) to match; (*Mus*) to tune; **s'accorder** *vi* to get on together; (*être d'accord*) to agree; (*couleurs, caractères*) to go together, match; (*Ling*) to agree; **je vous accorde que ...** I grant you that ...

accordeur [akɔʀdœʀ] nm (Mus) tuner

accoster [akɔste] vt (Navig) to draw alongside; (personne) to accost ▷ vi (Navig) to berth

accotement [akɔtmɑ̃] nm (de route) verge (Brit), shoulder; ~ **stabilisé/non stabilisé** hard shoulder/soft verge ou shoulder

accoter [akɔte] vt: ~ **qch contre/à** to lean ou rest sth against/on; **s'~ contre/à** to lean against/on

accouchement [akuʃmɑ̃] nm delivery, (child)birth; (travail) labour (Brit), labor (US); ~ **à terme** delivery at (full) term; ~ **sans douleur** natural childbirth

accoucher [akuʃe] vi to give birth, have a baby; (être en travail) to be in labour (Brit) ou labor (US) ▷ vt to deliver; ~ **d'un garçon** to give birth to a boy

accoucheur [akuʃœʀ] nm: (**médecin**) ~ obstetrician

accoucheuse [akuʃøz] nf midwife

accouder [akude]: **s'accouder** vi: **s'~ à/contre/sur** to rest one's elbows on/against/on; **accoudé à la fenêtre** leaning on the windowsill

accoudoir [akudwaʀ] nm armrest

accouplement [akupləmɑ̃] nm coupling; mating

accoupler [akuple] vt to couple; (pour la reproduction) to mate; **s'accoupler** vi to mate

accourir [akuʀiʀ] vi to rush ou run up

accoutrement [akutʀəmɑ̃] nm (péj) getup (Brit), outfit

accoutrer [akutʀe] (péj) vt to do ou get up; **s'accoutrer** to do ou get o.s. up

accoutumance [akutymɑ̃s] nf (gén) adaptation; (Méd) addiction

accoutumé, e [akutyme] adj (habituel) customary, usual; **comme à l'~e** as is customary ou usual

accoutumer [akutyme] vt: ~ **qn à qch/faire** to accustom sb to sth/to doing; **s'accoutumer à** to get accustomed ou used to

accréditer [akʀedite] vt (nouvelle) to substantiate; ~ **qn (auprès de)** to accredit sb (to)

accro [akʀo] nm/f (fam: = accroché(e)) addict

accroc [akʀo] nm (déchirure) tear; (fig) hitch, snag; **sans ~** without a hitch; **faire un ~ à** (vêtement) to make a tear in, tear; (fig: règle etc) to infringe

accrochage [akʀɔʃaʒ] nm hanging (up); hitching (up); (Auto) (minor) collision; (Mil) encounter, engagement; (dispute) clash, brush

accroche-cœur [akʀɔʃkœʀ] nm kiss-curl

accrocher [akʀɔʃe] vt (suspendre): ~ **qch à** to hang sth (up) on; (attacher: remorque) to hitch sth (up) to; (heurter) to catch; to hit; (déchirer): ~ **qch (à)** to catch sth (on); (Mil) to engage; (fig) to catch, attract ▷ vi to stick, get stuck; (fig: pourparlers etc) to hit a snag; (plaire: disque etc) to catch on; **s'accrocher** vi (se disputer) to have a clash ou brush; (ne pas céder) to hold one's own, hang on in (fam); **s'~ à** (rester pris à) to catch on;

(agripper, fig) to hang on ou cling to

accrocheur, -euse [akʀɔʃœʀ, -øz] adj (vendeur, concurrent) tenacious; (publicité) eye-catching; (titre) catchy, eye-catching

accroire [akʀwaʀ] vt: **faire ou laisser ~ à qn qch/que** to give sb to believe sth/that

accroîs [akʀwa], **accroissais** etc [akʀwasɛ] vb voir **accroître**

accroissement [akʀwasmɑ̃] nm increase

accroître [akʀwatʀ(ə)] vt, **s'accroître** vi to increase

accroupi, e [akʀupi] adj squatting, crouching (down)

accroupir [akʀupiʀ]: **s'accroupir** vi to squat, crouch (down)

accru, e [akʀy] pp de **accroître**

accu [aky] nm (fam: = accumulateur) accumulator, battery

accueil [akœj] nm welcome; (endroit) reception (desk); (: dans une gare) information kiosk; **comité/centre d'~** reception committee/centre

accueillant, e [akœjɑ̃, -ɑ̃t] adj welcoming, friendly

accueillir [akœjiʀ] vt to welcome; (loger) to accommodate

acculer [akyle] vt: ~ **qn à ou contre** to drive sb back against; ~ **qn dans** to corner sb in; ~ **qn à** (faillite) to drive sb to the brink of

accumulateur [akymylatœʀ] nm accumulator, battery

accumulation [akymylasjɔ̃] nf accumulation; **chauffage/radiateur à ~** (night-)storage heating/heater

accumuler [akymyle] vt to accumulate, amass; **s'accumuler** vi to accumulate; to pile up

accusateur, -trice [akyzatœʀ, -tʀis] nm/f accuser ▷ adj accusing; (document, preuve) incriminating

accusatif [akyzatif] nm (Ling) accusative

accusation [akyzasjɔ̃] nf (gén) accusation; (Jur) charge; (partie): **l'~** the prosecution; **mettre en ~** to indict; **acte d'~** bill of indictment

accusé, e [akyze] nm/f accused; (prévenu(e)) defendant ▷ nm: ~ **de réception** acknowledgement of receipt

accuser [akyze] vt to accuse; (fig) to emphasize, bring out; (: montrer) to show; **s'accuser** vi (s'accentuer) to become more marked; ~ **qn de** accuse sb of; (Jur) to charge sb with; ~ **qn/qch de qch** (rendre responsable) to blame sb/sth for sth; **s'~ de qch/d'avoir fait qch** to admit sth/having done sth; to blame o.s. for sth/for having done sth; ~ **réception de** to acknowledge receipt of; ~ **le coup** (aussi fig) to be visibly affected

acerbe [asɛʀb(ə)] adj caustic, acid

acéré, e [aseʀe] adj sharp

acétate [asetat] nm acetate

acétique [asetik] adj: **acide ~** acetic acid

acétone [asetɔn] nf acetone

acétylène [asetilɛn] nm acetylene

ach. *abr* = **achète**

acharné, e [aʃaʀne] *adj* (*lutte, adversaire*) fierce, bitter; (*travail*) relentless, unremitting

acharnement [aʃaʀnəmã] *nm* fierceness; relentlessness

acharner [aʃaʀne]: **s'acharner** *vi*: **s'~ sur** to go at fiercely, hound; **s'~ contre** to set o.s. against; to dog, pursue; (*malchance*) to hound; **s'~ à faire** to try doggedly to do; to persist in doing

achat [aʃa] *nm* buying *no pl*; (*article acheté*) purchase; **faire l'~ de** to buy, purchase; **faire des ~s** to do some shopping, buy a few things

acheminement [aʃminmã] *nm* conveyance

acheminer [aʃmine] *vt* (*courrier*) to forward, dispatch; (*troupes*) to convey, transport; (*train*) to route; **s'acheminer vers** to head for

acheter [aʃte] *vt* to buy, purchase; (*soudoyer*) to buy, bribe; **~ qch à** (*marchand*) to buy *ou* purchase sth from; (*ami etc: offrir*) to buy sth for; **~ à crédit** to buy on credit

acheteur, -euse [aʃtœʀ, -øz] *nm/f* buyer; shopper; (*Comm*) buyer; (*Jur*) vendee, purchaser

achevé, e [aʃve] *adj*: **d'un ridicule ~** thoroughly *ou* absolutely ridiculous; **d'un comique ~** absolutely hilarious

achèvement [aʃɛvmã] *nm* completion, finishing

achever [aʃve] *vt* to complete, finish; (*blessé*) to finish off; **s'achever** *vi* to end

achoppement [aʃɔpmã] *nm*: **pierre d'~** stumbling block

acide [asid] *adj* sour, sharp; (*ton*) acid, biting; (*Chimie*) acid(ic) ▷ *nm* acid

acidifier [asidifje] *vt* to acidify

acidité [asidite] *nf* sharpness; acidity

acidulé, e [asidyle] *adj* slightly acid; **bonbons ~s** acid drops (*Brit*), ≈ lemon drops (*US*)

acier [asje] *nm* steel; **~ inoxydable** stainless steel

aciérie [asjeʀi] *nf* steelworks *sg*

acné [akne] *nf* acne

acolyte [akɔlit] *nm* (*péj*) associate

acompte [akɔ̃t] *nm* deposit; (*versement régulier*) instalment; (*sur somme due*) payment on account; (*sur salaire*) advance; **un ~ de 10 euros** 10 euros on account

acoquiner [akɔkine]: **s'acoquiner avec** *vt* (*péj*) to team up with

Açores [asɔʀ] *nfpl*: **les ~** the Azores

à-côté [akote] *nm* side-issue; (*argent*) extra

à-coup [aku] *nm* (*du moteur*) (hic)cough; (*fig*) jolt; **sans ~s** smoothly; **par ~s** by fits and starts

acoustique [akustik] *nf* (*d'une salle*) acoustics *pl*; (*science*) acoustics *sg* ▷ *adj* acoustic

acquéreur [akeʀœʀ] *nm* buyer, purchaser; **se porter/se rendre ~ de qch** to announce one's intention to purchase/to purchase sth

acquérir [akeʀiʀ] *vt* to acquire; (*par achat*) to purchase, acquire; (*valeur*) to gain; (*résultats*) to achieve; **ce que ses efforts lui ont acquis** what his efforts have won *ou* gained (for) him

acquiers *etc* [akjɛʀ] *vb voir* **acquérir**

acquiescement [akjɛsmã] *nm* acquiescence, agreement

acquiescer [akjese] *vi* (*opiner*) to agree; (*consentir*): **~ (à qch)** to acquiesce *ou* assent (to sth)

acquis, e [aki, -iz] *pp de* **acquérir** ▷ *nm* (accumulated) experience; (*avantage*) gain ▷ *adj* (*voir acquérir*) acquired; gained; achieved; **être ~ à** (*plan, idée*) to be in full agreement with; **son aide nous est ~e** we can count on *ou* be sure of his help; **tenir qch pour ~** to take sth for granted

acquisition [akizisjɔ̃] *nf* acquisition; (*achat*) purchase; **faire l'~ de** to acquire; to purchase

acquit [aki] *vb voir* **acquérir** ▷ *nm* (*quittance*) receipt; **pour ~** received; **par ~ de conscience** to set one's mind at rest

acquittement [akitmã] *nm* acquittal; payment, settlement

acquitter [akite] *vt* (*Jur*) to acquit; (*facture*) to pay, settle; **s'acquitter de** to discharge; (*promesse, tâche*) to fulfil (*Brit*), fulfill (*US*), carry out

âcre [akʀ(ə)] *adj* acrid, pungent

âcreté [akʀəte] *nf* acridness, pungency

acrimonie [akʀimɔni] *nf* acrimony

acrobate [akʀɔbat] *nm/f* acrobat

acrobatie [akʀɔbasi] *nf* (*art*) acrobatics *sg*; (*exercice*) acrobatic feat; **~ aérienne** aerobatics *sg*

acrobatique [akʀɔbatik] *adj* acrobatic

acronyme [akʀɔnim] *nm* acronym

Acropole [akʀɔpɔl] *nf*: **l'~** the Acropolis

acrylique [akʀilik] *adj, nm* acrylic

acte [akt(ə)] *nm* act, action; (*Théât*) act; **actes** *nmpl* (*compte-rendu*) proceedings; **prendre ~ de** to note, take note of; **faire ~ de présence** to put in an appearance; **faire ~ de candidature** to submit an application; **~ d'accusation** charge (*Brit*), bill of indictment; **~ de baptême** baptismal certificate; **~ de mariage/naissance** marriage/birth certificate; **~ de vente** bill of sale

acteur [aktœʀ] *nm* actor

actif, -ive [aktif, -iv] *adj* active ▷ *nm* (*Comm*) assets *pl*; (*Ling*) active (voice); (*fig*): **avoir à son ~** to have to one's credit; **actifs** *nmpl* people in employment; **mettre à son ~** to add to one's list of achievements; **~ toxique** toxic asset; **l'~ et le passif** assets and liabilities; **prendre une part active à qch** to take an active part in sth; **population active** working population

action [aksjɔ̃] *nf* (*gén*) action; (*Comm*) share; **une bonne/mauvaise ~** a good/an unkind deed; **mettre en ~** to put into action; **passer à l'~** to take action; **sous l'~ de** under the effect of; **l'~ syndicale** (the) union action; **un film d'~** an action film *ou* movie; **~ en diffamation** libel action; **~ de grâce(s)** (*Rel*) thanksgiving

actionnaire [aksjɔnɛʀ] *nm/f* shareholder

actionner [aksjɔne] *vt* to work; to activate; to operate

active [aktiv] *adj f voir* **actif**

activement [aktivmɑ̃] *adv* actively

activer [aktive] *vt* to speed up; (*Chimie*) to activate; **s'activer** *vi* (*s'affairer*) to bustle about; (*se hâter*) to hurry up

activisme [aktivism(ə)] *nm* activism

activiste [aktivist(ə)] *nm/f* activist

activité [aktivite] *nf* activity; **en ~** (*volcan*) active; (*fonctionnaire*) in active life; (*militaire*) on active service

actrice [aktʀis] *nf* actress

actualiser [aktɥalize] *vt* to actualize; (*mettre à jour*) to bring up to date

actualité [aktɥalite] *nf* (*d'un problème*) topicality; (*événements*): **l'~** current events; **les ~s** (*Ciné, TV*) the news; **l'~ politique/sportive** the political/sports *ou* sporting news; **les ~s télévisées** the television news; **d'~** topical

actuel, le [aktɥɛl] *adj* (*présent*) present; (*d'actualité*) topical; (*non virtuel*) actual; **à l'heure ~le** at this moment in time, at the moment

actuellement [aktɥɛlmɑ̃] *adv* at present, at the present time

acuité [akɥite] *nf* acuteness

acuponcteur, acupuncteur [akypɔ̃ktœʀ] *nm* acupuncturist

acuponcture, acupuncture [akypɔ̃ktyʀ] *nf* acupuncture

adage [adaʒ] *nm* adage

adagio [ada(d)ʒjo] *adv, nm* adagio

adaptable [adaptabl(ə)] *adj* adaptable

adaptateur, -trice [adaptatœʀ, -tʀis] *nm/f* adapter

adaptation [adaptasjɔ̃] *nf* adaptation

adapter [adapte] *vt* to adapt; **s'adapter (à)** (*personne*) to adapt (to); (: *objet, prise etc*) to apply (to); **~ qch à** (*approprier*) to adapt sth to (fit); **~ qch sur/dans/à** (*fixer*) to fit sth on/into/to

addenda [adɛ̃da] *nm inv* addenda

Addis-Ababa [adisababa], **Addis-Abeba** [adisabəba] *n* Addis Ababa

additif [aditif] *nm* additional clause; (*substance*) additive; **~ alimentaire** food additive

addition [adisjɔ̃] *nf* addition; (*au café*) bill

additionnel, le [adisjɔnɛl] *adj* additional

additionner [adisjɔne] *vt* to add (up); **s'additionner** *vi* to add up; **~ un produit d'eau** to add water to a product

adduction [adyksjɔ̃] *nf* (*de gaz, d'eau*) conveyance

adepte [adɛpt(ə)] *nm/f* follower

adéquat, e [adekwa, -at] *adj* appropriate, suitable

adéquation [adekwasjɔ̃] *nf* appropriateness; (*Ling*) adequacy

adhérence [adeʀɑ̃s] *nf* adhesion

adhérent, e [adeʀɑ̃, -ɑ̃t] *nm/f* (*de club*) member

adhérer [adeʀe] *vi* (*coller*) to adhere, stick; **~ à** (*coller*) to adhere *ou* stick to; (*se rallier à: parti, club*) to join; to be a member of; (: *opinion, mouvement*) to support

adhésif, -ive [adezif, -iv] *adj* adhesive, sticky ▷ *nm* adhesive

adhésion [adezjɔ̃] *nf* (*à un club*) joining; membership; (*à une opinion*) support

ad hoc [adɔk] *adj* ad hoc

adieu, x [adjø] *excl* goodbye ▷ *nm* farewell; **dire ~ à qn** to say goodbye *ou* farewell to sb; **dire ~ à qch** (*renoncer*) to say *ou* wave goodbye to sth

adipeux, -euse [adipø, -øz] *adj* bloated, fat; (*Anat*) adipose

adjacent, e [adʒasɑ̃, -ɑ̃t] *adj*: **~ (à)** adjacent (to)

adjectif [adʒɛktif] *nm* adjective; **~ attribut** adjectival complement; **~ épithète** attributive adjective

adjectival, e, -aux [adʒɛktival, -o] *adj* adjectival

adjoignais *etc* [adʒwaɲɛ] *vb voir* **adjoindre**

adjoindre [adʒwɛ̃dʀ(ə)] *vt*: **~ qch à** to attach sth to; (*ajouter*) to add sth to; **~ qn à** (*personne*) to appoint sb as an assistant to; (*comité*) to appoint sb to, attach sb to; **s'adjoindre** *vt* (*collaborateur etc*) to take on, appoint

adjoint, e [adʒwɛ̃, -wɛ̃t] *pp de* **adjoindre** ▷ *nm/f* assistant; **directeur ~** assistant manager

adjonction [adʒɔ̃ksjɔ̃] *nf* (*voir adjoindre*) attaching; addition; appointment

adjudant [adʒydɑ̃] *nm* (*Mil*) warrant officer; **~-chef** ≈ warrant officer 1st class (*Brit*), ≈ chief warrant officer (*US*)

adjudicataire [adʒydikatɛʀ] *nm/f* successful bidder, purchaser; (*pour travaux*) successful tenderer (*Brit*) *ou* bidder (*US*)

adjudicateur, -trice [adʒydikatœʀ, -tʀis] *nm/f* (*aux enchères*) seller

adjudication [adʒydikasjɔ̃] *nf* sale by auction; (*pour travaux*) invitation to tender (*Brit*) *ou* bid (*US*)

adjuger [adʒyʒe] *vt* (*prix, récompense*) to award; (*lors d'une vente*) to auction (off); **s'adjuger** *vt* to take for o.s.; **adjugé!** (*vendu*) gone!, sold!

adjurer [adʒyʀe] *vt*: **~ qn de faire** to implore *ou* beg sb to do

adjuvant [adʒyvɑ̃] *nm* (*médicament*) adjuvant; (*additif*) additive; (*stimulant*) stimulant

admettre [admɛtʀ(ə)] *vt* (*visiteur, nouveau-venu*) to admit, let in; (*candidat: Scol*) to pass; (*Tech: gaz, eau, air*) to admit; (*tolérer*) to allow, accept; (*reconnaître*) to admit, acknowledge; (*supposer*) to suppose; **j'admets que ...** I admit that ...; **je n'admets pas que tu fasses cela** I won't allow you to do that; **admettons que ...** let's suppose that ...; **admettons** let's suppose so

administrateur, -trice [administʀatœʀ, -tʀis] *nm/f* (*Comm*) director; (*Admin*) administrator; **~ délégué** managing director; **~ judiciaire** receiver

administratif, -ive [administʀatif, -iv] *adj* administrative ▷ *nm* person in administration

administration [administʀasjɔ̃] *nf* administration; **l'A~** ≈ the Civil Service

administré, e [administʀe] *nm/f* ≈ citizen

administrer [administʀe] *vt* (*firme*) to manage, run; (*biens, remède, sacrement etc*) to administer

admirable [admiʀabl(ə)] *adj* admirable, wonderful

admirablement [admirabləmɑ̃] *adv* admirably
admirateur, -trice [admiratœr, -tris] *nm/f*
admirer
admiratif, -ive [admiratif, -iv] *adj* admiring
admiration [admirasjɔ̃] *nf* admiration; **être
en ~ devant** to be lost in admiration before
admirativement [admirativmɑ̃] *adv*
admiringly
admirer [admire] *vt* to admire
admis, e [admi, -iz] *pp de* **admettre**
admissibilité [admisibilite] *nf* eligibility;
admissibility, acceptability
admissible [admisibl(ə)] *adj* (*candidat*) eligible;
(*comportement*) admissible, acceptable; (*Jur*)
receivable
admission [admisjɔ̃] *nf* admission; **tuyau d'~**
intake pipe; **demande d'~** application for
membership; **service des ~s** admissions
admonester [admɔnɛste] *vt* to admonish
ADN *sigle m* (= *acide désoxyribonucléique*) DNA
ado [ado] *nm/f* (*fam*: = *adolescent(e)*) adolescent,
teenager
adolescence [adɔlesɑ̃s] *nf* adolescence
adolescent, e [adɔlesɑ̃, -ɑ̃t] *nm/f* adolescent,
teenager
adonner [adɔne]: **s'adonner à** *vt* (*sport*) to
devote o.s. to; (*boisson*) to give o.s. over to
adopter [adɔpte] *vt* to adopt; (*projet de loi etc*) to
pass
adoptif, -ive [adɔptif, -iv] *adj* (*parents*) adoptive;
(*fils, patrie*) adopted
adoption [adɔpsjɔ̃] *nf* adoption; **son pays/sa
ville d'~** his adopted country/town
adorable [adɔrabl(ə)] *adj* adorable
adoration [adɔrasjɔ̃] *nf* adoration; (*Rel*)
worship; **être en ~ devant** to be lost in
adoration before
adorer [adɔre] *vt* to adore; (*Rel*) to worship
adosser [adose] *vt*: **~ qch à** *ou* **contre** to stand
sth against; **s'~ à** *ou* **contre** to lean with one's
back against; **être adossé à** *ou* **contre** to be
leaning with one's back against
adoucir [adusir] *vt* (*goût, température*) to make
milder; (*avec du sucre*) to sweeten; (*peau, voix, eau*)
to soften; (*caractère, personne*) to mellow; (*peine*)
to soothe, allay; **s'adoucir** *vi* to become milder;
to soften; to mellow
adoucissement [adusismɑ̃] *nm* becoming
milder; sweetening; softening; mellowing;
soothing
adoucisseur [adusisœr] *nm*: **~ (d'eau)** water
softener
adr. *abr* = **adresse; adresser**
adrénaline [adrenalin] *nf* adrenaline
adresse [adrɛs] *nf* (*voir droit*) skill, dexterity;
(*domicile, Inform*) address; **à l'~ de** (*pour*) for the
benefit of
adresser [adrese] *vt* (*lettre: expédier*) to send;
(: *écrire l'adresse sur*) to address; (*injure, compliments*)
to address; **~ qn à un docteur/bureau** to refer
ou send sb to a doctor/an office; **~ la parole à qn**
to speak to *ou* address sb; **s'adresser à** (*parler à*)

to speak to, address; (*s'informer auprès de*) to go
and see, go and speak to; (: *bureau*) to enquire at;
(*livre, conseil*) to be aimed at
Adriatique [adrijatik] *nf*: **l'~** the Adriatic
adroit, e [adrwa, -wat] *adj* (*joueur, mécanicien*)
skilful (*Brit*), skillful (*US*), dext(e)rous; (*politicien
etc*) shrewd, skilled
adroitement [adrwatmɑ̃] *adv* skilfully (*Brit*),
skillfully (*US*), dext(e)rously; shrewdly
AdS *sigle f* = **Académie des Sciences**
ADSL *sigle m* (= *asymmetrical digital subscriber line*)
ADSL; **avoir l'~** to have broadband
aduler [adyle] *vt* to adulate
adulte [adylt(ə)] *nm/f* adult, grown-up ▷ *adj*
(*personne, attitude*) adult, grown-up; (*chien, arbre*)
fully-grown, mature; **l'âge ~** adulthood;
formation/film pour ~s adult training/film
adultère [adyltɛr] *adj* adulterous ▷ *nm/f*
adulterer/adulteress ▷ *nm* (*acte*) adultery
adultérin, e [adylterɛ̃, -in] *adj* born of adultery
advenir [advənir] *vi* to happen; **qu'est-il
advenu de ...?** what has become of ...?; **quoi
qu'il advienne** whatever befalls *ou* happens
adventiste [advɑ̃tist(ə)] *nm/f* (*Rel*) Adventist
adverbe [advɛrb(ə)] *nm* adverb; **~ de manière**
adverb of manner
adverbial, e, -aux [advɛrbjal, -o] *adj* adverbial
adversaire [advɛrsɛr] *nm/f* (*Sport, gén*)
opponent, adversary; (*Mil*) adversary, enemy
adverse [advɛrs(ə)] *adj* opposing
adversité [advɛrsite] *nf* adversity
AELE *sigle f* (= *Association européenne de libre-échange*)
EFTA (= *European Free Trade Association*)
AEN *sigle f* (= *Agence pour l'énergie nucléaire*) ≈ AEA
= **Atomic Energy Authority**
aérateur [aeratœr] *nm* ventilator
aération [aerasjɔ̃] *nf* airing; (*circulation de l'air*)
ventilation; **conduit d'~** ventilation shaft;
bouche d'~ air vent
aéré, e [aere] *adj* (*pièce, local*) airy, well-
ventilated; (*tissu*) loose-woven; **centre ~**
outdoor centre
aérer [aere] *vt* to air; (*fig*) to lighten; **s'aérer** *vi*
to get some (fresh) air
aérien, ne [aerjɛ̃, -ɛn] *adj* (*Aviat*) air *cpd*, aerial;
(*câble, métro*) overhead; (*fig*) light; **compagnie
~ne** (*company*); **ligne ~ne** airline
aérobic [aerɔbik] *nf* aerobics *sg*
aérobie [aerɔbi] *adj* aerobic
aéro-club [aerɔklœb] *nm* flying club
aérodrome [aerɔdrɔm] *nm* airfield, aerodrome
aérodynamique [aerɔdinamik] *adj*
aerodynamic, streamlined ▷ *nf*
aerodynamics *sg*
aérofrein [aerɔfrɛ̃] *nm* air brake
aérogare [aerɔgar] *nf* airport (buildings); (*en
ville*) air terminal
aéroglisseur [aerɔglisœr] *nm* hovercraft
aérogramme [aerɔgram] *nm* air letter,
aerogram(me)
aéromodélisme [aerɔmɔdelism(ə)] *nm* model
aircraft making

aéronaute [aeʀɔnot] *nm/f* aeronaut

aéronautique [aeʀɔnotik] *adj* aeronautical ▷ *nf* aeronautics *sg*

aéronaval, e [aeʀɔnaval] *adj* air and sea *cpd*

Aéronavale [aeʀɔnaval] *nf* ≈ Fleet Air Arm (*Brit*), ≈ Naval Air Force (*US*)

aéronef [aeʀɔnɛf] *nm* aircraft

aérophagie [aeʀɔfaʒi] *nf*: **il fait de l'~** he suffers from abdominal wind

aéroport [aeʀɔpɔʀ] *nm* airport; **~ d'embarquement** departure airport

aéroporté, e [aeʀɔpɔʀte] *adj* airborne, airlifted

aéroportuaire [aeʀɔpɔʀtɥeʀ] *adj* of an *ou* the airport, airport *cpd*

aéropostal, e, -aux [aeʀɔpɔstal, -o] *adj* airmail *cpd*

aérosol [aeʀɔsɔl] *nm* aerosol

aérospatial, e, -aux [aeʀɔspasjal, -o] *adj* aerospace ▷ *nf* the aerospace industry

aérostat [aeʀɔsta] *nm* aerostat

aérotrain [aeʀɔtʀɛ̃] *nm* hovertrain

AF *sigle fpl* = **allocations familiales** ▷ *sigle f* (*Suisse*) = **Assemblée fédérale**

AFAT [afat] *sigle m* (= *Auxiliaire féminin de l'armée de terre*) *member of the women's army*

affabilité [afabilite] *nf* affability

affable [afabl(ə)] *adj* affable

affabulateur, -trice [afabylatœʀ, -tʀis] *nm/f* storyteller

affabulation [afabylasjɔ̃] *nf* invention, fantasy

affabuler [afabyle] *vi* to make up stories

affacturage [afaktyʀaʒ] *nm* factoring

affadir [afadiʀ] *vt* to make insipid *ou* tasteless

affaiblir [afebliʀ] *vt* to weaken; **s'affaiblir** *vi* to weaken, grow weaker; (*vue*) to grow dim

affaiblissement [afeblismã] *nm* weakening

affaire [afɛʀ] *nf* (*problème, question*) matter; (*criminelle, judiciaire*) case; (*scandaleuse etc*) affair; (*entreprise*) business; (*marché, transaction*) (business) deal, (piece of) business *no pl*; (*occasion intéressante*) good deal; **affaires** *nfpl* affairs; (*activité commerciale*) business *sg*; (*effets personnels*) things, belongings; **~s de sport** sports gear; **tirer qn/se tirer d'~** to get sb/o.s. out of trouble; **ceci fera l'~** this will do (nicely); **avoir ~ à** (*comme adversaire*) to be faced with; (*en contact*) to be dealing with; **tu auras ~ à moi!** (*menace*) you'll have me to contend with!; **c'est une ~ de goût/d'argent** it's a question *ou* matter of taste/money; **c'est l'~ d'une minute/heure** it'll only take a minute/an hour; **ce sont mes ~s** (*cela me concerne*) that's my business; **toutes ~s cessantes** forthwith; **les ~s étrangères** (*Pol*) foreign affairs

affairé, e [afeʀe] *adj* busy

affairer [afeʀe]: **s'affairer** *vi* to busy o.s., bustle about

affairisme [afeʀism(ə)] *nm* (political) racketeering

affaissement [afesmã] *nm* subsidence; collapse

affaisser [afese]: **s'affaisser** *vi* (*terrain, immeuble*) to subside, sink; (*personne*) to collapse

affaler [afale]: **s'affaler** *vi*: **s'~ dans/sur** to collapse *ou* slump into/onto

affamé, e [afame] *adj* starving, famished

affamer [afame] *vt* to starve

affectation [afɛktasjɔ̃] *nf* (*voir affecter*) allotment; appointment; posting; (*voir affecté*) affectedness

affecté, e [afɛkte] *adj* affected

affecter [afɛkte] *vt* (*émouvoir*) to affect, move; (*feindre*) to affect, feign; (*telle ou telle forme etc*) to take on, assume; **~ qch à** to allocate *ou* allot sth to; **~ qn à** to appoint sb to; (*diplomate*) to post sb to; **~ qch de** (*de coefficient*) to modify sth by

affectif, -ive [afɛktif, -iv] *adj* emotional, affective

affection [afɛksjɔ̃] *nf* affection; (*mal*) ailment; **avoir de l'~ pour** to feel affection for; **prendre en ~** to become fond of

affectionner [afɛksjɔne] *vt* to be fond of

affectueusement [afɛktɥøzmã] *adv* affectionately

affectueux, -euse [afɛktɥø, -øz] *adj* affectionate

afférent, e [afeʀã, -ãt] *adj*: **~ à** pertaining *ou* relating to

affermir [afɛʀmiʀ] *vt* to consolidate, strengthen

affichage [afiʃaʒ] *nm* billposting, billsticking; (*électronique*) display; **"~ interdit"** "stick no bills", "billsticking prohibited"; **~ à cristaux liquides** liquid crystal display, LCD; **~ numérique** *ou* **digital** digital display

affiche [afiʃ] *nf* poster; (*officielle*) (public) notice; (*Théât*) bill; **être à l'~** (*Théât*) to be on; **tenir l'~** to run

afficher [afiʃe] *vt* (*affiche*) to put up, post up; (*réunion*) to put up a notice about; (*électroniquement*) to display; (*fig*) to exhibit, display; **s'afficher** *vi* (*péj*) to flaunt o.s.; **"défense d'~"** "stick no bills"

affichette [afiʃɛt] *nf* small poster *ou* notice

affilé, e [afile] *adj* sharp

affilée [afile]: **d'~** *adv* at a stretch

affiler [afile] *vt* to sharpen

affiliation [afiljasjɔ̃] *nf* affiliation

affilié, e [afilje] *adj*: **être ~ à** to be affiliated to ▷ *nm/f* affiliated party *ou* member

affilier [afilje] *vt*: **s'affilier à** to become affiliated to

affiner [afine] *vt* to refine; **s'affiner** *vi* to become (more) refined

affinité [afinite] *nf* affinity

affirmatif, -ive [afiʀmatif, -iv] *adj* affirmative ▷ *nf*: **répondre par l'affirmative** to reply in the affirmative; **dans l'affirmative** (*si oui*) if (the answer is) yes ..., if he does (*ou* you do *etc*) ...

affirmation [afiʀmasjɔ̃] *nf* assertion

affirmativement [afiʀmativmã] *adv* affirmatively, in the affirmative

affirmer [afiʀme] *vt* (*prétendre*) to maintain, assert; (*autorité etc*) to assert; **s'affirmer** *vi* to assert o.s.; to assert itself

affleurer [aflœʀe] vi to show on the surface
affliction [afliksjɔ̃] nf affliction
affligé, e [afliʒe] adj distressed, grieved; ~ **de** (maladie, tare) afflicted with
affligeant, e [afliʒɑ̃, -ɑ̃t] adj distressing
affliger [afliʒe] vt (peiner) to distress, grieve
affluence [aflyɑ̃s] nf crowds pl; **heures d'~** rush hour sg; **jours d'~** busiest days
affluent [aflyɑ̃] nm tributary
affluer [aflye] vi (secours, biens) to flood in, pour in; (sang) to rush, flow
afflux [afly] nm flood, influx; rush
affolant, e [afɔlɑ̃, -ɑ̃t] adj terrifying
affolé, e [afɔle] adj panic-stricken, panicky
affolement [afɔlmɑ̃] nm panic
affoler [afɔle] vt to throw into a panic; **s'affoler** vi to panic
affranchir [afʀɑ̃ʃiʀ] vt to put a stamp ou stamps on; (à la machine) to frank (Brit), meter (US); (esclave) to enfranchise, emancipate; (fig) to free, liberate; **s'affranchir de** to free o.s. from; **machine à ~** franking machine, postage meter
affranchissement [afʀɑ̃ʃismɑ̃] nm franking (Brit), metering (US); freeing; (Postes: prix payé) postage; **tarifs d'~** postage rates
affres [afʀ(ə)] nfpl: **dans les ~ de** in the throes of
affréter [afʀete] vt to charter
affreusement [afʀøzmɑ̃] adv dreadfully, awfully
affreux, -euse [afʀø, -øz] adj dreadful, awful
affriolant, e [afʀijɔlɑ̃, -ɑ̃t] adj tempting, enticing
affront [afʀɔ̃] nm affront
affrontement [afʀɔ̃tmɑ̃] nm (Mil, Pol) clash, confrontation
affronter [afʀɔ̃te] vt to confront, face; **s'affronter** to confront each other
affubler [afyble] vt (péj): ~ **qn de** to rig ou deck sb out in; (surnom) to attach to sb
affût [afy] nm (de canon) gun carriage; **à l'~ (de)** (gibier) lying in wait (for); (fig) on the look-out (for)
affûter [afyte] vt to sharpen, grind
afghan, e [afgɑ̃, -an] adj Afghan
Afghanistan [afganistɑ̃] nm: **l'~** Afghanistan
afin [afɛ̃]: ~ **que** conj so that, in order that; ~ **de faire** in order to do, so as to do
AFNOR [afnɔʀ] sigle f (= Association française de normalisation) industrial standards authority
a fortiori [afɔʀsjɔʀi] adv all the more, a fortiori
AFP sigle f = **Agence France-Presse**
AFPA sigle f = **Association pour la formation professionnelle des adultes**
africain, e [afʀikɛ̃, -ɛn] adj African ▷ nm/f: **Africain, e** African
afrikaans [afʀikɑ̃] nm, adj inv Afrikaans
Afrique [afʀik] nf: **l'~** Africa; **l'~ australe/du Nord/du Sud** southern/North/South Africa
afro [afʀo] adj inv: **coupe ~** afro hairstyle ▷ nm/f: **Afro** Afro
afro-américain, e [afʀoameʀikɛ̃, -ɛn] adj Afro-American

AG sigle f = **assemblée générale**
ag. abr = **agence**
agaçant, e [agasɑ̃, -ɑ̃t] adj irritating, aggravating
agacement [agasmɑ̃] nm irritation, aggravation
agacer [agase] vt to pester, tease; (involontairement) to irritate, aggravate; (aguicher) to excite, lead on
agapes [agap] nfpl (humoristique: festin) feast
agate [agat] nf agate
AGE sigle f = **assemblée générale extraordinaire**
âge [ɑʒ] nm age; **quel ~ as-tu?** how old are you?; **une femme d'un certain ~** a middle-aged woman, a woman who is getting on (in years); **bien porter son ~** to wear well; **prendre de l'~** to be getting on (in years), grow older; **limite d'~** age limit; **dispense d'~** special exemption from age limit; **troisième ~** (période) retirement; (personnes âgées) senior citizens; **l'~ ingrat** the awkward ou difficult age; ~ **légal** legal age; ~ **mental** mental age; **l'~ mûr** maturity, middle age; ~ **de raison** age of reason
âgé, e [ɑʒe] adj old, elderly; ~ **de 10 ans** 10 years old
agence [aʒɑ̃s] nf agency, office; (succursale) branch; ~ **immobilière** estate agent's (office) (Brit), real estate office (US); ~ **matrimoniale** marriage bureau; ~ **de placement** employment agency; ~ **de publicité** advertising agency; ~ **de voyages** travel agency
agencé, e [aʒɑ̃se] adj: **bien/mal ~** well/badly put together; well/badly laid out ou arranged
agencement [aʒɑ̃smɑ̃] nm putting together; arrangement, laying out
agencer [aʒɑ̃se] vt to put together; (local) to arrange, lay out
agenda [aʒɛ̃da] nm diary
agenouiller [aʒnuje]: **s'agenouiller** vi to kneel (down)
agent [aʒɑ̃] nm (aussi: **agent de police**) policeman; (Admin) official, officer; (fig: élément, facteur) agent; ~ **d'assurances** insurance broker; ~ **de change** stockbroker; ~ **commercial** sales representative; ~ **immobilier** estate agent (Brit), realtor (US); ~ **(secret)** (secret) agent
agglo [aglo] nm (fam) = **aggloméré**
agglomérat [aglɔmeʀa] nm (Géo) agglomerate
agglomération [aglɔmeʀasjɔ̃] nf town; (Auto) built-up area; **l'~ parisienne** the urban area of Paris
aggloméré [aglɔmeʀe] nm (bois) chipboard; (pierre) conglomerate
agglomérer [aglɔmeʀe] vt to pile up; (Tech: bois, pierre) to compress; **s'agglomérer** vi to pile up
agglutiner [aglytine] vt to stick together; **s'agglutiner** vi to congregate
aggravant, e [agʀavɑ̃, -ɑ̃t] adj: **circonstances ~es** aggravating circumstances

aggravation [agʀavasjɔ̃] *nf* worsening, aggravation; increase

aggraver [agʀave] *vt* to worsen, aggravate; (*Jur: peine*) to increase; **s'aggraver** *vi* to worsen; ~ **son cas** to make one's case worse

agile [aʒil] *adj* agile, nimble

agilement [aʒilmɑ̃] *adv* nimbly

agilité [aʒilite] *nf* agility, nimbleness

agio [aʒjo] *nm* (bank) charges *pl*

agir [aʒiʀ] *vi* (*se comporter*) to behave, act; (*faire quelque chose*) to act, take action; (*avoir de l'effet*) to act; **il s'agit de** it's a matter *ou* question of; it is about; (*il importe que*): **il s'agit de faire** we (*ou* you *etc*) must do; **de quoi s'agit-il?** what is it about?

agissements [aʒismɑ̃] *nmpl* (*gén péj*) schemes, intrigues

agitateur, -trice [aʒitatœʀ, -tʀis] *nm/f* agitator

agitation [aʒitasjɔ̃] *nf* (hustle and) bustle; (*trouble*) agitation, excitement; (*politique*) unrest, agitation

agité, e [aʒite] *adj* (*remuant*) fidgety, restless; (*troublé*) agitated, perturbed; (*journée*) hectic; (*mer*) rough; (*sommeil*) disturbed, broken

agiter [aʒite] *vt* (*bouteille, chiffon*) to shake; (*bras, mains*) to wave; (*préoccuper, exciter*) to trouble, perturb; **s'agiter** *vi* to bustle about; (*dormeur*) to toss and turn; (*enfant*) to fidget; (*Pol*) to grow restless; **"~ avant l'emploi"** "shake before use"

agneau, x [aɲo] *nm* lamb; (*toison*) lambswool

agnelet [aɲlɛ] *nm* little lamb

agnostique [agnɔstik] *adj, nm/f* agnostic

agonie [agɔni] *nf* mortal agony, death pangs *pl*; (*fig*) death throes *pl*

agonir [agɔniʀ] *vt*: ~ **qn d'injures** to hurl abuse at sb

agoniser [agɔnize] *vi* to be dying; (*fig*) to be in its death throes

agrafe [agʀaf] *nf* (*de vêtement*) hook, fastener; (*de bureau*) staple; (*Méd*) clip

agrafer [agʀafe] *vt* to fasten; to staple

agrafeuse [agʀaføz] *nf* stapler

agraire [agʀɛʀ] *adj* agrarian; (*mesure, surface*) land *cpd*

agrandir [agʀɑ̃diʀ] *vt* (*magasin, domaine*) to extend, enlarge; (*trou*) to enlarge, make bigger; (*Photo*) to enlarge, blow up; **s'agrandir** *vi* to be extended; to be enlarged

agrandissement [agʀɑ̃dismɑ̃] *nm* extension; enlargement; (*photographie*) enlargement

agrandisseur [agʀɑ̃disœʀ] *nm* (*Photo*) enlarger

agréable [agʀeabl(ə)] *adj* pleasant, nice

agréablement [agʀeabləmɑ̃] *adv* pleasantly

agréé, e [agʀee] *adj*: **concessionnaire ~** registered dealer; **magasin ~** registered dealer('s)

agréer [agʀee] *vt* (*requête*) to accept; ~ **à** *vt* to please, suit; **veuillez ~ ...** (*formule épistolaire*) yours faithfully

agrég [agʀɛg] *nf* (*fam*) = **agrégation**

agrégat [agʀega] *nm* aggregate

agrégation [agʀegasjɔ̃] *nf* highest teaching diploma in France; *see note*

● **AGRÉGATION**
●
● The *agrégation*, informally known as the
● "*agrég*", is a prestigious competitive
● examination for the recruitment of
● secondary school teachers in France. The
● number of candidates always far exceeds
● the number of vacant posts. Most teachers
● of 'classes préparatoires' and most
● university lecturers have passed the
● *agrégation*.

agrégé, e [agʀeʒe] *nm/f* holder of the *agrégation*

agréger [agʀeʒe]: **s'agréger** *vi* to aggregate

agrément [agʀemɑ̃] *nm* (*accord*) consent, approval; (*attraits*) charm, attractiveness; (*plaisir*) pleasure; **voyage d'~** pleasure trip

agrémenter [agʀemɑ̃te] *vt*: ~ **(de)** to embellish (with), adorn (with)

agrès [agʀɛ] *nmpl* (gymnastics) apparatus *sg*

agresser [agʀese] *vt* to attack

agresseur [agʀesœʀ] *nm* aggressor

agressif, -ive [agʀesif, -iv] *adj* aggressive

agression [agʀesjɔ̃] *nf* attack; (*Pol, Mil, Psych*) aggression

agressivement [agʀesivmɑ̃] *adv* aggressively

agressivité [agʀesivite] *nf* aggressiveness

agreste [agʀɛst(ə)] *adj* rustic

agricole [agʀikɔl] *adj* agricultural, farm *cpd*

agriculteur, -trice [agʀikyltœʀ, -tʀis] *nm/f* farmer

agriculture [agʀikyltyʀ] *nf* agriculture; farming

agripper [agʀipe] *vt* to grab, clutch; (*pour arracher*) to snatch, grab; **s'agripper à** to cling (on) to, clutch, grip

agroalimentaire [agʀɔalimɑ̃tɛʀ] *adj* farming *cpd* ▷ *nm*: **l'~** agribusiness

agronome [agʀɔnɔm] *nm/f* agronomist

agronomie [agʀɔnɔmi] *nf* agronomy

agronomique [agʀɔnɔmik] *adj* agronomic(al)

agrumes [agʀym] *nmpl* citrus fruit(s)

aguerrir [ageʀiʀ] *vt* to harden; **s'aguerrir (contre)** to become hardened (to)

aguets [agɛ]: **aux ~** *adv*: **être aux ~** to be on the look-out

aguichant, e [agiʃɑ̃, -ɑ̃t] *adj* enticing

aguicher [agiʃe] *vt* to entice

aguicheur, -euse [agiʃœʀ, -øz] *adj* enticing

ah [a] *excl* ah!; **ah bon?** really?, is that so?; **ah mais ...** yes, but ...; **ah non!** oh no!

ahuri, e [ayʀi] *adj* (*stupéfait*) flabbergasted; (*idiot*) dim-witted

ahurir [ayʀiʀ] *vt* to stupefy, stagger

ahurissant, e [ayʀisɑ̃, -ɑ̃t] *adj* stupefying, staggering, mind-boggling

ai [e] *vb voir* **avoir**

aide [ɛd] *nm/f* assistant ▷ *nf* assistance, help; (*secours financier*) aid; **à l'~ de** with the help *ou* aid of; **aller à l'~ de qn** to go to sb's aid, go to help sb; **venir en ~ à qn** to help sb, come to sb's assistance; **appeler (qn) à l'~** to call for help (from sb); **à l'~!** help!; **~ de camp** nm aide-de-camp; **~ comptable** nm accountant's assistant; **~ électricien** nm electrician's mate; **~ familiale** nf mother's help, ≈ home help; **judiciaire** nf legal aid; **~ de laboratoire** nm/f laboratory assistant; **~ ménagère** nf ≈ home help; **~ sociale** nf (assistance) state aid; **~ soignant, e** nm/f auxiliary nurse; **~ technique** nf ≈ VSO (Brit), ≈ Peace Corps (US)

aide-éducateur, -trice [ɛdmedykatœr, tʀis] nm/f classroom assistant

aide-mémoire [ɛdmemwaʀ] nm inv (key facts) handbook

aider [ede] vt to help; **~ à qch** to help (towards) sth; **~ qn à faire qch** to help sb to do sth; **s'aider de** (se servir de) to use, make use of

aide-soignant, e [ɛdswanjɑ̃, ɑ̃t] nm/f auxiliary nurse

aie etc [ɛ] vb voir **avoir**

aïe [aj] excl ouch!

AIEA sigle f (= Agence internationale de l'énergie atomique) IAEA (= International Atomic Energy Agency)

aïeul, e [ajœl] nm/f grandparent, grandfather/grandmother; (ancêtre) forebear

aïeux [ajø] nmpl grandparents; forebears, forefathers

aigle [ɛgl(ə)] nm eagle

aiglefin [ɛgləfɛ̃] nm = **églefin**

aigre [ɛgʀ(ə)] adj sour, sharp; (fig) sharp, cutting; **tourner à l'~** to turn sour

aigre-doux, -douce [ɛgʀədu, -dus] adj (fruit) bitter-sweet; (sauce) sweet and sour

aigrefin [ɛgʀəfɛ̃] nm swindler

aigrelet, te [ɛgʀəlɛ, -ɛt] adj (goût) sourish; (voix, son) sharpish

aigrette [ɛgʀɛt] nf (plume) feather

aigreur [ɛgʀœʀ] nf sourness; sharpness; **~s d'estomac** heartburn sg

aigri, e [egʀi] adj embittered

aigrir [egʀiʀ] vt (personne) to embitter; (caractère) to sour; **s'aigrir** vi to become embittered; to sour; (lait etc) to turn sour

aigu, ë [egy] adj (objet, arête) sharp, pointed; (son, voix) high-pitched, shrill; (note) high(-pitched); (douleur, intelligence) acute, sharp

aigue-marine [ɛgmaʀin] (pl **aigues-marines**) nf aquamarine

aiguillage [eguijaʒ] nm (Rail) points pl

aiguille [eguij] nf needle; (de montre) hand; **~ à tricoter** knitting needle

aiguiller [eguije] vt (orienter) to direct; (Rail) to shunt

aiguillette [eguijɛt] nf (Culin) aiguillette

aiguilleur [eguijœʀ] nm: **~ du ciel** air traffic controller

aiguillon [eguijɔ̃] nm (d'abeille) sting; (fig) spur, stimulus

aiguillonner [eguijɔne] vt to spur ou goad on

aiguiser [egize] vt to sharpen, grind; (fig) to stimulate; (: esprit) to sharpen; (: sens) to excite

aiguisoir [egizwaʀ] nm sharpener

aïkido [ajkido] nm aikido

ail [aj] nm garlic

aile [ɛl] nf wing; (de voiture) wing (Brit), fender (US); **battre de l'~** (fig) to be in a sorry state; **voler de ses propres ~s** to stand on one's own two feet; **~ libre** hang-glider

ailé, e [ele] adj winged

aileron [ɛlʀɔ̃] nm (de requin) fin; (d'avion) aileron

ailette [ɛlɛt] nf (Tech) fin; (: de turbine) blade

ailier [elje] nm (Sport) winger

aille etc [aj] vb voir **aller**

ailleurs [ajœʀ] adv elsewhere, somewhere else; **partout/nulle part ~** everywhere/nowhere else; **d'~** adv (du reste) moreover, besides; **par ~** adv (d'autre part) moreover, furthermore

ailloli [ajɔli] nm garlic mayonnaise

aimable [ɛmabl(ə)] adj kind, nice; **vous êtes bien ~** that's very nice ou kind of you, how kind (of you)!

aimablement [ɛmabləmɑ̃] adv kindly

aimant[1] [ɛmɑ̃] nm magnet

aimant[2], e [ɛmɑ̃, -ɑ̃t] adj loving, affectionate

aimanté, e [ɛmɑ̃te] adj magnetic

aimanter [ɛmɑ̃te] vt to magnetize

aimer [eme] vt to love; (d'amitié, affection, par goût) to like; (souhait): **j'aimerais ...** I would like ...; **s'aimer** to love each other; to like each other; **je n'aime pas beaucoup Paul** I don't like Paul much, I don't care much for Paul; **~ faire qch** to like doing sth, like to do sth; **aimeriez-vous que je vous accompagne?** would you like me to come with you?; **j'aimerais (bien) m'en aller** I should (really) like to go; **bien ~ qn/qch** to like sb/sth; **j'aime mieux Paul (que Pierre)** I prefer Paul (to Pierre); **j'aime mieux ou autant vous dire que** I may as well tell you that; **j'aimerais autant ou mieux y aller maintenant** I'd sooner ou rather go now; **j'aime assez aller au cinéma** I quite like going to the cinema

aine [ɛn] nf groin

aîné, e [ene] adj elder, older; (le plus âgé) eldest, oldest ▷ nm/f oldest child ou one, oldest boy ou son/girl ou daughter; **aînés** nmpl (fig: anciens) elders; **il est mon ~ (de 2 ans)** he's (2 years) older than me, he's (2 years) my senior

aînesse [enɛs] nf: **droit d'~** birthright

ainsi [ɛ̃si] adv (de cette façon) like this, in this way, thus; (ce faisant) thus ▷ conj thus, so; **~ que** (comme) (just) as; (et aussi) as well as; **pour ~ dire** so to speak, as it were; **~ donc** and so; **~ soit-il** (Rel) so be it; **et ~ de suite** and so on (and so forth)

aïoli [ajɔli] nm = **ailloli**

air [ɛʀ] nm air; (mélodie) tune; (expression) look, air; (atmosphère, ambiance): **dans l'~** in the air (fig); **prendre de grands ~s (avec qn)** to give o.s. airs (with sb); **en l'~** (up) into the air; **tirer en l'~** to fire shots in the air; **paroles/menaces**

en l'~ idle words/threats; **prendre l'~** to get some (fresh) air; *(avion)* to take off; **avoir l'~ triste** to look *ou* seem sad; **avoir l'~ de qch** to look like sth; **avoir l'~ de faire** to look as though one is doing, appear to be doing; **courant d'~** draught *(Brit)*, draft *(US)*; **le grand ~** the open air; **mal de l'~** air-sickness; **tête en l'~** scatterbrain; ~ **comprimé** compressed air; ~ **conditionné** air-conditioning

airbag [ɛʀbag] *nm* airbag

aire [ɛʀ] *nf (zone, fig, Math)* area; *(nid)* eyrie *(Brit)*, aerie *(US)*; ~ **d'atterrissage** landing strip; landing patch; ~ **de jeu** play area; ~ **de lancement** launching site; ~ **de stationnement** parking area

airelle [ɛʀɛl] *nf* bilberry

aisance [ɛzɑ̃s] *nf* ease; *(Couture)* easing, freedom of movement; *(richesse)* affluence; **être dans l'~** to be well-off *ou* affluent

aise [ɛz] *nf* comfort ▷ *adj*: **être bien ~ de/que** to be delighted to/that; **aises** *nfpl*: **aimer ses ~s** to like one's (creature) comforts; **prendre ses ~s** to make o.s. comfortable; **frémir d'~** to shudder with pleasure; **être à l'~** *ou* **à son ~** to be comfortable; *(pas embarrassé)* to be at ease; *(financièrement)* to be comfortably off; **se mettre à l'~** to make o.s. comfortable; **être mal à l'~** *ou* **à son ~** to be uncomfortable; *(gêné)* to be ill at ease; **mettre qn à l'~** to put sb at his *(ou* her) ease; **mettre qn mal à l'~** to make sb feel ill at ease; **à votre ~** please yourself, just as you like; **en faire à son ~** to do as one likes; **en prendre à son ~ avec qch** to be free and easy with sth, do as one likes with sth

aisé, e [eze] *adj* easy; *(assez riche)* well-to-do, well-off

aisément [ezemɑ̃] *adv* easily

aisselle [ɛsɛl] *nf* armpit

ait [ɛ] *vb voir* **avoir**

ajonc [aʒɔ̃] *nm* gorse *no pl*

ajouré, e [aʒuʀe] *adj* openwork *cpd*

ajournement [aʒuʀnəmɑ̃] *nm* adjournment; deferment, postponement

ajourner [aʒuʀne] *vt (réunion)* to adjourn; *(décision)* to defer, postpone; *(candidat)* to refer; *(conscrit)* to defer

ajout [aʒu] *nm* addition; **merci pour l'~** thanks for the add

ajouter [aʒute] *vt* to add; ~ **à** *(accroître)* to add to; **s'ajouter à** to add to; ~ **que** to add that; ~ **foi à** to lend *ou* give credence to

ajustage [aʒystaʒ] *nm* fitting

ajusté, e [aʒyste] *adj*: **bien ~** *(robe etc)* close-fitting

ajustement [aʒystəmɑ̃] *nm* adjustment

ajuster [aʒyste] *vt (régler)* to adjust; *(vêtement)* to alter; *(arranger)*: ~ **sa cravate** to adjust one's tie; *(coup de fusil)* to aim; *(cible)* to aim at; *(adapter)*: ~ **qch à** to fit sth to

ajusteur [aʒystœʀ] *nm* metal worker

alaise [alɛz] *nf* = **alèse**

alambic [alɑ̃bik] *nm* still

alambiqué, e [alɑ̃bike] *adj* convoluted, overcomplicated

alangui, e [alɑ̃gi] *adj* languid

alanguir [alɑ̃giʀ]: **s'alanguir** *vi* to grow languid

alarmant, e [alaʀmɑ̃, -ɑ̃t] *adj* alarming

alarme [alaʀm(ə)] *nf* alarm; **donner l'~** to give *ou* raise the alarm; **jeter l'~** to cause alarm

alarmer [alaʀme] *vt* to alarm; **s'alarmer** *vi* to become alarmed

alarmiste [alaʀmist(ə)] *adj* alarmist

Alaska [alaska] *nm*: **l'~** Alaska

albanais, e [albanɛ, -ɛz] *adj* Albanian ▷ *nm (Ling)* Albanian ▷ *nm/f*: **Albanais, e** Albanian

Albanie [albani] *nf*: **l'~** Albania

albâtre [albɑtʀ(ə)] *nm* alabaster

albatros [albatʀos] *nm* albatross

albigeois, e [albiʒwa, -waz] *adj* of *ou* from Albi

albinos [albinos] *nm/f* albino

album [albɔm] *nm* album; ~ **à colorier** colouring book; ~ **de timbres** stamp album

albumen [albymɛn] *nm* albumen

albumine [albymin] *nf* albumin; **avoir** *ou* **faire de l'~** to suffer from albuminuria

alcalin, e [alkalɛ̃, -in] *adj* alkaline

alchimie [alʃimi] *nf* alchemy

alchimiste [alʃimist(ə)] *nm* alchemist

alcool [alkɔl] *nm*: **l'~** alcohol; **un ~** a spirit, a brandy; ~ **à brûler** methylated spirits *(Brit)*, wood alcohol *(US)*; ~ **à 90°** surgical spirit; ~ **de prune** *etc* plum *etc* brandy

alcoolémie [alkɔlemi] *nf* blood alcohol level

alcoolique [alkɔlik] *adj, nm/f* alcoholic

alcoolisé, e [alkɔlize] *adj* alcoholic

alcoolisme [alkɔlism(ə)] *nm* alcoholism

alcootest®, alcotest® [alkɔtɛst] *nm (objet)* Breathalyser®; *(test)* breath-test; **faire subir l'alco(o)test à qn** to Breathalyse® sb

alcôve [alkov] *nf* alcove, recess

aléas [alea] *nmpl* hazards

aléatoire [aleatwaʀ] *adj* uncertain; *(Inform, Statistique)* random

alémanique [alemanik] *adj*: **la Suisse ~** German-speaking Switzerland

ALENA [alena] *sigle m (= Accord de libre-échange nord-américain)* NAFTA *(= North American Free Trade Agreement)*

alentour [alɑ̃tuʀ] *adv* around (about); **alentours** *nmpl* surroundings; **aux ~s de** in the vicinity *ou* neighbourhood of, around about; *(temps)* around about

alerte [alɛʀt(ə)] *adj* agile, nimble; *(style)* brisk, lively ▷ *nf* alert; warning; **donner l'~** to give the alert; **à la première ~** at the first sign of trouble *ou* danger; ~ **à la bombe** bomb scare

alerter [alɛʀte] *vt* to alert

alèse [alɛz] *nf (drap)* undersheet, drawsheet

aléser [aleze] *vt* to ream

alevin [alvɛ̃] *nm* alevin, young fish

alevinage [alvinaʒ] *nm* fish farming

Alexandrie [alɛksɑ̃dri] *n* Alexandria

alexandrin [alɛksɑ̃dʀɛ̃] *nm* alexandrine

alezan, e [alzɑ̃, -an] *adj* chestnut

algarade [algaʀad] *nf* row, dispute
algèbre [alʒɛbʀ(ə)] *nf* algebra
algébrique [alʒebʀik] *adj* algebraic
Alger [alʒe] *n* Algiers
Algérie [alʒeʀi] *nf*: **l'~** Algeria
algérien, ne [alʒeʀjɛ̃, -ɛn] *adj* Algerian ▷ *nm/f*:
   Algérien, ne Algerian
algérois, e [alʒeʀwa, -waz] *adj* of *ou* from
   Algiers ▷ *nm*: **l'A~** (*région*) the Algiers region
algorithme [algɔʀitm(ə)] *nm* algorithm
algue [alg(ə)] *nf* seaweed *no pl*
alias [aljas] *adv* alias
alibi [alibi] *nm* alibi
aliénation [aljenasjɔ̃] *nf* alienation
aliéné, e [aljene] *nm/f* insane person, lunatic
   (*péj*)
aliéner [aljene] *vt* to alienate; (*bien, liberté*) to
   give up; **s'aliéner** *vt* to alienate
alignement [aliɲmɑ̃] *nm* alignment, lining up;
   à l'~ in line
aligner [aliɲe] *vt* to align, line up; (*idées, chiffres*)
   to string together; (*adapter*): **~ qch sur** to bring
   sth into alignment with; **s'aligner** *vi* (*soldats
   etc*) to line up; **s'~ sur** (*Pol*) to align o.s. with
aliment [alimɑ̃] *nm* food; **~ complet** whole food
alimentaire [alimɑ̃tɛʀ] *adj* food *cpd*; (*péj: besogne*)
   done merely to earn a living; **produits ~s**
   foodstuffs, foods
alimentation [alimɑ̃tasjɔ̃] *nf* feeding;
   supplying, supply; (*commerce*) food trade;
   (*produits*) groceries *pl*; (*régime*) diet; (*Inform*) feed;
   ~ (générale) (general) grocer's; **~ de base**
   staple diet; **~ en feuilles/en continu/en
   papier** form/stream/sheet feed
alimenter [alimɑ̃te] *vt* to feed; (*Tech*): **~ (en)** to
   supply (with), feed (with); (*fig*) to sustain, keep
   going
alinéa [alinea] *nm* paragraph; **"nouvel ~"** "new
   line"
aliter [alite]: **s'aliter** *vi* to take to one's bed;
   infirme alité bedridden person *ou* invalid
alizé [alize] *adj, nm*: **(vent) ~** trade wind
allaitement [alɛtmɑ̃] *nm* feeding; **~ maternel/
   au biberon** breast-/bottle-feeding; **~ mixte**
   mixed feeding
allaiter [alete] *vt* (*femme*) to (breast-)feed, nurse;
   (*animal*) to suckle; **~ au biberon** to bottle-feed
allant [alɑ̃] *nm* drive, go
alléchant, e [aleʃɑ̃, -ɑ̃t] *adj* tempting, enticing
allécher [aleʃe] *vt*: **~ qn** to make sb's mouth
   water; to tempt sb, entice sb
allée [ale] *nf* (*de jardin*) path; (*en ville*) avenue,
   drive; **~s et venues** comings and goings
allégation [alegasjɔ̃] *nf* allegation
allégé, e [aleʒe] *adj* (*yaourt etc*) low-fat
alléger [aleʒe] *vt* (*voiture*) to make lighter;
   (*chargement*) to lighten; (*souffrance*) to alleviate,
   soothe
allégorie [alegɔʀi] *nf* allegory
allégorique [alegɔʀik] *adj* allegorical
allègre [alɛgʀ(ə)] *adj* lively, jaunty (*Brit*);
   (*personne*) gay, cheerful

allégresse [alegʀɛs] *nf* elation, gaiety
allegretto [al(l)egʀɛt(t)o] *adv, nm* allegretto
allegro [al(l)egʀo] *adv, nm* allegro
alléguer [alege] *vt* to put forward (as proof *ou* an
   excuse)
Allemagne [aləmaɲ] *nf*: **l'~** Germany; **l'~ de
   l'Est/Ouest** East/West Germany; **l'~ fédérale
   (RFA)** the Federal Republic of Germany (FRG)
allemand, e [almɑ̃, -ɑ̃d] *adj* German ▷ *nm* (*Ling*)
   German ▷ *nm/f*: **Allemand, e** German; **A~ de
   l'Est/l'Ouest** East/West German
aller [ale] *nm* (*trajet*) outward journey; (*billet*): **~
   (simple)** single (*Brit*) *ou* one-way ticket; **~ (et)
   retour (AR)** (*trajet*) return trip *ou* journey (*Brit*),
   round trip (*US*); (*billet*) return (*Brit*) *ou* round-
   trip (*US*) ticket ▷ *vi* (*gén*) to go; **~ à** (*convenir*) to
   suit; (*forme, pointure etc*) to fit; **cela me va**
   (*couleur*) that suits me; (*vêtement*) that suits me;
   that fits me; (*projet, disposition*) that suits me,
   that's fine *ou* OK by me; **~ à la chasse/pêche** to
   go hunting/fishing; **~ avec** (*couleurs, style etc*) to
   go (well) with; **je vais le faire/me fâcher** I'm
   going to do it/to get angry; **~ voir/chercher qn**
   to go and see/look for sb; **comment allez-
   vous?** how are you?; **comment ça va?** how are
   you?; (*affaires etc*) how are things?; **ça va? — oui
   (ça va)!** how are things? — fine!; **pour ~ à** how
   do I get to; **ça va (comme ça)** that's fine (as it
   is); **il va bien/mal** he's well/ not well, he's fine/
   ill; **ça va bien/mal** (*affaires etc*) it's going well/
   not going well; **tout va bien** everything's fine;
   ça ne va pas! (*mauvaise humeur etc*) that's not on!,
   hey, come on!; **ça ne va pas sans difficultés**
   it's not without difficulties; **~ mieux** to be
   better; **il y va de leur vie** their lives are at
   stake; **se laisser ~** to let o.s. go; **s'en aller** *vi*
   (*partir*) to be off, go, leave; (*disparaître*) to go away;
   ~ jusqu'à to go as far as; **ça va de soi, ça va
   sans dire** that goes without saying; **tu y vas
   un peu fort** you're going a bit (too) far; **allez!**
   go on!; come on!; **allons-y!** let's go!; **allez, au
   revoir!** right *ou* OK then, bye-bye!
allergène [alɛʀʒɛn] *nm* allergen
allergie [alɛʀʒi] *nf* allergy
allergique [alɛʀʒik] *adj* allergic; **~ à** allergic to
allez [ale] *vb voir* **aller**
alliage [aljaʒ] *nm* alloy
alliance [aljɑ̃s] *nf* (*Mil, Pol*) alliance; (*mariage*)
   marriage; (*bague*) wedding ring; **neveu par ~**
   nephew by marriage
allié, e [alje] *nm/f* ally; **parents et ~s** relatives
   and relatives by marriage
allier [alje] *vt* (*métaux*) to alloy; (*Pol, gén*) to ally;
   (*fig*) to combine; **s'allier** *vi* to become allies;
   (*éléments, caractéristiques*) to combine; **s'~ à** to
   become allied to *ou* with
alligator [aligatɔʀ] *nm* alligator
allitération [aliteʀasjɔ̃] *nf* alliteration
allô [alo] *excl* hullo, hallo
allocataire [alɔkatɛʀ] *nm/f* beneficiary
allocation [alɔkasjɔ̃] *nf* allowance; **~ (de)
   chômage** unemployment benefit; **~ (de)**

logement rent allowance; **~s familiales** ≈ child benefit *no pl*; **~s de maternité** maternity allowance

allocution [alɔkysjɔ̃] *nf* short speech

allongé, e [alɔ̃ʒe] *adj* (*étendu*): **être ~** to be stretched out *ou* lying down; (*long*) long; (*étiré*) elongated; (*oblong*) oblong; **rester ~** to be lying down; **mine ~e** long face

allonger [alɔ̃ʒe] *vt* to lengthen, make longer; (*étendre: bras, jambe*) to stretch (out); (*sauce*) to spin out, make go further; **s'allonger** *vi* to get longer; (*se coucher*) to lie down, stretch out; **~ le pas** to hasten one's step(s)

allouer [alwe] *vt*: **~ qch à** to allocate sth to, allot sth to

allumage [alymaʒ] *nm* (*Auto*) ignition

allume-cigare [alymsigaʀ] *nm inv* cigar lighter

allume-gaz [alymgɑz] *nm inv* gas lighter

allumer [alyme] *vt* (*lampe, phare, radio*) to put *ou* switch on; (*pièce*) to put *ou* switch the light(s) on in; (*feu, bougie, cigare, pipe, gaz*) to light; (*chauffage*) to put on; **s'allumer** *vi* (*lumière, lampe*) to come *ou* go on; **~ (la lumière *ou* l'électricité)** to put on the light

allumette [alymɛt] *nf* match; (*morceau de bois*) matchstick; (*Culin*): **~ au fromage** cheese straw; **~ de sûreté** safety match

allumeuse [alymøz] *nf* (*péj*) tease (*woman*)

allure [alyʀ] *nf* (*vitesse*) speed; (: *à pied*) pace; (*démarche*) walk; (*maintien*) bearing; (*aspect, air*) look; **avoir de l'~** to have style *ou* a certain elegance; **à toute ~** at top *ou* full speed

allusion [alyzjɔ̃] *nf* allusion; (*sous-entendu*) hint; **faire ~ à** to allude *ou* refer to; to hint at

alluvions [alyvjɔ̃] *nfpl* alluvial deposits, alluvium *sg*

almanach [almana] *nm* almanac

aloès [alɔɛs] *nm* (*Bot*) aloe

aloi [alwa] *nm*: **de bon/mauvais ~** of genuine/doubtful worth *ou* quality

○ **MOT-CLÉ**

alors [alɔʀ] *adv* **1** (*à ce moment-là*) then, at that time; **il habitait alors à Paris** he lived in Paris at that time; **jusqu'alors** up till *ou* until then
2 (*par conséquent*) then; **tu as fini? alors je m'en vais** have you finished? I'm going then
3 (*expressions*): **alors? quoi de neuf?** well *ou* so? what's new?; **et alors?** so (what)?; **ça alors!** (well) really!
▷ *conj*: **alors que 1** (*au moment où*) when, as; **il est arrivé alors que je partais** he arrived as I was leaving
2 (*pendant que*) while, when; **alors qu'il était à Paris, il a visité ...** while *ou* when he was in Paris, he visited ...
3 (*tandis que*) whereas, while; **alors que son frère travaillait dur, lui se reposait** while his brother was working hard, HE would rest

alouette [alwɛt] *nf* (sky)lark

alourdir [aluʀdiʀ] *vt* to weigh down, make heavy; **s'alourdir** *vi* to grow heavy *ou* heavier

aloyau [alwajo] *nm* sirloin

alpaga [alpaga] *nm* (*tissu*) alpaca

alpage [alpaʒ] *nm* high mountain pasture

Alpes [alp(ə)] *nfpl*: **les ~** the Alps

alpestre [alpɛstʀ(ə)] *adj* alpine

alphabet [alfabɛ] *nm* alphabet; (*livre*) ABC (book), primer

alphabétique [alfabetik] *adj* alphabetic(al); **par ordre ~** in alphabetical order

alphabétisation [alfabetizasjɔ̃] *nf* literacy teaching

alphabétiser [alfabetize] *vt* to teach to read and write; (*pays*) to eliminate illiteracy in

alphanumérique [alfanymeʀik] *adj* alphanumeric

alpin, e [alpɛ̃, -in] *adj* (*plante etc*) alpine; (*club*) climbing

alpinisme [alpinism(ə)] *nm* mountaineering, climbing

alpiniste [alpinist(ə)] *nm/f* mountaineer, climber

Alsace [alzas] *nf*: **l'~** Alsace

alsacien, ne [alzasjɛ̃, -ɛn] *adj* Alsatian

altercation [altɛʀkasjɔ̃] *nf* altercation

alter ego [altɛʀego] *nm* alter ego

altérer [altere] *vt* (*faits, vérité*) to falsify, distort; (*qualité*) to debase, impair; (*données*) to corrupt; (*donner soif à*) to make thirsty; **s'altérer** *vi* to deteriorate; to spoil

altermondialisme [altɛʀmɔ̃djalism] *nm* anti-globalism

altermondialiste [altɛʀmɔ̃djalist] *adj, nm/f* anti-globalist

alternance [altɛʀnɑ̃s] *nf* alternation; **en ~** alternately; **formation en ~** sandwich course

alternateur [altɛʀnatœʀ] *nm* alternator

alternatif, -ive [altɛʀnatif, -iv] *adj* alternating ▷ *nf* alternative

alternativement [altɛʀnativmɑ̃] *adv* alternately

alterner [altɛʀne] *vt* to alternate ▷ *vi*: **~ (avec)** to alternate (with); **(faire) ~ qch avec qch** to alternate sth with sth

Altesse [altɛs] *nf* Highness

altier, -ière [altje, -jɛʀ] *adj* haughty

altimètre [altimɛtʀ(ə)] *nm* altimeter

altiport [altipɔʀ] *nm* mountain airfield

altiste [altist(ə)] *nm/f* viola player, violist

altitude [altityd] *nf* altitude, height; **à 1000 m d'~** at a height *ou* an altitude of 1000 m; **en ~** at high altitudes; **perdre/prendre de l'~** to lose/gain height; **voler à haute/basse ~** to fly at a high/low altitude

alto [alto] *nm* (*instrument*) viola ▷ *nf* (*contr*)alto

altruisme [altʀyism(ə)] *nm* altruism

altruiste [altʀyist(ə)] *adj* altruistic

aluminium [alyminjɔm] *nm* aluminium (*Brit*), aluminum (*US*)

alun [alœ̃] *nm* alum

alunir [alyniʀ] *vi* to land on the moon

alunissage [alynisaʒ] *nm* (moon) landing
alvéole [alveɔl] *nm ou f* (*de ruche*) alveolus
alvéolé, e [alveɔle] *adj* honeycombed
AM *sigle f* = **assurance maladie**
amabilité [amabilite] *nf* kindness; **il a eu l'~ de**
he was kind *ou* good enough to
amadou [amadu] *nm* touchwood, amadou
amadouer [amadwe] *vt* to coax, cajole; (*adoucir*)
to mollify, soothe
amaigrir [amegRiR] *vt* to make thin *ou* thinner
amaigrissant, e [amegRisã, -ãt] *adj*: **régime ~**
slimming (*Brit*) *ou* weight-reduction (*US*) diet
amalgame [amalgam] *nm* amalgam; (*fig: de*
gens, d'idées) hotch-potch, mixture
amalgamer [amalgame] *vt* to amalgamate
amande [amãd] *nf* (*de l'amandier*) almond; (*de*
noyau de fruit) kernel; **en ~** (*yeux*) almond *cpd*,
almond-shaped
amandier [amãdje] *nm* almond (tree)
amanite [amanit] *nf* (*Bot*) mushroom of the genus
Amanita; **~ tue-mouches** fly agaric
amant [amã] *nm* lover
amarre [amaR] *nf* (*Navig*) (mooring) rope *ou* line;
amarres *nfpl* moorings
amarrer [amaRe] *vt* (*Navig*) to moor; (*gén*) to
make fast
amaryllis [amaRilis] *nf* amaryllis
amas [amɑ] *nm* heap, pile
amasser [amɑse] *vt* to amass; **s'amasser** *vi* to
pile up, accumulate; (*foule*) to gather
amateur [amatœR] *nm* amateur; **en ~** (*péj*)
amateurishly; **musicien/sportif ~** amateur
musician/sportsman; **~ de musique/sport** *etc*
music/sport *etc* lover
amateurisme [amatœRism(ə)] *nm*
amateurism; (*péj*) amateurishness
Amazone [amazon] *nf*: **l'~** the Amazon
amazone [amazɔn] *nf* horsewoman; **en ~** sidesaddle
Amazonie [amazɔni] *nf*: **l'~** Amazonia
ambages [ãbaʒ]: **sans ~** *adv* without beating
about the bush, plainly
ambassade [ãbasad] *nf* embassy; (*mission*): **en ~**
on a mission
ambassadeur, -drice [ãbasadœR, -dRis] *nm/f*
ambassador/ambassadress
ambiance [ãbjãs] *nf* atmosphere; **il y a de l'~**
everyone's having a good time
ambiant, e [ãbjã, -ãt] *adj* (*air, milieu*)
surrounding; (*température*) ambient
ambidextre [ãbidɛkstR(ə)] *adj* ambidextrous
ambigu, ë [ãbigy] *adj* ambiguous
ambiguïté [ãbiguite] *nf* ambiguousness *no pl*,
ambiguity
ambitieux, -euse [ãbisjø, -øz] *adj* ambitious
ambition [ãbisjɔ̃] *nf* ambition
ambitionner [ãbisjɔne] *vt* to have as one's aim
ou ambition
ambivalent, e [ãbivalã, -ãt] *adj* ambivalent
amble [ãbl(ə)] *nm*: **aller l'~** to amble
ambre [ãbR(ə)] *nm*: **~ (jaune)** amber; **~ gris**
ambergris

ambré, e [ãbRe] *adj* (*couleur*) amber; (*parfum*)
ambergris-scented
ambulance [ãbylãs] *nf* ambulance
ambulancier, -ière [ãbylãsje, -jɛR] *nm/f*
ambulanceman/woman (*Brit*), paramedic (*US*)
ambulant, e [ãbylã, -ãt] *adj* travelling,
itinerant
âme [ɑm] *nf* soul; **rendre l'~** to give up the
ghost; **bonne ~** (*aussi ironique*) kind soul; **un**
joueur/tricheur dans l'~ a gambler/cheat
through and through; **~ sœur** kindred spirit
amélioration [ameljɔRasjɔ̃] *nf* improvement
améliorer [ameljɔRe] *vt* to improve;
s'améliorer *vi* to improve, get better
aménagement [amenaʒmã] *nm* fitting out;
laying out; development; **aménagements** *nmpl*
developments; **l'~ du territoire** ≈ town and
country planning; **~s fiscaux** tax adjustments
aménager [amenaʒe] *vt* (*agencer: espace, local*) to
fit out; (: *terrain*) to lay out; (: *quartier, territoire*) to
develop; (*installer*) to fix up, put in; **ferme**
aménagée converted farmhouse
amende [amãd] *nf* fine; **mettre à l'~** to
penalize; **faire ~ honorable** to make amends
amendement [amãdmã] *nm* (*Jur*) amendment
amender [amãde] *vt* (*loi*) to amend; (*terre*) to
enrich; **s'amender** *vi* to mend one's ways
amène [amɛn] *adj* affable; **peu ~** unkind
amener [amne] *vt* to bring; (*causer*) to bring
about; (*baisser: drapeau, voiles*) to strike; **s'amener**
vi (*fam*) to show up, turn up; **~ qn à qch/à faire**
to lead sb to sth/to do
amenuiser [amənɥize]: **s'amenuiser** *vi* to
dwindle; (*chances*) to grow slimmer, lessen
amer, amère [amɛR] *adj* bitter
amèrement [amɛRmã] *adv* bitterly
américain, e [ameRikɛ̃, -ɛn] *adj* American ▷ *nm*
(*Ling*) American (English) ▷ *nm/f*: **Américain, e**
American; **en vedette ~e** as a special guest
(star)
américaniser [ameRikanize] *vt* to Americanize
américanisme [ameRikanism(ə)] *nm*
Americanism
amérindien, ne [ameRɛ̃djɛ̃, -ɛn] *adj*
Amerindian, American Indian
Amérique [ameRik] *nf* America; **l'~ centrale**
Central America; **l'~ latine** Latin America; **l'~**
du Nord North America; **l'~ du Sud** South
America
Amerloque [amɛRlɔk] *nm/f* (*fam*) Yank, Yankee
amerrir [ameRiR] *vi* to land (on the sea); (*capsule*
spatiale) to splash down
amerrissage [ameRisaʒ] *nm* landing (on the
sea); splash-down
amertume [amɛRtym] *nf* bitterness
améthyste [ametist(ə)] *nf* amethyst
ameublement [amœbləmã] *nm* furnishing;
(*meubles*) furniture; **articles d'~** furnishings;
tissus d'~ soft furnishings, furnishing fabrics
ameuter [amøte] *vt* (*badauds*) to draw a crowd
of; (*peuple*) to rouse, stir up
ami, e [ami] *nm/f* friend; (*amant/maîtresse*)

boyfriend/girlfriend ▷ adj: **pays/groupe ~** friendly country/group; **être (très) ~ avec qn** to be (very) friendly with sb; **être ~ de l'ordre** to be a lover of order; **un ~ des arts** a patron of the arts; **un ~ des chiens** a dog lover; **petit ~/ petite ~e** (fam) boyfriend/girlfriend

amiable [amjabl(ə)]: **à l'~** adv (Jur) out of court; (gén) amicably

amiante [amjɑ̃t] nm asbestos

amibe [amib] nf amoeba

amical, e, -aux [amikal, -o] adj friendly ▷ nf (club) association

amicalement [amikalmɑ̃] adv in a friendly way; (formule épistolaire) regards

amidon [amidɔ̃] nm starch

amidonner [amidɔne] vt to starch

amincir [amɛ̃siʀ] vt (objet) to thin (down); **s'amincir** vi to get thinner ou slimmer; **~ qn** to make sb thinner ou slimmer

amincissant, e [amɛ̃sisɑ̃, -ɑ̃t] adj slimming

aminé, e [amine] adj: **acide ~** amino acid

amiral, -aux [amiʀal, -o] nm admiral

amirauté [amiʀote] nf admiralty

amitié [amitje] nf friendship; **prendre en ~** to take a liking to; **faire** ou **présenter ses ~s à qn** to send sb one's best wishes; **~s** (formule épistolaire) (with) best wishes

ammoniac [amɔnjak] nm: **(gaz) ~** ammonia

ammoniaque [amɔnjak] nf ammonia (water)

amnésie [amnezi] nf amnesia

amnésique [amnezik] adj amnesic

Amnesty International [amnɛsti-] n Amnesty International

amniocentèse [amnjosɛ̃tɛz] nf amniocentesis

amnistie [amnisti] nf amnesty

amnistier [amnistje] vt to amnesty

amocher [amɔʃe] vt (fam) to mess up

amoindrir [amwɛ̃dʀiʀ] vt to reduce

amollir [amɔliʀ] vt to soften

amonceler [amɔ̃sle] vt: **s'amonceler** to pile ou heap up; (fig) to accumulate

amoncellement [amɔ̃sɛlmɑ̃] nm piling ou heaping up; accumulation; (tas) pile, heap; accumulation

amont [amɔ̃]: **en ~** adv upstream; (sur une pente) uphill; **en ~ de** prép upstream from; uphill from, above

amoral, e, -aux [amɔʀal, -o] adj amoral

amorce [amɔʀs(ə)] nf (sur un hameçon) bait; (explosif) cap; (tube) primer; (: contenu) priming; (fig: début) beginning(s), start

amorcer [amɔʀse] vt to bait; to prime; (commencer) to begin, start

amorphe [amɔʀf(ə)] adj passive, lifeless

amortir [amɔʀtiʀ] vt (atténuer: choc) to absorb, cushion; (bruit, douleur) to deaden; (Comm: dette) to pay off, amortize; (: mise de fonds, matériel) to write off; **~ un abonnement** to make a season ticket pay (for itself)

amortissable [amɔʀtisabl(ə)] adj (Comm) that can be paid off

amortissement [amɔʀtismɑ̃] nm (de matériel)

writing off; (d'une dette) paying off

amortisseur [amɔʀtisœʀ] nm shock absorber

amour [amuʀ] nm love; (liaison) love affair, love; (statuette etc) cupid; **un ~ de** a lovely little; **faire l'~** to make love

amouracher [amuʀaʃe]: **s'amouracher de** vt (péj) to become infatuated with

amourette [amuʀɛt] nf passing fancy

amoureusement [amuʀøzmɑ̃] adv lovingly

amoureux, -euse [amuʀø, -øz] adj (regard, tempérament) amorous; (vie, problèmes) love cpd; (personne): **~ (de qn)** in love (with sb) ▷ nm/f lover ▷ nmpl courting couple(s); **tomber ~ de qn** to fall in love with sb; **être ~ de qch** to be passionately fond of sth; **un ~ de la nature** a nature lover

amour-propre [amuʀpʀɔpʀ(ə)] (pl **amours-propres**) nm self-esteem

amovible [amɔvibl(ə)] adj removable, detachable

ampère [ɑ̃pɛʀ] nm amp(ere)

ampèremètre [ɑ̃pɛʀmɛtʀ(ə)] nm ammeter

amphétamine [ɑ̃fetamin] nf amphetamine

amphi [ɑ̃fi] nm (Scol fam: = amphithéâtre) lecture hall ou theatre

amphibie [ɑ̃fibi] adj amphibious

amphibien [ɑ̃fibjɛ̃] nm (Zool) amphibian

amphithéâtre [ɑ̃fiteatʀ(ə)] nm amphitheatre; (d'université) lecture hall ou theatre

amphore [ɑ̃fɔʀ] nf amphora

ample [ɑ̃pl(ə)] adj (vêtement) roomy, ample; (gestes, mouvement) broad; (ressources) ample; **jusqu'à plus ~ informé** (Admin) until further details are available

amplement [ɑ̃pləmɑ̃] adv amply; **~ suffisant** ample, more than enough

ampleur [ɑ̃plœʀ] nf scale, size; extent, magnitude

ampli [ɑ̃pli] nm (fam: = amplificateur) amplifier, amp

amplificateur [ɑ̃plifikatœʀ] nm amplifier

amplification [ɑ̃plifikasjɔ̃] nf amplification; expansion, increase

amplifier [ɑ̃plifje] vt (son, oscillation) to amplify; (fig) to expand, increase

amplitude [ɑ̃plityd] nf amplitude; (des températures) range

ampoule [ɑ̃pul] nf (électrique) bulb; (de médicament) phial; (aux mains, pieds) blister

ampoulé, e [ɑ̃pule] adj (péj) pompous, bombastic

amputation [ɑ̃pytasjɔ̃] nf amputation

amputer [ɑ̃pyte] vt (Méd) to amputate; (fig) to cut ou reduce drastically; **~ qn d'un bras/pied** to amputate sb's arm/foot

Amsterdam [amstɛʀdam] n Amsterdam

amulette [amylɛt] nf amulet

amusant, e [amyzɑ̃, -ɑ̃t] adj (divertissant, spirituel) entertaining, amusing; (comique) funny, amusing

amusé, e [amyze] adj amused

amuse-gueule [amyzgœl] nm inv appetizer,

snack

amusement [amyzmɑ̃] *nm* (*voir amusé*) amusement; (*voir amuser*) entertaining, amusing; (*jeu etc*) pastime, diversion

amuser [amyze] *vt* (*divertir*) to entertain, amuse; (*égayer, faire rire*) to amuse; (*détourner l'attention de*) to distract; **s'amuser** *vi* (*jouer*) to amuse o.s., play; (*se divertir*) to enjoy o.s., have fun; (*fig*) to mess around; **s'~ de qch** (*trouver comique*) to find sth amusing; **s'~ avec** *ou* **de qn** (*duper*) to make a fool of sb

amusette [amyzɛt] *nf* idle pleasure, trivial pastime

amuseur [amyzœR] *nm* entertainer; (*péj*) clown

amygdale [amidal] *nf* tonsil; **opérer qn des ~s** to take sb's tonsils out

amygdalite [amidalit] *nf* tonsillitis

AN *sigle f* = **Assemblée nationale**

an [ɑ̃] *nm* year; **être âgé de** *ou* **avoir 3 ans** to be 3 (years old); **en l'an 1980** in the year 1980; **le jour de l'an, le premier de l'an, le nouvel an** New Year's Day

anabolisant [anabɔlizɑ̃] *nm* anabolic steroid ·

anachronique [anakRɔnik] *adj* anachronistic

anachronisme [anakRɔnism(ə)] *nm* anachronism

anaconda [anakɔ̃da] *nm* (*Zool*) anaconda

anaérobie [anaeRɔbi] *adj* anaerobic

anagramme [anagRam] *nf* anagram

ANAH *sigle f* = **Agence nationale pour l'amélioration de l'habitat**

anal, e, -aux [anal, -o] *adj* anal

analgésique [analʒezik] *nm* analgesic

anallergique [analɛRʒik] *adj* hypoallergenic

analogie [analɔʒi] *nf* analogy

analogique [analɔʒik] *adj* (*Logique: raisonnement*) analogical; (*calculateur, montre etc*) analogue; (*Inform*) analog

analogue [analɔg] *adj*: **~ (à)** analogous (to), similar (to)

analphabète [analfabɛt] *nm/f* illiterate

analphabétisme [analfabetism(ə)] *nm* illiteracy

analyse [analiz] *nf* analysis; (*Méd*) test; **faire l'~ de** to analyse; **une ~ approfondie** an in-depth analysis; **en dernière ~** in the last analysis; **avoir l'esprit d'~** to have an analytical turn of mind; **~ grammaticale** grammatical analysis, parsing (*Scol*)

analyser [analize] *vt* to analyse; (*Méd*) to test

analyste [analist(ə)] *nm/f* analyst; (*psychanalyste*) (psycho)analyst

analyste-programmeur, -euse [analist-] (*pl* **analystes-programmeurs, -euses**) *nm/f* systems analyst

analytique [analitik] *adj* analytical

analytiquement [analitikmɑ̃] *adv* analytically

ananas [anana] *nm* pineapple

anarchie [anaRʃi] *nf* anarchy

anarchique [anaRʃik] *adj* anarchic

anarchisme [anaRʃism(ə)] *nm* anarchism

anarchiste [anaRʃist(ə)] *adj* anarchistic ▷ *nm/f* anarchist

anathème [anatɛm] *nm*: **jeter l'~ sur, lancer l'~ contre** to anathematize, curse

anatomie [anatɔmi] *nf* anatomy

anatomique [anatɔmik] *adj* anatomical

ancestral, e, -aux [ɑ̃sɛstRal, -o] *adj* ancestral

ancêtre [ɑ̃sɛtR(ə)] *nm/f* ancestor; (*fig*): **l'~ de** the forerunner of

anche [ɑ̃ʃ] *nf* reed

anchois [ɑ̃ʃwa] *nm* anchovy

ancien, ne [ɑ̃sjɛ̃, -ɛn] *adj* old; (*de jadis, de l'antiquité*) ancient; (*précédent, ex-*) former, old ▷ *nm* (*mobilier ancien*): **l'~** antiques *pl* ▷ *nm/f* (*dans une tribu etc*) elder; **un ~ ministre** a former minister; **mon ~ne voiture** my previous car; **être plus ~ que qn dans une maison** to have been in a firm longer than sb; (*dans la hiérarchie*) to be senior to sb in a firm; **~ combattant** ex-serviceman; **~ (élève)** (*Scol*) ex-pupil (*Brit*), alumnus (*US*)

anciennement [ɑ̃sjɛnmɑ̃] *adv* formerly

ancienneté [ɑ̃sjɛnte] *nf* oldness; antiquity; (*Admin*) (length of) service; seniority

ancrage [ɑ̃kRaʒ] *nm* anchoring; (*Navig*) anchorage; (*Constr*) anchor

ancre [ɑ̃kR(ə)] *nf* anchor; **jeter/lever l'~** to cast/weigh anchor; **à l'~** at anchor

ancrer [ɑ̃kRe] *vt* (*Constr*) to anchor; (*fig*) to fix firmly; **s'ancrer** *vi* (*Navig*) to (cast) anchor

andalou, -ouse [ɑ̃dalu, -uz] *adj* Andalusian

Andalousie [ɑ̃daluzi] *nf*: **l'~** Andalusia

andante [ɑ̃dɑ̃t] *adv, nm* andante

Andes [ɑ̃d] *nfpl*: **les ~** the Andes

Andorre [ɑ̃dɔR] *nf* Andorra

andouille [ɑ̃duj] *nf* (*Culin*) *sausage made of chitterlings*; (*fam*) clot, nit

andouillette [ɑ̃dujɛt] *nf* small andouille

âne [ɑn] *nm* donkey, ass; (*péj*) dunce, fool

anéantir [aneɑ̃tiR] *vt* to annihilate, wipe out; (*fig*) to obliterate, destroy; (*déprimer*) to overwhelm

anecdote [anɛkdɔt] *nf* anecdote

anecdotique [anɛkdɔtik] *adj* anecdotal

anémie [anemi] *nf* anaemia

anémié, e [anemje] *adj* anaemic; (*fig*) enfeebled

anémique [anemik] *adj* anaemic

anémone [anemɔn] *nf* anemone; **~ de mer** sea anemone

ânerie [ɑnRi] *nf* stupidity; (*parole etc*) stupid *ou* idiotic comment *etc*

anéroïde [aneRɔid] *adj voir* **baromètre**

ânesse [ɑnɛs] *nf* she-ass

anesthésie [anɛstezi] *nf* anaesthesia; **sous ~** under anaesthetic; **~ générale/locale** general/local anaesthetic; **faire une ~ locale à qn** to give sb a local anaesthetic

anesthésier [anɛstezje] *vt* to anaesthetize

anesthésique [anɛstezik] *adj* anaesthetic

anesthésiste [anɛstezist(ə)] *nm/f* anaesthetist

anfractuosité [ɑ̃fRaktɥozite] *nf* crevice

ange [ɑ̃ʒ] *nm* angel; **être aux ~s** to be over the moon; **~ gardien** guardian angel

angélique [ɑ̃ʒelik] *adj* angelic(al) ▷ *nf* angelica
angelot [ɑ̃ʒlo] *nm* cherub
angélus [ɑ̃ʒelys] *nm* angelus; (*cloches*) evening bells *pl*
angevin, e [ɑ̃ʒvɛ̃, -in] *adj* of *ou* from Anjou; of *ou* from Angers
angine [ɑ̃ʒin] *nf* sore throat, throat infection; ~ **de poitrine** angina (pectoris)
angiome [ɑ̃ʒjom] *nm* angioma
anglais, e [ɑ̃glɛ, -ɛz] *adj* English ▷ *nm* (*Ling*) English ▷ *nm/f*: **Anglais, e** Englishman/ woman; **les A~** the English; **filer à l'~e** to take French leave; **à l'~e** (*Culin*) boiled
anglaises [ɑ̃glɛz] *nfpl* (*cheveux*) ringlets
angle [ɑ̃gl(ə)] *nm* angle; (*coin*) corner; ~ **droit/ obtus/aigu/mort** right/obtuse/acute/dead angle
Angleterre [ɑ̃glətɛR] *nf*: **l'~** England
anglican, e [ɑ̃glikɑ̃, -an] *adj, nm/f* Anglican
anglicanisme [ɑ̃glikanism(ə)] *nm* Anglicanism
anglicisme [ɑ̃glisism(ə)] *nm* anglicism
angliciste [ɑ̃glisist(ə)] *nm/f* English scholar; (*étudiant*) student of English
anglo... [ɑ̃glɔ] *préfixe* Anglo-, anglo(-)
anglo-américain, e [ɑ̃glɔamerikɛ̃, -ɛn] *adj* Anglo-American ▷ *nm* (*Ling*) American English
anglo-arabe [ɑ̃glɔaRab] *adj* Anglo-Arab
anglo-canadien, ne [ɑ̃glɔkanadjɛ̃, -ɛn] *adj* Anglo-Canadian ▷ *nm* (*Ling*) Canadian English
anglo-normand, e [ɑ̃glɔnɔRmɑ̃, -ɑ̃d] *adj* Anglo-Norman; **les îles ~es** the Channel Islands
anglophile [ɑ̃glɔfil] *adj* anglophilic
anglophobe [ɑ̃glɔfɔb] *adj* anglophobic
anglophone [ɑ̃glɔfɔn] *adj* English-speaking
anglo-saxon, ne [ɑ̃glɔsaksɔ̃, -ɔn] *adj* Anglo-Saxon
angoissant, e [ɑ̃gwasɑ̃, -ɑ̃t] *adj* harrowing
angoisse [ɑ̃gwas] *nf*: **l'~** anguish *no pl*
angoissé, e [ɑ̃gwase] *adj* anguished; (*personne*) full of anxieties *ou* hang-ups (*fam*)
angoisser [ɑ̃gwase] *vt* to harrow, cause anguish to ▷ *vi* to worry, fret
Angola [ɑ̃gɔla] *nm*: **l'~** Angola
angolais, e [ɑ̃gɔlɛ, -ɛz] *adj* Angolan
angora [ɑ̃gɔRa] *adj, nm* angora
anguille [ɑ̃gij] *nf* eel; ~ **de mer** conger (eel); **il y a ~ sous roche** (*fig*) there's something going on, there's something beneath all this
angulaire [ɑ̃gylɛR] *adj* angular
anguleux, -euse [ɑ̃gylø, -øz] *adj* angular
anhydride [anidRid] *nm* anhydride
anicroche [anikRɔʃ] *nf* hitch, snag
animal, e, -aux [animal, -o] *adj, nm* animal; ~ **domestique/sauvage** domestic/wild animal
animalier [animalje] *adj*: **peintre ~** animal painter
animateur, -trice [animatœR, -tRis] *nm/f* (*de télévision*) host; (*de music-hall*) compère; (*de groupe*) leader, organizer; (*Ciné: technicien*) animator
animation [animasjɔ̃] *nf* (*voir animé*) busyness; liveliness; (*Ciné: technique*) animation; **animations** *nfpl* (*activité*) activities; **centre d'~**

≈ community centre
animé, e [anime] *adj* (*rue, lieu*) busy, lively; (*conversation, réunion*) lively, animated; (*opposé à inanimé, aussi Ling*) animate
animer [anime] *vt* (*ville, soirée*) to liven up, enliven; (*mettre en mouvement*) to drive; (*stimuler*) to drive, impel; **s'animer** *vi* to liven up, come to life
animosité [animozite] *nf* animosity
anis [ani] *nm* (*Culin*) aniseed; (*Bot*) anise
anisette [anizɛt] *nf* anisette
Ankara [ɑ̃kaRa] *n* Ankara
ankyloser [ɑ̃kiloze]: **s'ankyloser** *vi* to get stiff
annales [anal] *nfpl* annals
anneau, x [ano] *nm* ring; (*de chaîne*) link; (*Sport*): **exercices aux ~x** ring exercises
année [ane] *nf* year; **souhaiter la bonne ~ à qn** to wish sb a Happy New Year; **tout au long de l'~** all year long; **d'une ~ à l'autre** from one year to the next; **d'~ en ~** from year to year; **l'~ scolaire/fiscale** the school/tax year
année-lumière [anelymjɛR] (*pl* **années-lumières**) *nf* light year
annexe [anɛks(ə)] *adj* (*problème*) related; (*document*) appended; (*salle*) adjoining ▷ *nf* (*bâtiment*) annex(e); (*de document, ouvrage*) annex, appendix; (*jointe à une lettre, un dossier*) enclosure
annexer [anɛkse] *vt* to annex; **s'annexer** (*pays*) to annex; ~ **qch à** (*joindre*) to append sth to
annexion [anɛksjɔ̃] *nf* annexation
annihiler [aniile] *vt* to annihilate
anniversaire [anivɛRsɛR] *nm* birthday; (*d'un événement, bâtiment*) anniversary ▷ *adj*: **jour ~** anniversary
annonce [anɔ̃s] *nf* announcement; (*signe, indice*) sign; (*aussi*: **annonce publicitaire**) advertisement; (*Cartes*) declaration; ~ **personnelle** personal message; **les petites ~s** the small *ou* classified ads
annoncer [anɔ̃se] *vt* to announce; (*être le signe de*) to herald; (*Cartes*) to declare; **je vous annonce que ...** I wish to tell you that ...; **s'annoncer bien/difficile** *vi* to look promising/ difficult; ~ **la couleur** (*fig*) to lay one's cards on the table
annonceur, -euse [anɔ̃sœR, -øz] *nm/f* (*TV, Radio: speaker*) announcer; (*publicitaire*) advertiser
annonciateur, -trice [anɔ̃sjatœR, -tRis] *adj*: ~ **d'un événement** presaging an event
Annonciation [anɔ̃sjasjɔ̃] *nf*: **l'~** (*Rel*) the Annunciation; (*jour*) Annunciation Day
annotation [anɔtasjɔ̃] *nf* annotation
annoter [anɔte] *vt* to annotate
annuaire [anɥɛR] *nm* yearbook, annual; ~ **téléphonique** (telephone) directory, phone book
annuel, le [anɥɛl] *adj* annual, yearly
annuellement [anɥɛlmɑ̃] *adv* annually, yearly
annuité [anɥite] *nf* annual instalment
annulaire [anylɛR] *nm* ring *ou* third finger
annulation [anylasjɔ̃] *nf* cancellation; annulment; quashing, repeal

annuler [anyle] vt (rendez-vous, voyage) to cancel, call off; (mariage) to annul; (jugement) to quash (Brit), repeal (US); (résultats) to declare void; (Math, Physique) to cancel out; **s'annuler** to cancel each other out

anoblir [anɔbliʀ] vt to ennoble

anode [anɔd] nf anode

anodin, e [anɔdɛ̃, -in] adj harmless; (sans importance) insignificant, trivial

anomalie [anɔmali] nf anomaly

ânon [ɑnɔ̃] nm baby donkey; (petit âne) little donkey

ânonner [ɑnɔne] vi, vt to read in a drone; (hésiter) to read in a fumbling manner

anonymat [anɔnima] nm anonymity; **garder l'~** to remain anonymous

anonyme [anɔnim] adj anonymous; (fig) impersonal

anonymement [anɔnimmɑ̃] adv anonymously

anorak [anɔrak] nm anorak

anorexie [anɔʀɛksi] nf anorexia

anorexique [anɔʀɛksik] adj, nm/f anorexic

anormal, e, -aux [anɔrmal, -o] adj abnormal; (insolite) unusual, abnormal

anormalement [anɔrmalmɑ̃] adv abnormally; unusually

ANPE sigle f (= Agence nationale pour l'emploi) national employment agency (functions include job creation)

anse [ɑ̃s] nf handle; (Géo) cove

antagonisme [ɑ̃tagɔnism(ə)] nm antagonism

antagoniste [ɑ̃tagɔnist(ə)] adj antagonistic ▷ nm antagonist

antan [ɑ̃tɑ̃]: **d'~** adj of yesteryear, of long ago

antarctique [ɑ̃taʀktik] adj Antarctic ▷ nm: **l'A~** the Antarctic; **le cercle A~** the Antarctic Circle; **l'océan A~** the Antarctic Ocean

antécédent [ɑ̃tesedɑ̃] nm (Ling) antecedent; **antécédents** nmpl (Méd etc) past history sg; **~s professionnels** record, career to date

antédiluvien, ne [ɑ̃tedilyvjɛ̃, -ɛn] adj (fig) ancient, antediluvian

antenne [ɑ̃tɛn] nf (de radio, télévision) aerial; (d'insecte) antenna (pl -ae), feeler; (poste avancé) outpost; (petite succursale) sub-branch; **sur l'~** on the air; **passer à/avoir l'~** to go/be on the air; **deux heures d'~** two hours' broadcasting time; **hors ~** off the air; **~ chirurgicale** (Mil) advance surgical unit

antépénultième [ɑ̃tepenyltjɛm] adj antepenultimate

antérieur, e [ɑ̃teʀjœʀ] adj (d'avant) previous, earlier; (de devant) front; **~ à** prior ou previous to; **passé/futur ~** (Ling) past/future anterior

antérieurement [ɑ̃teʀjœʀmɑ̃] adv earlier; (précédemment) previously; **~ à** prior ou previous to

antériorité [ɑ̃teʀjɔʀite] nf precedence (in time)

anthologie [ɑ̃tɔlɔʒi] nf anthology

anthracite [ɑ̃tʀasit] nm anthracite ▷ adj: **(gris) ~ charcoal** (grey)

anthropologie [ɑ̃tʀɔpɔlɔʒi] nf anthropology

anthropologue [ɑ̃tʀɔpɔlɔg] nm/f anthropologist

anthropomorphisme [ɑ̃tʀɔpɔmɔʀfism(ə)] nm anthropomorphism

anthropophage [ɑ̃tʀɔpɔfaʒ] adj cannibalistic

anthropophagie [ɑ̃tʀɔpɔfaʒi] nf cannibalism, anthropophagy

anti... [ɑ̃ti] préfixe anti...

antiaérien, ne [ɑ̃tiaeʀjɛ̃, -ɛn] adj anti-aircraft; **abri ~** air-raid shelter

antialcoolique [ɑ̃tialkɔlik] adj anti-alcohol; **ligue ~** temperance league

antiatomique [ɑ̃tiatɔmik] adj: **abri ~** fallout shelter

antibiotique [ɑ̃tibjɔtik] nm antibiotic

antibrouillard [ɑ̃tibʀujaʀ] adj: **phare ~** fog lamp

antibruit [ɑ̃tibʀɥi] adj inv: **mur ~** (sur autoroute) sound-muffling wall

antibuée [ɑ̃tibɥe] adj inv: **dispositif ~** demister; **bombe ~** demister spray

anticancéreux, -euse [ɑ̃tikɑ̃seʀø, -øz] adj cancer cpd

anticasseur, anticasseurs [ɑ̃tikɑsœʀ] adj: **loi/mesure ~(s)** law/measure against damage done by demonstrators

antichambre [ɑ̃tiʃɑ̃bʀ(ə)] nf antechamber, anteroom; **faire ~** to wait (for an audience)

antichar [ɑ̃tiʃaʀ] adj antitank

antichoc [ɑ̃tiʃɔk] adj shockproof

anticipation [ɑ̃tisipasjɔ̃] nf anticipation; (Comm) payment in advance; **par ~** in anticipation, in advance; **livre/film d'~** science fiction book/film

anticipé, e [ɑ̃tisipe] adj (règlement, paiement) early, in advance; (joie etc) anticipated, early; **avec mes remerciements ~s** thanking you in advance ou anticipation

anticiper [ɑ̃tisipe] vt to anticipate, foresee; (paiement) to pay ou make in advance ▷ vi to look ou think ahead; (en racontant) to jump ahead; (prévoir) to anticipate; **~ sur** to anticipate

anticlérical, e, -aux [ɑ̃tikleʀikal, -o] adj anticlerical

anticoagulant, e [ɑ̃tikɔagylɑ̃, -ɑ̃t] adj, nm anticoagulant

anticolonialisme [ɑ̃tikɔlɔnjalism(ə)] nm anticolonialism

anticonceptionnel, le [ɑ̃tikɔ̃sɛpsjɔnɛl] adj contraceptive

anticonformisme [ɑ̃tikɔ̃fɔʀmism(ə)] nm nonconformism

anticonstitutionnel, le [ɑ̃tikɔ̃stitysjɔnɛl] adj unconstitutional

anticorps [ɑ̃tikɔʀ] nm antibody

anticyclone [ɑ̃tisiklɔn] nm anticyclone

antidater [ɑ̃tidate] vt to backdate, predate

antidémocratique [ɑ̃tidemɔkʀatik] adj antidemocratic; (peu démocratique) undemocratic

antidépresseur [ɑ̃tidepʀɛsœʀ] nm antidepressant

antidérapant, e [ɑ̃tideʀapɑ̃, -ɑ̃t] adj nonskid

antidopage [ɑ̃tidɔpaʒ], **antidoping** [ɑ̃tidɔpiŋ] *adj* (*lutte*) antidoping; (*contrôle*) dope *cpd*
antidote [ɑ̃tidɔt] *nm* antidote
antienne [ɑ̃tjɛn] *nf* (*fig*) chant, refrain
antigang [ɑ̃tigɑ̃g] *adj inv*: **brigade** ~ commando unit
antigel [ɑ̃tiʒɛl] *nm* antifreeze
antigène [ɑ̃tiʒɛn] *nm* antigen
antigouvernemental, e, -aux [ɑ̃tiguvɛrnəmɑ̃tal, -o] *adj* antigovernment
Antigua et Barbude [ɑ̃tigaebarbyd] *nf* Antigua and Barbuda
antihistaminique [ɑ̃tiistaminik] *nm* antihistamine
anti-inflammatoire [ɑ̃tiɛ̃flamatwar] *adj* anti-inflammatory
anti-inflationniste [ɑ̃tiɛ̃flasjɔnist(ə)] *adj* anti-inflationary
antillais, e [ɑ̃tijɛ, -ɛz] *adj* West Indian
Antilles [ɑ̃tij] *nfpl*: **les** ~ the West Indies; **les Grandes/Petites** ~ the Greater/Lesser Antilles
antilope [ɑ̃tilɔp] *nf* antelope
antimilitarisme [ɑ̃timilitarism(ə)] *nm* antimilitarism
antimilitariste [ɑ̃timilitarist(ə)] *adj* antimilitarist
antimissile [ɑ̃timisil] *adj* antimissile
antimite, antimites [ɑ̃timit] *adj, nm*: (**produit**) ~(**s**) mothproofer, moth repellent
antimondialisation [ɑ̃timɔ̃djalizasjɔ̃] *nf* anti-globalization
antinucléaire [ɑ̃tinykleɛr] *adj* antinuclear
antioxydant [ɑ̃tiɔksidɑ̃] *nm* antioxidant
antiparasite [ɑ̃tiparazit] *adj* (*Radio, TV*) anti-interference; **dispositif** ~ suppressor
antipathie [ɑ̃tipati] *nf* antipathy
antipathique [ɑ̃tipatik] *adj* unpleasant, disagreeable
antipelliculaire [ɑ̃tipelikylɛr] *adj* anti-dandruff
antiphrase [ɑ̃tifraz] *nf*: **par** ~ ironically
antipodes [ɑ̃tipɔd] *nmpl* (*Géo*): **les** ~ the antipodes; (*fig*): **être aux** ~ **de** to be the opposite extreme of
antipoison [ɑ̃tipwazɔ̃] *adj inv*: **centre** ~ poison centre
antipoliomyélitique [ɑ̃tipɔljɔmjelitik] *adj* polio *cpd*
antiquaire [ɑ̃tikɛr] *nm/f* antique dealer
antique [ɑ̃tik] *adj* antique; (*très vieux*) ancient, antiquated
antiquité [ɑ̃tikite] *nf* (*objet*) antique; **l'A~** Antiquity; **magasin/marchand d'~s** antique shop/dealer
antirabique [ɑ̃tirabik] *adj* rabies *cpd*
antiraciste [ɑ̃tirasist(ə)] *adj* antiracist, antiracialist
antireflet [ɑ̃tirəflɛ] *adj inv* (*verres*) antireflective
antirépublicain, e [ɑ̃tirepyblikɛ̃, -ɛn] *adj* antirepublican
antirides [ɑ̃tirid] *adj* (*crème*) antiwrinkle
antirouille [ɑ̃tiruj] *adj inv*: **peinture** ~ antirust paint; **traitement** ~ rustproofing

antisémite [ɑ̃tisemit] *adj* anti-Semitic
antisémitisme [ɑ̃tisemitism(ə)] *nm* anti-Semitism
antiseptique [ɑ̃tisɛptik] *adj, nm* antiseptic
antisocial, e, -aux [ɑ̃tisɔsjal, -o] *adj* antisocial
antispasmodique [ɑ̃tispasmɔdik] *adj, nm* antispasmodic
antisportif, -ive [ɑ̃tispɔrtif, -iv] *adj* unsporting; (*hostile au sport*) antisport
antitétanique [ɑ̃titetanik] *adj* tetanus *cpd*
antithèse [ɑ̃titɛz] *nf* antithesis
antitrust [ɑ̃titrœst] *adj inv* (*loi, mesures*) antimonopoly
antituberculeux, -euse [ɑ̃titybɛrkylø, -øz] *adj* tuberculosis *cpd*
antitussif, -ive [ɑ̃titysif, -iv] *adj* antitussive, cough *cpd*
antivariolique [ɑ̃tivarjɔlik] *adj* smallpox *cpd*
antiviral, e, -aux [ɑ̃tiviral, o] *adj* (*Méd*) antiviral
antivirus [ɑ̃tivirys] *nm* (*Inform*) antivirus (program)
antivol [ɑ̃tivɔl] *adj, nm*: (**dispositif**) ~ antitheft device; (*pour vélo*) padlock
antonyme [ɑ̃tɔnim] *nm* antonym
antre [ɑ̃tr(ə)] *nm* den, lair
anus [anys] *nm* anus
Anvers [ɑ̃vɛr] *n* Antwerp
anxiété [ɑ̃ksjete] *nf* anxiety
anxieusement [ɑ̃ksjøzmɑ̃] *adv* anxiously
anxieux, -euse [ɑ̃ksjø, -øz] *adj* anxious, worried; **être** ~ **de faire** to be anxious to do
AOC *sigle f* (= *Appellation d'origine contrôlée*) guarantee of quality of wine; *see note*

> ● **AOC**
> ●
> ● *AOC* ("appellation d'origine contrôlée") is
> ● the highest French wine classification. It
> ● indicates that the wine meets strict
> ● requirements concerning vineyard of
> ● origin, type of grape, method of production
> ● and alcoholic strength.

aorte [aɔrt(ə)] *nf* aorta
août [u] *nm* August; *voir aussi* **juillet; Assomption**
aoûtien, ne [ausjɛ̃, -ɛn] *nm/f* August holiday-maker
AP *sigle f* = **Assistance publique**
apaisant, e [apɛzɑ̃, -ɑ̃t] *adj* soothing
apaisement [apɛzmɑ̃] *nm* calming; soothing; (*aussi Pol*) appeasement; **apaisements** *nmpl* soothing reassurances; (*pour calmer*) pacifying words
apaiser [apeze] *vt* (*colère*) to calm, quell, soothe; (*faim*) to appease, assuage; (*douleur*) to soothe; (*personne*) to calm (down), pacify; **s'apaiser** *vi* (*tempête, bruit*) to die down, subside
apanage [apanaʒ] *nm*: **être l'~ de** to be the privilege *ou* prerogative of
aparté [aparte] *nm* (*Théât*) aside; (*entretien*) private conversation; **en** ~ *adv* in an aside (*Brit*);

(entretien) in private

apartheid [apaʀtɛd] nm apartheid

apathie [apati] nf apathy

apathique [apatik] adj apathetic

apatride [apatrid] nm/f stateless person

APCE sigle f (= Agence pour la création d'entreprises) business start-up agency

apercevoir [apɛʀsəvwaʀ] vt to see; **s'apercevoir de** vt to notice; **s'~ que** to notice that; **sans s'en ~** without realizing ou noticing

aperçu, e [apɛʀsy] pp de **apercevoir** ▷ nm (vue d'ensemble) general survey; (intuition) insight

apéritif, -ive [apeʀitif, -iv] adj which stimulates the appetite ▷ nm (boisson) aperitif; (réunion) (pre-lunch ou -dinner) drinks pl; **prendre l'~** to have drinks (before lunch ou dinner) ou an aperitif

apesanteur [apəzɑ̃tœʀ] nf weightlessness

à-peu-près [apøpʀɛ] nm inv (péj) vague approximation

apeuré, e [apœʀe] adj frightened, scared

aphasie [afazi] nf aphasia

aphone [afɔn] adj voiceless

aphorisme [afɔʀism(ə)] nm aphorism

aphrodisiaque [afʀɔdizjak] adj, nm aphrodisiac

aphte [aft(ə)] nm mouth ulcer

aphteuse [aftøz] adj f: **fièvre ~** foot-and-mouth disease

à-pic [apik] nm cliff, drop

apicole [apikɔl] adj beekeeping cpd

apiculteur, -trice [apikyltœʀ, -tʀis] nm/f beekeeper

apiculture [apikyltyʀ] nf beekeeping, apiculture

apitoiement [apitwamɑ̃] nm pity, compassion

apitoyer [apitwaje] vt to move to pity; **~ qn sur qn/qch** to move sb to pity for sb/over sth; **s'~ (sur qn/qch)** to feel pity ou compassion (for sb/over sth)

ap. J.-C. abr (= après Jésus-Christ) AD

APL sigle f (= aide personnalisée au logement) housing benefit

aplanir [aplaniʀ] vt to level; (fig) to smooth away, iron out

aplati, e [aplati] adj flat, flattened

aplatir [aplatiʀ] vt to flatten; **s'aplatir** vi to become flatter; (écrasé) to be flattened; (fig) to lie flat on the ground; (: fam) to fall flat on one's face; (: péj) to grovel

aplomb [aplɔ̃] nm (équilibre) balance, equilibrium; (fig) self-assurance; (: péj) nerve; **d'~** adv steady; (Constr) plumb

APN sigle m (appareil photo(graphique) numérique) digital camera

apocalypse [apɔkalips(ə)] nf apocalypse

apocalyptique [apɔkaliptik] adj (fig) apocalyptic

apocryphe [apɔkʀif] adj apocryphal

apogée [apɔʒe] nm (fig) peak, apogee

apolitique [apɔlitik] adj (indifférent) apolitical; (indépendant) unpolitical, non-political

apologie [apɔlɔʒi] nf praise; (Jur) vindication

apoplexie [apɔplɛksi] nf apoplexy

a posteriori [apɔsteʀjɔʀi] adv after the event, with hindsight, a posteriori

apostolat [apɔstɔla] nm (Rel) apostolate, discipleship; (gén) evangelism

apostolique [apɔstɔlik] adj apostolic

apostrophe [apɔstʀɔf] nf (signe) apostrophe; (appel) interpellation

apostropher [apɔstʀɔfe] vt (interpeller) to shout at, address sharply

apothéose [apɔteoz] nf pinnacle (of achievement); (Mus etc) grand finale

apothicaire [apɔtikɛʀ] nm apothecary

apôtre [apotʀ(ə)] nm apostle, disciple

apparaître [apaʀɛtʀ(ə)] vi to appear ▷ vb copule to appear, seem

apparat [apaʀa] nm: **tenue/dîner d'~** ceremonial dress/dinner

appareil [apaʀɛj] nm (outil, machine) piece of apparatus, device; (électrique etc) appliance; (politique, syndical) machinery; (avion) (aero)plane (Brit), (air)plane (US), aircraft inv; (téléphonique) telephone; (dentier) brace (Brit), braces (US); **~ digestif/reproducteur** digestive/reproductive system ou apparatus; **l'~ productif** the means of production; **qui est à l'~?** who's speaking?; **dans le plus simple ~** in one's birthday suit; **~ (photographique)** camera; **~ numérique** digital camera

appareillage [apaʀɛjaʒ] nm (appareils) equipment; (Navig) casting off, getting under way

appareiller [apaʀeje] vi (Navig) to cast off, get under way ▷ vt (assortir) to match up

appareil photo [apaʀɛjfɔtɔ] (pl **appareils photos**) nm camera

apparemment [apaʀamɑ̃] adv apparently

apparence [apaʀɑ̃s] nf appearance; **malgré les ~s** despite appearances; **en ~** apparently, seemingly

apparent, e [apaʀɑ̃, -ɑ̃t] adj visible; (évident) obvious; (superficiel) apparent; **poutres ~es** exposed beams

apparenté, e [apaʀɑ̃te] adj: **~ à** related to; (fig) similar to

apparenter [apaʀɑ̃te]: **s'apparenter à** vt to be similar to

apparier [apaʀje] vt (gants) to pair, match

appariteur [apaʀitœʀ] nm attendant, porter (in French universities)

apparition [apaʀisjɔ̃] nf appearance; (surnaturelle) apparition; **faire son ~** to appear

appartement [apaʀtəmɑ̃] nm flat (Brit), apartment (US)

appartenance [apaʀtənɑ̃s] nf: **~ à** belonging to, membership of

appartenir [apaʀtəniʀ]: **~ à** vt to belong to; (faire partie de) to belong to, be a member of; **il lui appartient de** it is up to him to

appartiendrai [apaʀtjɛ̃dʀe], **appartiens** etc [apaʀtjɛ̃] vb voir **appartenir**

apparu, e [apaʀy] pp de **apparaître**

appas [apɑ] nmpl (d'une femme) charms

appât [apɑ] *nm* (*Pêche*) bait; (*fig*) lure, bait

appâter [apɑte] *vt* (*hameçon*) to bait; (*poisson, fig*) to lure, entice

appauvrir [apovʀiʀ] *vt* to impoverish; **s'appauvrir** *vi* to grow poorer, become impoverished

appauvrissement [apovʀismɑ̃] *nm* impoverishment

appel [apɛl] *nm* call; (*nominal*) roll call; (: *Scol*) register; (*Mil: recrutement*) call-up; (*Jur*) appeal; **faire ~ à** (*invoquer*) to appeal to; (*avoir recours à*) to call on; (*nécessiter*) to call for, require; **faire** *ou* **interjeter ~** (*Jur*) to appeal, lodge an appeal; **faire l'~** to call the roll; to call the register; **indicatif d'~** call sign; **numéro d'~** (*Tél*) number; **produit d'~** (*Comm*) loss leader; **sans ~** (*fig*) final, irrevocable; **~ d'air** in-draught; **~ d'offres** (*Comm*) invitation to tender; **faire un ~ de phares** to flash one's headlights; **~ (téléphonique)** (tele)phone call

appelé [aple] *nm* (*Mil*) conscript

appeler [aple] *vt* to call, ring; (*Tél*) to call; (*faire venir: médecin etc*) to call, send for; (*fig: nécessiter*) to call for, demand; **~ au secours** to call for help; **~ qn à l'aide** *ou* **au secours** to call to sb to help; **~ qn à un poste/des fonctions** to appoint sb to a post/assign duties to sb; **être appelé à** (*fig*) to be destined to; **~ qn à comparaître** (*Jur*) to summon sb to appear; **en ~ à** to appeal to; **s'appeler**: **elle s'appelle Gabrielle** her name is Gabrielle, she's called Gabrielle; **comment ça s'appelle?** what is it *ou* that called?

appellation [apelɑsjɔ̃] *nf* designation, appellation; **vin d'~ contrôlée** "appellation contrôlée" wine, *wine guaranteed of a certain quality*

appelle *etc* [apɛl] *vb voir* **appeler**

appendice [apɛ̃dis] *nm* appendix

appendicite [apɑ̃disit] *nf* appendicitis

appentis [apɑ̃ti] *nm* lean-to

appert [apɛʀ] *vb*: **il ~ que** it appears that, it is evident that

appesantir [apzɑ̃tiʀ]: **s'appesantir** *vi* to grow heavier; **s'~ sur** (*fig*) to dwell at length on

appétissant, e [apetisɑ̃, -ɑ̃t] *adj* appetizing, mouth-watering

appétit [apeti] *nm* appetite; **couper l'~ à qn** to take away sb's appetite; **bon ~!** enjoy your meal!

applaudimètre [aplodimɛtʀ(ə)] *nm* applause meter

applaudir [aplodiʀ] *vt* to applaud ▷ *vi* to applaud, clap; **~ à** *vt* (*décision*) to applaud, commend

applaudissements [aplodismɑ̃] *nmpl* applause *sg*, clapping *sg*

applicable [aplikabl(ə)] *adj* applicable

applicateur [aplikatœʀ] *nm* applicator

application [aplikɑsjɔ̃] *nf* application; (*d'une loi*) enforcement; **mettre en ~** to implement

applique [aplik] *nf* wall lamp

appliqué, e [aplike] *adj* (*élève etc*) industrious, assiduous; (*science*) applied

appliquer [aplike] *vt* to apply; (*loi*) to enforce; (*donner: gifle, châtiment*) to give; **s'appliquer** *vi* (*élève etc*) to apply o.s.; **s'~ à** (*loi, remarque*) to apply to; **s'~ à faire qch** to apply o.s. to doing sth, take pains to do sth; **s'~ sur** (*coïncider avec*) to fit over

appoint [apwɛ̃] *nm* (extra) contribution *ou* help; **avoir/faire l'~** (*en payant*) to have/give the right change *ou* money; **chauffage d'~** extra heating

appointements [apwɛ̃tmɑ̃] *nmpl* salary *sg*, stipend

appointer [apwɛ̃te] *vt*: **être appointé à l'année/au mois** to be paid yearly/monthly

appontage [apɔ̃taʒ] *nm* landing (*on an aircraft carrier*)

appontement [apɔ̃tmɑ̃] *nm* landing stage, wharf

apponter [apɔ̃te] *vi* (*avion, hélicoptère*) to land

apport [apɔʀ] *nm* supply; (*argent, biens etc*) contribution

apporter [apɔʀte] *vt* to bring; (*preuve*) to give, provide; (*modification*) to make; (*remarque*) to contribute, add

apposer [apoze] *vt* to append; (*sceau etc*) to affix

apposition [apozisjɔ̃] *nf* appending; affixing; (*Ling*): **en ~** in apposition

appréciable [apʀesjabl(ə)] *adj* (*important*) appreciable, significant

appréciation [apʀesjɑsjɔ̃] *nf* appreciation; estimation, assessment; **appréciations** *nfpl* (*avis*) assessment *sg*, appraisal *sg*

apprécier [apʀesje] *vt* to appreciate; (*évaluer*) to estimate, assess; **j'~ais que tu ...** I should appreciate (it) if you ...

appréhender [apʀeɑ̃de] *vt* (*craindre*) to dread; (*arrêter*) to apprehend; **~ que** to fear that; **~ de faire** to dread doing

appréhensif, -ive [apʀeɑ̃sif, -iv] *adj* apprehensive

appréhension [apʀeɑ̃sjɔ̃] *nf* apprehension

apprendre [apʀɑ̃dʀ(ə)] *vt* to learn; (*événement, résultats*) to learn of, hear of; **~ qch à qn** (*informer*) to tell sb (of) sth; (*enseigner*) to teach sb sth; **tu me l'apprends!** that's news to me!; **~ à faire qch** to learn to do sth; **~ à qn à faire qch** to teach sb to do sth

apprenti, e [apʀɑ̃ti] *nm/f* apprentice; (*fig*) novice, beginner

apprentissage [apʀɑ̃tisaʒ] *nm* learning; (*Comm, Scol: période*) apprenticeship; **école** *ou* **centre d'~** training school *ou* centre; **faire l'~ de qch** (*fig*) to be initiated into sth

apprêt [apʀɛ] *nm* (*sur un cuir, une étoffe*) dressing; (*sur un mur*) size; (*sur un papier*) finish; **sans ~** (*fig*) without artifice, unaffectedly

apprêté, e [apʀete] *adj* (*fig*) affected

apprêter [apʀete] *vt* to dress, finish; **s'apprêter** *vi*: **s'~ à qch/à faire qch** to prepare for sth/for doing sth

appris, e [apʀi, -iz] *pp de* **apprendre**

apprivoisé, e [apʀivwaze] *adj* tame, tamed

apprivoiser [aprivwaze] *vt* to tame

approbateur, -trice [aprɔbatœr, -tris] *adj* approving

approbatif, -ive [aprɔbatif, -iv] *adj* approving

approbation [aprɔbasjɔ̃] *nf* approval; **digne d'~** (*conduite, travail*) praiseworthy, commendable

approchant, e [aprɔʃɑ̃, -ɑ̃t] *adj* similar, close; **quelque chose d'~** something similar

approche [aprɔʃ] *nf* approaching; (*arrivée, attitude*) approach; **approches** *nfpl* (*abords*) surroundings; **à l'~ du bateau/de l'ennemi** as the ship/enemy approached *ou* drew near; **l'~ d'un problème** the approach to a problem; **travaux d'~** (*fig*) manoeuvrings

approché, e [aprɔʃe] *adj* approximate

approcher [aprɔʃe] *vi* to approach, come near ▷ *vt* (*vedette, artiste*) to come close to, approach; (*rapprocher*): **~ qch (de qch)** to bring *ou* put *ou* move sth near (to sth); **~ de** *vt* to draw near to; (*quantité, moment*) to approach; **s'approcher de** *vt* to approach, go *ou* come *ou* move near to; **approchez-vous** come *ou* go nearer

approfondi, e [aprɔfɔ̃di] *adj* thorough, detailed

approfondir [aprɔfɔ̃dir] *vt* to deepen; (*question*) to go further into; **sans ~** without going too deeply into it

appropriation [aprɔprijasjɔ̃] *nf* appropriation

approprié, e [aprɔprije] *adj*: **~ (à)** appropriate (to), suited (to)

approprier [aprɔprije] *vt* (*adapter*) adapt; **s'approprier** *vt* to appropriate, take over

approuver [apruve] *vt* to agree with; (*autoriser: loi, projet*) to approve, pass; (*trouver louable*) to approve of; **je vous approuve entièrement/ne vous approuve pas** I agree with you entirely/ don't agree with you; **lu et approuvé** (read and) approved

approvisionnement [aprɔvizjɔnmɑ̃] *nm* supplying; (*provisions*) supply, stock

approvisionner [aprɔvizjɔne] *vt* to supply; (*compte bancaire*) to pay funds into; **~ qn en** to supply sb with; **s'approvisionner** *vi*: **s'~ dans un certain magasin/au marché** to shop in a certain shop/at the market; **s'~ en** to stock up with

approximatif, -ive [aprɔksimatif, -iv] *adj* approximate, rough; (*imprécis*) vague

approximation [aprɔksimasjɔ̃] *nf* approximation

approximativement [aprɔksimativmɑ̃] *adv* approximately, roughly; vaguely

appt *abr* = **appartement**

appui [apɥi] *nm* support; **prendre ~ sur** to lean on; (*objet*) to rest on; **point d'~** fulcrum; (*fig*) something to lean on; **à l'~ de** (*pour prouver*) in support of; **à l'~** *adv* to support one's argument; **l'~ de la fenêtre** the windowsill, the window ledge

appuie *etc* [apɥi] *vb voir* **appuyer**

appui-tête, appuie-tête [apɥitɛt] *nm inv* headrest

appuyé, e [apɥije] *adj* (*regard*) meaningful; (: *insistant*) intent, insistent; (*excessif: politesse, compliment*) exaggerated, overdone

appuyer [apɥije] *vt* (*poser*): **~ qch sur/contre/à** to lean *ou* rest sth on/against/on; (*soutenir: personne, demande*) to support, back (up) ▷ *vi*: **~ sur** (*bouton, frein*) to press, push; (*mot, détail*) to stress, emphasize; (*chose: peser sur*) to rest (heavily) on, press against; **s'appuyer sur** *vt* to lean on; (*compter sur*) to rely on; **s'~ sur qn** to lean on sb; **~ contre** (*toucher: mur, porte*) to lean *ou* rest against; **~ à droite** *ou* **sur sa droite** to bear (to the) right; **~ sur le champignon** to put one's foot down

apr. *abr* = **après**

âpre [ɑpr(ə)] *adj* acrid, pungent; (*fig*) harsh; (*lutte*) bitter; **~ au gain** grasping, greedy

après [aprɛ] *prép* after ▷ *adv* afterwards; **deux heures ~** two hours later; **~ qu'il est parti/ avoir fait** after he left/having done; **courir ~ qn** to run after sb; **crier ~ qn** to shout at sb; **être toujours ~ qn** (*critiquer etc*) to be always on at sb; **~ quoi** after which; **d'~** *prép* (*selon*) according to; **d'~ lui** according to him; **d'~ moi** in my opinion; **~ coup** *adv* after the event, afterwards; **~ tout** *adv* (*au fond*) after all; **et (puis) ~?** so what?

après-demain [aprɛdmɛ̃] *adv* the day after tomorrow

après-guerre [aprɛgɛr] *nm* post-war years *pl*; **d'~** *adj* post-war

après-midi [aprɛmidi] *nm ou f inv* afternoon

après-rasage [aprɛrazaʒ] *nm inv*: **(lotion) ~** after-shave (lotion)

après-shampooing [aprɛʃɑ̃pwɛ̃] *nm inv* conditioner

après-ski [aprɛski] *nm inv* (*chaussure*) snow boot; (*moment*) après-ski

après-soleil [aprɛsɔlej] *adj inv* after-sun *cpd* ▷ *nm* after-sun cream *ou* lotion

après-vente [aprɛvɑ̃t] *adj inv* after-sales *cpd*

âpreté [aprəte] *nf* (*voir âpre*) pungency; harshness; bitterness

à-propos [aprɔpo] *nm* (*d'une remarque*) aptness; **faire preuve d'~** to show presence of mind, do the right thing; **avec ~** suitably, aptly

apte [apt(ə)] *adj*: **~ à qch/faire qch** capable of sth/doing sth; **~ (au service)** (*Mil*) fit (for service)

aptitude [aptityd] *nf* ability, aptitude

apurer [apyre] *vt* (*Comm*) to clear

aquaculture [akwakyltyr] *nf* fish farming

aquaplanage [akwaplanaʒ] *nm* (*Auto*) aquaplaning

aquaplane [akwaplan] *nm* (*planche*) aquaplane; (*sport*) aquaplaning

aquaplaning [akwaplaniŋ] *nm* aquaplaning

aquarelle [akwarɛl] *nf* (*tableau*) watercolour (*Brit*), watercolor (*US*); (*genre*) watercolo(u)rs *pl*, aquarelle

aquarelliste [akwarelist(ə)] *nm/f* painter in watercolo(u)rs

aquarium [akwaʀjɔm] *nm* aquarium
aquatique [akwatik] *adj* aquatic, water *cpd*
aqueduc [akdyk] *nm* aqueduct
aqueux, -euse [akø, -øz] *adj* aqueous
aquilin [akilɛ̃] *adj m*: **nez ~** aquiline nose
AR *sigle m* = **accusé de réception; lettre/paquet avec AR** ≈ recorded delivery letter/parcel; (*Aviat, Rail etc*) = **aller (et) retour** ▷ *abr* (*Auto*) = **arrière**
arabe [aʀab] *adj* Arabic; (*désert, cheval*) Arabian; (*nation, peuple*) Arab ▷ *nm* (*Ling*) Arabic ▷ *nm/f*: **Arabe** Arab
arabesque [aʀabɛsk(ə)] *nf* arabesque
Arabie [aʀabi] *nf*: **l'~** Arabia; **l'~ Saoudite** *ou* **Séoudite** Saudi Arabia
arable [aʀabl(ə)] *adj* arable
arachide [aʀaʃid] *nf* groundnut (plant); (*graine*) peanut, groundnut
araignée [aʀeɲe] *nf* spider; **~ de mer** spider crab
araser [aʀaze] *vt* to level; (*en rabotant*) to plane (down)
aratoire [aʀatwaʀ] *adj*: **instrument ~** ploughing implement
arbalète [aʀbalɛt] *nf* crossbow
arbitrage [aʀbitʀaʒ] *nm* refereeing; umpiring; arbitration
arbitraire [aʀbitʀɛʀ] *adj* arbitrary
arbitre [aʀbitʀ(ə)] *nm* (*Sport*) referee; (: *Tennis, Cricket*) umpire; (*fig*) arbiter, judge; (*Jur*) arbitrator
arbitrer [aʀbitʀe] *vt* to referee; to umpire; to arbitrate
arborer [aʀbɔʀe] *vt* to bear, display; (*avec ostentation*) to sport
arborescence [aʀbɔʀesɑ̃s] *nf* tree structure
arboricole [aʀbɔʀikɔl] *adj* (*animal*) arboreal; (*technique*) arboricultural
arboriculture [aʀbɔʀikyltyʀ] *nf* arboriculture; **~ fruitière** fruit (tree) growing
arbre [aʀbʀ(ə)] *nm* tree; (*Tech*) shaft; **~ à cames** (*Auto*) camshaft; **~ fruitier** fruit tree; **~ généalogique** family tree; **~ de Noël** Christmas tree; **~ de transmission** (*Auto*) driveshaft
arbrisseau, x [aʀbʀiso] *nm* shrub
arbuste [aʀbyst(ə)] *nm* small shrub, bush
arc [aʀk] *nm* (*arme*) bow; (*Géom*) arc; (*Archit*) arch; **~ de cercle** arc of a circle; **en ~ de cercle** *adj* semi-circular
arcade [aʀkad] *nf* arch(way); **~s** arcade *sg*, arches; **~ sourcilière** arch of the eyebrows
arcanes [aʀkan] *nmpl* mysteries
arc-boutant [aʀkbutɑ̃] (*pl* **arcs-boutants**) *nm* flying buttress
arc-bouter [aʀkbute]: **s'arc-bouter** *vi*: **s'~ contre** to lean *ou* press against
arceau, x [aʀso] *nm* (*métallique etc*) hoop
arc-en-ciel [aʀkɑ̃sjɛl] (*pl* **arcs-en-ciel**) *nm* rainbow
archaïque [aʀkaik] *adj* archaic
archaïsme [aʀkaism(ə)] *nm* archaism
archange [aʀkɑ̃ʒ] *nm* archangel

arche [aʀʃ(ə)] *nf* arch; **~ de Noé** Noah's Ark
archéologie [aʀkeɔlɔʒi] *nf* arch(a)eology
archéologique [aʀkeɔlɔʒik] *adj* arch(a)eological
archéologue [aʀkeɔlɔg] *nm/f* arch(a)eologist
archer [aʀʃe] *nm* archer
archet [aʀʃɛ] *nm* bow
archevêché [aʀʃəveʃe] *nm* archbishopric; (*palais*) archbishop's palace
archevêque [aʀʃəvɛk] *nm* archbishop
archi... [aʀʃi] *préfixe* (*très*) dead, extra
archibondé, e [aʀʃibɔ̃de] *adj* chock-a-block (*Brit*), packed solid
archiduc [aʀʃidyk] *nm* archduke
archiduchesse [aʀʃidyʃɛs] *nf* archduchess
archipel [aʀʃipɛl] *nm* archipelago
archisimple [aʀʃisɛ̃pl(ə)] *adj* dead easy *ou* simple
architecte [aʀʃitɛkt(ə)] *nm* architect
architectural, e, -aux [aʀʃitɛktyʀal, -o] *adj* architectural
architecture [aʀʃitɛktyʀ] *nf* architecture
archive [aʀʃiv] *nf* file; **archives** *nfpl* archives
archiver [aʀʃive] *vt* to file
archiviste [aʀʃivist(ə)] *nm/f* archivist
arçon [aʀsɔ̃] *nm voir* **cheval**
arctique [aʀktik] *adj* Arctic ▷ *nm*: **l'A~** the Arctic; **le cercle A~** the Arctic Circle; **l'océan A~** the Arctic Ocean
ardemment [aʀdamɑ̃] *adv* ardently, fervently
ardent, e [aʀdɑ̃, -ɑ̃t] *adj* (*soleil*) blazing; (*fièvre*) raging; (*amour*) ardent, passionate; (*prière*) fervent
ardeur [aʀdœʀ] *nf* blazing heat; (*fig*) fervour, ardour
ardoise [aʀdwaz] *nf* slate
ardu, e [aʀdy] *adj* arduous, difficult; (*pente*) steep, abrupt
are [aʀ] *nm* are, 100 square metres
arène [aʀɛn] *nf* arena; (*fig*): **l'~ politique** the political arena; **arènes** *nfpl* bull-ring *sg*
arête [aʀɛt] *nf* (*de poisson*) bone; (*d'une montagne*) ridge; (*Géom etc*) edge (*where two faces meet*)
arg. *abr* = **argus**
argent [aʀʒɑ̃] *nm* (*métal*) silver; (*monnaie*) money; (*couleur*) silver; **en avoir pour son ~** to get value for money; **gagner beaucoup d'~** to earn a lot of money; **~ comptant** (hard) cash; **~ liquide** ready money, (ready) cash; **~ de poche** pocket money
argenté, e [aʀʒɑ̃te] *adj* silver(y); (*métal*) silver-plated
argenter [aʀʒɑ̃te] *vt* to silver(-plate)
argenterie [aʀʒɑ̃tʀi] *nf* silverware; (*en métal argenté*) silver plate
argentin, e [aʀʒɑ̃tɛ̃, -in] *adj* Argentinian, Argentine ▷ *nm/f*: **Argentin, e** Argentinian, Argentine
Argentine [aʀʒɑ̃tin] *nf*: **l'~** Argentina, the Argentine
argentique [aʀʒɑ̃tik] *adj* (*appareil-photo*) film *cpd*
argile [aʀʒil] *nf* clay

argileux, -euse [aʀʒilø, -øz] *adj* clayey
argot [aʀgo] *nm* slang; *see note*

● **ARGOT**
●
● *Argot* was the term originally used to
● describe the jargon of the criminal
● underworld, characterized by colourful
● images and distinctive intonation and
● designed to confuse the outsider. Some
● French authors write in *argot* and so have
● helped it spread and grow. More generally,
● the special vocabulary used by any social or
● professional group is also known as *argot*.

argotique [aʀgotik] *adj* slang *cpd*; *(très familier)*
slangy
arguer [aʀgɥe]: ~ **de** *vt* to put forward as a
pretext *ou* reason; ~ **que** to argue that
argument [aʀgymɑ̃] *nm* argument
argumentaire [aʀgymɑ̃tɛʀ] *nm* list of sales
points; *(brochure)* sales leaflet
argumentation [aʀgymɑ̃tasjɔ̃] *nf (fait
d'argumenter)* arguing; *(ensemble des arguments)*
argument
argumenter [aʀgymɑ̃te] *vi* to argue
argus [aʀgys] *nm* guide to second-hand car etc prices
arguties [aʀgysi] *nfpl* pettifoggery *sg* (Brit),
quibbles
aride [aʀid] *adj* arid
aridité [aʀidite] *nf* aridity
arien, ne [aʀjɛ̃, -ɛn] *adj* Arian
aristocrate [aʀistokʀat] *nm/f* aristocrat
aristocratie [aʀistokʀasi] *nf* aristocracy
aristocratique [aʀistokʀatik] *adj* aristocratic
arithmétique [aʀitmetik] *adj* arithmetic(al)
▷ *nf* arithmetic
armada [aʀmada] *nf (fig)* army
armagnac [aʀmaɲak] *nm* armagnac
armateur [aʀmatœʀ] *nm* shipowner
armature [aʀmatyʀ] *nf* framework; *(de tente etc)*
frame; *(de corset)* bone; *(de soutien-gorge)* wiring
arme [aʀm(ə)] *nf* weapon; *(section de l'armée)*
arm; **armes** *nfpl* weapons, arms; *(blason)* (coat
of) arms; **les ~s** *(profession)* soldiering *sg*; **à ~s
égales** on equal terms; **en ~s** up in arms;
passer par les ~s to execute (by firing squad);
prendre/présenter les ~s to take up/present
arms; **se battre à l'~ blanche** to fight with
blades; ~ **à feu** firearm; ~**s de destruction
massive** weapons of mass destruction
armé, e [aʀme] *adj* armed; ~ **de** armed with
armée [aʀme] *nf* army; ~ **de l'air** Air Force; **l'~
du Salut** the Salvation Army; ~ **de terre** Army
armement [aʀməmɑ̃] *nm (matériel)* arms *pl*,
weapons *pl*; *(: d'un pays)* arms *pl*, armament;
(action d'équiper un navire) fitting out; ~**s
nucléaires** nuclear armaments; **course aux ~s**
arms race
Arménie [aʀmeni] *nf*: **l'~** Armenia
arménien, ne [aʀmenjɛ̃, -ɛn] *adj* Armenian
▷ *nm (Ling)* Armenian ▷ *nm/f*: **Arménien, ne**
Armenian

armer [aʀme] *vt* to arm; *(arme à feu)* to cock;
(appareil-photo) to wind on; ~ **qch de** to fit sth
with; *(renforcer)* to reinforce sth with; ~ **qn de** to
arm *ou* equip sb with; **s'armer de** to arm o.s.
with
armistice [aʀmistis] *nm* armistice; **l'A~**
≈ Remembrance (Brit) *ou* Veterans (US) Day
armoire [aʀmwaʀ] *nf* (tall) cupboard; *(penderie)*
wardrobe (Brit), closet (US); ~ **à pharmacie**
medicine chest
armoiries [aʀmwaʀi] *nfpl* coat of arms *sg*
armure [aʀmyʀ] *nf* armour *no pl*, suit of armour
armurerie [aʀmyʀʀi] *nf* arms factory; *(magasin)*
gunsmith's (shop)
armurier [aʀmyʀje] *nm* gunsmith; *(Mil, d'armes
blanches)* armourer
ARN *sigle m* (= *acide ribonucléique*) RNA
arnaque [aʀnak] *nf*: **de l'~** daylight robbery
arnaquer [aʀnake] *vt* to do (*fam*), swindle; **se
faire ~** to be had (*fam*) *ou* done
arnaqueur [aʀnakœʀ] *nm* swindler
arnica [aʀnika] *nm*: **(teinture d')~** arnica
arobase [aʀobaz] *nf (Inform)* "at" symbol, @;
"paul ~ société point fr" "paul at société dot fr"
aromates [aʀomat] *nmpl* seasoning *sg*, herbs
(and spices)
aromathérapie [aʀomateʀapi] *nf* aromatherapy
aromatique [aʀomatik] *adj* aromatic
aromatisé, e [aʀomatize] *adj* flavoured
arôme [aʀom] *nm* aroma; *(d'une fleur etc)*
fragrance
arpège [aʀpɛʒ] *nm* arpeggio
arpentage [aʀpɑ̃taʒ] *nm* (land) surveying
arpenter [aʀpɑ̃te] *vt* to pace up and down
arpenteur [aʀpɑ̃tœʀ] *nm* land surveyor
arqué, e [aʀke] *adj* arched; *(jambes)* bow *cpd*,
bandy
arr. *abr* = **arrondissement**
arrachage [aʀaʃaʒ] *nm*: ~ **des mauvaises
herbes** weeding
arraché [aʀaʃe] *nm (Sport)* snatch; **obtenir à l'~**
(fig) to snatch
arrache-pied [aʀaʃpje]: **d'~** *adv* relentlessly
arracher [aʀaʃe] *vt* to pull out; *(page etc)* to tear
off, tear out; *(déplanter: légume)* to lift; *(: herbe,
souche)* to pull up; *(bras etc: par explosion)* to blow
off; *(: par accident)* to tear off; **s'arracher** *vt*
(article très recherché) to fight over; ~ **qch à qn** to
snatch sth from sb; *(fig)* to wring sth out of sb,
wrest sth from sb; ~ **qn à** *(solitude, rêverie)* to drag
sb out of; *(famille etc)* to tear *ou* wrench sb away
from; **se faire ~ une dent** to have a tooth out *ou*
pulled (US); **s'~ de** *(lieu)* to tear o.s. away from;
(habitude) to force o.s. out of
arraisonner [aʀezone] *vt* to board and search
arrangeant, e [aʀɑ̃ʒɑ̃, -ɑ̃t] *adj* accommodating,
obliging
arrangement [aʀɑ̃ʒmɑ̃] *nm* arrangement
arranger [aʀɑ̃ʒe] *vt* to arrange; *(réparer)* to fix,
put right; *(régler)* to settle, sort out; *(convenir à)* to
suit, be convenient for; **s'arranger** *vi (se mettre*

d'accord) to come to an agreement *ou* arrangement; (*s'améliorer: querelle, situation*) to be sorted out; (*se débrouiller*): **s'~ pour que ...** to arrange things so that ...; **je vais m'~** I'll manage; **ça va s'~** it'll sort itself out; **s'~ pour faire** to make sure that *ou* see to it that one can do

arrangeur [aʀɑ̃ʒœʀ] *nm* (*Mus*) arranger

arrestation [aʀɛstasjɔ̃] *nf* arrest

arrêt [aʀɛ] *nm* stopping; (*de bus etc*) stop; (*Jur*) judgment, decision; (*Football*) save; **arrêts** *nmpl* (*Mil*) arrest *sg*; **être à l'~** to be stopped, have come to a halt; **rester** *ou* **tomber en ~ devant** to stop short in front of; **sans ~** without stopping, non-stop; (*fréquemment*) continually; **~ d'autobus** bus stop; **~ facultatif** request stop; **~ de mort** capital sentence; **~ de travail** stoppage (of work)

arrêté, e [aʀete] *adj* (*idées*) firm, fixed ▷ *nm* order, decree; **~ municipal** ≈ bylaw, byelaw

arrêter [aʀete] *vt* to stop; (*chauffage etc*) to turn off, switch off; (*Comm: compte*) to settle; (*Couture: point*) to fasten off; (*fixer: date etc*) to appoint, decide on; (*criminel, suspect*) to arrest; **s'arrêter** *vi* to stop; (*s'interrompre*) to stop o.s.; **~ de faire** to stop doing; **arrête de te plaindre** stop complaining; **ne pas ~ de faire** to keep on doing; **s'~ de faire** to stop doing; **s'~ sur** (*choix, regard*) to fall on

arrhes [aʀ] *nfpl* deposit *sg*

arrière [aʀjɛʀ] *nm* back; (*Sport*) fullback ▷ *adj inv*: **siège/roue ~** back *ou* rear seat/wheel; **arrières** *nmpl* (*fig*): **protéger ses ~s** to protect the rear; **à l'~** *adv* behind, at the back; **en ~** *adv* behind; (*regarder*) back, behind; (*tomber, aller*) backwards; **en ~ de** *prép* behind

arriéré, e [aʀjere] *adj* (*péj*) backward ▷ *nm* (*d'argent*) arrears *pl*

arrière-boutique [aʀjɛʀbutik] *nf* back shop

arrière-cour [aʀjɛʀkuʀ] *nf* backyard

arrière-cuisine [aʀjɛʀkɥizin] *nf* scullery

arrière-garde [aʀjɛʀgaʀd(ə)] *nf* rearguard

arrière-goût [aʀjɛʀgu] *nm* aftertaste

arrière-grand-mère [aʀjɛʀgʀɑ̃mɛʀ] (*pl* **-s**) *nf* great-grandmother

arrière-grand-père [aʀjɛʀgʀɑ̃pɛʀ] (*pl* **arrière-grands-pères**) *nm* great-grandfather

arrière-grands-parents [aʀjɛʀgʀɑ̃paʀɑ̃] *nmpl* great-grandparents

arrière-pays [aʀjɛʀpei] *nm inv* hinterland

arrière-pensée [aʀjɛʀpɑ̃se] *nf* ulterior motive; (*doute*) mental reservation

arrière-petite-fille [aʀjɛʀpətitfij] (*pl* **arrière-petites-filles**) *nf* great-granddaughter

arrière-petit-fils [aʀjɛʀpətifis] (*pl* **arrière-petits-fils**) *nm* great-grandson

arrière-petits-enfants [aʀjɛʀpətizɑ̃fɑ̃] *nmpl* great-grandchildren

arrière-plan [aʀjɛʀplɑ̃] *nm* background; **d'~** *adj* (*Inform*) background *cpd*

arriérer [aʀjere]: **s'arriérer** *vi* (*Comm*) to fall into arrears

arrière-saison [aʀjɛʀsɛzɔ̃] *nf* late autumn

arrière-salle [aʀjɛʀsal] *nf* back room

arrière-train [aʀjɛʀtʀɛ̃] *nm* hindquarters *pl*

arrimer [aʀime] *vt* to stow; (*fixer*) to secure, fasten securely

arrivage [aʀivaʒ] *nm* arrival

arrivant, e [aʀivɑ̃, -ɑ̃t] *nm/f* newcomer

arrivée [aʀive] *nf* arrival; (*ligne d'arrivée*) finish; **~ d'air/de gaz** air/gas inlet; **courrier à l'~** incoming mail; **à mon ~** when I arrived

arriver [aʀive] *vi* to arrive; (*survenir*) to happen, occur; **j'arrive!** (I'm) just coming!; **il arrive à Paris à 8 h** he gets to *ou* arrives in Paris at 8; **~ à destination** to arrive at one's destination; **~ à** (*atteindre*) to reach; **~ à (faire) qch** (*réussir*) to manage (to do) sth; **~ à échéance** to fall due; **en ~ à faire ...** to end up doing ..., get to the point of doing ...; **il arrive que ...** it happens that ...; **il lui arrive de faire ...** he sometimes does ...

arrivisme [aʀivism(ə)] *nm* ambition, ambitiousness

arriviste [aʀivist(ə)] *nm/f* go-getter

arrogance [aʀɔgɑ̃s] *nf* arrogance

arrogant, e [aʀɔgɑ̃, -ɑ̃t] *adj* arrogant

arroger [aʀɔʒe]: **s'arroger** *vt* to assume (without right); **s'~ le droit de ...** to assume the right to ...

arrondi, e [aʀɔ̃di] *adj* round ▷ *nm* roundness

arrondir [aʀɔ̃diʀ] *vt* (*forme, objet*) to round; (*somme*) to round off; **s'arrondir** *vi* to become round(ed); **~ ses fins de mois** to supplement one's pay

arrondissement [aʀɔ̃dismɑ̃] *nm* (*Admin*) ≈ district

arrosage [aʀozaʒ] *nm* watering; **tuyau d'~** hose(pipe)

arroser [aʀoze] *vt* to water; (*victoire etc*) to celebrate (over a drink); (*Culin*) to baste

arroseur [aʀozœʀ] *nm* (*tourniquet*) sprinkler

arroseuse [aʀozøz] *nf* water cart

arrosoir [aʀozwaʀ] *nm* watering can

arrt *abr* = **arrondissement**

arsenal, -aux [aʀsənal, -o] *nm* (*Navig*) naval dockyard; (*Mil*) arsenal; (*fig*) gear, paraphernalia

art [aʀ] *nm* art; **avoir l'~ de faire** (*fig: personne*) to have a talent for doing; **les ~s** the arts; **livre/critique d'~** art book/ critic; **objet d'~** objet d'art; **~ dramatique** dramatic art; **~s martiaux** martial arts; **~s et métiers** applied arts and crafts; **~s ménagers** home economics *sg*; **~s plastiques** plastic arts

art. *abr* = **article**

artère [aʀtɛʀ] *nf* (*Anat*) artery; (*rue*) main road

artériel, le [aʀteʀjɛl] *adj* arterial

artériosclérose [aʀteʀjoskleʀoz] *nf* arteriosclerosis

arthrite [aʀtʀit] *nf* arthritis

arthrose [aʀtʀoz] *nf* (degenerative) osteoarthritis

artichaut [aʀtiʃo] *nm* artichoke

article [aʀtikl(ə)] *nm* article; (*Comm*) item, article; **faire l'~** (*Comm*) to do one's sales spiel; **faire l'~ de** (*fig*) to sing the praises of; **à l'~ de la mort** at the point of death; **~ défini/indéfini** definite/indefinite article; **~ de fond** (*Presse*) feature article; **~s de bureau** office equipment; **~s de voyage** travel goods *ou* items

articulaire [aʀtikylɛʀ] *adj* of the joints, articular

articulation [aʀtikylɑsjɔ̃] *nf* articulation; (*Anat*) joint

articulé, e [aʀtikyle] *adj* (*membre*) jointed; (*poupée*) with moving joints

articuler [aʀtikyle] *vt* to articulate; **s'articuler (sur)** *vi* (*Anat, Tech*) to articulate (with); **s'~ autour de** (*fig*) to centre around *ou* on, turn on

artifice [aʀtifis] *nm* device, trick

artificiel, le [aʀtifisjɛl] *adj* artificial

artificiellement [aʀtifisjɛlmɑ̃] *adv* artificially

artificier [aʀtifisje] *nm* pyrotechnist

artificieux, -euse [aʀtifisjø, -øz] *adj* guileful, deceitful

artillerie [aʀtijʀi] *nf* artillery, ordnance

artilleur [aʀtijœʀ] *nm* artilleryman, gunner

artisan [aʀtizɑ̃] *nm* artisan, (self-employed) craftsman; **l'~ de la victoire/du malheur** the architect of victory/of the disaster

artisanal, e, -aux [aʀtizanal, -o] *adj* of *ou* made by craftsmen; (*péj*) cottage industry *cpd*, unsophisticated

artisanalement [aʀtizanalmɑ̃] *adv* by craftsmen

artisanat [aʀtizana] *nm* arts and crafts *pl*

artiste [aʀtist(ə)] *nm/f* artist; (*Théât, Mus*) artist, performer; (: *de variétés*) entertainer

artistique [aʀtistik] *adj* artistic

artistiquement [aʀtistikmɑ̃] *adv* artistically

aryen, ne [aʀjɛ̃, -ɛn] *adj* Aryan

AS *sigle fpl* (*Admin*) = **assurances sociales** ▷ *sigle f* (*Sport*: = *Association sportive*) ≈ FC (= *Football Club*)

as *vb* [a] *voir* **avoir** ▷ *nm* [ɑs] ace

a/s *abr* (= *aux soins de*) c/o

ASBL *sigle f* (= *association sans but lucratif*) non-profit-making organization

asc. *abr* = **ascenseur**

ascendance [asɑ̃dɑ̃s] *nf* (*origine*) ancestry; (*Astrologie*) ascendant

ascendant, e [asɑ̃dɑ̃, -ɑ̃t] *adj* upward ▷ *nm* influence; **ascendants** *nmpl* ascendants

ascenseur [asɑ̃sœʀ] *nm* lift (*Brit*), elevator (*US*)

ascension [asɑ̃sjɔ̃] *nf* ascent; climb; **l'A~** (*Rel*) the Ascension; (: *jour férié*) Ascension (Day); *see note*; **(île de) l'A~** Ascension Island

> ● **L'ASCENSION**
>
> ● The *fête de l'Ascension* is a public holiday in
> ● France. It always falls on a Thursday, usually
> ● in May. Many French people take the
> ● following Friday off work too and enjoy a
> ● long weekend.

ascète [asɛt] *nm/f* ascetic

ascétique [asetik] *adj* ascetic

ascétisme [asetism(ə)] *nm* asceticism

ascorbique [askɔʀbik] *adj*: **acide ~** ascorbic acid

ASE *sigle f* (= *Agence spatiale européenne*) ESA (= *European Space Agency*)

asepsie [asɛpsi] *nf* asepsis

aseptique [asɛptik] *adj* aseptic

aseptisé, e [asɛptize] (*péj*) *adj* sanitized

asexué, e [asɛksɥe] *adj* asexual

asiatique [azjatik] *adj* Asian, Asiatic ▷ *nm/f*: **Asiatique** Asian

Asie [azi] *nf*: **l'~** Asia

asile [azil] *nm* (*refuge*) refuge, sanctuary; (*Pol*): **droit d'~** (political) asylum; (*pour malades, vieillards etc*) home; **accorder l'~ politique à qn** to grant *ou* give sb political asylum; **chercher/trouver ~ quelque part** to seek/find refuge somewhere

asocial, e, -aux [asɔsjal, -o] *adj* antisocial

aspect [aspɛ] *nm* appearance, look; (*fig*) aspect, side; (*Ling*) aspect; **à l'~ de** at the sight of

asperge [aspɛʀʒ(ə)] *nf* asparagus *no pl*

asperger [aspɛʀʒe] *vt* to spray, sprinkle

aspérité [asperite] *nf* excrescence, protruding bit (of rock *etc*)

aspersion [aspɛʀsjɔ̃] *nf* spraying, sprinkling

asphalte [asfalt(ə)] *nm* asphalt

asphyxiant, e [asfiksjɑ̃, -ɑ̃t] *adj* suffocating; **gaz ~** poison gas

asphyxie [asfiksi] *nf* suffocation, asphyxia, asphyxiation

asphyxier [asfiksje] *vt* to suffocate, asphyxiate; (*fig*) to stifle; **mourir asphyxié** to die of suffocation *ou* asphyxiation

aspic [aspik] *nm* (*Zool*) asp; (*Culin*) aspic

aspirant, e [aspirɑ̃, -ɑ̃t] *adj*: **pompe ~e** suction pump ▷ *nm* (*Navig*) midshipman

aspirateur [aspiʀatœʀ] *nm* vacuum cleaner, hoover®

aspiration [aspiʀɑsjɔ̃] *nf* inhalation, sucking (up); drawing up; **aspirations** *nfpl* (*ambitions*) aspirations

aspirer [aspiʀe] *vt* (*air*) to inhale; (*liquide*) to suck (up); (*appareil*) to suck *ou* draw up; **~ à** *vt* to aspire to

aspirine [aspiʀin] *nf* aspirin

assagir [asaʒiʀ] *vt*, **s'assagir** *vi* to quieten down, sober down

assaillant, e [asajɑ̃, -ɑ̃t] *nm/f* assailant, attacker

assaillir [asajiʀ] *vt* to assail, attack; **~ qn de** (*questions*) to assail *ou* bombard sb with

assainir [aseniʀ] *vt* to clean up; (*eau, air*) to purify

assainissement [asenismɑ̃] *nm* cleaning up; purifying

assaisonnement [asɛzɔnmɑ̃] *nm* seasoning

assaisonner [asɛzɔne] *vt* to season; **bien assaisonné** highly seasoned

assassin [asasɛ̃] *nm* murderer; assassin

assassinat [asasina] *nm* murder; assassination

assassiner [asasine] *vt* to murder; (*surtout Pol*) to assassinate

assaut [aso] *nm* assault, attack; **prendre d'~** to (take by) storm, assault; **donner l'~ (à)** to attack; **faire ~ de** (*rivaliser*) to vie with *ou* rival each other in

assèchement [asɛʃmã] *nm* draining, drainage

assécher [aseʃe] *vt* to drain

ASSEDIC [asedik] *sigle f* (= *Association pour l'emploi dans l'industrie et le commerce*) unemployment insurance scheme

assemblage [asãblaʒ] *nm* assembling; (*Menuiserie*) joint; **un ~ de** (*fig*) a collection of; **langage d'~** (*Inform*) assembly language

assemblée [asãble] *nf* (*réunion*) meeting; (*public, assistance*) gathering; assembled people; (*Pol*) assembly; (*Rel*): **l'~ des fidèles** the congregation; **l'A~ nationale (AN)** the (French) National Assembly; *see note*

● ASSEMBLÉE NATIONALE

The *Assemblée nationale* is the lower house of the French Parliament, the upper house being the "Sénat". It is housed in the Palais Bourbon in Paris. Its members, or "députés" are elected every five years.

assembler [asãble] *vt* (*joindre, monter*) to assemble, put together; (*amasser*) to gather (together), collect (together); **s'assembler** *vi* to gather, collect

assembleur [asãblœʀ] *nm* assembler, fitter; (*Inform*) assembler

assener, asséner [asene] *vt*: **~ un coup à qn** to deal sb a blow

assentiment [asãtimã] *nm* assent, consent; (*approbation*) approval

asseoir [aswaʀ] *vt* (*malade, bébé*) to sit up; (*personne debout*) to sit down; (*autorité, réputation*) to establish; **s'asseoir** *vi* to sit (o.s.) up; to sit (o.s.) down; **faire ~ qn** to ask sb to sit down; **asseyez-vous!, assieds-toi!** sit down!; **~ qch sur** to build sth on; (*appuyer*) to base sth on

assermenté, e [asɛʀmãte] *adj* sworn, on oath

assertion [asɛʀsjɔ̃] *nf* assertion

asservir [asɛʀviʀ] *vt* to subjugate, enslave

asservissement [asɛʀvismã] *nm* (*action*) enslavement; (*état*) slavery

assesseur [asesœʀ] *nm* (*Jur*) assessor

asseyais *etc* [asɛje] *vb voir* **asseoir**

assez [ase] *adv* (*suffisamment*) enough, sufficiently; (*passablement*) rather, quite, fairly; **~!** enough!, that'll do!; **~/pas ~ cuit** well enough done/underdone; **est-il ~ fort/rapide?** is he strong/fast enough?; **il est passé ~ vite** he went past rather *ou* quite *ou* fairly fast; **~ de pain/livres** enough *ou* sufficient bread/books; **vous en avez ~?** have you got enough?; **en avoir ~ de qch** (*en être fatigué*) to have had enough of sth; **travailler ~** to work (hard) enough

assidu, e [asidy] *adj* assiduous, painstaking; (*régulier*) regular; **~ auprès de qn** attentive towards sb

assiduité [asidɥite] *nf* assiduousness, painstaking regularity; attentiveness; **assiduités** *nfpl* assiduous attentions

assidûment [asidymã] *adv* assiduously, painstakingly; attentively

assied *etc* [asje] *vb voir* **asseoir**

assiégé, e [asjeʒe] *adj* under siege, besieged

assiéger [asjeʒe] *vt* to besiege, lay siege to; (*foule, touristes*) to mob, besiege

assiérai *etc* [asjeʀe] *vb voir* **asseoir**

assiette [asjɛt] *nf* plate; (*contenu*) plate(ful); (*équilibre*) seat; (*de colonne*) seating; (*de navire*) trim; **~ anglaise** assorted cold meats; **~ creuse** (soup) dish, soup plate; **~ à dessert** dessert *ou* side plate; **~ de l'impôt** basis of (tax) assessment; **~ plate** (dinner) plate

assiettée [asjete] *nf* plateful

assignation [asiɲasjɔ̃] *nf* assignation; (*Jur*) summons; (: *de témoin*) subpoena; **~ à résidence** compulsory order of residence

assigner [asiɲe] *vt*: **~ qch à** to assign *ou* allot sth to; (*valeur, importance*) to attach sth to; (*somme*) to allocate sth to; (*limites*) to set *ou* fix sth to; (*cause, effet*) to ascribe *ou* attribute sth to; **~ qn à** (*affecter*) to assign sb to; **~ qn à résidence** (*Jur*) to give sb a compulsory order of residence

assimilable [asimilabl(ə)] *adj* easily assimilated *ou* absorbed

assimilation [asimilasjɔ̃] *nf* assimilation, absorption

assimiler [asimile] *vt* to assimilate, absorb; (*comparer*): **~ qch/qn à** to liken *ou* compare sth/sb to; **s'assimiler** *vi* (*s'intégrer*) to be assimilated *ou* absorbed; **ils sont assimilés aux infirmières** (*Admin*) they are classed as nurses

assis, e [asi, -iz] *pp de* **asseoir** ▷ *adj* sitting (down), seated ▷ *nf* (*Constr*) course; (*Géo*) stratum (*pl* -a); (*fig*) basis (*pl* bases), foundation; **~ en tailleur** sitting cross-legged

assises [asiz] *nfpl* (*Jur*) assizes; (*congrès*) (annual) conference

assistanat [asistana] *nm* assistantship; (*à l'université*) probationary lectureship

assistance [asistãs] *nf* (*public*) audience; (*aide*) assistance; **porter** *ou* **prêter ~ à qn** to give sb assistance; **A~ publique (AP)** *public health service*; **enfant de l'A~ (publique)** child in care; **~ technique** technical aid

assistant, e [asistã, -ãt] *nm/f* assistant; (*d'université*) probationary lecturer; **les assistants** *nmpl* (*auditeurs etc*) those present; **~e sociale** social worker

assisté, e [asiste] *adj* (*Auto*) power assisted ▷ *nm/f* person receiving aid from the State

assister [asiste] *vt* to assist; **~ à** *vt* (*scène, événement*) to witness; (*conférence*) to attend, be (present) at; (*spectacle, match*) to be at, see

association [asɔsjasjɔ̃] *nf* association; (*Comm*) partnership; **~ d'idées/images** association of ideas/images

associé, e [asɔsje] *nm/f* associate; (*Comm*)

partner

associer [asɔsje] *vt* to associate; **~ qn à** (*profits*) to give sb a share of; (*affaire*) to make sb a partner in; (*joie, triomphe*) to include sb in; **~ qch à** (*joindre, allier*) to combine sth with; **s'associer** *vi* to join together; (*Comm*) to form a partnership ▷ *vt* (*collaborateur*) to take on (as a partner); **s'~ à** to be combined with; (*opinions, joie de qn*) to share in; **s'~ à** *ou* **avec qn pour faire** to join (forces) *ou* join together with sb to do

assoie *etc* [aswa] *vb voir* **asseoir**

assoiffé, e [aswafe] *adj* thirsty; (*fig*): **~ de** (*sang*) thirsting for; (*gloire*) thirsting after

assoirai [aswaʀe], **assois** *etc* [aswa] *vb voir* **asseoir**

assolement [asɔlmɑ̃] *nm* (systematic) rotation of crops

assombrir [asɔ̃bʀiʀ] *vt* to darken; (*fig*) to fill with gloom; **s'assombrir** *vi* to darken; (*devenir nuageux, fig: visage*) to cloud over; (*fig*) to become gloomy

assommer [asɔme] *vt* (*étourdir, abrutir*) to knock out, stun; (*fam: ennuyer*) to bore stiff

Assomption [asɔ̃psjɔ̃] *nf*: **l'~** the Assumption; *see note*

⬤ **L'ASSOMPTION**
⬤
⬤ The *fête de l'Assomption*, more commonly
⬤ known as "le 15 août" is a national holiday
⬤ in France. Traditionally, large numbers of
⬤ holidaymakers leave home on 15 August,
⬤ frequently causing chaos on the roads.

assorti, e [asɔʀti] *adj* matched, matching; **fromages/légumes ~s** assorted cheeses/ vegetables; **~ à** matching; **~ de** accompanied with; (*conditions, conseils*) coupled with; **bien/ mal ~** well/ill-matched

assortiment [asɔʀtimɑ̃] *nm* (*choix*) assortment, selection; (*harmonie de couleurs, formes*) arrangement; (*Comm: lot, stock*) selection

assortir [asɔʀtiʀ] *vt* to match; **s'assortir** *vi* to go well together, match; **~ qch à** to match sth with; **~ qch de** to accompany sth with; **s'~ de** to be accompanied by

assoupi, e [asupi] *adj* dozing, sleeping; (*fig*) (be)numbed; (*sens*) dulled

assoupir [asupiʀ]: **s'assoupir** *vi* (*personne*) to doze off; (*sens*) to go numb

assoupissement [asupismɑ̃] *nm* (*sommeil*) dozing; (*fig: somnolence*) drowsiness

assouplir [asupliʀ] *vt* to make supple, soften; (*membres, corps*) to limber up, make supple; (*fig*) to relax; (*: caractère*) to soften, make more flexible; **s'assouplir** *vi* to soften; to limber up; to relax; to become more flexible

assouplissant [asuplisɑ̃] *nm* (fabric) softener

assouplissement [asuplismɑ̃] *nm* softening; limbering up; relaxation; **exercices d'~** limbering up exercises

assourdir [asuʀdiʀ] *vt* (*bruit*) to deaden, muffle;

(*bruit*) to deafen

assourdissant, e [asuʀdisɑ̃, -ɑ̃t] *adj* (*bruit*) deafening

assouvir [asuviʀ] *vt* to satisfy, appease

assoyais *etc* [aswaje] *vb voir* **asseoir**

assujetti, e [asyʒeti] *adj*: **~ (à)** subject (to); (*Admin*): **~ à l'impôt** subject to tax(ation)

assujettir [asyʒetiʀ] *vt* to subject, subjugate; (*fixer: planches, tableau*) to fix securely; **~ qn à** (*règle, impôt*) to subject sb to

assujettissement [asyʒetismɑ̃] *nm* subjection, subjugation

assumer [asyme] *vt* (*fonction, emploi*) to assume, take on; (*accepter: conséquence, situation*) to accept

assurance [asyʀɑ̃s] *nf* (*certitude*) assurance; (*confiance en soi*) (self-)confidence; (*contrat*) insurance (policy); (*secteur commercial*) insurance; **prendre une ~ contre** to take out insurance *ou* an insurance policy against; **~ contre l'incendie** fire insurance; **~ contre le vol** insurance against theft; **société d'~**, **compagnie d'~s** insurance company; **~ maladie (AM)** health insurance; **~ au tiers** third party insurance; **~ tous risques** (*Auto*) comprehensive insurance; **~s sociales (AS)** ≈ National Insurance (*Brit*), ≈ Social Security (*US*)

assurance-vie [asyʀɑ̃svi] (*pl* **assurances-vie**) *nf* life assurance *ou* insurance

assurance-vol [asyʀɑ̃svɔl] (*pl* **assurances-vol**) *nf* insurance against theft

assuré, e [asyʀe] *adj* (*victoire etc*) certain, sure; (*démarche, voix*) assured, (self-)confident; (*certain*): **~ de** confident of; (*Assurances*) insured ▷ *nm/f* insured (person); **~ social** ≈ member of the National Insurance (*Brit*) *ou* Social Security (*US*) scheme

assurément [asyʀemɑ̃] *adv* assuredly, most certainly

assurer [asyʀe] *vt* (*Comm*) to insure; (*stabiliser*) to steady, stabilize; (*victoire etc*) to ensure, make certain; (*frontières, pouvoir*) to make secure; (*service, garde*) to provide, operate; **~ qch à qn** (*garantir*) to secure *ou* guarantee sth for sb; (*certifier*) to assure sb of sth; **~ à qn que** to assure sb that; **je vous assure que non/si** I assure you that that is not the case/is the case; **~ qn de** to assure sb of; **~ ses arrières** (*fig*) to be sure one has something to fall back on; **s'assurer (contre)** *vi* (*Comm*) to insure o.s. (against); **s'~ de/que** (*vérifier*) to make sure of/that; **s'~ (de)** (*aide de qn*) to secure; **s'~ sur la vie** to take out life insurance; **s'~ le concours/la collaboration de qn** to secure sb's aid/ collaboration

assureur [asyʀœʀ] *nm* insurance agent; (*société*) insurers *pl*

Assyrie [asiʀi] *nf*: **l'~** Assyria

astérisque [asteʀisk(ə)] *nm* asterisk

astéroïde [asteʀɔid] *nm* asteroid

asthmatique [asmatik] *adj* asthmatic

asthme [asm(ə)] *nm* asthma

asticot [astiko] *nm* maggot
asticoter [astikɔte] *vt (fam)* to needle, get at
astigmate [astigmat] *adj (Méd: personne)* astigmatic, having an astigmatism
astiquer [astike] *vt* to polish, shine
astrakan [astrakã] *nm* astrakhan
astral, e, -aux [astral, -o] *adj* astral
astre [astr(ə)] *nm* star
astreignant, e [astrɛɲã, -ãt] *adj* demanding
astreindre [astrɛ̃dr(ə)] *vt*: ~ **qn à qch** to force sth upon sb; ~ **qn à faire** to compel *ou* force sb to do; **s'astreindre à** to compel *ou* force o.s. to
astringent, e [astrɛ̃ʒã, -ãt] *adj* astringent
astrologie [astrɔlɔʒi] *nf* astrology
astrologique [astrɔlɔʒik] *adj* astrological
astrologue [astrɔlɔg] *nm/f* astrologer
astronaute [astronot] *nm/f* astronaut
astronautique [astronotik] *nf* astronautics *sg*
astronome [astronɔm] *nm/f* astronomer
astronomie [astronɔmi] *nf* astronomy
astronomique [astronɔmik] *adj* astronomic(al)
astrophysicien, ne [astrofizisjɛ̃, -ɛn] *nm/f* astrophysicist
astrophysique [astrofizik] *nf* astrophysics *sg*
astuce [astys] *nf* shrewdness, astuteness; *(truc)* trick, clever way; *(plaisanterie)* wisecrack
astucieusement [astysjøzmã] *adv* shrewdly, cleverly, astutely
astucieux, -euse [astysjø, -øz] *adj* shrewd, clever, astute
asymétrique [asimetrik] *adj* asymmetric(al)
AT *sigle m (= Ancien Testament)* OT
atavisme [atavism(ə)] *nm* atavism, heredity
atelier [atəlje] *nm* workshop; *(de peintre)* studio
atermoiements [atɛrmwamã] *nmpl* procrastination *sg*
atermoyer [atɛrmwaje] *vi* to temporize, procrastinate
athée [ate] *adj* atheistic ▷ *nm/f* atheist
athéisme [ateism(ə)] *nm* atheism
Athènes [atɛn] *n* Athens
athénien, ne [atenjɛ̃, -ɛn] *adj* Athenian
athlète [atlɛt] *nm/f (Sport)* athlete; *(costaud)* muscleman
athlétique [atletik] *adj* athletic
athlétisme [atletism(ə)] *nm* athletics *sg*; **faire de l'~** to do athletics; **tournoi d'~** athletics meeting
Atlantide [atlãtid] *nf*: **l'~** Atlantis
atlantique [atlãtik] *adj* Atlantic ▷ *nm*: **l'(océan) A~** the Atlantic (Ocean)
atlantiste [atlãtist(ə)] *adj, nm/f* Atlanticist
Atlas [atlas] *nm*: **l'~** the Atlas Mountains
atlas [atlas] *nm* atlas
atmosphère [atmosfɛr] *nf* atmosphere
atmosphérique [atmosferik] *adj* atmospheric
atoll [atɔl] *nm* atoll
atome [atom] *nm* atom
atomique [atomik] *adj* atomic, nuclear; *(usine)* nuclear; *(nombre, masse)* atomic
atomiseur [atomizœr] *nm* atomizer
atomiste [atomist(ə)] *nm/f (aussi:* **savant,**

ingénieur *etc* **atomiste)** atomic scientist
atone [aton] *adj* lifeless; *(Ling)* unstressed, unaccented
atours [atur] *nmpl* attire *sg*, finery *sg*
atout [atu] *nm* trump; *(fig)* asset; *(: plus fort)* trump card; **"~ pique/trèfle"** "spades/clubs are trumps"
ATP *sigle f (= Association des tennismen professionnels)* ATP (= Association of Tennis Professionals) ▷ *sigle mpl* = **arts et traditions populaires**; **musée des ~** ≈ folk museum
âtre [atr(ə)] *nm* hearth
atroce [atrɔs] *adj* atrocious, horrible
atrocement [atrɔsmã] *adv* atrociously, horribly
atrocité [atrɔsite] *nf* atrocity
atrophie [atrɔfi] *nf* atrophy
atrophier [atrɔfje]: **s'atrophier** *vi* to atrophy
attabler [atable]: **s'attabler** *vi* to sit down at (the) table; **s'~ à la terrasse** to sit down (at a table) on the terrace
ATTAC *sigle f (= Association pour la Taxation des Transactions pour l'Aide aux Citoyens)* ATTAC, organization critical of globalization originally set up to demand a tax on foreign currency speculation
attachant, e [ataʃã, -ãt] *adj* engaging, likeable
attache [ataʃ] *nf* clip, fastener; *(fig)* tie; **attaches** *nfpl (relations)* connections; **à l'~** *(chien)* tied up
attaché, e [ataʃe] *adj*: **être ~ à** *(aimer)* to be attached to ▷ *nm (Admin)* attaché; ~ **de presse/ d'ambassade** press/embassy attaché; ~ **commercial** commercial attaché
attaché-case [ataʃekɛz] *nm inv* attaché case *(Brit)*, briefcase
attachement [ataʃmã] *nm* attachment
attacher [ataʃe] *vt* to tie up; *(étiquette)* to attach, tie on; *(souliers)* to do up ▷ *vi (poêle, riz)* to stick; **s'attacher** *vi (robe etc)* to do up; **s'~ à** *(par affection)* to become attached to; **s'~ à faire qch** to endeavour to do sth; ~ **qch à** to tie *ou* fasten *ou* attach sth to; ~ **qn à** *(fig: lier)* to attach sb to; ~ **du prix/de l'importance à** to attach great value/attach importance to
attaquant [atakã] *nm (Mil)* attacker; *(Sport)* striker, forward
attaque [atak] *nf* attack; *(cérébrale)* stroke; *(d'épilepsie)* fit; **être/se sentir d'~** to be/feel on form; ~ **à main armée** armed attack
attaquer [atake] *vt* to attack; *(en justice)* to bring an action against, sue; *(travail)* to tackle, set about ▷ *vi* to attack; **s'attaquer à** *vt* to attack; *(épidémie, misère)* to tackle, attack
attardé, e [atarde] *adj (passants)* late; *(enfant)* backward; *(conceptions)* old-fashioned
attarder [atarde]: **s'attarder** *vi (sur qch, en chemin)* to linger; *(chez qn)* to stay on
atteignais *etc* [atɛɲɛ] *vb voir* **atteindre**
atteindre [atɛ̃dr(ə)] *vt* to reach; *(blesser)* to hit; *(contacter)* to reach, contact, get in touch with; *(émouvoir)* to affect
atteint, e [atɛ̃, -ɛ̃t] *pp de* **atteindre** ▷ *adj (Méd)*: **être ~ de** to be suffering from ▷ *nf* attack; **hors**

d'~e out of reach; **porter ~e à** to strike a blow at, undermine

attelage [atlaʒ] nm (de remorque etc) coupling (Brit), (trailer) hitch (US); (animaux) team; (harnachement) harness; (: de bœufs) yoke

atteler [atle] vt (cheval, bœufs) to hitch up; (wagons) to couple; **s'atteler à** (travail) to buckle down to

attelle [atɛl] nf splint

attenant, e [atnɑ̃, -ɑ̃t] adj: ~ (à) adjoining

attendant [atɑ̃dɑ̃]: **en ~** adv (dans l'intervalle) meanwhile, in the meantime

attendre [atɑ̃dʀ(ə)] vt to wait for; (être destiné ou réservé à) to await, be in store for ▷ vi to wait; **je n'attends plus rien (de la vie)** I expect nothing more (from life); **attendez que je réfléchisse** wait while I think; **s'~ à (ce que)** (escompter) to expect (that); **je ne m'y attendais pas** I didn't expect that; **ce n'est pas ce à quoi je m'attendais** that's not what I expected; **~ un enfant** to be expecting a baby; **~ de pied ferme** to wait determinedly; **~ de faire/d'être** to wait until one does/is; **~ que** to wait until; **~ qch de** to expect sth of; **faire ~ qn** to keep sb waiting; **se faire ~** to keep people (ou us etc) waiting; **en attendant** adv voir **attendant**

attendri, e [atɑ̃dʀi] adj tender

attendrir [atɑ̃dʀiʀ] vt to move (to pity); (viande) to tenderize; **s'attendrir (sur)** to be moved ou touched (by)

attendrissant, e [atɑ̃dʀisɑ̃, -ɑ̃t] adj moving, touching

attendrissement [atɑ̃dʀismɑ̃] nm (tendre) emotion; (apitoyé) pity

attendrisseur [atɑ̃dʀisœʀ] nm tenderizer

attendu, e [atɑ̃dy] pp de **attendre** ▷ adj long-awaited; (prévu) expected ▷ nm: **~s** reasons adduced for a judgment; **~ que** conj considering that, since

attentat [atɑ̃ta] nm (contre une personne) assassination attempt; (contre un bâtiment) attack; **~ à la bombe** bomb attack; **~ à la pudeur** (exhibitionnisme) indecent exposure no pl; (agression) indecent assault no pl; **~ suicide** suicide bombing

attente [atɑ̃t] nf wait; (espérance) expectation; **contre toute ~** contrary to (all) expectations

attenter [atɑ̃te]: **~ à** vt (liberté) to violate; **~ à la vie de qn** to make an attempt on sb's life; **~ à ses jours** to make an attempt on one's life

attentif, -ive [atɑ̃tif, -iv] adj (auditeur) attentive; (soin) scrupulous; (travail) careful; **~ à** paying attention to; (devoir) mindful of; **~ à faire** careful to do

attention [atɑ̃sjɔ̃] nf attention; (prévenance) attention, thoughtfulness no pl; **mériter ~** to be worthy of attention; **à l'~ de** for the attention of; **porter qch à l'~ de qn** to bring sth to sb's attention; **attirer l'~ de qn sur qch** to draw sb's attention to sth; **faire ~ (à)** to be careful (of); **faire ~ (à ce) que** to be ou make sure that; **~!** careful!, watch!, watch ou mind (Brit) out!; **~,**

si vous ouvrez cette lettre (sanction) just watch out, if you open that letter; **~, respectez les consignes de sécurité** be sure to observe the safety instructions

attentionné, e [atɑ̃sjɔne] adj thoughtful, considerate

attentisme [atɑ̃tism(ə)] nm wait-and-see policy

attentiste [atɑ̃tist(ə)] adj (politique) wait-and-see ▷ nm/f believer in a wait-and-see policy

attentivement [atɑ̃tivmɑ̃] adv attentively

atténuant, e [atenɥɑ̃, -ɑ̃t] adj: **circonstances ~es** extenuating circumstances

atténuer [atenɥe] vt to alleviate, ease; (diminuer) to lessen; (amoindrir) to mitigate the effects of; **s'atténuer** vi to ease; (violence etc) to abate

atterrer [ateʀe] vt to dismay, appal

atterrir [ateʀiʀ] vi to land

atterrissage [ateʀisaʒ] nm landing; **~ sur le ventre/sans visibilité/forcé** belly/blind/forced landing

attestation [atɛstasjɔ̃] nf certificate, testimonial; **~ médicale** doctor's certificate

attester [atɛste] vt to testify to, vouch for; (démontrer) to attest, testify to; **~ que** to testify that

attiédir [atjedir]: **s'attiédir** vi to become lukewarm; (fig) to cool down

attifé, e [atife] adj (fam) got up (Brit), decked out

attifer [atife] vt to get (Brit) ou do up, deck out

attique [atik] nm: **appartement en ~** penthouse (flat (Brit) ou apartment (US))

attirail [atiʀaj] nm gear; (péj) paraphernalia

attirance [atiʀɑ̃s] nf attraction; (séduction) lure

attirant, e [atiʀɑ̃, -ɑ̃t] adj attractive, appealing

attirer [atiʀe] vt to attract; (appâter) to lure, entice; **~ qn dans un coin/vers soi** to draw sb into a corner/towards one; **~ l'attention de qn** to attract sb's attention; **~ l'attention de qn sur qch** to draw sb's attention to sth; **~ des ennuis à qn** to make trouble for sb; **s'~ des ennuis** to bring trouble upon o.s., get into trouble

attiser [atize] vt (feu) to poke (up), stir up; (fig) to fan the flame of, stir up

attitré, e [atitʀe] adj qualified; (agréé) accredited, appointed

attitude [atityd] nf attitude; (position du corps) bearing

attouchements [atuʃmɑ̃] nmpl touching sg; (sexuels) fondling sg, stroking sg

attractif, -ive [atʀaktif, -iv] adj attractive

attraction [atʀaksjɔ̃] nf attraction; (de cabaret, cirque) number

attrait [atʀɛ] nm appeal, attraction; (plus fort) lure; **attraits** nmpl attractions; **éprouver de l'~ pour** to be attracted to

attrape [atʀap] nf voir **farce**

attrape-nigaud [atʀapnigo] nm con

attraper [atʀape] vt to catch; (habitude, amende) to get, pick up; (fam: duper) to take in (Brit), con

attrayant, e [atʀɛjɑ̃, -ɑ̃t] *adj* attractive

attribuer [atʀibɥe] *vt* (*prix*) to award; (*rôle, tâche*) to allocate, assign; (*imputer*): **~ qch à** to attribute sth to, ascribe sth to, put sth down to; **s'attribuer** *vt* (*s'approprier*) to claim for o.s.

attribut [atʀiby] *nm* attribute; (*Ling*) complement

attribution [atʀibysjɔ̃] *nf* (*voir attribuer*) awarding; allocation, assignment; attribution; **attributions** *nfpl* (*compétence*) attributions; **complément d'~** (*Ling*) indirect object

attristant, e [atʀistɑ̃, -ɑ̃t] *adj* saddening

attrister [atʀiste] *vt* to sadden; **s'~ de qch** to be saddened by sth

attroupement [atʀupmɑ̃] *nm* crowd, mob

attrouper [atʀupe]: **s'attrouper** *vi* to gather

au [o] *prép voir* **à**

aubade [obad] *nf* dawn serenade

aubaine [obɛn] *nf* godsend; (*financière*) windfall; (*Comm*) bonanza

aube [ob] *nf* dawn, daybreak; (*Rel*) alb; **à l'~** at dawn *ou* daybreak; **à l'~ de** (*fig*) at the dawn of

aubépine [obepin] *nf* hawthorn

auberge [obɛʀʒ(ə)] *nf* inn; **~ de jeunesse** youth hostel

aubergine [obɛʀʒin] *nf* aubergine (*Brit*), eggplant (*US*)

aubergiste [obɛʀʒist(ə)] *nm/f* inn-keeper, hotel-keeper

auburn [obœʀn] *adj inv* auburn

aucun, e [okœ̃, -yn] *adj, pron* no; (*positif*) any ▷ *pron* none; (*positif*) any(one); **il n'y a ~ livre** there isn't any book, there is no book; **je n'en vois ~ qui ...** I can't see any which ..., I (can) see none which ...; **~ homme** no man; **sans ~ doute** without any doubt; **sans ~e hésitation** without hesitation; **plus qu'~ autre** more than any other; **plus qu'~ de ceux qui ...** more than any of those who ...; **en ~e façon** in no way at all; **~ des deux** neither of the two; **~ d'entre eux** none of them; **d'~s** (*certains*) some

aucunement [okynmɑ̃] *adv* in no way, not in the least

audace [odas] *nf* daring, boldness; (*péj*) audacity; **il a eu l'~ de ...** he had the audacity to ...; **vous ne manquez pas d'~!** you're not lacking in nerve *ou* cheek!

audacieux, -euse [odasjø, -øz] *adj* daring, bold

au-dedans [odədɑ̃] *adv, prép* inside

au-dehors [odəɔʀ] *adv, prép* outside

au-delà [odla] *adv* beyond ▷ *nm*: **l'~** the hereafter; **~ de** *prép* beyond

au-dessous [odsu] *adv* underneath; below; **~ de** *prép* under(neath), below; (*limite, somme etc*) below, under; (*dignité, condition*) below

au-dessus [odsy] *adv* above; **~ de** *prép* above

au-devant [odvɑ̃]: **~ de** *prép*: **aller ~ de** to go (out) and meet; (*souhaits de qn*) to anticipate

audible [odibl(ə)] *adj* audible

audience [odjɑ̃s] *nf* audience; (*Jur: séance*) hearing; **trouver ~ auprès de** to arouse much interest among, get the (interested) attention of

audimat® [odimat] *nm* (*taux d'écoute*) ratings *pl*

audio-visuel, le [odjovizɥɛl] *adj* audio-visual ▷ *nm* (*équipement*) audio-visual aids *pl*; (*méthodes*) audio-visual methods *pl*; **l'~** radio and television

auditeur, -trice [oditœʀ, -tʀis] *nm/f* (*à la radio*) listener; (*à une conférence*) member of the audience, listener; **~ libre** unregistered student (*attending lectures*), auditor (*US*)

auditif, -ive [oditif, -iv] *adj* (*mémoire*) auditory; **appareil ~** hearing aid

audition [odisjɔ̃] *nf* (*ouïe, écoute*) hearing; (*Jur: de témoins*) examination; (*Mus, Théât: épreuve*) audition

auditionner [odisjɔne] *vt, vi* to audition

auditoire [oditwaʀ] *nm* audience

auditorium [oditɔʀjɔm] *nm* (*public*) studio

auge [oʒ] *nf* trough

augmentation [oɡmɑ̃tasjɔ̃] *nf* (*action*) increasing; raising; (*résultat*) increase; **~ (de salaire)** rise (in salary) (*Brit*), (pay) raise (*US*)

augmenter [oɡmɑ̃te] *vt* to increase, raise, put up; (*employé*) to increase the salary of, give a (salary) rise (*Brit*) *ou* (pay) raise (*US*) to ▷ *vi* to increase; **~ de poids/volume** to gain (in) weight/volume

augure [oɡyʀ] *nm* soothsayer, oracle; **de bon/mauvais ~** of good/ill omen

augurer [oɡyʀe] *vt*: **~ qch de** to foresee sth (coming) from *ou* out of; **~ bien de** to augur well for

auguste [oɡyst(ə)] *adj* august, noble, majestic

aujourd'hui [oʒuʀdɥi] *adv* today; **aujourd'hui en huit/quinze** a week/two weeks today, a week/two weeks from now; **à dater** *ou* **partir d'aujourd'hui** from today('s date)

aumône [omon] *nf* alms *sg* (*pl inv*); **faire l'~ (à qn)** to give alms (to sb); **faire l'~ de qch à qn** (*fig*) to favour sb with sth

aumônerie [omonʀi] *nf* chaplaincy

aumônier [omonje] *nm* chaplain

auparavant [opaʀavɑ̃] *adv* before(hand)

auprès [opʀɛ]: **~ de** *prép* next to, close to; (*recourir, s'adresser*) to; (*en comparaison de*) compared with, next to; (*dans l'opinion de*) in the opinion of

auquel [okɛl] *pron voir* **lequel**

aura *etc* [ɔʀa] *vb voir* **avoir**

aurai *etc* [ɔʀe] *vb voir* **avoir**

auréole [ɔʀeɔl] *nf* halo; (*tache*) ring

auréolé, e [ɔʀeɔle] *adj* (*fig*): **~ de gloire** crowned with *ou* in glory

auriculaire [ɔʀikylɛʀ] *nm* little finger

aurons *etc* [oʀɔ̃] *vb voir* **avoir**

aurore [ɔʀɔʀ] *nf* dawn, daybreak; **~ boréale** northern lights *pl*

ausculter [ɔskylte] *vt* to sound

auspices [ɔspis] *nmpl*: **sous les ~ de** under the patronage *ou* auspices of; **sous de bons/mauvais ~** under favourable/unfavourable auspices

aussi [osi] *adv* (*également*) also, too; (*de*

comparaison) as ▷ *conj* therefore, consequently; ~ **fort que** as strong as; **lui** ~ (*sujet*) he too; (*objet*) him too; ~ **bien que** (*de même que*) as well as

aussitôt [osito] *adv* straight away, immediately; ~ **que** as soon as; ~ **envoyé** as soon as it is (*ou* was) sent; ~ **fait** no sooner done

austère [ɔstɛR] *adj* austere; (*sévère*) stern

austérité [ɔsteRite] *nf* austerity; **plan/budget d'~** austerity plan/budget

austral, e [ɔstRal] *adj* southern; **l'océan A~** the Antarctic Ocean; **les Terres A~es** Antarctica

Australie [ɔstRali] *nf*: **l'~** Australia

australien, ne [ɔstRaljɛ̃, -ɛn] *adj* Australian ▷ *nm/f*: **Australien, ne** Australian

autant [otɑ̃] *adv* so much; (*comparatif*): ~ **(que)** as much (as); (*nombre*) as many (as); ~ **(de)** so much (*ou* many); as much (*ou* many); **n'importe qui aurait pu en faire** ~ anyone could have done the same *ou* as much; ~ **partir** we (*ou* you *etc*) may as well leave; ~ **ne rien dire** best not say anything; ~ **dire que ...** one might as well say that ...; **fort** ~ **que courageux** as strong as he is brave; **il n'est pas découragé pour** ~ he isn't discouraged for all that; **pour** ~ **que** *conj* assuming, as long as; **d'~** *adv* accordingly, in proportion; **d'~ plus/mieux (que)** all the more/the better (since)

autarcie [otaRsi] *nf* autarky, self-sufficiency

autel [otɛl] *nm* altar

auteur [otœR] *nm* author; **l'~ de cette remarque** the person who said that; **droit d'~** copyright

auteur-compositeur [otœRkɔ̃pozitœR] *nm/f* composer-songwriter

authenticité [otɑ̃tisite] *nf* authenticity

authentifier [otɑ̃tifje] *vt* to authenticate

authentique [otɑ̃tik] *adj* authentic, genuine

autiste [otist] *adj* autistic

auto [oto] *nf* car; **~s tamponneuses** bumper cars, dodgems

auto... [oto] *préfixe* auto..., self-

autobiographie [otɔbjɔgRafi] *nf* autobiography

autobiographique [otɔbjɔgRafik] *adj* autobiographical

autobronzant [otɔbRɔ̃zɑ̃] *nm* self-tanning cream (*or* lotion *etc*)

autobus [otɔbys] *nm* bus

autocar [otɔkaR] *nm* coach

autochtone [otɔktɔn] *nm/f* native

autocollant, e [otɔkɔlɑ̃, -ɑ̃t] *adj* self-adhesive; (*enveloppe*) self-seal ▷ *nm* sticker

auto-couchettes [otɔkuʃɛt] *adj inv*: **train** ~ car sleeper train, motorail® train (*Brit*)

autocratique [otɔkRatik] *adj* autocratic

autocritique [otɔkRitik] *nf* self-criticism

autocuiseur [otɔkwizœR] *nm* (*Culin*) pressure cooker

autodéfense [otɔdefɑ̃s] *nf* self-defence; **groupe d'~** vigilante committee

autodétermination [otɔdetɛRminasjɔ̃] *nf* self-determination

autodidacte [otɔdidakt(ə)] *nm/f* self-taught

person

autodiscipline [otɔdisiplin] *nf* self-discipline

autodrome [otɔdRom] *nm* motor-racing stadium

auto-école [otɔekɔl] *nf* driving school

autofinancement [otɔfinɑ̃smɑ̃] *nm* self-financing

autogéré, e [otɔʒeRe] *adj* self-managed, managed internally

autogestion [otɔʒɛstjɔ̃] *nf* joint worker-management control

autographe [otɔgRaf] *nm* autograph

autoguidé, e [otɔgide] *adj* self-guided

automate [otɔmat] *nm* (*robot*) automaton; (*machine*) (automatic) machine

automatique [otɔmatik] *adj, nm* automatic; **l'~** (*Tél*) ≈ direct dialling

automatiquement [otɔmatikmɑ̃] *adv* automatically

automatisation [otɔmatizasjɔ̃] *nf* automation

automatiser [otɔmatize] *vt* to automate

automédication [otɔmedikasjɔ̃] *nf* self-medication

automitrailleuse [otɔmitRajøz] *nf* armoured car

automnal, e, -aux [otɔnal, -o] *adj* autumnal

automne [otɔn] *nm* autumn (*Brit*), fall (*US*)

automobile [otɔmɔbil] *adj* motor *cpd* ▷ *nf* (motor) car; **l'~** motoring; (*industrie*) the car *ou* automobile (*US*) industry

automobiliste [otɔmɔbilist(ə)] *nm/f* motorist

autonettoyant, e [otɔnɛtwajɑ̃, -ɑ̃t] *adj*: **four** ~ self-cleaning oven

autonome [otɔnɔm] *adj* autonomous

autonomie [otɔnɔmi] *nf* autonomy; (*Pol*) self-government, autonomy; ~ **de vol** range

autonomiste [otɔnɔmist(ə)] *nm/f* separatist

autoportrait [otɔpɔRtRɛ] *nm* self-portrait

autopsie [otɔpsi] *nf* post-mortem (examination), autopsy

autopsier [otɔpsje] *vt* to carry out a post-mortem *ou* an autopsy on

autoradio [otɔRadjo] *nf* car radio

autorail [otɔRaj] *nm* railcar

autorisation [otɔRizasjɔ̃] *nf* permission, authorization; (*papiers*) permit; **donner à qn l'~ de** to give sb permission to, authorize sb to; **avoir l'~ de faire** to be allowed *ou* have permission to do, be authorized to do

autorisé, e [otɔRize] *adj* (*opinion, sources*) authoritative; (*permis*): ~ **à faire** authorized *ou* permitted to do; **dans les milieux ~s** in official circles

autoriser [otɔRize] *vt* to give permission for, authorize; (*fig*) to allow (of), sanction; ~ **qn à faire** to give permission to sb to do, authorize sb to do

autoritaire [otɔRitɛR] *adj* authoritarian

autoritarisme [otɔRitaRism(ə)] *nm* authoritarianism

autorité [otɔRite] *nf* authority; **faire** ~ to be authoritative; ~**s constituées** constitutional authorities

autoroute [ɔtɔʀut] *nf* motorway (Brit), expressway (US); **~ de l'information** (*Tél*) information highway

autoroutier, -ière [ɔtɔʀutje, -jɛʀ] *adj* motorway *cpd* (Brit), expressway *cpd* (US)

autosatisfaction [ɔtɔsatisfaksjɔ̃] *nf* self-satisfaction

auto-stop [ɔtɔstɔp] *nm*: **l'~** hitch-hiking; **faire de l'~** to hitch-hike; **prendre qn en ~** to give sb a lift

auto-stoppeur, -euse [ɔtɔstɔpœʀ, -øz] *nm/f* hitch-hiker, hitcher (Brit)

autosuffisant, e [ɔtɔsyfizɑ̃, -ɑ̃t] *adj* self-sufficient

autosuggestion [ɔtɔsygʒɛstjɔ̃] *nf* autosuggestion

autour [otuʀ] *adv* around; **~ de** *prép* around; (*environ*) around, about; **tout ~** *adv* all around

○ MOT-CLÉ

autre [otʀ(ə)] *adj* **1** (*différent*) other, different; **je préférerais un autre verre** I'd prefer another *ou* a different glass; **d'autres verres** different glasses; **se sentir autre** to feel different; **la difficulté est autre** the difficulty is *ou* lies elsewhere

2 (*supplémentaire*) other; **je voudrais un autre verre d'eau** I'd like another glass of water

3: **autre chose** something else; **autre part** somewhere else; **d'autre part** on the other hand

▷ *pron* **1**: **un autre** another (one); **nous/vous autres** us/you; **d'autres** others; **l'autre** the other (one); **les autres** the others; (*autrui*) others; **l'un et l'autre** both of them; **ni l'un ni l'autre** neither of them; **se détester l'un l'autre/les uns les autres** to hate each other *ou* one another; **d'une semaine/minute à l'autre** from one week/minute *ou* moment to the next; (*incessamment*) any week/minute *ou* moment now; **de temps à autre** from time to time; **entre autres** among other things

2 (*expressions*): **j'en ai vu d'autres** I've seen worse; **à d'autres!** pull the other one!

autrefois [otʀəfwa] *adv* in the past

autrement [otʀəmɑ̃] *adv* differently; (*d'une manière différente*) in another way; (*sinon*) otherwise; **je n'ai pas pu faire ~** I couldn't do anything else, I couldn't do otherwise; **~ dit** in other words; (*c'est-à-dire*) that is to say

Autriche [otʀiʃ] *nf*: **l'~** Austria

autrichien, ne [otʀiʃjɛ̃, -ɛn] *adj* Austrian ▷ *nm/f*: **Autrichien, ne** Austrian

autruche [otʀyʃ] *nf* ostrich; **faire l'~** (*fig*) to bury one's head in the sand

autrui [otʀɥi] *pron* others

auvent [ovɑ̃] *nm* canopy

auvergnat, e [ovɛʀɲa, -at] *adj* of *ou* from the Auvergne

Auvergne [ovɛʀɲ(ə)] *nf*: **l'~** the Auvergne

aux [o] *prép voir* **à**

auxiliaire [oksiljɛʀ] *adj*, *nm/f* auxiliary

auxquels, auxquelles [okɛl] *pron voir* **lequel**

AV *sigle m* (*Banque*: = *avis de virement*) *advice of bank transfer* ▷ *abr* (*Auto*) = **avant**

av. *abr* (= *avenue*) Av(e)

avachi, e [avaʃi] *adj* limp, flabby; (*chaussure, vêtement*) out-of-shape; (*personne*): **~ sur qch** slumped on *ou* across sth

avais *etc* [avɛ] *vb voir* **avoir**

aval [aval] *nm* (*accord*) endorsement, backing; (*Géo*): **en ~** downstream, downriver; (*sur une pente*) downhill; **en ~ de** downstream *ou* downriver from; downhill from

avalanche [avalɑ̃ʃ] *nf* avalanche; **~ poudreuse** powder snow avalanche

avaler [avale] *vt* to swallow

avaliser [avalize] *vt* (*plan, entreprise*) to back, support; (*Comm, Jur*) to guarantee

avance [avɑ̃s] *nf* (*de troupes etc*) advance; (*progrès*) progress; (*d'argent*) advance; (*opposé à retard*) lead; being ahead of schedule; **avances** *nfpl* overtures; (*amoureuses*) advances; **une ~ de 300 m/4 h** (*Sport*) a 300 m/4 hour lead; **(être) en ~** (to be) early; (*sur un programme*) (to be) ahead of schedule; **on n'est pas en ~!** we're kind of late!; **être en ~ sur qn** to be ahead of sb; **d'~, à l'~, par ~** in advance; **~ (du) papier** (*Inform*) paper advance

avancé, e [avɑ̃se] *adj* advanced; (*travail etc*) well on, well under way; (*fruit, fromage*) overripe ▷ *nf* projection; overhang; **il est ~ pour son âge** he is advanced for his age

avancement [avɑ̃smɑ̃] *nm* (*professionnel*) promotion; (*de travaux*) progress

avancer [avɑ̃se] *vi* to move forward, advance; (*projet, travail*) to make progress; (*être en saillie*) to overhang; to project; (*montre, réveil*) to be fast; (: *d'habitude*) to gain ▷ *vt* to move forward, advance; (*argent*) to advance; (*montre, pendule*) to put forward; (*faire progresser: travail etc*) to advance, move on; **s'avancer** *vi* to move forward, advance; (*fig*) to commit o.s.; (*faire saillie*) to overhang; to project; **j'avance (d'une heure)** I'm (an hour) fast

avanies [avani] *nfpl* snubs (Brit), insults

avant [avɑ̃] *prép* before ▷ *adv*: **trop/plus ~** too far/further forward ▷ *adj inv*: **siège/roue ~** front seat/wheel ▷ *nm* front; (*Sport: joueur*) forward; **~ qu'il parte/de partir** before he leaves/leaving; **~ qu'il (ne) pleuve** before it rains (*ou* rained); **~ tout** (*surtout*) above all; **à l'~** (*dans un véhicule*) in (the) front; **en ~** *adv* forward(s); **en ~ de** *prép* in front of; **aller de l'~** to steam ahead (*fig*), make good progress

avantage [avɑ̃taʒ] *nm* advantage; (*Tennis*): **service/dehors** advantage *ou* van (Brit) *ou* ad (US) in/out; **tirer ~ de** to take advantage of; **vous auriez ~ à faire** you would be well-advised to do, it would be to your advantage to do; **à l'~ de qn** to sb's advantage; **être à son ~**

to be at one's best; **~s en nature** benefits in kind; **~s sociaux** fringe benefits

avantager [avɑ̃taʒe] *vt* (*favoriser*) to favour; (*embellir*) to flatter

avantageux, -euse [avɑ̃taʒø, -øz] *adj* attractive; (*intéressant*) attractively priced; (*portrait, coiffure*) flattering; **conditions avantageuses** favourable terms

avant-bras [avɑ̃bʀa] *nm inv* forearm

avant-centre [avɑ̃sɑ̃tʀ(ə)] *nm* centre-forward

avant-coureur [avɑ̃kuʀœʀ] *adj inv* (*bruit etc*) precursory; **signe ~** advance indication *ou* sign

avant-dernier, -ière [avɑ̃dɛʀnje, -jɛʀ] *adj, nm/f* next to last, last but one

avant-garde [avɑ̃gaʀd(ə)] *nf* (*Mil*) vanguard; (*fig*) avant-garde; **d'~** avant-garde

avant-goût [avɑ̃gu] *nm* foretaste

avant-hier [avɑ̃tjɛʀ] *adv* the day before yesterday

avant-poste [avɑ̃pɔst(ə)] *nm* outpost

avant-première [avɑ̃pʀəmjɛʀ] *nf* (*de film*) preview; **en ~** as a preview, in a preview showing

avant-projet [avɑ̃pʀɔʒe] *nm* preliminary draft

avant-propos [avɑ̃pʀɔpo] *nm* foreword

avant-veille [avɑ̃vɛj] *nf*: **l'~** two days before

avare [avaʀ] *adj* miserly, avaricious ▷ *nm/f* miser; **~ de compliments** stingy *ou* sparing with one's compliments

avarice [avaʀis] *nf* avarice, miserliness

avarié, e [avaʀje] *adj* (*viande, fruits*) rotting, going off (*Brit*); (*Navig: navire*) damaged

avaries [avaʀi] *nfpl* (*Navig*) damage *sg*

avatar [avataʀ] *nm* misadventure; (*transformation*) metamorphosis

avec [avɛk] *prép* with; (*à l'égard de*) to(wards), with ▷ *adv* (*fam*) with it (*ou* him *etc*); **~ habileté/lenteur** skilfully/slowly; **~ eux/ces maladies** with them/these diseases; **~ ça** (*malgré ça*) for all that; **et ~ ça?** (*dans un magasin*) anything *ou* something else?

avenant, e [avnɑ̃, -ɑ̃t] *adj* pleasant ▷ *nm* (*Assurances*) additional clause; **à l'~** *adv* in keeping

avènement [avɛnmɑ̃] *nm* (*d'un roi*) accession, succession; (*d'un changement*) advent; (*d'une politique, idée*) coming

avenir [avniʀ] *nm*: **l'~** the future; **à l'~** in future; **sans ~** with no future, without a future; **carrière/politicien d'~** career/politician with prospects *ou* a future

Avent [avɑ̃] *nm*: **l'~** Advent

aventure [avɑ̃tyʀ] *nf*: **l'~** adventure; **une ~** an adventure; (*amoureuse*) an affair; **partir à l'~** to go off in search of adventure; (*au hasard*) to go where one's fancy takes one; **roman/film d'~** adventure story/film

aventurer [avɑ̃tyʀe] *vt* (*somme, réputation, vie*) to stake; (*remarque, opinion*) to venture; **s'aventurer** *vi* to venture; **s'~ à faire qch** to venture into sth

aventureux, -euse [avɑ̃tyʀø, -øz] *adj* adventurous, venturesome; (*projet*) risky, chancy

aventurier, -ière [avɑ̃tyʀje, -jɛʀ] *nm/f* adventurer ▷ *nf* (*péj*) adventuress

avenu, e [avny] *adj*: **nul et non ~** null and void

avenue [avny] *nf* avenue

avéré, e [aveʀe] *adj* recognized, acknowledged

avérer [aveʀe]: **s'avérer** *vr*: **s'~ faux/coûteux** to prove (to be) wrong/expensive

averse [avɛʀs(ə)] *nf* shower

aversion [avɛʀsjɔ̃] *nf* aversion, loathing

averti, e [avɛʀti] *adj* (well-)informed

avertir [avɛʀtiʀ] *vt*: **~ qn (de qch/que)** to warn sb (of sth/that); (*renseigner*) to inform sb (of sth/that); **~ qn de ne pas faire qch** to warn sb not to do sth

avertissement [avɛʀtismɑ̃] *nm* warning

avertisseur [avɛʀtisœʀ] *nm* horn, siren; **~ (d'incendie)** (fire) alarm

aveu, x [avø] *nm* confession; **passer aux ~x** to make a confession; **de l'~ de** according to

aveuglant, e [avœglɑ̃, -ɑ̃t] *adj* blinding

aveugle [avœgl(ə)] *adj* blind ▷ *nm/f* blind person; **les ~s** the blind; **test en (double) ~** (double) blind test

aveuglement [avœgləmɑ̃] *nm* blindness

aveuglément [avœglemɑ̃] *adv* blindly

aveugler [avœgle] *vt* to blind

aveuglette [avœglɛt]: **à l'~** *adv* groping one's way along; (*fig*) in the dark, blindly

avez [ave] *vb voir* **avoir**

aviateur, -trice [avjatœʀ, -tʀis] *nm/f* aviator, pilot

aviation [avjasjɔ̃] *nf* (*secteur commercial*) aviation; (*sport, métier de pilote*) flying; (*Mil*) air force; **terrain d'~** airfield; **~ de chasse** fighter force

aviculteur, -trice [avikyltœʀ, -tʀis] *nm/f* poultry farmer; bird breeder

aviculture [avikyltyʀ] *nf* (*de volailles*) poultry farming

avide [avid] *adj* eager; (*péj*) greedy, grasping; **~ de** (*sang etc*) thirsting for; **~ d'honneurs/d'argent** greedy for honours/money; **~ de connaître/d'apprendre** eager to know/learn

avidité [avidite] *nf* eagerness; greed

avilir [aviliʀ] *vt* to debase

avilissant, e [avilisɑ̃, -ɑ̃t] *adj* degrading

aviné, e [avine] *adj* drunken

avion [avjɔ̃] *nm* (*aero*)plane (*Brit*), (air)plane (*US*); **aller (quelque part) en ~** to go (somewhere) by plane, fly (somewhere); **par ~** by airmail; **~ de chasse** fighter; **~ de ligne** airliner; **~ à réaction** jet (plane)

avion-cargo [avjɔ̃kaʀgo] *nm* air freighter

avion-citerne [avjɔ̃sitɛʀn(ə)] *nm* air tanker

aviron [aviʀɔ̃] *nm* oar; (*sport*): **l'~** rowing

avis [avi] *nm* opinion; (*notification*) notice; (*Comm*): **~ de crédit/débit** credit/debit advice; **à mon ~** in my opinion; **je suis de votre ~** I share your opinion, I am of your opinion; **être d'~ que** to be of the opinion that; **changer d'~** to change one's mind; **sauf ~ contraire** unless you hear to the contrary; **sans ~ préalable**

without notice; **jusqu'à nouvel ~** until further notice; **~ de décès** death announcement

avisé, e [avize] *adj* sensible, wise; **être bien/mal ~ de faire** to be well-/ill-advised to do

aviser [avize] *vt* (*voir*) to notice, catch sight of; (*informer*): **~ qn de/que** to advise *ou* inform *ou* notify sb of/that ▷ *vi* to think about things, assess the situation; **s'~ de qch/que** to become suddenly aware of sth/that; **s'~ de faire** to take it into one's head to do

aviver [avive] *vt* (*douleur, chagrin*) to intensify; (*intérêt, désir*) to sharpen; (*colère, querelle*) to stir up; (*couleur*) to brighten up

av. J.-C. *abr* (= *avant Jésus-Christ*) BC

avocat, e [avɔka, -at] *nm/f* (*Jur*) ≈ barrister (*Brit*), lawyer; (*fig*) advocate, champion ▷ *nm* (*Culin*) avocado (pear); **se faire l'~ du diable** to be the devil's advocate; **l'~ de la défense/partie civile** the counsel for the defence/plaintiff; **~ d'affaires** business lawyer; **~ général** assistant public prosecutor

avocat-conseil [avɔkakɔ̃sɛj] (*pl* **avocats-conseils**) *nm* ≈ barrister (*Brit*)

avocat-stagiaire [avɔkastaʒjɛʀ] (*pl* **avocats-stagiaires**) *nm* ≈ barrister doing his articles (*Brit*)

avoine [avwan] *nf* oats *pl*

 MOT-CLÉ

avoir [avwaʀ] *nm* assets *pl*, resources *pl*; (*Comm*) credit; **avoir fiscal** tax credit
▷ *vt* **1** (*posséder*) to have; **elle a deux enfants/une belle maison** she has (got) two children/a lovely house; **il a les yeux bleus** he has (got) blue eyes
2 (*éprouver*): **qu'est-ce que tu as?, qu'as-tu?** what's wrong?, what's the matter?; *voir aussi* **faim, peur** *etc*
3 (*âge, dimensions*) to be; **il a 3 ans** he is 3 (years old); **le mur a 3 mètres de haut** the wall is 3 metres high
4 (*fam: duper*) to do, have; **on vous a eu!** you've been done *ou* had!
5: **en avoir contre qn** to have a grudge against sb; **en avoir assez** to be fed up; **j'en ai pour une demi-heure** it'll take me half an hour; **n'avoir que faire de qch** to have no use for sth
▷ *vb aux* **1** to have; **avoir mangé/dormi** to have eaten/slept; **hier je n'ai pas mangé** I didn't eat yesterday
2 (*avoir + à + infinitif*): **avoir à faire qch** to have to do sth; **vous n'avez qu'à lui demander** you only have to ask him; **tu n'as pas à me poser**

des questions it's not for you to ask me questions
▷ *vb impers* **1**: **il y a** (+*singulier*) there is; (+*pluriel*) there are; **qu'y-a-t-il?, qu'est-ce qu'il y a?** what's the matter?, what is it?; **il doit y avoir une explication** there must be an explanation; **il n'y a qu'à ...** we (*ou* you *etc*) will just have to ...; **il ne peut y en avoir qu'un** there can only be one
2 (*temporel*): **il y a 10 ans** 10 years ago; **il y a 10 ans/longtemps que je le connais** I've known him for 10 years/a long time; **il y a 10 ans qu'il est arrivé** it's 10 years since he arrived

avoisinant, e [avwazinɑ̃, -ɑ̃t] *adj* neighbouring

avoisiner [avwazine] *vt* to be near *ou* close to; (*fig*) to border *ou* verge on

avons [avɔ̃] *vb voir* **avoir**

avortement [avɔʀtəmɑ̃] *nm* abortion

avorter [avɔʀte] *vi* (*Méd*) to have an abortion; (*fig*) to fail; **faire ~** to abort; **se faire ~** to have an abortion

avouable [avwabl(ə)] *adj* respectable; **des pensées non ~s** unrepeatable thoughts

avoué, e [avwe] *adj* avowed ▷ *nm* (*Jur*) ≈ solicitor (*Brit*), lawyer

avouer [avwe] *vt* (*crime, défaut*) to confess (to) ▷ *vi* (*se confesser*) to confess; (*admettre*) to admit; **~ avoir fait/que** to admit *ou* confess to having done/that; **~ que oui/non** to admit that that is so/not so

avril [avʀil] *nm* April; *voir aussi* **juillet**

axe [aks(ə)] *nm* axis (*pl* axes); (*de roue etc*) axle; **dans l'~ de** directly in line with; (*fig*) main line; **~ routier** trunk road, main road

axer [akse] *vt*: **~ qch sur** to centre sth on

axial, e, -aux [aksjal, -o] *adj* axial

axiome [aksjom] *nm* axiom

ayant [ɛjɑ̃] *vb voir* **avoir** ▷ *nm*: **~ droit** assignee; **~ droit à** (*pension etc*) person eligible for *ou* entitled to

ayons *etc* [ɛjɔ̃] *vb voir* **avoir**

azalée [azale] *nf* azalea

Azerbaïdjan [azɛʀbaidʒɑ̃] *nm* Azerbaijan

azimut [azimyt] *nm* azimuth; **tous ~s** *adj* (*fig*) omnidirectional

azote [azɔt] *nm* nitrogen

azoté, e [azɔte] *adj* nitrogenous

AZT *sigle m* (= *azidothymidine*) AZT

aztèque [aztɛk] *adj* Aztec

azur [azyʀ] *nm* (*couleur*) azure, sky blue; (*ciel*) sky, skies *pl*

azyme [azim] *adj*: **pain ~** unleavened bread

Bb

B, b [be] *nm inv* B, b ▷ *abr* = **bien**; **B comme Bertha** B for Benjamin (*Brit*) *ou* Baker (*US*)

BA *sigle f* (= *bonne action*) good deed

baba [baba] *adj inv*: **en être ~** (*fam*) to be flabbergasted ▷ *nm*: **~ au rhum** rum baba

babil [babi] *nm* prattle

babillage [babijaʒ] *nm* chatter

babiller [babije] *vi* to prattle, chatter; (*bébé*) to babble

babines [babin] *nfpl* chops

babiole [babjɔl] *nf* (*bibelot*) trinket; (*vétille*) trifle

bâbord [babɔʀ] *nm*: **à** *ou* **par ~** to port, on the port side

babouin [babwɛ̃] *nm* baboon

baby-foot [babifut] *nm inv* table football

Babylone [babilɔn] *n* Babylon

babylonien, ne [babilɔnjɛ̃, -ɛn] *adj* Babylonian

baby-sitter [babisitœʀ] *nm/f* baby-sitter

baby-sitting [babisitiŋ] *nm* baby-sitting; **faire du ~** to baby-sit

bac [bak] *nm* (*Scol*) = **baccalauréat**; (*bateau*) ferry; (*récipient*) tub; (: *Photo etc*) tray; (: *Industrie*) tank; **~ à glace** ice-tray; **~ à légumes** vegetable compartment *ou* rack

baccalauréat [bakalɔʀea] *nm* ≈ A-levels *pl* (*Brit*), ≈ high school diploma (*US*); *see note*

⬤ **BACCALAURÉAT**
⬤
⬤ The *baccalauréat* or "bac" is the school-
⬤ leaving examination taken at a French
⬤ "lycée" at the age of 18; it marks the end of
⬤ seven years' secondary education. Several
⬤ subject combinations are available,
⬤ although in all cases a broad range is
⬤ studied. Successful candidates can go on to
⬤ university, if they so wish.

bâche [baʃ] *nf* tarpaulin, canvas sheet

bachelier, -ière [baʃəlje, -jɛʀ] *nm/f holder of the baccalauréat*

bâcher [baʃe] *vt* to cover (with a canvas sheet *ou* a tarpaulin)

bachot [baʃo] *nm* = **baccalauréat**

bachotage [baʃotaʒ] *nm* (*Scol*) cramming

bachoter [baʃote] *vi* (*Scol*) to cram (for an exam)

bacille [basil] *nm* bacillus

bâcler [bɑkle] *vt* to botch (up)

bacon [bekɔn] *nm* bacon

bactéricide [baktɛʀisid] *nm* (*Méd*) bactericide

bactérie [baktɛʀi] *nf* bacterium

bactérien, ne [baktɛʀjɛ̃, -ɛn] *adj* bacterial

bactériologie [baktɛʀjɔlɔʒi] *nf* bacteriology

bactériologique [baktɛʀjɔlɔʒik] *adj* bacteriological

bactériologiste [baktɛʀjɔlɔʒist(ə)] *nm/f* bacteriologist

badaud, e [bado, -od] *nm/f* idle onlooker

baderne [badɛʀn(ə)] *nf* (*péj*): **(vieille) ~** old fossil

badge [badʒ(ə)] *nm* badge

badigeon [badiʒɔ̃] *nm* distemper; colourwash

badigeonner [badiʒɔne] *vt* to distemper; to colourwash; (*péj: barbouiller*) to daub; (*Méd*) to paint

badin, e [badɛ̃, -in] *adj* light-hearted, playful

badinage [badinaʒ] *nm* banter

badine [badin] *nf* switch (*stick*)

badiner [badine] *vi*: **~ avec qch** to treat sth lightly; **ne pas ~ avec qch** not to trifle with sth

badminton [badmintɔn] *nm* badminton

BAFA [bafa] *sigle m* (= *Brevet d'aptitude aux fonctions d'animation*) diploma for youth leaders and workers

baffe [baf] *nf* (*fam*) slap, clout

Baffin [bafin] *nf*: **terre de ~** Baffin Island

baffle [bafl(ə)] *nm* baffle (board)

bafouer [bafwe] *vt* to deride, ridicule

bafouillage [bafujaʒ] *nm* (*fam: propos incohérents*) jumble of words

bafouiller [bafuje] *vi, vt* to stammer

bâfrer [bafʀe] *vi, vt* (*fam*) to guzzle, gobble

bagage [bagaʒ] *nm*: **~s** luggage *sg*, baggage *sg*; **faire ses ~s** to pack (one's bags); **~ littéraire** (stock of) literary knowledge; **~s à main** hand-luggage

bagarre [bagaʀ] *nf* fight, brawl; **il aime la ~** he loves a fight, he likes fighting

bagarrer [bagaʀe]: **se bagarrer** *vi* to (have a) fight

bagarreur, -euse [bagaʀœʀ, -øz] *adj* pugnacious ▷ *nm/f*: **il est ~** he loves a fight

bagatelle [bagatɛl] *nf* trifle, trifling sum (*ou* matter)

Bagdad, Baghdâd [bagdad] n Baghdad

bagnard [baɲaʀ] nm convict

bagne [baɲ] nm penal colony; **c'est le ~** (fig) it's forced labour

bagnole [baɲɔl] nf (fam) car, wheels pl (Brit)

bagout [bagu] nm glibness; **avoir du ~** to have the gift of the gab

bague [bag] nf ring; **~ de fiançailles** engagement ring; **~ de serrage** clip

baguenauder [bagnode]: **se baguenauder** vi to trail around, loaf around

baguer [bage] vt to ring

baguette [bagɛt] nf stick; (cuisine chinoise) chopstick; (de chef d'orchestre) baton; (pain) stick of (French) bread; (Constr: moulure) beading; **mener qn à la ~** to rule sb with a rod of iron; **~ magique** magic wand; **~ de sourcier** divining rod; **~ de tambour** drumstick

Bahamas [baamas] nfpl: **les (îles) ~** the Bahamas

Bahreïn [baʀɛn] nm Bahrain ou Bahrein

bahut [bay] nm chest

bai, e [bɛ] adj (cheval) bay

baie [bɛ] nf (Géo) bay; (fruit) berry; **~ (vitrée)** picture window

baignade [bɛɲad] nf (action) bathing; (bain) bathe; (endroit) bathing place

baigné, e [beɲe] adj: **~ de** bathed in; (trempé) soaked with; (inondé) flooded with

baigner [beɲe] vt (bébé) to bath ▷ vi: **~ dans son sang** to lie in a pool of blood; **~ dans la brume** to be shrouded in mist; **se baigner** vi to go swimming ou bathing; (dans une baignoire) to have a bath; **ça baigne!** (fam) everything's great!

baigneur, -euse [bɛɲœʀ, -øz] nm/f bather ▷ nm (poupée) baby doll

baignoire [bɛɲwaʀ] nf bath(tub); (Théât) ground-floor box

bail, baux [baj, bo] nm lease; **donner** ou **prendre qch à ~** to lease sth

bâillement [bajmɑ̃] nm yawn

bâiller [baje] vi to yawn; (être ouvert) to gape

bailleur [bajœʀ] nm: **~ de fonds** sponsor, backer; (Comm) sleeping ou silent partner

bâillon [bajɔ̃] nm gag

bâillonner [bajɔne] vt to gag

bain [bɛ̃] nm (dans une baignoire, Photo, Tech) bath; (dans la mer, une piscine) swim; **costume de ~** bathing costume (Brit), swimsuit; **prendre un ~** to have a bath; **se mettre dans le ~** (fig) to get into (the way of) it ou things; **~ de bouche** mouthwash; **~ de foule** walkabout; **~ de pieds** footbath; (au bord de la mer) paddle; **~ de siège** hip bath; **~ de soleil** sunbathing no pl; **prendre un ~ de soleil** to sunbathe; **~s de mer** sea bathing sg; **~s(-douches) municipaux** public baths

bain-marie [bɛ̃maʀi] (pl **bains-marie**) nm double boiler; **faire chauffer au ~** (boîte etc) to immerse in boiling water

baïonnette [bajɔnɛt] nf bayonet; (Élec): **douille à ~** bayonet socket; **ampoule à ~** bulb with a bayonet fitting

baisemain [bɛzmɛ̃] nm kissing a lady's hand

baiser [beze] nm kiss ▷ vt (main, front) to kiss; (fam!) to screw (!)

baisse [bɛs] nf fall, drop; (Comm): **"~ sur la viande"** "meat prices down"; **en ~** (cours, action) falling; **à la ~** downwards

baisser [bese] vt to lower; (radio, chauffage) to turn down; (Auto: phares) to dip (Brit), lower (US) ▷ vi to fall, drop, go down; **se baisser** vi to bend down

bajoues [baʒu] nfpl chaps, chops

bal [bal] nm dance; (grande soirée) ball; **~ costumé/masqué** fancy-dress/masked ball; **~ musette** dance (with accordion accompaniment)

balade [balad] nf walk, stroll; (en voiture) drive; **faire une ~** to go for a walk ou stroll; to go for a drive

balader [balade] vt (traîner) to trail around; **se balader** vi to go for a walk ou stroll; to go for a drive

baladeur [baladœʀ] nm personal stereo; **~ numérique** MP3 player

baladeuse [baladøz] nf inspection lamp

baladin [baladɛ̃] nm wandering entertainer

balafre [balafʀ(ə)] nf gash, slash; (cicatrice) scar

balafrer [balafʀe] vt to gash, slash

balai [balɛ] nm broom, brush; (Auto: d'essuie-glace) blade; (Mus: de batterie etc) brush; **donner un coup de ~** to give the floor a sweep; **~ mécanique** carpet sweeper

balai-brosse [balɛbʀɔs] (pl **balais-brosses**) nm (long-handled) scrubbing brush

balance [balɑ̃s] nf (à plateaux) scales pl; (de précision) balance; (Comm, Pol): **~ des comptes** ou **paiements** balance of payments; (signe): **la B~** Libra, the Scales; **être de la B~** to be Libra; **~ commerciale** balance of trade; **~ des forces** balance of power; **~ romaine** steelyard

balancelle [balɑ̃sɛl] nf garden hammock-seat

balancer [balɑ̃se] vt to swing; (lancer) to fling, chuck; (renvoyer, jeter) to chuck out ▷ vi to swing; **se balancer** vi to swing; (bateau) to rock; (branche) to sway; **se ~ de qch** (fam) not to give a toss about sth

balancier [balɑ̃sje] nm (de pendule) pendulum; (de montre) balance wheel; (perche) (balancing) pole

balançoire [balɑ̃swaʀ] nf swing; (sur pivot) seesaw

balayage [balɛjaʒ] nm sweeping; scanning

balayer [baleje] vt (feuilles etc) to sweep up, brush up; (pièce, cour) to sweep; (chasser) to sweep away ou aside; (radar) to scan; (: phares) to sweep across

balayette [balɛjɛt] nf small brush

balayeur, -euse [balɛjœʀ, -øz] nm/f road sweeper ▷ nf (engin) road sweeper

balayures [balɛjyʀ] nfpl sweepings

balbutiement [balbysimɑ̃] nm (paroles) stammering no pl; **balbutiements** nmpl (fig:

débuts) first faltering steps

balbutier [balbysje] *vi, vt* to stammer

balcon [balkɔ̃] *nm* balcony; (*Théât*) dress circle

baldaquin [baldakɛ̃] *nm* canopy

Bâle [bɑl] *n* Basle *ou* Basel

Baléares [baleaʀ] *nfpl*: **les ~** the Balearic Islands

baleine [balɛn] *nf* whale; (*de parapluie*) rib; (*de corset*) bone

baleinier [balenje] *nm* (*Navig*) whaler

baleinière [balenjɛʀ] *nf* whaleboat

balisage [balizaʒ] *nm* (*signaux*) beacons *pl*; buoys *pl*; runway lights *pl*; signs *pl*, markers *pl*

balise [baliz] *nf* (*Navig*) beacon, (marker) buoy; (*Aviat*) runway light, beacon; (*Auto, Ski*) sign

baliser [balize] *vt* to mark out (with beacons *ou* lights *etc*)

balistique [balistik] *adj* (*engin*) ballistic ▷ *nf* ballistics

balivernes [balivɛʀn(ə)] *nfpl* twaddle *sg* (*Brit*), nonsense *sg*

balkanique [balkanik] *adj* Balkan

Balkans [balkɑ̃] *nmpl*: **les ~** the Balkans

ballade [balad] *nf* ballad

ballant, e [balɑ̃, -ɑ̃t] *adj* dangling

ballast [balast] *nm* ballast

balle [bal] *nf* (*de fusil*) bullet; (*de sport*) ball; (*du blé*) chaff; (*paquet*) bale; (*fam: franc*) franc; **~ perdue** stray bullet

ballerine [balʀin] *nf* ballet dancer; (*chaussure*) pump, ballerina

ballet [balɛ] *nm* ballet; (*fig*): **~ diplomatique** diplomatic to-ings and fro-ings

ballon [balɔ̃] *nm* (*de sport*) ball; (*jouet, Aviat, de bande dessinée*) balloon; (*de vin*) glass; **~ d'essai** (*météorologique*) pilot balloon; (*fig*) feeler(s); **~ de football** football; **~ d'oxygène** oxygen bottle

ballonner [balɔne] *vt*: **j'ai le ventre ballonné** I feel bloated

ballon-sonde [balɔ̃sɔ̃d] (*pl* **ballons-sondes**) *nm* sounding balloon

ballot [balo] *nm* bundle; (*péj*) nitwit

ballottage [balɔtaʒ] *nm* (*Pol*) second ballot

ballotter [balɔte] *vi* to roll around; (*bateau etc*) to toss ▷ *vt* to shake *ou* throw about; to toss; **être ballotté entre** (*fig*) to be shunted between; (: *indécis*) to be torn between

ballottine [balɔtin] *nf* (*Culin*): **~ de volaille** meat loaf made with poultry

ball-trap [baltʀap] *nm* (*appareil*) trap; (*tir*) clay pigeon shooting

balluchon [balyʃɔ̃] *nm* bundle (of clothes)

balnéaire [balneɛʀ] *adj* seaside *cpd*

balnéothérapie [balneɔteʀapi] *nf* spa bath therapy

BALO *sigle m* (= *Bulletin des annonces légales obligatoires*) ≈ Public Notices (*in newspapers etc*)

balourd, e [baluʀ, -uʀd(ə)] *adj* clumsy ▷ *nm/f* clodhopper

balourdise [baluʀdiz] *nf* clumsiness; (*gaffe*) blunder

balte [balt] *adj* Baltic ▷ *nm/f*: **Balte** native of the Baltic States

baltique [baltik] *adj* Baltic ▷ *nf*: **la (mer) B~** the Baltic (Sea)

baluchon [balyʃɔ̃] *nm* = **balluchon**

balustrade [balystʀad] *nf* railings *pl*, handrail

bambin [bɑ̃bɛ̃] *nm* little child

bambou [bɑ̃bu] *nm* bamboo

ban [bɑ̃] *nm* round of applause, cheer; **être/mettre au ~ de** to be outlawed/to outlaw from; **le ~ et l'arrière-~ de sa famille** every last one of his relatives; **~s (de mariage)** banns, bans

banal, e [banal] *adj* banal, commonplace; (*péj*) trite; **four/moulin ~** village oven/mill

banalisé, e [banalize] *adj* (*voiture de police*) unmarked

banalité [banalite] *nf* banality; (*remarque*) truism, trite remark

banane [banan] *nf* banana

bananeraie [bananʀɛ] *nf* banana plantation

bananier [bananje] *nm* banana tree; (*bateau*) banana boat

banc [bɑ̃] *nm* seat, bench; (*de poissons*) shoal; **~ des accusés** dock; **~ d'essai** (*fig*) testing ground; **~ de sable** sandbank; **~ des témoins** witness box; **~ de touche** dugout

bancaire [bɑ̃kɛʀ] *adj* banking, bank *cpd*

bancal, e [bɑ̃kal] *adj* wobbly; (*personne*) bow-legged; (*fig: projet*) shaky

bandage [bɑ̃daʒ] *nm* bandaging; (*pansement*) bandage; **~ herniaire** truss

bande [bɑ̃d] *nf* (*de tissu etc*) strip; (*Méd*) bandage; (*motif, dessin*) stripe; (*Ciné*) film; (*Radio, groupe*) band; (*péj*): **une ~ de** a bunch *ou* crowd of; **par la ~** in a roundabout way; **donner de la ~** to list; **faire ~ à part** to keep to o.s.; **~ dessinée (BD)** strip cartoon (*Brit*), comic strip; **~ magnétique** magnetic tape; **~ passante** (*Inform*) bandwidth; **~ perforée** punched tape; **~ de roulement** (*de pneu*) tread; **~ sonore** sound track; **~ de terre** strip of land; **~ Velpeau®** (*Méd*) crêpe bandage

bandé, e [bɑ̃de] *adj* bandaged; **les yeux ~s** blindfold

bande-annonce [bɑ̃danɔ̃s] (*pl* **bandes-annonces**) *nf* (*Ciné*) trailer

bandeau, x [bɑ̃do] *nm* headband; (*sur les yeux*) blindfold; (*Méd*) head bandage

bandelette [bɑ̃dlɛt] *nf* strip of cloth, bandage

bander [bɑ̃de] *vt* to bandage; (*muscle*) to tense; (*arc*) to bend ▷ *vi* (*fam!*) to have a hard on (!); **~ les yeux à qn** to blindfold sb

banderole [bɑ̃dʀɔl] *nf* banderole; (*dans un défilé etc*) streamer

bande-son [bɑ̃dsɔ̃] (*pl* **bandes-son**) *nf* (*Ciné*) soundtrack

bandit [bɑ̃di] *nm* bandit

banditisme [bɑ̃ditism(ə)] *nm* violent crime, armed robberies *pl*

bandoulière [bɑ̃duljɛʀ] *nf*: **en ~** (slung *ou* worn) across the shoulder

Bangkok [bɑ̃kɔk] *n* Bangkok

Bangladesh [bɑ̃gladɛʃ] *nm*: **le ~** Bangladesh

banjo [bɑ̃(d)ʒo] *nm* banjo

banlieue [bɑ̃ljø] *nf* suburbs *pl*; **quartiers de ~** suburban areas; **trains de ~** commuter trains

banlieusard, e [bɑ̃ljøzaʀ, -aʀd(ə)] *nm/f* suburbanite

bannière [banjɛʀ] *nf* banner

bannir [baniʀ] *vt* to banish

banque [bɑ̃k] *nf* bank; (*activités*) banking; **~ des yeux/du sang** eye/blood bank; **~ d'affaires** merchant bank; **~ de dépôt** deposit bank; **~ de données** (*Inform*) data bank; **~ d'émission** bank of issue

banqueroute [bɑ̃kʀut] *nf* bankruptcy

banquet [bɑ̃kɛ] *nm* (*de club*) dinner; (*de noces*) reception; (*d'apparat*) banquet

banquette [bɑ̃kɛt] *nf* seat

banquier [bɑ̃kje] *nm* banker

banquise [bɑ̃kiz] *nf* ice field

bantou, e [bɑ̃tu] *adj* Bantu

baptême [batɛm] *nm* (*sacrement*) baptism; (*cérémonie*) christening, baptism; (*d'un navire*) launching; (*d'une cloche*) consecration, dedication; **~ de l'air** first flight

baptiser [batize] *vt* to christen; to baptize; to launch; to consecrate, dedicate

baptiste [batist(ə)] *adj, nm/f* Baptist

baquet [bakɛ] *nm* tub, bucket

bar [baʀ] *nm* bar; (*poisson*) bass

baragouin [baʀagwɛ̃] *nm* gibberish

baragouiner [baʀagwine] *vi* to gibber, jabber

baraque [baʀak] *nf* shed; (*fam*) house; **~ foraine** fairground stand

baraqué, e [baʀake] *adj* well-built, hefty

baraquements [baʀakmɑ̃] *nmpl* huts (*for refugees, workers etc*)

baratin [baʀatɛ̃] *nm* (*fam*) smooth talk, patter

baratiner [baʀatine] *vt* to chat up

baratte [baʀat] *nf* churn

Barbade [baʀbad] *nf*: **la ~** Barbados

barbant, e [baʀbɑ̃, -ɑ̃t] *adj* (*fam*) deadly (boring)

barbare [baʀbaʀ] *adj* barbaric ▷ *nm/f* barbarian

Barbarie [baʀbaʀi] *nf*: **la ~** the Barbary Coast

barbarie [baʀbaʀi] *nf* barbarism; (*cruauté*) barbarity

barbarisme [baʀbaʀism(ə)] *nm* (*Ling*) barbarism

barbe [baʀb(ə)] *nf* beard; (**au nez et) à la ~ de qn** (*fig*) under sb's very nose; **quelle ~!** (*fam*) what a drag *ou* bore!; **~ à papa** candy-floss (*Brit*), cotton candy (*US*)

barbecue [baʀbəkju] *nm* barbecue

barbelé [baʀbəle] *nm* barbed wire *no pl*

barber [baʀbe] *vt* (*fam*) to bore stiff

barbiche [baʀbiʃ] *nf* goatee

barbichette [baʀbiʃɛt] *nf* small goatee

barbiturique [baʀbityʀik] *nm* barbiturate

barboter [baʀbɔte] *vi* to paddle, dabble ▷ *vt* (*fam*) to filch

barboteuse [baʀbɔtøz] *nf* rompers *pl*

barbouiller [baʀbuje] *vt* to daub; (*péj: écrire, dessiner*) to scribble; **avoir l'estomac barbouillé** to feel queasy *ou* sick

barbu, e [baʀby] *adj* bearded

barbue [baʀby] *nf* (*poisson*) brill

Barcelone [baʀsələn] *n* Barcelona

barda [baʀda] *nm* (*fam*) kit, gear

barde [baʀd(ə)] *nf* (*Culin*) piece of fat bacon ▷ *nm* (*poète*) bard

bardé, e [baʀde] *adj*: **~ de médailles** *etc* bedecked with medals *etc*

bardeaux [baʀdo] *nmpl* shingle *no pl*

barder [baʀde] *vt* (*Culin: rôti, volaille*) to bard ▷ *vi* (*fam*): **ça va ~** sparks will fly

barème [baʀɛm] *nm* scale; (*liste*) table; **~ des salaires** salary scale

barge [baʀʒ] *nf* barge

baril [baʀil] *nm* (*tonneau*) barrel; (*de poudre*) keg

barillet [baʀijɛ] *nm* (*de revolver*) cylinder

bariolé, e [baʀjɔle] *adj* many-coloured, rainbow-coloured

barman [baʀman] *nm* barman

baromètre [baʀɔmɛtʀ(ə)] *nm* barometer; **~ anéroïde** aneroid barometer

baron [baʀɔ̃] *nm* baron

baronne [baʀɔn] *nf* baroness

baroque [baʀɔk] *adj* (*Art*) baroque; (*fig*) weird

baroud [baʀud] *nm*: **~ d'honneur** gallant last stand

baroudeur [baʀudœʀ] *nm* (*fam*) fighter

barque [baʀk(ə)] *nf* small boat

barquette [baʀkɛt] *nf* small boat-shaped tart; (*récipient: en aluminium*) tub; (: *en bois*) basket

barracuda [baʀakyda] *nm* barracuda

barrage [baʀaʒ] *nm* dam; (*sur route*) roadblock, barricade; **~ de police** police roadblock

barre [baʀ] *nf* (*de fer etc*) rod; (*Navig*) helm; (*écrite*) line, stroke; (*Danse*) barre; (*niveau*): **la livre a franchi la ~ des 1,70 euros** the pound has broken the 1.70 euros barrier; (*Jur*): **comparaître à la ~** to appear as a witness; **être à** *ou* **tenir la ~** (*Navig*) to be at the helm; **coup de ~** (*fig*): **c'est le coup de ~!** it's daylight robbery!; **j'ai le coup de ~!** I'm all in!; **~ fixe** (*Gym*) horizontal bar; **~ de mesure** (*Mus*) bar line; **~ à mine** crowbar; **~s parallèles/asymétriques** (*Gym*) parallel/asymmetric bars

barreau, x [baʀo] *nm* bar; (*Jur*): **le ~** the Bar

barrer [baʀe] *vt* (*route etc*) to block; (*mot*) to cross out; (*chèque*) to cross (*Brit*); (*Navig*) to steer; **se barrer** *vi* (*fam*) to clear off

barrette [baʀɛt] *nf* (*pour cheveux*) (hair) slide (*Brit*) *ou* clip (*US*); (*broche*) brooch

barreur [baʀœʀ] *nm* helmsman; (*aviron*) coxswain

barricade [baʀikad] *nf* barricade

barricader [baʀikade] *vt* to barricade; **se ~ chez soi** (*fig*) to lock o.s. in

barrière [baʀjɛʀ] *nf* fence; (*obstacle*) barrier; (*porte*) gate; **la Grande B~** the Great Barrier Reef; **~ de dégel** (*Admin: on roadsigns*) no heavy vehicles -- road liable to subsidence due to thaw; **~s douanières** trade barriers

barrique [baʀik] *nf* barrel, cask

barrir [baʀiʀ] *vi* to trumpet

bar-tabac [baʀtaba] *nm* bar (*which sells tobacco and stamps*)

baryton [baʀitɔ̃] *nm* baritone
bas, basse [ba, bas] *adj* low; (*action*) low, ignoble
▷ *nm* (*vêtement*) stocking; (*partie inférieure*): **le ~
de** the lower part *ou* foot *ou* bottom of ▷ *nf* (*Mus*)
bass ▷ *adv* low; (*parler*) softly; **plus ~** lower
down; more softly; (*dans un texte*) further on,
below; **la tête ~se** with lowered head; (*fig*)
with head hung low; **avoir la vue ~se** to be
short-sighted; **au ~ mot** at the lowest estimate;
enfant en ~ âge infant, young child; **en ~**
down below; at (*ou* to) the bottom; (*dans une
maison*) downstairs; **en ~ de** at the bottom of;
de ~ en haut upwards; from the bottom to the
top; **des hauts et des ~** ups and downs; **un ~
de laine** (*fam: économies*) money under the
mattress (*fig*); **mettre ~** *vi* (*animal*) to give birth;
à ~ la dictature! down with dictatorship!; **~
morceaux** (*viande*) cheap cuts
basalte [bazalt(ə)] *nm* basalt
basané, e [bazane] *adj* (*teint*) tanned, bronzed;
(*foncé; péj*) swarthy
bas-côté [bakote] *nm* (*de route*) verge (*Brit*),
shoulder (*US*); (*d'église*) (side) aisle
bascule [baskyl] *nf*: (**jeu de**) ~ seesaw; (**balance
à**) ~ scales *pl*; **fauteuil à ~** rocking chair;
système à ~ tip-over device; rocker device
basculer [baskyle] *vi* to fall over, topple (over);
(*benne*) to tip up ▷ *vt* (*aussi*: **faire basculer**) to
topple over; to tip out, tip up
base [baz] *nf* base; (*Pol*): **la ~** the rank and file,
the grass roots; (*fondement, principe*) basis (*pl
bases*); **jeter les ~s de** to lay the foundations of;
à la ~ de (*fig*) at the root of; **sur la ~ de** (*fig*) on
the basis of; **de ~** basic; **à ~ de café** *etc* coffee *etc*
-based; **~ de données** (*Inform*) database; **~ de
lancement** launching site
base-ball [bɛzbol] *nm* baseball
baser [baze] *vt*: **~ qch sur** to base sth on; **se ~
sur** (*données, preuves*) to base one's argument on;
être basé à/dans (*Mil*) to be based at/in
bas-fond [bafɔ̃] *nm* (*Navig*) shallow; **bas-fonds**
nmpl (*fig*) dregs
basilic [bazilik] *nm* (*Culin*) basil
basilique [bazilik] *nf* basilica
basket [baskɛt], **basket-ball** [baskɛtbol] *nm*
basketball
baskets [baskɛt] *nfpl* (*chaussures*) trainers (*Brit*),
sneakers (*US*)
basketteur, -euse [baskɛtœʀ, -øz] *nm/f*
basketball player
basquaise [baskɛz] *adj f* Basque ▷ *nf*: **B~** Basque
basque [bask(ə)] *adj, nm* (*Ling*) Basque ▷ *nm/f*:
Basque Basque; **le Pays ~** the Basque country
basques [bask(ə)] *nfpl* skirts; **pendu aux ~ de
qn** constantly pestering sb; (*mère etc*) hanging
on sb's apron strings
bas-relief [baʀəljɛf] *nm* bas-relief
basse [bas] *adj f, nf voir* **bas**
basse-cour [baskuʀ] (*pl* **basses-cours**) *nf*
farmyard; (*animaux*) farmyard animals
bassement [basmɑ̃] *adv* basely
bassesse [basɛs] *nf* baseness; (*acte*) base act

basset [basɛ] *nm* (*Zool*) basset (hound)
bassin [basɛ̃] *nm* (*cuvette*) bowl; (*pièce d'eau*) pond,
pool; (*de fontaine, Géo*) basin; (*Anat*) pelvis;
(*portuaire*) dock; **~ houiller** coalfield
bassine [basin] *nf* basin; (*contenu*) bowl, bowlful
bassiner [basine] *vt* (*plaie*) to bathe; (*lit*) to
warm with a warming pan; (*fam: ennuyer*) to
bore; (: *importuner*) to bug, pester
bassiste [basist(ə)] *nm/f* (double) bass player
basson [basɔ̃] *nm* bassoon
bastide [bastid] *nf* (*maison*) country house (*in
Provence*); (*ville*) walled town (*in SW France*)
bastion [bastjɔ̃] *nm* (*aussi fig, Pol*) bastion
bas-ventre [bavɑ̃tʀ(ə)] *nm* (lower part of the)
stomach
bât [ba] *nm* packsaddle
bataille [bataj] *nf* battle; **en ~** (*en travers*) at an
angle; (*en désordre*) awry; **~ rangée** pitched
battle
bataillon [batajɔ̃] *nm* battalion
bâtard, e [bataʀ, -aʀd(ə)] *adj* (*enfant*)
illegitimate; (*fig*) hybrid ▷ *nm/f* illegitimate
child, bastard (*péj*) ▷ *nm* (*Boulangerie*) ≈ Vienna
loaf; **chien ~** mongrel
batavia [batavja] *nf* ≈ Webb lettuce
bateau, x [bato] *nm* boat; (*grand*) ship ▷ *adj inv*
(*banal, rebattu*) hackneyed; **~ de pêche/à
moteur/à voiles** fishing/motor/sailing boat
bateau-citerne [batositɛʀn(ə)] *nm* tanker
bateau-mouche [batomuʃ] *nm* (passenger)
pleasure boat (*on the Seine*)
bateau-pilote [batopilɔt] *nm* pilot ship
bateleur, -euse [batlœʀ, -øz] *nm/f* street
performer
batelier, -ière [batəlje, -jɛʀ] *nm/f* ferryman/-
woman
bâti, e [bati] *adj* (*terrain*) developed ▷ *nm*
(*armature*) frame; (*Couture*) tacking; **bien ~**
(*personne*) well-built
batifoler [batifɔle] *vi* to frolic *ou* lark about
batik [batik] *nm* batik
bâtiment [batimɑ̃] *nm* building; (*Navig*) ship,
vessel; (*industrie*): **le ~** the building trade
bâtir [batiʀ] *vt* to build; (*Couture: jupe, ourlet*) to
tack; **fil à ~** (*Couture*) tacking thread
bâtisse [batis] *nf* building
bâtisseur, -euse [batisœʀ, -øz] *nm/f* builder
batiste [batist(ə)] *nf* (*Couture*) batiste, cambric
bâton [batɔ̃] *nm* stick; **mettre des ~s dans les
roues à qn** to put a spoke in sb's wheel; **à ~s
rompus** informally; **~ de rouge (à lèvres)**
lipstick; **~ de ski** ski stick
bâtonnet [batɔnɛ] *nm* short stick *ou* rod
bâtonnier [batɔnje] *nm* (*Jur*) ≈ President of the
Bar
batraciens [batʀasjɛ̃] *nmpl* amphibians
bats [ba] *vb voir* **battre**
battage [bataʒ] *nm* (*publicité*) (hard) plugging
battant, e [batɑ̃, -ɑ̃t] *vb voir* **battre** ▷ *adj*: **pluie
~e** lashing rain ▷ *nm* (*de cloche*) clapper; (*de
volets*) shutter, flap; (*de porte*) side; (*fig: personne*)
fighter; **porte à double ~** double door;

b

tambour ~ briskly

batte [bat] nf (Sport) bat

battement [batmɑ̃] nm (de cœur) beat; (intervalle) interval (between classes, trains etc); ~ **de paupières** blinking no pl (of eyelids); **un ~ de 10 minutes, 10 minutes de** ~ 10 minutes to spare

batterie [batʀi] nf (Mil, Élec) battery; (Mus) drums pl, drum kit; ~ **de cuisine** kitchen utensils pl; (casseroles etc) pots and pans pl; **une ~ de tests** a string of tests

batteur [batœʀ] nm (Mus) drummer; (appareil) whisk

batteuse [batøz] nf (Agr) threshing machine

battoir [batwaʀ] nm (à linge) beetle (for laundry); (à tapis) (carpet) beater

battre [batʀ(ə)] vt to beat; (pluie, vagues) to beat ou lash against; (œufs etc) to beat up, whisk; (blé) to thresh; (cartes) to shuffle; (passer au peigne fin) to scour ▷ vi (cœur) to beat; (volets etc) to bang, rattle; **se battre** vi to fight; ~ **la mesure** to beat time; ~ **en brèche** (Mil: mur) to batter; (fig: théorie) to demolish; (: institution etc) to attack; ~ **son plein** to be at its height, be going full swing; ~ **pavillon britannique** to fly the British flag; ~ **des mains** to clap one's hands; ~ **des ailes** to flap its wings; ~ **de l'aile** (fig) to be in a bad way ou in bad shape; ~ **la semelle** to stamp one's feet; ~ **en retraite** to beat a retreat

battu, e [baty] pp de **battre** ▷ nf (chasse) beat; (policière etc) search, hunt

baud [bo(d)] nm baud

baudruche [bodʀyʃ] nf: **ballon en** ~ (toy) balloon; (fig) windbag

baume [bom] nm balm

bauxite [boksit] nf bauxite

bavard, e [bavaʀ, -aʀd(ə)] adj (very) talkative; gossipy

bavardage [bavaʀdaʒ] nm chatter no pl; gossip no pl

bavarder [bavaʀde] vi to chatter; (indiscrètement) to gossip; (: révéler un secret) to blab

bavarois, e [bavaʀwa, -waz] adj Bavarian ▷ nm ou f (Culin) bavarois

bave [bav] nf dribble; (de chien etc) slobber, slaver (Brit), drool (US); (d'escargot) slime

baver [bave] vi to dribble; to slobber, slaver (Brit), drool (US); (encre, couleur) to run; **en** ~ (fam) to have a hard time (of it)

bavette [bavɛt] nf bib

baveux, -euse [bavø, -øz] adj dribbling; (omelette) runny

Bavière [bavjɛʀ] nf: **la** ~ Bavaria

bavoir [bavwaʀ] nm (de bébé) bib

bavure [bavyʀ] nf smudge; (fig) hitch; blunder

bayer [baje] vi: ~ **aux corneilles** to stand gaping

bazar [bazaʀ] nm general store; (fam) jumble

bazarder [bazaʀde] vt (fam) to chuck out

BCBG sigle adj (= bon chic bon genre) ≈ preppy

BCG sigle m (= bacille Calmette-Guérin) BCG

bcp abr = **beaucoup**

BD sigle f = **bande dessinée**; (= base de données) DB

bd abr = **boulevard**

b.d.c. abr (Typo: = bas de casse) l.c.

béant, e [beɑ̃, -ɑ̃t] adj gaping

béarnais, e [beaʀnɛ, -ɛz] adj of ou from the Béarn

béat, e [bea, -at] adj showing open-eyed wonder; (sourire etc) blissful

béatitude [beatityd] nf bliss

beau, bel, belle, beaux [bo, bɛl] adj beautiful, lovely; (homme) handsome ▷ nf (Sport) decider ▷ adv: **il fait** ~ the weather's fine ▷ nm: **avoir le sens du** ~ to have an aesthetic sense; **le temps est au** ~ the weather is set fair; **un ~ geste** (fig) a fine gesture; **un ~ salaire** a good salary; **un ~ gâchis/rhume** a fine mess/nasty cold; **en faire/dire de belles** to do/say (some) stupid things; **le ~ monde** high society; ~ **parleur** smooth talker; **un ~ jour** one (fine) day; **de plus belle** more than ever, even more; **bel et bien** well and truly; (vraiment) really (and truly); **le plus ~ c'est que ...** the best of it is that ...; **c'est du ~!** that's great, that is!; **on a ~ essayer** however hard ou no matter how hard we try; **il a ~ jeu de protester** etc it's easy for him to protest etc; **faire le ~** (chien) to sit up and beg

 MOT-CLÉ

beaucoup [boku] adv **1** a lot; **il boit beaucoup** he drinks a lot; **il ne boit pas beaucoup** he doesn't drink much ou a lot

2 (suivi de plus, trop etc) much, a lot, far; **il est beaucoup plus grand** he is much ou a lot ou far taller

3: **beaucoup de** (nombre) many, a lot of; (quantité) a lot of; **pas beaucoup de** (nombre) not many, not a lot of; (quantité) not much, not a lot of; **beaucoup d'étudiants/de touristes** a lot of ou many students/tourists; **beaucoup de courage** a lot of courage; **il n'a pas beaucoup d'argent** he hasn't got much ou a lot of money; **il n'y a pas beaucoup de touristes** there aren't many ou a lot of tourists

4: **de beaucoup** by far

▷ pron: **beaucoup le savent** lots of people know that

beau-fils [bofis] (pl **beaux-fils**) nm son-in-law; (remariage) stepson

beau-frère [bofʀɛʀ] (pl **beaux-frères**) nm brother-in-law

beau-père [bopɛʀ] (pl **beaux-pères**) nm father-in-law; (remariage) stepfather

beauté [bote] nf beauty; **de toute** ~ beautiful; **en** ~ adv with a flourish, brilliantly

beaux-arts [bozaʀ] nmpl fine arts

beaux-parents [bopaʀɑ̃] nmpl wife's/ husband's family, in-laws

bébé [bebe] nm baby

bébé-éprouvette [bebeepʀuvɛt] (pl **bébés-éprouvette**) nm test-tube baby

bec [bɛk] nm beak, bill; (de plume) nib; (de cafetière etc) spout; (de casserole etc) lip; (d'une clarinette etc)

43

mouthpiece; (*fam*) mouth; **clouer le ~ à qn**
(*fam*) to shut sb up; **ouvrir le ~** (*fam*) to open
one's mouth; **~ de gaz** (street) gaslamp; **~
verseur** pouring lip

bécane [bekan] *nf* (*fam*) bike

bécarre [bekaʀ] *nm* (*Mus*) natural

bécasse [bekas] *nf* (*Zool*) woodcock; (*fam*) silly
goose

bec-de-cane [bɛkdəkan] (*pl* **becs-de-cane**) *nm*
(*poignée*) door handle

bec-de-lièvre [bɛkdəljɛvʀ(ə)] (*pl* **becs-de-lièvre**)
nm harelip

béchamel [beʃamɛl] *nf*: (**sauce**) ~ white sauce,
bechamel sauce

bêche [bɛʃ] *nf* spade

bêcher [beʃe] *vt* (*terre*) to dig; (*personne: critiquer*)
to slate; (: *snober*) to look down on

bêcheur, -euse [beʃœʀ, -øz] *adj* (*fam*) stuck-up
▷ *nm/f* fault-finder; (*snob*) stuck-up person

bécoter [bekɔte]: **se bécoter** *vi* to smooch

becquée [beke] *nf*: **donner la ~ à** to feed

becqueter [bɛkte] *vt* (*fam*) to eat

bedaine [bədɛn] *nf* paunch

bédé [bede] *nf* (*fam*) = **bande dessinée**

bedeau, x [bədo] *nm* beadle

bedonnant, e [bədɔnɑ̃, -ɑ̃t] *adj* paunchy,
potbellied

bée [be] *adj*: **bouche ~** gaping

beffroi [befʀwa] *nm* belfry

bégaiement [begɛmɑ̃] *nm* stammering,
stuttering

bégayer [begeje] *vt, vi* to stammer

bégonia [begɔnja] *nm* (*Bot*) begonia

bègue [bɛg] *nm/f*: **être ~** to have a stammer

béqueule [begœl] *adj* prudish

beige [bɛʒ] *adj* beige

beignet [bɛɲɛ] *nm* fritter

bel [bɛl] *adj m* voir **beau**

bêler [bele] *vi* to bleat

belette [bəlɛt] *nf* weasel

belge [bɛlʒ(ə)] *adj* Belgian ▷ *nm/f*: **Belge**
Belgian; *see note*

● **FÊTE NATIONALE BELGE**
●
● The *fête nationale belge*, on 21 July, marks the
● day in 1831 when Leopold of Saxe-Coburg
● Gotha was crowned King Leopold I.

Belgique [bɛlʒik] *nf*: **la ~** Belgium

Belgrade [belgʀad] *n* Belgrade

bélier [belje] *nm* ram; (*engin*) (battering) ram;
(*signe*): **le B~** Aries, the Ram; **être du B~** to be
Aries

Bélize [beliz] *nm*: **le ~** Belize

bellâtre [belɑtʀ(ə)] *nm* dandy

belle [bɛl] *adj f, nf* voir **beau**

belle-famille [bɛlfamij] (*pl* **belles-familles**) *nf*
(*fam*) in-laws *pl*

belle-fille [bɛlfij] (*pl* **belles-filles**) *nf* daughter-
in-law; (*remariage*) stepdaughter

belle-mère [bɛlmɛʀ] (*pl* **belles-mères**) *nf*

mother-in-law; (*remariage*) stepmother

belle-sœur [bɛlsœʀ] (*pl* **belles-sœurs**) *nf* sister-
in-law

belliciste [belisist(ə)] *adj* warmongering

belligérance [beliʒeʀɑ̃s] *nf* belligerence

belligérant, e [beliʒeʀɑ̃, -ɑ̃t] *adj* belligerent

belliqueux, -euse [belikø, -øz] *adj* aggressive,
warlike

belote [bəlɔt] *nf* belote (*card game*)

belvédère [bɛlvedɛʀ] *nm* panoramic viewpoint
(*or small building there*)

bémol [bemɔl] *nm* (*Mus*) flat

ben [bɛ̃] *excl* (*fam*) well

bénédiction [benediksjɔ̃] *nf* blessing

bénéfice [benefis] *nm* (*Comm*) profit; (*avantage*)
benefit; **au ~ de** in aid of

bénéficiaire [benefisjɛʀ] *nm/f* beneficiary

bénéficier [benefisje] *vi*: **~ de** to enjoy; (*profiter*)
to benefit by *ou* from; (*obtenir*) to get, be given

bénéfique [benefik] *adj* beneficial

Bénélux [benelyks] *nm*: **le ~** Benelux, the
Benelux countries

benêt [bənɛ] *nm* simpleton

bénévolat [benevɔla] *nm* voluntary service *ou*
work

bénévole [benevɔl] *adj* voluntary, unpaid

bénévolement [benevɔlmɑ̃] *adv* voluntarily

Bengale [bɛ̃gal] *nm*: **le ~** Bengal; **le golfe du ~**
the Bay of Bengal

bengali [bɛ̃gali] *adj* Bengali, Bengalese ▷ *nm*
(*Ling*) Bengali

Bénin [benɛ̃] *nm*: **le ~** Benin

bénin, -igne [benɛ̃, -iɲ] *adj* minor, mild;
(*tumeur*) benign

bénir [beniʀ] *vt* to bless

bénit, e [beni, -it] *adj* consecrated; **eau ~e** holy
water

bénitier [benitje] *nm* stoup, font (*for holy water*)

benjamin, e [bɛ̃ʒamɛ̃, -in] *nm/f* youngest child;
(*Sport*) under-13

benne [bɛn] *nf* skip; (*de téléphérique*) (cable) car; **~
basculante** tipper (*Brit*), dump *ou* dumper truck

benzine [bɛ̃zin] *nf* benzine

béotien, ne [beɔsjɛ̃, -ɛn] *nm/f* philistine

BEP *sigle m* (= *Brevet d'études professionnelles*) school-
leaving diploma, taken at approx. 18 years

BEPC *sigle m* (= *Brevet d'études du premier cycle*) former
school certificate (taken at approx. 16 years)

béquille [bekij] *nf* crutch; (*de bicyclette*) stand

berbère [bɛʀbɛʀ] *adj* Berber ▷ *nm* (*Ling*) Berber
▷ *nm/f*: **Berbère** Berber

bercail [bɛʀkaj] *nm* fold

berceau, x [bɛʀso] *nm* cradle, crib

bercer [bɛʀse] *vt* to rock, cradle; (*musique etc*) to
lull; **~ qn de** (*promesses etc*) to delude sb with

berceur, -euse [bɛʀsœʀ, -øz] *adj* soothing ▷ *nf*
(*chanson*) lullaby

BERD [bɛʀd] *sigle f* (= *Banque européenne pour la
reconstruction et le développement*) EBRD

béret [beʀɛ], **béret basque** [beʀɛbask(ə)] *nm*
beret

bergamote [bɛʀgamɔt] *nf* (*Bot*) bergamot

berge [bɛʀʒ(ə)] nf bank
berger, -ère [bɛʀʒe, -ɛʀ] nm/f shepherd/
shepherdess; **~ allemand** (chien) alsatian (dog)
(Brit), German shepherd (dog) (US)
bergerie [bɛʀʒəʀi] nf sheep pen
bergeronnette [bɛʀʒəʀɔnɛt] nf wagtail
béribéri [beʀibeʀi] nm beriberi
Berlin [bɛʀlɛ̃] n Berlin; **~-Est/-Ouest** East/West
Berlin
berline [bɛʀlin] nf (Auto) saloon (car) (Brit),
sedan (US)
berlingot [bɛʀlɛ̃go] nm (emballage) carton
(pyramid shaped); (bonbon) lozenge
berlinois, e [bɛʀlinwa, -waz] adj of ou from
Berlin ▷ nm/f: **Berlinois, e** Berliner
berlue [bɛʀly] nf: **j'ai la ~** I must be seeing
things
bermuda [bɛʀmyda] nm (short) Bermuda shorts
Bermudes [bɛʀmyd] nfpl: **les (îles) ~** Bermuda
Berne [bɛʀn(ə)] n Bern
berne [bɛʀn(ə)] nf: **en ~** at half-mast; **mettre
en ~** to fly at half-mast
berner [bɛʀne] vt to fool
bernois, e [bɛʀnwa, -waz] adj Bernese
berrichon, ne [beʀiʃɔ̃, -ɔn] adj of ou from the
Berry
besace [bəzas] nf beggar's bag
besogne [bəzɔɲ] nf work no pl, job
besogneux, -euse [bəzɔɲø, -øz] adj hard-
working
besoin [bəzwɛ̃] nm need; (pauvreté): **le ~** need,
want; **le ~ d'argent/de gloire** the need for
money/glory; **~s (naturels)** nature's needs;
faire ses ~s to relieve o.s.; **avoir ~ de qch/faire
qch** to need sth/to do sth; **il n'y a pas ~ de
(faire)** there is no need to (do); **au ~, si ~ est** if
need be; **pour les ~s de la cause** for the
purpose in hand
bestial, e, -aux [bɛstjal, -o] adj bestial, brutish
▷ nmpl cattle
bestiole [bɛstjɔl] nf (tiny) creature
bétail [betaj] nm livestock, cattle pl
bétaillère [betajɛʀ] nf livestock truck
bête [bɛt] nf animal; (bestiole) insect, creature
▷ adj stupid, silly; **les ~s** (the) animals;
chercher la petite ~ to nit-pick; **~ noire** pet
hate, bugbear (Brit); **~ sauvage** wild beast; **~ de
somme** beast of burden
bêtement [bɛtmɑ̃] adv stupidly; **tout ~** quite
simply
Bethléem [bɛtleɛm] n Bethlehem
bêtifier [betifje] vi to talk nonsense
bêtise [betiz] nf stupidity; (action, remarque)
stupid thing (to say ou do); (bonbon) type of mint
sweet (Brit) ou candy (US); **faire/dire une ~** to
do/say something stupid
béton [betɔ̃] nm concrete; **(en) ~** (fig: alibi,
argument) cast iron; **~ armé** reinforced concrete;
~ précontraint prestressed concrete
bétonner [betɔne] vt to concrete (over)
bétonnière [betɔnjɛʀ] nf cement mixer
bette [bɛt] nf (Bot) (Swiss) chard

betterave [bɛtʀav] nf (rouge) beetroot (Brit), beet
(US); **~ fourragère** mangel-wurzel; **~ sucrière**
sugar beet
beugler [bøgle] vi to low; (péj: radio etc) to blare
▷ vt (péj: chanson etc) to bawl out
Beur [bœʀ] adj, nm/f see note

● BEUR
Beur is a term used to refer to a person born
in France of North African immigrant
parents. It is not racist and is often used by
the media, anti-racist groups and second-
generation North Africans themselves. The
word itself comes from back slang or
"verlan".

beurre [bœʀ] nm butter; **mettre du ~ dans les
épinards** (fig) to add a little to the kitty; **~ de
cacao** cocoa butter; **~ noir** brown butter (sauce)
beurrer [bœʀe] vt to butter
beurrier [bœʀje] nm butter dish
beuverie [bœvʀi] nf drinking session
bévue [bevy] nf blunder
Beyrouth [beʀut] n Beirut
Bhoutan [butɑ̃] nm: **le ~** Bhutan
bi... [bi] préfixe bi..., two-
Biafra [bjafʀa] nm: **le ~** Biafra
biafrais, e [bjafʀɛ, -ɛz] adj Biafran
biais [bjɛ] nm (moyen) device, expedient; (aspect)
angle; (bande de tissu) piece of cloth cut on the
bias; **en ~, de ~** (obliquement) at an angle; (fig)
indirectly
biaiser [bjeze] vi (fig) to sidestep the issue
biathlon [biatlɔ̃] nm biathlon
bibelot [biblo] nm trinket, curio
biberon [bibʀɔ̃] nm (feeding) bottle; **nourrir au
~** to bottle-feed
bible [bibl(ə)] nf bible
bibliobus [biblijɔbys] nm mobile library van
bibliographie [biblijɔgʀafi] nf bibliography
bibliophile [biblijɔfil] nm/f book-lover
bibliothécaire [biblijɔtekɛʀ] nm/f librarian
bibliothèque [biblijɔtɛk] nf library; (meuble)
bookcase; **~ municipale** public library
biblique [biblik] adj biblical
bic® [bik] nm Biro®
bicarbonate [bikaʀbɔnat] nm: **~ (de soude)**
bicarbonate of soda
bicentenaire [bisɑ̃tnɛʀ] nm bicentenary
biceps [bisɛps] nm biceps
biche [biʃ] nf doe
bichonner [biʃɔne] vt to groom
bicolore [bikɔlɔʀ] adj two-coloured (Brit), two-
colored (US)
bicoque [bikɔk] nf (péj) shack, dump
bicorne [bikɔʀn(ə)] nm cocked hat
bicyclette [bisiklɛt] nf bicycle
bidasse [bidas] nm (fam) squaddie (Brit)
bide [bid] nm (fam: ventre) belly; (Théât) flop
bidet [bidɛ] nm bidet
bidoche [bidɔʃ] nf (fam) meat

bidon [bidɔ̃] *nm* can ▷ *adj inv* (*fam*) phoney
bidonnant, e [bidɔnɑ̃, -ɑ̃t] *adj* (*fam*) hilarious
bidonville [bidɔ̃vil] *nm* shanty town
bidule [bidyl] *nm* (*fam*) thingamajig
bielle [bjɛl] *nf* connecting rod; (*Auto*) track rod
biélorusse [bjelɔrys] *adj* Belarussian ▷ *nm/f*:
   Biélorusse Belarussian
Biélorussie [bjelɔrysi] *nf* Belorussia

 MOT-CLÉ

bien [bjɛ̃] *nm* **1** (*avantage, profit*): **faire le bien** to
do good; **faire du bien à qn** to do sb good; **ça
fait du bien de faire** it does you good to do;
dire du bien de to speak well of; **c'est pour
son bien** it's for his own good; **changer en
bien** to change for the better; **le bien public**
the public good; **vouloir du bien à qn** (*vouloir
aider*) to have sb's (best) interests at heart; **je te
veux du bien** (*pour mettre en confiance*) I don't
wish you any harm
2 (*possession, patrimoine*) possession, property;
son bien le plus précieux his most treasured
possession; **avoir du bien** to have property;
biens (**de consommation** *etc*) (consumer *etc*)
goods; **biens durables** (consumer) durables
3 (*moral*): **le bien** good; **distinguer le bien du
mal** to tell good from evil
▷ *adv* **1** (*de façon satisfaisante*) well; **elle travaille/
mange bien** she works/eats well; **aller** *or* **se
porter bien** to be well; **croyant bien faire, je/
il** ... thinking I/he was doing the right thing, I/
he ...
2 (*valeur intensive*) quite; **bien jeune** quite
young; **bien assez** quite enough; **bien mieux**
(very) much better; **bien du temps/des gens**
quite a time/a number of people; **j'espère bien
y aller** I do hope to go; **je veux bien le faire**
(*concession*) I'm quite willing to do it; **il faut
bien le faire** it has to be done; **il y a bien deux
ans** at least two years ago; **il semble bien que**
it really seems that; **peut-être bien** it could
well be; **aimer bien** to like; **Paul est bien
venu, n'est-ce pas?** Paul HAS come, hasn't
he?; **où peut-il bien être passé?** where on
earth can he have got to?
3 (*conséquence, résultat*): **si bien que** with the
result that; **on verra bien** we'll see; **faire bien
de ...** to be right to ...
▷ *excl* right!, OK!, fine!; **eh bien!** well!; (**c'est**)
bien fait! it serves you (*ou* him *etc*) right!; **bien
sûr!, bien entendu!** certainly!, of course!
▷ *adj inv* **1** (*en bonne forme, à l'aise*): **je me sens
bien, je suis bien** I feel fine; **je ne me sens pas
bien, je ne suis pas bien** I don't feel well; **on
est bien dans ce fauteuil** this chair is very
comfortable
2 (*joli, beau*) good-looking; **tu es bien dans
cette robe** you look good in that dress
3 (*satisfaisant*) good; **elle est bien, cette
maison/secrétaire** it's a good house/she's a
good secretary; **c'est très bien** (**comme ça**) it's

fine (like that); **ce n'est pas si bien que ça** it's
not as good *ou* great as all that; **c'est bien?** is
that all right?
4 (*moralement*) right; (: *personne*) good, nice;
(*respectable*) respectable; **ce n'est pas bien de ...**
it's not right to ...; **elle est bien, cette femme**
she's a nice woman, she's a good sort; **des gens
bien** respectable people
5 (*en bons termes*): **être bien avec qn** to be on
good terms with sb

bien-aimé, e [bjɛ̃neme] *adj, nm/f* beloved
bien-être [bjɛ̃nɛtʀ(ə)] *nm* well-being
bienfaisance [bjɛ̃fəzɑ̃s] *nf* charity
bienfaisant, e [bjɛ̃fəzɑ̃, -ɑ̃t] *adj* (*chose*) beneficial
bienfait [bjɛ̃fɛ] *nm* act of generosity,
benefaction; (*de la science etc*) benefit
bienfaiteur, -trice [bjɛ̃fɛtœʀ, -tʀis] *nm/f*
benefactor/benefactress
bien-fondé [bjɛ̃fɔ̃de] *nm* soundness
bien-fonds [bjɛ̃fɔ̃] *nm* property
bienheureux, -euse [bjɛ̃nœʀø, -øz] *adj* happy;
(*Rel*) blessed, blest
biennal, e, -aux [bjenal, -o] *adj* biennial
bien-pensant, e [bjɛ̃pɑ̃sɑ̃, -ɑ̃t] *adj* right-
thinking ▷ *nm/f*: **les ~s** right-minded people
bien que [bjɛ̃k(ə)] *conj* although
bienséance [bjɛ̃seɑ̃s] *nf* propriety, decorum *no
pl*; **les ~s** (*convenances*) the proprieties
bienséant, e [bjɛ̃seɑ̃, -ɑ̃t] *adj* proper, seemly
bientôt [bjɛ̃to] *adv* soon; **à ~** see you soon
bienveillance [bjɛ̃vɛjɑ̃s] *nf* kindness
bienveillant, e [bjɛ̃vɛjɑ̃, -ɑ̃t] *adj* kindly
bienvenu, e [bjɛ̃vny] *adj* welcome ▷ *nm/f*: **être
le ~/la ~e** to be welcome ▷ *nf*: **souhaiter la ~e
à** to welcome; **~e à** welcome to
bière [bjɛʀ] *nf* (*boisson*) beer; (*cercueil*) bier; **~
blonde** lager; **~ brune** brown ale; **~ (à la)
pression** draught beer
biffer [bife] *vt* to cross out
bifteck [biftɛk] *nm* steak
bifurcation [bifyʀkasjɔ̃] *nf* fork (*in road*); (*fig*)
new direction
bifurquer [bifyʀke] *vi* (*route*) to fork; (*véhicule*) to
turn off
bigame [bigam] *adj* bigamous
bigamie [bigami] *nf* bigamy
bigarré, e [bigaʀe] *adj* multicoloured (*Brit*),
multicolored (*US*); (*disparate*) motley
bigarreau, x [bigaʀo] *nm* type of cherry
bigleux, -euse [biglø, -øz] *adj* (*fam: qui louche*)
cross-eyed; (: *qui voit mal*) short-sighted; **il est
complètement ~** he's as blind as a bat
bigorneau, x [bigɔʀno] *nm* winkle
bigot, e [bigo, -ɔt] (*péj*) *adj* bigoted ▷ *nm/f* bigot
bigoterie [bigɔtʀi] *nf* bigotry
bigoudi [bigudi] *nm* curler
bigrement [bigʀəmɑ̃] *adv* (*fam*) fantastically
bijou, x [biʒu] *nm* jewel
bijouterie [biʒutʀi] *nf* (*magasin*) jeweller's
(shop) (*Brit*), jewelry store (*US*); (*bijoux*)
jewellery, jewelry

bijoutier, -ière [biʒutje, -jɛʀ] nm/f jeweller
(Brit), jeweler (US)
bikini [bikini] nm bikini
bilan [bilɑ̃] nm (Comm) balance sheet(s); (annuel)
end of year statement; (fig) (net) outcome; (: de
victimes) toll; **faire le ~ de** to assess; to review;
déposer son ~ to file a bankruptcy statement;
~ de santé (Méd) check-up; **~ social** statement of a
firm's policies towards its employees
bilatéral, e, -aux [bilateʀal, -o] adj bilateral
bilboquet [bilbɔkɛ] nm (jouet) cup-and-ball
game
bile [bil] nf bile; **se faire de la ~** (fam) to worry
o.s. sick
biliaire [biljɛʀ] adj biliary
bilieux, -euse [biljø, -øz] adj bilious; (fig:
colérique) testy
bilingue [bilɛ̃g] adj bilingual
bilinguisme [bilɛ̃gɥism(ə)] nm bilingualism
billard [bijaʀ] nm billiards sg; (table) billiard
table; **c'est du ~** (fam) it's a cinch; **passer sur
le ~** (fam) to have an (ou one's) operation; **~
électrique** pinball
bille [bij] nf ball; (du jeu de billes) marble; (de bois)
log; **jouer aux ~s** to play marbles
billet [bijɛ] nm (aussi: **billet de banque**)
(bank)note; (de cinéma, de bus etc) ticket; (courte
lettre) note; **~ à ordre** ou **de commerce** (Comm)
promissory note, IOU; **~ d'avion/de train**
plane/train ticket; **~ circulaire** round-trip
ticket; **~ doux** love letter; **~ de faveur**
complimentary ticket; **~ de loterie** lottery
ticket; **~ de quai** platform ticket; **~
électronique** e-ticket
billetterie [bijɛtʀi] nf ticket office; (distributeur)
ticket dispenser; (Banque) cash dispenser
billion [biljɔ̃] nm billion (Brit), trillion (US)
billot [bijo] nm block
bimbeloterie [bɛ̃blɔtʀi] nf (objets) fancy goods
bimensuel, le [bimɑ̃sɥɛl] adj bimonthly, twice-
monthly
bimestriel, le [bimɛstʀijɛl] adj bimonthly, two-
monthly
bimoteur [bimɔtœʀ] adj twin-engined
binaire [binɛʀ] adj binary
biner [bine] vt to hoe
binette [binɛt] nf (outil) hoe
binoclard, e [binɔklaʀ, -aʀd(ə)] (fam) adj specky
▷ nm/f four-eyes
binocle [binɔkl(ə)] nm pince-nez
binoculaire [binɔkylɛʀ] adj binocular
binôme [binom] nm binomial
bio [bjo] adj (fam) = **biologique**; (produits, aliments)
organic
bio... [bjɔ] préfixe bio...
biocarburant [bjokaʀbyʀɑ̃] nm biofuel
biochimie [bjɔʃimi] nf biochemistry
biochimique [bjɔʃimik] adj biochemical
biochimiste [bjɔʃimist(ə)] nm/f biochemist
biodégradable [bjɔdegʀadabl(ə)] adj
biodegradable
biodiversité [bjodivɛʀsite] nf biodiversity

bioéthique [bjoetik] nf bioethics sg
biographe [bjɔgʀaf] nm/f biographer
biographie [bjɔgʀafi] nf biography
biographique [bjɔgʀafik] adj biographical
biologie [bjɔlɔʒi] nf biology
biologique [bjɔlɔʒik] adj biological
biologiste [bjɔlɔʒist(ə)] nm/f biologist
biomasse [bjomas] nf biomass
biopsie [bjɔpsi] nf (Méd) biopsy
biosphère [bjɔsfɛʀ] nf biosphere
biotechnologie [bjotɛknɔlɔʒi] nf biotechnology
bioterrorisme [bjotɛʀɔʀism] nm bioterrorism
bioterroriste [bjotɛʀɔʀist] nm/f bioterrorist
biotope [bjɔtɔp] nm biotope
bipartisme [bipaʀtism(ə)] nm two-party
system
bipartite [bipaʀtit] adj (Pol) two-party,
bipartisan
bipède [bipɛd] nm biped, two-footed creature
biphasé, e [bifaze] adj (Élec) two-phase
biplace [biplas] adj, nm (avion) two-seater
biplan [biplɑ̃] nm biplane
bique [bik] nf nanny goat; (péj) old hag
biquet, te [bikɛ, -ɛt] nm/f: **mon ~** (fam) my lamb
BIRD [biʀd] sigle f (= Banque internationale pour la
reconstruction et le développement) IBRD
biréacteur [biʀeaktœʀ] nm twin-engined jet
birman, e [biʀmɑ̃, -an] adj Burmese
Birmanie [biʀmani] nf: **la ~** Burma
bis, e [bi, biz] adj (couleur) greyish brown ▷ adv
[bis]: **12 ~ 12a** ou A ▷ excl, nm [bis] encore ▷ nf
(baiser) kiss; (vent) North wind; **faire une** ou **la
~e à qn** to kiss sb
bisaïeul, e [bizajœl] nm/f great-grandfather/
great-grandmother
bisannuel, le [bizanɥɛl] adj biennial
bisbille [bisbij] nf: **être en ~ avec qn** to be at
loggerheads with sb
Biscaye [biske] nf: **le golfe de ~** the Bay of
Biscay
biscornu, e [biskɔʀny] adj crooked; (bizarre)
weird(-looking)
biscotte [biskɔt] nf (breakfast) rusk
biscuit [biskɥi] nm biscuit (Brit), cookie (US);
(gateau) sponge cake; **~ à la cuiller** sponge
finger
biscuiterie [biskɥitʀi] nf biscuit
manufacturing
bise [biz] adj f, nf voir **bis**
biseau, x [bizo] nm bevelled edge; **en ~** bevelled
biseauter [bizote] vt to bevel
bisexué, e [bisɛksɥe] adj bisexual
bisexuel, le [bisɛksɥɛl] adj, nm/f bisexual
bismuth [bismyt] nm bismuth
bison [bizɔ̃] nm bison
bisou [bizu] nm (fam) kiss
bisque [bisk(ə)] nf: **~ d'écrevisses** shrimp
bisque
bissectrice [bisɛktʀis] nf bisector
bisser [bise] vt (faire rejouer: artiste, chanson) to
encore; (rejouer: morceau) to give an encore of
bissextile [bisɛkstil] adj: **année ~** leap year

bistouri [bistuʀi] *nm* lancet
bistre [bistʀ(ə)] *adj* (*couleur*) bistre; (*peau, teint*) tanned
bistro, bistrot [bistʀo] *nm* bistro, café
BIT *sigle m* (= *Bureau international du travail*) ILO
bit [bit] *nm* (*Inform*) bit
biterrois, e [biteʀwa, -waz] *adj* of *ou* from Béziers
bitte [bit] *nf*: ~ **d'amarrage** bollard (*Naut*)
bitume [bitym] *nm* asphalt
bitumer [bityme] *vt* to asphalt
bivalent, e [bivalɑ̃, -ɑ̃t] *adj* bivalent
bivouac [bivwak] *nm* bivouac
bizarre [bizaʀ] *adj* strange, odd
bizarrement [bizaʀmɑ̃] *adv* strangely, oddly
bizarrerie [bizaʀʀi] *nf* strangeness, oddness
blackbouler [blakbule] *vt* (*à une élection*) to blackball
blafard, e [blafaʀ, -aʀd(ə)] *adj* wan
blague [blag] *nf* (*propos*) joke; (*farce*) trick; **sans ~!** no kidding!; ~ **à tabac** tobacco pouch
blaguer [blage] *vi* to joke ▷ *vt* to tease
blagueur, -euse [blagœʀ, -øz] *adj* teasing ▷ *nm/f* joker
blair [blɛʀ] *nm* (*fam*) conk
blaireau, x [blɛʀo] *nm* (*Zool*) badger; (*brosse*) shaving brush
blairer [blɛʀe] *vt*: **je ne peux pas le ~** I can't bear *ou* stand him
blâmable [blɑmabl(ə)] *adj* blameworthy
blâme [blɑm] *nm* blame; (*sanction*) reprimand
blâmer [blɑme] *vt* (*réprouver*) to blame; (*réprimander*) to reprimand
blanc, blanche [blɑ̃, blɑ̃ʃ] *adj* white; (*non imprimé*) blank; (*innocent*) pure ▷ *nm/f* white, white man/woman ▷ *nm* (*couleur*) white; (*linge*): **le ~** whites *pl*; (*espace non écrit*) blank; (*aussi*: **blanc d'œuf**) (egg-)white; (*aussi*: **blanc de poulet**) breast, white meat; (*aussi*: **vin blanc**) white wine ▷ *nf* (*Mus*) minim (*Brit*), half-note (*US*); (*fam*: *drogue*) smack; **d'une voix blanche** in a toneless voice; **aux cheveux ~s** white-haired; **le ~ de l'œil** the white of the eye; **laisser en ~** to leave blank; **chèque en ~** blank cheque; **à ~** *adv* (*chauffer*) white-hot; (*tirer, charger*) with blanks; **saigner à ~** to bleed white; **~ cassé** off-white
blanc-bec [blɑ̃bɛk] (*pl* **blancs-becs**) *nm* greenhorn
blanchâtre [blɑ̃ʃɑtʀ(ə)] *adj* (*teint, lumière*) whitish
blancheur [blɑ̃ʃœʀ] *nf* whiteness
blanchir [blɑ̃ʃiʀ] *vt* (*gén*) to whiten; (*linge, fig*: *argent*) to launder; (*Culin*) to blanch; (*fig*: *disculper*) to clear ▷ *vi* to grow white; (*cheveux*) to go white; **blanchi à la chaux** whitewashed
blanchissage [blɑ̃ʃisaʒ] *nm* (*du linge*) laundering
blanchisserie [blɑ̃ʃisʀi] *nf* laundry
blanchisseur, -euse [blɑ̃ʃisœʀ, -øz] *nm/f* launderer
blanc-seing [blɑ̃sɛ̃] (*pl* **blancs-seings**) *nm* signed blank paper

blanquette [blɑ̃kɛt] *nf* (*Culin*): ~ **de veau** veal in a white sauce, blanquette de veau
blasé, e [blaze] *adj* blasé
blaser [blaze] *vt* to make blasé
blason [blazɔ̃] *nm* coat of arms
blasphémateur, -trice [blasfematœʀ, -tʀis] *nm/f* blasphemer
blasphématoire [blasfematwaʀ] *adj* blasphemous
blasphème [blasfɛm] *nm* blasphemy
blasphémer [blasfeme] *vi* to blaspheme ▷ *vt* to blaspheme against
blatte [blat] *nf* cockroach
blazer [blazɛʀ] *nm* blazer
blé [ble] *nm* wheat; ~ **en herbe** wheat on the ear; ~ **noir** buckwheat
bled [blɛd] *nm* (*péj*) hole; (*en Afrique du Nord*): **le ~** the interior
blême [blɛm] *adj* pale
blêmir [blemiʀ] *vi* (*personne*) to (turn) pale; (*lueur*) to grow pale
blennorragie [blenɔʀaʒi] *nf* blennorrhoea
blessant, e [blesɑ̃, -ɑ̃t] *adj* hurtful
blessé, e [blese] *adj* injured ▷ *nm/f* injured person, casualty; **un ~ grave**, **un grand ~** a seriously injured *ou* wounded person
blesser [blese] *vt* to injure; (*délibérément: Mil etc*) to wound; (*souliers etc, offenser*) to hurt; **se blesser** to injure o.s.; **se ~ au pied** *etc* to injure one's foot *etc*
blessure [blesyʀ] *nf* injury; wound
blet, te [blɛ, blɛt] *adj* overripe
blette [blɛt] *nf* = **bette**
bleu, e [blø] *adj* blue; (*bifteck*) very rare ▷ *nm* (*couleur*) blue; (*novice*) greenhorn; (*contusion*) bruise; (*vêtement: aussi:* **bleus**) overalls *pl* (*Brit*), coveralls *pl* (*US*); **avoir une peur ~e** to be scared stiff; **zone ~e** ≈ restricted parking area; **fromage ~** blue cheese; **au ~** (*Culin*) au bleu; ~ (**de lessive**) ≈ blue bag; ~ **de méthylène** (*Méd*) methylene blue; ~ **marine/nuit/roi** navy/ midnight/royal blue
bleuâtre [bløɑtʀ(ə)] *adj* (*fumée etc*) bluish, blueish
bleuet [bløɛ] *nm* cornflower
bleuir [bløiʀ] *vt, vi* to turn blue
bleuté, e [bløte] *adj* blue-shaded
blindage [blɛ̃daʒ] *nm* armo(u)r-plating
blindé, e [blɛ̃de] *adj* armoured (*Brit*), armored (*US*); (*fig*) hardened ▷ *nm* armoured *ou* armored car; (*char*) tank
blinder [blɛ̃de] *vt* to armour (*Brit*), armor (*US*); (*fig*) to harden
blizzard [blizaʀ] *nm* blizzard
bloc [blɔk] *nm* (*de pierre etc, Inform*) block; (*de papier à lettres*) pad; (*ensemble*) group, block; **serré à ~** tightened right down; **en ~** as a whole; wholesale; **faire ~** to unite; ~ **opératoire** operating *ou* theatre block; ~ **sanitaire** toilet block; ~ **sténo** shorthand notebook
blocage [blɔkaʒ] *nm* (*voir bloquer*) blocking; jamming; freezing; (*Psych*) hang-up

bloc-cuisine [blɔkkɥizin] (pl **blocs-cuisines**) nm kitchen unit

bloc-cylindres [blɔksilɛ̃dʀ(ə)] (pl **blocs-cylindres**) nm cylinder block

bloc-évier [blɔkevje] (pl **blocs-éviers**) nm sink unit

bloc-moteur [blɔkmɔtœʀ] (pl **blocs-moteurs**) nm engine block

bloc-notes [blɔknɔt] (pl **blocs-notes**) nm note pad

blocus [blɔkys] nm blockade

blog, blogue [blɔg] nm blog

blogging [blɔgiŋ] nm blogging

bloguer [blɔge] vi to blog

blond, e [blɔ̃, -ɔ̃d] adj fair; (plus clair) blond; (sable, blés) golden ▷ nm/f fair-haired ou blond man/woman; **~ cendré** ash blond

blondeur [blɔ̃dœʀ] nf fairness; blondness

blondin, e [blɔ̃dɛ̃, -in] nm/f fair-haired ou blond child ou young person

blondinet, te [blɔ̃dinɛ, -ɛt] nm/f blondy

blondir [blɔ̃diʀ] vi (personne, cheveux) to go fair ou blond

bloquer [blɔke] vt (passage) to block; (pièce mobile) to jam; (crédits, compte) to freeze; (personne, négociations etc) to hold up; (regrouper) to group; **~ les freins** to jam on the brakes

blottir [blɔtiʀ]: **se blottir** vi to huddle up

blousant, e [bluzɑ̃, ɑ̃t] adj blousing out

blouse [bluz] nf overall

blouser [bluze] vi to blouse out

blouson [bluzɔ̃] nm blouson (jacket); **~ noir** (fig) ≈ rocker

blue-jean [bludʒin], **blue-jeans** [bludʒins] nm jeans

blues [bluz] nm blues pl

bluet [blyɛ] nm = **bleuet**

bluff [blœf] nm bluff

bluffer [blœfe] vi, vt to bluff

BNF sigle f = **Bibliothèque nationale de France**

boa [bɔa] nm (Zool): **~ (constricteur)** boa (constrictor); (tour de cou) (feather ou fur) boa

bobard [bɔbaʀ] nm (fam) tall story

bobèche [bɔbɛʃ] nf candle-ring

bobine [bɔbin] nf (de fil) reel; (de machine à coudre) spool; (de machine à écrire) ribbon; (Élec) coil; **~ (d'allumage)** (Auto) coil; **~ de pellicule** (Photo) roll of film

bobo [bobo] nm sore spot

bobsleigh [bɔbslɛg] nm bob(sleigh)

bocage [bɔkaʒ] nm (Géo) bocage, farmland crisscrossed by hedges and trees; (bois) grove, copse (Brit)

bocal, -aux [bɔkal, -o] nm jar

bock [bɔk] nm (beer) glass; (contenu) glass of beer

body [bɔdi] nm body(suit); (Sport) leotard

bœuf [bœf, pl bø] nm ox, steer; (Culin) beef; (Mus: fam) jam session

bof [bɔf] excl (fam: indifférence) don't care!, meh; (: pas terrible) nothing special

Bogota [bɔgɔta] n Bogotá

bogue [bɔg] nf (Bot) husk ▷ nm (Inform) bug

Bohème [bɔɛm] nf: **la ~** Bohemia

bohème [bɔɛm] adj happy-go-lucky, unconventional

bohémien, ne [bɔemjɛ̃, -ɛn] adj Bohemian ▷ nm/f gipsy

boire [bwaʀ] vt to drink; (s'imprégner de) to soak up; **~ un coup** to have a drink

bois [bwa] vb voir **boire** ▷ nm wood; (Zool) antler; (Mus): **les ~** the woodwind; **de ~, en ~** wooden; **~ vert** green wood; **~ mort** deadwood; **~ de lit** bedstead

boisé, e [bwaze] adj woody, wooded

boiser [bwaze] vt (galerie de mine) to timber; (chambre) to panel; (terrain) to plant with trees

boiseries [bwazʀi] nfpl panelling sg

boisson [bwasɔ̃] nf drink; **pris de ~** drunk, intoxicated; **~s alcoolisées** alcoholic beverages ou drinks; **~s non alcoolisées** soft drinks

boit [bwa] vb voir **boire**

boîte [bwat] nf box; (fam: entreprise) firm, company; **aliments en ~** canned ou tinned (Brit) foods; **~ de sardines/petits pois** can ou tin (Brit) of sardines/peas; **mettre qn en ~** (fam) to have a laugh at sb's expense; **~ d'allumettes** box of matches; (vide) matchbox; **~ de conserves** can ou tin (Brit) (of food); **~ crânienne** cranium; **~ à gants** glove compartment; **~ aux lettres** letter box, mailbox (US); (Inform) mailbox; **~ à musique** musical box; **~ noire** (Aviat) black box; **~ de nuit** night club; **~ à ordures** dustbin (Brit), trash can (US); **~ postale (BP)** PO box; **~ de vitesses** gear box; **~ vocale** voice mail

boiter [bwate] vi to limp; (fig) to wobble; (raisonnement) to be shaky

boiteux, -euse [bwatø, -øz] adj lame; wobbly; shaky

boîtier [bwatje] nm case; (d'appareil photo) body; **~ de montre** watch case

boitiller [bwatije] vi to limp slightly, have a slight limp

boive etc [bwav] vb voir **boire**

bol [bɔl] nm bowl; (contenu): **un ~ de café** etc a bowl of coffee etc; **un ~ d'air** a breath of fresh air; **en avoir ras le ~** (fam) to have had a bellyful

bolée [bɔle] nf bowlful

boléro [bɔleʀo] nm bolero

bolet [bɔlɛ] nm boletus (mushroom)

bolide [bɔlid] nm racing car; **comme un ~** like a rocket

Bolivie [bɔlivi] nf: **la ~** Bolivia

bolivien, ne [bɔlivjɛ̃, -ɛn] adj Bolivian ▷ nm/f: **Bolivien, ne** Bolivian

bolognais, e [bɔlɔɲɛ, -ɛz] adj Bolognese

Bologne [bɔlɔɲ] n Bologna

bombance [bɔ̃bɑ̃s] nf: **faire ~** to have a feast, revel

bombardement [bɔ̃baʀdəmɑ̃] nm bombing

bombarder [bɔ̃baʀde] vt to bomb; **~ qn de** (cailloux, lettres) to bombard sb with; **~ qn directeur** to thrust sb into the director's seat

bombardier [bɔ̃baʀdje] nm (avion) bomber; (aviateur) bombardier

bombe [bɔ̃b] *nf* bomb; (*atomiseur*) (aerosol) spray; (*Équitation*) riding cap; **faire la ~** (*fam*) to go on a binge; **~ atomique** atomic bomb; **~ à retardement** time bomb

bombé, e [bɔ̃be] *adj* rounded; (*mur*) bulging; (*front*) domed; (*route*) steeply cambered

bomber [bɔ̃be] *vi* to bulge; (*route*) to camber ▷ *vt*: **~ le torse** to swell out one's chest

🔵 **MOT-CLÉ**

bon, bonne [bɔ̃, bɔn] *adj* **1** (*agréable, satisfaisant*) good; **un bon repas/restaurant** a good meal/restaurant; **être bon en maths** to be good at maths

2 (*charitable*): **être bon (envers)** to be good (to), to be kind (to); **vous êtes trop bon** you're too kind

3 (*correct*) right; **le bon numéro/moment** the right number/moment

4 (*souhaits*): **bon anniversaire** happy birthday; **bon courage** good luck; **bon séjour** enjoy your stay; **bon voyage** have a good trip; **bon week-end** have a good weekend; **bonne année** happy New Year; **bonne chance** good luck; **bonne fête** happy holiday; **bonne nuit** good night

5 (*approprié*): **bon à/pour** fit to/for; **bon à jeter** fit for the bin; **c'est bon à savoir** that's useful to know; **à quoi bon (...)?** what's the point *ou* use (of ...)?

6 (*intensif*): **ça m'a pris deux bonnes heures** it took me a good two hours; **un bon nombre de** a good number of

7: **bon enfant** *adj inv* accommodating, easy-going; **bonne femme** (*péj*) woman; **de bonne heure** early; **bon marché** cheap; **bon mot** witticism; **pour faire bon poids** ... to make up for it ...; **bon sens** common sense; **bon vivant** jovial chap; **bonnes œuvres** charitable works, charities; **bonne sœur** nun

▷ *nm* **1** (*billet*) voucher; (*aussi*: **bon cadeau**) gift voucher; **bon de caisse** cash voucher; **bon d'essence** petrol coupon; **bon à tirer** pass for press; **bon du Trésor** Treasury bond

2: **avoir du bon** to have its good points; **il y a du bon dans ce qu'il dit** there's some sense in what he says; **pour de bon** for good

▷ *nm/f*: **un bon à rien** a good-for-nothing

▷ *adv*: **il fait bon** it's *ou* the weather is fine; **sentir bon** to smell good; **tenir bon** to stand firm; **juger bon de faire** ... to think fit to do ...

▷ *excl* right!, good!; **ah bon?** really?; **bon, je reste** right, I'll stay; *voir aussi* **bonne**

bonasse [bɔnas] *adj* soft, meek

bonbon [bɔ̃bɔ̃] *nm* (boiled) sweet

bonbonne [bɔ̃bɔn] *nf* demijohn; carboy

bonbonnière [bɔ̃bɔnjɛʀ] *nf* sweet (*Brit*) *ou* candy (*US*) box

bond [bɔ̃] *nm* leap; (*d'une balle*) rebound, ricochet; **faire un ~** to leap in the air; **d'un seul ~** in one bound, with one leap; **~ en avant**

(*fig: progrès*) leap forward

bonde [bɔ̃d] *nf* (*d'évier etc*) plug; (: *trou*) plughole; (*de tonneau*) bung; bunghole

bondé, e [bɔ̃de] *adj* packed (full)

bondieuserie [bɔ̃djøzʀi] *nf* (*péj: objet*) religious knick-knack

bondir [bɔ̃diʀ] *vi* to leap; **~ de joie** (*fig*) to jump for joy; **~ de colère** (*fig*) to be hopping mad

bonheur [bɔnœʀ] *nm* happiness; **avoir le ~ de** to have the good fortune to; **porter ~ (à qn)** to bring (sb) luck; **au petit ~** haphazardly; **par ~** fortunately

bonhomie [bɔnɔmi] *nf* good-naturedness

bonhomme [bɔnɔm] (*pl* **bonshommes** [bɔ̃zɔm]) *nm* fellow ▷ *adj* good-natured; **un vieux ~** an old chap; **aller son ~ de chemin** to carry on in one's own sweet way; **~ de neige** snowman

boni [bɔni] *nm* profit

bonification [bɔnifikasjɔ̃] *nf* bonus

bonifier [bɔnifje]: **se bonifier** *vi* to improve

boniment [bɔnimɑ̃] *nm* patter *no pl*

bonjour [bɔ̃ʒuʀ] *excl, nm* hello; (*selon l'heure*) good morning (*ou* afternoon); **donner** *ou* **souhaiter le ~ à qn** to bid sb good morning *ou* afternoon

Bonn [bɔn] *n* Bonn

bonne [bɔn] *adj f voir* **bon** ▷ *nf* (*domestique*) maid; **~ à tout faire** general help; **~ d'enfant** nanny

bonne-maman [bɔnmamɑ̃] (*pl* **bonnes-mamans**) *nf* granny, grandma, gran

bonnement [bɔnmɑ̃] *adv*: **tout** ~ quite simply

bonnet [bɔnɛ] *nm* bonnet, hat; (*de soutien-gorge*) cup; **~ d'âne** dunce's cap; **~ de bain** bathing cap; **~ de nuit** nightcap

bonneterie [bɔnɛtʀi] *nf* hosiery

bon-papa [bɔ̃papa] (*pl* **bons-papas**) *nm* grandpa, grandad

bonsoir [bɔ̃swaʀ] *excl* good evening

bonté [bɔ̃te] *nf* kindness *no pl*; **avoir la ~ de** to be kind *ou* good enough to

bonus [bɔnys] *nm* (*Assurances*) no-claims bonus

bonze [bɔ̃z] *nm* (*Rel*) bonze

boomerang [bumʀɑ̃g] *nm* boomerang

boots [buts] *nfpl* boots

borborygme [bɔʀbɔʀigm(ə)] *nm* rumbling noise

bord [bɔʀ] *nm* (*de table, verre, falaise*) edge; (*de rivière, lac*) bank; (*de route*) side; (*de vêtement*) edge, border; (*de chapeau*) brim; **(monter) à ~** (to go) on board; **jeter par-dessus ~** to throw overboard; **le commandant de ~/les hommes du ~** the ship's master/crew; **du même ~** (*fig*) of the same opinion; **au ~ de la mer/route** at the seaside/roadside; **être au ~ des larmes** to be on the verge of tears; **virer de ~** (*Navig*) to tack; **sur les ~s** (*fig*) slightly; **de tous ~s** on all sides; **~ du trottoir** kerb (*Brit*), curb (*US*)

bordeaux [bɔʀdo] *nm* Bordeaux ▷ *adj inv* maroon

bordée [bɔʀde] *nf* broadside; **une ~ d'injures** a volley of abuse; **tirer une ~** to go out on the town

bordel [bɔʀdɛl] *nm* brothel; (*fam!*) bloody (*Brit*)

b

ou goddamn (US) mess (!) ▷ *excl* hell!

bordelais, e [bɔʀdəlɛ, -ɛz] *adj* of *ou* from Bordeaux

border [bɔʀde] *vt* (*être le long de*) to border, line; (*garnir*): **~ qch de** to line sth with; to trim sth with; (*qn dans son lit*) to tuck up

bordereau, x [bɔʀdəʀo] *nm* docket, slip

bordure [bɔʀdyʀ] *nf* border; (*sur un vêtement*) trim(ming), border; **en ~ de** on the edge of

boréal, e, aux [bɔʀeal, -o] *adj* boreal, northern

borgne [bɔʀɲ(ə)] *adj* one-eyed; **hôtel ~** shady hotel; **fenêtre ~** obstructed window

bornage [bɔʀnaʒ] *nm* (*d'un terrain*) demarcation

borne [bɔʀn(ə)] *nf* boundary stone; (*aussi:* **borne kilométrique**) kilometre-marker, ≈ milestone; **bornes** *nfpl* (*fig*) limits; **dépasser les ~s** to go too far; **sans ~(s)** boundless

borné, e [bɔʀne] *adj* narrow; (*obtus*) narrow-minded

Bornéo [bɔʀneo] *nm*: **le ~** Borneo

borner [bɔʀne] *vt* (*délimiter*) to limit; (*limiter*) to confine; **se ~ à faire** to content o.s. with doing; to limit o.s. to doing

bosniaque [bɔznjak] *adj* Bosnian ▷ *nm/f*: **Bosniaque** Bosnian

Bosnie [bɔsni] *nf* Bosnia

Bosnie-Herzégovine [bɔsniɛʀzegɔvin] *nf* Bosnia-Herzegovina

bosnien, ne [bɔznjɛ̃, -ɛn] *adj* Bosnian ▷ *nm/f*: **Bosnien, ne** Bosnian

Bosphore [bɔsfɔʀ] *nm*: **le ~** the Bosphorus

bosquet [bɔskɛ] *nm* copse (Brit), grove

bosse [bɔs] *nf* (*de terrain etc*) bump; (*enflure*) lump; (*du bossu, du chameau*) hump; **avoir la ~ des maths** *etc* to have a gift for maths *etc*; **il a roulé sa ~** he's been around

bosseler [bɔsle] *vt* (*ouvrer*) to emboss; (*abîmer*) to dent

bosser [bɔse] *vi* (*fam*) to work; (: *dur*) to slog (hard) (Brit), slave (away)

bosseur, -euse [bɔsœʀ, -øz] *nm/f* (hard) worker, slogger (Brit)

bossu, e [bɔsy] *nm/f* hunchback

bot [bo] *adj m*: **pied ~** club foot

botanique [bɔtanik] *nf* botany ▷ *adj* botanic(al)

botaniste [bɔtanist(ə)] *nm/f* botanist

Botswana [bɔtswana] *nm*: **le ~** Botswana

botte [bɔt] *nf* (*soulier*) (high) boot; (*Escrime*) thrust; (*gerbe*): **~ de paille** bundle of straw; **~ de radis/d'asperges** bunch of radishes/asparagus; **~s de caoutchouc** wellington boots

botter [bɔte] *vt* to put boots on; (*donner un coup de pied à*) to kick; (*fam*): **ça me botte** I fancy that

bottier [bɔtje] *nm* bootmaker

bottillon [bɔtijɔ̃] *nm* bootee

bottin® [bɔtɛ̃] *nm* directory

bottine [bɔtin] *nf* ankle boot

botulisme [bɔtylism(ə)] *nm* botulism

bouc [buk] *nm* goat; (*barbe*) goatee; **~ émissaire** scapegoat

boucan [bukɑ̃] *nm* din, racket

bouche [buʃ] *nf* mouth; **une ~ à nourrir** a mouth to feed; **les ~s inutiles** the non-productive members of the population; **faire du ~ à ~ à qn** to give sb the kiss of life (Brit), give sb mouth-to-mouth resuscitation; **de ~ à oreille** confidentially; **pour la bonne ~** (*pour la fin*) till last; **faire venir l'eau à la ~** to make one's mouth water; **~ cousue!** mum's the word!; **~ d'aération** air vent; **~ de chaleur** hot air vent; **~ d'égout** manhole; **~ d'incendie** fire hydrant; **~ de métro** métro entrance

bouché, e [buʃe] *adj* (*flacon etc*) stoppered; (*temps, ciel*) overcast; (*carrière*) blocked; (*péj: personne*) thick; (*trompette*) muted; **avoir le nez ~** to have a blocked(-up) nose

bouchée [buʃe] *nf* mouthful; **ne faire qu'une ~ de** (*fig*) to make short work of; **pour une ~ de pain** (*fig*) for next to nothing; **~s à la reine** chicken vol-au-vents

boucher [buʃe] *nm* butcher ▷ *vt* (*pour colmater*) to stop up; to fill up; (*obstruer*) to block (up); **se boucher** (*tuyau etc*) to block up, get blocked up; **se ~ le nez** to hold one's nose

bouchère [buʃɛʀ] *nf* butcher; (*femme du boucher*) butcher's wife

boucherie [buʃʀi] *nf* butcher's (shop); (*métier*) butchery; (*fig*) slaughter, butchery

bouche-trou [buʃtʀu] *nm* (*fig*) stop-gap

bouchon [buʃɔ̃] *nm* (*en liège*) cork; (*autre matière*) stopper; (*fig: embouteillage*) holdup; (*Pêche*) float; **~ doseur** measuring cap

bouchonner [buʃɔne] *vt* to rub down ▷ *vi* to form a traffic jam

bouchot [buʃo] *nm* mussel bed

bouclage [buklaʒ] *nm* sealing off

boucle [bukl(ə)] *nf* (*forme, figure, aussi Inform*) loop; (*objet*) buckle; **~ (de cheveux)** curl; **~ d'oreilles** earring

bouclé, e [bukle] *adj* curly; (*tapis*) uncut

boucler [bukle] *vt* (*fermer: ceinture etc*) to fasten; (: *magasin*) to shut; (*terminer*) to finish off; (: *circuit*) to complete; (*budget*) to balance; (*enfermer*) to shut away; (: *condamné*) to lock up; (: *quartier*) to seal off ▷ *vi* to curl; **faire ~** (*cheveux*) to curl; **~ la boucle** (Aviat) to loop the loop

bouclette [buklɛt] *nf* small curl

bouclier [buklije] *nm* shield

bouddha [buda] *nm* Buddha

bouddhisme [budism(ə)] *nm* Buddhism

bouddhiste [budist(ə)] *nm/f* Buddhist

bouder [bude] *vi* to sulk ▷ *vt* (*chose*) to turn one's nose up at; (*personne*) to refuse to have anything to do with

bouderie [budʀi] *nf* sulking *no pl*

boudeur, -euse [budœʀ, -øz] *adj* sullen, sulky

boudin [budɛ̃] *nm* (Culin) black pudding; (Tech) roll; **~ blanc** white pudding

boudiné, e [budine] *adj* (*doigt*) podgy; (*serré*): **~ dans** (*vêtement*) bulging out of

boudoir [budwaʀ] *nm* boudoir; (*biscuit*) sponge finger

boue [bu] *nf* mud

bouée [bwe] *nf* buoy; (*de baigneur*) rubber ring; **~**

(de sauvetage) lifebuoy; *(fig)* lifeline

boueux, -euse [bwø, -øz] *adj* muddy ▷ *nm (fam)* refuse *(Brit)* ou garbage *(US)* collector

bouffant, e [bufã, -ãt] *adj* puffed out

bouffe [buf] *nf (fam)* grub, food

bouffée [bufe] *nf* puff; **~ de chaleur** *(gén)* blast of hot air; *(Méd)* hot flush *(Brit)* ou flash *(US)*; **~ de fièvre/de honte** flush of fever/shame; **~ d'orgueil** fit of pride

bouffer [bufe] *vi (fam)* to eat; *(Couture)* to puff out ▷ *vt (fam)* to eat

bouffi, e [bufi] *adj* swollen

bouffon, ne [bufɔ̃, -ɔn] *adj* farcical, comical ▷ *nm* jester

bouge [buʒ] *nm (bar louche)* (low) dive; *(taudis)* hovel

bougeoir [buʒwaʀ] *nm* candlestick

bougeotte [buʒɔt] *nf*: **avoir la ~** to have the fidgets

bouger [buʒe] *vi* to move; *(dent etc)* to be loose; *(changer)* to alter; *(agir)* to stir ▷ *vt* to move; **se bouger** *(fam)* to move (oneself)

bougie [buʒi] *nf* candle; *(Auto)* spark(ing) plug

bougon, ne [bugɔ̃, -ɔn] *adj* grumpy

bougonner [bugɔne] *vi, vt* to grumble

bougre [bugʀ(ə)] *nm* chap; *(fam)*: **ce ~ de ...** that confounded ...

boui-boui [bwibwi] *nm (fam)* greasy spoon

bouillabaisse [bujabɛs] *nf type of fish soup*

bouillant, e [bujã, -ãt] *adj (qui bout)* boiling; *(très chaud)* boiling (hot); *(fig: ardent)* hot-headed; **~ de colère** *etc* seething with anger *etc*

bouille [buj] *nf (fam)* mug

bouilleur [bujœʀ] *nm*: **~ de cru** (home) distiller

bouillie [buji] *nf* gruel; *(de bébé)* cereal; **en ~** *(fig)* crushed

bouillir [bujiʀ] *vi* to boil ▷ *vt (aussi:* **faire bouillir**: *Culin)* to boil; **~ de colère** *etc* to seethe with anger *etc*

bouilloire [bujwaʀ] *nf* kettle

bouillon [bujɔ̃] *nm (Culin)* stock *no pl*; *(bulles, écume)* bubble; **~ de culture** culture medium

bouillonnement [bujɔnmã] *nm (d'un liquide)* bubbling; *(des idées)* ferment

bouillonner [bujɔne] *vi* to bubble; *(fig)* to bubble up; *(torrent)* to foam

bouillotte [bujɔt] *nf* hot-water bottle

boulanger, -ère [bulãʒe, -ɛʀ] *nm/f* baker ▷ *nf (femme du boulanger)* baker's wife

boulangerie [bulãʒʀi] *nf* bakery, baker's (shop); *(commerce)* bakery; **~ industrielle** bakery

boulangerie-pâtisserie [bulãʒʀipatisʀi] *(pl* **boulangeries-pâtisseries**) *nf* baker's and confectioner's (shop)

boule [bul] *nf (gén)* ball; *(pour jouer)* bowl; *(de machine à écrire)* golf ball; **roulé en ~** curled up in a ball; **se mettre en ~** *(fig)* to fly off the handle, blow one's top; **perdre la ~** *(fig: fam)* to go off one's rocker; **~ de gomme** *(bonbon)* gum(drop), pastille; **~ de neige** snowball; **faire ~ de neige** *(fig)* to snowball

bouleau, x [bulo] *nm* (silver) birch

bouledogue [buldɔg] *nm* bulldog

bouler [bule] *vi (fam)*: **envoyer ~ qn** to send sb packing; **je me suis fait ~** *(à un examen)* they flunked me

boulet [bulɛ] *nm (aussi:* **boulet de canon**) cannonball; *(de bagnard)* ball and chain; *(charbon)* (coal) nut

boulette [bulɛt] *nf* ball

boulevard [bulvaʀ] *nm* boulevard

bouleversant, e [bulvɛʀsã, -ãt] *adj (récit)* deeply distressing; *(nouvelle)* shattering

bouleversé, e [bulvɛʀse] *adj (ému)* deeply distressed; shattered

bouleversement [bulvɛʀsəmã] *nm (politique, social)* upheaval

bouleverser [bulvɛʀse] *vt (émouvoir)* to overwhelm; *(causer du chagrin à)* to distress; *(pays, vie)* to disrupt; *(papiers, objets)* to turn upside down, upset

boulier [bulje] *nm* abacus; *(de jeu)* scoring board

boulimie [bulimi] *nf* bulimia; compulsive eating

boulimique [bulimik] *adj* bulimic

boulingrin [bulɛ̃gʀɛ̃] *nm* lawn

bouliste [bulist(ə)] *nm/f* bowler

boulocher [bulɔʃe] *vi (laine etc)* to develop little snarls

boulodrome [bulɔdʀɔm] *nm* bowling pitch

boulon [bulɔ̃] *nm* bolt

boulonner [bulɔne] *vt* to bolt

boulot [bulo] *nm (fam: travail)* work

boulot, te [bulo, -ɔt] *adj* plump, tubby

boum [bum] *nm* bang ▷ *nf* party

bouquet [bukɛ] *nm (de fleurs)* bunch (of flowers), bouquet; *(de persil etc)* bunch; *(parfum)* bouquet; *(fig)* crowning piece; **c'est le ~!** that's the last straw!; **~ garni** *(Culin)* bouquet garni

bouquetin [buktɛ̃] *nm* ibex

bouquin [bukɛ̃] *nm (fam)* book

bouquiner [bukine] *vi (fam)* to read

bouquiniste [bukinist(ə)] *nm/f* bookseller

bourbeux, -euse [buʀbø, -øz] *adj* muddy

bourbier [buʀbje] *nm (quag)mire*

bourde [buʀd(ə)] *nf (erreur)* howler; *(gaffe)* blunder

bourdon [buʀdɔ̃] *nm* bumblebee

bourdonnement [buʀdɔnmã] *nm* buzzing *no pl*, buzz; **avoir des ~s d'oreilles** to have a buzzing (noise) in one's ears

bourdonner [buʀdɔne] *vi* to buzz; *(moteur)* to hum

bourg [buʀ] *nm* small market town *(ou village)*

bourgade [buʀgad] *nf* township

bourgeois, e [buʀʒwa, -waz] *adj (péj)* ≈ (upper) middle class; bourgeois; *(maison etc)* very comfortable ▷ *nm/f (autrefois)* burgher

bourgeoisie [buʀʒwazi] *nf* ≈ upper middle classes *pl*; bourgeoisie; **petite ~** middle classes

bourgeon [buʀʒɔ̃] *nm* bud

bourgeonner [buʀʒɔne] *vi* to bud

Bourgogne [buʀgɔɲ] *nf*: **la ~** Burgundy ▷ *nm*: **bourgogne** Burgundy (wine)

bourguignon, ne [buʀɡiɲɔ̃, -ɔn] *adj* of *ou* from Burgundy, Burgundian; **bœuf ~** bœuf bourguignon

bourlinguer [buʀlɛ̃ɡe] *vi* to knock about a lot, get around a lot

bourrade [buʀad] *nf* shove, thump

bourrage [buʀaʒ] *nm* (*papier*) jamming; **~ de crâne** brainwashing; (*Scol*) cramming

bourrasque [buʀask(ə)] *nf* squall

bourratif, -ive [buʀatif, -iv] *adj* filling, stodgy

bourre [buʀ] *nf* (*de coussin, matelas etc*) stuffing

bourré, e [buʀe] *adj* (*rempli*): **~ de** crammed full of; (*fam: ivre*) pickled, plastered

bourreau, x [buʀo] *nm* executioner; (*fig*) torturer; **~ de travail** workaholic, glutton for work

bourrelé, e [buʀle] *adj*: **être ~ de remords** to be racked by remorse

bourrelet [buʀlɛ] *nm* draught (*Brit*) *ou* draft (*US*) excluder; (*de peau*) fold *ou* roll (of flesh)

bourrer [buʀe] *vt* (*pipe*) to fill; (*poêle*) to pack; (*valise*) to cram (full); **~ de** to cram (full) with, stuff with; **~ de coups** to hammer blows on, pummel; **~ le crâne à qn** to pull the wool over sb's eyes; (*endoctriner*) to brainwash sb

bourricot [buʀiko] *nm* small donkey

bourrique [buʀik] *nf* (*âne*) ass

bourru, e [buʀy] *adj* surly, gruff

bourse [buʀs(ə)] *nf* (*subvention*) grant; (*porte-monnaie*) purse; **sans ~ délier** without spending a penny; **la B~** the Stock Exchange; **~ du travail** ≈ trades union council (regional headquarters)

boursicoter [buʀsikɔte] *vi* (*Comm*) to dabble on the Stock Market

boursier, -ière [buʀsje, -jɛʀ] *adj* (*Comm*) Stock Market *cpd* ▷ *nm/f* (*Scol*) grant-holder

boursouflé, e [buʀsufle] *adj* swollen, puffy; (*fig*) bombastic, turgid

boursoufler [buʀsufle] *vt* to puff up, bloat; **se boursoufler** *vi* (*visage*) to swell *ou* puff up; (*peinture*) to blister

boursouflure [buʀsuflyʀ] *nf* (*du visage*) swelling, puffiness; (*de la peinture*) blister; (*fig: du style*) pomposity

bous [bu] *vb voir* **bouillir**

bousculade [buskylad] *nf* (*hâte*) rush; (*poussée*) crush

bousculer [buskyle] *vt* to knock over; to knock into; (*fig*) to push, rush

bouse [buz] *nf*: **~ (de vache)** (cow) dung *no pl* (*Brit*), manure *no pl*

bousiller [buzije] *vt* (*fam*) to wreck

boussole [busɔl] *nf* compass

bout [bu] *vb voir* **bouillir** ▷ *nm* bit; (*extrémité: d'un bâton etc*) tip; (: *d'une ficelle, table, rue, période*) end; **au ~ de** at the end of, after; **au ~ du compte** at the end of the day; **pousser qn à ~** to push sb to the limit (of his patience); **venir à ~ de** to manage to finish (off) *ou* overcome; **~ à ~** end to end; **à tout ~ de champ** at every turn; **d'un ~ à l'autre, de ~ en ~** from one end to the other; **à ~**

portant at point-blank range; **un ~ de chou** (*enfant*) a little tot; **~ d'essai** (*Ciné etc*) screen test; **~ filtre** filter tip

boutade [butad] *nf* quip, sally

boute-en-train [butɑ̃tʀɛ̃] *nm inv* live wire (*fig*)

bouteille [butɛj] *nf* bottle; (*de gaz butane*) cylinder

boutiquaire [butikɛʀ] *adj*: **niveau ~** shopping level

boutique [butik] *nf* shop (*Brit*), store (*US*); (*de grand couturier, de mode*) boutique

boutiquier, -ière [butikje, -jɛʀ] *nm/f* shopkeeper (*Brit*), storekeeper (*US*)

boutoir [butwaʀ] *nm*: **coup de ~** (*choc*) thrust; (*fig: propos*) barb

bouton [butɔ̃] *nm* (*de vêtement, électrique etc*) button; (*Bot*) bud; (*sur la peau*) spot; (*de porte*) knob; **~ de manchette** cuff-link; **~ d'or** buttercup

boutonnage [butɔnaʒ] *nm* (*action*) buttoning(-up); **un manteau à double ~** a coat with two rows of buttons

boutonner [butɔne] *vt* to button up, do up; **se boutonner** to button one's clothes up

boutonneux, -euse [butɔnø, -øz] *adj* spotty

boutonnière [butɔnjɛʀ] *nf* buttonhole

bouton-poussoir [butɔ̃puswaʀ] (*pl* **boutons-poussoirs**) *nm* pushbutton

bouton-pression [butɔ̃pʀesjɔ̃] (*pl* **boutons-pression**) *nm* press stud, snap fastener

bouture [butyʀ] *nf* cutting; **faire des ~s** to take cuttings

bouvreuil [buvʀœj] *nm* bullfinch

bovidé [bɔvide] *nm* bovine

bovin, e [bɔvɛ̃, -in] *adj* bovine ▷ *nm*: **~s** cattle

bowling [bɔliŋ] *nm* (tenpin) bowling; (*salle*) bowling alley

box [bɔks] *nm* lock-up (garage); (*de salle, dortoir*) cubicle; (*d'écurie*) loose-box; (*aussi*: **box-calf**) box calf; **le ~ des accusés** the dock

boxe [bɔks(ə)] *nf* boxing

boxer [bɔkse] *vi* to box ▷ *nm* [bɔksɛʀ] (*chien*) boxer

boxeur [bɔksœʀ] *nm* boxer

boyau, x [bwajo] *nm* (*corde de raquette etc*) (cat) gut; (*galerie*) passage(way); (*narrow*) gallery; (*pneu de bicyclette*) tubeless tyre ▷ *nmpl* (*viscères*) entrails, guts

boyaux [bwajo] *nmpl* (*viscères*) entrails, guts

boycottage [bɔjkɔtaʒ] *nm* (*d'un produit*) boycotting

boycotter [bɔjkɔte] *vt* to boycott

BP *sigle f* = **boîte postale**

brabançon, ne [bʀabɑ̃sɔ̃, -ɔn] *adj* of *ou* from Brabant

Brabant [bʀabɑ̃] *nm*: **le ~** Brabant

bracelet [bʀaslɛ] *nm* bracelet

bracelet-montre [bʀaslɛmɔ̃tʀ(ə)] *nm* wristwatch

braconnage [bʀakɔnaʒ] *nm* poaching

braconner [bʀakɔne] *vi* to poach

braconnier [bʀakɔnje] *nm* poacher

brader [bʀade] *vt* to sell off, sell cheaply
braderie [bʀadʀi] *nf* clearance sale; *(par des particuliers)* ≈ car boot sale *(Brit)*, ≈ garage sale *(US)*; *(magasin)* discount store; *(sur marché)* cut-price *(Brit) ou* cut-rate *(US)* stall
braguette [bʀagɛt] *nf* fly, flies *pl (Brit)*, zipper *(US)*
braillard, e [bʀajaʀ, -aʀd] *adj (fam)* bawling, yelling
braille [bʀaj] *nm* Braille
braillement [bʀajmɑ̃] *nm (cri)* bawling *no pl*, yelling *no pl*
brailler [bʀaje] *vi* to bawl, yell ▷ *vt* to bawl out, yell out
braire [bʀɛʀ] *vi* to bray
braise [bʀɛz] *nf* embers *pl*
braiser [bʀeze] *vt* to braise; **bœuf braisé** braised steak
bramer [bʀame] *vi* to bell; *(fig)* to wail
brancard [bʀɑ̃kaʀ] *nm (civière)* stretcher; *(bras, perche)* shaft
brancardier [bʀɑ̃kaʀdje] *nm* stretcher-bearer
branchages [bʀɑ̃ʃaʒ] *nmpl* branches, boughs
branche [bʀɑ̃ʃ] *nf* branch; *(de lunettes)* side(-piece)
branché, e [bʀɑ̃ʃe] *adj (fam)* switched-on, trendy ▷ *nm/f (fam)* trendy
branchement [bʀɑ̃ʃmɑ̃] *nm* connection
brancher [bʀɑ̃ʃe] *vt* to connect (up); *(en mettant la prise)* to plug in; ~ **qn/qch sur** *(fig)* to get sb/sth launched onto
branchies [bʀɑ̃ʃi] *nfpl* gills
brandade [bʀɑ̃dad] *nf* brandade *(cod dish)*
brandebourgeois, e [bʀɑ̃dəbuʀʒwa, -waz] *adj* of *ou* from Brandenburg
brandir [bʀɑ̃diʀ] *vt (arme)* to brandish, wield; *(document)* to flourish, wave
brandon [bʀɑ̃dɔ̃] *nm* firebrand
branlant, e [bʀɑ̃lɑ̃, -ɑ̃t] *adj (mur, meuble)* shaky
branle [bʀɑ̃l] *nm:* **mettre en ~** to set swinging; **donner le ~ à** to set in motion
branle-bas [bʀɑ̃lba] *nm inv* commotion
branler [bʀɑ̃le] *vi* to be shaky, be loose ▷ *vt:* ~ **la tête** to shake one's head
braquage [bʀakaʒ] *nm (fam)* stick-up, hold-up; *(Auto):* **rayon de** ~ turning circle
braque [bʀak] *nm (Zool)* pointer
braquer [bʀake] *vi (Auto)* to turn (the wheel) ▷ *vt (revolver etc):* ~ **qch sur** to aim sth at, point sth at; *(mettre en colère):* ~ **qn** to antagonize sb, put sb's back up; ~ **son regard sur** to fix one's gaze on; **se braquer** *vi:* **se** ~ **(contre)** to take a stand (against)
bras [bʀa] *nm* arm; *(de fleuve)* branch ▷ *nmpl (fig: travailleurs)* labour *sg (Brit)*, labor *sg (US)*, hands; ~ **dessus ~ dessous** arm in arm; **à ~ raccourcis** with fists flying; **à tour de** ~ with all one's might; **baisser les** ~ to give up; ~ **droit** *(fig)* right hand man; ~ **de fer** arm-wrestling; **une partie de ~ de fer** *(fig)* a trial of strength; ~ **de levier** lever arm; ~ **de mer** arm of the sea, sound
brasero [bʀazeʀo] *nm* brazier

brasier [bʀazje] *nm* blaze, (blazing) inferno; *(fig)* inferno
Brasilia [bʀazilja] *n* Brasilia
bras-le-corps [bʀalkɔʀ]: **à ~** *adv* (a)round the waist
brassage [bʀasaʒ] *nm (de la bière)* brewing; *(fig)* mixing
brassard [bʀasaʀ] *nm* armband
brasse [bʀas] *nf (nage)* breast-stroke; *(mesure)* fathom; ~ **papillon** butterfly(-stroke)
brassée [bʀase] *nf* armful; **une ~ de** *(fig)* a number of
brasser [bʀase] *vt (bière)* to brew; *(remuer: salade)* to toss; *(: cartes)* to shuffle; *(fig)* to mix; ~ **l'argent/les affaires** to handle a lot of money/business
brasserie [bʀasʀi] *nf (restaurant)* bar *(selling food)*, brasserie; *(usine)* brewery
brasseur [bʀasœʀ] *nm (de bière)* brewer; ~ **d'affaires** big businessman
brassière [bʀasjɛʀ] *nf* (baby's) vest *(Brit) ou* undershirt *(US)*; *(de sauvetage)* life jacket
bravache [bʀavaʃ] *nm* blusterer, braggart
bravade [bʀavad] *nf:* **par ~** out of bravado
brave [bʀav] *adj (courageux)* brave; *(bon, gentil)* good, kind
bravement [bʀavmɑ̃] *adv* bravely; *(résolument)* boldly
braver [bʀave] *vt* to defy
bravo [bʀavo] *excl* bravo! ▷ *nm* cheer
bravoure [bʀavuʀ] *nf* bravery
BRB *sigle f (Police:* = *Brigade de répression du banditisme)* ≈ serious crime squad
break [bʀɛk] *nm (Auto)* estate car *(Brit)*, station wagon *(US)*
brebis [bʀəbi] *nf* ewe; ~ **galeuse** black sheep
brèche [bʀɛʃ] *nf* breach, gap; **être sur la ~** *(fig)* to be on the go
bredouille [bʀəduj] *adj* empty-handed
bredouiller [bʀəduje] *vi, vt* to mumble, stammer
bref, brève [bʀɛf, bʀɛv] *adj* short, brief ▷ *adv* in short ▷ *nf (voyelle)* short vowel; *(information)* brief news item; **d'un ton ~** sharply, curtly; **en ~** in short, in brief; **à ~ délai** shortly
brelan [bʀəlɑ̃] *nm:* **un ~** three of a kind; **un ~ d'as** three aces
breloque [bʀəlɔk] *nf* charm
brème [bʀɛm] *nf* bream
Brésil [bʀezil] *nm:* **le ~** Brazil
brésilien, ne [bʀeziljɛ̃, -ɛn] *adj* Brazilian ▷ *nm/f:* **Brésilien, ne** Brazilian
bressan, e [bʀesɑ̃, -an] *adj* of *ou* from Bresse
Bretagne [bʀətaɲ] *nf:* **la ~** Brittany
bretelle [bʀətɛl] *nf (de fusil etc)* sling; *(de vêtement)* strap; *(d'autoroute)* slip road *(Brit)*, entrance ou exit ramp *(US)*; **bretelles** *nfpl (pour pantalon)* braces *(Brit)*, suspenders *(US)*; ~ **de contournement** *(Auto)* bypass; ~ **de raccordement** *(Auto)* access road
breton, ne [bʀətɔ̃, -ɔn] *adj* Breton ▷ *nm (Ling)* Breton ▷ *nm/f:* **Breton, ne** Breton

breuvage [bʀœvaʒ] *nm* beverage, drink
brève [bʀɛv] *adj f, nf voir* **bref**
brevet [bʀəvɛ] *nm* diploma, certificate; ~
(**d'invention**) patent; ~ **d'apprentissage**
certificate of apprenticeship; ~ (**des collèges**)
school certificate, taken at approx. 16 years
breveté, e [bʀəvte] *adj* patented; (*diplômé*)
qualified
breveter [bʀəvte] *vt* to patent
bréviaire [bʀevjɛʀ] *nm* breviary
BRGM *sigle m* = **Bureau de recherches**
géologiques et minières
briard, e [bʀijaʀ, -aʀd(ə)] *adj* of *ou* from Brie
▷ *nm* (*chien*) briard
bribes [bʀib] *nfpl* bits, scraps; (*d'une conversation*)
snatches; **par** ~ piecemeal
bric [bʀik]: **de** ~ **et de broc** *adv* with any old
thing
bric-à-brac [bʀikabʀak] *nm inv* bric-a-brac,
jumble
bricolage [bʀikɔlaʒ] *nm*: **le** ~ do-it-yourself
(jobs); (*péj*) patched-up job
bricole [bʀikɔl] *nf* (*babiole, chose insignifiante*)
trifle; (*petit travail*) small job
bricoler [bʀikɔle] *vi* to do odd jobs; (*en amateur*)
to do DIY jobs; (*passe-temps*) to potter about ▷ *vt*
(*réparer*) to fix up; (*mal réparer*) to tinker with;
(*trafiquer: voiture etc*) to doctor, fix
bricoleur, -euse [bʀikɔlœʀ, -øz] *nm/f*
handyman/woman, DIY enthusiast
bride [bʀid] *nf* bridle; (*d'un bonnet*) string, tie; **à** ~
abattue flat out, hell for leather; **tenir en** ~ to
keep in check; **lâcher la** ~ **à**, **laisser la** ~ **sur le**
cou à to give free rein to
bridé, e [bʀide] *adj*: **yeux** ~**s** slit eyes
brider [bʀide] *vt* (*réprimer*) to keep in check;
(*cheval*) to bridle; (*Culin: volaille*) to truss
bridge [bʀidʒ(ə)] *nm* bridge
brie [bʀi] *nm* Brie (*cheese*)
brièvement [bʀijɛvmɑ̃] *adv* briefly
brièveté [bʀijɛvte] *nf* brevity
brigade [bʀigad] *nf* squad; (*Mil*) brigade
brigadier [bʀigadje] *nm* (*Police*) ≈ sergeant; (*Mil*)
bombardier; corporal
brigadier-chef [bʀigadjeʃɛf] (*pl* **brigadiers-**
chefs) *nm* ≈ lance-sergeant
brigand [bʀigɑ̃] *nm* brigand
brigandage [bʀigɑ̃daʒ] *nm* robbery
briguer [bʀige] *vt* to aspire to; (*suffrages*) to
canvass
brillamment [bʀijamɑ̃] *adv* brilliantly
brillant, e [bʀijɑ̃, -ɑ̃t] *adj* brilliant; bright;
(*luisant*) shiny, shining ▷ *nm* (*diamant*) brilliant
briller [bʀije] *vi* to shine
brimade [bʀimad] *nf* vexation, harassment *no*
pl; bullying *no pl*
brimbaler [bʀɛ̃bale] *vb* = **bringuebaler**
brimer [bʀime] *vt* to harass; to bully
brin [bʀɛ̃] *nm* (*de laine, ficelle etc*) strand; (*fig*): **un** ~
de a bit of; **un** ~ **mystérieux** *etc* (*fam*) a weeny
bit mysterious *etc*; ~ **d'herbe** blade of grass; ~
de muguet sprig of lily of the valley; ~ **de**

paille wisp of straw
brindille [bʀɛ̃dij] *nf* twig
bringue [bʀɛ̃g] *nf* (*fam*): **faire la** ~ to go on a
binge
bringuebaler [bʀɛ̃gbale] *vi* to shake (about) ▷ *vt*
to cart about
brio [bʀijo] *nm* brilliance; (*Mus*) brio; **avec** ~
brilliantly, with panache
brioche [bʀijɔʃ] *nf* brioche (bun); (*fam: ventre*)
paunch
brioché, e [bʀijɔʃe] *adj* brioche-style
brique [bʀik] *nf* brick; (*fam*) 10 000 francs ▷ *adj*
inv brick red
briquer [bʀike] *vt* (*fam*) to polish up
briquet [bʀikɛ] *nm* (*cigarette*) lighter
briqueterie [bʀiktʀi] *nf* brickyard
bris [bʀi] *nm*: ~ **de clôture** (*Jur*) breaking in; ~ **de**
glaces (*Auto*) breaking of windows
brisant [bʀizɑ̃] *nm* reef; (*vague*) breaker
brise [bʀiz] *nf* breeze
brisé, e [bʀize] *adj* broken; ~ (**de fatigue**)
exhausted; **d'une voix** ~**e** in a voice broken
with emotion; **pâte** ~**e** shortcrust pastry
brisées [bʀize] *nfpl*: **aller** *ou* **marcher sur les** ~
de qn to compete with sb in his own province
brise-glace, brise-glaces [bʀizglas] *nm inv*
(*navire*) icebreaker
brise-jet [bʀizʒɛ] *nm inv* tap swirl
brise-lames [bʀizlam] *nm inv* breakwater
briser [bʀize] *vt* to break; **se briser** *vi* to break
brise-tout [bʀiztu] *nm inv* wrecker
briseur, -euse [bʀizœʀ, -øz] *nm/f*: ~ **de grève**
strike-breaker
brise-vent [bʀizvɑ̃] *nm inv* windbreak
bristol [bʀistɔl] *nm* (*carte de visite*) visiting card
britannique [bʀitanik] *adj* British ▷ *nm/f*:
Britannique Briton, British person; **les B**~**s** the
British
broc [bʀo] *nm* pitcher
brocante [bʀɔkɑ̃t] *nf* (*objets*) secondhand goods
pl, junk; (*commerce*) secondhand trade; junk
dealing
brocanteur, -euse [bʀɔkɑ̃tœʀ, -øz] *nm/f* junk
shop owner; junk dealer
brocart [bʀɔkaʀ] *nm* brocade
broche [bʀɔʃ] *nf* brooch; (*Culin*) spit; (*fiche*)
spike, peg; (*Méd*) pin; **à la** ~ spit-roasted,
roasted on a spit
broché, e [bʀɔʃe] *adj* (*livre*) paper-backed; (*tissu*)
brocaded
brochet [bʀɔʃɛ] *nm* pike *inv*
brochette [bʀɔʃɛt] *nf* skewer; ~ **de décorations**
row of medals
brochure [bʀɔʃyʀ] *nf* pamphlet, brochure,
booklet
brocoli [bʀɔkɔli] *nm* broccoli
brodequins [bʀɔdkɛ̃] *nmpl* (*de marche*) (lace-up)
boots
broder [bʀɔde] *vt* to embroider ▷ *vi*: ~ (**sur des**
faits *ou* **une histoire**) to embroider the facts
broderie [bʀɔdʀi] *nf* embroidery
bromure [bʀɔmyʀ] *nm* bromide

broncher [bʀɔ̃ʃe] vi: **sans ~** without flinching, without turning a hair

bronches [bʀɔ̃ʃ] nfpl bronchial tubes

bronchite [bʀɔ̃ʃit] nf bronchitis

broncho-pneumonie [bʀɔ̃kɔpnømɔni] nf broncho-pneumonia no pl

bronzage [bʀɔ̃zaʒ] nm (hâle) (sun)tan

bronze [bʀɔ̃z] nm bronze

bronzé, e [bʀɔ̃ze] adj tanned

bronzer [bʀɔ̃ze] vt to tan ▷ vi to get a tan; **se bronzer** to sunbathe

brosse [bʀɔs] nf brush; **donner un coup de ~ à qch** to give sth a brush; **coiffé en ~** with a crewcut; **~ à cheveux** hairbrush; **~ à dents** toothbrush; **~ à habits** clothesbrush

brosser [bʀɔse] vt (nettoyer) to brush; (fig: tableau etc) to paint; to draw; **se brosser** vt, vi to brush one's clothes; **se ~ les dents** to brush one's teeth; **tu peux te ~!** (fam) you can sing for it!

brou [bʀu] nm: **~ de noix** (pour bois) walnut stain; (liqueur) walnut liqueur

brouette [bʀuɛt] nf wheelbarrow

brouhaha [bʀuaa] nm hubbub

brouillage [bʀujaʒ] nm (d'une émission) jamming

brouillard [bʀujaʀ] nm fog; **être dans le ~** (fig) to be all at sea

brouille [bʀuj] nf quarrel

brouillé, e [bʀuje] adj (fâché): **il est ~ avec ses parents** he has fallen out with his parents; (teint) muddy

brouiller [bʀuje] vt to mix up; to confuse; (Radio) to cause interference to; (: délibérément) to jam; (rendre trouble) to cloud; (désunir: amis) to set at odds; **se brouiller** vi (ciel, vue) to cloud over; (détails) to become confused; **se ~ (avec)** to fall out (with); **~ les pistes** to cover one's tracks; (fig) to confuse the issue

brouillon, ne [bʀujɔ̃, -ɔn] adj disorganized, unmethodical ▷ nm (first) draft; **cahier de ~** rough (work) book

broussailles [bʀusaj] nfpl undergrowth sg

broussailleux, -euse [bʀusajø, -øz] adj bushy

brousse [bʀus] nf: **la ~** the bush

brouter [bʀute] vt to graze on ▷ vi to graze; (Auto) to judder

broutille [bʀutij] nf trifle

broyer [bʀwaje] vt to crush; **~ du noir** to be down in the dumps

bru [bʀy] nf daughter-in-law

brucelles [bʀysɛl] nfpl: **(pinces) ~** tweezers

brugnon [bʀyɲɔ̃] nm nectarine

bruine [bʀɥin] nf drizzle

bruiner [bʀɥine] vb impers: **il bruine** it's drizzling, there's a drizzle

bruire [bʀɥiʀ] vi (eau) to murmur; (feuilles, étoffe) to rustle

bruissement [bʀɥismɑ̃] nm murmuring; rustling

bruit [bʀɥi] nm: **un ~** a noise, a sound; (fig: rumeur) a rumour (Brit), a rumor (US); **le ~** noise; **pas/trop de ~** no/too much noise; **sans ~** without a sound, noiselessly; **faire du ~** to

make a noise; **~ de fond** background noise

bruitage [bʀɥitaʒ] nm sound effects pl

bruiteur, -euse [bʀɥitœʀ, -øz] nm/f sound-effects engineer

brûlant, e [bʀylɑ̃, -ɑ̃t] adj burning (hot); (liquide) boiling (hot); (regard) fiery; (sujet) red-hot

brûlé, e [bʀyle] adj (fig: démasqué) blown; (: homme politique etc) discredited ▷ nm: **odeur de ~** smell of burning

brûle-pourpoint [bʀylpuʀpwɛ̃]: **à ~** adv point-blank

brûler [bʀyle] vt to burn; (eau bouillante) to scald; (consommer: électricité, essence) to use; (feu rouge, signal) to go through (without stopping) ▷ vi to burn; (jeu): **tu brûles** you're getting warm ou hot; **se brûler** to burn o.s.; to scald o.s.; **se ~ la cervelle** to blow one's brains out; **~ les étapes** to make rapid progress; (aller trop vite) to cut corners; **~ (d'impatience) de faire qch** to burn with impatience to do sth, be dying to do sth

brûleur [bʀylœʀ] nm burner

brûlot [bʀylo] nm (Culin) flaming brandy; **un ~ de contestation** (fig) a hotbed of dissent

brûlure [bʀylyʀ] nf (lésion) burn; (sensation) burning no pl, burning sensation; **~s d'estomac** heartburn sg

brume [bʀym] nf mist

brumeux, -euse [bʀymø, -øz] adj misty; (fig) hazy

brumisateur [bʀymizatœʀ] nm atomizer

brun, e [bʀœ̃, -yn] adj brown; (cheveux, personne) dark ▷ nm (couleur) brown ▷ nf (cigarette) cigarette made of dark tobacco; (bière) ≈ brown ale, ≈ stout

brunâtre [bʀynɑtʀ(ə)] adj brownish

brunch [bʀœntʃ] nm brunch

Brunei [bʀynei] nm: **le ~** Brunei

brunir [bʀyniʀ] vi: **se brunir** to get a tan ▷ vt to tan

brushing [bʀœʃiŋ] nm blow-dry

brusque [bʀysk(ə)] adj (soudain) abrupt, sudden; (rude) abrupt, brusque

brusquement [bʀyskəmɑ̃] adv (soudainement) abruptly, suddenly

brusquer [bʀyske] vt to rush

brusquerie [bʀyskəʀi] nf abruptness, brusqueness

brut, e [bʀyt] adj raw, crude, rough; (diamant) uncut; (soie, minéral, Inform: données) raw; (Comm) gross ▷ nf brute; **(champagne) ~** brut champagne; **(pétrole) ~** crude (oil)

brutal, e, -aux [bʀytal, -o] adj brutal

brutalement [bʀytalmɑ̃] adv brutally

brutaliser [bʀytalize] vt to handle roughly, manhandle

brutalité [bʀytalite] nf brutality no pl

brute [bʀyt] adj f, nf voir **brut**

Bruxelles [bʀysɛl] n Brussels

bruxellois, e [bʀysɛlwa, -waz] adj of ou from Brussels ▷ nm/f: **Bruxellois, e** inhabitant ou native of Brussels

bruyamment [bʀɥijamɑ̃] adv noisily

bruyant, e [bʀɥijɑ̃, -ɑ̃t] adj noisy

bruyère [bʀyjɛʀ] *nf* heather

BT *sigle m* (= *Brevet de technicien*) *vocational training certificate, taken at approx. 18 years*

BTA *sigle m* (= *Brevet de technicien agricole*) *agricultural training certificate, taken at approx. 18 years*

BTP *sigle mpl* (= *Bâtiments et travaux publics*) *public buildings and works sector*

BTS *sigle m* (= *Brevet de technicien supérieur*) *vocational training certificate taken at end of two-year higher education course*

BU *sigle f* = **Bibliothèque universitaire**

bu, e [by] *pp de* **boire**

buanderie [bɥɑ̃dʀi] *nf* laundry

Bucarest [bykaʀɛst] *n* Bucharest

buccal, e, -aux [bykal, -o] *adj*: **par voie ~e** orally

bûche [byʃ] *nf* log; **prendre une ~** (*fig*) to come a cropper (*Brit*), fall flat on one's face; **~ de Noël** Yule log

bûcher [byʃe] *nm* pyre; bonfire ▷ *vi* (*fam: étudier*) to swot (*Brit*), grind (*US*) ▷ *vt* to swot up (*Brit*), cram

bûcheron [byʃʀɔ̃] *nm* woodcutter

bûchette [byʃɛt] *nf* (*de bois*) stick, twig; (*pour compter*) rod

bûcheur, -euse [byʃœʀ, -øz] *nm/f* (*fam: étudiant*) swot (*Brit*), grind (*US*)

bucolique [bykɔlik] *adj* bucolic, pastoral

Budapest [bydapɛst] *n* Budapest

budget [bydʒɛ] *nm* budget

budgétaire [bydʒetɛʀ] *adj* budgetary, budget cpd

budgétiser [bydʒetize] *vt* to budget (for)

buée [bɥe] *nf* (*sur une vitre*) mist; (*de l'haleine*) steam

Buenos Aires [bwenɔzɛʀ] *n* Buenos Aires

buffet [byfɛ] *nm* (*meuble*) sideboard; (*de réception*) buffet; **~ (de gare)** (station) buffet, snack bar

buffle [byfl(ə)] *nm* buffalo

buis [bɥi] *nm* box tree; (*bois*) box(wood)

buisson [bɥisɔ̃] *nm* bush

buissonnière [bɥisɔnjɛʀ] *adj f*: **faire l'école ~** to play truant (*Brit*), skip school

bulbe [bylb(ə)] *nm* (*Bot, Anat*) bulb; (*coupole*) onion-shaped dome

bulgare [bylgaʀ] *adj* Bulgarian ▷ *nm* (*Ling*) Bulgarian ▷ *nm/f*: **Bulgare** Bulgarian, Bulgar

Bulgarie [bylgaʀi] *nf*: **la ~** Bulgaria

bulldozer [buldozœʀ] *nm* bulldozer

bulle [byl] *adj, nm*: **(papier) ~** manil(l)a paper ▷ *nf* bubble; (*de bande dessinée*) balloon; (*papale*) bull; **~ de savon** soap bubble

bulletin [byltɛ̃] *nm* (*communiqué, journal*) bulletin; (*papier*) form; (: *de bagages*) ticket; (*Scol*) report; **~ d'informations** news bulletin; **~ météorologique** weather report; **~ de naissance** birth certificate; **~ de salaire** pay slip; **~ de santé** medical bulletin; **~ (de vote)** ballot paper

buraliste [byʀalist(ə)] *nm/f* (*de bureau de tabac*) tobacconist; (*de poste*) clerk

bure [byʀ] *nf* homespun; (*de moine*) frock

bureau, x [byʀo] *nm* (*meuble*) desk; (*pièce, service*) office; **~ de change** (foreign) exchange office *ou* bureau; **~ d'embauche** ≈ job centre; **~ d'études** design office; **~ de location** box office; **~ des objets trouvés** lost property office (*Brit*), lost and found (*US*); **~ de placement** employment agency; **~ de poste** post office; **~ de tabac** tobacconist's (shop), smoke shop (*US*); **~ de vote** polling station

bureaucrate [byʀokʀat] *nm* bureaucrat

bureaucratie [byʀokʀasi] *nf* bureaucracy

bureaucratique [byʀokʀatik] *adj* bureaucratic

bureautique [byʀotik] *nf* office automation

burette [byʀɛt] *nf* (*de mécanicien*) oilcan; (*de chimiste*) burette

burin [byʀɛ̃] *nm* cold chisel; (*Art*) burin

buriné, e [byʀine] *adj* (*fig: visage*) craggy, seamed

Burkina [byʀkina], **Burkina-Faso** [byʀkinafaso] *nm*: **le ~(-Faso)** Burkina Faso

burlesque [byʀlɛsk(ə)] *adj* ridiculous; (*Littérature*) burlesque

burnous [byʀnu(s)] *nm* burnous

Burundi [buʀundi] *nm*: **le ~** Burundi

bus *vb* [by] *voir* **boire** ▷ *nm* [bys] (*véhicule, aussi Inform*) bus

busard [byzaʀ] *nm* harrier

buse [byz] *nf* buzzard

busqué, e [byske] *adj*: **nez ~** hook(ed) nose

buste [byst(ə)] *nm* (*Anat*) chest; (: *de femme*) bust; (*sculpture*) bust

bustier [bystje] *nm* (*soutien-gorge*) long-line bra

but [by] *vb voir* **boire** ▷ *nm* (*cible*) target; (*fig*) goal, aim; (*Football etc*) goal; **de ~ en blanc** point-blank; **avoir pour ~ de faire** to aim to do; **dans le ~ de** with the intention of

butane [bytan] *nm* butane; (*domestique*) calor gas® (*Brit*), butane

buté, e [byte] *adj* stubborn, obstinate ▷ *nf* (*Archit*) abutment; (*Tech*) stop

buter [byte] *vi*: **~ contre** *ou* **sur** to bump into; (*trébucher*) to stumble against ▷ *vt* to antagonize; **se buter** *vi* to get obstinate, dig in one's heels

buteur [bytœʀ] *nm* striker

butin [bytɛ̃] *nm* booty, spoils *pl*; (*d'un vol*) loot

butiner [bytine] *vi* to gather nectar

butor [bytɔʀ] *nm* (*fig*) lout

butte [byt] *nf* mound, hillock; **être en ~ à** to be exposed to

buvable [byvabl(ə)] *adj* (*eau, vin*) drinkable; (*Méd: ampoule etc*) to be taken orally; (*fig: roman etc*) reasonable

buvais *etc* [byvɛ] *vb voir* **boire**

buvard [byvaʀ] *nm* blotter

buvette [byvɛt] *nf* refreshment room *ou* stall; (*comptoir*) bar

buveur, -euse [byvœʀ, -øz] *nm/f* drinker

buvons *etc* [byvɔ̃] *vb voir* **boire**

BVP *sigle m* (= *Bureau de vérification de la publicité*) *advertising standards authority*

Byzance [bizɑ̃s] *n* Byzantium

byzantin, e [bizɑ̃tɛ̃, -in] *adj* Byzantine

BZH *abr* (= *Breizh*) Brittany

Cc

C, c [se] *nm inv* C, c ▷ *abr* (= *centime*) c; (= *Celsius*) C;
C comme Célestin C for Charlie

c' [s] *pron voir* **ce**

CA *sigle m* = **chiffre d'affaires; conseil
d'administration; corps d'armée** ▷ *sigle f* =
chambre d'agriculture

ça [sa] *pron* (*pour désigner*) this; (: *plus loin*) that;
(*comme sujet indéfini*) it; **ça m'étonne que** it
surprises me that; **ça va?** how are you?; how
are things?; (*d'accord?*) OK?, all right?; **ça alors!**
(*désapprobation*) well!, really!; (*étonnement*)
heavens!; **c'est ça** that's right

çà [sa] *adv*: **çà et là** here and there

cabale [kabal] *nf* (*Théât, Pol*) cabal, clique

caban [kabã] *nm* reefer jacket, donkey jacket

cabane [kaban] *nf* hut, cabin

cabanon [kabanɔ̃] *nm* chalet, (country) cottage

cabaret [kabaʀɛ] *nm* night club

cabas [kaba] *nm* shopping bag

cabestan [kabɛstã] *nm* capstan

cabillaud [kabijo] *nm* cod *inv*

cabine [kabin] *nf* (*de bateau*) cabin; (*de plage*)
(beach) hut; (*de piscine etc*) cubicle; (*de camion,
train*) cab; (*d'avion*) cockpit; **~ (d'ascenseur)** lift
cage; **~ d'essayage** fitting room; **~ de
projection** projection room; **~ spatiale** space
capsule; **~ (téléphonique)** call *ou* (tele)phone
box, (tele)phone booth

cabinet [kabinɛ] *nm* (*petite pièce*) closet; (*de
médecin*) surgery (*Brit*), office (*US*); (*de notaire etc*)
office; (: *clientèle*) practice; (*Pol*) cabinet; (*d'un
ministre*) advisers *pl*; **cabinets** *nmpl* (*w.-c.*) toilet
sg; **~ d'affaires** business consultants' (bureau),
business partnership; **~ de toilette** toilet; **~ de
travail** study

câble [kɑbl(ə)] *nm* cable; **le ~** (*TV*) cable
television, cablevision (*US*)

câblé, e [kɑble] *adj* (*fam*) switched on; (*Tech*)
linked to cable television

câbler [kɑble] *vt* to cable; **~ un quartier** (*TV*) to
put cable television into an area

cabosser [kabɔse] *vt* to dent

cabot [kabo] *nm* (*péj: chien*) mutt

cabotage [kabɔtaʒ] *nm* coastal navigation

caboteur [kabɔtœʀ] *nm* coaster

cabotin, e [kabɔtɛ̃, -in] *nm/f* (*péj: personne
maniérée*) poseur; (: *acteur*) ham ▷ *adj* dramatic,
theatrical

cabotinage [kabɔtinaʒ] *nm* playacting; third-
rate acting, ham acting

cabrer [kabʀe]: **se cabrer** *vi* (*cheval*) to rear up;
(*avion*) to nose up; (*fig*) to revolt, rebel; to jib

cabri [kabʀi] *nm* kid

cabriole [kabʀijɔl] *nf* caper; (*gymnastique etc*)
somersault

cabriolet [kabʀijɔlɛ] *nm* convertible

CAC [kak] *sigle f* = **Compagnie des agents de
change; indice ~** ≈ FT index (*Brit*), ≈ Dow Jones
average (*US*)

caca [kaka] *nm* (*langage enfantin*) pooh; (*couleur*):
~ d'oie greeny-yellow; **faire ~** (*fam*) to do a pooh

cacahuète [kakaɥɛt] *nf* peanut

cacao [kakao] *nm* cocoa (powder); (*boisson*) cocoa

cachalot [kaʃalo] *nm* sperm whale

cache [kaʃ] *nm* mask, card (*for masking*) ▷ *nf*
hiding place

cache-cache [kaʃkaʃ] *nm*: **jouer à ~** to play
hide-and-seek

cache-col [kaʃkɔl] *nm* scarf

cachemire [kaʃmiʀ] *nm* cashmere ▷ *adj*: **dessin
~** paisley pattern; **le C~** Kashmir

cache-nez [kaʃne] *nm inv* scarf, muffler

cache-pot [kaʃpo] *nm inv* flower-pot holder

cache-prise [kaʃpʀiz] *nm inv* socket cover

cacher [kaʃe] *vt* to hide, conceal; **~ qch à qn** to
hide *ou* conceal sth from sb; **se cacher** to hide;
to be hidden *ou* concealed; **il ne s'en cache pas**
he makes no secret of it

cache-sexe [kaʃsɛks] *nm inv* G-string

cachet [kaʃɛ] *nm* (*comprimé*) tablet; (*sceau: du roi*)
seal; (: *de la poste*) postmark; (*rétribution*) fee; (*fig*)
style, character

cacheter [kaʃte] *vt* to seal; **vin cacheté** vintage
wine

cachette [kaʃɛt] *nf* hiding place; **en ~** on the sly,
secretly

cachot [kaʃo] *nm* dungeon

cachotterie [kaʃɔtʀi] *nf* mystery; **faire des ~s**
to be secretive

cachottier, -ière [kaʃɔtje, -jɛʀ] *adj* secretive

cachou [kaʃu] *nm*: **pastille de ~** cachou (*sweet*)

cacophonie [kakɔfɔni] *nf* cacophony, din

cacophonique [kakɔfɔnik] *adj* cacophonous
cactus [kaktys] *nm* cactus
c.-à-d. *abr* (= *c'est-à-dire*) i.e.
cadastre [kadastʀ(ə)] *nm* land register
cadavéreux, -euse [kadaveʀø, -øz] *adj* (*teint, visage*) deathly pale
cadavérique [kadaveʀik] *adj* deathly (pale), deadly pale
cadavre [kadavʀ(ə)] *nm* corpse, (dead) body
Caddie® [kadi] *nm* (supermarket) trolley
cadeau, x [kado] *nm* present, gift; **faire un ~ à qn** to give sb a present *ou* gift; **faire ~ de qch à qn** to make a present of sth to sb, give sb sth as a present
cadenas [kadna] *nm* padlock
cadenasser [kadnase] *vt* to padlock
cadence [kadɑ̃s] *nf* (*Mus*) cadence; (: *rythme*) rhythm; (*de travail etc*) rate; **cadences** *nfpl* (*en usine*) production rate *sg*; **en ~** rhythmically; in time
cadencé, e [kadɑ̃se] *adj* rhythmic(al); **au pas ~** (*Mil*) in quick time
cadet, te [kadɛ, -ɛt] *adj* younger; (*le plus jeune*) youngest ▷ *nm/f* youngest child *ou* one, youngest boy *ou* son/girl *ou* daughter; **il est mon ~ de deux ans** he's two years younger than me, he's two years my junior; **les ~s** (*Sport*) the minors (*15–17 years*); **le ~ de mes soucis** the least of my worries
cadrage [kadʀaʒ] *nm* framing (*of shot*)
cadran [kadʀɑ̃] *nm* dial; **~ solaire** sundial
cadre [kadʀ(ə)] *nm* frame; (*environnement*) surroundings *pl*; (*limites*) scope ▷ *nm/f* (*Admin*) managerial employee, executive ▷ *adj*: **loi ~** outline *ou* blueprint law; **~ moyen/supérieur** (*Admin*) middle/senior management employee, junior/senior executive; **rayer qn des ~s** to discharge sb; to dismiss sb; **dans le ~ de** (*fig*) within the framework *ou* context of
cadrer [kadʀe] *vi*: **~ avec** to tally *ou* correspond with ▷ *vt* (*Ciné, Photo*) to frame
cadreur, -euse [kadʀœʀ, -øz] *nm/f* (*Ciné*) cameraman/woman
caduc, -uque [kadyk] *adj* obsolete; (*Bot*) deciduous
CAF *sigle f* (= *Caisse d'allocations familiales*) family allowance office
caf *abr* (*coût, assurance, fret*) cif
cafard [kafaʀ] *nm* cockroach; **avoir le ~** to be down in the dumps, be feeling low
cafardeux, -euse [kafaʀdø, -øz] *adj* (*personne, ambiance*) depressing, melancholy
café [kafe] *nm* coffee; (*bistro*) café ▷ *adj inv* coffee *cpd*; **~ crème** coffee with cream; **~ au lait** white coffee; **~ noir** black coffee; **~ en grains** coffee beans; **~ en poudre** instant coffee; **~ tabac** tobacconist's or newsagent's also serving coffee and spirits; **~ liégeois** coffee ice cream with whipped cream
café-concert [kafekɔ̃sɛʀ] (*pl* **cafés-concerts**) *nm* (*aussi*: **caf'conc'**) café with a cabaret
caféine [kafein] *nf* caffeine
cafétéria [kafeteʀja] *nf* cafeteria

café-théâtre [kafeteatʀ(ə)] (*pl* **cafés-théâtres**) *nm* café used as a venue by (experimental) theatre groups
cafetière [kaftjɛʀ] *nf* (*pot*) coffee-pot
cafouillage [kafujaʒ] *nm* shambles *sg*
cafouiller [kafuje] *vi* to get in a shambles; (*machine etc*) to work in fits and starts
cage [kaʒ] *nf* cage; **~ (des buts)** goal; **en ~** in a cage, caged up *ou* in; **~ d'ascenseur** lift shaft; **~ d'escalier** (stair)well; **~ thoracique** rib cage
cageot [kaʒo] *nm* crate
cagibi [kaʒibi] *nm* shed
cagneux, -euse [kaɲø, -øz] *adj* knock-kneed
cagnotte [kaɲɔt] *nf* kitty
cagoule [kagul] *nf* cowl; hood; (*Ski etc*) cagoule
cahier [kaje] *nm* notebook; (*Typo*) signature; (*revue*): **~s** journal; **~ de revendications/doléances** list of claims/grievances; **~ de brouillons** rough book, jotter; **~ des charges** specification; **~ d'exercices** exercise book
cahin-caha [kaɛ̃kaa] *adv*: **aller ~** to jog along; (*fig*) to be so-so
cahot [kao] *nm* jolt, bump
cahoter [kaɔte] *vi* to bump along, jog along
cahoteux, -euse [kaɔtø, -øz] *adj* bumpy
cahute [kayt] *nf* shack, hut
caïd [kaid] *nm* big chief, boss
caillasse [kajas] *nf* (*pierraille*) loose stones *pl*
caille [kaj] *nf* quail
caillé, e [kaje] *adj*: **lait ~** curdled milk, curds *pl*
caillebotis [kajbɔti] *nm* duckboard
cailler [kaje] *vi* (*lait*) to curdle; (*sang*) to clot; (*fam*) to be cold
caillot [kajo] *nm* (blood) clot
caillou, x [kaju] *nm* (little) stone
caillouter [kajute] *vt* (*chemin*) to metal
caillouteux, -euse [kajutø, -øz] *adj* stony; pebbly
cailloutis [kajuti] *nm* (*petits graviers*) gravel
caïman [kaimɑ̃] *nm* cayman
Caïmans [kaimɑ̃] *nfpl*: **les ~** the Cayman Islands
Caire [kɛʀ] *nm*: **le ~** Cairo
caisse [kɛs] *nf* box; (*où l'on met la recette*) cashbox; (: *machine*) till; (*où l'on paye*) cash desk (*Brit*), checkout counter; (: *au supermarché*) checkout; (*de banque*) cashier's desk; (*Tech*) case, casing; **faire sa ~** (*Comm*) to count the takings; **~ claire** (*Mus*) side *ou* snare drum; **~ éclair** express checkout; **~ enregistreuse** cash register; **~ d'épargne (CE)** savings bank; **~ noire** slush fund; **~ de retraite** pension fund; **~ de sortie** checkout; *voir* **grosse**
caissier, -ière [kesje, -jɛʀ] *nm/f* cashier
caisson [kesɔ̃] *nm* box, case
cajoler [kaʒɔle] *vt* to wheedle, coax; to surround with love and care, make a fuss of
cajoleries [kaʒɔlʀi] *nfpl* coaxing *sg*, flattery *sg*
cajou [kaʒu] *nm* cashew nut
cake [kɛk] *nm* fruit cake
CAL *sigle m* (= *Comité d'action lycéen*) pupils' action group seeking to reform school system
cal [kal] *nm* callus
cal. *abr* = **calorie**

59

calamar [kalamaʀ] *nm* = **calmar**

calaminé, e [kalamine] *adj* (*Auto*) coked up

calamité [kalamite] *nf* calamity, disaster

calandre [kalɑ̃dʀ(ə)] *nf* radiator grill; (*machine*) calender, mangle

calanque [kalɑ̃k] *nf* rocky inlet

calcaire [kalkɛʀ] *nm* limestone ▷ *adj* (*eau*) hard; (*Géo*) limestone *cpd*

calciné, e [kalsine] *adj* burnt to ashes

calcium [kalsjɔm] *nm* calcium

calcul [kalkyl] *nm* calculation; **le ~** (*Scol*) arithmetic; **~ différentiel/intégral** differential/integral calculus; **~ mental** mental arithmetic; **~** (**biliaire**) (gall)stone; **~** (**rénal**) (kidney) stone; **d'après mes ~s** by my reckoning

calculateur [kalkylatœʀ] *nm*, **calculatrice** [kalkylatʀis] *nf* calculator

calculé, e [kalkyle] *adj*: **risque ~** calculated risk

calculer [kalkyle] *vt* to calculate, work out, reckon; (*combiner*) to calculate; **~ qch de tête** to work sth out in one's head

calculette [kalkylɛt] *nf* (pocket) calculator

cale [kal] *nf* (*de bateau*) hold; (*en bois*) wedge, chock; **~ sèche** *ou* **de radoub** dry dock

calé, e [kale] *adj* (*fam*) clever, bright

calebasse [kalbas] *nf* calabash, gourd

calèche [kalɛʃ] *nf* horse-drawn carriage

caleçon [kalsɔ̃] *nm* pair of underpants, trunks *pl*; **~ de bain** bathing trunks *pl*

calembour [kalɑ̃buʀ] *nm* pun

calendes [kalɑ̃d] *nfpl*: **renvoyer aux ~ grecques** to postpone indefinitely

calendrier [kalɑ̃dʀije] *nm* calendar; (*fig*) timetable

cale-pied [kalpje] *nm inv* toe clip

calepin [kalpɛ̃] *nm* notebook

caler [kale] *vt* to wedge, chock up; **~ (son moteur/véhicule)** to stall (one's engine/vehicle); **se ~ dans un fauteuil** to make o.s. comfortable in an armchair

calfater [kalfate] *vt* to caulk

calfeutrage [kalføtʀaʒ] *nm* draughtproofing (*Brit*), draftproofing (*US*)

calfeutrer [kalføtʀe] *vt* to (make) draughtproof (*Brit*) *ou* draftproof (*US*); **se calfeutrer** *vi* to make o.s. snug and comfortable

calibre [kalibʀ(ə)] *nm* (*d'un fruit*) grade; (*d'une arme*) bore, calibre (*Brit*), caliber (*US*); (*fig*) calibre, caliber

calibrer [kalibʀe] *vt* to grade

calice [kalis] *nm* (*Rel*) chalice; (*Bot*) calyx

calicot [kaliko] *nm* (*tissu*) calico

calife [kalif] *nm* caliph

Californie [kalifɔʀni] *nf*: **la ~** California

californien, ne [kalifɔʀnjɛ̃, -ɛn] *adj* Californian

califourchon [kalifuʀʃɔ̃]: **à ~** *adv* astride; **à ~ sur** astride, straddling

câlin, e [kalɛ̃, -in] *adj* cuddly, cuddlesome; tender

câliner [kaline] *vt* to fondle, cuddle

câlineries [kalinʀi] *nfpl* cuddles

calisson [kalisɔ̃] *nm* diamond-shaped sweet or candy made with ground almonds

calleux, -euse [kalø, -øz] *adj* horny, callous

calligraphie [kaligʀafi] *nf* calligraphy

callosité [kalozite] *nf* callus

calmant [kalmɑ̃] *nm* tranquillizer, sedative; (*contre la douleur*) painkiller

calmar [kalmaʀ] *nm* squid

calme [kalm(ə)] *adj* calm, quiet ▷ *nm* calm(ness), quietness; **sans perdre son ~** without losing one's cool *ou* calmness; **~ plat** (*Navig*) dead calm

calmement [kalməmɑ̃] *adv* calmly, quietly

calmer [kalme] *vt* to calm (down); (*douleur, inquiétude*) to ease, soothe; **se calmer** *vi* to calm down

calomniateur, -trice [kalɔmnjatœʀ, -tʀis] *nm/f* slanderer; libeller

calomnie [kalɔmni] *nf* slander; (*écrite*) libel

calomnier [kalɔmnje] *vt* to slander; to libel

calomnieux, -euse [kalɔmnjø, -øz] *adj* slanderous; libellous

calorie [kalɔʀi] *nf* calorie

calorifère [kalɔʀifɛʀ] *nm* stove

calorifique [kalɔʀifik] *adj* calorific

calorifuge [kalɔʀifyʒ] *adj* (heat-)insulating, heat-retaining

calot [kalo] *nm* forage cap

calotte [kalɔt] *nf* (*coiffure*) skullcap; (*gifle*) slap; **la ~** (*péj: clergé*) the cloth, the clergy; **~ glaciaire** icecap

calque [kalk(ə)] *nm* (*aussi*: **papier calque**) tracing paper; (*dessin*) tracing; (*fig*) carbon copy

calquer [kalke] *vt* to trace; (*fig*) to copy exactly

calvados [kalvados] *nm* Calvados (*apple brandy*)

calvaire [kalvɛʀ] *nm* (*croix*) wayside cross, calvary; (*souffrances*) suffering, martyrdom

calvitie [kalvisi] *nf* baldness

camaïeu [kamajø] *nm*: **(motif en) ~** monochrome motif

camarade [kamaʀad] *nm/f* friend, pal; (*Pol*) comrade

camaraderie [kamaʀadʀi] *nf* friendship

camarguais, e [kamaʀgɛ, -ɛz] *adj* of *ou* from the Camargue

Camargue [kamaʀg] *nf*: **la ~** the Camargue

cambiste [kɑ̃bist(ə)] *nm* (*Comm*) foreign exchange dealer, exchange agent

Cambodge [kɑ̃bɔdʒ] *nm*: **le ~** Cambodia

cambodgien, ne [kɑ̃bɔdʒjɛ̃, -ɛn] *adj* Cambodian ▷ *nm/f*: **Cambodgien, ne** Cambodian

cambouis [kɑ̃bwi] *nm* dirty oil *ou* grease

cambré, e [kɑ̃bʀe] *adj*: **avoir les reins ~s** to have an arched back; **avoir le pied très ~** to have very high arches *ou* insteps

cambrer [kɑ̃bʀe] *vt* to arch; **se cambrer** *vi* to arch one's back; **~ la taille** *ou* **les reins** to arch one's back

cambriolage [kɑ̃bʀijɔlaʒ] *nm* burglary

cambrioler [kɑ̃bʀijɔle] *vt* to burgle (*Brit*), burglarize (*US*)

cambrioleur, -euse [kɑ̃bʀijɔlœʀ, -øz] *nm/f*

burglar

cambrure [kɑ̄bʀyʀ] nf (du pied) arch; (de la route) camber; **~ des reins** small of the back

cambuse [kɑ̄byz] nf storeroom

came [kam] nf: **arbre à ~s** camshaft; **arbre à ~s en tête** overhead camshaft

camée [kame] nm cameo

caméléon [kameleɔ̄] nm chameleon

camélia [kamelja] nm camellia

camelot [kamlo] nm street pedlar

camelote [kamlɔt] nf rubbish, trash, junk

camembert [kamɑ̄bɛʀ] nm Camembert (cheese)

caméra [kameʀa] nf (Ciné, TV) camera; (d'amateur) cine-camera

caméraman [kameʀaman] nm cameraman/-woman

Cameroun [kamʀun] nm: **le ~** Cameroon

camerounais, e [kamʀunɛ, -ɛz] adj Cameroonian

caméscope® [kameskɔp] nm camcorder

camion [kamjɔ̄] nm lorry (Brit), truck; (plus petit, fermé) van; (charge): **~ de sable/cailloux** lorry-load (Brit) ou truck-load of sand/stones; **~ de dépannage** breakdown (Brit) ou tow (US) truck

camion-citerne [kamjɔ̄sitɛʀn(ə)] (pl **camions-citernes**) nm tanker

camionnage [kamjɔnaʒ] nm haulage (Brit), trucking (US); **frais/entreprise de ~** haulage costs/business

camionnette [kamjɔnɛt] nf (small) van

camionneur [kamjɔnœʀ] nm (entrepreneur) haulage contractor (Brit), trucker (US); (chauffeur) lorry (Brit) ou truck driver; van driver

camisole [kamizɔl] nf: **~ (de force)** straitjacket

camomille [kamɔmij] nf camomile; (boisson) camomile tea

camouflage [kamuflaʒ] nm camouflage

camoufler [kamufle] vt to camouflage; (fig) to conceal, cover up

camouflet [kamuflɛ] nm (fam) snub

camp [kɑ̄] nm camp; (fig) side; **~ de nudistes/vacances** nudist/holiday camp; **~ de concentration** concentration camp

campagnard, e [kɑ̄paɲaʀ, -aʀd(ə)] adj country cpd ▷ nm/f countryman/woman

campagne [kɑ̄paɲ] nf country, countryside; (Mil, Pol, Comm) campaign; **en ~** (Mil) in the field; **à la ~** in/to the country; **faire ~ pour** to campaign for; **~ électorale** election campaign; **~ de publicité** advertising campaign

campanile [kɑ̄panil] nm (tour) bell tower

campé, e [kɑ̄pe] adj: **bien ~** (personnage, tableau) well-drawn

campement [kɑ̄pmɑ̄] nm camp, encampment

camper [kɑ̄pe] vi to camp ▷ vt (chapeau etc) to pull ou put on firmly; (dessin) to sketch; **se ~ devant** to plant o.s. in front of

campeur, -euse [kɑ̄pœʀ, -øz] nm/f camper

camphre [kɑ̄fʀ(ə)] nm camphor

camphré, e [kɑ̄fʀe] adj camphorated

camping [kɑ̄piŋ] nm camping; **(terrain de) ~** campsite, camping site; **faire du ~** to go

camping; **faire du ~ sauvage** to camp rough

camping-car [kɑ̄piŋkaʀ] nm caravanette, camper (US)

camping-gaz® [kɑ̄piŋgaz] nm inv camp(ing) stove

campus [kɑ̄pys] nm campus

camus, e [kamy, -yz] adj: **nez ~** pug nose

Canada [kanada] nm: **le ~** Canada

canadair® [kanadɛʀ] nm fire-fighting plane

canadien, ne [kanadjɛ̄, -ɛn] adj Canadian ▷ nm/f: **Canadien, ne** Canadian ▷ nf (veste) fur-lined jacket

canaille [kanaj] nf (péj) scoundrel; (populace) riff-raff ▷ adj raffish, rakish

canal, -aux [kanal, -o] nm canal; (naturel) channel; (Admin): **par le ~ de** through (the medium of), via; **~ de distribution/télévision** distribution/television channel; **~ de Panama/Suez** Panama/Suez Canal

canalisation [kanalizasjɔ̄] nf (tuyau) pipe

canaliser [kanalize] vt to canalize; (fig) to channel

canapé [kanape] nm settee, sofa; (Culin) canapé, open sandwich

canapé-lit [kanapeli] (pl **canapés-lits**) nm sofa bed

canaque [kanak] adj of ou from New Caledonia ▷ nm/f: **Canaque** native of New Caledonia

canard [kanaʀ] nm duck

canari [kanaʀi] nm canary

Canaries [kanaʀi] nfpl: **les (îles) ~** the Canary Islands, the Canaries

cancaner [kɑ̄kane] vi to gossip (maliciously); (canard) to quack

cancanier, -ière [kɑ̄kanje, -jɛʀ] adj gossiping

cancans [kɑ̄kɑ̄] nmpl (malicious) gossip sg

cancer [kɑ̄sɛʀ] nm cancer; (signe): **le C~** Cancer, the Crab; **être du C~** to be Cancer; **il a un ~** he has cancer

cancéreux, -euse [kɑ̄seʀø, -øz] adj cancerous; (personne) suffering from cancer

cancérigène [kɑ̄seʀiʒɛn] adj carcinogenic

cancérologue [kɑ̄seʀɔlɔg] nm/f cancer specialist

cancre [kɑ̄kʀ(ə)] nm dunce

cancrelat [kɑ̄kʀəla] nm cockroach

candélabre [kɑ̄delɑbʀ(ə)] nm candelabrum; (lampadaire) street lamp, lamppost

candeur [kɑ̄dœʀ] nf ingenuousness

candi [kɑ̄di] adj inv: **sucre ~** (sugar-)candy

candidat, e [kɑ̄dida, -at] nm/f candidate; (à un poste) applicant, candidate

candidature [kɑ̄didatyʀ] nf candidacy; application; **poser sa ~** to submit an application, apply; **~ spontanée** unsolicited job application

candide [kɑ̄did] adj ingenuous, guileless, naïve

cane [kan] nf (female) duck

caneton [kantɔ̄] nm duckling

canette [kanɛt] nf (de bière) (flip-top) bottle; (de machine à coudre) spool

canevas [kanva] nm (Couture) canvas (for tapestry work); (fig) framework, structure

caniche [kaniʃ] *nm* poodle

caniculaire [kanikylɛʀ] *adj* (*chaleur, jour*) scorching

canicule [kanikyl] *nf* scorching heat; midsummer heat, dog days *pl*

canif [kanif] *nm* penknife, pocket knife

canin, e [kanɛ̃, -in] *adj* canine ▷ *nf* canine (tooth), eye tooth; **exposition ~e** dog show

caniveau, x [kanivo] *nm* gutter

cannabis [kanabis] *nm* cannabis

canne [kan] *nf* (walking) stick; **~ à pêche** fishing rod; **~ à sucre** sugar cane; **les ~s blanches** (*les aveugles*) the blind

canné, e [kane] *adj* (*chaise*) cane *cpd*

cannelé, e [kanle] *adj* fluted

cannelle [kanɛl] *nf* cinnamon

cannelure [kanlyʀ] *nf* fluting *no pl*

canner [kane] *vt* (*chaise*) to make *ou* repair with cane

cannibale [kanibal] *nm/f* cannibal

cannibalisme [kanibalism(ə)] *nm* cannibalism

canoë [kanɔe] *nm* canoe; (*sport*) canoeing; **~ (kayak)** kayak

canon [kanɔ̃] *nm* (*arme*) gun; (*Hist*) cannon; (*d'une arme: tube*) barrel; (*fig*) model; (*Mus*) canon ▷ *adj*: **droit ~** canon law; **~ rayé** rifled barrel

cañon [kaɲɔ̃] *nm* canyon

canonique [kanɔnik] *adj*: **âge ~** respectable age

canoniser [kanɔnize] *vt* to canonize

canonnade [kanɔnad] *nf* cannonade

canonnier [kanɔnje] *nm* gunner

canonnière [kanɔnjɛʀ] *nf* gunboat

canot [kano] *nm* boat, ding(h)y; **~ pneumatique** rubber *ou* inflatable ding(h)y; **~ de sauvetage** lifeboat

canotage [kanɔtaʒ] *nm* rowing

canoter [kanɔte] *vi* to go rowing

canoteur, -euse [kanɔtœʀ, -øz] *nm/f* rower

canotier [kanɔtje] *nm* boater

Cantal [kɑ̃tal] *nm*: **le ~** Cantal

cantate [kɑ̃tat] *nf* cantata

cantatrice [kɑ̃tatʀis] *nf* (opera) singer

cantilène [kɑ̃tilɛn] *nf* (*Mus*) cantilena

cantine [kɑ̃tin] *nf* canteen; (*réfectoire d'école*) dining hall

cantique [kɑ̃tik] *nm* hymn

canton [kɑ̃tɔ̃] *nm* district (*consisting of several communes*); *see note*; (*en Suisse*) canton

CANTON

A French *canton* is the administrative division represented by a councillor in the "Conseil général". It comprises a number of "communes" and is, in turn, a subdivision of an "arrondissement". In Switzerland the *cantons* are the 23 autonomous political divisions which make up the Swiss confederation.

cantonade [kɑ̃tɔnad]: **à la ~** *adv* to everyone in general; (*crier*) from the rooftops

cantonais, e [kɑ̃tɔnɛ, -ɛz] *adj* Cantonese ▷ *nm* (*Ling*) Cantonese

cantonal, e, -aux [kɑ̃tɔnal, -o] *adj* cantonal, ≈ district

cantonnement [kɑ̃tɔnmɑ̃] *nm* (*lieu*) billet; (*action*) billeting

cantonner [kɑ̃tɔne] *vt* (*Mil*) to billet (*Brit*), quarter; to station; **se ~ dans** to confine o.s. to

cantonnier [kɑ̃tɔnje] *nm* roadmender

canular [kanylaʀ] *nm* hoax

CAO *sigle f* (= *conception assistée par ordinateur*) CAD

caoutchouc [kautʃu] *nm* rubber; **~ mousse** foam rubber; **en ~** rubber *cpd*

caoutchouté, e [kautʃute] *adj* rubberized

caoutchouteux, -euse [kautʃutø, -øz] *adj* rubbery

CAP *sigle m* (= *Certificat d'aptitude professionnelle*) vocational training certificate taken at secondary school

cap [kap] *nm* (*Géo*) cape; headland; (*fig*) hurdle; watershed; (*Navig*): **changer de ~** to change course; **mettre le ~ sur** to head *ou* steer for; **doubler** *ou* **passer le ~** (*fig*) to get over the worst; **Le C~** Cape Town; **le ~ de Bonne Espérance** the Cape of Good Hope; **le ~ Horn** Cape Horn; **les îles du C~ Vert** (*aussi*: **le Cap-Vert**) the Cape Verde Islands

capable [kapabl(ə)] *adj* able, capable; **~ de qch/faire** capable of sth/doing; **il est ~ d'oublier** he could easily forget; **spectacle ~ d'intéresser** show likely to be of interest

capacité [kapasite] *nf* (*compétence*) ability; (*Jur, Inform, d'un récipient*) capacity; **~ (en droit)** basic legal qualification

caparaçonner [kapaʀasɔne] *vt* (*fig*) to clad

cape [kap] *nf* cape, cloak; **rire sous ~** to laugh up one's sleeve

capeline [kaplin] *nf* wide-brimmed hat

CAPES [kapɛs] *sigle m* (= *Certificat d'aptitude au professorat de l'enseignement du second degré*) secondary teaching diploma; *see note*

CAPES

The French CAPES ("certificat d'aptitude au professorat de l'enseignement du second degré") is a competitive examination sat by prospective secondary school teachers after the 'licence'. Successful candidates become fully qualified teachers ("professeurs certifiés").

capésien, ne [kapesjɛ̃, -ɛn] *nm/f* person who holds the CAPES

CAPET [kapɛt] *sigle m* (= *Certificat d'aptitude au professorat de l'enseignement technique*) technical teaching diploma

capharnaüm [kafaʀnaɔm] *nm* shambles *sg*

capillaire [kapilɛʀ] *adj* (*soins, lotion*) hair *cpd*; (*vaisseau etc*) capillary; **artiste ~** hair artist *ou* designer

capillarité [kapilaʀite] *nf* capillary action

capilotade [kapilɔtad]: **en ~** *adv* crushed to a

pulp; smashed to pieces

capitaine [kapitɛn] *nm* captain; **~ des pompiers** fire chief (*Brit*), fire marshal (*US*); **~ au long cours** master mariner

capitainerie [kapitɛnʀi] *nf* (*du port*) harbour (*Brit*) *ou* harbor (*US*) master's (office)

capital, e, -aux [kapital, -o] *adj* major; fundamental; (*Jur*) capital ▷ *nm* capital; (*fig*) stock; asset ▷ *nf* (*ville*) capital; (*lettre*) capital (letter) ▷ *nmpl* (*fonds*) capital *sg*, money *sg*; **les sept péchés capitaux** the seven deadly sins; **peine ~e** capital punishment; **~ (social)** authorized capital; **~ d'exploitation** working capital

capitaliser [kapitalize] *vt* to amass, build up; (*Comm*) to capitalize ▷ *vi* to save

capitalisme [kapitalism(ə)] *nm* capitalism

capitaliste [kapitalist(ə)] *adj, nm/f* capitalist

capiteux, -euse [kapitø, -øz] *adj* (*vin, parfum*) heady; (*sensuel*) sensuous, alluring

capitonnage [kapitɔnaʒ] *nm* padding

capitonné, e [kapitɔne] *adj* padded

capitonner [kapitɔne] *vt* to pad

capitulation [kapitylasjɔ̃] *nf* capitulation

capituler [kapityle] *vi* to capitulate

caporal, -aux [kapɔʀal, -o] *nm* lance corporal

caporal-chef [kapɔʀalʃɛf, kapɔʀo-] (*pl* **caporaux-chefs**) *nm* corporal

capot [kapo] *nm* (*Auto*) bonnet (*Brit*), hood (*US*)

capote [kapɔt] *nf* (*de voiture*) hood (*Brit*), top (*US*); (*de soldat*) greatcoat; **~ (anglaise)** (*fam*) rubber, condom

capoter [kapɔte] *vi* to overturn; (*négociations*) to founder

câpre [kɑpʀ(ə)] *nf* caper

caprice [kapʀis] *nm* whim, caprice; passing fancy; **caprices** *nmpl* (*de la mode etc*) vagaries; **faire un ~** to throw a tantrum; **faire des ~s** to be temperamental

capricieux, -euse [kapʀisjø, -øz] *adj* capricious; whimsical; temperamental

Capricorne [kapʀikɔʀn] *nm*: **le ~** Capricorn, the Goat; **être du ~** to be Capricorn

capsule [kapsyl] *nf* (*de bouteille*) cap; (*amorce*) primer; cap; (*Bot etc, spatiale*) capsule

captage [kaptaʒ] *nm* (*d'une émission de radio*) picking-up; (*d'énergie, d'eau*) harnessing

capter [kapte] *vt* (*ondes radio*) to pick up; (*eau*) to harness; (*fig*) to win, capture

capteur [kaptœʀ] *nm*: **~ solaire** solar collector

captieux, -euse [kapsjø, -øz] *adj* specious

captif, -ive [kaptif, -iv] *adj, nm/f* captive

captivant, e [kaptivɑ̃, -ɑ̃t] *adj* captivating

captiver [kaptive] *vt* to captivate

captivité [kaptivite] *nf* captivity; **en ~** in captivity

capture [kaptyʀ] *nf* capture, catching *no pl*; catch

capturer [kaptyʀe] *vt* to capture, catch

capuche [kapyʃ] *nf* hood

capuchon [kapyʃɔ̃] *nm* hood; (*de stylo*) cap, top

capucin [kapysɛ̃] *nm* Capuchin monk

capucine [kapysin] *nf* (*Bot*) nasturtium

Cap-Vert [kabvɛʀ] *nm*: **le ~** Cape Verde

caquelon [kaklɔ̃] *nm* (*ustensile de cuisson*) fondue pot

caquet [kakɛ] *nm*: **rabattre le ~ à qn** to bring sb down a peg or two

caqueter [kakte] *vi* (*poule*) to cackle; (*fig*) to prattle

car [kaʀ] *nm* coach (*Brit*), bus ▷ *conj* because, for; **~ de police** police van; **~ de reportage** broadcasting *ou* radio van

carabine [kaʀabin] *nf* carbine, rifle; **~ à air comprimé** airgun

carabiné, e [kaʀabine] *adj* violent; (*cocktail, amende*) stiff

Caracas [kaʀakas] *n* Caracas

caracoler [kaʀakɔle] *vi* to caracole, prance

caractère [kaʀaktɛʀ] *nm* (*gén*) character; **en ~s gras** in bold type; **en petits ~s** in small print; **en ~s d'imprimerie** in block capitals; **avoir du ~** to have character; **avoir bon/mauvais ~** to be good-/ill-natured *ou* tempered; **~ de remplacement** wild card (*Inform*); **~s/seconde (cps)** characters per second (cps)

caractériel, le [kaʀakteʀjɛl] *adj* (*enfant*) (emotionally) disturbed ▷ *nm/f* problem child; **troubles ~s** emotional problems

caractérisé, e [kaʀakteʀize] *adj*: **c'est une grippe/de l'insubordination ~e** it is a clear(-cut) case of flu/insubordination

caractériser [kaʀakteʀize] *vt* to characterize; **se ~ par** to be characterized *ou* distinguished by

caractéristique [kaʀakteʀistik] *adj, nf* characteristic

carafe [kaʀaf] *nf* decanter; carafe

carafon [kaʀafɔ̃] *nm* small carafe

caraïbe [kaʀaib] *adj* Caribbean; **les Caraïbes** *nfpl* the Caribbean (Islands); **la mer des C~s** the Caribbean Sea

carambolage [kaʀɑ̃bɔlaʒ] *nm* multiple crash, pileup

caramel [kaʀamɛl] *nm* (*bonbon*) caramel, toffee; (*substance*) caramel

caraméliser [kaʀamelize] *vt* to caramelize

carapace [kaʀapas] *nf* shell

carapater [kaʀapate]: **se carapater** *vi* to take to one's heels, scram

carat [kaʀa] *nm* carat; **or à 18 ~s** 18-carat gold

caravane [kaʀavan] *nf* caravan

caravanier [kaʀavanje] *nm* caravanner

caravaning [kaʀavaniŋ] *nm* caravanning; (*emplacement*) caravan site

caravelle [kaʀavɛl] *nf* caravel

carbonate [kaʀbɔnat] *nm* (*Chimie*) **~ de soude** sodium carbonate

carbone [kaʀbɔn] *nm* carbon; (*feuille*) carbon, sheet of carbon paper; (*double*) carbon (copy)

carbonique [kaʀbɔnik] *adj*: **gaz ~** carbon dioxide; **neige ~** dry ice

carbonisé, e [kaʀbɔnize] *adj* charred; **mourir ~** to be burned to death

carboniser [kaʀbɔnize] *vt* to carbonize; (*brûler*

complètement) to burn down, reduce to ashes

carburant [kaʀbyʀɑ̃] *nm* (motor) fuel

carburateur [kaʀbyʀatœʀ] *nm* carburettor

carburation [kaʀbyʀasjɔ̃] *nf* carburation

carburer [kaʀbyʀe] *vi* (*moteur*): **bien/mal ~** to be well/badly tuned

carcan [kaʀkɑ̃] *nm* (*fig*) yoke, shackles *pl*

carcasse [kaʀkas] *nf* carcass; (*de véhicule etc*) shell

carcéral, e, -aux [kaʀseʀal, -o] *adj* prison *cpd*

carcinogène [kaʀsinoʒɛn] *adj* carcinogenic

cardan [kaʀdɑ̃] *nm* universal joint

carder [kaʀde] *vt* to card

cardiaque [kaʀdjak] *adj* cardiac, heart *cpd* ▷ *nm/f* heart patient; **être ~** to have a heart condition

cardigan [kaʀdigɑ̃] *nm* cardigan

cardinal, e, -aux [kaʀdinal, -o] *adj* cardinal ▷ *nm* (*Rel*) cardinal

cardiologie [kaʀdjɔlɔʒi] *nf* cardiology

cardiologue [kaʀdjɔlɔg] *nm/f* cardiologist, heart specialist

cardio-vasculaire [kaʀdjovaskylɛʀ] *adj* cardiovascular

cardon [kaʀdɔ̃] *nm* cardoon

carême [kaʀɛm] *nm*: **le C~** Lent

carence [kaʀɑ̃s] *nf* incompetence, inadequacy; (*manque*) deficiency; **~ vitaminique** vitamin deficiency

carène [kaʀɛn] *nf* hull

caréner [kaʀene] *vt* (*Navig*) to careen; (*carrosserie*) to streamline

caressant, e [kaʀɛsɑ̃, -ɑ̃t] *adj* affectionate; caressing, tender

caresse [kaʀɛs] *nf* caress

caresser [kaʀese] *vt* to caress, stroke, fondle; (*fig: projet, espoir*) to toy with

cargaison [kaʀgɛzɔ̃] *nf* cargo, freight

cargo [kaʀgo] *nm* cargo boat, freighter; **~ mixte** cargo and passenger ship

cari [kaʀi] *nm* = **curry**

caricatural, e, -aux [kaʀikatyʀal, -o] *adj* caricatural, caricature-like

caricature [kaʀikatyʀ] *nf* caricature; (*politique etc*) (satirical) cartoon

caricaturer [kaʀikatyʀe] *vt* (*personne*) to caricature; (*politique etc*) to satirize

caricaturiste [kaʀikatyʀist(ə)] *nm/f* caricaturist, (satirical) cartoonist

carie [kaʀi] *nf*: **la ~ (dentaire)** tooth decay; **une ~** a bad tooth

carié, e [kaʀje] *adj*: **dent ~e** bad *ou* decayed tooth

carillon [kaʀijɔ̃] *nm* (*d'église*) bells *pl*; (*de pendule*) chimes *pl*; (*de porte*): **~ (électrique)** (electric) door chime *ou* bell

carillonner [kaʀijone] *vi* to ring, chime, peal

caritatif, -ive [kaʀitatif, -iv] *adj* charitable

carlingue [kaʀlɛ̃g] *nf* cabin

carmélite [kaʀmelit] *nf* Carmelite nun

carmin [kaʀmɛ̃] *adj inv* crimson

carnage [kaʀnaʒ] *nm* carnage, slaughter

carnassier, -ière [kaʀnasje, -jɛʀ] *adj*

carnivorous ▷ *nm* carnivore

carnation [kaʀnasjɔ̃] *nf* complexion; **carnations** *nfpl* (*Peinture*) flesh tones

carnaval [kaʀnaval] *nm* carnival

carné, e [kaʀne] *adj* meat *cpd*, meat-based

carnet [kaʀnɛ] *nm* (*calepin*) notebook; (*de tickets, timbres etc*) book; (*d'école*) school report; (*journal intime*) diary; **~ d'adresses** address book; **~ de chèques** cheque book (*Brit*), checkbook (*US*); **~ de commandes** order book; **~ de notes** (*Scol*) (school) report; **~ à souches** counterfoil book

carnier [kaʀnje] *nm* gamebag

carnivore [kaʀnivɔʀ] *adj* carnivorous ▷ *nm* carnivore

Carolines [kaʀolin] *nfpl*: **les ~** the Caroline Islands

carotide [kaʀotid] *nf* carotid (artery)

carotte [kaʀot] *nf* (*aussi fig*) carrot

Carpates [kaʀpat] *nfpl*: **les ~** the Carpathians, the Carpathian Mountains

carpe [kaʀp(ə)] *nf* carp

carpette [kaʀpɛt] *nf* rug

carquois [kaʀkwa] *nm* quiver

carre [kaʀ] *nf* (*de ski*) edge

carré, e [kaʀe] *adj* square; (*fig: franc*) straightforward ▷ *nm* (*de terrain, jardin*) patch, plot; (*Navig: salle*) wardroom; (*Math*) square; **~ blanc** (*TV*) "adults only" symbol; (*Cartes*): **~ d'as/de rois** four aces/kings; **élever un nombre au ~** to square a number; **mètre/ kilomètre ~** square metre/kilometre; **~ de soie** silk headsquare *ou* headscarf; **~ d'agneau** loin of lamb

carreau, x [kaʀo] *nm* (*en faïence etc*) (floor) tile, (wall) tile; (*window*) pane; (*motif*) check, square; (*Cartes: couleur*) diamonds *pl*; (: *carte*) diamond; **tissu à ~x** checked fabric; **papier à ~x** squared paper

carrefour [kaʀfuʀ] *nm* crossroads *sg*

carrelage [kaʀlaʒ] *nm* tiling; (tiled) floor

carreler [kaʀle] *vt* to tile

carrelet [kaʀlɛ] *nm* (*poisson*) plaice

carreleur [kaʀlœʀ] *nm* (floor) tiler

carrément [kaʀemɑ̃] *adv* (*franchement*) straight out, bluntly; (*sans détours, sans hésiter*) straight; (*nettement*) definitely; **il l'a ~ mis à la porte** he threw him straight out

carrer [kaʀe]: **se carrer** *vi*: **se ~ dans un fauteuil** to settle o.s. comfortably *ou* ensconce o.s. in an armchair

carrier [kaʀje] *nm*: **(ouvrier) ~** quarryman, quarrier

carrière [kaʀjɛʀ] *nf* (*de roches*) quarry; (*métier*) career; **militaire de ~** professional soldier; **faire ~ dans** to make one's career in

carriériste [kaʀjeʀist(ə)] *nm/f* careerist

carriole [kaʀjɔl] *nf* (*péj*) old cart

carrossable [kaʀosabl(ə)] *adj* suitable for (motor) vehicles

carrosse [kaʀos] *nm* (horse-drawn) coach

carrosserie [kaʀosʀi] *nf* body, bodywork *no pl* (*Brit*); (*activité, commerce*) coachwork (*Brit*), (car) body manufacturing; **atelier de ~** (*pour réparations*) body shop, panel beaters' (yard) (*Brit*)

carrossier [kaʀɔsje] *nm* coachbuilder (*Brit*), (car) body repairer; (*dessinateur*) car designer

carrousel [kaʀuzɛl] *nm* (*Équitation*) carousel; (*fig*) merry-go-round

carrure [kaʀyʀ] *nf* build; (*fig*) stature

cartable [kaʀtabl(ə)] *nm* (*d'écolier*) satchel, (school)bag

carte [kaʀt(ə)] *nf* (*de géographie*) map; (*marine, du ciel*) chart; (*de fichier, d'abonnement etc, à jouer*) card; (*au restaurant*) menu; (*aussi:* **carte postale**) (post)card; (*aussi:* **carte de visite**) (visiting) card; **avoir/donner ~ blanche** to have/give carte blanche *ou* a free hand; **tirer les ~s à qn** to read sb's cards; **jouer aux ~s** to play cards; **jouer ~s sur table** (*fig*) to put one's cards on the table; **à la ~** (*au restaurant*) à la carte; **~ à circuit imprimé** printed circuit; **~ à puce** smartcard, chip and PIN card; **~ bancaire** cash card; **C~ Bleue**® debit card; **~ de crédit** credit card; **~ d'état-major** ≈ Ordnance (*Brit*) *ou* Geological (*US*) Survey map; **la ~ grise** (*Auto*) ≈ the (car) registration document; **~ d'identité** identity card; **~ jeune** young person's railcard; **~ mémoire** (*d'appareil photo numérique*) memory card; **~ perforée** punch(ed) card; **~ routière** road map; **~ de séjour** residence permit; **~ SIM** SIM card; **~ téléphonique** phonecard; **la ~ verte** (*Auto*) the green card; **la ~ des vins** the wine list

cartel [kaʀtɛl] *nm* cartel

carte-lettre [kaʀtəlɛtʀ(ə)] (*pl* **cartes-lettres**) *nf* letter-card

carte-mère [kaʀtəmɛʀ] (*pl* **cartes-mères**) *nf* (*Inform*) mother board

carter [kaʀtɛʀ] *nm* (*Auto: d'huile*) sump (*Brit*), oil pan (*US*); (: *de la boîte de vitesses*) casing; (*de bicyclette*) chain guard

carte-réponse [kaʀt(ə)ʀepɔ̃s] (*pl* **cartes-réponses**) *nf* reply card

cartésien, ne [kaʀtezjɛ̃, -ɛn] *adj* Cartesian

Carthage [kaʀtaʒ] *n* Carthage

cartilage [kaʀtilaʒ] *nm* (*Anat*) cartilage

cartilagineux, -euse [kaʀtilaʒinø, -øz] *adj* (*viande*) gristly

cartographe [kaʀtɔgʀaf] *nm/f* cartographer

cartographie [kaʀtɔgʀafi] *nf* cartography, map-making

cartomancie [kaʀtɔmɑ̃si] *nf* fortune-telling, card-reading

cartomancien, ne [kaʀtɔmɑ̃sjɛ̃, -ɛn] *nm/f* fortune-teller (*with cards*)

carton [kaʀtɔ̃] *nm* (*matériau*) cardboard; (*boîte*) (cardboard) box; (*d'invitation*) invitation card; (*Art*) sketch; cartoon; **en ~** cardboard *cpd*; **faire un ~** (*au tir*) to have a go at the rifle range; to score a hit; **~ (à dessin)** portfolio

cartonnage [kaʀtɔnaʒ] *nm* cardboard (packing)

cartonné, e [kaʀtɔne] *adj* (*livre*) hardback, cased

carton-pâte [kaʀtɔ̃pɑt] *nm* pasteboard; **de ~** (*fig*) cardboard *cpd*

cartouche [kaʀtuʃ] *nf* cartridge; (*de cigarettes*) carton

cartouchière [kaʀtuʃjɛʀ] *nf* cartridge belt

cas [kɑ] *nm* case; **faire peu de ~/grand ~ de** to attach little/great importance to; **le ~ échéant** if need be; **en aucun ~** on no account, under no circumstances (whatsoever); **au ~ où** in case; **dans ce ~** in that case; **en ~ de** in case of, in the event of; **en ~ de besoin** if need be; **en ~ d'urgence** in an emergency; **en ce ~** in that case; **en tout ~** in any case, at any rate; **~ de conscience** matter of conscience; **~ de force majeure** case of absolute necessity; (*Assurances*) act of God; **~ limite** borderline case; **~ social** social problem

Casablanca [kazablɑ̃ka] *n* Casablanca

casanier, -ière [kazanje, -jɛʀ] *adj* stay-at-home

casaque [kazak] *nf* (*de jockey*) blouse

cascade [kaskad] *nf* waterfall, cascade; (*fig*) stream, torrent

cascadeur, -euse [kaskadœʀ, -øz] *nm/f* stuntman/girl

case [kɑz] *nf* (*hutte*) hut; (*compartiment*) compartment; (*pour le courrier*) pigeonhole; (*de mots croisés, d'échiquier*) square; (*sur un formulaire*) box

casemate [kazmat] *nf* blockhouse

caser [kɑze] *vt* (*mettre*) to put; (*loger*) to put up; (*péj*) to find a job for; to marry off; **se caser** *vi* (*personne*) to settle down

caserne [kazɛʀn(ə)] *nf* barracks

casernement [kazɛʀnəmɑ̃] *nm* barrack buildings *pl*

cash [kaʃ] *adv*: **payer ~** to pay cash down

casier [kɑzje] *nm* (*à journaux etc*) rack; (*de bureau*) filing cabinet; (: *à cases*) set of pigeonholes; (*case*) compartment; pigeonhole; (: *à clef*) locker; (*Pêche*) lobster pot; **~ à bouteilles** bottle rack; **~ judiciaire** police record

casino [kazino] *nm* casino

casque [kask(ə)] *nm* helmet; (*chez le coiffeur*) (hair-)dryer; (*pour audition*) (head-)phones *pl*, headset; **les C~s bleus** the UN peacekeeping force

casquer [kaske] *vi* (*fam*) to cough up, stump up (*Brit*)

casquette [kaskɛt] *nf* cap

cassable [kasabl(ə)] *adj* (*fragile*) breakable

cassant, e [kasɑ̃, -ɑ̃t] *adj* brittle; (*fig*) brusque, abrupt

cassate [kasat] *nf*: **(glace) ~** cassata

cassation [kasasjɔ̃] *nf*: **se pourvoir en ~** to lodge an appeal; **recours en ~** appeal to the Supreme Court

casse [kɑs] *nf* (*pour voitures*): **mettre à la ~** to scrap, send to the breakers (*Brit*); (*dégâts*): **il y a eu de la ~** there were a lot of breakages; (*Typo*): **haut/bas de ~** upper/lower case

cassé, e [kase] *adj* (*voix*) cracked; (*vieillard*) bent

casse-cou [kasku] *adj inv* daredevil, reckless; **crier ~ à qn** to warn sb (*against a risky undertaking*)

casse-croûte [kaskʀut] *nm inv* snack

casse-noisettes [kasnwazɛt], **casse-noix** [kasnwa] *nm inv* nutcrackers *pl*

casse-pieds [kaspje] *adj, nm/f inv* (*fam*): **il est ~, c'est un ~** he's a pain (in the neck)

casser [kase] *vt* to break; (*Admin*: *gradé*) to demote; (*Jur*) to quash; (*Comm*): **~ les prix** to slash prices; **se casser** *vi* to break; (*fam*) to go, leave ▷ *vt*: **se ~ la jambe/une jambe** to break one's leg/a leg; **à tout ~** fantastic, brilliant; **se ~ net** to break clean off

casserole [kasʀɔl] *nf* saucepan; **à la ~** (*Culin*) braised

casse-tête [kastɛt] *nm inv* (*fig*) brain teaser; (*difficultés*) headache (*fig*)

cassette [kasɛt] *nf* (*bande magnétique*) cassette; (*coffret*) casket; **~ numérique** digital compact cassette; **~ vidéo** video

casseur [kasœʀ] *nm* hooligan; rioter

cassis [kasis] *nm* blackcurrant; (*de la route*) dip, bump

cassonade [kasɔnad] *nf* brown sugar

cassoulet [kasulɛ] *nm* *sausage and bean hotpot*

cassure [kasyʀ] *nf* break, crack

castagnettes [kastaɲɛt] *nfpl* castanets

caste [kast(ə)] *nf* caste

castillan, e [kastijɑ̃, -an] *adj* Castilian ▷ *nm* (*Ling*) Castilian

Castille [kastij] *nf*: **la ~** Castile

castor [kastɔʀ] *nm* beaver

castrer [kastʀe] *vt* (*mâle*) to castrate; (*femelle*) to spay; (*cheval*) to geld; (*chat, chien*) to doctor (*Brit*), fix (*US*)

cataclysme [kataklism(ə)] *nm* cataclysm

catacombes [katakɔ̃b] *nfpl* catacombs

catadioptre [katadjɔptʀ(ə)] *nm* = **cataphote**

catafalque [katafalk(ə)] *nm* catafalque

catalan, e [katalɑ̃, -an] *adj* Catalan, Catalonian ▷ *nm* (*Ling*) Catalan

Catalogne [katalɔɲ] *nf*: **la ~** Catalonia

catalogue [katalɔg] *nm* catalogue

cataloguer [katalɔge] *vt* to catalogue, list; (*péj*) to put a label on

catalyse [kataliz] *nf* catalysis

catalyser [katalize] *vt* to catalyze

catalyseur [katalizœʀ] *nm* catalyst

catalytique [katalitik] *adj* catalytic

catamaran [katamaʀɑ̃] *nm* (*voilier*) catamaran

cataphote [katafɔt] *nm* reflector

cataplasme [kataplasm(ə)] *nm* poultice

catapulte [katapylt(ə)] *nf* catapult

catapulter [katapylte] *vt* to catapult

cataracte [kataʀakt(ə)] *nf* cataract; **opérer qn de la ~** to operate on sb for a cataract

catarrhe [kataʀ] *nm* catarrh

catarrheux, -euse [kataʀø, -øz] *adj* catarrhal

catastrophe [katastʀɔf] *nf* catastrophe, disaster; **atterrir en ~** to make an emergency landing; **partir en ~** to rush away

catastropher [katastʀɔfe] *vt* (*personne*) to shatter

catastrophique [katastʀɔfik] *adj* catastrophic, disastrous

catch [katʃ] *nm* (all-in) wrestling

catcheur, -euse [katʃœʀ, -øz] *nm/f* (all-in) wrestler

catéchiser [kateʃize] *vt* to indoctrinate; to lecture

catéchisme [kateʃism(ə)] *nm* catechism

catéchumène [katekymɛn] *nm/f* catechumen, *person attending religious instruction prior to baptism*

catégorie [kategɔʀi] *nf* category; (*Boucherie*): **morceaux de première/deuxième ~** prime/second cuts

catégorique [kategɔʀik] *adj* categorical

catégoriquement [kategɔʀikmɑ̃] *adv* categorically

catégoriser [kategɔʀize] *vt* to categorize

caténaire [katenɛʀ] *nf* (*Rail*) catenary

cathédrale [katedʀal] *nf* cathedral

cathéter [katetɛʀ] *nm* (*Méd*) catheter

cathode [katɔd] *nf* cathode

cathodique [katɔdik] *adj*: **rayons ~s** cathode rays; **tube/écran ~** cathode-ray tube/screen

catholicisme [katɔlisism(ə)] *nm* (Roman) Catholicism

catholique [katɔlik] *adj, nm/f* (Roman) Catholic; **pas très ~** a bit shady *ou* fishy

catimini [katimini]: **en ~** *adv* on the sly, on the quiet

catogan [katɔgɑ̃] *nm* bow (*tying hair on neck*)

Caucase [kokaz] *nm*: **le ~** the Caucasus (Mountains)

caucasien, ne [kokazjɛ̃, -ɛn] *adj* Caucasian

cauchemar [koʃmaʀ] *nm* nightmare

cauchemardesque [koʃmaʀdɛsk(ə)] *adj* nightmarish

causal, e [kozal] *adj* causal

causalité [kozalite] *nf* causality

causant, e [kozɑ̃, -ɑ̃t] *adj* chatty, talkative

cause [koz] *nf* cause; (*Jur*) lawsuit, case; brief; **faire ~ commune avec qn** to take sides with sb; **être ~ de** to be the cause of; **à ~ de** because of, owing to; **pour ~ de** on account of; owing to; **(et) pour ~** and for (a very) good reason; **être en ~** (*intérêts*) to be at stake; (*personne*) to be involved; (*qualité*) to be in question; **mettre en ~** to implicate; to call into question; **remettre en ~** to challenge, call into question; **c'est hors de ~** it's out of the question; **en tout état de ~** in any case

causer [koze] *vt* to cause ▷ *vi* to chat, talk

causerie [kozʀi] *nf* talk

causette [kozɛt] *nf*: **faire la** *ou* **un brin de ~** to have a chat

caustique [kostik] *adj* caustic

cauteleux, -euse [kotlø, -øz] *adj* wily

cautériser [koteʀize] *vt* to cauterize

caution [kosjɔ̃] *nf* guarantee, security; deposit; (*Jur*) bail (bond); (*fig*) backing, support; **payer la ~ de qn** to stand bail for sb; **se porter ~ pour qn** to stand security for sb; **libéré sous ~** released on bail; **sujet à ~** unconfirmed

cautionnement [kosjɔnmɑ̃] *nm* (*somme*) guarantee, security

cautionner [kosjɔne] vt to guarantee; (soutenir) to support

cavalcade [kavalkad] nf (fig) stampede

cavale [kaval] nf: **en ~** on the run

cavalerie [kavalʀi] nf cavalry

cavalier, -ière [kavalje, -jɛʀ] adj (désinvolte) offhand ▷ nm/f rider; (au bal) partner ▷ nm (Échecs) knight; **faire ~ seul** to go it alone; **allée** ou **piste cavalière** riding path

cavalièrement [kavaljɛʀmɑ̃] adv offhandedly

cave [kav] nf cellar; (cabaret) (cellar) nightclub ▷ adj: **yeux ~s** sunken eyes; **joues ~s** hollow cheeks

caveau, x [kavo] nm vault

caverne [kavɛʀn(ə)] nf cave

caverneux, -euse [kavɛʀnø, -øz] adj cavernous

caviar [kavjaʀ] nm caviar(e)

cavité [kavite] nf cavity

Cayenne [kajɛn] n Cayenne

CB [sibi] sigle f (= citizens' band, canaux banalisés) CB = **carte bancaire**

CC sigle m = **corps consulaire**; **compte courant**

CCI sigle f = **Chambre de commerce et d'industrie**

CCP sigle m = **compte chèque postal**

CD sigle m (= chemin départemental) secondary road, ≈ B road (Brit); (= compact disc) CD; (= comité directeur) steering committee; (Pol) = **corps diplomatique**

CDD sigle m (= contrat à durée déterminée) fixed-term contract

CDI sigle m (= Centre de documentation et d'information) school library; (= contrat à durée indéterminée) permanent ou open-ended contract

CD-ROM [sedeʀɔm] nm inv (= Compact Disc Read Only Memory) CD-Rom

CDS sigle m (= Centre des démocrates sociaux) political party

CE sigle f (= Communauté européenne) EC; (Comm) = **caisse d'épargne** ▷ sigle m (Industrie) = **comité d'entreprise**; (Scol) = **cours élémentaire**

○ **MOT-CLÉ**

ce, cette [sə, sɛt] (devant nm **cet** + voyelle ou h aspiré; pl **ces**) adj dém (proximité) this; these pl; (non-proximité) that; those pl; **cette maison(-ci/là)** this/that house; **cette nuit** (qui vient) tonight; (passée) last night
▷ pron 1: **c'est** it's, it is; **c'est petit/grand/un livre** it's ou it is small/big/a book; **c'est un peintre** he's ou he is a painter; **ce sont des peintres** they're ou they are painters; **c'est le facteur** etc (à la porte) it's the postman etc; **qui est-ce?** who is it?; (en désignant) who is he/she?; **qu'est-ce?** what is it?; **c'est toi qui lui as parlé** it was you who spoke to him
2: **c'est que: c'est qu'il est lent/qu'il n'a pas faim** the fact is, he's slow/he's not hungry
3 (expressions): **c'est ça** (correct) that's it, that's right; **c'est toi qui le dis!** that's what YOU say!; voir aussi **c'est-à-dire**; voir **-ci**; **est-ce que**;

n'est-ce pas
4: **ce qui, ce que** what; (chose qui): **il est bête, ce qui me chagrine** he's stupid, which saddens me; **tout ce qui bouge** everything that ou which moves; **tout ce que je sais** all I know; **ce dont j'ai parlé** what I talked about; **ce que c'est grand!** it's so big!

CEA sigle m (= Commissariat à l'énergie atomique) ≈ AEA (= Atomic Energy Authority) (Brit) ≈ AEC = **Atomic Energy Commission** (US)

CECA [seka] sigle f (= Communauté européenne du charbon et de l'acier) ECSC (= European Coal and Steel Community)

ceci [səsi] pron this

cécité [sesite] nf blindness

céder [sede] vt to give up ▷ vi (pont, barrage) to give way; (personne) to give in; **~ à** to yield to, give in to

cédérom [sedeʀɔm] nm CD-ROM

CEDEX [sedɛks] sigle m (= courrier d'entreprise à distribution exceptionnelle) accelerated postal service for bulk users

cédille [sedij] nf cedilla

cèdre [sɛdʀ(ə)] nm cedar

CEE sigle f (= Communauté économique européenne) EEC

CEI sigle f (= Communauté des États indépendants) CIS

ceindre [sɛ̃dʀ(ə)] vt (mettre) to put on; (entourer): **~ qch de qch** to put sth round sth

ceinture [sɛ̃tyʀ] nf belt; (taille) waist; (fig) ring; belt; circle; **~ de sauvetage** lifebelt (Brit), life preserver (US); **~ de sécurité** safety ou seat belt; **~ (de sécurité) à enrouleur** inertia reel seat belt; **~ verte** green belt

ceinturer [sɛ̃tyʀe] vt (saisir) to grasp (round the waist); (entourer) to surround

ceinturon [sɛ̃tyʀɔ̃] nm belt

cela [səla] pron that; (comme sujet indéfini) it; **~ m'étonne que** it surprises me that; **quand/où ~?** when/where (was that)?

célébrant [selebʀɑ̃] nm (Rel) celebrant

célébration [selebʀasjɔ̃] nf celebration

célèbre [selɛbʀ(ə)] adj famous

célébrer [selebʀe] vt to celebrate; (louer) to extol

célébrité [selebʀite] nf fame; (star) celebrity

céleri [sɛlʀi] nm: **~(-rave)** celeriac; **~ (en branche)** celery

célérité [seleʀite] nf speed, swiftness

céleste [selɛst(ə)] adj celestial; heavenly

célibat [seliba] nm celibacy, bachelor/spinsterhood

célibataire [selibatɛʀ] adj single, unmarried ▷ nm/f bachelor/unmarried ou single woman; **mère ~** single ou unmarried mother

celle, celles [sɛl] pron voir **celui**

cellier [selje] nm storeroom

cellophane® [selɔfan] nf cellophane

cellulaire [selylɛʀ] adj (Bio) cell cpd, cellular; **voiture** ou **fourgon ~** prison ou police van; **régime ~** confinement

cellule [selyl] nf (gén) cell; **~ (photo-électrique)**

electronic eye
cellulite [selylit] *nf* cellulite
celluloïd® [selylɔid] *nm* Celluloid
cellulose [selyloz] *nf* cellulose
celte [sɛlt(ə)], **celtique** [sɛltik] *adj* Celt, Celtic

⊙ MOT-CLÉ

celui, celle [səlɥi, sɛl] (*mpl* **ceux**, *fpl* **celles**) *pron*
1: **celui-ci/là, celle-ci/là** this one/that one;
ceux-ci, celles-ci these (ones); **ceux-là, celles-là** those (ones); **celui de mon frère** my brother's; **celui du salon/du dessous** the one in (*ou* from) the lounge/below
2: **celui qui bouge** the one which *ou* that moves; (*personne*) the one who moves; **celui que je vois** the one (which *ou* that) I see; (*personne*) the one (whom) I see; **celui dont je parle** the one I'm talking about
3 (*valeur indéfinie*): **celui qui veut** whoever wants

cénacle [senakl(ə)] *nm* (literary) coterie *ou* set
cendre [sādʀ(ə)] *nf* ash; ~**s** (*d'un foyer*) ash(es), cinders; (*volcaniques*) ash *sg*; (*d'un défunt*) ashes; **sous la ~** (*Culin*) in (the) embers
cendré, e [sādʀe] *adj* (*couleur*) ashen; (**piste**) ~**e** cinder track
cendreux, -euse [sādʀø, -øz] *adj* (*terrain, substance*) cindery; (*teint*) ashen
cendrier [sādʀije] *nm* ashtray
cène [sɛn] *nf*: **la ~** (Holy) Communion; (*Art*) the Last Supper
censé, e [sāse] *adj*: **être ~ faire** to be supposed to do
censément [sāsemā] *adv* supposedly
censeur [sāsœʀ] *nm* (*Scol*) deputy head (*Brit*), vice-principal (*US*); (*Ciné, Pol*) censor
censure [sāsyʀ] *nf* censorship
censurer [sāsyʀe] *vt* (*Ciné, Presse*) to censor; (*Pol*) to censure
cent [sā] *num* a hundred, one hundred; **pour ~** (%) per cent (%); **faire les ~ pas** to pace up and down ▷ *nm* (*US, Canada, partie de l'euro etc*) cent
centaine [sātɛn] *nf*: **une ~ (de)** about a hundred, a hundred or so; (*Comm*) a hundred; **plusieurs ~s (de)** several hundred; **des ~s (de)** hundreds (of)
centenaire [sātnɛʀ] *adj* hundred-year-old ▷ *nm/f* centenarian ▷ *nm* (*anniversaire*) centenary
centième [sātjɛm] *num* hundredth
centigrade [sātigʀad] *nm* centigrade
centigramme [sātigʀam] *nm* centigramme
centilitre [sātilitʀ(ə)] *nm* centilitre (*Brit*), centiliter (*US*)
centime [sātim] *nm* centime; ~ **d'euro** euro cent
centimètre [sātimɛtʀ(ə)] *nm* centimetre (*Brit*), centimeter (*US*); (*ruban*) tape measure, measuring tape
centrafricain, e [sātʀafʀikɛ̃, -ɛn] *adj* of *ou* from the Central African Republic

central, e, -aux [sātʀal, -o] *adj* central ▷ *nm*: ~ (**téléphonique**) (telephone) exchange ▷ *nf*: ~**e d'achat** (*Comm*) central buying service; ~**e électrique/nucléaire** electric/nuclear power station; ~**e syndicale** group of affiliated trade unions
centralisation [sātʀalizasjɔ̃] *nf* centralization
centraliser [sātʀalize] *vt* to centralize
centralisme [sātʀalism(ə)] *nm* centralism
centraméricain, e [sātʀameʀikɛ̃, -ɛn] *adj* Central American
centre [sātʀ(ə)] *nm* centre (*Brit*), center (*US*); ~ **commercial/sportif/culturel** shopping/ sports/arts centre; ~ **aéré** outdoor centre; ~ **d'appels** call centre; ~ **d'apprentissage** training college; ~ **d'attraction** centre of attraction; ~ **de gravité** centre of gravity; ~ **de loisirs** leisure centre; ~ **d'enfouissement des déchets** landfill site; ~ **hospitalier** hospital complex; ~ **de tri** (*Postes*) sorting office; ~**s nerveux** (*Anat*) nerve centres
centrer [sātʀe] *vt* to centre (*Brit*), center (*US*) ▷ *vi* (*Football*) to centre the ball
centre-ville [sātʀəvil] (*pl* **centres-villes**) *nm* town centre (*Brit*) *ou* center (*US*), downtown (area) (*US*)
centrifuge [sātʀifyʒ] *adj*: **force ~** centrifugal force
centrifuger [sātʀifyʒe] *vt* to centrifuge
centrifugeuse [sātʀifyʒøz] *nf* (*pour fruits*) juice extractor
centripète [sātʀipɛt] *adj*: **force ~** centripetal force
centrisme [sātʀism(ə)] *nm* centrism
centriste [sātʀist(ə)] *adj, nm/f* centrist
centuple [sātypl(ə)] *nm*: **le ~ de qch** a hundred times sth; **au ~** a hundredfold
centupler [sātyple] *vi, vt* to increase a hundredfold
CEP *sigle m* = **Certificat d'études (primaires)**
cep [sɛp] *nm* (vine) stock
cépage [sepaʒ] *nm* (type of) vine
cèpe [sɛp] *nm* (edible) boletus
cependant [səpādā] *adv* however, nevertheless
céramique [seʀamik] *adj* ceramic ▷ *nf* ceramic; (*art*) ceramics *sg*
céramiste [seʀamist(ə)] *nm/f* ceramist
cerbère [sɛʀbɛʀ] *nm* (*fig: péj*) bad-tempered doorkeeper
cerceau, x [sɛʀso] *nm* (*d'enfant, de tonnelle*) hoop
cercle [sɛʀkl(ə)] *nm* circle; (*objet*) band, hoop; **décrire un ~** (*avion*) to circle; (*projectile*) to describe a circle; ~ **d'amis** circle of friends; ~ **de famille** family circle; ~ **vicieux** vicious circle
cercler [sɛʀkle] *vt*: **lunettes cerclées d'or** gold-rimmed glasses
cercueil [sɛʀkœj] *nm* coffin
céréale [seʀeal] *nf* cereal
céréalier, -ière [seʀealje, -jɛʀ] *adj* (*production, cultures*) cereal *cpd*
cérébral, e, -aux [seʀebʀal, -o] *adj* (*Anat*) cerebral, brain *cpd*; (*fig*) mental, cerebral

cérémonial [seremɔnjal] *nm* ceremonial
cérémonie [seremɔni] *nf* ceremony;
  cérémonies *nfpl* (*péj*) fuss *sg*, to-do *sg*
cérémonieux, -euse [seremɔnjø, -øz] *adj*
  ceremonious, formal
cerf [sɛʀ] *nm* stag
cerfeuil [sɛʀfœj] *nm* chervil
cerf-volant [sɛʀvɔlɑ̃] *nm* kite; **jouer au ~** to fly
  a kite
cerisaie [səʀize] *nf* cherry orchard
cerise [səʀiz] *nf* cherry
cerisier [səʀizje] *nm* cherry (tree)
CERN [sɛʀn] *sigle m* (= *Centre européen de recherche
  nucléaire*) CERN
cerné, e [sɛʀne] *adj*: **les yeux ~s** with dark rings
  ou shadows under the eyes
cerner [sɛʀne] *vt* (*Mil etc*) to surround; (*fig:
  problème*) to delimit, define
cernes [sɛʀn(ə)] *nfpl* (dark) rings, shadows
  (under the eyes)
certain, e [sɛʀtɛ̃, -ɛn] *adj* certain; (*sûr*): **~ (de/
  que)** certain *ou* sure (of/ that); **d'un ~ âge** past
  one's prime, not so young; **un ~ temps** (quite)
  some time; **sûr et ~** absolutely certain; **~s** *pron*
  some
certainement [sɛʀtɛnmɑ̃] *adv* (*probablement*)
  most probably *ou* likely; (*bien sûr*) certainly, of
  course
certes [sɛʀt(ə)] *adv* admittedly; of course;
  indeed (yes)
certificat [sɛʀtifika] *nm* certificate; **C~
  d'études (primaires)** *former school leaving
  certificate* (taken at the end of primary education); **C~
  de fin d'études secondaires** school leaving
  certificate
certifié, e [sɛʀtifje] *adj*: **professeur ~** qualified
  teacher; (*Admin*): **copie ~e conforme (à
  l'original)** certified copy (of the original)
certifier [sɛʀtifje] *vt* to certify, guarantee; **~ à
  qn que** to assure sb that, guarantee to sb that; **~
  qch à qn** to guarantee sth to sb
certitude [sɛʀtityd] *nf* certainty
cérumen [seʀymɛn] *nm* (ear)wax
cerveau, x [sɛʀvo] *nm* brain; **~ électronique**
  electronic brain
cervelas [sɛʀvəla] *nm* saveloy
cervelle [sɛʀvɛl] *nf* (*Anat*) brain; (*Culin*) brain(s);
  se creuser la ~ to rack one's brains
cervical, e, -aux [sɛʀvikal, -o] *adj* cervical
cervidés [sɛʀvide] *nmpl* cervidae
CES *sigle m* (= *Collège d'enseignement secondaire*)
  ≈ (junior) secondary school (*Brit*), ≈ junior high
  school (*US*)
ces [se] *adj dém voir* **ce**
césarienne [sezaʀjɛn] *nf* caesarean (*Brit*) *ou*
  cesarean (*US*) (section)
cessantes [sesɑ̃t] *adj fpl*: **toutes affaires ~**
  forthwith
cessation [sesasjɔ̃] *nf*: **~ des hostilités**
  cessation of hostilities; **~ de paiements/
  commerce** suspension of payments/trading
cesse [ses]: **sans ~** *adv* continually, constantly;

continuously; **il n'avait de ~ que** he would not
rest until
cesser [sese] *vt* to stop ▷ *vi* to stop, cease; **~ de
  faire** to stop doing; **faire ~ (**bruit, scandale**)** to put
  a stop to
cessez-le-feu [seselfø] *nm inv* ceasefire
cession [sesjɔ̃] *nf* transfer
c'est [sɛ] *voir* **ce**
c'est-à-dire [sɛtadiʀ] *adv* that is (to say);
  (*demander de préciser*): **c'est-à-dire?** what does
  that mean?; **c'est-à-dire que ...** (*en conséquence*)
  which means that ...; (*manière d'excuse*) well, in
  fact ...
CET *sigle m* (= *Collège d'enseignement technique*)
  (*formerly*) technical school
cet [sɛt] *adj dém voir* **ce**
cétacé [setase] *nm* cetacean
cette [sɛt] *adj dém voir* **ce**
ceux [sø] *pron voir* **celui**
cévenol, e [sevnɔl] *adj* of *ou* from the Cévennes
  region
cf. *abr* (= *confer*) cf, cp
CFAO *sigle f* (= *conception de fabrication assistée par
  ordinateur*) CAM
CFC *sigle mpl* (= *chlorofluorocarbures*) CFC
CFDT *sigle f* (= *Confédération française démocratique du
  travail*) trade union
CFF *sigle m* (= *Chemins de fer fédéraux*) Swiss railways
CFL *sigle m* (= *Chemins de fer luxembourgeois*)
  Luxembourg railways
CFP *sigle m* = **Centre de formation
  professionnelle** ▷ *sigle f* = **Compagnie française
  des pétroles**
CFTC *sigle f* (= *Confédération française des travailleurs
  chrétiens*) trade union
CGC *sigle f* (= *Confédération générale des cadres*)
  management union
CGPME *sigle f* = **Confédération générale des
  petites et moyennes entreprises**
CGT *sigle f* (= *Confédération générale du travail*) *trade
  union*
CH *abr* (= *Confédération helvétique*) CH
ch. *abr* = **charges**; **chauffage**; **cherche**
chacal [ʃakal] *nm* jackal
chacun, e [ʃakœ̃, -yn] *pron* each; (*indéfini*)
  everyone, everybody
chagrin, e [ʃagʀɛ̃, -in] *adj* morose ▷ *nm* grief,
  sorrow; **avoir du ~** to be grieved *ou* sorrowful
chagriner [ʃagʀine] *vt* to grieve, distress;
  (*contrarier*) to bother, worry
chahut [ʃay] *nm* uproar
chahuter [ʃayte] *vt* to rag, bait ▷ *vi* to make an
  uproar
chahuteur, -euse [ʃaytœʀ, -øz] *nm/f* rowdy
chai [ʃɛ] *nm* wine and spirit store(house)
chaîne [ʃɛn] *nf* chain; (*Radio, TV*) channel;
  (*Inform*) string; **chaînes** *nfpl* (*liens, asservissement*)
  fetters, bonds; **travail à la ~** production line
  work; **réactions en ~** chain reactions; **faire la
  ~** to form a (human) chain; **~ alimentaire** food
  chain; **~ compacte** music centre; **~ d'entraide**
  mutual aid association; **~ (haute-fidélité** *ou*

hi-fi) hi-fi system; ~ **(de montage** *ou* **de fabrication)** production *ou* assembly line; ~ **(de montagnes)** (mountain) range; ~ **de solidarité** solidarity network; ~ **(stéréo** *ou* **audio)** stereo (system)

chaînette [ʃɛnɛt] *nf* (small) chain

chaînon [ʃɛnɔ̃] *nm* link

chair [ʃɛʀ] *nf* flesh ▷ *adj*: **(couleur)** ~ flesh-coloured; **avoir la ~ de poule** to have goose pimples *ou* goose flesh; **bien en** ~ plump, well-padded; **en** ~ **et en os** in the flesh; ~ **à saucisses** sausage meat

chaire [ʃɛʀ] *nf* (*d'église*) pulpit; (*d'université*) chair

chaise [ʃɛz] *nf* chair; ~ **de bébé** high chair; ~ **électrique** electric chair; ~ **longue** deckchair

chaland [ʃalɑ̃] *nm* (*bateau*) barge

châle [ʃal] *nm* shawl

chalet [ʃalɛ] *nm* chalet

chaleur [ʃalœʀ] *nf* heat; (*fig*) warmth; fire, fervour (*Brit*), fervor (*US*); heat; **en** ~ (*Zool*) on heat

chaleureusement [ʃalœʀøzmɑ̃] *adv* warmly

chaleureux, -euse [ʃalœʀø, -øz] *adj* warm

challenge [ʃalɑ̃ʒ] *nm* contest, tournament

challenger [ʃalɑ̃ʒɛʀ] *nm* (*Sport*) challenger

chaloupe [ʃalup] *nf* launch; (*de sauvetage*) lifeboat

chalumeau, x [ʃalymo] *nm* blowlamp (*Brit*), blowtorch

chalut [ʃaly] *nm* trawl (net); **pêcher au** ~ to trawl

chalutier [ʃalytje] *nm* trawler; (*pêcheur*) trawlerman

chamade [ʃamad] *nf*: **battre la** ~ to beat wildly

chamailler [ʃamaje]: **se chamailler** *vi* to squabble, bicker

chamarré, e [ʃamaʀe] *adj* richly brocaded

chambard [ʃɑ̃baʀ] *nm* rumpus

chambardement [ʃɑ̃baʀdəmɑ̃] *nm*: **c'est le grand** ~ everything has been (*ou* is being) turned upside down

chambarder [ʃɑ̃baʀde] *vt* to turn upside down

chamboulement [ʃɑ̃bulmɑ̃] *nm* disruption

chambouler [ʃɑ̃bule] *vt* to disrupt, turn upside down

chambranle [ʃɑ̃bʀɑ̃l] *nm* (door) frame

chambre [ʃɑ̃bʀ(ə)] *nf* bedroom; (*Tech*) chamber; (*Pol*) chamber, house; (*Jur*) court; (*Comm*) chamber; federation; **faire** ~ **à part** to sleep in separate rooms; **stratège/alpiniste en** ~ armchair strategist/mountaineer; ~ **à un lit/ deux lits** single/twin-bedded room; ~ **pour une/deux personne(s)** single/double room; ~ **d'accusation** court of criminal appeal; ~ **d'agriculture** (CA) *body responsible for the agricultural interests of a département*; ~ **à air** (*de pneu*) (inner) tube; ~ **d'amis** spare *ou* guest room; ~ **de combustion** combustion chamber; ~ **de commerce et d'industrie (CCI)** chamber of commerce and industry; ~ **à coucher** bedroom; **la C~ des députés** the Chamber of Deputies, ≈ the House (of Commons) (*Brit*), ≈ the House of Representatives (*US*); ~ **forte** strongroom; ~ **froide** *ou* **frigorifique** cold room; ~ **à gaz** gas chamber; ~ **d'hôte** ≈ bed and breakfast (*in private home*); ~ **des machines** engine-room; ~ **des métiers** (CM) *chamber of commerce for trades*; ~ **meublée** bedsit(ter) (*Brit*), furnished room; ~ **noire** (*Photo*) dark room

chambrée [ʃɑ̃bʀe] *nf* room

chambrer [ʃɑ̃bʀe] *vt* (*vin*) to bring to room temperature

chameau, x [ʃamo] *nm* camel

chamois [ʃamwa] *nm* chamois ▷ *adj*: **(couleur)** ~ fawn, buff

champ [ʃɑ̃] *nm* (*aussi Inform*) field; (*Photo: aussi:* **dans le champ**) in the picture; **prendre du** ~ to draw back; **laisser le** ~ **libre à qn** to leave sb a clear field; ~ **d'action** sphere of operation(s); ~ **de bataille** battlefield; ~ **de courses** racecourse; ~ **d'honneur** field of honour; ~ **de manœuvre** (*Mil*) parade ground; ~ **de mines** minefield; ~ **de tir** shooting *ou* rifle range; ~ **visuel** field of vision

Champagne [ʃɑ̃paɲ] *nf*: **la** ~ Champagne, the Champagne region

champagne [ʃɑ̃paɲ] *nm* champagne

champenois, e [ʃɑ̃pənwa, -waz] *adj* of *ou* from Champagne; (*vin*): **méthode ~e** champagne-type

champêtre [ʃɑ̃pɛtʀ(ə)] *adj* country *cpd*, rural

champignon [ʃɑ̃piɲɔ̃] *nm* mushroom; (*terme générique*) fungus; (*fam: accélérateur*) accelerator, gas pedal (*US*); ~ **de couche** *ou* **de Paris** button mushroom; ~ **vénéneux** toadstool, poisonous mushroom

champion, ne [ʃɑ̃pjɔ̃, -ɔn] *adj, nm/f* champion

championnat [ʃɑ̃pjɔna] *nm* championship

chance [ʃɑ̃s] *nf*: **la** ~ luck; **une** ~ a stroke *ou* piece of luck *ou* good fortune; (*occasion*) a lucky break; **chances** *nfpl* (*probabilités*) chances; **avoir de la** ~ to be lucky; **il a des** ~ **de gagner** he has a chance of winning; **il y a de fortes** ~**s pour que Paul soit malade** it's highly probable that Paul is ill; **bonne ~!** good luck!; **encore une** ~ **que tu viennes!** it's lucky you're coming!; **je n'ai pas de** ~ I'm out of luck; (*toujours*) I never have any luck; **donner sa** ~ **à qn** to give sb a chance

chancelant, e [ʃɑ̃slɑ̃, -ɑ̃t] *adj* (*personne*) tottering; (*santé*) failing

chanceler [ʃɑ̃sle] *vi* to totter

chancelier [ʃɑ̃səlje] *nm* (*allemand*) chancellor; (*d'ambassade*) secretary

chancellerie [ʃɑ̃sɛlʀi] *nf* (*en France*) ministry of justice; (*en Allemagne*) chancellery; (*d'ambassade*) chancery

chanceux, -euse [ʃɑ̃sø, -øz] *adj* lucky, fortunate

chancre [ʃɑ̃kʀ(ə)] *nm* canker

chandail [ʃɑ̃daj] *nm* (thick) jumper *ou* sweater

Chandeleur [ʃɑ̃dlœʀ] *nf*: **la** ~ Candlemas

chandelier [ʃɑ̃dəlje] *nm* candlestick; (*à plusieurs branches*) candelabra

chandelle [ʃɑ̃dɛl] *nf* (tallow) candle; (*Tennis*):

faire une ~ to lob; (Aviat): **monter en ~** to climb vertically; **tenir la ~** to play gooseberry; **dîner aux ~s** candlelight dinner

change [ʃɑ̃ʒ] nm (Comm) exchange; **opérations de ~** (foreign) exchange transactions; **contrôle des ~s** exchange control; **gagner/perdre au ~** to be better/worse off (for it); **donner le ~ à qn** (fig) to lead sb up the garden path

changeant, e [ʃɑ̃ʒɑ̃, -ɑ̃t] adj changeable, fickle

changement [ʃɑ̃ʒmɑ̃] nm change; **~ de vitesse** (dispositif) gears pl; (action) gear change

changer [ʃɑ̃ʒe] vt (modifier) to change, alter; (remplacer, Comm, rhabiller) to change ▷ vi to change, alter; **se changer** vi to change (o.s.); **~ de** (remplacer: adresse, nom, voiture etc) to change one's; **~ de train** to change trains; **~ d'air** to get a change of air; **~ de couleur/direction** to change colour/direction; **~ d'idée** to change one's mind; **~ de place avec qn** to change places with sb; **~ de vitesse** (Auto) to change gear; **~ qn/qch de place** to move sb/sth to another place; **~ (de bus** etc) to change (buses etc); **~ qch en** to change sth into

changeur [ʃɑ̃ʒœR] nm (personne) moneychanger; **~ automatique** change machine; **~ de disques** record changer, autochange

chanoine [ʃanwan] nm canon

chanson [ʃɑ̃sɔ̃] nf song

chansonnette [ʃɑ̃sɔnɛt] nf ditty

chansonnier [ʃɑ̃sɔnje] nm cabaret artist (specializing in political satire); (recueil) song book

chant [ʃɑ̃] nm song; (art vocal) singing; (d'église) hymn; (de poème) canto; (Tech): **posé de** ou **sur ~** placed edgeways; **~ de Noël** Christmas carol

chantage [ʃɑ̃taʒ] nm blackmail; **faire du ~** to use blackmail; **soumettre qn à un ~** to blackmail sb

chantant, e [ʃɑ̃tɑ̃, -ɑ̃t] adj (accent, voix) sing-song

chanter [ʃɑ̃te] vt, vi to sing; **~ juste/faux** to sing in tune/out of tune; **si cela lui chante** (fam) if he feels like it ou fancies it

chanterelle [ʃɑ̃tRɛl] nf chanterelle (edible mushroom)

chanteur, -euse [ʃɑ̃tœR, -øz] nm/f singer; **~ de charme** crooner

chantier [ʃɑ̃tje] nm (building) site; (sur une route) roadworks pl; **mettre en ~** to start work on; **~ naval** shipyard

chantilly [ʃɑ̃tiji] nf voir **crème**

chantonner [ʃɑ̃tɔne] vi, vt to sing to oneself, hum

chantre [ʃɑ̃tR(ə)] nm (fig) eulogist

chanvre [ʃɑ̃vR(ə)] nm hemp

chaos [kao] nm chaos

chaotique [kaɔtik] adj chaotic

chap. abr (= chapitre) ch

chapardage [ʃapaRdaʒ] nm pilfering

chaparder [ʃapaRde] vt to pinch

chapeau, x [ʃapo] nm hat; (Presse) introductory paragraph; **~!** well done!; **~ melon** bowler hat; **~ mou** trilby; **~x de roues** hub caps

chapeauter [ʃapote] vt (Admin) to head, oversee

chapelain [ʃaplɛ̃] nm (Rel) chaplain

chapelet [ʃaplɛ] nm (Rel) rosary; (fig): **un ~ de** a string of; **dire son ~** to tell one's beads

chapelier, -ière [ʃapəlje, -jɛR] nm/f hatter; milliner

chapelle [ʃapɛl] nf chapel; **~ ardente** chapel of rest

chapellerie [ʃapɛlRi] nf (magasin) hat shop; (commerce) hat trade

chapelure [ʃaplyR] nf (dried) breadcrumbs pl

chaperon [ʃapRɔ̃] nm chaperon

chaperonner [ʃapRɔne] vt to chaperon

chapiteau, x [ʃapito] nm (Archit) capital; (de cirque) marquee, big top

chapitre [ʃapitR(ə)] nm chapter; (fig) subject, matter; **avoir voix au ~** to have a say in the matter

chapitrer [ʃapitRe] vt to lecture, reprimand

chapon [ʃapɔ̃] nm capon

chaque [ʃak] adj each, every; (indéfini) every

char [ʃaR] nm (à foin etc) cart, waggon; (de carnaval) float; **~ (d'assaut)** tank

charabia [ʃaRabja] nm (péj) gibberish, gobbledygook (Brit)

charade [ʃaRad] nf riddle; (mimée) charade

charbon [ʃaRbɔ̃] nm coal; **~ de bois** charcoal

charbonnage [ʃaRbɔnaʒ] nm: **les ~s de France** the (French) Coal Board sg

charbonnier [ʃaRbɔnje] nm coalman

charcuterie [ʃaRkytRi] nf (magasin) pork butcher's shop and delicatessen; (produits) cooked pork meats pl

charcutier, -ière [ʃaRkytje, -jɛR] nm/f pork butcher

chardon [ʃaRdɔ̃] nm thistle

chardonneret [ʃaRdɔnRɛ] nm goldfinch

charentais, e [ʃaRɑ̃tɛ, -ɛz] adj of ou from Charente ▷ nf (pantoufle) slipper

charge [ʃaRʒ(ə)] nf (fardeau) load; (explosif, Élec, Mil, Jur) charge; (rôle, mission) responsibility; **charges** nfpl (du loyer) service charges; **à la ~ de** (dépendant de) dependent upon, supported by; (aux frais de) chargeable to, payable by; **j'accepte, à ~ de revanche** I accept, provided I can do the same for you (in return) one day; **prendre en ~** to take charge of; (véhicule) to take on; (dépenses) to take care of; **~ utile** (Auto) live load; (Comm) payload; **~s sociales** social security contributions

chargé [ʃaRʒe] adj (voiture, animal, personne) laden; (fusil, batterie, caméra) loaded; (occupé: emploi du temps, journée) busy, full; (estomac) heavy, full; (langue) furred; (décoration, style) heavy, ornate ▷ nm: **~ d'affaires** chargé d'affaires; **~ de cours** ≈ lecturer; **~ de** (responsable de) responsible for

chargement [ʃaRʒəmɑ̃] nm (action) loading; charging; (objets) load

charger [ʃaRʒe] vt (voiture, fusil, caméra) to load; (batterie) to charge ▷ vi (Mil etc) to charge; **se ~ de** vt to see to, take care of; **~ qn de qch/faire qch** to give sb the responsibility for sth/of doing sth; to put sb in charge of sth/doing sth;

se ~ **de faire qch** to take it upon o.s. to do sth

chargeur [ʃaʀʒœʀ] nm (dispositif: d'arme à feu) magazine; (: Photo) cartridge; ~ **de batterie** (Élec) battery charger

chariot [ʃaʀjo] nm trolley; (charrette) waggon; ~ **élévateur** fork-lift truck

charisme [kaʀism(ə)] nm charisma

charitable [ʃaʀitabl(ə)] adj charitable; kind

charité [ʃaʀite] nf charity; **faire la** ~ to give to charity; to do charitable works; **faire la** ~ **à** to give (something) to; **fête/vente de** ~ fête/sale in aid of charity

charivari [ʃaʀivaʀi] nm hullabaloo

charlatan [ʃaʀlatɑ̃] nm charlatan

charlotte [ʃaʀlɔt] nf (Culin) charlotte

charmant, e [ʃaʀmɑ̃, -ɑ̃t] adj charming

charme [ʃaʀm(ə)] nm charm; **charmes** nmpl (appas) charms; **c'est ce qui en fait le** ~ that is its attraction; **faire du** ~ to be charming, turn on the charm; **aller** ou **se porter comme un** ~ to be in the pink

charmer [ʃaʀme] vt to charm; **je suis charmé de ...** I'm delighted to ...

charmeur, -euse [ʃaʀmœʀ, -øz] nm/f charmer; ~ **de serpents** snake charmer

charnel, le [ʃaʀnɛl] adj carnal

charnier [ʃaʀnje] nm mass grave

charnière [ʃaʀnjɛʀ] nf hinge; (fig) turning-point

charnu, e [ʃaʀny] adj fleshy

charogne [ʃaʀɔɲ] nf carrion no pl; (fam!) bastard (!)

charolais, e [ʃaʀɔlɛ, -ez] adj of ou from the Charolais

charpente [ʃaʀpɑ̃t] nf frame(work); (fig) structure, framework; (carrure) build, frame

charpenté, e [ʃaʀpɑ̃te] adj: **bien** ou **solidement** ~ (personne) well-built; (texte) well-constructed

charpenterie [ʃaʀpɑ̃tʀi] nf carpentry

charpentier [ʃaʀpɑ̃tje] nm carpenter

charpie [ʃaʀpi] nf: **en** ~ (fig) in shreds ou ribbons

charretier [ʃaʀtje] nm carter; **de** ~ (péj: langage, manières) uncouth

charrette [ʃaʀɛt] nf cart

charrier [ʃaʀje] vt to carry (along); to cart, carry ▷ vi (fam) to exaggerate

charrue [ʃaʀy] nf plough (Brit), plow (US)

charte [ʃaʀt(ə)] nf charter

charter [tʃaʀtœʀ] nm (vol) charter flight; (avion) charter plane

chasse [ʃas] nf hunting; (au fusil) shooting; (poursuite) chase; (aussi: **chasse d'eau**) flush; **la** ~ **est ouverte** the hunting season is open; **la** ~ **est fermée** it is the close (Brit) ou closed (US) season; **aller à la** ~ to go hunting; **prendre en** ~, **donner la** ~ **à** to give chase to; **tirer la** ~ **(d'eau)** to flush the toilet, pull the chain; ~ **aérienne** aerial pursuit; ~ **à courre** hunting; ~ **à l'homme** manhunt; ~ **gardée** private hunting grounds pl; ~ **sous-marine** underwater fishing

châsse [ʃas] nf reliquary, shrine

chassé-croisé [ʃasekʀwaze] (pl **chassés-croisés**) nm (Danse) chassé-croisé; (fig) mix-up (where people miss each other in turn)

chasse-neige [ʃasnɛʒ] nm inv snowplough (Brit), snowplow (US)

chasser [ʃase] vt to hunt; (expulser) to chase away ou out, drive away ou out; (dissiper) to chase ou sweep away; to dispel, drive away

chasseur, -euse [ʃasœʀ, -øz] nm/f hunter ▷ nm (avion) fighter; (domestique) page (boy), messenger (boy); ~ **d'images** roving photographer; ~ **de têtes** (fig) headhunter; ~s **alpins** mountain infantry

chassieux, -euse [ʃasjø, -øz] adj sticky, gummy

châssis [ʃasi] nm (Auto) chassis; (cadre) frame; (de jardin) cold frame

chaste [ʃast(ə)] adj chaste

chasteté [ʃastəte] nf chastity

chasuble [ʃazybl(ə)] nf chasuble; **robe** ~ pinafore dress (Brit), jumper (US)

chat¹ [ʃa] nm cat; ~ **sauvage** wildcat

chat² [tʃat] nm (Internet: salon) chat room (: conversation) chat

châtaigne [ʃatɛɲ] nf chestnut

châtaignier [ʃatɛɲe] nm chestnut (tree)

châtain [ʃatɛ̃] adj inv chestnut (brown); (personne) chestnut-haired

château, x [ʃato] nm castle; ~ **d'eau** water tower; ~ **fort** stronghold, fortified castle; ~ **de sable** sand castle

châtelain, e [ʃatlɛ̃, -ɛn] nm/f lord/lady of the manor ▷ nf (ceinture) chatelaine

châtier [ʃatje] vt to punish, castigate; (fig: style) to polish, refine

chatière [ʃatjɛʀ] nf (porte) cat flap

châtiment [ʃatimɑ̃] nm punishment, castigation; ~ **corporel** corporal punishment

chatoiement [ʃatwamɑ̃] nm shimmer(ing)

chaton [ʃatɔ̃] nm (Zool) kitten; (Bot) catkin; (de bague) bezel; stone

chatouillement [ʃatujmɑ̃] nm (gén) tickling; (dans le nez, la gorge) tickle

chatouiller [ʃatuje] vt to tickle; (l'odorat, le palais) to titillate

chatouilleux, -euse [ʃatujø, -øz] adj ticklish; (fig) touchy, over-sensitive

chatoyant, e [ʃatwajɑ̃, -ɑ̃t] adj (reflet, étoffe) shimmering; (couleurs) sparkling

chatoyer [ʃatwaje] vi to shimmer

châtrer [ʃatʀe] vt (mâle) to castrate; (femelle) to spay; (cheval) to geld; (chat, chien) to doctor (Brit), fix (US); (fig) to mutilate

chatte [ʃat] nf (she-)cat

chatter [tʃate] vi (Internet) to chat

chatterton [ʃatɛʀtɔn] nm (ruban isolant: Élec) (adhesive) insulating tape

chaud, e [ʃo, -od] adj (gén) warm; (très chaud) hot; (fig: félicitations) hearty; (discussion) heated; **il fait** ~ it's warm; it's hot; **manger** ~ to have something hot to eat; **avoir** ~ to be warm; to be hot; **tenir** ~ to keep hot; **ça me tient** ~ it keeps me warm; **tenir au** ~ to keep in a warm place;

rester au ~ to stay in the warm

chaudement [ʃodmɑ̃] *adv* warmly; (*fig*) hotly

chaudière [ʃodjɛR] *nf* boiler

chaudron [ʃodRɔ̃] *nm* cauldron

chaudronnerie [ʃodRɔnRi] *nf* (*usine*) boilerworks; (*activité*) boilermaking; (*boutique*) coppersmith's workshop

chauffage [ʃofaʒ] *nm* heating; ~ **au gaz/à l'électricité/au charbon** gas/electric/solid fuel heating; ~ **central** central heating; ~ **par le sol** underfloor heating

chauffagiste [ʃofaʒist(ə)] *nm* (*installateur*) heating engineer

chauffant, e [ʃofɑ̃, -ɑ̃t] *adj*: **couverture ~e** electric blanket; **plaque ~e** hotplate

chauffard [ʃofaR] *nm* (*péj*) reckless driver; road hog; (*après un accident*) hit-and-run driver

chauffe-bain [ʃofbɛ̃] *nm* = **chauffe-eau**

chauffe-biberon [ʃofbibRɔ̃] *nm* (baby's) bottle warmer

chauffe-eau [ʃofo] *nm inv* water heater

chauffe-plats [ʃofpla] *nm inv* dish warmer

chauffer [ʃofe] *vt* to heat ▷ *vi* to heat up, warm up; (*trop chauffer: moteur*) to overheat; **se chauffer** *vi* (*se mettre en train*) to warm up; (*au soleil*) to warm o.s.

chaufferie [ʃofRi] *nf* boiler room

chauffeur [ʃofœR] *nm* driver; (*privé*) chauffeur; **voiture avec/sans ~** chauffeur-driven/self-drive car; ~ **de taxi** taxi driver

chauffeuse [ʃoføz] *nf* fireside chair

chauler [ʃole] *vt* (*mur*) to whitewash

chaume [ʃom] *nm* (*du toit*) thatch; (*tiges*) stubble

chaumière [ʃomjɛR] *nf* (thatched) cottage

chaussée [ʃose] *nf* road(way); (*digue*) causeway

chausse-pied [ʃospje] *nm* shoe-horn

chausser [ʃose] *vt* (*bottes, skis*) to put on; (*enfant*) to put shoes on; (*soulier*) to fit; ~ **du 38/42** to take size 38/42; ~ **grand/bien** to be big-/well-fitting; **se chausser** to put one's shoes on

chausse-trappe [ʃostRap] *nf* trap

chaussette [ʃosɛt] *nf* sock

chausseur [ʃosœR] *nm* (*marchand*) footwear specialist, shoemaker

chausson [ʃosɔ̃] *nm* slipper; (*de bébé*) bootee; ~ **(aux pommes)** (apple) turnover

chaussure [ʃosyR] *nf* shoe; (*commerce*): **la ~** the shoe industry *ou* trade; **~s basses** flat shoes; **~s montantes** ankle boots; **~s de ski** ski boots

chaut [ʃo] *vb*: **peu me ~** it matters little to me

chauve [ʃov] *adj* bald

chauve-souris [ʃovsuRi] (*pl* **chauves-souris**) *nf* bat

chauvin, e [ʃovɛ̃, -in] *adj* chauvinistic; jingoistic

chauvinisme [ʃovinism(ə)] *nm* chauvinism; jingoism

chaux [ʃo] *nf* lime; **blanchi à la ~** whitewashed

chavirer [ʃaviRe] *vi* to capsize, overturn

chef [ʃɛf] *nm* head, leader; (*patron*) boss; (*de cuisine*) chef; **au premier ~** extremely, to the nth degree; **de son propre ~** on his *ou* her own initiative; **général/commandant en ~**

general-/commander-in-chief; ~ **d'accusation** (*Jur*) charge, count (of indictment); ~ **d'atelier** (shop) foreman; ~ **de bureau** head clerk; ~ **de clinique** senior hospital lecturer; ~ **d'entreprise** company head; ~ **d'équipe** team leader; ~ **d'état** head of state; ~ **de famille** head of the family; ~ **de file** (*de parti etc*) leader; ~ **de gare** station master; ~ **d'orchestre** conductor (*Brit*), leader (*US*), ~ **de rayon** department(al) supervisor; ~ **de service** departmental head

chef-d'œuvre [ʃɛdœvR(ə)] (*pl* **chefs-d'œuvre**) *nm* masterpiece

chef-lieu [ʃɛfljø] (*pl* **chefs-lieux**) *nm* county town

cheftaine [ʃɛftɛn] *nf* (guide) captain

cheik, cheikh [ʃɛk] *nm* sheik

chemin [ʃəmɛ̃] *nm* path; (*itinéraire, direction, trajet*) way; **en ~**, ~ **faisant** on the way; ~ **de fer** railway (*Brit*), railroad (*US*); **par ~ de fer** by rail; **les ~s de fer** the railways (*Brit*), the railroad (*US*), ~ **de terre** dirt track

cheminée [ʃəmine] *nf* chimney; (*à l'intérieur*) chimney piece, fireplace; (*de bateau*) funnel

cheminement [ʃəminmɑ̃] *nm* progress; course

cheminer [ʃəmine] *vi* to walk (along)

cheminot [ʃəmino] *nm* railwayman (*Brit*), railroad worker (*US*)

chemise [ʃəmiz] *nf* shirt; (*dossier*) folder; ~ **de nuit** nightdress

chemiserie [ʃəmizRi] *nf* (gentlemen's) outfitters'

chemisette [ʃəmizɛt] *nf* short-sleeved shirt

chemisier [ʃəmizje] *nm* blouse

chenal, -aux [ʃənal, -o] *nm* channel

chenapan [ʃənapɑ̃] *nm* (*garnement*) rascal; (*péj: vaurien*) rogue

chêne [ʃɛn] *nm* oak (tree); (*bois*) oak

chenet [ʃənɛ] *nm* fire-dog, andiron

chenil [ʃənil] *nm* kennels *pl*

chenille [ʃənij] *nf* (*Zool*) caterpillar; (*Auto*) caterpillar track; **véhicule à ~s** tracked vehicle, caterpillar

chenillette [ʃənijɛt] *nf* tracked vehicle

cheptel [ʃɛptɛl] *nm* livestock

chèque [ʃɛk] *nm* cheque (*Brit*), check (*US*); **faire/toucher un ~** to write/cash a cheque; **par ~** by cheque; ~ **barré/sans provision** crossed (*Brit*) / bad cheque; ~ **en blanc** blank cheque; ~ **au porteur** cheque to bearer; ~ **postal** post office cheque, ≈ giro cheque (*Brit*); ~ **de voyage** traveller's cheque

chèque-cadeau [ʃɛkkado] (*pl* **chèques-cadeaux**) *nm* gift token

chèque-repas (*pl* **chèques-repas**) [ʃɛkRəpa], **chèque-restaurant** (*pl* **chèques-restaurant**) [ʃɛkRɛstoRɑ̃] *nm* ≈ luncheon voucher

chéquier [ʃekje] *nm* cheque book (*Brit*), checkbook (*US*)

cher, -ère [ʃɛR] *adj* (*aimé*) dear; (*coûteux*) expensive, dear ▷ *adv*: **coûter/payer ~** to cost/pay a lot ▷ *nf*: **la bonne chère** good food; **cela**

coûte ~ it's expensive, it costs a lot of money; **mon ~, ma chère** my dear

chercher [ʃɛrʃe] *vt* to look for; *(gloire etc)* to seek; **~ des ennuis/la bagarre** to be looking for trouble/a fight; **aller ~** to go for, go and fetch; **~ à faire** to try to do

chercheur, -euse [ʃɛrʃœr, -øz] *nm/f* researcher, research worker; **~ de** seeker of; hunter of; **~ d'or** gold digger

chère [ʃɛr] *adj f, nf voir* **cher**

chèrement [ʃɛrmã] *adv* dearly

chéri, e [ʃeri] *adj* beloved, dear; **(mon) ~** darling

chérir [ʃerir] *vt* to cherish

cherté [ʃɛrte] *nf:* **la ~ de la vie** the high cost of living

chérubin [ʃerybɛ̃] *nm* cherub

chétif, -ive [ʃetif, -iv] *adj* puny, stunted

cheval, -aux [ʃəval, -o] *nm* horse; *(Auto):* **~ (vapeur) (CV)** horsepower *no pl*; **50 chevaux (au frein)** 50 brake horsepower, 50 b.h.p.; **10 chevaux (fiscaux)** 10 horsepower *(for tax purposes)*; **faire du ~** to ride; **à ~** on horseback; **à ~ sur** astride, straddling; *(fig)* overlapping; **~ d'arçons** vaulting horse; **~ à bascule** rocking horse; **~ de bataille** charger; *(fig)* hobby-horse; **~ de course** race horse; **chevaux de bois** *(des manèges)* wooden (fairground) horses; *(manège)* merry-go-round

chevaleresque [ʃəvalrɛsk(ə)] *adj* chivalrous

chevalerie [ʃəvalri] *nf* chivalry; knighthood

chevalet [ʃəvalɛ] *nm* easel

chevalier [ʃəvalje] *nm* knight; **~ servant** escort

chevalière [ʃəvaljɛr] *nf* signet ring

chevalin, e [ʃəvalɛ̃, -in] *adj* of horses, equine; *(péj)* horsy; **boucherie ~e** horse-meat butcher's

cheval-vapeur [ʃəvalvapœr, ʃəvo-] *(pl* **chevaux-vapeur)** *nm voir* **cheval**

chevauchée [ʃəvoʃe] *nf* ride; cavalcade

chevauchement [ʃəvoʃmã] *nm* overlap

chevaucher [ʃəvoʃe] *vi (aussi:* **se chevaucher)** to overlap (each other) ▷ *vt* to be astride, straddle

chevaux [ʃəvo] *nmpl voir* **cheval**

chevelu, e [ʃəvly] *adj* with a good head of hair, hairy *(péj)*

chevelure [ʃəvlyr] *nf* hair *no pl*

chevet [ʃəve] *nm:* **au ~ de qn** at sb's bedside; **lampe de ~** bedside lamp

cheveu, x [ʃəvø] *nm* hair ▷ *nmpl (chevelure)* hair *sg*; **avoir les ~x courts/en brosse** to have short hair/a crew cut; **se faire couper les ~x** to get ou have one's hair cut; **tiré par les ~x** *(histoire)* far-fetched

cheville [ʃəvij] *nf (Anat)* ankle; *(de bois)* peg; *(pour enfoncer une vis)* plug; **être en ~ avec qn** to be in cahoots with sb; **~ ouvrière** *(fig)* kingpin

chèvre [ʃɛvr(ə)] *nf* (she-)goat; **ménager la ~ et le chou** to try to please everyone

chevreau, x [ʃəvro] *nm* kid

chèvrefeuille [ʃɛvrəfœj] *nm* honeysuckle

chevreuil [ʃəvrœj] *nm* roe deer *inv*; *(Culin)* venison

chevron [ʃəvrõ] *nm (poutre)* rafter; *(motif)*

chevron, v(-shape); **à ~s** chevron-patterned; *(petits)* herringbone

chevronné, e [ʃəvrɔne] *adj* seasoned, experienced

chevrotant, e [ʃəvrɔtã, -ãt] *adj* quavering

chevroter [ʃəvrɔte] *vi (personne, voix)* to quaver

chevrotine [ʃəvrɔtin] *nf* buckshot *no pl*

chewing-gum [ʃwiŋgɔm] *nm* chewing gum

 MOT-CLÉ

chez [ʃe] *prép* **1** *(à la demeure de)* at; *(: direction)* to; **chez qn** at/to sb's house ou place; **chez moi** at home; *(direction)* home
2 *(à l'entreprise de):* **il travaille chez Renault** he works for Renault, he works at Renault('s)
3 *(+profession)* at; *(: direction)* to; **chez le boulanger/dentiste** at ou to the baker's/dentist's
4 *(dans le caractère, l'œuvre de)* in; **chez les renards/Racine** in foxes/Racine; **chez les Français** among the French; **chez lui, c'est un devoir** for him, it's a duty
▷ *nm inv:* **mon chez moi/ton chez toi** *etc* my/your *etc* home ou place

chez-soi [ʃeswa] *nm inv* home

Chf. cent. *abr (= chauffage central)* c.h

chiadé, e [ʃjade] *adj (fam: fignolé, soigné)* wicked

chialer [ʃjale] *vi (fam)* to blubber; **arrête de ~!** stop blubbering!

chiant, e [ʃjã, -ãt] *adj (fam!)* bloody annoying *(vulgar: Brit)* damn annoying; **qu'est-ce qu'il est ~!** he's such a bloody pain! *(!)*

chic [ʃik] *adj inv* chic, smart; *(généreux)* nice, decent ▷ *nm* stylishness; **avoir le ~ de** ou **pour** to have the knack of ou for; **de ~** *adv* off the cuff; **~!** great!, terrific!

chicane [ʃikan] *nf (obstacle)* zigzag; *(querelle)* squabble

chicaner [ʃikane] *vi (ergoter):* **~ sur** to quibble about

chiche [ʃiʃ] *adj (mesquin)* niggardly, mean; *(pauvre)* meagre *(Brit)*, meager *(US)* ▷ *excl (en réponse à un défi)* you're on!; **tu n'es pas ~ de lui parler!** you wouldn't (dare) speak to her!

chichement [ʃiʃmã] *adv (pauvrement)* meagrely *(Brit)*, meagerly *(US)*; *(mesquinement)* meanly

chichi [ʃiʃi] *nm (fam)* fuss; **faire des ~s** to make a fuss

chichis [ʃiʃi] *(fam) nmpl* fuss *sg*

chicorée [ʃikɔre] *nf (café)* chicory; *(salade)* endive; **~ frisée** curly endive

chicot [ʃiko] *nm* stump

chien [ʃjɛ̃] *nm* dog; *(de pistolet)* hammer; **temps de ~** rotten weather; **vie de ~** dog's life; **couché en ~ de fusil** curled up; **~ d'aveugle** guide dog; **~ de chasse** gun dog; **~ de garde** guard dog; **~ policier** police dog; **~ de race** pedigree dog; **~ de traîneau** husky

chiendent [ʃjɛ̃dã] *nm* couch grass

chien-loup [ʃjɛ̃lu] *(pl* **chiens-loups)** *nm*

wolfhound

chienne [ʃjɛn] nf (she-)dog, bitch

chier [ʃje] vi (fam!) to crap (!), shit (!); **faire ~ qn** (importuner) to bug sb; (causer des ennuis à) to piss sb around (!); **se faire ~** (s'ennuyer) to be bored rigid

chiffe [ʃif] nf: **il est mou comme une ~, c'est une ~ molle** he's spineless ou wet

chiffon [ʃifɔ̃] nm (piece of) rag

chiffonné, e [ʃifone] adj (fatigué: visage) worn-looking

chiffonner [ʃifone] vt to crumple, crease; (tracasser) to concern

chiffonnier [ʃifonje] nm ragman, rag-and-bone man; (meuble) chiffonier

chiffrable [ʃifʀabl(ə)] adj numerable

chiffre [ʃifʀ(ə)] nm (représentant un nombre) figure; numeral; (montant, total) total, sum; (d'un code) code, cipher; **~s romains/arabes** roman/arabic figures ou numerals; **en ~s ronds** in round figures; **écrire un nombre en ~s** to write a number in figures; **~ d'affaires (CA)** turnover; **~ de ventes** sales figures

chiffrer [ʃifʀe] vt (dépense) to put a figure to, assess; (message) to (en)code, cipher ▷ vi: **~ à, se ~ à** to add up to

chignole [ʃiɲɔl] nf drill

chignon [ʃiɲɔ̃] nm chignon, bun

chiite [ʃiit] adj Shiite ▷ nm/f: **Chiite** Shiite

Chili [ʃili] nm: **le ~** Chile

chilien, ne [ʃiljɛ̃, -ɛn] adj Chilean ▷ nm/f: **Chilien, ne** Chilean

chimère [ʃimɛʀ] nf (wild) dream, pipe dream, idle fancy

chimérique [ʃimeʀik] adj (utopique) fanciful

chimie [ʃimi] nf chemistry

chimio [ʃimjo], **chimiothérapie** [ʃimjoteʀapi] nf chemotherapy

chimique [ʃimik] adj chemical; **produits ~s** chemicals

chimiste [ʃimist(ə)] nm/f chemist

chimpanzé [ʃɛ̃pɑ̃ze] nm chimpanzee

chinchilla [ʃɛ̃ʃila] nm chinchilla

Chine [ʃin] nf: **la ~** China; **la ~ libre, la république de ~** the Republic of China, Nationalist China (Taiwan)

chine [ʃin] nm rice paper; (porcelaine) china (vase)

chiné, e [ʃine] adj flecked

chinois, e [ʃinwa, -waz] adj Chinese; (fig: péj) pernickety, fussy ▷ nm (Ling) Chinese ▷ nm/f: **Chinois, e** Chinese

chinoiserie [ʃinwazʀi], **chinoiseries** nf(pl) (péj) red tape, fuss

chiot [ʃjo] nm pup(py)

chiper [ʃipe] vt (fam) to pinch

chipie [ʃipi] nf shrew

chipolata [ʃipolata] nf chipolata

chipoter [ʃipote] vi (manger) to nibble; (ergoter) to quibble, haggle

chips [ʃips] nfpl (aussi: **pommes chips**) crisps (Brit), (potato) chips (US)

chique [ʃik] nf quid, chew

chiquenaude [ʃiknod] nf flick, flip

chiquer [ʃike] vi to chew tobacco

chiromancie [kiʀomɑ̃si] nf palmistry

chiromancien, ne [kiʀomɑ̃sjɛ̃, -ɛn] nm/f palmist

chiropracteur [kiʀopʀaktœʀ] nm, **chiropraticien, ne** [kiʀopʀatisjɛ̃, -ɛn] nm/f chiropractor

chirurgical, e, -aux [ʃiʀyʀʒikal, -o] adj surgical

chirurgie [ʃiʀyʀʒi] nf surgery; **~ esthétique** cosmetic ou plastic surgery

chirurgien [ʃiʀyʀʒjɛ̃] nm surgeon; **~ dentiste** dental surgeon

chiure [ʃjyʀ] nf: **~s de mouche** fly specks

ch.-l. abr = **chef-lieu**

chlore [klɔʀ] nm chlorine

chloroforme [klɔʀofɔʀm(ə)] nm chloroform

chlorophylle [klɔʀofil] nf chlorophyll

chlorure [klɔʀyʀ] nm chloride

choc [ʃɔk] nm impact; shock; crash; (moral) shock; (affrontement) clash ▷ adj: **prix ~** amazing ou incredible price/prices; **de ~** (troupe, traitement) shock cpd; (patron etc) high-powered; **~ opératoire/nerveux** post-operative/nervous shock; **~ en retour** return shock; (fig) backlash

chocolat [ʃokola] nm chocolate; (boisson) (hot) chocolate; **~ chaud** hot chocolate; **~ à cuire** cooking chocolate; **~ au lait** milk chocolate; **~ en poudre** drinking chocolate

chocolaté, e [ʃokolate] adj chocolate cpd, chocolate-flavoured

chocolaterie [ʃokolatʀi] nf (fabrique) chocolate factory

chocolatier, -ière [ʃokolatje, -jɛʀ] nm/f chocolate maker

chœur [kœʀ] nm (chorale) choir; (Opéra, Théât) chorus; (Archit) choir, chancel; **en ~** in chorus

choir [ʃwaʀ] vi to fall

choisi, e [ʃwazi] adj (de premier choix) carefully chosen; select; **textes ~s** selected writings

choisir [ʃwaziʀ] vt to choose; (entre plusieurs) to choose, select; **~ de faire qch** to choose ou opt to do sth

choix [ʃwa] nm choice; selection; **avoir le ~** to have the choice; **je n'avais pas le ~** I had no choice; **de premier ~** (Comm) class ou grade one; **de ~** choice cpd, selected; **au ~** as you wish ou prefer; **de mon/son ~** of my/his ou her choosing

choléra [kɔleʀa] nm cholera

cholestérol [kɔlɛsteʀɔl] nm cholesterol

chômage [ʃomaʒ] nm unemployment; **mettre au ~** to make redundant, put out of work; **être au ~** to be unemployed ou out of work; **~ partiel** short-time working; **~ structurel** structural unemployment; **~ technique** lay-offs pl

chômer [ʃome] vi to be unemployed, be idle; **jour chômé** public holiday

chômeur, -euse [ʃomœʀ, -øz] nm/f unemployed person, person out of work

chope [ʃop] nf tankard

choper [ʃope] (fam) vt (objet, maladie) to catch

choquant, e [ʃokɑ̃, -ɑ̃t] adj shocking

choquer [ʃɔke] vt (offenser) to shock; (commotionner) to shake (up)

choral, e [kɔʀal] adj choral ▷ nf choral society, choir

chorégraphe [kɔʀegʀaf] nm/f choreographer

chorégraphie [kɔʀegʀafi] nf choreography

choriste [kɔʀist(ə)] nm/f choir member; (Opéra) chorus member

chorus [kɔʀys] nm: **faire ~ (avec)** to voice one's agreement (with)

chose [ʃoz] nf thing ▷ nm (fam: machin) thingamajig ▷ adj inv: **être/se sentir tout ~** (bizarre) to be/feel a bit odd; (malade) to be/feel out of sorts; **dire bien des ~s à qn** to give sb's regards to sb; **parler de ~(s) et d'autre(s)** to talk about one thing and another; **c'est peu de ~** it's nothing much

chou, x [ʃu] nm cabbage ▷ adj inv cute; **mon petit ~** (my) sweetheart; **faire ~ blanc** to draw a blank; **feuille de ~** (fig: journal) rag; **~ à la crème** cream bun (made of choux pastry); **~ de Bruxelles** Brussels sprout

choucas [ʃuka] nm jackdaw

chouchou, te [ʃuʃu, -ut] nm/f (Scol) teacher's pet

chouchouter [ʃuʃute] vt to pet

choucroute [ʃukʀut] nf sauerkraut; **~ garnie** sauerkraut with cooked meats and potatoes

chouette [ʃwɛt] nf owl ▷ adj (fam) great, smashing

chou-fleur [ʃuflœʀ] (pl **choux-fleurs**) nm cauliflower

chou-rave [ʃuʀav] (pl **choux-raves**) nm kohlrabi

choyer [ʃwaje] vt to cherish; to pamper

CHR sigle m = **Centre hospitalier régional**

chrétien, ne [kʀetjɛ̃, -ɛn] adj, nm/f Christian

chrétiennement [kʀetjɛnmɑ̃] adv in a Christian way ou spirit

chrétienté [kʀetjɛ̃te] nf Christendom

Christ [kʀist] nm: **le ~** Christ; **christ** (crucifix etc) figure of Christ; **Jésus ~** Jesus Christ

christianiser [kʀistjanize] vt to convert to Christianity

christianisme [kʀistjanism(ə)] nm Christianity

chromatique [kʀɔmatik] adj chromatic

chrome [kʀom] nm chromium; (revêtement) chrome, chromium

chromé, e [kʀome] adj chrome-plated, chromium-plated

chromosome [kʀɔmozom] nm chromosome

chronique [kʀɔnik] adj chronic ▷ nf (de journal) column, page; (historique) chronicle; (Radio, TV): **la ~ sportive/théâtrale** the sports/theatre review; **la ~ locale** local news and gossip

chroniqueur [kʀɔnikœʀ] nm columnist; chronicler

chrono [kʀɔno] nm (fam) = **chronomètre**

chronologie [kʀɔnɔlɔʒi] nf chronology

chronologique [kʀɔnɔlɔʒik] adj chronological

chronologiquement [kʀɔnɔlɔʒikmɑ̃] adv chronologically

chronomètre [kʀɔnɔmɛtʀ(ə)] nm stopwatch

chronométrer [kʀɔnɔmetʀe] vt to time

chronométreur [kʀɔnɔmetʀœʀ] nm timekeeper

chrysalide [kʀizalid] nf chrysalis

chrysanthème [kʀizɑ̃tɛm] nm chrysanthemum

CHU sigle m (= Centre hospitalo-universitaire) ≈ (teaching) hospital

chu, e [ʃy] pp de **choir**

chuchotement [ʃyʃɔtmɑ̃] nm whisper

chuchoter [ʃyʃɔte] vt, vi to whisper

chuintement [ʃɥɛ̃tmɑ̃] nm hiss

chuinter [ʃɥɛ̃te] vi to hiss

chut excl [ʃyt] sh! ▷ vb [ʃy] voir **choir**

chute [ʃyt] nf fall; (de bois, papier: déchet) scrap; **la ~ des cheveux** hair loss; **faire une ~ (de 10 m)** to fall (10 m); **~s de pluie/neige** rain/snowfalls; **~ (d'eau)** waterfall; **~ du jour** nightfall; **~ libre** free fall; **~ des reins** small of the back

Chypre [ʃipʀ] nm Cyprus

chypriote [ʃipʀiɔt] adj, nm/f = **cypriote**

-ci, ci- [si] adv voir **par; ci-contre; ci-joint** etc ▷ adj dém: **ce garçon~/-là** this/that boy; **ces femmes~/-là** these/those women

CIA sigle f CIA

cial abr = **commercial**

ciao [tʃao] excl (fam) (bye-)bye

ci-après [siapʀɛ] adv hereafter

cibiste [sibist(ə)] nm CB enthusiast

cible [sibl(ə)] nf target

cibler [sible] vt to target

ciboire [sibwaʀ] nm ciborium (vessel)

ciboule [sibul] nf (large) chive

ciboulette [sibulɛt] nf (small) chive

ciboulot [sibulo] nm (fam) head, nut; **il n'a rien dans le ~** he's got nothing between his ears

cicatrice [sikatʀis] nf scar

cicatriser [sikatʀize] vt to heal; **se cicatriser** to heal (up), form a scar

ci-contre [sikɔ̃tʀ(ə)] adv opposite

CICR sigle m (= Comité international de la Croix-Rouge) ICRC

ci-dessous [sidəsu] adv below

ci-dessus [sidəsy] adv above

ci-devant [sidəvɑ̃] nm/f inv aristocrat who lost his/ her title in the French Revolution

CIDJ sigle m (= Centre d'information et de documentation de la jeunesse) careers advisory service

cidre [sidʀ(ə)] nm cider

cidrerie [sidʀəʀi] nf cider factory

Cie abr (= compagnie) Co

ciel [sjɛl] nm sky; (Rel) heaven; **ciels** nmpl (Peinture etc) skies; **cieux** nmpl sky sg, skies; (Rel) heaven sg; **à ~ ouvert** open-air; (mine) opencast; **tomber du ~** (arriver à l'improviste) to appear out of the blue; (être stupéfait) to be unable to believe one's eyes; **C~!** good heavens!; **~ de lit** canopy

cierge [sjɛʀʒ(ə)] nm candle; **~ pascal** Easter candle

cieux [sjø] nmpl voir **ciel**

cigale [sigal] nf cicada

cigare [sigaʀ] nm cigar

cigarette [sigaʀɛt] nf cigarette; **~ (à) bout**

filtre filter cigarette
ci-gît [siʒi] *adv* here lies
cigogne [sigɔɲ] *nf* stork
ciguë [sigy] *nf* hemlock
ci-inclus, e [siɛ̃kly, -yz] *adj, adv* enclosed
ci-joint, e [siʒwɛ̃, -ɛ̃t] *adj, adv* enclosed; **veuillez trouver** ~ please find enclosed
cil [sil] *nm* (eye)lash
ciller [sije] *vi* to blink
cimaise [simɛz] *nf* picture rail
cime [sim] *nf* top; (*montagne*) peak
ciment [simɑ̃] *nm* cement; ~ **armé** reinforced concrete
cimenter [simɑ̃te] *vt* to cement
cimenterie [simɑ̃tri] *nf* cement works *sg*
cimetière [simtjɛʀ] *nm* cemetery; (*d'église*) churchyard; ~ **de voitures** scrapyard
cinéaste [sineast(ə)] *nm/f* film-maker
ciné-club [sineklœb] *nm* film club; film society
cinéma [sinema] *nm* cinema; **aller au** ~ to go to the cinema *ou* pictures *ou* movies; ~ **d'animation** cartoon (film)
cinémascope® [sinemaskɔp] *nm* Cinemascope®
cinémathèque [sinematɛk] *nf* film archives *pl ou* library
cinématographie [sinematɔgʀafi] *nf* cinematography
cinématographique [sinematɔgʀafik] *adj* film *cpd*, cinema *cpd*
cinéphile [sinefil] *nm/f* film buff
cinérama® [sinerama] *nm*: **en** ~ in Cinerama®
cinétique [sinetik] *adj* kinetic
cingalais, cinghalais, e [sɛ̃galɛ, -ɛz] *adj* Sin(g)halese
cinglant, e [sɛ̃glɑ̃, -ɑ̃t] *adj* (*propos, ironie*) scathing, biting; (*échec*) crushing
cinglé, e [sɛ̃gle] *adj* (*fam*) crazy
cingler [sɛ̃gle] *vt* to lash; (*fig*) to sting ▷ *vi* (*Navig*): ~ **vers** to make *ou* head for
cinq [sɛ̃k] *num* five
cinquantaine [sɛ̃kɑ̃tɛn] *nf*: **une** ~ **(de)** about fifty; **avoir la** ~ (*âge*) to be around fifty
cinquante [sɛ̃kɑ̃t] *num* fifty
cinquantenaire [sɛ̃kɑ̃tnɛʀ] *adj, nm/f* fifty-year-old
cinquantième [sɛ̃kɑ̃tjɛm] *num* fiftieth
cinquième [sɛ̃kjɛm] *num* fifth
cinquièmement [sɛ̃kjɛmmɑ̃] *adv* fifthly
cintre [sɛ̃tʀ(ə)] *nm* coat-hanger; (*Archit*) arch; **plein** ~ semicircular arch
cintré, e [sɛ̃tre] *adj* curved; (*chemise*) fitted, slim-fitting
CIO *sigle m* (= Comité international olympique) IOC (= International Olympic Committee); (= centre d'information et d'orientation) careers advisory centre
cirage [siʀaʒ] *nm* (shoe) polish
circoncis, e [siʀkɔ̃si, -iz] *adj* circumcized
circoncision [siʀkɔ̃sizjɔ̃] *nf* circumcision
circonférence [siʀkɔ̃feʀɑ̃s] *nf* circumference

circonflexe [siʀkɔ̃flɛks(ə)] *adj*: **accent** ~ circumflex accent
circonlocution [siʀkɔ̃lɔkysjɔ̃] *nf* circumlocution
circonscription [siʀkɔ̃skʀipsjɔ̃] *nf* district; ~ **électorale** (*d'un député*) constituency; ~ **militaire** military area
circonscrire [siʀkɔ̃skʀiʀ] *vt* to define, delimit; (*incendie*) to contain; (*propriété*) to mark out; (*sujet*) to define
circonspect, e [siʀkɔ̃spɛkt] *adj* circumspect, cautious
circonspection [siʀkɔ̃spɛksjɔ̃] *nf* circumspection, caution
circonstance [siʀkɔ̃stɑ̃s] *nf* circumstance; (*occasion*) occasion; **œuvre de** ~ occasional work; **air de** ~ fitting air; **tête de** ~ appropriate demeanour (*Brit*) *ou* demeanor (*US*); ~**s atténuantes** mitigating circumstances
circonstancié, e [siʀkɔ̃stɑ̃sje] *adj* detailed
circonstanciel, le [siʀkɔ̃stɑ̃sjɛl] *adj*: **complément/proposition** ~**(le)** adverbial phrase/clause
circonvenir [siʀkɔ̃vniʀ] *vt* to circumvent
circonvolutions [siʀkɔ̃vɔlysjɔ̃] *nfpl* twists, convolutions
circuit [siʀkɥi] *nm* (*trajet*) tour, (round) trip; (*Élec, Tech*) circuit; ~ **automobile** motor circuit; ~ **de distribution** distribution network; ~ **fermé** closed circuit; ~ **intégré** integrated circuit
circulaire [siʀkylɛʀ] *adj, nf* circular
circulation [siʀkylɑsjɔ̃] *nf* circulation; (*Auto*): **la** ~ (the) traffic; **bonne/mauvaise** ~ good/bad circulation; **mettre en** ~ to put into circulation
circulatoire [siʀkylatwaʀ] *adj*: **avoir des troubles** ~**s** to have problems with one's circulation
circuler [siʀkyle] *vi* to drive (along); to walk along; (*train etc*) to run; (*sang, devises*) to circulate; **faire** ~ (*nouvelle*) to spread (about), circulate; (*badauds*) to move on
cire [siʀ] *nf* wax; ~ **à cacheter** sealing wax
ciré [siʀe] *nm* oilskin
cirer [siʀe] *vt* to wax, polish
cireur [siʀœʀ] *nm* shoeshine boy
cireuse [siʀøz] *nf* floor polisher
cireux, -euse [siʀø, -øz] *adj* (*fig*: *teint*) sallow, waxen
cirque [siʀk(ə)] *nm* circus; (*arène*) amphitheatre (*Brit*), amphitheater (*US*); (*Géo*) cirque; (*fig*: *désordre*) chaos, bedlam; (: *chichis*) carry-on
cirrhose [siʀoz] *nf*: ~ **du foie** cirrhosis of the liver
cisaille [sizaj], **cisailles** *nf(pl)* (gardening) shears *pl*
cisailler [sizaje] *vt* to clip
ciseau, x [sizo] *nm*: ~ **(à bois)** chisel ▷ *nmpl* (pair of) scissors; **sauter en** ~**x** to do a scissors jump; ~ **à froid** cold chisel
ciseler [sizle] *vt* to chisel, carve
ciselure [sizlyʀ] *nf* engraving; (*bois*) carving

Cisjordanie [sisʒɔʀdani] *nf*: **la ~** the West Bank (of Jordan)

citadelle [sitadɛl] *nf* citadel

citadin, e [sitadɛ̃, -in] *nm/f* city dweller ▷ *adj* town *cpd*, city *cpd*, urban

citation [sitasjɔ̃] *nf* (*d'auteur*) quotation; (*Jur*) summons *sg*; (*Mil: récompense*) mention

cité [site] *nf* town; (*plus grande*) city; **~ ouvrière** (workers') housing estate; **~ universitaire** students' residences *pl*

cité-dortoir [sitedɔʀtwaʀ] (*pl* **cités-dortoirs**) *nf* dormitory town

cité-jardin [siteʒaʀdɛ̃] (*pl* **cités-jardins**) *nf* garden city

citer [site] *vt* (*un auteur*) to quote (from); (*nommer*) to name; (*Jur*) to summon; **~ (en exemple)** (*personne*) to hold up (as an example); **je ne veux ~ personne** I don't want to name names

citerne [sitɛʀn(ə)] *nf* tank

cithare [sitaʀ] *nf* zither

citoyen, ne [sitwajɛ̃, -ɛn] *nm/f* citizen

citoyenneté [sitwajɛnte] *nf* citizenship

citrique [sitʀik] *adj*: **acide ~** citric acid

citron [sitʀɔ̃] *nm* lemon; **~ pressé** (fresh) lemon juice; **~ vert** lime

citronnade [sitʀɔnad] *nf* lemonade

citronné, e [sitʀɔne] *adj* (*boisson*) lemon-flavoured (*Brit*) *ou* -flavored (*US*); (*eau de toilette*) lemon-scented

citronnelle [sitʀɔnɛl] *nf* citronella

citronnier [sitʀɔnje] *nm* lemon tree

citrouille [sitʀuj] *nf* pumpkin

cive [siv] *nf* chive

civet [sivɛ] *nm* stew; **~ de lièvre** jugged hare

civette [sivɛt] *nf* (*Bot*) chives *pl*; (*Zool*) civet (cat)

civière [sivjɛʀ] *nf* stretcher

civil, e [sivil] *adj* (*Jur, Admin, poli*) civil; (*non militaire*) civilian ▷ *nm* civilian; **en ~** in civilian clothes; **dans le ~** in civilian life

civilement [sivilmɑ̃] *adv* (*poliment*) civilly; **se marier ~** to have a civil wedding

civilisation [sivilizasjɔ̃] *nf* civilization

civilisé, e [sivilize] *adj* civilized

civiliser [sivilize] *vt* to civilize

civilité [sivilite] *nf* civility; **présenter ses ~s** to present one's compliments

civique [sivik] *adj* civic; **instruction ~** (*Scol*) civics *sg*

civisme [sivism(ə)] *nm* public-spiritedness

cl. *abr* (= *centilitre*) cl

clafoutis [klafuti] *nm* batter pudding (*containing fruit*)

claie [klɛ] *nf* grid, riddle

clair, e [klɛʀ] *adj* light; (*chambre*) light, bright; (*eau, son, fig*) clear ▷ *adv*: **voir ~** to see clearly ▷ *nm*: **mettre au ~** (*notes etc*) to tidy up; **tirer qch au ~** to clear sth up, clarify sth; **bleu ~** light blue; **pour être ~** so as to make it plain; **y voir ~** (*comprendre*) to understand, see; **le plus ~ de son temps/argent** the better part of his time/money; **en ~** (*non codé*) in clear; **~ de lune** moonlight

claire [klɛʀ] *nf*: (**huître de**) **~** fattened oyster

clairement [klɛʀmɑ̃] *adv* clearly

claire-voie [klɛʀvwa]: **à ~** *adj* letting the light through; openwork *cpd*

clairière [klɛʀjɛʀ] *nf* clearing

clair-obscur [klɛʀɔpskyʀ] (*pl* **clairs-obscurs**) *nm* half-light; (*fig*) uncertainty

clairon [klɛʀɔ̃] *nm* bugle

claironner [klɛʀɔne] *vt* (*fig*) to trumpet, shout from the rooftops

clairsemé, e [klɛʀsəme] *adj* sparse

clairvoyance [klɛʀvwajɑ̃s] *nf* clear-sightedness

clairvoyant, e [klɛʀvwajɑ̃, -ɑ̃t] *adj* perceptive, clear-sighted

clam [klam] *nm* (*Zool*) clam

clamer [klame] *vt* to proclaim

clameur [klamœʀ] *nf* clamour (*Brit*), clamor (*US*)

clan [klɑ̃] *nm* clan

clandestin, e [klɑ̃dɛstɛ̃, -in] *adj* clandestine, covert; (*Pol*) underground, clandestine; **passager ~** stowaway

clandestinement [klɑ̃dɛstinmɑ̃] *adv* secretly; **s'embarquer ~** to stow away

clandestinité [klɑ̃dɛstinite] *nf*: **dans la ~** (*en secret*) under cover; (*en se cachant: vivre*) underground; **entrer dans la ~** to go underground

clapet [klapɛ] *nm* (*Tech*) valve

clapier [klapje] *nm* (rabbit) hutch

clapotement [klapɔtmɑ̃] *nm* lap(ping)

clapoter [klapɔte] *vi* to lap

clapotis [klapɔti] *nm* lap(ping)

claquage [klakaʒ] *nm* pulled *ou* strained muscle

claque [klak] *nf* (*gifle*) slap; (*Théât*) claque ▷ *nm* (*chapeau*) opera hat

claquement [klakmɑ̃] *nm* (*de porte: bruit répété*) banging; (*: bruit isolé*) slam

claquemurer [klakmyʀe]: **se claquemurer** *vi* to shut o.s. away, closet o.s

claquer [klake] *vi* (*drapeau*) to flap; (*porte*) to bang, slam; (*coup de feu*) to ring out ▷ *vt* (*porte*) to slam, bang; (*doigts*) to snap; **elle claquait des dents** her teeth were chattering; **se ~ un muscle** to pull *ou* strain a muscle

claquettes [klakɛt] *nfpl* tap-dancing *sg*

clarification [klaʀifikasjɔ̃] *nf* (*fig*) clarification

clarifier [klaʀifje] *vt* (*fig*) to clarify

clarinette [klaʀinɛt] *nf* clarinet

clarinettiste [klaʀinetist(ə)] *nm/f* clarinettist

clarté [klaʀte] *nf* lightness; brightness; (*d'un son, de l'eau*) clearness; (*d'une explication*) clarity

classe [klɑs] *nf* class; (*Scol: local*) class(room); (*: leçon*) class; (*: élèves*) class, form; **1ère/2ème ~** 1st/2nd class; **un (soldat de) deuxième ~** (*Mil: armée de terre*) ≈ private (soldier); (*: armée de l'air*) ≈ aircraftman (*Brit*), ≈ airman basic (*US*); **de ~** luxury *cpd*; **faire ses ~s** (*Mil*) to do one's (recruit's) training; **faire la ~** (*Scol*) to be a *ou* the teacher; to teach; **aller en ~** to go to school; **aller en ~ verte/de neige/de mer** to go to the countryside/skiing/to the seaside with the school; ~ **préparatoire** *class which prepares students for the Grandes Écoles entry exams; see note;* ~ **sociale** *social class;* ~ **touriste** *economy class*

⬤ **CLASSES PRÉPARATOIRES**
⬤
⬤ *Classes préparatoires* are the two years of
⬤ intensive study which coach students for
⬤ the competitive entry examinations to the
⬤ "grandes écoles". These extremely
⬤ demanding courses follow the
⬤ "baccalauréat" and are usually done at a
⬤ "lycée". Schools which provide such classes
⬤ are more highly regarded than those which
⬤ do not.

classement [klasmɑ̃] *nm* classifying; filing; grading; closing; (*rang: Scol*) place; (: *Sport*) placing; (*liste: Scol*) class list (in order of merit); (: *Sport*) placings *pl*; **premier au ~ général** (*Sport*) first overall

classer [klase] *vt* (*idées, livres*) to classify; (*papiers*) to file; (*candidat, concurrent*) to grade; (*personne: juger: péj*) to rate; (*Jur: affaire*) to close; **se ~ premier/dernier** to come first/last; (*Sport*) to finish first/last

classeur [klasœʀ] *nm* file; (*meuble*) filing cabinet; ~ **à feuillets mobiles** ring binder

classification [klasifikasjɔ̃] *nf* classification

classifier [klasifje] *vt* to classify

classique [klasik] *adj* classical; (*habituel*) standard, classic ▷ *nm* classic; classical author; **études ~s** classical studies, classics

claudication [klodikasjɔ̃] *nf* limp

clause [kloz] *nf* clause

claustrer [klostʀe] *vt* to confine

claustrophobie [klostʀɔfɔbi] *nf* claustrophobia

clavecin [klavsɛ̃] *nm* harpsichord

claveciniste [klavsinist(ə)] *nm/f* harpsichordist

clavicule [klavikyl] *nf* clavicle, collarbone

clavier [klavje] *nm* keyboard

clé, clef [kle] *nf* key; (*Mus*) clef; (*de mécanicien*) spanner (*Brit*), wrench (*US*) ▷ *adj*: **problème/ position** ~ key problem/position; **mettre sous** ~ to place under lock and key; **prendre la ~ des champs** to run away, make off; **prix ~s en main** (*d'une voiture*) on-the-road price; (*d'un appartement*) price with immediate entry; ~ **de sol/de fa/d'ut** treble/bass/alto clef; **livre/film** *etc* **à** ~ book/film *etc* in which real people are depicted under fictitious names; **à la** ~ (*à la fin*) at the end of it all; ~ **anglaise** = **clé à molette**; ~ **de contact** ignition key; ~ **à molette** adjustable spanner (*Brit*) *ou* wrench, monkey wrench; ~ **USB** USB key; ~ **de voûte** keystone

clématite [klematit] *nf* clematis

clémence [klemɑ̃s] *nf* mildness; leniency

clément, e [klemɑ̃, -ɑ̃t] *adj* (*temps*) mild; (*indulgent*) lenient

clémentine [klemɑ̃tin] *nf* (*Bot*) clementine

clenche [klɑ̃ʃ] *nf* latch

cleptomane [klɛptɔman] *nm/f* = **kleptomane**

clerc [klɛʀ] *nm*: ~ **de notaire** *ou* **d'avoué** lawyer's clerk

clergé [klɛʀʒe] *nm* clergy

clérical, e, -aux [kleʀikal, -o] *adj* clerical

cliché [kliʃe] *nm* (*Photo*) negative; print; (*Typo*) (printing) plate; (*Ling*) cliché

client, e [klijɑ̃, -ɑ̃t] *nm/f* (*acheteur*) customer, client; (*d'hôtel*) guest, patron; (*du docteur*) patient; (*de l'avocat*) client

clientèle [klijɑ̃tɛl] *nf* (*du magasin*) customers *pl*, clientèle; (*du docteur, de l'avocat*) practice; **accorder sa ~ à** to give one's custom to; **retirer sa ~ à** to take one's business away from

cligner [kliɲe] *vi*: ~ **des yeux** to blink (one's eyes); ~ **de l'œil** to wink

clignotant [kliɲɔtɑ̃] *nm* (*Auto*) indicator

clignoter [kliɲɔte] *vi* (*étoiles etc*) to twinkle; (*lumière: à intervalles réguliers*) to flash; (: *vaciller*) to flicker; (*yeux*) to blink

climat [klima] *nm* climate

climatique [klimatik] *adj* climatic

climatisation [klimatizasjɔ̃] *nf* air conditioning

climatisé, e [klimatize] *adj* air-conditioned

climatiseur [klimatizœʀ] *nm* air conditioner

clin d'œil [klɛ̃dœj] *nm* wink; **en un clin d'œil** in a flash

clinique [klinik] *adj* clinical ▷ *nf* nursing home, (private) clinic

clinquant, e [klɛ̃kɑ̃, -ɑ̃t] *adj* flashy

clip [klip] *nm* (*pince*) clip; (*vidéo*) pop (*ou* promotional) video

clique [klik] *nf* (*péj: bande*) clique, set; **prendre ses ~s et ses claques** to pack one's bags

cliquer [klike] *vi* (*Inform*) to click; ~ **deux fois** to double-click

cliqueter [klikte] *vi* to clash; (*ferraille, clefs, monnaie*) to jangle, jingle; (*verres*) to chink

cliquetis [klikti] *nm* jangle; jingle; chink

clitoris [klitɔʀis] *nm* clitoris

clivage [klivaʒ] *nm* cleavage; (*fig*) rift, split

cloaque [klɔak] *nm* (*fig*) cesspit

clochard, e [klɔʃaʀ, -aʀd(ə)] *nm/f* tramp

cloche [klɔʃ] *nf* (*d'église*) bell; (*fam*) clot; (*chapeau*) cloche (hat); ~ **à fromage** cheese-cover

cloche-pied [klɔʃpje]: **à ~** *adv* on one leg, hopping (along)

clocher [klɔʃe] *nm* church tower; (*en pointe*) steeple ▷ *vi* (*fam*) to be *ou* go wrong; **de ~** (*péj*) parochial

clocheton [klɔʃtɔ̃] *nm* pinnacle

clochette [klɔʃɛt] *nf* bell

clodo [klɔdo] *nm* (*fam: = clochard*) tramp

cloison [klwazɔ̃] *nf* partition (wall); ~ **étanche** (*fig*) impenetrable barrier, brick wall (*fig*)

cloisonner [klwazɔne] *vt* to partition (off), to divide up; (*fig*) to compartmentalize

cloître [klwatʀ(ə)] *nm* cloister

cloîtrer [klwatʀe] *vt*: **se cloîtrer** to shut o.s. away; (*Rel*) to enter a convent *ou* monastery

clonage [klɔnaʒ] *nm* cloning

clone [klɔn] *nm* clone

79

cloner [klone] vt to clone
clope [klɔp] (fam) nm ou f fag (Brit), cigarette
clopin-clopant [klɔpɛ̃klɔpɑ̃] adv hobbling
along; (fig) so-so
clopiner [klɔpine] vi to hobble along
cloporte [klɔpɔʀt(ə)] nm woodlouse
cloque [klɔk] nf blister
cloqué, e [klɔke] adj: **étoffe ~e** seersucker
cloquer [klɔke] vi (peau, peinture) to blister
clore [klɔʀ] vt to close; **~ une session** (Inform) to
log out
clos, e [klo, -oz] pp de **clore** ▷ adj voir **maison**;
huis; vase ▷ nm (enclosed) field
clôt [klo] vb voir **clore**
clôture [klotyʀ] nf closure, closing; (barrière)
enclosure, fence
clôturer [klotyʀe] vt (terrain) to enclose, close
off; (festival, débats) to close
clou [klu] nm nail; (Méd) boil; **clous** nmpl =
passage clouté; pneus à ~s studded tyres; **le ~
du spectacle** the highlight of the show; **~ de
girofle** clove
clouer [klue] vt to nail down (ou up); (fig): **~ sur/
contre** to pin to/against
clouté, e [klute] adj studded
clown [klun] nm clown; **faire le ~** (fig) to clown
(about), play the fool
clownerie [klunʀi] nf clowning no pl; **faire des
~s** to clown around
club [klœb] nm club
CM sigle f = **chambre des métiers** ▷ sigle m =
conseil municipal; (Scol) = **cours moyen**
cm. abr (= centimètre) cm
CMU sigle f (= couverture maladie universelle) system of
free health care for those on low incomes
CNAT sigle f (= Commission nationale d'aménagement
du territoire) national development agency
CNC sigle m (= Conseil national de la consommation)
national consumers' council
CNDP sigle m = **Centre national de
documentation pédagogique**
CNE sigle m (= Contrat nouvelles embauches) less
stringent type of employment contract for use by small
companies
CNED sigle m (= Centre national d'enseignement à
distance) ≈ Open University
CNIL sigle f (= Commission nationale de l'informatique
et des libertés) board which enforces law on data
protection
CNIT sigle m (= Centre national des industries et des
techniques) exhibition centre in Paris
CNJA sigle m (= Centre national des jeunes agriculteurs)
farmers' union
CNL sigle f (= Confédération nationale du logement)
consumer group for housing
CNRS sigle m = **Centre national de la recherche
scientifique**
c/o abr (= care of) c/o
coagulant [kɔagylɑ̃] nm (Méd) coagulant
coaguler [kɔagyle]: **se coaguler** vi to coagulate
coaliser [kɔalize]: **se coaliser** vi to unite, join
forces

coalition [kɔalisjɔ̃] nf coalition
coasser [kɔase] vi to croak
coauteur [kɔotœʀ] nm co-author
coaxial, e, -aux [kɔaksjal, -o] adj coaxial
cobaye [kɔbaj] nm guinea-pig
cobra [kɔbʀa] nm cobra
coca® [kɔka] nm Coke®
cocagne [kɔkaɲ] nf: **pays de ~** land of plenty;
mât de ~ greasy pole (fig)
cocaïne [kɔkain] nf cocaine
cocarde [kɔkaʀd(ə)] nf rosette
cocardier, -ière [kɔkaʀdje, -jɛʀ] adj jingoistic,
chauvinistic; militaristic
cocasse [kɔkas] adj comical, funny
coccinelle [kɔksinɛl] nf ladybird (Brit), ladybug
(US)
coccyx [kɔksis] nm coccyx
cocher [kɔʃe] nm coachman ▷ vt to tick off;
(entailler) to notch
cochère [kɔʃɛʀ] adj f voir **porte**
cochon, ne [kɔʃɔ̃, -ɔn] nm pig ▷ nm/f (péj: sale)
(filthy) pig; (: méchant) swine ▷ adj (fam) dirty,
smutty; **~ d'Inde** guinea-pig; **~ de lait** (Culin)
sucking pig
cochonnaille [kɔʃɔnaj] nf (péj: charcuterie) (cold)
pork
cochonnerie [kɔʃɔnʀi] nf (fam: saleté) filth;
(: marchandises) rubbish, trash
cochonnet [kɔʃɔnɛ] nm (Boules) jack
cocker [kɔkɛʀ] nm cocker spaniel
cocktail [kɔktɛl] nm cocktail; (réception) cocktail
party
coco [kɔko] nm voir **noix**; (fam) bloke (Brit), dude
(US)
cocon [kɔkɔ̃] nm cocoon
cocorico [kɔkɔʀiko] excl, nm cock-a-doodle-do
cocotier [kɔkɔtje] nm coconut palm
cocotte [kɔkɔt] nf (en fonte) casserole; **ma ~** (fam)
sweetie (pie); **~ (minute)**® pressure cooker; **~
en papier** paper shape
cocu [kɔky] nm cuckold
code [kɔd] nm code; **se mettre en ~(s)** to dip
(Brit) ou dim (US) one's (head)lights; **~ à barres**
bar code; **~ de caractère** (Inform) character
code; **~ civil** Common Law; **~ machine**
machine code; **~ pénal** penal code; **~ postal**
(numéro) postcode (Brit), zip code (US); **~ de la
route** highway code; **~ secret** cipher
codéine [kɔdein] nf codeine
coder [kɔde] vt to (en)code
codétenu, e [kɔdɛtny] nm/f fellow prisoner ou
inmate
codicille [kɔdisil] nm codicil
codifier [kɔdifje] vt to codify
codirecteur, -trice [kɔdiʀɛktœʀ, -tʀis] nm/f co-
director
coéditeur, -trice [kɔeditœʀ, -tʀis] nm/f co-
publisher; (rédacteur) co-editor
coefficient [kɔefisjɑ̃] nm coefficient; **~
d'erreur** margin of error
coéquipier, -ière [kɔekipje, -jɛʀ] nm/f team-
mate, partner

coercition [kɔɛʀsisjɔ̃] *nf* coercion

cœur [kœʀ] *nm* heart; (*Cartes: couleur*) hearts *pl*; (: *carte*) heart; (*Culin*): ~ **de laitue/d'artichaut** lettuce/artichoke heart; (*fig*): ~ **du débat** heart of the debate; ~ **de l'été** height of summer; ~ **de la forêt** depths *pl* of the forest; **affaire de** ~ love affair; **avoir bon** ~ to be kind-hearted; **avoir mal au** ~ to feel sick; **contre** *ou* **sur son** ~ to one's breast; **opérer qn à** ~ **ouvert** to perform open-heart surgery on sb; **recevoir qn à** ~ **ouvert** to welcome sb with open arms; **parler à** ~ **ouvert** to open one's heart; **de tout son** ~ with all one's heart; **avoir le** ~ **gros** *ou* **serré** to have a heavy heart; **en avoir le** ~ **net** to be clear in one's own mind (about it); **par** ~ by heart; **de bon** ~ willingly; **avoir à** ~ **de faire** to be very keen to do; **cela lui tient à** ~ that's (very) close to his heart; **prendre les choses à** ~ to take things to heart; **à** ~ -**joie** to one's heart's content; **être de tout** ~ **avec qn** to be (completely) in accord with sb

coexistence [kɔɛgzistɑ̃s] *nf* coexistence
coexister [kɔɛgziste] *vi* to coexist
coffrage [kɔfʀaʒ] *nm* (*Constr: dispositif*) form(work)
coffre [kɔfʀ(ə)] *nm* (*meuble*) chest; (*coffre-fort*) safe; (*d'auto*) boot (*Brit*), trunk (*US*); **avoir du** ~ (*fam*) to have a lot of puff
coffre-fort [kɔfʀəfɔʀ] (*pl* **coffres-forts**) *nm* safe
coffrer [kɔfʀe] *vt* (*fam*) to put inside, lock up
coffret [kɔfʀɛ] *nm* casket; ~ **à bijoux** jewel box
cogérant, e [kɔʒeʀɑ̃, -ɑ̃t] *nm/f* joint manager/manageress
cogestion [kɔʒestjɔ̃] *nf* joint management
cogiter [kɔʒite] *vi* to cogitate
cognac [kɔɲak] *nm* brandy, cognac
cognement [kɔɲmɑ̃] *nm* knocking
cogner [kɔɲe] *vi* to knock, bang; **se cogner** *vi* to bump o.s.
cohabitation [kɔabitasjɔ̃] *nf* living together; (*Pol, Jur*) cohabitation
cohabiter [kɔabite] *vi* to live together
cohérence [kɔeʀɑ̃s] *nf* coherence
cohérent, e [kɔeʀɑ̃, -ɑ̃t] *adj* coherent
cohésion [kɔezjɔ̃] *nf* cohesion
cohorte [kɔɔʀt(ə)] *nf* troop
cohue [kɔy] *nf* crowd
coi, coite [kwa, kwat] *adj*: **rester** ~ to remain silent
coiffe [kwaf] *nf* headdress
coiffé, e [kwafe] *adj*: **bien/mal** ~ with tidy/untidy hair; ~ **d'un béret** wearing a beret; ~ **en arrière** with one's hair brushed *ou* combed back; ~ **en brosse** with a crew cut
coiffer [kwafe] *vt* (*fig*) to cover, top; ~ **qn** to do sb's hair; ~ **qn d'un béret** to put a beret on sb; **se coiffer** *vi* to do one's hair; to put on a *ou* one's hat
coiffeur, -euse [kwafœʀ, -øz] *nm/f* hairdresser ▷ *nf* (*table*) dressing table
coiffure [kwafyʀ] *nf* (*cheveux*) hairstyle, hairdo; (*chapeau*) hat, headgear *no pl*; (*art*): **la** ~ hairdressing

coin [kwɛ̃] *nm* corner; (*pour graver*) die; (*pour coincer*) wedge; (*poinçon*) hallmark; **l'épicerie du** ~ the local grocer; **dans le** ~ (*aux alentours*) in the area, around about; locally; **au** ~ **du feu** by the fireside; **du** ~ **de l'œil** out of the corner of one's eye; **regard en** ~ side(ways) glance; **sourire en** ~ half-smile
coincé, e [kwɛ̃se] *adj* stuck, jammed; (*fig: inhibé*) inhibited, with hang-ups
coincer [kwɛ̃se] *vt* to jam; (*fam*) to catch (out); to nab; **se coincer** *vi* to get stuck *ou* jammed
coïncidence [kɔɛ̃sidɑ̃s] *nf* coincidence
coïncider [kɔɛ̃side] *vi*: ~ (**avec**) to coincide (with); (*correspondre: témoignage etc*) to correspond *ou* tally (with)
coin-coin [kwɛ̃kwɛ̃] *nm inv* quack
coing [kwɛ̃] *nm* quince
coït [kɔit] *nm* coitus
coite [kwat] *adj f voir* **coi**
coke [kɔk] *nm* coke
col [kɔl] *nm* (*de chemise*) collar; (*encolure, cou*) neck; (*de montagne*) pass; ~ **roulé** polo-neck; ~ **de l'utérus** cervix
coléoptère [kɔleɔptɛʀ] *nm* beetle
colère [kɔlɛʀ] *nf* anger; **une** ~ a fit of anger; **être en** ~ (**contre qn**) to be angry (with sb); **mettre qn en** ~ to make sb angry; **se mettre en** ~ to get angry
coléreux, -euse [kɔleʀø, -øz] *adj*, **colérique** [kɔleʀik] ▷ *adj* quick-tempered, irascible
colibacille [kɔlibasil] *nm* colon bacillus
colibacillose [kɔlibasiloz] *nf* colibacillosis
colifichet [kɔlifiʃɛ] *nm* trinket
colimaçon [kɔlimasɔ̃] *nm*: **escalier en** ~ spiral staircase
colin [kɔlɛ̃] *nm* hake
colin-maillard [kɔlɛ̃majaʀ] *nm* (*jeu*) blind man's buff
colique [kɔlik] *nf* diarrhoea (*Brit*), diarrhea (*US*); (*douleurs*) colic (pains *pl*); (*fam: personne ou chose ennuyeuse*) pain
colis [kɔli] *nm* parcel; **par** ~ **postal** by parcel post
colistier, -ière [kɔlistje, -jɛʀ] *nm/f* fellow candidate
colite [kɔlit] *nf* colitis
coll. *abr* = **collection**; (= *collaborateurs*): **et** ~ et al
collaborateur, -trice [kɔlabɔʀatœʀ, -tʀis] *nm/f* (*aussi Pol*) collaborator; (*d'une revue*) contributor
collaboration [kɔlabɔʀasjɔ̃] *nf* collaboration
collaborer [kɔlabɔʀe] *vi* to collaborate; (*aussi:* **collaborer à**) to collaborate on; (*revue*) to contribute to
collage [kɔlaʒ] *nm* (*Art*) collage
collagène [kɔlaʒɛn] *nm* collagen
collant, e [kɔlɑ̃, -ɑ̃t] *adj* sticky; (*robe etc*) clinging, skintight; (*péj*) clinging ▷ *nm* (*bas*) tights *pl*
collatéral, e, -aux [kɔlateʀal, -o] *nm/f* collateral
collation [kɔlasjɔ̃] *nf* light meal
colle [kɔl] *nf* glue; (*à papiers peints*) (wallpaper)

C

paste; (*devinette*) teaser, riddle; (*Scol fam*) detention; **~ forte** superglue®

collecte [kɔlɛkt(ə)] *nf* collection; **faire une ~** to take up a collection

collecter [kɔlɛkte] *vt* to collect

collecteur [kɔlɛktœʀ] *nm* (*égout*) main sewer

collectif, -ive [kɔlɛktif, -iv] *adj* collective; (*visite, billet etc*) group *cpd* ▷ *nm*: **~ budgétaire** mini-budget (*Brit*), mid-term budget; **immeuble ~** block of flats

collection [kɔlɛksjɔ̃] *nf* collection; (*Édition*) series; **pièce de ~** collector's item; **faire (la) ~ de** to collect; **(toute) une ~ de ...** (*fig*) a (complete) set of ...

collectionner [kɔlɛksjɔne] *vt* (*tableaux, timbres*) to collect

collectionneur, -euse [kɔlɛksjɔnœʀ, -øz] *nm/f* collector

collectivement [kɔlɛktivmɑ̃] *adv* collectively

collectiviser [kɔlɛktivize] *vt* to collectivize

collectivisme [kɔlɛktivism(ə)] *nm* collectivism

collectiviste [kɔlɛktivist(ə)] *adj* collectivist

collectivité [kɔlɛktivite] *nf* group; **la ~** the community, the collectivity; **les ~s locales** local authorities

collège [kɔlɛʒ] *nm* (*école*) (secondary) school; *see note*; (*assemblée*) body; **~ électoral** electoral college

COLLÈGE

A *collège* is a state secondary school for children between 11 and 15 years of age. Pupils follow a national curriculum which prescribes a common core along with several options. Schools are free to arrange their own timetable and choose their own teaching methods. Before leaving this phase of their education, students are assessed by examination and course work for their "brevet des collèges".

collégial, e, -aux [kɔleʒjal, -o] *adj* collegiate

collégien, ne [kɔleʒjɛ̃, -ɛn] *nm/f* secondary school pupil (*Brit*), high school student (*US*)

collègue [kɔlɛg] *nm/f* colleague

coller [kɔle] *vt* (*papier, timbre*) to stick (on); (*affiche*) to stick up; (*appuyer, placer contre*): **~ son front à la vitre** to press one's face to the window; (*enveloppe*) to stick down; (*morceaux*) to stick *ou* glue together; (*fam: mettre, fourrer*) to stick, shove; (*Scol fam*) to keep in, give detention to ▷ *vi* (*être collant*) to be sticky; (*adhérer*) to stick; **~ qch sur** to stick (*ou* paste *ou* glue) sth on(to); **~ à** to stick to; (*fig*) to cling to

collerette [kɔlʀɛt] *nf* ruff; (*Tech*) flange

collet [kɔlɛ] *nm* (*piège*) snare, noose; (*cou*): **prendre qn au ~** to grab sb by the throat; **~ monté** *adj inv* straight-laced

colleter [kɔlte] *vt* (*adversaire*) to collar, grab by the throat; **se ~ avec** to wrestle with

colleur [kɔlœʀ] *nm*: **~ d'affiches** bill-poster

collier [kɔlje] *nm* (*bijou*) necklace; (*de chien, Tech*) collar; **~ (de barbe), barbe en ~** narrow beard along the line of the jaw; **~ de serrage** choke collar

collimateur [kɔlimatœʀ] *nm*: **être dans le ~** (*fig*) to be in the firing line; **avoir qn/qch dans le ~** (*fig*) to have sb/sth in one's sights

colline [kɔlin] *nf* hill

collision [kɔlizjɔ̃] *nf* collision, crash; **entrer en ~ (avec)** to collide (with)

colloque [kɔlɔk] *nm* colloquium, symposium

collusion [kɔlyzjɔ̃] *nf* collusion

collutoire [kɔlytwaʀ] *nm* (*Méd*) oral medication; (*en bombe*) throat spray

collyre [kɔliʀ] *nm* (*Méd*) eye lotion

colmater [kɔlmate] *vt* (*fuite*) to seal off; (*brèche*) to plug, fill in

Cologne [kɔlɔɲ] *n* Cologne

colombage [kɔlɔ̃baʒ] *nm* half-timbering; **une maison à ~s** a half-timbered house

colombe [kɔlɔ̃b] *nf* dove

Colombie [kɔlɔ̃bi] *nf*: **la ~** Colombia

colombien, ne [kɔlɔ̃bjɛ̃, -ɛn] *adj* Colombian ▷ *nm/f*: **Colombien, ne** Colombian

colon [kɔlɔ̃] *nm* settler; (*enfant*) boarder (*in children's holiday camp*)

côlon [kolɔ̃] *nm* colon (*Méd*)

colonel [kɔlɔnɛl] *nm* colonel; (*de l'armée de l'air*) group captain

colonial, e, -aux [kɔlɔnjal, -o] *adj* colonial

colonialisme [kɔlɔnjalism(ə)] *nm* colonialism

colonialiste [kɔlɔnjalist(ə)] *adj, nm/f* colonialist

colonie [kɔlɔni] *nf* colony; **~ (de vacances)** holiday camp (*for children*)

colonisation [kɔlɔnizasjɔ̃] *nf* colonization

coloniser [kɔlɔnize] *vt* to colonize

colonnade [kɔlɔnad] *nf* colonnade

colonne [kɔlɔn] *nf* column; **se mettre en ~ par deux/quatre** to get into twos/fours; **en ~ par deux** in double file; **~ de secours** rescue party; **~ (vertébrale)** spine, spinal column

colonnette [kɔlɔnɛt] *nf* small column

colophane [kɔlɔfan] *nf* rosin

colorant [kɔlɔʀɑ̃] *nm* colo(u)ring

coloration [kɔlɔʀasjɔ̃] *nf* colour(ing) (*Brit*), color(ing) (*US*); **se faire faire une ~** (*chez le coiffeur*) to have one's hair dyed

coloré, e [kɔlɔʀe] *adj* (*fig*) colo(u)rful

colorer [kɔlɔʀe] *vt* to colour (*Brit*), color (*US*); **se colorer** *vi* to turn red; to blush

coloriage [kɔlɔʀjaʒ] *nm* colo(u)ring

colorier [kɔlɔʀje] *vt* to colo(u)r (in); **album à ~** colouring book

coloris [kɔlɔʀi] *nm* colo(u)r, shade

coloriste [kɔlɔʀist(ə)] *nm/f* colo(u)rist

colossal, e, -aux [kɔlɔsal, -o] *adj* colossal, huge

colosse [kɔlɔs] *nm* giant

colostrum [kɔlɔstʀɔm] *nm* colostrum

colporter [kɔlpɔʀte] *vt* to peddle

colporteur, -euse [kɔlpɔʀtœʀ, -øz] *nm/f*

hawker, pedlar

colt [kɔlt] *nm* revolver, Colt®

coltiner [kɔltine] *vt* to lug about

colza [kɔlza] *nm* rape(seed)

coma [kɔma] *nm* coma; **être dans le ~** to be in a coma

comateux, -euse [kɔmatø, -øz] *adj* comatose

combat [kɔ̃ba] *vb voir* **combattre** ▷ *nm* fight; fighting *no pl*; **~ de boxe** boxing match; **~ de rues** street fighting *no pl*; **~ singulier** single combat

combatif, -ive [kɔ̃batif, -iv] *adj* with a lot of fight

combativité [kɔ̃bativite] *nf* fighting spirit

combattant [kɔ̃batɑ̃] *vb voir* **combattre** ▷ *nm* combatant; (*d'une rixe*) brawler; **ancien ~** war veteran

combattre [kɔ̃batR(ə)] *vi* to fight ▷ *vt* to fight; (*épidémie, ignorance*) to combat

combien [kɔ̃bjɛ̃] *adv* (*quantité*) how much; (*nombre*) how many; (*exclamatif*) how; **~ de** how much; how many; **~ de temps** how long, how much time; **c'est ~?, ça fait ~?** how much is it?; **~ coûte/pèse ceci?** how much does this cost/weigh?; **vous mesurez ~?** what size are you?; **ça fait ~ en largeur?** how wide is that?

combinaison [kɔ̃binɛzɔ̃] *nf* combination; (*astuce*) device, scheme; (*de femme*) slip; (*d'aviateur*) flying suit; (*d'homme-grenouille*) wetsuit; (*bleu de travail*) boilersuit (Brit), coveralls *pl* (US)

combine [kɔ̃bin] *nf* trick; (*péj*) scheme, fiddle (Brit)

combiné [kɔ̃bine] *nm* (*aussi:* **combiné téléphonique**) receiver; (*Ski*) combination (event); (*vêtement de femme*) corselet

combiner [kɔ̃bine] *vt* to combine; (*plan, horaire*) to work out, devise

comble [kɔ̃bl(ə)] *adj* (*salle*) packed (full) ▷ *nm* (*du bonheur, plaisir*) height; **combles** *nmpl* (*Constr*) attic *sg*, loft *sg*; **de fond en ~** from top to bottom; **pour ~ de malchance** to cap it all; **c'est le ~!** that beats everything!, that takes the biscuit! (Brit); **sous les ~s** in the attic

combler [kɔ̃ble] *vt* (*trou*) to fill in; (*besoin, lacune*) to fill; (*déficit*) to make good; (*satisfaire*) to gratify, fulfil (Brit), fulfill (US); **~ qn de joie** to fill sb with joy; **~ qn d'honneurs** to shower sb with honours

combustible [kɔ̃bystibl(ə)] *adj* combustible ▷ *nm* fuel

combustion [kɔ̃bystjɔ̃] *nf* combustion

COMECON [kɔmekɔn] *sigle m* Comecon

comédie [kɔmedi] *nf* comedy; (*fig*) playacting *no pl*; **jouer la ~** (*fig*) to put on an act; **la C~ française**; *see note*; **~ musicale** musical

● mainly performs in the Palais Royal in
● Paris, tending to concentrate on classical
● French drama.

comédien, ne [kɔmedjɛ̃, -ɛn] *nm/f* actor/actress; (*comique*) comedy actor/actress, comedian/comedienne; (*fig*) sham

comestible [kɔmɛstibl(ə)] *adj* edible; **comestibles** *nmpl* foods

comète [kɔmɛt] *nf* comet

comice [kɔmis] *nm*: **~ agricole** agricultural show

comique [kɔmik] *adj* (*drôle*) comical; (*Théât*) comic ▷ *nm* (*artiste*) comic, comedian; **le ~ de qch** the funny *ou* comical side of sth

comité [kɔmite] *nm* committee; **petit ~** select group; **~ directeur** management committee; **~ d'entreprise (CE)** works council; **~ des fêtes** festival committee

commandant [kɔmɑ̃dɑ̃] *nm* (*gén*) commander, commandant; (*Mil: grade*) major; (: *armée de l'air*) squadron leader; (*Navig*) captain; **~ (de bord)** (*Aviat*) captain

commande [kɔmɑ̃d] *nf* (*Comm*) order; (*Inform*) command; **commandes** *nfpl* (*Aviat etc*) controls; **passer une ~ (de)** to put in an order (for); **sur ~** to order; **~ à distance** remote control; **véhicule à double ~** vehicle with dual controls

commandement [kɔmɑ̃dmɑ̃] *nm* command; (*ordre*) command, order; (*Rel*) commandment

commander [kɔmɑ̃de] *vt* (*Comm*) to order; (*diriger, ordonner*) to command; **~ à** (*Mil*) to command; (*contrôler, maîtriser*) to have control over; **~ à qn de faire** to command *ou* order sb to do

commanditaire [kɔmɑ̃ditɛR] *nm* sleeping (Brit) *ou* silent (US) partner

commandite [kɔmɑ̃dit] *nf*: **(société en) ~** limited partnership

commanditer [kɔmɑ̃dite] *vt* (*Comm*) to finance, back; to commission

commando [kɔmɑ̃do] *nm* commando (squad)

⬤ **MOT-CLÉ**

comme [kɔm] *prép* **1** (*comparaison*) like; **tout comme son père** just like his father; **fort comme un bœuf** as strong as an ox; **joli comme tout** ever so pretty

2 (*manière*) like; **faites-le comme ça** do it like this, do it this way; **comme ça** *ou* **cela on n'aura pas d'ennuis** that way we won't have any problems; **comme ci, comme ça** so-so, middling; **comment ça va? — comme ça** how are things? — OK; **comme on dit** as they say

3 (*en tant que*) as a; **donner comme prix** to give as a prize; **travailler comme secrétaire** to work as a secretary

4: **comme quoi** (*d'où il s'ensuit que*) which shows that; **il a écrit une lettre comme quoi il ...** he's written a letter saying that ...

5: **comme il faut** *adv* properly

▷ *adj* (*correct*) proper, correct
▷ *conj* **1** (*ainsi que*) as; **elle écrit comme elle parle** she writes as she talks; **comme si** as if **2** (*au moment où, alors que*) as; **il est parti comme j'arrivais** he left as I arrived **3** (*parce que, puisque*) as, since; **comme il était en retard, il ...** as he was late, he ...
▷ *adv:* **comme il est fort/c'est bon!** he's so strong/it's so good!; **il est malin comme c'est pas permis** he's as smart as anything

commémoratif, -ive [kɔmemɔʀatif, -iv] *adj* commemorative; **un monument ~** a memorial
commémoration [kɔmemɔʀasjɔ̃] *nf* commemoration
commémorer [kɔmemɔʀe] *vt* to commemorate
commencement [kɔmɑ̃smɑ̃] *nm* beginning, start, commencement; **commencements** *nmpl* (*débuts*) beginnings
commencer [kɔmɑ̃se] *vt* to begin, start, commence ▷ *vi* to begin, start, commence; **~ à** *ou* **de faire** to begin *ou* start doing; **~ par qch** to begin with sth; **~ par faire qch** to begin by doing sth
commensal, e, -aux [kɔmɑ̃sal, -o] *nm/f* companion at table
comment [kɔmɑ̃] *adv* how; **~?** (*que dites-vous*) (I beg your) pardon?; **~!** what! ▷ *nm:* **le ~ et le pourquoi** the whys and wherefores; **et ~!** and how!; **~ donc!** of course!; **~ faire?** how will we do it?; **~ se fait-il que ...?** how is it that ...?
commentaire [kɔmɑ̃tɛʀ] *nm* comment; remark; **~ (de texte)** (*Scol*) commentary; **~ sur image** voice-over
commentateur, -trice [kɔmɑ̃tatœʀ, -tʀis] *nm/f* commentator
commenter [kɔmɑ̃te] *vt* (*jugement, événement*) to comment (up)on; (*Radio, TV: match, manifestation*) to cover, give a commentary on
commérages [kɔmeʀaʒ] *nmpl* gossip *sg*
commerçant, e [kɔmɛʀsɑ̃, -ɑ̃t] *adj* commercial; trading; (*rue*) shopping *cpd*; (*personne*) commercially shrewd ▷ *nm/f* shopkeeper, trader
commerce [kɔmɛʀs(ə)] *nm* (*activité*) trade, commerce; (*boutique*) business; **le petit ~** small shop owners *pl*, small traders *pl*; **faire ~ de** to trade in; (*fig: péj*) to trade on; **chambre de ~** Chamber of Commerce; **livres de ~** (account) books; **vendu dans le ~** sold in the shops; **vendu hors-~** sold directly to the public; **~ en** *ou* **de gros/détail** wholesale/retail trade; **~ électronique** e-commerce; **~ équitable** fair trade; **~ intérieur/extérieur** home/foreign trade
commercer [kɔmɛʀse] *vi:* **~ avec** to trade with
commercial, e, -aux [kɔmɛʀsjal, -o] *adj* commercial, trading; (*péj*) commercial ▷ *nm:* **les commerciaux** the commercial people
commercialisable [kɔmɛʀsjalizabl(ə)] *adj* marketable
commercialisation [kɔmɛʀsjalizasjɔ̃] *nf*

marketing
commercialiser [kɔmɛʀsjalize] *vt* to market
commère [kɔmɛʀ] *nf* gossip
commettant [kɔmetɑ̃] *vb voir* **commettre** ▷ *nm* (*Jur*) principal
commettre [kɔmɛtʀ(ə)] *vt* to commit; **se commettre** *vi* to compromise one's good name
commis¹ [kɔmi] *nm* (*de magasin*) (shop) assistant (*Brit*), sales clerk (*US*); (*de banque*) clerk; **~ voyageur** commercial traveller (*Brit*) *ou* traveler (*US*)
commis², e [kɔmi, -iz] *pp de* **commettre**
commisération [kɔmizeʀasjɔ̃] *nf* commiseration
commissaire [kɔmisɛʀ] *nm* (*de police*) ≈ (police) superintendent (*Brit*), ≈ (police) captain (*US*); (*de rencontre sportive etc*) steward; **~ du bord** (*Navig*) purser; **~ aux comptes** (*Admin*) auditor
commissaire-priseur [kɔmisɛʀpʀizœʀ] (*pl* **commissaires-priseurs**) *nm* (official) auctioneer
commissariat [kɔmisaʀja] *nm:* **~ (de police)** police station; (*Admin*) commissionership
commission [kɔmisjɔ̃] *nf* (*comité, pourcentage*) commission; (*message*) message; (*course*) errand; **commissions** *nfpl* (*achats*) shopping *sg*; **~ d'examen** examining board
commissionnaire [kɔmisjɔnɛʀ] *nm* delivery boy (*ou* man); messenger; (*Transports*) (forwarding) agent
commissure [kɔmisyʀ] *nf:* **les ~s des lèvres** the corners of the mouth
commode [kɔmɔd] *adj* (*pratique*) convenient, handy; (*facile*) easy; (*air, personne*) easy-going; (*personne*): **pas ~** awkward (to deal with) ▷ *nf* chest of drawers
commodité [kɔmɔdite] *nf* convenience
commotion [kɔmɔsjɔ̃] *nf:* **~ (cérébrale)** concussion
commotionné, e [kɔmɔsjɔne] *adj* shocked, shaken
commuer [kɔmɥe] *vt* to commute
commun, e [kɔmœ̃, -yn] *adj* common; (*pièce*) communal, shared; (*réunion, effort*) joint ▷ *nf* (*Admin*) commune, ≈ district; (: *urbaine*) ≈ borough; **communs** *nmpl* (*bâtiments*) outbuildings; **cela sort du ~** it's out of the ordinary; **le ~ des mortels** the common run of people; **sans ~e mesure** incomparable; **être ~ à** (*chose*) to be shared by; **en ~** (*faire*) jointly; **mettre en ~** to pool, share; **peu ~** unusual; **d'un ~ accord** of one accord, with one accord
communal, e, -aux [kɔmynal, -o] *adj* (*Admin*) of the commune, ≈ (district *ou* borough) council *cpd*
communard, e [kɔmynaʀ, -aʀd(ə)] *nm/f* (*Hist*) Communard; (*péj: communiste*) commie
communautaire [kɔmynotɛʀ] *adj* community *cpd*
communauté [kɔmynote] *nf* community; (*Jur*): **régime de la ~** communal estate settlement
commune [kɔmyn] *adj f, nf voir* **commun**

communément [kɔmynemɑ̃] *adv* commonly

Communes [kɔmyn] *nfpl* (*en Grande-Bretagne: parlement*) Commons

communiant, e [kɔmynjɑ̃, -ɑ̃t] *nm/f* communicant; **premier** ~ child taking his first communion

communicant, e [kɔmynikɑ̃, -ɑ̃t] *adj* communicating

communicatif, -ive [kɔmynikatif, -iv] *adj* (*personne*) communicative; (*rire*) infectious

communication [kɔmynikasjɔ̃] *nf* communication; ~ (**téléphonique**)(telephone) call; **avoir la** ~ (**avec**) to get *ou* be through (to); **vous avez la** ~ you're through; **donnez-moi la** ~ **avec** put me through to; **mettre qn en** ~ **avec qn** (*en contact*) to put sb in touch with sb; (*au téléphone*) to connect sb with sb; ~ **interurbaine** long-distance call; ~ **en PCV** reverse charge (Brit) *ou* collect (US) call; ~ **avec préavis** personal call

communier [kɔmynje] *vi* (*Rel*) to receive communion; (*fig*) to be united

communion [kɔmynjɔ̃] *nf* communion

communiqué [kɔmynike] *nm* communiqué; ~ **de presse** press release

communiquer [kɔmynike] *vt* (*nouvelle, dossier*) to pass on, convey; (*maladie*) to pass on; (*peur etc*) to communicate; (*chaleur, mouvement*) to transmit ▷ *vi* to communicate; ~ **avec** (*salle*) to communicate with; **se** ~ **à** (*se propager*) to spread to

communisme [kɔmynism(ə)] *nm* communism

communiste [kɔmynist(ə)] *adj, nm/f* communist

commutateur [kɔmytatœR] *nm* (*Élec*) (change-over) switch, commutator

commutation [kɔmytasjɔ̃] *nf* (*Inform*): ~ **de messages** message switching; ~ **de paquets** packet switching

Comores [kɔmɔR] *nfpl*: **les** (**îles**) ~ the Comoros (Islands)

comorien, ne [kɔmɔRjɛ̃, -ɛn] *adj* of *ou* from the Comoros

compact, e [kɔ̃pakt] *adj* dense; compact

compagne [kɔ̃paɲ] *nf* companion

compagnie [kɔ̃paɲi] *nf* (*firme, Mil*) company; (*groupe*) gathering; (*présence*): **la** ~ **de qn** sb's company; **homme/femme de** ~ escort; **tenir** ~ **à qn** to keep sb company; **fausser** ~ **à qn** to give sb the slip, slip *ou* sneak away from sb; **en** ~ **de** in the company of; **Dupont et** ~, **Dupont et Cie** Dupont and Company, Dupont and Co; ~ **aérienne** airline (company)

compagnon [kɔ̃paɲɔ̃] *nm* companion; (*autrefois: ouvrier*) craftsman; journeyman

comparable [kɔ̃paRabl(ə)] *adj*: ~ (**à**) comparable (to)

comparaison [kɔ̃paRɛzɔ̃] *nf* comparison; (*métaphore*) simile; **en** ~ (**de**) in comparison (with); **par** ~ (**à**) by comparison (with)

comparaître [kɔ̃paRɛtR(ə)] *vi*: ~ (**devant**) to appear (before)

comparatif, -ive [kɔ̃paRatif, -iv] *adj, nm* comparative

comparativement [kɔ̃paRativmɑ̃] *adv* comparatively; ~ **à** by comparison with

comparé, e [kɔ̃paRe] *adj*: **littérature** *etc* ~**e** comparative literature *etc*

comparer [kɔ̃paRe] *vt* to compare; ~ **qch/qn à** *ou* **et** (*pour choisir*) to compare sth/sb with *ou* and; (*pour établir une similitude*) to compare sth/sb to *ou* and

comparse [kɔ̃paRs(ə)] *nm/f* (*péj*) associate, stooge

compartiment [kɔ̃paRtimɑ̃] *nm* compartment

compartimenté, e [kɔ̃paRtimɑ̃te] *adj* partitioned; (*fig*) compartmentalized

comparu, e [kɔ̃paRy] *pp de* **comparaître**

comparution [kɔ̃paRysjɔ̃] *nf* appearance

compas [kɔ̃pa] *nm* (*Géom*) (pair of) compasses *pl*; (*Navig*) compass

compassé, e [kɔ̃pase] *adj* starchy, formal

compassion [kɔ̃pasjɔ̃] *nf* compassion

compatibilité [kɔ̃patibilite] *nf* compatibility

compatible [kɔ̃patibl(ə)] *adj*: ~ (**avec**) compatible (with)

compatir [kɔ̃patiR] *vi*: ~ (**à**) to sympathize (with)

compatissant, e [kɔ̃patisɑ̃, -ɑ̃t] *adj* sympathetic

compatriote [kɔ̃patRijɔt] *nm/f* compatriot, fellow countryman/woman

compensateur, -trice [kɔ̃pɑ̃satœR, -tRis] *adj* compensatory

compensation [kɔ̃pɑ̃sasjɔ̃] *nf* compensation; (*Banque*) clearing; **en** ~ in *ou* as compensation

compensé, e [kɔ̃pɑ̃se] *adj*: **semelle** ~**e** platform sole

compenser [kɔ̃pɑ̃se] *vt* to compensate for, make up for

compère [kɔ̃pɛR] *nm* accomplice; fellow musician *ou* comedian *etc*

compétence [kɔ̃petɑ̃s] *nf* competence

compétent, e [kɔ̃petɑ̃, -ɑ̃t] *adj* (*apte*) competent, capable; (*Jur*) competent

compétitif, -ive [kɔ̃petitif, -iv] *adj* competitive

compétition [kɔ̃petisjɔ̃] *nf* (*gén*) competition; (*Sport: épreuve*) event; **la** ~ competitive sport; **être en** ~ **avec** to be competing with; **la** ~ **automobile** motor racing

compétitivité [kɔ̃petitivite] *nf* competitiveness

compilateur [kɔ̃pilatœR] *nm* (*Inform*) compiler

compiler [kɔ̃pile] *vt* to compile

complainte [kɔ̃plɛ̃t] *nf* lament

complaire [kɔ̃plɛR]: **se complaire** *vi*: **se** ~ **dans/ parmi** to take pleasure in/in being among

complaisais *etc* [kɔ̃plɛzɛ] *vb voir* **complaire**

complaisamment [kɔ̃plɛzamɑ̃] *adv* kindly; complacently

complaisance [kɔ̃plɛzɑ̃s] *nf* kindness; (*péj*) indulgence; (: *fatuité*) complacency; **attestation de** ~ *certificate produced to oblige a patient etc*; **pavillon de** ~ flag of convenience

complaisant, e [kɔ̃plɛzɑ̃, -ɑ̃t] *vb voir* **complaire**

▷ *adj* (*aimable*) kind; obliging; (*péj*) accommodating; (: *fat*) complacent

complaît [kɔ̃plɛ] *vb voir* **complaire**

complément [kɔ̃plemɑ̃] *nm* complement; (*reste*) remainder; (*Ling*) complement; ~ **d'information** (*Admin*) supplementary *ou* further information; ~ **d'agent** agent; ~ **(d'objet) direct/indirect** direct/indirect object; ~ **(circonstanciel) de lieu/temps** adverbial phrase of place/time; ~ **de nom** possessive phrase

complémentaire [kɔ̃plemɑ̃tɛʀ] *adj* complementary; (*additionnel*) supplementary

complet, -ète [kɔ̃plɛ, -ɛt] *adj* complete; (*plein: hôtel etc*) full ▷ *nm* (*aussi:* **complet-veston**) suit; **au (grand)** ~ all together

complètement [kɔ̃plɛtmɑ̃] *adv* (*en entier*) completely; (*absolument: fou, faux etc*) absolutely; (*à fond: étudier etc*) fully, in depth

compléter [kɔ̃plete] *vt* (*porter à la quantité voulue*) to complete; (*augmenter*) to complement, supplement; to add to; **se compléter** *vi* (*personnes*) to complement one another; (*collection etc*) to become complete

complexe [kɔ̃plɛks(ə)] *adj* complex ▷ *nm* (*Psych*) complex, hang-up; (*bâtiments*): ~ **hospitalier/industriel** hospital/industrial complex

complexé, e [kɔ̃plɛkse] *adj* mixed-up, hung-up

complexité [kɔ̃plɛksite] *nf* complexity

complication [kɔ̃plikasjɔ̃] *nf* complexity, intricacy; (*difficulté, ennui*) complication; **complications** *nfpl* (*Méd*) complications

complice [kɔ̃plis] *nm* accomplice

complicité [kɔ̃plisite] *nf* complicity

compliment [kɔ̃plimɑ̃] *nm* (*louange*) compliment; **compliments** *nmpl* (*félicitations*) congratulations

complimenter [kɔ̃plimɑ̃te] *vt*: ~ **qn (sur** *ou* **de)** to congratulate *ou* compliment sb (on)

compliqué, e [kɔ̃plike] *adj* complicated, complex, intricate; (*personne*) complicated

compliquer [kɔ̃plike] *vt* to complicate; **se compliquer** *vi* (*situation*) to become complicated; **se ~ la vie** to make life difficult *ou* complicated for o.s

complot [kɔ̃plo] *nm* plot

comploter [kɔ̃plɔte] *vi, vt* to plot

complu, e [kɔ̃ply] *pp de* **complaire**

comportement [kɔ̃pɔʀtəmɑ̃] *nm* behaviour (*Brit*), behavior (*US*); (*Tech: d'une pièce, d'un véhicule*) behavio(u)r, performance

comporter [kɔ̃pɔʀte] *vt* to be composed of, consist of, comprise; (*être équipé de*) to have; (*impliquer*) to entail, involve; **se comporter** *vi* to behave; (*Tech*) to behave, perform

composant [kɔ̃pozɑ̃] *nm* component, constituent

composante [kɔ̃pozɑ̃t] *nf* component

composé, e [kɔ̃poze] *adj* (*visage, air*) studied; (*Bio, Chimie, Ling*) compound ▷ *nm* (*Chimie, Ling*) compound; ~ **de** made up of

composer [kɔ̃poze] *vt* (*musique, texte*) to compose; (*mélange, équipe*) to make up; (*faire partie de*) to make up, form; (*Typo*) to (type)set ▷ *vi* (*Scol*) to sit *ou* do a test; (*transiger*) to come to terms; **se ~ de** to be composed of, be made up of; ~ **un numéro** (*au téléphone*) to dial a number

composite [kɔ̃pozit] *adj* heterogeneous

compositeur, -trice [kɔ̃pozitœʀ, -tʀis] *nm/f* (*Mus*) composer; (*Typo*) compositor, typesetter

composition [kɔ̃pozisjɔ̃] *nf* composition; (*Scol*) test; (*Typo*) (type)setting, composition; **de bonne ~** (*accommodant*) easy to deal with; **amener qn à ~** to get sb to come to terms; ~ **française** (*Scol*) French essay

compost [kɔ̃pɔst] *nm* compost

composter [kɔ̃pɔste] *vt* to date-stamp; to punch

composteur [kɔ̃pɔstœʀ] *nm* date stamp; punch; (*Typo*) composing stick

compote [kɔ̃pɔt] *nf* stewed fruit *no pl*; ~ **de pommes** stewed apples

compotier [kɔ̃pɔtje] *nm* fruit dish *ou* bowl

compréhensible [kɔ̃pʀeɑ̃sibl(ə)] *adj* comprehensible; (*attitude*) understandable

compréhensif, -ive [kɔ̃pʀeɑ̃sif, -iv] *adj* understanding

compréhension [kɔ̃pʀeɑ̃sjɔ̃] *nf* understanding; comprehension

comprendre [kɔ̃pʀɑ̃dʀ(ə)] *vt* to understand; (*se composer de*) to comprise, consist of; (*inclure*) to include; **se faire ~** to make o.s. understood; to get one's ideas across; **mal ~** to misunderstand

compresse [kɔ̃pʀɛs] *nf* compress

compresser [kɔ̃pʀese] *vt* to squash in, crush together; (*Inform*) to zip

compresseur [kɔ̃pʀesœʀ] *adj m voir* **rouleau**

compressible [kɔ̃pʀesibl(ə)] *adj* (*Physique*) compressible; (*dépenses*) reducible

compression [kɔ̃pʀesjɔ̃] *nf* compression; (*d'un crédit etc*) reduction

comprimé, e [kɔ̃pʀime] *adj*: **air ~** compressed air ▷ *nm* tablet

comprimer [kɔ̃pʀime] *vt* to compress; (*fig: crédit etc*) to reduce, cut down

compris, e [kɔ̃pʀi, -iz] *pp de* **comprendre** ▷ *adj* (*inclus*) included; ~? understood?, is that clear?; ~ **entre** (*situé*) contained between; **la maison ~e/non ~e, y/non ~ la maison** including/excluding the house; **service ~** service (charge) included; **100 euros tout ~** 100 euros all inclusive *ou* all-in

compromettant, e [kɔ̃pʀɔmetɑ̃, -ɑ̃t] *adj* compromising

compromettre [kɔ̃pʀɔmetʀ(ə)] *vt* to compromise

compromis [kɔ̃pʀɔmi] *vb voir* **compromettre** ▷ *nm* compromise

compromission [kɔ̃pʀɔmisjɔ̃] *nf* compromise, deal

comptabiliser [kɔ̃tabilize] *vt* (*valeur*) to post; (*fig*) to evaluate

comptabilité [kɔ̃tabilite] *nf* (*activité, technique*) accounting, accountancy; (*d'une société: comptes*) accounts *pl*, books *pl*; (: *service*) accounts office *ou* department; **~ à partie double** double-entry book-keeping

comptable [kɔ̃tabl(ə)] *nm/f* accountant ▷ *adj* accounts *cpd*, accounting

comptant [kɔ̃tɑ̃] *adv*: **payer ~** to pay cash; **acheter ~** to buy for cash

compte [kɔ̃t] *nm* count, counting; (*total, montant*) count, (right) number; (*bancaire, facture*) account; **comptes** *nmpl* accounts, books; (*fig*) explanation *sg*; **ouvrir un ~** to open an account; **rendre des ~s à qn** (*fig*) to be answerable to sb; **faire le ~ de** to count up, make a count of; **tout ~ fait** on the whole; **à ce ~-là** (*dans ce cas*) in that case; (*à ce train-là*) at that rate; **en fin de ~** (*fig*) all things considered, weighing it all up; **au bout du ~** in the final analysis; **à bon ~** at a favourable price; (*fig*) lightly; **avoir son ~** (*fig: fam*) to have had it; **pour le ~ de** on behalf of; **pour son propre ~** for one's own benefit; **sur le ~ de qn** (*à son sujet*) about sb; **travailler à son ~** to work for oneself; **mettre qch sur le ~ de qn** (*le rendre responsable*) to attribute sth to sb; **prendre qch à son ~** to take responsibility for sth; **trouver son ~ à qch** to do well out of sth; **régler un ~** (*s'acquitter de qch*) to settle an account; (*se venger*) to get one's own back; **rendre ~ (à qn) de qch** to give (sb) an account of sth; **tenir ~ de qch** to take sth into account; **~ tenu de** taking into account; **~ en banque** bank account; **~ chèque(s)** current account; **~ chèque postal (CCP)** Post Office account; **~ client** (*sur bilan*) accounts receivable; **~ courant (CC)** current account; **~ de dépôt** deposit account; **~ d'exploitation** operating account; **~ fournisseur** (*sur bilan*) accounts payable; **~ à rebours** countdown; **~ rendu** account, report; (*de film, livre*) review; *voir aussi* **rendre**

compte-gouttes [kɔ̃tgut] *nm inv* dropper

compter [kɔ̃te] *vt* to count; (*facturer*) to charge for; (*avoir à son actif, comporter*) to have; (*prévoir*) to allow, reckon; (*tenir compte de, inclure*) to include; (*penser, espérer*): **~ réussir/revenir** to expect to succeed/return ▷ *vi* to count; (*être économe*) to economize; (*être non négligeable*) to count, matter; (*valoir*): **~ pour** to count for; (*figurer*): **~ parmi** to be *ou* rank among; **~ sur** to count (up)on; **~ avec qch/qn** to reckon with *ou* take account of sth/sb; **~ sans qch/qn** to reckon without sth/sb; **sans ~ que** besides which; **à ~ du 10 janvier** (*Comm*) (as) from 10th January

compte-tours [kɔ̃ttuʀ] *nm inv* rev(olution) counter

compteur [kɔ̃tœʀ] *nm* meter; **~ de vitesse** speedometer

comptine [kɔ̃tin] *nf* nursery rhyme

comptoir [kɔ̃twaʀ] *nm* (*de magasin*) counter; (*de café*) counter, bar; (*colonial*) trading post

compulser [kɔ̃pylse] *vt* to consult

comte, comtesse [kɔ̃t, kɔ̃tɛs] *nm/f* count/countess

con, ne [kɔ̃, kɔn] *adj* (*fam!*) bloody (*Brit*) *ou* damned stupid (!)

concasser [kɔ̃kase] *vt* (*pierre, sucre*) to crush; (*poivre*) to grind

concave [kɔ̃kav] *adj* concave

concéder [kɔ̃sede] *vt* to grant; (*défaite, point*) to concede; **~ que** to concede that

concentration [kɔ̃sɑ̃tʀasjɔ̃] *nf* concentration

concentrationnaire [kɔ̃sɑ̃tʀasjɔnɛʀ] *adj* of *ou* in concentration camps

concentré [kɔ̃sɑ̃tʀe] *nm* concentrate; **~ de tomates** tomato purée

concentrer [kɔ̃sɑ̃tʀe] *vt* to concentrate; **se concentrer** to concentrate

concentrique [kɔ̃sɑ̃tʀik] *adj* concentric

concept [kɔ̃sɛpt] *nm* concept

concepteur, -trice [kɔ̃sɛptœʀ, -tʀis] *nm/f* designer

conception [kɔ̃sɛpsjɔ̃] *nf* conception; (*d'une machine etc*) design

concernant [kɔ̃sɛʀnɑ̃] *prép* (*se rapportant à*) concerning; (*en ce qui concerne*) as regards

concerner [kɔ̃sɛʀne] *vt* to concern; **en ce qui me concerne** as far as I am concerned; **en ce qui concerne ceci** as far as this is concerned, with regard to this

concert [kɔ̃sɛʀ] *nm* concert; **de ~** *adv* in unison; together

concertation [kɔ̃sɛʀtasjɔ̃] *nf* (*échange de vues*) dialogue; (*rencontre*) meeting

concerter [kɔ̃sɛʀte] *vt* to devise; **se concerter** *vi* (*collaborateurs etc*) to put our (*ou* their *etc*) heads together, consult (each other)

concertiste [kɔ̃sɛʀtist(ə)] *nm/f* concert artist

concerto [kɔ̃sɛʀto] *nm* concerto

concession [kɔ̃sesjɔ̃] *nf* concession

concessionnaire [kɔ̃sesjɔnɛʀ] *nm/f* agent, dealer

concevable [kɔ̃svabl(ə)] *adj* conceivable

concevoir [kɔ̃svwaʀ] *vt* (*idée, projet*) to conceive (of); (*méthode, plan d'appartement, décoration etc*) to plan, design; (*enfant*) to conceive; **maison bien/mal conçue** well-/badly-designed *ou* -planned house

concierge [kɔ̃sjɛʀʒ(ə)] *nm/f* caretaker; (*d'hôtel*) head porter

conciergerie [kɔ̃sjɛʀʒəʀi] *nf* caretaker's lodge

concile [kɔ̃sil] *nm* council, synod

conciliable [kɔ̃siljabl(ə)] *adj* (*opinions etc*) reconcilable

conciliabules [kɔ̃siljabyl] *nmpl* (private) discussions, confabulations (*Brit*)

conciliant, e [kɔ̃siljɑ̃, -ɑ̃t] *adj* conciliatory

conciliateur, -trice [kɔ̃siljatœʀ, -tʀis] *nm/f* mediator, go-between

conciliation [kɔ̃siljasjɔ̃] *nf* conciliation

concilier [kɔ̃silje] *vt* to reconcile; **se concilier qn/l'appui de qn** to win sb over/sb's support

concis, e [kɔ̃si, -iz] *adj* concise

concision [kɔ̃sizjɔ̃] *nf* concision, conciseness

concitoyen, ne [kɔ̃sitwajɛ̃, -ɛn] *nm/f* fellow citizen

conclave [kɔ̃klav] *nm* conclave
concluant, e [kɔ̃klyɑ̃, -ɑ̃t] *vb voir* **conclure** ▷ *adj* conclusive
conclure [kɔ̃klyʀ] *vt* to conclude; (*signer: accord, pacte*) to enter into; (*déduire*): ~ **qch de qch** to deduce sth from sth; ~ **à l'acquittement** to decide in favour of an acquittal; ~ **au suicide** to come to the conclusion (*ou* (Jur) to pronounce) that it is a case of suicide; ~ **un marché** to clinch a deal; **j'en conclus que** from that I conclude that
conclusion [kɔ̃klyzjɔ̃] *nf* conclusion; **conclusions** *nfpl* (*Jur*) submissions; findings; **en** ~ in conclusion
concocter [kɔ̃kɔkte] *vt* to concoct
conçois [kɔ̃swa], **conçoive** *etc* [kɔ̃swav] *vb voir* **concevoir**
concombre [kɔ̃kɔ̃bʀ(ə)] *nm* cucumber
concomitant, e [kɔ̃kɔmitɑ̃, -ɑ̃t] *adj* concomitant
concordance [kɔ̃kɔʀdɑ̃s] *nf* concordance; **la ~ des temps** (*Ling*) the sequence of tenses
concordant, e [kɔ̃kɔʀdɑ̃, -ɑ̃t] *adj* (*témoignages, versions*) corroborating
concorde [kɔ̃kɔʀd(ə)] *nf* concord
concorder [kɔ̃kɔʀde] *vi* to tally, agree
concourir [kɔ̃kuʀiʀ] *vi* (*Sport*) to compete; ~ **à** *vt* (*effet etc*) to work towards
concours [kɔ̃kuʀ] *vb voir* **concourir** ▷ *nm* competition; (*Scol*) competitive examination; (*assistance*) aid, help; **recrutement par voie de** ~ recruitment by (competitive) examination; **apporter son** ~ **à** to give one's support to; ~ **de circonstances** combination of circumstances; ~ **hippique** horse show; *voir* **hors-concours**
concret, -ète [kɔ̃kʀɛ, -ɛt] *adj* concrete
concrètement [kɔ̃kʀɛtmɑ̃] *adv* in concrete terms
concrétisation [kɔ̃kʀetizasjɔ̃] *nf* realization
concrétiser [kɔ̃kʀetize] *vt* to realize; **se concrétiser** *vi* to materialize
conçu, e [kɔ̃sy] *pp de* **concevoir**
concubin, e [kɔ̃kybɛ̃, -in] *nm/f* (*Jur*) cohabitant
concubinage [kɔ̃kybinaʒ] *nm* (*Jur*) cohabitation
concupiscence [kɔ̃kypisɑ̃s] *nf* concupiscence
concurremment [kɔ̃kyʀamɑ̃] *adv* concurrently; jointly
concurrence [kɔ̃kyʀɑ̃s] *nf* competition; **jusqu'à ~ de** up to; ~ **déloyale** unfair competition
concurrencer [kɔ̃kyʀɑ̃se] *vt* to compete with; **ils nous concurrencent dangereusement** they are a serious threat to us
concurrent, e [kɔ̃kyʀɑ̃, -ɑ̃t] *adj* competing ▷ *nm/f* (*Sport, Écon etc*) competitor; (*Scol*) candidate
concurrentiel, le [kɔ̃kyʀɑ̃sjɛl] *adj* competitive
conçus [kɔ̃sy] *vb voir* **concevoir**
condamnable [kɔ̃danabl(ə)] *adj* (*action, opinion*) reprehensible
condamnation [kɔ̃danasjɔ̃] *nf* (*action*) condemnation; sentencing; (*peine*) sentence;

conviction; ~ **à mort** death sentence
condamné, e [kɔ̃dane] *nm/f* (*Jur*) convict
condamner [kɔ̃dane] *vt* (*blâmer*) to condemn; (*Jur*) to sentence; (*porte, ouverture*) to fill in, block up; (*malade*) to give up (hope for); (*obliger*): ~ **qn à qch/à faire** to condemn sb to sth/to do; ~ **qn à deux ans de prison** to sentence sb to two years' imprisonment; ~ **qn à une amende** to impose a fine on sb
condensateur [kɔ̃dɑ̃satœʀ] *nm* condenser
condensation [kɔ̃dɑ̃sasjɔ̃] *nf* condensation
condensé [kɔ̃dɑ̃se] *nm* digest
condenser [kɔ̃dɑ̃se]: **se condenser** *vi* to condense
condescendance [kɔ̃desɑ̃dɑ̃s] *nf* condescension
condescendant, e [kɔ̃desɑ̃dɑ̃, -ɑ̃t] *adj* (*personne, attitude*) condescending
condescendre [kɔ̃desɑ̃dʀ(ə)] *vi*: ~ **à** to condescend to
condiment [kɔ̃dimɑ̃] *nm* condiment
condisciple [kɔ̃disipl(ə)] *nm/f* school fellow, fellow student
condition [kɔ̃disjɔ̃] *nf* condition; **conditions** *nfpl* (*tarif, prix*) terms; (*circonstances*) conditions; **sans** ~ *adj* unconditional ▷ *adv* unconditionally; **sous** ~ **que** on condition that; **à** ~ **de** *ou* **que** provided that; **en bonne** ~ in good condition; **mettre en** ~ (*Sport etc*) to get fit; (*Psych*) to condition (mentally); ~**s de vie** living conditions
conditionnel, le [kɔ̃disjɔnɛl] *adj* conditional ▷ *nm* conditional (tense)
conditionnement [kɔ̃disjɔnmɑ̃] *nm* (*emballage*) packaging; (*fig*) conditioning
conditionner [kɔ̃disjɔne] *vt* (*déterminer*) to determine; (*Comm: produit*) to package; (*fig: personne*) to condition; **air conditionné** air conditioning; **réflexe conditionné** conditioned reflex
condoléances [kɔ̃dɔleɑ̃s] *nfpl* condolences
conducteur, -trice [kɔ̃dyktœʀ, -tʀis] *adj* (*Élec*) conducting ▷ *nm/f* (*Auto etc*) driver; (*d'une machine*) operator ▷ *nm* (*Élec etc*) conductor
conduire [kɔ̃dɥiʀ] *vt* (*véhicule, passager*) to drive; (*délégation, troupeau*) to lead; **se conduire** *vi* to behave; ~ **vers/à** to lead towards/to; ~ **qn quelque part** to take sb somewhere; to drive sb somewhere
conduit, e [kɔ̃dɥi, -it] *pp de* **conduire** ▷ *nm* (*Tech*) conduit, pipe; (*Anat*) duct, canal
conduite [kɔ̃dɥit] *nf* (*en auto*) driving; (*comportement*) behaviour (*Brit*), behavior (*US*); (*d'eau, de gaz*) pipe; **sous la** ~ **de** led by; ~ **forcée** pressure pipe; ~ **à gauche** left-hand drive; ~ **intérieure** saloon (car)
cône [kon] *nm* cone; **en forme de** ~ cone-shaped
conf. *abr* = **confort**; **tt** ~ all mod cons (*Brit*)
confection [kɔ̃fɛksjɔ̃] *nf* (*fabrication*) making; (*Couture*): **la** ~ the clothing industry, the rag trade (*fam*); **vêtement de** ~ ready-to-wear *ou*

off-the-peg garment

confectionner [kɔ̃fɛksjɔne] vt to make

confédération [kɔ̃federasjɔ̃] nf confederation

conférence [kɔ̃ferɑ̃s] nf (exposé) lecture; (pourparlers) conference; ~ **de presse** press conference; ~ **au sommet** summit (conference)

conférencier, -ière [kɔ̃ferɑ̃sje, -jɛr] nm/f lecturer

conférer [kɔ̃fere] vt: ~ **à qn** (titre, grade) to confer on sb; ~ **à qch/qn** (aspect etc) to endow sth/sb with, give (to) sth/sb

confesser [kɔ̃fese] vt to confess; **se confesser** vi (Rel) to go to confession

confesseur [kɔ̃fesœr] nm confessor

confession [kɔ̃fesjɔ̃] nf confession; (culte: catholique etc) denomination

confessionnal, -aux [kɔ̃fesjɔnal, -o] nm confessional

confessionnel, le [kɔ̃fesjɔnɛl] adj denominational

confetti [kɔ̃feti] nm confetti no pl

confiance [kɔ̃fjɑ̃s] nf confidence, trust; faith; **avoir ~ en** to have confidence ou faith in, trust; **faire ~ à** to trust; **en toute ~** with complete confidence; **de ~** trustworthy, reliable; **mettre qn en ~** to win sb's trust; **vote de ~** (Pol) vote of confidence; **inspirer ~ à** to inspire confidence in; ~ **en soi** self-confidence; voir **question**

confiant, e [kɔ̃fjɑ̃, -ɑ̃t] adj confident; trusting

confidence [kɔ̃fidɑ̃s] nf confidence

confident, e [kɔ̃fidɑ̃, -ɑ̃t] nm/f confidant/ confidante

confidentiel, le [kɔ̃fidɑ̃sjɛl] adj confidential

confidentiellement [kɔfidɑ̃sjɛlmɑ̃] adv in confidence, confidentially

confier [kɔ̃fje] vt: ~ **à qn** (objet en dépôt, travail etc) to entrust to sb; (secret, pensée) to confide to sb; **se confier à qn** to confide in sb

configuration [kɔ̃figyrasjɔ̃] nf configuration, layout; (Inform) configuration

configurer [kɔ̃figyre] vt to configure

confiné, e [kɔ̃fine] adj enclosed; (air) stale

confiner [kɔ̃fine] vt: ~ **à** to confine to; (toucher) to border on; **se ~ dans** ou **à** to confine o.s. to

confins [kɔ̃fɛ̃] nmpl: **aux ~ de** on the borders of

confirmation [kɔ̃firmasjɔ̃] nf confirmation

confirmer [kɔ̃firme] vt to confirm; ~ **qn dans une croyance/ses fonctions** to strengthen sb in a belief/his duties

confiscation [kɔ̃fiskasjɔ̃] nf confiscation

confiserie [kɔ̃fizri] nf (magasin) confectioner's ou sweet shop (Brit), candy store (US); **confiseries** nfpl (bonbons) confectionery sg, sweets, candy no pl

confiseur, -euse [kɔ̃fizœr, -øz] nm/f confectioner

confisquer [kɔ̃fiske] vt to confiscate

confit, e [kɔ̃fi, -it] adj: **fruits ~s** crystallized fruits ▷ nm: ~ **d'oie** potted goose

confiture [kɔ̃fityr] nf jam; ~ **d'oranges** (orange) marmalade

conflagration [kɔ̃flagrasjɔ̃] nf cataclysm

conflictuel, le [kɔ̃fliktɥel] adj full of clashes ou conflicts

conflit [kɔ̃fli] nm conflict

confluent [kɔ̃flyɑ̃] nm confluence

confondre [kɔ̃fɔ̃dr(ə)] vt (jumeaux, faits) to confuse, mix up; (témoin, menteur) to confound; **se confondre** vi to merge; **se ~ en excuses** to offer profuse apologies, apologize profusely; ~ **qch/qn avec qch/qn d'autre** to mistake sth/sb for sth/sb else

confondu, e [kɔ̃fɔ̃dy] pp de **confondre** ▷ adj (stupéfait) speechless, overcome; **toutes catégories ~es** taking all categories together

conformation [kɔ̃fɔrmasjɔ̃] nf conformation

conforme [kɔ̃fɔrm(ə)] adj: ~ **à** (en accord avec) in accordance with, in keeping with; (identique à) true to; **copie certifiée ~** (Admin) certified copy; ~ **à la commande** as per order

conformé, e [kɔ̃fɔrme] adj: **bien ~** well-formed

conformément [kɔ̃fɔrmemɑ̃] adv: ~ **à** in accordance with

conformer [kɔ̃fɔrme] vt: ~ **qch à** to model sth on; **se ~ à** to conform to

conformisme [kɔ̃fɔrmism(ə)] nm conformity

conformiste [kɔ̃fɔrmist(ə)] adj, nm/f conformist

conformité [kɔ̃fɔrmite] nf conformity; agreement; **en ~ avec** in accordance with

confort [kɔ̃fɔr] nm comfort; **tout ~** (Comm) with all mod cons (Brit) ou modern conveniences

confortable [kɔ̃fɔrtabl(ə)] adj comfortable

confortablement [kɔ̃fɔrtabləmɑ̃] adv comfortably

conforter [kɔ̃fɔrte] vt to reinforce, strengthen

confrère [kɔ̃frɛr] nm colleague; fellow member

confrérie [kɔ̃freri] nf brotherhood

confrontation [kɔ̃frɔ̃tasjɔ̃] nf confrontation

confronté, e [kɔ̃frɔ̃te] adj: ~ **à** confronted by, facing

confronter [kɔ̃frɔ̃te] vt to confront; (textes) to compare, collate

confus, e [kɔ̃fy, -yz] adj (vague) confused; (embarrassé) embarrassed

confusément [kɔ̃fyzemɑ̃] adv (distinguer, ressentir) vaguely; (parler) confusedly

confusion [kɔ̃fyzjɔ̃] nf (voir confus) confusion; embarrassment; (voir confondre) confusion; mixing up; (erreur) confusion; ~ **des peines** (Jur) concurrency of sentences

congé [kɔ̃ʒe] nm (vacances) holiday; (arrêt de travail) time off no pl, leave no pl; (Mil) leave no pl; (avis de départ) notice; **en ~** on holiday; off (work); on leave; **semaine/jour de ~** week/day off; **prendre ~ de qn** to take one's leave of sb; **donner son ~ à** to hand ou give in one's notice to; ~ **de maladie** sick leave; ~ **de maternité** maternity leave; ~**s payés** paid holiday ou leave

congédier [kɔ̃ʒedje] vt to dismiss

congélateur [kɔ̃ʒelatœr] nm freezer, deep freeze

congélation [kɔ̃ʒelasjɔ̃] nf freezing; (de l'huile)

congealing

congeler [kɔ̃ʒle]: **se congeler** vi to freeze

congénère [kɔ̃ʒenɛʀ] nm/f fellow (bear ou lion etc), fellow creature

congénital, e, -aux [kɔ̃ʒenital, -o] adj congenital

congère [kɔ̃ʒɛʀ] nf snowdrift

congestion [kɔ̃ʒɛstjɔ̃] nf congestion; ~ **cérébrale** stroke; ~ **pulmonaire** congestion of the lungs

congestionner [kɔ̃ʒɛstjɔne] vt to congest; (Méd) to flush

conglomérat [kɔ̃ɡlɔmeʀa] nm conglomerate

Congo [kɔ̃go] nm: **le ~** (pays, fleuve) the Congo

congolais, e [kɔ̃ɡɔlɛ, -ɛz] adj Congolese ▷ nm/f: **Congolais, e** Congolese

congratuler [kɔ̃ɡʀatyle] vt to congratulate

congre [kɔ̃ɡʀ(ə)] nm conger (eel)

congrégation [kɔ̃ɡʀegasjɔ̃] nf (Rel) congregation; (gén) assembly; gathering

congrès [kɔ̃ɡʀɛ] nm congress

congressiste [kɔ̃ɡʀesist(ə)] nm/f delegate, participant (at a congress)

congru, e [kɔ̃ɡʀy] adj: **la portion ~e** the smallest ou meanest share

conifère [kɔnifɛʀ] nm conifer

conique [kɔnik] adj conical

conjecture [kɔ̃ʒɛktyʀ] nf conjecture, speculation no pl

conjecturer [kɔ̃ʒɛktyʀe] vt, vi to conjecture

conjoint, e [kɔ̃ʒwɛ̃, -wɛ̃t] adj joint ▷ nm/f spouse

conjointement [kɔ̃ʒwɛ̃tmɑ̃] adv jointly

conjonctif, -ive [kɔ̃ʒɔ̃ktif, -iv] adj: **tissu ~** connective tissue

conjonction [kɔ̃ʒɔ̃ksjɔ̃] nf (Ling) conjunction

conjonctivite [kɔ̃ʒɔ̃ktivit] nf conjunctivitis

conjoncture [kɔ̃ʒɔ̃ktyʀ] nf circumstances pl; **la ~ (économique)** the economic climate ou situation

conjoncturel, le [kɔ̃ʒɔ̃ktyʀɛl] adj: **variations/ tendances ~les** economic fluctuations/trends

conjugaison [kɔ̃ʒyɡɛzɔ̃] nf (Ling) conjugation

conjugal, e, -aux [kɔ̃ʒyɡal, -o] adj conjugal; married

conjugué, e [kɔ̃ʒyɡe] adj combined

conjuguer [kɔ̃ʒyɡe] vt (Ling) to conjugate; (efforts etc) to combine

conjuration [kɔ̃ʒyʀasjɔ̃] nf conspiracy

conjuré, e [kɔ̃ʒyʀe] nm/f conspirator

conjurer [kɔ̃ʒyʀe] vt (sort, maladie) to avert; (implorer): ~ **qn de faire qch** to beseech ou entreat sb to do sth

connais [kɔnɛ], **connaissais** etc [kɔnɛsɛ] vb voir **connaître**

connaissance [kɔnɛsɑ̃s] nf (savoir) knowledge no pl; (personne connue) acquaintance; (conscience) consciousness; **connaissances** nfpl knowledge no pl; **être sans ~** to be unconscious; **perdre/ reprendre ~** to lose/regain consciousness; **à ma/sa ~** to (the best of) my/his knowledge; **faire ~ avec qn** ou **la ~ de qn** (rencontrer) to meet

sb; (apprendre à connaître) to get to know sb; **avoir ~ de** to be aware of; **prendre ~ de** (document etc) to peruse; **en ~ de cause** with full knowledge of the facts; **de ~** (personne, visage) familiar

connaissant etc [kɔnɛsɑ̃] vb voir **connaître**

connaissement [kɔnɛsmɑ̃] nm bill of lading

connaisseur, -euse [kɔnɛsœʀ, -øz] nm/f connoisseur ▷ adj expert

connaître [kɔnɛtʀ(ə)] vt to know; (éprouver) to experience; (avoir) to have; to enjoy; ~ **de nom/ vue** to know by name/sight; **se connaître** vi to know each other; (soi-même) to know o.s.; **ils se sont connus à Genève** they (first) met in Geneva; **s'y ~ en qch** to know about sth

connasse [kɔnas] nf (fam!) stupid bitch (!) ou cow (!)

connecté, e [kɔnɛkte] adj (Inform) on line

connecter [kɔnɛkte] vt to connect; **se connecter à Internet** to log onto the internet

connerie [kɔnʀi] nf (fam) (bloody) stupid (Brit) ou damn-fool (US) thing to do ou say

connexe [kɔnɛks(ə)] adj closely related

connexion [kɔnɛksjɔ̃] nf connection

connivence [kɔnivɑ̃s] nf connivance

connotation [kɔnɔtasjɔ̃] nf connotation

connu, e [kɔny] pp de **connaître** ▷ adj (célèbre) well-known

conque [kɔ̃k] nf (coquille) conch (shell)

conquérant, e [kɔ̃keʀɑ̃, -ɑ̃t] nm/f conqueror

conquérir [kɔ̃keʀiʀ] vt to conquer, win

conquerrai etc [kɔ̃keʀʀe] vb voir **conquérir**

conquête [kɔ̃kɛt] nf conquest

conquière, conquiers etc [kɔ̃kjɛʀ] vb voir **conquérir**

conquis, e [kɔ̃ki, -iz] pp de **conquérir**

consacrer [kɔ̃sakʀe] vt (Rel): ~ **qch (à)** to consecrate sth (to); (fig: usage etc) to sanction, establish; (employer): ~ **qch à** to devote ou dedicate sth to; **se consacrer à qch/faire** to dedicate ou devote o.s. to sth/to doing

consanguin, e [kɔ̃sɑ̃ɡɛ̃, -in] adj between blood relations; **frère ~** half-brother (on father's side); **mariage ~** intermarriage

consciemment [kɔ̃sjamɑ̃] adv consciously

conscience [kɔ̃sjɑ̃s] nf conscience; (perception) consciousness; **avoir/prendre ~ de** to be/ become aware of; **perdre/reprendre ~** to lose/ regain consciousness; **avoir bonne/mauvaise ~** to have a clear/guilty conscience; **en (toute) ~** in all conscience

consciencieux, -euse [kɔ̃sjɑ̃sjø, -øz] adj conscientious

conscient, e [kɔ̃sjɑ̃, -ɑ̃t] adj conscious; ~ **de** aware ou conscious of

conscription [kɔ̃skʀipsjɔ̃] nf conscription

conscrit [kɔ̃skʀi] nm conscript

consécration [kɔ̃sekʀasjɔ̃] nf consecration

consécutif, -ive [kɔ̃sekytif, -iv] adj consecutive; ~ **à** following upon

consécutivement [kɔ̃sekytivmɑ̃] adv consecutively; ~ **à** following on

conseil [kɔ̃sɛj] nm (avis) piece of advice, advice no

pl; (*assemblée*) council; (*expert*): **~ en
recrutement** recruitment consultant ▷ *adj*:
ingénieur-~ engineering consultant; **tenir ~**
to hold a meeting; to deliberate; **donner un ~
ou des ~s à qn** to give sb (a piece of) advice;
demander ~ à qn to ask sb's advice; **prendre ~
(auprès de qn)** to take advice (from sb); **~
d'administration (CA)** board (of directors); **~
de classe** (*Scol*) *meeting of teachers, parents and class
representatives to discuss pupils' progress*; **~ de
discipline** disciplinary committee; **~ général**
regional council; *see note*; **~ de guerre** court-
martial; **le ~ des ministres** ≈ the Cabinet; **~
municipal (CM)** town council; **~ régional**
regional board of elected representatives; **~ de
révision** recruitment *ou* draft (US) board

● **CONSEIL GÉNÉRAL**

Each "département" of France is run by a
Conseil général, whose remit covers personnel,
transport infrastructure, housing, school
grants and economic development. The
council is made up of "conseillers
généraux", each of whom represents a
"canton" and is elected for a six-year term.
Half of the council's membership are
elected every three years.

conseiller[1] [kɔ̃seje] *vt* (*personne*) to advise;
(*méthode, action*) to recommend, advise; **~ qch à
qn** to recommend sth to sb; **~ à qn de faire qch**
to advise sb to do sth
conseiller[2]**, -ière** [kɔ̃seje, -ɛʀ] *nm/f* adviser; **~
général** regional councillor; **~ matrimonial**
marriage guidance counsellor; **~ municipal**
town councillor; **~ d'orientation** (*Scol*) careers
adviser (Brit), (school) counselor (US)
consensuel, le [kɔ̃sɑ̃sɥɛl] *adj* consensual
consensus [kɔ̃sɛ̃sys] *nm* consensus
consentement [kɔ̃sɑ̃tmɑ̃] *nm* consent
consentir [kɔ̃sɑ̃tiʀ] *vt*: **~ (à qch/faire)** to agree
ou consent (to sth/to doing); **~ qch à qn** to grant
sb sth
conséquence [kɔ̃sekɑ̃s] *nf* consequence,
outcome; **conséquences** *nfpl* consequences,
repercussions; **en ~** (*donc*) consequently; (*de
façon appropriée*) accordingly; **ne pas tirer à ~** to
be unlikely to have any repercussions; **sans ~**
unimportant; **de ~** important
conséquent, e [kɔ̃sekɑ̃, -ɑ̃t] *adj* logical,
rational; (*fam: important*) substantial; **par ~**
consequently
conservateur, -trice [kɔ̃sɛʀvatœʀ, -tʀis] *adj*
conservative ▷ *nm/f* (*Pol*) conservative; (*de
musée*) curator
conservation [kɔ̃sɛʀvasjɔ̃] *nf* retention;
keeping; preservation
conservatisme [kɔ̃sɛʀvatism(ə)] *nm*
conservatism
conservatoire [kɔ̃sɛʀvatwaʀ] *nm* academy;
(*Écologie*) conservation area

conserve [kɔ̃sɛʀv(ə)] *nf* (*gén pl*) canned *ou* tinned
(Brit) food; **~s de poisson** canned *ou* tinned (Brit)
fish; **en ~** canned, tinned (Brit); **de ~** (*ensemble*)
in concert; (*naviguer*) in convoy
conservé, e [kɔ̃sɛʀve] *adj*: **bien ~** (*personne*) well-
preserved
conserver [kɔ̃sɛʀve] *vt* (*faculté*) to retain, keep;
(*habitude*) to keep up; (*amis, livres*) to keep;
(*préserver, Culin*) to preserve; **se conserver** *vi*
(*aliments*) to keep; (*aussi*: **"conserver au frais"**)
"store in a cool place"
conserverie [kɔ̃sɛʀvəʀi] *nf* canning factory
considérable [kɔ̃sideʀabl(ə)] *adj* considerable,
significant, extensive
considération [kɔ̃sideʀasjɔ̃] *nf* consideration;
(*estime*) esteem, respect; **considérations** *nfpl*
(*remarques*) reflections; **prendre en ~** to take
into consideration *ou* account; **ceci mérite ~**
this is worth considering; **en ~ de** given,
because of
considéré, e [kɔ̃sideʀe] *adj* respected; **tout
bien ~** all things considered
considérer [kɔ̃sideʀe] *vt* to consider; (*regarder*)
to consider, study; **~ qch comme** to regard sth
as
consigne [kɔ̃siɲ] *nf* (*Comm*) deposit; (*de gare*) left
luggage (office) (Brit), checkroom (US); (*punition*:
Scol) detention; (: *Mil*) confinement to barracks;
(*ordre, instruction*) instructions *pl*; **~
automatique** left-luggage locker; **~s de
sécurité** safety instructions
consigné, e [kɔ̃siɲe] *adj* (*Comm: bouteille,
emballage*) returnable; **non ~** non-returnable
consigner [kɔ̃siɲe] *vt* (*note, pensée*) to record;
(*marchandises*) to deposit; (*punir: Mil*) to confine
to barracks; (: *élève*) to put in detention; (*Comm*)
to put a deposit on
consistance [kɔ̃sistɑ̃s] *nf* consistency
consistant, e [kɔ̃sistɑ̃, -ɑ̃t] *adj* thick; solid
consister [kɔ̃siste] *vi*: **~ en/dans/à faire** to
consist of/in/in doing
consœur [kɔ̃sœʀ] *nf* (lady) colleague; fellow
member
consolation [kɔ̃sɔlasjɔ̃] *nf* consolation *no pl*,
comfort *no pl*
console [kɔ̃sɔl] *nf* console; **~ graphique** *ou* **de
visualisation** (*Inform*) visual display unit, VDU;
~ de jeux games console
consoler [kɔ̃sɔle] *vt* to console; **se ~ (de qch)** to
console o.s. (for sth)
consolider [kɔ̃sɔlide] *vt* to strengthen,
reinforce; (*fig*) to consolidate; **bilan consolidé**
consolidated balance sheet
consommateur, -trice [kɔ̃sɔmatœʀ, -tʀis] *nm/f*
(*Écon*) consumer; (*dans un café*) customer
consommation [kɔ̃sɔmasjɔ̃] *nf* consumption;
(*Jur*) consummation; (*boisson*) drink; **~ aux 100
km** (*Auto*) (fuel) consumption per 100 km,
≈ miles per gallon (mpg), ≈ gas mileage (US); **de
~** (*biens, société*) consumer *cpd*
consommé, e [kɔ̃sɔme] *adj* consummate ▷ *nm*
consommé

consommer [kɔ̃sɔme] vt (personne) to eat ou drink, consume; (voiture, usine, poêle) to use, consume; (Jur) to consummate ▷ vi (dans un café) to (have a) drink

consonance [kɔ̃sɔnɑ̃s] nf consonance; **nom à ~ étrangère** foreign-sounding name

consonne [kɔ̃sɔn] nf consonant

consortium [kɔ̃sɔrsjɔm] nm consortium

consorts [kɔ̃sɔr] nmpl: **et ~** (péj) and company, and his bunch ou like

conspirateur, -trice [kɔ̃spiratœr, -tris] nm/f conspirator, plotter

conspiration [kɔ̃spirasjɔ̃] nf conspiracy

conspirer [kɔ̃spire] vi to conspire, plot; **~ à** (tendre à) to conspire to

conspuer [kɔ̃spɥe] vt to boo, shout down

constamment [kɔ̃stamɑ̃] adv constantly

constance [kɔ̃stɑ̃s] nf permanence, constancy; (d'une amitié) steadfastness; **travailler avec ~** to work steadily; **il faut de la ~ pour la supporter** (fam) you need a lot of patience to put up with her

constant, e [kɔ̃stɑ̃, -ɑ̃t] adj constant; (personne) steadfast ▷ nf constant

Constantinople [kɔ̃stɑ̃tinɔpl(ə)] n Constantinople

constat [kɔ̃sta] nm (d'huissier) certified report (by bailiff); (de police) report; (observation) (observed) fact, observation; (affirmation) statement; **~ (à l'amiable)** (jointly agreed) statement for insurance purposes

constatation [kɔ̃statasjɔ̃] nf noticing; certifying; (remarque) observation

constater [kɔ̃state] vt (remarquer) to note, notice; (Admin, Jur: attester) to certify; (dégâts) to note; **~ que** (dire) to state that

constellation [kɔ̃stelasjɔ̃] nf constellation

constellé, e [kɔ̃stele] adj: **~ de** (étoiles) studded ou spangled with; (taches) spotted with

consternant, e [kɔ̃stɛrnɑ̃ -ɑ̃t] adj (nouvelle) dismaying; (attristant, étonnant: bêtise) appalling

consternation [kɔ̃stɛrnasjɔ̃] nf consternation, dismay

consterner [kɔ̃stɛrne] vt to dismay

constipation [kɔ̃stipasjɔ̃] nf constipation

constipé, e [kɔ̃stipe] adj constipated; (fig) stiff

constituant, e [kɔ̃stitɥɑ̃, -ɑ̃t] adj (élément) constituent; **assemblée ~e** (Pol) constituent assembly

constitué, e [kɔ̃stitɥe] adj: **~ de** made up ou composed of; **bien ~** of sound constitution; well-formed

constituer [kɔ̃stitɥe] vt (comité, équipe) to set up, form; (dossier, collection) to put together, build up; (éléments, parties: composer) to make up, constitute; (représenter, être) to constitute; **se ~ prisonnier** to give o.s. up; **se ~ partie civile** to bring an independent action for damages

constitution [kɔ̃stitysjɔ̃] nf setting up; building up; (composition) composition, make-up; (santé, Pol) constitution

constitutionnel, le [kɔ̃stitysjɔnɛl] adj constitutional

constructeur [kɔ̃stryktœr] nm manufacturer, builder

constructif, -ive [kɔ̃stryktif, -iv] adj (positif) constructive

construction [kɔ̃stryksjɔ̃] nf construction, building

construire [kɔ̃strɥir] vt to build, construct; **se construire** vi: **l'immeuble s'est construit très vite** the building went up ou was built very quickly

consul [kɔ̃syl] nm consul

consulaire [kɔ̃sylɛr] adj consular

consulat [kɔ̃syla] nm consulate

consultant, e [kɔ̃syltɑ̃, -ɑ̃t] adj consultant

consultatif, -ive [kɔ̃syltatif, -iv] adj advisory

consultation [kɔ̃syltasjɔ̃] nf consultation; **consultations** nfpl (Pol) talks; **être en ~** (délibération) to be in consultation; (médecin) to be consulting; **aller à la ~** (Méd) to go to the surgery (Brit) ou doctor's office (US); **heures de ~** (Méd) surgery (Brit) ou office (US) hours

consulter [kɔ̃sylte] vt to consult ▷ vi (médecin) to hold surgery (Brit), be in (the office) (US); **se consulter** vi to confer

consumer [kɔ̃syme] vt to consume; **se consumer** vi to burn; **se ~ de chagrin/douleur** to be consumed with sorrow/grief

consumérisme [kɔ̃symerism(ə)] nm consumerism

contact [kɔ̃takt] nm contact; **au ~ de** (air, peau) on contact with; (gens) through contact with; **mettre/couper le ~** (Auto) to switch on/off the ignition; **entrer en ~** (fils, objets) to come into contact, make contact; **se mettre en ~ avec** (Radio) to make contact with; **prendre ~ avec** (relation d'affaires, connaissance) to get in touch ou contact with

contacter [kɔ̃takte] vt to contact, get in touch with

contagieux, -euse [kɔ̃taʒjø, -øz] adj contagious; infectious

contagion [kɔ̃taʒjɔ̃] nf contagion

container [kɔ̃tɛnɛr] nm container

contamination [kɔ̃taminasjɔ̃] nf infection; contamination

contaminer [kɔ̃tamine] vt (par un virus) to infect; (par des radiations) to contaminate

conte [kɔ̃t] nm tale; **~ de fées** fairy tale

contemplatif, -ive [kɔ̃tɑ̃platif, -iv] adj contemplative

contemplation [kɔ̃tɑ̃plasjɔ̃] nf contemplation; (Rel, Philosophie) meditation

contempler [kɔ̃tɑ̃ple] vt to contemplate, gaze at

contemporain, e [kɔ̃tɑ̃pɔrɛ̃, -ɛn] adj, nm/f contemporary

contenance [kɔ̃tnɑ̃s] nf (d'un récipient) capacity; (attitude) bearing, attitude; **perdre ~** to lose one's composure; **se donner une ~** to give the impression of composure; **faire bonne ~ (devant)** to put on a bold front (in the face of)

conteneur [kɔ̃tnœr] nm container; **~ (de**

bouteilles) bottle bank

conteneurisation [kɔ̃tnœʀizasjɔ̃] *nf*
containerization

contenir [kɔ̃tniʀ] *vt* to contain; *(avoir une capacité de)* to hold; **se contenir** *vi (se retenir)* to control o.s. *ou* one's emotions, contain o.s.

content, e [kɔ̃tã, -ãt] *adj* pleased, glad; ~ **de** pleased with; **je serais** ~ **que tu ...** I would be pleased if you ...

contentement [kɔ̃tãtmã] *nm* contentment, satisfaction

contenter [kɔ̃tãte] *vt* to satisfy, please; *(envie)* to satisfy; **se** ~ **de** to content o.s. with

contentieux [kɔ̃tãsjø] *nm (Comm)* litigation; *(: service)* litigation department; *(Pol etc)* contentious issues *pl*

contenu, e [kɔ̃tny] *pp de* **contenir** ▷ *nm (d'un bol)* contents *pl*; *(d'un texte)* content

conter [kɔ̃te] *vt* to recount, relate; **en** ~ **de belles à qn** to tell tall stories to sb

contestable [kɔ̃tɛstabl(ə)] *adj* questionable

contestataire [kɔ̃tɛstatɛʀ] *adj (journal, étudiant)* anti-establishment ▷ *nm/f* (anti-establishment) protester

contestation [kɔ̃tɛstasjɔ̃] *nf* questioning, contesting; *(Pol)*: **la** ~ anti-establishment activity, protest

conteste [kɔ̃tɛst(ə)]: **sans** ~ *adv* unquestionably, indisputably

contesté, e [kɔ̃tɛste] *adj (roman, écrivain)* controversial

contester [kɔ̃tɛste] *vt* to question, contest ▷ *vi (Pol: gén)* to protest, rebel (against established authority)

conteur, -euse [kɔ̃tœʀ, -øz] *nm/f* story-teller

contexte [kɔ̃tɛkst(ə)] *nm* context

contiendrai [kɔ̃tjɛ̃dʀe], **contiens** etc [kɔ̃tjɛ̃] *vb voir* **contenir**

contigu, ë [kɔ̃tigy] *adj*: ~ **(à)** adjacent (to)

continent [kɔ̃tinã] *nm* continent

continental, e, -aux [kɔ̃tinãtal, -o] *adj* continental

contingences [kɔ̃tɛ̃ʒãs] *nfpl* contingencies

contingent [kɔ̃tɛ̃ʒã] *nm (Mil)* contingent; *(Comm)* quota

contingenter [kɔ̃tɛ̃ʒãte] *vt (Comm)* to fix a quota on

contins etc [kɔ̃tɛ̃] *vb voir* **contenir**

continu, e [kɔ̃tiny] *adj* continuous; **(courant)** ~ direct current, DC

continuation [kɔ̃tinɥasjɔ̃] *nf* continuation

continuel, le [kɔ̃tinɥɛl] *adj (qui se répète)* constant, continual; *(continu)* continuous

continuellement [kɔ̃tinɥɛlmã] *adv* continually; continuously

continuer [kɔ̃tinɥe] *vt (travail, voyage etc)* to continue (with), carry on (with), go on with; *(prolonger: alignement, rue)* to continue ▷ *vi (pluie, vie, bruit)* to continue, go on; *(voyageur)* to go on; **se continuer** *vi* to carry on; ~ **à** *ou* **de faire** to go on *ou* continue doing

continuité [kɔ̃tinɥite] *nf* continuity;

continuation

contondant, e [kɔ̃tɔ̃dã, -ãt] *adj*: **arme** ~**e** blunt instrument

contorsion [kɔ̃tɔʀsjɔ̃] *nf* contortion

contorsionner [kɔ̃tɔʀsjɔne]: **se contorsionner** *vi* to contort o.s., writhe about

contorsionniste [kɔ̃tɔʀsjɔnist(ə)] *nm/f* contortionist

contour [kɔ̃tuʀ] *nm* outline, contour; **contours** *nmpl (d'une rivière etc)* windings

contourner [kɔ̃tuʀne] *vt* to bypass, walk *ou* drive) round

contraceptif, -ive [kɔ̃tʀasɛptif, -iv] *adj, nm* contraceptive

contraception [kɔ̃tʀasɛpsjɔ̃] *nf* contraception

contracté, e [kɔ̃tʀakte] *adj (muscle)* tense, contracted; *(personne: tendu)* tense, tensed up; **article** ~ *(Ling)* contracted article

contracter [kɔ̃tʀakte] *vt (muscle etc)* to tense, contract; *(maladie, dette, obligation)* to contract; *(assurance)* to take out; **se contracter** *vi (métal, muscles)* to contract

contraction [kɔ̃tʀaksjɔ̃] *nf* contraction

contractuel, le [kɔ̃tʀaktɥɛl] *adj* contractual ▷ *nm/f (agent)* traffic warden; *(employé)* contract employee

contradiction [kɔ̃tʀadiksjɔ̃] *nf* contradiction

contradictoire [kɔ̃tʀadiktwaʀ] *adj* contradictory, conflicting; **débat** ~ (open) debate

contraignant, e [kɔ̃tʀɛɲã, -ãt] *vb voir* **contraindre** ▷ *adj* restricting

contraindre [kɔ̃tʀɛ̃dʀ(ə)] *vt*: ~ **qn à faire** to force *ou* compel sb to do

contraint, e [kɔ̃tʀɛ̃, -ɛ̃t] *pp de* **contraindre** ▷ *adj (mine, air)* constrained, forced ▷ *nf* constraint; **sans** ~**e** unrestrainedly, unconstrainedly

contraire [kɔ̃tʀɛʀ] *adj, nm* opposite; ~ **à** contrary to; **au** ~ *adv* on the contrary

contrairement [kɔ̃tʀɛʀmã] *adv*: ~ **à** contrary to, unlike

contralto [kɔ̃tʀalto] *nm* contralto

contrariant, e [kɔ̃tʀaʀjã, -ãt] *adj (personne)* contrary, perverse; *(incident)* annoying

contrarier [kɔ̃tʀaʀje] *vt (personne)* to annoy, bother; *(fig)* to impede; to thwart, frustrate

contrariété [kɔ̃tʀaʀjete] *nf* annoyance

contraste [kɔ̃tʀast(ə)] *nm* contrast

contraster [kɔ̃tʀaste] *vt, vi* to contrast

contrat [kɔ̃tʀa] *nm* contract; *(fig: accord, pacte)* agreement; ~ **de travail** employment contract

contravention [kɔ̃tʀavãsjɔ̃] *nf (infraction)*: ~ **à** contravention of; *(amende)* fine; *(PV pour stationnement interdit)* parking ticket; **dresser** ~ **à** *(automobiliste)* to book; to write out a parking ticket for

contre [kɔ̃tʀ(ə)] *prép* against; *(en échange)* (in exchange) for; **par** ~ on the other hand

contre-amiral, -aux [kɔ̃tʀamiʀal, -o] *nm* rear admiral

contre-attaque [kɔ̃tʀatak] *nf* counterattack

contre-attaquer [kɔ̃tʀatake] *vi* to

counterattack

contre-balancer [kɔ̃tRəbalɑ̃se] vt to counterbalance; (fig) to offset

contrebande [kɔ̃tRəbɑ̃d] nf (trafic) contraband, smuggling; (marchandise) contraband, smuggled goods pl; **faire la ~ de** to smuggle

contrebandier, -ière [kɔ̃tRəbɑ̃dje, -jɛR] nm/f smuggler

contrebas [kɔ̃tRəba]: **en ~** adv (down) below

contrebasse [kɔ̃tRəbas] nf (double) bass

contrebassiste [kɔ̃tRəbasist(ə)] nm/f (double) bass player

contre-braquer [kɔ̃tRəbRake] vi to steer into a skid

contrecarrer [kɔ̃tRəkaRe] vt to thwart

contrechamp [kɔ̃tRəʃɑ̃] nm (Ciné) reverse shot

contrecœur [kɔ̃tRəkœR]: **à ~** adv (be)grudgingly, reluctantly

contrecoup [kɔ̃tRəku] nm repercussions pl; **par ~** as an indirect consequence

contre-courant [kɔ̃tRəkuRɑ̃]: **à ~** adv against the current

contredire [kɔ̃tRədiR] vt (personne) to contradict; (témoignage, assertion, faits) to refute; **se contredire** vi to contradict o.s.

contredit, e [kɔ̃tRədi, -it] pp de **contredire** ▷ nm: **sans ~** without question

contrée [kɔ̃tRe] nf region; land

contre-écrou [kɔ̃tRekRu] nm lock nut

contre-enquête [kɔ̃tRɑ̃kɛt] nf counter-inquiry

contre-espionnage [kɔ̃tRɛspjɔnaʒ] nm counter-espionage

contre-exemple [kɔ̃tRɛgzɑ̃pl(ə)] nf counter-example

contre-expertise [kɔ̃tRɛkspɛRtiz] nf second (expert) assessment

contrefaçon [kɔ̃tRəfasɔ̃] nf forgery; **~ de brevet** patent infringement

contrefaire [kɔ̃tRəfɛR] vt (document, signature) to forge, counterfeit; (personne, démarche) to mimic; (dénaturer: sa voix etc) to disguise

contrefait, e [kɔ̃tRəfɛ, -ɛt] pp de **contrefaire** ▷ adj misshapen, deformed

contrefasse [kɔ̃tRəfas], **contreferai** etc [kɔ̃tRəfRe] vb voir **contrefaire**

contre-filet [kɔ̃tRəfilɛ] nm (Culin) sirloin

contreforts [kɔ̃tRəfɔR] nmpl foothills

contre-haut [kɔ̃tRəo]: **en ~** adv (up) above

contre-indication [kɔ̃tRɛ̃dikasjɔ̃] nf contraindication

contre-indiqué, e [kɔ̃tRɛ̃dike] adj (Méd) contraindicated

contre-interrogatoire [kɔ̃tRɛ̃teRɔgatwaR] nm: **faire subir un ~ à qn** to cross-examine sb

contre-jour [kɔ̃tRəʒuR]: **à ~** adv against the light

contremaître [kɔ̃tRəmɛtR(ə)] nm foreman

contre-manifestant, e [kɔ̃tRəmanifɛstɑ̃, -ɑ̃t] nm/f counter-demonstrator

contre-manifestation [kɔ̃tRəmanifɛstasjɔ̃] nf counter-demonstration

contremarque [kɔ̃tRəmaRk(ə)] nf (ticket) pass-out ticket

contre-offensive [kɔ̃tRɔfɑ̃siv] nf counteroffensive

contre-ordre [kɔ̃tRɔRdR(ə)] nm = **contrordre**

contrepartie [kɔ̃tRəpaRti] nf compensation; **en ~** in compensation; in return

contre-performance [kɔ̃tRəpɛRfɔRmɑ̃s] nf below-average performance

contrepèterie [kɔ̃tRəpetRi] nf spoonerism

contre-pied [kɔ̃tRəpje] nm (inverse, opposé): **le ~ de ...** the exact opposite of ...; **prendre le ~ de** to take the opposing view of; to take the opposite course to; **prendre qn à ~** (Sport) to wrong-foot sb

contre-plaqué [kɔ̃tRəplake] nm plywood

contre-plongée [kɔ̃tRəplɔ̃ʒe] nf low-angle shot

contrepoids [kɔ̃tRəpwa] nm counterweight, counterbalance; **faire ~** to act as a counterbalance

contrepoil [kɔ̃tRəpwal]: **à ~** adv the wrong way

contrepoint [kɔ̃tRəpwɛ̃] nm counterpoint

contrepoison [kɔ̃tRəpwazɔ̃] nm antidote

contrer [kɔ̃tRe] vt to counter

contre-révolution [kɔ̃tRəRevɔlysjɔ̃] nf counter-revolution

contre-révolutionnaire [kɔ̃tRəRevɔlysjɔnɛR] nm/f counter-revolutionary

contresens [kɔ̃tRəsɑ̃s] nm misinterpretation; (mauvaise traduction) mistranslation; (absurdité) nonsense no pl; **à ~** adv the wrong way

contresigner [kɔ̃tRəsiɲe] vt to countersign

contretemps [kɔ̃tRətɑ̃] nm hitch, contretemps; **à ~** adv (Mus) out of time; (fig) at an inopportune moment

contre-terrorisme [kɔ̃tRəteRɔRism(ə)] nm counter-terrorism

contre-terroriste [kɔ̃tRəteRɔRist(ə)] nm/f counter-terrorist

contre-torpilleur [kɔ̃tRətɔRpijœR] nm destroyer

contrevenant, e [kɔ̃tRəvnɑ̃, -ɑ̃t] vb voir **contrevenir** ▷ nm/f offender

contrevenir [kɔ̃tRəvniR]: **~ à** vt to contravene

contre-voie [kɔ̃tRəvwa]: **à ~** adv (en sens inverse) on the wrong track; (du mauvais côté) on the wrong side

contribuable [kɔ̃tRibɥabl(ə)] nm/f taxpayer

contribuer [kɔ̃tRibɥe]: **~ à** vt to contribute towards

contribution [kɔ̃tRibysjɔ̃] nf contribution; **les ~s** (bureaux) the tax office; **mettre à ~** to call upon; **~s directes/indirectes** direct/indirect taxation

contrit, e [kɔ̃tRi, -it] adj contrite

contrôlable [kɔ̃tRolabl(ə)] adj (maîtrisable: situation, débit) controllable; (alibi, déclarations) verifiable

contrôle [kɔ̃tRol] nm checking no pl, check; supervision; monitoring; (test) test, examination; **perdre le ~ de son véhicule** to lose control of one's vehicle; **~ des changes** (Comm) exchange controls; **~ continu** (Scol)

continuous assessment; **~ d'identité** identity
check; **~ des naissances** birth control; **~ des
prix** price control

contrôler [kɔ̃trole] vt (vérifier) to check;
(surveiller) to supervise; to monitor, control;
(maîtriser, Comm: firme) to control; **se contrôler** vi
to control o.s.

contrôleur, -euse [kɔ̃trolœr, -øz] nm/f (de train)
(ticket) inspector; (de bus) (bus) conductor/tress;
~ de la navigation aérienne, ~ aérien air
traffic controller; **~ financier** financial
controller

contrordre [kɔ̃trɔrdr(ə)] nm counter-order,
countermand; **sauf ~** unless otherwise
directed

controverse [kɔ̃trɔvɛrs(ə)] nf controversy
controversé, e [kɔ̃trɔvɛrse] adj (personnage,
question) controversial

contumace [kɔ̃tymas]: **par ~** adv in absentia
contusion [kɔ̃tyzjɔ̃] nf bruise, contusion
contusionné, e [kɔ̃tyzjone] adj bruised
conurbation [kɔnyrbasjɔ̃] nf conurbation
convaincant, e [kɔ̃vɛ̃kɑ̃, -ɑ̃t] vb voir **convaincre**
▷ adj convincing

convaincre [kɔ̃vɛ̃kr(ə)] vt: **~ qn (de qch)** to
convince sb (of sth); **~ qn (de faire)** to persuade
sb (to do); **~ qn de** (Jur: délit) to convict sb of
convaincu, e [kɔ̃vɛ̃ky] pp de **convaincre** ▷ adj:
d'un ton ~ with conviction

convainquais etc [kɔ̃vɛ̃kɛ] vb voir **convaincre**
convalescence [kɔ̃valesɑ̃s] nf convalescence;
maison de ~ convalescent home

convalescent, e [kɔ̃valesɑ̃, -ɑ̃t] adj, nm/f
convalescent

convenable [kɔ̃vnabl(ə)] adj suitable; (décent)
acceptable, proper; (assez bon) decent,
acceptable; adequate, passable

convenablement [kɔ̃vnabləmɑ̃] adv (placé,
choisi) suitably; (s'habiller, s'exprimer) properly;
(payé, logé) decently

convenance [kɔ̃vnɑ̃s] nf: **à ma/votre ~** to my/
your liking; **convenances** nfpl proprieties

convenir [kɔ̃vnir] vt to be suitable; **~ à** to suit;
il convient de it is advisable to; (bienséant) it is
right ou proper to; **~ de** (bien-fondé de qch) to
admit (to), acknowledge; (date, somme etc) to
agree upon; **~ que** (admettre) to admit that,
acknowledge the fact that; **~ de faire qch** to
agree to do sth; **il a été convenu que** it has
been agreed that; **comme convenu** as agreed

convention [kɔ̃vɑ̃sjɔ̃] nf convention;
conventions nfpl (convenances) convention sg,
social conventions; **de ~** conventional; **~
collective** (Écon) collective agreement

conventionnalisme [kɔ̃vɑ̃sjɔnalism(ə)] nm (des
idées) conventionality

conventionné, e [kɔ̃vɑ̃sjone] adj (Admin) applying
charges laid down by the state

conventionnel, le [kɔ̃vɑ̃sjɔnɛl] adj conventional
conventionnellement [kɔ̃vɑ̃sjɔnɛlmɑ̃] adv
conventionally

conventuel, le [kɔ̃vɑ̃tɥɛl] adj monastic;

monastery cpd, conventual, convent cpd
convenu, e [kɔ̃vny] pp de **convenir** ▷ adj agreed
convergent, e [kɔ̃vɛrʒɑ̃, -ɑ̃t] adj convergent
converger [kɔ̃vɛrʒe] vi to converge; **~ vers** ou
sur to converge on

conversation [kɔ̃vɛrsasjɔ̃] nf conversation;
avoir de la ~ to be a good conversationalist
converser [kɔ̃vɛrse] vi to converse
conversion [kɔ̃vɛrsjɔ̃] nf conversion; (Ski) kick
turn

convertible [kɔ̃vɛrtibl(ə)] adj (Écon) convertible;
(canapé) ~ sofa bed

convertir [kɔ̃vɛrtir] vt: **~ qn (à)** to convert sb
(to); **~ qch en** to convert sth into; **se ~ (à)** to be
converted (to)

convertisseur [kɔ̃vɛrtisœr] nm (Élec) converter
convexe [kɔ̃vɛks(ə)] adj convex
conviction [kɔ̃viksjɔ̃] nf conviction
conviendrai [kɔ̃vjɛ̃dre], **conviens** etc [kɔ̃vjɛ̃] vb
voir **convenir**

convier [kɔ̃vje] vt: **~ qn à** (dîner etc) to (cordially)
invite sb to; **~ qn à faire** to urge sb to do
convint etc [kɔ̃vɛ̃] vb voir **convenir**
convive [kɔ̃viv] nm/f guest (at table)
convivial, e [kɔ̃vivjal] adj (Inform) user-friendly
convocation [kɔ̃vɔkasjɔ̃] nf (voir convoquer)
convening, convoking; summoning;
invitation; (document) notification to attend;
summons sg

convoi [kɔ̃vwa] nm (de voitures, prisonniers) convoy;
(train) train; **~ (funèbre)** funeral procession
convoiter [kɔ̃vwate] vt to covet
convoitise [kɔ̃vwatiz] nf covetousness; (sexuelle)
lust, desire

convoler [kɔ̃vɔle] vi: **~ (en justes noces)** to be
wed

convoquer [kɔ̃vɔke] vt (assemblée) to convene,
convoke; (subordonné, témoin) to summon;
(candidat) to ask to attend; **~ qn (à)** (réunion) to
invite sb (to attend)

convoyer [kɔ̃vwaje] vt to escort
convoyeur [kɔ̃vwajœr] nm (Navig) escort ship;
~ de fonds security guard

convulsé, e [kɔ̃vylse] adj (visage) distorted
convulsif, -ive [kɔ̃vylsif, -iv] adj convulsive
convulsions [kɔ̃vylsjɔ̃] nfpl convulsions
cookie [kuki] nm (Inform) cookie
coopérant [kɔɔperɑ̃] nm ≈ person doing
Voluntary Service Overseas (Brit), ≈ member of
the Peace Corps (US)

coopératif, -ive [kɔɔperatif, -iv] adj, nf cooperative

coopération [kɔɔperasjɔ̃] nf co-operation;
(Admin): **la C~** ≈ Voluntary Service Overseas
(Brit) ou the Peace Corps (US) (done as alternative to
military service)

coopérer [kɔɔpere] vi: **~ (à)** to co-operate (in)
coordination [kɔɔrdinasjɔ̃] nf coordination
coordonnateur, -trice [kɔɔrdɔnatœr, -tris] adj
coordinating ▷ nm/f coordinator
coordonné, e [kɔɔrdɔne] adj coordinated ▷ nf
(Ling) coordinate clause; **coordonnés** nmpl

(*vêtements*) coordinates; **coordonnées** *nfpl* (*Math*) coordinates; (*détails personnels*) address, phone number, schedule *etc*; whereabouts; **donnez-moi vos ~** (*fam*) can I have your details please?

coordonner [kɔɔrdɔne] *vt* to coordinate

copain, copine [kɔpɛ̃, kɔpin] *nm/f* mate (*Brit*), pal ▷ *adj*: **être ~ avec** to be pally with

copeau, x [kɔpo] *nm* shaving; (*de métal*) turning

Copenhague [kɔpənag] *n* Copenhagen

copie [kɔpi] *nf* copy; (*Scol*) script, paper; exercise; **~ certifiée conforme** certified copy; **~ papier** (*Inform*) hard copy

copier [kɔpje] *vt, vi* to copy; **~ sur** to copy from

copieur [kɔpjœr] *nm* (photo)copier

copieusement [kɔpjøzmɑ̃] *adv* copiously

copieux, -euse [kɔpjø, -øz] *adj* copious, hearty

copilote [kɔpilɔt] *nm* (*Aviat*) co-pilot; (*Auto*) co-driver, navigator

copinage [kɔpinaʒ] *nm*: **obtenir qch par ~** to get sth through contacts

copine [kɔpin] *nf voir* **copain**

copiste [kɔpist(ə)] *nm/f* copyist, transcriber

coproduction [kɔprɔdyksjɔ̃] *nf* coproduction, joint production

copropriétaire [kɔprɔprijetɛr] *nm/f* co-owner

copropriété [kɔprɔprijete] *nf* co-ownership, joint ownership; **acheter en ~** to buy on a co-ownership basis

copulation [kɔpylasjɔ̃] *nf* copulation

copyright [kɔpirajt] *nm* copyright

coq [kɔk] *nm* cockerel, rooster ▷ *adj inv* (*Boxe*): **poids ~** bantamweight; **~ de bruyère** grouse; **~ du village** (*fig: péj*) ladykiller; **~ au vin** coq au vin

coq-à-l'âne [kɔkalan] *nm inv* abrupt change of subject

coque [kɔk] *nf* (*de noix, mollusque*) shell; (*de bateau*) hull; **à la ~** (*Culin*) (soft-)boiled

coquelet [kɔklɛ] *nm* (*Culin*) cockerel

coquelicot [kɔkliko] *nm* poppy

coqueluche [kɔklyʃ] *nf* whooping-cough; (*fig*): **être la ~ de qn** to be sb's flavour of the month

coquet, te [kɔkɛ, -ɛt] *adj* appearance-conscious; (*joli*) pretty

coquetier [kɔktje] *nm* egg-cup

coquettement [kɔkɛtmɑ̃] *adv* (*s'habiller*) attractively; (*meubler*) prettily

coquetterie [kɔkɛtri] *nf* appearance-consciousness

coquillage [kɔkijaʒ] *nm* (*mollusque*) shellfish *inv*; (*coquille*) shell

coquille [kɔkij] *nf* shell; (*Typo*) misprint; **~ de beurre** shell of butter; **~ d'œuf** *adj* (*couleur*) eggshell; **~ de noix** nutshell; **~ St Jacques** scallop

coquillettes [kɔkijɛt] *nfpl* pasta shells

coquin, e [kɔkɛ̃, -in] *adj* mischievous, roguish; (*polisson*) naughty ▷ *nm/f* (*péj*) rascal

cor [kɔr] *nm* (*Mus*) horn; (*Méd*): **~ (au pied)** corn; **réclamer à ~ et à cri** to clamour for; **~ anglais** cor anglais; **~ de chasse** hunting horn

corail, -aux [kɔraj, -o] *nm* coral *no pl*

Coran [kɔrɑ̃] *nm*: **le ~** the Koran

coraux [kɔro] *nmpl de* **corail**

corbeau, x [kɔrbo] *nm* crow

corbeille [kɔrbɛj] *nf* basket; (*Inform*) recycle bin; (*Bourse*): **la ~** ≈ the floor (of the Stock Exchange); **~ de mariage** (*fig*) wedding presents *pl*; **~ à ouvrage** work-basket; **~ à pain** breadbasket; **~ à papier** waste paper basket *ou* bin

corbillard [kɔrbijar] *nm* hearse

cordage [kɔrdaʒ] *nm* rope; **cordages** *nmpl* (*de voilure*) rigging *sg*

corde [kɔrd(ə)] *nf* rope; (*de violon, raquette, d'arc*) string; (*trame*): **la ~** the thread; (*Athlétisme, Auto*): **la ~** the rails *pl*; **les ~s** (*Boxe*) the ropes; **les (instruments à) ~s** (*Mus*) the strings, the stringed instruments; **semelles de ~** rope soles; **tenir la ~** (*Athlétisme, Auto*) to be in the inside lane; **tomber des ~s** to rain cats and dogs; **tirer sur la ~** to go too far; **la ~ sensible** the right chord; **usé jusqu'à la ~** threadbare; **~ à linge** washing *ou* clothes line; **~ lisse** (climbing) rope; **~ à nœuds** knotted climbing rope; **~ raide** tightrope; **~ à sauter** skipping rope; **~s vocales** vocal cords

cordeau, x [kɔrdo] *nm* string, line; **tracé au ~** as straight as a die

cordée [kɔrde] *nf* (*d'alpinistes*) rope, roped party

cordelière [kɔrdəljɛr] *nf* cord (belt)

cordial, e, aux [kɔrdjal, -o] *adj* warm, cordial ▷ *nm* cordial, pick-me-up

cordialement [kɔrdjalmɑ̃] *adv* cordially, heartily; (*formule épistolaire*) (kind) regards

cordialité [kɔrdjalite] *nf* warmth, cordiality

cordillère [kɔrdijɛr] *nf*: **la ~ des Andes** the Andes cordillera *ou* range

cordon [kɔrdɔ̃] *nm* cord, string; **~ sanitaire/de police** sanitary/police cordon; **~ littoral** sandbank, sandbar; **~ ombilical** umbilical cord

cordon-bleu [kɔrdɔ̃blø] *adj, nm/f* cordon bleu

cordonnerie [kɔrdɔnri] *nf* shoe repairer's *ou* mender's (shop)

cordonnier [kɔrdɔnje] *nm* shoe repairer *ou* mender, cobbler

cordouan, e [kɔrduɑ̃, -an] *adj* Cordovan

Cordoue [kɔrdu] *n* Cordoba

Corée [kɔre] *nf*: **la ~** Korea; **la ~ du Sud/du Nord** South/North Korea; **la République (démocratique populaire) de ~** the (Democratic People's) Republic of Korea

coréen, ne [kɔreɛ̃, -ɛn] *adj* Korean ▷ *nm* (*Ling*) Korean ▷ *nm/f*: **Coréen, ne** Korean

coreligionnaire [kɔrəliʒjɔnɛr] *nm/f* fellow Christian/Muslim/Jew *etc*

Corfou [kɔrfu] *n* Corfu

coriace [kɔrjas] *adj* tough

coriandre [kɔrjɑ̃dr(ə)] *nf* coriander

Corinthe [kɔrɛ̃t] *n* Corinth

cormoran [kɔrmɔrɑ̃] *nm* cormorant

cornac [kɔrnak] *nm* elephant driver

corne [kɔrn(ə)] *nf* horn; (*de cerf*) antler; (*de la peau*) callus; **~ d'abondance** horn of plenty; **~**

de brume (*Navig*) foghorn

cornée [kɔʀne] *nf* cornea

corneille [kɔʀnɛj] *nf* crow

cornélien, ne [kɔʀneljɛ̃, -ɛn] *adj* (*débat etc*) where love and duty conflict

cornemuse [kɔʀnəmyz] *nf* bagpipes *pl*; **joueur de** ~ piper

corner¹ [kɔʀnɛʀ] *nm* (*Football*) corner (kick)

corner² [kɔʀne] *vt* (*pages*) to make dog-eared ▷ *vi* (*klaxonner*) to blare out

cornet [kɔʀnɛ] *nm* (*paper*) cone; (*de glace*) cornet, cone; ~ **à pistons** cornet

cornette [kɔʀnɛt] *nf* cornet (*headgear*)

corniaud [kɔʀnjo] *nm* (*chien*) mongrel; (*péj*) twit, clot

corniche [kɔʀniʃ] *nf* (*de meuble, neigeuse*) cornice; (*route*) coast road

cornichon [kɔʀniʃɔ̃] *nm* gherkin

Cornouailles [kɔʀnwaj] *nf(pl)* Cornwall

cornue [kɔʀny] *nf* retort

corollaire [kɔʀɔlɛʀ] *nm* corollary

corolle [kɔʀɔl] *nf* corolla

coron [kɔʀɔ̃] *nm* mining cottage; mining village

coronaire [kɔʀɔnɛʀ] *adj* coronary

corporation [kɔʀpɔʀasjɔ̃] *nf* corporate body; (*au Moyen-Âge*) guild

corporel, le [kɔʀpɔʀɛl] *adj* bodily; (*punition*) corporal; **soins ~s** care *sg* of the body

corps [kɔʀ] *nm* (*gén*) body; (*cadavre*) (dead) body; **à son ~ défendant** against one's will; **à ~ perdu** headlong; **perdu ~ et biens** lost with all hands; **prendre ~** to take shape; **faire ~ avec** to be joined to; to form one body with; ~ **d'armée** (**CA**) army corps; ~ **de ballet** corps de ballet; ~ **constitués** (*Pol*) constitutional bodies; **le ~ consulaire** (**CC**) the consular corps; ~ **à ~** *adv* hand-to-hand ▷ *nm* clinch; **le ~ du délit** (*Jur*) corpus delicti; **le ~ diplomatique** (**CD**) the diplomatic corps; **le ~ électoral** the electorate; **le ~ enseignant** the teaching profession; ~ **étranger** (*Méd*) foreign body; ~ **expéditionnaire** task force; ~ **de garde** guardroom; ~ **législatif** legislative body; **le ~ médical** the medical profession

corpulence [kɔʀpylɑ̃s] *nf* build; (*embonpoint*) stoutness (*Brit*), corpulence; **de forte ~** of large build

corpulent, e [kɔʀpylɑ̃, -ɑ̃t] *adj* stout (*Brit*), corpulent

corpus [kɔʀpys] *nm* (*Ling*) corpus

correct, e [kɔʀɛkt] *adj* (*exact*) accurate, correct; (*bienséant, honnête*) correct; (*passable*) adequate

correctement [kɔʀɛktəmɑ̃] *adv* accurately; correctly; adequately

correcteur, -trice [kɔʀɛktœʀ, -tʀis] *nm/f* (*Scol*) examiner, marker; (*Typo*) proofreader

correctif, -ive [kɔʀɛktif, -iv] *adj* corrective ▷ *nm* (*mise au point*) rider, qualification

correction [kɔʀɛksjɔ̃] *nf* (*voir corriger*) correction; marking; (*voir correct*) correctness; (*rature, surcharge*) correction, emendation; (*coups*) thrashing; ~ **sur écran** (*Inform*) screen editing;

~ **(des épreuves)** proofreading

correctionnel, le [kɔʀɛksjɔnɛl] *adj* (*Jur*): **tribunal ~** ≈ criminal court

corrélation [kɔʀelasjɔ̃] *nf* correlation

correspondance [kɔʀɛspɔ̃dɑ̃s] *nf* correspondence; (*de train, d'avion*) connection; **ce train assure la ~ avec l'avion de 10 heures** this train connects with the 10 o'clock plane; **cours par ~** correspondence course; **vente par** ~ mail-order business

correspondancier, -ière [kɔʀɛspɔ̃dɑ̃sje, -jɛʀ] *nm/f* correspondence clerk

correspondant, e [kɔʀɛspɔ̃dɑ̃, -ɑ̃t] *nm/f* correspondent; (*Tél*) person phoning (*ou* being phoned)

correspondre [kɔʀɛspɔ̃dʀ(ə)] *vi* (*données, témoignages*) to correspond, tally; (*chambres*) to communicate; ~ **à** to correspond to; ~ **avec qn** to correspond with sb

Corrèze [kɔʀɛz] *nf*: **la ~** the Corrèze

corrézien, ne [kɔʀezjɛ̃, -ɛn] *adj* of *ou* from the Corrèze

corrida [kɔʀida] *nf* bullfight

corridor [kɔʀidɔʀ] *nm* corridor, passage

corrigé [kɔʀiʒe] *nm* (*Scol*) correct version; fair copy

corriger [kɔʀiʒe] *vt* (*devoir*) to correct, mark; (*texte*) to correct, emend; (*erreur, défaut*) to correct, put right; (*punir*) to thrash; ~ **qn de** (*défaut*) to cure sb of; **se ~ de** to cure o.s. of

corroborer [kɔʀɔbɔʀe] *vt* to corroborate

corroder [kɔʀɔde] *vt* to corrode

corrompre [kɔʀɔ̃pʀ(ə)] *vt* (*dépraver*) to corrupt; (*acheter: témoin etc*) to bribe

corrompu, e [kɔʀɔ̃py] *adj* corrupt

corrosif, -ive [kɔʀozif, -iv] *adj* corrosive

corrosion [kɔʀozjɔ̃] *nf* corrosion

corruption [kɔʀypsjɔ̃] *nf* corruption; bribery

corsage [kɔʀsaʒ] *nm* (*d'une robe*) bodice; (*chemisier*) blouse

corsaire [kɔʀsɛʀ] *nm* pirate, corsair; privateer

corse [kɔʀs(ə)] *adj* Corsican ▷ *nm/f*: **Corse** Corsican ▷ *nf*: **la C~** Corsica

corsé, e [kɔʀse] *adj* vigorous; (*café etc*) full-flavoured (*Brit*) *ou* -flavored (*US*); (*goût*) full; (*fig*) spicy; tricky

corselet [kɔʀsəlɛ] *nm* corselet

corser [kɔʀse] *vt* (*difficulté*) to aggravate; (*intrigue*) to liven up; (*sauce*) to add spice to

corset [kɔʀsɛ] *nm* corset; (*d'une robe*) bodice; ~ **orthopédique** surgical corset

corso [kɔʀso] *nm*: ~ **fleuri** procession of floral floats

cortège [kɔʀtɛʒ] *nm* procession

cortisone [kɔʀtizon] *nf* (*Méd*) cortisone

corvée [kɔʀve] *nf* chore, drudgery *no pl*; (*Mil*) fatigue (duty)

cosaque [kɔzak] *nm* cossack

cosignataire [kɔsiɲatɛʀ] *adj, nm/f* co-signatory

cosinus [kɔsinys] *nm* (*Math*) cosine

cosmétique [kɔsmetik] *nm* (*pour les cheveux*) hair-oil; (*produit de beauté*) beauty care product

cosmétologie [kɔsmetɔlɔʒi] *nf* beauty care
cosmique [kɔsmik] *adj* cosmic
cosmonaute [kɔsmɔnot] *nm/f* cosmonaut, astronaut
cosmopolite [kɔsmɔpɔlit] *adj* cosmopolitan
cosmos [kɔsmɔs] *nm* outer space; cosmos
cosse [kɔs] *nf* (Bot) pod, hull
cossu, e [kɔsy] *adj* opulent-looking, well-to-do
Costa Rica [kɔstaʀika] *nm*: **le ~** Costa Rica
costaricien, ne [kɔstaʀisjɛ̃, -ɛn] *adj* Costa Rican
▷ *nm/f*: **Costaricien, ne** Costa Rican
costaud, e [kɔsto, -od] *adj* strong, sturdy
costume [kɔstym] *nm* (d'homme) suit; (de théâtre) costume
costumé, e [kɔstyme] *adj* dressed up
costumier, -ière [kɔstymje, -jɛʀ] *nm/f* (fabricant, loueur) costumier; (Théât) wardrobe master/mistress
cotangente [kɔtɑ̃ʒɑ̃t] *nf* (Math) cotangent
cotation [kɔtasjɔ̃] *nf* quoted value
cote [kɔt] *nf* (en Bourse etc) quotation; quoted value; (d'un cheval): **la ~ de** the odds *pl* on; (d'un candidat etc) rating; (mesure: sur une carte) spot height; (: sur un croquis) dimension; (de classement) (classification) mark; reference number; **avoir la ~** to be very popular; **inscrit à la ~** quoted on the Stock Exchange; **~ d'alerte** danger *ou* flood level; **~ mal taillée** (fig) compromise; **~ de popularité** popularity rating
coté, e [kɔte] *adj*: **être ~** to be listed *ou* quoted; **être ~ en Bourse** to be quoted on the Stock Exchange; **être bien/mal ~** to be highly/poorly rated
côte [kot] *nf* (rivage) coast(line); (pente) slope; (: sur une route) hill; (Anat) rib; (d'un tricot, tissu) rib, ribbing *no pl*; **~ à ~** *adv* side by side; **la C~ (d'Azur)** the (French) Riviera; **la C~ d'Ivoire** the Ivory Coast; **~ de porc** pork chop
côté [kote] *nm* (gén) side; (direction) way, direction; **de chaque ~ (de)** on each side of; **de tous les ~s** from all directions; **de quel ~ est-il parti?** which way *ou* in which direction did he go?; **de ce/de l'autre ~** this/the other way; **d'un ~ ... de l'autre ~ ...** (alternative) on (the) one hand ... on the other (hand) ...; **du ~ de** (provenance) from; (direction) towards; **du ~ de Lyon** (proximité) near Lyons; **du ~ gauche** on the left-hand side; **de ~** *adv* sideways; on one side; to one side; aside; **laisser de ~** to leave on one side; **mettre de ~** to put on one side, put aside; **de mon ~** (quant à moi) for my part; **à ~** *adv* (right) nearby; beside next door; (d'autre part) besides; **à ~ de** beside; next to; (fig) in comparison to; **à ~ (de la cible)** off target, wide (of the mark); **être aux ~s de** to be by the side of
coteau, x [kɔto] *nm* hill
côtelé, e [kotle] *adj* ribbed; **pantalon en velours ~** corduroy trousers *pl*
côtelette [kotlɛt] *nf* chop
coter [kɔte] *vt* (Bourse) to quote

coterie [kɔtʀi] *nf* set
côtier, -ière [kotje, -jɛʀ] *adj* coastal
cotisation [kɔtizasjɔ̃] *nf* subscription, dues *pl*; (pour une pension) contributions *pl*
cotiser [kɔtize] *vi*: **~ (à)** to pay contributions (to); (à une association) to subscribe (to); **se cotiser** to club together
coton [kɔtɔ̃] *nm* cotton; **~ hydrophile** cotton wool (Brit), absorbent cotton (US)
cotonnade [kɔtɔnad] *nf* cotton (fabric)
Coton-Tige® [kɔtɔ̃tiʒ] *nm* cotton bud®
côtoyer [kotwaje] *vt* to be close to; (rencontrer) to rub shoulders with; (longer) to run alongside; (fig: friser) to be bordering *ou* verging on
cotte [kɔt] *nf*: **~ de mailles** coat of mail
cou [ku] *nm* neck
couac [kwak] *nm* (fam) bum note
couard, e [kwaʀ, -aʀd(ə)] *adj* cowardly
couchage [kuʃaʒ] *nm voir* **sac**
couchant [kuʃɑ̃] *adj*: **soleil ~** setting sun
couche [kuʃ] *nf* (strate: gén, Géo) layer, stratum (pl -a); (de peinture, vernis) coat; (de poussière, crème) layer; (de bébé) nappy (Brit), diaper (US); **~ d'ozone** ozone layer; **couches** *nfpl* (Méd) confinement *sg*; **~s sociales** social levels *ou* strata
couché, e [kuʃe] *adj* (étendu) lying down; (au lit) in bed
couche-culotte [kuʃkylɔt] (pl **couches-culottes**) *nf* (plastic-coated) disposable nappy (Brit) *ou* diaper (US)
coucher [kuʃe] *nm* (du soleil) setting ▷ *vt* (personne) to put to bed; (: loger) to put up; (objet) to lay on its side; (écrire) to inscribe, couch ▷ *vi* (dormir) to sleep, spend the night; **~ avec qn** to sleep with sb, go to bed with sb; **se coucher** *vi* (pour dormir) to go to bed; (pour se reposer) to lie down; (soleil) to set, go down; **à prendre avant le ~** (Méd) take at night *ou* before going to bed; **~ de soleil** sunset
couchette [kuʃɛt] *nf* couchette; (de marin) bunk
coucheur [kuʃœʀ] *nm*: **mauvais ~** awkward customer
couci-couça [kusikusa] *adv* (fam) so-so
coucou [kuku] *nm* cuckoo ▷ *excl* peek-a-boo
coude [kud] *nm* (Anat) elbow; (de tuyau, de la route) bend; **~ à ~** *adv* shoulder to shoulder, side by side
coudée [kude] *nf*: **avoir ses ~s franches** (fig) to have a free rein
cou-de-pied [kudpje] (pl **cous-de-pied**) *nm* instep
coudoyer [kudwaje] *vt* to brush past *ou* against; (fig) to rub shoulders with
coudre [kudʀ(ə)] *vt* (bouton) to sew on; (robe) to sew (up) ▷ *vi* to sew
couenne [kwan] *nf* (de lard) rind
couette [kwɛt] *nf* duvet, (continental) quilt; **couettes** *nfpl* (cheveux) bunches
couffin [kufɛ̃] *nm* Moses basket; (straw) basket
couilles [kuj] *nfpl* (fam!) balls (!)
couiner [kwine] *vi* to squeal

coulage [kulaʒ] *nm* (*Comm*) loss of stock (*due to theft or negligence*)

coulant, e [kulã, -ãt] *adj* (*indulgent*) easy-going; (*fromage etc*) runny

coulée [kule] *nf* (*de lave, métal en fusion*) flow; ~ **de neige** snowslide

couler [kule] *vi* to flow, run; (*fuir: stylo, récipient*) to leak; (*sombrer: bateau*) to sink ▷ *vt* (*cloche, sculpture*) to cast; (*bateau*) to sink; (*fig*) to ruin, bring down; (: *passer*): ~ **une vie heureuse** to enjoy a happy life; **se ~ dans** (*interstice etc*) to slip into; **faire ~** (*eau*) to run; **faire ~ un bain** to run a bath; **il a coulé une bielle** (*Auto*) his big end went; ~ **de source** to follow on naturally; ~ **à pic** to sink *ou* go straight to the bottom

couleur [kulœR] *nf* colour (*Brit*), color (*US*); (*Cartes*) suit; **couleurs** *nfpl* (*du teint*) colo(u)r *sg*; **les ~s** (*Mil*) the colo(u)rs; **en ~s** (*film*) in colo(u)r; **télévision en ~s** colo(u)r television; **de ~** (*homme, femme*) colo(u)red; **sous ~ de** on the pretext of; **de quelle ~** of what colo(u)r

couleuvre [kulœvR(ə)] *nf* grass snake

coulisse [kulis] *nf* (*Tech*) runner; **coulisses** *nfpl* (*Théât*) wings; (*fig*): **dans les ~s** behind the scenes; **porte à ~** sliding door

coulisser [kulise] *vi* to slide, run

couloir [kulwaR] *nm* corridor, passage; (*d'avion*) aisle; (*de bus*) gangway; (: *sur la route*) bus lane; (*Sport: de piste*) lane; (*Géo*) gully; ~ **aérien** air corridor *ou* lane; ~ **de navigation** shipping lane

coulpe [kulp(ə)] *nf*: **battre sa ~** to repent openly

coup [ku] *nm* (*heurt, choc*) knock; (*affectif*) blow, shock; (*agressif*) blow; (*avec arme à feu*) shot; (*de l'horloge*) chime; (*Sport*) stroke; shot; blow; (*fam: fois*) time; (*Échecs*) move; ~ **de coude/genou** nudge (with the elbow)/ with the knee; **à ~s de hache/marteau** (hitting) with an axe/a hammer; ~ **de tonnerre** clap of thunder; ~ **de sonnette** ring of the bell; ~ **de crayon/pinceau** stroke of the pencil/brush; **donner un ~ de balai** to sweep up, give the floor a sweep; **donner un ~ de chiffon** to go round with the duster; **avoir le ~** (*fig*) to have the knack; **être dans le/hors du ~** to be in/not to be in on it; **boire un ~** to have a drink; **d'un seul ~** (*subitement*) suddenly; (*à la fois*) at one go; in one blow; **du ~** so (you see); **du premier ~** first time *ou* go, at the first attempt; **du même ~** at the same time; **à ~ sûr** definitely, without fail; **après ~** afterwards; ~ **sur ~** in quick succession; **être sur un ~** to be on to something; **sur le ~** outright; **sous le ~ de** (*surprise etc*) under the influence of; **tomber sous le ~ de la loi** to constitute a statutory offence; **à tous les ~s** every time; **il a raté son ~** he missed his turn; **pour le ~** for once; ~ **bas** (*fig*): **donner un ~ bas à qn** to hit sb below the belt; ~ **de chance** stroke of luck; ~ **de chapeau** (*fig*) pat on the back; ~ **de couteau** stab (of a knife); ~ **dur** hard blow; ~ **d'éclat** (great) feat; ~ **d'envoi** kick-off; ~ **d'essai** first attempt; ~ **d'état** coup d'état; ~ **de feu** shot; ~ **de filet**

(*Police*) haul; ~ **de foudre** (*fig*) love at first sight; ~ **fourré** stab in the back; ~ **franc** free kick; ~ **de frein** (*sharp*) braking *no pl*; ~ **de fusil** rifle shot; ~ **de grâce** coup de grâce; ~ **du lapin** (*Auto*) whiplash; ~ **de main**: **donner un ~ de main à qn** to give sb a (helping) hand; ~ **de maître** master stroke; ~ **d'œil** glance; ~ **de pied** kick; ~ **de poing** punch; ~ **de soleil** sunburn *no pl*; ~ **de téléphone** phone call; ~ **de tête** (*fig*) (sudden) impulse; ~ **de théâtre** (*fig*) dramatic turn of events; ~ **de vent** gust of wind; **en ~ de vent** (*rapidement*) in a tearing hurry

coupable [kupabl(ə)] *adj* guilty; (*pensée*) guilty, culpable ▷ *nm/f* (*gén*) culprit; (*Jur*) guilty party; ~ **de** guilty of

coupant, e [kupã, -ãt] *adj* (*lame*) sharp; (*fig: voix, ton*) cutting

coupe [kup] *nf* (*verre*) goblet; (*à fruits*) dish; (*Sport*) cup; (*de cheveux, de vêtement*) cut; (*graphique, plan*) (cross) section; **être sous la ~ de** to be under the control of; **faire des ~s sombres dans** to make drastic cuts in

coupé, e [kupe] *adj* (*communications, route*) cut, blocked; (*vêtement*): **bien/mal ~** well/badly cut ▷ *nm* (*Auto*) coupé ▷ *nf* (*Navig*) gangway

coupe-circuit [kupsiRkɥi] *nm inv* cutout, circuit breaker

coupe-feu [kupfø] *nm inv* firebreak

coupe-gorge [kupgɔRʒ(ə)] *nm inv* cut-throats' den

coupe-ongles [kupɔ̃gl(ə)] *nm inv* (*pince*) nail clippers; (*ciseaux*) nail scissors

coupe-papier [kuppapje] *nm inv* paper knife

couper [kupe] *vt* to cut; (*retrancher*) to cut (out), take out; (*route, courant*) to cut off; (*appétit*) to take away; (*fièvre*) to take down, reduce; (*vin, cidre*) to blend; (: *à table*) to dilute (with water) ▷ *vi* to cut; (*prendre un raccourci*) to take a short-cut; (*Cartes: diviser le paquet*) to cut; (: *avec l'atout*) to trump; **se couper** *vi* (*se blesser*) to cut o.s.; (*en témoignant etc*) to give o.s. away; ~ **l'appétit à qn** to spoil sb's appetite; ~ **la parole à qn** to cut sb short; ~ **les vivres à qn** to cut off sb's vital supplies; ~ **le contact** *ou* **l'allumage** (*Auto*) to turn off the ignition; ~ **les ponts avec qn** to break with sb; **se faire ~ les cheveux** to have *ou* get one's hair cut

couperet [kupRɛ] *nm* cleaver, chopper

couperosé, e [kupRoze] *adj* blotchy

couple [kupl(ə)] *nm* couple; ~ **de torsion** torque

coupler [kuple] *vt* to couple (together)

couplet [kuplɛ] *nm* verse

coupleur [kuplœR] *nm*: ~ **acoustique** acoustic coupler

coupole [kupɔl] *nf* dome; cupola

coupon [kupɔ̃] *nm* (*ticket*) coupon; (*de tissu*) remnant; roll

coupon-réponse [kupɔ̃repɔ̃s] (*pl* **coupons-réponses**) *nm* reply coupon

coupure [kupyR] *nf* cut; (*billet de banque*) note; (*de journal*) cutting; ~ **de courant** power cut

C

cour [kuʀ] *nf* (*de ferme, jardin*) (court)yard;
(*d'immeuble*) back yard; (*Jur, royale*) court; **faire la
~ à qn** to court sb; **~ d'appel** appeal court (*Brit*),
appellate court (*US*); **~ d'assises** court of
assizes, ≈ Crown Court (*Brit*); **~ de cassation**
final court of appeal; **~ des comptes** (*Admin*)
revenue court; **~ martiale** court-martial; **~ de
récréation** (*Scol*) schoolyard, playground

courage [kuʀaʒ] *nm* courage, bravery

courageusement [kuʀaʒøzmɑ̃] *adv* bravely,
courageously

courageux, -euse [kuʀaʒø, -øz] *adj* brave,
courageous

couramment [kuʀamɑ̃] *adv* commonly; (*parler*)
fluently

courant, e [kuʀɑ̃, -ɑ̃t] *adj* (*fréquent*) common;
(*Comm, gén: normal*) standard; (*en cours*) current
▷ *nm* current; (*fig*) movement; trend; **être au ~
(de)** (*fait, nouvelle*) to know (about); **mettre qn
au ~ (de)** (*fait, nouvelle*) to tell sb (about); (*nouveau
travail etc*) to teach sb the basics (of), brief sb
(about); **se tenir au ~ (de)** (*techniques etc*) to keep
o.s. up-to-date (on); **dans le ~ de** (*pendant*) in
the course of; **~ octobre** *etc* in the course of
October *etc*; **le 10 ~** (*Comm*) the 10th inst.; **~
d'air** draught (*Brit*), draft (*US*); **~ électrique**
(electric) current, power

courbature [kuʀbatyʀ] *nf* ache

courbaturé, e [kuʀbatyʀe] *adj* aching

courbe [kuʀb(ə)] *adj* curved ▷ *nf* curve; **~ de
niveau** contour line

courber [kuʀbe] *vt* to bend; **~ la tête** to bow
one's head; **se courber** *vi* (*branche etc*) to bend,
curve; (*personne*) to bend (down)

courbette [kuʀbɛt] *nf* low bow

coure *etc* [kuʀ] *vb voir* **courir**

coureur, -euse [kuʀœʀ, -øz] *nm/f* (*Sport*) runner
(*ou* driver); (*péj*) womanizer/manhunter; **~
cycliste/automobile** racing cyclist/driver

courge [kuʀʒ(ə)] *nf* (*Bot*) gourd; (*Culin*) marrow

courgette [kuʀʒɛt] *nf* courgette (*Brit*), zucchini
(*US*)

courir [kuʀiʀ] *vi* (*gén*) to run; (*se dépêcher*) to rush;
(*fig: rumeurs*) to go round; (*Comm: intérêt*) to
accrue ▷ *vt* (*Sport: épreuve*) to compete in; (*risque*)
to run; (*danger*) to face; **~ les cafés/bals** to do
the rounds of the cafés/dances; **le bruit court
que** the rumour is going round that; **par les
temps qui courent** at the present time; **~
après qn** to run after sb, chase (after) sb;
laisser ~ to let things alone; **faire ~ qn** to make
sb run around (all over the place); **tu peux
(toujours) ~!** you've got a hope!

couronne [kuʀɔn] *nf* crown; (*de fleurs*) wreath,
circlet; **~ (funéraire** *ou* **mortuaire)** (funeral)
wreath

couronnement [kuʀɔnmɑ̃] *nm* coronation,
crowning; (*fig*) crowning achievement

couronner [kuʀɔne] *vt* to crown

courons [kuʀɔ̃], **courrai** *etc* [kuʀe] *vb voir* **courir**

courre [kuʀ] *vb voir* **chasse**

courriel [kuʀjɛl] *nm* email; **envoyer qch par ~**
to email sth

courrier [kuʀje] *nm* mail, post; (*lettres à écrire*)
letters *pl*; (*rubrique*) column; **qualité ~** letter
quality; **long/moyen ~** *adj* (*Aviat*) long-/
medium-haul; **~ du cœur** problem page; **~
électronique** electronic mail, E-mail

courroie [kuʀwa] *nf* strap; (*Tech*) belt; **~ de
transmission/de ventilateur** driving/fan belt

courrons *etc* [kuʀɔ̃] *vb voir* **courir**

courroucé, e [kuʀuse] *adj* wrathful

cours [kuʀ] *vb voir* **courir** ▷ *nm* (*leçon*) lesson;
class; (*série de leçons*) course; (*cheminement*)
course; (*écoulement*) flow; (*avenue*) walk; (*Comm*)
rate; price; (*Bourse*) quotation; **donner libre ~ à**
to give free expression to; **avoir ~** (*monnaie*) to be
legal tender; (*fig*) to be current; (*Scol*) to have a
class *ou* lecture; **en ~** (*année*) current; (*travaux*) in
progress; **en ~ de route** on the way; **au ~ de** in
the course of, during; **le ~ du change** the
exchange rate; **~ d'eau** waterway; **~
élémentaire (CE)** *2nd and 3rd years of primary
school;* **~ moyen (CM)** *4th and 5th years of primary
school;* **~ préparatoire** ≈ infants' class (*Brit*),
≈ 1st grade (*US*); **~ du soir** night school

course [kuʀs(ə)] *nf* running; (*Sport: épreuve*) race;
(*trajet: du soleil*) course; (*: d'un projectile*) flight;
(*: d'une pièce mécanique*) travel; (*excursion*) outing;
climb; (*d'un taxi, autocar*) journey, trip; (*petite
mission*) errand; **courses** *nfpl* (*achats*) shopping
sg; (*Hippisme*) races; **faire les** *ou* **ses ~s** to go
shopping; **jouer aux ~s** to bet on the races; **à
bout de ~** (*épuisé*) exhausted; **~ automobile** car
race; **~ de côte** (*Auto*) hill climb; **~ par étapes**
ou **d'étapes** race in stages; **~ d'obstacles**
obstacle race; **~ à pied** walking race; **~ de
vitesse** sprint; **~s de chevaux** horse racing

coursier, -ière [kuʀsje, -jɛʀ] *nm/f* courier

court, e [kuʀ, kuʀt(ə)] *adj* short ▷ *adv* short
▷ *nm*: **~ (de tennis)** (tennis) court; **tourner ~** to
come to a sudden end; **couper ~ à** to cut short;
à ~ de short of; **prendre qn de ~** to catch sb
unawares; **pour faire ~** briefly, to cut a long
story short; **ça fait ~** that's not very long; **tirer
à la ~e paille** to draw lots; **faire la ~e échelle à
qn** to give sb a leg up; **~ métrage** (*Ciné*) short
(film)

court-bouillon [kuʀbujɔ̃] (*pl* **courts-bouillons**)
nm court-bouillon

court-circuit [kuʀsiʀkɥi] (*pl* **courts-circuits**)
nm short-circuit

court-circuiter [kuʀsiʀkɥite] *vt* (*fig*) to bypass

courtier, -ière [kuʀtje, -jɛʀ] *nm/f* broker

courtisan [kuʀtizɑ̃] *nm* courtier

courtisane [kuʀtizan] *nf* courtesan

courtiser [kuʀtize] *vt* to court, woo

courtois, e [kuʀtwa, -waz] *adj* courteous

courtoisement [kuʀtwazmɑ̃] *adv* courteously

courtoisie [kuʀtwazi] *nf* courtesy

couru, e [kuʀy] *pp de* **courir** ▷ *adj* (*spectacle etc*)
popular; **c'est ~ (d'avance)!** (*fam*) it's a safe bet!

cousais *etc* [kuzɛ] *vb voir* **coudre**

couscous [kuskus] *nm* couscous

cousin, e [kuzɛ̃, -in] *nm/f* cousin ▷ *nm* (*Zool*) mosquito; **~ germain** first cousin

cousons *etc* [kuzɔ̃] *vb voir* **coudre**

coussin [kusɛ̃] *nm* cushion; **~ d'air** (*Tech*) air cushion

cousu, e [kuzy] *pp de* **coudre** ▷ *adj*: **~ d'or** rolling in riches

coût [ku] *nm* cost; **le ~ de la vie** the cost of living

coûtant [kutɑ̃] *adj m*: **au prix ~** at cost price

couteau, x [kuto] *nm* knife; **~ à cran d'arrêt** flick-knife; **~ de cuisine** kitchen knife; **~ à pain** bread knife; **~ de poche** pocket knife

couteau-scie [kutosi] (*pl* **couteaux-scies**) *nm* serrated(-edged) knife

coutelier, -ière [kutəlje, -jɛʀ] *adj*: **l'industrie coutelière** the cutlery industry ▷ *nm/f* cutler

coutellerie [kutɛlʀi] *nf* cutlery shop; cutlery

coûter [kute] *vt* to cost ▷ *vi*: **~ à qn** to cost sb a lot; **~ cher** to be expensive; **~ cher à qn** (*fig*) to cost sb dear *ou* dearly; **combien ça coûte?** how much is it?, what does it cost?; **coûte que coûte** at all costs

coûteux, -euse [kutø, -øz] *adj* costly, expensive

coutume [kutym] *nf* custom; **de ~** usual, customary

coutumier, -ière [kutymje, -jɛʀ] *adj* customary; **elle est coutumière du fait** that's her usual trick

couture [kutyʀ] *nf* sewing; dress-making; (*points*) seam

couturier [kutyʀje] *nm* fashion designer, couturier

couturière [kutyʀjɛʀ] *nf* dressmaker

couvée [kuve] *nf* brood, clutch

couvent [kuvɑ̃] *nm* (*de sœurs*) convent; (*de frères*) monastery; (*établissement scolaire*) convent (school)

couver [kuve] *vt* to hatch; (*maladie*) to be sickening for ▷ *vi* (*feu*) to smoulder (*Brit*), smolder (*US*); (*révolte*) to be brewing; **~ qn/qch des yeux** to look lovingly at sb/sth; (*convoiter*) to look longingly at sb/sth

couvercle [kuvɛʀkl(ə)] *nm* lid; (*de bombe aérosol etc, qui se visse*) cap, top

couvert, e [kuvɛʀ, -ɛʀt(ə)] *pp de* **couvrir** ▷ *adj* (*ciel*) overcast; (*coiffé d'un chapeau*) wearing a hat ▷ *nm* place setting; (*place à table*) place; (*au restaurant*) cover charge; **couverts** *nmpl* place settings; cutlery *sg*; **~ de** covered with *ou* in; **bien ~** (*habillé*) well wrapped up; **mettre le ~** to lay the table; **à ~** under cover; **sous le ~ de** under the shelter of; (*fig*) under cover of

couverture [kuvɛʀtyʀ] *nf* (*de lit*) blanket; (*de bâtiment*) roofing; (*de livre, fig: d'un espion etc, Assurances*) cover; (*Presse*) coverage; **de ~** (*lettre etc*) covering; **~ chauffante** electric blanket

couveuse [kuvøz] *nf* (*à poules*) sitter, brooder; (*de maternité*) incubator

couvre *etc* [kuvʀ(ə)] *vb voir* **couvrir**

couvre-chef [kuvʀəʃɛf] *nm* hat

couvre-feu, x [kuvʀəfø] *nm* curfew

couvre-lit [kuvʀəli] *nm* bedspread

couvre-pieds [kuvʀəpje] *nm inv* quilt

couvreur [kuvʀœʀ] *nm* roofer

couvrir [kuvʀiʀ] *vt* to cover; (*dominer, étouffer: voix, pas*) to drown out; (*erreur*) to cover up; (*Zool: s'accoupler à*) to cover; **se couvrir** *vi* (*ciel*) to cloud over; (*s'habiller*) to cover up, wrap up; (*se coiffer*) to put on one's hat; (*par une assurance*) to cover o.s.; **se ~** (*fleurs, boutons*) to become covered in

cover-girl [kɔvœʀg[ʷœ]ʀl] *nf* model

cow-boy [kobɔj] *nm* cowboy

coyote [kɔjɔt] *nm* coyote

CP *sigle m* = **cours préparatoire**

CPAM *sigle f* (= *Caisse primaire d'assurances maladie*) health insurance office

cps *abr* (= *caractères par seconde*) cps

cpt *abr* = **comptant**

CQFD *abr* (= *ce qu'il fallait démontrer*) QED = **quod erat demonstrandum**

CR *sigle m* = **compte rendu**

crabe [kʀab] *nm* crab

crachat [kʀaʃa] *nm* spittle *no pl*, spit *no pl*

craché, e [kʀaʃe] *adj*: **son père tout ~** the spitting image of his (*ou* her) father

cracher [kʀaʃe] *vi* to spit ▷ *vt* to spit out; (*fig: lave etc*) to belch (out); **~ du sang** to spit blood

crachin [kʀaʃɛ̃] *nm* drizzle

crachiner [kʀaʃine] *vi* to drizzle

crachoir [kʀaʃwaʀ] *nm* spittoon; (*de dentiste*) bowl

crachotement [kʀaʃɔtmɑ̃] *nm* crackling *no pl*

crachoter [kʀaʃɔte] *vi* (*haut-parleur, radio*) to crackle

crack [kʀak] *nm* (*intellectuel*) whiz kid; (*sportif*) ace; (*poulain*) hot favourite (*Brit*) *ou* favorite (*US*)

Cracovie [kʀakɔvi] *n* Cracow

cradingue [kʀadɛ̃g] *adj* (*fam*) disgustingly dirty, filthy-dirty

craie [kʀɛ] *nf* chalk

craignais *etc* [kʀɛɲɛ] *vb voir* **craindre**

craindre [kʀɛ̃dʀ(ə)] *vt* to fear, be afraid of; (*être sensible à: chaleur, froid*) to be easily damaged by; **~ de/que** to be afraid of/that; **je crains qu'il (ne) vienne** I am afraid he may come

crainte [kʀɛ̃t] *nf* fear; **de ~ de/que** for fear of/that

craintif, -ive [kʀɛ̃tif, -iv] *adj* timid

craintivement [kʀɛ̃tivmɑ̃] *adv* timidly

cramer [kʀame] *vi* (*fam*) to burn

cramoisi, e [kʀamwazi] *adj* crimson

crampe [kʀɑ̃p] *nf* cramp; **~ d'estomac** stomach cramp

crampon [kʀɑ̃pɔ̃] *nm* (*de semelle*) stud; (*Alpinisme*) crampon

cramponner [kʀɑ̃pɔne]: **se cramponner** *vi*: **se ~ (à)** to hang *ou* cling on to

cran [kʀɑ̃] *nm* (*entaille*) notch; (*de courroie*) hole; (*courage*) guts *pl*; **~ d'arrêt/de sûreté** safety catch; **~ de mire** bead

crâne [kʀɑn] *nm* skull

crâner [kʀɑne] *vi* (*fam*) to swank, show off

crânien, ne [kʀɑnjɛ̃, -ɛn] *adj* cranial, skull *cpd*,

brain *cpd*

crapaud [kʀapo] *nm* toad

crapule [kʀapyl] *nf* villain

crapuleux, -euse [kʀapylø, -øz] *adj*: **crime ~** villainous crime

craquelure [kʀaklyʀ] *nf* crack; crackle *no pl*

craquement [kʀakmɑ̃] *nm* crack, snap; *(du plancher)* creak, creaking *no pl*

craquer [kʀake] *vi (bois, plancher)* to creak; *(fil, branche)* to snap; *(couture)* to come apart, burst; *(fig)* to break down, fall apart; *(: être enthousiasmé)* to go wild ▷ *vt*: **~ une allumette** to strike a match

crasse [kʀas] *nf* grime, filth ▷ *adj (fig: ignorance)* crass

crasseux, -euse [kʀasø, øz] *adj* filthy

crassier [kʀasje] *nm* slag heap

cratère [kʀatɛʀ] *nm* crater

cravache [kʀavaʃ] *nf (riding)* crop

cravacher [kʀavaʃe] *vt* to use the crop on

cravate [kʀavat] *nf* tie

cravater [kʀavate] *vt* to put a tie on; *(fig)* to grab round the neck

crawl [kʀol] *nm* crawl

crawlé, e [kʀole] *adj*: **dos ~** backstroke

crayeux, -euse [kʀɛjø, -øz] *adj* chalky

crayon [kʀɛjɔ̃] *nm* pencil; *(de rouge à lèvres etc)* stick, pencil; **écrire au ~** to write in pencil; **~ à bille** ball-point pen; **~ de couleur** crayon; **~ optique** light pen

crayon-feutre [kʀɛjɔ̃føtʀ(ə)] *(pl* **crayons-feutres**) *nm* felt(-tip) pen

crayonner [kʀɛjɔne] *vt* to scribble, sketch

CRDP *sigle m (= Centre régional de documentation pédagogique)* teachers' resource centre

créance [kʀeɑ̃s] *nf (Comm)* (financial) claim, (recoverable) debt; **donner ~ à qch** to lend credence to sth

créancier, -ière [kʀeɑ̃sje, -jɛʀ] *nm/f* creditor

créateur, -trice [kʀeatœʀ, -tʀis] *adj* creative ▷ *nm/f* creator; **le C~** *(Rel)* the Creator

créatif, -ive [kʀeatif, -iv] *adj* creative

création [kʀeasjɔ̃] *nf* creation

créativité [kʀeativite] *nf* creativity

créature [kʀeatyʀ] *nf* creature

crécelle [kʀesɛl] *nf* rattle

crèche [kʀɛʃ] *nf (de Noël)* crib; *see note; (garderie)* crèche, day nursery

● **CRÈCHE**
●
● In France the Christmas crib (*crèche*) usually
● contains figurines representing a miller, a
● wood-cutter and other villagers as well as
● the Holy Family and the traditional cow,
● donkey and shepherds. The Three Wise Men
● are added to the nativity scene at Epiphany
● (6 January, Twelfth Night).

crédence [kʀedɑ̃s] *nf* (small) sideboard

crédibilité [kʀedibilite] *nf* credibility

crédible [kʀedibl(ə)] *adj* credible

crédit [kʀedi] *nm (gén)* credit; **crédits** *nmpl* funds; **acheter à ~** to buy on credit *ou* on easy terms; **faire ~ à qn** to give sb credit; **~ municipal** pawnshop; **~ relais** bridging loan

crédit-bail [kʀedibaj] *(pl* **crédits-bails**) *nm (Écon)* leasing

créditer [kʀedite] *vt*: **~ un compte (de)** to credit an account (with)

créditeur, -trice [kʀeditœʀ, -tʀis] *adj* in credit, credit *cpd* ▷ *nm/f* customer in credit

credo [kʀedo] *nm* credo, creed

crédule [kʀedyl] *adj* credulous, gullible

crédulité [kʀedylite] *nf* credulity, gullibility

créer [kʀee] *vt* to create; *(Théât: pièce)* to produce (for the first time); *(: rôle)* to create

crémaillère [kʀemajɛʀ] *nf (Rail)* rack; *(tige crantée)* trammel; **direction à ~** *(Auto)* rack and pinion steering; **pendre la ~** to have a house-warming party

crémation [kʀemasjɔ̃] *nf* cremation

crématoire [kʀematwaʀ] *adj*: **four ~** crematorium

crématorium [kʀematɔʀjɔm] *nm* crematorium

crème [kʀɛm] *nf* cream; *(entremets)* cream dessert ▷ *adj inv* cream; **un (café) ~ =** a white coffee; **~ chantilly** whipped cream, crème Chantilly; **~ fouettée** whipped cream; **~ glacée** ice cream; **~ à raser** shaving cream; **~ solaire** sun cream

crémerie [kʀemʀi] *nf* dairy; *(tearoom)* teashop

crémeux, -euse [kʀemø, -øz] *adj* creamy

crémier, -ière [kʀemje, -jɛʀ] *nm/f* dairyman/-woman

créneau, x [kʀeno] *nm (de fortification)* crenel(le); *(fig, aussi Comm)* gap, slot; *(Auto)*: **faire un ~** to reverse into a parking space *(between cars alongside the kerb)*

créole [kʀeɔl] *adj, nm/f* Creole

crêpe [kʀɛp] *nf (galette)* pancake ▷ *nm (tissu)* crêpe; *(de deuil)* black mourning crêpe; *(ruban)* black armband *(ou* hatband *ou* ribbon); **semelle (de) ~** crêpe sole; **~ de Chine** crêpe de Chine

crêpé, e [kʀepe] *adj (cheveux)* backcombed

crêperie [kʀepʀi] *nf* pancake shop *ou* restaurant

crépi [kʀepi] *nm* roughcast

crépir [kʀepiʀ] *vt* to roughcast

crépitement [kʀepitmɑ̃] *nm (du feu)* crackling *no pl; (d'une arme automatique)* rattle *no pl*

crépiter [kʀepite] *vi* to sputter, splutter, crackle

crépon [kʀepɔ̃] *nm* seersucker

CREPS [kʀɛps] *sigle m (= Centre régional d'éducation physique et sportive) =* sports *ou* leisure centre

crépu, e [kʀepy] *adj* frizzy, fuzzy

crépuscule [kʀepyskyl] *nm* twilight, dusk

crescendo [kʀeʃɛndo] *nm, adv (Mus)* crescendo; **aller ~** *(fig)* to rise higher and higher, grow ever greater

cresson [kʀesɔ̃] *nm* watercress

Crète [kʀɛt] *nf*: **la ~** Crete

crête [kʀɛt] *nf (de coq)* comb; *(de vague, montagne)* crest

crétin, e [kʀetɛ̃, -in] *nm/f* cretin

crétois, e [kʀetwa, -waz] adj Cretan

cretonne [kʀətɔn] nf cretonne

creuser [kʀøze] vt (trou, tunnel) to dig; (sol) to dig a hole in; (bois) to hollow out; (fig) to go (deeply) into; **ça creuse** that gives you a real appetite; **se ~ (la cervelle)** to rack one's brains

creuset [kʀøzε] nm crucible; (fig) melting pot, (severe) test

creux, -euse [kʀø, -øz] adj hollow ▷ nm hollow; (fig: sur graphique etc) trough; **heures creuses** slack periods; off-peak periods; **le ~ de l'estomac** the pit of the stomach

crevaison [kʀəvεzɔ̃] nf puncture, flat

crevant, e [kʀəva, -ãt] adj (fam: fatigant) knackering; (: très drôle) priceless

crevasse [kʀəvas] nf (dans le sol) crack, fissure; (de glacier) crevasse; (de la peau) crack

crevé, e [kʀəve] adj (fam: fatigué) worn out, dead beat

crève-cœur [kʀεvkœʀ] nm inv heartbreak

crever [kʀəve] vt (papier) to tear, break; (tambour, ballon) to burst ▷ vi (pneu) to burst; (automobiliste) to have a puncture (Brit) ou a flat (tire) (US); (abcès, outre, nuage) to burst (open); (fam) to die; **cela lui a crevé un œil** it blinded him in one eye; **~ l'écran** to have real screen presence

crevette [kʀəvεt] nf: **~ (rose)** prawn; **~ grise** shrimp

CRF sigle f (= Croix-Rouge française) French Red Cross

cri [kʀi] nm cry, shout; (d'animal: spécifique) cry, call; **à grands ~s** at the top of one's voice; **c'est le dernier ~** (fig) it's the latest fashion

criant, e [kʀija, -ãt] adj (injustice) glaring

criard, e [kʀijaʀ, -aʀd(ə)] adj (couleur) garish, loud; (voix) yelling

crible [kʀibl(ə)] nm riddle; (mécanique) screen, jig; **passer qch au ~** to put sth through a riddle; (fig) to go over sth with a fine-tooth comb

criblé, e [kʀible] adj: **~ de** riddled with

cric [kʀik] nm (Auto) jack

cricket [kʀikεt] nm cricket

criée [kʀije] nf: **(vente à la) ~** (sale by) auction

crier [kʀije] vi (pour appeler) to shout, cry (out); (de peur, de douleur etc) to scream, yell; (fig: grincer) to squeal, screech ▷ vt (ordre, injure) to shout (out), yell (out); **sans ~ gare** without warning; **~ grâce** to cry for mercy; **~ au secours** to shout for help

crieur, -euse [kʀijœʀ, -øz] nm/f: **~ de journaux** newspaper seller

crime [kʀim] nm crime; (meurtre) murder

Crimée [kʀime] nf: **la ~** the Crimea

criminalité [kʀiminalite] nf criminality, crime

criminel, le [kʀiminεl] adj criminal ▷ nm/f criminal; murderer; **~ de guerre** war criminal

criminologie [kʀiminɔlɔʒi] nf criminology

criminologiste [kʀiminɔlɔʒist(ə)] nm/f criminologist

criminologue [kʀiminɔlɔg] nm/f criminologist

crin [kʀɛ̃] nm hair no pl; (fibre) horsehair; **à tous**

~s, à tout ~ diehard, out-and-out

crinière [kʀinjεʀ] nf mane

crique [kʀik] nf creek, inlet

criquet [kʀikε] nm grasshopper

crise [kʀiz] nf crisis (pl crises); (Méd) attack; fit; **~ cardiaque** heart attack; **~ de foi** crisis of belief; **~ de foie** bilious attack; **~ de nerfs** attack of nerves

crispant, e [kʀispã, -ãt] adj annoying, irritating

crispation [kʀispasjɔ̃] nf (spasme) twitch; (contraction) contraction; tenseness

crispé, e [kʀispe] adj tense, nervous

crisper [kʀispe] vt to tense; (poings) to clench; **se crisper** to tense; to clench; (personne) to get tense

crissement [kʀismã] nm crunch; rustle; screech

crisser [kʀise] vi (neige) to crunch; (tissu) to rustle; (pneu) to screech

cristal, -aux [kʀistal, -o] nm crystal; **crystaux** nmpl (objets) crystal(ware) sg; **~ de plomb** (lead) crystal; **~ de roche** rock-crystal; **cristaux de soude** washing soda sg

cristallin, e [kʀistalɛ̃, -in] adj crystal-clear ▷ nm (Anat) crystalline lens

cristalliser [kʀistalize] vi, vt, **se cristalliser** vi to crystallize

critère [kʀitεʀ] nm criterion (pl -ia)

critiquable [kʀitikabl(ə)] adj open to criticism

critique [kʀitik] adj critical ▷ nm/f (de théâtre, musique) critic ▷ nf criticism; (Théât etc: article) review; **la ~** (activité) criticism; (personnes) the critics pl

critiquer [kʀitike] vt (dénigrer) to criticize; (évaluer, juger) to assess, examine (critically)

croasser [kʀɔase] vi to caw

croate [kʀɔat] adj Croatian ▷ nm (Ling) Croat, Croatian

Croatie [kʀɔasi] nf: **la ~** Croatia

croc [kʀo] nm (dent) fang; (de boucher) hook

croc-en-jambe [kʀɔkãʒãb] (pl **crocs-en-jambe**) nm: **faire un ~ à qn** to trip sb up

croche [kʀɔʃ] nf (Mus) quaver (Brit), eighth note (US); **double ~** semiquaver (Brit), sixteenth note (US)

croche-pied [kʀɔʃpje] nm = **croc-en-jambe**

crochet [kʀɔʃε] nm hook; (clef) picklock; (détour) detour; (Boxe): **~ du gauche** left hook; (Tricot: aiguille) crochet hook; (: technique) crochet; **crochets** nmpl (Typo) square brackets; **vivre aux ~s de qn** to live ou sponge off sb

crocheter [kʀɔʃte] vt (serrure) to pick

crochu, e [kʀɔʃy] adj hooked; claw-like

crocodile [kʀɔkɔdil] nm crocodile

crocus [kʀɔkys] nm crocus

croire [kʀwaʀ] vt to believe; **~ qn honnête** to believe sb (to be) honest; **se ~ fort** to think one is strong; **~ que** to believe ou think that; **vous croyez?** do you think so?; **~ être/faire** to think one is/does; **~ à, ~ en** to believe in

croîs etc [kʀwa] vb voir **croître**

croisade [kʀwazad] nf crusade

croisé, e [kʀwaze] *adj* (*veston*) double-breasted ▷ *nm* (*guerrier*) crusader ▷ *nf* (*fenêtre*) window, casement; **~e d'ogives** intersecting ribs; **à la ~e des chemins** at the crossroads

croisement [kʀwazmɑ̃] *nm* (*carrefour*) crossroads *sg*; (*Bio*) crossing; crossbreed

croiser [kʀwaze] *vt* (*personne, voiture*) to pass; (*route*) to cross, cut across; (*Bio*) to cross ▷ *vi* (*Navig*) to cruise; **~ les jambes/bras** to cross one's legs/fold one's arms; **se croiser** *vi* (*personnes, véhicules*) to pass each other; (*routes*) to cross, intersect; (*lettres*) to cross (in the post); (*regards*) to meet; **se ~ les bras** (*fig*) to twiddle one's thumbs

croiseur [kʀwazœʀ] *nm* cruiser (*warship*)

croisière [kʀwazjɛʀ] *nf* cruise; **vitesse de ~** (*Auto etc*) cruising speed

croisillon [kʀwazijɔ̃] *nm*: **motif/fenêtre à ~s** lattice pattern/window

croissais *etc* [kʀwasɛ] *vb voir* **croître**

croissance [kʀwasɑ̃s] *nf* growing, growth; **troubles de la ~** growing pains; **maladie de ~** growth disease; **~ économique** economic growth

croissant, e [kʀwasɑ̃, -ɑ̃t] *vb voir* **croître** ▷ *adj* growing; rising ▷ *nm* (*à manger*) croissant; (*motif*) crescent; **~ de lune** crescent moon

croître [kʀwatʀ(ə)] *vi* to grow; (*lune*) to wax

croix [kʀwa] *nf* cross; **en ~** *adj, adv* in the form of a cross; **la C~ Rouge** the Red Cross

croquant, e [kʀɔkɑ̃, -ɑ̃t] *adj* crisp, crunchy ▷ *nm/f* (*péj*) yokel, (country) bumpkin

croque-madame [kʀɔkmadam] *nm inv* toasted cheese sandwich with a fried egg on top

croque-mitaine [kʀɔkmitɛn] *nm* bog(e)y-man (*pl* -men)

croque-monsieur [kʀɔkməsjø] *nm inv* toasted ham and cheese sandwich

croque-mort [kʀɔkmɔʀ] *nm* (*péj*) pallbearer

croquer [kʀɔke] *vt* (*manger*) to crunch; to munch; (*dessiner*) to sketch ▷ *vi* to be crisp *ou* crunchy; **chocolat à ~** plain dessert chocolate

croquet [kʀɔkɛ] *nm* croquet

croquette [kʀɔkɛt] *nf* croquette

croquis [kʀɔki] *nm* sketch

cross [kʀɔs], **cross-country** [kʀɔskuntʀi] (*pl* -(-countries)) *nm* cross-country race *ou* run; cross-country racing *ou* running

crosse [kʀɔs] *nf* (*de fusil*) butt; (*de revolver*) grip; (*d'évêque*) crook, crosier; (*de hockey*) hockey stick

crotale [kʀɔtal] *nm* rattlesnake

crotte [kʀɔt] *nf* droppings *pl*; **~!** (*fam*) damn!

crotté, e [kʀɔte] *adj* muddy, mucky

crottin [kʀɔtɛ̃] *nm*: **~ (de cheval)** (horse) dung *ou* manure

croulant, e [kʀulɑ̃, -ɑ̃t] *nm/f* (*fam*) old fogey

crouler [kʀule] *vi* (*s'effondrer*) to collapse; (*être délabré*) to be crumbling

croupe [kʀup] *nf* croup, rump; **en ~** pillion

croupier [kʀupje] *nm* croupier

croupion [kʀupjɔ̃] *nm* (*d'un oiseau*) rump; (*Culin*) parson's nose

croupir [kʀupiʀ] *vi* to stagnate

CROUS [kʀus] *sigle m* (= *Centre régional des œuvres universitaires et scolaires*) students' representative body

croustade [kʀustad] *nf* (*Culin*) croustade

croustillant, e [kʀustijɑ̃, -ɑ̃t] *adj* crisp; (*fig*) spicy

croustiller [kʀustije] *vi* to be crisp *ou* crusty

croûte [kʀut] *nf* crust; (*du fromage*) rind; (*de vol-au-vent*) case; (*Méd*) scab; **en ~** (*Culin*) in pastry, in a pie; **~ aux champignons** mushrooms on toast; **~ au fromage** cheese on toast *no pl*; **~ de pain** (*morceau*) crust (of bread); **~ terrestre** earth's crust

croûton [kʀutɔ̃] *nm* (*Culin*) crouton; (*bout du pain*) crust, heel

croyable [kʀwajabl(ə)] *adj* believable, credible

croyais *etc* [kʀwaje] *vb voir* **croire**

croyance [kʀwajɑ̃s] *nf* belief

croyant, e [kʀwajɑ̃, -ɑ̃t] *vb voir* **croire** ▷ *adj*: **être/ne pas être ~** to be/not to be a believer ▷ *nm/f* believer

Crozet [kʀɔzɛ] *n*: **les îles ~** the Crozet Islands

CRS *sigle fpl* (= *Compagnies républicaines de sécurité*) state security police force ▷ *sigle m* member of the CRS

cru, e [kʀy] *pp de* **croire** ▷ *adj* (*non cuit*) raw; (*lumière, couleur*) harsh; (*description*) crude; (*paroles, langage: franc*) blunt; (: *grossier*) crude ▷ *nm* (*vignoble*) vineyard; (*vin*) wine ▷ *nf* (*d'un cours d'eau*) swelling, rising; **de son (propre) ~** (*fig*) of his own devising; **monter à ~** to ride bareback; **du ~** local; **en ~e** in spate

crû [kʀy] *pp de* **croître**

cruauté [kʀyote] *nf* cruelty

cruche [kʀyʃ] *nf* pitcher, (earthenware) jug

crucial, e, -aux [kʀysjal, -o] *adj* crucial

crucifier [kʀysifje] *vt* to crucify

crucifix [kʀysifi] *nm* crucifix

crucifixion [kʀysifiksjɔ̃] *nf* crucifixion

cruciforme [kʀysifɔʀm(ə)] *adj* cruciform, cross-shaped

cruciverbiste [kʀysivɛʀbist(ə)] *nm/f* crossword puzzle enthusiast

crudité [kʀydite] *nf* crudeness *no pl*; harshness *no pl*; **crudités** *nfpl* (*Culin*) mixed salads (*as hors-d'œuvre*)

crue [kʀy] *nf voir* **cru**

cruel, le [kʀyɛl] *adj* cruel

cruellement [kʀyɛlmɑ̃] *adv* cruelly

crûment [kʀymɑ̃] *adv* (*voir cru*) harshly; bluntly; crudely

crus, crûs *etc* [kʀy] *vb voir* **croire**; **croître**

crustacés [kʀystase] *nmpl* shellfish

crypte [kʀipt(ə)] *nf* crypt

CSA *sigle f* (= *Conseil supérieur de l'audiovisuel*) French broadcasting regulatory body, ≈ IBA (Brit), ≈ FCC (US)

cse *abr* = **cause**

CSEN *sigle f* (= *Confédération syndicale de l'éducation nationale*) group of teachers' unions

CSG *sigle f* (= *contribution sociale généralisée*) supplementary social security contribution in aid of the underprivileged

CSM *sigle m* (= *Conseil supérieur de la magistrature*)

French magistrates' council

Cte abr = **Comtesse**

CU sigle f = **communauté urbaine**

Cuba [kyba] nm: **le ~** Cuba

cubage [kybaʒ] nm cubage, cubic content

cubain, e [kybɛ̃, -ɛn] adj Cuban ▷ nm/f: **Cubain, e** Cuban

cube [kyb] nm cube; (jouet) brick, building block; **gros ~** powerful motorbike; **mètre ~** cubic metre; **2 au ~ = 8** 2 cubed is 8; **élever au ~** to cube

cubique [kybik] adj cubic

cubisme [kybism(ə)] nm cubism

cubiste [kybist(ə)] adj, nm/f cubist

cubitus [kybitys] nm ulna

cueillette [kœjɛt] nf picking, gathering; harvest ou crop (of fruit)

cueillir [kœjiʀ] vt (fruits, fleurs) to pick, gather; (fig) to catch

cuiller, cuillère [kɥijɛʀ] nf spoon; **~ à café** coffee spoon; (Culin) ≈ teaspoonful; **~ à soupe** soup spoon; (Culin) ≈ tablespoonful

cuillerée [kɥijʀe] nf spoonful; (Culin): **~ à soupe/café** tablespoonful/teaspoonful

cuir [kɥiʀ] nm leather; (avant tannage) hide; **~ chevelu** scalp

cuirasse [kɥiʀas] nf breastplate

cuirassé [kɥiʀase] nm (Navig) battleship

cuire [kɥiʀ] vt: **(faire) ~** (aliments) to cook; (au four) to bake; (poterie) to fire ▷ vi to cook; (picoter) to smart, sting, burn; **bien cuit** well done; **trop cuit** overdone; **pas assez cuit** underdone; **cuit à point** medium done; done to a turn

cuisant, e [kɥizɑ̃, -ɑ̃t] vb voir **cuire** ▷ adj (douleur) smarting, burning; (fig: souvenir, échec) bitter

cuisine [kɥizin] nf (pièce) kitchen; (art culinaire) cookery, cooking; (nourriture) cooking, food; **faire la ~** to cook

cuisiné, e [kɥizine] adj: **plat ~** ready-made meal ou dish

cuisiner [kɥizine] vt to cook; (fam) to grill ▷ vi to cook

cuisinette [kɥizinɛt] nf kitchenette

cuisinier, -ière [kɥizinje, -jɛʀ] nm/f cook ▷ nf (poêle) cooker; **cuisinière électrique/à gaz** electric/gas cooker

cuisis etc [kɥizi] vb voir **cuire**

cuissardes [kɥisaʀd] nfpl (de pêcheur) waders; (de femme) thigh boots

cuisse [kɥis] nf (Anat) thigh; (Culin) leg

cuisson [kɥisɔ̃] nf cooking; (de poterie) firing

cuissot [kɥiso] nm haunch

cuistre [kɥistʀ(ə)] nm prig

cuit, e [kɥi, -it] pp de **cuire** ▷ nf (fam): **prendre une ~** to get plastered ou smashed

cuivre [kɥivʀ(ə)] nm copper; **les ~s** (Mus) the brass; **~ rouge** copper; **~ jaune** brass

cuivré, e [kɥivʀe] adj coppery; (peau) bronzed

cul [ky] nm (fam!) arse (Brit !), ass (US !), bum (Brit); **~ de bouteille** bottom of a bottle

culasse [kylas] nf (Auto) cylinder-head; (de

fusil) breech

culbute [kylbyt] nf somersault; (accidentelle) tumble, fall

culbuter [kylbyte] vi to (take a) tumble, fall (head over heels)

culbuteur [kylbytœʀ] nm (Auto) rocker arm

cul-de-jatte [kydʒat] (pl **culs-de-jatte**) nm/f legless cripple

cul-de-sac [kydsak] (pl **culs-de-sac**) nm cul-de-sac

culinaire [kylinɛʀ] adj culinary

culminant, e [kylminɑ̃, -ɑ̃t] adj: **point ~** highest point; (fig) height, climax

culminer [kylmine] vi to reach its highest point; to tower

culot [kylo] nm (d'ampoule) cap; (effronterie) cheek, nerve

culotte [kylɔt] nf (de femme) panties pl, knickers pl (Brit); (d'homme) underpants pl; (pantalon) trousers pl (Brit), pants pl (US); **~ de cheval** riding breeches pl

culotté, e [kylɔte] adj (pipe) seasoned; (cuir) mellowed; (effronté) cheeky

culpabiliser [kylpabilize] vt: **~ qn** to make sb feel guilty

culpabilité [kylpabilite] nf guilt

culte [kylt(ə)] adj: **livre/film ~** cult film/book ▷ nm (religion) religion; (hommage, vénération) worship; (protestant) service

cultivable [kyltivabl(ə)] adj cultivable

cultivateur, -trice [kyltivatœʀ, -tʀis] nm/f farmer

cultivé, e [kyltive] adj (personne) cultured, cultivated

cultiver [kyltive] vt to cultivate; (légumes) to grow, cultivate

culture [kyltyʀ] nf cultivation; growing; (connaissances etc) culture; **(champs de) ~s** land(s) under cultivation; **~ physique** physical training

culturel, le [kyltyʀɛl] adj cultural

culturisme [kyltyʀism(ə)] nm body-building

culturiste [kyltyʀist(ə)] nm/f body-builder

cumin [kymɛ̃] nm (Culin) cumin

cumul [kymyl] nm (voir cumuler) holding (ou drawing) concurrently; **~ de peines** sentences to run consecutively

cumulable [kymylabl(ə)] adj (fonctions) which may be held concurrently

cumuler [kymyle] vt (emplois, honneurs) to hold concurrently; (salaires) to draw concurrently; (Jur: droits) to accumulate

cupide [kypid] adj greedy, grasping

cupidité [kypidite] nf greed

curable [kyʀabl(ə)] adj curable

Curaçao [kyʀaso] n Curaçao ▷ nm: **curaçao** curaçao

curare [kyʀaʀ] nm curare

curatif, -ive [kyʀatif, -iv] adj curative

cure [kyʀ] nf (Méd) course of treatment; (Rel) cure, ≈ living; presbytery, ≈ vicarage; **faire une ~ de fruits** to go on a fruit cure ou diet; **faire**

une ~ **thermale** to take the waters; **n'avoir ~ de** to pay no attention to; ~ **d'amaigrissement** slimming course; ~ **de repos** rest cure; ~ **de sommeil** sleep therapy *no pl*

curé [kyʀe] *nm* parish priest; **M le ~** ≈ Vicar

cure-dent [kyʀdɑ̃] *nm* toothpick

curée [kyʀe] *nf* (*fig*) scramble for the pickings

cure-ongles [kyʀɔ̃gl(ə)] *nm inv* nail cleaner

cure-pipe [kyʀpip] *nm* pipe cleaner

curer [kyʀe] *vt* to clean out; **se ~ les dents** to pick one's teeth

curetage [kyʀtaʒ] *nm* (*Méd*) curettage

curieusement [kyʀjøzmɑ̃] *adv* oddly

curieux, -euse [kyʀjø, -øz] *adj* (*étrange*) strange, curious; (*indiscret*) curious, inquisitive; (*intéressé*) inquiring, curious ▷ *nmpl* (*badauds*) onlookers, bystanders

curiosité [kyʀjozite] *nf* curiosity, inquisitiveness; (*objet*) curio(sity); (*site*) unusual feature *ou* sight

curiste [kyʀist(ə)] *nm/f person taking the waters at a spa*

curriculum vitae [kyʀikylɔmvite] *nm inv* curriculum vitae

curry [kyʀi] *nm* curry; **poulet au ~** curried chicken, chicken curry

curseur [kyʀsœʀ] *nm* (*Inform*) cursor; (*de règle*) slide; (*de fermeture-éclair*) slider

cursif, -ive [kyʀsif, -iv] *adj*: **écriture cursive** cursive script

cursus [kyʀsys] *nm* degree course

curviligne [kyʀviliɲ] *adj* curvilinear

cutané, e [kytane] *adj* cutaneous, skin *cpd*

cuti-réaction [kytiʀeaksjɔ̃] *nf* (*Méd*) skin-test

cuve [kyv] *nf* vat; (*à mazout etc*) tank

cuvée [kyve] *nf* vintage

cuvette [kyvɛt] *nf* (*récipient*) bowl, basin; (*du lavabo*) (wash)basin; (*des w.-c.*) pan; (*Géo*) basin

CV *sigle m* (*Auto*) = **cheval vapeur**; (*Admin*) = **curriculum vitae**

CVS *sigle adj* (= *corrigées des variations saisonnières*) seasonally adjusted

cx *abr* (= *coefficient de pénétration dans l'air*) drag coefficient

cyanure [sjanyʀ] *nm* cyanide

cybercafé [sibɛʀkafe] *nm* cybercafé

cyberculture [sibɛʀkyltyʀ] *nf* cyberculture

cyberespace [sibɛʀɛspas] *nm* cyberspace

cybernaute [sibɛʀnot] *nm/f* Internet user

cybernétique [sibɛʀnetik] *nf* cybernetics *sg*

cyclable [siklabl(ə)] *adj*: **piste ~** cycle track

cyclamen [siklamɛn] *nm* cyclamen

cycle [sikl(ə)] *nm* cycle; (*Scol*): **premier/second ~** ≈ middle/upper school (*Brit*), ≈ junior/senior high school (*US*)

cyclique [siklik] *adj* cyclic(al)

cyclisme [siklism(ə)] *nm* cycling

cycliste [siklist(ə)] *nm/f* cyclist ▷ *adj* cycle *cpd*; **coureur ~** racing cyclist

cyclo-cross [siklɔkʀɔs] *nm* (*Sport*) cyclo-cross; (*épreuve*) cyclo-cross race

cyclomoteur [siklɔmɔtœʀ] *nm* moped

cyclomotoriste [siklɔmɔtɔʀist(ə)] *nm/f* moped rider

cyclone [siklon] *nm* hurricane

cyclotourisme [siklɔtuʀism(ə)] *nm* (bi)cycle touring

cygne [siɲ] *nm* swan

cylindre [silɛ̃dʀ(ə)] *nm* cylinder; **moteur à 4 ~s en ligne** straight-4 engine

cylindrée [silɛ̃dʀe] *nf* (*Auto*) (cubic) capacity; **une (voiture de) grosse ~** a big-engined car

cylindrique [silɛ̃dʀik] *adj* cylindrical

cymbale [sɛ̃bal] *nf* cymbal

cynique [sinik] *adj* cynical

cyniquement [sinikmɑ̃] *adv* cynically

cynisme [sinism(ə)] *nm* cynicism

cyprès [sipʀɛ] *nm* cypress

cypriote [sipʀijɔt] *adj* Cypriot ▷ *nm/f*: **Cypriote** Cypriot

cyrillique [siʀilik] *adj* Cyrillic

cystite [sistit] *nf* cystitis

cytise [sitiz] *nm* laburnum

cytologie [sitɔlɔʒi] *nf* cytology

Dd

D, d [de] *nm inv* D, d ▷ *abr:* **D** (*Météorologie:*
= *dépression*) low, depression; **D comme Désiré**
D for David (*Brit*) *ou* Dog (*US*); *voir* **système**
d' *prép, art voir* **de**
Dacca [daka] *n* Dacca
dactylo [daktilo] *nf* (*aussi:* **dactylographe**)
typist; (*aussi:* **dactylographie**) typing,
typewriting
dactylographier [daktilɔgʀafje] *vt* to type (out)
dada [dada] *nm* hobby-horse
dadais [dadɛ] *nm* ninny, lump
dague [dag] *nf* dagger
dahlia [dalja] *nm* dahlia
dahoméen, ne [daɔmeɛ̃, -ɛn] *adj* Dahomean
Dahomey [daɔme] *nm:* **le ~** Dahomey
daigner [deɲe] *vt* to deign
daim [dɛ̃] *nm* (fallow) deer *inv*; (*peau*) buckskin;
(*imitation*) suede
dais [dɛ] *nm* (*tenture*) canopy
Dakar [dakaʀ] *n* Dakar
dal. *abr* (= *décalitre*) dal.
dallage [dalaʒ] *nm* paving
dalle [dal] *nf* slab; (*au sol*) paving stone,
flag(stone); **que ~** nothing at all, damn all (*Brit*)
daller [dale] *vt* to pave
dalmatien, ne [dalmasjɛ̃, -ɛn] *nm/f* (*chien*)
Dalmatian
daltonien, ne [daltɔnjɛ̃, -ɛn] *adj* colour-blind
(*Brit*), color-blind (*US*)
daltonisme [daltɔnism(ə)] *nm* colour (*Brit*) *ou*
color (*US*) blindness
dam [dam] *nm:* **au grand ~ de** much to the
detriment (*ou* annoyance) of
Damas [dama] *n* Damascus
damas [dama] *nm* (*étoffe*) damask
damassé, e [damase] *adj* damask *cpd*
dame [dam] *nf* lady; (*Cartes, Échecs*) queen;
dames *nfpl* (*jeu*) draughts *sg* (*Brit*), checkers *sg*
(*US*); **les (toilettes des) ~s** the ladies' (toilets);
~ de charité benefactress; **~ de compagnie**
lady's companion
dame-jeanne [damʒan] (*pl* **dames-jeannes**) *nf*
demijohn
damer [dame] *vt* to ram *ou* pack down; **~ le pion
à** (*fig*) to get the better of
damier [damje] *nm* draughts board (*Brit*),

checkerboard (*US*); (*dessin*) check (pattern); **en ~**
check
damner [dane] *vt* to damn
dancing [dãsiŋ] *nm* dance hall
dandiner [dãdine]: **se dandiner** *vi* to sway
about; (*en marchant*) to waddle along
Danemark [danmaʀk] *nm:* **le ~** Denmark
danger [dãʒe] *nm* danger; **mettre en ~** to
endanger, put in danger; **être en ~ de mort** to
be in peril of one's life; **être hors de ~** to be out
of danger
dangereusement [dãʒʀøzmã] *adv* dangerously
dangereux, -euse [dãʒʀø, -øz] *adj* dangerous
danois, e [danwa, -waz] *adj* Danish ▷ *nm* (*Ling*)
Danish ▷ *nm/f:* **Danois, e** Dane

 MOT-CLÉ

dans [dã] *prép* **1** (*position*) in; (*à l'intérieur de*)
inside; **c'est dans le tiroir/le salon** it's in the
drawer/lounge; **dans la boîte** in *ou* inside the
box; **marcher dans la ville/la rue** to walk
about the town/along the street; **je l'ai lu dans
le journal** I read it in the newspaper; **être
dans les meilleurs** to be among *ou* one of the
best

2 (*direction*) into; **elle a couru dans le salon** she
ran into the lounge

3 (*provenance*) out of, from; **je l'ai pris dans le
tiroir/salon** I took it out of *ou* from the drawer/
lounge; **boire dans un verre** to drink out of *ou*
from a glass

4 (*temps*) in; **dans deux mois** in two months, in
two months' time

5 (*approximation*) about; **dans les 20 euros**
about 20 euros

dansant, e [dãsã, -ãt] *adj:* **soirée ~e** evening of
dancing; (*bal*) dinner dance
danse [dãs] *nf:* **la ~** dancing; (*classique*) (ballet)
dancing; **une ~** a dance; **~ du ventre** belly
dancing
danser [dãse] *vi, vt* to dance
danseur, -euse [dãsœʀ, -øz] *nm/f* ballet dancer;
(*au bal etc*) dancer; (: *cavalier*) partner; **~ de
claquettes** tap-dancer; **en danseuse** (*à vélo*)

standing on the pedals

Danube [danyb] *nm*: **le ~** the Danube

DAO *sigle m* (= *dessin assisté par ordinateur*) CAD

dard [daʀ] *nm* sting (*organ*)

darder [daʀde] *vt* to shoot, send forth

dare-dare [daʀdaʀ] *adv* in double quick time

Dar-es-Salaam, Dar-es-Salam [daʀɛsalam] *n* Dar-es-Salaam

darne [daʀn] *nf* steak (*of fish*)

darse [daʀs(ə)] *nf* sheltered dock (*in a Mediterranean port*)

dartre [daʀtʀ(ə)] *nf* (*Méd*) sore

datation [datasjɔ̃] *nf* dating

date [dat] *nf* date; **faire ~** to mark a milestone; **de longue ~** *adj* longstanding; **~ de naissance** date of birth; **~ limite** deadline; (*d'un aliment: aussi*: **date limite de vente**) sell-by date

dater [date] *vt, vi* to date; **~ de** to date from, go back to; **à ~ de** (as) from

dateur [datœʀ] *nm* (*de montre*) date indicator; **timbre ~** date stamp

datif [datif] *nm* dative

datte [dat] *nf* date

dattier [datje] *nm* date palm

daube [dob] *nf*: **bœuf en ~** beef casserole

dauphin [dofɛ̃] *nm* (*Zool*) dolphin; (*du roi*) dauphin; (*fig*) heir apparent

Dauphiné [dofine] *nm*: **le ~** the Dauphiné

dauphinois, e [dofinwa, -waz] *adj* of *ou* from the Dauphiné

daurade [dɔʀad] *nf* sea bream

davantage [davɑ̃taʒ] *adv* more; (*plus longtemps*) longer; **~ de** more; **~ que** more than

DB *sigle f* (*Mil*) = **division blindée**

DCA *sigle f* (= *défense contre avions*) anti-aircraft defence

DCT *sigle m* (= *diphtérie coqueluche tétanos*) DPT

DDASS [das] *sigle f* (= *Direction départementale d'action sanitaire et sociale*) ≈ DWP (= *Department of Work and Pensions* (*Brit*)), ≈ SSA (= *Social Security Administration* (*US*))

DDT *sigle m* (= *dichloro-diphénol-trichloréthane*) DDT

 MOT-CLÉ

de, d' (*de* + *le* = **du**, *de* + *les* = **des**) *prép* **1** (*appartenance*) of; **le toit de la maison** the roof of the house; **la voiture d'Elisabeth/de mes parents** Elizabeth's/my parents' car

2 (*provenance*) from; **il vient de Londres** he comes from London; **de Londres à Paris** from London to Paris; **elle est sortie du cinéma** she came out of the cinema

3 (*moyen*) with; **je l'ai fait de mes propres mains** I did it with my own two hands

4 (*caractérisation, mesure*): **un mur de brique/bureau d'acajou** a brick wall/mahogany desk; **un billet de 10 euros** a 10 euro note; **une pièce de 2 m de large** *ou* **large de 2 m** a room 2 m wide, a 2m-wide room; **un bébé de 10 mois** a 10-month-old baby; **12 mois de crédit/travail** 12 months' credit/work; **elle est payée 20**

euros de l'heure she's paid 20 euros an hour *ou* per hour; **augmenter de 10 euros** to increase by 10 euros; **trois jours de libres** three free days, three days free; **un verre d'eau** a glass of water; **il mange de tout** he'll eat anything

5 (*rapport*) from; **de quatre à six** from four to six

6 (*de la part de*): **estimé de ses collègues** respected by his colleagues

7 (*cause*): **mourir de faim** to die of hunger; **rouge de colère** red with fury

8 (*vb* + *de* + *infin*) to; **il m'a dit de rester** he told me to stay

9 (*en apposition*): **cet imbécile de Paul** that idiot Paul; **le terme de franglais** the term "franglais"

▷ *art* **1** (*phrases affirmatives*) some (*souvent omis*); **du vin, de l'eau, des pommes** (some) wine, (some) water, (some) apples; **des enfants sont venus** some children came; **pendant des mois** for months

2 (*phrases interrogatives et négatives*) any; **a-t-il du vin?** has he got any wine?; **il n'a pas de pommes/d'enfants** he hasn't (got) any apples/children, he has no apples/children

dé [de] *nm* (*à jouer*) die *ou* dice; (*aussi*: **dé à coudre**) thimble; **dés** *nmpl* (*jeu*) (game of) dice; **un coup de dés** a throw of the dice; **couper en dés** (*Culin*) to dice

DEA *sigle m* (= *Diplôme d'études approfondies*) postgraduate diploma

dealer [dilœʀ] *nm* (*fam*) (drug) pusher

déambulateur [deɑ̃bylatœʀ] *nm* zimmer®

déambuler [deɑ̃byle] *vi* to stroll about

déb. *abr* = **débutant**; (*Comm*) = **à débattre**

débâcle [debɑkl(ə)] *nf* rout

déballage [debalaʒ] *nm* (*de marchandises*) display (*of loose goods*); (*fig: fam*) outpourings *pl*

déballer [debale] *vt* to unpack

débandade [debɑ̃dad] *nf* scattering; (*déroute*) rout

débander [debɑ̃de] *vt* to unbandage

débaptiser [debatize] *vt* (*rue*) to rename

débarbouiller [debaʀbuje] *vt* to wash; **se débarbouiller** *vi* to wash (one's face)

débarcadère [debaʀkadɛʀ] *nm* landing stage (*Brit*), wharf

débardeur [debaʀdœʀ] *nm* docker, stevedore; (*maillot*) slipover, tank top

débarquement [debaʀkəmɑ̃] *nm* unloading, landing; disembarkation; (*Mil*) landing; **le D~** the Normandy landings

débarquer [debaʀke] *vt* to unload, land ▷ *vi* to disembark; (*fig*) to turn up

débarras [debaʀa] *nm* lumber room; (*placard*) junk cupboard; (*remise*) outhouse; **bon ~!** good riddance!

débarrasser [debaʀase] *vt* to clear ▷ *vi* (*enlever le couvert*) to clear away; **~ qn de** (*vêtements, paquets*) to relieve sb of; (*habitude, ennemi*) to rid sb of; **~ qch de** (*fouillis etc*) to clear sth of; **se débarrasser**

de vt to get rid of; to rid o.s. of

débat [deba] vb voir **débattre** ▷ nm discussion, debate; **débats** nmpl (Pol) proceedings, debates

débattre [debatʀ(ə)] vt to discuss, debate; **se débattre** vi to struggle

débauchage [deboʃaʒ] nm (licenciement) laying off (of staff); (par un concurrent) poaching

débauche [deboʃ] nf debauchery; **une ~ de** (fig) a profusion of; (: de couleurs) a riot of

débauché, e [deboʃe] adj debauched ▷ nm/f profligate

débaucher [deboʃe] vt (licencier) to lay off, dismiss; (salarié d'une autre entreprise) to poach; (entraîner) to lead astray, debauch; (inciter à la grève) to incite

débile [debil] adj weak, feeble; (fam: idiot) dim-witted ▷ nm/f: **~ mental, e** mental defective

débilitant, e [debilitā, -āt] adj debilitating

débilité [debilite] nf debility; (fam: idiotie) stupidity; **~ mentale** mental debility

débiner [debine]: **se débiner** vi to do a bunk (Brit), clear out

débit [debi] nm (d'un liquide, fleuve) (rate of) flow; (d'un magasin) turnover (of goods); (élocution) delivery; (bancaire) debit; **avoir un ~ de 10 euros** to be 10 euros in debit; **~ de boissons** drinking establishment; **~ de tabac** tobacconist's (shop) (Brit), tobacco ou smoke shop (US)

débiter [debite] vt (compte) to debit; (liquide, gaz) to yield, produce, give out; (couper: bois, viande) to cut up; (vendre) to retail; (péj: paroles etc) to come out with, churn out

débiteur, -trice [debitœʀ, -tʀis] nm/f debtor ▷ adj in debit; (compte) debit cpd

déblai [deblɛ] nm (nettoyage) clearing; **déblais** nmpl (terre) earth; (décombres) rubble

déblaiement [deblɛmā] nm clearing; **travaux de ~** earth moving sg

déblatérer [deblateʀe] vi: **~ contre** to go on about

déblayer [debleje] vt to clear; **~ le terrain** (fig) to clear the ground

déblocage [deblɔkaʒ] nm (des prix, cours) unfreezing

débloquer [deblɔke] vt (frein, fonds) to release; (prix) to unfreeze ▷ vi (fam) to talk rubbish

débobiner [debɔbine] vt to unwind

déboires [debwaʀ] nmpl setbacks

déboisement [debwazmā] nm deforestation

déboiser [debwaze] vt to clear of trees; (région) to deforest; **se déboiser** vi (colline, montagne) to become bare of trees

déboîter [debwate] vt (Auto) to pull out; **se ~ le genou** etc to dislocate one's knee etc

débonnaire [debɔnɛʀ] adj easy-going, good-natured

débordant, e [debɔʀdā, -āt] adj (joie) unbounded; (activité) exuberant

débordé, e [debɔʀde] adj: **être ~ de** (travail, demandes) to be snowed under with

débordement [debɔʀdəmā] nm overflowing

déborder [debɔʀde] vi to overflow; (lait etc) to boil over ▷ vt (Mil, Sport) to outflank; **~ (de) qch** (dépasser) to extend beyond sth; **~ de** (joie, zèle) to be brimming over with ou bursting with

débouché [debuʃe] nm (pour vendre) outlet; (perspective d'emploi) opening; (sortie): **au ~ de la vallée** where the valley opens out (onto the plain)

déboucher [debuʃe] vt (évier, tuyau etc) to unblock; (bouteille) to uncork, open ▷ vi: **~ de** to emerge from, come out of; **~ sur** to come out onto; to open out onto; (fig) to arrive at, lead up to

débouler [debule] vi to go (ou come) tumbling down; (sans tomber) to come careering down ▷ vt: **~ l'escalier** to belt down the stairs

déboulonner [debulɔne] vt to dismantle; (fig: renvoyer) to dismiss; (: détruire le prestige de) to discredit

débours [debuʀ] nmpl outlay

débourser [debuʀse] vt to pay out, lay out

déboussoler [debusɔle] vt to disorientate, disorient

debout [dəbu] adv: **être ~** (personne) to be standing, stand; (: levé, éveillé) to be up (and about); (chose) to be upright; **être encore ~** (fig: en état) to be still going; to be still standing; to be still up; **mettre qn ~** to get sb to his feet; **mettre qch ~** to stand sth up; **se mettre ~** to get up (on one's feet); **se tenir ~** to stand; **~!** get up!; **cette histoire ne tient pas ~** this story doesn't hold water

débouter [debute] vt (Jur) to dismiss; **~ qn de sa demande** to dismiss sb's petition

déboutonner [debutɔne] vt to undo, unbutton; **se déboutonner** vi to come undone ou unbuttoned

débraillé, e [debʀaje] adj slovenly, untidy

débrancher [debʀāʃe] vt (appareil électrique) to unplug; (téléphone, courant électrique) to disconnect, cut off

débrayage [debʀɛjaʒ] nm (Auto) clutch; (: action) disengaging the clutch; (grève) stoppage; **faire un double ~** to double-declutch

débrayer [debʀeje] vi (Auto) to declutch, disengage the clutch; (cesser le travail) to stop work

débridé, e [debʀide] adj unbridled, unrestrained

débrider [debʀide] vt (cheval) to unbridle; (Culin: volaille) to untruss

débris [debʀi] nm (fragment) fragment ▷ nmpl (déchets) pieces, debris sg; rubbish sg (Brit), garbage sg (US)

débrouillard, e [debʀujaʀ, -aʀd(ə)] adj smart, resourceful

débrouillardise [debʀujaʀdiz] nf smartness, resourcefulness

débrouiller [debʀuje] vt to disentangle, untangle; (fig) to sort out, unravel; **se débrouiller** vi to manage

débroussailler [debʀusaje] vt to clear (of

brushwood)

débusquer [debyske] *vt* to drive out (from cover)

début [deby] *nm* beginning, start; **débuts** *nmpl* beginnings; (*de carrière*) début *sg*; **faire ses ~s** to start out; **au ~ in** *ou* at the beginning, at first; **au ~ de** at the beginning *ou* start of; **dès le ~** from the start

débutant, e [debytã, -ãt] *nm/f* beginner, novice

débuter [debyte] *vi* to begin, start; (*faire ses débuts*) to start out

deçà [dəsa]: **en ~ de** *prép* this side of; **en ~** *adv* on this side

décacheter [dekaʃte] *vt* to unseal, open

décade [dekad] *nf* (*10 jours*) (period of) ten days; (*10 ans*) decade

décadence [dekadãs] *nf* decadence; decline

décadent, e [dekadã, -ãt] *adj* decadent

décaféiné, e [dekafeine] *adj* decaffeinated, caffeine-free

décalage [dekalaʒ] *nm* move forward *ou* back; shift forward *ou* back; (*écart*) gap; (*désaccord*) discrepancy; **~ horaire** time difference (between time zones), time-lag

décalaminer [dekalamine] *vt* to decoke

décalcification [dekalsifikasjõ] *nf* decalcification

décalcifier [dekalsifje]: **se décalcifier** *vr* to decalcify

décalcomanie [dekalkɔmani] *nf* transfer

décaler [dekale] *vt* (*dans le temps: avancer*) to bring forward; (: *retarder*) to put back; (*changer de position*) to shift forward *ou* back; **~ de 10 cm** to move forward *ou* back by 10 cm; **~ de deux heures** to bring *ou* move forward two hours; to put back two hours

décalitre [dekalitr(ə)] *nm* decalitre (*Brit*), decaliter (*US*)

décalogue [dekalɔg] *nm* Decalogue

décalquer [dekalke] *vt* to trace; (*par pression*) to transfer

décamètre [dekametr(ə)] *nm* decametre (*Brit*), decameter (*US*)

décamper [dekãpe] *vi* to clear out *ou* off

décan [dekã] *nm* (*Astrologie*) decan

décanter [dekãte] *vt* to (allow to) settle (and decant); **se décanter** *vi* to settle

décapage [dekapaʒ] *nm* stripping; scouring; sanding

décapant [dekapã] *nm* acid solution; scouring agent; paint stripper

décaper [dekape] *vt* to strip; (*avec abrasif*) to scour; (*avec papier de verre*) to sand

décapiter [dekapite] *vt* to behead; (*par accident*) to decapitate; (*fig*) to cut the top off; (: *organisation*) to remove the top people from

décapotable [dekapɔtabl(ə)] *adj* convertible

décapoter [dekapɔte] *vt* to put down the top of

décapsuler [dekapsyle] *vt* to take the cap *ou* top off

décapsuleur [dekapsylœr] *nm* bottle-opener

décarcasser [dekarkase] *vt*: **se ~ pour qn/pour faire qch** (*fam*) to slog one's guts out for sb/to do sth

décathlon [dekatlõ] *nm* decathlon

décati, e [dekati] *adj* faded, aged

décédé, e [desede] *adj* deceased

décéder [desede] *vi* to die

décelable [des(ə)labl(ə)] *adj* discernible

déceler [desle] *vt* to discover, detect; (*révéler*) to indicate, reveal

décélération [deselerasjõ] *nf* deceleration

décélérer [deselere] *vi* to decelerate, slow down

décembre [desãbr(ə)] *nm* December; *voir aussi* **juillet**

décemment [desamã] *adv* decently

décence [desãs] *nf* decency

décennal, e, -aux [desenal, -o] *adj* (*qui dure dix ans*) having a term of ten years, ten-year; (*qui revient tous les dix ans*) ten-yearly

décennie [desni] *nf* decade

décent, e [desã, -ãt] *adj* decent

décentralisation [desãtralizasjõ] *nf* decentralization

décentraliser [desãtralize] *vt* to decentralize

décentrer [desãtre] *vt* to throw off centre; **se décentrer** *vi* to move off-centre

déception [desεpsjõ] *nf* disappointment

décerner [deserne] *vt* to award

décès [desε] *nm* death, decease; **acte de ~** death certificate

décevant, e [desvã, -ãt] *adj* disappointing

décevoir [desvwar] *vt* to disappoint

déchaîné, e [deʃene] *adj* unbridled, raging

déchaînement [deʃenmã] *nm* (*de haine, violence*) outbreak, outburst

déchaîner [deʃene] *vt* (*passions, colère*) to unleash; (*rires etc*) to give rise to, arouse; **se déchaîner** *vi* to be unleashed; (*rires*) to burst out; (*se mettre en colère*) to fly into a rage; **se ~ contre qn** to unleash one's fury on sb

déchanter [deʃãte] *vi* to become disillusioned

décharge [deʃarʒ(ə)] *nf* (*dépôt d'ordures*) rubbish tip *ou* dump; (*électrique*) electrical discharge; (*salve*) volley of shots; **à la ~ de** in defence of

déchargement [deʃarʒəmã] *nm* unloading

décharger [deʃarʒe] *vt* (*marchandise, véhicule*) to unload; (*Élec*) to discharge; (*arme: neutraliser*) to unload; (: *faire feu*) to discharge, fire; **~ qn de** (*responsabilité*) to relieve sb of, release sb from; **sa colère (sur)** to vent one's anger (on); **~ sa conscience** to unburden one's conscience; **se ~ dans** (*se déverser*) to flow into; **se ~ d'une affaire sur qn** to hand a matter over to sb

décharné, e [deʃarne] *adj* bony, emaciated, fleshless

déchaussé, e [deʃose] *adj* (*dent*) loose

déchausser [deʃose] *vt* (*personne*) to take the shoes off; (*skis*) to take off; **se déchausser** *vi* to take off one's shoes; (*dent*) to come *ou* work loose

dèche [dεʃ] *nf* (*fam*): **être dans la ~** to be flat broke

déchéance [deʃeãs] *nf* (*déclin*) degeneration,

decay, decline; (*chute*) fall

déchet [deʃɛ] *nm* (*de bois, tissu etc*) scrap; (*perte: gén Comm*) wastage, waste; **déchets** *nmpl* (*ordures*) refuse *sg*, rubbish *sg* (Brit), garbage *sg* (US); **~s radioactifs** radioactive waste

déchiffrage [deʃifraʒ] *nm* sight-reading

déchiffrer [deʃifʀe] *vt* to decipher

déchiqueté, e [deʃikte] *adj* jagged(-edged), ragged

déchiqueter [deʃikte] *vt* to tear *ou* pull to pieces

déchirant, e [deʃiʀɑ̃, -ɑ̃t] *adj* heart-breaking, heart-rending

déchiré, e [deʃiʀe] *adj* torn; (*fig*) heart-broken

déchirement [deʃiʀmɑ̃] *nm* (*chagrin*) wrench, heartbreak; (*gén pl: conflit*) rift, split

déchirer [deʃiʀe] *vt* to tear, rip; (*mettre en morceaux*) to tear up; (*pour ouvrir*) to tear off; (*arracher*) to tear out; (*fig*) to tear apart; **se déchirer** *vi* to tear, rip; **se ~ un muscle/tendon** to tear a muscle/tendon

déchirure [deʃiʀyʀ] *nf* (*accroc*) tear, rip; **~ musculaire** torn muscle

déchoir [deʃwaʀ] *vi* (*personne*) to lower o.s., demean o.s.; **~ de** to fall from

déchu, e [deʃy] *pp de* **déchoir** ▷ *adj* fallen; (*roi*) deposed

décibel [desibɛl] *nm* decibel

décidé, e [deside] *adj* (*personne, air*) determined; **c'est ~** it's decided; **être ~ à faire** to be determined to do

décidément [desidemɑ̃] *adv* undoubtedly; really

décider [deside] *vt*: **~ qch** to decide on sth; **~ de faire/que** to decide to do/that; **~ qn (à faire qch)** to persuade *ou* induce sb (to do sth); **~ de qch** to decide upon sth; (*chose*) to determine sth; **se décider** *vi* (*personne*) to decide, make up one's mind; (*problème, affaire*) to be resolved; **se ~ à qch** to decide on sth; **se ~ à faire** to decide *ou* make up one's mind to do; **se ~ pour qch** to decide on *ou* in favour of sth

décideur [desidœʀ] *nm* decision-maker

décilitre [desilitʀ(ə)] *nm* decilitre (Brit), deciliter (US)

décimal, e, -aux [desimal, -o] *adj, nf* decimal

décimalisation [desimalizasjɔ̃] *nf* decimalization

décimaliser [desimalize] *vt* to decimalize

décimer [desime] *vt* to decimate

décimètre [desimɛtʀ(ə)] *nm* decimetre (Brit), decimeter (US); **double ~** (20 cm) ruler

décisif, -ive [desizif, -iv] *adj* decisive; (*qui l'emporte*): **le facteur/l'argument ~** the deciding factor/argument

décision [desizjɔ̃] *nf* decision; (*fermeté*) decisiveness, decision; **prendre une ~** to make a decision; **prendre la ~ de faire** to take the decision to do; **emporter** *ou* **faire la ~** to be decisive

déclamation [deklamasjɔ̃] *nf* declamation; (*péj*) ranting, spouting

déclamatoire [deklamatwaʀ] *adj* declamatory

déclamer [deklame] *vt* to declaim; (*péj*) to spout ▷ *vi*: **~ contre** to rail against

déclarable [deklaʀabl(ə)] *adj* (*marchandise*) dutiable; (*revenus*) declarable

déclaration [deklaʀasjɔ̃] *nf* declaration; registration; (*discours: Pol etc*) statement; (*compte rendu*) report; **fausse ~** misrepresentation; **~ (d'amour)** declaration; **~ de décès** registration of death; **~ de guerre** declaration of war; **~ (d'impôts)** statement of income, tax declaration, ≈ tax return; **~ (de sinistre)** (insurance) claim; **~ de revenus** statement of income

déclaré, e [deklaʀe] *adj* (*juré*) avowed

déclarer [deklaʀe] *vt* to declare, announce; (*revenus, employés, marchandises*) to declare; (*décès, naissance*) to register; (*vol etc: à la police*) to report; **rien à ~** nothing to declare; **se déclarer** *vi* (*feu, maladie*) to break out; **~ la guerre** to declare war

déclassé, e [deklase] *adj* relegated, downgraded; (*matériel*) (to be) sold off

déclassement [deklasmɑ̃] *nm* relegation, downgrading; (*Rail etc*) change of class

déclasser [deklase] *vt* to relegate, downgrade; (*déranger: fiches, livres*) to get out of order

déclenchement [deklɑ̃ʃmɑ̃] *nm* release; setting off

déclencher [deklɑ̃ʃe] *vt* (*mécanisme etc*) to release; (*sonnerie*) to set off, activate; (*attaque, grève*) to launch; (*provoquer*) to trigger off; **se déclencher** *vi* to release itself; to go off

déclencheur [deklɑ̃ʃœʀ] *nm* release mechanism

déclic [deklik] *nm* trigger mechanism; (*bruit*) click

déclin [deklɛ̃] *nm* decline

déclinaison [deklinɛzɔ̃] *nf* declension

décliner [dekline] *vi* to decline ▷ *vt* (*invitation*) to decline, refuse; (*responsabilité*) to refuse to accept; (*nom, adresse*) to state; (*Ling*) to decline; **se décliner** (*Ling*) to decline

déclivité [deklivite] *nf* slope, incline; **en ~** sloping, on the incline

décloisonner [deklwazɔne] *vt* to decompartmentalize

déclouer [deklue] *vt* to unnail

décocher [dekɔʃe] *vt* to hurl; (*flèche, regard*) to shoot

décoction [dekɔksjɔ̃] *nf* decoction

décodage [dekɔdaʒ] *nm* deciphering, decoding

décoder [dekɔde] *vt* to decipher, decode

décodeur [dekɔdœʀ] *nm* decoder

décoiffé, e [dekwafe] *adj*: **elle est toute ~e** her hair is in a mess

décoiffer [dekwafe] *vt*: **~ qn** to disarrange *ou* mess up sb's hair; to take sb's hat off; **se décoiffer** *vi* to take off one's hat

décoincer [dekwɛ̃se] *vt* to unjam, loosen

déçois *etc* [deswa], **déçoive** *etc* [deswav] *vb voir* **décevoir**

décolérer [dekɔleʀe] *vi*: **il ne décolère pas** he's still angry, he hasn't calmed down

décollage [dekɔlaʒ] *nm* (*Aviat, Écon*) takeoff
décollé, e [dekɔle] *adj*: **oreilles ~es** sticking-out ears
décollement [dekɔlmɑ̃] *nm* (*Méd*): **~ de la rétine** retinal detachment
décoller [dekɔle] *vt* to unstick ▷ *vi* to take off; (*projet, entreprise*) to take off, get off the ground; **se décoller** *vi* to come unstuck
décolleté, e [dekɔlte] *adj* low-necked, low-cut; (*femme*) wearing a low-cut dress ▷ *nm* low neck(line); (*épaules*) (bare) neck and shoulders; (*plongeant*) cleavage
décolleter [dekɔlte] *vt* (*vêtement*) to give a low neckline to; (*Tech*) to cut
décolonisation [dekɔlɔnizasjɔ̃] *nf* decolonization
décoloniser [dekɔlɔnize] *vt* to decolonize
décolorant [dekɔlɔrɑ̃] *nm* decolorant, bleaching agent
décoloration [dekɔlɔrasjɔ̃] *nf*: **se faire faire une ~** (*chez le coiffeur*) to have one's hair bleached *ou* lightened
décoloré, e [dekɔlɔre] *adj* (*vêtement*) faded; (*cheveux*) bleached
décolorer [dekɔlɔre] *vt* (*tissu*) to fade; (*cheveux*) to bleach, lighten; **se décolorer** *vi* to fade
décombres [dekɔ̃bʀ(ə)] *nmpl* rubble *sg*, debris *sg*
décommander [dekɔmɑ̃de] *vt* to cancel; (*invités*) to put off; **se décommander** *vi* to cancel, cry off
décomposé, e [dekɔ̃poze] *adj* (*pourri*) decomposed; (*visage*) haggard, distorted
décomposer [dekɔ̃poze] *vt* to break up; (*Chimie*) to decompose; (*Math*) to factorize; **se décomposer** *vi* to decompose
décomposition [dekɔ̃pozisjɔ̃] *nf* breaking up; decomposition; factorization; **en ~** (*organisme*) in a state of decay, decomposing
décompresser [dekɔ̃prese] *vi* (*fam: se détendre*) to unwind
décompresseur [dekɔ̃presœʀ] *nm* decompressor
décompression [dekɔ̃presjɔ̃] *nf* decompression
décomprimer [dekɔ̃prime] *vt* to decompress
décompte [dekɔ̃t] *nm* deduction; (*facture*) breakdown (of an account), detailed account
décompter [dekɔ̃te] *vt* to deduct
déconcentration [dekɔ̃sɑ̃trasjɔ̃] *nf* (*des industries etc*) dispersal; **~ des pouvoirs** devolution
déconcentré, e [dekɔ̃sɑ̃tre] *adj* (*sportif etc*) who has lost (his/her) concentration
déconcentrer [dekɔ̃sɑ̃tre] *vt* (*Admin*) to disperse; **se déconcentrer** *vi* to lose (one's) concentration
déconcertant, e [dekɔ̃sɛʀtɑ̃, -ɑ̃t] *adj* disconcerting
déconcerter [dekɔ̃sɛʀte] *vt* to disconcert, confound
déconditionner [dekɔ̃disjɔne] *vt*: **~ l'opinion américaine** to change the way the Americans have been forced to think

déconfit, e [dekɔ̃fi, -it] *adj* crestfallen, downcast
déconfiture [dekɔ̃fityʀ] *nf* collapse, ruin; (*morale*) defeat
décongélation [dekɔ̃ʒelasjɔ̃] *nf* defrosting, thawing
décongeler [dekɔ̃ʒle] *vt* to thaw (out)
décongestionner [dekɔ̃ʒɛstjɔne] *vt* (*Méd*) to decongest; (*rues*) to relieve congestion in
déconnecter [dekɔnɛkte] *vt* to disconnect
déconner [dekɔne] *vi* (*fam!: en parlant*) to talk (a load of) rubbish (*Brit*) *ou* garbage (*US*); (: *faire des bêtises*) to muck about; **sans ~** no kidding
déconseiller [dekɔ̃seje] *vt*: **~ qch (à qn)** to advise (sb) against sth; **à qn de faire** to advise sb against doing; **c'est déconseillé** it's not advised *ou* advisable
déconsidérer [dekɔ̃sidere] *vt* to discredit
décontamination [dekɔ̃taminasjɔ̃] *nf* decontamination
décontaminer [dekɔ̃tamine] *vt* to decontaminate
décontenancer [dekɔ̃tnɑ̃se] *vt* to disconcert, discountenance
décontracté, e [dekɔ̃trakte] *adj* relaxed
décontracter [dekɔ̃trakte] *vt*, **se décontracter** *vi* to relax
décontraction [dekɔ̃traksjɔ̃] *nf* relaxation
déconvenue [dekɔ̃vny] *nf* disappointment
décor [dekɔʀ] *nm* décor; (*paysage*) scenery; **décors** *nmpl* (*Théât*) scenery *sg*, decor *sg*; (*Ciné*) set *sg*; **changement de ~** (*fig*) change of scene; **entrer dans le ~** (*fig*) to run off the road; **en ~ naturel** (*Ciné*) on location
décorateur, -trice [dekɔratœr, -tris] *nm/f* (interior) decorator; (*Ciné*) set designer
décoratif, -ive [dekɔratif, -iv] *adj* decorative
décoration [dekɔrasjɔ̃] *nf* decoration
décorer [dekɔre] *vt* to decorate
décortiqué, e [dekɔrtike] *adj* shelled; hulled
décortiquer [dekɔrtike] *vt* to shell; (*riz*) to hull; (*fig*) to dissect
décorum [dekɔrɔm] *nm* decorum; etiquette
décote [dekɔt] *nf* tax relief
découcher [dekuʃe] *vi* to spend the night away
découdre [dekudʀ(ə)] *vt* (*vêtement, couture*) to unpick, take the stitching out of; (*bouton*) to take off; **se découdre** *vi* to come unstitched; (*bouton*) to come off; **en ~** (*fig*) to fight, do battle
découler [dekule] *vi*: **~ de** to ensue *ou* follow from
découpage [dekupaʒ] *nm* cutting up; carving; (*image*) cut-out (figure); **~ électoral** division into constituencies
découper [dekupe] *vt* (*papier, tissu etc*) to cut up; (*volaille, viande*) to carve; (*détacher: manche, article*) to cut out; **se ~ sur** (*ciel, fond*) to stand out against
découplé, e [dekuple] *adj*: **bien ~** well-built, well-proportioned
découpure [dekupyʀ] *nf*: **~s** (*morceaux*) cut-out bits; (*d'une côte, arête*) indentations, jagged

outline sg

décourageant, e [dekuraʒɑ̃, ɑ̃t] adj discouraging; (personne, attitude) discouraging, negative

découragement [dekuraʒmɑ̃] nm discouragement, despondency

décourager [dekuraʒe] vt to discourage, dishearten; (dissuader) to discourage, put off; **se décourager** vi to lose heart, become discouraged; **~ qn de faire/de qch** to discourage sb from doing/from sth, put sb off doing/sth

décousu, e [dekuzy] pp de **découdre** ▷ adj unstitched; (fig) disjointed, disconnected

découvert, e [dekuvɛr, -ɛrt(ə)] pp de **découvrir** ▷ adj (tête) bare, uncovered; (lieu) open, exposed ▷ nm (bancaire) overdraft ▷ nf discovery; **à ~** adv (Mil) exposed, without cover; (fig) openly ▷ adj (Comm) overdrawn; **à visage ~** openly; **aller à la ~e de** to go in search of

découvrir [dekuvrir] vt to discover; (apercevoir) to see; (enlever ce qui couvre ou protège) to uncover; (montrer, dévoiler) to reveal; **se découvrir** vi to take off one's hat; (se déshabiller) to take something off; (au lit) to uncover o.s.; (ciel) to clear; **se ~ des talents** to find hidden talents in o.s.

décrasser [dekrase] vt to clean

décrêper [dekrepe] vt (cheveux) to straighten

décrépi, e [dekrepi] adj peeling; with roughcast rendering removed

décrépit, e [dekrepi, -it] adj decrepit

décrépitude [dekrepityd] nf decrepitude; decay

decrescendo [dekreʃɛndo] nm (Mus) decrescendo; **aller ~** (fig) to decline, be on the wane

décret [dekrɛ] nm decree

décréter [dekrete] vt to decree; (ordonner) to order

décret-loi [dekrɛlwa] nm statutory order

décrié, e [dekrije] adj disparaged

décrire [dekrir] vt to describe; (courbe, cercle) to follow, describe

décrisper [dekrispe] vt to defuse

décrit, e [dekri, -it] pp de **décrire**

décrivais etc [dekrive] vb voir **décrire**

décrochage [dekrɔʃaʒ] nm: **~ scolaire** (Scol) ≈ truancy

décrochement [dekrɔʃmɑ̃] nm (d'un mur etc) recess

décrocher [dekrɔʃe] vt (dépendre) to take down; (téléphone) to take off the hook; (: pour répondre): **~ (le téléphone)** to pick up ou lift the receiver; (fig: contrat etc) to get, land ▷ vi to drop out; to switch off; **se décrocher** vi (tableau, rideau) to fall down

décroîs etc [dekrwa] vb voir **décroître**

décroiser [dekrwaze] vt (bras) to unfold; (jambes) to uncross

décroissant, e [dekrwasɑ̃, -ɑ̃t] vb voir **décroître** ▷ adj decreasing, declining, diminishing; **par ordre ~** in descending order

décroître [dekrwatr(ə)] vi to decrease,

decline diminish

décrotter [dekrɔte] vt (chaussures) to clean the mud from; **se ~ le nez** to pick one's nose

décru, e [dekry] pp de **décroître**

décrue [dekry] nf drop in level (of the waters)

décrypter [dekripte] vt to decipher

déçu, e [desy] pp de **décevoir** ▷ adj disappointed

déculotter [dekylɔte] vt: **~ qn** to take off ou down sb's trousers; **se déculotter** vi to take off ou down one's trousers

déculpabiliser [dekylpabilize] vt (personne) to relieve of guilt; (chose) to decriminalize

décuple [dekypl(ə)] nm: **le ~ de** ten times; **au ~** tenfold

décupler [dekyple] vt, vi to increase tenfold

déçut etc [desy] vb voir **décevoir**

dédaignable [dedɛɲabl(ə)] adj: **pas ~** not to be despised

dédaigner [dedɛɲe] vt to despise, scorn; (négliger) to disregard, spurn; **~ de faire** to consider it beneath one to do, not deign to do

dédaigneusement [dedɛɲøzmɑ̃] adv scornfully, disdainfully

dédaigneux, -euse [dedɛɲø, -øz] adj scornful, disdainful

dédain [dedɛ̃] nm scorn, disdain

dédale [dedal] nm maze

dedans [dədɑ̃] adv inside; (pas en plein air) indoors, inside ▷ nm inside; **au ~** on the inside; inside; **en ~ (vers l'intérieur)** inwards; voir aussi **là**

dédicace [dedikas] nf (imprimée) dedication; (manuscrite, sur une photo etc) inscription

dédicacer [dedikase] vt: **~ (à qn)** to sign (for sb), autograph (for sb), inscribe (to sb)

dédié, e [dedje] adj: **ordinateur ~** dedicated computer

dédier [dedje] vt to dedicate

dédire [dedir]: **se dédire** vi to go back on one's word; (se rétracter) to retract, recant

dédit, e [dedi, -it] pp de **dédire** ▷ nm (Comm) forfeit, penalty

dédommagement [dedɔmaʒmɑ̃] nm compensation

dédommager [dedɔmaʒe] vt: **~ qn (de)** to compensate sb (for); (fig) to repay sb (for)

dédouaner [dedwane] vt to clear through customs

dédoublement [dedubləmɑ̃] nm splitting; (Psych): **~ de la personnalité** split ou dual personality

dédoubler [deduble] vt (classe, effectifs) to split (into two); (couverture etc) to unfold; (manteau) to remove the lining of; **~ un train/les trains** to run a relief train/additional trains; **se dédoubler** vi (Psych) to have a split personality

dédramatiser [dedramatize] vt (situation) to defuse; (événement) to play down

déductible [dedyktibl(ə)] adj deductible

déduction [dedyksjɔ̃] nf (d'argent) deduction; (raisonnement) deduction, inference

déduire [deduir] vt: **~ qch (de)** (ôter) to deduct sth (from); (conclure) to deduce ou infer sth (from)

déesse [deɛs] *nf* goddess

DEFA *sigle m* (= *Diplôme d'État relatif aux fonctions d'animation*) *diploma for senior youth leaders*

défaillance [defajɑ̃s] *nf* (*syncope*) blackout; (*fatigue*) (sudden) weakness *no pl*; (*technique*) fault, failure; (*morale etc*) weakness; **~ cardiaque** heart failure

défaillant, e [defajɑ̃, -ɑ̃t] *adj* defective; (*Jur: témoin*) defaulting

défaillir [defajiʀ] *vi* to faint; to feel faint; (*mémoire etc*) to fail

défaire [defɛʀ] *vt* (*installation, échafaudage*) to take down, dismantle; (*paquet etc, nœud, vêtement*) to undo; (*bagages*) to unpack; (*ouvrage*) to undo, unpick; (*cheveux*) to take out; **se défaire** *vi* to come undone; **se ~ de** *vt* (*se débarrasser de*) to get rid of; (*se séparer de*) to part with; **~ le lit** (*pour changer les draps*) to strip the bed; (*pour se coucher*) to turn back the bedclothes

défait, e [defɛ, -ɛt] *pp de* **défaire** ▷ *adj* (*visage*) haggard, ravaged ▷ *nf* defeat

défaites [defɛt] *vb voir* **défaire**

défaitisme [defetism(ə)] *nm* defeatism

défaitiste [defetist(ə)] *adj, nm/f* defeatist

défalcation [defalkɑsjɔ̃] *nf* deduction

défalquer [defalke] *vt* to deduct

défasse *etc* [defas] *vb voir* **défaire**

défausser [defose] *vt* to get rid of; **se défausser** *vi* (*Cartes*) to discard

défaut [defo] *nm* (*moral*) fault, failing, defect; (*d'étoffe, métal*) fault, flaw, defect; (*manque, carence*): **~ de** lack of; shortage of; (*Inform*) bug; **~ de la cuirasse** (*fig*) chink in the armour (*Brit*) *ou* armor (*US*); **en ~** at fault; in the wrong; **faire ~** (*manquer*) to be lacking; **à ~** *adv* failing that; **à ~ de** for lack *ou* want of; **par ~** (*Jur*) in his (*ou* her *etc*) absence

défaveur [defavœʀ] *nf* disfavour (*Brit*), disfavor (*US*)

défavorable [defavɔʀabl(ə)] *adj* unfavourable (*Brit*), unfavorable (*US*)

défavoriser [defavɔʀize] *vt* to put at a disadvantage

défectif, -ive [defɛktif, -iv] *adj*: **verbe ~** defective verb

défection [defɛksjɔ̃] *nf* defection, failure to give support *ou* assistance; failure to appear; **faire ~** (*d'un parti etc*) to withdraw one's support, leave

défectueux, -euse [defɛktɥø, -øz] *adj* faulty, defective

défectuosité [defɛktɥozite] *nf* defectiveness *no pl*; (*défaut*) defect, fault

défendable [defɑ̃dabl(ə)] *adj* defensible

défendeur, -eresse [defɑ̃dœʀ, -dʀɛs] *nm/f* (*Jur*) defendant

défendre [defɑ̃dʀ(ə)] *vt* to defend; (*interdire*) to forbid; **~ à qn qch/de faire** to forbid sb sth/to do; **il est défendu de cracher** spitting (is) prohibited *ou* is not allowed; **c'est défendu** it is forbidden; **se défendre** *vi* to defend o.s.; **il se défend** (*fig*) he can hold his own; **ça se défend**

(*fig*) it holds together; **se ~ de/contre** (*se protéger*) to protect o.s. from/against; **se ~ de** (*se garder de*) to refrain from; (*nier*): **se ~ de vouloir** to deny wanting

défenestrer [defənɛstʀe] *vt* to throw out of the window

défense [defɑ̃s] *nf* defence (*Brit*), defense (*US*); (*d'éléphant etc*) tusk; **ministre de la ~** Minister of Defence (*Brit*), Defence Secretary; **la ~ nationale** defence, the defence of the realm (*Brit*); **la ~ contre avions** anti-aircraft defence; **"~ de fumer/cracher"** "no smoking/spitting", "smoking/spitting prohibited"; **prendre la ~ de qn** to stand up for sb; **~ des consommateurs** consumerism

défenseur [defɑ̃sœʀ] *nm* defender; (*Jur*) counsel for the defence

défensif, -ive [defɑ̃sif, -iv] *adj, nf* defensive; **être sur la défensive** to be on the defensive

déféquer [defeke] *vi* to defecate

déferai *etc* [defʀe] *vb voir* **défaire**

déférence [defeʀɑ̃s] *nf* deference

déférent, e [defeʀɑ̃, -ɑ̃t] *adj* (*poli*) deferential, deferent

déférer [defeʀe] *vt* (*Jur*) to refer; **~ à** *vt* (*requête, décision*) to defer to; **~ qn à la justice** to hand sb over to justice

déferlant, e [defɛʀlɑ̃, -ɑ̃t] *adj*: **vague ~e** breaker

déferlement [defɛʀləmɑ̃] *nm* breaking; surge

déferler [defɛʀle] *vi* (*vagues*) to break; (*fig*) to surge

défi [defi] *nm* (*provocation*) challenge; (*bravade*) defiance; **mettre qn au ~ de faire qch** to challenge sb to do sth; **relever un ~** to take up *ou* accept a challenge

défiance [defjɑ̃s] *nf* mistrust, distrust

déficeler [defisle] *vt* (*paquet*) to undo, untie

déficience [defisjɑ̃s] *nf* deficiency

déficient, e [defisjɑ̃, -ɑ̃t] *adj* deficient

déficit [defisit] *nm* (*Comm*) deficit; (*Psych etc: manque*) defect; **~ budgétaire** budget deficit; **être en ~** to be in deficit

déficitaire [defisitɛʀ] *adj* (*année, récolte*) bad; **entreprise/budget ~** business/budget in deficit

défier [defje] *vt* (*provoquer*) to challenge; (*fig*) to defy, brave; **se ~ de** (*se méfier de*) to distrust, mistrust; **~ qn de faire** to challenge *ou* defy sb to do; **~ qn à** to challenge sb to; **~ toute comparaison/concurrence** to be incomparable/unbeatable

défigurer [defigyʀe] *vt* to disfigure; (*boutons etc*) to mar *ou* spoil (the looks of); (*fig: œuvre*) to mutilate, deface

défilé [defile] *nm* (*Géo*) (narrow) gorge *ou* pass; (*soldats*) parade; (*manifestants*) procession, march; **un ~ de** (*voitures, visiteurs etc*) a stream of

défiler [defile] *vi* (*troupes*) to march past; (*sportifs*) to parade; (*manifestants*) to march; (*visiteurs*) to pour, stream; **se défiler** *vi* (*se dérober*) to slip away, sneak off; **faire ~** (*bande, film*) to put on; (*Inform*) to scroll

défini, e [defini] *adj* definite
définir [definiʀ] *vt* to define
définissable [definisabl(ə)] *adj* definable
définitif, -ive [definitif, -iv] *adj* (*final*) final,
  definitive; (*pour longtemps*) permanent,
  definitive; (*sans appel*) final, definite ▷ *nf*: **en**
  définitive eventually; (*somme toute*) when all is
  said and done
définition [definisjɔ̃] *nf* definition; (*de mots
  croisés*) clue; (*TV*) (*picture*) resolution
définitivement [definitivmɑ̃] *adv* definitively;
  permanently; definitely
défit *etc* [defi] *vb voir* **défaire**
déflagration [deflagʀasjɔ̃] *nf* explosion
déflation [deflasjɔ̃] *nf* deflation
déflationniste [deflasjɔnist(ə)] *adj*
  deflationist, deflationary
déflecteur [deflɛktœʀ] *nm* (*Auto*) quarterlight
  (*Brit*), deflector (*US*)
déflorer [deflɔʀe] *vt* (*jeune fille*) to deflower; (*fig*)
  to spoil the charm of
défoncé, e [defɔ̃se] *adj* smashed in; broken
  down; (*route*) full of potholes ▷ *nm/f* addict
défoncer [defɔ̃se] *vt* (*caisse*) to stave in; (*porte*) to
  smash in *ou* down; (*lit, fauteuil*) to burst (the
  springs of); (*terrain, route*) to rip *ou* plough up; **se**
  défoncer *vi* (*se donner à fond*) to give it all one's
  got
défont [defɔ̃] *vb voir* **défaire**
déformant, e [defɔʀmɑ̃, -ɑ̃t] *adj*: **glace ~e** *ou*
  miroir ~ distorting mirror
déformation [defɔʀmasjɔ̃] *nf* loss of shape;
  deformation; distortion; **~ professionnelle**
  conditioning by one's job
déformer [defɔʀme] *vt* to put out of shape;
  (*corps*) to deform; (*pensée, fait*) to distort; **se**
  déformer *vi* to lose its shape
défoulement [defulmɑ̃] *nm* release of tension;
  unwinding
défouler [defule]: **se défouler** *vi* (*Psych*) to work
  off one's tensions, release one's pent-up
  feelings; (*gén*) to unwind, let off steam
défraîchi, e [defʀeʃi] *adj* faded; (*article à vendre*)
  shop-soiled
défraîchir [defʀeʃiʀ]: **se défraîchir** *vi* to fade; to
  become shop-soiled
défrayer [defʀeje] *vt*: **~ qn** to pay sb's expenses;
  ~ la chronique to be in the news; **~ la**
  conversation to be the main topic of
  conversation
défrichement [defʀiʃmɑ̃] *nm* clearance
défricher [defʀiʃe] *vt* to clear (for cultivation)
défriser [defʀize] *vt* (*cheveux*) to straighten; (*fig*)
  to annoy
défroisser [defʀwase] *vt* to smooth out
défroque [defʀɔk] *nf* cast-off
défroqué [defʀɔke] *nm* former monk (*ou* priest)
défroquer [defʀɔke] *vi* (*aussi*: **se défroquer**) to
  give up the cloth, renounce one's vows
défunt, e [defœ̃, -œ̃t] *adj*: **son ~ père** his late
  father ▷ *nm/f* deceased
dégagé, e [degaʒe] *adj* clear; (*ton, air*) casual,
  jaunty

dégagement [degaʒmɑ̃] *nm* emission; freeing;
  clearing; (*espace libre*) clearing; passage;
  clearance; (*Football*) clearance; **voie de ~** slip
  road; **itinéraire de ~** alternative route (*to relieve
  traffic congestion*)
dégager [degaʒe] *vt* (*exhaler*) to give off, emit;
  (*délivrer*) to free, extricate; (*Mil: troupes*) to relieve;
  (*désencombrer*) to clear; (*isoler, mettre en valeur*) to
  bring out; (*crédits*) to release; **se dégager** *vi*
  (*odeur*) to emanate, be given off; (*passage, ciel*) to
  clear; **~ qn de** (*engagement, parole etc*) to release *ou*
  free sb from; **se ~ de** (*fig: engagement etc*) to get
  out of; (: *promesse*) to go back on
dégaine [degɛn] *nf* awkward way of walking
dégainer [degene] *vt* to draw
dégarni, e [degaʀni] *adj* bald
dégarnir [degaʀniʀ] *vt* (*vider*) to empty, clear; **se**
  dégarnir *vi* to empty; to be cleaned out *ou*
  cleared; (*tempes, crâne*) to go bald
dégâts [dega] *nmpl* damage *sg*; **faire des ~** to
  damage
dégauchir [degoʃiʀ] *vt* (*Tech*) to surface
dégazer [degaze] *vi* (*pétrolier*) to clean its tanks
dégel [deʒɛl] *nm* thaw; (*fig: des prix etc*)
  unfreezing
dégeler [deʒle] *vt* to thaw (out); (*fig*) to unfreeze
  ▷ *vi* to thaw (out); **se dégeler** *vi* (*fig*) to thaw out
dégénéré, e [deʒeneʀe] *adj, nm/f* degenerate
dégénérer [deʒeneʀe] *vi* to degenerate; (*empirer*)
  to go from bad to worse; (*devenir*): **~ en** to
  degenerate into
dégénérescence [deʒeneʀesɑ̃s] *nf*
  degeneration
dégingandé, e [deʒɛ̃gɑ̃de] *adj* gangling, lanky
dégivrage [deʒivʀaʒ] *nm* defrosting; de-icing
dégivrer [deʒivʀe] *vt* (*frigo*) to defrost; (*vitres*) to
  de-ice
dégivreur [deʒivʀœʀ] *nm* defroster; de-icer
déglinguer [deglɛ̃ge] *vt* to bust
déglutir [deglytiʀ] *vt, vi* to swallow
déglutition [deglytisjɔ̃] *nf* swallowing
dégonflé, e [degɔ̃fle] *adj* (*pneu*) flat; (*fam*)
  chicken ▷ *nm/f* (*fam*) chicken
dégonfler [degɔ̃fle] *vt* (*pneu, ballon*) to let down,
  deflate ▷ *vi* (*désenfler*) to go down; **se dégonfler**
  vi (*fam*) to chicken out
dégorger [degɔʀʒe] *vi* (*Culin*): **faire ~** to leave to
  sweat; (*aussi*: **se dégorger**: *rivière*): **~ dans** to flow
  into ▷ *vt* to disgorge
dégoter [degɔte] *vt* (*fam*) to dig up, find
dégouliner [deguline] *vi* to trickle, drip; **~ de** to
  be dripping with
dégoupiller [degupije] *vt* (*grenade*) to take the
  pin out of
dégourdi, e [deguʀdi] *adj* smart, resourceful
dégourdir [deguʀdiʀ] *vt* to warm (up); **se ~ (les**
  jambes) to stretch one's legs
dégoût [degu] *nm* disgust, distaste
dégoûtant, e [degutɑ̃, -ɑ̃t] *adj* disgusting
dégoûté, e [degute] *adj* disgusted; **~ de** sick of
dégoûter [degute] *vt* to disgust; **cela me**

d

dégoûte I find this disgusting *ou* revolting; ~ **qn de qch** to put sb off sth; **se ~ de** to get *ou* become sick of

dégoutter [degute] *vi* to drip; **~ de** to be dripping with

dégradant, e [degʁadɑ̃, -ɑ̃t] *adj* degrading

dégradation [degʁadasjɔ̃] *nf* reduction in rank; defacement; degradation, debasement; deterioration; (*aussi*: **dégradations**: *dégâts*) damage *no pl*

dégradé, e [degʁade] *adj* (*couleur*) shaded off; (*teintes*) faded; (*cheveux*) layered ▷ *nm* (*Peinture*) gradation

dégrader [degʁade] *vt* (*Mil*: *officier*) to degrade; (*abîmer*) to damage, deface; (*avilir*) to degrade, debase; **se dégrader** *vi* (*relations, situation*) to deteriorate

dégrafer [degʁafe] *vt* to unclip, unhook, unfasten

dégraissage [degʁesaʒ] *nm* (*Écon*) cutbacks *pl*; **~ et nettoyage à sec** dry cleaning

dégraissant [degʁesɑ̃] *nm* spot remover

dégraisser [degʁese] *vt* (*soupe*) to skim; (*vêtement*) to take the grease marks out of; (*Écon*) to cut back; (: *entreprise*) to slim down

degré [dəgʁe] *nm* degree; (*d'escalier*) step; **brûlure au 1er/2ème ~** 1st/2nd degree burn; **équation du 1er/2ème ~** linear/quadratic equation; **le premier ~** (*Scol*) primary level; **alcool à 90 ~s** surgical spirit; **vin de 10 ~s** 10° wine (*on Gay-Lussac scale*); **par ~(s)** *adv* by degrees, gradually

dégressif, -ive [degʁesif, -iv] *adj* on a decreasing scale, degressive; **tarif ~** decreasing rate of charge

dégrèvement [degʁɛvmɑ̃] *nm* tax relief

dégrever [degʁəve] *vt* to grant tax relief to; to reduce the tax burden on

dégriffé, e [degʁife] *adj* (*vêtement*) sold without the designer's label; **voyage ~** discount holiday

dégringolade [degʁɛ̃gɔlad] *nf* tumble; (*fig*) collapse

dégringoler [degʁɛ̃gɔle] *vi* to tumble (down); (*fig*: *prix, monnaie etc*) to collapse

dégriser [degʁize] *vt* to sober up

dégrossir [degʁosiʁ] *vt* (*bois*) to trim; (*fig*) to work out roughly; (: *personne*) to knock the rough edges off

déguenillé, e [dɛgnije] *adj* ragged, tattered

déguerpir [degɛʁpiʁ] *vi* to clear off

dégueulasse [degœlas] *adj* (*fam*) disgusting

dégueuler [degœle] *vi* (*fam*) to puke, throw up

déguisé, e [degize] *adj* disguised; dressed up; ~ **en** disguised (*ou* dressed up) as

déguisement [degizmɑ̃] *nm* disguise; (*habits*: *pour s'amuser*) dressing-up clothes; (: *pour tromper*) disguise

déguiser [degize] *vt* to disguise; **se déguiser (en)** *vi* (*se costumer*) to dress up (as); (*pour tromper*) to disguise o.s. (as)

dégustation [degystasjɔ̃] *nf* tasting; sampling; savouring (*Brit*), savoring (*US*); (*séance*): **~ de vin(s)** wine-tasting

déguster [degyste] *vt* (*vins*) to taste; (*fromages etc*) to sample; (*savourer*) to enjoy, savour (*Brit*), savor (*US*)

déhancher [deɑ̃ʃe]: **se déhancher** *vi* to sway one's hips; to lean (one's weight) on one hip

dehors [dəɔʁ] *adv* outside; (*en plein air*) outdoors, outside ▷ *nm* outside ▷ *nmpl* (*apparences*) appearances, exterior *sg*; **mettre** *ou* **jeter ~** to throw out; **au ~** outside; (*en apparence*) outwardly; **au ~ de** outside; **de ~** from outside; **en ~** outside; outwards; **en ~ de** apart from

déifier [deifje] *vt* to deify

déjà [deʒa] *adv* already; (*auparavant*) before, already; **as-tu ~ été en France?** have you been to France before?; **c'est ~ pas mal** that's not too bad (at all); **c'est ~ quelque chose** (at least) it's better than nothing; **quel nom, ~?** what was the name again?

déjanter [deʒɑ̃te]: **se déjanter** *vi* (*pneu*) to come off the rim

déjà-vu [deʒavy] *nm*: **c'est du ~** there's nothing new in that

déjeté, e [deʒte] *adj* lop-sided, crooked

déjeuner [deʒœne] *vi* to (have) lunch; (*le matin*) to have breakfast ▷ *nm* lunch; (*petit déjeuner*) breakfast; **~ d'affaires** business lunch

déjouer [deʒwe] *vt* to elude, to foil, thwart

déjuger [deʒyʒe]: **se déjuger** *vi* to go back on one's opinion

delà [dəla] *adv*: **par ~, en ~ (de), au ~ (de)** beyond

délabré, e [delabʁe] *adj* dilapidated, broken-down

délabrement [delabʁəmɑ̃] *nm* decay, dilapidation

délabrer [delabʁe]: **se délabrer** *vi* to fall into decay, become dilapidated

délacer [delase] *vt* to unlace, undo

délai [delɛ] *nm* (*attente*) waiting period; (*sursis*) extension (of time); (*temps accordé*: *aussi*: **délais**) time limit; **sans ~** without delay; **à bref ~** shortly, very soon; at short notice; **dans les ~s** within the time limit; **un ~ de 30 jours** a period of 30 days; **comptez un ~ de livraison de 10 jours** allow 10 days for delivery

délaissé, e [delese] *adj* abandoned, deserted; neglected

délaisser [delese] *vt* (*abandonner*) to abandon, desert; (*négliger*) to neglect

délassant, e [delasɑ̃, -ɑ̃t] *adj* relaxing

délassement [delasmɑ̃] *nm* relaxation

délasser [delase] *vt* (*reposer*) to relax; (*divertir*) to divert, entertain; **se délasser** *vi* to relax

délateur, -trice [delatœʁ, -tʁis] *nm/f* informer

délation [delasjɔ̃] *nf* denouncement, informing

délavé, e [delave] *adj* faded

délayage [delɛjaʒ] *nm* mixing; thinning down

délayer [deleje] *vt* (*Culin*) to mix (with water *etc*); (*peinture*) to thin down; (*fig*) to pad out, spin out

delco® [dɛlko] *nm* (*Auto*) distributor; **tête de delco** distributor cap

délectation [delɛktasjɔ̃] *nf* delight

délecter [delɛkte]: **se délecter** vi: **se ~ de** to revel ou delight in

délégation [delegɑsjɔ̃] nf delegation; **~ de pouvoir** delegation of power

délégué, e [delege] adj delegated ▷ nm/f delegate; representative; **ministre ~ à** minister with special responsibility for

déléguer [delege] vt to delegate

délestage [delɛstaʒ] nm: **itinéraire de ~** alternative route (to relieve traffic congestion)

délester [delɛste] vt (navire) to unballast; **~ une route** to relieve traffic congestion on a road by diverting traffic

Delhi [dɛli] n Delhi

délibérant, e [deliberɑ̃, -ɑ̃t] adj: **assemblée ~e** deliberative assembly

délibératif, -ive [deliberatif, -iv] adj: **avoir voix délibérative** to have voting rights

délibération [deliberɑsjɔ̃] nf deliberation

délibéré, e [delibere] adj (conscient) deliberate; (déterminé) determined, resolute; **de propos ~** (à dessein, exprès) intentionally

délibérément [deliberemɑ̃] adv deliberately; (résolument) resolutely

délibérer [delibere] vi to deliberate

délicat, e [delika, -at] adj delicate; (plein de tact) tactful; (attentionné) thoughtful; (exigeant) fussy, particular; **procédés peu ~s** unscrupulous methods

délicatement [delikatmɑ̃] adv delicately; (avec douceur) gently

délicatesse [delikatɛs] nf delicacy; tactfulness; thoughtfulness; **délicatesses** nfpl attentions, consideration sg

délice [delis] nm delight

délicieusement [delisjøzmɑ̃] adv deliciously; delightfully

délicieux, -euse [delisjø, -øz] adj (au goût) delicious; (sensation, impression) delightful

délictueux, -euse [deliktɥø, -øz] adj criminal

délié, e [delje] adj nimble, agile; (mince) slender, fine ▷ nm: **les ~s** the upstrokes (in handwriting)

délier [delje] vt to untie; **~ qn de** (serment etc) to free ou release sb from

délimitation [delimitɑsjɔ̃] nf delimitation

délimiter [delimite] vt to delimit

délinquance [delɛ̃kɑ̃s] nf criminality; **~ juvénile** juvenile delinquency

délinquant, e [delɛ̃kɑ̃, -ɑ̃t] adj, nm/f delinquent

déliquescence [delikesɑ̃s] nf: **en ~** in a state of decay

déliquescent, e [delikesɑ̃, -ɑ̃t] adj decaying

délirant, e [delirɑ̃, -ɑ̃t] adj (Méd: fièvre) delirious; (imagination) frenzied; (fam: déraisonnable) crazy

délire [delir] nm (fièvre) delirium; (fig) frenzy; (: folie) lunacy

délirer [delire] vi to be delirious; (fig) to be raving

délit [deli] nm (criminal) offence; **~ de droit commun** violation of common law; **~ de fuite** failure to stop after an accident; **~ d'initiés** insider dealing ou trading; **~ de presse** violation of the press laws

délivrance [delivrɑ̃s] nf freeing, release; (sentiment) relief

délivrer [delivre] vt (prisonnier) to (set) free, release; (passeport, certificat) to issue; **~ qn de** (ennemis) to set sb free from, deliver ou free sb from; (fig) to rid sb of

délocalisation [delɔkalizɑsjɔ̃] nf relocation

délocaliser [delɔkalize] vt (entreprise, emplois) relocate

déloger [delɔʒe] vt (locataire) to turn out; (objet coincé, ennemi) to dislodge

déloyal, e, -aux [delwajal, -o] adj (personne, conduite) disloyal; (procédé) unfair

Delphes [dɛlf] n Delphi

delta [dɛlta] nm (Géo) delta

deltaplane® [dɛltaplan] nm hang-glider

déluge [delyʒ] nm (biblique) Flood, Deluge; (grosse pluie) downpour, deluge; (grand nombre): **~ de** flood of

déluré, e [delyre] adj smart, resourceful; (péj) forward, pert

démagnétiser [demaɲetize] vt to demagnetize

démagogie [demagɔʒi] nf demagogy

démagogique [demagɔʒik] adj demagogic, popularity-seeking; (Pol) vote-catching

démagogue [demagɔg] adj demagogic ▷ nm demagogue

démaillé, e [demaje] adj (bas) laddered (Brit), with a run (ou runs)

demain [dəmɛ̃] adv tomorrow; **~ matin/soir** tomorrow morning/evening; **~ midi** tomorrow at midday; **à ~!** see you tomorrow!

demande [dəmɑ̃d] nf (requête) request; (revendication) demand; (Admin, formulaire) application; (Écon): **la ~** demand; **"~s d'emploi"** "situations wanted"; **à la ~ générale** by popular request; **~ en mariage** (marriage) proposal; **faire sa ~ (en mariage)** to propose (marriage); **~ de naturalisation** application for naturalization; **~ de poste** job application

demandé, e [dəmɑ̃de] adj (article etc): **très ~** (very) much in demand

demander [dəmɑ̃de] vt to ask for; (question: date, heure, chemin) to ask; (requérir, nécessiter) to require, demand; **~ qch à qn** to ask sb for sth, ask sb sth; **ils demandent deux secrétaires et un ingénieur** they're looking for two secretaries and an engineer; **~ la main de qn** to ask for sb's hand (in marriage); **~ pardon à qn** to apologize to sb; **~ à ou de voir/faire** to ask to see/ask if one can do; **~ à qn de faire** to ask sb to do; **~ que/pourquoi** to ask that/why; **se ~ si/pourquoi** etc to wonder if/why etc; (sens purement réfléchi) to ask o.s. if/why etc; **on vous demande au téléphone** you're wanted on the phone, there's someone for you on the phone; **il ne demande que ça** that's all he wants; **je ne demande pas mieux** I'm asking nothing more; **il ne demande qu'à faire** all he wants is to do

demandeur, -euse [dəmɑ̃dœr, -øz] nm/f: **~**

d'emploi job-seeker

démangeaison [demɑ̃ʒɛzɔ̃] nf itching

démanger [demɑ̃ʒe] vi to itch; **la main me démange** my hand is itching; **l'envie** ou **ça me démange de faire** I'm itching to do

démantèlement [demɑ̃tɛlmɑ̃] nm breaking up

démanteler [demɑ̃tle] vt to break up; to demolish

démaquillant [demakijɑ̃] nm make-up remover

démaquiller [demakije] vt: **se démaquiller** to remove one's make-up

démarcage [demaʀkaʒ] nm = **démarquage**

démarcation [demaʀkasjɔ̃] nf demarcation

démarchage [demaʀʃaʒ] nm (Comm) door-to-door selling

démarche [demaʀʃ(ə)] nf (allure) gait, walk; (intervention) step; approach; (fig: intellectuelle) thought processes pl; approach; **faire** ou **entreprendre des ~s** to take action; **faire des ~s auprès de qn** to approach sb

démarcheur, -euse [demaʀʃœʀ, -øz] nm/f (Comm) door-to-door salesman/woman; (Pol etc) canvasser

démarquage [demaʀkaʒ] nm marking down

démarque [demaʀk(ə)] nf (Comm: d'un article) mark-down

démarqué, e [demaʀke] adj (Football) unmarked; (Comm) reduced; **prix ~s** marked-down prices

démarquer [demaʀke] vt (prix) to mark down; (joueur) to stop marking; **se démarquer** vi (Sport) to shake off one's marker

démarrage [demaʀaʒ] nm starting no pl, start; **~ en côte** hill start

démarrer [demaʀe] vt to start up ▷ vi (conducteur) to start (up); (véhicule) to move off; (travaux, affaire) to get moving; (coureur: accélérer) to pull away

démarreur [demaʀœʀ] nm (Auto) starter

démasquer [demaske] vt to unmask; **se démasquer** to unmask; (fig) to drop one's mask

démâter [demate] vt to dismast ▷ vi to be dismasted

démêlant, e [demɛlɑ̃, -ɑ̃t] adj: **baume ~, crème ~e** (hair) conditioner

démêler [demele] vt to untangle, disentangle

démêlés [demele] nmpl problems

démembrement [demɑ̃bʀəmɑ̃] nm dismemberment

démembrer [demɑ̃bʀe] vt to dismember

déménagement [demenaʒmɑ̃] nm (du point de vue du locataire etc) move; (: du déménageur) removal (Brit), moving (US); **entreprise/camion de ~** removal (Brit) ou moving (US) firm/van

déménager [demenaʒe] vt (meubles) to (re)move ▷ vi to move (house)

déménageur [demenaʒœʀ] nm removal man (Brit), (furniture) mover (US); (entrepreneur) furniture remover

démence [demɑ̃s] nf madness, insanity; (Méd)

dementia

démener [demne]: **se démener** vi to thrash about; (fig) to exert o.s.

dément, e [demɑ̃, -ɑ̃t] vb voir **démentir** ▷ adj (fou) mad (Brit), crazy; (fam) brilliant, fantastic

démenti [demɑ̃ti] nm refutation

démentiel, le [demɑ̃sjɛl] adj insane

démentir [demɑ̃tiʀ] vt (nouvelle, témoin) to refute; (faits etc) to belie, refute; **~ que** to deny that; **ne pas se ~** not to fail, keep up

démerder [demɛʀde]: **se démerder** vi (fam!) to bloody well manage for o.s.

démériter [demeʀite] vi: **~ auprès de qn** to come down in sb's esteem

démesure [deməzyʀ] nf immoderation, immoderateness

démesuré, e [deməzyʀe] adj immoderate, disproportionate

démesurément [deməzyʀemɑ̃] adv disproportionately

démettre [demɛtʀ(ə)] vt: **~ qn de** (fonction, poste) to dismiss sb from; **se ~ (de ses fonctions)** to resign (from) one's duties; **se ~ l'épaule** etc to dislocate one's shoulder etc

demeurant [dəmœʀɑ̃]: **au ~** adv for all that

demeure [dəmœʀ] nf residence; **dernière ~** (fig) last resting place; **mettre qn en ~ de faire** to enjoin ou order sb to do; **à ~** adv permanently

demeuré, e [dəmœʀe] adj backward ▷ nm/f backward person

demeurer [dəmœʀe] vi (habiter) to live; (séjourner) to stay; (rester) to remain; **en ~ là** (personne) to leave it at that; (: choses) to be left at that

demi, e [dəmi] adj: **et ~, trois heures/bouteilles et ~es** three and a half hours/bottles, three hours/bottles and a half ▷ nm (bière: = 0.25 litre) ≈ half-pint; (Football) half-back; **il est 2 heures et ~e** it's half past 2; **il est midi et ~** it's half past 12; **~ de mêlée/d'ouverture** (Rugby) scrum/fly half; **à ~** adv half-; **ouvrir à ~** to half-open; **faire les choses à ~** to do things by halves; **à la ~e** (heure) on the half-hour

demi... [dəmi] préfixe half-, semi..., demi-

demi-bas [dəmiba] nm inv (chaussette) knee-sock

demi-bouteille [dəmibutɛj] nf half-bottle

demi-cercle [dəmisɛʀkl(ə)] nm semicircle; **en ~** adj semicircular ▷ adv in a semicircle

demi-douzaine [dəmiduzɛn] nf half-dozen, half a dozen

demi-finale [dəmifinal] nf semifinal

demi-finaliste [dəmifinalist(ə)] nm/f semifinalist

demi-fond [dəmifɔ̃] nm (Sport) medium-distance running

demi-frère [dəmifʀɛʀ] nm half-brother

demi-gros [dəmigʀo] nm inv wholesale trade

demi-heure [dəmijœʀ] nf: **une ~** a half-hour, half an hour

demi-jour [dəmiʒuʀ] nm half-light

demi-journée [dəmiʒuʀne] nf half-day, half a day

démilitariser [demilitaʀize] vt to demilitarize
demi-litre [dəmilitʀ(ə)] nm half-litre (Brit), half-liter (US), half a litre ou liter
demi-livre [dəmilivʀ(ə)] nf half-pound, half a pound
demi-longueur [dəmilɔ̃gœʀ] nf (Sport) half-length, half a length
demi-lune [dəmilyn]: **en ~** adj inv semicircular
demi-mal [dəmimal] nm: **il n'y a que ~** there's not much harm done
demi-mesure [dəmimzyʀ] nf half-measure
demi-mot [dəmimo]: **à ~** adv without having to spell things out
déminer [demine] vt to clear of mines
démineur [deminœʀ] nm bomb disposal expert
demi-pension [dəmipɑ̃sjɔ̃] nf half-board; **être en ~** (Scol) to take school meals
demi-pensionnaire [dəmipɑ̃sjɔnɛʀ] nm/f (Scol) half-boarder
demi-place [dəmiplas] nf half-price; (Transports) half-fare
démis, e [demi, -iz] pp de **démettre** ▷ adj (épaule etc) dislocated
demi-saison [dəmisɛzɔ̃] nf: **vêtements de ~** spring ou autumn clothing
demi-sel [dəmisɛl] adj inv slightly salted
demi-sœur [dəmisœʀ] nf half-sister
demi-sommeil [dəmisɔmɛj] nm doze
demi-soupir [dəmisupiʀ] nm (Mus) quaver (Brit) ou eighth note (US) rest
démission [demisjɔ̃] nf resignation; **donner sa ~** to give ou hand in one's notice, hand in one's resignation
démissionnaire [demisjɔnɛʀ] adj outgoing ▷ nm/f person resigning
démissionner [demisjɔne] vi (de son poste) to resign, give ou hand in one's notice
demi-tarif [dəmitaʀif] nm half-price; (Transports) half-fare
demi-ton [dəmitɔ̃] nm (Mus) semitone
demi-tour [dəmituʀ] nm about-turn; **faire un ~** (Mil etc) to make an about-turn; **faire ~** to turn (and go) back; (Auto) to do a U-turn
démobilisation [demɔbilizasjɔ̃] nf demobilization; (fig) demotivation, demoralization
démobiliser [demɔbilize] vt to demobilize; (fig) to demotivate, demoralize
démocrate [demɔkʀat] adj democratic ▷ nm/f democrat
démocrate-chrétien, ne [demɔkʀatkʀetjɛ̃, -ɛn] nm/f Christian Democrat
démocratie [demɔkʀasi] nf democracy; **~ populaire/libérale** people's/liberal democracy
démocratique [demɔkʀatik] adj democratic
démocratiquement [demɔkʀatikmɑ̃] adv democratically
démocratisation [demɔkʀatizasjɔ̃] nf democratization
démocratiser [demɔkʀatize] vt to democratize
démodé, e [demɔde] adj old-fashioned
démoder [demɔde]: **se démoder** vi to go out of fashion

démographe [demɔgʀaf] nm/f demographer
démographie [demɔgʀafi] nf demography
démographique [demɔgʀafik] adj demographic; **poussée ~** increase in population
demoiselle [dəmwazɛl] nf (jeune fille) young lady; (célibataire) single lady, maiden lady; **~ d'honneur** bridesmaid
démolir [demɔliʀ] vt to demolish; (fig: personne) to do for
démolisseur [demɔlisœʀ] nm demolition worker
démolition [demɔlisjɔ̃] nf demolition
démon [demɔ̃] nm demon, fiend; evil spirit; (enfant turbulent) devil, demon; **le ~ du jeu/des femmes** a mania for gambling/women; **le D~** the Devil
démonétiser [demɔnetize] vt to demonetize
démoniaque [demɔnjak] adj fiendish
démonstrateur, -trice [demɔ̃stʀatœʀ, -tʀis] nm/f demonstrator
démonstratif, -ive [demɔ̃stʀatif, -iv] adj, nm (aussi Ling) demonstrative
démonstration [demɔ̃stʀasjɔ̃] nf demonstration; (aérienne, navale) display
démontable [demɔ̃tabl(ə)] adj folding
démontage [demɔ̃taʒ] nm dismantling
démonté, e [demɔ̃te] adj (fig) raging, wild
démonte-pneu [demɔ̃təpnø] nm tyre lever (Brit), tire iron (US)
démonter [demɔ̃te] vt (machine etc) to take down, dismantle; (pneu, porte) to take off; (cavalier) to throw, unseat; (fig: personne) to disconcert; **se démonter** vi (personne) to lose countenance
démontrable [demɔ̃tʀabl(ə)] adj demonstrable
démontrer [demɔ̃tʀe] vt to demonstrate, show
démoralisant, e [demɔʀalizɑ̃, -ɑ̃t] adj demoralizing
démoralisateur, -trice [demɔʀalizatœʀ, -tʀis] adj demoralizing
démoraliser [demɔʀalize] vt to demoralize
démordre [demɔʀdʀ] vi (aussi: **ne pas démordre de**) to refuse to give up, stick to
démouler [demule] vt (gâteau) to turn out
démultiplication [demyltiplikasjɔ̃] nf reduction; reduction ratio
démuni, e [demyni] adj (sans argent) impoverished; **~ de** without, lacking in
démunir [demyniʀ] vt: **~ qn de** to deprive sb of; **se ~ de** to part with, give up
démuseler [demyzle] vt to unmuzzle
démystifier [demistifje] vt to demystify
démythifier [demitifje] vt to demythologize
dénatalité [denatalite] nf fall in the birth rate
dénationalisation [denasjɔnalizasjɔ̃] nf denationalization
dénationaliser [denasjɔnalize] vt to denationalize
dénaturé, e [denatyʀe] adj (alcool) denaturized; (goûts) unnatural

dénaturer [denatyʀe] vt (goût) to alter (completely); (pensée, fait) to distort, misrepresent

dénégations [denegasjɔ̃] nfpl denials

déneigement [denɛʒmɑ̃] nm snow clearance

déneiger [deneʒe] vt to clear snow from

déni [deni] nm: ~ **(de justice)** denial of justice

déniaiser [denjeze] vt: ~ **qn** to teach sb about life

dénicher [denife] vt to unearth

dénicotinisé, e [denikɔtinize] adj nicotine-free

denier [dənje] nm (monnaie) formerly, a coin of small value; (de bas) denier; ~ **du culte** contribution to parish upkeep; **~s publics** public money; **de ses (propres) ~s** out of one's own pocket

dénier [denje] vt to deny; ~ **qch à qn** to deny sb sth

dénigrement [denigʀəmɑ̃] nm denigration; **campagne de ~** smear campaign

dénigrer [denigʀe] vt to denigrate, run down

dénivelé, e [denivle] adj (chaussée) on a lower level ▷ nm difference in height

déniveler [denivle] vt to make uneven; to put on a lower level

dénivellation [denivɛlasjɔ̃] nf, **dénivellement** [denivɛlmɑ̃] ▷ nm difference in level; (pente) ramp; (creux) dip

dénombrer [denɔ̃bʀe] vt (compter) to count; (énumérer) to enumerate, list

dénominateur [denɔminatœʀ] nm denominator; ~ **commun** common denominator

dénomination [denɔminasjɔ̃] nf designation, appellation

dénommé, e [denɔme] adj: **le ~ Dupont** the man by the name of Dupont

dénommer [denɔme] vt to name

dénoncer [denɔ̃se] vt to denounce; **se dénoncer** vi to give o.s. up, come forward

dénonciation [denɔ̃sjasjɔ̃] nf denunciation

dénoter [denɔte] vt to denote

dénouement [denumɑ̃] nm outcome, conclusion; (Théât) dénouement

dénouer [denwe] vt to unknot, undo

dénoyauter [denwajote] vt to stone; **appareil à ~** stoner

dénoyauteur [denwajotœʀ] nm stoner

denrée [dɑ̃ʀe] nf commodity; (aussi: **denrée alimentaire**) food(stuff)

dense [dɑ̃s] adj dense

densité [dɑ̃site] nf denseness; (Physique) density

dent [dɑ̃] nf tooth; **avoir/garder une ~ contre qn** to have/hold a grudge against sb; **se mettre qch sous la ~** to eat sth; **être sur les ~s** to be on one's last legs; **faire ses ~s** to teethe, cut (one's) teeth; **en ~s de scie** serrated; (irrégulier) jagged; **avoir les ~s longues** (fig) to be ruthlessly ambitious; ~ **de lait/sagesse** milk/wisdom tooth

dentaire [dɑ̃tɛʀ] adj dental; **cabinet ~** dental surgery; **école ~** dental school

denté, e [dɑ̃te] adj: **roue ~e** cog wheel

dentelé, e [dɑ̃tle] adj jagged, indented

dentelle [dɑ̃tɛl] nf lace no pl

dentelure [dɑ̃tlyʀ] nf (aussi: **dentelures**) jagged outline

dentier [dɑ̃tje] nm denture

dentifrice [dɑ̃tifʀis] adj, nm: **(pâte) ~** toothpaste; **eau ~** mouthwash

dentiste [dɑ̃tist(ə)] nm/f dentist

dentition [dɑ̃tisjɔ̃] nf teeth pl, dentition

dénucléariser [denykleaʀize] vt to make nuclear-free

dénudé, e [denyde] adj bare

dénuder [denyde] vt to bare; **se dénuder** (personne) to strip

dénué, e [denɥe] adj: ~ **de** lacking in; (intérêt) devoid of

dénuement [denymɑ̃] nm destitution

dénutrition [denytʀisjɔ̃] nf undernourishment

déodorant [deodɔʀɑ̃] nm deodorant

déodoriser [deodɔʀize] vt to deodorize

déontologie [deɔ̃tɔlɔʒi] nf code of ethics; (professionnelle) (professional) code of practice

dép. abr (= département) dept; (= départ) dep.

dépannage [depanaʒ] nm: **service/camion de ~** (Auto) breakdown service/truck

dépanner [depane] vt (voiture, télévision) to fix, repair; (fig) to bail out, help out

dépanneur [depanœʀ] nm (Auto) breakdown mechanic; (TV) television engineer

dépanneuse [depanøz] nf breakdown lorry (Brit), tow truck (US)

dépareillé, e [depaʀeje] adj (collection, service) incomplete; (gant, volume, objet) odd

déparer [depaʀe] vt to spoil, mar

départ [depaʀ] nm leaving no pl, departure; (Sport) start; (sur un horaire) departure; **à son ~** when he left; **au ~** (au début) initially, at the start; **courrier au ~** outgoing mail

départager [depaʀtaʒe] vt to decide between

département [depaʀtəmɑ̃] nm department; see note

○ **DÉPARTEMENTS**
○
○ France is divided into 96 administrative
○ units called départements. These local
○ government divisions are headed by a state-
○ appointed 'préfet', and administered by an
○ elected 'Conseil général'. Départements are
○ usually named after prominent
○ geographical features such as rivers or
○ mountain ranges.

---

départemental, e, -aux [depaʀtəmɑ̃tal, -o] adj departmental

départementaliser [depaʀtəmɑ̃talize] vt to devolve authority to

départir [depaʀtiʀ]: **se ~ de** vt to abandon, depart from

dépassé, e [depɑse] adj superseded, outmoded; (fig) out of one's depth

dépassement [depɑsmɑ̃] nm (Auto)

overtaking *no pl*

dépasser [depase] *vt* (*véhicule, concurrent*) to overtake; (*endroit*) to pass, go past; (*somme, limite*) to exceed; (*fig: en beauté etc*) to surpass, outshine; (*être en saillie sur*) to jut out above (*ou* in front of); (*dérouter*): **cela me dépasse** it's beyond me ▷ *vi* (*Auto*) to overtake; (*jupon*) to show; **se dépasser** *vi* to excel o.s.

dépassionner [depasjɔne] *vt* (*débat etc*) to take the heat out of

dépaver [depave] *vt* to remove the cobblestones from

dépaysé, e [depeize] *adj* disorientated

dépaysement [depeizmɑ̃] *nm* disorientation; change of scenery

dépayser [depeize] *vt* (*désorienter*) to disorientate; (*changer agréablement*) to provide with a change of scenery.

dépecer [depəse] *vt* (*boucher*) to joint, cut up; (*animal*) to dismember

dépêche [depɛʃ] *nf* dispatch; **~ (télégraphique)** telegram, wire

dépêcher [depeʃe] *vt* to dispatch; **se dépêcher** *vi* to hurry; **se ~ de faire qch** to hasten to do sth, hurry (in order) to do sth

dépeindre [depɛ̃dʀ(ə)] *vt* to depict

dépénalisation [depenalizasjɔ̃] *nf* decriminalization

dépendance [depɑ̃dɑ̃s] *nf* (*interdépendance*) dependence *no pl*, dependency; (*bâtiment*) outbuilding

dépendant, e [depɑ̃dɑ̃, -ɑ̃t] *vb voir* **dépendre** ▷ *adj* (*financièrement*) dependent

dépendre [depɑ̃dʀ(ə)] *vt* (*tableau*) to take down; **~ de** *vt* to depend on, to be dependent on; (*appartenir*) to belong to; **ça dépend** it depends

dépens [depɑ̃] *nmpl*: **aux ~ de** at the expense of

dépense [depɑ̃s] *nf* spending *no pl*, expense, expenditure *no pl*; (*fig*) consumption; (*: de temps, de forces*) expenditure; **pousser qn à la ~** to make sb incur an expense; **~ physique** (physical) exertion; **~s de fonctionnement** revenue expenditure; **~s d'investissement** capital expenditure; **~s publiques** public expenditure

dépenser [depɑ̃se] *vt* to spend; (*gaz, eau*) to use; (*fig*) to expend, use up; **se dépenser** *vi* (*se fatiguer*) to exert o.s.

dépensier, -ière [depɑ̃sje, -jɛʀ] *adj*: **il est ~** he's a spendthrift

déperdition [depɛʀdisjɔ̃] *nf* loss

dépérir [depeʀiʀ] *vi* (*personne*) to waste away; (*plante*) to wither

dépersonnaliser [depɛʀsɔnalize] *vt* to depersonalize

dépêtrer [depetʀe] *vt*: **se ~ de** (*situation*) to extricate o.s. from

dépeuplé, e [depœple] *adj* depopulated

dépeuplement [depœpləmɑ̃] *nm* depopulation

dépeupler [depœple] *vt* to depopulate; **se dépeupler** *vi* to be depopulated

déphasage [defazaʒ] *nm* (*fig*) being out of touch

déphasé, e [defaze] *adj* (*Élec*) out of phase; (*fig*) out of touch

déphaser [defaze] *vt* (*fig*) to put out of touch

dépilation [depilasjɔ̃] *nf* hair loss; hair removal

dépilatoire [depilatwaʀ] *adj* depilatory, hair-removing

dépiler [depile] *vt* (*épiler*) to depilate, remove hair from

dépistage [depistaʒ] *nm* (*Méd*) screening

dépister [depiste] *vt* to detect; (*Méd*) to screen; (*voleur*) to track down; (*poursuivants*) to throw off the scent

dépit [depi] *nm* vexation, frustration; **en ~ de** *prép* in spite of; **en ~ du bon sens** contrary to all good sense

dépité, e [depite] *adj* vexed, frustrated

dépiter [depite] *vt* to vex, frustrate

déplacé, e [deplase] *adj* (*propos*) out of place, uncalled-for; **personne ~e** displaced person

déplacement [deplasmɑ̃] *nm* moving; shifting; transfer; (*voyage*) trip, travelling *no pl* (*Brit*), traveling *no pl* (*US*); **en ~** away (on a trip); **~ d'air** displacement of air; **~ de vertèbre** slipped disc

déplacer [deplase] *vt* (*table, voiture*) to move, shift; (*employé*) to transfer, move; **se déplacer** *vi* (*objet*) to move; (*organe*) to become displaced; (*personne: bouger*) to move, walk; (*: voyager*) to travel ▷ *vt* (*vertèbre etc*) to displace

déplaire [deplɛʀ] *vi*: **ceci me déplaît** I don't like this, I dislike this; **il cherche à nous ~** he's trying to displease us *ou* be disagreeable to us; **se ~ quelque part** to dislike it *ou* be unhappy somewhere

déplaisant, e [deplɛzɑ̃, -ɑ̃t] *vb voir* **déplaire** ▷ *adj* disagreeable, unpleasant

déplaisir [deplɛziʀ] *nm* displeasure, annoyance

déplaît [deplɛ] *vb voir* **déplaire**

dépliant [deplijɑ̃] *nm* leaflet

déplier [deplije] *vt* to unfold; **se déplier** *vi* (*parachute*) to open

déplisser [deplise] *vt* to smooth out

déploiement [deplwamɑ̃] *nm* (*voir déployer*) deployment; display

déplomber [deplɔ̃be] *vt* (*caisse, compteur*) to break (open) the seal of; (*Inform*) to hack into

déplorable [deplɔʀabl(ə)] *adj* deplorable; lamentable

déplorer [deplɔʀe] *vt* (*regretter*) to deplore; (*pleurer sur*) to lament

déployer [deplwaje] *vt* to open out, spread; (*Mil*) to deploy; (*montrer*) to display, exhibit

déplu [deply] *pp de* **déplaire**

dépointer [depwɛ̃te] *vi* to clock out

dépoli, e [depoli] *adj*: **verre ~** frosted glass

dépolitiser [depolitize] *vt* to depoliticize

dépopulation [depɔpylasjɔ̃] *nf* depopulation

déportation [depɔʀtasjɔ̃] *nf* deportation

déporté, e [depɔʀte] *nm/f* deportee; (*1939–45*) concentration camp prisoner

déporter [depɔʀte] *vt* (*Pol*) to deport; (*dévier*) to carry off course; **se déporter** *vi* (*voiture*) to swerve

déposant, e [depozɑ̃, -ɑ̃t] nm/f (épargnant) depositor

dépose [depoz] nf taking out; taking down

déposé, e [depoze] adj registered; voir aussi **marque**

déposer [depoze] vt (gén: mettre, poser) to lay down, put down, set down; (à la banque, à la consigne) to deposit; (caution) to put down; (passager) to drop (off), set down; (démonter: serrure, moteur) to take out; (: rideau) to take down; (roi) to depose; (Admin: faire enregistrer) to file; to register ▷ vi to form a sediment ou deposit; (Jur): ~ **(contre)** to testify ou give evidence (against); **se déposer** vi to settle; ~ **son bilan** (Comm) to go into (voluntary) liquidation

dépositaire [depoziteʀ] nm/f (Jur) depository; (Comm) agent; ~ **agréé** authorized agent

déposition [depozisjɔ̃] nf (Jur) deposition

déposséder [deposede] vt to dispossess

dépôt [depo] nm (à la banque, sédiment) deposit; (entrepôt, réserve) warehouse, store; (gare) depot; (prison) cells pl; ~ **d'ordures** rubbish (Brit) ou garbage (US) dump, tip (Brit); ~ **de bilan** (voluntary) liquidation; ~ **légal** registration of copyright

dépoter [depote] vt (plante) to take from the pot, transplant

dépotoir [depotwaʀ] nm dumping ground, rubbish (Brit) ou garbage (US) dump; ~ **nucléaire** nuclear (waste) dump

dépouille [depuj] nf (d'animal) skin, hide; (humaine): ~ **(mortelle)** mortal remains pl

dépouillé, e [depuje] adj (fig) bare, bald; ~ **de** stripped of; lacking in

dépouillement [depujmɑ̃] nm (de scrutin) count, counting no pl

dépouiller [depuje] vt (animal) to skin; (spolier) to deprive of one's possessions; (documents) to go through, peruse; ~ **qn/qch de** to strip sb/sth of; ~ **le scrutin** to count the votes

dépourvu, e [depuʀvy] adj: ~ **de** lacking in, without; **au** ~ adv: **prendre qn au** ~ to catch sb unawares

dépoussiérer [depusjeʀe] vt to remove dust from

dépravation [depʀavasjɔ̃] nf depravity

dépravé, e [depʀave] adj depraved

dépraver [depʀave] vt to deprave

dépréciation [depʀesjasjɔ̃] nf depreciation

déprécier [depʀesje] vt to reduce the value of; **se déprécier** vi to depreciate

déprédations [depʀedasjɔ̃] nfpl damage sg

dépressif, -ive [depʀesif, -iv] adj depressive

dépression [depʀesjɔ̃] nf depression; ~ **(nerveuse)** (nervous) breakdown

déprimant, e [depʀimɑ̃, -ɑ̃t] adj depressing

déprime [depʀim] nf (fam): **la** ~ depression

déprimé, e [depʀime] adj (découragé) depressed

déprimer [depʀime] vt to depress

déprogrammer [depʀɔgʀame] vt (supprimer) to cancel

DEPS sigle (= dernier entré premier sorti) LIFO (= last in first out)

dépt abr (= département) dept

dépuceler [depysle] vt (fam) to take the virginity of

 MOT-CLÉ

depuis [dəpɥi] prép **1** (point de départ dans le temps) since; **il habite Paris depuis 1983/l'an dernier** he has been living in Paris since 1983/last year; **depuis quand?** since when?; **depuis quand le connaissez-vous?** how long have you known him?; **depuis lors** since then

2 (temps écoulé) for; **il habite Paris depuis cinq ans** he has been living in Paris for five years; **je le connais depuis trois ans** I've known him for three years; **depuis combien de temps êtes-vous ici?** how long have you been here?

3 (lieu): **il a plu depuis Metz** it's been raining since Metz; **elle a téléphoné depuis Valence** she rang from Valence

4 (quantité, rang) from; **depuis les plus petits jusqu'aux plus grands** from the youngest to the oldest

▷ adv (temps) since (then); **je ne lui ai pas parlé depuis** I haven't spoken to him since (then); **depuis que** conj (ever) since; **depuis qu'il m'a dit ça** (ever) since he said that to me

dépuratif, -ive [depyʀatif, -iv] adj depurative, purgative

députation [depytasjɔ̃] nf deputation; (fonction) position of deputy, ≈ parliamentary seat (Brit), ≈ seat in Congress (US)

député, e [depyte] nm/f (Pol) deputy, ≈ Member of Parliament (Brit), ≈ Congressman/woman (US)

députer [depyte] vt to delegate; ~ **qn auprès de** to send sb (as a representative) to

déracinement [deʀasinmɑ̃] nm (gén) uprooting; (d'un préjugé) eradication

déraciner [deʀasine] vt to uproot

déraillement [deʀajmɑ̃] nm derailment

dérailler [deʀaje] vi (train) to be derailed, go off ou jump the rails; (fam) to be completely off the track; **faire** ~ to derail

dérailleur [deʀajœʀ] nm (de vélo) dérailleur gears pl

déraison [deʀezɔ̃] nf unreasonableness

déraisonnable [deʀezɔnabl(ə)] adj unreasonable

déraisonner [deʀezɔne] vi to talk nonsense, rave

dérangement [deʀɑ̃ʒmɑ̃] nm (gêne, déplacement) trouble; (gastrique etc) disorder; (mécanique) breakdown; **en** ~ (téléphone) out of order

déranger [deʀɑ̃ʒe] vt (personne) to trouble, bother, disturb; (projets) to disrupt, upset; (objets, vêtements) to disarrange; **se déranger** to put o.s. out; (se déplacer) to (take the trouble to) come (ou go) out; **est-ce que cela vous dérange si ...?** do you mind if ...?; **ça te**

dérangerait de faire ...? would you mind doing ...?; **ne vous dérangez pas** don't go to any trouble; don't disturb yourself

dérapage [deʀapaʒ] *nm* skid, skidding *no pl*; going out of control

déraper [deʀape] *vi* (*voiture*) to skid; (*personne, semelles, couteau*) to slip; (*fig: économie etc*) to go out of control

dératé, e [deʀate] *nm/f*: **courir comme un ~** to run like the clappers

dératiser [deʀatize] *vt* to rid of rats

déréglé, e [deʀegle] *adj* (*mœurs*) dissolute

dérèglement [deʀɛgləmɑ̃] *nm* upsetting *no pl*, upset

déréglementation [deʀɛgləmɑ̃tasjɔ̃] *nf* deregulation

dérégler [deʀegle] *vt* (*mécanisme*) to put out of order, cause to break down; (*estomac*) to upset; **se dérégler** *vi* to break down, go wrong

dérider [deʀide] *vt*, **se dérider** *vi* to cheer up

dérision [deʀizjɔ̃] *nf* derision; **tourner en ~** to deride; **par ~** in mockery

dérisoire [deʀizwaʀ] *adj* derisory

dérivatif [deʀivatif] *nm* distraction

dérivation [deʀivasjɔ̃] *nf* derivation; diversion

dérive [deʀiv] *nf* (*de dériveur*) centre-board; **aller à la ~** (*Navig, fig*) to drift; **~ des continents** (*Géo*) continental drift

dérivé, e [deʀive] *adj* derived ▷ *nm* (*Ling*) derivative; (*Tech*) by-product ▷ *nf* (*Math*) derivative

dériver [deʀive] *vt* (*Math*) to derive; (*cours d'eau etc*) to divert ▷ *vi* (*bateau*) to drift; **~ de** to derive from

dériveur [deʀivœʀ] *nm* sailing dinghy

dermatite [dɛʀmatit] *nf* dermatitis

dermato [dɛʀmato] *nm/f* (*fam: = dermatologue*) dermatologist

dermatologie [dɛʀmatɔlɔʒi] *nf* dermatology

dermatologue [dɛʀmatɔlɔg] *nm/f* dermatologist

dermatose [dɛʀmatoz] *nf* dermatosis

dermite [dɛʀmit] *nf* = **dermatite**

dernier, -ière [dɛʀnje, -jɛʀ] *adj* (*dans le temps, l'espace*) last; (*le plus récent: gén avant n*) latest, last; (*final, ultime: effort*) final; (*échelon, grade*) top, highest ▷ *nm* (*étage*) top floor; **lundi/le mois ~** last Monday/month; **du ~ chic** extremely smart; **le ~ cri** the last word (in fashion); **les ~s honneurs** the last tribute; **le ~ soupir, rendre le ~ soupir** to breathe one's last; **en ~** *adv* last; **ce ~, cette dernière** the latter

dernièrement [dɛʀnjɛʀmɑ̃] *adv* recently

dernier-né, dernière-née [dɛʀnjene, dɛʀnjɛʀne] *nm/f* (*enfant*) last-born

dérobade [deʀɔbad] *nf* side-stepping *no pl*

dérobé, e [deʀɔbe] *adj* (*porte*) secret, hidden; **à la ~e** surreptitiously

dérober [deʀɔbe] *vt* to steal; (*cacher*): **~ qch à (la vue de) qn** to conceal *ou* hide sth from sb('s view); **se dérober** *vi* (*s'esquiver*) to slip away; (*fig*) to shy away; **se ~ sous** (*s'effondrer*) to give way

beneath; **se ~ à** (*justice, regards*) to hide from; (*obligation*) to shirk

dérogation [deʀɔgasjɔ̃] *nf* (special) dispensation

déroger [deʀɔʒe]: **~ à** *vt* to go against, depart from

dérouiller [deʀuje] *vt*: **se ~ les jambes** to stretch one's legs

déroulement [deʀulmɑ̃] *nm* (*d'une opération etc*) progress

dérouler [deʀule] *vt* (*ficelle*) to unwind; (*papier*) to unroll; **se dérouler** *vi* to unwind; to unroll, come unrolled; (*avoir lieu*) to take place; (*se passer*) to go

déroutant, e [deʀutɑ̃, -ɑ̃t] *adj* disconcerting

déroute [deʀut] *nf* (*Mil*) rout; (*fig*) total collapse; **mettre en ~** to rout; **en ~** routed

dérouter [deʀute] *vt* (*avion, train*) to reroute, divert; (*étonner*) to disconcert, throw (out)

derrick [deʀik] *nm* derrick (*over oil well*)

derrière [dɛʀjɛʀ] *adv, prép* behind ▷ *nm* (*d'une maison*) back; (*postérieur*) behind, bottom; **les pattes de ~** the back legs, the hind legs; **par ~** from behind; (*fig*) in an underhand way, behind one's back

derviche [dɛʀviʃ] *nm* dervish

DES *sigle m* (= *diplôme d'études supérieures*) *university post-graduate degree*

des [de] *art voir* **de**

dès [dɛ] *prép* from; **~ que** *conj* as soon as; **~ à présent** here and now; **~ son retour** as soon as he was (*ou* is) back; **~ réception** upon receipt; **~ lors** *adv* from then on; **~ lors que** *conj* from the moment (that)

désabusé, e [dezabyze] *adj* disillusioned

désaccord [dezakɔʀ] *nm* disagreement

désaccordé, e [dezakɔʀde] *adj* (*Mus*) out of tune

désacraliser [desakʀalize] *vt* to deconsecrate; (*fig: profession, institution*) to take the mystique out of

désaffecté, e [dezafɛkte] *adj* disused

désaffection [dezafɛksjɔ̃] *nf*: **~ pour** estrangement from

désagréable [dezagʀeablə] *adj* unpleasant, disagreeable

désagréablement [dezagʀeabləmɑ̃] *adv* disagreeably, unpleasantly

désagrégation [dezagʀegasjɔ̃] *nf* disintegration

désagréger [dezagʀeʒe]: **se désagréger** *vi* to disintegrate, break up

désagrément [dezagʀemɑ̃] *nm* annoyance, trouble *no pl*

désaltérant, e [dezalteʀɑ̃, -ɑ̃t] *adj* thirst-quenching

désaltérer [dezalteʀe] *vt*: **se désaltérer** to quench one's thirst; **ça désaltère** it's thirst-quenching, it quenches your thirst

désamorcer [dezamɔʀse] *vt* to remove the primer from; (*fig*) to defuse; (: *prévenir*) to forestall

désappointé, e [dezapwɛte] *adj* disappointed

désapprobateur, -trice [dezapʀɔbatœʀ, -tʀis] *adj* disapproving

désapprobation [dezapʀɔbasjɔ̃] *nf* disapproval

désapprouver [dezapʀuve] *vt* to disapprove of

désarçonner [dezaʀsɔne] *vt* to unseat, throw; *(fig)* to throw, nonplus *(Brit)*, disconcert

désargenté, e [dezaʀʒɑ̃te] *adj* impoverished

désarmant, e [dezaʀmɑ̃, -ɑ̃t] *adj* disarming

désarmé, e [dezaʀme] *adj (fig)* disarmed

désarmement [dezaʀməmɑ̃] *nm* disarmament

désarmer [dezaʀme] *vt (Mil, aussi fig)* to disarm; *(Navig)* to lay up; *(fusil)* to unload; (: *mettre le cran de sûreté*) to put the safety catch on ▷ *vi (pays)* to disarm; *(haine)* to wane; *(personne)* to give up

désarroi [dezaʀwa] *nm* helplessness, disarray

désarticulé, e [dezaʀtikyle] *adj (pantin, corps)* dislocated

désarticuler [dezaʀtikyle] *vt*: **se désarticuler** to contort (o.s.)

désassorti, e [dezasɔʀti] *adj* non-matching, unmatched; *(magasin, marchand)* sold out

désastre [dezastʀ(ə)] *nm* disaster

désastreux, -euse [dezastʀø, -øz] *adj* disastrous

désavantage [dezavɑ̃taʒ] *nm* disadvantage; *(inconvénient)* drawback, disadvantage

désavantager [dezavɑ̃taʒe] *vt* to put at a disadvantage

désavantageux, -euse [dezavɑ̃taʒø, -øz] *adj* unfavourable, disadvantageous

désaveu [dezavø] *nm* repudiation; *(déni)* disclaimer

désavouer [dezavwe] *vt* to disown, repudiate, disclaim

désaxé, e [dezakse] *adj (fig)* unbalanced

désaxer [dezakse] *vt (roue)* to put out of true; *(personne)* to throw off balance

desceller [desele] *vt (pierre)* to pull free

descendance [desɑ̃dɑ̃s] *nf (famille)* descendants *pl*, issue; *(origine)* descent

descendant, e [desɑ̃dɑ̃, -ɑ̃t] *vb voir* **descendre** ▷ *nm/f* descendant

descendeur, -euse [desɑ̃dœʀ, -øz] *nm/f (Sport)* downhiller

descendre [desɑ̃dʀ(ə)] *vt (escalier, montagne)* to go *(ou* come) down; *(valise, paquet)* to take *ou* get down; *(étagère etc)* to lower; *(fam: abattre)* to shoot down; (: *boire*) to knock back ▷ *vi* to go *(ou* come) down; *(passager: s'arrêter)* to get out, alight; *(niveau, température)* to go *ou* come down, fall, drop; *(marée)* to go out; **à pied/en voiture** to walk/drive down, go down on foot/by car; **~ de** *(famille)* to be descended from; **~ du train** to get out of *ou* off the train; **~ d'un arbre** to climb down from a tree; **~ de cheval** to dismount, get off one's horse; **~ à l'hôtel** to stay at a hotel; **~ dans la rue** *(manifester)* to take to the streets; **~ en ville** to go into town, go down town

descente [desɑ̃t] *nf* descent, going down; *(chemin)* way down; *(Ski)* downhill (race); **au milieu de la ~** halfway down; **freinez dans les ~s** use the brakes going downhill; **~ de lit**

bedside rug; **~ (de police)** *(police)* raid

descriptif, -ive [dɛskʀiptif, -iv] *adj* descriptive ▷ *nm* explanatory leaflet

description [dɛskʀipsjɔ̃] *nf* description

désembourber [dezɑ̃buʀbe] *vt* to pull out of the mud

désembourgeoiser [dezɑ̃buʀʒwaze] *vt*: **~ qn** to get sb out of his *(ou* her) middle-class attitudes

désembuer [dezɑ̃bɥe] *vt* to demist

désemparé, e [dezɑ̃paʀe] *adj* bewildered, distraught; *(bateau, avion)* crippled

désemparer [dezɑ̃paʀe] *vi*: **sans ~** without stopping

désemplir [dezɑ̃pliʀ] *vi*: **ne pas ~** to be always full

désenchanté, e [dezɑ̃ʃɑ̃te] *adj* disenchanted, disillusioned

désenchantement [dezɑ̃ʃɑ̃tmɑ̃] *nm* disenchantment, disillusion

désenclaver [dezɑ̃klave] *vt* to open up

désencombrer [dezɑ̃kɔ̃bʀe] *vt* to clear

désenfler [dezɑ̃fle] *vi* to become less swollen

désengagement [dezɑ̃ɡaʒmɑ̃] *nm (Pol)* disengagement

désensabler [dezɑ̃sable] *vt* to pull out of the sand

désensibiliser [desɑ̃sibilize] *vt (Méd)* to desensitize

désenvenimer [dezɑ̃vnime] *vt (plaie)* to remove the poison from; *(fig)* to take the sting out of

désépaissir [dezepesiʀ] *vt* to thin (out)

déséquilibre [dezekilibʀ(ə)] *nm (position)*: **être en ~** to be unsteady; *(fig: des forces, du budget)* imbalance; *(Psych)* unbalance

déséquilibré, e [dezekilibʀe] *nm/f (Psych)* unbalanced person

déséquilibrer [dezekilibʀe] *vt* to throw off balance

désert, e [dezɛʀ, -ɛʀt(ə)] *adj* deserted ▷ *nm* desert

déserter [dezɛʀte] *vi, vt* to desert

déserteur [dezɛʀtœʀ] *nm* deserter

désertion [dezɛʀsjɔ̃] *nf* desertion

désertique [dezɛʀtik] *adj* desert *cpd*; *(inculte)* barren, empty

désescalade [dezɛskalad] *nf (Mil)* de-escalation

désespérant, e [dezɛspeʀɑ̃, -ɑ̃t] *adj* hopeless, despairing

désespéré, e [dezɛspeʀe] *adj* desperate; *(regard)* despairing; **état ~** *(Méd)* hopeless condition

désespérément [dezɛspeʀemɑ̃] *adv* desperately

désespérer [dezɛspeʀe] *vt* to drive to despair ▷ *vi*, **se désespérer** *vi* to despair; **~ de** to despair of

désespoir [dezɛspwaʀ] *nm* despair; **être** *ou* **faire le ~ de qn** to be the despair of sb; **en ~ de cause** in desperation

déshabillé, e [dezabije] *adj* undressed ▷ *nm* négligée

déshabiller [dezabije] *vt* to undress; **se déshabiller** *vi* to undress (o.s.)

déshabituer [dezabitɥe] *vt*: **se ~ de** to get out of

the habit of

désherbant [dezɛʀbɑ̃] nm weed-killer

désherber [dezɛʀbe] vt to weed

déshérité, e [dezerite] adj disinherited ▷ nm/f: **les ~s** (pauvres) the underprivileged, the deprived

déshériter [dezerite] vt to disinherit

déshonneur [dezɔnœʀ] nm dishonour (Brit), dishonor (US), disgrace

déshonorer [dezɔnɔʀe] vt to dishonour (Brit), dishonor (US), bring disgrace upon; **se déshonorer** vi to bring dishono(u)r on o.s.

déshumaniser [dezymanize] vt to dehumanize

déshydratation [dezidʀatasjɔ̃] nf dehydration

déshydraté, e [dezidʀate] adj dehydrated

déshydrater [dezidʀate] vt to dehydrate

desiderata [deziderata] nmpl requirements

design [dizajn] adj (mobilier) designer cpd ▷ nm (industrial) design

désignation [deziɲasjɔ̃] nf naming, appointment; (signe, mot) name, designation

designer [dizajnɛʀ] nm designer

désigner [deziɲe] vt (montrer) to point out, indicate; (dénommer) to denote, refer to; (nommer: candidat etc) to name, appoint

désillusion [dezilyzjɔ̃] nf disillusion(ment)

désillusionner [dezilyzjɔne] vt to disillusion

désincarné, e [dezɛ̃kaʀne] adj disembodied

désinence [dezinɑ̃s] nf ending, inflexion

désinfectant, e [dezɛ̃fɛktɑ̃, -ɑ̃t] adj, nm disinfectant

désinfecter [dezɛ̃fɛkte] vt to disinfect

désinfection [dezɛ̃fɛksjɔ̃] nf disinfection

désinformation [dezɛ̃fɔʀmasjɔ̃] nf disinformation

désintégration [dezɛ̃tegʀasjɔ̃] nf disintegration

désintégrer [dezɛ̃tegʀe] vt to break up; **se désintégrer** vi to disintegrate

désintéressé, e [dezɛ̃terese] adj (généreux, bénévole) disinterested, unselfish

désintéressement [dezɛ̃teʀɛsmɑ̃] nm (générosité) disinterestedness

désintéresser [dezɛ̃terese] vt: **se désintéresser (de)** to lose interest (in)

désintérêt [dezɛ̃teʀɛ] nm (indifférence) disinterest

désintoxication [dezɛ̃tɔksikasjɔ̃] nf treatment for alcoholism (ou drug addiction); **faire une cure de ~** to have ou undergo treatment for alcoholism (ou drug addiction)

désintoxiquer [dezɛ̃tɔksike] vt to treat for alcoholism (ou drug addiction)

désinvolte [dezɛ̃vɔlt(ə)] adj casual, off-hand

désinvolture [dezɛ̃vɔltyʀ] nf casualness

désir [deziʀ] nm wish; (fort, sensuel) desire

désirable [deziʀabl(ə)] adj desirable

désirer [dezire] vt to want, wish for; (sexuellement) to desire; **je désire ...** (formule de politesse) I would like ...; **il désire que tu l'aides** he would like ou he wants you to help him; **~ faire** to want ou wish to do; **ça laisse à ~** it

leaves something to be desired

désireux, -euse [deziʀø, -øz] adj: **~ de faire** anxious to do

désistement [dezistəmɑ̃] nm withdrawal

désister [deziste]: **se désister** vi to stand down, withdraw

désobéir [dezɔbeiʀ] vi: **~ (à qn/qch)** to disobey (sb/sth)

désobéissance [dezɔbeisɑ̃s] nf disobedience

désobéissant, e [dezɔbeisɑ̃, -ɑ̃t] adj disobedient

désobligeant, e [dezɔbliʒɑ̃, -ɑ̃t] adj disagreeable, unpleasant

désobliger [dezɔbliʒe] vt to offend

désodorisant [dezɔdɔʀizɑ̃] nm air freshener, deodorizer

désodoriser [dezɔdɔʀize] vt to deodorize

désœuvré, e [dezœvʀe] adj idle

désœuvrement [dezœvʀəmɑ̃] nm idleness

désolant, e [dezɔlɑ̃, -ɑ̃t] adj distressing

désolation [dezɔlasjɔ̃] nf (affliction) distress, grief; (d'un paysage etc) desolation, devastation

désolé, e [dezɔle] adj (paysage) desolate; **je suis ~** I'm sorry

désoler [dezɔle] vt to distress, grieve; **se désoler** vi to be upset

désolidariser [desɔlidaʀize] vt: **se ~ de** ou **d'avec** to dissociate o.s. from

désopilant, e [dezɔpilɑ̃, -ɑ̃t] adj screamingly funny, hilarious

désordonné, e [dezɔʀdɔne] adj untidy, disorderly

désordre [dezɔʀdʀ(ə)] nm disorder(liness), untidiness; (anarchie) disorder; **désordres** nmpl (Pol) disturbances, disorder sg; **en ~** in a mess, untidy

désorganiser [dezɔʀganize] vt to disorganize

désorienté, e [dezɔʀjɑ̃te] adj disorientated; (fig) bewildered

désorienter [dezɔʀjɑ̃te] vt (fig) to confuse

désormais [dezɔʀmɛ] adv in future, from now on

désosser [dezɔse] vt to bone

despote [dɛspɔt] nm despot; (fig) tyrant

despotique [dɛspɔtik] adj despotic

despotisme [dɛspɔtism(ə)] nm despotism

desquamer [dɛskwame]: **se desquamer** vi to flake off

desquels, desquelles [dekɛl] prép + pron voir lequel

DESS sigle m (= Diplôme d'études supérieures spécialisées) post-graduate diploma

dessaisir [deseziʀ] vt: **~ un tribunal d'une affaire** to remove a case from a court; **se ~ de** vt to give up, part with

dessaler [desale] vt (eau de mer) to desalinate; (Culin: morue etc) to soak; (fig fam: délurer): **~ qn** to teach sb a thing or two ▷ vi (voilier) to capsize

Desse abr = **duchesse**

desséché, e [deseʃe] adj dried up

dessèchement [desɛʃmɑ̃] nm drying out; dryness; hardness

dessécher [deseʃe] vt (terre, plante) to dry out,

parch; (*peau*) to dry out; (*volontairement: aliments etc*) to dry, dehydrate; (*fig: cœur*) to harden; **se dessécher** vi to dry out; (*peau, lèvres*) to go dry

dessein [desɛ̃] *nm* design; **dans le ~ de** with the intention of; **à ~** intentionally, deliberately

desseller [desele] *vt* to unsaddle

desserrer [desere] *vt* to loosen; (*frein*) to release; (*poing, dents*) to unclench; (*objets alignés*) to space out; **ne pas ~ les dents** not to open one's mouth

dessert [desɛʀ] *vb voir* **desservir** ▷ *nm* dessert, pudding

desserte [desɛʀt(ə)] *nf* (*table*) side table; (*transport*): **la ~ du village est assurée par autocar** there is a coach service to the village; **chemin** *ou* **voie de ~** service road

desservir [desɛʀviʀ] *vt* (*ville, quartier*) to serve; (: *voie de communication*) to lead into; (*vicaire: paroisse*) to serve; (*nuire à: personne*) to do a disservice to; (*débarrasser*): **~ (la table)** to clear the table

dessiller [desije] *vt* (*fig*): **~ les yeux à qn** to open sb's eyes

dessin [desɛ̃] *nm* (*œuvre, art*) drawing; (*motif*) pattern, design; (*contour*) (out)line; **le ~ industriel** draughtsmanship (*Brit*), draftsmanship (*US*); **~ animé** cartoon (film); **~ humoristique** cartoon

dessinateur, -trice [desinatœʀ, -tʀis] *nm/f* drawer; (*de bandes dessinées*) cartoonist; (*industriel*) draughtsman (*Brit*), draftsman (*US*); **dessinatrice de mode** fashion designer

dessiner [desine] *vt* to draw; (*concevoir: carrosserie, maison*) to design; (*robe: taille*) to show off; **se dessiner** vi (*forme*) to be outlined; (*fig: solution*) to emerge

dessoûler [desule] *vt, vi* to sober up

dessous [dəsu] *adv* underneath, beneath ▷ *nm* underside; (*étage inférieur*): **les voisins du ~** the downstairs neighbours ▷ *nmpl* (*sous-vêtements*) underwear *sg*; (*fig*) hidden aspects; **en ~** underneath; below; (*fig: en catimini*) slyly, on the sly; **par ~** underneath; below; **de ~ le lit** from under the bed; **au-~** *adv* below; **au-~ de** *prép* below; (*peu digne de*) beneath; **au-~ de tout** the (absolute) limit; **avoir le ~** to get the worst of it

dessous-de-bouteille [dəsudbutɛj] *nm* bottle mat

dessous-de-plat [dəsudpla] *nm inv* tablemat

dessous-de-table [dəsudtabl(ə)] *nm* (*fig*) bribe, under-the-counter payment

dessus [dəsy] *adv* on top; (*collé, écrit*) on it ▷ *nm* top; (*étage supérieur*): **les voisins/ l'appartement du ~** the upstairs neighbours/ flat; **en ~** above; **par ~** *adv* over it ▷ *prép* over; **au-~** above; **au-~ de** above; **avoir/prendre le ~** to have/get the upper hand; **reprendre le ~** to get over it; **bras ~ bras dessous** arm in arm; **sens ~ dessous** upside down; *voir* **ci-**; **là-**

dessus-de-lit [dəsydli] *nm inv* bedspread

déstabiliser [destabilize] *vt* (*Pol*) to destabilize

destin [destɛ̃] *nm* fate; (*avenir*) destiny

destinataire [dɛstinatɛʀ] *nm/f* (*Postes*) addressee; (*d'un colis*) consïgnee; (*d'un mandat*) payee; **aux risques et périls du ~** at owner's risk

destination [dɛstinasjɔ̃] *nf* (*lieu*) destination; (*usage*) purpose; **à ~ de** (*avion etc*) bound for; (*voyageur*) bound for, travelling to

destinée [dɛstine] *nf* fate; (*existence, avenir*) destiny

destiner [dɛstine] *vt*: **~ qn à** (*poste, sort*) to destine sb for; **~ qn/qch à** (*prédestiner*) to mark sb/sth out for; **~ qch à** (*envisager d'affecter*) to intend to use sth for; **~ qch à qn** (*envisager de donner*) to intend to give sth to sb, intend sb to have sth; (*adresser*) to intend sth for sb; **se ~ à l'enseignement** to intend to become a teacher; **être destiné à** (*sort*) to be destined to + *verbe*; (*usage*) to be intended *ou* meant for; (*sort*) to be in store for

destituer [dɛstitɥe] *vt* to depose; **~ qn de ses fonctions** to relieve sb of his duties

destitution [dɛstitysjɔ̃] *nf* deposition

destructeur, -trice [dɛstʀyktœʀ, -tʀis] *adj* destructive

destructif, -ive [dɛstʀyktif, -iv] *adj* destructive

destruction [dɛstʀyksjɔ̃] *nf* destruction

déstructuré, e [dɛstʀyktyʀe] *adj*: **vêtements ~s** casual clothes

déstructurer [destʀyktyʀe] *vt* to break down, take to pieces

désuet, -ète [desɥɛ, -ɛt] *adj* outdated, outmoded

désuétude [desɥetyd] *nf*: **tomber en ~** to fall into disuse, become obsolete

désuni, e [dezyni] *adj* divided, disunited

désunion [dezynjɔ̃] *nf* disunity

désunir [dezyniʀ] *vt* to disunite; **se désunir** vi (*athlète*) to get out of one's stride

détachable [detaʃabl(ə)] *adj* (*coupon etc*) tear-off *cpd*; (*capuche etc*) detachable

détachant [detaʃɑ̃] *nm* stain remover

détaché, e [detaʃe] *adj* (*fig*) detached ▷ *nm/f* (*représentant*) person on secondment (*Brit*) *ou* a posting

détachement [detaʃmɑ̃] *nm* detachment; (*fonctionnaire, employé*): **être en ~** to be on secondment (*Brit*) *ou* a posting

détacher [detaʃe] *vt* (*enlever*) to detach, remove; (*délier*) to untie; (*Admin*): **~ qn (auprès de** *ou* **à)** to send sb on secondment (to) (*Brit*), post sb (to); (*Mil*) to detail; (*vêtement: nettoyer*) to remove the stains from; **se détacher** vi (*tomber*) to come off; to come out; (*se défaire*) to come undone; (*Sport*) to pull *ou* break away; (*se délier: chien, prisonnier*) to break loose; **se ~ sur** to stand out against; **se ~ de** (*se désintéresser*) to grow away from

détail [detaj] *nm* detail; (*Comm*): **le ~** retail; **prix de ~** retail price; **au ~** *adv* (*Comm*) retail; (: *individuellement*) separately; **donner le ~ de** to give a detailed account of; (*compte*) to give a breakdown of; **en ~** in detail

détaillant, e [detajɑ̃, -ɑ̃t] *nm/f* retailer

détaillé, e [detaje] *adj* (*récit*) detailed

détailler [detaje] *vt* (*Comm*) to sell retail; to sell separately; (*expliquer*) to explain in detail; to detail; (*examiner*) to look over, examine

détaler [detale] *vi* (*lapin*) to scamper off; (*fam: personne*) to make off, scarper (*fam*)

détartrant [detaʀtʀɑ̃] *nm* descaling agent (*Brit*), scale remover

détartrer [detaʀtʀe] *vt* to descale; (*dents*) to scale

détaxe [detaks(ə)] *nf* (*réduction*) reduction in tax; (*suppression*) removal of tax; (*remboursement*) tax refund

détaxer [detakse] *vt* (*réduire*) to reduce the tax on; (*ôter*) to remove the tax on

détecter [detɛkte] *vt* to detect

détecteur [detɛktœʀ] *nm* detector, sensor; **~ de mensonges** lie detector; **~ (de mines)** mine detector

détection [detɛksjɔ̃] *nf* detection

détective [detɛktiv] *nm* detective; **~ (privé)** private detective *ou* investigator

déteindre [detɛ̃dʀ(ə)] *vi* to fade; (*fig*): **~ sur** to rub off on

déteint, e [detɛ̃, -ɛ̃t] *pp de* **déteindre**

dételer [detle] *vt* to unharness; (*voiture, wagon*) to unhitch ▷ *vi* (*fig: s'arrêter*) to leave off (working)

détendeur [detɑ̃dœʀ] *nm* (*de bouteille à gaz*) regulator

détendre [detɑ̃dʀ(ə)] *vt* (*fil*) to slacken, loosen; (*personne, atmosphère*) to relax; (: *situation*) to relieve; **se détendre** *vi* to lose its tension; to relax

détendu, e [detɑ̃dy] *adj* relaxed

détenir [detniʀ] *vt* (*fortune, objet, secret*) to be in possession of; (*prisonnier*) to detain; (*record*) to hold; **~ le pouvoir** to be in power

détente [detɑ̃t] *nf* relaxation; (*Pol*) détente; (*d'une arme*) trigger; (*d'un athlète qui saute*) spring

détenteur, -trice [detɑ̃tœʀ, -tʀis] *nm/f* holder

détention [detɑ̃sjɔ̃] *nf* (*voir détenir*) possession; detention; holding; **~ préventive** (pre-trial) custody

détenu, e [detny] *pp de* **détenir** ▷ *nm/f* prisoner

détergent [detɛʀʒɑ̃] *nm* detergent

détérioration [deteʀjɔʀasjɔ̃] *nf* damaging; deterioration

détériorer [deteʀjɔʀe] *vt* to damage; **se détériorer** *vi* to deteriorate

déterminant, e [detɛʀminɑ̃, -ɑ̃t] *adj*: **un facteur ~** à determining factor ▷ *nm* (*Ling*) determiner

détermination [detɛʀminasjɔ̃] *nf* determining; (*résolution*) decision; (*fermeté*) determination

déterminé, e [detɛʀmine] *adj* (*résolu*) determined; (*précis*) specific, definite

déterminer [detɛʀmine] *vt* (*fixer*) to determine; (*décider*): **~ qn à faire** to decide sb to do; **se ~ à faire** to make up one's mind to do

déterminisme [detɛʀminism(ə)] *nm* determinism

déterré, e [detere] *nm/f*: **avoir une mine de ~** to look like death warmed up (*Brit*) *ou* warmed over (*US*)

déterrer [detere] *vt* to dig up

détersif, -ive [detɛʀsif, -iv] *adj, nm* detergent

détestable [detɛstabl(ə)] *adj* foul, detestable

détester [detɛste] *vt* to hate, detest

détiendrai [detjɛ̃dʀe], **détiens** *etc* [detjɛ̃] *vb voir* **détenir**

détonant, e [detɔnɑ̃, -ɑ̃t] *adj*: **mélange ~** explosive mixture

détonateur [detɔnatœʀ] *nm* detonator

détonation [detɔnasjɔ̃] *nf* detonation, bang, report (of a gun)

détoner [detɔne] *vi* to detonate, explode

détonner [detɔne] *vi* (*Mus*) to go out of tune; (*fig*) to clash

détordre [detɔʀdʀ(ə)] *vt* to untwist, unwind

détour [detuʀ] *nm* detour; (*tournant*) bend, curve; (*fig: subterfuge*) roundabout means; **sans ~** (*fig*) plainly

détourné, e [deturne] *adj* (*sentier, chemin, moyen*) roundabout

détournement [detuʀnəmɑ̃] *nm* diversion, rerouting; **~ d'avion** hijacking; **~ (de fonds)** embezzlement *ou* misappropriation (of funds); **~ de mineur** corruption of a minor

détourner [deturne] *vt* to divert; (*avion*) to divert, reroute; (: *par la force*) to hijack; (*yeux, tête*) to turn away; (*de l'argent*) to embezzle, misappropriate; **se détourner** to turn away; **~ la conversation** to change the subject; **~ qn de son devoir** to divert sb from his duty; **~ l'attention (de qn)** to distract *ou* divert (sb's) attention

détracteur, -trice [detʀaktœʀ, -tʀis] *nm/f* disparager, critic

détraqué, e [detʀake] *adj* (*machine, santé*) broken-down ▷ *nm/f* (*fam*): **c'est un ~** he's unhinged

détraquer [detʀake] *vt* to put out of order; (*estomac*) to upset; **se détraquer** *vi* to go wrong

détrempe [detʀɑ̃p] *nf* (*Art*) tempera

détrempé, e [detʀɑ̃pe] *adj* (*sol*) sodden, waterlogged

détremper [detʀɑ̃pe] *vt* (*peinture*) to water down

détresse [detʀɛs] *nf* distress; **en ~** (*avion etc*) in distress; **appel/signal de ~** distress call/signal

détriment [detʀimɑ̃] *nm*: **au ~ de** to the detriment of

détritus [detʀitys] *nmpl* rubbish *sg*, refuse *sg*, garbage *sg* (*US*)

détroit [detʀwa] *nm* strait; **le ~ de Bering** *ou* **Behring** the Bering Strait; **le ~ de Gibraltar** the Straits of Gibraltar; **le ~ du Bosphore** the Bosphorus; **le ~ de Magellan** the Strait of Magellan, the Magellan Strait

détromper [detʀɔ̃pe] *vt* to disabuse; **se détromper** *vi*: **détrompez-vous** don't believe it

détrôner [detʀone] *vt* to dethrone, depose; (*fig*) to oust, dethrone

détrousser [detʀuse] *vt* to rob

détruire [detʀ̩iʀ] *vt* to destroy; *(fig: santé, réputation)* to ruin; *(documents)* to shred
détruit, e [detʀ̩i, -it] *pp de* **détruire**
dette [dɛt] *nf* debt; ~ **publique** *ou* **de l'État** national debt
DEUG [døg] *sigle m* = **Diplôme d'études universitaires générales**; *see note*

● DEUG

French students sit their DEUG ('diplôme d'études universitaires générales') after two years at university. They can then choose to leave university altogether, or go on to study for their 'licence'. The certificate specifies the student's major subject and may be awarded with distinction.

deuil [dœj] *nm (perte)* bereavement; *(période)* mourning; *(chagrin)* grief; **porter le ~** to wear mourning; **prendre le/être en ~** to go into/be in mourning
DEUST [dœst] *sigle m* = **Diplôme d'études universitaires scientifiques et techniques**
deux [dø] *num* two; **les ~** both; **ses ~ mains** both his hands, his two hands; **à ~ pas** a short distance away; **tous les ~ mois** every two months, every other month; **~ points** colon *sg*
deuxième [døzjɛm] *num* second
deuxièmement [døzjɛmmɑ̃] *adv* secondly, in the second place
deux-pièces [døpjɛs] *nm inv (tailleur)* two-piece (suit); *(de bain)* two-piece (swimsuit); *(appartement)* two-roomed flat (Brit) *ou* apartment (US)
deux-roues [døʀu] *nm* two-wheeled vehicle
deux-temps [døtɑ̃] *adj* two-stroke
devais *etc* [dəvɛ] *vb voir* **devoir**
dévaler [devale] *vt* to hurtle down
dévaliser [devalize] *vt* to rob, burgle
dévalorisant, e [devalɔʀizɑ̃, -ɑ̃t] *adj* depreciatory
dévalorisation [devalɔʀizasjɔ̃] *nf* depreciation
dévaloriser [devalɔʀize] *vt* to reduce the value of; **se dévaloriser** *vi* to depreciate
dévaluation [devalɥasjɔ̃] *nf* depreciation; *(Écon: mesure)* devaluation
dévaluer [devalɥe] *vt*, **se dévaluer** *vi* to devalue
devancer [dəvɑ̃se] *vt* to be ahead of; *(distancer)* to get ahead of; *(arriver avant)* to arrive before; *(prévenir)* to anticipate; **~ l'appel** *(Mil)* to enlist before call-up
devancier, -ière [dəvɑ̃sje, -jɛʀ] *nm/f* precursor
devant [dəvɑ̃] *vb voir* **devoir** ▷ *adv* in front; *(à distance: en avant)* ahead ▷ *prép* in front of; ahead of; *(avec mouvement: passer)* past; *(fig)* before, in front of; *(: face à)* faced with, in the face of; *(: vu)* in view of ▷ *nm* front; **prendre les ~s** to make the first move; **de ~** *(roue, porte)* front; **les pattes de ~** the front legs, the forelegs; **par ~** *(boutonner)* at the front; *(entrer)* the front way; **par-~ notaire** in the presence of a notary; **aller**

au-~ de qn to go out to meet sb; **aller au-~ de** *(désirs de qn)* to anticipate; **aller au-~ des ennuis** *ou* **difficultés** to be asking for trouble
devanture [dəvɑ̃tyʀ] *nf (façade)* (shop) front; *(étalage)* display; (shop) window
dévastateur, -trice [devastatœʀ, -tʀis] *adj* devastating
dévastation [devastasjɔ̃] *nf* devastation
dévaster [devaste] *vt* to devastate
déveine [devɛn] *nf* rotten luck *no pl*
développement [devlɔpmɑ̃] *nm* development
développer [devlɔpe] *vt*, **se développer** *vi* to develop
devenir [dəvniʀ] *vi* to become; **~ instituteur** to become a teacher; **que sont-ils devenus?** what has become of them?
devenu, e [dəvny] *pp de* **devenir**
dévergondé, e [devɛʀgɔ̃de] *adj* wild, shameless
dévergonder [devɛʀgɔ̃de] *vt*, **se dévergonder** *vi* to get into bad ways
déverrouiller [devɛʀuje] *vt* to unbolt
devers [dəvɛʀ] *adv*: **par ~ soi** to oneself
déverser [devɛʀse] *vt (liquide)* to pour (out); *(ordures)* to tip (out); **se ~ dans** *(fleuve, mer)* to flow into
déversoir [devɛʀswaʀ] *nm* overflow
dévêtir [devetiʀ] *vt*, **se dévêtir** *vi* to undress
devez [dəve] *vb voir* **devoir**
déviation [devjasjɔ̃] *nf* deviation; *(Auto)* diversion *(Brit)*, detour *(US)*; **~ de la colonne (vertébrale)** curvature of the spine
dévider [devide] *vt* to unwind
dévidoir [devidwaʀ] *nm* reel
deviendrai [dəvjɛ̃dʀe], **deviens** *etc* [dəvjɛ̃] *vb voir* **devenir**
dévier [devje] *vt (fleuve, circulation)* to divert; *(coup)* to deflect ▷ *vi* to veer (off course); **(faire) ~** *(projectile)* to deflect; *(véhicule)* to push off course
devin [dəvɛ̃] *nm* soothsayer, seer
deviner [dəvine] *vt* to guess; *(prévoir)* to foretell, foresee; *(apercevoir)* to distinguish
devinette [dəvinɛt] *nf* riddle
devint *etc* [dəvɛ̃] *vb voir* **devenir**
devis [dəvi] *nm* estimate, quotation; **~ descriptif/estimatif** detailed/preliminary estimate
dévisager [devizaʒe] *vt* to stare at
devise [dəviz] *nf (formule)* motto, watchword; *(Écon: monnaie)* currency; **devises** *nfpl (argent)* currency *sg*
deviser [dəvize] *vi* to converse
dévisser [devise] *vt* to unscrew, undo; **se dévisser** *vi* to come unscrewed
de visu [devizy] *adv*: **se rendre compte de qch ~** to see sth for o.s.
dévitaliser [devitalize] *vt (dent)* to remove the nerve from
dévoiler [devwale] *vt* to unveil
devoir [dəvwaʀ] *nm* duty; *(Scol)* piece of homework, homework *no pl*; *(: en classe)* exercise ▷ *vt (argent, respect)*: **~ qch (à qn)** to owe (sb) sth;

(suivi de l'infinitif: obligation): **il doit le faire** he has to do it, he must do it; *(: fatalité)*: **cela devait arriver un jour** it was bound to happen; *(: intention)*: **il doit partir demain** he is (due) to leave tomorrow; *(: probabilité)*: **il doit être tard** it must be late; **se faire un ~ de faire qch** to make it one's duty to do sth; **~s de vacances** homework set for the holidays; **se ~ de faire qch** to be duty bound to do sth; **je devrais faire** I ought to *ou* should do; **tu n'aurais pas dû** you ought not to have *ou* shouldn't have; **comme il se doit** *(comme il faut)* as is right and proper

dévolu, e [devɔly] *adj*: **~ à** allotted to ▷ *nm*: **jeter son ~ sur** to fix one's choice on

devons [dəvɔ̃] *vb voir* **devoir**

dévorant, e [devɔʀɑ̃, -ɑ̃t] *adj (faim, passion)* raging

dévorer [devɔʀe] *vt* to devour; *(feu, soucis)* to consume; **~ qn/qch des yeux** *ou* **du regard** *(fig)* to eye sb/sth intently; *(: convoitise)* to eye sb/sth greedily

dévot, e [devo, -ɔt] *adj* devout, pious ▷ *nm/f* devout person; **un faux ~** a falsely pious person

dévotion [devɔsjɔ̃] *nf* devoutness; **être à la ~ de qn** to be totally devoted to sb; **avoir une ~ pour qn** to worship sb

dévoué, e [devwe] *adj* devoted

dévouement [devumɑ̃] *nm* devotion, dedication

dévouer [devwe]: **se dévouer** *vi (se sacrifier)*: **se ~ (pour)** to sacrifice o.s. (for); *(se consacrer)*: **se ~ à** to devote *ou* dedicate o.s. to

dévoyé, e [devwaje] *adj* delinquent

dévoyer [devwaje] *vt* to lead astray; **se dévoyer** *vi* to go off the rails; **~ l'opinion publique** to influence public opinion

devrai *etc* [dəvʀe] *vb voir* **devoir**

dextérité [dɛksteʀite] *nf* skill, dexterity

dézipper [dezipe] *vt (Inform)* to unzip

dfc *abr (= désire faire connaissance)* in personal column of newspaper

DG *sigle m* = **directeur général**

dg. *abr (= décigramme)* dg.

DGE *sigle f (= Dotation globale d'équipement)* state contribution to local government budget

DGSE *sigle f (= Direction générale de la sécurité extérieure)* ≈ MI6 *(Brit)*, ≈ CIA *(US)*

diabète [djabɛt] *nm* diabetes *sg*

diabétique [djabetik] *nm/f* diabetic

diable [djabl(ə)] *nm* devil; **une musique du ~** an unholy racket; **il fait une chaleur du ~** it's fiendishly hot; **avoir le ~ au corps** to be the very devil

diablement [djabləmɑ̃] *adv* fiendishly

diableries [djabləʀi] *nfpl (d'enfant)* devilment *sg*, mischief *sg*

diablesse [djablɛs] *nf (petite fille)* little devil

diablotin [djablɔtɛ̃] *nm* imp; *(pétard)* cracker

diabolique [djabɔlik] *adj* diabolical

diabolo [djabɔlo] *nm (jeu)* diabolo; *(boisson)* lemonade and fruit cordial; **~(-menthe)** lemonade and mint cordial

diacre [djakʀ(ə)] *nm* deacon

diadème [djadɛm] *nm* diadem

diagnostic [djagnɔstik] *nm* diagnosis *sg*

diagnostiquer [djagnɔstike] *vt* to diagnose

diagonal, e, -aux [djagɔnal, -o] *adj, nf* diagonal; **en ~e** diagonally; **lire en ~e** *(fig)* to skim through

diagramme [djagʀam] *nm* chart, graph

dialecte [djalɛkt(ə)] *nm* dialect

dialectique [djalɛktik] *adj* dialectic(al)

dialogue [djalɔg] *nm* dialogue; **~ de sourds** dialogue of the deaf

dialoguer [djalɔge] *vi* to converse; *(Pol)* to have a dialogue

dialoguiste [djalɔgist(ə)] *nm/f* dialogue writer

dialyse [djaliz] *nf* dialysis

diamant [djamɑ̃] *nm* diamond

diamantaire [djamɑ̃tɛʀ] *nm* diamond dealer

diamétralement [djametʀalmɑ̃] *adv* diametrically; **~ opposés** *(opinions)* diametrically opposed

diamètre [djamɛtʀ(ə)] *nm* diameter

diapason [djapazɔ̃] *nm* tuning fork; *(fig)*: **être/se mettre au ~ (de)** to be/get in tune (with)

diaphane [djafan] *adj* diaphanous

diaphragme [djafʀagm(ə)] *nm (Anat, Photo)* diaphragm; *(contraceptif)* diaphragm, cap; **ouverture du ~** *(Photo)* aperture

diapo [djapo], **diapositive** [djapozitiv] *nf* transparency, slide

diaporama [djapɔʀama] *nm* slide show

diapré, e [djapʀe] *adj* many-coloured *(Brit)*, many-colored *(US)*

diarrhée [djaʀe] *nf* diarrhoea *(Brit)*, diarrhea *(US)*

diatribe [djatʀib] *nf* diatribe

dichotomie [dikɔtɔmi] *nf* dichotomy

dictaphone [diktafɔn] *nm* Dictaphone®

dictateur [diktatœʀ] *nm* dictator

dictatorial, e, -aux [diktatɔʀjal, -o] *adj* dictatorial

dictature [diktatyʀ] *nf* dictatorship

dictée [dikte] *nf* dictation; **prendre sous ~** to take down *(sth dictated)*

dicter [dikte] *vt* to dictate

diction [diksjɔ̃] *nf* diction, delivery; **cours de ~** speech production lesson(s)

dictionnaire [diksjɔnɛʀ] *nm* dictionary; **~ géographique** gazetteer

dicton [diktɔ̃] *nm* saying, dictum

didacticiel [didaktisjɛl] *nm* educational software

didactique [didaktik] *adj* didactic

dièse [djɛz] *nm (Mus)* sharp

diesel [djezɛl] *nm, adj inv* diesel

diète [djɛt] *nf* diet; **être à la ~** to be on a diet

diététicien, ne [djetetisjɛ̃, -ɛn] *nm/f* dietician

diététique [djetetik] *nf* dietetics *sg* ▷ *adj*: **magasin ~** health food shop *(Brit)* ou store *(US)*

dieu, x [djø] *nm* god; **D~** God; **le bon D~** the good Lord; **mon D~!** good heavens!

diffamant, e [difamɑ̃, -ɑ̃t] *adj* slanderous, defamatory; libellous

diffamation [difamasjɔ̃] *nf* slander; (*écrite*) libel; **attaquer qn en ~** to sue sb for slander (*ou* libel)

diffamatoire [difamatwaʀ] *adj* slanderous, defamatory; libellous

diffamer [difame] *vt* to slander, defame; to libel

différé [difeʀe] *adj* (*Inform*): **traitement ~** batch processing; **crédit ~** deferred credit ▷ *nm* (*TV*): **en ~** (pre-)recorded

différemment [difeʀamɑ̃] *adv* differently

différence [difeʀɑ̃s] *nf* difference; **à la ~ de** unlike

différenciation [difeʀɑ̃sjasjɔ̃] *nf* differentiation

différencier [difeʀɑ̃sje] *vt* to differentiate; **se différencier** *vi* (*organisme*) to become differentiated; **se ~ de** to differentiate o.s. from; (*être différent*) to differ from

différend [difeʀɑ̃] *nm* difference (of opinion), disagreement

différent, e [difeʀɑ̃, -ɑ̃t] *adj*: **~ (de)** different (from); **~s objets** different *ou* various objects; **à ~es reprises** on various occasions

différentiel, le [difeʀɑ̃sjɛl] *adj, nm* differential

différer [difeʀe] *vt* to postpone, put off ▷ *vi*: **~ (de)** to differ (from); **~ de faire** (*tarder*) to delay doing

difficile [difisil] *adj* difficult; (*exigeant*) hard to please, difficult (to please); **faire le** *ou* **la ~** to be hard to please, be difficult

difficilement [difisilmɑ̃] *adv* (*marcher, s'expliquer etc*) with difficulty; **~ lisible/compréhensible** difficult *ou* hard to read/understand

difficulté [difikylte] *nf* difficulty; **en ~** (*bateau, alpiniste*) in trouble *ou* difficulties; **avoir de la ~ à faire** to have difficulty (in) doing

difforme [difɔʀm(ə)] *adj* deformed, misshapen

difformité [difɔʀmite] *nf* deformity

diffracter [difʀakte] *vt* to diffract

diffus, e [dify, -yz] *adj* diffuse

diffuser [difyze] *vt* (*chaleur, bruit, lumière*) to diffuse; (*émission, musique*) to broadcast; (*nouvelle, idée*) to circulate; (*Comm: livres, journaux*) to distribute

diffuseur [difyzœʀ] *nm* diffuser; distributor

diffusion [difyzjɔ̃] *nf* diffusion, broadcast(ing); circulation; distribution

digérer [diʒeʀe] *vt* (*personne*) to digest; (*: machine*) to process; (*fig: accepter*) to stomach, put up with

digeste [diʒɛst(ə)] *adj* easily digestible

digestible [diʒɛstibl(ə)] *adj* digestible

digestif, -ive [diʒɛstif, -iv] *adj* digestive ▷ *nm* (after-dinner) liqueur

digestion [diʒɛstjɔ̃] *nf* digestion

digit [didʒit] *nm*: **~ binaire** binary digit

digital, e, -aux [diʒital, -o] *adj* digital

digitale [diʒital] *nf* digitalis, foxglove

digne [diɲ] *adj* dignified; **~ de** worthy of; **~ de foi** trustworthy

dignitaire [diɲitɛʀ] *nm* dignitary

dignité [diɲite] *nf* dignity

digression [digʀesjɔ̃] *nf* digression

digue [dig] *nf* dike, dyke; (*pour protéger la côte*) sea wall

dijonnais, e [diʒɔnɛ, -ɛz] *adj* of *ou* from Dijon ▷ *nm/f*: **Dijonnais, e** inhabitant *ou* native of Dijon

diktat [diktat] *nm* diktat

dilapidation [dilapidasjɔ̃] *nf* (*voir vb*) squandering; embezzlement, misappropriation

dilapider [dilapide] *vt* to squander, waste; (*détourner: biens, fonds publics*) to embezzle, misappropriate

dilater [dilate] *vt* to dilate; (*gaz, métal*) to cause to expand; (*ballon*) to distend; **se dilater** *vi* to expand

dilemme [dilɛm] *nm* dilemma

dilettante [diletɑ̃t] *nm/f* dilettante; **en ~** in a dilettantish way

dilettantisme [diletɑ̃tism(ə)] *nm* dilettant(e)ism

diligence [diliʒɑ̃s] *nf* stagecoach, diligence; (*empressement*) despatch; **faire ~** to make haste

diligent, e [diliʒɑ̃, -ɑ̃t] *adj* prompt and efficient; diligent

diluant [dilɥɑ̃] *nm* thinner(s)

diluer [dilɥe] *vt* to dilute

dilution [dilysjɔ̃] *nf* dilution

diluvien, ne [dilyvjɛ̃, -ɛn] *adj*: **pluie ~ne** torrential rain

dimanche [dimɑ̃ʃ] *nm* Sunday; **le ~ des Rameaux/de Pâques** Palm/Easter Sunday; *voir aussi* **lundi**

dîme [dim] *nf* tithe

dimension [dimɑ̃sjɔ̃] *nf* (*grandeur*) size; (*gén pl: cotes, Math: de l'espace*) dimension

diminué, e [diminɥe] *adj* (*personne: physiquement*) run-down; (*: mentalement*) less alert

diminuer [diminɥe] *vt* to reduce, decrease; (*ardeur etc*) to lessen; (*personne: physiquement*) to undermine; (*dénigrer*) to belittle ▷ *vi* to decrease, diminish

diminutif [diminytif] *nm* (*Ling*) diminutive; (*surnom*) pet name

diminution [diminysjɔ̃] *nf* decreasing, diminishing

dînatoire [dinatwaʀ] *adj*: **goûter ~** ≈ high tea (*Brit*); **apéritif ~** ≈ evening buffet

dinde [dɛ̃d] *nf* turkey; (*femme stupide*) goose

dindon [dɛ̃dɔ̃] *nm* turkey

dindonneau, x [dɛ̃dɔno] *nm* turkey poult

dîner [dine] *nm* dinner ▷ *vi* to have dinner; **~ d'affaires/de famille** business/family dinner

dînette [dinɛt] *nf* (*jeu*): **jouer à la ~** to play at tea parties

dingue [dɛ̃g] *adj* (*fam*) crazy

dinosaure [dinozɔʀ] *nm* dinosaur

diocèse [djɔsɛz] *nm* diocese

diode [djɔd] *nf* diode

diphasé, e [difaze] *adj* (*Élec*) two-phase

diphtérie [difteʀi] *nf* diphtheria

diphtongue [diftɔ̃g] *nf* diphthong

diplomate [diplɔmat] *adj* diplomatic ▷ *nm* diplomat; (*fig: personne habile*) diplomatist; (*Culin: gâteau*) dessert made of sponge cake, candied fruit and custard, ≈ trifle (*Brit*)

diplomatie [diplɔmasi] *nf* diplomacy

diplomatique [diplɔmatik] *adj* diplomatic

diplôme [diplom] *nm* diploma certificate; (*examen*) (diploma) examination

diplômé, e [diplome] *adj* qualified

dire [diʀ] *nm*: **au ~ de** according to; **leurs ~s** what they say ▷ *vt* to say; (*secret, mensonge*) to tell; **~ l'heure/la vérité** to tell the time/the truth; **dis pardon/merci** say sorry/thank you; **~ qch à qn** to tell sb sth; **~ à qn qu'il fasse** *ou* **de faire** to tell sb to do; **~ que** to say that; **on dit que** they say that; **comme on dit** as they say; **on dirait que** it looks (*ou* sounds *etc*) as though; **on dirait du vin** you'd *ou* one would think it was wine; **que dites-vous de** (*penser*) what do you think of; **si cela lui dit** if he feels like it, if he fancies it; **cela ne me dit rien** that doesn't appeal to me; **à vrai ~** truth to tell; **pour ainsi ~** so to speak; **cela va sans ~** that goes without saying; **dis donc!, dites donc!** (*pour attirer l'attention*) hey!; (*au fait*) by the way; **et ~ que ...** and to think that ...; **ceci** *ou* **cela dit** that being said; (*à ces mots*) whereupon; **c'est dit, voilà qui est dit** so that's settled; **il n'y a pas à ~** there's no getting away from it; **c'est ~ si ...** that just shows that ...; **c'est beaucoup/peu ~** that's saying a lot/not saying much; **se dire** *vi* (*à soi-même*) to say to oneself; (*se prétendre*): **se ~ malade** *etc* to say (that) one is ill *etc*; **ça se dit ... en anglais** that is ... in English; **cela ne se dit pas comme ça** you don't say it like that; **se ~ au revoir** to say goodbye (to each other)

direct, e [diʀɛkt] *adj* direct ▷ *nm* (*train*) through train; **en ~** (*émission*) live; **train/bus ~** express train/bus

directement [diʀɛktəmɑ̃] *adv* directly

directeur, -trice [diʀɛktœʀ, -tʀis] *nm/f* (*d'entreprise*) director; (*de service*) manager/eress; (*d'école*) head(teacher) (*Brit*), principal (*US*); **comité ~** management *ou* steering committee; **~ général** general manager; **~ de thèse** ≈ PhD supervisor

direction [diʀɛksjɔ̃] *nf* management; conducting; supervision; (*Auto*) steering; (*sens*) direction; **sous la ~ de** (*Mus*) conducted by; **en ~ de** (*avion, train, bateau*) for; **"toutes ~s"** (*Auto*) "all routes"

directive [diʀɛktiv] *nf* directive, instruction

directorial, e, -aux [diʀɛktɔʀjal, -o] *adj* (*bureau*) director's; manager's; head teacher's

directrice [diʀɛktʀis] *adj f, nf voir* **directeur**

dirent [diʀ] *vb voir* **dire**

dirigeable [diʀiʒabl(ə)] *adj, nm*: (**ballon) ~** dirigible

dirigeant, e [diʀiʒɑ̃, -ɑ̃t] *adj* managerial; (*classes*) ruling ▷ *nm/f* (*d'un parti etc*) leader; (*d'entreprise*) manager, member of the management

diriger [diʀiʒe] *vt* (*entreprise*) to manage, run; (*véhicule*) to steer; (*orchestre*) to conduct; (*recherches, travaux*) to supervise, be in charge of; (*braquer: regard, arme*): **~ sur** to point *ou* level *ou* aim at; (*fig: critiques*): **~ contre** to aim at; **se diriger** *vi* (*s'orienter*) to find one's way; **se ~ vers** *ou* **sur** to make *ou* head for

dirigisme [diʀiʒism(ə)] *nm* (*Écon*) state intervention, interventionism

dirigiste [diʀiʒist(ə)] *adj* interventionist

dis [di], **disais** *etc* [dize] *vb voir* **dire**

discal, e, -aux [diskal, -o] *adj* (*Méd*): **hernie ~e** slipped disc

discernement [disɛʀnəmɑ̃] *nm* discernment, judgment

discerner [disɛʀne] *vt* to discern, make out

disciple [disipl(ə)] *nm/f* disciple

disciplinaire [disiplinɛʀ] *adj* disciplinary

discipline [disiplin] *nf* discipline

discipliné, e [disipline] *adj* (well-)disciplined

discipliner [disipline] *vt* to discipline; (*cheveux*) to control

discobole [diskɔbɔl] *nm/f* discus thrower

discographie [diskɔgʀafi] *nf* discography

discontinu, e [diskɔ̃tiny] *adj* intermittent; (*bande: sur la route*) broken

discontinuer [diskɔ̃tinɥe] *vi*: **sans ~** without stopping, without a break

disconvenir [diskɔ̃vniʀ] *vi*: **ne pas ~ de qch/que** not to deny sth/that

discophile [diskɔfil] *nm/f* record enthusiast

discordance [diskɔʀdɑ̃s] *nf* discordance; conflict

discordant, e [diskɔʀdɑ̃, -ɑ̃t] *adj* discordant; conflicting

discorde [diskɔʀd(ə)] *nf* discord, dissension

discothèque [diskɔtɛk] *nf* (*disques*) record collection; (*: dans une bibliothèque*): **~ (de prêt)** record library; (*boîte de nuit*) disco(thèque)

discourais *etc* [diskuʀe] *vb voir* **discourir**

discourir [diskuʀiʀ] *vi* to discourse, hold forth

discours [diskuʀ] *vb voir* **discourir** ▷ *nm* speech; **~ direct/indirect** (*Ling*) direct/indirect *ou* reported speech

discourtois, e [diskuʀtwa, waz] *adj* discourteous

discrédit [diskʀedi] *nm*: **jeter le ~ sur** to discredit

discréditer [diskʀedite] *vt* to discredit

discret, -ète [diskʀɛ, -ɛt] *adj* discreet; (*fig: musique, style*) unobtrusive; (*: endroit*) quiet

discrètement [diskʀɛtmɑ̃] *adv* discreetly

discrétion [diskʀesjɔ̃] *nf* discretion; **à la ~ de qn** at sb's discretion; in sb's hands; **à ~** (*boisson etc*) unlimited, as much as one wants

discrétionnaire [diskʀesjɔnɛʀ] *adj* discretionary

discrimination [diskʀiminasjɔ̃] *nf* discrimination; **sans ~** indiscriminately

discriminatoire [diskʀiminatwaʀ] *adj* discriminatory

disculper [diskylpe] *vt* to exonerate

discussion [diskysjɔ̃] *nf* discussion
discutable [diskytabl(ə)] *adj* (*contestable*)
doubtful; (*à débattre*) debatable
discuté, e [diskyte] *adj* controversial
discuter [diskyte] *vt* (*contester*) to question,
dispute; (*débattre: prix*) to discuss ▷ *vi* to talk;
(*ergoter*) to argue; **~ de** to discuss
dise *etc* [diz] *vb voir* **dire**
disert, e [dizɛʀ, -ɛʀt(ə)] *adj* loquacious
disette [dizɛt] *nf* food shortage
diseuse [dizøz] *nf*: **~ de bonne aventure**
fortune-teller
disgrâce [disgʀɑs] *nf* disgrace; **être en ~** to be
in disgrace
disgracié, e [disgʀasje] *adj* (*en disgrâce*) disgraced
disgracieux, -euse [disgʀasjø, -øz] *adj*
ungainly, awkward
disjoindre [disʒwɛ̃dʀ(ə)] *vt* to take apart; **se
disjoindre** *vi* to come apart
disjoint, e [disʒwɛ̃, -wɛ̃t] *pp de* **disjoindre** ▷ *adj*
loose
disjoncteur [disʒɔ̃ktœʀ] *nm* (*Élec*) circuit
breaker
dislocation [dislɔkasjɔ̃] *nf* dislocation
disloquer [dislɔke] *vt* (*membre*) to dislocate;
(*chaise*) to dismantle; (*troupe*) to disperse; **se
disloquer** *vi* (*parti, empire*) to break up; **se ~
l'épaule** to dislocate one's shoulder
disons *etc* [dizɔ̃] *vb voir* **dire**
disparaître [dispaʀɛtʀ(ə)] *vi* to disappear; (*à la
vue*) to vanish, disappear; to be hidden *ou*
concealed; (*être manquant*) to go missing,
disappear; (*se perdre: traditions etc*) to die out;
(*personne: mourir*) to die; **faire ~** (*objet, tache, trace*)
to remove; (*personne*) to get rid of
disparate [dispaʀat] *adj* disparate; (*couleurs*) ill-
assorted
disparité [dispaʀite] *nf* disparity
disparition [dispaʀisjɔ̃] *nf* disappearance
disparu, e [dispaʀy] *pp de* **disparaître** ▷ *nm/f*
missing person; (*défunt*) departed; **être porté ~**
to be reported missing
dispendieux, -euse [dispɑ̃djø, -øz] *adj*
extravagant, expensive
dispensaire [dispɑ̃sɛʀ] *nm* community clinic
dispense [dispɑ̃s] *nf* exemption; (*permission*)
special permission; **~ d'âge** special exemption
from age limit
dispenser [dispɑ̃se] *vt* (*donner*) to lavish, bestow;
(*exempter*): **~ qn de** to exempt sb from; **se ~ de** *vt*
to avoid, get out of
disperser [dispɛʀse] *vt* to scatter; (*fig: son
attention*) to dissipate; **se disperser** *vi* to scatter;
(*fig*) to dissipate one's efforts
dispersion [dispɛʀsjɔ̃] *nf* scattering; (*des efforts*)
dissipation
disponibilité [dispɔnibilite] *nf* availability;
(*Admin*): **être en ~** to be on leave of absence;
disponibilités *nfpl* (*Comm*) liquid assets
disponible [dispɔnibl(ə)] *adj* available
dispos [dispo] *adj m*: **(frais et) ~** fresh (as a
daisy)

disposé, e [dispoze] *adj* (*d'une certaine manière*)
arranged, laid-out; **bien/mal ~** (*humeur*) in a
good/bad mood; **bien/mal ~ pour** *ou* **envers qn**
well/badly disposed towards sb; **~ à** (*prêt à*)
willing *ou* prepared to
disposer [dispoze] *vt* (*arranger, placer*) to arrange;
(*inciter*): **~ qn à qch/faire qch** to dispose *ou*
incline sb towards sth/to do sth ▷ *vi*: **vous
pouvez ~** you may leave; **~ de** *vt* to have (at
one's disposal); **se ~ à faire** to prepare to do, be
about to do
dispositif [dispozitif] *nm* device; (*fig*) system,
plan of action; set-up; (*d'un texte de loi*) operative
part; **~ de sûreté** safety device
disposition [dispozisjɔ̃] *nf* (*arrangement*)
arrangement, layout; (*humeur*) mood; (*tendance*)
tendency; **dispositions** *nfpl* (*mesures*) steps,
measures; (*préparatifs*) arrangements; (*de loi,
testament*) provisions; (*aptitudes*) bent *sg*,
aptitude *sg*; **à la ~ de qn** at sb's disposal
disproportion [dispʀɔpɔʀsjɔ̃] *nf* disproportion
disproportionné, e [dispʀɔpɔʀsjɔne] *adj*
disproportionate, out of all proportion
dispute [dispyt] *nf* quarrel, argument
disputer [dispyte] *vt* (*match*) to play; (*combat*) to
fight; (*course*) to run; **se disputer** *vi* to quarrel,
have a quarrel; (*match, combat, course*) to take
place; **~ qch à qn** to fight with sb for *ou* over sth
disquaire [diskɛʀ] *nm/f* record dealer
disqualification [diskalifikasjɔ̃] *nf*
disqualification
disqualifier [diskalifje] *vt* to disqualify; **se
disqualifier** *vi* to bring discredit on o.s.
disque [disk(ə)] *nm* (*Mus*) record; (*Inform*) disk,
disc; (*forme, pièce*) disc; (*Sport*) discus; **~ compact**
compact disc; **~ compact interactif** CD-I®; **~
dur** hard disk; **~ d'embrayage** (*Auto*) clutch
plate; **~ laser** compact disc; **~ de
stationnement** parking disc; **~ système**
system disk
disquette [diskɛt] *nf* diskette, floppy (disk)
dissection [disɛksjɔ̃] *nf* dissection
dissemblable [disɑ̃blabl(ə)] *adj* dissimilar
dissemblance [disɑ̃blɑ̃s] *nf* dissimilarity,
difference
dissémination [diseminasjɔ̃] *nf* (*voir vb*)
scattering; dispersal; (*des armes*) proliferation
disséminer [disemine] *vt* to scatter; (*troupes: sur
un territoire*) to disperse
dissension [disɑ̃sjɔ̃] *nf* dissension; **dissensions**
nfpl dissension
disséquer [diseke] *vt* to dissect
dissertation [disɛʀtasjɔ̃] *nf* (*Scol*) essay
disserter [disɛʀte] *vi*: **~ sur** to discourse upon
dissidence [disidɑ̃s] *nf* (*concept*) dissidence;
rejoindre la ~ to join the dissidents
dissident, e [disidɑ̃, -ɑ̃t] *adj, nm/f* dissident
dissimilitude [disimilityd] *nf* dissimilarity
dissimulateur, -trice [disimyltœʀ, -tʀis] *adj*
dissembling ▷ *nm/f* dissembler
dissimulation [disimylasjɔ̃] *nf* concealing;
(*duplicité*) dissimulation; **~ de bénéfices/de**

revenus concealment of profits/income
dissimulé, e [disimyle] *adj* (*personne: secret*) secretive; (*: fourbe, hypocrite*) deceitful
dissimuler [disimyle] *vt* to conceal; **se dissimuler** *vi* to conceal o.s.; to be concealed
dissipation [disipasjɔ̃] *nf* squandering; unruliness; (*débauche*) dissipation
dissipé, e [disipe] *adj* (*indiscipliné*) unruly
dissiper [disipe] *vt* to dissipate; (*fortune*) to squander, fritter away; **se dissiper** *vi* (*brouillard*) to clear, disperse; (*doutes*) to disappear, melt away; (*élève*) to become undisciplined *ou* unruly
dissociable [disɔsjabl(ə)] *adj* separable
dissocier [disɔsje] *vt* to dissociate; **se dissocier** *vi* (*éléments, groupe*) to break up, split up; **se ~ de** (*groupe, point de vue*) to dissociate o.s. from
dissolu, e [disɔly] *adj* dissolute
dissoluble [disɔlybl(ə)] *adj* (*Pol: assemblée*) dissolvable
dissolution [disɔlysjɔ̃] *nf* dissolving; (*Pol, Jur*) dissolution
dissolvant, e [disɔlvɑ̃, -ɑ̃t] *vb voir* **dissoudre** ▷ *nm* (*Chimie*) solvent; **~ (gras)** nail polish remover
dissonant, e [disɔnɑ̃, -ɑ̃t] *adj* discordant
dissoudre [disudʀ(ə)] *vt*, **se dissoudre** *vi* to dissolve
dissous, -oute [disu, -ut] *pp de* **dissoudre**
dissuader [disɥade] *vt*: **~ qn de faire/de qch** to dissuade sb from doing/from sth
dissuasif, -ive [disɥazif, iv] *adj* dissuasive
dissuasion [disɥazjɔ̃] *nf* dissuasion; **force de ~** deterrent power
distance [distɑ̃s] *nf* distance; (*fig: écart*) gap; **à ~** at *ou* from a distance; (*mettre en marche, commander*) by remote control; **(situé) à ~** (*Inform*) remote; **tenir qn à ~** to keep sb at a distance; **se tenir à ~** to keep one's distance; **à une ~ de 10 km, à 10 km de ~** 10 km away, at a distance of 10 km; **à deux ans de ~** with a gap of two years; **prendre ses ~s** to space out; **garder ses ~s** to keep one's distance; **tenir la ~** (*Sport*) to cover the distance, last the course; **~ focale** (*Photo*) focal length
distancer [distɑ̃se] *vt* to outdistance, leave behind
distancier [distɑ̃sje]: **se distancier** *vi* to distance o.s.
distant, e [distɑ̃, -ɑ̃t] *adj* (*réservé*) distant, aloof; (*éloigné*) distant, far away; **~ de** (*lieu*) far away *ou* a long way from; **~ de 5 km (d'un lieu)** 5 km away (from a place)
distendre [distɑ̃dʀ(ə)] *vt*, **se distendre** *vi* to distend
distillation [distilasjɔ̃] *nf* distillation, distilling
distillé, e [distile] *adj*: **eau ~e** distilled water
distiller [distile] *vt* to distil; (*fig*) to exude; to elaborate
distillerie [distilʀi] *nf* distillery
distinct, e [distɛ̃(kt), distɛ̃kt(ə)] *adj* distinct
distinctement [distɛ̃ktəmɑ̃] *adv* distinctly
distinctif, -ive [distɛ̃ktif, -iv] *adj* distinctive

distinction [distɛ̃ksjɔ̃] *nf* distinction
distingué, e [distɛ̃ge] *adj* distinguished
distinguer [distɛ̃ge] *vt* to distinguish; **se distinguer** *vi* (*s'illustrer*) to distinguish o.s.; (*différer*): **se ~ (de)** to distinguish o.s. *ou* be distinguished (from)
distinguo [distɛ̃go] *nm* distinction
distorsion [distɔʀsjɔ̃] *nf* (*gén*) distortion; (*fig: déséquilibre*) disparity, imbalance
distraction [distʀaksjɔ̃] *nf* (*manque d'attention*) absent-mindedness; (*oubli*) lapse (in concentration *ou* attention); (*détente*) diversion, recreation; (*passe-temps*) distraction, entertainment
distraire [distʀɛʀ] *vt* (*déranger*) to distract; (*divertir*) to entertain, divert; (*détourner: somme d'argent*) to divert, misappropriate; **se distraire** *vi* to amuse *ou* enjoy o.s.
distrait, e [distʀɛ, -ɛt] *pp de* **distraire** ▷ *adj* absent-minded
distraitement [distʀɛtmɑ̃] *adv* absent-mindedly
distrayant, e [distʀɛjɑ̃, -ɑ̃t] *vb voir* **distraire** ▷ *adj* entertaining
distribuer [distʀibɥe] *vt* to distribute; to hand out; (*Cartes*) to deal (out); (*courrier*) to deliver
distributeur [distʀibytœʀ] *nm* (*Auto, Comm*) distributor; (*automatique*) (vending) machine; **~ de billets** (*Rail*) ticket machine; (*Banque*) cash dispenser
distribution [distʀibysjɔ̃] *nf* distribution; (*postale*) delivery; (*choix d'acteurs*) casting; **circuits de ~** (*Comm*) distribution network; **~ des prix** (*Scol*) prize giving
district [distʀik(t)] *nm* district
dit, e [di, dit] *pp de* **dire** ▷ *adj* (*fixé*): **le jour ~** the arranged day; (*surnommé*): **X, ~ Pierrot** X, known as *ou* called Pierrot
dites [dit] *vb voir* **dire**
dithyrambique [ditiʀɑ̃bik] *adj* eulogistic
DIU *sigle m* (= *dispositif intra-utérin*) IUD
diurétique [djyʀetik] *adj, nm* diuretic
diurne [djyʀn(ə)] *adj* diurnal, daytime *cpd*
divagations [divagasjɔ̃] *nfpl* ramblings; ravings
divaguer [divage] *vi* to ramble; (*malade*) to rave
divan [divɑ̃] *nm* divan
divan-lit [divɑ̃li] *nm* divan (bed)
divergence [divɛʀʒɑ̃s] *nf* divergence; **des ~s d'opinion au sein de ...** differences of opinion within ...
divergent, e [divɛʀʒɑ̃, -ɑ̃t] *adj* divergent
diverger [divɛʀʒe] *vi* to diverge
divers, e [divɛʀ, -ɛʀs(ə)] *adj* (*varié*) diverse, varied; (*différent*) different, various; **(frais) ~** (*Comm*) sundries, miscellaneous (expenses); **"~"** (*rubrique*) "miscellaneous"
diversement [divɛʀsəmɑ̃] *adv* in various *ou* diverse ways
diversification [divɛʀsifikasjɔ̃] *nf* diversification
diversifier [divɛʀsifje] *vt*, **se diversifier** *vi* to

diversify

diversion [divɛRsjɔ̃] *nf* diversion; **faire ~** to create a diversion

diversité [divɛRsite] *nf* diversity, variety

divertir [divɛRtiR] *vt* to amuse, entertain; **se divertir** *vi* to amuse *ou* enjoy o.s.

divertissant, e [divɛRtisɑ̃, -ɑ̃t] *adj* entertaining

divertissement [divɛRtismɑ̃] *nm* entertainment; (*Mus*) divertimento, divertissement

dividende [dividɑ̃d] *nm* (*Math, Comm*) dividend

divin, e [divɛ̃, -in] *adj* divine; (*fig: excellent*) heavenly, divine

divinateur, -trice [divinatœR, -tRis] *adj* perspicacious

divinatoire [divinatwaR] *adj* (*art, science*) divinatory; **baguette ~** divining rod

diviniser [divinize] *vt* to deify

divinité [divinite] *nf* divinity

divisé, e [divize] *adj* divided

diviser [divize] *vt* (*gén, Math*) to divide; (*morceler, subdiviser*) to divide (up), split (up); **se ~ en** to divide into; **~ par** to divide by

diviseur [divizœR] *nm* (*Math*) divisor

divisible [divizibl(ə)] *adj* divisible

division [divizjɔ̃] *nf* (*gén*) division; **~ du travail** (*Écon*) division of labour

divisionnaire [divizjɔnɛR] *adj*: **commissaire ~** ≈ chief superintendent (*Brit*), ≈ police chief (*US*)

divorce [divɔRs(ə)] *nm* divorce

divorcé, e [divɔRse] *nm/f* divorcee

divorcer [divɔRse] *vi* to get a divorce, get divorced; **~ de** *ou* **d'avec qn** to divorce sb

divulgation [divylgasjɔ̃] *nf* disclosure

divulguer [divylge] *vt* to divulge, disclose

dix [di, dis, diz] *num* ten

dix-huit [dizɥit] *num* eighteen

dix-huitième [dizɥitjɛm] *num* eighteenth

dixième [dizjɛm] *num* tenth

dix-neuf [diznœf] *num* nineteen

dix-neuvième [diznœvjɛm] *num* nineteenth

dix-sept [disɛt] *num* seventeen

dix-septième [disɛtjɛm] *num* seventeenth

dizaine [dizɛn] *nf* (10) ten; (*environ 10*): **une ~ (de)** about ten, ten or so

Djakarta [dʒakaRta] *n* Djakarta

Djibouti [dʒibuti] *n* Djibouti

dl *abr* (= *décilitre*) dl

DM *abr* (= *Deutschmark*) DM

dm. *abr* (= *décimètre*) dm.

do [do] *nm* (*note*) C; (*en chantant la gamme*) do(h)

docile [dɔsil] *adj* docile

docilement [dɔsilmɑ̃] *adv* docilely

docilité [dɔsilite] *nf* docility

dock [dɔk] *nm* dock; (*hangar, bâtiment*) warehouse

docker [dɔkɛR] *nm* docker

docte [dɔkt(ə)] *adj* (*péj*) learned

docteur, e [dɔktœR] *nm/f* doctor; **~ en médecine** doctor of medicine

doctoral, e, -aux [dɔktɔRal, -o] *adj* pompous, bombastic

doctorat [dɔktɔRa] *nm*: **~ (d'Université)**

≈ doctorate; **~ d'État** ≈ PhD; **~ de troisième cycle** ≈ doctorate

doctoresse [dɔktɔRɛs] *nf* lady doctor

doctrinaire [dɔktRinɛR] *adj* doctrinaire; (*sentencieux*) pompous, sententious

doctrinal, e, -aux [dɔktRinal, o] *adj* doctrinal

doctrine [dɔktRin] *nf* doctrine

document [dɔkymɑ̃] *nm* document

documentaire [dɔkymɑ̃tɛR] *adj, nm* documentary

documentaliste [dɔkymɑ̃talist(ə)] *nm/f* archivist; (*Presse, TV*) researcher

documentation [dɔkymɑ̃tasjɔ̃] *nf* documentation, literature; (*Presse, TV: service*) research

documenté, e [dɔkymɑ̃te] *adj* well-informed, well-documented; well-researched

documenter [dɔkymɑ̃te] *vt*: **se ~ (sur)** to gather information *ou* material (on *ou* about)

Dodécanèse [dɔdekanɛz] *nm* Dodecanese (Islands)

dodeliner [dɔdline] *vi*: **~ de la tête** to nod one's head gently

dodo [dɔdo] *nm*: **aller faire ~** to go to beddy-byes

dodu, e [dɔdy] *adj* plump

dogmatique [dɔgmatik] *adj* dogmatic

dogmatisme [dɔgmatism(ə)] *nm* dogmatism

dogme [dɔgm(ə)] *nm* dogma

dogue [dɔg] *nm* mastiff

doigt [dwa] *nm* finger; **à deux ~s de** within an ace (*Brit*) *ou* an inch of; **un ~ de lait/whisky** a drop of milk/whisky; **désigner** *ou* **montrer du ~** to point at; **au ~ et à l'œil** to the letter; **connaître qch sur le bout du ~** to know sth backwards; **mettre le ~ sur la plaie** (*fig*) to find the sensitive spot; **~ de pied** toe

doigté [dwate] *nm* (*Mus*) fingering; (*fig: habileté*) diplomacy, tact

doigtier [dwatje] *nm* fingerstall

dois *etc* [dwa] *vb voir* **devoir**

doit *etc* [dwa] *vb voir* **devoir**

doive *etc* [dwav] *vb voir* **devoir**

doléances [dɔleɑ̃s] *nfpl* complaints; (*réclamations*) grievances

dolent, e [dɔlɑ̃, -ɑ̃t] *adj* doleful, mournful

dollar [dɔlaR] *nm* dollar

dolmen [dɔlmɛn] *nm* dolmen

DOM [dɔm] *sigle m ou mpl* = **Département(s) d'outre-mer**

domaine [dɔmɛn] *nm* estate, property; (*fig*) domain, field; **tomber dans le ~ public** (*livre etc*) to be out of copyright; **dans tous les ~s** in all areas

domanial, e, -aux [dɔmanjal, -o] *adj* national, state *cpd*

dôme [dom] *nm* dome

domestication [dɔmɛstikasjɔ̃] *nf* (*voir domestiquer*) domestication; harnessing

domesticité [dɔmɛstisite] *nf* (domestic) staff

domestique [dɔmɛstik] *adj* domestic ▷ *nm/f* servant, domestic

domestiquer [dɔmɛstike] *vt* to domesticate;
(*vent, marées*) to harness

domicile [dɔmisil] *nm* home, place of residence;
à ~ at home; **élire ~ à** to take up residence in;
sans ~ fixe of no fixed abode; **~ conjugal**
marital home; **~ légal** domicile

domicilié, e [dɔmisilje] *adj*: **être ~ à** to have
one's home in *ou* at

dominant, e [dɔminɑ̃, -ɑ̃t] *adj* dominant; (*plus
important*) predominant ▷ *nf* (*caractéristique*)
dominant characteristic; (*couleur*) dominant
colour

dominateur, -trice [dɔminatœR, -tRis] *adj*
dominating; (*qui aime à dominer*) domineering

domination [dɔminasjɔ̃] *nf* domination

dominer [dɔmine] *vt* to dominate; (*passions etc*)
to control, master; (*surpasser*) to outclass,
surpass; (*surplomber*) to tower above, dominate
▷ *vi* to be in the dominant position; **se dominer**
vi to control o.s.

dominicain, e [dɔminikɛ̃, -ɛn] *adj* Dominican

dominical, e, -aux [dɔminikal, -o] *adj* Sunday
cpd, dominical

Dominique [dɔminik] *nf*: **la ~** Dominica

domino [dɔmino] *nm* domino; **dominos** *nmpl*
(*jeu*) dominoes *sg*

dommage [dɔmaʒ] *nm* (*préjudice*) harm, injury;
(*dégâts, pertes*) damage *no pl*; **c'est ~ de faire/que**
it's a shame *ou* pity to do/that; **quel ~!** what a
pity *ou* shame!; **~s corporels** physical injury

dommages-intérêts [dɔmaʒ(əz)ɛ̃teRɛ] *nmpl*
damages

dompter [dɔ̃te] *vt* to tame

dompteur, -euse [dɔ̃tœR, -øz] *nm/f* trainer; (*de
lion*) lion tamer

DOM-ROM [dɔmRɔm], **DOM-TOM** [dɔmtɔm]
sigle m ou mpl (= Département(s) et Régions/
Territoire(s) d'outre-mer) French overseas departments
and regions; *see note*

DOM-TOM, ROM ET COM

There are four "Départements d'outre-mer"
or DOMs: Guadeloupe, Martinique, La
Réunion and French Guyana. They are run
in the same way as metropolitan
"départements" and their inhabitants are
French citizens. In administrative terms
they are also "Régions", and in this regard
are also referred to as "ROM" (Régions
d'outre-mer). The term "DOM-TOM" is still
commonly used, but the term "Territoire
d'outre-mer" has been superseded by that of
"Collectivité d'outre-mer" (COM). The COMs
include French Polynesia, Wallis-and-
Futuna, New Caledonia and polar
territories. They are independent, but each
is supervised by a representative of the
French government.

don [dɔ̃] *nm* (*cadeau*) gift; (*charité*) donation;
(*aptitude*) gift, talent; **avoir des ~s pour** to have

a gift *ou* talent for; **faire ~ de** to make a gift of;
~ en argent cash donation

donateur, -trice [dɔnatœR, -tRis] *nm/f* donor

donation [dɔnasjɔ̃] *nf* donation

donc [dɔ̃k] *conj* therefore, so; (*après une digression*)
so, then; (*intensif*): **voilà ~ la solution** so there's
the solution; **je disais ~ que ...** as I was saying,
...; **venez ~ dîner à la maison** do come for
dinner; **allons ~!** come now!; **faites ~** go ahead

donjon [dɔ̃ʒɔ̃] *nm* keep

don Juan [dɔ̃ʒɥɑ̃] *nm* Don Juan

donnant, e [dɔnɑ̃, -ɑ̃t] *adj*: **~, ~** fair's fair

donne [dɔn] *nf* (*Cartes*): **il y a mauvaise** *ou*
fausse ~ there's been a misdeal

donné, e [dɔne] *adj* (*convenu*) given; (*pas cher*)
very cheap ▷ *nf* (*Math, Inform, gén*) datum; **c'est
~** it's a gift; **étant ~ ...** given ...

données [dɔne] *nfpl* data

donner [dɔne] *vt* to give; (*vieux habits etc*) to give
away; (*spectacle*) to put on; (*film*) to show; **~ qch
à qn** to give sb sth, give sth to sb; **~ sur** (*fenêtre,
chambre*) to look (out) onto; **~ dans** (*piège etc*) to
fall into; **faire ~ l'infanterie** (*Mil*) to send in
the infantry; **~ l'heure à qn** to tell sb the time;
~ le ton (*fig*) to set the tone; **~ à penser/
entendre que ...** to make one think/give one to
understand that ...; **se ~ à fond (à son travail)**
to give one's all (to one's work); **se ~ du mal** *ou*
de la peine (pour faire qch) to go to a lot of
trouble (to do sth); **s'en ~ à cœur joie** (*fam*) to
have a great time (of it)

donneur, -euse [dɔnœR, -øz] *nm/f* (*Méd*) donor;
(*Cartes*) dealer; **~ de sang** blood donor

 MOT-CLÉ

dont [dɔ̃] *pron relatif* **1** (*appartenance: objets*) whose,
of which; (*: êtres animés*) whose; **la maison dont
le toit est rouge** the house the roof of which is
red, the house whose roof is red; **l'homme
dont je connais la sœur** the man whose sister
I know
2 (*parmi lesquel(le)s*): **deux livres, dont l'un
est ...** two books, one of which is ...; **il y avait
plusieurs personnes, dont Gabrielle** there
were several people, among them Gabrielle; **10
blessés, dont 2 grièvement** 10 injured, 2 of
them seriously
3 (*complément d'adjectif, de verbe*): **le fils dont il
est si fier** the son he's so proud of; **ce dont je
parle** what I'm talking about; **la façon dont il
l'a fait** the way (in which) he did it

donzelle [dɔ̃zɛl] *nf* (*péj*) young madam

dopage [dɔpaʒ] *nm* doping

dopant [dɔpɑ̃] *nm* dope

doper [dɔpe] *vt* to dope; **se doper** *vi* to take dope

doping [dɔpiŋ] *nm* doping; (*excitant*) dope

dorade [dɔRad] *nf* = **daurade**

doré, e [dɔRe] *adj* golden; (*avec dorure*) gilt, gilded

dorénavant [dɔRenavɑ̃] *adv* from now on,
henceforth

dorer [dɔʀe] vt (cadre) to gild; (faire) ~ (Culin) to brown; (: gâteau) to glaze; **se ~ au soleil** to sunbathe; ~ **la pilule à qn** to sugar the pill for sb

dorloter [dɔʀlɔte] vt to pamper, cosset (Brit); **se faire ~** to be pampered ou cosseted

dormant, e [dɔʀmɑ̃, -ɑ̃t] adj: **eau ~e** still water

dorme etc [dɔʀm(ə)] vb voir **dormir**

dormeur, -euse [dɔʀmœʀ, -øz] nm/f sleeper

dormir [dɔʀmiʀ] vi to sleep; (être endormi) to be asleep; ~ **à poings fermés** to sleep very soundly

dorsal, e, -aux [dɔʀsal, -o] adj dorsal; voir **rouleau**

dortoir [dɔʀtwaʀ] nm dormitory

dorure [dɔʀyʀ] nf gilding

doryphore [dɔʀifɔʀ] nm Colorado beetle

dos [do] nm back; (de livre) spine; **"voir au ~"** "see over"; **robe décolletée dans le ~** low-backed dress; **de ~** from the back, from behind; ~ **à ~** back to back; **sur le ~** on one's back; **à ~ de chameau** riding on a camel; **avoir bon ~** to be a good excuse; **se mettre qn à ~** to turn sb against one

dosage [dozaʒ] nm mixture

dos-d'âne [dodɑn] nm humpback; **pont en dos-d'âne** humpbacked bridge

dose [doz] nf (Méd) dose; **forcer la ~** (fig) to overstep the mark

doser [doze] vt to measure out; (mélanger) to mix in the correct proportions; (fig) to expend in the right amounts ou proportions; to strike a balance between

doseur [dozœʀ] nm measure; **bouchon ~** measuring cap

dossard [dosaʀ] nm number (worn by competitor)

dossier [dosje] nm (renseignements, fichier) file; (enveloppe) folder, file; (de chaise) back; (Presse) feature; **le ~ social/monétaire** (fig) the social/financial question; ~ **suspendu** suspension file

dot [dɔt] nf dowry

dotation [dɔtasjɔ̃] nf block grant; endowment

doté, e [dɔte] adj: ~ **de** equipped with

doter [dɔte] vt: ~ **qn/qch de** to equip sb/sth with

douairière [dwɛʀjɛʀ] nf dowager

douane [dwan] nf (poste, bureau) customs pl; (taxes) (customs) duty; **passer la ~** to go through customs; **en ~** (marchandises, entrepôt) bonded

douanier, -ière [dwanje, -jɛʀ] adj customs cpd ▷ nm customs officer

doublage [dublaʒ] nm (Ciné) dubbing

double [dubl(ə)] adj, adv double ▷ nm (2 fois plus): **le ~ (de)** twice as much (ou many) (as), double the amount (ou number) (of); (autre exemplaire) duplicate, copy; (sosie) double; (Tennis) doubles sg; **voir ~** to see double; **en ~ (exemplaire)** in duplicate; **faire ~ emploi** to be redundant; **à ~ sens** with a double meaning; **à ~ tranchant** two-edged; ~ **carburateur** twin carburettor; **à ~s commandes** dual-control; ~ **messieurs/mixte** men's/mixed doubles sg; ~ **toit** (de tente)

fly sheet; ~ **vue** second sight

doublé, e [duble] adj (vêtement): ~ **(de)** lined (with)

double-cliquer [dubl(ə)klike] vi (Inform) to double-click

doublement [dubləmɑ̃] nm doubling; twofold increase ▷ adv doubly; (pour deux raisons) in two ways, on two counts

doubler [duble] vt (multiplier par 2) to double; (vêtement) to line; (dépasser) to overtake, pass; (film) to dub; (acteur) to stand in for ▷ vi to double, increase twofold; **se ~ de** to be coupled with; ~ **(la classe)** (Scol) to repeat a year; ~ **un cap** (Navig) to round a cape; (fig) to get over a hurdle

doublure [dublyʀ] nf lining; (Ciné) stand-in

douce [dus] adj f voir **doux**

douceâtre [dusɑtʀ(ə)] adj sickly sweet

doucement [dusmɑ̃] adv gently; (à voix basse) softly; (lentement) slowly

doucereux, -euse [dusʀø, -øz] adj (péj) sugary

douceur [dusœʀ] nf softness; sweetness; mildness; gentleness; **douceurs** nfpl (friandises) sweets (Brit), candy sg (US); **en ~** gently

douche [duʃ] nf shower; **douches** nfpl shower room sg; **prendre une ~** to have ou take a shower; ~ **écossaise** (fig): ~ **froide** (fig) let-down

doucher [duʃe] vt: ~ **qn** to give sb a shower; (mouiller) to drench sb; (fig) to give sb a telling-off; **se doucher** vi to have ou take a shower

doudoune [dudun] nf padded jacket; (fam) boob

doué, e [dwe] adj gifted, talented; ~ **de** endowed with; **être ~ pour** to have a gift for

douille [duj] nf (Élec) socket; (de projectile) case

douillet, te [dujɛ, -ɛt] adj cosy; (péj) soft

douleur [dulœʀ] nf pain; (chagrin) grief, distress; **ressentir des ~s** to feel pain; **il a eu la ~ de perdre son père** he suffered the grief of losing his father

douloureux, -euse [duluʀø, -øz] adj painful

doute [dut] nm doubt; **sans ~** adv no doubt; (probablement) probably; **sans nul** ou **aucun ~** without (a) doubt; **hors de ~** beyond doubt; **nul ~ que** there's no doubt that; **mettre en ~** to call into question; **mettre en ~ que** to question whether

douter [dute] vt to doubt; ~ **de** vt (allié) to doubt, have (one's) doubts about; (résultat) to be doubtful of; ~ **que** to doubt whether ou if; **j'en doute** I have my doubts; **se ~ de qch/que** to suspect sth/that; **je m'en doutais** I suspected as much; **il ne se doutait de rien** he didn't suspect a thing

douteux, -euse [dutø, -øz] adj (incertain) doubtful; (discutable) dubious, questionable; (péj) dubious-looking

douve [duv] nf (de château) moat; (de tonneau) stave

Douvres [duvʀ(ə)] n Dover

doux, douce [du, dus] adj (lisse, moelleux, pas vif: couleur, non calcaire: eau) soft; (sucré, agréable) sweet; (peu fort: moutarde etc, clément: climat) mild;

(*pas brusque*) gentle; **en douce** (*partir etc*) on the quiet

douzaine [duzɛn] *nf* (12) dozen; (*environ 12*): **une ~ (de)** a dozen or so, twelve or so

douze [duz] *num* twelve; **les D~** (*membres de la CEE*) the Twelve

douzième [duzjɛm] *num* twelfth

doyen, ne [dwajɛ̃, -ɛn] *nm/f* (*en âge, ancienneté*) most senior member; (*de faculté*) dean

DPLG *sigle* (= *diplômé par le gouvernement*) *extra certificate for architects, engineers etc*

Dr *abr* (= *docteur*) Dr

dr. *abr* (= *droit(e)*) R, r

draconien, ne [drakɔnjɛ̃, -ɛn] *adj* draconian, stringent

dragage [dragaʒ] *nm* dredging

dragée [draʒe] *nf* sugared almond; (*Méd*) (sugar-coated) pill

dragéifié, e [draʒeifje] *adj* (*Méd*) sugar-coated

dragon [dragɔ̃] *nm* dragon

drague [drag] *nf* (*filet*) dragnet; (*bateau*) dredger

draguer [drage] *vt* (*rivière: pour nettoyer*) to dredge; (*: pour trouver qch*) to drag; (*fam*) to try and pick up, chat up (*Brit*) ▷ *vi* (*fam*) to try and pick sb up, chat up (*Brit*)

dragueur [dragœr] *nm* (*aussi:* **dragueur de mines**) minesweeper; (*fam*): **quel ~!** he's a great one for picking up girls!

drain [drɛ̃] *nm* (*Méd*) drain

drainage [drɛnaʒ] *nm* drainage

drainer [drene] *vt* to drain; (*fig: visiteurs, région*) to drain off

dramatique [dramatik] *adj* dramatic; (*tragique*) tragic ▷ *nf* (*TV*) (television) drama

dramatisation [dramatizasjɔ̃] *nf* dramatization

dramatiser [dramatize] *vt* to dramatize

dramaturge [dramatyrʒ(ə)] *nm* dramatist, playwright

drame [dram] *nm* (*Théât*) drama; (*catastrophe*) drama, tragedy; **~ familial** family drama

drap [dra] *nm* (*de lit*) sheet; (*tissu*) woollen fabric; **~ de plage** beach towel

drapé [drape] *nm* (*d'un vêtement*) hang

drapeau, x [drapo] *nm* flag; **sous les ~x** with the colours (*Brit*) *ou* colors (*US*), in the army

draper [drape] *vt* to drape; (*robe, jupe*) to arrange

draperies [drapri] *nfpl* hangings

drap-housse [draus] (*pl* **draps-housses**) *nm* fitted sheet

drapier [drapje] *nm* (*woollen*) cloth manufacturer; (*marchand*) clothier

drastique [drastik] *adj* drastic

dressage [drɛsaʒ] *nm* training

dresser [drese] *vt* (*mettre vertical, monter: tente*) to put up, erect; (*fig: liste, bilan, contrat*) to draw up; (*animal*) to train; **se dresser** *vi* (*falaise, obstacle*) to stand; (*avec grandeur, menace*) to tower (up); (*personne*) to draw o.s. up; **~ l'oreille** to prick up one's ears; **~ la table** to set *ou* lay the table; **~ qn contre qn d'autre** to set sb against sb else; **~ un procès-verbal** *ou* **une contravention à qn**

to book sb

dresseur, -euse [drɛsœr, -øz] *nm/f* trainer

dressoir [dreswar] *nm* dresser

dribbler [drible] *vt, vi* (*Sport*) to dribble

drille [drij] *nm*: **joyeux ~** cheerful sort

drogue [drɔg] *nf* drug; **la ~** drugs *pl*; **~ dure/douce** hard/soft drugs *pl*

drogué, e [drɔge] *nm/f* drug addict

droguer [drɔge] *vt* (*victime*) to drug; (*malade*) to give drugs to; **se droguer** *vi* (*aux stupéfiants*) to take drugs; (*péj: de médicaments*) to dose o.s. up

droguerie [drɔgri] *nf* ≈ hardware shop (*Brit*) *ou* store (*US*)

droguiste [drɔgist(ə)] *nm* ≈ keeper (*ou* owner) of a hardware shop *ou* store

droit, e [drwa, drwat] *adj* (*non courbe*) straight; (*vertical*) upright, straight; (*fig: loyal, franc*) upright, straight(forward); (*opposé à gauche*) right, right-hand ▷ *adv* straight ▷ *nm* (*prérogative, Boxe*) right; (*taxe*) duty, tax; (*: d'inscription*) fee; (*lois, branche*): **le ~** law ▷ *nf* (Pol) right (wing); (*ligne*) straight line; **~ au but** *ou* **au fait/cœur** straight to the point/heart; **avoir le ~ de** to be allowed to; **avoir ~ à** to be entitled to; **être en ~ de** to have a *ou* the right to; **faire ~ à** to grant, accede to; **être dans son ~** to be within one's rights; **à bon ~** (*justement*) with good reason; **de quel ~?** by what right?; **à qui de ~** to whom it may concern; **à ~e** on the right; (*direction*) (to the) right; **à ~e de** to the right of; **de ~e, sur votre ~e** on your right; (Pol) right-wing; **~ d'auteur** copyright; **avoir ~ de cité (dans)** (*fig*) to belong (to); **~ coutumier** common law; **~ de regard** right of access *ou* inspection; **~ de réponse** right to reply; **~ de visite** (right of) access; **~ de vote** (right to) vote; **~s d'auteur** royalties; **~s de douane** customs duties; **~s de l'homme** human rights; **~s d'inscription** enrolment *ou* registration fees

droitement [drwatmɑ̃] *adv* (*agir*) uprightly

droitier, -ière [drwatje, -jɛr] *nm/f* right-handed person

droiture [drwatyr] *nf* uprightness, straightness

drôle [drol] *adj* (*amusant*) funny, amusing; (*bizarre*) funny, peculiar; **un ~ de ...** (*bizarre*) a strange *ou* funny ...; (*intensif*) an incredible ..., a terrific ...

drôlement [drolmɑ̃] *adv* funnily; peculiarly; (*très*) terribly, awfully; **il fait ~ froid** it's awfully cold

drôlerie [drolri] *nf* funniness; funny thing

dromadaire [drɔmadɛr] *nm* dromedary

dru, e [dry] *adj* (*cheveux*) thick, bushy; (*pluie*) heavy ▷ *adv* (*pousser*) thickly; (*tomber*) heavily

drugstore [drœgstɔr] *nm* drugstore

druide [drɥid] *nm* Druid

ds *abr* = **dans**

DST *sigle f* (= *Direction de la surveillance du territoire*) *internal security service*, ≈ MI5 (*Brit*)

DT *sigle m* (= *diphtérie tétanos*) *vaccine*

DTCP *sigle m* (= *diphtérie tétanos coqueluche polio*) vaccine

DTP *sigle m* (= *diphtérie tétanos polio*) vaccine

DTTAB *sigle m* (= *diphtérie tétanos typhoïde A et B*) vaccine

du [dy] *art voir* **de**

dû, due [dy] *pp de* **devoir** ▷ *adj* (*somme*) owing, owed; (: *venant à échéance*) due; (*causé par*): **dû à** due to ▷ *nm* due; (*somme*) dues *pl*

dualisme [dɥalism(ə)] *nm* dualism

Dubaï, Dubay [dybaj] *n* Dubai

dubitatif, -ive [dybitatif, -iv] *adj* doubtful, dubious

Dublin [dyblɛ̃] *n* Dublin

duc [dyk] *nm* duke

duché [dyʃe] *nm* dukedom, duchy

duchesse [dyʃɛs] *nf* duchess

duel [dɥɛl] *nm* duel

duettiste [dɥetist(ə)] *nm/f* duettist

duffel-coat [dœfœlkot] *nm* duffel coat

dûment [dymɑ̃] *adv* duly

dumping [dœmpiŋ] *nm* dumping

dune [dyn] *nf* dune

Dunkerque [dœ̃kɛrk] *n* Dunkirk

duo [dɥo] *nm* (*Mus*) duet; (*fig: couple*) duo, pair

dupe [dyp] *nf* dupe ▷ *adj*: (**ne pas**) **être ~ de** (not) to be taken in by

duper [dype] *vt* to dupe, deceive

duperie [dypri] *nf* deception, dupery

duplex [dyplɛks] *nm* (*appartement*) split-level apartment, duplex; (*TV*): **émission en ~** link-up

duplicata [dyplikata] *nm* duplicate

duplicateur [dyplikatœr] *nm* duplicator; **~ à alcool** spirit duplicator

duplicité [dyplisite] *nf* duplicity

duquel [dykɛl] *prép* + *pron voir* **lequel**

dur, e [dyr] *adj* (*pierre, siège, travail, problème*) hard; (*lumière, voix, climat*) harsh; (*sévère*) hard, harsh; (*cruel*) hard(-hearted); (*porte, col*) stiff; (*viande*) tough ▷ *adv* hard ▷ *nf*: **à la ~e** rough; **mener la vie ~e à qn** to give sb a hard time; **~ d'oreille** hard of hearing

durabilité [dyrabilite] *nf* durability

durable [dyrabl(ə)] *adj* lasting

durablement [dyrabləmɑ̃] *adv* for the long term

durant [dyrɑ̃] *prép* (*au cours de*) during; (*pendant*) for; **~ des mois, des mois ~** for months

durcir [dyrsir] *vt, vi,* **se durcir** *vi* to harden

durcissement [dyrsismɑ̃] *nm* hardening

durée [dyre] *nf* length; (*d'une pile etc*) life; (*déroulement: des opérations etc*) duration; **pour une ~ illimitée** for an unlimited length of time; **de courte ~** (*séjour, répit*) brief, short-term; **de longue ~** (*effet*) long-term; **pile de longue ~** long-life battery

durement [dyrmɑ̃] *adv* harshly

durent [dyr] *vb voir* **devoir**

durer [dyre] *vi* to last

dureté [dyrte] *nf* (*voir dur*) hardness; harshness; stiffness; toughness

durillon [dyrijɔ̃] *nm* callus

durit® [dyrit] *nf* (*car radiator*) hose

DUT *sigle m* = **Diplôme universitaire de technologie**

dut *etc* [dy] *vb voir* **devoir**

duvet [dyvɛ] *nm* down; (**sac de couchage en**) **~** down-filled sleeping bag

duveteux, -euse [dyvtø, -øz] *adj* downy

DVD *sigle m* (= *digital versatile disc*) DVD

dynamique [dinamik] *adj* dynamic

dynamiser [dinamize] *vt* to pep up, enliven; (*équipe, service*) to inject some dynamism into

dynamisme [dinamism(ə)] *nm* dynamism

dynamite [dinamit] *nf* dynamite

dynamiter [dinamite] *vt* to (blow up with) dynamite

dynamo [dinamo] *nf* dynamo

dynastie [dinasti] *nf* dynasty

dysenterie [disɑ̃tri] *nf* dysentery

dyslexie [dislɛksi] *nf* dyslexia, word blindness

dyslexique [dislɛksik] *adj* dyslexic

dyspepsie [dispɛpsi] *nf* dyspepsia

Ee

E, e [ə] *nm inv* E, e ▷ *abr* (= *Est*) E; **E comme Eugène** E for Edward (*Brit*) *ou* Easy (*US*)

EAO *sigle m* (= *enseignement assisté par ordinateur*) CAL (= *computer-aided learning*)

EAU *sigle mpl* (= *Émirats arabes unis*) UAE (= *United Arab Emirates*)

eau, x [o] *nf* water ▷ *nfpl* waters; **prendre l'~** (*chaussure etc*) to leak, let in water; **prendre les ~x** to take the waters; **faire ~** to leak; **tomber à l'~** (*fig*) to fall through; **à l'~ de rose** slushy, sentimental; **~ bénite** holy water; **~ de Cologne** eau de Cologne; **~ courante** running water; **~ distillée** distilled water; **~ douce** fresh water; **~ de Javel** bleach; **~ lourde** heavy water; **~ minérale** mineral water; **~ oxygénée** hydrogen peroxide; **~ plate** still water; **~ de pluie** rainwater; **~ salée** salt water; **~ de toilette** toilet water; **~x ménagères** dirty water (*from washing up etc*); **~x territoriales** territorial waters; **~x usées** liquid waste

eau-de-vie [odvi] (*pl* **eaux-de-vie**) *nf* brandy

eau-forte [ofɔʀt(ə)] (*pl* **eaux-fortes**) *nf* etching

ébahi, e [ebai] *adj* dumbfounded, flabbergasted

ébahir [ebaiʀ] *vt* to astonish, astound

ébats [eba] *vb voir* **ébattre** ▷ *nmpl* frolics, gambols

ébattre [ebatʀ(ə)]: **s'ébattre** *vi* to frolic

ébauche [eboʃ] *nf* (rough) outline, sketch

ébaucher [eboʃe] *vt* to sketch out, outline; (*fig*): **~ un sourire/geste** to give a hint of a smile/ make a slight gesture; **s'ébaucher** *vi* to take shape

ébène [ebɛn] *nf* ebony

ébéniste [ebenist(ə)] *nm* cabinetmaker

ébénisterie [ebenistʀi] *nf* cabinetmaking; (*bâti*) cabinetwork

éberlué, e [ebɛʀlɥe] *adj* astounded, flabbergasted

éblouir [ebluiʀ] *vt* to dazzle

éblouissant, e [ebluisɑ̃, -ɑ̃t] *adj* dazzling

éblouissement [ebluismɑ̃] *nm* dazzle; (*faiblesse*) dizzy turn

ébonite [ebɔnit] *nf* vulcanite

éborgner [ebɔʀɲe] *vt*: **~ qn** to blind sb in one eye

éboueur [ebwœʀ] *nm* dustman (*Brit*), garbage man (*US*)

ébouillanter [ebujɑ̃te] *vt* to scald; (*Culin*) to blanch; **s'ébouillanter** *vi* to scald o.s

éboulement [ebulmɑ̃] *nm* falling rocks *pl*, rock fall; (*amas*) heap of boulders *etc*

ébouler [ebule]: **s'ébouler** *vi* to crumble, collapse

éboulis [ebuli] *nmpl* fallen rocks

ébouriffé, e [ebuʀife] *adj* tousled, ruffled

ébouriffer [ebuʀife] *vt* to tousle, ruffle

ébranlement [ebʀɑ̃lmɑ̃] *nm* shaking

ébranler [ebʀɑ̃le] *vt* to shake; (*rendre instable: mur, santé*) to weaken; **s'ébranler** *vi* (*partir*) to move off

ébrécher [ebʀeʃe] *vt* to chip

ébriété [ebʀijete] *nf*: **en état d'~** in a state of intoxication

ébrouer [ebʀue]: **s'ébrouer** *vi* (*souffler*) to snort; (*s'agiter*) to shake o.s.

ébruiter [ebʀɥite] *vt*, **s'ébruiter** *vi* to spread

ébullition [ebylisjɔ̃] *nf* boiling point; **en ~** boiling; (*fig*) in an uproar

écaille [ekaj] *nf* (*de poisson*) scale; (*de coquillage*) shell; (*matière*) tortoiseshell; (*de roc etc*) flake

écaillé, e [ekaje] *adj* (*peinture*) flaking

écailler [ekaje] *vt* (*poisson*) to scale; (*huître*) to open; **s'écailler** *vi* to flake *ou* peel (off)

écarlate [ekaʀlat] *adj* scarlet

écarquiller [ekaʀkije] *vt*: **~ les yeux** to stare wide-eyed

écart [ekaʀ] *nm* gap; (*embardée*) swerve; (*saut*) sideways leap; (*fig*) departure, deviation; **à l'~** *adv* out of the way; **à l'~ de** *prép* away from; (*fig*) out of; **faire le grand ~** (*Danse, Gymnastique*) to do the splits; **~ de conduite** misdemeanour

écarté, e [ekaʀte] *adj* (*lieu*) out-of-the-way, remote; (*ouvert*): **les jambes ~es** legs apart; **les bras ~s** arms outstretched

écarteler [ekaʀtəle] *vt* to quarter; (*fig*) to tear apart

écartement [ekaʀtəmɑ̃] *nm* space, gap; (*Rail*) gauge

écarter [ekaʀte] *vt* (*séparer*) to move apart, separate; (*éloigner*) to push back, move away; (*ouvrir: bras, jambes*) to spread, open; (: *rideau*) to draw (back); (*éliminer: candidat, possibilité*) to dismiss; (*Cartes*) to discard; **s'écarter** *vi* to part; (*personne*) to move away; **s'~ de** to wander from

ecchymose [ekimoz] *nf* bruise

ecclésiastique [eklezjastik] *adj* ecclesiastical
▷ *nm* ecclesiastic

écervelé, e [esεrvəle] *adj* scatterbrained,
featherbrained

ECG *sigle m* (= *électrocardiogramme*) ECG

échafaud [eʃafo] *nm* scaffold

échafaudage [eʃafodaʒ] *nm* scaffolding; (*fig*)
heap, pile

échafauder [eʃafode] *vt* (*plan*) to construct

échalas [eʃala] *nm* stake, pole; (*personne*)
beanpole

échalote [eʃalɔt] *nf* shallot

échancré, e [eʃɑ̃kre] *adj* (*robe, corsage*) low-
necked; (*côte*) indented

échancrure [eʃɑ̃kryr] *nf* (*de robe*) scoop neckline;
(*de côte, arête rocheuse*) indentation

échange [eʃɑ̃ʒ] *nm* exchange; **en ~** in exchange;
en ~ de in exchange *ou* return for; **libre ~** free
trade; **~ de lettres/politesses/vues** exchange
of letters/civilities/views; **~s commerciaux**
trade; **~s culturels** cultural exchanges

échangeable [eʃɑ̃zabl(ə)] *adj* exchangeable

échanger [eʃɑ̃ʒe] *vt*: **~ qch (contre)** to exchange
sth (for)

échangeur [eʃɑ̃ʒœr] *nm* (*Auto*) interchange

échantillon [eʃɑ̃tijɔ̃] *nm* sample

échantillonnage [eʃɑ̃tijɔnaʒ] *nm* selection of
samples

échappatoire [eʃapatwar] *nf* way out

échappée [eʃape] *nf* (*vue*) vista; (*Cyclisme*)
breakaway

échappement [eʃapmɑ̃] *nm* (*Auto*) exhaust; **~
libre** cutout

échapper [eʃape]: **~ à** *vt* (*gardien*) to escape
(from); (*punition, péril*) to escape; **~ à qn** (*détail,
sens*) to escape sb; (*objet qu'on tient: aussi:*
échapper des mains de qn) to slip out of sb's
hands; **laisser ~** to let fall; (*cri etc*) to let out;
s'échapper *vi* to escape; **l'~ belle** to have a
narrow escape

écharde [eʃard(ə)] *nf* splinter (of wood)

écharpe [eʃarp(ə)] *nf* scarf; (*de maire*) sash; (*Méd*)
sling; **prendre en ~** (*dans une collision*) to hit
sideways on

écharper [eʃarpe] *vt* to tear to pieces

échasse [eʃas] *nf* stilt

échassier [eʃasje] *nm* wader

échauder [eʃode] *vt*: **se faire ~** (*fig*) to get one's
fingers burnt

échauffement [eʃofmɑ̃] *nm* overheating; (*Sport*)
warm-up

échauffer [eʃofe] *vt* (*métal, moteur*) to overheat;
(*fig: exciter*) to fire, excite; **s'échauffer** *vi* (*Sport*)
to warm up; (*discussion*) to become heated

échauffourée [eʃofure] *nf* clash, brawl; (*Mil*)
skirmish

échéance [eʃeɑ̃s] *nf* (*d'un paiement: date*)
settlement date; (*: somme due*) financial
commitment(s); (*fig*) deadline; **à brève/longue
~** *adj* short-/long-term ▷ *adv* in the short/long
term

échéancier [eʃeɑ̃sje] *nm* schedule

échéant [eʃeɑ̃]: **le cas ~** *adv* if the case arises

échec [eʃεk] *nm* failure; (*Échecs*): **~ et mat/au
roi** checkmate/check; **échecs** *nmpl* (*jeu*) chess
sg; **mettre en ~** to put in check; **tenir en ~** to
hold in check; **faire ~ à** to foil, thwart

échelle [eʃεl] *nf* ladder; (*fig, d'une carte*) scale; **à
l'~ de** on the scale of; **sur une grande/petite ~**
on a large/small scale; **faire la courte ~ à qn** to
give sb a leg up; **~ de corde** rope ladder

échelon [eʃlɔ̃] *nm* (*d'échelle*) rung; (*Admin*) grade

échelonner [eʃlɔne] *vt* to space out, spread out;
(versement) échelonné (payment) by
instalments

écheveau, x [εʃvo] *nm* skein, hank

échevelé, e [eʃəvle] *adj* tousled, dishevelled;
(*fig*) wild, frenzied

échine [eʃin] *nf* backbone, spine

échiner [eʃine]: **s'échiner** *vi* (*se fatiguer*) to work
o.s. to the bone

échiquier [eʃikje] *nm* chessboard

écho [eko] *nm* echo; **échos** *nmpl* (*potins*) gossip
sg, rumours; (*Presse: rubrique*) "news in brief";
rester sans ~ (*suggestion etc*) to come to nothing;
se faire l'~ de to repeat, spread about

échographie [ekɔgrafi] *nf* ultrasound (scan)

échoir [eʃwar] *vi* (*dette*) to fall due; (*délais*) to
expire; **~ à** *vt* to fall to

échoppe [eʃɔp] *nf* stall, booth

échouer [eʃwe] *vi* to fail; (*débris etc: sur la plage*) to
be washed up; (*aboutir: personne dans un café etc*) to
arrive ▷ *vt* (*bateau*) to ground; **s'échouer** *vi* to
run aground

échu, e [eʃy] *pp de* **échoir** ▷ *adj* due, mature

échut *etc* [eʃy] *vb voir* **échoir**

éclabousser [eklabuse] *vt* to splash; (*fig*) to
tarnish

éclaboussure [eklabusyr] *nf* splash; (*fig*) stain

éclair [eklεr] *nm* (*d'orage*) flash of lightning,
lightning *no pl*; (*Photo: de flash*) flash; (*fig*) flash,
spark; (*gâteau*) éclair

éclairage [eklεraʒ] *nm* lighting

éclairagiste [eklεraʒist(ə)] *nm/f* lighting
engineer

éclaircie [eklεrsi] *nf* bright *ou* sunny interval

éclaircir [eklεrsir] *vt* to lighten; (*fig*) to clear up,
clarify; (*Culin*) to thin (down); **s'éclaircir** *vi* (*ciel*)
to brighten up, clear; (*cheveux*) to go thin;
(*situation etc*) to become clearer; **s'~ la voix** to
clear one's throat

éclaircissement [eklεrsismɑ̃] *nm* clearing up,
clarification

éclairer [eklere] *vt* (*lieu*) to light (up); (*personne:
avec une lampe de poche etc*) to light the way for;
(*fig: instruire*) to enlighten; (*: rendre compréhensible*)
to shed light on ▷ *vi*: **~ mal/bien** to give a poor/
good light; **s'éclairer** *vi* (*phare, rue*) to light up;
(*situation etc*) to become clearer; **s'~ à la bougie/
l'électricité** to use candlelight/have electric
lighting

éclaireur, -euse [eklεrœr, -øz] *nm/f* (*scout*) (boy)
scout/(girl) guide ▷ *nm* (*Mil*) scout; **partir en ~**

to go off to reconnoitre

éclat [ekla] *nm* (*de bombe, de verre*) fragment; (*du soleil, d'une couleur etc*) brightness, brilliance; (*d'une cérémonie*) splendour; (*scandale*): **faire un ~** to cause a commotion; **action d' ~** outstanding action; **voler en ~s** to shatter; **des ~s de verre** broken glass; flying glass; **~ de rire** burst *ou* roar of laughter; **~ de voix** shout

éclatant, e [eklatã, -ãt] *adj* brilliant, bright; (*succès*) resounding; (*revanche*) devastating

éclater [eklate] *vi* (*pneu*) to burst; (*bombe*) to explode; (*guerre, épidémie*) to break out; (*groupe, parti*) to break up; **~ de rire/en sanglots** to burst out laughing/sobbing

éclectique [eklɛktik] *adj* eclectic

éclipse [eklips(ə)] *nf* eclipse

éclipser [eklipse] *vt* to eclipse; **s'éclipser** *vi* to slip away

éclopé, e [eklɔpe] *adj* lame

éclore [eklɔʀ] *vi* (*œuf*) to hatch; (*fleur*) to open (out)

éclosion [eklozjɔ̃] *nf* blossoming

écluse [eklyz] *nf* lock

éclusier [eklyzje] *nm* lock keeper

éco- [eko] *préfixe* eco-

écœurant, e [ekœrã, -ãt] *adj* sickening; (*gâteau etc*) sickly

écœurement [ekœrmã] *nm* disgust

écœurer [ekœre] *vt*: **~ qn** to make sb feel sick; (*fig: démoraliser*) to disgust sb

école [ekɔl] *nf* school; **aller à l'~** to go to school; **faire ~** to collect a following; **les grandes ~s** *prestige university-level colleges with competitive entrance examinations*; **~ maternelle** nursery school; *see note*; **~ primaire** primary (*Brit*) *ou* grade (*US*) school; **~ secondaire** secondary (*Brit*) *ou* high (*US*) school; **~ privée/publique/élémentaire** private/state/elementary school; **~ de dessin/danse/musique** art/dancing/music school; **~ hôtelière** catering college; **~ normale (d'instituteurs) (ENI)** *primary school teachers' training college*; **~ normale supérieure (ENS)** *grande école for training secondary school teachers*; **~ de secrétariat** secretarial college

● ÉCOLE MATERNELLE

Nursery school (kindergarten) (*l'école maternelle*) is publicly funded in France and, though not compulsory, is attended by most children between the ages of three and six. Statutory education begins with primary (grade) school (*l'école primaire*) and is attended by children between the ages of six and 10 or 11.

écolier, -ière [ekɔlje, -jɛʀ] *nm/f* schoolboy/girl

écolo [ekɔlo] *nm/f* (*fam*) ecologist ▷ *adj* ecological

écologie [ekɔlɔʒi] *nf* ecology; (*sujet scolaire*) environmental studies *pl*

écologique [ekɔlɔʒik] *adj* ecological; environmental

écologiste [ekɔlɔʒist(ə)] *nm/f* ecologist; environmentalist

éconduire [ekɔ̃dɥiʀ] *vt* to dismiss

économat [ekɔnɔma] *nm* (*fonction*) bursarship (*Brit*), treasurership (*US*); (*bureau*) bursar's office (*Brit*), treasury (*US*)

économe [ekɔnɔm] *adj* thrifty ▷ *nm/f* (*de lycée etc*) bursar (*Brit*), treasurer (*US*)

économétrie [ekɔnɔmetri] *nf* econometrics *sg*

économie [ekɔnɔmi] *nf* (*vertu*) economy, thrift; (*gain: d'argent, de temps etc*) saving; (*science*) economics *sg*; (*situation économique*) economy; **économies** *nfpl* (*pécule*) savings; **faire des ~s** to save up; **une ~ de temps/d'argent** a saving in time/of money; **~ dirigée** planned economy; **~ de marché** market economy

économique [ekɔnɔmik] *adj* (*avantageux*) economical; (*Écon*) economic

économiquement [ekɔnɔmikmã] *adv* economically; **les ~ faibles** (*Admin*) the low-paid, people on low incomes

économiser [ekɔnɔmize] *vt, vi* to save

économiseur [ekɔnɔmizər] *nm*: **~ d'écran** (*Inform*) screen saver

économiste [ekɔnɔmist(ə)] *nm/f* economist

écoper [ekɔpe] *vi* to bale out; (*fig*) to cop it; **~ (de)** *vt* to get

écorce [ekɔʀs(ə)] *nf* bark; (*de fruit*) peel

écorcer [ekɔʀse] *vt* to bark

écorché, e [ekɔʀʃe] *adj*: **~ vif** flayed alive ▷ *nm* cut-away drawing

écorcher [ekɔʀʃe] *vt* (*animal*) to skin; (*égratigner*) to graze; **~ une langue** to speak a language brokenly; **s'~ le genou** *etc* to scrape *ou* graze one's knee *etc*

écorchure [ekɔʀʃyʀ] *nf* graze

écorner [ekɔʀne] *vt* (*taureau*) to dehorn; (*livre*) to make dog-eared

écossais, e [ekɔsɛ, -ɛz] *adj* Scottish, Scots; (*whisky, confiture*) Scotch; (*écharpe, tissu*) tartan ▷ *nm* (*Ling*) Scots; (: *gaélique*) Gaelic; (*tissu*) tartan (cloth) ▷ *nm/f*: **Écossais, e** Scot, Scotsman/woman; **les É~** the Scots

Écosse [ekɔs] *nf*: **l'~** Scotland

écosser [ekɔse] *vt* to shell

écosystème [ekɔsistɛm] *nm* ecosystem

écot [eko] *nm*: **payer son ~** to pay one's share

écoulement [ekulmã] *nm* (*de faux billets*) circulation; (*de stock*) selling

écouler [ekule] *vt* to dispose of; **s'écouler** *vi* (*eau*) to flow (out); (*foule*) to drift away; (*jours, temps*) to pass (by)

écourter [ekuʀte] *vt* to curtail, cut short

écoute [ekut] *nf* (*Navig: cordage*) sheet; (*Radio, TV*): **temps d'~** (listening *ou* viewing) time; **heure de grande ~** peak listening *ou* viewing time; **prendre l'~** to tune in; **rester à l'~ (de)** to stay tuned in (to); **~s téléphoniques** phone tapping *sg*

écouter [ekute] *vt* to listen to

écouteur [ekutœʀ] *nm* (*Tél*) (additional)

earpiece; **écouteurs** *nmpl* (*Radio*) headphones, headset *sg*

écoutille [ekutij] *nf* hatch

écr. *abr* = **écrire**

écrabouiller [ekʀabuje] *vt* to squash, crush

écran [ekʀɑ̃] *nm* screen; (*Inform*) screen, VDU; ~ **de fumée/d'eau** curtain of smoke/water; **porter à l'~** (*Ciné*) to adapt for the screen; **le petit** ~ television, the small screen

écrasant, e [ekʀazɑ̃, -ɑ̃t] *adj* overwhelming

écraser [ekʀaze] *vt* to crush; (*piéton*) to run over; (*Inform*) to overwrite; **se faire** ~ to be run over; **écrase(-toi)!** shut up!; **s'~** (**au sol**) to crash; **s'~ contre** to crash into

écrémé, e [ekʀeme] *adj* (*lait*) skimmed

écrémer [ekʀeme] *vt* to skim

écrevisse [ekʀəvis] *nf* crayfish *inv*

écrier [ekʀije]: **s'écrier** *vi* to exclaim

écrin [ekʀɛ̃] *nm* case, box

écrire [ekʀiʀ] *vt, vi* to write ▷ *vi*: **ça s'écrit comment?** how is it spelt?; ~ **à qn que** to write and tell sb that; **s'écrire** *vi* to write to one another

écrit, e [ekʀi, -it] *pp de* **écrire** ▷ *adj*: **bien/mal** ~ well/badly written ▷ *nm* document; (*examen*) written paper; **par** ~ in writing

écriteau, x [ekʀito] *nm* notice, sign

écritoire [ekʀitwaʀ] *nf* writing case

écriture [ekʀityʀ] *nf* writing; (*Comm*) entry; **écritures** *nfpl* (*Comm*) accounts, books; **l'É~ (sainte)**, **les É~s** the Scriptures

écrivain [ekʀivɛ̃] *nm* writer

écrivais *etc* [ekʀivɛ] *vb voir* **écrire**

écrou [ekʀu] *nm* nut

écrouer [ekʀue] *vt* to imprison; (*provisoirement*) to remand in custody

écroulé, e [ekʀule] *adj* (*de fatigue*) exhausted; (*par un malheur*) overwhelmed; ~ (**de rire**) in stitches

écroulement [ekʀulmɑ̃] *nm* collapse

écrouler [ekʀule]: **s'écrouler** *vi* to collapse

écru, e [ekʀy] *adj* (*toile*) raw, unbleached; (*couleur*) off-white, écru

écu [eky] *nm* (*bouclier*) shield; (*monnaie: ancienne*) crown; (: *de la CEE*) ecu

écueil [ekœj] *nm* reef; (*fig*) pitfall; stumbling block

écuelle [ekɥɛl] *nf* bowl

éculé, e [ekyle] *adj* (*chaussure*) down-at-heel; (*fig: péj*) hackneyed

écume [ekym] *nf* foam; (*Culin*) scum; ~ **de mer** meerschaum

écumer [ekyme] *vt* (*Culin*) to skim; (*fig*) to plunder ▷ *vi* (*mer*) to foam; (*fig*) to boil with rage

écumoire [ekymwaʀ] *nf* skimmer

écureuil [ekyʀœj] *nm* squirrel

écurie [ekyʀi] *nf* stable

écusson [ekysɔ̃] *nm* badge

écuyer, -ère [ekɥije, -ɛʀ] *nm/f* rider

eczéma [ɛgzema] *nm* eczema

éd. *abr* = **édition**

édam [edam] *nm* (*fromage*) edam

edelweiss [edɛlvajs] *nm inv* edelweiss

éden [edɛn] *nm* Eden

édenté, e [edɑ̃te] *adj* toothless

EDF *sigle f* (= *Électricité de France*) *national electricity company*

édifiant, e [edifjɑ̃, -ɑ̃t] *adj* edifying

édification [edifikasjɔ̃] *nf* (*d'un bâtiment*) building, erection

édifice [edifis] *nm* building, edifice

édifier [edifje] *vt* to build, erect; (*fig*) to edify

édiles [edil] *nmpl* city fathers

Édimbourg [edɛ̃buʀ] *n* Edinburgh

édit [edi] *nm* edict

édit. *abr* = **éditeur**

éditer [edite] *vt* (*publier*) to publish; (: *disque*) to produce; (*préparer: texte, Inform*) to edit

éditeur, -trice [editœʀ, -tʀis] *nm/f* publisher; editor; ~ **de textes** (*Inform*) text editor

édition [edisjɔ̃] *nf* editing *no pl*; (*série d'exemplaires*) edition; (*industrie du livre*): **l'~** publishing; ~ **sur écran** (*Inform*) screen editing

édito [edito] *nm* (*fam: éditorial*) editorial, leader

éditorial, -aux [editɔʀjal, -o] *nm* editorial, leader

éditorialiste [editɔʀjalist(ə)] *nm/f* editorial *ou* leader writer

édredon [edʀədɔ̃] *nm* eiderdown, comforter (*US*)

éducateur, -trice [edykatœʀ, -tʀis] *nm/f* teacher; ~ **spécialisé** specialist teacher

éducatif, -ive [edykatif, -iv] *adj* educational

éducation [edykasjɔ̃] *nf* education; (*familiale*) upbringing; (*manières*) (good) manners *pl*; **bonne/mauvaise** ~ good/bad upbringing; **sans** ~ bad-mannered, ill-bred; **l'É~** (**nationale**) ≈ the Department for Education; ~ **permanente** continuing education; ~ **physique** physical education

édulcorant [edylkɔʀɑ̃] *nm* sweetener

édulcorer [edylkɔʀe] *vt* to sweeten; (*fig*) to tone down

éduquer [edyke] *vt* to educate; (*élever*) to bring up; (*faculté*) to train; **bien/mal éduqué** well/ badly brought up

EEG *sigle m* (= *électroencéphalogramme*) EEG

effacé, e [efase] *adj* (*fig*) retiring, unassuming

effacer [efase] *vt* to erase, rub out; (*bande magnétique*) to erase; (*Inform: fichier, fiche*) to delete; **s'effacer** *vi* (*inscription etc*) to wear off; (*pour laisser passer*) to step aside; ~ **le ventre** to pull one's stomach in

effarant, e [efaʀɑ̃, -ɑ̃t] *adj* alarming

effaré, e [efaʀe] *adj* alarmed

effarement [efaʀmɑ̃] *nm* alarm

effarer [efaʀe] *vt* to alarm

effarouchement [efaʀuʃmɑ̃] *nm* alarm

effaroucher [efaʀuʃe] *vt* to frighten *ou* scare away; (*personne*) to alarm

effectif, -ive [efɛktif, -iv] *adj* real; effective ▷ *nm* (*Mil*) strength; (*Scol*) total number of pupils, size; ~**s** numbers, strength *sg*; (*Comm*) manpower *sg*; **réduire l'~ de** to downsize

effectivement [efɛktivmɑ̃] *adv* effectively;

(*réellement*) actually, really; (*en effet*) indeed

effectuer [efɛktɥe] *vt* (*opération, mission*) to carry out; (*déplacement, trajet*) to make, complete; (*mouvement*) to execute, make; **s'effectuer** *vi* to be carried out

efféminé, e [efemine] *adj* effeminate

effervescence [efɛrvesãs] *nf* (*fig*): **en ~** in a turmoil

effervescent, e [efɛrvesã, -ãt] *adj* (*cachet, boisson*) effervescent; (*fig*) agitated, in a turmoil

effet [efɛ] *nm* (*résultat, artifice*) effect; (*impression*) impression; (*Comm*) bill; (*Jur: d'une loi, d'un jugement*): **avec ~ rétroactif** applied retrospectively; **effets** *nmpl* (*vêtements etc*) things; **~ de style/couleur/lumière** stylistic/colour/lighting effect; **~s de voix** dramatic effects with one's voice; **faire de l'~** (*médicament, menace*) to have an effect, be effective; **sous l'~ de** under the effect of; **donner de l'~ à une balle** (*Tennis*) to put some spin on a ball; **à cet ~** to that end; **en ~** *adv* indeed; **~ (de commerce)** bill of exchange; **~ de serre** greenhouse effect; **~s spéciaux** (*Ciné*) special effects

effeuiller [efœje] *vt* to remove the leaves (*ou* petals) from

efficace [efikas] *adj* (*personne*) efficient; (*action, médicament*) effective

efficacité [efikasite] *nf* efficiency; effectiveness

effigie [efiʒi] *nf* effigy; **brûler qn en ~** to burn an effigy of sb

effilé, e [efile] *adj* slender; (*pointe*) sharp; (*carrosserie*) streamlined

effiler [efile] *vt* (*cheveux*) to thin (out); (*tissu*) to fray

effilocher [efilɔʃe]: **s'effilocher** *vi* to fray

efflanqué, e [eflãke] *adj* emaciated

effleurement [eflœrmã] *nm*: **touche à ~** touch-sensitive control *ou* key

effleurer [eflœre] *vt* to brush (against); (*sujet*) to touch upon; (*idée, pensée*): **~ qn** to cross sb's mind

effluves [eflyv] *nmpl* exhalation(s)

effondré, e [efɔ̃dre] *adj* (*abattu: par un malheur, échec*) overwhelmed

effondrement [efɔ̃drəmã] *nm* collapse

effondrer [efɔ̃dre]: **s'effondrer** *vi* to collapse

efforcer [efɔrse]: **s'efforcer de** *vt*: **s'~ de faire** to try hard to do

effort [efɔr] *nm* effort; **faire un ~** to make an effort; **faire tous ses ~s** to try one's hardest; **faire l'~ de ...** to make the effort to ...; **sans ~** *adj* effortless ▷ *adv* effortlessly; **~ de mémoire** attempt to remember; **~ de volonté** effort of will

effraction [efraksjɔ̃] *nf* breaking-in; **s'introduire par ~ dans** to break into

effrangé, e [efrãʒe] *adj* fringed; (*effiloché*) frayed

effrayant, e [efrɛjã, -ãt] *adj* frightening, fearsome; (*sens affaibli*) dreadful

effrayer [efreje] *vt* to frighten, scare; (*rebuter*) to put off; **s'effrayer (de)** *vi* to be frightened *ou* scared (by)

effréné, e [efrene] *adj* wild

effritement [efritmã] *nm* crumbling; erosion; slackening off

effriter [efrite]: **s'effriter** *vi* to crumble; (*monnaie*) to be eroded; (*valeurs*) to slacken off

effroi [efrwa] *nm* terror, dread *no pl*

effronté, e [efrɔ̃te] *adj* insolent

effrontément [efrɔ̃temã] *adv* insolently

effronterie [efrɔ̃tri] *nf* insolence

effroyable [efrwajabl(ə)] *adj* horrifying, appalling

effusion [efyzjɔ̃] *nf* effusion; **sans ~ de sang** without bloodshed

égailler [egaje]: **s'égailler** *vi* to scatter, disperse

égal, e, -aux [egal, -o] *adj* (*identique, ayant les mêmes droits*) equal; (*plan: surface*) even, level; (*constant: vitesse*) steady; (*équitable*) even ▷ *nm/f* equal; **être ~ à** (*prix, nombre*) to be equal to; **ça m'est ~** it's all the same to me, it doesn't matter to me, I don't mind; **c'est ~, ...** all the same, ...; **sans ~** matchless, unequalled; **à l'~ de** (*comme*) just like; **d'~ à ~** as equals

également [egalmã] *adv* equally; evenly; steadily; (*aussi*) too, as well

égaler [egale] *vt* to equal

égalisateur, -trice [egalizatœr, -tris] *adj* (*Sport*): **but ~** equalizing goal, equalizer

égalisation [egalizasjɔ̃] *nf* (*Sport*) equalization

égaliser [egalize] *vt* (*sol, salaires*) to level (out); (*chances*) to equalize ▷ *vi* (*Sport*) to equalize

égalitaire [egalitɛr] *adj* egalitarian

égalitarisme [egalitarism(ə)] *nm* egalitarianism

égalité [egalite] *nf* equality; evenness; steadiness; (*Math*) identity; **être à ~ (de points)** to be level; **~ de droits** equality of rights; **~ d'humeur** evenness of temper

égard [egar] *nm*: **~s** *nmpl* consideration *sg*; **à cet ~** in this respect; **à certains ~s/tous ~s** in certain respects/all respects; **eu ~ à** in view of; **par ~ pour** out of consideration for; **sans ~ pour** without regard for; **à l'~ de** *prép* towards; (*en ce qui concerne*) concerning, as regards

égaré, e [egare] *adj* lost

égarement [egarmã] *nm* distraction; aberration

égarer [egare] *vt* (*objet*) to mislay; (*moralement*) to lead astray; **s'égarer** *vi* to get lost, lose one's way; (*objet*) to go astray; (*fig: dans une discussion*) to wander

égayer [egeje] *vt* (*personne*) to amuse; (: *remonter*) to cheer up; (*récit, endroit*) to brighten up, liven up

Égée [eʒe] *adj*: **la mer ~** the Aegean (Sea)

égéen, ne [eʒeɛ̃, -ɛn] *adj* Aegean

égérie [eʒeri] *nf*: **l'~ de qn/qch** the brains behind sb/sth

égide [eʒid] *nf*: **sous l'~ de** under the aegis of

églantier [eglãtje] *nm* wild *ou* dog rose(-bush)

églantine [eglãtin] *nf* wild *ou* dog rose

églefin [egləfɛ̃] *nm* haddock

église [egliz] *nf* church

égocentrique [egɔsɑ̃tʀik] *adj* egocentric, self-centred

égocentrisme [egɔsɑ̃tʀism(ə)] *nm* egocentricity

égoïne [egɔin] *nf* handsaw

égoïsme [egɔism(ə)] *nm* selfishness, egoism

égoïste [egɔist(ə)] *adj* selfish, egoistic ▷ *nm/f* egoist

égoïstement [egɔistəmɑ̃] *adv* selfishly

égorger [egɔʀʒe] *vt* to cut the throat of

égosiller [egozije]: **s'égosiller** *vi* to shout o.s. hoarse

égotisme [egɔtism(ə)] *nm* egotism, egoism

égout [egu] *nm* sewer; **eaux d'~** sewage

égoutier [egutje] *nm* sewer worker

égoutter [egute] *vt* (*linge*) to wring out; (*vaisselle, fromage*) to drain ▷ *vi*, **s'égoutter** *vi* to drip

égouttoir [egutwaʀ] *nm* draining board; (*mobile*) draining rack

égratigner [egʀatiɲe] *vt* to scratch; **s'égratigner** *vi* to scratch o.s.

égratignure [egʀatiɲyʀ] *nf* scratch

égrener [egʀəne] *vt*: **~ une grappe, ~ des raisins** to pick grapes off a bunch; **s'égrener** *vi* (*fig: heures etc*) to pass by; (: *notes*) to chime out

égrillard, e [egʀijaʀ, -aʀd(ə)] *adj* ribald, bawdy

Égypte [eʒipt] *nf*: **l'~** Egypt

égyptien, ne [eʒipsjɛ̃, -ɛn] *adj* Egyptian ▷ *nm/f*: **Égyptien, ne** Egyptian

égyptologue [eʒiptɔlɔg] *nm/f* Egyptologist

eh [e] *excl* hey!; **eh bien** well

éhonté, e [eɔ̃te] *adj* shameless, brazen (*Brit*)

éjaculation [eʒakylasjɔ̃] *nf* ejaculation

éjaculer [eʒakyle] *vi* to ejaculate

éjectable [eʒɛktabl(ə)] *adj*: **siège ~** ejector seat

éjecter [eʒɛkte] *vt* (*Tech*) to eject; (*fam*) to kick *ou* chuck out

éjection [eʒɛksjɔ̃] *nf* ejection

élaboration [elabɔʀasjɔ̃] *nf* elaboration

élaboré, e [elabɔʀe] *adj* (*complexe*) elaborate

élaborer [elabɔʀe] *vt* to elaborate; (*projet, stratégie*) to work out; (*rapport*) to draft

élagage [elagaʒ] *nm* pruning

élaguer [elage] *vt* to prune

élan [elɑ̃] *nm* (*Zool*) elk, moose; (*Sport: avant le saut*) run up; (*de véhicule*) momentum; (*fig: de tendresse etc*) surge; **prendre son ~/de l'~** to take a run up/gather speed; **perdre son ~** to lose one's momentum

élancé, e [elɑ̃se] *adj* slender

élancement [elɑ̃smɑ̃] *nm* shooting pain

élancer [elɑ̃se]: **s'élancer** *vi* to dash, hurl o.s.; (*fig: arbre, clocher*) to soar (upwards)

élargir [elaʀʒiʀ] *vt* to widen; (*vêtement*) to let out; (*Jur*) to release; **s'élargir** *vi* to widen; (*vêtement*) to stretch

élargissement [elaʀʒismɑ̃] *nm* widening; letting out

élasticité [elastisite] *nf* (*aussi Écon*) elasticity; **~ de l'offre/de la demande** flexibility of supply/demand

élastique [elastik] *adj* elastic ▷ *nm* (*de bureau*) rubber band; (*pour la couture*) elastic *no pl*

élastomère [elastɔmɛʀ] *nm* elastomer

Elbe [ɛlb] *nf*: **l'île d'~** (the Island of) Elba; (*fleuve*): **l'~** the Elbe

eldorado [ɛldɔʀado] *nm* Eldorado

électeur, -trice [elɛktœʀ, -tʀis] *nm/f* elector, voter

électif, -ive [elɛktif, -iv] *adj* elective

élection [elɛksjɔ̃] *nf* election; **élections** *nfpl* (*Pol*) election(s); **sa terre/patrie d'~** the land/country of one's choice; **~ partielle** ≈ by-election; **~s législatives/présidentielles** general/presidential election *sg*; *see note*

⬤ **ÉLECTIONS LÉGISLATIVES**

⬤ *Élections législatives* are held in France every
⬤ five years to elect "députés" to the
⬤ "Assemblée nationale". The president is
⬤ chosen in the "élection présidentielle",
⬤ which also comes round every five years.
⬤ Voting is by direct universal suffrage and is
⬤ divided into two rounds. The ballots always
⬤ take place on a Sunday.

électoral, e, -aux [elɛktɔʀal, -o] *adj* electoral, election *cpd*

électoralisme [elɛktɔʀalism(ə)] *nm* electioneering

électorat [elɛktɔʀa] *nm* electorate

électricien, ne [elɛktʀisjɛ̃, -ɛn] *nm/f* electrician

électricité [elɛktʀisite] *nf* electricity; **allumer/éteindre l'~** to put on/off the light; **~ statique** static electricity

électrification [elɛktʀifikasjɔ̃] *nf* (*Rail*) electrification; (*d'un village etc*) laying on of electricity

électrifier [elɛktʀifje] *vt* (*Rail*) to electrify

électrique [elɛktʀik] *adj* electric(al)

électriser [elɛktʀize] *vt* to electrify

électro... [elɛktʀɔ] *préfixe* electro...

électro-aimant [elɛktʀɔɛmɑ̃] *nm* electromagnet

électrocardiogramme [elɛktʀɔkaʀdjɔgʀam] *nm* electrocardiogram

électrocardiographe [elɛktʀɔkaʀdjɔgʀaf] *nm* electrocardiograph

électrochoc [elɛktʀɔʃɔk] *nm* electric shock treatment

électrocuter [elɛktʀɔkyte] *vt* to electrocute

électrocution [elɛktʀɔkysjɔ̃] *nf* electrocution

électrode [elɛktʀɔd] *nf* electrode

électro-encéphalogramme [elɛktʀɔɑ̃sefalɔgʀam] *nm* electroencephalogram

électrogène [elɛktʀɔʒɛn] *adj*: **groupe ~** generating set

électrolyse [elɛktʀɔliz] *nf* electrolysis *sg*

électromagnétique [elɛktʀɔmaɲetik] *adj* electromagnetic

électroménager [elɛktʀɔmenaʒe] *adj*:

appareils ~s domestic (electrical) appliances ▷ *nm*: **l'~** household appliances
électron [elεktrɔ̃] *nm* electron
électronicien, ne [elεktrɔnisjɛ̃, -εn] *nm/f* electronics (Brit) *ou* electrical (US) engineer
électronique [elεktrɔnik] *adj* electronic ▷ *nf* (*science*) electronics *sg*
électronucléaire [elεktrɔnykleεr] *adj* nuclear power *cpd* ▷ *nm*: **l'~** nuclear power
électrophone [elεktrɔfɔn] *nm* record player
électrostatique [elεktrɔstatik] *adj* electrostatic ▷ *nf* electrostatics *sg*
élégamment [elegamɑ̃] *adv* elegantly
élégance [elegɑ̃s] *nf* elegance
élégant, e [elegɑ̃, -ɑ̃t] *adj* elegant; (*solution*) neat, elegant; (*attitude, procédé*) courteous, civilized
élément [elemɑ̃] *nm* element; (*pièce*) component, part; **éléments** *nmpl* elements
élémentaire [elemɑ̃tεr] *adj* elementary; (*Chimie*) elemental
éléphant [elefɑ̃] *nm* elephant; **~ de mer** elephant seal
éléphanteau, x [elefɑ̃to] *nm* baby elephant
éléphantesque [elefɑ̃tεsk(ə)] *adj* elephantine
élevage [εlvaʒ] *nm* breeding; (*de bovins*) cattle breeding *ou* rearing; (*ferme*) cattle farm
élévateur [elevatœr] *nm* elevator
élévation [elevasjɔ̃] *nf* (*gén*) elevation; (*voir élever*) raising; (*voir s'élever*) rise
élevé, e [εlve] *adj* (*prix, sommet*) high; (*fig: noble*) elevated; **bien/mal ~** well-/ill-mannered
élève [elεv] *nm/f* pupil; **~ infirmière** student nurse
élever [εlve] *vt* (*enfant*) to bring up, raise; (*bétail, volaille*) to breed; (*abeilles*) to keep; (*hausser: taux, niveau*) to raise; (*fig: âme, esprit*) to elevate; (*édifier: monument*) to put up, erect; **s'élever** *vi* (*avion, alpiniste*) to go up; (*niveau, température, aussi: cri etc*) to rise; (*survenir: difficultés*) to arise; **s'~ à** (*frais, dégâts*) to amount to, add up to; **s'~ contre** to rise up against; **~ une protestation/critique** to raise a protest/make a criticism; **~ qn au rang de** to raise *ou* elevate sb to the rank of; **~ un nombre au carré/au cube** to square/cube a number
éleveur, -euse [εlvœr, -øz] *nm/f* stock breeder
elfe [εlf(ə)] *nm* elf
élidé, e [elide] *adj* elided
élider [elide] *vt* to elide
éligibilité [eliʒibilite] *nf* eligibility
éligible [eliʒibl(ə)] *adj* eligible
élimé, e [elime] *adj* worn (thin), threadbare
élimination [eliminasjɔ̃] *nf* elimination
éliminatoire [eliminatwar] *adj* eliminatory; (*Sport*) disqualifying ▷ *nf* (*Sport*) heat
éliminer [elimine] *vt* to eliminate
élire [elir] *vt* to elect; **~ domicile à** to take up residence in *ou* at
élision [elizjɔ̃] *nf* elision
élite [elit] *nf* elite; **tireur d'~** crack rifleman; **chercheur d'~** top-notch researcher

élitisme [elitism(ə)] *nm* elitism
élitiste [elitist(ə)] *adj* elitist
élixir [eliksir] *nm* elixir
elle [εl] *pron* (*sujet*) she; (: *chose*) it; (*complément*) her; it; **~s** (*sujet*) they; (*complément*) them; **~-même** herself; itself; **~s-mêmes** themselves; *voir* **il**
ellipse [elips(ə)] *nf* ellipse; (*Ling*) ellipsis *sg*
elliptique [eliptik] *adj* elliptical
élocution [elɔkysjɔ̃] *nf* delivery; **défaut d'~** speech impediment
éloge [elɔʒ] *nm* praise *gen no pl*; **faire l'~ de** to praise
élogieusement [elɔʒjøzmɑ̃] *adv* very favourably
élogieux, -euse [elɔʒjø, -øz] *adj* laudatory, full of praise
éloigné, e [elwaɲe] *adj* distant, far-off
éloignement [elwaɲmɑ̃] *nm* removal; putting off; estrangement; (*fig: distance*) distance
éloigner [elwaɲe] *vt* (*objet*): **~ qch (de)** to move *ou* take sth away (from); (*personne*): **~ qn (de)** to take sb away *ou* remove sb (from); (*échéance*) to put off, postpone; (*soupçons, danger*) to ward off; **s'éloigner (de)** *vi* (*personne*) to go away (from); (*véhicule*) to move away (from); (*affectivement*) to become estranged (from)
élongation [elɔ̃gasjɔ̃] *nf* strained muscle
éloquence [elɔkɑ̃s] *nf* eloquence
éloquent, e [elɔkɑ̃, -ɑ̃t] *adj* eloquent
élu, e [ely] *pp de* **élire** ▷ *nm/f* (*Pol*) elected representative
élucider [elyside] *vt* to elucidate
élucubrations [elykybrasjɔ̃] *nfpl* wild imaginings
éluder [elyde] *vt* to evade
élus *etc* [ely] *vb voir* **élire**
élusif, -ive [elyzif, -iv] *adj* elusive
Élysée [elize] *nm*: **(le palais de) l'~** the Élysée palace; *see note*; **les Champs ~s** the Champs Élysées

● **L'ÉLYSÉE**
●
● The *palais de l'Élysée*, situated in the heart of
● Paris just off the Champs Élysées, is the
● official residence of the French President.
● Built in the eighteenth century, it has
● performed its present function since 1876.
● A shorter form of its name, "l'Élysée" is
● frequently used to refer to the presidency
● itself.

émacié, e [emasje] *adj* emaciated
émail, -aux [emaj, -o] *nm* enamel
e-mail [imεl] *nm* email; **envoyer qch par ~** to email sth
émaillé, e [emaje] *adj* enamelled; (*fig*): **~ de** dotted with
émailler [emaje] *vt* to enamel
émanation [emanasjɔ̃] *nf* emanation
émancipation [emɑ̃sipasjɔ̃] *nf* emancipation

émancipé, e [emɑ̃sipe] *adj* emancipated
émanciper [emɑ̃sipe] *vt* to emancipate;
s'émanciper (*fig*) to become emancipated *ou*
liberated
émaner [emane]: **~ de** *vt* to emanate from;
(*Admin*) to proceed from
émarger [emaʀʒe] *vt* to sign; **~ de 1000 euros
à un budget** to receive 1000 euros out of a
budget
émasculer [emaskyle] *vt* to emasculate
emballage [ɑ̃balaʒ] *nm* wrapping; packing;
(*papier*) wrapping; (*carton*) packaging
emballer [ɑ̃bale] *vt* to wrap (up); (*dans un carton*)
to pack (up); (*fig: fam*) to thrill (to bits);
s'emballer *vi* (*moteur*) to race; (*cheval*) to bolt;
(*fig: personne*) to get carried away
emballeur, -euse [ɑ̃balœʀ, -øz] *nm/f* packer
embarcadère [ɑ̃baʀkadɛʀ] *nm* landing stage
(*Brit*), pier
embarcation [ɑ̃baʀkasjɔ̃] *nf* (small) boat,
(small) craft *inv*
embardée [ɑ̃baʀde] *nf* swerve; **faire une ~** to
swerve
embargo [ɑ̃baʀgo] *nm* embargo; **mettre l'~ sur**
to put an embargo on, embargo
embarquement [ɑ̃baʀkəmɑ̃] *nm* embarkation;
loading; boarding
embarquer [ɑ̃baʀke] *vt* (*personne*) to embark;
(*marchandise*) to load; (*fam*) to cart off; (*: arrêter*) to
nick ▷ *vi* (*passager*) to board; (*Navig*) to ship
water; **s'embarquer** *vi* to board; **s'~ dans**
(*affaire, aventure*) to embark upon
embarras [ɑ̃baʀa] *nm* (*obstacle*) hindrance;
(*confusion*) embarrassment; (*ennuis*): **être dans
l'~** to be in a predicament *ou* an awkward
position; (*gêne financière*) to be in difficulties; **~
gastrique** stomach upset
embarrassant, e [ɑ̃baʀasɑ̃, -ɑ̃t] *adj*
cumbersome; embarrassing; awkward
embarrassé, e [ɑ̃baʀase] *adj* (*encombré*)
encumbered; (*gêné*) embarrassed; (*explications
etc*) awkward
embarrasser [ɑ̃baʀase] *vt* (*encombrer*) to clutter
(up); (*gêner*) to hinder, hamper; (*fig*) to cause
embarrassment to; to put in an awkward
position; **s'embarrasser de** *vi* to burden o.s.
with
embauche [ɑ̃boʃ] *nf* hiring; **bureau d'~** labour
office
embaucher [ɑ̃boʃe] *vt* to take on, hire;
s'embaucher comme *vi* to get (o.s.) a job as
embauchoir [ɑ̃boʃwaʀ] *nm* shoetree
embaumer [ɑ̃bome] *vt* to embalm; (*parfumer*) to
fill with its fragrance; **~ la lavande** to be
fragrant with (the scent of) lavender
embellie [ɑ̃beli] *nf* bright spell, brighter
period
embellir [ɑ̃beliʀ] *vt* to make more attractive;
(*une histoire*) to embellish ▷ *vi* to grow lovelier *ou*
more attractive
embellissement [ɑ̃belismɑ̃] *nm*
embellishment

embêtant, e [ɑ̃bɛtɑ̃, -ɑ̃t] *adj* annoying
embêtement [ɑ̃bɛtmɑ̃] *nm* problem, difficulty;
embêtements *nmpl* trouble *sg*
embêter [ɑ̃bɛte] *vt* to bother; **s'embêter** *vi*
(*s'ennuyer*) to be bored; **ça m'embête** it bothers
me; **il ne s'embête pas!** (*ironique*) he does all
right for himself!
emblée [ɑ̃ble]: **d'~** *adv* straightaway
emblème [ɑ̃blɛm] *nm* emblem
embobiner [ɑ̃bɔbine] *vt* (*enjôler*): **~ qn** to get
round sb
emboîtable [ɑ̃bwatabl(ə)] *adj* interlocking
emboîter [ɑ̃bwate] *vt* to fit together;
s'emboîter dans to fit into; **s'~ (l'un dans
l'autre)** to fit together; **~ le pas à qn** to follow
in sb's footsteps
embolie [ɑ̃bɔli] *nf* embolism
embonpoint [ɑ̃bɔ̃pwɛ̃] *nm* stoutness (*Brit*),
corpulence; **prendre de l'~** to grow stout (*Brit*)
ou corpulent
embouché, e [ɑ̃buʃe] *adj*: **mal ~** foul-mouthed
embouchure [ɑ̃buʃyʀ] *nf* (*Géo*) mouth; (*Mus*)
mouthpiece
embourber [ɑ̃buʀbe]: **s'embourber** *vi* to get
stuck in the mud; (*fig*): **s'~ dans** to sink into
embourgeoiser [ɑ̃buʀʒwaze]: **s'embourgeoiser**
vi to adopt a middle-class outlook
embout [ɑ̃bu] *nm* (*de canne*) tip; (*de tuyau*) nozzle
embouteillage [ɑ̃butejaʒ] *nm* traffic jam,
(traffic) holdup (*Brit*)
embouteiller [ɑ̃buteje] *vt* (*véhicules etc*) to block
emboutir [ɑ̃butiʀ] *vt* (*Tech*) to stamp; (*heurter*) to
crash into, ram
embranchement [ɑ̃bʀɑ̃ʃmɑ̃] *nm* (*routier*)
junction; (*classification*) branch
embrancher [ɑ̃bʀɑ̃ʃe] *vt* (*tuyaux*) to join; **~ qch
sur** to join sth to
embraser [ɑ̃bʀaze]: **s'embraser** *vi* to flare up
embrassade [ɑ̃bʀasad] *nf* (*gén pl*) hugging and
kissing *no pl*
embrasse [ɑ̃bʀas] *nf* (*de rideau*) tie-back, loop
embrasser [ɑ̃bʀase] *vt* to kiss; (*sujet, période*) to
embrace, encompass; (*carrière*) to embark on;
(*métier*) to go in for, take up; **~ du regard** to
take in (*with eyes*); **s'embrasser** *vi* to kiss (each
other)
embrasure [ɑ̃bʀazyʀ] *nf*: **dans l'~ de la porte**
in the door(way)
embrayage [ɑ̃bʀɛjaʒ] *nm* clutch
embrayer [ɑ̃bʀeje] *vi* (*Auto*) to let in the clutch
▷ *vt* (*fig: affaire*) to set in motion; **~ sur qch** to
begin on sth
embrigader [ɑ̃bʀigade] *vt* to recruit
embrocher [ɑ̃bʀɔʃe] *vt* to (put on a) spit (*ou*
skewer)
embrouillamini [ɑ̃bʀujamini] *nm* (*fam*) muddle
embrouillé, e [ɑ̃bʀuje] *adj* (*affaire*) confused,
muddled
embrouiller [ɑ̃bʀuje] *vt* (*fils*) to tangle (up);
(*fiches, idées, personne*) to muddle up;
s'embrouiller *vi* to get in a muddle
embroussaillé, e [ɑ̃bʀusaje] *adj* overgrown,

scrubby; (*cheveux*) bushy, shaggy

embruns [ɑ̃bʀœ̃] *nmpl* sea spray *sg*

embryologie [ɑ̃bʀijɔlɔʒi] *nf* embryology

embryon [ɑ̃bʀijɔ̃] *nm* embryo

embryonnaire [ɑ̃bʀijɔnɛʀ] *adj* embryonic

embûches [ɑ̃byʃ] *nfpl* pitfalls, traps

embué, e [ɑ̃bɥe] *adj* misted up; **yeux ~s de larmes** eyes misty with tears

embuscade [ɑ̃byskad] *nf* ambush; **tendre une ~ à** to lay an ambush for

embusqué, e [ɑ̃byske] *adj* in ambush ▷ *nm* (*péj*) shirker, skiver (*Brit*)

embusquer [ɑ̃byske]: **s'embusquer** *vi* to take up position (for an ambush)

éméché, e [emeʃe] *adj* tipsy, merry

émeraude [ɛmʀod] *nf* emerald ▷ *adj inv* emerald-green

émergence [emɛʀʒɑ̃s] *nf* (*fig*) emergence

émerger [emɛʀʒe] *vi* to emerge; (*faire saillie, aussi fig*) to stand out

émeri [ɛmʀi] *nm*: **toile** *ou* **papier ~** emery paper

émérite [emeʀit] *adj* highly skilled

émerveillement [emɛʀvɛjmɑ̃] *nm* wonderment

émerveiller [emɛʀveje] *vt* to fill with wonder; **s'émerveiller de** *vi* to marvel at

émet *etc* [emɛ] *vb voir* **émettre**

émétique [emetik] *nm* emetic

émetteur, -trice [emɛtœʀ, -tʀis] *adj* transmitting; **(poste) ~** transmitter

émetteur-récepteur [emetœʀʀesɛptœʀ] (*pl* **émetteurs-récepteurs**) *nm* transceiver

émettre [emɛtʀ(ə)] *vt* (*son, lumière*) to give out, emit; (*message etc: Radio*) to transmit; (*billet, timbre, emprunt, chèque*) to issue; (*hypothèse, avis*) to voice, put forward; (*vœu*) to express ▷ *vi*: **~ sur ondes courtes** to broadcast on short wave

émeus *etc* [emø] *vb voir* **émouvoir**

émeute [emøt] *nf* riot

émeutier, -ière [emøtje, -jɛʀ] *nm/f* rioter

émeuve *etc* [emœv] *vb voir* **émouvoir**

émietter [emjete] *vt* (*pain, terre*) to crumble; (*fig*) to split up, disperse; **s'émietter** *vi* (*pain, terre*) to crumble

émigrant, e [emigʀɑ̃, -ɑ̃t] *nm/f* emigrant

émigration [emigʀasjɔ̃] *nf* emigration

émigré, e [emigʀe] *nm/f* expatriate

émigrer [emigʀe] *vi* to emigrate

émincer [emɛ̃se] *vt* (*Culin*) to slice thinly

éminemment [eminamɑ̃] *adv* eminently

éminence [eminɑ̃s] *nf* distinction; (*colline*) knoll, hill; **Son É~** His Eminence; **~ grise** éminence grise

éminent, e [eminɑ̃, -ɑ̃t] *adj* distinguished

émir [emiʀ] *nm* emir

émirat [emiʀa] *nm* emirate; **les É~s arabes unis (EAU)** the United Arab Emirates (UAE)

émis, e [emi, -iz] *pp de* **émettre**

émissaire [emisɛʀ] *nm* emissary

émission [emisjɔ̃] *nf* (*voir émettre*) emission; transmission; issue; (*Radio, TV*) programme, broadcast

émit *etc* [emi] *vb voir* **émettre**

emmagasinage [ɑ̃magazinaʒ] *nm* storage; storing away

emmagasiner [ɑ̃magazine] *vt* to (put into) store; (*fig*) to store up

emmailloter [ɑ̃majɔte] *vt* to wrap up

emmanchure [ɑ̃mɑ̃ʃyʀ] *nf* armhole

emmêlement [ɑ̃mɛlmɑ̃] *nm* (*état*) tangle

emmêler [ɑ̃mele] *vt* to tangle (up); (*fig*) to muddle up; **s'emmêler** *vi* to get into a tangle

emménagement [ɑ̃menaʒmɑ̃] *nm* settling in

emménager [ɑ̃menaʒe] *vi* to move in; **~ dans** to move into

emmener [ɑ̃mne] *vt* to take (with one); (*comme otage, capture*) to take away; **~ qn au concert** to take sb to a concert

emmental, emmenthal [emɛ̃tal] *nm* (*fromage*) Emmenthal

emmerder [ɑ̃mɛʀde] (*fam!*) *vt* to bug, bother; **s'emmerder** *vi* (*s'ennuyer*) to be bored stiff; **je t'emmerde!** to hell with you!

emmitoufler [ɑ̃mitufle] *vt* to wrap up (warmly); **s'emmitoufler** to wrap (o.s.) up (warmly)

emmurer [ɑ̃myʀe] *vt* to wall up, immure

émoi [emwa] *nm* (*agitation, effervescence*) commotion; (*trouble*) agitation; **en ~** (*sens*) excited, stirred

émollient, e [emɔljɑ̃, -ɑ̃t] *adj* (*Méd*) emollient

émoluments [emɔlymɑ̃] *nmpl* remuneration *sg*, fee *sg*

émonder [emɔ̃de] *vt* (*arbre etc*) to prune; (*amande etc*) to blanch

émoticone [emɔticon] *nm* (*Inform*) smiley

émotif, -ive [emɔtif, -iv] *adj* emotional

émotion [emɔsjɔ̃] *nf* emotion; **avoir des ~s** (*fig*) to get a fright; **donner des ~s à** to give a fright to; **sans ~** without emotion, coldly

émotionnant, e [emɔsjɔnɑ̃, -ɑ̃t] *adj* upsetting

émotionnel, le [emɔsjɔnɛl] *adj* emotional

émotionner [emɔsjɔne] *vt* to upset

émoulu, e [emuly] *adj*: **frais ~ de** fresh from, just out of

émoussé, e [emuse] *adj* blunt

émousser [emuse] *vt* to blunt; (*fig*) to dull

émoustiller [emustije] *vt* to titillate, arouse

émouvant, e [emuvɑ̃, -ɑ̃t] *adj* moving

émouvoir [emuvwaʀ] *vt* (*troubler*) to stir, affect; (*toucher, attendrir*) to move; (*indigner*) to rouse; (*effrayer*) to disturb, worry; **s'émouvoir** *vi* to be affected; to be moved; to be roused; to be disturbed *ou* worried

empailler [ɑ̃paje] *vt* to stuff

empailleur, -euse [ɑ̃pajœʀ, -øz] *nm/f* (*d'animaux*) taxidermist

empaler [ɑ̃pale] *vt* to impale

empaquetage [ɑ̃paktaʒ] *nm* packing, packaging

empaqueter [ɑ̃pakte] *vt* to pack up

emparer [ɑ̃paʀe]: **s'emparer de** *vt* (*objet*) to seize, grab; (*comme otage, Mil*) to seize; (*peur etc*) to take hold of

empâter [ɑ̃pate]: **s'empâter** vi to thicken out

empattement [ɑ̃patmɑ̃] nm (Auto) wheelbase; (Typo) serif

empêché, e [ɑ̃peʃe] adj detained

empêchement [ɑ̃pɛʃmɑ̃] nm (unexpected) obstacle, hitch

empêcher [ɑ̃peʃe] vt to prevent; **~ qn de faire** to prevent ou stop sb (from) doing; **~ que qch (n')arrive/qn (ne) fasse** to prevent sth from happening/sb from doing; **il n'empêche que** nevertheless, be that as it may; **il n'a pas pu s'~ de rire** he couldn't help laughing

empêcheur [ɑ̃peʃœʀ] nm: **~ de danser en rond** spoilsport, killjoy (Brit)

empeigne [ɑ̃pɛɲ] nf upper (of shoe)

empennage [ɑ̃pɛnaʒ] nm (Aviat) tailplane

empereur [ɑ̃pʀœʀ] nm emperor

empesé, e [ɑ̃pəze] adj (fig) stiff, starchy

empeser [ɑ̃pəze] vt to starch

empester [ɑ̃pɛste] vt (lieu) to stink out ▷ vi to stink, reek; **~ le tabac/le vin** to stink ou reek of tobacco/wine

empêtrer [ɑ̃petʀe] vt: **s'empêtrer dans** (fils etc, aussi fig) to get tangled up in

emphase [ɑ̃faz] nf pomposity, bombast; **avec ~** pompously

emphatique [ɑ̃fatik] adj emphatic

empiècement [ɑ̃pjɛsmɑ̃] nm (Couture) yoke

empierrer [ɑ̃pjere] vt (route) to metal

empiéter [ɑ̃pjete]: **~ sur** vt to encroach upon

empiffrer [ɑ̃pifʀe]: **s'empiffrer** vi (péj) to stuff o.s.

empiler [ɑ̃pile] vt to pile (up), stack (up); **s'empiler** vi to pile up

empire [ɑ̃piʀ] nm empire; (fig) influence; **style E~** Empire style; **sous l'~ de** in the grip of

empirer [ɑ̃piʀe] vi to worsen, deteriorate

empirique [ɑ̃piʀik] adj empirical

empirisme [ɑ̃piʀism(ə)] nm empiricism

emplacement [ɑ̃plasmɑ̃] nm site; **sur l'~ de** on the site of

emplâtre [ɑ̃plɑtʀ(ə)] nm plaster; (fam) twit

emplette [ɑ̃plɛt] nf: **faire l'~ de** to purchase; **emplettes** shopping sg; **faire des ~s** to go shopping

emplir [ɑ̃pliʀ] vt to fill; **s'emplir (de)** vi to fill (with)

emploi [ɑ̃plwa] nm use; (Comm, Écon): **l'~** employment; (poste) job, situation; **d'~ facile** easy to use; **le plein ~** full employment; **~ du temps** timetable, schedule

emploie etc [ɑ̃plwa] vb voir **employer**

employé, e [ɑ̃plwaje] nm/f employee; **~ de bureau/banque** office/bank employee ou clerk; **~ de maison** domestic (servant)

employer [ɑ̃plwaje] vt (outil, moyen, méthode, mot) to use; (ouvrier, main-d'œuvre) to employ; **s'~ à qch/à faire** to apply ou devote o.s. to sth/to doing

employeur, -euse [ɑ̃plwajœʀ, -øz] nm/f employer

empocher [ɑ̃pɔʃe] vt to pocket

empoignade [ɑ̃pwaɲad] nf row, set-to

empoigne [ɑ̃pwaɲ] nf: **foire d'~** free-for-all

empoigner [ɑ̃pwaɲe] vt to grab; **s'empoigner** vi (fig) to have a row ou set-to

empois [ɑ̃pwa] nm starch

empoisonnement [ɑ̃pwazɔnmɑ̃] nm poisoning; (fam: ennui) annoyance, irritation

empoisonner [ɑ̃pwazɔne] vt to poison; (empester: air, pièce) to stink out; (fam): **~ qn** to drive sb mad; **s'empoisonner** vi to poison o.s.; **~ l'atmosphère** (aussi fig) to poison the atmosphere; (aussi: **il nous empoisonne l'existence**) he's the bane of our life

empoissonner [ɑ̃pwasɔne] vt (étang, rivière) to stock with fish

emporté, e [ɑ̃pɔʀte] adj (personne, caractère) fiery

emportement [ɑ̃pɔʀtəmɑ̃] nm fit of rage, anger no pl

emporte-pièce [ɑ̃pɔʀtəpjɛs] nm inv (Tech) punch; **à l'~** adj (fig) incisive

emporter [ɑ̃pɔʀte] vt to take (with one); (en dérobant ou enlevant, emmener: blessés, voyageurs) to take away; (entraîner) to carry away ou along; (arracher) to tear off; (rivière, vent) to carry away; (Mil: position) to take; (avantage, approbation) to win; **s'emporter** vi (de colère) to fly into a rage, lose one's temper; **la maladie qui l'a emporté** the illness which caused his death; **l'~** to gain victory; **l'~ (sur)** to get the upper hand (of); (méthode etc) to prevail (over); **boissons à ~** take-away drinks

empoté, e [ɑ̃pɔte] adj (maladroit) clumsy

empourpré, e [ɑ̃puʀpʀe] adj crimson

empreint, e [ɑ̃pʀɛ̃, -ɛ̃t] adj: **~ de** marked with; tinged with ▷ nf (de pied, main) print; (fig) stamp, mark; **~e (digitale)** fingerprint; **~e écologique** carbon footprint

empressé, e [ɑ̃pʀese] adj attentive; (péj) overanxious to please, overattentive

empressement [ɑ̃pʀɛsmɑ̃] nm eagerness

empresser [ɑ̃pʀese]: **s'empresser** vi: **s'~ auprès de qn** to surround sb with attentions; **s'~ de faire** to hasten to do

emprise [ɑ̃pʀiz] nf hold, ascendancy; **sous l'~ de** under the influence of

emprisonnement [ɑ̃pʀizɔnmɑ̃] nm imprisonment

emprisonner [ɑ̃pʀizɔne] vt to imprison, jail

emprunt [ɑ̃pʀɛ̃] nm borrowing no pl, loan (from debtor's point of view); (Ling etc) borrowing; **nom d'~** assumed name; **~ d'État** government ou state loan; **~ public à 5%** 5% public loan

emprunté, e [ɑ̃pʀɛ̃te] adj (fig) ill-at-ease, awkward

emprunter [ɑ̃pʀɛ̃te] vt to borrow; (itinéraire) to take, follow; (style, manière) to adopt, assume

emprunteur, -euse [ɑ̃pʀɛ̃tœʀ, -øz] nm/f borrower

empuantir [ɑ̃pɥɑ̃tiʀ] vt to stink out

EMT sigle f (= éducation manuelle et technique) handwork as a school subject

ému, e [emy] *pp de* **émouvoir** ▷ *adj* excited; touched; moved

émulation [emylɑsjɔ̃] *nf* emulation

émule [emyl] *nm/f* imitator

émulsion [emylsjɔ̃] *nf* emulsion; (*cosmétique*) (water-based) lotion

émut *etc* [emy] *vb voir* **émouvoir**

EN *sigle f* = **Éducation nationale**; *voir* **éducation**

○ MOT-CLÉ

en [ɑ̃] *prép* **1** (*endroit, pays*) in; (*direction*) to; **habiter en France/ville** to live in France/town; **aller en France/ville** to go to France/town **2** (*moment, temps*) in; **en été/juin** in summer/June; **en 3 jours/20 ans** in 3 days/20 years **3** (*moyen*) by; **en avion/taxi** by plane/taxi **4** (*composition*) made of; **c'est en verre/coton/laine** it's (made of) glass/cotton/wool; **en métal/plastique** made of metal/plastic; **un collier en argent** a silver necklace; **en deux volumes/une pièce** in two volumes/one piece **5** (*description, état*): **une femme (habillée) en rouge** a woman (dressed) in red; **peindre qch en rouge** to paint sth red; **en T/étoile** T-/star-shaped; **en chemise/chaussettes** in one's shirt sleeves/socks; **en soldat** as a soldier; **en civil** in civilian clothes; **cassé en plusieurs morceaux** broken into several pieces; **en réparation** being repaired, under repair; **en vacances** on holiday; **en bonne santé** healthy, in good health; **en deuil** in mourning; **le même en plus grand** the same but *ou* only bigger **6** (*avec gérondif*) while; on; **en dormant** while sleeping, as one sleeps; **en sortant** on going out, as he *etc* went out; **sortir en courant** to run out; **en apprenant la nouvelle, il s'est évanoui** he fainted at the news *ou* when he heard the news **7** (*matière*): **fort en math** good at maths; **expert en** expert in **8** (*conformité*): **en tant que** as; **en bon politicien, il ...** good politician that he is, he ..., like a good *ou* true politician, he ...; **je te parle en ami** I'm talking to you as a friend ▷ *pron* **1** (*indéfini*): **j'en ai/veux** I have/want some; **en as-tu?** have you got any?; **il n'y en a pas** there isn't *ou* aren't any; **je n'en veux pas** I don't want any; **j'en ai deux** I've got two; **combien y en a-t-il?** how many (of them) are there?; **j'en ai assez** I've got enough (of it *ou* them); (*j'en ai marre*) I've had enough; **où en étais-je?** where was I? **2** (*provenance*) from there; **j'en viens** I've come from there **3** (*cause*): **il en est malade/perd le sommeil** he is ill/can't sleep because of it **4** (*de la part de*): **elle en est aimée** she is loved by him (*ou* them *etc*) **5** (*complément de nom, d'adjectif, de verbe*): **j'en connais les dangers** I know its *ou* the dangers;

j'en suis fier/ai besoin I am proud of it/need it; **il en est ainsi** *ou* **de même pour moi** it's the same for me, same here

ENA [ena] *sigle f* (= *École nationale d'administration*) *grande école for training civil servants*

énarque [enaʀk(ə)] *nm/f* former ENA student

encablure [ɑ̃kablyʀ] *nf* (*Navig*) cable's length

encadrement [ɑ̃kadʀəmɑ̃] *nm* framing; training; (*de porte*) frame; ~ **du crédit** credit restrictions

encadrer [ɑ̃kadʀe] *vt* (*tableau, image*) to frame; (*fig: entourer*) to surround; (*personnel, soldats etc*) to train; (*Comm: crédit*) to restrict

encadreur [ɑ̃kadʀœʀ] *nm* (picture) framer

encaisse [ɑ̃kɛs] *nf* cash in hand; ~ **or/métallique** gold/gold and silver reserves

encaissé, e [ɑ̃kese] *adj* (*vallée*) steep-sided; (*rivière*) with steep banks

encaisser [ɑ̃kese] *vt* (*chèque*) to cash; (*argent*) to collect; (*fig: coup, défaite*) to take

encaisseur [ɑ̃kesœʀ] *nm* collector (*of debts etc*)

encan [ɑ̃kɑ̃] : **à l'~** *adv* by auction

encanailler [ɑ̃kanaje]: **s'encanailler** *vi* to become vulgar *ou* common; to mix with the riff-raff

encart [ɑ̃kaʀ] *nm* insert; ~ **publicitaire** publicity insert

encarter [ɑ̃kaʀte] *vt* to insert

en-cas [ɑ̃kɑ] *nm inv* snack

encastrable [ɑ̃kastʀabl(ə)] *adj* (*four, élément*) that can be built in

encastré, e [ɑ̃kastʀe] *adj* (*four, baignoire*) built-in

encastrer [ɑ̃kastʀe] *vt*: ~ **qch dans** (*mur*) to embed sth in(to); (*boîtier*) to fit sth into; **s'encastrer dans** *vi* to fit into; (*heurter*) to crash into

encaustique [ɑ̃kɔstik] *nf* polish, wax

encaustiquer [ɑ̃kɔstike] *vt* to polish, wax

enceinte [ɑ̃sɛ̃t] *adj f*: ~ **(de six mois)** (six months) pregnant ▷ *nf* (*mur*) wall; (*espace*) enclosure; ~ **(acoustique)** speaker

encens [ɑ̃sɑ̃] *nm* incense

encenser [ɑ̃sɑ̃se] *vt* to (in)cense; (*fig*) to praise to the skies

encensoir [ɑ̃sɑ̃swaʀ] *nm* thurible (*Brit*), censer

encéphalogramme [ɑ̃sefalɔgʀam] *nm* encephalogram

encercler [ɑ̃sɛʀkle] *vt* to surround

enchaîné [ɑ̃ʃene] *nm* (*Ciné*) link shot

enchaînement [ɑ̃ʃenmɑ̃] *nm* (*fig*) linking

enchaîner [ɑ̃ʃene] *vt* to chain up; (*mouvements, séquences*) to link (together) ▷ *vi* to carry on

enchanté, e [ɑ̃ʃɑ̃te] *adj* (*ravi*) delighted; (*ensorcelé*) enchanted; ~ **(de faire votre connaissance)** pleased to meet you, how do you do?

enchantement [ɑ̃ʃɑ̃tmɑ̃] *nm* delight; (*magie*) enchantment; **comme par ~** as if by magic

enchanter [ɑ̃ʃɑ̃te] *vt* to delight

enchanteur, -teresse [ɑ̃ʃɑ̃tœʀ, -tʀɛs] *adj* enchanting

enchâsser [ɑ̃ʃase] vt: ~ **qch (dans)** to set sth (in)
enchère [ɑ̃ʃɛʀ] nf bid; **faire une ~** to (make a) bid; **mettre/vendre aux ~s** to put up for (sale by)/sell by auction; **les ~s montent** the bids are rising; **faire monter les ~s** (fig) to raise the bidding
enchérir [ɑ̃ʃeʀiʀ] vi: ~ **sur qn** (aux enchères, aussi fig) to outbid sb
enchérisseur, -euse [ɑ̃ʃeʀisœʀ, -øz] nm/f bidder
enchevêtrement [ɑ̃ʃvɛtʀəmɑ̃] nm tangle
enchevêtrer [ɑ̃ʃvetʀe] vt to tangle (up)
enclave [ɑ̃klav] nf enclave
enclaver [ɑ̃klave] vt to enclose, hem in
enclencher [ɑ̃klɑ̃ʃe] vt (mécanisme) to engage; (fig: affaire) to set in motion; **s'enclencher** vi to engage
enclin, e [ɑ̃klɛ̃, -in] adj: ~ **à qch/à faire** inclined ou prone to sth/to do
enclore [ɑ̃klɔʀ] vt to enclose
enclos [ɑ̃klo] nm enclosure; (clôture) fence
enclume [ɑ̃klym] nf anvil
encoche [ɑ̃kɔʃ] nf notch
encoder [ɑ̃kɔde] vt to encode
encodeur [ɑ̃kɔdœʀ] nm encoder
encoignure [ɑ̃kɔɲyʀ] nf corner
encoller [ɑ̃kɔle] vt to paste
encolure [ɑ̃kɔlyʀ] nf (tour de cou) collar size; (col, cou) neck
encombrant, e [ɑ̃kɔ̃bʀɑ̃, -ɑ̃t] adj cumbersome, bulky
encombre [ɑ̃kɔ̃bʀ(ə)]: **sans ~** adv without mishap ou incident
encombré, e [ɑ̃kɔ̃bʀe] adj (pièce, passage) cluttered; (lignes téléphoniques) engaged; (marché) saturated
encombrement [ɑ̃kɔ̃bʀəmɑ̃] nm (d'un lieu) cluttering (up); (d'un objet: dimensions) bulk
encombrer [ɑ̃kɔ̃bʀe] vt to clutter (up); (gêner) to hamper; **s'encombrer de** vi (bagages etc) to load ou burden o.s. with; ~ **le passage** to block ou obstruct the way
encontre [ɑ̃kɔ̃tʀ(ə)]: **à l'~ de** prép against, counter to
encorbellement [ɑ̃kɔʀbɛlmɑ̃] nm: **fenêtre en ~** oriel window
encorder [ɑ̃kɔʀde] vt: **s'encorder** (Alpinisme) to rope up

 MOT-CLÉ

encore [ɑ̃kɔʀ] adv **1** (continuation) still; **il y travaille encore** he's still working on it; **pas encore** not yet
2 (de nouveau) again; **j'irai encore demain** I'll go again tomorrow; **encore une fois** (once) again; **encore un effort** one last effort; **encore deux jours** two more days
3 (intensif) even, still; **encore plus fort/mieux** even louder/better, louder/better still; **hier encore** even yesterday; **non seulement ..., mais encore ...** not only ..., but also ...; **encore!** (insatisfaction) not again!; **quoi encore?**

what now?
4 (restriction) even so ou then, only; **encore pourrais-je le faire si ...** even so, I might be able to do it if ...; **si encore** if only; **encore que** conj although

encourageant, e [ɑ̃kuʀaʒɑ̃, -ɑ̃t] adj encouraging
encouragement [ɑ̃kuʀaʒmɑ̃] nm encouragement; (récompense) incentive
encourager [ɑ̃kuʀaʒe] vt to encourage; ~ **qn à faire qch** to encourage sb to do sth
encourir [ɑ̃kuʀiʀ] vt to incur
encrasser [ɑ̃kʀase] vt to foul up; (Auto etc) to soot up
encre [ɑ̃kʀ(ə)] nf ink; ~ **de Chine** Indian ink; ~ **indélébile** indelible ink; ~ **sympathique** invisible ink
encrer [ɑ̃kʀe] vt to ink
encreur [ɑ̃kʀœʀ] adj m: **rouleau ~** inking roller
encrier [ɑ̃kʀije] nm inkwell
encroûter [ɑ̃kʀute]: **s'encroûter** vi (fig) to get into a rut, get set in one's ways
encyclique [ɑ̃siklik] nf encyclical
encyclopédie [ɑ̃siklɔpedi] nf encyclopaedia (Brit), encyclopedia (US)
encyclopédique [ɑ̃siklɔpedik] adj encyclopaedic (Brit), encyclopedic (US)
endémique [ɑ̃demik] adj endemic
endetté, e [ɑ̃dete] adj in debt; (fig): **très ~ envers qn** deeply indebted to sb
endettement [ɑ̃dɛtmɑ̃] nm debts pl
endetter [ɑ̃dete] vt, **s'endetter** vi to get into debt
endeuiller [ɑ̃dœje] vt to plunge into mourning; **manifestation endeuillée par** event over which a tragic shadow was cast by
endiablé, e [ɑ̃djable] adj furious; (enfant) boisterous
endiguer [ɑ̃dige] vt to dyke (up); (fig) to check, hold back
endimanché, e [ɑ̃dimɑ̃ʃe] adj in one's Sunday best
endimancher [ɑ̃dimɑ̃ʃe] vt: **s'endimancher** to put on one's Sunday best; **avoir l'air endimanché** to be all done up to the nines (fam)
endive [ɑ̃div] nf chicory no pl
endocrine [ɑ̃dɔkʀin] adj f: **glande ~** endocrine (gland)
endoctrinement [ɑ̃dɔktʀinmɑ̃] nm indoctrination
endoctriner [ɑ̃dɔktʀine] vt to indoctrinate
endolori, e [ɑ̃dɔlɔʀi] adj painful
endommager [ɑ̃dɔmaʒe] vt to damage
endormant, e [ɑ̃dɔʀmɑ̃, -ɑ̃t] adj dull, boring
endormi, e [ɑ̃dɔʀmi] pp de endormir ▷ adj (personne) asleep; (fig: indolent, lent) sluggish; (engourdi: main, pied) numb
endormir [ɑ̃dɔʀmiʀ] vt to put to sleep; (chaleur etc) to send to sleep; (Méd: dent, nerf) to anaesthetize; (fig: soupçons) to allay; **s'endormir**

vi to fall asleep, go to sleep

endoscope [ɑ̃dɔskɔp] *nm* (*Méd*) endoscope

endoscopie [ɑ̃dɔskɔpi] *nf* endoscopy

endosser [ɑ̃dose] *vt* (*responsabilité*) to take, shoulder; (*chèque*) to endorse; (*uniforme, tenue*) to put on, don

endroit [ɑ̃dʀwa] *nm* place; (*localité*): **les gens de l'~** the local people; (*opposé à l'envers*) right side; **à cet ~** in this place; **à l'~** right side out; the right way up; (*vêtement*) the right way out; **à l'~ de** *prép* regarding, with regard to; **par ~s** in places

enduire [ɑ̃dɥiʀ] *vt* to coat; **~ qch de** to coat sth with

enduit, e [ɑ̃dɥi, -it] *pp de* **enduire** ▷ *nm* coating

endurance [ɑ̃dyʀɑ̃s] *nf* endurance

endurant, e [ɑ̃dyʀɑ̃, -ɑ̃t] *adj* tough, hardy

endurcir [ɑ̃dyʀsiʀ] *vt* (*physiquement*) to toughen; (*moralement*) to harden; **s'endurcir** *vi* to become tougher; to become hardened

endurer [ɑ̃dyʀe] *vt* to endure, bear

énergétique [enɛʀʒetik] *adj* (*ressources etc*) energy *cpd*; (*aliment*) energizing

énergie [enɛʀʒi] *nf* (*Physique*) energy; (*Tech*) power; (*fig: physique*) energy; (*: morale*) vigour, spirit; **~ éolienne/solaire** wind/solar power

énergique [enɛʀʒik] *adj* energetic; vigorous; (*mesures*) drastic, stringent

énergiquement [enɛʀʒikmɑ̃] *adv* energetically; drastically

énergisant, e [enɛʀʒizɑ̃, -ɑ̃t] *adj* energizing

énergumène [enɛʀgymɛn] *nm* rowdy character *ou* customer

énervant, e [enɛʀvɑ̃, -ɑ̃t] *adj* irritating

énervé, e [enɛʀve] *adj* nervy, on edge; (*agacé*) irritated

énervement [enɛʀvəmɑ̃] *nm* nerviness; irritation

énerver [enɛʀve] *vt* to irritate, annoy; **s'énerver** *vi* to get excited, get worked up

enfance [ɑ̃fɑ̃s] *nf* (*âge*) childhood; (*fig*) infancy; (*enfants*) children *pl*; **c'est l'~ de l'art** it's child's play; **petite ~** infancy; **souvenir/ami d'~** childhood memory/friend; **retomber en ~** to lapse into one's second childhood

enfant [ɑ̃fɑ̃] *nm/f* child; **~ adoptif/naturel** adopted/natural child; **bon ~** *adj* good-natured, easy-going; **~ de chœur** *nm* (*Rel*) altar boy; **~ prodige** child prodigy; **~ unique** only child

enfanter [ɑ̃fɑ̃te] *vi* to give birth ▷ *vt* to give birth to

enfantillage [ɑ̃fɑ̃tijaʒ] *nm* (*péj*) childish behaviour *no pl*

enfantin, e [ɑ̃fɑ̃tɛ̃, -in] *adj* childlike; (*péj*) childish; (*langage*) child *cpd*

enfer [ɑ̃fɛʀ] *nm* hell; **allure/bruit d'~** horrendous speed/noise

enfermer [ɑ̃fɛʀme] *vt* to shut up; (*à clef, interner*) to lock up; **s'enfermer** *vi* to shut o.s. away; **s'~ à clé** to lock o.s. in; **s'~ dans la solitude/le mutisme** to retreat into solitude/silence

enferrer [ɑ̃feʀe]: **s'enferrer** *vi*: **s'~ dans** to tangle o.s. up in

enfiévré, e [ɑ̃fjevʀe] *adj* (*fig*) feverish

enfilade [ɑ̃filad] *nf*: **une ~ de** a series *ou* line of; **prendre des rues en ~** to cross directly from one street into the next

enfiler [ɑ̃file] *vt* (*vêtement*): **~ qch** to slip sth on, slip into sth; (*insérer*): **~ qch dans** to stick sth into; (*rue, couloir*) to take; (*perles*) to string; (*aiguille*) to thread; **s'enfiler dans** *vi* to disappear into

enfin [ɑ̃fɛ̃] *adv* at last; (*en énumérant*) lastly; (*de restriction, résignation*) still; (*eh bien*) well; (*pour conclure*) in a word

enflammé, e [ɑ̃flame] *adj* (*torche, allumette*) burning; (*Méd: plaie*) inflamed; (*fig: nature, discours, déclaration*) fiery

enflammer [ɑ̃flame] *vt* to set fire to; (*Méd*) to inflame; **s'enflammer** *vi* to catch fire; to become inflamed

enflé, e [ɑ̃fle] *adj* swollen; (*péj: style*) bombastic, turgid

enfler [ɑ̃fle] *vi* to swell (up); **s'enfler** *vi* to swell

enflure [ɑ̃flyʀ] *nf* swelling

enfoncé, e [ɑ̃fɔ̃se] *adj* staved-in, smashed-in; (*yeux*) deep-set

enfoncement [ɑ̃fɔ̃smɑ̃] *nm* (*recoin*) nook

enfoncer [ɑ̃fɔ̃se] *vt* (*clou*) to drive in; (*faire pénétrer*): **~ qch dans** to push (*ou* drive) sth into; (*forcer: porte*) to break open; (*: plancher*) to cause to cave in; (*défoncer: côtes etc*) to smash; (*fam: surpasser*) to lick, beat (hollow) ▷ *vi* (*dans la vase etc*) to sink in; (*sol, surface porteuse*) to give way; **s'enfoncer** *vi* to sink; **s'~ dans** to sink into; (*forêt, ville*) to disappear into; **~ un chapeau sur la tête** to cram *ou* jam a hat on one's head; **~ qn dans la dette** to drag sb into debt

enfouir [ɑ̃fwiʀ] *vt* (*dans le sol*) to bury; (*dans un tiroir etc*) to tuck away; **s'enfouir dans/sous** to bury o.s. in/under

enfourcher [ɑ̃fuʀʃe] *vt* to mount; **~ son dada** (*fig*) to get on one's hobby-horse

enfourner [ɑ̃fuʀne] *vt* to put in the oven; (*poterie*) to put in the kiln; **~ qch dans** to shove *ou* stuff sth into; **s'enfourner dans** (*personne*) to dive into

enfreignais *etc* [ɑ̃fʀɛɲɛ] *vb voir* **enfreindre**

enfreindre [ɑ̃fʀɛ̃dʀ(ə)] *vt* to infringe, break

enfuir [ɑ̃fɥiʀ]: **s'enfuir** *vi* to run away *ou* off

enfumer [ɑ̃fyme] *vt* to smoke out

enfuyais *etc* [ɑ̃fɥijɛ] *vb voir* **enfuir**

engagé, e [ɑ̃gaʒe] *adj* (*littérature etc*) engagé, committed

engageant, e [ɑ̃gaʒɑ̃, -ɑ̃t] *adj* attractive, appealing

engagement [ɑ̃gaʒmɑ̃] *nm* taking on, engaging; starting; investing; (*promesse*) commitment; (*Mil: combat*) engagement; (*: recrutement*) enlistment; (*Sport*) entry; **prendre l'~ de faire** to undertake to do; **sans ~** (*Comm*) without obligation

engager [ɑ̃gaʒe] *vt* (*embaucher*) to take on,

engage; (commencer) to start; (lier) to bind, commit; (impliquer, entraîner) to involve; (investir) to invest, lay out; (faire intervenir) to engage; (Sport: concurrents, chevaux) to enter; (inciter): **~ qn à faire** to urge sb to do; (faire pénétrer): **~ qch dans** to insert sth into; **~ qn à qch** to urge sth on sb; **s'engager** vi to get taken on; (Mil) to enlist; (promettre, politiquement) to commit o.s.; (débuter) to start (up); **s'~ à faire** to undertake to do; **s'~ dans** (rue, passage) to enter, turn into; (s'emboîter) to engage ou fit into; (fig: affaire, discussion) to enter into, embark on

engazonner [ãgazɔne] vt to turf

engeance [ãʒãs] nf mob

engelures [ãʒlyʀ] nfpl chilblains

engendrer [ãʒãdʀe] vt to father; (fig) to create, breed

engin [ãʒɛ̃] nm machine instrument; vehicle; (péj) gadget; (Aviat: avion) aircraft inv; (: missile) missile; **~ blindé** armoured vehicle; **~ (explosif)** (explosive) device; **~s (spéciaux)** missiles

englober [ãglɔbe] vt to include

engloutir [ãglutiʀ] vt to swallow up; (fig: dépenses) to devour; **s'engloutir** vi to be engulfed

englué, e [ãglye] adj sticky

engoncé, e [ãgɔ̃se] adj: **~ dans** cramped in

engorgement [ãgɔʀʒəmã] nm blocking; (Méd) engorgement

engorger [ãgɔʀʒe] vt to obstruct, block; **s'engorger** vi to become blocked

engouement [ãgumã] nm (sudden) passion

engouffrer [ãgufʀe] vt to swallow up, devour; **s'engouffrer dans** to rush into

engourdi, e [ãguʀdi] adj numb

engourdir [ãguʀdiʀ] vt to numb; (fig) to dull, blunt; **s'engourdir** vi to go numb

engrais [ãgʀɛ] nm manure; **~ (chimique)** (chemical) fertilizer; **~ organique/ inorganique** organic/inorganic fertilizer

engraisser [ãgʀese] vt to fatten (up); (terre: fertiliser) to fertilize ▷ vi (péj) to get fat(ter)

engranger [ãgʀãʒe] vt (foin) to bring in; (fig) to store away

engrenage [ãgʀənaʒ] nm gears pl, gearing; (fig) chain

engueuler [ãgœle] vt (fam) to bawl at ou out

enguirlander [ãgiʀlãde] vt (fam) to give sb a bawling out, bawl at

enhardir [ãaʀdiʀ]: **s'enhardir** vi to grow bolder

ENI [eni] sigle f = **école normale (d'instituteurs)**

énième [enjɛm] adj = **nième**

énigmatique [enigmatik] adj enigmatic

énigmatiquement [enigmatikmã] adv enigmatically

énigme [enigm(ə)] nf riddle

enivrant, e [ãnivʀã, -ãt] adj intoxicating

enivrer [ãnivʀe] vt: **s'enivrer** to get drunk; **s'~ de** (fig) to become intoxicated with

enjambée [ãʒãbe] nf stride; **d'une ~** with one stride

enjamber [ãʒãbe] vt to stride over; (pont etc) to span, straddle

enjeu, x [ãʒø] nm stakes pl

enjoindre [ãʒwɛ̃dʀ(ə)] vt: **~ à qn de faire** to enjoin ou order sb to do

enjôler [ãʒole] vt to coax, wheedle

enjôleur, -euse [ãʒolœʀ, -øz] adj (sourire, paroles) winning

enjolivement [ãʒɔlivmã] nm embellishment

enjoliver [ãʒɔlive] vt to embellish

enjoliveur [ãʒɔlivœʀ] nm (Auto) hub cap

enjoué, e [ãʒwe] adj playful

enlacer [ãlase] vt (étreindre) to embrace, hug; (lianes) to wind round, entwine

enlaidir [ãlediʀ] vt to make ugly ▷ vi to become ugly

enlevé, e [ãlve] adj (morceau de musique) played brightly

enlèvement [ãlɛvmã] nm removal; (rapt) abduction, kidnapping; **l'~ des ordures ménagères** refuse collection

enlever [ãlve] vt (ôter: gén) to remove; (: vêtement, lunettes) to take off; (: Méd: organe) to remove; (emporter: ordures etc) to collect, take away; (kidnapper) to abduct, kidnap; (obtenir: prix, contrat) to win; (Mil: position) to take; (morceau de piano etc) to execute with spirit ou brio; (prendre): **~ qch à qn** to take sth (away) from sb; **s'enlever** vi (tache) to come out ou off; **la maladie qui nous l'a enlevé** (euphémisme) the illness which took him from us

enliser [ãlize]: **s'enliser** vi to sink, get stuck; (dialogue etc) to get bogged down

enluminure [ãlyminyʀ] nf illumination

ENM sigle f (= École nationale de la magistrature) grande école for law students

enneigé, e [ãneʒe] adj snowy; (col) snowed-up; (maison) snowed-in

enneigement [ãnɛʒmã] nm depth of snow, snowfall; **bulletin d'~** snow report

ennemi, e [ɛnmi] adj hostile; (Mil) enemy cpd ▷ nm/f enemy; **être ~ de** to be strongly averse ou opposed to

ennième [ɛnjɛm] adj = **nième**

ennoblir [ãnɔbliʀ] vt to ennoble

ennui [ãnɥi] nm (lassitude) boredom; (difficulté) trouble no pl; **avoir des ~s** to have problems; **s'attirer des ~s** to cause problems for o.s.

ennuie etc [ãnɥi] vb voir **ennuyer**

ennuyé, e [ãnɥije] adj (air, personne) preoccupied, worried

ennuyer [ãnɥije] vt to bother; (lasser) to bore; **s'ennuyer** vi to be bored; (s'ennuyer de: regretter) to miss; **si cela ne vous ennuie pas** if it's no trouble to you

ennuyeux, -euse [ãnɥijø, -øz] adj boring, tedious; (agaçant) annoying

énoncé [enɔse] nm terms pl; wording; (Ling) utterance

énoncer [enɔse] vt to say, express; (conditions) to set out, lay down, state

énonciation [enɔsjasjɔ̃] nf statement

enorgueillir [ãnɔʀgœjiʀ]: **s'enorgueillir de** vt to

pride o.s. on; to boast

énorme [enɔʀm(ə)] *adj* enormous, huge

énormément [enɔʀmemɑ̃] *adv* enormously, tremendously; ~ **de neige/gens** an enormous amount of snow/number of people

énormité [enɔʀmite] *nf* enormity, hugeness; (*propos*) outrageous remark

en part. *abr* (= *en particulier*) esp.

enquérir [ɑ̃keʀiʀ]: **s'enquérir de** *vt* to inquire about

enquête [ɑ̃kɛt] *nf* (*de journaliste, de police*) investigation; (*judiciaire, administrative*) inquiry; (*sondage d'opinion*) survey

enquêter [ɑ̃kete] *vi* to investigate; to hold an inquiry; (*faire un sondage*): ~ (**sur**) to do a survey (on), carry out an opinion poll (on)

enquêteur, -euse *ou* **-trice** [ɑ̃kɛtœʀ, -øz, -tʀis] *nm/f* officer in charge of an investigation; person conducting a survey; pollster

enquiers, enquière *etc* [ɑ̃kjɛʀ] *vb voir* **enquérir**

enquiquiner [ɑ̃kikine] *vt* to rile, irritate

enquis, e [ɑ̃ki, -iz] *pp de* **enquérir**

enraciné, e [ɑ̃ʀasine] *adj* deep-rooted

enragé, e [ɑ̃ʀaʒe] *adj* (*Méd*) rabid, with rabies; (*furieux*) furiously angry; (*fig*) fanatical; ~ **de** wild about

enrageant, e [ɑ̃ʀaʒɑ̃, -ɑ̃t] *adj* infuriating

enrager [ɑ̃ʀaʒe] *vi* to be furious, be in a rage; **faire** ~ **qn** to make sb wild with anger

enrayer [ɑ̃ʀeje] *vt* to check, stop; **s'enrayer** *vi* (*arme à feu*) to jam

enrégimenter [ɑ̃ʀeʒimɑ̃te] *vt* (*péj*) to enlist

enregistrement [ɑ̃ʀʒistʀəmɑ̃] *nm* recording; (*Admin*) registration; ~ **des bagages** (*à l'aéroport*) baggage check-in; ~ **magnétique** tape-recording

enregistrer [ɑ̃ʀʒistʀe] *vt* (*Mus*) to record; (*Inform*) to save; (*remarquer, noter*) to note, record; (*Comm: commande*) to note, enter; (*fig: mémoriser*) to make a mental note of; (*Admin*) to register; (*aussi*: **faire enregistrer**: *bagages: par train*) to register; (: *à l'aéroport*) to check in

enregistreur, -euse [ɑ̃ʀʒistʀœʀ, -øz] *adj* (*machine*) recording *cpd* ▷ *nm* (*appareil*): ~ **de vol** (*Aviat*) flight recorder

enrhumé, e [ɑ̃ʀyme] *adj*: **il est** ~ he has a cold

enrhumer [ɑ̃ʀyme]: **s'enrhumer** *vi* to catch a cold

enrichir [ɑ̃ʀiʃiʀ] *vt* to make rich(er); (*fig*) to enrich; **s'enrichir** *vi* to get rich(er)

enrichissant, e [ɑ̃ʀiʃisɑ̃, -ɑ̃t] *adj* instructive

enrichissement [ɑ̃ʀiʃismɑ̃] *nm* enrichment

enrober [ɑ̃ʀɔbe] *vt*: ~ **qch de** to coat sth with; (*fig*) to wrap sth up in

enrôlement [ɑ̃ʀolmɑ̃] *nm* enlistment

enrôler [ɑ̃ʀole] *vt* to enlist; **s'enrôler (dans)** *vi* to enlist (in)

enroué, e [ɑ̃ʀwe] *adj* hoarse

enrouer [ɑ̃ʀwe]: **s'enrouer** *vi* to go hoarse

enrouler [ɑ̃ʀule] *vt* (*fil, corde*) to wind (up); **s'enrouler** to coil up; ~ **qch autour de** to wind sth (a)round

enrouleur, -euse [ɑ̃ʀulœʀ, -øz] *adj* (*Tech*) winding ▷ *nm voir* **ceinture**

enrubanné, e [ɑ̃ʀybane] *adj* trimmed with ribbon

ENS *sigle f* = **école normale supérieure**

ensabler [ɑ̃sable] *vt* (*port, canal*) to silt up, sand up; (*embarcation*) to strand (on a sandbank); **s'ensabler** *vi* to silt up; to get stranded

ensacher [ɑ̃saʃe] *vt* to pack into bags

ENSAM *sigle f* (= *École nationale supérieure des arts et métiers*) *grande école for engineering students*

ensanglanté, e [ɑ̃sɑ̃glɑ̃te] *adj* covered with blood

enseignant, e [ɑ̃sɛɲɑ̃, -ɑ̃t] *adj* teaching ▷ *nm/f* teacher

enseigne [ɑ̃sɛɲ] *nf* sign ▷ *nm*: ~ **de vaisseau** lieutenant; **à telle ~ que** so much so that; **être logés à la même** ~ (*fig*) to be in the same boat; ~ **lumineuse** neon sign

enseignement [ɑ̃sɛɲmɑ̃] *nm* teaching; ~ **ménager** home economics; ~ **primaire** primary (*Brit*) *ou* grade school (*US*) education; ~ **secondaire** secondary (*Brit*) *ou* high school (*US*) education

enseigner [ɑ̃seɲe] *vt, vi* to teach; ~ **qch à qn/à qn que** to teach sb sth/sb that

ensemble [ɑ̃sɑ̃bl(ə)] *adv* together ▷ *nm* (*assemblage, Math*) set; (*totalité*): **l'~ du/de la** the whole *ou* entire; (*vêtement féminin*) ensemble, suit; (*unité, harmonie*) unity; (*résidentiel*) housing development; **aller** ~ to go together; **impression/idée d'~** overall *ou* general impression/idea; **dans l'~** (*en gros*) on the whole; **dans son** ~ overall, in general; ~ **vocal/musical** vocal/musical ensemble

ensemblier [ɑ̃sɑ̃blije] *nm* interior designer

ensemencer [ɑ̃smɑ̃se] *vt* to sow

enserrer [ɑ̃seʀe] *vt* to hug (tightly)

ENSET [ɑ̃sɛt] *sigle f* (= *École normale supérieure de l'enseignement technique*) *grande école for training technical teachers*

ensevelir [ɑ̃səvliʀ] *vt* to bury

ensilage [ɑ̃silaʒ] *nm* (*aliment*) silage

ensoleillé, e [ɑ̃sɔleje] *adj* sunny

ensoleillement [ɑ̃sɔlɛjmɑ̃] *nm* period *ou* hours *pl* of sunshine

ensommeillé, e [ɑ̃sɔmeje] *adj* sleepy, drowsy

ensorceler [ɑ̃sɔʀsəle] *vt* to enchant, bewitch

ensuite [ɑ̃sɥit] *adv* then, next; (*plus tard*) afterwards, later; ~ **de quoi** after which

ensuivre [ɑ̃sɥivʀ(ə)]: **s'ensuivre** *vi* to follow, ensue; **il s'ensuit que ...** it follows that ...; **et tout ce qui s'ensuit** and all that goes with it

entaché, e [ɑ̃taʃe] *adj*: ~ **de** marred by; ~ **de nullité** null and void

entacher [ɑ̃taʃe] *vt* to soil

entaille [ɑ̃taj] *nf* (*encoche*) notch; (*blessure*) cut; **se faire une** ~ to cut o.s.

entailler [ɑ̃taje] *vt* to notch; to cut; **s'~ le doigt** to cut one's finger

entamer [ɑ̃tame] *vt* to start; (*hostilités, pourparlers*) to open; (*fig: altérer*) to make a dent in; to damage

entartrer [ɑ̃taʀtʀe]: **s'entartrer** vi to fur up; (dents) to become covered with plaque

entassement [ɑ̃tasmɑ̃] nm (tas) pile, heap

entasser [ɑ̃tase] vt (empiler) to pile up, heap up; (tenir à l'étroit) to cram together; **s'entasser** vi to pile up; to cram; **s'~ dans** to cram into

entendement [ɑ̃tɑ̃dmɑ̃] nm understanding

entendre [ɑ̃tɑ̃dʀ(ə)] vt to hear; (comprendre) to understand; (vouloir dire) to mean; (vouloir): **~ être obéi/que** to intend ou mean to be obeyed/that; **j'ai entendu dire que** I've heard (it said) that; **je suis heureux de vous l'~ dire** I'm pleased to hear you say it; **~ parler de** to hear of; **laisser ~ que, donner à ~ que** to let it be understood that; **~ raison** to see sense, listen to reason; **qu'est-ce qu'il ne faut pas ~!** whatever next!; **j'ai mal entendu** I didn't catch what was said; **je vous entends très mal** I can hardly hear you; **s'entendre** vi (sympathiser) to get on; (se mettre d'accord) to agree; **s'~ à qch/à faire** (être compétent) to be good at sth/doing; **ça s'entend** (est audible) it's audible; **je m'entends** I mean; **entendons-nous!** let's be clear what we mean

entendu, e [ɑ̃tɑ̃dy] pp de **entendre** ▷ adj (réglé) agreed; (au courant: air) knowing; **étant ~ que** since (it's understood ou agreed that); **(c'est) ~** all right, agreed; **c'est ~** (concession) all right, granted; **bien ~** of course

entente [ɑ̃tɑ̃t] nf (entre amis, pays) understanding, harmony; (accord, traité) agreement, understanding; **à double ~** (sens) with a double meaning

entériner [ɑ̃teʀine] vt to ratify, confirm

entérite [ɑ̃teʀit] nf enteritis no pl

enterrement [ɑ̃tɛʀmɑ̃] nm burying; (cérémonie) funeral, burial; (cortège funèbre) funeral procession

enterrer [ɑ̃teʀe] vt to bury

entêtant, e [ɑ̃tɛtɑ̃, -ɑ̃t] adj heady

en-tête [ɑ̃tɛt] nm heading; (de papier à lettres) letterhead; **papier à ~** headed notepaper

entêté, e [ɑ̃tete] adj stubborn

entêtement [ɑ̃tɛtmɑ̃] nm stubbornness

entêter [ɑ̃tete]: **s'entêter** vi: **s'~ (à faire)** to persist (in doing)

enthousiasmant, e [ɑ̃tuzjasmɑ̃, -ɑ̃t] adj exciting

enthousiasme [ɑ̃tuzjasm(ə)] nm enthusiasm; **avec ~** enthusiastically

enthousiasmé, e [ɑ̃tuzjasme] adj filled with enthusiasm

enthousiasmer [ɑ̃tuzjasme] vt to fill with enthusiasm; **s'~ (pour qch)** to get enthusiastic (about sth)

enthousiaste [ɑ̃tuzjast(ə)] adj enthusiastic

enticher [ɑ̃tiʃe]: **s'enticher de** vt to become infatuated with

entier, -ière [ɑ̃tje, -jɛʀ] adj (non entamé, en totalité) whole; (total, complet) complete; (fig: caractère) unbending, averse to compromise ▷ nm (Math)

whole; **en ~** totally; in its entirety; **se donner tout ~ à qch** to devote o.s. completely to sth; **lait ~** full-cream milk; **pain ~** wholemeal bread; **nombre ~** whole number

entièrement [ɑ̃tjɛʀmɑ̃] adv entirely, completely, wholly

entité [ɑ̃tite] nf entity

entomologie [ɑ̃tɔmɔlɔʒi] nf entomology

entonner [ɑ̃tɔne] vt (chanson) to strike up

entonnoir [ɑ̃tɔnwaʀ] nm (ustensile) funnel; (trou) shell-hole, crater

entorse [ɑ̃tɔʀs(ə)] nf (Méd) sprain; (fig): **~ à la loi/au règlement** infringement of the law/rule; **se faire une ~ à la cheville/au poignet** to sprain one's ankle/wrist

entortiller [ɑ̃tɔʀtije] vt (envelopper): **~ qch dans/avec** to wrap sth in/with; (enrouler): **~ qch autour de** to twist ou wind sth (a)round; (fam): **~ qn** to get (a)round sb; (: duper) to hoodwink sb (Brit), trick sb; **s'entortiller dans** vi (draps) to roll o.s. up in; (fig: réponses) to get tangled up in

entourage [ɑ̃tuʀaʒ] nm circle; family (circle); (d'une vedette etc) entourage; (ce qui enclôt) surround

entouré, e [ɑ̃tuʀe] adj (recherché, admiré) popular; **~ de** surrounded by

entourer [ɑ̃tuʀe] vt to surround; (apporter son soutien à) to rally round; **~ de** to surround with; (trait) to encircle with; **s'entourer de** vi to surround o.s. with; **s'~ de précautions** to take all possible precautions

entourloupette [ɑ̃tuʀlupɛt] nf mean trick

entournures [ɑ̃tuʀnyʀ] nfpl: **gêné aux ~** in financial difficulties; (fig) a bit awkward

entracte [ɑ̃tʀakt(ə)] nm interval

entraide [ɑ̃tʀɛd] nf mutual aid ou assistance

entraider [ɑ̃tʀede]: **s'entraider** vi to help each other

entrailles [ɑ̃tʀɑj] nfpl entrails; (humaines) bowels

entrain [ɑ̃tʀɛ̃] nm spirit; **avec ~** (répondre, travailler) energetically; **faire qch sans ~** to do sth half-heartedly ou without enthusiasm

entraînant, e [ɑ̃tʀɛnɑ̃, -ɑ̃t] adj (musique) stirring, rousing

entraînement [ɑ̃tʀɛnmɑ̃] nm training; (Tech): **à chaîne/galet** chain/wheel drive; **manquer d'~** to be unfit; **~ par ergots/friction** (Inform) tractor/friction feed

entraîner [ɑ̃tʀene] vt (tirer: wagons) to pull; (charrier) to carry ou drag along; (Tech) to drive; (emmener: personne) to take (off); (mener à l'assaut, influencer) to lead; (Sport) to train; (impliquer) to entail; (causer) to lead to, bring about; **~ qn à faire** (inciter) to lead sb to do; **s'entraîner** vi (Sport) to train; **s'~ à qch/à faire** to train o.s. for sth/to do

entraîneur [ɑ̃tʀɛnœʀ] nm (Sport) coach, trainer; (Hippisme) trainer

entraîneuse [ɑ̃tʀɛnøz] nf (de bar) hostess

entrapercevoir [ɑ̃tʀapɛʀsəvwaʀ] vt to catch a glimpse of

entrave [ɑ̃tʀav] *nf* hindrance
entraver [ɑ̃tʀave] *vt* (*circulation*) to hold up; (*action, progrès*) to hinder, hamper
entre [ɑ̃tʀ(ə)] *prép* between; (*parmi*) among(st); **l'un d'~ eux/nous** one of them/us; **le meilleur d'~ eux/nous** the best of them/us; **ils préfèrent rester ~ eux** they prefer to keep to themselves; **~ autres (choses)** among other things; **~ nous, ...** between ourselves ..., between you and me ...; **ils se battent ~ eux** they are fighting among(st) themselves
entrebâillé, e [ɑ̃tʀəbaje] *adj* half-open, ajar
entrebâillement [ɑ̃tʀəbajmɑ̃] *nm*: **dans l'~ (de la porte)** in the half-open door
entrebâiller [ɑ̃tʀəbaje] *vt* to half open
entrechat [ɑ̃tʀəʃa] *nm* leap
entrechoquer [ɑ̃tʀəʃɔke]: **s'entrechoquer** *vi* to knock *ou* bang together
entrecôte [ɑ̃tʀəkot] *nf* entrecôte *ou* rib steak
entrecoupé, e [ɑ̃tʀəkupe] *adj* (*paroles, voix*) broken
entrecouper [ɑ̃tʀəkupe] *vt*: **~ qch de** to intersperse sth with; **~ un récit/voyage de** to interrupt a story/journey with; **s'entrecouper** *vi* (*traits, lignes*) to cut across each other
entrecroiser [ɑ̃tʀəkʀwaze] *vt*, **s'entrecroiser** *vi* to intertwine
entrée [ɑ̃tʀe] *nf* entrance; (*accès: au cinéma etc*) admission; (*billet*) (admission) ticket; (*Culin*) first course; (*Comm: de marchandises*) entry; (*Inform*) entry, input; **entrées** *nfpl*: **avoir ses ~s chez** *ou* **auprès de** to be a welcome visitor to; **d'~** *adv* from the outset; **erreur d'~** input error; **"~ interdite"** "no admittance *ou* entry"; **~ des artistes** stage door; **~ en matière** introduction; **~ principale** main entrance; **~ en scène** entrance; **~ de service** service entrance
entrefaites [ɑ̃tʀəfɛt]: **sur ces ~** *adv* at this juncture
entrefilet [ɑ̃tʀəfilɛ] *nm* (*article*) paragraph, short report
entregent [ɑ̃tʀəʒɑ̃] *nm*: **avoir de l'~** to have an easy manner
entrejambes [ɑ̃tʀəʒɑ̃b] *nm inv* crotch
entrelacement [ɑ̃tʀəlasmɑ̃] *nm*: **un ~ de ...** a network of ...
entrelacer [ɑ̃tʀəlase] *vt*, **s'entrelacer** *vi* to intertwine
entrelarder [ɑ̃tʀəlaʀde] *vt* to lard; (*fig*): **entrelardé de** interspersed with
entremêler [ɑ̃tʀəmele] *vt*: **~ qch de** to (inter)mingle sth with
entremets [ɑ̃tʀəmɛ] *nm* (cream) dessert
entremetteur, -euse [ɑ̃tʀəmɛtœʀ, -øz] *nm/f* go-between
entremettre [ɑ̃tʀəmɛtʀ(ə)]: **s'entremettre** *vi* to intervene
entremise [ɑ̃tʀəmiz] *nf* intervention; **par l'~ de** through
entrepont [ɑ̃tʀəpɔ̃] *nm* steerage; **dans l'~** in steerage

entreposer [ɑ̃tʀəpoze] *vt* to store, put into storage
entrepôt [ɑ̃tʀəpo] *nm* warehouse
entreprenant, e [ɑ̃tʀəpʀənɑ̃, -ɑ̃t] *vb voir* **entreprendre** ⊳ *adj* (*actif*) enterprising; (*trop galant*) forward
entreprendre [ɑ̃tʀəpʀɑ̃dʀ(ə)] *vt* (*se lancer dans*) to undertake; (*commencer*) to begin *ou* start (upon); (*personne*) to buttonhole; **~ qn sur un sujet** to tackle sb on a subject; **~ de faire** to undertake to do
entrepreneur [ɑ̃tʀəpʀənœʀ] *nm*: **~ (en bâtiment)** (building) contractor; **~ de pompes funèbres** funeral director, undertaker
entreprenne *etc* [ɑ̃tʀəpʀɛn] *vb voir* **entreprendre**
entrepris, e [ɑ̃tʀəpʀi, -iz] *pp de* **entreprendre** ⊳ *nf* (*société*) firm, business; (*action*) undertaking, venture
entrer [ɑ̃tʀe] *vi* to go (*ou* come) in, enter ⊳ *vt* (*Inform*) to input, enter; (**faire**) **~ qch dans** to get sth into; **~ dans** (*gén*) to enter; (*pièce*) to go (*ou* come) into, enter; (*club*) to join; (*heurter*) to run into; (*partager: vues, craintes de qn*) to share; (*être une composante de*) to go into; (*faire partie de*) to form part of; **~ au couvent** to enter a convent; **~ à l'hôpital** to go into hospital; **~ dans le système** (*Inform*) to log in; **~ en fureur** to become angry; **~ en ébullition** to start to boil; **~ en scène** to come on stage; **laisser ~ qn/qch** to let sb/sth in; **faire ~** (*visiteur*) to show in
entresol [ɑ̃tʀəsɔl] *nm* entresol, mezzanine
entre-temps [ɑ̃tʀətɑ̃] *adv* meanwhile, (in the) meantime
entretenir [ɑ̃tʀətniʀ] *vt* to maintain; (*amitié*) to keep alive; (*famille, maîtresse*) to support, keep; **~ qn (de)** to speak to sb (about); **s'entretenir (de)** to converse (about); **~ qn dans l'erreur** to let sb remain in ignorance
entretenu, e [ɑ̃tʀətny] *pp de* **entretenir** ⊳ *adj* (*femme*) kept; **bien/mal ~** (*maison, jardin*) well/badly kept
entretien [ɑ̃tʀətjɛ̃] *nm* maintenance; (*discussion*) discussion, talk; (*audience*) interview; **frais d'~** maintenance charges
entretiendrai [ɑ̃tʀətjɛ̃dʀe], **entretiens** *etc* [ɑ̃tʀətjɛ̃] *vb voir* **entretenir**
entretuer [ɑ̃tʀətɥe]: **s'entretuer** *vi* to kill one another
entreverrai [ɑ̃tʀəveʀe], **entrevit** *etc* [ɑ̃tʀəvi] *vb voir* **entrevoir**
entrevoir [ɑ̃tʀəvwaʀ] *vt* (*à peine*) to make out; (*brièvement*) to catch a glimpse of
entrevu, e [ɑ̃tʀəvy] *pp de* **entrevoir** ⊳ *nf* meeting; (*audience*) interview
entrouvert, e [ɑ̃tʀuvɛʀ, -ɛʀt(ə)] *pp de* **entrouvrir** ⊳ *adj* half-open
entrouvrir [ɑ̃tʀuvʀiʀ] *vt*, **s'entrouvrir** *vi* to half open
énumération [enymeʀasjɔ̃] *nf* enumeration
énumérer [enymeʀe] *vt* to list, enumerate
envahir [ɑ̃vaiʀ] *vt* to invade; (*inquiétude, peur*) to

e

come over

envahissant, e [ãvaisã, -ãt] *adj* (*péj: personne*) interfering, intrusive

envahissement [ãvaismã] *nm* invasion

envahisseur [ãvaisœʀ] *nm* (*Mil*) invader

envasement [ãnvazmã] *nm* silting up

envaser [ãvaze]: **s'envaser** *vi* to get bogged down (in the mud)

enveloppe [ãvlɔp] *nf* (*de lettre*) envelope; (*Tech*) casing; outer layer; **mettre sous** ~ to put in an envelope; ~ **autocollante** self-seal envelope; ~ **budgétaire** budget; ~ **à fenêtre** window envelope

envelopper [ãvlɔpe] *vt* to wrap; (*fig*) to envelop, shroud; **s'~ dans un châle/une couverture** to wrap o.s. in a shawl/blanket

envenimer [ãvnime] *vt* to aggravate; **s'envenimer** *vi* (*plaie*) to fester; (*situation, relations*) to worsen

envergure [ãvɛʀgyʀ] *nf* (*d'un oiseau, avion*) wingspan; (*fig: étendue*) scope; (: *valeur*) calibre

enverrai *etc* [ãvɛʀe] *vb voir* **envoyer**

envers [ãvɛʀ] *prép* towards, to ▷ *nm* other side; (*d'une étoffe*) wrong side; **à l'**~ upside down; back to front; (*vêtement*) inside out; ~ **et contre tous** *ou* **tout** against all opposition

enviable [ãvjabl(ə)] *adj* enviable; **peu** ~ unenviable

envie [ãvi] *nf* (*sentiment*) envy; (*souhait*) desire, wish; (*tache sur la peau*) birthmark; (*filet de peau*) hangnail; **avoir** ~ **de** to feel like; (*désir plus fort*) to want; **avoir** ~ **de faire** to feel like doing; to want to do; **avoir** ~ **que** to wish that; **donner à qn l'**~ **de faire** to make sb want to do; **ça lui fait** ~ he would like that

envier [ãvje] *vt* to envy; ~ **qch à qn** to envy sb sth; **n'avoir rien à** ~ **à** to have no cause to be envious of

envieux, -euse [ãvjø, -øz] *adj* envious

environ [ãviʀɔ̃] *adv*: ~ **3 h/2 km, 3 h/2km** ~ (around) about 3 o'clock/2 km, 3 o'clock/2 km or so

environnant, e [ãviʀɔnã, -ãt] *adj* surrounding

environnement [ãviʀɔnmã] *nm* environment

environnementaliste [ãviʀɔnmãtalist(ə)] *nm/f* environmentalist

environner [ãviʀɔne] *vt* to surround

environs [ãviʀɔ̃] *nmpl* surroundings; **aux** ~ **de** around

envisageable [ãvizaʒabl(ə)] *adj* conceivable

envisager [ãvizaʒe] *vt* (*examiner, considérer*) to view, contemplate; (*avoir en vue*) to envisage; ~ **de faire** to consider doing

envoi [ãvwa] *nm* sending; (*paquet*) parcel, consignment; ~ **contre remboursement** (*Comm*) cash on delivery

envoie *etc* [ãvwa] *vb voir* **envoyer**

envol [ãvɔl] *nm* takeoff

envolée [ãvɔle] *nf* (*fig*) flight

envoler [ãvɔle]: **s'envoler** *vi* (*oiseau*) to fly away *ou* off; (*avion*) to take off; (*papier, feuille*) to blow away; (*fig*) to vanish (into thin air)

envoûtant, e [ãvutã, -ãt] *adj* enchanting

envoûtement [ãvutmã] *nm* bewitchment

envoûter [ãvute] *vt* to bewitch

envoyé, e [ãvwaje] *nm/f* (*Pol*) envoy; (*Presse*) correspondent ▷ *adj*: **bien** ~ (*remarque, réponse*) well-aimed

envoyer [ãvwaje] *vt* to send; (*lancer*) to hurl, throw; ~ **une gifle/un sourire à qn** to aim a blow/flash a smile at sb; ~ **les couleurs** to run up the colours; ~ **chercher** to send for; ~ **par le fond** (*bateau*) to send to the bottom

envoyeur, -euse [ãvwajœʀ, -øz] *nm/f* sender

enzyme [ãzim] *nf ou m* enzyme

éolien, ne [eɔljɛ̃, -ɛn] *adj* wind *cpd* ▷ *nf* wind turbine; **pompe** ~**ne** windpump

EOR *sigle m* (= *élève officier de réserve*) ≈ military cadet

éosine [eɔzin] *nf* eosin (*antiseptic used in France to treat skin ailments*)

épagneul, e [epaɲœl] *nm/f* spaniel

épais, se [epɛ, -ɛs] *adj* thick

épaisseur [epɛsœʀ] *nf* thickness

épaissir [epesiʀ] *vt*, **s'épaissir** *vi* to thicken

épaississement [epesismã] *nm* thickening

épanchement [epãʃmã] *nm*: **un** ~ **de synovie** water on the knee; **épanchements** *nmpl* (*fig*) (sentimental) outpourings

épancher [epãʃe] *vt* to give vent to; **s'épancher** *vi* to open one's heart; (*liquide*) to pour out

épandage [epãdaʒ] *nm* manure spreading

épanoui, e [epanwi] *adj* (*éclos, ouvert, développé*) blooming; (*radieux*) radiant

épanouir [epanwiʀ]: **s'épanouir** *vi* (*fleur*) to bloom, open out; (*visage*) to light up; (*fig: se développer*) to blossom (out); (: *mentalement*) to open up

épanouissement [epanwismã] *nm* blossoming; opening up

épargnant, e [epaʀɲã, -ãt] *nm/f* saver, investor

épargne [epaʀɲ(ə)] *nf* saving; **l'**~**-logement** property investment

épargner [epaʀɲe] *vt* to save; (*ne pas tuer ou endommager*) to spare ▷ *vi* to save; ~ **qch à qn** to spare sb sth

éparpillement [epaʀpijmã] *nm* (*de papier*) scattering; (*des efforts*) dissipation

éparpiller [epaʀpije] *vt* to scatter; (*pour répartir*) to disperse; (*fig: efforts*) to dissipate; **s'éparpiller** *vi* to scatter; (*fig*) to dissipate one's efforts

épars, e [epaʀ, -aʀs(ə)] *adj* (*maisons*) scattered; (*cheveux*) sparse

épatant, e [epatã, -ãt] *adj* (*fam*) super, splendid

épaté, e [epate] *adj*: **nez** ~ flat nose (with wide nostrils)

épater [epate] *vt* to amaze; (*impressionner*) to impress

épaule [epol] *nf* shoulder

épaulé-jeté [epoleʒəte] (*pl* **épaulés-jetés**) *nm* (*Sport*) clean-and-jerk

épaulement [epolmã] *nm* escarpment; (*mur*) retaining wall

épauler [epole] *vt* (*aider*) to back up, support;

(*arme*) to raise (to one's shoulder) ▷ *vi* to (take) aim

épaulette [epolɛt] *nf* (*Mil*, *d'un veston*) epaulette; (*de combinaison*) shoulder strap

épave [epav] *nf* wreck

épée [epe] *nf* sword

épeler [eple] *vt* to spell

éperdu, e [epɛʀdy] *adj* (*personne*) overcome; (*sentiment*) passionate; (*fuite*) frantic

éperdument [epɛʀdymã] *adv* (*aimer*) wildly; (*espérer*) fervently

éperlan [epɛʀlã] *nm* (*Zool*) smelt

éperon [epʀɔ̃] *nm* spur

éperonner [epʀɔne] *vt* to spur (on); (*navire*) to ram

épervier [epɛʀvje] *nm* (*Zool*) sparrowhawk; (*Pêche*) casting net

éphèbe [efɛb] *nm* beautiful young man

éphémère [efemɛʀ] *adj* ephemeral, fleeting

éphéméride [efemeʀid] *nf* block *ou* tear-off calendar

épi [epi] *nm* (*de blé, d'orge*) ear; **~ de cheveux** tuft of hair; **stationnement/se garer en ~** parking/to park at an angle to the kerb

épice [epis] *nf* spice

épicé, e [epise] *adj* highly spiced, spicy; (*fig*) spicy

épicéa [episea] *nm* spruce

épicentre [episãtʀ(ə)] *nm* epicentre

épicer [epise] *vt* to spice; (*fig*) to add spice to

épicerie [episʀi] *nf* (*magasin*) grocer's shop; (*denrées*) groceries *pl*; **~ fine** delicatessen (shop)

épicier, -ière [episje, -jɛʀ] *nm/f* grocer

épicurien, ne [epikyʀjɛ̃, -ɛn] *adj* epicurean

épidémie [epidemi] *nf* epidemic

épidémique [epidemik] *adj* epidemic

épiderme [epidɛʀm(ə)] *nm* skin, epidermis

épidermique [epidɛʀmik] *adj* skin *cpd*, epidermic

épier [epje] *vt* to spy on, watch closely; (*occasion*) to look out for

épieu, x [epjø] *nm* (hunting-)spear

épigramme [epigʀam] *nf* epigram

épigraphe [epigʀaf] *nf* epigraph

épilation [epilasjɔ̃] *nf* removal of unwanted hair

épilatoire [epilatwaʀ] *adj* depilatory, hair-removing

épilepsie [epilɛpsi] *nf* epilepsy

épileptique [epilɛptik] *adj*, *nm/f* epileptic

épiler [epile] *vt* (*jambes*) to remove the hair from; (*sourcils*) to pluck; **s'~ les jambes** to remove the hair from one's legs; **s'~ les sourcils** to pluck one's eyebrows; **se faire ~** to get unwanted hair removed; **crème à ~** hair-removing *ou* depilatory cream; **pince à ~** eyebrow tweezers

épilogue [epilɔg] *nm* (*fig*) conclusion, dénouement

épiloguer [epilɔge] *vi*: **~ sur** to hold forth on

épinards [epinaʀ] *nmpl* spinach *sg*

épine [epin] *nf* thorn, prickle; (*d'oursin etc*) spine, prickle; **~ dorsale** backbone

épineux, -euse [epinø, -øz] *adj* thorny, prickly

épinglage [epɛ̃glaʒ] *nm* pinning

épingle [epɛ̃gl(ə)] *nf* pin; **tirer son ~ du jeu** to play one's game well; **tiré à quatre ~s** well turned-out; **monter qch en ~** to build sth up, make a thing of sth (*fam*); **~ à chapeau** hatpin; **~ à cheveux** hairpin; **virage en ~ à cheveux** hairpin bend; **~ de cravate** tie pin; **~ de nourrice** *ou* **de sûreté** *ou* **double** safety pin, nappy (*Brit*) *ou* diaper (*US*) pin

épingler [epɛ̃gle] *vt* (*badge, décoration*): **~ qch sur** to pin sth on(to); (*Couture: tissu, robe*) to pin together; (*fam*) to catch, nick

épinière [epinjɛʀ] *adj f voir* **moelle**

Épiphanie [epifani] *nf* Epiphany

épique [epik] *adj* epic

épiscopal, e, -aux [episkɔpal, -o] *adj* episcopal

épiscopat [episkɔpa] *nm* bishopric, episcopate

épisiotomie [epizjɔtɔmi] *nf* (*Méd*) episiotomy

épisode [epizɔd] *nm* episode; **film/roman à ~s** serialized film/novel, serial

épisodique [epizɔdik] *adj* occasional

épisodiquement [epizɔdikmã] *adv* occasionally

épissure [episyʀ] *nf* splice

épistémologie [epistemɔlɔʒi] *nf* epistemology

épistolaire [epistɔlɛʀ] *adj* epistolary; **être en relations ~s avec qn** to correspond with sb

épitaphe [epitaf] *nf* epitaph

épithète [epitɛt] *nf* (*nom, surnom*) epithet; **adjectif ~** attributive adjective

épître [epitʀ(ə)] *nf* epistle

éploré, e [eplɔʀe] *adj* in tears, tearful

épluchage [eplyʃaʒ] *nm* peeling; (*de dossier etc*) careful reading *ou* analysis

épluche-légumes [eplyʃlegym] *nm inv* potato peeler

éplucher [eplyʃe] *vt* (*fruit, légumes*) to peel; (*comptes, dossier*) to go over with a fine-tooth comb

éplucheur [eplyʃœʀ] *nm* (automatic) peeler

épluchures [eplyʃyʀ] *nfpl* peelings

épointer [epwɛ̃te] *vt* to blunt

éponge [epɔ̃ʒ] *nf* sponge; **passer l'~ (sur)** (*fig*) to let bygones be bygones (with regard to); **jeter l'~** (*fig*) to throw in the towel; **~ métallique** scourer

éponger [epɔ̃ʒe] *vt* (*liquide*) to mop *ou* sponge up; (*surface*) to sponge; (*fig: déficit*) to soak up, absorb; **s'~ le front** to mop one's brow

épopée [epɔpe] *nf* epic

époque [epɔk] *nf* (*de l'histoire*) age, era; (*de l'année, la vie*) time; **d'~** *adj* (*meuble*) period *cpd*; **à cette ~** at this (*ou* that) time *ou* period; **faire ~** to make history

épouiller [epuje] *vt* to pick lice off; (*avec un produit*) to delouse

époumoner [epumɔne]: **s'époumoner** *vi* to shout (*ou* sing) o.s. hoarse

épouse [epuz] *nf* wife

épouser [epuze] *vt* to marry; (*fig: idées*) to espouse; (*: forme*) to fit

époussetage [epustaʒ] *nm* dusting
épousseter [epuste] *vt* to dust
époustouflant, e [epustuflɑ̃, -ɑ̃t] *adj* staggering, mind-boggling
époustoufler [epustufle] *vt* to flabbergast, astound
épouvantable [epuvɑ̃tabl(ə)] *adj* appalling, dreadful
épouvantablement [epuvɑ̃tabləmɑ̃] *adj* terribly, dreadfully
épouvantail [epuvɑ̃taj] *nm* (*à moineaux*) scarecrow; (*fig*) bog(e)y; bugbear
épouvante [epuvɑ̃t] *nf* terror; **film d'~** horror film
épouvanter [epuvɑ̃te] *vt* to terrify
époux [epu] *nm* husband ▷ *nmpl*: **les ~** the (married) couple, the husband and wife
éprendre [eprɑ̃dr(ə)]: **s'éprendre de** *vt* to fall in love with
épreuve [eprœv] *nf* (*d'examen*) test; (*malheur, difficulté*) trial, ordeal; (*Photo*) print; (*Typo*) proof; (*Sport*) event; **à l'~ des balles/du feu** (*vêtement*) bulletproof/fireproof; **à toute ~** unfailing; **mettre à l'~** to put to the test; **~ de force** trial of strength; (*fig*) showdown; **~ de résistance** test of resistance; **~ de sélection** (*Sport*) heat
épris, e [epri, -iz] *vb voir* **éprendre** ▷ *adj*: **~ de** in love with
éprouvant, e [epruvɑ̃, -ɑ̃t] *adj* trying
éprouvé, e [epruve] *adj* tested, proven
éprouver [epruve] *vt* (*tester*) to test; (*mettre à l'épreuve*) to put to the test; (*marquer, faire souffrir*) to afflict, distress; (*ressentir*) to experience
éprouvette [epruvɛt] *nf* test tube
EPS *sigle f* (= *Éducation physique et sportive*) ≈ PE
épuisant, e [epɥizɑ̃, -ɑ̃t] *adj* exhausting
épuisé, e [epɥize] *adj* exhausted; (*livre*) out of print
épuisement [epɥizmɑ̃] *nm* exhaustion; **jusqu'à ~ des stocks** while stocks last
épuiser [epɥize] *vt* (*fatiguer*) to exhaust, wear *ou* tire out; (*stock, sujet*) to exhaust; **s'épuiser** *vi* to wear *ou* tire o.s. out, exhaust o.s.; (*stock*) to run out
épuisette [epɥizɛt] *nf* landing net; shrimping net
épuration [epyrasjɔ̃] *nf* purification; purging; refinement
épure [epyr] *nf* working drawing
épurer [epyre] *vt* (*liquide*) to purify; (*parti, administration*) to purge; (*langue, texte*) to refine
équarrir [ekarir] *vt* (*pierre, arbre*) to square (off); (*animal*) to quarter
équateur [ekwatœr] *nm* equator; **(la république de) l'É~** Ecuador
équation [ekwasjɔ̃] *nf* equation; **mettre en ~** to equate; **~ du premier/second degré** simple/quadratic equation
équatorial, e, -aux [ekwatɔrjal, -o] *adj* equatorial
équatorien, ne [ekwatɔrjɛ̃, -ɛn] *adj* Ecuadorian ▷ *nm/f*: **Équatorien, ne** Ecuadorian

équerre [ekɛr] *nf* (*à dessin*) (set) square; (*pour fixer*) brace; **en ~** at right angles; **à l'~, d'~** straight; **double ~** T-square
équestre [ekɛstr(ə)] *adj* equestrian
équeuter [ekøte] *vt* (*Culin*) to remove the stalk(s) from
équidé [ekide] *nm* (*Zool*) member of the horse family
équidistance [ekɥidistɑ̃s] *nf*: **à ~ (de)** equidistant (from)
équidistant, e [ekɥidistɑ̃, -ɑ̃t] *adj*: **~ (de)** equidistant (from)
équilatéral, e, -aux [ekɥilateral, -o] *adj* equilateral
équilibrage [ekilibraʒ] *nm* (*Auto*): **~ des roues** wheel balancing
équilibre [ekilibr(ə)] *nm* balance; (*d'une balance*) equilibrium; **~ budgétaire** balanced budget; **garder/perdre l'~** to keep/lose one's balance; **être en ~** to be balanced; **mettre en ~** to make steady; **avoir le sens de l'~** to be well-balanced
équilibré, e [ekilibre] *adj* (*fig*) well-balanced, stable
équilibrer [ekilibre] *vt* to balance; **s'équilibrer** *vi* (*poids*) to balance; (*fig: défauts etc*) to balance each other out
équilibriste [ekilibrist(ə)] *nm/f* tightrope walker
équinoxe [ekinɔks] *nm* equinox
équipage [ekipaʒ] *nm* crew; **en grand ~** in great array
équipe [ekip] *nf* team; (*bande: parfois péj*) bunch; **travailler par ~s** to work in shifts; **travailler en ~** to work as a team; **faire ~ avec** to team up with; **~ de chercheurs** research team; **~ de secours** *ou* **de sauvetage** rescue team
équipé, e [ekipe] *adj* (*cuisine etc*) equipped, fitted(-out) ▷ *nf* escapade
équipement [ekipmɑ̃] *nm* equipment; **équipements** *nmpl* amenities, facilities; installations; **biens/dépenses d'~** capital goods/expenditure; **ministère de l'É~** department of public works; **~s sportifs/collectifs** sports/community facilities *ou* resources
équiper [ekipe] *vt* to equip; (*voiture, cuisine*) to equip, fit out; **~ qn/qch de** to equip sb/sth with; **s'équiper** *vi* (*sportif*) to equip o.s., kit o.s. out
équipier, -ière [ekipje, -jɛr] *nm/f* team member
équitable [ekitabl(ə)] *adj* fair
équitablement [ekitabləmɑ̃] *adv* fairly, equitably
équitation [ekitasjɔ̃] *nf* (horse-)riding; **faire de l'~** to go (horse-)riding
équité [ekite] *nf* equity
équivaille *etc* [ekivaj] *vb voir* **équivaloir**
équivalence [ekivalɑ̃s] *nf* equivalence
équivalent, e [ekivalɑ̃, -ɑ̃t] *adj, nm* equivalent
équivaloir [ekivalwar]: **~ à** *vt* to be equivalent to; (*représenter*) to amount to
équivaut *etc* [ekivo] *vb voir* **équivaloir**
équivoque [ekivɔk] *adj* equivocal, ambiguous;

(*louche*) dubious ▷ *nf* ambiguity
érable [eRabl(ə)] *nm* maple
éradication [eRadikasjɔ̃] *nf* eradication
éradiquer [eRadike] *vt* to eradicate
érafler [eRafle] *vt* to scratch; **s'~ la main/les jambes** to scrape *ou* scratch one's hand/legs
éraflure [eRaflyR] *nf* scratch
éraillé, e [eRaje] *adj* (*voix*) rasping, hoarse
ère [eR] *nf* era; **en l'an 1050 de notre ~** in the year 1050 A.D.
érection [eReksjɔ̃] *nf* erection
éreintant, e [eRẽtɑ̃, -ɑ̃t] *adj* exhausting
éreinté, e [eRẽte] *adj* exhausted
éreintement [eRẽtmɑ̃] *nm* exhaustion
éreinter [eRẽte] *vt* to exhaust, wear out; (*fig: critiquer*) to slate; **s'~ (à faire qch/à qch)** to wear o.s. out (doing sth/with sth)
ergonomie [eRgɔnɔmi] *nf* ergonomics *sg*
ergonomique [eRgɔnɔmik] *adj* ergonomic
ergot [eRgo] *nm* (*de coq*) spur; (*Tech*) lug
ergoter [eRgɔte] *vi* to split hairs, argue over details
ergoteur, -euse [eRgɔtœR, -øz] *nm/f* hairsplitter
ériger [eRiʒe] *vt* (*monument*) to erect; **~ qch en principe/loi** to make sth a principle/law; **s'~ en critique (de)** to set o.s. up as a critic (of)
ermitage [eRmitaʒ] *nm* retreat
ermite [eRmit] *nm* hermit
éroder [eRɔde] *vt* to erode
érogène [eRɔʒɛn] *adj* erogenous
érosion [eRozjɔ̃] *nf* erosion
érotique [eRɔtik] *adj* erotic
érotiquement [eRɔtikmɑ̃] *adv* erotically
érotisme [eRɔtism(ə)] *nm* eroticism
errance [eRɑ̃s] *nf* wandering
errant, e [eRɑ̃, -ɑ̃t] *adj*: **un chien ~** a stray dog
erratum [eRatɔm, -a] (*pl* **errata**) *nm* erratum
errements [eRmɑ̃] *nmpl* misguided ways
errer [eRe] *vi* to wander
erreur [eRœR] *nf* mistake, error; (*Inform*) error; (*morale*): **~s** *nfpl* errors; **être dans l'~** to be wrong; **induire qn en ~** to mislead sb; **par ~** by mistake; **sauf ~** unless I'm mistaken; **faire ~** to be mistaken; **~ de date** mistake in the date; **~ de fait** error of fact; **~ d'impression** (*Typo*) misprint; **~ judiciaire** miscarriage of justice; **~ de jugement** error of judgment; **~ matérielle** *ou* **d'écriture** clerical error; **~ tactique** tactical error
erroné, e [eRɔne] *adj* wrong, erroneous
ersatz [eRzats] *nm* substitute, ersatz; **~ de café** coffee substitute
éructer [eRykte] *vi* to belch
érudit, e [eRydi, -it] *adj* erudite, learned ▷ *nm/f* scholar
érudition [eRydisjɔ̃] *nf* erudition, scholarship
éruptif, -ive [eRyptif, -iv] *adj* eruptive
éruption [eRypsjɔ̃] *nf* eruption; (*cutanée*) outbreak; (*: boutons*) rash; (*fig: de joie, colère, folie*) outburst
E/S *abr* (= *entrée/sortie*) I/O (= in/out)
es [ɛ] *vb voir* **être**

ès [ɛs] *prép*: **licencié ès lettres/sciences** ≈ Bachelor of Arts/Science; **docteur ès lettres** ≈ doctor of philosophy, ≈ PhD
esbroufe [ɛsbRuf] *nf*: **faire de l'~** to have people on
escabeau, x [ɛskabo] *nm* (*tabouret*) stool; (*échelle*) stepladder
escadre [ɛskadR(ə)] *nf* (*Navig*) squadron; (*Aviat*) wing
escadrille [ɛskadRij] *nf* (*Aviat*) flight
escadron [ɛskadRɔ̃] *nm* squadron
escalade [ɛskalad] *nf* climbing *no pl*; (*Pol etc*) escalation
escalader [ɛskalade] *vt* to climb, scale
escalator [ɛskalatɔR] *nm* escalator
escale [ɛskal] *nf* (*Navig*) call; (*: port*) port of call; (*Aviat*) stop(over); **faire ~ à** to put in at, call in at; to stop over at; **~ technique** (*Aviat*) refuelling stop
escalier [ɛskalje] *nm* stairs *pl*; **dans l'~** *ou* **les ~s** on the stairs; **descendre l'~** *ou* **les ~s** to go downstairs; **~ mécanique** *ou* **roulant** escalator; **~ de secours** fire escape; **~ de service** backstairs; **~ à vis** *ou* **en colimaçon** spiral staircase
escalope [ɛskalɔp] *nf* escalope
escamotable [ɛskamɔtabl(ə)] *adj* (*train d'atterrissage, antenne*) retractable; (*table, lit*) fold-away
escamoter [ɛskamɔte] *vt* (*esquiver*) to get round, evade; (*faire disparaître*) to conjure away; (*dérober: portefeuille etc*) to snatch; (*train d'atterrissage*) to retract; (*mots*) to miss out
escapade [ɛskapad] *nf*: **faire une ~** to go on a jaunt; (*s'enfuir*) to run away *ou* off
escarbille [ɛskaRbij] *nf* bit of grit
escarcelle [ɛskaRsɛl] *nf*: **faire tomber dans l'~** (*argent*) to bring in
escargot [ɛskaRgo] *nm* snail
escarmouche [ɛskaRmuʃ] *nf* (*Mil*) skirmish; (*fig: propos hostiles*) angry exchange
escarpé, e [ɛskaRpe] *adj* steep
escarpement [ɛskaRpəmɑ̃] *nm* steep slope
escarpin [ɛskaRpɛ̃] *nm* flat(-heeled) shoe
escarre [ɛskaR] *nf* bedsore
Escaut [ɛsko] *nm*: **l'~** the Scheldt
escient [esjɑ̃] *nm*: **à bon ~** advisedly
esclaffer [ɛsklafe]: **s'esclaffer** *vi* to guffaw
esclandre [ɛsklɑ̃dR(ə)] *nm* scene, fracas
esclavage [ɛsklavaʒ] *nm* slavery
esclavagiste [ɛsklavaʒist(ə)] *adj* pro-slavery ▷ *nm/f* supporter of slavery
esclave [ɛsklav] *nm/f* slave; **être ~ de** (*fig*) to be a slave of
escogriffe [ɛskɔgRif] *nm* (*péj*) beanpole
escompte [ɛskɔ̃t] *nm* discount
escompter [ɛskɔ̃te] *vt* (*Comm*) to discount; (*espérer*) to expect, reckon upon; **~ que** to reckon *ou* expect that
escorte [ɛskɔRt(ə)] *nf* escort; **faire ~ à** to escort
escorter [ɛskɔRte] *vt* to escort
escorteur [ɛskɔRtœR] *nm* (*Navig*) escort (ship)

159

escouade [ɛskwad] *nf* squad; *(fig: groupe de personnes)* group

escrime [ɛskRim] *nf* fencing; **faire de l'~** to fence

escrimer [ɛskRime]: **s'escrimer** *vi*: **s'~ à faire** to wear o.s. out doing

escrimeur, -euse [ɛskRimœR, -øz] *nm/f* fencer

escroc [ɛskRo] *nm* swindler, con-man

escroquer [ɛskRɔke] *vt*: **~ qn (de qch)/qch à qn** to swindle sb (out of sth)/sth out of sb

escroquerie [ɛskRɔkRi] *nf* swindle

ésotérique [ezɔteRik] *adj* esoteric

espace [ɛspas] *nm* space; **~ publicitaire** advertising space; **~ vital** living space

espacé, e [ɛspase] *adj* spaced out

espacement [ɛspasmã] *nm*: **~ proportionnel** proportional spacing *(on printer)*

espacer [ɛspase] *vt* to space out; **s'espacer** *vi* *(visites etc)* to become less frequent

espadon [ɛspadɔ̃] *nm* swordfish *inv*

espadrille [ɛspadRij] *nf* rope-soled sandal

Espagne [ɛspaɲ(ə)] *nf*: **l'~** Spain

espagnol, e [ɛspaɲɔl] *adj* Spanish ▷ *nm* *(Ling)* Spanish ▷ *nm/f*: **Espagnol, e** Spaniard

espagnolette [ɛspaɲɔlɛt] *nf* (window) catch; **fermé à l'~** resting on the catch

espalier [ɛspalje] *nm* *(arbre fruitier)* espalier

espèce [ɛspɛs] *nf* *(Bio, Bot, Zool)* species *inv*; *(gén: sorte)* sort, kind, type; *(péj)*: **~ de maladroit/de brute!** you clumsy oaf/you brute!; **espèces** *nfpl* *(Comm)* cash *sg*; *(Rel)* species; **de toute ~** of all kinds *ou* sorts; **en l'~** *adv* in the case in point; **payer en ~s** to pay (in) cash; **cas d'~** individual case; **l'~ humaine** humankind

espérance [ɛspeRãs] *nf* hope; **~ de vie** life expectancy

espéranto [ɛspeRãto] *nm* Esperanto

espérer [ɛspeRe] *vt* to hope for; **j'espère (bien)** I hope so; **~ que/faire** to hope that/to do; **~ en** to trust in

espiègle [ɛspjɛgl(ə)] *adj* mischievous

espièglerie [ɛspjɛgləRi] *nf* mischievousness; *(tour, farce)* piece of mischief, prank

espion, ne [ɛspjɔ̃, -ɔn] *nm/f* spy; **avion ~** spy plane

espionnage [ɛspjɔnaʒ] *nm* espionage, spying; **film/roman d'~** spy film/novel

espionner [ɛspjɔne] *vt* to spy (up)on

esplanade [ɛsplanad] *nf* esplanade

espoir [ɛspwaR] *nm* hope; **l'~ de qch/de faire qch** the hope of sth/of doing sth; **avoir bon ~ que ...** to have high hopes that ...; **garder l'~ que ...** to remain hopeful that ...; **un ~ de la boxe/du ski** one of boxing's/skiing's hopefuls, one of the hopes of boxing/skiing; **sans ~** *adj* hopeless

esprit [ɛspRi] *nm* *(pensée, intellect)* mind; *(humour, ironie)* wit; *(mentalité, d'une loi etc, fantôme etc)* spirit; **l'~ d'équipe/de compétition** team/competitive spirit; **faire de l'~** to try to be witty; **reprendre ses ~s** to come to; **perdre l'~** to lose one's mind; **avoir bon/mauvais ~** to be

of a good/bad disposition; **avoir l'~ à faire qch** to have a mind to do sth; **avoir l'~ critique** to be critical; **~ de contradiction** contrariness; **~ de corps** esprit de corps; **~ de famille** family loyalty; **l'~ malin** *(le diable)* the Evil One; **~s chagrins** fault-finders

esquif [ɛskif] *nm* skiff

esquimau, de, -x [ɛskimo, -od] *adj* Eskimo ▷ *nm* *(Ling)* Eskimo; *(glace)*: **E~®** ice lolly *(Brit)*, popsicle *(US)* ▷ *nm/f*: **Esquimau, de** Eskimo; **chien ~** husky

esquinter [ɛskɛ̃te] *vt* *(fam)* to mess up; **s'esquinter** *vi*: **s'~ à faire qch** to knock o.s. out doing sth

esquisse [ɛskis] *nf* sketch; **l'~ d'un sourire/ changement** a hint of a smile/of change

esquisser [ɛskise] *vt* to sketch; **s'esquisser** *vi* *(amélioration)* to begin to be detectable; **~ un sourire** to give a hint of a smile

esquive [ɛskiv] *nf* *(Boxe)* dodging; *(fig)* sidestepping

esquiver [ɛskive] *vt* to dodge; **s'esquiver** *vi* to slip away

essai [esɛ] *nm* trying; *(tentative)* attempt, try; *(Rugby)* try; *(Littérature)* essay; **essais** *nmpl* *(Auto)* trials; **à l'~** on a trial basis; **~ gratuit** *(Comm)* free trial

essaim [esɛ̃] *nm* swarm

essaimer [eseme] *vi* to swarm; *(fig)* to spread, expand

essayage [esɛjaʒ] *nm* *(d'un vêtement)* trying on, fitting; **salon d'~** fitting room; **cabine d'~** fitting room *(cubicle)*

essayer [eseje] *vt* *(gén)* to try; *(vêtement, chaussures)* to try (on); *(restaurant, méthode, voiture)* to try (out) ▷ *vi* to try; **~ de faire** to try *ou* attempt to do; **s'~ à faire** to try one's hand at doing; **essayez un peu!** *(menace)* just you try!

essayeur, -euse [esɛjœR, -øz] *nm/f* *(chez un tailleur etc)* fitter

essayiste [esejist(ə)] *nm/f* essayist

ESSEC [ɛsɛk] *sigle f* (= *École supérieure des sciences économiques et sociales*) *grande école for management and business studies*

essence [esɑ̃s] *nf* *(de voiture)* petrol *(Brit)*, gas(oline) *(US)*; *(extrait de plante, Philosophie)* essence; *(espèce: d'arbre)* species *inv*; **prendre de l'~** to get (some) petrol *ou* gas; **par ~** *(essentiellement)* essentially; **~ de citron/rose** lemon/rose oil; **~ sans plomb** unleaded petrol; **~ de térébenthine** turpentine

essentiel, le [esɑ̃sjɛl] *adj* essential ▷ *nm*: **l'~ d'un discours/d'une œuvre** the essence of a speech/work of art; **emporter l'~** to take the essentials; **c'est l'~** *(ce qui importe)* that's the main thing; **l'~ de** *(la majeure partie)* the main part of

essentiellement [esɑ̃sjɛlmɑ̃] *adv* essentially

esseulé, e [esœle] *adj* forlorn

essieu, x [esjø] *nm* axle

essor [esɔR] *nm* *(de l'économie etc)* rapid expansion; **prendre son ~** *(oiseau)* to fly off

essorage [esɔʀaʒ] *nm* wringing out; spin-drying; spinning; shaking

essorer [esɔʀe] *vt* (*en tordant*) to wring (out); (*par la force centrifuge*) to spin-dry; (*salade*) to spin; (: *en secouant*) to shake dry

essoreuse [esɔʀøz] *nf* mangle, wringer; (*à tambour*) spin-dryer

essoufflé, e [esufle] *adj* out of breath, breathless

essouffler [esufle] *vt* to make breathless; **s'essouffler** *vi* to get out of breath; (*fig: économie*) to run out of steam

essuie *etc* [esɥi] *vb voir* **essuyer**

essuie-glace [esɥiglas] *nm* windscreen (*Brit*) *ou* windshield (*US*) wiper

essuie-mains [esɥimɛ̃] *nm inv* hand towel

essuierai *etc* [esɥiʀe] *vb voir* **essuyer**

essuie-tout [esɥitu] *nm inv* kitchen paper

essuyer [esɥije] *vt* to wipe; (*fig: subir*) to suffer; **s'essuyer** (*après le bain*) to dry o.s.; **~ la vaisselle** to dry up, dry the dishes

est [ɛ] *vb voir* **être** ▷ *nm* [ɛst]: **l'~** the east ▷ *adj inv* east; (*région*) east(ern); **à l'~** in the east; (*direction*) to the east, east(wards); **à l'~ de** (to the) east of; **les pays de l'E~** the eastern countries

estafette [ɛstafɛt] *nf* (*Mil*) dispatch rider

estafilade [ɛstafilad] *nf* gash, slash

est-allemand, e [ɛstalmɑ̃, -ɑ̃d] *adj* East German

estaminet [ɛstaminɛ] *nm* tavern

estampe [ɛstɑ̃p] *nf* print, engraving

estamper [ɛstɑ̃pe] *vt* (*monnaies etc*) to stamp; (*fam: escroquer*) to swindle

estampille [ɛstɑ̃pij] *nf* stamp

est-ce que [ɛskə] *adv*: **~ c'est cher/c'était bon?** is it expensive/was it good?; **quand est-ce qu'il part?** when does he leave?, when is he leaving?; **où est-ce qu'il va?** where's he going?; *voir aussi* **que**

este [ɛst(ə)] *adj* Estonian ▷ *nm/f*: **Este** Estonian

esthète [ɛstɛt] *nm/f* aesthete

esthéticienne [ɛstetisjɛn] *nf* beautician

esthétique [ɛstetik] *adj* (*sens, jugement*) aesthetic; (*beau*) attractive, aesthetically pleasing ▷ *nf* aesthetics *sg*; **l'~ industrielle** industrial design

esthétiquement [ɛstetikmɑ̃] *adv* aesthetically

estimable [ɛstimabl(ə)] *adj* respected

estimatif, -ive [ɛstimatif, -iv] *adj* estimated

estimation [ɛstimasjɔ̃] *nf* valuation; assessment; **d'après mes ~s** according to my calculations

estime [ɛstim] *nf* esteem, regard; **avoir de l'~ pour qn** to think highly of sb

estimer [ɛstime] *vt* (*respecter*) to esteem, hold in high regard; (*expertiser*) to value; (*évaluer*) to assess, estimate; (*penser*): **~ que/être** to consider that/o.s. to be; **s'estimer satisfait/ heureux** *vi* to feel satisfied/happy; **j'estime la distance à 10 km** I reckon the distance to be 10 km

estival, e, -aux [ɛstival, -o] *adj* summer *cpd*;

station **~e** (summer) holiday resort

estivant, e [ɛstivɑ̃, -ɑ̃t] *nm/f* (summer) holiday-maker

estoc [ɛstɔk] *nm*: **frapper d'~ et de taille** to cut and thrust

estocade [ɛstɔkad] *nf* death-blow

estomac [ɛstɔma] *nm* stomach; **avoir mal à l'~** to have stomach ache; **avoir l'~ creux** to have an empty stomach

estomaqué, e [ɛstɔmake] *adj* flabbergasted

estompe [ɛstɔ̃p] *nf* stump; (*dessin*) stump drawing

estompé, e [ɛstɔ̃pe] *adj* blurred

estomper [ɛstɔ̃pe] *vt* (*Art*) to shade off; (*fig*) to blur, dim; **s'estomper** *vi* (*sentiments*) to soften; (*contour*) to become blurred

Estonie [ɛstɔni] *nf*: **l'~** Estonia

estonien, ne [ɛstɔnjɛ̃, -ɛn] *adj* Estonian ▷ *nm* (*Ling*) Estonian ▷ *nm/f*: **Estonien, ne** Estonian

estrade [ɛstʀad] *nf* platform, rostrum

estragon [ɛstʀagɔ̃] *nm* tarragon

estropié, e [ɛstʀɔpje] *nm/f* cripple

estropier [ɛstʀɔpje] *vt* to cripple, maim; (*fig*) to twist, distort

estuaire [ɛstɥɛʀ] *nm* estuary

estudiantin, e [ɛstydjɑ̃tɛ̃, -in] *adj* student *cpd*

esturgeon [ɛstyʀʒɔ̃] *nm* sturgeon

et [e] *conj* and; **et lui?** what about him?; **et alors?, et (puis) après?** so what?; (*ensuite*) and then?

ét. *abr* = **étage**

ETA [eta] *sigle m* (*Pol*) ETA

étable [etabl(ə)] *nf* cowshed

établi, e [etabli] *adj* established ▷ *nm* (work)bench

établir [etabliʀ] *vt* (*papiers d'identité, facture*) to make out; (*liste, programme*) to draw up; (*gouvernement, artisan etc: aider à s'installer*) to set up, establish; (*entreprise, atelier, camp*) to set up; (*réputation, usage, fait, culpabilité, relations*) to establish; (*Sport: record*) to set; **s'établir** *vi* (*se faire: entente etc*) to be established; **s'~ (à son compte)** to set up in business; **s'~ à/près de** to settle in/near

établissement [etablismɑ̃] *nm* making out; drawing up; setting up, establishing; (*entreprise, institution*) establishment; **~ de crédit** credit institution; **~ hospitalier** hospital complex; **~ industriel** industrial plant, factory; **~ scolaire** school, educational establishment

étage [etaʒ] *nm* (*d'immeuble*) storey (*Brit*), story (*US*), floor; (*de fusée*) stage; (*Géo: de culture, végétation*) level; **au 2ème ~** on the 2nd (*Brit*) *ou* 3rd (*US*) floor; **à l'~** upstairs; **maison à deux ~s** two-storey *ou* -story house; **de bas ~** *adj* low-born; (*médiocre*) inferior

étager [etaʒe] *vt* (*cultures*) to lay out in tiers; **s'étager** *vi* (*prix*) to range; (*zones, cultures*) to lie on different levels

étagère [etaʒɛʀ] *nf* (*rayon*) shelf; (*meuble*) shelves *pl*, set of shelves

étai [etɛ] *nm* stay, prop

e

étain [etɛ̃] *nm* tin; (*Orfèvrerie*) pewter *no pl*
étais *etc* [etɛ] *vb voir* **être**
étal [etal] *nm* stall
étalage [etalaʒ] *nm* display; (*vitrine*) display window; **faire ~ de** to show off, parade
étalagiste [etalaʒist(ə)] *nm/f* window-dresser
étale [etal] *adj* (*mer*) slack
étalement [etalmɑ̃] *nm* spreading; (*échelonnement*) staggering
étaler [etale] *vt* (*carte, nappe*) to spread (out); (*peinture, liquide*) to spread; (*échelonner: paiements, dates, vacances*) to spread, stagger; (*exposer: marchandises*) to display; (*richesses, connaissances*) to parade; **s'étaler** *vi* (*liquide*) to spread out; (*fam*) to come a cropper (*Brit*), fall flat on one's face; **s'~ sur** (*paiements etc*) to be spread over
étalon [etalɔ̃] *nm* (*mesure*) standard; (*cheval*) stallion; **l'~-or** the gold standard
étalonner [etalɔne] *vt* to calibrate
étamer [etame] *vt* (*casserole*) to tin(plate); (*glace*) to silver
étamine [etamin] *nf* (*Bot*) stamen; (*tissu*) butter muslin
étanche [etɑ̃ʃ] *adj* (*récipient, aussi fig*) watertight; (*montre, vêtement*) waterproof; **~ à l'air** airtight
étanchéité [etɑ̃ʃeite] *nf* watertightness; airtightness
étancher [etɑ̃ʃe] *vt* (*liquide*) to stop (flowing); **~ sa soif** to quench *ou* slake one's thirst
étançon [etɑ̃sɔ̃] *nm* (*Tech*) prop
étançonner [etɑ̃sɔne] *vt* to prop up
étang [etɑ̃] *nm* pond
étant [etɑ̃] *vb voir* **être; donné**
étape [etap] *nf* stage; (*lieu d'arrivée*) stopping place; (*Cyclisme*) staging point; **faire ~ à** to stop off at; **brûler les ~s** (*fig*) to cut corners
état [eta] *nm* (*Pol, condition*) state; (*d'un article d'occasion etc*) condition, state; (*liste*) inventory, statement; (*condition: professionnelle*) profession, trade; (: *sociale*) status; **en bon/mauvais ~** in good/poor condition; **en ~ (de marche)** in (working) order; **remettre en ~** to repair; **hors d'~** out of order; **être en ~/hors d'~ de faire** to be in a state/in no fit state to do; **en tout ~ de cause** in any event; **être dans tous ses ~s** to be in a state; **faire ~ de** (*alléguer*) to put forward; **en ~ d'arrestation** under arrest; **~ de grâce** (*Rel*) state of grace; (*fig*) honeymoon period; **en ~ de grâce** (*fig*) inspired; **en ~ d'ivresse** under the influence of drink; **~ de choses** (*situation*) state of affairs; **~ civil** civil status; (*bureau*) registry office (*Brit*); **~ d'esprit** frame of mind; **~ des lieux** inventory of fixtures; **~ de santé** state of health; **~ de siège/d'urgence** state of siege/emergency; **~ de veille** (*Psych*) waking state; **~s d'âme** moods; **les É~s barbaresques** the Barbary States; **les É~s du Golfe** the Gulf States; **~s de service** service record *sg*
étatique [etatik] *adj* state *cpd*, State *cpd*
étatisation [etatizasjɔ̃] *nf* nationalization
étatiser [etatize] *vt* to bring under state control
étatisme [etatism(ə)] *nm* state control

étatiste [etatist(ə)] *adj* (*doctrine etc*) of state control ▷ *nm/f* partisan of state control
état-major [etamaʒɔʀ] (*pl* **états-majors**) *nm* (*Mil*) staff; (*d'un parti etc*) top advisers *pl*; (*d'une entreprise*) top management
État-providence [etapʀɔvidɑ̃s] *nm* welfare state
États-Unis [etazyni] *nmpl*: **les ~ (d'Amérique)** the United States (of America)
étau, x [eto] *nm* vice (*Brit*), vise (*US*)
étayer [eteje] *vt* to prop *ou* shore up; (*fig*) to back up
et cætera, et cetera [ɛtsetera], **etc.** *adv* et cetera, and so on, etc
été [ete] *pp de* **être** ▷ *nm* summer; **en ~** in summer
éteignais *etc* [etɛɲɛ] *vb voir* **éteindre**
éteignoir [etɛɲwaʀ] *nm* (*candle*) snuffer; (*péj*) killjoy, wet blanket
éteindre [etɛ̃dʀ(ə)] *vt* (*lampe, lumière, radio, chauffage*) to turn *ou* switch off; (*cigarette, incendie, bougie*) to put out, extinguish; (*Jur: dette*) to extinguish; **s'éteindre** *vi* to go off; to go out; (*mourir*) to pass away
éteint, e [etɛ̃, -ɛ̃t] *pp de* **éteindre** ▷ *adj* (*fig*) lacklustre, dull; (*volcan*) extinct; **tous feux ~s** (*Auto: rouler*) without lights
étendard [etɑ̃daʀ] *nm* standard
étendre [etɑ̃dʀ(ə)] *vt* (*appliquer: pâte, liquide*) to spread; (*déployer: carte etc*) to spread out; (*sur un fil: lessive, linge*) to hang up *ou* out; (*bras, jambes, par terre: blessé*) to stretch out; (*diluer*) to dilute, thin; (*fig: agrandir*) to extend; (*fam: adversaire*) to floor; **s'étendre** *vi* (*augmenter, se propager*) to spread; (*terrain, forêt etc*): **s'~ jusqu'à/de ... à** to stretch as far as/from ... to; **s'~ (sur)** (*s'allonger*) to stretch out (upon); (*se coucher*) to lie down (on); (*fig: expliquer*) to elaborate *ou* enlarge (upon)
étendu, e [etɑ̃dy] *adj* extensive ▷ *nf* (*d'eau, de sable*) stretch, expanse; (*importance*) extent
éternel, le [etɛʀnɛl] *adj* eternal; **les neiges ~les** perpetual snow
éternellement [etɛʀnɛlmɑ̃] *adv* eternally
éterniser [etɛʀnize]: **s'éterniser** *vi* to last for ages; (*personne*) to stay for ages
éternité [etɛʀnite] *nf* eternity; **il y a** *ou* **ça fait une ~ que** it's ages since; **de toute ~** from time immemorial
éternuement [etɛʀnymɑ̃] *nm* sneeze
éternuer [etɛʀnɥe] *vi* to sneeze
êtes [ɛt] *vb voir* **être**
étêter [etete] *vt* (*arbre*) to poll(ard); (*clou, poisson*) to cut the head off
éther [etɛʀ] *nm* ether
éthéré, e [etere] *adj* ethereal
Éthiopie [etjɔpi] *nf*: **l'~** Ethiopia
éthiopien, ne [etjɔpjɛ̃, -ɛn] *adj* Ethiopian
éthique [etik] *adj* ethical ▷ *nf* ethics *sg*
ethnie [ɛtni] *nf* ethnic group
ethnique [ɛtnik] *adj* ethnic
ethnographe [ɛtnɔgraf] *nm/f* ethnographer
ethnographie [ɛtnɔgrafi] *nf* ethnography

ethnographique [ɛtnɔgʀafik] *adj* ethnographic(al)

ethnologie [ɛtnɔlɔʒi] *nf* ethnology

ethnologique [ɛtnɔlɔʒik] *adj* ethnological

ethnologue [ɛtnɔlɔg] *nm/f* ethnologist

éthylique [etilik] *adj* alcoholic

éthylisme [etilism(ə)] *nm* alcoholism

étiage [etjaʒ] *nm* low water

étiez [etje] *vb voir* **être**

étincelant, e [etēslɑ̃, -ɑ̃t] *adj* sparkling

étinceler [etēsle] *vi* to sparkle

étincelle [etēsɛl] *nf* spark

étioler [etjɔle]: **s'étioler** *vi* to wilt

étions [etjɔ̃] *vb voir* **être**

étique [etik] *adj* skinny, bony

étiquetage [etiktaʒ] *nm* labelling

étiqueter [etikte] *vt* to label

étiquette [etikɛt] *vb voir* **étiqueter** ▷ *nf* label; (*protocole*): **l'~** etiquette

étirer [etiʀe] *vt* to stretch; (*ressort*) to stretch out; **s'étirer** *vi* (*personne*) to stretch; (*convoi, route*): **s'~ sur** to stretch out over

étoffe [etɔf] *nf* material, fabric; **avoir l'~ d'un chef** *etc* to be cut out to be a leader *etc*; **avoir de l'~** to be a forceful personality

étoffer [etɔfe] *vt* to flesh out; **s'étoffer** *vi* to fill out

étoile [etwal] *nf* star ▷ *adj*: **danseuse** *ou* **danseur ~** leading dancer; **la bonne/mauvaise ~ de qn** sb's lucky/unlucky star; **à la belle ~** (out) in the open; **~ filante** shooting star; **~ de mer** starfish; **~ polaire** pole star

étoilé, e [etwale] *adj* starry

étole [etɔl] *nf* stole

étonnamment [etɔnamɑ̃] *adv* amazingly

étonnant, e [etɔnɑ̃, -ɑ̃t] *adj* surprising

étonné, e [etɔne] *adj* surprised

étonnement [etɔnmɑ̃] *nm* surprise; **à mon grand ~ ...** to my great surprise *ou* amazement ...

étonner [etɔne] *vt* to surprise; **s'étonner que/de** to be surprised that/at; **cela m'~ait (que)** (*j'en doute*) I'd be (very) surprised (if)

étouffant, e [etufɑ̃, -ɑ̃t] *adj* stifling

étouffé, e [etufe] *adj* (*asphyxié*) suffocated; (*assourdi: cris, rires*) smothered ▷ *nf*: **à l'~e** (*Culin: poisson, légumes*) steamed; (*: viande*) braised

étouffement [etufmɑ̃] *nm* suffocation

étouffer [etufe] *vt* to suffocate; (*bruit*) to muffle; (*scandale*) to hush up ▷ *vi* to suffocate; (*avoir trop chaud; aussi fig*) to feel stifled; **s'étouffer** *vi* (*en mangeant etc*) to choke

étouffoir [etufwaʀ] *nm* (*Mus*) damper

étourderie [etuʀdəʀi] *nf* heedlessness *no pl*; thoughtless blunder; **faute d'~** careless mistake

étourdi, e [etuʀdi] *adj* (*distrait*) scatterbrained, heedless

étourdiment [etuʀdimɑ̃] *adv* rashly

étourdir [etuʀdiʀ] *vt* (*assommer*) to stun, daze; (*griser*) to make dizzy *ou* giddy

étourdissant, e [etuʀdisɑ̃, -ɑ̃t] *adj* staggering

étourdissement [etuʀdismɑ̃] *nm* dizzy spell

étourneau, x [etuʀno] *nm* starling

étrange [etʀɑ̃ʒ] *adj* strange

étrangement [etʀɑ̃ʒmɑ̃] *adv* strangely

étranger, -ère [etʀɑ̃ʒe, -ɛʀ] *adj* foreign; (*pas de la famille, non familier*) strange ▷ *nm/f* foreigner; stranger ▷ *nm*: **l'~** foreign countries; **à l'~** abroad; **de l'~** from abroad; **~ à** (*mal connu*) unfamiliar to; (*sans rapport*) irrelevant to

étrangeté [etʀɑ̃ʒte] *nf* strangeness

étranglé, e [etʀɑ̃gle] *adj*: **d'une voix ~e** in a strangled voice

étranglement [etʀɑ̃gləmɑ̃] *nm* (*d'une vallée etc*) constriction, narrow passage

étrangler [etʀɑ̃gle] *vt* to strangle; (*fig: presse, libertés*) to stifle; **s'étrangler** *vi* (*en mangeant etc*) to choke; (*se resserrer*) to make a bottleneck

étrave [etʀav] *nf* stem

 MOT-CLÉ

être [ɛtʀ(ə)] *nm* being; **être humain** human being

▷ *vb copule* **1** (*état, description*) to be; **il est instituteur** he is *ou* he's a teacher; **vous êtes grand/intelligent/fatigué** you are *ou* you're tall/clever/tired

2 (+à: *appartenir*) to be; **le livre est à Paul** the book is Paul's *ou* belongs to Paul; **c'est à moi/eux** it is *ou* it's mine/theirs

3 (+de: *provenance*): **il est de Paris** he is from Paris; (*appartenance*;): **il est des nôtres** he is one of us

4 (*date*): **nous sommes le 10 janvier** it's the 10th of January (today)

▷ *vi* to be; **je ne serai pas ici demain** I won't be here tomorrow

▷ *vb aux* **1** to have; to be; **être arrivé/allé** to have arrived/gone; **il est parti** he has left, he has gone

2 (*forme passive*) to be; **être fait par** to be made by; **il a été promu** he has been promoted

3 (+à +inf: *obligation, but*): **c'est à réparer** it needs repairing; **c'est à essayer** it should be tried; **il est à espérer que ...** it is *ou* it's to be hoped that ...

▷ *vb impers* **1**: **il est** (*avec adjectif*) it is; **il est impossible de le faire** it's impossible to do it

2 (*heure, date*): **il est 10 heures** it is *ou* it's 10 o'clock

3 (*emphatique*): **c'est moi** it's me; **c'est à lui de le faire** it's up to him to do it; *voir aussi* **est-ce que; n'est-ce pas; c'est-à-dire; ce**

étreindre [etʀēdʀ(ə)] *vt* to clutch, grip; (*amoureusement, amicalement*) to embrace; **s'étreindre** to embrace

étreinte [etʀēt] *nf* clutch, grip; embrace; **resserrer son ~ autour de** (*fig*) to tighten one's grip on *ou* around

étrenner [etʀene] *vt* to use (*ou* wear) for the first time

étrennes [etʀɛn] *nfpl* (*cadeaux*) New Year's present; (*gratifications*) ≈ Christmas box *sg*, ≈ Christmas bonus

étrier [etʀije] *nm* stirrup

étriller [etʀije] *vt* (*cheval*) to curry; (*fam: battre*) to slaughter (*fig*)

étriper [etʀipe] *vt* to gut; (*fam*): ~ **qn** to tear sb's guts out

étriqué, e [etʀike] *adj* skimpy

étroit, e [etʀwa, -wat] *adj* narrow; (*vêtement*) tight; (*fig: serré*) close, tight; **à l'~** cramped; ~ **d'esprit** narrow-minded

étroitement [etʀwatmɑ̃] *adv* closely

étroitesse [etʀwatɛs] *nf* narrowness; ~ **d'esprit** narrow-mindedness

étrusque [etʀysk(ə)] *adj* Etruscan

étude [etyd] *nf* studying; (*ouvrage, rapport, Mus*) study; (*de notaire: bureau*) office; (: *charge*) practice; (*Scol: salle de travail*) study room; **études** *nfpl* (*Scol*) studies; **être à l'~** (*projet etc*) to be under consideration; **faire des ~s (de droit/médecine)** to study (law/medicine); **~s secondaires/supérieures** secondary/higher education; **~ de cas** case study; **~ de faisabilité** feasibility study; **~ de marché** (*Écon*) market research

étudiant, e [etydjɑ̃, -ɑ̃t] *adj, nm/f* student

étudié, e [etydje] *adj* (*démarche*) studied; (*système*) carefully designed; (*prix*) keen

étudier [etydje] *vt, vi* to study

étui [etɥi] *nm* case

étuve [etyv] *nf* steamroom; (*appareil*) sterilizer

étuvée [etyve]: **à l'~** *adv* braised

étymologie [etimɔlɔʒi] *nf* etymology

étymologique [etimɔlɔʒik] *adj* etymological

eu, eue [y] *pp de* **avoir**

EU *sigle mpl* (= *États-Unis*) US

EUA *sigle mpl* (= *États-Unis d'Amérique*) USA

eucalyptus [økaliptys] *nm* eucalyptus

Eucharistie [økaʀisti] *nf*: **l'~** the Eucharist, the Lord's Supper

eucharistique [økaʀistik] *adj* eucharistic

euclidien, ne [øklidjɛ̃, -ɛn] *adj* Euclidian

eugénique [øʒenik] *adj* eugenic ▷ *nf* eugenics *sg*

eugénisme [øʒenism(ə)] *nm* eugenics *sg*

euh [ø] *excl* er

eunuque [ønyk] *nm* eunuch

euphémique [øfemik] *adj* euphemistic

euphémisme [øfemism(ə)] *nm* euphemism

euphonie [øfɔni] *nf* euphony

euphorbe [øfɔʀb(ə)] *nf* (*Bot*) spurge

euphorie [øfɔʀi] *nf* euphoria

euphorique [øfɔʀik] *adj* euphoric

euphorisant, e [øfɔʀizɑ̃, -ɑ̃t] *adj* exhilarating

eurafricain, e [øʀafʀikɛ̃, -ɛn] *adj* Eurafrican

eurasiatique [øʀazjatik] *adj* Eurasiatic

Eurasie [øʀazi] *nf*: **l'~** Eurasia

eurasien, ne [øʀazjɛ̃, -ɛn] *adj* Eurasian

EURATOM [øʀatɔm] *sigle f* Euratom

eurent [yʀ(ə)] *vb voir* **avoir**

euro [øʀo] *nm* euro

euro- [øʀo] *préfixe* Euro-

eurocrate [øʀɔkʀat] *nm/f* (*péj*) Eurocrat

eurodevise [øʀodəviz] *nf* Eurocurrency

eurodollar [øʀodɔlaʀ] *nm* Eurodollar

Euroland [øʀɔlɑ̃d] *nm* Euroland

euromonnaie [øʀomɔnɛ] *nf* Eurocurrency

Europe [øʀɔp] *nf*: **l'~** Europe; **l'~ centrale** Central Europe; **l'~ verte** European agriculture

européanisation [øʀɔpeanizasjɔ̃] *nf* Europeanization

européaniser [øʀɔpeanize] *vt* to Europeanize

européen, ne [øʀɔpeɛ̃, -ɛn] *adj* European ▷ *nm/f*: **Européen, ne** European

eurosceptique [øʀosɛptik] *nm/f* Eurosceptic

Eurovision [øʀovizjɔ̃] *nf* Eurovision; **émission en ~** Eurovision broadcast

eus *etc* [y] *vb voir* **avoir**

euthanasie [øtanazi] *nf* euthanasia

eux [ø] *pron* (*sujet*) they; (*objet*) them; ~, **ils ont fait ...** THEY did ...

évacuation [evakɥasjɔ̃] *nf* evacuation

évacué, e [evakɥe] *nm/f* evacuee

évacuer [evakɥe] *vt* (*salle, région*) to evacuate, clear; (*occupants, population*) to evacuate; (*toxine etc*) to evacuate, discharge

évadé, e [evade] *adj* escaped ▷ *nm/f* escapee

évader [evade]: **s'évader** *vi* to escape

évaluation [evalɥasjɔ̃] *nf* assessment, evaluation

évaluer [evalɥe] *vt* to assess, evaluate

évanescent, e [evanesɑ̃, -ɑ̃t] *adj* evanescent

évangélique [evɑ̃ʒelik] *adj* evangelical

évangélisation [evɑ̃ʒelizasjɔ̃] *nf* evangelization

évangéliser [evɑ̃ʒelize] *vt* to evangelize

évangéliste [evɑ̃ʒelist(ə)] *nm* evangelist

évangile [evɑ̃ʒil] *nm* gospel; (*texte de la Bible*): **É~** Gospel; **ce n'est pas l'É~** (*fig*) it's not gospel

évanoui, e [evanwi] *adj* in a faint; **tomber ~** to faint

évanouir [evanwiʀ]: **s'évanouir** *vi* to faint, pass out; (*disparaître*) to vanish, disappear

évanouissement [evanwismɑ̃] *nm* (*syncope*) fainting fit; (*Méd*) loss of consciousness

évaporation [evapɔʀasjɔ̃] *nf* evaporation

évaporé, e [evapɔʀe] *adj* giddy, scatterbrained

évaporer [evapɔʀe]: **s'évaporer** *vi* to evaporate

évasé, e [evaze] *adj* (*jupe etc*) flared

évaser [evaze] *vt* (*tuyau*) to widen, open out; (*jupe, pantalon*) to flare; **s'évaser** *vi* to widen, open out

évasif, -ive [evazif, -iv] *adj* evasive

évasion [evazjɔ̃] *nf* escape; **littérature d'~** escapist literature; **~ des capitaux** (*Écon*) flight of capital; **~ fiscale** tax avoidance

évasivement [evazivmɑ̃] *adv* evasively

évêché [eveʃe] *nm* (*fonction*) bishopric; (*palais*) bishop's palace

éveil [evɛj] *nm* awakening; **être en ~** to be alert; **mettre qn en ~, donner l'~ à qn** to arouse sb's suspicions; **activités d'~** early-learning activities

éveillé, e [eveje] *adj* awake; (*vif*) alert, sharp
éveiller [eveje] *vt* to (a)waken; **s'éveiller** *vi* to (a)waken; (*fig*) to be aroused
événement [evɛnmã] *nm* event
éventail [evãtaj] *nm* fan; (*choix*) range; **en ~** fanned out; fan-shaped
éventaire [evãtɛʀ] *nm* stall, stand
éventé, e [evãte] *adj* (*parfum, vin*) stale
éventer [evãte] *vt* (*secret, complot*) to uncover; (*avec un éventail*) to fan; **s'éventer** *vi* (*parfum, vin*) to go stale
éventrer [evãtʀe] *vt* to disembowel; (*fig*) to tear *ou* rip open
éventualité [evãtɥalite] *nf* eventuality; possibility; **dans l'~ de** in the event of; **parer à toute ~** to guard against all eventualities
éventuel, le [evãtɥɛl] *adj* possible
éventuellement [evãtɥɛlmã] *adv* possibly
évêque [evɛk] *nm* bishop
Everest [ɛvʀɛst] *nm*: **(mont) ~** (Mount) Everest
évertuer [evɛʀtɥe]: **s'évertuer** *vi*: **s'~ à faire** to try very hard to do
éviction [eviksjɔ̃] *nf* ousting, supplanting; (*de locataire*) eviction
évidemment [evidamã] *adv* obviously
évidence [evidãs] *nf* obviousness; (*fait*) obvious fact; **se rendre à l'~** to bow before the evidence; **nier l'~** to deny the evidence; **à l'~** evidently; **de toute ~** quite obviously *ou* evidently; **en ~** conspicuous; **mettre en ~** to bring to the fore
évident, e [evidã, -ãt] *adj* obvious, evident; **ce n'est pas ~** (*cela pose des problèmes*) it's not (all that) straightforward, it's not as simple as all that
évider [evide] *vt* to scoop out
évier [evje] *nm* (kitchen) sink
évincer [evɛ̃se] *vt* to oust, supplant
évitable [evitabl(ə)] *adj* avoidable
évitement [evitmã] *nm*: **place d'~** (*Auto*) passing place
éviter [evite] *vt* to avoid; **~ de faire/que qch ne se passe** to avoid doing/sth happening; **~ qch à qn** to spare sb sth
évocateur, -trice [evɔkatœʀ, -tʀis] *adj* evocative, suggestive
évocation [evɔkasjɔ̃] *nf* evocation
évolué, e [evɔlɥe] *adj* advanced; (*personne*) broad-minded
évoluer [evɔlɥe] *vi* (*enfant, maladie*) to develop; (*situation, moralement*) to evolve, develop; (*aller et venir: danseur etc*) to move about, circle
évolutif, -ive [evɔlytif, -iv] *adj* evolving
évolution [evɔlysjɔ̃] *nf* development; evolution; **évolutions** *nfpl* movements
évolutionnisme [evɔlysjɔnism(ə)] *nm* evolutionism
évoquer [evɔke] *vt* to call to mind, evoke; (*mentionner*) to mention
ex. *abr* (= *exemple*) ex.
ex- [ɛks] *préfixe* ex-
exacerbé, e [ɛgzasɛʀbe] *adj* (*orgueil, sensibilité*) exaggerated

exacerber [ɛgzasɛʀbe] *vt* to exacerbate
exact, e [ɛgzakt] *adj* (*précis*) exact, accurate, precise; (*correct*) correct; (*ponctuel*) punctual; **l'heure ~e** the right *ou* exact time
exactement [ɛgzaktəmã] *adv* exactly, accurately, precisely; correctly; (*c'est cela même*) exactly
exaction [ɛgzaksjɔ̃] *nf* (*d'argent*) exaction; (*gén pl: actes de violence*) abuse(s)
exactitude [ɛgzaktityd] *nf* exactitude, accurateness, precision
ex aequo [ɛgzeko] *adj* equally placed; **classé 1er ~** placed equal first
exagération [ɛgzaʒeʀasjɔ̃] *nf* exaggeration
exagéré, e [ɛgzaʒeʀe] *adj* (*prix etc*) excessive
exagérément [ɛgzaʒeʀemã] *adv* excessively
exagérer [ɛgzaʒeʀe] *vt* to exaggerate ▷ *vi* (*abuser*) to go too far; (*dépasser les bornes*) to overstep the mark; (*déformer les faits*) to exaggerate; **s'exagérer qch** to exaggerate sth
exaltant, e [ɛgzaltã, -ãt] *adj* exhilarating
exaltation [ɛgzaltasjɔ̃] *nf* exaltation
exalté, e [ɛgzalte] *adj* (over)excited ▷ *nm/f* (*péj*) fanatic
exalter [ɛgzalte] *vt* (*enthousiasmer*) to excite, elate; (*glorifier*) to exalt
examen [ɛgzamɛ̃] *nm* examination; (*Scol*) exam, examination; **à l'~** (*dossier, projet*) under consideration; (*Comm*) on approval; **~ blanc** mock exam(ination); **~ de la vue** sight test
examinateur, -trice [ɛgzaminatœʀ, -tʀis] *nm/f* examiner
examiner [ɛgzamine] *vt* to examine
exaspérant, e [ɛgzaspeʀã, -ãt] *adj* exasperating
exaspération [ɛgzaspeʀasjɔ̃] *nf* exasperation
exaspéré, e [ɛgzaspeʀe] *adj* exasperated
exaspérer [ɛgzaspeʀe] *vt* to exasperate; (*aggraver*) to exacerbate
exaucer [ɛgzose] *vt* (*vœu*) to grant, fulfil; **~ qn** to grant sb's wishes
ex cathedra [ɛkskatedʀa] *adj, adv* ex cathedra
excavateur [ɛkskavatœʀ] *nm* excavator, mechanical digger
excavation [ɛkskavasjɔ̃] *nf* excavation
excavatrice [ɛkskavatʀis] *nf* = **excavateur**
excédent [ɛksedã] *nm* surplus; **en ~** surplus; **payer 60 euros d'~** (*de bagages*) to pay 60 euros excess baggage; **~ de bagages** excess baggage; **~ commercial** trade surplus
excédentaire [ɛksedãtɛʀ] *adj* surplus, excess
excéder [ɛksede] *vt* (*dépasser*) to exceed; (*agacer*) to exasperate; **excédé de fatigue** exhausted; **excédé de travail** worn out with work
excellence [ɛksɛlãs] *nf* excellence; (*titre*) Excellency; **par ~** par excellence
excellent, e [ɛksɛlã, -ãt] *adj* excellent
exceller [ɛksele] *vi*: **~ (dans)** to excel (in)
excentricité [ɛksãtʀisite] *nf* eccentricity
excentrique [ɛksãtʀik] *adj* eccentric; (*quartier*) outlying ▷ *nm/f* eccentric
excentriquement [ɛksãtʀikmã] *adv* eccentrically

excepté, e [ɛksɛpte] *adj, prép*: **les élèves ~s**, **~ les élèves** except for *ou* apart from the pupils; **~ si/ quand** except if/when; **~ que** except that

excepter [ɛksɛpte] *vt* to except

exception [ɛksɛpsjɔ̃] *nf* exception; **faire ~** to be an exception; **faire une ~** to make an exception; **sans ~** without exception; **à l'~ de** except for, with the exception of; **d'~** (*mesure, loi*) special, exceptional

exceptionnel, le [ɛksɛpsjɔnɛl] *adj* exceptional; (*prix*) special

exceptionnellement [ɛksɛpsjɔnɛlmɑ̃] *adv* exceptionally; (*par exception*) by way of an exception, on this occasion

excès [ɛksɛ] *nm* surplus ▷ *nmpl* excesses; **à l'~** (*méticuleux, généreux*) to excess; **avec ~** to excess; **sans ~** in moderation; **tomber dans l'~ inverse** to go to the opposite extreme; **~ de langage** immoderate language; **~ de pouvoir** abuse of power; **~ de vitesse** speeding *no pl*, exceeding the speed limit; **~ de zèle** overzealousness *no pl*

excessif, -ive [ɛksesif, -iv] *adj* excessive

excessivement [ɛksesivmɑ̃] *adv* (*trop: cher*) excessively, inordinately; (*très: riche, laid*) extremely, incredibly; **manger/boire ~** to eat/ drink to excess

exciper [ɛksipe]: **~ de** *vt* to plead

excipient [ɛksipjɑ̃] *nm* (*Méd*) inert base, excipient

exciser [ɛksize] *vt* (*Méd*) to excise

excision [ɛksizjɔ̃] *nf* (*Méd*) excision; (*rituelle*) circumcision

excitant, e [ɛksitɑ̃, -ɑ̃t] *adj* exciting ▷ *nm* stimulant

excitation [ɛksitasjɔ̃] *nf* (*état*) excitement

excité, e [ɛksite] *adj* excited

exciter [ɛksite] *vt* to excite; (*café etc*) to stimulate; **s'exciter** *vi* to get excited; **~ qn à** (*révolte etc*) to incite sb to

exclamation [ɛksklamasjɔ̃] *nf* exclamation

exclamer [ɛksklame]: **s'exclamer** *vi* to exclaim

exclu, e [ɛkskly] *pp de* **exclure** ▷ *adj*: **il est/n'est pas ~ que** ... it's out of the question/not impossible that ...; **ce n'est pas ~** it's not impossible, I don't rule that out

exclure [ɛksklyʀ] *vt* (*faire sortir*) to expel; (*ne pas compter*) to exclude, leave out; (*rendre impossible*) to exclude, rule out

exclusif, -ive [ɛksklyzif, -iv] *adj* exclusive; **avec la mission exclusive/dans le but ~ de ...** with the sole mission/aim of ...; **agent ~** sole agent

exclusion [ɛksklyzjɔ̃] *nf* expulsion; **à l'~ de** with the exclusion *ou* exception of

exclusivement [ɛksklyzivmɑ̃] *adv* exclusively

exclusivité [ɛksklyzivite] *nf* exclusiveness; (*Comm*) exclusive rights *pl*; **passer en ~** (*film*) to go on general release

excommunier [ɛkskɔmynje] *vt* to excommunicate

excréments [ɛkskʀemɑ̃] *nmpl* excrement *sg*, faeces

excréter [ɛkskʀete] *vt* to excrete

excroissance [ɛkskʀwasɑ̃s] *nf* excrescence, outgrowth

excursion [ɛkskyʀsjɔ̃] *nf* (*en autocar*) excursion, trip; (*à pied*) walk, hike; **faire une ~** to go on an excursion *ou* a trip; to go on a walk *ou* hike

excursionniste [ɛkskyʀsjɔnist(ə)] *nm/f* tripper; hiker

excusable [ɛkskyzabl(ə)] *adj* excusable

excuse [ɛkskyz] *nf* excuse; **excuses** *nfpl* apology *sg*, apologies; **faire des ~s** to apologize; **faire ses ~s** to offer one's apologies; **mot d'~** (*Scol*) note from one's parent(s) (*to explain absence etc*); **lettre d'~s** letter of apology

excuser [ɛkskyze] *vt* to excuse; **~ qn de qch** (*dispenser*) to excuse sb from sth; **s'excuser (de)** to apologize (for); **"excusez-moi"** "I'm sorry"; (*pour attirer l'attention*) "excuse me"; **se faire ~** to ask to be excused

exécrable [ɛgzekʀabl(ə)] *adj* atrocious

exécrer [ɛgzekʀe] *vt* to loathe, abhor

exécutant, e [ɛgzekytɑ̃, -ɑ̃t] *nm/f* performer

exécuter [ɛgzekyte] *vt* (*prisonnier*) to execute; (*tâche etc*) to execute, carry out; (*Mus: jouer*) to perform, execute; (*Inform*) to run; **s'exécuter** *vi* to comply

exécuteur, -trice [ɛgzekytœʀ, -tʀis] *nm/f* (*testamentaire*) executor ▷ *nm* (*bourreau*) executioner

exécutif, -ive [ɛgzekytif, -iv] *adj, nm* (*Pol*) executive

exécution [ɛgzekysjɔ̃] *nf* execution; carrying out; **mettre à ~** to carry out

exécutoire [ɛgzekytwaʀ] *adj* (*Jur*) (legally) binding

exégèse [ɛgzeʒɛz] *nf* exegesis

exégète [ɛgzeʒɛt] *nm* exegete

exemplaire [ɛgzɑ̃plɛʀ] *adj* exemplary ▷ *nm* copy

exemple [ɛgzɑ̃pl(ə)] *nm* example; **par ~** for instance, for example; (*valeur intensive*) really!; **sans ~** (*bêtise, gourmandise etc*) unparalleled; **donner l'~** to set an example; **prendre ~ sur** to take as a model; **à l'~ de** just like; **pour l'~** (*punir*) as an example

exempt, e [ɛgzɑ̃, -ɑ̃t] *adj*: **~ de** (*dispensé de*) exempt from; (*sans*) free from; **~ de taxes** tax-free

exempter [ɛgzɑ̃te] *vt*: **~ de** to exempt from

exercé, e [ɛgzɛʀse] *adj* trained

exercer [ɛgzɛʀse] *vt* (*pratiquer*) to exercise, practise; (*faire usage de: prérogative*) to exercise; (*effectuer: influence, contrôle, pression*) to exert; (*former*) to exercise, train ▷ *vi* (*médecin*) to be in practice; **s'exercer** (*sportif, musicien*) to practise; (*se faire sentir: pression etc*): **s'~ (sur** *ou* **contre)** to be exerted (on); **s'~ à faire qch** to train o.s. to do sth

exercice [ɛgzɛʀsis] *nm* practice; exercising; (*tâche, travail*) exercise; (*Comm, Admin: période*) accounting period; **l'~** (*sportive etc*) exercise; (*Mil*) drill; **en ~** (*juge*) in office; (*médecin*) practising; **dans l'~ de ses fonctions** in the discharge of his duties; **~s d'assouplissement** limbering-up (exercises)

exergue [ɛgzɛʀg(ə)] nm: **mettre en ~** (inscription) to inscribe; **porter en ~** to be inscribed with

exhalaison [ɛgzalɛzɔ̃] nf exhalation

exhaler [ɛgzale] vt (parfum) to exhale; (souffle, son, soupir) to utter, breathe; **s'exhaler** vi to rise (up)

exhausser [ɛgzose] vt to raise (up)

exhausteur [ɛgzostœʀ] nm extractor fan

exhaustif, -ive [ɛgzostif, -iv] adj exhaustive

exhiber [ɛgzibe] vt (montrer: papiers, certificat) to present, produce; (péj) to display, flaunt; **s'exhiber** (personne) to parade; (exhibitionniste) to expose o.s.

exhibitionnisme [ɛgzibisjɔnism(ə)] nm exhibitionism

exhibitionniste [ɛgzibisjɔnist(ə)] nm/f exhibitionist

exhortation [ɛgzɔʀtasjɔ̃] nf exhortation

exhorter [ɛgzɔʀte] vt: **~ qn à faire** to urge sb to do

exhumer [ɛgzyme] vt to exhume

exigeant, e [ɛgziʒɑ̃, -ɑ̃t] adj demanding; (péj) hard to please

exigence [ɛgziʒɑ̃s] nf demand, requirement

exiger [ɛgziʒe] vt to demand, require

exigible [ɛgziʒibl(ə)] adj (Comm, Jur) payable

exigu, ë [ɛgzigy] adj cramped, tiny

exiguïté [ɛgziguite] nf (d'un lieu) cramped nature

exil [ɛgzil] nm exile; **en ~** in exile

exilé, e [ɛgzile] nm/f exile

exiler [ɛgzile] vt to exile; **s'exiler** to go into exile

existant, e [ɛgzistɑ̃, -ɑ̃t] adj (actuel, présent) existing

existence [ɛgzistɑ̃s] nf existence; **dans l'~** in life

existentialisme [ɛgzistɑ̃sjalism(ə)] nm existentialism

existentiel, le [ɛgzistɑ̃sjɛl] adj existential

exister [ɛgziste] vi to exist; **il existe un/des** there is a/are (some)

exode [ɛgzɔd] nm exodus

exonération [ɛgzɔneʀasjɔ̃] nf exemption

exonéré, e [ɛgzɔneʀe] adj: **~ de TVA** zero-rated (for VAT)

exonérer [ɛgzɔneʀe] vt: **~ de** to exempt from

exorbitant, e [ɛgzɔʀbitɑ̃, -ɑ̃t] adj exorbitant

exorbité, e [ɛgzɔʀbite] adj: **yeux ~s** bulging eyes

exorciser [ɛgzɔʀsize] vt to exorcize

exorde [ɛgzɔʀd(ə)] nm introduction

exotique [ɛgzɔtik] adj exotic

exotisme [ɛgzɔtism(ə)] nm exoticism

expansif, -ive [ɛkspɑ̃sif, -iv] adj expansive, communicative

expansion [ɛkspɑ̃sjɔ̃] nf expansion

expansionniste [ɛkspɑ̃sjɔnist(ə)] adj expansionist

expansivité [ɛkspɑ̃sivite] nf expansiveness

expatrié, e [ɛkspatʀije] nm/f expatriate

expatrier [ɛkspatʀije] vt (argent) to take ou send

out of the country; **s'expatrier** to leave one's country

expectative [ɛkspɛktativ] nf: **être dans l'~** to be waiting to see

expectorant, e [ɛkspɛktɔʀɑ̃, -ɑ̃t] adj: **sirop ~** expectorant (syrup)

expectorer [ɛkspɛktɔʀe] vi to expectorate

expédient [ɛkspedjɑ̃] nm (parfois péj) expedient; **vivre d'~s** to live by one's wits

expédier [ɛkspedje] vt (lettre, paquet) to send; (troupes, renfort) to dispatch; (péj: travail etc) to dispose of, dispatch

expéditeur, -trice [ɛkspeditœʀ, -tʀis] nm/f (Postes) sender

expéditif, -ive [ɛkspeditif, -iv] adj quick, expeditious

expédition [ɛkspedisjɔ̃] nf sending; (scientifique, sportive, Mil) expedition; **~ punitive** punitive raid

expéditionnaire [ɛkspedisjɔnɛʀ] adj: **corps ~** (Mil) task force

expérience [ɛkspeʀjɑ̃s] nf (de la vie, des choses) experience; (scientifique) experiment; **avoir de l'~** to have experience, be experienced; **avoir l'~ de** to have experience of; **faire l'~ de qch** to experience sth; **~ de chimie/d'électricité** chemical/electrical experiment

expérimental, e, -aux [ɛkspeʀimɑ̃tal, -o] adj experimental

expérimentalement [ɛkspeʀimɑ̃talmɑ̃] adv experimentally

expérimenté, e [ɛkspeʀimɑ̃te] adj experienced

expérimenter [ɛkspeʀimɑ̃te] vt (machine, technique) to test out, experiment with

expert, e [ɛkspɛʀ, -ɛʀt(ə)] adj: **~ en** expert in ▷ nm (spécialiste) expert; **~ en assurances** insurance valuer

expert-comptable [ɛkspɛʀkɔ̃tabl(ə)] (pl **experts-comptables**) nm ≈ chartered (Brit) ou certified public (US) accountant

expertise [ɛkspɛʀtiz] nf valuation; assessment; valuer's (ou assessor's) report; (Jur) (forensic) examination

expertiser [ɛkspɛʀtize] vt (objet de valeur) to value; (voiture accidentée etc) to assess damage to

expier [ɛkspje] vt to expiate, atone for

expiration [ɛkspiʀasjɔ̃] nf expiry (Brit), expiration; breathing out no pl

expirer [ɛkspiʀe] vi (prendre fin, littéraire: mourir) to expire; (respirer) to breathe out

explétif, -ive [ɛkspletif, -iv] adj (Ling) expletive

explicable [ɛksplikabl(ə)] adj: **pas ~** inexplicable

explicatif, -ive [ɛksplikatif, -iv] adj (mot, texte, note) explanatory

explication [ɛksplikasjɔ̃] nf explanation; (discussion) discussion; **~ de texte** (Scol) critical analysis (of a text)

explicite [ɛksplisit] adj explicit

explicitement [ɛksplisitmɑ̃] adv explicitly

expliciter [ɛksplisite] vt to make explicit

expliquer [ɛksplike] vt to explain; **~ (à qn)**

comment/que to point out *ou* explain (to sb) how/that; **s'expliquer** (*se faire comprendre: personne*) to explain o.s.; (*discuter*) to discuss things; (*se disputer*) to have it out; (*comprendre*): **je m'explique son retard/absence** I understand his lateness/absence; **son erreur s'explique** one can understand his mistake

exploit [ɛksplwa] *nm* exploit, feat

exploitable [ɛskplwatabl(ə)] *adj* (*gisement etc*) that can be exploited; **~ par une machine** machine-readable

exploitant [ɛksplwatã] *nm* farmer

exploitation [ɛksplwatasjɔ̃] *nf* exploitation; running; (*entreprise*): **~ agricole** farming concern

exploiter [ɛksplwate] *vt* to exploit; (*entreprise, ferme*) to run, operate

exploiteur, -euse [ɛksplwatœr, -øz] *nm/f* (*péj*) exploiter

explorateur, -trice [ɛksplɔratœr, -tris] *nm/f* explorer

exploration [ɛksplɔrasjɔ̃] *nf* exploration

explorer [ɛksplɔre] *vt* to explore

exploser [ɛksploze] *vi* to explode, blow up; (*engin explosif*) to go off; (*fig: joie, colère*) to burst out, explode; (: *personne: de colère*) to explode, flare up; **faire ~** (*bombe*) to explode, detonate; (*bâtiment, véhicule*) to blow up

explosif, -ive [ɛksplozif, -iv] *adj, nm* explosive

explosion [ɛksplozjɔ̃] *nf* explosion; **~ de joie/colère** outburst of joy/rage; **~ démographique** population explosion

exponentiel, le [ɛkspɔnãsjɛl] *adj* exponential

exportateur, -trice [ɛkspɔrtatœr, -tris] *adj* exporting ▷ *nm* exporter

exportation [ɛkspɔrtasjɔ̃] *nf* export

exporter [ɛkspɔrte] *vt* to export

exposant [ɛkspozã] *nm* exhibitor; (*Math*) exponent

exposé, e [ɛkspoze] *nm* (*écrit*) exposé; (*oral*) talk ▷ *adj*: **~ au sud** facing south, with a southern aspect; **bien ~** well situated; **très ~** very exposed

exposer [ɛkspoze] *vt* (*montrer: marchandise*) to display; (: *peinture*) to exhibit, show; (*parler de: problème, situation*) to explain, expose, set out; (*mettre en danger, orienter: maison etc*) to expose; **~ qn/qch à** to expose sb/sth to; **~ sa vie** to risk one's life; **s'exposer à** (*soleil, danger*) to expose o.s. to; (*critiques, punition*) to lay o.s. open to

exposition [ɛkspozisjɔ̃] *nf* (*voir exposer*) displaying; exhibiting; explanation, exposition; exposure; (*voir exposé*) aspect, situation; (*manifestation*) exhibition; (*Photo*) exposure; (*introduction*) exposition

exprès¹ [ɛksprɛ] *adv* (*délibérément*) on purpose; (*spécialement*) specially; **faire ~ de faire qch** to do sth on purpose

exprès², -esse [ɛksprɛs] *adj* (*ordre, défense*) express, formal ▷ *adj inv, adv* (*Postes*) express; **envoyer qch en ~** to send sth express

express [ɛksprɛs] *adj, nm*: (**café**) **~** espresso;

(**train**) **~** fast train

expressément [ɛksprɛsemã] *adv* expressly, specifically

expressif, -ive [ɛksprɛsif, -iv] *adj* expressive

expression [ɛksprɛsjɔ̃] *nf* expression; **réduit à sa plus simple ~** reduced to its simplest terms; **liberté/moyens d'~** freedom/means of expression; **~ toute faite** set phrase

expressionnisme [ɛksprɛsjɔnism(ə)] *nm* expressionism

expressivité [ɛksprɛsivite] *nf* expressiveness

exprimer [ɛksprime] *vt* (*sentiment, idée*) to express; (*faire sortir: jus, liquide*) to press out; **s'exprimer** *vi* (*personne*) to express o.s.

expropriation [ɛksprɔprijasjɔ̃] *nf* expropriation; **frapper d'~** to put a compulsory purchase order on

exproprier [ɛksprɔprije] *vt* to buy up (*ou* buy the property of) by compulsory purchase, expropriate

expulser [ɛkspylse] *vt* (*d'une salle, d'un groupe*) to expel; (*locataire*) to evict; (*Football*) to send off

expulsion [ɛkspylsjɔ̃] *nf* expulsion; eviction; sending off

expurger [ɛkspyrʒe] *vt* to expurgate, bowdlerize

exquis, e [ɛkski, -iz] *adj* (*gâteau, parfum, élégance*) exquisite; (*personne, temps*) delightful

exsangue [ɛksãg] *adj* bloodless, drained of blood

exsuder [ɛksyde] *vt* to exude

extase [ɛkstaz] *nf* ecstasy; **être en ~** to be in raptures

extasier [ɛkstazje]: **s'extasier** *vi*: **s'~ sur** to go into raptures over

extatique [ɛkstatik] *adj* ecstatic

extenseur [ɛkstãsœr] *nm* (*Sport*) chest expander

extensible [ɛkstãsibl(ə)] *adj* extensible

extensif, -ive [ɛkstãsif, -iv] *adj* extensive

extension [ɛkstãsjɔ̃] *nf* (*d'un muscle, ressort*) stretching; (*Méd*): **à l'~** in traction; (*fig*) extension; expansion

exténuant, e [ɛkstenɥã, -ãt] *adj* exhausting

exténuer [ɛkstenɥe] *vt* to exhaust

extérieur, e [ɛksterjœr] *adj* (*de dehors: porte, mur etc*) outer, outside; (: *commerce, politique*) foreign; (: *influences, pressions*) external; (*au dehors: escalier, w.-c.*) outside; (*apparent: calme, gaieté etc*) outer ▷ *nm* (*d'une maison, d'un récipient etc*) outside, exterior; (*d'une personne: apparence*) exterior; (*d'un pays, d'un groupe social*): **l'~** the outside world; **à l'~** (*dehors*) outside; (*fig: à l'étranger*) abroad

extérieurement [ɛksterjœrmã] *adv* (*de dehors*) on the outside; (*en apparence*) on the surface

extérioriser [ɛksterjɔrize] *vt* to exteriorize

extermination [ɛkstɛrminasjɔ̃] *nf* extermination, wiping out

exterminer [ɛkstɛrmine] *vt* to exterminate, wipe out

externat [ɛkstɛrna] *nm* day school

externe [ɛkstɛrn(ə)] *adj* external, outer ▷ *nm/f* (*Méd*) non-resident medical student, extern

(US); (Scol) day pupil

extincteur [ɛkstɛ̃ktœʀ] nm (fire) extinguisher

extinction [ɛkstɛ̃ksjɔ̃] nf extinction; (Jur: d'une dette) extinguishment; ~ **de voix** (Méd) loss of voice

extirper [ɛkstiʀpe] vt (tumeur) to extirpate; (plante) to root out, pull up; (préjugés) to eradicate

extorquer [ɛkstɔʀke] vt (de l'argent, un renseignement): ~ **qch à qn** to extort sth from sb

extorsion [ɛkstɔʀsjɔ̃] nf: ~ **de fonds** extortion of money

extra [ɛkstʀa] adj inv first-rate; (marchandises) top-quality ▷ nm inv extra help ▷ préfixe extra(-)

extraction [ɛkstʀaksjɔ̃] nf extraction

extrader [ɛkstʀade] vt to extradite

extradition [ɛkstʀadisjɔ̃] nf extradition

extra-fin, e [ɛkstʀafɛ̃, -in] adj extra-fine

extra-fort, e [ɛkstʀafɔʀ] adj extra strong

extraire [ɛkstʀɛʀ] vt to extract

extrait, e [ɛkstʀɛ, -ɛt] pp de **extraire** ▷ nm (de plante) extract; (de film, livre) extract, excerpt; ~ **de naissance** birth certificate

extra-lucide [ɛkstʀalysid] adj: **voyante** ~ clairvoyant

extraordinaire [ɛkstʀaɔʀdinɛʀ] adj extraordinary; (Pol, Admin) special; **ambassadeur** ~ ambassador extraordinary; **assemblée** ~ extraordinary meeting; **par** ~ by some unlikely chance

extraordinairement [ɛkstʀaɔʀdinɛʀmɑ̃] adv extraordinarily

extrapoler [ɛkstʀapɔle] vt, vi to extrapolate

extra-sensoriel, le [ɛkstʀasɑ̃sɔʀjɛl] adj extrasensory

extra-terrestre [ɛkstʀatɛʀɛstʀ(ə)] nm/f extraterrestrial

extra-utérin, e [ɛkstʀayteʀɛ̃, -in] adj extrauterine

extravagance [ɛkstʀavagɑ̃s] nf extravagance no pl; extravagant behaviour no pl

extravagant, e [ɛkstʀavagɑ̃, -ɑ̃t] adj (personne, attitude) extravagant; (idée) wild

extraverti, e [ɛkstʀavɛʀti] adj extrovert

extrayais etc [ɛkstʀɛjɛ] vb voir **extraire**

extrême [ɛkstʀɛm] adj, nm extreme; (intensif): **d'une ~ simplicité/brutalité** extremely simple/brutal; **d'un ~ à l'autre** from one extreme to another; **à l'~** in the extreme; **à l'~ rigueur** in the absolute extreme

extrêmement [ɛkstʀɛmmɑ̃] adv extremely

extrême-onction [ɛkstʀɛmɔ̃ksjɔ̃] (pl **extrêmes-onctions**) nf (Rel) last rites pl, Extreme Unction

Extrême-Orient [ɛkstʀɛmɔʀjɑ̃] nm: **l'~** the Far East

extrême-oriental, e, -aux [ɛkstʀɛmɔʀjɑ̃tal, -o] adj Far Eastern

extrémisme [ɛkstʀemism(ə)] nm extremism

extrémiste [ɛkstʀemist(ə)] adj, nm/f extremist

extrémité [ɛkstʀemite] nf (bout) end; (situation) straits pl, plight; (geste désespéré) extreme action; **extrémités** nfpl (pieds et mains) extremities; **à la dernière ~** (à l'agonie) on the point of death

extroverti, e [ɛkstʀɔvɛʀti] adj = **extraverti**

exubérance [ɛgzybeʀɑ̃s] nf exuberance

exubérant, e [ɛgzybeʀɑ̃, -ɑ̃t] adj exuberant

exulter [ɛgzylte] vi to exult

exutoire [ɛgzytwaʀ] nm outlet, release

ex-voto [ɛksvoto] nm inv ex-voto

eye-liner [ajlajnœʀ] nm eyeliner

Ff

F, f [ɛf] *nm inv* F, f ▷ *abr* = **féminin**; (= *franc*) fr.;
(= *Fahrenheit*) F; (= *frère*) Br(o).; (= *femme*) W;
(*appartement*): **un F2/F3** a 2-/3-roomed flat (*Brit*)
ou apartment (*US*); **F comme François** F for
Frederick (*Brit*) *ou* Fox (*US*)

fa [fɑ] *nm inv* (*Mus*) F; (*en chantant la gamme*) fa

fable [fɑbl(ə)] *nf* fable; (*mensonge*) story, tale

fabricant [fabʀikɑ̃] *nm* manufacturer, maker

fabrication [fabʀikasjɔ̃] *nf* manufacture,
making

fabrique [fabʀik] *nf* factory

fabriquer [fabʀike] *vt* to make; (*industriellement*)
to manufacture, make; (*construire: voiture*)
to manufacture, build; (: *maison*) to build; (*fig:
inventer: histoire, alibi*) to make up; (*fam*): **qu'est-
ce qu'il fabrique?** what is he up to?; **~ en série**
to mass-produce

fabulateur, -trice [fabylatœʀ, -tʀis] *nm/f*: **c'est
un ~** he fantasizes, he makes up stories

fabulation [fabylasjɔ̃] *nf* (*Psych*) fantasizing

fabuleusement [fabyløzmɑ̃] *adv* fabulously,
fantastically

fabuleux, -euse [fabylø, -øz] *adj* fabulous,
fantastic

fac [fak] *abr f* (*fam*: = *faculté*) Uni (*Brit: fam*)
≈ college (*US*)

façade [fasad] *nf* front, façade; (*fig*) façade

face [fas] *nf* face; (*fig: aspect*) side ▷ *adj*: **le côté ~**
heads; **perdre/sauver la ~** to lose/save face;
regarder qn en ~ to look sb in the face; **la
maison/le trottoir d'en ~** the house/pavement
opposite; **en ~ de** *prép* opposite; (*fig*) in front of;
de ~ *adv* from the front; face on; **~ à** *prép*
facing; (*fig*) faced with, in the face of; **faire ~ à**
to face; **faire ~ à la demande** (*Comm*) to meet
the demand; **~ à ~** *adv* facing each other ▷ *nm
inv* encounter

face-à-main [fasamɛ̃] (*pl* **faces-à-main**) *nm*
lorgnette

facéties [fasesi] *nfpl* jokes, pranks

facétieux, -euse [fasesjø, -øz] *adj* mischievous

facette [faset] *nf* facet

fâché, e [fɑʃe] *adj* angry; (*désolé*) sorry

fâcher [fɑʃe] *vt* to anger; **se fâcher** *vi* to get
angry; **se ~ avec** (*se brouiller*) to fall out with

fâcherie [fɑʃʀi] *nf* quarrel

fâcheusement [fɑʃøzmɑ̃] *adv* unpleasantly;
(*impressionné etc*) badly; **avoir ~ tendance à** to
have an irritating tendency to

fâcheux, -euse [fɑʃø, -øz] *adj* unfortunate,
regrettable

facho [faʃo] *adj, nm/f* (*fam*: = *fasciste*) fascist

facial, e, -aux [fasjal, -o] *adj* facial

faciès [fasjɛs] *nm* (*visage*) features *pl*

facile [fasil] *adj* easy; (*accommodant*) easy-going

facilement [fasilmɑ̃] *adv* easily

facilité [fasilite] *nf* easiness; (*disposition, don*)
aptitude; (*moyen, occasion, possibilité*): **il a la ~ de
rencontrer les gens** he has every opportunity
to meet people; **facilités** *nfpl* facilities; (*Comm*)
terms; **~s de crédit** credit terms; **~s de
paiement** easy terms

faciliter [fasilite] *vt* to make easier

façon [fasɔ̃] *nf* (*manière*) way; (*d'une robe etc*)
making-up; cut; (: *main-d'œuvre*) labour (*Brit*),
labor (*US*); (*imitation*): **châle ~ cachemire**
cashmere-style shawl; **façons** *nfpl* (*péj*) fuss *sg*;
faire des ~s (*péj: être affecté*) to be affected; (: *faire
des histoires*) to make a fuss; **de quelle ~?** (in)
what way?; **sans ~** *adv* without fuss ▷ *adj*
unaffected; **d'une autre ~** in another way; **en
aucune ~** in no way; **de ~ à so as to; de ~ à ce
que, de (telle) ~ que** so that; **de toute ~**
anyway, in any case; (**c'est une) ~ de parler** it's
a way of putting it; **travail à ~** tailoring

façonner [fasɔne] *vt* (*fabriquer*) to manufacture;
(*travailler: matière*) to shape, fashion; (*fig*) to
mould, shape

fac-similé [faksimile] *nm* facsimile

facteur, -trice [faktœʀ, -tʀis] *nm/f* postman/
woman (*Brit*), mailman/woman (*US*) ▷ *nm*
(*Math, gén*) factor; **~ d'orgues** organ builder; **~
de pianos** piano maker; **~ rhésus** rhesus factor

factice [faktis] *adj* artificial

faction [faksjɔ̃] *nf* (*groupe*) faction; (*Mil*) guard *ou*
sentry (duty); watch; **en ~** on guard; standing
watch

factionnaire [faksjɔnɛʀ] *nm* guard, sentry

factoriel, le [faktɔʀjɛl] *adj, nf* factorial

factotum [faktɔtɔm] *nm* odd-job man,
dogsbody (*Brit*)

factuel, le [faktɥɛl] *adj* factual

facturation [faktyʀɑsjɔ̃] *nf* invoicing; (*bureau*) invoicing (office)

facture [faktyʀ] *nf* (*à payer: gén*) bill; (: *Comm*) invoice; (*d'un artisan, artiste*) technique, workmanship

facturer [faktyʀe] *vt* to invoice

facturier, -ière [faktyʀje, -jɛʀ] *nm/f* invoice clerk

facultatif, -ive [fakyltatif, -iv] *adj* optional; (*arrêt de bus*) request *cpd*

faculté [fakylte] *nf* (*intellectuelle, d'université*) faculty; (*pouvoir, possibilité*) power

fadaises [fadɛz] *nfpl* twaddle *sg*

fade [fad] *adj* insipid

fading [fadiŋ] *nm* (*Radio*) fading

fagot [fago] *nm* (*de bois*) bundle of sticks

fagoté, e [faɡɔte] *adj* (*fam*): **drôlement ~** oddly dressed

faible [fɛbl(ə)] *adj* weak; (*voix, lumière, vent*) faint; (*élève, copie*) poor; (*rendement, intensité, revenu etc*) low ▷ *nm* weak point; (*pour quelqu'un*) weakness, soft spot; **~ d'esprit** feeble-minded

faiblement [fɛbləmɑ̃] *adv* weakly; (*peu: éclairer etc*) faintly

faiblesse [fɛblɛs] *nf* weakness

faiblir [febliʀ] *vi* to weaken; (*lumière*) to dim; (*vent*) to drop

faïence [fajɑ̃s] *nf* earthenware *no pl*; (*objet*) piece of earthenware

faignant, e [fɛɲɑ̃, -ɑ̃t] *nm/f* = **fainéant, e**

faille [faj] *vb voir* **falloir** ▷ *nf* (*Géo*) fault; (*fig*) flaw, weakness

failli, e [faji] *adj, nm/f* bankrupt

faillible [fajibl(ə)] *adj* fallible

faillir [fajiʀ] *vi*: **j'ai failli tomber/lui dire** I almost *ou* nearly fell/told him; **~ à une promesse/un engagement** to break a promise/an agreement

faillite [fajit] *nf* bankruptcy; (*échec: d'une politique etc*) collapse; **être en ~** to be bankrupt; **faire ~** to go bankrupt

faim [fɛ̃] *nf* hunger; (*fig*): **~ d'amour/de richesse** hunger *ou* yearning for love/wealth; **avoir ~** to be hungry; **rester sur sa ~** (*aussi fig*) to be left wanting more

fainéant, e [fɛneɑ̃, -ɑ̃t] *nm/f* idler, loafer

fainéantise [feneɑ̃tiz] *nf* idleness, laziness

⬤ MOT-CLÉ

faire [fɛʀ] *vt* **1** (*fabriquer, être l'auteur de*) to make; (*produire*) to produce; (*construire: maison, bateau*) to build; **faire du vin/une offre/un film** to make wine/an offer/a film; **faire du bruit** to make a noise

2 (*effectuer: travail, opération*) to do; **que faites-vous?** (*quel métier etc*) what do you do?; (*quelle activité: au moment de la question*) what are you doing?; **que faire?** what are we going to do?, what can be done (about it)?; **faire la lessive/le ménage** to do the washing/the housework

3 (*études*) to do; (*sport, musique*) to play; **faire du droit/du français** to do law/French; **faire du rugby/piano** to play rugby/the piano; **faire du cheval/du ski** to go riding/skiing

4 (*visiter*): **faire les magasins** to go shopping; **faire l'Europe** to tour *ou* do Europe

5 (*simuler*): **faire le malade/l'ignorant** to act the invalid/the fool

6 (*transformer, avoir un effet sur*): **faire de qn un frustré/avocat** to make sb frustrated/a lawyer; **ça ne me fait rien** (*m'est égal*) I don't care *ou* mind; (*me laisse froid*) it has no effect on me; **ça ne fait rien** it doesn't matter; **faire que** (*impliquer*) to mean that

7 (*calculs, prix, mesures*): **deux et deux font quatre** two and two are *ou* make four; **ça fait 10 m/15 euros** it's 10 m/15 euros; **je vous le fais 10 euros** I'll let you have it for 10 euros

8 (*vb +de*): **qu'a-t-il fait de sa valise/de sa sœur?** what has he done with his case/his sister?

9: **ne faire que**: **il ne fait que critiquer** (*sans cesse*) all he (ever) does is criticize; (*seulement*) he's only criticizing

10 (*dire*) to say; **vraiment? fit-il** really? he said

11 (*maladie*) to have; **faire du diabète/de la tension** to have diabetes *sg*/high blood pressure

▷ *vi* **1** (*agir, s'y prendre*) to act, do; **il faut faire vite** we (*ou* you *etc*) must act quickly; **comment a-t-il fait pour?** how did he manage to?; **faites comme chez vous** make yourself at home; **je n'ai pas pu faire autrement** there was nothing else I could do

2 (*paraître*) to look; **faire vieux/démodé** to look old/old-fashioned; **ça fait bien** it looks good; **tu fais jeune dans cette robe** that dress makes you look young(er)

3 (*remplaçant un autre verbe*) to do; **ne le casse pas comme je l'ai fait** don't break it as I did; **je peux le voir? — faites!** can I see it? — please do!; **remets-le en place — je viens de le faire** put it back in its place — I just have (done)

▷ *vb impers* **1**: **il fait beau** *etc* the weather is fine *etc*; *voir aussi* **jour**; **froid** *etc*

2 (*temps écoulé, durée*): **ça fait deux ans qu'il est parti** it's two years since he left; **ça fait deux ans qu'il y est** he's been there for two years

▷ *vb aux* **1**: **faire** (+*infinitif: action directe*) to make; **faire tomber/bouger qch** to make sth fall/move; **faire démarrer un moteur/chauffer de l'eau** to start up an engine/heat some water; **cela fait dormir** it makes you sleep; **faire travailler les enfants** to make the children work *ou* get the children to work; **il m'a fait traverser la rue** he helped me to cross the road

2 (*indirectement, par un intermédiaire*): **faire réparer qch** to get *ou* have sth repaired; **faire punir les enfants** to have the children punished; **il m'a fait ouvrir la porte** he got me to open the door

se faire *vi* **1** (*vin, fromage*) to mature

2: **cela se fait beaucoup/ne se fait pas** it's

done a lot/not done

3 (+*nom ou pron*): **se faire une jupe** to make o.s. a skirt; **se faire des amis** to make friends; **se faire du souci** to worry; **se faire des illusions** to delude o.s.; **se faire beaucoup d'argent** to make a lot of money; **il ne s'en fait pas** he doesn't worry

4 (+*adj*: *devenir*): **se faire vieux** to be getting old; (*délibérément*): **se faire beau** to do o.s. up

5: **se faire à** (*s'habituer*) to get used to; **je n'arrive pas à me faire à la nourriture/au climat** I can't get used to the food/climate

6 (+*infinitif*): **se faire examiner la vue/opérer** to have one's eyes tested/have an operation; **se faire couper les cheveux** to get one's hair cut; **il va se faire tuer/punir** he's going to get himself killed/get (himself) punished; **il s'est fait aider** he got somebody to help him; **il s'est fait aider par Simon** he got Simon to help him; **se faire faire un vêtement** to get a garment made for o.s.

7 (*impersonnel*): **comment se fait-il/faisait-il que?** how is it/was it that?; **il peut se faire que nous utilisions ...** it's possible that we could use ...

faire-part [fɛʀpaʀ] *nm inv* announcement (*of birth, marriage etc*)
fair-play [fɛʀplɛ] *adj inv* fair play
fais [fɛ] *vb voir* **faire**
faisabilité [fəzabilite] *nf* feasibility
faisable [fəzabl(ə)] *adj* feasible
faisais *etc* [fəzɛ] *vb voir* **faire**
faisan, e [fəzɑ̃, -an] *nm/f* pheasant
faisandé, e [fəzɑ̃de] *adj* high (*bad*); (*fig péj*) corrupt, decadent
faisceau, x [fɛso] *nm* (*de lumière etc*) beam; (*de branches etc*) bundle
faiseur, -euse [fəzœʀ, -øz] *nm/f* (*gén: péj*): **~ de** maker of ▷ *nm* (bespoke) tailor; **~ d'embarras** fusspot; **~ de projets** schemer
faisons *etc* [fəzɔ̃] *vb voir* **faire**
faisselle [fɛsɛl] *nf* cheese strainer
fait¹ [fɛ] *vb voir* **faire** ▷ *nm* (*événement*) event, occurrence; (*réalité, donnée*) fact; **le ~ que/de manger** the fact that/of eating; **être le ~ de** (*causé par*) to be the work of; **être au ~ (de)** to be informed (of); **mettre qn au ~** to inform sb, put sb in the picture; **au ~** (*à propos*) by the way; **en venir au ~** to get to the point; **de ~** *adj* (*opposé à: de droit*) de facto ▷ *adv* in fact; **du ~ de ceci/qu'il a menti** because of *ou* on account of this/his having lied; **de ce ~** therefore, for this reason; **en ~** in fact; **en ~ de repas** by way of a meal; **prendre ~ et cause pour qn** to support sb, side with sb; **prendre qn sur le ~** to catch sb in the act; **dire à qn son ~** to give sb a piece of one's mind; **hauts ~s** (*exploits*) exploits; **~ d'armes** feat of arms; **~ divers** (short) news item; **les ~s et gestes de qn** sb's actions *ou* doings
fait², e [fɛ, fɛt] *pp de* **faire** ▷ *adj* (*mûr: fromage,*

melon) ripe; (*maquillé: yeux*) made-up; (*vernis: ongles*) painted, polished; **un homme ~** a grown man; **tout(e) ~(e)** (*préparé à l'avance*) ready-made; **c'en est ~ de notre tranquillité** that's the end of our peace; **c'est bien ~ (pour lui** *ou* **eux** *etc*) it serves him (*ou* them *etc*) right
faîte [fɛt] *nm* top; (*fig*) pinnacle, height
faites [fɛt] *vb voir* **faire**
faîtière [fɛtjɛʀ] *nf* (*de tente*) ridge pole
faitout [fɛtu] *nm* stewpot
fakir [fakiʀ] *nm* (*Théât*) wizard
falaise [falɛz] *nf* cliff
falbalas [falbala] *nmpl* fripperies, frills
fallacieux, -euse [falasjø, -øz] *adj* (*raisonnement*) fallacious; (*apparences*) deceptive; (*espoir*) illusory
falloir [falwaʀ] *vb impers*: **il faut faire les lits** we (*ou* you *etc*) have to *ou* must make the beds; **il faut que je fasse les lits** I have to *ou* must make the beds; **il a fallu qu'il parte** he had to leave; **il faudrait qu'elle rentre** she ought to go home; **il va ~ 10 euros** we'll (*ou* I'll *etc*) need 10 euros; **il doit ~ du temps** that must take time; **il vous faut tourner à gauche après l'église** you have to turn left past the church; **nous avons ce qu'il (nous) faut** we have what we need; **il faut qu'il ait oublié** he must have forgotten; **il a fallu qu'il l'apprenne** he would have to hear about it; **il ne fallait pas** (*pour remercier*) you shouldn't have (done); **faut le faire!** (it) takes some doing! ▷ *vi*: **s'en falloir**: **il s'en est fallu de 10 euros/5 minutes** we (*ou* they *etc*) were 10 euros short/5 minutes late (*ou* early); **il s'en faut de beaucoup qu'il soit ...** he is far from being ...; **il s'en est fallu de peu que cela n'arrive** it very nearly happened; **ou peu s'en faut** or just about, or as good as; **comme il faut** *adj* proper ▷ *adv* properly
fallu [faly] *pp de* **falloir**
falot, e [falo, -ɔt] *adj* dreary, colourless (*Brit*), colorless (*US*) ▷ *nm* lantern
falsification [falsifikasjɔ̃] *nf* falsification
falsifier [falsifje] *vt* to falsify
famé, e [fame] *adj*: **mal ~** disreputable, of ill repute
famélique [famelik] *adj* half-starved
fameux, -euse [famø, -øz] *adj* (*illustre: parfois péj*) famous; (*bon: repas, plat etc*) first-rate, first-class; (*intensif*): **un ~ problème** *etc* a real problem *etc*; **pas ~** not great, not much good
familial, e, -aux [familjal, -o] *adj* family *cpd* ▷ *nf* (*Auto*) family estate car (*Brit*), station wagon (*US*)
familiariser [familjaʀize] *vt*: **~ qn avec** to familiarize sb with; **se ~ avec** to familiarize o.s. with
familiarité [familjaʀite] *nf* familiarity; informality; **familiarités** *nfpl* familiarities; **~ avec** (*sujet, science*) familiarity with
familier, -ière [familje, -jɛʀ] *adj* (*connu, impertinent*) familiar; (*dénotant une certaine intimité*) informal, friendly; (*Ling*) informal,

colloquial ▷ *nm* regular (visitor)

familièrement [familjɛʀmɑ̃] *adv* (*sans façon: s'entretenir*) informally; (*cavalièrement*) familiarly

famille [famij] *nf* family; **il a de la ~ à Paris** he has relatives in Paris

famine [famin] *nf* famine

fan [fan] *nm/f* fan

fana [fana] *adj, nm/f* (*fam*) = **fanatique**

fanal, -aux [fanal, -o] *nm* beacon; lantern

fanatique [fanatik] *adj:* ~ **(de)** fanatical (about) ▷ *nm/f* fanatic

fanatisme [fanatism(ə)] *nm* fanaticism

fane [fan] *nf* top

fané, e [fane] *adj* faded

faner [fane]: **se faner** *vi* to fade

faneur, -euse [fanœʀ, -øz] *nm/f* haymaker ▷ *nf* (*Tech*) tedder

fanfare [fɑ̃faʀ] *nf* (*orchestre*) brass band; (*musique*) fanfare; **en ~** (*avec bruit*) noisily

fanfaron, ne [fɑ̃faʀɔ̃, -ɔn] *nm/f* braggart

fanfaronnades [fɑ̃faʀɔnad] *nfpl* bragging *no pl*

fanfreluches [fɑ̃fʀəlyʃ] *nfpl* trimming *no pl*

fange [fɑ̃ʒ] *nf* mire

fanion [fanjɔ̃] *nm* pennant

fanon [fanɔ̃] *nm* (*de baleine*) plate of baleen; (*repli de peau*) dewlap, wattle

fantaisie [fɑ̃tezi] *nf* (*spontanéité*) fancy, imagination; (*caprice*) whim; extravagance; (*Mus*) fantasia ▷ *adj:* **bijou (de)** ~ (piece of) costume jewellery (*Brit*) *ou* jewelry (*US*); **pain (de)** ~ fancy bread

fantaisiste [fɑ̃tezist(ə)] *adj* (*péj*) unorthodox, eccentric ▷ *nm/f* (*de music-hall*) variety artist *ou* entertainer

fantasmagorique [fɑ̃tasmagɔʀik] *adj* phantasmagorical

fantasme [fɑ̃tasm(ə)] *nm* fantasy

fantasmer [fɑ̃tasme] *vi* to fantasize

fantasque [fɑ̃task(ə)] *adj* whimsical, capricious; fantastic

fantassin [fɑ̃tasɛ̃] *nm* infantryman

fantastique [fɑ̃tastik] *adj* fantastic

fantoche [fɑ̃tɔʃ] *nm* (*péj*) puppet

fantomatique [fɑ̃tɔmatik] *adj* ghostly

fantôme [fɑ̃tom] *nm* ghost, phantom

FAO *sigle f* (= Food and Agricultural Organization) FAO

faon [fɑ̃] *nm* fawn (*deer*)

FAQ *abr f* (= foire aux questions) FAQ *pl* (= frequently asked questions)

faramineux, -euse [faʀaminø, -øz] *adj* (*fam*) fantastic

farandole [faʀɑ̃dɔl] *nf* farandole

farce [faʀs(ə)] *nf* (*viande*) stuffing; (*blague*) (practical) joke; (*Théât*) farce; **faire une ~ à qn** to play a (practical) joke on sb; **~s et attrapes** jokes and novelties

farceur, -euse [faʀsœʀ, -øz] *nm/f* practical joker; (*fumiste*) clown

farci, e [faʀsi] *adj* (*Culin*) stuffed

farcir [faʀsiʀ] *vt* (*viande*) to stuff; (*fig*): ~ **qch de** to stuff sth with; **se farcir** (*fam*): **je me suis farci la vaisselle** I've got stuck *ou* landed with the washing-up

fard [faʀ] *nm* make-up; ~ **à joues** blusher

fardeau, x [faʀdo] *nm* burden

farder [faʀde] *vt* to make up; (*vérité*) to disguise; **se farder** to make o.s. up

farfelu, e [faʀfəly] *adj* wacky (*fam*), hare-brained

farfouiller [faʀfuje] *vi* (*péj*) to rummage around

fariboles [faʀibɔl] *nfpl* nonsense *no pl*

farine [faʀin] *nf* flour; ~ **de blé** wheatflour; ~ **de maïs** cornflour (*Brit*), cornstarch (*US*); ~ **lactée** (*pour bouillie*) baby cereal

fariner [faʀine] *vt* to flour

farineux, -euse [faʀinø, -øz] *adj* (*sauce, pomme*) floury ▷ *nmpl* (*aliments*) starchy foods

farniente [faʀnjɛnte] *nm* idleness

farouche [faʀuʃ] *adj* shy, timid; (*sauvage*) savage, wild; (*violent*) fierce

farouchement [faʀuʃmɑ̃] *adv* fiercely

fart [faʀ(t)] *nm* (ski) wax

farter [faʀte] *vt* to wax

fascicule [fasikyl] *nm* volume

fascinant, e [fasinɑ̃, -ɑ̃t] *adj* fascinating

fascination [fasinasjɔ̃] *nf* fascination

fasciner [fasine] *vt* to fascinate

fascisant, e [faʃizɑ̃, -ɑ̃t] *adj* fascistic

fascisme [faʃism(ə)] *nm* fascism

fasciste [faʃist(ə)] *adj, nm/f* fascist

fasse *etc* [fas] *vb voir* **faire**

faste [fast(ə)] *nm* splendour (*Brit*), splendor (*US*) ▷ *adj:* **c'est un jour ~** it's his (*ou* our *etc*) lucky day

fastidieux, -euse [fastidjø, -øz] *adj* tedious, tiresome

fastueux, -euse [fastɥø, -øz] *adj* sumptuous, luxurious

fat [fa] *adj m* conceited, smug

fatal, e [fatal] *adj* fatal; (*inévitable*) inevitable

fatalement [fatalmɑ̃] *adv* inevitably

fatalisme [fatalism(ə)] *nm* fatalism

fataliste [fatalist(ə)] *adj* fatalistic

fatalité [fatalite] *nf* (*destin*) fate; (*coïncidence*) fateful coincidence; (*caractère inévitable*) inevitability

fatidique [fatidik] *adj* fateful

fatigant, e [fatigɑ̃, -ɑ̃t] *adj* tiring; (*agaçant*) tiresome

fatigue [fatig] *nf* tiredness, fatigue; (*détérioration*) fatigue; **les ~s du voyage** the wear and tear of the journey

fatigué, e [fatige] *adj* tired

fatiguer [fatige] *vt* to tire, make tired; (*Tech*) to put a strain on, strain; (*fig: importuner*) to wear out ▷ *vi* (*moteur*) to labour (*Brit*), labor (*US*), strain; **se fatiguer** *vi* to get tired; to tire o.s. (out); **se ~ à faire qch** to tire o.s. out doing sth

fatras [fatʀa] *nm* jumble, hotchpotch

fatuité [fatɥite] *nf* conceitedness, smugness

faubourg [fobuʀ] *nm* suburb

faubourien, ne [fobuʀjɛ̃, -ɛn] *adj* (*accent*) working-class

fauché, e [foʃe] *adj* (*fam*) broke

faucher [foʃe] vt (herbe) to cut; (champs, blés) to reap; (fig) to cut down; to mow down; (fam: voler) to pinch, nick

faucheur, -euse [foʃœʀ, -øz] nm/f reaper, mower

faucille [fosij] nf sickle

faucon [fokɔ̃] nm falcon, hawk

faudra etc [fodʀa] vb voir **falloir**

faufil [fofil] nm (Couture) tacking thread

faufilage [fofilaʒ] nm (Couture) tacking

faufiler [fofile] vt to tack, baste; **se faufiler** vi: **se ~ dans** to edge one's way into; **se ~ parmi/entre** to thread one's way among/between

faune [fon] nf (Zool) wildlife, fauna; (fig péj) set, crowd ▷ nm faun; **~ marine** marine (animal) life

faussaire [fosɛʀ] nm/f forger

fausse [fos] adj f voir **faux**

faussement [fosmɑ̃] adv (accuser) wrongly, wrongfully; (croire) falsely, erroneously

fausser [fose] vt (objet) to bend, buckle; (fig) to distort; **~ compagnie à qn** to give sb the slip

fausset [fosɛ] nm: **voix de ~** falsetto voice

fausseté [foste] nf wrongness; falseness

faut [fo] vb voir **falloir**

faute [fot] nf (erreur) mistake, error; (péché, manquement) misdemeanour; (Football etc) offence; (Tennis) fault; (responsabilité): **par la ~ de** through the fault of, because of; **c'est de sa/ma ~** it's his/my fault; **être en ~** to be in the wrong; **prendre qn en ~** to catch sb out; **~ de** (temps, argent) for ou through lack of; **~ de mieux** for want of anything ou something better; **sans ~** adv without fail; **~ de frappe** typing error; **~ d'inattention** careless mistake; **~ d'orthographe** spelling mistake; **~ professionnelle** professional misconduct no pl

fauteuil [fotœj] nm armchair; **~ à bascule** rocking chair; **~ club** (big) easy chair; **~ d'orchestre** seat in the front stalls (Brit) ou the orchestra (US); **~ roulant** wheelchair

fauteur [fotœʀ] nm: **~ de troubles** trouble-maker

fautif, -ive [fotif, -iv] adj (incorrect) incorrect, inaccurate; (responsable) at fault, in the wrong; (coupable) guilty ▷ nm/f culprit

fauve [fov] nm wildcat; (peintre) Fauve ▷ adj (couleur) fawn

fauvette [fovɛt] nf warbler

fauvisme [fovism(ə)] nm (Art) Fauvism

faux¹ [fo] nf scythe

faux², fausse [fo, fos] adj (inexact) wrong; (piano, voix) out of tune; (falsifié) fake, forged; (sournois, postiche) false ▷ adv (Mus) out of tune ▷ nm (copie) fake, forgery; (opposé au vrai): **le ~** falsehood; **le ~ numéro/la fausse clé** the wrong number/key; **faire fausse route** to go the wrong way; **faire ~ bond à qn** to let sb down; **~ ami** (Ling) faux ami; **~ col** detachable collar; **~ départ** (Sport, fig) false start; **~ frais** nmpl extras, incidental expenses; **~ frère** (fig péj) false friend; **~ mouvement** awkward

movement; **~ nez** false nose; **~ nom** assumed name; **~ pas** tripping no pl; (fig) faux pas; **~ témoignage** (délit) perjury; **fausse alerte** false alarm; **fausse clé** skeleton key; **fausse couche** (Méd) miscarriage; **fausse joie** vain joy; **fausse note** wrong note

faux-filet [fofilɛ] nm sirloin

faux-fuyant [fofɥijɑ̃] nm equivocation

faux-monnayeur [fomɔnɛjœʀ] nm counterfeiter, forger

faux-semblant [fosɑ̃blɑ̃] nm pretence (Brit), pretense (US)

faux-sens [fosɑ̃s] nm mistranslation

faveur [favœʀ] nf favour (Brit), favor (US); **traitement de ~** preferential treatment; **à la ~ de** under cover of; (grâce à) thanks to; **en ~ de** in favo(u)r of

favorable [favɔʀabl(ə)] adj favo(u)rable

favori, te [favɔʀi, -it] adj, nm/f favo(u)rite

favoris [favɔʀi] nmpl (barbe) sideboards (Brit), sideburns

favoriser [favɔʀize] vt to favour (Brit), favor (US)

favoritisme [favɔʀitism(ə)] nm (péj) favo(u)ritism

fax [faks] nm fax

faxer vt to fax

fayot [fajo] nm (fam) crawler

FB abr (= franc belge) BF, FB

FBI sigle m FBI

FC sigle m (= Football Club) FC

fébrile [febʀil] adj feverish, febrile; **capitaux ~s** (Écon) hot money

fébrilement [febʀilmɑ̃] adv feverishly

fécal, e, -aux [fekal, -o] adj voir **matière**

fécond, e [fekɔ̃, -ɔ̃d] adj fertile

fécondation [fekɔ̃dasjɔ̃] nf fertilization

féconder [fekɔ̃de] vt to fertilize

fécondité [fekɔ̃dite] nf fertility

fécule [fekyl] nf potato flour

féculent [fekylɑ̃] nm starchy food

fédéral, e, -aux [federal, -o] adj federal

fédéralisme [federalism(ə)] nm federalism

fédéraliste [federalist(ə)] adj federalist

fédération [federasjɔ̃] nf federation; **la F~ française de football** the French football association

fée [fe] nf fairy

féerie [feʀi] nf enchantment

féerique [feʀik] adj magical, fairytale cpd

feignant, e [fɛɲɑ̃, -ɑ̃t] nm/f = **fainéant, e**

feindre [fɛ̃dʀ(ə)] vt to feign ▷ vi to dissemble; **~ de faire** to pretend to do

feint, e [fɛ̃, fɛ̃t] pp de **feindre** ▷ adj feigned ▷ nf (Sport: escrime) feint; (: Football, Rugby) dummy (Brit), fake (US); (fam: ruse) sham

feinter [fɛ̃te] vi (Sport: escrime) to feint; (: Football, Rugby) to dummy (Brit), fake (US) ▷ vt (fam: tromper) to fool

fêlé, e [fele] adj (aussi fig) cracked

fêler [fele] vt to crack

félicitations [felisitasjɔ̃] nfpl congratulations

félicité [felisite] nf bliss

féliciter [felisite] *vt:* ~ **qn (de)** to congratulate sb (on)

félin, e [felɛ̃, -in] *adj* feline ▷ *nm* (big) cat

félon, ne [felɔ̃, -ɔn] *adj* perfidious, treacherous

félonie [feloni] *nf* treachery

fêlure [felyʀ] *nf* crack

femelle [fəmɛl] *adj (aussi Élec, Tech)* female ▷ *nf* female

féminin, e [feminɛ̃, -in] *adj* feminine; *(sexe)* female; *(équipe, vêtements etc)* women's; *(parfois péj: homme)* effeminate ▷ *nm (Ling)* feminine

féminiser [feminize] *vt* to feminize; *(rendre efféminé)* to make effeminate; **se féminiser** *vi:* **cette profession se féminise** this profession is attracting more women

féminisme [feminism(ə)] *nm* feminism

féministe [feminist(ə)] *adj, nf* feminist

féminité [feminite] *nf* femininity

femme [fam] *nf* woman; *(épouse)* wife; **être très ~** to be very much a woman; **devenir ~** to attain womanhood; **~ d'affaires** businesswoman; **~ de chambre** chambermaid; **~ fatale** femme fatale; **~ au foyer** housewife; **~ d'intérieur** (real) homemaker; **~ de ménage** domestic help, cleaning lady; **~ du monde** society woman; **~-objet** sex object; **~ de tête** determined, intellectual woman

fémoral, e, -aux [femoʀal, -o] *adj* femoral

fémur [femyʀ] *nm* femur, thighbone

FEN [fɛn] *sigle f* (= *Fédération de l'Éducation nationale*) teachers' trades union

fenaison [fənɛzɔ̃] *nf* haymaking

fendillé, e [fɑ̃dije] *adj (terre etc)* crazed

fendre [fɑ̃dʀ(ə)] *vt (couper en deux)* to split; *(fissurer)* to crack; *(fig: traverser)* to cut through; to push one's way through; **se fendre** *vi* to crack

fendu, e [fɑ̃dy] *adj (sol, mur)* cracked; *(jupe)* slit

fenêtre [fənɛtʀ(ə)] *nf* window; **~ à guillotine** sash window

fennec [fenɛk] *nm* fennec

fenouil [fənuj] *nm* fennel

fente [fɑ̃t] *nf* slit; *(fissure)* crack

féodal, e, -aux [feodal, -o] *adj* feudal

féodalisme [feodalism(ə)] *nm* feudalism

féodalité [feodalite] *nf* feudalism

fer [fɛʀ] *nm* iron; *(de cheval)* shoe; **fers** *nmpl (Méd)* forceps; **mettre aux ~s** *(enchaîner)* to put in chains; **au ~ rouge** with a red-hot iron; **santé/main de ~** iron constitution/hand; **~ à cheval** horseshoe; **en ~ à cheval** *(fig)* horseshoe-shaped; **~ forgé** wrought iron; **~ à friser** curling tongs; **~ de lance** spearhead; **~ (à repasser)** iron; **~ à souder** soldering iron

ferai etc [fəʀe] *vb voir* **faire**

fer-blanc [fɛʀblɑ̃] *nm* tin(plate)

ferblanterie [fɛʀblɑ̃tʀi] *nf* tinplate making; *(produit)* tinware

ferblantier [fɛʀblɑ̃tje] *nm* tinsmith

férié, e [feʀje] *adj:* **jour ~** public holiday

ferions etc [fəʀjɔ̃] *vb voir* **faire**

férir [feʀiʀ]: **sans coup ~** *adv* without meeting any opposition

fermage [fɛʀmaʒ] *nm* tenant farming

ferme [fɛʀm(ə)] *adj* firm ▷ *adv (travailler etc)* hard; *(discuter)* ardently ▷ *nf (exploitation)* farm; *(maison)* farmhouse; **tenir ~** to stand firm

fermé, e [fɛʀme] *adj* closed, shut; *(gaz, eau etc)* off; *(fig: personne)* uncommunicative; *(: milieu)* exclusive

fermement [fɛʀməmɑ̃] *adv* firmly

ferment [fɛʀmɑ̃] *nm* ferment

fermentation [fɛʀmɑ̃tasjɔ̃] *nf* fermentation

fermenter [fɛʀmɑ̃te] *vi* to ferment

fermer [fɛʀme] *vt* to close, shut; *(cesser l'exploitation de)* to close down, shut down; *(eau, lumière, électricité, robinet)* to put off, turn off; *(aéroport, route)* to close ▷ *vi* to close, shut; to close down, shut down; **se fermer** *vi (yeux)* to close, shut; *(fleur, blessure)* to close up; **~ à clef** to lock; **~ au verrou** to bolt; **~ les yeux (sur qch)** *(fig)* to close one's eyes (to sth); **se ~ à** *(pitié, amour)* to close one's heart ou mind to

fermeté [fɛʀməte] *nf* firmness

fermette [fɛʀmɛt] *nf* farmhouse

fermeture [fɛʀmətyʀ] *nf* closing; shutting; closing ou shutting down; putting ou turning off; *(dispositif)* catch; fastening, fastener; **heure de ~** *(Comm)* closing time; **jour de ~** *(Comm)* day on which the shop *(etc)* is closed; **~ éclair**® *ou* **à glissière** zip (fastener) (Brit), zipper; *voir* **fermer**

fermier, -ière [fɛʀmje, -jɛʀ] *nm/f* farmer ▷ *nf (femme de fermier)* farmer's wife ▷ *adj:* **beurre/cidre ~** farm butter/cider

fermoir [fɛʀmwaʀ] *nm* clasp

féroce [feʀɔs] *adj* ferocious, fierce

férocement [feʀɔsmɑ̃] *adv* ferociously

férocité [feʀɔsite] *nf* ferocity, ferociousness

ferons etc [fəʀɔ̃] *vb voir* **faire**

ferraille [feʀaj] *nf* scrap iron; **mettre à la ~** to scrap; **bruit de ~** clanking

ferrailler [feʀaje] *vi* to clank

ferrailleur [feʀajœʀ] *nm* scrap merchant

ferrant [feʀɑ̃] *adj m voir* **maréchal-ferrant**

ferré, e [feʀe] *adj (chaussure)* hobnailed; *(canne)* steel-tipped; **~ sur** *(fam: savant)* well up on

ferrer [feʀe] *vt (cheval)* to shoe; *(chaussure)* to nail; *(canne)* to tip; *(poisson)* to strike

ferreux, -euse [feʀø, -øz] *adj* ferrous

ferronnerie [feʀɔnʀi] *nf* ironwork; **~ d'art** wrought iron work

ferronnier [feʀɔnje] *nm* craftsman in wrought iron; *(marchand)* ironware merchant

ferroviaire [feʀɔvjɛʀ] *adj* rail *cpd*, railway *cpd* (Brit), railroad *cpd* (US)

ferrugineux, -euse [feʀyʒinø, -øz] *adj* ferruginous

ferrure [feʀyʀ] *nf (ornamental)* hinge

ferry [feʀe], **ferry-boat** [feʀebot] *nm* ferry

fertile [fɛʀtil] *adj* fertile; **~ en incidents** eventful, packed with incidents

fertilisant [fɛʀtilizɑ̃] *nm* fertilizer

fertilisation [fɛʀtilizasjɔ̃] *nf* fertilization

fertiliser [fɛʀtilize] *vt* to fertilize

fertilité [fɛʀtilite] *nf* fertility

féru, e [feʁy] *adj*: ~ **de** with a keen interest in

férule [feʁyl] *nf*: **être sous la** ~ **de qn** to be under sb's (iron) rule

fervent, e [fɛʁvɑ̃, -ɑ̃t] *adj* fervent

ferveur [fɛʁvœʁ] *nf* fervour (*Brit*), fervor (*US*)

fesse [fɛs] *nf* buttock; **les ~s** the bottom *sg*, the buttocks

fessée [fese] *nf* spanking

fessier [fesje] *nm* (*fam*) behind

festin [fɛstɛ̃] *nm* feast

festival [fɛstival] *nm* festival

festivalier [fɛstivalje] *nm* festival-goer

festivités [fɛstivite] *nfpl* festivities, merrymaking *sg*

feston [fɛstɔ̃] *nm* (*Archit*) festoon; (*Couture*) scallop

festoyer [fɛstwaje] *vi* to feast

fêtard [fɛtaʁ] *nm* (*péj*) high liver, merrymaker

fête [fɛt] *nf* (*religieuse*) feast; (*publique*) holiday; (*en famille etc*) celebration; (*kermesse*) fête, fair, festival; (*du nom*) feast day, name day; **faire la ~** to live it up; **faire ~ à qn** to give sb a warm welcome; **se faire une ~ de** to look forward to; to enjoy; **ça va être sa ~!** (*fam*) he's going to get it!; **jour de ~** holiday; **les ~s (de fin d'année)** the festive season; **la salle/le comité des ~s** the village hall/festival committee; **la ~ des Mères/Pères** Mother's/Father's Day; **~ de charité** charity fair *ou* fête; **~ foraine** (fun)fair; **la ~ de la musique**; *see note*; **~ mobile** movable feast (day); **la F~ Nationale** the national holiday

● **FÊTE DE LA MUSIQUE**

The *fête de la musique* is a music festival which has taken place every year since 1981. On 21 June throughout France local musicians perform free of charge in parks, streets and squares.

Fête-Dieu [fɛtdjø] *nf*: **la ~** Corpus Christi

fêter [fete] *vt* to celebrate; (*personne*) to have a celebration for

fétiche [fetiʃ] *nm* fetish; **animal ~, objet ~** mascot

fétichisme [fetiʃism(ə)] *nm* fetishism

fétichiste [fetiʃist(ə)] *adj* fetishist

fétide [fetid] *adj* fetid

fétu [fety] *nm*: **~ de paille** wisp of straw

feu¹ [fø] *adj inv*: **~ son père** his late father

feu², x [fø] *nm* (*gén*) fire; (*signal lumineux*) light; (*de cuisinière*) ring; (*sensation de brûlure*) burning (sensation); **feux** *nmpl* fire *sg*; (*Auto*) (traffic) lights; **tous ~x éteints** (*Navig, Auto*) without lights; **au ~!** (*incendie*) fire!; **à ~ doux/vif** over a slow/brisk heat; **à petit ~** (*Culin*) over a gentle heat; (*fig*) slowly; **faire ~** to fire; **ne pas faire long ~** (*fig*) not to last long; **commander le ~** (*Mil*) to give the order to (open) fire; **tué au ~** (*Mil*) killed in action; **mettre à ~** (*fusée*) to fire off; **pris entre deux ~x** caught in the crossfire;

en ~ on fire; **être tout ~ tout flamme (pour)** (*passion*) to be aflame with passion (for); (*enthousiasme*) to be fired with enthusiasm (for); **prendre ~** to catch fire; **mettre le ~ à** to set fire to, set on fire; **faire du ~** to make a fire; **avez-vous du ~?** (*pour cigarette*) have you (got) a light?; **~ rouge/vert/orange** (*Auto*) red/green/amber (*Brit*) *ou* yellow (*US*) light; **donner le ~ vert à qch/qn** (*fig*) to give sth/sb the go-ahead *ou* green light; **~ arrière** (*Auto*) rear light; **~ d'artifice** firework; (*spectacle*) fireworks *pl*; **~ de camp** campfire; **~ de cheminée** chimney fire; **~ de joie** bonfire; **~ de paille** (*fig*) flash in the pan; **~x de brouillard** (*Auto*) fog lights *ou* lamps; **~x de croisement** (*Auto*) dipped (*Brit*) *ou* dimmed (*US*) headlights; **~x de position** (*Auto*) sidelights; **~x de route** (*Auto*) headlights (on full (*Brit*) *ou* high (*US*) beam); **~x de stationnement** parking lights

feuillage [fœja3] *nm* foliage, leaves *pl*

feuille [fœj] *nf* (*d'arbre*) leaf; **~ (de papier)** sheet (of paper); **rendre ~ blanche** (*Scol*) to give in a blank paper; **~ d'or/de métal** gold/metal leaf; **~ de chou** (*péj: journal*) rag; **~ d'impôts** tax form; **~ de maladie** medical expenses claim form; **~ morte** dead leaf; **~ de paye** pay slip; **~ de présence** attendance sheet; **~ de température** temperature chart; **~ de vigne** (*Bot*) vine leaf; (*sur statue*) fig leaf; **~ volante** loose sheet

feuillet [fœjɛ] *nm* leaf, page

feuilletage [fœjta3] *nm* (*aspect feuilleté*) flakiness

feuilleté, e [fœjte] *adj* (*Culin*) flaky; (*verre*) laminated

feuilleter [fœjte] *vt* (*livre*) to leaf through

feuilleton [fœjtɔ̃] *nm* serial

feuillette *etc* [fœjɛt] *vb voir* **feuilleter**

feuillu, e [fœjy] *adj* leafy ▷ *nm* broad-leaved tree

feulement [følmɑ̃] *nm* growl

feutre [føtʁ(ə)] *nm* felt; (*chapeau*) felt hat; (*stylo*) felt-tip(ped pen)

feutré, e [føtʁe] *adj* feltlike; (*pas, voix*) muffled

feutrer [føtʁe] *vt* to felt; (*fig: bruits*) to muffle ▷ *vi*, **se feutrer** *vi* (*tissu*) to felt

feutrine [føtʁin] *nf* (lightweight) felt

fève [fɛv] *nf* broad bean; (*dans la galette des Rois*) charm (*hidden in cake eaten on Twelfth Night*)

février [fevʁije] *nm* February; *voir aussi* **juillet**

fez [fɛz] *nm* fez

FF *abr* (= *franc français*) FF

FFA *sigle fpl* (= *Forces françaises en Allemagne*) French forces in Germany

FFF *abr* = **Fédération française de football**

FFI *sigle fpl* = **Forces françaises de l'intérieur (1942–45)** ▷ *sigle m* member of the FFI

FFL *sigle fpl* (= *Forces françaises libres*) Free French Army

Fg *abr* = **faubourg**

FGA *sigle m* (= *Fonds de garantie automobile*) fund financed through insurance premiums, to compensate victims of uninsured losses

FGEN *sigle f* (= *Fédération générale de l'éducation nationale*) teachers' trade union

fi [fi] *excl*: **faire fi de** to snap one's fingers at
fiabilité [fjabilite] *nf* reliability
fiable [fjabl(ə)] *adj* reliable
fiacre [fjakʀ(ə)] *nm* (hackney) cab *ou* carriage
fiançailles [fjɑ̃saj] *nfpl* engagement *sg*
fiancé, e [fjɑ̃se] *nm/f* fiancé (fiancée) ▷ *adj*: **être ~ (à)** to be engaged (to)
fiancer [fjɑ̃se]: **se fiancer** *vi*: **se ~ (avec)** to become engaged (to)
fiasco [fjasko] *nm* fiasco
fibranne [fibʀan] *nf* bonded fibre *ou* fiber (US)
fibre [fibʀ(ə)] *nf* fibre, fiber (US); **avoir la ~ paternelle/militaire** to be a born father/soldier; **~ optique** optical fibre *ou* fiber; **~ de verre** fibreglass (Brit), fiberglass (US), glass fibre *ou* fiber
fibreux, -euse [fibʀø, -øz] *adj* fibrous; (viande) stringy
fibrome [fibʀom] *nm* (Méd) fibroma
ficelage [fisla3] *nm* tying (up)
ficelé, e [fisle] *adj* (fam): **être mal ~** (habillé) to be badly got up; **bien/mal ~** (conçu: roman, projet) well/badly put together
ficeler [fisle] *vt* to tie up
ficelle [fisɛl] *nf* string *no pl*; (morceau) piece *ou* length of string; (pain) stick of French bread; **ficelles** *nfpl* (fig) strings; **tirer sur la ~** (fig) to go too far
fiche [fiʃ] *nf* (carte) (index) card; (formulaire) form; (Élec) plug; **~ de paye** pay slip; **~ signalétique** (Police) identification card; **~ technique** data sheet, specification *ou* spec sheet
ficher [fiʃe] *vt* (dans un fichier) to file; (: Police) to put on file; (fam) to do; (: donner) to give; (: mettre) to stick *ou* shove; (planter): **~ qch dans** to stick *ou* drive sth into; **~ qn à la porte** (fam) to chuck sb out; **fiche(-moi) le camp** (fam) clear off; **fiche-moi la paix** (fam) leave me alone; **se ~ dans** (s'enfoncer) to get stuck in, embed itself in; **se ~ de** (fam) to make fun of; not to care about
fichier [fiʃje] *nm* (gén, Inform) file; (à cartes) card index; **~ actif** *ou* **en cours d'utilisation** (Inform) active file; **~ d'adresses** mailing list; **~ d'archives** (Inform) archive file
fichu, e [fiʃy] *pp de* **ficher** (fam) ▷ *adj* (fam: fini, inutilisable) bust, done for; (: intensif) wretched, darned ▷ *nm* (foulard) (head)scarf; **être ~ de** to be capable of; **mal ~** feeling lousy; useless; **bien ~** great
fictif, -ive [fiktif, -iv] *adj* fictitious
fiction [fiksjɔ̃] *nf* fiction; (fait imaginé) invention
fictivement [fiktivmɑ̃] *adv* fictitiously
fidèle [fidɛl] *adj*: **~ (à)** faithful (to) ▷ *nm/f* (Rel): **les ~s** the faithful; (à l'église) the congregation
fidèlement [fidɛlmɑ̃] *adv* faithfully
fidélité [fidelite] *nf* faithfulness
Fidji [fidʒi] *nfpl*: **(les îles) ~** Fiji
fiduciaire [fidysjɛʀ] *adj* fiduciary; **héritier ~** heir, trustee; **monnaie ~** flat money
fief [fjɛf] *nm* fief; (fig) preserve; stronghold
fieffé, e [fjefe] *adj* (ivrogne, menteur) arrant, out-and-out

fiel [fjɛl] *nm* gall
fiente [fjɑ̃t] *nf* (bird) droppings *pl*
fier¹ [fje]: **se ~ à** *vt* to trust
fier², fière [fjɛʀ] *adj* proud; **~ de** proud of; **avoir fière allure** to cut a fine figure
fièrement [fjɛʀmɑ̃] *adv* proudly
fierté [fjɛʀte] *nf* pride
fièvre [fjɛvʀ(ə)] *nf* fever; **avoir de la ~/39 de ~** to have a high temperature/a temperature of 39° C; **~ typhoïde** typhoid fever
fiévreusement [fjevʀøzmɑ̃] *adv* (fig) feverishly
fiévreux, -euse [fjevʀø, -øz] *adj* feverish
FIFA [fifa] *sigle f* (= Fédération internationale de Football association) FIFA
fifre [fifʀ(ə)] *nm* fife; (personne) fife-player
fig *abr* (= figure) fig
figé, e [fiʒe] *adj* (manières) stiff; (société) rigid; (sourire) set
figer [fiʒe] *vt* to congeal; (fig: personne) to freeze, root to the spot; **se figer** *vi* to congeal; to freeze; (institutions etc) to become set, stop evolving
fignoler [fiɲɔle] *vt* to put the finishing touches to
figue [fig] *nf* fig
figuier [figje] *nm* fig tree
figurant, e [figyʀɑ̃, -ɑ̃t] *nm/f* (Théât) walk-on; (Ciné) extra
figuratif, -ive [figyʀatif, -iv] *adj* representational, figurative
figuration [figyʀasjɔ̃] *nf* walk-on parts *pl*; extras *pl*
figure [figyʀ] *nf* (visage) face; (image, tracé, forme, personnage) figure; (illustration) picture, diagram; **faire ~ de** to look like; **faire bonne ~** to put up a good show; **faire triste ~** to be a sorry sight; **~ de rhétorique** figure of speech
figuré, e [figyʀe] *adj* (sens) figurative
figurer [figyʀe] *vi* to appear ▷ *vt* to represent; **se ~ que** to imagine that; **figurez-vous que ...** would you believe that ...?
figurine [figyʀin] *nf* figurine
fil [fil] *nm* (brin, fig: d'une histoire) thread; (du téléphone) cable, wire; (textile de lin) linen; (d'un couteau: tranchant) edge; **au ~ des années** with the passing of the years; **au ~ de l'eau** with the stream *ou* current; **de ~ en aiguille** one thing leading to another; **ne tenir qu'à un ~** (vie, réussite etc) to hang by a thread; **donner du ~ à retordre à qn** to make life difficult for sb; **donner/recevoir un coup de ~** to make/get a phone call; **~ à coudre** (sewing) thread *ou* yarn; **~ dentaire** dental floss; **~ électrique** electric wire; **~ de fer** wire; **~ de fer barbelé** barbed wire; **~ à pêche** fishing line; **~ à plomb** plumb line; **~ à souder** soldering wire
filament [filamɑ̃] *nm* (Élec) filament; (de liquide) trickle, thread
filandreux, -euse [filɑ̃dʀø, -øz] *adj* stringy
filant, e [filɑ̃, -ɑ̃t] *adj*: **étoile ~e** shooting star
filasse [filas] *adj inv* white blond
filature [filatyʀ] *nf* (fabrique) mill; (policière)

shadowing *no pl*, tailing *no pl*; **prendre qn en ~** to shadow *ou* tail sb

file [fil] *nf* line; **~ (d'attente)** queue (*Brit*), line (*US*); **prendre la ~** to join the (end of the) queue *ou* line; **prendre la ~ de droite** (*Auto*) to move into the right-hand lane; **se mettre en ~** to form a line; (*Auto*) to get into lane; **stationner en double ~** (*Auto*) to double-park; **à la ~** *adv* (*d'affilée*) in succession; (*à la suite*) one after another; **à la** *ou* **en ~ indienne** in single file

filer [file] *vt* (*tissu, toile, verre*) to spin; (*dérouler: câble etc*) to pay ou let out; (*prendre en filature*) to shadow, tail; (*fam: donner*): **~ qch à qn** to slip sth ▷ *vi* (*bas, maille, liquide, pâte*) to run; (*aller vite*) to fly past *ou* by; (*fam: partir*) to make off; **~ à l'anglaise** to take French leave; **~ doux** to behave o.s., toe the line; **~ un mauvais coton** to be in a bad way

filet [file] *nm* net; (*Culin*) fillet; (*d'eau, de sang*) trickle; **tendre un ~** (*police*) to set a trap; **~ (à bagages)** (*Rail*) luggage rack; **~ (à provisions)** string bag

filetage [filtaʒ] *nm* threading; thread

fileter [filte] *vt* to thread

filial, e, -aux [filjal, -o] *adj* filial ▷ *nf* (*Comm*) subsidiary; affiliate

filiation [filjasjɔ̃] *nf* filiation

filière [filjɛR] *nf*: **passer par la ~** to go through the (administrative) channels; **suivre la ~** to work one's way up (through the hierarchy)

filiforme [filifɔRm(ə)] *adj* spindly; threadlike

filigrane [filigRan] *nm* (*d'un billet, timbre*) watermark; **en ~** (*fig*) showing just beneath the surface

filin [filɛ̃] *nm* (*Navig*) rope

fille [fij] *nf* girl; (*opposé à fils*) daughter; **vieille ~** old maid; **~ de joie** prostitute; **~ de salle** waitress

fille-mère [fijmɛR] (*pl* **filles-mères**) *nf* unmarried mother

fillette [fijɛt] *nf* (little) girl

filleul, e [fijœl] *nm/f* godchild, godson (goddaughter)

film [film] *nm* (*pour photo*) (roll of) film; (*œuvre*) film, picture, movie; (*couche*) film; **~ muet/parlant** silent/talking picture *ou* movie; **~ alimentaire** clingfilm; **~ d'amour/d'animation/d'horreur** romantic/animated/horror film; **~ comique** comedy; **~ policier** thriller

filmer [filme] *vt* to film

filon [filɔ̃] *nm* vein, lode; (*fig*) lucrative line, money-spinner

filou [filu] *nm* (*escroc*) swindler

fils [fis] *nm* son; **~ de famille** moneyed young man; **~ à papa** (*péj*) daddy's boy

filtrage [filtRaʒ] *nm* filtering

filtrant, e [filtRɑ̃, -ɑ̃t] *adj* (*huile solaire etc*) filtering

filtre [filtR(ə)] *nm* filter; **"~ ou sans ~?"** (*cigarettes*) "tipped or plain?"; **~ à air** air filter

filtrer [filtRe] *vt* to filter; (*fig: candidats, visiteurs*) to screen ▷ *vi* to filter (through)

fin¹ [fɛ̃] *nf* end; **fins** *nfpl* (*but*) ends; **à (la) ~ mai**, **~ mai** at the end of May; **en ~ de semaine** at the end of the week; **prendre ~** to come to an end; **toucher à sa ~** to be drawing to a close; **mettre ~ à** to put an end to; **mener à bonne ~** to bring to a successful conclusion; **à cette ~** to this end; **à toutes ~s utiles** for your information; **à la ~** in the end, eventually; **sans ~** *adj* endless ▷ *adv* endlessly; **~ de non-recevoir** (*Jur, Admin*) objection; **~ de section** (*de ligne d'autobus*) (fare) stage

fin², e [fɛ̃, fin] *adj* (*papier, couche, fil*) thin; (*cheveux, poudre, pointe, visage*) fine; (*taille*) neat, slim; (*esprit, remarque*) subtle; shrewd ▷ *adv* (*moudre, couper*) finely ▷ *nm*: **vouloir jouer au plus ~ (avec qn)** to try to outsmart sb ▷ *nf* (*alcool*) liqueur brandy; **c'est ~!** (*ironique*) how clever!; **~ prêt/soûl** quite ready/drunk; **un ~ gourmet** a gourmet; **un ~ tireur** a crack shot; **avoir la vue/l'ouïe ~e** to have sharp eyes/ears, have keen eyesight/hearing; **or/linge/vin ~** fine gold/linen/wine; **le ~ fond de** the very depths of; **le ~ mot de** the real story behind; **la ~e fleur de** the flower of; **une ~e mouche** (*fig*) a sly customer; **~es herbes** mixed herbs

final, e [final] *adj, nf* final ▷ *nm* (*Mus*) finale; **quarts de ~e** quarter finals; **8èmes/16èmes de ~e** 2nd/1st round (*in 5 round knock-out competition*)

finalement [finalmɑ̃] *adv* finally, in the end; (*après tout*) after all

finaliste [finalist(ə)] *nm/f* finalist

finalité [finalite] *nf* (*but*) aim, goal; (*fonction*) purpose

finance [finɑ̃s] *nf* finance; **finances** *nfpl* (*situation financière*) finances; (*activités financières*) finance *sg*; **moyennant ~** for a fee *ou* consideration

financement [finɑ̃smɑ̃] *nm* financing

financer [finɑ̃se] *vt* to finance

financier, -ière [finɑ̃sje, -jɛR] *adj* financial ▷ *nm* financier

financièrement [finɑ̃sjɛRmɑ̃] *adv* financially

finasser [finase] *vi* (*péj*) to wheel and deal

finaud, e [fino, -od] *adj* wily

fine [fin] *adj f, nf voir* **fin, e**

finement [finmɑ̃] *adv* thinly; finely; neatly, slimly; subtly; shrewdly

finesse [finɛs] *nf* thinness; fineness; neatness, slimness; subtlety; shrewdness; **finesses** *nfpl* (*subtilités*) niceties; finer points

fini, e [fini] *adj* finished; (*Math*) finite; (*intensif*): **un menteur ~** a liar through and through ▷ *nm* (*d'un objet manufacturé*) finish

finir [finiR] *vt* to finish ▷ *vi* to finish, end; **~ quelque part** to end *ou* finish up somewhere; **~ de faire** to finish doing; (*cesser*) to stop doing; **~ par faire** to end *ou* finish up doing; **il finit par m'agacer** he's beginning to get on my nerves; **~ en pointe/tragédie** to end in a point/in tragedy; **en ~ avec** to be *ou* have done with; **à n'en plus ~** (*route, discussions*) never-ending; **il**

va mal ~ he will come to a bad end; **c'est bientôt fini?** (reproche) have you quite finished?

finish [finiʃ] nm (Sport) finish

finissage [finisaʒ] nm finishing

finisseur, -euse [finisœʀ, -øz] nm/f (Sport) strong finisher

finition [finisjɔ̃] nf finishing; finish

finlandais, e [fɛ̃lɑ̃dɛ, -ɛz] adj Finnish ▷ nm/f: **Finlandais, e** Finn

Finlande [fɛ̃lɑ̃d] nf: **la** ~ Finland

finnois, e [finwa, -waz] adj Finnish ▷ nm (Ling) Finnish

fiole [fjɔl] nf phial

fiord [fjɔʀ(d)] nm = **fjord**

fioriture [fjɔʀityʀ] nf embellishment, flourish

fioul [fjul] nm fuel oil

firent [fiʀ] vb voir **faire**

firmament [fiʀmamɑ̃] nm firmament, skies pl

firme [fiʀm(ə)] nf firm

fis [fi] vb voir **faire**

fisc [fisk] nm tax authorities pl, ≈ Inland Revenue (Brit), ≈ Internal Revenue Service (US)

fiscal, e, -aux [fiskal, -o] adj tax cpd, fiscal

fiscaliser [fiskalize] vt to subject to tax

fiscaliste [fiskalist(ə)] nm/f tax specialist

fiscalité [fiskalite] nf tax system; (charges) taxation

fissible [fisibl(ə)] adj fissile

fission [fisjɔ̃] nf fission

fissure [fisyʀ] nf crack

fissurer [fisyʀe] vt, **se fissurer** vi to crack

fiston [fistɔ̃] nm (fam) son, lad

fit [fi] vb voir **faire**

FIV sigle f (= fécondation in vitro) IVF

fixage [fiksaʒ] nm (Photo) fixing

fixateur [fiksatœʀ] nm (Photo) fixer; (pour cheveux) hair cream

fixatif [fiksatif] nm fixative

fixation [fiksasjɔ̃] nf fixing; fastening; setting; (de ski) binding; (Psych) fixation

fixe [fiks(ə)] adj fixed; (emploi) steady, regular ▷ nm (salaire) basic salary; **à heure** ~ at a set time; **menu à prix** ~ set menu

fixé, e [fikse] adj (heure, jour) appointed; **être** ~ **(sur)** to have made up one's mind (about); to know for certain (about)

fixement [fiksəmɑ̃] adv fixedly, steadily

fixer [fikse] vt (attacher): ~ **qch (à/sur)** to fix ou fasten sth (to/onto); (déterminer) to fix, set; (Chimie, Photo) to fix; (poser son regard sur) to look hard at, stare at; **se fixer** (s'établir) to settle down; ~ **son choix sur qch** to decide on sth; **se** ~ **sur** (attention) to focus on

fixité [fiksite] nf fixedness

fjord [fjɔʀ(d)] nm fjord, fiord

fl. abr (= fleuve) r, R; (= florin) fl

flacon [flakɔ̃] nm bottle

flagada [flagada] adj inv (fam: fatigué) shattered

flagellation [flaʒelasjɔ̃] nf flogging

flageller [flaʒele] vt to flog, scourge

flageoler [flaʒɔle] vi to have knees like jelly

flageolet [flaʒɔlɛ] nm (Mus) flageolet; (Culin) dwarf kidney bean

flagornerie [flagɔʀnəʀi] nf toadying, fawning

flagorneur, -euse [flagɔʀnœʀ, -øz] nm/f toady, fawner

flagrant, e [flagʀɑ̃, -ɑ̃t] adj flagrant, blatant; **en** ~ **délit** in the act, in flagrante delicto

flair [flɛʀ] nm sense of smell; (fig) intuition

flairer [fleʀe] vt (humer) to sniff (at); (détecter) to scent

flamand, e [flamɑ̃, -ɑ̃d] adj Flemish ▷ nm (Ling) Flemish ▷ nm/f: **Flamand, e** Fleming; **les F~s** the Flemish

flamant [flamɑ̃] nm flamingo

flambant [flɑ̃bɑ̃] adv: ~ **neuf** brand new

flambé, e [flɑ̃be] adj (Culin) flambé ▷ nf blaze; (fig) flaring-up, explosion

flambeau, x [flɑ̃bo] nm (flaming) torch; **se passer le** ~ (fig) to hand down the (ou a) tradition

flambée [flɑ̃be] nf (feu) blaze; (Comm): ~ **des prix** (sudden) shooting up of prices

flamber [flɑ̃be] vi to blaze (up) ▷ vt (poulet) to singe; (aiguille) to sterilize

flambeur, -euse [flɑ̃bœʀ, -øz] nm/f big-time gambler

flamboyant, e [flɑ̃bwajɑ̃, -ɑ̃t] adj blazing; flaming

flamboyer [flɑ̃bwaje] vi to blaze (up); (fig) to flame

flamenco [flamɛnko] nm flamenco

flamingant, e [flamɛ̃gɑ̃, -ɑ̃t] adj Flemish-speaking ▷ nm/f: **Flamingant, e** Flemish speaker; (Pol) Flemish nationalist

flamme [flam] nf flame; (fig) fire, fervour; **en** ~**s** on fire, ablaze

flammèche [flamɛʃ] nf (flying) spark

flammerole [flamʀɔl] nf will-o'-the-wisp

flan [flɑ̃] nm (Culin) custard tart ou pie

flanc [flɑ̃] nm side; (Mil) flank; **à** ~ **de colline** on the hillside; **prêter le** ~ **à** (fig) to lay o.s. open to

flancher [flɑ̃ʃe] vi (cesser de fonctionner) to fail, pack up; (armée) to quit

Flandre [flɑ̃dʀ(ə)] nf: **la** ~ (aussi: **les Flandres**) Flanders

flanelle [flanɛl] nf flannel

flâner [flɑne] vi to stroll

flânerie [flɑnʀi] nf stroll

flâneur, -euse [flɑnœʀ, -øz] adj idle ▷ nm/f stroller

flanquer [flɑ̃ke] vt to flank; (fam: jeter): ~ **par terre/à la porte** to fling to the ground/chuck out; (: donner): ~ **la frousse à qn** to put the wind up sb, give sb an awful fright

flapi, e [flapi] adj dog-tired

flaque [flak] nf (d'eau) puddle; (d'huile, de sang etc) pool

flash [flaʃ] (pl **-es**) nm (Photo) flash; ~ **(d'information)** newsflash

flasque [flask(ə)] adj flabby ▷ nf (flacon) flask

flatter [flate] vt to flatter; (caresser) to stroke; **se** ~ **de qch** to pride o.s. on sth

flatterie [flatʀi] nf flattery

flatteur, -euse [flatœʀ, -øz] *adj* flattering ▷ *nm/ f* flatterer

flatulence [flatylɑ̃s], **flatuosité** [flatɥozite] *nf* (*Méd*) flatulence, wind

FLB *abr* (= *franco long du bord*) FAS ▷ *sigle m* (*Pol*) = **Front de libération de la Bretagne**

FLC *sigle m* = **Front de libération de la Corse**

fléau, x [fleo] *nm* scourge, curse; (*de balance*) beam; (*pour le blé*) flail

fléchage [fleʃaʒ] *nm* (*d'un itinéraire*) signposting

flèche [flɛʃ] *nf* arrow; (*de clocher*) spire; (*de grue*) jib; (*trait d'esprit, critique*) shaft; **monter en ~** (*fig*) to soar, rocket; **partir en ~** (*fig*) to be off like a shot; **à ~ variable** (*avion*) swing-wing *cpd*

flécher [fleʃe] *vt* to arrow, mark with arrows

fléchette [fleʃɛt] *nf* dart; **fléchettes** *nfpl* (*jeu*) darts *sg*

fléchir [fleʃiʀ] *vt* (*corps, genou*) to bend; (*fig*) to sway, weaken ▷ *vi* (*poutre*) to sag, bend; (*fig*) to weaken, flag; (: *baisser: prix*) to fall off

fléchissement [fleʃismɑ̃] *nm* bending; sagging; flagging; (*de l'économie*) dullness

flegmatique [flɛgmatik] *adj* phlegmatic

flegme [flɛgm(ə)] *nm* composure

flemmard, e [flemaʀ, -aʀd(ə)] *nm/f* lazybones *sg*, loafer

flemme [flɛm] *nf* (*fam*): **j'ai la ~ de le faire** I can't be bothered

flétan [fletɑ̃] *nm* (*Zool*) halibut

flétrir [fletʀiʀ] *vt* to wither; (*stigmatiser*) to condemn (in the most severe terms); **se flétrir** *vi* to wither

fleur [flœʀ] *nf* flower; (*d'un arbre*) blossom; **être en ~** (*arbre*) to be in blossom; **tissu à ~s** flowered *ou* flowery fabric; **la (fine) ~ de** (*fig*) the flower of; **être ~ bleue** to be soppy *ou* sentimental; **à ~ de terre** just above the ground; **faire une ~ à qn** to do sb a favour (*Brit*) *ou* favor (*US*); **~ de lis** fleur-de-lis

fleurer [flœʀe] *vt*: **~ la lavande** to have the scent of lavender

fleuret [flœʀe] *nm* (*arme*) foil; (*sport*) fencing

fleurette [flœʀɛt] *nf*: **conter ~ à qn** to whisper sweet nothings to sb

fleuri, e [flœʀi] *adj* in flower *ou* bloom; surrounded by flowers; (*fig: style*) flowery; (: *teint*) glowing

fleurir [flœʀiʀ] *vi* (*rose*) to flower; (*arbre*) to blossom; (*fig*) to flourish ▷ *vt* (*tombe*) to put flowers on; (*chambre*) to decorate with flowers

fleuriste [flœʀist(ə)] *nm/f* florist

fleuron [flœʀɔ̃] *nm* jewel (*fig*)

fleuve [flœv] *nm* river; **roman-~** saga; **discours-~** interminable speech

flexibilité [flɛksibilite] *nf* flexibility

flexible [flɛksibl(ə)] *adj* flexible

flexion [flɛksjɔ̃] *nf* flexing, bending; (*Ling*) inflection

flibustier [flibystje] *nm* buccaneer

flic [flik] *nm* (*fam: péj*) cop

flingue [flɛ̃g] *nm* (*fam*) shooter

flipper *nm* [flipœʀ] pinball (machine) ▷ *vi*

[flipe] (*fam: être déprimé*) to feel down, be on a downer; (: *être exalté*) to freak out

flirt [flœʀt] *nm* flirting; (*personne*) boyfriend, girlfriend

flirter [flœʀte] *vi* to flirt

FLN *sigle m* = **Front de libération nationale (during the Algerian war)**

FLNKS *sigle m* (= *Front de libération nationale kanak et socialiste*) political movement in New Caledonia

flocon [flɔkɔ̃] *nm* flake; (*de laine etc: boulette*) flock; **~s d'avoine** oat flakes, porridge oats

floconneux, -euse [flɔkɔnø, -øz] *adj* fluffy, fleecy

flonflons [flɔ̃flɔ̃] *nmpl* blare *sg*

flopée [flɔpe] *nf*: **une ~ de** loads of

floraison [flɔʀɛzɔ̃] *nf* flowering; blossoming; flourishing; *voir* **fleurir**

floral, e, -aux [flɔʀal, -o] *adj* floral, flower *cpd*

floralies [flɔʀali] *nfpl* flower show *sg*

flore [flɔʀ] *nf* flora

Florence [flɔʀɑ̃s] *n* (*ville*) Florence

florentin, e [flɔʀɑ̃tɛ̃, -in] *adj* Florentine

floriculture [flɔʀikyltyʀ] *nf* flower-growing

florissant, e [flɔʀisɑ̃, -ɑ̃t] *vb voir* **fleurir** ▷ *adj* flourishing; (*santé, teint, mine*) blooming

flot [flo] *nm* flood, stream; (*marée*) flood tide; **flots** *nmpl* (*de la mer*) waves; **être à ~** (*Navig*) to be afloat; (*fig*) to be on an even keel; **à ~s** (*couler*) in torrents; **entrer à ~s** to stream *ou* pour in

flottage [flɔtaʒ] *nm* (*du bois*) floating

flottaison [flɔtɛzɔ̃] *nf*: **ligne de ~** waterline

flottant, e [flɔtɑ̃, -ɑ̃t] *adj* (*vêtement*) loose(-fitting); (*cours, barème*) floating

flotte [flɔt] *nf* (*Navig*) fleet; (*fam*) water; rain

flottement [flɔtmɑ̃] *nm* (*fig*) wavering, hesitation; (*Écon*) floating

flotter [flɔte] *vi* to float; (*nuage, odeur*) to drift; (*drapeau*) to fly; (*vêtements*) to hang loose ▷ *vb impers* (*fam: pleuvoir*): **il flotte** it's raining ▷ *vt* to float; **faire ~** to float

flotteur [flɔtœʀ] *nm* float

flottille [flɔtij] *nf* flotilla

flou, e [flu] *adj* fuzzy, blurred; (*fig*) woolly (*Brit*), vague; (*non ajusté: robe*) loose(-fitting)

flouer [flue] *vt* to swindle

FLQ *abr* (= *franco long du quai*) FAQ

fluctuant, e [flyktɥɑ̃, -ɑ̃t] *adj* (*prix, cours*) fluctuating; (*opinions*) changing

fluctuation [flyktɥasjɔ̃] *nf* fluctuation

fluctuer [flyktɥe] *vi* to fluctuate

fluet, te [flyɛ, -ɛt] *adj* thin, slight; (*voix*) thin

fluide [flyid] *adj* fluid; (*circulation etc*) flowing freely ▷ *nm* fluid; (*force*) (mysterious) power

fluidifier [flyidifje] *vt* to make fluid

fluidité [flyidite] *nf* fluidity; free flow

fluor [flyɔʀ] *nm* fluorine

fluoré, e [flyɔʀe] *adj* fluoridated

fluorescent, e [flyɔʀesɑ̃, -ɑ̃t] *adj* fluorescent

flûte [flyt] *nf* (*aussi*: **flûte traversière**) flute; (*verre*) flute glass; (*pain*) long loaf; **petite ~** piccolo; **~!** drat it!; **~ (à bec)** recorder; **~ de Pan** panpipes *pl*

flûtiste [flytist(ə)] *nm/f* flautist, flute player
fluvial, e, -aux [flyvjal, -o] *adj* river *cpd*, fluvial
flux [fly] *nm* incoming tide; (*écoulement*) flow; **le ~ et le re~** the ebb and flow
fluxion [flyksjɔ̃] *nf*: **~ de poitrine** pneumonia
FM *sigle f* (= *frequency modulation*) FM
Fme *abr* (= *femme*) W
FMI *sigle m* (= *Fonds monétaire international*) IMF
FN *sigle m* (= *Front national*) ≈ NF (= *National Front*)
FNAC [fnak] *sigle f* (= *Fédération nationale des achats des cadres*) chain of discount shops (hi-fi, photo etc)
FNSEA *sigle f* (= *Fédération nationale des syndicats d'exploitants agricoles*) farmers' union
FO *sigle f* (= *Force ouvrière*) trades union
foc [fɔk] *nm* jib
focal, e, -aux [fɔkal, -o] *adj* focal ▷ *nf* focal length
focaliser [fɔkalize] *vt* to focus
foehn [føn] *nm* foehn, föhn
fœtal, e, -aux [fetal, -o] *adj* fetal, foetal (*Brit*)
fœtus [fetys] *nm* fetus, foetus (*Brit*)
foi [fwa] *nf* faith; **sous la ~ du serment** under *ou* on oath; **ajouter ~ à** to lend credence to; **faire ~** (*prouver*) to be evidence; **digne de ~** reliable; **sur la ~ de** on the word *ou* strength of; **être de bonne/mauvaise ~** to be in good faith/not to be in good faith; **ma ~!** well!
foie [fwa] *nm* liver; **~ gras** foie gras
foin [fwɛ̃] *nm* hay; **faire les ~s** to make hay; **faire du ~** (*fam*) to kick up a row
foire [fwaR] *nf* fair; (*fête foraine*) (fun) fair; (*fig: désordre, confusion*) bear garden; **~ aux questions** (*Internet*) frequently asked questions; **faire la ~** to whoop it up; **~ (exposition)** trade fair
fois [fwa] *nf* time; **une/deux ~** once/twice; **trois/vingt ~** three/twenty times; **deux ~ deux** twice two; **deux/quatre ~ plus grand (que)** twice/four times as big (as); **une ~** (*passé*) once; (*futur*) sometime; **une (bonne) ~ pour toutes** once and for all; **encore une ~** again, once more; **il était une ~** once upon a time; **une ~ que c'est fait** once it's done; **une ~ parti** once he (*ou* I *etc*) had left; **des ~** (*parfois*) sometimes; **si des ~ ...** (*fam*) if ever ...; **non mais des ~!** (*fam*) (now) look here!; **à la ~** (*ensemble*) (all) at once; **à la ~ grand et beau** both tall and handsome
foison [fwazɔ̃] *nf*: **une ~ de** an abundance of; **à ~** *adv* in plenty
foisonnant, e [fwazɔnɑ̃, -ɑ̃t] *adj* teeming
foisonnement [fwazɔnmɑ̃] *nm* profusion, abundance
foisonner [fwazɔne] *vi* to abound; **~ en** *ou* **de** to abound in
fol [fɔl] *adj m voir* **fou**
folâtre [fɔlɑtR(ə)] *adj* playful
folâtrer [fɔlɑtRe] *vi* to frolic (about)
folichon, ne [fɔliʃɔ̃, -ɔn] *adj*: **ça n'a rien de ~** it's not a lot of fun
folie [fɔli] *nf* (*d'une décision, d'un acte*) madness, folly; (*état*) madness, insanity; (*acte*) folly; **la ~ des grandeurs** delusions of grandeur; **faire des ~s** (*en dépenses*) to be extravagant

folklore [fɔlklɔR] *nm* folklore
folklorique [fɔlklɔRik] *adj* folk *cpd*; (*fam*) weird
folle [fɔl] *adj f, nf voir* **fou**
follement [fɔlmɑ̃] *adv* (*très*) madly, wildly
follet [fɔlɛ] *adj m*: **feu ~** will-o'-the-wisp
fomentateur, -trice [fɔmɑ̃tatœR, -tRis] *nm/f* agitator
fomenter [fɔmɑ̃te] *vt* to stir up, foment
foncé, e [fɔ̃se] *adj* dark; **bleu ~** dark blue
foncer [fɔ̃se] *vt* to make darker; (*Culin: moule etc*) to line ▷ *vi* to go darker; (*fam: aller vite*) to tear *ou* belt along; **~ sur** to charge at
fonceur, -euse [fɔ̃sœR, -øz] *nm/f* whizz kid
foncier, -ière [fɔ̃sje, -jɛR] *adj* (*honnêteté etc*) basic, fundamental; (*malhonnêteté*) deep-rooted; (*Comm*) real estate *cpd*
foncièrement [fɔ̃sjɛRmɑ̃] *adv* basically; (*absolument*) thoroughly
fonction [fɔ̃ksjɔ̃] *nf* (*rôle, Math, Ling*) function; (*emploi, poste*) post, position; **fonctions** *nfpl* (*professionnelles*) duties; **entrer en ~s** to take up one's post *ou* duties; to take up office; **voiture de ~** company car; **être ~ de** (*dépendre de*) to depend on; **en ~ de** (*par rapport à*) according to; **faire ~ de** to serve as; **la ~ publique** the state *ou* civil (*Brit*) service
fonctionnaire [fɔ̃ksjɔnɛR] *nm/f* state employee *ou* official; (*dans l'administration*) ≈ civil servant (*Brit*)
fonctionnariser [fɔ̃ksjɔnaRize] *vt* (*Admin: personne*) to give the status of a state employee to
fonctionnel, le [fɔ̃ksjɔnɛl] *adj* functional
fonctionnellement [fɔ̃ksjɔnɛlmɑ̃] *adv* functionally
fonctionnement [fɔ̃ksjɔnmɑ̃] *nm* working; functioning; operation
fonctionner [fɔ̃ksjɔne] *vi* to work, function; (*entreprise*) to operate, function; **faire ~** to work, operate
fond [fɔ̃] *nm voir aussi* **fonds**; (*d'un récipient, trou*) bottom; (*d'une salle, scène*) back; (*d'un tableau, décor*) background; (*opposé à la forme*) content; (*petite quantité*): **un ~ de verre** a drop; (*Sport*): **le ~** long distance (running); **course/épreuve de ~** long-distance race/trial; **au ~ de** at the bottom of; at the back of; **aller au ~ des choses** to get to the root of things; **le ~ de sa pensée** his (*ou* her) true thoughts *ou* feelings; **sans ~** *adj* bottomless; **envoyer par le ~** (*Navig: couler*) to sink, scuttle; **à ~** *adv* (*connaître, soutenir*) thoroughly; (*appuyer, visser*) right down *ou* home; **à ~ (de train)** *adv* (*fam*) full tilt; **dans le ~, au ~** *adv* (*en somme*) basically, really; **de ~ en comble** *adv* from top to bottom; **~ sonore** background noise; background music; **~ de teint** foundation
fondamental, e, -aux [fɔ̃damɑ̃tal, -o] *adj* fundamental
fondamentalement [fɔ̃damɑ̃talmɑ̃] *adv* fundamentally
fondamentalisme [fɔ̃damɑ̃talism(ə)] *nm* fundamentalism

fondamentaliste [fɔ̃damɑ̃talist(ə)] *adj, nm/f* fundamentalist

fondant, e [fɔ̃dɑ̃, -ɑ̃t] *adj (neige)* melting; *(poire)* that melts in the mouth; *(chocolat)* fondant

fondateur, -trice [fɔ̃datœʀ, -tʀis] *nm/f* founder; **membre ~** founder *(Brit) ou* founding *(US)* member

fondation [fɔ̃dasjɔ̃] *nf* founding; *(établissement)* foundation; **fondations** *nfpl (d'une maison)* foundations; **travail de ~** foundation works *pl*

fondé, e [fɔ̃de] *adj (accusation etc)* well-founded ▷ *nm*: **~ de pouvoir** authorized representative; **mal ~** unfounded; **être ~ à croire** to have grounds for believing *ou* good reason to believe

fondement [fɔ̃dmɑ̃] *nm (derrière)* behind; **fondements** *nmpl* foundations; **sans ~** *adj (rumeur etc)* groundless, unfounded

fonder [fɔ̃de] *vt* to found; *(fig)*: **~ qch sur** to base sth on; **se ~ sur** *(personne)* to base o.s. on; **~ un foyer** *(se marier)* to set up home

fonderie [fɔ̃dʀi] *nf* smelting works *sg*

fondeur, -euse [fɔ̃dœʀ, -øz] *nm/f (skieur)* long-distance skier ▷ *nm*: **(ouvrier) ~** caster

fondre [fɔ̃dʀ(ə)] *vt* to melt; *(dans l'eau: sucre, sel)* to dissolve; *(fig: mélanger)* to merge, blend ▷ *vi* to melt; to dissolve; *(fig)* to melt away; *(se précipiter)*: **~ sur** to swoop down on; **se fondre** *vi (se combiner, se confondre)* to merge into each other; to dissolve; **~ en larmes** to dissolve into tears

fondrière [fɔ̃dʀijɛʀ] *nf* rut

fonds [fɔ̃] *nm (de bibliothèque)* collection; *(Comm)*: **~ (de commerce)** business; *(fig)*: **~ de probité** *etc* fund of integrity *etc* ▷ *nmpl (argent)* funds; **à ~ perdus** *adv* with little or no hope of getting the money back; **être en ~** to be in funds; **mise de ~** investment, (capital) outlay; **F~ monétaire international (FMI)** International Monetary Fund (IMF); **~ de roulement** *nm* float

fondu, e [fɔ̃dy] *adj (beurre, neige)* melted; *(métal)* molten ▷ *nm (Ciné)*: **~ (enchaîné)** dissolve ▷ *nf (Culin)* fondue

fongicide [fɔ̃ʒisid] *nm* fungicide

font [fɔ̃] *vb voir* **faire**

fontaine [fɔ̃tɛn] *nf* fountain; *(source)* spring

fontanelle [fɔ̃tanɛl] *nf* fontanelle

fonte [fɔ̃t] *nf* melting; *(métal)* cast iron; **la ~ des neiges** the (spring) thaw

fonts baptismaux [fɔ̃batismo] *nmpl* (baptismal) font *sg*

foot [fut], **football** [futbol] *nm* football, soccer

footballeur, -euse [futbolœʀ, -øz] *nm/f* footballer *(Brit)*, football *ou* soccer player

footing [futiŋ] *nm* jogging; **faire du ~** to go jogging

for [fɔʀ] *nm*: **dans** *ou* **en son ~ intérieur** in one's heart of hearts

forage [fɔʀaʒ] *nm* drilling, boring

forain, e [fɔʀɛ̃, -ɛn] *adj* fairground *cpd* ▷ *nm (marchand)* stallholder; *(acteur etc)* fairground entertainer

forban [fɔʀbɑ̃] *nm (pirate)* pirate; *(escroc)* crook

forçat [fɔʀsa] *nm* convict

force [fɔʀs(ə)] *nf* strength; *(puissance: surnaturelle etc)* power; *(Physique, Mécanique)* force; **forces** *nfpl (physiques)* strength *sg*; *(Mil)* forces; *(effectifs)*: **d'importantes ~s de police** large contingents of police; **avoir de la ~** to be strong; **être à bout de ~** to have no strength left; **à la ~ du poignet** *(fig)* by the sweat of one's brow; **à ~ de faire** by dint of doing; **arriver en ~** *(nombreux)* to arrive in force; **cas de ~ majeure** case of absolute necessity; *(Assurances)* act of God; **~ de la nature** natural force; **de ~** *adv* forcibly, by force; **de toutes mes/ses ~s** with all my/his strength; **par la ~** using force; **par la ~ des choses/d'habitude** by force of circumstances/habit; **à toute ~** *(absolument)* at all costs; **faire ~ de rames/voiles** to ply the oars/cram on sail; **être de ~ à faire** to be up to doing; **de première ~** first class; **la ~ armée** *(les troupes)* the army; **~ d'âme** fortitude; **~ de frappe** strike force; **~ d'inertie** force of inertia; **la ~ publique** the authorities responsible for public order; **~s d'intervention** *(Mil, Police)* peace-keeping force *sg*; **les ~s de l'ordre** the police

forcé, e [fɔʀse] *adj* forced; *(bain)* unintended; *(inévitable)*: **c'est ~!** it's inevitable!, it HAS to be!

forcément [fɔʀsemɑ̃] *adv* necessarily; inevitably; *(bien sûr)* of course

forcené, e [fɔʀsəne] *adj* frenzied ▷ *nm/f* maniac

forceps [fɔʀsɛps] *nm* forceps *pl*

forcer [fɔʀse] *vt (contraindre)*: **~ qn à faire** to force sb to do; *(porte, serrure, plante)* to force; *(moteur, voix)* to strain ▷ *vi (Sport)* to overtax o.s.; **se ~ à faire qch** to force o.s. to do sth; **~ la dose/l'allure** to overdo it/increase the pace; **~ l'attention/le respect** to command attention/respect; **~ la consigne** to bypass orders

forcing [fɔʀsiŋ] *nm (Sport)*: **faire le ~** to pile on the pressure

forcir [fɔʀsiʀ] *vi (grossir)* to broaden out; *(vent)* to freshen

forclore [fɔʀklɔʀ] *vt (Jur: personne)* to debar

forclusion [fɔʀklyzjɔ̃] *nf (Jur)* debarment

forer [fɔʀe] *vt* to drill, bore

forestier, -ière [fɔʀɛstje, -jɛʀ] *adj* forest *cpd*

foret [fɔʀe] *nm* drill

forêt [fɔʀe] *nf* forest; **Office National des F~s** *(Admin)* ≈ Forestry Commission *(Brit)*, ≈ National Forest Service *(US)*; **la F~ Noire** the Black Forest

foreuse [fɔʀøz] *nf* (electric) drill

forfait [fɔʀfɛ] *nm (Comm)* fixed *ou* set price; all-in deal *ou* price; *(crime)* infamy; **déclarer ~** to withdraw; **gagner par** to win by a walkover; **travailler à ~** to work for a lump sum

forfaitaire [fɔʀfɛtɛʀ] *adj* set; inclusive

forfait-vacances [fɔʀfɛvakɑ̃s] *(pl* **forfaits-vacances)** *nm* package holiday

forfanterie [fɔʀfɑ̃tʀi] *nf* boastfulness *no pl*

forge [fɔʀʒ(ə)] *nf* forge, smithy

forgé, e [fɔʀʒe] *adj*: **~ de toutes pièces** *(histoire)* completely fabricated

forger [fɔʀʒe] vt to forge; (fig: personnalité) to form; (: prétexte) to contrive, make up
forgeron [fɔʀʒəʀɔ̃] nm (black)smith
formaliser [fɔʀmalize]: **se formaliser** vi: **se ~ (de)** to take offence (at)
formalisme [fɔʀmalism(ə)] nm formality
formalité [fɔʀmalite] nf formality
format [fɔʀma] nm size; **petit ~** small size; (Photo) 35 mm (film)
formater [fɔʀmate] vt (disque) to format; **non formaté** unformatted
formateur, -trice [fɔʀmatœʀ, -tʀis] adj formative
formation [fɔʀmasjɔ̃] nf forming; (éducation) training; (Mus) group; (Mil, Aviat, Géo) formation; **la ~ permanente** ou **continue** continuing education; **la ~ professionnelle** vocational training
forme [fɔʀm(ə)] nf (gén) form; (d'un objet) shape, form; **formes** nfpl (bonnes manières) proprieties; (d'une femme) figure sg; **en ~ de poire** pear-shaped, in the shape of a pear; **sous ~ de** in the form of; in the guise of; **sous ~ de cachets** in the form of tablets; **être en (bonne** ou **pleine) ~**, **avoir la ~** (Sport etc) to be on form; **en bonne et due ~** in due form; **pour la ~** for the sake of form; **sans autre ~ de procès** (fig) without further ado; **prendre ~** to take shape
formel, le [fɔʀmɛl] adj (preuve, décision) definite, positive; (logique) formal
formellement [fɔʀmɛlmɑ̃] adv (interdit) strictly
former [fɔʀme] vt (gén) to form; (éduquer: soldat, ingénieur etc) to train; **se former** to form; to train
formidable [fɔʀmidabl(ə)] adj tremendous
formidablement [fɔʀmidabləmɑ̃] adv tremendously
formol [fɔʀmɔl] nm formalin, formol
formosan, e [fɔʀmozɑ̃, -an] adj Formosan
Formose [fɔʀmoz] nm Formosa
formulaire [fɔʀmylɛʀ] nm form
formulation [fɔʀmylasjɔ̃] nf formulation; expression; voir **formuler**
formule [fɔʀmyl] nf (gén) formula; (formulaire) form; **selon la ~ consacrée** as one says; **~ de politesse** polite phrase; (en fin de lettre) letter ending
formuler [fɔʀmyle] vt (émettre: réponse, vœux) to formulate; (expliciter: sa pensée) to express
forniquer [fɔʀnike] vi to fornicate
fort, e [fɔʀ, fɔʀt(ə)] adj strong; (intensité, rendement) high, great; (corpulent) large; (doué): **être ~ (en)** to be good (at) ▷ adv (serrer, frapper) hard; (sonner) loud(ly); (beaucoup) greatly, very much; (très) very ▷ nm (édifice) fort; (point fort) strong point, forte; (gén pl: personne, pays): **le ~**, **les ~s** the strong; **c'est un peu ~!** it's a bit much!; **à plus ~e raison** even more so, all the more reason; **avoir ~ à faire avec qn** to have a hard job with sb; **se faire ~ de faire** to claim one can do; **~ bien/peu** very well/few; **au plus ~ de** (au milieu de) in the thick of, at the height of; **~e tête** rebel

fortement [fɔʀtəmɑ̃] adv strongly; (s'intéresser) deeply
forteresse [fɔʀtəʀɛs] nf fortress
fortifiant [fɔʀtifjɑ̃] nm tonic
fortifications [fɔʀtifikasjɔ̃] nfpl fortifications
fortifier [fɔʀtifje] vt to strengthen, fortify; (Mil) to fortify; **se fortifier** vi (personne, santé) to grow stronger
fortin [fɔʀtɛ̃] nm (small) fort
fortiori [fɔʀtjɔʀi]: **à ~** adv all the more so
FORTRAN [fɔʀtʀɑ̃] nm FORTRAN
fortuit, e [fɔʀtɥi, -it] adj fortuitous, chance cpd
fortuitement [fɔʀtɥitmɑ̃] adv fortuitously
fortune [fɔʀtyn] nf fortune; **faire ~** to make one's fortune; **de ~** adj makeshift; (compagnon) chance cpd
fortuné, e [fɔʀtyne] adj wealthy, well-off
forum [fɔʀɔm] nm forum
fosse [fos] nf (grand trou) pit; (tombe) grave; **la ~ aux lions/ours** the lions' den/bear pit; **~ commune** common ou communal grave; **~ (d'orchestre)** (orchestra) pit; **~ à purin** cesspit; **~ septique** septic tank; **~s nasales** nasal fossae
fossé [fose] nm ditch; (fig) gulf, gap
fossette [fosɛt] nf dimple
fossile [fosil] nm fossil ▷ adj fossilized, fossil cpd
fossilisé, e [fosilize] adj fossilized
fossoyeur [foswajœʀ] nm gravedigger
fou, fol, folle [fu, fɔl] adj mad, crazy; (déréglé etc) wild, erratic; (mèche) stray; (herbe) wild; (fam: extrême, très grand) terrific, tremendous ▷ nm/f madman/woman ▷ nm (du roi) jester, fool; (Échecs) bishop; **~ à lier, ~ furieux (folle furieuse)** raving mad; **être ~ de** to be mad ou crazy about; (chagrin, joie, colère) to be wild with; **faire le ~** to play ou act the fool; **avoir le ~ rire** to have the giggles
foucade [fukad] nf caprice
foudre [fudʀ(ə)] nf lightning; **foudres** nfpl (fig: colère) wrath sg
foudroyant, e [fudʀwajɑ̃, -ɑ̃t] adj devastating; (maladie, poison) violent
foudroyer [fudʀwaje] vt to strike down; **~ qn du regard** to look daggers at sb; **il a été foudroyé** he was struck by lightning
fouet [fwɛ] nm whip; (Culin) whisk; **de plein ~** adv head on
fouettement [fwɛtmɑ̃] nm lashing no pl
fouetter [fwete] vt to whip; to whisk
fougasse [fugas] nf type of flat pastry
fougère [fuʒɛʀ] nf fern
fougue [fug] nf ardour (Brit), ardor (US), spirit
fougueusement [fugøzmɑ̃] adv ardently
fougueux, -euse [fugø, -øz] adj fiery, ardent
fouille [fuj] nf search; **fouilles** nfpl (archéologiques) excavations; **passer à la ~** to be searched
fouillé, e [fuje] adj detailed
fouiller [fuje] vt to search; (creuser) to dig; (: archéologue) to excavate; (approfondir: étude etc) to go into ▷ vi (archéologue) to excavate; **~ dans/parmi** to rummage in/among

fouillis [fuji] *nm* jumble, muddle

fouine [fwin] *nf* stone marten

fouiner [fwine] *vi* (*péj*): ~ **dans** to nose around *ou* about in

fouineur, -euse [fwinœʀ, -øz] *adj* nosey ▷ *nm/f* nosey parker, snooper

fouir [fwiʀ] *vt* to dig

fouisseur, -euse [fwisœʀ, -øz] *adj* burrowing

foulage [fulaʒ] *nm* pressing

foulante [fulãt] *adj f*: **pompe ~** force pump

foulard [fulaʀ] *nm* scarf

foule [ful] *nf* crowd; **une ~ de** masses of; **venir en ~** to come in droves

foulée [fule] *nf* stride; **dans la ~ de** on the heels of

fouler [fule] *vt* to press; (*sol*) to tread upon; **se fouler** *vi* (*fam*) to overexert o.s.; **se ~ la cheville** to sprain one's ankle; ~ **aux pieds** to trample underfoot

foulure [fulyʀ] *nf* sprain

four [fuʀ] *nm* oven; (*de potier*) kiln; (*Théât: échec*) flop; **allant au ~** ovenproof

fourbe [fuʀb(ə)] *adj* deceitful

fourberie [fuʀbəʀi] *nf* deceit

fourbi [fuʀbi] *nm* (*fam*) gear, junk

fourbir [fuʀbiʀ] *vt*: ~ **ses armes** (*fig*) to get ready for the fray

fourbu, e [fuʀby] *adj* exhausted

fourche [fuʀʃ(ə)] *nf* pitchfork; (*de bicyclette*) fork

fourcher [fuʀʃe] *vi*: **ma langue a fourché** it was a slip of the tongue

fourchette [fuʀʃɛt] *nf* fork; (*Statistique*) bracket, margin

fourchu, e [fuʀʃy] *adj* split; (*arbre etc*) forked

fourgon [fuʀgɔ̃] *nm* van; (*Rail*) wag(g)on; ~ **mortuaire** hearse

fourgonnette [fuʀgɔnɛt] *nf* (delivery) van

fourmi [fuʀmi] *nf* ant; **avoir des ~s** (*fig*) to have pins and needles

fourmilière [fuʀmiljɛʀ] *nf* ant-hill; (*fig*) hive of activity

fourmillement [fuʀmijmã] *nm* (*démangeaison*) pins and needles *pl*; (*grouillement*) swarming *no pl*

fourmiller [fuʀmije] *vi* to swarm; ~ **de** to be teeming with, be swarming with

fournaise [fuʀnɛz] *nf* blaze; (*fig*) furnace, oven

fourneau, x [fuʀno] *nm* stove

fournée [fuʀne] *nf* batch

fourni, e [fuʀni] *adj* (*barbe, cheveux*) thick; (*magasin*): **bien ~ (en)** well stocked (with)

fournil [fuʀni] *nm* bakehouse

fournir [fuʀniʀ] *vt* to supply; (*preuve, exemple*) to provide, supply; (*effort*) to put in; ~ **qch à qn** to supply sth to sb, supply *ou* provide sb with sth; ~ **qn en** (*Comm*) to supply sb with; **se ~ chez** to shop at

fournisseur, -euse [fuʀnisœʀ, -øz] *nm/f* supplier; (*Internet*): ~ **d'accès à Internet** (Internet) service provider

fourniture [fuʀnityʀ] *nf* supply(ing); **fournitures** *nfpl* supplies; ~**s de bureau** office supplies, stationery; ~**s scolaires** school stationery

fourrage [fuʀaʒ] *nm* fodder

fourrager¹ [fuʀaʒe] *vi*: ~ **dans/parmi** to rummage through/among

fourrager², -ère [fuʀaʒe, -ɛʀ] *adj* fodder *cpd* ▷ *nf* (*Mil*) fourragère

fourré, e [fuʀe] *adj* (*bonbon, chocolat*) filled; (*manteau, botte*) fur-lined ▷ *nm* thicket

fourreau, x [fuʀo] *nm* sheath; (*de parapluie*) cover; **robe ~** figure-hugging dress

fourrer [fuʀe] *vt* (*fam*): ~ **qch dans** to stick *ou* shove sth into; **se ~ dans/sous** to get into/under; **se ~ dans** (*une mauvaise situation*) to land o.s. in

fourre-tout [fuʀtu] *nm inv* (*sac*) holdall; (*péj*) junk room (*ou* cupboard); (*fig*) rag-bag

fourreur [fuʀœʀ] *nm* furrier

fourrière [fuʀjɛʀ] *nf* pound

fourrure [fuʀyʀ] *nf* fur; (*sur l'animal*) coat; **manteau/col de ~** fur coat/collar

fourvoyer [fuʀvwaje]: **se fourvoyer** *vi* to go astray, stray; **se ~ dans** to stray into

foutre [futʀ(ə)] *vt* (*fam!*) = **ficher#**; (*fam*)

foutu, e [futy] *adj* (*fam!*) = **fichu**

foyer [fwaje] *nm* (*de cheminée*) hearth; (*fig*) seat, centre; (*famille*) family; (*domicile*) home; (*local de réunion*) (social) club; (*résidence*) hostel; (*salon*) foyer; (*Optique, Photo*) focus; **lunettes à double ~** bi-focal glasses

FP *sigle f* (= *franchise postale*) exemption from postage

FPA *sigle f* (= *Formation professionnelle pour adultes*) adult education

FPLP *sigle m* (= *Front populaire de la libération de la Palestine*) PFLP (= *Popular Front for the Liberation of Palestine*)

fracas [fʀaka] *nm* din; crash

fracassant, e [fʀakasã, -ãt] *adj* sensational, staggering

fracasser [fʀakase] *vt* to smash; **se fracasser contre** *ou* **sur** to crash against

fraction [fʀaksjɔ̃] *nf* fraction

fractionnement [fʀaksjɔnmã] *nm* division

fractionner [fʀaksjɔne] *vt* to divide (up), split (up)

fracture [fʀaktyʀ] *nf* fracture; ~ **du crâne** fractured skull; ~ **de la jambe** broken leg

fracturer [fʀaktyʀe] *vt* (*coffre, serrure*) to break open; (*os, membre*) to fracture

fragile [fʀaʒil] *adj* fragile, delicate; (*fig*) frail

fragiliser [fʀaʒilize] *vt* to weaken, make fragile

fragilité [fʀaʒilite] *nf* fragility

fragment [fʀagmã] *nm* (*d'un objet*) fragment, piece; (*d'un texte*) passage, extract

fragmentaire [fʀagmãtɛʀ] *adj* sketchy

fragmenter [fʀagmãte] *vt* to split up

frai [fʀɛ] *nm* spawn; (*ponte*) spawning

fraîche [fʀɛʃ] *adj f voir* **frais**

fraîchement [fʀɛʃmã] *adv* (*sans enthousiasme*) coolly; (*récemment*) freshly, newly

fraîcheur [fʀɛʃœʀ] *nf* coolness; freshness; *voir* **frais**

fraîchir [fʀɛʃiʀ] vi to get cooler; (vent) to freshen
frais, fraîche [fʀɛ, fʀɛʃ] adj (air, eau, accueil) cool; (petit pois, œufs, nouvelles, couleur, troupes) fresh; **le voilà ~!** he's in a (right) mess! ▷ adv (récemment) newly, fresh(ly); **il fait ~** it's cool; **servir ~** chill before serving, serve chilled ▷ nm: **mettre au ~** to put in a cool place; **prendre le ~** to take a breath of cool air ▷ nmpl (débours) expenses; (Comm) costs; charges; **faire des ~** to spend; to go to a lot of expense; **faire les ~ de** to bear the brunt of; **faire les ~ de la conversation** (parler) to do most of the talking; (en être le sujet) to be the topic of conversation; **il en a été pour ses ~** he could have spared himself the trouble; **rentrer dans ses ~** to recover one's expenses; **~ de déplacement** travel(ling) expenses; **~ d'entretien** upkeep; **~ généraux** overheads; **~ de scolarité** school fees, tuition (US)

fraise [fʀɛz] nf strawberry; (Tech) countersink (bit); (de dentiste) drill; **~ des bois** wild strawberry

fraiser [fʀeze] vt to countersink; (Culin: pâte) to knead

fraiseuse [fʀezøz] nf (Tech) milling machine

fraisier [fʀezje] nm strawberry plant

framboise [fʀɑ̃bwaz] nf raspberry

framboisier [fʀɑ̃bwazje] nm raspberry bush

franc, franche [fʀɑ̃, fʀɑ̃ʃ] adj (personne) frank, straightforward; (visage) open; (net: refus, couleur) clear; (: coupure) clean; (intensif) downright; (exempt): **~ de port** post free, postage paid; (zone, port) free; (boutique) duty-free ▷ adv: **parler ~** to be frank ou candid ▷ nm franc

français, e [fʀɑ̃sɛ, -ɛz] adj French ▷ nm (Ling) French ▷ nm/f: **Français, e** Frenchman/woman; **les F~** the French

franc-comtois, e (mpl **francs-comtois**) [fʀɑ̃kɔ̃twa, -waz] adj of ou from (the) Franche-Comté

France [fʀɑ̃s] nf: **la ~** France; **en ~** in France; **~ 2, ~ 3** public-sector television channels; see note

⬤ **FRANCE TÉLÉVISION**
⬤
⬤
⬤ France 2 and France 3 are public-sector
⬤ television channels. France 2 is a national
⬤ general interest and entertainment
⬤ channel; France 3 provides regional news
⬤ and information as well as programmes for
⬤ the national network.

Francfort [fʀɑ̃kfɔʀ] n Frankfurt

franche [fʀɑ̃ʃ] adj f voir **franc**

Franche-Comté [fʀɑ̃ʃkɔ̃te] nf Franche-Comté

franchement [fʀɑ̃ʃmɑ̃] adv frankly; clearly; (tout à fait) downright ▷ excl well, really!; voir **franc**

franchir [fʀɑ̃ʃiʀ] vt (obstacle) to clear, get over; (seuil, ligne, rivière) to cross; (distance) to cover

franchisage [fʀɑ̃ʃizaʒ] nm (Comm) franchising

franchise [fʀɑ̃ʃiz] nf frankness; (douanière, d'impôt) exemption; (Assurances) excess; (Comm)

franchise; **~ de bagages** baggage allowance

franchissable [fʀɑ̃ʃisabl(ə)] adj (obstacle) surmountable

francilien, ne [fʀɑ̃siljɛ̃, -ɛn] adj of ou from the Île-de-France region ▷ nm/f: **Francilien, ne** person from the Île-de-France region

franciscain, e [fʀɑ̃siskɛ̃, -ɛn] adj Franciscan

franciser [fʀɑ̃size] vt to gallicize, Frenchify

franc-jeu [fʀɑ̃ʒø] nm: **jouer ~** to play fair

franc-maçon [fʀɑ̃masɔ̃] (pl **francs-maçons**) nm Freemason

franc-maçonnerie [fʀɑ̃masɔnʀi] nf Freemasonry

franco [fʀɑ̃ko] adv (Comm): **~ (de port)** postage paid

franco... [fʀɑ̃ko] préfixe franco-

franco-canadien [fʀɑ̃kɔkanadjɛ̃] nm (Ling) Canadian French

francophile [fʀɑ̃kɔfil] adj Francophile

francophobe [fʀɑ̃kɔfɔb] adj Francophobe

francophone [fʀɑ̃kɔfɔn] adj French-speaking ▷ nm/f French speaker

francophonie [fʀɑ̃kɔfɔni] nf French-speaking communities pl

franco-québécois [fʀɑ̃kɔkebekwa] nm (Ling) Quebec French

franc-parler [fʀɑ̃paʀle] nm inv outspokenness

franc-tireur [fʀɑ̃tiʀœʀ] nm (Mil) irregular; (fig) freelance

frange [fʀɑ̃ʒ] nf fringe; (cheveux) fringe (Brit), bangs (US)

frangé, e [fʀɑ̃ʒe] adj (tapis, nappe): **~ de** trimmed with

frangin [fʀɑ̃ʒɛ̃] nm (fam) brother

frangine [fʀɑ̃ʒin] nf (fam) sis, sister

frangipane [fʀɑ̃ʒipan] nf almond paste

franglais [fʀɑ̃glɛ] nm Franglais

franquette [fʀɑ̃kɛt]: **à la bonne ~** adv without any fuss

frappant, e [fʀapɑ̃, -ɑ̃t] adj striking

frappe [fʀap] nf (d'une dactylo, pianiste, machine à écrire) touch; (Boxe) punch; (péj) hood, thug

frappé, e [fʀape] adj (Culin) iced; **~ de panique** panic-stricken; **~ de stupeur** thunderstruck, dumbfounded

frapper [fʀape] vt to hit, strike; (étonner) to strike; (monnaie) to strike, stamp; **se frapper** vi (s'inquiéter) to get worked up; **~ à la porte** to knock at the door; **~ dans ses mains** to clap one's hands; **~ du poing sur** to bang one's fist on; **~ un grand coup** (fig) to strike a blow

frasques [fʀask(ə)] nfpl escapades; **faire des ~** to get up to mischief

fraternel, le [fʀatɛʀnɛl] adj brotherly, fraternal

fraternellement [fʀatɛʀnɛlmɑ̃] adv in a brotherly way

fraterniser [fʀatɛʀnize] vi to fraternize

fraternité [fʀatɛʀnite] nf brotherhood

fratricide [fʀatʀisid] adj fratricidal

fraude [fʀod] nf fraud; (Scol) cheating; **passer qch en ~** to smuggle sth in (ou out); **~ fiscale** tax evasion

f

frauder [fʀode] vi, vt to cheat; ~ **le fisc** to evade paying tax(es)

fraudeur, -euse [fʀodœʀ, -øz] nm/f person guilty of fraud; (candidat) candidate who cheats; (au fisc) tax evader

frauduleusement [fʀodyløzmã] adv fraudulently

frauduleux, -euse [fʀodylø, -øz] adj fraudulent

frayer [fʀeje] vt to open up, clear ▷ vi to spawn; (fréquenter): ~ **avec** to mix ou associate with; **se ~ un passage dans** to clear o.s. a path through, force one's way through

frayeur [fʀɛjœʀ] nf fright

fredaines [fʀədɛn] nfpl mischief sg, escapades

fredonner [fʀədɔne] vt to hum

freezer [fʀizœʀ] nm freezing compartment

frégate [fʀegat] nf frigate

frein [fʀɛ̃] nm brake; **mettre un ~ à** (fig) to put a brake on, check; **sans ~** (sans limites) unchecked; **~ à main** handbrake; **~ moteur** engine braking; **~s à disques** disc brakes; **~s à tambour** drum brakes

freinage [fʀɛnaʒ] nm braking; **distance de ~** braking distance; **traces de ~** tyre (Brit) ou tire (US) marks

freiner [fʀene] vi to brake ▷ vt (progrès etc) to check

frelaté, e [fʀəlate] adj adulterated; (fig) tainted

frêle [fʀɛl] adj frail, fragile

frelon [fʀəlɔ̃] nm hornet

freluquet [fʀəlykɛ] nm (péj) whippersnapper

frémir [fʀemiʀ] vi (de froid, de peur) to tremble, shiver; (de joie) to quiver; (eau) to (begin to) bubble

frémissement [fʀemismã] nm shiver; quiver; bubbling no pl

frêne [fʀɛn] nm ash (tree)

frénésie [fʀenezi] nf frenzy

frénétique [fʀenetik] adj frenzied, frenetic

frénétiquement [fʀenetikmã] adv frenetically

fréon® [fʀeɔ̃] nm Freon®

fréquemment [fʀekamã] adv frequently

fréquence [fʀekãs] nf frequency

fréquent, e [fʀekã, -ãt] adj frequent

fréquentable [fʀekãtabl(ə)] adj: **il est peu ~** he's not the type one can associate oneself with

fréquentation [fʀekãtasjɔ̃] nf frequenting; seeing; **fréquentations** nfpl company sg

fréquenté, e [fʀekãte] adj: **très ~** (very) busy; **mal ~** patronized by disreputable elements

fréquenter [fʀekãte] vt (lieu) to frequent; (personne) to see; **se fréquenter** to see a lot of each other

frère [fʀɛʀ] nm brother ▷ adj: **partis/pays ~s** sister parties/countries

fresque [fʀɛsk(ə)] nf (Art) fresco

fret [fʀɛ] nm freight

fréter [fʀete] vt to charter

frétiller [fʀetije] vi to wriggle; to quiver; ~ **de la queue** to wag its tail

fretin [fʀətɛ̃] nm: **le menu ~** the small fry

freudien, ne [fʀødjɛ̃, -ɛn] adj Freudian

freux [fʀø] nm (Zool) rook

friable [fʀijabl(ə)] adj crumbly

friand, e [fʀijã, -ãd] adj: ~ **de** very fond of ▷ nm (Culin) small minced-meat (Brit) ou ground-meat (US) pie; (: sucré) small almond cake

friandise [fʀijãdiz] nf sweet

fric [fʀik] nm (fam) cash, bread

fricassée [fʀikase] nf fricassee

fric-frac [fʀikfʀak] nm break-in

friche [fʀiʃ]: **en ~** adj, adv (lying) fallow

friction [fʀiksjɔ̃] nf (massage) rub, rub-down; (chez le coiffeur) scalp massage; (Tech, fig) friction

frictionner [fʀiksjɔne] vt to rub (down); to massage

frigidaire® [fʀiʒidɛʀ] nm refrigerator

frigide [fʀiʒid] adj frigid

frigidité [fʀiʒidite] nf frigidity

frigo [fʀigo] nm (= frigidaire) fridge

frigorifier [fʀigɔʀifje] vt to refrigerate; (fig: personne) to freeze

frigorifique [fʀigɔʀifik] adj refrigerating

frileusement [fʀiløzmã] adv with a shiver

frileux, -euse [fʀilø, -øz] adj sensitive to (the) cold; (fig) overcautious

frimas [fʀima] nmpl wintry weather sg

frime [fʀim] nf (fam): **c'est de la ~** it's all put on; **pour la ~** just for show

frimer [fʀime] vi to put on an act

frimeur, -euse [fʀimœʀ, -øz] nm/f poser

frimousse [fʀimus] nf (sweet) little face

fringale [fʀɛ̃gal] nf: **avoir la ~** to be ravenous

fringant, e [fʀɛ̃gã, -ãt] adj dashing

fringues [fʀɛ̃g] nfpl (fam) clothes, gear no pl

fripé, e [fʀipe] adj crumpled

friperie [fʀipʀi] nf (commerce) secondhand clothes shop; (vêtements) secondhand clothes

fripes [fʀip] nfpl secondhand clothes

fripier, -ière [fʀipje, -jɛʀ] nm/f secondhand clothes dealer

fripon, ne [fʀipɔ̃, -ɔn] adj roguish, mischievous ▷ nm/f rascal, rogue

fripouille [fʀipuj] nf scoundrel

frire [fʀiʀ] vt (aussi: **faire frire**) ▷ vi to fry

Frisbee® [fʀizbi] nm Frisbee®

frise [fʀiz] nf frieze

frisé, e [fʀize] adj curly, curly-haired ▷ nf: (**chicorée**) **~e** curly endive

friser [fʀize] vt to curl; (fig: surface) to skim, graze; (: mort) to come within a hair's breadth of; (: hérésie) to verge on ▷ vi (cheveux) to curl; (personne) to have curly hair; **se faire ~** to have one's hair curled

frisette [fʀizɛt] nf little curl

frisotter [fʀizɔte] vi (cheveux) to curl tightly

frisquet [fʀiskɛ] adj m chilly

frisson [fʀisɔ̃], **frissonnement** [fʀisɔnmã] nm shudder, shiver; quiver

frissonner [fʀisɔne] vi (personne) to shudder, shiver; (feuilles) to quiver

frit, e [fʀi, fʀit] pp de **frire** ▷ adj fried ▷ nf: (**pommes**) **~es** chips (Brit), French fries

friterie [fʀitʀi] nf ≈ chip shop (Brit),

≈ hamburger stand (US)

friteuse [fritøz] *nf* chip pan (Brit), deep (fat) fryer

friture [frityr] *nf* (*huile*) (deep) fat; (*plat*): ~ **(de poissons)** fried fish; (*Radio*) crackle, crackling *no pl*; **fritures** *nfpl* (*aliments frits*) fried food *sg*

frivole [frivɔl] *adj* frivolous

frivolité [frivolite] *nf* frivolity

froc [frɔk] *nm* (*Rel*) habit; (*fam: pantalon*) trousers *pl*, pants *pl*

froid, e [frwa, frwad] *adj* cold ▷ *nm* cold; (*absence de sympathie*) coolness *no pl*; **il fait ~** it's cold; **avoir ~** to be cold; **prendre ~** to catch a chill *ou* cold; **à ~** *adv* (*démarrer*) (from) cold; **(pendant) les grands ~s** (in) the depths of winter, (during) the cold season; **jeter un ~** (*fig*) to cast a chill; **être en ~ avec** to be on bad terms with; **battre ~ à qn** to give sb the cold shoulder

froidement [frwadmɑ̃] *adv* (*accueillir*) coldly; (*décider*) coolly

froideur [frwadœr] *nf* coolness *no pl*

froisser [frwase] *vt* to crumple (up), crease; (*fig*) to hurt, offend; **se froisser** *vi* to crumple, crease; to take offence (Brit) *ou* offense (US); **se ~ un muscle** to strain a muscle

frôlement [frolmɑ̃] *nm* (*contact*) light touch

frôler [frole] *vt* to brush against; (*projectile*) to skim past; (*fig*) to come within a hair's breadth of, come very close to

fromage [frɔmaʒ] *nm* cheese; ~ **blanc** soft white cheese; ~ **de tête** pork brawn

fromager, -ère [frɔmaʒe, -ɛr] *nm/f* cheese merchant ▷ *adj* (*industrie*) cheese *cpd*

fromagerie [frɔmaʒri] *nf* cheese dairy

froment [frɔmɑ̃] *nm* wheat

fronce [frɔ̃s] *nf* (*de tissu*) gather

froncement [frɔ̃smɑ̃] *nm*: ~ **de sourcils** frown

froncer [frɔ̃se] *vt* to gather; ~ **les sourcils** to frown

frondaisons [frɔ̃dɛzɔ̃] *nfpl* foliage *sg*

fronde [frɔ̃d] *nf* sling; (*fig*) rebellion, rebelliousness

frondeur, -euse [frɔ̃dœr, -øz] *adj* rebellious

front [frɔ̃] *nm* forehead, brow; (*Mil, Météorologie, Pol*) front; **avoir le ~ de faire** to have the effrontery to do; **de ~** *adv* (*se heurter*) head-on; (*rouler*) together (*2 or 3 abreast*); (*simultanément*) at once; **faire ~ à** to face up to; ~ **de mer** (sea) front

frontal, e, -aux [frɔ̃tal, -o] *adj* frontal

frontalier, -ière [frɔ̃talje, -jɛr] *adj* border *cpd*, frontier *cpd* ▷ *nm/f*: **(travailleurs) ~s** workers who cross the border to go to work, commuters from across the border

frontière [frɔ̃tjɛr] *nf* (*Géo, Pol*) frontier, border; (*fig*) frontier, boundary

frontispice [frɔ̃tispis] *nm* frontispiece

fronton [frɔ̃tɔ̃] *nm* pediment; (*de pelote basque*) (front) wall

frottement [frɔtmɑ̃] *nm* rubbing, scraping; **frottements** *nmpl* (*fig: difficultés*) friction *sg*

frotter [frɔte] *vi* to rub, scrape ▷ *vt* to rub; (*pour nettoyer*) to rub (up); (: *avec une brosse*) to scrub; ~ **une allumette** to strike a match; **se ~ à qn** to cross swords with sb; **se ~ à qch** to come up against sth; **se ~ les mains** (*fig*) to rub one's hands (gleefully)

frottis [frɔti] *nm* (*Méd*) smear

frottoir [frɔtwar] *nm* (*d'allumettes*) friction strip; (*pour encaustiquer*) (long-handled) brush

frou-frou [frufru] (*pl* **frous-frous**) *nm* rustle

frousse [frus] *nf* (*fam: peur*): **avoir la ~** to be in a blue funk

fructifier [fryktifje] *vi* to yield a profit; **faire ~** to turn to good account

fructueux, -euse [fryktɥø, -øz] *adj* fruitful; profitable

frugal, e, -aux [frygal, -o] *adj* frugal

frugalement [frygalmɑ̃] *adv* frugally

frugalité [frygalite] *nf* frugality

fruit [frɥi] *nm* fruit *gen no pl*; ~**s de mer** (*Culin*) seafood(s); ~**s secs** dried fruit *sg*

fruité, e [frɥite] *adj* (*vin*) fruity

fruiterie [frɥitri] *nf* (*boutique*) greengrocer's (Brit), fruit (and vegetable) store (US)

fruitier, -ière [frɥitje, -jɛr] *adj*: **arbre ~** fruit tree ▷ *nm/f* fruiterer (Brit), fruit merchant (US)

fruste [fryst(ə)] *adj* unpolished, uncultivated

frustrant, e [frystrɑ̃, -ɑ̃t] *adj* frustrating

frustration [frystrɑsjɔ̃] *nf* frustration

frustré, e [frystre] *adj* frustrated

frustrer [frystre] *vt* to frustrate; (*priver*): ~ **qn de qch** to deprive sb of sth

FS *abr* (= *franc suisse*) FS, SF

FSE *sigle m* (= *foyer socio-éducatif*) community home

FTP *sigle mpl* (= *Francs-tireurs et partisans*) Communist Resistance in 1940–45

fuchsia [fyʃja] *nm* fuchsia

fuel [fjul], **fuel-oil** [fjulɔjl] *nm* fuel oil; (*pour chauffer*) heating oil

fugace [fygas] *adj* fleeting

fugitif, -ive [fyʒitif, -iv] *adj* (*lueur, amour*) fleeting; (*prisonnier etc*) runaway ▷ *nm/f* fugitive, runaway

fugue [fyg] *nf* (*d'un enfant*) running away *no pl*; (*Mus*) fugue; **faire une ~** to run away, abscond

fuir [fɥir] *vt* to flee from; (*éviter*) to shun ▷ *vi* to run away; (*gaz, robinet*) to leak

fuite [fɥit] *nf* flight; (*écoulement*) leak, leakage; (*divulgation*) leak; **être en ~** to be on the run; **mettre en ~** to put to flight; **prendre la ~** to take flight

fulgurant, e [fylgyrɑ̃, -ɑ̃t] *adj* lightning *cpd*, dazzling

fulminant, e [fylminɑ̃, -ɑ̃t] *adj* (*lettre, regard*) furious; ~ **de colère** raging with anger

fulminer [fylmine] *vi*: ~ **(contre)** to thunder forth (against)

fumant, e [fymɑ̃, -ɑ̃t] *adj* smoking; (*liquide*) steaming; **un coup ~** (*fam*) a master stroke

fumé, e [fyme] *adj* (*Culin*) smoked; (*verre*) tinted ▷ *nf* smoke; **partir en ~e** to go up in smoke

fume-cigarette [fymsigaret] *nm inv* cigarette

holder

fumer [fyme] *vi* to smoke; *(liquide)* to steam ▷ *vt* to smoke; *(terre, champ)* to manure

fumerie [fymʀi] *nf*: ~ **d'opium** opium den

fumerolles [fymʀɔl] *nfpl* gas and smoke *(from volcano)*

fûmes [fym] *vb voir* **être**

fumet [fymɛ] *nm* aroma

fumeur, -euse [fymœʀ, -øz] *nm/f* smoker; **(compartiment)** ~s smoking compartment

fumeux, -euse [fymø, -øz] *adj (péj)* woolly (Brit), hazy

fumier [fymje] *nm* manure

fumigation [fymigasjɔ̃] *nf* fumigation

fumigène [fymiʒɛn] *adj* smoke *cpd*

fumiste [fymist(ə)] *nm (ramoneur)* chimney sweep ▷ *nm/f (péj: paresseux)* shirker; *(charlatan)* phoney

fumisterie [fymistəʀi] *nf (péj)* fraud, con

fumoir [fymwaʀ] *nm* smoking room

funambule [fynɑ̃byl] *nm* tightrope walker

funèbre [fynɛbʀ(ə)] *adj* funeral *cpd*; *(fig)* doleful; funereal

funérailles [fyneʀaj] *nfpl* funeral *sg*

funéraire [fyneʀɛʀ] *adj* funeral *cpd*, funerary

funeste [fynɛst(ə)] *adj* disastrous; deathly

funiculaire [fynikylɛʀ] *nm* funicular (railway)

FUNU [fyny] *sigle f* (= Force d'urgence des Nations unies) UNEF (= United Nations Emergency Forces)

fur [fyʀ]: **au ~ et à mesure** *adv* as one goes along; **au ~ et à mesure que** as; **au ~ et à mesure de leur progression** as they advance *(ou* advanced)

furax [fyʀaks] *adj inv (fam)* livid

furent [fyʀ] *vb voir* **être**

furet [fyʀɛ] *nm* ferret

fureter [fyʀte] *vi (péj)* to nose about

fureur [fyʀœʀ] *nf* fury; *(passion)*: ~ **de** passion for; **faire** ~ to be all the rage

furibard, e [fyʀibaʀ, -aʀd(ə)] *adj (fam)* livid, absolutely furious

furibond, e [fyʀibɔ̃, -ɔ̃d] *adj* livid, absolutely furious

furie [fyʀi] *nf* fury; *(femme)* shrew, vixen; **en ~** *(mer)* raging

furieusement [fyʀjøzmɑ̃] *adv* furiously

furieux, -euse [fyʀjø, -øz] *adj* furious

furoncle [fyʀɔ̃kl(ə)] *nm* boil

furtif, -ive [fyʀtif, -iv] *adj* furtive

furtivement [fyʀtivmɑ̃] *adv* furtively

fus [fy] *vb voir* **être**

fusain [fyzɛ̃] *nm (Bot)* spindle-tree; *(Art)* charcoal

fuseau, x [fyzo] *nm (pantalon)* (ski-)pants *pl*; *(pour filer)* spindle; **en ~** *(jambes)* tapering; *(colonne)* bulging; ~ **horaire** time zone

fusée [fyze] *nf* rocket; ~ **éclairante** flare

fuselage [fyzlaʒ] *nm* fuselage

fuselé, e [fyzle] *adj* slender; *(galbé)* tapering

fuser [fyze] *vi (rires etc)* to burst forth

fusible [fyzibl(ə)] *nm (Élec: fil)* fuse wire; (: *fiche)* fuse

fusil [fyzi] *nm (de guerre, à canon rayé)* rifle, gun; *(de chasse, à canon lisse)* shotgun, gun; ~ **à deux coups** double-barrelled rifle *ou* shotgun; ~ **sous-marin** spear-gun

fusilier [fyzilje] *nm (Mil)* rifleman

fusillade [fyzijad] *nf* gunfire *no pl*, shooting *no pl*; *(combat)* gun battle

fusiller [fyzije] *vt* to shoot; ~ **qn du regard** to look daggers at sb

fusil-mitrailleur [fyzimitʀajœʀ] *(pl* **fusils-mitrailleurs)** *nm* machine gun

fusion [fyzjɔ̃] *nf* fusion, melting; *(fig)* merging; *(Comm)* merger; **en ~** *(métal, roches)* molten

fusionnement [fyzjɔnmɑ̃] *nm* merger

fusionner [fyzjɔne] *vi* to merge

fustiger [fystiʒe] *vt* to denounce

fut [fy] *vb voir* **être**

fût [fy] *vb voir* **être** ▷ *nm (tonneau)* barrel, cask; *(de canon)* stock; *(d'arbre)* bole, trunk; *(de colonne)* shaft

futaie [fytɛ] *nf* forest, plantation

futé, e [fyte] *adj* crafty

fûtes [fyt] *vb voir* **être**

futile [fytil] *adj (inutile)* futile; *(frivole)* frivolous

futilement [fytilmɑ̃] *adv* frivolously

futilité [fytilite] *nf* futility; frivolousness; *(chose futile)* futile pursuit *(ou* thing *etc)*

futon [fytɔ̃] *nm* futon

futur, e [fytyʀ] *adj, nm* future; **son ~ époux** her husband-to-be; **au ~** *(Ling)* in the future

futuriste [fytyʀist(ə)] *adj* futuristic

futurologie [fytyʀɔlɔʒi] *nf* futurology

fuyant, e [fɥijɑ̃, -ɑ̃t] *vb voir* **fuir** ▷ *adj (regard etc)* evasive; *(lignes etc)* receding; *(perspective)* vanishing

fuyard, e [fɥijaʀ, -aʀd(ə)] *nm/f* runaway

fuyons *etc* [fɥijɔ̃] *vb voir* **fuir**

G g

G, g [ʒe] nm inv G, g ▷ abr (= gramme) g; (= gauche)
L, l; **G comme Gaston** G for George; **le G8** (Pol)
the G8 nations, the Group of Eight
gabardine [gabaʀdin] nf gabardine
gabarit [gabaʀi] nm (fig: dimension, taille) size;
(: valeur) calibre; (Tech) template; **du même ~**
(fig) of the same type, of that ilk
gabegie [gabʒi] nf (péj) chaos
Gabon [gabɔ̃] nm: **le ~** Gabon
gabonais, e [gabɔnɛ, -ɛz] adj Gabonese
gâcher [gaʃe] vt (gâter) to spoil, ruin; (gaspiller) to
waste; (plâtre) to temper; (mortier) to mix
gâchette [gaʃɛt] nf trigger
gâchis [gaʃi] nm (désordre) mess; (gaspillage)
waste no pl
gadget [gadʒɛt] nm thingumajig; (nouveauté)
gimmick
gadin [gadɛ̃] nm (fam): **prendre un ~** to come a
cropper (Brit)
gadoue [gadu] nf sludge
gaélique [gaelik] adj Gaelic ▷ nm (Ling) Gaelic
gaffe [gaf] nf (instrument) boat hook; (fam: erreur)
blunder; **faire ~** (fam) to watch out
gaffer [gafe] vi to blunder
gaffeur, -euse [gafœʀ, -øz] nm/f blunderer
gag [gag] nm gag
gaga [gaga] adj (fam) gaga
gage [gaʒ] nm (dans un jeu) forfeit; (fig: de fidélité)
token; **gages** nmpl (salaire) wages; (garantie)
guarantee sg; **mettre en ~** to pawn; **laisser en
~** to leave as security
gager [gaʒe] vt: **~ que** to bet ou wager that
gageure [gaʒyʀ] nf: **c'est une ~** it's attempting
the impossible
gagnant, e [gaɲɑ̃, -ɑ̃t] adj: **billet/numéro ~**
winning ticket/number ▷ adv: **jouer ~** (aux
courses) to be bound to win ▷ nm/f winner
gagne-pain [gaɲpɛ̃] nm inv job
gagne-petit [gaɲpəti] nm inv low wage earner
gagner [gaɲe] vt (concours, procès, pari) to win;
(somme d'argent, revenu) to earn; (aller vers, atteindre)
to reach; (s'emparer de) to overcome; (envahir) to
spread to; (se concilier): **~ qn** to win sb over ▷ vi
to win; (fig) to gain; **~ du temps/de la place** to
gain time/save space; **~ sa vie** to earn one's
living; **~ du terrain** (aussi fig) to gain ground; **~
qn de vitesse** to outstrip sb; (aussi fig): **~ à faire**
(s'en trouver bien) to be better off doing; **il y gagne**
it's in his interest, it's to his advantage
gagneur [gaɲœʀ] nm winner
gai, e [ge] adj cheerful; (livre, pièce de théâtre)
light-hearted; (un peu ivre) merry
gaiement [gemɑ̃] adv cheerfully
gaieté [gete] nf cheerfulness; **gaietés** nfpl
(souvent ironique) delights; **de ~ de cœur** with a
light heart
gaillard, e [gajaʀ, -aʀd(ə)] adj (robuste) sprightly;
(grivois) bawdy, ribald ▷ nm/f (strapping) fellow/
wench
gaillardement [gajaʀdəmɑ̃] adv cheerfully
gain [gɛ̃] nm (revenu) earnings pl; (bénéfice: gén pl)
profits pl; (au jeu: gén pl) winnings pl; (fig: de
temps, place) saving; (: avantage) benefit; (: lucre)
gain; **avoir ~ de cause** to win the case; (fig) to
be proved right; **obtenir ~ de cause** (fig) to win
out
gaine [gɛn] nf (corset) girdle; (fourreau) sheath;
(de fil électrique etc) outer covering
gaine-culotte [gɛnkylɔt] (pl **gaines-culottes**) nf
pantie girdle
gainer [gene] vt to cover
gala [gala] nm official reception; **soirée de ~**
gala evening
galamment [galamɑ̃] adv courteously
galant, e [galɑ̃, -ɑ̃t] adj (courtois) courteous,
gentlemanly; (entreprenant) flirtatious, gallant;
(aventure, poésie) amorous; **en ~e compagnie**
(homme) with a lady friend; (femme) with a
gentleman friend
galanterie [galɑ̃tʀi] nf gallantry
galantine [galɑ̃tin] nf galantine
Galapagos [galapagɔs] nfpl: **les (îles) ~** the
Galapagos Islands
galaxie [galaksi] nf galaxy
galbe [galb(ə)] nm curve(s); shapeliness
galbé, e [galbe] adj (jambes) (well-)rounded;
bien ~ shapely
gale [gal] nf (Méd) scabies sg; (de chien) mange
galéjade [galeʒad] nf tall story
galère [galɛʀ] nf galley
galérer [galere] vi (fam) to work hard, slave
(away)

galerie [galʀi] nf gallery; (Théât) circle; (de voiture) roof rack; (fig: spectateurs) audience; ~ **marchande** shopping mall; ~ **de peinture** (private) art gallery

galérien [galeʀjɛ̃] nm galley slave

galet [galɛ] nm pebble; (Tech) wheel; **galets** nmpl pebbles, shingle sg

galette [galɛt] nf (gâteau) flat pastry cake; (crêpe) savoury pancake; **la ~ des Rois** cake traditionally eaten on Twelfth Night

galeux, -euse [galø, -øz] adj: **un chien ~** a mangy dog

Galice [galis] nf: **la ~** Galicia (in Spain)

Galicie [galisi] nf: **la ~** Galicia; (in Central Europe)

galiléen, ne [galileɛ̃, -ɛn] adj Galilean

galimatias [galimatja] nm (péj) gibberish

galipette [galipɛt] nf: **faire des ~s** to turn somersaults

Galles [gal] nfpl: **le pays de ~** Wales

gallicisme [galisism(ə)] nm French idiom; (tournure fautive) gallicism

gallois, e [galwa, -waz] adj Welsh ▷ nm (Ling) Welsh ▷ nm/f: **Gallois, e** Welshman(-woman)

gallo-romain, e [galoʀɔmɛ̃, -ɛn] adj Gallo-Roman

galoche [galɔʃ] nf clog

galon [galɔ̃] nm (Mil) stripe; (décoratif) piece of braid; **prendre du ~** to be promoted

galop [galo] nm gallop; **au ~** at a gallop; ~ **d'essai** (fig) trial run

galopade [galɔpad] nf stampede

galopant, e [galɔpɑ̃, -ɑ̃t] adj: **inflation ~e** galloping inflation; **démographie ~e** exploding population

galoper [galɔpe] vi to gallop

galopin [galɔpɛ̃] nm urchin, ragamuffin

galvaniser [galvanize] vt to galvanize

galvaudé, e [galvode] adj (expression) hackneyed; (mot) clichéd

galvauder [galvode] vt to debase

gambade [gɑ̃bad] nf: **faire des ~s** to skip ou frisk about

gambader [gɑ̃bade] vi to skip ou frisk about

gamberger [gɑ̃bɛʀʒe] (fam) vi to (have a) think ▷ vt to dream up

Gambie [gɑ̃bi] nf: **la ~** (pays) Gambia; (fleuve) the Gambia

gamelle [gamɛl] nf mess tin; billy can; (fam): **ramasser une ~** to fall flat on one's face

gamin, e [gamɛ̃, -in] nm/f kid ▷ adj mischievous, playful

gaminerie [gaminʀi] nf mischievousness, playfulness

gamme [gam] nf (Mus) scale; (fig) range

gammé, e [game] adj: **croix ~e** swastika

Gand [gɑ̃] n Ghent

Gange [gɑ̃ʒ] nm: **le ~** the Ganges

gang [gɑ̃g] nm gang

ganglion [gɑ̃glijɔ̃] nm ganglion; (lymphatique) gland; **avoir des ~s** to have swollen glands

gangrène [gɑ̃gʀɛn] nf gangrene; (fig) corruption; corrupting influence

gangster [gɑ̃gstɛʀ] nm gangster

gangstérisme [gɑ̃gstɛʀism(ə)] nm gangsterism

gangue [gɑ̃g] nf coating

ganse [gɑ̃s] nf braid

gant [gɑ̃] nm glove; **prendre des ~s** (fig) to handle the situation with kid gloves; **relever le ~** (fig) to take up the gauntlet; ~ **de crin** massage glove; ~ **de toilette** (face) flannel (Brit), face cloth; ~**s de boxe** boxing gloves; ~**s de caoutchouc** rubber gloves

ganté, e [gɑ̃te] adj: ~ **de blanc** wearing white gloves

ganterie [gɑ̃tʀi] nf glove trade; (magasin) glove shop

garage [gaʀaʒ] nm garage; ~ **à vélos** bicycle shed

garagiste [gaʀaʒist(ə)] nm/f (propriétaire) garage owner; (mécanicien) garage mechanic

garant, e [gaʀɑ̃, -ɑ̃t] nm/f guarantor ▷ nm guarantee; **se porter ~ de** to vouch for; to be answerable for

garantie [gaʀɑ̃ti] nf guarantee, warranty; (gage) security, surety; **(bon de) ~** guarantee ou warranty slip; ~ **de bonne exécution** performance bond

garantir [gaʀɑ̃tiʀ] vt to guarantee; (protéger): ~ **de** to protect from; **je vous garantis que** I can assure you that; **garanti pure laine/2 ans** guaranteed pure wool/for 2 years

garce [gaʀs(ə)] nf (péj) bitch

garçon [gaʀsɔ̃] nm boy; (célibataire) bachelor; (jeune homme) boy, lad; (aussi: **garçon de café**) waiter; ~ **boucher/coiffeur** butcher's/hairdresser's assistant; ~ **de courses** messenger; ~ **d'écurie** stable lad; ~ **manqué** tomboy

garçonnet [gaʀsɔnɛ] nm small boy

garçonnière [gaʀsɔnjɛʀ] nf bachelor flat

garde [gaʀd(ə)] nm (de prisonnier) guard; (de domaine etc) warden; (soldat, sentinelle) guardsman ▷ nf guarding; looking after; (soldats, Boxe, Escrime) guard; (faction) watch; (d'une arme) hilt; (Typo: aussi: **page** ou **feuille de garde**) flyleaf; (: collée) endpaper; **de ~** adj, adv on duty; **monter la ~** to stand guard; **être sur ses ~s** to be on one's guard; **mettre en ~** to warn; **mise en ~** warning; **prendre ~ (à)** to be careful (of); **avoir la ~ des enfants** (après divorce) to have custody of the children; ~ **champêtre** nm rural policeman; ~ **du corps** nm bodyguard; ~ **d'enfants** nf child minder; ~ **forestier** nm forest warden; ~ **mobile** nm, nf mobile guard; ~ **des Sceaux** nm ≈ Lord Chancellor (Brit), ≈ Attorney General (US); ~ **à vue** (Jur) ≈ police custody

garde-à-vous [gaʀdavu] nm inv: **être/se mettre au ~** to be at/stand to attention; ~ **(fixe)!** (Mil) attention!

garde-barrière [gaʀdəbaʀjɛʀ] (pl **gardes-barrière(s)**) nm/f level-crossing keeper

garde-boue [gaʀdəbu] nm inv mudguard

garde-chasse [gaʀdəʃas] (pl **gardes-chasse(s)**)

garde-côte [gaʀdəkot] *nm* (*vaisseau*) coastguard boat

garde-feu [gaʀdəfø] *nm inv* fender

garde-fou [gaʀdəfu] *nm* railing, parapet

garde-malade [gaʀdəmalad] (*pl* **gardes-malade(s)**) *nf* home nurse

garde-manger [gaʀdmãʒe] *nm inv* (*boîte*) meat safe; (*placard*) pantry, larder

garde-meuble [gaʀdəmœbl(ə)] *nm* furniture depository

garde-pêche [gaʀdəpɛʃ] *nm inv* (*personne*) water bailiff; (*navire*) fisheries protection ship

garder [gaʀde] *vt* (*conserver*) to keep; (: *sur soi: vêtement, chapeau*) to keep on; (*surveiller: enfants*) to look after; (: *immeuble, lieu, prisonnier*) to guard; **se garder** *vi* (*aliment: se conserver*) to keep; **se ~ de faire** to be careful not to do; **~ le lit/la chambre** to stay in bed/indoors; **~ le silence** to keep silent *ou* quiet; **~ la ligne** to keep one's figure; **~ à vue** to keep in custody; **pêche/chasse gardée** private fishing/hunting (ground)

garderie [gaʀdəʀi] *nf* day nursery, crèche

garde-robe [gaʀdəʀɔb] *nf* wardrobe

gardeur, -euse [gaʀdœʀ, -øz] *nm/f* (*de vaches*) cowherd; (*de chèvres*) goatherd

gardian [gaʀdjã] *nm* cowboy (*in the Camargue*)

gardien, ne [gaʀdjɛ̃, -ɛn] *nm/f* (*garde*) guard; (*de prison*) warder; (*de domaine, réserve*) warden; (*de musée etc*) attendant; (*de phare, cimetière*) keeper; (*d'immeuble*) caretaker; (*fig*) guardian; **~ de but** goalkeeper; **~ de nuit** night watchman; **~ de la paix** policeman

gardiennage [gaʀdjɛnaʒ] *nm* (*emploi*) caretaking; **société de ~** security firm

gardon [gaʀdõ] *nm* roach

gare [gaʀ] *nf* (*railway*) station, train station (*US*) ▷ *excl*: **~ à ...** mind ...!, watch out for ...!; **~ à ne pas ...** mind you don't ...!; **~ à toi!** watch out!; **sans crier ~** without warning; **~ maritime** harbour station; **~ routière** coach (*Brit*) *ou* bus station; (*de camions*) haulage (*Brit*) *ou* trucking (*US*) depot; **~ de triage** marshalling yard

garenne [gaʀɛn] *nf voir* **lapin**

garer [gaʀe] *vt* to park; **se garer** to park; (*pour laisser passer*) to draw into the side

gargantuesque [gaʀgãtɥɛsk(ə)] *adj* gargantuan

gargariser [gaʀgaʀize]: **se gargariser** *vi* to gargle; **se ~ de** (*fig*) to revel in

gargarisme [gaʀgaʀism(ə)] *nm* gargling *no pl*; (*produit*) gargle

gargote [gaʀgɔt] *nf* cheap restaurant, greasy spoon (*fam*)

gargouille [gaʀguj] *nf* gargoyle

gargouillement [gaʀgujmã] *nm* = **gargouillis**

gargouiller [gaʀguje] *vi* (*estomac*) to rumble; (*eau*) to gurgle

gargouillis [gaʀguji] *nm* (*gén pl: voir vb*) rumbling; gurgling

garnement [gaʀnəmã] *nm* rascal, scallywag

garni, e [gaʀni] *adj* (*plat*) served with vegetables (*and chips, pasta or rice*) ▷ *nm* (*appartement*) furnished accommodation *no pl* (*Brit*) *ou* accommodations *pl* (*US*)

garnir [gaʀniʀ] *vt* to decorate; (*remplir*) to fill; (*recouvrir*) to cover; **se garnir** *vi* (*pièce, salle*) to fill up; **~ qch de** (*orner*) to decorate sth with; to trim sth with; (*approvisionner*) to fill *ou* stock sth with; (*protéger*) to fit sth with; (*Culin*) to garnish sth with

garnison [gaʀnizõ] *nf* garrison

garniture [gaʀnityʀ] *nf* (*Culin: légumes*) vegetables *pl*; (: *persil etc*) garnish; (: *farce*) filling; (*décoration*) trimming; (*protection*) fittings *pl*; **~ de cheminée** mantelpiece ornaments *pl*; **~ de frein** (*Auto*) brake lining; **~ intérieure** (*Auto*) interior trim; **~ périodique** sanitary towel (*Brit*) *ou* napkin (*US*)

garrigue [gaʀig] *nf* scrubland

garrot [gaʀo] *nm* (*Méd*) tourniquet; (*torture*) garrotte

garrotter [gaʀote] *vt* to tie up; (*fig*) to muzzle

gars [ga] *nm* lad; (*type*) guy

Gascogne [gaskɔɲ] *nf*: **la ~** Gascony

gascon, ne [gaskõ, -ɔn] *adj* Gascon ▷ *nm*: **G~** (*hâbleur*) braggart

gas-oil [gazɔjl] *nm* diesel oil

gaspillage [gaspijaʒ] *nm* waste

gaspiller [gaspije] *vt* to waste

gaspilleur, -euse [gaspijœʀ, -øz] *adj* wasteful

gastrique [gastʀik] *adj* gastric, stomach *cpd*

gastro-entérite [gastʀoãteʀit] *nf* (*Méd*) gastro-enteritis

gastro-intestinal, e, -aux [gastʀoɛ̃testinal, -o] *adj* gastrointestinal

gastronome [gastʀonɔm] *nm/f* gourmet

gastronomie [gastʀonɔmi] *nf* gastronomy

gastronomique [gastʀonɔmik] *adj*: **menu ~** gourmet menu

gâteau, x [gato] *nm* cake ▷ *adj inv* (*fam: trop indulgent*): **papa-/maman-~** doting father/mother; **~ d'anniversaire** birthday cake; **~ de riz** ≈ rice pudding; **~ sec** biscuit

gâter [gate] *vt* to spoil; **se gâter** *vi* (*dent, fruit*) to go bad; (*temps, situation*) to change for the worse

gâterie [gatʀi] *nf* little treat

gâteux, -euse [gatø, -øz] *adj* senile

gâtisme [gatism(ə)] *nm* senility

GATT [gat] *sigle m* (= *General Agreement on Tariffs and Trade*) GATT

gauche [goʃ] *adj* left, left-hand; (*maladroit*) awkward, clumsy ▷ *nf* (*Pol*) left (wing); (*Boxe*) left; **à ~** on the left; (*direction*) (to the) left; **à ~ de** (on *ou* to the) left of; **à la ~ de** to the left of; **sur votre ~** on your left; **de ~** (*Pol*) left-wing

gauchement [goʃmã] *adv* awkwardly, clumsily

gaucher, -ère [goʃe, -ɛʀ] *adj* left-handed

gaucherie [goʃʀi] *nf* awkwardness, clumsiness

gauchir [goʃiʀ] *vt* (*planche, objet*) to warp; (*fig: fait, idée*) to distort

gauchisant, e [goʃizã, -ãt] *adj* with left-wing tendencies

gauchisme [goʃism(ə)] *nm* leftism
gauchiste [goʃist(ə)] *adj, nm/f* leftist
gaufre [gofʀ(ə)] *nf* (*pâtisserie*) waffle; (*de cire*) honeycomb
gaufrer [gofʀe] *vt* (*papier*) to emboss; (*tissu*) to goffer
gaufrette [gofʀɛt] *nf* wafer
gaufrier [gofʀije] *nm* (*moule*) waffle iron
Gaule [gol] *nf*: **la ~** Gaul
gaule [gol] *nf* (*perche*) (long) pole; (*canne à pêche*) fishing rod
gauler [gole] *vt* (*arbre*) to beat (*using a long pole to bring down fruit*); (*fruits*) to beat down (*with a pole*)
gaullisme [golism(ə)] *nm* Gaullism
gaulliste [golist(ə)] *adj, nm/f* Gaullist
gaulois, e [golwa, -waz] *adj* Gallic; (*grivois*) bawdy ▷ *nm/f*: **Gaulois, e** Gaul
gauloiserie [golwazʀi] *nf* bawdiness
gausser [gose]: **se ~ de** *vt* to deride
gaver [gave] *vt* to force-feed; (*fig*): **~ de** to cram with, fill up with; (*personne*): **se ~ de** to stuff o.s. with
gay [gɛ] *adj, nm* (*fam*) gay
gaz [gɑz] *nm inv* gas; **mettre les ~** (*Auto*) to put one's foot down; **chambre/masque à ~** gas chamber/mask; **~ en bouteille** bottled gas; **~ butane** Calor gas® (*Brit*), butane gas; **~ carbonique** carbon dioxide; **~ hilarant** laughing gas; **~ lacrymogène** tear gas; **~ naturel** natural gas; **~ de ville** town gas (*Brit*), manufactured domestic gas
gaze [gɑz] *nf* gauze
gazéifié, e [gazeifje] *adj* carbonated, aerated
gazelle [gazɛl] *nf* gazelle
gazer [gɑze] *vt* to gas ▷ *vi* (*fam*) to be going *ou* working well
gazette [gazɛt] *nf* news sheet
gazeux, -euse [gɑzø, -øz] *adj* gaseous; (*eau*) sparkling; (*boisson*) fizzy
gazoduc [gazɔdyk] *nm* gas pipeline
gazole [gazɔl] *nm* = **gas-oil**
gazomètre [gazɔmɛtʀ(ə)] *nm* gasometer
gazon [gɑzɔ̃] *nm* (*herbe*) turf, grass; (*pelouse*) lawn
gazonner [gɑzɔne] *vt* (*terrain*) to grass over
gazouillement [gazujmɑ̃] *nm* (*voir vb*) chirping; babbling
gazouiller [gazuje] *vi* (*oiseau*) to chirp; (*enfant*) to babble
gazouillis [gazuji] *nmpl* chirp *sg*
GB *sigle f* (= *Grande Bretagne*) GB
gd *abr* (= *grand*) L
GDF *sigle m* (= *Gaz de France*) national gas company
geai [ʒɛ] *nm* jay
géant, e [ʒeɑ̃, -ɑ̃t] *adj* gigantic, giant; (*Comm*) giant-size ▷ *nm/f* giant
geignement [ʒɛɲmɑ̃] *nm* groaning, moaning
geindre [ʒɛ̃dʀ(ə)] *vi* to groan, moan
gel [ʒɛl] *nm* frost; (*de l'eau*) freezing; (*fig: des salaires, prix*) freeze; freezing; (*produit de beauté*) gel; **~ douche** shower gel
gélatine [ʒelatin] *nf* gelatine

gélatineux, -euse [ʒelatinø, -øz] *adj* jelly-like, gelatinous
gelé, e [ʒəle] *adj* frozen ▷ *nf* jelly; (*gel*) frost; **~ blanche** hoarfrost, white frost
geler [ʒəle] *vt, vi* to freeze; **il gèle** it's freezing
gélule [ʒelyl] *nf* capsule
gelures [ʒəlyʀ] *nfpl* frostbite *sg*
Gémeaux [ʒemo] *nmpl*: **les ~** Gemini, the Twins; **être des ~** to be Gemini
gémir [ʒemiʀ] *vi* to groan, moan
gémissement [ʒemismɑ̃] *nm* groan, moan
gemme [ʒɛm] *nf* gem(stone)
gémonies [ʒemɔni] *nfpl*: **vouer qn aux ~** to subject sb to public scorn
gén. *abr* (= *généralement*) gen.
gênant, e [ʒenɑ̃, -ɑ̃t] *adj* (*objet*) awkward, in the way; (*histoire, personne*) embarrassing
gencive [ʒɑ̃siv] *nf* gum
gendarme [ʒɑ̃daʀm(ə)] *nm* gendarme
gendarmer [ʒɑ̃daʀme]: **se gendarmer** *vi* to kick up a fuss
gendarmerie [ʒɑ̃daʀməʀi] *nf* military police force in countryside and small towns; their police station or barracks
gendre [ʒɑ̃dʀ(ə)] *nm* son-in-law
gène [ʒɛn] *nm* (*Bio*) gene
gêne [ʒɛn] *nf* (*à respirer, bouger*) discomfort, difficulty; (*dérangement*) bother, trouble; (*manque d'argent*) financial difficulties *pl ou* straits *pl*; (*confusion*) embarrassment; **sans ~** *adj* inconsiderate
gêné, e [ʒene] *adj* embarrassed; (*dépourvu d'argent*) short (of money)
généalogie [ʒenealɔʒi] *nf* genealogy
généalogique [ʒenealɔʒik] *adj* genealogical
gêner [ʒene] *vt* (*incommoder*) to bother; (*encombrer*) to hamper; (*bloquer le passage*) to be in the way of; (*déranger*) to bother; (*embarrasser*): **~ qn** to make sb feel ill-at-ease; **se gêner** to put o.s. out; **ne vous gênez pas!** (*ironique*) go right ahead!, don't mind me!; **je vais me ~!** (*ironique*) why should I care?
général, e, -aux [ʒeneʀal, -o] *adj, nm* general ▷ *nf*: (*répétition*) **~e** final dress rehearsal; **en ~** usually, in general; **à la satisfaction ~e** to everyone's satisfaction
généralement [ʒeneʀalmɑ̃] *adv* generally
généralisable [ʒeneʀalizabl(ə)] *adj* generally applicable
généralisation [ʒeneʀalizasjɔ̃] *nf* generalization
généraliser [ʒeneʀalize] *vt, vi* to generalize; **se généraliser** *vi* to become widespread
généraliste [ʒeneʀalist(ə)] *nm/f* (*Méd*) general practitioner, GP
généralité [ʒeneʀalite] *nf*: **la ~ des ...** the majority of ...; **généralités** *nfpl* generalities; (*introduction*) general points
générateur, -trice [ʒeneʀatœʀ, -tʀis] *adj*: **~ de** which causes *ou* brings about ▷ *nf* (*Élec*) generator
génération [ʒeneʀasjɔ̃] *nf* generation

généreusement [ʒenerøzmã] *adv* generously
généreux, -euse [ʒenerø, -øz] *adj* generous
générique [ʒenerik] *adj* generic ▷ *nm* (*Ciné, TV*) credits *pl*, credit titles *pl*
générosité [ʒenerozite] *nf* generosity
Gênes [ʒɛn] *n* Genoa
genèse [ʒənɛz] *nf* genesis
genêt [ʒənɛ] *nm* (*Bot*) broom *no pl*
généticien, ne [ʒenetisjɛ̃, -ɛn] *nm/f* geneticist
génétique [ʒenetik] *adj* genetic ▷ *nf* genetics *sg*
génétiquement [ʒenetikmã] *adv* genetically
gêneur, -euse [ʒɛnœr, -øz] *nm/f* (*personne qui gêne*) obstacle; (*importun*) intruder
Genève [ʒənɛv] *n* Geneva
genevois, e [ʒənəvwa, -waz] *adj* Genevan
genévrier [ʒənevrije] *nm* juniper
génial, e, -aux [ʒenjal, -o] *adj* of genius; (*fam*) fantastic, brilliant
génie [ʒeni] *nm* genius; (*Mil*): **le ~** ≈ the Engineers *pl*; **avoir du ~** to have genius; **~ civil** civil engineering; **~ génétique** genetic engineering
genièvre [ʒənjɛvr(ə)] *nm* (*Bot*) juniper (tree); (*boisson*) Dutch gin; **grain de ~** juniper berry
génisse [ʒenis] *nf* heifer; **foie de ~** ox liver
génital, e, -aux [ʒenital, -o] *adj* genital
génitif [ʒenitif] *nm* genitive
génocide [ʒenɔsid] *nm* genocide
génois, e [ʒenwa, -waz] *adj* Genoese ▷ *nf* (*gâteau*) ≈ sponge cake
genou, x [ʒnu] *nm* knee; **à ~x** on one's knees; **se mettre à ~x** to kneel down
genouillère [ʒənujɛr] *nf* (*Sport*) kneepad
genre [ʒãr] *nm* (*espèce, sorte*) kind, type, sort; (*allure*) manner; (*Ling*) gender; (*Art*) genre; (*Zool etc*) genus; **se donner du ~** to give o.s. airs; **avoir bon ~** to have style; **avoir mauvais ~** to be ill-mannered
gens [ʒã] *nmpl* (*f in some phrases*) people *pl*; **les ~ d'Église** the clergy; **les ~ du monde** society people; **~ de maison** domestics
gentiane [ʒãsjan] *nf* gentian
gentil, le [ʒãti, -ij] *adj* kind; (*enfant: sage*) good; (*sympa: endroit etc*) nice; **c'est très ~ à vous** it's very kind *ou* good *ou* nice of you
gentilhommière [ʒãtijɔmjɛr] *nf* (small) manor house *ou* country seat
gentillesse [ʒãtijɛs] *nf* kindness
gentillet, te [ʒãtijɛ, -ɛt] *adj* nice little
gentiment [ʒãtimã] *adv* kindly
génuflexion [ʒenyflɛksjɔ̃] *nf* genuflexion
géo *abr* (= *géographie*) geography
géodésique [ʒeodezik] *adj* geodesic
géographe [ʒeograf] *nm/f* geographer
géographie [ʒeografi] *nf* geography
géographique [ʒeografik] *adj* geographical
geôlier [ʒolje] *nm* jailer
géologie [ʒeɔlɔʒi] *nf* geology
géologique [ʒeɔlɔʒik] *adj* geological
géologiquement [ʒeɔlɔʒikmã] *adv* geologically
géologue [ʒeɔlɔg] *nm/f* geologist
géomètre [ʒeomɛtr(ə)] *nm*: (**arpenteur-)~** (land) surveyor
géométrie [ʒeometri] *nf* geometry; **à ~ variable** (*Aviat*) swing-wing
géométrique [ʒeometrik] *adj* geometric
géophysique [ʒeofizik] *nf* geophysics *sg*
géopolitique [ʒeopolitik] *nf* geopolitics *sg*
Géorgie [ʒeorʒi] *nf*: **la ~** (*URSS, USA*) Georgia; **la ~ du Sud** South Georgia
géorgien, ne [ʒeorʒjɛ̃, -ɛn] *adj* Georgian
géostationnaire [ʒeostasjɔnɛr] *adj* geostationary
géothermique [ʒeotɛrmik] *adj*: **énergie ~** geothermal energy
gérance [ʒerãs] *nf* management; **mettre en ~** to appoint a manager for; **prendre en ~** to take over (the management of)
géranium [ʒeranjɔm] *nm* geranium
gérant, e [ʒerã, -ãt] *nm/f* manager/manageress; **~ d'immeuble** managing agent
gerbe [ʒɛrb(ə)] *nf* (*de fleurs, d'eau*) spray; (*de blé*) sheaf; (*fig*) shower, burst
gercé, e [ʒɛrse] *adj* chapped
gercer [ʒɛrse] *vi*, **se gercer** *vi* to chap
gerçure [ʒɛrsyr] *nf* crack
gérer [ʒere] *vt* to manage
gériatrie [ʒerjatri] *nf* geriatrics *sg*
gériatrique [ʒerjatrik] *adj* geriatric
germain, e [ʒɛrmɛ̃, -ɛn] *adj*: **cousin ~** first cousin
germanique [ʒɛrmanik] *adj* Germanic
germaniste [ʒɛrmanist(ə)] *nm/f* German scholar
germe [ʒɛrm(ə)] *nm* germ
germer [ʒɛrme] *vi* to sprout; (*semence, aussi fig*) to germinate
gérondif [ʒerɔ̃dif] *nm* gerund; (*en latin*) gerundive
gérontologie [ʒerɔ̃tɔlɔʒi] *nf* gerontology
gérontologue [ʒerɔ̃tɔlɔg] *nm/f* gerontologist
gésier [ʒezje] *nm* gizzard
gésir [ʒezir] *vi* to be lying (down); *voir aussi* **ci-gît**
gestation [ʒɛstasjɔ̃] *nf* gestation
geste [ʒɛst(ə)] *nm* gesture; move; motion; **il fit un ~ de la main pour m'appeler** he signed to me to come over, he waved me over; **ne faites pas un ~** (*ne bougez pas*) don't move
gesticuler [ʒɛstikyle] *vi* to gesticulate
gestion [ʒɛstjɔ̃] *nf* management; **~ des disques** (*Inform*) housekeeping; **~ de fichier(s)** (*Inform*) file management
gestionnaire [ʒɛstjɔnɛr] *nm/f* administrator; **~ de fichiers** (*Inform*) file manager
geyser [ʒezɛr] *nm* geyser
Ghana [gana] *nm*: **le ~** Ghana
ghetto [gɛto] *nm* ghetto
gibecière [ʒibsjɛr] *nf* (*de chasseur*) gamebag; (*sac en bandoulière*) shoulder bag
gibelotte [ʒiblɔt] *nf* rabbit fricassee in white wine
gibet [ʒibɛ] *nm* gallows *pl*
gibier [ʒibje] *nm* (*animaux*) game; (*fig*) prey
giboulée [ʒibule] *nf* sudden shower
giboyeux, -euse [ʒibwajø, -øz] *adj* well-stocked

with game

Gibraltar [ʒibʀaltaʀ] *nm* Gibraltar

gibus [ʒibys] *nm* opera hat

giclée [ʒikle] *nf* spurt, squirt

gicler [ʒikle] *vi* to spurt, squirt

gicleur [ʒiklœʀ] *nm* (*Auto*) jet

GIE *sigle m* = **groupement d'intérêt économique**

gifle [ʒifl(ə)] *nf* slap (in the face)

gifler [ʒifle] *vt* to slap (in the face)

gigantesque [ʒigɑ̃tɛsk(ə)] *adj* gigantic

gigantisme [ʒigɑ̃tism(ə)] *nm* (*Méd*) gigantism; (*des mégalopoles*) vastness

gigaoctet [ʒigaɔktɛ] *nm* gigabyte

GIGN *sigle m* (= *Groupe d'intervention de la gendarmerie nationale*) special crack force of the gendarmerie, ≈ SAS (*Brit*)

gigogne [ʒigɔɲ] *adj*: **lits ~s** truckle (*Brit*) *ou* trundle (*US*) beds; **tables/poupées ~s** nest of tables/dolls

gigolo [ʒigɔlo] *nm* gigolo

gigot [ʒigo] *nm* leg (of mutton *ou* lamb)

gigoter [ʒigɔte] *vi* to wriggle (about)

gilet [ʒilɛ] *nm* waistcoat; (*pull*) cardigan; (*de corps*) vest; **~ pare-balles** bulletproof jacket; **~ de sauvetage** life jacket

gin [dʒin] *nm* gin

gingembre [ʒɛ̃ʒɑ̃bʀ(ə)] *nm* ginger

gingivite [ʒɛ̃ʒivit] *nf* inflammation of the gums, gingivitis

ginseng [ʒinsɛŋ] *nm* ginseng

girafe [ʒiʀaf] *nf* giraffe

giratoire [ʒiʀatwaʀ] *adj*: **sens ~** roundabout

girofle [ʒiʀɔfl(ə)] *nm*: **clou de ~** clove

giroflée [ʒiʀɔfle] *nf* wallflower

girolle [ʒiʀɔl] *nf* chanterelle

giron [ʒiʀɔ̃] *nm* (*genoux*) lap; (*fig: sein*) bosom

Gironde [ʒiʀɔ̃d] *nf*: **la ~** the Gironde

girophare [ʒiʀɔfaʀ] *nm* revolving (flashing) light

girouette [ʒiʀwɛt] *nf* weather vane *ou* cock

gis [ʒi], **gisais** *etc* [ʒize] *vb voir* **gésir**

gisement [ʒizmɑ̃] *nm* deposit

gît [ʒi] *vb voir* **gésir**

gitan, e [ʒitɑ̃, -an] *nm/f* gipsy

gîte [ʒit] *nm* home; shelter; (*du lièvre*) form; **~ (rural)** (country) holiday cottage *ou* apartment

gîter [ʒite] *vi* (*Navig*) to list

givrage [ʒivʀaʒ] *nm* icing

givrant, e [ʒivʀɑ̃, -ɑ̃t] *adj*: **brouillard ~** freezing fog

givre [ʒivʀ(ə)] *nm* (hoar)frost

givré, e [ʒivʀe] *adj*: **citron ~/orange ~e** lemon/orange sorbet (*served in fruit skin*)

glabre [glabʀ(ə)] *adj* hairless; (*menton*) clean-shaven

glaçage [glasaʒ] *nm* (*au sucre*) icing; (*au blanc d'œuf, de la viande*) glazing

glace [glas] *nf* ice; (*crème glacée*) ice cream; (*verre*) sheet of glass; (*miroir*) mirror; (*de voiture*) window; **glaces** *nfpl* (*Géo*) ice sheets, ice *sg*; **de ~** (*fig: accueil, visage*) frosty, icy; **rester de ~** to remain unmoved

glacé, e [glase] *adj* icy; (*boisson*) iced

glacer [glase] *vt* to freeze; (*boisson*) to chill, ice; (*gâteau*) to ice (*Brit*), frost (*US*); (*papier, tissu*) to glaze; (*fig*): **~ qn** to chill sb; (*fig*) to make sb's blood run cold

glaciaire [glasjɛʀ] *adj* (*période*) ice *cpd*; (*relief*) glacial

glacial, e [glasjal] *adj* icy

glacier [glasje] *nm* (*Géo*) glacier; (*marchand*) ice-cream maker

glacière [glasjɛʀ] *nf* icebox

glaçon [glasɔ̃] *nm* icicle; (*pour boisson*) ice cube

gladiateur [gladjatœʀ] *nm* gladiator

glaïeul [glajœl] *nm* gladiola

glaire [glɛʀ] *nf* (*Méd*) phlegm *no pl*

glaise [glɛz] *nf* clay

glaive [glɛv] *nm* two-edged sword

gland [glɑ̃] *nm* (*de chêne*) acorn; (*décoration*) tassel; (*Anat*) glans

glande [glɑ̃d] *nf* gland

glander [glɑ̃de] *vi* (*fam*) to fart around (*Brit*) (!); screw around (*US*) (!)

glaner [glane] *vt, vi* to glean

glapir [glapiʀ] *vi* to yelp

glapissement [glapismɑ̃] *nm* yelping

glas [gla] *nm* knell, toll

glauque [glok] *adj* dull blue-green

glissade [glisad] *nf* (*par jeu*) slide; (*chute*) slip; (*dérapage*) skid; **faire une ~s** to slide

glissant, e [glisɑ̃, -ɑ̃t] *adj* slippery

glisse [glis] *nf*: **sports de ~** sports involving sliding or gliding (*eg skiing, surfing, windsurfing*)

glissement [glismɑ̃] *nm* sliding; (*fig*) shift; **~ de terrain** landslide

glisser [glise] *vi* (*avancer*) to glide *ou* slide along; (*coulisser, tomber*) to slide; (*déraper*) to slip; (*être glissant*) to be slippery ▷ *vt*: **~ qch sous/dans/à** to slip sth under/into/to; **~ sur** (*fig: détail etc*) to skate over; **se ~ dans/entre** to slip into/between

glissière [glisjɛʀ] *nf* slide channel; **à ~** (*porte, fenêtre*) sliding; **~ de sécurité** (*Auto*) crash barrier

glissoire [gliswaʀ] *nf* slide

global, e, -aux [glɔbal, -o] *adj* overall

globalement [glɔbalmɑ̃] *adv* taken as a whole

globe [glɔb] *nm* globe; **sous ~** under glass; **~ oculaire** eyeball; **le ~ terrestre** the globe

globe-trotter [glɔbtʀɔtœʀ] *nm* globe-trotter

globule [glɔbyl] *nm* (*du sang*): **~ blanc/rouge** white/red corpuscle

globuleux, -euse [glɔbylø, -øz] *adj*: **yeux ~** protruding eyes

gloire [glwaʀ] *nf* glory; (*mérite*) distinction, credit; (*personne*) celebrity

glorieux, -euse [glɔʀjø, -øz] *adj* glorious

glorifier [glɔʀifje] *vt* to glorify, extol; **se ~ de** to glory in

gloriole [glɔʀjɔl] *nf* vainglory

glose [gloz] *nf* gloss

glossaire [glɔsɛʀ] *nm* glossary

glotte [glɔt] *nf* (*Anat*) glottis

glouglouter [gluglute] *vi* to gurgle

gloussement [glusmɑ̃] nm (de poule) cluck; (rire) chuckle

glousser [gluse] vi to cluck; (rire) to chuckle

glouton, ne [glutɔ̃, -ɔn] adj gluttonous, greedy

gloutonnerie [glutɔnʀi] nf gluttony

glu [gly] nf birdlime

gluant, e [glyɑ̃, -ɑ̃t] adj sticky, gummy

glucide [glysid] nm carbohydrate

glucose [glykoz] nm glucose

gluten [glytɛn] nm gluten

glycérine [gliseʀin] nf glycerine

glycine [glisin] nf wisteria

GMT sigle adj (= Greenwich Mean Time) GMT

gnangnan [ɲɑ̃ɲɑ̃] adj inv (fam: livre, film) soppy

GNL sigle m (= gaz naturel liquéfié) LNG (= liquefied natural gas)

gnôle [njol] nf (fam) booze no pl; **un petit verre de ~** a drop of the hard stuff

gnome [gnom] nm gnome

gnon [ɲɔ̃] nm (fam: coup de poing) bash; (: marque) dent

GO sigle fpl (= grandes ondes) LW ▷ sigle m (= gentil organisateur) title given to leaders on Club Méditerranée holidays; extended to refer to easy-going leader of any group

Go abr (= gigaoctet) GB

go [go]: **tout de go** adv straight out

goal [gol] nm goalkeeper

gobelet [gɔblɛ] nm (en métal) tumbler; (en plastique) beaker; (à dés) cup

gober [gɔbe] vt to swallow

goberger [gɔbɛʀʒe]: **se goberger** vi to cosset o.s.

Gobi [gɔbi] n: **désert de ~** Gobi Desert

godasse [gɔdas] nf (fam) shoe

godet [gɔdɛ] nm pot; (Couture) unpressed pleat

godiller [gɔdije] vi (Navig) to scull; (Ski) to wedeln

goéland [gɔelɑ̃] nm (sea)gull

goélette [gɔelɛt] nf schooner

goémon [gɔemɔ̃] nm wrack

gogo [gɔgo] nm (péj) mug, sucker; **à ~** adv galore

goguenard, e [gɔgnaʀ, -aʀd(ə)] adj mocking

goguette [gɔgɛt] nf: **en ~** on the binge

goinfre [gwɛ̃fʀ(ə)] nm glutton

goinfrer [gwɛ̃fʀe]: **se goinfrer** vi to make a pig of o.s.; **se ~ de** to guzzle

goitre [gwatʀ(ə)] nm goitre

golf [gɔlf] nm (jeu) golf; (terrain) golf course; **~ miniature** crazy ou miniature golf

golfe [gɔlf(ə)] nm gulf; bay; **le ~ d'Aden** the Gulf of Aden; **le ~ de Gascogne** the Bay of Biscay; **le ~ du Lion** the Gulf of Lions; **le ~ Persique** the Persian Gulf

golfeur, -euse [gɔlfœʀ, -øz] nm/f golfer

gominé, e [gɔmine] adj slicked down

gomme [gɔm] nf (à effacer) rubber (Brit), eraser; (résine) gum; **boule** ou **pastille de ~** throat pastille

gommé, e [gɔme] adj: **papier ~** gummed paper

gommer [gɔme] vt (effacer) to rub out (Brit), erase; (enduire de gomme) to gum

gond [gɔ̃] nm hinge; **sortir de ses ~s** (fig) to fly off the handle

gondole [gɔ̃dɔl] nf gondola; (pour l'étalage) shelves pl, gondola

gondoler [gɔ̃dɔle]: **se gondoler** vi to warp, buckle; (fam: rire) to hoot with laughter; to be in stitches

gondolier [gɔ̃dɔlje] nm gondolier

gonflable [gɔ̃flabl(ə)] adj inflatable

gonflage [gɔ̃flaʒ] nm inflating, blowing up

gonflé, e [gɔ̃fle] adj swollen; (ventre) bloated; (fam: culotté): **être ~** to have a nerve

gonflement [gɔ̃fləmɑ̃] nm inflation; (Méd) swelling

gonfler [gɔ̃fle] vt (pneu, ballon) to inflate, blow up; (nombre, importance) to inflate ▷ vi (pied etc) to swell (up); (Culin: pâte) to rise

gonfleur [gɔ̃flœʀ] nm air pump

gong [gɔ̃g] nm gong

gonzesse [gɔ̃zɛs] nf (fam) chick, bird (Brit)

goret [gɔʀɛ] nm piglet

gorge [gɔʀʒ(ə)] nf (Anat) throat; (poitrine) breast; (Géo) gorge; (rainure) groove; **avoir mal à la ~** to have a sore throat; **avoir la ~ serrée** to have a lump in one's throat

gorgé, e [gɔʀʒe] adj: **~ de** filled with; (eau) saturated with ▷ nf mouthful; sip; gulp; **boire à petites/grandes ~es** to take little sips/big gulps

gorille [gɔʀij] nm gorilla; (fam) bodyguard

gosier [gozje] nm throat

gosse [gɔs] nm/f kid

gothique [gɔtik] adj gothic

gouache [gwaʃ] nf gouache

gouaille [gwaj] nf street wit, cocky humour (Brit) ou humor (US)

goudron [gudʀɔ̃] nm (asphalte) tar(mac) (Brit), asphalt; (du tabac) tar

goudronner [gudʀɔne] vt to tar(mac) (Brit), asphalt

gouffre [gufʀ(ə)] nm abyss, gulf

goujat [guʒa] nm boor

goujon [guʒɔ̃] nm gudgeon

goulée [gule] nf gulp

goulet [gulɛ] nm bottleneck

goulot [gulo] nm neck; **boire au ~** to drink from the bottle

goulu, e [guly] adj greedy

goulûment [gulymɑ̃] adv greedily

goupille [gupij] nf (metal) pin

goupiller [gupije] vt to pin (together)

goupillon [gupijɔ̃] nm (Rel) sprinkler; (brosse) bottle brush; **le ~** (fig) the cloth, the clergy

gourd, e [guʀ, guʀd(ə)] adj numb (with cold); (fam) oafish

gourde [guʀd(ə)] nf (récipient) flask; (fam) (clumsy) clot ou oaf

gourdin [guʀdɛ̃] nm club, bludgeon

gourer [guʀe] (fam): **se gourer** vi to boob

gourmand, e [guʀmɑ̃, -ɑ̃d] adj greedy

gourmandise [guʀmɑ̃diz] nf greed; (bonbon) sweet (Brit), piece of candy (US)

gourmet [guʀmɛ] nm epicure

gourmette [guʀmɛt] nf chain bracelet

gourou [guʀu] nm guru

gousse [gus] *nf* (*de vanille etc*) pod; **~ d'ail** clove of garlic

gousset [gusɛ] *nm* (*de gilet*) fob

goût [gu] *nm* taste; (*fig: appréciation*) taste, liking; **le (bon) ~** good taste; **de bon ~** in good taste, tasteful; **de mauvais ~** in bad taste, tasteless; **avoir bon/mauvais ~** (*aliment*) to taste nice/nasty; (*personne*) to have good/bad taste; **avoir du/manquer de ~** to have/lack taste; **avoir du ~ pour** to have a liking for; **prendre ~ à** to develop a taste *ou* a liking for

goûter [gute] *vt* (*essayer*) to taste; (*apprécier*) to enjoy ▷ *vi* to have (afternoon) tea ▷ *nm* (afternoon) tea; **~ à** to taste, sample; **~ de** to have a taste of; **~ d'enfants/d'anniversaire** children's tea/birthday party

goutte [gut] *nf* drop; (*Méd*) gout; (*alcool*) nip (*Brit*), tot (*Brit*), drop (*US*); **gouttes** *nfpl* (*Méd*) drops; **~ à ~** *adv* a drop at a time; **tomber ~ à ~** to drip

goutte-à-goutte [gutagut] *nm inv* (*Méd*) drip; **alimenter au ~** to drip-feed

gouttelette [gutlɛt] *nf* droplet

goutter [gute] *vi* to drip

gouttière [gutjɛʀ] *nf* gutter

gouvernail [guvɛʀnaj] *nm* rudder; (*barre*) helm, tiller

gouvernant, e [guvɛʀnɑ̃, -ɑ̃t] *adj* ruling *cpd* ▷ *nf* housekeeper; (*d'un enfant*) governess

gouverne [guvɛʀn(ə)] *nf*: **pour sa ~** for his guidance

gouvernement [guvɛʀnəmɑ̃] *nm* government

gouvernemental, e, -aux [guvɛʀnəmɑ̃tal, -o] *adj* (*politique*) government *cpd*; (*journal, parti*) pro-government

gouverner [guvɛʀne] *vt* to govern; (*diriger*) to steer; (*fig*) to control

gouverneur [guvɛʀnœʀ] *nm* governor; (*Mil*) commanding officer

goyave [gɔjav] *nf* guava

GPL *sigle m* (= *gaz de pétrole liquéfié*) LPG (= *liquefied petroleum gas*)

GQG *sigle m* (= *grand quartier général*) GHQ

grabataire [gʀabatɛʀ] *adj* bedridden ▷ *nm/f* bedridden invalid

grâce [gʀɑs] *nf* grace; (*faveur*) favour; (*Jur*) pardon; **grâces** *nfpl* (*Rel*) grace *sg*; **de bonne/mauvaise ~** with (a) good/bad grace; **dans les bonnes ~s de qn** in favour with sb; **faire ~ à qn de qch** to spare sb sth; **rendre ~(s) à** to give thanks to; **demander ~** to beg for mercy; **droit de ~** right of reprieve; **recours en ~** plea for pardon; **~ à** *prép* thanks to

gracier [gʀasje] *vt* to pardon

gracieusement [gʀasjøzmɑ̃] *adv* graciously, kindly; (*gratuitement*) freely; (*avec grâce*) gracefully

gracieux, -euse [gʀasjø, -øz] *adj* (*charmant, élégant*) graceful; (*aimable*) gracious, kind; **à titre ~** free of charge

gracile [gʀasil] *adj* slender

gradation [gʀadasjɔ̃] *nf* gradation

grade [gʀad] *nm* (*Mil*) rank; (*Scol*) degree; **monter en ~** to be promoted

gradé [gʀade] *nm* (*Mil*) officer

gradin [gʀadɛ̃] *nm* (*dans un théâtre*) tier; (*de stade*) step; **gradins** *nmpl* (*de stade*) terracing *no pl* (*Brit*), standing area; **en ~s** terraced

graduation [gʀadɥasjɔ̃] *nf* graduation

gradué, e [gʀadɥe] *adj* (*exercices*) graded (for difficulty); (*thermomètre, verre*) graduated

graduel, le [gʀadɥɛl] *adj* gradual; progressive

graduer [gʀadɥe] *vt* (*effort etc*) to increase gradually; (*règle, verre*) to graduate

graffiti [gʀafiti] *nmpl* graffiti

grain [gʀɛ̃] *nm* (*gén*) grain; (*de chapelet*) bead; (*Navig*) squall; (*averse*) heavy shower; (*fig: petite quantité*): **un ~ de** a touch of; **~ de beauté** beauty spot; **~ de café** coffee bean; **~ de poivre** peppercorn; **~ de poussière** speck of dust; **~ de raisin** grape

graine [gʀɛn] *nf* seed; **mauvaise ~** (*mauvais sujet*) bad lot; **une ~ de voyou** a hooligan in the making

graineterie [gʀɛntʀi] *nf* seed merchant's (shop)

grainetier, -ière [gʀɛntje, -jɛʀ] *nm/f* seed merchant

graissage [gʀɛsaʒ] *nm* lubrication, greasing

graisse [gʀɛs] *nf* fat; (*lubrifiant*) grease; **~ saturée** saturated fat

graisser [gʀese] *vt* to lubricate, grease; (*tacher*) to make greasy

graisseux, -euse [gʀesø, -øz] *adj* greasy; (*Anat*) fatty

grammaire [gʀamɛʀ] *nf* grammar

grammatical, e, -aux [gʀamatikal, -o] *adj* grammatical

gramme [gʀam] *nm* gramme

grand, e [gʀɑ̃, gʀɑ̃d] *adj* (*haut*) tall; (*gros, vaste, large*) big, large; (*long*) long; (*sens abstraits*) great ▷ *adv*: **~ ouvert** wide open; **un ~ buveur** a heavy drinker; **un ~ homme** a great man; **son ~ frère** his big *ou* older brother; **avoir ~ besoin de** to be in dire *ou* desperate need of; **il est ~ temps de** it's high time to; **il est assez ~ pour** he's big *ou* old enough to; **voir ~** to think big; **en ~** on a large scale; **au ~ air** in the open (air); **les ~s blessés/brûlés** the severely injured/burned; **de ~ matin** at the crack of dawn; **~ écart** splits *pl*; **~ ensemble** housing scheme; **~ jour** broad daylight; **~ livre** (*Comm*) ledger; **~ magasin** department store; **~ malade** very sick person; **~ public** general public; **~e personne** grown-up; **~e surface** hypermarket, superstore; **~es écoles** *prestige university-level colleges with competitive entrance examinations; see note*; **~es lignes** (*Rail*) main lines; **~es vacances** summer holidays

● GRANDES ÉCOLES

The *grandes écoles* are highly-respected institutes of higher education which train students for specific careers. Students who have spent two years after the "baccalauréat" in the "classes préparatoires" are recruited by competitive entry examination. The prestigious *grandes écoles* have a strong corporate identity and tend to furnish France with its intellectual, administrative and political élite.

grand-angle [gʀɑ̃tɑ̃gl(ə)] (*pl* **grands-angles**) *nm* (Photo) wide-angle lens

grand-angulaire [gʀɑ̃tɑ̃gylɛʀ] (*pl* **grands-angulaires**) *nm* (Photo) wide-angle lens

grand-chose [gʀɑ̃ʃoz] *nm/f inv*: **pas** ~ not much

Grande-Bretagne [gʀɑ̃dbʀətaɲ] *nf*: **la** ~ (Great) Britain; **en** ~ in (Great) Britain

grandement [gʀɑ̃dmɑ̃] *adv* (tout à fait) greatly; (largement) easily; (généreusement) lavishly

grandeur [gʀɑ̃dœʀ] *nf* (dimension) size; (fig: ampleur, importance) magnitude; (: gloire, puissance) greatness; ~ **nature** *adj* life-size

grand-guignolesque [gʀɑ̃giɲɔlɛsk(ə)] *adj* gruesome

grandiloquent, e [gʀɑ̃dilɔkɑ̃, -ɑ̃t] *adj* bombastic, grandiloquent

grandiose [gʀɑ̃djoz] *adj* (paysage, spectacle) imposing

grandir [gʀɑ̃diʀ] *vi* (enfant, arbre) to grow; (bruit, hostilité) to increase, grow ▷ *vt*: ~ **qn** (vêtement, chaussure) to make sb look taller; (fig) to make sb grow in stature

grandissant, e [gʀɑ̃disɑ̃, -ɑ̃t] *adj* growing

grand-mère [gʀɑ̃mɛʀ] (*pl* **grand(s)-mères**) *nf* grandmother

grand-messe [gʀɑ̃mɛs] *nf* high mass

grand-oncle [gʀɑ̃tɔ̃kl(ə), gʀɑ̃zɔ̃kl(ə)] (*pl* **grands-oncles**) *nm* great-uncle

grand-peine [gʀɑ̃pɛn]: **à** ~ *adv* with (great) difficulty

grand-père [gʀɑ̃pɛʀ] (*pl* **grands-pères**) *nm* grandfather

grand-route [gʀɑ̃ʀut] *nf* main road

grand-rue [gʀɑ̃ʀy] *nf* high street

grands-parents [gʀɑ̃paʀɑ̃] *nmpl* grandparents

grand-tante [gʀɑ̃tɑ̃t] (*pl* **grand(s)-tantes**) *nf* great-aunt

grand-voile [gʀɑ̃vwal] *nf* mainsail

grange [gʀɑ̃ʒ] *nf* barn

granit, granite [gʀanit] *nm* granite

granitique [gʀanitik] *adj* granite; (terrain) granitic

granule [gʀanyl] *nm* small pill

granulé [gʀanyle] *nm* granule

granuleux, -euse [gʀanylø, -øz] *adj* granular

graphe [gʀaf] *nm* graph

graphie [gʀafi] *nf* written form

graphique [gʀafik] *adj* graphic ▷ *nm* graph

graphisme [gʀafism(ə)] *nm* graphic arts *pl*; graphics *sg*; (écriture) handwriting

graphiste [gʀafist(ə)] *nm/f* graphic designer

graphologie [gʀafɔlɔʒi] *nf* graphology

graphologue [gʀafɔlɔg] *nm/f* graphologist

grappe [gʀap] *nf* cluster; ~ **de raisin** bunch of grapes

grappiller [gʀapije] *vt* to glean

grappin [gʀapɛ̃] *nm* grapnel; **mettre le** ~ **sur** (fig) to get one's claws on

gras, se [gʀa, gʀas] *adj* (viande, soupe) fatty; (personne) fat; (surface, main, cheveux) greasy; (terre) sticky; (toux) loose, phlegmy; (rire) throaty; (plaisanterie) coarse; (crayon) soft-lead; (Typo) bold ▷ *nm* (Culin) fat; **faire la** ~**se matinée** to have a lie-in (Brit), sleep late; **matière** ~**se** fat (content)

gras-double [gʀadubl(ə)] *nm* (Culin) tripe

grassement [gʀasmɑ̃] *adv* (généreusement): ~ **payé** handsomely paid; (grossièrement: rire) coarsely

grassouillet, te [gʀasujɛ, -ɛt] *adj* podgy, plump

gratifiant, e [gʀatifjɑ̃, -ɑ̃t] *adj* gratifying, rewarding

gratification [gʀatifikasjɔ̃] *nf* bonus

gratifier [gʀatifje] *vt*: ~ **qn de** to favour (Brit) *ou* favor (US) sb with; to reward sb with; (sourire etc) to favo(u)r sb with

gratin [gʀatɛ̃] *nm* (Culin) cheese- (*ou* crumb-)topped dish; (: croûte) topping; **au** ~ au gratin; **tout le** ~ **parisien** all the best people of Paris

gratiné [gʀatine] *adj* (Culin) au gratin; (fam) hellish ▷ *nf* (soupe) onion soup au gratin

gratis [gʀatis] *adv, adj* free

gratitude [gʀatityd] *nf* gratitude

gratte-ciel [gʀatsjɛl] *nm inv* skyscraper

grattement [gʀatmɑ̃] *nm* (bruit) scratching (noise)

gratte-papier [gʀatpapje] *nm inv* (péj) penpusher

gratter [gʀate] *vt* (frotter) to scrape; (enlever) to scrape off; (bras, bouton) to scratch; **se gratter** to scratch o.s.

grattoir [gʀatwaʀ] *nm* scraper

gratuit, e [gʀatɥi, -ɥit] *adj* (entrée) free; (billet) free, complimentary; (fig) gratuitous

gratuité [gʀatɥite] *nf* being free (of charge); gratuitousness

gratuitement [gʀatɥitmɑ̃] *adv* (sans payer) free; (sans preuve, motif) gratuitously

gravats [gʀava] *nmpl* rubble *sg*

grave [gʀav] *adj* (dangereux: maladie, accident) serious, bad; (sérieux: sujet, problème) serious, grave; (personne, air) grave, solemn; (voix, son) deep, low-pitched ▷ *nm* (Mus) low register; **ce n'est pas** ~! it's all right, don't worry; **blessé** ~ seriously injured person

graveleux, -euse [gʀavlø, -øz] *adj* (terre) gravelly; (fruit) gritty; (contes, propos) smutty

gravement [gʀavmɑ̃] *adv* seriously; badly; gravely

graver [gʀave] *vt* (plaque, nom) to engrave; (CD, DVD) to burn; (fig): ~ **qch dans son esprit/sa mémoire** to etch sth in one's mind/memory

graveur [gʀavœʀ] *nm* engraver; ~ **de CD/DVD** CD/DVD burner *or* writer

gravier [gʀavje] *nm* (loose) gravel *no pl*

gravillons [gʀavijɔ̃] *nmpl* gravel *sg*, loose

g

chippings *ou* gravel

gravir [gʀaviʀ] *vt* to climb (up)

gravitation [gʀavitasjɔ̃] *nf* gravitation

gravité [gʀavite] *nf* (*voir grave*) seriousness; gravity; (*Physique*) gravity

graviter [gʀavite] *vi*: ~ **autour de** to revolve around

gravure [gʀavyʀ] *nf* engraving; (*reproduction*) print; plate

gré [gʀe] *nm*: **à son** ~ *adj* to his liking ▷ *adv* as he pleases; **au ~ de** according to, following; **contre le ~ de qn** against sb's will; **de son (plein)** ~ of one's own free will; **de ~ ou de force** whether one likes it or not; **de bon** ~ willingly; **bon ~ mal** ~ like it or not; willy-nilly; **de ~ à** ~ (*Comm*) by mutual agreement; **savoir (bien)** ~ **à qn de qch** to be (most) grateful to sb for sth

grec, grecque [gʀɛk] *adj* Greek; (*classique: vase etc*) Grecian ▷ *nm* (*Ling*) Greek ▷ *nm/f*: **Grec, Grecque** Greek

Grèce [gʀɛs] *nf*: **la** ~ Greece

gredin, e [gʀədɛ̃, -in] *nm/f* rogue, rascal

gréement [gʀemɑ̃] *nm* rigging

greffe [gʀɛf] *nf* graft; transplant ▷ *nm* (*Jur*) office

greffer [gʀefe] *vt* (*Bot, Méd: tissu*) to graft; (*Méd: organe*) to transplant

greffier [gʀefje] *nm* clerk of the court

grégaire [gʀegɛʀ] *adj* gregarious

grège [gʀɛʒ] *adj*: **soie** ~ raw silk

grêle [gʀɛl] *adj* (very) thin ▷ *nf* hail

grêlé, e [gʀele] *adj* pockmarked

grêler [gʀele] *vb impers*: **il grêle** it's hailing ▷ *vt*: **la région a été grêlée** the region was damaged by hail

grêlon [gʀelɔ̃] *nm* hailstone

grelot [gʀəlo] *nm* little bell

grelottant, e [gʀəlɔtɑ̃, -ɑ̃t] *adj* shivering, shivery

grelotter [gʀəlɔte] *vi* (*trembler*) to shiver

Grenade [gʀənad] *n* Granada ▷ *nf* (*île*) Grenada

grenade [gʀənad] *nf* (*explosive*) grenade; (*Bot*) pomegranate; ~ **lacrymogène** teargas grenade

grenadier [gʀənadje] *nm* (*Mil*) grenadier; (*Bot*) pomegranate tree

grenadine [gʀənadin] *nf* grenadine

grenat [gʀəna] *adj inv* dark red

grenier [gʀənje] *nm* (*de maison*) attic; (*de ferme*) loft

grenouille [gʀənuj] *nf* frog

grenouillère [gʀənujɛʀ] *nf* (*de bébé*) leggings; (*: combinaison*) sleepsuit

grenu, e [gʀəny] *adj* grainy, grained

grès [gʀɛ] *nm* (*roche*) sandstone; (*poterie*) stoneware

grésil [gʀezi] *nm* (fine) hail

grésillement [gʀezijmɑ̃] *nm* sizzling; crackling

grésiller [gʀezije] *vi* to sizzle; (*Radio*) to crackle

grève [gʀɛv] *nf* (*d'ouvriers*) strike; (*plage*) shore; **se mettre en/faire** ~ to go on/be on strike; ~ **bouchon** partial strike (*in key areas of a company*);

~ **de la faim** hunger strike; ~ **perlée** go-slow (*Brit*), slowdown (*US*); ~ **sauvage** wildcat strike; ~ **de solidarité** sympathy strike; ~ **surprise** lightning strike; ~ **sur le tas** sit down strike; ~ **tournante** strike by rota; ~ **du zèle** work-to-rule (*Brit*), slowdown (*US*)

grever [gʀəve] *vt* (*budget, économie*) to put a strain on; **grevé d'impôts** crippled by taxes; **grevé d'hypothèques** heavily mortgaged

gréviste [gʀevist(ə)] *nm/f* striker

gribouillage [gʀibujaʒ] *nm* scribble, scrawl

gribouiller [gʀibuje] *vt* to scribble, scrawl ▷ *vi* to doodle

gribouillis [gʀibuji] *nm* (*dessin*) doodle; (*action*) doodling *no pl*; (*écriture*) scribble

grief [gʀijɛf] *nm* grievance; **faire** ~ **à qn de** to reproach sb for

grièvement [gʀijɛvmɑ̃] *adv* seriously

griffe [gʀif] *nf* claw; (*fig*) signature; (*: d'un couturier, parfumeur*) label, signature

griffé, e [gʀife] *adj* designer(-label) *cpd*

griffer [gʀife] *vt* to scratch

griffon [gʀifɔ̃] *nm* (*chien*) griffon

griffonnage [gʀifɔnaʒ] *nm* scribble

griffonner [gʀifɔne] *vt* to scribble

griffure [gʀifyʀ] *nf* scratch

grignoter [gʀiɲɔte] *vt, vi* to nibble

gril [gʀil] *nm* steak *ou* grill pan

grillade [gʀijad] *nf* grill

grillage [gʀijaʒ] *nm* (*treillis*) wire netting; (*clôture*) wire fencing

grillager [gʀijaʒe] *vt* (*objet*) to put wire netting on; (*périmètre, jardin*) to put wire fencing around

grille [gʀij] *nf* (*portail*) (metal) gate; (*clôture*) railings *pl*; (*d'égout*) (metal) grate; (*fig*) grid

grille-pain [gʀijpɛ̃] *nm inv* toaster

griller [gʀije] *vt* (*aussi*: **faire griller**: *pain*) to toast; (*: viande*) to grill (*Brit*), broil (*US*); (*: café*) to roast; (*fig: ampoule etc*) to burn out, blow; ~ **un feu rouge** to jump the lights (*Brit*), run a stoplight (*US*) ▷ *vi* (*brûler*) to be roasting

grillon [gʀijɔ̃] *nm* (*Zool*) cricket

grimace [gʀimas] *nf* grimace; (*pour faire rire*): **faire des** ~**s** to pull *ou* make faces

grimacer [gʀimase] *vi* to grimace

grimacier, -ière [gʀimasje, -jɛʀ] *adj*: **c'est un enfant** ~ that child is always pulling faces

grimer [gʀime] *vt* to make up

grimoire [gʀimwaʀ] *nm* (*illisible*) unreadable scribble; (*livre de magie*) book of magic spells

grimpant, e [gʀɛ̃pɑ̃, -ɑ̃t] *adj*: **plante** ~**e** climbing plant, climber

grimper [gʀɛ̃pe] *vi, vt* to climb ▷ *nm*: **le** ~ (*Sport*) rope-climbing; ~ **à/sur** to climb (up)/climb onto

grimpeur, -euse [gʀɛ̃pœʀ, -øz] *nm/f* climber

grinçant, e [gʀɛ̃sɑ̃, -ɑ̃t] *adj* grating

grincement [gʀɛ̃smɑ̃] *nm* grating (noise); creaking (noise)

grincer [gʀɛ̃se] *vi* (*porte, roue*) to grate; (*plancher*) to creak; ~ **des dents** to grind one's teeth

grincheux, -euse [gʀɛ̃ʃø, -øz] *adj* grumpy

gringalet [gʀɛ̃galɛ] *adj m* puny ▷ *nm* weakling
griotte [gʀijɔt] *nf* Morello cherry
grippal, e, -aux [gʀipal, -o] *adj* (*état*) flu-like
grippe [gʀip] *nf* flu, influenza; **avoir la ~** to have (the) flu; **prendre qn/qch en ~** (*fig*) to take a sudden dislike to sb/sth; **~ aviaire** bird flu; **~ porcine** swine flu
grippé, e [gʀipe] *adj*: **être ~** to have (the) flu; (*moteur*) to have seized up (*Brit*) *ou* jammed
gripper [gʀipe] *vt, vi* to jam
grippe-sou [gʀipsu] *nm/f* penny pincher
gris, e [gʀi, gʀiz] *adj* grey (*Brit*), gray (*US*); (*ivre*) tipsy ▷ *nm* (*couleur*) grey (*Brit*), gray (*US*); **il fait ~** it's a dull *ou* grey day; **faire ~e mine** to look miserable *ou* morose; **faire ~e mine à qn** to give sb a cool reception
grisaille [gʀizaj] *nf* greyness (*Brit*), grayness (*US*), dullness
grisant, e [gʀizã, -ãt] *adj* intoxicating, exhilarating
grisâtre [gʀizɑtʀ(ə)] *adj* greyish (*Brit*), grayish (*US*)
griser [gʀize] *vt* to intoxicate; **se ~ de** (*fig*) to become intoxicated with
griserie [gʀizʀi] *nf* intoxication
grisonnant, e [gʀizɔnã, -ãt] *adj* greying (*Brit*), graying (*US*)
grisonner [gʀizɔne] *vi* to be going grey (*Brit*) *ou* gray (*US*)
Grisons [gʀizɔ̃] *nmpl*: **les ~** Graubünden
grisou [gʀizu] *nm* firedamp
gris-vert [gʀivɛʀ] *adj* grey-green
grive [gʀiv] *nf* (*Zool*) thrush
grivois, e [gʀivwa, -waz] *adj* saucy
grivoiserie [gʀivwazʀi] *nf* sauciness
Groenland [gʀɔɛnlɑ̃d] *nm*: **le ~** Greenland
grog [gʀɔg] *nm* grog
groggy [gʀɔgi] *adj inv* dazed
grogne [gʀɔɲ] *nf* grumble
grognement [gʀɔɲmã] *nm* grunt; growl
grogner [gʀɔɲe] *vi* to growl; (*fig*) to grumble
grognon, ne [gʀɔɲɔ̃, -ɔn] *adj* grumpy, grouchy
groin [gʀwɛ̃] *nm* snout
grommeler [gʀɔmle] *vi* to mutter to o.s.
grondement [gʀɔ̃dmã] *nm* rumble; growl
gronder [gʀɔ̃de] *vi* (*canon, moteur, tonnerre*) to rumble; (*animal*) to growl; (*fig: révolte*) to be brewing ▷ *vt* to scold
groom [gʀum] *nm* page, bellhop (*US*)
gros, se [gʀo, gʀos] *adj* big, large; (*obèse*) fat; (*problème, quantité*) great; (*travaux, dégâts*) extensive; (*large: trait, fil*) thick, heavy ▷ *adv*: **risquer/gagner ~** to risk/win a lot ▷ *nm* (*Comm*): **le ~** the wholesale business; **écrire ~** to write in big letters; **prix de ~** wholesale price; **par ~ temps/~se mer** in rough weather/heavy seas; **le ~ de** the main body of; (*du travail etc*) the bulk of; **en avoir ~ sur le cœur** to be upset; **en ~** roughly; (*Comm*) wholesale; **~ lot** jackpot; **~ mot** coarse word, vulgarity; **~ œuvre** shell (of building); **~ plan** (*Photo*) close-up; **~ porteur** wide-bodied aircraft, jumbo (jet); **~ sel** cooking

salt; **~ titre** headline; **~se caisse** big drum
groseille [gʀozɛj] *nf*: **~ (rouge)/(blanche)** red/ white currant; **~ à maquereau** gooseberry
groseillier [gʀozeje] *nm* red *ou* white currant bush; gooseberry bush
grosse [gʀos] *adj f voir* **gros** ▷ *nf* (*Comm*) gross
grossesse [gʀosɛs] *nf* pregnancy; **~ nerveuse** phantom pregnancy
grosseur [gʀosœʀ] *nf* size; fatness; (*tumeur*) lump
grossier, -ière [gʀosje, -jɛʀ] *adj* coarse; (*travail*) rough; crude; (*évident: erreur*) gross
grossièrement [gʀosjɛʀmã] *adv* coarsely; roughly; crudely; (*en gros*) roughly
grossièreté [gʀosjɛʀte] *nf* coarseness; rudeness
grossir [gʀosiʀ] *vi* (*personne*) to put on weight; (*fig*) to grow, get bigger; (*rivière*) to swell ▷ *vt* to increase; (*exagérer*) to exaggerate; (*au microscope*) to magnify, enlarge; (*vêtement*): **~ qn** to make sb look fatter
grossissant, e [gʀosisã, -ãt] *adj* magnifying, enlarging
grossissement [gʀosismã] *nm* (*optique*) magnification
grossiste [gʀosist(ə)] *nm/f* wholesaler
grosso modo [gʀosomɔdo] *adv* roughly
grotesque [gʀɔtɛsk(ə)] *adj* grotesque
grotte [gʀɔt] *nf* cave
grouiller [gʀuje] *vi* (*foule*) to mill about; (*fourmis*) to swarm about; **~ de** to be swarming with
groupe [gʀup] *nm* group; **cabinet de ~** group practice; **médecine de ~** group practice; **~ électrogène** generator; **~ de parole** support group; **~ de pression** pressure group; **~ sanguin** blood group; **~ scolaire** school complex
groupement [gʀupmã] *nm* grouping; (*groupe*) group; **~ d'intérêt économique (GIE)** ≈ trade association
grouper [gʀupe] *vt* to group; (*ressources, moyens*) to pool; **se grouper** to get together
groupuscule [gʀupyskyl] *nm* clique
gruau [gʀyo] *nm*: **pain de ~** wheaten bread
grue [gʀy] *nf* crane; **faire le pied de ~** (*fam*) to hang around (waiting), kick one's heels (*Brit*)
gruger [gʀyʒe] *vt* to cheat, dupe
grumeaux [gʀymo] *nmpl* (*Culin*) lumps
grumeleux, -euse [gʀymlø, -øz] *adj* (*sauce etc*) lumpy; (*peau etc*) bumpy
grutier [gʀytje] *nm* crane driver
gruyère [gʀyjɛʀ] *nm* gruyère (*Brit*) *ou* Swiss cheese
Guadeloupe [gwadlup] *nf*: **la ~** Guadeloupe
guadeloupéen, ne [gwadlupeɛ̃, -ɛn] *adj* Guadelupian
Guatémala [gwatemala] *nm*: **le ~** Guatemala
guatémalien, ne [gwatemaljɛ̃, -ɛn] *adj* Guatemalan
guatémaltèque [gwatemaltɛk] *adj* Guatemalan
gué [ge] *nm* ford; **passer à ~** to ford
guenilles [gənij] *nfpl* rags

guenon [gənɔ̃] *nf* female monkey

guépard [gepaʀ] *nm* cheetah

guêpe [gɛp] *nf* wasp

guêpier [gepje] *nm* (*fig*) trap

guère [gɛʀ] *adv* (*avec adjectif, adverbe*): **ne ... ~** hardly; (*avec verbe*): **ne ... ~** (*tournure négative*) much; hardly ever; (*very*) long; **il n'y a ~ que/de** there's hardly anybody (*ou* anything) but/hardly any

guéridon [geʀidɔ̃] *nm* pedestal table

guérilla [geʀija] *nf* guerrilla warfare

guérillero [geʀijeʀo] *nm* guerrilla

guérir [geʀiʀ] *vt* (*personne, maladie*) to cure; (*membre, plaie*) to heal ▷ *vi* (*personne*) to recover, be cured; (*plaie, chagrin*) to heal; **~ de** to be cured of, recover from; **~ qn de** to cure sb of

guérison [geʀizɔ̃] *nf* curing; healing; recovery

guérissable [geʀisabl(ə)] *adj* curable

guérisseur, -euse [geʀisœʀ, -øz] *nm/f* healer

guérite [geʀit] *nf* (*Mil*) sentry box; (*sur un chantier*) (workman's) hut

Guernesey [gɛʀnəzɛ] *nf* Guernsey

guernesiais, e [gɛʀnəzjɛ, -ez] *adj* of *ou* from Guernsey

guerre [gɛʀ] *nf* war; (*méthode*): **~ atomique/de tranchées** atomic/trench warfare *no pl*; **en ~** at war; **faire la ~ à** to wage war against; **de ~ lasse** (*fig*) tired of fighting *ou* resisting; **de bonne ~** fair and square; **~ civile/mondiale** civil/world war; **~ froide/sainte** cold/holy war; **~ d'usure** war of attrition

guerrier, -ière [geʀje, -jɛʀ] *adj* warlike ▷ *nm/f* warrior

guerroyer [gɛʀwaje] *vi* to wage war

guet [gɛ] *nm*: **faire le ~** to be on the watch *ou* look-out

guet-apens [gɛtapɑ̃] (*pl* **guets-apens**) *nm* ambush

guêtre [gɛtʀ(ə)] *nf* gaiter

guetter [gete] *vt* (*épier*) to watch (intently); (*attendre*) to watch (out) for; (: *pour surprendre*) to be lying in wait for

guetteur [gɛtœʀ] *nm* look-out

gueule [gœl] *nf* mouth; (*fam: visage*) mug; (: *bouche*) gob (!), mouth; **ta ~!** (*fam*) shut up!; **~ de bois** (*fam*) hangover

gueule-de-loup [gœldəlu] (*pl* **gueules-de-loup**) *nf* snapdragon

gueuler [gœle] *vi* (*fam*) to bawl

gueuleton [gœltɔ̃] *nm* (*fam*) blowout (*Brit*), big meal

gueux [gø] *nm* beggar; (*coquin*) rogue

gui [gi] *nm* mistletoe

guibole [gibɔl] *nf* (*fam*) leg

guichet [giʃɛ] *nm* (*de bureau, banque*) counter, window; (*d'une porte*) wicket, hatch; **les ~s** (*à la gare, au théâtre*) the ticket office; **jouer à ~s fermés** to play to a full house

guichetier, -ière [giʃtje, -jɛʀ] *nm/f* counter clerk

guide [gid] *nm* guide; (*livre*) guide(book) ▷ *nf*

(*fille scout*) (girl) guide (*Brit*), girl scout (*US*); **guides** *nfpl* (*d'un cheval*) reins

guider [gide] *vt* to guide

guidon [gidɔ̃] *nm* handlebars *pl*

guigne [giɲ] *nf* (*fam*): **avoir la ~** to be jinxed

guignol [giɲɔl] *nm* ≈ Punch and Judy show; (*fig*) clown

guillemets [gijmɛ] *nmpl*: **entre ~** in inverted commas *ou* quotation marks; **~ de répétition** ditto marks

guilleret, te [gijʀɛ, -ɛt] *adj* perky, bright

guillotine [gijɔtin] *nf* guillotine

guillotiner [gijɔtine] *vt* to guillotine

guimauve [gimov] *nf* (*Bot*) marshmallow; (*fig*) sentimentality, sloppiness

guimbarde [gɛ̃baʀd(ə)] *nf* old banger (*Brit*), jalopy

guindé, e [gɛ̃de] *adj* stiff, starchy

Guinée [gine] *nf*: **la (République de) ~** (the Republic of) Guinea; **la ~ équatoriale** Equatorial Guinea

Guinée-Bissau [ginebiso] *nf*: **la ~** Guinea-Bissau

guinéen, ne [gineɛ̃, -ɛn] *adj* Guinean

guingois [gɛ̃gwa]: **de ~** *adv* askew

guinguette [gɛ̃gɛt] *nf* open-air café or dance hall

guirlande [giʀlɑ̃d] *nf* garland; (*de papier*) paper chain; **~ lumineuse** lights *pl*, fairy lights *pl* (*Brit*); **~ de Noël** tinsel *no pl*

guise [giz] *nf*: **à votre ~** as you wish *ou* please; **en ~ de** by way of

guitare [gitaʀ] *nf* guitar

guitariste [gitaʀist(ə)] *nm/f* guitarist, guitar player

gustatif, -ive [gystatif, -iv] *adj* gustatory; *voir* **papille**

guttural, e, -aux [gytyʀal, -o] *adj* guttural

guyanais, e [gɥijanɛ, -ez] *adj* Guyanese, Guyanan; (*français*) Guianese, Guianan

Guyane [gɥijan] *nf*: **la ~** Guyana; **la ~ (française)** (French) Guiana

gvt *abr* (= *gouvernement*) govt

gym [ʒim] *nf* (*exercices*) gym

gymkhana [ʒimkana] *nm* rally; **~ motocycliste** (motorbike) scramble (*Brit*), motocross

gymnase [ʒimnɑz] *nm* gym(nasium)

gymnaste [ʒimnast(ə)] *nm/f* gymnast

gymnastique [ʒimnastik] *nf* gymnastics *sg*; (*au réveil etc*) keep-fit exercises *pl*; **~ corrective** remedial gymnastics

gynécologie [ʒinekɔlɔʒi] *nf* gynaecology (*Brit*), gynecology (*US*)

gynécologique [ʒinekɔlɔʒik] *adj* gynaecological (*Brit*), gynecological (*US*)

gynécologue [ʒinekɔlɔg] *nm/f* gynaecologist (*Brit*), gynecologist (*US*)

gypse [ʒips(ə)] *nm* gypsum

gyrophare [ʒiʀɔfaʀ] *nm* (*sur une voiture*) revolving (flashing) light

Hh

H, h [aʃ] *nm inv* H, h ▷ *abr* (= *homme*) M;
  (= *hydrogène*) H = **heure**; **à l'heure H** at zero
  hour; **bombe H** H bomb; **H comme Henri** H
  for Harry (*Brit*) *ou* How (*US*)
ha. *abr* (= *hectare*) ha.
hab. *abr* = **habitant**
habile [abil] *adj* skilful; (*malin*) clever
habilement [abilmɑ̃] *adv* skilfully; cleverly
habileté [abilte] *nf* skill, skilfulness; cleverness
habilité, e [abilite] *adj*: **~ à faire** entitled to do,
  empowered to do
habiliter [abilite] *vt* to empower, entitle
habillage [abijaʒ] *nm* dressing
habillé, e [abije] *adj* dressed; (*chic*) dressy;
  (*Tech*): **~ de** covered with; encased in
habillement [abijmɑ̃] *nm* clothes *pl*; (*profession*)
  clothing industry
habiller [abije] *vt* to dress; (*fournir en vêtements*) to
  clothe; **s'habiller** to dress (o.s.); (*se déguiser,
  mettre des vêtements chic*) to dress up; **s'~ de/en** to
  dress in/dress up as; **s'~ chez/à** to buy one's
  clothes from/at
habilleuse [abijøz] *nf* (*Ciné, Théât*) dresser
habit [abi] *nm* outfit; **habits** *nmpl* (*vêtements*)
  clothes; **~ (de soirée)** tails *pl*; evening dress;
  prendre l'~ (*Rel: entrer en religion*) to enter (holy)
  orders
habitable [abitabl(ə)] *adj* (in)habitable
habitacle [abitakl(ə)] *nm* cockpit; (*Auto*)
  passenger cell
habitant, e [abitɑ̃, -ɑ̃t] *nm/f* inhabitant; (*d'une
  maison*) occupant, occupier; **loger chez l'~** to
  stay with the locals
habitat [abita] *nm* housing conditions *pl*; (*Bot,
  Zool*) habitat
habitation [abitɑsjɔ̃] *nf* living; (*demeure*)
  residence, home; (*maison*) house; **~s à loyer
  modéré (HLM)** low-rent, state-owned housing,
  ≈ council housing *sg* (*Brit*), ≈ public housing
  units (*US*)
habité, e [abite] *adj* inhabited; lived in
habiter [abite] *vt* to live in; (*sentiment*) to dwell
  in ▷ *vi*: **~ à/dans** to live in *ou* at/in; **~ chez** *ou*
  avec qn to live with sb; **~ 16 rue Montmartre**
  to live at number 16 rue Montmartre; **~ rue
  Montmartre** to live in rue Montmartre

habitude [abityd] *nf* habit; **avoir l'~ de faire** to
  be in the habit of doing; **avoir l'~ des enfants**
  to be used to children; **prendre l'~ de faire qch**
  to get into the habit of doing sth; **perdre une ~**
  to get out of a habit; **d'~** usually; **comme d'~** as
  usual; **par ~** out of habit
habitué, e [abitɥe] *adj*: **être ~ à** to be used *ou*
  accustomed to ▷ *nm/f* regular visitor; (*client*)
  regular (customer)
habituel, le [abitɥɛl] *adj* usual
habituellement [abitɥɛlmɑ̃] *adv* usually
habituer [abitɥe] *vt*: **~ qn à** to get sb used to;
  s'habituer à to get used to
'hâbleur, -euse ['ɑblœʀ, -øz] *adj* boastful
'hache ['aʃ] *nf* axe
'haché, e ['aʃe] *adj* minced (*Brit*), ground (*US*);
  (*persil*) chopped; (*fig*) jerky
'hache-légumes ['aʃlegym] *nm inv* vegetable
  chopper
'hacher ['aʃe] *vt* (*viande*) to mince (*Brit*), grind
  (*US*); (*persil*) to chop; **~ menu** to mince *ou* grind
  finely; to chop finely
'hachette ['aʃɛt] *nf* hatchet
'hache-viande ['aʃvjɑ̃d] *nm inv* (*meat*) mincer
  (*Brit*) *ou* grinder (*US*); (*couteau*) (*meat*) cleaver
'hachis ['aʃi] *nm* mince *no pl* (*Brit*), hamburger
  meat (*US*); **~ de viande** minced (*Brit*) *ou* ground
  (*US*) meat
'hachisch ['aʃiʃ] *nm* hashish
'hachoir ['aʃwaʀ] *nm* chopper; (*meat*) mincer
  (*Brit*) *ou* grinder (*US*); (*planche*) chopping board
'hachurer ['aʃyʀe] *vt* to hatch
'hachures ['aʃyʀ] *nfpl* hatching *sg*
'hagard, e ['agaʀ, -aʀd(ə)] *adj* wild, distraught
'haie ['ɛ] *nf* hedge; (*Sport*) hurdle; (*fig: rang*) line,
  row; **200 m ~s** 200 m hurdles; **~ d'honneur**
  guard of honour
'haillons ['ajɔ̃] *nmpl* rags
'haine ['ɛn] *nf* hatred
'haineux, -euse ['ɛnø, -øz] *adj* full of hatred
'haïr ['aiʀ] *vt* to detest, hate; **se 'haïr** to hate
  each other
'hais ['ɛ], **'haïs** *etc* ['ai] *vb voir* **'haïr**
'haïssable ['aisabl(ə)] *adj* detestable
Haïti [aiti] *n* Haiti
haïtien, ne [aisjɛ̃, -ɛn] *adj* Haitian

'halage ['alaʒ] *nm*: **chemin de ~** towpath
'hâle ['al] *nm* (sun)tan
'hâlé, e ['ale] *adj* (sun)tanned, sunburnt
haleine [alɛn] *nf* breath; **perdre ~** to get out of breath; **à perdre ~** until one is gasping for breath; **avoir mauvaise ~** to have bad breath; **reprendre ~** to get one's breath back; **hors d'~** out of breath; **tenir en ~** to hold spellbound; (*en attente*) to keep in suspense; **de longue ~** *adj* long-term
'haler ['ale] *vt* to haul in; (*remorquer*) to tow
'haleter ['alte] *vi* to pant
'hall ['ol] *nm* hall
hallali [alali] *nm* kill
'halle ['al] *nf* (covered) market; **'halles** *nfpl* central food market *sg*
'hallebarde ['albaʀd] *nf* halberd; **il pleut des ~s** (*fam*) it's bucketing down
hallucinant, e [alysinɑ̃, -ɑ̃t] *adj* staggering
hallucination [alysinasjɔ̃] *nf* hallucination
hallucinatoire [alysinatwaʀ] *adj* hallucinatory
halluciné, e [alysine] *nm/f* person suffering from hallucinations; (*fou*) (raving) lunatic
hallucinogène [a(l)lysinɔʒɛn] *adj* hallucinogenic ▷ *nm* hallucinogen
'halo ['alo] *nm* halo
halogène [alɔʒɛn] *nm*: **lampe (à) ~** halogen lamp
'halte ['alt(ə)] *nf* stop, break; (*escale*) stopping place; (*Rail*) halt ▷ *excl* stop!; **faire ~** to stop
'halte-garderie ['altgaʀdəʀi] (*pl* **'haltes-garderies**) *nf* crèche
haltère [altɛʀ] *nm* (*à boules, disques*) dumbbell, barbell; (**poids et**) **~s** weightlifting
haltérophile [alteʀɔfil] *nm/f* weightlifter
haltérophilie [alteʀɔfili] *nf* weightlifting
'hamac ['amak] *nm* hammock
'Hambourg ['ɑ̃buʀ] *n* Hamburg
'hamburger ['ɑ̃buʀgœʀ] *nm* hamburger
'hameau, x ['amo] *nm* hamlet
hameçon [amsɔ̃] *nm* (fish) hook
'hampe ['ɑ̃p] *nf* (*de drapeau etc*) pole; (*de lance*) shaft
'hamster ['amstɛʀ] *nm* hamster
'hanche ['ɑ̃ʃ] *nf* hip
'hand-ball ['ɑ̃dbal] *nm* handball
'handballeur, -euse ['ɑ̃dbalœʀ, -øz] *nm/f* handball player
'handicap ['ɑ̃dikap] *nm* handicap
'handicapé, e ['ɑ̃dikape] *adj* handicapped ▷ *nm/f* physically (*ou* mentally) handicapped person; **~ moteur** spastic
'handicaper ['ɑ̃dikape] *vt* to handicap
'hangar ['ɑ̃gaʀ] *nm* shed; (*Aviat*) hangar
'hanneton ['antɔ̃] *nm* cockchafer
'Hanovre ['anɔvʀ(ə)] *n* Hanover
'hanter ['ɑ̃te] *vt* to haunt
'hantise ['ɑ̃tiz] *nf* obsessive fear
'happer ['ape] *vt* to snatch; (*train etc*) to hit
'harangue ['aʀɑ̃g] *nf* harangue
'haranguer ['aʀɑ̃ge] *vt* to harangue
'haras ['aʀɑ] *nm* stud farm

'harassant, e ['aʀasɑ̃, -ɑ̃t] *adj* exhausting
'harcèlement ['aʀsɛlmɑ̃] *nm* harassment; **~ sexuel** sexual harassment
'harceler ['aʀsəle] *vt* (*Mil, Chasse*) to harass, harry; (*importuner*) to plague
'hardes ['aʀd(ə)] *nfpl* rags
'hardi, e ['aʀdi] *adj* bold, daring
'hardiesse ['aʀdjɛs] *nf* audacity; **avoir la ~ de** to have the audacity *ou* effrontery to
'harem ['aʀɛm] *nm* harem
'hareng ['aʀɑ̃] *nm* herring
'hargne ['aʀɲ(ə)] *nf* aggressivity, aggressiveness
'hargneusement ['aʀɲøzmɑ̃] *adv* belligerently, aggressively
'hargneux, -euse ['aʀɲø, -øz] *adj* (*propos, personne*) belligerent, aggressive; (*chien*) fierce
'haricot ['aʀiko] *nm* bean; **~ blanc/rouge** haricot/kidney bean; **~ vert** French (*Brit*) *ou* green bean
harmonica [aʀmɔnika] *nm* mouth organ
harmonie [aʀmɔni] *nf* harmony
harmonieux, -euse [aʀmɔnjø, -øz] *adj* harmonious
harmonique [aʀmɔnik] *adj, nm ou f* harmonic
harmoniser [aʀmɔnize] *vt* to harmonize; **s'harmoniser** (*couleurs, teintes*) to go well together
harmonium [aʀmɔnjɔm] *nm* harmonium
'harnaché, e ['aʀnaʃe] *adj* (*fig*) rigged out
'harnachement ['aʀnaʃmɑ̃] *nm* (*habillement*) rig-out; (*équipement*) harness, equipment
'harnacher ['aʀnaʃe] *vt* to harness
'harnais ['aʀnɛ] *nm* harness
'haro ['aʀo] *nm*: **crier ~ sur qn/qch** to inveigh against sb/sth
'harpe ['aʀp(ə)] *nf* harp
'harpie ['aʀpi] *nf* harpy
'harpiste ['aʀpist(ə)] *nm/f* harpist
'harpon ['aʀpɔ̃] *nm* harpoon
'harponner ['aʀpɔne] *vt* to harpoon; (*fam*) to collar
'hasard ['azaʀ] *nm*: **le ~** chance, fate; **un ~** a coincidence; (*aubaine, chance*) a stroke of luck; **au ~** (*sans but*) aimlessly; (*à l'aveuglette*) at random, haphazardly; **par ~** by chance; **comme par ~** as if by chance; **à tout ~** on the off chance; (*en cas de besoin*) just in case
'hasarder ['azaʀde] *vt* (*mot*) to venture; (*fortune*) to risk; **se ~ à faire** to risk doing, venture to do
'hasardeux, -euse ['azaʀdø, -øz] *adj* hazardous, risky; (*hypothèse*) rash
'haschisch ['aʃiʃ] *nm* hashish
'hâte ['at] *nf* haste; **à la ~** hurriedly, hastily; **en ~** posthaste, with all possible speed; **avoir ~ de** to be eager *ou* anxious to
'hâter ['ate] *vt* to hasten; **se 'hâter** to hurry; **se ~ de** to hurry *ou* hasten to
'hâtif, -ive ['atif, -iv] *adj* (*travail*) hurried; (*décision*) hasty; (*légume*) early
'hâtivement ['ativmɑ̃] *adv* hurriedly; hastily
'hauban ['obɑ̃] *nm* (*Navig*) shroud
'hausse ['os] *nf* rise, increase; (*de fusil*) backsight

adjuster; **à la ~** upwards; **en ~** rising

'hausser ['ose] *vt* to raise; **~ les épaules** to shrug (one's shoulders); **se ~ sur la pointe des pieds** to stand (up) on tiptoe *ou* tippy-toe (US)

'haut, e ['o, 'ot] *adj* high; (*grand*) tall; (*son, voix*) high(-pitched) ▷ *adv* high ▷ *nm* top (part); **de 3 m de ~, ~ de 3 m** 3 m high, 3 m in height; **en ~e montagne** high up in the mountains; **en ~ lieu** in high places; **à ~e voix, (tout) ~** aloud, out loud; **des ~s et des bas** ups and downs; **du ~ de** from the top of; **tomber de ~** to fall from a height; (*fig*) to have one's hopes dashed; **dire qch bien ~** to say sth plainly; **prendre qch de (très) ~** to react haughtily to sth; **traiter qn de ~ ~** to treat sb with disdain; **de ~ en bas** from top to bottom; downwards; **~ en couleur** (*chose*) highly coloured; (*personne*): **un personnage ~ en couleur** a colourful character; **plus ~** higher up, further up; (*dans un texte*) above; (*parler*) louder; **en ~** up above; at (*ou* to) the top; (*dans une maison*) upstairs; **en ~ de** at the top of; **~ les mains!** hands up!, stick 'em up!; **la ~e couture/coiffure** haute couture/coiffure; **~ débit** (*Inform*) broadband; **~e fidélité** hi-fi, high fidelity; **la ~e finance** high finance; **~e trahison** high treason

'hautain, e ['otɛ̃, -ɛn] *adj* (*personne, regard*) haughty

'hautbois ['obwɑ] *nm* oboe

'hautboïste ['oboist(ə)] *nm/f* oboist

'haut-de-forme ['odfɔʀm(ə)] (*pl* **'hauts-de-forme**) *nm* top hat

'haute-contre ['otkɔ̃tʀ(ə)] (*pl* **'hautes-contre**) *nf* counter-tenor

'hautement ['otmɑ̃] *adv* (*ouvertement*) openly; (*supérieurement*): **~ qualifié** highly qualified

'hauteur ['otœʀ] *nf* height; (*Géo*) height, hill; (*fig*) loftiness; haughtiness; **à ~ de** up to (the level of); **à ~ des yeux** at eye level; **à la ~ de** (*sur la même ligne*) level with; by; (*fig*) equal to; **à la ~** (*fig*) up to it, equal to the task

'Haute-Volta ['otvɔlta] *nf*: **la ~** Upper Volta

'haut-fond ['ofɔ̃] (*pl* **'hauts-fonds**) *nm* shallow

'haut-fourneau ['ofuʀno] (*pl* **'hauts-fourneaux**) *nm* blast *ou* smelting furnace

'haut-le-cœur ['olkœʀ] *nm inv* retch, heave

'haut-le-corps ['olkɔʀ] *nm inv* start, jump

'haut-parleur ['opaʀlœʀ] (*pl* **-s**) *nm* (loud)speaker

'hauturier, -ière ['otyʀje, -jɛʀ] *adj* (*Navig*) deep-sea

'havanais, e ['avanɛ, -ɛz] *adj* of *ou* from Havana

'Havane ['avan] *nf*: **la ~** Havana ▷ *nm*: **'havane** (*cigare*) Havana

'hâve ['av] *adj* gaunt

'havrais, e ['avʀɛ, -ɛz] *adj* of *ou* from Le Havre

'havre ['avʀ(ə)] *nm* haven

'havresac ['avʀəsak] *nm* haversack

Hawaï [awai] *n* Hawaii; **les îles ~** the Hawaiian Islands

hawaïen, ne [awajɛ̃, -ɛn] *adj* Hawaiian ▷ *nm* (*Ling*) Hawaiian

'Haye ['ɛ] *n*: **la ~** the Hague

'hayon ['ɛjɔ̃] *nm* tailgate

HCR *sigle m* (= *Haut-Commissariat des Nations unies pour les réfugiés*) UNHCR

hdb. *abr* (= *heures de bureau*) o.h. = **office hours**

'hé ['e] *excl* hey!

hebdo [ɛbdo] *nm* (*fam*) weekly

hebdomadaire [ɛbdɔmadɛʀ] *adj, nm* weekly

hébergement [ebɛʀʒəmɑ̃] *nm* accommodation, lodging; taking in

héberger [ebɛʀʒe] *vt* to accommodate, lodge; (*réfugiés*) to take in

hébergeur [ebɛʀʒœʀ] *nm* (*Internet*) host

hébété, e [ebete] *adj* dazed

hébétude [ebetyd] *nf* stupor

hébraïque [ebʀaik] *adj* Hebrew, Hebraic

hébreu, x [ebʀø] *adj m, nm* Hebrew

Hébrides [ebʀid] *nf*: **les ~** the Hebrides

HEC *sigle fpl* (= *École des hautes études commerciales*) *grande école for management and business studies*

hécatombe [ekatɔ̃b] *nf* slaughter

hectare [ɛktaʀ] *nm* hectare, 10,000 square metres

hecto... [ɛkto] *préfixe* hecto...

hectolitre [ɛktɔlitʀ(ə)] *nm* hectolitre

hédoniste [edɔnist(ə)] *adj* hedonistic

hégémonie [eʒemɔni] *nf* hegemony

'hein ['ɛ̃] *excl* eh?; (*sollicitant l'approbation*): **tu m'approuves, ~?** so I did the right thing then?; **Paul est venu, ~?** Paul came, did he?; **que fais-tu, ~?** hey! what are you doing?

'hélas ['elɑs] *excl* alas! ▷ *adv* unfortunately

'héler ['ele] *vt* to hail

hélice [elis] *nf* propeller

hélicoïdal, e, -aux [elikɔidal, -o] *adj* helical; helicoid

hélicoptère [elikɔptɛʀ] *nm* helicopter

héliogravure [eljɔgʀavyʀ] *nf* heliogravure

héliomarin, e [eljɔmaʀɛ̃, -in] *adj*: **centre ~** *centre offering sea and sun therapy*

héliotrope [eljɔtʀɔp] *nm* (*Bot*) heliotrope

héliport [elipɔʀ] *nm* heliport

héliporté, e [elipɔʀte] *adj* transported by helicopter

hélium [eljɔm] *nm* helium

hellénique [elenik] *adj* Hellenic

hellénisant, e [elenizɑ̃, -ɑ̃t], **helléniste** [elenist(ə)] *nm/f* hellenist

Helsinki [ɛlzinki] *n* Helsinki

helvète [ɛlvɛt] *adj* Helvetian ▷ *nm/f*: **Helvète** Helvetian

Helvétie [ɛlvesi] *nf*: **la ~** Helvetia

helvétique [ɛlvetik] *adj* Swiss

hématologie [ematɔlɔʒi] *nf* (*Méd*) haematology.

hématome [ematom] *nm* haematoma

hémicycle [emisikl(ə)] *nm* semicircle; (*Pol*): **l'~** the benches (in French parliament)

hémiplégie [emipleʒi] *nf* paralysis of one side, hemiplegia

hémisphère [emisfɛʀ] *nf*: **~ nord/sud** northern/southern hemisphere

hémisphérique [emisfeʀik] *adj* hemispherical

hémoglobine [emɔglɔbin] *nf* haemoglobin (*Brit*), hemoglobin (*US*)

hémophile [emɔfil] *adj* haemophiliac (*Brit*), hemophiliac (*US*)

hémophilie [emɔfili] *nf* haemophilia (*Brit*), hemophilia (*US*)

hémorragie [emɔraʒi] *nf* bleeding *no pl*, haemorrhage (*Brit*), hemorrhage (*US*); ~ **cérébrale** cerebral haemorrhage; ~ **interne** internal bleeding *ou* haemorrhage

hémorroïdes [emɔrɔid] *nfpl* piles, haemorrhoids (*Brit*), hemorrhoids (*US*)

hémostatique [emɔstatik] *adj* haemostatic (*Brit*), hemostatic (*US*)

'henné ['ene] *nm* henna

'hennir ['enir] *vi* to neigh, whinny

'hennissement ['enismɑ̃] *nm* neighing, whinnying

'hep ['ɛp] *excl* hey!

hépatite [epatit] *nf* hepatitis, liver infection

héraldique [eraldik] *adj* heraldry

herbacé, e [ɛrbase] *adj* herbaceous

herbage [ɛrbaʒ] *nm* pasture

herbe [ɛrb(ə)] *nf* grass; (*Culin, Méd*) herb; **en ~** unripe; (*fig*) budding; **touffe/brin d'~** clump/blade of grass

herbeux, -euse [ɛrbø, -øz] *adj* grassy

herbicide [ɛrbisid] *nm* weed-killer

herbier [ɛrbje] *nm* herbarium

herbivore [ɛrbivɔr] *nm* herbivore

herboriser [ɛrbɔrize] *vi* to collect plants

herboriste [ɛrbɔrist(ə)] *nm/f* herbalist

herboristerie [ɛrbɔristri] *nf* (*magasin*) herbalist's shop; (*commerce*) herb trade

herculéen, ne [ɛrkyleɛ̃, -ɛn] *adj* (*fig*) herculean

'hère ['ɛr] *nm*: **pauvre ~** poor wretch

héréditaire [ereditɛr] *adj* hereditary

hérédité [eredite] *nf* heredity

hérésie [erezi] *nf* heresy

hérétique [eretik] *nm/f* heretic

'hérissé, e ['erise] *adj* bristling; ~ **de** spiked with; (*fig*) bristling with

'hérisser ['erise] *vt*: ~ **qn** (*fig*) to ruffle sb; **se 'hérisser** *vi* to bristle, bristle up

'hérisson ['erisɔ̃] *nm* hedgehog

héritage [eritaʒ] *nm* inheritance; (*fig*) heritage; (: *legs*) legacy; **faire un (petit) ~** to come into (a little) money

hériter [erite] *vi*: ~ **de qch (de qn)** to inherit sth (from sb); ~ **de qn** to inherit sb's property

héritier, -ière [eritje, -jɛr] *nm/f* heir/heiress

hermaphrodite [ɛrmafrɔdit] *adj* (*Bot, Zool*) hermaphrodite

hermétique [ɛrmetik] *adj* (à l'*air*) airtight; (à l'*eau*) watertight; (*fig: écrivain, style*) abstruse; (: *visage*) impenetrable

hermétiquement [ɛrmetikmɑ̃] *adv* hermetically

hermine [ɛrmin] *nf* ermine

'hernie ['ɛrni] *nf* hernia

héroïne [erɔin] *nf* heroine; (*drogue*) heroin

héroïnomane [erɔinɔman] *nm/f* heroin addict

héroïque [erɔik] *adj* heroic

héroïquement [erɔikmɑ̃] *adv* heroically

héroïsme [erɔism(ə)] *nm* heroism

'héron ['erɔ̃] *nm* heron

'héros ['ero] *nm* hero

herpès [ɛrpɛs] *nm* herpes

'herse ['ɛrs(ə)] *nf* harrow; (*de château*) portcullis

hertz [ɛrts] *nm* (*Élec*) hertz

hertzien, ne [ɛrtsjɛ̃, -ɛn] *adj* (*Élec*) Hertzian

hésitant, e [ezitɑ̃, -ɑ̃t] *adj* hesitant

hésitation [ezitasjɔ̃] *nf* hesitation

hésiter [ezite] *vi*: ~ **(à faire)** to hesitate (to do); ~ **sur qch** to hesitate over sth

hétéro [etero] *adj inv* (*hétérosexuel(le)*) hetero

hétéroclite [eterɔklit] *adj* heterogeneous; (*objets*) sundry

hétérogène [eterɔʒɛn] *adj* heterogeneous

hétérosexuel, le [eterɔsɛkɥɛl] *adj* heterosexual

'hêtre ['ɛtr(ə)] *nm* beech

heure [œr] *nf* hour; (*Scol*) period; (*moment, moment fixé*) time; **c'est l'~** it's time; **pourriez-vous me donner l'~, s'il vous plaît?** could you tell me the time, please?; **quelle ~ est-il?** what time is it?; **2 ~s (du matin)** 2 o'clock (in the morning); **à la bonne ~!** (*parfois ironique*) splendid!; **être à l'~** to be on time; (*montre*) to be right; **le bus passe à l'~** the bus runs on the hour; **mettre à l'~** to set right; **100 km à l'~** ≈ 60 miles an *ou* per hour; **à toute ~** at any time; **24 ~s sur 24** round the clock, 24 hours a day; **à l'~ qu'il est** at this time (of day); (*fig*) now; **à l'~ actuelle** at the present time; **sur l'~** at once; **pour l'~** for the time being; **d'~ en ~** from one hour to the next; (*régulièrement*) hourly; **d'une ~ à l'autre** from hour to hour; **de bonne ~** early; **deux ~s de marche/travail** two hours' walking/work; **une ~ d'arrêt** an hour's break *ou* stop; ~ **d'été** summer time (*Brit*), daylight saving time (*US*); ~ **de pointe** rush hour; ~**s de bureau** office hours; ~**s supplémentaires** overtime *sg*

heureusement [œrøzmɑ̃] *adv* (*par bonheur*) fortunately, luckily; ~ **que ...** it's a good job that ..., fortunately ...

heureux, -euse [œrø, -øz] *adj* happy; (*chanceux*) lucky, fortunate; (*judicieux*) felicitous, fortunate; **être ~ de qch** to be pleased *ou* happy about sth; **être ~ de faire/que** to be pleased *ou* happy to do/that; **s'estimer ~ de qch/que** to consider o.s. fortunate with sth/that; **encore ~ que ...** just as well that ...

'heurt ['œr] *nm* (*choc*) collision; **'heurts** *nmpl* (*fig*) clashes

'heurté, e ['œrte] *adj* (*fig*) jerky, uneven; (: *couleurs*) clashing

'heurter ['œrte] *vt* (*mur*) to strike, hit; (*personne*) to collide with; (*fig*) to go against, upset; **se 'heurter** (*couleurs, tons*) to clash; **se ~ à** to collide with; (*fig*) to come up against; ~ **qn de front** to clash head-on with sb

'heurtoir ['œrtwar] *nm* door knocker

hévéa [evea] *nm* rubber tree

hexagonal, e, -aux [ɛgzagɔnal, -o] *adj*
hexagonal; *(français)* French *(see note at hexagone)*
hexagone [ɛgzagɔn] *nm* hexagon; *(la France)*
France *(because of its roughly hexagonal shape)*
HF *sigle f* (= *haute fréquence*) HF
hiatus [jatys] *nm* hiatus
hibernation [ibɛrnasjɔ̃] *nf* hibernation
hiberner [ibɛrne] *vi* to hibernate
hibiscus [ibiskys] *nm* hibiscus
'hibou, x ['ibu] *nm* owl
'hic ['ik] *nm (fam)* snag
'hideusement ['idøzmã] *adv* hideously
'hideux, -euse ['idø, -øz] *adj* hideous
hier [jɛr] *adv* yesterday; **~ matin/soir/midi**
yesterday morning/evening/at midday; **toute
la journée d'~** all day yesterday; **toute la
matinée d'~** all yesterday morning
'hiérarchie ['jerarʃi] *nf* hierarchy
'hiérarchique ['jerarʃik] *adj* hierarchic
'hiérarchiquement ['jerarʃikmã] *adv*
hierarchically
'hiérarchiser ['jerarʃize] *vt* to organize into a
hierarchy
'hiéroglyphe ['jeroglif] *nm* hieroglyphic
'hiéroglyphique ['jeroglifik] *adj* hieroglyphic
'hi-fi ['ifi] *nf inv* hi-fi
hilarant, e [ilarã, -ãt] *adj* hilarious
hilare [ilar] *adj* mirthful
hilarité [ilarite] *nf* hilarity, mirth
Himalaya [imalaja] *nm*: **l'~** the Himalayas *pl*
himalayen, ne [imalajɛ̃, -ɛn] *adj* Himalayan
hindou, e [ɛ̃du] *adj, nm/f* Hindu; *(Indien)* Indian
hindouisme [ɛ̃duism(ə)] *nm* Hinduism
Hindoustan [ɛ̃dustã] *nm*: **l'~** Hindustan
'hippie ['ipi] *nm/f* hippy
hippique [ipik] *adj* equestrian, horse *cpd*
hippisme [ipism(ə)] *nm* (horse-)riding
hippocampe [ipokãp] *nm* sea horse
hippodrome [ipodrom] *nm* racecourse
hippophagique [ipofaʒik] *adj*: **boucherie ~**
horse butcher's
hippopotame [ipopotam] *nm* hippopotamus
hirondelle [irɔ̃dɛl] *nf* swallow
hirsute [irsyt] *adj (personne)* hairy; *(barbe)*
shaggy; *(tête)* tousled
hispanique [ispanik] *adj* Hispanic
hispanisant, e [ispanizã, -ãt], **hispaniste**
[ispanist(ə)] *nm/f* Hispanist
hispano-américain, e [ispanoamerikɛ̃, -ɛn] *adj*
Spanish-American
hispano-arabe [ispanoarab] *adj* Hispano-
Moresque
'hisser ['ise] *vt* to hoist, haul up; **se 'hisser sur**
to haul o.s. up onto
histoire [istwar] *nf (science, événements)* history;
(anecdote, récit, mensonge) story; *(affaire)* business
no pl; *(chichis: gén pl)* fuss *no pl*; **histoires** *nfpl*
(ennuis) trouble *sg*; **l'~ de France** French history,
the history of France; **l'~ sainte** biblical
history; **~ géo** humanities *pl*; **une ~ de** *(fig)* a
question of
histologie [istɔlɔʒi] *nf* histology

historien, ne [istɔrjɛ̃, -ɛn] *nm/f* historian
historique [istɔrik] *adj* historical; *(important)*
historic ▷ *nm (exposé, récit)*: **faire l'~ de** to give
the background to
historiquement [istɔrikmã] *adv* historically
'hit-parade ['itparad] *nm*: **le ~** the charts
HIV *sigle m* (= *human immunodeficiency virus*) HIV
hiver [ivɛr] *nm* winter; **en ~** in winter
hivernal, e, -aux [ivɛrnal, -o] *adj (de l'hiver)*
winter *cpd*; *(comme en hiver)* wintry
hivernant, e [ivɛrnã, -ãt] *nm/f* winter holiday-
maker
hiverner [ivɛrne] *vi* to winter
HLM *sigle m ou f* (= *habitations à loyer modéré*) low-
rent, state-owned housing; **un(e) ~** ≈ a council flat
(ou house) (Brit), ≈ a public housing unit (US)
Hme *abr* (= *homme*) M
HO *abr* (= *hors œuvre*) labour not included *(on
invoices)*
'hobby ['ɔbi] *nm* hobby
'hochement ['ɔʃmã] *nm*: **~ de tête** nod; shake of
the head
'hocher ['ɔʃe] *vt*: **~ la tête** to nod; *(signe négatif ou
dubitatif)* to shake one's head
'hochet ['ɔʃɛ] *nm* rattle
'hockey ['ɔkɛ] *nm*: **~ (sur glace/gazon)** (ice/
field) hockey
'hockeyeur, -euse ['ɔkɛjœr, -øz] *nm/f* hockey
player
'holà ['ɔla] *nm*: **mettre le ~ à qch** to put a stop to
sth
'holding ['ɔldiŋ] *nm* holding company
'hold-up ['ɔldœp] *nm inv* hold-up
'hollandais, e ['ɔlãdɛ, -ɛz] *adj* Dutch ▷ *nm (Ling)*
Dutch ▷ *nm/f*: **'Hollandais, e** Dutchman/
woman; **les 'Hollandais** the Dutch
'Hollande ['ɔlãd] *nf*: **la ~** Holland ▷ *nm*:
'hollande *(fromage)* Dutch cheese
holocauste [ɔlɔkost(ə)] *nm* holocaust
hologramme [ɔlɔgram] *nm* hologram
'homard ['ɔmar] *nm* lobster
homéopathe [ɔmeɔpat] *n* homoeopath
homéopathie [ɔmeɔpati] *nf* homoeopathy
homéopathique [ɔmeɔpatik] *adj* homoeopathic
homérique [ɔmerik] *adj* Homeric
homicide [ɔmisid] *nm* murder ▷ *nm/f*
murderer/eress; **~ involontaire** manslaughter
hommage [ɔmaʒ] *nm* tribute; **hommages** *nmpl*:
présenter ses ~s to pay one's respects; **rendre
~ à** to pay tribute *ou* homage to; **en ~ de** as a
token of; **faire ~ de qch à qn** to present sb with
sth
homme [ɔm] *nm* man; *(espèce humaine)*: **l'~** man,
mankind; **~ d'affaires** businessman; **~ des
cavernes** caveman; **~ d'Église** churchman,
clergyman; **~ d'État** statesman; **~ de loi**
lawyer; **~ de main** hired man; **~ de paille**
stooge; **~ politique** politician; **l'~ de la rue** the
man in the street; **~ à tout faire** odd-job man
homme-grenouille [ɔmgrənuj] *(pl hommes-
grenouilles)* *nm* frogman
homme-orchestre [ɔmɔrkɛstr(ə)] *(pl hommes-*

h

orchestres) *nm* one-man band

homme-sandwich [ɔmsɑ̃dwitʃ] (*pl* **hommes-sandwichs**) *nm* sandwich (board) man

homo [ɔmo] *adj*, *nm/f* = **homosexuel**

homogène [ɔmɔʒɛn] *adj* homogeneous

homogénéisé, e [ɔmɔʒeneize] *adj*: **lait ~** homogenized milk

homogénéité [ɔmɔʒeneite] *nf* homogeneity

homologation [ɔmɔlɔɡasjɔ̃] *nf* ratification; official recognition

homologue [ɔmɔlɔɡ] *nm/f* counterpart, opposite number

homologué, e [ɔmɔlɔɡe] *adj* (*Sport*) officially recognized, ratified; (*tarif*) authorized

homologuer [ɔmɔlɔɡe] *vt* (*Jur*) to ratify; (*Sport*) to recognize officially, ratify

homonyme [ɔmɔnim] *nm* (*Ling*) homonym; (*d'une personne*) namesake

homosexualité [ɔmɔsɛksɥalite] *nf* homosexuality

homosexuel, le [ɔmɔsɛksɥɛl] *adj* homosexual

'Honduras [ʼɔ̃dyras] *nm*: **le ~** Honduras

'hondurien, ne [ʼɔ̃dyrjɛ̃, -ɛn] *adj* Honduran

'Hong-Kong [ʼɔ̃ɡkɔ̃ɡ] *n* Hong Kong

'hongre [ʼɔ̃ɡʀ(ə)] *adj* (*cheval*) gelded ▷ *nm* gelding

'Hongrie [ʼɔ̃ɡʀi] *nf*: **la ~** Hungary

'hongrois, e [ʼɔ̃ɡʀwa, -waz] *adj* Hungarian ▷ *nm* (*Ling*) Hungarian ▷ *nm/f*: **'Hongrois, e** Hungarian

honnête [ɔnɛt] *adj* (*intègre*) honest; (*juste, satisfaisant*) fair

honnêtement [ɔnɛtmɑ̃] *adv* honestly

honnêteté [ɔnɛtte] *nf* honesty

honneur [ɔnœʀ] *nm* honour; (*mérite*): **l'~ lui revient** the credit is his; **à qui ai-je l'~?** to whom have I the pleasure of speaking?; **"j'ai l'~ de ..."** "I have the honour of ..."; **en l'~ de** (*personne*) in honour of; (*événement*) on the occasion of; **faire ~ à** (*engagements*) to honour; (*famille, professeur*) to be a credit to; (*fig: repas etc*) to do justice to; **être à l'~** to be in the place of honour; **être en ~** to be in favour; **membre d'~** honorary member; **table d'~** top table

Honolulu [ɔnɔlyly] *n* Honolulu

honorable [ɔnɔʀabl(ə)] *adj* worthy, honourable; (*suffisant*) decent

honorablement [ɔnɔʀabləmɑ̃] *adv* honourably; decently

honoraire [ɔnɔʀɛʀ] *adj* honorary; **honoraires** *nmpl* fees; **professeur ~** professor emeritus

honorer [ɔnɔʀe] *vt* to honour; (*estimer*) to hold in high regard; (*faire honneur à*) to do credit to; **~ qn de** to honour sb with; **s'honorer de** to pride o.s. upon

honorifique [ɔnɔʀifik] *adj* honorary

'honte [ʼɔ̃t] *nf* shame; **avoir ~ de** to be ashamed of; **faire ~ à qn** to make sb (feel) ashamed

'honteusement [ʼɔ̃tøzmɑ̃] *adv* ashamedly; shamefully

'honteux, -euse [ʼɔ̃tø, -øz] *adj* ashamed; (*conduite, acte*) shameful, disgraceful

hôpital, -aux [ɔpital, -o] *nm* hospital

'hoquet [ʼɔkɛ] *nm* hiccough; **avoir le ~** to have (the) hiccoughs

'hoqueter [ʼɔkte] *vi* to hiccough

horaire [ɔʀɛʀ] *adj* hourly ▷ *nm* timetable, schedule; **horaires** *nmpl* (*heures de travail*) hours; **~ flexible** *ou* **mobile** *ou* **à la carte** *ou* **souple** flex(i)time

'horde [ʼɔʀd(ə)] *nf* horde

'horions [ʼɔʀjɔ̃] *nmpl* blows

horizon [ɔʀizɔ̃] *nm* horizon; (*paysage*) landscape, view; **sur l'~** on the skyline *ou* horizon

horizontal, e, -aux [ɔʀizɔ̃tal, -o] *adj* horizontal ▷ *nf*: **à l'~e** on the horizontal

horizontalement [ɔʀizɔ̃talmɑ̃] *adv* horizontally

horloge [ɔʀlɔʒ] *nf* clock; **l'~ parlante** the speaking clock; **~ normande** grandfather clock; **~ physiologique** biological clock

horloger, -ère [ɔʀlɔʒe, -ɛʀ] *nm/f* watchmaker; clockmaker

horlogerie [ɔʀlɔʒʀi] *nf* watchmaking; watchmaker's (shop); clockmaker's (shop); **pièces d'~** watch parts *ou* components

'hormis [ʼɔʀmi] *prép* save

hormonal, e, -aux [ɔʀmɔnal, -o] *adj* hormonal

hormone [ɔʀmɔn] *nf* hormone

horodaté, e [ɔʀodate] *adj* (*ticket*) time- and date-stamped; (*stationnement*) pay and display

horodateur, -trice [ɔʀodatœʀ, -tris] *adj* (*appareil*) for stamping the time and date ▷ *nm/f* (parking) ticket machine

horoscope [ɔʀɔskɔp] *nm* horoscope

horreur [ɔʀœʀ] *nf* horror; **avoir ~ de** to loathe, detest; **quelle ~!** how awful!; **cela me fait ~** I find that awful

horrible [ɔʀibl(ə)] *adj* horrible

horriblement [ɔʀibləmɑ̃] *adv* horribly

horrifiant, e [ɔʀifjɑ̃, -ɑ̃t] *adj* horrifying

horrifier [ɔʀifje] *vt* to horrify

horrifique [ɔʀifik] *adj* horrific

horripilant, e [ɔʀipilɑ̃, -ɑ̃t] *adj* exasperating

horripiler [ɔʀipile] *vt* to exasperate

'hors [ʼɔʀ] *prép* except (for); **~ de** out of; **~ ligne** (*Inform*) off line; **~ pair** outstanding; **~ de propos** inopportune; **~ série** (*sur mesure*) made-to-order; (*exceptionnel*) exceptional; **~ service (HS)**, **~ d'usage** out of service; **être ~ de soi** to be beside o.s.

'hors-bord [ʼɔʀbɔʀ] *nm inv* outboard motor; (*canot*) speedboat (with outboard motor)

'hors-concours [ʼɔʀkɔ̃kuʀ] *adj inv* ineligible to compete; (*fig*) in a class of one's own

'hors-d'œuvre [ʼɔʀdœvʀ(ə)] *nm inv* hors d'œuvre

'hors-jeu [ʼɔʀʒø] *nm inv* being offside *no pl*

'hors-la-loi [ʼɔʀlalwa] *nm inv* outlaw

'hors-piste, **'hors-pistes** [ʼɔʀpist] *nm inv* (*Ski*) cross-country

hors-taxe [ʼɔʀtaks] *adj* (*sur une facture, prix*) excluding VAT; (*boutique, marchandises*) duty-free

'hors-texte [ʼɔʀtɛkst(ə)] *nm inv* plate

hortensia [ɔʀtɑ̃sja] *nm* hydrangea
horticole [ɔʀtikɔl] *adj* horticultural
horticulteur, -trice [ɔʀtikyltœʀ, -tʀis] *nm/f*
horticulturalist (Brit), horticulturist (US)
horticulture [ɔʀtikyltyʀ] *nf* horticulture
hospice [ɔspis] *nm* (*de vieillards*) home; (*asile*)
hospice
hospitalier, -ière [ɔspitalje, -jɛʀ] *adj* (*accueillant*)
hospitable; (*Méd: service, centre*) hospital *cpd*
hospitalisation [ɔspitalizasjɔ̃] *nf*
hospitalization
hospitaliser [ɔspitalize] *vt* to take (*ou* send) to
hospital, hospitalize
hospitalité [ɔspitalite] *nf* hospitality
hospitalo-universitaire [ɔspitalɔynivɛʀsitɛʀ]
adj: **centre ~ (CHU)** ≈ (teaching) hospital
hostie [ɔsti] *nf* host; (*Rel*)
hostile [ɔstil] *adj* hostile
hostilité [ɔstilite] *nf* hostility; **hostilités** *nfpl*
hostilities
hôte [ot] *nm* (*maître de maison*) host; (*client*)
patron; (*fig*) inhabitant, occupant ▷ *nm/f* (*invité*)
guest; **~ payant** paying guest
hôtel [otɛl] *nm* hotel; **aller à l'~** to stay in a
hotel; **~ (particulier)** (private) mansion; **~ de
ville** town hall
hôtelier, -ière [otəlje, -jɛʀ] *adj* hotel *cpd* ▷ *nm/f*
hotelier, hotel-keeper
hôtellerie [otɛlʀi] *nf* (*profession*) hotel business;
(*auberge*) inn
hôtesse [otɛs] *nf* hostess; **~ de l'air** flight
attendant; **~ (d'accueil)** receptionist
'hotte [ɔt] *nf* (*panier*) basket (*carried on the back*);
(*de cheminée*) hood; **~ aspirante** cooker hood
'houblon [ublɔ̃] *nm* (*Bot*) hop; (*pour la bière*)
hops *pl*
'houe [u] *nf* hoe
'houille [uj] *nf* coal; **~ blanche** hydroelectric
power
'houiller, -ère [uje, -ɛʀ] *adj* coal *cpd*; (*terrain*)
coal-bearing ▷ *nf* coal mine
'houle [ul] *nf* swell
'houlette [ulɛt] *nf*: **sous la ~ de** under the
guidance of
'houleux, -euse [ulø, -øz] *adj* heavy, swelling;
(*fig*) stormy, turbulent
'houppe [up], **'houppette** [upɛt] *nf* powder
puff; (*cheveux*) tuft
'hourra [uʀa] *nm* cheer ▷ *excl* hurrah!
'houspiller [uspije] *vt* to scold
'housse [us] *nf* cover; (*pour protéger provisoirement*)
dust cover; (*pour recouvrir à neuf*) loose *ou* stretch
cover; **~ (penderie)** hanging wardrobe
'houx [u] *nm* holly
hovercraft [ovœʀkʀaft] *nm* hovercraft
HS *abr* = **hors service**
HT *abr* = **'hors taxe**
'hublot [yblo] *nm* porthole
'huche [yʃ] *nf*: **à pain** bread bin
'huées [ɥe] *nfpl* boos
'huer [ɥe] *vt* to boo; (*hibou, chouette*) to hoot
huile [ɥil] *nf* oil; (*Art*) oil painting; (*fam*) bigwig;

mer d'~ (*très calme*) glassy sea, sea of glass; **faire
tache d'~** (*fig*) to spread; **~ d'arachide**
groundnut oil; **~ essentielle** essential oil; **~ de
foie de morue** cod-liver oil; **~ de ricin** castor
oil; **~ solaire** suntan oil; **~ de table** salad oil
huiler [ɥile] *vt* to oil
huilerie [ɥilʀi] *nf* (*usine*) oil-works
huileux, -euse [ɥilø, -øz] *adj* oily
huilier [ɥilje] *nm* (oil and vinegar) cruet
huis [ɥi] *nm*: **à ~ clos** in camera
huissier [ɥisje] *nm* usher; (*Jur*) ≈ bailiff
'huit [ɥi(t)] *num* eight; **samedi en ~** a week on
Saturday; **dans ~ jours** in a week('s time)
'huitaine [ɥitɛn] *nf*: **une ~ de** about eight,
eight or so; **une ~ de jours** a week or so
'huitante [ɥitɑ̃t] *num* (*Suisse*) eighty
'huitième [ɥitjɛm] *num* eighth
huître [ɥitʀ(ə)] *nf* oyster
'hululement [ylylmɑ̃] *nm* hooting
'hululer [ylyle] *vi* to hoot
humain, e [ymɛ̃, -ɛn] *adj* human; (*compatissant*)
humane ▷ *nm* human (being)
humainement [ymɛnmɑ̃] *adv* humanly;
humanely
humanisation [ymanizasjɑ̃] *nf* humanization
humaniser [ymanize] *vt* to humanize
humaniste [ymanist(ə)] *nm/f* (*Ling*) classicist;
humanist
humanitaire [ymanitɛʀ] *adj* humanitarian
humanitarisme [ymanitaʀism(ə)] *nm*
humanitarianism
humanité [ymanite] *nf* humanity
humanoïde [ymanɔid] *nm/f* humanoid
humble [œ̃bl(ə)] *adj* humble
humblement [œ̃bləmɑ̃] *adv* humbly
humecter [ymɛkte] *vt* to dampen; **s'~ les
lèvres** to moisten one's lips
'humer [yme] *vt* to inhale; (*pour sentir*) to smell
humérus [ymeʀys] *nm* (*Anat*) humerus
humeur [ymœʀ] *nf* mood; (*tempérament*) temper;
(*irritation*) bad temper; **de bonne/mauvaise ~** in
a good/bad mood; **être d'~ à faire qch** to be in
the mood for doing sth
humide [ymid] *adj* (*linge*) damp; (*main, yeux*)
moist; (*climat, chaleur*) humid; (*saison, route*) wet
humidificateur [ymidifikatœʀ] *nm* humidifier
humidifier [ymidifje] *vt* to humidify
humidité [ymidite] *nf* humidity; dampness;
traces d'~ traces of moisture *ou* damp
humiliant, e [ymiljɑ̃, -ɑ̃t] *adj* humiliating
humiliation [ymiljasjɔ̃] *nf* humiliation
humilier [ymilje] *vt* to humiliate; **s'~ devant
qn** to humble o.s. before sb
humilité [ymilite] *nf* humility
humoriste [ymɔʀist(ə)] *nm/f* humorist
humoristique [ymɔʀistik] *adj* humorous;
humoristic
humour [ymuʀ] *nm* humour; **avoir de l'~** to
have a sense of humour; **~ noir** sick humour
humus [ymys] *nm* humus
'huppé, e [ype] *adj* crested; (*fam*) posh
'hurlement [yʀləmɑ̃] *nm* howling *no pl*, howl;

h

yelling *no pl*, yell

'**hurler** ['yʀle] *vi* to howl, yell; (*fig*: *vent*) to howl; (: *couleurs etc*) to clash; ~ **à la mort** (*chien*) to bay at the moon

hurluberlu [yʀlybɛʀly] *nm* (*péj*) crank ▷ *adj* cranky

'**hutte** ['yt] *nf* hut

hybride [ibʀid] *adj* hybrid

hydratant, e [idʀatɑ̃, -ɑ̃t] *adj* (*crème*) moisturizing

hydrate [idʀat] *nm*: ~**s de carbone** carbohydrates

hydrater [idʀate] *vt* to hydrate

hydraulique [idʀolik] *adj* hydraulic

hydravion [idʀavjɔ̃] *nm* seaplane, hydroplane

hydro... [idʀɔ] *préfixe* hydro...

hydrocarbure [idʀɔkaʀbyʀ] *nm* hydrocarbon

hydrocution [idʀɔkysjɔ̃] *nf* immersion syncope

hydro-électrique [idʀɔelɛktʀik] *adj* hydroelectric

hydrogène [idʀɔʒɛn] *nm* hydrogen

hydroglisseur [idʀɔglisœʀ] *nm* hydroplane

hydrographie [idʀɔgʀafi] *nf* (*fleuves*) hydrography

hydrophile [idʀɔfil] *adj voir* **coton**

hyène [jɛn] *nf* hyena

hygiène [iʒjɛn] *nf* hygiene; ~ **intime** personal hygiene

hygiénique [iʒenik] *adj* hygienic

hymne [imn(ə)] *nm* hymn; ~ **national** national anthem

hyper... [ipɛʀ] *préfixe* hyper...

hyperlien [ipɛʀljɛ̃] *nm* (*Inform*) hyperlink

hypermarché [ipɛʀmaʀʃe] *nm* hypermarket

hypermétrope [ipɛʀmetʀɔp] *adj* long-sighted

hypernerveux, -euse [ipɛʀnɛʀvø, -øz] *adj* highly-strung

hypersensible [ipɛʀsɑ̃sibl(ə)] *adj* hypersensitive

hypertendu, e [ipɛʀtɑ̃dy] *adj* having high blood pressure, hypertensive

hypertension [ipɛʀtɑ̃sjɔ̃] *nf* high blood pressure, hypertension

hypertexte [ipɛʀtɛkst] *nm* (*Inform*) hypertext

hypertrophié, e [ipɛʀtʀɔfje] *adj* hypertrophic

hypnose [ipnoz] *nf* hypnosis

hypnotique [ipnɔtik] *adj* hypnotic

hypnotiser [ipnɔtize] *vt* to hypnotize

hypnotiseur [ipnɔtizœʀ] *nm* hypnotist

hypnotisme [ipnɔtism(ə)] *nm* hypnotism

hypocondriaque [ipɔkɔ̃dʀijak] *adj* hypochondriac

hypocrisie [ipɔkʀizi] *nf* hypocrisy

hypocrite [ipɔkʀit] *adj* hypocritical ▷ *nm/f* hypocrite

hypocritement [ipɔkʀitmɑ̃] *adv* hypocritically

hypotendu, e [ipɔtɑ̃dy] *adj* having low blood pressure, hypotensive

hypotension [ipɔtɑ̃sjɔ̃] *nf* low blood pressure, hypotension

hypoténuse [ipɔtenyz] *nf* hypotenuse

hypothécaire [ipɔtekɛʀ] *adj* mortgage; **garantie/prêt** ~ mortgage security/loan

hypothèque [ipɔtɛk] *nf* mortgage

hypothéquer [ipɔteke] *vt* to mortgage

hypothermie [ipɔtɛʀmi] *nf* hypothermia

hypothèse [ipɔtɛz] *nf* hypothesis; **dans l'**~ **où** assuming that

hypothétique [ipɔtetik] *adj* hypothetical

hypothétiquement [ipɔtetikmɑ̃] *adv* hypothetically

hystérectomie [isteʀɛktɔmi] *nf* hysterectomy

hystérie [isteʀi] *nf* hysteria; ~ **collective** mass hysteria

hystérique [isteʀik] *adj* hysterical

Hz *abr* (= Hertz) Hz

Ii

I, i [i] *nm inv* I, i; **I comme Irma** I for Isaac (*Brit*) *ou* Item (*US*)
IAC *sigle f* (= *insémination artificielle entre conjoints*) AIH
IAD *sigle f* (= *insémination artificielle par donneur extérieur*) AID
ibère [ibɛʀ] *adj* Iberian ▷ *nm/f*: **Ibère** Iberian
ibérique [ibeʀik] *adj*: **la péninsule ~** the Iberian peninsula
ibid. [ibid] *abr* (= *ibidem*) ibid., ib.
iceberg [isbɛʀg] *nm* iceberg
ici [isi] *adv* here; **jusqu'~** as far as this; (*temporel*) until now; **d'~ là** by then; (*en attendant*) in the meantime; **d'~ peu** before long
icône [ikon] *nf* (*aussi Inform*) icon
iconoclaste [ikɔnɔklast(ə)] *nm/f* iconoclast
iconographie [ikɔnɔgʀafi] *nf* iconography; (*illustrations*) (collection of) illustrations
id. [id] *abr* (=*idem*) id.
idéal, e, -aux [ideal, -o] *adj* ideal ▷ *nm* ideal; (*système de valeurs*) ideals *pl*
idéalement [idealmã] *adv* ideally
idéalisation [idealizasjɔ̃] *nf* idealization
idéaliser [idealize] *vt* to idealize
idéalisme [idealism(ə)] *nm* idealism
idéaliste [idealist(ə)] *adj* idealistic ▷ *nm/f* idealist
idée [ide] *nf* idea; (*illusion*): **se faire des ~s** to imagine things, get ideas into one's head; **avoir dans l'~ que** to have an idea that; **mon ~, c'est que ...** I suggest that ..., I think that ...; **à l'~ de/que** at the idea of/that, at the thought of/that; **je n'ai pas la moindre ~** I haven't the faintest idea; **avoir ~ que** to have an idea that; **avoir des ~s larges/étroites** to be broad-/narrow-minded; **venir à l'~ de qn** to occur to sb; **en voilà des ~s!** the very idea!; **~ fixe** idée fixe, obsession; **~s noires** black *ou* dark thoughts; **~s reçues** accepted ideas *ou* wisdom
identifiable [idɑ̃tifjabl(ə)] *adj* identifiable
identifiant [idɑ̃tifjɑ̃] *nm* (*Inform*) login
identification [idɑ̃tifikasjɔ̃] *nf* identification
identifier [idɑ̃tifje] *vt* to identify; **~ qch/qn à** to identify sth/sb with; **s'~ avec** *ou* **à qn/qch** (*héros etc*) to identify with sb/sth
identique [idɑ̃tik] *adj*: **~ (à)** identical (to)

identité [idɑ̃tite] *nf* identity; **~ judiciaire** (*Police*) ≈ Criminal Records Office
idéogramme [ideɔgʀam] *nm* ideogram
idéologie [ideɔlɔʒi] *nf* ideology
idéologique [ideɔlɔʒik] *adj* ideological
idiomatique [idjɔmatik] *adj*: **expression ~** idiom, idiomatic expression
idiome [idjom] *nm* (*Ling*) idiom
idiot, e [idjo, idjɔt] *adj* idiotic ▷ *nm/f* idiot
idiotie [idjɔsi] *nf* idiocy; (*propos*) idiotic remark
idiotisme [idjɔtism(ə)] *nm* idiom, idiomatic phrase
idoine [idwan] *adj* fitting
idolâtrer [idɔlɑtʀe] *vt* to idolize
idolâtrie [idɔlɑtʀi] *nf* idolatry
idole [idɔl] *nf* idol
idylle [idil] *nf* idyll
idyllique [idilik] *adj* idyllic
if [if] *nm* yew
IFOP [ifɔp] *sigle m* (= *Institut français d'opinion publique*) French market research institute
IGH *sigle m* = **immeuble de grande hauteur**
igloo [iglu] *nm* igloo
IGN *sigle m* = **Institut géographique national**
ignare [iɲaʀ] *adj* ignorant
ignifuge [iɲify3] *adj* fireproofing ▷ *nm* fireproofing (substance)
ignifuger [iɲify3e] *vt* to fireproof
ignoble [iɲɔbl(ə)] *adj* vile
ignominie [iɲɔmini] *nf* ignominy; (*acte*) ignominious *ou* base act
ignominieux, -euse [iɲɔminjø, øz] *adj* ignominious
ignorance [iɲɔʀɑ̃s] *nf* ignorance; **dans l'~ de** in ignorance of, ignorant of
ignorant, e [iɲɔʀɑ̃, -ɑ̃t] *adj* ignorant ▷ *nm/f*: **faire l'~** to pretend one doesn't know; **~ de** ignorant of, not aware of; **~ en** ignorant of, knowing nothing of
ignoré, e [iɲɔʀe] *adj* unknown
ignorer [iɲɔʀe] *vt* (*ne pas connaître*) not to know, be unaware *ou* ignorant of; (*être sans expérience de*: *plaisir, guerre etc*) not to know about, have no experience of; (*bouder: personne*) to ignore; **j'ignore comment/si** I do not know how/if; **~ que** to be unaware that, not to know that; **je**

n'ignore pas que ... I'm not forgetting that ...,
I'm not unaware that ...; **je l'ignore** I don't
know

IGPN sigle f (= Inspection générale de la police nationale)
police disciplinary body

IGS sigle f (= Inspection générale des services) police
disciplinary body for Paris

iguane [igwan] nm iguana

il [il] pron he; (animal, chose, en tournure
impersonnelle) it; NB: en anglais les navires et les pays
sont en général assimilés aux femelles, et les bébés aux
choses, si le sexe n'est pas spécifié; **ils** they; **il neige**
it's snowing; voir aussi **avoir**

île [il] nf island; **les Î~s** the West Indies; **l'~ de
Beauté** Corsica; **l'~ Maurice** Mauritius; **les ~s
anglo-normandes** the Channel Islands; **les ~s
Britanniques** the British Isles; **les ~s Cocos** ou
Keeling the Cocos ou Keeling Islands; **les ~s
Cook** the Cook Islands; **les ~s Scilly** the Scilly
Isles, the Scillies; **les ~s Shetland** the Shetland
Islands, Shetland; **les ~s Sorlingues**; = **les îles
Scilly**; **les ~s Vierges** the Virgin Islands

iliaque [iljak] adj (Anat): **os/artère ~** iliac bone/
artery

illégal, e, -aux [ilegal, -o] adj illegal, unlawful
(Admin)

illégalement [ilegalmɑ̃] adv illegally

illégalité [ilegalite] nf illegality; unlawfulness;
être dans l'~ to be outside the law

illégitime [ileʒitim] adj illegitimate; (optimisme,
sévérité) unjustified, unwarranted

illégitimement [ileʒitimmɑ̃] adv illegitimately

illégitimité [ileʒitimite] nf illegitimacy;
gouverner dans l'~ to rule illegally

illettré, e [iletʀe] adj, nm/f illiterate

illicite [ilisit] adj illicit

illicitement [ilisitmɑ̃] adv illicitly

illico [iliko] adv (fam) pronto

illimité, e [ilimite] adj (immense) boundless,
unlimited; (congé, durée) indefinite, unlimited

illisible [ilizibl(ə)] adj illegible; (roman)
unreadable

illisiblement [iliziblǝmɑ̃] adv illegibly

illogique [iloʒik] adj illogical

illogisme [iloʒism(ə)] nm illogicality

illumination [ilyminɑsjɔ̃] nf illumination,
floodlighting; (inspiration) flash of inspiration;
illuminations nfpl illuminations, lights

illuminé, e [ilymine] adj lit up; illuminated,
floodlit ▷ nm/f (fig: péj) crank

illuminer [ilymine] vt to light up; (monument,
rue: pour une fête) to illuminate, floodlight;
s'illuminer vi to light up

illusion [ilyzjɔ̃] nf illusion; **se faire des ~s** to
delude o.s.; **faire ~** to delude ou fool people; **~
d'optique** optical illusion

illusionner [ilyzjɔne] vt to delude; **s'~ (sur qn/
qch)** to delude o.s. (about sb/sth)

illusionnisme [ilyzjɔnism(ə)] nm conjuring

illusionniste [ilyzjɔnist(ə)] nm/f conjuror

illusoire [ilyzwaʀ] adj illusory, illusive

illustrateur [ilystʀatœʀ] nm illustrator

illustratif, -ive [ilystʀatif, -iv] adj illustrative

illustration [ilystʀɑsjɔ̃] nf illustration; (d'un
ouvrage: photos) illustrations pl

illustre [ilystʀ(ə)] adj illustrious, renowned

illustré, e [ilystʀe] adj illustrated ▷ nm
illustrated magazine; (pour enfants) comic

illustrer [ilystʀe] vt to illustrate; **s'illustrer** to
become famous, win fame

îlot [ilo] nm small island, islet; (de maisons)
block; (petite zone): **un ~ de verdure** an island of
greenery, a patch of green

ils [il] pron voir **il**

image [imaʒ] nf (gén) picture; (comparaison,
ressemblance, Optique) image; **~ de** picture ou
image of; **~ d'Épinal** (social) stereotype; **~ de
marque** brand image; (d'une personne) (public)
image; (d'une entreprise) corporate image; **~
pieuse** holy picture

imagé, e [imaʒe] adj full of imagery

imaginable [imaʒinabl(ə)] adj imaginable;
difficilement ~ hard to imagine

imaginaire [imaʒinɛʀ] adj imaginary

imaginatif, -ive [imaʒinatif, -iv] adj
imaginative

imagination [imaʒinɑsjɔ̃] nf imagination;
(chimère) fancy, imagining; **avoir de l'~** to be
imaginative, have a good imagination

imaginer [imaʒine] vt to imagine; (croire):
qu'allez-vous ~ là? what on earth are you
thinking of?; (inventer: expédient, mesure) to
devise, think up; **s'imaginer** vt (se figurer: scène
etc) to imagine, picture; **s'~ à 60 ans** to picture
ou imagine o.s. at 60; **s'~ que** to imagine that;
s'~ pouvoir faire qch to think one can do sth;
j'imagine qu'il a voulu plaisanter I suppose
he was joking; **~ de faire** (se mettre dans l'idée de)
to dream up the idea of doing

imbattable [ɛ̃batabl(ə)] adj unbeatable

imbécile [ɛ̃besil] adj idiotic ▷ nm/f idiot; (Méd)
imbecile

imbécillité [ɛ̃besilite] nf idiocy; imbecility;
idiotic action (ou remark etc)

imberbe [ɛ̃bɛʀb(ə)] adj beardless

imbiber [ɛ̃bibe] vt: **~ qch de** to moisten ou wet
sth with; **s'imbiber de** to become saturated
with; **imbibé(e) d'eau** (chaussures, étoffe)
saturated; (terre) waterlogged

imbriqué, e [ɛ̃bʀike] adj overlapping

imbriquer [ɛ̃bʀike]: **s'imbriquer** vi to overlap
(each other); (fig) to become interlinked ou
interwoven

imbroglio [ɛ̃bʀɔljo] nm imbroglio

imbu, e [ɛ̃by] adj: **~ de** full of; **~ de soi-même/sa
supériorité** full of oneself/one's superiority

imbuvable [ɛ̃byvabl(ə)] adj undrinkable

imitable [imitabl(ə)] adj imitable; **facilement
~** easily imitated

imitateur, -trice [imitatœʀ, -tʀis] nm/f (gén)
imitator; (Music-Hall: d'une personnalité)
impersonator

imitation [imitɑsjɔ̃] nf imitation;
impersonation; **sac ~ cuir** bag in imitation ou

simulated leather; **à l'~ de** in imitation of
imiter [imite] *vt* to imitate; (*personne*) to imitate, impersonate; (*contrefaire: signature, document*) to forge, copy; (*ressembler à*) to look like; **il se leva et je l'imitai** he got up and I did likewise
imm. *abr* = **immeuble**
immaculé, e [imakyle] *adj* spotless, immaculate; **l'I~e Conception** (*Rel*) the Immaculate Conception
immanent, e [imanã, -ãt] *adj* immanent
immangeable [ɛ̃mãʒabl(ə)] *adj* inedible, uneatable
immanquable [ɛ̃mãkabl(ə)] *adj* (*cible*) impossible to miss; (*fatal, inévitable*) bound to happen, inevitable
immanquablement [ɛ̃mãkabləmã] *adv* inevitably
immatériel, le [imateʀjɛl] *adj* ethereal; (*Philosophie*) immaterial
immatriculation [imatʀikylasjɔ̃] *nf* registration
immatriculer [imatʀikyle] *vt* to register; **faire/ se faire ~** to register; **voiture immatriculée dans la Seine** car with a Seine registration (number)
immature [imatyʀ] *adj* immature
immaturité [imatyʀite] *nf* immaturity
immédiat, e [imedja, -at] *adj* immediate ▷ *nm*: **dans l'~** for the time being; **dans le voisinage ~ de** in the immediate vicinity of
immédiatement [imedjatmã] *adv* immediately
immémorial, e, -aux [imemɔʀjal, -o] *adj* ancient, age-old
immense [imãs] *adj* immense
immensément [imãsemã] *adv* immensely
immensité [imãsite] *nf* immensity
immerger [imɛʀʒe] *vt* to immerse, submerge; (*câble etc*) to lay under water; (*déchets*) to dump at sea; **s'immerger** *vi* (*sous-marin*) to dive, submerge
immérité, e [imeʀite] *adj* undeserved
immersion [imɛʀsjɔ̃] *nf* immersion
immettable [ɛ̃mɛtabl(ə)] *adj* unwearable
immeuble [imœbl(ə)] *nm* building ▷ *adj* (*Jur*) immovable, real; **~ locatif** block of rented flats (*Brit*), rental building (*US*); **~ de rapport** investment property
immigrant, e [imigʀã, -ãt] *nm/f* immigrant
immigration [imigʀasjɔ̃] *nf* immigration
immigré, e [imigʀe] *nm/f* immigrant
immigrer [imigʀe] *vi* to immigrate
imminence [iminãs] *nf* imminence
imminent, e [iminã, -ãt] *adj* imminent, impending
immiscer [imise]: **s'immiscer** *vi*: **s'~ dans** to interfere in *ou* with
immixtion [imiksjɔ̃] *nf* interference
immobile [imɔbil] *adj* still, motionless; (*pièce de machine*) fixed; (*fig*) unchanging; **rester/se tenir ~** to stay/keep still
immobilier, -ière [imɔbilje, -jɛʀ] *adj* property

cpd, in real property ▷ *nm*: **l'~** the property *ou* the real estate business
immobilisation [imɔbilizasjɔ̃] *nf* immobilization; **immobilisations** *nfpl* (*Jur*) fixed assets
immobiliser [imɔbilize] *vt* (*gén*) to immobilize; (*circulation, véhicule, affaires*) to bring to a standstill; **s'immobiliser** (*personne*) to stand still; (*machine, véhicule*) to come to a halt *ou* a standstill
immobilisme [imɔbilism(ə)] *nm* strong resistance *ou* opposition to change
immobilité [imɔbilite] *nf* immobility
immodéré, e [imɔdeʀe] *adj* immoderate, inordinate
immodérément [imɔdeʀemã] *adv* immoderately
immoler [imɔle] *vt* to sacrifice
immonde [imɔ̃d] *adj* foul; (*sale: ruelle, taudis*) squalid
immondices [imɔ̃dis] *nfpl* (*ordures*) refuse *sg*; (*saletés*) filth *sg*
immoral, e, -aux [imɔʀal, -o] *adj* immoral
immoralisme [imɔʀalism(ə)] *nm* immoralism
immoralité [imɔʀalite] *nf* immorality
immortaliser [imɔʀtalize] *vt* to immortalize
immortel, le [imɔʀtɛl] *adj* immortal ▷ *nf* (*Bot*) everlasting (flower)
immuable [imɥabl(ə)] *adj* (*inébranlable*) immutable; (*qui ne change pas*) unchanging; (*personne*): **~ dans ses convictions** immoveable (in one's convictions)
immunisation [imynizasjɔ̃] *nf* immunization
immunisé, e [im(m)ynize] *adj*: **~ contre** immune to
immuniser [imynize] *vt* (*Méd*) to immunize; **~ qn contre** to immunize sb against; (*fig*) to make sb immune to
immunitaire [imynitɛʀ] *adj* immune
immunité [imynite] *nf* immunity; **~ diplomatique** diplomatic immunity; **~ parlementaire** parliamentary privilege
immunologie [imynɔlɔʒi] *nf* immunology
immutabilité [imytabilite] *nf* immutability
impact [ɛ̃pakt] *nm* impact; **point d'~** point of impact
impair, e [ɛ̃pɛʀ] *adj* odd ▷ *nm* faux pas, blunder; **numéros ~s** odd numbers
impalpable [ɛ̃palpabl(ə)] *adj* impalpable
impaludation [ɛ̃palydasjɔ̃] *nf* inoculation against malaria
imparable [ɛ̃paʀabl(ə)] *adj* unstoppable
impardonnable [ɛ̃paʀdɔnabl(ə)] *adj* unpardonable, unforgivable; **vous êtes ~ d'avoir fait cela** it's unforgivable of you to have done that
imparfait, e [ɛ̃paʀfɛ, -ɛt] *adj* imperfect ▷ *nm* (*Ling*) imperfect (tense)
imparfaitement [ɛ̃paʀfɛtmã] *adv* imperfectly
impartial, e, -aux [ɛ̃paʀsjal, -o] *adj* impartial, unbiased
impartialité [ɛ̃paʀsjalite] *nf* impartiality

impartir [ɛ̃paʀtiʀ] *vt*: ~ **qch à qn** to assign sth to sb; (*dons*) to bestow sth upon sb; **dans les délais impartis** in the time allowed

impasse [ɛ̃pas] *nf* dead-end, cul-de-sac; (*fig*) deadlock; **être dans l'~** (*négociations*) to have reached deadlock; ~ **budgétaire** budget deficit

impassibilité [ɛ̃pasibilite] *nf* impassiveness

impassible [ɛ̃pasibl(ə)] *adj* impassive

impassiblement [ɛ̃pasibləmɑ̃] *adv* impassively

impatiemment [ɛ̃pasjamɑ̃] *adv* impatiently

impatience [ɛ̃pasjɑ̃s] *nf* impatience

impatient, e [ɛ̃pasjɑ̃, -ɑ̃t] *adj* impatient; ~ **de faire qch** keen *ou* impatient to do sth

impatienter [ɛ̃pasjɑ̃te] *vt* to irritate, annoy; **s'impatienter** *vi* to get impatient; **s'~ de/ contre** to lose patience at/with, grow impatient at/with

impayable [ɛ̃pɛjabl(ə)] *adj* (*drôle*) priceless

impayé, e [ɛ̃peje] *adj* unpaid, outstanding

impeccable [ɛ̃pekabl(ə)] *adj* faultless, impeccable; (*propre*) spotlessly clean; (*chic*) impeccably dressed; (*fam*) smashing

impeccablement [ɛ̃pekabləmɑ̃] *adv* impeccably

impénétrable [ɛ̃penetrabl(ə)] *adj* impenetrable

impénitent, e [ɛ̃penitɑ̃, -ɑ̃t] *adj* unrepentant

impensable [ɛ̃pɑ̃sabl(ə)] *adj* unthinkable, unbelievable

imper [ɛ̃pɛʀ] *nm* (*imperméable*) mac

impératif, -ive [ɛ̃peʀatif, -iv] *adj* imperative; (*Jur*) mandatory ▷ *nm* (*Ling*) imperative; **impératifs** *nmpl* requirements; demands

impérativement [ɛ̃peʀativmɑ̃] *adv* imperatively

impératrice [ɛ̃peʀatʀis] *nf* empress

imperceptible [ɛ̃pɛʀsɛptibl(ə)] *adj* imperceptible

imperceptiblement [ɛ̃pɛʀsɛptibləmɑ̃] *adv* imperceptibly

imperdable [ɛ̃pɛʀdabl(ə)] *adj* that cannot be lost

imperfectible [ɛ̃pɛʀfɛktibl(ə)] *adj* which cannot be perfected

imperfection [ɛ̃pɛʀfɛksjɔ̃] *nf* imperfection

impérial, e, -aux [ɛ̃peʀjal, -o] *adj* imperial ▷ *nf* upper deck; **autobus à ~e** double-decker bus

impérialisme [ɛ̃peʀjalism(ə)] *nm* imperialism

impérialiste [ɛ̃peʀjalist(ə)] *adj* imperialist

impérieusement [ɛ̃peʀjøzmɑ̃] *adv*: **avoir ~ besoin de qch** to have urgent need of sth

impérieux, -euse [ɛ̃peʀjø, -øz] *adj* (*caractère, ton*) imperious; (*obligation, besoin*) pressing, urgent

impérissable [ɛ̃peʀisabl(ə)] *adj* undying, imperishable

imperméabilisation [ɛ̃pɛʀmeabilizasjɔ̃] *nf* waterproofing

imperméabiliser [ɛ̃pɛʀmeabilize] *vt* to waterproof

imperméable [ɛ̃pɛʀmeabl(ə)] *adj* waterproof; (*Géo*) impermeable; (*fig*): ~ **à** impervious to ▷ *nm* raincoat; ~ **à l'air** airtight

impersonnel, le [ɛ̃pɛʀsɔnɛl] *adj* impersonal

impertinemment [ɛ̃pɛʀtinamɑ̃] *adv* impertinently

impertinence [ɛ̃pɛʀtinɑ̃s] *nf* impertinence

impertinent, e [ɛ̃pɛʀtinɑ̃, -ɑ̃t] *adj* impertinent

imperturbable [ɛ̃pɛʀtyʀbabl(ə)] *adj* (*personne*) imperturbable; (*sang-froid*) unshakeable; **rester ~** to remain unruffled

imperturbablement [ɛ̃pɛʀtyʀbabləmɑ̃] *adv* imperturbably; unshakeably

impétrant, e [ɛ̃petʀɑ̃, -ɑ̃t] *nm/f* (*Jur*) applicant

impétueux, -euse [ɛ̃petɥø, -øz] *adj* fiery

impétuosité [ɛ̃petɥozite] *nf* fieriness

impie [ɛ̃pi] *adj* impious, ungodly

impiété [ɛ̃pjete] *nf* impiety

impitoyable [ɛ̃pitwajabl(ə)] *adj* pitiless, merciless

impitoyablement [ɛ̃pitwajabləmɑ̃] *adv* mercilessly

implacable [ɛ̃plakabl(ə)] *adj* implacable

implacablement [ɛ̃plakabləmɑ̃] *adv* implacably

implant [ɛ̃plɑ̃] *nm* (*Méd*) implant

implantation [ɛ̃plɑ̃tasjɔ̃] *nf* establishment; settling; implantation

implanter [ɛ̃plɑ̃te] *vt* (*usine, industrie, usage*) to establish; (*colons etc*) to settle; (*idée, préjugé*) to implant; **s'implanter dans** *vi* to be established in; to settle in; to become implanted in

implémenter [ɛ̃plemɑ̃te] *vt* (*aussi Inform*) to implement

implication [ɛ̃plikasjɔ̃] *nf* implication

implicite [ɛ̃plisit] *adj* implicit

implicitement [ɛ̃plisitmɑ̃] *adv* implicitly

impliquer [ɛ̃plike] *vt* to imply; ~ **qn (dans)** to implicate sb (in)

implorant, e [ɛ̃plɔʀɑ̃, -ɑ̃t] *adj* imploring

implorer [ɛ̃plɔʀe] *vt* to implore

imploser [ɛ̃ploze] *vi* to implode

implosion [ɛ̃plozjɔ̃] *nf* implosion

impoli, e [ɛ̃pɔli] *adj* impolite, rude

impoliment [ɛ̃pɔlimɑ̃] *adv* impolitely

impolitesse [ɛ̃pɔlitɛs] *nf* impoliteness, rudeness; (*propos*) impolite *ou* rude remark

impondérable [ɛ̃pɔ̃deʀabl(ə)] *nm* imponderable

impopulaire [ɛ̃pɔpylɛʀ] *adj* unpopular

impopularité [ɛ̃pɔpylaʀite] *nf* unpopularity

importable [ɛ̃pɔʀtabl(ə)] *adj* (*Comm: marchandise*) importable; (*vêtement: immettable*) unwearable

importance [ɛ̃pɔʀtɑ̃s] *nf* importance; **avoir de l'~** to be important; **sans ~** unimportant; **d'~** important, considerable; **quelle ~?** what does it matter?

important, e [ɛ̃pɔʀtɑ̃, -ɑ̃t] *adj* important; (*en quantité*) considerable, sizeable; (*: gamme, dégâts*) extensive; (*péj: airs, ton*) self-important ▷ *nm*: **l'~** the important thing

importateur, -trice [ɛ̃pɔʀtatœʀ, -tʀis] *adj* importing ▷ *nm/f* importer; **pays ~ de blé** wheat-importing country

importation [ɛ̃pɔʀtasjɔ̃] *nf* import; introduction; (*produit*) import

importer [ɛ̃pɔʀte] *vt* (*Comm*) to import;

import-export [ɛ̃pɔʀɛkspɔʀ] *nm* import-export business

importun, e [ɛ̃pɔʀtœ̃, -yn] *adj* irksome, importunate; (*arrivée, visite*) inopportune, ill-timed ▷ *nm* intruder

importuner [ɛ̃pɔʀtyne] *vt* to bother

imposable [ɛ̃pozabl(ə)] *adj* taxable

imposant, e [ɛ̃pozɑ̃, -ɑ̃t] *adj* imposing

imposé, e [ɛ̃poze] *adj* (*soumis à l'impôt*) taxed; (*Gym etc: figures*) set

imposer [ɛ̃poze] *vt* (*taxer*) to tax; (*Rel*): ~ **les mains** to lay on hands; ~ **qch à qn** to impose sth on sb; **s'imposer** *vi* (*être nécessaire*) to be imperative; (*montrer sa proéminence*) to stand out, emerge; (*artiste: se faire connaître*) to win recognition, come to the fore; **en** ~ to be imposing; **en** ~ **à** to impress; **ça s'impose** it's essential, it's vital

imposition [ɛ̃pozisjɔ̃] *nf* (*Admin*) taxation

impossibilité [ɛ̃posibilite] *nf* impossibility; **être dans l'** ~ **de faire** to be unable to do, find it impossible to do

impossible [ɛ̃posibl(ə)] *adj* impossible ▷ *nm*: **l'** ~ the impossible; ~ **à faire** impossible to do; **il m'est** ~ **de le faire** it is impossible for me to do it, I can't possibly do it; **faire l'** ~ **(pour que)** to do one's utmost (so that); **si, par** ~ ... if, by some miracle ...

imposteur [ɛ̃pɔstœʀ] *nm* impostor

imposture [ɛ̃pɔstyʀ] *nf* imposture, deception

impôt [ɛ̃po] *nm* tax; (*taxes*) taxation, taxes *pl*; **impôts** *nmpl* (*contributions*) (income) tax *sg*; **payer 1000 euros d'** ~**s** to pay 1,000 euros in tax; ~ **direct/indirect** direct/indirect tax; ~ **sur le chiffre d'affaires** tax on turnover; ~ **foncier** land tax; ~ **sur la fortune** wealth tax; ~ **sur les plus-values** capital gains tax; ~ **sur le revenu** income tax; ~ **sur le RPP** personal income tax; ~ **sur les sociétés** tax on companies; ~**s locaux** rates, local taxes (US), ≈ council tax (*Brit*)

impotence [ɛ̃pɔtɑ̃s] *nf* disability

impotent, e [ɛ̃pɔtɑ̃, -ɑ̃t] *adj* disabled

impraticable [ɛ̃pʀatikabl(ə)] *adj* (*projet*) impracticable, unworkable; (*piste*) impassable

imprécation [ɛ̃pʀekasjɔ̃] *nf* imprecation

imprécis, e [ɛ̃pʀesi, -iz] *adj* (*contours, souvenir*) imprecise, vague; (*tir*) inaccurate, imprecise

imprécision [ɛ̃pʀesizjɔ̃] *nf* imprecision

imprégner [ɛ̃pʀeɲe] *vt* (*tissu, tampon*): ~ **(de)** to soak *ou* impregnate (with); (*lieu, air*): ~ **(de)** to fill (with); (*amertume, ironie*) to pervade; **s'imprégner de** *vi* to become impregnated with; to be filled with; (*fig*) to absorb

imprenable [ɛ̃pʀənabl(ə)] *adj* (*forteresse*)

impregnable; **vue** ~ unimpeded outlook

impresario [ɛ̃pʀesaʀjo] *nm* manager, impresario

impression [ɛ̃pʀesjɔ̃] *nf* impression; (*d'un ouvrage, tissu*) printing; (*Photo*) exposure; **faire bonne** ~ to make a good impression; **donner une** ~ **de/l'** ~ **que** to give the impression of/that; **avoir l'** ~ **de/que** to have the impression of/that; **faire** ~ to make an impression; ~**s de voyage** impressions of one's journey

impressionnable [ɛ̃pʀesjɔnabl(ə)] *adj* impressionable

impressionnant, e [ɛ̃pʀesjɔnɑ̃, -ɑ̃t] *adj* impressive; upsetting

impressionner [ɛ̃pʀesjɔne] *vt* (*frapper*) to impress; (*troubler*) to upset; (*Photo*) to expose

impressionnisme [ɛ̃pʀesjɔnism(ə)] *nm* impressionism

impressionniste [ɛ̃pʀesjɔnist(ə)] *adj, nm/f* impressionist

imprévisible [ɛ̃pʀevizibl(ə)] *adj* unforeseeable; (*réaction, personne*) unpredictable

imprévoyance [ɛ̃pʀevwajɑ̃s] *nf* lack of foresight

imprévoyant, e [ɛ̃pʀevwajɑ̃, -ɑ̃t] *adj* lacking in foresight; (*en matière d'argent*) improvident

imprévu, e [ɛ̃pʀevy] *adj* unforeseen, unexpected ▷ *nm* unexpected incident; **l'** ~ the unexpected; **en cas d'** ~ if anything unexpected happens; **sauf** ~ barring anything unexpected

imprimante [ɛ̃pʀimɑ̃t] *nf* (*Inform*) printer; ~ **à bulle d'encre** bubblejet printer; ~ **à jet d'encre** ink-jet printer; ~ **à laser** laser printer; ~ **(ligne par) ligne** line printer; ~ **à marguerite** daisy-wheel printer

imprimé [ɛ̃pʀime] *nm* (*formulaire*) printed form; (*Postes*) printed matter *no pl*; (*tissu*) printed fabric; **un** ~ **à fleurs/pois** (*tissu*) a floral/polka-dot print

imprimer [ɛ̃pʀime] *vt* to print; (*Inform*) to print (out); (*apposer: visa, cachet*) to stamp; (*empreinte etc*) to imprint; (*publier*) to publish; (*communiquer: mouvement, impulsion*) to impart, transmit

imprimerie [ɛ̃pʀimʀi] *nf* printing; (*établissement*) printing works *sg*; (*atelier*) printing house, printery

imprimeur [ɛ̃pʀimœʀ] *nm* printer; ~**-éditeur/- libraire** printer and publisher/bookseller

improbable [ɛ̃pʀɔbabl(ə)] *adj* unlikely, improbable

improductif, -ive [ɛ̃pʀɔdyktif, -iv] *adj* unproductive

impromptu, e [ɛ̃pʀɔ̃pty] *adj* impromptu; (*départ*) sudden

imprononçable [ɛ̃pʀɔnɔ̃sabl(ə)] *adj* unpronounceable

impropre [ɛ̃pʀɔpʀ(ə)] *adj* inappropriate; ~ **à** unsuitable for

improprement [ɛ̃pʀɔpʀəmɑ̃] *adv* improperly

impropriété [ɛ̃pʀɔpʀijete] *nf*: ~ **(de langage)** incorrect usage *no pl*

improvisation [ɛ̃pʀɔvizasjɔ̃] *nf* improvization

improvisé, e [ɛ̃pʀɔvize] *adj* makeshift, improvized; *(jeu etc)* scratch, improvized; **avec des moyens ~s** using whatever comes to hand

improviser [ɛ̃pʀɔvize] *vt, vi* to improvize; **s'improviser** *(secours, réunion)* to be improvized; **s'~ cuisinier** to (decide to) act as cook; **~ qn cuisinier** to get sb to act as cook

improviste [ɛ̃pʀɔvist(ə)]: **à l'~** *adv* unexpectedly, without warning

imprudemment [ɛ̃pʀydamɑ̃] *adv* carelessly; unwisely, imprudently

imprudence [ɛ̃pʀydɑ̃s] *nf* carelessness *no pl*; imprudence *no pl*; act of carelessness; (:) foolish *ou* unwise action

imprudent, e [ɛ̃pʀydɑ̃, -ɑ̃t] *adj* (*conducteur, geste, action*) careless; (*remarque*) unwise, imprudent; (*projet*) foolhardy

impubère [ɛ̃pybɛʀ] *adj* below the age of puberty

impubliable [ɛ̃pyblijabl(ə)] *adj* unpublishable

impudemment [ɛ̃pydamɑ̃] *adv* impudently

impudence [ɛ̃pydɑ̃s] *nf* impudence

impudent, e [ɛ̃pydɑ̃, -ɑ̃t] *adj* impudent

impudeur [ɛ̃pydœʀ] *nf* shamelessness

impudique [ɛ̃pydik] *adj* shameless

impuissance [ɛ̃pɥisɑ̃s] *nf* helplessness; ineffectualness; impotence

impuissant, e [ɛ̃pɥisɑ̃, -ɑ̃t] *adj* helpless; (*sans effet*) ineffectual; (*sexuellement*) impotent ▷ *nm* impotent man; **~ à faire qch** powerless to do sth

impulsif, -ive [ɛ̃pylsif, -iv] *adj* impulsive

impulsion [ɛ̃pylsjɔ̃] *nf* (*Élec, instinct*) impulse; (*élan, influence*) impetus

impulsivement [ɛ̃pylsivmɑ̃] *adv* impulsively

impulsivité [ɛ̃pylsivite] *nf* impulsiveness

impunément [ɛ̃pynemɑ̃] *adv* with impunity

impuni, e [ɛ̃pyni] *adj* unpunished

impunité [ɛ̃pynite] *nf* impunity

impur, e [ɛ̃pyʀ] *adj* impure

impureté [ɛ̃pyʀte] *nf* impurity

imputable [ɛ̃pytabl(ə)] *adj* (*attribuable*): **~ à** imputable to, ascribable to; (*Comm: somme*): **~ sur** chargeable to

imputation [ɛ̃pytasjɔ̃] *nf* imputation, charge

imputer [ɛ̃pyte] *vt* (*attribuer*): **~ qch à** to ascribe *ou* impute sth to; (*Comm*): **~ qch à** *ou* **sur** to charge sth to

imputrescible [ɛ̃pytʀesibl(ə)] *adj* rotproof

in [in] *adj inv* in, trendy

INA [ina] *sigle m* (= *Institut national de l'audio-visuel*) library of television archives

inabordable [inabɔʀdabl(ə)] *adj* (*lieu*) inaccessible; (*cher*) prohibitive

inaccentué, e [inaksɑ̃tɥe] *adj* (*Ling*) unstressed

inacceptable [inaksɛptabl(ə)] *adj* unacceptable

inaccessible [inaksesibl(ə)] *adj* inaccessible; (*objectif*) unattainable; (*insensible*): **~ à** impervious to

inaccoutumé, e [inakutyme] *adj* unaccustomed

inachevé, e [inaʃve] *adj* unfinished

inactif, -ive [inaktif, -iv] *adj* inactive, idle

inaction [inaksjɔ̃] *nf* inactivity

inactivité [inaktivite] *nf* (*Admin*): **en ~** out of active service

inadaptation [inadaptasjɔ̃] *nf* (*Psych*) maladjustment

inadapté, e [inadapte] *adj* (*Psych: adulte, enfant*) maladjusted ▷ *nm/f* (*péj: adulte: asocial*) misfit; **~ à** not adapted to, unsuited to

inadéquat, e [inadekwa, wat] *adj* inadequate

inadéquation [inadekwasjɔ̃] *nf* inadequacy

inadmissible [inadmisibl(ə)] *adj* inadmissible

inadvertance [inadvɛʀtɑ̃s]: **par ~** *adv* inadvertently

inaliénable [inaljenabl(ə)] *adj* inalienable

inaltérable [inalteʀabl(ə)] *adj* (*matière*) stable; (*fig*) unchanging; **~ à** unaffected by; **couleur ~ (au lavage/à la lumière)** fast colour/fade-resistant colour

inamovible [inamɔvibl(ə)] *adj* fixed; (*Jur*) irremovable

inanimé, e [inanime] *adj* (*matière*) inanimate; (*évanoui*) unconscious; (*sans vie*) lifeless

inanité [inanite] *nf* futility

inanition [inanisjɔ̃] *nf*: **tomber d'~** to faint with hunger (and exhaustion)

inaperçu, e [inapɛʀsy] *adj*: **passer ~** to go unnoticed

inappétence [inapetɑ̃s] *nf* lack of appetite

inapplicable [inaplikabl(ə)] *adj* inapplicable

inapplication [inaplikasjɔ̃] *nf* lack of application

inappliqué, e [inaplike] *adj* lacking in application

inappréciable [inapʀesjabl(ə)] *adj* (*service*) invaluable; (*différence, nuance*) inappreciable

inapte [inapt(ə)] *adj*: **~ à** incapable of; (*Mil*) unfit for

inaptitude [inaptityd] *nf* inaptitude; unfitness

inarticulé, e [inaʀtikyle] *adj* inarticulate

inassimilable [inasimilabl(ə)] *adj* that cannot be assimilated

inassouvi, e [inasuvi] *adj* unsatisfied, unfulfilled

inattaquable [inatakabl(ə)] *adj* (*Mil*) unassailable; (*texte, preuve*) irrefutable

inattendu, e [inatɑ̃dy] *adj* unexpected ▷ *nm*: **l'~** the unexpected

inattentif, -ive [inatɑ̃tif, -iv] *adj* inattentive; **~ à** (*dangers, détails*) heedless of

inattention [inatɑ̃sjɔ̃] *nf* inattention; (*inadvertance*): **une minute d'~** a minute of inattention, a minute's carelessness; **par ~** inadvertently; **faute d'~** careless mistake

inaudible [inodibl(ə)] *adj* inaudible

inaugural, e, -aux [inogyʀal, -o] *adj* (*cérémonie*) inaugural, opening; (*vol, voyage*) maiden

inauguration [inogyʀasjɔ̃] *nf* unveiling; opening; **discours/cérémonie d'~** inaugural speech/ceremony

inaugurer [inogyʀe] *vt* (*monument*) to unveil; (*exposition, usine*) to open; (*fig*) to inaugurate

inauthenticité [inotɑ̃tisite] *nf* inauthenticity

inavouable [inavwabl(ə)] *adj* undisclosable; (*honteux*) shameful
inavoué, e [inavwe] *adj* unavowed
INC *sigle m* (= *Institut national de la consommation*) consumer research organization
inca [ɛ̃ka] *adj inv* Inca ▷ *nm/f*: **Inca** Inca
incalculable [ɛ̃kalkylabl(ə)] *adj* incalculable; **un nombre ~ de** countless numbers of
incandescence [ɛ̃kɑ̃desɑ̃s] *nf* incandescence; **en ~** incandescent, white-hot; **porter à ~** to heat white-hot; **lampe/manchon à ~** incandescent lamp/(gas) mantle
incandescent, e [ɛ̃kɑ̃desɑ̃, -ɑ̃t] *adj* incandescent, white-hot
incantation [ɛ̃kɑ̃tɑsjɔ̃] *nf* incantation
incantatoire [ɛ̃kɑ̃tatwaʀ] *adj*: **formule ~** incantation
incapable [ɛ̃kapabl(ə)] *adj* incapable; **~ de faire** incapable of doing; (*empêché*) unable to do
incapacitant, e [ɛ̃kapasitɑ̃, -ɑ̃t] *adj* (*Mil*) incapacitating
incapacité [ɛ̃kapasite] *nf* incapability; (*Jur*) incapacity; **être dans l'~ de faire** to be unable to do; **~ permanente/de travail** permanent/industrial disablement; **~ électorale** ineligibility to vote
incarcération [ɛ̃kaʀseʀɑsjɔ̃] *nf* incarceration
incarcérer [ɛ̃kaʀseʀe] *vt* to incarcerate
incarnat, e [ɛ̃kaʀna, -at] *adj* (*rosy*) pink
incarnation [ɛ̃kaʀnɑsjɔ̃] *nf* incarnation
incarné, e [ɛ̃kaʀne] *adj* incarnate; (*ongle*) ingrown
incarner [ɛ̃kaʀne] *vt* to embody, personify; (*Théât*) to play; (*Rel*) to incarnate; **s'incarner dans** *vi* (*Rel*) to be incarnate in
incartade [ɛ̃kaʀtad] *nf* prank, escapade
incassable [ɛ̃kasabl(ə)] *adj* unbreakable
incendiaire [ɛ̃sɑ̃djɛʀ] *adj* incendiary; (*fig: discours*) inflammatory ▷ *nm/f* fire-raiser, arsonist
incendie [ɛ̃sɑ̃di] *nm* fire; **~ criminel** arson *no pl*; **~ de forêt** forest fire
incendier [ɛ̃sɑ̃dje] *vt* (*mettre le feu à*) to set fire to, set alight; (*brûler complètement*) to burn down
incertain, e [ɛ̃sɛʀtɛ̃, -ɛn] *adj* uncertain; (*temps*) uncertain, unsettled; (*imprécis: contours*) indistinct, blurred
incertitude [ɛ̃sɛʀtityd] *nf* uncertainty
incessamment [ɛ̃sesamɑ̃] *adv* very shortly
incessant, e [ɛ̃sesɑ̃, -ɑ̃t] *adj* incessant, unceasing
incessible [ɛ̃sesibl(ə)] *adj* (*Jur*) non-transferable
inceste [ɛ̃sɛst(ə)] *nm* incest
incestueux, -euse [ɛ̃sɛstɥø, -øz] *adj* incestuous
inchangé, e [ɛ̃ʃɑ̃ʒe] *adj* unchanged, unaltered
inchantable [ɛ̃ʃɑ̃tabl(ə)] *adj* unsingable
inchauffable [ɛ̃ʃofabl(ə)] *adj* impossible to heat
incidemment [ɛ̃sidamɑ̃] *adv* in passing
incidence [ɛ̃sidɑ̃s] *nf* (*effet, influence*) effect; (*Physique*) incidence
incident [ɛ̃sidɑ̃] *nm* incident; **~ de frontière** border incident; **~ de parcours** minor hitch *ou*

setback; **~ technique** technical difficulties *pl*, technical hitch
incinérateur [ɛ̃sineʀatœʀ] *nm* incinerator
incinération [ɛ̃sineʀɑsjɔ̃] *nf* (*d'ordures*) incineration; (*crémation*) cremation
incinérer [ɛ̃sineʀe] *vt* (*ordures*) to incinerate; (*mort*) to cremate
incise [ɛ̃siz] *nf* (*Ling*) interpolated clause
inciser [ɛ̃size] *vt* to make an incision in; (*abcès*) to lance
incisif, -ive [ɛ̃sizif, -iv] *adj* incisive, cutting ▷ *nf* incisor
incision [ɛ̃sizjɔ̃] *nf* incision; (*d'un abcès*) lancing
incitation [ɛ̃sitɑsjɔ̃] *nf* (*encouragement*) incentive; (*provocation*) incitement
inciter [ɛ̃site] *vt*: **~ qn à (faire) qch** to prompt *ou* encourage sb to do sth; (*à la révolte etc*) to incite sb to do sth
incivil, e [ɛ̃sivil] *adj* uncivil
incivilité [ɛ̃sivilite] *nf* (*grossièreté*) incivility; **incivilités** *nfpl* antisocial behaviour *sg*
inclinable [ɛ̃klinabl(ə)] *adj* (*dossier etc*) tilting; **siège à dossier ~** reclining seat
inclinaison [ɛ̃klinɛzɔ̃] *nf* (*déclivité: d'une route etc*) incline; (: *d'un toit*) slope; (*état penché: d'un mur*) lean; (: *de la tête*) tilt; (: *d'un navire*) list
inclination [ɛ̃klinɑsjɔ̃] *nf* (*penchant*) inclination, tendency; **montrer de l'~ pour les sciences** *etc* to show an inclination for the sciences *etc*; **~s égoïstes/altruistes** egoistic/altruistic tendencies; **~ de (la) tête** nod (of the head); **~ (de buste)** bow
incliner [ɛ̃kline] *vt* (*bouteille*) to tilt; (*tête*) to incline; (*inciter*): **~ qn à qch/à faire** to encourage sb towards sth/to do ▷ *vi*: **~ à qch/à faire** (*tendre à, pencher pour*) to incline towards sth/doing, tend towards sth/to do; **s'incliner** *vi* (*route*) to slope; (*toit*) to be sloping; **s'~ (devant)** to bow (before)
inclure [ɛ̃klyʀ] *vt* to include; (*joindre à un envoi*) to enclose; **jusqu'au 10 mars inclus** until 10th March inclusive
inclus, e [ɛ̃kly, -yz] *pp de* **inclure** ▷ *adj* (*joint à un envoi*) enclosed; (*compris: frais, dépense*) included; (*Math: ensemble*): **~ dans** included in; **jusqu'au troisième chapitre ~** up to and including the third chapter
inclusion [ɛ̃klyzjɔ̃] *nf* (*voir inclure*) inclusion; enclosing
inclusivement [ɛ̃klyzivmɑ̃] *adv* inclusively
inclut [ɛ̃kly] *vb voir* **inclure**
incoercible [ɛ̃kɔɛʀsibl(ə)] *adj* uncontrollable
incognito [ɛ̃kɔɲito] *adv* incognito ▷ *nm*: **garder l'~** to remain incognito
incohérence [ɛ̃kɔeʀɑ̃s] *nf* inconsistency; incoherence
incohérent, e [ɛ̃kɔeʀɑ̃, -ɑ̃t] *adj* inconsistent; incoherent
incollable [ɛ̃kɔlabl(ə)] *adj* (*riz*) that does not stick; (*fam: personne*): **il est ~** he's got all the answers
incolore [ɛ̃kɔlɔʀ] *adj* colourless

incomber [ɛ̃kɔ̃be]: **~ à** vt (devoirs, responsabilité) to rest ou be incumbent upon; (: frais, travail) to be the responsibility of

incombustible [ɛ̃kɔ̃bystibl(ə)] adj incombustible

incommensurable [ɛ̃kɔmɑ̃syrabl(ə)] adj immeasurable

incommodant, e [ɛ̃kɔmɔdɑ̃, -ɑ̃t] adj (bruit) annoying; (chaleur) uncomfortable

incommode [ɛ̃kɔmɔd] adj inconvenient; (posture, siège) uncomfortable

incommodément [ɛ̃kɔmɔdemɑ̃] adv (installé, assis) uncomfortably; (logé, situé) inconveniently

incommoder [ɛ̃kɔmɔde] vt: **~ qn** to bother ou inconvenience sb; (embarrasser) to make sb feel uncomfortable ou ill at ease

incommodité [ɛ̃kɔmɔdite] nf inconvenience

incommunicable [ɛ̃kɔmynikabl(ə)] adj (Jur: droits, privilèges) non-transferable; (pensée) incommunicable

incomparable [ɛ̃kɔ̃parabl(ə)] adj not comparable; (inégalable) incomparable, matchless

incomparablement [ɛ̃kɔ̃parabləmɑ̃] adv incomparably

incompatibilité [ɛ̃kɔ̃patibilite] nf incompatibility; **~ d'humeur** (mutual) incompatibility

incompatible [ɛ̃kɔ̃patibl(ə)] adj incompatible

incompétence [ɛ̃kɔ̃petɑ̃s] nf lack of expertise; incompetence

incompétent, e [ɛ̃kɔ̃petɑ̃, -ɑ̃t] adj (ignorant) inexpert; (incapable) incompetent, not competent

incomplet, -ète [ɛ̃kɔ̃plɛ, -ɛt] adj incomplete

incomplètement [ɛ̃kɔ̃plɛtmɑ̃] adv not completely, incompletely

incompréhensible [ɛ̃kɔ̃preɑ̃sibl(ə)] adj incomprehensible

incompréhensif, -ive [ɛ̃kɔ̃preɑ̃sif, -iv] adj lacking in understanding, unsympathetic

incompréhension [ɛ̃kɔ̃preɑ̃sjɔ̃] nf lack of understanding

incompressible [ɛ̃kɔ̃presibl(ə)] adj (Physique) incompressible; (fig: dépenses) that cannot be reduced; (Jur: peine) irreducible

incompris, e [ɛ̃kɔ̃pri, -iz] adj misunderstood

inconcevable [ɛ̃kɔ̃svabl(ə)] adj (conduite etc) inconceivable; (mystère) incredible

inconciliable [ɛ̃kɔ̃siljabl(ə)] adj irreconcilable

inconditionnel, le [ɛ̃kɔ̃disjɔnɛl] adj unconditional; (partisan) unquestioning ▷ nm/f (partisan) unquestioning supporter

inconditionnellement [ɛ̃kɔ̃disjɔnɛlmɑ̃] adv unconditionally

inconduite [ɛ̃kɔ̃dɥit] nf bad ou unsuitable behaviour no pl

inconfort [ɛ̃kɔ̃fɔr] nm lack of comfort, discomfort

inconfortable [ɛ̃kɔ̃fɔrtabl(ə)] adj uncomfortable

inconfortablement [ɛ̃kɔ̃fɔrtabləmɑ̃] adv uncomfortably

incongru, e [ɛ̃kɔ̃gry] adj unseemly; (remarque) ill-chosen, incongruous

incongruité [ɛ̃kɔ̃gryite] nf unseemliness; incongruity; (parole incongrue) ill-chosen remark

inconnu, e [ɛ̃kɔny] adj unknown; (sentiment, plaisir) new, strange ▷ nm/f stranger; unknown person (ou artist etc) ▷ nm: **l'~** the unknown ▷ nf (Math) unknown; (fig) unknown factor

inconsciemment [ɛ̃kɔ̃sjamɑ̃] adv unconsciously

inconscience [ɛ̃kɔ̃sjɑ̃s] nf unconsciousness; recklessness

inconscient, e [ɛ̃kɔ̃sjɑ̃, -ɑ̃t] adj unconscious; (irréfléchi) reckless ▷ nm (Psych): **l'~** the subconscious, the unconscious; **~ de** unaware of

inconséquence [ɛ̃kɔ̃sekɑ̃s] nf inconsistency; thoughtlessness; (action, parole) thoughtless thing to do (ou say)

inconséquent, e [ɛ̃kɔ̃sekɑ̃, -ɑ̃t] adj (illogique) inconsistent; (irréfléchi) thoughtless

inconsidéré, e [ɛ̃kɔ̃sidere] adj ill-considered

inconsidérément [ɛ̃kɔ̃sideremɑ̃] adv thoughtlessly

inconsistant, e [ɛ̃kɔ̃sistɑ̃, -ɑ̃t] adj flimsy, weak; (crème etc) runny

inconsolable [ɛ̃kɔ̃sɔlabl(ə)] adj inconsolable

inconstance [ɛ̃kɔ̃stɑ̃s] nf inconstancy, fickleness

inconstant, e [ɛ̃kɔ̃stɑ̃, -ɑ̃t] adj inconstant, fickle

inconstitutionnel, le [ɛ̃kɔ̃stitysjɔnɛl] adj unconstitutional

incontestable [ɛ̃kɔ̃tɛstabl(ə)] adj unquestionable, indisputable

incontestablement [ɛ̃kɔ̃tɛstabləmɑ̃] adv unquestionably, indisputably

incontesté, e [ɛ̃kɔ̃tɛste] adj undisputed

incontinence [ɛ̃kɔ̃tinɑ̃s] nf (Méd) incontinence

incontinent, e [ɛ̃kɔ̃tinɑ̃, -ɑ̃t] adj (Méd) incontinent ▷ adv (tout de suite) forthwith

incontournable [ɛ̃kɔ̃turnabl(ə)] adj unavoidable

incontrôlable [ɛ̃kɔ̃trolabl(ə)] adj unverifiable

incontrôlé, e [ɛ̃kɔ̃trole] adj uncontrolled

inconvenance [ɛ̃kɔ̃vnɑ̃s] nf (parole, action) impropriety

inconvenant, e [ɛ̃kɔ̃vnɑ̃, -ɑ̃t] adj unseemly, improper

inconvénient [ɛ̃kɔ̃venjɑ̃] nm (d'une situation, d'un projet) disadvantage, drawback; (d'un remède, changement etc) risk, inconvenience; **si vous n'y voyez pas d'~** if you have no objections; **y a-t-il un ~ à …?** (risque) isn't there a risk in …?; (objection) is there any objection to …?

inconvertible [ɛ̃kɔ̃vɛrtibl(ə)] adj inconvertible

incorporation [ɛ̃kɔrpɔrasjɔ̃] nf (Mil) call-up

incorporé, e [ɛ̃kɔrpɔre] adj (micro etc) built-in

incorporel, le [ɛ̃kɔrpɔrɛl] adj (Jur): **biens ~s** intangible property

incorporer [ɛ̃kɔrpɔre] vt: **~ (à)** to mix in (with); (paragraphe etc): **~ (dans)** to incorporate (in);

(*territoire, immigrants*): ~ **(dans)** to incorporate (into); (*Mil: appeler*) to recruit, call up; (: *affecter*): ~ **qn dans** to enlist sb into

incorrect, e [ɛ̃kɔrɛkt] *adj* (*impropre, inconvenant*) improper; (*défectueux*) faulty; (*inexact*) incorrect; (*impoli*) impolite; (*déloyal*) underhand

incorrectement [ɛ̃kɔrɛktəmɑ̃] *adv* improperly; faultily; incorrectly; impolitely; in an underhand way

incorrection [ɛ̃kɔrɛksjɔ̃] *nf* impropriety; incorrectness; underhand nature; (*terme impropre*) impropriety; (*action, remarque*) improper behaviour (*ou* remark)

incorrigible [ɛ̃kɔriʒibl(ə)] *adj* incorrigible

incorruptible [ɛ̃kɔryptibl(ə)] *adj* incorruptible

incrédibilité [ɛ̃kredibilite] *nf* incredibility

incrédule [ɛ̃kredyl] *adj* incredulous; (*Rel*) unbelieving

incrédulité [ɛ̃kredylite] *nf* incredulity; **avec ~** incredulously

increvable [ɛ̃krəvabl(ə)] *adj* (*pneu*) puncture-proof; (*fam*) tireless

incriminer [ɛ̃krimine] *vt* (*personne*) to incriminate; (*action, conduite*) to bring under attack; (*bonne foi, honnêteté*) to call into question; **livre/article incriminé** offending book/article

incrochetable [ɛ̃krɔʃtabl(ə)] *adj* (*serrure*) that can't be picked, burglarproof

incroyable [ɛ̃krwajabl(ə)] *adj* incredible, unbelievable

incroyablement [ɛ̃krwajabləmɑ̃] *adv* incredibly, unbelievably

incroyant, e [ɛ̃krwajɑ̃, -ɑ̃t] *nm/f* non-believer

incrustation [ɛ̃krystasjɔ̃] *nf* inlaying *no pl*; inlay; (*dans une chaudière etc*) fur *no pl*, scale *no pl*

incruster [ɛ̃kryste] *vt* (*Art*): ~ **qch dans/qch de** to inlay sth into/sth with; (*radiateur etc*) to coat with scale *ou* fur; **s'incruster** *vi* (*invité*) to take root; (*radiateur etc*) to become coated with scale *ou* fur; **s'~ dans** (*corps étranger, caillou*) to become embedded in

incubateur [ɛ̃kybatœr] *nm* incubator

incubation [ɛ̃kybasjɔ̃] *nf* incubation

inculpation [ɛ̃kylpasjɔ̃] *nf* charging *no pl*; charge; **sous l'~ de** on a charge of

inculpé, e [ɛ̃kylpe] *nm/f* accused

inculper [ɛ̃kylpe] *vt*: ~ **(de)** to charge (with)

inculquer [ɛ̃kylke] *vt*: ~ **qch à** to inculcate sth in, instil sth into

inculte [ɛ̃kylt(ə)] *adj* uncultivated; (*esprit, peuple*) uncultured; (*barbe*) unkempt

incultivable [ɛ̃kyltivabl(ə)] *adj* (*terrain*) unworkable

inculture [ɛ̃kyltyr] *nf* lack of education

incurable [ɛ̃kyrabl(ə)] *adj* incurable

incurie [ɛ̃kyri] *nf* carelessness

incursion [ɛ̃kyrsjɔ̃] *nf* incursion, foray

incurvé, e [ɛ̃kyrve] *adj* curved

incurver [ɛ̃kyrve] *vt* (*barre de fer*) to bend into a curve; **s'incurver** *vi* (*planche, route*) to bend

Inde [ɛ̃d] *nf*: **l'~** India

indécemment [ɛ̃desamɑ̃] *adv* indecently

indécence [ɛ̃desɑ̃s] *nf* indecency; (*propos, acte*) indecent remark (*ou* act *etc*)

indécent, e [ɛ̃desɑ̃, -ɑ̃t] *adj* indecent

indéchiffrable [ɛ̃deʃifrabl(ə)] *adj* indecipherable

indéchirable [ɛ̃deʃirabl(ə)] *adj* tear-proof

indécis, e [ɛ̃desi, -iz] *adj* indecisive; (*perplexe*) undecided

indécision [ɛ̃desizjɔ̃] *nf* indecision, indecisiveness

indéclinable [ɛ̃deklinabl(ə)] *adj* (*Ling: mot*) indeclinable

indécomposable [ɛ̃dekɔ̃pozabl(ə)] *adj* that cannot be broken down

indécrottable [ɛ̃dekrɔtabl(ə)] *adj* (*fam*) hopeless

indéfectible [ɛ̃defɛktibl(ə)] *adj* (*attachement*) indestructible

indéfendable [ɛ̃defɑ̃dabl(ə)] *adj* indefensible

indéfini, e [ɛ̃defini] *adj* (*imprécis, incertain*) undefined; (*illimité, Ling*) indefinite

indéfiniment [ɛ̃definimɑ̃] *adv* indefinitely

indéfinissable [ɛ̃definisabl(ə)] *adj* indefinable

indéformable [ɛ̃defɔrmabl(ə)] *adj* that keeps its shape

indélébile [ɛ̃delebil] *adj* indelible

indélicat, e [ɛ̃delika, -at] *adj* tactless; (*malhonnête*) dishonest

indélicatesse [ɛ̃delikatɛs] *nf* tactlessness; dishonesty

indémaillable [ɛ̃demajabl(ə)] *adj* run-resist

indemne [ɛ̃dɛmn(ə)] *adj* unharmed

indemnisable [ɛ̃dɛmnizabl(ə)] *adj* entitled to compensation

indemnisation [ɛ̃dɛmnizasjɔ̃] *nf* (*somme*) indemnity, compensation

indemniser [ɛ̃dɛmnize] *vt*: ~ **qn (de)** to compensate sb (for); **se faire ~** to get compensation

indemnité [ɛ̃dɛmnite] *nf* (*dédommagement*) compensation *no pl*; (*allocation*) allowance; ~ **de licenciement** redundancy payment; ~ **de logement** housing allowance; ~ **parlementaire** ≈ MP's (*Brit*) *ou* Congressman's (*US*) salary

indémontable [ɛ̃demɔ̃tabl(ə)] *adj* (*meuble etc*) that cannot be dismantled, in one piece

indéniable [ɛ̃denjabl(ə)] *adj* undeniable, indisputable

indéniablement [ɛ̃denjabləmɑ̃] *adv* undeniably

indépendamment [ɛ̃depɑ̃damɑ̃] *adv* independently; ~ **de** independently of; (*abstraction faite de*) irrespective of; (*en plus de*) over and above

indépendance [ɛ̃depɑ̃dɑ̃s] *nf* independence; ~ **matérielle** financial independence

indépendant, e [ɛ̃depɑ̃dɑ̃, -ɑ̃t] *adj* independent; ~ **de** independent of; **chambre ~e** room with private entrance; **travailleur ~** self-employed worker

indépendantiste [ɛ̃depɑ̃dɑ̃tist(ə)] *adj, nm/f* separatist

indéracinable [ɛ̃deʀasinabl(ə)] *adj* (*fig: croyance etc*) ineradicable

indéréglable [ɛ̃deʀeglabl(ə)] *adj* which will not break down

indescriptible [ɛ̃deskʀiptibl(ə)] *adj* indescribable

indésirable [ɛ̃deziʀabl(ə)] *adj* undesirable

indestructible [ɛ̃destʀyktibl(ə)] *adj* indestructible; (*marque, impression*) indelible

indéterminable [ɛ̃detɛʀminabl(ə)] *adj* indeterminable

indétermination [ɛ̃detɛʀminasjɔ̃] *nf* indecision, indecisiveness

indéterminé, e [ɛ̃detɛʀmine] *adj* unspecified; indeterminate; indeterminable

index [ɛ̃dɛks] *nm* (*doigt*) index finger; (*d'un livre etc*) index; **mettre à l'~** to blacklist

indexation [ɛ̃dɛksasjɔ̃] *nf* indexing

indexé, e [ɛ̃dɛkse] *adj* (*Écon*): ~ (**sur**) index-linked (to)

indexer [ɛ̃dɛkse] *vt* (*salaire, emprunt*): ~ (**sur**) to index (on)

indicateur [ɛ̃dikatœʀ] *nm* (*Police*) informer; (*livre*) guide; (*: liste*) directory; (*Tech*) gauge; indicator; (*Écon*) indicator ▷ *adj*: **poteau** ~ signpost; **tableau** ~ indicator (board); ~ **des chemins de fer** railway timetable; ~ **de direction** (*Auto*) indicator; ~ **immobilier** property gazette; ~ **de niveau** level, gauge; ~ **de pression** pressure gauge; ~ **de rues** street directory; ~ **de vitesse** speedometer

indicatif, -ive [ɛ̃dikatif, -iv] *adj*: **à titre** ~ for (your) information ▷ *nm* (*Ling*) indicative; (*d'une émission*) theme *ou* signature tune; (*Tél*) dialling code; ~ **d'appel** (*Radio*) call sign

indication [ɛ̃dikasjɔ̃] *nf* indication; (*renseignement*) information *no pl*; **indications** *nfpl* (*directives*) instructions; ~ **d'origine** (*Comm*) place of origin

indice [ɛ̃dis] *nm* (*marque, signe*) indication, sign; (*Police: lors d'une enquête*) clue; (*Jur: présomption*) piece of evidence; (*Science, Écon, Tech*) index; (*Admin*) grading; rating; ~ **du coût de la vie** cost-of-living index; ~ **inférieur** subscript; ~ **d'octane** octane rating; ~ **des prix** price index; ~ **de traitement** salary grading

indicible [ɛ̃disibl(ə)] *adj* inexpressible

indien, ne [ɛ̃djɛ̃, -ɛn] *adj* Indian ▷ *nm/f*: **Indien, ne** (*d'Amérique*) Native American; (*d'Inde*) Indian

indifféremment [ɛ̃difeʀamɑ̃] *adv* (*sans distinction*) equally; indiscriminately

indifférence [ɛ̃difeʀɑ̃s] *nf* indifference

indifférencié, e [ɛ̃difeʀɑ̃sje] *adj* undifferentiated

indifférent, e [ɛ̃difeʀɑ̃, -ɑ̃t] *adj* (*peu intéressé*) indifferent; ~ **à** (*insensible à*) indifferent to, unconcerned about; (*peu intéressant pour*) indifferent to; immaterial to; **ça m'est** ~ (**que ...**) it doesn't matter to me (whether ...)

indifférer [ɛ̃difeʀe] *vt*: **cela m'indiffère** I'm indifferent about it

indigence [ɛ̃diʒɑ̃s] *nf* poverty; **être dans l'**~ to be destitute

indigène [ɛ̃diʒɛn] *adj* native, indigenous; (*de la région*) local ▷ *nm/f* native

indigent, e [ɛ̃diʒɑ̃, -ɑ̃t] *adj* destitute, poverty-stricken; (*fig*) poor

indigeste [ɛ̃diʒɛst(ə)] *adj* indigestible

indigestion [ɛ̃diʒɛstjɔ̃] *nf* indigestion *no pl*; **avoir une** ~ to have indigestion

indignation [ɛ̃diɲasjɔ̃] *nf* indignation; **avec** ~ indignantly

indigne [ɛ̃diɲ] *adj*: ~ (**de**) unworthy (of)

indigné, e [ɛ̃diɲe] *adj* indignant

indignement [ɛ̃diɲmɑ̃] *adv* shamefully

indigner [ɛ̃diɲe] *vt* to make indignant; **s'indigner (de/contre)** *vi* to be (*ou* become) indignant (at)

indignité [ɛ̃diɲite] *nf* unworthiness *no pl*; (*acte*) shameful act

indigo [ɛ̃digo] *nm* indigo

indiqué, e [ɛ̃dike] *adj* (*date, lieu*) given, appointed; (*adéquat*) appropriate, suitable; (*conseillé*) advisable; (*remède, traitement*) appropriate

indiquer [ɛ̃dike] *vt* (*désigner*): ~ **qch/qn à qn** to point sth/sb out to sb; (*pendule, aiguille*) to show; (*étiquette, plan*) to show, indicate; (*faire connaître: médecin, lieu*): ~ **qch/qn à qn** to tell sb of sth/sb; (*renseigner sur*) to point out, tell; (*déterminer: date, lieu*) to give, state; (*dénoter*) to indicate, point to; ~ **du doigt** to point out; ~ **de la main** to indicate with one's hand; ~ **du regard** to glance towards *ou* in the direction of; **pourriez-vous m'**~ **les toilettes/l'heure?** could you direct me to the toilets/tell me the time?

indirect, e [ɛ̃diʀɛkt] *adj* indirect

indirectement [ɛ̃diʀɛktəmɑ̃] *adv* indirectly; (*apprendre*) in a roundabout way

indiscernable [ɛ̃disɛʀnabl(ə)] *adj* undiscernable

indiscipline [ɛ̃disiplin] *nf* lack of discipline

indiscipliné, e [ɛ̃disipline] *adj* undisciplined; (*fig*) unmanageable

indiscret, -ète [ɛ̃diskʀɛ, -ɛt] *adj* indiscreet

indiscrétion [ɛ̃diskʀesjɔ̃] *nf* indiscretion; **sans** ~, ... without wishing to be indiscreet, ...

indiscutable [ɛ̃diskytabl(ə)] *adj* indisputable

indiscutablement [ɛ̃diskytabləmɑ̃] *adv* indisputably

indiscuté, e [ɛ̃diskyte] *adj* (*incontesté: droit, chef*) undisputed

indispensable [ɛ̃dispɑ̃sabl(ə)] *adj* indispensable, essential; ~ **à qn/pour faire qch** essential for sb/to do sth

indisponibilité [ɛ̃disponibilite] *nf* unavailability

indisponible [ɛ̃disponibl(ə)] *adj* unavailable

indisposé, e [ɛ̃dispoze] *adj* indisposed, unwell

indisposer [ɛ̃dispoze] *vt* (*incommoder*) to upset; (*déplaire à*) to antagonize

indisposition [ɛ̃dispozisjɔ̃] *nf* (slight) illness, indisposition

indissociable [ɛ̃disɔsjabl(ə)] *adj* indissociable
indissoluble [ɛ̃disɔlybl(ə)] *adj* indissoluble
indissolublement [ɛ̃disɔlyblǝmɑ̃] *adv*
  indissolubly
indistinct, e [ɛ̃distɛ̃, -ɛ̃kt(ə)] *adj* indistinct
indistinctement [ɛ̃distɛ̃ktǝmɑ̃] *adv* (*voir,
  prononcer*) indistinctly; (*sans distinction*) without
  distinction, indiscriminately
individu [ɛ̃dividy] *nm* individual
individualiser [ɛ̃dividɥalize] *vt* to
  individualize; (*personnaliser*) to tailor to
  individual requirements; **s'individualiser** *vi* to
  develop one's own identity
individualisme [ɛ̃dividɥalism(ə)] *nm*
  individualism
individualiste [ɛ̃dividɥalist(ə)] *nm/f*
  individualist
individualité [ɛ̃dividɥalite] *nf* individuality
individuel, le [ɛ̃dividɥɛl] *adj* (*gén*) individual;
  (*opinion, livret, contrôle, avantages*) personal;
  chambre ~le single room; **maison ~le**
  detached house; **propriété ~le** personal *ou*
  private property
individuellement [ɛ̃dividɥɛlmɑ̃] *adv*
  individually
indivis, e [ɛ̃divi, -iz] *adj* (Jur: *bien, succession*)
  indivisible; (: *cohéritiers, propriétaires*) joint
indivisible [ɛ̃divizibl(ə)] *adj* indivisible
Indochine [ɛ̃dɔʃin] *nf*: **l'~** Indochina
indochinois, e [ɛ̃dɔʃinwa, -waz] *adj*
  Indochinese
indocile [ɛ̃dɔsil] *adj* unruly
indo-européen, ne [ɛ̃dɔøʀɔpeɛ̃, -ɛn] *adj* Indo-
  European ▷ *nm* (Ling) Indo-European
indolence [ɛ̃dɔlɑ̃s] *nf* indolence
indolent, e [ɛ̃dɔlɑ̃, -ɑ̃t] *adj* indolent
indolore [ɛ̃dɔlɔʀ] *adj* painless
indomptable [ɛ̃dɔ̃tabl(ə)] *adj* untameable; (*fig*)
  invincible, indomitable
indompté, e [ɛ̃dɔ̃te] *adj* (*cheval*) unbroken
Indonésie [ɛ̃dɔnezi] *nf*: **l'~** Indonesia
indonésien, ne [ɛ̃dɔnezjɛ̃, -ɛn] *adj* Indonesian
  ▷ *nm/f*: **Indonésien, ne** Indonesian
indu, e [ɛ̃dy] *adj*: **à des heures ~es** at an
  ungodly hour
indubitable [ɛ̃dybitabl(ə)] *adj* indubitable
indubitablement [ɛ̃dybitablǝmɑ̃] *adv*
  indubitably
induction [ɛ̃dyksjɔ̃] *nf* induction
induire [ɛ̃dɥiʀ] *vt*: **~ qch de** to induce sth from;
  ~ qn en erreur to lead sb astray, mislead sb
indulgence [ɛ̃dylʒɑ̃s] *nf* indulgence; leniency;
  avec ~ indulgently; leniently
indulgent, e [ɛ̃dylʒɑ̃, -ɑ̃t] *adj* (*parent, regard*)
  indulgent; (*juge, examinateur*) lenient
indûment [ɛ̃dymɑ̃] *adv* without due cause;
  (*illégitimement*) wrongfully
industrialisation [ɛ̃dystʀijalizasjɔ̃] *nf*
  industrialization
industrialisé, e [ɛ̃dystʀijalize] *adj*
  industrialized
industrialiser [ɛ̃dystʀijalize] *vt* to

industrialize; **s'industrialiser** *vi* to become
  industrialized
industrie [ɛ̃dystʀi] *nf* industry; **~ automobile/
  textile** car/textile industry; **~ du spectacle**
  entertainment business
industriel, le [ɛ̃dystʀijɛl] *adj* industrial; (*produit
  industriellement: pain etc*) mass-produced, factory-
  produced ▷ *nm* industrialist; (*fabricant*)
  manufacturer
industriellement [ɛ̃dystʀijɛlmɑ̃] *adv*
  industrially
industrieux, -euse [ɛ̃dystʀijø, -øz] *adj*
  industrious
inébranlable [inebʀɑ̃labl(ə)] *adj* (*masse, colonne*)
  solid; (*personne, certitude, foi*) steadfast,
  unwavering
inédit, e [inedi, -it] *adj* (*correspondance etc*)
  (hitherto) unpublished; (*spectacle, moyen*) novel,
  original
ineffable [inefabl(ə)] *adj* inexpressible,
  ineffable
ineffaçable [inefasabl(ə)] *adj* indelible
inefficace [inefikas] *adj* (*remède, moyen*)
  ineffective; (*machine, employé*) inefficient
inefficacité [inefikasite] *nf* ineffectiveness;
  inefficiency
inégal, e, -aux [inegal, -o] *adj* unequal;
  (*irrégulier*) uneven
inégalable [inegalabl(e)] *adj* matchless
inégalé, e [inegale] *adj* unmatched, unequalled
inégalement [inegalmɑ̃] *adv* unequally
inégalité [inegalite] *nf* inequality; unevenness
  no pl; **~ de deux hauteurs** difference *ou*
  disparity between two heights; **~s de terrain**
  uneven ground
inélégance [inelegɑ̃s] *nf* inelegance
inélégant, e [inelegɑ̃, -ɑ̃t] *adj* inelegant;
  (*indélicat*) discourteous
inéligible [ineliʒibl(ə)] *adj* ineligible
inéluctable [inelyktabl(ə)] *adj* inescapable
inéluctablement [inelyktablǝmɑ̃] *adv*
  inescapably
inemployable [inɑ̃plwajabl(ə)] *adj* unusable
inemployé, e [inɑ̃plwaje] *adj* unused
inénarrable [inenaʀabl(ə)] *adj* hilarious
inepte [inɛpt(ə)] *adj* inept
ineptie [inɛpsi] *nf* ineptitude; (*propos*)
  nonsense *no pl*
inépuisable [inepɥizabl(ə)] *adj* inexhaustible
inéquitable [inekitabl(ə)] *adj* inequitable
inerte [inɛʀt(ə)] *adj* lifeless; (*apathique*) passive,
  inert; (*Physique, Chimie*) inert
inertie [inɛʀsi] *nf* inertia
inescompté, e [inɛskɔ̃te] *adj* unexpected,
  unhoped-for
inespéré, e [inɛspeʀe] *adj* unhoped-for,
  unexpected
inesthétique [inɛstetik] *adj* unsightly
inestimable [inɛstimabl(e)] *adj* priceless; (*fig:
  bienfait*) invaluable
inévitable [inevitabl(ə)] *adj* unavoidable; (*fatal,
  habituel*) inevitable

inévitablement [inevitabləmã] *adv* inevitably
inexact, e [inɛgzakt] *adj* inaccurate, inexact; (*non ponctuel*) unpunctual
inexactement [inɛgzaktəmã] *adv* inaccurately
inexactitude [inɛgzaktityd] *nf* inaccuracy
inexcusable [inɛkskyzabl(ə)] *adj* inexcusable, unforgivable
inexécutable [inɛgzekytabl(ə)] *adj* impracticable, unworkable; (*Mus*) unplayable
inexistant, e [inɛgzistã, -ãt] *adj* non-existent
inexorable [inɛgzɔrabl(ə)] *adj* inexorable; (*personne: dur*): **~ (à)** unmoved (by)
inexorablement [inɛgzɔrabləmã] *adv* inexorably
inexpérience [inɛkspɛrjãs] *nf* inexperience, lack of experience
inexpérimenté, e [inɛkspɛrimãte] *adj* inexperienced; (*arme, procédé*) untested
inexplicable [inɛksplikabl(ə)] *adj* inexplicable
inexplicablement [inɛksplikabləmã] *adv* inexplicably
inexpliqué, e [inɛksplike] *adj* unexplained
inexploitable [inɛksplwatabl(ə)] *adj* (*gisement, richesse*) unexploitable; (*données, renseignements*) unusable
inexploité, e [inɛksplwate] *adj* unexploited, untapped
inexploré, e [inɛksplɔre] *adj* unexplored
inexpressif, -ive [inɛkspresif, -iv] *adj* inexpressive; (*regard etc*) expressionless
inexpressivité [inɛkspresivite] *nf* expressionlessness
inexprimable [inɛksprimabl(ə)] *adj* inexpressible
inexprimé, e [inɛksprime] *adj* unspoken, unexpressed
inexpugnable [inɛkspygnabl(ə)] *adj* impregnable
inextensible [inɛkstãsibl(ə)] *adj* (*tissu*) non-stretch
in extenso [inɛkstɛso] *adv* in full
inextinguible [inɛkstɛ̃gibl(ə)] *adj* (*soif*) unquenchable; (*rire*) uncontrollable
in extremis [inɛkstremis] *adv* at the last minute ▷ *adj* last-minute; (*testament*) death bed *cpd*
inextricable [inɛkstrikabl(ə)] *adj* inextricable
inextricablement [inɛkstrikabləmã] *adv* inextricably
infaillibilité [ɛ̃fajibilite] *nf* infallibility
infaillible [ɛ̃fajibl(ə)] *adj* infallible; (*instinct*) infallible, unerring
infailliblement [ɛ̃fajibləmã] *adv* (*certainement*) without fail
infaisable [ɛ̃fəzabl(ə)] *adj* (*travail etc*) impossible, impractical
infamant, e [ɛ̃famã, -ãt] *adj* libellous, defamatory
infâme [ɛ̃fam] *adj* vile
infamie [ɛ̃fami] *nf* infamy
infanterie [ɛ̃fãtri] *nf* infantry
infanticide [ɛ̃fãtisid] *nm/f* child-murderer, murderess ▷ *nm* (*meurtre*) infanticide
infantile [ɛ̃fãtil] *adj* (*Méd*) infantile, child *cpd*; (*péj: ton, réaction*) infantile, childish
infantilisme [ɛ̃fãtilism(ə)] *nm* infantilism
infarctus [ɛ̃farktys] *nm*: **~ (du myocarde)** coronary (thrombosis)
infatigable [ɛ̃fatigabl(ə)] *adj* tireless, indefatigable
infatigablement [ɛ̃fatigabləmã] *adv* tirelessly, indefatigably
infatué, e [ɛ̃fatɥe] *adj* conceited; **~ de** full of
infécond, e [ɛ̃fekɔ̃, -ɔ̃d] *adj* infertile, barren
infect, e [ɛ̃fɛkt] *adj* vile, foul; (*repas, vin*) revolting, foul
infecter [ɛ̃fɛkte] *vt* (*atmosphère, eau*) to contaminate; (*Méd*) to infect; **s'infecter** *vi* to become infected *ou* septic
infectieux, -euse [ɛ̃fɛksjø, -øz] *adj* infectious
infection [ɛ̃fɛksjɔ̃] *nf* infection
inféoder [ɛ̃feɔde] *vt*: **s'inféoder à** to pledge allegiance to
inférer [ɛ̃fere] *vt*: **~ qch de** to infer sth from
inférieur, e [ɛ̃ferjœr] *adj* lower; (*en qualité, intelligence*) inferior ▷ *nm/f* inferior; **~ à** (*somme, quantité*) less *ou* smaller than; (*moins bon que*) inferior to; (*tâche: pas à la hauteur de*) unequal to
infériorité [ɛ̃ferjɔrite] *nf* inferiority; **~ en nombre** inferiority in numbers
infernal, e, -aux [ɛ̃fɛrnal, -o] *adj* (*chaleur, rythme*) infernal; (*méchanceté, complot*) diabolical
infester [ɛ̃fɛste] *vt* to infest; **infesté de moustiques** infested with mosquitoes, mosquito-ridden
infidèle [ɛ̃fidɛl] *adj* unfaithful; (*Rel*) infidel
infidélité [ɛ̃fidelite] *nf* unfaithfulness *no pl*
infiltration [ɛ̃filtrasjɔ̃] *nf* infiltration
infiltrer [ɛ̃filtre]: **s'infiltrer** *vi*: **s'~ dans** to penetrate into; (*liquide*) to seep into; (*fig: noyauter*) to infiltrate
infime [ɛ̃fim] *adj* minute, tiny; (*inférieur*) lowly
infini, e [ɛ̃fini] *adj* infinite ▷ *nm* infinity; **à l'~** (*Math*) to infinity; (*discourir*) ad infinitum, endlessly; (*agrandir, varier*) infinitely; (*à perte de vue*) endlessly (into the distance)
infiniment [ɛ̃finimã] *adv* infinitely; **~ grand/petit** (*Math*) infinitely great/infinitesimal
infinité [ɛ̃finite] *nf*: **une ~ de** an infinite number of
infinitésimal, e, -aux [ɛ̃finitezimal, -o] *adj* infinitesimal
infinitif, -ive [ɛ̃finitif, -iv] *adj, nm* infinitive
infirme [ɛ̃firm(ə)] *adj* disabled ▷ *nm/f* disabled person; **~ de guerre** war cripple; **~ du travail** industrially disabled person
infirmer [ɛ̃firme] *vt* to invalidate
infirmerie [ɛ̃firməri] *nf* sick bay
infirmier, -ière [ɛ̃firmje, -jɛr] *nm/f* nurse ▷ *adj*: **élève ~** student nurse; **infirmière chef** sister; **infirmière diplômée** registered nurse; **infirmière visiteuse** visiting nurse, ≈ district nurse (*Brit*)
infirmité [ɛ̃firmite] *nf* disability

inflammable [ɛ̃flamabl(ə)] *adj* (in)flammable
inflammation [ɛ̃flamasjɔ̃] *nf* inflammation
inflammatoire [ɛ̃flamatwaʀ] *adj* (*Méd*) inflammatory
inflation [ɛ̃flasjɔ̃] *nf* inflation; **~ rampante/ galopante** creeping/galloping inflation
inflationniste [ɛ̃flasjɔnist(ə)] *adj* inflationist
infléchir [ɛ̃fleʃiʀ] *vt* (*fig: politique*) to reorientate, redirect; **s'infléchir** *vi* (*poutre, tringle*) to bend, sag
inflexibilité [ɛ̃flɛksibilite] *nf* inflexibility
inflexible [ɛ̃flɛksibl(ə)] *adj* inflexible
inflexion [ɛ̃flɛksjɔ̃] *nf* inflexion; **~ de la tête** slight nod (of the head)
infliger [ɛ̃fliʒe] *vt*: **~ qch (à qn)** to inflict sth (on sb); (*amende, sanction*) to impose sth (on sb)
influençable [ɛ̃flyɑ̃sabl(ə)] *adj* easily influenced
influence [ɛ̃flyɑ̃s] *nf* influence; (*d'un médicament*) effect
influencer [ɛ̃flyɑ̃se] *vt* to influence
influent, e [ɛ̃flyɑ̃, -ɑ̃t] *adj* influential
influer [ɛ̃flye]: **~ sur** *vt* to have an influence upon
influx [ɛ̃fly] *nm*: **~ nerveux** (nervous) impulse
infobulle [ɛ̃fobyl] *nf* (*Inform*) help bubble
infographie [ɛ̃fɔgʀafi] *nf* computer graphics *sg*
informateur, -trice [ɛ̃fɔʀmatœʀ, -tʀis] *nm/f* informant
informaticien, ne [ɛ̃fɔʀmatisjɛ̃, -ɛn] *nm/f* computer scientist
informatif, -ive [ɛ̃fɔʀmatif, -iv] *adj* informative
information [ɛ̃fɔʀmasjɔ̃] *nf* (*renseignement*) piece of information; (*Presse, TV: nouvelle*) item of news; (*diffusion de renseignements, Inform*) information; (*Jur*) inquiry, investigation; **informations** *nfpl* (TV) news *sg*; **voyage d'~** fact-finding trip; **agence d'~** news agency; **journal d'~** quality (*Brit*) *ou* serious newspaper
informatique [ɛ̃fɔʀmatik] *nf* (*technique*) data processing; (*science*) computer science ▷ *adj* computer *cpd*
informatisation [ɛ̃fɔʀmatizasjɔ̃] *nf* computerization
informatiser [ɛ̃fɔʀmatize] *vt* to computerize
informe [ɛ̃fɔʀm(ə)] *adj* shapeless
informé, e [ɛ̃fɔʀme] *adj*: **jusqu'à plus ample ~** until further information is available
informel, le [ɛ̃fɔʀmɛl] *adj* informal
informer [ɛ̃fɔʀme] *vt*: **~ qn (de)** to inform sb (of) ▷ *vi* (*Jur*): **~ contre qn/sur qch** to initiate inquiries about sb/sth; **s'informer (sur)** to inform o.s. (about); **s'~ (de qch/si)** to inquire *ou* find out (about sth/whether *ou* if)
informulé, e [ɛ̃fɔʀmyle] *adj* unformulated
infortune [ɛ̃fɔʀtyn] *nf* misfortune
infos [ɛ̃fo] *nfpl* (= *informations*) news
infraction [ɛ̃fʀaksjɔ̃] *nf* offence; **~ à** violation *ou* breach of; **être en ~** to be in breach of the law
infranchissable [ɛ̃fʀɑ̃ʃisabl(ə)] *adj* impassable; (*fig*) insuperable
infrarouge [ɛ̃fʀaʀuʒ] *adj, nm* infrared
infrason [ɛ̃fʀasɔ̃] *nm* infrasonic vibration

infrastructure [ɛ̃fʀastʀyktyʀ] *nf* (*d'une route etc*) substructure; (*Aviat, Mil*) ground installations *pl*; (*touristique etc*) facilities *pl*
infréquentable [ɛ̃fʀekɑ̃tabl(ə)] *adj* not to be associated with
infroissable [ɛ̃fʀwasabl(ə)] *adj* crease-resistant
infructueux, -euse [ɛ̃fʀyktɥø, -øz] *adj* fruitless, unfruitful
infus, e [ɛ̃fy, -yz] *adj*: **avoir la science ~e** to have innate knowledge
infuser [ɛ̃fyze] *vt* (*aussi*: **faire infuser**: *thé*) to brew; (: *tisane*) to infuse ▷ *vi* to brew; to infuse; **laisser ~** (to leave) to brew
infusion [ɛ̃fyzjɔ̃] *nf* (*tisane*) infusion, herb tea
ingambe [ɛ̃gɑ̃b] *adj* spry, nimble
ingénier [ɛ̃ʒenje]: **s'ingénier** *vi*: **s'~ à faire** to strive to do
ingénierie [ɛ̃ʒeniʀi] *nf* engineering
ingénieur [ɛ̃ʒenjœʀ] *nm* engineer; **~ agronome/chimiste** agricultural/chemical engineer; **~ conseil** consulting engineer; **~ du son** sound engineer
ingénieusement [ɛ̃ʒenjøzmɑ̃] *adv* ingeniously
ingénieux, -euse [ɛ̃ʒenjø, -øz] *adj* ingenious, clever
ingéniosité [ɛ̃ʒenjozite] *nf* ingenuity
ingénu, e [ɛ̃ʒeny] *adj* ingenuous, artless ▷ *nf* (*Théât*) ingénue
ingénuité [ɛ̃ʒenɥite] *nf* ingenuousness
ingénument [ɛ̃ʒenymɑ̃] *adv* ingenuously
ingérence [ɛ̃ʒeʀɑ̃s] *nf* interference
ingérer [ɛ̃ʒeʀe]: **s'ingérer** *vi*: **s'~ dans** to interfere in
ingouvernable [ɛ̃guvɛʀnabl(ə)] *adj* ungovernable
ingrat, e [ɛ̃gʀa, -at] *adj* (*personne*) ungrateful; (*sol*) poor; (*travail, sujet*) arid, thankless; (*visage*) unprepossessing
ingratitude [ɛ̃gʀatityd] *nf* ingratitude
ingrédient [ɛ̃gʀedjɑ̃] *nm* ingredient
inguérissable [ɛ̃geʀisabl(ə)] *adj* incurable
ingurgiter [ɛ̃gyʀʒite] *vt* to swallow; **faire ~ qch à qn** to make sb swallow sth; (*fig: connaissances*) to force sth into sb
inhabile [inabil] *adj* clumsy; (*fig*) inept
inhabitable [inabitabl(ə)] *adj* uninhabitable
inhabité, e [inabite] *adj* (*régions*) uninhabited; (*maison*) unoccupied
inhabituel, le [inabitɥɛl] *adj* unusual
inhalateur [inalatœʀ] *nm* inhaler; **~ d'oxygène** oxygen mask
inhalation [inalasjɔ̃] *nf* (*Méd*) inhalation; **faire des ~s** to use an inhalation bath
inhaler [inale] *vt* to inhale
inhérent, e [ineʀɑ̃, -ɑ̃t] *adj*: **~ à** inherent in
inhiber [inibe] *vt* to inhibit
inhibition [inibisjɔ̃] *nf* inhibition
inhospitalier, -ière [inɔspitalje, -jɛʀ] *adj* inhospitable
inhumain, e [inymɛ̃, -ɛn] *adj* inhuman
inhumation [inymasjɔ̃] *nf* interment, burial
inhumer [inyme] *vt* to inter, bury

inimaginable [inimaʒinabl(ə)] *adj* unimaginable

inimitable [inimitabl(ə)] *adj* inimitable

inimitié [inimitje] *nf* enmity

ininflammable [inɛ̃flamabl(ə)] *adj* non-flammable

inintelligent, e [inɛ̃teliʒɑ̃, -ɑ̃t] *adj* unintelligent

inintelligible [inɛ̃teliʒibl(ə)] *adj* unintelligible

inintelligiblement [inɛ̃teliʒibləmɑ̃] *adv* unintelligibly

inintéressant, e [inɛ̃teresɑ̃, -ɑ̃t] *adj* uninteresting

ininterrompu, e [inɛ̃terɔ̃py] *adj* (*file, série*) unbroken; (*flot, vacarme*) uninterrupted, non-stop; (*effort*) unremitting, continuous

iniquité [inikite] *nf* iniquity

initial, e, -aux [inisjal, -o] *adj, nf* initial; **initiales** *nfpl* initials

initialement [inisjalmɑ̃] *adv* initially

initialiser [inisjalize] *vt* to initialize

initiateur, -trice [inisjatœr, -tris] *nm/f* initiator; (*d'une mode, technique*) innovator, pioneer

initiation [inisjasjɔ̃] *nf* initiation

initiatique [inisjatik] *adj* (*rites, épreuves*) initiatory

initiative [inisjativ] *nf* initiative; **prendre l'~ de qch/de faire** to take the initiative for sth/of doing; **avoir de l'~** to have initiative, show enterprise; **esprit/qualités d'~** spirit/qualities of initiative; **à** *ou* **sur l'~ de qn** on sb's initiative; **de sa propre ~** on one's own initiative

initié, e [inisje] *adj* initiated ▷ *nm/f* initiate

initier [inisje] *vt* to initiate; **~ qn à** to initiate sb into; (*faire découvrir: art, jeu*) to introduce sb to; **s'initier à** *vi* (*métier, profession, technique*) to become initiated into

injectable [ɛ̃ʒɛktabl(ə)] *adj* injectable

injecté, e [ɛ̃ʒɛkte] *adj*: **yeux ~s de sang** bloodshot eyes

injecter [ɛ̃ʒɛkte] *vt* to inject

injection [ɛ̃ʒɛksjɔ̃] *nf* injection; **à ~** (*Auto*) fuel injection *cpd*

injonction [ɛ̃ʒɔ̃ksjɔ̃] *nf* injunction, order; **~ de payer** (*Jur*) order to pay

injouable [ɛ̃ʒwabl(ə)] *adj* unplayable

injure [ɛ̃ʒyr] *nf* insult, abuse *no pl*

injurier [ɛ̃ʒyrje] *vt* to insult, abuse

injurieux, -euse [ɛ̃ʒyrjø, -øz] *adj* abusive, insulting

injuste [ɛ̃ʒyst(ə)] *adj* unjust, unfair

injustement [ɛ̃ʒystəmɑ̃] *adv* unjustly, unfairly

injustice [ɛ̃ʒystis] *nf* injustice

injustifiable [ɛ̃ʒystifjabl(ə)] *adj* unjustifiable

injustifié, e [ɛ̃ʒystifje] *adj* unjustified, unwarranted

inlassable [ɛ̃lɑsabl(ə)] *adj* tireless, indefatigable

inlassablement [ɛ̃lɑsabləmɑ̃] *adv* tirelessly

inné, e [ine] *adj* innate, inborn

innocemment [inɔsamɑ̃] *adv* innocently

innocence [inɔsɑ̃s] *nf* innocence

innocent, e [inɔsɑ̃, -ɑ̃t] *adj* innocent ▷ *nm/f* innocent person; **faire l'~** to play *ou* come the innocent

innocenter [inɔsɑ̃te] *vt* to clear, prove innocent

innocuité [inɔkɥite] *nf* innocuousness

innombrable [inɔ̃brabl(ə)] *adj* innumerable

innommable [inɔmabl(ə)] *adj* unspeakable

innovateur, -trice [inɔvatœr, -tris] *adj* innovatory

innovation [inɔvasjɔ̃] *nf* innovation

innover [inɔve] *vi*: **~ en matière d'art** to break new ground in the field of art

inobservance [inɔpsɛrvɑ̃s] *nf* non-observance

inobservation [inɔpsɛrvasjɔ̃] *nf* non-observation, inobservance

inoccupé, e [inɔkype] *adj* unoccupied

inoculer [inɔkyle] *vt*: **~ qch à qn** (*volontairement*) to inoculate sb with sth; (*accidentellement*) to infect sb with sth; **~ qn contre** to inoculate sb against

inodore [inɔdɔr] *adj* (*gaz*) odourless; (*fleur*) scentless

inoffensif, -ive [inɔfɑ̃sif, -iv] *adj* harmless, innocuous

inondable [inɔ̃dabl(ə)] *adj* (*zone etc*) liable to flooding

inondation [inɔ̃dɑsjɔ̃] *nf* flooding *no pl*; (*torrent, eau*) flood

inonder [inɔ̃de] *vt* to flood; (*fig*) to inundate, overrun; **~ de** (*fig*) to flood *ou* swamp with

inopérable [inɔperabl(ə)] *adj* inoperable

inopérant, e [inɔperɑ̃, -ɑ̃t] *adj* inoperative, ineffective

inopiné, e [inɔpine] *adj* unexpected, sudden

inopinément [inɔpinemɑ̃] *adv* unexpectedly

inopportun, e [inɔpɔrtœ̃, -yn] *adj* ill-timed, untimely; inappropriate; (*moment*) inopportune

inorganisation [inɔrganizasjɔ̃] *nf* lack of organization

inorganisé, e [inɔrganize] *adj* (*travailleurs*) non-organized

inoubliable [inublijabl(ə)] *adj* unforgettable

inouï, e [inwi] *adj* unheard-of, extraordinary

inox [inɔks] *adj, nm* (= *inoxydable*) stainless (steel)

inoxydable [inɔksidabl(ə)] *adj* stainless; (*couverts*) stainless steel *cpd*

inqualifiable [ɛ̃kalifjabl(ə)] *adj* unspeakable

inquiet, -ète [ɛ̃kjɛ, -ɛt] *adj* (*par nature*) anxious; (*momentanément*) worried; **~ de qch/au sujet de qn** worried about sth/sb

inquiétant, e [ɛ̃kjetɑ̃, -ɑ̃t] *adj* worrying, disturbing

inquiéter [ɛ̃kjete] *vt* to worry, disturb; (*harceler*) to harass; **s'inquiéter** to worry, become anxious; **s'~ de** to worry about; (*s'enquérir de*) to inquire about

inquiétude [ɛ̃kjetyd] *nf* anxiety; **donner de l'~** *ou* **des ~s à** to worry; **avoir de l'~** *ou* **des ~s au sujet de** to feel anxious *ou* worried about

inquisiteur, -trice [ɛ̃kizitœr, -tris] *adj* (*regards, questions*) inquisitive, prying

inquisition [ɛ̃kizisjɔ̃] *nf* inquisition
INRA [inʀa] *sigle m* = **Institut national de la recherche agronomique**
inracontable [ɛ̃ʀakɔ̃tabl(ə)] *adj* (*trop osé*) unrepeatable; (*trop compliqué*): **l'histoire est ~** the story is too complicated to relate
insaisissable [ɛ̃sezisabl(ə)] *adj* elusive
insalubre [ɛ̃salybʀ(ə)] *adj* unhealthy, insalubrious
insalubrité [ɛ̃salybʀite] *nf* unhealthiness, insalubrity
insanité [ɛ̃sanite] *nf* madness *no pl*, insanity *no pl*
insatiable [ɛ̃sasjabl(ə)] *adj* insatiable
insatisfaction [ɛ̃satisfaksjɔ̃] *nf* dissatisfaction
insatisfait, e [ɛ̃satisfɛ, -ɛt] *adj* (*non comblé*) unsatisfied; (: *passion, envie*) unfulfilled; (*mécontent*) dissatisfied
inscription [ɛ̃skʀipsjɔ̃] *nf* (*sur un mur, écriteau etc*) inscription; (*à une institution: voir s'inscrire*) enrolment; registration
inscrire [ɛ̃skʀiʀ] *vt* (*marquer: sur son calepin etc*) to note *ou* write down; (: *sur un mur, une affiche etc*) to write; (: *dans la pierre, le métal*) to inscribe; (*mettre: sur une liste, un budget etc*) to put down; (*enrôler: soldat*) to enlist; **~ qn à** (*club, école etc*) to enrol sb at; **s'inscrire** *vi* (*pour une excursion etc*) to put one's name down; **s'~ (à)** (*club, parti*) to join; (*université*) to register *ou* enrol (at); (*examen, concours*) to register *ou* enter (for); **s'~ dans** (*se situer: négociations etc*) to come within the scope of; **s'~ en faux contre** to deny (strongly); (*Jur*) to challenge
inscrit, e [ɛ̃skʀi, it] *pp de* **inscrire** ▷ *adj* (*étudiant, électeur etc*) registered
insécable [ɛ̃sekabl(ə)] *adj* (*Inform*) indivisible; **espace ~** hard space
insecte [ɛ̃sɛkt(ə)] *nm* insect
insecticide [ɛ̃sɛktisid] *nm* insecticide
insécurité [ɛ̃sekyʀite] *nf* insecurity, lack of security
INSEE [inse] *sigle m* (= *Institut national de la statistique et des études économiques*) national institute of statistical and economic information
insémination [ɛ̃seminasjɔ̃] *nf* insemination
insensé, e [ɛ̃sɑ̃se] *adj* insane, mad
insensibiliser [ɛ̃sɑ̃sibilize] *vt* to anaesthetize; (*à une allergie*) to desensitize; **~ à qch** (*fig*) to cause to become insensitive to sth
insensibilité [ɛ̃sɑ̃sibilite] *nf* insensitivity
insensible [ɛ̃sɑ̃sibl(ə)] *adj* (*nerf, membre*) numb; (*dur, indifférent*) insensitive; (*imperceptible*) imperceptible
insensiblement [ɛ̃sɑ̃sibləmɑ̃] *adv* (*doucement, peu à peu*) imperceptibly
inséparable [ɛ̃sepaʀabl(ə)] *adj*: **~ (de)** inseparable (from) ▷ *nmpl*: **~s** (*oiseaux*) lovebirds
insérer [ɛ̃seʀe] *vt* to insert; **s'~ dans** to fit into; (*fig*) to come within
INSERM [ɛ̃sɛʀm] *sigle m* (= *Institut national de la santé et de la recherche médicale*) national institute for medical research

insert [ɛ̃sɛʀ] *nm* enclosed fireplace burning solid fuel
insertion [ɛ̃sɛʀsjɔ̃] *nf* (*d'une personne*) integration
insidieusement [ɛ̃sidjøzmɑ̃] *adv* insidiously
insidieux, -euse [ɛ̃sidjø, -øz] *adj* insidious
insigne [ɛ̃siɲ] *nm* (*d'un parti, club*) badge ▷ *adj* distinguished; **insignes** *nmpl* (*d'une fonction*) insignia *pl*
insignifiant, e [ɛ̃siɲifjɑ̃, -ɑ̃t] *adj* insignificant; (*somme, affaire, détail*) trivial, insignificant
insinuant, e [ɛ̃sinɥɑ̃, -ɑ̃t] *adj* ingratiating
insinuation [ɛ̃sinɥasjɔ̃] *nf* innuendo, insinuation
insinuer [ɛ̃sinɥe] *vt* to insinuate, imply; **s'insinuer dans** *vi* to seep into; (*fig*) to worm one's way into, creep into
insipide [ɛ̃sipid] *adj* insipid
insistance [ɛ̃sistɑ̃s] *nf* insistence; **avec ~** insistently
insistant, e [ɛ̃sistɑ̃, -ɑ̃t] *adj* insistent
insister [ɛ̃siste] *vi* to insist; (*s'obstiner*) to keep on; **~ sur** (*détail, note*) to stress; **~ pour qch/ pour faire qch** to be insistent about sth/about doing sth
insociable [ɛ̃sɔsjabl(ə)] *adj* unsociable
insolation [ɛ̃sɔlasjɔ̃] *nf* (*Méd*) sunstroke *no pl*; (*ensoleillement*) period of sunshine
insolence [ɛ̃sɔlɑ̃s] *nf* insolence *no pl*; **avec ~** insolently
insolent, e [ɛ̃sɔlɑ̃, -ɑ̃t] *adj* insolent
insolite [ɛ̃sɔlit] *adj* strange, unusual
insoluble [ɛ̃sɔlybl(ə)] *adj* insoluble
insolvable [ɛ̃sɔlvabl(ə)] *adj* insolvent
insomniaque [ɛ̃sɔmnjak] *adj, nm/f* insomniac
insomnie [ɛ̃sɔmni] *nf* insomnia *no pl*, sleeplessness *no pl*; **avoir des ~s** to suffer from insomnia
insondable [ɛ̃sɔ̃dabl(ə)] *adj* unfathomable
insonore [ɛ̃sɔnɔʀ] *adj* soundproof
insonorisation [ɛ̃sɔnɔʀizasjɔ̃] *nf* soundproofing
insonoriser [ɛ̃sɔnɔʀize] *vt* to soundproof
insouciance [ɛ̃susjɑ̃s] *nf* carefree attitude; heedless attitude
insouciant, e [ɛ̃susjɑ̃, -ɑ̃t] *adj* carefree; (*imprévoyant*) heedless
insoumis, e [ɛ̃sumi, -iz] *adj* (*caractère, enfant*) rebellious, refractory; (*contrée, tribu*) unsubdued; (*Mil: soldat*) absent without leave ▷ *nm* (*Mil: soldat*) absentee
insoumission [ɛ̃sumisjɔ̃] *nf* rebelliousness; (*Mil*) absence without leave
insoupçonnable [ɛ̃supsɔnabl(ə)] *adj* above suspicion
insoupçonné, e [ɛ̃supsɔne] *adj* unsuspected
insoutenable [ɛ̃sutnabl(ə)] *adj* (*argument*) untenable; (*chaleur*) unbearable
inspecter [ɛ̃spɛkte] *vt* to inspect
inspecteur, -trice [ɛ̃spɛktœʀ, -tʀis] *nm/f* inspector; (*des assurances*) assessor; **~ d'Académie** (regional) director of education; **~ (de l'enseignement) primaire** primary school inspector; **~ des finances** ≈ tax inspector (*Brit*),

≈ Internal Revenue Service agent (US); **~ (de police)** (police) inspector

inspection [ɛ̃spɛksjɔ̃] *nf* inspection

inspirateur, -trice [ɛ̃spiRatœR, -tRis] *nm/f* (*instigateur*) instigator; (*animateur*) inspirer

inspiration [ɛ̃spiRɑsjɔ̃] *nf* inspiration; breathing in *no pl*; (*idée*) flash of inspiration, brainwave; **sous l'~ de** prompted by

inspiré, e [ɛ̃spiRe] *adj*: **être bien/mal ~ de faire qch** to be well-advised/ill-advised to do sth

inspirer [ɛ̃spiRe] *vt* (*gén*) to inspire ▷ *vi* (*aspirer*) to breathe in; **s'inspirer de** (*artiste*) to draw one's inspiration from; (*tableau*) to be inspired by; **~ qch à qn** (*œuvre, projet, action*) to inspire sb with sth; (*dégoût, crainte, horreur*) to fill sb with sth; **ça ne m'inspire pas** I'm not keen on the idea

instabilité [ɛ̃stabilite] *nf* instability

instable [ɛ̃stabl(ə)] *adj* (*meuble, équilibre*) unsteady; (*population, temps*) unsettled; (*paix, régime, caractère*) unstable

installateur [ɛ̃stalatœR] *nm* fitter

installation [ɛ̃stalɑsjɔ̃] *nf* installation; putting in *ou* up; fitting out; settling in; (*appareils etc*) fittings *pl*, installations *pl*; **installations** *nfpl* installations; (*industrielles*) plant *sg*; (*de loisirs*) facilities

installé, e [ɛ̃stale] *adj*: **bien/mal ~** well/poorly equipped; (*personne*) well/not very well set up *ou* organized

installer [ɛ̃stale] *vt* (*loger*): **~ qn** to get sb settled, install sb; (*asseoir, coucher*) to settle (down); (*placer*) to put, place; (*meuble*) to put in; (*rideau, étagère, tente*) to put up; (*gaz, électricité etc*) to put in, install; (*appartement*) to fit out; (*aménager*): **~ une salle de bains dans une pièce** to fit out a room with a bathroom suite; **s'installer** *vi* (*s'établir: artisan, dentiste etc*) to set o.s. up; (*se loger*): **s'~ à l'hôtel/chez qn** to move into a hotel/in with sb; (*emménager*) to settle in; (*sur un siège, à un emplacement*) to settle (down); (*fig: maladie, grève*) to take a firm hold *ou* grip

instamment [ɛ̃stamɑ̃] *adv* urgently

instance [ɛ̃stɑ̃s] *nf* (*Jur: procédure*) (legal) proceedings *pl*; (*Admin: autorité*) authority; **instances** *nfpl* (*prières*) entreaties; **affaire en ~** matter pending; **courrier en ~** mail ready for posting; **être en ~ de divorce** to be awaiting a divorce; **train en ~ de départ** train on the point of departure; **tribunal de première ~** court of first instance; **en seconde ~** on appeal

instant [ɛ̃stɑ̃] *nm* moment, instant; **dans un ~** in a moment; **à l'~** this instant; **je l'ai vu à l'~** I've just this minute seen him, I saw him a moment ago; **à l'~ (même) où** at the (very) moment that *ou* when, (just) as; **à chaque ~, à tout ~** at any moment; constantly; **pour l'~** for the moment, for the time being; **par ~s** at times; **de tous les ~s** perpetual; **dès l'~ où** *ou* **que ...** from the moment when ..., since that moment when ...

instantané, e [ɛ̃stɑ̃tane] *adj* (*lait, café*) instant;

(*explosion, mort*) instantaneous ▷ *nm* snapshot

instantanément [ɛ̃stɑ̃tanemɑ̃] *adv* instantaneously

instar [ɛ̃staR]: **à l'~ de** *prép* following the example of, like

instaurer [ɛ̃stɔRe] *vt* to institute; **s'instaurer** *vi* to set o.s. up; (*collaboration etc*) to be established

instigateur, -trice [ɛ̃stigatœR, -tRis] *nm/f* instigator

instigation [ɛ̃stigɑsjɔ̃] *nf*: **à l'~ de qn** at sb's instigation

instiller [ɛ̃stile] *vt* to instil, apply

instinct [ɛ̃stɛ̃] *nm* instinct; **d'~** (*spontanément*) instinctively; **~ grégaire** herd instinct; **~ de conservation** instinct of self-preservation

instinctif, -ive [ɛ̃stɛ̃ktif, -iv] *adj* instinctive

instinctivement [ɛ̃stɛ̃ktivmɑ̃] *adv* instinctively

instit [ɛ̃stit] (*fam*) *nm/f* (primary school) teacher

instituer [ɛ̃stitɥe] *vt* to institute, set up; **s'~ défenseur d'une cause** to set o.s up as defender of a cause

institut [ɛ̃stity] *nm* institute; **~ de beauté** beauty salon; **~ médico-légal** mortuary; **I~ universitaire de technologie (IUT)** technical college

instituteur, -trice [ɛ̃stitytœR, -tRis] *nm/f* (primary (*Brit*) *ou* grade (*US*) school) teacher

institution [ɛ̃stitysjɔ̃] *nf* institution; (*collège*) private school

institutionnaliser [ɛ̃stitysjɔnalize] *vt* to institutionalize

instructeur, -trice [ɛ̃stRyktœR, -tRis] *adj* (*Mil*): **sergent ~** drill sergeant; (*Jur*): **juge ~** examining (*Brit*) *ou* committing (*US*) magistrate ▷ *nm/f* instructor

instructif, -ive [ɛ̃stRyktif, -iv] *adj* instructive

instruction [ɛ̃stRyksjɔ̃] *nf* (*enseignement, savoir*) education; (*Jur*) (preliminary) investigation and hearing; (*directive*) instruction; (*Admin: document*) directive; **instructions** *nfpl* instructions; (*mode d'emploi*) directions, instructions; **~ civique** civics *sg*; **~ primaire/publique** primary/public education; **~ religieuse** religious education; **~ professionnelle** vocational training

instruire [ɛ̃stRɥiR] *vt* (*élèves*) to teach; (*recrues*) to train; (*Jur: affaire*) to conduct the investigation for; **s'instruire** to educate o.s.; **s'~ auprès de qn de qch** (*s'informer*) to find sth out from sb; **~ qn de qch** (*informer*) to inform *ou* advise sb of sth; **~ contre qn** (*Jur*) to investigate sb

instruit, e [ɛ̃stRɥi, -it] *pp de* **instruire** ▷ *adj* educated

instrument [ɛ̃stRymɑ̃] *nm* instrument; **~ à cordes/vent** stringed/wind instrument; **~ de mesure** measuring instrument; **~ de musique** musical instrument; **~ de travail** (working) tool

instrumental, e, -aux [ɛ̃stRymɑ̃tal, -o] *adj* instrumental

instrumentation [ɛ̃stRymɑ̃tɑsjɔ̃] *nf* instrumentation

instrumentiste [ɛ̃stʀymɑ̃tist(ə)] nm/f
instrumentalist
insu [ɛ̃sy] nm: **à l'~ de qn** without sb knowing
insubmersible [ɛ̃sybmɛʀsibl(ə)] adj unsinkable
insubordination [ɛ̃sybɔʀdinɑsjɔ̃] nf
rebelliousness; (Mil) insubordination
insubordonné, e [ɛ̃sybɔʀdɔne] adj
insubordinate
insuccès [ɛ̃syksɛ] nm failure
insuffisamment [ɛ̃syfizamɑ̃] adv insufficiently
insuffisance [ɛ̃syfizɑ̃s] nf insufficiency;
inadequacy; **insuffisances** nfpl (lacunes)
inadequacies; **~ cardiaque** cardiac
insufficiency no pl; **~ hépatique** liver deficiency
insuffisant, e [ɛ̃syfizɑ̃, -ɑ̃t] adj insufficient;
(élève, travail) inadequate
insuffler [ɛ̃syfle] vt: **~ qch dans** to blow sth into;
~ qch à qn to inspire sb with sth
insulaire [ɛ̃sylɛʀ] adj island cpd; (attitude)
insular
insularité [ɛ̃sylaʀite] nf insularity
insuline [ɛ̃sylin] nf insulin
insultant, e [ɛ̃syltɑ̃, -ɑ̃t] adj insulting
insulte [ɛ̃sylt(ə)] nf insult
insulter [ɛ̃sylte] vt to insult
insupportable [ɛ̃sypɔʀtabl(ə)] adj unbearable
insurgé, e [ɛ̃syʀʒe] adj, nm/f insurgent, rebel
insurger [ɛ̃syʀʒe]: **s'insurger** vi: **s'~ (contre)** to
rise up ou rebel (against)
insurmontable [ɛ̃syʀmɔ̃tabl(ə)] adj (difficulté)
insuperable; (aversion) unconquerable
insurpassable [ɛ̃syʀpɑsabl(ə)] adj
unsurpassable, unsurpassed
insurrection [ɛ̃syʀɛksjɔ̃] nf insurrection, revolt
insurrectionnel, le [ɛ̃syʀɛksjɔnɛl] adj
insurrectionary
intact, e [ɛ̃takt] adj intact
intangible [ɛ̃tɑ̃ʒibl(ə)] adj intangible; (principe)
inviolable
intarissable [ɛ̃taʀisabl(ə)] adj inexhaustible
intégral, e, -aux [ɛ̃tegʀal, -o] adj complete ▷ nf
(Math) integral; (œuvres complètes) complete
works
intégralement [ɛ̃tegʀalmɑ̃] adv in full, fully
intégralité [ɛ̃tegʀalite] nf (d'une somme, d'un
revenu) whole (ou full) amount; **dans son ~** in its
entirety
intégrant, e [ɛ̃tegʀɑ̃, -ɑ̃t] adj: **faire partie ~e de**
to be an integral part of, be part and parcel of
intégration [ɛ̃tegʀasjɔ̃] nf integration
intégrationniste [ɛ̃tegʀasjɔnist(ə)] adj, nm/f
integrationist
intégré, e [ɛ̃tegʀe] adj: **circuit ~** integrated
circuit
intègre [ɛ̃tɛgʀ(ə)] adj perfectly honest, upright
intégrer [ɛ̃tegʀe] vt: **~ qch à** ou **dans** to
integrate sth into; **s'~ à** ou **dans** to become
integrated into
intégrisme [ɛ̃tegʀism(ə)] nm fundamentalism
intégriste [ɛ̃tegʀist(ə)] adj, nm/f
fundamentalist
intégrité [ɛ̃tegʀite] nf integrity

intellect [ɛ̃telɛkt] nm intellect
intellectuel, le [ɛ̃telɛktɥɛl] adj, nm/f
intellectual; (péj) highbrow
intellectuellement [ɛ̃telɛktɥɛlmɑ̃] adv
intellectually
intelligemment [ɛ̃teliʒamɑ̃] adv intelligently
intelligence [ɛ̃teliʒɑ̃s] nf intelligence;
(compréhension): **l'~ de** the understanding of;
(complicité): **regard d'~** glance of complicity,
meaningful ou knowing look; (accord): **vivre en
bonne ~ avec qn** to be on good terms with sb;
intelligences nfpl (Mil, fig) secret contacts; **être
d'~** to have an understanding; **~ artificielle**
artificial intelligence (A.I.)
intelligent, e [ɛ̃teliʒɑ̃, -ɑ̃t] adj intelligent;
(capable): **~ en affaires** competent in business
intelligentsia [ɛ̃telidʒɛnsja] nf intelligentsia
intelligible [ɛ̃teliʒibl(ə)] adj intelligible
intello [ɛ̃telo] adj, nm/f (fam) highbrow
intempérance [ɛ̃tɑ̃peʀɑ̃s] nf overindulgence no
pl; intemperance no pl
intempérant, e [ɛ̃tɑ̃peʀɑ̃, -ɑ̃t] adj
overindulgent; (moralement) intemperate
intempéries [ɛ̃tɑ̃peʀi] nfpl bad weather sg
intempestif, -ive [ɛ̃tɑ̃pɛstif, -iv] adj untimely
intenable [ɛ̃tnabl(ə)] adj unbearable
intendance [ɛ̃tɑ̃dɑ̃s] nf (Mil) supply corps;
(: bureau) supplies office; (Scol) bursar's office
intendant, e [ɛ̃tɑ̃dɑ̃, -ɑ̃t] nm/f (Mil)
quartermaster; (Scol) bursar; (d'une propriété)
steward
intense [ɛ̃tɑ̃s] adj intense
intensément [ɛ̃tɑ̃semɑ̃] adv intensely
intensif, -ive [ɛ̃tɑ̃sif, -iv] adj intensive; **cours ~**
crash course; **~ en main-d'œuvre** labour-
intensive; **~ en capital** capital-intensive
intensification [ɛ̃tɑ̃sifikasjɔ̃] nf intensification
intensifier [ɛ̃tɑ̃sifje] vt, **s'intensifier** vi to
intensify
intensité [ɛ̃tɑ̃site] nf intensity
intensivement [ɛ̃tɑ̃sivmɑ̃] adv intensively
intenter [ɛ̃tɑ̃te] vt: **~ un procès contre** ou **à qn**
to start proceedings against sb
intention [ɛ̃tɑ̃sjɔ̃] nf intention; (Jur) intent;
avoir l'~ de faire to intend to do, have the
intention of doing; **dans l'~ de faire qch** with
a view to doing sth; **à l'~ de** prép for;
(renseignement) for the benefit ou information of;
(film, ouvrage) aimed at; **à cette ~** with this aim
in view; **sans ~** unintentionally; **faire qch
sans mauvaise ~** to do sth without ill intent;
agir dans une bonne ~ to act with good
intentions
intentionné, e [ɛ̃tɑ̃sjɔne] adj: **bien ~** well-
meaning ou -intentioned; **mal ~** ill-
intentioned
intentionnel, le [ɛ̃tɑ̃sjɔnɛl] adj intentional,
deliberate
intentionnellement [ɛ̃tɑ̃sjɔnɛlmɑ̃] adv
intentionally, deliberately
inter [ɛ̃tɛʀ] nm (Tél: interurbain) long-distance
call service; (Sport): **~ gauche/droit** inside-

left/-right

interactif, -ive [ɛ̃tɛʀaktif, -iv] *adj* (*aussi Inform*) interactive

interaction [ɛ̃tɛʀaksjɔ̃] *nf* interaction

interbancaire [ɛ̃tɛʀbɑ̃kɛʀ] *adj* interbank

intercalaire [ɛ̃tɛʀkalɛʀ] *adj, nm*: (**feuillet**) ~ insert; (**fiche**) ~ divider

intercaler [ɛ̃tɛʀkale] *vt* to insert; **s'intercaler entre** *vi* to come in between; to slip in between

intercéder [ɛ̃tɛʀsede] *vi*: ~ (**pour qn**) to intercede (on behalf of sb)

intercepter [ɛ̃tɛʀsɛpte] *vt* to intercept; (*lumière, chaleur*) to cut off

intercepteur [ɛ̃tɛʀsɛptœʀ] *nm* (*Aviat*) interceptor

interception [ɛ̃tɛʀsɛpsjɔ̃] *nf* interception; **avion d'**~ interceptor

intercession [ɛ̃tɛʀsesjɔ̃] *nf* intercession

interchangeable [ɛ̃tɛʀʃɑ̃ʒabl(ə)] *adj* interchangeable

interclasse [ɛ̃tɛʀklas] *nm* (*Scol*) break (between classes)

interclubs [ɛ̃tɛʀklœb] *adj inv* interclub

intercommunal, e, -aux [ɛ̃tɛʀkɔmynal, -o] *adj* intervillage, intercommunity

intercommunautaire [ɛ̃tɛʀkɔmynotɛʀ] *adj* intercommunity

intercontinental, e, -aux [ɛ̃tɛʀkɔ̃tinɑ̃tal, -o] *adj* intercontinental

intercostal, e, -aux [ɛ̃tɛʀkɔstal, -o] *adj* intercostal, between the ribs

interdépartemental, e, -aux [ɛ̃tɛʀdepaʀtəmɑ̃tal, -o] *adj* interdepartmental

interdépendance [ɛ̃tɛʀdepɑ̃dɑ̃s] *nf* interdependence

interdépendant, e [ɛ̃tɛʀdepɑ̃dɑ̃, -ɑ̃t] *adj* interdependent

interdiction [ɛ̃tɛʀdiksjɔ̃] *nf* ban; ~ **de faire qch** ban on doing sth; ~ **de séjour** (*Jur*) order banning ex-prisoner from frequenting specified places

interdire [ɛ̃tɛʀdiʀ] *vt* to forbid; (*Admin: stationnement, meeting, passage*) to ban, prohibit; (*: journal, livre*) to ban; ~ **qch à qn** to forbid sb sth; ~ **à qn de faire** to forbid sb to do, prohibit sb from doing; (*empêchement*) to prevent *ou* preclude sb from doing; **s'interdire qch** *vi* (*éviter*) to refrain *ou* abstain from sth; (*se refuser*): **il s'interdit d'y penser** he doesn't allow himself to think about it

interdisciplinaire [ɛ̃tɛʀdisiplinɛʀ] *adj* interdisciplinary

interdit, e [ɛ̃tɛʀdi, -it] *pp de* **interdire** ▷ *adj* (*stupéfait*) taken aback; (*défendu*) forbidden, prohibited ▷ *nm* interdict, prohibition; **film ~ aux moins de 18/13 ans** ≈ 18-/PG-rated film; **sens ~** one way; **stationnement ~** no parking; ~ **de chéquier** having cheque book facilities suspended; ~ **de séjour** subject to an "interdiction de séjour"

intéressant, e [ɛ̃teʀesɑ̃, -ɑ̃t] *adj* interesting; **faire l'**~ to draw attention to o.s.

intéressé, e [ɛ̃teʀese] *adj* (*parties*) involved, concerned; (*amitié, motifs*) self-interested ▷ *nm*: **l'**~ the interested party; **les ~s** those concerned *ou* involved

intéressement [ɛ̃teʀesmɑ̃] *nm* (*Comm*) profit-sharing

intéresser [ɛ̃teʀese] *vt* to interest; (*toucher*) to be of interest *ou* concern to; (*Admin: concerner*) to affect, concern; (*Comm: travailleur*) to give a share in the profits to; (*: partenaire*) to interest (in the business); **s'intéresser à** *vi* to take an interest in, be interested in; ~ **qn à qch** to get sb interested in sth

intérêt [ɛ̃teʀɛ] *nm* (*aussi Comm*) interest; (*égoïsme*) self-interest; **porter de l'**~ **à qn** to take an interest in sb; **agir par** ~ to act out of self-interest; **avoir des ~s dans** (*Comm*) to have a financial interest *ou* a stake in; **avoir ~ à faire** to do well to do; **il y a ~ à ...** it would be a good thing to ...; ~ **composé** compound interest

interface [ɛ̃tɛʀfas] *nf* (*Inform*) interface

interférence [ɛ̃tɛʀfeʀɑ̃s] *nf* interference

interférer [ɛ̃tɛʀfeʀe] *vi*: ~ (**avec**) to interfere (with)

intergouvernemental, e, -aux [ɛ̃tɛʀguvɛʀnəmɑ̃tal, -o] *adj* intergovernmental

intérieur, e [ɛ̃teʀjœʀ] *adj* (*mur, escalier, poche*) inside; (*commerce, politique*) domestic; (*cour, calme, vie*) inner; (*navigation*) inland ▷ *nm* (*d'une maison, d'un récipient etc*) inside; (*d'un pays, aussi: décor, mobilier*) interior; (*Pol*): **l'I~** (the Department of) the Interior, ≈ the Home Office (*Brit*); **à l'**~ (**de**) inside; (*fig*) within; **de l'**~ (*fig*) from the inside; **en** ~ (*Ciné*) in the studio; **vêtement d'**~ indoor garment

intérieurement [ɛ̃teʀjœʀmɑ̃] *adv* inwardly

intérim [ɛ̃teʀim] *nm* (*période*) interim period; (*travail*) temping; **agence d'**~ temping agency; **assurer l'**~ (**de**) to deputize (for); **président par** ~ interim president; **travailler en** ~ to temp

intérimaire [ɛ̃teʀimɛʀ] *adj* temporary, interim ▷ *nm/f* (*secrétaire etc*) temporary, temp (*Brit*); (*suppléant*) deputy

intérioriser [ɛ̃teʀjɔʀize] *vt* to internalize

interjection [ɛ̃tɛʀʒɛksjɔ̃] *nf* interjection

interjeter [ɛ̃tɛʀʒəte] *vt* (*Jur*): ~ **appel** to lodge an appeal

interligne [ɛ̃tɛʀliɲ] *nm* inter-line space ▷ *nf* (*Typo*) lead, leading; **simple/double** ~ single/double spacing

interlocuteur, -trice [ɛ̃tɛʀlɔkytœʀ, -tʀis] *nm/f* speaker; (*Pol*): ~ **valable** valid representative; **son** ~ the person he *ou* she was speaking to

interlope [ɛ̃tɛʀlɔp] *adj* illicit; (*milieu, bar*) shady

interloquer [ɛ̃tɛʀlɔke] *vt* to take aback

interlude [ɛ̃tɛʀlyd] *nm* interlude

intermède [ɛ̃tɛʀmɛd] *nm* interlude

intermédiaire [ɛ̃tɛʀmedjɛʀ] *adj* intermediate; middle; half-way ▷ *nm/f* intermediary; (*Comm*) middleman; **sans** ~ directly; **par l'**~ **de** through

interminable [ɛ̃tɛʀminabl(ə)] *adj* never-ending

interminablement [ɛ̃tɛʀminabləmɑ̃] *adv* interminably

interministériel, le [ɛ̃tɛʀministeʀjɛl] *adj:* **comité ~** interdepartmental committee

intermittence [ɛ̃tɛʀmitɑ̃s] *nf:* **par ~** intermittently, sporadically

intermittent, e [ɛ̃tɛʀmitɑ̃, -ɑ̃t] *adj* intermittent, sporadic

internat [ɛ̃tɛʀna] *nm* (*Scol*) boarding school

international, e, -aux [ɛ̃tɛʀnasjɔnal, -o] *adj, nm/f* international

internationalisation [ɛ̃tɛʀnasjɔnalizasjɔ̃] *nf* internationalization

internationaliser [ɛ̃tɛʀnasjɔnalize] *vt* to internationalize

internationalisme [ɛ̃tɛʀnasjɔnalism(ə)] *nm* internationalism

internaute [ɛ̃tɛʀnot] *nm/f* Internet user

interne [ɛ̃tɛʀn(ə)] *adj* internal ▷ *nm/f* (*Scol*) boarder; (*Méd*) houseman (*Brit*), intern (*US*)

internement [ɛ̃tɛʀnəmɑ̃] *nm* (*Pol*) internment; (*Méd*) confinement

interner [ɛ̃tɛʀne] *vt* (*Pol*) to intern; (*Méd*) to confine to a mental institution

Internet [ɛ̃tɛʀnɛt] *nm:* **l'~** the Internet

interparlementaire [ɛ̃tɛʀpaʀləmɑ̃tɛʀ] *adj* interparliamentary

interpellation [ɛ̃tɛʀpelasjɔ̃] *nf* interpellation; (*Pol*) question

interpeller [ɛ̃tɛʀpele] *vt* (*appeler*) to call out to; (*apostropher*) to shout at; (*Police*) to take in for questioning; (*Pol*) to question; **s'interpeller** *vi* to exchange insults

interphone [ɛ̃tɛʀfɔn] *nm* intercom

interplanétaire [ɛ̃tɛʀplanetɛʀ] *adj* interplanetary

Interpol [ɛ̃tɛʀpɔl] *sigle m* Interpol

interpoler [ɛ̃tɛʀpɔle] *vt* to interpolate

interposer [ɛ̃tɛʀpoze] *vt* to interpose; **s'interposer** *vi* to intervene; **par personnes interposées** through a third party

interprétariat [ɛ̃tɛʀpʀetaʀja] *nm* interpreting

interprétation [ɛ̃tɛʀpʀetasjɔ̃] *nf* interpretation

interprète [ɛ̃tɛʀpʀɛt] *nm/f* interpreter; (*porte-parole*) spokesman

interpréter [ɛ̃tɛʀpʀete] *vt* to interpret

interprofessionnel, le [ɛ̃tɛʀpʀɔfesjɔnɛl] *adj* interprofessional

interrogateur, -trice [ɛ̃tɛʀɔgatœʀ, -tʀis] *adj* questioning, inquiring ▷ *nm/f* (*Scol*) (oral) examiner

interrogatif, -ive [ɛ̃tɛʀɔgatif, -iv] *adj* (*Ling*) interrogative

interrogation [ɛ̃tɛʀɔgasjɔ̃] *nf* question; (*Scol*) (written *ou* oral) test

interrogatoire [ɛ̃tɛʀɔgatwaʀ] *nm* (*Police*) questioning *no pl*; (*Jur*) cross-examination, interrogation

interroger [ɛ̃tɛʀɔʒe] *vt* to question; (*Inform*) to search; (*Scol: candidat*) to test; **~ qn (sur qch)** to question sb (about sth); **~ qn du regard** to look questioningly at sb, give sb a questioning look;

s'~ sur qch to ask o.s. about sth, ponder (about) sth

interrompre [ɛ̃tɛʀɔ̃pʀ(ə)] *vt* (*gén*) to interrupt; (*travail, voyage*) to break off, interrupt; **s'interrompre** *vi* to break off

interrupteur [ɛ̃tɛʀyptœʀ] *nm* switch

interruption [ɛ̃tɛʀypsjɔ̃] *nf* interruption; **sans ~** without a break; **~ de grossesse** termination of pregnancy; **~ volontaire de grossesse** voluntary termination of pregnancy, abortion

interscolaire [ɛ̃tɛʀskɔlɛʀ] *adj* interschool(s)

intersection [ɛ̃tɛʀsɛksjɔ̃] *nf* intersection

intersidéral, e, -aux [ɛ̃tɛʀsideʀal, -o] *adj* interstellar

interstice [ɛ̃tɛʀstis] *nm* crack, slit

intersyndical, e, -aux [ɛ̃tɛʀsɛ̃dikal, -o] *adj* interunion

interurbain [ɛ̃tɛʀyʀbɛ̃] (*Tél*) *nm* long-distance call service ▷ *adj* long-distance

intervalle [ɛ̃tɛʀval] *nm* (*espace*) space; (*de temps*) interval; **dans l'~** in the meantime; **à deux mois d'~** after a space of two months; **à ~s rapprochés** at close intervals; **par ~s** at intervals

intervenant, e [ɛ̃tɛʀvənɑ̃, -ɑ̃t] *vb voir* **intervenir** ▷ *nm/f* speaker (*at conference*)

intervenir [ɛ̃tɛʀvəniʀ] *vi* (*gén*) to intervene; (*survenir*) to take place; (*faire une conférence*) to give a talk *ou* lecture; **~ auprès de/en faveur de qn** to intervene with/on behalf of sb; **la police a dû ~** police had to step in *ou* intervene; **les médecins ont dû ~** the doctors had to operate

intervention [ɛ̃tɛʀvɑ̃sjɔ̃] *nf* intervention; (*conférence*) talk, paper; **~ (chirurgicale)** operation

interventionnisme [ɛ̃tɛʀvɑ̃sjɔnism(ə)] *nm* interventionism

interventionniste [ɛ̃tɛʀvɑ̃sjɔnist(ə)] *adj* interventionist

intervenu, e [ɛ̃tɛʀv(ə)ny] *pp de* **intervenir**

intervertible [ɛ̃tɛʀvɛʀtibl(ə)] *adj* interchangeable

intervertir [ɛ̃tɛʀvɛʀtiʀ] *vt* to invert (the order of), reverse

interviendrai [ɛ̃tɛʀvjɛ̃dʀe], **interviens** *etc* [ɛ̃tɛʀvjɛ̃] *vb voir* **intervenir**

interview [ɛ̃tɛʀvju] *nf* interview

interviewer [ɛ̃tɛʀvjuve] *vt* to interview ▷ *nm* [ɛ̃tɛʀvjuvœʀ] (*journaliste*) interviewer

intervins *etc* [ɛ̃tɛʀvɛ̃] *vb voir* **intervenir**

intestat [ɛ̃tɛsta] *adj* (*Jur*): **décéder ~** to die intestate

intestin, e [ɛ̃tɛstɛ̃, -in] *adj* internal ▷ *nm* intestine; **~ grêle** small intestine

intestinal, e, -aux [ɛ̃tɛstinal, -o] *adj* intestinal

intime [ɛ̃tim] *adj* intimate; (*vie, journal*) private; (*convictions*) inmost; (*dîner, cérémonie*) held among friends, quiet ▷ *nm/f* close friend

intimement [ɛ̃timmɑ̃] *adv* (*profondément*) deeply, firmly; (*étroitement*) intimately

intimer [ɛ̃time] *vt* (*Jur*) to notify; **~ à qn l'ordre de faire** to order sb to do

intimidant, e [ɛ̃timidɑ̃, -ɑ̃t] *adj* intimidating
intimidation [ɛ̃timidasjɔ̃] *nf* intimidation; **manœuvres d'~** (*action*) acts of intimidation; (*stratégie*) intimidatory tactics
intimider [ɛ̃timide] *vt* to intimidate
intimité [ɛ̃timite] *nf* intimacy; (*vie privée*) privacy; private life; **dans l'~** in private; (*sans formalités*) with only a few friends, quietly
intitulé [ɛ̃tityle] *nm* title
intituler [ɛ̃tityle] *vt*: **comment a-t-il intitulé son livre?** what title did he give his book?; **s'intituler** *vi* to be entitled; (*personne*) to call o.s.
intolérable [ɛ̃tɔlerabl(ə)] *adj* intolerable
intolérance [ɛ̃tɔlerɑ̃s] *nf* intolerance; **~ aux antibiotiques** intolerance to antibiotics
intolérant, e [ɛ̃tɔlerɑ̃, -ɑ̃t] *adj* intolerant
intonation [ɛ̃tɔnasjɔ̃] *nf* intonation
intouchable [ɛ̃tuʃabl(ə)] *adj* (*fig*) above the law, sacrosanct; (*Rel*) untouchable
intox [ɛ̃tɔks] (*fam*) *nf* brainwashing
intoxication [ɛ̃tɔksikasjɔ̃] *nf* poisoning *no pl*; (*toxicomanie*) drug addiction; (*fig*) brainwashing; **~ alimentaire** food poisoning
intoxiqué, e [ɛ̃tɔksike] *nm/f* addict
intoxiquer [ɛ̃tɔksike] *vt* to poison; (*fig*) to brainwash; **s'intoxiquer** to poison o.s.
intradermique [ɛ̃tradɛrmik] *adj, nf*: **(injection)** ~ intradermal *ou* intracutaneous injection
intraduisible [ɛ̃traduizibl(ə)] *adj* untranslatable; (*fig*) inexpressible
intraitable [ɛ̃trɛtabl(ə)] *adj* inflexible, uncompromising
intramusculaire [ɛ̃tramyskylɛr] *adj, nf*: **(injection)** ~ intramuscular injection
intranet [ɛ̃tranɛt] *nm* intranet
intransigeance [ɛ̃trɑ̃ziʒɑ̃s] *nf* intransigence
intransigeant, e [ɛ̃trɑ̃ziʒɑ̃, -ɑ̃t] *adj* intransigent; (*morale, passion*) uncompromising
intransitif, -ive [ɛ̃trɑ̃zitif, -iv] *adj* (*Ling*) intransitive
intransportable [ɛ̃trɑ̃spɔrtabl(ə)] *adj* (*blessé*) unable to travel
intraveineux, -euse [ɛ̃travɛnø, -øz] *adj* intravenous
intrépide [ɛ̃trepid] *adj* dauntless, intrepid
intrépidité [ɛ̃trepidite] *nf* dauntlessness
intrigant, e [ɛ̃trigɑ̃, -ɑ̃t] *nm/f* schemer
intrigue [ɛ̃trig] *nf* intrigue; (*scénario*) plot
intriguer [ɛ̃trige] *vi* to scheme ▷ *vt* to puzzle, intrigue
intrinsèque [ɛ̃trɛ̃sɛk] *adj* intrinsic
introductif, -ive [ɛ̃trɔdyktif, -iv] *adj* introductory
introduction [ɛ̃trɔdyksjɔ̃] *nf* introduction; **paroles/chapitre d'~** introductory words/chapter; **lettre/mot d'~** letter/note of introduction
introduire [ɛ̃trɔduir] *vt* to introduce; (*visiteur*) to show in; (*aiguille, clef*): **~ qch dans** to insert *ou* introduce sth into; (*personne*): **~ à qch** to introduce to sth; (: *présenter*): **~ qn à qn/dans un**

club to introduce sb to sb/to a club; **s'introduire** *vi* (*techniques, usages*) to be introduced; **s'~ dans** to gain entry into; to get o.s. accepted into; (*eau, fumée*) to get into; **~ au clavier** to key in
introduit, e [ɛ̃trɔdui, -it] *pp de* **introduire** ▷ *adj*: **bien ~** (*personne*) well-received
introniser [ɛ̃trɔnize] *vt* to enthrone
introspection [ɛ̃trɔspɛksjɔ̃] *nf* introspection
introuvable [ɛ̃truvabl(ə)] *adj* which cannot be found; (*Comm*) unobtainable
introverti, e [ɛ̃trɔvɛrti] *nm/f* introvert
intrus, e [ɛ̃try, -yz] *nm/f* intruder
intrusion [ɛ̃tryzjɔ̃] *nf* intrusion; (*ingérence*) interference
intuitif, -ive [ɛ̃tuitif, -iv] *adj* intuitive
intuition [ɛ̃tuisjɔ̃] *nf* intuition; **avoir une ~** to have a feeling; **avoir l'~ de qch** to have an intuition of sth; **avoir de l'~** to have intuition
intuitivement [ɛ̃tuitivmɑ̃] *adv* intuitively
inusable [inyzabl(ə)] *adj* hard-wearing
inusité, e [inyzite] *adj* rarely used
inutile [inytil] *adj* useless; (*superflu*) unnecessary
inutilement [inytilmɑ̃] *adv* needlessly
inutilisable [inytilizabl(ə)] *adj* unusable
inutilisé, e [inytilize] *adj* unused
inutilité [inytilite] *nf* uselessness
invaincu, e [ɛ̃vɛ̃ky] *adj* unbeaten; (*armée, peuple*) unconquered
invalide [ɛ̃valid] *adj* disabled ▷ *nm/f*: **~ de guerre** disabled ex-serviceman; **~ du travail** industrially disabled person
invalider [ɛ̃valide] *vt* to invalidate
invalidité [ɛ̃validite] *nf* disability
invariable [ɛ̃varjabl(ə)] *adj* invariable
invariablement [ɛ̃varjabləmɑ̃] *adv* invariably
invasion [ɛ̃vazjɔ̃] *nf* invasion
invective [ɛ̃vɛktiv] *nf* invective
invectiver [ɛ̃vɛktive] *vt* to hurl abuse at ▷ *vi*: **~ contre** to rail against
invendable [ɛ̃vɑ̃dabl(ə)] *adj* unsaleable, unmarketable
invendu, e [ɛ̃vɑ̃dy] *adj* unsold ▷ *nm* return; **invendus** *nmpl* unsold goods
inventaire [ɛ̃vɑ̃tɛr] *nm* inventory; (*Comm*: *liste*) stocklist; (: *opération*) stocktaking *no pl*; (*fig*) survey; **faire un ~** to make an inventory; (*Comm*) to take stock; **faire** *ou* **procéder à l'~** to take stock
inventer [ɛ̃vɑ̃te] *vt* to invent; (*subterfuge*) to devise, invent; (*histoire, excuse*) to make up, invent; **~ de faire** to hit on the idea of doing
inventeur, -trice [ɛ̃vɑ̃tœr, -tris] *nm/f* inventor
inventif, -ive [ɛ̃vɑ̃tif, -iv] *adj* inventive
invention [ɛ̃vɑ̃sjɔ̃] *nf* invention; (*imagination, inspiration*) inventiveness
inventivité [ɛ̃vɑ̃tivite] *nf* inventiveness
inventorier [ɛ̃vɑ̃tɔrje] *vt* to make an inventory of
invérifiable [ɛ̃verifjabl(ə)] *adj* unverifiable
inverse [ɛ̃vɛrs(ə)] *adj* (*ordre*) reverse; (*sens*) opposite; (*rapport*) inverse ▷ *nm* reverse; inverse;

en proportion ~ in inverse proportion; **dans le sens** ~ **des aiguilles d'une montre** anticlockwise; **en sens** ~ in (*ou* from) the opposite direction; **à l'**~ conversely
inversement [ɛ̃vɛʀsəmɑ̃] *adv* conversely
inverser [ɛ̃vɛʀse] *vt* to reverse, invert; (*Élec*) to reverse
inversion [ɛ̃vɛʀsjɔ̃] *nf* reversal; inversion
invertébré, e [ɛ̃vɛʀtebʀe] *adj, nm* invertebrate
inverti, e [ɛ̃vɛʀti] *nm/f* homosexual
investigation [ɛ̃vɛstigasjɔ̃] *nf* investigation, inquiry
investir [ɛ̃vɛstiʀ] *vt* to invest; **s'investir** *vi* (*Psych*) to involve o.s.; ~ **qn de** to vest *ou* invest sb with
investissement [ɛ̃vɛstismɑ̃] *nm* investment; (*Psych*) involvement
investisseur [ɛ̃vɛstisœʀ] *nm* investor
investiture [ɛ̃vɛstityʀ] *nf* investiture; (*à une élection*) nomination
invétéré, e [ɛ̃vetere] *adj* (*habitude*) ingrained; (*bavard, buveur*) inveterate
invincible [ɛ̃vɛ̃sibl(ə)] *adj* invincible, unconquerable
invinciblement [ɛ̃vɛ̃sibləmɑ̃] *adv* (*fig*) invincibly
inviolabilité [ɛ̃vjɔlabilite] *nf*: ~ **parlementaire** parliamentary immunity
inviolable [ɛ̃vjɔlabl(ə)] *adj* inviolable
invisible [ɛ̃vizibl(ə)] *adj* invisible; (*fig: personne*) not available
invitation [ɛ̃vitasjɔ̃] *nf* invitation; **à/sur l'**~ **de qn** at/on sb's invitation; **carte/lettre d'**~ invitation card/letter
invite [ɛ̃vit] *nf* invitation
invité, e [ɛ̃vite] *nm/f* guest
inviter [ɛ̃vite] *vt* to invite; ~ **qn à faire qch** to invite sb to do sth; (*chose*) to induce *ou* tempt sb to do sth
invivable [ɛ̃vivabl(ə)] *adj* unbearable, impossible
involontaire [ɛ̃vɔlɔ̃tɛʀ] *adj* (*mouvement*) involuntary; (*insulte*) unintentional; (*complice*) unwitting
involontairement [ɛ̃vɔlɔ̃tɛʀmɑ̃] *adv* involuntarily
invoquer [ɛ̃vɔke] *vt* (*Dieu, muse*) to call upon, invoke; (*prétexte*) to put forward (as an excuse); (*témoignage*) to call upon; (*loi, texte*) to refer to; ~ **la clémence de qn** to beg sb *ou* appeal to sb for clemency
invraisemblable [ɛ̃vʀɛsɑ̃blabl(ə)] *adj* unlikely, improbable; (*bizarre*) incredible
invraisemblance [ɛ̃vʀɛsɑ̃blɑ̃s] *nf* unlikelihood *no pl*, improbability
invulnérable [ɛ̃vylneʀabl(ə)] *adj* invulnerable
iode [jɔd] *nm* iodine
iodé, e [jɔde] *adj* iodized
ion [jɔ̃] *nm* ion
ionique [jɔnik] *adj* (*Archit*) Ionic; (*Science*) ionic
ioniseur [jɔnizœʀ] *nm* ionizer
iota [jɔta] *nm*: **sans changer un** ~ without changing one iota *ou* the tiniest bit

IPC *sigle m* (= *Indice des prix à la consommation*) CPI
iPod® [aɪpɔd] *nm* iPod®
IR. *abr* = **infrarouge**
IRA *sigle f* (= *Irish Republican Army*) IRA
irai *etc* [iʀe] *vb voir* **aller**
Irak [iʀak] *nm*: **l'**~ Iraq *ou* Irak
irakien, ne [iʀakjɛ̃, -ɛn] *adj* Iraqi ▷ *nm/f*: **Irakien, ne** Iraqi
Iran [iʀɑ̃] *nm*: **l'**~ Iran
iranien, ne [iʀanjɛ̃, -ɛn] *adj* Iranian ▷ *nm* (*Ling*) Iranian ▷ *nm/f*: **Iranien, ne** Iranian
Iraq [iʀak] *nm* = **Irak**
iraquien, ne [iʀakjɛ̃, -ɛn] *adj, nm/f* = **irakien, ne**
irascible [iʀasibl(ə)] *adj* short-tempered, irascible
irions *etc* [iʀjɔ̃] *vb voir* **aller**
iris [iʀis] *nm* iris
irisé, e [iʀize] *adj* iridescent
irlandais, e [iʀlɑ̃dɛ, -ez] *adj, nm* (*Ling*) Irish ▷ *nm/f*: **Irlandais, e** Irishman/woman; **les I**~ the Irish
Irlande [iʀlɑ̃d] *nf*: **l'**~ (*pays*) Ireland; (*état*) the Irish Republic, the Republic of Ireland, Eire; ~ **du Nord** Northern Ireland, Ulster; ~ **du Sud** Southern Ireland, Irish Republic, Eire; **la mer d'**~ the Irish Sea
ironie [iʀɔni] *nf* irony
ironique [iʀɔnik] *adj* ironical
ironiquement [iʀɔnikmɑ̃] *adv* ironically
ironiser [iʀɔnize] *vi* to be ironical
irons *etc* [iʀɔ̃] *vb voir* **aller**
IRPP *sigle m* (= *impôt sur le revenu des personnes physiques*) income tax
irradiation [iʀadjasjɔ̃] *nf* irradiation
irradier [iʀadje] *vi* to radiate ▷ *vt* to irradiate
irraisonné, e [iʀɛzɔne] *adj* irrational, unreasoned
irrationnel, le [iʀasjɔnɛl] *adj* irrational
irrattrapable [iʀatʀapabl(ə)] *adj* (*retard*) that cannot be made up; (*bévue*) that cannot be made good
irréalisable [iʀealizabl(ə)] *adj* unrealizable; (*projet*) impracticable
irréalisme [iʀealism(ə)] *nm* lack of realism
irréaliste [iʀealist(ə)] *adj* unrealistic
irréalité [iʀealite] *nf* unreality
irrecevable [iʀsəvabl(ə)] *adj* unacceptable
irréconciliable [iʀekɔ̃siljabl(ə)] *adj* irreconcilable
irrécouvrable [iʀekuvʀabl(ə)] *adj* irrecoverable
irrécupérable [iʀekypeʀabl(ə)] *adj* unreclaimable, beyond repair; (*personne*) beyond redemption *ou* recall
irrécusable [iʀekyzabl(ə)] *adj* (*témoignage*) unimpeachable; (*preuve*) incontestable, indisputable
irréductible [iʀedyktibl(ə)] *adj* indomitable, implacable; (*Math: fraction, équation*) irreducible
irréductiblement [iʀedyktibləmɑ̃] *adv* implacably
irréel, le [iʀeɛl] *adj* unreal
irréfléchi, e [iʀefleʃi] *adj* thoughtless
irréfutable [iʀefytabl(ə)] *adj* irrefutable

irréfutablement [iʀefytabləmã] *adv*
irrefutably

irrégularité [iʀegylaʀite] *nf* irregularity;
unevenness *no pl*

irrégulier, -ière [iʀegylje, -jɛʀ] *adj* irregular;
(*surface, rythme, écriture*) uneven, irregular; (*élève,
athlète*) erratic

irrégulièrement [iʀegyljɛʀmã] *adv* irregularly

irrémédiable [iʀemedjabl(ə)] *adj* irreparable

irrémédiablement [iʀemedjabləmã] *adv*
irreparably

irremplaçable [iʀãplasabl(ə)] *adj* irreplaceable

irréparable [iʀepaʀabl(ə)] *adj* beyond repair,
irreparable; (*fig*) irreparable

irrépréhensible [iʀepʀeãsibl(ə)] *adj*
irreproachable

irrépressible [iʀepʀesibl(ə)] *adj* irrepressible

irréprochable [iʀepʀɔʃabl(ə)] *adj*
irreproachable, beyond reproach; (*tenue, toilette*)
impeccable

irrésistible [iʀezistibl(ə)] *adj* irresistible;
(*preuve, logique*) compelling

irrésistiblement [iʀezistibləmã] *adv*
irresistibly

irrésolu, e [iʀezɔly] *adj* irresolute

irrésolution [iʀezɔlysjɔ̃] *nf* irresoluteness

irrespectueux, -euse [iʀɛspɛktɥø, -øz] *adj*
disrespectful

irrespirable [iʀɛspiʀabl(ə)] *adj* unbreathable;
(*fig*) oppressive, stifling

irresponsabilité [iʀɛspɔ̃sabilite] *nf*
irresponsibility

irresponsable [iʀɛspɔ̃sabl(ə)] *adj* irresponsible

irrévérencieux, -euse [iʀeveʀãsjø, -øz] *adj*
irreverent

irréversible [iʀevɛʀsibl(ə)] *adj* irreversible

irréversiblement [iʀevɛʀsibləmã] *adv*
irreversibly

irrévocable [iʀevɔkabl(ə)] *adj* irrevocable

irrévocablement [iʀevɔkabləmã] *adv*
irrevocably

irrigation [iʀigasjɔ̃] *nf* irrigation

irriguer [iʀige] *vt* to irrigate

irritabilité [iʀitabilite] *nf* irritability

irritable [iʀitabl(ə)] *adj* irritable

irritant, e [iʀitã, -ãt] *adj* irritating; (*Méd*)
irritant

irritation [iʀitasjɔ̃] *nf* irritation

irrité, e [iʀite] *adj* irritated

irriter [iʀite] *vt* (*agacer*) to irritate, annoy; (*Méd:
enflammer*) to irritate; **s'~ contre qn/de qch** to
get annoyed *ou* irritated with sb/at sth

irruption [iʀypsjɔ̃] *nf* irruption *no pl*; **faire ~
dans** to burst into

ISBN *sigle m* (= *International Standard Book Number*)
ISBN

ISF *sigle m* (= *impôt de solidarité sur la fortune*) wealth tax

Islam [islam] *nm* Islam

islamique [islamik] *adj* Islamic

islamiste [islamist(ə)] *adj, nm/f* Islamic

islandais, e [islãdɛ, -ɛz] *adj* Icelandic ▷ *nm* (*Ling*)
Icelandic ▷ *nm/f*: **I~, e** Icelander

Islande [islãd] *nf*: **l'~** Iceland

ISMH *sigle m* = **Inventaire supplémentaire des
monuments historiques; monument inscrit
à l'~** = listed building

isocèle [izɔsɛl] *adj* isoceles

isolant, e [izɔlã, -ãt] *adj* insulating; (*insonorisant*)
soundproofing ▷ *nm* insulator

isolateur [izɔlatœʀ] *nm* (*Élec*) insulator

isolation [izɔlasjɔ̃] *nf* insulation; **~
acoustique/thermique** sound/thermal
insulation

isolationnisme [izɔlasjɔnism(ə)] *nm*
isolationism

isolé, e [izɔle] *adj* isolated; (*Élec*) insulated

isolement [izɔlmã] *nm* isolation; solitary
confinement

isolément [izɔlemã] *adv* in isolation

isoler [izɔle] *vt* to isolate; (*prisonnier*) to put in
solitary confinement; (*ville*) to cut off, isolate;
(*Élec*) to insulate

isoloir [izɔlwaʀ] *nm* polling booth

isorel® [izɔʀɛl] *nm* hardboard

isotherme [izɔtɛʀm(ə)] *adj* (*camion*) refrigerated

Israël [isʀaɛl] *nm*: **l'~** Israel

israélien, ne [isʀaeljɛ̃, -ɛn] *adj* Israeli ▷ *nm/f*:
Israélien, ne Israeli

israélite [isʀaelit] *adj* Jewish; (*dans l'Ancien
Testament*) Israelite ▷ *nm/f*: **Israélite** Jew/Jewess;
Israelite

issu, e [isy] *adj*: **~ de** descended from; (*fig*)
stemming from ▷ *nf* (*ouverture, sortie*) exit;
(*solution*) way out, solution; (*dénouement*)
outcome; **à l'~e de** at the conclusion *ou* close of;
rue sans ~e dead end, no through road (*Brit*), no
outlet (*US*); **~e de secours** emergency exit

Istamboul, Istanbul [istãbul] *n* Istanbul

isthme [ism(ə)] *nm* isthmus

Italie [itali] *nf*: **l'~** Italy

italien, ne [italjɛ̃, -ɛn] *adj* Italian ▷ *nm* (*Ling*)
Italian ▷ *nm/f*: **Italien, ne** Italian

italique [italik] *nm*: **en ~(s)** in italics

item [itɛm] *nm* item; (*question*) question, test

itinéraire [itineʀɛʀ] *nm* itinerary, route

itinérant, e [itineʀã, -ãt] *adj* itinerant,
travelling

ITP *sigle m* (= *ingénieur des travaux publics*) civil
engineer

IUT *sigle m* = **Institut universitaire de
technologie**

IVG *sigle f* (= *interruption volontaire de grossesse*)
abortion

ivoire [ivwaʀ] *nm* ivory

ivoirien, ne [ivwaʀjɛ̃, -ɛn] *adj* of *ou* from the
Ivory Coast

ivraie [ivʀɛ] *nf*: **séparer le bon grain de l'~** (*fig*)
to separate the wheat from the chaff

ivre [ivʀ(ə)] *adj* drunk; **~ de** (*colère*) wild with;
(*bonheur*) drunk *ou* intoxicated with; **~ mort**
dead drunk

ivresse [ivʀɛs] *nf* drunkenness; (*euphorie*)
intoxication

ivrogne [ivʀɔɲ] *nm/f* drunkard

Jj

J, j [ʒi] *nm inv* J, j ▷ *abr* = **jour**; **jour J** D-day;
(= *Joule*) J; **J comme Joseph** J for Jack (*Brit*) *ou* Jig
(*US*)

j' [ʒ] *pron voir* **je**

jabot [ʒabo] *nm* (*Zool*) crop; (*de vêtement*) jabot

jacasser [ʒakase] *vi* to chatter

jachère [ʒaʃɛʀ] *nf*: (**être**) **en ~** (to lie) fallow

jacinthe [ʒasɛ̃t] *nf* hyacinth; **~ des bois**
bluebell

jack [dʒak] *nm* jack plug

jacquard [ʒakaʀ] *adj inv* Fair Isle

jacquerie [ʒakʀi] *nf* riot

jade [ʒad] *nm* jade

jadis [ʒadis] *adv* in times past, formerly

jaguar [ʒagwaʀ] *nm* (*Zool*) jaguar

jaillir [ʒajiʀ] *vi* (*liquide*) to spurt out, gush out;
(*lumière*) to flood out; (*fig*) to rear up; to burst out

jaillissement [ʒajismɑ̃] *nm* spurt, gush

jais [ʒɛ] *nm* jet; (**d'un noir**) **de ~** jet-black

jalon [ʒalɔ̃] *nm* range pole; (*fig*) milestone;
poser des ~s (*fig*) to pave the way

jalonner [ʒalɔne] *vt* to mark out; (*fig*) to mark,
punctuate

jalousement [ʒaluzmɑ̃] *adv* jealously

jalouser [ʒaluze] *vt* to be jealous of

jalousie [ʒaluzi] *nf* jealousy; (*store*) (venetian)
blind

jaloux, -ouse [ʒalu, -uz] *adj* jealous; **être ~ de
qn/qch** to be jealous of sb/sth

jamaïquain, e [ʒamaikɛ̃, -ɛn] *adj* Jamaican

Jamaïque [ʒamaik] *nf*: **la ~** Jamaica

jamais [ʒamɛ] *adv* never; (*sans négation*) ever;
ne ... ~ never; **~ de la vie!** never!; **si ... ~** if ever ...;
à (tout) ~, **pour ~** for ever, for ever and ever

jambage [ʒɑ̃baʒ] *nm* (*de lettre*) downstroke; (*de
porte*) jamb

jambe [ʒɑ̃b] *nf* leg; **à toutes ~s** as fast as one's
legs can carry one

jambières [ʒɑ̃bjɛʀ] *nfpl* legwarmers; (*Sport*) shin
pads

jambon [ʒɑ̃bɔ̃] *nm* ham

jambonneau, x [ʒɑ̃bɔno] *nm* knuckle of ham

jante [ʒɑ̃t] *nf* (wheel) rim

janvier [ʒɑ̃vje] *nm* January; *voir aussi* **juillet**

Japon [ʒapɔ̃] *nm*: **le ~** Japan

japonais, e [ʒapɔnɛ, -ɛz] *adj* Japanese ▷ *nm*
(*Ling*) Japanese ▷ *nm/f*: **Japonais, e** Japanese

japonaiserie [ʒapɔnɛzʀi] *nf* (*bibelot*) Japanese
curio

jappement [ʒapmɑ̃] *nm* yap, yelp

japper [ʒape] *vi* to yap, yelp

jaquette [ʒakɛt] *nf* (*de cérémonie*) morning coat;
(*de femme*) jacket; (*de livre*) dust cover, (dust)
jacket

jardin [ʒaʀdɛ̃] *nm* garden; **~ d'acclimatation**
zoological gardens *pl*; **~ botanique** botanical
gardens *pl*; **~ d'enfants** nursery school; **~
potager** vegetable garden; **~ public** (public)
park, public gardens *pl*; **~s suspendus** hanging
gardens; **~ zoologique** zoological gardens

jardinage [ʒaʀdinaʒ] *nm* gardening

jardiner [ʒaʀdine] *vi* to garden, do some
gardening

jardinet [ʒaʀdinɛ] *nm* little garden

jardinier, -ière [ʒaʀdinje, -jɛʀ] *nm/f* gardener
▷ *nf* (*de fenêtre*) window box; **jardinière
d'enfants** nursery school teacher; **jardinière
(de légumes)** (*Culin*) mixed vegetables

jargon [ʒaʀgɔ̃] *nm* (*charabia*) gibberish;
(*publicitaire, scientifique etc*) jargon

jarre [ʒaʀ] *nf* (earthenware) jar

jarret [ʒaʀɛ] *nm* back of knee; (*Culin*) knuckle,
shin

jarretelle [ʒaʀtɛl] *nf* suspender (*Brit*), garter (*US*)

jarretière [ʒaʀtjɛʀ] *nf* garter

jars [ʒaʀ] *nm* (*Zool*) gander

jaser [ʒaze] *vi* to chatter, prattle; (*indiscrètement*)
to gossip

jasmin [ʒasmɛ̃] *nm* jasmine

jaspe [ʒasp(ə)] *nm* jasper

jaspé, e [ʒaspe] *adj* marbled, mottled

jatte [ʒat] *nf* basin, bowl

jauge [ʒoʒ] *nf* (*capacité*) capacity, tonnage;
(*instrument*) gauge; **~ (de niveau) d'huile**
dipstick

jauger [ʒoʒe] *vt* to gauge the capacity of; (*fig*) to
size up; **~ 3 000 tonneaux** to measure 3,000
tons

jaunâtre [ʒonɑtʀ(ə)] *adj* (*couleur, teint*) yellowish

jaune [ʒon] *adj, nm* yellow ▷ *nm/f* Asiatic; (*briseur
de grève*) blackleg ▷ *adv* (*fam*): **rire ~** to laugh on
the other side of one's face; **~ d'œuf** (egg) yolk

jaunir [ʒoniʀ] *vi, vt* to turn yellow
jaunisse [ʒonis] *nf* jaundice
Java [ʒava] *nf* Java
java [ʒava] *nf (fam)*: **faire la ~** to live it up, have a
real party
javanais, e [ʒavanɛ, -ɛz] *adj* Javanese
Javel [ʒavɛl] *nf voir* **eau**
javelliser [ʒavelize] *vt (eau)* to chlorinate
javelot [ʒavlo] *nm* javelin; *(Sport)*: **faire du ~** to
throw the javelin
jazz [dʒaz] *nm* jazz
J.-C. *abr* = **Jésus-Christ**
je, j' [ʒ(ə)] *pron* I
jean [dʒin] *nm* jeans *pl*
jeannette [ʒanɛt] *nf (planchette)* sleeve board;
(petite fille scout) Brownie
jeep® [(d)ʒip] *nf (Auto)* Jeep®
jérémiades [ʒeʀemjad] *nfpl* moaning *sg*
jerrycan [ʒeʀikan] *nm* jerry can
Jersey [ʒɛʀzɛ] *nf* Jersey
jersey [ʒɛʀzɛ] *nm* jersey; *(Tricot)*: **pointe de ~**
stocking stitch
jersiais, e [ʒɛʀzjɛ, -ɛz] *adj* Jersey *cpd*, of *ou* from
Jersey
Jérusalem [ʒeʀyzalɛm] *n* Jerusalem
jésuite [ʒezɥit] *nm* Jesuit
Jésus-Christ [ʒezykʀi(st)] *n* Jesus Christ; **600
avant/après ~** *ou* **J.-C.** 600 B.C./A.D.
jet¹ [ʒɛ] *nm (lancer)* throwing *no pl*, throw;
(jaillissement) jet; spurt; *(de tuyau)* nozzle; *(fig)*:
premier ~ *(ébauche)* rough outline; **arroser au
~** to hose; **d'un (seul) ~** *(d'un seul coup)* at *(ou* in)
one go; **du premier ~** at the first attempt *ou*
shot; **~ d'eau** spray; *(fontaine)* fountain
jet² [dʒɛt] *nm (avion)* jet
jetable [ʒətabl(ə)] *adj* disposable
jeté [ʒəte] *nm (Tricot)*: **un ~** make one; **~ de table**
(table) runner; **~ de lit** bedspread
jetée [ʒəte] *nf* jetty; pier
jeter [ʒəte] *vt (gén)* to throw; *(se défaire de)* to
throw away *ou* out; *(son, lueur etc)* to give out; **~
qch à qn** to throw sth to sb; *(de façon agressive)* to
throw sth at sb; *(Navig)*: **~ l'ancre** to cast
anchor; **~ un coup d'œil (à)** to take a look (at);
~ les bras en avant/la tête en arrière to throw
one's arms forward/one's head back(ward); **~
l'effroi parmi** to spread fear among; **~ un sort
à qn** to cast a spell on sb; **~ qn dans la misère**
to reduce sb to poverty; **~ qn dehors/en prison**
to throw sb out/into prison; **~ l'éponge** *(fig)* to
throw in the towel; **~ des fleurs à qn** *(fig)* to say
lovely things to sb; **~ la pierre à qn** *(accuser,
blâmer)* to accuse sb; **se ~ sur** to throw o.s. onto;
se ~ dans *(fleuve)* to flow into; **se ~ par la
fenêtre** to throw o.s. out of the window; **se ~ à
l'eau** *(fig)* to take the plunge
jeton [ʒətɔ̃] *nm (au jeu)* counter; *(de téléphone)*
token; **~s de présence** (director's) fees
jette *etc* [ʒɛt] *vb voir* **jeter**
jeu, x [ʒø] *nm (divertissement, Tech: d'une pièce)* play;
*(défini par des règles, Tennis: partie, Football etc: façon
de jouer)* game; *(Théât etc)* acting; *(fonctionnement)*

working, interplay; *(série d'objets, jouet)* set;
(Cartes) hand; *(au casino)*: **le ~** gambling; **cacher
son ~** *(fig)* to keep one's cards hidden, conceal
one's hand; **c'est un ~ d'enfant!** *(fig)* it's child's
play!; **en ~** at stake; at work; *(Football)* in play;
remettre en ~ to throw in; **entrer/mettre en
~** to come/bring into play; **par ~** *(pour s'amuser)*
for fun; **d'entrée de ~** *(tout de suite, dès le début)*
from the outset; **entrer dans le ~/le ~ de qn**
(fig) to play the game/sb's game; **jouer gros ~** to
play for high stakes; **se piquer/se prendre au
~** to get excited over/get caught up in the game;
~ d'arcade video game; **~ de boules** game of
bowls; *(endroit)* bowling pitch; *(boules)* set of
bowls; **~ de cartes** card game; *(paquet)* pack of
cards; **~ de construction** building set; **~
d'échecs** chess set; **~ d'écritures** *(Comm)* paper
transaction; **~ électronique** electronic game;
~ de hasard game of chance; **~ de mots** pun; **le
~ de l'oie** snakes and ladders *sg*; **~ d'orgue(s)**
organ stop; **~ de patience** puzzle; **~ de
physionomie** facial expressions *pl*; **~ de
société** parlour game; **~ télévisé** television
game; **~ vidéo** computer game; **~x de lumière**
lighting effects; **J~x olympiques (JO)** Olympic
Games
jeu-concours [ʒøkɔ̃kuʀ] *(pl* **jeux-concours**) *nm*
competition
jeudi [ʒødi] *nm* Thursday; **~ saint** Maundy
Thursday; *voir aussi* **lundi**
jeun [ʒœ̃] **à ~** *adv* on an empty stomach
jeune [ʒœn] *adj* young ▷ *adv*: **faire/s'habiller ~**
to look/dress young; **les ~s** young people, the
young; **~ fille** *nf* girl; **~ homme** *nm* young
man; **~ loup** *nm (Pol, Écon)* young go-getter; **~
premier** leading man; **~s gens** *nmpl* young
people; **~s mariés** *nmpl* newly weds
jeûne [ʒøn] *nm* fast
jeûner [ʒøne] *vt* to fast, go without food
jeunesse [ʒœnɛs] *nf* youth; *(aspect)*
youthfulness; *(jeunes)* young people *pl*, youth
jf *sigle f* = **jeune fille**
jh *sigle m* = **jeune homme**
JI *sigle m* = **juge d'instruction**
jiu-jitsu [ʒyʒitsy] *nm inv (Sport)* jujitsu
JMF *sigle f (= Jeunesses musicales de France)* association
to promote music among the young
JO *sigle m* = **Journal officiel** ▷ *sigle mpl* = **Jeux
olympiques**
joaillerie [ʒoajʀi] *nf* jewel trade; jewellery *(Brit)*,
jewelry *(US)*
joaillier, -ière [ʒoaje, -jɛʀ] *nm/f* jeweller *(Brit)*,
jeweler *(US)*
job [dʒɔb] *nm* job
jobard [ʒobaʀ] *nm (péj)* sucker, mug
jockey [ʒokɛ] *nm* jockey
jodler [ʒodle] *vi* to yodel
jogging [dʒogiŋ] *nm* tracksuit *(Brit)*, sweatsuit
(US); **faire du ~** to jog, go jogging
joie [ʒwa] *nf* joy
joignais *etc* [ʒwaɲɛ] *vb voir* **joindre**
joindre [ʒwɛ̃dʀ(ə)] *vt* to join; **~ qch à** *(à une lettre)*

to enclose sth with; (à un mail) to attach sth to; (contacter) to contact, get in touch with; ~ **les mains/talons** to put one's hands/heels together; ~ **les deux bouts** (fig: du mois) to make ends meet; **se joindre** (mains etc) to come together; **se ~ à qn** to join sb; **se ~ à qch** to join in sth

joint, e [ʒwɛ̃, -ɛ̃t] pp de **joindre** ▷ adj: ~ (**à**) (lettre, paquet) attached (to), enclosed (with); **pièce ~e** (de lettre) enclosure; (de mail) attachment ▷ nm joint; (ligne) join; (de ciment etc) pointing no pl; **chercher/trouver le ~** (fig) to look for/come up with the answer; ~ **de cardan** cardan joint; ~ **de culasse** cylinder head gasket; ~ **de robinet** washer; ~ **universel** universal joint

jointure [ʒwɛ̃tyʀ] nf (Anat: articulation) joint; (Tech: assemblage) joint; (: ligne) join

joker [ʒɔkɛʀ] nm (Cartes) joker; (Inform): (**caractère**) ~ wild card

joli, e [ʒɔli] adj pretty, attractive; **une ~e somme/situation** a nice little sum/situation; **un ~ gâchis** etc a nice mess etc; **c'est du ~!** that's very nice!; **tout ça, c'est bien ~ mais …** that's all very well but …

joliment [ʒɔlimɑ̃] adv prettily, attractively; (fam: très) pretty

jonc [ʒɔ̃] nm (bul)rush; (bague, bracelet) band

joncher [ʒɔ̃ʃe] vt (choses) to be strewed on; **jonché de** strewn with

jonction [ʒɔ̃ksjɔ̃] nf joining; (**point de**) ~ (de routes) junction; (de fleuves) confluence; **opérer une ~** (Mil etc) to rendez-vous

jongler [ʒɔ̃gle] vi to juggle; (fig): ~ **avec** to juggle with, play with

jongleur, -euse [ʒɔ̃glœʀ, -øz] nm/f juggler

jonquille [ʒɔ̃kij] nf daffodil

Jordanie [ʒɔʀdani] nf: **la ~** Jordan

jordanien, ne [ʒɔʀdanjɛ̃, -ɛn] adj Jordanian ▷ nm/f: **Jordanien, ne** Jordanian

jouable [ʒwabl(ə)] adj playable

joue [ʒu] nf cheek; **mettre en ~** to take aim at

jouer [ʒwe] vt (partie, carte, coup, Mus: morceau) to play; (somme d'argent, réputation) to stake, wager; (pièce, rôle) to perform; (film) to show; (simuler: sentiment) to affect, feign ▷ vi to play; (Théât, Ciné) to act, perform; (bois, porte: se voiler) to warp; (clef, pièce: avoir du jeu) to be loose; (entrer ou être en jeu) to come into play, come into it; ~ **sur** (miser) to gamble on; ~ **de** (Mus) to play; ~ **du couteau/ des coudes** to use knives/one's elbows; ~ **à** (jeu, sport, roulette) to play; ~ **au héros** to act ou play the hero; ~ **avec** (risquer) to gamble with; **se ~ de** (difficultés) to make light of; **se ~ de qn** to deceive ou dupe sb; ~ **un tour à qn** to play a trick on sb; ~ **la comédie** (fig) to put on an act, put it on; ~ **aux courses** to back horses, bet on horses; ~ **à la baisse/hausse** (Bourse) to play for a fall/rise; ~ **serré** to play a close game; ~ **de malchance** to be dogged with ill-luck; ~ **sur les mots** to play with words; **à toi/nous de ~** it's your/our go ou turn

jouet [ʒwɛ] nm toy; **être le ~ de** (illusion etc) to be

the victim of

joueur, -euse [ʒwœʀ, -øz] nm/f player ▷ adj (enfant, chat) playful; **être beau/mauvais ~** to be a good/bad loser

joufflu, e [ʒufly] adj chubby(-cheeked)

joug [ʒu] nm yoke

jouir [ʒwiʀ]: ~ **de** vt to enjoy

jouissance [ʒwisɑ̃s] nf pleasure; (Jur) use

jouisseur, -euse [ʒwisœʀ, -øz] nm/f sensualist

joujou [ʒuʒu] nm (fam) toy

jour [ʒuʀ] nm day; (opposé à la nuit) day, daytime; (clarté) daylight; (fig: aspect): **sous un ~ favorable/nouveau** in a favourable/new light; (ouverture) opening; (Couture) openwork no pl; **au ~ le ~** from day to day; **de nos ~s** these days, nowadays; **tous les ~s** every day; **de ~ en ~** day by day; **d'un ~ à l'autre** from one day to the next; **du ~ au lendemain** overnight; **il fait ~** it's daylight; **en plein ~** in broad daylight; **au ~** in daylight; **au petit ~** at daybreak; **au grand ~** (fig) in the open; **mettre au ~** to uncover, disclose; **être à ~** to be up to date; **mettre à ~** to bring up to date, update; **mise à ~** updating; **donner le ~ à** to give birth to; **voir le ~** to be born; **se faire ~** (fig) to become clear; ~ **férié** public holiday; **le J ~** D-day; ~ **ouvrable** working day

Jourdain [ʒuʀdɛ̃] nm: **le ~** the (River) Jordan

journal, -aux [ʒuʀnal, -o] nm (news)paper; (personnel) journal, diary; ~ **de bord** log; ~ **de mode** fashion magazine; **le J~ officiel (de la République française) (JO)** bulletin giving details of laws and official announcements; ~ **parlé/télévisé** radio/television news sg

journalier, -ière [ʒuʀnalje, -jɛʀ] adj daily; (banal) everyday ▷ nm day labourer

journalisme [ʒuʀnalism(ə)] nm journalism

journaliste [ʒuʀnalist(ə)] nm/f journalist

journalistique [ʒuʀnalistik] adj journalistic

journée [ʒuʀne] nf day; **la ~ continue** the 9 to 5 working day (with short lunch break)

journellement [ʒuʀnɛlmɑ̃] adv (tous les jours) daily; (souvent) every day

joute [ʒut] nf (tournoi) duel; (verbale) duel, battle of words

jouvence [ʒuvɑ̃s] nf: **bain de ~** rejuvenating experience

jouxter [ʒukste] vt to adjoin

jovial [ʒɔvjal] adj jovial, jolly

jovialité [ʒɔvjalite] nf joviality

joyau, x [ʒwajo] nm gem, jewel

joyeusement [ʒwajøzmɑ̃] adv joyfully, gladly

joyeux, -euse [ʒwajø, -øz] adj joyful, merry; ~ **Noël!** Merry ou Happy Christmas!; **joyeuses Pâques!** Happy Easter!; ~ **anniversaire!** many happy returns!

JT sigle m = **journal télévisé**

jubilation [ʒybilasjɔ̃] nf jubilation

jubilé [ʒybile] nm jubilee

jubiler [ʒybile] vi to be jubilant, exult

jucher [ʒyʃe] vt: ~ **qch sur** to perch sth (up)on ▷ vi (oiseau): ~ **sur** to perch (up)on; **se ~ sur** to perch o.s. (up)on

judaïque [ʒydaik] *adj (loi)* Judaic; *(religion)* Jewish

judaïsme [ʒydaism(ə)] *nm* Judaism

judas [ʒyda] *nm (trou)* spy-hole

Judée [ʒyde] *nf*: **la ~** Jud(a)ea

judéo- [ʒydeo] *préfixe* Judeo-

judéo-allemand, e [ʒydeɔalmɑ̃, -ɑ̃d] *adj, nm* Yiddish

judéo-chrétien, ne [ʒydeɔkretjɛ̃, -ɛn] *adj* Judeo-Christian

judiciaire [ʒydisjɛʀ] *adj* judicial

judicieusement [ʒydisjøzmɑ̃] *adv* judiciously

judicieux, -euse [ʒydisjø, -øz] *adj* judicious

judo [ʒydo] *nm* judo

judoka [ʒydɔka] *nm/f* judoka

juge [ʒyʒ] *nm* judge; **~ d'instruction** examining *(Brit)* ou committing *(US)* magistrate; **~ de paix** justice of the peace; **~ de touche** linesman

jugé [ʒyʒe]: **au ~** *adv* by guesswork

jugement [ʒyʒmɑ̃] *nm* judgment; *(Jur: au pénal)* sentence; *(: au civil)* decision; **~ de valeur** value judgment

jugeote [ʒyʒɔt] *nf (fam)* gumption

juger [ʒyʒe] *vt* to judge ▷ *nm*: **au ~** by guesswork; **~ qn/qch satisfaisant** to consider sb/sth (to be) satisfactory; **~ que** to think ou consider that; **~ bon de faire** to consider it a good idea to do, see fit to do; **~ de** *vt* to judge; **jugez de ma surprise** imagine my surprise

jugulaire [ʒygylɛʀ] *adj* jugular ▷ *nf (Mil)* chinstrap

juguler [ʒygyle] *vt (maladie)* to halt; *(révolte)* to suppress; *(inflation etc)* to control, curb

juif, -ive [ʒɥif, -iv] *adj* Jewish ▷ *nm/f*: **Juif, ive** Jew/Jewess ou Jewish woman

juillet [ʒɥijɛ] *nm* July; **le premier ~** the first of July *(Brit)*, July first *(US)*; **le deux/onze ~** the second/eleventh of July, July second/eleventh; **il est venu le 5 ~** he came on 5th July ou July 5th; **en ~** in July; **début/fin ~** at the beginning/end of July; *see note*

● **Le 14 juillet**

● *Le 14 juillet* is a national holiday in France and
● commemorates the storming of the Bastille
● during the French Revolution. Throughout
● the country there are celebrations, which
● feature parades, music, dancing and
● firework displays. In Paris a military parade
● along the Champs-Élysées is attended by
● the President.

juin [ʒɥɛ̃] *nm* June; *voir aussi* **juillet**

juive [ʒɥiv] *adj, nf voir* **juif**

jumeau, -elle, -x [ʒymo, -ɛl] *adj, nm/f* twin; **maisons jumelles** semidetached houses

jumelage [ʒymlaʒ] *nm* twinning

jumeler [ʒymle] *vt* to twin; **roues jumelées** double wheels; **billets de loterie jumelés**

double series lottery tickets; **pari jumelé** double bet

jumelle [ʒymɛl] *adj f, nf voir* **jumeau** ▷ *vb voir* **jumeler**

jumelles [ʒymɛl] *nfpl* binoculars

jument [ʒymɑ̃] *nf* mare

jungle [ʒɔ̃gl(ə)] *nf* jungle

junior [ʒynjɔʀ] *adj* junior

junte [ʒɔ̃t] *nf* junta

jupe [ʒyp] *nf* skirt

jupe-culotte [ʒypkylɔt] *(pl* **jupes-culottes***) nf* divided skirt, culotte(s)

jupette [ʒypɛt] *nf* short skirt

jupon [ʒypɔ̃] *nm* waist slip ou petticoat

Jura [ʒyʀɑ] *nm*: **le ~** the Jura (Mountains)

jurassien, ne [ʒyʀasjɛ̃, -ɛn] *adj* of ou from the Jura Mountains

juré, e [ʒyʀe] *nm/f* juror ▷ *adj*: **ennemi ~** sworn ou avowed enemy

jurer [ʒyʀe] *vt (obéissance etc)* to swear, vow ▷ *vi (dire des jurons)* to swear, curse; *(dissoner)*: **~ (avec)** to clash (with); *(s'engager)*: **~ de faire/que** to swear ou vow to do/that; *(affirmer)*: **~ que** to swear ou vouch that; **~ de qch** *(s'en porter garant)* to swear to sth; **ils ne jurent que par lui** they swear by him; **je vous jure!** honestly!

juridiction [ʒyʀidiksjɔ̃] *nf* jurisdiction; *(tribunal, tribunaux)* court(s) of law

juridique [ʒyʀidik] *adj* legal

juridiquement [ʒyʀidikmɑ̃] *adv (devant la justice)* juridically; *(du point de vue du droit)* legally

jurisconsulte [ʒyʀikɔ̃sylt(ə)] *nm* jurisconsult

jurisprudence [ʒyʀispʀydɑ̃s] *nf (Jur: décisions)* (legal) precedents; *(principes juridiques)* jurisprudence; **faire ~** *(faire autorité)* to set a precedent

juriste [ʒyʀist(ə)] *nm/f* jurist; lawyer

juron [ʒyʀɔ̃] *nm* curse, swearword

jury [ʒyʀi] *nm (Jur)* jury; *(Scol)* board (of examiners), jury

jus [ʒy] *nm* juice; *(de viande)* gravy, (meat) juice; **~ de fruits** fruit juice; **~ de raisin/tomates** grape/tomato juice

jusant [ʒyzɑ̃] *nm* ebb (tide)

jusqu'au-boutiste [ʒyskobutist(ə)] *nm/f* extremist, hardliner

jusque [ʒysk(ə)]: **jusqu'à** *prép (endroit)* as far as, (up) to; *(moment)* until, till; *(limite)* up to; **~ sur/dans** up to, as far as; *(y compris)* even on/in; **~ vers** until about; **jusqu'à ce que** *conj* until; **~- là** *(temps)* until then; *(espace)* up to there; **jusqu'ici** *(temps)* until now; *(espace)* up to here; **jusqu'à présent** until now, so far

justaucorps [ʒystokɔʀ] *nm inv (Danse, Sport)* leotard

juste [ʒyst(ə)] *adj (équitable)* just, fair; *(légitime)* just, justified; *(exact, vrai)* right; *(étroit, insuffisant)* tight ▷ *adv* right; tight; *(chanter)* in tune; *(seulement)* just; **~ assez/au-dessus** just enough/above; **pouvoir tout ~ faire** to be only just able to do; **au ~** exactly, actually; **comme de ~** of course, naturally; **le ~ milieu** the happy medium; **à ~ titre** rightfully

justement [ʒystəmã] *adv* rightly; justly; (*précisément*): **c'est ~ ce qu'il fallait faire** that's just *ou* precisely what needed doing

justesse [ʒystɛs] *nf* (*précision*) accuracy; (*d'une remarque*) aptness; (*d'une opinion*) soundness; **de ~** just, by a narrow margin

justice [ʒystis] *nf* (*équité*) fairness, justice; (*Admin*) justice; **rendre la ~** to dispense justice; **traduire en ~** to bring before the courts; **obtenir ~** to obtain justice; **rendre ~ à qn** to do sb justice; **se faire ~** to take the law into one's own hands; (*se suicider*) to take one's life

justiciable [ʒystisjabl(ə)] *adj*: **~ de** (*Jur*) answerable to

justicier, -ière [ʒystisje, -jɛʀ] *nm/f* judge, righter of wrongs

justifiable [ʒystifjabl(ə)] *adj* justifiable

justificatif, -ive [ʒystifikatif, -iv] *adj* (*document etc*) supporting ▷ *nm* supporting proof

justification [ʒystifikasjɔ̃] *nf* justification

justifier [ʒystifje] *vt* to justify; **~ de** *vt* to prove; **non justifié** unjustified; **justifié à droite/ gauche** ranged right/left

jute [ʒyt] *nm* jute

juteux, -euse [ʒytø, -øz] *adj* juicy

juvénile [ʒyvenil] *adj* young, youthful

juxtaposer [ʒykstapoze] *vt* to juxtapose

juxtaposition [ʒykstapozisjɔ̃] *nf* juxtaposition

K, k [ka] *nm inv* K, k ▷ *abr* (= *kilo*) kg; **K comme Kléber** K for King

K 7 [kasɛt] *nf* cassette

Kaboul, Kabul [kabul] *n* Kabul

kabyle [kabil] *adj* Kabyle ▷ *nm* (*Ling*) Kabyle ▷ *nm/f*: **Kabyle** Kabyle

Kabylie [kabili] *nf*: **la ~** Kabylia

kafkaïen, ne [kafkajɛ̃, -ɛn] *adj* Kafkaesque

kaki [kaki] *adj inv* khaki

Kalahari [kalaaʀi] *n*: **désert de ~** Kalahari Desert

kaléidoscope [kaleidɔskɔp] *nm* kaleidoscope

Kampala [kɑ̃pala] *n* Kampala

Kampuchéa [kɑ̃putʃea] *nm*: **le ~ (démocratique)** (the People's Republic of) Kampuchea

kangourou [kɑ̃guʀu] *nm* kangaroo

kaolin [kaɔlɛ̃] *nm* kaolin

kapok [kapɔk] *nm* kapok

karaoke [kaʀaoke] *nm* karaoke

karaté [kaʀate] *nm* karate

kart [kaʀt] *nm* go-cart

karting [kaʀtiŋ] *nm* go-carting, karting

kascher [kaʃɛʀ] *adj inv* kosher

kayak [kajak] *nm* kayak

Kazakhstan [kaʒakstɑ̃] *nm* Kazakhstan

Kenya [kenja] *nm*: **le ~** Kenya

kenyan, e [kenjɑ̃, -an] *adj* Kenyan ▷ *nm/f*: **Kenyan, e** Kenyan

képi [kepi] *nm* kepi

Kerguelen [kɛʀgelɛn] *nfpl*: **les (îles) ~** Kerguelen

kermesse [kɛʀmɛs] *nf* bazaar, (charity) fête; village fair

kérosène [keʀozɛn] *nm* jet fuel; rocket fuel

kg *abr* (= *kilogramme*) kg

KGB *sigle m* KGB

khmer, -ère [kmɛʀ] *adj* Khmer ▷ *nm* (*Ling*) Khmer

khôl [kol] *nm* khol

kibboutz [kibuts] *nm* kibbutz

kidnapper [kidnape] *vt* to kidnap

kidnappeur, -euse [kidnapœʀ, -øz] *nm/f* kidnapper

kidnapping [kidnapiŋ] *nm* kidnapping

Kilimandjaro [kilimɑ̃dʒaʀo] *nm*: **le ~** Mount Kilimanjaro

kilo [kilo] *nm* kilo

kilogramme [kilɔgʀam] *nm* kilogramme (*Brit*), kilogram (*US*)

kilométrage [kilɔmetʀaʒ] *nm* number of kilometres travelled, ≈ mileage

kilomètre [kilɔmɛtʀ(ə)] *nm* kilometre (*Brit*), kilometer (*US*); **~s-heure** kilometres per hour

kilométrique [kilɔmetʀik] *adj* (*distance*) in kilometres; **compteur ~** ≈ mileage indicator

kilooctet [kilɔɔktɛ] *nm* kilobyte

kilowatt [kilɔwat] *nm* kilowatt

kinésithérapeute [kineziteʀapøt] *nm/f* physiotherapist

kinésithérapie [kineziteʀapi] *nf* physiotherapy

kiosque [kjɔsk(ə)] *nm* kiosk, stall; (*Tél etc*) *telephone and/or videotext information service*; **~ à journaux** newspaper kiosk

kir [kiʀ] *nm* kir (*white wine with blackcurrant liqueur*)

Kirghizistan [kiʀgizistɑ̃] *nm* Kirghizia

kirsch [kiʀʃ] *nm* kirsch

kit [kit] *nm* kit; **~ piéton** *ou* **mains libres** hands-free kit; **en ~** in kit form

kitchenette [kitʃ(ə)nɛt] *nf* kitchenette

kiwi [kiwi] *nm* (*Zool*) kiwi; (*Bot*) kiwi (fruit)

klaxon [klaksɔn] *nm* horn

klaxonner [klaksone] *vi, vt* to hoot (*Brit*), honk (one's horn) (*US*)

kleptomane [klɛptɔman] *nm/f* kleptomaniac

km *abr* (= *kilomètre*) km

km/h *abr* = **kilomètres/heure**

knock-out [nɔkawt] *nm* knock-out

Ko *abr* (*Inform*: = *kilooctet*) kB

K.-O. [kao] *adj inv* (knocked) out, out for the count

koala [kɔala] *nm* koala (bear)

kolkhoze [kɔlkoz] *nm* kolkhoz

Kosovo [kɔsɔvo] *nm*: **le ~** Kosovo

Koweit [kɔwɛt] *nm*: **le ~** Kuwait, Koweit

koweitien, ne [kɔwɛtjɛ̃, -ɛn] *adj* Kuwaiti ▷ *nm/f*: **Koweitien, ne** Kuwaiti

krach [kʀak] *nm* (*Écon*) crash

kraft [kʀaft] *nm* brown *ou* kraft paper

Kremlin [kʀɛmlɛ̃] *nm*: **le ~** the Kremlin

Kuala Lumpur [kwalalympuʀ] *n* Kuala

Lumpur
kurde [kyʀd(ə)] *adj* Kurdish ▷ *nm* (*Ling*) Kurdish
▷ *nm/f*: **Kurde** Kurd
Kurdistan [kyʀdistã] *nm*: **le ~** Kurdistan
Kuweit [kɔwɛt] *nm* = **Koweit**

kW *abr* (= *kilowatt*) kW
k-way® [kawɛ] *nm* (lightweight nylon) cagoule
kW/h *abr* (= *kilowatt/heure*) kW/h
kyrielle [kiʀjɛl] *nf*: **une ~ de** a stream of
kyste [kist(ə)] *nm* cyst

k

Ll

L, l [ɛl] *nm inv* L, l ▷ *abr* (= *litre*) l; (*Scol*): **L ès L = Licence ès Lettres; L en D = Licence en Droit; L comme Louis** L for Lucy (*Brit*) *ou* Love (*US*)

l' [l] *art déf voir* **le**

la [la] *art déf, pron voir* **le** ▷ *nm* (*Mus*) A; (*en chantant la gamme*) la

là [la] *adv voir aussi* **-ci; celui** there; (*ici*) here; (*dans le temps*) then; **est-ce que Catherine est là?** is Catherine there (*ou* here)?; **c'est là que** this is where; **là où** where; **de là** (*fig*) hence; **par là** (*fig*) by that; **tout est là** (*fig*) that's what it's all about

là-bas [laba] *adv* there

label [labɛl] *nm* stamp, seal

labeur [labœR] *nm* toil *no pl*, toiling *no pl*

labo [labo] *nm* (= *laboratoire*) lab

laborantin, e [labɔRɑ̃tɛ̃, -in] *nm/f* laboratory assistant

laboratoire [labɔRatwaR] *nm* laboratory; **~ de langues/d'analyses** language/(medical) analysis laboratory

laborieusement [labɔRjøzmɑ̃] *adv* laboriously

laborieux, -euse [labɔRjø, -øz] *adj* (*tâche*) laborious; **classes laborieuses** working classes

labour [labuR] *nm* ploughing *no pl* (*Brit*), plowing *no pl* (*US*); **labours** *nmpl* (*champs*) ploughed fields; **cheval de ~** plough- *ou* cart-horse; **bœuf de ~** ox

labourage [labuRaʒ] *nm* ploughing (*Brit*), plowing (*US*)

labourer [labuRe] *vt* to plough (*Brit*), plow (*US*); (*fig*) to make deep gashes *ou* furrows in

laboureur [labuRœR] *nm* ploughman (*Brit*), plowman (*US*)

labrador [labRadɔR] *nm* (*chien*) labrador; (*Géo*): **le L~** Labrador

labyrinthe [labiRɛ̃t] *nm* labyrinth, maze

lac [lak] *nm* lake; **le ~ Léman** Lake Geneva; **les Grands L~s** the Great Lakes; *voir aussi* **lacs**

lacer [lase] *vt* to lace *ou* do up

lacérer [laseRe] *vt* to tear to shreds

lacet [lasɛ] *nm* (*de chaussure*) lace; (*de route*) sharp bend; (*piège*) snare; **chaussures à ~s** lace-up *ou* lacing shoes

lâche [laʃ] *adj* (*poltron*) cowardly; (*desserré*) loose, slack; (*morale, mœurs*) lax ▷ *nm/f* coward

lâchement [laʃmɑ̃] *adv* (*par peur*) like a coward; (*par bassesse*) despicably

lâcher [laʃe] *nm* (*de ballons, oiseaux*) release ▷ *vt* to let go of; (*ce qui tombe, abandonner*) to drop; (*oiseau, animal: libérer*) to release, set free; (*fig: mot, remarque*) to let slip, come out with; (*Sport: distancer*) to leave behind ▷ *vi* (*fil, amarres*) to break, give way; (*freins*) to fail; **~ les amarres** (*Navig*) to cast off (the moorings); **~ prise** to let go

lâcheté [laʃte] *nf* cowardice; (*bassesse*) lowness

lacis [lasi] *nm* (*de ruelles*) maze

laconique [lakɔnik] *adj* laconic

laconiquement [lakɔnikmɑ̃] *adv* laconically

lacrymal, e, aux [lakRimal, -o] *adj* (*canal, glande*) tear *cpd*

lacrymogène [lakRimɔʒɛn] *adj*: **grenade/gaz ~** tear gas grenade/tear gas

lacs [la] *nm* (*piège*) snare

lactation [laktasjɔ̃] *nf* lactation

lacté, e [lakte] *adj* milk *cpd*

lactique [laktik] *adj*: **acide/ferment ~** lactic acid/ferment

lactose [laktoz] *nm* lactose, milk sugar

lacune [lakyn] *nf* gap

lacustre [lakystR(ə)] *adj* lake *cpd*, lakeside *cpd*

lad [lad] *nm* stable-lad

là-dedans [ladədɑ̃] *adv* inside (there), in it; (*fig*) in that

là-dehors [ladəɔR] *adv* out there

là-derrière [ladɛRjɛR] *adv* behind there; (*fig*) behind that

là-dessous [ladsu] *adv* underneath, under there; (*fig*) behind that

là-dessus [ladsy] *adv* on there; (*fig*) at that point; (: *à ce sujet*) about that

là-devant [ladvɑ̃] *adv* there (in front)

ladite [ladit] *adj voir* **ledit**

ladre [ladR(ə)] *adj* miserly

lagon [lagɔ̃] *nm* lagoon

Lagos [lagɔs] *n* Lagos

lagune [lagyn] *nf* lagoon

là-haut [lao] *adv* up there

laïc [laik] *adj, nm/f* = **laïque**

laïciser [laisize] *vt* to secularize

laïcité [laisite] *nf* secularity, secularism
laid, e [lɛ, lɛd] *adj* ugly; (*fig: acte*) mean, cheap
laideron [lɛdRɔ̃] *nm* ugly girl
laideur [lɛdœR] *nf* ugliness *no pl*; meanness *no pl*
laie [lɛ] *nf* wild sow
lainage [lɛnaʒ] *nm* woollen garment; (*étoffe*) woollen material
laine [lɛn] *nf* wool; **~ peignée** worsted (wool); **~ à tricoter** knitting wool; **~ de verre** glass wool; **~ vierge** new wool
laineux, -euse [lɛnø, -øz] *adj* woolly
lainier, -ière [lɛnje, -jɛR] *adj* (*industrie etc*) woollen
laïque [laik] *adj* lay, civil; (*Scol*) state *cpd* (*as opposed to private and Roman Catholic*) ▷ *nm/f* layman(-woman)
laisse [lɛs] *nf* (*de chien*) lead, leash; **tenir en ~** to keep on a lead *ou* leash
laissé-pour-compte, laissée-, laissés- [lesepuRkɔ̃t] *adj* (*Comm*) unsold; (: *refusé*) returned ▷ *nm/f* (*fig*) reject; **les laissés-pour-compte de la reprise économique** those who are left out of the economic upturn
laisser [lɛse] *vt* to leave ▷ *vb aux:* **~ qn faire** to let sb do; **se ~ exploiter** to let o.s. be exploited; **se ~ aller** to let o.s. go; **~ qn tranquille** to let *ou* leave sb alone; **laisse-toi faire** let me (*ou* him) do it; **rien ne laisse penser que ...** there is no reason to think that ...; **cela ne laisse pas de surprendre** nonetheless it is surprising
laisser-aller [leseale] *nm* carelessness, slovenliness
laisser-faire [lesefɛR] *nm* laissez-faire
laissez-passer [lesepase] *nm inv* pass
lait [lɛ] *nm* milk; **frère/sœur de ~** foster brother/sister; **~ écrémé/concentré/condensé** skimmed/condensed/evaporated milk; **~ en poudre** powdered milk, milk powder; **~ de chèvre/vache** goat's/cow's milk; **~ maternel** mother's milk; **~ démaquillant/de beauté** cleansing/beauty lotion
laitage [lɛtaʒ] *nm* milk product
laiterie [lɛtRi] *nf* dairy
laiteux, -euse [lɛtø, -øz] *adj* milky
laitier, -ière [lɛtje, -jɛR] *adj* dairy ▷ *nm/f* milkman (dairywoman)
laiton [lɛtɔ̃] *nm* brass
laitue [lety] *nf* lettuce
laïus [lajys] *nm* (*péj*) spiel
lama [lama] *nm* llama
lambeau, x [lɑ̃bo] *nm* scrap; **en ~x** in tatters, tattered
lambin, e [lɑ̃bɛ̃, -in] *adj* (*péj*) slow
lambiner [lɑ̃bine] *vi* (*péj*) to dawdle
lambris [lɑ̃bRi] *nm* panelling *no pl*
lambrissé, e [lɑ̃bRise] *adj* panelled
lame [lam] *nf* blade; (*vague*) wave; (*lamelle*) strip; **~ de fond** ground swell *no pl*; **~ de rasoir** razor blade
lamé [lame] *nm* lamé
lamelle [lamɛl] *nf* (*lame*) small blade; (*morceau*) sliver; (*de champignon*) gill; **couper en ~s** to slice

thinly
lamentable [lamɑ̃tabl(ə)] *adj* (*déplorable*) appalling; (*pitoyable*) pitiful
lamentablement [lamɑ̃tabləmɑ̃] *adv* (*échouer*) miserably; (*se conduire*) appallingly
lamentation [lamɑ̃tasjɔ̃] *nf* wailing *no pl*, lamentation; moaning *no pl*
lamenter [lamɑ̃te]: **se lamenter** *vi:* **se ~ (sur)** to moan (over)
laminage [laminaʒ] *nm* lamination
laminer [lamine] *vt* to laminate; (*fig: écraser*) to wipe out
laminoir [laminwaR] *nm* rolling mill; **passer au ~** (*fig*) to go (*ou* put) through the mill
lampadaire [lɑ̃padɛR] *nm* (*de salon*) standard lamp; (*dans la rue*) street lamp
lampe [lɑ̃p(ə)] *nf* lamp; (*Tech*) valve; **~ à alcool** spirit lamp; **~ à bronzer** sunlamp; **~ de poche** torch (*Brit*), flashlight (*US*); **~ à souder** blowlamp; **~ témoin** warning light
lampée [lɑ̃pe] *nf* gulp, swig
lampe-tempête [lɑ̃ptɑ̃pɛt] (*pl* **lampes-tempête**) *nf* storm lantern
lampion [lɑ̃pjɔ̃] *nm* Chinese lantern
lampiste [lɑ̃pist(ə)] *nm* light (maintenance) man; (*fig*) underling
lamproie [lɑ̃pRwa] *nf* lamprey
lance [lɑ̃s] *nf* spear; **~ d'arrosage** garden hose; **~ à eau** water hose; **~ d'incendie** fire hose
lancée [lɑ̃se] *nf:* **être/continuer sur sa ~** to be under way/keep going
lance-flammes [lɑ̃sflam] *nm inv* flamethrower
lance-fusées [lɑ̃sfyze] *nm inv* rocket launcher
lance-grenades [lɑ̃sgRənad] *nm inv* grenade launcher
lancement [lɑ̃smɑ̃] *nm* launching *no pl*, launch; **offre de ~** introductory offer
lance-missiles [lɑ̃smisil] *nm inv* missile launcher
lance-pierres [lɑ̃spjɛR] *nm inv* catapult
lancer [lɑ̃se] *nm* (*Sport*) throwing *no pl*, throw; (*Pêche*) rod and reel fishing ▷ *vt* to throw; (*émettre, projeter*) to throw out, send out; (*produit, fusée, bateau, artiste*) to launch; (*injure*) to hurl, fling; (*proclamation, mandat d'arrêt*) to issue; (*emprunt*) to float; (*moteur*) to send roaring away; **~ qch à qn** to throw sth to sb; (*de façon agressive*) to throw sth at sb; **~ un cri** *ou* **un appel** to shout *ou* call out; **se lancer** *vi* (*prendre de l'élan*) to build up speed; (*se précipiter*): **se ~ sur** *ou* **contre** to rush at; **se ~ dans** (*discussion*) to launch into; (*aventure*) to embark on; (*les affaires, la politique*) to go into; **~ du poids** *nm* putting the shot
lance-roquettes [lɑ̃sRɔkɛt] *nm inv* rocket launcher
lance-torpilles [lɑ̃stɔRpij] *nm inv* torpedo tube
lanceur, -euse [lɑ̃sœR, -øz] *nm/f* bowler; (*Baseball*) pitcher ▷ *nm* (*Espace*) launcher
lancinant, e [lɑ̃sinɑ̃, -ɑ̃t] *adj* (*regrets etc*) haunting; (*douleur*) shooting
lanciner [lɑ̃sine] *vi* to throb; (*fig*) to nag

landais, e [lɑ̃dɛ, -ɛz] *adj* of *ou* from the Landes
landau [lɑ̃do] *nm* pram (*Brit*), baby carriage (*US*)
lande [lɑ̃d] *nf* moor
Landes [lɑ̃d] *nfpl*: **les ~** the Landes
langage [lɑ̃gaʒ] *nm* language; **~ d'assemblage** (*Inform*) assembly language; **~ du corps** body language; **~ évolué/machine** (*Inform*) high-level/machine language; **~ de programmation** (*Inform*) programming language
lange [lɑ̃ʒ] *nm* flannel blanket; **langes** *nmpl* swaddling clothes
langer [lɑ̃ʒe] *vt* to change (the nappy (*Brit*) *ou* diaper (*US*) of); **table à ~** changing table
langoureusement [lɑ̃guʀøzmɑ̃] *adv* languorously
langoureux, -euse [lɑ̃guʀø, -øz] *adj* languorous
langouste [lɑ̃gust(ə)] *nf* crayfish *inv*
langoustine [lɑ̃gustin] *nf* Dublin Bay prawn
langue [lɑ̃g] *nf* (*Anat, Culin*) tongue; (*Ling*) language; (*bande*): **~ de terre** spit of land; **tirer la ~ (à)** to stick out one's tongue (at); **donner sa ~ au chat** to give up, give in; **de ~ française** French-speaking; **~ de bois** officialese; **~ maternelle** native language, mother tongue; **~ verte** slang; **~ vivante** modern language
langue-de-chat [lɑ̃gdəʃa] *nf* finger biscuit
languedocien, ne [lɑ̃gdɔsjɛ̃, -ɛn] *adj* of *ou* from the Languedoc
languette [lɑ̃gɛt] *nf* tongue
langueur [lɑ̃gœʀ] *nf* languidness
languir [lɑ̃giʀ] *vi* to languish; (*conversation*) to flag; **se languir** *vi* to be languishing; **faire ~ qn** to keep sb waiting
languissant, e [lɑ̃gisɑ̃, -ɑ̃t] *adj* languid
lanière [lanjɛʀ] *nf* (*de fouet*) lash; (*de valise, bretelle*) strap
lanoline [lanɔlin] *nf* lanolin
lanterne [lɑ̃tɛʀn(ə)] *nf* (*portable*) lantern; (*électrique*) light, lamp; (*de voiture*) (side)light; **~ rouge** (*fig*) tail-ender; **~ vénitienne** Chinese lantern
lanterneau, x [lɑ̃tɛʀno] *nm* skylight
lanterner [lɑ̃tɛʀne] *vi*: **faire ~ qn** to keep sb hanging around
Laos [laɔs] *nm*: **le ~** Laos
laotien, ne [laɔsjɛ̃, -ɛn] *adj* Laotian
lapalissade [lapalisad] *nf* statement of the obvious
La Paz [lapaz] *n* La Paz
laper [lape] *vt* to lap up
lapereau, x [lapʀo] *nm* young rabbit
lapidaire [lapidɛʀ] *adj* stone *cpd*; (*fig*) terse
lapider [lapide] *vt* to stone
lapin [lapɛ̃] *nm* rabbit; (*fourrure*) cony; **coup du ~** rabbit punch; **poser un ~ à qn** to stand sb up; **~ de garenne** wild rabbit
lapis [lapis], **lapis-lazuli** [lapislazyli] *nm inv* lapis lazuli
lapon, e [lapɔ̃, -ɔn] *adj* Lapp, Lappish ▷ *nm* (*Ling*)

Lapp, Lappish ▷ *nm/f*: **Lapon, e** Lapp, Laplander
Laponie [lapɔni] *nf*: **la ~** Lapland
laps [laps] *nm*: **~ de temps** space of time, time *no pl*
lapsus [lapsys] *nm* slip
laquais [lakɛ] *nm* lackey
laque [lak] *nf* lacquer; (*brute*) shellac; (*pour cheveux*) hair spray ▷ *nm* lacquer; piece of lacquer ware
laqué, e [lake] *adj* lacquered
laquelle [lakɛl] *pron voir* **lequel**
larbin [laʀbɛ̃] *nm* (*péj*) flunkey
larcin [laʀsɛ̃] *nm* theft
lard [laʀ] *nm* (*graisse*) fat; (*bacon*) (streaky) bacon
larder [laʀde] *vt* (*Culin*) to lard
lardon [laʀdɔ̃] *nm* (*Culin*) piece of chopped bacon; (*fam: enfant*) kid
large [laʀʒ(ə)] *adj* wide; broad; (*fig*) generous ▷ *adv*: **calculer/voir ~** to allow extra/think big ▷ *nm* (*largeur*): **5 m de ~** 5 m wide *ou* in width; (*mer*): **le ~** the open sea; **en ~** *adv* sideways; **au ~ de** off; **~ d'esprit** broad-minded; **ne pas en mener ~** to have one's heart in one's boots
largement [laʀʒəmɑ̃] *adv* widely; (*de loin*) greatly; (*amplement, au minimum*) easily; (*sans compter: donner etc*) generously
largesse [laʀʒɛs] *nf* generosity; **largesses** *nfpl* liberalities
largeur [laʀʒœʀ] *nf* (*qu'on mesure*) width; (*impression visuelle*) wideness, width; breadth; broadness
larguer [laʀge] *vt* to drop; (*fam: se débarrasser de*) to get rid of; **~ les amarres** to cast off (the moorings)
larme [laʀm(ə)] *nf* tear; (*fig*): **une ~ de** a drop of; **en ~s** in tears; **pleurer à chaudes ~s** to cry one's eyes out, cry bitterly
larmoyant, e [laʀmwajɑ̃, -ɑ̃t] *adj* tearful
larmoyer [laʀmwaje] *vi* (*yeux*) to water; (*se plaindre*) to whimper
larron [laʀɔ̃] *nm* thief
larve [laʀv(ə)] *nf* (*Zool*) larva; (*fig*) worm
larvé, e [laʀve] *adj* (*fig*) latent
laryngite [laʀɛ̃ʒit] *nf* laryngitis
laryngologiste [laʀɛ̃gɔlɔʒist(ə)] *nm/f* throat specialist
larynx [laʀɛ̃ks] *nm* larynx
las, lasse [lɑ, lɑs] *adj* weary
lasagne [lazaɲ] *nf* lasagne
lascar [laskaʀ] *nm* character; (*malin*) rogue
lascif, -ive [lasif, -iv] *adj* lascivious
laser [lazɛʀ] *nm*: (**rayon**) **~** laser (beam); **chaîne** *ou* **platine ~** compact disc (player); **disque ~** compact disc
lassant, e [lɑsɑ̃, -ɑ̃t] *adj* tiresome, wearisome
lasse [lɑs] *adj f voir* **las**
lasser [lɑse] *vt* to weary, tire; **se ~ de** to grow weary *ou* tired of
lassitude [lɑsityd] *nf* lassitude, weariness
lasso [laso] *nm* lasso; **prendre au ~** to lasso
latent, e [latɑ̃, -ɑ̃t] *adj* latent

latéral, e, aux [lateʀal, -o] *adj* side *cpd*, lateral
latéralement [lateʀalmã] *adv* edgeways;
(*arriver, souffler*) from the side
latex [latɛks] *nm inv* latex
latin, e [latɛ̃, -in] *adj* Latin ▷ *nm* (*Ling*) Latin
▷ *nm/f*: **Latin, e** Latin; **j'y perds mon ~** it's all
Greek to me
latiniste [latinist(ə)] *nm/f* Latin scholar (*ou*
student)
latino-américain, e [latinoameʀikɛ̃, -ɛn] *adj*
Latin-American
latitude [latityd] *nf* latitude; (*fig*): **avoir la ~ de
faire** to be left free *ou* be at liberty to do; **à 48°
de ~ Nord** at latitude 48° North; **sous toutes
les ~s** (*fig*) world-wide, throughout the world
latrines [latʀin] *nfpl* latrines
latte [lat] *nf* lath, slat; (*de plancher*) board
lattis [lati] *nm* lathwork
laudanum [lodanɔm] *nm* laudanum
laudatif, -ive [lodatif, -iv] *adj* laudatory
lauréat, e [lɔʀea, -at] *nm/f* winner
laurier [lɔʀje] *nm* (*Bot*) laurel; (*Culin*) bay leaves
pl; **lauriers** *nmpl* (*fig*) laurels
laurier-rose [lɔʀjeʀoz] (*pl* **lauriers-roses**) *nm*
oleander
laurier-tin [lɔʀjetɛ̃] (*pl* **lauriers-tins**) *nm*
laurustinus
lavable [lavabl(ə)] *adj* washable
lavabo [lavabo] *nm* washbasin; **lavabos** *nmpl*
toilet *sg*
lavage [lavaʒ] *nm* washing *no pl*, wash; **~
d'estomac/d'intestin** stomach/intestinal
wash; **~ de cerveau** brainwashing *no pl*
lavande [lavãd] *nf* lavender
lavandière [lavãdjɛʀ] *nf* washerwoman
lave [lav] *nf* lava *no pl*
lave-glace [lavglas] *nm* (*Auto*) windscreen (*Brit*)
ou windshield (*US*) washer
lave-linge [lavlɛ̃ʒ] *nm inv* washing machine
lavement [lavmã] *nm* (*Méd*) enema
laver [lave] *vt* to wash; (*tache*) to wash off; (*fig:
affront*) to avenge; **se laver** to have a wash,
wash; **se ~ les mains/dents** to wash one's
hands/clean one's teeth; **~ la vaisselle/le linge**
to wash the dishes/clothes; **~ qn de** (*accusation*)
to clear sb of
laverie [lavʀi] *nf*: **~ (automatique)**
launderette
lavette [lavɛt] *nf* (*chiffon*) dish cloth; (*brosse*) dish
mop; (*fam: homme*) wimp, drip
laveur, -euse [lavœʀ, -øz] *nm/f* cleaner
lave-vaisselle [lavvɛsɛl] *nm inv* dishwasher
lavis [lavi] *nm* (*technique*) washing; (*dessin*) wash
drawing
lavoir [lavwaʀ] *nm* wash house; (*bac*) washtub
laxatif, -ive [laksatif, -iv] *adj, nm* laxative
laxisme [laksism(ə)] *nm* laxity
laxiste [laksist(ə)] *adj* lax
layette [lɛjɛt] *nf* layette
layon [lɛjɔ̃] *nm* trail
lazaret [lazaʀɛ] *nm* quarantine area
lazzi [ladzi] *nm* gibe

LCR *sigle f* (= *Ligue communiste révolutionnaire*)
political party

 MOT-CLÉ

le, l', la [l(ə)] (*pl* **les**) *art déf* **1** the; **le livre/la
pomme/l'arbre** the book/the apple/the tree;
les étudiants the students
2 (*noms abstraits*): **le courage/l'amour/la
jeunesse** courage/love/youth
3 (*indiquant la possession*): **se casser la jambe** *etc*
to break one's leg *etc*; **levez la main** put your
hand up; **avoir les yeux gris/le nez rouge** to
have grey eyes/a red nose
4 (*temps*): **le matin/soir** in the morning/
evening; mornings/evenings; **le jeudi** *etc*
(*d'habitude*) on Thursdays *etc*; (*ce jeudi-là etc*) on
(the) Thursday; **nous venons le 3 décembre**
(*parlé*) we're coming on the 3rd of December *ou*
on December the 3rd; (*écrit*) we're coming (on)
3rd *ou* 3 December
5 (*distribution, évaluation*) a, an; **trois euros le
mètre/kilo** three euros a *ou* per metre/kilo; **le
tiers/quart de** a third/quarter of
▷ *pron* **1** (*personne: mâle*) him; (*: femelle*) her;
(*: pluriel*) them; **je le/la/les vois** I can see him/
her/them
2 (*animal, chose: singulier*) it; (*: pluriel*) them; **je le
(ou la) vois** I can see it; **je les vois** I can see
them
3 (*remplaçant une phrase*): **je ne le savais pas** I
didn't know (about it); **il était riche et ne l'est
plus** he was once rich but no longer is

lé [le] *nm* (*de tissu*) width; (*de papier peint*) strip,
length
leader [lidœʀ] *nm* leader
leadership [lidœʀʃip] *nm* (*Pol*) leadership
leasing [liziŋ] *nm* leasing
lèche-bottes [lɛʃbɔt] *nm inv* bootlicker
lèchefrite [lɛʃfʀit] *nf* dripping pan *ou* tray
lécher [leʃe] *vt* to lick; (*laper: lait, eau*) to lick *ou*
lap up; (*finir, polir*) to over-refine; **~ les vitrines**
to go window-shopping; **se ~ les doigts/lèvres**
to lick one's fingers/lips
lèche-vitrines [lɛʃvitʀin] *nm inv*: **faire du ~** to
go window-shopping
leçon [ləsɔ̃] *nf* lesson; **faire la ~** to teach; **faire
la ~ à** (*fig*) to give a lecture to; **~s de conduite**
driving lessons; **~s particulières** private
lessons *ou* tuition *sg* (*Brit*)
lecteur, -trice [lɛktœʀ, -tʀis] *nm/f* reader;
(*d'université*) (foreign language) assistant (*Brit*),
(foreign) teaching assistant (*US*) ▷ *nm* (*Tech*): **~
de cassettes** cassette player; **~ de CD/DVD**
(*Inform: d'ordinateur*) CD/DVD drive; (*de salon*) CD/
DVD player; **~ MP3** MP3 player
lectorat [lɛktɔʀa] *nm* (foreign language *ou*
teaching) assistantship
lecture [lɛktyʀ] *nf* reading
LED [lɛd] *sigle f* (= *light emitting diode*) LED
ledit [lədi], **ladite** [ladit] (*mpl* **lesdits** [ledi]) (*fpl*

lesdites [ledit]) adj the aforesaid
légal, e, -aux [legal, -o] adj legal
légalement [legalmã] adv legally
légalisation [legalizasjɔ̃] nf legalization
légaliser [legalize] vt to legalize
légalité [legalite] nf legality, lawfulness; **être dans/sortir de la ~** to be within/step outside the law
légat [lega] nm (Rel) legate
légataire [legatɛʀ] nm legatee
légendaire [leʒɑ̃dɛʀ] adj legendary
légende [leʒɑ̃d] nf (mythe) legend; (de carte, plan) key, legend; (de dessin) caption
léger, -ère [leʒe, -ɛʀ] adj light; (bruit, retard) slight; (boisson, parfum) weak; (couche, étoffe) thin; (superficiel) thoughtless; (volage) free and easy; flighty; (peu sérieux) lightweight; **blessé ~** slightly injured person; **à la légère** adv (parler, agir) rashly, thoughtlessly
légèrement [leʒɛʀmɑ̃] adv lightly; thoughtlessly, rashly; **~ plus grand** slightly bigger
légèreté [leʒɛʀte] nf lightness; thoughtlessness
légiférer [leʒifeʀe] vi to legislate
légion [leʒjɔ̃] nf legion; **la L~ étrangère** the Foreign Legion; **la L~ d'honneur** the Legion of Honour; see note

LÉGION D'HONNEUR

Created by Napoleon in 1802 to reward services to the French nation, the Légion d'honneur is a prestigious group of men and women headed by the President of the Republic, "the Grand Maître". Members receive a nominal tax-free payment each year.

légionnaire [leʒjɔnɛʀ] nm (Mil) legionnaire; (de la Légion d'honneur) holder of the Legion of Honour
législateur [leʒislatœʀ] nm legislator, lawmaker
législatif, -ive [leʒislatif, -iv] adj legislative; **législatives** nfpl general election sg
législation [leʒislasjɔ̃] nf legislation
législature [leʒislatyʀ] nf legislature; (période) term (of office)
légiste [leʒist(ə)] nm jurist ▷ adj: **médecin ~** forensic scientist (Brit), medical examiner (US)
légitime [leʒitim] adj (Jur) lawful, legitimate; (enfant) legitimate; (fig) rightful, legitimate; **en état de ~ défense** in self-defence
légitimement [leʒitimmɑ̃] adv lawfully; legitimately; rightfully
légitimer [leʒitime] vt (enfant) to legitimize; (justifier: conduite etc) to justify
légitimité [leʒitimite] nf (Jur) legitimacy
legs [lɛg] nm legacy
léguer [lege] vt: **~ qch à qn** (Jur) to bequeath sth to sb; (fig) to hand sth down ou pass sth on to sb
légume [legym] nm vegetable; **~s verts** green

vegetables; **~s secs** pulses
légumier [legymje] nm vegetable dish
leitmotiv [lejtmɔtiv] nm leitmotiv, leitmotif
Léman [lemɑ̃] nm voir lac
lendemain [lɑ̃dmɛ̃] nm: **le ~** the next ou following day; **le ~ matin/soir** the next ou following morning/evening; **le ~ de** the day after; **au ~ de** in the days following; in the wake of; **penser au ~** to think of the future; **sans ~** short-lived; **de beaux ~s** bright prospects; **des ~s qui chantent** a rosy future
lénifiant, e [lenifjɑ̃, -ɑ̃t] adj soothing
léniniste [leninist(ə)] adj, nm/f Leninist
lent, e [lɑ̃, lɑ̃t] adj slow
lente [lɑ̃t] nf nit
lentement [lɑ̃tmɑ̃] adv slowly
lenteur [lɑ̃tœʀ] nf slowness no pl; **lenteurs** nfpl (actions, décisions lentes) slowness sg
lentille [lɑ̃tij] nf (Optique) lens sg; (Bot) lentil; **~ d'eau** duckweed; **~s de contact** contact lenses
léonin, e [leɔnɛ̃, -in] adj (fig: contrat etc) one-sided
léopard [leɔpaʀ] nm leopard
LEP [lɛp] sigle m (= lycée d'enseignement professionnel) secondary school for vocational training, pre-1986
lèpre [lɛpʀ(ə)] nf leprosy
lépreux, -euse [lepʀø, -øz] nm/f leper ▷ adj (fig) flaking, peeling

MOT-CLÉ

lequel, laquelle [ləkɛl, lakɛl] (mpl **lesquels**, fpl **lesquelles**) [à + lequel = **auquel**, de + lequel = **duquel**] pron **1** (interrogatif) which, which one **2** (relatif: personne: sujet) who; (: objet, après préposition) whom; (sujet: possessif) whose; (: chose) which; **je l'ai proposé au directeur, lequel est d'accord** I suggested it to the director, who agrees; **la femme à laquelle j'ai acheté mon chien** the woman from whom I bought my dog; **le pont sur lequel nous sommes passés** the bridge (over) which we crossed; **un homme sur la compétence duquel on peut compter** a man whose competence one can count on ▷ adj: **auquel cas** in which case

les [le] art déf, pron voir le
lesbienne [lɛsbjɛn] nf lesbian
lesdits [ledi], **lesdites** [ledit] adj voir ledit
lèse-majesté [lɛzmaʒɛste] nf inv: **crime de ~** crime of lese-majesty
léser [leze] vt to wrong; (Méd) to injure
lésiner [lezine] vt: **~ (sur)** to skimp (on)
lésion [lezjɔ̃] nf lesion, damage no pl; **~s cérébrales** brain damage
Lesotho [lezɔto] nm: **le ~** Lesotho
lesquels, lesquelles [lekɛl] pron voir lequel
lessivable [lesivabl(ə)] adj washable
lessive [lesiv] nf (poudre) washing powder; (linge) washing no pl, wash; (opération) washing no pl; **faire la ~** to do the washing
lessivé, e [lesive] adj (fam) washed out
lessiver [lesive] vt to wash

lessiveuse [lesivøz] *nf* (*récipient*) washtub
lessiviel [lesivjɛl] *adj* detergent
lest [lɛst] *nm* ballast; **jeter** *ou* **lâcher du ~** (*fig*) to make concessions
leste [lɛst(ə)] *adj* (*personne, mouvement*) sprightly, nimble; (*désinvolte: manières*) offhand; (*osé: plaisanterie*) risqué
lestement [lɛstəmɑ̃] *adv* nimbly
lester [lɛste] *vt* to ballast
letchi [lɛtʃi] *nm* = **litchi**
léthargie [letaʀʒi] *nf* lethargy
léthargique [letaʀʒik] *adj* lethargic
letton, ne [lɛtɔ̃, -ɔn] *adj* Latvian, Lett
Lettonie [lɛtɔni] *nf*: **la ~** Latvia
lettre [lɛtʀ(ə)] *nf* letter; **lettres** *nfpl* (*étude, culture*) literature *sg*; (*Scol*) arts (subjects); **à la ~** (*au sens propre*) literally; (*ponctuellement*) to the letter; **en ~s majuscules** *ou* **capitales** in capital letters, in capitals; **en toutes ~s** in words, in full; **~ de change** bill of exchange; **~ piégée** letter bomb; **~ de voiture (aérienne)** (air) waybill, (air) bill of lading; **~s de noblesse** pedigree
lettré, e [letʀe] *adj* well-read, scholarly
lettre-transfert [lɛtʀətʀɑ̃sfɛʀ] (*pl* **lettres-transferts**) *nf* (pressure) transfer
leu [lø] *nm voir* **queue**
leucémie [løsemi] *nf* leukaemia

○ MOT-CLÉ

leur [lœʀ] *adj poss* their; **leur maison** their house; **leurs amis** their friends; **à leur approche** as they came near; **à leur vue** at the sight of them
▷ *pron* **1** (*objet indirect*) (to) them; **je leur ai dit la vérité** I told them the truth; **je le leur ai donné** I gave it to them, I gave them it
2 (*possessif*): **le (la) leur, les leurs** theirs

leurre [lœʀ] *nm* (*appât*) lure; (*fig*) delusion; (*: piège*) snare
leurrer [lœʀe] *vt* to delude, deceive
leurs [lœʀ] *adj voir* **leur**
levain [ləvɛ̃] *nm* leaven; **sans ~** unleavened
levant, e [ləvɑ̃, -ɑ̃t] *adj*: **soleil ~** rising sun ▷ *nm*: **le L~** the Levant; **au soleil ~** at sunrise
levantin, e [ləvɑ̃tɛ̃, -in] *adj* Levantine ▷ *nm/f*: **Levantin, e** Levantine
levé, e [ləve] *adj*: **être ~** to be up ▷ *nm*: **~ de terrain** land survey; **à mains ~es** (*vote*) by a show of hands; **au pied ~** at a moment's notice
levée [ləve] *nf* (*Postes*) collection; (*Cartes*) trick; **~ de boucliers** general outcry; **~ du corps** *collection of the body from house of the deceased, before funeral*; **~ d'écrou** release from custody; **~ de terre** levee; **~ de troupes** levy
lever [ləve] *vt* (*vitre, bras etc*) to raise; (*soulever de terre, supprimer: interdiction, siège*) to lift; (*: difficulté*) to remove; (*séance*) to close; (*impôts, armée*) to levy; (*Chasse: lièvre*) to start; (*: perdrix*) to flush;

(*fam: fille*) to pick up ▷ *vi* (*Culin*) to rise ▷ *nm*: **au ~** on getting up; **se lever** *vi* to get up; (*soleil*) to rise; (*jour*) to break; (*brouillard*) to lift; **levez-vous!, lève-toi!** stand up!, get up!; **ça va se ~** the weather will clear; **~ du jour** daybreak; **~ du rideau** (*Théât*) curtain; **~ de rideau** (*pièce*) curtain raiser; **~ de soleil** sunrise
lève-tard [lɛvtaʀ] *nm/f inv* late riser
lève-tôt [lɛvto] *nm/f inv* early riser, early bird
levier [ləvje] *nm* lever; **faire ~ sur** to lever up (*ou* off); **~ de changement de vitesse** gear lever
lévitation [levitasjɔ̃] *nf* levitation
levraut [ləvʀo] *nm* (*Zool*) leveret
lèvre [lɛvʀ(ə)] *nf* lip; **lèvres** *nfpl* (*d'une plaie*) edges; **petites/grandes ~s** labia minora/majora; **du bout des ~s** half-heartedly
lévrier [levʀije] *nm* greyhound
levure [ləvyʀ] *nf* yeast; **~ chimique** baking powder
lexical, e, -aux [lɛksikal, -o] *adj* lexical
lexicographe [lɛksikɔgʀaf] *nm/f* lexicographer
lexicographie [lɛksikɔgʀafi] *nf* lexicography, dictionary writing
lexicologie [lɛksikɔlɔʒi] *nf* lexicology
lexique [lɛksik] *nm* vocabulary, lexicon; (*glossaire*) vocabulary
lézard [lezaʀ] *nm* lizard; (*peau*) lizard skin
lézarde [lezaʀd(ə)] *nf* crack
lézarder [lezaʀde]: **se lézarder** *vi* to crack
liaison [ljɛzɔ̃] *nf* (*rapport*) connection, link; (*Rail, Aviat etc*) link; (*relation: d'amitié*) friendship; (*: d'affaires*) relationship; (*: amoureuse*) affair; (*Culin, Phonétique*) liaison; **entrer/être en ~ avec** to get/be in contact with; **~ radio** radio contact; **~ (de transmission de données)** (*Inform*) data link
liane [ljan] *nf* creeper
liant, e [ljɑ̃, -ɑ̃t] *adj* sociable
liasse [ljas] *nf* wad, bundle
Liban [libɑ̃] *nm*: **le ~** (the) Lebanon
libanais [libanɛ, -ɛz] *adj* Lebanese ▷ *nm/f*: **Libanais, e** Lebanese
libations [libasjɔ̃] *nfpl* libations
libelle [libɛl] *nm* lampoon
libellé [libele] *nm* wording
libeller [libele] *vt* (*chèque, mandat*): **~ (au nom de)** to make out (to); (*lettre*) to word
libellule [libelyl] *nf* dragonfly
libéral, e, -aux [liberal, -o] *adj, nm/f* liberal; **les professions ~es** the professions
libéralement [libeʀalmɑ̃] *adv* liberally
libéralisation [liberalizasjɔ̃] *nf* liberalization; **~ du commerce** easing of trade restrictions
libéraliser [liberalize] *vt* to liberalize
libéralisme [liberalism(ə)] *nm* liberalism
libéralité [liberalite] *nf* liberality *no pl*, generosity *no pl*
libérateur, -trice [liberatœʀ, -tʀis] *adj* liberating ▷ *nm/f* liberator
libération [liberasjɔ̃] *nf* liberation, freeing; release; discharge; **~ conditionnelle** release on

parole

libéré, e [libeʀe] *adj* liberated; **~ de** freed from; **être ~ sous caution/sur parole** to be released on bail/on parole

libérer [libeʀe] *vt* (*délivrer*) to free, liberate; (: *moralement, Psych*) to liberate; (*relâcher: prisonnier*) to release; (: *soldat*) to discharge; (*dégager: gaz, cran d'arrêt*) to release; (*Écon: échanges commerciaux*) to ease restrictions on; **se libérer** (*de rendez-vous*) to try and be free, get out of previous engagements; **~ qn de** (*liens, dette*) to free sb from; (*promesse*) to release sb from

Libéria [libeʀja] *nm*: **le ~** Liberia

libérien, ne [libeʀjɛ̃, -ɛn] *adj* Liberian ▷ *nm/f*: **Libérien, ne** Liberian

libéro [libeʀo] *nm* (*Football*) sweeper

libertaire [libɛʀtɛʀ] *adj* libertarian

liberté [libɛʀte] *nf* freedom; (*loisir*) free time; **libertés** *nfpl* (*privautés*) liberties; **mettre/être en ~** to set/be free; **en ~ provisoire/surveillée/conditionnelle** on bail/probation/parole; **~ d'association** right of association; **~ de conscience** freedom of conscience; **~ du culte** freedom of worship; **~ d'esprit** independence of mind; **~ d'opinion** freedom of thought; **~ de la presse** freedom of the press; **~ de réunion** right to hold meetings; **~ syndicale** union rights *pl*; **~s individuelles** personal freedom *sg*; **~s publiques** civil rights

libertin, e [libɛʀtɛ̃, -in] *adj* libertine, licentious

libertinage [libɛʀtinaʒ] *nm* licentiousness

libidineux, -euse [libidinø, -øz] *adj* lustful

libido [libido] *nf* libido

libraire [libʀɛʀ] *nm/f* bookseller

libraire-éditeur [libʀɛʀeditœʀ] (*pl* **libraires-éditeurs**) *nm* publisher and bookseller

librairie [libʀeʀi] *nf* bookshop

librairie-papeterie [libʀeʀipapetʀi] (*pl* **librairies-papeteries**) *nf* bookseller's and stationer's

libre [libʀ(ə)] *adj* free; (*route*) clear; (*place etc*) vacant, free; (*fig: propos, manières*) open; (*Scol*) private and Roman Catholic (*as opposed to "laïque"*); **de ~** (*place*) free; **~ de qch/de faire** free from sth/to do; **vente ~** (*Comm*) unrestricted sale; **~ arbitre** free will; **~ concurrence** free-market economy; **~ entreprise** free enterprise

libre-échange [libʀeʃɑ̃ʒ] *nm* free trade

librement [libʀəmɑ̃] *adv* freely

libre-penseur, -euse [libʀəpɑ̃sœʀ, -øz] *nm/f* free thinker

libre-service [libʀəsɛʀvis] *nm inv* (*magasin*) self-service store; (*restaurant*) self-service restaurant

librettiste [libʀetist(ə)] *nm/f* librettist

Libye [libi] *nf*: **la ~** Libya

libyen, ne [libjɛ̃, -ɛn] *adj* Libyan ▷ *nm/f*: **Libyen, ne** Libyan

lice [lis] *nf*: **entrer en ~** (*fig*) to enter the lists

licence [lisɑ̃s] *nf* (*permis*) permit; (*diplôme*) (first) degree; *see note*; (*liberté*) liberty; (*poétique, orthographique*) licence (Brit), license (US); (*des*

mœurs) licentiousness; **~ ès lettres/en droit** arts/law degree

licencié, e [lisɑ̃sje] *nm/f* (*Scol*): **~ ès lettres/en droit** ≈ Bachelor of Arts/Law, arts/law graduate; (*Sport*) permit-holder

licenciement [lisɑ̃simɑ̃] *nm* dismissal; redundancy; laying off *no pl*

licencier [lisɑ̃sje] *vt* (*renvoyer*) to dismiss; (*débaucher*) to make redundant; to lay off

licencieux, -euse [lisɑ̃sjø, -øz] *adj* licentious

lichen [likɛn] *nm* lichen

licite [lisit] *adj* lawful

licorne [likɔʀn(ə)] *nf* unicorn

licou [liku] *nm* halter

lie [li] *nf* dregs *pl*, sediment

lié, e [lje] *adj*: **très ~ avec** (*fig*) very friendly with *ou* close to; **~ par** (*serment, promesse*) bound by; **avoir partie ~e (avec qn)** to be involved (with sb)

Liechtenstein [liʃtɛnʃtajn] *nm*: **le ~** Liechtenstein

lie-de-vin [lidvɛ̃] *adj inv* wine(-coloured)

liège [ljɛʒ] *nm* cork

liégeois, e [ljeʒwa, -waz] *adj* of *ou* from Liège ▷ *nm/f*: **Liégeois, e** inhabitant *ou* native of Liège; **café/chocolat ~** coffee/chocolate ice cream topped with whipped cream

lien [ljɛ̃] *nm* (*corde, fig: affectif, culturel*) bond; (*rapport*) link, connection; (*analogie*) link; **~ de parenté** family tie

lier [lje] *vt* (*attacher*) to tie up; (*joindre*) to link up; (*fig: unir, engager*) to bind; (*Culin*) to thicken; **~ qch à** (*attacher*) to tie sth to; (*associer*) to link sth to; **~ conversation (avec)** to strike up a conversation (with); **se lier avec** to make friends with

lierre [ljɛʀ] *nm* ivy

liesse [ljɛs] *nf*: **être en ~** to be jubilant

lieu, x [ljø] *nm* place; **lieux** *nmpl* (*locaux*) premises; (*endroit: d'un accident etc*) scene *sg*; **en ~ sûr** in a safe place; **en haut ~** in high places; **vider** *ou* **quitter les ~x** to leave the premises; **arriver/être sur les ~x** to arrive/be on the scene; **en premier ~** in the first place; **en dernier ~** lastly; **avoir ~** to take place; **avoir ~ de faire** to have grounds *ou* good reason for doing; **tenir ~ de** to take the place of; (*servir de*) to serve as; **donner ~ à** to give rise to, give cause for; **au ~ de** instead of; **au ~ qu'il y aille** instead of him going; **~ commun** commonplace; **~ géométrique** locus; **~ de naissance** place of birth

lieu-dit [ljødi] (*pl* **lieux-dits**) *nm* locality

lieue [ljø] *nf* league

lieutenant [ljøtnɑ̃] *nm* lieutenant; ~ **de vaisseau** (*Navig*) lieutenant

lieutenant-colonel [ljøtnɑ̃kɔlɔnɛl] (*pl* **lieutenants-colonels**) *nm* (*armée de terre*) lieutenant colonel; (*armée de l'air*) wing commander (*Brit*), lieutenant colonel (*US*)

lièvre [ljɛvʀ(ə)] *nm* hare; (*coureur*) pacemaker; **lever un ~** (*fig*) to bring up a prickly subject

liftier, -ière [liftje, -jɛʀ] *nm,f* lift (*Brit*) *ou* elevator (*US*) attendant

lifting [liftiŋ] *nm* face lift

ligament [ligamɑ̃] *nm* ligament

ligature [ligatyʀ] *nf* ligature

lige [liʒ] *adj*: **homme ~** (*péj*) henchman

ligne [liɲ] *nf* (*gén*) line; (*Transports: liaison*) service; (*: trajet*) route; (*silhouette*): **garder la ~** to keep one's figure; **en ~** (*Inform*) on line; **en ~ droite** as the crow flies; **"à la ~"** "new paragraph"; **entrer en ~ de compte** to be taken into account; to come into it; **~ de but/médiane** goal/halfway line; **~ d'arrivée/de départ** finishing/starting line; **~ de conduite** course of action; **~ directrice** guiding line; **~ fixe** (*Tél*) fixed line (phone); **~ d'horizon** skyline; **~ de mire** line of sight; **~ de touche** touchline

ligné, e [liɲe] *adj*: **papier ~** ruled paper ▷ *nf* (*race, famille*) line, lineage; (*postérité*) descendants *pl*

ligneux, -euse [liɲø, -øz] *adj* ligneous, woody

lignite [liɲit] *nm* lignite

ligoter [ligɔte] *vt* to tie up

ligue [lig] *nf* league

liguer [lige]: **se liguer** *vi* to form a league; **se ~ contre** (*fig*) to combine against

lilas [lila] *nm* lilac

lillois, e [lilwa, -waz] *adj* of *ou* from Lille

Lima [lima] *n* Lima

limace [limas] *nf* slug

limaille [limaj] *nf*: **~ de fer** iron filings *pl*

limande [limɑ̃d] *nf* dab

limande-sole [limɑ̃dsɔl] *nf* lemon sole

limbes [lɛ̃b] *nmpl* limbo *sg*; **être dans les ~** (*fig: projet etc*) to be up in the air

lime [lim] *nf* (*Tech*) file; (*Bot*) lime; **~ à ongles** nail file

limer [lime] *vt* (*bois, métal*) to file (down); (*ongles*) to file; (*fig: prix*) to pare down

limier [limje] *nm* (*Zool*) bloodhound; (*détective*) sleuth

liminaire [liminɛʀ] *adj* (*propos*) introductory

limitatif, -ive [limitatif, -iv] *adj* restrictive

limitation [limitasjɔ̃] *nf* limitation, restriction; **sans ~ de temps** with no time limit; **~ des naissances** birth control; **~ de vitesse** speed limit

limite [limit] *nf* (*de terrain*) boundary; (*partie ou point extrême*) limit; **dans la ~ de** within the limits of; **à la ~** (*au pire*) if the worst comes (*ou* came) to the worst; **sans ~s** (*bêtise, richesse, pouvoir*) limitless, boundless; **vitesse/charge ~** maximum speed/load; **cas ~** borderline case; **date ~** deadline; **date ~ de vente/**

consommation sell-by/best-before date; **prix ~** upper price limit; **~ d'âge** maximum age, age limit

limiter [limite] *vt* (*restreindre*) to limit, restrict; (*délimiter*) to border, form the boundary of; **se ~ (à qch/à faire)** (*personne*) to limit *ou* confine o.s. (to sth/to doing sth); **se ~ à** (*chose*) to be limited to

limitrophe [limitʀɔf] *adj* border *cpd*; **~ de** bordering on

limogeage [limɔʒaʒ] *nm* dismissal

limoger [limɔʒe] *vt* to dismiss

limon [limɔ̃] *nm* silt

limonade [limɔnad] *nf* lemonade (*Brit*), (lemon) soda (*US*)

limonadier, -ière [limɔnadje, -jɛʀ] *nm/f* (*commerçant*) café owner; (*fabricant de limonade*) soft drinks manufacturer

limoneux, -euse [limɔnø, -øz] *adj* muddy

limousin, e [limuzɛ̃, -in] *adj* of *ou* from Limousin ▷ *nm* (*région*): **le L~** the Limousin ▷ *nf* limousine

limpide [lɛ̃pid] *adj* limpid

lin [lɛ̃] *nm* (*Bot*) flax; (*tissu, toile*) linen

linceul [lɛ̃sœl] *nm* shroud

linéaire [lineɛʀ] *adj* linear ▷ *nm*: **~ (de vente)** shelves *pl*

linéament [lineamɑ̃] *nm* outline

linge [lɛ̃ʒ] *nm* (*serviettes etc*) linen; (*pièce de tissu*) cloth; (*aussi*: **linge de corps**) underwear; (*aussi*: **linge de toilette**) towel; (*lessive*) washing; **~ sale** dirty linen

lingère [lɛ̃ʒɛʀ] *nf* linen maid

lingerie [lɛ̃ʒʀi] *nf* lingerie, underwear

lingot [lɛ̃go] *nm* ingot

linguiste [lɛ̃gɥist(ə)] *nm/f* linguist

linguistique [lɛ̃gɥistik] *adj* linguistic ▷ *nf* linguistics *sg*

lino [lino], **linoléum** [linɔleɔm] *nm* lino(leum)

linotte [linɔt] *nf*: **tête de ~** bird brain

linteau, x [lɛ̃to] *nm* lintel

lion, ne [ljɔ̃, ljɔn] *nm/f* lion (lioness); (*signe*): **le L~** Leo, the Lion; **être du L~** to be Leo; **~ de mer** sea lion

lionceau, x [ljɔ̃so] *nm* lion cub

liposuccion [liposyksjɔ̃] *nf* liposuction

lippu, e [lipy] *adj* thick-lipped

liquéfier [likefje] *vt* to liquefy; **se liquéfier** *vi* (*gaz etc*) to liquefy; (*fig: personne*) to succumb

liqueur [likœʀ] *nf* liqueur

liquidateur, -trice [likidatœʀ, -tʀis] *nm/f* (*Jur*) receiver; **~ judiciaire** official liquidator

liquidation [likidasjɔ̃] *nf* liquidation; (*Comm*) clearance (sale); **~ judiciaire** compulsory liquidation

liquide [likid] *adj* liquid ▷ *nm* liquid; (*Comm*): **en ~** in ready money *ou* cash

liquider [likide] *vt* (*société, biens, témoin gênant*) to liquidate; (*compte, problème*) to settle; (*Comm: articles*) to clear, sell off

liquidités [likidite] *nfpl* (*Comm*) liquid assets

liquoreux, -euse [likɔrø, -øz] *adj* syrupy

I

lire [liʀ] *nf (monnaie)* lira ▷ *vt, vi* to read; **~ qch à qn** to read sth (out) to sb

lis *vb* [li] *voir* **lire** ▷ *nm* [lis] = **lys**

lisais *etc* [lizɛ] *vb voir* **lire**

Lisbonne [lizbɔn] *n* Lisbon

lise *etc* [liz] *vb voir* **lire**

liseré [lizʀe] *nm* border, edging

liseron [lizʀɔ̃] *nm* bindweed

liseuse [lizøz] *nf* book-cover; *(veste)* bed jacket

lisible [lizibl(ə)] *adj* legible; *(digne d'être lu)* readable

lisiblement [lizibləmɑ̃] *adv* legibly

lisière [lizjɛʀ] *nf (de forêt)* edge; *(de tissu)* selvage

lisons [lizɔ̃] *vb voir* **lire**

lisse [lis] *adj* smooth

lisser [lise] *vt* to smooth

lisseur [lisœʀ] *nm* straighteners *pl*

listage [listaʒ] *nm (Inform)* listing

liste [list(ə)] *nf* list; *(Inform)* listing; **faire la ~ de** to list, make out a list of; **~ d'attente** waiting list; **~ civile** civil list; **~ électorale** electoral roll; **~ de mariage** wedding (present) list; **~ noire** hit list

lister [liste] *vt* to list

listéria [listeʀja] *nf* listeria

listing [listiŋ] *nm (Inform)* listing; **qualité ~** draft quality

lit [li] *nm (gén)* bed; **faire son ~** to make one's bed; **aller/se mettre au ~** to go to/get into bed; **chambre avec un grand ~** room with a double bed; **prendre le ~** to take to one's bed; **d'un premier ~** *(Jur)* of a first marriage; **~ de camp** camp bed *(Brit)*, cot *(US)*; **~ d'enfant** cot *(Brit)*, crib *(US)*

litanie [litani] *nf* litany

lit-cage [likaʒ] *(pl* **lits-cages)** *nm* folding bed

litchi [litʃi] *nm* lychee

literie [litʀi] *nf* bedding; *(linge)* bedding, bedclothes *pl*

litho [lito], **lithographie** [litɔgʀafi] *nf* litho(graphy); *(épreuve)* litho(graph)

litière [litjɛʀ] *nf* litter

litige [litiʒ] *nm* dispute; **en ~** in contention

litigieux, -euse [litiʒjø, -øz] *adj* litigious, contentious

litote [litɔt] *nf* understatement

litre [litʀ(ə)] *nm* litre; *(récipient)* litre measure

littéraire [liteʀɛʀ] *adj* literary

littéral, e, -aux [liteʀal, -o] *adj* literal

littéralement [liteʀalmɑ̃] *adv* literally

littérature [liteʀatyʀ] *nf* literature

littoral, e, -aux [litɔʀal, -o] *adj* coastal ▷ *nm* coast

Lituanie [litɥani] *nf*: **la ~** Lithuania

lituanien, ne [litɥanjɛ̃, -ɛn] *adj* Lithuanian ▷ *nm (Ling)* Lithuanian ▷ *nm/f*: **Lituanien, ne** Lithuanian

liturgie [lityʀʒi] *nf* liturgy

liturgique [lityʀʒik] *adj* liturgical

livide [livid] *adj* livid, pallid

living [liviŋ], **living-room** [liviŋʀum] *nm* living room

livrable [livʀabl(ə)] *adj (Comm)* that can be delivered

livraison [livʀɛzɔ̃] *nf* delivery; **~ à domicile** home delivery (service)

livre [livʀ(ə)] *nm* book; *(imprimerie etc)*: **le ~** the book industry ▷ *nf (poids, monnaie)* pound; **traduire qch à ~ ouvert** to translate sth off the cuff *ou* at sight; **~ blanc** official report *(on war, natural disaster etc, prepared by independent body)*; **~ de bord** *(Navig)* logbook; **~ de comptes** account(s) book; **~ de cuisine** cookery book *(Brit)*, cookbook; **~ de messe** mass *ou* prayer book; **~ d'or** visitors' book; **~ de poche** paperback *(small and cheap)*; **~ sterling** pound sterling; **~ verte** green pound

livré, e [livʀe] *nf* livery ▷ *adj*: **~ à** *(l'anarchie etc)* given over to; **~ à soi-même** left to oneself *ou* one's own devices

livrer [livʀe] *vt (Comm)* to deliver; *(otage, coupable)* to hand over; *(secret, information)* to give away; **se ~ à** *(se confier)* to confide in; *(se rendre)* to give o.s. up to; *(s'abandonner à: débauche etc)* to give o.s. up *ou* over to; *(faire: pratiques, actes)* to indulge in; *(travail)* to be engaged in, engage in; *(: sport)* to practise; *(: enquête)* to carry out; **~ bataille** to give battle

livresque [livʀɛsk(ə)] *adj (péj)* bookish

livret [livʀɛ] *nm* booklet; *(d'opéra)* libretto; **~ de caisse d'épargne** (savings) bank-book; **~ de famille** (official) family record book; **~ scolaire** (school) report book

livreur, -euse [livʀœʀ, -øz] *nm/f* delivery boy *ou* man/girl *ou* woman

LO *sigle f* (= Lutte ouvrière) *political party*

lob [lɔb] *nm* lob

lobe [lɔb] *nm*: **~ de l'oreille** ear lobe

lober [lɔbe] *vt* to lob

local, e, -aux [lɔkal, -o] *adj* local ▷ *nm (salle)* premises *pl* ▷ *nmpl* premises

localement [lɔkalmɑ̃] *adv* locally

localisé, e [lɔkalize] *adj* localized

localiser [lɔkalize] *vt (repérer)* to locate, place; *(limiter)* to localize, confine

localité [lɔkalite] *nf* locality

locataire [lɔkatɛʀ] *nm/f* tenant; *(de chambre)* lodger

locatif, -ive [lɔkatif, -iv] *adj (charges, réparations)* incumbent upon the tenant; *(valeur)* rental; *(immeuble)* with rented flats, used as a letting *ou* rental *(US)* concern

location [lɔkasjɔ̃] *nf (par le locataire)* renting; *(par l'usager: de voiture etc)* hiring *(Brit)*, renting *(US)*; *(par le propriétaire)* renting out, letting; hiring out *(Brit)*; *(de billets, places)* booking; *(bureau)* booking office; **"~ de voitures"** "car hire *(Brit)* ou rental *(US)*"

location-vente [lɔkasjɔ̃vɑ̃t] *nf* form of hire purchase *(Brit)* ou installment plan *(US)*

lock-out [lɔkawt] *nm inv* lockout

locomoteur, -trice [lɔkɔmɔtœʀ, -tʀis] *adj, nf* locomotive

locomotion [lɔkɔmosjɔ̃] *nf* locomotion

locomotive [lɔkɔmɔtiv] *nf* locomotive, engine; *(fig)* pacesetter, pacemaker

locuteur, -trice [lɔkytœR, -tRis] *nm/f (Ling)* speaker

locution [lɔkysjɔ̃] *nf* phrase

loden [lɔdɛn] *nm* loden

lofer [lɔfe] *vi (Navig)* to luff

logarithme [lɔgaRitm(ə)] *nm* logarithm

loge [lɔʒ] *nf (Théât: d'artiste)* dressing room; *(: de spectateurs)* box; *(de concierge, franc-maçon)* lodge

logeable [lɔʒabl(ə)] *adj* habitable; *(spacieux)* roomy

logement [lɔʒmɑ̃] *nm* flat *(Brit)*, apartment *(US)*; accommodation *no pl (Brit)*, accommodations *pl (US)*; **le ~** housing; **chercher un ~** to look for a flat *ou* apartment, look for accommodation(s); **construire des ~s bon marché** to build cheap housing *sg*; **crise du ~** housing shortage; **~ de fonction** *(Admin)* company flat *ou* apartment, accommodation(s) provided with one's job

loger [lɔʒe] *vt* to accommodate ▷ *vi* to live; **se loger: trouver à se ~** to find accommodation; **se ~ dans** *(balle, flèche)* to lodge itself in

logeur, -euse [lɔʒœR, -øz] *nm/f* landlord (landlady)

loggia [lɔdʒja] *nf* loggia

logiciel [lɔʒisjɛl] *nm (Inform)* piece of software

logicien, ne [lɔʒisjɛ̃, -ɛn] *nm/f* logician

logique [lɔʒik] *adj* logical ▷ *nf* logic; **c'est ~** it stands to reason

logiquement [lɔʒikmɑ̃] *adv* logically

logis [lɔʒi] *nm* home; abode, dwelling

logisticien, ne [lɔʒistisjɛ̃, -ɛn] *nm/f* logistician

logistique [lɔʒistik] *nf* logistics *sg* ▷ *adj* logistic

logo [lɔgo], **logotype** [lɔgɔtip] *nm* logo

loi [lwa] *nf* law; **faire la ~** to lay down the law; **les ~s de la mode** *(fig)* the dictates of fashion; **proposition de ~** (private member's) bill; **projet de ~** (government) bill

loi-cadre [lwakadR(ə)] *(pl* **lois-cadres)** *nf (Pol)* blueprint law

loin [lwɛ̃] *adv* far; *(dans le temps: futur)* a long way off; *(: passé)* a long time ago; **plus ~** further; **moins ~ (que)** not as far (as); **~ de** far from; **d'ici** a long way from here; **pas ~ de 100 euros** not far off 100 euros; **au ~** far off; **de ~** *adv* from a distance; *(fig: de beaucoup)* by far; **il vient de ~** he's come a long way; he comes from a long way away; **de ~ en ~** here and there; *(de temps en temps)* (every) now and then; **~ de là** *(au contraire)* far from it

lointain, e [lwɛ̃tɛ̃, -ɛn] *adj* faraway, distant; *(dans le futur, passé)* distant, far-off; *(cause, parent)* remote, distant ▷ *nm:* **dans le ~** in the distance

loi-programme [lwapRɔgRam] *(pl* **lois-programmes)** *nf (Pol)* act providing framework for government programme

loir [lwaR] *nm* dormouse

Loire [lwaR] *nf:* **la ~** the Loire

loisible [lwazibl(ə)] *adj:* **il vous est ~ de ...** you are free to ...

loisir [lwaziR] *nm:* **heures de ~** spare time;

loisirs *nmpl* leisure *sg*; *(activités)* leisure activities; **avoir le ~ de faire** to have the time *ou* opportunity to do; **(tout) à ~** *(en prenant son temps)* at leisure; *(autant qu'on le désire)* at one's pleasure

lombaire [lɔ̃bɛR] *adj* lumbar

lombalgie [lɔ̃balʒi] *nf* back pain

londonien, ne [lɔ̃dɔnjɛ̃, -ɛn] *adj* London *cpd*, of London ▷ *nm/f:* **Londonien, ne** Londoner

Londres [lɔ̃dR(ə)] *n* London

long, longue [lɔ̃, lɔ̃g] *adj* long ▷ *adv:* **en savoir ~** to know a great deal ▷ *nm:* **de 3 m de ~** 3 m long, 3 m in length ▷ *nf:* **à la longue** in the end; **faire ~ feu** to fizzle out; **ne pas faire ~ feu** not to last long; **au ~ cours** *(Navig)* ocean *cpd*, ocean-going; **de longue date** *adj* long-standing; **longue durée** *adj* long-term; **de longue haleine** *adj* long-term; **être ~ à faire** to take a long time to do; **en ~** *adv* lengthwise, lengthways; **(tout) le ~ de** (all) along; **tout au ~ de** *(année, vie)* throughout; **de ~ en large** *(marcher)* to and fro, up and down; **en ~ et en large** *(fig)* in every detail

longanimité [lɔ̃ganimite] *nf* forbearance

long-courrier [lɔ̃kuRje] *nm (Aviat)* long-haul aircraft

longe [lɔ̃ʒ] *nf (corde: pour attacher)* tether; *(pour mener)* lead; *(Culin)* loin

longer [lɔ̃ʒe] *vt* to go *(ou* walk *ou* drive) along(side); *(mur, route)* to border

longévité [lɔ̃ʒevite] *nf* longevity

longiligne [lɔ̃ʒiliɲ] *adj* long-limbed

longitude [lɔ̃ʒityd] *nf* longitude; **à 45° de ~ ouest** at 45° longitude west

longitudinal, e, -aux [lɔ̃ʒitydinal, -o] *adj* longitudinal, lengthways; *(entaille, vallée)* running lengthways

longtemps [lɔ̃tɑ̃] *adv* (for) a long time, (for) long; **ça ne va pas durer ~** it won't last long; **avant ~** before long; **pour/pendant ~** for a long time; **je n'en ai pas pour ~** I shan't be long; **mettre ~ à faire** to take a long time to do; **il en a pour ~** he'll be a long time; **il y a ~ que je travaille** I have been working (for) a long time; **il n'y a pas ~ que je l'ai rencontré** it's not long since I met him

longue [lɔ̃g] *adj f voir* **long**

longuement [lɔ̃gmɑ̃] *adv (longtemps: parler, regarder)* for a long time; *(en détail: expliquer, raconter)* at length

longueur [lɔ̃gœR] *nf* length; **longueurs** *nfpl (fig: d'un film etc)* tedious parts; **sur une ~ de 10 km** for *ou* over 10 km; **en ~** *adv* lengthwise, lengthways; **tirer en ~** to drag on; **à ~ de journée** all day long; **d'une ~** *(gagner)* by a length; **~ d'onde** wavelength

longue-vue [lɔ̃gvy] *nf* telescope

look [luk] *(fam)* *nm* look, image

looping [lupiŋ] *nm (Aviat):* **faire des ~s** to loop the loop

lopin [lɔpɛ̃] *nm:* **~ de terre** patch of land

loquace [lɔkas] *adj* talkative, loquacious

loque [lɔk] *nf* (*personne*) wreck; **loques** *nfpl*
(*habits*) rags; **être** *ou* **tomber en ~s** to be in rags

loquet [lɔkɛ] *nm* latch

lorgner [lɔʀɲe] *vt* to eye; (*convoiter*) to have one's
eye on

lorgnette [lɔʀɲɛt] *nf* opera glasses *pl*

lorgnon [lɔʀɲɔ̃] *nm* (*face-à-main*) lorgnette;
(*pince-nez*) pince-nez

loriot [lɔʀjo] *nm* (golden) oriole

lorrain, e [lɔʀɛ̃, -ɛn] *adj* of *ou* from Lorraine;
quiche ~e quiche

lors [lɔʀ]: **~ de** *prép* (*au moment de*) at the time of;
(*pendant*) during; **~ même que** even though

lorsque [lɔʀsk(ə)] *conj* when, as

losange [lɔzɑ̃ʒ] *nm* diamond; (*Géom*) lozenge;
en ~ diamond-shaped

lot [lo] *nm* (*part*) share; (*de loterie*) prize; (*fig:
destin*) fate, lot; (*Comm, Inform*) batch; **~ de
consolation** consolation prize

loterie [lɔtʀi] *nf* lottery; (*tombola*) raffle; **L~
nationale** French national lottery

loti, e [lɔti] *adj*: **bien/mal ~** well-/badly off,
lucky/unlucky

lotion [losjɔ̃] *nf* lotion; **~ après rasage** after-
shave (lotion); **~ capillaire** hair lotion

lotir [lɔtiʀ] *vt* (*terrain: diviser*) to divide into plots;
(:*vendre*) to sell by lots

lotissement [lɔtismɑ̃] *nm* (*groupe de maisons,
d'immeubles*) housing development; (*parcelle*)
(building) plot, lot

loto [lɔto] *nm* lotto

lotte [lɔt] *nf* (*Zool: de rivière*) burbot; (:*de mer*)
monkfish

louable [lwabl(ə)] *adj* (*appartement, garage*)
rentable; (*action, personne*) praiseworthy,
commendable

louage [lwaʒ] *nm*: **voiture de ~** hired (*Brit*) *ou*
rented (*US*) car; (*à louer*) hire (*Brit*) *ou* rental (*US*)
car

louange [lwɑ̃ʒ] *nf*: **à la ~ de** in praise of;
louanges *nfpl* praise *sg*

loubar, loubard [lubaʀ] *nm* (*fam*) lout

louche [luʃ] *adj* shady, dubious ▷ *nf* ladle

loucher [luʃe] *vi* to squint; (*fig*): **~ sur** to have
one's (beady) eye on

louer [lwe] *vt* (*maison: propriétaire*) to let, rent
(out); (:*locataire*) to rent; (*voiture etc*) to hire out
(*Brit*), rent (out); to hire (*Brit*), rent; (*réserver*) to
book; (*faire l'éloge de*) to praise; **"à ~"** "to let"
(*Brit*), "for rent" (*US*); **~ qn de** to praise sb for; **se
~ de** to congratulate o.s. on

loufoque [lufɔk] *adj* (*fam*) crazy, zany

loukoum [lukum] *nm* Turkish delight

loulou [lulu] *nm* (*chien*) spitz; **~ de Poméranie**
Pomeranian (dog)

loup [lu] *nm* wolf; (*poisson*) bass; (*masque*) (eye)
mask; **jeune ~** young go-getter; **~ de mer**
(*marin*) old seadog

loupe [lup] *nf* magnifying glass; **~ de noyer**
burr walnut; **à la ~** (*fig*) in minute detail

louper [lupe] *vt* (*fam: manquer*) to miss; (:*gâcher*)
to mess up, bungle

lourd, e [luʀ, luʀd(ə)] *adj* heavy; (*chaleur, temps*)
sultry; (*fig: personne, style*) heavy-handed ▷ *adv*:
peser ~ to be heavy; **~ de** (*menaces*) charged
with; (*conséquences*) fraught with; **artillerie/
industrie ~e** heavy artillery/industry

lourdaud, e [luʀdo, -od] *adj* oafish

lourdement [luʀdəmɑ̃] *adv* heavily; **se
tromper ~** to make a big mistake

lourdeur [luʀdœʀ] *nf* heaviness; **~ d'estomac**
indigestion *no pl*

loustic [lustik] *nm* (*fam péj*) joker

loutre [lutʀ(ə)] *nf* otter; (*fourrure*) otter skin

louve [luv] *nf* she-wolf

louveteau, x [luvto] *nm* (*Zool*) wolf-cub; (*scout*)
cub (scout)

louvoyer [luvwaje] *vi* (*Navig*) to tack; (*fig*) to
hedge, evade the issue

lover [lɔve]: **se lover** *vi* to coil up

loyal, e, -aux [lwajal, -o] *adj* (*fidèle*) loyal,
faithful; (*fair-play*) fair

loyalement [lwajalmɑ̃] *adv* loyally, faithfully;
fairly

loyalisme [lwajalism(ə)] *nm* loyalty

loyauté [lwajote] *nf* loyalty, faithfulness;
fairness

loyer [lwaje] *nm* rent; **~ de l'argent** interest
rate

LP *sigle m* (= *lycée professionnel*) *secondary school for
vocational training*

LPO *sigle f* (= *Ligue pour la protection des oiseaux*) *bird
protection society*

LSD *sigle m* (= *Lyserg Säure Diäthylamid*) LSD

lu, e [ly] *pp de* **lire**

lubie [lybi] *nf* whim, craze

lubricité [lybʀisite] *nf* lust

lubrifiant [lybʀifjɑ̃] *nm* lubricant

lubrifier [lybʀifje] *vt* to lubricate

lubrique [lybʀik] *adj* lecherous

lucarne [lykaʀn(ə)] *nf* skylight

lucide [lysid] *adj* (*conscient*) lucid, conscious;
(*perspicace*) clear-headed

lucidité [lysidite] *nf* lucidity

luciole [lysjɔl] *nf* firefly

lucratif, -ive [lykʀatif, -iv] *adj* lucrative;
profitable; **à but non ~** non profit-making

ludique [lydik] *adj* play *cpd*, playing

ludothèque [lydɔtɛk] *nf* toy library

luette [lɥɛt] *nf* uvula

lueur [lɥœʀ] *nf* (*chatoyante*) glimmer *no pl*;
(*métallique, mouillée*) gleam *no pl*; (*rougeoyante*)
glow *no pl*; (*pâle*) (faint) light; (*fig*) spark;
(:*d'espérance*) glimmer, gleam

luge [lyʒ] *nf* sledge (*Brit*), sled (*US*); **faire de la ~**
to sledge (*Brit*), sled (*US*), toboggan

lugubre [lygybʀ(ə)] *adj* gloomy; dismal

 MOT-CLÉ

lui [lɥi] *pp de* **luire**
▷ *pron* **1** (*objet indirect: mâle*) (to) him; (:*femelle*)
(to) her; (:*chose, animal*) (to) it; **je lui ai parlé** I
have spoken to him (*ou* to her); **il lui a offert**

un cadeau he gave him (*ou* her) a present; **je le lui ai donné** I gave it to him (*ou* her)
2 (*après préposition, comparatif: personne*) him; (*: chose, animal*) it; **elle est contente de lui** she is pleased with him; **je la connais mieux que lui** I know her better than he does; **cette voiture est à lui** this car belongs to him, this is HIS car
3 (*sujet, forme emphatique*) he; **lui, il est à Paris** HE is in Paris; **c'est lui qui l'a fait** HE did it

lui-même [lɥimɛm] *pron* (*personne*) himself; (*chose*) itself
luire [lɥiʀ] *vi* (*gén*) to shine, gleam; (*surface mouillée*) to glisten; (*reflets chauds, cuivrés*) to glow
luisant, e [lɥizɑ̃, -ɑ̃t] *vb voir* **luire** ▷ *adj* shining, gleaming
lumbago [lɔ̃bago] *nm* lumbago
lumière [lymjɛʀ] *nf* light; **lumières** *nfpl* (*d'une personne*) knowledge *sg*, wisdom *sg*; **à la ~ de** by the light of; (*fig: événements*) in the light of; **fais de la ~** let's have some light, give us some light; **faire (toute) la ~ sur** (*fig*) to clarify (completely); **mettre en ~** (*fig*) to highlight; **~ du jour/soleil** day/sunlight
luminaire [lyminɛʀ] *nm* lamp, light
lumineux, -euse [lyminø, -øz] *adj* (*émettant de la lumière*) luminous; (*éclairé*) illuminated; (*ciel, journée, couleur*) bright; (*relatif à la lumière: rayon etc*) of light, light *cpd*; (*fig: regard*) radiant
luminosité [lyminozite] *nf* (*Tech*) luminosity
lump [lœp] *nm*: **œufs de ~** lump-fish roe
lunaire [lynɛʀ] *adj* lunar, moon *cpd*
lunatique [lynatik] *adj* whimsical, temperamental
lunch [lœntʃ] *nm* (*réception*) buffet lunch
lundi [lœdi] *nm* Monday; **on est ~** it's Monday; **le ~ 20 août** Monday 20th August; **il est venu ~** he came on Monday; **le(s) ~(s)** on Mondays; **à ~!** see you (on) Monday!; **~ de Pâques** Easter Monday; **~ de Pentecôte** Whit Monday (*Brit*)
lune [lyn] *nf* moon; **pleine/nouvelle ~** full/new moon; **être dans la ~** (*distrait*) to have one's head in the clouds; **~ de miel** honeymoon
luné, e [lyne] *adj*: **bien/mal ~** in a good/bad mood
lunette [lynɛt] *nf*: **~s** *nfpl* glasses, spectacles; (*protectrices*) goggles; **~ d'approche** telescope; **~ arrière** (*Auto*) rear window; **~s noires** dark glasses; **~s de soleil** sunglasses
lurent [lyʀ] *vb voir* **lire**
lurette [lyʀɛt] *nf*: **il y a belle ~** ages ago
luron, ne [lyʀɔ̃, -ɔn] *nm/f* lad/lass; **joyeux** *ou* **gai ~** gay dog
lus *etc* [ly] *vb voir* **lire**
lustre [lystʀ(ə)] *nm* (*de plafond*) chandelier; (*fig: éclat*) lustre
lustrer [lystʀe] *vt*: **~ qch** (*faire briller*) to make sth shine; (*user*) to make sth shiny
lut [ly] *vb voir* **lire**
luth [lyt] *nm* lute
luthier [lytje] *nm* (stringed-)instrument maker

lutin [lytɛ̃] *nm* imp, goblin
lutrin [lytʀɛ̃] *nm* lectern
lutte [lyt] *nf* (*conflit*) struggle; (*Sport*): **la ~** wrestling; **de haute ~** after a hard-fought struggle; **~ des classes** class struggle; **~ libre** (*Sport*) all-in wrestling
lutter [lyte] *vi* to fight, struggle; (*Sport*) to wrestle
lutteur, -euse [lytœʀ, -øz] *nm/f* (*Sport*) wrestler; (*fig*) battler, fighter
luxation [lyksasjɔ̃] *nf* dislocation
luxe [lyks(ə)] *nm* luxury; **un ~ de** (*détails, précautions*) a wealth of; **de ~** *adj* luxury *cpd*
Luxembourg [lyksɑ̃buʀ] *nm*: **le ~** Luxembourg
luxembourgeois, e [lyksɑ̃buʀʒwa, -waz] *adj* of *ou* from Luxembourg ▷ *nm/f*: **Luxembourgeois, e** inhabitant *ou* native of Luxembourg
luxer [lykse] *vt*: **se ~ l'épaule** to dislocate one's shoulder
luxueusement [lyksɥøzmɑ̃] *adv* luxuriously
luxueux, -euse [lyksɥø, -øz] *adj* luxurious
luxure [lyksyʀ] *nf* lust
luxuriant, e [lyksyʀjɑ̃, -ɑ̃t] *adj* luxuriant, lush
luzerne [lyzɛʀn(ə)] *nf* lucerne, alfalfa
lycée [lise] *nm* (state) secondary (*Brit*) *ou* high (US) school; **~ technique** technical secondary *ou* high school; *see note*

⬤ **LYCÉE**

French pupils spend the last three years of their secondary education at a *lycée*, where they sit their "baccalauréat" before leaving school or going on to higher education. There are various types of *lycée*, including the "lycées d'enseignement technologique", providing technical courses, and "lycées d'enseignement professionnel", providing vocational courses. Some *lycées*, particularly those with a wide catchment area or those which run specialist courses, have boarding facilities.

lycéen, ne [liseɛ̃, -ɛn] *nm/f* secondary school pupil
Lycra® [likʀa] *nm* Lycra®
lymphatique [lɛ̃fatik] *adj* (*fig*) lethargic, sluggish
lymphe [lɛ̃f] *nf* lymph
lyncher [lɛ̃ʃe] *vt* to lynch
lynx [lɛ̃ks] *nm* lynx
Lyon [ljɔ̃] *n* Lyons
lyonnais, e [ljɔnɛ, -ɛz] *adj* of *ou* from Lyons; (*Culin*) Lyonnaise
lyophilisé, e [ljɔfilize] *adj* freeze-dried
lyre [liʀ] *nf* lyre
lyrique [liʀik] *adj* lyrical; (*Opéra*) lyric; **artiste ~** opera singer; **comédie ~** comic opera; **théâtre ~** opera house (*for light opera*)
lyrisme [liʀism(ə)] *nm* lyricism
lys [lis] *nm* lily

Mm

M, m [ɛm] *nm inv* M, m ▷ *abr* = **majeur;**
masculin; mètre; Monsieur; (= *million*) M; **M**
comme Marcel M for Mike
m' [m] *pron voir* **me**
MA *sigle m* = **maître auxiliaire**
ma [ma] *adj poss voir* **mon**
maboul, e [mabul] *adj* (*fam*) loony
macabre [makɑbʀ(ə)] *adj* macabre, gruesome
macadam [makadam] *nm* tarmac (*Brit*), asphalt
macaron [makaʀɔ̃] *nm* (*gâteau*) macaroon;
(*insigne*) (round) badge
macaroni [makaʀɔni] *nm*, **macaronis** *nmpl*
macaroni *sg*; **~(s) au gratin** macaroni cheese
(*Brit*), macaroni and cheese (*US*)
Macédoine [masedwan] *nf* Macedonia
macédoine [masedwan] *nf*: **~ de fruits** fruit
salad; **~ de légumes** mixed vegetables *pl*
macérer [maseʀe] *vi, vt* to macerate
mâchefer [maʃfɛʀ] *nm* clinker, cinders *pl*
mâcher [maʃe] *vt* to chew; **ne pas ~ ses mots**
not to mince one's words; **~ le travail à qn** (*fig*)
to spoon-feed sb, do half sb's work for him
machiavélique [makjavelik] *adj* Machiavellian
machin [maʃɛ̃] *nm* (*fam*) thingamajig, thing;
(*personne*): **M~** what's-his-name
machinal, e, -aux [maʃinal, -o] *adj* mechanical,
automatic
machinalement [maʃinalmmɑ̃] *adv*
mechanically, automatically
machination [maʃinasjɔ̃] *nf* scheming, frame-
up
machine [maʃin] *nf* machine; (*locomotive; de*
navire etc) engine; (*fig: rouages*) machinery; (*fam:*
personne): **M~** what's-her-name; **faire ~ arrière**
(*Navig*) to go astern; (*fig*) to back-pedal; **~ à**
laver/coudre/tricoter washing/sewing/
knitting machine; **~ à écrire** typewriter; **~ à**
sous fruit machine; **~ à vapeur** steam engine
machine-outil [maʃinuti] (*pl* **machines-outils**)
nf machine tool
machinerie [maʃinʀi] *nf* machinery, plant;
(*d'un navire*) engine room
machinisme [maʃinism(ə)] *nm* mechanization
machiniste [maʃinist(ə)] *nm* (*Théât*) scene
shifter; (*de bus, métro*) driver
macho [matʃo] (*fam*) *nm* male chauvinist

mâchoire [maʃwaʀ] *nf* jaw; **~ de frein** brake
shoe
mâchonner [maʃone] *vt* to chew (at)
maçon [masɔ̃] *nm* bricklayer; (*constructeur*)
builder
mâcon [mɑkɔ̃] *nm* Mâcon wine
maçonner [masone] *vt* (*revêtir*) to face, render
(with cement); (*boucher*) to brick up
maçonnerie [masonʀi] *nf* (*murs: de brique*)
brickwork; (: *de pierre*) masonry, stonework;
(*activité*) bricklaying; building; **~ de béton**
concrete
maçonnique [masonik] *adj* masonic
macramé [makʀame] *nm* macramé
macrobiotique [makʀɔbjɔtik] *adj* macrobiotic
macrocosme [makʀɔkɔsm(ə)] *nm* macrocosm
macro-économie [makʀɔekɔnɔmi] *nf*
macroeconomics *sg*
maculer [makyle] *vt* to stain; (*Typo*) to mackle
Madagascar [madagaskaʀ] *nf* Madagascar
Madame [madam] (*pl* **Mesdames** [medam]) *nf*:
~ X Mrs X; **occupez-vous de ~/Monsieur/**
Mademoiselle please serve this lady/
gentleman/(young) lady; **bonjour ~/**
Monsieur/Mademoiselle good morning; (*ton*
déférent) good morning Madam/Sir/Madam; (*le*
nom est connu) good morning Mrs X/Mr X/Miss X;
~/Monsieur/Mademoiselle! (*pour appeler*)
excuse me!; (*ton déférent*) Madam/Sir/Miss!; **~/**
Monsieur/Mademoiselle (*sur lettre*) Dear
Madam/Sir/Madam; **chère ~/cher Monsieur/**
chère Mademoiselle Dear Mrs X/Mr X/Miss X;
~ la Directrice the director; the manageress;
the head teacher; **Mesdames** Ladies
Madeleine [madlɛn]: **îles de la ~** *nfpl* Magdalen
Islands
madeleine [madlɛn] *nf* madeleine, ≈ sponge
finger cake
Mademoiselle [madmwazɛl] (*pl*
Mesdemoiselles [medmwazɛl]) *nf* Miss; *voir*
aussi **Madame**
Madère [madɛʀ] *nf* Madeira ▷ *nm*: **madère**
Madeira (wine)
madone [madon] *nf* Madonna
madré, e [madʀe] *adj* crafty, wily
Madrid [madʀid] *n* Madrid

madrier [madʀije] *nm* beam
madrigal, -aux [madʀigal, -o] *nm* madrigal
madrilène [madʀilɛn] *adj* of *ou* from Madrid
maestria [maɛstʀija] *nf* (masterly) skill
maestro [maɛstʀo] *nm* maestro
mafia, maffia [mafja] *nf* Maf(f)ia
magasin [magazɛ̃] *nm* (*boutique*) shop; (*entrepôt*) warehouse; (*d'arme, appareil-photo*) magazine; **en ~** (*Comm*) in stock; **faire les ~s** to go (a)round the shops, do the shops; **~ d'alimentation** grocer's (shop) (*Brit*), grocery store (*US*)
magasinier [magazinje] *nm* warehouseman
magazine [magazin] *nm* magazine
mage [maʒ] *nm*: **les Rois M~s** the Magi, the (Three) Wise Men
Maghreb [magʀɛb] *nm*: **le ~** the Maghreb, North(-West) Africa
maghrébin, e [magʀebɛ̃, -in] *adj* of *ou* from the Maghreb ▷ *nm/f*: **Maghrébin, e** North African, Maghrebi
magicien, ne [maʒisjɛ̃, -ɛn] *nm/f* magician
magie [maʒi] *nf* magic; **~ noire** black magic
magique [maʒik] *adj* (*occulte*) magic; (*fig*) magical
magistral, e, -aux [maʒistʀal, -o] *adj* (*œuvre, adresse*) masterly; (*ton*) authoritative; (*gifle etc*) sound, resounding; (*ex cathedra*): **enseignement ~** lecturing, lectures *pl*; **cours ~** lecture
magistrat [maʒistʀa] *nm* magistrate
magistrature [maʒistʀatyʀ] *nf* magistracy, magistrature; **~ assise** judges *pl*, bench; **~ debout** state prosecutors *pl*
magma [magma] *nm* (*Géo*) magma; (*fig*) jumble
magnanime [maɲanim] *adj* magnanimous
magnanimité [maɲanimite] *nf* magnanimity
magnat [magna] *nm* tycoon, magnate
magner [maɲe]: **se magner** *vi* (*fam*) to get a move on
magnésie [maɲezi] *nf* magnesia
magnésium [maɲezjɔm] *nm* magnesium
magnétique [maɲetik] *adj* magnetic
magnétiser [maɲetize] *vt* to magnetize; (*fig*) to mesmerize, hypnotize
magnétiseur, -euse [maɲetizœʀ, -øz] *nm/f* hypnotist
magnétisme [maɲetism(ə)] *nm* magnetism
magnéto [maɲeto] *nm* (*à cassette*) cassette deck; (*magnétophone*) tape recorder
magnétophone [maɲetɔfɔn] *nm* tape recorder; **~ à cassettes** cassette recorder
magnétoscope [maɲetɔskɔp] *nm*: **~ (à cassette)** video (recorder)
magnificence [maɲifisɑ̃s] *nf* (*faste*) magnificence, splendour (*Brit*), splendor (*US*); (*générosité*) munificence, lavishness
magnifier [maɲifje] *vt* (*glorifier*) to glorify; (*idéaliser*) to idealize
magnifique [maɲifik] *adj* magnificent
magnifiquement [maɲifikmɑ̃] *adv* magnificently
magnolia [maɲɔlja] *nm* magnolia

magnum [magnɔm] *nm* magnum
magot [mago] *nm* (*argent*) pile (of money); (*économies*) nest egg
magouille [maguj] *nf* (*fam*) scheming
magret [magʀɛ] *nm*: **~ de canard** duck breast
mahométan, e [maɔmetɑ̃, -an] *adj* Mohammedan, Mahometan
mai [mɛ] *nm* May; *see note*; *voir aussi* **juillet**

LE PREMIER MAI

Le premier mai is a public holiday in France and commemorates the trades union demonstrations in the United States in 1886 when workers demanded the right to an eight-hour working day. Sprigs of lily of the valley are traditionally exchanged. *Le 8 mai* is also a public holiday and commemorates the surrender of the German army to Eisenhower on 7 May, 1945. It is marked by parades of ex-servicemen and ex-servicewomen in most towns. The social upheavals of May and June 1968, with their student demonstrations, workers' strikes and general rioting, are usually referred to as "les événements de mai 68". De Gaulle's Government survived, but reforms in education and a move towards decentralization ensued.

maigre [mɛgʀ(ə)] *adj* (very) thin, skinny; (*viande*) lean; (*fromage*) low-fat; (*végétation*) thin, sparse; (*fig*) poor, meagre, skimpy ▷ *adv*: **faire ~** not to eat meat; **jours ~s** days of abstinence, fish days
maigrelet, te [mɛgʀəlɛ, -ɛt] *adj* skinny, scrawny
maigreur [mɛgʀœʀ] *nf* thinness
maigrichon, ne [megʀiʃɔ̃, -ɔn] *adj* = **maigrelet, te**
maigrir [megʀiʀ] *vi* to get thinner, lose weight ▷ *vt*: **~ qn** (*vêtement*) to make sb look slim(mer)
mail [mɛl] *nm* email
mailing [mɛliŋ] *nm* direct mail *no pl*; **un ~** a mailshot
maille [maj] *nf* (*boucle*) stitch; (*ouverture*) hole (in the mesh); **avoir ~ à partir avec qn** to have a brush with sb; **~ à l'endroit/à l'envers** knit one/purl one; (*boucle*) plain/purl stitch
maillechort [majʃɔʀ] *nm* nickel silver
maillet [majɛ] *nm* mallet
maillon [majɔ̃] *nm* link
maillot [majo] *nm* (*aussi*: **maillot de corps**) vest; (*de danseur*) leotard; (*de sportif*) jersey; **~ de bain** bathing costume (*Brit*), swimsuit; (*d'homme*) bathing trunks *pl*; **~ deux pièces** two-piece swimsuit, bikini; **~ jaune** yellow jersey
main [mɛ̃] *nf* hand; **la ~ dans la ~** hand in hand; **à deux ~s** with both hands; **à une ~** with one hand; **à la ~** (*tenir, avoir*) in one's hand; (*faire, tricoter etc*) by hand; **se donner la ~** to hold hands; **donner** *ou* **tendre la ~ à qn** to hold out one's hand to sb; **se serrer la ~** to shake hands;

serrer la ~ à qn to shake hands with sb; **sous la ~** to *ou* at hand; **haut les ~s!** hands up!; **à ~ levée** (*Art*) freehand; **à ~s levées** (*voter*) with a show of hands; **attaque à ~ armée** armed attack; **à ~ droite/gauche** to the right/left; **à remettre en ~s propres** to be delivered personally; **de première ~** (*renseignement*) first-hand; (*Comm: voiture etc*) with only one previous owner; **faire ~ basse sur** to help o.s. to; **mettre la dernière ~ à** to put the finishing touches to; **mettre la ~ à la pâte** (*fig*) to lend a hand; **avoir/ passer la ~** (*Cartes*) to lead/hand over the lead; **s'en laver les ~s** (*fig*) to wash one's hands of it; **se faire/perdre la ~** to get one's hand in/lose one's touch; **avoir qch bien en ~** to have got the hang of sth; **en un tour de ~** (*fig*) in the twinkling of an eye; **~ courante** handrail
mainate [mɛnat] *nm* myna(h) bird
main-d'œuvre [mɛ̃dœvʀ(ə)] *nf* manpower, labour (*Brit*), labor (*US*)
main-forte [mɛ̃fɔʀt(ə)] *nf*: **prêter ~ à qn** to come to sb's assistance
mainmise [mɛ̃miz] *nf* seizure; (*fig*): **avoir la ~ sur** to have a grip *ou* stranglehold on
mains-libres [mɛ̃libʀ] *adj inv* (*téléphone, kit*) hands-free
maint, e [mɛ̃, mɛ̃t] *adj* many a; **~s** many; **à ~es reprises** time and (time) again
maintenance [mɛ̃tnãs] *nf* maintenance, servicing
maintenant [mɛ̃tnã] *adv* now; (*actuellement*) nowadays
maintenir [mɛ̃tniʀ] *vt* (*retenir, soutenir*) to support; (*contenir: foule etc*) to keep in check, hold back; (*conserver*) to maintain, uphold; (*affirmer*) to maintain; **se maintenir** *vi* (*paix, temps*) to hold; (*préjugé*) to persist; (*malade*) to remain stable
maintien [mɛ̃tjɛ̃] *nm* maintaining, upholding; (*attitude*) bearing; **~ de l'ordre** maintenance of law and order
maintiendrai [mɛ̃tjɛ̃dʀe], **maintiens** *etc* [mɛ̃tjɛ̃] *vb voir* **maintenir**
maire [mɛʀ] *nm* mayor
mairie [meʀi] *nf* (*endroit*) town hall; (*administration*) town council
mais [mɛ] *conj* but; **~ non!** of course not!; **~ enfin** but after all; (*indignation*) look here!; **~ encore?** is that all?
maïs [mais] *nm* maize (*Brit*), corn (*US*)
maison [mɛzõ] *nf* (*bâtiment*) house; (*chez-soi*) home; (*Comm*) firm; (*famille*): **ami de la ~** friend of the family ▷ *adj inv* (*Culin*) home-made; (: *au restaurant*) made by the chef; (*Comm*) in-house, own; (*fam*) first-rate; **à la ~** at home; (*direction*) home; **~ d'arrêt** (short-stay) prison; **~ centrale** prison; **~ close** brothel; **~ de correction** ≈ remand home (*Brit*), ≈ reformatory (*US*); **~ de la culture** ≈ arts centre; **~ des jeunes** ≈ youth club; **~ mère** parent company; **~ de passe**; = **maison close**; **~ de repos** convalescent home; **~ de retraite** old people's home; **~ de santé** mental home
Maison-Blanche [mɛzõblãʃ] *nf*: **la ~** the White House
maisonnée [mɛzɔne] *nf* household, family
maisonnette [mɛzɔnɛt] *nf* small house
maître, -esse [mɛtʀ(ə), mɛtʀɛs] *nm/f* master (mistress); (*Scol*) teacher, schoolmaster(-mistress) ▷ *nm* (*peintre etc*) master; (*titre*): **M~ (Me)** Maître, *term of address for lawyers etc* ▷ *nf* (*amante*) mistress ▷ *adj* (*principal, essentiel*) main; **maison de ~** family seat; **être ~ de** (*soi-même, situation*) to be in control of; **se rendre ~ de** (*pays, ville*) to gain control of; (*situation, incendie*) to bring under control; **être passé ~ dans l'art de** to be a (past) master in the art of; **une maîtresse femme** a forceful woman; **~ d'armes** fencing master; **~ auxiliaire (MA)** (*Scol*) temporary teacher; **~ chanteur** blackmailer; **~ de chapelle** choirmaster; **~ de conférences** ≈ senior lecturer (*Brit*), ≈ assistant professor (*US*); **~/ maîtresse d'école** teacher, schoolmaster/-mistress; **~ d'hôtel** (*domestique*) butler; (*d'hôtel*) head waiter; **~ de maison** host; **~ nageur** lifeguard; **~ d'œuvre** (*Constr*) project manager; **~ d'ouvrage** (*Constr*) client; **~ queux** chef; **maîtresse de maison** hostess; (*ménagère*) housewife
maître-assistant, e [mɛtʀasistã, -ãt] (*pl* **maîtres-assistants, es**) *nm/f* ≈ lecturer
maîtrise [metʀiz] *nf* (*aussi*: **maîtrise de soi**) self-control; (*habileté*) skill, mastery; (*suprématie*) mastery, command; (*diplôme*) ≈ master's degree; *see note*; (*chefs d'équipe*) supervisory staff

⬤ **MAÎTRISE**
⬤
⬤ The *maîtrise* is a French degree which is
⬤ awarded to university students if they
⬤ successfully complete two more years' study
⬤ after the "DEUG". Students wishing to go on
⬤ to do research or to take the "agrégation"
⬤ must hold a *maîtrise*.

maîtriser [metʀize] *vt* (*cheval, incendie*) to (bring under) control; (*sujet*) to master; (*émotion*) to control; **se maîtriser** to control o.s.
majesté [maʒɛste] *nf* majesty
majestueux, -euse [maʒɛstɥø, -øz] *adj* majestic
majeur, e [maʒœʀ] *adj* (*important*) major; (*Jur*) of age; (*fig*) adult ▷ *nm/f* (*Jur*) person who has come of age *ou* attained his (*ou* her) majority ▷ *nm* (*doigt*) middle finger; **en ~e partie** for the most part; **la ~e partie de** the major part of
major [maʒɔʀ] *nm* adjutant; (*Scol*): **~ de la promotion** first in one's year
majoration [maʒɔʀasjõ] *nf* increase
majordome [maʒɔʀdɔm] *nm* major-domo
majorer [maʒɔʀe] *vt* to increase
majorette [maʒɔʀɛt] *nf* majorette
majoritaire [maʒɔʀitɛʀ] *adj* majority *cpd*;

système/scrutin ~ majority system/ballot
majorité [maʒɔʀite] *nf* (*gén*) majority; (*parti*) party in power; **en** ~ (*composé etc*) mainly
Majorque [maʒɔʀk(ə)] *nf* Majorca
majuscule [maʒyskyl] *adj, nf*: (**lettre**) ~ capital (letter)
mal, maux [mal, mo] *nm* (*opposé au bien*) evil; (*tort, dommage*) harm; (*douleur physique*) pain, ache; (*maladie*) illness, sickness *no pl*; (*difficulté, peine*) trouble; (*souffrance morale*) pain ▷ *adv* badly ▷ *adj*: **c'est** ~ (**de faire**) it's bad *ou* wrong (to do); **être** ~ to be uncomfortable; **être** ~ **avec qn** to be on bad terms with sb; **être au plus** ~ (*malade*) to be very bad; (*brouillé*) to be at daggers drawn; **il comprend** ~ he has difficulty in understanding; **il a** ~ **compris** he misunderstood; ~ **tourner** to go wrong; **dire/penser du** ~ **de** to speak/think ill of; **ne vouloir de** ~ **à personne** to wish nobody any ill; **il n'a rien fait de** ~ he has done nothing wrong; **avoir du** ~ **à faire qch** to have trouble doing sth; **se donner du** ~ **pour faire qch** to go to a lot of trouble to do sth; **ne voir aucun** ~ **à** to see no harm in, see nothing wrong in; **craignant** ~ **faire** fearing he *etc* was doing the wrong thing; **sans penser** *ou* **songer à** ~ without meaning any harm; **faire du** ~ **à qn** to hurt sb; to harm sb; **se faire** ~ to hurt o.s.; **se faire** ~ **au pied** to hurt one's foot; **ça fait** ~ it hurts; **j'ai** ~ (**ici**) it hurts (here); **j'ai** ~ **au dos** my back aches, I've got a pain in my back; **avoir** ~ **à la tête/à la gorge** to have a headache/a sore throat; **avoir** ~ **aux dents/à l'oreille** to have toothache/earache; **avoir le** ~ **de l'air** to be airsick; **avoir le** ~ **du pays** to be homesick; ~ **de mer** seasickness; ~ **de la route** carsickness; ~ **en point** *adj inv* in a bad state; **maux de ventre** stomach ache *sg*; *voir aussi* **cœur**
malabar [malabaʀ] *nm* (*fam*) muscle man
malade [malad] *adj* ill, sick; (*poitrine, jambe*) bad; (*plante*) diseased; (*fig: entreprise, monde*) ailing ▷ *nm/f* invalid, sick person; (*à l'hôpital etc*) patient; **tomber** ~ to fall ill; **être** ~ **du cœur** to have heart trouble *ou* a bad heart; **grand** ~ seriously ill person; ~ **mental** mentally sick *ou* ill person
maladie [maladi] *nf* (*spécifique*) disease, illness; (*mauvaise santé*) illness, sickness; (*fig: manie*) mania; **être rongé par la** ~ to be wasting away (through illness); ~ **d'Alzheimer** Alzheimer's disease; ~ **de peau** skin disease
maladif, -ive [maladif, -iv] *adj* sickly; (*curiosité, besoin*) pathological
maladresse [maladʀɛs] *nf* clumsiness *no pl*; (*gaffe*) blunder
maladroit, e [maladʀwa, -wat] *adj* clumsy
maladroitement [maladʀwatmɑ̃] *adv* clumsily
mal-aimé, e [maleme] *nm/f* unpopular person; (*de la scène politique, de la société*) persona non grata
malais, e [malɛ, -ɛz] *adj* Malay, Malayan ▷ *nm* (Ling) Malay ▷ *nm/f*: **Malais, e** Malay, Malayan
malaise [malɛz] *nm* (*Méd*) feeling of faintness;

feeling of discomfort; (*fig*) uneasiness, malaise; **avoir un** ~ to feel faint *ou* dizzy
malaisé, e [maleze] *adj* difficult
Malaisie [malɛzi] *nf*: **la** ~ Malaya, West Malaysia; **la péninsule de** ~ the Malay Peninsula
malappris, e [malapʀi, -iz] *nm/f* ill-mannered *ou* boorish person
malaria [malaʀja] *nf* malaria
malavisé, e [malavize] *adj* ill-advised, unwise
Malawi [malawi] *nm*: **le** ~ Malawi
malaxer [malakse] *vt* (*pétrir*) to knead; (*mêler*) to mix
Malaysia [malɛzja] *nf*: **la** ~ Malaysia
malbouffe [malbuf] *nf* (*fam*): **la** ~ junk food
malchance [malʃɑ̃s] *nf* misfortune, ill luck *no pl*; **par** ~ unfortunately; **quelle** ~! what bad luck!
malchanceux, -euse [malʃɑ̃sø, -øz] *adj* unlucky
malcommode [malkɔmɔd] *adj* impractical, inconvenient
Maldives [maldiv] *nfpl*: **les** ~ the Maldive Islands
maldonne [maldɔn] *nf* (*Cartes*) misdeal; **il y a** ~ (*fig*) there's been a misunderstanding
mâle [mɑl] *adj* (*Élec, Tech*) male; (*viril: voix, traits*) manly ▷ *nm* male
malédiction [malediksjɔ̃] *nf* curse
maléfice [malefis] *nm* evil spell
maléfique [malefik] *adj* evil, baleful
malencontreusement [malɑ̃kɔ̃tʀøzmɑ̃] *adv* (*arriver*) at the wrong moment; (*rappeler, mentionner*) inopportunely
malencontreux, -euse [malɑ̃kɔ̃tʀø, -øz] *adj* unfortunate, untoward
malentendant, e [malɑ̃tɑ̃dɑ̃, -ɑ̃t] *nm/f*: **les** ~**s** the hard of hearing
malentendu [malɑ̃tɑ̃dy] *nm* misunderstanding
malfaçon [malfasɔ̃] *nf* fault
malfaisant, e [malfəzɑ̃, -ɑ̃t] *adj* evil, harmful
malfaiteur [malfɛtœʀ] *nm* lawbreaker, criminal; (*voleur*) thief
malfamé, e [malfame] *adj* disreputable, of ill repute
malfrat [malfʀa] *nm* villain, crook
malgache [malgaʃ] *adj* Malagasy, Madagascan ▷ *nm* (Ling) Malagasy ▷ *nm/f*: **Malgache** Malagasy, Madagascan
malgré [malgʀe] *prép* in spite of, despite; ~ **tout** *adv* in spite of everything
malhabile [malabil] *adj* clumsy
malheur [malœʀ] *nm* (*situation*) adversity, misfortune; (*événement*) misfortune; (*: plus fort*) disaster, tragedy; **par** ~ unfortunately; **quel** ~! what a shame *ou* pity!; **faire un** ~ (*fam: un éclat*) to do something desperate; (*: avoir du succès*) to be a smash hit
malheureusement [malœʀøzmɑ̃] *adv* unfortunately
malheureux, -euse [malœʀø, -øz] *adj* (*triste*) unhappy, miserable; (*infortuné, regrettable*) unfortunate; (*malchanceux*) unlucky; (*insignifiant*) wretched ▷ *nm/f* (*infortuné, misérable*) poor soul; (*indigent, miséreux*) unfortunate

m

creature; **les ~** the destitute; **avoir la main
malheureuse** (au jeu) to be unlucky; (tout casser)
to be ham-fisted
malhonnête [malɔnɛt] adj dishonest
malhonnêtement [malɔnɛtmã] adv
dishonestly
malhonnêteté [malɔnɛtte] nf dishonesty;
rudeness no pl
Mali [mali] nm: **le ~** Mali
malice [malis] nf mischievousness;
(méchanceté): **par ~** out of malice ou spite; **sans ~**
guileless
malicieusement [malisjøzmã] adv
mischievously
malicieux, -euse [malisjø, -øz] adj mischievous
malien, ne [maljɛ̃, -ɛn] adj Malian
malignité [maliɲite] nf (d'une tumeur, d'un mal)
malignancy
malin, -igne [malɛ̃, -iɲ] adj (futé: f gén: **maline**)
smart, shrewd; (: sourire) knowing; (Méd,
influence) malignant; **faire le ~** to show off;
éprouver un ~ plaisir à to take malicious
pleasure in
malingre [malɛ̃gʀ(ə)] adj puny
malintentionné, e [malɛ̃tãsjɔne] adj ill-
intentioned, malicious
malle [mal] nf trunk; (Auto): **~ (arrière)** boot
(Brit), trunk (US)
malléable [maleabl(ə)] adj malleable
malle-poste [malpɔst(ə)] (pl **malles-poste**) nf
mail coach
mallette [malɛt] nf (valise) (small) suitcase;
(aussi: **mallette de voyage**) overnight case; (pour
documents) attaché case
malmener [malməne] vt to manhandle; (fig) to
give a rough ride to
malnutrition [malnytʀisjɔ̃] nf malnutrition
malodorant, e [malɔdɔʀã, -ãt] adj foul-
smelling
malotru [malɔtʀy] nm lout, boor
Malouines [malwin] nfpl: **les ~** the Falklands,
the Falkland Islands
malpoli, e [malpɔli] nm/f rude individual
malpropre [malpʀɔpʀ(ə)] adj (personne, vêtement)
dirty; (travail) slovenly; (histoire, plaisanterie)
unsavory (Brit), unsavory (US), smutty;
(malhonnête) dishonest
malpropreté [malpʀɔpʀəte] nf dirtiness
malsain, e [malsɛ̃, -ɛn] adj unhealthy
malséant, e [malseã, -ãt] adj unseemly,
unbecoming
malsonnant, e [malsɔnã, -ãt] adj offensive
malt [malt] nm malt; **pur ~** (whisky) malt
(whisky)
maltais, e [maltɛ, -ɛz] adj Maltese
Malte [malt(ə)] nf Malta
malté, e [malte] adj (lait etc) malted
maltraiter [maltʀete] vt (brutaliser) to
manhandle, ill-treat; (critiquer, éreinter) to slate
(Brit), roast
malus [malys] nm (Assurances) car insurance
weighting, penalty

malveillance [malvɛjãs] nf (animosité) ill will;
(intention de nuire) malevolence; (Jur) malicious
intent no pl
malveillant, e [malvɛjã, -ãt] adj malevolent,
malicious
malvenu, e [malvəny] adj: **être ~ de** ou **à faire
qch** not to be in a position to do sth
malversation [malvɛʀsasjɔ̃] nf embezzlement,
misappropriation (of funds)
mal-vivre [malvivʀ] nm inv malaise
maman [mamã] nf mum(my) (Brit), mom (US)
mamelle [mamɛl] nf teat
mamelon [mamlɔ̃] nm (Anat) nipple; (colline)
knoll, hillock
mamie [mami] nf (fam) granny
mammifère [mamifɛʀ] nm mammal
mammouth [mamut] nm mammoth
manager [manadʒɛʀ] nm (Sport) manager;
(Comm): **~ commercial** commercial director
manche [mãʃ] nf (de vêtement) sleeve; (d'un jeu,
tournoi) round; (Géo): **la M~** the (English)
Channel ▷ nm (d'outil, casserole) handle; (de pelle,
pioche etc) shaft; (de violon, guitare) neck; (fam)
clumsy oaf; **faire la ~** to pass the hat; **~ à air** nf
(Aviat) wind-sock; **~ à balai** nm broomstick;
(Aviat, Inform) joystick
manchette [mãʃɛt] nf (de chemise) cuff; (coup)
forearm blow; (titre) headline
manchon [mãʃɔ̃] nm (de fourrure) muff; **~ à
incandescence** incandescent (gas) mantle
manchot [mãʃo] nm one-armed man; armless
man; (Zool) penguin
mandarine [mãdaʀin] nf mandarin (orange),
tangerine
mandat [mãda] nm (postal) postal ou money
order; (d'un député etc) mandate; (procuration)
power of attorney, proxy; (Police) warrant; **~
d'amener** summons sg; **~ d'arrêt** warrant for
arrest; **~ de dépôt** committal order; **~ de
perquisition** (Police) search warrant
mandataire [mãdatɛʀ] nm/f (représentant,
délégué) representative; (Jur) proxy
mandat-carte [mãdakaʀt(ə)] (pl **mandats-
cartes**) nm money order (in postcard form)
mandater [mãdate] vt (personne) to appoint;
(Pol: député) to elect
mandat-lettre [mãdalɛtʀ(ə)] (pl **mandats-
lettres**) nm money order (with space for
correspondence)
mandchou, e [mãtʃu] adj Manchu,
Manchurian ▷ nm (Ling) Manchu ▷ nm/f:
Mandchou, e Manchu
Mandchourie [mãtʃuʀi] nf: **la ~** Manchuria
mander [mãde] vt to summon
mandibule [mãdibyl] nf mandible
mandoline [mãdɔlin] nf mandolin(e)
manège [manɛʒ] nm riding school; (à la foire)
roundabout (Brit), merry-go-round; (fig) game,
ploy; **faire un tour de ~** to go for a ride on a ou
the roundabout etc; **~ (de chevaux de bois)**
roundabout (Brit), merry-go-round
manette [manɛt] nf lever, tap; **~ de jeu** (Inform)

joystick

manganèse [mɑ̃ganɛz] nm manganese

mangeable [mɑ̃ʒabl(ə)] adj edible, eatable

mangeaille [mɑ̃ʒaj] nf (péj) grub

mangeoire [mɑ̃ʒwaʀ] nf trough, manger

manger [mɑ̃ʒe] vt to eat; (ronger: rouille etc) to eat into ou away; (utiliser, consommer) to eat up ▷ vi to eat

mange-tout [mɑ̃ʒtu] nm inv mange-tout

mangeur, -euse [mɑ̃ʒœʀ, -øz] nm/f eater

mangouste [mɑ̃gust(ə)] nf mongoose

mangue [mɑ̃g] nf mango

maniabilité [manjabilite] nf (d'un outil) handiness; (d'un véhicule, voilier) manoeuvrability

maniable [manjabl(ə)] adj (outil) handy; (voiture, voilier) easy to handle; manoeuvrable (Brit), maneuverable (US); (fig: personne) easily influenced, manipulable

maniaque [manjak] adj (pointilleux, méticuleux) finicky, fussy; (atteint de manie) suffering from a mania ▷ nm/f maniac

manie [mani] nf mania; (tic) odd habit

maniement [manimɑ̃] nm handling; ~ d'armes arms drill

manier [manje] vt to handle; **se manier** vi (fam) to get a move on

maniéré, e [manjeʀe] adj affected

manière [manjɛʀ] nf (façon) way, manner; (genre, style) style; **manières** nfpl (attitude) manners; (chichis) fuss sg; **de ~ à** so as to; **de telle ~ que** in such a way that; **de cette ~** in this way ou manner; **d'une ~ générale** generally speaking, as a general rule; **de toute ~** in any case; **d'une certaine ~** in a (certain) way; **faire des ~s** to put on airs; **employer la ~ forte** to use strong-arm tactics

manif [manif] nf (manifestation) demo

manifestant, e [manifɛstɑ̃, -ɑ̃t] nm/f demonstrator

manifestation [manifɛstasjɔ̃] nf (de joie, mécontentement) expression, demonstration; (symptôme) outward sign; (fête etc) event; (Pol) demonstration

manifeste [manifɛst(ə)] adj obvious, evident ▷ nm manifesto

manifestement [manifɛstəmɑ̃] adv obviously

manifester [manifɛste] vt (volonté, intentions) to show, indicate; (joie, peur) to express, show ▷ vi (Pol) to demonstrate; **se manifester** vi (émotion) to show ou express itself; (difficultés) to arise; (symptômes) to appear; (témoin etc) to come forward

manigance [manigɑ̃s] nf scheme

manigancer [manigɑ̃se] vt to plot, devise

Manille [manij] n Manila

manioc [manjɔk] nm cassava, manioc

manipulateur, -trice [manipylatœʀ, -tʀis] nm/f (technicien) technician, operator; (prestidigitateur) conjurer; (péj) manipulator

manipulation [manipylasjɔ̃] nf handling; manipulation

manipuler [manipyle] vt to handle; (fig) to manipulate

manivelle [manivɛl] nf crank

manne [man] nf (Rel) manna; (fig) godsend

mannequin [mankɛ̃] nm (Couture) dummy; (Mode) model

manœuvrable [manœvʀabl(ə)] adj (bateau, véhicule) manoeuvrable (Brit), maneuverable (US)

manœuvre [manœvʀ(ə)] nf (gén) manoeuvre (Brit), maneuver (US) ▷ nm (ouvrier) labourer (Brit), laborer (US)

manœuvrer [manœvʀe] vt to manoeuvre (Brit), maneuver (US); (levier, machine) to operate; (personne) to manipulate ▷ vi to manoeuvre ou maneuver

manoir [manwaʀ] nm manor ou country house

manomètre [manɔmɛtʀ(ə)] nm gauge, manometer

manquant, e [mɑ̃kɑ̃, -ɑ̃t] adj missing

manque [mɑ̃k] nm (insuffisance): ~ **de** lack of; (vide) emptiness, gap; (Méd) withdrawal; **manques** nmpl (lacunes) faults, defects; **par ~ de** for want of; ~ **à gagner** loss of profit ou earnings

manqué [mɑ̃ke] adj failed; **garçon ~** tomboy

manquement [mɑ̃kmɑ̃] nm: ~ **à** (discipline, règle) breach of

manquer [mɑ̃ke] vi (faire défaut) to be lacking; (être absent) to be missing; (échouer) to fail ▷ vt to miss ▷ vb impers: **il (nous) manque encore 10 euros** we are still 10 euros short; **il manque des pages (au livre)** there are some pages missing ou some pages are missing (from the book); **l'argent qui leur manque** the money they need ou are short of; **le pied/la voix lui manqua** he missed his footing/his voice failed him; ~ **à qn** (absent etc): **il/cela me manque** I miss him/that; ~ **à** vt (règles etc) to be in breach of, fail to observe; ~ **de** vt to lack; (Comm) to be out of (stock of); **ne pas ~ de faire: il n'a pas manqué de le dire** he certainly said it; ~ **(de) faire: il a manqué (de) se tuer** he very nearly got killed; **il ne manquerait plus qu'il fasse** all we need now is for him to do; **je n'y manquerai pas** leave it to me, I'll definitely do it

mansarde [mɑ̃saʀd(ə)] nf attic

mansardé, e [mɑ̃saʀde] adj attic cpd

mansuétude [mɑ̃sɥetyd] nf leniency

mante [mɑ̃t] nf: ~ **religieuse** praying mantis

manteau, x [mɑ̃to] nm coat; ~ **de cheminée** mantelpiece; **sous le ~** (fig) under cover

mantille [mɑ̃tij] nf mantilla

manucure [manykyʀ] nf manicurist

manuel, le [manɥɛl] adj manual ▷ nm/f manually gifted pupil (as opposed to intellectually gifted) ▷ nm (ouvrage) manual, handbook

manuellement [manɥɛlmɑ̃] adv manually

manufacture [manyfaktyʀ] nf (établissement) factory; (fabrication) manufacture

manufacturé, e [manyfaktyʀe] adj manufactured

manufacturier, -ière [manyfaktyʀje, -jɛʀ] *nm/f*
factory owner

manuscrit, e [manyskʀi, -it] *adj* handwritten
▷ *nm* manuscript

manutention [manytɑ̃sjɔ̃] *nf* (*Comm*) handling;
(*local*) storehouse

manutentionnaire [manytɑ̃sjɔnɛʀ] *nm/f*
warehouseman(-woman), packer

manutentionner [manytɑ̃sjɔne] *vt* to handle

mappemonde [mapmɔ̃d] *nf* (*plane*) map of the
world; (*sphère*) globe

maquereau, x [makʀo] *nm* mackerel *inv*; (*fam:
proxénète*) pimp

maquerelle [makʀɛl] *nf* (*fam*) madam

maquette [makɛt] *nf* (*d'un décor, bâtiment,
véhicule*) (scale) model; (*Typo*) mockup; (: *d'une
page illustrée, affiche*) paste-up; (: *prêt à la
reproduction*) artwork

maquignon [makiɲɔ̃] *nm* horse-dealer

maquillage [makijaʒ] *nm* making up; faking;
(*produits*) make-up

maquiller [makije] *vt* (*personne, visage*) to make
up; (*truquer: passeport, statistique*) to fake; (: *voiture
volée*) to do over (*respray etc*); **se maquiller** to
make o.s. up

maquilleur, -euse [makijœʀ, -øz] *nm/f* make-
up artist

maquis [maki] *nm* (*Géo*) scrub; (*fig*) tangle; (*Mil*)
maquis, underground fighting *no pl*

maquisard, e [makizaʀ, -aʀd(ə)] *nm/f* maquis,
member of the Resistance

marabout [maʀabu] *nm* (*Zool*) marabou(t)

maraîcher, -ère [maʀeʃe, maʀeʃɛʀ] *adj*:
cultures maraîchères market gardening *sg*
▷ *nm/f* market gardener

marais [maʀɛ] *nm* marsh, swamp; **~ salant**
saltworks

marasme [maʀasm(ə)] *nm* (*Pol, Écon*)
stagnation, sluggishness; (*accablement*)
dejection, depression

marathon [maʀatɔ̃] *nm* marathon

marâtre [maʀɑtʀ(ə)] *nf* cruel mother

maraude [maʀod] *nf* pilfering, thieving (*of
poultry, crops*); (*dans un verger*) scrumping;
(*vagabondage*) prowling; **en ~** on the prowl; (*taxi*)
cruising

maraudeur, -euse [maʀodœʀ, -øz] *nm/f*
marauder; prowler

marbre [maʀbʀ(ə)] *nm* (*pierre, statue*) marble;
(*d'une table, commode*) marble top; (*Typo*) stone,
bed; **rester de ~** to remain stonily indifferent

marbrer [maʀbʀe] *vt* to mottle, blotch; (*Tech:
papier*) to marble

marbrerie [maʀbʀəʀi] *nf* (*atelier*) marble
mason's workshop; (*industrie*) marble industry

marbrures [maʀbʀyʀ] *nfpl* blotches *pl*; (*Tech*)
marbling *sg*

marc [maʀ] *nm* (*de raisin, pommes*) marc; **~ de café**
coffee grounds *pl ou* dregs *pl*

marcassin [maʀkasɛ̃] *nm* young wild boar

marchand, e [maʀʃɑ̃, -ɑ̃d] *nm/f* shopkeeper,
tradesman(-woman); (*au marché*) stallholder;
(*spécifique*): **~ de cycles/tapis** bicycle/carpet
dealer; **~ de charbon/vins** coal/wine merchant
▷ *adj*: **prix/valeur ~(e)** market price/value;
qualité ~e standard quality; **~ en gros/au
détail** wholesaler/retailer; **~ de biens** real
estate agent; **~ de canons** (*péj*) arms dealer; **~
de couleurs** ironmonger (*Brit*), hardware
dealer (*US*); **~/e de fruits** fruiterer (*Brit*), fruit
seller (*US*); **~/e de journaux** newsagent; **~/e de
légumes** greengrocer (*Brit*), produce dealer
(*US*); **~/e de poisson** fishmonger (*Brit*), fish
seller (*US*); **~/e de(s) quatre-saisons**
costermonger (*Brit*), street vendor (selling fresh
fruit and vegetables); **~ de sable** (*fig*) sandman;
~ de tableaux art dealer

marchandage [maʀʃɑ̃daʒ] *nm* bargaining; (*péj:
électoral*) bargaining, manoeuvring

marchander [maʀʃɑ̃de] *vt* (*article*) to bargain *ou*
haggle over; (*éloges*) to be sparing with ▷ *vi* to
bargain, haggle

marchandisage [maʀʃɑ̃dizaʒ] *nm*
merchandizing

marchandise [maʀʃɑ̃diz] *nf* goods *pl*,
merchandise *no pl*

marche [maʀʃ(ə)] *nf* (*d'escalier*) step; (*activité*)
walking; (*promenade, trajet, allure*) walk;
(*démarche*) walk, gait; (*Mil etc, Mus*) march;
(*fonctionnement*) running; (*progression*) progress;
course; **à une heure de ~** an hour's walk
(away); **ouvrir/fermer la ~** to lead the way/
bring up the rear; **dans le sens de la ~** (*Rail*)
facing the engine; **en ~** (*monter etc*) while the
vehicle is moving *ou* in motion; **mettre en ~** to
start; **remettre qch en ~** to set *ou* start sth
going again; **se mettre en ~** (*personne*) to get
moving; (*machine*) to start; **~ arrière** (*Auto*)
reverse (gear); **faire ~ arrière** (*Auto*) to reverse;
(*fig*) to backtrack, back-pedal; **~ à suivre**
(correct) procedure; (*sur notice*) (step by step)
instructions *pl*

marché [maʀʃe] *nm* (*lieu, Comm, Écon*) market;
(*ville*) trading centre; (*transaction*) bargain, deal;
par-dessus le ~ into the bargain; **faire son ~** to
do one's shopping; **mettre le ~ en main à qn**
to tell sb to take it or leave it; **~ au comptant**
(*Bourse*) spot market; **~ aux fleurs** flower
market; **~ noir** black market; **faire du ~ noir** to
buy and sell on the black market; **~ aux puces**
flea market; **~ à terme** (*Bourse*) forward market;
~ du travail labour market

marchepied [maʀʃəpje] *nm* (*Rail*) step; (*Auto*)
running board; (*fig*) stepping stone

marcher [maʀʃe] *vi* to walk; (*Mil*) to march;
(*aller: voiture, train, affaires*) to go; (*prospérer*) to go
well; (*fonctionner*) to work, run; (*fam*) to go
along, agree; (: *croire naïvement*) to be taken in; **~
sur** to walk on; (*mettre le pied sur*) to step on *ou* in;
(*Mil*) to march upon; **~ dans** (*herbe etc*) to walk in
ou on; (*flaque*) to step in; **faire ~ qn** (*pour rire*) to
pull sb's leg; (*pour tromper*) to lead sb up the
garden path

marcheur, -euse [maʀʃœʀ, -øz] *nm/f* walker

mardi [maʀdi] *nm* Tuesday; **M~ gras** Shrove Tuesday; *voir aussi* **lundi**

mare [maʀ] *nf* pond; **~ de sang** pool of blood

marécage [maʀekaʒ] *nm* marsh, swamp

marécageux, -euse [maʀekaʒø, -øz] *adj* marshy, swampy

maréchal, -aux [maʀeʃal, -o] *nm* marshal; **~ des logis** (*Mil*) sergeant

maréchal-ferrant [maʀeʃalfeʀɑ̃, maʀeʃo-] (*pl* **maréchaux-ferrants**) *nm* blacksmith

maréchaussée [maʀeʃose] *nf* (*humoristique:* *gendarmes*) constabulary (*Brit*), police

marée [maʀe] *nf* tide; (*poissons*) fresh (sea) fish; **~ haute/basse** high/low tide; **~ montante/descendante** rising/ebb tide; **~ noire** oil slick

marelle [maʀɛl] *nf*: (**jouer à**) **la ~** (to play) hopscotch

marémotrice [maʀemɔtʀis] *adj f* tidal

mareyeur, -euse [maʀɛjœʀ, -øz] *nm/f* wholesale (sea) fish merchant

margarine [maʀgaʀin] *nf* margarine

marge [maʀʒ(ə)] *nf* margin; **en ~** in the margin; **en ~ de** (*fig*) on the fringe of; (*en dehors de*) cut off from; (*qui se rapporte à*) connected with; **~ bénéficiaire** profit margin, mark-up; **~ de sécurité** safety margin

margelle [maʀʒɛl] *nf* coping

margeur [maʀʒœʀ] *nm* margin stop

marginal, e, -aux [maʀʒinal, -o] *adj* marginal ▷ *nm/f* dropout

marguerite [maʀgəʀit] *nf* marguerite, (oxeye) daisy

marguillier [maʀgije] *nm* churchwarden

mari [maʀi] *nm* husband

mariage [maʀjaʒ] *nm* (*union, état, fig*) marriage; (*noce*) wedding; **~ civil/religieux** registry office (*Brit*) *ou* civil/church wedding; **un ~ de raison/d'amour** a marriage of convenience/a love match; **~ blanc** unconsummated marriage; **~ en blanc** white wedding

marié, e [maʀje] *adj* married ▷ *nm/f* (bride)groom/bride; **les ~s** the bride and groom; **les (jeunes) ~s** the newly-weds

marier [maʀje] *vt* to marry; (*fig*) to blend; **se ~ (avec)** to marry, get married (to); (*fig*) to blend (with)

marijuana [maʀiʒwana] *nf* marijuana

marin, e [maʀɛ̃, -in] *adj* sea *cpd*, marine ▷ *nm* sailor ▷ *nf* navy; (*Art*) seascape; (*couleur*) navy (blue); **avoir le pied ~** to be a good sailor; (*garder son équilibre*) to have one's sea legs; **~e de guerre** navy; **~e marchande** merchant navy; **~e à voiles** sailing ships *pl*

marina [maʀina] *nf* marina

marinade [maʀinad] *nf* marinade

marine [maʀin] *adj f, nf voir* **marin** ▷ *adj inv* navy (blue) ▷ *nm* (*Mil*) marine

mariner [maʀine] *vi, vt* to marinate, marinade

marinier [maʀinje] *nm* bargee

marinière [maʀinjɛʀ] *nf* (*blouse*) smock ▷ *adj inv*: **moules ~** (*Culin*) mussels in white wine

marionnette [maʀjɔnɛt] *nf* puppet

marital, e, -aux [maʀital, -o] *adj*: **autorisation ~e** husband's permission

maritalement [maʀitalmɑ̃] *adv*: **vivre ~** to live together (as husband and wife)

maritime [maʀitim] *adj* sea *cpd*, maritime; (*ville*) coastal, seaside; (*droit*) shipping, maritime

marjolaine [maʀʒɔlɛn] *nf* marjoram

marketing [maʀkətiŋ] *nm* (*Comm*) marketing

marmaille [maʀmɑj] *nf* (*péj*) (gang of) brats *pl*

marmelade [maʀməlad] *nf* (*compote*) stewed fruit, compote; **~ d'oranges** (orange) marmalade; **en ~** (*fig*) crushed (to a pulp)

marmite [maʀmit] *nf* (cooking-)pot

marmiton [maʀmitɔ̃] *nm* kitchen boy

marmonner [maʀmɔne] *vt, vi* to mumble, mutter

marmot [maʀmo] *nm* (*fam*) brat

marmotte [maʀmɔt] *nf* marmot

marmotter [maʀmɔte] *vt* (*prière*) to mumble, mutter

marne [maʀn(ə)] *nf* (*Géo*) marl

Maroc [maʀɔk] *nm*: **le ~** Morocco

marocain, e [maʀɔkɛ̃, -ɛn] *adj* Moroccan ▷ *nm/f*: **Marocain, e** Moroccan

maroquin [maʀɔkɛ̃] *nm* (*peau*) morocco (leather); (*fig*) (minister's) portfolio

maroquinerie [maʀɔkinʀi] *nf* (*industrie*) leather craft; (*commerce*) leather shop; (*articles*) fine leather goods *pl*

maroquinier [maʀɔkinje] *nm* (*fabricant*) leather craftsman; (*marchand*) leather dealer

marotte [maʀɔt] *nf* fad

marquant, e [maʀkɑ̃, -ɑ̃t] *adj* outstanding

marque [maʀk(ə)] *nf* mark; (*Sport, Jeu*) score; (*Comm: de produits*) brand, make; (: *de disques*) label; (*insigne: d'une fonction*) badge; (*fig*): **~ d'affection** token of affection; **~ de joie** sign of joy; **à vos ~s!** (*Sport*) on your marks!; **de ~** *adj* (*Comm*) brand-name *cpd*; proprietary; (*fig*) high-class; (: *personnage, hôte*) distinguished; **produit de ~** quality product; **~ déposée** registered trademark; **~ de fabrique** trademark

marqué, e [maʀke] *adj* marked

marquer [maʀke] *vt* to mark; (*inscrire*) to write down; (*bétail*) to brand; (*Sport: but etc*) to score; (: *joueur*) to mark; (*accentuer: taille etc*) to emphasize; (*manifester: refus, intérêt*) to show ▷ *vi* (*événement, personnalité*) to stand out, be outstanding; (*Sport*) to score; **~ qn de son influence/empreinte** to have an influence/leave its impression on sb; **~ un temps d'arrêt** to pause momentarily; **~ le pas** (*fig*) to mark time; **il a marqué ce jour-là d'une pierre blanche** that was a red-letter day for him; **~ les points** (*tenir la marque*) to keep the score

marqueté, e [maʀkəte] *adj* inlaid

marqueterie [maʀkətʀi] *nf* inlaid work, marquetry

marqueur, -euse [maʀkœʀ, -øz] *nm/f* (*Sport: de but*) scorer ▷ *nm* (*crayon feutre*) marker pen

marquis, e [maʀki, -iz] *nm/f* marquis *ou* marquess (marchioness) ▷ *nf* (*auvent*) glass canopy *ou* awning

Marquises [maʀkiz] *nfpl*: **les (îles)** ~ the Marquesas Islands

marraine [maʀɛn] *nf* godmother; (*d'un navire, d'une rose etc*) namer

Marrakech [maʀakɛʃ] *n* Marrakech *ou* Marrakesh

marrant, e [maʀɑ̃, -ɑ̃t] *adj* (*fam*) funny

marre [maʀ] *adv* (*fam*): **en avoir ~ de** to be fed up with

marrer [maʀe]: **se marrer** *vi* (*fam*) to have a (good) laugh

marron, ne [maʀɔ̃, -ɔn] *nm* (*fruit*) chestnut ▷ *adj inv* brown ▷ *adj* (*péj*) crooked; (: *faux*) bogus; **~s glacés** marrons glacés

marronnier [maʀɔnje] *nm* chestnut (tree)

Mars [maʀs] *nm ou f* Mars

mars [maʀs] *nm* March; *voir aussi* **juillet**

marseillais, e [maʀsɛjɛ, -ɛz] *adj* of *ou* from Marseilles ▷ *nf*: **la M~e** *the French national anthem*; *see note*

● LA MARSEILLAISE

The *Marseillaise* has been France's national anthem since 1879. The words of the "Chant de guerre de l'armée du Rhin", as the song was originally called, were written to an anonymous tune by an army captain called Rouget de Lisle in 1792. Adopted as a marching song by the Marseille battalion, it was finally popularized as the *Marseillaise*.

Marseille [maʀsɛj] *n* Marseilles

marsouin [maʀswɛ̃] *nm* porpoise

marsupiaux [maʀsypjo] *nmpl* marsupials

marteau, x [maʀto] *nm* hammer; (*de porte*) knocker; **~ pneumatique** pneumatic drill

marteau-pilon [maʀtopilɔ̃] (*pl* **marteaux-pilons**) *nm* power hammer

marteau-piqueur [maʀtopikœʀ] (*pl* **marteaux-piqueurs**) *nm* pneumatic drill

martel [maʀtɛl] *nm*: **se mettre ~ en tête** to worry o.s.

martèlement [maʀtɛlmɑ̃] *nm* hammering

marteler [maʀtəle] *vt* to hammer; (*mots, phrases*) to rap out

martial, e, -aux [maʀsjal, -o] *adj* martial; **cour ~e** court-martial

martien, ne [maʀsjɛ̃, -ɛn] *adj* Martian, of *ou* from Mars

martinet [maʀtinɛ] *nm* (*fouet*) small whip; (*Zool*) swift

martingale [maʀtɛ̃gal] *nf* (*Couture*) half-belt; (*Jeu*) winning formula

martiniquais, e [maʀtinikɛ, -ɛz] *adj* of *ou* from Martinique

Martinique [maʀtinik] *nf*: **la ~** Martinique

martin-pêcheur (*pl* **martins-pêcheurs**) [maʀtɛ̃pɛʃœʀ] *nm* kingfisher

martre [maʀtʀ(ə)] *nf* marten; **~ zibeline** sable

martyr, e [maʀtiʀ] *nm/f* martyr ▷ *adj* martyred;

enfants ~s battered children

martyre [maʀtiʀ] *nm* martyrdom; (*fig: sens affaibli*) agony, torture; **souffrir le ~** to suffer agonies

martyriser [maʀtiʀize] *vt* (*Rel*) to martyr; (*fig*) to bully; (: *enfant*) to batter

mas [mɑ(s)] *nm* *traditional house or farm in Provence*

mascara [maskaʀa] *nm* mascara

mascarade [maskaʀad] *nf* masquerade

mascotte [maskɔt] *nf* mascot

masculin, e [maskylɛ̃, -in] *adj* masculine; (*sexe, population*) male; (*équipe, vêtements*) men's; (*viril*) manly ▷ *nm* masculine

masochisme [mazɔʃism(ə)] *nm* masochism

masochiste [mazɔʃist(ə)] *adj* masochistic ▷ *nm/f* masochist

masque [mask(ə)] *nm* mask; **~ de beauté** face pack; **~ à gaz** gas mask; **~ de plongée** diving mask

masqué, e [maske] *adj* masked

masquer [maske] *vt* (*cacher: porte, goût*) to hide, conceal; (*dissimuler: vérité, projet*) to mask, obscure

massacrant, e [masakʀɑ̃, -ɑ̃t] *adj*: **humeur ~e** foul temper

massacre [masakʀ(ə)] *nm* massacre, slaughter; **jeu de ~** (*fig*) wholesale slaughter

massacrer [masakʀe] *vt* to massacre, slaughter; (*fig: adversaire*) to slaughter; (: *texte etc*) to murder

massage [masaʒ] *nm* massage

masse [mas] *nf* mass; (*péj*): **la ~** the masses *pl*; (*Élec*) earth; (*maillet*) sledgehammer; **masses** *nfpl* masses; **une ~ de**, **des ~s de** (*fam*) masses *ou* loads of; **en ~** *adv* (*en bloc*) in bulk; (*en foule*) en masse ▷ *adj* (*exécutions, production*) mass *cpd*; **~ monétaire** (*Écon*) money supply; **~ salariale** (*Comm*) wage(s) bill

massepain [maspɛ̃] *nm* marzipan

masser [mase] *vt* (*assembler*) to gather; (*pétrir*) to massage; **se masser** *vi* to gather

masseur, -euse [masœʀ, -øz] *nm/f* (*personne*) masseur(-euse) ▷ *nm* (*appareil*) massager

massicot [masiko] *nm* (*Typo*) guillotine

massif, -ive [masif, -iv] *adj* (*porte*) solid, massive; (*visage*) heavy, large; (*bois, or*) solid; (*dose*) massive; (*déportations etc*) mass *cpd* ▷ *nm* (*montagneux*) massif; (*de fleurs*) clump, bank

massivement [masivmɑ̃] *adv* (*répondre*) en masse; (*administrer, injecter*) in massive doses

massue [masy] *nf* club, bludgeon ▷ *adj inv*: **argument ~** sledgehammer argument

mastectomie [mastɛktɔmi] *nf* mastectomy

mastic [mastik] *nm* (*pour vitres*) putty; (*pour fentes*) filler

masticage [mastikaʒ] *nm* (*d'une fente*) filling; (*d'une vitre*) puttying

mastication [mastikasjɔ̃] *nf* chewing, mastication

mastiquer [mastike] *vt* (*aliment*) to chew, masticate; (*fente*) to fill; (*vitre*) to putty

mastoc [mastɔk] *adj inv* hefty

mastodonte [mastɔdɔ̃t] *nm* monster (*fig*)

masturbation [mastyʀbasjɔ̃] *nf* masturbation
masturber [mastyʀbe] *vt*: **se masturber** to masturbate
m'as-tu-vu [matyvy] *nm/f inv* show-off
masure [mazyʀ] *nf* tumbledown cottage
mat, e [mat] *adj (couleur, métal)* mat(t); *(bruit, son)* dull ▷ *adj inv (Échecs)*: **être ~** to be checkmate
mât [mɑ] *nm (Navig)* mast; *(poteau)* pole, post
matamore [matamɔʀ] *nm* braggart, blusterer
match [matʃ] *nm* match; **~ nul** draw, tie (US); **faire ~ nul** to draw (Brit), tie (US); **~ aller** first leg; **~ retour** second leg, return match
matelas [matla] *nm* mattress; **~ pneumatique** air bed *ou* mattress; **~ à ressorts** spring *ou* interior-sprung mattress
matelassé, e *adj* padded; *(tissu)* quilted
matelasser [matlase] *vt* to pad
matelot [matlo] *nm* sailor, seaman
mater [mate] *vt (personne)* to bring to heel, subdue; *(révolte)* to put down; *(fam)* to watch, look at
matérialisation [mateʀjalizasjɔ̃] *nf* materialization
matérialiser [mateʀjalize]: **se matérialiser** *vi* to materialize
matérialisme [mateʀjalism(ə)] *nm* materialism
matérialiste [mateʀjalist(ə)] *adj* materialistic ▷ *nm/f* materialist
matériau, x [mateʀjo] *nm* material; **matériaux** *nmpl* material(s); **~x de construction** building materials
matériel, le [mateʀjɛl] *adj* material; *(organisation, aide, obstacle)* practical; *(fig: péj: personne)* materialistic ▷ *nm* equipment *no pl; (de camping etc)* gear *no pl; (Inform)* hardware; **il n'a pas le temps ~ de le faire** he doesn't have the time (needed) to do it; **~ d'exploitation** *(Comm)* plant; **~ roulant** rolling stock
matériellement [mateʀjɛlmɑ̃] *adv (financièrement)* materially; **~ à l'aise** comfortably off; **je n'en ai ~ pas le temps** I simply do not have the time
maternel, le [matɛʀnɛl] *adj (amour, geste)* motherly, maternal; *(grand-père, oncle)* maternal ▷ *nf (aussi:* **école maternelle)** (state) nursery school
materner [matɛʀne] *vt (personne)* to mother
maternisé, e [matɛʀnize] *adj*: **lait ~** (infant) formula
maternité [matɛʀnite] *nf (établissement)* maternity hospital; *(état de mère)* motherhood, maternity; *(grossesse)* pregnancy
math [mat] *nfpl* maths (Brit), math (US)
mathématicien, ne [matematisjɛ̃, -ɛn] *nm/f* mathematician
mathématique [matematik] *adj* mathematical
mathématiques [matematik] *nfpl* mathematics *sg*
matheux, -euse [matø, -øz] *nm/f (fam)* maths (Brit) *ou* math (US) student; *(fort en math)* mathematical genius

maths [mat] *nfpl* maths (Brit), math (US)
matière [matjɛʀ] *nf (Physique)* matter; *(Comm, Tech)* material; matter *no pl; (fig: d'un livre etc)* subject matter; *(Scol)* subject; **en ~ de** as regards; **donner ~ à** to give cause to; **~ plastique** plastic; **~s fécales** faeces; **~s grasses** fat (content) *sg*; **~s premières** raw materials
MATIF [matif] *sigle m (= Marché à terme des instruments financiers)* body which regulates the activities of the French Stock Exchange
Matignon [matiɲɔ̃] *nm*: **(l'hôtel) ~** the French Prime Minister's residence; *see note*

○ **HÔTEL MATIGNON**
○
○ The *hôtel Matignon* is the Paris office and
○ residence of the French Prime Minister. By
○ extension, the term "Matignon" is often
○ used to refer to the Prime Minister and his
○ or her staff.

matin [matɛ̃] *nm, adv* morning; **le ~** *(pendant le matin)* in the morning; **demain ~** tomorrow morning; **le lendemain ~** (the) next morning; **du ~ au soir** from morning till night; **une heure du ~** one o'clock in the morning; **de grand** *ou* **bon ~** early in the morning
matinal, e, -aux [matinal, -o] *adj (toilette, gymnastique)* morning *cpd; (de bonne heure)* early; **être ~** *(personne)* to be up early; *(: habituellement)* to be an early riser
matinée [matine] *nf* morning; *(spectacle)* matinée, afternoon performance
matois, e [matwa, -waz] *adj* wily
matou [matu] *nm* tom(cat)
matraquage [matʀakaʒ] *nm* beating up; **~ publicitaire** plug, plugging
matraque [matʀak] *nf (de malfaiteur)* cosh (Brit), club; *(de policier)* truncheon (Brit), billy (US)
matraquer [matʀake] *vt* to beat up (with a truncheon *ou* billy); to cosh (Brit), club; *(fig: touristes etc)* to rip off; *(: disque)* to plug
matriarcal, e, -aux [matʀijaʀkal, -o] *adj* matriarchal
matrice [matʀis] *nf (Anat)* womb; *(Tech)* mould; *(Math etc)* matrix
matricule [matʀikyl] *nf (aussi:* **registre matricule)** roll, register ▷ *nm (aussi:* **numéro matricule)**: *Mil)* regimental number; *(: Admin)* reference number
matrimonial, e, -aux [matʀimɔnjal, -o] *adj* marital, marriage *cpd*
matrone [matʀɔn] *nf* matron
mâture [mɑtyʀ] *nf* masts *pl*
maturité [matyʀite] *nf* maturity; *(d'un fruit)* ripeness, maturity
maudire [modiʀ] *vt* to curse
maudit, e [modi, -it] *adj (fam: satané)* blasted, confounded
maugréer [mogʀee] *vi* to grumble
mauresque [mɔʀɛsk(ə)] *adj* Moorish
Maurice [mɔʀis] *nf*: **(l'île) ~** Mauritius

m

mauricien, ne [mɔrisjɛ̃, -ɛn] *adj* Mauritian
Mauritanie [mɔritani] *nf:* **la ~** Mauritania
mauritanien, ne [mɔritanjɛ̃, -ɛn] *adj*
Mauritanian
mausolée [mozɔle] *nm* mausoleum
maussade [mosad] *adj* (*air, personne*) sullen; (*ciel, temps*) dismal
mauvais, e [mɔvɛ, -ɛz] *adj* bad; (*méchant, malveillant*) malicious, spiteful; (*faux*): **le ~ numéro** the wrong number ▷ *nm:* **le ~** the bad side ▷ *adv:* **il fait ~** the weather is bad; **sentir ~** to have a nasty smell, smell bad *ou* nasty; **la mer est ~e** the sea is rough; **~ coucheur** awkward customer; **~ coup** (*fig*) criminal venture; **~ garçon** tough; **~ pas** tight spot; **~ plaisant** hoaxer; **~ traitements** ill treatment *sg*; **~e herbe** weed; **~e langue** gossip, scandalmonger (*Brit*); **~e passe** difficult situation; (*période*) bad patch; **~e tête** rebellious *ou* headstrong customer
mauve [mov] *adj* (*couleur*) mauve ▷ *nf* (*Bot*) mallow
mauviette [movjɛt] *nf* (*péj*) weakling
maux [mo] *nmpl voir* **mal**
max. *abr* (= *maximum*) max
maximal, e, -aux [maksimal, -o] *adj* maximal
maxime [maksim] *nf* maxim
maximum [maksimɔm] *adj, nm* maximum; **atteindre un/son ~** to reach a/his peak; **au ~** *adv* (*le plus possible*) to the full; as much as one can; (*tout au plus*) at the (very) most *ou* maximum
Mayence [majɑ̃s] *n* Mainz
mayonnaise [majɔnɛz] *nf* mayonnaise
Mayotte [majɔt] *nf* Mayotte
mazout [mazut] *nm* (*fuel*) oil; **chaudière/ poêle à ~** oil-fired boiler/stove
mazouté, e [mazute] *adj* oil-polluted
MDM *sigle mpl* (= *Médecins du Monde*) medical association for aid to Third World countries
Me *abr* = **Maître**
me, m' [m(ə)] *pron* me; (*réfléchi*) myself
méandres [meɑ̃dʀ(ə)] *nmpl* meanderings
mec [mɛk] *nm* (*fam*) guy, bloke (*Brit*)
mécanicien, ne [mekanisjɛ̃, -ɛn] *nm/f* mechanic; (*Rail*) (train *ou* engine) driver; **~ navigant** *ou* **de bord** (*Aviat*) flight engineer
mécanique [mekanik] *adj* mechanical ▷ *nf* (*science*) mechanics *sg*; (*technologie*) mechanical engineering; (*mécanisme*) mechanism; engineering; works *pl*; **ennui ~** engine trouble *no pl*; **s'y connaître en ~** to be mechanically minded; **~ hydraulique** hydraulics *sg*; **~ ondulatoire** wave mechanics *sg*
mécaniquement [mekanikmɑ̃] *adv* mechanically
mécanisation [mekanizasjɔ̃] *nf* mechanization
mécaniser [mekanize] *vt* to mechanize
mécanisme [mekanism(ə)] *nm* mechanism; **~ des taux de change** exchange rate mechanism
mécano [mekano] *nm* (*fam*) mechanic
mécène [mesɛn] *nm* patron
méchamment [meʃamɑ̃] *adv* nastily,
maliciously; spitefully; viciously
méchanceté [meʃɑ̃ste] *nf* (*d'une personne, d'une parole*) nastiness, maliciousness, spitefulness; (*parole, action*) nasty *ou* spiteful *ou* malicious remark (*ou* action)
méchant, e [meʃɑ̃, -ɑ̃t] *adj* nasty, malicious, spiteful; (*enfant: pas sage*) naughty; (*animal*) vicious; (*avant le nom: péjorative*) nasty
mèche [mɛʃ] *nf* (*de lampe, bougie*) wick; (*d'un explosif*) fuse; (*Méd*) pack, dressing; (*de vilebrequin, perceuse*) bit; (*de dentiste*) drill; (*de fouet*) lash; (*de cheveux*) lock; **se faire faire des ~s** (*chez le coiffeur*) to have one's hair streaked, have highlights put in one's hair; **vendre la ~** to give the game away; **de ~ avec** in league with
méchoui [meʃwi] *nm* whole sheep barbecue
mécompte [mekɔ̃t] *nm* (*erreur*) miscalculation; (*déception*) disappointment
méconnais *etc* [mekɔnɛ] *vb voir* **méconnaître**
méconnaissable [mekɔnɛsabl(ə)] *adj* unrecognizable
méconnaissais *etc* [mekɔnɛsɛ] *vb voir* **méconnaître**
méconnaissance [mekɔnɛsɑ̃s] *nf* ignorance
méconnaître [mekɔnɛtʀ(ə)] *vt* (*ignorer*) to be unaware of; (*mésestimer*) to misjudge
méconnu, e [mekɔny] *pp de* **méconnaître** ▷ *adj* (*génie etc*) unrecognized
mécontent, e [mekɔ̃tɑ̃, -ɑ̃t] *adj:* **~ (de)** (*insatisfait*) discontented *ou* dissatisfied *ou* displeased (with); (*contrarié*) annoyed (at) ▷ *nm/f* malcontent, dissatisfied person
mécontentement [mekɔ̃tɑ̃tmɑ̃] *nm* dissatisfaction, discontent, displeasure; annoyance
mécontenter [mekɔ̃tɑ̃te] *vt* to displease
Mecque [mɛk] *nf:* **la ~** Mecca
mécréant, e [mekreɑ̃, -ɑ̃t] *adj* (*peuple*) infidel; (*personne*) atheistic
méd. *abr* = **médecin**
médaille [medaj] *nf* medal
médaillé, e [medaje] *nm/f* (*Sport*) medal-holder
médaillon [medajɔ̃] *nm* (*portrait*) medallion; (*bijou*) locket; (*Culin*) médaillon; **en ~** *adj* (*carte etc*) inset
médecin [medsɛ̃] *nm* doctor; **~ du bord** (*Navig*) ship's doctor; **~ généraliste** general practitioner, GP; **~ légiste** forensic scientist (*Brit*), medical examiner (*US*); **~ traitant** family doctor, GP
médecine [medsin] *nf* medicine; **~ générale** general medicine; **~ infantile** paediatrics *sg* (*Brit*), pediatrics *sg* (*US*); **~ légale** forensic medicine; **~ préventive** preventive medicine; **~ du travail** occupational *ou* industrial medicine; **~s parallèles** *ou* **douces** alternative medicine
MEDEF [medɛf] *sigle m* (= *Mouvement des entreprises de France*) French employers' confederation
médian, e [medjɑ̃, -an] *adj* median
médias [medja] *nmpl:* **les ~** the media
médiateur, -trice [medjatœʀ, -tʀis] *nm/f voir*

médiation mediator; arbitrator

médiathèque [medjatɛk] *nf* media library

médiation [medjasjɔ̃] *nf* mediation; (*dans conflit social etc*) arbitration

médiatique [medjatik] *adj* media *cpd*

médiatisé, e [medjatize] *adj* reported in the media; **ce procès a été très ~** (*péj*) this trial was turned into a media event

médiator [medjatɔR] *nm* plectrum

médical, e, -aux [medikal, -o] *adj* medical; **visiteur** *ou* **délégué ~** medical rep *ou* representative

médicalement [medikalmɑ̃] *adv* medically

médicament [medikamɑ̃] *nm* medicine, drug

médicamenteux, -euse [medikamɑ̃tø, -øz] *adj* medicinal

médication [medikasjɔ̃] *nf* medication

médicinal, e, -aux [medisinal, -o] *adj* medicinal

médico-légal, e, -aux [medikolegal, -o] *adj* forensic

médico-social, e, -aux [medikɔsɔsjal, -o] *adj*: **assistance ~e** medical and social assistance

médiéval, e, -aux [medjeval, -o] *adj* medieval

médiocre [medjɔkR(ə)] *adj* mediocre, poor

médiocrité [medjɔkRite] *nf* mediocrity

médire [mediR] *vi*: **~ de** to speak ill of

médisance [medizɑ̃s] *nf* scandalmongering *no pl* (*Brit*), mud-slinging *no pl*; (*propos*) piece of scandal *ou* malicious gossip

médisant, e [medizɑ̃, -ɑ̃t] *vb voir* **médire** ▷ *adj* slanderous, malicious

médit, e [medi, -it] *pp de* **médire**

méditatif, -ive [meditatif, -iv] *adj* thoughtful

méditation [meditasjɔ̃] *nf* meditation

méditer [medite] *vt* (*approfondir*) to meditate on, ponder (over); (*combiner*) to meditate ▷ *vi* to meditate; **~ de faire** to contemplate doing, plan to do

Méditerranée [meditɛRane] *nf*: **la (mer) ~** the Mediterranean (Sea)

méditerranéen, ne [meditɛRaneɛ̃, -ɛn] *adj* Mediterranean ▷ *nm/f*: **Méditerranéen, ne** Mediterranean

médium [medjɔm] *nm* medium (*spiritualist*)

médius [medjys] *nm* middle finger

méduse [medyz] *nf* jellyfish

méduser [medyze] *vt* to dumbfound

meeting [mitiŋ] *nm* (*Pol, Sport*) rally, meeting; **~ d'aviation** air show

méfait [mefɛ] *nm* (*faute*) misdemeanour, wrongdoing; **méfaits** *nmpl* (*ravages*) ravages

méfiance [mefjɑ̃s] *nf* mistrust, distrust

méfiant, e [mefjɑ̃, -ɑ̃t] *adj* mistrustful, distrustful

méfier [mefje]: **se méfier** *vi* to be wary; (*faire attention*) to be careful; **se ~ de** *vt* to mistrust, distrust, be wary of; to be careful about

mégalomane [megaloman] *adj* megalomaniac

mégalomanie [megalomani] *nf* megalomania

mégalopole [megalopɔl] *nf* megalopolis

méga-octet [megaɔktɛ] *nm* megabyte

mégarde [megaRd(ə)] *nf*: **par ~** accidentally;

(*par erreur*) by mistake

mégatonne [megatɔn] *nf* megaton

mégère [meʒɛR] *nf* (*péj: femme*) shrew

mégot [mego] *nm* cigarette end *ou* butt

mégoter [megote] *vi* to nitpick

meilleur, e [mɛjœR] *adj, adv* better; (*valeur superlative*) best ▷ *nm*: **le ~** (*celui qui ...*) the best (one); (*ce qui ...*) the best ▷ *nf*: **la ~e** the best (one); **le ~ des deux** the better of the two; **de ~e heure** earlier; **~ marché** cheaper

méjuger [meʒyʒe] *vt* to misjudge

mél [mɛl] *nm* email

mélancolie [melɑ̃kɔli] *nf* melancholy, gloom

mélancolique [melɑ̃kɔlik] *adj* melancholy, gloomy

mélange [melɑ̃ʒ] *nm* (*opération*) mixing; blending; (*résultat*) mixture; blend; **sans ~** unadulterated

mélanger [melɑ̃ʒe] *vt* (*substances*) to mix; (*vins, couleurs*) to blend; (*mettre en désordre, confondre*) to mix up, muddle (up); **se mélanger** (*liquides, couleurs*) to blend, mix

mélanine [melanin] *nf* melanin

mélasse [melas] *nf* treacle, molasses *sg*

mêlée [mele] *nf* (*bataille, cohue*) mêlée, scramble; (*lutte, conflit*) tussle, scuffle; (*Rugby*) scrum(mage)

mêler [mele] *vt* (*substances, odeurs, races*) to mix; (*embrouiller*) to muddle (up), mix up; **se mêler** to mix; (*se joindre, s'allier*) to mingle; **se ~ à** (*personne*) to join; to mix with; (: *odeurs etc*) to mingle with; **se ~ de** (*personne*) to meddle with, interfere in; **mêle-toi de tes affaires!** mind your own business!; **~ à** *ou* **avec** *ou* **de** to mix with; to mingle with; **~ qn à** (*affaire*) to get sb mixed up *ou* involved in

mélo [melo] *nm adj* = **mélodrame**; **mélodramatique**

mélodie [melɔdi] *nf* melody

mélodieux, -euse [melɔdjø, -øz] *adj* melodious, tuneful

mélodique [melɔdik] *adj* melodic

mélodramatique [melɔdRamatik] *adj* melodramatic

mélodrame [melɔdRam] *nm* melodrama

mélomane [meloman] *nm/f* music lover

melon [məlɔ̃] *nm* (*Bot*) (honeydew) melon; (*aussi*: **chapeau melon**) bowler (hat); **~ d'eau** watermelon

mélopée [melɔpe] *nf* monotonous chant

membrane [mɑ̃bRan] *nf* membrane

membre [mɑ̃bR(ə)] *nm* (*Anat*) limb; (*personne, pays, élément*) member ▷ *adj* member; **être ~ de** to be a member of; **~ (viril)** (male) organ

mémé [meme] *nf* (*fam*) granny; (: *vieille femme*) old dear

⊙ **MOT-CLÉ**

même [mɛm] *adj* **1** (*avant le nom*) same; **en même temps** at the same time; **ils ont les mêmes goûts** they have the same *ou* similar tastes

2 (*après le nom: renforcement*): **il est la loyauté même** he is loyalty itself; **ce sont ses paroles/celles-là même** they are his very words/the very ones

▷ *pron*: **le (la) même** the same one

▷ *adv* **1** (*renforcement*): **il n'a même pas pleuré** he didn't even cry; **même lui l'a dit** even HE said it; **ici même** at this very place; **même si** even if

2: **à même**: **à même la bouteille** straight from the bottle; **à même la peau** next to the skin; **être à même de faire** to be in a position to do, be able to do; **mettre qn à même de faire** to enable sb to do

3: **de même** likewise; **faire de même** to do likewise *ou* the same; **lui de même** so does (*ou* did *ou* is) he; **de même que** just as; **il en va de même pour** the same goes for

mémento [memɛ̄to] *nm* (*agenda*) appointments diary; (*ouvrage*) summary

mémo [memo] (*fam*) *nm* memo

mémoire [memwaʀ] *nf* memory ▷ *nm* (*Admin, Jur*) memorandum; (*Scol*) dissertation, paper; **avoir la ~ des visages/chiffres** to have a (good) memory for faces/figures; **n'avoir aucune ~** to have a terrible memory; **avoir de la ~** to have a good memory; **à la ~ de** to the *ou* in memory of; **pour ~** *adv* for the record; **de ~** *adv* from memory; **de ~ d'homme** in living memory; **mettre en ~** (*Inform*) to store; **~ morte** ROM; **~ vive** RAM

mémoires [memwaʀ] *nmpl* memoirs

mémorable [memɔʀabl(ə)] *adj* memorable

mémorandum [memɔʀɑ̃dɔm] *nm* memorandum; (*carnet*) notebook

mémorial, -aux [memɔʀjal, -o] *nm* memorial

mémoriser [memɔʀize] *vt* to memorize; (*Inform*) to store

menaçant, e [mənasɑ̃, -ɑ̃t] *adj* threatening, menacing

menace [mənas] *nf* threat; **~ en l'air** empty threat

menacer [mənase] *vt* to threaten; **~ qn de qch/de faire qch** to threaten sb with sth/to do sth

ménage [menaʒ] *nm* (*travail*) housekeeping, housework; (*couple*) (married) couple; (*famille, Admin*) household; **faire le ~** to do the housework; **faire des ~s** to work as a cleaner (*in private homes*); **monter son ~** to set up house; **se mettre en ~ (avec)** to set up house (with); **heureux en ~** happily married; **faire bon ~ avec** to get on well with; **~ de poupée** doll's kitchen set; **~ à trois** love triangle

ménagement [menaʒmɑ̃] *nm* care and attention; **ménagements** *nmpl* (*égards*) consideration *sg*, attention *sg*

ménager¹ [menaʒe] *vt* (*traiter avec mesure*) to handle with tact; to treat considerately; (*utiliser*) to use with care; (: *avec économie*) to use sparingly; (*prendre soin de*) to take (great) care of,

look after; (*organiser*) to arrange; (*installer*) to put in; to make; **se ménager** to look after o.s.; **~ qch à qn** (*réserver*) to have sth in store for sb

ménager², -ère [menaʒe, -ɛʀ] *adj* household *cpd*, domestic ▷ *nf* (*femme*) housewife; (*couverts*) canteen (of cutlery)

ménagerie [menaʒʀi] *nf* menagerie

mendiant, e [mɑ̃djɑ̃, -ɑ̃t] *nm/f* beggar

mendicité [mɑ̃disite] *nf* begging

mendier [mɑ̃dje] *vi* to beg ▷ *vt* to beg (for); (*fig: éloges, compliments*) to fish for

menées [məne] *nfpl* intrigues, manœuvres (*Brit*), maneuvers (*US*); (*Comm*) activities

mener [məne] *vt* to lead; (*enquête*) to conduct; (*affaires*) to manage, conduct, run ▷ *vi*: **~ (à la marque)** to lead, be in the lead; **~ à/dans** (*emmener*) to take to/into; **~ qch à bonne fin** *ou* **à terme** *ou* **à bien** to see sth through (to a successful conclusion), complete sth successfully

meneur, -euse [mənœʀ, -øz] *nm/f* leader; (*péj: agitateur*) ringleader; **~ d'hommes** born leader; **~ de jeu** host, quizmaster (*Brit*)

menhir [meniʀ] *nm* standing stone

méningite [menɛ̄ʒit] *nf* meningitis *no pl*

ménisque [menisk] *nm* (*Anat*) meniscus

ménopause [menɔpoz] *nf* menopause

menotte [mənɔt] *nf* (*langage enfantin*) handie; **menottes** *nfpl* handcuffs; **passer les ~s à** to handcuff

mens [mɑ̃] *vb voir* **mentir**

mensonge [mɑ̃sɔ̄ʒ] *nm*: **le ~** lying *no pl*; **un ~** a lie

mensonger, -ère [mɑ̃sɔ̄ʒe, -ɛʀ] *adj* false

menstruation [mɑ̃stʀyasjɔ̄] *nf* menstruation

menstruel, le [mɑ̃stʀyɛl] *adj* menstrual

mensualiser [mɑ̃syalize] *vt* to pay monthly

mensualité [mɑ̃syalite] *nf* (*somme payée*) monthly payment; (*somme perçue*) monthly salary

mensuel, le [mɑ̃syɛl] *adj* monthly ▷ *nm/f* (*employé*) employee paid monthly ▷ *nm* (*Presse*) monthly

mensuellement [mɑ̃syɛlmɑ̃] *adv* monthly

mensurations [mɑ̃syʀasjɔ̄] *nfpl* measurements

mentais *etc* [mɑ̃tɛ] *vb voir* **mentir**

mental, e, -aux [mɑ̃tal, -o] *adj* mental

mentalement [mɑ̃talmɑ̃] *adv* in one's head, mentally

mentalité [mɑ̃talite] *nf* mentality

menteur, -euse [mɑ̃tœʀ, -øz] *nm/f* liar

menthe [mɑ̃t] *nf* mint; **~ (à l'eau)** peppermint cordial

mentholé, e [mɑ̃tɔle] *adj* menthol *cpd*, mentholated

mention [mɑ̃sjɔ̄] *nf* (*note*) note, comment; (*Scol*): **~ (très) bien/passable** (very) good/satisfactory pass; **faire ~ de** to mention; **"rayer la ~ inutile"** "delete as appropriate"

mentionner [mɑ̃sjɔne] *vt* to mention

mentir [mɑ̃tiʀ] *vi* to lie

menton [mɑ̃tɔ̄] *nm* chin

mentonnière [mãtɔnjɛʀ] *nf* chin strap

menu, e [məny] *adj* (*mince*) thin; (*petit*) tiny; (*frais, difficulté*) minor ▷ *adv* (*couper, hacher*) very fine ▷ *nm* menu; **par le ~** (*raconter*) in minute detail; **~ touristique** popular *ou* tourist menu; **~e monnaie** small change

menuet [mənɥɛ] *nm* minuet

menuiserie [mənɥizʀi] *nf* (*travail*) joinery, carpentry; (*d'amateur*) woodwork; (*local*) joiner's workshop; (*ouvrages*) woodwork *no pl*

menuisier [mənɥizje] *nm* joiner, carpenter

méprendre [mepʀãdʀ(ə)]: **se méprendre** *vi*: **se méprendre sur** to be mistaken about

mépris, e [mepʀi, -iz] *pp de* **méprendre** ▷ *nm* (*dédain*) contempt, scorn; (*indifférence*): **le ~ de** contempt *ou* disregard for; **au ~ de** regardless of, in defiance of

méprisable [mepʀizabl(ə)] *adj* contemptible, despicable

méprisant, e [mepʀizã, -ãt] *adj* contemptuous, scornful

méprise [mepʀiz] *nf* mistake, error; (*malentendu*) misunderstanding

mépriser [mepʀize] *vt* to scorn, despise; (*gloire, danger*) to scorn, spurn

mer [mɛʀ] *nf* sea; (*marée*) tide; **~ fermée** inland sea; **en ~** at sea; **prendre la ~** to put out to sea; **en haute** *ou* **pleine ~** off shore, on the open sea; **la ~ Adriatique** the Adriatic (Sea); **la ~ des Antilles** *ou* **des Caraïbes** the Caribbean (Sea); **la ~ Baltique** the Baltic (Sea); **la ~ Caspienne** the Caspian Sea; **la ~ de Corail** the Coral Sea; **la ~ Égée** the Aegean (Sea); **la ~ Ionienne** the Ionian Sea; **la ~ Morte** the Dead Sea; **la ~ Noire** the Black Sea; **la ~ du Nord** the North Sea; **la ~ Rouge** the Red Sea; **la ~ des Sargasses** the Sargasso Sea; **les ~s du Sud** the South Seas; **la ~ Tyrrhénienne** the Tyrrhenian Sea

mercantile [mɛʀkãtil] *adj* (*péj*) mercenary

mercantilisme [mɛʀkãtilism(ə)] *nm* (*esprit mercantile*) mercenary attitude

mercenaire [mɛʀsənɛʀ] *nm* mercenary

mercerie [mɛʀsəʀi] *nf* (*Couture*) haberdashery (*Brit*), notions *pl* (*US*); (*boutique*) haberdasher's (shop) (*Brit*), notions store (*US*)

merci [mɛʀsi] *excl* thank you ▷ *nf*: **à la ~ de qn/qch** at sb's mercy/the mercy of sth; **~ beaucoup** thank you very much; **~ de** *ou* **pour** thank you for; **sans ~** *adj* merciless ▷ *adv* mercilessly

mercier, -ière [mɛʀsje, -jɛʀ] *nm/f* haberdasher

mercredi [mɛʀkʀədi] *nm* Wednesday; **~ des Cendres** Ash Wednesday; *voir aussi* **lundi**

mercure [mɛʀkyʀ] *nm* mercury

merde [mɛʀd(ə)] (*fam!*) *nf* shit (!) ▷ *excl* (bloody) hell (!)

merdeux, -euse [mɛʀdø, -øz] *nm/f* (*fam!*) little bugger (*Brit*) (!), little devil

mère [mɛʀ] *nf* mother ▷ *adj inv* mother *cpd*; **~ célibataire** single parent, unmarried mother

merguez [mɛʀgɛz] *nf* spicy North African sausage

méridien [meʀidjɛ̃] *nm* meridian

méridional, e, -aux [meʀidjɔnal, -o] *adj*

southern; (*du midi de la France*) Southern (French) ▷ *nm/f* Southerner

meringue [məʀɛ̃g] *nf* meringue

mérinos [meʀinos] *nm* merino

merisier [məʀizje] *nm* wild cherry (tree)

méritant, e [meʀitã, -ãt] *adj* deserving

mérite [meʀit] *nm* merit; **le ~ (de ceci) lui revient** the credit (for this) is his

mériter [meʀite] *vt* to deserve; **~ de réussir** to deserve to succeed; **il mérite qu'on fasse ...** he deserves people to do ...

méritocratie [meʀitɔkʀasi] *nf* meritocracy

méritoire [meʀitwaʀ] *adj* praiseworthy, commendable

merlan [mɛʀlã] *nm* whiting

merle [mɛʀl(ə)] *nm* blackbird

mérou [meʀu] *nm* grouper (*fish*)

merveille [mɛʀvɛj] *nf* marvel, wonder; **faire ~** *ou* **des ~s** to work wonders; **à ~** perfectly, wonderfully

merveilleux, -euse [mɛʀvɛjø, -øz] *adj* marvellous, wonderful

mes [me] *adj poss voir* **mon**

mésalliance [mezaljãs] *nf* misalliance, mismatch

mésallier [mezalje]: **se mésallier** *vi* to marry beneath (*ou* above) o.s.

mésange [mezãʒ] *nf* tit(mouse); **~ bleue** bluetit

mésaventure [mezavãtyʀ] *nf* misadventure, misfortune

Mesdames [medam] *nfpl voir* **Madame**

Mesdemoiselles [medmwazɛl] *nfpl voir* **Mademoiselle**

mésentente [mezãtãt] *nf* dissension, disagreement

mésestimer [mezɛstime] *vt* to underestimate, underrate

Mésopotamie [mezɔpɔtami] *nf*: **la ~** Mesopotamia

mesquin, e [mɛskɛ̃, -in] *adj* mean, petty

mesquinerie [mɛskinʀi] *nf* meanness *no pl*, pettiness *no pl*

mess [mɛs] *nm* mess

message [mesaʒ] *nm* message; **~ d'erreur** (*Inform*) error message; **~ électronique** (*Inform*) email; **~ publicitaire** ad, advertisement; **~ téléphoné** telegram dictated by telephone

messager, -ère [mesaʒe, -ɛʀ] *nm/f* messenger

messagerie [mesaʒʀi] *nf*: **~ électronique** electronic mail, email; **~ instantanée** instant messaging, IM; **~ rose** *lonely hearts and contact service on videotext*; **~s aériennes/maritimes** air freight/shipping service *sg*; **~s de presse** press distribution service; **~ vocale** voice mail

messe [mɛs] *nf* mass; **aller à la ~** to go to mass; **~ de minuit** midnight mass; **faire des ~s basses** (*fig, péj*) to mutter

messie [mesi] *nm*: **le M~** the Messiah

Messieurs [mesjø] *nmpl voir* **Monsieur**

mesure [məzyʀ] *nf* (*évaluation, dimension*) measurement; (*étalon, récipient, contenu*) measure; (*Mus: cadence*) time, tempo; (: *division*) bar; (*retenue*) moderation; (*disposition*) measure, step; **unité/système de ~** unit/system of measurement; **sur ~** (*costume*) made-to-measure; (*fig*) personally adapted; **à la ~ de** (*fig*: *personne*) worthy of; (*chambre etc*) on the same scale as; **dans la ~ où** insofar as, inasmuch as; **dans une certaine ~** to some *ou* a certain extent; **à ~ que** as; **en ~** (*Mus*) in time *ou* tempo; **être en ~ de** to be in a position to; **dépasser la ~** (*fig*) to overstep the mark

mesuré, e [məzyʀe] *adj* (*ton, effort*) measured; (*personne*) restrained

mesurer [məzyʀe] *vt* to measure; (*juger*) to weigh up, assess; (*limiter*) to limit, ration; (*modérer*) to moderate; (*proportionner*): **~ qch à** to match sth to, gear sth to; **se ~ avec** to have a confrontation with; to tackle; **il mesure 1 m 80** he's 1 m 80 tall

met [mɛ] *vb voir* **mettre**

métabolisme [metabɔlism(ə)] *nm* metabolism

métairie [meteʀi] *nf* smallholding

métal, -aux [metal, -o] *nm* metal

métalangage [metalɑ̃gaʒ] *nm* metalanguage

métallique [metalik] *adj* metallic

métallisé, e [metalize] *adj* metallic

métallurgie [metalyʀʒi] *nf* metallurgy

métallurgique [metalyʀʒik] *adj* steel *cpd*, metal *cpd*

métallurgiste [metalyʀʒist(ə)] *nm/f* (*ouvrier*) steel *ou* metal worker; (*industriel*) metallurgist

métamorphose [metamɔʀfoz] *nf* metamorphosis

métamorphoser [metamɔʀfoze] *vt* to transform

métaphore [metafɔʀ] *nf* metaphor

métaphorique [metafɔʀik] *adj* metaphorical, figurative

métaphoriquement [metafɔʀikmɑ̃] *adv* metaphorically

métaphysique [metafizik] *nf* metaphysics *sg* ▷ *adj* metaphysical

métapsychique [metapsiʃik] *adj* psychic, parapsychological

métayer, -ère [meteje, metɛjɛʀ] *nm/f* (tenant) farmer

météo [meteo] *nf* (*bulletin*) (weather) forecast; (*service*) ≈ Met Office (*Brit*), ≈ National Weather Service (*US*)

météore [meteɔʀ] *nm* meteor

météorite [meteɔʀit] *nm ou f* meteorite

météorologie [meteɔʀɔlɔʒi] *nf* (*étude*) meteorology; (*service*) ≈ Meteorological Office (*Brit*), ≈ National Weather Service (*US*)

météorologique [meteɔʀɔlɔʒik] *adj* meteorological, weather *cpd*

météorologue [meteɔʀɔlɔg], **météorologiste** [meteɔʀɔlɔʒist(ə)] *nm/f* meteorologist, weather forecaster

métèque [metɛk] *nm* (*péj*) wop (!)

méthane [metan] *nm* methane

méthanier [metanje] *nm* (*bateau*) (liquefied) gas carrier *ou* tanker

méthode [metɔd] *nf* method; (*livre, ouvrage*) manual, tutor

méthodique [metɔdik] *adj* methodical

méthodiquement [metɔdikmɑ̃] *adv* methodically

méthodiste [metɔdist(ə)] *adj, nm/f* (*Rel*) Methodist

méthylène [metilɛn] *nm*: **bleu de ~** *nm* methylene blue

méticuleux, -euse [metikylø, -øz] *adj* meticulous

métier [metje] *nm* (*profession: gén*) job; (: *manuel*) trade; (: *artisanal*) craft; (*technique, expérience*) (acquired) skill *ou* technique; (*aussi*: **métier à tisser**) (weaving) loom; **être du ~** to be in the trade *ou* profession

métis, se [metis] *adj, nm/f* half-caste, half-breed

métisser [metise] *vt* to cross(breed)

métrage [metʀaʒ] *nm* (*de tissu*) length; (*Ciné*) footage, length; **long/moyen/court ~** feature *ou* full-length/medium-length/short film

mètre [mɛtʀ(ə)] *nm* metre (*Brit*), meter (*US*); (*règle*) (metre *ou* meter) rule; (*ruban*) tape measure; **~ carré/cube** square/cubic metre *ou* meter

métrer [metʀe] *vt* (*Tech*) to measure (in metres *ou* meters); (*Constr*) to survey

métreur, -euse [metʀœʀ, -øz] *nm/f*: **~ (vérificateur), métreuse (vérificatrice)** (quantity) surveyor

métrique [metʀik] *adj* metric ▷ *nf* metrics *sg*

métro [metʀo] *nm* underground (*Brit*), subway (*US*)

métronome [metʀɔnɔm] *nm* metronome

métropole [metʀɔpɔl] *nf* (*capitale*) metropolis; (*pays*) home country

métropolitain, e [metʀɔpɔlitɛ̃, -ɛn] *adj* metropolitan

mets [mɛ] *nm* dish ▷ *vb voir* **mettre**

mettable [metabl(ə)] *adj* fit to be worn, decent

metteur [metœʀ] *nm*: **~ en scène** (*Théât*) producer; (*Ciné*) director; **~ en ondes** (*Radio*) producer

 MOT-CLÉ

mettre [metʀ(ə)] *vt* **1** (*placer*) to put; **mettre en bouteille/en sac** to bottle/put in bags *ou* sacks; **mettre qch à la poste** to post sth (*Brit*), mail sth (*US*); **mettre en examen (pour)** to charge (with) (*Brit*), indict (for) (*US*); **mettre une note gaie/amusante** to inject a cheerful/an amusing note; **mettre qn debout/assis** to help sb up *ou* to their feet/help sb to sit down

2 (*vêtements: revêtir*) to put on; (: *porter*) to wear; **mets ton gilet** put your cardigan on; **je ne mets plus mon manteau** I no longer wear my coat

3 (*faire fonctionner: chauffage, électricité*) to put on; (: *réveil, minuteur*) to set; (*installer: gaz, eau*) to put in, lay on; **mettre en marche** to start up

4 (*consacrer*): **mettre du temps/deux heures à**

faire qch to take time/two hours to do sth; **y mettre du sien** to pull one's weight

5 (*noter, écrire*) to say, put (down); **qu'est-ce qu'il a mis sur la carte?** what did he say *ou* write on the card?; **mettez au pluriel ...** put ... into the plural

6 (*supposer*): **mettons que ...** let's suppose *ou* say that ...

7 (*faire + vb*): **faire mettre le gaz/l'électricité** to have gas/electricity put in *ou* installed
se mettre *vi* **1** (*se placer*): **vous pouvez vous mettre là** you can sit (*ou* stand) there; **où ça se met?** where does it go?; **se mettre au lit** to get into bed; **se mettre au piano** to sit down at the piano; **se mettre à l'eau** to get into the water; **se mettre de l'encre sur les doigts** to get ink on one's fingers

2 (*s'habiller*): **se mettre en maillot de bain** to get into *ou* put on a swimsuit; **n'avoir rien à se mettre** to have nothing to wear

3 (*dans rapports*): **se mettre bien/mal avec qn** to get on the right/wrong side of sb; **se mettre qn à dos** to get on sb's bad side; **se mettre avec qn** (*prendre parti*) to side with sb; (*faire équipe*) to team up with sb; (*en ménage*) to move in with sb

4: **se mettre à** to begin, start; **se mettre à faire** to begin *ou* start doing *ou* to do; **se mettre au piano** to start learning the piano; **se mettre au régime** to go on a diet; **se mettre au travail/à l'étude** to get down to work/one's studies; **il est temps de s'y mettre** it's time we got down to it *ou* got on with it

meublant, e [mœblã, -ãt] *adj* (*tissus etc*) effective (in the room)

meuble [mœbl(ə)] *nm* (*objet*) piece of furniture; (*ameublement*) furniture *no pl* ▷ *adj* (*terre*) loose, friable; (*Jur*): **biens ~s** movables

meublé [mœble] *nm* (*pièce*) furnished room; (*appartement*) furnished flat (*Brit*) *ou* apartment (*US*)

meubler [mœble] *vt* to furnish; (*fig*): **~ qch (de)** to fill sth (with); **se meubler** to furnish one's house

meuf [mœf] *nf* (*fam*) woman

meugler [møgle] *vi* to low, moo

meule [møl] *nf* (*à broyer*) millstone; (*à aiguiser*) grindstone; (*à polir*) buff wheel; (*de foin, blé*) stack; (*de fromage*) round

meunerie [mønʀi] *nf* (*industrie*) flour trade; (*métier*) milling

meunier, -ière [mønje, -jɛʀ] *nm* miller ▷ *nf* miller's wife ▷ *adj f* (*Culin*) meunière

meurs *etc* [mœʀ] *vb voir* **mourir**

meurtre [mœʀtʀ(ə)] *nm* murder

meurtrier, -ière [mœʀtʀije, -jɛʀ] *adj* (*arme, épidémie, combat*) deadly; (*accident*) fatal; (*carrefour, route*) lethal; (*fureur, instincts*) murderous ▷ *nm/f* murderer(-ess) ▷ *nf* (*ouverture*) loophole

meurtrir [mœʀtʀiʀ] *vt* to bruise; (*fig*) to wound

meurtrissure [mœʀtʀisyʀ] *nf* bruise; (*fig*) scar

meus *etc* [mœ] *vb voir* **mouvoir**

Meuse [mœz] *nf*: **la ~** the Meuse

meute [møt] *nf* pack

meuve *etc* [mœv] *vb voir* **mouvoir**

mévente [mevãt] *nf* slump (in sales)

mexicain, e [mɛksikɛ̃, -ɛn] *adj* Mexican ▷ *nm/f*: **Mexicain, e** Mexican

Mexico [mɛksiko] *n* Mexico City

Mexique [mɛksik] *nm*: **le ~** Mexico

mezzanine [mɛdzanin] *nf* mezzanine (floor)

MF *sigle mpl* = **millions de francs** ▷ *sigle f* (*Radio*: = *modulation de fréquence*) FM

Mgr *abr* = **Monseigneur**

mi [mi] *nm* (*Mus*) E; (*en chantant la gamme*) mi

mi... [mi] *préfixe* half(-), mid-; **à la mi-janvier** in mid-January; **mi-bureau, mi-chambre** half office, half bedroom; **à mi-jambes/-corps** (up *ou* down) to the knees/waist; **à mi-hauteur/-pente** halfway up (*ou* down)/up (*ou* down) the hill

miaou [mjau] *nm* miaow

miaulement [mjolmã] *nm* (*cri*) miaow; (*continu*) miaowing *no pl*

miauler [mjole] *vi* to miaow

mi-bas [miba] *nm inv* knee-length sock

mica [mika] *nm* mica

mi-carême [mikaʀɛm] *nf*: **la ~** the third Thursday in Lent

miche [miʃ] *nf* round *ou* cob loaf

mi-chemin [miʃmɛ̃]: **à ~** *adv* halfway, midway

mi-clos, e [miklo, -kloz] *adj* half-closed

micmac [mikmak] *nm* (*péj*) carry-on

mi-côte [mikot]: **à ~** *adv* halfway up (*ou* down) the hill

mi-course [mikuʀs]: **à ~** *adv* halfway through the race

micro [mikʀo] *nm* mike, microphone; **~ cravate** lapel mike

microbe [mikʀob] *nm* germ, microbe

microbiologie [mikʀobjɔlɔʒi] *nf* microbiology

microchirurgie [mikʀoʃiʀyʀʒi] *nf* microsurgery

microclimat [mikʀoklima] *nm* microclimate

microcosme [mikʀokɔsm(ə)] *nm* microcosm

micro-édition [mikʀoedisjɔ̃] *nf* desk-top publishing

micro-électronique [mikʀoelɛktʀɔnik] *nf* microelectronics *sg*

microfiche [mikʀofiʃ] *nf* microfiche

microfilm [mikʀofilm] *nm* microfilm

micro-onde [mikʀoɔ̃d] *nf*: **four à ~s** microwave oven

micro-ordinateur [mikʀoɔʀdinatœʀ] *nm* microcomputer

micro-organisme [mikʀoɔʀganism(ə)] *nm* micro-organism

microphone [mikʀofɔn] *nm* microphone

microplaquette [mikʀoplakɛt] *nf* microchip

microprocesseur [mikʀopʀosɛsœʀ] *nm* microprocessor

microscope [mikʀoskɔp] *nm* microscope; **au ~** under *ou* through the microscope

microscopique [mikʀoskɔpik] *adj* microscopic

microsillon [mikʀosijɔ̃] *nm* long-playing record

MIDEM [midɛm] *sigle m* (= *Marché international du disque et de l'édition musicale*) music industry trade fair

midi [midi] *nm* (*milieu du jour*) midday, noon; (*moment du déjeuner*) lunchtime; (*sud*) south; (: *de la France*): **le M~** the South (of France), the Midi; **à ~** at 12 (o'clock) *ou* midday *ou* noon; **tous les ~s** every lunchtime; **le repas de ~** lunch; **en plein ~** (right) in the middle of the day; (*sud*) facing south

midinette [midinɛt] *nf* silly young townie

mie [mi] *nf* inside (of the loaf)

miel [mjɛl] *nm* honey; **être tout ~** (*fig*) to be all sweetness and light

mielleux, -euse [mjɛlø, -øz] *adj* (*péj*) sugary, honeyed

mien, ne [mjɛ̃, mjɛn] *adj, pron*: **le (la) ~(ne), les ~s** mine; **les ~s** (*ma famille*) my family

miette [mjɛt] *nf* (*de pain, gâteau*) crumb; (*fig: de la conversation etc*) scrap; **en ~s** (*fig*) in pieces *ou* bits

 MOT-CLÉ

mieux [mjø] *adv* **1** (*d'une meilleure façon*): **mieux (que)** better (than); **elle travaille/mange mieux** she works/eats better; **aimer mieux** to prefer; **j'attendais mieux de vous** I expected better of you; **elle va mieux** she is better; **de mieux en mieux** better and better
2 (*de la meilleure façon*) best; **ce que je sais le mieux** what I know best; **les livres les mieux faits** the best made books
3 (*intensif*): **vous feriez mieux de faire ...** you would be better to do ...; **crier à qui mieux mieux** to try to shout each other down
▷ *adj* **1** (*plus à l'aise, en meilleure forme*) better; **se sentir mieux** to feel better
2 (*plus satisfaisant*) better; **c'est mieux ainsi** it's better like this; **c'est le mieux des deux** it's the better of the two; **le/la mieux, les mieux** the best; **demandez-lui, c'est le mieux** ask him, it's the best thing
3 (*plus joli*) better-looking; (*plus gentil*) nicer; **il est mieux que son frère** (*plus beau*) he's better-looking than his brother; (*plus gentil*) he's nicer than his brother; **il est mieux sans moustache** he looks better without a moustache
4: **au mieux** at best; **au mieux avec** on the best of terms with; **pour le mieux** for the best; **qui mieux est** even better, better still
▷ *nm* **1** (*progrès*) improvement
2: **de mon/ton mieux** as best I/you can (*ou* could); **faire de son mieux** to do one's best; **du mieux qu'il peut** the best he can; **faute de mieux** for lack *ou* want of anything better, failing anything better

mieux-être [mjøzɛtr(ə)] *nm* greater well-being; (*financier*) improved standard of living

mièvre [mjɛvr(ə)] *adj* sickly sentimental

mignon, ne [miɲɔ̃, -ɔn] *adj* sweet, cute

migraine [migrɛn] *nf* headache; migraine

migrant, e [migrɑ̃, -ɑ̃t] *adj, nm/f* migrant

migrateur, -trice [migratœr, -tris] *adj* migratory

migration [migrasjɔ̃] *nf* migration

mijaurée [miʒɔre] *nf* pretentious (young) madam

mijoter [miʒɔte] *vt* to simmer; (*préparer avec soin*) to cook lovingly; (*affaire, projet*) to plot, cook up ▷ *vi* to simmer

mil [mil] *num* = **mille**

Milan [milɑ̃] *n* Milan

milanais, e [milanɛ, -ɛz] *adj* Milanese

mildiou [mildju] *nm* mildew

milice [milis] *nf* militia

milicien, ne [milisjɛ̃, -ɛn] *nm/f* militiaman(-woman)

milieu, x [miljø] *nm* (*centre*) middle; (*fig*) middle course *ou* way; (*aussi*: **juste milieu**) happy medium; (*Bio, Géo*) environment; (*entourage social*) milieu; (*familial*) background; circle; (*pègre*): **le ~** the underworld; **au ~ de** in the middle of; **au beau** *ou* **en plein ~ (de)** right in the middle (of); **~ de terrain** (*Football: joueur*) midfield player; (: *joueurs*) midfield

militaire [militɛr] *adj* military ▷ *nm* serviceman; **service ~** military service

militant, e [militɑ̃, -ɑ̃t] *adj, nm/f* militant

militantisme [militɑ̃tism(ə)] *nm* militancy

militariser [militarize] *vt* to militarize

militarisme [militarism(ə)] *nm* (*péj*) militarism

militer [milite] *vi* to be a militant; **~ pour/contre** to militate in favour of/against

milk-shake [milkʃɛk] *nm* milk shake

mille [mil] *num* a *ou* one thousand ▷ *nm* (*mesure*): **~ (marin)** nautical mile; **mettre dans le ~** to hit the bull's-eye; (*fig*) to be bang on (target)

millefeuille [milfœj] *nm* cream *ou* vanilla slice

millénaire [milenɛr] *nm* millennium ▷ *adj* thousand-year-old; (*fig*) ancient

mille-pattes [milpat] *nm inv* centipede

millésime [milezim] *nm* year

millésimé, e [milezime] *adj* vintage *cpd*

millet [mijɛ] *nm* millet

milliard [miljar] *nm* milliard, thousand million (*Brit*), billion (*US*)

milliardaire [miljardɛr] *nm/f* multimillionaire (*Brit*), billionaire (*US*)

millième [miljɛm] *num* thousandth

millier [milje] *nm* thousand; **un ~ (de)** a thousand or so, about a thousand; **par ~s** in (their) thousands, by the thousand

milligramme [miligram] *nm* milligramme (*Brit*), milligram (*US*)

millimétré, e [milimetre] *adj*: **papier ~** graph paper

millimètre [milimetr(ə)] *nm* millimetre (*Brit*), millimeter (*US*)

million [miljɔ̃] *nm* million; **deux ~s de** two million; **riche à ~s** worth millions

millionième [miljɔnjɛm] *num* millionth

millionnaire [miljɔnɛr] *nm/f* millionaire

mi-lourd [milur] *adj m, nm* light heavyweight

mime [mim] *nm/f* (*acteur*) mime(r); (*imitateur*) mimic ▷ *nm* (*art*) mime, miming

mimer [mime] *vt* to mime; (*singer*) to mimic, take off

mimétisme [mimetism(ə)] *nm* (*Bio*) mimicry

mimique [mimik] *nf* (*funny face*); (*signes*) gesticulations *pl*, sign language *no pl*

mimosa [mimoza] *nm* mimosa

mi-moyen [mimwajɛ̃] *adj m, nm* welterweight

MIN *sigle m* (= *Marché d'intérêt national*) *wholesale market for fruit, vegetables and agricultural produce*

min. *abr* (= *minimum*) min

minable [minabl(ə)] *adj* (*personne*) shabby (-looking); (*travail*) pathetic

minaret [minaʀɛ] *nm* minaret

minauder [minode] *vi* to mince, simper

minauderies [minodʀi] *nfpl* simpering *sg*

mince [mɛ̃s] *adj* thin; (*personne, taille*) slim; (*fig: profit, connaissances*) slight, small; (: *prétexte*) weak ▷ *excl*: ~ **(alors)!** darn it!

minceur [mɛ̃sœʀ] *nf* thinness slimness, slenderness

mincir [mɛ̃siʀ] *vi* to get slimmer *ou* thinner

mine [min] *nf* (*physionomie*) expression, look; (*extérieur*) exterior, appearance; (*de crayon*) lead; (*gisement, exploitation, explosif*) mine; **mines** *nfpl* (*péj*) simpering airs; **les M~s** (*Admin*) the national mining and geological service, the government vehicle testing department; **avoir bonne ~** (*personne*) to look well; (*ironique*) to look an utter idiot; **avoir mauvaise ~** to look unwell; **faire ~ de faire** to make a pretence of doing; **ne pas payer de ~** to be not much to look at; **~ de rien** *adv* with a casual air; although you wouldn't think so; **~ de charbon** coal mine; **~ à ciel ouvert** opencast (*Brit*) *ou* open-air (*US*) mine

miner [mine] *vt* (*saper*) to undermine, erode; (*Mil*) to mine

minerai [minʀɛ] *nm* ore

minéral, e, -aux [mineʀal, -o] *adj* mineral; (*Chimie*) inorganic ▷ *nm* mineral

minéralier [mineʀalje] *nm* (*bateau*) ore tanker

minéralisé, e [mineʀalize] *adj* mineralized

minéralogie [mineʀalɔʒi] *nf* mineralogy

minéralogique [mineʀalɔʒik] *adj* mineralogical; **plaque ~** number (*Brit*) *ou* license (*US*) plate; **numéro ~** registration (*Brit*) *ou* license (*US*) number

minet, te [minɛ, -ɛt] *nm/f* (*chat*) pussy-cat; (*péj*) young trendy

mineur, e [minœʀ] *adj* minor ▷ *nm/f* (*Jur*) minor ▷ *nm* (*travailleur*) miner; (*Mil*) sapper; **~ de fond** face worker

miniature [minjatyʀ] *adj, nf* miniature

miniaturisation [minjatyʀizɑsjɔ̃] *nf* miniaturization

miniaturiser [minjatyʀize] *vt* to miniaturize

minibus [minibys] *nm* minibus

mini-cassette [minikasɛt] *nf* cassette (recorder)

minichaîne [miniʃɛn] *nf* mini system

minier, -ière [minje, -jɛʀ] *adj* mining

mini-jupe [miniʒyp] *nf* mini-skirt

minimal, e, -aux [minimal, -o] *adj* minimum

minimaliste [minimalist(ə)] *adj* (*Art*) minimalist

minime [minim] *adj* minor, minimal ▷ *nm/f* (*Sport*) junior

minimiser [minimize] *vt* to minimize; (*fig*) to play down

minimum [minimɔm] *adj, nm* minimum; **au ~** at the very least; **~ vital** (*salaire*) living wage; (*niveau de vie*) subsistence level

mini-ordinateur [miniɔʀdinatœʀ] *nm* minicomputer

ministère [ministɛʀ] *nm* (*cabinet*) government; (*département*) ministry (*Brit*), department; (*Rel*) ministry; **~ public** (*Jur*) Prosecution, State Prosecutor

ministériel, le [ministeʀjɛl] *adj* government *cpd*; ministerial, departmental; (*partisan*) pro-government

ministrable [ministʀabl(ə)] *adj* (*Pol*): **il est ~** he's a potential minister

ministre [ministʀ(ə)] *nm* minister (*Brit*), secretary; (*Rel*) minister; **~ d'État** senior minister *ou* secretary

Minitel® [minitɛl] *nm* videotext terminal and service

minium [minjɔm] *nm* red lead paint

minois [minwa] *nm* little face

minorer [minɔʀe] *vt* to cut, reduce

minoritaire [minɔʀitɛʀ] *adj* minority *cpd*

minorité [minɔʀite] *nf* minority; **être en ~** to be in the *ou* a minority; **mettre en ~** (*Pol*) to defeat

Minorque [minɔʀk] *nf* Minorca

minorquin, e [minɔʀkɛ̃, -in] *adj* Minorcan

minoterie [minɔtʀi] *nf* flour-mill

minuit [minɥi] *nm* midnight

minuscule [minyskyl] *adj* minute, tiny ▷ *nf*: **(lettre) ~** small letter

minutage [minytaʒ] *nm* timing

minute [minyt] *nf* minute; (*Jur: original*) minute, draft ▷ *excl* just a minute!, hang on!; **à la ~** (*présent*) (just) this instant; (*passé*) there and then; **entrecôte** *ou* **steak ~** minute steak

minuter [minyte] *vt* to time

minuterie [minytʀi] *nf* time switch

minuteur [minytœʀ] *nm* timer

minutie [minysi] *nf* meticulousness; minute detail; **avec ~** meticulously; in minute detail

minutieusement [minysjøzmɑ̃] *adv* (*organiser, travailler*) meticulously; (*examiner*) minutely

minutieux, -euse [minysjø, -øz] *adj* (*personne*) meticulous; (*inspection*) minutely detailed; (*travail*) requiring painstaking attention to detail

mioche [mjɔʃ] *nm* (*fam*) nipper, brat

mirabelle [miʀabɛl] *nf* (*fruit*) (cherry) plum; (*eau-de-vie*) plum brandy

miracle [miʀakl(ə)] *nm* miracle

miraculé, e [miʀakyle] *adj* who has been miraculously cured (*ou* rescued)

miraculeux, -euse [miʀakylø, -øz] *adj*

m

miraculous

mirador [miʀadɔʀ] nm (Mil) watchtower

mirage [miʀaʒ] nm mirage

mire [miʀ] nf (d'un fusil) sight; (TV) test card; **point de ~** target; (fig) focal point; **ligne de ~** line of sight

mirent [miʀ] vb voir **mettre**

mirer [miʀe] vt (œufs) to candle; **se mirer** vi: **se ~ dans** (personne) to gaze at one's reflection in; (: chose) to be mirrored in

mirifique [miʀifik] adj wonderful

mirobolant, e [miʀɔbɔlɑ̃, -ɑ̃t] adj fantastic

miroir [miʀwaʀ] nm mirror

miroiter [miʀwate] vi to sparkle, shimmer; **faire ~ qch à qn** to paint sth in glowing colours for sb, dangle sth in front of sb's eyes

miroiterie [miʀwatʀi] nf (usine) mirror factory; (magasin) mirror dealer's (shop)

Mis abr = **marquis**

mis, e [mi, miz] pp de **mettre** ▷ adj (couvert, table) set, laid; (personne): **bien ~** well dressed ▷ nf (argent: au jeu) stake; (tenue) clothing; attire; **être de ~e** to be acceptable ou in season; **~e en bouteilles** bottling; **~e en examen** charging, indictment; **~e à feu** blast-off; **~e de fonds** capital outlay; **~e à jour** (Inform) update; **~e à mort** kill; **~e à pied** (d'un employé) suspension; lay-off; **~e sur pied** (d'une affaire, entreprise) setting up; **~e en plis** set; **~e au point** (Photo) focusing; (fig) clarification; **~e à prix** reserve (Brit) ou upset price; **~e en scène** production

misaine [mizɛn] nf: **mât de ~** foremast

misanthrope [mizɑ̃tʀɔp] nm/f misanthropist

Mise abr = **marquise**

mise [miz] adj f, nf voir **mis**

miser [mize] vt (enjeu) to stake, bet; **~ sur** vt (cheval, numéro) to bet on; (fig) to bank ou count on

misérable [mizeʀabl(ə)] adj (lamentable, malheureux) pitiful, wretched; (pauvre) poverty-stricken; (insignifiant, mesquin) miserable ▷ nm/f wretch; (miséreux) poor wretch

misère [mizɛʀ] nf (pauvreté) (extreme) poverty, destitution; **misères** nfpl (malheurs) woes, miseries; (ennuis) little troubles; **être dans la ~** to be destitute ou poverty-stricken; **salaire de ~** starvation wage; **faire des ~s à qn** to torment sb; **~ noire** utter destitution, abject poverty

miséreux, -euse [mizeʀø, -øz] adj poverty-stricken ▷ nm/f down-and-out

miséricorde [mizeʀikɔʀd(ə)] nf mercy, forgiveness

miséricordieux, -euse [mizeʀikɔʀdjø, -øz] adj merciful, forgiving

misogyne [mizɔʒin] adj misogynous ▷ nm/f misogynist

missel [misɛl] nm missal

missile [misil] nm missile

mission [misjɔ̃] nf mission; **partir en ~** (Admin, Pol) to go on an assignment

missionnaire [misjɔnɛʀ] nm/f missionary

missive [misiv] nf missive

mistral [mistʀal] nm mistral (wind)

mit [mi] vb voir **mettre**

mitaine [mitɛn] nf mitt(en)

mite [mit] nf clothes moth

mité, e [mite] adj moth-eaten

mi-temps [mitɑ̃] nf inv (Sport: période) half; (: pause) half-time; **à ~** adj, adv part-time

miteux, -euse [mitø, -øz] adj seedy, shabby

mitigé, e [mitiʒe] adj (conviction, ardeur) lukewarm; (sentiments) mixed

mitonner [mitɔne] vt (préparer) to cook with loving care; (fig) to cook up quietly

mitoyen, ne [mitwajɛ̃, -ɛn] adj common, party cpd; **maisons ~nes** semi-detached houses; (plus de deux) terraced (Brit) ou row (US) houses

mitraille [mitʀaj] nf (balles de fonte) grapeshot; (décharge d'obus) shellfire

mitrailler [mitʀaje] vt to machine-gun; (fig: photographier) to snap away at; **~ qn de** to pelt ou bombard sb with

mitraillette [mitʀajɛt] nf submachine gun

mitrailleur [mitʀajœʀ] nm machine gunner ▷ adj m: **fusil ~** machine gun

mitrailleuse [mitʀajøz] nf machine gun

mitre [mitʀ(ə)] nf mitre

mitron [mitʀɔ̃] nm baker's boy

mi-voix [mivwa]: **à ~** adv in a low ou hushed voice

mixage [miksaʒ] nm (Ciné) (sound) mixing

mixer, mixeur [miksœʀ] nm (Culin) (food) mixer

mixité [miksite] nf (Scol) coeducation

mixte [mikst(ə)] adj (gén) mixed; (Scol) mixed, coeducational; **à usage ~** dual-purpose; **cuisinière ~** combined gas and electric cooker; **équipe ~** combined team

mixture [mikstyʀ] nf mixture; (fig) concoction

MJC sigle f (= maison des jeunes et de la culture) community arts centre and youth club

ml abr (= millilitre) ml

MLF sigle m (= Mouvement de libération de la femme) Women's Movement

Mlle (pl **-s**) abr = **Mademoiselle**

MM abr = **Messieurs**; voir **Monsieur**

Mme (pl **-s**) abr = **Madame**

MMS sigle m (= Multimedia messaging service) MMS

mn. abr (= minute) min

mnémotechnique [mnemɔtɛknik] adj mnemonic

MNS sigle m (= maître nageur sauveteur) ≈ lifeguard

MO sigle f (= main-d'œuvre) labour costs (on invoices)

Mo abr = **méga-octet**; **métro**

mobile [mɔbil] adj mobile; (amovible) loose, removable; (pièce de machine) moving; (élément de meuble etc) movable ▷ nm (motif) motive; (œuvre d'art) mobile; (Physique) moving object ou body; **(téléphone) ~** mobile (phone) (Brit), cell (phone) (US)

mobilier, -ière [mɔbilje, -jɛʀ] adj (Jur) personal ▷ nm (meubles) furniture; **valeurs mobilières** transferable securities; **vente mobilière** sale of personal property ou chattels

mobilisation [mɔbilizasjɔ̃] *nf* mobilization
mobiliser [mɔbilize] *vt* (*Mil*, *gén*) to mobilize
mobilité [mɔbilite] *nf* mobility
mobylette® [mɔbilɛt] *nf* moped
mocassin [mɔkasɛ̃] *nm* moccasin
moche [mɔʃ] *adj* (*fam: laid*) ugly; (: *mauvais*, *méprisable*) rotten
modalité [mɔdalite] *nf* form, mode; **modalités** *nfpl* (*d'un accord etc*) clauses, terms; **~s de paiement** methods of payment
mode [mɔd] *nf* fashion; (*commerce*) fashion trade *ou* industry ▷ *nm* (*manière*) form, mode; method; (*Ling*) mood; (*Inform*, *Mus*) mode; **travailler dans la ~** to be in the fashion business; **à la ~** fashionable, in fashion; **~ dialogué** (*Inform*) interactive *ou* conversational mode; **~ d'emploi** directions *pl* (for use); **~ de vie** way of life
modelage [mɔdlaʒ] *nm* modelling
modelé [mɔdle] *nm* (*Géo*) relief; (*du corps etc*) contours *pl*
modèle [mɔdɛl] *adj* model ▷ *nm* model; (*qui pose: de peintre*) sitter; (*type*) type; (*gabarit*, *patron*) pattern; **~ courant** *ou* **de série** (*Comm*) production model; **~ déposé** registered design; **~ réduit** small-scale model
modeler [mɔdle] *vt* (*Art*) to model, mould; (*vêtement*, *érosion*) to mould, shape; **~ qch sur/ d'après** to model sth on
modélisation [mɔdelizasjɔ̃] *nf* (*Math*) modelling
modéliste [mɔdelist(ə)] *nm/f* (*Couture*) designer; (*de modèles réduits*) model maker
modem [mɔdɛm] *nm* (*Inform*) modem
modérateur, -trice [mɔdeRatœR, -tRis] *adj* moderating ▷ *nm/f* moderator
modération [mɔdeRasjɔ̃] *nf* moderation; **~ de peine** reduction of sentence
modéré, e [mɔdeRe] *adj*, *nm/f* moderate
modérément [mɔdeRemɑ̃] *adv* moderately, in moderation
modérer [mɔdeRe] *vt* to moderate; **se modérer** *vi* to restrain o.s
moderne [mɔdɛRn(ə)] *adj* modern ▷ *nm* (*Art*) modern style; (*ameublement*) modern furniture
modernisation [mɔdɛRnizasjɔ̃] *nf* modernization
moderniser [mɔdɛRnize] *vt* to modernize
modernisme [mɔdɛRnism(ə)] *nm* modernism
modernité [mɔdɛRnite] *nf* modernity
modeste [mɔdɛst(ə)] *adj* modest; (*origine*) humble, lowly
modestement [mɔdɛstəmɑ̃] *adv* modestly
modestie [mɔdɛsti] *nf* modesty; **fausse ~** false modesty
modicité [mɔdisite] *nf*: **la ~ des prix** *etc* the low prices *etc*
modificatif, -ive [mɔdifikatif, -iv] *adj* modifying
modification [mɔdifikasjɔ̃] *nf* modification
modifier [mɔdifje] *vt* to modify, alter; (*Ling*) to modify; **se modifier** *vi* to alter

modique [mɔdik] *adj* (*salaire*, *somme*) modest
modiste [mɔdist(ə)] *nf* milliner
modulaire [mɔdylɛR] *adj* modular
modulation [mɔdylasjɔ̃] *nf* modulation; **~ de fréquence (FM** *ou* **MF**) frequency modulation (FM)
module [mɔdyl] *nm* module
moduler [mɔdyle] *vt* to modulate; (*air*) to warble
moelle [mwal] *nf* marrow; (*fig*) pith, core; **~ épinière** spinal chord
moelleux, -euse [mwalø, -øz] *adj* soft; (*au goût*, *à l'ouïe*) mellow; (*gracieux*, *souple*) smooth
moellon [mwalɔ̃] *nm* rubble stone
mœurs [mœR] *nfpl* (*conduite*) morals; (*manières*) manners; (*pratiques sociales*) habits; (*mode de vie*) life style *sg*; (*d'une espèce animale*) behaviour *sg* (*Brit*), behavior *sg* (*US*); **femme de mauvaises ~** loose woman; **passer dans les ~** to become the custom; **contraire aux bonnes ~** contrary to proprieties
mohair [mɔɛR] *nm* mohair
moi [mwa] *pron* me; (*emphatique*): **~, je ...** for my part, I ..., I myself ... ▷ *nm inv* (*Psych*) ego, self; **à ~!** (*à l'aide*) help (me)!
moignon [mwaɲɔ̃] *nm* stump
moi-même [mwamɛm] *pron* myself; (*emphatique*) I myself
moindre [mwɛ̃dR(ə)] *adj* lesser; lower; **le (la) ~**, **les ~s** the least; the slightest; **le (la) ~ de** least of; **c'est la ~ des choses** it's nothing at all
moindrement [mwɛ̃dRəmɑ̃] *adv*: **pas le ~** not in the least
moine [mwan] *nm* monk, friar
moineau, x [mwano] *nm* sparrow

 MOT-CLÉ

moins [mwɛ̃] *adv* **1** (*comparatif*): **moins (que)** less (than); **moins grand que** less tall than, not as tall as; **il a trois ans de moins que moi** he's three years younger than me; **il est moins intelligent que moi** he's not as clever as me, he's less clever than me; **moins je travaille, mieux je me porte** the less I work, the better I feel
2 (*superlatif*): **le moins** (the) least; **c'est ce que j'aime le moins** it's what I like (the) least; **le(la) moins doué(e)** the least gifted; **au moins, du moins** at least; **pour le moins** at the very least
3: **moins de** (*quantité*) less (than); (*nombre*) fewer (than); **moins de sable/d'eau** less sand/water; **moins de livres/gens** fewer books/people; **moins de deux ans** less than two years; **moins de midi** not yet midday
4: **de moins, en moins: 100 euros/3 jours de moins** 100 euros/3 days less; **trois livres en moins** three books fewer; three books too few; **de l'argent en moins** less money; **le soleil en moins** but for the sun, minus the sun; **de moins en moins** less and less; **en moins de**

269

deux in a flash *ou* a trice
5: **à moins de**, **à moins que** unless; **à moins de faire** unless we do (*ou* he does *etc*); **à moins que tu ne fasses** unless you do; **à moins d'un accident** barring any accident
▷ *prép*: **quatre moins deux** four minus two; **dix heures moins cinq** five to ten; **il fait moins cinq** it's five (degrees) below (freezing), it's minus five; **il est moins cinq** it's five to
▷ *nm* (*signe*) minus sign

moins-value [mwɛ̃valy] *nf* (*Écon, Comm*) depreciation
moire [mwaʀ] *nf* moiré
moiré, e [mwaʀe] *adj* (*tissu, papier*) moiré, watered; (*reflets*) shimmering
mois [mwa] *nm* month; (*salaire, somme dû*) (monthly) pay *ou* salary; **treizième ~, double ~** extra month's salary
moïse [mɔiz] *nm* Moses basket
moisi, e [mwazi] *adj* mouldy (*Brit*), moldy (*US*), mildewed ▷ *nm* mould, mold, mildew; **odeur de ~** musty smell
moisir [mwaziʀ] *vi* to go mouldy (*Brit*) *ou* moldy (*US*); (*fig*) to rot; (*personne*) to hang about ▷ *vt* to make mouldy *ou* moldy
moisissure [mwazisyʀ] *nf* mould *no pl* (*Brit*), mold *no pl* (*US*)
moisson [mwasɔ̃] *nf* harvest; (*époque*) harvest (time); (*fig*): **faire une ~ de** to gather a wealth of
moissonner [mwasɔne] *vt* to harvest, reap; (*fig*) to collect
moissonneur, -euse [mwasɔnœʀ, -øz] *nm/f* harvester, reaper ▷ *nf* (*machine*) harvester
moissonneuse-batteuse [mwasɔnøzbatøz] (*pl* **moissonneuses-batteuses**) *nf* combine harvester
moite [mwat] *adj* (*peau, mains*) sweaty, sticky; (*atmosphère*) muggy
moitié [mwatje] *nf* half; (*épouse*): **sa ~** his better half; **la ~** half; **la ~ de** half (of), half the amount (*ou* number) of; **la ~ du temps/des gens** half the time/the people; **à la ~ de** halfway through; **~ moins grand** half as tall; **~ plus long** half as long again, longer by half; **à ~** half (*avant le verbe*), half- (*avant l'adjectif*); **à ~ prix** (at) half price, half-price; **de ~** by half; **~ ~** half-and-half
moka [mɔka] *nm* (*café*) mocha coffee; (*gâteau*) mocha cake
mol [mɔl] *adj m voir* **mou**
molaire [mɔlɛʀ] *nf* molar
moldave [mɔldav] *adj* Moldavian
Moldavie [mɔldavi] *nf*: **la ~** Moldavia
môle [mol] *nm* jetty
moléculaire [mɔlekylɛʀ] *adj* molecular
molécule [mɔlekyl] *nf* molecule
moleskine [mɔlɛskin] *nf* imitation leather
molester [mɔlɛste] *vt* to manhandle, maul (about)
molette [mɔlɛt] *nf* toothed *ou* cutting wheel
mollasse [mɔlas] *adj* (*péj: sans énergie*) sluggish;

(: *flasque*) flabby
molle [mɔl] *adj f voir* **mou**
mollement [mɔlmɑ̃] *adv* softly; (*péj*) sluggishly; (*protester*) feebly
mollesse [mɔlɛs] *nf* (*voir mou*) softness; flabbiness; limpness; sluggishness; feebleness
mollet [mɔlɛ] *nm* calf ▷ *adj m*: **œuf ~** soft-boiled egg
molletière [mɔltjɛʀ] *adj f*: **bande ~** puttee
molleton [mɔltɔ̃] *nm* (*Textiles*) felt
molletonné, e [mɔltɔne] *adj* (*gants etc*) fleece-lined
mollir [mɔliʀ] *vi* (*jambes*) to give way; (*Navig: vent*) to drop, die down; (*fig: personne*) to relent; (: *courage*) to fail, flag
mollusque [mɔlysk(ə)] *nm* (*Zool*) mollusc; (*fig: personne*) lazy lump
molosse [mɔlɔs] *nm* big ferocious dog
môme [mom] *nm/f* (*fam: enfant*) brat; (: *fille*) bird (*Brit*), chick
moment [mɔmɑ̃] *nm* moment; (*occasion*): **profiter du ~** to take (advantage of) the opportunity; **ce n'est pas le ~** this is not the right time; **à un certain ~** at some point; **à un ~ donné** at a certain point; **à quel ~?** when exactly?; **au même ~** at the same time; (*instant*) at the same moment; **pour un bon ~** for a good while; **pour le ~** for the moment, for the time being; **au ~ de** at the time of; **au ~ où** as; at a time when; **à tout ~** at any time *ou* moment; (*continuellement*) constantly, continually; **en ce ~** at the moment; (*aujourd'hui*) at present; **sur le ~** at the time; **par ~s** now and then, at times; **d'un ~ à l'autre** any time (now); **du ~ où** *ou* **que** seeing that, since; **n'avoir pas un ~ à soi** not to have a minute to oneself
momentané, e [mɔmɑ̃tane] *adj* temporary, momentary
momentanément [mɔmɑ̃tanemɑ̃] *adv* for a moment, for a while
momie [mɔmi] *nf* mummy
mon [mɔ̃], **ma** [ma] (*pl* **mes** [me]) *adj poss* my
monacal, e, -aux [mɔnakal, -o] *adj* monastic
Monaco [mɔnako] *nm*: **le ~** Monaco
monarchie [mɔnaʀʃi] *nf* monarchy
monarchiste [mɔnaʀʃist(ə)] *adj, nm/f* monarchist
monarque [mɔnaʀk(ə)] *nm* monarch
monastère [mɔnastɛʀ] *nm* monastery
monastique [mɔnastik] *adj* monastic
monceau, x [mɔ̃so] *nm* heap
mondain, e [mɔ̃dɛ̃, -ɛn] *adj* (*soirée, vie*) society *cpd*; (*obligations*) social; (*peintre, écrivain*) fashionable; (*personne*) society *cpd* ▷ *nm/f* society man/woman, socialite ▷ *nf*: **la Mondaine, la police ~e** ≈ the vice squad
mondanités [mɔ̃danite] *nfpl* (*vie mondaine*) society life *sg*; (*paroles*) (society) small talk *sg*; (*Presse*) (society) gossip column *sg*
monde [mɔ̃d] *nm* world; (*personnes mondaines*): **le ~** (high) society; (*milieu*): **être du même ~** to move in the same circles; (*gens*): **il y a du ~**

(*beaucoup de gens*) there are a lot of people; (*quelques personnes*) there are some people; **y a-t-il du ~ dans le salon?** is there anybody in the lounge?; **beaucoup/peu de ~** many/few people; **le meilleur** *etc* **du ~** the best *etc* in the world; **mettre au ~** to bring into the world; **pas le moins du ~** not in the least; **se faire un ~ de qch** to make a great deal of fuss about sth; **tour du ~** round-the-world trip; **homme/femme du ~** society man/woman

mondial, e, -aux [mɔ̃djal, -o] *adj* (*population*) world *cpd*; (*influence*) world-wide

mondialement [mɔ̃djalmɑ̃] *adv* throughout the world

mondialisation [mɔ̃djalizasjɔ̃] *nf* (*d'une technique*) global application; (*d'un conflit*) global spread

mondovision [mɔ̃dovizjɔ̃] *nf* (world coverage by) satellite television

monégasque [monegask(ə)] *adj* Monegasque, of *ou* from Monaco ▷ *nm/f*: **Monégasque** Monegasque

monétaire [monetɛʀ] *adj* monetary

monétarisme [monetaʀism(ə)] *nm* monetarism

monétique [monetik] *nf* electronic money

mongol, e [mɔ̃gɔl] *adj* Mongol, Mongolian ▷ *nm* (*Ling*) Mongolian ▷ *nm/f*: **Mongol, e** (*Méd*) Mongol, Mongoloid; (*de la Mongolie*) Mongolian

Mongolie [mɔ̃gɔli] *nf*: **la ~** Mongolia

mongolien, ne [mɔ̃gɔljɛ̃, -ɛn] *adj, nm/f* mongol

mongolisme [mɔ̃gɔlism(ə)] *nm* mongolism, Down's syndrome

moniteur, -trice [monitœʀ, -tʀis] *nm/f* (*Sport*) instructor (instructress); (*de colonie de vacances*) supervisor ▷ *nm* (*écran*) monitor; **~ cardiaque** cardiac monitor; **~ d'auto-école** driving instructor

monitorage [monitoʀaʒ] *nm* monitoring

monitorat [monitoʀa] *nm* (*formation*) instructor's training (course); (*fonction*) instructorship

monnaie [monɛ] *nf* (*pièce*) coin; (*Écon: gén: moyen d'échange*) currency; (*petites pièces*): **avoir de la ~** to have (some) change; **faire de la ~** to get (some) change; **avoir/faire la ~ de 20 euros** to have change of/get change for 20 euros; **faire** *ou* **donner à qn la ~ de 20 euros** to give sb change for 20 euros, change 20 euros for sb; **rendre à qn la ~ (sur 20 euros)** to give sb the change (from *ou* out of 20 euros); **servir de ~ d'échange** (*fig*) to be used as a bargaining counter *ou* as bargaining counters; **payer en ~ de singe** to fob (sb) off with empty promises; **c'est ~ courante** it's a common occurrence; **~ légale** legal tender

monnayable [monɛjabl(ə)] *adj* (*vendable*) convertible into cash; **mes services sont ~s** my services are worth money

monnayer [monɛje] *vt* to convert into cash; (*talent*) to capitalize on

monnayeur [monɛjœʀ] *nm voir* **faux**

mono [mono] *nf* (*monophonie*) mono ▷ *nm* (*monoski*) monoski

monochrome [monokʀom] *adj* monochrome

monocle [monokl(ə)] *nm* monocle, eyeglass

monocoque [monokɔk] *adj* (*voiture*) monocoque ▷ *nm* (*voilier*) monohull

monocorde [monokɔʀd(ə)] *adj* monotonous

monoculture [monokyltyʀ] *nf* single-crop farming, monoculture

monogamie [monogami] *nf* monogamy

monogramme [monogʀam] *nm* monogram

monokini [monokini] *nm* one-piece bikini, bikini pants *pl*

monolingue [monolɛ̃g] *adj* monolingual

monolithique [monolitik] *adj* (*lit, fig*) monolithic

monologue [monolɔg] *nm* monologue, soliloquy; **~ intérieur** stream of consciousness

monologuer [monologe] *vi* to soliloquize

monôme [monom] *nm* (*Math*) monomial; (*d'étudiants*) students' rag procession

monoparental, e, -aux [monopaʀɑ̃tal, -o] *adj*: **famille ~e** single-parent *ou* one-parent family

monophasé, e [monofaze] *adj* single-phase *cpd*

monophonie [monofoni] *nf* monophony

monoplace [monoplas] *adj, nm, nf* single-seater, one-seater

monoplan [monoplɑ̃] *nm* monoplane

monopole [monopɔl] *nm* monopoly

monopolisation [monopolizasjɔ̃] *nf* monopolization

monopoliser [monopolize] *vt* to monopolize

monorail [monoʀaj] *nm* monorail; monorail train

monoski [monoski] *nm* monoski

monosyllabe [monosilab] *nm* monosyllable, word of one syllable

monosyllabique [monosilabik] *adj* monosyllabic

monotone [monotɔn] *adj* monotonous

monotonie [monotoni] *nf* monotony

monseigneur [mɔ̃sɛɲœʀ] *nm* (*archevêque, évêque*) Your (*ou* His) Grace; (*cardinal*) Your (*ou* His) Eminence; **M~ Thomas** Bishop Thomas; Cardinal Thomas

Monsieur [məsjø] (*pl* **Messieurs** [mesjø]) *nm* (*titre*) Mr; (*homme quelconque*): **un/le monsieur** a/the gentleman; *voir aussi* **Madame**

monstre [mɔ̃stʀ(ə)] *nm* monster ▷ *adj* (*fam: effet, publicité*) massive; **un travail ~** a fantastic amount of work; an enormous job; **~ sacré** superstar

monstrueux, -euse [mɔ̃stʀyø, -øz] *adj* monstrous

monstruosité [mɔ̃stʀyozite] *nf* monstrosity

mont [mɔ̃] *nm*: **par ~s et par vaux** up hill and down dale; **le M~ Blanc** Mont Blanc; **~ de Vénus** mons veneris

montage [mɔ̃taʒ] *nm* putting up; (*d'un bijou*) mounting, setting; (*d'une machine etc*) assembly; (*Photo*) photomontage; (*Ciné*) editing; **~ sonore** sound editing

montagnard, e [mɔ̃taɲaʀ, -aʀd(ə)] *adj* mountain *cpd* ▷ *nm/f* mountain-dweller

montagne [mɔ̃taɲ] *nf* (*cime*) mountain; (*région*): **la ~** the mountains *pl*; **la haute ~** the high mountains; **les ~s Rocheuses** the Rocky Mountains, the Rockies; **~s russes** big dipper *sg*, switchback *sg*

montagneux, -euse [mɔ̃taɲø, -øz] *adj* mountainous; hilly

montant, e [mɔ̃tɑ̃, -ɑ̃t] *adj* (*mouvement, marée*) rising; (*chemin*) uphill; (*robe, corsage*) high-necked ▷ *nm* (*somme, total*) (sum) total, (total) amount; (*de fenêtre*) upright; (*de lit*) post

mont-de-piété [mɔ̃dpjete] (*pl* **monts-de-piété**) *nm* pawnshop

monte [mɔ̃t] *nf* (*accouplement*): **la ~** stud; (*d'un jockey*) seat

monté, e [mɔ̃te] *adj*: **être ~ contre qn** to be angry with sb; (*fourni, équipé*): **~ en** equipped with

monte-charge [mɔ̃tʃaʀʒ(ə)] *nm inv* goods lift, hoist

montée [mɔ̃te] *nf* rising, rise; (*escalade*) ascent, climb; (*chemin*) way up; (*côte*) hill; **au milieu de la ~** halfway up; **le moteur chauffe dans les ~s** the engine overheats going uphill

Monténégro [mɔ̃tenegʀo] *nm*: **le ~** Montenegro

monte-plats [mɔ̃tpla] *nm inv* service lift

monter [mɔ̃te] *vt* (*escalier, côte*) to go (*ou* come) up; (*valise, paquet*) to take (*ou* bring) up; (*cheval*) to mount; (*femelle*) to cover, serve; (*tente, échafaudage*) to put up; (*machine*) to assemble; (*bijou*) to mount, set; (*Couture*) to sew on; (: *manche*) to set in; (*Ciné*) to edit; (*Théât*) to put on, stage; (*société, coup etc*) to set up; (*fournir, équiper*) to equip ▷ *vi* to go (*ou* come) up; (*avion, voiture*) to climb, go up; (*chemin, niveau, température, voix, prix*) to go up, rise; (*brouillard, bruit*) to rise, come up; (*passager*) to get on; (*à cheval*): **~ bien/mal** to ride well/badly; **~ à cheval/bicyclette** to get on *ou* mount a horse/bicycle; (*faire du cheval etc*) to ride (a horse), to (ride a) bicycle; **~ à pied/en voiture** to walk/drive up, go up on foot/by car; **~ dans le train/l'avion** to get into the train/plane, board the train/plane; **~ sur** to climb up onto; **~ sur** *ou* **un arbre/une échelle** to climb (up) a tree/ladder; **~ à bord** to (get on) board; **~ à la tête de qn** to go to sb's head; **~ sur les planches** to go on the stage; **~ en grade** to be promoted; **se monter** (*s'équiper*) to equip o.s., get kitted out (*Brit*); **se ~ à** (*frais etc*) to add up to, come to; **~ qn contre qn** to set sb against sb; **~ la tête à qn** to give sb ideas

monteur, -euse [mɔ̃tœʀ, -øz] *nm/f* (*Tech*) fitter; (*Ciné*) (film) editor

montgolfière [mɔ̃gɔlfjɛʀ] *nf* hot-air balloon

monticule [mɔ̃tikyl] *nm* mound

montmartrois, e [mɔ̃maʀtʀwa, -waz] *adj* of *ou* from Montmartre

montre [mɔ̃tʀ(ə)] *nf* watch; (*ostentation*): **pour la ~** for show; **~ en main** exactly, to the minute;

faire ~ de to show, display; **contre la ~** (*Sport*) against the clock; **~ de plongée** diver's watch

montréalais, e [mɔ̃ʀealɛ, -ɛz] *adj* of *ou* from Montreal ▷ *nm/f*: **Montréalais, e** Montrealer

montre-bracelet [mɔ̃tʀəbʀaslɛ] (*pl* **montres-bracelets**) *nf* wrist watch

montrer [mɔ̃tʀe] *vt* to show; **se montrer** to appear; **~ qch à qn** to show sb sth; **~ qch du doigt** to point to sth, point one's finger at sth; **se ~ intelligent** to prove (to be) intelligent

montreur, -euse [mɔ̃tʀœʀ, -øz] *nm/f*: **~ de marionnettes** puppeteer

monture [mɔ̃tyʀ] *nf* (*bête*) mount; (*d'une bague*) setting; (*de lunettes*) frame

monument [mɔnymɑ̃] *nm* monument; **~ aux morts** war memorial

monumental, e, -aux [mɔnymɑ̃tal, -o] *adj* monumental

moquer [mɔke]: **se ~ de** *vt* to make fun of, laugh at; (*fam: se désintéresser de*) not to care about; (*tromper*): **se ~ de qn** to take sb for a ride

moquerie [mɔkʀi] *nf* mockery *no pl*

moquette [mɔkɛt] *nf* fitted carpet, wall-to-wall carpeting *no pl*

moquetter [mɔkete] *vt* to carpet

moqueur, -euse [mɔkœʀ, -øz] *adj* mocking

moral, e, -aux [mɔʀal, -o] *adj* moral ▷ *nm* morale ▷ *nf* (*conduite*) morals *pl* (*règles*), moral code, ethic; (*valeurs*) moral standards *pl*, morality; (*science*) ethics *sg*, moral philosophy; (*conclusion: d'une fable etc*) moral; **au ~**, **sur le plan ~** morally; **avoir le ~ à zéro** to be really down; **faire la ~e à** to lecture, preach at

moralement [mɔʀalmɑ̃] *adv* morally

moralisateur, -trice [mɔʀalizatœʀ, -tʀis] *adj* moralizing, sanctimonious ▷ *nm/f* moralizer

moraliser [mɔʀalize] *vt* (*sermonner*) to lecture, preach at

moraliste [mɔʀalist(ə)] *nm/f* moralist ▷ *adj* moralistic

moralité [mɔʀalite] *nf* (*d'une action, attitude*) morality; (*conduite*) morals *pl*; (*conclusion, enseignement*) moral

moratoire [mɔʀatwaʀ] *adj m*: **intérêts ~s** (*Écon*) interest on arrears

morbide [mɔʀbid] *adj* morbid

morceau, x [mɔʀso] *nm* piece, bit; (*d'une œuvre*) passage, extract; (*Mus*) piece; (*Culin: de viande*) cut; **mettre en ~x** to pull to pieces *ou* bits

morceler [mɔʀsəle] *vt* to break up, divide up

morcellement [mɔʀsɛlmɑ̃] *nm* breaking up

mordant, e [mɔʀdɑ̃, -ɑ̃t] *adj* scathing, cutting; (*froid*) biting ▷ *nm* (*dynamisme, énergie*) spirit; (*fougue*) bite, punch

mordicus [mɔʀdikys] *adv* (*fam*) obstinately, stubbornly

mordiller [mɔʀdije] *vt* to nibble at, chew at

mordoré, e [mɔʀdɔʀe] *adj* lustrous bronze

mordre [mɔʀdʀ(ə)] *vt* to bite; (*lime, vis*) to bite into ▷ *vi* (*poisson*) to bite; **~ dans** to bite into; **~ sur** (*fig*) to go over into, overlap into; **~ à qch** (*comprendre, aimer*) to take to; **~ à l'hameçon** to bite, rise to the bait

mordu, e [mɔʀdy] *pp de* **mordre** ▷ *adj* (*amoureux*) smitten ▷ *nm/f*: **un ~ du jazz/de la voile** a jazz/sailing fanatic *ou* buff

morfondre [mɔʀfɔ̃dʀ(ə)]: **se morfondre** *vi* to mope

morgue [mɔʀg(ə)] *nf* (*arrogance*) haughtiness; (*lieu: de la police*) morgue; (: *à l'hôpital*) mortuary

moribond, e [mɔʀibɔ̃, -ɔ̃d] *adj* dying, moribund

morille [mɔʀij] *nf* morel (*mushroom*)

mormon, e [mɔʀmɔ̃, -ɔn] *adj, nm/f* Mormon

morne [mɔʀn(ə)] *adj* (*personne, visage*) glum, gloomy; (*temps, vie*) dismal, dreary

morose [mɔʀoz] *adj* sullen, morose; (*marché*) sluggish

morphine [mɔʀfin] *nf* morphine

morphinomane [mɔʀfinɔman] *nm/f* morphine addict

morphologie [mɔʀfɔlɔʒi] *nf* morphology

morphologique [mɔʀfɔlɔʒik] *adj* morphological

mors [mɔʀ] *nm* bit

morse [mɔʀs(ə)] *nm* (*Zool*) walrus; (*Tél*) Morse (code)

morsure [mɔʀsyʀ] *nf* bite

mort[1] [mɔʀ] *nf* death; **se donner la ~** to take one's own life; **de ~** (*silence, pâleur*) deathly; **blessé à ~** fatally wounded *ou* injured; **à la vie, à la ~** for better, for worse; **~ clinique** brain death; **~ subite du nourrisson, ~ au berceau** cot death

mort[2] [mɔʀ, mɔʀt(ə)] *pp de* **mourir** ▷ *adj* dead ▷ *nm/f* (*défunt*) dead man/woman; (*victime*): **il y a eu plusieurs ~s** several people were killed, there were several killed ▷ *nm* (*Cartes*) dummy; **~ ou vif** dead or alive; **~ de peur/fatigue** frightened to death/dead tired; **~s et blessés** casualties; **faire le ~** to play dead; (*fig*) to lie low

mortadelle [mɔʀtadɛl] *nf* mortadella

mortalité [mɔʀtalite] *nf* mortality, death rate

mort-aux-rats [mɔʀtoʀa] *nfinv* rat poison

mortel, le [mɔʀtɛl] *adj* (*poison etc*) deadly, lethal; (*accident, blessure*) fatal; (*Rel: danger, frayeur*) mortal; (*fig: froid*) deathly; (: *ennui, soirée*) deadly (*boring*) ▷ *nm/f* mortal

mortellement [mɔʀtɛlmɑ̃] *adv* (*blessé etc*) fatally, mortally; (*pâle etc*) deathly; (*fig: ennuyeux etc*) deadly

morte-saison [mɔʀtəsɛzɔ̃] (*pl* **mortes-saisons**) *nf* slack *ou* off season

mortier [mɔʀtje] *nm* (*gén*) mortar

mortifier [mɔʀtifje] *vt* to mortify

mort-né, e [mɔʀne] *adj* (*enfant*) stillborn; (*fig*) abortive

mortuaire [mɔʀtɥɛʀ] *adj* funeral *cpd*; **avis ~s** death announcements, intimations; **chapelle ~** mortuary chapel; **couronne ~** (funeral) wreath; **domicile ~** house of the deceased; **drap ~** pall

morue [mɔʀy] *nf* (*Zool*) cod *inv*; (*Culin: salée*) salt-cod

morvandeau, -elle, x [mɔʀvɑ̃do, -ɛl] *adj* of *ou* from the Morvan region

morveux, -euse [mɔʀvø, -øz] *adj* (*fam*) snotty-nosed

mosaïque [mɔzaik] *nf* (*Art*) mosaic; (*fig*) patchwork

Moscou [mɔsku] *n* Moscow

moscovite [mɔskɔvit] *adj* of *ou* from Moscow, Moscow *cpd* ▷ *nm/f*: **Moscovite** Muscovite

mosquée [mɔske] *nf* mosque

mot [mo] *nm* word; (*message*) line, note; (*bon mot etc*) saying; **le ~ de la fin** the last word; **~ à ~** *adj, adv* word for word; **~ pour ~** word for word, verbatim; **sur *ou* à ces ~s** with these words; **en un ~** in a word; **à ~s couverts** in veiled terms; **prendre qn au ~** to take sb at his word; **se donner le ~** to send the word round; **avoir son ~ à dire** to have a say; **~ d'ordre** watchword; **~ de passe** password; **~s croisés** crossword (puzzle) *sg*

motard [mɔtaʀ] *nm* biker; (*policier*) motorcycle cop

motel [mɔtɛl] *nm* motel

moteur, -trice [mɔtœʀ, -tʀis] *adj* (*Anat, Physiol*) motor; (*Tech*) driving; (*Auto*): **à 4 roues motrices** 4-wheel drive ▷ *nm* engine, motor; (*fig*) mover, mainspring; **à ~** power-driven, motor *cpd*; **~ à deux temps** two-stroke engine; **~ à explosion** internal combustion engine; **~ à réaction** jet engine; **~ de recherche** search engine; **~ thermique** heat engine

motif [mɔtif] *nm* (*cause*) motive; (*décoratif*) design, pattern, motif; (*d'un tableau*) subject, motif; (*Mus*) figure, motif; **motifs** *nmpl* (*Jur*) grounds *pl*; **sans ~** *adj* groundless

motion [mosjɔ̃] *nf* motion; **~ de censure** motion of censure, vote of no confidence

motivation [mɔtivasjɔ̃] *nf* motivation

motivé, e [mɔtive] *adj* (*acte*) justified; (*personne*) motivated

motiver [mɔtive] *vt* (*justifier*) to justify, account for; (*Admin, Jur, Psych*) to motivate

moto [mɔto] *nf* (motor)bike; **~ verte *ou* de trial** trail (*Brit*) *ou* dirt (*US*) bike

moto-cross [mɔtokʀɔs] *nm* motocross

motoculteur [mɔtokyltœʀ] *nm* (motorized) cultivator

motocyclette [mɔtosiklɛt] *nf* motorbike, motorcycle

motocyclisme [mɔtosiklism(ə)] *nm* motorcycle racing

motocycliste [mɔtosiklist(ə)] *nm/f* motorcyclist

motoneige [mɔtonɛʒ] *nf* snow bike

motorisé, e [mɔtoʀize] *adj* (*troupe*) motorized; (*personne*) having one's own transport

motrice [mɔtʀis] *adjf voir* **moteur**

motte [mɔt] *nf*: **~ de terre** lump of earth, clod (of earth); **~ de gazon** turf, sod; **~ de beurre** lump of butter

motus [mɔtys] *excl*: **~ (et bouche cousue)!** mum's the word!

mou, mol, molle [mu, mɔl] *adj* soft; (*péj: visage,*

traits) flabby; (: *geste*) limp; (: *personne*) sluggish; (: *résistance, protestations*) feeble ▷ *nm* (*homme mou*) wimp; (*abats*) lights *pl*, lungs *pl*; (*de la corde*): **avoir du ~** to be slack; **donner du ~** to slacken, loosen; **avoir les jambes molles** to be weak at the knees

mouchard, e [muʃaʀ, -aʀd(ə)] *nm/f* (*péj: Scol*) sneak; (: *Police*) stool pigeon, grass (*Brit*) ▷ *nm* (*appareil*) control device; (: *de camion*) tachograph

mouche [muʃ] *nf* fly; (*Escrime*) button; (*de taffetas*) patch; **prendre la ~** to go into a huff; **faire ~** to score a bull's-eye

moucher [muʃe] *vt* (*enfant*) to blow the nose of; (*chandelle*) to snuff (out); **se moucher** to blow one's nose

moucheron [muʃʀɔ̃] *nm* midge

moucheté, e [muʃte] *adj* (*cheval*) dappled; (*laine*) flecked; (*Escrime*) buttoned

mouchoir [muʃwaʀ] *nm* handkerchief, hanky; **~ en papier** tissue, paper hanky

moudre [mudʀ(ə)] *vt* to grind

moue [mu] *nf* pout; **faire la ~** to pout; (*fig*) to pull a face

mouette [mwɛt] *nf* (sea)gull

moufette, mouffette [mufɛt] *nf* skunk

moufle [mufl(ə)] *nf* (*gant*) mitt(en); (*Tech*) pulley block

mouflon [muflɔ̃] *nm* mouf(f)lon

mouillage [mujaʒ] *nm* (*Navig: lieu*) anchorage, moorings *pl*

mouillé, e [muje] *adj* wet

mouiller [muje] *vt* (*humecter*) to wet, moisten; (*tremper*): **~ qn/qch** to make sb/sth wet; (*Culin: ragoût*) to add stock *ou* wine to; (*couper, diluer*) to water down; (*mine etc*) to lay ▷ *vi* (*Navig*) to lie *ou* be at anchor; **se mouiller** to get wet; (*fam*) to commit o.s; to get (o.s.) involved; **~ l'ancre** to drop *ou* cast anchor

mouillette [mujɛt] *nf* (bread) finger

mouillure [mujyʀ] *nf* wet *no pl*; (*tache*) wet patch

moulage [mulaʒ] *nm* moulding (*Brit*), molding (*US*); (*objet*) cast

moulais *etc* [mulɛ] *vb voir* **moudre**

moulant, e [mulɑ̃, -ɑ̃t] *adj* figure-hugging

moule [mul] *vb voir* **moudre** ▷ *nf* (*mollusque*) mussel ▷ *nm* (*creux, Culin*) mould (*Brit*), mold (*US*); (*modèle plein*) cast; **~ à gâteau** *nm* cake tin (*Brit*) *ou* pan (*US*); **~ à gaufre** *nm* waffle iron; **~ à tarte** *nm* pie *ou* flan dish

moulent [mul] *vb voir* **moudre; mouler**

mouler [mule] *vt* (*brique*) to mould (*Brit*), mold (*US*); (*statue*) to cast; (*visage, bas-relief*) to make a cast of; (*lettre*) to shape with care; (*vêtement*) to hug, fit closely round; **~ qch sur** (*fig*) to model sth on

moulin [mulɛ̃] *nm* mill; (*fam*) engine; **~ à café** coffee mill; **~ à eau** watermill; **~ à légumes** (vegetable) shredder; **~ à paroles** (*fig*) chatterbox; **~ à poivre** pepper mill; **~ à prières** prayer wheel; **~ à vent** windmill

mouliner [muline] *vt* to shred

moulinet [mulinɛ] *nm* (*de treuil*) winch; (*de canne*

à pêche) reel; (*mouvement*): **faire des ~s avec qch** to whirl sth around

moulinette® [mulinɛt] *nf* (vegetable) shredder

moulons *etc* [mulɔ̃] *vb voir* **moudre**

moulu, e [muly] *pp de* **moudre** ▷ *adj* (*café*) ground

moulure [mulyʀ] *nf* (*ornement*) moulding (*Brit*), molding (*US*)

mourant, e [muʀɑ̃, -ɑ̃t] *vb voir* **mourir** ▷ *adj* dying ▷ *nm/f* dying man/woman

mourir [muʀiʀ] *vi* to die; (*civilisation*) to die out; **~ assassiné** to be murdered; **~ de froid/faim/ vieillesse** to die of exposure/hunger/old age; **~ de faim/d'ennui** (*fig*) to be starving/be bored to death; **~ d'envie de faire** to be dying to do; **s'ennuyer à ~** to be bored to death

mousquetaire [muskətɛʀ] *nm* musketeer

mousqueton [muskətɔ̃] *nm* (*fusil*) carbine; (*anneau*) snap-link, karabiner

moussant, e [musɑ̃, -ɑ̃t] *adj* foaming; **bain ~** foam *ou* bubble bath, bath foam

mousse [mus] *nf* (*Bot*) moss; (*écume: sur eau, bière*) froth, foam; (: *shampooing*) lather; (*de champagne*) bubbles *pl*; (*Culin*) mousse; (*en caoutchouc etc*) foam ▷ *nm* (*Navig*) ship's boy; **bain de ~** bubble bath; **bas ~** stretch stockings; **balle ~** rubber ball; **~ carbonique** (fire-fighting) foam; **~ de nylon** nylon foam; (*tissu*) stretch nylon; **~ à raser** shaving foam

mousseline [muslin] *nf* (*Textiles*) muslin; chiffon; **pommes ~** (*Culin*) creamed potatoes

mousser [muse] *vi* to foam; to lather

mousseux, -euse [musø, -øz] *adj* (*chocolat*) frothy; (*eau*) foamy, frothy; (*vin*) sparkling ▷ *nm*: (**vin**) **~** sparkling wine

mousson [musɔ̃] *nf* monsoon

moussu, e [musy] *adj* mossy

moustache [mustaʃ] *nf* moustache; **moustaches** *nfpl* (*d'animal*) whiskers *pl*

moustachu, e [mustaʃy] *adj* wearing a moustache

moustiquaire [mustikɛʀ] *nf* (*rideau*) mosquito net; (*chassis*) mosquito screen

moustique [mustik] *nm* mosquito

moutarde [mutaʀd(ə)] *nf* mustard ▷ *adj inv* mustard(-coloured)

moutardier [mutaʀdje] *nm* mustard jar

mouton [mutɔ̃] *nm* (*Zool, péj*) sheep *inv*; (*peau*) sheepskin; (*Culin*) mutton

mouture [mutyʀ] *nf* grinding; (*péj*) rehash

mouvant, e [muvɑ̃, -ɑ̃t] *adj* unsettled; changing; shifting

mouvement [muvmɑ̃] *nm* (*gen, aussi: mécanisme*) movement; (*ligne courbe*) contours *pl*; (*fig: tumulte, agitation*) activity, bustle; (: *impulsion*) impulse; reaction; (*geste*) gesture; (*Mus: rythme*) tempo; **en ~** in motion; on the move; **mettre qch en ~** to set sth in motion, set sth going; **~ d'humeur** fit *ou* burst of temper; **~ d'opinion** trend of (public) opinion; **le ~ perpétuel** perpetual motion

mouvementé, e [muvmɑ̃te] *adj* (*vie, poursuite*)

eventful; (*réunion*) turbulent

mouvoir [muvwaʀ] *vt* (*levier, membre*) to move; (*machine*) to drive; **se mouvoir** to move

moyen, ne [mwajɛ̃, -ɛn] *adj* average; (*tailles, prix*) medium; (*de grandeur moyenne*) medium-sized ▷ *nm* (*façon*) means *sg*, way ▷ *nf* average; (*Statistique*) mean; (*Scol*: *à l'examen*) pass mark; (*Auto*) average speed; **moyens** *nmpl* (*capacités*) means; **au ~ de** by means of; **y a-t-il ~ de ...?** is it possible to ...?, can one ...?; **par quel ~?** how?, which way?, by which means?; **par tous les ~s** by every possible means, every possible way; **avec les ~s du bord** (*fig*) with what's available *ou* what comes to hand; **employer les grands ~s** to resort to drastic measures; **par ses propres ~s** all by oneself; **en ~ne** on (an) average; **faire la ~ne** to work out the average; **~ de locomotion/d'expression** means of transport/expression; **~ âge** Middle Ages; **~ de transport** means of transport; **~ne d'âge** average age; **~ne entreprise** (*Comm*) medium-sized firm

moyenâgeux, -euse [mwajɛnaʒø, -øz] *adj* medieval

moyen-courrier [mwajɛ̃kuʀje] *nm* (*Aviat*) medium-haul aircraft

moyennant [mwajɛnɑ̃] *prép* (*somme*) for; (*service, conditions*) in return for; (*travail, effort*) with

moyennement [mwajɛnmɑ̃] *adv* fairly, moderately; (*faire*) fairly *ou* moderately well

Moyen-Orient [mwajɛnɔʀjɑ̃] *nm*: **le ~** the Middle East

moyeu, x [mwajø] *nm* hub

mozambicain, e [mɔzɑ̃bikɛ̃, -ɛn] *adj* Mozambican

Mozambique [mɔzɑ̃bik] *nm*: **le ~** Mozambique

MRAP *sigle m* = **Mouvement contre le racisme et pour l'amitié entre les peuples**

MRG *sigle m* (= *Mouvement des radicaux de gauche*) political party

ms *abr* (= *manuscrit*) MS., ms

MSF *sigle mpl* = **Médecins sans frontières**

MST *sigle f* (= *maladie sexuellement transmissible*) STD (= *sexually transmitted disease*)

mû, mue [my] *pp de* **mouvoir**

mucosité [mykozite] *nf* mucus *no pl*

mucus [mykys] *nm* mucus *no pl*

mue [my] *pp de* **mouvoir** ▷ *nf* moulting (*Brit*), molting (*US*); sloughing; breaking of the voice

muer [mɥe] *vi* (*oiseau, mammifère*) to moult (*Brit*), molt (*US*); (*serpent*) to slough (its skin); (*jeune garçon*): **il mue** his voice is breaking; **se ~ en** to transform into

muet, te [mɥɛ, -ɛt] *adj* dumb; (*fig*): **~ d'admiration** *etc* speechless with admiration *etc*; (*joie, douleur, Ciné*) silent; (*Ling*: *lettre*) silent, mute; (*carte*) blank ▷ *nm/f* mute ▷ *nm*: **le ~** (*Ciné*) the silent cinema *ou* (*esp US*) movies

mufle [myfl(ə)] *nm* muzzle; (*goujat*) boor ▷ *adj* boorish

mugir [myʒiʀ] *vi* (*bœuf*) to bellow; (*vache*) to low, moo; (*fig*) to howl

mugissement [myʒismɑ̃] *nm* (*voir mugir*) bellowing; lowing, mooing; howling

muguet [mygɛ] *nm* (*Bot*) lily of the valley; (*Méd*) thrush

mulâtre, tresse [mylɑtʀ(ə), -tʀɛs] *nm/f* mulatto

mule [myl] *nf* (*Zool*) (she-)mule

mules [myl] *nfpl* (*pantoufles*) mules

mulet [mylɛ] *nm* (*Zool*) (he-)mule; (*poisson*) mullet

muletier, -ière [myltje, -jɛʀ] *adj*: **sentier** *ou* **chemin ~** mule track

mulot [mylo] *nm* fieldmouse

multicolore [myltikɔlɔʀ] *adj* multicoloured (*Brit*), multicolored (*US*)

multicoque [myltikɔk] *nm* multihull

multidisciplinaire [myltidisiplinɛʀ] *adj* multidisciplinary

multiforme [myltifɔʀm(ə)] *adj* many-sided

multilatéral, e, -aux [myltilateʀal, -o] *adj* multilateral

multimilliardaire [myltimiljaʀdɛʀ], **multimillionnaire** [myltimiljɔnɛʀ] *adj, nm/f* multimillionaire

multinational, e, -aux [myltinasjɔnal, -o] *adj*, *nf* multinational

multiple [myltipl(ə)] *adj* multiple, numerous; (*varié*) many, manifold ▷ *nm* (*Math*) multiple

multiplex [myltiplɛks] *nm* (*Radio*) live link-up

multiplicateur [myltiplikatœʀ] *nm* multiplier

multiplication [myltiplikasjɔ̃] *nf* multiplication

multiplicité [myltiplisite] *nf* multiplicity

multiplier [myltiplije] *vt* to multiply; **se multiplier** *vi* to multiply; (*fig*: *personne*) to be everywhere at once

multiprogrammation [myltipʀɔgʀamasjɔ̃] *nf* (*Inform*) multiprogramming

multipropriété [myltipʀɔpʀijete] *nf* timesharing *no pl*

multirisque [myltiʀisk] *adj*: **assurance ~** multiple-risk insurance

multisalles [myltisal] *adj*: (**cinéma**) **~** multiplex (cinema)

multitraitement [myltitʀɛtmɑ̃] *nm* (*Inform*) multiprocessing

multitude [myltityd] *nf* multitude; mass; **une ~ de** a vast number of, a multitude of

Munich [mynik] *n* Munich

munichois, e [mynikwa, -waz] *adj* of *ou* from Munich

municipal, e, -aux [mynisipal, -o] *adj* municipal; town *cpd*

municipalité [mynisipalite] *nf* (*corps municipal*) town council, corporation; (*commune*) town, municipality

munificence [mynifisɑ̃s] *nf* munificence

munir [myniʀ] *vt*: **~ qn/qch de** to equip sb/sth with; **se ~ de** to provide o.s. with

munitions [mynisjɔ̃] *nfpl* ammunition *sg*

muqueuse [mykøz] *nf* mucous membrane

mur [myʀ] *nm* wall; (*fig*) stone *ou* brick wall;

m

faire le ~ (interne, soldat) to jump the wall; **~ du son** sound barrier

mûr, e [myʀ] adj ripe; (personne) mature ▷ nf (de la ronce) blackberry; (du mûrier) mulberry

muraille [myʀaj] nf (high) wall

mural, e, -aux [myʀal, -o] adj wall cpd ▷ nm (Art) mural

mûre [myʀ] nf voir **mûr**

mûrement [myʀmɑ̃] adv: **ayant ~ réfléchi** having given the matter much thought

murène [myʀɛn] nf moray (eel)

murer [myʀe] vt (enclos) to wall (in); (porte, issue) to wall up; (personne) to wall up ou in

muret [myʀɛ] nm low wall

mûrier [myʀje] nm mulberry tree; (ronce) blackberry bush

mûrir [myʀiʀ] vi (fruit, blé) to ripen; (abcès, furoncle) to come to a head; (fig: idée, personne) to mature; (projet) to develop ▷ vt (fruit, blé) to ripen; (personne) to (make) mature; (pensée, projet) to nurture

murmure [myʀmyʀ] nm murmur; **murmures** nmpl (plaintes) murmurings, mutterings

murmurer [myʀmyʀe] vi to murmur; (se plaindre) to mutter, grumble

mus etc [my] vb voir **mouvoir**

musaraigne [myzaʀɛɲ] nf shrew

musarder [myzaʀde] vi to idle (about); (en marchant) to dawdle (along)

musc [mysk] nm musk

muscade [myskad] nf (aussi: **noix muscade**) nutmeg

muscat [myska] nm (raisin) muscat grape; (vin) muscatel (wine)

muscle [myskl(ə)] nm muscle

musclé, e [myskle] adj (personne, corps) muscular; (fig: politique, régime etc) strong-arm cpd

muscler [myskle] vt to develop the muscles of

musculaire [myskylɛʀ] adj muscular

musculation [myskylasjɔ̃] nf: **exercices de ~** muscle-developing exercises

musculature [myskylatyʀ] nf muscle structure, muscles pl, musculature

muse [myz] nf muse

museau, x [myzo] nm muzzle

musée [myze] nm museum; (de peinture) art gallery

museler [myzle] vt to muzzle

muselière [myzəljɛʀ] nf muzzle

musette [myzɛt] nf (sac) lunch bag ▷ adj inv (orchestre etc) accordion cpd

muséum [myzeɔm] nm museum

musical, e, -aux [myzikal, -o] adj musical

music-hall [myzikol] nm variety theatre; (genre) variety

musicien, ne [myzisjɛ̃, -ɛn] adj musical ▷ nm/f musician

musique [myzik] nf music; (fanfare) band; **faire de la ~** to make music; (jouer d'un instrument) to play an instrument; **~ de chambre** chamber music; **~ de fond** background music

musqué, e [myske] adj musky

must [mœst] nm must

musulman, e [myzylmɑ̃, -an] adj, nm/f Moslem, Muslim

mutant, e [mytɑ̃, -ɑ̃t] nm/f mutant

mutation [mytasjɔ̃] nf (Admin) transfer; (Bio) mutation

muter [myte] vt (Admin) to transfer

mutilation [mytilasjɔ̃] nf mutilation

mutilé, e [mytile] nm/f disabled person (through loss of limbs); **~ de guerre** disabled ex-serviceman; **grand ~** severely disabled person

mutiler [mytile] vt to mutilate, maim; (fig) to mutilate, deface

mutin, e [mytɛ̃, -in] adj (enfant, air, ton) mischievous, impish ▷ nm/f (Mil, Navig) mutineer

mutiner [mytine]: **se mutiner** vi to mutiny

mutinerie [mytinʀi] nf mutiny

mutisme [mytism(ə)] nm silence

mutualiste [mytɥalist(ə)] adj: **société ~** mutual benefit society, ≈ Friendly Society

mutualité [mytɥalite] nf (assurance) mutual (benefit) insurance scheme

mutuel, le [mytɥɛl] adj mutual ▷ nf mutual benefit society

mutuellement [mytɥɛlmɑ̃] adv each other, one another

Myanmar [mjanmaʀ] nm Myanmar

myocarde [mjɔkaʀd(ə)] nm voir **infarctus**

myope [mjɔp] adj short-sighted

myopie [mjɔpi] nf short-sightedness, myopia

myosotis [mjozɔtis] nm forget-me-not

myriade [miʀjad] nf myriad

myrtille [miʀtij] nf bilberry (Brit), blueberry (US), whortleberry

mystère [mistɛʀ] nm mystery

mystérieusement [misteʀjøzmɑ̃] adv mysteriously

mystérieux, -euse [misteʀjø, -øz] adj mysterious

mysticisme [mistisism(ə)] nm mysticism

mystificateur, -trice [mistifikatœʀ, -tʀis] nm/f hoaxer, practical joker

mystification [mistifikasjɔ̃] nf (tromperie, mensonge) hoax; (mythe) mystification

mystifier [mistifje] vt to fool, take in; (tromper) to mystify

mystique [mistik] adj mystic, mystical ▷ nm/f mystic

mythe [mit] nm myth

mythifier [mitifje] vt to turn into a myth, mythologize

mythique [mitik] adj mythical

mythologie [mitɔlɔʒi] nf mythology

mythologique [mitɔlɔʒik] adj mythological

mythomane [mitɔman] adj, nm/f mythomaniac

Nn

N, n [ɛn] *nm inv* N, n ▷ *abr* (= *nord*) N; **N comme Nicolas** N for Nelly (*Brit*) *ou* Nan (*US*)

n' [n] *adv voir* **ne**

nabot [nabo] *nm* dwarf

nacelle [nasɛl] *nf* (*de ballon*) basket

nacre [nakʀ(ə)] *nf* mother-of-pearl

nacré, e [nakʀe] *adj* pearly

nage [naʒ] *nf* swimming; (*manière*) style of swimming, stroke; **traverser/s'éloigner à la ~** to swim across/away; **en ~** bathed in perspiration; **~ indienne** sidestroke; **~ libre** freestyle; **~ papillon** butterfly

nageoire [naʒwaʀ] *nf* fin

nager [naʒe] *vi* to swim; (*fig: ne rien comprendre*) to be all at sea; **~ dans** to be swimming in; (*vêtements*) to be lost in; **~ dans le bonheur** to be overjoyed

nageur, -euse [naʒœʀ, -øz] *nm/f* swimmer

naguère [nagɛʀ] *adv* (*il y a peu de temps*) not long ago; (*autrefois*) formerly

naïf, -ïve [naif, naiv] *adj* naïve

nain, e [nɛ̃, nɛn] *adj, nm/f* dwarf

Nairobi [naiʀɔbi] *n* Nairobi

nais [nɛ], **naissais** *etc* [nɛsɛ] *vb voir* **naître**

naissance [nɛsɑ̃s] *nf* birth; **donner ~ à** to give birth to; (*fig*) to give rise to; **prendre ~** to originate; **aveugle de ~** born blind; **Français de ~** French by birth; **à la ~ des cheveux** at the roots of the hair; **lieu de ~** place of birth

naissant, e [nɛsɑ̃, -ɑ̃t] *vb voir* **naître** ▷ *adj* budding, incipient; (*jour*) dawning

naît [nɛ] *vb voir* **naître**

naître [nɛtʀ(ə)] *vi* to be born; (*conflit, complications*): **~ de** to arise from, be born out of; **~ à** (*amour, poésie*) to awaken to; **je suis né en 1960** I was born in 1960; **il naît plus de filles que de garçons** there are more girls born than boys; **faire ~** (*fig*) to give rise to, arouse

naïvement [naivmɑ̃] *adv* naïvely

naïveté [naivte] *nf* naivety

nana [nana] *nf* (*fam: fille*) bird (*Brit*), chick

nantais, e [nɑ̃tɛ, -ɛz] *adj* of *ou* from Nantes

nantir [nɑ̃tiʀ] *vt*: **~ qn de** to provide sb with; **les nantis** (*péj*) the well-to-do

napalm [napalm] *nm* napalm

naphtaline [naftalin] *nf*: **boules de ~** mothballs

Naples [napl(ə)] *n* Naples

napolitain, e [napɔlitɛ̃, -ɛn] *adj* Neapolitan; **tranche ~e** Neapolitan ice cream

nappe [nap] *nf* tablecloth; (*fig*) sheet; layer; **~ de mazout** oil slick; **~ (phréatique)** water table

napper [nape] *vt*: **~ qch de** to coat sth with

napperon [napʀɔ̃] *nm* table-mat; **~ individuel** place mat

naquis *etc* [naki] *vb voir* **naître**

narcisse [naʀsis] *nm* narcissus

narcissique [naʀsisik] *adj* narcissistic

narcissisme [naʀsisism(ə)] *nm* narcissism

narcodollars [naʀkodɔlaʀ] *nmpl* drug money *no pl*

narcotique [naʀkɔtik] *adj, nm* narcotic

narguer [naʀge] *vt* to taunt

narine [naʀin] *nf* nostril

narquois, e [naʀkwa, -waz] *adj* derisive, mocking

narrateur, -trice [naʀatœʀ, -tʀis] *nm/f* narrator

narration [naʀasjɔ̃] *nf* narration, narrative; (*Scol*) essay

narrer [naʀe] *vt* to tell the story of, recount

NASA [naza] *sigle f* (= *National Aeronautics and Space Administration*) NASA

nasal, e, -aux [nazal, -o] *adj* nasal

naseau, x [nazo] *nm* nostril

nasillard, e [nazijaʀ, -aʀd(ə)] *adj* nasal

nasiller [nazije] *vi* to speak with a (nasal) twang

nasse [nas] *nf* fish-trap

natal, e [natal] *adj* native

nataliste [natalist(ə)] *adj* supporting a rising birth rate

natalité [natalite] *nf* birth rate

natation [natasjɔ̃] *nf* swimming; **faire de la ~** to go swimming (*regularly*)

natif, -ive [natif, -iv] *adj* native

nation [nasjɔ̃] *nf* nation; **les N~s unies (NU)** the United Nations (UN)

national, e, -aux [nasjɔnal, -o] *adj* national ▷ *nf*: **(route) ~e** A road (*Brit*), ≈ state highway (*US*); **obsèques ~es** state funeral

nationalisation [nasjɔnalizasjɔ̃] *nf* nationalization

nationaliser [nasjɔnalize] *vt* to nationalize

nationalisme [nasjɔnalism(ə)] *nm* nationalism

nationaliste [nasjɔnalist(ə)] *adj, nm/f* nationalist

nationalité [nasjɔnalite] *nf* nationality; **de ~ française** of French nationality

natte [nat] *nf* (*tapis*) mat; (*cheveux*) plait

natter [nate] *vt* (*cheveux*) to plait

naturalisation [natyralizasjɔ̃] *nf* naturalization

naturaliser [natyralize] *vt* to naturalize; (*empailler*) to stuff

naturaliste [natyralist(ə)] *nm/f* naturalist; (*empailleur*) taxidermist

nature [natyr] *nf* nature ▷ *adj, adv* (*Culin*) plain, without seasoning or sweetening; (*café, thé: sans lait*) black; (: *sans sucre*) without sugar; **payer en ~** to pay in kind; **peint d'après ~** painted from life; **être de ~ à faire qch** (*propre à*) to be the sort of thing (*ou* person) to do sth; **~ morte** still-life

naturel, le [natyrɛl] *adj* natural ▷ *nm* naturalness; (*caractère*) disposition, nature; (*autochtone*) native; (*aussi*: **au naturel**: *Culin*) in water; in its own juices

naturellement [natyrɛlmɑ̃] *adv* naturally; (*bien sûr*) of course

naturisme [natyrism(ə)] *nm* naturism

naturiste [natyrist(ə)] *nm/f* naturist

naufrage [nofraʒ] *nm* (ship)wreck; (*fig*) wreck; **faire ~** to be shipwrecked

naufragé, e [nofraʒe] *nm/f* shipwreck victim, castaway

nauséabond, e [nozeabɔ̃, -ɔ̃d] *adj* foul, nauseous

nausée [noze] *nf* nausea; **avoir la ~** to feel sick; **avoir des ~s** to have waves of nausea, feel nauseous *ou* sick

nautique [nɔtik] *adj* nautical, water *cpd*; **sports ~s** water sports

nautisme [nɔtism(ə)] *nm* water sports *pl*

naval, e [naval] *adj* naval

navarrais, e [navarɛ, -ɛz] *adj* Navarrese

navet [navɛ] *nm* turnip; (*péj*) third-rate film

navette [navɛt] *nf* shuttle; (*en car etc*) shuttle (service); **faire la ~ (entre)** to go to and fro (between), shuttle (between); **~ spatiale** space shuttle

navigabilité [navigabilite] *nf* (*d'un navire*) seaworthiness; (*d'un avion*) airworthiness

navigable [navigabl(ə)] *adj* navigable

navigant, e [navigɑ̃, -ɑ̃t] *adj* (*Aviat: personnel*) flying ▷ *nm/f*: **les ~s** the flying staff *ou* personnel

navigateur [navigatœr] *nm* (*Navig*) seafarer, sailor; (*Aviat*) navigator; (*Inform*) browser

navigation [navigasjɔ̃] *nf* navigation, sailing; (*Comm*) shipping; **compagnie de ~** shipping company; **~ spatiale** space navigation

naviguer [navige] *vi* to navigate, sail

navire [navir] *nm* ship; **~ de guerre** warship; **~ marchand** merchantman

navire-citerne [navirsitɛrn(ə)] (*pl* **navires-citernes**) *nm* tanker

navire-hôpital [navirɔpital, -to] (*pl* **navires-hôpitaux**) *nm* hospital ship

navrant, e [navrɑ̃, -ɑ̃t] *adj* (*affligeant*) upsetting; (*consternant*) annoying

navrer [navre] *vt* to upset, distress; **je suis navré (de/de faire/que)** I'm so sorry (for/for doing/that)

NB *abr* (= *nota bene*) NB

nbr. *abr* = **nombreux**

nbses *abr* = **nombreuses**

ND *sigle f* = **Notre Dame**

NDA *sigle f* = **note de l'auteur**

NDE *sigle f* = **note de l'éditeur**

NDLR *sigle f* = **note de la rédaction**

NDT *sigle f* = **note du traducteur**

ne, n' [n(ə)] *adv voir* **pas**; **plus**; **jamais** *etc*; (*explétif*) *non traduit*

né, e [ne] *pp de* **naître**; **né en 1960** born in 1960; **née Scott** née Scott; **né(e) de ... et de ...** son/daughter of ... and of ...; **né d'une mère française** having a French mother; **né pour commander** born to lead ▷ *adj*: **un comédien né** a born comedian

néanmoins [neɑ̃mwɛ̃] *adv* nevertheless, yet

néant [neɑ̃] *nm* nothingness; **réduire à ~** to bring to nought; (*espoir*) to dash

nébuleux, -euse [nebylø, -øz] *adj* (*ciel*) cloudy; (*fig*) nebulous ▷ *nf* (*Astronomie*) nebula

nébuliser [nebylize] *vt* (*liquide*) to spray

nébulosité [nebylozite] *nf* cloud cover; **~ variable** cloudy in places

nécessaire [nesesɛr] *adj* necessary ▷ *nm* necessary; (*sac*) kit; **faire le ~** to do the necessary; **n'emporter que le strict ~** to take only what is strictly necessary; **~ de couture** sewing kit; **~ de toilette** toilet bag; **~ de voyage** overnight bag

nécessairement [nesesɛrmɑ̃] *adv* necessarily

nécessité [nesesite] *nf* necessity; **se trouver dans la ~ de faire qch** to find it necessary to do sth; **par ~** out of necessity

nécessiter [nesesite] *vt* to require

nécessiteux, -euse [nesesitø, -øz] *adj* needy

nec plus ultra [nɛkplysyltra] *nm*: **le ~ de** the last word in

nécrologie [nekrɔlɔʒi] *nf* obituary

nécrologique [nekrɔlɔʒik] *adj*: **article ~** obituary; **rubrique ~** obituary column

nécromancie [nekrɔmɑ̃si] *nf* necromancy

nécrose [nekroz] *nf* necrosis

nectar [nɛktar] *nm* nectar

nectarine [nɛktarin] *nf* nectarine

néerlandais, e [neɛrlɑ̃dɛ, -ɛz] *adj* Dutch, of the Netherlands ▷ *nm* (*Ling*) Dutch ▷ *nm/f*: **Néerlandais, e** Dutchman/woman; **les N~** the Dutch

nef [nɛf] *nf* (*d'église*) nave

néfaste [nefast(ə)] *adj* baneful; ill-fated

négatif, -ive [negatif, iv] *adj* negative ▷ *nm* (*Photo*) negative

négation [negasjɔ̃] *nf* denial; (*Ling*) negation

négativement [negativmɑ̃] *adv*: **répondre ~** to give a negative response

négligé, e [negliʒe] *adj* (*en désordre*) slovenly ▷ *nm* (*tenue*) negligee

négligeable [negliʒabl(ə)] *adj* insignificant,

negligible

négligemment [negliʒamɑ̃] *adv* carelessly

négligence [negliʒɑ̃s] *nf* carelessness *no pl*; (*faute*) careless omission

négligent, e [negliʒɑ̃, -ɑ̃t] *adj* careless; (*Jur etc*) negligent

négliger [negliʒe] *vt* (*épouse, jardin*) to neglect; (*tenue*) to be careless about; (*avis, précautions*) to disregard, overlook; ~ **de faire** to fail to do, not bother to do; **se négliger** to neglect o.s

négoce [negɔs] *nm* trade

négociable [negɔsjabl(ə)] *adj* negotiable

négociant [negɔsjɑ̃] *nm* merchant

négociateur [negɔsjatœʀ] *nm* negotiator

négociation [negɔsjasjɔ̃] *nf* negotiation; **~s collectives** collective bargaining *sg*

négocier [negɔsje] *vi, vt* to negotiate

nègre [nɛgʀ(ə)] *nm* (*péj*) Negro; (*péj: écrivain*) ghost writer ▷ *adj* (*péj*) Negro

négresse [negʀɛs] *nf* (*péj*) Negress

négrier [negʀije] *nm* (*fig*) slave driver

neige [nɛʒ] *nf* snow; **battre les œufs en ~** (*Culin*) to whip *ou* beat the egg whites until stiff; ~ **carbonique** dry ice; ~ **fondue** (*par terre*) slush; (*qui tombe*) sleet; ~ **poudreuse** powdery snow

neiger [neʒe] *vi* to snow

neigeux, -euse [nɛʒø, -øz] *adj* snowy, snow-covered

nénuphar [nenyfaʀ] *nm* water-lily

néo-calédonien, ne [neɔkaledɔnjɛ̃, -ɛn] *adj* New Caledonian ▷ *nm/f*: **Néo-calédonien, ne** native of New Caledonia

néocapitalisme [neokapitalism(ə)] *nm* neocapitalism

néo-colonialisme [neokɔlɔnjalism(ə)] *nm* neocolonialism

néologisme [neɔlɔʒism(ə)] *nm* neologism

néon [neɔ̃] *nm* neon

néo-natal, e [neɔnatal] *adj* neonatal

néophyte [neɔfit] *nm/f* novice

néo-zélandais, e [neozelɑ̃dɛ, -ɛz] *adj* New Zealand *cpd* ▷ *nm/f*: **Néo-zélandais, e** New Zealander

Népal [nepal] *nm*: **le ~** Nepal

népalais, e [nepalɛ, -ɛz] *adj* Nepalese, Nepali ▷ *nm* (*Ling*) Nepalese, Nepali ▷ *nm/f*: **Népalais, e** Nepalese, Nepali

néphrétique [nefʀetik] *adj* (*Méd: colique*) nephritic

néphrite [nefʀit] *nf* (*Méd*) nephritis

népotisme [nepɔtism(ə)] *nm* nepotism

nerf [nɛʀ] *nm* nerve; (*fig*) spirit; (: *forces*) stamina; **nerfs** *nmpl* nerves; **être** *ou* **vivre sur les ~s** to live on one's nerves; **être à bout de ~s** to be at the end of one's tether; **passer ses ~s sur qn** to take it out on sb

nerveusement [nɛʀvøzmɑ̃] *adv* nervously

nerveux, -euse [nɛʀvø, -øz] *adj* nervous; (*cheval*) highly-strung; (*voiture*) nippy, responsive; (*tendineux*) sinewy

nervosité [nɛʀvozite] *nf* nervousness; (*émotivité*) excitability

nervure [nɛʀvyʀ] *nf* (*de feuille*) vein; (*Archit, Tech*) rib

n'est-ce pas [nɛspa] *adv* isn't it?, won't you? *etc* (*selon le verbe qui précède*); **c'est bon, n'est-ce pas?** it's good, isn't it?; **il a peur, n'est-ce pas?** he's afraid, isn't he?; **n'est-ce pas que c'est bon?** don't you think it's good?; **lui, n'est-ce pas, il peut se le permettre** he, of course, can afford to do that, can't he?

net, nette [nɛt] *adj* (*sans équivoque, distinct*) clear; (*photo*) sharp; (*évident*) definite; (*propre*) neat, clean; (*Comm: prix, salaire, poids*) net ▷ *adv* (*refuser*) flatly ▷ *nm*: **mettre au ~** to copy out; **s'arrêter ~** to stop dead; **la lame a cassé ~** the blade snapped clean through; **faire place nette** to make a clean sweep; **~ d'impôt** tax free

Net [nɛt] *nm* (*Internet*): **le ~** the Net

netiquette [nɛtikɛt] *nf* netiquette

nettement [nɛtmɑ̃] *adv* (*distinctement*) clearly; (*évidemment*) definitely; (*avec comparatif, superlatif*): **~ mieux** definitely *ou* clearly better

netteté [nɛtte] *nf* clearness

nettoie *etc* [nɛtwa] *vb voir* **nettoyer**

nettoiement [netwamɑ̃] *nm* (*Admin*) cleaning; **service du ~** refuse collection

nettoierai *etc* [nɛtwaʀe] *vb voir* **nettoyer**

nettoyage [nɛtwajaʒ] *nm* cleaning; **~ à sec** dry cleaning

nettoyant [nɛtwajɑ̃] *nm* (*produit*) cleaning agent

nettoyer [nɛtwaje] *vt* to clean; (*fig*) to clean out

neuf¹ [nœf] *num* nine

neuf², neuve [nœf, nœv] *adj* new ▷ *nm*: **repeindre à ~** to redecorate; **remettre à ~** to do up (as good as new), refurbish; **n'acheter que du ~** to buy everything new; **quoi de ~?** what's new?

neurasthénique [nøʀastenik] *adj* neurasthenic

neurochirurgie [nøʀoʃiʀyʀʒi] *nf* neurosurgery

neurochirurgien [nøʀoʃiʀyʀʒjɛ̃] *nm* neurosurgeon

neuroleptique [nøʀɔlɛptik] *adj* neuroleptic

neurologie [nøʀɔlɔʒi] *nf* neurology

neurologique [nøʀɔlɔʒik] *adj* neurological

neurologue [nøʀɔlɔg] *nm/f* neurologist

neurone [nøʀɔn] *nm* neuron(e)

neuropsychiatre [nøʀopsikjatʀ(ə)] *nm/f* neuropsychiatrist

neutralisation [nøtʀalizasjɔ̃] *nf* neutralization

neutraliser [nøtʀalize] *vt* to neutralize

neutralisme [nøtʀalism(ə)] *nm* neutralism

neutralité [nøtʀalite] *nf* neutrality

neutre [nøtʀ(ə)] *adj, nm* (*Ling*) neutral

neutron [nøtʀɔ̃] *nm* neutron

neuve [nœv] *adj f voir* **neuf**

neuvième [nœvjɛm] *num* ninth

neveu, x [nəvø] *nm* nephew

névralgie [nevʀalʒi] *nf* neuralgia

névralgique [nevʀalʒik] *adj* (*fig: sensible*) sensitive; **centre ~** nerve centre

névrite [nevʀit] *nf* neuritis

névrose [nevʀoz] *nf* neurosis

névrosé, e [nevʀoze] *adj, nm/f* neurotic

névrotique [nevʀɔtik] *adj* neurotic

n

New York [njujɔʀk] *n* New York
new-yorkais, e [njujɔʀkɛ, -ɛz] *adj* of *ou* from
New York, New York *cpd* ▷ *nm/f*: **New-Yorkais, e**
New Yorker
nez [ne] *nm* nose; **rire au ~ de qn** to laugh in
sb's face; **avoir du ~** to have flair; **avoir le ~ fin**
to have foresight; **~ à ~ avec** face to face with; **à
vue de ~** roughly
NF *sigle mpl* = **nouveaux francs** ▷ *sigle f* (*Industrie*:
= *norme française*) industrial standard
ni [ni] *conj*: **ni l'un ni l'autre ne sont** *ou* **n'est**
neither one nor the other is; **il n'a rien dit ni**
fait he hasn't said or done anything
Niagara [njagaʀa] *nm*: **les chutes du ~** the
Niagara Falls
niais, e [njɛ, -ɛz] *adj* silly, thick
niaiserie [njɛzʀi] *nf* gullibility; (*action, propos,*
futilité) silliness
Nicaragua [nikaʀagwa] *nm*: **le ~** Nicaragua
nicaraguayen, ne [nikaʀagwajɛ̃, -ɛn] *adj*
Nicaraguan ▷ *nm/f*: **Nicaraguayen, ne**
Nicaraguan
Nice [nis] *n* Nice
niche [niʃ] *nf* (*du chien*) kennel; (*de mur*) recess,
niche; (*farce*) trick
nichée [niʃe] *nf* brood, nest
nicher [niʃe] *vi* to nest; **se ~ dans** (*personne: se*
blottir) to snuggle into; (: *se cacher*) to hide in;
(*objet*) to lodge itself in
nichon [niʃɔ̃] *nm* (*fam*) boob, tit
nickel [nikɛl] *nm* nickel
niçois, e [niswa, -waz] *adj* of *ou* from Nice;
(*Culin*) Nicoise
nicotine [nikɔtin] *nf* nicotine
nid [ni] *nm* nest; (*fig: repaire etc*) den, lair; **~**
d'abeilles (*Couture, Textile*) honeycomb stitch; **~**
de poule pothole
nièce [njɛs] *nf* niece
nième [ɛnjɛm] *adj*: **la ~ fois** the nth *ou*
umpteenth time
nier [nje] *vt* to deny
nigaud, e [nigo, -od] *nm/f* booby, fool
Niger [niʒɛʀ] *nm*: **le ~** Niger; (*fleuve*) the Niger
Nigéria [niʒeʀja] *nm ou f* Nigeria
nigérian, e [niʒeʀjɑ̃, -an] *adj* Nigerian ▷ *nm/f*:
Nigérian, e Nigerian
nigérien, ne [niʒeʀjɛ̃, -ɛn] *adj* of *ou* from Niger
night-club [najtklœb] *nm* nightclub
nihilisme [niilism(ə)] *nm* nihilism
nihiliste [niilist(ə)] *adj* nihilist, nihilistic
Nil [nil] *nm*: **le ~** the Nile
n'importe [nɛ̃pɔʀt(ə)] *adv*: **n'importe!** no
matter!; **n'importe qui/quoi/où** anybody/
anything/anywhere; **n'importe quoi!** (*fam*:
désapprobation) what rubbish!; **n'importe**
quand any time; **n'importe quel/quelle** any;
n'importe lequel/laquelle any (one);
n'importe comment (*sans soin*) carelessly;
n'importe comment, il part ce soir he's
leaving tonight in any case
nippes [nip] *nfpl* (*fam*) togs
nippon, e *ou* **ne** [nipɔ̃, -ɔn] *adj* Japanese

nique [nik] *nf*: **faire la ~ à** to thumb one's nose
at (*fig*)
nitouche [nituʃ] *nf* (*péj*): **c'est une sainte ~** she
looks as if butter wouldn't melt in her mouth
nitrate [nitʀat] *nm* nitrate
nitrique [nitʀik] *adj*: **acide ~** nitric acid
nitroglycérine [nitʀogliseʀin] *nf*
nitroglycerin(e)
niveau, x [nivo] *nm* level; (*des élèves, études*)
standard; **au ~ de** at the level of; (*personne*) on a
level with; **de ~ (avec)** level (with); **le ~ de la**
mer sea level; **~ (à bulle)** spirit level; **~ (d'eau)**
water level; **~ de vie** standard of living
niveler [nivle] *vt* to level
niveleuse [nivløz] *nf* (*Tech*) grader
nivellement [nivɛlmɑ̃] *nm* levelling
nivernais, e [nivɛʀnɛ, -ɛz] *adj* of *ou* from Nevers
(and region) ▷ *nm/f*: **Nivernais, e** inhabitant *ou*
native of Nevers (and region)
NL *sigle f* = **nouvelle lune**
NN *abr* (= *nouvelle norme*) revised standard of hotel
classification
n° *abr* (*numéro*) no
nobiliaire [nɔbiljɛʀ] *adj f voir* **particule**
noble [nɔbl(ə)] *adj* noble; (*de qualité: métal etc*)
precious ▷ *nm/f* noble(man/-woman)
noblesse [nɔblɛs] *nf* (*classe sociale*) nobility;
(*d'une action etc*) nobleness
noce [nɔs] *nf* wedding; (*gens*) wedding party (*ou*
guests *pl*); **il l'a épousée en secondes ~s** she
was his second wife; **faire la ~** (*fam*) to go on a
binge; **~s d'or/d'argent/de diamant** golden/
silver/diamond wedding
noceur [nɔsœʀ] *nm* (*fam*): **c'est un sacré ~** he's
a real party animal
nocif, -ive [nɔsif, -iv] *adj* harmful, noxious
noctambule [nɔktɑ̃byl] *nm* night-bird
nocturne [nɔktyʀn(ə)] *adj* nocturnal ▷ *nf* (*Sport*)
floodlit fixture; (*d'un magasin*) late opening
Noël [nɔɛl] *nm* Christmas; **la (fête de) ~**
Christmas time
nœud [nø] *nm* (*de corde, du bois, Navig*) knot;
(*ruban*) bow; (*fig: liens*) bond, tie; (: *d'une question*)
crux; (*Théât etc*): **le ~ de l'action** the web of
events; **~ coulant** noose; **~ gordien** Gordian
knot; **~ papillon** bow tie
noie *etc* [nwa] *vb voir* **noyer**
noir, e [nwaʀ] *adj* black; (*obscur, sombre*) dark
▷ *nm/f* black man/woman ▷ *nm*: **dans le ~** in
the dark ▷ *nf* (*Mus*) crotchet (*Brit*), quarter note
(*US*); **il fait ~** it is dark; **au ~** *adv* (*acheter, vendre*)
on the black market; **travail au ~**
moonlighting
noirâtre [nwaʀatʀ(ə)] *adj* (*teinte*) blackish
noirceur [nwaʀsœʀ] *nf* blackness; darkness
noircir [nwaʀsiʀ] *vt, vi* to blacken
noise [nwaz] *nf*: **chercher ~ à** to try and pick a
quarrel with
noisetier [nwaztje] *nm* hazel (tree)
noisette [nwazɛt] *nf* hazelnut; (*morceau: de*
beurre etc) small knob ▷ *adj* (*yeux*) hazel
noix [nwa] *nf* walnut; (*fam*) twit; (*Culin*): **une ~**

de beurre a knob of butter; **à la ~** *(fam)* worthless; **~ de cajou** cashew nut; **~ de coco** coconut; **~ muscade** nutmeg; **~ de veau** *(Culin)* round fillet of veal

nom [nɔ̃] *nm* name; *(Ling)* noun; **connaître qn de ~** to know sb by name; **au ~ de** in the name of; **~ d'une pipe** *ou* **d'un chien!** *(fam)* for goodness' sake!; **~ de Dieu!** *(fam!)* bloody hell! *(Brit)*, my God!; **~ commun/propre** common/proper noun; **~ composé** *(Ling)* compound noun; **~ déposé** trade name; **~ d'emprunt** assumed name; **~ de famille** surname; **~ de fichier** file name; **~ de jeune fille** maiden name

nomade [nɔmad] *adj* nomadic ▷ *nm/f* nomad

nombre [nɔ̃bʀ(ə)] *nm* number; **venir en ~** to come in large numbers; **depuis ~ d'années** for many years; **ils sont au ~ de trois** there are three of them; **au ~ de mes amis** among my friends; **sans ~** countless; **(bon) ~ de** *(beaucoup, plusieurs)* a (large) number of; **~ premier/entier** prime/whole number

nombreux, -euse [nɔ̃bʀø, -øz] *adj* many, numerous; *(avec nom sg: foule etc)* large; **peu ~** few; small; **de ~ cas** many cases

nombril [nɔ̃bʀi] *nm* navel

nomenclature [nɔmɑ̃klatyʀ] *nf* wordlist; list of items

nominal, e, -aux [nɔminal, -o] *adj* nominal; *(appel, liste)* of names

nominatif, -ive [nɔminatif, -iv] *nm* *(Ling)* nominative ▷ *adj*: **liste nominative** list of names; **carte nominative** calling card; **titre ~** registered name

nomination [nɔminasjɔ̃] *nf* nomination

nommément [nɔmemɑ̃] *adv* *(désigner)* by name

nommer [nɔme] *vt* *(baptiser)* to name, give a name to; *(qualifier)* to call; *(mentionner)* to name, give the name of; *(élire)* to appoint, nominate; **se nommer: il se nomme Pascal** his name's Pascal, he's called Pascal

non [nɔ̃] *adv* *(réponse)* no; *(suivi d'un adjectif, adverbe)* not; **Paul est venu, ~?** Paul came, didn't he?; **répondre** *ou* **dire que ~** to say no; **~ pas que** not that; **~ plus: moi ~ plus** neither do I, I don't either; **je préférerais que ~** I would prefer not; **il se trouve que ~** perhaps not; **je pense que ~** I don't think so; **~ mais!** well really!; **~ mais des fois!** you must be joking!; **~ alcoolisé** non-alcoholic; **~ loin/seulement** not far/only

nonagénaire [nɔnaʒenɛʀ] *nm/f* nonagenarian

non-agression [nɔnagʀesjɔ̃] *nf*: **pacte de ~** non-aggression pact

nonante [nɔnɑ̃t] *num* *(Belgique, Suisse)* ninety

non-assistance [nɔnasistɑ̃s] *nf* *(Jur)*: **~ à personne en danger** failure to render assistance to a person in danger

nonce [nɔ̃s] *nm* *(Rel)* nuncio

nonchalamment [nɔ̃ʃalamɑ̃] *adv* nonchalantly

nonchalance [nɔ̃ʃalɑ̃s] *nf* nonchalance, casualness

nonchalant, e [nɔ̃ʃalɑ̃, -ɑ̃t] *adj* nonchalant, casual

non-conformisme [nɔ̃kɔ̃fɔʀmism(ə)] *nm* nonconformism

non-conformiste [nɔ̃kɔ̃fɔʀmist(ə)] *adj, nm/f* non-conformist

non-conformité [nɔ̃kɔ̃fɔʀmite] *nf* nonconformity

non-croyant, e [nɔ̃kʀwajɑ̃, -ɑ̃t] *nm/f* *(Rel)* non-believer

non-engagé, e [nɔ̃nɑ̃gaʒe] *adj* non-aligned

non-fumeur [nɔ̃fymœʀ] *nm* non-smoker

non-ingérence [nɔnɛ̃ʒeʀɑ̃s] *nf* non-interference

non-initié, e [nɔ̃ninisje] *nm/f* lay person; **les ~s** the uninitiated

non-inscrit, e [nɔnɛ̃skʀi, -it] *nm/f* *(Pol: député)* independent

non-intervention [nɔnɛ̃tɛʀvɑ̃sjɔ̃] *nf* non-intervention

non-lieu [nɔ̃ljø] *nm*: **il y a eu ~** the case was dismissed

nonne [nɔn] *nf* nun

nonobstant [nɔnɔpstɑ̃] *prép* notwithstanding

non-paiement [nɔ̃pɛmɑ̃] *nm* non-payment

non-prolifération [nɔ̃pʀɔlifeʀasjɔ̃] *nf* non-proliferation

non-résident [nɔ̃residɑ̃] *nm* *(Écon)* non-resident

non-retour [nɔ̃ʀətuʀ] *nm*: **point de ~** point of no return

non-sens [nɔ̃sɑ̃s] *nm* absurdity

non-spécialiste [nɔ̃spesjalist(ə)] *nm/f* non-specialist

non-stop [nɔnstɔp] *adj inv* nonstop

non-syndiqué, e [nɔ̃sɛ̃dike] *nm/f* non-union member

non-violence [nɔ̃vjɔlɑ̃s] *nf* nonviolence

non-violent, e [nɔ̃vjɔlɑ̃, -ɑ̃t] *adj* non-violent

nord [nɔʀ] *nm* North ▷ *adj* northern; north; **au ~** *(situation)* in the north; *(direction)* to the north; **au ~ de** north of, to the north of; **perdre le ~** to lose one's way *(fig)*

nord-africain, e [nɔʀafʀikɛ̃, -ɛn] *adj* North-African ▷ *nm/f*: **Nord-Africain, e** North African

nord-américain, e [nɔʀamerikɛ̃, -ɛn] *adj* North American ▷ *nm/f*: **Nord-Américain, e** North American

nord-coréen, ne [nɔʀkɔʀeɛ̃, -ɛn] *adj* North Korean ▷ *nm/f*: **Nord-Coréen, ne** North Korean

nord-est [nɔʀɛst] *nm* North-East

nordique [nɔʀdik] *adj* *(pays, race)* Nordic; *(langues)* Scandinavian, Nordic ▷ *nm/f*: **Nordique** Scandinavian

nord-ouest [nɔʀwɛst] *nm* North-West

nord-vietnamien, ne [nɔʀvjɛtnamjɛ̃, -ɛn] *adj* North Vietnamese ▷ *nm/f*: **Nord-Vietnamien, ne** North Vietnamese

normal, e, -aux [nɔʀmal, -o] *adj* normal ▷ *nf*: **la ~e** the norm, the average

normalement [nɔʀmalmɑ̃] *adv* *(en général)* normally; *(comme prévu)*: **~, il le fera demain** he should be doing it tomorrow, he's supposed to do it tomorrow

normalien, ne [nɔʁmaljɛ̃, -ɛn] *nm/f student of École normale supérieure*

normalisation [nɔʁmalizasjɔ̃] *nf* standardization; normalization

normaliser [nɔʁmalize] *vt* (*Comm, Tech*) to standardize; (*Pol*) to normalize

normand, e [nɔʁmɑ̃, -ɑ̃d] *adj* (*de Normandie*) Norman ▷ *nm/f*: **Normand, e** (*de Normandie*) Norman

Normandie [nɔʁmɑ̃di] *nf*: **la** ~ Normandy

norme [nɔʁm(ə)] *nf* norm; (*Tech*) standard

Norvège [nɔʁvɛʒ] *nf*: **la** ~ Norway

norvégien, ne [nɔʁveʒjɛ̃, -ɛn] *adj* Norwegian ▷ *nm* (*Ling*) Norwegian ▷ *nm/f*: **Norvégien, ne** Norwegian

nos [no] *adj poss voir* **notre**

nostalgie [nɔstalʒi] *nf* nostalgia

nostalgique [nɔstalʒik] *adj* nostalgic

notable [nɔtabl(ə)] *adj* notable, noteworthy; (*marqué*) noticeable, marked ▷ *nm* prominent citizen

notablement [nɔtabləmɑ̃] *adv* notably; (*sensiblement*) noticeably

notaire [nɔtɛʁ] *nm* notary; solicitor

notamment [nɔtamɑ̃] *adv* in particular, among others

notariat [nɔtaʁja] *nm* profession of notary (*ou* solicitor)

notarié, e [nɔtaʁje] *adj*: **acte** ~ deed drawn up by a notary (*ou* solicitor)

notation [nɔtasjɔ̃] *nf* notation

note [nɔt] *nf* (*écrite, Mus*) note; (*Scol*) mark (*Brit*), grade; (*facture*) bill; **prendre des** ~s to take notes; **prendre** ~ **de** to note; (*par écrit*) to note, write down; **dans la** ~ exactly right; **forcer la** ~ to exaggerate; **une** ~ **de tristesse/de gaieté** a sad/happy note; ~ **de service** memorandum

noté, e [nɔte] *adj*: **être bien/mal** ~ (*employé etc*) to have a good/bad record

noter [nɔte] *vt* (*écrire*) to write down, note; (*remarquer*) to note, notice; (*Scol, Admin: donner une appréciation*) to mark, give a grade to; **notez bien que ...** (please) note that ...

notice [nɔtis] *nf* summary, short article; (*brochure*): ~ **explicative** explanatory leaflet, instruction booklet

notification [nɔtifikasjɔ̃] *nf* notification

notifier [nɔtifje] *vt*: ~ **qch à qn** to notify sb of sth, notify sth to sb

notion [nosjɔ̃] *nf* notion, idea; **notions** *nfpl* (*rudiments*) rudiments

notoire [nɔtwaʁ] *adj* widely known; (*en mal*) notorious; **le fait est** ~ the fact is common knowledge

notoriété [nɔtɔʁjete] *nf*: **c'est de** ~ **publique** it's common knowledge

notre, nos [nɔtʁ(ə), no] *adj poss* our

nôtre [notʁ(ə)] *adj* ours ▷ *pron*: **le/la** ~ ours; **les** ~**s** ours; (*alliés etc*) our own people; **soyez des** ~**s** join us

nouba [nuba] *nf* (*fam*): **faire la** ~ to live it up

nouer [nwe] *vt* to tie, knot; (*fig: alliance etc*) to strike up; ~ **la conversation** to start a conversation; **se nouer** *vi*: **c'est là où l'intrigue se noue** it's at that point that the strands of the plot come together; **ma gorge se noua** a lump came to my throat

noueux, -euse [nwø, -øz] *adj* gnarled

nougat [nuga] *nm* nougat

nougatine [nugatin] *nf* kind of nougat

nouille [nuj] *nf* (*fam*) noodle (*Brit*), fathead; **nouilles** *nfpl* (*pâtes*) noodles; pasta *sg*

nounou [nunu] *nf* nanny

nounours [nunuʁs] *nm* teddy (bear)

nourri, e [nuʁi] *adj* (*feu etc*) sustained

nourrice [nuʁis] *nf* ≈ baby-minder; (*autrefois*) wet-nurse

nourrir [nuʁiʁ] *vt* to feed; (*fig: espoir*) to harbour, nurse; **logé nourri** with board and lodging; ~ **au sein** to breast-feed; **se** ~ **de légumes** to live on vegetables

nourrissant, e [nuʁisɑ̃, -ɑ̃t] *adj* nourishing, nutritious

nourrisson [nuʁisɔ̃] *nm* (*unweaned*) infant

nourriture [nuʁityʁ] *nf* food

nous [nu] *pron* (*sujet*) we; (*objet*) us

nous-mêmes [numɛm] *pron* ourselves

nouveau, nouvel, -elle, x [nuvo, -ɛl] *adj* new; (*original*) novel ▷ *nm/f* new pupil (*ou* employee) ▷ *nm*: **il y a du** ~ there's something new ▷ *nf* (piece of) news *sg*; (*Littérature*) short story; **nouvelles** *nfpl* (*Presse, TV*) news; **de** ~ **à** ~ again; **je suis sans nouvelles de lui** I haven't heard from him; **Nouvel An** New Year; ~ **venu, nouvelle venue** newcomer; -**x mariés** newlyweds; **nouvelle vague** new wave

nouveau-né, e [nuvone] *nm/f* newborn (baby)

nouveauté [nuvote] *nf* novelty; (*chose nouvelle*) innovation, something new; (*Comm*) new film (*ou* book *ou* creation *etc*)

nouvel *adj m*, **nouvelle** *adj f, nf* [nuvɛl] *voir* **nouveau**

Nouvelle-Angleterre [nuvɛlɑ̃glətɛʁ] *nf*: **la** ~ New England

Nouvelle-Calédonie [nuvɛlkaledɔni] *nf*: **la** ~ New Caledonia

Nouvelle-Écosse [nuvɛlekɔs] *nf*: **la** ~ Nova Scotia

Nouvelle-Galles du Sud [nuvɛlgaldysyd] *nf*: **la** ~ New South Wales

Nouvelle-Guinée [nuvɛlgine] *nf*: **la** ~ New Guinea

nouvellement [nuvɛlmɑ̃] *adv* (*arrivé etc*) recently, newly

Nouvelle-Orléans [nuvɛlɔʁleɑ̃] *nf*: **la** ~ New Orleans

Nouvelles-Hébrides [nuvɛlsebʁid] *nfpl*: **les** ~ the New Hebrides

Nouvelle-Zélande [nuvɛlzelɑ̃d] *nf*: **la** ~ New Zealand

nouvelliste [nuvelist(ə)] *nm/f* editor *ou* writer of short stories

novateur, -trice [nɔvatœʁ, -tʁis] *adj* innovative ▷ *nm/f* innovator

novembre [nɔvɑ̃bʀ(ə)] *nm* November; *see note*; *voir aussi* **juillet**

⬤ **LE 11 NOVEMBRE**

⬤
⬤ *Le 11 novembre* is a public holiday in France
⬤ and commemorates the signing of the
⬤ armistice, near Compiègne, at the end of the
⬤ First World War.

novice [nɔvis] *adj* inexperienced ▷ *nm/f* novice
noviciat [nɔvisja] *nm* (*Rel*) noviciate
noyade [nwajad] *nf* drowning *no pl*
noyau, x [nwajo] *nm* (*de fruit*) stone; (*Bio, Physique*) nucleus; (*Élec, Géo, fig: centre*) core; (*fig: d'artistes etc*) group; (: *de résistants etc*) cell
noyautage [nwajotaʒ] *nm* (*Pol*) infiltration
noyauter [nwajote] *vt* (*Pol*) to infiltrate
noyé, e [nwaje] *nm/f* drowning (*ou* drowned) man/woman ▷ *adj* (*fig: dépassé*) out of one's depth
noyer [nwaje] *nm* walnut (tree); (*bois*) walnut ▷ *vt* to drown; (*fig*) to flood; to submerge; (*Auto: moteur*) to flood; **se noyer** to be drowned, drown; (*suicide*) to drown o.s.; ~ **son chagrin** to drown one's sorrows; ~ **le poisson** to duck the issue
NSP *sigle m* (*Rel*) = **Notre Saint Père**; (*dans les sondages*: = *ne sais pas*) don't know
NT *sigle m* (= *Nouveau Testament*) NT
NU *sigle fpl* (= *Nations unies*) UN
nu, e [ny] *adj* naked; (*membres*) naked, bare; (*chambre, fil, plaine*) bare ▷ *nm* (*Art*) nude; **le nu intégral** total nudity; **se mettre nu** to strip; **mettre à nu** to bare
nuage [nɥaʒ] *nm* cloud; **être dans les ~s** (*distrait*) to have one's head in the clouds; ~ **de lait** drop of milk
nuageux, -euse [nɥaʒø, -øz] *adj* cloudy
nuance [nɥɑ̃s] *nf* (*de couleur, sens*) shade; **il y a une ~ (entre)** there's a slight difference (between); **une ~ de tristesse** a tinge of sadness
nuancé, e [nɥɑ̃se] *adj* (*opinion*) finely-shaded, subtly differing; **être ~ dans ses opinions** to have finely-shaded opinions
nuancer [nɥɑ̃se] *vt* (*pensée, opinion*) to qualify
nubile [nybil] *adj* nubile
nucléaire [nykleɛʀ] *adj* nuclear ▷ *nm* nuclear power
nudisme [nydism(ə)] *nm* nudism
nudiste [nydist(ə)] *adj, nm/f* nudist
nudité [nydite] *nf voir* **nu** nudity, nakedness; bareness
nuée [nɥe] *nf*: **une ~ de** a cloud *ou* host *ou* swarm of
nues [ny] *nfpl*: **tomber des ~** to be taken aback; **porter qn aux ~** to praise sb to the skies
nui [nɥi] *pp de* **nuire**
nuire [nɥiʀ] *vi* to be harmful; ~ **à** to harm, do damage to
nuisance [nɥizɑ̃s] *nf* nuisance; **nuisances** *nfpl* pollution *sg*
nuisible [nɥizibl(ə)] *adj* harmful; (**animal**) ~ pest
nuisis *etc* [nɥizi] *vb voir* **nuire**
nuit [nɥi] *nf* night; **payer sa** ~ to pay for one's overnight accommodation; **il fait** ~ it's dark; **cette** ~ (*hier*) last night; (*aujourd'hui*) tonight; **de** ~ (*vol, service*) night *cpd*; ~ **blanche** sleepless night; ~ **de noces** wedding night; ~ **de Noël** Christmas Eve
nuitamment [nɥitamɑ̃] *adv* by night
nuitées [nɥite] *nfpl* overnight stays, beds occupied (*in statistics*)
nul, nulle [nyl] *adj* (*aucun*) no; (*minime*) nil, non-existent; (*non valable*) null; (*péj*) useless, hopeless ▷ *pron* none, no one; **résultat ~**, **match ~** draw; **nulle part** *adv* nowhere
nullement [nylmɑ̃] *adv* by no means
nullité [nylite] *nf* nullity; (*péj*) hopelessness; (: *personne*) hopeless individual, nonentity
numéraire [nymeʀɛʀ] *nm* cash; metal currency
numéral, e, -aux [nymeʀal, -o] *adj* numeral
numérateur [nymeʀatœʀ] *nm* numerator
numération [nymeʀasjɔ̃] *nf*: ~ **décimale/binaire** decimal/binary notation; ~ **globulaire** blood count
numérique [nymeʀik] *adj* numerical; (*Inform*) digital
numériquement [nymeʀikmɑ̃] *adv* numerically; (*Inform*) digitally
numériser [nymeʀize] *vt* (*Inform*) to digitize
numéro [nymeʀo] *nm* number; (*spectacle*) act, turn; **faire** *ou* **composer un** ~ to dial a number; ~ **d'identification personnel** personal identification number (PIN); ~ **d'immatriculation** *ou* **minéralogique** *ou* **de police** registration (*Brit*) *ou* license (*US*) number; ~ **de téléphone** (tele)phone number; ~ **vert** ≈ Freefone® number (*Brit*), ≈ toll-free number (*US*)
numérotage [nymeʀotaʒ] *nm* numbering
numérotation [nymeʀotasjɔ̃] *nf* numeration
numéroter [nymeʀote] *vt* to number
numerus clausus [nymeʀysklozys] *nm inv* restriction *ou* limitation of numbers
numismate [nymismat] *nm/f* numismatist, coin collector
nu-pieds [nypje] *nm inv* sandal ▷ *adj inv* barefoot
nuptial, e, -aux [nypsjal, -o] *adj* nuptial; wedding *cpd*
nuptialité [nypsjalite] *nf*: **taux de** ~ marriage rate
nuque [nyk] *nf* nape of the neck
nu-tête [nytɛt] *adj inv* bareheaded
nutritif, -ive [nytʀitif, -iv] *adj* nutritional; (*aliment*) nutritious, nourishing
nutrition [nytʀisjɔ̃] *nf* nutrition
nutritionnel, le [nytʀisjɔnɛl] *adj* nutritional
nutritionniste [nytʀisjɔnist(ə)] *nm/f* nutritionist
nylon [nilɔ̃] *nm* nylon
nymphomane [nɛ̃fɔman] *adj, nf* nymphomaniac

n

Oo

O, o [o] *nm inv* O, o ▷ *abr* (= *ouest*) W; **O comme Oscar** O for Oliver (*Brit*) *ou* Oboe (*US*)

OAS *sigle f* (= *Organisation de l'armée secrète*) organization opposed to Algerian independence (1961–63)

oasis [ɔazis] *nf ou m* oasis

obédience [ɔbedjãs] *nf* allegiance

obéir [ɔbeiʀ] *vi* to obey; **~ à** to obey; (*moteur, véhicule*) to respond to

obéissance [ɔbeisãs] *nf* obedience

obéissant, e [ɔbeisã, -ãt] *adj* obedient

obélisque [ɔbelisk(ə)] *nm* obelisk

obèse [ɔbɛz] *adj* obese

obésité [ɔbezite] *nf* obesity

objecter [ɔbʒɛkte] *vt* (*prétexter*) to plead, put forward as an excuse; **~ qch à** (*argument*) to put forward sth against; **~ (à qn) que** to object (to sb) that

objecteur [ɔbʒɛktœʀ] *nm*: **~ de conscience** conscientious objector

objectif, -ive [ɔbʒɛktif, -iv] *adj* objective ▷ *nm* (*Optique, Photo*) lens *sg*; (*Mil: fig*) objective; **~ grand angulaire/à focale variable** wide-angle/zoom lens

objection [ɔbʒɛksjõ] *nf* objection; **~ de conscience** conscientious objection

objectivement [ɔbʒɛktivmã] *adv* objectively

objectivité [ɔbʒɛktivite] *nf* objectivity

objet [ɔbʒɛ] *nm* (*chose*) object; (*d'une discussion, recherche*) subject; **être** *ou* **faire l'~ de** (*discussion*) to be the subject of; (*soins*) to be given *ou* shown; **sans ~** *adj* purposeless; (*sans fondement*) groundless; **~ d'art** objet d'art; **~s personnels** personal items; **~s de toilette** toiletries; **~s trouvés** lost property *sg* (*Brit*), lost-and-found *sg* (*US*); **~s de valeur** valuables

obligataire [ɔbligatɛʀ] *adj* bond *cpd* ▷ *nm/f* bondholder, debenture holder

obligation [ɔbligasjõ] *nf* obligation; (*gén pl: devoir*) duty; (*Comm*) bond, debenture; **sans ~ d'achat** with no obligation (to buy); **être dans l'~ de faire** to be obliged to do; **avoir l'~ de faire** to be under an obligation to do; **~s familiales** family obligations *ou* responsibilities; **~s militaires** military obligations *ou* duties

obligatoire [ɔbligatwaʀ] *adj* compulsory, obligatory

obligatoirement [ɔbligatwaʀmã] *adv* compulsorily; (*fatalement*) necessarily

obligé, e [ɔbliʒe] *adj* (*redevable*): **être très ~ à qn** to be most obliged to sb; (*contraint*): **je suis (bien) ~ (de le faire)** I have to (do it); (*nécessaire: conséquence*) necessary; **c'est ~!** it's inevitable!

obligeamment [ɔbliʒamã] *adv* obligingly

obligeance [ɔbliʒãs] *nf*: **avoir l'~ de** to be kind *ou* good enough to

obligeant, e [ɔbliʒã, -ãt] *adj* obliging; kind

obliger [ɔbliʒe] *vt* (*contraindre*): **~ qn à faire** to force *ou* oblige sb to do; (*Jur: engager*) to bind; (*rendre service à*) to oblige

oblique [ɔblik] *adj* oblique; **regard ~** sidelong glance; **en ~** *adv* diagonally

obliquer [ɔblike] *vi*: **~ vers** to turn off towards

oblitération [ɔbliteʀasjõ] *nf* cancelling *no pl*, cancellation; obstruction

oblitérer [ɔbliteʀe] *vt* (*timbre-poste*) to cancel; (*Méd: canal, vaisseau*) to obstruct

oblong, oblongue [ɔblõ, ɔblõg] *adj* oblong

obnubiler [ɔbnybile] *vt* to obsess

obole [ɔbɔl] *nf* offering

obscène [ɔpsɛn] *adj* obscene

obscénité [ɔpsenite] *nf* obscenity

obscur, e [ɔpskyʀ] *adj* (*sombre*) dark; (*fig: raisons*) obscure; (: *sentiment, malaise*) vague; (: *personne, vie*) humble, lowly

obscurcir [ɔpskyʀsiʀ] *vt* to darken; (*fig*) to obscure; **s'obscurcir** *vi* to grow dark

obscurité [ɔpskyʀite] *nf* darkness; **dans l'~** in the dark, in darkness; (*anonymat, médiocrité*) in obscurity

obsédant, e [ɔpsedã, -ãt] *adj* obsessive

obsédé, e [ɔpsede] *nm/f* fanatic; **~(e) sexuel(le)** sex maniac

obséder [ɔpsede] *vt* to obsess, haunt

obsèques [ɔpsɛk] *nfpl* funeral *sg*

obséquieux, -euse [ɔpsekjø, -øz] *adj* obsequious

observance [ɔpsɛʀvãs] *nf* observance

observateur, -trice [ɔpsɛʀvatœʀ, -tʀis] *adj* observant, perceptive ▷ *nm/f* observer

observation [ɔpsɛʀvasjõ] *nf* observation; (*d'un règlement etc*) observance; (*commentaire*) observation, remark; (*reproche*) reproof; **en ~** (*Méd*) under observation

observatoire [ɔpsɛʀvatwaʀ] *nm* observatory; (*lieu élevé*) observation post, vantage point

observer [ɔpsɛʀve] *vt* (*regarder*) to observe, watch; (*examiner*) to examine; (*scientifiquement, aussi: règlement, jeûne etc*) to observe; (*surveiller*) to watch; (*remarquer*) to observe, notice; **faire ~ qch à qn** (*dire*) to point out sth to sb; **s'observer** *vi* (*se surveiller*) to keep a check on o.s.

obsession [ɔpsesjɔ̃] *nf* obsession; **avoir l'~ de** to have an obsession with

obsessionnel, le [ɔpsesjɔnɛl] *adj* obsessive

obsolescent, e [ɔpsɔlesɑ̃, -ɑ̃t] *adj* obsolescent

obstacle [ɔpstakl(ə)] *nm* obstacle; (*Équitation*) jump, hurdle; **faire ~ à** (*lumière*) to block out; (*projet*) to hinder, put obstacles in the path of; **~s antichars** tank defences

obstétricien, ne [ɔpstetʀisjɛ̃, -ɛn] *nm/f* obstetrician

obstétrique [ɔpstetʀik] *nf* obstetrics *sg*

obstination [ɔpstinasjɔ̃] *nf* obstinacy

obstiné, e [ɔpstine] *adj* obstinate

obstinément [ɔpstinemɑ̃] *adv* obstinately

obstiner [ɔpstine]: **s'obstiner** *vi* to insist, dig one's heels in; **s'~ à faire** to persist (obstinately) in doing; **s'~ sur qch** to keep working at sth, labour away at sth

obstruction [ɔpstʀyksjɔ̃] *nf* obstruction, blockage; (*Sport*) obstruction; **faire de l'~** (*fig*) to be obstructive

obstruer [ɔpstʀye] *vt* to block, obstruct; **s'obstruer** *vi* to become blocked

obtempérer [ɔptɑ̃peʀe] *vi* to obey; **~ à** to obey, comply with

obtenir [ɔptəniʀ] *vt* to obtain, get; (*total*) to arrive at, reach; (*résultat*) to achieve, obtain; **~ de pouvoir faire** to obtain permission to do; **~ qch à qn** to obtain sth for sb; **~ de qn qu'il fasse** to get sb to agree to do(ing)

obtention [ɔptɑ̃sjɔ̃] *nf* obtaining

obtenu, e [ɔpt(ə)ny] *pp de* **obtenir**

obtiendrai [ɔptjɛ̃dʀe], **obtiens** [ɔptjɛ̃], **obtint** *etc* [ɔptɛ̃] *vb voir* **obtenir**

obturateur [ɔptyʀatœʀ] *nm* (*Photo*) shutter; **~ à rideau** focal plane shutter

obturation [ɔptyʀasjɔ̃] *nf* closing (up); **~ (dentaire)** filling; **vitesse d'~** (*Photo*) shutter speed

obturer [ɔptyʀe] *vt* to close (up); (*dent*) to fill

obtus, e [ɔpty, -yz] *adj* obtuse

obus [ɔby] *nm* shell; **~ explosif** high-explosive shell; **~ incendiaire** incendiary device, fire bomb

obvier [ɔbvje]: **~ à** *vt* to obviate

OC *sigle fpl* (= *ondes courtes*) SW

occasion [ɔkazjɔ̃] *nf* (*aubaine, possibilité*) opportunity; (*circonstance*) occasion; (*Comm: article non neuf*) secondhand buy; (: *acquisition avantageuse*) bargain; **à plusieurs ~s** on several occasions; **à la première ~** at the first *ou* earliest opportunity; **avoir l'~ de faire** to have

the opportunity to do; **être l'~ de** to occasion, give rise to; **à l'~** *adv* sometimes, on occasions; (*un jour*) some time; **à l'~ de** on the occasion of; **d'~** *adj, adv* secondhand

occasionnel, le [ɔkazjɔnɛl] *adj* (*fortuit*) chance *cpd*; (*non régulier*) occasional; (: *travail*) casual

occasionnellement [ɔkazjɔnɛlmɑ̃] *adv* occasionally, from time to time

occasionner [ɔkazjɔne] *vt* to cause, bring about; **~ qch à qn** to cause sb sth

occident [ɔksidɑ̃] *nm*: **l'O** the West

occidental, e, -aux [ɔksidɑtal, -o] *adj* western; (*Pol*) Western ▷ *nm/f* Westerner

occidentaliser [ɔksidɑtalize] *vt* (*coutumes, mœurs*) to westernize

occiput [ɔksipyt] *nm* back of the head, occiput

occire [ɔksiʀ] *vt* to slay

occitan, e [ɔksitɑ̃, -an] *adj* of the langue d'oc, of Provençal French

occlusion [ɔklyzjɔ̃] *nf*: **~ intestinale** obstruction of the bowel

occulte [ɔkylt(ə)] *adj* occult, supernatural

occulter [ɔkylte] *vt* (*fig*) to overshadow

occupant, e [ɔkypɑ̃, -ɑ̃t] *adj* occupying ▷ *nm/f* (*d'un appartement*) occupier, occupant; (*d'un véhicule*) occupant ▷ *nm* (*Mil*) occupying forces *pl*; (*Pol: d'usine etc*) occupier

occupation [ɔkypasjɔ̃] *nf* occupation; **l'O~** the Occupation (of France)

occupationnel, le [ɔkypasjɔnɛl] *adj*: **thérapie ~le** occupational therapy

occupé, e [ɔkype] *adj* (*Mil, Pol*) occupied; (*personne: affairé, pris*) busy; (*esprit: absorbé*) occupied; (*place, sièges*) taken; (*toilettes, ligne*) engaged

occuper [ɔkype] *vt* to occupy; (*poste, fonction*) to hold; (*main-d'œuvre*) to employ; **s'~ (à qch)** to occupy o.s ou keep o.s. busy (with sth); **s'~ de** (*être responsable de*) to be in charge of; (*se charger de: affaire*) to take charge of, deal with; (: *clients etc*) to attend to; (*s'intéresser à, pratiquer: politique etc*) to be involved in; **ça occupe trop de place** it takes up too much room

occurrence [ɔkyʀɑ̃s] *nf*: **en l'~** in this case

OCDE *sigle f* (= *Organisation de coopération et de développement économique*) OECD

océan [ɔseɑ̃] *nm* ocean; **l'~ Indien** the Indian Ocean

Océanie [ɔseani] *nf*: **l'O~** Oceania, South Sea Islands

océanique [ɔseanik] *adj* oceanic

océanographe [ɔseanɔgraf] *nm/f* oceanographer

océanographie [ɔseanɔgrafi] *nf* oceanography

océanologie [ɔseanɔlɔʒi] *nf* oceanology

ocelot [ɔslo] *nm* (*Zool*) ocelot; (*fourrure*) ocelot fur

ocre [ɔkʀ(ə)] *adj inv* ochre

octane [ɔktan] *nm* octane

octante [ɔktɑ̃t] *num* (*Belgique, Suisse*) eighty

octave [ɔktav] *nf* octave

octet [ɔktɛ] *nm* byte

octobre [ɔktɔbʀ(ə)] *nm* October; *voir aussi* **juillet**

o

octogénaire [ɔktɔʒenɛʀ] *adj, nm/f* octogenarian
octogonal, e, -aux [ɔktɔgɔnal, -o] *adj* octagonal
octogone [ɔktɔgɔn] *nm* octagon
octroi [ɔktʀwa] *nm* granting
octroyer [ɔktʀwaje] *vt*: ~ **qch à qn** to grant sth to sb, grant sb sth
oculaire [ɔkylɛʀ] *adj* ocular, eye *cpd* ▷ *nm* (*de microscope*) eyepiece
oculiste [ɔkylist(ə)] *nm/f* eye specialist, oculist
ode [ɔd] *nf* ode
odeur [ɔdœʀ] *nf* smell
odieusement [ɔdjøzmɑ̃] *adv* odiously
odieux, -euse [ɔdjø, -øz] *adj* odious, hateful
odontologie [ɔdɔ̃tɔlɔʒi] *nf* odontology
odorant, e [ɔdɔʀɑ̃, -ɑ̃t] *adj* sweet-smelling, fragrant
odorat [ɔdɔʀa] *nm* (sense of) smell; **avoir l'~ fin** to have a keen sense of smell
odoriférant, e [ɔdɔʀiferɑ̃, -ɑ̃t] *adj* sweet-smelling, fragrant
odyssée [ɔdise] *nf* odyssey
OEA *sigle f* (= *Organisation des États américains*) OAS
œcuménique [ekymenik] *adj* ecumenical
œdème [edɛm] *nm* oedema (*Brit*), edema (*US*)
œil [œj] (*pl* **yeux** [jø]) *nm* eye; **avoir un ~ poché** *ou* **au beurre noir** to have a black eye; **à l'~** (*fam*) for free; **à l'~ nu** with the naked eye; **tenir qn à l'~** to keep an eye *ou* a watch on sb; **avoir l'~ à** to keep an eye on; **faire de l'~ à qn** to make eyes at sb; **voir qch d'un bon/mauvais ~** to view sth in a favourable/an unfavourable light; **à l'~ vif** with a lively expression; **à mes/ses yeux** in my/his eyes; **de ses propres yeux** with his own eyes; **fermer les yeux (sur)** (*fig*) to turn a blind eye (to); **les yeux fermés** (*aussi fig*) with one's eyes shut; **fermer l'~** to get a moment's sleep; **~ pour ~, dent pour dent** an eye for an eye, a tooth for a tooth; **pour les beaux yeux de qn** (*fig*) for love of sb; **~ de verre** glass eye
œil-de-bœuf [œjdəbœf] (*pl* **œils-de-bœuf**) *nm* bull's-eye (window)
œillade [œjad] *nf*: **lancer une ~ à qn** to wink at sb, give sb a wink; **faire des ~s à** to make eyes at
œillères [œjɛʀ] *nfpl* blinkers (*Brit*), blinders (*US*); **avoir des ~** (*fig*) to be blinkered, wear blinders
œillet [œjɛ] *nm* (*Bot*) carnation; (*trou*) eyelet
œnologue [enɔlɔg] *nm/f* wine expert
œsophage [ezɔfaʒ] *nm* oesophagus (*Brit*), esophagus (*US*)
œstrogène [ɛstʀɔʒɛn] *adj* oestrogen (*Brit*), estrogen (*US*)
œuf [œf] *nm* egg; **étouffer dans l'~** to nip in the bud; **~ à la coque/dur/mollet** boiled/hard-boiled/soft-boiled egg; **~ au plat/poché** fried/poached egg; **~s brouillés** scrambled eggs; **~ de Pâques** Easter egg; **~ à repriser** darning egg
œuvre [œvʀ(ə)] *nf* (*tâche*) task, undertaking; (*ouvrage achevé, livre, tableau etc*) work; (*ensemble de la production artistique*) works *pl*; (*organisation charitable*) charity ▷ *nm* (*d'un artiste*) works *pl*; (*Constr*): **le gros ~** the shell; **œuvres** *nfpl* (*actes*)

deeds, works; **être/se mettre à l'~** to be at/get (down) to work; **mettre en ~** (*moyens*) to make use of; (*plan, loi, projet etc*) to implement; **~ d'art** work of art; **bonnes ~s** good works *ou* deeds; **~s de bienfaisance** charitable works
OFCE *sigle m* (= *Observatoire français des conjonctures économiques*) economic research institute
offensant, e [ɔfɑ̃sɑ̃, -ɑ̃t] *adj* offensive, insulting
offense [ɔfɑ̃s] *nf* (*affront*) insult; (*Rel: péché*) transgression, trespass
offenser [ɔfɑ̃se] *vt* to offend, hurt; (*principes, Dieu*) to offend against; **s'offenser de** *vi* to take offence (*Brit*) *ou* offense (*US*) at
offensif, -ive [ɔfɑ̃sif, -iv] *adj* (*armes, guerre*) offensive ▷ *nf* offensive; (*fig: du froid, de l'hiver*) onslaught; **passer à l'offensive** to go into the attack *ou* offensive
offert, e [ɔfɛʀ, -ɛʀt(ə)] *pp de* **offrir**
offertoire [ɔfɛʀtwaʀ] *nm* offertory
office [ɔfis] *nm* (*charge*) office; (*agence*) bureau, agency; (*Rel*) service ▷ *nm ou f* (*pièce*) pantry; **faire ~ de** to act as; to do duty as; **d'~** *adv* automatically; **bons ~s** (*Pol*) good offices; **~ du tourisme** tourist bureau
officialiser [ɔfisjalize] *vt* to make official
officiel, le [ɔfisjɛl] *adj, nm/f* official
officiellement [ɔfisjɛlmɑ̃] *adv* officially
officier [ɔfisje] *nm* officer ▷ *vi* (*Rel*) to officiate; **~ de l'état-civil** registrar; **~ ministériel** member of the legal profession; **~ de police** ≈ police officer
officieusement [ɔfisjøzmɑ̃] *adv* unofficially
officieux, -euse [ɔfisjø, -øz] *adj* unofficial
officinal, e, -aux [ɔfisinal, -o] *adj*: **plantes ~es** medicinal plants
officine [ɔfisin] *nf* (*de pharmacie*) dispensary; (*Admin: pharmacie*) pharmacy; (*gén péj: bureau*) agency, office
offrais *etc* [ɔfʀɛ] *vb voir* **offrir**
offrande [ɔfʀɑ̃d] *nf* offering
offrant [ɔfʀɑ̃] *nm*: **au plus ~** to the highest bidder
offre [ɔfʀ(ə)] *vb voir* **offrir** ▷ *nf* offer; (*aux enchères*) bid; (*Admin: soumission*) tender; (*Écon*): **l'~** supply; **~ d'emploi** job advertised; **"~s d'emploi"** "situations vacant"; **~ publique d'achat (OPA)** takeover bid; **~s de service** offer of service
offrir [ɔfʀiʀ] *vt*: **~ (à qn)** to offer (to sb); (*faire cadeau*) to give to (sb); **s'offrir** *vi* (*se présenter: occasion, paysage*) to present itself ▷ *vt* (*se payer: vacances, voiture*) to treat o.s. to; **~ (à qn) de faire qch** to offer to do sth (for sb); **~ à boire à qn** to offer sb a drink; **s'~ à faire qch** to offer *ou* volunteer to do sth; **s'~ comme guide/en otage** to offer one's services as (a) guide/offer o.s. as (a) hostage; **s'~ aux regards** (*personne*) to expose o.s. to the public gaze
offset [ɔfsɛt] *nm* offset (printing)
offusquer [ɔfyske] *vt* to offend; **s'offusquer de** to take offence (*Brit*) *ou* offense (*US*) at, be offended by

ogive [ɔʒiv] *nf* (*Archit*) diagonal rib; (*d'obus, de missile*) nose cone; **voûte en ~** rib vault; **arc en ~** lancet arch; **~ nucléaire** nuclear warhead

OGM *sigle m* GMO

ogre [ɔgʀ(ə)] *nm* ogre

oh [o] *excl* oh!; **oh la la!** oh (dear)!; **pousser des oh! et des ah!** to gasp with admiration

oie [wa] *nf* (*Zool*) goose; **~ blanche** (*fig*) young innocent

oignon [ɔɲɔ̃] *nm* (*Culin*) onion; (*de tulipe etc: bulbe*) bulb; (*Méd*) bunion; **ce ne sont pas tes ~s** (*fam*) that's none of your business

oindre [wɛ̃dʀ(ə)] *vt* to anoint

oiseau, x [wazo] *nm* bird; **~ de proie** bird of prey

oiseau-mouche [wazomuʃ] (*pl* **oiseaux-mouches**) *nm* hummingbird

oiseleur [wazlœʀ] *nm* bird-catcher

oiselier, -ière [wazəlje, -jɛʀ] *nm/f* bird-seller

oisellerie [wazɛlʀi] *nf* bird shop

oiseux, -euse [wazø, -øz] *adj* pointless, idle; (*sans valeur, importance*) trivial

oisif, -ive [wazif, -iv] *adj* idle ▷ *nm/f* (*péj*) man/lady of leisure

oisillon [wazijɔ̃] *nm* little *ou* baby bird

oisiveté [wazivte] *nf* idleness

OIT *sigle f* (= *Organisation internationale du travail*) ILO

OK [okɛ] *excl* OK!, all right!

OL *sigle fpl* (= *ondes longues*) LW

oléagineux, -euse [ɔleaʒinø, -øz] *adj* oleaginous, oil-producing

oléiculture [ɔleikyltyʀ] *nm* olive growing

oléoduc [ɔleodyk] *nm* (oil) pipeline

olfactif, -ive [ɔlfaktif, -iv] *adj* olfactory

olibrius [ɔlibʀijys] *nm* oddball

oligarchie [ɔligaʀʃi] *nf* oligarchy

oligo-élément [ɔligoelemɑ̃] *nm* trace element

oligopole [ɔligɔpɔl] *nm* oligopoly

olivâtre [ɔlivatʀ(ə)] *adj* olive-greenish; (*teint*) sallow

olive [ɔliv] *nf* (*Bot*) olive ▷ *adj inv* olive-green

oliveraie [ɔlivʀɛ] *nf* olive grove

olivier [ɔlivje] *nm* olive (tree); (*bois*) olive (wood)

olographe [ɔlɔgʀaf] *adj*: **testament ~** will written, dated and signed by the testator

OLP *sigle f* (= *Organisation de libération de la Palestine*) PLO

olympiade [ɔlɛ̃pjad] *nf* (*période*) Olympiad; **les ~s** (*jeux*) the Olympiad *sg*

olympien, ne [ɔlɛ̃pjɛ̃, -ɛn] *adj* Olympian, of Olympian aloofness

olympique [ɔlɛ̃pik] *adj* Olympic

OM *sigle fpl* (= *ondes moyennes*) MW

Oman [ɔman] *nm*: **l'~, le sultanat d'~** (the Sultanate of) Oman

ombilical, e, -aux [ɔ̃bilikal, -o] *adj* umbilical

ombrage [ɔ̃bʀaʒ] *nm* (*ombre*) (leafy) shade; (*fig*): **prendre ~ de** to take umbrage at; **faire** *ou* **porter ~ à qn** to offend sb

ombragé, e [ɔ̃bʀaʒe] *adj* shaded, shady

ombrageux, -euse [ɔ̃bʀaʒø, -øz] *adj* (*cheval*) skittish, nervous; (*personne*) touchy, easily offended

ombre [ɔ̃bʀ(ə)] *nf* (*espace non ensoleillé*) shade; (*ombre portée, tache*) shadow; **à l'~** in the shade; (*fam: en prison*) behind bars; **à l'~ de** in the shade of; (*tout près de, fig*) in the shadow of; **tu me fais de l'~** you're in my light; **ça nous donne de l'~** it gives us (some) shade; **il n'y a pas l'~ d'un doute** there's not the shadow of a doubt; **dans l'~** in the shade; **vivre dans l'~** (*fig*) to live in obscurity; **laisser dans l'~** (*fig*) to leave in the dark; **~ à paupières** eye shadow; **~ portée** shadow; **~s chinoises** (*spectacle*) shadow show *sg*

ombrelle [ɔ̃bʀɛl] *nf* parasol, sunshade

ombrer [ɔ̃bʀe] *vt* to shade

OMC *sigle f* (= *organisation mondiale du commerce*) WTO

omelette [ɔmlɛt] *nf* omelette; **~ baveuse** runny omelette; **~ au fromage/au jambon** cheese/ham omelette; **~ aux herbes** omelette with herbs; **~ norvégienne** baked Alaska

omettre [ɔmɛtʀ(ə)] *vt* to omit, leave out; **~ de faire** to fail *ou* omit to do

omis, e [ɔmi, -iz] *pp de* **omettre**

omission [ɔmisjɔ̃] *nf* omission

omnibus [ɔmnibys] *nm* slow *ou* stopping train

omnipotent, e [ɔmnipɔtɑ̃, -ɑ̃t] *adj* omnipotent

omnipraticien, ne [ɔmnipʀatisjɛ̃, -ɛn] *nm/f* (*Méd*) general practitioner

omniprésent, e [ɔmnipʀezɑ̃, -ɑ̃t] *adj* omnipresent

omniscient, e [ɔmnisjɑ̃, -ɑ̃t] *adj* omniscient

omnisports [ɔmnispɔʀ] *adj inv* (*club*) general sports *cpd*; (*salle*) multi-purpose *cpd*; (*terrain*) all-purpose *cpd*

omnium [ɔmnjɔm] *nm* (*Comm*) corporation; (*Cyclisme*) omnium; (*Courses*) open handicap

omnivore [ɔmnivɔʀ] *adj* omnivorous

omoplate [ɔmɔplat] *nf* shoulder blade

OMS *sigle f* (= *Organisation mondiale de la santé*) WHO

 MOT-CLÉ

on [ɔ̃] *pron* **1** (*indéterminé*) you, one; **on peut le faire ainsi** you *ou* one can do it like this, it can be done like this; **on dit que ...** they say that ..., it is said that ..

2 (*quelqu'un*): **on les a attaqués** they were attacked; **on vous demande au téléphone** there's a phone call for you, you're wanted on the phone; **on frappe à la porte** someone's knocking at the door

3 (*nous*) we; **on va y aller demain** we're going tomorrow

4 (*les gens*) they; **autrefois, on croyait ...** they used to believe ..

5: **on ne peut plus** *adv*: **on ne peut plus stupide** as stupid as can be

once [ɔ̃s] *nf*: **une ~ de** an ounce of

oncle [ɔ̃kl(ə)] nm uncle
onction [ɔ̃ksjɔ̃] nf voir **extrême-onction**
onctueux, -euse [ɔ̃ktɥø, -øz] adj creamy,
smooth; (fig) smooth, unctuous
onde [ɔ̃d] nf (Physique) wave; **sur l'~** on the
waters; **sur les ~s** on the radio; **mettre en ~s**
to produce for the radio; **~ de choc** shock wave;
~s courtes (OC) short wave sg; **petites ~s (PO)**,
~s moyennes (OM) medium wave sg; **grandes
~s (GO)**, **~s longues (OL)** long wave sg; **~s
sonores** sound waves
ondée [ɔ̃de] nf shower
on-dit [ɔ̃di] nm inv rumour
ondoyer [ɔ̃dwaje] vi to ripple, wave ▷ vt (Rel) to
baptize (in an emergency)
ondulant, e [ɔ̃dylɑ̃, -ɑ̃t] adj (démarche) swaying;
(ligne) undulating
ondulation [ɔ̃dylasjɔ̃] nf undulation; wave
ondulé, e [ɔ̃dyle] adj undulating; wavy
onduler [ɔ̃dyle] vi to undulate; (cheveux) to wave
onéreux, -euse [ɔnerø, -øz] adj costly; **à titre ~**
in return for payment
ONF sigle m (= Office national des forêts) ≈ Forestry
Commission (Brit), ≈ National Forest Service
(US)
ONG sigle f (= organisation non-gouvernemental) NGO
ongle [ɔ̃gl(ə)] nm (Anat) nail; **manger** ou **ronger
ses ~s** to bite one's nails; **se faire les ~s** to do
one's nails
onglet [ɔ̃glɛ] nm (rainure) (thumbnail) groove;
(bande de papier) tab
onguent [ɔ̃gɑ̃] nm ointment
onirique [ɔnirik] adj dreamlike, dream cpd
onirisme [ɔnirism(ə)] nm dreams pl
onomatopée [ɔnɔmatɔpe] nf onomatopoeia
ont [ɔ̃] vb voir **avoir**
ontarien, ne [ɔ̃tarjɛ̃, -ɛn] adj Ontarian
ONU [ɔny] sigle f (= Organisation des Nations unies)
UN(O)
onusien, ne [ɔnyzjɛ̃, -ɛn] adj of the UN(O), of
the United Nations (Organization)
onyx [ɔniks] nm onyx
onze [ɔ̃z] num eleven
onzième [ɔ̃zjɛm] num eleventh
op [ɔp] nf (opération): **salle d'op** (operating)
theatre
OPA sigle f = **offre publique d'achat**
opacité [ɔpasite] nf opaqueness
opale [ɔpal] nf opal
opalescent, e [ɔpalesɑ̃, -ɑ̃t] adj opalescent
opalin, e [ɔpalɛ̃, -in] adj, nf opaline
opaque [ɔpak] adj (vitre, verre) opaque; (brouillard,
nuit) impenetrable
OPE sigle f (= offre publique d'échange) take-over bid
where bidder offers shares in his company in exchange for
shares in target company
OPEP [ɔpɛp] sigle f (= Organisation des pays
exportateurs de pétrole) OPEC
opéra [ɔpera] nm opera; (édifice) opera house
opérable [ɔperabl(ə)] adj operable
opéra-comique [ɔperakɔmik] (pl **opéras-
comiques**) nm light opera, opéra comique

opérant, e [ɔperɑ̃, -ɑ̃t] adj (mesure) effective
opérateur, -trice [ɔperatœr, -tris] nm/f
operator; **~ (de prise de vues)** cameraman
opération [ɔperasjɔ̃] nf operation; (Comm)
dealing; **salle/table d'~** operating theatre/
table; **~ de sauvetage** rescue operation; **~ à
cœur ouvert** open-heart surgery no pl
opérationnel, le [ɔperasjɔnel] adj operational
opératoire [ɔperatwar] adj (manœuvre, méthode)
operating; (choc etc) post-operative
opéré, e [ɔpere] nm/f post-operative patient
opérer [ɔpere] vt (Méd) to operate on; (faire,
exécuter) to carry out, make ▷ vi (remède: faire effet)
to act, work; (procéder) to proceed; (Méd) to
operate; **s'opérer** vi (avoir lieu) to occur, take
place; **se faire ~** to have an operation; **se faire
~ des amygdales/du cœur** to have one's tonsils
out/have a heart operation
opérette [ɔperɛt] nf operetta, light opera
ophtalmique [ɔftalmik] adj ophthalmic
ophtalmologie [ɔftalmɔlɔʒi] nf ophthalmology
ophtalmologue [ɔftalmɔlɔg] nm/f
ophthalmologist
opiacé, e [ɔpjase] adj opiate
opiner [ɔpine] vi: **~ de la tête** to nod assent ▷ vt:
~ à to consent to
opiniâtre [ɔpinjɑtr(ə)] adj stubborn
opiniâtreté [ɔpinjɑtrəte] nf stubbornness
opinion [ɔpinjɔ̃] nf opinion; **l'~ (publique)**
public opinion; **avoir bonne/mauvaise ~ de** to
have a high/low opinion of
opiomane [ɔpjɔman] nm/f opium addict
opium [ɔpjɔm] nm opium
OPJ sigle m (= officier de police judiciaire) ≈ DC
(= Detective Constable)
opportun, e [ɔpɔrtœ̃, -yn] adj timely,
opportune; **en temps ~** at the appropriate time
opportunément [ɔpɔrtynemɑ̃] adv
opportunely
opportunisme [ɔpɔrtynism(ə)] nm
opportunism
opportuniste [ɔpɔrtynist(ə)] adj, nm/f
opportunist
opportunité [ɔpɔrtynite] nf timeliness,
opportuneness
opposant, e [ɔpozɑ̃, -ɑ̃t] adj opposing ▷ nm/f
opponent
opposé, e [ɔpoze] adj (direction, rive) opposite;
(faction) opposing; (couleurs) contrasting;
(opinions, intérêts) conflicting; (contre): **~ à**
opposed to, against ▷ nm: **l'~** the other ou
opposite side (ou direction); (contraire) the
opposite; **être ~ à** to be opposed to; **à l'~** (fig) on
the other hand; **à l'~ de** on the other ou
opposite side from; (fig) contrary to, unlike
opposer [ɔpoze] vt (meubles, objets) to place
opposite each other; (personnes, armées, équipes) to
oppose; (couleurs, termes, tons) to contrast;
(comparer: livres, avantages) to contrast; **~ qch à**
(comme obstacle, défense) to set sth against; (comme
objection) to put sth forward against; (en
contraste) to set sth opposite; to match sth with;

s'opposer vi (sens réciproque) to conflict; to clash; to face each other; to contrast; **s'~ à** (interdire, empêcher) to oppose; (tenir tête à) to rebel against; **sa religion s'y oppose** it's against his religion; **s'~ à ce que qn fasse** to be opposed to sb's doing

opposition [ɔpozisjɔ̃] nf opposition; **par ~** in contrast; **par ~ à** as opposed to, in contrast with; **entrer en ~ avec** to come into conflict with; **être en ~ avec** (idées, conduite) to be at variance with; **faire ~ à un chèque** to stop a cheque

oppressant, e [ɔpʀesɑ̃, -ɑ̃t] adj oppressive

oppresser [ɔpʀese] vt to oppress; **se sentir oppressé** to feel breathless

oppresseur [ɔpʀesœʀ] nm oppressor

oppressif, -ive [ɔpʀesif, -iv] adj oppressive

oppression [ɔpʀesjɔ̃] nf oppression; (malaise) feeling of suffocation

opprimer [ɔpʀime] vt (asservir: peuple, faibles) to oppress; (étouffer: liberté, opinion) to suppress, stifle; (chaleur etc) to suffocate, oppress

opprobre [ɔpʀɔbʀ(ə)] nm disgrace

opter [ɔpte] vi: **~ pour** to opt for; **~ entre** to choose between

opticien, ne [ɔptisjɛ̃, -ɛn] nm/f optician

optimal, e, -aux [ɔptimal, -o] adj optimal

optimisation [ɔptimizasjɔ̃] nf optimization

optimiser [ɔptimize] vt to optimize

optimisme [ɔptimism(ə)] nm optimism

optimiste [ɔptimist(ə)] adj optimistic ▷ nm/f optimist

optimum [ɔptimɔm] adj, nm optimum

option [ɔpsjɔ̃] nf option; (Auto: supplément) optional extra; **matière à ~** (Scol) optional subject (Brit), elective (US); **prendre une ~ sur** to take (out) an option on; **~ par défaut** (Inform) default (option)

optionnel, le [ɔpsjɔnɛl] adj optional

optique [ɔptik] adj (nerf) optic; (verres) optical ▷ nf (Photo: lentilles etc) optics pl; (science, industrie) optics sg; (fig: manière de voir) perspective

opulence [ɔpylɑ̃s] nf wealth, opulence

opulent, e [ɔpylɑ̃, -ɑ̃t] adj wealthy, opulent; (formes, poitrine) ample, generous

OPV sigle f (= offre publique de vente) public offer of sale

or [ɔʀ] nm gold ▷ conj now, but; **d'or** (fig) golden; **en or** gold cpd; (occasion) golden; **un mari/ enfant en or** a treasure; **une affaire en or** (achat) a real bargain; (commerce) a gold mine; **plaqué or** gold-plated; **or noir** black gold

oracle [ɔʀakl(ə)] nm oracle

orage [ɔʀaʒ] nm (thunder)storm

orageux, -euse [ɔʀaʒø, -øz] adj stormy

oraison [ɔʀɛzɔ̃] nf orison, prayer; **~ funèbre** funeral oration

oral, e, -aux [ɔʀal, -o] adj (déposition, promesse) oral, verbal; (Méd): **par voie ~e** by mouth, orally ▷ nm (Scol) oral

oralement [ɔʀalmɑ̃] adv orally

orange [ɔʀɑ̃ʒ] adj inv, nf orange; **~ sanguine**

blood orange; **~ pressée** freshly-squeezed orange juice

orangé, e [ɔʀɑ̃ʒe] adj orangey, orange-coloured

orangeade [ɔʀɑ̃ʒad] nf orangeade

oranger [ɔʀɑ̃ʒe] nm orange tree

orangeraie [ɔʀɑ̃ʒʀɛ] nf orange grove

orangerie [ɔʀɑ̃ʒʀi] nf orangery

orang-outan, orang-outang [ɔʀɑ̃utɑ̃] nm orang-utan

orateur [ɔʀatœʀ] nm speaker; orator

oratoire [ɔʀatwaʀ] nm (lieu, chapelle) oratory; (au bord du chemin) wayside shrine ▷ adj oratorical

oratorio [ɔʀatɔʀjo] nm oratorio

orbital, e, -aux [ɔʀbital, -o] adj orbital; **station ~e** space station

orbite [ɔʀbit] nf (Anat) (eye-)socket; (Physique) orbit; **mettre sur ~** to put into orbit; (fig) to launch; **dans l'~ de** (fig) within the sphere of influence of

Orcades [ɔʀkad] nfpl: **les ~** the Orkneys, the Orkney Islands

orchestral, e, -aux [ɔʀkɛstʀal, -o] adj orchestral

orchestrateur, -trice [ɔʀkɛstʀatœʀ, -tʀis] nm/f orchestrator

orchestration [ɔʀkɛstʀasjɔ̃] nf orchestration

orchestre [ɔʀkɛstʀ(ə)] nm orchestra; (de jazz, danse) band; (places) stalls pl (Brit), orchestra (US)

orchestrer [ɔʀkɛstʀe] vt (Mus) to orchestrate; (fig) to mount, stage-manage

orchidée [ɔʀkide] nf orchid

ordinaire [ɔʀdinɛʀ] adj ordinary; (coutumier: maladresse etc) usual; (de tous les jours) everyday; (modèle, qualité) standard ▷ nm ordinary; (menus) everyday fare ▷ nf (essence) ≈ two-star (petrol) (Brit), ≈ regular (gas) (US); **d'~** usually, normally; **à l'~** usually, ordinarily

ordinairement [ɔʀdinɛʀmɑ̃] adv ordinarily, usually

ordinal, e, -aux [ɔʀdinal, -o] adj ordinal

ordinateur [ɔʀdinatœʀ] nm computer; **mettre sur ~** to computerize, put on computer; **~ de bureau** desktop computer; **~ individuel** ou **personnel** personal computer; **~ portable** laptop (computer)

ordination [ɔʀdinasjɔ̃] nf ordination

ordonnance [ɔʀdɔnɑ̃s] nf organization; (groupement, disposition) layout; (Méd) prescription; (Jur) order; (Mil) orderly, batman (Brit); **d'~** (Mil) regulation cpd; **officier d'~** aide-de-camp

ordonnateur, -trice [ɔʀdɔnatœʀ, -tʀis] nm/f (d'une cérémonie, fête) organizer; **~ des pompes funèbres** funeral director

ordonné, e [ɔʀdɔne] adj tidy, orderly; (Math) ordered ▷ nf (Math) Y-axis, ordinate

ordonner [ɔʀdɔne] vt (agencer) to organize, arrange; (: meubles, appartement) to lay out, arrange; (donner un ordre): **~ à qn de faire** to order sb to do; (Math) to (arrange in) order; (Rel) to ordain; (Méd) to prescribe; (Jur) to order; **s'ordonner** vi (faits) to organize themselves

ordre [ɔʀdʀ(ə)] *nm* (*gén*) order; (*propreté et soin*) orderliness, tidiness; (*association professionnelle, honorifique*) association; (*Comm*): **à l'~ de** payable to; (*nature*): **d'~ pratique** of a practical nature; **ordres** *nmpl* (*Rel*) holy orders; **avoir de l'~** to be tidy *ou* orderly; **mettre en ~** to tidy (up), put in order; **mettre bon ~ à** to put to rights, sort out; **procéder par ~** to take things one at a time; **être aux ~s de qn/sous les ~s de qn** to be at sb's disposal/under sb's command; **rappeler qn à l'~** to call sb to order; **jusqu'à nouvel ~** until further notice; **dans le même ~ d'idées** in this connection; **par ~ d'entrée en scène** in order of appearance; **un ~ de grandeur** some idea of the size (*ou* amount); **de premier ~** first-rate; **~ de grève** strike call; **~ du jour** (*d'une réunion*) agenda; (*Mil*) order of the day; **à l'~ du jour** on the agenda; (*fig*) topical; (*Mil: citer*) in dispatches; **~ de mission** (*Mil*) orders *pl*; **~ public** law and order; **~ de route** marching orders *pl*

ordure [ɔʀdyʀ] *nf* filth *no pl*; (*propos, écrit*) obscenity, (piece of) filth; **ordures** *nfpl* (*balayures, déchets*) rubbish *sg*, refuse *sg*; **~s ménagères** household refuse

ordurier, -ière [ɔʀdyʀje, -jɛʀ] *adj* lewd, filthy

oreille [ɔʀɛj] *nf* (*Anat*) ear; (*de marmite, tasse*) handle; (*Tech: d'un écrou*) wing; **avoir de l'~** to have a good ear (for music); **avoir l'~ fine** to have good *ou* sharp ears; **l'~ basse** crestfallen, dejected; **se faire tirer l'~** to take a lot of persuading; **dire qch à l'~ de qn** to have a word in sb's ear (about sth)

oreiller [ɔʀeje] *nm* pillow

oreillette [ɔʀɛjɛt] *nf* (*Anat*) auricle

oreillons [ɔʀɛjɔ̃] *nmpl* mumps *sg*

ores [ɔʀ]: **d'~ et déjà** *adv* already

orfèvre [ɔʀfɛvʀ(ə)] *nm* goldsmith; silversmith

orfèvrerie [ɔʀfɛvʀəʀi] *nf* (*art, métier*) goldsmith's (*ou* silversmith's) trade; (*ouvrage*) (silver *ou* gold) plate

orfraie [ɔʀfʀɛ] *nm* white-tailed eagle; **pousser des cris d'~** to yell at the top of one's voice

organe [ɔʀgan] *nm* organ; (*véhicule, instrument*) instrument; (*voix*) voice; (*porte-parole*) representative, mouthpiece; **~s de commande** (*Tech*) controls; **~s de transmission** (*Tech*) transmission system *sg*

organigramme [ɔʀganigʀam] *nm* (*hiérarchique, structure*) organization chart; (*des opérations*) flow chart

organique [ɔʀganik] *adj* organic

organisateur, -trice [ɔʀganizatœʀ, -tʀis] *nm/f* organizer

organisation [ɔʀganizasjɔ̃] *nf* organization; **O~ des Nations unies (ONU)** United Nations (Organization) (UN, UNO); **O~ mondiale de la santé (OMS)** World Health Organization (WHO); **O~ du traité de l'Atlantique Nord (OTAN)** North Atlantic Treaty Organization (NATO)

organisationnel, le [ɔʀganizasjɔnɛl] *adj* organizational

organiser [ɔʀganize] *vt* to organize; (*mettre sur pied: service etc*) to set up; **s'organiser** *vi* to get organized

organisme [ɔʀganism(ə)] *nm* (*Bio*) organism; (*corps humain*) body; (*Admin, Pol etc*) body, organism

organiste [ɔʀganist(ə)] *nm/f* organist

orgasme [ɔʀgasm(ə)] *nm* orgasm, climax

orge [ɔʀʒ(ə)] *nf* barley

orgeat [ɔʀʒa] *nm*: **sirop d'~** barley water

orgelet [ɔʀʒəlɛ] *nm* sty(e)

orgie [ɔʀʒi] *nf* orgy

orgue [ɔʀg(ə)] *nm* organ; **orgues** *nfpl* organ *sg*; **~ de Barbarie** barrel *ou* street organ

orgueil [ɔʀgœj] *nm* pride

orgueilleux, -euse [ɔʀgœjø, -øz] *adj* proud

Orient [ɔʀjɑ̃] *nm*: **l'~** the East, the Orient

orientable [ɔʀjɑ̃tabl(ə)] *adj* (*phare, lampe etc*) adjustable

oriental, e, -aux [ɔʀjɑ̃tal, -o] *adj* oriental, eastern; (*frontière*) eastern ▷ *nm/f*: **Oriental, e** Oriental

orientation [ɔʀjɑ̃tasjɔ̃] *nf* positioning; adjustment; orientation; direction; (*d'une maison etc*) aspect; (*d'un journal*) leanings *pl*; **avoir le sens de l'~** to have a (good) sense of direction; **course d'~** orienteering exercise; **~ professionnelle** careers advice *ou* guidance; (*service*) careers advisory service

orienté, e [ɔʀjɑ̃te] *adj* (*fig: article, journal*) slanted; **bien/mal ~** (*appartement*) well/badly positioned; **~ au sud** facing south, with a southern aspect

orienter [ɔʀjɑ̃te] *vt* (*situer*) to position; (*placer, disposer: pièce mobile*) to adjust, position; (*tourner*) to direct, turn; (*voyageur, touriste, recherches*) to direct; (*fig: élève*) to orientate; **s'orienter** *vi* (*se repérer*) to find one's bearings; **s'~ vers** (*fig*) to turn towards

orienteur, -euse [ɔʀjɑ̃tœʀ, -øz] *nm/f* (*Scol*) careers adviser

orifice [ɔʀifis] *nm* opening, orifice

oriflamme [ɔʀiflam] *nf* banner, standard

origan [ɔʀigɑ̃] *nm* oregano

originaire [ɔʀiʒinɛʀ] *adj* original; **être ~ de** (*pays, lieu*) to be a native of; (*provenir de*) to originate from; to be native to

original, e, -aux [ɔʀiʒinal, -o] *adj* original; (*bizarre*) eccentric ▷ *nm/f* (*fam: excentrique*) eccentric; (: *fantaisiste*) joker ▷ *nm* (*document etc, Art*) original; (*dactylographie*) top copy

originalité [ɔʀiʒinalite] *nf* (*d'un nouveau modèle*) originality *no pl*; (*excentricité, bizarrerie*) eccentricity

origine [ɔʀiʒin] *nf* origin; (*d'un message, appel téléphonique*) source; (*d'une révolution, réussite*) root; **origines** *nfpl* (*d'une personne*) origins; **d'~** of origin; (*pneus etc*) original; (*bureau postal*) dispatching; **d'~ française** of French origin; **dès l'~** at *ou* from the outset; **à l'~** originally; **avoir son ~ dans** to have its origins in, originate in

originel, le [ɔʀiʒinɛl] *adj* original
originellement [ɔʀiʒinɛlmã] *adv* (*à l'origine*)
originally; (*dès l'origine*) from the beginning
oripeaux [ɔʀipo] *nmpl* rags
ORL *sigle f* (= *oto-rhino-laryngologie*) ENT ▷ *sigle m/f*
(= *oto-rhino-laryngologiste*) ENT specialist; **être en**
~ (*malade*) to be in the ENT hospital *ou*
department
orme [ɔʀm(ə)] *nm* elm
orné, e [ɔʀne] *adj* ornate; **~ de** adorned *ou*
decorated with
ornement [ɔʀnəmã] *nm* ornament; (*fig*)
embellishment, adornment; **~s sacerdotaux**
vestments
ornemental, e, -aux [ɔʀnəmãtal, -o] *adj*
ornamental
ornementer [ɔʀnəmãte] *vt* to ornament
orner [ɔʀne] *vt* to decorate, adorn; **~ qch de** to
decorate sth with
ornière [ɔʀnjɛʀ] *nf* rut; (*fig*): **sortir de l'~**
(*routine*) to get out of the rut; (*impasse*) to get out
of a spot
ornithologie [ɔʀnitɔlɔʒi] *nf* ornithology
ornithologue [ɔʀnitɔlɔg] *nm/f* ornithologist; **~**
amateur birdwatcher
orphelin, e [ɔʀfəlɛ̃, -in] *adj* orphan(ed) ▷ *nm/f*
orphan; **~ de père/mère** fatherless/motherless
orphelinat [ɔʀfəlina] *nm* orphanage
ORSEC [ɔʀsɛk] *sigle f* = **Organisation des**
secours; **le plan ~** *disaster contingency plan*
ORSECRAD [ɔʀsɛkʀad] *sigle m* = **ORSEC en cas**
d'accident nucléaire
orteil [ɔʀtɛj] *nm* toe; **gros ~** big toe
ORTF *sigle m* (= *Office de radio-diffusion télévision*
française) (*former*) French broadcasting corporation
orthodontiste [ɔʀtɔdõtist(ə)] *nm/f*
orthodontist
orthodoxe [ɔʀtɔdɔks(ə)] *adj* orthodox
orthodoxie [ɔʀtɔdɔksi] *nf* orthodoxy
orthogénie [ɔʀtɔʒeni] *nf* family planning
orthographe [ɔʀtɔgʀaf] *nf* spelling
orthographier [ɔʀtɔgʀafje] *vt* to spell; **mal**
orthographié misspelt
orthopédie [ɔʀtɔpedi] *nf* orthopaedics *sg* (*Brit*),
orthopedics *sg* (*US*)
orthopédique [ɔʀtɔpedik] *adj* orthopaedic
(*Brit*), orthopedic (*US*)
orthopédiste [ɔʀtɔpedist(ə)] *nm/f* orthopaedic
(*Brit*) *ou* orthopedic (*US*) specialist
orthophonie [ɔʀtɔfɔni] *nf* (*Méd*) speech
therapy; (*Ling*) correct pronunciation
orthophoniste [ɔʀtɔfɔnist(ə)] *nm/f* speech
therapist
ortie [ɔʀti] *nf* (stinging) nettle; **~ blanche**
white dead-nettle
OS *sigle m* = **ouvrier spécialisé**
os [ɔs] *nm* bone; **sans os** (*Boucherie*) off the bone,
boned; **os à moelle** marrowbone
oscillation [ɔsilasjõ] *nf* oscillation; **oscillations**
nfpl (*fig*) fluctuations
osciller [ɔsile] *vi* (*pendule*) to swing; (*au vent etc*)
to rock; (*Tech*) to oscillate; (*fig*): **~ entre** to

waver *ou* fluctuate between
osé, e [oze] *adj* daring, bold
oseille [ozɛj] *nf* sorrel
oser [oze] *vi, vt* to dare; **~ faire** to dare (to) do
osier [ozje] *nm* (*Bot*) willow; **d'~, en ~**
wicker(work) *cpd*
Oslo [ɔslo] *n* Oslo
osmose [ɔsmoz] *nf* osmosis
ossature [ɔsatyʀ] *nf* (*Anat: squelette*) frame,
skeletal structure; (: *du visage*) bone structure;
(*fig*) framework
osselet [ɔslɛ] *nm* (*Anat*) ossicle; **jouer aux ~s** to
play jacks
ossements [ɔsmã] *nmpl* bones
osseux, -euse [ɔsø, -øz] *adj* bony; (*tissu, maladie,*
greffe) bone *cpd*
ossifier [ɔsifje]: **s'ossifier** *vi* to ossify
ossuaire [ɔsɥɛʀ] *nm* ossuary
Ostende [ɔstãd] *n* Ostend
ostensible [ɔstãsibl(ə)] *adj* conspicuous
ostensiblement [ɔstãsibləmã] *adv*
conspicuously
ostensoir [ɔstãswaʀ] *nm* monstrance
ostentation [ɔstãtasjõ] *nf* ostentation; **faire ~**
de to parade, make a display of
ostentatoire [ɔstãtatwaʀ] *adj* ostentatious
ostracisme [ɔstʀasism(ə)] *nm* ostracism;
frapper d'~ to ostracize
ostréicole [ɔstʀeikɔl] *adj* oyster *cpd*
ostréiculture [ɔstʀeikyltyʀ] *nf* oyster-farming
otage [ɔtaʒ] *nm* hostage; **prendre qn comme ~**
to take sb hostage
OTAN [ɔtã] *sigle f* (= *Organisation du traité de*
l'Atlantique Nord) NATO
otarie [ɔtaʀi] *nf* sea-lion
ôter [ote] *vt* to remove; (*soustraire*) to take away;
~ qch à qn to take sth (away) from sb; **~ qch de**
to remove sth from; **six ôté de dix égale**
quatre six from ten equals *ou* is four
otite [ɔtit] *nf* ear infection
oto-rhino [ɔtoʀino(-)], **oto-rhino-**
laryngologiste *nm/f* ear, nose and throat
specialist.
ottomane [ɔtɔman] *nf* ottoman
ou [u] *conj* or; **ou ... ou** either ... or; **ou bien** or
(else)

 MOT-CLÉ

où [u] *pron relatif* **1** (*position, situation*) where, that
(*souvent omis*); **la chambre où il était** the room
(that) he was in, the room where he was; **la**
ville où je l'ai rencontré the town where I met
him; **la pièce d'où il est sorti** the room he
came out of; **le village d'où je viens** the village
I come from; **les villes par où il est passé** the
towns he went through
2 (*temps, état*) that (*souvent omis*); **le jour où il est**
parti the day (that) he left; **au prix où c'est** at
the price it is
▷ *adv* **1** (*interrogation*) where; **où est-il/va-t-il?**
where is he/is he going?; **par où?** which way?;

d'où vient que ...? how come ...?
2 (*position*) where; **je sais où il est** I know
where he is; **où que l'on aille** wherever you go

OUA *sigle f* (= *Organisation de l'unité africaine*) OAU
(= *Organization of African Unity*)

ouais [wɛ] *excl* yeah

ouate [wat] *nf* cotton wool (*Brit*), cotton (*US*);
(*bourre*) padding, wadding; **~ (hydrophile)**
cotton wool (*Brit*), (absorbent) cotton (*US*)

ouaté, e [wate] *adj* cotton-wool; (*doublé*)
padded; (*fig: atmosphère*) cocoon-like; (: *pas, bruit*)
muffled

oubli [ubli] *nm* (*acte*): **l'~ de** forgetting;
(*étourderie*) forgetfulness *no pl*; (*négligence*)
omission, oversight; (*absence de souvenirs*)
oblivion; **~ de soi** self-effacement, self-
negation

oublier [ublije] *vt* (*gén*) to forget; (*ne pas voir:
erreurs etc*) to miss; (*ne pas mettre: virgule, nom*) to
leave out, forget; (*laisser quelque part: chapeau etc*)
to leave behind; **s'oublier** *vi* to forget o.s.;
(*enfant, animal*) to have an accident (*euphemism*); **~
l'heure** to forget (about) the time

oubliettes [ublijɛt] *nfpl* dungeon *sg*; **(jeter) aux
~** (*fig*) (to put) completely out of mind

oublieux, -euse [ublijø, -øz] *adj* forgetful

oued [wɛd] *nm* wadi

ouest [wɛst] *nm* west ▷ *adj inv* west; (*région*)
western; **à l'~** in the west, (to the) west,
westwards; **à l'~ de** (to the) west of; **vent d'~**
westerly wind

ouest-allemand, e [wɛstalmã, -ãd] *adj* West
German

ouf [uf] *excl* phew!

Ouganda [ugãda] *nm*: **l'~** Uganda

ougandais, e [ugãdɛ, -ɛz] *adj* Ugandan

oui [wi] *adv* yes; **répondre (par) ~** to answer
yes; **mais ~, bien sûr** yes, of course; **je pense
que ~** I think so; **pour un ~ ou pour un non** for
no apparent reason

ouï-dire [widir]: **par ~** *adv* by hearsay

ouïe [wi] *nf* hearing; **ouïes** *nfpl* (*de poisson*) gills;
(*de violon*) sound-hole *sg*

ouïr [wir] *vt* to hear; **avoir ouï dire que** to have
heard it said that

ouistiti [wistiti] *nm* marmoset

ouragan [uragã] *nm* hurricane; (*fig*) storm

Oural [ural] *nm*: **l'~** (*fleuve*) the Ural; (*aussi:* **les
monts Oural**) the Urals, the Ural Mountains

ourdir [urdir] *vt* (*complot*) to hatch

ourdou [urdu] *adj inv* Urdu ▷ *nm* (*Ling*) Urdu

ourlé, e [urle] *adj* hemmed; (*fig*) rimmed

ourler [urle] *vt* to hem

ourlet [urlɛ] *nm* hem; (*de l'oreille*) rim; **faire un
~ à** to hem

ours [urs] *nm* bear; **~ brun/blanc** brown/polar
bear; **~ marin** fur seal; **~ mal léché** uncouth
fellow; **~ (en peluche)** teddy (bear)

ourse [urs(ə)] *nf* (*Zool*) she-bear; **la Grande/
Petite O~** the Great/Little Bear, Ursa Major/
Minor

oursin [ursɛ̃] *nm* sea urchin

ourson [ursɔ̃] *nm* (bear-)cub

ouste [ust(ə)] *excl* hop it!

outil [uti] *nm* tool

outillage [utijaʒ] *nm* set of tools; (*d'atelier*)
equipment *no pl*

outiller [utije] *vt* (*ouvrier, usine*) to equip

outrage [utraʒ] *nm* insult; **faire subir les
derniers ~s à** (*femme*) to ravish; **~ aux bonnes
mœurs** (*Jur*) outrage to public decency; **~ à
magistrat** (*Jur*) contempt of court; **~ à la
pudeur** (*Jur*) indecent behaviour *no pl*

outragé, e [utraʒe] *adj* offended; outraged

outrageant, e [utraʒã, -ãt] *adj* offensive

outrager [utraʒe] *vt* to offend gravely; (*fig:
contrevenir à*) to outrage, insult

outrageusement [utraʒøzmã] *adv*
outrageously

outrance [utrãs] *nf* excessiveness *no pl*, excess;
à ~ *adv* excessively, to excess

outrancier, -ière [utrãsje, -jɛr] *adj* extreme

outre [utr(ə)] *nf* goatskin, water skin ▷ *prép*
besides ▷ *adv*: **passer ~** to carry on regardless;
passer ~ à to disregard, take no notice of; **en ~**
besides, moreover; **~ que** apart from the fact
that; **~ mesure** immoderately; unduly

outré, e [utre] *adj* (*flatterie, éloge*) excessive,
exaggerated; (*indigné, scandalisé*) outraged

outre-Atlantique [utratlãtik] *adv* across the
Atlantic

outrecuidance [utrəkɥidãs] *nf*
presumptuousness *no pl*

outre-Manche [utrəmãʃ] *adv* across the
Channel

outremer [utrəmɛr] *adj inv* ultramarine

outre-mer [utrəmɛr] *adv* overseas; **d'~**
overseas

outrepasser [utrəpase] *vt* to go beyond, exceed

outrer [utre] *vt* (*pensée, attitude*) to exaggerate;
(*indigner: personne*) to outrage

outre-Rhin [utrərɛ̃] *adv* across the Rhine, in
Germany

outsider [awtsajdœr] *nm* outsider

ouvert, e [uvɛr, -ɛrt(ə)] *pp de* **ouvrir** ▷ *adj* open;
(*robinet, gaz etc*) on; **à bras ~s** with open arms

ouvertement [uvɛrtəmã] *adv* openly

ouverture [uvɛrtyr] *nf* opening; (*Mus*)
overture; (*Pol*): **l'~** the widening of the political
spectrum; (*Photo*): **~ (du diaphragme)**
aperture; **ouvertures** *nfpl* (*propositions*)
overtures; **~ d'esprit** open-mindedness;
heures d'~ (*Comm*) opening hours; **jours d'~**
(*Comm*) days of opening

ouvrable [uvrabl(ə)] *adj*: **jour ~** working day,
weekday; **heures ~s** business hours

ouvrage [uvraʒ] *nm* (*tâche, de tricot etc, Mil*) work
no pl; (*objet: Couture, Art*) (piece of) work; (*texte,
livre*) work; **panier ou corbeille à ~** work basket;
~ d'art (*Génie Civil*) bridge or tunnel etc

ouvragé, e [uvraʒe] *adj* finely embroidered (*ou*
worked *ou* carved)

ouvrant, e [uvrã, -ãt] *vb voir* **ouvrir** ▷ *adj*: **toit ~**

sunroof

ouvré, e [uvʀe] *adj* finely-worked; **jour ~** working day

ouvre-boîte, ouvre-boîtes [uvʀəbwat] *nm inv* tin (*Brit*) *ou* can opener

ouvre-bouteille, ouvre-bouteilles [uvʀəbutɛj] *nm inv* bottle-opener

ouvreuse [uvʀøz] *nf* usherette

ouvrier, -ière [uvʀije, -jɛʀ] *nm/f* worker ▷ *nf* (*Zool*) worker (bee) ▷ *adj* working-class; (*problèmes, conflit*) industrial, labour *cpd* (*Brit*), labor *cpd* (*US*); (*revendications*) workers'; **classe ouvrière** working class; **~ agricole** farmworker; **~ qualifié** skilled worker; **~ spécialisé (OS)** semiskilled worker; **~ d'usine** factory worker

ouvrir [uvʀiʀ] *vt* (*gén*) to open; (*brèche, passage*) to open up; (*commencer l'exploitation de, créer*) to open (up); (*eau, électricité, chauffage, robinet*) to turn on; (*Méd: abcès*) to open up, cut open ▷ *vi* to open; to open up; (*Cartes*): **~ à trèfle** to open in clubs; **s'ouvrir** *vi* to open; **s'~ à** (*art etc*) to open one's mind to; **s'~ à qn (de qch)** to open one's heart to sb (about sth); **s'~ les veines** to slash *ou* cut one's wrists; **~ sur** to open onto; **~ l'appétit à qn** to whet sb's appetite; **~ des horizons** to open up new horizons; **~ l'esprit** to broaden one's horizons; **~ une session** (*Inform*) to log in

ouvroir [uvʀwaʀ] *nm* workroom, sewing room

ovaire [ɔvɛʀ] *nm* ovary

ovale [ɔval] *adj* oval

ovation [ɔvasjɔ̃] *nf* ovation

ovationner [ɔvasjɔne] *vt*: **~ qn** to give sb an ovation

ovin, e [ɔvɛ̃, -in] *adj* ovine

OVNI [ɔvni] *sigle m* (= objet volant non identifié) UFO

ovoïde [ɔvɔid] *adj* egg-shaped

ovulation [ɔvylasjɔ̃] *nf* (*Physiol*) ovulation

ovule [ɔvyl] *nm* (*Physiol*) ovum; (*Méd*) pessary

oxfordien, ne [ɔksfɔʀdjɛ̃, -ɛn] *adj* Oxonian ▷ *nm/f*: **Oxfordien, ne** Oxonian

oxydable [ɔksidabl(ə)] *adj* liable to rust

oxyde [ɔksid] *nm* oxide; **~ de carbone** carbon monoxide

oxyder [ɔkside]: **s'oxyder** *vi* to become oxidized

oxygéné, e [ɔksiʒene] *adj*: **eau ~e** hydrogen peroxide; **cheveux ~s** bleached hair

oxygène [ɔksiʒɛn] *nm* oxygen; (*fig*): **cure d'~** fresh air cure

ozone [ozɔn] *nm* ozone; **trou dans la couche d'~** hole in the ozone layer

O

Pp

P, p [pe] *nm inv* P, p ▷ *abr* (= *Père*) Fr; (= *page*) p; **P comme Pierre** P for Peter

PA *sigle fpl* = **petites annonces**

PAC *sigle f* (= *Politique agricole commune*) CAP

pacage [pakaʒ] *nm* grazing, pasture

pacemaker [pɛsmɛkœʀ] *nm* pacemaker

pachyderme [paʃidɛʀm(ə)] *nm* pachyderm; elephant

pacificateur, -trice [pasifikatœʀ, -tʀis] *adj* pacificatory

pacification [pasifikɑsjɔ̃] *nf* pacification

pacifier [pasifje] *vt* to pacify

pacifique [pasifik] *adj* (*personne*) peaceable; (*intentions, coexistence*) peaceful ▷ *nm*: **le P~, l'océan P~** the Pacific (Ocean)

pacifiquement [pasifikmɑ̃] *adv* peaceably; peacefully

pacifisme [pasifism(ə)] *nm* pacifism

pacifiste [pasifist(ə)] *nm/f* pacifist

pack [pak] *nm* pack

pacotille [pakɔtij] *nf* (*péj*) cheap goods *pl*; **de ~** cheap

PACS [paks] *sigle m* (= *pacte civil de solidarité*) ≈ civil partnership

pacser [pakse]: **se pacser** *vi* ≈ to form a civil partnership

pacte [pakt(ə)] *nm* pact, treaty

pactiser [paktize] *vi*: **~ avec** to come to terms with

pactole [paktɔl] *nm* gold mine (*fig*)

paddock [padɔk] *nm* paddock

Padoue [padu] *n* Padua

PAF *sigle f* (= *Police de l'air et des frontières*) police authority responsible for civil aviation, border control etc ▷ *sigle m* (= *paysage audiovisuel français*) French broadcasting scene

pagaie [pagɛ] *nf* paddle

pagaille [pagaj] *nf* mess, shambles *sg*; **il y en a en ~** there are loads *ou* heaps of them

paganisme [paganism(ə)] *nm* paganism

pagayer [pageje] *vi* to paddle

page [paʒ] *nf* page; (*passage: d'un roman*) passage ▷ *nm* page (boy); **mettre en ~s** to make up (into pages); **mise en ~** layout; **à la ~** (*fig*) up-to-date; **~ d'accueil** (*Inform*) home page; **~ blanche** blank page; **~ de garde** endpaper; **~ Web** (*Inform*) web page

page-écran [paʒekʀɑ̃] (*pl* **pages-écrans**) *nf* (*Inform*) screen page

pagination [paʒinasjɔ̃] *nf* pagination

paginer [paʒine] *vt* to paginate

pagne [paɲ] *nm* loincloth

pagode [pagɔd] *nf* pagoda

paie [pɛ] *nf* = **paye**

paiement [pɛmɑ̃] *nm* = **payement**

païen, ne [pajɛ̃, -ɛn] *adj, nm/f* pagan, heathen

paillard, e [pajaʀ, -aʀd(ə)] *adj* bawdy

paillasse [pajas] *nf* (*matelas*) straw mattress; (*d'un évier*) draining board

paillasson [pajasɔ̃] *nm* doormat

paille [pɑj] *nf* straw; (*défaut*) flaw; **être sur la ~** to be ruined; **~ de fer** steel wool

paillé, e [pɑje] *adj* with a straw seat

pailleté, e [pajte] *adj* sequined

paillette [pajɛt] *nf* speck, flake; **paillettes** *nfpl* (*décoratives*) sequins, spangles; **lessive en ~s** soapflakes *pl*

pain [pɛ̃] *nm* (*substance*) bread; (*unité*) loaf (of bread); (*morceau*): **~ de cire** *etc* bar of wax *etc*; (*Culin*): **~ de poisson/légumes** fish/vegetable loaf; **petit ~** (bread) roll; **~ bis/complet** brown/wholemeal (*Brit*) *ou* wholewheat (*US*) bread; **~ de campagne** farmhouse bread; **~ d'épice** ≈ gingerbread; **~ grillé** toast; **~ de mie** sandwich loaf; **~ perdu** French toast; **~ de seigle** rye bread; **~ de sucre** sugar loaf

pair, e [pɛʀ] *adj* (*nombre*) even ▷ *nm* peer; **aller de ~ (avec)** to go hand in hand *ou* together (with); **au ~** (*Finance*) at par; **valeur au ~** par value; **jeune fille au ~** au pair

paire [pɛʀ] *nf* pair; **une ~ de lunettes/tenailles** a pair of glasses/pincers; **faire la ~**: **les deux font la ~** they are two of a kind

pais [pɛ] *vb voir* **paître**

paisible [pezibl(ə)] *adj* peaceful, quiet

paisiblement [peziblmɑ̃] *adv* peacefully, quietly

paître [pɛtʀ(ə)] *vi* to graze

paix [pɛ] *nf* peace; (*fig*) peacefulness, peace; **faire la ~ avec** to make peace with; **avoir la ~** to have peace (and quiet)

Pakistan [pakistɑ̃] *nm*: **le ~** Pakistan

pakistanais, e [pakistanɛ, -ɛz] *adj* Pakistani
PAL *sigle m* (= *Phase Alternation Line*) PAL
palabrer [palabʀe] *vi* to argue endlessly
palabres [palabʀ(ə)] *nfpl ou mpl* endless
  discussions
palace [palas] *nm* luxury hotel
palais [palɛ] *nm* palace; (*Anat*) palate; **le P~
  Bourbon** *the seat of the French National Assembly*; **le
  P~ de l'Élysée** the Élysée Palace; **~ des
  expositions** exhibition centre; **le P~ de
  Justice** the Law Courts *pl*
palan [palɑ̃] *nm* hoist
pale [pal] *nf* (*d'hélice*) blade; (*de roue*) paddle
pâle [pal] *adj* pale; (*fig*): **une ~ imitation** a pale
  imitation; **bleu ~** pale blue; **~ de colère** white
  ou pale with anger
palefrenier [palfʀənje] *nm* groom (*for horses*)
paléontologie [paleɔ̃tɔlɔʒi] *nf* paleontology
paléontologiste [paleɔ̃tɔlɔʒist(ə)],
  paléontologue [paleɔ̃tɔlɔg] *nm/f*
  paleontologist
Palerme [palɛʀm(ə)] *n* Palermo
Palestine [palɛstin] *nf*: **la ~** Palestine
palestinien, ne [palɛstinjɛ̃, -ɛn] *adj* Palestinian
  ▷ *nm/f*: **Palestinien, ne** Palestinian
palet [palɛ] *nm* disc; (*Hockey*) puck
paletot [palto] *nm* (short) coat
palette [palɛt] *nf* palette; (*de produits*) range
palétuvier [paletyvje] *nm* mangrove
pâleur [pɑlœʀ] *nf* paleness
palier [palje] *nm* (*d'escalier*) landing; (*fig*) level,
  plateau; (: *phase stable*) levelling (*Brit*) *ou* leveling
  (*US*) off, new level; (*Tech*) bearing; **nos voisins
  de ~** our neighbo(u)rs across the landing (*Brit*)
  ou the hall (*US*); **en ~** *adv* level; **par ~s** in stages
palière [paljɛʀ] *adj f* landing *cpd*
pâlir [pɑliʀ] *vi* to turn *ou* go pale; (*couleur*) to
  fade; **faire ~ qn** (*de jalousie*) to make sb green
  (with envy)
palissade [palisad] *nf* fence
palissandre [palisɑ̃dʀ(ə)] *nm* rosewood
palliatif [paljatif] *nm* palliative; (*expédient*)
  stopgap measure
pallier [palje] *vt*: **~ à** *vt* to offset, make up for
palmarès [palmaʀɛs] *nm* record (of
  achievements); (*Scol*) prize list; (*Sport*) list of
  winners
palme [palm(ə)] *nf* (*Bot*) palm leaf; (*symbole*)
  palm; (*de plongeur*) flipper; **~s (académiques)**
  decoration for services to education
palmé, e [palme] *adj* (*pattes*) webbed
palmeraie [palməʀɛ] *nf* palm grove
palmier [palmje] *nm* palm tree
palmipède [palmipɛd] *nm* palmiped,
  webfooted bird
palois, e [palwa, -waz] *adj* of *ou* from Pau ▷ *nm/f*:
  Palois, e inhabitant *ou* native of Pau
palombe [palɔ̃b] *nf* woodpigeon, ringdove
pâlot, te [pɑlo, -ɔt] *adj* pale, peaky
palourde [paluʀd(ə)] *nf* clam
palpable [palpabl(ə)] *adj* tangible, palpable
palper [palpe] *vt* to feel, finger

palpitant, e [palpitɑ̃, -ɑ̃t] *adj* thrilling, gripping
palpitation [palpitasjɔ̃] *nf* palpitation
palpiter [palpite] *vi* (*cœur, pouls*) to beat; (: *plus
  fort*) to pound, throb; (*narines, chair*) to quiver
paludisme [palydism(ə)] *nm* malaria
palustre [palystʀ(ə)] *adj* (*coquillage etc*) marsh
  cpd; (*fièvre*) malarial
pâmer [pɑme]: **se pâmer** *vi* to swoon; (*fig*): **se ~
  devant** to go into raptures over
pâmoison [pɑmwazɔ̃] *nf*: **tomber en ~** to
  swoon
pampa [pɑ̃pa] *nf* pampas *pl*
pamphlet [pɑ̃flɛ] *nm* lampoon, satirical tract
pamphlétaire [pɑ̃fletɛʀ] *nm/f* lampoonist
pamplemousse [pɑ̃pləmus] *nm* grapefruit
pan [pɑ̃] *nm* section, piece; (*côté: d'un prisme, d'une
  tour*) side, face ▷ *excl* bang!; **~ de chemise** shirt
  tail; **~ de mur** section of wall
panacée [panase] *nf* panacea
panachage [panaʃaʒ] *nm* blend, mix; (*Pol*) *voting
  for candidates from different parties instead of for the set
  list of one party*
panache [panaʃ] *nm* plume; (*fig*) spirit, panache
panaché, e [panaʃe] *adj*: **œillet ~** variegated
  carnation; **glace ~e** mixed ice cream; **salade ~e**
  mixed salad; **bière ~e** shandy
panais [panɛ] *nm* parsnip
Panama [panama] *nm*: **le ~** Panama
panaméen, ne [panameɛ̃, -ɛn] *adj* Panamanian
  ▷ *nm/f*: **Panaméen, ne** Panamanian
panaris [panaʀi] *nm* whitlow
pancarte [pɑ̃kaʀt(ə)] *nf* sign, notice; (*dans un
  défilé*) placard
pancréas [pɑ̃kʀeas] *nm* pancreas
panda [pɑ̃da] *nm* panda
pandémie [pɑ̃demi] *nf* pandemic
pané, e [pane] *adj* fried in breadcrumbs
panégyrique [paneʒiʀik] *nm*: **faire le ~ de qn**
  to extol sb's merits *ou* virtues
panier [panje] *nm* basket; (*à diapositives*)
  magazine; **mettre au ~** to chuck away; **~ de
  crabes: c'est un ~ de crabes** (*fig*) they're
  constantly at one another's throats; **~ percé**
  (*fig*) spendthrift; **~ à provisions** shopping
  basket; **~ à salade** (*Culin*) salad shaker; (*Police*)
  paddy wagon, police van
panier-repas [panjeʀ(ə)pa] (*pl* **paniers-repas**)
  nm packed lunch
panification [panifikasjɔ̃] *nf* bread-making
panique [panik] *adj* panicky ▷ *nf* panic
paniquer [panike] *vi* to panic
panne [pan] *nf* (*d'un mécanisme, moteur*)
  breakdown; **être/tomber en ~** to have broken
  down/break down; **être en ~ d'essence** *ou* **en ~
  sèche** to have run out of petrol (*Brit*) *ou* gas (*US*);
  mettre en ~ (*Navig*) to bring to; **~ d'électricité**
  ou **de courant** power *ou* electrical failure
panneau, x [pano] *nm* (*écriteau*) sign, notice; (*de
  boiserie, de tapisserie etc*) panel; **tomber dans le ~**
  (*fig*) to walk into the trap; **~ d'affichage** notice
  (*Brit*) *ou* bulletin (*US*) board; **~ électoral** board
  for election poster; **~ indicateur** signpost; **~**

P

publicitaire hoarding (Brit), billboard (US); ~ **de signalisation** roadsign; ~ **solaire** solar panel

panonceau, x [panɔso] nm (de magasin etc) sign; (de médecin etc) plaque

panoplie [panɔpli] nf (jouet) outfit; (d'armes) display; (fig) array

panorama [panɔrama] nm (vue) all-round view, panorama; (peinture) panorama; (fig: étude complète) complete overview

panoramique [panɔramik] adj panoramic; (carrosserie) with panoramic windows ▷ nm (Ciné, TV) panoramic shot

panse [pɑs] nf paunch

pansement [pɑsmɑ] nm dressing, bandage; ~ **adhésif** sticking plaster (Brit), bandaid® (US)

panser [pɑse] vt (plaie) to dress, bandage; (bras) to put a dressing on, bandage; (cheval) to groom

pantacourt [pɑtakur] nm cropped trousers pl

pantalon [pɑtalɔ] nm trousers pl (Brit), pants pl (US), pair of trousers ou pants; ~ **de ski** ski pants pl

pantalonnade [pɑtalɔnad] nf slapstick (comedy)

pantelant, e [pɑtlɑ, -ɑt] adj gasping for breath, panting

panthère [pɑter] nf panther

pantin [pɑte] nm (jouet) jumping jack; (péj: personne) puppet

pantois [pɑtwa] adj m: **rester** ~ to be flabbergasted

pantomime [pɑtɔmim] nf mime; (pièce) mime show; (péj) fuss, carry-on

pantouflard, e [pɑtuflar, -ard(ə)] adj (péj) stay-at-home

pantoufle [pɑtufl(ə)] nf slipper

panure [panyr] nf breadcrumbs pl

PAO sigle f (= publication assistée par ordinateur) DTP

paon [pɑ] nm peacock

papa [papa] nm dad(dy)

papauté [papote] nf papacy

papaye [papaj] nf pawpaw

pape [pap] nm pope

paperasse [papras] nf (péj) bumf no pl, papers pl; forms pl

paperasserie [paprasri] nf (péj) red tape no pl; paperwork no pl

papeterie [papetri] nf (fabrication du papier) paper-making (industry); (usine) paper mill; (magasin) stationer's (shop (Brit)); (articles) stationery

papetier, -ière [paptje, -jer] nm/f paper-maker; stationer

papetier-libraire [paptjelibrer] (pl **papetiers-libraires**) nm bookseller and stationer

papi [papi] nm (fam) granddad

papier [papje] nm paper; (feuille) sheet ou piece of paper; (article) article; (écrit officiel) document; **papiers** nmpl (aussi: **papiers d'identité**) (identity) papers; **sur le** ~ (théoriquement) on paper; **noircir du** ~ to write page after page; ~ **couché/glacé** art/glazed paper; ~

(d')aluminium aluminium (Brit) ou aluminum (US) foil, tinfoil; ~ **d'Arménie** incense paper; ~ **bible** India ou bible paper; ~ **de brouillon** rough ou scrap paper; ~ **bulle** manil(l)a paper; ~ **buvard** blotting paper; ~ **calque** tracing paper; ~ **carbone** carbon paper; ~ **collant** Sellotape® (Brit), Scotch tape® (US), sticky tape; ~ **en continu** continuous stationery; ~ **à dessin** drawing paper; ~ **d'emballage** wrapping paper; ~ **gommé** gummed paper; ~ **hygiénique** toilet paper; ~ **journal** newsprint; (pour emballer) newspaper; ~ **à lettres** writing paper, notepaper; ~ **mâché** papier-mâché; ~ **machine** typing paper; ~ **peint** wallpaper; ~ **pelure** India paper; ~ **à pliage accordéon** fanfold paper; ~ **de soie** tissue paper; ~ **thermique** thermal paper; ~ **de tournesol** litmus paper; ~ **de verre** sandpaper

papier-filtre [papjefiltr(ə)] (pl **papiers-filtres**) nm filter paper

papier-monnaie [papjemɔnɛ] (pl **papiers-monnaies**) nm paper money

papille [papij] nf: ~**s gustatives** taste buds

papillon [papijɔ] nm butterfly; (fam: contravention) (parking) ticket; (Tech: écrou) wing ou butterfly nut; ~ **de nuit** moth

papillonner [papijɔne] vi to flit from one thing (ou person) to another

papillote [papijɔt] nf (pour cheveux) curlpaper; (de gigot) (paper) frill

papilloter [papijɔte] vi (yeux) to blink; (paupières) to flutter; (lumière) to flicker

papotage [papɔtaʒ] nm chitchat

papoter [papɔte] vi to chatter

papou, e [papu] adj Papuan

Papouasie-Nouvelle-Guinée [papwazinuvɛlgine] nf: **la** ~ Papua-New-Guinea

paprika [paprika] nm paprika

papyrus [papirys] nm papyrus

pâque [pak] nf: **la** ~ Passover; voir aussi **Pâques**

paquebot [pakbo] nm liner

pâquerette [pakrɛt] nf daisy

Pâques [pak] nm, nfpl: **faire ses** ~ to do one's Easter duties; **l'île de** ~ Easter Island

paquet [pakɛ] nm packet; (colis) parcel; (ballot) bundle; (dans négociations) package (deal); (fig: tas): ~ **de** pile ou heap of; **paquets** nmpl (bagages) bags; **mettre le** ~ (fam) to give one's all; ~ **de mer** big wave

paquetage [paktaʒ] nm (Mil) kit, pack

paquet-cadeau [pakɛkado] (pl **paquets-cadeaux**) nm gift-wrapped parcel

par [par] prép by; **finir** etc ~ to end etc with; ~ **amour** out of love; **passer** ~ **Lyon/la côte** to go via ou through Lyons/along by the coast; ~ **la fenêtre** (jeter, regarder) out of the window; **trois** ~ **jour/personne** three a ou per day/head; **deux** ~ **deux** two at a time; (marcher etc) in twos; ~ **où?** which way?; ~ **ici** this way; (dans le coin) round here; ~**-ci**, ~**-là** here and there

para [para] nm (parachutiste) para

parabole [parabɔl] nf (Rel) parable; (Géom)

parabola

parabolique [paʀabɔlik] *adj* parabolic;
antenne ~ satellite dish

parachever [paʀaʃve] *vt* to perfect

parachutage [paʀaʃytaʒ] *nm* (*de soldats, vivres*)
parachuting-in; **nous sommes contre le ~
d'un candidat parisien dans notre
circonscription** (*Pol, fig*) we are against a
Parisian candidate being landed on us

parachute [paʀaʃyt] *nm* parachute

parachuter [paʀaʃyte] *vt* (*soldat etc*) to
parachute; (*fig*) to pitchfork; **il a été
parachuté à la tête de l'entreprise** he was
brought in from outside as head of the
company

parachutisme [paʀaʃytism(ə)] *nm* parachuting

parachutiste [paʀaʃytist(ə)] *nm/f* parachutist;
(*Mil*) paratrooper

parade [paʀad] *nf* (*spectacle, défilé*) parade;
(*Escrime, Boxe*) parry; (*ostentation*): **faire ~ de** to
display, show off; (*défense, riposte*): **trouver la ~
à une attaque** to find the answer to an attack;
de ~ *adj* ceremonial; (*superficiel*) superficial,
outward

parader [paʀade] *vi* to swagger (around), show
off

paradis [paʀadi] *nm* heaven, paradise; **P~
terrestre** (*Rel*) Garden of Eden; (*fig*) heaven on
earth

paradisiaque [paʀadizjak] *adj* heavenly, divine

paradoxal, e, -aux [paʀadɔksal, -o] *adj*
paradoxical

paradoxalement [paʀadɔksalmɑ̃] *adv*
paradoxically

paradoxe [paʀadɔks(ə)] *nm* paradox

parafe [paʀaf] *nm*, **parafer** [paʀafe] ▷ *vt* =
paraphe; parapher

paraffine [paʀafin] *nf* paraffin; paraffin wax

paraffiné, e [paʀafine] *adj*: **papier ~** wax(ed)
paper

parafoudre [paʀafudʀ(ə)] *nm* (*Élec*) lightning
conductor

parages [paʀaʒ] *nmpl* (*Navig*) waters; **dans les ~
(de)** in the area *ou* vicinity (of)

paragraphe [paʀagʀaf] *nm* paragraph

Paraguay [paʀagwɛ] *nm*: **le ~** Paraguay

paraguayen, ne [paʀagwajɛ̃, -ɛn] *adj*
Paraguayan ▷ *nm/f*: **Paraguayen, ne**
Paraguayan

paraître [paʀɛtʀ(ə)] *vb copule* to seem, look,
appear ▷ *vi* to appear; (*être visible*) to show;
(*Presse, Édition*) to be published, come out,
appear; (*briller*) to show off; **laisser ~ qch** to let
(sth) show ▷ *vb impers*: **il paraît que** it seems *ou*
appears that; **il me paraît que** it seems to me
that; **il paraît absurde de** it seems absurd to;
il ne paraît pas son âge he doesn't look his
age; **~ en justice** to appear before the court(s);
~ en scène/en public/à l'écran to appear on
stage/in public/on the screen

parallèle [paʀalɛl] *adj* parallel; (*police, marché*)
unofficial; (*société, énergie*) alternative ▷ *nm*

(*comparaison*): **faire un ~ entre** to draw a
parallel between; (*Géo*) parallel ▷ *nf* parallel
(line); **en ~** in parallel; **mettre en ~** (*choses
opposées*) to compare; (*choses semblables*) to
parallel

parallèlement [paʀalɛlmɑ̃] *adv* in parallel; (*fig:
en même temps*) at the same time

parallélépipède [paʀalelepipɛd] *nm*
parallelepiped

parallélisme [paʀalelism(ə)] *nm* parallelism;
(*Auto*) wheel alignment

parallélogramme [paʀalelɔgʀam] *nm*
parallelogram

paralyser [paʀalize] *vt* to paralyze

paralysie [paʀalizi] *nf* paralysis

paralytique [paʀalitik] *adj, nm/f* paralytic

paramédical, e, -aux [paʀamedikal, -o] *adj*
paramedical

paramètre [paʀamɛtʀ(ə)] *nm* parameter

paramilitaire [paʀamilitɛʀ] *adj* paramilitary

paranoïa [paʀanɔja] *nf* paranoia

paranoïaque [paʀanɔjak] *nm/f* paranoiac

paranormal, e, -aux [paʀanɔʀmal, -o] *adj*
paranormal

parapet [paʀapɛ] *nm* parapet

paraphe [paʀaf] *nm* (*trait*) flourish; (*signature*)
initials *pl*; signature

parapher [paʀafe] *vt* to initial; to sign

paraphrase [paʀafʀɑz] *nf* paraphrase

paraphraser [paʀafʀɑze] *vt* to paraphrase

paraplégie [paʀapleʒi] *nf* paraplegia

paraplégique [paʀapleʒik] *adj, nm/f* paraplegic

parapluie [paʀaplɥi] *nm* umbrella; **~ atomique
ou nucléaire** nuclear umbrella; **~ pliant**
telescopic umbrella

parapsychique [paʀapsiʃik] *adj*
parapsychological

parapsychologie [paʀapsikɔlɔʒi] *nf*
parapsychology

parapublic, -ique [paʀapyblik] *adj* partly state-
controlled

parascolaire [paʀaskɔlɛʀ] *adj* extracurricular

parasitaire [paʀazitɛʀ] *adj* parasitic(al)

parasite [paʀazit] *nm* parasite ▷ *adj* (*Bot, Bio*)
parasitic(al); **parasites** *nmpl* (*Tél*)
interference *sg*

parasitisme [paʀazitism(ə)] *nm* parasitism

parasol [paʀasɔl] *nm* parasol, sunshade

paratonnerre [paʀatɔnɛʀ] *nm* lightning
conductor

paravent [paʀavɑ̃] *nm* folding screen; (*fig*)
screen

parc [paʀk] *nm* (*public*) park, gardens *pl*; (*de
château etc*) grounds *pl*; (*pour le bétail*) pen,
enclosure; (*d'enfant*) playpen; (*Mil: entrepôt*)
depot; (*ensemble d'unités*) stock; (*de voitures etc*)
fleet; **~ d'attractions** amusement park; **~
automobile** (*d'un pays*) number of cars on the
roads; **~ à huîtres** oyster bed; **~ à thème** theme
park; **~ national** national park; **~ naturel**
nature reserve; **~ de stationnement** car park;
~ zoologique zoological gardens *pl*

P

parcelle [paʀsɛl] nf fragment, scrap; (de terrain) plot, parcel

parcelliser [paʀselize] vt to divide ou split up

parce que [paʀsk(ə)] conj because

parchemin [paʀʃəmɛ̃] nm parchment

parcheminé, e [paʀʃəmine] adj wrinkled; (papier) with a parchment finish

parcimonie [paʀsimɔni] nf parsimony, parsimoniousness

parcimonieux, -euse [paʀsimɔnjø, -øz] adj parsimonious, miserly

parcmètre [paʀkmɛtʀ(ə)], **parcomètre** [paʀkɔmɛtʀ(ə)] nm parking meter

parcotrain [paʀkɔtʀɛ̃] nm station car park (Brit) ou parking lot (US), park-and-ride car park (Brit)

parcourir [paʀkuʀiʀ] vt (trajet, distance) to cover; (article, livre) to skim ou glance through; (lieu) to go all over, travel up and down; (frisson, vibration) to run through; **~ des yeux** to run one's eye over

parcours [paʀkuʀ] vb voir **parcourir** ▷ nm (trajet) journey; (itinéraire) route; (Sport: terrain) course; (: tour) round; run; lap; **~ du combattant** assault course

parcouru, e [paʀkuʀy] pp de **parcourir**

par-delà [paʀdəla] prép beyond

par-dessous [paʀdəsu] prép, adv under(neath)

pardessus [paʀdəsy] nm overcoat

par-dessus [paʀdəsy] prép over (the top of) ▷ adv over (the top); **~ le marché** on top of it all

par-devant [paʀdəvɑ̃] prép in the presence of, before ▷ adv at the front; round the front

pardon [paʀdɔ̃] nm forgiveness no pl ▷ excl (excuses) (I'm) sorry; (pour interpeller etc) excuse me; (demander de répéter etc) (I beg your) pardon? (Brit), pardon me? (US)

pardonnable [paʀdɔnabl(ə)] adj forgivable, excusable

pardonner [paʀdɔne] vt to forgive; **~ qch à qn** to forgive sb for sth; **qui ne pardonne pas** (maladie, erreur) fatal

paré, e [paʀe] adj ready, prepared

pare-balles [paʀbal] adj inv bulletproof

pare-boue [paʀbu] nm inv mudflap

pare-brise [paʀbʀiz] nm inv windscreen (Brit), windshield (US)

pare-chocs [paʀʃɔk] nm inv bumper (Brit), fender (US)

pare-étincelles [paʀetɛ̃sɛl] nm inv fireguard

pare-feu [paʀfø] nm inv firebreak ▷ adj inv: **portes ~** fire (resistant) doors

pareil, le [paʀɛj] adj (identique) the same, alike; (similaire) similar; (tel) such; **un courage/livre ~** such courage/a book, courage/a book like this; **de ~s livres** such books ▷ adv: **habillés ~** dressed the same (way), dressed alike; **faire ~** to do the same (thing); **j'en veux un ~** I'd like one just like it; **rien de ~** no (ou any) such thing, nothing (ou anything) like it; **ses ~s** one's fellow men; one's peers; **ne pas avoir son (sa) ~(le)** to be second to none; **~ à** the same as; similar to; **sans ~** unparalleled, unequalled;

c'est du ~ au même it comes to the same thing, it's six (of one) and half-a-dozen (of the other); **en ~ cas** in such a case; **rendre la ~le à qn** to pay sb back in his own coin

pareillement [paʀɛjmɑ̃] adv the same, alike; in such a way; (également) likewise

parement [paʀmɑ̃] nm (Constr: revers d'un col, d'une manche) facing; (Rel): **~ d'autel** antependium

parent, e [paʀɑ̃, -ɑ̃t] nm/f: **un/une ~/e** a relative ou relation ▷ adj: **être ~ de** to be related to; **parents** nmpl (père et mère) parents; (famille, proches) relatives, relations; **~ unique** lone parent; **~s par alliance** relatives ou relations by marriage; **~s en ligne directe** blood relations

parental, e, -aux [paʀɑ̃tal, -o] adj parental

parenté [paʀɑ̃te] nf (lien) relationship; (personnes) relatives pl, relations pl

parenthèse [paʀɑ̃tɛz] nf (ponctuation) bracket, parenthesis; (Math) bracket; (digression) parenthesis, digression; **ouvrir/fermer la ~** to open/close brackets; **entre ~s** in brackets; (fig) incidentally

parer [paʀe] vt to adorn; (Culin) to dress, trim; (éviter) to ward off; **~ à** (danger) to ward off; (inconvénient) to deal with; **se ~ de** (fig: qualité, titre) to assume; **~ à toute éventualité** to be ready for every eventuality; **~ au plus pressé** to attend to what's most urgent

pare-soleil [paʀsɔlɛj] nm inv sun visor

paresse [paʀɛs] nf laziness

paresser [paʀese] vi to laze around

paresseusement [paʀɛsøzmɑ̃] adv lazily; sluggishly

paresseux, -euse [paʀɛsø, -øz] adj lazy; (fig) slow, sluggish ▷ nm (Zool) sloth

parfaire [paʀfɛʀ] vt to perfect, complete

parfait, e [paʀfɛ, -ɛt] pp de **parfaire** ▷ adj perfect ▷ nm (Ling) perfect (tense); (Culin) parfait ▷ excl fine, excellent

parfaitement [paʀfɛtmɑ̃] adv perfectly ▷ excl (most) certainly

parfaites [paʀfɛt], **parfasse** [paʀfas], **parferai** etc [paʀfʀe] vb voir **parfaire**

parfois [paʀfwa] adv sometimes

parfum [paʀfœ̃] nm (produit) perfume, scent; (odeur: de fleur) scent, fragrance; (: de tabac, vin) aroma; (goût: de glace, milk-shake) flavour (Brit), flavor (US)

parfumé, e [paʀfyme] adj (fleur, fruit) fragrant; (papier à lettres etc) scented; (femme) wearing perfume ou scent, perfumed; (aromatisé): **~ au café** coffee-flavoured (Brit) ou -flavored (US)

parfumer [paʀfyme] vt (odeur, bouquet) to perfume; (mouchoir) to put scent ou perfume on; (crème, gâteau) to flavour (Brit), flavor (US); **se parfumer** to put on (some) perfume ou scent; (d'habitude) to use perfume ou scent

parfumerie [paʀfymʀi] nf (commerce) perfumery; (produits) perfumes; (boutique) perfume shop (Brit) ou store (US)

pari [paʀi] nm bet, wager; (Sport) bet; **~ mutuel urbain (PMU)** system of betting on horses

paria [paʀja] *nm* outcast

parier [paʀje] *vt* to bet; **j'aurais parié que si/non** I'd have said he (*ou* you *etc*) would/wouldn't

parieur [paʀjœʀ] *nm* (*turfiste etc*) punter

Paris [paʀi] *n* Paris

parisien, ne [paʀizjɛ̃, -ɛn] *adj* Parisian; (*Géo, Admin*) Paris *cpd* ▷ *nm/f*: **Parisien, ne** Parisian

paritaire [paʀitɛʀ] *adj*: **commission** ~ joint commission

parité [paʀite] *nf* parity; ~ **de change** (*Écon*) exchange parity

parjure [paʀʒyʀ] *nm* (*faux serment*) false oath, perjury; (*violation de serment*) breach of oath, perjury ▷ *nm/f* perjurer

parjurer [paʀʒyʀe]: **se parjurer** *vi* to perjure o.s

parka [paʀka] *nf* parka

parking [paʀkiŋ] *nm* (*lieu*) car park (*Brit*), parking lot (*US*)

parlant, e [paʀlɑ̃, -ɑ̃t] *adj* (*fig*) graphic, vivid; (: *comparaison, preuve*) eloquent; (*Ciné*) talking ▷ *adv*: **généralement** ~ generally speaking

parlé, e [paʀle] *adj*: **langue ~e** spoken language

parlement [paʀləmɑ̃] *nm* parliament; **le P~ européen** the European Parliament

parlementaire [paʀləmɑ̃tɛʀ] *adj* parliamentary ▷ *nm/f* (*député*) ≈ Member of Parliament (*Brit*) *ou* Congress (*US*); parliamentarian; (*négociateur*) negotiator, mediator

parlementarisme [paʀləmɑ̃taʀism(ə)] *nm* parliamentary government

parlementer [paʀləmɑ̃te] *vi* (*ennemis*) to negotiate, parley; (*s'entretenir, discuter*) to argue at length, have lengthy talks

parler [paʀle] *nm* speech; dialect ▷ *vi* to speak, talk; (*avouer*) to talk; ~ (**à qn**) **de** to talk *ou* speak (to sb) about; ~ **pour qn** (*intercéder*) to speak for sb; ~ **en l'air** to say the first thing that comes into one's head; ~ **le/en français** to speak French/in French; ~ **affaires** to talk business; ~ **en dormant/du nez** to talk in one's sleep/ through one's nose; **sans** ~ **de** (*fig*) not to mention, to say nothing of; **tu parles!** you must be joking!; **n'en parlons plus!** let's forget it!

parleur [paʀlœʀ] *nm*: **beau** ~ fine talker

parloir [paʀlwaʀ] *nm* (*d'une prison, d'un hôpital*) visiting room; (*Rel*) parlour (*Brit*), parlor (*US*)

parlote [paʀlɔt] *nf* chitchat

Parme [paʀm(ə)] *n* Parma

parme [paʀm(ə)] *adj* violet (blue)

parmesan [paʀməzɑ̃] *nm* Parmesan (cheese)

parmi [paʀmi] *prép* among(st)

parodie [paʀɔdi] *nf* parody

parodier [paʀɔdje] *vt* (*œuvre, auteur*) to parody

paroi [paʀwa] *nf* wall; (*cloison*) partition; ~ **rocheuse** rock face

paroisse [paʀwas] *nf* parish

paroissial, e, -aux [paʀwasjal, -o] *adj* parish *cpd*

paroissien, ne [paʀwasjɛ̃, -ɛn] *nm/f* parishioner ▷ *nm* prayer book

parole [paʀɔl] *nf* (*faculté*): **la** ~ speech; (*mot, promesse*) word; (*Rel*): **la bonne** ~ the word of God; **paroles** *nfpl* (*Mus*) words, lyrics; **tenir** ~ to keep one's word; **avoir la** ~ to have the floor; **n'avoir qu'une** ~ to be true to one's word; **donner la** ~ **à qn** to hand over to sb; **prendre la** ~ to speak; **demander la** ~ to ask for permission to speak; **perdre la** ~ to lose the power of speech; (*fig*) to lose one's tongue; **je le crois sur** ~ I'll take his word for it, I'll take him at his word; **temps de** ~ (*TV, Radio etc*) discussion time; **ma ~!** my word!, good heavens!; ~ **d'honneur** word of honour (*Brit*) *ou* honor (*US*)

parolier, -ière [paʀɔlje, -jɛʀ] *nm/f* lyricist; (*Opéra*) librettist

paroxysme [paʀɔksism(ə)] *nm* height, paroxysm

parpaing [paʀpɛ̃] *nm* bond-stone, parpen

parquer [paʀke] *vt* (*voiture, matériel*) to park; (*bestiaux*) to pen (in *ou* up); (*prisonniers*) to pack in

parquet [paʀkɛ] *nm* (*plancher*) floor; (*Jur: bureau*) public prosecutor's office; **le** ~ (**général**) (*magistrats*) ≈ the Bench

parqueter [paʀkəte] *vt* to lay a parquet floor in

parrain [paʀɛ̃] *nm* godfather; (*d'un navire*) namer; (*d'un nouvel adhérent*) sponsor, proposer

parrainage [paʀɛnaʒ] *nm* sponsorship

parrainer [paʀene] *vt* (*nouvel adhérent*) to sponsor, propose; (*entreprise*) to promote, sponsor

parricide [paʀisid] *nm, nf* parricide

pars [paʀ] *vb voir* **partir**

parsemer [paʀsəme] *vt* (*feuilles, papiers*) to be scattered over; ~ **qch de** to scatter sth with

parsi, e [paʀsi] *adj* Parsee

part [paʀ] *vb voir* **partir** ▷ *nf* (*qui revient à qn*) share; (*fraction, partie*) part; (*de gâteau, fromage*) portion; (*Finance*) (non-voting) share; **prendre** ~ **à** (*débat etc*) to take part in; (*soucis, douleur de qn*) to share in; **faire** ~ **de qch à qn** to announce sth to sb, inform sb of sth; **pour ma** ~ as for me, as far as I'm concerned; **à** ~ **entière** *adj* full; **de la** ~ **de** (*au nom de*) on behalf of; (*donné par*) from; **c'est de la** ~ **de qui?** (*au téléphone*) who's calling *ou* speaking (please)?; **de toute(s)** ~(**s**) from all sides *ou* quarters; **de** ~ **et d'autre** on both sides, on either side; **de** ~ **en** ~ right through; **d'une** ~ **... d'autre** ~ on the one hand ... on the other hand; **nulle/autre/quelque** ~ nowhere/ elsewhere/somewhere; **à** ~ *adv* separately; (*de côté*) aside ▷ *prép* apart from, except for ▷ *adj* exceptional, special; **pour une large** *ou* **bonne** ~ to a great extent; **prendre qch en bonne/ mauvaise** ~ to take sth well/badly; **faire la** ~ **des choses** to make allowances; **faire la** ~ **du feu** (*fig*) to cut one's losses; **faire la** ~ (**trop**) **belle à qn** to give sb more than his (*ou* her) share

part. *abr* = **particulier**

partage [paʀtaʒ] *nm voir* **partager** sharing (out) *no pl*, share-out; sharing; dividing up; (*Pol: de suffrages*) share; **recevoir qch en** ~ to receive sth as one's share (*ou* lot); **sans** ~ undivided

partagé, e [paʀtaʒe] *adj* (*opinions etc*) divided; (*amour*) shared; **être ~ entre** to be shared between; **être ~ sur** to be divided about

partager [paʀtaʒe] *vt* to share; (*distribuer, répartir*) to share (out); (*morceler, diviser*) to divide (up); **se partager** *vt* (*héritage etc*) to share between themselves (*ou* ourselves *etc*)

partance [paʀtɑ̃s]: **en ~** *adv* outbound, due to leave; **en ~ pour** (bound) for

partant, e [paʀtɑ̃, -ɑ̃t] *vb voir* **partir** ▷ *adj*: **être ~ pour qch** (*d'accord pour*) to be quite ready for sth ▷ *nm* (*Sport*) starter; (*Hippisme*) runner

partenaire [paʀtənɛʀ] *nm/f* partner; **~s sociaux** management and workforce

parterre [paʀtɛʀ] *nm* (*de fleurs*) (flower) bed, border; (*Théât*) stalls *pl*

parti [paʀti] *nm* (*Pol*) party; (*décision*) course of action; (*personne à marier*) match; **tirer ~ de** to take advantage of, turn to good account; **prendre le ~ de faire** to make up one's mind to do, resolve to do; **prendre le ~ de qn** to stand up for sb, side with sb; **prendre ~ (pour/contre)** to take sides *ou* a stand (for/against); **prendre son ~ de** to come to terms with; **~ pris** bias

partial, e, -aux [paʀsjal, -o] *adj* biased, partial

partialement [paʀsjalmɑ̃] *adv* in a biased way

partialité [paʀsjalite] *nf* bias, partiality

participant, e [paʀtisipɑ̃, -ɑ̃t] *nm/f* participant; (*à un concours*) entrant; (*d'une société*) member

participation [paʀtisipasjɔ̃] *nf* participation; sharing; (*Comm*) interest; **la ~ aux bénéfices** profit-sharing; **la ~ ouvrière** worker participation; **"avec la ~ de ..."** "featuring ..."

participe [paʀtisip] *nm* participle; **~ passé/présent** past/present participle

participer [paʀtisipe]: **~ à** *vt* (*course, réunion*) to take part in; (*profits etc*) to share in; (*frais etc*) to contribute to; (*entreprise: financièrement*) to cooperate in; (*chagrin, succès de qn*) to share (in); **~ de** *vt* to partake of.

particulariser [paʀtikylaʀize] *vt*: **se particulariser** to mark o.s. (*ou* itself) out

particularisme [paʀtikylaʀism(ə)] *nm* sense of identity

particularité [paʀtikylaʀite] *nf* particularity; (*distinctive*) characteristic, feature

particule [paʀtikyl] *nf* particle; **~ (nobiliaire)** nobiliary particle

particulier, -ière [paʀtikylje, -jɛʀ] *adj* (*personnel, privé*) private; (*spécial*) special, particular; (*caractéristique*) characteristic, distinctive; (*spécifique*) particular ▷ *nm* (*individu: Admin*) private individual; **"~ vend ..."** (*Comm*) "for sale privately ...", "for sale by owner ..." (*US*); **~ à** peculiar to; **en ~** *adv* (*surtout*) in particular, particularly; (*à part*) separately; (*en privé*) in private

particulièrement [paʀtikyljɛʀmɑ̃] *adv* particularly

partie [paʀti] *nf* (*gén*) part; (*profession, spécialité*) field, subject; (*Jur etc: protagonistes*) party; (*de*

cartes, tennis etc*) game; (*fig: lutte, combat*) struggle, fight; **une ~ de campagne/de pêche** an outing in the country/a fishing party *ou* trip; **en ~** *adv* partly, in part; **faire ~ de** to belong to; (*chose*) to be part of; **prendre qn à ~** to take sb to task; (*malmener*) to set on sb; **en grande ~** largely, in the main; **ce n'est que ~ remise** it will be for another time *ou* the next time; **avoir ~ liée avec qn** to be in league with sb; **~ civile** (*Jur*) *party claiming damages in a criminal case*

partiel, le [paʀsjɛl] *adj* partial ▷ *nm* (*Scol*) class exam

partiellement [paʀsjɛlmɑ̃] *adv* partially, partly

partir [paʀtiʀ] *vi* (*gén*) to go; (*quitter*) to go, leave; (*s'éloigner*) to go (*ou* drive *etc*) away *ou* off; (*moteur*) to start; (*pétard*) to go off; (*bouchon*) to come out; (*bouton*) to come off; **~ de** (*lieu: quitter*) to leave; (: *commencer à*) to start from; (*date*) to run *ou* start from; **~ pour/à** (*lieu, pays etc*) to leave for/go off to; **à ~ de** from

partisan, e [paʀtizɑ̃, -an] *nm/f* partisan; (*d'un parti, régime etc*) supporter ▷ *adj* (*lutte, querelle*) partisan, one-sided; **être ~ de qch/faire** to be in favour (*Brit*) *ou* favor (*US*) of sth/doing

partitif, -ive [paʀtitif, -iv] *adj*: **article ~** partitive article

partition [paʀtisjɔ̃] *nf* (*Mus*) score

partout [paʀtu] *adv* everywhere; **~ où il allait** everywhere *ou* wherever he went; **trente ~** (*Tennis*) thirty all

paru [paʀy] *pp de* **paraître**

parure [paʀyʀ] *nf* (*bijoux etc*) finery *no pl*; jewellery *no pl* (*Brit*), jewelry *no pl* (*US*); (*assortiment*) set

parus *etc* [paʀy] *vb voir* **paraître**

parution [paʀysjɔ̃] *nf* publication, appearance

parvenir [paʀvəniʀ]: **~ à** *vt* (*atteindre*) to reach; (*obtenir, arriver à*) to attain; (*réussir*): **à faire** to manage to do, succeed in doing; **faire ~ qch à qn** to have sth sent to sb

parvenu, e [paʀvəny] *pp de* **parvenir** ▷ *nm/f* (*péj*) parvenu, upstart

parviendrai [paʀvjɛ̃dʀe], **parviens** *etc* [paʀvjɛ̃] *vb voir* **parvenir**

parvis [paʀvi] *nm* square (*in front of a church*)

 MOT-CLÉ

pas¹ [pɑ] *adv* **1** (*en corrélation avec ne, non etc*) not; **il ne pleure pas** (*habituellement*) he does not *ou* doesn't cry; (*maintenant*) he's not *ou* isn't crying; **je ne mange pas de viande** I don't *ou* do not eat meat; **il n'a pas pleuré/ne pleurera pas** he did not *ou* didn't/will not *ou* won't cry; **ils n'ont pas de voiture/d'enfants** they haven't got a car/any children, they have no car/children; **il m'a dit de ne pas le faire** he told me not to do it; **non pas que ...** not that ..

2 (*employé sans ne etc*): **pas moi** not me, not I, I don't (*ou* can't *etc*); **elle travaille, (mais) lui pas** *ou* **pas lui** she works but he doesn't *ou* does not; **une pomme pas mûre** an apple which

isn't ripe; **pas plus tard qu'hier** only
yesterday; **pas du tout** not at all; **pas de
sucre, merci** no sugar, thanks; **ceci est à vous
ou pas?** is this yours or not?, is this yours or
isn't it?
3: **pas mal** (*joli: personne, maison*) not bad; **pas
mal fait** not badly done *ou* made; **comment ça
va? — pas mal** how are things? — not bad; **pas
mal de** quite a lot of

pas² [pɑ] *nm* (*allure, mesure*) pace; (*démarche*)
tread; (*enjambée, Danse, fig: étape*) step; (*bruit*)
(foot)step; (*trace*) footprint; (*allure*) pace; (*d'un
cheval*) walk; (*mesure*) pace; (*Tech: de vis, d'écrou*)
thread; **~ à ~** step by step; **au ~** at a walking
pace; **de ce ~** (*à l'instant même*) straightaway, at
once; **marcher à grands ~** to stride along;
mettre qn au ~ to bring sb to heel; **au ~ de
gymnastique/de course** at a jog trot/at a run;
à ~ de loup stealthily; **faire les cent ~** to pace
up and down; **faire les premiers ~** to make the
first move; **retourner** *ou* **revenir sur ses ~** to
retrace one's steps; **se tirer d'un mauvais ~** to
get o.s. out of a tight spot; **sur le ~ de la porte**
on the doorstep; **le ~ de Calais** (*détroit*) the
Straits *pl* of Dover; **~ de porte** (*fig*) key money
pascal, e, -aux [paskal, -o] *adj* Easter *cpd*
passable [pɑsabl(ə)] *adj* passable, tolerable
passablement [pɑsabləmɑ̃] *adv* (*pas trop mal*)
reasonably well; (*beaucoup*) quite a lot
passade [pɑsad] *nf* passing fancy, whim
passage [pɑsaʒ] *nm* (*fait de passer*) *voir* **passer**;
(*lieu, prix de la traversée, extrait de livre etc*) passage;
(*chemin*) way; (*itinéraire*) **sur le ~ du cortège**
along the route of the procession; **"laissez/
n'obstruez pas le ~"** "keep clear/do not
obstruct"; **au ~** (*en passant*) as I (*ou* he *etc*) went
by; **de ~** (*touristes*) passing through; (*amants etc*)
casual; **~ clouté** pedestrian crossing; **"~
interdit"** "no entry"; **~ à niveau** level (*Brit*) *ou*
grade (*US*) crossing; **"~ protégé"** right of way over
secondary road(s) on your right; **~ souterrain**
subway (*Brit*), underpass; **~ à tabac** beating-up;
~ à vide (*fig*) bad patch
passager, -ère [pɑsaʒe, -ɛʀ] *adj* passing; (*hôte*)
short-stay *cpd*; (*oiseau*) migratory ▷ *nm/f*
passenger; **~ clandestin** stowaway
passagèrement [pɑsaʒɛʀmɑ̃] *adv* temporarily,
for a short time
passant, e [pɑsɑ̃, -ɑ̃t] *adj* (*rue, endroit*) busy ▷ *nm/f*
passer-by ▷ *nm* (*pour ceinture etc*) loop; **en ~:
remarquer qch en ~** to notice sth in passing
passation [pɑsasjɔ̃] *nf* (*Jur: d'un acte*) signing; **~
des pouvoirs** transfer *ou* handover of power
passe [pɑs] *nf* (*Sport, magnétique*) pass; (*Navig*)
channel ▷ *nm* (*passe-partout*) master *ou* skeleton
key; **être en ~ de faire** to be on the way to
doing; **être dans une mauvaise ~** (*fig*) to be
going through a bad patch; **être dans une
bonne ~** (*fig*) to be in a healthy situation; **~
d'armes** (*fig*) heated exchange
passé, e [pɑse] *adj* (*événement, temps*) past;

(*couleur, tapisserie*) faded; (*précédent*): **dimanche ~**
last Sunday ▷ *prép* after ▷ *nm* past; (*Ling*) past
(tense); **il est ~ midi** *ou* **midi ~** it's gone (*Brit*) *ou*
past twelve; **~ de mode** out of fashion; **~
composé** perfect (tense); **~ simple** past
historic
passe-droit [pɑsdʀwa] *nm* special privilege
passéiste [pɑseist(ə)] *adj* backward-looking
passementerie [pɑsmɑ̃tʀi] *nf* trimmings *pl*
passe-montagne [pɑsmɔ̃taɲ] *nm* balaclava
passe-partout [pɑspaʀtu] *nm inv* master *ou*
skeleton key ▷ *adj inv* all-purpose
passe-passe [pɑspɑs] *nm*: **tour de ~** trick,
sleight of hand *no pl*
passe-plat [pɑspla] *nm* serving hatch
passeport [pɑspɔʀ] *nm* passport
passer [pɑse] *vi* (*se rendre, aller*) to go; (*voiture,
piétons: défiler*) to pass (by), go by; (*faire une halte
rapide: facteur, laitier etc*) to come, call; (: *pour rendre
visite*) to call *ou* drop in; (*courant, air, lumière,
franchir un obstacle etc*) to get through; (*accusé,
projet de loi*): **~ devant** to come before; (*film,
émission*) to be on; (*temps, jours*) to pass, go by;
(*liquide, café*) to go through; (*être digéré, avalé*) to go
down; (*couleur, papier*) to fade; (*mode*) to die out;
(*douleur*) to pass, go away; (*Cartes*) to pass; (*Scol*)
to go up (to the next class); (*devenir*): **~
président** to be appointed *ou* become president
▷ *vt* (*frontière, rivière etc*) to cross; (*douane*) to go
through; (*examen*) to sit, take; (*visite médicale etc*)
to have; (*journée, temps*) to spend; (*donner*): **~ qch
à qn** to pass sth to sb; to give sb sth;
(*transmettre*): **~ qch à qn** to pass sth on to sb;
(*enfiler: vêtement*) to slip on; (*faire entrer, mettre*):
(faire) ~ qch dans/par to get sth into/through;
(*café*) to pour the water on; (*thé, soupe*) to strain;
(*film, pièce*) to show, put on; (*disque*) to play, put
on; (*marché, accord*) to agree on; (*tolérer*): **~ qch à
qn** to let sb get away with sth; **se passer** *vi*
(*avoir lieu: scène, action*) to take place; (*se dérouler:
entretien etc*) to go; (*arriver*): **que s'est-il passé?**
what happened?; (*s'écouler: semaine etc*) to pass,
go by; **se ~ de** *vt* to go *ou* do without; **se ~ les
mains sous l'eau/de l'eau sur le visage** to put
one's hands under the tap/run water over one's
face; **en passant** in passing; **~ par** to go
through; **passez devant/par ici** go in front/
this way; **~ sur** *vt* (*faute, détail inutile*) to pass
over; **~ dans les mœurs/l'usage** to become the
custom/normal usage; **~ avant qch/qn** (*fig*) to
come before sth/sb; **laisser ~** (*air, lumière,
personne*) to let through; (*occasion*) to let slip,
miss; (*erreur*) to overlook; **faire ~** (*message*) to get
over *ou* across; **faire ~ à qn le goût de qch** to
cure sb of his (*ou* her) taste for sth; **~ à la radio/
fouille** to be X-rayed/searched; **~ à la radio/
télévision** to be on the radio/on television; **~ à
table** to sit down to eat; **~ au salon** to go
through to *ou* into the sitting room; **~ à
l'opposition** to go over to the opposition; **~ aux
aveux** to confess, make a confession; **~ à
l'action** to go into action; **~ pour riche** to be

taken for a rich man; **il passait pour avoir** he was said to have; **faire ~ qn/qch pour** to make sb/sth out to be; **passe encore de le penser, mais de le dire!** it's one thing to think it, but to say it!; **passons!** let's say no more (about it); **et j'en passe!** and that's not all!; **~ en seconde, ~ la seconde** (Auto) to change into second; **~ qch en fraude** to smuggle sth in (ou out); **~ la main par la portière** to stick one's hand out of the door; **~ le balai/l'aspirateur** to sweep up/hoover; **~ commande/la parole à qn** to hand over to sb; **je vous passe M. X** (je vous mets en communication avec lui) I'm putting you through to Mr X; (je lui passe l'appareil) here is Mr X, I'll hand you over to Mr X; **~ prendre** to (come and) collect

passereau, x [pɑsʀo] nm sparrow

passerelle [pɑsʀɛl] nf footbridge; (de navire, avion) gangway; (Navig): **~ (de commandement)** bridge

passe-temps [pɑstɑ̃] nm inv pastime

passette [pɑsɛt] nf (tea-)strainer

passeur, -euse [pɑsœʀ, -øz] nm/f smuggler

passible [pɑsibl(ə)] adj: **~ de** liable to

passif, -ive [pɑsif, -iv] adj passive ▷ nm (Ling) passive; (Comm) liabilities pl

passion [pɑsjɔ̃] nf passion; **avoir la ~ de** to have a passion for; **fruit de la ~** passion fruit

passionnant, e [pɑsjɔnɑ̃, -ɑ̃t] adj fascinating

passionné, e [pɑsjɔne] adj (personne, tempérament) passionate; (description) impassioned ▷ nm/f: **c'est un ~ d'échecs** he's a chess fanatic; **être ~ de** ou **pour qch** to have a passion for sth

passionnel, le [pɑsjɔnɛl] adj of passion

passionnément [pɑsjɔnemɑ̃] adv passionately

passionner [pɑsjɔne] vt (personne) to fascinate, grip; (débat, discussion) to inflame; **se ~ pour** to take an avid interest in; to have a passion for

passivement [pɑsivmɑ̃] adv passively

passivité [pɑsivite] nf passivity, passiveness

passoire [pɑswaʀ] nf sieve; (à légumes) colander; (à thé) strainer

pastel [pɑstɛl] nm, adj inv (Art) pastel

pastèque [pɑstɛk] nf watermelon

pasteur [pɑstœʀ] nm (protestant) minister, pastor

pasteurisation [pɑstœʀizasjɔ̃] nf pasteurization

pasteurisé, e [pɑstœʀize] adj pasteurized

pasteuriser [pɑstœʀize] vt to pasteurize

pastiche [pɑstiʃ] nm pastiche

pastille [pɑstij] nf (à sucer) lozenge, pastille; (de papier etc) (small) disc; **~s pour la toux** cough drops ou lozenges

pastis [pɑstis] nm anise-flavoured alcoholic drink

pastoral, e, -aux [pɑstɔʀal, -o] adj pastoral

patagon, ne [pataɡɔ̃, -ɔn] adj Patagonian

Patagonie [pataɡɔni] nf: **la ~** Patagonia

patate [patat] nf spud; **~ douce** sweet potato

pataud, e [pato, -od] adj lumbering

patauger [patoʒe] vi (pour s'amuser) to splash about; (avec effort) to wade about; (fig) to flounder; **~ dans** (en marchant) to wade through

patch [patʃ] nm nicotine patch

patchouli [patʃuli] nm patchouli

patchwork [patʃwœʀk] nm patchwork

pâte [pat] nf (à tarte) pastry; (à pain) dough; (à frire) batter; (substance molle) paste; cream; **pâtes** nfpl (macaroni etc) pasta sg; **fromage à ~ dure/molle** hard/soft cheese; **~ d'amandes** almond paste; **~ brisée** shortcrust (Brit) ou pie crust (US) pastry; **~ à choux/feuilletée** choux/puff ou flaky (Brit) pastry; **~ de fruits** crystallized fruit no pl; **~ à modeler** modelling clay, Plasticine® (Brit); **~ à papier** paper pulp

pâté [pate] nm (charcuterie: terrine) pâté; (tache) ink blot; (de sable) sandpie; **~ (en croûte)** ≈ meat pie; **~ de foie** liver pâté; **~ de maisons** block (of houses)

pâtée [pate] nf mash, feed

patelin [patlɛ̃] nm little place

patente [patɑ̃t] nf (Comm) trading licence (Brit) ou license (US)

patenté, e [patɑ̃te] adj (Comm) licensed; (fig: attitré) registered, (officially) recognized

patère [patɛʀ] nf (coat-)peg

paternalisme [patɛʀnalism(ə)] nm paternalism

paternaliste [patɛʀnalist(ə)] adj paternalistic

paternel, le [patɛʀnɛl] adj (amour, soins) fatherly; (ligne, autorité) paternal

paternité [patɛʀnite] nf paternity, fatherhood

pâteux, -euse [patø, -øz] adj thick; pasty; **avoir la bouche** ou **langue pâteuse** to have a furred (Brit) ou coated tongue

pathétique [patetik] adj pathetic, moving

pathologie [patɔlɔʒi] nf pathology

pathologique [patɔlɔʒik] adj pathological

patibulaire [patibylɛʀ] adj sinister

patiemment [pasjamɑ̃] adv patiently

patience [pasjɑ̃s] nf patience; **être à bout de ~** to have run out of patience; **perdre/prendre ~** to lose (one's)/have patience

patient, e [pasjɑ̃, -ɑ̃t] adj, nm/f patient

patienter [pasjɑ̃te] vi to wait

patin [patɛ̃] nm skate; (sport) skating; (de traîneau, luge) runner; (pièce de tissu) cloth pad (used as slippers to protect polished floor); **~ (de frein)** brake block; **~s (à glace)** (ice) skates; **~s à roulettes** roller skates

patinage [patinaʒ] nm skating; **~ artistique/de vitesse** figure/speed skating

patine [patin] nf sheen

patiner [patine] vi to skate; (embrayage) to slip; (roue, voiture) to spin; **se patiner** vi (meuble, cuir) to acquire a sheen, become polished

patineur, -euse [patinœʀ, -øz] nm/f skater

patinoire [patinwaʀ] nf skating rink, (ice) rink

patio [patjo] nm patio

pâtir [patiʀ] **~ de** vt to suffer because of

pâtisserie [patisʀi] nf (boutique) cake shop; (métier) confectionery; (à la maison) pastry- ou cake-making, baking; **pâtisseries** nfpl (gâteaux)

pastries, cakes
pâtissier, -ière [pɑtisje, -jɛʀ] *nm/f* pastrycook;
confectioner
patois [patwa] *nm* dialect, patois
patraque [patʀak] *(fam) adj* peaky, off-colour
patriarche [patʀijaʀʃ(ə)] *nm* patriarch
patrie [patʀi] *nf* homeland
patrimoine [patʀimwan] *nm* inheritance,
patrimony; *(culture)* heritage; **~ génétique** *ou*
héréditaire genetic inheritance
patriote [patʀijɔt] *adj* patriotic ▷ *nm/f* patriot
patriotique [patʀijɔtik] *adj* patriotic
patriotisme [patʀijɔtism(ə)] *nm* patriotism
patron, ne [patʀɔ̃, -ɔn] *nm/f (chef)* boss,
manager(-ess); *(propriétaire)* owner,
proprietor(-tress); *(employeur)* employer; *(Méd)*
≈ senior consultant; *(Rel)* patron saint ▷ *nm*
(Couture) pattern; **~ de thèse** supervisor (of
postgraduate thesis)
patronage [patʀɔnaʒ] *nm* patronage;
(organisation, club) (parish) youth club; (parish)
children's club
patronal, e, -aux [patʀɔnal, -o] *adj (syndicat,*
intérêts) employers'
patronat [patʀɔna] *nm* employers *pl*
patronner [patʀɔne] *vt* to sponsor, support
patronnesse [patʀɔnɛs] *adj f:* **dame ~** patroness
patronyme [patʀɔnim] *nm* name
patronymique [patʀɔnimik] *adj:* **nom ~**
patronymic (name)
patrouille [patʀuj] *nf* patrol
patrouiller [patʀuje] *vi* to patrol, be on patrol
patrouilleur [patʀujœʀ] *nm (Aviat)* scout
(plane); *(Navig)* patrol boat
patte [pat] *nf (jambe)* leg; *(pied: de chien, chat)* paw;
(: d'oiseau) foot; *(languette)* strap; *(: de poche)* flap;
(favoris): **~s (de lapin)** (short) sideburns; **à ~s**
d'éléphant *adj (pantalon)* flared; **~s de mouche**
(fig) spidery scrawl *sg*; **~s d'oie** *(fig)* crow's feet
pattemouille [patmuj] *nf* damp cloth *(for*
ironing)
pâturage [pɑtyʀaʒ] *nm* pasture
pâture [pɑtyʀ] *nf* food
paume [pom] *nf* palm
paumé, e [pome] *nm/f (fam)* drop-out
paumer [pome] *vt (fam)* to lose
paupérisation [popeʀizasjɔ̃] *nf* pauperization
paupérisme [popeʀism(ə)] *nm* pauperism
paupière [popjɛʀ] *nf* eyelid
paupiette [popjɛt] *nf:* **~s de veau** veal olives
pause [poz] *nf (arrêt)* break; *(en parlant, Mus)*
pause; **~ de midi** lunch break
pause-café [pozkafe] *(pl* **pauses-café***) nf*
coffee-break
pauvre [povʀ(ə)] *adj* poor ▷ *nm/f* poor man/
woman; **les ~s** the poor; **~ en calcium** low in
calcium
pauvrement [povʀəmɑ̃] *adv* poorly
pauvreté [povʀəte] *nf (état)* poverty; **pauvreté**
énergétique fuel poverty
pavage [pavaʒ] *nm* paving; cobbles *pl*
pavaner [pavane]: **se pavaner** *vi* to strut about

pavé, e [pave] *adj (cour)* paved; *(rue)* cobbled
▷ *nm (bloc)* paving stone; cobblestone; *(pavage)*
paving; *(bifteck)* slab of steak; *(fam: livre)* hefty
tome; **être sur le ~** *(sans domicile)* to be on the
streets; *(sans emploi)* to be out of a job; **~**
numérique *(Inform)* keypad
pavillon [pavijɔ̃] *nm (de banlieue)* small
(detached) house; *(kiosque)* lodge; pavilion;
(d'hôpital) ward; *(Mus: de cor etc)* bell; *(Anat: de*
l'oreille) pavilion, pinna; *(Navig)* flag; **~ de**
complaisance flag of convenience
pavoiser [pavwaze] *vt* to deck with flags ▷ *vi* to
put out flags; *(fig)* to rejoice, exult
pavot [pavo] *nm* poppy
payable [pɛjabl(ə)] *adj* payable
payant, e [pɛjɑ̃, -ɑ̃t] *adj (spectateurs etc)* paying;
(billet) that you pay for, to be paid for; *(fig:*
entreprise) profitable; **c'est ~** you have to pay,
there is a charge
paye [pɛj] *nf* pay, wages *pl*
payement [pɛjmɑ̃] *nm* payment
payer [peje] *vt (créancier, employé, loyer)* to pay;
(achat, réparations, fig: faute) to pay for ▷ *vi* to pay;
(métier) to pay, be well-paid; *(effort, tactique etc)* to
pay off; **être bien/mal payé** to be well/badly
paid; **il me l'a fait ~ 10 euros** he charged me 10
euros for it; **~ qn de** *(ses efforts, peines)* to reward
sb for; **~ qch à qn** to buy sth for sb, buy sb sth;
ils nous ont payé le voyage they paid for our
trip; **~ de sa personne** to give of oneself; **~**
d'audace to act with great daring; **~ cher qch**
to pay dear(ly) for sth; **cela ne paie pas de**
mine it doesn't look much; **se ~ qch** to buy o.s.
sth; **se ~ de mots** to shoot one's mouth off; **se**
~ la tête de qn to take the mickey out of sb (Brit),
make a fool of sb; *(duper)* to take sb for a ride
payeur, -euse [pɛjœʀ, -øz] *adj (organisme, bureau)*
payments *cpd* ▷ *nm/f* payer
pays [pei] *nm (territoire, habitants)* country, land;
(région) region; *(village)* village; **du ~** *adj* local; **le**
~ de Galles Wales
paysage [peizaʒ] *nm* landscape
paysager, -ère [peizaʒe, -ɛʀ] *adj (jardin, parc)*
landscaped
paysagiste [peizaʒist(ə)] *nm/f (de jardin)*
landscape gardener; *(Art)* landscapist,
landscape painter
paysan, ne [peizɑ̃, -an] *nm/f* countryman/-
woman; farmer; *(péj)* peasant ▷ *adj* country *cpd*,
farming, farmers'
paysannat [peizana] *nm* peasantry
Pays-Bas [peiba] *nmpl:* **les ~** the Netherlands
PC *sigle m (Pol)* = **parti communiste**; *(Inform:*
= *personal computer)* PC; *(= prêt conventionné)* type of
loan for house purchase; *(Constr)* = **permis de**
construire; *(Mil)* = **poste de commandement**
pcc *abr (= pour copie conforme)* c.c
Pce *abr* = **prince**
Pcesse *abr* = **princesse**
PCV *abr* = **percevoir**; *voir* **communication**
PDA *sigle m (= personal digital assistant)* PDA
p de p *abr* = **pas de porte**

p

PDG *sigle m* = **président directeur général**

p.-ê. *abr* = **peut-être**

PEA *sigle m* (= *plan d'épargne en actions*) *building society savings plan*

péage [pea3] *nm* toll; (*endroit*) tollgate; **pont à ~** toll bridge

peau, x [po] *nf* skin; (*cuir*): **gants de ~** leather gloves; **être bien/mal dans sa ~** to be at ease/odds with oneself; **se mettre dans la ~ de qn** to put o.s. in sb's place *ou* shoes; **faire ~ neuve** (*se renouveler*) to change one's image; **~ de chamois** (*chiffon*) chamois leather, shammy; **~ d'orange** orange peel

peaufiner [pofine] *vt* to polish (up)

Peau-Rouge [poru3] *nm/f* Red Indian, red skin

peccadille [pekadij] *nf* trifle, peccadillo

péché [pefe] *nm* sin; **~ mignon** weakness

pêche [pɛʃ] *nf* (*sport, activité*) fishing; (*poissons pêchés*) catch; (*fruit*) peach; **aller à la ~** to go fishing; **avoir la ~** (*fam*) to be on (top) form; **~ à la ligne** (*en rivière*) angling; **~ sous-marine** deep-sea fishing

pêche-abricot [pɛʃabriko] (*pl* **pêches-abricots**) *nf* yellow peach

pécher [pefe] *vi* (*Rel*) to sin; (*fig: personne*) to err; (: *chose*) to be flawed; **~ contre la bienséance** to break the rules of good behaviour

pêcher [pefe] *nm* peach tree ▷ *vi* to go fishing; (*en rivière*) to go angling ▷ *vt* (*attraper*) to catch, land; (*chercher*) to fish for; **~ au chalut** to trawl

pécheur, -eresse [peʃœr, peʃrɛs] *nm/f* sinner

pêcheur [pɛʃœr] *nm voir* **pêcher** fisherman; angler; **~ de perles** pearl diver

pectine [pɛktin] *nf* pectin

pectoral, e, -aux [pɛktɔral, -o] *adj* (*Anat*) pectoral; (*sirop*) throat *cpd*, cough *cpd* ▷ *nmpl* pectoral muscles

pécule [pekyl] *nm* savings *pl*, nest egg; (*d'un détenu*) earnings *pl* (*paid on release*)

pécuniaire [pekynjɛr] *adj* financial

pédagogie [pedagɔʒi] *nf* educational methods *pl*, pedagogy

pédagogique [pedagɔʒik] *adj* educational; **formation ~** teacher training

pédagogue [pedagɔg] *nm/f* teacher, education(al)ist

pédale [pedal] *nf* pedal; **mettre la ~ douce** to soft-pedal

pédaler [pedale] *vi* to pedal

pédalier [pedalje] *nm* pedal and gear mechanism

pédalo [pedalo] *nm* pedalo, pedal-boat

pédant, e [pedã, -ãt] *adj* (*péj*) pedantic ▷ *nm/f* pedant

pédantisme [pedãtism(ə)] *nm* pedantry

pédéraste [pederast(ə)] *nm* homosexual, pederast

pédérastie [pederasti] *nf* homosexuality, pederasty

pédestre [pedɛstr(ə)] *adj*: **tourisme ~** hiking; **randonnée ~** (*activité*) rambling; (*excursion*) ramble

pédiatre [pedjatr(ə)] *nm/f* paediatrician (*Brit*), pediatrician *ou* pediatrist (*US*), child specialist

pédiatrie [pedjatri] *nf* paediatrics *sg* (*Brit*), pediatrics *sg* (*US*)

pédicure [pedikyr] *nm/f* chiropodist

pedigree [pedigre] *nm* pedigree

peeling [piliŋ] *nm* exfoliation treatment

PEEP *sigle f* = **Fédération des parents d'élèves de l'enseignement public**

pègre [pɛgr(ə)] *nf* underworld

peignais *etc* [pɛɲɛ] *vb voir* **peindre**

peigne [pɛɲ] *vb voir* **peindre; peigner** ▷ *nm* comb

peigné, e [pɛɲe] *adj*: **laine ~e** wool worsted; combed wool

peigner [pɛɲe] *vt* to comb (the hair of); **se peigner** to comb one's hair

peignez *etc* [pɛɲe] *vb voir* **peindre**

peignoir [pɛɲwar] *nm* dressing gown; **~ de bain** bathrobe; **~ de plage** beach robe

peignons [pɛɲɔ̃] *vb voir* **peindre**

peinard, e [penar, -ard(ə)] *adj* (*emploi*) cushy (*Brit*), easy; (*personne*): **on est ~ ici** we're left in peace here

peindre [pɛ̃dr(ə)] *vt* to paint; (*fig*) to portray, depict

peine [pɛn] *nf* (*affliction*) sorrow, sadness *no pl*; (*mal, effort*) trouble *no pl*, effort; (*difficulté*) difficulty; (*punition, châtiment*) punishment; (*Jur*) sentence; **faire de la ~ à qn** to distress *ou* upset sb; **prendre la ~ de faire** to go to the trouble of doing; **se donner de la ~** to make an effort; **ce n'est pas la ~ de faire** there's no point in doing, it's not worth doing; **ce n'est pas la ~ que vous fassiez** there's no point (in) you doing; **avoir de la ~ à faire** to have difficulty doing; **donnez-vous** *ou* **veuillez-vous donner la ~ d'entrer** please do come in; **c'est ~ perdue** it's a waste of time (and effort); **à ~** *adv* scarcely, hardly, barely; **à ~ ... que** hardly ... than; **c'est à ~ si ...** it's (*ou* it was) a job to ...; **sous ~**: **sous ~ d'être puni** for fear of being punished; **défense d'afficher sous ~ d'amende** billposters will be fined; **~ capitale** capital punishment; **~ de mort** death sentence *ou* penalty

peiner [pene] *vi* to work hard; to struggle; (*moteur, voiture*) to labour (*Brit*), labor (*US*) ▷ *vt* to grieve, sadden

peint, e [pɛ̃, pɛ̃t] *pp de* **peindre**

peintre [pɛ̃tr(ə)] *nm* painter; **~ en bâtiment** house painter, painter and decorator; **~ d'enseignes** signwriter

peinture [pɛ̃tyr] *nf* painting; (*couche de couleur, couleur*) paint; (*surfaces peintes: aussi:* **peintures**) paintwork; **je ne peux pas le voir en ~** I can't stand the sight of him; **~ mate/brillante** matt/gloss paint; **"~ fraîche"** "wet paint"

péjoratif, -ive [peʒɔratif, -iv] *adj* pejorative, derogatory

Pékin [pekɛ̃] *n* Peking

pékinois, e [pekinwa, -waz] *adj* Pekin(g)ese ▷ *nm* (*chien*) peke, pekin(g)ese; (*Ling*) Mandarin,

Pekin(g)ese ▷ nm/f: **Pékinois, e** Pekin(g)ese

PEL sigle m (= plan d'épargne logement) savings scheme providing lower-interest mortgages

pelade [pəlad] nf alopecia

pelage [pəlaʒ] nm coat, fur

pelé, e [pəle] adj (chien) hairless; (vêtement) threadbare; (terrain) bare

pêle-mêle [pɛlmɛl] adv higgledy-piggledy

peler [pəle] vt, vi to peel

pèlerin [pɛlʀɛ̃] nm pilgrim

pèlerinage [pɛlʀinaʒ] nm (voyage) pilgrimage; (lieu) place of pilgrimage, shrine

pèlerine [pɛlʀin] nf cape

pélican [pelikɑ̃] nm pelican

pelisse [pəlis] nf fur-lined cloak

pelle [pɛl] nf shovel; (d'enfant, de terrassier) spade; **~ à gâteau** cake slice; **~ mécanique** mechanical digger

pelletée [pɛlte] nf shovelful; spadeful

pelleter [pɛlte] vt to shovel (up)

pelleteuse [pɛltøz] nf mechanical digger, excavator

pelletier [pɛltje] nm furrier

pellicule [pelikyl] nf film; **pellicules** nfpl (Méd) dandruff sg

Péloponnèse [pelɔpɔnɛz] nm: **le ~** the Peloponnese

pelote [pəlɔt] nf (de fil, laine) ball; (d'épingles) pin cushion; **~ basque** pelota

peloter [pəlɔte] vt (fam) to feel (up); **se peloter** vi to pet

peloton [pəlɔtɔ̃] nm (groupe: de personnes) group; (: de pompiers, gendarmes) squad; (: Sport) pack; (de laine) ball; **~ d'exécution** firing squad

pelotonner [pəlɔtɔne]: **se pelotonner** vi to curl (o.s.) up

pelouse [pəluz] nf lawn; (Hippisme) spectating area inside racetrack

peluche [pəlyʃ] nf (bit of) fluff; **animal en ~** soft toy, fluffy animal

pelucher [p(ə)lyʃe] vi to become fluffy, fluff up

pelucheux, -euse [p(ə)lyʃø, -øz] adj fluffy

pelure [pəlyʀ] nf peeling, peel no pl; **~ d'oignon** onion skin

pénal, e, -aux [penal, -o] adj penal

pénalisation [penalizasjɔ̃] nf (Sport) sanction, penalty

pénaliser [penalize] vt to penalize

pénalité [penalite] nf penalty

penalty, ies [penalti, -z] nm (Sport) penalty (kick)

pénard, e [penaʀ, -aʀd(ə)] adj = **peinard**

pénates [penat] nmpl: **regagner ses ~** to return to the bosom of one's family

penaud, e [pəno, -od] adj sheepish, contrite

penchant [pɑ̃ʃɑ̃] nm: **un ~ à faire/à qch** a tendency to do/to sth; **un ~ pour qch** a liking ou fondness for sth

penché, e [pɑ̃ʃe] adj slanting

pencher [pɑ̃ʃe] vi to tilt, lean over ▷ vt to tilt; **se pencher** vi to lean over; (se baisser) to bend down; **se ~ sur** to bend over; (fig: problème) to

look into; **se ~ au dehors** to lean out; **~ pour** to be inclined to favour (Brit) ou favor (US)

pendable [pɑ̃dabl(ə)] adj: **tour ~** rotten trick; **c'est un cas ~!** he (ou she) deserves to be shot!

pendaison [pɑ̃dɛzɔ̃] nf hanging

pendant, e [pɑ̃dɑ̃, -ɑ̃t] adj hanging (out); (Admin, Jur) pending ▷ nm counterpart; matching piece ▷ prép during; **faire ~ à** to match; to be the counterpart of; **~ que** while; **~s d'oreilles** drop ou pendant earrings

pendeloque [pɑ̃dlɔk] nf pendant

pendentif [pɑ̃dɑ̃tif] nm pendant

penderie [pɑ̃dʀi] nf wardrobe; (placard) walk-in cupboard

pendiller [pɑ̃dije] vi to flap (about)

pendre [pɑ̃dʀ(ə)] vt, vi to hang; **se ~ (à)** (se suicider) to hang o.s. (on); **~ à** to hang (down) from; **~ qch à** (mur) to hang sth (up) on; (plafond) to hang sth (up) from; **se ~ à** (se suspendre) to hang from

pendu, e [pɑ̃dy] pp de **pendre** ▷ nm/f hanged man (ou woman)

pendulaire [pɑ̃dylɛʀ] adj pendular, of a pendulum

pendule [pɑ̃dyl] nf clock ▷ nm pendulum

pendulette [pɑ̃dylɛt] nf small clock

pêne [pɛn] nm bolt

pénétrant, e [penetʀɑ̃, -ɑ̃t] adj (air, froid) biting; (pluie) that soaks right through you; (fig: odeur) noticeable; (œil, regard) piercing; (clairvoyant, perspicace) perceptive ▷ nf (route) expressway

pénétration [penetʀasjɔ̃] nf (fig: d'idées etc) penetration; (perspicacité) perception

pénétré, e [penetʀe] adj (air, ton) earnest; **être ~ de soi-même/son importance** to be full of oneself/one's own importance

pénétrer [penetʀe] vi to come ou get in ▷ vt to penetrate; **~ dans** to enter; (froid, projectile) to penetrate; (: air, eau) to come into, get into; (mystère, secret) to fathom; **se ~ de qch** to get sth firmly set in one's mind

pénible [penibl(ə)] adj (astreignant) hard; (affligeant) painful; (personne, caractère) tiresome; **il m'est ~ de ...** I'm sorry to ...

péniblement [penibləmɑ̃] adv with difficulty

péniche [peniʃ] nf barge; **~ de débarquement** landing craft inv

pénicilline [penisilin] nf penicillin

péninsulaire [penɛ̃sylɛʀ] adj peninsular

péninsule [penɛ̃syl] nf peninsula

pénis [penis] nm penis

pénitence [penitɑ̃s] nf (repentir) penitence; (peine) penance; (punition, châtiment) punishment; **mettre un enfant en ~** ≈ to make a child stand in the corner; **faire ~** to do a penance

pénitencier [penitɑ̃sje] nm prison, penitentiary (US)

pénitent, e [penitɑ̃, -ɑ̃t] adj penitent

pénitentiaire [penitɑ̃sjɛʀ] adj prison cpd, penitentiary (US)

pénombre [penɔ̃bʀ(ə)] nf half-light

P

pensable [pɑ̃sabl(ə)] *adj*: **ce n'est pas ~** it's unthinkable

pensant, e [pɑ̃sɑ̃, -ɑ̃t] *adj*: **bien ~** right-thinking

pense-bête [pɑ̃sbɛt] *nm* aide-mémoire, mnemonic device

pensée [pɑ̃se] *nf* thought; (*démarche, doctrine*) thinking *no pl*; (*Bot*) pansy; **se représenter qch par la ~** to conjure up a mental picture of sth; **en ~** in one's mind

penser [pɑ̃se] *vi* to think ▷ *vt* to think; (*concevoir: problème, machine*) to think out; **~ à** to think of; (*songer à: ami, vacances*) to think of *ou* about; (*réfléchir à: problème, offre*): **~ à qch** to think about sth, think sth over; **~ à faire qch** to think of doing sth; **~ faire qch** to be thinking of doing sth, intend to do sth; **faire ~ à** to remind one of; **n'y pensons plus** let's forget it; **vous n'y pensez pas!** don't let it bother you!; **sans ~ à mal** without meaning any harm; **je le pense aussi** I think so too; **je pense que oui/non** I think so/don't think so

penseur [pɑ̃sœʀ] *nm* thinker; **libre ~** free-thinker

pensif, -ive [pɑ̃sif, -iv] *adj* pensive, thoughtful

pension [pɑ̃sjɔ̃] *nf* (*allocation*) pension; (*prix du logement*) board and lodging, bed and board; (*maison particulière*) boarding house; (*hôtel*) guesthouse, hotel; (*école*) boarding school; **prendre ~ chez** to take board and lodging at; **prendre qn en ~** to take sb (in) as a lodger; **mettre en ~** to send to boarding school; **~ alimentaire** (*d'étudiant*) living allowance; (*de divorcée*) maintenance allowance; alimony; **~ complète** full board; **~ de famille** boarding house, guesthouse; **~ de guerre/d'invalidité** war/disablement pension

pensionnaire [pɑ̃sjɔnɛʀ] *nm/f* boarder; guest

pensionnat [pɑ̃sjɔna] *nm* boarding school

pensionné, e [pɑ̃sjɔne] *nm/f* pensioner

pensivement [pɑ̃sivmɑ̃] *adv* pensively, thoughtfully

pensum [pɛ̃sɔm] *nm* (*Scol*) punishment exercise; (*fig*) chore

pentagone [pɛ̃tagɔn] *nm* pentagon; **le P~** the Pentagon

pentathlon [pɛ̃tatlɔ̃] *nm* pentathlon

pente [pɑ̃t] *nf* slope; **en ~** *adj* sloping

Pentecôte [pɑ̃tkot] *nf*: **la ~** Whitsun (*Brit*), Pentecost; (*dimanche*) Whitsunday (*Brit*); **lundi de ~** Whit Monday (*Brit*)

pénurie [penyʀi] *nf* shortage; **~ de main-d'œuvre** undermanning

PEP [pɛp] *sigle m* (= *plan d'épargne populaire*) individual savings plan

pépé [pepe] *nm* (*fam*) grandad

pépère [pepɛʀ] *adj* (*fam*) cushy; (*fam*) quiet ▷ *nm* (*fam*) grandad

pépier [pepje] *vi* to chirp, tweet

pépin [pepɛ̃] *nm* (*Bot: graine*) pip; (*fam: ennui*) snag, hitch; (*: parapluie*) brolly (*Brit*), umbrella

pépinière [pepinjɛʀ] *nf* nursery; (*fig*) nest, breeding-ground

pépiniériste [pepinjeʀist(ə)] *nm* nurseryman

pépite [pepit] *nf* nugget

PEPS *abr* (= *premier entré premier sorti*) first in first out

PER [pɛʀ] *sigle m* (= *plan d'épargne retraite*) type of personal pension plan

perçant, e [pɛʀsɑ̃, -ɑ̃t] *adj* (*vue, regard, yeux*) sharp, keen; (*cri, voix*) piercing, shrill

percée [pɛʀse] *nf* (*trouée*) opening; (*Mil, Comm: fig*) breakthrough; (*Sport*) break

perce-neige [pɛʀsənɛʒ] *nm ou f inv* snowdrop

perce-oreille [pɛʀsɔʀɛj] *nm* earwig

percepteur [pɛʀsɛptœʀ] *nm* tax collector

perceptible [pɛʀsɛptibl(ə)] *adj* (*son, différence*) perceptible; (*impôt*) payable, collectable

perception [pɛʀsɛpsjɔ̃] *nf* perception; (*d'impôts etc*) collection; (*bureau*) tax (collector's) office

percer [pɛʀse] *vt* to pierce; (*ouverture etc*) to make; (*mystère, énigme*) to penetrate ▷ *vi* to come through; (*réussir*) to break through; **~ une dent** to cut a tooth

perceuse [pɛʀsøz] *nf* drill; **~ à percussion** hammer drill

percevable [pɛʀsəvabl(ə)] *adj* collectable, payable

percevoir [pɛʀsəvwaʀ] *vt* (*distinguer*) to perceive, detect; (*taxe, impôt*) to collect; (*revenu, indemnité*) to receive

perche [pɛʀʃ(ə)] *nf* (*Zool*) perch; (*bâton*) pole; **~ à son** (*sound*) boom

percher [pɛʀʃe] *vt*: **~ qch sur** to perch sth on ▷ *vi*, **se percher** *vi* (*oiseau*) to perch

perchiste [pɛʀʃist(ə)] *nm/f* (*Sport*) pole vaulter; (*TV etc*) boom operator

perchoir [pɛʀʃwaʀ] *nm* perch; (*fig*) presidency of the French National Assembly

perclus, e [pɛʀkly, -yz] *adj*: **~ de** (*rhumatismes*) crippled with

perçois *etc* [pɛʀswa] *vb voir* **percevoir**

percolateur [pɛʀkɔlatœʀ] *nm* percolator

perçu, e [pɛʀsy] *pp de* **percevoir**

percussion [pɛʀkysjɔ̃] *nf* percussion

percussionniste [pɛʀkysjɔnist(ə)] *nm/f* percussionist

percutant, e [pɛʀkytɑ̃, -ɑ̃t] *adj* (*article etc*) resounding, forceful

percuter [pɛʀkyte] *vt* to strike; (*véhicule*) to crash into ▷ *vi*: **~ contre** to crash into

percuteur [pɛʀkytœʀ] *nm* firing pin, hammer

perdant, e [pɛʀdɑ̃, -ɑ̃t] *nm/f* loser ▷ *adj* losing

perdition [pɛʀdisjɔ̃] *nf* (*morale*) ruin; **en ~** (*Navig*) in distress; **lieu de ~** den of vice

perdre [pɛʀdʀ(ə)] *vt* to lose; (*gaspiller: temps, argent*) to waste; (*: occasion*) to waste, miss; (*personne: moralement etc*) to ruin ▷ *vi* to lose; (*sur une vente etc*) to lose out; (*récipient*) to leak; **se perdre** *vi* (*s'égarer*) to get lost, lose one's way; (*fig: se gâter*) to go to waste; (*disparaître*) to disappear, vanish; **il ne perd rien pour attendre** it can wait, it'll keep

perdreau, x [pɛʀdʀo] *nm* (young) partridge

perdrix [pɛʀdʀi] *nf* partridge

perdu, e [pɛʀdy] *pp de* **perdre** ▷ *adj* (*enfant, cause, objet*) lost; (*isolé*) out-of-the-way; (*Comm: emballage*) non-returnable; (*récolte etc*) ruined; (*malade*): **il est ~** there's no hope left for him; **à vos moments ~s** in your spare time

père [pɛʀ] *nm* father; **pères** *nmpl* (*ancêtres*) forefathers; **de ~ en fils** from father to son; **~ de famille** father; family man; **mon ~** (*Rel*) Father; **le ~ Noël** Father Christmas

pérégrinations [peʀegʀinɑsjɔ̃] *nfpl* travels

péremption [peʀɑ̃psjɔ̃] *nf*: **date de ~** expiry date

péremptoire [peʀɑ̃ptwaʀ] *adj* peremptory

pérennité [peʀenite] *nf* durability, lasting quality

péréquation [peʀekwɑsjɔ̃] *nf* (*des salaires*) realignment; (*des prix, impôts*) equalization

perfectible [pɛʀfɛktibl(ə)] *adj* perfectible

perfection [pɛʀfɛksjɔ̃] *nf* perfection; **à la ~** *adv* to perfection

perfectionné, e [pɛʀfɛksjone] *adj* sophisticated

perfectionnement [pɛʀfɛksjɔnmɑ̃] *nm* improvement

perfectionner [pɛʀfɛksjone] *vt* to improve, perfect; **se ~ en anglais** to improve one's English

perfectionniste [pɛʀfɛksjɔnist(ə)] *nm/f* perfectionist

perfide [pɛʀfid] *adj* perfidious, treacherous

perfidie [pɛʀfidi] *nf* treachery

perforant, e [pɛʀfɔʀɑ̃, -ɑ̃t] *adj* (*balle*) armour-piercing (*Brit*), armor-piercing (*US*)

perforateur, -trice [pɛʀfɔʀatœʀ, -tʀis] *nm/f* punch-card operator ▷ *nm* (*perceuse*) borer; drill ▷ *nf* (*perceuse*) borer; drill; (*pour cartes*) card-punch; (*de bureau*) punch

perforation [pɛʀfɔʀɑsjɔ̃] *nf* perforation; punching; (*trou*) hole

perforatrice [pɛʀfɔʀatʀis] *nf voir* **perforateur**

perforé, e [pɛʀfɔʀe] *adj*: **bande ~** punched tape; **carte ~** punch card

perforer [pɛʀfɔʀe] *vt* to perforate, punch a hole *ou* holes in; (*ticket, bande, carte*) to punch

perforeuse [pɛʀfɔʀøz] *nf* (*machine*) (card) punch; (*personne*) card punch operator

performance [pɛʀfɔʀmɑ̃s] *nf* performance

performant, e [pɛʀfɔʀmɑ̃, -ɑ̃t] *adj* (*Écon: produit, entreprise*) high-return *cpd*; (*Tech: appareil, machine*) high-performance *cpd*

perfusion [pɛʀfyzjɔ̃] *nf* perfusion; **faire une ~ à qn** to put sb on a drip

péricliter [peʀiklite] *vi* to go downhill

péridurale [peʀidyʀal] *nf* epidural

périgourdin, e [peʀiguʀdɛ̃, -in] *adj* of *ou* from the Perigord

péril [peʀil] *nm* peril; **au ~ de sa vie** at the risk of his life; **à ses risques et ~s** at his (*ou* her) own risk

périlleux, -euse [peʀijø, -øz] *adj* perilous

périmé, e [peʀime] *adj* (out)dated; (*Admin*) out-of-date, expired

périmètre [peʀimɛtʀ(ə)] *nm* perimeter

périnatal, e [peʀinatal] *adj* perinatal

période [peʀjɔd] *nf* period

périodique [peʀjɔdik] *adj* (*phases*) periodic; (*publication*) periodical; (*Math: fraction*) recurring ▷ *nm* periodical; **garniture** *ou* **serviette ~** sanitary towel (*Brit*) *ou* napkin (*US*)

périodiquement [peʀjɔdikmɑ̃] *adv* periodically

péripéties [peʀipesi] *nfpl* events, episodes

périphérie [peʀifeʀi] *nf* periphery; (*d'une ville*) outskirts *pl*

périphérique [peʀifeʀik] *adj* (*quartiers*) outlying; (*Anat, Tech*) peripheral; (*station de radio*) operating from a neighbouring country ▷ *nm* (*Inform*) peripheral; (*Auto*): (**boulevard**) **~** ring road (*Brit*), beltway (*US*)

périphrase [peʀifʀaz] *nf* circumlocution

périple [peʀipl(ə)] *nm* journey

périr [peʀiʀ] *vi* to die, perish

périscolaire [peʀiskɔlɛʀ] *adj* extracurricular

périscope [peʀiskɔp] *nm* periscope

périssable [peʀisabl(ə)] *adj* perishable

péristyle [peʀistil] *nm* peristyle

péritonite [peʀitɔnit] *nf* peritonitis

perle [pɛʀl(ə)] *nf* pearl; (*de plastique, métal, sueur*) bead; (*personne, chose*) gem, treasure; (*erreur*) gem, howler

perlé, e [pɛʀle] *adj* (*rire*) rippling, tinkling; (*travail*) exquisite; (*orge*) pearl *cpd*; **grève ~e** go-slow, selective strike (action)

perler [pɛʀle] *vi* to form in droplets

perlier, -ière [pɛʀlje, -jɛʀ] *adj* pearl *cpd*

permanence [pɛʀmanɑ̃s] *nf* permanence; (*local*) (duty) office, strike headquarters; (*service des urgences*) emergency service; (*Scol*) study room; **assurer une ~** (*service public, bureaux*) to operate *ou* maintain a basic service; **être de ~** to be on call *ou* duty; **en ~** *adv* (*toujours*) permanently; (*continûment*) continuously

permanent, e [pɛʀmanɑ̃, -ɑ̃t] *adj* permanent; (*spectacle*) continuous; (*armée, comité*) standing ▷ *nf* perm ▷ *nm/f* (*d'un syndicat, parti*) paid official

perméable [pɛʀmeabl(ə)] *adj* (*terrain*) permeable; **~ à** (*fig*) receptive *ou* open to

permettre [pɛʀmɛtʀ(ə)] *vt* to allow, permit; **~ à qn de faire/qch** to allow sb to do/sth; **se ~ de faire qch** to take the liberty of doing sth; **permettez!** excuse me!

permis, e [pɛʀmi, -iz] *pp de* **permettre** ▷ *nm* permit, licence (*Brit*), license (*US*); **~ de chasse** hunting permit; **~ (de conduire)** (driving) licence (*Brit*), (driver's) license (*US*); **~ de construire** planning permission (*Brit*), building permit (*US*); **~ d'inhumer** burial certificate; **~ poids lourds** ≈ HGV (driving) licence (*Brit*), ≈ class E (driver's) license (*US*); **~ de séjour** residence permit; **~ de travail** work permit

permissif, -ive [pɛʀmisif, -iv] *adj* permissive

permission [pɛʀmisjɔ̃] *nf* permission; (*Mil*) leave; (: *papier*) pass; **en ~** on leave; **avoir la ~ de faire** to have permission to do, be allowed to do

permissionnaire [pɛʀmisjɔnɛʀ] *nm* soldier on leave

permutable [pɛʁmytabl(ə)] *adj* which can be changed *ou* switched around

permuter [pɛʁmyte] *vt* to change around, permutate ▷ *vi* to change, swap

pernicieux, -euse [pɛʁnisjø, -øz] *adj* pernicious

péroné [peʁɔne] *nm* fibula

pérorer [peʁɔʁe] *vi* to hold forth

Pérou [peʁu] *nm*: **le ~** Peru

perpendiculaire [pɛʁpɑ̃dikylɛʁ] *adj, nf* perpendicular

perpendiculairement [pɛʁpɑ̃dikylɛʁmɑ̃] *adv* perpendicularly

perpète [pɛʁpɛt] *nf*: **à ~** (*fam: loin*) miles away; (*: longtemps*) forever

perpétrer [pɛʁpetʁe] *vt* to perpetrate

perpétuel, le [pɛʁpetɥɛl] *adj* perpetual; (*Admin etc*) permanent; for life

perpétuellement [pɛʁpetɥɛlmɑ̃] *adv* perpetually, constantly

perpétuer [pɛʁpetɥe] *vt* to perpetuate; **se perpétuer** (*usage, injustice*) to be perpetuated; (*espèces*) to survive

perpétuité [pɛʁpetɥite] *nf*: **à ~** *adj, adv* for life; **être condamné à ~** to be sentenced to life imprisonment, receive a life sentence

perplexe [pɛʁplɛks(ə)] *adj* perplexed, puzzled

perplexité [pɛʁplɛksite] *nf* perplexity

perquisition [pɛʁkizisjɔ̃] *nf* (*police*) search

perquisitionner [pɛʁkizisjɔne] *vi* to carry out a search

perron [peʁɔ̃] *nm* steps *pl* (*in front of mansion etc*)

perroquet [peʁɔkɛ] *nm* parrot

perruche [peʁyʃ] *nf* budgerigar (*Brit*), budgie (*Brit*), parakeet (*US*)

perruque [peʁyk] *nf* wig

persan, e [pɛʁsɑ̃, -an] *adj* Persian ▷ *nm* (*Ling*) Persian

perse [pɛʁs(ə)] *adj* Persian ▷ *nm* (*Ling*) Persian ▷ *nm/f*: **Perse** Persian ▷ *nf*: **la P~** Persia

persécuter [pɛʁsekyte] *vt* to persecute

persécution [pɛʁsekysjɔ̃] *nf* persecution

persévérance [pɛʁseveʁɑ̃s] *nf* perseverance

persévérant, e [pɛʁseveʁɑ̃, -ɑ̃t] *adj* persevering

persévérer [pɛʁseveʁe] *vi* to persevere; **~ à croire que** to continue to believe that

persiennes [pɛʁsjɛn] *nfpl* (slatted) shutters

persiflage [pɛʁsiflaʒ] *nm* mockery *no pl*

persifleur, -euse [pɛʁsiflœʁ, -øz] *adj* mocking

persil [pɛʁsi] *nm* parsley

persillé, e [pɛʁsije] *adj* (sprinkled) with parsley; (*fromage*) veined; (*viande*) marbled, with fat running through

Persique [pɛʁsik] *adj*: **le golfe ~** the (Persian) Gulf

persistance [pɛʁsistɑ̃s] *nf* persistence

persistant, e [pɛʁsistɑ̃, -ɑ̃t] *adj* persistent; (*feuilles*) evergreen; **à feuillage ~** evergreen

persister [pɛʁsiste] *vi* to persist; **~ à faire qch** to persist in doing sth

personnage [pɛʁsɔnaʒ] *nm* (*notable*) personality; figure; (*individu*) character, individual; (*Théât*) character; (*Peinture*) figure

personnaliser [pɛʁsɔnalize] *vt* to personalize; (*appartement*) to give a personal touch to

personnalité [pɛʁsɔnalite] *nf* personality; (*personnage*) prominent figure

personne [pɛʁsɔn] *nf* person ▷ *pron* nobody, no one; (*quelqu'un*) anybody, anyone; **personnes** *nfpl* people *pl*; **il n'y a ~** there's nobody in *ou* there, there isn't anybody in *ou* there; **10 euros par ~** 10 euros per person *ou* a head; **en ~** personally, in person; **~ âgée** elderly person; **~ à charge** (*Jur*) dependent; **~ morale** *ou* **civile** (*Jur*) legal entity

personnel, le [pɛʁsɔnɛl] *adj* personal; (*égoïste: personne*) selfish, self-centred; (*idée, opinion*): **j'ai des idées ~les à ce sujet** I have my own ideas about that ▷ *nm* personnel, staff; **service du ~** personnel department

personnellement [pɛʁsɔnɛlmɑ̃] *adv* personally

personnification [pɛʁsɔnifikasjɔ̃] *nf* personification; **c'est la ~ de la cruauté** he's cruelty personified

personnifier [pɛʁsɔnifje] *vt* to personify; to typify; **c'est l'honnêteté personnifiée** he (*ou* she *etc*) is honesty personified

perspective [pɛʁspɛktiv] *nf* (*Art*) perspective; (*vue, coup d'œil*) view; (*point de vue*) viewpoint, angle; (*chose escomptée, envisagée*) prospect; **en ~** in prospect

perspicace [pɛʁspikas] *adj* clear-sighted, gifted with *ou* showing) insight

perspicacité [pɛʁspikasite] *nf* insight, perspicacity

persuader [pɛʁsɥade] *vt*: **~ qn (de/de faire)** to persuade sb (of/to do); **j'en suis persuadé** I'm quite sure *ou* convinced (of it)

persuasif, -ive [pɛʁsɥazif, -iv] *adj* persuasive

persuasion [pɛʁsɥazjɔ̃] *nf* persuasion

perte [pɛʁt(ə)] *nf* loss; (*de temps*) waste; (*fig: morale*) ruin; **pertes** *nfpl* losses; **à ~** (*Comm*) at a loss; **à ~ de vue** as far as the eye can (*ou* could) see; (*fig*) interminably; **en pure ~** for absolutely nothing; **courir à sa ~** to be on the road to ruin; **être en ~ de vitesse** (*fig*) to be losing momentum; **avec ~ et fracas** forcibly; **~ de chaleur** heat loss; **~ sèche** dead loss; **~s blanches** (vaginal) discharge *sg*

pertinemment [pɛʁtinamɑ̃] *adv* to the point; (*savoir*) perfectly well, full well

pertinence [pɛʁtinɑ̃s] *nf* pertinence, relevance; discernment

pertinent, e [pɛʁtinɑ̃, -ɑ̃t] *adj* (*remarque*) apt, pertinent, relevant; (*analyse*) discerning, judicious

perturbateur, -trice [pɛʁtyʁbatœʁ, -tʁis] *adj* disruptive

perturbation [pɛʁtyʁbasjɔ̃] *nf* (*dans un service public*) disruption; (*agitation, trouble*) perturbation; **~ (atmosphérique)** atmospheric disturbance

perturber [pɛʁtyʁbe] *vt* to disrupt; (*Psych*) to perturb, disturb

péruvien, ne [peʁyvjɛ̃, -ɛn] *adj* Peruvian ▷ *nm/f*:

Péruvien, ne Peruvian

pervenche [pɛʀvɑ̃ʃ] *nf* periwinkle; (*fam*) traffic warden (*Brit*), meter maid (*US*)

pervers, e [pɛʀvɛʀ, -ɛʀs(ə)] *adj* perverted, depraved; (*malfaisant*) perverse

perversion [pɛʀvɛʀsjɔ̃] *nf* perversion

perversité [pɛʀvɛʀsite] *nf* depravity; perversity

perverti, e [pɛʀvɛʀti] *nm/f* pervert

pervertir [pɛʀvɛʀtiʀ] *vt* to pervert

pesage [pəzaʒ] *nm* weighing; (*Hippisme: action*) weigh-in; (*: salle*) weighing room; (*: enceinte*) enclosure

pesamment [pəzamɑ̃] *adv* heavily

pesant, e [pəzɑ̃, -ɑ̃t] *adj* heavy; (*fig*) burdensome ▷ *nm*: **valoir son ~ de** to be worth one's weight in

pesanteur [pəzɑ̃tœʀ] *nf* gravity

pèse-bébé [pɛzbebe] *nm* (baby) scales *pl*

pesée [pəze] *nf* weighing; (*Boxe*) weigh-in; (*pression*) pressure

pèse-lettre [pɛzlɛtʀ(ə)] *nm* letter scales *pl*

pèse-personne [pɛzpɛʀsɔn] *nm* (bathroom) scales *pl*

peser [pəze] *vt* to weigh; (*considérer, comparer*) to weigh up ▷ *vi* to be heavy; (*fig*) to carry weight; **~ sur** (*levier, bouton*) to press, push; (*fig: accabler*) to lie heavy on; (*: influencer*) to influence; **~ à qn** to weigh heavy on sb

pessaire [pɛsɛʀ] *nm* pessary

pessimisme [pesimism(ə)] *nm* pessimism

pessimiste [pesimist(ə)] *adj* pessimistic ▷ *nm/f* pessimist

peste [pɛst(ə)] *nf* plague; (*fig*) pest, nuisance

pester [pɛste] *vi*: **~ contre** to curse

pesticide [pɛstisid] *nm* pesticide

pestiféré, e [pɛstifeʀe] *nm/f* plague victim

pestilentiel, le [pɛstilɑ̃sjɛl] *adj* foul

pet [pɛ] *nm* (*fam!*) fart (!)

pétale [petal] *nm* petal

pétanque [petɑ̃k] *nf* type of bowls; *see note*

● **PÉTANQUE**

Pétanque is a version of the game of "boules", played on a variety of hard surfaces. Standing with their feet together, players throw steel bowls at a wooden jack. *Pétanque* originated in the South of France and is still very much associated with that area.

pétarade [petaʀad] *nf* backfiring *no pl*

pétarader [petaʀade] *vi* to backfire

pétard [petaʀ] *nm* (*feu d'artifice*) banger (*Brit*), firecracker; (*de cotillon*) cracker; (*Rail*) detonator

pet-de-nonne [pɛdnɔn] (*pl* **pets-de-nonne**) *nm* ≈ choux bun

péter [pete] *vi* (*fam: casser, sauter*) to burst; to bust; (*fam!*) to fart (!)

pète-sec [pɛtsɛk] *adj inv* abrupt, sharp (-tongued)

pétillant, e [petijɑ̃, -ɑ̃t] *adj* sparkling

pétiller [petije] *vi* (*flamme, bois*) to crackle;

(*mousse, champagne*) to bubble; (*pierre, métal*) to glisten; (*yeux*) to sparkle; (*fig*): **~ d'esprit** to sparkle with wit

petit, e [pəti, -it] *adj* (*gén*) small; (*main, objet, colline, en âge: enfant*) small, little; (*mince, fin: personne, taille, pluie*) slight; (*voyage*) short, little; (*bruit etc*) faint, slight; (*mesquin*) mean; (*peu important*) minor ▷ *nm/f* (*petit enfant*) little one, child; **petits** *nmpl* (*d'un animal*) young *pl*; **faire des ~s** to have kittens (*ou* puppies *etc*); **en ~** in miniature; **mon ~** son; little one; **ma ~** dear; little one; **pauvre ~** poor little thing; **la classe des ~s** the infant class; **pour ~s et grands** for children and adults; **les tout-~s** the little ones, the tiny tots; **~ à ~** bit by bit, gradually; **~(e) ami/e** boyfriend/girlfriend; **les ~es annonces** the small ads; **~ déjeuner** breakfast; **~ doigt** little finger; **le ~ écran** the small screen; **~ four** petit four; **~ pain** (bread) roll; **~e monnaie** small change; **~e vérole** smallpox; **~s pois** petit pois *pl*, garden peas; **~es gens** people of modest means

petit-beurre [pətibœʀ] (*pl* **petits-beurre**) *nm* sweet butter biscuit (*Brit*) *ou* cookie (*US*)

petit-bourgeois, petite-bourgeoise [pətibuʀʒwa, pətitbuʀʒwaz] (*pl* **petit(e)s-bourgeois(es)**) *adj* (*péj*) petit-bourgeois, middle-class

petite-fille [pətitfij] (*pl* **petites-filles**) *nf* granddaughter

petitement [pətitmɑ̃] *adv* poorly; meanly; **être logé ~** to be in cramped accommodation

petitesse [pətitɛs] *nf* smallness; (*d'un salaire, de revenus*) modestness; (*mesquinerie*) meanness

petit-fils [pətifis] (*pl* **petits-fils**) *nm* grandson

pétition [petisjɔ̃] *nf* petition; **faire signer une ~** to get up a petition

pétitionnaire [petisjɔnɛʀ] *nm/f* petitioner

pétitionner [petisjɔne] *vi* to petition

petit-lait [pətilɛ] (*pl* **petits-laits**) *nm* whey *no pl*

petit-nègre [pətinɛgʀ(ə)] *nm* (*péj*) pidgin French

petits-enfants [pətizɑ̃fɑ̃] *nmpl* grandchildren

petit-suisse [pətisɥis] (*pl* **petits-suisses**) *nm* small individual pot of cream cheese

pétoche [petɔʃ] *nf* (*fam*): **avoir la ~** to be scared out of one's wits

pétri, e [petʀi] *adj*: **~ d'orgueil** filled with pride

pétrifier [petʀifje] *vt* to petrify; (*fig*) to paralyze, transfix

pétrin [petʀɛ̃] *nm* kneading-trough; (*fig*): **dans le ~** in a jam *ou* fix

pétrir [petʀiʀ] *vt* to knead

pétrochimie [petʀɔʃimi] *nf* petrochemistry

pétrochimique [petʀɔʃimik] *adj* petrochemical

pétrodollar [petʀɔdɔlaʀ] *nm* petrodollar

pétrole [petʀɔl] *nm* oil; (*aussi*: **pétrole lampant**) paraffin (*Brit*), kerosene (*US*)

pétrolier, -ière [petʀɔlje, -jɛʀ] *adj* oil *cpd*; (*pays*) oil-producing ▷ *nm* (*navire*) oil tanker; (*financier*) oilman; (*technicien*) petroleum engineer

pétrolifère [petʀɔlifɛʀ] *adj* oil(-bearing)

P et T *sigle fpl* = **postes et télécommunications**

pétulant, e [petylɑ̃, -ɑ̃t] *adj* exuberant

 MOT-CLÉ

peu [pø] *adv* **1** (*modifiant verbe, adjectif, adverbe*): **il boit peu** he doesn't drink (very) much; **il est peu bavard** he's not very talkative; **peu avant/après** shortly before/afterwards; **pour peu qu'il fasse** if he should do, if by any chance he does

2 (*modifiant nom*): **peu de: peu de gens/d'arbres** few *ou* not (very) many people/trees; **il a peu d'espoir** he hasn't (got) much hope, he has little hope; **pour peu de temps** for (only) a short while; **à peu de frais** for very little cost

3: **peu à peu** little by little; **à peu près** just about, more or less; **à peu près 10 kg/10 euros** approximately 10 kg/10 euros

▷ *nm* **1**: **le peu de gens qui** the few people who; **le peu de sable qui** what little sand, the little sand which

2: **un peu** a little; **un petit peu** a little bit; **un peu d'espoir** a little hope; **elle est un peu bavarde** she's rather talkative; **un peu plus/moins de** slightly more/less (*ou* fewer) than; **pour un peu il ...**, **un peu plus et il ...** he very nearly *ou* all but ...; **essayez un peu!** have a go!, just try it!

▷ *pron*: **peu le savent** few know (it); **avant** *ou* **sous peu** shortly, before long; **depuis peu** for a short *ou* little while; (*au passé*) a short *ou* little while ago; **de peu** (only) just; **c'est peu de chose** it's nothing; **il est de peu mon cadet** he's just a little *ou* bit younger than me

peuplade [pœplad] *nf* (*horde, tribu*) tribe, people
peuple [pœpl(ə)] *nm* people; (*masse*): **un ~ de vacanciers** a crowd of holiday-makers; **il y a du ~** there are a lot of people
peuplé, e [pœple] *adj*: **très/peu ~** densely/sparsely populated
peupler [pœple] *vt* (*pays, région*) to populate; (*étang*) to stock; (*hommes, poissons*) to inhabit; (*fig: imagination, rêves*) to fill; **se peupler** *vi* (*ville, région*) to become populated; (*fig: s'animer*) to fill (up), be filled
peuplier [pøplije] *nm* poplar (tree)
peur [pœʀ] *nf* fear; **avoir ~ (de/de faire/que)** to be frightened *ou* afraid (of/of doing/that); **prendre ~** to take fright; **faire ~ à** to frighten; **de ~ de/que** for fear of/that; **j'ai ~ qu'il ne soit trop tard** I'm afraid it might be too late; **j'ai ~ qu'il (ne) vienne (pas)** I'm afraid he may (not) come
peureux, -euse [pœʀø, -øz] *adj* fearful, timorous
peut [pø] *vb voir* **pouvoir**
peut-être [pøtɛtʀ(ə)] *adv* perhaps, maybe; **~ que** perhaps, maybe; **~ bien qu'il fera/est** he may well do/be
peuvent [pœv], **peux** *etc* [pø] *vb voir* **pouvoir**
p. ex. *abr* (= *par exemple*) e.g.

phalange [falɑ̃ʒ] *nf* (*Anat*) phalanx; (*Mil: fig*) phalanx
phallique [falik] *adj* phallic
phallocrate [falɔkʀat] *nm* male chauvinist
phallocratie [falɔkʀasi] *nf* male chauvinism
phallus [falys] *nm* phallus
pharaon [faʀaɔ̃] *nm* Pharaoh
phare [faʀ] *nm* (*en mer*) lighthouse; (*d'aéroport*) beacon; (*de véhicule*) headlight, headlamp (*Brit*)
▷ *adj*: **produit ~** leading product; **se mettre en ~s, mettre ses ~s** to put on one's headlights; **~s de recul** reversing (*Brit*) *ou* back-up (*US*) lights
pharmaceutique [faʀmasøtik] *adj* pharmaceutic(al)
pharmacie [faʀmasi] *nf* (*science*) pharmacology; (*magasin*) chemist's (*Brit*), pharmacy; (*officine*) dispensary; (*produits*) pharmaceuticals *pl*; (*armoire*) medicine chest *ou* cupboard, first-aid cupboard
pharmacien, ne [faʀmasjɛ̃, -ɛn] *nm/f* pharmacist, chemist (*Brit*)
pharmacologie [faʀmakɔlɔʒi] *nf* pharmacology
pharyngite [faʀɛ̃ʒit] *nf* pharyngitis *no pl*
pharynx [faʀɛ̃ks] *nm* pharynx
phase [faz] *nf* phase
phénoménal, e, -aux [fenɔmenal, -o] *adj* phenomenal
phénomène [fenɔmɛn] *nm* phenomenon; (*monstre*) freak
philanthrope [filɑ̃tʀɔp] *nm/f* philanthropist
philanthropie [filɑ̃tʀɔpi] *nf* philanthropy
philanthropique [filɑ̃tʀɔpik] *adj* philanthropic
philatélie [filateli] *nf* philately, stamp collecting
philatélique [filatelik] *adj* philatelic
philatéliste [filatelist(ə)] *nm/f* philatelist, stamp collector
philharmonique [filaʀmɔnik] *adj* philharmonic
philippin, e [filipɛ̃, -in] *adj* Filipino
Philippines [filipin] *nfpl*: **les ~** the Philippines
philistin [filistɛ̃] *nm* philistine
philo [filo] *nf* (*fam: = philosophie*) philosophy
philosophe [filɔzɔf] *nm/f* philosopher ▷ *adj* philosophical
philosopher [filɔzɔfe] *vi* to philosophize
philosophie [filɔzɔfi] *nf* philosophy
philosophique [filɔzɔfik] *adj* philosophical
philosophiquement [filɔzɔfikmɑ̃] *adv* philosophically
philtre [filtʀ(ə)] *nm* philtre, love potion
phlébite [flebit] *nf* phlebitis
phlébologue [flebɔlɔg] *nm/f* vein specialist
phobie [fɔbi] *nf* phobia
phonétique [fɔnetik] *adj* phonetic ▷ *nf* phonetics *sg*
phonétiquement [fɔnetikmɑ̃] *adv* phonetically
phonographe [fɔnɔgʀaf] *nm* (wind-up) gramophone
phoque [fɔk] *nm* seal; (*fourrure*) sealskin

phosphate [fɔsfat] *nm* phosphate
phosphaté, e [fɔsfate] *adj* phosphate-enriched
phosphore [fɔsfɔʀ] *nm* phosphorus
phosphoré, e [fɔsfɔʀe] *adj* phosphorous
phosphorescent, e [fɔsfɔʀesɑ̃, -ɑ̃t] *adj* luminous
phosphorique [fɔsfɔʀik] *adj*: **acide ~** phosphoric acid
photo [fɔto] *nf* (*photographie*) photo ▷ *adj*: **appareil/pellicule ~** camera/film; **en ~** in *ou* on a photo; **prendre en ~** to take a photo of; **aimer la/faire de la ~** to like taking/take photos; **~ en couleurs** colour photo; **~ d'identité** passport photo
photo... [fɔto] *préfixe* photo...
photocopie [fɔtɔkɔpi] *nf* (*procédé*) photocopying; (*document*) photocopy
photocopier [fɔtɔkɔpje] *vt* to photocopy
photocopieur [fɔtɔkɔpjœʀ] *nm*, **photocopieuse** [fɔtɔkɔpjøz] *nf* (photo)copier
photo-électrique [fɔtɔelɛktʀik] *adj* photo-electric
photo-finish [fɔtofiniʃ] (*pl* **photos-finish**) *nf* (*appareil*) photo finish camera; (*photo*) photo finish picture; **il y a eu ~ pour la troisième place** there was a photo finish for third place
photogénique [fɔtɔʒenik] *adj* photogenic
photographe [fɔtɔgʀaf] *nm/f* photographer
photographie [fɔtɔgʀafi] *nf* (*procédé, technique*) photography; (*cliché*) photograph; **faire de la ~** to do photography as a hobby; (*comme métier*) to be a photographer
photographier [fɔtɔgʀafje] *vt* to photograph, take
photographique [fɔtɔgʀafik] *adj* photographic
photogravure [fɔtɔgʀavyʀ] *nf* photoengraving
photomaton® [fɔtɔmatɔ̃] *nm* photo-booth, photomat
photomontage [fɔtɔmɔ̃taʒ] *nm* photomontage
photophone [fɔtɔfɔn] *nm* camera phone
photo-robot [fɔtɔʀɔbo] *nf* Identikit® (picture)
photosensible [fɔtɔsɑ̃sibl(ə)] *adj* photosensitive
photostat [fɔtɔsta] *nm* photostat
phrase [fʀaz] *nf* (*Ling*) sentence; (*propos, Mus*) phrase; **phrases** *nfpl* (*péj*) flowery language *sg*
phraséologie [fʀazeɔlɔʒi] *nf* phraseology; (*rhétorique*) flowery language
phraseur, -euse [fʀazœʀ, -øz] *nm/f*: **c'est un ~** he uses such flowery language
phrygien, ne [fʀiʒjɛ̃, -ɛn] *adj*: **bonnet ~** Phrygian cap
phtisie [ftizi] *nf* consumption
phylloxéra [filɔkseʀa] *nm* phylloxera
physicien, ne [fizisjɛ̃, -ɛn] *nm/f* physicist
physiologie [fizjɔlɔʒi] *nf* physiology
physiologique [fizjɔlɔʒik] *adj* physiological
physiologiquement [fizjɔlɔʒikmɑ̃] *adv* physiologically
physionomie [fizjɔnɔmi] *nf* face; (*d'un paysage etc*) physiognomy

physionomiste [fizjɔnɔmist(ə)] *nm/f* good judge of faces; person who has a good memory for faces
physiothérapie [fizjɔteʀapi] *nf* natural medicine, alternative medicine
physique [fizik] *adj* physical ▷ *nm* physique ▷ *nf* physics *sg*; **au ~** physically
physiquement [fizikmɑ̃] *adv* physically
phytothérapie [fitɔteʀapi] *nf* herbal medicine
p.i. *abr* = **par intérim**; *voir* **intérim**
piaffer [pjafe] *vi* to stamp
piaillement [pjajmɑ̃] *nm* squawking *no pl*
piailler [pjaje] *vi* to squawk
pianiste [pjanist(ə)] *nm/f* pianist
piano [pjano] *nm* piano; **~ à queue** grand piano
pianoter [pjanɔte] *vi* to tinkle away (at the piano); (*tapoter*): **~ sur** to drum one's fingers on
piaule [pjol] *nf* (*fam*) pad
piauler [pjole] *vi* (*enfant*) to whimper; (*oiseau*) to cheep
PIB *sigle m* (= *produit intérieur brut*) GDP
pic [pik] *nm* (*instrument*) pick(axe); (*montagne*) peak; (*Zool*) woodpecker; **à ~** *adv* vertically; (*fig*) just at the right time; **couler à ~** (*bateau*) to go straight down; **~ à glace** ice pick
picard, e [pikaʀ, -aʀd(ə)] *adj* of *ou* from Picardy
Picardie [pikaʀdi] *nf*: **la ~** Picardy
picaresque [pikaʀɛsk(ə)] *adj* picaresque
piccolo [pikɔlo] *nm* piccolo
pichenette [piʃnɛt] *nf* flick
pichet [piʃɛ] *nm* jug
pickpocket [pikpɔkɛt] *nm* pickpocket
pick-up [pikœp] *nm inv* record player
picorer [pikɔʀe] *vt* to peck
picot [piko] *nm* sprocket; **entraînement par roue à ~s** sprocket feed
picotement [pikɔtmɑ̃] *nm* smarting *no pl*, prickling *no pl*
picoter [pikɔte] *vt* (*oiseau*) to peck ▷ *vi* (*irriter*) to smart, prickle
pictural, e, -aux [piktyʀal, -o] *adj* pictorial
pie [pi] *nf* magpie; (*fig*) chatterbox ▷ *adj inv*: **cheval ~** piebald; **vache ~** black and white cow
pièce [pjɛs] *nf* (*d'un logement*) room; (*Théât*) play; (*de mécanisme, machine*) part; (*de monnaie*) coin; (*Couture*) patch; (*document*) document; (*de drap, fragment, d'une collection*) piece; (*de bétail*) head; **mettre en ~s** to smash to pieces; **deux euros ~** two euros each; **vendre à la ~** to sell separately *ou* individually; **travailler/payer à la ~** to do piecework/pay piece rate; **de toutes ~s: c'est inventé de toutes ~s** it's a complete fabrication; **un maillot une ~** a one-piece swimsuit; **un deux-~s cuisine** a two-room(ed) flat (*Brit*) *ou* apartment (*US*) with kitchen; **tout d'une ~** (*personne: franc*) blunt; (: *sans souplesse*) inflexible; **~ à conviction** exhibit; **~ d'eau** ornamental lake *ou* pond; **~ d'identité: avez-vous une ~ d'identité?** have you got any (means of) identification?; **~ jointe** (*Inform*) attachment; **~ montée** tiered cake; **~ de rechange** spare (part); **~ de résistance** pièce de

P

résistance; (*plat*) main dish; **~s détachées** spares, (spare) parts; **en ~s détachées** (*à monter*) in kit form; **~s justificatives** supporting documents

pied [pje] *nm* foot; (*de verre*) stem; (*de table*) leg; (*de lampe*) base; (*plante*) plant; **~s nus** barefoot; **à ~ on foot**; **à ~ sec** without getting one's feet wet; **à ~ d'œuvre** ready to start (work); **au ~ de la lettre** literally; **au ~ levé** at a moment's notice; **de ~ en cap** from head to foot; **en ~** (*portrait*) full-length; **avoir ~** to be able to touch the bottom, not to be out of one's depth; **avoir le ~ marin** to be a good sailor; **perdre ~** to lose one's footing; (*fig*) to get out of one's depth; **sur ~** (*Agr*) on the stalk, uncut; (*debout, rétabli*) up and about; **mettre sur ~** (*entreprise*) to set up; **mettre à ~** to suspend; to lay off; **mettre qn au ~ du mur** to get sb with his (*ou* her) back to the wall; **sur le ~ de guerre** ready for action; **sur un ~ d'égalité** on an equal footing; **sur ~ d'intervention** on stand-by; **faire du ~ à qn** (*prévenir*) to give sb a (warning) kick; (*galamment*) to play footsie with sb; **mettre les ~s quelque part** to set foot somewhere; **faire des ~s et des mains** (*fig*) to move heaven and earth, pull out all the stops; **c'est le ~!** (*fam*) it's terrific!; **se lever du bon ~/du ~ gauche** to get out of bed on the right/wrong side; **~ de lit** footboard; **~ de nez: faire un ~ de nez à** to thumb one's nose at; **~ de vigne** vine

pied-à-terre [pjetatɛʀ] *nm inv* pied-à-terre

pied-bot [pjebo] (*pl* **pieds-bots**) *nm* person with a club foot

pied-de-biche [pjedbiʃ] (*pl* **pieds-de-biche**) *nm* claw; (*Couture*) presser foot

pied-de-poule [pjedpul] *adj inv* hound's-tooth

piédestal, -aux [pjedɛstal, -o] *nm* pedestal

pied-noir [pjenwaʀ] (*pl* **pieds-noirs**) *nm* Algerian-born Frenchman

piège [pjɛʒ] *nm* trap; **prendre au ~** to trap

piéger [pjeʒe] *vt* (*animal, fig*) to trap; (*avec une bombe*) to booby-trap; **lettre/voiture piégée** letter-/car-bomb

piercing [pjɛʀsiŋ] *nm* piercing

pierraille [pjɛʀɑj] *nf* loose stones *pl*

pierre [pjɛʀ] *nf* stone; **première ~** (*d'un édifice*) foundation stone; **mur de ~s sèches** drystone wall; **faire d'une ~ deux coups** to kill two birds with one stone; **~ à briquet** flint; **~ fine** semiprecious stone; **~ ponce** pumice stone; **~ de taille** freestone *no pl*; **~ tombale** tombstone, gravestone; **~ de touche** touchstone

pierreries [pjɛʀʀi] *nfpl* gems, precious stones

pierreux, -euse [pjɛʀø, -øz] *adj* stony

piété [pjete] *nf* piety

piétinement [pjetinmɑ̃] *nm* stamping *no pl*

piétiner [pjetine] *vi* (*trépigner*) to stamp (one's foot); (*marquer le pas*) to stand about; (*fig*) to be at a standstill ▷ *vt* to trample on

piéton, ne [pjetɔ̃, -ɔn] *nm/f* pedestrian ▷ *adj* pedestrian *cpd*

piétonnier, -ière [pjetɔnje, -jɛʀ] *adj* pedestrian *cpd*

piètre [pjɛtʀ(ə)] *adj* poor, mediocre

pieu, x [pjø] *nm* (*piquet*) post; (*pointu*) stake; (*fam: lit*) bed

pieusement [pjøzmɑ̃] *adv* piously

pieuvre [pjœvʀ(ə)] *nf* octopus

pieux, -euse [pjø, -øz] *adj* pious

pif [pif] *nm* (*fam*) conk (*Brit*), beak; **au ~ = au pifomètre**

piffer [pife] *vt* (*fam*): **je ne peux pas le ~** I can't stand him

pifomètre [pifɔmɛtʀ(ə)] *nm* (*fam*): **choisir** *etc* **au ~** to follow one's nose when choosing *etc*

pige [piʒ] *nf* piecework rate

pigeon [piʒɔ̃] *nm* pigeon; **~ voyageur** homing pigeon

pigeonnant, e [piʒɔnɑ̃, -ɑ̃t] *adj* full, well-developed

pigeonneau, x [piʒɔno] *nm* young pigeon

pigeonnier [piʒɔnje] *nm* pigeon loft, dovecot(e)

piger [piʒe] *vi* (*fam*) to get it ▷ *vt* (*fam*) to get, understand

pigiste [piʒist(ə)] *nm/f* (*typographe*) typesetter on piecework; (*journaliste*) freelance journalist (*paid by the line*)

pigment [pigmɑ̃] *nm* pigment

pignon [piɲɔ̃] *nm* (*de mur*) gable; (*d'engrenage*) cog(wheel), gearwheel; (*graine*) pine kernel; **avoir ~ sur rue** (*fig*) to have a prosperous business

pile [pil] *nf* (*tas, pilier*) pile; (*Élec*) battery ▷ *adj*: **le côté ~** tails ▷ *adv* (*net, brusquement*) dead; (*à temps, à point nommé*) just at the right time; **à deux heures ~** at two on the dot; **jouer à ~ ou face** to toss up (for it); **~ ou face?** heads or tails?

piler [pile] *vt* to crush, pound

pileux, -euse [pilø, -øz] *adj*: **système ~** (body) hair

pilier [pilje] *nm* (*colonne, support*) pillar; (*personne*) mainstay; (*Rugby*) prop (forward)

pillage [pijaʒ] *nm* pillaging, plundering, looting

pillard, e [pijaʀ, -aʀd(ə)] *nm/f* looter; plunderer

piller [pije] *vt* to pillage, plunder, loot

pilleur, -euse [pijœʀ, -øz] *nm/f* looter

pilon [pilɔ̃] *nm* (*instrument*) pestle; (*de volaille*) drumstick; **mettre un livre au ~** to pulp a book

pilonner [pilɔne] *vt* to pound

pilori [pilɔʀi] *nm*: **mettre** *ou* **clouer au ~** to pillory

pilotage [pilɔtaʒ] *nm* piloting; flying; **~ automatique** automatic piloting; **~ sans visibilité** blind flying

pilote [pilɔt] *nm* pilot; (*de char, voiture*) driver ▷ *adj* pilot *cpd*; **usine/ferme ~** experimental factory/farm; **~ de chasse/d'essai/de ligne** fighter/test/airline pilot; **~ de course** racing driver

piloter [pilɔte] *vt* (*navire*) to pilot; (*avion*) to fly; (*automobile*) to drive; (*fig*): **~ qn** to guide sb round

pilotis [pilɔti] *nm* pile; stilt

pilule [pilyl] *nf* pill; **prendre la ~** to be on the

pill; ~ **du lendemain** morning-after pill

pimbêche [pɛ̃bɛʃ] *nf* (*péj*) stuck-up girl

piment [pimɑ̃] *nm* (*Bot*) pepper, capsicum; (*fig*) spice, piquancy; ~ **rouge** (*Culin*) chilli

pimenté, e [pimɑ̃te] *adj* hot and spicy

pimenter [pimɑ̃te] *vt* (*plat*) to season (with peppers *ou* chillis); (*fig*) to add *ou* give spice to

pimpant, e [pɛ̃pɑ̃, -ɑ̃t] *adj* spruce

pin [pɛ̃] *nm* pine (tree); (*bois*) pine(wood)

pinacle [pinakl(ə)] *nm*: **porter qn au** ~ (*fig*) to praise sb to the skies

pinard [pinaʀ] *nm* (*fam*) (cheap) wine, plonk (*Brit*)

pince [pɛ̃s] *nf* (*outil*) pliers *pl*; (*de homard, crabe*) pincer, claw; (*Couture: pli*) dart; ~ **à sucre/glace** sugar/ice tongs *pl*; ~ **à épiler** tweezers *pl*; ~ **à linge** clothes peg (*Brit*) *ou* pin (*US*); ~ **universelle** (universal) pliers *pl*; ~**s de cycliste** bicycle clips

pincé, e [pɛ̃se] *adj* (*air*) stiff; (*mince: bouche*) pinched ▷ *nf*: **une ~e de** a pinch of

pinceau, x [pɛ̃so] *nm* (paint)brush

pincement [pɛ̃smɑ̃] *nm*: ~ **au cœur** twinge of regret

pince-monseigneur [pɛ̃smɔ̃sɛɲœʀ] (*pl* **pinces-monseigneur**) *nf* crowbar

pince-nez [pɛ̃sne] *nm inv* pince-nez

pincer [pɛ̃se] *vt* to pinch; (*Mus: cordes*) to pluck; (*Couture*) to dart, put darts in; (*fam*) to nab; **se ~ le doigt** to squeeze *ou* nip one's finger; **se ~ le nez** to hold one's nose

pince-sans-rire [pɛ̃ssɑ̃ʀiʀ] *adj inv* deadpan

pincettes [pɛ̃sɛt] *nfpl* tweezers; (*pour le feu*) (fire) tongs

pinçon [pɛ̃sɔ̃] *nm* pinch mark

pinède [pinɛd] *nf* pinewood, pine forest

pingouin [pɛ̃gwɛ̃] *nm* penguin

ping-pong [piŋpɔ̃g] *nm* table tennis

pingre [pɛ̃gʀ(ə)] *adj* niggardly

pinson [pɛ̃sɔ̃] *nm* chaffinch

pintade [pɛ̃tad] *nf* guinea-fowl

pin up [pinœp] *nf inv* pin-up (girl)

pioche [pjɔʃ] *nf* pickaxe

piocher [pjɔʃe] *vt* to dig up (with a pickaxe); (*fam*) to swot (*Brit*) *ou* grind (*US*) at; ~ **dans** to dig into

piolet [pjɔlɛ] *nm* ice axe

pion, ne [pjɔ̃, pjɔn] *nm/f* (*Scol: péj*) student paid to supervise schoolchildren ▷ *nm* (*Échecs*) pawn; (*Dames*) piece, draught (*Brit*), checker (*US*)

pionnier [pjɔnje] *nm* pioneer

pipe [pip] *nf* pipe; **fumer la** *ou* **une** ~ to smoke a pipe; ~ **de bruyère** briar pipe

pipeau, x [pipo] *nm* (reed-)pipe

pipe-line [piplin] *nm* pipeline

piper [pipe] *vt* (*dé*) to load; (*carte*) to mark; **sans** ~ **mot** (*fam*) without a squeak; **les dés sont pipés** (*fig*) the dice are loaded

pipette [pipɛt] *nf* pipette

pipi [pipi] *nm* (*fam*): **faire** ~ to have a wee

piquant, e [pikɑ̃, -ɑ̃t] *adj* (*barbe, rosier etc*) prickly; (*saveur, sauce*) hot, pungent; (*fig: description, style*) racy; (: *mordant, caustique*) biting ▷ *nm* (*épine*) thorn, prickle; (*de hérisson*) quill, spine; (*fig*) spiciness, spice

pique [pik] *nf* (*arme*) pike; (*fig*): **envoyer** *ou* **lancer des** ~**s à qn** to make cutting remarks to sb ▷ *nm* (*Cartes: couleur*) spades *pl*; (: *carte*) spade

piqué, e [pike] *adj* (*Couture*) (machine-)stitched; quilted; (*livre, glace*) mildewed; (*vin*) sour; (*Mus: note*) staccato; (*fam: personne*) nuts ▷ *nm* (*Aviat*) dive; (*Textiles*) piqué

pique-assiette [pikasjɛt] *nm/f inv* (*péj*) scrounger, sponger

pique-fleurs [pikflœʀ] *nm inv* flower holder

pique-nique [piknik] *nm* picnic

pique-niquer [piknike] *vi* to (have a) picnic

pique-niqueur, -euse [piknikœʀ, -øz] *nm/f* picnicker

piquer [pike] *vt* (*percer*) to prick; (*Méd*) to give an injection to; (: *animal blessé etc*) to put to sleep; (*insecte, fumée, ortie*) to sting; (: *poivre*) to burn; (: *froid*) to bite; (*Couture*) to machine (stitch); (*intérêt etc*) to arouse; (*fam: prendre*) to pick up; (: *voler*) to pinch; (: *arrêter*) to nab; (*planter*): ~ **qch dans** to stick sth into; (*fixer*): ~ **qch à** *ou* **sur** to pin sth onto ▷ *vi* (*oiseau, avion*) to go into a dive; (*saveur*) to be pungent; to be sour; **se piquer** (*avec une aiguille*) to prick o.s.; (*se faire une piqûre*) to inject o.s.; (*se vexer*) to get annoyed; **se ~ de faire** to pride o.s. on doing; ~ **sur** to swoop down on; to head straight for; ~ **du nez** (*avion*) to go into a nose-dive; ~ **une tête** (*plonger*) to dive headfirst; ~ **un galop/un cent mètres** to break into a gallop/put on a sprint; ~ **une crise** to throw a fit; ~ **au vif** (*fig*) to sting

piquet [pikɛ] *nm* (*pieu*) post, stake; (*de tente*) peg; **mettre un élève au** ~ to make a pupil stand in the corner; ~ **de grève** (strike) picket; ~ **d'incendie** fire-fighting squad

piqueté, e [pikte] *adj*: ~ **de** dotted with

piquette [pikɛt] *nf* (*fam*) cheap wine, plonk (*Brit*)

piqûre [pikyʀ] *nf* (*d'épingle*) prick; (*d'ortie*) sting; (*de moustique*) bite; (*Méd*) injection, shot (*US*); (*Couture*) (straight) stitch; straight stitching; (*de ver*) hole; (*tache*) (spot of) mildew; **faire une** ~ **à qn** to give sb an injection

piranha [piʀana] *nm* piranha

piratage [piʀataʒ] *nm* (*Inform*) piracy

pirate [piʀat] *adj* pirate *cpd* ▷ *nm* pirate; (*fig: escroc*) crook, shark; (*Inform*) hacker; ~ **de l'air** hijacker

pirater [piʀate] *vi* (*Inform*) to hack ▷ *vt* (*Inform*) to hack into

piraterie [piʀatʀi] *nf* (act of) piracy; ~ **aérienne** hijacking

pire [piʀ] *adj* (*comparatif*) worse; (*superlatif*): **le (la)** ~ ... the worst ... ▷ *nm*: **le** ~ **(de)** the worst (of)

Pirée [piʀe] *n* Piraeus

pirogue [piʀɔg] *nf* dugout (canoe)

pirouette [piʀwɛt] *nf* pirouette; (*fig: volte-face*) about-turn

pis [pi] *nm* (*de vache*) udder; (*pire*): **le** ~ the worst

p

▷ *adj, adv* worse; **qui ~ est** what is worse; **au ~ aller** if the worst comes to the worst, at worst

pis-aller [pizale] *nm inv* stopgap

pisciculture [pisikyltyʀ] *nf* fish farming

piscine [pisin] *nf* (swimming) pool; **~ couverte** indoor (swimming) pool

Pise [piz] *n* Pisa

pissenlit [pisɑ̃li] *nm* dandelion

pisser [pise] *vi* (fam!) to pee

pissotière [pisɔtjɛʀ] *nf* (fam) public urinal

pistache [pistaʃ] *nf* pistachio (nut)

pistard [pistaʀ] *nm* (Cyclisme) track cyclist

piste [pist(ə)] *nf* (d'un animal, sentier) track, trail; (indice) lead; (de stade, de magnétophone: de cirque) ring; (de danse) floor; (de patinage) rink; (de ski) run; (Aviat) runway; **~ cavalière** bridle path; **~ cyclable** cycle track, bikeway (US); **~ sonore** sound track

pister [piste] *vt* to track, trail

pisteur [pistœʀ] *nm* (Ski) member of the ski patrol

pistil [pistil] *nm* pistil

pistolet [pistɔlɛ] *nm* (arme) pistol, gun; (à peinture) spray gun; **~ à bouchon/air comprimé** popgun/airgun; **~ à eau** water pistol

pistolet-mitrailleur [pistɔlɛmitʀajœʀ] (*pl* **pistolets-mitrailleurs**) *nm* submachine gun

piston [pistɔ̃] *nm* (Tech) piston; (Mus) valve; (fig: appui) string-pulling

pistonner [pistɔne] *vt* (candidat) to pull strings for

pitance [pitɑ̃s] *nf* (péj) (means of) sustenance

piteusement [pitøzmɑ̃] *adv* (échouer) miserably

piteux, -euse [pitø, -øz] *adj* pitiful, sorry (avant le nom); **en ~ état** in a sorry state

pitié [pitje] *nf* pity; **sans ~** *adj* pitiless, merciless; **faire ~** to inspire pity; **il me fait ~** I pity him, I feel sorry for him; **avoir ~ de** (compassion) to pity, feel sorry for; (merci) to have pity ou mercy on; **par ~!** for pity's sake!

piton [pitɔ̃] *nm* (clou) peg, bolt; **~ rocheux** rocky outcrop

pitoyable [pitwajabl(ə)] *adj* pitiful

pitre [pitʀ(ə)] *nm* clown

pitrerie [pitʀəʀi] *nf* tomfoolery *no pl*

pittoresque [pitɔʀɛsk(ə)] *adj* picturesque; (expression, détail) colourful (Brit), colorful (US)

pivert [pivɛʀ] *nm* green woodpecker

pivoine [pivwan] *nf* peony

pivot [pivo] *nm* pivot; (d'une dent) post

pivoter [pivɔte] *vi* (fauteuil) to swivel; (porte) to revolve; **~ sur ses talons** to swing round

pixel [piksɛl] *nm* pixel

pizza [pidza] *nf* pizza

PJ *sigle f* = **police judiciaire** ▷ *sigle fpl* (= **pièces jointes**) encl

PL *sigle m* (Auto) = **poids lourd**

Pl. *abr* = **place**

placage [plakaʒ] *nm* (bois) veneer

placard [plakaʀ] *nm* (armoire) cupboard; (affiche) poster, notice; (Typo) galley; **~ publicitaire** display advertisement

placarder [plakaʀde] *vt* (affiche) to put up; (mur) to stick posters on

place [plas] *nf* (emplacement, situation, classement) place; (de ville, village) square; (Écon): **~ financière/boursière** money/stock market; (espace libre) room, space; (de parking) space; (siège: de train, cinéma, voiture) seat; (prix: au cinéma etc) price; (: dans un bus, taxi) fare; (emploi) job; **en ~** (mettre) in its place; **de ~ en ~, par ~s** here and there, in places; **sur ~** on the spot; **faire ~ à** to give way to; **faire de la ~ à** to make room for; **ça prend de la ~** it takes up a lot of room ou space; **prendre ~** to take one's place; **remettre qn à sa ~** to put sb in his (ou her) place; **ne pas rester** ou **tenir en ~** to be always on the go; **à la ~ de** in place of, instead of; **une quatre ~s** (Auto) a four-seater; **il y a 20 ~s assises/debout** there are 20 seats/there is standing room for 20; **~ forte** fortified town; **~ d'honneur** place (ou seat) of honour (Brit) ou honor (US)

placé, e [plase] *adj* (Hippisme) placed; **haut ~** (fig) high-ranking; **être bien/mal ~** to be well/badly placed; (spectateur) to have a good/bad seat; **être bien/mal ~ pour faire** to be in/not to be in a position to do

placebo [plasebo] *nm* placebo

placement [plasmɑ̃] *nm* placing; (Finance) investment; **agence** ou **bureau de ~** employment agency

placenta [plasɑ̃ta] *nm* placenta

placer [plase] *vt* to place, put; (convive, spectateur) to seat; (capital, argent) to place, invest; (dans la conversation) to put ou get in; **~ qn chez** to get sb a job at (ou with); **se ~ au premier rang** to go and stand (ou sit) in the first row

placide [plasid] *adj* placid

placidité [plasidite] *nf* placidity

placier, -ière [plasje, -jɛʀ] *nm/f* commercial rep(resentative), salesman/woman

Placoplâtre® [plakoplatʀ] *nm* plasterboard

plafond [plafɔ̃] *nm* ceiling

plafonner [plafɔne] *vt* (pièce) to put a ceiling (up) in ▷ *vi* to reach one's (ou a) ceiling

plafonnier [plafɔnje] *nm* ceiling light; (Auto) interior light

plage [plaʒ] *nf* beach; (station) (seaside) resort; (fig) band, bracket; (de disque) track, band; **~ arrière** (Auto) parcel ou back shelf

plagiaire [plaʒjɛʀ] *nm/f* plagiarist

plagiat [plaʒja] *nm* plagiarism

plagier [plaʒje] *vt* to plagiarize

plagiste [plaʒist(ə)] *nm/f* beach attendant

plaid [plɛd] *nm* (tartan) car rug, lap robe (US)

plaidant, e [plɛdɑ̃, -ɑ̃t] *adj* litigant

plaider [plede] *vi* (avocat) to plead; (plaignant) to go to court, litigate ▷ *vt* to plead; **~ pour** (fig) to speak for

plaideur, -euse [plɛdœʀ, -øz] *nm/f* litigant

plaidoirie [plɛdwaʀi] *nf* (Jur) speech for the defence (Brit) ou defense (US)

plaidoyer [plɛdwaje] *nm* (Jur) speech for the defence (Brit) ou defense (US); (fig) plea

plaie [plɛ] nf wound

plaignant, e [plɛɲɑ̃, -ɑ̃t] vb voir **plaindre** ▷ nm/f plaintiff

plaindre [plɛ̃dʀ(ə)] vt to pity, feel sorry for; **se plaindre** vi (gémir) to moan; (protester, rouspéter): **se ~ (à qn) (de)** to complain (to sb) (about); (souffrir): **se ~ de** to complain of

plaine [plɛn] nf plain

plain-pied [plɛ̃pje]: **de ~** adv at street-level; (fig) straight; **de ~ (avec)** on the same level (as)

plaint, e [plɛ̃, -ɛ̃t] pp de **plaindre** ▷ nf (gémissement) moan, groan; (doléance) complaint; **porter ~e** to lodge a complaint

plaintif, -ive [plɛ̃tif, -iv] adj plaintive

plaire [plɛʀ] vi to be a success, be successful; to please; **~ à**: **cela me plaît** I like it; **essayer de ~ à qn** (en étant serviable etc) to try and please sb; **elle plaît aux hommes** she's a success with men, men like her; **se ~ quelque part** to like being somewhere, like it somewhere; **se ~ à faire** to take pleasure in doing; **ce qu'il vous plaira** what(ever) you like ou wish; **s'il vous/te plaît** please

plaisamment [plɛzamɑ̃] adv pleasantly

plaisance [plɛzɑ̃s] nf (aussi: **navigation de plaisance**) (pleasure) sailing, yachting

plaisancier [plɛzɑ̃sje] nm amateur sailor, yachting enthusiast

plaisant, e [plɛzɑ̃, -ɑ̃t] adj pleasant; (histoire, anecdote) amusing

plaisanter [plɛzɑ̃te] vi to joke ▷ vt (personne) to tease, make fun of; **pour ~** for a joke; **on ne plaisante pas avec cela** that's no joking matter; **tu plaisantes!** you're joking ou kidding!

plaisanterie [plɛzɑ̃tʀi] nf joke; joking no pl

plaisantin [plɛzɑ̃tɛ̃] nm joker; (fumiste) fly-by-night

plaise etc [plɛz] vb voir **plaire**

plaisir [pleziʀ] nm pleasure; **faire ~ à qn** (délibérément) to be nice to sb, please sb; (cadeau, nouvelle etc): **ceci me fait ~** I'm delighted ou very pleased with this; **prendre ~ à/à faire** to take pleasure in/in doing; **j'ai le ~ de ...** it is with great pleasure that I ...; **M. et Mme X ont le ~ de vous faire part de ...** M. and Mme X are pleased to announce ...; **se faire un ~ de faire qch** to be (only too) pleased to do sth; **faites-moi le ~ de ...** would you mind ..., would you be kind enough to ...; **à ~** freely; for the sake of it; **au ~ (de vous revoir)** (I hope to) see you again; **pour le** ou **pour son** ou **par ~** for pleasure

plaît [plɛ] vb voir **plaire**

plan, e [plɑ̃, -an] adj flat ▷ nm plan; (Géom) plane; (fig) level, plane; (Ciné) shot; **au premier/second ~** in the foreground/middle distance; **à l'arrière ~** in the background; **mettre qch au premier ~** (fig) to consider sth to be of primary importance; **sur le ~ sexuel** sexually, as far as sex is concerned; **laisser/rester en ~** to abandon/be abandoned; **~ d'action** plan of action; **~ directeur** (Écon)

master plan; **~ d'eau** lake; pond; **~ de travail** work-top, work surface; **~ de vol** (Aviat) flight plan

planche [plɑ̃ʃ] nf (pièce de bois) plank, (wooden) board; (illustration) plate; (de salades, radis, poireaux) bed; (d'un plongeoir) (diving) board; **les ~s** (Théât) the boards; **en ~s** adj wooden; **faire la ~** (dans l'eau) to float on one's back; **avoir du pain sur la ~** to have one's work cut out; **~ à découper** chopping board; **~ à dessin** drawing board; **~ à pain** breadboard; **~ à repasser** ironing board; **~ (à roulettes)** (planche) skateboard; (sport) skateboarding; **~ de salut** (fig) sheet anchor; **~ à voile** (planche) windsurfer, sailboard; (sport) windsurfing

plancher [plɑ̃ʃe] nm floor; (planches) floorboards pl; (fig) minimum level ▷ vi to work hard

planchiste [plɑ̃ʃist(ə)] nm/f windsurfer

plancton [plɑ̃ktɔ̃] nm plankton

planer [plane] vi (oiseau, avion) to glide; (fumée, vapeur) to float, hover; (drogué) to be (on a) high; **~ sur** (fig) to hang over; to hover above

planétaire [planetɛʀ] adj planetary

planétarium [planetaʀjɔm] nm planetarium

planète [planɛt] nf planet

planeur [planœʀ] nm glider

planification [planifikasjɔ̃] nf (economic) planning

planifier [planifje] vt to plan

planisphère [planisfɛʀ] nm planisphere

planning [planiŋ] nm programme (Brit), program (US), schedule; **~ familial** family planning

planque [plɑ̃k] nf (fam: combine, filon) cushy (Brit) ou easy number; (: cachette) hideout

planquer [plɑ̃ke] vt (fam) to hide (away), stash away; **se planquer** to hide

plant [plɑ̃] nm seedling, young plant

plantage [plɑ̃taʒ] nm (d'ordinateur) crash

plantaire [plɑ̃tɛʀ] adj voir **voûte**

plantation [plɑ̃tasjɔ̃] nf planting; (de fleurs, légumes) bed; (exploitation) plantation

plante [plɑ̃t] nf plant; **~ d'appartement** house ou pot plant; **~ du pied** sole (of the foot); **~ verte** house plant

planter [plɑ̃te] vt (plante) to plant; (enfoncer) to hammer ou drive in; (tente) to put up, pitch; (drapeau, échelle, décors) to put up; (fam: mettre) to dump; (: abandonner): **~ là** to ditch; **se planter** vi (fam: se tromper) to get it wrong; (ordinateur) to crash; **~ qch dans** to hammer ou drive sth into; to stick sth into; **se ~ dans** to sink into; to get stuck in; **se ~ devant** to plant o.s. in front of

planteur [plɑ̃tœʀ] nm planter

planton [plɑ̃tɔ̃] nm orderly

plantureux, -euse [plɑ̃tyʀø, -øz] adj (repas) copious, lavish; (femme) buxom

plaquage [plakaʒ] nm (Rugby) tackle

plaque [plak] nf plate; (de verre) sheet; (de verglas, d'eczéma) patch; (dentaire) plaque; (avec inscription) plaque; **~ (minéralogique** ou **de police** ou **d'immatriculation)** number (Brit) ou license

P

315

(US) plate; **~ de beurre** slab of butter; **~ chauffante** hotplate; **~ de chocolat** bar of chocolate; **~ de cuisson** hob; **~ d'identité** identity disc; **~ tournante** (fig) centre (Brit), center (US)

plaqué, e [plake] adj: **~ or/argent** gold-/silver-plated ▷ nm: **~ or/argent** gold/silver plate; **~ acajou** with a mahogany veneer

plaquer [plake] vt (bijou) to plate; (bois) to veneer; (aplatir): **~ qch sur/contre** to make sth stick ou cling to; (Rugby) to bring down; (fam: laisser tomber) to drop, ditch; **se ~ contre** to flatten o.s. against; **~ qn contre** to pin sb to

plaquette [plakɛt] nf tablet; (de chocolat) bar; (de beurre) slab, packet; (livre) small volume; (Méd: de pilules, gélules) pack, packet; **~ de frein** (Auto) brake pad

plasma [plasma] nm plasma

plastic [plastik] nm plastic explosive

plastifié, e [plastifje] adj plastic-coated

plastifier [plastifje] vt (document, photo) to laminate

plastiquage [plastikaʒ] nm bombing, bomb attack

plastique [plastik] adj plastic ▷ nm plastic ▷ nf plastic arts pl; (d'une statue) modelling

plastiquer [plastike] vt to blow up

plastiqueur [plastikœʀ] nm terrorist (planting a plastic bomb)

plastron [plastʀɔ̃] nm shirt front

plastronner [plastʀɔne] vi to swagger

plat, e [pla, -at] adj flat; (fade: vin) flat-tasting, insipid; (personne, livre) dull ▷ nm (récipient, Culin) dish; (d'un repas): **le premier ~** the first course; (partie plate): **le ~ de la main** the flat of the hand; (: d'une route) flat (part); **à ~ ventre** adv face down; (tomber) flat on one's face; **à ~** adj (pneu, batterie) flat; (fam: fatigué) dead beat, tired out; **~ cuisiné** pre-cooked meal (ou dish); **~ du jour** dish of the day; **~ principal** ou **de résistance** main course; **~s préparés** convenience food(s)

platane [platan] nm plane tree

plateau, x [plato] nm (support) tray; (d'une table) top; (d'une balance) pan; (Géo) plateau; (de tourne-disques) turntable; (Ciné) set; (TV): **nous avons deux journalistes sur le ~ ce soir** we have two journalists with us tonight; **~ à fromages** cheeseboard

plateau-repas [platoʀəpa] (pl **plateaux-repas**) nm tray meal, TV dinner (US)

plate-bande [platbɑ̃d] (pl **plates-bandes**) nf flower bed

platée [plate] nf dish(ful)

plate-forme [platfɔʀm(ə)] (pl **plates-formes**) nf platform; **~ de forage/pétrolière** drilling/oil rig

platine [platin] nm platinum ▷ nf (d'un tourne-disque) turntable; **~ disque/cassette** record/cassette deck; **~ laser** ou **compact-disc** compact disc (player)

platitude [platityd] nf platitude

platonique [platɔnik] adj platonic

plâtras [plɑtʀa] nm rubble no pl

plâtre [plɑtʀ(ə)] nm (matériau) plaster; (statue) plaster statue; (Méd) (plaster) cast; **plâtres** nmpl plasterwork sg; **avoir un bras dans le ~** to have an arm in plaster

plâtrer [plɑtʀe] vt to plaster; (Méd) to set ou put in a (plaster) cast

plâtrier [plɑtʀije] nm plasterer

plausible [plozibl(ə)] adj plausible

play-back [plɛbak] nm miming

play-boy [plɛbɔj] nm playboy

plébiscite [plebisit] nm plebiscite

plébisciter [plebisite] vt (approuver) to give overwhelming support to; (élire) to elect by an overwhelming majority

plectre [plɛktʀ(ə)] nm plectrum

plein, e [plɛ̃, -ɛn] adj full; (porte, roue) solid; (chienne, jument) big (with young) ▷ nm: **faire le ~ (d'essence)** to fill up (with petrol (Brit) ou gas (US)) ▷ prép: **avoir de l'argent ~ les poches** to have loads of money; **~ de** full of; **avoir les mains ~es** to have one's hands full; **à ~es mains** (ramasser) in handfuls; (empoigner) firmly; **à ~ régime** at maximum revs; (fig) at full speed; **à ~ temps** full-time; **en ~ air** in the open air; **jeux en ~ air** outdoor games; **en ~e mer** on the open sea; **en ~ soleil** in direct sunlight; **en ~e nuit/rue** in the middle of the night/street; **en ~ milieu** right in the middle; **en ~ jour** in broad daylight; **les ~s** the downstrokes (in handwriting); **faire le ~ des voix** to get the maximum number of votes possible; **en ~ sur** right on; **en avoir ~ le dos** (fam) to have had it up to here

pleinement [plɛnmɑ̃] adv fully; to the full

plein-emploi [plɛnɑ̃plwa] nm full employment

plénière [plenjɛʀ] adj f: **assemblée ~** plenary assembly

plénipotentiaire [plenipɔtɑ̃sjɛʀ] nm plenipotentiary

plénitude [plenityd] nf fullness

pléthore [pletɔʀ] nf: **~ de** overabundance ou plethora of

pléthorique [pletɔʀik] adj (classes) overcrowded; (documentation) excessive

pleurer [plœʀe] vi to cry; (yeux) to water ▷ vt to mourn (for); **~ sur** vt to lament (over), bemoan; **~ de rire** to laugh till one cries

pleurésie [plœʀezi] nf pleurisy

pleureuse [plœʀøz] nf professional mourner

pleurnicher [plœʀniʃe] vi to snivel, whine

pleurs [plœʀ] nmpl: **en ~** in tears

pleut [plø] vb voir **pleuvoir**

pleutre [pløtʀ(ə)] adj cowardly

pleuvait etc [pløvɛ] vb voir **pleuvoir**

pleuviner [pløvine] vb impers to drizzle

pleuvoir [pløvwaʀ] vb impers to rain ▷ vi (fig): **~ (sur)** to shower down (upon), be showered upon; **il pleut** it's raining; **il pleut des cordes** ou **à verse** ou **à torrents** it's pouring (down), it's raining cats and dogs

pleuvra etc [plØvRa] vb voir **pleuvoir**
plexiglas® [plɛksiglas] nm Plexiglas® (US)
pli [pli] nm fold; (de jupe) pleat; (de pantalon) crease; (aussi: **faux pli**) crease; (enveloppe) envelope; (lettre) letter; (Cartes) trick; **prendre le ~ de faire** to get into the habit of doing; **ça ne fait pas un ~!** don't you worry!; **~ d'aisance** inverted pleat
pliable [plijabl(ə)] adj pliable, flexible
pliage [plija3] nm folding; (Art) origami
pliant, e [plijã, -ãt] adj folding ▷ nm folding stool, campstool
plier [plije] vt to fold; (pour ranger) to fold up; (table pliante) to fold down; (genou, bras) to bend ▷ vi to bend; (fig) to yield; **se ~ à** to submit to; **~ bagages** (fig) to pack up (and go)
plinthe [plɛ̃t] nf skirting board
plissé, e [plise] adj (jupe, robe) pleated; (peau) wrinkled; (Géo) folded ▷ nm (Couture) pleats pl
plissement [plismã] nm (Géo) fold
plisser [plise] vt (chiffonner: papier, étoffe) to crease; (rider: front) to furrow, wrinkle; (: bouche) to pucker; (jupe) to put pleats in; **se plisser** vi (vêtement, étoffe) to crease
pliure [plijyR] nf (du bras, genou) bend; (d'un ourlet) fold
plomb [plɔ̃] nm (métal) lead; (d'une cartouche) (lead) shot; (Pêche) sinker; (sceau) (lead) seal; (Élec) fuse; **de ~** (soleil) blazing; **sans ~** (essence) unleaded; **sommeil de ~** heavy ou very deep sleep; **mettre à ~** to plumb
plombage [plɔ̃ba3] nm (de dent) filling
plomber [plɔ̃be] vt (canne, ligne) to weight (with lead); (colis, wagon) to put a lead seal on; (Tech: mur) to plumb; (dent) to fill (Brit), stop (US); (Inform) to protect
plomberie [plɔ̃bRi] nf plumbing
plombier [plɔ̃bje] nm plumber
plonge [plɔ̃3] nf: **faire la ~** to be a washer-up (Brit) ou dishwasher (person)
plongeant, e [plɔ̃3ã, -ãt] adj (vue) from above; (tir, décolleté) plunging
plongée [plɔ̃3e] nf (Sport) diving no pl; (: sans scaphandre) skin diving; (de sous-marin) submersion, dive; **en ~** (sous-marin) submerged; (prise de vue) high angle
plongeoir [plɔ̃3waR] nm diving board
plongeon [plɔ̃3ɔ̃] nm dive
plonger [plɔ̃3e] vi to dive ▷ vt: **~ qch dans** to plunge sth into; **~ dans un sommeil profond** to sink straight into a deep sleep; **~ qn dans l'embarras** to throw sb into a state of confusion
plongeur, -euse [plɔ̃3œR, -øz] nm/f diver; (de café) washer-up (Brit), dishwasher (person)
plot [plo] nm (Élec) contact
ploutocratie [plutɔkRasi] nf plutocracy
ploutocratique [plutɔkRatik] adj plutocratic
ployer [plwaje] vt to bend ▷ vi to bend; (plancher) to sag
plu [ply] pp de **plaire**; **pleuvoir**
pluie [plɥi] nf rain; (averse, ondée): **une ~ brève** a

shower; (fig): **~ de** shower of; **une ~ fine** fine rain; **retomber en ~** to shower down; **sous la ~** in the rain
plumage [plyma3] nm plumage no pl, feathers pl
plume [plym] nf feather; (pour écrire) (pen) nib; (fig) pen; **dessin à la ~** pen and ink drawing
plumeau, x [plymo] nm feather duster
plumer [plyme] vt to pluck
plumet [plymɛ] nm plume
plumier [plymje] nm pencil box
plupart [plypaR]: **la ~** pron the majority, most (of them); **la ~ des** most, the majority of; **la ~ du temps/d'entre nous** most of the time/of us; **pour la ~** adv for the most part, mostly
pluralisme [plyRalism(ə)] nm pluralism
pluralité [plyRalite] nf plurality
pluridisciplinaire [plyRidisiplinɛR] adj multidisciplinary
pluriel [plyRjɛl] nm plural; **au ~** in the plural
plus¹ [ply] vb voir **plaire**

⬤ MOT-CLÉ

plus² [ply] adv **1** (forme négative): **ne ... plus** no more, no longer; **je n'ai plus d'argent** I've got no more money ou no money left; **il ne travaille plus** he's no longer working, he doesn't work any more
2 [ply, plyz] (+voyelle: comparatif) more, ...+er; (superlatif): **le plus** the most, the ...+est; **plus grand/intelligent (que)** bigger/more intelligent (than); **le plus grand/intelligent** the biggest/most intelligent; **tout au plus** at the very most
3 [plys] (davantage) more; **il travaille plus (que)** he works more (than); **plus il travaille, plus il est heureux** the more he works, the happier he is; **plus de pain** more bread; **plus de 10 personnes/trois heures/quatre kilos** more than ou over 10 people/three hours/four kilos; **trois heures de plus que** three hours more than; **plus de minuit** after ou past midnight; **de plus** what's more, moreover; **il a trois ans de plus que moi** he's three years older than me; **trois kilos en plus** three kilos more; **en plus de** in addition to; **de plus en plus** more and more; **en plus de cela ...** what is more ...; **plus ou moins** more or less; **ni plus ni moins** no more, no less; **sans plus** (but) no more than that, (but) that's all; **qui plus est** what is more
▷ prép [plys]: **quatre plus deux** four plus two

plusieurs [plyzjœR] adj, pron several; **ils sont ~** there are several of them
plus-que-parfait [plyskəpaRfɛ] nm pluperfect, past perfect
plus-value [plyvaly] nf (d'un bien) appreciation; (bénéfice) capital gain; (budgétaire) surplus
plut [ply] vb voir **plaire**; **pleuvoir**
plutonium [plytɔnjɔm] nm plutonium
plutôt [plyto] adv rather; **je ferais ~ ceci** I'd rather ou sooner do this; **fais ~ comme ça** try

this way instead; **~ que (de) faire** rather than *ou* instead of doing

pluvial, e, -aux [plyvjal, -o] *adj* (*eaux*) rain *cpd*

pluvieux, -euse [plyvjø, -øz] *adj* rainy, wet

pluviosité [plyvjɔzite] *nf* rainfall

PM *sigle f* = **Police militaire**

p.m. *abr* (= *pour mémoire*) for the record

PME *sigle fpl* = **petites et moyennes entreprises**

PMI *sigle fpl* = **petites et moyennes industries**
▷ *sigle f* = **protection maternelle et infantile**

PMU *sigle m* = **pari mutuel urbain**; (*café*) betting agency; *see note*

PMU

The PMU ("pari mutuel urbain") is a Government-regulated network of betting counters run from bars displaying the PMU sign. Punters buy fixed-price tickets predicting winners or finishing positions in horse races. The traditional bet is the "tiercé", a triple bet, although other multiple bets ("quarté" and so on) are becoming increasingly popular.

PNB *sigle m* (= *produit national brut*) GNP

pneu [pnø] *nm* (*de roue*) tyre (*Brit*), tire (*US*); (*message*) letter sent by pneumatic tube

pneumatique [pnømatik] *adj* pneumatic; (*gonflable*) inflatable ▷ *nm* tyre (*Brit*), tire (*US*)

pneumonie [pnømɔni] *nf* pneumonia

PO *sigle fpl* (= *petites ondes*) MW

po [po] *abr voir* **science**

p.o. *abr* (= *par ordre*) p.p. (*on letters etc*)

Pô [po] *nm*: **le Pô** the Po

poche [pɔʃ] *nf* pocket; (*déformation*): **faire une/ des ~(s)** to bag; (*sous les yeux*) bag, pouch; (*Zool*) pouch ▷ *nm* (*livre de poche*) (pocket-size) paperback; **de ~** pocket *cpd*; **en être de sa ~** to be out of pocket; **c'est dans la ~** it's in the bag

poché, e [pɔʃe] *adj*: **œuf ~** poached egg; **œil ~** black eye

pocher [pɔʃe] *vt* (*Culin*) to poach; (*Art*) to sketch ▷ *vi* (*vêtement*) to bag

poche-revolver [pɔʃʀəvɔlvɛʀ] (*pl* **poches-revolver**) *nf* hip pocket

pochette [pɔʃɛt] *nf* (*de timbres*) wallet, envelope; (*d'aiguilles etc*) case; (*sac: de femme*) clutch bag, purse; (*: d'homme*) bag; (*sur veston*) breast pocket; (*mouchoir*) breast pocket handkerchief; **~ d'allumettes** book of matches; **~ de disque** record sleeve; **~ surprise** lucky bag

pochoir [pɔʃwaʀ] *nm* (*Art: cache*) stencil; (*: tampon*) transfer

podcast [pɔdkast] *nm* (*Inform*) podcast

podcaster [pɔdkaste] *vi* (*Inform*) to podcast

podium [pɔdjɔm] *nm* podium

poêle [pwal] *nm* stove ▷ *nf*: **~ (à frire)** frying pan

poêlon [pwalɔ̃] *nm* casserole

poème [pɔɛm] *nm* poem

poésie [pɔezi] *nf* (*poème*) poem; (*art*): **la ~** poetry

poète [pɔɛt] *nm* poet; (*fig*) dreamer ▷ *adj* poetic

poétique [pɔetik] *adj* poetic

pognon [pɔɲɔ̃] *nm* (*fam: argent*) dough

poids [pwa] *nm* weight; (*Sport*) shot; **vendre au ~** to sell by weight; **de ~** *adj* (*argument etc*) weighty; **prendre du ~** to put on weight; **faire le ~** (*fig*) to measure up; **~ plume/mouche/coq/ moyen** (*Boxe*) feather/fly/bantam/ middleweight; **~ et haltères** weight lifting *sg*; **~ lourd** (*Boxe*) heavyweight; (*camion: aussi*: **PL**) (big) lorry (*Brit*), truck (*US*); (*: Admin*) large goods vehicle (*Brit*), truck (*US*); **~ mort** dead weight; **~ utile** net weight

poignant, e [pwaɲɑ̃, -ɑ̃t] *adj* poignant, harrowing

poignard [pwaɲaʀ] *nm* dagger

poignarder [pwaɲaʀde] *vt* to stab, knife

poigne [pwaɲ] *nf* grip; (*fig*) firm-handedness; **à ~** firm-handed

poignée [pwaɲe] *nf* (*de sel etc, fig*) handful; (*de couvercle, porte*) handle; **~ de main** handshake

poignet [pwaɲɛ] *nm* (*Anat*) wrist; (*de chemise*) cuff

poil [pwal] *nm* (*Anat*) hair; (*de pinceau, brosse*) bristle; (*de tapis, tissu*) strand; (*pelage*) coat; (*ensemble des poils*): **avoir du ~ sur la poitrine** to have hair(s) on one's chest, have a hairy chest; **à ~** *adj* (*fam*) starkers; **au ~** *adj* (*fam*) hunky-dory; **de tout ~** of all kinds; **être de bon/ mauvais ~** to be in a good/bad mood; **~ à gratter** itching powder

poilu, e [pwaly] *adj* hairy

poinçon [pwɛ̃sɔ̃] *nm* awl; bodkin; (*marque*) hallmark

poinçonner [pwɛ̃sɔne] *vt* (*marchandise*) to stamp; (*bijou etc*) to hallmark; (*billet, ticket*) to clip, punch

poinçonneuse [pwɛ̃sɔnøz] *nf* (*outil*) punch

poindre [pwɛ̃dʀ(ə)] *vi* (*fleur*) to come up; (*aube*) to break; (*jour*) to dawn

poing [pwɛ̃] *nm* fist; **dormir à ~s fermés** to sleep soundly

point [pwɛ̃] *vb voir* **poindre** ▷ *nm* (*marque, signe*) dot; (*: de ponctuation*) full stop, period (*US*); (*moment, de score etc, fig: question*) point; (*endroit*) spot; (*Couture, Tricot*) stitch ▷ *adv* = **pas**; **ne ... ~** not (at all); **faire le ~** (*Navig*) to take a bearing; (*fig*) to take stock (of the situation); **faire le ~ sur** to review; **en tout ~** in every respect; **sur le ~ de faire** (just) about to do; **au ~ que, à tel que** so much so that; **mettre au ~** (*mécanisme, procédé*) to develop; (*appareil photo*) to focus; (*affaire*) to settle; **à ~** (*Culin*) just right; (*: viande*) medium; **à ~ (nommé)** just at the right time; **~ de croix/tige/chaînette** (*Couture*) cross/stem/ chain stitch; **~ mousse/jersey** (*Tricot*) garter/ stocking stitch; **~ de départ/d'arrivée/d'arrêt** departure/arrival/stopping point; **~ chaud** (*Mil, Pol*) hot spot; **~ de chute** landing place; (*fig*) stopping-off point; **~ (de côté)** stitch (*pain*); **~ culminant** summit; (*fig*) height, climax; **~ d'eau** spring, water point; **~ d'exclamation**

exclamation mark; **~ faible** weak spot; **~ final** full stop, period (US); **~ d'interrogation** question mark; **au ~ mort** (Auto) in neutral; (affaire, entreprise) at a standstill; **~ noir** (sur le visage) blackhead; (Auto) accident black spot; **~ de non-retour** point of no return; **~ de repère** landmark; (dans le temps) point of reference; **~ de vente** retail outlet; **~ de vue** viewpoint; (fig: opinion) point of view; **du ~ de vue de** from the point of view of; **~s cardinaux** points of the compass, cardinal points; **~s de suspension** suspension points

pointage [pwɛtaʒ] nm ticking off; checking in

pointe [pwɛt] nf point; (de la côte) headland; (allusion) dig; sally; (fig) **une ~ d'ail/d'accent** a touch ou hint of garlic/of an accent; **pointes** nfpl (Danse) points, point shoes; **être à la ~ de** (fig) to be in the forefront of; **faire** ou **pousser une ~ jusqu'à ...** to press on as far as ...; **sur la ~ des pieds** on tiptoe; **en ~** adv (tailler) into a point ▷ adj pointed, tapered; **de ~** adj (technique etc) leading; (vitesse) maximum, top; **heures/ jours de ~** peak hours/days; **faire du 180 en ~** (Auto) to have a top ou maximum speed of 180; **faire des ~s** (Danse) to dance on points; **~ d'asperge** asparagus tip; **~ de courant** surge (of current); **~ de vitesse** burst of speed

pointer [pwɛte] vt (cocher) to tick off; (employés etc) to check in; (diriger: canon, longue-vue, doigt): **~ vers qch** to point at sth; (Mus: note) to dot ▷ vi (employé) to clock in ou on; (pousses) to come through; (jour) to break; **~ les oreilles** (chien) to prick up its ears

pointeur, -euse [pwɛtœʀ, -øz] nm/f time-keeper ▷ nf timeclock ▷ nm (Inform) cursor

pointillé [pwɛtije] nm (trait) dotted line; (Art) stippling no pl

pointilleux, -euse [pwɛtijø, -øz] adj particular, pernickety

pointu, e [pwɛty] adj pointed; (clou) sharp; (voix) shrill; (analyse) precise

pointure [pwɛtyʀ] nf size

point-virgule [pwɛviʀgyl] (pl **points-virgules**) nm semi-colon

poire [pwaʀ] nf pear; (fam: péj) mug; **~ électrique** (pear-shaped) switch; **~ à injections** syringe

poireau, x [pwaʀo] nm leek

poireauter [pwaʀote] vi (fam) to hang about (waiting)

poirier [pwaʀje] nm pear tree; (Sport): **faire le ~** to do a headstand

pois [pwa] nm (Bot) pea; (sur une étoffe) dot, spot; **à ~** (cravate etc) spotted, polka-dot cpd; **~ chiche** chickpea; **~ de senteur** sweet pea; **~ cassés** split peas

poison [pwazɔ̃] nm poison

poisse [pwas] nf rotten luck

poisser [pwase] vt to make sticky

poisseux, -euse [pwasø, -øz] adj sticky

poisson [pwasɔ̃] nm fish gen inv; **les P~s** (signe)

Pisces, the Fish; **être des P~s** to be Pisces; **pêcher** ou **prendre du ~** ou **des ~s** to fish; **~ d'avril** April fool; (blague) April fool's day trick; see note; **~ rouge** goldfish

● **POISSON D'AVRIL**

The traditional April Fools' Day prank in France involves attaching a cut-out paper fish, known as a "poisson d'avril", to the back of one's victim, without being caught.

poisson-chat [pwasɔ̃ʃa] (pl **poissons-chats**) nm catfish

poissonnerie [pwasɔnʀi] nf fishmonger's (Brit), fish store (US)

poissonneux, -euse [pwasɔnø, -øz] adj abounding in fish

poissonnier, -ière [pwasɔnje, -jɛʀ] nm/f fishmonger (Brit), fish merchant (US) ▷ nf (ustensile) fish kettle

poisson-scie [pwasɔ̃si] (pl **poissons-scies**) nm sawfish

poitevin, e [pwatvɛ̃, -in] adj (région) of ou from Poitou; (ville) of ou from Poitiers

poitrail [pwatʀaj] nm (d'un cheval etc) breast

poitrine [pwatʀin] nf (Anat) chest; (seins) bust, bosom; (Culin) breast; **~ de bœuf** brisket

poivre [pwavʀ(ə)] nm pepper; **~ en grains/ moulu** whole/ground pepper; **~ de cayenne** cayenne (pepper); **~ et sel** adj (cheveux) pepper-and-salt

poivré, e [pwavʀe] adj peppery

poivrer [pwavʀe] vt to pepper

poivrier [pwavʀije] nm (Bot) pepper plant

poivrière [pwavʀijɛʀ] nf pepperpot, pepper shaker (US)

poivron [pwavʀɔ̃] nm pepper, capsicum; **~ vert/ rouge** green/red pepper

poix [pwa] nf pitch (tar)

poker [pɔkɛʀ] nm: **le ~** poker; **partie de ~** (fig) gamble; **~ d'as** four aces

polaire [pɔlɛʀ] adj polar

polar [pɔlaʀ] (fam) nm detective novel

polarisation [pɔlaʀizasjɔ̃] nf (Physique, Élec) polarization; (fig) focusing

polariser [pɔlaʀize] vt to polarize; (fig: attirer) to attract; (: réunir, concentrer) to focus; **être polarisé sur** (personne) to be completely bound up with ou absorbed by

pôle [pol] nm (Géo, Élec) pole; **le ~ Nord/Sud** the North/South Pole; **~ d'attraction** (fig) centre of attraction

polémique [pɔlemik] adj controversial, polemic(al) ▷ nf controversy

polémiquer [pɔlemike] vi to be involved in controversy

polémiste [pɔlemist(ə)] nm/f polemist, polemicist

poli, e [pɔli] adj polite; (lisse) smooth; polished

police [pɔlis] nf police; (discipline): **assurer la ~ de** ou **dans** to keep order in; **peine de simple ~**

sentence given by a magistrates' or police court; ~
(**d'assurance**) (insurance) policy; ~ (**de
caractères**) (Typo, Inform) font, typeface; ~
judiciaire (**PJ**) ≈ Criminal Investigation
Department (CID) (Brit), ≈ Federal Bureau of
Investigation (FBI) (US); ~ **des mœurs** ≈ vice
squad; ~ **secours** ≈ emergency services pl
polichinelle [pɔliʃinɛl] nm Punch; (péj) buffoon;
secret de ~ open secret
policier, -ière [pɔlisje, -jɛʀ] adj police cpd ▷ nm
policeman; (aussi: **roman policier**) detective
novel
policlinique [pɔliklinik] nf ≈ outpatients sg
(clinic)
poliment [pɔlimɑ̃] adv politely
polio [pɔljo] nf (aussi: **poliomyélite**) polio ▷ nm/f
(aussi: **poliomyélitique**) polio patient ou case
poliomyélite [pɔljɔmjelit] nf poliomyelitis
poliomyélitique [pɔljɔmjelitik] nm/f polio
patient ou case
polir [pɔliʀ] vt to polish
polisson, ne [pɔlisɔ̃, -ɔn] adj naughty
politesse [pɔlitɛs] nf politeness; **politesses** nfpl
(exchange of) courtesies; **rendre une ~ à qn** to
return sb's favour (Brit) ou favor (US)
politicard [pɔlitikaʀ] nm (péj) politico, political
schemer
politicien, ne [pɔlitisjɛ̃, -ɛn] adj political ▷ nm/f
politician
politique [pɔlitik] adj political ▷ nf (science,
activité) politics sg; (principes, tactique) policy,
policies pl ▷ nm (politicien) politician; ~
étrangère/intérieure foreign/domestic policy
politique-fiction [pɔlitikfiksjɔ̃] nf political
fiction
politiquement [pɔlitikmɑ̃] adv politically
politisation [pɔlitizasjɔ̃] nf politicization
politiser [pɔlitize] vt to politicize; ~ **qn** to make
sb politically aware
pollen [pɔlɛn] nm pollen
polluant, e [pɔlɥɑ̃, -ɑ̃t] adj polluting ▷ nm
polluting agent, pollutant
polluer [pɔlɥe] vt to pollute
pollueur, -euse [pɔlɥœʀ, -øz] nm/f polluter
pollution [pɔlysjɔ̃] nf pollution
polo [pɔlo] nm (sport) polo; (tricot) polo shirt
Pologne [pɔlɔɲ] nf: **la** ~ Poland
polonais, e [pɔlɔnɛ, -ez] adj Polish ▷ nm (Ling)
Polish ▷ nm/f: **Polonais, e** Pole
poltron, ne [pɔltʀɔ̃, -ɔn] adj cowardly
poly... [pɔli] préfixe poly...
polyamide [pɔliamid] nf polyamide
polychrome [pɔlikʀom] adj polychrome,
polychromatic
polyclinique [pɔliklinik] nf (private) clinic
(treating different illnesses)
polycopie [pɔlikɔpi] nf (procédé) duplicating;
(reproduction) duplicated copy
polycopié, e [pɔlikɔpje] adj duplicated ▷ nm
handout, duplicated notes pl
polycopier [pɔlikɔpje] vt to duplicate
polyculture [pɔlikyltyʀ] nf mixed farming

polyester [pɔliɛstɛʀ] nm polyester
polyéthylène [pɔlietilɛn] nm polyethylene
polygame [pɔligam] adj polygamous
polygamie [pɔligami] nf polygamy
polyglotte [pɔliglɔt] adj polyglot
polygone [pɔligɔn] nm polygon
Polynésie [pɔlinezi] nf: **la** ~ Polynesia; **la** ~
française French Polynesia
polynésien, ne [pɔlinezjɛ̃, -ɛn] adj Polynesian
polynôme [pɔlinom] nm polynomial
polype [pɔlip] nm polyp
polystyrène [pɔlistiʀɛn] nm polystyrene
polytechnicien, ne [pɔlitɛknisjɛ̃, -ɛn] nm/f
student or former student of the École polytechnique
Polytechnique [pɔliteknik] nf: (**École**) ~
prestigious military academy producing high-ranking
officers and engineers
polyvalent, e [pɔlivalɑ̃, -ɑ̃t] adj (vaccin)
polyvalent; (personne) versatile; (salle) multi-
purpose ▷ nm ≈ tax inspector
pomélo [pɔmelo] nm pomelo, grapefruit
pommade [pɔmad] nf ointment, cream
pomme [pɔm] nf (Bot) apple; (boule décorative)
knob; (pomme de terre): **steak ~s (frites)** steak
and chips (Brit) ou (French) fries (US); **tomber
dans les ~s** (fam) to pass out; ~ **d'Adam** Adam's
apple; **~s allumettes** French fries (thin-cut); ~
d'arrosoir (sprinkler) rose; ~ **de pin** pine ou fir
cone; ~ **de terre** potato; **~s vapeur** boiled
potatoes
pommé, e [pɔme] adj (chou etc) firm
pommeau, x [pɔmo] nm (boule) knob; (de selle)
pommel
pommelé, e [pɔmle] adj: **gris ~** dapple grey
pommette [pɔmɛt] nf cheekbone
pommier [pɔmje] nm apple tree
pompe [pɔ̃p] nf pump; (faste) pomp (and
ceremony); ~ **à eau/essence** water/petrol
pump; ~ **à huile** oil pump; ~ **à incendie** fire
engine (apparatus); **~s funèbres** undertaker's sg,
funeral parlour sg (Brit), mortician's sg (US)
Pompéi [pɔ̃pei] n Pompeii
pompéien, ne [pɔ̃pejɛ̃, -ɛn] adj Pompeiian
pomper [pɔ̃pe] vt to pump; (évacuer) to pump
out; (aspirer) to pump up; (absorber) to soak up
▷ vi to pump
pompeusement [pɔ̃pøzmɑ̃] adv pompously
pompeux, -euse [pɔ̃pø, -øz] adj pompous
pompier [pɔ̃pje] nm fireman ▷ adj m (style)
pretentious, pompous
pompiste [pɔ̃pist(ə)] nm/f petrol (Brit) ou gas (US)
pump attendant
pompon [pɔ̃pɔ̃] nm pompom, bobble
pomponner [pɔ̃pɔne] vt to titivate (Brit),
dress up
ponce [pɔ̃s] nf: **pierre ~** pumice stone
poncer [pɔ̃se] vt to sand (down)
ponceuse [pɔ̃søz] nf sander
poncif [pɔ̃sif] nm cliché
ponction [pɔ̃ksjɔ̃] nf (d'argent etc) withdrawal;
~ **lombaire** lumbar puncture
ponctualité [pɔ̃ktɥalite] nf punctuality

ponctuation [põktɥasjõ] *nf* punctuation
ponctuel, le [põktɥɛl] *adj* (*à l'heure, Tech*) punctual; (*fig: opération etc*) one-off, single; (*scrupuleux*) punctilious, meticulous
ponctuellement [põktɥɛlmɑ̃] *adv* punctually; punctiliously, meticulously
ponctuer [põktɥe] *vt* to punctuate; (*Mus*) to phrase
pondéré, e [põdeRe] *adj* level-headed, composed
pondérer [põdeRe] *vt* to balance
pondeuse [põdøz] *nf* layer, laying hen
pondre [põdR(ə)] *vt* to lay; (*fig*) to produce ▷ *vi* to lay
poney [pɔnɛ] *nm* pony
pongiste [põʒist(ə)] *nm/f* table tennis player
pont [põ] *nm* bridge; (*Auto*) ~ **arrière/avant** rear/front axle; (*Navig*) deck; **faire le** ~ to take the extra day off; *see note*; **faire un** ~ **d'or à qn** to offer sb a fortune to take a job; ~ **aérien** airlift; ~ **basculant** bascule bridge; ~ **d'envol** flight deck; ~ **élévateur** hydraulic ramp; ~ **de graissage** ramp (*in garage*); ~ **à péage** tollbridge; ~ **roulant** travelling crane; ~ **suspendu** suspension bridge; ~ **tournant** swing bridge; **P~s et Chaussées** highways department

⬤ **FAIRE LE PONT**

⬤ The expression "faire le pont" refers to the
⬤ practice of taking a Monday or Friday off to
⬤ make a long weekend if a public holiday
⬤ falls on a Tuesday or Thursday. The French
⬤ commonly take an extra day off work to give
⬤ four consecutive days' holiday at
⬤ "l'Ascension", "le 14 juillet" and the "15 août".

ponte [põt] *nf* laying; (*œufs pondus*) clutch ▷ *nm* (*fam*) big shot
pontife [põtif] *nm* pontiff
pontifier [põtifje] *vi* to pontificate
pont-levis [põlvi] (*pl* **ponts-levis**) *nm* drawbridge
ponton [põtõ] *nm* pontoon (*on water*)
pop [pɔp] *adj inv* pop ▷ *nm*: **le** ~ pop (*music*)
pop-corn [pɔpkɔRn] *nm* popcorn
popeline [pɔplin] *nf* poplin
populace [pɔpylas] *nf* (*péj*) rabble
populaire [pɔpylɛR] *adj* popular; (*manifestation*) mass *cpd*, of the people; (*milieux, clientèle*) working-class; (*Ling: mot etc*) used by the lower classes (of society)
populariser [pɔpylaRize] *vt* to popularize
popularité [pɔpylaRite] *nf* popularity
population [pɔpylasjõ] *nf* population; ~ **active/agricole** working/farming population
populeux, -euse [pɔpylø, -øz] *adj* densely populated
porc [pɔR] *nm* (*Zool*) pig; (*Culin*) pork; (*peau*) pigskin
porcelaine [pɔRsəlɛn] *nf* (*substance*) porcelain, china; (*objet*) piece of china(ware)

porcelet [pɔRsəlɛ] *nm* piglet
porc-épic [pɔRkepik] (*pl* **porcs-épics**) *nm* porcupine
porche [pɔRʃ(ə)] *nm* porch
porcher, -ère [pɔRʃe, -ɛR] *nm/f* pig-keeper
porcherie [pɔRʃəRi] *nf* pigsty
porcin, e [pɔRsɛ̃, -in] *adj* (*race*) porcine; (*élevage*) pig *cpd*; (*fig*) piglike
pore [pɔR] *nm* pore
poreux, -euse [pɔRø, -øz] *adj* porous
porno [pɔRno] *adj* porno ▷ *nm* porn
pornographie [pɔRnɔgrafi] *nf* pornography
pornographique [pɔRnɔgrafik] *adj* pornographic
port [pɔR] *nm* (*Navig*) harbour (*Brit*), harbor (*US*), port; (*ville, Inform*) port; (*de l'uniforme etc*) wearing; (*pour lettre*) postage; (*pour colis, aussi: posture*) carriage; ~ **de commerce/de pêche** commercial/fishing port; **arriver à bon** ~ to arrive safe and sound; ~ **d'arme** (*Jur*) carrying of a firearm; ~ **d'attache** (*Navig*) port of registry; (*fig*) home base; ~ **d'escale** port of call; ~ **franc** free port
portable [pɔRtabl(ə)] *adj* (*vêtement*) wearable; (*portatif*) portable; (*téléphone*) mobile (*Brit*), cell (*US*) ▷ *nm* (*Inform*) laptop (computer); (*téléphone*) mobile (phone) (*Brit*), cell (phone) (*US*)
portail [pɔRtaj] *nm* gate; (*de cathédrale*) portal
portant, e [pɔRtɑ̃, -ɑ̃t] *adj* (*murs*) structural, supporting; (*roues*) running; **bien/mal** ~ in good/poor health
portatif, -ive [pɔRtatif, -iv] *adj* portable
porte [pɔRt(ə)] *nf* door; (*de ville, forteresse, Ski*) gate; **mettre à la** ~ to throw out; **prendre la** ~ to leave, go away; **à ma/sa** ~ (*tout près*) on my/his (*ou* her) doorstep; ~ (**d'embarquement**) (*Aviat*) (departure) gate; ~ **d'entrée** front door; ~ **à** ~ *nm* door-to-door selling; ~ **de secours** emergency exit; ~ **de service** service entrance
porté, e [pɔRte] *adj*: **être** ~ **à faire qch** to be apt to do sth, tend to do sth; **être** ~ **sur qch** to be partial to sth
porte-à-faux [pɔRtafo] *nm*: **en** ~ cantilevered; (*fig*) in an awkward position
porte-aiguilles [pɔRtegɥij] *nm inv* needle case
porte-avions [pɔRtavjõ] *nm inv* aircraft carrier
porte-bagages [pɔRtbagaʒ] *nm inv* luggage rack (*ou* basket *etc*)
porte-bébé [pɔRtbebe] *nm* baby sling *ou* carrier
porte-bonheur [pɔRtbɔnœR] *nm inv* lucky charm
porte-bouteilles [pɔRtbutɛj] *nm inv* bottle carrier; (*à casiers*) wine rack
porte-cartes [pɔRtəkaRt(ə)] *nm inv* (*de cartes d'identité*) card holder; (*de cartes géographiques*) map wallet
porte-cigarettes [pɔRtsigaRɛt] *nm inv* cigarette case
porte-clefs [pɔRtəkle] *nm inv* key ring
porte-conteneurs [pɔRtəkõtnœR] *nm inv* container ship
porte-couteau, x [pɔRtkuto] *nm* knife rest

P

porte-crayon [pɔʀtkʀɛjɔ̃] nm pencil holder
porte-documents [pɔʀtdɔkymɑ̃] nm inv
attaché ou document case
porte-drapeau, x [pɔʀtdʀapo] nm standard
bearer
portée [pɔʀte] nf (d'une arme) range; (fig:
importance) impact, import; (: capacités) scope,
capability; (de chatte etc) litter; (Mus) stave, staff;
à/hors de ~ (de) within/out of reach (of); **à ~ de
(la) main** within (arm's) reach; **à ~ de voix**
within earshot; **à la ~ de qn** (fig) at sb's level,
within sb's capabilities; **à la ~ de toutes les
bourses** to suit every pocket, within everyone's
means
portefaix [pɔʀtəfɛ] nm inv porter
porte-fenêtre [pɔʀtfənɛtʀ(ə)] (pl **portes-
fenêtres**) nf French window
portefeuille [pɔʀtəfœj] nm wallet; (Pol, Bourse)
portfolio; **faire un lit en ~** to make an apple-
pie bed
porte-jarretelles [pɔʀtʒaʀtɛl] nm inv suspender
belt (Brit), garter belt (US)
porte-jupe [pɔʀtəʒyp] nm skirt hanger
portemanteau, x [pɔʀtmɑ̃to] nm coat rack
porte-mine [pɔʀtəmin] nm propelling (Brit) ou
mechanical (US) pencil
porte-monnaie [pɔʀtmɔnɛ] nm inv purse
porte-parapluies [pɔʀtparaplɥi] nm inv
umbrella stand
porte-parole [pɔʀtparɔl] nm inv spokesperson
porte-plume [pɔʀtəplym] nm inv penholder
porter [pɔʀte] vt (charge ou sac etc, aussi: fœtus) to
carry; (sur soi: vêtement, barbe, bague) to wear; (fig:
responsabilité etc) to bear, carry; (inscription, marque,
titre, patronyme: arbre: fruits, fleurs) to bear;
(jugement) to pass; (apporter): **~ qch quelque
part/à qn** to take sth somewhere/to sb;
(inscrire): **~ qch sur** to put sth down on; to enter
sth in ▷ vi (voix, regard, canon) to carry; (coup,
argument) to hit home; **se porter** vi (se sentir): **se
~ bien/mal** to be well/unwell; (aller): **se ~ vers**
to go towards; **~ sur** (peser) to rest on; (accent) to
fall on; (conférence etc) to concern; (heurter) to
strike; **être porté à faire** to be apt ou inclined
to do; **elle portait le nom de Rosalie** she was
called Rosalie; **~ qn au pouvoir** to bring sb to
power; **~ bonheur à qn** to bring sb luck; **~ qn à
croire** to lead sb to believe; **~ son âge** to look
one's age; **~ un toast** to drink a toast; **~ de
l'argent au crédit d'un compte** to credit an
account with some money; **se ~ partie civile** to
associate in a court action with the public prosecutor; **se
~ garant de qch** to guarantee sth, vouch for
sth; **se ~ candidat à la députation** ≈ to stand
for Parliament (Brit), ≈ run for Congress (US); **se
faire ~ malade** to report sick; **~ la main à son
chapeau** to raise one's hand to one's hat; **~ son
effort sur** to direct one's efforts towards; **~ un
fait à la connaissance de qn** to bring a fact to
sb's attention ou notice
porte-savon [pɔʀtsavɔ̃] nm soap dish
porte-serviettes [pɔʀtsɛʀvjɛt] nm inv towel rail

portes-ouvertes [pɔʀtuvɛʀt(ə)] adj inv:
journée ~ open day
porteur, -euse [pɔʀtœʀ, -øz] adj (Comm) strong,
promising; (nouvelle, chèque etc): **être ~ de** to be
the bearer of ▷ nm/f (de messages) bearer ▷ nm (de
bagages) porter; (Comm: de chèque) bearer;
(: d'actions) holder; **(avion) gros ~** wide-bodied
aircraft, jumbo (jet)
porte-voix [pɔʀtəvwa] nm inv megaphone,
loudhailer (Brit)
portier [pɔʀtje] nm doorman,
commissionnaire (Brit)
portière [pɔʀtjɛʀ] nf door
portillon [pɔʀtijɔ̃] nm gate
portion [pɔʀsjɔ̃] nf (part) portion, share; (partie)
portion, section
portique [pɔʀtik] nm (Sport) crossbar; (Archit)
portico; (Rail) gantry
porto [pɔʀto] nm port (wine)
portoricain, e [pɔʀtɔʀikɛ̃, -ɛn] adj Puerto Rican
Porto Rico [pɔʀtɔʀiko] nf Puerto Rico
portrait [pɔʀtʀɛ] nm portrait; (photographie)
photograph; (fig): **elle est le ~ de sa mère** she's
the image of her mother
portraitiste [pɔʀtʀetist(ə)] nm/f portrait
painter
portrait-robot [pɔʀtʀɛʀɔbo] nm Identikit® ou
Photo-fit ® (Brit) picture
portuaire [pɔʀtɥɛʀ] adj port cpd, harbour cpd
(Brit), harbor cpd (US)
portugais, e [pɔʀtygɛ, -ɛz] adj Portuguese ▷ nm
(Ling) Portuguese ▷ nm/f: **Portugais, e**
Portuguese
Portugal [pɔʀtygal] nm: **le ~** Portugal
POS sigle m (= plan d'occupation des sols) zoning
ordinances ou regulations
pose [poz] nf (de moquette) laying; (de rideaux,
papier peint) hanging; (attitude, d'un modèle) pose;
(Photo) exposure
posé, e [poze] adj calm, unruffled
posément [pozemɑ̃] adv calmly
posemètre [pozmɛtʀ(ə)] nm exposure meter
poser [poze] vt (déposer): **~ qch (sur)/qn à** to put
sth down (on)/drop sb at; (placer): **~ qch sur/
quelque part** to put sth on/somewhere;
(installer: moquette, carrelage) to lay; (rideaux, papier
peint) to hang; (Math: chiffre) to put (down);
(question) to ask; (principe, conditions) to lay ou set
down; (problème) to formulate; (difficulté) to
pose; (personne: mettre en valeur) to give standing
to ▷ vi (modèle) to pose; to sit; **se poser** (oiseau,
avion) to land; (question) to arise; **se ~ en** to pass
o.s off as, pose as; **~ son** ou **un regard sur qn/
qch** to turn one's gaze on sb/sth; **~ sa
candidature** to apply; (Pol) to put o.s. up for
election
poseur, -euse [pozœʀ, -øz] nm/f (péj) show-off,
poseur; **~ de parquets/carrelages** floor/tile
layer
positif, -ive [pozitif, -iv] adj positive
position [pozisjɔ̃] nf position; **prendre ~** (fig) to
take a stand

positionner [pozisjɔne] *vt* to position; (*compte en banque*) to calculate the balance of

positivement [pozitivmɑ̃] *adv* positively

posologie [pozɔlɔʒi] *nf* directions *pl* for use, dosage

possédant, e [posedɑ̃, -ɑ̃t] *adj* (*classe*) wealthy ▷ *nm/f*: **les ~s** the haves, the wealthy

possédé, e [posede] *nm/f* person possessed

posséder [posede] *vt* to own, possess; (*qualité, talent*) to have, possess; (*bien connaître: métier, langue*) to have mastered, have a thorough knowledge of; (*sexuellement, aussi: suj: colère*) to possess; (*fam: duper*) to take in

possesseur [posesœr] *nm* owner

possessif, -ive [posesif, -iv] *adj, nm* (*Ling*) possessive

possession [posesjɔ̃] *nf* ownership *no pl*; possession; (*aussi*: **être/entrer en possession de qch**) to be in/take possession of sth

possibilité [posibilite] *nf* possibility; **possibilités** *nfpl* (*moyens*) means; (*potentiel*) potential *sg*; **avoir la ~ de faire** to be in a position to do; to have the opportunity to do

possible [posibl(ə)] *adj* possible; (*projet, entreprise*) feasible ▷ *nm*: **faire son ~** to do all one can, do one's utmost; (**ce n'est) pas ~!** impossible!; **le plus/moins de livres ~** as many/few books as possible; **dès que ~** as soon as possible; **gentil** *etc* **au ~** as nice *etc* as it is possible to be

postal, e, -aux [postal, -o] *adj* postal, post office *cpd*; **sac ~** mailbag, postbag

postdater [postdate] *vt* to postdate

poste [post(ə)] *nf* (*service*) post, postal service; (*administration, bureau*) post office ▷ *nm* (*fonction, Mil*) post; (*Tél*) extension; (*de radio etc*) set; (*de budget*) item; **postes** *nfpl* post office *sg*; **P~s télécommunications et télédiffusion (PTT)** postal and telecommunications service; **agent** *ou* **employé des ~s** post office worker; **mettre à la ~ to** post; **~ de commandement (PC)** *nm* (*Mil etc*) headquarters; **~ de contrôle** *nm* checkpoint; **~ de douane** *nm* customs post; **~ émetteur** *nm* transmitting set; **~ d'essence** *nm* filling station; **~ d'incendie** *nm* fire point; **~ de péage** *nm* tollgate; **~ de pilotage** *nm* cockpit; **~ (de police)** *nm* police station; **~ de radio** *nm* radio set; **~ restante (PR)** *nf* poste restante (*Brit*), general delivery (*US*); **~ de secours** *nm* first-aid post; **~ de télévision** *nm* television set; **~ de travail** *nm* work station

poster *vt* [poste] to post ▷ *nm* [postɛr] poster; **se poster** to position o.s

postérieur, e [posterjœr] *adj* (*date*) later; (*partie*) back ▷ *nm* (*fam*) behind

postérieurement [posterjœrmɑ̃] *adv* later, subsequently; **~ à** after

posteriori [posterjɔri]: **a ~** *adv* with hindsight, a posteriori

postérité [posterite] *nf* posterity

postface [postfas] *nf* appendix

posthume [postym] *adj* posthumous

postiche [postiʃ] *adj* false ▷ *nm* hairpiece

postier, -ière [postje, -jɛr] *nm/f* post office worker

postillon [postijɔ̃] *nm*: **envoyer des ~s** to splutter

postillonner [postijone] *vi* to splutter

post-natal, e [postnatal] *adj* postnatal

postopératoire [postɔperatwar] *adj* post-operative

postscolaire [postskɔlɛr] *adj* further, continuing

post-scriptum [postskriptom] *nm inv* postscript

postsynchronisation [postsɛ̃krɔnizasjɔ̃] *nf* dubbing

postsynchroniser [postsɛ̃krɔnize] *vt* to dub

postulant, e [postylɑ̃, -ɑ̃t] *nm/f* (*candidat*) applicant; (*Rel*) postulant

postulat [postyla] *nm* postulate

postuler [postyle] *vt* (*emploi*) to apply for, put in for

posture [postyr] *nf* posture, position; (*fig*) position

pot [po] *nm* jar, pot; (*en plastique, carton*) carton; (*en métal*) tin; (*fam*): **avoir du ~** to be lucky; **boire** *ou* **prendre un ~** (*fam*) to have a drink; **découvrir le ~ aux roses** to find out what's been going on; **~ catalytique** catalytic converter; **~ (de chambre)** (chamber)pot; **~ d'échappement** exhaust pipe; **~ de fleurs** plant pot, flowerpot; (*plante*) pot plant; **~ à tabac** tobacco jar

potable [potabl(ə)] *adj* (*fig: boisson*) drinkable; (: *travail, devoir*) decent; **eau (non) ~** (not) drinking water

potache [potaʃ] *nm* schoolboy

potage [potaʒ] *nm* soup

potager, -ère [potaʒe, -ɛr] *adj* (*plante*) edible, vegetable *cpd*; (**jardin**) ~ kitchen *ou* vegetable garden

potasse [potas] *nf* potassium hydroxide; (*engrais*) potash

potasser [potase] *vt* (*fam*) to swot up (*Brit*), cram

potassium [potasjom] *nm* potassium

pot-au-feu [potofø] *nm inv* (beef) stew; (*viande*) stewing beef ▷ *adj* (*fam: personne*) stay-at-home

pot-de-vin [podvɛ̃] (*pl* **pots-de-vin**) *nm* bribe

pote [pot] *nm* (*fam*) mate (*Brit*), pal

poteau, x [poto] *nm* post; **~ de départ/arrivée** starting/finishing post; **~ (d'exécution)** execution post, stake; **~ indicateur** signpost; **~ télégraphique** telegraph pole; **~x (de but)** goal-posts

potée [pote] *nf* hotpot (*of pork and cabbage*)

potelé, e [potle] *adj* plump, chubby

potence [potɑ̃s] *nf* gallows *sg*; **en ~** T-shaped

potentat [potɑ̃ta] *nm* potentate; (*fig: péj*) despot

potentiel, le [potɑ̃sjɛl] *adj, nm* potential

potentiellement [potɑ̃sjɛlmɑ̃] *adv* potentially

poterie [potri] *nf* (*fabrication*) pottery; (*objet*) piece of pottery

potiche [potiʃ] *nf* large vase

potier [potje] *nm* potter

potins [potɛ̃] *nmpl* gossip *sg*

p

potion [posjɔ̃] *nf* potion
potiron [pɔtiʀɔ̃] *nm* pumpkin
pot-pourri [popuʀi] (*pl* **pots-pourris**) *nm* (*Mus*) medley
pou, x [pu] *nm* louse
pouah [pwa] *excl* ugh!, yuk!
poubelle [pubɛl] *nf* (dust)bin
pouce [pus] *nm* thumb; **se tourner** *ou* **se rouler les ~s** (*fig*) to twiddle one's thumbs; **manger sur le ~** to eat on the run, snatch something to eat
poudre [pudʀ(ə)] *nf* powder; (*fard*) (face) powder; (*explosif*) gunpowder; **en ~: café en ~** instant coffee; **savon en ~** soap powder; **lait en ~** dried *ou* powdered milk; **~ à canon** gunpowder; **~ à éternuer** sneezing powder; **~ à récurer** scouring powder; **~ de riz** face powder
poudrer [pudʀe] *vt* to powder
poudreux, -euse [pudʀø, -øz] *adj* dusty; (*neige*) powdery, powder *cpd*
poudrier [pudʀije] *nm* (powder) compact
poudrière [pudʀijɛʀ] *nf* powder magazine; (*fig*) powder keg
pouf [puf] *nm* pouffe
pouffer [pufe] *vi*: **~ (de rire)** to snigger; to giggle
pouffiasse [pufjas] *nf* (*fam*) fat cow; (*prostituée*) tart
pouilleux, -euse [pujø, -øz] *adj* flea-ridden; (*fig*) seedy
poulailler [pulaje] *nm* henhouse; (*Théât*): **le ~** the gods *sg*
poulain [pulɛ̃] *nm* foal; (*fig*) protégé
poularde [pulaʀd(ə)] *nf* fatted chicken
poule [pul] *nf* (*Zool*) hen; (*Culin*) (boiling) fowl; (*Sport*) (round-robin) tournament; (*Rugby*) group; (*fam*) bird (*Brit*), chick, broad (*US*); (*prostituée*) tart; **~ d'eau** moorhen; **~ mouillée** coward; **~ pondeuse** laying hen, layer; **~ au riz** chicken and rice
poulet [pulɛ] *nm* chicken; (*fam*) cop
poulette [pulɛt] *nf* (*jeune poule*) pullet
pouliche [puliʃ] *nf* filly
poulie [puli] *nf* pulley
poulpe [pulp(ə)] *nm* octopus
pouls [pu] *nm* pulse; (*Anat*): **prendre le ~ de qn** to take sb's pulse
poumon [pumɔ̃] *nm* lung; **~ d'acier** *ou* **artificiel** iron *ou* artificial lung
poupe [pup] *nf* stern; **en ~** astern
poupée [pupe] *nf* doll; **jouer à la ~** to play with one's doll (*ou* dolls); **de ~** (*très petit*): **jardin de ~** doll's garden, pocket-handkerchief-sized garden
poupin, e [pupɛ̃, -in] *adj* chubby
poupon [pupɔ̃] *nm* babe-in-arms
pouponner [pupɔne] *vi* to fuss (around)
pouponnière [pupɔnjɛʀ] *nf* crèche, day nursery
pour [puʀ] *prép* for ▷ *nm*: **le ~ et le contre** the pros and cons; **~ faire** (so as) to do, in order to do; **~ avoir fait** for having done; **~ que** so that, in order that; **~ moi** (*à mon avis, pour ma part*) for my part, personally; **~ riche qu'il soit** rich though he may be; **~ 20 euros d'essence** 20 euros' worth of petrol; **~ cent** per cent; **~ ce qui est de** as for; **y être ~ quelque chose** to have something to do with it
pourboire [puʀbwaʀ] *nm* tip
pourcentage [puʀsɑ̃taʒ] *nm* percentage; **travailler au ~** to work on commission
pourchasser [puʀʃase] *vt* to pursue
pourfendeur [puʀfɑ̃dœʀ] *nm* sworn opponent
pourfendre [puʀfɑ̃dʀ(ə)] *vt* to assail
pourlécher [puʀleʃe]: **se pourlécher** *vi* to lick one's lips
pourparlers [puʀpaʀle] *nmpl* talks, negotiations; **être en ~ avec** to be having talks with
pourpre [puʀpʀ(ə)] *adj* crimson
pourquoi [puʀkwa] *adv, conj* why ▷ *nm inv*: **le ~ (de)** the reason (for)
pourrai *etc* [puʀe] *vb voir* **pouvoir**
pourri, e [puʀi] *adj* rotten; (*roche, pierre*) crumbling; (*temps, climat*) filthy, foul ▷ *nm*: **sentir le ~** to smell rotten
pourriel [puʀjɛl] *nm* (*Inform*) spam
pourrir [puʀiʀ] *vi* to rot; (*fruit*) to go rotten *ou* bad; (*fig: situation*) to deteriorate ▷ *vt* to rot; (*fig: corrompre: personne*) to corrupt; (: *gâter: enfant*) to spoil thoroughly
pourrissement [puʀismɑ̃] *nm* deterioration
pourriture [puʀityʀ] *nf* rot
pourrons *etc* [puʀɔ̃] *vb voir* **pouvoir**
poursuis *etc* [puʀsɥi] *vb voir* **poursuivre**
poursuite [puʀsɥit] *nf* pursuit, chase; **poursuites** *nfpl* (*Jur*) legal proceedings; (**course**) **~ track** race; (*fig*) chase
poursuivant, e [puʀsɥivɑ̃, -ɑ̃t] *vb voir* **poursuivre** ▷ *nm/f* pursuer; (*Jur*) plaintiff
poursuivre [puʀsɥivʀ(ə)] *vt* to pursue, chase (after); (*relancer*) to hound, harry; (*obséder*) to haunt; (*Jur*) to bring proceedings against, prosecute; (: *au civil*) to sue; (*but*) to strive towards; (*voyage, études*) to carry on with, continue ▷ *vi* to carry on, go on; **se poursuivre** *vi* to go on, continue
pourtant [puʀtɑ̃] *adv* yet; **mais ~** but nevertheless, but even so; **c'est ~ facile** (and) yet it's easy
pourtour [puʀtuʀ] *nm* perimeter
pourvoi [puʀvwa] *nm* appeal
pourvoir [puʀvwaʀ] *nm* (*Comm*) supply ▷ *vt*: **~ qch/qn de** to equip sth/sb with ▷ *vi*: **~ à** to provide for; (*emploi*) to fill; **se pourvoir** *vi* (*Jur*): **se ~ en cassation** to take one's case to the Court of Appeal
pourvoyeur, -euse [puʀvwajœʀ, -øz] *nm/f* supplier
pourvu, e [puʀvy] *pp de* **pourvoir** ▷ *adj*: **~ de** equipped with; **~ que** *conj* (*si*) provided that, so long as; (*espérons que*) let's hope (that)
pousse [pus] *nf* growth; (*bourgeon*) shoot
poussé, e [puse] *adj* sophisticated, advanced; (*moteur*) souped-up
pousse-café [puskafe] *nm inv* (after-dinner)

liqueur

poussée [puse] nf thrust; (coup) push; (Méd) eruption; (fig) upsurge

pousse-pousse [puspus] nm inv rickshaw

pousser [puse] vt to push; (acculer) to drive sb to do sth; (moteur, voiture) to drive hard; (émettre: cri etc) to give; (stimuler) to urge on; to drive hard; (poursuivre) to carry on; (inciter): ~ **qn à faire qch** to urge ou press sb to do sth ▷ vi to push; (croître) to grow; (aller): ~ **plus loin** to push on a bit further; **se pousser** vi to move over; **faire ~** (plante) to grow; ~ **le dévouement** etc **jusqu'à ...** to take devotion etc as far as ...

poussette [puset] nf (voiture d'enfant) pushchair (Brit), stroller (US)

poussette-canne [pusetkan] (pl **poussettes-cannes**) nf baby buggy (Brit), (folding) stroller (US)

poussier [pusje] nm coaldust

poussière [pusjɛʀ] nf dust; (grain) speck of dust; **et des ~s** (fig) and a bit; ~ **de charbon** coaldust

poussiéreux, -euse [pusjeʀø, -øz] adj dusty

poussif, -ive [pusif, -iv] adj wheezy, wheezing

poussin [pusɛ̃] nm chick

poussoir [puswaʀ] nm button

poutre [putʀ(ə)] nf beam; (en fer, ciment armé) girder; ~**s apparentes** exposed beams

poutrelle [putʀɛl] nf (petite poutre) small beam; (barre d'acier) girder

---

⊙ MOT-CLÉ

pouvoir [puvwaʀ] nm power; (Pol: dirigeants): **le pouvoir** those in power; **les pouvoirs publics** the authorities; **avoir pouvoir de faire** (autorisation) to have (the) authority to do; (droit) to have the right to do; **pouvoir absolu** absolute power; **pouvoir absorbant** absorbency; **pouvoir d'achat** purchasing power; **pouvoir calorifique** calorific value ▷ vb semi-aux **1** (être en état de) can, be able to; **je ne peux pas le réparer** I can't ou I am not able to repair it; **déçu de ne pas pouvoir le faire** disappointed not to be able to do it **2** (avoir la permission) can, may, be allowed to; **vous pouvez aller au cinéma** you can ou may go to the pictures **3** (probabilité, hypothèse) may, might, could; **il a pu avoir un accident** he may ou might ou could have had an accident; **il aurait pu le dire!** he might ou could have said (so)! **4** (expressions): **tu ne peux pas savoir!** you have no idea!; **tu peux le dire!** you can say that again! ▷ vb impers may, might, could; **il peut arriver que** it may ou might ou could happen that; **il pourrait pleuvoir** it might rain ▷ vt **1** can, be able to; **j'ai fait tout ce que j'ai pu** I did all I could; **je n'en peux plus** (épuisé) I'm exhausted; (à bout) I can't take any more **2** (vb +adj ou adv comparatif): **je me porte on ne peut mieux** I'm absolutely fine, I couldn't be better; **elle est on ne peut plus gentille** she couldn't be nicer, she's as nice as can be

se pouvoir vi: **il se peut que** it may ou might be that; **cela se pourrait** that's quite possible

---

PP sigle f (= préventive de la pellagre: vitamine) niacin ▷ abr (= pages) pp

p.p. abr (= par procuration) p.p.

p.p.c.m. sigle m (Math: = plus petit commun multiple) LCM (= lowest common multiple)

PQ sigle f (Canada: = province de Québec) PQ

PR sigle m = **parti républicain** ▷ sigle f = **poste restante**

pr abr = **pour**

pragmatique [pʀagmatik] adj pragmatic

pragmatisme [pʀagmatism(ə)] nm pragmatism

Prague [pʀag] n Prague

prairie [pʀeʀi] nf meadow

praline [pʀalin] nf (bonbon) sugared almond; (au chocolat) praline

praliné, e [pʀaline] adj (amande) sugared; (chocolat, glace) praline cpd

praticable [pʀatikabl(ə)] adj (route etc) passable, practicable; (projet) practicable

praticien, ne [pʀatisjɛ̃, -ɛn] nm/f practitioner

pratiquant, e [pʀatikɑ̃, -ɑ̃t] adj practising (Brit), practicing (US)

pratique [pʀatik] nf practice ▷ adj practical; (commode: horaire etc) convenient; (: outil) handy, useful; **dans la ~** in (actual) practice; **mettre en ~** to put into practice

pratiquement [pʀatikmɑ̃] adv (dans la pratique) in practice; (pour ainsi dire) practically, virtually

pratiquer [pʀatike] vt to practise (Brit), practice (US); (Sport etc) to go in for, play; (appliquer: méthode, théorie) to apply; (intervention, opération) to carry out; (ouverture, abri) to make ▷ vi (Rel) to be a churchgoer

pré [pʀe] nm meadow

préados [pʀeado] nmpl pre-teens

préalable [pʀealabl(ə)] adj preliminary; **condition ~ (de)** precondition (for), prerequisite (for); **sans avis ~** without prior ou previous notice; **au ~** first, beforehand

préalablement [pʀealabləmɑ̃] adv first, beforehand

Préalpes [pʀealp(ə)] nfpl: **les ~** the Pre-Alps

préalpin, e [pʀealpɛ̃, -in] adj of the Pre-Alps

préambule [pʀeɑ̃byl] nm preamble; (fig) prelude; **sans ~** straight away

préau, x [pʀeo] nm (d'une cour d'école) covered playground; (d'un monastère, d'une prison) inner courtyard

préavis [pʀeavi] nm notice; ~ **de congé** notice; **communication avec ~** (Tél) personal ou person-to-person call

prébende [pʀebɑ̃d] nf (péj) remuneration

précaire [pʀekɛʀ] adj precarious

précaution [pʀekosjɔ̃] nf precaution; **avec ~** cautiously; **prendre des** ou **ses ~s** to take precautions; **par ~** as a precaution; **pour plus**

P

de ~ to be on the safe side; **~s oratoires** carefully phrased remarks

précautionneux, -euse [pʀekosjɔnø, -øz] *adj* cautious, careful

précédemment [pʀesedamɑ̃] *adv* before, previously

précédent, e [pʀesedɑ̃, -ɑ̃t] *adj* previous ▷ *nm* precedent; **sans ~** unprecedented; **le jour ~** the day before, the previous day

précéder [pʀesede] *vt* to precede; (*marcher ou rouler devant*) to be in front of; (*arriver avant*) to get ahead of

précepte [pʀesɛpt(ə)] *nm* precept

précepteur, -trice [pʀesɛptœʀ, -tʀis] *nm/f* (private) tutor

préchauffer [pʀeʃofe] *vt* to preheat

prêcher [pʀeʃe] *vt, vi* to preach

prêcheur, -euse [pʀeʃœʀ, -øz] *adj* moralizing ▷ *nm/f* (*Rel*) preacher; (*fig*) moralizer

précieusement [pʀesjøzmɑ̃] *adv* (*avec soin*) carefully; (*avec préciosité*) preciously

précieux, -euse [pʀesjø, -øz] *adj* precious; (*collaborateur, conseils*) invaluable; (*style, écrivain*) précieux, precious

préciosité [pʀesjozite] *nf* preciosity, preciousness

précipice [pʀesipis] *nm* drop, chasm; (*fig*) abyss; **au bord du ~** at the edge of the precipice

précipitamment [pʀesipitamɑ̃] *adv* hurriedly, hastily

précipitation [pʀesipitasjɔ̃] *nf* (*hâte*) haste; **~s (atmosphériques)** precipitation *sg*

précipité, e [pʀesipite] *adj* (*respiration*) fast; (*pas*) hurried; (*départ*) hasty

précipiter [pʀesipite] *vt* (*faire tomber*): **~ qn/qch du haut de** to throw *ou* hurl sb/sth off *ou* from; (*hâter: marche*) to quicken; (: *départ*) to hasten; **se précipiter** *vi* (*événements*) to move faster; (*respiration*) to speed up; **se ~ sur/vers** to rush at/ towards; **se ~ au-devant de qn** to throw o.s. before sb

précis, e [pʀesi, -iz] *adj* precise; (*tir, mesures*) accurate, precise ▷ *nm* handbook

précisément [pʀesizemɑ̃] *adv* precisely; **ma vie n'est pas ~ distrayante** my life is not exactly entertaining

préciser [pʀesize] *vt* (*expliquer*) to be more specific about, clarify; (*spécifier*) to state, specify; **se préciser** *vi* to become clear(er)

précision [pʀesizjɔ̃] *nf* precision; accuracy; (*détail*) point *ou* detail (*made clear or to be clarified*); **précisions** *nfpl* further details

précoce [pʀekɔs] *adj* early; (*enfant*) precocious; (*calvitie*) premature

précocité [pʀekɔsite] *nf* earliness; precociousness

préconçu, e [pʀekɔ̃sy] *adj* preconceived

préconiser [pʀekɔnize] *vt* to advocate

précuit, e [pʀekɥi, -it] *adj* precooked

précurseur [pʀekyʀsœʀ] *adj m* precursory ▷ *nm* forerunner, precursor

prédateur [pʀedatœʀ] *nm* predator

prédécesseur [pʀedesesœʀ] *nm* predecessor

prédécoupé, e [pʀedekupe] *adj* pre-cut

prédestiner [pʀedɛstine] *vt*: **~ qn à qch/à faire** to predestine sb for sth/to do

prédicateur [pʀedikatœʀ] *nm* preacher

prédiction [pʀediksjɔ̃] *nf* prediction

prédilection [pʀedilɛksjɔ̃] *nf*: **avoir une ~ pour** to be partial to; **de ~** favourite (*Brit*), favorite (*US*)

prédire [pʀediʀ] *vt* to predict

prédisposer [pʀedispoze] *vt*: **~ qn à qch/à faire** to predispose sb to sth/to do

prédisposition [pʀedispozisjɔ̃] *nf* predisposition

prédit, e [pʀedi, -it] *pp de* **prédire**

prédominance [pʀedɔminɑ̃s] *nf* predominance

prédominant, e [pʀedɔminɑ̃, -ɑ̃t] *adj* predominant; prevailing

prédominer [pʀedɔmine] *vi* to predominate; (*avis*) to prevail

pré-électoral, e, -aux [pʀeelɛktɔʀal, -o] *adj* pre-election *cpd*

pré-emballé, e [pʀeɑ̃bale] *adj* pre-packed

prééminent, e [pʀeeminɑ̃, -ɑ̃t] *adj* pre-eminent

préemption [pʀeɑ̃psjɔ̃] *nf*: **droit de ~** (*Jur*) pre-emptive right

pré-encollé, e [pʀeɑ̃kɔle] *adj* pre-pasted

préétabli, e [pʀeetabli] *adj* pre-established

préexistant, e [pʀeɛgzistɑ̃, -ɑ̃t] *adj* pre-existing

préfabriqué, e [pʀefabʀike] *adj* prefabricated; (*péj: sourire*) artificial ▷ *nm* prefabricated material

préface [pʀefas] *nf* preface

préfacer [pʀefase] *vt* to write a preface for

préfectoral, e, -aux [pʀefɛktɔʀal, -o] *adj* prefectorial

préfecture [pʀefɛktyʀ] *nf* prefecture; *see note*; **~ de police** police headquarters

préférable [pʀefeʀabl(ə)] *adj* preferable

préféré, e [pʀefeʀe] *adj, nm/f* favourite (*Brit*), favorite (*US*)

préférence [pʀefeʀɑ̃s] *nf* preference; **de ~** preferably; **de** *ou* **par ~ à** in preference to, rather than; **donner la ~ à qn** to give preference to sb; **par ordre de ~** in order of preference; **obtenir la ~ sur** to have preference over

préférentiel, le [pʀefeʀɑ̃sjɛl] *adj* preferential

préférer [pʀefeʀe] *vt*: **~ qn/qch (à)** to prefer sb/ sth (to), like sb/sth better (than); **~ faire** to prefer to do; **je préférerais du thé** I would rather have tea, I'd prefer tea

préfet [pʀefɛ] *nm* prefect; **~ de police** ≈ Chief Constable (*Brit*), ≈ Police Commissioner (*US*)

préfigurer [pʀefigyʀe] *vt* to prefigure

préfixe [pʀefiks(ə)] *nm* prefix

préhistoire [pʀeistwaʀ] *nf* prehistory

préhistorique [pʀeistɔʀik] *adj* prehistoric

préjudice [pʀeʒydis] *nm* (*matériel*) loss; (*moral*) harm *no pl*; **porter ~ à** to harm, be detrimental to; **au ~ de** at the expense of

préjudiciable [pʀeʒydisjabl(ə)] *adj*: **~ à** prejudicial *ou* harmful to

préjugé [pʀeʒyʒe] *nm* prejudice; **avoir un ~ contre** to be prejudiced against; **bénéficier d'un ~ favorable** to be viewed favourably

préjuger [pʀeʒyʒe]: **~ de** *vt* to prejudge

prélasser [pʀelase]: **se prélasser** *vi* to lounge

prélat [pʀela] *nm* prelate

prélavage [pʀelavaʒ] *nm* pre-wash

prélèvement [pʀelɛvmɑ̃] *nm* deduction; withdrawal; **faire un ~ de sang** to take a blood sample

prélever [pʀelve] *vt* (*échantillon*) to take; **~ (sur)** (*argent*) to deduct (from); (*: sur son compte*) to withdraw (from)

préliminaire [pʀeliminɛʀ] *adj* preliminary; **préliminaires** *nmpl* preliminaries; (*négociations*) preliminary talks

prélude [pʀelyd] *nm* prelude; (*avant le concert*) warm-up

prématuré, e [pʀematyʀe] *adj* premature; (*retraite*) early ▷ *nm* premature baby

prématurément [pʀematyʀemɑ̃] *adv* prematurely

préméditation [pʀemeditasjɔ̃] *nf*: **avec ~** *adj* premeditated ▷ *adv* with intent

préméditer [pʀemedite] *vt* to premeditate, plan

prémices [pʀemis] *nfpl* beginnings

premier, -ière [pʀəmje, -jɛʀ] *adj* first; (*branche, marche, grade*) bottom; (*fig: fondamental*) basic; prime; (*en importance*) first, foremost ▷ *nm* (*premier étage*) first (*Brit*) *ou* second (*US*) floor ▷ *nf* (*Auto*) first (gear); (*Rail, Aviat etc*) first class; (*Scol: classe*) penultimate school year (*age 16–17*); (*Théât*) first night; (*Ciné*) première; (*exploit*) first; **au ~ abord** at first sight; **au** *ou* **du ~ coup** at the first attempt *ou* go; **de ~ ordre** first-class, first-rate; **de première qualité, de ~ choix** best *ou* top quality; **de première importance** of the highest importance; **de première nécessité** absolutely essential; **le ~ venu** the first person to come along; **jeune ~** leading man; **le ~ de l'an** New Year's Day; **enfant du ~ lit** child of a first marriage; **en ~ lieu** in the first place; **~ âge** (*d'un enfant*) the first three months (of life); **P~ Ministre** Prime Minister

premièrement [pʀəmjɛʀmɑ̃] *adv* firstly

première-née [pʀəmjɛʀne] (*pl* **premières-nées**) *nf* first-born

premier-né [pʀəmjene] (*pl* **premiers-nés**) *nm* first-born

prémisse [pʀemis] *nf* premise

prémolaire [pʀemɔlɛʀ] *nf* premolar

prémonition [pʀemɔnisjɔ̃] *nf* premonition

prémonitoire [pʀemɔnitwaʀ] *adj* premonitory

prémunir [pʀemyniʀ]: **se prémunir** *vi*: **se ~ contre** to protect o.s. from, guard against

prenant, e [pʀənɑ̃, -ɑ̃t] *vb voir* **prendre** ▷ *adj* absorbing, engrossing

prénatal, e [pʀenatal] *adj* (*Méd*) antenatal; (*allocation*) maternity *cpd*

prendre [pʀɑ̃dʀ(ə)] *vt* to take; (*aller chercher*) to get, fetch; (*se procurer*) to get; (*réserver: place*) to book; (*acquérir: du poids, de la valeur*) to put on, gain; (*malfaiteur, poisson*) to catch; (*passager*) to pick up; (*personnel, aussi: couleur, goût*) to take on; (*locataire*) to take in; (*traiter: enfant, problème*) to handle; (*voix, ton*) to put on; (*prélever: pourcentage, argent*) to take off; (*ôter*): **~ qch à** to take sth from; (*coincer*): **se ~ les doigts dans** to get one's fingers caught in ▷ *vi* (*liquide, ciment*) to set; (*greffe, vaccin*) to take; (*mensonge*) to be successful; (*feu: foyer*) to go; (*: incendie*) to start; (*allumette*) to light; (*se diriger*): **~ à gauche** to turn (to the) left; **~ son origine** *ou* **sa source** (*mot, rivière*) to have its source; **~ qn pour** to take sb for; **se ~ pour** to think one is; **~ sur soi de faire qch** to take it upon o.s. to do sth; **~ qn en sympathie/horreur** to get to like/loathe sb; **à tout ~** all things considered; **s'en ~ à** (*agresser*) to set about; (*passer sa colère sur*) to take it out on; (*critiquer*) to attack; (*remettre en question*) to challenge; **se ~ d'amitié/d'affection pour** to befriend/become fond of; **s'y ~** (*procéder*) to set about it; **s'y ~ à l'avance** to see to it in advance; **s'y ~ à deux fois** to try twice, make two attempts

preneur [pʀənœʀ] *nm*: **être ~** to be willing to buy; **trouver ~** to find a buyer

preniez [pʀənje] *vb voir* **prendre**

prenne *etc* [pʀɛn] *vb voir* **prendre**

prénom [pʀenɔ̃] *nm* first name

prénommer [pʀenɔme] *vt*: **elle se prénomme Claude** her (first) name is Claude

prénuptial, e, -aux [pʀenypsjal, -o] *adj* premarital

préoccupant, e [pʀeɔkypɑ̃, -ɑ̃t] *adj* worrying

préoccupation [pʀeɔkypasjɔ̃] *nf* (*souci*) concern; (*idée fixe*) preoccupation

préoccupé, e [pʀeɔkype] *adj* concerned; preoccupied

préoccuper [pʀeɔkype] *vt* (*tourmenter, tracasser*) to concern; (*absorber, obséder*) to preoccupy; **se ~ de qch** to be concerned about sth; to show concern about sth

préparateur, -trice [pʀepaʀatœʀ, -tʀis] *nm/f* assistant

préparatifs [pʀepaʀatif] *nmpl* preparations

préparation [pʀepaʀasjɔ̃] *nf* preparation; (*Scol*) piece of homework

préparatoire [pʀepaʀatwaʀ] *adj* preparatory

préparer [pʀepaʀe] *vt* to prepare; (*café, repas*) to

make; (*examen*) to prepare for; (*voyage, entreprise*) to plan; **se préparer** vi (*orage, tragédie*) to brew, be in the air; **se ~ (à qch/à faire)** to prepare (o.s.) *ou* get ready (for sth/to do); **~ qch à qn** (*surprise etc*) to have sth in store for sb; **~ qn à qch** (*nouvelle etc*) to prepare sb for sth

prépondérance [pʀepɔ̃deʀɑ̃s] *nf*: **~ (sur)** predominance (over)

prépondérant, e [pʀepɔ̃deʀɑ̃, -ɑ̃t] *adj* major, dominating; **voix ~e** casting vote

préposé, e [pʀepoze] *adj*: **~ à** in charge of ▷ *nm/f* (*gén: employé*) employee; (*Admin: facteur*) postman/woman (*Brit*), mailman/woman (*US*); (*de la douane etc*) official; (*de vestiaire*) attendant

préposer [pʀepoze] *vt*: **~ qn à qch** to appoint sb to sth

préposition [pʀepozisjɔ̃] *nf* preposition

prérentrée [pʀeʀɑ̃tʀe] *nf* in-service training period before start of school term

préretraite [pʀeʀətʀɛt] *nf* early retirement

prérogative [pʀeʀɔgativ] *nf* prerogative

près [pʀɛ] *adv* near, close; **~ de** *prép* near (to), close to; (*environ*) nearly, almost; **~ d'ici** near here; **de ~** *adv* closely; **à cinq kg ~** to within about five kg; **à cela ~ que** apart from the fact that; **je ne suis pas ~ de lui pardonner** I'm nowhere near ready to forgive him; **on n'est pas à un jour ~** one day (either way) won't make any difference, we're not going to quibble over the odd day

présage [pʀezaʒ] *nm* omen

présager [pʀezaʒe] *vt* (*prévoir*) to foresee; (*annoncer*) to portend

pré-salé [pʀesale] (*pl* **prés-salés**) *nm* (*Culin*) salt-meadow lamb

presbyte [pʀɛsbit] *adj* long-sighted (*Brit*), far-sighted (*US*)

presbytère [pʀɛsbitɛʀ] *nm* presbytery

presbytérien, ne [pʀɛsbiteʀjɛ̃, -ɛn] *adj, nm/f* Presbyterian

presbytie [pʀɛsbisi] *nf* long-sightedness (*Brit*), far-sightedness (*US*)

prescience [pʀesjɑ̃s] *nf* prescience, foresight

préscolaire [pʀeskɔlɛʀ] *adj* preschool *cpd*

prescription [pʀɛskʀipsjɔ̃] *nf* (*instruction*) order, instruction; (*Méd, Jur*) prescription

prescrire [pʀɛskʀiʀ] *vt* to prescribe; **se prescrire** vi (*Jur*) to lapse

prescrit, e [pʀɛskʀi, -it] *pp de* **prescrire** ▷ *adj* (*date etc*) stipulated

préséance [pʀeseɑ̃s] *nf* precedence *no pl*

présélection [pʀeseleksjɔ̃] *nf* (*de candidats*) short-listing; **effectuer une ~** to draw up a shortlist

présélectionner [pʀeseleksjɔne] *vt* to preselect; (*dispositif*) to preset; (*candidats*) to make an initial selection from among, short-list (*Brit*)

présence [pʀezɑ̃s] *nf* presence; (*au bureau etc*) attendance; **en ~** face to face; **en ~ de** in (the) presence of; (*fig*) in the face of; **faire acte de ~** to put in a token appearance; **~ d'esprit** presence of mind

présent, e [pʀezɑ̃, -ɑ̃t] *adj, nm* present; (*Admin, Comm*): **la ~e lettre/loi** this letter/law ▷ *nm/f*: **les ~s** (*personnes*) those present ▷ *nf* (*Comm: lettre*): **la ~e** this letter; **à ~** now, at present; **dès à ~** here and now; **jusqu'à ~** up till now, until now; **à ~ que** now that

présentable [pʀezɑ̃tabl(ə)] *adj* presentable

présentateur, -trice [pʀezɑ̃tatœʀ, -tʀis] *nm/f* presenter

présentation [pʀezɑ̃tasjɔ̃] *nf* presentation; introduction; (*allure*) appearance

présenter [pʀezɑ̃te] *vt* to present; (*invité, candidat*) to introduce; (*félicitations, condoléances*) to offer; (*montrer: billet, pièce d'identité*) to show, produce; (*faire inscrire: candidat*) to put forward; (*soumettre*) to submit ▷ *vi*: **~ mal/bien** to have an unattractive/a pleasing appearance; **se présenter** vi (*sur convocation*) to report, come; (*se faire connaître*) to come forward; (*à une élection*) to stand; (*occasion*) to arise; **se ~ à un examen** to sit an exam; **se ~ bien/mal** to look good/not too good

présentoir [pʀezɑ̃twaʀ] *nm* (*étagère*) display shelf; (*vitrine*) showcase; (*étal*) display stand

préservatif [pʀezɛʀvatif] *nm* condom, sheath

préservation [pʀezɛʀvasjɔ̃] *nf* protection, preservation

préserver [pʀezɛʀve] *vt*: **~ de** (*protéger*) to protect from; (*sauver*) to save from

présidence [pʀezidɑ̃s] *nf* presidency; chairmanship

président [pʀezidɑ̃] *nm* (*Pol*) president; (*d'une assemblée, Comm*) chairman; **~ directeur général (PDG)** chairman and managing director (*Brit*), chairman and president (*US*); **~ du jury** (*Jur*) foreman of the jury; (*d'examen*) chief examiner

présidente [pʀezidɑ̃t] *nf* president; (*femme du président*) president's wife; (*d'une réunion*) chairwoman

présidentiable [pʀezidɑ̃sjabl(ə)] *adj, nm/f* potential president

présidentiel, le [pʀezidɑ̃sjɛl] *adj* presidential; **présidentielles** *nfpl* presidential election(s)

présider [pʀezide] *vt* to preside over; (*dîner*) to be the guest of honour (*Brit*) *ou* honor (*US*) at; **~ à** *vt* to direct; to govern

présomption [pʀezɔ̃psjɔ̃] *nf* presumption

présomptueux, -euse [pʀezɔ̃ptɥø, -øz] *adj* presumptuous

presque [pʀɛsk(ə)] *adv* almost, nearly; **~ rien** hardly anything; **~ pas** hardly (at all); **~ pas de** hardly any; **personne, ou ~** next to nobody, hardly anyone; **la ~ totalité (de)** almost *ou* nearly all

presqu'île [pʀɛskil] *nf* peninsula

pressant, e [pʀɛsɑ̃, -ɑ̃t] *adj* urgent; (*personne*) insistent; **se faire ~** to become insistent

presse [pʀɛs] *nf* press; (*affluence*): **heures de ~** busy times; **sous ~** gone to press; **mettre sous ~** to send to press; **avoir une bonne/mauvaise ~** to have a good/bad press; **~ féminine**

women's magazines *pl*; ~ **d'information** quality newspapers *pl*

pressé, e [prese] *adj* in a hurry; (*air*) hurried; (*besogne*) urgent ▷ *nm*: **aller au plus** ~ to see to first things first; **être ~ de faire qch** to be in a hurry to do sth; **orange ~e** freshly squeezed orange juice

presse-citron [prɛsitrɔ̃] *nm inv* lemon squeezer

presse-fruits [prɛsfrɥi] *nm inv* lemon squeezer

pressentiment [prɛsɑ̃timɑ̃] *nm* foreboding, premonition

pressentir [prɛsɑ̃tir] *vt* to sense; (*prendre contact avec*) to approach

presse-papiers [prɛspapje] *nm inv* paperweight

presse-purée [prɛspyre] *nm inv* potato masher

presser [prese] *vt* (*fruit, éponge*) to squeeze; (*interrupteur, bouton*) to press, push; (*allure, affaire*) to speed up; (*débiteur etc*) to press; (*inciter*): ~ **qn de faire** to urge *ou* press sb to do ▷ *vi* to be urgent; **se presser** (*se hâter*) to hurry (up); (*se grouper*) to crowd; **rien ne presse** there's no hurry; **se ~ contre qn** to squeeze up against sb; ~ **le pas** to quicken one's step; ~ **qn entre ses bras** to squeeze sb tight

pressing [presiŋ] *nm* (*repassage*) steam-pressing; (*magasin*) dry-cleaner's

pression [prɛsjɔ̃] *nf* pressure; (*bouton*) press stud (*Brit*), snap fastener; **faire ~ sur** to put pressure on; **sous ~** pressurized, under pressure; (*fig*) keyed up; ~ **artérielle** blood pressure

pressoir [prɛswar] *nm* (*wine ou oil etc*) press

pressurer [prɛsyre] *vt* (*fig*) to squeeze

pressurisé, e [prɛsyrize] *adj* pressurized

prestance [prɛstɑ̃s] *nf* presence, imposing bearing

prestataire [prɛstatɛr] *nm/f* person receiving benefits; (*Comm*): ~ **de services** provider of services

prestation [prɛstasjɔ̃] *nf* (*allocation*) benefit; (*d'une assurance*) cover *no pl*; (*d'une entreprise*) service provided; (*d'un joueur, artiste*) performance; ~ **de serment** taking the oath; ~ **de service** provision of a service; **~s familiales** ≈ child benefit

preste [prɛst(ə)] *adj* nimble

prestement [prɛstəmɑ̃] *adv* nimbly

prestidigitateur, -trice [prɛstidiʒitatœr, -tris] *nm/f* conjurer

prestidigitation [prɛstidiʒitasjɔ̃] *nf* conjuring

prestige [prɛstiʒ] *nm* prestige

prestigieux, -euse [prɛstiʒjø, -øz] *adj* prestigious

présumer [prezyme] *vt*: ~ **que** to presume *ou* assume that; ~ **de** to overrate; ~ **qn coupable** to presume sb guilty

présupposé [presypoze] *nm* presupposition

présupposer [presypoze] *vt* to presuppose

présupposition [presypozisjɔ̃] *nf* presupposition

présure [prezyr] *nf* rennet

prêt, e [prɛ, prɛt] *adj* ready ▷ *nm* lending *no pl*; (*somme prêtée*) loan; ~ **à faire** ready to do; ~ **à tout** ready for anything; ~ **sur gages** pawnbroking *no pl*

prêt-à-porter [prɛtaporte] (*pl* **prêts-à-porter**) *nm* ready-to-wear *ou* off-the-peg (*Brit*) clothes *pl*

prétendant [pretɑ̃dɑ̃] *nm* pretender; (*d'une femme*) suitor

prétendre [pretɑ̃dr(ə)] *vt* (*affirmer*): ~ **que** to claim that; (*avoir l'intention de*): ~ **faire qch** to mean *ou* intend to do sth; ~ **à** *vt* (*droit, titre*) to lay claim to

prétendu, e [pretɑ̃dy] *adj* (*supposé*) so-called

prétendument [pretɑ̃dymɑ̃] *adv* allegedly

prête-nom [prɛtnɔ̃] *nm* (*péj*) figurehead; (*Comm etc*) dummy

prétentieux, -euse [pretɑ̃sjø, -øz] *adj* pretentious

prétention [pretɑ̃sjɔ̃] *nf* pretentiousness; (*exigence, ambition*) claim; **sans ~** unpretentious

prêter [prete] *vt* (*livres, argent*): ~ **qch (à)** to lend sth (to); (*supposer*): ~ **à qn** (*caractère, propos*) to attribute to sb ▷ *vi*: **se prêter** (*tissu, cuir*) to give; ~ **à** (*commentaires etc*) to be open to, give rise to; **se ~ à** to lend o.s. (*ou* itself) to; (*manigances etc*) to go along with; ~ **assistance à** to give help to; ~ **attention** to pay attention; ~ **serment** to take the oath; ~ **l'oreille** to listen

prêteur, -euse [prɛtœr, -øz] *nm/f* moneylender; ~ **sur gages** pawnbroker

prétexte [pretɛkst(ə)] *nm* pretext, excuse; **sous aucun ~** on no account; **sous (le) ~ que/de** on the pretext that/of

prétexter [pretɛkste] *vt* to give as a pretext *ou* an excuse

prêtre [prɛtr(ə)] *nm* priest

prêtre-ouvrier [prɛtruvrije] (*pl* **prêtres-ouvriers**) *nm* worker-priest

prêtrise [prɛtriz] *nf* priesthood

preuve [prœv] *nf* proof; (*indice*) proof, evidence *no pl*; **jusqu'à ~ du contraire** until proved otherwise; **faire ~ de** to show; **faire ses ~s** to prove o.s. (*ou* itself); ~ **matérielle** material evidence

prévaloir [prevalwar] *vi* to prevail; **se ~ de** *vt* to take advantage of; (*tirer vanité de*) to pride o.s. on

prévarication [prevarikasjɔ̃] *nf* maladministration

prévaut *etc* [prevo] *vb voir* **prévaloir**

prévenances [prevnɑ̃s] *nfpl* thoughtfulness *sg*, kindness *sg*

prévenant, e [prevnɑ̃, -ɑ̃t] *adj* thoughtful, kind

prévenir [prevnir] *vt* (*éviter*) to avoid, prevent; (*anticiper*) to anticipate; ~ **qn (de)** (*avertir*) to warn sb (about); (*informer*) to tell *ou* inform sb (about); ~ **qn contre** (*influencer*) to prejudice sb against

préventif, -ive [prevɑ̃tif, -iv] *adj* preventive

prévention [prevɑ̃sjɔ̃] *nf* prevention; (*préjugé*) prejudice; (*Jur*) custody, detention; ~ **routière** road safety

prévenu, e [pʀevny] nm/f (Jur) defendant, accused

prévisible [pʀeviziblə)] adj foreseeable

prévision [pʀevizjɔ̃] nf: ~s predictions; (météorologiques, économiques) forecast sg; **en ~ de** in anticipation of; ~s **météorologiques** ou **du temps** weather forecast sg

prévisionnel, le [pʀevizjɔnɛl] adj concerned with future requirements

prévit etc [pʀevi] vb voir **prévoir**

prévoir [pʀevwaʀ] vt (deviner) to foresee; (s'attendre à) to expect, reckon on; (prévenir) to anticipate; (organiser) to plan; (préparer, réserver) to allow; **prévu pour quatre personnes** designed for four people; **prévu pour 10 h** scheduled for 10 o'clock

prévoyance [pʀevwajɑ̃s] nf foresight; **société/ caisse de** ~ provident society/contingency fund

prévoyant, e [pʀevwajɑ̃, -ɑ̃t] vb voir **prévoir** ▷ adj gifted with (ou showing) foresight, far-sighted

prévu, e [pʀevy] pp de **prévoir**

prier [pʀije] vi to pray ▷ vt (Dieu) to pray to; (implorer) to beg; (demander): ~ **qn de faire** to ask sb to do; (inviter): ~ **qn à dîner** to invite sb to dinner; **se faire** ~ to need coaxing ou persuading; **je vous en prie** (allez-y) please do; (de rien) don't mention it; **je vous prie de faire** please (would you) do

prière [pʀijɛʀ] nf prayer; (demande instante) plea, entreaty; **"~ de faire ..."** "please do ..."

primaire [pʀimɛʀ] adj primary; (péj: personne) simple-minded; (: idées) simplistic ▷ nm (Scol) primary education

primauté [pʀimote] nf (fig) primacy

prime [pʀim] nf (bonification) bonus; (subside) allowance; (Comm: cadeau) free gift; (Assurances, Bourse) premium ▷ adj: **de ~ abord** at first glance; ~ **de risque** danger money no pl; ~ **de transport** travel allowance

primer [pʀime] vt (l'emporter sur) to prevail over; (récompenser) to award a prize to ▷ vi to dominate, prevail

primesautier, -ière [pʀimsotje, -jɛʀ] adj impulsive

primeur [pʀimœʀ] nf: **avoir la ~ de** to be the first to hear (ou see etc); **primeurs** nfpl (fruits, légumes) early fruits and vegetables; **marchand de** ~ greengrocer (Brit), produce dealer (US)

primevère [pʀimvɛʀ] nf primrose

primitif, -ive [pʀimitif, -iv] adj primitive; (originel) original ▷ nm/f primitive

primo [pʀimo] adv first (of all), firstly

primordial, e, -aux [pʀimɔʀdjal, -o] adj essential, primordial

prince [pʀɛ̃s] nm prince; ~ **charmant** Prince Charming; ~ **de Galles** nm inv (tissu) check cloth; ~ **héritier** crown prince

princesse [pʀɛ̃sɛs] nf princess

princier, -ière [pʀɛ̃sje, -jɛʀ] adj princely

principal, e, -aux [pʀɛ̃sipal, -o] adj principal, main ▷ nm (Scol) head (teacher) (Brit), principal

(US); (essentiel) main thing ▷ nf (Ling): **(proposition)** ~**e** main clause

principalement [pʀɛ̃sipalmɑ̃] adv principally, mainly

principauté [pʀɛ̃sipote] nf principality

principe [pʀɛ̃sip] nm principle; **partir du** ~ **que** to work on the principle ou assumption that; **pour le** ~ on principle, for the sake of it; **de** ~ adj (hostilité) automatic; (accord) in principle; **par** ~ on principle; **en** ~ (habituellement) as a rule; (théoriquement) in principle

printanier, -ière [pʀɛ̃tanje, -jɛʀ] adj spring, spring-like

printemps [pʀɛ̃tɑ̃] nm spring; **au** ~ in spring

priori [pʀijɔʀi]: **a** ~ adv at first glance, initially; a priori

prioritaire [pʀijɔʀitɛʀ] adj having priority; (Auto) having right of way; (Inform) foreground

priorité [pʀijɔʀite] nf (Auto): **avoir la** ~ **(sur)** to have right of way (over); ~ **à droite** right of way to vehicles coming from the right; **en** ~ as a (matter of) priority

pris, e [pʀi, pʀiz] pp de **prendre** ▷ adj (place) taken; (billets) sold; (journée, mains) full; (personne) busy; (crème, ciment) set; (Méd: enflammé): **avoir le nez/la gorge** ~**(e)** to have a stuffy nose/a bad throat; (saisi): **être** ~ **de peur/ de fatigue** to be stricken with fear/overcome with fatigue

prise [pʀiz] nf (d'une ville) capture; (Pêche, Chasse) catch; (de judo ou catch, point d'appui ou pour empoigner) hold; (Élec: fiche) plug; (: femelle) socket; (: au mur) point; **en** ~ (Auto) in gear; **être aux** ~**s avec** to be grappling with; to be battling with; **lâcher** ~ to let go; **donner** ~ **à** (fig) to give rise to; **avoir** ~ **sur qn** to have a hold over sb; ~ **en charge** (taxe) pick-up charge; (par la sécurité sociale) undertaking to reimburse costs; ~ **de contact** initial meeting, first contact; ~ **de courant** power point; ~ **d'eau** water (supply) point; tap; ~ **multiple** adaptor; ~ **d'otages** hostage-taking; ~ **à partie** (Jur) action against a judge; ~ **de sang** blood test; ~ **de son** sound recording; ~ **de tabac** pinch of snuff; ~ **de terre** earth; ~ **de vue** (photo) shot; (action): ~ **de vue(s)** filming, shooting

priser [pʀize] vt (tabac, héroïne) to take; (estimer) to prize, value ▷ vi to take snuff

prisme [pʀismə)] nm prism

prison [pʀizɔ̃] nf prison; **aller/être en** ~ to go to/be in prison ou jail; **faire de la** ~ to serve time; **être condamné à cinq ans de** ~ to be sentenced to five years' imprisonment ou five years in prison

prisonnier, -ière [pʀizɔnje, -jɛʀ] nm/f prisoner ▷ adj captive; **faire qn** ~ to take sb prisoner

prit [pʀi] vb voir **prendre**

privatif, -ive [pʀivatif, -iv] adj (jardin etc) private; (peine) which deprives one of one's liberties

privations [pʀivasjɔ̃] nfpl privations, hardships

privatisation [pʀivatizasjɔ̃] nf privatization

privatiser [pʀivatize] vt to privatize

privautés [pʀivote] *nfpl* liberties
privé, e [pʀive] *adj* private; *(dépourvu)*: ~ **de** without, lacking; **en** ~, **dans le** ~ in private
priver [pʀive] *vt*: ~ **qn de** to deprive sb of; **se** ~ **de** to go *ou* do without; **ne pas se** ~ **de faire** not to refrain from doing
privilège [pʀivilɛʒ] *nm* privilege
privilégié, e [pʀivileʒje] *adj* privileged
privilégier [pʀivileʒje] *vt* to favour (*Brit*), favor (*US*)
prix [pʀi] *nm* (*valeur*) price; (*récompense, Scol*) prize; **mettre à** ~ to set a reserve (*Brit*) *ou* an upset (*US*) price on; **au** ~ **fort** at a very high price; **acheter qch à** ~ **d'or** to pay a (small) fortune for sth; **hors de** ~ exorbitantly priced; **à aucun** ~ not at any price; **à tout** ~ at all costs; **grand** ~ (*Sport*) Grand Prix; ~ **d'achat/de vente/ de revient** purchasing/selling/cost price; ~ **conseillé** manufacturer's recommended price (MRP)
pro [pʀo] *nm* (= *professionnel*) pro
probabilité [pʀobabilite] *nf* probability; **selon toute** ~ in all probability
probable [pʀobabl(ə)] *adj* likely, probable
probablement [pʀobabləmɑ̃] *adv* probably
probant, e [pʀobɑ̃, -ɑ̃t] *adj* convincing
probatoire [pʀobatwaʀ] *adj* (*examen, test*) preliminary; (*stage*) probationary, trial *cpd*
probité [pʀobite] *nf* integrity, probity
problématique [pʀoblematik] *adj* problematic(al) ▷ *nf* problematics *sg*; (*problème*) problem
problème [pʀoblɛm] *nm* problem
procédé [pʀosede] *nm* (*méthode*) process; (*comportement*) behaviour *no pl* (*Brit*), behavior *no pl* (*US*)
procéder [pʀosede] *vi* to proceed; to behave; ~ **à** *vt* to carry out
procédure [pʀosedyʀ] *nf* (*Admin, Jur*) procedure
procès [pʀosɛ] *nm* (*Jur*) trial; (: *poursuites*) proceedings *pl*; **être en** ~ **avec** to be involved in a lawsuit with; **faire le** ~ **de qn/qch** (*fig*) to put sb/sth on trial; **sans autre forme de** ~ without further ado
processeur [pʀosesœʀ] *nm* processor
procession [pʀosesjɔ̃] *nf* procession
processus [pʀosesys] *nm* process
procès-verbal, -aux [pʀosɛvɛʀbal, -o] *nm* (*constat*) statement; (*aussi*: **PV**): **avoir un** ~ to get a parking ticket; to be booked; (*de réunion*) minutes *pl*
prochain, e [pʀoʃɛ̃, -ɛn] *adj* next; (*proche*) impending; near ▷ *nm* fellow man; **la** ~**e fois/ semaine** ~**e** next time/week; **à la** ~**e!** (*fam*): **à la** ~**e fois** see you!, till the next time!; **un** ~ **jour** (some day) soon
prochainement [pʀoʃɛnmɑ̃] *adv* soon, shortly
proche [pʀoʃ] *adj* nearby; (*dans le temps*) imminent; close at hand; (*parent, ami*) close; **proches** *nmpl* (*parents*) close relatives, next of kin; (*amis*): **l'un de ses** ~**s** one of those close to him (*ou* her); **être** ~ (**de**) to be near, be close (to);

de ~ **en** ~ gradually
Proche-Orient [pʀoʃoʀjɑ̃] *nm*: **le** ~ the Near East
proclamation [pʀoklamasjɔ̃] *nf* proclamation
proclamer [pʀoklame] *vt* to proclaim; (*résultat d'un examen*) to announce
procréer [pʀokʀee] *vt* to procreate
procuration [pʀokyʀasjɔ̃] *nf* proxy; power of attorney; **voter par** ~ to vote by proxy
procurer [pʀokyʀe] *vt* (*fournir*): ~ **qch à qn** to get *ou* obtain sth for sb; (*causer: plaisir etc*): ~ **qch à qn** to bring *ou* give sb sth; **se procurer** *vt* to get
procureur [pʀokyʀœʀ] *nm* public prosecutor; ~ **général** public prosecutor (*in appeal court*)
prodigalité [pʀodigalite] *nf* (*générosité*) generosity; (*extravagance*) extravagance, wastefulness
prodige [pʀodiʒ] *nm* (*miracle, merveille*) marvel, wonder; (*personne*) prodigy
prodigieusement [pʀodiʒjøzmɑ̃] *adv* tremendously
prodigieux, -euse [pʀodiʒjø, -øz] *adj* prodigious; phenomenal
prodigue [pʀodig] *adj* (*généreux*) generous; (*dépensier*) extravagant, wasteful; **fils** ~ prodigal son
prodiguer [pʀodige] *vt* (*argent, biens*) to be lavish with; (*soins, attentions*): ~ **qch à qn** to lavish sth on sb
producteur, -trice [pʀodyktœʀ, -tʀis] *adj*: ~ **de blé** wheat-producing; (*Ciné*): **société productrice** film *ou* movie company ▷ *nm/f* producer
productif, -ive [pʀodyktif, -iv] *adj* productive
production [pʀodyksjɔ̃] *nf* (*gén*) production; (*rendement*) output; (*produits*) products *pl*, goods *pl*; (*œuvres*): **la** ~ **dramatique du XVIIe siècle** the plays of the 17th century
productivité [pʀodyktivite] *nf* productivity
produire [pʀodɥiʀ] *vt, vi* to produce; **se produire** *vi* (*acteur*) to perform, appear; (*événement*) to happen, occur
produit, e [pʀodɥi, -it] *pp de* **produire** ▷ *nm* (*gén*) product; ~ **d'entretien** cleaning product; ~ **national brut (PNB)** gross national product (GNP); ~ **net** net profit; ~ **pour la vaisselle** washing-up (*Brit*) *ou* dish-washing (*US*) liquid; ~ **des ventes** income from sales; ~**s agricoles** farm produce *sg*; ~**s alimentaires** foodstuffs; ~**s de beauté** beauty products, cosmetics
proéminent, e [pʀoeminɑ̃, -ɑ̃t] *adj* prominent
prof [pʀof] *nm* (*fam*: = *professeur*) teacher; professor; lecturer
prof. [pʀof] *abr* = **professeur; professionnel**
profane [pʀofan] *adj* (*Rel*) secular; (*ignorant, non initié*) uninitiated ▷ *nm/f* layman
profaner [pʀofane] *vt* to desecrate; (*fig: sentiment*) to defile; (: *talent*) to debase
proférer [pʀofeʀe] *vt* to utter
professer [pʀofese] *vt* to profess
professeur, e [pʀofesœʀ] *nm/f* teacher; (*titulaire d'une chaire*) professor; ~ (**de faculté**) (university) lecturer

P

profession [pʀɔfɛsjɔ̃] nf (libérale) profession; (gén) occupation; **faire ~ de** (opinion, religion) to profess; **de ~** by profession; **"sans ~"** "unemployed"; (femme mariée) "housewife"

professionnel, le [pʀɔfɛsjɔnɛl] adj professional ▷ nm/f professional; (ouvrier qualifié) skilled worker

professoral, e, -aux [pʀɔfɛsɔʀal, -o] adj professorial; **le corps ~** the teaching profession

professorat [pʀɔfɛsɔʀa] nm: **le ~** the teaching profession

profil [pʀɔfil] nm profile; (d'une voiture) line, contour; **de ~** in profile

profilé, e [pʀɔfile] adj shaped; (aile etc) streamlined

profiler [pʀɔfile] vt to streamline; **se profiler** vi (arbre, tour) to stand out, be silhouetted

profit [pʀɔfi] nm (avantage) benefit, advantage; (Comm, Finance) profit; **au ~ de** in aid of; **tirer** ou **retirer ~ de** to profit from; **mettre à ~** to take advantage of; to turn to good account; **~s et pertes** (Comm) profit and loss(es)

profitable [pʀɔfitabl(ə)] adj beneficial; profitable

profiter [pʀɔfite] vi: **~ de** to take advantage of; to make the most of; **~ de ce que ...** to take advantage of the fact that ...; **~ à** to be of benefit to, benefit; to be profitable to

profiteur, -euse [pʀɔfitœʀ, -øz] nm/f (péj) profiteer

profond, e [pʀɔfɔ̃, -ɔ̃d] adj deep; (méditation, mépris) profound; **peu ~** (eau, vallée, puits) shallow; (coupure) superficial; **au plus ~ de** in the depths of, at the (very) bottom of; **la France ~e** the heartlands of France

profondément [pʀɔfɔ̃demã] adv deeply; profoundly

profondeur [pʀɔfɔ̃dœʀ] nf depth

profusément [pʀɔfyzemã] adv profusely

profusion [pʀɔfyzjɔ̃] nf profusion; **à ~** in plenty

progéniture [pʀɔʒenityʀ] nf offspring inv

progiciel [pʀɔʒisjɛl] nm (Inform) (software) package; **~ d'application** applications package, applications software no pl

progouvernemental, e, -aux [pʀɔguvɛʀnəmãtal, -o] adj pro-government cpd

programmable [pʀɔgʀamabl(ə)] adj programmable

programmateur, -trice [pʀɔgʀamatœʀ, -tʀis] nm/f (Ciné, TV) programme (Brit) ou program (US) planner ▷ nm (de machine à laver etc) timer

programmation [pʀɔgʀamasjɔ̃] nf programming

programme [pʀɔgʀam] nm programme (Brit), program (US); (TV, Radio) program(me)s pl; (Scol) syllabus, curriculum; (Inform) program; **au ~ de ce soir** (TV) among tonight's program(me)s

programmé, e [pʀɔgʀame] adj: **enseignement ~** programmed learning

programmer [pʀɔgʀame] vt (TV, Radio) to put on, show; (organiser, prévoir) to schedule; (Inform) to program

programmeur, -euse [pʀɔgʀamœʀ, -øz] nm/f (computer) programmer

progrès [pʀɔgʀɛ] nm progress no pl; **faire des/ être en ~** to make/be making progress

progresser [pʀɔgʀese] vi to progress; (troupes etc) to make headway ou progress

progressif, -ive [pʀɔgʀesif, -iv] adj progressive

progression [pʀɔgʀesjɔ̃] nf progression; (d'une troupe etc) advance, progress

progressiste [pʀɔgʀesist(ə)] adj progressive

progressivement [pʀɔgʀesivmã] adv progressively

prohiber [pʀɔibe] vt to prohibit, ban

prohibitif, -ive [pʀɔibitif, -iv] adj prohibitive

prohibition [pʀɔibisjɔ̃] nf ban, prohibition; (Hist) Prohibition

proie [pʀwa] nf prey no pl; **être la ~ de** to fall prey to; **être en ~ à** (doutes, sentiment) to be prey to; (douleur, mal) to be suffering

projecteur [pʀɔʒɛktœʀ] nm projector; (de théâtre, cirque) spotlight

projectile [pʀɔʒɛktil] nm missile; (d'arme) projectile, bullet (ou shell etc)

projection [pʀɔʒɛksjɔ̃] nf projection; showing; **conférence avec ~s** lecture with slides (ou a film)

projectionniste [pʀɔʒɛksjɔnist(ə)] nm/f (Ciné) projectionist

projet [pʀɔʒɛ] nm plan; (ébauche) draft; **faire des ~s** to make plans; **~ de loi** bill

projeter [pʀɔʒte] vt (envisager) to plan; (film, photos) to project; (passer) to show; (ombre, lueur) to throw, cast, project; (jeter) to throw up (ou off ou out); **~ de faire qch** to plan to do sth

prolétaire [pʀɔletɛʀ] adj, nm/f proletarian

prolétariat [pʀɔletaʀja] nm proletariat

prolétarien, -ne [pʀɔletaʀjɛ̃, -ɛn] adj proletarian

prolifération [pʀɔlifeʀasjɔ̃] nf proliferation

proliférer [pʀɔlifeʀe] vi to proliferate

prolifique [pʀɔlifik] adj prolific

prolixe [pʀɔliks(ə)] adj verbose

prolo [pʀɔlo] nm/f (fam: = prolétaire) prole (péj)

prologue [pʀɔlɔg] nm prologue

prolongateur [pʀɔlɔ̃gatœʀ] nm (Élec) extension cable

prolongation [pʀɔlɔ̃gasjɔ̃] nf prolongation; extension; **prolongations** nfpl (Football) extra time sg

prolongement [pʀɔlɔ̃ʒmã] nm extension; **prolongements** nmpl (fig) repercussions, effects; **dans le ~ de** running on from

prolonger [pʀɔlɔ̃ʒe] vt (débat, séjour) to prolong; (délai, billet, rue) to extend; (chose) to be a continuation ou an extension of; **se prolonger** vi to go on

promenade [pʀɔmnad] nf walk (ou drive ou ride); **faire une ~** to go for a walk; **une ~ (à pied)/en voiture/à vélo** a walk/drive/(bicycle) ride

promener [pʀɔmne] vt (personne, chien) to take out for a walk; (fig) to carry around; to trail

round; (*doigts, regard*): ~ **qch sur** to run sth over;
se promener *vi* (*à pied*) to go for (*ou* be out for) a
walk; (*en voiture*) to go for (*ou* be out for) a drive;
(*fig*): **se** ~ **sur** to wander over
promeneur, -euse [pʀɔmnœʀ, -øz] *nm/f*
walker, stroller
promenoir [pʀɔmənwaʀ] *nm* gallery, (covered)
walkway
promesse [pʀɔmɛs] *nf* promise; ~ **d'achat**
commitment to buy
prometteur, -euse [pʀɔmɛtœʀ, -øz] *adj*
promising
promettre [pʀɔmɛtʀ(ə)] *vt* to promise ▷ *vi*
(*récolte, arbre*) to look promising; (*enfant, musicien*)
to be promising; **se** ~ **de faire** to resolve *ou*
mean to do; ~ **à qn de faire** to promise sb that
one will do
promeus *etc* [pʀɔmø] *vb voir* **promouvoir**
promis, e [pʀɔmi, -iz] *pp de* **promettre** ▷ *adj*:
être ~ **à qch** (*destiné*) to be destined for sth
promiscuité [pʀɔmiskɥite] *nf* crowding; lack of
privacy
promit [pʀɔmi] *vb voir* **promettre**
promontoire [pʀɔmɔ̃twaʀ] *nm* headland
promoteur, -trice [pʀɔmɔtœʀ, -tʀis] *nm/f*
(*instigateur*) instigator, promoter; ~
(**immobilier**) property developer (*Brit*), real
estate promoter (*US*)
promotion [pʀɔmɔsjɔ̃] *nf* (*avancement*)
promotion; (*Scol*) year (*Brit*), class; **en** ~ (*Comm*)
on promotion, on (special) offer
promotionnel, le [pʀɔmɔsjɔnɛl] *adj* (*article*) on
promotion, on (special) offer; (*vente*)
promotional
promouvoir [pʀɔmuvwaʀ] *vt* to promote
prompt, e [pʀɔ̃, pʀɔ̃t] *adj* swift, rapid;
(*intervention, changement*) sudden; ~ **à faire qch**
quick to do sth
promptement [pʀɔ̃ptəmã] *adv* swiftly
prompteur® [pʀɔ̃tœʀ] *nm* Autocue® (*Brit*),
Teleprompter® (*US*)
promptitude [pʀɔ̃tityd] *nf* swiftness, rapidity
promu, e [pʀɔmy] *pp de* **promouvoir**
promulguer [pʀɔmylge] *vt* to promulgate
prôner [pʀone] *vt* (*louer*) to laud, extol;
(*préconiser*) to advocate, commend
pronom [pʀɔnɔ̃] *nm* pronoun
pronominal, e, -aux [pʀɔnɔminal, -o] *adj*
pronominal; (*verbe*) reflexive, pronominal
prononcé, e [pʀɔnɔ̃se] *adj* pronounced, marked
prononcer [pʀɔnɔ̃se] *vt* (*son, mot, jugement*) to
pronounce; (*dire*) to utter; (*allocution*) to deliver
▷ *vi* (*Jur*) to deliver *ou* give a verdict; ~ **bien/mal**
to have good/poor pronunciation; **se**
prononcer *vi* to reach a decision, give a verdict;
se ~ **sur** to give an opinion on; **se** ~ **contre** to
come down against; **ça se prononce**
comment? how do you pronounce this?
prononciation [pʀɔnɔ̃sjasjɔ̃] *nf* pronunciation
pronostic [pʀɔnɔstik] *nm* (*Méd*) prognosis; (*fig:
aussi*: **pronostics**) forecast
pronostiquer [pʀɔnɔstike] *vt* (*Méd*) to

prognosticate; (*annoncer, prévoir*) to forecast,
foretell
pronostiqueur, -euse [pʀɔnɔstikœʀ, -øz] *nm/f*
forecaster
propagande [pʀɔpagãd] *nf* propaganda; **faire
de la** ~ **pour qch** to plug *ou* push sth
propagandiste [pʀɔpagãdist(ə)] *nm/f*
propagandist
propagation [pʀɔpagasjɔ̃] *nf* propagation
propager [pʀɔpaʒe] *vt* to spread; **se propager** *vi*
to spread; (*Physique*) to be propagated
propane [pʀɔpan] *nm* propane
propension [pʀɔpãsjɔ̃] *nf*: ~ **à (faire) qch**
propensity to (do) sth
prophète [pʀɔfɛt], **prophétesse** [pʀɔfetɛs]
nm/f prophet(ess)
prophétie [pʀɔfesi] *nf* prophecy
prophétique [pʀɔfetik] *adj* prophetic
prophétiser [pʀɔfetize] *vt* to prophesy
prophylactique [pʀɔfilaktik] *adj* prophylactic
propice [pʀɔpis] *adj* favourable (*Brit*),
favorable (*US*)
proportion [pʀɔpɔʀsjɔ̃] *nf* proportion; **il n'y a
aucune** ~ **entre le prix demandé et le prix
réel** the asking price bears no relation to the
real price; **à** ~ **de** proportionally to, in
proportion to; **en** ~ **(de)** in proportion (to); **hors
de** ~ out of proportion; **toute(s)** ~**(s) gardée(s)**
making due allowance(s)
proportionné, e [pʀɔpɔʀsjɔne] *adj*: **bien** ~ well-
proportioned; ~ **à** proportionate to
proportionnel, le [pʀɔpɔʀsjɔnɛl] *adj*
proportional; ~ **à** proportional to ▷ *nf*
proportional representation
proportionnellement [pʀɔpɔʀsjɔnɛlmã] *adv*
proportionally, proportionately
proportionner [pʀɔpɔʀsjɔne] *vt*: ~ **qch à** to
proportion *ou* adjust sth to
propos [pʀɔpo] *nm* (*paroles*) talk *no pl*, remark;
(*intention, but*) intention, aim; (*sujet*): **à quel** ~?
what about?; **à** ~ **de** about, regarding; **à tout** ~
for no reason at all; **à ce** ~ on that subject, in
this connection; **à** ~ *adv* by the way;
(*opportunément*) (just) at the right moment; **hors
de** ~, **mal à** ~ *adv* at the wrong moment
proposer [pʀɔpoze] *vt* (*suggérer*): ~ **qch (à qn)/de
faire** to suggest sth (to sb)/doing, propose sth
(to sb)/(to) do; (*offrir*): ~ **qch à qn/de faire** to
offer sb sth/to do; (*candidat*) to nominate, put
forward; (*loi, motion*) to propose; **se** ~ (**pour
faire**) to offer one's services (to do); **se** ~ **de
faire** to intend *ou* propose to do
proposition [pʀɔpozisjɔ̃] *nf* suggestion;
proposal; offer; (*Ling*) clause; **sur la** ~ **de** at the
suggestion of; ~ **de loi** private bill
propre [pʀɔpʀ(ə)] *adj* clean; (*net*) neat, tidy; (*qui
ne salit pas: chien, chat*) house-trained; (: *enfant*)
toilet-trained; (*fig: honnête*) honest; (*possessif*)
own; (*sens*) literal; (*particulier*): ~ **à** peculiar to,
characteristic of; (*approprié*): ~ **à** suitable *ou*
appropriate for; (*de nature à*): ~ **à faire** likely to
do, that will do ▷ *nm*: **recopier au** ~ to make a

fair copy of; (*particularité*): **le ~ de** the peculiarity of, the distinctive feature of; **au ~** (*Ling*) literally; **appartenir à qn en ~** to belong to sb (exclusively); **~ à rien** *nm/f* (*péj*) good-for-nothing

proprement [prɔprəmã] *adv* cleanly; neatly, tidily; **à ~ parler** strictly speaking; **le village ~ dit** the actual village, the village itself

propret, te [prɔprɛ, -ɛt] *adj* neat and tidy, spick-and-span

propreté [prɔprəte] *nf* cleanliness, cleanness; neatness, tidiness

propriétaire [prɔprijetɛr] *nm/f* owner; (*d'hôtel etc*) proprietor(-tress), owner; (*pour le locataire*) landlord(-lady); **~ (immobilier)** house-owner; householder; **~ récoltant** grower; **~ (terrien)** landowner

propriété [prɔprijete] *nf* (*droit*) ownership; (*objet, immeuble etc*) property *gen no pl*; (*villa*) residence, property; (*terres*) property *gen no pl*, land *gen no pl*; (*qualité, Chimie, Math*) property; (*correction*) appropriateness, suitability; **~ artistique et littéraire** artistic and literary copyright; **~ industrielle** patent rights *pl*

propulser [prɔpylse] *vt* (*missile*) to propel; (*projeter*) to hurl, fling

propulsion [prɔpylsjɔ̃] *nf* propulsion

prorata [prɔrata] *nm inv*: **au ~ de** in proportion to, on the basis of

prorogation [prɔrɔgasjɔ̃] *nf* deferment; extension; adjournment

proroger [prɔrɔʒe] *vt* to put back, defer; (*prolonger*) to extend; (*assemblée*) to adjourn, prorogue

prosaïque [prɔzaik] *adj* mundane, prosaic

proscription [prɔskripsjɔ̃] *nf* banishment; (*interdiction*) banning; prohibition

proscrire [prɔskrir] *vt* (*bannir*) to banish; (*interdire*) to ban, prohibit

prose [proz] *nf* prose (*style*)

prosélyte [prɔzelit] *nm/f* proselyte, convert

prospecter [prɔspɛkte] *vt* to prospect; (*Comm*) to canvass

prospecteur-placier [prɔspɛktœrplasje] (*pl* **prospecteurs-placiers**) *nm* placement officer

prospectif, -ive [prɔspɛktif, -iv] *adj* prospective

prospectus [prɔspɛktys] *nm* (*feuille*) leaflet; (*dépliant*) brochure, leaflet

prospère [prɔspɛr] *adj* prosperous; (*santé, entreprise*) thriving, flourishing

prospérer [prɔspere] *vi* to thrive

prospérité [prɔsperite] *nf* prosperity

prostate [prɔstat] *nf* prostate (gland)

prosterner [prɔstɛrne]: **se prosterner** *vi* to bow low, prostrate o.s

prostituée [prɔstitɥe] *nf* prostitute

prostitution [prɔstitysjɔ̃] *nf* prostitution

prostré, e [prɔstre] *adj* prostrate

protagoniste [prɔtagɔnist(ə)] *nm* protagonist

protecteur, -trice [prɔtɛktœr, -tris] *adj* protective; (*air, ton*: *péj*) patronizing ▷ *nm/f* (*défenseur*) protector; (*des arts*) patron

protection [prɔtɛksjɔ̃] *nf* protection; (*d'un personnage influent*: *aide*) patronage; **écran de ~** protective screen; **~ civile** state-financed civilian rescue service; **~ maternelle et infantile (PMI)** social service concerned with child welfare

protectionnisme [prɔtɛksjɔnism(ə)] *nm* protectionism

protectionniste [prɔtɛksjɔnist(ə)] *adj* protectionist

protégé, e [prɔteʒe] *nm/f* protégé(e)

protège-cahier [prɔtɛʒkaje] *nm* exercise book cover

protéger [prɔteʒe] *vt* to protect; (*aider, patronner*: *personne, arts*) to be a patron of; (: *carrière*) to further; **se ~ de/contre** to protect o.s. from

protège-slip [prɔtɛʒslip] *nm* panty liner

protéine [prɔtein] *nf* protein

protestant, e [prɔtɛstã, -ãt] *adj, nm/f* Protestant

protestantisme [prɔtɛstãtism(ə)] *nm* Protestantism

protestataire [prɔtɛstatɛr] *nm/f* protestor

protestation [prɔtɛstasjɔ̃] *nf* (*plainte*) protest; (*déclaration*) protestation, profession

protester [prɔtɛste] *vi*: **~ (contre)** to protest (against *ou* about); **~ de** (*son innocence, sa loyauté*) to protest

prothèse [prɔtɛz] *nf* artificial limb, prosthesis; **~ dentaire** (*appareil*) denture; (*science*) dental engineering

protocolaire [prɔtɔkɔlɛr] *adj* formal; (*questions, règles*) of protocol

protocole [prɔtɔkɔl] *nm* protocol; (*fig*) etiquette; **~ d'accord** draft treaty; **~ opératoire** (*Méd*) operating procedure

prototype [prɔtɔtip] *nm* prototype

protubérance [prɔtyberãs] *nf* bulge, protuberance

protubérant, e [prɔtyberã, -ãt] *adj* protruding, bulging, protuberant

proue [pru] *nf* bow(s *pl*), prow

prouesse [pruɛs] *nf* feat

prouver [pruve] *vt* to prove

provenance [prɔvnãs] *nf* origin; (*de mot, coutume*) source; **avion en ~ de** plane (arriving) from

provençal, e, -aux [prɔvãsal, -o] *adj* Provençal ▷ *nm* (*Ling*) Provençal

Provence [prɔvãs] *nf*: **la ~** Provence

provenir [prɔvnir]: **~ de** *vt* to come from; (*résulter de*) to be due to, be the result of

proverbe [prɔvɛrb(ə)] *nm* proverb

proverbial, e, -aux [prɔvɛrbjal, -o] *adj* proverbial

providence [prɔvidãs] *nf*: **la ~** providence

providentiel, le [prɔvidãsjɛl] *adj* providential

province [prɔvɛ̃s] *nf* province

provincial, e, -aux [prɔvɛ̃sjal, -o] *adj, nm/f* provincial

proviseur [prɔvizœr] *nm* ≈ head (teacher) (*Brit*), ≈ principal (*US*)

provision [prɔvizjɔ̃] *nf* (*réserve*) stock, supply; (*avance*: *à un avocat, avoué*) retainer, retaining fee;

(*Comm*) funds *pl* (in account); reserve;
provisions *nfpl* (*vivres*) provisions, food *no pl*;
  faire ~ de to stock up with; **placard** *ou* **armoire**
  à ~s food cupboard
provisoire [prɔvizwar] *adj* temporary; (*Jur*)
  provisional; **mise en liberté ~** release on bail
provisoirement [prɔvizwarmɑ̃] *adv*
  temporarily, for the time being
provocant, e [prɔvɔkɑ̃, -ɑ̃t] *adj* provocative
provocateur, -trice [prɔvɔkatœr, -tris] *adj*
  provocative ▷ *nm* (*meneur*) agitator
provocation [prɔvɔkasjɔ̃] *nf* provocation
provoquer [prɔvɔke] *vt* (*défier*) to provoke;
  (*causer*) to cause, bring about; (: *curiosité*) to
  arouse, give rise to; (: *aveux*) to prompt, elicit;
  (*inciter*): **~ qn à** to incite sb to
prox. *abr* = **proximité**
proxénète [prɔksenɛt] *nm* procurer
proxénétisme [prɔksenetism(ə)] *nm* procuring
proximité [prɔksimite] *nf* nearness, closeness,
  proximity; (*dans le temps*) imminence, closeness;
  à ~ near *ou* close by; **à ~ de** near (to), close to
prude [pryd] *adj* prudish
prudemment [prydamɑ̃] *adv* (*voir prudent*)
  carefully; cautiously; prudently; wisely, sensibly
prudence [prydɑ̃s] *nf* carefulness; caution;
  prudence; **avec ~** carefully; cautiously; wisely;
  par (mesure de) ~ as a precaution
prudent, e [prydɑ̃, -ɑ̃t] *adj* (*pas téméraire*) careful,
  cautious, prudent; (: *en général*) safety-
  conscious; (*sage, conseillé*) wise, sensible; (*réservé*)
  cautious; **ce n'est pas ~** it's risky; it's not
  sensible; **soyez ~** take care, be careful
prune [pryn] *nf* plum
pruneau, x [pryno] *nm* prune
prunelle [prynɛl] *nf* pupil; (*œil*) eye; (*Bot*) sloe;
  (*eau de vie*) sloe gin
prunier [prynje] *nm* plum tree
Prusse [prys] *nf*: **la ~** Prussia
PS *sigle m* = **parti socialiste**; (= *post-scriptum*) PS
psalmodier [psalmɔdje] *vt* to chant; (*fig*) to
  drone out
psaume [psom] *nm* psalm
pseudonyme [psødɔnim] *nm* (*gén*) fictitious
  name; (*d'écrivain*) pseudonym, pen name; (*de
  comédien*) stage name
PSIG *sigle m* (= *Peloton de surveillance et d'intervention
  de gendarmerie*) type of police commando squad
PSU *sigle m* = **parti socialiste unifié**
psy [psi] *nm/f* (*fam*: = *psychiatre, psychologue*) shrink
psychanalyse [psikanaliz] *nf* psychoanalysis
psychanalyser [psikanalize] *vt* to
  psychoanalyze; **se faire ~** to undergo
  (psycho)analysis
psychanalyste [psikanalist(ə)] *nm/f*
  psychoanalyst
psychanalytique [psikanalitik] *adj*
  psychoanalytical
psychédélique [psikedelik] *adj* psychedelic
psychiatre [psikjatr(ə)] *nm/f* psychiatrist
psychiatrie [psikjatri] *nf* psychiatry
psychiatrique [psikjatrik] *adj* psychiatric;

(*hôpital*) mental, psychiatric
psychique [psiʃik] *adj* psychological
psychisme [psiʃism(ə)] *nm* psyche
psychologie [psikɔlɔʒi] *nf* psychology
psychologique [psikɔlɔʒik] *adj* psychological
psychologiquement [psikɔlɔʒikmɑ̃] *adv*
  psychologically
psychologue [psikɔlɔg] *nm/f* psychologist;
  être ~ (*fig*) to be a good psychologist
psychomoteur, -trice [psikɔmɔtœr, -tris] *adj*
  psychomotor
psychopathe [psikɔpat] *nm/f* psychopath
psychopédagogie [psikɔpedagɔʒi] *nf*
  educational psychology
psychose [psikoz] *nf* (*Méd*) psychosis; (*obsession,
  idée fixe*) obsessive fear
psychosomatique [psikɔsɔmatik] *adj*
  psychosomatic
psychothérapie [psikɔterapi] *nf*
  psychotherapy
psychotique [psikɔtik] *adj* psychotic
PTCA *sigle m* = **poids total en charge autorisé**
Pte *abr* = **Porte**
pte *abr* (= *pointe*) pt
PTMA *sigle m* (= *poids total maximum autorisé*)
  maximum loaded weight
PTT *sigle fpl* = **poste**
pu [py] *pp de* **pouvoir**
puanteur [pɥɑ̃tœr] *nf* stink, stench
pub [pyb] *nf* (*fam*) = **publicité**; **la ~** advertising
pubère [pyber] *adj* pubescent
puberté [pyberte] *nf* puberty
pubis [pybis] *nm* (*bas-ventre*) pubes *pl*; (*os*) pubis
public, -ique [pyblik] *adj* public; (*école,
  instruction*) state *cpd*; (*scrutin*) open ▷ *nm* public;
  (*assistance*) audience; **en ~** in public; **le grand ~**
  the general public
publication [pyblikasjɔ̃] *nf* publication
publiciste [pyblisist(ə)] *nm/f* adman
publicitaire [pyblisiter] *adj* advertising *cpd*;
  (*film, voiture*) publicity *cpd*; (*vente*) promotional
  ▷ *nm* adman; **rédacteur ~** copywriter
publicité [pyblisite] *nf* (*méthode, profession*)
  advertising; (*annonce*) advertisement;
  (*révélations*) publicity
publier [pyblije] *vt* to publish; (*nouvelle*) to
  publicize, make public
publipostage [pybliposta3] *nm* mailshot,
  (mass) mailing
publique [pyblik] *adj f voir* **public**
publiquement [pyblikmɑ̃] *adv* publicly
puce [pys] *nf* flea; (*Inform*) chip; (**marché aux**)
  ~s flea market *sg*; **mettre la ~ à l'oreille de qn**
  to give sb something to think about
puceau, x [pyso] *adj m*: **être ~** to be a virgin
pucelle [pysɛl] *adj f*: **être ~** to be a virgin
puceron [pysrɔ̃] *nm* aphid
pudeur [pydœr] *nf* modesty
pudibond, e [pydibɔ̃, -ɔ̃d] *adj* prudish
pudique [pydik] *adj* (*chaste*) modest; (*discret*)
  discreet
pudiquement [pydikmɑ̃] *adv* modestly

P

puer [pɥe] (*péj*) *vi* to stink ▷ *vt* to stink of, reek of

puéricultrice [pɥeʀikyltʀis] *nf* ≈ nursery nurse

puériculture [pɥeʀikyltyʀ] *nf* infant care

puéril, e [pɥeʀil] *adj* childish

puérilement [pɥeʀilmɑ̃] *adv* childishly

puérilité [pɥeʀilite] *nf* childishness; (*acte, idée*) childish thing

pugilat [pyʒila] *nm* (*fist*) fight

puis [pɥi] *vb voir* **pouvoir** ▷ *adv* (*ensuite*) then; (*dans une énumération*) next; (*en outre*): **et** ~ and (then); **et** ~ **(après** *ou* **quoi)?** so (what)?

puisard [pɥizaʀ] *nm* (*égout*) cesspool

puiser [pɥize] *vt*: ~ **(dans)** to draw (from); ~ **dans qch** to dip into sth

puisque [pɥisk(ə)] *conj* since; (*valeur intensive*): ~ **je te le dis!** I'm telling you!

puissamment [pɥisamɑ̃] *adv* powerfully

puissance [pɥisɑ̃s] *nf* power; **en** ~ *adj* potential; **deux (à la)** ~ **cinq** two to the power (of) five

puissant, e [pɥisɑ̃, -ɑ̃t] *adj* powerful

puisse *etc* [pɥis] *vb voir* **pouvoir**

puits [pɥi] *nm* well; ~ **artésien** artesian well; ~ **de mine** mine shaft; ~ **de science** fount of knowledge

pull [pyl], **pull-over** [pylɔvœʀ] *nm* sweater, jumper (*Brit*)

pulluler [pylyle] *vi* to swarm; (*fig: erreurs*) to abound, proliferate

pulmonaire [pylmɔnɛʀ] *adj* lung *cpd*; (*artère*) pulmonary

pulpe [pylp(ə)] *nf* pulp

pulsation [pylsasjɔ̃] *nf* (*Méd*) beat

pulsé [pylse] *adj m*: **chauffage à air** ~ warm air heating

pulsion [pylsjɔ̃] *nf* (*Psych*) drive, urge

pulvérisateur [pylveʀizatœʀ] *nm* spray

pulvérisation [pylveʀizasjɔ̃] *nf* spraying

pulvériser [pylveʀize] *vt* (*solide*) to pulverize; (*liquide*) to spray; (*fig: anéantir: adversaire*) to pulverize; (: *record*) to smash, shatter; (: *argument*) to demolish

puma [pyma] *nm* puma, cougar

punaise [pynɛz] *nf* (*Zool*) bug; (*clou*) drawing pin (*Brit*), thumb tack (*US*)

punch [pɔ̃ʃ] *nm* (*boisson*) punch [pœnʃ] (*Boxe*) punching ability; (*fig*) punch

punching-ball [pœnʃiŋbol] *nm* punchball

punir [pyniʀ] *vt* to punish; ~ **qn de qch** to punish sb for sth

punitif, -ive [pynitif, -iv] *adj* punitive

punition [pynisjɔ̃] *nf* punishment

pupille [pypij] *nf* (*Anat*) pupil ▷ *nm/f* (*enfant*) ward; ~ **de l'État** child in care; ~ **de la Nation** war orphan

pupitre [pypitʀ(ə)] *nm* (*Scol*) desk; (*Rel*) lectern; (*de chef d'orchestre*) rostrum; ~ **de commande** control panel

pur, e [pyʀ] *adj* pure; (*vin*) undiluted; (*whisky*) neat; (*intentions*) honourable (*Brit*), honorable (*US*) ▷ *nm* (*personne*) hard-liner; **en ~e perte** fruitlessly, to no avail

purée [pyʀe] *nf*: ~ **(de pommes de terre)** ≈ mashed potatoes *pl*; ~ **de marrons** chestnut purée; ~ **de pois** (*fig*) peasoup(er)

purement [pyʀmɑ̃] *adv* purely

pureté [pyʀte] *nf* purity

purgatif [pyʀgatif] *nm* purgative, purge

purgatoire [pyʀgatwaʀ] *nm* purgatory

purge [pyʀʒ(ə)] *nf* (*Pol*) purge; (*Méd*) purging *no pl*; purge

purger [pyʀʒe] *vt* (*radiateur*) to flush (out), drain; (*circuit hydraulique*) to bleed; (*Méd, Pol*) to purge; (*Jur: peine*) to serve

purification [pyʀifikasjɔ̃] *nf* (*de l'eau*) purification; ~ **ethnique** ethnic cleansing

purifier [pyʀifje] *vt* to purify; (*Tech: métal*) to refine

purin [pyʀɛ̃] *nm* liquid manure

puriste [pyʀist(ə)] *nm/f* purist

puritain, e [pyʀitɛ̃, -ɛn] *adj, nm/f* Puritan

puritanisme [pyʀitanism(ə)] *nm* Puritanism

pur-sang [pyʀsɑ̃] *nm inv* thoroughbred, pure-bred

purulent, e [pyʀylɑ̃, -ɑ̃t] *adj* purulent

pus [py] *vb voir* **pouvoir** ▷ *nm* pus

pusillanime [pyzilanim] *adj* fainthearted

pustule [pystyl] *nf* pustule

putain [pytɛ̃] *nf* (*fam!*) whore (*!*); **ce/cette ~ de ...** this bloody (*Brit*) *ou* goddamn (*US*) ... (*!*)

putois [pytwa] *nm* polecat; **crier comme un ~** to yell one's head off

putréfaction [pytʀefaksjɔ̃] *nf* putrefaction

putréfier [pytʀefje] *vt*, **se putréfier** *vi* to putrefy, rot

putride [pytʀid] *adj* putrid

putsch [putʃ] *nm* (*Pol*) putsch

puzzle [pœzl(ə)] *nm* jigsaw (puzzle)

PV *sigle m* = **procès-verbal**

PVC *sigle f* (= *polychlorure de vinyle*) PVC

PVD *sigle mpl* (= *pays en voie de développement*) developing countries

Px *abr* = **prix**

pygmée [pigme] *nm* pygmy

pyjama [piʒama] *nm* pyjamas *pl*, pair of pyjamas

pylône [pilon] *nm* pylon

pyramide [piʀamid] *nf* pyramid

pyrénéen, ne [piʀeneɛ̃, -ɛn] *adj* Pyrenean

Pyrénées [piʀene] *nfpl*: **les ~** the Pyrenees

pyrex® [piʀɛks] *nm* Pyrex®

pyrogravure [piʀɔgʀavyʀ] *nf* poker-work

pyromane [piʀɔman] *nm/f* arsonist

python [pitɔ̃] *nm* python

Qq

Q, q [ky] *nm inv* Q, q ▷ *abr* (= *quintal*) q; **Q comme Quintal** Q for Queen

Qatar [katar] *nm*: **le ~** Qatar

QCM *sigle m* (= *questionnaire à choix multiples*) multiple-choice test

QG *sigle m* (= *quartier général*) HQ

QHS *sigle m* (= *quartier de haute sécurité*) high-security wing *ou* prison

QI *sigle m* (= *quotient intellectuel*) IQ

qqch. *abr* (= *quelque chose*) sth

qqe *abr* = **quelque**

qqes *abr* = **quelques**

qqn *abr* (= *quelqu'un*) sb, s.o.

quadra [k(w)adra] (*fam*) *nm/f* (= *quadragénaire*) person in his (*ou* her) forties; **les ~s** forty somethings (*fam*)

quadragénaire [kadraʒenɛr] *nm/f* (*de quarante ans*) forty-year-old; (*de quarante à cinquante ans*) man/woman in his/her forties

quadrangulaire [kwadrãgylɛr] *adj* quadrangular

quadrature [kwadratyr] *nf*: **c'est la ~ du cercle** it's like trying to square the circle

quadrichromie [kwadrikrɔmi] *nf* four-colour (*Brit*) *ou* -color (*US*) printing

quadrilatère [k(w)adrilatɛr] *nm* (*Géom, Mil*) quadrilateral; (*terrain*) four-sided area

quadrillage [kadrijaʒ] *nm* (*lignes etc*) square pattern, criss-cross pattern

quadrillé, e [kadrije] *adj* (*papier*) squared

quadriller [kadrije] *vt* (*papier*) to mark out in squares; (*Police: ville, région etc*) to keep under tight control, be positioned throughout

quadrimoteur [k(w)adrimɔtœr] *nm* four-engined plane

quadripartite [kwadripartit] *adj* (*entre pays*) four-power; (*entre partis*) four-party

quadriphonie [kadrifɔni] *nf* quadraphony

quadriréacteur [k(w)adrireaktœr] *nm* four-engined jet

quadrupède [k(w)adrypɛd] *nm* quadruped

quadruple [k(w)adrypl(ə)] *nm*: **le ~ de** four times as much as

quadrupler [k(w)adryple] *vt, vi* to quadruple, increase fourfold

quadruplés, -ées [k(w)adryple] *nm/fpl* quadruplets, quads

quai [ke] *nm* (*de port*) quay; (*de gare*) platform; (*de cours d'eau, canal*) embankment; **être à ~** (*navire*) to be alongside; (*train*) to be in the station; **le Q~ d'Orsay** *offices of the French Ministry for Foreign Affairs*; **le Q~ des Orfèvres** *central police headquarters*

qualifiable [kalifjabl(ə)] *adj*: **ce n'est pas ~** it defies description

qualificatif, -ive [kalifikatif, -iv] *adj* (*Ling*) qualifying ▷ *nm* (*terme*) term; (*Ling*) qualifier

qualification [kalifikasjɔ̃] *nf* qualification

qualifié, e [kalifje] *adj* qualified; (*main d'œuvre*) skilled

qualifier [kalifje] *vt* to qualify; (*appeler*): **~ qch/qn de** to describe sth/sb as; **se qualifier** *vi* (*Sport*) to qualify; **être qualifié pour** to be qualified for

qualitatif, -ive [kalitatif, -iv] *adj* qualitative

qualité [kalite] *nf* quality; (*titre, fonction*) position; **en ~ de** in one's capacity as; **ès ~s** in an official capacity; **avoir ~ pour** to have authority to; **de ~** *adj* quality *cpd*; **rapport ~-prix** value (for money)

quand [kã] *conj, adv* when; **~ je serai riche** when I'm rich; **~ même** (*cependant, pourtant*) nevertheless; (*tout de même*) all the same; really; **~ bien même** even though

quant [kã]: **~ à** *prép* (*pour ce qui est de*) as for, as to; (*au sujet de*) regarding

quant-à-soi [kãtaswa] *nm*: **rester sur son ~** to remain aloof

quantième [kãtjɛm] *nm* date, day (of the month)

quantifiable [kãtifjabl(ə)] *adj* quantifiable

quantifier [kãtifje] *vt* to quantify

quantitatif, -ive [kãtitatif, -iv] *adj* quantitative

quantitativement [kãtitativmã] *adv* quantitatively

quantité [kãtite] *nf* quantity, amount; (*Science*) quantity; (*grand nombre*): **une** *ou* **des ~(s) de** a great deal of; a lot of; **en grande ~** in large quantities; **en ~s industrielles** in vast amounts; **du travail en ~** a great deal of work; **~ de** many

quarantaine [karãtɛn] *nf* (*isolement*)

quarantine; (*âge*): **avoir la ~** to be around forty; (*nombre*): **une ~ (de)** forty or so, about forty; **mettre en ~** to put into quarantine; (*fig*) to send to Coventry (*Brit*), ostracize

quarante [kaʀɑ̃t] *num* forty

quarantième [kaʀɑ̃tjɛm] *num* fortieth

quark [kwaʀk] *nm* quark

quart [kaʀ] *nm* (*fraction*) quarter; (*surveillance*) watch; (*partie*): **un ~ de poulet/fromage** a chicken quarter/a quarter of a cheese; **un ~ de beurre** a quarter kilo of butter, ≈ a half pound of butter; **un ~ de vin** a quarter litre of wine; **une livre un ~** *ou* **et ~** one and a quarter pounds; **le ~ de** a quarter of; **~ d'heure** quarter of an hour; **deux heures et** *ou* **un ~** (a) quarter past two, (a) quarter after two (*US*); **il est le ~** it's (a) quarter past *ou* after (*US*); **une heure moins le ~** (a) quarter to one, (a) quarter of one (*US*); **il est moins le ~** it's (a) quarter to; **être de/prendre le ~** to keep/take the watch; **~ de tour** quarter turn; **au ~ de tour** (*fig*) straight off; **~s de finale** (*Sport*) quarter finals

quarté [kaʀte] *nm* (*Courses*) system of forecast betting giving first four horses

quarteron [kaʀtəʀɔ̃] *nm* (*péj*) small bunch, handful

quartette [kwaʀtɛt] *nm* quartet(te)

quartier [kaʀtje] *nm* (*de ville*) district, area; (*de bœuf, de la lune*) quarter; (*de fruit, fromage*) piece; **quartiers** *nmpl* (*Mil, Blason*) quarters; **cinéma/salle de ~** local cinema/hall; **avoir ~ libre** to be free; (*Mil*) to have leave from barracks; **ne pas faire de ~** to spare no one, give no quarter; **~ commerçant/résidentiel** shopping/residential area; **~ général (QG)** headquarters (HQ)

quartier-maître [kaʀtjemɛtʀ(ə)] *nm* ≈ leading seaman

quartz [kwaʀts] *nm* quartz

quasi [kazi] *adv* almost, nearly ▷ *préfixe*: **~certitude** near certainty

quasiment [kazimɑ̃] *adv* almost, very nearly

quaternaire [kwatɛʀnɛʀ] *adj* (*Géo*) Quaternary

quatorze [katɔʀz(ə)] *num* fourteen

quatorzième [katɔʀzjɛm] *num* fourteenth

quatrain [katʀɛ̃] *nm* quatrain

quatre [katʀ(ə)] *num* four; **à ~ pattes** on all fours; **tiré à ~ épingles** dressed up to the nines; **faire les ~ cent coups** to be a bit wild; **se mettre en ~ pour qn** to go out of one's way for sb; **~ à ~** (*monter, descendre*) four at a time; **à ~ mains** (*jouer*) four-handed

quatre-vingt-dix [katʀəvɛ̃dis] *num* ninety

quatre-vingts [katʀəvɛ̃] *num* eighty

quatre-vingt-un *num* eighty-one

quatrième [katʀijɛm] *num* fourth

quatuor [kwatɥɔʀ] *nm* quartet(te)

 MOT-CLÉ

que [kə] *conj* **1** (*introduisant complétive*) that; **il sait que tu es là** he knows (that) you're here; **je**

veux que tu acceptes I want you to accept; **il a dit que oui** he said he would (*ou* it was *etc*)

2 (*reprise d'autres conjonctions*): **quand il rentrera et qu'il aura mangé** when he gets back and (when) he has eaten; **si vous y allez ou que vous ...** if you go there or if you ...

3 (*en tête de phrase: hypothèse, souhait etc*): **qu'il veuille ou non** whether he likes it or not; **qu'il fasse ce qu'il voudra!** let him do as he pleases!

4 (*but*): **tenez-le qu'il ne tombe pas** hold it so (that) it doesn't fall

5 (*après comparatif*) than; as; *voir aussi* **plus; aussi; autant** *etc*

6 (*seulement*): **ne ... que** only; **il ne boit que de l'eau** he only drinks water

7 (*temps*): **elle venait à peine de sortir qu'il se mit à pleuvoir** she had just gone out when it started to rain, no sooner had she gone out than it started to rain; **il y a quatre ans qu'il est parti** it is four years since he left, he left four years ago

▷ *adv* (*exclamation*): **qu'il** *ou* **qu'est-ce qu'il est bête/court vite!** he's so silly!/he runs so fast!; **que de livres!** what a lot of books!

▷ *pron* **1** (*relatif: personne*) whom; (: *chose*) that, which; **l'homme que je vois** the man (whom) I see; **le livre que tu vois** the book (that *ou* which) you see; **un jour que j'étais ...** a day when I was ..

2 (*interrogatif*) what; **que fais-tu?**, **qu'est-ce que tu fais?** what are you doing?; **qu'est-ce que c'est?** what is it?, what's that?; **que faire?** what can one do?; **que préfères-tu, celui-ci ou celui-là?** which (one) do you prefer, this one or that one?

Québec [kebɛk] *n* (*ville*) Quebec ▷ *nm*: **le ~** Quebec (Province)

québécois, e [kebekwa, -waz] *adj* Quebec *cpd* ▷ *nm* (*Ling*) Quebec French ▷ *nm/f*: **Québécois, e** Quebecois, Quebec(k)er

 MOT-CLÉ

quel, quelle [kɛl] *adj* **1** (*interrogatif: personne*) who; (: *chose*) what; which; **quel est cet homme?** who is this man?; **quel est ce livre?** what is this book?; **quel livre/homme?** what book/man?; (*parmi un certain choix*) which book/man?; **quels acteurs préférez-vous?** which actors do you prefer?; **dans quels pays êtes-vous allé?** which *ou* what countries did you go to?

2 (*exclamatif*): **quelle surprise/coïncidence!** what a surprise/coincidence!

3: **quel(le) que soit le coupable** whoever is guilty; **quel que soit votre avis** whatever your opinion (may be)

quelconque [kɛlkɔ̃k] *adj* (*médiocre*) indifferent, poor; (*sans attrait*) ordinary, plain; (*indéfini*): **un ami/prétexte ~** some friend/pretext or other;

un livre ~ **suffira** any book will do; **pour une raison** ~ for some reason (or other)

○ MOT-CLÉ

quelque [kɛlkə] *adj* **1** some; a few; (*tournure interrogative*) any; **quelque espoir** some hope; **il a quelques amis** he has a few *ou* some friends; **a-t-il quelques amis?** has he any friends?; **les quelques livres qui** the few books which; **20 kg et quelque(s)** a bit over 20 kg; **il habite à quelque distance d'ici** he lives some distance *ou* way (away) from here
2: quelque ... que whatever, whichever; **quelque livre qu'il choisisse** whatever (*ou* whichever) book he chooses; **par quelque temps qu'il fasse** whatever the weather
3: quelque chose something; (*tournure interrogative*) anything; **quelque chose d'autre** something else; anything else; **y être pour quelque chose** to have something to do with it; **faire quelque chose à qn** to have an effect on sb, do something to sb; **quelque part** somewhere; anywhere; **en quelque sorte** as it were
▷ *adv* **1** (*environ*): **quelque 100 mètres** some 100 metres
2: quelque peu rather, somewhat

quelquefois [kɛlkəfwa] *adv* sometimes
quelques-uns, --unes [kɛlkəzœ̃, -yn] *pron* some, a few; ~ **des lecteurs** some of the readers
quelqu'un [kɛlkœ̃] *pron* someone, somebody; (*tournure interrogative ou négative+*) anyone *ou* anybody; **quelqu'un d'autre** someone *ou* somebody else; anybody else
quémander [kemɑ̃de] *vt* to beg for
qu'en dira-t-on [kɑ̃diratɔ̃] *nm inv*: **le qu'en dira-t-on** gossip, what people say
quenelle [kənɛl] *nf* quenelle
quenouille [kənuj] *nf* distaff
querelle [kərɛl] *nf* quarrel; **chercher ~ à qn** to pick a quarrel with sb
quereller [kərele]: **se quereller** *vi* to quarrel
querelleur, -euse [kərɛlœr, -øz] *adj* quarrelsome
qu'est-ce que [kɛskə] *voir* **que**
qu'est-ce qui [kɛski] *voir* **qui**
question [kɛstjɔ̃] *nf* (*gén*) question; (*fig*) matter; issue; **il a été ~ de** we (*ou* they) spoke about; **il est ~ de les emprisonner** there's talk of them being jailed; **c'est une ~ de temps** it's a matter *ou* question of time; **de quoi est-il ~?** what is it about?; **il n'en est pas ~** there's no question of it; **en ~** in question; **hors de ~** out of the question; **je ne me suis jamais posé la ~** I've never thought about it; **(re)mettre en ~** (*autorité, science*) to question; **poser la ~ de confiance** (*Pol*) to ask for a vote of confidence; ~ **piège** (*d'apparence facile*) trick question; (*pour nuire*) loaded question; ~ **subsidiaire** tiebreaker
questionnaire [kɛstjɔnɛr] *nm* questionnaire

questionner [kɛstjɔne] *vt* to question
quête [kɛt] *nf* (*collecte*) collection; (*recherche*) quest, search; **faire la ~** (*à l'église*) to take the collection; (*artiste*) to pass the hat round; **se mettre en ~ de qch** to go in search of sth
quêter [kete] *vi* (*à l'église*) to take the collection; (*dans la rue*) to collect money (for charity) ▷ *vt* to seek
quetsche [kwɛtʃ(ə)] *nf* damson
queue [kø] *nf* tail; (*fig: du classement*) bottom; (: *de poêle*) handle; (: *de fruit, feuille*) stalk; (: *de train, colonne, file*) rear; (*file: de personnes*) queue (*Brit*), line (*US*); **en ~ (de train)** at the rear of the train); **faire la ~** to queue (up) (*Brit*), line up (*US*); **se mettre à la ~** to join the queue *ou* line; **histoire sans ~ ni tête** cock and bull story; **à la ~ leu leu** in single file; (*fig*) one after the other; ~ **de cheval** ponytail; ~ **de poisson**: **faire une ~ de poisson à qn** (*Auto*) to cut in front of sb; **finir en ~ de poisson** (*film*) to come to an abrupt end
queue-de-pie [kødpi] (*pl* **queues-de-pie**) *nf* (*habit*) tails *pl*, tail coat
queux [kø] *adj m voir* **maître**
qui [ki] *pron* (*personne*) who; (*avec préposition*) whom; (*chose, animal*) which, that; (*interrogatif indirect: sujet*): **je me demande ~ est là?** I wonder who is there?; (: *objet*): **elle ne sait à ~ se plaindre** she doesn't know who to complain to *ou* to whom to complain; **qu'est-ce ~ est sur la table?** what is on the table?; **à ~ est ce sac?** whose bag is this?; **à ~ parlais-tu?** who were you talking to?, to whom were you talking?; **chez ~ allez-vous?** whose house are you going to?; **amenez ~ vous voulez** bring who(ever) you like; ~ **est-ce ~ ...?** who?; ~ **est-ce que ...?** who?; whom?; ~ **que ce soit** whoever it may be
quiche [kiʃ] *nf* quiche; ~ **lorraine** quiche Lorraine
quiconque [kikɔ̃k] *pron* (*celui qui*) whoever, anyone who; (*n'importe qui, personne*) anyone, anybody
quidam [kɥidam] *nm* (*hum*) fellow
quiétude [kjetyd] *nf* (*d'un lieu*) quiet, tranquillity; (*d'une personne*) peace (of mind), serenity; **en toute ~** in complete peace; (*mentale*) with complete peace of mind
quignon [kiɲɔ̃] *nm*: ~ **de pain** (*croûton*) crust of bread; (*morceau*) hunk of bread
quille [kij] *nf* ninepin, skittle (*Brit*); (*Navig: d'un bateau*) keel; **(jeu de) ~s** ninepins *sg*, skittles *sg* (*Brit*)
quincaillerie [kɛ̃kajri] *nf* (*ustensiles, métier*) hardware, ironmongery (*Brit*); (*magasin*) hardware shop *ou* store (*US*), ironmonger's (*Brit*)
quincaillier, -ière [kɛ̃kaje, -jɛr] *nm/f* hardware dealer, ironmonger (*Brit*)
quinconce [kɛ̃kɔ̃s] *nm*: **en ~** in staggered rows
quinine [kinin] *nf* quinine
quinqua [kɛ̃ka] (*fam*) *nm/f* (= *quinquagénaire*) person in his (*ou* her) fifties; **les ~s** fifty somethings (*fam*)

q

quinquagénaire [kɛ̃kaʒenɛʀ] *nm/f* (*de cinquante ans*) fifty-year old; (*de cinquante à soixante ans*) man/woman in his/her fifties

quinquennal, e, -aux [kɛ̃kenal, -o] *adj* five-year, quinquennial

quinquennat [kɛ̃kena] *nm* five year term of office (*of French President*)

quintal, -aux [kɛ̃tal, -o] *nm* quintal (*100 kg*)

quinte [kɛ̃t] *nf*: ~ **(de toux)** coughing fit

quintessence [kɛ̃tesɑ̃s] *nf* quintessence, very essence

quintette [kɛ̃tɛt] *nm* quintet(te)

quintuple [kɛ̃typl(ə)] *nm*: **le** ~ **de** five times as much as

quintupler [kɛ̃typle] *vt*, *vi* to increase fivefold

quintuplés, -ées [kɛ̃typle] *nm/fpl* quintuplets, quins

quinzaine [kɛ̃zɛn] *nf*: **une** ~ **(de)** about fifteen, fifteen or so; **une** ~ **(de jours)** (*deux semaines*) a fortnight (*Brit*), two weeks; ~ **publicitaire** *ou* **commerciale** (two-week) sale

quinze [kɛ̃z] *num* fifteen; **demain en** ~ a fortnight (*Brit*) *ou* two weeks tomorrow; **dans** ~ **jours** in a fortnight('s time) (*Brit*), in two weeks(' time)

quinzième [kɛ̃zjɛm] *num* fifteenth

quiproquo [kipʀɔko] *nm* (*méprise sur une personne*) mistake; (*malentendu sur un sujet*) misunderstanding; (*Théât*) (case of) mistaken identity

Quito [kito] *n* Quito

quittance [kitɑ̃s] *nf* (*reçu*) receipt; (*facture*) bill

quitte [kit] *adj*: **être** ~ **envers qn** to be no longer in sb's debt; (*fig*) to be quits with sb; **être** ~ **de** (*obligation*) to be clear of; **en être** ~ **à bon compte** to have got off lightly; ~ **à faire** even if it means doing; ~ **ou double** (*jeu*) double or quits; (*fig*): **c'est du** ~ **ou double** it's a big risk

quitter [kite] *vt* to leave; (*espoir, illusion*) to give up; (*vêtement*) to take off; **se quitter** (*couples, interlocuteurs*) to part; **ne quittez pas** (*au téléphone*) hold the line; **ne pas** ~ **qn d'une semelle** to stick to sb like glue

quitus [kitys] *nm* final discharge; **donner** ~ **à** to discharge

qui-vive [kiviv] *nm inv*: **être sur le** ~ to be on the alert

quoi [kwa] *pron* (*interrogatif*) what; ~ **de neuf** *ou* **de nouveau?** what's new *ou* the news?; **as-tu de** ~ **écrire?** have you anything to write with?; **il n'a pas de** ~ **se l'acheter** he can't afford it, he hasn't got the money to buy it; **il y a de** ~ **être fier** that's something to be proud of; **"il n'y a pas de** ~**"** "(please) don't mention it", "not at all"; ~ **qu'il arrive** whatever happens; ~ **qu'il en soit** be that as it may; ~ **que ce soit** anything at all; **en** ~ **puis-je vous aider?** how can I help you?; **à** ~ **bon?** what's the use *ou* point?; **et puis** ~ **encore!** what(ever) next!; ~ **faire?** what's to be done?; **sans** ~ (*ou sinon*) otherwise

quoique [kwak(ə)] *conj* (al)though

quolibet [kɔlibɛ] *nm* gibe, jeer

quorum [kɔʀɔm] *nm* quorum

quota [kwɔta] *nm* quota

quote-part [kɔtpaʀ] *nf* share

quotidien, ne [kɔtidjɛ̃, -ɛn] *adj* (*journalier*) daily; (*banal*) ordinary, everyday ▷ *nm* (*journal*) daily (paper); (*vie quotidienne*) daily life, day-to-day existence; **les grands ~s** the big (national) dailies

quotidiennement [kɔtidjɛnmɑ̃] *adv* daily, every day

quotient [kɔsjɑ̃] *nm* (*Math*) quotient; ~ **intellectuel (QI)** intelligence quotient (IQ)

quotité [kɔtite] *nf* (*Finance*) quota

Rr

R, r [ɛʀ] *nm inv* R, ʀ ▷ *abr* = **route**; **rue**; **R comme Raoul** R for Robert (*Brit*) *ou* Roger (*US*)

rab [ʀab] (*fam*), **rabiot** [ʀabjo] *nm* extra, more

rabâcher [ʀabaʃe] *vi* to harp on ▷ *vt* keep on repeating

rabais [ʀabɛ] *nm* reduction, discount; **au ~** at a reduction *ou* discount

rabaisser [ʀabese] *vt* (*rabattre*) to reduce; (*dénigrer*) to belittle

rabane [ʀaban] *nf* raffia (matting)

Rabat [ʀaba(t)] *n* Rabat

rabat [ʀaba] *vb voir* **rabattre** ▷ *nm* flap

rabat-joie [ʀabaʒwa] *nm/f inv* killjoy (*Brit*), spoilsport

rabatteur, -euse [ʀabatœʀ, -øz] *nm/f* (*de gibier*) beater; (*péj*) tout

rabattre [ʀabatʀ(ə)] *vt* (*couvercle, siège*) to pull down; (*col*) to turn down; (*couture*) to stitch down; (*gibier*) to drive; (*somme d'un prix*) to deduct, take off; (*orgueil, prétentions*) to humble; (*Tricot*) to decrease; **se rabattre** *vi* (*bords, couvercle*) to fall shut; (*véhicule, coureur*) to cut in; **se ~ sur** (*accepter*) to fall back on

rabattu, e [ʀabaty] *pp de* **rabattre** ▷ *adj* turned down

rabbin [ʀabɛ̃] *nm* rabbi

rabique [ʀabik] *adj* rabies *cpd*

râble [ʀabl(ə)] *nm* back; (*Culin*) saddle

râblé, e [ʀable] *adj* broad-backed, stocky

rabot [ʀabo] *nm* plane

raboter [ʀabɔte] *vt* to plane (down)

raboteux, -euse [ʀabɔtø, -øz] *adj* uneven, rough

rabougri, e [ʀabugʀi] *adj* stunted

rabrouer [ʀabʀue] *vt* to snub, rebuff

racaille [ʀakɑj] *nf* (*péj*) rabble, riffraff

raccommodage [ʀakɔmɔdaʒ] *nm* mending *no pl*, repairing *no pl*; darning *no pl*

raccommoder [ʀakɔmɔde] *vt* to mend, repair; (*chaussette etc*) to darn; (*fam: réconcilier: amis, ménage*) to bring together again; **se ~ (avec)** (*fam*) to patch it up (with)

raccompagner [ʀakɔ̃paɲe] *vt* to take *ou* see back

raccord [ʀakɔʀ] *nm* link; **~ de maçonnerie** pointing *no pl*; **~ de peinture** join; touch-up

raccordement [ʀakɔʀdəmɑ̃] *nm* joining up; connection

raccorder [ʀakɔʀde] *vt* to join (up), link up; (*pont etc*) to connect, link; **se ~ à** to join up with; (*fig: se rattacher à*) to tie in with; **~ au réseau du téléphone** to connect to the telephone service

raccourci [ʀakuʀsi] *nm* short cut; **en ~** in brief

raccourcir [ʀakuʀsiʀ] *vt* to shorten ▷ *vi* (*vêtement*) to shrink

raccroc [ʀakʀo]: **par ~** *adv* by chance

raccrocher [ʀakʀɔʃe] *vt* (*tableau, vêtement*) to hang back up; (*récepteur*) to put down; (*fig: affaire*) to save ▷ *vi* (*Tél*) to hang up, ring off; **se ~ à** *vt* to cling to, hang on to; **ne raccrochez pas** (*Tél*) hold on, don't hang up

race [ʀas] *nf* race; (*d'animaux, fig: espèce*) breed; (*ascendance, origine*) stock, race; **de ~** *adj* purebred, pedigree

racé, e [ʀase] *adj* thoroughbred

rachat [ʀaʃa] *nm* buying; buying back; redemption; atonement

racheter [ʀaʃte] *vt* (*article perdu*) to buy another; (*davantage*): **~ du lait/trois œufs** to buy more milk/another three eggs *ou* three more eggs; (*après avoir vendu*) to buy back; (*d'occasion*) to buy; (*Comm: part, firme*) to buy up; (: *pension, rente*) to redeem; (*Rel: pécheur*) to redeem; (: *péché*) to atone for, expiate; (*mauvaise conduite, oubli, défaut*) to make up for; **se racheter** (*Rel*) to redeem o.s.; (*gén*) to make amends, make up for it

rachitique [ʀaʃitik] *adj* suffering from rickets; (*fig*) scraggy, scrawny

rachitisme [ʀaʃitism(ə)] *nm* rickets *sg*

racial, e, -aux [ʀasjal, -o] *adj* racial

racine [ʀasin] *nf* root; (*fig: attache*) roots *pl*; **~ carrée/cubique** square/cube root; **prendre ~** (*fig*) to take root; to put down roots

racisme [ʀasism(ə)] *nm* racism, racialism

raciste [ʀasist(ə)] *adj, nm/f* racist, racialist

racket [ʀakɛt] *nm* racketeering *no pl*

racketteur [ʀakɛtœʀ] *nm* racketeer

raclée [ʀakle] *nf* (*fam*) hiding, thrashing

raclement [ʀakləmɑ̃] *nm* (*bruit*) scraping (noise)

racler [ʀakle] *vt* (*os, plat*) to scrape; (*tache, boue*) to scrape off; (*fig: instrument*) to scrape on; (*chose: frotter contre*) to scrape (against)

raclette [Raklɛt] *nf* (*Culin*) raclette (*Swiss cheese dish*)

racloir [RaklwaR] *nm* (*outil*) scraper

racolage [Rakɔlaʒ] *nm* soliciting; touting

racoler [Rakɔle] *vt* (*attirer: prostituée*) to solicit; (*: parti, marchand*) to tout for; (*attraper*) to pick up

racoleur, -euse [RakɔlœR, -øz] *adj* (*péj*) cheap and alluring ▷ *nm* (*péj: de clients etc*) tout ▷ *nf* streetwalker

racontars [Rakɔ̃taR] *nmpl* stories, gossip *sg*

raconter [Rakɔ̃te] *vt*: ~ (**à qn**) (*décrire*) to relate (to sb), tell (sb) about; (*dire*) to tell (sb)

racorni, e [RakɔRni] *adj* hard(ened)

racornir [RakɔRniR] *vt* to harden

radar [RadaR] *nm* radar; **système** ~ radar system; **écran** ~ radar screen

rade [Rad] *nf* (natural) harbour; **en ~ de Toulon** in Toulon harbour; **rester en ~** (*fig*) to be left stranded

radeau, x [Rado] *nm* raft; ~ **de sauvetage** life raft

radial, e, -aux [Radjal, -o] *adj* radial

radiant, e [Radjɑ̃, -ɑ̃t] *adj* radiant

radiateur [RadjatœR] *nm* radiator, heater; (*Auto*) radiator; ~ **électrique/à gaz** electric/gas heater *ou* fire

radiation [Radjasjɔ̃] *nf* (*d'un nom etc*) striking off *no pl*; (*Physique*) radiation

radical, e, -aux [Radikal, -o] *adj* radical ▷ *nm* (*Ling*) stem; (*Math*) root sign; (*Pol*) radical

radicalement [Radikalmɑ̃] *adv* radically, completely

radicaliser [Radikalize] *vt* (*durcir: opinions etc*) to harden; **se radicaliser** *vi* (*mouvement etc*) to become more radical

radicalisme [Radikalism(ə)] *nm* (*Pol*) radicalism

radier [Radje] *vt* to strike off

radiesthésie [Radjɛstezi] *nf* divination (by radiation)

radiesthésiste [Radjɛstezist(ə)] *nm/f* diviner

radieux, -euse [Radjø, -øz] *adj* (*visage, personne*) radiant; (*journée, soleil*) brilliant, glorious

radin, e [Radɛ̃, -in] *adj* (*fam*) stingy

radio [Radjo] *nf* radio; (*Méd*) X-ray ▷ *nm* (*personne*) radio operator; **à la ~** on the radio; **avoir la ~** to have a radio; **passer à la ~** to be on the radio; **se faire faire une ~/une ~ des poumons** to have an X-ray/a chest X-ray

radio... [Radjɔ] *préfixe* radio...

radioactif, -ive [Radjɔaktif, -iv] *adj* radioactive

radioactivité [Radjɔaktivite] *nf* radioactivity

radioamateur [RadjɔamatœR] *nm* (radio) ham

radiobalise [Radjɔbaliz] *nf* radio beacon

radiocassette [Radjɔkasɛt] *nf* cassette radio

radiodiffuser [Radjɔdifyze] *vt* to broadcast

radiodiffusion [Radjɔdifyzjɔ̃] *nf* (radio) broadcasting

radioélectrique [RadjɔelɛktRik] *adj* radio *cpd*

radiographie [Radjɔgrafi] *nf* radiography; (*photo*) X-ray photograph, radiograph

radiographier [Radjɔgrafje] *vt* to X-ray; **se faire** ~ to have an X-ray

radioguidage [Radjɔgidaʒ] *nm* (*Navig, Aviat*) radio control; (*Auto*) (broadcast of) traffic information

radioguider [Radjɔgide] *vt* (*Navig, Aviat*) to guide by radio, control by radio

radiologie [Radjɔlɔʒi] *nf* radiology

radiologique [Radjɔlɔʒik] *adj* radiological

radiologue [Radjɔlɔg] *nm/f* radiologist

radiophonique [Radjɔfɔnik] *adj*: **programme/ émission/jeu** ~ radio programme/broadcast/ game

radio-réveil [RadjɔRevɛj] *nm* clock radio

radioscopie [Radjɔskɔpi] *nf* radioscopy

radio-taxi [Radjɔtaksi] *nm* radiotaxi

radiotélescope [Radjɔtelɛskɔp] *nm* radiotelescope

radiotélévisé, e [Radjɔtelevize] *adj* broadcast on radio and television

radiothérapie [Radjɔterapi] *nf* radiotherapy

radis [Radi] *nm* radish; ~ **noir** horseradish *no pl*

radium [Radjɔm] *nm* radium

radoter [Radɔte] *vi* to ramble on

radoub [Radu] *nm*: **bassin** *ou* **cale de** ~ dry dock

radouber [Radube] *vt* to repair, refit

radoucir [RadusiR]: **se radoucir** *vi* (*se réchauffer*) to become milder; (*se calmer*) to calm down; to soften

radoucissement [Radusismɑ̃] *nm* milder period, better weather

rafale [Rafal] *nf* (*vent*) gust (of wind); (*de balles, d'applaudissements*) burst; ~ **de mitrailleuse** burst of machine-gun fire

raffermir [RafɛRmiR] *vt*, **se raffermir** *vi* (*tissus, muscle*) to firm up; (*fig*) to strengthen

raffermissement [RafɛRmismɑ̃] *nm* (*fig*) strengthening

raffinage [Rafinaʒ] *nm* refining

raffiné, e [Rafine] *adj* refined

raffinement [Rafinmɑ̃] *nm* refinement

raffiner [Rafine] *vt* to refine

raffinerie [RafinRi] *nf* refinery

raffoler [Rafɔle]: ~ **de** *vt* to be very keen on

raffut [Rafy] *nm* (*fam*) row, racket

rafiot [Rafjo] *nm* tub

rafistoler [Rafistɔle] *vt* (*fam*) to patch up

rafle [Rafl(ə)] *nf* (*de police*) roundup, raid

rafler [Rafle] *vt* (*fam*) to swipe, nick

rafraîchir [RafReʃiR] *vt* (*atmosphère, température*) to cool (down); (*aussi*: **mettre à rafraîchir**) to chill; (*air, eau*) to freshen up; (*: boisson*) to refresh; (*fig: rénover*) to brighten up ▷ *vi*: **mettre du vin/une boisson à** ~ to chill wine/a drink; **se rafraîchir** to grow cooler; to freshen up; (*personne: en buvant etc*) to refresh o.s.; ~ **la mémoire à qn** to refresh sb's memory

rafraîchissant, e [RafReʃisɑ̃, -ɑ̃t] *adj* refreshing

rafraîchissement [RafReʃismɑ̃] *nm* cooling; (*boisson*) cool drink; **rafraîchissements** *nmpl* (*boissons, fruits etc*) refreshments

ragaillardir [RagajaRdiR] *vt* (*fam*) to perk *ou* buck up

rage [Raʒ] *nf* (*Méd*): **la** ~ rabies; (*fureur*) rage, fury; **faire ~** to rage; **~ de dents** (raging) toothache

rager [Raʒe] *vi* to fume (with rage); **faire ~ qn** to enrage sb, get sb mad

rageur, -euse [RaʒœR, -øz] *adj* snarling; ill-tempered

raglan [Raglɑ̃] *adj inv* raglan

ragot [Rago] *nm* (*fam*) malicious gossip *no pl*

ragoût [Ragu] *nm* (*plat*) stew

ragoûtant, e [Ragutɑ̃, -ɑ̃t] *adj*: **peu ~** unpalatable

rai [Rɛ] *nm*: **un ~ de soleil/lumière** a shaft of sunlight/light

raid [Rɛd] *nm* (*Mil*) raid; (*attaque aérienne*) air raid; (*Sport*) long-distance trek

raide [Rɛd] *adj* (*tendu*) taut, tight; (*escarpé*) steep; (*droit: cheveux*) straight; (*ankylosé, dur, guindé*) stiff; (*fam: cher*) steep, stiff; (*: sans argent*) flat broke; (*osé, licencieux*) daring ▷ *adv* (*en pente*) steeply; **~ mort** stone dead

raideur [RɛdœR] *nf* steepness; stiffness

raidir [Redir] *vt* (*muscles*) to stiffen; (*câble*) to pull taut, tighten; **se raidir** *vi* to stiffen; to become taut; (*personne: se crisper*) to tense up; (*: devenir intransigeant*) to harden

raidissement [Redismɑ̃] *nm* stiffening; tightening; hardening

raie [Rɛ] *nf* (*Zool*) skate, ray; (*rayure*) stripe; (*des cheveux*) parting

raifort [RɛfɔR] *nm* horseradish

rail [Raj] *nm* (*barre d'acier*) rail; (*chemins de fer*) railways *pl* (*Brit*), railroads *pl* (*US*); **les ~s** (*la voie ferrée*) the rails, the track *sg*; **par ~** by rail; **~ conducteur** live *ou* conductor rail

railler [Raje] *vt* to scoff at, jeer at

raillerie [RajRi] *nf* mockery

railleur, -euse [RajœR, -øz] *adj* mocking

rainurage [RenyRaʒ] *nm* (*Auto*) uneven road surface

rainure [RenyR] *nf* groove; slot

rais [Rɛ] *nm inv* = **rai**

raisin [Rɛzɛ̃] *nm* (*aussi*: **raisins**) grapes *pl*; (*variété*): **~ blanc/noir** white (*ou* green)/black grape; **~ muscat** muscat grape; **~s secs** raisins

raison [Rɛzɔ̃] *nf* reason; **avoir ~** to be right; **donner ~ à** (*personne*) to agree with sb; (*fait*) to prove sb right; **avoir ~ de qn/qch** to get the better of sb/sth; **se faire une ~** to learn to live with it; **perdre la ~** to become insane; (*fig*) to take leave of one's senses; **recouvrer la ~** to come to one's senses; **ramener qn à la ~** to make sb see sense; **demander ~ à qn de** (*affront etc*) to demand satisfaction from sb for; **entendre ~** to listen to reason, see reason; **plus que de ~** too much, more than is reasonable; **~ de plus** all the more reason; **à plus forte ~** all the more so; **en ~ de** (*à cause de*) because of; (*à proportion de*) in proportion to; **à ~ de** at the rate of; **~ d'État** reason of state; **~ d'être** raison d'être; **~ sociale** corporate name

raisonnable [Rɛzɔnabl(ə)] *adj* reasonable, sensible

raisonnablement [Rɛzɔnabləmɑ̃] *adv* reasonably

raisonné, e [Rɛzɔne] *adj* reasoned

raisonnement [Rɛzɔnmɑ̃] *nm* reasoning; arguing; argument

raisonner [Rɛzɔne] *vi* (*penser*) to reason; (*argumenter, discuter*) to argue ▷ *vt* (*personne*) to reason with; (*attitude: justifier*) to reason out; **se raisonner** to reason with oneself

raisonneur, -euse [RɛzɔnœR, -øz] *adj* (*péj*) quibbling

rajeunir [RaʒœniR] *vt* (*coiffure, robe*): **~ qn** to make sb look younger; (*cure etc*) to rejuvenate; (*fig: rafraîchir*) to brighten up; (*: moderniser*) to give a new look to; (*: en recrutant*) to inject new blood into ▷ *vi* (*personne*) to become (*ou* look) younger; (*entreprise, quartier*) to be modernized

rajout [Raʒu] *nm* addition

rajouter [Raʒute] *vt* (*commentaire*) to add; **~ du sel/un œuf** to add some more salt/another egg; **~ que** to add that; **en ~** to lay it on thick

rajustement [Raʒystəmɑ̃] *nm* adjustment

rajuster [Raʒyste] *vt* (*vêtement*) to straighten, tidy; (*salaires*) to adjust; (*machine*) to readjust; **se rajuster** to tidy *ou* straighten o.s. up

râle [Rɑl] *nm* groan; **~ d'agonie** death rattle

ralenti [Ralɑ̃ti] *nm*: **au ~** (*Ciné*) in slow motion; (*fig*) at a slower pace; **tourner au ~** (*Auto*) to tick over, idle

ralentir [Ralɑ̃tiR] *vt, vi*, **se ralentir** *vi* to slow down

ralentissement [Ralɑ̃tism] *nm* slowing down

râler [Rɑle] *vi* to groan; (*fam*) to grouse, moan (and groan)

ralliement [Ralimɑ̃] *nm* (*rassemblement*) rallying; (*adhésion: à une cause, une opinion*) winning over; **point/signe de ~** rallying point/sign

rallier [Ralje] *vt* (*rassembler*) to rally; (*rejoindre*) to rejoin; (*gagner à sa cause*) to win over; **se ~ à** (*avis*) to come over *ou* round to

rallonge [Ralɔ̃ʒ] *nf* (*de table*) (extra) leaf; (*argent etc*) extra *no pl*; (*Élec*) extension (cable *ou* flex); (*fig: de crédit etc*) extension

rallonger [Ralɔ̃ʒe] *vt* to lengthen

rallumer [Ralyme] *vt* to light up again, relight; (*fig*) to revive; **se rallumer** *vi* (*lumière*) to come on again

rallye [Rali] *nm* rally; (*Pol*) march

ramages [Ramaʒ] *nmpl* (*dessin*) leaf pattern *sg*; (*chants*) songs

ramassage [Ramasaʒ] *nm*: **~ scolaire** school bus service

ramassé, e [Ramase] *adj* (*trapu*) squat, stocky; (*concis: expression etc*) compact

ramasse-miettes [Ramasmjɛt] *nm inv* table-tidy

ramasser [Ramase] *vt* (*objet tombé ou par terre*: *fam*) to pick up; (*recueillir*) to collect; (*récolter*) to gather; (*: pommes de terre*) to lift; **se ramasser** *vi* (*sur soi-même*) to huddle up; to crouch

ramasseur, -euse [RamasœR, -øz] *nm/f*: **~ de balles** ballboy/girl

r

ramassis [ʀamɑsi] *nm* (*péj: de gens*) bunch; (:*de choses*) jumble

rambarde [ʀɑ̃baʀd(ə)] *nf* guardrail

rame [ʀam] *nf* (*aviron*) oar; (*de métro*) train; (*de papier*) ream; **~ de haricots** bean support; **faire force de ~s** to row hard

rameau, x [ʀamo] *nm* (small) branch; (*fig*) branch; **les R~x** (*Rel*) Palm Sunday *sg*

ramener [ʀamne] *vt* to bring back; (*reconduire*) to take back; (*rabattre: couverture, visière*): **~ qch sur** to pull sth back over; **~ qch à** (*réduire à, Math*) to reduce sth to; **~ qn à la vie/raison** to bring sb back to life/bring sb to his (*ou* her) senses; **se ramener** *vi* (*fam*) to roll *ou* turn up; **se ~ à** (*se réduire à*) to come *ou* boil down to

ramequin [ʀamkɛ̃] *nm* ramekin

ramer [ʀame] *vi* to row

rameur, -euse [ʀamœʀ, -øz] *nm/f* rower

rameuter [ʀamøte] *vt* to gather together

ramier [ʀamje] *nm*: **(pigeon) ~** woodpigeon

ramification [ʀamifikasjɔ̃] *nf* ramification

ramifier [ʀamifje]: **se ramifier** *vi* (*tige, secte, réseau*): **se ~ (en)** to branch out (into); (*veines, nerfs*) to ramify

ramolli, e [ʀamɔli] *adj* soft

ramollir [ʀamɔliʀ] *vt* to soften; **se ramollir** *vi* (*os, tissus*) to get (*ou* go) soft; (*beurre, asphalte*) to soften

ramonage [ʀamɔnaʒ] *nm* (chimney-)sweeping

ramoner [ʀamɔne] *vt* (*cheminée*) to sweep; (*pipe*) to clean

ramoneur [ʀamɔnœʀ] *nm* (chimney) sweep

rampe [ʀɑ̃p] *nf* (*d'escalier*) banister(s *pl*); (*dans un garage, d'un terrain*) ramp; (*Théât*): **la ~** the footlights *pl*; (*lampes: lumineuse, de balisage*) floodlights *pl*; **passer la ~** (*toucher le public*) to get across to the audience; **~ de lancement** launching pad

ramper [ʀɑ̃pe] *vi* (*reptile, animal*) to crawl; (*plante*) to creep

rancard [ʀɑ̃kaʀ] *nm* (*fam*) date; tip

rancart [ʀɑ̃kaʀ] *nm*: **mettre au ~** (*article, projet*) to scrap; (*personne*) to put on the scrapheap

rance [ʀɑ̃s] *adj* rancid

rancir [ʀɑ̃siʀ] *vi* to go off, go rancid

rancœur [ʀɑ̃kœʀ] *nf* rancour (*Brit*), rancor (*US*), resentment

rançon [ʀɑ̃sɔ̃] *nf* ransom; (*fig*): **la ~ du succès** *etc* the price of success *etc*

rançonner [ʀɑ̃sɔne] *vt* to hold to ransom

rancune [ʀɑ̃kyn] *nf* grudge, rancour (*Brit*), rancor (*US*); **garder ~ à qn (de qch)** to bear sb a grudge (for sth); **sans ~!** no hard feelings!

rancunier, -ière [ʀɑ̃kynje, -jɛʀ] *adj* vindictive, spiteful

randonnée [ʀɑ̃dɔne] *nf* ride; (*à pied*) walk, ramble; hike, hiking *no pl*

randonneur, -euse [ʀɑ̃dɔnœʀ, -øz] *nm/f* hiker

rang [ʀɑ̃] *nm* (*rangée*) row; (*de perles*) row, string, rope; (*grade, condition sociale, classement*) rank; **rangs** *nmpl* (*Mil*) ranks; **se mettre en ~s/sur un ~** to get into *ou* form rows/a line; **sur trois ~s** (lined up) three deep; **se mettre en ~s par quatre** to form fours *ou* rows of four; **se mettre sur les ~s** (*fig*) to get into the running; **au premier ~** in the first row; (*fig*) ranking first; **rentrer dans le ~** to get into line; **au ~ de** (*au nombre de*) among (the ranks of); **avoir ~ de** to hold the rank of

rangé, e [ʀɑ̃ʒe] *adj* (*sérieux*) orderly, steady

rangée [ʀɑ̃ʒe] *nf* row

rangement [ʀɑ̃ʒmɑ̃] *nm* tidying-up, putting-away; **faire des ~s** to tidy up

ranger [ʀɑ̃ʒe] *vt* (*classer, grouper*) to order, arrange; (*mettre à sa place*) to put away; (*voiture dans la rue*) to park; (*mettre de l'ordre dans*) to tidy up; (*arranger, disposer: en cercle etc*) to arrange; (*fig: classer*): **~ qn/qch parmi** to rank sb/sth among; **se ranger** *vi* (*se placer, se disposer: autour d'une table etc*) to take one's place, sit round; (*véhicule, conducteur: s'écarter*) to pull over; (:*s'arrêter*) to pull in; (*piéton*) to step aside; (*s'assagir*) to settle down; **se ~ à** (*avis*) to come round to, fall in with

ranimer [ʀanime] *vt* (*personne évanouie*) to bring round; (*revigorer: forces, courage*) to restore; (*réconforter: troupes etc*) to kindle new life in; (*douleur, souvenir*) to revive; (*feu*) to rekindle

rap [ʀap] *nm* rap (music)

rapace [ʀapas] *nm* bird of prey ▷ *adj* (*péj*) rapacious, grasping; **~ diurne/nocturne** diurnal/nocturnal bird of prey

rapatrié, e [ʀapatʀije] *nm/f* repatriate (*esp French North African settler*)

rapatriement [ʀapatʀimɑ̃] *nm* repatriation

rapatrier [ʀapatʀije] *vt* to repatriate; (*capitaux*) to bring (back) into the country

râpe [ʀɑp] *nf* (*Culin*) grater; (*à bois*) rasp

râpé, e [ʀɑpe] *adj* (*tissu*) threadbare; (*Culin*) grated

râper [ʀɑpe] *vt* (*Culin*) to grate; (*gratter, râcler*) to rasp

rapetasser [ʀaptase] *vt* (*fam*) to patch up

rapetisser [ʀaptise] *vt*: **~ qch** to shorten sth; to make sth look smaller ▷ *vi*, **se rapetisser** *vi* to shrink

râpeux, -euse [ʀapø, -øz] *adj* rough

raphia [ʀafja] *nm* raffia

rapide [ʀapid] *adj* fast; (*prompt*) quick; (*intelligence*) quick ▷ *nm* express (train); (*de cours d'eau*) rapid

rapidement [ʀapidmɑ̃] *adv* fast; quickly

rapidité [ʀapidite] *nf* speed; quickness

rapiécer [ʀapjese] *vt* to patch

rappel [ʀapɛl] *nm* (*d'un ambassadeur, Mil*) recall; (*Théât*) curtain call; (*Méd: vaccination*) booster; (*Admin: de salaire*) back pay *no pl*; (*d'une aventure, d'un nom*) reminder; (*de limitation de vitesse: sur écriteau*) speed limit sign (reminder); (*Tech*) return; (*Navig*) sitting out; (*Alpinisme: aussi:* **rappel de corde**) abseiling *no pl*, roping down *no pl*; abseil; **~ à l'ordre** call to order

rappeler [ʀaple] *vt* (*pour faire revenir, retéléphoner*) to call back; (*ambassadeur, Mil*) to recall; (*acteur*) to call back (onto the stage); (*faire se souvenir*): **~**

qch à qn to remind sb of sth; **se rappeler** *vt* (*se souvenir de*) to remember, recall; **~ qn à la vie** to bring sb back to life; **~ qn à la décence** to recall sb to a sense of decency; **ça rappelle la Provence** it's reminiscent of Provence, it reminds you of Provence; **se ~ que...** to remember that...

rappelle *etc* [Rapɛl] *vb voir* **rappeler**

rappliquer [Raplike] *vi* (*fam*) to turn up

rapport [RapɔR] *nm* (*compte rendu*) report; (*profit*) yield, return; revenue; (*lien, analogie*) relationship; (*corrélation*) connection; (*proportion: Math, Tech*) ratio; **rapports** *nmpl* (*entre personnes, pays*) relations; **avoir ~ à** to have something to do with, concern; **être en ~ avec** (*idée de corrélation*) to be related to; **être/se mettre en ~ avec qn** to be/get in touch with sb; **par ~ à** (*comparé à*) in relation to; (*à propos de*) with regard to; **sous le ~ de** from the point of view of; **sous tous (les) ~s** in all respects; **~s (sexuels)** (sexual) intercourse *sg*; **~ qualité-prix** value (for money)

rapporté, e [RapɔRte] *adj*: **pièce ~e** (*Couture*) patch

rapporter [RapɔRte] *vt* (*rendre, ramener*) to bring back; (*apporter davantage*) to bring more; (*Couture*) to sew on; (*investissement*) to yield; (: *activité*) to bring in; (*relater*) to report; (*Jur: annuler*) to revoke ▷ *vi* (*investissement*) to give a good return *ou* yield; (*activité*) to be very profitable; (*péj: moucharder*) to tell; **~ qch à** (*fig: rattacher*) to relate sth to; **se ~ à** (*correspondre à*) to relate to; **s'en ~ à** to rely on

rapporteur, -euse [RapɔRtœR, -øz] *nm/f* (*de procès, commission*) reporter; (*péj*) telltale ▷ *nm* (*Géom*) protractor

rapproché, e [RapRoʃe] *adj* (*proche*) near, close at hand; **~s** (*l'un de l'autre*) at close intervals

rapprochement [RapRoʃmɑ̃] *nm* (*réconciliation: de nations, familles*) reconciliation; (*analogie, rapport*) parallel

rapprocher [RapRoʃe] *vt* (*chaise d'une table*): **~ qch (de)** to bring sth closer (to); (*deux objets*) to bring closer together; (*réunir*) to bring together; (*comparer*) to establish a parallel between; **se rapprocher** *vi* to draw closer *ou* nearer; (*fig: familles, pays*) to come together; to come closer together; **se ~ de** to come closer to; (*présenter une analogie avec*) to be close to

rapt [Rapt] *nm* abduction

raquette [Rakɛt] *nf* (*de tennis*) racket; (*de ping-pong*) bat; (*à neige*) snowshoe

rare [RaR] *adj* rare; (*main-d'œuvre, denrées*) scarce; (*cheveux, herbe*) sparse; **il est ~ que** it's rare that, it's unusual that; **se faire ~** to become scarce; (*fig: personne*) to make oneself scarce

raréfaction [RaRefaksjɔ̃] *nf* scarcity; (*de l'air*) rarefaction

raréfier [RaRefje]: **se raréfier** *vi* to grow scarce; (*air*) to rarefy

rarement [RaRmɑ̃] *adv* rarely, seldom

rareté [RaRte] *nf voir* **rare** rarity; scarcity

rarissime [RaRisim] *adj* extremely rare

RAS *abr* = **rien à signaler**

ras, e [Ra, Raz] *adj* (*tête, cheveux*) close-cropped; (*poil, herbe*) short; (*mesure, cuillère*) level ▷ *adv* short; **faire table ~e** to make a clean sweep; **en ~e campagne** in open country; **à ~ bords** to the brim; **au ~ de** level with; **en avoir ~ le bol** (*fam*) to be fed up; **~ du cou** *adj* (*pull, robe*) crew-neck

rasade [Razad] *nf* glassful

rasant, e [Razɑ̃, ɑ̃t] *adj* (*Mil: balle, tir*) grazing; (*fam*) boring

rascasse [Raskas] *nf* (*Zool*) scorpion fish

rasé, e [Raze] *adj*: **~ de frais** freshly shaven; **~ de près** close-shaven

rase-mottes [Razmɔt] *nm inv*: **faire du ~** to hedgehop; **vol en ~** hedgehopping

raser [Raze] *vt* (*barbe, cheveux*) to shave off; (*menton, personne*) to shave; (*fam: ennuyer*) to bore; (*démolir*) to raze (to the ground); (*frôler*) to graze, skim; **se raser** to shave; (*fam*) to be bored (to tears)

rasoir [RazwaR] *nm* razor; **~ électrique** electric shaver *ou* razor; **~ mécanique** *ou* **de sûreté** safety razor

rassasier [Rasazje] *vt* to satisfy; **être rassasié** (*dégoûté*) to be sated; to have had more than enough

rassemblement [Rasɑ̃bləmɑ̃] *nm* (*groupe*) gathering; (*Pol*) union; association; (*Mil*): **le ~** parade

rassembler [Rasɑ̃ble] *vt* (*réunir*) to assemble, gather; (*regrouper, amasser*) to gather together, collect; **se rassembler** *vi* to gather; **~ ses idées/ses esprits/son courage** to collect one's thoughts/gather one's wits/screw up one's courage

rasseoir [RaswaR]: **se rasseoir** *vi* to sit down again

rassir [RasiR] *vi* to go stale

rassis, e [Rasi, -iz] *adj* (*pain*) stale

rassurant, e [RasyRɑ̃, -ɑ̃t] *adj* (*nouvelles etc*) reassuring

rassuré, e [RasyRe] *adj*: **ne pas être très ~** to be rather ill at ease

rassurer [RasyRe] *vt* to reassure; **se rassurer** to be reassured; **rassure-toi** don't worry

rat [Ra] *nm* rat; **~ d'hôtel** hotel thief; **~ musqué** muskrat

ratatiné, e [Ratatine] *adj* shrivelled (up), wrinkled

ratatiner [Ratatine] *vt* to shrivel; (*peau*) to wrinkle; **se ratatiner** *vi* to shrivel; to become wrinkled

ratatouille [Ratatuj] *nf* (*Culin*) ratatouille

rate [Rat] *nf* female rat; (*Anat*) spleen

raté, e [Rate] *adj* (*tentative*) unsuccessful, failed ▷ *nm/f* failure ▷ *nm* misfiring *no pl*

râteau, x [Rato] *nm* rake

râtelier [Ratəlje] *nm* rack; (*fam*) false teeth *pl*

rater [Rate] *vi* (*ne pas partir: coup de feu*) to fail to go off; (*affaire, projet etc*) to go wrong, fail ▷ *vt* (*cible, train, occasion*) to miss; (*démonstration, plat*) to spoil; (*examen*) to fail; **~ son coup** to fail, not to bring it off

raticide [Ratisid] *nm* rat poison

ratification [Ratifikasjɔ̃] *nf* ratification

ratifier [Ratifje] *vt* to ratify

ratio [Rasjo] *nm* ratio

ration [Rasjɔ̃] *nf* ration; (*fig*) share; **~ alimentaire** food intake

rationalisation [Rasjɔnalizasjɔ̃] *nf* rationalization

rationaliser [Rasjɔnalize] *vt* to rationalize

rationnel, le [Rasjɔnɛl] *adj* rational

rationnellement [Rasjɔnɛlmɑ̃] *adv* rationally

rationnement [Rasjɔnmɑ̃] *nm* rationing; **ticket de ~** ration coupon

rationner [Rasjɔne] *vt* to ration; (*personne*) to put on rations; **se rationner** to ration o.s.

ratisser [Ratise] *vt* (*allée*) to rake; (*feuilles*) to rake up; (*armée, police*) to comb; **~ large** to cast one's net wide

raton [Ratɔ̃] *nm*: **~ laveur** raccoon

RATP *sigle f* (= *Régie autonome des transports parisiens*) *Paris transport authority*

rattacher [Ratafe] *vt* (*animal, cheveux*) to tie up again; (*incorporer: Admin etc*): **~ qch à** to join sth to, unite sth with; (*fig: relier*): **~ qch à** to link sth with, relate sth to; (*: lier*): **~ qn à** to bind *ou* tie sb to; **se ~ à** (*fig: avoir un lien avec*) to be linked (*ou* connected) with

rattrapage [RatRapaʒ] *nm* (*Scol*) remedial classes *pl*; (*Écon*) catching up

rattraper [RatRape] *vt* (*fugitif*) to recapture; (*retenir, empêcher de tomber*) to catch (hold of); (*atteindre, rejoindre*) to catch up with; (*réparer: erreur*) to make up for; **se rattraper** *vi* (*regagner: du temps*) to make up for lost time; (*: de l'argent etc*) to make good one's losses; (*réparer une gaffe etc*) to make up for it; **se ~ (à)** (*se raccrocher*) to stop o.s. falling (by catching hold of); **~ son retard/le temps perdu** to make up (for) lost time

rature [RatyR] *nf* deletion, erasure

raturer [RatyRe] *vt* to cross out, delete, erase

rauque [Rok] *adj* raucous; hoarse

ravagé, e [Ravaʒe] *adj* (*visage*) harrowed

ravager [Ravaʒe] *vt* to devastate, ravage

ravages [Ravaʒ] *nmpl* ravages; **faire des ~** to wreak havoc; (*fig: séducteur*) to break hearts

ravalement [Ravalmɑ̃] *nm* restoration

ravaler [Ravale] *vt* (*mur, façade*) to restore; (*déprécier*) to lower; (*avaler de nouveau*) to swallow again; **~ sa colère/son dégoût** to stifle one's anger/swallow one's distaste

ravauder [Ravode] *vt* to repair, mend

rave [Rav] *nf* (*Bot*) rape

ravi, e [Ravi] *adj* delighted; **être ~ de/que** to be delighted with/that

ravier [Ravje] *nm* hors d'œuvre dish

ravigote [Ravigɔt] *adj*: **sauce ~** oil and vinegar dressing with shallots

ravigoter [Ravigɔte] *vt* (*fam*) to buck up

ravin [Ravɛ̃] *nm* gully, ravine

raviner [Ravine] *vt* to furrow, gully

ravioli [Ravjɔli] *nmpl* ravioli *sg*

ravir [RaviR] *vt* (*enchanter*) to delight; (*enlever*): **~ qch à qn** to rob sb of sth; **à ~** *adv* delightfully, beautifully; **être beau à ~** to be ravishingly beautiful

raviser [Ravize]: **se raviser** *vi* to change one's mind

ravissant, e [Ravisɑ̃, -ɑ̃t] *adj* delightful

ravissement [Ravismɑ̃] *nm* (*enchantement, délice*) rapture

ravisseur, -euse [Ravisœr, -øz] *nm/f* abductor, kidnapper

ravitaillement [Ravitajmɑ̃] *nm* resupplying; refuelling; (*provisions*) supplies *pl*; **aller au ~** to go for fresh supplies; **~ en vol** (*Aviat*) in-flight refuelling

ravitailler [Ravitaje] *vt* to resupply; (*véhicule*) to refuel; **se ravitailler** *vi* to get fresh supplies

raviver [Ravive] *vt* (*feu*) to rekindle, revive; (*douleur*) to revive; (*couleurs*) to brighten up

ravoir [RavwaR] *vt* to get back

rayé, e [Reje] *adj* (*à rayures*) striped; (*éraflé*) scratched

rayer [Reje] *vt* (*érafler*) to scratch; (*barrer*) to cross *ou* score out; (*d'une liste: radier*) to cross *ou* strike off

rayon [Rɛjɔ̃] *nm* (*de soleil etc*) ray; (*Géom*) radius; (*de roue*) spoke; (*étagère*) shelf; (*de grand magasin*) department; (*fig: domaine*) responsibility, concern; (*de ruche*) (honey)comb; **dans un ~ de** within a radius of; **rayons** *nmpl* (*radiothérapie*) radiation; **~ d'action** range; **~ de braquage** (*Auto*) turning circle; **~ laser** laser beam; **~ de soleil** sunbeam, ray of sunlight *ou* sunshine; **~s X** X-rays

rayonnage [Rɛjɔnaʒ] *nm* set of shelves

rayonnant, e [Rɛjɔnɑ̃, -ɑ̃t] *adj* radiant

rayonne [Rɛjɔn] *nf* rayon

rayonnement [Rɛjɔnmɑ̃] *nm* radiation; (*fig: éclat*) radiance; (*: influence*) influence

rayonner [Rɛjɔne] *vi* (*chaleur, énergie*) to radiate; (*fig: émotion*) to shine forth; (*: visage*) to be radiant; (*avenues, axes*) to radiate; (*touriste*) to go touring (*from one base*)

rayure [RejyR] *nf* (*motif*) stripe; (*éraflure*) scratch; (*rainure, d'un fusil*) groove; **à ~s** striped

raz-de-marée [Radmare] *nm inv* tidal wave

razzia [Razja] *nf* raid, foray

RBE *sigle m* (= *revenu brut d'exploitation*) gross profit (*of a farm*)

R-D *sigle f* (= *Recherche-Développement*) R & D

RDA *sigle f* (= *République démocratique allemande*) GDR

rdc *abr* = **rez-de-chaussée**

ré [Re] *nm* (*Mus*) D; (*en chantant la gamme*) re

réabonnement [Reabɔnmɑ̃] *nm* renewal of subscription

réabonner [Reabɔne] *vt*: **~ qn à** to renew sb's subscription to; **se ~ (à)** to renew one's subscription (to)

réac [Reak] *adj, nm/f* (*fam*: = *réactionnaire*)

reactionary

réacteur [ʀeaktœʀ] *nm* jet engine; **~ nucléaire** nuclear reactor

réactif [ʀeaktif] *nm* reagent

réaction [ʀeaksjɔ̃] *nf* reaction; **par ~** jet-propelled; **avion/moteur à ~** jet (plane)/jet engine; **~ en chaîne** chain reaction

réactionnaire [ʀeaksjɔnɛʀ] *adj, nm/f* reactionary

réactualiser [ʀeaktɥalize] *vt* to update, bring up to date

réadaptation [ʀeadaptasjɔ̃] *nf* readjustment; rehabilitation

réadapter [ʀeadapte] *vt* to readjust; (*Méd*) to rehabilitate; **se ~ (à)** to readjust (to)

réaffirmer [ʀeafiʀme] *vt* to reaffirm, reassert

réagir [ʀeaʒiʀ] *vi* to react

réajuster [ʀeaʒyste] *vt* = **rajuster**

réalisable [ʀealizabl(ə)] *adj* (*projet, plan*) feasible; (*Comm: valeur*) realizable

réalisateur, -trice [ʀealizatœʀ, -tʀis] *nm/f* (TV, *Ciné*) director

réalisation [ʀealizasjɔ̃] *nf* carrying out; realization; fulfilment; achievement; production; (*œuvre*) production, work; (*création*) creation

réaliser [ʀealize] *vt* (*projet, opération*) to carry out, realize; (*rêve, souhait*) to realize, fulfil; (*exploit*) to achieve; (*achat, vente*) to make; (*film*) to produce; (*se rendre compte de, Comm: bien, capital*) to realize; **se réaliser** *vi* to be realized

réalisme [ʀealism(ə)] *nm* realism

réaliste [ʀealist(ə)] *adj* realistic; (*peintre, roman*) realist ▷ *nm/f* realist

réalité [ʀealite] *nf* reality; **en ~** in (actual) fact; **dans la ~** in reality; **~ virtuelle** virtual reality

réanimation [ʀeanimasjɔ̃] *nf* resuscitation; **service de ~** intensive care unit

réanimer [ʀeanime] *vt* (*Méd*) to resuscitate

réapparaître [ʀeapaʀɛtʀ(ə)] *vi* to reappear

réapparition [ʀeapaʀisjɔ̃] *nf* reappearance

réapprovisionner [ʀeapʀɔvizjɔne] *vt* (*magasin*) to restock; **se ~ (en)** to restock (with)

réarmement [ʀeaʀmemɑ̃] *nm* rearmament

réarmer [ʀeaʀme] *vt* (*arme*) to reload ▷ *vi* (*état*) to rearm

réassortiment [ʀeasɔʀtimɑ̃] *nm* (*Comm*) restocking

réassortir [ʀeasɔʀtiʀ] *vt* to match up

réassurance [ʀeasyʀɑ̃s] *nf* reinsurance

réassurer [ʀeasyʀe] *vt* to reinsure

rebaptiser [ʀəbatize] *vt* (*rue*) to rename

rébarbatif, -ive [ʀebaʀbatif, -iv] *adj* forbidding; (*style*) off-putting (*Brit*), crabbed

rebattre [ʀəbatʀ(ə)] *vt*: **~ les oreilles à qn de qch** to keep harping on to sb about sth

rebattu, e [ʀəbaty] *pp de* **rebattre** ▷ *adj* hackneyed

rebelle [ʀəbɛl] *nm/f* rebel ▷ *adj* (*troupes*) rebel; (*enfant*) rebellious; (*mèche etc*) unruly; **~ à qch** unamenable to sth; **~ à faire** unwilling to do

rebeller [ʀəbele]: **se rebeller** *vi* to rebel

rébellion [ʀebeljɔ̃] *nf* rebellion; (*rebelles*) rebel forces *pl*

rebiffer [ʀəbife]: **se rebiffer** *vr* to fight back

reboisement [ʀəbwazmɑ̃] *nm* reafforestation

reboiser [ʀəbwaze] *vt* to replant with trees, reafforest

rebond [ʀəbɔ̃] *nm* (*voir rebondir*) bounce; rebound

rebondi, e [ʀəbɔ̃di] *adj* (*ventre*) rounded; (*joues*) chubby, well-rounded

rebondir [ʀəbɔ̃diʀ] *vi* (*ballon: au sol*) to bounce; (*: contre un mur*) to rebound; (*fig: procès, action, conversation*) to get moving again, be suddenly revived

rebondissement [ʀəbɔ̃dismɑ̃] *nm* new development

rebord [ʀəbɔʀ] *nm* edge

reboucher [ʀəbuʃe] *vt* (*flacon*) to put the stopper (*ou* top) back on, recork; (*trou*) to stop up

rebours [ʀəbuʀ]: **à ~** *adv* the wrong way

rebouteux, -euse [ʀəbutø, -øz] *nm/f* (*péj*) bonesetter

reboutonner [ʀəbutɔne] *vt* (*vêtement*) to button up (again)

rebrousse-poil [ʀəbʀuspwal]: **à ~** *adv* the wrong way

rebrousser [ʀəbʀuse] *vt* (*cheveux, poils*) to brush back, brush up; **~ chemin** to turn back

rebuffade [ʀəbyfad] *nf* rebuff

rébus [ʀebys] *nm inv* (*jeu d'esprit*) rebus; (*fig*) puzzle

rebut [ʀəby] *nm*: **mettre au ~** to scrap, discard

rebutant, e [ʀəbytɑ̃, -ɑ̃t] *adj* (*travail, démarche*) off-putting, disagreeable

rebuter [ʀəbyte] *vt* to put off

récalcitrant, e [ʀekalsitʀɑ̃, -ɑ̃t] *adj* refractory, recalcitrant

recaler [ʀəkale] *vt* (*Scol*) to fail

récapitulatif, -ive [ʀekapitylatif, -iv] *adj* (*liste, tableau*) summary *cpd*, that sums up

récapituler [ʀekapityle] *vt* to recapitulate; (*résumer*) to sum up

recel [ʀəsɛl] *nm* receiving (stolen goods)

receler [ʀəsəle] *vt* (*produit d'un vol*) to receive; (*malfaiteur*) to harbour; (*fig*) to conceal

receleur, -euse [ʀəsəlœʀ, -øz] *nm/f* receiver

récemment [ʀesamɑ̃] *adv* recently

recensement [ʀəsɑ̃smɑ̃] *nm* census; inventory

recenser [ʀəsɑ̃se] *vt* (*population*) to take a census of; (*inventorier*) to make an inventory of; (*dénombrer*) to list

récent, e [ʀesɑ̃, -ɑ̃t] *adj* recent

récépissé [ʀesepise] *nm* receipt

réceptacle [ʀesɛptakl(ə)] *nm* (*où les choses aboutissent*) recipient; (*où les choses sont stockées*) repository; (*Bot*) receptacle

récepteur, -trice [ʀesɛptœʀ, -tʀis] *adj* receiving ▷ *nm* receiver; **~ (de radio)** radio set *ou* receiver

réceptif, -ive [ʀesɛptif, -iv] *adj*: **~ (à)** receptive (to)

réception [ʀesɛpsjɔ̃] *nf* receiving *no pl*; (*d'une marchandise, commande*) receipt; (*accueil*) reception, welcome; (*bureau*) reception (desk);

r

(*réunion mondaine*) reception, party; (*pièces*) reception rooms *pl*; (*Sport: après un saut*) landing; (*du ballon*) catching *no pl*; **jour/heures de ~** day/hours for receiving visitors (*ou* students *etc*)

réceptionner [resɛpsjɔne] *vt* (*Comm*) to take delivery of; (*Sport: ballon*) to catch (and control)

réceptionniste [resɛpsjɔnist(ə)] *nm/f* receptionist

réceptivité [resɛptivite] *nf* (*à une influence*) receptiveness; (*à une maladie*) susceptibility

récessif, -ive [resesif, -iv] *adj* (*Biol*) recessive

récession [resesjɔ̃] *nf* recession

recette [rəsɛt] *nf* (*Culin*) recipe; (*fig*) formula, recipe; (*Comm*) takings *pl*; (*Admin: bureau*) tax *ou* revenue office; **recettes** *nfpl* (*Comm: rentrées*) receipts; **faire ~** (*spectacle, exposition*) to be a winner

receveur, -euse [rəsvœr, -øz] *nm/f* (*des contributions*) tax collector; (*des postes*) postmaster/mistress; (*d'autobus*) conductor/conductress; (*Méd: de sang, organe*) recipient

recevoir [rəsvwar] *vt* to receive; (*lettre, prime*) to receive, get; (*client, patient, représentant*) to see; (*jour, soleil: pièce*) to get; (*Scol: candidat*) to pass ▷ *vi* to receive visitors; to give parties; to see patients *etc*; **se recevoir** *vi* (*athlète*) to land; **~ qn à dîner** to invite sb to dinner; **il reçoit de huit à 10** he's at home from eight to 10, he will see visitors from eight to 10; (*docteur, dentiste etc*) he sees patients from eight to 10; **être reçu** (*à un examen*) to pass; **être bien/mal reçu** to be well/badly received

rechange [rəʃɑ̃ʒ]: **de ~** *adj* (*pièces, roue*) spare; (*fig: solution*) alternative; **des vêtements de ~** a change of clothes

rechaper [rəʃape] *vt* to remould (*Brit*), remold (*US*), retread

réchapper [reʃape]: **~ de** *ou* **à** *vt* (*accident, maladie*) to come through; **va-t-il en ~?** is he going to get over it?, is he going to come through (it)?

recharge [rəʃarʒ(ə)] *nf* refill

rechargeable [rəʃarʒabl(ə)] *adj* refillable; rechargeable

recharger [rəʃarʒe] *vt* (*camion, fusil, appareil photo*) to reload; (*briquet, stylo*) to refill; (*batterie*) to recharge

réchaud [reʃo] *nm* (*portable*) stove, plate-warmer

réchauffé [reʃofe] *nm* (*nourriture*) reheated food; (*fig*) stale news (*ou* joke *etc*)

réchauffement [reʃofmɑ̃] *nm* warming (up); **le ~ de la planète** global warming

réchauffer [reʃofe] *vt* (*plat*) to reheat; (*mains, personne*) to warm; **se réchauffer** *vi* to get warmer; **se ~ les doigts** to warm (up) one's fingers

rêche [rɛʃ] *adj* rough

recherche [rəʃɛrʃ(ə)] *nf* (*action*): **la ~ de** the search for; (*raffinement*) affectedness, studied elegance; (*scientifique etc*): **la ~** research; **recherches** *nfpl* (*de la police*) investigations;

(*scientifiques*) research *sg*; **être/se mettre à la ~ de** to be/go in search of

recherché, e [rəʃɛrʃe] *adj* (*rare, demandé*) much sought-after; (*entouré: acteur, femme*) in demand; (*raffiné*) studied, affected

rechercher [rəʃɛrʃe] *vt* (*objet égaré, personne*) to look for, search for; (*témoins, coupable, main-d'œuvre*) to look for; (*causes d'un phénomène, nouveau procédé*) to try to find; (*bonheur etc, l'amitié de qn*) to seek; **"~ et remplacer"** (*Inform*) "find and replace"

rechigner [rəʃiɲe] *vi*: **~ (à)** to balk (at)

rechute [rəʃyt] *nf* (*Méd*) relapse; (*dans le péché, le vice*) lapse; **faire une ~** to have a relapse

rechuter [rəʃyte] *vi* (*Méd*) to relapse

récidive [residiv] *nf* (*Jur*) second (*ou* subsequent) offence; (*fig*) repetition; (*Méd*) recurrence

récidiver [residive] *vi* to commit a second (*ou* subsequent) offence; (*fig*) to do it again

récidiviste [residivist(ə)] *nm/f* second (*ou* habitual) offender, recidivist

récif [resif] *nm* reef

récipiendaire [resipjɑ̃dɛr] *nm* recipient (*of diploma etc*); (*d'une société*) newly elected member

récipient [resipjɑ̃] *nm* container

réciproque [resiprɔk] *adj* reciprocal ▷ *nf*: **la ~** (*l'inverse*) the converse

réciproquement [resiprɔkmɑ̃] *adv* reciprocally; **et ~** and vice versa

récit [resi] *nm* (*action de narrer*) telling; (*conte, histoire*) story

récital [resital] *nm* recital

récitant, e [resitɑ̃, -ɑ̃t] *nm/f* narrator

récitation [resitasjɔ̃] *nf* recitation

réciter [resite] *vt* to recite

réclamation [reklamasjɔ̃] *nf* complaint; **réclamations** *nfpl* (*bureau*) complaints department *sg*

réclame [reklam] *nf*: **la ~** advertising; **une ~** an ad(vertisement), an advert (*Brit*); **faire de la ~ (pour qch/qn)** to advertise (sth/sb); **article en ~** special offer

réclamer [reklame] *vt* (*aide, nourriture etc*) to ask for; (*revendiquer: dû, part, indemnité*) to claim, demand; (*nécessiter*) to demand, require ▷ *vi* to complain; **se ~ de** to give as one's authority; to claim filiation with

reclassement [rəklasmɑ̃] *nm* reclassifying; regrading; rehabilitation

reclasser [rəklase] *vt* (*fiches, dossiers*) to reclassify; (*fig: fonctionnaire etc*) to regrade; (*: ouvrier licencié*) to place, rehabilitate

reclus, e [rəkly, -yz] *nm/f* recluse

réclusion [reklyzjɔ̃] *nf* imprisonment; **~ à perpétuité** life imprisonment

recoiffer [rəkwafe] *vt*: **~ un enfant** to do a child's hair again; **se recoiffer** to do one's hair again

recoin [rəkwɛ̃] *nm* nook, corner; (*fig*) hidden recess

reçois *etc* [rəswa] *vb voir* **recevoir**

reçoive *etc* [rəswav] *vb voir* **recevoir**

recoller [Rəkɔle] vt (enveloppe) to stick back down

récolte [Rekɔlt(ə)] nf harvesting, gathering; (produits) harvest, crop; (fig) crop, collection; (: d'observations) findings

récolter [Rekɔlte] vt to harvest, gather (in); (fig) to get

recommandable [Rəkɔmɑ̃dabl(ə)] adj commendable; **peu** ~ not very commendable

recommandation [Rəkɔmɑ̃dasjɔ̃] nf recommendation

recommandé [Rəkɔmɑ̃de] nm (méthode etc) recommended; (Postes): **en** ~ by registered mail

recommander [Rəkɔmɑ̃de] vt to recommend; (qualités etc) to commend; (Postes) to register; ~ **qch à qn** to recommend sth to sb; ~ **à qn de faire** to recommend sb to do; ~ **qn auprès de qn** ou **à qn** to recommend sb to sb; **il est recommandé de faire ...** it is recommended that one does ...; **se** ~ **à qn** to commend o.s. to sb; **se** ~ **de qn** to give sb's name as a reference

recommencer [Rəkɔmɑ̃se] vt (reprendre: lutte, séance) to resume, start again; (refaire: travail, explications) to start afresh, start (over) again; (récidiver: erreur) to make again ▷ vi to start again; (récidiver) to do it again; ~ **à faire** to start doing again; **ne recommence pas!** don't do that again!

récompense [Rekɔ̃pɑ̃s] nf reward; (prix) award; **recevoir qch en** ~ to get sth as a reward, be rewarded with sth

récompenser [Rekɔ̃pɑ̃se] vt: ~ **qn (de** ou **pour)** to reward sb (for)

réconciliation [Rekɔ̃siljɑsjɔ̃] nf reconciliation

réconcilier [Rekɔ̃silje] vt to reconcile; ~ **qn avec qn** to reconcile sb with sb; ~ **qn avec qch** to reconcile sb to sth; **se réconcilier (avec)** to be reconciled (with)

reconductible [Rəkɔ̃dyktibl(ə)] adj (Jur: contrat, bail) renewable

reconduction [Rəkɔ̃dyksjɔ̃] nf renewal; (Pol: d'une politique) continuation

reconduire [Rəkɔ̃dɥir] vt (raccompagner) to take ou see back; (: à la porte) to show out; (: à son domicile) to see home, take home; (Jur, Pol: renouveler) to renew

réconfort [Rekɔ̃fɔr] nm comfort

réconfortant, e [Rekɔ̃fɔrtɑ̃, -ɑ̃t] adj (idée, paroles) comforting; (boisson) fortifying

réconforter [Rekɔ̃fɔrte] vt (consoler) to comfort; (revigorer) to fortify

reconnais etc [R(ə)kɔnɛ] vb voir **reconnaître**

reconnaissable [Rəkɔnɛsabl(ə)] adj recognizable

reconnaissance [Rəkɔnɛsɑ̃s] nf recognition; acknowledgement; (gratitude) gratitude, gratefulness; (Mil) reconnaissance, recce; **en** ~ (Mil) on reconnaissance; ~ **de dette** acknowledgement of a debt, IOU

reconnaissant, e [Rəkɔnɛsɑ̃, -ɑ̃t] vb voir **reconnaître** ▷ adj grateful; **je vous serais** ~ **de bien vouloir** I should be most grateful if you would (kindly)

reconnaître [RəkɔnɛtR(ə)] vt to recognize; (Mil: lieu) to reconnoitre; (Jur: enfant, dette, droit) to acknowledge; ~ **que** to admit ou acknowledge that; ~ **qn/qch à** (l'identifier grâce à) to recognize sb/sth by; ~ **à qn: je lui reconnais certaines qualités** I recognize certain qualities in him; **se** ~ **quelque part** (s'y retrouver) to find one's way around (a place)

reconnu, e [R(ə)kɔny] pp de **reconnaître** ▷ adj (indiscuté, connu) recognized

reconquérir [Rəkɔ̃keRiR] vt to reconquer, recapture; (sa dignité etc) to recover

reconquête [Rəkɔ̃kɛt] nf recapture; recovery

reconsidérer [Rəkɔ̃sidere] vt to reconsider

reconstituant, e [Rəkɔ̃stitɥɑ̃, -ɑ̃t] adj (régime) strength-building ▷ nm tonic, pick-me-up

reconstituer [Rəkɔ̃stitɥe] vt (monument ancien) to recreate, build a replica of; (fresque, vase brisé) to piece together, reconstitute; (événement, accident) to reconstruct; (fortune, patrimoine) to rebuild; (Bio: tissus etc) to regenerate

reconstitution [Rəkɔ̃stitysjɔ̃] nf (d'un accident etc) reconstruction

reconstruction [Rəkɔ̃stRyksjɔ̃] nf rebuilding, reconstruction

reconstruire [Rəkɔ̃stRɥiR] vt to rebuild, reconstruct

reconversion [Rəkɔ̃vɛRsjɔ̃] nf (du personnel) redeployment

reconvertir [Rəkɔ̃vɛRtiR] vt (usine) to reconvert; (personnel, troupes etc) to redeploy; **se** ~ **dans** (un métier, une branche) to move into, be redeployed into

recopier [Rəkɔpje] vt (transcrire) to copy out again, write out again; (mettre au propre: devoir) to make a clean ou fair copy of

record [Rəkɔr] nm, adj record; ~ **du monde** world record

recoucher [Rəkuʃe] vt (enfant) to put back to bed

recoudre [RəkudR(ə)] vt (bouton) to sew back on; (plaie, incision) to sew (back) up, stitch up

recoupement [Rəkupmɑ̃] nm: **faire un** ~ ou **des** ~**s** to cross-check; **par** ~ by cross-checking

recouper [Rəkupe] vt (tranche) to cut again; (vêtement) to recut ▷ vi (Cartes) to cut again; **se recouper** vi (témoignages) to tie ou match up

recourais etc [RəkuRɛ] vb voir **recourir**

recourbé, e [RəkuRbe] adj curved; hooked; bent

recourber [RəkuRbe] vt (branche, tige de métal) to bend

recourir [RəkuRiR] vi (courir de nouveau) to run again; (refaire une course) to race again; ~ **à** vt (ami, agence) to turn ou appeal to; (force, ruse, emprunt) to resort to, have recourse to

recours [RəkuR] vb voir **recourir** ▷ nm (Jur) appeal; **avoir** ~ **à**; = **recourir à**; **dernier** ~ as a last resort; **sans** ~ final; with no way out; ~ **en grâce** plea for clemency (ou pardon)

recouru, e [RəkuRy] pp de **recourir**

recousu, e [Rəkuzy] pp de **recoudre**

recouvert, e [RəkuvɛR, -ɛRt(ə)] pp de **recouvrir**

recouvrable [RəkuvRabl(ə)] adj (somme)

r

recoverable

recouvrais etc [ʀəkuvʀɛ] vb voir **recouvrer**; **recouvrir**

recouvrement [ʀəkuvʀəmɑ̃] nm recovery

recouvrer [ʀəkuvʀe] vt (vue, santé etc) to recover, regain; (impôts) to collect; (créance) to recover

recouvrir [ʀəkuvʀiʀ] vt (couvrir à nouveau) to re-cover; (couvrir entièrement: aussi fig) to cover; (cacher, masquer) to conceal, hide; **se recouvrir** (se superposer) to overlap

recracher [ʀəkʀaʃe] vt to spit out

récréatif, -ive [ʀekʀeatif, -iv] adj of entertainment; recreational

récréation [ʀekʀeasjɔ̃] nf recreation, entertainment; (Scol) break

recréer [ʀəkʀee] vt to recreate

récrier [ʀekʀije]: **se récrier** vi to exclaim

récriminations [ʀekʀiminasjɔ̃] nfpl remonstrations, complaints

récriminer [ʀekʀimine] vi: ~ **contre qn/qch** to remonstrate against sb/sth

recroqueviller [ʀəkʀɔkvije]: **se recroqueviller** vi (feuilles) to curl ou shrivel up; (personne) to huddle up

recru, e [ʀəkʀy] adj: ~ **de fatigue** exhausted ▷ nf recruit

recrudescence [ʀəkʀydesɑ̃s] nf fresh outbreak

recrutement [ʀəkʀytmɑ̃] nm recruiting, recruitment

recruter [ʀəkʀyte] vt to recruit

rectal, e, -aux [ʀɛktal, -o] adj: **par voie ~e** rectally

rectangle [ʀɛktɑ̃gl(ə)] nm rectangle

rectangulaire [ʀɛktɑ̃gylɛʀ] adj rectangular

recteur [ʀɛktœʀ] nm ≈ (regional) director of education (Brit), ≈ state superintendent of education (US)

rectificatif, -ive [ʀɛktifikatif, -iv] adj corrected ▷ nm correction

rectification [ʀɛktifikasjɔ̃] nf correction

rectifier [ʀɛktifje] vt (tracé, virage) to straighten; (calcul, adresse) to correct; (erreur, faute) to rectify, put right

rectiligne [ʀɛktiliɲ] adj straight; (Géom) rectilinear

rectitude [ʀɛktityd] nf rectitude, uprightness

recto [ʀɛkto] nm front (of a sheet of paper)

rectorat [ʀɛktɔʀa] nm (fonction) position of recteur; (bureau) recteur's office; voir aussi **recteur**

rectum [ʀɛktɔm] nm rectum

reçu, e [ʀəsy] pp de **recevoir** ▷ adj (admis, consacré) accepted ▷ nm (Comm) receipt

recueil [ʀəkœj] nm collection

recueillement [ʀəkœjmɑ̃] nm meditation, contemplation

recueilli, e [ʀəkœji] adj contemplative

recueillir [ʀəkœjiʀ] vt to collect; (voix, suffrages) to win; (accueillir: réfugiés, chat) to take in; **se recueillir** vi to gather one's thoughts; to meditate

recuire [ʀəkɥiʀ] vi: **faire ~** to recook

recul [ʀəkyl] nm retreat; recession; decline;

(d'arme à feu) recoil, kick; **avoir un mouvement de** ~ to recoil, start back; **prendre du** ~ to stand back; **avec le** ~ with the passing of time, in retrospect

reculade [ʀəkylad] nf (péj) climb-down

reculé, e [ʀəkyle] adj remote

reculer [ʀəkyle] vi to move back, back away; (Auto) to reverse, back (up); (fig: civilisation, épidémie) to (be on the) decline; (: se dérober) to shrink back ▷ vt to move back; to reverse, back (up); (fig: possibilités, limites) to extend; (: date, décision) to postpone; ~ **devant** (danger, difficulté) to shrink from; ~ **pour mieux sauter** (fig) to postpone the evil day

reculons [ʀəkylɔ̃]: **à** ~ adv backwards

récupérable [ʀekypeʀabl(ə)] adj (créance) recoverable; (heures) which can be made up; (ferraille) salvageable

récupération [ʀekypeʀasjɔ̃] nf (de métaux etc) salvage, reprocessing; (Pol) bringing into line

récupérer [ʀekypeʀe] vt (rentrer en possession de) to recover, get back; (: forces) to recover; (déchets etc) to salvage (for reprocessing); (remplacer: journée, heures de travail) to make up; (délinquant etc) to rehabilitate; (Pol) to bring into line ▷ vi to recover

récurer [ʀekyʀe] vt to scour; **poudre à** ~ scouring powder

reçus etc [ʀəsy] vb voir **recevoir**

récusable [ʀekyzabl(ə)] adj (témoin) challengeable; (témoignage) impugnable

récuser [ʀekyze] vt to challenge; **se récuser** to decline to give an opinion

recyclage [ʀəsiklaʒ] nm reorientation; retraining; recycling; **cours de** ~ retraining course

recycler [ʀəsikle] vt (Scol) to reorientate; (employés) to retrain; (matériau) to recycle; **se recycler** to retrain; to go on a retraining course

rédacteur, -trice [ʀedaktœʀ, -tʀis] nm/f (journaliste) writer; subeditor; (d'ouvrage de référence) editor, compiler; ~ **en chef** chief editor; ~ **publicitaire** copywriter

rédaction [ʀedaksjɔ̃] nf writing; (rédacteurs) editorial staff; (bureau) editorial office(s); (Scol: devoir) essay, composition

reddition [ʀedisjɔ̃] nf surrender

redéfinir [ʀədefiniʀ] vt to redefine

redemander [ʀədmɑ̃de] vt (renseignement) to ask again for; (nourriture): ~ **de** to ask for more (ou another); (objet prêté): ~ **qch** to ask for sth back

redémarrer [ʀədemaʀe] vi (véhicule) to start again, get going again; (fig: industrie etc) to get going again

rédemption [ʀedɑ̃psjɔ̃] nf redemption

redéploiement [ʀədeplwamɑ̃] nm redeployment

redescendre [ʀədesɑ̃dʀ(ə)] vi (à nouveau) to go back down; (après la montée) to go down (again) ▷ vt (pente etc) to go down

redevable [ʀədvabl(ə)] adj: **être** ~ **de qch à qn** (somme) to owe sb sth; (fig) to be indebted to sb for sth

redevance [ʀədvɑ̃s] *nf* (*Tél*) rental charge; (*TV*) licence (*Brit*) *ou* license (*US*) fee

redevenir [ʀədvəniʀ] *vi* to become again

rédhibitoire [ʀedibitwaʀ] *adj*: **vice ~** (*Jur*) latent defect in merchandise that renders the sales contract void; (*fig*: *défaut*) crippling

rediffuser [ʀədifyze] *vt* (*Radio, TV*) to repeat, broadcast again

rediffusion [ʀədifyzjɔ̃] *nf* repeat (programme)

rédiger [ʀediʒe] *vt* to write; (*contrat*) to draw up

redire [ʀədiʀ] *vt* to repeat; **trouver à ~ à** to find fault with

redistribuer [ʀədistʀibɥe] *vt* (*cartes etc*) to deal again; (*richesses, tâches, revenus*) to redistribute

redite [ʀədit] *nf* (needless) repetition

redondance [ʀədɔ̃dɑ̃s] *nf* redundancy

redonner [ʀədɔne] *vt* (*restituer*) to give back, return; (*du courage, des forces*) to restore

redoublé, e [ʀəduble] *adj*: **à coups ~s** even harder, twice as hard

redoubler [ʀəduble] *vi* (*tempête, violence*) to intensify, get even stronger *ou* fiercer *etc*; (*Scol*) to repeat a year ▷ *vt* (*Scol: classe*) to repeat; (*Ling: lettre*) to double; **le vent redouble de violence** the wind is blowing twice as hard

redoutable [ʀədutabl(ə)] *adj* formidable, fearsome

redouter [ʀədute] *vt* to fear; (*appréhender*) to dread; **~ de faire** to dread doing

redoux [ʀədu] *nm* milder spell

redressement [ʀədʀɛsmɑ̃] *nm* (*de l'économie etc*) putting right; **maison de ~** reformatory; **~ fiscal** repayment of back taxes

redresser [ʀədʀese] *vt* (*arbre, mât*) to set upright, right; (*pièce tordue*) to straighten out; (*Aviat, Auto*) to straighten up; (*situation, économie*) to put right; **se redresser** *vi* (*objet penché*) to right itself; to straighten up; (*personne*) to sit (*ou* stand) up; to sit (*ou* stand) up straight; (*fig: pays, situation*) to recover; **~ (les roues)** (*Auto*) to straighten up

redresseur [ʀədʀesœʀ] *nm*: **~ de torts** righter of wrongs

réducteur, -trice [ʀedyktœʀ, -tʀis] *adj* simplistic

réduction [ʀedyksjɔ̃] *nf* reduction; **en ~** *adv* in miniature, scaled-down

réduire [ʀedɥiʀ] *vt* (*gén, Culin, Math*) to reduce; (*prix, dépenses*) to cut, reduce; (*carte*) to scale down, reduce; (*Méd: fracture*) to set; **~ qn/qch à** to reduce sb/sth to; **se ~ à** (*revenir à*) to boil down to; **se ~ en** (*se transformer en*) to be reduced to; **en être réduit à** to be reduced to

réduit, e [ʀedɥi, -it] *pp de* **réduire** ▷ *adj* (*prix, tarif, échelle*) reduced; (*mécanisme*) scaled-down; (*vitesse*) reduced ▷ *nm* tiny room; recess

rééditer [ʀeedite] *vt* to republish

réédition [ʀeedisjɔ̃] *nf* new edition

rééducation [ʀeedykasjɔ̃] *nf* (*d'un membre*) re-education; (*de délinquants, d'un blessé*) rehabilitation; **~ de la parole** speech therapy;

centre de ~ physiotherapy *ou* physical therapy (*US*) centre

rééduquer [ʀeedyke] *vt* to reeducate; to rehabilitate

réel, le [ʀeel] *adj* real ▷ *nm*: **le ~** reality

réélection [ʀeelɛksjɔ̃] *nf* re-election

rééligible [ʀeeliʒibl(ə)] *adj* re-eligible

réélire [ʀeeliʀ] *vt* to re-elect

réellement [ʀeelmɑ̃] *adv* really

réembaucher [ʀeɑ̃boʃe] *vt* to take on again

réemploi [ʀeɑ̃plwa] *nm* = **remploi**

réemployer [ʀeɑ̃plwaje] *vt* (*méthode, produit*) to re-use; (*argent*) to reinvest; (*personnel, employé*) to re-employ

rééquilibrer [ʀeekilibʀe] *vt* (*budget*) to balance (again)

réescompte [ʀeeskɔ̃t] *nm* rediscount

réessayer [ʀeeseje] *vt* to try on again

réévaluation [ʀeevalɥasjɔ̃] *nf* revaluation

réévaluer [ʀeevalɥe] *vt* to revalue

réexaminer [ʀeegzamine] *vt* to re-examine

réexpédier [ʀeekspedje] *vt* (*à l'envoyeur*) to return, send back; (*au destinataire*) to send on, forward

réexporter [ʀeekspɔʀte] *vt* to re-export

réf. *abr* = **référence(s)**; **V/~.** Your ref

refaire [ʀəfɛʀ] *vt* (*faire de nouveau, recommencer*) to do again; (*réparer, restaurer*) to do up; **se refaire** *vi* (*en argent*) to make up one's losses; **se ~ une santé** to recuperate; **se ~ à qch** (*se réhabituer à*) to get used to sth again

refasse *etc* [ʀəfas] *vb voir* **refaire**

réfection [ʀefɛksjɔ̃] *nf* repair; **en ~** under repair

réfectoire [ʀefɛktwaʀ] *nm* refectory

referai *etc* [ʀ(ə)fʀe] *vb voir* **refaire**

référé [ʀefeʀe] *nm* (*Jur*) emergency interim proceedings *ou* ruling

référence [ʀefeʀɑ̃s] *nf* reference; **références** *nfpl* (*recommandations*) reference *sg*; **faire ~ à** to refer to; **ouvrage de ~** reference work; **ce n'est pas une ~** (*fig*) that's no recommendation

référendum [ʀefeʀɑ̃dɔm] *nm* referendum

référer [ʀefeʀe]: **se ~ à** *vt* to refer to; **en ~ à qn** to refer the matter to sb

refermer [ʀəfɛʀme] *vt* to close again, shut again

refiler [ʀəfile] *vt* (*fam*): **~ qch à qn** to palm (*Brit*) *ou* fob sth off on sb; to pass sth on to sb

refit *etc* [ʀəfi] *vb voir* **refaire**

réfléchi, e [ʀefleʃi] *adj* (*caractère*) thoughtful; (*action*) well-thought-out; (*Ling*) reflexive

réfléchir [ʀefleʃiʀ] *vt* to reflect ▷ *vi* to think; **~ à** *ou* **sur** to think about; **c'est tout réfléchi** my mind's made up

réflecteur [ʀeflektœʀ] *nm* (*Auto*) reflector

reflet [ʀəflɛ] *nm* reflection; (*sur l'eau etc*) sheen *no pl*, glint; **reflets** *nmpl* gleam *sg*

refléter [ʀəflete] *vt* to reflect; **se refléter** *vi* to be reflected

réflex [ʀeflɛks] *adj inv* (*Photo*) reflex

réflexe [ʀeflɛks(ə)] *adj, nm* reflex; **~ conditionné** conditioned reflex

r

réflexion [Reflɛksjɔ̃] nf (de la lumière etc, pensée) reflection; (fait de penser) thought; (remarque) remark; **réflexions** nfpl (méditations) thought sg, reflection sg; **sans ~** without thinking; **~ faite, à la ~** après réflexion, on reflection; **délai de ~** cooling-off period; **groupe de ~** think tank

réflexologie [Reflɛksɔlɔʒi] nf reflexology

refluer [Rəflye] vi to flow back; (foule) to surge back

reflux [Rəfly] nm (de la mer) ebb; (fig) backward surge

refondre [Rəfɔ̃dR(ə)] vt (texte) to recast

refont [R(ə)fɔ̃] vb voir **refaire**

reformater [Rəfɔrmate] vt to reformat

réformateur, -trice [Refɔrmatœr, -tris] nm/f reformer ▷ adj (mesures) reforming

Réformation [Refɔrmasjɔ̃] nf: **la ~** the Reformation

réforme [Refɔrm(ə)] nf reform; (Mil) declaration of unfitness for service; discharge (on health grounds); (Rel): **la R~** the Reformation

réformé, e [Refɔrme] adj, nm/f (Rel) Protestant

reformer [Rəfɔrme] vt, **se reformer** vi to reform; **~ les rangs** (Mil) to fall in again

réformer [Refɔrme] vt to reform; (Mil: recrue) to declare unfit for service; (: soldat) to discharge, invalid out; (matériel) to scrap

réformisme [Refɔrmism(ə)] nm reformism, policy of reform

réformiste [Refɔrmist(ə)] adj, nm/f (Pol) reformist

refoulé, e [Rəfule] adj (Psych) repressed

refoulement [Rəfulmɑ̃] nm (d'une armée) driving back; (Psych) repression

refouler [Rəfule] vt (envahisseurs) to drive back, repulse; (liquide) to force back; (fig) to suppress; (Psych) to repress

réfractaire [Refrakter] adj (minerai) refractory; (brique) fire cpd; (maladie) which is resistant to treatment; (prêtre) non-juring; **soldat ~** draft evader; **être ~ à** to resist

réfracter [Refrakte] vt to refract

réfraction [Refraksjɔ̃] nf refraction

refrain [Rəfrɛ̃] nm (Mus) refrain, chorus; (air, fig) tune

refréner, réfréner [Rəfrene, Refrene] vt to curb, check

réfrigérant, e [Refriʒerɑ̃, -ɑ̃t] adj refrigerant, cooling

réfrigérateur [Refriʒeratœr] nm refrigerator; **~-congélateur** fridge-freezer

réfrigération [Refriʒerasjɔ̃] nf refrigeration

réfrigéré, e [Refriʒere] adj (camion, wagon) refrigerated

réfrigérer [Refriʒere] vt to refrigerate; (fam: glacer: aussi fig) to cool

refroidir [Rəfrwadir] vt to cool; (fig) to have a cooling effect on ▷ vi to cool (down); **se refroidir** vi (prendre froid) to catch a chill; (temps) to get cooler ou colder; (fig) to cool (off)

refroidissement [Rəfrwadismɑ̃] nm cooling; (grippe etc) chill

refuge [Rəfyʒ] nm refuge; (pour piétons) (traffic) island; **demander ~ à qn** to ask sb for refuge

réfugié, e [Refyʒje] adj, nm/f refugee

réfugier [Refyʒje]: **se réfugier** vi to take refuge

refus [Rəfy] nm refusal; **ce n'est pas de ~** I won't say no, it's very welcome

refuser [Rəfyze] vt to refuse; (Scol: candidat) to fail ▷ vi to refuse; **~ qch à qn/de faire** to refuse sb sth/to do; **~ du monde** to have to turn people away; **se ~ à qch** ou **à faire qch** to refuse to do sth; **il ne se refuse rien** he doesn't stint himself; **se ~ à qn** to refuse sb

réfutable [Refytabl(ə)] adj refutable

réfuter [Refyte] vt to refute

regagner [Rəgaɲe] vt (argent, faveur) to win back; (lieu) to get back to; **~ le temps perdu** to make up for lost time; **~ du terrain** to regain ground

regain [Rəgɛ̃] nm (herbe) second crop of hay; (renouveau): **~ de qch** renewed sth

régal [Regal] nm treat; **un ~ pour les yeux** a pleasure ou delight to look at

régalade [Regalad] adv: **à la ~** from the bottle (held away from the lips)

régaler [Regale] vt: **~ qn** to treat sb to a delicious meal; **~ qn de** to treat sb to; **se régaler** vi to have a delicious meal; (fig) to enjoy o.s

regard [Rəgar] nm (coup d'œil) look, glance; (expression) look (in one's eye); **parcourir/menacer du ~** to cast an eye over/look threateningly at; **au ~ de** (loi, morale) from the point of view of; **en ~** (vis à vis) opposite; **en ~ de** in comparison with

regardant, e [Rəgardɑ̃, -ɑ̃t] adj: **très/peu ~ (sur)** quite fussy/very free (about); (économe) very tight-fisted/quite generous (with)

regarder [Rəgarde] vt (examiner, observer, lire) to look at; (film, télévision, match) to watch; (envisager: situation, avenir) to view; (considérer: son intérêt etc) to be concerned with; (être orienté vers): **~ (vers)** to face; (concerner) to concern ▷ vi to look; **~ à** vt (dépense, qualité, détails) to be fussy with ou over; **~ à faire** to hesitate to do; **dépenser sans ~** to spend freely; **~ qn/qch comme** to regard sb/sth as; **~ (qch) dans le dictionnaire** to look (sth up) in the dictionary; **~ par la fenêtre** to look out of the window; **cela me regarde** it concerns me, it's my business

régate [Regat], **régates** nf(pl) regatta

régénérer [Reʒenere] vt to regenerate; (fig) to revive

régent [Reʒɑ̃] nm regent

régenter [Reʒɑ̃te] vt to rule over; to dictate to

régie [Reʒi] nf (Comm, Industrie) state-owned company; (Théât, Ciné) production; (Radio, TV) control room; **la ~ de l'État** state control

regimber [Rəʒɛ̃be] vi to balk, jib

régime [Reʒim] nm (Pol Géo) régime; (Admin: carcéral, fiscal etc) system; (Méd) diet; (Tech) (engine) speed; (fig) rate, pace; (de bananes, dattes) bunch; **se mettre au/suivre un ~** to go on/be on a diet; **~ sans sel** salt-free diet; **à bas/**

haut ~ (*Auto*) at low/high revs; **à plein ~** flat out, at full speed; **~ matrimonial** marriage settlement

régiment [Reʒimɑ̃] *nm* (*Mil: unité*) regiment; (*fig: fam*): **un ~ de** an army of; **un copain de ~** a pal from military service *ou* (one's) army days

région [Reʒjɔ̃] *nf* region; **la ~ parisienne** the Paris area

régional, e, -aux [Reʒjɔnal, -o] *adj* regional

régionalisation [Reʒjɔnalizasjɔ̃] *nf* regionalization

régionalisme [Reʒjɔnalism(ə)] *nm* regionalism

régir [ReʒiR] *vt* to govern

régisseur [ReʒisœR] *nm* (*d'un domaine*) steward; (*Ciné, TV*) assistant director; (*Théât*) stage manager

registre [RəʒistR(ə)] *nm* (*livre*) register; logbook; ledger; (*Mus, Ling*) register; (*d'orgue*) stop; **~ de comptabilité** ledger; **~ de l'état civil** register of births, marriages and deaths

réglable [Reglabl(ə)] *adj* (*siège, flamme etc*) adjustable; (*achat*) payable

réglage [Reglaʒ] *nm* (*d'une machine*) adjustment; (*d'un moteur*) tuning

réglé, e [Regle] *adj* well-ordered; stable, steady; (*papier*) ruled; (*arrangé*) settled

règle [Regl(ə)] *nf* (*instrument*) ruler; (*loi, prescription*) rule; **règles** *nfpl* (*Physiol*) period *sg*; **avoir pour ~ de** to make it a rule that *ou* to; **en ~** (*papiers d'identité*) in order; **être/se mettre en ~** to be/put o.s. straight with the authorities; **en ~ générale** as a (general) rule; **être la ~** to be the rule; **être de ~** to be usual; **~ à calcul** slide rule; **~ de trois** (*Math*) rule of three

règlement [Reglǝmɑ̃] *nm* settling; (*paiement*) settlement; (*arrêté*) regulation; (*règles, statuts*) regulations *pl*, rules *pl*; **~ à la commande** cash with order; **~ de compte(s)** settling of scores; **~ en espèces/par chèque** payment in cash/by cheque; **~ intérieur** (*Scol*) school rules *pl*; (*Admin*) by-laws *pl*; **~ judiciaire** compulsory liquidation

réglementaire [Reglǝmɑ̃tɛR] *adj* conforming to the regulations; (*tenue, uniforme*) regulation *cpd*

réglementation [Reglǝmɑ̃tasjɔ̃] *nf* regulation, control; (*règlements*) regulations *pl*

réglementer [Reglǝmɑ̃te] *vt* to regulate, control

régler [Regle] *vt* (*mécanisme, machine*) to regulate, adjust; (*moteur*) to tune; (*thermostat etc*) to set, adjust; (*emploi du temps etc*) to organize, plan; (*question, conflit, facture, dette*) to settle; (*fournisseur*) to settle up with, pay; (*papier*) to rule; **~ qch sur** to model sth on; **~ son compte** to sort sb out, settle sb; **~ un compte** to settle a score with sb

réglisse [Reglis] *nf ou m* liquorice; **bâton de ~** liquorice stick

règne [Rɛɲ] *nm* (*d'un roi etc, fig*) reign; (*Bio*): **le ~ végétal/animal** the vegetable/animal kingdom

régner [Reɲe] *vi* (*roi*) to rule, reign; (*fig*) to reign

regonfler [R(ə)gɔ̃fle] *vt* (*ballon, pneu*) to reinflate, blow up again

regorger [RəgɔRʒe] *vi* to overflow; **~ de** to overflow with, be bursting with

régresser [Regrese] *vi* (*phénomène*) to decline; (*enfant, malade*) to regress

régressif, -ive [Regresif, -iv] *adj* regressive

régression [Regresjɔ̃] *nf* decline; regression; **être en ~** to be on the decline

regret [RəgrɛR] *nm* regret; **à ~** with regret; **avec ~** regretfully; **être au ~ de devoir/ne pas pouvoir faire** to regret to have to/that one is unable to do; **j'ai le ~ de vous informer que …** I regret to inform you that …

regrettable [Rəgrɛtabl(ə)] *adj* regrettable

regretter [Rəgrɛte] *vt* to regret; (*personne*) to miss; **~ d'avoir fait** to regret doing; **~ que** to regret that, be sorry that; **non, je regrette** no, I'm sorry

regroupement [R(ə)grupmɑ̃] *nm* grouping together; (*groupe*) group

regrouper [Rəgrupe] *vt* (*grouper*) to group together; (*contenir*) to include, comprise; **se regrouper** *vi* to gather (together)

régularisation [Regylarizasjɔ̃] *nf* (*de papiers, passeport*) putting in order; (*de sa situation: par le mariage*) regularization; (*d'un mécanisme*) regulation

régulariser [Regylarize] *vt* (*fonctionnement, trafic*) to regulate; (*passeport, papiers*) to put in order; (*sa situation*) to straighten out, regularize

régularité [Regylarite] *nf* regularity

régulateur, -trice [Regylatœr, -tris] *adj* regulating ▷ *nm* (*Tech*): **~ de vitesse/de température** speed/temperature regulator

régulation [Regylasjɔ̃] *nf* (*du trafic*) regulation; **~ des naissances** birth control

régulier, -ière [Regylje, -jɛR] *adj* (*gén*) regular; (*vitesse, qualité*) steady; (*répartition, pression*) even; (*Transports: ligne, service*) scheduled, regular; (*légal, réglementaire*) lawful, in order; (*fam: correct*) straight, on the level

régulièrement [RegyljɛRmɑ̃] *adv* regularly; steadily; evenly; normally

régurgiter [Regyrʒite] *vt* to regurgitate

réhabiliter [Reabilite] *vt* to rehabilitate; (*fig*) to restore to favour (*Brit*) *ou* favor (*US*)

réhabituer [Reabitɥe] *vt*: **se ~ à qch/à faire qch** to get used to sth again/to doing sth again

rehausser [Rəose] *vt* to heighten, raise; (*fig*) to set off, enhance

réimporter [Reɛ̃pɔrte] *vt* to reimport

réimposer [Reɛ̃poze] *vt* (*Finance*) to reimpose; to tax again

réimpression [Reɛ̃presjɔ̃] *nf* reprinting; (*ouvrage*) reprint

réimprimer [Reɛ̃prime] *vt* to reprint

Reims [Rɛ̃s] *n* Rheims

rein [Rɛ̃] *nm* kidney; **reins** *nmpl* (*dos*) back *sg*; **avoir mal aux ~s** to have backache; **~ artificiel** kidney machine

réincarnation [Reɛ̃karnasjɔ̃] *nf* reincarnation

réincarner [Reɛ̃karne]: **se réincarner** *vr* to be reincarnated

reine [ʀɛn] *nf* queen

reine-claude [ʀɛnklod] *nf* greengage

reinette [ʀɛnɛt] *nf* rennet, pippin

réinitialisation [ʀeinisjalizasjɔ̃] *nf* (*Inform*) reset

réinscriptible [ʀeɛ̃skʀiptibl] *adj* (CD, DVD) rewritable

réinsérer [ʀeɛ̃seʀe] *vt* (*délinquant, handicapé etc*) to rehabilitate

réinsertion [ʀeɛ̃sɛʀsjɔ̃] *nf* rehabilitation

réintégrer [ʀeɛ̃tegʀe] *vt* (*lieu*) to return to; (*fonctionnaire*) to reinstate

réitérer [ʀeiteʀe] *vt* to repeat, reiterate

rejaillir [ʀəʒajiʀ] *vi* to splash up; ~ **sur** to splash up onto; (*fig*) to rebound on; to fall upon

rejet [ʀəʒɛ] *nm* (*action, aussi Méd*) rejection; (*Poésie*) enjambement, rejet; (*Bot*) shoot

rejeter [ʀəʒte] *vt* (*relancer*) to throw back; (*vomir*) to bring *ou* throw up; (*écarter*) to reject; (*déverser*) to throw out, discharge; (*reporter*): ~ **un mot à la fin d'une phrase** to transpose a word to the end of a sentence; **se ~ sur qch** (*accepter faute de mieux*) to fall back on sth; ~ **la tête/les épaules en arrière** to throw one's head/pull one's shoulders back; ~ **la responsabilité de qch sur qn** to lay the responsibility for sth at sb's door

rejeton [ʀəʒtɔ̃] *nm* offspring

rejette *etc* [ʀ(ə)ʒɛt] *vb voir* **rejeter**

rejoignais *etc* [ʀ(ə)ʒwaɲɛ] *vb voir* **rejoindre**

rejoindre [ʀəʒwɛ̃dʀ(ə)] *vt* (*famille, régiment*) to rejoin, return to; (*lieu*) to get (back) to; (*route etc*) to meet, join; (*rattraper*) to catch up (with); **se rejoindre** *vi* to meet; **je te rejoins au café** I'll see *ou* meet you at the café

réjoui, e [ʀeʒwi] *adj* joyous

réjouir [ʀeʒwiʀ] *vt* to delight; **se réjouir** *vi* to be delighted; **se ~ de qch/de faire** to be delighted about sth/to do; **se ~ que** to be delighted that

réjouissances [ʀeʒwisɑ̃s] *nfpl* (*joie*) rejoicing *sg*; (*fête*) festivities, merry-making *sg*

réjouissant, e [ʀeʒwisɑ̃, -ɑ̃t] *adj* heartening, delightful

relâche [ʀəlɑʃ]: **faire ~** *vi* (*navire*) to put into port; (*Ciné*) to be closed; **c'est le jour de ~** (*Ciné*) it's closed today; **sans ~** *adv* without respite *ou* a break

relâché, e [ʀəlɑʃe] *adj* loose, lax

relâchement [ʀəlɑʃmɑ̃] *nm* (*d'un prisonnier*) release; (*de la discipline, musculaire*) relaxation

relâcher [ʀəlɑʃe] *vt* (*ressort, prisonnier*) to release; (*étreinte, cordes*) to loosen; (*discipline*) to relax ▷ *vi* (*Navig*) to put into port; **se relâcher** *vi* to loosen; (*discipline*) to become slack *ou* lax; (*élève etc*) to slacken off

relais [ʀəlɛ] *nm* (*Sport*): (**course de**) ~ relay (race); (*Radio, TV*) relay; (*intermédiaire*) go-between; **équipe de** ~ shift team; (*Sport*) relay team; **prendre le** ~ (**de**) to take over (from); ~ **de poste** post house, coaching inn; ~ **routier** ≈ transport café (*Brit*), ≈ truck stop (US)

relance [ʀəlɑ̃s] *nf* boosting, revival; (*Écon*)

reflation

relancer [ʀəlɑ̃se] *vt* (*balle*) to throw back (again); (*moteur*) to restart; (*fig*) to boost, revive; (*personne*): ~ **qn** to pester sb; to get on to sb again

relater [ʀəlate] *vt* to relate, recount

relatif, -ive [ʀəlatif, -iv] *adj* relative

relation [ʀəlasjɔ̃] *nf* (*récit*) account, report; (*rapport*) relation(ship); **relations** *nfpl* (*rapports*) relations; relationship; (*connaissances*) connections; **être/entrer en ~(s) avec** to be in contact *ou* be dealing/get in contact with; **mettre qn en ~(s) avec** to put sb in touch with; ~**s internationales** international relations; ~**s publiques** public relations; ~**s (sexuelles)** sexual relations, (sexual) intercourse *sg*

relativement [ʀəlativmɑ̃] *adv* relatively; ~ **à** in relation to

relativiser [ʀəlativize] *vt* to see in relation to; to put into context

relativité [ʀəlativite] *nf* relativity

relax [ʀəlaks] *adj inv*, **relaxe** [ʀəlaks(ə)] ▷ *adj* relaxed, informal, casual; easy-going; (**fauteuil-**)~ *nm* reclining chair

relaxant, e [ʀəlaksɑ̃, -ɑ̃t] *adj* (*cure, médicament*) relaxant; (*ambiance*) relaxing

relaxation [ʀ(ə)laksasjɔ̃] *nf* relaxation

relaxer [ʀəlakse] *vt* to relax; (*Jur*) to discharge; **se relaxer** *vi* to relax

relayer [ʀəleje] *vt* (*collaborateur, coureur etc*) to relieve, take over from; (*Radio, TV*) to relay; **relayer** (*dans une activité*) to take it in turns

relecture [ʀ(ə)lɛktyʀ] *nf* rereading

relégation [ʀəlegasjɔ̃] *nf* (*Sport*) relegation

reléguer [ʀəlege] *vt* to relegate; ~ **au second plan** to push into the background

relent [ʀəlɑ̃], **relents** *nm(pl)* stench *sg*

relevé, e [ʀəlve] *adj* (*bord de chapeau*) turned-up; (*manches*) rolled-up; (*fig: style*) elevated; (: *sauce*) highly-seasoned ▷ *nm* (*lecture*) reading; (*de cotes*) plotting; (*liste*) statement; list; (*facture*) account; ~ **de compte** bank statement; ~ **d'identité bancaire** (**RIB**) (bank) account number

relève [ʀəlɛv] *nf* relief; (*équipe*) relief team (*ou* troops *pl*); **prendre la** ~ to take over

relèvement [ʀəlɛvmɑ̃] *nm* (*d'un taux, niveau*) raising

relever [ʀəlve] *vt* (*statue, meuble*) to stand up again; (*personne tombée*) to help up; (*vitre, plafond, niveau de vie*) to raise; (*pays, économie, entreprise*) to put back on its feet; (*col*) to turn up; (*style, conversation*) to elevate; (*plat, sauce*) to season; (*sentinelle, équipe*) to relieve; (*souligner: fautes, points*) to pick out; (*constater: traces etc*) to find, pick up; (*répliquer à: remarque*) to react to, reply to; (: *défi*) to accept, take up; (*noter: adresse etc*) to take down, note; (: *plan*) to sketch; (: *cotes etc*) to plot; (*compteur*) to read; (*ramasser: cahiers, copies*) to collect, take in ▷ *vi* (*jupe, bord*) to ride up; ~ **de** *vt* (*maladie*) to be recovering from; (*être du ressort de*) to be a matter for; (*Admin: dépendre de*) to come under; (*fig*) to pertain to; **se relever** *vi* (*se* remettre debout) to get up; (fig): **se ~ (de)** to recover (from); **~ qn de** (vœux) to release sb from; (fonctions) to relieve sb of; **~ la tête** to look up; to hold up one's head

relief [Rəljɛf] nm relief; (de pneu) tread pattern; **reliefs** nmpl (restes) remains; **en ~** in relief; (photographie) three-dimensional; **mettre en ~** (fig) to bring out, highlight

relier [Rəlje] vt to link up; (livre) to bind; **~ qch à** to link sth to; **livre relié cuir** leather-bound book

relieur, -euse [RəljœR, -øz] nm/f (book)binder

religieusement [R(ə)liʒjøzmɑ̃] adv religiously; (enterré, mariés) in church; **vivre ~** to lead a religious life

religieux, -euse [Rəliʒjø, -øz] adj religious ▷ nm monk ▷ nf nun; (gâteau) cream bun

religion [Rəliʒjɔ̃] nf religion; (piété, dévotion) faith; **entrer en ~** to take one's vows

reliquaire [RəlikɛR] nm reliquary

reliquat [Rəlika] nm (d'une somme) balance; (Jur: de succession) residue

relique [Rəlik] nf relic

relire [RəliR] vt (à nouveau) to reread, read again; (vérifier) to read over; **se relire** to read through what one has written

reliure [RəljyR] nf binding; (art, métier): **la ~** book-binding

reloger [R(ə)lɔʒe] vt (locataires, sinistrés) to rehouse

relooker [Rəluke] vt: ~ qn to give sb a makeover

relu, e [Rəly] pp de **relire**

reluire [RəlɥiR] vi to gleam

reluisant, e [Rəlɥizɑ̃, -ɑ̃t] vb voir **reluire** ▷ adj gleaming; **peu ~** (fig) unattractive; unsavoury (Brit), unsavory (US)

reluquer [R(ə)lyke] vt (fam) to eye (up), ogle

remâcher [Rəmɑʃe] vt to chew or ruminate over

remailler [Rəmaje] vt (tricot) to darn; (filet) to mend

remaniement [Rəmanimɑ̃] nm: **~ ministériel** Cabinet reshuffle

remanier [Rəmanje] vt to reshape, recast; (Pol) to reshuffle

remarier [R(ə)maRje]: **se remarier** vi to remarry, get married again

remarquable [Rəmarkabl(ə)] adj remarkable

remarquablement [R(ə)markabləmɑ̃] adv remarkably

remarque [Rəmark(ə)] nf remark; (écrite) note

remarquer [Rəmarke] vt (voir) to notice; (dire): ~ **que** to remark that; **se ~** to be noticeable; **se faire ~** to draw attention to o.s.; **faire ~ (à qn) que** to point out (to sb) that; **faire ~ qch (à qn)** to point sth out (to sb); **remarquez, ...** mark you, ..., mind you, ...

remballer [Rɑ̃bale] vt to wrap up (again); (dans un carton) to pack up (again)

rembarrer [Rɑ̃baRe] vt: ~ **qn** (repousser) to rebuff sb; (remettre à sa place) to put sb in his (ou her) place

remblai [Rɑ̃blɛ] nm embankment

remblayer [Rɑ̃bleje] vt to bank up; (fossé) to fill in

rembobiner [Rɑ̃bɔbine] vt to rewind

rembourrage [Rɑ̃buRaʒ] nm stuffing; padding

rembourré, e [Rɑ̃buRe] adj padded

rembourrer [Rɑ̃buRe] vt to stuff; (dossier, vêtement, souliers) to pad

remboursable [Rɑ̃buRsabl(ə)] adj repayable

remboursement [Rɑ̃buRsəmɑ̃] nm repayment; **envoi contre ~** cash on delivery

rembourser [Rɑ̃buRse] vt to pay back, repay

rembrunir [RɑbRyniR]: **se rembrunir** vi to grow sombre (Brit) ou somber (US)

remède [Rəmɛd] nm (médicament) medicine; (traitement, fig) remedy, cure; **trouver un ~ à** (Méd, fig) to find a cure for

remédier [Rəmedje]: ~ **à** vt to remedy

remembrement [RəmɑbRəmɑ̃] nm (Agr) regrouping of lands

remémorer [RəmemɔRe]: **se remémorer** vt to recall, recollect

remerciements [RəmɛRsimɑ̃] nmpl thanks; **(avec) tous mes ~** (with) grateful ou many thanks

remercier [RəmɛRsje] vt to thank; (congédier) to dismiss; **~ qn de/d'avoir fait** to thank sb for/ for having done; **non, je vous remercie** no thank you

remettre [RəmɛtR(ə)] vt (vêtement): **~ qch** to put sth back on, put sth on again; (replacer): **~ qch quelque part** to put sth back somewhere; (ajouter): **~ du sel/un sucre** to add more salt/ another lump of sugar; (rétablir: personne): **~ qn** to set sb back on his (ou her) feet; (rendre, restituer): **~ qch à qn** to give sth back to sb, return sth to sb; (donner, confier: paquet, argent): **~ qch à qn** to hand sth over to sb, deliver sth to sb; (prix, décoration): **~ qch à qn** to present sb with sth; (ajourner): **~ qch (à)** to postpone sth ou put sth off (until); **se remettre** vi to get better, recover; **se ~ de** to recover from, get over; **s'en à** to leave it (up) to; **se ~ à faire/qch** to start doing/sth again; **~ un moteur/une machine en marche** to get an engine/a machine going again; **~ en état/en ordre** to repair/sort out; **~ en cause/question** to challenge/question again; **~ sa démission** to hand in one's notice; **~ qch à neuf** to make sth as good as new; **~ qn à sa place** (fig) to put sb in his (ou her) place

réminiscence [Reminisɑ̃s] nf reminiscence

remis, e [Rəmi, -iz] pp de **remettre** ▷ nf delivery; presentation; (rabais) discount; (local) shed; **~ en marche/en ordre** starting up again/sorting out; **~ en cause/question** calling into question/challenging; **~ de fonds** remittance; **~ en jeu** (Football) throw-in; **~ à neuf** restoration; **~ de peine** remission of sentence

remiser [Rəmize] vt to put away

rémission [Remisjɔ̃]: **sans ~** adj irremediable adv unremittingly

remodeler [Rəmɔdle] vt to remodel; (fig: restructurer) to restructure

rémois, e [Remwa, -waz] *adj* of *ou* from Rheims
▷ *nm/f*: **Rémois, e** inhabitant *ou* native of Rheims

remontant [Rəmɔ̃tɑ̃] *nm* tonic, pick-me-up

remontée [Rəmɔ̃te] *nf* rising; ascent; **~s mécaniques** (*Ski*) ski lifts, ski tows

remonte-pente [Rəmɔ̃tpɑ̃t] *nm* ski lift, (ski) tow

remonter [Rəmɔ̃te] *vi* (*à nouveau*) to go back up; (*à cheval*) to remount; (*après une descente*) to go up (again); (*en voiture*) to get back in; (*jupe*) to ride up ▷ *vt* (*pente*) to go up; (*fleuve*) to sail (*ou swim etc*) up; up; (*manches, pantalon*) to roll up; (*col*) to turn up; (*niveau, limite*) to raise; (*fig: personne*) to buck up; (*moteur, meuble*) to put back together, reassemble; (*garde-robe etc*) to renew, replenish; (*montre, mécanisme*) to wind up; **~ le moral à qn** to raise sb's spirits; **~ à** (*dater de*) to date *ou* go back to; **~ en voiture** to get back into the car

remontoir [Rəmɔ̃twaR] *nm* winding mechanism, winder

remontrance [Rəmɔ̃tRɑ̃s] *nf* reproof, reprimand

remontrer [Rəmɔ̃tRe] *vt* (*montrer de nouveau*): **~ qch (à qn)** to show sth again (to sb); (*fig*): **en ~ à** to prove one's superiority over

remords [RəmɔR] *nm* remorse *no pl*; **avoir des ~** to feel remorse, be conscience-stricken

remorque [RəmɔRk(ə)] *nf* trailer; **prendre/être en ~** to tow/be on tow; **être à la ~** (*fig*) to tag along (behind)

remorquer [RəmɔRke] *vt* to tow

remorqueur [RəmɔRkœR] *nm* tug(boat)

rémoulade [Remulad] *nf dressing with mustard and herbs*

rémouleur [RemulœR] *nm* (knife- *ou* scissor-) grinder

remous [Rəmu] *nm* (*d'un navire*) (back)wash *no pl*; (*de rivière*) swirl, eddy *pl*; (*fig*) stir *sg*

rempailler [Rɑ̃paje] *vt* to reseat (*with straw*)

rempart [Rɑ̃paR] *nm* rampart; **faire à qn un ~ de son corps** to shield sb with one's (own) body

remparts [Rɑ̃paR] *nmpl* walls, ramparts

rempiler [Rɑ̃pile] *vt* (*dossiers, livres etc*) to pile up again ▷ *vi* (*Mil: fam*) to join up again

remplaçant, e [Rɑ̃plasɑ̃, -ɑ̃t] *nm/f* replacement, substitute, stand-in; (*Théât*) understudy; (*Scol*) supply (*Brit*) *ou* substitute (*US*) teacher

remplacement [Rɑ̃plasmɑ̃] *nm* replacement; (*job*) replacement work *no pl*; (*suppléance: Scol*) supply (*Brit*) *ou* substitute (*US*) teacher; **assurer le ~ de qn** (*remplaçant*) to stand in *ou* substitute for sb; **faire des ~s** (*professeur*) to do supply *ou* substitute teaching; (*médecin*) to do locum work

remplacer [Rɑ̃plase] *vt* to replace; (*prendre temporairement la place de*) to stand in for; (*tenir lieu de*) to take the place of, act as a substitute for; **~ qch/qn par** to replace sth/sb with

rempli, e [Rɑ̃pli] *adj* (*emploi du temps*) full, busy; **~ de** full of, filled with

remplir [Rɑ̃pliR] *vt* to fill (up); (*questionnaire*) to fill out *ou* up; (*obligations, fonction, condition*) to fulfil; **se remplir** *vi* to fill up; **~ qch de** to fill sth with

remplissage [Rɑ̃plisaʒ] *nm* (*fig: péj*) padding

remploi [Rɑ̃plwa] *nm* re-use

rempocher [Rɑ̃pɔʃe] *vt* to put back into one's pocket

remporter [Rɑ̃pɔRte] *vt* (*marchandise*) to take away; (*fig*) to win, achieve

rempoter [Rɑ̃pɔte] *vt* to repot

remuant, e [Rəmɥɑ̃, -ɑ̃t] *adj* restless

remue-ménage [Rəmymenaʒ] *nm inv* commotion

remuer [Rəmɥe] *vt* to move; (*café, sauce*) to stir ▷ *vi* to move; (*fig: opposants*) to show signs of unrest; **se remuer** *vi* to move; (*se démener*) to stir o.s.; (*fam*) to get a move on

rémunérateur, -trice [RemyneRatœR, -tRis] *adj* remunerative, lucrative

rémunération [RemyneRasjɔ̃] *nf* remuneration

rémunérer [RemyneRe] *vt* to remunerate, pay

renâcler [Rənɑkle] *vi* to snort; (*fig*) to grumble, balk

renaissance [Rənɛsɑ̃s] *nf* rebirth, revival; **la R~** the Renaissance

renaître [RənɛtR(ə)] *vi* to be revived; **~ à la vie** to take on a new lease of life; **~ à l'espoir** to find fresh hope

rénal, e, -aux [Renal, -o] *adj* renal, kidney *cpd*

renard [RənaR] *nm* fox

renardeau [Rənardo] *nm* fox cub

rencard [Rɑ̃kaR] *nm* = **rancard**

rencart [Rɑ̃kaR] *nm* = **rancart**

renchérir [Rɑ̃ʃeRiR] *vi* to become more expensive; (*fig*): **~ (sur)** to add something (to)

renchérissement [Rɑ̃ʃeRismɑ̃] *nm* increase (in the cost *ou* price of)

rencontre [Rɑ̃kɔ̃tR(ə)] *nf* (*de cours d'eau*) confluence; (*de véhicules*) collision; (*entrevue, congrès, match etc*) meeting; (*imprévue*) encounter; **faire la ~ de qn** to meet sb; **aller à la ~ de qn** to go and meet sb; **amours de ~** casual love affairs

rencontrer [Rɑ̃kɔ̃tRe] *vt* to meet; (*mot, expression*) to come across; (*difficultés*) to meet with; **se rencontrer** to meet; (*véhicules*) to collide

rendement [Rɑ̃dmɑ̃] *nm* (*d'un travailleur, d'une machine*) output; (*d'une culture*) yield; (*d'un investissement*) return; **à plein ~** at full capacity

rendez-vous [Rɑ̃devu] *nm* (*rencontre*) appointment; (: *d'amoureux*) date; (*lieu*) meeting place; **donner ~ à qn** to arrange to meet sb; **recevoir sur ~** to have an appointment system; **fixer un ~ à qn** to give sb an appointment; **avoir/prendre ~ (avec)** to have/make an appointment (with); **prendre ~ chez le médecin** to make an appointment with the doctor; **~ spatial** *ou* **orbital** docking (in space)

rendormir [Rɑ̃dɔRmiR]: **se rendormir** *vr* to go back to sleep

rendre [Rɑ̃dR(ə)] *vt* (*livre, argent etc*) to give back, return; (*otages, visite, politesse, Jur: verdict*) to return; (*honneurs*) to pay; (*sang, aliments*) to bring up; (*sons: instrument*) to produce, make; (*exprimer, traduire*) to render; (*jugement*) to pronounce, render; (*faire devenir*): **~ qn célèbre/qch possible** to make sb famous/sth possible; **se rendre** *vi* (*capituler*) to surrender, give o.s. up; (*aller*): **se ~ quelque part** to go somewhere; **se ~ à** (*arguments etc*) to bow to; (*ordres*) to comply with; **se ~ compte de qch** to realize sth; **~ la vue/la santé à qn** to restore sb's sight/health; **~ la liberté à qn** to set sb free; **~ la monnaie** to give change; **se ~ insupportable/malade** to become unbearable/make o.s. ill

rendu, e [Rɑ̃dy] *pp de* **rendre** ▷ *adj* (*fatigué*) exhausted

renégat, e [Rənega, -at] *nm/f* renegade

renégocier [Rənegɔsje] *vt* to renegociate

rênes [Rɛn] *nfpl* reins

renfermé, e [Rɑ̃fɛrme] *adj* (*fig*) withdrawn ▷ *nm*: **sentir le ~** to smell stuffy

renfermer [Rɑ̃fɛrme] *vt* to contain; **se renfermer (sur soi-même)** to withdraw into o.s

renfiler [Rɑ̃file] *vt* (*collier*) to rethread; (*pull*) to slip on

renflé, e [Rɑ̃fle] *adj* bulging, bulbous

renflement [Rɑ̃fləmɑ̃] *nm* bulge

renflouer [Rɑ̃flue] *vt* to refloat; (*fig*) to set back on its (*ou* his/her *etc*) feet (again)

renfoncement [Rɑ̃fɔ̃smɑ̃] *nm* recess

renforcer [Rɑ̃fɔrse] *vt* to reinforce; **~ qn dans ses opinions** to confirm sb's opinion

renfort [Rɑ̃fɔr]: **~s** *nmpl* reinforcements; **en ~** as a back-up; **à grand ~ de** with a great deal of

renfrogné, e [Rɑ̃frɔɲe] *adj* sullen, scowling

renfrogner [Rɑ̃frɔɲe]: **se renfrogner** *vi* to scowl

rengager [Rɑ̃gaʒe] *vt* (*personnel*) to take on again; **se rengager** (*Mil*) to re-enlist

rengaine [Rɑ̃gɛn] *nf* (*péj*) old tune

rengainer [Rɑ̃gene] *vt* (*revolver*) to put back in its holster; (*épée*) to sheathe; (*fam: compliment, discours*) to save, withhold

rengorger [Rɑ̃gɔrʒe]: **se rengorger** *vi* (*fig*) to puff o.s up

renier [Rənje] *vt* (*parents*) to disown, repudiate; (*engagements*) to go back on; (*foi*) to renounce

renifler [Rənifle] *vi* to sniff ▷ *vt* (*tabac*) to sniff up; (*odeur*) to sniff

rennais, e [Rɛnɛ, -ɛz] *adj* of *ou* from Rennes ▷ *nm/f*: **Rennais, e** inhabitant *ou* native of Rennes

renne [Rɛn] *nm* reindeer *inv*

renom [Rənɔ̃] *nm* reputation; (*célébrité*) renown; **vin de grand ~** highly renowned wine

renommé, e [R(ə)nɔme] *adj* celebrated, renowned ▷ *nf* fame

renoncement [Rənɔ̃smɑ̃] *nm* abnegation, renunciation

renoncer [Rənɔ̃se] *vi*: **~ à** *vt* to give up; **~ à faire** to give up the idea of doing; **j'y renonce!** I give up!

renouer [Rənwe] *vt* (*cravate etc*) to retie; (*fig: conversation, liaison*) to renew, resume; **~ avec** (*tradition*) to revive; (*habitude*) to take up again; **~ avec qn** to take up with sb again

renouveau, x [Rənuvo] *nm* revival; **~ de succès** renewed success

renouvelable [R(ə)nuvlabl(ə)] *adj* (*contrat, bail, énergie*) renewable; (*expérience*) which can be renewed

renouveler [Rənuvle] *vt* to renew; (*exploit, méfait*) to repeat; **se renouveler** *vi* (*incident*) to recur, happen again, be repeated; (*cellules etc*) to be renewed *ou* replaced; (*artiste, écrivain*) to try something new

renouvellement [R(ə)nuvɛlmɑ̃] *nm* renewal; recurrence

rénovation [Renɔvasjɔ̃] *nf* renovation; restoration; reform(ing); redevelopment

rénover [Renɔve] *vt* (*immeuble*) to renovate, do up; (*meuble*) to restore; (*enseignement*) to reform; (*quartier*) to redevelop

renseignement [Rɑ̃sɛɲmɑ̃] *nm* information *no pl*, piece of information; (*Mil*) intelligence *no pl*; **prendre des ~s sur** to make inquiries about, ask for information about; **(guichet des) ~s** information desk; **(service des) ~s** (*Tél*) directory inquiries (*Brit*), information (*US*); **service de ~s** (*Mil*) intelligence service; **les ~s généraux** ≈ the secret police

renseigner [Rɑ̃sɛɲe] *vt*: **~ qn (sur)** to give information to sb (about); **se renseigner** *vi* to ask for information, make inquiries

rentabiliser [Rɑ̃tabilize] *vt* (*capitaux, production*) to make profitable

rentabilité [Rɑ̃tabilite] *nf* profitability; cost-effectiveness; (*d'un investissement*) return; **seuil de ~** break-even point

rentable [Rɑ̃tabl(ə)] *adj* profitable; cost-effective

rente [Rɑ̃t] *nf* income; (*pension*) pension; (*titre*) government stock *ou* bond; **~ viagère** life annuity

rentier, -ière [Rɑ̃tje, -jɛr] *nm/f* person of private *ou* independent means

rentrée [Rɑ̃tre] *nf*: **~ (d'argent)** cash *no pl* coming in; **la ~ (des classes *ou* scolaire)** the start of the new school year; **la ~ (parlementaire)** the reopening *ou* reassembly of parliament; **faire sa ~** (*artiste, acteur*) to make a comeback

rentrer [Rɑ̃tre] *vi* (*entrer de nouveau*) to go (*ou* come) back in; (*entrer*) to go (*ou* come) in; (*revenir chez soi*) to go (*ou* come) (back) home; (*air, clou: pénétrer*) to go in; (*revenu, argent*) to come in ▷ *vt* (*foins*) to bring in; (*véhicule*) to put away; (*chemise dans pantalon etc*) to tuck in; (*griffes*) to draw in; (*train d'atterrissage*) to raise; (*fig: larmes, colère etc*) to hold back; **~ le ventre** to pull in one's stomach; **~ dans** to go (*ou* come) back into; to go (*ou* come) into; (*famille, patrie*) to go back *ou* return to; (*heurter*) to crash into; (*appartenir à*) to be included in; (: *catégorie etc*) to fall into; **~ dans l'ordre** to get back to normal; **~ dans ses frais** to recover one's expenses (*ou* initial outlay)

renverrai *etc* [Rɑ̃vere] *vb voir* **renvoyer**

renversant, e [Rɑ̃vɛrsɑ̃, -ɑ̃t] *adj* amazing, astounding

renverse [Rɑ̃vɛrs(ə)]: **à la ~** *adv* backwards

renversé, e [Rɑ̃vɛʀse] *adj (écriture)* backhand; *(image)* reversed; *(stupéfait)* staggered

renversement [Rɑ̃vɛʀsəmɑ̃] *nm (d'un régime, des traditions)* overthrow; ~ **de la situation** reversal of the situation

renverser [Rɑ̃vɛʀse] *vt (faire tomber: chaise, verre)* to knock over, overturn; *(piéton)* to knock down; *(liquide, contenu)* to spill, upset; *(retourner: verre, image)* to turn upside down, invert; *(: ordre des mots etc)* to reverse; *(fig: gouvernement etc)* to overthrow; *(stupéfier)* to bowl over, stagger; **se renverser** *vi* to fall over; to overturn; to spill; **se ~ (en arrière)** to lean back; ~ **la tête/le corps (en arrière)** to tip one's head back/throw oneself back; ~ **la vapeur** *(fig)* to change course

renvoi [Rɑ̃vwa] *nm* dismissal; return; reflection; postponement; *(référence)* cross-reference; *(éructation)* belch

renvoyer [Rɑ̃vwaje] *vt* to send back; *(congédier)* to dismiss; *(Tennis)* to return; *(lumière)* to reflect; *(son)* to echo; *(ajourner)*: ~ **qch (à)** to postpone sth (until); ~ **qch à qn** *(rendre)* to return sth to sb; ~ **qn à** *(fig)* to refer sb to

réorganisation [ReɔRganizasjɔ̃] *nf* reorganization

réorganiser [ReɔRganize] *vt* to reorganize

réorienter [ReɔRjɑ̃te] *vt* to reorient(ate), redirect

réouverture [Reuvɛʀtyʀ] *nf* reopening

repaire [Rəpɛʀ] *nm* den

repaître [RəpɛtR(ə)] *vt* to feast; to feed; **se ~ de** *vt (animal)* to feed on; *(fig)* to wallow *ou* revel in

répandre [Repɑ̃dR(ə)] *vt (renverser)* to spill; *(étaler, diffuser)* to spread; *(lumière)* to shed; *(chaleur, odeur)* to give off; **se répandre** *vi* to spill; to spread; **se ~ en** *(injures etc)* to pour out

répandu, e [Repɑ̃dy] *pp de* **répandre** ▷ *adj (opinion, usage)* widespread

réparable [Reparabl(ə)] *adj (montre etc)* repairable; *(perte etc)* which can be made up for

reparaître [RəparɛtR(ə)] *vi* to reappear

réparateur, -trice [Reparatœr, -tris] *nm/f* repairer

réparation [Reparasjɔ̃] *nf* repairing *no pl*, repair; **en ~** *(machine etc)* under repair; **demander à qn ~ de** *(offense etc)* to ask sb to make amends for

réparer [Repare] *vt* to repair; *(fig: offense)* to make up for, atone for; *(: oubli, erreur)* to put right

reparler [Rəparle] *vi*: ~ **de qn/qch** to talk about sb/sth again; ~ **à qn** to speak to sb again

repars *etc* [Rəpar] *vb voir* **repartir**

repartie [Rəparti] *nf* retort; **avoir de la ~** to be quick at repartee

repartir [RəpartiR] *vi* to set off again; to leave again; *(fig)* to get going again, pick up again; ~ **à zéro** to start from scratch (again)

répartir [RepartiR] *vt (pour attribuer)* to share out; *(pour disperser, disposer)* to divide up; *(poids, chaleur)* to distribute; *(étaler: dans le temps)*: ~ **sur** to spread over; *(classer, diviser)*: ~ **en** to divide into,

split up into; **se répartir** *vt (travail, rôles)* to share out between themselves

répartition [Repartisjɔ̃] *nf* sharing out; dividing up; distribution

repas [Rəpa] *nm* meal; **à l'heure des ~** at mealtimes

repassage [Rəpasaʒ] *nm* ironing

repasser [Rəpase] *vi* to come *(ou* go*)* back ▷ *vt (vêtement, tissu)* to iron; *(examen)* to retake, resit; *(film)* to show again; *(lame)* to sharpen; *(leçon, rôle: revoir)* to go over (again); *(plat, pain)*: ~ **qch à qn** to pass sth back to sb

repasseuse [Rəpasøz] *nf (machine)* ironing machine

repayer [Rəpeje] *vt* to pay again

repêchage [Rəpɛʃaʒ] *nm (Scol)*: **question de ~** question to give candidates a second chance

repêcher [Rəpeʃe] *vt (noyé)* to recover the body of, fish out; *(fam: candidat)* to pass *(by inflating marks)*; to give a second chance to

repeindre [RəpɛdR(ə)] *vt* to repaint

repentir [Rəpɑ̃tiR] *nm* repentance; **se repentir** *vi*: **se ~ (de)** to repent (of)

répercussions [Repɛrkysjɔ̃] *nfpl* repercussions

répercuter [Repɛrkyte] *vt (réfléchir, renvoyer: son, voix)* to reflect; *(faire transmettre: consignes, charges etc)* to pass on; **se répercuter** *vi (bruit)* to reverberate; *(fig)*: **se ~ sur** to have repercussions on

repère [Rəpɛr] *nm* mark; *(monument etc)* landmark; **(point de) ~** point of reference

repérer [Rəpere] *vt (erreur, connaissance)* to spot; *(abri, ennemi)* to locate; **se repérer** *vi* to get one's bearings; **se faire ~** to be spotted

répertoire [Repɛrtwar] *nm (liste)* (alphabetical) list; *(carnet)* index notebook; *(Inform)* directory; *(de carnet)* thumb index; *(indicateur)* directory, index; *(d'un théâtre, artiste)* repertoire

répertorier [Repɛrtɔrje] *vt* to itemize, list

répéter [Repete] *vt* to repeat; *(préparer: leçon)* ▷ *aussi vi* to learn, go over; *(Théât)* to rehearse; **se répéter** *(redire)* to repeat o.s.; *(se reproduire)* to be repeated, recur

répéteur [Repetœr] *nm (Tél)* repeater

répétitif, -ive [Repetitif, -iv] *adj* repetitive

répétition [Repetisjɔ̃] *nf* repetition; *(Théât)* rehearsal; **répétitions** *nfpl (leçons)* private coaching *sg*; **armes à ~** repeater weapons; ~ **générale** final dress rehearsal

repeupler [Rəpœple] *vt* to repopulate; *(forêt, rivière)* to restock

repiquage [Rəpikaʒ] *nm* pricking out, planting out; re-recording

repiquer [Rəpike] *vt (plants)* to prick out, plant out; *(enregistrement)* to re-record

répit [Repi] *nm* respite; **sans ~** without letting up

replacer [Rəplase] *vt* to replace, put back

replanter [Rəplɑ̃te] *vt* to replant

replat [Rəpla] *nm* ledge

replâtrer [RəplɑtRe] *vt (mur)* to replaster

replet, -ète [Rəplɛ, -ɛt] *adj* chubby, fat

repli [Rəpli] *nm* (*d'une étoffe*) fold; (*Mil, fig*) withdrawal

replier [Rəplije] *vt* (*rabattre*) to fold down *ou* over; **se replier** *vi* (*armée*) to withdraw, fall back; **se ~ sur soi-même** to withdraw into oneself

réplique [Replik] *nf* (*repartie, fig*) reply; (*objection*) retort; (*Théât*) line; (*copie*) replica; **donner la ~ à** to play opposite; **sans ~** *adj* no-nonsense; irrefutable

répliquer [Replike] *vi* to reply; (*avec impertinence*) to answer back; (*riposter*) to retaliate

replonger [Rəplɔ̃ʒe] *vt*: **~ qch dans** to plunge sth back into; **se ~ dans** (*journal etc*) to immerse o.s. in again

répondant, e [Repɔ̃dɑ̃, -ɑ̃t] *nm/f* (*garant*) guarantor, surety

répondeur [Repɔ̃dœR] *nm* answering machine

répondre [Repɔ̃dR(ə)] *vi* to answer, reply; (*freins, mécanisme*) to respond; **~ à** *vt* to reply to, answer; (*avec impertinence*): **~ à qn** to answer sb back; (*invitation, convocation*) to reply to; (*affection, salut*) to return; (*provocation: mécanisme etc*) to respond to; (*correspondre à: besoin*) to answer; (*: conditions*) to meet; (*: description*) to match; **~ que** to answer *ou* reply that; **~ de** to answer for

réponse [Repɔ̃s] *nf* answer, reply; **avec ~ payée** (*Postes*) reply-paid, post-paid (*US*); **avoir ~ à tout** to have an answer for everything; **en ~ à** in reply to; **carte-/bulletin-~** reply card/slip

report [RəpɔR] *nm* postponement; transfer; **~ d'incorporation** (*Mil*) deferment

reportage [RəpɔRtaʒ] *nm* (*bref*) report; (*écrit: documentaire*) story; article; (*en direct*) commentary; (*genre, activité*): **le ~** reporting

reporter *nm* [RəpɔRtɛR] reporter ▷ *vt* [RəpɔRte] (*total*): **~ qch sur** to carry sth forward *ou* over to; (*ajourner*): **~ qch (à)** to postpone sth (until); (*transférer*): **~ qch sur** to transfer sth to; **se ~ à** (*époque*) to think back to; (*document*) to refer to

repos [Rəpo] *nm* rest; (*fig*) peace (and quiet); (*mental*) peace of mind; (*Mil*): **~!** (stand) at ease!; **en ~** at rest; **au ~** at rest; (*soldat*) at ease; **de tout ~** safe

reposant, e [R(ə)pozɑ̃, -ɑ̃t] *adj* restful; (*sommeil*) refreshing

repose [Rəpoz] *nf* refitting

reposé, e [Rəpoze] *adj* fresh, rested; **à tête ~e** in a leisurely way, taking time to think

repose-pied [Rəpozpje] *nm inv* footrest

reposer [Rəpoze] *vt* (*verre, livre*) to put down; (*rideaux, carreaux*) to put back; (*délasser*) to rest; (*problème*) to reformulate ▷ *vi* (*liquide, pâte*) to settle, rest; (*personne*): **ici repose ...** here lies ...; **~ sur** to be built on; (*fig*) to rest on; **se reposer** *vi* to rest; **se ~ sur qn** to rely on sb

repoussant, e [Rəpusɑ̃, -ɑ̃t] *adj* repulsive

repoussé, e [Rəpuse] *adj* (*cuir*) embossed (by hand)

repousser [Rəpuse] *vi* to grow again ▷ *vt* to repel, repulse; (*offre*) to turn down, reject; (*tiroir, personne*) to push back; (*différer*) to put back

répréhensible [RepReɑ̃sibl(ə)] *adj* reprehensible

reprendre [RəpRɑ̃dR(ə)] *vt* (*prisonnier, ville*) to recapture; (*objet prêté, donné*) to take back; (*chercher*): **je viendrai te ~ à 4 h** I'll come and fetch you *ou* I'll come back for you at 4; (*se resservir de*): **~ du pain/un œuf** to take (*ou* eat) more bread/another egg; (*Comm: article usagé*) to take back; to take in part exchange; (*firme, entreprise*) to take over; (*travail, promenade*) to resume; (*emprunter: argument, idée*) to take up, use; (*refaire: article etc*) to go over again; (*jupe etc*) to alter; (*émission, pièce*) to put on again; (*réprimander*) to tell off; (*corriger*) to correct ▷ *vi* (*classes, pluie*) to start (up) again; (*activités, travaux, combats*) to resume, start (up) again; (*affaires, industrie*) to pick up; (*dire*): **reprit-il** he went on; **se reprendre** (*se ressaisir*) to recover, pull o.s. together; **s'y ~** to make another attempt; **~ des forces** to recover one's strength; **~ courage** to take new heart; **~ ses habitudes/sa liberté** to get back into one's old habits/regain one's freedom; **~ la route** to resume one's journey, set off again; **~ connaissance** to come to, regain consciousness; **~ haleine** *ou* **son souffle** to get one's breath back; **~ la parole** to speak again

repreneur [RəpRənœR] *nm* company fixer *ou* doctor

reprenne *etc* [RəpRɛn] *vb voir* **reprendre**

représailles [RəpRezaj] *nfpl* reprisals, retaliation *sg*

représentant, e [RəpRezɑ̃tɑ̃, -ɑ̃t] *nm/f* representative

représentatif, -ive [RəpRezɑ̃tatif, -iv] *adj* representative

représentation [RəpRezɑ̃tasjɔ̃] *nf* representation; performing; (*symbole, image*) representation; (*spectacle*) performance; (*Comm*): **la ~** commercial travelling; sales representation; **frais de ~** (*d'un diplomate*) entertainment allowance

représenter [RəpRezɑ̃te] *vt* to represent; (*donner: pièce, opéra*) to perform; **se représenter** *vt* (*se figurer*) to imagine; to visualize ▷ *vi*: **se ~ à** (*Pol*) to stand *ou* run again at; (*Scol*) to resit

répressif, -ive [Represif, -iv] *adj* repressive

répression [Represjɔ̃] *nf voir* **réprimer** suppression; repression; (*Pol*): **la ~** repression; **mesures de ~** repressive measures

réprimande [Reprimɑ̃d] *nf* reprimand, rebuke

réprimander [Reprimɑ̃de] *vt* to reprimand, rebuke

réprimer [Reprime] *vt* (*émotions*) to suppress; (*peuple etc*) repress

repris, e [RəpRi, -iz] *pp de* **reprendre** ▷ *nm*: **~ de justice** ex-prisoner, ex-convict

reprise [RəpRiz] *nf* (*recommencement*) resumption; (*économique*) recovery; (*TV*) repeat; (*Ciné*) rerun; (*Boxe etc*) round; (*Auto*) acceleration *no pl*; (*Comm*) trade-in, part exchange; (*de location*) sum asked for any extras or improvements made to the property; (*raccommodage*) darn; mend; **la ~ des hostilités** the resumption of hostilities; **à**

plusieurs ~s on several occasions, several times

repriser [Rəprize] vt to darn; to mend; **aiguille/ coton à ~** darning needle/thread

réprobateur, -trice [Reprobatœr, -tris] adj reproving

réprobation [Reprobasjɔ̃] nf reprobation

reproche [Rəprɔʃ] nm (remontrance) reproach; **ton/air de ~** reproachful tone/look; **faire des ~s à qn** to reproach sb; **faire ~ à qn de qch** to reproach sb for sth; **sans ~(s)** beyond ou above reproach

reprocher [Rəprɔʃe] vt: **~ qch à qn** to reproach ou blame sb for sth; **~ qch à** (machine, théorie) to have sth against; **se ~ qch/d'avoir fait qch** to blame o.s for sth/for doing sth

reproducteur, -trice [Rəprɔdyktœr, -tris] adj reproductive

reproduction [Rəprɔdyksjɔ̃] nf reproduction; **~ interdite** all rights (of reproduction) reserved

reproduire [Rəprɔdɥir] vt to reproduce; **se reproduire** vi (Bio) to reproduce; (recommencer) to recur, re-occur

reprographie [Rəprɔgrafi] nf (photo)copying

réprouvé, e [Repruve] nm/f reprobate

réprouver [Repruve] vt to reprove

reptation [Rɛptasjɔ̃] nf crawling

reptile [Rɛptil] nm reptile

repu, e [Rəpy] pp de **repaître** ▷ adj satisfied, sated

républicain, e [Repyblikɛ̃, -ɛn] adj, nm/f republican

république [Repyblik] nf republic; **R~ arabe du Yémen** Yemen Arab Republic; **R~ Centrafricaine** Central African Republic; **R~ de Corée** South Korea; **R~ dominicaine** Dominican Republic; **R~ d'Irlande** Irish Republic, Eire; **R~ populaire de Chine** People's Republic of China; **R~ populaire démocratique de Corée** Democratic People's Republic of Korea; **R~ populaire du Yémen** People's Democratic Republic of Yemen

répudier [Repydje] vt (femme) to repudiate; (doctrine) to renounce

répugnance [Repyɲɑ̃s] nf repugnance, loathing; **avoir ou éprouver de la ~ pour** (médicament, comportement, travail etc) to have an aversion to; **avoir ou éprouver de la ~ à faire qch** to be reluctant to do sth

répugnant, e [Repyɲɑ̃, -ɑ̃t] adj repulsive, loathsome

répugner [Repyɲe]: **~ à** vt: **~ à qn** to repel ou disgust sb; **~ à faire** to be loath ou reluctant to do

répulsion [Repylsjɔ̃] nf repulsion

réputation [Repytasjɔ̃] nf reputation; **avoir la ~ d'être ...** to have a reputation for being ...; **connaître qn/qch de ~** to know sb/sth by repute; **de ~ mondiale** world-renowned

réputé, e [Repyte] adj renowned; **être ~ pour** to have a reputation for, be renowned for

requérir [Rəkerir] vt (nécessiter) to require, call

for; (au nom de la loi) to call upon; (Jur: peine) to call for, demand

requête [Rəkɛt] nf request, petition; (Jur) petition

requiem [Rekɥijɛm] nm requiem

requiers etc [Rəkjɛr] vb voir **requérir**

requin [Rəkɛ̃] nm shark

requinquer [Rəkɛ̃ke] vt to set up, pep up

requis, e [Rəki, -iz] pp de **requérir** ▷ adj required

réquisition [Rekizisjɔ̃] nf requisition

réquisitionner [Rekizisjɔne] vt to requisition

réquisitoire [Rekizitwar] nm (Jur) closing speech for the prosecution; (fig): **~ contre** indictment of

RER sigle m (= Réseau express régional) Greater Paris high speed train service

rescapé, e [Rɛskape] nm/f survivor

rescousse [Rɛskus] nf: **aller à la ~ de qn** to go to sb's aid ou rescue; **appeler qn à la ~** to call on sb for help

réseau, x [Rezo] nm network

réséda [Rezeda] nm (Bot) reseda, mignonette

réservation [Rezɛrvasjɔ̃] nf reservation; booking

réserve [Rezɛrv(ə)] nf (retenue) reserve; (entrepôt) storeroom; (restriction, aussi: d'Indiens) reservation; (de pêche, chasse) preserve; (restrictions): **faire des ~s** to have reservations; **officier de ~** reserve officer; **sous toutes ~s** with all reserve; (dire) with reservations; **sous ~** subject to; **sans ~** adv unreservedly; **en ~** in reserve; **de ~** (provisions etc) in reserve

réservé, e [Rezɛrve] adj (discret) reserved; (chasse, pêche) private; **~ à ou pour** reserved for

réserver [Rezɛrve] vt (gén) to reserve; (chambre, billet etc) to book, reserve; (mettre de côté, garder): **~ qch pour ou à** to keep ou save sth for; **~ qch à qn** to reserve (ou book) sth for sb; (fig: destiner) to have sth in store for sb; **se ~ le droit de faire** to reserve the right to do

réserviste [Rezɛrvist(ə)] nm reservist

réservoir [Rezɛrvwar] nm tank

résidence [Rezidɑ̃s] nf residence; **~ principale/ secondaire** main/second home; **~ universitaire** hall of residence; **(en) ~ surveillée** (under) house arrest

résident, e [Rezidɑ̃, -ɑ̃t] nm/f (ressortissant) foreign resident; (d'un immeuble) resident ▷ adj (Inform) resident

résidentiel, le [Rezidɑ̃sjɛl] adj residential

résider [Rezide] vi: **~ à ou dans ou en** to reside in; **~ dans** (fig) to lie in

résidu [Rezidy] nm residue no pl

résiduel, le [Rezidɥɛl] adj residual

résignation [Reziɲasjɔ̃] nf resignation

résigné, e [Reziɲe] adj resigned

résigner [Reziɲe] vt to relinquish, resign; **se résigner** vi: **se ~ (à qch/à faire)** to resign o.s. (to sth/to doing)

résiliable [Reziljabl(ə)] adj which can be terminated

résilier [Rezilje] vt to terminate

résille [Rezij] nf (hair)net

résine [Rezin] nf resin

résiné, e [Rezine] adj: **vin ~** retsina

résineux, -euse [Rezinø, -øz] adj resinous ▷ nm coniferous tree

résistance [Rezistɑ̃s] nf resistance; (de réchaud, bouilloire: fil) element

résistant, e [Rezistɑ̃, -ɑ̃t] adj (personne) robust, tough; (matériau) strong, hard-wearing ▷ nm/f (patriote) Resistance worker ou fighter

résister [Reziste] vi to resist; **~ à** vt (assaut, tentation) to resist; (effort, souffrance) to withstand; (matériau, plante) to stand up to, withstand; (personne: désobéir à) to stand up to, oppose

résolu, e [Rezɔly] pp de **résoudre** ▷ adj (ferme) resolute; **être ~ à qch/faire** to be set upon sth/doing

résolument [Rezɔlymɑ̃] adv resolutely, steadfastly; **~ contre qch** firmly against sth

résolution [Rezɔlysjɔ̃] nf solving; (fermeté, décision, Inform) resolution; **prendre la ~ de** to make a resolution to

résolvais etc [Rezɔlvɛ] vb voir **résoudre**

résonance [Rezɔnɑ̃s] nf resonance

résonner [Rezɔne] vi (cloche, pas) to reverberate, resound; (salle) to be resonant; **~ de** to resound with

résorber [Rezɔrbe]: **se résorber** vi (Méd) to be resorbed; (fig) to be absorbed

résoudre [Rezudr(ə)] vt to solve; **~ qn à faire qch** to get sb to make up his (ou her) mind to do sth; **~ de faire** to resolve to do; **se ~ à faire** to bring o.s. to do

respect [Rɛspɛ] nm respect; **tenir en ~** to keep at bay

respectabilité [Rɛspɛktabilite] nf respectability

respectable [Rɛspɛktabl(ə)] adj respectable

respecter [Rɛspɛkte] vt to respect; **faire ~** to enforce; **le lexicographe qui se respecte** (fig) any self-respecting lexicographer

respectif, -ive [Rɛspɛktif, -iv] adj respective

respectivement [Rɛspɛktivmɑ̃] adv respectively

respectueusement [Rɛspɛktɥøzmɑ̃] adv respectfully

respectueux, -euse [Rɛspɛktɥø, -øz] adj respectful; **~ de** respectful of

respirable [Rɛspirabl(ə)] adj: **peu ~** unbreathable

respiration [Rɛspirasjɔ̃] nf breathing no pl; **faire une ~ complète** to breathe in and out; **retenir sa ~** to hold one's breath; **~ artificielle** artificial respiration

respiratoire [Rɛspiratwar] adj respiratory

respirer [Rɛspire] vi to breathe; (fig: se reposer) to get one's breath, have a break; (: être soulagé) to breathe again ▷ vt to breathe (in), inhale; (manifester: santé, calme etc) to exude

resplendir [Rɛsplɑ̃dir] vi to shine; (fig): **~ (de)** to be radiant (with)

resplendissant, e [Rɛsplɑ̃disɑ̃, -ɑ̃t] adj radiant

responsabilité [Rɛspɔ̃sabilite] nf responsibility; (légale) liability; **refuser la ~ de** to deny responsibility (ou liability) for; **prendre ses ~s** to assume responsibility for one's actions; **~ civile** civil liability; **~ pénale/morale/collective** criminal/moral/collective responsibility

responsable [Rɛspɔ̃sabl(ə)] adj responsible ▷ nm/f (du ravitaillement etc) person in charge; (de parti, syndicat) official; **~ de** responsible for; (légalement: de dégâts etc) liable for; (chargé de) in charge of, responsible for

resquiller [Rɛskije] vi (au cinéma, au stade) to get in on the sly; (dans le train) to fiddle a free ride

resquilleur, -euse [Rɛskijœr, -øz] nm/f (qui n'est pas invité) gatecrasher; (qui ne paie pas) fare dodger

ressac [Rəsak] nm backwash

ressaisir [Rəsezir]: **se ressaisir** vi to regain one's self-control; (équipe sportive) to rally

ressasser [Rəsase] vt (remâcher) to keep turning over; (redire) to keep trotting out

ressemblance [Rəsɑ̃blɑ̃s] nf (visuelle) resemblance, similarity, likeness; (: Art) likeness; (analogie, trait commun) similarity

ressemblant, e [Rəsɑ̃blɑ̃, -ɑ̃t] adj (portrait) lifelike, true to life

ressembler [Rəsɑ̃ble]: **~ à** vt to be like, resemble; (visuellement) to look like; **se ressembler** vi to be (ou look) alike

ressemeler [Rəsəmle] vt to (re)sole

ressens etc [R(ə)sɑ̃] vb voir **ressentir**

ressentiment [Rəsɑ̃timɑ̃] nm resentment

ressentir [Rəsɑ̃tir] vt to feel; **se ~ de** to feel (ou show) the effects of

resserre [Rəsɛr] nf shed

resserrement [R(ə)sɛrmɑ̃] nm narrowing; strengthening; (goulet) narrow part

resserrer [Rəsɛre] vt (pores) to close; (nœud, boulon) to tighten (up); (fig: liens) to strengthen; **se resserrer** vi (route, vallée) to narrow; (liens) to strengthen; **se ~ (autour de)** to draw closer (around), to close in (on)

ressers etc [R(ə)sɛr] vb voir **resservir**

resservir [Rəsɛrvir] vi to do ou serve again ▷ vt: **~ qch (à qn)** to serve sth up again (to sb); **~ de qch (à qn)** to give (sb) a second helping of sth; **~ qn (d'un plat)** to give sb a second helping (of a dish); **se ~ de** (plat) to take a second helping of; (outil etc) to use again

ressort [Rəsɔr] vb voir **ressortir** ▷ nm (pièce) spring; (force morale) spirit; (recours): **en dernier ~** as a last resort; (compétence): **être du ~ de** to fall within the competence of

ressortir [Rəsɔrtir] vi to go (ou come) out (again); (contraster) to stand out; **~ de** (résulter de): **il ressort de ceci que** it emerges from this that; **~ à** (Jur) to come under the jurisdiction of; (Admin) to be the concern of; **faire ~** (fig: souligner) to bring out

ressortissant, e [Rəsɔrtisɑ̃, -ɑ̃t] nm/f national

ressouder [Rəsude] vt to solder together again

ressource [Rəsurs(ə)] nf: **avoir la ~ de** to have

the possibility of; **ressources** *nfpl* resources; (*fig*) possibilities; **leur seule ~ était de** the only course open to them was to; **~s d'énergie** energy resources

ressusciter [Resysite] *vt* to resuscitate, restore to life; (*fig*) to revive, bring back ▷ *vi* to rise (from the dead); (*fig: pays*) to come back to life

restant, e [Restɑ̃, -ɑ̃t] *adj* remaining ▷ *nm*: **le ~ (de)** the remainder (of); **un ~ (de trop)** some leftover; (*fig: vestige*) a remnant *ou* last trace of

restaurant [Restɔrɑ̃] *nm* restaurant; **manger au ~** to eat out; **~ d'entreprise** staff canteen *ou* cafeteria (*US*); **~ universitaire (RU)** university refectory *ou* cafeteria (*US*)

restaurateur, -trice [Restɔratœr, -tris] *nm/f* restaurant owner, restaurateur; (*de tableaux*) restorer

restauration [Restɔrasjɔ̃] *nf* restoration; (*hôtellerie*) catering; **~ rapide** fast food

restaurer [Restɔre] *vt* to restore; **se restaurer** *vi* to have something to eat

restauroute [Restɔrut] *nm* = **restoroute**

reste [Rɛst(ə)] *nm* (*restant*): **le ~ (de)** the rest (of); (*de trop*): **un ~ (de)** some leftover; (*vestige*): **un ~ de** a remnant *ou* last trace of; (*Math*) remainder; **restes** *nmpl* leftovers; (*d'une cité etc, dépouille mortelle*) remains; **avoir du temps de ~** to have time to spare; **ne voulant pas être en ~** not wishing to be outdone; **partir sans attendre** *ou* **demander son ~** (*fig*) to leave without waiting to hear more; **du ~, au ~** *adv* besides, moreover; **pour le ~, quant au ~** *adv* as for the rest

rester [Rɛste] *vi* (*dans un lieu, un état, une position*) to stay, remain; (*subsister*) to remain, be left; (*durer*) to last, live on ▷ *vb impers*: **il reste du pain/deux œufs** there's some bread/there are two eggs left (over); **il reste du temps/10 minutes** there's some time/there are 10 minutes left; **il me reste assez de temps** I have enough time left; **voilà tout ce qui (me) reste** that's all I've got left; **ce qui reste à faire** what remains to be done; **ce qui me reste à faire** what remains for me to do; (**il**) **reste à savoir/établir si ...** it remains to be seen/established if *ou* whether ...; **il n'en reste pas moins que ...** the fact remains that ..., it's nevertheless a fact that ...; **en ~ à** (*stade, menaces*) to go no further than, only go as far as; **restons-en là** let's leave it at that; **~ sur une impression** to retain an impression; **y ~: il a failli y ~** he nearly met his end

restituer [Rɛstitɥe] *vt* (*objet, somme*): **~ qch (à qn)** to return *ou* restore sth (to sb); (*énergie*) to release; (*son*) to reproduce

restitution [Rɛstitysjɔ̃] *nf* restoration

restoroute [Rɛstɔrut] *nm* motorway (*Brit*) *ou* highway (*US*) restaurant

restreindre [Rɛstrɛ̃dr(ə)] *vt* to restrict, limit; **se restreindre** (*dans ses dépenses etc*) to cut down; (*champ de recherches*) to narrow

restreint, e [Rɛstrɛ̃, -ɛ̃t] *pp de* **restreindre** ▷ *adj* restricted, limited

restrictif, -ive [Rɛstriktif, -iv] *adj* restrictive, limiting

restriction [Rɛstriksjɔ̃] *nf* restriction; (*condition*) qualification; **restrictions** *nfpl* (*mentales*) reservations; **sans ~** *adv* unreservedly

restructuration [Rəstryktyrasjɔ̃] *nf* restructuring

restructurer [Rəstryktyre] *vt* to restructure

résultante [Rezyltɑ̃t] *nf* (*conséquence*) result, consequence

résultat [Rezylta] *nm* result; (*conséquence*) outcome *no pl*, result; (*d'élection etc*) results *pl*; **résultats** *nmpl* (*d'une enquête*) findings; **~s sportifs** sports results

résulter [Rezylte]: **~ de** *vt* to result from, be the result of; **il résulte de ceci que ...** the result of this is that ...

résumé [Rezyme] *nm* summary, résumé; **faire le ~ de** to summarize; **en ~** *adv* in brief; (*pour conclure*) to sum up

résumer [Rezyme] *vt* (*texte*) to summarize; (*récapituler*) to sum up; (*fig*) to epitomize, typify; **se résumer** *vi* (*personne*) to sum up (one's ideas); **se ~ à** to come down to

resurgir [Rəsyrʒir] *vi* to reappear, re-emerge

résurrection [Rezyrɛksjɔ̃] *nf* resurrection; (*fig*) revival

rétablir [Retablir] *vt* to restore, re-establish; (*personne: traitement*): **~ qn** to restore sb to health, help sb recover; (*Admin*): **~ qn dans son emploi/ses droits** to reinstate sb in his post/restore sb's rights; **se rétablir** *vi* (*guérir*) to recover; (*silence, calme*) to return, be restored; (*Gym etc*): **se ~ (sur)** to pull o.s. up (onto)

rétablissement [Retablismɑ̃] *nm* restoring; recovery; pull-up

rétamer [Retame] *vt* to re-coat, re-tin

rétameur [Retamœr] *nm* tinker

retaper [Rətape] *vt* (*maison, voiture etc*) to do up; (*fam: revigorer*) to buck up; (*redactylographier*) to retype

retard [Rətar] *nm* (*d'une personne attendue*) lateness *no pl*; (*sur l'horaire, un programme, une échéance*) delay; (*fig: scolaire, mental etc*) backwardness; **être en ~** (*pays*) to be backward; (*dans paiement, travail*) to be behind; **en ~ (de deux heures)** (two hours) late; **avoir un ~ de deux km** (*Sport*) to be two km behind; **rattraper son ~** to catch up; **avoir du ~** to be late; (*sur un programme*) to be behind (schedule); **prendre du ~** (*train, avion*) to be delayed; (*montre*) to lose (time); **sans ~** *adv* without delay; **~ à l'allumage** (*Auto*) retarded spark; **~ scolaire** backwardness at school

retardataire [Rətardatɛr] *adj* late; (*enfant, idées*) backward ▷ *nm/f* latecomer; backward child

retardé, e [Rətarde] *adj* backward

retardement [Rətardəmɑ̃]: **à ~** *adj* delayed action *cpd*; **bombe à ~** time bomb

retarder [Rətarde] *vt* (*sur un horaire*): **~ qn (d'une heure)** to delay sb (an hour); (*sur un programme*): **~ qn (de trois mois)** to set sb back *ou* delay sb (three months); (*départ, date*): ~ **qch (de deux jours)** to put sth back (two days), delay sth (for *ou* by two days); (*horloge*) to put back ▷ *vi* (*montre*) to be slow; (: *habituellement*) to lose (time); **je retarde (d'une heure)** I'm (an hour) slow

retendre [ʀətɑ̃dʀ(ə)] *vt* (*câble etc*) to stretch again; (*Mus*: *cordes*) to retighten

retenir [ʀətniʀ] *vt* (*garder, retarder*) to keep, detain; (*maintenir: objet qui glisse, fig: colère, larmes, rire*) to hold back; (: *objet suspendu*) to hold; (: *chaleur, odeur*) to retain; (*fig: empêcher d'agir*): ~ **qn (de faire)** to hold sb back (from doing); (*se rappeler*) to retain; (*réserver*) to reserve; (*accepter*) to accept; (*prélever*): ~ **qch (sur)** to deduct sth (from); **se retenir** (*euphémisme*) to hold on; (*se raccrocher*): **se ~ à** to hold onto; (*se contenir*): **se ~ de faire** to restrain o.s. from doing; ~ **son souffle** *ou* **haleine** to hold one's breath; ~ **qn à dîner** to ask sb to stay for dinner; **je pose trois et je retiens deux** put down three and carry two

rétention [ʀetɑ̃sjɔ̃] *nf*: ~ **d'urine** urine retention

retentir [ʀətɑ̃tiʀ] *vi* to ring out; (*salle*): ~ **de** to ring *ou* resound with; ~ **sur** *vt* (*fig*) to have an effect upon

retentissant, e [ʀətɑ̃tisɑ̃, -ɑ̃t] *adj* resounding; (*fig*) impact-making

retentissement [ʀətɑ̃tismɑ̃] *nm* (*retombées*) repercussions *pl*; effect, impact

retenu, e [ʀətny] *pp de* **retenir** ▷ *adj* (*place*) reserved; (*personne: empêché*) held up; (*propos: contenu, discret*) restrained ▷ *nf* (*prélèvement*) deduction; (*Math*) number to carry over; (*Scol*) detention; (*modération*) (self-)restraint; (*réserve*) reserve, reticence; (*Auto*) tailback

réticence [ʀetisɑ̃s] *nf* reticence *no pl*, reluctance *no pl*; **sans ~** without hesitation

réticent, e [ʀetisɑ̃, -ɑ̃t] *adj* reticent, reluctant

retiendrai [ʀətjɛ̃dʀe], **retiens** *etc* [ʀətjɛ̃] *vb voir* **retenir**

rétif, -ive [ʀetif, -iv] *adj* restive

rétine [ʀetin] *nf* retina

retint *etc* [ʀətɛ̃] *vb voir* **retenir**

retiré, e [ʀətiʀe] *adj* (*solitaire*) secluded; (*éloigné*) remote

retirer [ʀətiʀe] *vt* to withdraw; (*vêtement, lunettes*) to take off, remove; (*enlever*): ~ **qch à qn** to take sth from sb; (*extraire*): ~ **qn/qch de** to take sb away from/sth out of, remove sb/sth from; (*reprendre: bagages, billets*) to collect, pick up; ~ **des avantages de** to derive advantages from; **se retirer** *vi* (*partir, reculer*) to withdraw; (*prendre sa retraite*) to retire; **se ~ de** to withdraw from; to retire from

retombées [ʀətɔ̃be] *nfpl* (*radioactives*) fallout *sg*; (*fig*) fallout; spin-offs

retomber [ʀətɔ̃be] *vi* (*à nouveau*) to fall again; (*rechuter*): ~ **malade/dans l'erreur** to fall ill again/fall back into error; (*atterrir: après un saut etc*) to land; (*tomber, redescendre*) to fall back; (*pendre*) to fall, hang (down); (*échoir*): ~ **sur qn** to

fall on sb

retordre [ʀətɔʀdʀ(ə)] *vt*: **donner du fil à ~ à qn** to make life difficult for sb

rétorquer [ʀetɔʀke] *vt*: ~ **(à qn) que** to retort (to sb) that

retors, e [ʀətɔʀ, -ɔʀs(ə)] *adj* wily

rétorsion [ʀetɔʀsjɔ̃] *nf*: **mesures de ~** reprisals

retouche [ʀətuʃ] *nf* touching up *no pl*; alteration; **faire une ~** *ou* **des ~s à** to touch up

retoucher [ʀətuʃe] *vt* (*photographie, tableau*) to touch up; (*texte, vêtement*) to alter

retour [ʀətuʀ] *nm* return; **au ~** (*en arrivant*) when we (*ou* they *etc*) get (*ou* got) back; (*en route*) on the way back; **pendant le ~** on the way *ou* journey back; **à mon/ton ~** on my/your return; **au ~ de** on the return of; **être de ~ (de)** to be back (from); **de ~ à .../chez moi** back at .../back home; **en ~** *adv* in return; **par ~ du courrier** by return of post; **par un juste ~ des choses** by a favourable twist of fate; **match ~** return match; ~ **en arrière** (*Ciné*) flashback; (*mesure*) backward step; ~ **de bâton** kickback; ~ **de chariot** carriage return; ~ **à l'envoyeur** (*Postes*) return to sender; ~ **de flamme** backfire; ~ **(automatique) à la ligne** (*Inform*) wordwrap; ~ **de manivelle** (*fig*) backfire; ~ **offensif** renewed attack; ~ **aux sources** (*fig*) return to basics

retournement [ʀətuʀnəmɑ̃] *nm* (*d'une personne: revirement*) turning (round); ~ **de la situation** reversal of the situation

retourner [ʀətuʀne] *vt* (*dans l'autre sens: matelas, crêpe*) to turn (over); (: *caisse*) to turn upside down; (: *sac, vêtement*) to turn inside out; (*fig: argument*) to turn back; (*en remuant: terre, sol, foin*) to turn over; (*émouvoir: personne*) to shake; (*renvoyer, restituer*): ~ **qch à qn** to return sth to sb ▷ *vi* (*aller, revenir*): ~ **quelque part/à** to go back *ou* return somewhere/to; ~ **à** (*état, activité*) to return to, go back to; **se retourner** *vi* to turn over; (*tourner la tête*) to turn round; **s'en ~** to go back; **se retourner contre** (*fig*) to turn against; **savoir de quoi il retourne** to know what it is all about; ~ **sa veste** (*fig*) to turn one's coat; ~ **en arrière** *ou* **sur ses pas** to turn back, retrace one's steps; ~ **aux sources** to go back to basics

retracer [ʀətʀase] *vt* to relate, recount

rétracter [ʀetʀakte] *vt*, **se rétracter** *vi* to retract

retraduire [ʀətʀaduiʀ] *vt* to translate again; (*dans la langue de départ*) to translate back

retrait [ʀətʀɛ] *nm voir* **retirer** withdrawal; collection; *voir* **se retirer** withdrawal; (*rétrécissement*) shrinkage; **en ~** *adj* set back; **écrire en ~** to indent; ~ **du permis (de conduire)** disqualification from driving (*Brit*), revocation of driver's license (*US*)

retraite [ʀətʀɛt] *nf* (*d'une armée, Rel, refuge*) retreat; (*d'un employé*) retirement; (*revenu*) (retirement) pension; **être/mettre à la ~** to be retired/pension off *ou* retire; **prendre sa ~** to retire; ~ **anticipée** early retirement; ~ **aux flambeaux** torchlight tattoo

retraité, e [RətRete] adj retired ▷ nm/f (old age) pensioner

retraitement [RətRetmā] nm reprocessing

retraiter [RətRete] vt to reprocess

retranchement [RətRāʃmā] nm entrenchment; **poursuivre qn dans ses derniers ~s** to drive sb into a corner

retrancher [RətRāʃe] vt (passage, détails) to take out, remove; (nombre, somme): **~ qch de** to take ou deduct sth from; (couper) to cut off; **se ~ derrière/dans** to entrench o.s. behind/in; (fig) to take refuge behind/in

retranscrire [RətRāskRiR] vt to retranscribe

retransmettre [RətRāsmɛtR(ə)] vt (Radio) to broadcast, relay; (TV) to show

retransmission [RətRāsmisjɔ̃] nf broadcast; showing

retravailler [Rətravaje] vi to start work again ▷ vt to work on again

retraverser [RətRavɛRse] vt (dans l'autre sens) to cross back over

rétréci, e [RetResi] adj (idées, esprit) narrow

rétrécir [RetResiR] vt (vêtement) to take in ▷ vi to shrink; **se rétrécir** vi to narrow

rétrécissement [RetResismā] nm narrowing

retremper [RətRāpe] vt: **se ~ dans** (fig) to reimmerse o.s. in

rétribuer [Retribɥe] vt (travail) to pay for; (personne) to pay

rétribution [Retribysjɔ̃] nf payment

rétro [RetRo] adj inv old-style ▷ nm (rétroviseur) (rear-view) mirror; **la mode ~** the nostalgia vogue

rétroactif, -ive [Retroaktif, -iv] adj retroactive

rétrocéder [Retrosede] vt to retrocede

rétrocession [Retrosesjɔ̃] nf retrocession

rétrofusée [Retrofyze] nf retrorocket

rétrograde [RetRogRad] adj reactionary, backward-looking

rétrograder [RetRogRade] vi (élève) to fall back; (économie) to regress; (Auto) to change down

rétroprojecteur [Retropro3ɛktœR] nm overhead projector

rétrospectif, -ive [Retrospɛktif, -iv] adj, nf retrospective

rétrospectivement [Retrospɛktivmā] adv in retrospect

retroussé, e [Rətruse] adj: **nez ~** turned-up nose

retrousser [Rətruse] vt to roll up; (fig: nez) to wrinkle; (: lèvres) to curl

retrouvailles [Rətruvaj] nfpl reunion sg

retrouver [Rətruve] vt (fugitif, objet perdu) to find; (occasion) to find again; (calme, santé) to regain; (reconnaître: expression, style) to recognize; (revoir) to see again; (rejoindre) to meet (again), join; **se retrouver** vi to meet; (s'orienter) to find one's way; **se ~ quelque part** to find o.s. somewhere; to end up somewhere; **se ~ seul/sans argent** to find o.s. alone/with no money; **se ~ dans** (calculs, dossiers, désordre) to make sense of; **s'y ~** (rentrer dans ses frais) to break even

rétroviseur [RetrovizœR] nm (rear-view) mirror

réunifier [Reynifje] vt to reunify

Réunion [Reynjɔ̃] nf: **la ~, l'île de la ~** Réunion

réunion [Reynjɔ̃] nf bringing together; joining; (séance) meeting

réunionnais, e [Reynjonɛ, -ɛz] adj of ou from Réunion

réunir [ReyniR] vt (convoquer) to call together; (rassembler) to gather together; (cumuler) to combine; (rapprocher) to bring together (again), reunite; (rattacher) to join (together); **se réunir** vi (se rencontrer) to meet; (s'allier) to unite

réussi, e [Reysi] adj successful

réussir [ReysiR] vi to succeed, be successful; (à un examen) to pass; (plante, culture) to thrive, do well ▷ vt to make a success of; to bring off; **~ à faire** to succeed in doing; **~ à qn** to go right for sb; (aliment) to agree with sb; **le travail/le mariage lui réussit** work/married life agrees with him

réussite [Reysit] nf success; (Cartes) patience

réutiliser [Reytilize] vt to re-use

revaloir [RəvalwaR] vt: **je vous revaudrai cela** I'll repay you some day; (en mal) I'll pay you back for this

revalorisation [Rəvalorizasjɔ̃] nf revaluation; raising

revaloriser [Rəvalorize] vt (monnaie) to revalue; (salaires, pensions) to raise the level of; (institution, tradition) to reassert the value of

revanche [Rəvāʃ] nf revenge; **prendre sa ~ (sur)** to take one's revenge (on); **en ~ (par contre)** on the other hand; (en compensation) in return

rêvasser [Rɛvase] vi to daydream

rêve [Rɛv] nm dream; (activité psychique): **le ~** dreaming; **paysage/silence de ~** dreamlike landscape/silence; **~ éveillé** daydreaming no pl, daydream

rêvé, e [Reve] adj (endroit, mari etc) ideal

revêche [Rəvɛʃ] adj surly, sour-tempered

réveil [Revɛj] nm (d'un dormeur) waking up no pl; (fig) awakening; (pendule) alarm (clock); **au ~** when I (ou you etc) wake (ou woke) up, on waking (up); **sonner le ~** (Mil) to sound the reveille

réveille-matin [Revɛjmatɛ̃] nm inv alarm clock

réveiller [Reveje] vt (personne) to wake up; (fig) to awaken, revive; **se réveiller** vi to wake up; (fig) to be revived, reawaken

réveillon [Revɛjɔ̃] nm Christmas Eve; (de la Saint-Sylvestre) New Year's Eve; Christmas Eve (ou New Year's Eve) party ou dinner

réveillonner [Revɛjone] vi to celebrate Christmas Eve (ou New Year's Eve)

révélateur, -trice [RevelatœR, -tris] adj: **~ (de qch)** revealing (sth) ▷ nm (Photo) developer

révélation [Revelasjɔ̃] nf revelation

révéler [Revele] vt (gén) to reveal; (divulguer) to disclose, reveal; (dénoter) to reveal, show; (faire connaître au public): **~ qn/qch** to make sb/sth widely known, bring sb/sth to the public's notice; **se révéler** vi to be revealed, reveal itself; **se ~ facile/faux** to prove (to be) easy/ false; **se ~ cruel/un allié sûr** to show o.s. to be cruel/a trustworthy ally

revenant, e [ʀəvnɑ̃, -ɑ̃t] *nm/f* ghost

revendeur, -euse [ʀəvɑ̃dœʀ, -øz] *nm/f* (*détaillant*) retailer; (*d'occasions*) secondhand dealer

revendicatif, -ive [ʀəvɑ̃dikatif, -iv] *adj* (*mouvement*) protest *cpd*

revendication [ʀəvɑ̃dikasjɔ̃] *nf* claim, demand; **journée de ~** day of action (in support of one's claims)

revendiquer [ʀəvɑ̃dike] *vt* to claim, demand; (*responsabilité*) to claim ▷ *vi* to agitate in favour of one's claims

revendre [ʀəvɑ̃dʀ(ə)] *vt* (*d'occasion*) to resell; (*détailler*) to sell; (*vendre davantage de*): **~ du sucre/ un foulard/deux bagues** to sell more sugar/ another scarf/another two rings; **à ~** *adv* (*en abondance*) to spare

revenir [ʀəvniʀ] *vi* to come back; (*Culin*): **faire ~** to brown; (*coûter*): **~ cher/à 100 euros (à qn)** to cost (sb) a lot/100 euros; **~ à** (*études, projet*) to return to, go back to; (*équivaloir à*) to amount to; **~ à qn** (*rumeur, nouvelle*) to get back to sb, reach sb's ears; (*part, honneur*) to go to sb, be sb's; (*souvenir, nom*) to come back to sb; **~ de** (*fig: maladie, étonnement*) to recover from; **~ sur** (*question, sujet*) to go back over; (*engagement*) to go back on; **~ à la charge** to return to the attack; **~ à soi** to come round; **n'en pas ~: je n'en reviens** I can't get over it; **~ sur ses pas** to retrace one's steps; **cela revient à dire que/au même** it amounts to saying that/to the same thing; **~ de loin** (*fig*) to have been at death's door

revente [ʀəvɑ̃t] *nf* resale

revenu, e [ʀəvny] *pp de* **revenir** ▷ *nm* income; (*de l'État*) revenue; (*d'un capital*) yield; **revenus** *nmpl* income *sg*; **~ national brut** gross national income

rêver [ʀeve] *vi, vt* to dream; (*rêvasser*) to (day)dream; **~ de** (*voir en rêve*) to dream of *ou* about; **~ de qch/de faire** to dream of sth/of doing; **~ à** to dream of

réverbération [ʀevɛʀbeʀasjɔ̃] *nf* reflection

réverbère [ʀevɛʀbɛʀ] *nm* street lamp *ou* light

réverbérer [ʀevɛʀbeʀe] *vt* to reflect

reverdir [ʀəvɛʀdiʀ] *vi* (*arbre etc*) to turn green again

révérence [ʀeveʀɑ̃s] *nf* (*vénération*) reverence; (*salut: d'homme*) bow; (: *de femme*) curtsey

révérencieux, -euse [ʀeveʀɑ̃sjø, -øz] *adj* reverent

révérend, e [ʀeveʀɑ̃, -ɑ̃d] *adj*: **le ~ père Pascal** the Reverend Father Pascal

révérer [ʀeveʀe] *vt* to revere

rêverie [ʀɛvʀi] *nf* daydreaming *no pl*, daydream

reverrai *etc* [ʀəveʀe] *vb voir* **revoir**

revers [ʀəvɛʀ] *nm* (*de feuille, main*) back; (*d'étoffe*) wrong side; (*de pièce, médaille*) back, reverse; (*Tennis, Ping-Pong*) backhand; (*de veston*) lapel; (*de*

pantalon) turn-up; (*fig: échec*) setback; **~ de fortune** reverse of fortune; **d'un ~ de main** with the back of one's hand; **le ~ de la médaille** (*fig*) the other side of the coin; **prendre à ~** (*Mil*) to take from the rear

reverser [ʀəvɛʀse] *vt* (*reporter: somme etc*): **~ sur** to put back into; (*liquide*): **~ (dans)** to pour some more (into)

réversible [ʀevɛʀsibl(ə)] *adj* reversible

revêtement [ʀəvɛtmɑ̃] *nm* (*de paroi*) facing; (*des sols*) flooring; (*de chaussée*) surface; (*de tuyau etc: enduit*) coating

revêtir [ʀəvetiʀ] *vt* (*habit*) to don, put on; (*fig*) to take on; **~ qn de** to dress sb in; (*fig*) to endow *ou* invest sb with; **~ qch de** to cover sth with; (*fig*) to cloak sth in; **~ d'un visa** to append a visa to

rêveur, -euse [ʀevœʀ, -øz] *adj* dreamy ▷ *nm/f* dreamer

reviendrai *etc* [ʀəvjɛ̃dʀe] *vb voir* **revenir**

revienne *etc* [ʀəvjɛn] *vb voir* **revenir**

revient [ʀəvjɛ̃] *vb voir* **revenir** ▷ *nm*: **prix de ~** cost price

revigorer [ʀəvigɔʀe] *vt* to invigorate, revive, buck up

revint *etc* [ʀəvɛ̃] *vb voir* **revenir**

revirement [ʀəviʀmɑ̃] *nm* change of mind; (*d'une situation*) reversal

revis *etc* [ʀəvi] *vb voir* **revoir**

révisable [ʀevizabl(ə)] *adj* (*procès, taux etc*) reviewable, subject to review

réviser [ʀevize] *vt* (*texte, Scol: matière*) to revise; (*comptes*) to audit; (*machine, installation, moteur*) to overhaul, service; (*Jur: procès*) to review

révision [ʀevizjɔ̃] *nf* revision; auditing *no pl*; overhaul, servicing *no pl*; review; **conseil de ~** (*Mil*) recruiting board; **faire ses ~s** (*Scol*) to do one's revision (Brit), revise (Brit), review (US); **la ~ des 10 000 km** (*Auto*) the 10,000 km service

révisionnisme [ʀevizjɔnism(ə)] *nm* revisionism

revisser [ʀəvise] *vt* to screw back again

revit [ʀəvi] *vb voir* **revoir**

revitaliser [ʀəvitalize] *vt* to revitalize

revivifier [ʀəvivifje] *vt* to revitalize

revivre [ʀəvivʀ(ə)] *vi* (*reprendre des forces*) to come alive again; (*traditions*) to be revived ▷ *vt* (*épreuve, moment*) to relive; **faire ~** (*mode, institution, usage*) to bring back to life

révocable [ʀevɔkabl(ə)] *adj* (*délégué*) dismissible; (*contrat*) revocable

révocation [ʀevɔkasjɔ̃] *nf* dismissal; revocation

revoir [ʀəvwaʀ] *vt* to see again; (*réviser*) to revise (Brit), review (US) ▷ *nm*: **au ~** goodbye; **dire au ~ à qn** to say goodbye to sb; **se revoir** (*amis*) to meet (again), see each other again

révoltant, e [ʀevɔltɑ̃, -ɑ̃t] *adj* revolting

révolte [ʀevɔlt(ə)] *nf* rebellion, revolt

révolter [ʀevɔlte] *vt* to revolt, outrage; **se révolter** *vi*: **se ~ (contre)** to rebel (against); **se ~ (à)** to be outraged (by)

révolu, e [ʀevɔly] *adj* past; (*Admin*): **âgé de 18 ans ~s** over 18 years of age; **après trois ans ~s**

r

when three full years have passed

révolution [ʀevɔlysjɔ̃] *nf* revolution; **être en ~** (*pays etc*) to be in revolt; **la ~ industrielle** the industrial revolution

révolutionnaire [ʀevɔlysjɔnɛʀ] *adj, nm/f* revolutionary

révolutionner [ʀevɔlysjɔne] *vt* to revolutionize; (*fig*) to stir up

revolver [ʀevɔlvɛʀ] *nm* gun; (*à barillet*) revolver

révoquer [ʀevɔke] *vt* (*fonctionnaire*) to dismiss, remove from office; (*arrêt, contrat*) to revoke

revoyais *etc* [ʀəvwaje] *vb voir* **revoir**

revu, e [ʀəvy] *pp de* **revoir** ▷ *nf* (*inventaire, examen*) review; (*Mil: défilé*) review, march past; (*: inspection*) inspection, review; (*périodique*) review, magazine; (*pièce satirique*) revue; (*de music-hall*) variety show; **passer en ~** to review, inspect; (*fig*) to review; **~ de (la) presse** press review

révulsé, e [ʀevylse] *adj* (*yeux*) rolled upwards; (*visage*) contorted

Reykjavik [ʀekjavik] *n* Reykjavik

rez-de-chaussée [ʀedʃose] *nm inv* ground floor

rez-de-jardin [ʀedʒaʀdɛ̃] *nm inv* garden level

RF *sigle f* = **République française**

RFA *sigle f* (= *République fédérale d'Allemagne*) FRG

RFO *sigle f* (= *Radio-Télévision Française d'Outre-mer*) French overseas broadcasting service

RG *sigle mpl* (= *renseignements généraux*) security section of the police force

rhabiller [ʀabije] *vt*: **se rhabiller** to get dressed again, put one's clothes on again

rhapsodie [ʀapsɔdi] *nf* rhapsody

rhéostat [ʀeɔsta] *nm* rheostat

rhésus [ʀezys] *adj, nm* rhesus; **~ positif/négatif** rhesus positive/negative

rhétorique [ʀetɔʀik] *nf* rhetoric ▷ *adj* rhetorical

Rhin [ʀɛ̃] *nm*: **le ~** the Rhine

rhinite [ʀinit] *nf* rhinitis

rhinocéros [ʀinɔseʀɔs] *nm* rhinoceros

rhinopharyngite [ʀinɔfaʀɛ̃ʒit] *nf* throat infection

rhodanien, ne [ʀɔdanjɛ̃, -ɛn] *adj* Rhône *cpd*, of the Rhône

Rhodes [ʀɔd] *n*: **(l'île de) ~** (the island of) Rhodes

Rhodésie [ʀɔdezi] *nf*: **la ~** Rhodesia

rhodésien, ne [ʀɔdezjɛ̃, -ɛn] *adj* Rhodesian

rhododendron [ʀɔdɔdɛ̃dʀɔ̃] *nm* rhododendron

Rhône [ʀon] *nm*: **le ~** the Rhone

rhubarbe [ʀybaʀb(ə)] *nf* rhubarb

rhum [ʀɔm] *nm* rum

rhumatisant, e [ʀymatizɑ̃, -ɑ̃t] *adj, nm/f* rheumatic

rhumatismal, e, -aux [ʀymatismal, -o] *adj* rheumatic

rhumatisme [ʀymatism(ə)] *nm* rheumatism *no pl*

rhumatologie [ʀymatɔlɔʒi] *nf* rheumatology

rhumatologue [ʀymatɔlɔg] *nm/f* rheumatologist

rhume [ʀym] *nm* cold; **~ de cerveau** head cold;

le ~ des foins hay fever

rhumerie [ʀɔmʀi] *nf* (*distillerie*) rum distillery

RI *sigle m* (*Mil*) = **régiment d'infanterie**

ri [ʀi] *pp de* **rire**

riant, e [ʀjɑ̃, -ɑ̃t] *vb voir* **rire** ▷ *adj* smiling, cheerful; (*campagne, paysage*) pleasant

RIB *sigle m* = **relevé d'identité bancaire**

ribambelle [ʀibɑ̃bɛl] *nf*: **une ~ de** a herd *ou* swarm of

ricain, e [ʀikɛ̃, -ɛn] *adj* (*fam*) Yank, Yankee

ricanement [ʀikanmɑ̃] *nm* snigger; giggle

ricaner [ʀikane] *vi* (*avec méchanceté*) to snigger; (*bêtement, avec gêne*) to giggle

riche [ʀiʃ] *adj* (*gén*) rich; (*personne, pays*) rich, wealthy; **~ en** rich in; **~ de** full of; rich in

richement [ʀiʃmɑ̃] *adv* richly

richesse [ʀiʃɛs] *nf* wealth; (*fig*) richness; **richesses** *nfpl* wealth *sg*; treasures; **~ en vitamines** high vitamin content

richissime [ʀiʃisim] *adj* extremely rich *ou* wealthy

ricin [ʀisɛ̃] *nm*: **huile de ~** castor oil

ricocher [ʀikɔʃe] *vi*: **~ (sur)** to rebound (off); (*sur l'eau*) to bounce (on *ou* off); **faire ~** (*galet*) to skim

ricochet [ʀikɔʃe] *nm* rebound; bounce; **faire ~** to rebound, bounce; (*fig*) to rebound; **faire des ~s** to skip stones; **par ~** *adv* on the rebound; (*fig*) as an indirect result

rictus [ʀiktys] *nm* grin, (snarling) grimace

ride [ʀid] *nf* wrinkle; (*fig*) ripple

ridé, e [ʀide] *adj* wrinkled

rideau, x [ʀido] *nm* curtain; **tirer/ouvrir les ~x** to draw/open the curtains; **~ de fer** metal shutter; (*Pol*): **le ~ de fer** the Iron Curtain

ridelle [ʀidɛl] *nf* slatted side (*of truck*)

rider [ʀide] *vt* to wrinkle; (*fig*) to ripple, ruffle the surface of; **se rider** *vi* to become wrinkled

ridicule [ʀidikyl] *adj* ridiculous ▷ *nm* ridiculousness *no pl*; **le ~** ridicule; (*travers: gén pl*) absurdities *pl*; **tourner en ~** to ridicule

ridiculement [ʀidikylmɑ̃] *adv* ridiculously

ridiculiser [ʀidikylize] *vt* to ridicule; **se ridiculiser** to make a fool of o.s

ridule [ʀidyl] *nf* (*euph: ride*) little wrinkle

rie *etc* [ʀi] *vb voir* **rire**

 MOT-CLÉ

rien [ʀjɛ̃] *pron* **1**: **(ne)... rien** nothing; (*tournure négative*) anything; **qu'est-ce que vous avez? — rien** what have you got? — nothing; **il n'a rien dit/fait** he said/did nothing, he hasn't said/ done anything; **il n'a rien** (*n'est pas blessé*) he's all right; **ça ne fait rien** it doesn't matter; **il n'y est pour rien** he's got nothing to do with it

2 (*quelque chose*): **a-t-il jamais rien fait pour nous?** has he ever done anything for us?

3: **rien de**: **rien d'intéressant** nothing interesting; **rien d'autre** nothing else; **rien du tout** nothing at all; **il n'a rien d'un champion** he's no champion, there's nothing of the champion about him

4: **rien que** just, only; nothing but; **rien que pour lui faire plaisir** only *ou* just to please him; **rien que la vérité** nothing but the truth; **rien que cela** that alone
▷ *excl*: **de rien!** not at all!, don't mention it!; **il n'en est rien!** nothing of the sort!; **rien à faire!** it's no good!, it's no use!
▷ *nm*: **un petit rien** (*cadeau*) a little something; **des riens** trivia *pl*; **un rien de** a hint of; **en un rien de temps** in no time at all; **avoir peur d'un rien** to be frightened of the slightest thing

rieur, -euse [ʀjœʀ, -øz] *adj* cheerful
rigide [ʀiʒid] *adj* stiff; (*fig*) rigid; (*moralement*) strict
rigidité [ʀiʒidite] *nf* stiffness; **la ~ cadavérique** rigor mortis
rigolade [ʀigɔlad] *nf*: **la ~** fun; (*fig*): **c'est de la ~** it's a big farce; (*c'est facile*) it's a cinch
rigole [ʀigɔl] *nf* (*conduit*) channel; (*filet d'eau*) rivulet
rigoler [ʀigɔle] *vi* (*rire*) to laugh; (*s'amuser*) to have (some) fun; (*plaisanter*) to be joking *ou* kidding
rigolo, ote [ʀigɔlo, -ɔt] *adj* (*fam*) funny ▷ *nm/f* comic; (*péj*) fraud, phoney
rigorisme [ʀigɔʀism(ə)] *nm* (moral) rigorism
rigoriste [ʀigɔʀist(ə)] *adj* rigorist
rigoureusement [ʀiguʀøzmɑ̃] *adv* rigorously; **~ vrai/interdit** strictly true/forbidden
rigoureux, -euse [ʀiguʀø, -øz] *adj* (*morale*) rigorous, strict; (*personne*) stern, strict; (*climat, châtiment*) rigorous, harsh, severe; (*interdiction, neutralité*) strict; (*preuves, analyse, méthode*) rigorous
rigueur [ʀiguʀ] *nf* rigour (*Brit*), rigor (*US*); strictness; harshness; **"tenue de soirée de ~"** "evening dress (to be worn)"; **être de ~** to be the usual thing, be the rule; **à la ~** at a pinch; possibly; **tenir ~ à qn de qch** to hold sth against sb
riions *etc* [ʀijɔ̃] *vb voir* **rire**
rillettes [ʀijɛt] *nfpl* ≈ potted meat *sg*
rime [ʀim] *nf* rhyme; **n'avoir ni ~ ni raison** to have neither rhyme nor reason
rimer [ʀime] *vi*: **~ (avec)** to rhyme (with); **ne ~ à rien** not to make sense
Rimmel® [ʀimɛl] *nm* mascara
rinçage [ʀɛ̃saʒ] *nm* rinsing (out); (*opération*) rinse
rince-doigts [ʀɛ̃sdwa] *nm inv* finger-bowl
rincer [ʀɛ̃se] *vt* to rinse; (*récipient*) to rinse out; **se ~ la bouche** to rinse one's mouth out
ring [ʀiŋ] *nm* (boxing) ring; **monter sur le ~** (*aussi fig*) to enter the ring; (: *faire carrière de boxeur*) to take up boxing
ringard, e [ʀɛ̃gaʀ, -aʀd(ə)] *adj* (*péj*) old-fashioned
Rio de Janeiro [ʀiodʒaneʀ(o)] *n* Rio de Janeiro
rions [ʀiɔ̃] *vb voir* **rire**
ripaille [ʀipaj] *nf*: **faire ~** to feast
riper [ʀipe] *vi* to slip, slide

ripoliné, e [ʀipoline] *adj* enamel-painted
riposte [ʀipɔst(ə)] *nf* retort, riposte; (*fig*) counter-attack, reprisal
riposter [ʀipɔste] *vi* to retaliate ▷ *vt*: **~ que** to retort that; **~ à** *vt* to counter; to reply to
ripper [ʀipe] *vt* (*Inform*) to rip
rire [ʀiʀ] *vi* to laugh; (*se divertir*) to have fun; (*plaisanter*) to joke ▷ *nm* laugh; **le ~** laughter; **~ de** *vt* to laugh at; **se ~ de** to make light of; **tu veux ~!** you must be joking!; **~ aux éclats/aux larmes** to roar with laughter/laugh until one cries; **~ jaune** to force oneself to laugh; **~ sous cape** to laugh up one's sleeve; **~ au nez de qn** to laugh in sb's face; **pour ~** (*pas sérieusement*) for a joke *ou* a laugh
ris [ʀi] *vb voir* **rire** ▷ *nm*: **~ de veau** (calf) sweetbread
risée [ʀize] *nf*: **être la ~ de** to be the laughing stock of
risette [ʀizɛt] *nf*: **faire ~ (à)** to give a nice little smile (to)
risible [ʀizibl(ə)] *adj* laughable, ridiculous
risque [ʀisk(ə)] *nm* risk; **l'attrait du ~** the lure of danger; **prendre des ~s** to take risks; **à ses ~s et périls** at his own risk; **au ~ de** at the risk of; **~ d'incendie** fire risk; **~ calculé** calculated risk
risqué, e [ʀiske] *adj* risky; (*plaisanterie*) risqué, daring
risquer [ʀiske] *vt* to risk; (*allusion, question*) to venture, hazard; **tu risques qu'on te renvoie** you risk being dismissed; **ça ne risque rien** it's quite safe; **~ de: il risque de se tuer** he could get *ou* risks getting himself killed; **il a risqué de se tuer** he almost got himself killed; **ce qui risque de se produire** what might *ou* could well happen; **il ne risque pas de recommencer** there's no chance of him doing that again; **se risquer dans** (*s'aventurer*) to venture into; **se risquer à faire** (*tenter*) to dare to do; **~ le tout pour le tout** to risk the lot
risque-tout [ʀiskətu] *nm/f inv* daredevil
rissoler [ʀisɔle] *vi, vt*: **(faire) ~** to brown
ristourne [ʀistuʀn(ə)] *nf* rebate; discount
rit *etc* [ʀi] *vb voir* **rire**
rite [ʀit] *nm* rite; (*fig*) ritual
ritournelle [ʀituʀnɛl] *nf* (*fig*) tune; **c'est toujours la même ~** (*fam*) it's always the same old story
rituel, le [ʀituɛl] *adj, nm* ritual
rituellement [ʀituɛlmɑ̃] *adv* religiously
riv. *abr* (= *rivière*) R
rivage [ʀivaʒ] *nm* shore
rival, e, -aux [ʀival, -o] *adj, nm/f* rival; **sans ~** *adj* unrivalled
rivaliser [ʀivalize] *vi*: **~ avec** to rival, vie with; (*être comparable*) to hold its own against, compare with; **~ avec qn de** (*élégance etc*) to vie with *ou* rival sb in
rivalité [ʀivalite] *nf* rivalry
rive [ʀiv] *nf* shore; (*de fleuve*) bank
river [ʀive] *vt* (*clou, pointe*) to clinch; (*plaques*) to

r

rivet together; **être rivé sur/à** to be riveted on/to

riverain, e [ʀivʀɛ̃, -ɛn] *adj* riverside *cpd*; lakeside *cpd*; roadside *cpd* ▷ *nm/f* riverside (*ou* lakeside) resident; local *ou* roadside resident

rivet [ʀivɛ] *nm* rivet

riveter [ʀivte] *vt* to rivet (together)

Riviera [ʀivjɛʀa] *nf*: **la ~ (italienne)** the Italian Riviera

rivière [ʀivjɛʀ] *nf* river; **~ de diamants** diamond rivière

rixe [ʀiks(ə)] *nf* brawl, scuffle

Riyad [ʀijad] *n* Riyadh

riz [ʀi] *nm* rice; **~ au lait** ≈ rice pudding

rizière [ʀizjɛʀ] *nf* paddy field

RMC *sigle f* = **Radio Monte Carlo**

RMI *sigle m* (= *revenu minimum d'insertion*) ≈ income support (*Brit*), ≈ welfare (*US*)

RN *sigle f* = **route nationale**

robe [ʀɔb] *nf* dress; (*de juge, d'ecclésiastique*) robe; (*de professeur*) gown; (*pelage*) coat; **~ de soirée/de mariée** evening/wedding dress; **~ de baptême** christening robe; **~ de chambre** dressing gown; **~ de grossesse** maternity dress

robinet [ʀɔbinɛ] *nm* tap, faucet (*US*); **~ du gaz** gas tap; **~ mélangeur** mixer tap

robinetterie [ʀɔbinɛtʀi] *nf* taps *pl*, plumbing

roboratif, -ive [ʀɔbɔʀatif, -iv] *adj* bracing, invigorating

robot [ʀɔbo] *nm* robot; **~ de cuisine** food processor

robotique [ʀɔbɔtik] *nf* robotics *sg*

robotiser [ʀɔbɔtize] *vt* (*personne, travailleur*) to turn into a robot; (*monde, vie*) to automate

robuste [ʀɔbyst(ə)] *adj* robust, sturdy

robustesse [ʀɔbystɛs] *nf* robustness, sturdiness

roc [ʀɔk] *nm* rock

rocade [ʀɔkad] *nf* (*Auto*) bypass

rocaille [ʀɔkaj] *nf* (*pierres*) loose stones *pl*; (*terrain*) rocky *ou* stony ground; (*jardin*) rockery, rock garden ▷ *adj* (*style*) rocaille

rocailleux, -euse [ʀɔkajø, -øz] *adj* rocky, stony; (*voix*) harsh

rocambolesque [ʀɔkɑ̃bɔlɛsk(ə)] *adj* fantastic, incredible

roche [ʀɔʃ] *nf* rock

rocher [ʀɔʃe] *nm* rock; (*Anat*) petrosal bone

rochet [ʀɔʃɛ] *nm*: **roue à ~** ratchet wheel

rocheux, -euse [ʀɔʃø, -øz] *adj* rocky; **les (montagnes) Rocheuses** the Rockies, the Rocky Mountains

rock [ʀɔk], **rock and roll** [ʀɔkɛnʀɔl] *nm* (*musique*) rock(-'n'-roll); (*danse*) rock

rocker [ʀɔkœʀ] *nm* (*chanteur*) rock musician; (*adepte*) rock fan

rocking-chair [ʀɔkiŋ(t)ʃɛʀ] *nm* rocking chair

rococo [ʀɔkɔko] *nm* rococo ▷ *adj* rococo

rodage [ʀɔdaʒ] *nm* running in (*Brit*), breaking in (*US*); **en ~** (*Auto*) running *ou* breaking in

rodé, e [ʀɔde] *adj* run in (*Brit*), broken in (*US*); (*personne*): **~ à qch** having got the hang of sth

rodéo [ʀɔdeo] *nm* rodeo

roder [ʀɔde] *vt* (*moteur, voiture*) to run in (*Brit*), break in (*US*); **~ un spectacle** to iron out the initial problems of a show

rôder [ʀode] *vi* to roam *ou* wander about; (*de façon suspecte*) to lurk (about *ou* around)

rôdeur, -euse [ʀodœʀ, -øz] *nm/f* prowler

rodomontades [ʀɔdɔmɔ̃tad] *nfpl* bragging *sg*; sabre rattling *sg*

rogatoire [ʀɔgatwaʀ] *adj*: **commission ~** letters rogatory

rogne [ʀɔɲ] *nf*: **être en ~** to be mad *ou* in a temper; **se mettre en ~** to get mad *ou* in a temper

rogner [ʀɔɲe] *vt* to trim; (*fig*) to whittle down; **~ sur** (*fig*) to cut down *ou* back on

rognons [ʀɔɲɔ̃] *nmpl* kidneys

rognures [ʀɔɲyʀ] *nfpl* trimmings

rogue [ʀɔg] *adj* arrogant

roi [ʀwa] *nm* king; **les R~s mages** the Three Wise Men, the Magi; **le jour** *ou* **la fête des R~s**, **les R~s** Twelfth Night; *see note*

● **FÊTE DES ROIS**

● The *'fête des Rois'* is celebrated on 6 January.
● Figurines representing the Three Wise Men
● are traditionally added to the Christmas
● crib ('crèche') and people eat 'galette des
● Rois', a flat cake in which a porcelain charm
● ('la fève') is hidden. Whoever finds the
● charm is king or queen for the day and can
● choose a partner.

---

roitelet [ʀwatlɛ] *nm* wren; (*péj*) kinglet

rôle [ʀol] *nm* role; (*contribution*) part

rollers [ʀɔlœʀ] *nmpl* Rollerblades®

rollmops [ʀɔlmɔps] *nm* rollmop

romain, e [ʀɔmɛ̃, -ɛn] *adj* Roman ▷ *nm/f*: **Romain, e** Roman ▷ *nf* (*Culin*) cos (lettuce)

roman, e [ʀɔmɑ̃, -an] *adj* (*Archit*) Romanesque; (*Ling*) Romance *cpd*, Romanic ▷ *nm* novel; **~ d'amour** love story; **~ d'espionnage** spy novel *ou* story; **~ noir** thriller; **~ policier** detective novel

romance [ʀɔmɑ̃s] *nf* ballad

romancer [ʀɔmɑ̃se] *vt* to romanticize

romanche [ʀɔmɑ̃ʃ] *adj*, *nm* Romansh

romancier, -ière [ʀɔmɑ̃sje, -jɛʀ] *nm/f* novelist

romand, e [ʀɔmɑ̃, -ɑ̃d] *adj* of *ou* from French-speaking Switzerland ▷ *nm/f*: **Romand, e** French-speaking Swiss

romanesque [ʀɔmanɛsk(ə)] *adj* (*fantastique*) fantastic; storybook *cpd*; (*sentimental*) romantic; (*Littérature*) novelistic

roman-feuilleton [ʀɔmɑ̃fœjtɔ̃] (*pl* **romans-feuilletons**) *nm* serialized novel

roman-fleuve [ʀɔmɑ̃flœv] (*pl* **romans-fleuves**) *nm* saga, roman-fleuve

romanichel, le [ʀɔmaniʃɛl] *nm/f* gipsy

roman-photo [ʀɔmɑ̃fɔto] (*pl* **romans-photos**) *nm* (romantic) picture story

romantique [ʀɔmɑ̃tik] *adj* romantic

romantisme [ʀɔmɑ̃tism(ə)] *nm* romanticism

romarin [ʀɔmaʀɛ̃] *nm* rosemary

rombière [ʀɔ̃bjɛʀ] *nf* (*péj*) old bag

Rome [ʀɔm] *n* Rome

rompre [ʀɔ̃pʀ(ə)] *vt* to break; (*entretien, fiançailles*) to break off ▷ *vi* (*fiancés*) to break it off; **se rompre** *vi* to break; (*Méd*) to burst, rupture; **se ~ les os** *ou* **le cou** to break one's neck; **~ avec** to break with; **à tout ~** *adv* wildly; **applaudir à tout ~** to bring down the house, applaud wildly; **~ la glace** (*fig*) to break the ice; **rompez (les rangs)!** (*Mil*) dismiss!, fall out!

rompu, e [ʀɔ̃py] *pp de* **rompre** ▷ *adj* (*fourbu*) exhausted, worn out; **~ à** with wide experience of; inured to

romsteck [ʀɔmstɛk] *nm* rump steak *no pl*

ronce [ʀɔ̃s] *nf* (*Bot*) bramble branch; (*Menuiserie*): **~ de noyer** burr walnut; **ronces** *nfpl* brambles, thorns

ronchonner [ʀɔ̃ʃɔne] *vi* (*fam*) to grouse, grouch

rond, e [ʀɔ̃, ʀɔ̃d] *adj* round; (*joues, mollets*) well-rounded; (*fam: ivre*) tight; (*sincère, décidé*): **être ~ en affaires** to be on the level in business, do an honest deal ▷ *nm* (*cercle*) ring; (*fam: sou*): **je n'ai plus un ~** I haven't a penny left ▷ *nf* (*gén: de surveillance*) rounds *pl*, patrol; (*danse*) round (dance); (*Mus*) semibreve (*Brit*), whole note (*US*) ▷ *adv*: **tourner ~** (*moteur*) to run smoothly; **ça ne tourne pas ~** (*fig*) there's something not quite right about it; **pour faire un compte ~** to make (it) a round figure, to round (it) off; **avoir le dos ~** to be round-shouldered; **en ~** (*s'asseoir, danser*) in a ring; **à la ~e** (*alentour*): **à 10 km à la ~e** for 10 km round; (*à chacun son tour*): **passer qch à la ~e** to pass sth (a)round; **faire des ~s de jambe** to bow and scrape; **~ de serviette** napkin ring

rond-de-cuir [ʀɔ̃dkɥiʀ] (*pl* **ronds-de-cuir**) *nm* (*péj*) penpusher

rondelet, te [ʀɔ̃dlɛ, -ɛt] *adj* plump; (*fig: somme*) tidy; (: *bourse*) well-lined, fat

rondelle [ʀɔ̃dɛl] *nf* (*Tech*) washer; (*tranche*) slice, round

rondement [ʀɔ̃dmɑ̃] *adv* (*avec décision*) briskly; (*loyalement*) frankly

rondeur [ʀɔ̃dœʀ] *nf* (*d'un bras, des formes*) plumpness; (*bonhomie*) friendly straightforwardness; **rondeurs** *nfpl* (*d'une femme*) curves

rondin [ʀɔ̃dɛ̃] *nm* log

rond-point [ʀɔ̃pwɛ̃] (*pl* **ronds-points**) *nm* roundabout (*Brit*), traffic circle (*US*)

ronflant, e [ʀɔ̃flɑ̃, -ɑ̃t] *adj* (*péj*) high-flown, grand

ronflement [ʀɔ̃fləmɑ̃] *nm* snore, snoring *no pl*

ronfler [ʀɔ̃fle] *vi* to snore; (*moteur, poêle*) to hum; (: *plus fort*) to roar

ronger [ʀɔ̃ʒe] *vt* to gnaw (at); (*vers, rouille*) to eat into; **~ son frein** to champ (at) the bit; (*fig*): **se ~ de souci, se ~ les sangs** to worry o.s. sick, fret; **se ~ les ongles** to bite one's nails

rongeur, -euse [ʀɔ̃ʒœʀ, -øz] *nm/f* rodent

ronronnement [ʀɔ̃ʀɔnmɑ̃] *nm* purring; (*bruit*) purr

ronronner [ʀɔ̃ʀɔne] *vi* to purr

roque [ʀɔk] *nm* (*Échecs*) castling

roquefort [ʀɔkfɔʀ] *nm* Roquefort

roquer [ʀɔke] *vi* to castle

roquet [ʀɔkɛ] *nm* nasty little lap-dog

roquette [ʀɔkɛt] *nf* rocket; **~ antichar** antitank rocket

rosace [ʀozas] *nf* (*vitrail*) rose window, rosace; (*motif: de plafond etc*) rose

rosaire [ʀozɛʀ] *nm* rosary

rosbif [ʀɔsbif] *nm*: **du ~** roasting beef; (*cuit*) roast beef; **un ~** a joint of (roasting) beef

rose [ʀoz] *nf* rose; (*vitrail*) rose window ▷ *adj* pink; **~ bonbon** *adj inv* candy pink; **~ des vents** compass card

rosé, e [ʀoze] *adj* pinkish; (*vin*) **~** rosé (wine)

roseau, x [ʀozo] *nm* reed

rosée [ʀoze] *adj f voir* **rosé** ▷ *nf*: **goutte de ~** dewdrop

roseraie [ʀozʀɛ] *nf* rose garden; (*plantation*) rose nursery

rosette [ʀozɛt] *nf* rosette (*gen of the Légion d'honneur*)

rosier [ʀozje] *nm* rosebush, rose tree

rosir [ʀoziʀ] *vi* to go pink

rosse [ʀɔs] *nf* (*péj: cheval*) nag ▷ *adj* nasty, vicious

rosser [ʀɔse] *vt* (*fam*) to thrash

rossignol [ʀɔsiɲɔl] *nm* (*Zool*) nightingale; (*crochet*) picklock

rot [ʀo] *nm* belch; (*de bébé*) burp

rotatif, -ive [ʀɔtatif, -iv] *adj* rotary ▷ *nf* rotary press

rotation [ʀɔtasjɔ̃] *nf* rotation; (*fig*) rotation, swap-around; (*renouvellement*) turnover; **par ~** on a rota (*Brit*) *ou* rotation (*US*) basis; **~ des cultures** crop rotation; **~ des stocks** stock turnover

rotatoire [ʀɔtatwaʀ] *adj*: **mouvement ~** rotary movement

roter [ʀɔte] *vi* (*fam*) to burp, belch

rôti [ʀoti] *nm*: **du ~** roasting meat; (*cuit*) roast meat; **un ~ de bœuf/porc** a joint of (roasting) beef/pork

rotin [ʀɔtɛ̃] *nm* rattan (cane); **fauteuil en ~** cane (arm)chair

rôtir [ʀotiʀ] *vt* (*aussi*: **faire rôtir**) to roast ▷ *vi* to roast; **se ~ au soleil** to bask in the sun

rôtisserie [ʀotisʀi] *nf* (*restaurant*) steakhouse; (*comptoir, magasin*) roast meat counter (*ou* shop)

rôtissoire [ʀotiswaʀ] *nf* (roasting) spit

rotonde [ʀɔtɔ̃d] *nf* (*Archit*) rotunda; (*Rail*) engine shed

rotondité [ʀɔtɔ̃dite] *nf* roundness

rotor [ʀɔtɔʀ] *nm* rotor

Rotterdam [ʀɔtɛʀdam] *n* Rotterdam

rotule [ʀɔtyl] *nf* kneecap, patella

roturier, -ière [ʀɔtyʀje, -jɛʀ] *nm/f* commoner

rouage [ʀwaʒ] *nm* cog(wheel), gearwheel; (*de montre*) part; (*fig*) cog; **rouages** *nmpl* (*fig*) internal structure *sg*

Rouanda [ʀwɑ̃da] *nm*: **le ~** Rwanda

roubaisien, ne [ʀubɛzjɛ̃, -ɛn] *adj* of *ou* from Roubaix

roublard, e [ʀublaʀ, -aʀd(ə)] *adj* (*péj*) crafty, wily

rouble [ʀubl(ə)] *nm* rouble

roucoulement [ʀukulmɑ̃] *nm* (*de pigeons, fig*) coo, cooing

roucouler [ʀukule] *vi* to coo; (*fig: péj*) to warble; (: *amoureux*) to bill and coo

roue [ʀu] *nf* wheel; **faire la ~** (*paon*) to spread *ou* fan its tail; (*Gym*) to do a cartwheel; **descendre en ~ libre** to freewheel *ou* coast down; **pousser à la ~** to put one's shoulder to the wheel; **grande ~** (*à la foire*) big wheel; **~ à aubes** paddle wheel; **~ dentée** cogwheel; **~ de secours** spare wheel

roué, e [ʀwe] *adj* wily

rouennais, e [ʀwanɛ, -ɛz] *adj* of *ou* from Rouen

rouer [ʀwe] *vt*: **~ qn de coups** to give sb a thrashing

rouet [ʀwɛ] *nm* spinning wheel

rouge [ʀuʒ] *adj, nm/f* red ▷ *nm* red; (*fard*) rouge; (**vin**) **~** red wine; **passer au ~** (*signal*) to go red; (*automobiliste*) to go through a red light; **porter au ~** (*métal*) to bring to red heat; **sur la liste ~** (*Tél*) ex-directory (*Brit*), unlisted (*US*); **~ de honte/colère** red with shame/anger; **se fâcher tout/voir ~** to blow one's top/see red; **~ (à lèvres)** lipstick

rougeâtre [ʀuʒatʀ(ə)] *adj* reddish

rougeaud, e [ʀuʒo, -od] *adj* (*teint*) red; (*personne*) red-faced

rouge-gorge [ʀuʒgɔʀʒ(ə)] *nm* robin (redbreast)

rougeoiement [ʀuʒwamɑ̃] *nm* reddish glow

rougeole [ʀuʒɔl] *nf* measles *sg*

rougeoyant, e [ʀuʒwajɑ̃, -ɑ̃t] *adj* (*ciel, braises*) glowing; (*aube, reflets*) glowing red

rougeoyer [ʀuʒwaje] *vi* to glow red

rouget [ʀuʒɛ] *nm* mullet

rougeur [ʀuʒœʀ] *nf* redness; (*du visage*) red face; **rougeurs** *nfpl* (*Méd*) red blotches

rougir [ʀuʒiʀ] *vi* (*de honte, timidité*) to blush, flush; (*de plaisir, colère*) to flush; (*fraise, tomate*) to go *ou* turn red; (*ciel*) to redden

rouille [ʀuj] *adj inv* rust-coloured, rusty ▷ *nf* rust; (*Culin*) spicy (Provençal) sauce served with fish dishes

rouillé, e [ʀuje] *adj* rusty

rouiller [ʀuje] *vt* to rust ▷ *vi* to rust, go rusty; **se rouiller** *vi* to rust; (*fig: mentalement*) to become rusty; (: *physiquement*) to grow stiff

roulade [ʀulad] *nf* (*Gym*) roll; (*Culin*) rolled meat *no pl*; (*Mus*) roulade, run

roulage [ʀulaʒ] *nm* (*transport*) haulage

roulant, e [ʀulɑ̃, -ɑ̃t] *adj* (*meuble*) on wheels; (*surface, trottoir*) moving; **matériel ~** (*Rail*) rolling stock; **personnel ~** (*Rail*) train crews *pl*

roulé, e [ʀule] *adj*: **bien ~e** (*fam: femme*) shapely, curvy

rouleau, x [ʀulo] *nm* (*de papier, tissu, pièces de monnaie, Sport*) roll; (*de machine à écrire*) roller, platen; (*à mise en plis, à peinture, vague*) roller; **être au bout du ~** (*fig*) to be at the end of the line; **~**

compresseur steamroller; **~ à pâtisserie** rolling pin; **~ de pellicule** roll of film

roulé-boulé [ʀulebule] (*pl* **roulés-boulés**) (*Sport*) roll

roulement [ʀulmɑ̃] *nm* (*bruit*) rumbling *no pl*, rumble; (*rotation*) rotation; turnover; (: *de capitaux*) circulation; **par ~** on a rota (*Brit*) *ou* rotation (*US*) basis; **~ (à billes)** ball bearings *pl*; **~ de tambour** drum roll; **~ d'yeux** roll(ing) of the eyes

rouler [ʀule] *vt* to roll; (*papier, tapis*) to roll up; (*Culin: pâte*) to roll out; (*fam*) to do, con ▷ *vi* (*bille, boule*) to roll; (*voiture, train*) to go, run; (*automobiliste*) to drive; (*cycliste*) to ride; (*bateau*) to roll; (*tonnerre*) to rumble, roll; (*dégringoler*): **~ en bas de** to roll down; **~ sur** (*conversation*) to turn on; **se ~ dans** (*boue*) to roll in; (*couverture*) to roll o.s. (up) in; **~ dans la farine** (*fam*) to con; **~ les épaules/hanches** to sway one's shoulders/wiggle one's hips; **~ les "r"** to roll one's r's; **~ sur l'or** to be rolling in money, be rolling in it; **~ (sa bosse)** to go places

roulette [ʀulɛt] *nf* (*de table, fauteuil*) castor; (*de pâtissier*) pastry wheel; (*jeu*): **la ~** roulette; **à ~s** on castors; **la ~ russe** Russian roulette

roulis [ʀuli] *nm* roll(ing)

roulotte [ʀulɔt] *nf* caravan

roumain, e [ʀumɛ̃, -ɛn] *adj* Rumanian, Romanian ▷ *nm* (*Ling*) Rumanian, Romanian ▷ *nm/f*: **Roumain, e** Rumanian, Romanian

Roumanie [ʀumani] *nf*: **la ~** Rumania, Romania

roupiller [ʀupije] *vi* (*fam*) to sleep

rouquin, e [ʀukɛ̃, -in] *nm/f* (*péj*) redhead

rouspéter [ʀuspete] *vi* (*fam*) to moan, grouse

rousse [ʀus] *adj f voir* **roux**

rousseur [ʀusœʀ] *nf*: **tache de ~** freckle

roussi [ʀusi] *nm*: **ça sent le ~** there's a smell of burning; (*fig*) I can smell trouble

roussir [ʀusiʀ] *vt* to scorch ▷ *vi* (*feuilles*) to go *ou* turn brown; (*Culin*): **faire ~** to brown

routage [ʀutaʒ] *nm* (*collective*) mailing

routard, e [ʀutaʀ, -aʀd(ə)] *nm/f* traveller

route [ʀut] *nf* road; (*fig: chemin*) way; (*itinéraire, parcours*) route; (*fig: voie*) road, path; **par (la) ~** by road; **il y a trois heures de ~** it's a three-hour ride *ou* journey; **en ~** *adv* on the way; **en ~!** let's go!; **en cours de ~** en route; **mettre en ~** to start up; **se mettre en ~** to set off; **faire ~ vers** to head towards; **faire fausse ~** (*fig*) to be on the wrong track; **~ nationale (RN)** ≈ A-road (*Brit*), ≈ state highway (*US*)

routier, -ière [ʀutje, -jɛʀ] *adj* road *cpd* ▷ *nm* (*camionneur*) (long-distance) lorry (*Brit*) *ou* truck driver; (*restaurant*) ≈ transport café (*Brit*), ≈ truck stop (*US*); (*scout*) ≈ rover; (*cycliste*) road racer ▷ *nf* (*voiture*) touring car; **vieux ~** old stager; **carte routière** road map

routine [ʀutin] *nf* routine; **visite/contrôle de ~** routine visit/check

routinier, -ière [ʀutinje, -jɛʀ] *adj* (*péj: travail*) humdrum, routine; (: *personne*) addicted to routine

rouvert, e [ʀuvɛʀ, -ɛʀt(ə)] *pp de* **rouvrir**

rouvrir [ʀuvʀiʀ] *vt, vi* to reopen, open again; **se rouvrir** *vi* (*blessure*) to open up again

roux, rousse [ʀu, ʀus] *adj* red; (*personne*) red-haired ▷ *nm/f* redhead ▷ *nm* (*Culin*) roux

royal, e, -aux [ʀwajal, -o] *adj* royal; (*fig*) fit for a king, princely; blissful; thorough

royalement [ʀwajalmɑ̃] *adv* royally

royaliste [ʀwajalist(ə)] *adj, nm/f* royalist

royaume [ʀwajom] *nm* kingdom; (*fig*) realm; **le ~ des cieux** the kingdom of heaven

Royaume-Uni [ʀwajomyni] *nm*: **le ~** the United Kingdom

royauté [ʀwajote] *nf* (*dignité*) kingship; (*régime*) monarchy

RP *sigle f* (= *recette principale*) ≈ main post office = **région parisienne** ▷ *sigle fpl* (= *relations publiques*) PR

RPR *sigle m* (= *Rassemblement pour la République*) political party

R.S.V.P. *abr* (= *répondez s'il vous plaît*) R.S.V.P

RTB *sigle f* = **Radio-Télévision belge**

Rte *abr* = **route**

RTL *sigle f* = **Radio-Télévision Luxembourg**

RU [ʀy] *sigle m* = **restaurant universitaire**

ruade [ʀyad] *nf* kick

Ruanda [ʀwɑ̃da] *nm*: **le ~** Rwanda

ruban [ʀybɑ̃] *nm* (*gén*) ribbon; (*pour ourlet, couture*) binding; (*de téléscripteur etc*) tape; (*d'acier*) strip; **~ adhésif** adhesive tape; **~ carbone** carbon ribbon

rubéole [ʀybeɔl] *nf* German measles *sg*, rubella

rubicond, e [ʀybikɔ̃, -ɔ̃d] *adj* rubicund, ruddy

rubis [ʀybi] *nm* ruby; (*Horlogerie*) jewel; **payer ~ sur l'ongle** to pay cash on the nail

rubrique [ʀybʀik] *nf* (*titre, catégorie*) heading, rubric; (*Presse: article*) column

ruche [ʀyʃ] *nf* hive

rucher [ʀyʃe] *nm* apiary

rude [ʀyd] *adj* (*barbe, toile*) rough; (*métier, tâche*) hard, tough; (*climat*) severe, harsh; (*bourru*) harsh, rough; (*fruste*) rugged, tough; (*fam*) jolly good; **être mis à ~ épreuve** to be put through the mill

rudement [ʀydmɑ̃] *adv* (*tomber, frapper*) hard; (*traiter, reprocher*) harshly; (*fam: très*) terribly; (: *beaucoup*) terribly hard

rudesse [ʀydɛs] *nf* roughness; toughness; severity; harshness

rudimentaire [ʀydimɑ̃tɛʀ] *adj* rudimentary, basic

rudiments [ʀydimɑ̃] *nmpl* rudiments; basic knowledge *sg*; basic principles

rudoyer [ʀydwaje] *vt* to treat harshly

rue [ʀy] *nf* street; **être/jeter qn à la ~** to be on the streets/throw sb out onto the street

ruée [ʀɥe] *nf* rush; **la ~ vers l'or** the gold rush

ruelle [ʀɥɛl] *nf* alley(way)

ruer [ʀɥe] *vi* (*cheval*) to kick out; **se ruer** *vi*: **se ~ sur** to pounce on; **se ~ vers/dans/hors de** to rush *ou* dash towards/into/out of; **~ dans les brancards** to become rebellious

rugby [ʀygbi] *nm* rugby (football); **~ à treize/quinze** rugby league/union

rugir [ʀyʒiʀ] *vi* to roar

rugissement [ʀyʒismɑ̃] *nm* roar, roaring *no pl*

rugosité [ʀygozite] *nf* roughness; (*aspérité*) rough patch

rugueux, -euse [ʀygø, -øz] *adj* rough

ruine [ʀɥin] *nf* ruin; **ruines** *nfpl* ruins; **tomber en ~** to fall into ruin(s)

ruiner [ʀɥine] *vt* to ruin

ruineux, -euse [ʀɥinø, -øz] *adj* terribly expensive to buy (*ou* run), ruinous; extravagant

ruisseau, x [ʀɥiso] *nm* stream, brook; (*caniveau*) gutter; (*fig*): **~x de larmes/sang** floods of tears/streams of blood

ruisselant, e [ʀɥislɑ̃, -ɑ̃t] *adj* streaming

ruisseler [ʀɥisle] *vi* to stream; **~ (d'eau)** to be streaming (with water); **~ de lumière** to stream with light

ruissellement [ʀɥisɛlmɑ̃] *nm* streaming; **~ de lumière** stream of light

rumeur [ʀymœʀ] *nf* (*bruit confus*) rumbling; hubbub *no pl*; (*protestation*) murmur(ing); (*nouvelle*) rumour (*Brit*), rumor (*US*)

ruminer [ʀymine] *vt* (*herbe*) to ruminate; (*fig*) to ruminate on *ou* over, chew over ▷ *vi* (*vache*) to chew the cud, ruminate

rumsteck [ʀɔ̃mstɛk] *nm* = **romsteck**

rupestre [ʀypɛstʀ(ə)] *adj* (*plante*) rock *cpd*; (*art*) wall *cpd*

rupture [ʀyptyʀ] *nf* (*de câble, digue*) breaking; (*de tendon*) rupture, tearing; (*de négociations etc*) breakdown; (*de contrat*) breach; (*séparation, désunion*) break-up, split; **en ~ de ban** at odds with authority; **en ~ de stock** (*Comm*) out of stock

rural, e, -aux [ʀyʀal, -o] *adj* rural, country *cpd* ▷ *nmpl*: **les ruraux** country people

ruse [ʀyz] *nf*: **la ~** cunning, craftiness; trickery; **une ~** a trick, a ruse; **par ~** by trickery

rusé, e [ʀyze] *adj* cunning, crafty

russe [ʀys] *adj* Russian ▷ *nm* (*Ling*) Russian ▷ *nm/f*: **Russe** Russian

Russie [ʀysi] *nf*: **la ~** Russia; **la ~ blanche** White Russia; **la ~ soviétique** Soviet Russia

rustine [ʀystin] *nf* repair patch (*for bicycle inner tube*)

rustique [ʀystik] *adj* rustic; (*plante*) hardy

rustre [ʀystʀ(ə)] *nm* boor

rut [ʀyt] *nm*: **être en ~** (*animal domestique*) to be in *ou* on heat; (*animal sauvage*) to be rutting

rutabaga [ʀytabaga] *nm* swede

rutilant, e [ʀytilɑ̃, -ɑ̃t] *adj* gleaming

RV *sigle m* = **rendez-vous**

Rwanda [ʀwɑ̃da] *nm*: **le ~** Rwanda

rythme [ʀitm(ə)] *nm* rhythm; (*vitesse*) rate; (: *de la vie*) pace, tempo; **au ~ de 10 par jour** at the rate of 10 a day

rythmé, e [ʀitme] *adj* rhythmic(al)

rythmer [ʀitme] *vt* to give rhythm to

rythmique [ʀitmik] *adj* rhythmic(al) ▷ *nf* rhythmics *sg*

r

Ss

S, s [ɛs] *nm inv* S, s ▷ *abr* (= *sud*) S; (= *seconde*) sec; (= *siècle*) c., century; **S comme Suzanne** S for Sugar

s' [s] *pron voir* **se**

s/ *abr* = **sur**

SA *sigle f* = **société anonyme**; (= *Son Altesse*) HH

sa [sa] *adj possessif voir* **son**

sabbatique [sabatik] *adj*: **année ~** sabbatical year

sable [sabl(ə)] *nm* sand; **~s mouvants** quicksand(s)

sablé [sable] *adj* (*allée*) sandy ▷ *nm* shortbread biscuit; **pâte ~e** (*Culin*) shortbread dough

sabler [sable] *vt* to sand; (*contre le verglas*) to grit; **~ le champagne** to drink champagne

sableux, -euse [sablø, -øz] *adj* sandy

sablier [sablije] *nm* hourglass; (*de cuisine*) egg timer

sablière [sablijɛʀ] *nf* sand quarry

sablonneux, -euse [sablɔnø, -øz] *adj* sandy

saborder [sabɔʀde] *vt* (*navire*) to scuttle; (*fig*) to wind up, shut down

sabot [sabo] *nm* clog; (*de cheval, bœuf*) hoof; **~ (de Denver)** (wheel) clamp; **~ de frein** brake shoe

sabotage [sabotaʒ] *nm* sabotage

saboter [sabote] *vt* (*travail, morceau de musique*) to botch, make a mess of; (*machine, installation, négociation etc*) to sabotage

saboteur, -euse [sabotœʀ, -øz] *nm/f* saboteur

sabre [sabʀ(ə)] *nm* sabre; **le ~** (*fig*) the sword, the army

sabrer [sabʀe] *vt* to cut down

sac [sak] *nm* bag; (*à charbon etc*) sack; (*pillage*) sack(ing); **mettre à ~** to sack; **~ à provisions/ de voyage** shopping/travelling bag; **~ de couchage** sleeping bag; **~ à dos** rucksack; **~ à main** handbag; **~ de plage** beach bag

saccade [sakad] *nf* jerk; **par ~s** jerkily; haltingly

saccadé, e [sakade] *adj* jerky

saccage [sakaʒ] *nm* havoc

saccager [sakaʒe] *vt* (*piller*) to sack, lay waste; (*dévaster*) to create havoc in, wreck

saccharine [sakaʀin] *nf* saccharin(e)

saccharose [sakaʀoz] *nm* sucrose

SACEM [sasɛm] *sigle f* (= *Société des auteurs, compositeurs et éditeurs de musique*) body responsible for collecting and distributing royalties

sacerdoce [sasɛʀdɔs] *nm* priesthood; (*fig*) calling, vocation

sacerdotal, e, -aux [sasɛʀdɔtal, -o] *adj* priestly, sacerdotal

sachant *etc* [saʃɑ̃] *vb voir* **savoir**

sache *etc* [saʃ] *vb voir* **savoir**

sachet [saʃɛ] *nm* (small) bag; (*de lavande, poudre, shampooing*) sachet; **thé en ~s** tea bags; **~ de thé** tea bag

sacoche [sakɔʃ] *nf* (*gén*) bag; (*de bicyclette*) saddlebag; (*du facteur*) (post)bag; (*d'outils*) toolbag

sacquer [sake] *vt* (*fam: candidat, employé*) to sack; (: *réprimander, mal noter*) to plough

sacraliser [sakʀalize] *vt* to make sacred

sacre [sakʀ(ə)] *nm* coronation; consecration

sacré, e [sakʀe] *adj* sacred; (*fam: satané*) blasted; (: *fameux*): **un ~ ...** a heck of a ...; (*Anat*) sacral

sacrement [sakʀəmɑ̃] *nm* sacrament; **les derniers ~s** the last rites

sacrer [sakʀe] *vt* (*roi*) to crown; (*évêque*) to consecrate ▷ *vi* to curse, swear

sacrifice [sakʀifis] *nm* sacrifice; **faire le ~ de** to sacrifice

sacrificiel, le [sakʀifisjɛl] *adj* sacrificial

sacrifier [sakʀifje] *vt* to sacrifice; **~ à** *vt* to conform to; **se sacrifier** to sacrifice o.s; **articles sacrifiés** (*Comm*) items sold at rock-bottom *ou* give-away prices

sacrilège [sakʀilɛʒ] *nm* sacrilege ▷ *adj* sacrilegious

sacristain [sakʀistɛ̃] *nm* sexton; sacristan

sacristie [sakʀisti] *nf* sacristy; (*culte protestant*) vestry

sacro-saint, e [sakʀosɛ̃, -ɛ̃t] *adj* sacrosanct

sadique [sadik] *adj* sadistic ▷ *nm/f* sadist

sadisme [sadism(ə)] *nm* sadism

sadomasochisme [sadɔmazoʃism(ə)] *nm* sadomasochism

sadomasochiste [sadɔmazoʃist(ə)] *nm/f* sadomasochist

safari [safari] *nm* safari; **faire un ~** to go on safari

safari-photo [safarifɔto] *nm* photographic

safari

SAFER [safɛʀ] *sigle f* (= *Société d'aménagement foncier et d'établissement rural*) *organization with the right to buy land in order to retain it for agricultural use*

safran [safʀɑ̃] *nm* saffron

saga [saga] *nf* saga

sagace [sagas] *adj* sagacious, shrewd

sagacité [sagasite] *nf* sagacity, shrewdness

sagaie [sagɛ] *nf* assegai

sage [saʒ] *adj* wise; (*enfant*) good ▷ *nm* wise man; sage

sage-femme [saʒfam] *nf* midwife

sagement [saʒmɑ̃] *adv* (*raisonnablement*) wisely, sensibly; (*tranquillement*) quietly

sagesse [saʒɛs] *nf* wisdom

Sagittaire [saʒitɛʀ] *nm*: **le ~** Sagittarius, the Archer; **être du ~** to be Sagittarius

Sahara [saaʀa] *nm*: **le ~** the Sahara (Desert); **le ~ occidental** (*pays*) Western Sahara

saharien, ne [saaʀjɛ̃, -ɛn] *adj* Saharan ▷ *nf* safari jacket

Sahel [saɛl] *nm*: **le ~** the Sahel

sahélien, ne [saeljɛ̃, -ɛn] *adj* Sahelian

saignant, e [sɛɲɑ̃, -ɑ̃t] *adj* (*viande*) rare; (*blessure, plaie*) bleeding

saignée [seɲe] *nf* (*Méd*) bleeding *no pl*, bloodletting *no pl*; (*Anat*): **la ~ du bras** the bend of the arm; (*fig: Mil*) heavy losses *pl*; (: *prélèvement*) savage cut

saignement [sɛɲmɑ̃] *nm* bleeding; **~ de nez** nosebleed

saigner [seɲe] *vi* to bleed ▷ *vt* to bleed; (*animal*) to bleed to death; **~ qn à blanc** (*fig*) to bleed sb white; **~ du nez** to have a nosebleed

Saigon [sajgɔ̃] *n* Saigon

saillant, e [sajɑ̃, -ɑ̃t] *adj* (*pommettes, menton*) prominent; (*corniche etc*) projecting; (*fig*) salient, outstanding

saillie [saji] *nf* (*sur un mur etc*) projection; (*trait d'esprit*) witticism; (*accouplement*) covering, serving; **faire ~** to project, stick out; **en ~**, **formant ~** projecting, overhanging

saillir [sajiʀ] *vi* to project, stick out; (*veine, muscle*) to bulge ▷ *vt* (*Élevage*) to cover, serve

sain, e [sɛ̃, sɛn] *adj* healthy; (*dents, constitution*) healthy, sound; (*lectures*) wholesome; **~ et sauf** safe and sound, unharmed; **~ d'esprit** sound in mind, sane

saindoux [sɛ̃du] *nm* lard

sainement [sɛnmɑ̃] *adv* (*vivre*) healthily; (*raisonner*) soundly

saint, e [sɛ̃, sɛ̃t] *adj* holy; (*fig*) saintly ▷ *nm/f* saint; **la S~e Vierge** the Blessed Virgin

saint-bernard [sɛ̃bɛʀnaʀ] *nm inv* (*chien*) St Bernard

Sainte-Hélène [sɛ̃telɛn] *nf* St Helena

Sainte-Lucie [sɛ̃tlysi] *nf* Saint Lucia

Saint-Esprit [sɛ̃tɛspʀi] *nm*: **le ~** the Holy Spirit *ou* Ghost

sainteté [sɛ̃te] *nf* holiness; saintliness

Saint-Laurent [sɛ̃loʀɑ̃] *nm*: **le ~** the St Lawrence

Saint-Marin [sɛ̃maʀɛ̃] *nm*: **le ~** San Marino

Saint-Père [sɛ̃pɛʀ] *nm*: **le ~** the Holy Father, the Pontiff

Saint-Pierre [sɛ̃pjɛʀ] *nm* Saint Peter; (*église*) Saint Peter's

Saint-Pierre-et-Miquelon [sɛ̃pjɛʀemiklɔ̃] *nm* Saint Pierre and Miquelon

Saint-Siège [sɛ̃sjɛʒ] *nm*: **le ~** the Holy See

Saint-Sylvestre [sɛ̃silvɛstʀ(ə)] *nf*: **la ~** New Year's Eve

Saint-Thomas [sɛ̃tɔma] *nf* Saint Thomas

Saint-Vincent et les Grenadines [sɛ̃vɛ̃sɑ̃elegʀənadin] *nm* St Vincent and the Grenadines

sais *etc* [sɛ] *vb voir* **savoir**

saisie [sezi] *nf* seizure; **à la ~** (*texte*) being keyed; **~ (de données)** (data) capture

saisine [sezin] *nf* (*Jur*) *submission of a case to the court*

saisir [seziʀ] *vt* to take hold of, grab; (*fig: occasion*) to seize; (*comprendre*) to grasp; (*entendre*) to get, catch; (*émotions*) to take hold of, come over; (*Inform*) to capture, keyboard; (*Culin*) to fry quickly; (*Jur: biens, publication*) to seize; (: *juridiction*): **~ un tribunal d'une affaire** to submit *ou* refer a case to a court; **se ~ de** *vt* to seize; **être saisi** (*frappé de*) to be overcome

saisissant, e [sezisɑ̃, -ɑ̃t] *adj* startling, striking; (*froid*) biting

saisissement [sezismɑ̃] *nm*: **muet/figé de ~** speechless/frozen with emotion

saison [sɛzɔ̃] *nf* season; **la belle/mauvaise ~** the summer/winter months; **être de ~** to be in season; **en/hors ~** in/out of season; **haute/basse/morte ~** high/low/slack season; **la ~ des pluies/des amours** the rainy/mating season

saisonnier, -ière [sɛzɔnje, -jɛʀ] *adj* seasonal ▷ *nm* (*travailleur*) seasonal worker; (*vacancier*) seasonal holidaymaker

sait [sɛ] *vb voir* **savoir**

salace [salas] *adj* salacious

salade [salad] *nf* (*Bot*) lettuce *etc* (*generic term*); (*Culin*) (green) salad; (*fam*) tangle, muddle; **salades** *nfpl* (*fam*): **raconter des ~s** to tell tales (*fam*); **haricots en ~** bean salad; **~ de concombres** cucumber salad; **~ de fruits** fruit salad; **~ niçoise** salade niçoise; **~ russe** Russian salad; **~ de tomates** tomato salad; **~ verte** green salad

saladier [saladje] *nm* (*salad*) bowl

salaire [salɛʀ] *nm* (*annuel, mensuel*) salary; (*hebdomadaire, journalier*) pay, wages *pl*; (*fig*) reward; **~ de base** basic salary (*ou* wage); **~ de misère** starvation wage; **~ minimum interprofessionnel de croissance (SMIC)** *index-linked guaranteed minimum wage*

salaison [salɛzɔ̃] *nf* salting; **salaisons** *nfpl* salt meat *sg*

salamandre [salamɑ̃dʀ(ə)] *nf* salamander

salami [salami] *nm* salami *no pl*, salami sausage

salant [salɑ̃] *adj m*: **marais ~** salt pan

salarial, e, -aux [salaʀjal, -o] *adj* salary *cpd*, wage(s) *cpd*

S

salariat [salaʀja] *nm* salaried staff
salarié, e [salaʀje] *adj* salaried; wage-earning
▷ *nm/f* salaried employee; wage-earner
salaud [salo] *nm* (*fam!*) sod (!), bastard (!)
sale [sal] *adj* dirty; (*fig: avant le nom*) nasty
salé, e [sale] *adj* (*liquide, saveur*) salty; (*Culin*)
salted, salt *cpd*; (*fig*) spicy, juicy; (: *note, facture*)
steep, stiff ▷ *nm* (*porc salé*) salt pork; **petit ~**
≈ boiling bacon
salement [salmɑ̃] *adv* (*manger etc*) dirtily,
messily
saler [sale] *vt* to salt
saleté [salte] *nf* (*état*) dirtiness; (*crasse*) dirt,
filth; (*tache etc*) dirt *no pl*, something dirty, dirty
mark; (*fig: tour*) filthy trick; (: *chose sans valeur*)
rubbish *no pl*; (: *obscénité*) filth *no pl*; (: *microbe etc*)
bug; **vivre dans la ~** to live in squalor
salière [saljɛʀ] *nf* saltcellar
saligaud [saligo] *nm* (*fam!*) bastard (!), sod (!)
salin, e [salɛ̃, -in] *adj* saline ▷ *nf* saltworks *sg*
salinité [salinite] *nf* salinity, salt-content
salir [saliʀ] *vt* to (make) dirty; (*fig*) to soil the
reputation of; **se salir** to get dirty
salissant, e [salisɑ̃, -ɑ̃t] *adj* (*tissu*) which shows
the dirt; (*métier*) dirty, messy
salissure [salisyʀ] *nf* dirt *no pl*; (*tache*) dirty
mark
salive [saliv] *nf* saliva
saliver [salive] *vi* to salivate
salle [sal] *nf* room; (*d'hôpital*) ward; (*de restaurant*)
dining room; (*d'un cinéma*) auditorium; (: *public*)
audience; **faire ~ comble** to have a full house;
~ d'armes (*pour l'escrime*) arms room; **~
d'attente** waiting room; **~ de bain(s)**
bathroom; **~ de bal** ballroom; **~ de cinéma**
cinema; **~ de classe** classroom; **~ commune**
(*d'hôpital*) ward; **~ de concert** concert hall; **~ de
consultation** consulting room (*Brit*), office
(*US*); **~ de danse** dance hall; **~ de douches**
shower-room; **~ d'eau** shower-room; **~
d'embarquement** (*à l'aéroport*) departure
lounge; **~ d'exposition** showroom; **~ de jeux**
games room; playroom; **~ des machines**
engine room; **~ à manger** dining room;
(*mobilier*) dining room suite; **~ obscure** cinema
(*Brit*), movie theater (*US*); **~ d'opération**
(*d'hôpital*) operating theatre; **~ des professeurs**
staffroom; **~ de projection** film theatre; **~ de
séjour** living room; **~ de spectacle** theatre;
cinema; **~ des ventes** saleroom
salmonellose [salmɔneloz] *nf* (*Méd*) salmonella
poisoning
Salomon [salɔmɔ̃]: **les îles ~** the Solomon
Islands
salon [salɔ̃] *nm* lounge, sitting room; (*mobilier*)
lounge suite; (*exposition*) exhibition, show;
(*mondain, littéraire*) salon; **~ de coiffure**
hairdressing salon; **~ de discussion** (*Inform*)
chatroom; **~ de thé** tearoom
salopard [salɔpaʀ] *nm* (*fam!*) bastard (!)
salope [salɔp] *nf* (*fam!*) bitch (!)
saloper [salɔpe] *vt* (*fam!*) to muck up, mess up

saloperie [salɔpʀi] *nf* (*fam!*) filth *no pl*; dirty
trick, rubbish *no pl*
salopette [salɔpɛt] *nf* dungarees *pl*; (*d'ouvrier*)
overall(s)
salpêtre [salpɛtʀ(ə)] *nm* saltpetre
salsifis [salsifi] *nm* salsify, oyster plant
SALT [salt] *sigle* (= *Strategic Arms Limitation Talks ou
Treaty*) SALT
saltimbanque [saltɛ̃bɑ̃k] *nm/f* (travelling)
acrobat
salubre [salybʀ(ə)] *adj* healthy, salubrious
salubrité [salybʀite] *nf* healthiness, salubrity;
~ publique public health
saluer [salɥe] *vt* (*pour dire bonjour, fig*) to greet;
(*pour dire au revoir*) to take one's leave; (*Mil*) to
salute
salut [saly] *nm* (*sauvegarde*) safety; (*Rel*)
salvation; (*geste*) wave; (*parole*) greeting; (*Mil*)
salute ▷ *excl* (*fam: pour dire bonjour*) hi (there);
(: *pour dire au revoir*) see you!, bye!
salutaire [salytɛʀ] *adj* (*remède*) beneficial;
(*conseils*) salutary
salutations [salytɑsjɔ̃] *nfpl* greetings; **recevez
mes ~ distinguées** *ou* **respectueuses** yours
faithfully
salutiste [salytist(ə)] *nm/f* Salvationist
Salvador [salvadɔʀ] *nm*: **le ~** El Salvador
salve [salv(ə)] *nf* salvo; volley of shots; **~
d'applaudissements** burst of applause
Samarie [samaʀi] *nf*: **la ~** Samaria
samaritain [samaʀitɛ̃] *nm*: **le bon S~** the Good
Samaritan
samedi [samdi] *nm* Saturday; *voir aussi* **lundi**
Samoa [samɔa] *nfpl*: **les (îles) ~** Samoa, the
Samoa Islands
SAMU [samy] *sigle m* (= *service d'assistance médicale
d'urgence*) ≈ ambulance (service) (*Brit*),
≈ paramedics (*US*)
sanatorium [sanatɔʀjɔm] *nm* sanatorium
sanctifier [sɑ̃ktifje] *vt* to sanctify
sanction [sɑ̃ksjɔ̃] *nf* sanction; (*fig*) penalty;
prendre des ~s contre to impose sanctions on
sanctionner [sɑ̃ksjɔne] *vt* (*loi, usage*) to
sanction; (*punir*) to punish
sanctuaire [sɑ̃ktɥɛʀ] *nm* sanctuary
sandale [sɑ̃dal] *nf* sandal; **~s à lanières** strappy
sandals
sandalette [sɑ̃dalɛt] *nf* sandal
sandwich [sɑ̃dwitʃ] *nm* sandwich; **pris en ~**
sandwiched
sang [sɑ̃] *nm* blood; **en ~** covered in blood;
jusqu'au ~ (*mordre, pincer*) till the blood comes;
se faire du mauvais ~ to fret, get in a state
sang-froid [sɑ̃fʀwa] *nm* calm, sangfroid;
garder/perdre/reprendre son ~ to keep/lose/
regain one's cool; **de ~** in cold blood
sanglant, e [sɑ̃glɑ̃, -ɑ̃t] *adj* bloody, covered in
blood; (*combat*) bloody; (*fig: reproche, affront*) cruel
sangle [sɑ̃gl(ə)] *nf* strap; **sangles** *nfpl* (*pour lit etc*)
webbing *sg*
sangler [sɑ̃gle] *vt* to strap up; (*animal*) to girth
sanglier [sɑ̃glije] *nm* (wild) boar

sanglot [sɑ̃glo] *nm* sob
sangloter [sɑ̃glɔte] *vi* to sob
sangsue [sɑ̃sy] *nf* leech
sanguin, e [sɑ̃gɛ̃, -in] *adj* blood *cpd*; (*fig*) fiery
▷ *nf* blood orange; (*Art*) red pencil drawing
sanguinaire [sɑ̃ginɛʀ] *adj* (*animal, personne*) bloodthirsty; (*lutte*) bloody
sanguinolent, e [sɑ̃ginɔlɑ̃, -ɑ̃t] *adj* streaked with blood
Sanisette® [sanizɛt] *nf* coin-operated public lavatory
sanitaire [sanitɛʀ] *adj* health *cpd*; **sanitaires** *nmpl* (*salle de bain et w.-c.*) bathroom *sg*; **installation/appareil** ~ bathroom plumbing/appliance
sans [sɑ̃] *prép* without; ~ **qu'il s'en aperçoive** without him *ou* his noticing; ~ **scrupules** unscrupulous; ~ **manches** sleeveless
sans-abri [sɑ̃zabʀi] *nmpl* homeless
sans-emploi [sɑ̃zɑ̃plwa] *nmpl* jobless
sans-façon [sɑ̃fasɔ̃] *adj inv* fuss-free; free and easy
sans-gêne [sɑ̃ʒɛn] *adj inv* inconsiderate ▷ *nm inv* (*attitude*) lack of consideration
sans-logis [sɑ̃lɔʒi] *nmpl* homeless
sans-souci [sɑ̃susi] *adj inv* carefree
sans-travail [sɑ̃tʀavaj] *nmpl* unemployed, jobless
santal [sɑ̃tal] *nm* sandal(wood)
santé [sɑ̃te] *nf* health; **avoir une ~ de fer** to be bursting with health; **être en bonne ~** to be in good health, be healthy; **boire à la ~ de qn** to drink (to) sb's health; **"à la ~ de"** "here's to"; **à ta** *ou* **votre ~!** cheers!; **service de ~** (*dans un port etc*) quarantine service; **la ~ publique** public health
Santiago [sɑ̃tjago], **Santiago du Chili** [sɑ̃tjagodyʃili] *n* Santiago (de Chile)
santon [sɑ̃tɔ̃] *nm ornamental figure at a Christmas crib*
saoudien, ne [saudjɛ̃, -ɛn] *adj* Saudi (Arabian) ▷ *nm/f*: **Saoudien, ne** Saudi (Arabian)
saoul, e [su, sul] *adj* = **soûl, e**
sape [sap] *nf*: **travail de ~** (*Mil*) sap; (*fig*) insidious undermining process *ou* work; **sapes** *nfpl* (*fam*) gear *sg*, togs
saper [sape] *vt* to undermine, sap; **se saper** *vi* (*fam*) to dress
sapeur [sapœʀ] *nm* sapper
sapeur-pompier [sapœʀpɔ̃pje] *nm* fireman
saphir [safiʀ] *nm* sapphire; (*d'électrophone*) needle, sapphire
sapin [sapɛ̃] *nm* fir (tree); (*bois*) fir; ~ **de Noël** Christmas tree
sapinière [sapinjɛʀ] *nf* fir plantation *ou* forest
SAR *sigle f* (= *Son Altesse Royale*) HRH
sarabande [saʀabɑ̃d] *nf* saraband; (*fig*) hullabaloo; whirl
sarbacane [saʀbakan] *nf* blowpipe, blowgun; (*jouet*) peashooter
sarcasme [saʀkasm(ə)] *nm* sarcasm *no pl*; (*propos*) piece of sarcasm

sarcastique [saʀkastik] *adj* sarcastic
sarcastiquement [saʀkastikmɑ̃] *adv* sarcastically
sarclage [saʀklaʒ] *nm* weeding
sarcler [saʀkle] *vt* to weed
sarcloir [saʀklwaʀ] *nm* (weeding) hoe, spud
sarcophage [saʀkɔfaʒ] *nm* sarcophagus
Sardaigne [saʀdɛɲ] *nf*: **la ~** Sardinia
sarde [saʀd(ə)] *adj* Sardinian
sardine [saʀdin] *nf* sardine; ~**s à l'huile** sardines in oil
sardinerie [saʀdinʀi] *nf* sardine cannery
sardinier, -ière [saʀdinje, -jɛʀ] *adj* (*pêche, industrie*) sardine *cpd* ▷ *nm* (*bateau*) sardine boat
sardonique [saʀdɔnik] *adj* sardonic
sari [saʀi] *nm* sari
SARL [saʀl] *sigle f* = **société à responsabilité limitée**
sarment [saʀmɑ̃] *nm*: ~ **(de vigne)** vine shoot
sarrasin [saʀazɛ̃] *nm* buckwheat
sarrau [saʀo] *nm* smock
Sarre [saʀ] *nf*: **la ~** the Saar
sarriette [saʀjɛt] *nf* savory
sarrois, e [saʀwa, -waz] *adj* Saar *cpd* ▷ *nm/f*: **Sarrois, e** inhabitant *ou* native of the Saar
sas [sas] *nm* (*de sous-marin, d'engin spatial*) airlock; (*d'écluse*) lock
satané, e [satane] *adj* (*fam*) confounded
satanique [satanik] *adj* satanic, fiendish
satelliser [satelize] *vt* (*fusée*) to put into orbit; (*fig: pays*) to make into a satellite
satellite [satelit] *nm* satellite; **pays ~** satellite country
satellite-espion [satelitɛspjɔ̃] (*pl* **satellites-espions**) *nm* spy satellite
satellite-observatoire [satelitɔpsɛʀvatwaʀ] (*pl* **satellites-observatoires**) *nm* observation satellite
satellite-relais [satelitʀəlɛ] (*pl* **satellites-relais**) *nm* (TV) relay satellite
satiété [sasjete]: **à ~** *adv* to satiety *ou* satiation; (*répéter*) ad nauseam
satin [satɛ̃] *nm* satin
satiné, e [satine] *adj* satiny; (*peau*) satin-smooth
satinette [satinɛt] *nf* satinet, sateen
satire [satiʀ] *nf* satire; **faire la ~** to satirize
satirique [satiʀik] *adj* satirical
satiriser [satiʀize] *vt* to satirize
satiriste [satiʀist(ə)] *nm/f* satirist
satisfaction [satisfaksjɔ̃] *nf* satisfaction; **à ma grande ~** to my great satisfaction; **obtenir ~** to obtain *ou* get satisfaction; **donner ~ (à)** to give satisfaction (to)
satisfaire [satisfɛʀ] *vt* to satisfy; **se satisfaire de** to be satisfied *ou* content with; ~ **à** *vt* (*engagement*) to fulfil; (*revendications, conditions*) to satisfy, meet
satisfaisant, e [satisfəzɑ̃, -ɑ̃t] *vb voir* **satisfaire** ▷ *adj* satisfactory; (*qui fait plaisir*) satisfying
satisfait, e [satisfɛ, -ɛt] *pp de* **satisfaire** ▷ *adj* satisfied; ~ **de** happy *ou* satisfied with

S

satisfasse [satisfas], **satisferai** etc [satisfʀe] vb voir **satisfaire**

saturation [satyʀasjɔ̃] nf saturation; **arriver à ~** to reach saturation point

saturer [satyʀe] vt to saturate; **~ qn/qch de** to saturate sb/sth with

saturnisme [satyʀnism(ə)] nm (Méd) lead poisoning

satyre [satiʀ] nm satyr; (péj) lecher

sauce [sos] nf sauce; (avec un rôti) gravy; **en ~** in a sauce; **~ blanche** white sauce; **~ chasseur** sauce chasseur; **~ tomate** tomato sauce

saucer [sose] vt (assiette) to soak up the sauce from

saucière [sosjɛʀ] nf sauceboat; gravy boat

saucisse [sosis] nf sausage

saucisson [sosisɔ̃] nm (slicing) sausage; **~ à l'ail** garlic sausage

saucissonner [sosisɔne] vt to cut up, slice ▷ vi to picnic

sauf[1] [sof] prép except; **~ si** (à moins que) unless; **~ avis contraire** unless you hear to the contrary; **~ empêchement** barring (any) problems; **~ erreur** if I'm not mistaken; **~ imprévu** unless anything unforeseen arises, barring accidents

sauf[2], **sauve** [sof, sov] adj unharmed, unhurt; (fig: honneur) intact, saved; **laisser la vie sauve à qn** to spare sb's life

sauf-conduit [sofkɔ̃dɥi] nm safe-conduct

sauge [soʒ] nf sage

saugrenu, e [soɡʀəny] adj preposterous, ludicrous

saule [sol] nm willow (tree); **~ pleureur** weeping willow

saumâtre [somatʀ(ə)] adj briny; (désagréable: plaisanterie) unsavoury (Brit), unsavory (US)

saumon [somɔ̃] nm salmon inv ▷ adj inv salmon (pink)

saumoné, e [somɔne] adj: **truite ~e** salmon trout

saumure [somyʀ] nf brine

sauna [sona] nm sauna

saupoudrer [sopudʀe] vt: **~ qch de** to sprinkle sth with

saupoudreuse [sopudʀøz] nf dredger

saur [soʀ] adj m: **hareng ~** smoked ou red herring, kipper

saurai etc [soʀe] vb voir **savoir**

saut [so] nm jump; (discipline sportive) jumping; **faire un ~** to (make a) jump ou leap; **faire un ~ chez qn** to pop over to sb's (place); **au ~ du lit** on getting out of bed; **~ en hauteur/longueur** high/long jump; **~ à la corde** skipping; **~ de page/ligne** (Inform) page/line break; **~ en parachute** parachuting no pl; **~ à la perche** pole vaulting; **~ à l'élastique** bungee jumping; **~ périlleux** somersault

saute [sot] nf: **~ de vent/température** sudden change of wind direction/in the temperature; **avoir des ~s d'humeur** to have sudden changes of mood

sauté, e [sote] adj (Culin) sauté ▷ nm: **~ de veau** sauté of veal

saute-mouton [sotmutɔ̃] nm: **jouer à ~** to play leapfrog

sauter [sote] vi to jump, leap; (exploser) to blow up, explode; (: fusibles) to blow; (se rompre) to snap, burst; (se détacher) to pop out (ou off) ▷ vt to jump (over), leap (over); (fig: omettre) to skip, miss (out); **faire ~** to blow up; to burst open; (Culin) to sauté; **~ à pieds joints/à cloche-pied** to make a standing jump/to hop; **~ en parachute** to make a parachute jump; **~ à la corde** to skip; **~ de joie** to jump for joy; **~ de colère** to be hopping with rage ou hopping mad; **~ au cou de qn** to fly into sb's arms; **~ aux yeux** to be quite obvious; **~ au plafond** (fig) to hit the roof

sauterelle [sotʀɛl] nf grasshopper

sauterie [sotʀi] nf party, hop

sauteur, -euse [sotœʀ, -øz] nm/f (athlète) jumper ▷ nf (casserole) shallow pan, frying pan; **~ à la perche** pole vaulter; **~ à skis** ski jumper

sautillement [sotijmɑ̃] nm hopping; skipping

sautiller [sotije] vi to hop; to skip

sautoir [sotwaʀ] nm chain; (Sport: emplacement) jumping pit; **~ (de perles)** string of pearls

sauvage [sovaʒ] adj (gén) wild; (peuplade) savage; (farouche) unsociable; (barbare) wild, savage; (non officiel) unauthorized, unofficial ▷ nm/f savage; (timide) unsociable type, recluse

sauvagement [sovaʒmɑ̃] adv savagely

sauvageon, ne [sovaʒɔ̃, -ɔn] nm/f little savage

sauvagerie [sovaʒʀi] nf wildness; savagery; unsociability

sauve [sov] adj f voir **sauf**

sauvegarde [sovɡaʀd(ə)] nf safeguard; **sous la ~ de** under the protection of; **disquette/fichier de ~** (Inform) backup disk/file

sauvegarder [sovɡaʀde] vt to safeguard; (Inform: enregistrer) to save; (: copier) to back up

sauve-qui-peut [sovkipø] nm inv stampede, mad rush ▷ excl run for your life!

sauver [sove] vt to save; (porter secours à) to rescue; (récupérer) to salvage, rescue; **se sauver** vi (s'enfuir) to run away; (fam: partir) to be off; **~ qn de** to save sb from; **~ la vie à qn** to save sb's life; **~ les apparences** to keep up appearances

sauvetage [sovtaʒ] nm rescue; **~ en montagne** mountain rescue; **ceinture de ~** lifebelt (Brit), life preserver (US); **brassière** ou **gilet de ~** lifejacket (Brit), life preserver (US)

sauveteur [sovtœʀ] nm rescuer

sauvette [sovɛt]: **à la ~** adv (vendre) without authorization; (se marier etc) hastily, hurriedly; **vente à la ~** (unauthorized) street trading, (street) peddling

sauveur [sovœʀ] nm saviour (Brit), savior (US)

SAV sigle m = **service après-vente**

savais etc [save] vb voir **savoir**

savamment [savamɑ̃] adv (avec érudition) learnedly; (habilement) skilfully, cleverly

savane [savan] nf savannah

savant, e [savɑ̃, -ɑ̃t] adj scholarly, learned; (calé)

clever ▷ *nm* scientist; **animal ~** performing animal

savate [savat] *nf* worn-out shoe; (*Sport*) French boxing

saveur [savœʀ] *nf* flavour (*Brit*), flavor (*US*); (*fig*) savour (*Brit*), savor (*US*)

Savoie [savwa] *nf*: **la ~** Savoy

savoir [savwaʀ] *vt* to know; (*être capable de*): **il sait nager** he knows how to swim, he can swim ▷ *nm* knowledge; **se savoir** (*être connu*) to be known; **se savoir malade/incurable** to know that one is ill/incurably ill; **il est petit: tu ne peux pas ~!** you won't believe how small he is!; **vous n'êtes pas sans ~ que** you are not *ou* will not be unaware of the fact that; **je crois ~ que ...** I believe that ..., I think I know that ...; **je n'en sais rien** I (really) don't know; **à ~ (que)** that is, namely; **faire ~ qch à qn** to inform sb about sth, let sb know sth; **pas que je sache** not as far as I know; **sans le ~** *adv* unknowingly, unwittingly; **en ~ long** to know a lot

savoir-faire [savwaʀfɛʀ] *nm inv* savoir-faire, know-how

savoir-vivre [savwaʀvivʀ(ə)] *nm inv*: **le ~** savoir-faire, good manners *pl*

savon [savɔ̃] *nm* (*produit*) soap; (*morceau*) bar *ou* tablet of soap; (*fam*): **passer un ~ à qn** to give sb a good dressing-down

savonner [savɔne] *vt* to soap

savonnerie [savɔnʀi] *nf* soap factory

savonnette [savɔnɛt] *nf* bar *ou* tablet of soap

savonneux, -euse [savɔnø, -øz] *adj* soapy

savons [savɔ̃] *vb voir* **savoir**

savourer [savuʀe] *vt* to savour (*Brit*), savor (*US*)

savoureux, -euse [savuʀø, -øz] *adj* tasty; (*fig*) spicy, juicy

savoyard, e [savwajaʀ, -aʀd(ə)] *adj* Savoyard

Saxe [saks(ə)] *nf*: **la ~** Saxony

saxo [saksɔ], **saxophone** [saksɔfɔn] *nm* sax(ophone)

saxophoniste [saksɔfɔnist(ə)] *nm/f* saxophonist, sax(ophone) player

saynète [sɛnɛt] *nf* playlet

SBB *sigle f* (= *Schweizerische Bundesbahn*) *Swiss federal railways*

sbire [sbiʀ] *nm* (*péj*) henchman

sc. *abr* = **scène**

s/c *abr* (= *sous couvert de*) ≈ c/o

scabreux, -euse [skabʀø, -øz] *adj* risky; (*indécent*) improper, shocking

scalpel [skalpɛl] *nm* scalpel

scalper [skalpe] *vt* to scalp

scampi [skãpi] *nmpl* scampi

scandale [skãdal] *nm* scandal; (*tapage*): **faire du ~** to make a scene, create a disturbance; **faire ~** to scandalize people; **au grand ~ de ...** to the great indignation of ...

scandaleusement [skãdaløzmã] *adv* scandalously, outrageously

scandaleux, -euse [skãdalø, -øz] *adj* scandalous, outrageous

scandaliser [skãdalize] *vt* to scandalize; **se ~ (de)** to be scandalized (by)

scander [skãde] *vt* (*vers*) to scan; (*mots, syllabes*) to stress separately; (*slogans*) to chant

scandinave [skãdinav] *adj* Scandinavian ▷ *nm/f*: **Scandinave** Scandinavian

Scandinavie [skãdinavi] *nf*: **la ~** Scandinavia

scanner [skanɛʀ] *nm* (*Méd*) scanner

scanographie [skanɔgʀafi] *nf* (*Méd*) scanning; (*image*) scan

scaphandre [skafãdʀ(ə)] *nm* (*de plongeur*) diving suit; (*de cosmonaute*) spacesuit; **~ autonome** aqualung

scaphandrier [skafãdʀije] *nm* diver

scarabée [skaʀabe] *nm* beetle

scarlatine [skaʀlatin] *nf* scarlet fever

scarole [skaʀɔl] *nf* endive

scatologique [skatɔlɔʒik] *adj* scatological, lavatorial

sceau, x [so] *nm* seal; (*fig*) stamp, mark; **sous le ~ du secret** under the seal of secrecy

scélérat, e [selera, -at] *nm/f* villain, blackguard ▷ *adj* villainous, blackguardly

sceller [sele] *vt* to seal

scellés [sele] *nmpl* seals

scénario [senaʀjo] *nm* (*Ciné*) screenplay, script; (: *idée, plan*) scenario; (*fig*) pattern; scenario

scénariste [senaʀist(ə)] *nm/f* scriptwriter

scène [sɛn] *nf* (*gén*) scene; (*estrade, fig: théâtre*) stage; **entrer en ~** to come on stage; **mettre en ~** (*Théât*) to stage; (*Ciné*) to direct; (*fig*) to present, introduce; **sur le devant de la ~** (*en pleine actualité*) in the forefront; **porter à la ~** to adapt for the stage; **faire une ~ (à qn)** to make a scene (with sb); **~ de ménage** domestic fight *ou* scene

scénique [senik] *adj* (*effets*) theatrical; (*art*) scenic

scepticisme [sɛptisism(ə)] *nm* scepticism

sceptique [sɛptik] *adj* sceptical ▷ *nm/f* sceptic

sceptre [sɛptʀ(ə)] *nm* sceptre

schéma [ʃema] *nm* (*diagramme*) diagram, sketch; (*fig*) outline

schématique [ʃematik] *adj* diagrammatic(al), schematic; (*fig*) oversimplified

schématiquement [ʃematikmã] *adv* schematically, diagrammatically

schématisation [ʃematizasjɔ̃] *nf* schematization; oversimplification

schématiser [ʃematize] *vt* to schematize; to (over)simplify

schismatique [ʃismatik] *adj* schismatic

schisme [ʃism(ə)] *nm* schism; rift, split

schiste [ʃist(ə)] *nm* schist

schizophrène [skizɔfʀɛn] *nm/f* schizophrenic

schizophrénie [skizɔfʀeni] *nf* schizophrenia

sciatique [sjatik] *adj*: **nerf ~** sciatic nerve ▷ *nf* sciatica

scie [si] *nf* saw; (*fam*: *rengaine*) catch-tune; (: *personne*) bore; **~ à bois** wood saw; **~ circulaire** circular saw; **~ à découper** fretsaw; **~ à métaux** hacksaw; **~ sauteuse** jigsaw

S

sciemment [sjamɑ̃] *adv* knowingly, wittingly

science [sjɑ̃s] *nf* science; (*savoir*) knowledge; (*savoir-faire*) art, skill; **~s économiques** economics; **~s humaines/sociales** social sciences; **~s naturelles** natural science *sg*, biology *sg*; **~s po** political studies

science-fiction [sjɑ̃sfiksjɔ̃] *nf* science fiction

scientifique [sjɑ̃tifik] *adj* scientific ▷ *nm/f* (*savant*) scientist; (*étudiant*) science student

scientifiquement [sjɑ̃tifikmɑ̃] *adv* scientifically

scier [sje] *vt* to saw; (*retrancher*) to saw off

scierie [siRi] *nf* sawmill

scieur [sjœR] *nm*: **~ de long** pit sawyer

Scilly [sili]: **les îles ~** the Scilly Isles, the Scillies, the Isles of Scilly

scinder [sɛ̃de] *vt*, **se scinder** *vi* to split (up)

scintillant, e [sɛ̃tijɑ̃, -ɑ̃t] *adj* sparkling

scintillement [sɛ̃tijmɑ̃] *nm* sparkling *no pl*

scintiller [sɛ̃tije] *vi* to sparkle

scission [sisjɔ̃] *nf* split

sciure [sjyR] *nf*: **~ (de bois)** sawdust

sclérose [skleRoz] *nf* sclerosis; (*fig*) ossification; **~ en plaques (SEP)** multiple sclerosis (MS)

sclérosé, e [skleRoze] *adj* sclerosed, sclerotic; ossified

scléroser [skleRoze]: **se scléroser** *vi* to become sclerosed; (*fig*) to become ossified

scolaire [skɔlɛR] *adj* school *cpd*; (*péj*) schoolish; **l'année ~** the school year; (*à l'université*) the academic year; **en âge ~** of school age

scolarisation [skɔlaRizasjɔ̃] *nf* (*d'un enfant*) schooling; **la ~ d'une région** the provision of schooling in a region; **le taux de ~** the proportion of children in full-time education

scolariser [skɔlaRize] *vt* to provide with schooling (*ou* schools)

scolarité [skɔlaRite] *nf* schooling; **frais de ~** school fees (*Brit*), tuition (*US*)

scolastique [skɔlastik] *adj* (*péj*) scholastic

scoliose [skɔljoz] *nf* curvature of the spine, scoliosis

scoop [skup] *nm* (*Presse*) scoop, exclusive

scooter [skutœR] *nm* (motor) scooter

scorbut [skɔRbyt] *nm* scurvy

score [skɔR] *nm* score; (*électoral etc*) result

scories [skɔRi] *nfpl* scoria *pl*

scorpion [skɔRpjɔ̃] *nm* (*signe*): **le S~** Scorpio, the Scorpion; **être du S~** to be Scorpio

scotch [skɔtʃ] *nm* (*whisky*) scotch, whisky; (*adhésif*) Sellotape® (*Brit*), Scotch tape® (*US*)

scotcher [skɔtʃe] *vt* to sellotape® (*Brit*), scotchtape® (*US*)

scout, e [skut] *adj, nm* scout

scoutisme [skutism(ə)] *nm* (boy) scout movement; (*activités*) scouting

scribe [skRib] *nm* scribe; (*péj*) penpusher

scribouillard [skRibujaR] *nm* penpusher

script [skRipt(ə)] *nm* printing; (*Ciné*) (shooting) script

scripte [skRipt(ə)] *nf* continuity girl

script-girl [skRiptgœRl] *nf* continuity girl

scriptural, e, -aux [skRiptyRal, -o] *adj*: **monnaie ~e** bank money

scrupule [skRypyl] *nm* scruple; **être sans ~s** to be unscrupulous; **se faire un ~ de qch** to have scruples *ou* qualms about doing sth

scrupuleusement [skRypyløzmɑ̃] *adv* scrupulously

scrupuleux, -euse [skRypylø, -øz] *adj* scrupulous

scrutateur, -trice [skRytatœR, -tRis] *adj* searching ▷ *nm/f* scrutineer

scruter [skRyte] *vt* to search, scrutinize; (*l'obscurité*) to peer into; (*motifs, comportement*) to examine, scrutinize

scrutin [skRytɛ̃] *nm* (*vote*) ballot; (*ensemble des opérations*) poll; **~ proportionnel/majoritaire** election on a proportional/majority basis; **~ à deux tours** poll with two ballots *ou* rounds; **~ de liste** list system

sculpter [skylte] *vt* to sculpt; (*érosion*) to carve

sculpteur [skyltœR] *nm* sculptor

sculptural, e, -aux [skyltyRal, -o] *adj* sculptural; (*fig*) statuesque

sculpture [skyityR] *nf* sculpture; **~ sur bois** wood carving

sdb. *abr* = **salle de bain**

SDF *sigle m* (= *sans domicile fixe*) homeless person; **les ~** the homeless

SDN *sigle f* (= *Société des Nations*) League of Nations

SE *sigle f* (= *Son Excellence*) HE

⬤ **MOT-CLÉ**

se, s' [s(ə)] *pron* **1** (*emploi réfléchi*) oneself; (: *masc*) himself; (: *fém*) herself; (: *sujet non humain*) itself; (: *pl*) themselves; **se voir comme l'on est** to see o.s. as one is

2 (*réciproque*) one another, each other; **ils s'aiment** they love one another *ou* each other

3 (*passif*): **cela se répare facilement** it is easily repaired

4 (*possessif*): **se casser la jambe/laver les mains** to break one's leg/wash one's hands

séance [seɑ̃s] *nf* (*d'assemblée, récréative*) meeting, session; (*de tribunal*) sitting, session; (*musicale, Ciné, Théât*) performance; **ouvrir/lever la ~** to open/close the meeting; **~ tenante** forthwith

séant, e [seɑ̃, -ɑ̃t] *adj* seemly, fitting ▷ *nm* posterior

seau, x [so] *nm* bucket, pail; **~ à glace** ice bucket

sébum [sebɔm] *nm* sebum

sec, sèche [sɛk, sɛʃ] *adj* dry; (*raisins, figues*) dried; (*cœur, personne: insensible*) hard, cold; (*maigre, décharné*) spare, lean; (*réponse, ton*) sharp, curt; (*démarrage*) sharp, sudden ▷ *nm*: **tenir au ~** to keep in a dry place ▷ *adv* hard; (*démarrer*) sharply; **boire ~** to be a heavy drinker; **je le bois ~** I drink it straight *ou* neat; **à pied ~** without getting one's feet wet; **à ~** *adj* dried up; (*à court d'argent*) broke

SECAM [sekam] *sigle m* (= *procédé séquentiel à*

mémoire) SECAM

sécante [sekɑ̃t] *nf* secant

sécateur [sekatœʀ] *nm* secateurs *pl* (*Brit*), shears *pl*, pair of secateurs *ou* shears

sécession [sesesjɔ̃] *nf*: **faire** ~ to secede; **la guerre de S**~ the American Civil War

séchage [seʃaʒ] *nm* drying; (*de bois*) seasoning

sèche [sɛʃ] *adj f voir* **sec** ▷ *nf* (*fam*) cigarette, fag (*Brit*)

sèche-cheveux [sɛʃʃəvø] *nm inv* hair-drier

sèche-linge [sɛʃlɛ̃ʒ] *nm inv* drying cabinet

sèche-mains [sɛʃmɛ̃] *nm inv* hand drier

sèchement [sɛʃmɑ̃] *adv* (*frapper etc*) sharply; (*répliquer etc*) drily, sharply

sécher [seʃe] *vt* to dry; (*dessécher: peau, blé*) to dry (out); (: *étang*) to dry up; (*bois*) to season; (*fam: classe, cours*) to skip, miss ▷ *vi* to dry; to dry out; to dry up; (*fam: candidat*) to be stumped; **se sécher** (*après le bain*) to dry o.s.

sécheresse [seʃʀɛs] *nf* dryness; (*absence de pluie*) drought

séchoir [seʃwaʀ] *nm* drier

second, e [səgɔ̃, -ɔ̃d] *adj* second ▷ *nm* (*assistant*) second in command; (*étage*) second floor (*Brit*), third floor (*US*); (*Navig*) first mate ▷ *nf* second; (*Scol*) ≈ fifth form (*Brit*), ≈ tenth grade (*US*); **en** ~ (*en second rang*) in second place; **voyager en** ~**e** to travel second-class; **doué de** ~**e vue** having (the gift of) second sight; **trouver son** ~**souffle** (*Sport, fig*) to get one's second wind; **être dans un état** ~ to be in a daze (*ou* trance); **de** ~**e main** second-hand

secondaire [səgɔ̃dɛʀ] *adj* secondary

seconder [səgɔ̃de] *vt* to assist; (*favoriser*) to back

secouer [səkwe] *vt* to shake; (*passagers*) to rock; (*traumatiser*) to shake (up); **se secouer** (*chien*) to shake itself; (*fam: se démener*) to shake o.s. up; ~ **la poussière d'un tapis** to shake the dust off a carpet; ~ **la tête** to shake one's head

secourable [səkuʀabl(ə)] *adj* helpful

secourir [səkuʀiʀ] *vt* (*aller sauver*) to (go and) rescue; (*prodiguer des soins à*) to help, assist; (*venir en aide à*) to assist, aid

secourisme [səkuʀism(ə)] *nm* (*premiers soins*) first aid; (*sauvetage*) life saving

secouriste [səkuʀist(ə)] *nm/f* first-aid worker

secourons *etc* [səkuʀɔ̃] *vb voir* **secourir**

secours [səkuʀ] *vb voir* **secourir** ▷ *nm* help, aid, assistance ▷ *nmpl* aid *sg*; **cela lui a été d'un grand** ~ this was a great help to him; **au** ~! help!; **appeler au** ~ to shout *ou* call for help; **appeler qn à son** ~ to call sb to one's assistance; **porter** ~ **à qn** to give sb assistance, help sb; **les premiers** ~ first aid *sg*; **le** ~ **en montagne** mountain rescue

secouru, e [səkuʀy] *pp de* **secourir**

secousse [səkus] *nf* jolt, bump; (*électrique*) shock; (*fig: psychologique*) jolt, shock; ~ **sismique** *ou* **tellurique** earth tremor

secret, -ète [səkʀɛ, -ɛt] *adj* secret; (*fig: renfermé*) reticent, reserved ▷ *nm* secret; (*discrétion absolue*): **le** ~ secrecy; **en** ~ in secret, secretly; **au** ~ in solitary confinement; ~ **de fabrication** trade secret; ~ **professionnel** professional secrecy

secrétaire [səkʀetɛʀ] *nm/f* secretary ▷ *nm* (*meuble*) writing desk, secretaire; ~ **d'ambassade** embassy secretary; ~ **de direction** private *ou* personal secretary; ~ **d'État** ≈ junior minister; ~ **général (SG)** Secretary-General; (*Comm*) company secretary; ~ **de mairie** town clerk; ~ **médicale** medical secretary; ~ **de rédaction** sub-editor

secrétariat [s(ə)kʀetaʀja] *nm* (*profession*) secretarial work; (*bureau: d'entreprise, d'école*) (secretary's) office; (: *d'organisation internationale*) secretariat; (*Pol etc: fonction*) secretaryship, office of Secretary

secrètement [səkʀɛtmɑ̃] *adv* secretly

sécréter [sekʀete] *vt* to secrete

sécrétion [sekʀesjɔ̃] *nf* secretion

sectaire [sɛktɛʀ] *adj* sectarian, bigoted

sectarisme [sɛktaʀism(ə)] *nm* sectarianism

secte [sɛkt(ə)] *nf* sect

secteur [sɛktœʀ] *nm* sector; (*Admin*) district; (*Élec*): **branché sur le** ~ plugged into the mains (supply); **fonctionne sur pile et** ~ battery or mains operated; **le** ~ **privé/public** (*Écon*) the private/public sector; **le** ~ **primaire/tertiaire** the primary/tertiary sector

section [sɛksjɔ̃] *nf* section; (*de parcours d'autobus*) fare stage; (*Mil: unité*) platoon; ~ **rythmique** rhythm section

sectionner [sɛksjɔne] *vt* to sever; **se sectionner** *vi* to be severed

sectionneur [sɛksjɔnœʀ] *nm* (*Élec*) isolation switch

sectoriel, le [sɛktɔʀjɛl] *adj* sector-based

sectorisation [sɛktɔʀizasjɔ̃] *nf* division into sectors

sectoriser [sɛktɔʀize] *vt* to divide into sectors

sécu [seky] *nf* (*fam: = sécurité sociale*) ≈ dole (*Brit*), ≈ Welfare (*US*)

séculaire [sekylɛʀ] *adj* secular; (*très vieux*) age-old

séculariser [sekylaʀize] *vt* to secularize

séculier, -ière [sekylje, -jɛʀ] *adj* secular

sécurisant, e [sekyʀizɑ̃, -ɑ̃t] *adj* secure, giving a sense of security

sécuriser [sekyʀize] *vt* to give a sense of security to

sécurité [sekyʀite] *nf* security; (*absence de danger*) safety; **impression de** ~ sense of security; **la** ~ **internationale** international security; **système de** ~ security (*ou* safety) system; **être en** ~ to be safe; **la** ~ **de l'emploi** job security; **la** ~ **routière** road safety; **la** ~ **sociale** ≈ (the) Social Security (*Brit*), ≈ (the) Welfare (*US*)

sédatif, -ive [sedatif, -iv] *adj, nm* sedative

sédentaire [sedɑ̃tɛʀ] *adj* sedentary

sédiment [sedimɑ̃] *nm* sediment; **sédiments** *nmpl* (*alluvions*) sediment *sg*

sédimentaire [sedimɑ̃tɛʀ] *adj* sedimentary

sédimentation [sedimɑ̃tasjɔ̃] *nf*

S

sedimentation

séditieux, -euse [sedisjø, -øz] *adj* insurgent; seditious

sédition [sedisjɔ̃] *nf* insurrection; sedition

séducteur, -trice [sedyktœr, -tris] *adj* seductive ▷ *nm/f* seducer (seductress)

séduction [sedyksjɔ̃] *nf* seduction; (*charme, attrait*) appeal, charm

séduire [sedɥir] *vt* to charm; (*femme: abuser de*) to seduce; (*chose*) to appeal to

séduisant, e [sedɥizɑ̃, -ɑ̃t] *vb voir* **séduire** ▷ *adj* (*femme*) seductive; (*homme, offre*) very attractive

séduit, e [sedɥi, -it] *pp de* **séduire**

segment [sɛgmɑ̃] *nm* segment; (*Auto*): **~ (de piston)** piston ring; **~ de frein** brake shoe

segmenter [sɛgmɑ̃te] *vt*, **se segmenter** *vi* to segment

ségrégation [segregasjɔ̃] *nf* segregation

ségrégationnisme [segregasjɔnism(ə)] *nm* segregationism

ségrégationniste [segregasjɔnist(ə)] *adj* segregationist

seiche [sɛʃ] *nf* cuttlefish

séide [seid] *nm* (*péj*) henchman

seigle [sɛgl(ə)] *nm* rye

seigneur [sɛɲœr] *nm* lord; **le S~** the Lord

seigneurial, e, -aux [sɛɲœrjal, -o] *adj* lordly, stately

sein [sɛ̃] *nm* breast; (*entrailles*) womb; **au ~ de** *prép* (*équipe, institution*) within; (*flots, bonheur*) in the midst of; **donner le ~ à** (*bébé*) to feed (at the breast); to breast-feed; **nourrir au ~** to breast-feed

Seine [sɛn] *nf*: **la ~** the Seine

séisme [seism(ə)] *nm* earthquake

séismique *etc* [seismik] *voir* **sismique** *etc*

SEITA [seita] *sigle f* = **Société d'exploitation industrielle des tabacs et allumettes**

seize [sɛz] *num* sixteen

seizième [sɛzjɛm] *num* sixteenth

séjour [seʒur] *nm* stay; (*pièce*) living room

séjourner [seʒurne] *vi* to stay

sel [sɛl] *nm* salt; (*fig*) wit; spice; **~ de cuisine/de table** cooking/table salt; **~ gemme** rock salt; **~s de bain** bathsalts

sélect, e [selɛkt] *adj* select

sélectif, -ive [selɛktif, -iv] *adj* selective

sélection [selɛksjɔ̃] *nf* selection; **faire/opérer une ~ parmi** to make a selection from among; **épreuve de ~** (*Sport*) trial (for selection); **~ naturelle** natural selection; **~ professionnelle** professional recruitment

sélectionné, e [selɛksjɔne] *adj* (*joueur*) selected; (*produit*) specially selected

sélectionner [selɛksjɔne] *vt* to select

sélectionneur, -euse [selɛksjɔnœr, -øz] *nm/f* selector

sélectivement [selɛktivmɑ̃] *adv* selectively

sélectivité [selɛktivite] *nf* selectivity

self [sɛlf] *nm* (*fam*) self-service

self-service [sɛlfsɛrvis] *adj* self-service ▷ *nm* self-service (restaurant); (*magasin*) self-service

shop

selle [sɛl] *nf* saddle; **selles** *nfpl* (*Méd*) stools; **aller à la ~** (*Méd*) to have a bowel movement; **se mettre en ~** to mount, get into the saddle

seller [sele] *vt* to saddle

sellette [sɛlɛt] *nf*: **être sur la ~** to be on the carpet (*fig*)

sellier [selje] *nm* saddler

selon [səlɔ̃] *prép* according to; (*en se conformant à*) in accordance with; **~ moi** as I see it; **~ que** according to, depending on whether

SEm *sigle f* (= *Son Éminence*) HE

semailles [səmaj] *nfpl* sowing *sg*

semaine [səmɛn] *nf* week; (*salaire*) week's wages *ou* pay, weekly wages *ou* pay; **en ~** during the week, on weekdays; **à la petite ~** from day to day; **la ~ sainte** Holy Week

semainier [səmenje] *nm* (*bracelet*) bracelet made up of seven bands; (*calendrier*) desk diary; (*meuble*) chest of (seven) drawers

sémantique [semɑ̃tik] *adj* semantic ▷ *nf* semantics *sg*

sémaphore [semafɔr] *nm* (*Rail*) semaphore signal

semblable [sɑ̃blabl(ə)] *adj* similar; (*de ce genre*): **de ~s mésaventures** such mishaps ▷ *nm* fellow creature *ou* man; **~ à** similar to, like

semblant [sɑ̃blɑ̃] *nm*: **un ~ de vérité** a semblance of truth; **faire ~ (de faire)** to pretend (to do)

sembler [sɑ̃ble] *vb copule* to seem ▷ *vb impers*: **il semble (bien) que/inutile de** it (really) seems *ou* appears that/useless to; **il me semble (bien) que** it (really) seems to me that, I (really) think that; **il me semble le connaître** I think *ou* I've a feeling I know him; **~ être** to seem to be; **comme bon lui semble** as he sees fit; **me semble-t-il, à ce qu'il me semble** it seems to me, to my mind

semelle [səmɛl] *nf* sole; (*intérieure*) insole, inner sole; **battre la ~** to stamp one's feet (to keep them warm); (*fig*) to hang around (waiting); **~s compensées** platform soles

semence [səmɑ̃s] *nf* (*graine*) seed; (*clou*) tack

semer [səme] *vt* to sow; (*fig: éparpiller*) to scatter; (*confusion*) to spread; (*: poursuivants*) to lose, shake off; **~ la discorde parmi** to sow discord among; **semé de** (*difficultés*) riddled with

semestre [səmɛstr(ə)] *nm* half-year; (*Scol*) semester

semestriel, le [səmɛstrijɛl] *adj* half-yearly; semestral

semeur, -euse [səmœr, -øz] *nm/f* sower

semi-automatique [səmiɔtɔmatik] *adj* semiautomatic

semiconducteur [səmikɔ̃dyktœr] *nm* (*Inform*) semiconductor

semi-conserve [səmikɔ̃sɛrv(ə)] *nf* semi-perishable foodstuff

semi-fini [səmifini] *adj m* (*produit*) semi-finished

semi-liberté [səmilibɛrte] *nf* (*Jur*) partial release from prison (*in order to follow a profession or* *undergo medical treatment)*

sémillant, e [semijã, -ãt] *adj* vivacious; dashing
séminaire [seminɛʀ] *nm* seminar; (*Rel*)
seminary
séminariste [seminaʀist(ə)] *nm* seminarist
sémiologie [semjɔlɔʒi] *nf* semiology
semi-public, -ique [səmipyblik] *adj* (*Jur*)
semipublic
semi-remorque [səmiʀəmɔʀk(ə)] *nf* trailer
▷ *nm* articulated lorry (*Brit*), semi(trailer) (*US*)
semis [səmi] *nm* (*terrain*) seedbed, seed plot;
(*plante*) seedling
sémite [semit] *adj* Semitic
sémitique [semitik] *adj* Semitic
semoir [səmwaʀ] *nm* seed-bag; seeder
semonce [səmɔ̃s] *nf:* **un coup de ~** a shot across
the bows
semoule [səmul] *nf* semolina; **~ de riz** ground
rice
sempiternel, le [sɛ̃pitɛʀnɛl] *adj* eternal, never-
ending
sénat [sena] *nm* senate; *see note*

● SÉNAT

The *Sénat* is the upper house of the French
parliament and is housed in the Palais du
Luxembourg in Paris. One-third of its
members, "sénateurs" are elected for a
nine-year term every three years by an
electoral college consisting of the "députés"
and other elected representatives. The *Sénat*
has a wide range of powers but can be
overridden by the lower house, the
"Assemblée nationale" in case of dispute.

sénateur [senatœʀ] *nm* senator
sénatorial, e, -aux [senatɔʀjal, -o] *adj*
senatorial, Senate *cpd*
Sénégal [senegal] *nm:* **le ~** Senegal
sénégalais, e [senegalɛ, -ez] *adj* Senegalese
sénevé [sɛnve] *nm* (*Bot*) mustard; (*graine*)
mustard seed
sénile [senil] *adj* senile
sénilité [senilite] *nf* senility
senior [senjɔʀ] *nm/f* (*Sport*) senior
sens [sã] *vb voir* **sentir** ▷ *nm* [sãs] (*Physiol, instinct*)
sense; (*signification*) meaning, sense; (*direction*)
direction, way ▷ *nmpl* (*sensualité*) senses;
reprendre ses ~ to regain consciousness; **avoir
le ~ des affaires/de la mesure** to have
business sense/a sense of moderation; **ça n'a
pas de ~** that doesn't make (any) sense; **en
dépit du bon ~** contrary to all good sense;
tomber sous le ~ to stand to reason, be
perfectly obvious; **en un ~, dans un ~** in a way;
en ce ~ que in the sense that; **à mon ~** to my
mind; **dans le ~ des aiguilles d'une montre**
clockwise; **dans le ~ de la longueur/largeur**
lengthways/widthways; **dans le mauvais ~**
the wrong way; in the wrong direction; **bon ~**
good sense; **~ commun** common sense; **~**

dessus dessous upside down; **~ interdit, ~
unique** one-way street
sensass [sãsas] *adj* (*fam*) fantastic
sensation [sãsasjɔ̃] *nf* sensation; **faire ~** to
cause a sensation, create a stir; **à ~** (*péj*)
sensational
sensationnel, le [sãsasjɔnɛl] *adj* sensational
sensé, e [sãse] *adj* sensible
sensibilisation [sãsibilizasjɔ̃] *nf*
consciousness-raising; **une campagne de ~
de l'opinion** a campaign to raise public
awareness
sensibiliser [sãsibilize] *vt* to sensitize; **~ qn (à)**
to make sb sensitive (to)
sensibilité [sãsibilite] *nf* sensitivity; (*affectivité,
émotivité*) sensitivity, sensibility
sensible [sãsibl(ə)] *adj* sensitive; (*aux sens*)
perceptible; (*appréciable: différence, progrès*)
appreciable, noticeable; (*quartier*) problem *cpd*; **~
à** sensitive to
sensiblement [sãsibləmã] *adv* (*notablement*)
appreciably, noticeably; (*à peu près*): **ils ont ~ le
même poids** they weigh approximately the
same
sensiblerie [sãsibləʀi] *nf* sentimentality;
squeamishness
sensitif, -ive [sãsitif, -iv] *adj* (*nerf*) sensory;
(*personne*) oversensitive
sensoriel, le [sãsɔʀjɛl] *adj* sensory, sensorial
sensualité [sãsɥalite] *nf* sensuality,
sensuousness
sensuel, le [sãsɥɛl] *adj* sensual; sensuous
sent [sã] *vb voir* **sentir**
sente [sãt] *nf* path
sentence [sãtãs] *nf* (*jugement*) sentence; (*adage*)
maxim
sentencieusement [sãtãsjøzmã] *adv*
sententiously
sentencieux, -euse [sãtãsjø, -øz] *adj*
sententious
senteur [sãtœʀ] *nf* scent, perfume
senti, e [sãti] *adj:* **bien ~** (*mots etc*) well-chosen
sentier [sãtje] *nm* path
sentiment [sãtimã] *nm* feeling; (*conscience,
impression*): **avoir le ~ de/que** to be aware of/
have the feeling that; **recevez mes ~s
respectueux** yours faithfully; **faire du ~** (*péj*)
to be sentimental; **si vous me prenez par les
~s** if you appeal to my feelings
sentimental, e, -aux [sãtimãtal, -o] *adj*
sentimental; (*vie, aventure*) love *cpd*
sentimentalisme [sãtimãtalism(ə)] *nm*
sentimentalism
sentimentalité [sãtimãtalite] *nf*
sentimentality
sentinelle [sãtinɛl] *nf* sentry; **en ~** standing
guard; (*soldat: en faction*) on sentry duty
sentir [sãtiʀ] *vt* (*par l'odorat*) to smell; (*par le goût*)
to taste; (*au toucher, fig*) to feel; (*répandre une odeur
de*) to smell of; (*: ressemblance*) to smell like; (*avoir
la saveur de*) to taste of; to taste like; (*fig: dénoter,
annoncer*) to be indicative of; to smack of; to

S

foreshadow ▷ vi to smell; ~ **mauvais** to smell bad; **se ~ bien** to feel good; **se ~ mal** (*être indisposé*) to feel unwell *ou* ill; **se ~ le courage/la force de faire** to feel brave/strong enough to do; **ne plus se ~ de joie** to be beside o.s. with joy; **il ne peut pas le ~** (*fam*) he can't stand him

seoir [swaR]: **~ à** vt to become, befit; **comme il (leur) sied** as it is fitting (to them)

Séoul [seul] n Seoul

SEP sigle f (= *sclérose en plaques*) MS

séparation [sepaRasjɔ̃] nf separation; (*cloison*) division, partition; **~ de biens** division of property (*in marriage settlement*); **~ de corps** legal separation

séparatisme [sepaRatism(ə)] nm separatism

séparatiste [sepaRatist(ə)] adj, nm/f (*Pol*) separatist

séparé, e [sepaRe] adj (*appartements, pouvoirs*) separate; (*époux*) separated; **~ de** separate from; separated from

séparément [sepaRemã] adv separately

séparer [sepaRe] vt (*gén*) to separate; (*divergences etc*) to divide; to drive apart; (: *différences, obstacles*) to stand between; (*détacher*): **~ qch de** to pull sth (off) from; (*dissocier*) to distinguish between; (*diviser*): **~ qch par** to divide sth (up) with; **~ une pièce en deux** to divide a room into two; **se séparer** (*époux*) to separate, part; (*prendre congé: amis etc*) to part, leave each other; (*adversaires*) to separate; (*se diviser: route, tige etc*) to divide; (*se détacher*): **se ~ (de)** to split off (from); to come off; **se ~ de** (*époux*) to separate *ou* part from; (*employé, objet personnel*) to part with

sépia [sepja] nf sepia

sept [sɛt] num seven

septante [sɛptɑ̃t] num (*Belgique, Suisse*) seventy

septembre [sɛptɑ̃bR(ə)] nm September; *voir aussi* **juillet**

septennal, e, -aux [sɛptenal, -o] adj seven-year; (*festival*) seven-year, septennial

septennat [sɛptena] nm seven-year term (of office)

septentrional, e, -aux [sɛptɑ̃tRijɔnal, -o] adj northern

septicémie [sɛptisemi] nf blood poisoning, septicaemia

septième [sɛtjɛm] num seventh; **être au ~ ciel** to be on cloud nine

septique [sɛptik] adj: **fosse ~** septic tank

septuagénaire [sɛptɥaʒenɛR] adj, nm/f septuagenarian

sépulcral, e, -aux [sepylkRal, -o] adj (*voix*) sepulchral

sépulcre [sepylkR(ə)] nm sepulchre

sépulture [sepyltyR] nf burial; (*tombeau*) burial place, grave

séquelles [sekɛl] nfpl after-effects; (*fig*) aftermath sg; consequences

séquence [sekɑ̃s] nf sequence

séquentiel, le [sekɑ̃sjɛl] adj sequential

séquestration [sekɛstRasjɔ̃] nf illegal confinement; impounding

séquestre [sekɛstR(ə)] nm impoundment; **mettre sous ~** to impound

séquestrer [sekɛstRe] vt (*personne*) to confine illegally; (*biens*) to impound

serai etc [səRe] vb voir **être**

sérail [seRaj] nm seraglio; harem; **rentrer au ~** to return to the fold

serbe [sɛRb(ə)] adj Serbian ▷ nm (*Ling*) Serbian ▷ nm/f: **Serbe** Serb

Serbie [sɛRbi] nf: **la ~** Serbia

serbo-croate [sɛRbɔkRɔat] adj Serbo-Croat, Serbo-Croatian ▷ nm (*Ling*) Serbo-Croat

serein, e [səRɛ̃, -ɛn] adj serene; (*jugement*) dispassionate

sereinement [səRɛnmã] adv serenely

sérénade [seRenad] nf serenade; (*fam*) hullabaloo

sérénité [seRenite] nf serenity

serez [səRe] vb voir **être**

serf, serve [sɛR, sɛRv(ə)] nm/f serf

serfouette [sɛRfwɛt] nf weeding hoe

serge [sɛRʒ(ə)] nf serge

sergent [sɛRʒã] nm sergeant

sergent-chef [sɛRʒãʃɛf] nm staff sergeant

sergent-major [sɛRʒãmaʒɔR] nm ≈ quartermaster sergeant

sériciculture [seRisikyltyR] nf silkworm breeding, sericulture

série [seRi] nf (*de questions, d'accidents, TV*) series inv; (*de clés, casseroles, outils*) set; (*catégorie: Sport*) rank; class; **en ~** in quick succession; (*Comm*) mass cpd; **de ~** adj standard; **hors ~** (*Comm*) custom-built; (*fig*) outstanding; **imprimante ~** (*Inform*) serial printer; **soldes de fin de ~s** end of line special offers; **~ noire** nm (crime) thriller ▷ nf (*suite de malheurs*) run of bad luck

sérier [seRje] vt to classify, sort out

sérieusement [seRjøzmã] adv seriously; reliably; responsibly; **il parle ~** he's serious, he means it; **~?** are you serious?, do you mean it?

sérieux, -euse [seRjø, -øz] adj serious; (*élève, employé*) reliable, responsible; (*client, maison*) reliable, dependable; (*offre, proposition*) genuine, serious; (*grave, sévère*) serious, solemn; (*maladie, situation*) serious, grave; (*important*) considerable ▷ nm seriousness; reliability; **ce n'est pas ~** (*raisonnable*) that's not on; **garder son ~** to keep a straight face; **manquer de ~** not to be very responsible (*ou* reliable); **prendre qch/qn au ~** to take sth/sb seriously

sérigraphie [seRigRafi] nf silk screen printing

serin [səRɛ̃] nm canary

seriner [səRine] vt: **~ qch à qn** to drum sth into sb

seringue [səRɛ̃g] nf syringe

serions etc [səRjɔ̃] vb voir **être**

serment [sɛRmã] nm (*juré*) oath; (*promesse*) pledge, vow; **prêter ~** to take the *ou* an oath; **faire le ~ de** to take a vow to, swear to; **sous ~** on *ou* under oath

sermon [sɛRmɔ̃] nm sermon; (*péj*) sermon, lecture

sermonner [sɛʀmɔne] vt to lecture

SERNAM [sɛʀnam] sigle m (= Service national de messageries) rail delivery service

sérologie [seʀɔlɔʒi] nf serology

séronégatif, -ive [seʀonegatif, -iv] adj HIV negative

séropositif, -ive [seʀopozitif, -iv] adj HIV positive

serpe [sɛʀp(ə)] nf billhook

serpent [sɛʀpɑ̃] nm snake; ~ **à sonnettes** rattlesnake; ~ **monétaire (européen)** (European) monetary snake

serpenter [sɛʀpɑ̃te] vi to wind

serpentin [sɛʀpɑ̃tɛ̃] nm (tube) coil; (ruban) streamer

serpillière [sɛʀpijɛʀ] nf floorcloth

serrage [seʀaʒ] nm tightening; **collier de ~** clamp

serre [sɛʀ] nf (Agr) greenhouse; ~ **chaude** hothouse; ~ **froide** unheated greenhouse

serré, e [seʀe] adj (tissu) closely woven; (réseau) dense; (écriture) close; (habits) tight; (fig: lutte, match) tight, close-fought; (passagers etc) (tightly) packed; (café) strong ▷ adv: **jouer ~** to play it close, play a close game; **écrire ~** to write a cramped hand; **avoir la gorge ~e** to have a lump in one's throat

serre-livres [sɛʀlivʀ(ə)] nm inv book ends pl

serrement [sɛʀmɑ̃] nm: ~ **de main** handshake; ~ **de cœur** pang of anguish

serrer [seʀe] vt (tenir) to grip ou hold tight; (comprimer, coincer) to squeeze; (poings, mâchoires) to clench; (vêtement) to be too tight for; to fit tightly; (rapprocher) to close up, move closer together; (ceinture, nœud, frein, vis) to tighten ▷ vi: ~ **à droite** to keep to the right; to move into the right-hand lane; **se serrer** (se rapprocher) to squeeze up; **se ~ contre qn** to huddle up to sb; **se ~ les coudes** to stick together, back one another up; **se ~ la ceinture** to tighten one's belt; ~ **la main à qn** to shake sb's hand; ~ **qn dans ses bras** to hug sb, clasp sb in one's arms; ~ **la gorge à qn** (chagrin) to bring a lump to sb's throat; ~ **les dents** to clench ou grit one's teeth; ~ **qn de près** to follow close behind sb; ~ **le trottoir** to hug the kerb; ~ **sa droite** to keep well to the right; ~ **la vis à qn** to crack down harder on sb; ~ **les rangs** to close ranks

serres [sɛʀ] nfpl (griffes) claws, talons

serre-tête [sɛʀtɛt] nm inv (bandeau) headband; (bonnet) skullcap

serrure [seʀyʀ] nf lock

serrurerie [seʀyʀʀi] nf (métier) locksmith's trade; (ferronnerie) ironwork; ~ **d'art** ornamental ironwork

serrurier [seʀyʀje] nm locksmith

sers, sert [sɛʀ] vb voir **servir**

sertir [sɛʀtiʀ] vt (pierre) to set; (pièces métalliques) to crimp

sérum [seʀɔm] nm serum; ~ **antivenimeux** snakebite serum; ~ **sanguin** (blood) serum

servage [sɛʀvaʒ] nm serfdom

servant [sɛʀvɑ̃] nm server

servante [sɛʀvɑ̃t] nf (maid)servant

serve [sɛʀv] nf voir **serf** ▷ vb voir **servir**

serveur, -euse [sɛʀvœʀ, -øz] nm/f waiter (waitress) ▷ nm (Inform) server ▷ adj: **centre ~** (Inform) service centre

servi, e [sɛʀvi] adj: **être bien ~** to get a large helping (ou helpings); **vous êtes ~?** are you being served?

serviable [sɛʀvjabl(ə)] adj obliging, willing to help

service [sɛʀvis] nm (gén) service; (série de repas): **premier ~** first sitting; (pourboire) service (charge); (assortiment de vaisselle) set, service; (linge de table) set; (bureau: de la vente etc) department, section; (travail): **pendant le ~** on duty; **services** nmpl (travail, Écon) services, inclusive/exclusive of service; **faire le ~** to serve; **être en ~ chez qn** (domestique) to be in sb's service; **être au ~ de** (patron, patrie) to be in the service of; **être au ~ de qn** (collaborateur, voiture) to be at sb's service; **porte de ~** tradesman's entrance; **rendre ~ à** to help; **il aime rendre ~** he likes to help; **rendre un ~ à qn** to do sb a favour; **heures de ~** hours of duty; **être de ~** to be on duty; **reprendre du ~** to get back into action; **avoir 25 ans de ~** to have completed 25 years' service; **être/mettre en ~** to be in/put into service ou operation; **hors ~** not in use; out of order; ~ **à thé/café** tea/coffee set ou service; ~ **après-vente (SAV)** after-sales service; **en ~ commandé** on an official assignment; ~ **funèbre** funeral service; ~ **militaire** military service; see note; ~ **d'ordre** police (ou stewards) in charge of maintaining order; ~**s publics** public services, (public) utilities; ~**s secrets** secret service sg; ~**s sociaux** social services

---

🔵 SERVICE MILITAIRE

Until 1997, French men over the age of 18 who were passed as fit, and who were not in full-time higher education, were required to do ten months' "service militaire". Conscientious objectors were required to do two years' community service. Since 1997, military service has been suspended in France. However, all sixteen-year-olds, both male and female, are required to register for a compulsory one-day training course, the "JAPD" ("journée d'appel de préparation à la défense"), which covers basic information on the principles and organization of defence in France, and also advises on career opportunities in the military and in the voluntary sector. Young people must attend the training day before their eighteenth birthday.

---

serviette [sɛʀvjɛt] nf (de table) (table) napkin, serviette; (de toilette) towel; (porte-documents) briefcase; **~ éponge** terry towel; **~ hygiénique** sanitary towel

servile [sɛʀvil] *adj* servile

servir [sɛʀviʀ] *vt* (*gén*) to serve; (*dîneur: au restaurant*) to wait on; (*client: au magasin*) to serve, attend to; (*fig: aider*): **~ qn** to aid sb; to serve sb's interests; to stand sb in good stead; (*Comm: rente*) to pay ▷ *vi* (*Tennis*) to serve; (*Cartes*) to deal; (*être militaire*) to serve; **~ qch à qn** to serve sb with sth, help sb to sth; **qu'est-ce que je vous sers?** what can I get you?; **se servir** (*prendre d'un plat*) to help o.s.; (*s'approvisionner*): **se ~ chez** to shop at; **se ~ de** (*plat*) to help o.s. to; (*voiture, outil, relations*) to use; **~ à qn** (*diplôme, livre*) to be of use to sb; **ça m'a servi pour faire** it was useful to me when I did; I used it to do; **~ à qch/à faire** (*outil etc*) to be used for sth/for doing; **ça peut ~** it may come in handy; **à quoi cela sert-il (de faire)?** what's the use (of doing)?; **cela ne sert à rien** it's no use; **~ (à qn) de ...** to serve as ... (for sb); **~ à dîner (à qn)** to serve dinner (to sb)

serviteur [sɛʀvitœʀ] *nm* servant

servitude [sɛʀvityd] *nf* servitude; (*fig*) constraint; (*Jur*) easement

servofrein [sɛʀvɔfʀɛ̃] *nm* servo(-assisted) brake

servomécanisme [sɛʀvɔmekanism(ə)] *nm* servo system

ses [se] *adj possessif voir* **son**

sésame [sezam] *nm* (*Bot*) sesame; (*graine*) sesame seed

session [sesjɔ̃] *nf* session

set [sɛt] *nm* set; (*napperon*) placemat; **~ de table** set of placemats

seuil [sœj] *nm* doorstep; (*fig*) threshold; **sur le ~ de la maison** in the doorway of his house, on his doorstep; **au ~ de** (*fig*) on the threshold *ou* brink *ou* edge of; **~ de rentabilité** (*Comm*) breakeven point

seul, e [sœl] *adj* (*sans compagnie*) alone; (*avec nuance affective: isolé*) lonely; (*unique*): **un ~ livre** only one book, a single book; **le ~ livre** the only book; **~ ce livre, ce livre ~** this book alone, only this book; **d'un ~ coup** (*soudainement*) all at once; (*à la fois*) at one blow ▷ *adv* (*vivre*) alone, on one's own; **parler tout ~** to talk to oneself; **faire qch (tout) ~** to do sth (all) on one's own *ou* (all) by oneself ▷ *nm, nf*: **il en reste un(e) ~(e)** there's only one left; **pas un(e) ~(e)** not a single; **à lui (tout) ~** single-handed, on his own; **à ~** in private

seulement [sœlmɑ̃] *adv* (*pas davantage*): **~ cinq**, **cinq ~** only five; (*exclusivement*): **~ eux** only them, them alone; (*pas avant*): **~ hier/à 10h** only yesterday/at 10 o'clock; (*mais, toutefois*): **il consent, ~ il demande des garanties** he agrees, only he wants guarantees; **non ~ ... mais aussi** *ou* **encore** not only ... but also

sève [sɛv] *nf* sap

sévère [sevɛʀ] *adj* severe

sévèrement [sevɛʀmɑ̃] *adv* severely

sévérité [severite] *nf* severity

sévices [sevis] *nmpl* (physical) cruelty *sg*, ill treatment *sg*

Séville [sevil] *n* Seville

sévir [seviʀ] *vi* (*punir*) to use harsh measures, crack down; (*fléau*) to rage, be rampant; **~ contre** (*abus*) to deal ruthlessly with, crack down on

sevrage [səvʀaʒ] *nm* weaning; deprivation; (*d'un toxicomane*) withdrawal

sevrer [səvʀe] *vt* to wean; (*fig*): **~ qn de** to deprive sb of

sexagénaire [sɛgzaʒenɛʀ] *adj, nm/f* sexagenarian

SExc *sigle f* (= *Son Excellence*) HE

sexe [sɛks(ə)] *nm* sex; (*organe mâle*) member

sexisme [sɛksism(ə)] *nm* sexism

sexiste [sɛksist(ə)] *adj, nm* sexist

sexologie [sɛksɔlɔʒi] *nf* sexology

sexologue [sɛksɔlɔg] *nm/f* sexologist, sex specialist

sextant [sɛkstɑ̃] *nm* sextant

sexualité [sɛksɥalite] *nf* sexuality

sexué, e [sɛksɥe] *adj* sexual

sexuel, le [sɛksɥɛl] *adj* sexual; **acte ~** sex act

sexuellement [sɛksɥɛlmɑ̃] *adv* sexually

seyait [sejɛ] *vb voir* **seoir**

seyant, e [sɛjɑ̃, -ɑ̃t] *vb voir* **seoir** ▷ *adj* becoming

Seychelles [seʃɛl] *nfpl*: **les ~** the Seychelles

SG *sigle m* = **secrétaire général**

SGEN *sigle m* (= *Syndicat général de l'éducation nationale*) trades union

shaker [ʃɛkœʀ] *nm* (cocktail) shaker

shampooiner [ʃɑ̃pwine] *vt* to shampoo

shampooineur, -euse [ʃɑ̃pwinœʀ, -øz] *nm/f* (*personne*) junior (*who does the shampooing*)

shampooing [ʃɑ̃pwɛ̃] *nm* shampoo; **se faire un ~** to shampoo one's hair; **~ colorant** (colour) rinse; **~ traitant** medicated shampoo

Shetland [ʃɛtlɑ̃d] *n*: **les îles ~** the Shetland Islands, Shetland

shoot [ʃut] *nm* (*Football*) shot

shooter [ʃute] *vi* (*Football*) to shoot; **se shooter** (*drogué*) to mainline

shopping [ʃɔpiŋ] *nm*: **faire du ~** to go shopping

short [ʃɔʀt] *nm* (pair of) shorts *pl*

SI *sigle m* = **syndicat d'initiative**

 MOT-CLÉ

si [si] *nm* (*Mus*) B; (*en chantant la gamme*) ti ▷ *adv* **1** (*oui*) yes; **"Paul n'est pas venu"** — **"si!"** "Paul hasn't come" — "Yes he has!"; **je vous assure que si** I assure you he did/she is *etc* **2** (*tellement*) so; **si gentil/rapidement** so kind/ fast; (*tant et*) **si bien que** so much so that; **si rapide qu'il soit** however fast he may be ▷ *conj* if; **si tu veux** if you want; **je me demande si** I wonder if *ou* whether; **si j'étais toi** if I were you; **si seulement** if only; **si ce n'est que** apart from; **une des plus belles, si**

ce n'est la plus belle one of the most beautiful, if not THE most beautiful; **s'il est aimable, eux par contre ...** while *ou* whereas he's nice, they (on the other hand) ...

siamois, e [sjamwa, -waz] *adj* Siamese; **frères/ sœurs ~(es)** Siamese twins

Sibérie [siberi] *nf*: **la ~** Siberia

sibérien, ne [siberjɛ̃, -ɛn] *adj* Siberian ▷ *nm/f*: **Sibérien, ne** Siberian

sibyllin, e [sibilɛ̃, -in] *adj* sibylline

SICAV [sikav] *sigle f* (= *société d'investissement à capital variable*) open-ended investment trust, share in such a trust

Sicile [sisil] *nf*: **la ~** Sicily

sicilien, ne [sisiljɛ̃, -ɛn] *adj* Sicilian

sida [sida] *nm* (= *syndrome immuno-déficitaire acquis*) AIDS *sg*

sidéral, e, -aux [sideral, -o] *adj* sideral

sidérant, e [siderɑ̃, -ɑ̃t] *adj* staggering

sidéré, e [sidere] *adj* staggered

sidérurgie [sideryrʒi] *nf* steel industry

sidérurgique [sideryrʒik] *adj* steel *cpd*

sidérurgiste [sideryrʒist(ə)] *nm/f* steel worker

siècle [sjɛkl(ə)] *nm* century; (*époque*): **le ~ des lumières/de l'atome** the age of enlightenment/atomic age; (*Rel*): **le ~** the world

sied [sje] *vb voir* **seoir**

siège [sjɛʒ] *nm* seat; (*d'entreprise*) head office; (*d'organisation*) headquarters *pl*; (*Mil*) siege; **lever le ~** to raise the siege; **mettre le ~ devant** to besiege; **présentation par le ~** (*Méd*) breech presentation; **~ avant/arrière** (*Auto*) front/back seat; **~ baquet** bucket seat; **~ social** registered office

siéger [sjeʒe] *vi* (*assemblée, tribunal*) to sit; (*résider, se trouver*) to lie, be located

sien, ne [sjɛ̃, sjɛn] *pron*: **le(la) ~(ne), les ~s(~nes)**; his; hers; (*d'une chose*) its; **y mettre du ~** to pull one's weight; **faire des ~nes** (*fam*) to be up to one's (usual) tricks; **les ~s** (*sa famille*) one's family

siérait *etc* [sjere] *vb voir* **seoir**

Sierra Leone [sjeraleɔne] *nf*: **la ~** Sierra Leone

sieste [sjɛst(ə)] *nf* (afternoon) snooze *ou* nap, siesta; **faire la ~** to have a snooze *ou* nap

sieur [sjœr] *nm*: **le ~ Thomas** Mr Thomas; (*en plaisantant*) Master Thomas

sifflant, e [siflɑ̃, -ɑ̃t] *adj* (*bruit*) whistling; (*toux*) wheezing; **(consonne) ~e** sibilant

sifflement [sifləmɑ̃] *nm* whistle, whistling *no pl*; wheezing *no pl*; hissing *no pl*

siffler [sifle] *vi* (*gén*) to whistle; (*avec un sifflet*) to blow (on) one's whistle; (*en respirant*) to wheeze; (*serpent, vapeur*) to hiss ▷ *vt* (*chanson*) to whistle; (*chien etc*) to whistle for; (*fille*) to whistle at; (*pièce, orateur*) to hiss, boo; (*faute*) to blow one's whistle at; (*fin du match, départ*) to blow one's whistle for; (*fam: verre, bouteille*) to guzzle, knock back (*Brit*)

sifflet [siflɛ] *nm* whistle; **sifflets** *nmpl* (*de mécontentement*) whistles, boos; **coup de ~** whistle

siffloter [siflɔte] *vi, vt* to whistle

sigle [sigl(ə)] *nm* acronym, (set of) initials *pl*

signal, -aux [siɲal, -o] *nm* (*signe convenu, appareil*) signal; (*indice, écriteau*) sign; **donner le ~ de** to give the signal for; **~ d'alarme** alarm signal; **~ d'alerte/de détresse** warning/distress signal; **~ horaire** time signal; **~ optique/sonore** warning light/sound; visual/acoustic signal; **signaux (lumineux)** (*Auto*) traffic signals; **signaux routiers** road signs; (*lumineux*) traffic lights

signalement [siɲalmɑ̃] *nm* description, particulars *pl*

signaler [siɲale] *vt* to indicate; to announce; to report; (*être l'indice de*) to indicate; (*faire remarquer*): **~ qch à qn/à qn que** to point out sth to sb/to sb that; (*appeler l'attention sur*): **~ qn à la police** to bring sb to the notice of the police; **se ~ par** to distinguish o.s. by; **se ~ à l'attention de qn** to attract sb's attention

signalétique [siɲaletik] *adj*: **fiche ~** identification sheet

signalisation [siɲalizasjɔ̃] *nf* signalling, signposting; signals *pl*; roadsigns *pl*; **panneau de ~** roadsign

signaliser [siɲalize] *vt* to put up roadsigns on; to put signals on

signataire [siɲatɛr] *nm/f* signatory

signature [siɲatyr] *nf* signature; (*action*) signing

signe [siɲ] *nm* sign; (*Typo*) mark; **ne pas donner ~ de vie** to give no sign of life; **c'est bon ~** it's a good sign; **c'est ~ que** it's a sign that; **faire un ~ de la main/tête** to give a sign with one's hand/shake one's head; **faire ~ à qn** (*fig*) to get in touch with sb; **faire ~ à qn d'entrer** to motion (to) sb to come in; **en ~ de** as a sign *ou* mark of; **le ~ de la croix** the sign of the Cross; **~ de ponctuation** punctuation mark; **~ du zodiaque** sign of the zodiac; **~s particuliers** distinguishing marks

signer [siɲe] *vt* to sign; **se signer** *vi* to cross o.s

signet [siɲɛ] *nm* bookmark

significatif, -ive [siɲifikatif, -iv] *adj* significant

signification [siɲifikasjɔ̃] *nf* meaning

signifier [siɲifje] *vt* (*vouloir dire*) to mean, signify; (*faire connaître*): **~ qch (à qn)** to make sth known (to sb); (*Jur*): **~ qch à qn** to serve notice of sth on sb

silence [silɑ̃s] *nm* silence; (*Mus*) rest; **garder le ~ (sur qch)** to keep silent (about sth), say nothing (about sth); **passer sous ~** to pass over (in silence); **réduire au ~** to silence

silencieusement [silɑ̃sjøzmɑ̃] *adv* silently

silencieux, -euse [silɑ̃sjø, -øz] *adj* quiet, silent ▷ *nm* silencer (*Brit*), muffler (*US*)

silex [silɛks] *nm* flint

silhouette [silwɛt] *nf* outline, silhouette;

(*lignes, contour*) outline; (*figure*) figure

silice [silis] *nf* silica

siliceux, -euse [silisø, -øz] *adj* (*terrain*) chalky

silicium [silisjɔm] *nm* silicon; **plaquette de ~** silicon chip

silicone [silikon] *nf* silicone

silicose [silikoz] *nf* silicosis, dust disease

sillage [sijaʒ] *nm* wake; (*fig*) trail; **dans le ~ de** (*fig*) in the wake of

sillon [sijɔ̃] *nm* (*d'un champ*) furrow; (*de disque*) ˙groove

sillonner [sijɔne] *vt* (*creuser*) to furrow; (*traverser*) to cross, criss-cross

silo [silo] *nm* silo

simagrées [simagʀe] *nfpl* fuss *sg*; airs and graces

simiesque [simjɛsk(ə)] *adj* monkey-like, ape-like

similaire [similɛʀ] *adj* similar

similarité [similaʀite] *nf* similarity

simili [simili] *nm* imitation; (*Typo*) half-tone ▷ *nf* half-tone engraving

simili... [simili] *préfixe* imitation *cpd*, artificial

similicuir [similikɥiʀ] *nm* imitation leather

similigravure [similigʀavyʀ] *nf* half-tone engraving

similitude [similityd] *nf* similarity

simple [sɛ̃pl(ə)] *adj* (*gén*) simple; (*non multiple*) single; **simples** *nmpl* (*Méd*) medicinal plants; **~ messieurs** *nm* (*Tennis*) men's singles *sg*; **un ~ particulier** an ordinary citizen; **une ~ formalité** a mere formality; **cela varie du ~ au double** it can double, it can double the price *etc*; **dans le plus ~ appareil** in one's birthday suit; **~ course** *adj* single; **~ d'esprit** *nm/f* simpleton; **~ soldat** private

simplement [sɛ̃pləmɑ̃] *adv* simply

simplet, te [sɛ̃plɛ, -ɛt] *adj* (*personne*) simple-minded

simplicité [sɛ̃plisite] *nf* simplicity; **en toute ~** quite simply

simplification [sɛ̃plifikasjɔ̃] *nf* simplification

simplifier [sɛ̃plifje] *vt* to simplify

simpliste [sɛ̃plist(ə)] *adj* simplistic

simulacre [simylakʀ(ə)] *nm* enactment; (*péj*): **un ~ de** a pretence of, a sham

simulateur, -trice [simylatœʀ, -tʀis] *nm/f* shammer, pretender; (*qui se prétend malade*) malingerer ▷ *nm*: **~ de vol** flight simulator

simulation [simylasjɔ̃] *nf* shamming, simulation; malingering

simuler [simyle] *vt* to sham, simulate

simultané, e [simyltane] *adj* simultaneous

simultanéité [simyltaneite] *nf* simultaneity

simultanément [simyltanemɑ̃] *adv* simultaneously

Sinaï [sinai] *nm*: **le ~** Sinai

sinapisme [sinapism(ə)] *nm* (*Méd*) mustard poultice

sincère [sɛ̃sɛʀ] *adj* sincere; genuine; heartfelt; **mes ~s condoléances** my deepest sympathy

sincèrement [sɛ̃sɛʀmɑ̃] *adv* sincerely; genuinely

sincérité [sɛ̃seʀite] *nf* sincerity; **en toute ~** in all sincerity

sinécure [sinekyʀ] *nf* sinecure

sine die [sinedje] *adv* sine die, indefinitely

sine qua non [sinekwanɔn] *adj*: **condition ~** indispensable condition

Singapour [sɛ̃gapuʀ] *nm*: **le ~** Singapore

singe [sɛ̃ʒ] *nm* monkey; (*de grande taille*) ape

singer [sɛ̃ʒe] *vt* to ape, mimic

singeries [sɛ̃ʒʀi] *nfpl* antics; (*simagrées*) airs and graces

singulariser [sɛ̃gylaʀize] *vt* to mark out; **se singulariser** to call attention to o.s.

singularité [sɛ̃gylaʀite] *nf* peculiarity

singulier, -ière [sɛ̃gylje, -jɛʀ] *adj* remarkable, singular; (*Ling*) singular ▷ *nm* singular

singulièrement [sɛ̃gyljɛʀmɑ̃] *adv* singularly, remarkably

sinistre [sinistʀ(ə)] *adj* sinister; (*intensif*): **un ~ imbécile** an incredible idiot ▷ *nm* (*incendie*) blaze; (*catastrophe*) disaster; (*Assurances*) damage (*giving rise to a claim*)

sinistré, e [sinistʀe] *adj* disaster-stricken ▷ *nm/f* disaster victim

sinistrose [sinistʀoz] *nf* pessimism

sino... [sino] *préfixe*: **sino-indien** Sino-Indian, Chinese-Indian

sinon [sinɔ̃] *conj* (*autrement, sans quoi*) otherwise, or else; (*sauf*) except, other than; (*si ce n'est*) if not

sinueux, -euse [sinɥø, -øz] *adj* winding; (*fig*) tortuous

sinuosités [sinɥozite] *nfpl* winding *sg*, curves

sinus [sinys] *nm* (*Anat*) sinus; (*Géom*) sine

sinusite [sinyzit] *nf* sinusitis, sinus infection

sinusoïdal, e, -aux [sinyzoidal, -o] *adj* sinusoidal

sinusoïde [sinyzoid] *nf* sinusoid

sionisme [sjonism(ə)] *nm* Zionism

sioniste [sjonist(ə)] *adj, nm/f* Zionist

siphon [sifɔ̃] *nm* (*tube, d'eau gazeuse*) siphon; (*d'évier etc*) U-bend

siphonner [sifone] *vt* to siphon

sire [siʀ] *nm* (*titre*): **S~** Sire; **un triste ~** an unsavoury individual

sirène [siʀɛn] *nf* siren; **~ d'alarme** fire alarm; (*pendant la guerre*) air-raid siren

sirop [siʀo] *nm* (*à diluer: de fruit etc*) syrup, cordial; (*Brit*); (*boisson*) fruit drink; (*pharmaceutique*) syrup, mixture; **~ de menthe** mint syrup *ou* cordial; **~ contre la toux** cough syrup *ou* mixture

siroter [siʀote] *vt* to sip

sirupeux, -euse [siʀypø, -øz] *adj* syrupy

sis, e [si, siz] *adj*: **~ rue de la Paix** located in the rue de la Paix

sisal [sizal] *nm* (*Bot*) sisal

sismique [sismik] *adj* seismic

sismographe [sismogʀaf] *nm* seismograph

sismologie [sismoloʒi] *nf* seismology

site [sit] *nm* (*paysage, environnement*) setting;

(*d'une ville etc*: *emplacement*) site; ~ **(pittoresque)** beauty spot; ~**s touristiques** places of interest; ~**s naturels/historiques** natural/historic sites; ~ **web** (*Inform*) website

sitôt [sito] *adv*: ~ **parti** as soon as he *etc* had left; ~ **après** straight after; **pas de** ~ not for a long time; ~ **(après) que** as soon as

situation [sitɥasjɔ̃] *nf* (*gén*) situation; (*d'un édifice, d'une ville*) situation, position; (*emplacement*) location; **être en** ~ **de faire qch** to be in a position to do sth; ~ **de famille** marital status

situé, e [sitɥe] *adj*: **bien** ~ well situated, in a good location; ~ **à/près de** situated at/near

situer [sitɥe] *vt* to site, situate; (*en pensée*) to set, place; **se situer** *vi*: **se** ~ **à/près de** to be situated at/near

SIVOM [sivɔm] *sigle m* (= *Syndicat intercommunal à vocation multiple*) association of "communes"

six [sis] *num* six

sixième [sizjɛm] *num* sixth; **en** ~ (*Scol*: *classe*) first form (*Brit*), sixth grade (*US*)

skaï® [skaj] *nm* ≈ Leatherette®

skate [sket], **skate-board** [sketbɔrd] *nm* (*sport*) skateboarding; (*planche*) skateboard

sketch [skɛtʃ] *nm* (*variety*) sketch

ski [ski] *nm* (*objet*) ski; (*sport*) skiing; **faire du** ~ to ski; ~ **alpin** Alpine skiing; ~ **court** short ski; ~ **évolutif** short ski method; ~ **de fond** cross-country skiing; ~ **nautique** water-skiing; ~ **de piste** downhill skiing; ~ **de randonnée** cross-country skiing

ski-bob [skibɔb] *nm* skibob

skier [skje] *vi* to ski

skieur, -euse [skjœr, -øz] *nm/f* skier

skif, skiff [skif] *nm* skiff

slalom [slalɔm] *nm* slalom; **faire du** ~ **entre** to slalom between

slalomer [slalɔme] *vi* (*entre des obstacles*) to weave in and out; (*Ski*) to slalom

slalomeur, -euse [slalɔmœr, -øz] *nm/f* (*Ski*) slalom skier

slave [slav] *adj* Slav(onic), Slavic ▷ *nm* (*Ling*) Slavonic ▷ *nm/f*: **Slave** Slav

slip [slip] *nm* (*sous-vêtement*) underpants *pl*, pants *pl* (*Brit*), briefs *pl*; (*de bain: d'homme*) (bathing *ou* swimming) trunks *pl*; (: *du bikini*) (bikini) briefs *pl ou* bottoms *pl*

slogan [slɔgɑ̃] *nm* slogan

slovaque [slɔvak] *adj* Slovak ▷ *nm* (*Ling*) Slovak ▷ *nm/f*: **Slovaque** Slovak

Slovaquie [slɔvaki] *nf*: **la** ~ Slovakia

slovène [slɔvɛn] *adj* Slovene ▷ *nm* (*Ling*) Slovene ▷ *nm/f*: **Slovène** Slovene

Slovénie [slɔveni] *nf*: **la** ~ Slovenia

slow [slo] *nm* (*danse*) slow number

SM *sigle f* (= *Sa Majesté*) HM

SMAG [smag] *sigle m* = **salaire minimum agricole garanti**

smasher [smaʃe] *vi* to smash the ball ▷ *vt* (*balle*) to smash

SMIC [smik] *sigle m* = **salaire minimum**

interprofessionnel de croissance; *see note*

● **SMIC**
●
● In France, the *SMIC* ("salaire minimum
● interprofessionnel de croissance") is the
● minimum hourly rate which workers over
● the age of 18 must legally be paid. It is index-
● linked and is raised each time the cost of
● living rises by 2 per cent.

smicard, e [smikar, -ard(ə)] *nm/f* minimum wage earner

smocks [smɔk] *nmpl* (*Couture*) smocking *no pl*

smoking [smɔkiŋ] *nm* dinner *ou* evening suit

SMS *sigle m* = **short message service**; (*message*) text (message)

SMUR [smyr] *sigle m* (= *service médical d'urgence et de réanimation*) specialist mobile emergency unit

snack [snak] *nm* snack bar

SNC *abr* = **service non compris**

SNCB *sigle f* (= *Société nationale des chemins de fer belges*) Belgian railways

SNCF *sigle f* (= *Société nationale des chemins de fer français*) French railways

SNES [snɛs] *sigle m* (= *Syndicat national de l'enseignement secondaire*) secondary teachers' union

SNE-sup [ɛsɛnəsyp] *sigle m* (= *Syndicat national de l'enseignement supérieur*) university teachers' union

SNJ *sigle m* (= *Syndicat national des journalistes*) journalists' union

snob [snɔb] *adj* snobbish ▷ *nm/f* snob

snober [snɔbe] *vt*: ~ **qn** to give sb the cold shoulder, treat sb with disdain

snobinard, e [snɔbinar, -ard(ə)] *nm/f* snooty *ou* stuck-up person

snobisme [snɔbism(ə)] *nm* snobbery

SNSM *sigle f* (= *Société nationale de sauvetage en mer*) national sea-rescue association

s.o. *abr* (= *sans objet*) no longer applicable

sobre [sɔbr(ə)] *adj* temperate, abstemious; (*élégance, style*) restrained, sober; ~ **de** (*gestes, compliments*) sparing of

sobrement [sɔbrəmɑ̃] *adv* in moderation, abstemiously; soberly

sobriété [sɔbrijete] *nf* temperance, abstemiousness; sobriety

sobriquet [sɔbrikɛ] *nm* nickname

soc [sɔk] *nm* ploughshare

sociabilité [sɔsjabilite] *nf* sociability

sociable [sɔsjabl(ə)] *adj* sociable

social, e, -aux [sɔsjal, -o] *adj* social

socialisant, e [sɔsjalizɑ̃, -ɑ̃t] *adj* with socialist tendencies

socialisation [sɔsjalizasjɔ̃] *nf* socialisation

socialiser [sɔsjalize] *vt* to socialize

socialisme [sɔsjalism(ə)] *nm* socialism

socialiste [sɔsjalist(ə)] *adj, nm/f* socialist

sociétaire [sɔsjetɛr] *nm/f* member

société [sɔsjete] *nf* society; (*d'abeilles, de fourmis*) colony; (*sportive*) club; (*Comm*) company; **la bonne** ~ polite society; **se plaire dans la** ~ **de**

to enjoy the society of; **l'archipel de la S~** the Society Islands; **la ~ d'abondance/de consommation** the affluent/consumer society; **~ par actions** joint stock company; **~ anonyme (SA)** ≈ limited company (Ltd) (Brit), ≈ incorporated company (Inc.) (US); **~ d'investissement à capital variable (SICAV)** ≈ investment trust (Brit), ≈ mutual fund (US); **~ à responsabilité limitée (SARL)** *type of limited liability company (with non-negotiable shares)*; **~ savante** learned society; **~ de services** service company

socioculturel, le [sɔsjokyltyʀɛl] *adj* sociocultural

socio-économique [sɔsjoekɔnɔmik] *adj* socioeconomic

socio-éducatif, --ive [sɔsjoedykatif, -iv] *adj* socioeducational

sociolinguistique [sɔsjolɛ̃gɥistik] *adj* sociolinguistic

sociologie [sɔsjɔlɔʒi] *nf* sociology

sociologique [sɔsjɔlɔʒik] *adj* sociological

sociologue [sɔsjɔlɔg] *nm/f* sociologist

socio-professionnel, le [sɔsjoprɔfɛsjɔnɛl] *adj* socioprofessional

socle [sɔkl(ə)] *nm* (*de colonne, statue*) plinth, pedestal; (*de lampe*) base

socquette [sɔkɛt] *nf* ankle sock

soda [sɔda] *nm* (*boisson*) fizzy drink, soda (US)

sodium [sɔdjɔm] *nm* sodium

sodomie [sɔdɔmi] *nf* sodomy; buggery

sodomiser [sɔdɔmize] *vt* to sodomize; to bugger

sœur [sœʀ] *nf* sister; (*religieuse*) nun, sister; **~ Élisabeth** (Rel) Sister Elizabeth; **~ de lait** foster sister

sofa [sɔfa] *nm* sofa

Sofia [sɔfja] *n* Sofia

SOFRES [sɔfʀɛs] *sigle f* (= *Société française d'enquête par sondage*) *company which conducts opinion polls*

soi [swa] *pron* oneself; **cela va de ~** that *ou* it goes without saying, it stands to reason

soi-disant [swadizã] *adj inv* so-called ▷ *adv* supposedly

soie [swa] *nf* silk; (*de porc, sanglier: poil*) bristle

soient [swa] *vb voir* **être**

soierie [swaʀi] *nf* (*industrie*) silk trade; (*tissu*) silk

soif [swaf] *nf* thirst; (*fig*): **~ de** thirst *ou* craving for; **avoir ~** to be thirsty; **donner ~ à qn** to make sb thirsty

soigné, e [swaɲe] *adj* (*tenue*) well-groomed, neat; (*travail*) careful, meticulous; (*fam*) whopping; stiff

soigner [swaɲe] *vt* (*malade, maladie: docteur*) to treat; (: *infirmière, mère*) to nurse, look after; (*blessé*) to tend; (*travail, détails*) to take care over; (*jardin, chevelure, invités*) to look after

soigneur [swaɲœʀ] *nm* (Cyclisme, Football) trainer; (Boxe) second

soigneusement [swaɲøzmã] *adv* carefully

soigneux, -euse [swaɲø, -øz] *adj* (*propre*) tidy, neat; (*méticuleux*) painstaking, careful; **~ de** careful with

soi-même [swamɛm] *pron* oneself

soin [swɛ̃] *nm* (*application*) care; (*propreté, ordre*) tidiness, neatness; (*responsabilité*): **le ~ de qch** the care of sth; **soins** *nmpl* (*à un malade, blessé*) treatment *sg*, medical attention *sg*; (*attentions, prévenance*) care and attention *sg*; (*hygiène*) care *sg*; **~s de la chevelure/de beauté** hair/beauty care; **~s du corps/ménage** care of one's body/the home; **avoir** *ou* **prendre ~ de** to take care of, look after; **avoir** *ou* **prendre ~ de faire** to take care to do; **faire qch avec (grand) ~** to do sth (very) carefully; **sans ~** *adj* careless; untidy; **les premiers ~s** first aid *sg*; **aux bons ~s de** c/o, care of; **être aux petits ~s pour qn** to wait on sb hand and foot, see to sb's every need; **confier qn aux ~s de qn** to hand sb over to sb's care

soir [swaʀ] *nm, adv* evening; **le ~** in the evening(s); **ce ~** this evening, tonight; **à ce ~!** see you this evening (*ou* tonight)!; **la veille au ~** the previous evening; **sept/dix heures du ~** seven in the evening/ten at night; **le repas/journal du ~** the evening meal/newspaper; **dimanche ~** Sunday evening; **hier ~** yesterday evening; **demain ~** tomorrow evening, tomorrow night

soirée [swaʀe] *nf* evening; (*réception*) party; **donner en ~** (*film, pièce*) to give an evening performance of

soit [swa] *vb voir* **être** ▷ *conj* (*à savoir*) namely, to wit; (*ou*): **~ ... ~ ...** either ... or ▷ *adv* so be it, very well; **~ un triangle ABC** let ABC be a triangle; **~ que ... ~ que** *ou* **ou que** whether ... or whether

soixantaine [swasɑ̃tɛn] *nf*: **une ~ (de)** sixty or so, about sixty; **avoir la ~** to be around sixty

soixante [swasɑ̃t] *num* sixty

soixante-dix [swasɑ̃tdis] *num* seventy

soixante-dixième [swasɑ̃tdizjɛm] *num* seventieth

soixante-huitard, e [swazɑ̃tɥitaʀ, -aʀd(ə)] *adj* relating to the demonstrations of May 1968 ▷ *nm/f* participant in the demonstrations of May 1968

soixantième [swasɑ̃tjɛm] *num* sixtieth

soja [sɔʒa] *nm* soya; (*graines*) soya beans *pl*; **germes de ~** beansprouts

sol [sɔl] *nm* ground; (*de logement*) floor; (*revêtement*) flooring *no pl*; (*territoire, Agr, Géo*) soil; (*Mus*) G; (: *en chantant la gamme*) so(h)

solaire [sɔlɛʀ] *adj* solar, sun *cpd*

solarium [sɔlaʀjɔm] *nm* solarium

soldat [sɔlda] *nm* soldier; **S~ inconnu** Unknown Warrior *ou* Soldier; **~ de plomb** tin *ou* toy soldier

solde [sɔld(ə)] *nf* pay ▷ *nm* (Comm) balance; **soldes** *nmpl ou nfpl* (Comm) sales; (*articles*) sale goods; **à la ~ de qn** (*péj*) in sb's pay; **~ créditeur/débiteur** credit/debit balance; **~ à payer** balance outstanding; **en ~** at sale price; **aux ~s** at the sales

solder [sɔlde] *vt* (*compte*) to settle; (*marchandise*) to sell at sale price, sell off; **se ~ par** (*fig*) to end

in; **article soldé (à) 10 euros** item reduced to
10 euros
soldeur, -euse [sɔldœʀ, -øz] *nm/f (Comm)*
discounter
sole [sɔl] *nf* sole *inv (fish)*
soleil [sɔlɛj] *nm* sun; *(lumière)* sun(light); *(temps
ensoleillé)* sun(shine); *(feu d'artifice)* Catherine
wheel; *(d'acrobate)* grand circle; *(Bot)* sunflower;
il y a *ou* **il fait du ~** it's sunny; **au ~** in the sun;
en plein ~ in full sun; **le ~ levant/couchant**
the rising/setting sun; **le ~ de minuit** the
midnight sun
solennel, le [sɔlanɛl] *adj* solemn; ceremonial
solennellement [sɔlanɛlmɑ̃] *adv* solemnly
solennité [sɔlanite] *nf (d'une fête)* solemnity;
solennités *nfpl (formalités)* formalities
solénoïde [sɔlenɔid] *nm (Élec)* solenoid
solfège [sɔlfɛʒ] *nm* rudiments *pl* of music;
(exercices) ear training *no pl*
solfier [sɔlfje] *vt:* **~ un morceau** to sing a piece
using the sol-fa
soli [sɔli] *nmpl de* **solo**
solidaire [sɔlidɛʀ] *adj (personnes)* who stand
together, who show solidarity; *(pièces
mécaniques)* interdependent; *(Jur: engagement)*
binding on all parties; *(: débiteurs)* jointly liable;
être ~ de *(collègues)* to stand by; *(mécanisme)* to be
bound up with, be dependent on
solidairement [sɔlidɛʀmɑ̃] *adv* jointly
solidariser [sɔlidaʀize]: **se ~ avec** *vt* to show
solidarity with
solidarité [sɔlidaʀite] *nf (entre personnes)*
solidarity; *(de mécanisme, phénomènes)*
interdependence; **par ~ (avec)** *(cesser le travail
etc)* in sympathy (with)
solide [sɔlid] *adj* solid; *(mur, maison, meuble)* solid,
sturdy; *(connaissances, argument)* sound; *(personne)*
robust, sturdy; *(estomac)* strong ▷ *nm* solid;
avoir les reins ~s *(fig)* to be in a good financial
position; to have sound financial backing
solidement [sɔlidmɑ̃] *adv* solidly; *(fermement)*
firmly
solidifier [sɔlidifje] *vt,* **se solidifier** *vi* to solidify
solidité [sɔlidite] *nf* solidity; sturdiness
soliloque [sɔlilɔk] *nm* soliloquy
soliste [sɔlist(ə)] *nm/f* soloist
solitaire [sɔlitɛʀ] *adj (sans compagnie)* solitary,
lonely; *(isolé)* solitary, isolated, lone; *(lieu)*
lonely ▷ *nm/f* recluse; loner ▷ *nm (diamant, jeu)*
solitaire
solitude [sɔlityd] *nf* loneliness; *(paix)* solitude
solive [sɔliv] *nf* joist
sollicitations [sɔlisitasjɔ̃] *nfpl (requêtes)*
entreaties, appeals; *(attractions)* enticements;
(Tech) stress *sg*
solliciter [sɔlisite] *vt (personne)* to appeal to;
(emploi, faveur) to seek; *(moteur)* to prompt;
(occupations, attractions etc): **~ qn** to appeal to sb's
curiosity *etc;* to entice sb; to make demands on
sb's time; **~ qn de faire** to appeal to sb *ou*
request sb to do
sollicitude [sɔlisityd] *nf* concern

solo [sɔlo] *nm (pl* **soli** [sɔli]) *(Mus)* solo
sol-sol [sɔlsɔl] *adj inv* surface-to-surface
solstice [sɔlstis] *nm* solstice; **~ d'hiver/d'été**
winter/summer solstice
solubilisé, e [sɔlybilize] *adj* soluble
solubilité [sɔlybilite] *nf* solubility
soluble [sɔlybl(ə)] *adj (sucre, cachet)* soluble;
(problème etc) soluble, solvable
soluté [sɔlyte] *nm* solution
solution [sɔlysjɔ̃] *nf* solution; **~ de continuité**
gap, break; **~ de facilité** easy way out
solutionner [sɔlysjɔne] *vt* to solve, find a
solution for
solvabilité [sɔlvabilite] *nf* solvency
solvable [sɔlvabl(ə)] *adj* solvent
solvant [sɔlvɑ̃] *nm* solvent
Somalie [sɔmali] *nf:* **la ~** Somalia
somalien, ne [sɔmaljɛ̃, -ɛn] *adj* Somalian
somatique [sɔmatik] *adj* somatic
sombre [sɔ̃bʀ(ə)] *adj* dark; *(fig)* sombre, gloomy;
(sinistre) awful, dreadful
sombrer [sɔ̃bʀe] *vi (bateau)* to sink, go down; **~
corps et biens** to go down with all hands; **~
dans** *(misère, désespoir)* to sink into
sommaire [sɔmɛʀ] *adj (simple)* basic; *(expéditif)*
summary ▷ *nm* summary; **faire le ~ de** to
make a summary of, summarize; **exécution ~**
summary execution
sommairement [sɔmɛʀmɑ̃] *adv* basically;
summarily
sommation [sɔmasjɔ̃] *nf (Jur)* summons *sg*;
(avant de faire feu) warning
somme [sɔm] *nf (Math)* sum; *(fig)* amount;
(argent) sum, amount ▷ *nm:* **faire un ~** to have a
(short) nap; **faire la ~ de** to add up; **en ~, ~
toute** *adv* all in all
sommeil [sɔmɛj] *nm* sleep; **avoir ~** to be sleepy;
avoir le ~ léger to be a light sleeper; **en ~** *(fig)*
dormant
sommeiller [sɔmeje] *vi* to doze; *(fig)* to lie
dormant
sommelier [sɔməlje] *nm* wine waiter
sommer [sɔme] *vt:* **~ qn de faire** to command
ou order sb to do; *(Jur)* to summon sb to do
sommes [sɔm] *vb voir* **être**; *voir aussi* **somme**
sommet [sɔmɛ] *nm* top; *(d'une montagne)*
summit, top; *(fig: de la perfection, gloire)* height;
(Géom: d'angle) vertex; *(conférence)* summit
(conference)
sommier [sɔmje] *nm* bed base, bedspring (US);
(Admin: registre) register; **~ à ressorts** (interior
sprung) divan base (Brit), box spring (US); **~ à
lattes** slatted bed base
sommité [sɔmite] *nf* prominent person,
leading light
somnambule [sɔmnɑ̃byl] *nm/f* sleepwalker
somnambulisme [sɔmnɑ̃bylism(ə)] *nm*
sleepwalking
somnifère [sɔmnifɛʀ] *nm* sleeping drug;
(comprimé) sleeping pill *ou* tablet
somnolence [sɔmnɔlɑ̃s] *nf* drowsiness
somnolent, e [sɔmnɔlɑ̃, -ɑ̃t] *adj* sleepy, drowsy

somnoler [sɔmnɔle] vi to doze
somptuaire [sɔ̃ptɥɛʀ] adj: **lois ~s** sumptuary laws; **dépenses ~s** extravagant expenditure sg
somptueusement [sɔ̃ptɥøzmɑ̃] adv sumptuously
somptueux, -euse [sɔ̃ptɥø, -øz] adj sumptuous; (cadeau) lavish
somptuosité [sɔ̃ptɥozite] nf sumptuousness; (d'un cadeau) lavishness
son¹ [sɔ̃], **sa** [sa] (pl **ses** [se]) adj possessif (antécédent humain mâle) his; (: femelle) her; (: valeur indéfinie) one's, his (her); (: non humain) its; voir **il**
son² [sɔ̃] nm sound; (de blé etc) bran; **~ et lumière** adj inv son et lumière
sonar [sɔnaʀ] nm (Navig) sonar
sonate [sɔnat] nf sonata
sondage [sɔ̃daʒ] nm (de terrain) boring, drilling; (de mer, atmosphère) sounding; probe; (enquête) survey, sounding out of opinion; **~ (d'opinion)** (opinion) poll
sonde [sɔ̃d] nf (Navig) lead ou sounding line; (Météorologie) sonde; (Méd) probe; catheter; (d'alimentation) feeding tube; (Tech) borer, driller; (de forage, sondage) drill; (pour fouiller etc) probe; **~ à avalanche** pole (for probing snow and locating victims); **~ spatiale** probe
sonder [sɔ̃de] vt (Navig) to sound; (atmosphère, plaie, bagages etc) to probe; (Tech) to bore, drill; (fig: personne) to sound out; (: opinion) to probe; **~ le terrain** (fig) to see how the land lies
songe [sɔ̃ʒ] nm dream
songer [sɔ̃ʒe] vi to dream; **~ à** (rêver à) to muse over, think over; (penser à) to think of; (envisager) to contemplate, think of, consider; **~ que** to consider that; to think that
songerie [sɔ̃ʒʀi] nf reverie
songeur, -euse [sɔ̃ʒœʀ, -øz] adj pensive; **ça me laisse ~** that makes me wonder
sonnailles [sɔnaj] nfpl jingle of bells
sonnant, e [sɔnɑ̃, -ɑ̃t] adj: **en espèces ~es et trébuchantes** in coin of the realm; **à huit heures ~es** on the stroke of eight
sonné, e [sɔne] adj (fam) cracked; (passé): **il est midi ~** it's gone twelve; **il a quarante ans bien ~s** he's well into his forties
sonner [sɔne] vi (retentir) to ring; (donner une impression) to sound ▷ vt (cloche) to ring; (glas, tocsin) to sound; (portier, infirmière) to ring for; (messe) to ring the bell for; (fam: choc, coup) to knock out; **~ du clairon** to sound the bugle; **~ bien/mal/creux** to sound good/bad/hollow; **~ faux** (instrument) to sound out of tune; (rire) to ring false; **~ les heures** to strike the hours; **minuit vient de ~** midnight has just struck; **~ chez qn** to ring sb's doorbell, ring at sb's door
sonnerie [sɔnʀi] nf (son) ringing; (sonnette) bell; (mécanisme d'horloge) striking mechanism; (de téléphone portable) ringtone; **~ d'alarme** alarm bell; **~ de clairon** bugle call
sonnet [sɔnɛ] nm sonnet
sonnette [sɔnɛt] nf bell; **~ d'alarme** alarm bell;

~ de nuit night-bell
sono [sɔno] nf (= sonorisation) PA (system); (d'une discothèque) sound system
sonore [sɔnɔʀ] adj (voix) sonorous, ringing; (salle, métal) resonant; (ondes, film, signal) sound cpd; (Ling) voiced; **effets ~s** sound effects
sonorisation [sɔnɔʀizasjɔ̃] nf (installations) public address system; (d'une discothèque) sound system
sonoriser [sɔnɔʀize] vt (film, spectacle) to add the sound track to; (salle) to fit with a public address system
sonorité [sɔnɔʀite] nf (de piano, violon) tone; (de voix, mot) sonority; (d'une salle) resonance; acoustics pl
sonothèque [sɔnɔtɛk] nf sound library
sont [sɔ̃] vb voir **être**
sophisme [sɔfism(ə)] nm sophism
sophiste [sɔfist(ə)] nm/f sophist
sophistication [sɔfistikasjɔ̃] nf sophistication
sophistiqué, e [sɔfistike] adj sophisticated
soporifique [sɔpɔʀifik] adj soporific
soprano [sɔpʀano] nm/f soprano
sorbet [sɔʀbɛ] nm water ice, sorbet
sorbetière [sɔʀbətjɛʀ] nf ice-cream maker
sorbier [sɔʀbje] nm service tree
sorcellerie [sɔʀsɛlʀi] nf witchcraft no pl, sorcery no pl
sorcier, -ière [sɔʀsje, -jɛʀ] nm/f sorcerer (witch ou sorceress) ▷ adj: **ce n'est pas ~** (fam) it's as easy as pie
sordide [sɔʀdid] adj sordid; squalid
Sorlingues [sɔʀlɛ̃g] nfpl: **les (îles) ~** the Scilly Isles, the Isles of Scilly, the Scillies
sornettes [sɔʀnɛt] nfpl twaddle sg
sort [sɔʀ] vb voir **sortir** ▷ nm (fortune, destinée) fate; (condition, situation) lot; (magique): **jeter un ~** to cast a spell; **un coup du ~** a blow dealt by fate; **le ~ en est jeté** the die is cast; **tirer au ~** to draw lots; **tirer qch au ~** to draw lots for sth
sortable [sɔʀtabl(ə)] adj: **il n'est pas ~** you can't take him anywhere
sortant, e [sɔʀtɑ̃, -ɑ̃t] vb voir **sortir** ▷ adj (numéro) which comes up (in a draw etc); (député, président) outgoing
sorte [sɔʀt(ə)] vb voir **sortir** ▷ nf sort, kind; **une ~ de** a sort of; **de la ~** adv in that way; **en quelque ~** in a way; **de ~ à** so as to, in order to; **de (telle) ~ que, en ~ que** (de manière que) so that; (si bien que) so much so that; **faire en ~ que** to see to it that
sortie [sɔʀti] nf (issue) way out, exit; (Mil) sortie; (fig: verbale) outburst; sally; (: parole incongrue) odd remark; (d'un gaz, de l'eau) outlet; (promenade) outing; (le soir: au restaurant etc) night out; (de produits) export; (de capitaux) outflow; (Comm: somme): **~s** items of expenditure; outgoings; (Inform) output; (d'imprimante) printout; **à sa ~** as he went out ou left; **à la ~ de l'école/l'usine** (moment) after school/work; when school/the factory comes out; (lieu) at the school/factory gates; **à la ~ de ce nouveau modèle** when this

new model comes (*ou* came) out, when they bring (*ou* brought) out this new model; **~ de bain** (*vêtement*) bathrobe; **"~ de camions"** "vehicle exit"; **~ papier** hard copy; **~ de secours** emergency exit

sortilège [sɔʀtilɛʒ] *nm* (magic) spell

sortir [sɔʀtiʀ] *vi* (*gén*) to come out; (*partir, se promener, aller au spectacle etc*) to go out; (*bourgeon, plante, numéro gagnant*) to come up ▷ *vt* (*gén*) to take out; (*produit, ouvrage, modèle*) to bring out; (*boniments, incongruités*) to come out with; (*Inform*) to output; (: *sur papier*) to print out; (*fam: expulser*) to throw out ▷ *nm*: **au ~ de l'hiver/l'enfance** as winter/childhood nears its end; **~ qch de** to take sth out of; **~ qn d'embarras** to get sb out of trouble; **~ de** (*gén*) to leave; (*endroit*) to go (*ou* come) out of, leave; (*rainure etc*) to come out of; (*maladie*) to get over; (*époque*) to get through; (*cadre, compétence*) to be outside; (*provenir de: famille etc*) to come from; **~ de table** to leave the table; **~ du système** (*Inform*) to log out; **~ de ses gonds** (*fig*) to fly off the handle; **se ~ de** (*affaire, situation*) to get out of; **s'en ~** (*malade*) to pull through; (*d'une difficulté etc*) to come through all right; to get through, be able to manage

SOS *sigle m* mayday, SOS

sosie [sɔzi] *nm* double

sot, sotte [so, sɔt] *adj* silly, foolish ▷ *nm/f* fool

sottement [sɔtmɑ̃] *adv* foolishly

sottise [sɔtiz] *nf* silliness *no pl*, foolishness *no pl*; (*propos, acte*) silly *ou* foolish thing (to do *ou* say)

sou [su] *nm*: **près de ses ~s** tight-fisted; **sans le ~** penniless; **à ~** penny by penny; **pas un ~ de bon sens** not a scrap *ou* an ounce of good sense; **de quatre ~s** worthless

souahéli, e [swaeli] *adj* Swahili ▷ *nm* (*Ling*) Swahili

soubassement [subasmɑ̃] *nm* base

soubresaut [subʀəso] *nm* (*de peur etc*) start; (*cahot: d'un véhicule*) jolt

soubrette [subʀɛt] *nf* soubrette, maidservant

souche [suʃ] *nf* (*d'arbre*) stump; (*de carnet*) counterfoil (*Brit*), stub; **dormir comme une ~** to sleep like a log; **de vieille ~** of old stock

souci [susi] *nm* (*inquiétude*) worry; (*préoccupation*) concern; (*Bot*) marigold; **se faire du ~** to worry; **avoir (le) ~ de** to have concern for; **par ~ de** for the sake of, out of concern for

soucier [susje]: **se ~ de** *vt* to care about

soucieux, -euse [susjø, -øz] *adj* concerned, worried; **~ de** concerned about; **peu ~ de/que** caring little about/whether

soucoupe [sukup] *nf* saucer; **~ volante** flying saucer

soudain, e [sudɛ̃, -ɛn] *adj* (*douleur, mort*) sudden ▷ *adv* suddenly, all of a sudden

soudainement [sudɛnmɑ̃] *adv* suddenly

soudaineté [sudɛnte] *nf* suddenness

Soudan [sudɑ̃] *nm*: **le ~** the Sudan

soudanais, e [sudanɛ, -ɛz] *adj* Sudanese

soude [sud] *nf* soda

soudé, e [sude] *adj* (*fig: pétales, organes*) joined

(together)

souder [sude] *vt* (*avec fil à souder*) to solder; (*par soudure autogène*) to weld; (*fig*) to bind *ou* knit together; to fuse (together); **se souder** *vi* (*os*) to knit (together)

soudeur, -euse [sudœʀ, -øz] *nm/f* (*ouvrier*) welder

soudoyer [sudwaje] *vt* (*péj*) to bribe, buy over

soudure [sudyʀ] *nf* soldering; welding; (*joint*) soldered joint; weld; **faire la ~** (*Comm*) to fill a gap; (*fig: assurer une transition*) to bridge the gap

souffert, e [sufɛʀ, -ɛʀt(ə)] *pp de* **souffrir**

soufflage [suflaʒ] *nm* (*du verre*) glass-blowing

souffle [sufl(ə)] *nm* (*en expirant*) breath; (*en soufflant*) puff, blow; (*respiration*) breathing; (*d'explosion, de ventilateur*) blast; (*du vent*) blowing; (*fig*) inspiration; **retenir son ~** to hold one's breath; **avoir du/manquer de ~** to have a lot of puff/be short of breath; **être à bout de ~** to be out of breath; **avoir le ~ court** to be short-winded; **un ~ d'air** *ou* **de vent** a breath of air, a puff of wind; **~ au cœur** (*Méd*) heart murmur

soufflé, e [sufle] *adj* (*Culin*) soufflé; (*fam: ahuri, stupéfié*) staggered ▷ *nm* (*Culin*) soufflé

souffler [sufle] *vi* (*gén*) to blow; (*haleter*) to puff (and blow) ▷ *vt* (*feu, bougie*) to blow out; (*chasser: poussière etc*) to blow away; (*Tech: verre*) to blow; (*explosion*) to destroy (with its blast); (*dire*): **~ qch à qn** to whisper sth to sb; (*fam: voler*): **~ qch à qn** to pinch sth from sb; **~ son rôle à qn** to prompt sb; **ne pas ~ mot** not to breathe a word; **laisser ~ qn** (*fig*) to give sb a breather

soufflet [suflɛ] *nm* (*instrument*) bellows *pl*; (*entre wagons*) vestibule; (*Couture*) gusset; (*gifle*) slap (in the face)

souffleur, -euse [suflœʀ, -øz] *nm/f* (*Théât*) prompter; (*Tech*) glass-blower

souffrance [sufʀɑ̃s] *nf* suffering; **en ~** (*marchandise*) awaiting delivery; (*affaire*) pending

souffrant, e [sufʀɑ̃, -ɑ̃t] *adj* unwell

souffre-douleur [sufʀədulœʀ] *nm inv* whipping boy (*Brit*), butt, underdog

souffreteux, -euse [sufʀətø, -øz] *adj* sickly

souffrir [sufʀiʀ] *vi* to suffer; (*éprouver des douleurs*) to be in pain ▷ *vt* to suffer, endure; (*supporter*) to bear, stand; (*admettre: exception etc*) to allow *ou* admit of; **~ de** (*maladie, froid*) to suffer from; **~ des dents** to have trouble with one's teeth; **ne pas pouvoir ~ qch/que ...** not to be able to endure *ou* bear sth/that ...; **faire ~ qn** (*personne*) to make sb suffer; (: *dents, blessure etc*) to hurt sb

soufre [sufʀ(ə)] *nm* sulphur (*Brit*), sulfur (*US*)

soufrer [sufʀe] *vt* (*vignes*) to treat with sulphur *ou* sulfur

souhait [swɛ] *nm* wish; **tous nos ~s de** good wishes *ou* our best wishes for; **riche** *etc* **à ~** as rich *etc* as one could wish; **à vos ~s!** bless you!

souhaitable [swɛtabl(ə)] *adj* desirable

souhaiter [swete] *vt* to wish for; **~ le bonjour à qn** to bid sb good day; **~ la bonne année à qn** to wish sb a happy New Year; **il est à ~ que** it is to

S

be hoped that

souiller [suje] *vt* to dirty, soil; (*fig*) to sully, tarnish

souillure [sujyʀ] *nf* stain

soûl, e [su, sul] *adj* drunk; (*fig*): **~ de musique/plaisirs** drunk with music/pleasure ▷ *nm*: **tout son ~** to one's heart's content

soulagement [sulaʒmɑ̃] *nm* relief

soulager [sulaʒe] *vt* to relieve; **~ qn de** to relieve sb of

soûler [sule] *vt*: **~ qn** to get sb drunk; (*boisson*) to make sb drunk; (*fig*) to make sb's head spin *ou* reel; **se soûler** to get drunk; **se ~ de** (*fig*) to intoxicate o.s with

soûlerie [sulʀi] *nf* (*péj*) drunken binge

soulèvement [sulɛvmɑ̃] *nm* uprising; (*Géo*) upthrust

soulever [sulve] *vt* to lift; (*vagues, poussière*) to send up; (*peuple*) to stir up (to revolt); (*enthousiasme*) to arouse; (*question, débat, protestations, difficultés*) to raise; **se soulever** *vi* (*peuple*) to rise up; (*personne couchée*) to lift o.s. up; (*couvercle etc*) to lift; **cela me soulève le cœur** it makes me feel sick

soulier [sulje] *nm* shoe; **~s bas** low-heeled shoes; **~s plats/à talons** flat/heeled shoes

souligner [suliɲe] *vt* to underline; (*fig*) to emphasize, stress

soumettre [sumɛtʀ(ə)] *vt* (*pays*) to subject, subjugate; (*rebelles*) to put down, subdue; **~ qn/qch à** to subject sb/sth to; **~ qch à qn** (*projet etc*) to submit sth to sb; **se ~ (à)** (*se rendre, obéir*) to submit (to); **se ~ à** (*formalités etc*) to submit to; (*régime etc*) to submit o.s. to

soumis, e [sumi, -iz] *pp de* **soumettre** ▷ *adj* submissive; **revenus ~ à l'impôt** taxable income

soumission [sumisjɔ̃] *nf* (*voir se soumettre*) submission; (*docilité*) submissiveness; (*Comm*) tender

soumissionner [sumisjɔne] *vt* (*Comm: travaux*) to bid for, tender for

soupape [supap] *nf* valve; **~ de sûreté** safety valve

soupçon [supsɔ̃] *nm* suspicion; (*petite quantité*): **un ~ de** a hint *ou* touch of; **avoir ~ de** to suspect; **au dessus de tout ~** above (all) suspicion

soupçonner [supsɔne] *vt* to suspect; **~ qn de qch/d'être** to suspect sb of sth/of being

soupçonneux, -euse [supsɔnø, -øz] *adj* suspicious

soupe [sup] *nf* soup; **~ au lait** *adj inv* quick-tempered; **~ à l'oignon/de poisson** onion/fish soup; **~ populaire** soup kitchen

soupente [supɑ̃t] *nf* (*mansarde*) attic; (*placard*) cupboard (*Brit*) *ou* closet (*US*) under the stairs

souper [supe] *vi* to have supper ▷ *nm* supper; **avoir soupé de** (*fam*) to be sick and tired of

soupeser [supəze] *vt* to weigh in one's hand(s), feel the weight of; (*fig*) to weigh up

soupière [supjɛʀ] *nf* (soup) tureen

soupir [supiʀ] *nm* sigh; (*Mus*) crotchet rest (*Brit*),

quarter note rest (*US*); **rendre le dernier ~** to breathe one's last

soupirail, -aux [supiʀaj, -o] *nm* (small) basement window

soupirant [supiʀɑ̃] *nm* (*péj*) suitor, wooer

soupirer [supiʀe] *vi* to sigh; **~ après qch** to yearn for sth

souple [supl(ə)] *adj* supple; (*col*) soft; (*fig: règlement, caractère*) flexible; (*: démarche, taille*) lithe, supple

souplesse [suplɛs] *nf* suppleness; flexibility

source [suʀs(ə)] *nf* (*point d'eau*) spring; (*d'un cours d'eau, fig*) source; **prendre sa ~ à/dans** (*cours d'eau*) to have its source at/in; **tenir qch de bonne ~/de ~ sûre** to have sth on good authority/from a reliable source; **~ thermale/d'eau minérale** hot *ou* thermal/mineral spring

sourcier, -ière [suʀsje, -jɛʀ] *nm* water diviner

sourcil [suʀsij] *nm* (eye)brow

sourcilière [suʀsiljɛʀ] *adj f voir* **arcade**

sourciller [suʀsije] *vi*: **sans ~** without turning a hair *ou* batting an eyelid

sourcilleux, -euse [suʀsijø, -øz] *adj* (*hautain, sévère*) haughty, supercilious; (*pointilleux*) finicky, pernickety

sourd, e [suʀ, suʀd(ə)] *adj* deaf; (*bruit, voix*) muffled; (*couleur*) muted; (*douleur*) dull; (*lutte*) silent, hidden; (*Ling*) voiceless ▷ *nm/f* deaf person; **être ~ à** to be deaf to

sourdement [suʀdəmɑ̃] *adv* (*avec un bruit sourd*) dully; (*secrètement*) silently

sourdine [suʀdin] *nf* (*Mus*) mute; **en ~** *adv* softly, quietly; **mettre une ~ à** (*fig*) to tone down

sourd-muet, sourde-muette [suʀmyɛ, suʀdmyɛt] *adj* deaf-and-dumb ▷ *nm/f* deaf-mute

sourdre [suʀdʀ(ə)] *vi* (*eau*) to spring up; (*fig*) to rise

souriant, e [suʀjɑ̃, -ɑ̃t] *vb voir* **sourire** ▷ *adj* cheerful

souricière [suʀisjɛʀ] *nf* mousetrap; (*fig*) trap

sourie *etc* [suʀi] *vb voir* **sourire**

sourire [suʀiʀ] *nm* smile ▷ *vi* to smile; **~ à qn** to smile at sb; (*fig*) to appeal to sb; (*: chance*) to smile on sb; **faire un ~ à qn** to give sb a smile; **garder le ~** to keep smiling

souris [suʀi] *nf* (*aussi Inform*) mouse

sournois, e [suʀnwa, -waz] *adj* deceitful, underhand

sournoisement [suʀnwazmɑ̃] *adv* deceitfully

sournoiserie [suʀnwazʀi] *nf* deceitfulness, underhandedness

sous [su] *prép* (*gén*) under; **~ la pluie/le soleil** in the rain/sunshine; **~ mes yeux** before my eyes; **~ terre** *adj, adv* underground; **~ vide** *adj, adv* vacuum-packed; **~ l'influence/l'action de** under the influence of/by the action of; **~ antibiotiques/perfusion** on antibiotics/a drip; **~ cet angle/ce rapport** from this angle/in this respect; **~ peu** *adv* shortly, before long

sous... [su, suz + *vowel*] *préfixe* sub-; under...

sous-alimentation [suzalimɑ̃tasjɔ̃] *nf*
undernourishment
sous-alimenté, e [suzalimɑ̃te] *adj*
undernourished
sous-bois [subwa] *nm inv* undergrowth
sous-catégorie [sukategɔri] *nf* subcategory
sous-chef [suʃɛf] *nm* deputy chief, second in
command; ~ **de bureau** deputy head clerk
sous-comité [sukɔmite] *nm* subcommittee
sous-commission [sukɔmisjɔ̃] *nf*
subcommittee
sous-continent [sukɔ̃tinɑ̃] *nm* subcontinent
sous-couche [sukuʃ] *nf (de peinture)* undercoat
souscripteur, -trice [suskriptœr, -tris] *nm/f*
subscriber
souscription [suskripsjɔ̃] *nf* subscription;
offert en ~ available on subscription
souscrire [suskrir]: ~ **à** *vt* to subscribe to
sous-cutané, e [sukytane] *adj* subcutaneous
sous-développé, e [sudevlɔpe] *adj*
underdeveloped
sous-développement [sudevlɔpmɑ̃] *nm*
underdevelopment
sous-directeur, -trice [sudirɛktœr, -tris] *nm/f*
assistant manager/manageress, submanager/
manageress
sous-emploi [suzɑ̃plwa] *nm* underemployment
sous-employé, e [suzɑ̃plwaje] *adj*
underemployed
sous-ensemble [suzɑ̃sɑ̃bl(ə)] *nm* subset
sous-entendre [suzɑ̃tɑ̃dr(ə)] *vt* to imply, infer
sous-entendu, e [suzɑ̃tɑ̃dy] *adj* implied; *(Ling)*
understood ▷ *nm* innuendo, insinuation
sous-équipé, e [suzekipe] *adj* under-equipped;
~ **en infrastructures industrielles** *(Écon: pays,
région)* with an insufficient industrial
infrastructure
sous-estimer [suzɛstime] *vt* to underestimate
sous-exploiter [suzɛksplwate] *vt* to
underexploit
sous-exposer [suzɛkspoze] *vt* to underexpose
sous-fifre [sufifr(ə)] *nm (péj)* underling
sous-groupe [sugrup] *nm* subgroup
sous-homme [suzɔm] *nm* sub-human
sous-jacent, e [suʒasɑ̃, -ɑ̃t] *adj* underlying
sous-lieutenant [suljøtnɑ̃] *nm* sub-lieutenant
sous-locataire [sulɔkatɛr] *nm/f* subtenant
sous-location [sulɔkasjɔ̃] *nf* subletting
sous-louer [sulwe] *vt* to sublet
sous-main [sumɛ̃] *nm inv* desk blotter; **en** ~ *adv*
secretly
sous-marin, e [sumarɛ̃, -in] *adj (flore, volcan)*
submarine; *(navigation, pêche, explosif)*
underwater ▷ *nm* submarine
sous-médicalisé, e [sumedikalize] *adj* lacking
adequate medical care
sous-nappe [sunap] *nf* undercloth
sous-officier [suzɔfisje] *nm* ≈ non-
commissioned officer (NCO)
sous-ordre [suzɔrdr(ə)] *nm* subordinate;
créancier en ~ creditor's creditor
sous-payé, e [supeje] *adj* underpaid

sous-préfecture [suprefɛktyr] *nf* sub-
prefecture
sous-préfet [suprefɛ] *nm* sub-prefect
sous-production [suprɔdyksjɔ̃] *nf*
underproduction
sous-produit [suprɔdɥi] *nm* by-product; *(fig:
péj)* pale imitation
sous-programme [suprɔgram] *nm (Inform)*
subroutine
sous-pull [supul] *nm* thin poloneck sweater
sous-secrétaire [susəkretɛr] *nm:* ~ **d'État**
Under-Secretary of State
soussigné, e [susiɲe] *adj:* **je** ~ I the undersigned
sous-sol [susɔl] *nm* basement; *(Géo)* subsoil
sous-tasse [sutas] *nf* saucer
sous-tendre [sutɑ̃dr(ə)] *vt* to underlie
sous-titre [sutitr(ə)] *nm* subtitle
sous-titré, e [sutitre] *adj* with subtitles
soustraction [sustraksjɔ̃] *nf* subtraction
soustraire [sustrɛr] *vt* to subtract, take away;
(dérober): ~ **qch à qn** to remove sth from sb; ~ **qn
à** *(danger)* to shield sb from; **se** ~ **à** *(autorité,
obligation, devoir)* to elude, escape from
sous-traitance [sutrɛtɑ̃s(ə)] *nf* subcontracting
sous-traitant [sutrɛtɑ̃] *nm* subcontractor
sous-traiter [sutrete] *vt, vi* to subcontract
soustrayais *etc* [sustrɛjɛ] *vb voir* **soustraire**
sous-verre [suver] *nm inv* glass mount
sous-vêtement [suvɛtmɑ̃] *nm* undergarment,
item of underwear; **sous-vêtements** *nmpl*
underwear *sg*
soutane [sutan] *nf* cassock, soutane
soute [sut] *nf* hold; ~ **à bagages** baggage hold
soutenable [sutnabl(ə)] *adj (opinion)* tenable,
defensible
soutenance [sutnɑ̃s] *nf:* ~ **de thèse** ≈ viva (voce)
soutènement [sutɛnmɑ̃] *nm:* **mur de** ~
retaining wall
souteneur [sutnœr] *nm* procurer
soutenir [sutnir] *vt* to support; *(assaut, choc,
regard)* to stand up to, withstand; *(intérêt, effort)*
to keep up; *(assurer):* ~ **que** to maintain that; **se
soutenir** *(dans l'eau etc)* to hold o.s. up; *(être
soutenable: point de vue)* to be tenable; *(s'aider
mutuellement)* to stand by each other; ~ **la
comparaison avec** to bear *ou* stand comparison
with; ~ **le regard de qn** to be able to look sb in
the face
soutenu, e [sutny] *pp de* **soutenir** ▷ *adj (efforts)*
sustained, unflagging; *(style)* elevated; *(couleur)*
strong
souterrain, e [sutɛrɛ̃, -ɛn] *adj* underground;
(fig) subterranean ▷ *nm* underground passage
soutien [sutjɛ̃] *nm* support; **apporter son** ~ **à**
to lend one's support to; ~ **de famille**
breadwinner
soutiendrai *etc* [sutjɛ̃dre] *vb voir* **soutenir**
soutien-gorge [sutjɛ̃gɔrʒ(ə)] *(pl* **soutiens-
gorge)** *nm* bra; *(de maillot de bain)* top
soutiens [sutjɛ̃], **soutint** *etc* [sutɛ̃] *vb voir*
soutenir
soutirer [sutire] *vt:* ~ **qch à qn** to squeeze *ou* get

S

sth out of sb

souvenance [suvnɑ̃s] *nf*: **avoir ~ de** to recollect

souvenir [suvniʀ] *nm* (*réminiscence*) memory; (*cadeau*) souvenir, keepsake; (*de voyage*) souvenir ▷ *vb*: **se ~ de** *vt* to remember; **se ~ que** to remember that; **garder le ~ de** to retain the memory of; **en ~ de** in memory *ou* remembrance of; **avec mes affectueux/meilleurs ~s, ...** with love from, .../regards, ...

souvent [suvɑ̃] *adv* often; **peu ~** seldom, infrequently; **le plus ~** more often than not, most often

souvenu, e [suvəny] *pp de* **se souvenir**

souverain, e [suvʀɛ̃, -ɛn] *adj* sovereign; (*fig: mépris*) supreme ▷ *nm/f* sovereign, monarch

souverainement [suvʀɛnmɑ̃] *adv* (*sans appel*) with sovereign power; (*extrêmement*) supremely, intensely

souveraineté [suvʀɛnte] *nf* sovereignty

souviendrai [suvjɛ̃dʀe], **souviens** [suvjɛ̃], **souvint** *etc* [suvɛ̃] *vb voir* **se souvenir**

soviétique [sɔvjetik] *adj* Soviet ▷ *nm/f*: **Soviétique** Soviet citizen

soviétologue [sɔvjetɔlɔg] *nm/f* Kremlinologist

soyeux, -euse [swajø, -øz] *adj* silky

soyez *etc* [swaje] *vb voir* **être**

soyons *etc* [swajɔ̃] *vb voir* **être**

SPA *sigle f* (= *Société protectrice des animaux*) ≈ RSPCA (*Brit*), ≈ SPCA (*US*)

spacieux, -euse [spasjø, -øz] *adj* spacious; roomy

spaciosité [spasjozite] *nf* spaciousness

spaghettis [spageti] *nmpl* spaghetti *sg*

sparadrap [spaʀadʀa] *nm* adhesive *ou* sticking (*Brit*) plaster, bandaid® (*US*)

Sparte [spaʀt(ə)] *nf* Sparta

spartiate [spaʀsjat] *adj* Spartan; **spartiates** *nfpl* (*sandales*) Roman sandals

spasme [spazm(ə)] *nm* spasm

spasmodique [spazmɔdik] *adj* spasmodic

spatial, e, -aux [spasjal, -o] *adj* (*Aviat*) space *cpd*; (*Psych*) spatial

spatule [spatyl] *nf* (*ustensile*) slice; spatula; (*bout*) tip

speaker, ine [spikœʀ, -kʀin] *nm/f* announcer

spécial, e, -aux [spesjal, -o] *adj* special; (*bizarre*) peculiar

spécialement [spesjalmɑ̃] *adv* especially, particularly; (*tout exprès*) specially; **pas ~** not particularly

spécialisation [spesjalizasjɔ̃] *nf* specialization

spécialisé, e [spesjalize] *adj* specialised; **ordinateur ~** dedicated computer

spécialiser [spesjalize]: **se spécialiser** *vi* to specialize

spécialiste [spesjalist(ə)] *nm/f* specialist

spécialité [spesjalite] *nf* speciality; (*Scol*) special field; **~ pharmaceutique** patent medicine

spécieux, -euse [spesjø, -øz] *adj* specious

spécification [spesifikasjɔ̃] *nf* specification

spécificité [spesifisite] *nf* specificity

spécifier [spesifje] *vt* to specify, state

spécifique [spesifik] *adj* specific

spécifiquement [spesifikmɑ̃] *adv* (*typiquement*) typically; (*tout exprès*) specifically

spécimen [spesimɛn] *nm* specimen; (*revue etc*) specimen *ou* sample copy

spectacle [spɛktakl(ə)] *nm* (*tableau, scène*) sight; (*représentation*) show; (*industrie*) show business, entertainment; **se donner en ~** (*péj*) to make a spectacle *ou* an exhibition of o.s.; **pièce/revue à grand ~** spectacular (play/revue); **au ~ de ...** at the sight of ...

spectaculaire [spɛktakylɛʀ] *adj* spectacular

spectateur, -trice [spɛktatœʀ, -tʀis] *nm/f* (*Ciné etc*) member of the audience; (*Sport*) spectator; (*d'un événement*) onlooker, witness

spectre [spɛktʀ(ə)] *nm* (*fantôme, fig*) spectre; (*Physique*) spectrum; **~ solaire** solar spectrum

spéculateur, -trice [spekylatœʀ, -tʀis] *nm/f* speculator

spéculatif, -ive [spekylatif, -iv] *adj* speculative

spéculation [spekylasjɔ̃] *nf* speculation

spéculer [spekyle] *vi* to speculate; **~ sur** (*Comm*) to speculate in; (*réfléchir*) to speculate on; (*tabler sur*) to bank *ou* rely on

spéléologie [speleɔlɔʒi] *nf* (*étude*) speleology; (*activité*) potholing

spéléologue [speleɔlɔg] *nm/f* speleologist; potholer

spermatozoïde [spɛʀmatozoid] *nm* sperm, spermatozoon

sperme [spɛʀm(ə)] *nm* semen, sperm

spermicide [spɛʀmisid] *adj, nm* spermicide

sphère [sfɛʀ] *nf* sphere

sphérique [sferik] *adj* spherical

sphincter [sfɛ̃ktɛʀ] *nm* sphincter

sphinx [sfɛ̃ks] *nm inv* sphinx; (*Zool*) hawkmoth

spiral, -aux [spiʀal, -o] *nm* hairspring

spirale [spiʀal] *nf* spiral; **en ~** in a spiral

spire [spiʀ] *nf* (*d'une spirale*) turn; (*d'une coquille*) whorl

spiritisme [spiʀitism(ə)] *nm* spiritualism, spiritism

spirituel, le [spiʀitɥɛl] *adj* spiritual; (*fin, piquant*) witty; **musique ~le** sacred music; **concert ~** concert of sacred music

spirituellement [spiʀitɥɛlmɑ̃] *adv* spiritually; wittily

spiritueux [spiʀitɥø] *nm* spirit

splendeur [splɑ̃dœʀ] *nf* splendour (*Brit*), splendor (*US*)

splendide [splɑ̃did] *adj* splendid, magnificent

spolier [spɔlje] *vt*: **~ qn (de)** to despoil sb (of)

spongieux, -euse [spɔ̃ʒjø, -øz] *adj* spongy

sponsor [spɔ̃sɔʀ] *nm* sponsor

sponsoriser [spɔ̃sɔʀize] *vt* to sponsor

spontané, e [spɔ̃tane] *adj* spontaneous

spontanéité [spɔ̃taneite] *nf* spontaneity

spontanément [spɔ̃tanemɑ̃] *adv* spontaneously

sporadique [spɔʀadik] *adj* sporadic

sporadiquement [spɔʀadikmɑ̃] *adv*

sporadically

sport [spɔʀ] nm sport ▷ adj inv (vêtement) casual; (fair-play) sporting; **faire du ~** to do sport; **~ individuel/d'équipe** individual/team sport; **~ de combat** combative sport; **~s d'hiver** winter sports

sportif, -ive [spɔʀtif, -iv] adj (journal, association, épreuve) sports cpd; (allure, démarche) athletic; (attitude, esprit) sporting; **les résultats ~s** the sports results

sportivement [spɔʀtivmã] adv sportingly

sportivité [spɔʀtivite] nf sportsmanship

spot [spɔt] nm (lampe) spot(light); (annonce): **~ (publicitaire)** commercial (break)

spray [spʀɛ] nm spray, aerosol

sprint [spʀint] nm sprint; **piquer un ~** to put on a (final) spurt

sprinter nm [spʀintœʀ] sprinter ▷ vi [spʀinte] to sprint

squale [skwal] nm (type of) shark

square [skwaʀ] nm public garden(s)

squash [skwaʃ] nm squash

squat [skwat] nm (lieu) squat

squatter nm [skwatœʀ] squatter ▷ vt [skwate] to squat

squelette [skəlɛt] nm skeleton

squelettique [skəletik] adj scrawny; (fig) skimpy

SRAS sigle m (= syndrome respiratoire aigu sévère) SARS

Sri Lanka [sʀilãka] nm Sri Lanka

sri-lankais, e [sʀilãkɛ, -ɛz] adj Sri-Lankan

SS sigle f = **sécurité sociale**; (= Sa Sainteté) HH

ss abr = **sous**

SSR sigle f (= Société suisse romande) the Swiss French-language broadcasting company

St, Ste abr (= Saint(e)) St

stabilisateur, -trice [stabilizatœʀ, -tʀis] adj stabilizing ▷ nm stabilizer; (d'un véhicule) anti-roll device; (d'un avion) tailplane

stabiliser [stabilize] vt to stabilize; (terrain) to consolidate

stabilité [stabilite] nf stability

stable [stabl(ə)] adj stable, steady

stade [stad] nm (Sport) stadium; (phase, niveau) stage

stadier [stadje] nm steward (working in a stadium), stage

stage [staʒ] nm training period; training course; (d'avocat stagiaire) articles pl; **~ en entreprise** work experience placement

stagiaire [staʒjɛʀ] nm/f, adj trainee (cpd)

stagnant, e [stagnã, -ãt] adj stagnant

stagnation [stagnasjɔ̃] nf stagnation

stagner [stagne] vi to stagnate

stalactite [stalaktit] nf stalactite

stalagmite [stalagmit] nf stalagmite

stalle [stal] nf stall, box

stand [stãd] nm (d'exposition) stand; (de foire) stall; **~ de tir** (à la foire, Sport) shooting range; **~ de ravitaillement** pit

standard [stãdaʀ] adj inv standard ▷ nm (type,

norme) standard; (téléphonique) switchboard

standardisation [stãdaʀdizasjɔ̃] nf standardization

standardiser [stãdaʀdize] vt to standardize

standardiste [stãdaʀdist(ə)] nm/f switchboard operator

standing [stãdiŋ] nm standing; **immeuble de grand ~** block of luxury flats (Brit), condo(minium) (US)

star [staʀ] nf star

starlette [staʀlɛt] nf starlet

starter [staʀtɛʀ] nm (Auto) choke; (Sport: personne) starter; **mettre le ~** to pull out the choke

station [stasjɔ̃] nf station; (de bus) stop; (de villégiature) resort; (posture): **la ~ debout** standing, an upright posture; **~ balnéaire** seaside resort; **~ de graissage** lubrication bay; **~ de lavage** carwash; **~ de ski** ski resort; **~ de sports d'hiver** winter sports resort; **~ de taxis** taxi rank (Brit) ou stand (US); **~ thermale** thermal spa; **~ de travail** workstation

stationnaire [stasjɔnɛʀ] adj stationary

stationnement [stasjɔnmã] nm parking; **zone de ~ interdit** no parking area; **~ alterné** parking on alternate sides

stationner [stasjɔne] vi to park

station-service [stasjɔ̃sɛʀvis] nf service station

statique [statik] adj static

statisticien, ne [statistisjɛ̃, -ɛn] nm/f statistician

statistique [statistik] nf (science) statistics sg; (rapport, étude) statistic ▷ adj statistical; **statistiques** nfpl (données) statistics pl

statistiquement [statistikmã] adv statistically

statue [staty] nf statue

statuer [statɥe] vi: **~ sur** to rule on, give a ruling on

statuette [statɥɛt] nf statuette

statu quo [statykwo] nm status quo

stature [statyʀ] nf stature; **de haute ~** of great stature

statut [staty] nm status; **statuts** nmpl (Jur, Admin) statutes

statutaire [statytɛʀ] adj statutory

Sté abr (= société) soc

steak [stɛk] nm steak

stèle [stɛl] nf stela, stele

stellaire [stelɛʀ] adj stellar

stencil [stɛnsil] nm stencil

sténo [stenɔ] nm/f (aussi: **sténographe**) shorthand typist (Brit), stenographer (US) ▷ nf (aussi: **sténographie**) shorthand; **prendre en ~** to take down in shorthand

sténodactylo [stenɔdaktilo] nm/f shorthand typist (Brit), stenographer (US)

sténodactylographie [stenɔdaktilɔgʀafi] nf shorthand typing (Brit), stenography (US)

sténographe [stenɔgʀaf] nm/f shorthand typist (Brit), stenographer (US)

sténographie [stenɔgʀafi] nf shorthand; **prendre en ~** to take down in shorthand

S

sténographier [stenɔgʀafje] *vt* to take down in shorthand

sténographique [stenɔgʀafik] *adj* shorthand *cpd*

stentor [stɑ̃tɔʀ] *nm*: **voix de ~** stentorian voice

step® [stɛp] *nm* step aerobics *sg*®, step Reebok®

stéphanois, e [stefanwa, -waz] *adj* of *ou* from Saint-Étienne

steppe [stɛp] *nf* steppe

stère [stɛʀ] *nm* stere

stéréo *nf* (*aussi*: **stéréophonie**) stereo; **émission en ~** stereo broadcast ▷ *adj* (*aussi*: **stéréophonique**) stereo

stéréophonie [steʀeɔfɔni] *nf* stereo(phony); **émission en ~** stereo broadcast

stéréophonique [steʀeɔfɔnik] *adj* stereo(phonic)

stéréoscope [steʀeɔskɔp] *nm* stereoscope

stéréoscopique [steʀeɔskɔpik] *adj* stereoscopic

stéréotype [steʀeɔtip] *nm* stereotype

stéréotypé, e [steʀeɔtipe] *adj* stereotyped

stérile [steʀil] *adj* sterile; (*terre*) barren; (*fig*) fruitless, futile

stérilement [steʀilmɑ̃] *adv* fruitlessly

stérilet [steʀilɛ] *nm* coil, loop

stérilisateur [steʀilizatœʀ] *nm* sterilizer

stérilisation [steʀilizasjɔ̃] *nf* sterilization

stériliser [steʀilize] *vt* to sterilize

stérilité [steʀilite] *nf* sterility

sternum [stɛʀnɔm] *nm* breastbone, sternum

stéthoscope [stetɔskɔp] *nm* stethoscope

stick [stik] *nm* stick

stigmates [stigmat] *nmpl* scars, marks; (*Rel*) stigmata *pl*

stigmatiser [stigmatize] *vt* to denounce, stigmatize

stimulant, e [stimylɑ̃, -ɑ̃t] *adj* stimulating ▷ *nm* (*Méd*) stimulant; (*fig*) stimulus, incentive

stimulateur [stimylatœʀ] *nm*: **~ cardiaque** pacemaker

stimulation [stimylasjɔ̃] *nf* stimulation

stimuler [stimyle] *vt* to stimulate

stimulus [stimylys] *nm* (*pl* **stimuli** [stimyli]) stimulus

stipulation [stipylasjɔ̃] *nf* stipulation

stipuler [stipyle] *vt* to stipulate, specify

stock [stɔk] *nm* stock; **en ~** in stock

stockage [stɔkaʒ] *nm* stocking; storage

stocker [stɔke] *vt* to stock; (*déchets*) to store

Stockholm [stɔkɔlm] *n* Stockholm

stockiste [stɔkist(ə)] *nm* stockist

stoïcisme [stɔisism(ə)] *nm* stoicism

stoïque [stɔik] *adj* stoic, stoical

stoïquement [stɔikmɑ̃] *adv* stoically

stomacal, e, -aux [stɔmakal, -o] *adj* gastric, stomach *cpd*

stomatologie [stɔmatɔlɔʒi] *nf* stomatology

stomatologue [stɔmatɔlɔg] *nm/f* stomatologist

stop [stɔp] *nm* (*Auto*: *écriteau*) stop sign; (: *signal*) brake-light; (*dans un télégramme*) stop ▷ *excl* stop!

stoppage [stɔpaʒ] *nm* invisible mending

stopper [stɔpe] *vt* to stop, halt; (*Couture*) to mend ▷ *vi* to stop, halt

store [stɔʀ] *nm* blind; (*de magasin*) shade, awning

strabisme [stʀabism(ə)] *nm* squint(ing)

strangulation [stʀɑ̃gylasjɔ̃] *nf* strangulation

strapontin [stʀapɔ̃tɛ̃] *nm* jump *ou* foldaway seat

Strasbourg [stʀazbuʀ] *n* Strasbourg

strass [stʀas] *nm* paste, strass

stratagème [stʀataʒɛm] *nm* stratagem

strate [stʀat] *nf* (*Géo*) stratum, layer

stratège [stʀatɛʒ] *nm* strategist

stratégie [stʀateʒi] *nf* strategy

stratégique [stʀateʒik] *adj* strategic

stratégiquement [stʀateʒikmɑ̃] *adv* strategically

stratifié, e [stʀatifje] *adj* (*Géo*) stratified; (*Tech*) laminated

stratosphère [stʀatɔsfɛʀ] *nf* stratosphere

stress [stʀɛs] *nm inv* stress

stressant, e [stʀɛsɑ̃, -ɑ̃t] *adj* stressful

stresser [stʀɛse] *vt* to stress, cause stress in

strict, e [stʀikt(ə)] *adj* strict; (*tenue, décor*) severe, plain; **son droit le plus ~** his most basic right; **dans la plus ~e intimité** strictly in private; **le ~ nécessaire/minimum** the bare essentials/minimum

strictement [stʀiktəmɑ̃] *adv* strictly; plainly

strident, e [stʀidɑ̃, -ɑ̃t] *adj* shrill, strident

stridulations [stʀidylasjɔ̃] *nfpl* stridulations, chirrings

strie [stʀi] *nf* streak; (*Anat, Géo*) stria

strier [stʀije] *vt* to streak; to striate

strip-tease [stʀiptiz] *nm* striptease

strip-teaseuse [stʀiptizøz] *nf* stripper, striptease artist

striures [stʀijyʀ] *nfpl* streaking *sg*

strophe [stʀɔf] *nf* verse, stanza

structure [stʀyktyʀ] *nf* structure; **~s d'accueil/touristiques** reception/tourist facilities

structurer [stʀyktyʀe] *vt* to structure

strychnine [stʀiknin] *nf* strychnine

stuc [styk] *nm* stucco

studieusement [stydjøzmɑ̃] *adv* studiously

studieux, -euse [stydjø, -øz] *adj* (*élève*) studious; (*vacances*) study *cpd*

studio [stydjo] *nm* (*logement*) studio flat (*Brit*) *ou* apartment (*US*); (*d'artiste, TV etc*) studio

stupéfaction [stypefaksjɔ̃] *nf* stupefaction, astonishment

stupéfait, e [stypefɛ, -ɛt] *adj* astonished

stupéfiant, e [stypefjɑ̃, -ɑ̃t] *adj* stunning, astonishing ▷ *nm* (*Méd*) drug, narcotic

stupéfier [stypefje] *vt* to stupefy; (*étonner*) to stun, astonish

stupeur [stypœʀ] *nf* (*inertie, insensibilité*) stupor; (*étonnement*) astonishment, amazement

stupide [stypid] *adj* stupid; (*hébété*) stunned

stupidement [stypidmɑ̃] *adv* stupidly

stupidité [stypidite] *nf* stupidity *no pl*; (*propos, action*) stupid thing (to say *ou* do)

stups [styp] *nmpl* = **stupéfiants**; **brigade des ~** narcotics bureau *ou* squad

style [stil] *nm* style; **meuble/robe de ~** piece of period furniture/period dress; **~ de vie** lifestyle

stylé, e [stile] *adj* well-trained

stylet [stilɛ] *nm* (*poignard*) stiletto; (*Chirurgie*) stylet

stylisé, e [stilize] *adj* stylized

styliste [stilist(ə)] *nm/f* designer; stylist

stylistique [stilistik] *nf* stylistics *sg* ▷ *adj* stylistic

stylo [stilo] *nm*: **~ (à encre)** (fountain) pen; **~ (à) bille** ballpoint pen

stylo-feutre [stilɔføtʀ(ə)] *nm* felt-tip pen

su, e [sy] *pp de* **savoir** ▷ *nm*: **au su de** with the knowledge of

suaire [sɥɛʀ] *nm* shroud

suant, e [sɥɑ̃, -ɑ̃t] *adj* sweaty

suave [sɥav] *adj* (*odeur*) sweet; (*voix*) suave, smooth; (*coloris*) soft, mellow

subalterne [sybaltɛʀn(ə)] *adj* (*employé, officier*) junior; (*rôle*) subordinate, subsidiary ▷ *nm/f* subordinate, inferior

subconscient [sypkɔ̃sjɑ̃] *nm* subconscious

subdiviser [sybdivize] *vt* to subdivide

subdivision [sybdivizjɔ̃] *nf* subdivision

subir [sybiʀ] *vt* (*affront, dégâts, mauvais traitements*) to suffer; (*influence, charme*) to be under, be subjected to; (*traitement, opération, châtiment*) to undergo; (*personne*) to suffer, be subjected to

subit, e [sybi, -it] *adj* sudden

subitement [sybitmɑ̃] *adv* suddenly, all of a sudden

subjectif, -ive [sybʒɛktif, -iv] *adj* subjective

subjectivement [sybʒɛktivmɑ̃] *adv* subjectively

subjectivité [sybʒɛktivite] *nf* subjectivity

subjonctif [sybʒɔ̃ktif] *nm* subjunctive

subjuguer [sybʒyge] *vt* to subjugate

sublime [syblim] *adj* sublime

sublimer [syblime] *vt* to sublimate

submergé, e [sybmɛʀʒe] *adj* submerged; (*fig*): **~ de** snowed under with; overwhelmed with

submerger [sybmɛʀʒe] *vt* to submerge; (*foule*) to engulf; (*fig*) to overwhelm

submersible [sybmɛʀsibl(ə)] *nm* submarine

subordination [sybɔʀdinasjɔ̃] *nf* subordination

subordonné, e [sybɔʀdɔne] *adj, nm/f* subordinate; **~ à** (*personne*) subordinate to; (*résultats etc*) subject to, depending on

subordonner [sybɔʀdɔne] *vt*: **~ qn/qch à** to subordinate sb/sth to

subornation [sybɔʀnasjɔ̃] *nf* bribing

suborner [sybɔʀne] *vt* to bribe

subrepticement [sybʀɛptismɑ̃] *adv* surreptitiously

subroger [sybʀɔʒe] *vt* (*Jur*) to subrogate

subside [sypsid] *nm* grant

subsidiaire [sypsidjɛʀ] *adj* subsidiary; **question ~** deciding question

subsistance [sybzistɑ̃s] *nf* subsistence; **pourvoir à la ~ de qn** to keep sb, provide for sb's subsistence *ou* keep

subsister [sybziste] *vi* (*rester*) to remain, subsist; (*vivre*) to live; (*survivre*) to live on

subsonique [sybsɔnik] *adj* subsonic

substance [sypstɑ̃s] *nf* substance; **en ~** in substance

substantiel, le [sypstɑ̃sjɛl] *adj* substantial

substantif [sypstɑ̃tif] *nm* noun, substantive

substantiver [sypstɑ̃tive] *vt* to nominalize

substituer [sypstitɥe] *vt*: **~ qn/qch à** to substitute sb/sth for; **se ~ à qn** (*représenter*) to substitute for sb; (*évincer*) to substitute o.s. for sb

substitut [sypstity] *nm* (*Jur*) deputy public prosecutor; (*succédané*) substitute

substitution [sypstitysjɔ̃] *nf* substitution

subterfuge [sybtɛʀfyʒ] *nm* subterfuge

subtil, e [syptil] *adj* subtle

subtilement [syptilmɑ̃] *adv* subtly

subtiliser [syptilize] *vt*: **~ qch (à qn)** to spirit sth away (from sb)

subtilité [syptilite] *nf* subtlety

subtropical, e, -aux [sybtʀɔpikal, -o] *adj* subtropical

suburbain, e [sybyʀbɛ̃, -ɛn] *adj* suburban

subvenir [sybvəniʀ] : **~ à** *vt* to meet

subvention [sybvɑ̃sjɔ̃] *nf* subsidy, grant

subventionner [sybvɑ̃sjɔne] *vt* to subsidize

subversif, -ive [sybvɛʀsif, -iv] *adj* subversive

subversion [sybvɛʀsjɔ̃] *nf* subversion

suc [syk] *nm* (Bot) sap; (*de viande, fruit*) juice; **~s gastriques** gastric juices

succédané [syksedane] *nm* substitute

succéder [syksede]: **~ à** *vt* (*directeur, roi etc*) to succeed; (*venir après: dans une série*) to follow, succeed; **se succéder** *vi* (*accidents, années*) to follow one another

succès [syksɛ] *nm* success; **avec ~** successfully; **sans ~** unsuccessfully; **avoir du ~** to be a success, be successful; **à ~** successful; **livre à ~** bestseller; **~ de librairie** bestseller; **~ (féminins)** conquests

successeur [syksesœʀ] *nm* successor

successif, -ive [syksesif, -iv] *adj* successive

succession [syksesjɔ̃] *nf* (*série, Pol*) succession; (*Jur: patrimoine*) estate, inheritance; **prendre la ~ de** (*directeur*) to succeed, take over from; (*entreprise*) to take over

successivement [syksesivmɑ̃] *adv* successively

succinct, e [syksɛ̃, -ɛ̃t] *adj* succinct

succinctement [syksɛ̃tmɑ̃] *adv* succinctly

succion [syksjɔ̃] *nf*: **bruit de ~** sucking noise

succomber [sykɔ̃be] *vi* to die, succumb; (*fig*): **~ à** to give way to, succumb to

succulent, e [sykylɑ̃, -ɑ̃t] *adj* succulent

succursale [sykyʀsal] *nf* branch; **magasin à ~s multiples** chain *ou* multiple store

sucer [syse] *vt* to suck

sucette [sysɛt] *nf* (*bonbon*) lollipop; (*de bébé*) dummy (Brit), comforter, pacifier (US)

suçoter [sysɔte] *vt* to suck

sucre [sykʀ(ə)] *nm* (*substance*) sugar; (*morceau*) lump of sugar, sugar lump *ou* cube; **~ de canne/**

betterave cane/beet sugar; **~ en morceaux/ cristallisé/en poudre** lump *ou* cube/ granulated/caster sugar; **~ glace** icing sugar; **~ d'orge** barley sugar

sucré, e [sykʀe] *adj* (*produit alimentaire*) sweetened; (*au goût*) sweet; (*péj*) sugary, honeyed

sucrer [sykʀe] *vt* (*thé, café*) to sweeten, put sugar in; **~ qn** to put sugar in sb's tea (*ou* coffee *etc*); **se sucrer** to help o.s. to sugar, have some sugar; (*fam*) to line one's pocket(s)

sucrerie [sykʀəʀi] *nf* (*usine*) sugar refinery; **sucreries** *nfpl* (*bonbons*) sweets, sweet things

sucrier, -ière [sykʀije, -jɛʀ] *adj* (*industrie*) sugar *cpd*; (*région*) sugar-producing ▷ *nm* (*fabricant*) sugar producer; (*récipient*) sugar bowl *ou* basin

sud [syd] *nm*: **le ~** the south ▷ *adj inv* south; (*côte*) south, southern; **au ~** (*situation*) in the south; (*direction*) to the south; **au ~ de** (to the) south of

sud-africain, e [sydafʀikɛ̃, -ɛn] *adj* South African ▷ *nm/f*: **Sud-Africain, e** South African

sud-américain, e [sydameʀikɛ̃, -ɛn] *adj* South American ▷ *nm/f*: **Sud-Américain, e** South American

sudation [sydasjɔ̃] *nf* sweating, sudation

sud-coréen, ne [sydkɔʀeɛ̃, -ɛn] *adj* South Korean ▷ *nm/f*: **Sud-Coréen, ne** South Korean

sud-est [sydɛst] *nm, adj inv* south-east

sud-ouest [sydwɛst] *nm, adj inv* south-west

sud-vietnamien, ne [sydvjɛtnamjɛ̃, -ɛn] *adj* South Vietnamese ▷ *nm/f*: **Sud-Vietnamien, ne** South Vietnamese

Suède [sɥɛd] *nf*: **la ~** Sweden

suédois, e [sɥedwa, -waz] *adj* Swedish ▷ *nm* (*Ling*) Swedish ▷ *nm/f*: **Suédois, e** Swede

suer [sɥe] *vi* to sweat; (*suinter*) to ooze ▷ *vt* (*fig*) to exude; **~ à grosses gouttes** to sweat profusely

sueur [sɥœʀ] *nf* sweat; **en ~** sweating, in a sweat; **avoir des ~s froides** to be in a cold sweat

suffire [syfiʀ] *vi* (*être assez*): **~ (à qn/pour qch/ pour faire)** to be enough *ou* sufficient (for sb/ for sth/to do); (*satisfaire*): **cela lui suffit** he's content with this, this is enough for him; **se suffire** *vi* to be self-sufficient; **cela suffit pour les irriter/qu'ils se fâchent** it's enough to annoy them/for them to get angry; **il suffit d'une négligence/qu'on oublie pour que ...** it only takes one act of carelessness/one only needs to forget for ...; **ça suffit!** that's enough!, that'll do!

suffisamment [syfizamɑ̃] *adv* sufficiently, enough; **~ de** sufficient, enough

suffisance [syfizɑ̃s] *nf* (*vanité*) self-importance, bumptiousness; (*quantité*): **en ~** in plenty

suffisant, e [syfizɑ̃, -ɑ̃t] *adj* (*temps, ressources*) sufficient; (*résultats*) satisfactory; (*vaniteux*) self-important, bumptious

suffisons *etc* [syfizɔ̃] *vb voir* **suffire**

suffixe [syfiks(ə)] *nm* suffix

suffocant, e [syfɔkɑ̃, -ɑ̃t] *adj* (*étouffant*) suffocating; (*stupéfiant*) staggering

suffocation [syfɔkasjɔ̃] *nf* suffocation

suffoquer [syfɔke] *vt* to choke, suffocate; (*stupéfier*) to stagger, astound ▷ *vi* to choke, suffocate; **~ de colère/d'indignation** to choke with anger/indignation

suffrage [syfʀaʒ] *nm* (*Pol: voix*) vote; (: *méthode*): **~ universel/direct/indirect** universal/direct/ indirect suffrage; (*du public etc*) approval *no pl*; **~s exprimés** valid votes

suggérer [syɡʒeʀe] *vt* to suggest; **~ que/de faire** to suggest that/doing

suggestif, -ive [syɡʒɛstif, -iv] *adj* suggestive

suggestion [syɡʒɛstjɔ̃] *nf* suggestion

suggestivité [syɡʒɛstivite] *nf* suggestiveness, suggestive nature

suicidaire [sɥisidɛʀ] *adj* suicidal

suicide [sɥisid] *nm* suicide ▷ *adj*: **opération ~** suicide mission

suicidé, e [sɥiside] *nm/f* suicide

suicider [sɥiside]: **se suicider** *vi* to commit suicide

suie [sɥi] *nf* soot

suif [sɥif] *nm* tallow

suinter [sɥɛte] *vi* to ooze

suis [sɥi] *vb voir* **être**; **suivre**

suisse [sɥis] *adj* Swiss ▷ *nm* (*bedeau*) ≈ verger ▷ *nm/f*: **Suisse** Swiss *pl inv* ▷ *nf*: **la S~** Switzerland; **la S~ romande/allemande** French-speaking/German-speaking Switzerland; **~ romand** Swiss French

suisse-allemand, e [sɥisalmɑ̃, -ɑ̃d] *adj, nm/f* Swiss German

Suissesse [sɥisɛs] *nf* Swiss (woman *ou* girl)

suit [sɥi] *vb voir* **suivre**

suite [sɥit] *nf* (*continuation: d'énumération etc*) rest, remainder; (: *de feuilleton*) continuation; (: *second film etc sur le même thème*) sequel; (*série: de maisons, succès*): **une ~ de** a series *ou* succession of; (*Math*) series *sg*; (*conséquence*) result; (*ordre, liaison logique*) coherence; (*appartement, Mus*) suite; (*escorte*) retinue, suite; **suites** *nfpl* (*d'une maladie etc*) effects; **prendre la ~ de** (*directeur etc*) to succeed, take over from; **donner ~ à** (*requête, projet*) to follow up; **faire ~ à** to follow; (**faisant**) **~ à votre lettre du** further to your letter of the; **sans ~** *adj* incoherent, disjointed ▷ *adv* incoherently, disjointedly; **de ~** *adv* (*d'affilée*) in succession; (*immédiatement*) at once; **par la ~** afterwards, subsequently; **à la ~** *adv* one after the other; **à la ~ de** (*derrière*) behind; (*en conséquence de*) following; **par ~ de** owing to, as a result of; **avoir de la ~ dans les idées** to show great singleness of purpose; **attendre la ~ des événements** to (wait and see) what happens

suivant, e [sɥivɑ̃, -ɑ̃t] *vb voir* **suivre** ▷ *adj* next, following; (*ci-après*): **l'exercice ~** the following exercise ▷ *prép* (*selon*) according to; **~ que** according to whether; **au ~!** next!

suive *etc* [sɥiv] *vb voir* **suivre**

suiveur [sɥivœʀ] *nm* (*Cyclisme*) (official) follower; (*péj*) (camp) follower

suivi, e [sɥivi] *pp de* **suivre** ▷ *adj* (*régulier*) regular; (*Comm: article*) in general production; (*cohérent*) consistent; coherent ▷ *nm* follow-up; **très/peu** ~ (*cours*) well-/poorly-attended; (*mode*) widely/not widely adopted; (*feuilleton etc*) widely/not widely followed

suivre [sɥivʀ(ə)] *vt* (*gén*) to follow; (*Scol: cours*) to attend; (: *leçon*) to follow, attend to; (: *programme*) to keep up with; (*Comm: article*) to continue to stock ▷ *vi* to follow; (*élève: écouter*) to attend, pay attention; (: *assimiler le programme*) to keep up, follow; **se suivre** (*accidents, personnes, voitures etc*) to follow one after the other; (*raisonnement*) to be coherent; ~ **des yeux** to follow with one's eyes; **faire** ~ (*lettre*) to forward; ~ **son cours** (*enquête etc*) to run *ou* take its course; "**à** ~" "to be continued"

sujet, te [syʒɛ, -ɛt] *adj*: **être** ~ **à** (*accidents*) to be prone to; (*vertige etc*) to be liable *ou* subject to ▷ *nm/f* (*d'un souverain*) subject ▷ *nm* subject; **un** ~ **de dispute/discorde/mécontentement** a cause for argument/dissension/dissatisfaction; **c'est à quel** ~? what is it about?; **avoir** ~ **de se plaindre** to have cause for complaint; **au** ~ **de** *prép* about; ~ **à caution** *adj* questionable; ~ **de conversation** topic *ou* subject of conversation; ~ **d'examen** (*Scol*) examination question; examination paper; ~ **d'expérience** (*Bio etc*) experimental subject

sujétion [syʒesjɔ̃] *nf* subjection; (*fig*) constraint

sulfater [sylfate] *vt* to spray with copper sulphate

sulfureux, -euse [sylfyʀø, -øz] *adj* sulphurous (*Brit*), sulfurous (*US*)

sulfurique [sylfyʀik] *adj*: **acide** ~ sulphuric (*Brit*) *ou* sulfuric (*US*) acid

sulfurisé, e [sylfyʀize] *adj*: **papier** ~ greaseproof (*Brit*) *ou* wax (*US*) paper

Sumatra [symatʀa] *nf* Sumatra

summum [sɔmɔm] *nm*: **le** ~ **de** the height of

super [sypɛʀ] *adj inv* great, fantastic ▷ *nm* (= *supercarburant*) ≈ 4-star (*Brit*), ≈ premium (*US*)

superbe [sypɛʀb(ə)] *adj* magnificent, superb ▷ *nf* arrogance

superbement [sypɛʀbəmɑ̃] *adv* superbly

supercarburant [sypɛʀkaʀbyʀɑ̃] *nm* ≈ 4-star petrol (*Brit*), ≈ premium gas (*US*)

supercherie [sypɛʀʃəʀi] *nf* trick, trickery *no pl*; (*fraude*) fraud

supérette [sypeʀɛt] *nf* minimarket

superfétatoire [sypɛʀfetatwaʀ] *adj* superfluous

superficie [sypɛʀfisi] *nf* (*surface*) area; (*fig*) surface

superficiel, le [sypɛʀfisjɛl] *adj* superficial

superficiellement [sypɛʀfisjɛlmɑ̃] *adv* superficially

superflu, e [sypɛʀfly] *adj* superfluous ▷ *nm*: **le** ~ the superfluous

superforme [sypɛʀfɔʀm(ə)] *nf* (*fam*) top form, excellent shape

super-grand [sypɛʀgʀɑ̃] *nm* superpower

super-huit [sypɛʀɥit] *adj*: **camera/film** ~ super-eight camera/film

supérieur, e [sypeʀjœʀ] *adj* (*lèvre, étages, classes*) upper; (*plus élevé: température, niveau*): ~ (**à**) higher (than); (*meilleur: qualité, produit*): ~ (**à**) superior (to); (*excellent, hautain*) superior ▷ *nm/f* superior; **Mère** ~**e** Mother Superior; **à l'étage** ~ on the next floor up; ~ **en nombre** superior in number

supérieurement [sypeʀjœʀmɑ̃] *adv* exceptionally well; (*avec adjectif*) exceptionally

supériorité [sypeʀjɔʀite] *nf* superiority

superlatif [sypɛʀlatif] *nm* superlative

supermarché [sypɛʀmaʀʃe] *nm* supermarket

supernova [sypɛʀnɔva] *nf* supernova

superposable [sypɛʀpozabl(ə)] *adj* (*figures*) that may be superimposed; (*lits*) stackable

superposer [sypɛʀpoze] *vt* to superpose; (*meubles, caisses*) to stack; (*faire chevaucher*) to superimpose; **se superposer** (*images, souvenirs*) to be superimposed; **lits superposés** bunk beds

superposition [sypɛʀpozisjɔ̃] *nf* superposition; superimposition

superpréfet [sypɛʀpʀefɛ] *nm* *prefect in charge of a region*

superproduction [sypɛʀpʀɔdyksjɔ̃] *nf* (*film*) spectacular

superpuissance [sypɛʀpɥisɑ̃s] *nf* superpower

supersonique [sypɛʀsɔnik] *adj* supersonic

superstitieux, -euse [sypɛʀstisjø, -øz] *adj* superstitious

superstition [sypɛʀstisjɔ̃] *nf* superstition

superstructure [sypɛʀstʀyktyʀ] *nf* superstructure

supertanker [sypɛʀtɑ̃kœʀ] *nm* supertanker

superviser [sypɛʀvize] *vt* to supervise

supervision [sypɛʀvizjɔ̃] *nf* supervision

suppl. *abr* = **supplément**

supplanter [syplɑ̃te] *vt* to supplant

suppléance [sypleɑ̃s] *nf* (*poste*) supply post (*Brit*), substitute teacher's post (*US*)

suppléant, e [sypleɑ̃, -ɑ̃t] *adj* (*juge, fonctionnaire*) deputy *cpd*; (*professeur*) supply *cpd* (*Brit*), substitute *cpd* (*US*) ▷ *nm/f* deputy; supply *ou* substitute teacher; **médecin** ~ locum

suppléer [syplee] *vt* (*ajouter: mot manquant etc*) to supply, provide; (*compenser: lacune*) to fill in; (: *défaut*) to make up for; (*remplacer: professeur*) to stand in for; (: *juge*) to deputize for; ~ **à** *vt* to make up for; to substitute for

supplément [syplemɑ̃] *nm* supplement; **un** ~ **de travail** extra *ou* additional work; **un** ~ **de frites** *etc* an extra portion of chips *etc*; **un** ~ **de 10 euros** a supplement of 10 euros, an extra *ou* additional 10 euros; **ceci est en** ~ (*au menu etc*) this is extra, there is an extra charge for this; ~ **d'information** additional information

supplémentaire [syplemɑ̃tɛʀ] *adj* additional, further; (*train, bus*) relief *cpd*, extra

supplétif, -ive [sypletif, -iv] *adj* (*Mil*) auxiliary

suppliant, e [syplijɑ̃, -ɑ̃t] *adj* imploring

supplication [syplikasjɔ̃] *nf* (*Rel*) supplication;
supplications *nfpl* (*adjurations*) pleas, entreaties
supplice [syplis] *nm* (*peine corporelle*) torture *no pl*;
form of torture; (*douleur physique, morale*) torture,
agony; **être au ~** to be in agony
supplier [syplije] *vt* to implore, beseech
supplique [syplik] *nf* petition
support [sypɔʀ] *nm* support; (*pour livre, outils*)
stand; **~ audio-visuel** audio-visual aid; **~
publicitaire** advertising medium
supportable [sypɔʀtabl(ə)] *adj* (*douleur,
température*) bearable; (*procédé, conduite*)
tolerable
supporter *nm* [sypɔʀtɛʀ] supporter, fan ▷ *vt*
[sypɔʀte] (*poids, poussée, Sport: concurrent, équipe*) to
support; (*conséquences, épreuve*) to bear, endure;
(*défauts, personne*) to tolerate, put up with; (*chose:
chaleur etc*) to withstand; (*personne: chaleur, vin*) to
take
supposé, e [sypoze] *adj* (*nombre*) estimated;
(*auteur*) supposed
supposer [sypoze] *vt* to suppose; (*impliquer*) to
presuppose; **en supposant** *ou* **à ~ que**
supposing (that)
supposition [sypozisjɔ̃] *nf* supposition
suppositoire [sypozitwaʀ] *nm* suppository
suppôt [sypo] *nm* (*péj*) henchman
suppression [sypʀesjɔ̃] *nf* (*voir supprimer*)
removal; deletion; cancellation; suppression
supprimer [sypʀime] *vt* (*cloison, cause, anxiété*) to
remove; (*clause, mot*) to delete; (*congés, service
d'autobus etc*) to cancel; (*publication, article*) to
suppress; (*emplois, privilèges, témoin gênant*) to do
away with; **~ qch à qn** to deprive sb of sth
suppurer [sypyʀe] *vi* to suppurate
supputations [sypytasjɔ̃] *nfpl* calculations,
reckonings
supputer [sypyte] *vt* to calculate, reckon
supranational, e, -aux [sypʀanasjɔnal, -o] *adj*
supranational
suprématie [sypʀemasi] *nf* supremacy
suprême [sypʀɛm] *adj* supreme
suprêmement [sypʀɛmmɑ̃] *adv* supremely

◯ **MOT-CLÉ**

sur¹ [syʀ] *prép* **1** (*position*) on; (*pardessus*) over; (*au-
dessus*) above; **pose-le sur la table** put it on the
table; **je n'ai pas d'argent sur moi** I haven't
any money on me
2 (*direction*) towards; **en allant sur Paris** going
towards Paris; **sur votre droite** on *ou* to your
right
3 (*à propos de*) on, about; **un livre/une
conférence sur Balzac** a book/lecture on *ou*
about Balzac
4 (*proportion, mesures*) out of; by; **un sur 10** one in
10; (*Scol*) one out of 10; **sur 20, deux sont
venus** out of 20, two came; **4 m sur 2** 4 m by 2;
avoir accident sur accident to have one
accident after another
5 (*cause*): **sur sa recommandation** on *ou* at his

recommendation; **sur son invitation** at his
invitation
6: **sur ce** *adv* whereupon; **sur ce, il faut que
je vous quitte** and now I must leave you

sur², e [syʀ] *adj* sour
sûr, e [syʀ] *adj* sure, certain; (*digne de confiance*)
reliable; (*sans danger*) safe; **peu ~** unreliable; **~
de qch** sure *ou* certain of sth; **être ~ de qn** to be
sure of sb; **~ et certain** absolutely certain; **~ de
soi** self-assured, self-confident; **le plus ~ est
de** the safest thing is to
surabondance [syʀabɔ̃dɑ̃s] *nf* overabundance
surabondant, e [syʀabɔ̃dɑ̃, -ɑ̃t] *adj*
overabundant
surabonder [syʀabɔ̃de] *vi* to be overabundant;
~ de to abound with, have an overabundance of
suractivité [syʀaktivite] *nf* hyperactivity
suraigu, ë [syʀegy] *adj* very shrill
surajouter [syʀaʒute] *vt*: **~ qch à** to add sth to
suralimentation [syʀalimɑ̃tasjɔ̃] *nf*
overfeeding; (*Tech: d'un moteur*) supercharging
suralimenté, e [syʀalimɑ̃te] *adj* (*personne*)
overfed; (*moteur*) supercharged
suranné, e [syʀane] *adj* outdated, outmoded
surarmement [syʀaʀməmɑ̃] *nm* (*excess*)
stockpiling of arms (*ou* weapons)
surbaissé, e [syʀbese] *adj* lowered, low
surcapacité [syʀkapasite] *nf* overcapacity
surcharge [syʀʃaʀʒ(ə)] *nf* (*de passagers,
marchandises*) excess load; (*de détails, d'ornements*)
overabundance, excess; (*correction*) alteration;
(*Postes*) surcharge; **prendre des passagers en ~**
to take on excess *ou* extra passengers; **~ de
bagages** excess luggage; **~ de travail** extra
work
surchargé, e [syʀʃaʀʒe] *adj* (*décoration, style*)
over-elaborate, overfussy; (*voiture, emploi du
temps*) overloaded
surcharger [syʀʃaʀʒe] *vt* to overload; (*timbre-
poste*) to surcharge; (*décoration*) to overdo
surchauffe [syʀʃof] *nf* overheating
surchauffé, e [syʀʃofe] *adj* overheated; (*fig:
imagination*) overactive
surchoix [syʀʃwa] *adj inv* top-quality
surclasser [syʀklase] *vt* to outclass
surconsommation [syʀkɔ̃sɔmasjɔ̃] *nf* (*Écon*)
overconsumption
surcoté, e [syʀkɔte] *adj* overpriced
surcouper [syʀkupe] *vt* to overtrump
surcroît [syʀkʀwa] *nm*: **~ de qch** additional sth;
par *ou* **de ~** moreover; **en ~** in addition
surdi-mutité [syʀdimytite] *nf*: **atteint de ~**
deaf and dumb
surdité [syʀdite] *nf* deafness; **atteint de ~
totale** profoundly deaf
surdoué, e [syʀdwe] *adj* gifted
sureau, x [syʀo] *nm* elder (tree)
sureffectif [syʀefɛktif] *nm* overmanning
surélever [syʀelve] *vt* to raise, heighten
sûrement [syʀmɑ̃] *adv* reliably; safely, securely;
(*certainement*) certainly; **~ pas** certainly not

suremploi [syʀɑ̃plwa] *nm* (*Écon*) overemployment

surenchère [syʀɑ̃ʃɛʀ] *nf* (*aux enchères*) higher bid; (*sur prix fixe*) overbid; (*fig*) overstatement; outbidding tactics *pl*; ~ **de violence** build-up of violence; ~ **électorale** political (*ou* electoral) one-upmanship

surenchérir [syʀɑ̃ʃeʀiʀ] *vi* to bid higher; to raise one's bid; (*fig*) to try and outbid each other

surendettement [syʀɑ̃dɛtmɑ̃] *nm* excessive debt

surent [syʀ] *vb voir* **savoir**

surentraîné, e [syʀɑ̃tʀene] *adj* overtrained

suréquipé, e [syʀekipe] *adj* overequipped

surestimer [syʀɛstime] *vt* (*tableau*) to overvalue; (*possibilité, personne*) to overestimate

sûreté [syʀte] *nf* (*voir sûr*) reliability; safety; (*Jur*) guaranty; surety; **mettre en ~** to put in a safe place; **pour plus de ~** as an extra precaution; to be on the safe side; **la ~ de l'État** State security; **la S~ (nationale)** division of the Ministère de l'Intérieur heading all police forces except the gendarmerie and the Paris préfecture de police

surexcité, e [syʀɛksite] *adj* overexcited

surexciter [syʀɛksite] *vt* (*personne*) to overexcite; **cela surexcite ma curiosité** it really rouses my curiosity

surexploiter [syʀɛksplwate] *vt* to overexploit

surexposer [syʀɛkspoze] *vt* to overexpose

surf [sœʀf] *nm* surfing; **faire du ~** to go surfing

surface [syʀfas] *nf* surface; (*superficie*) surface area; **faire ~** to surface; **en ~** *adv* near the surface; (*fig*) superficially; **la pièce fait 100 m² de ~** the room has a surface area of 100m²; ~ **de réparation** (*Sport*) penalty area; ~ **porteuse** *ou* **de sustentation** (*Aviat*) aerofoil

surfait, e [syʀfɛ, -ɛt] *adj* overrated

surfer [sœʀfe] *vi* to surf; ~ **sur Internet** to surf the Internet

surfeur, -euse [sœʀfœʀ, -øz] *nm/f* surfer

surfiler [syʀfile] *vt* (*Couture*) to oversew

surfin, e [syʀfɛ̃, -in] *adj* superfine

surgélateur [syʀʒelatœʀ] *nm* deep freeze

surgélation [syʀʒelasjɔ̃] *nf* deep-freezing

surgelé, e [syʀʒəle] *adj* (deep-)frozen

surgeler [syʀʒəle] *vt* to (deep-)freeze

surgir [syʀʒiʀ] *vi* (*personne, véhicule*) to appear suddenly; (*jaillir*) to shoot up; (*montagne etc*) to rise up, loom up; (*fig: problème, conflit*) to arise

surhomme [syʀɔm] *nm* superman

surhumain, e [syʀymɛ̃, -ɛn] *adj* superhuman

surimposer [syʀɛ̃poze] *vt* to overtax

surimpression [syʀɛ̃pʀesjɔ̃] *nf* (*Photo*) double exposure; **en ~** superimposed

surimprimer [syʀɛ̃pʀime] *vt* to overstrike, overprint

Surinam [syʀinam] *nm*: **le ~** Surinam

surinfection [syʀɛ̃fɛksjɔ̃] *nf* (*Méd*) secondary infection

surjet [syʀʒɛ] *nm* (*Couture*) overcast seam

sur-le-champ [syʀləʃɑ̃] *adv* immediately

surlendemain [syʀlɑ̃dmɛ̃] *nm*: **le ~ (soir)** two days later (in the evening); **le ~ de** two days after

surligneur [syʀliɲœʀ] *nm* (*feutre*) highlighter (pen)

surmenage [syʀmənaʒ] *nm* overwork; **le ~ intellectuel** mental fatigue

surmené, e [syʀməne] *adj* overworked

surmener [syʀməne] *vt*, **se surmener** *vi* to overwork

surmonter [syʀmɔ̃te] *vt* (*coupole etc*) to surmount, top; (*vaincre*) to overcome, surmount

surmultiplié, e [syʀmyltiplije] *adj, nf*: (**vitesse**) ~**e** overdrive

surnager [syʀnaʒe] *vi* to float

surnaturel, le [syʀnatyʀɛl] *adj, nm* supernatural

surnom [syʀnɔ̃] *nm* nickname

surnombre [syʀnɔ̃bʀ(ə)] *nm*: **être en ~** to be too many (*ou* one too many)

surnommer [syʀnɔme] *vt* to nickname

surnuméraire [syʀnymeʀɛʀ] *nm/f* supernumerary

suroît [syʀwa] *nm* sou'wester

surpasser [syʀpase] *vt* to surpass; **se surpasser** *vi* to surpass o.s., excel o.s.

surpayer [syʀpeje] *vt* (*personne*) to overpay; (*article etc*) to pay too much for

surpeuplé, e [syʀpœple] *adj* overpopulated

surpeuplement [syʀpœpləmɑ̃] *nm* overpopulation

surpiquer [syʀpike] *vt* (*Couture*) to overstitch

surpiqûre [syʀpikyʀ] *nf* (*Couture*) overstitching

surplace [syʀplas] *nm*: **faire du ~** to mark time

surplis [syʀpli] *nm* surplice

surplomb [syʀplɔ̃] *nm* overhang; **en ~** overhanging

surplomber [syʀplɔ̃be] *vi* to be overhanging ▷ *vt* to overhang; (*dominer*) to tower above

surplus [syʀply] *nm* (*Comm*) surplus; (*reste*): ~ **de bois** wood left over; **au ~** moreover; ~ **américains** American army surplus *sg*

surpopulation [syʀpɔpylasjɔ̃] *nf* overpopulation

surprenant, e [syʀpʀənɑ̃, -ɑ̃t] *vb voir* **surprendre** ▷ *adj* amazing

surprendre [syʀpʀɑ̃dʀ(ə)] *vt* (*étonner, prendre à l'improviste*) to amaze, surprise; (*secret*) to discover; (*tomber sur: intrus etc*) to catch; (*fig*) to detect; to chance *ou* happen upon; (*clin d'œil*) to intercept; (*conversation*) to overhear; (*orage, nuit etc*) to catch out, take by surprise; ~ **la vigilance/bonne foi de qn** to catch sb out/betray sb's good faith; **se ~ à faire** to catch *ou* find o.s. doing

surprime [syʀpʀim] *nf* additional premium

surpris, e [syʀpʀi, -iz] *pp de* **surprendre** ▷ *adj*: ~ (**de/que**) amazed *ou* surprised (at/that)

surprise [syʀpʀiz] *nf* surprise; **faire une ~ à qn** to give sb a surprise; **voyage sans ~s** uneventful journey; **par ~** *adv* by surprise

surprise-partie [syʀpʀizpaʀti] *nf* party

surprit [syʀpʀi] *vb voir* **surprendre**

S

surproduction [syʀpʀɔdyksjɔ̃] *nf* overproduction

surréaliste [syʀʀealist(ə)] *adj, nm/f* surrealist

sursaut [syʀso] *nm* start, jump; **~ de** (*énergie, indignation*) sudden fit *ou* burst of; **en ~** *adv* with a start

sursauter [syʀsote] *vi* to (give a) start, jump

surseoir [syʀswaʀ]: **~ à** *vt* to defer; (*Jur*) to stay

sursis [syʀsi] *nm* (*Jur: gén*) suspended sentence; (*à l'exécution capitale, aussi fig*) reprieve; (*Mil*): **~ (d'appel ou d'incorporation)** deferment; **condamné à cinq mois (de prison) avec ~** given a five-month suspended (prison) sentence

sursitaire [syʀsitɛʀ] *nm* (*Mil*) deferred conscript

sursois [syʀswa], **sursoyais** *etc* [syʀswaje] *vb voir* **surseoir**

surtaxe [syʀtaks(ə)] *nf* surcharge

surtension [syʀtɑ̃sjɔ̃] *nf* (*Élec*) overvoltage

surtout [syʀtu] *adv* (*avant tout, d'abord*) above all; (*spécialement, particulièrement*) especially; **il aime le sport, ~ le football** he likes sport, especially football; **cet été, il a ~ fait de la pêche** this summer he went fishing more than anything (else); **~ pas d'histoires!** no fuss now!; **~, ne dites rien!** whatever you do – don't say anything!; **~ pas!** certainly *ou* definitely not!; **~ que ...** especially as ...

survécu, e [syʀveky] *pp de* **survivre**

surveillance [syʀvɛjɑ̃s] *nf* watch; (*Police, Mil*) surveillance; **sous ~ médicale** under medical supervision; **la ~ du territoire** internal security; *voir aussi* **DST**

surveillant, e [syʀvɛjɑ̃, -ɑ̃t] *nm/f* (*de prison*) warder; (*Scol*) monitor; (*de travaux*) supervisor, overseer

surveiller [syʀveje] *vt* (*enfant, élèves, bagages*) to watch, keep an eye on; (*malade*) to watch over; (*prisonnier, suspect*) to keep (a) watch on; (*territoire, bâtiment*) to (keep) watch over; (*travaux, cuisson*) to supervise; (*Scol: examen*) to invigilate; **se surveiller** to keep a check *ou* watch on o.s.; **~ son langage/sa ligne** to watch one's language/figure

survenir [syʀvəniʀ] *vi* (*incident, retards*) to occur, arise; (*événement*) to take place; (*personne*) to appear, arrive

survenu, e [syʀv(ə)ny] *pp de* **survenir**

survêt [syʀvɛt], **survêtement** [syʀvɛtmɑ̃] *nm* tracksuit (*Brit*), sweat suit (*US*)

survie [syʀvi] *nf* survival; (*Rel*) afterlife; **équipement de ~** survival equipment; **une ~ de quelques mois** a few more months of life

surviens [syʀvjɛ̃], **survint** *etc* [syʀvɛ̃] *vb voir* **survenir**

survit *etc* [syʀvi] *vb voir* **survivre**

survitrage [syʀvitʀaʒ] *nm* double-glazing

survivance [syʀvivɑ̃s] *nf* relic

survivant, e [syʀvivɑ̃, -ɑ̃t] *vb voir* **survivre** ▷ *nm/f* survivor

survivre [syʀvivʀ(ə)] *vi* to survive; **~ à** *vt* (*accident etc*) to survive; (*personne*) to outlive; **la**

victime a peu de chance de ~ the victim has little hope of survival

survol [syʀvɔl] *nm* flying over

survoler [syʀvɔle] *vt* to fly over; (*fig: livre*) to skim through; (: *question, problèmes*) to skim over

survolté, e [syʀvɔlte] *adj* (*Élec*) stepped up, boosted; (*fig*) worked up

sus [sy(s)]: **en ~ de** *prép* in addition to, over and above; **en ~** *adv* in addition; **~ à** *excl*: **~ au tyran!** at the tyrant! *vb* [sy] *voir* **savoir**

susceptibilité [syseptibilite] *nf* sensitivity *no pl*

susceptible [syseptibl(ə)] *adj* touchy, sensitive; **~ d'amélioration** *ou* **d'être amélioré** that can be improved, open to improvement; **~ de faire** (*capacité*) able to do; (*probabilité*) liable to do

susciter [sysite] *vt* (*admiration*) to arouse; (*obstacles, ennuis*): **~ (à qn)** to create (for sb)

susdit, e [sysdi, -dit] *adj* foresaid

susmentionné, e [sysmɑ̃sjɔne] *adj* above-mentioned

susnommé, e [sysnɔme] *adj* above-named

suspect, e [syspɛ(kt), -ɛkt(ə)] *adj* suspicious; (*témoignage, opinions, vin etc*) suspect ▷ *nm/f* suspect; **peu ~ de** most unlikely to be suspected of

suspecter [syspɛkte] *vt* to suspect; (*honnêteté de qn*) to question, have one's suspicions about; **~ qn d'être/d'avoir fait qch** to suspect sb of being/having done sth

suspendre [syspɑ̃dʀ(ə)] *vt* (*accrocher: vêtement*): **~ qch (à)** to hang sth up (on); (*fixer: lustre etc*): **~ qch à** to hang sth from; (*interrompre, démettre*) to suspend; (*remettre*) to defer; **se ~ à** to hang from

suspendu, e [syspɑ̃dy] *pp de* **suspendre** ▷ *adj* (*accroché*): **~ à** hanging on (*ou* from); (*perché*): **~ au-dessus de** suspended over; (*Auto*): **bien/mal ~** with good/poor suspension; **être ~ aux lèvres de qn** to hang upon sb's every word

suspens [syspɑ̃]: **en ~** *adv* (*affaire*) in abeyance; **tenir en ~** to keep in suspense

suspense [syspɑ̃s] *nm* suspense

suspension [syspɑ̃sjɔ̃] *nf* suspension; deferment; (*Auto*) suspension; (*lustre*) pendant light fitting; **en ~** in suspension, suspended; **~ d'audience** adjournment

suspicieux, -euse [syspisjø, -øz] *adj* suspicious

suspicion [syspisjɔ̃] *nf* suspicion

sustentation [systɑ̃tasjɔ̃] *nf* (*Aviat*) lift; **base** *ou* **polygone de ~** support polygon

sustenter [systɑ̃te]: **se sustenter** *vi* to take sustenance

susurrer [sysyʀe] *vt* to whisper

sut [sy] *vb voir* **savoir**

suture [sytyʀ] *nf*: **point de ~** stitch

suturer [sytyʀe] *vt* to stitch up, suture

suzeraineté [syzʀɛnte] *nf* suzerainty

svelte [svɛlt(ə)] *adj* slender, svelte

SVP *sigle* (= *s'il vous plaît*) please

Swaziland [swazilɑ̃d] *nm*: **le ~** Swaziland

sweat [swit] *nm* (*fam*) sweatshirt

sweat-shirt [switʃœʀt] (*pl* **-s**) *nm* sweatshirt

syllabe [silab] *nf* syllable

sylphide [silfid] nf (fig): **sa taille de ~** her sylph-like figure

sylvestre [silvɛstʀ(ə)] adj: **pin ~** Scots pine, Scotch fir

sylvicole [silvikɔl] adj forestry cpd

sylviculteur [silvikyltœʀ] nm forester

sylviculture [silvikyltyʀ] nf forestry, sylviculture

symbole [sɛ̃bɔl] nm symbol

symbolique [sɛ̃bɔlik] adj symbolic; (geste, offrande) token cpd; (salaire, dommages-intérêts) nominal

symboliquement [sɛ̃bɔlikmɑ̃] adv symbolically

symboliser [sɛ̃bɔlize] vt to symbolize

symétrie [simetʀi] nf symmetry

symétrique [simetʀik] adj symmetrical

symétriquement [simetʀikmɑ̃] adv symmetrically

sympa [sɛ̃pa] adj inv (= sympathique) nice; friendly; good

sympathie [sɛ̃pati] nf (inclination) liking; (affinité) fellow feeling; (condoléances) sympathy; **accueillir avec ~** (projet) to receive favourably; **avoir de la ~ pour qn** to like sb, have a liking for sb; **témoignages de ~** expressions of sympathy; **croyez à toute ma ~** you have my deepest sympathy

sympathique [sɛ̃patik] adj (personne, figure) nice, friendly, likeable; (geste) friendly; (livre) good; (déjeuner) nice; (réunion, endroit) pleasant, nice

sympathisant, e [sɛ̃patizɑ̃, -ɑ̃t] nm/f sympathizer

sympathiser [sɛ̃patize] vi (voisins etc: s'entendre) to get on (Brit) ou along (US) (well); (: se fréquenter) to socialize, see each other; **~ avec** to get on ou along (well) with, to see, socialize with

symphonie [sɛ̃fɔni] nf symphony

symphonique [sɛ̃fɔnik] adj (orchestre, concert) symphony cpd; (musique) symphonic

symposium [sɛ̃pozjɔm] nm symposium

symptomatique [sɛ̃ptɔmatik] adj symptomatic

symptôme [sɛ̃ptom] nm symptom

synagogue [sinagɔg] nf synagogue

synchrone [sɛ̃kʀɔn] adj synchronous

synchronique [sɛ̃kʀɔnik] adj: **tableau ~** synchronic table of events

synchronisation [sɛ̃kʀɔnizasjɔ̃] nf synchronization; (Auto): **~ des vitesses** synchromesh

synchronisé, e [sɛ̃kʀɔnize] adj synchronized

synchroniser [sɛ̃kʀɔnize] vt to synchronize

syncope [sɛ̃kɔp] nf (Méd) blackout; (Mus) syncopation; **tomber en ~** to faint, pass out

syncopé, e [sɛ̃kɔpe] adj syncopated

syndic [sɛ̃dik] nm managing agent

syndical, e, -aux [sɛ̃dikal, -o] adj (trade-)union cpd; **centrale ~e** group of affiliated trade unions

syndicalisme [sɛ̃dikalism(ə)] nm (mouvement) trade unionism; (activités) union(ist) activities pl

syndicaliste [sɛ̃dikalist(ə)] nm/f trade unionist

syndicat [sɛ̃dika] nm (d'ouvriers, employés) (trade(s)) union; (autre association d'intérêts) union, association; **~ d'initiative (SI)** tourist office ou bureau; **~ patronal** employers' syndicate, federation of employers; **~ de propriétaires** association of property owners

syndiqué, e [sɛ̃dike] adj belonging to a (trade) union; **non ~** non-union

syndiquer [sɛ̃dike]: **se syndiquer** vi to form a trade union; (adhérer) to join a trade union

syndrome [sɛ̃dʀom] nm syndrome; **~ prémenstruel** premenstrual syndrome (PMS)

synergie [sinɛʀʒi] nf synergy

synode [sinɔd] nm synod

synonyme [sinɔnim] adj synonymous ▷ nm synonym; **~ de** synonymous with

synopsis [sinɔpsis] nm ou nf synopsis

synoptique [sinɔptik] adj: **tableau ~** synoptic table

synovie [sinɔvi] nf synovia; **épanchement de ~** water on the knee

syntaxe [sɛ̃taks(ə)] nf syntax

synthèse [sɛ̃tɛz] nf synthesis; **faire la ~ de** to synthesize

synthétique [sɛ̃tetik] adj synthetic

synthétiser [sɛ̃tetize] vt to synthesize

synthétiseur [sɛ̃tetizœʀ] nm (Mus) synthesizer

syphilis [sifilis] nf syphilis

Syrie [siʀi] nf: **la ~** Syria

syrien, ne [siʀjɛ̃, -ɛn] adj Syrian ▷ nm/f: **Syrien, ne** Syrian

systématique [sistematik] adj systematic

systématiquement [sistematikmɑ̃] adv systematically

systématiser [sistematize] vt to systematize

système [sistɛm] nm system; **le ~ D** resourcefulness; **~ décimal** decimal system; **~ expert** expert system; **~ d'exploitation** (Inform) operating system; **~ immunitaire** immune system; **~ métrique** metric system; **~ solaire** solar system

S

Tt

T, t [te] *nm inv* T, t ▷ *abr* (= *tonne*) t; **T comme Thérèse** T for Tommy

t' [t(ə)] *pron voir* **te**

ta [ta] *adj poss voir* **ton**

tabac [taba] *nm* tobacco; (*aussi:* **débit** *ou* **bureau de tabac**) tobacconist's (shop) ▷ *adj inv:* (**couleur**) **~** buff, tobacco *cpd;* **passer qn à ~** to beat sb up; **faire un ~** (*fam*) to be a big hit; **~ blond/brun** light/dark tobacco; **~ gris** shag; **~ à priser** snuff

tabagie [tabaʒi] *nf* smoke den

tabagisme [tabaʒism(ə)] *nm* nicotine addiction; **~ passif** passive smoking

tabasser [tabase] *vt* to beat up

tabatière [tabatjɛʀ] *nf* snuffbox

tabernacle [tabɛʀnakl(ə)] *nm* tabernacle

table [tabl(ə)] *nf* table; **avoir une bonne ~** to keep a good table; **à ~!** dinner *etc* is ready!; **se mettre à ~** to sit down to eat; (*fig: fam*) to come clean; **mettre** *ou* **dresser/desservir la ~** to lay *ou* set/clear the table; **faire ~ rase de** to make a clean sweep of; **~ basse** coffee table; **~ de cuisson** (*à l'électricité*) hotplate; (*au gaz*) gas ring; **~ d'écoute** wire-tapping set; **~ d'harmonie** sounding board; **~ d'hôte** set menu; **~ de lecture** turntable; **~ des matières** (table of) contents *pl;* **~ de multiplication** multiplication table; **~ des négociations** negotiating table; **~ de nuit** *ou* **de chevet** bedside table; **~ ronde** (*débat*) round table; **~ roulante** (tea) trolley; **~ de toilette** washstand; **~ traçante** (*Inform*) plotter

tableau, x [tablo] *nm* (*Art*) painting; (*reproduction, fig*) picture; (*panneau*) board; (*schéma*) table, chart; **~ d'affichage** notice board; **~ de bord** dashboard; (*Aviat*) instrument panel; **~ de chasse** tally; **~ de contrôle** console, control panel; **~ de maître** masterpiece; **~ noir** blackboard

tablée [table] *nf* (*personnes*) table

tabler [table] *vi:* **~ sur** to count *ou* bank on

tablette [tablɛt] *nf* (*planche*) shelf; **~ de chocolat** bar of chocolate

tableur [tablœʀ] *nm* (*Inform*) spreadsheet

tablier [tablije] *nm* apron; (*de pont*) roadway; (*de cheminée*) (flue-)shutter

tabou, e [tabu] *adj, nm* taboo

tabouret [tabuʀɛ] *nm* stool

tabulateur [tabylatœʀ] *nm* (*Tech*) tabulator

tac [tak] *nm:* **du ~ au ~** tit for tat

tache [taʃ] *nf* (*saleté*) stain, mark; (*Art: de couleur, lumière*) spot; splash, patch; **faire ~ d'huile** to spread, gain ground; **~ de rousseur** *ou* **de son** freckle; **~ de vin** (*sur la peau*) strawberry mark

tâche [taʃ] *nf* task; **travailler à la ~** to do piecework

tacher [taʃe] *vt* to stain, mark; (*fig*) to sully, stain; **se tacher** *vi* (*fruits*) to become marked

tâcher [taʃe] *vi:* **~ de faire** to try to do, endeavour (*Brit*) *ou* endeavor (*US*) to do

tâcheron [taʃʀɔ̃] *nm* (*fig*) drudge

tacheté, e [taʃte] *adj:* **~ de** speckled *ou* spotted with

tachisme [taʃism(ə)] *nm* (*Peinture*) tachisme

tachygraphe [takigʀaf] *nm* tachograph

tachymètre [takimɛtʀ(ə)] *nm* tachometer

tacite [tasit] *adj* tacit

tacitement [tasitmɑ̃] *adv* tacitly

taciturne [tasityʀn(ə)] *adj* taciturn

tacot [tako] *nm* (*péj: voiture*) banger (*Brit*), clunker (*US*)

tact [takt] *nm* tact; **avoir du ~** to be tactful, have tact

tacticien, ne [taktisjɛ̃, -ɛn] *nm/f* tactician

tactile [taktil] *adj* tactile

tactique [taktik] *adj* tactical ▷ *nf* (*technique*) tactics *nsg;* (*plan*) tactic

Tadjikistan [tadʒikistɑ̃] *nm* Tajikistan

taffetas [tafta] *nm* taffeta

Tage [taʒ] *nm:* **le ~** the (river) Tagus

Tahiti [taiti] *nf* Tahiti

tahitien, ne [taisjɛ̃, -ɛn] *adj* Tahitian

taie [tɛ] *nf:* **~ (d'oreiller)** pillowslip, pillowcase

taillader [tɑjade] *vt* to gash

taille [tɑj] *nf* cutting; pruning; (*milieu du corps*) waist; (*hauteur*) height; (*grandeur*) size; **de ~ à faire** capable of doing; **de ~** *adj* sizeable; **quelle ~ faites- vous?** what size are you?

taillé, e [tɑje] *adj* (*moustache, ongles, arbre*) trimmed; **~ pour** (*fait pour, apte à*) cut out for; tailor-made for; **~ en pointe** sharpened to a point

taille-crayon, taille-crayons [tɑjkʀɛjɔ̃] *nm inv* pencil sharpener

tailler [tɑje] *vt* (*pierre, diamant*) to cut; (*arbre, plante*) to prune; (*vêtement*) to cut out; (*crayon*) to sharpen; **se tailler** *vt* (*ongles, barbe*) to trim, cut; (*fig: réputation*) to gain, win ▷ *vi* (*fam: s'enfuir*) to beat it; **~ dans** (*chair, bois*) to cut into; **~ grand/petit** to be on the large/small side

tailleur [tɑjœʀ] *nm* (*couturier*) tailor; (*vêtement*) suit, costume; **en ~** (*assis*) cross-legged; **~ de diamants** diamond-cutter

taillis [tɑji] *nm* copse

tain [tɛ̃] *nm* silvering; **glace sans ~** two-way mirror

taire [tɛʀ] *vt* to keep to o.s., conceal ▷ *vi*: **faire ~ qn** to make sb be quiet; (*fig*) to silence sb; **se taire** *vi* (*s'arrêter de parler*) to fall silent, stop talking; (*ne pas parler*) to be silent *ou* quiet; (*s'abstenir de s'exprimer*) to keep quiet; (*bruit, voix*) to disappear; **tais-toi!**, **taisez-vous!** be quiet!

Taiwan [tajwan] *nf* Taiwan

talc [talk] *nm* talc, talcum powder

talé, e [tale] *adj* (*fruit*) bruised

talent [talɑ̃] *nm* talent; **avoir du ~** to be talented, have talent

talentueux, -euse [talɑ̃tɥø, -øz] *adj* talented

talion [taljɔ̃] *nm*: **la loi du ~** an eye for an eye

talisman [talismɑ̃] *nm* talisman

talkie-walkie [tɔkiwɔki] *nm* walkie-talkie

taloche [talɔʃ] *nf* (*fam: claque*) slap; (*Tech*) plaster float

talon [talɔ̃] *nm* heel; (*de chèque, billet*) stub, counterfoil (Brit); **~s plats/aiguilles** flat/stiletto heels; **être sur les ~s de qn** to be on sb's heels; **tourner les ~s** to turn on one's heel; **montrer les ~s** (*fig*) to show a clean pair of heels

talonner [talɔne] *vt* to follow hard behind; (*fig*) to hound; (*Rugby*) to heel

talonnette [talɔnɛt] *nf* (*de chaussure*) heelpiece; (*de pantalon*) stirrup

talquer [talke] *vt* to put talc(um powder) on

talus [taly] *nm* embankment; **~ de remblai/déblai** embankment/excavation slope

tamarin [tamaʀɛ̃] *nm* (*Bot*) tamarind

tambour [tɑ̃buʀ] *nm* (*Mus, also Tech*) drum; (*musicien*) drummer; (*porte*) revolving door(*s pl*); **sans ~ ni trompette** unobtrusively

tambourin [tɑ̃buʀɛ̃] *nm* tambourine

tambouriner [tɑ̃buʀine] *vi*: **~ contre** to drum against *ou* on

tambour-major [tɑ̃buʀmaʒɔʀ] (*pl* **tambours-majors**) *nm* drum major

tamis [tami] *nm* sieve

Tamise [tamiz] *nf*: **la ~** the Thames

tamisé, e [tamize] *adj* (*fig*) subdued, soft

tamiser [tamize] *vt* to sieve, sift

tampon [tɑ̃pɔ̃] *nm* (*de coton, d'ouate*) pad; (*aussi*: **tampon hygiénique** *ou* **périodique**) tampon; (*amortisseur, Inform: aussi*: **mémoire tampon**) buffer; (*bouchon*) plug, stopper; (*cachet, timbre*) stamp; (*Chimie*) buffer; **~ encreur** inking pad; **~**

(à récurer) scouring pad

tamponné, e [tɑ̃pɔne] *adj*: **solution ~e** buffer solution

tamponner [tɑ̃pɔne] *vt* (*timbres*) to stamp; (*heurter*) to crash *ou* ram into; (*essuyer*) to mop up; **se tamponner** (*voitures*) to crash (into each other)

tamponneuse [tɑ̃pɔnøz] *adj f*: **autos ~s** dodgems, bumper cars

tam-tam [tamtam] *nm* tomtom

tancer [tɑ̃se] *vt* to scold

tanche [tɑ̃ʃ] *nf* tench

tandem [tɑ̃dɛm] *nm* tandem; (*fig*) duo, pair

tandis [tɑ̃di]: **~ que** *conj* while

tangage [tɑ̃gaʒ] *nm* pitching (and tossing)

tangent, e [tɑ̃ʒɑ̃, -ɑ̃t] *adj* (*Math*): **~ à** tangential to; (*fam: de justesse*) close ▷ *nf* (*Math*) tangent

Tanger [tɑ̃ʒe] *n* Tangier

tango [tɑ̃go] *nm* (*Mus*) tango ▷ *adj inv* (*couleur*) dark orange

tanguer [tɑ̃ge] *vi* to pitch (and toss)

tanière [tanjɛʀ] *nf* lair, den

tanin [tanɛ̃] *nm* tannin

tank [tɑ̃k] *nm* tank

tanker [tɑ̃kɛʀ] *nm* tanker

tankini [tɑ̃kini] *nm* tankini

tanné, e [tane] *adj* weather-beaten

tanner [tane] *vt* to tan

tannerie [tanʀi] *nf* tannery

tanneur [tanœʀ] *nm* tanner

tant [tɑ̃] *adv* so much; **~ de** (*sable, eau*) so much; (*gens, livres*) so many; **~ que** *conj* as long as; **~ que** (*comparatif*) as much as; **~ mieux** that's great; so much the better; **~ mieux pour lui** good for him; **~ pis** too bad; **un ~ soit peu** (*un peu*) a little bit; (*même un peu*) (even) remotely; **~ bien que mal** as well as can be expected; **~ s'en faut** far from it, not by a long way

tante [tɑ̃t] *nf* aunt

tantinet [tɑ̃tinɛ]: **un ~** *adv* a tiny bit

tantôt [tɑ̃to] *adv* (*parfois*): **~ ... ~** now ... now; (*cet après-midi*) this afternoon

Tanzanie [tɑ̃zani] *nf*: **la ~** Tanzania

tanzanien, ne [tɑ̃zanjɛ̃, -ɛn] *adj* Tanzanian

TAO *sigle f* (= *traduction assistée par ordinateur*) MAT (= *machine-aided translation*)

taon [tɑ̃] *nm* horsefly, gadfly

tapage [tapaʒ] *nm* uproar, din; (*fig*) fuss, row; **~ nocturne** (*Jur*) disturbance of the peace (*at night*)

tapageur, -euse [tapaʒœʀ, -øz] *adj* (*bruyant: enfants etc*) noisy; (*toilette*) loud, flashy; (*publicité*) obtrusive

tape [tap] *nf* slap

tape-à-l'œil [tapalœj] *adj inv* flashy, showy

taper [tape] *vt* (*personne*) to clout; (*porte*) to bang, slam; (*dactylographier*) to type (out); (*Inform*) to key(board); (*fam: emprunter*): **~ qn de 10 euros** to touch sb for 10 euros, cadge 10 euros off sb ▷ *vi* (*soleil*) to beat down; **se taper** *vt* (*fam: travail*) to get landed with; (: *boire, manger*) to down; **~ sur qn** to thump sb; (*fig*) to run sb down; **~ sur qch**

(*clou etc*) to hit sth; (*table etc*) to bang on sth; ~ **à** (*porte etc*) to knock on; ~ **dans** (*se servir*) to dig into; ~ **des mains/pieds** to clap one's hands/ stamp one's feet; ~ **(à la machine)** to type

tapi, e [tapi] *adj*: ~ **dans/derrière** (*blotti*) crouching *ou* cowering in/behind; (*caché*) hidden away in/behind

tapinois [tapinwa]: **en** ~ *adv* stealthily

tapioca [tapjɔka] *nm* tapioca

tapir [tapiʀ]: **se tapir** *vi* to hide away

tapis [tapi] *nm* carpet; (*de table*) cloth; **mettre sur le** ~ (*fig*) to bring up for discussion; **aller au** ~ (*Boxe*) to go down; **envoyer au** ~ (*Boxe*) to floor; ~ **roulant** conveyor belt; ~ **de sol** (*de tente*) groundsheet; ~ **de souris** (*Inform*) mouse mat

tapis-brosse [tapibʀɔs] *nm* doormat

tapisser [tapise] *vt* (*avec du papier peint*) to paper; (*recouvrir*): ~ **qch (de)** to cover sth (with)

tapisserie [tapisʀi] *nf* (*tenture, broderie*) tapestry; (: *travail*) tapestry-making; (: *ouvrage*) tapestry work; (*papier peint*) wallpaper; (*fig*): **faire** ~ to sit out, be a wallflower

tapissier, -ière [tapisje, -jɛʀ] *nm/f*: ~- **décorateur** upholsterer and decorator

tapoter [tapɔte] *vt* to pat, tap

taquet [takɛ] *nm* (*cale*) wedge; (*cheville*) peg

taquin, e [takɛ̃, -in] *adj* teasing

taquiner [takine] *vt* to tease

taquinerie [takinʀi] *nf* teasing *no pl*

tarabiscoté, e [taʀabiskɔte] *adj* over-ornate, fussy

tarabuster [taʀabyste] *vt* to bother, worry

tarama [taʀama] *nm* (*Culin*) taramasalata

tarauder [taʀode] *vt* (*Tech*) to tap; to thread; (*fig*) to pierce

tard [taʀ] *adv* late; **au plus** ~ at the latest; **plus** ~ later (on) ▷ *nm*: **sur le** ~ (*à une heure avancée*) late in the day; (*vers la fin de la vie*) late in life

tarder [taʀde] *vi* (*chose*) to be a long time coming; (*personne*): ~ **à faire** to delay doing; **il me tarde d'être** I am longing to be; **sans** (**plus**) ~ without (further) delay

tardif, -ive [taʀdif, -iv] *adj* (*heure, repas, fruit*) late; (*talent, goût*) late in developing

tardivement [taʀdivmɑ̃] *adv* late

tare [taʀ] *nf* (*Comm*) tare; (*fig*) defect; blemish

taré, e [taʀe] *nm/f* cretin

targette [taʀʒɛt] *nf* (*verrou*) bolt

targuer [taʀge]: **se** ~ **de** *vt* to boast about

tarif [taʀif] *nm* (*liste*) price list, tariff (Brit); (*barème*) rate, rates *pl*, tariff (Brit); (: *de taxis etc*) fares *pl*; **voyager à plein** ~/**à** ~ **réduit** to travel at full/reduced fare

tarifaire [taʀifɛʀ] *adj* (*voir tarif*) relating to price lists *etc*

tarifé, e [taʀife] *adj*: ~ **10 euros** priced at 10 euros

tarifer [taʀife] *vt* to fix the price *ou* rate for

tarification [taʀifikasjɔ̃] *nf* fixing of a price scale

tarir [taʀiʀ] *vi* to dry up, run dry ▷ *vt* to dry up

tarot [taʀo], **tarots** *nm(pl)* tarot cards

tartare [taʀtaʀ] *adj* (*Culin*) tartar(e)

tarte [taʀt(ə)] *nf* tart; ~ **aux pommes/à la crème** apple/custard tart

tartelette [taʀtəlɛt] *nf* tartlet

tartine [taʀtin] *nf* slice of bread (and butter (*ou* jam)); ~ **de miel** slice of bread and honey; ~ **beurrée** slice of bread and butter

tartiner [taʀtine] *vt* to spread; **fromage à** ~ cheese spread

tartre [taʀtʀ(ə)] *nm* (*des dents*) tartar; (*de chaudière*) fur, scale

tas [ta] *nm* heap, pile; (*fig*): **un** ~ **de** heaps of, lots of; **en** ~ in a heap *ou* pile; **dans le** ~ (*fig*) in the crowd; among them; **formé sur le** ~ trained on the job

Tasmanie [tasmani] *nf*: **la** ~ Tasmania

tasmanien, ne [tasmanjɛ̃, -ɛn] *adj* Tasmanian

tasse [tas] *nf* cup; **boire la** ~ (*en se baignant*) to swallow a mouthful; ~ **à café/thé** coffee/ teacup

tassé, e [tase] *adj*: **bien** ~ (*café etc*) strong

tasseau, x [taso] *nm* length of wood

tassement [tasmɑ̃] *nm* (*de vertèbres*) compression; (*Écon, Pol*: *ralentissement*) fall-off, slowdown; (*Bourse*) dullness

tasser [tase] *vt* (*terre, neige*) to pack down; (*entasser*): ~ **qch dans** to cram sth into; **se tasser** *vi* (*terrain*) to settle; (*personne: avec l'âge*) to shrink; (*fig*) to sort itself out, settle down

tâter [tate] *vt* to feel; (*fig*) to sound out; ~ **de** (*prison etc*) to have a taste of; **se tâter** (*hésiter*) to be in two minds; ~ **le terrain** (*fig*) to test the ground

tatillon, ne [tatijɔ̃, -ɔn] *adj* pernickety

tâtonnement [tatɔnmɑ̃] *nm*: **par** ~**s** (*fig*) by trial and error

tâtonner [tatɔne] *vi* to grope one's way along; (*fig*) to grope around (in the dark)

tâtons [tatɔ̃]: **à** ~ *adv*: **chercher/avancer à** ~ to grope around for/grope one's way forward

tatouage [tatwaʒ] *nm* tattooing; (*dessin*) tattoo

tatouer [tatwe] *vt* to tattoo

taudis [todi] *nm* hovel, slum

taule [tol] *nf* (*fam*) nick (Brit), jail

taupe [top] *nf* mole; (*peau*) moleskin

taupinière [topinjɛʀ] *nf* molehill

taureau, x [tɔʀo] *nm* bull; (*signe*): **le T**~ Taurus, the Bull; **être du T**~ to be Taurus

taurillon [tɔʀijɔ̃] *nm* bull-calf

tauromachie [tɔʀɔmaʃi] *nf* bullfighting

taux [to] *nm* rate; (*d'alcool*) level; ~ **d'escompte** discount rate; ~ **d'intérêt** interest rate; ~ **de mortalité** mortality rate

tavelé, e [tavle] *adj* marked

taverne [tavɛʀn(ə)] *nf* inn, tavern

taxable [taksabl(ə)] *adj* taxable

taxation [taksasjɔ̃] *nf* taxation; (*Tél*) charges *pl*

taxe [taks(ə)] *nf* tax; (*douanière*) duty; **toutes** ~**s comprises (TTC)** inclusive of tax; ~ **de base** (*Tél*) unit charge; ~ **de séjour** tourist tax; ~ **à** *ou* **sur la valeur ajoutée (TVA)** value added tax (VAT)

taxer [takse] *vt* (*personne*) to tax; (*produit*) to put a tax on, tax; **~ qn de qch** (*qualifier*) to call sb sth; (*accuser*) to accuse sb of sth, tax sb with sth

taxi [taksi] *nm* taxi

taxidermie [taksidɛʀmi] *nf* taxidermy

taxidermiste [taksidɛʀmist(ə)] *nm/f* taxidermist

taximètre [taksimɛtʀ(ə)] *nm* (taxi)meter

taxiphone [taksifɔn] *nm* pay phone

TB *abr* = **très bien, très bon**

tbe *abr* (= *très bon état*) VGC, vgc

TCF *sigle m* (= *Touring Club de France*) ≈ AA *ou* RAC (*Brit*), ≈ AAA (*US*)

Tchad [tʃad] *nm*: **le ~** Chad

tchadien, ne [tʃadjɛ̃, -ɛn] *adj* Chad(ian), of *ou* from Chad

tchao [tʃao] *excl* (*fam*) bye(-bye)!

tchécoslovaque [tʃekɔslɔvak] *adj* Czechoslovak(ian) ▷ *nm/f*: **Tchécoslovaque** Czechoslovak(ian)

Tchécoslovaquie [tʃekɔslɔvaki] *nf*: **la ~** Czechoslovakia

tchèque [tʃɛk] *adj* Czech ▷ *nm* (*Ling*) Czech ▷ *nm/f*: **Tchèque** Czech; **la République ~** the Czech Republic

Tchétchénie [tʃetʃeni] *nf*: **la ~** Chechnya

TCS *sigle m* (= *Touring Club de Suisse*) ≈ AA *ou* RAC (*Brit*), ≈ AAA (*US*)

TD *sigle mpl* = **travaux dirigés**

te, t' [t(ə)] *pron* you; (*réfléchi*) yourself

té [te] *nm* T-square

technicien, ne [tɛknisjɛ̃, -ɛn] *nm/f* technician

technicité [tɛknisite] *nf* technical nature

technico-commercial, e, -aux [tɛknikokɔmɛʀsjal, -o] *adj*: **agent ~** sales technician

technique [tɛknik] *adj* technical ▷ *nf* technique

techniquement [tɛknikmɑ̃] *adv* technically

techno [tɛkno] *nf* (*fam*: *Mus*): **la (musique) ~** techno (music); (*fam*) = **technologie**

technocrate [tɛknɔkrat] *nm/f* technocrat

technocratie [tɛknɔkrasi] *nf* technocracy

technologie [tɛknɔlɔʒi] *nf* technology

technologique [tɛknɔlɔʒik] *adj* technological

technologue [tɛknɔlɔg] *nm/f* technologist

teck [tɛk] *nm* teak

teckel [tekɛl] *nm* dachshund

tee-shirt [tiʃœrt] *nm* T-shirt, tee-shirt

Téhéran [teeʀɑ̃] *n* Teheran

teigne [tɛɲ] *vb voir* **teindre** ▷ *nf* (*Zool*) moth; (*Méd*) ringworm

teigneux, -euse [tɛɲø, -øz] *adj* (*péj*) nasty, scabby

teindre [tɛ̃dʀ(ə)] *vt* to dye; **se ~ (les cheveux)** to dye one's hair

teint, e [tɛ̃, tɛ̃t] *pp de* **teindre** ▷ *adj* dyed ▷ *nm* (*du visage: permanent*) complexion, colouring (*Brit*), coloring (*US*); (*momentané*) colour (*Brit*), color (*US*) ▷ *nf* shade, colour, color; (*fig: petite dose*): **une ~e de** a hint of; **grand ~** *adj inv* colourfast; **bon ~** *adj inv* (*couleur*) fast; (*tissu*) colourfast; (*personne*) staunch, firm

teinté, e [tɛ̃te] *adj* (*verres*) tinted; (*bois*) stained; **~ acajou** mahogany-stained; **~ de** (*fig*) tinged with

teinter [tɛ̃te] *vt* to tint; (*bois*) to stain; (*fig: d'ironie etc*) to tinge

teinture [tɛ̃tyʀ] *nf* dyeing; (*substance*) dye; (*Méd*): **~ d'iode** tincture of iodine

teinturerie [tɛ̃tyʀʀi] *nf* dry cleaner's

teinturier, -ière [tɛ̃tyʀje, -jɛʀ] *nm/f* dry cleaner

tel, telle [tɛl] *adj* (*pareil*) such; (*indéfini*) such-and-such a, a given; (*comme*): **~ un/des ...** like a/like ...; (*intensif*): **un ~/de ~s ...** such (a)/such ...; **rien de ~** nothing like it, no such thing; **~ que** *conj* like, such as; **~ quel** as it is *ou* stands (*ou* was *etc*)

tél. *abr* = **téléphone**

Tel Aviv [tɛlaviv] *n* Tel Aviv

télé [tele] *nf* (*télévision*) TV, telly (*Brit*); **à la ~** on TV *ou* telly

télébenne [teleben] *nm, nf* telecabine, gondola

télécabine [telekabin] *nm, nf* telecabine, gondola

télécarte [telekart(ə)] *nf* phonecard

téléchargeable [teleʃaʀʒabl] *adj* downloadable

téléchargement [teleʃaʀʒemɑ̃] *nm* (*action*) downloading; (*fichier*) download

télécharger [teleʃaʀʒe] *vt* (*Inform*) to download

TELECOM [telekɔm] *abr* (= *Télécommunications*) ≈ Telecom.

télécommande [telekɔmɑ̃d] *nf* remote control

télécommander [telekɔmɑ̃de] *vt* to operate by remote control, radio-control

télécommunications [telekɔmynikɑsjɔ̃] *nfpl* telecommunications

télécopie [telekɔpi] *nf* fax, telefax

télécopieur [telekɔpjœʀ] *nm* fax (machine)

télédétection [teledetɛksjɔ̃] *nf* remote sensing

télédiffuser [teledifyze] *vt* to broadcast (on television)

télédiffusion [teledifyzjɔ̃] *nf* television broadcasting

télédistribution [teledistʀibysjɔ̃] *nf* cable TV

téléenseignement [teleɑ̃sɛɲmɑ̃] *nm* distance teaching (*ou* learning)

téléférique [teleferik] *nm* = **téléphérique**

téléfilm [telefilm] *nm* film made for TV, TV film

télégramme [telegram] *nm* telegram

télégraphe [telegraf] *nm* telegraph

télégraphie [telegrafi] *nf* telegraphy

télégraphier [telegrafje] *vt* to telegraph, cable

télégraphique [telegrafik] *adj* telegraph *cpd*, telegraphic; (*fig*) telegraphic

télégraphiste [telegrafist(ə)] *nm/f* telegraphist

téléguider [telegide] *vt* to operate by remote control, radio-control

téléinformatique [teleɛ̃fɔʀmatik] *nf* remote access computing

téléjournal, -aux [teleʒurnal, -o] *nm* television news magazine programme

télématique [telematik] *nf* telematics *nsg* ▷ *adj* telematic

téléobjectif [teleɔbʒɛktif] *nm* telephoto lens *nsg*

t

téléopérateur, trice [teleɔpeʀatœʀ, tʀis] *nm/f* call-centre operator

télépathie [telepati] *nf* telepathy

téléphérique [telefeʀik] *nm* cable-car

téléphone [telefɔn] *nm* telephone; **avoir le** ~ to be on the (tele)phone; **au** ~ on the phone; ~ **arabe** bush telegraph; ~ **à carte** cardphone; ~ **avec appareil photo** cameraphone; ~ **mobile** *ou* **portable** mobile (phone) (*Brit*), cell (phone) (*US*); ~ **rouge** hotline; ~ **sans fil** cordless (tele)phone

téléphoner [telefɔne] *vt* to telephone ▷ *vi* to telephone; to make a phone call; ~ **à** to phone up, ring up, call up

téléphonie [telefɔni] *nf* telephony

téléphonique [telefɔnik] *adj* telephone *cpd*, phone *cpd*; **cabine** ~ call box (*Brit*), (tele)phone box (*Brit*) *ou* booth; **conversation/appel** ~ (tele)phone conversation/call

téléphoniste [telefɔnist(ə)] *nm/f* telephonist, telephone operator; (*d'entreprise*) switchboard operator

téléport [telepɔʀ] *nm* teleport

téléprospection [teleprɔspɛksjɔ̃] *nf* telesales

téléréalité [teleʀealite] *nf* reality TV

télescopage [telɛskɔpaʒ] *nm* crash

télescope [telɛskɔp] *nm* telescope

télescoper [telɛskɔpe] *vt* to smash up; **se télescoper** (*véhicules*) to collide, crash into each other

télescopique [telɛskɔpik] *adj* telescopic

téléscripteur [teleskʀiptœʀ] *nm* teleprinter

télésiège [telesjɛʒ] *nm* chairlift

téléski [teleski] *nm* ski-tow; ~ **à archets** T-bar tow; ~ **à perche** button lift

téléspectateur, -trice [telespɛktatœʀ, -tʀis] *nm/f* (television) viewer

télétexte® [teletɛkst] *nm* Teletext®

téléthon [teletɔ̃] *nm* telethon

télétransmission [teletʀɑ̃smisjɔ̃] *nf* remote transmission

télétype [teletip] *nm* teleprinter

télévente [televɑ̃t] *nf* telesales

téléviser [televize] *vt* to televise

téléviseur [televizœʀ] *nm* television set

télévision [televizjɔ̃] *nf* television; **(poste de)** ~ television (set); **avoir la** ~ to have a television; **à la** ~ on television; ~ **par câble/satellite** cable/satellite television

télex [telɛks] *nm* telex

télexer [telɛkse] *vt* to telex

télexiste [telɛksist(ə)] *nm/f* telex operator

telle [tɛl] *adj f voir* **tel**

tellement [tɛlmɑ̃] *adv* (*tant*) so much; (*si*) so; ~ **plus grand (que)** so much bigger (than); ~ **de** (*sable, eau*) so much; (*gens, livres*) so many; **il s'est endormi** ~ **il était fatigué** he was so tired (that) he fell asleep; **pas** ~ not really; **pas** ~ **fort/lentement** not (all) that strong/slowly; **il ne mange pas** ~ he doesn't eat (all that) much

tellurique [telyʀik] *adj:* **secousse** ~ earth tremor

téméraire [temeʀɛʀ] *adj* reckless, rash

témérité [temeʀite] *nf* recklessness, rashness

témoignage [temwaɲaʒ] *nm* (*Jur: déclaration*) testimony *no pl*, evidence *no pl*; (*: faits*) evidence *no pl*; (*gén: rapport, récit*) account; (*fig: d'affection etc*) token, mark; expression

témoigner [temwaɲe] *vt* (*manifester: intérêt, gratitude*) to show ▷ *vi* (*Jur*) to testify, give evidence; ~ **que** to testify that; (*fig: démontrer*) to reveal that, testify to the fact that; ~ **de** *vt* (*confirmer*) to bear witness to, testify to

témoin [temwɛ̃] *nm* witness; (*fig*) testimony; (*Sport*) baton; (*Constr*) telltale ▷ *adj* control *cpd*, test *cpd*; ~ **le fait que ...** (as) witness the fact that ...; **appartement-**~ show flat (*Brit*), model apartment (*US*); **être** ~ **de** (*voir*) to witness; **prendre à** ~ to call to witness; ~ **à charge** witness for the prosecution; ~ **de connexion** (*Inform*) cookie; **T-** **de Jehovah** Jehovah's Witness; ~ **de moralité** character reference; ~ **oculaire** eyewitness

tempe [tɑ̃p] *nf* (*Anat*) temple

tempérament [tɑ̃peʀamɑ̃] *nm* temperament, disposition; (*santé*) constitution; **à** ~ (*vente*) on deferred (payment) terms; (*achat*) by instalments, hire purchase *cpd*; **avoir du** ~ to be hot-blooded

tempérance [tɑ̃peʀɑ̃s] *nf* temperance; **société de** ~ temperance society

tempérant, e [tɑ̃peʀɑ̃, -ɑ̃t] *adj* temperate

température [tɑ̃peʀatyʀ] *nf* temperature; **prendre la** ~ **de** to take the temperature of; (*fig*) to gauge the feeling of; **avoir** *ou* **faire de la** ~ to be running *ou* have a temperature

tempéré, e [tɑ̃peʀe] *adj* temperate

tempérer [tɑ̃peʀe] *vt* to temper

tempête [tɑ̃pɛt] *nf* storm; ~ **de sable/neige** sand/snowstorm; **vent de** ~ gale

tempêter [tɑ̃pete] *vi* to rant and rave

temple [tɑ̃pl(ə)] *nm* temple; (*protestant*) church

tempo [tɛmpo] *nm* tempo

temporaire [tɑ̃pɔʀɛʀ] *adj* temporary

temporairement [tɑ̃pɔʀɛʀmɑ̃] *adv* temporarily

temporel, le [tɑ̃pɔʀɛl] *adj* temporal

temporisateur, -trice [tɑ̃pɔʀizatœʀ, -tʀis] *adj* temporizing, delaying

temporisation [tɑ̃pɔʀizasjɔ̃] *nf* temporizing, playing for time

temporiser [tɑ̃pɔʀize] *vi* to temporize, play for time

temps [tɑ̃] *nm* (*atmosphérique*) weather; (*durée*) time; (*époque*) time, times *pl*; (*Ling*) tense; (*Mus*) beat; (*Tech*) stroke; **les** ~ **changent/sont durs** times are changing/hard; **il fait beau/mauvais** ~ the weather is fine/bad; **avoir le** ~/ **tout le** ~/**juste le** ~ to have time/plenty of time/ just enough time; **avoir fait son** ~ (*fig*) to have had its (*ou* his *etc*) day; **en** ~ **de paix/guerre** in peacetime/wartime; **en** ~ **utile** *ou* **voulu** in due time *ou* course; **de** ~ **en** ~, **de** ~ **à autre** from time to time, now and again; **en même** ~ at the same time; **à** ~ (*partir, arriver*) in time; **à plein/ mi-**~ *adv, adj* full-/part-time; **à** ~ **partiel** *adv, adj* part-time; **dans le ~** at one time; **de tout ~** always; **du ~ que** at the time when, in the days when; **dans le** *ou* **du** *ou* **au ~ où** at the time when; **pendant ce ~** in the meantime; **~ d'accès** (*Inform*) access time; **~ d'arrêt** pause, halt; **~ mort** (*Sport*) stoppage (time); (*Comm*) slack period; **~ partagé** (*Inform*) time-sharing; **~ réel** (*Inform*) real time

tenable [tənabl(ə)] *adj* bearable

tenace [tənas] *adj* tenacious, persistent

ténacité [tenasite] *nf* tenacity, persistence

tenailler [tənaje] *vt* (*fig*) to torment, torture

tenailles [tənaj] *nfpl* pincers

tenais *etc* [t(ə)nɛ] *vb voir* **tenir**

tenancier, -ière [tənɑ̃sje, -jɛʀ] *nm/f* (*d'hôtel, de bistro*) manager (manageress)

tenant, e [tənɑ̃, -ɑ̃t] *adj f voir* **séance** ▷ *nm/f* (*Sport*): **~ du titre** title-holder ▷ *nm*: **d'un seul ~** in one piece; **les ~s et les aboutissants** (*fig*) the ins and outs

tendance [tɑ̃dɑ̃s] *nf* (*opinions*) leanings *pl*, sympathies *pl*; (*inclination*) tendency; (*évolution*) trend; **~ à la hausse/baisse** upward/downward trend; **avoir ~ à** to have a tendency to, tend to

tendancieux, -euse [tɑ̃dɑ̃sjø, -øz] *adj* tendentious

tendeur [tɑ̃dœʀ] *nm* (*de vélo*) chain-adjuster; (*de câble*) wire-strainer; (*de tente*) runner; (*attache*) elastic strap

tendinite [tɑ̃dinit] *nf* tendinitis, tendonitis

tendon [tɑ̃dɔ̃] *nm* tendon, sinew; **~ d'Achille** Achilles' tendon

tendre [tɑ̃dʀ(ə)] *adj* (*viande, légumes*) tender; (*bois, roche, couleur*) soft; (*affectueux*) tender, loving ▷ *vt* (*élastique, peau*) to stretch, draw tight; (*muscle*) to tense; (*donner*): **~ qch à qn** to hold sth out to sb; to offer sb sth; (*fig: piège*) to set, lay; (*tapisserie*): **tendu de soie** hung with silk, with silk hangings; **se tendre** *vi* (*corde*) to tighten; (*relations*) to become strained; **~ à qch/à faire** to tend towards sth/to do; **~ l'oreille** to prick up one's ears; **~ la main/le bras** to hold out one's hand/stretch out one's arm; **~ la perche à qn** (*fig*) to throw sb a line

tendrement [tɑ̃dʀəmɑ̃] *adv* tenderly, lovingly

tendresse [tɑ̃dʀɛs] *nf* tenderness; **tendresses** *nfpl* (*caresses etc*) tenderness *no pl*, caresses

tendu, e [tɑ̃dy] *pp de* **tendre** ▷ *adj* tight; tensed; strained

ténèbres [tenɛbʀ(ə)] *nfpl* darkness *nsg*

ténébreux, -euse [tenebʀø, -øz] *adj* obscure, mysterious; (*personne*) saturnine

Ténérife [tenerif] *nf* Tenerife

teneur [tənœʀ] *nf* content, substance; (*d'une lettre*) terms *pl*, content; **~ en cuivre** copper content

ténia [tenja] *nm* tapeworm

tenir [təniʀ] *vt* to hold; (*magasin, hôtel*) to run; (*promesse*) to keep ▷ *vi* to hold; (*neige, gel*) to last; (*survivre*) to survive; **se tenir** *vi* (*avoir lieu*) to be held, take place; (*être: personne*) to stand; **se ~ droit** to stand up (*ou* sit up) straight; **bien se ~**

to behave well; **se ~ à qch** to hold on to sth; **s'en ~ à qch** to confine o.s. to sth; to stick to sth; **~ à** *vt* to be attached to, care about (*ou* for); (*avoir pour cause*) to be due to, stem from; **~ à faire** to want to do, be keen to do; **~ à ce que qn fasse qch** to be anxious that sb should do sth; **~ de** *vt* to partake of; (*ressembler à*) to take after; **ça ne tient qu'à lui** it is entirely up to him; **~ qn pour** to take sb for; **~ qch de qn** (*histoire*) to have heard *ou* learnt sth from sb; (*qualité, défaut*) to have inherited *ou* got sth from sb; **~ les comptes** to keep the books; **~ un rôle** to play a part; **~ de la place** to take up space *ou* room; **~ l'alcool** to be able to hold a drink; **~ le coup** to hold out; **~ bon** to stand *ou* hold fast; **~ trois jours/deux mois** (*résister*) to hold out *ou* last three days/two months; **~ au chaud/à l'abri** to keep hot/under shelter *ou* cover; **~ prêt** to have ready; **~ sa langue** (*fig*) to hold one's tongue; **tiens** (*ou* **tenez**), **voilà le stylo** there's the pen!; **tiens, Alain!** look, here's Alain!; **tiens?** (*surprise*) really?; **tiens-toi bien!** (*pour informer*) brace yourself!, take a deep breath!

tennis [tenis] *nm* tennis; (*aussi:* **court de tennis**) tennis court ▷ *nmpl ou fpl* (*aussi:* **chaussures de tennis**) tennis *ou* gym shoes; **~ de table** table tennis

tennisman [tenisman] *nm* tennis player

ténor [tenɔʀ] *nm* tenor

tension [tɑ̃sjɔ̃] *nf* tension; (*fig: des relations, de la situation*) tension; (*: concentration, effort*) strain; (*Méd*) blood pressure; **faire** *ou* **avoir de la ~** to have high blood pressure; **~ nerveuse/raciale** nervous/racial tension

tentaculaire [tɑ̃takylɛʀ] *adj* (*fig*) sprawling

tentacule [tɑ̃takyl] *nm* tentacle

tentant, e [tɑ̃tɑ̃, -ɑ̃t] *adj* tempting

tentateur, -trice [tɑ̃tatœʀ, -tʀis] *adj* tempting ▷ *nm* (*Rel*) tempter

tentation [tɑ̃tasjɔ̃] *nf* temptation

tentative [tɑ̃tativ] *nf* attempt, bid; **~ d'évasion** escape bid; **~ de suicide** suicide attempt

tente [tɑ̃t] *nf* tent; **~ à oxygène** oxygen tent

tenter [tɑ̃te] *vt* (*éprouver, attirer*) to tempt; (*essayer*): **~ qch/de faire** to attempt *ou* try sth/to do; **être tenté de** to be tempted to; **~ sa chance** to try one's luck

tenture [tɑ̃tyʀ] *nf* hanging

tenu, e [təny] *pp de* **tenir** ▷ *adj* (*maison, comptes*): **bien ~** well-kept; (*obligé*): **~ de faire** under an obligation to do ▷ *nf* (*action de tenir*) running; keeping; holding; (*vêtements*) clothes *pl*, gear; (*allure*) dress *no pl*, appearance; (*comportement*) manners *pl*, behaviour (*Brit*), behavior (*US*); **être en ~e** to be dressed (up); **se mettre en ~e** to dress (up); **en grande ~e** in full dress; **en petite ~e** scantily dressed *ou* clad; **avoir de la ~e** to have good manners; (*journal*) to have a high standard; **~e de combat** combat gear *ou* dress; **~e de pompier** fireman's uniform; **~e de route** (*Auto*) road-holding; **~e de soirée** evening dress; **~e de sport/voyage** sports/

t

409

travelling clothes *pl ou* gear *no pl*

ténu, e [teny] *adj* (*indice, nuance*) tenuous, subtle; (*fil, objet*) fine; (*voix*) thin

TER *abr m* (= *Train Régional Express*) local train

ter [tɛʀ] *adj*: **16** ≈ 16b *ou* B

térébenthine [teʀebɑ̃tin] *nf*: (**essence de**) ~ (oil of) turpentine

tergal® [tɛʀgal] *nm* Terylene®

tergiversations [tɛʀʒivɛʀsasjɔ̃] *nfpl* shilly-shallying *no pl*

tergiverser [tɛʀʒivɛʀse] *vi* to shilly-shally

terme [tɛʀm(ə)] *nm* term; (*fin*) end; **être en bons/mauvais ~s avec qn** to be on good/bad terms with sb; **vente/achat à** ~ (*Comm*) forward sale/purchase; **au ~ de** at the end of; **en d'autres ~s** in other words; **moyen** ~ (*solution intermédiaire*) middle course; **à court/long** ~ *adj* short-/long-term *ou* -range ▷ *adv* in the short/long term; **à** ~ *adj* (*Méd*) full-term ▷ *adv* sooner or later, eventually; (*Méd*) at term; **avant** ~ (*Méd*) ▷ *adj* premature ▷ *adv* prematurely; **mettre un** ~ **à** to put an end *ou* a stop to; **toucher à son** ~ to be nearing its end

terminaison [tɛʀminɛzɔ̃] *nf* (*Ling*) ending

terminal, e, -aux [tɛʀminal, -o] *adj* (*partie, phase*) final; (*Méd*) terminal ▷ *nm* terminal ▷ *nf* (*Scol*) ≈ sixth form *ou* year (*Brit*), ≈ twelfth grade (*US*)

terminer [tɛʀmine] *vt* to end; (*travail, repas*) to finish; **se terminer** *vi* to end; **se** ~ **par** to end with

terminologie [tɛʀminɔlɔʒi] *nf* terminology

terminus [tɛʀminys] *nm* terminus; ~! all change!

termite [tɛʀmit] *nm* termite, white ant

termitière [tɛʀmitjɛʀ] *nf* ant-hill

ternaire [tɛʀnɛʀ] *adj* compound

terne [tɛʀn(ə)] *adj* dull

ternir [tɛʀniʀ] *vt* to dull; (*fig*) to sully, tarnish; **se ternir** *vi* to become dull

terrain [tɛʀɛ̃] *nm* (*sol, fig*) ground; (*Comm*) land *no pl*, plot (of land); (: *à bâtir*) site; **sur le** ~ (*fig*) on the field; ~ **de football/rugby** football/rugby pitch (*Brit*) *ou* field (*US*); ~ **d'atterrissage** landing strip; ~ **d'aviation** airfield; ~ **de camping** campsite; **un** ~ **d'entente** an area of agreement; ~ **de golf** golf course; ~ **de jeu** playground; (*Sport*) games field; ~ **de sport** sports ground; ~ **vague** waste ground *no pl*

terrasse [tɛʀas] *nf* terrace; (*de café*) pavement area, terrasse; **à la** ~ (*café*) outside

terrassement [tɛʀasmɑ̃] *nm* earth-moving, earthworks *pl*; embankment

terrasser [tɛʀase] *vt* (*adversaire*) to floor, bring down; (*maladie etc*) to lay low

terrassier [tɛʀasje] *nm* navvy, roadworker

terre [tɛʀ] *nf* (*gén, aussi Élec*) earth; (*substance*) soil, earth; (*opposé à mer*) land *no pl*; (*contrée*) land; **terres** *nfpl* (*terrains*) lands, land *nsg*; **travail de la** ~ work on the land; **en** ~ (*pipe, poterie*) clay *cpd*; **mettre en** ~ (*plante etc*) to plant; (*personne: enterrer*) to bury; **à** *ou* **par** ~ (*mettre, être*) on the ground (*ou* floor); (*jeter, tomber*) to the ground,

down; ~ **à** ~ *adj inv* down-to-earth, matter-of-fact; **la T~ Adélie** Adélie Coast *ou* Land; ~ **de bruyère** (heath-)peat; ~ **cuite** earthenware; terracotta; **la** ~ **ferme** dry land, terra firma; **la T~ de Feu** Tierra del Fuego; ~ **glaise** clay; **la T~ promise** the Promised Land; **la T~ Sainte** the Holy Land

terreau [tɛʀo] *nm* compost

Terre-Neuve [tɛʀnœv] *nf*: **la** ~ (*aussi*: **l'île de Terre-Neuve**) Newfoundland

terre-plein [tɛʀplɛ̃] *nm* platform

terrer [tɛʀe]: **se terrer** *vi* to hide away; to go to ground

terrestre [tɛʀɛstʀ(ə)] *adj* (*surface*) earth's, of the earth; (*Bot, Zool, Mil*) land *cpd*; (*Rel*) earthly, worldly

terreur [tɛʀœʀ] *nf* terror *no pl*, fear

terreux, -euse [tɛʀø, -øz] *adj* muddy; (*goût*) earthy

terrible [tɛʀibl(ə)] *adj* terrible, dreadful; (*fam: fantastique*) terrific

terriblement [tɛʀibləmɑ̃] *adv* (*très*) terribly, awfully

terrien, ne [tɛʀjɛ̃, -ɛn] *adj*: **propriétaire** ~ landowner ▷ *nm/f* countryman/woman, man/woman of the soil; (*non martien etc*) earthling; (*non marin*) landsman

terrier [tɛʀje] *nm* burrow, hole; (*chien*) terrier

terrifiant, e [tɛʀifjɑ̃, -ɑ̃t] *adj* (*effrayant*) terrifying; (*extraordinaire*) terrible, awful

terrifier [tɛʀifje] *vt* to terrify

terril [tɛʀil] *nm* slag heap

terrine [tɛʀin] *nf* (*récipient*) terrine; (*Culin*) pâté

territoire [tɛʀitwaʀ] *nm* territory; **T~ des Afars et des Issas** French Territory of Afars and Issas

territorial, e, -aux [tɛʀitɔʀjal, -o] *adj* territorial; **eaux ~es** territorial waters; **armée ~e** regional defence force, ≈ Territorial Army (*Brit*); **collectivités ~es** local and regional authorities

terroir [tɛʀwaʀ] *nm* (*Agr*) soil; (*région*) region; **accent du** ~ country *ou* rural accent

terroriser [tɛʀɔʀize] *vt* to terrorize

terrorisme [tɛʀɔʀism(ə)] *nm* terrorism

terroriste [tɛʀɔʀist(ə)] *nm/f* terrorist

tertiaire [tɛʀsjɛʀ] *adj* tertiary ▷ *nm* (*Écon*) tertiary sector, service industries *pl*

tertiarisation [tɛʀsjaʀizasjɔ̃] *nf* expansion or development of the service sector

tertre [tɛʀtʀ(ə)] *nm* hillock, mound

tes [te] *adj poss voir* **ton**

tesson [tesɔ̃] *nm*: ~ **de bouteille** piece of broken bottle

test [tɛst] *nm* test; ~ **de grossesse** pregnancy test

testament [tɛstamɑ̃] *nm* (*Jur*) will; (*fig*) legacy; (*Rel*): **T~ Testament**; **faire son** ~ to make one's will

testamentaire [tɛstamɑ̃tɛʀ] *adj* of a will

tester [tɛste] *vt* to test

testicule [tɛstikyl] *nm* testicle

tétanie [tetani] *nf* tetany

tétanos [tetanos] *nm* tetanus

têtard [tɛtaʀ] *nm* tadpole

tête [tɛt] *nf* head; (*cheveux*) hair *no pl*; (*visage*) face; (*longueur*) **gagner d'une (courte) ~** to win by a (short) head; (*Football*) header; **de ~** *adj* (*wagon etc*) front *cpd*; (*concurrent*) leading ▷ *adv* (*calculer*) in one's head, mentally; **par ~** (*par personne*) per head; **se mettre en ~ que** to get it into one's head that; **se mettre en ~ de faire** to take it into one's head to do; **prendre la ~ de qch** to take the lead in sth; **perdre la ~** (*fig: s'affoler*) to lose one's head; (: *devenir fou*) to go off one's head; **ça ne va pas, la ~?** (*fam*) are you crazy?; **tenir ~ à qn** to stand up to *ou* defy sb; **la ~ en bas** with one's head down; **la ~ la première** (*tomber*) head-first; **la ~ basse** hanging one's head; **avoir la ~ dure** (*fig*) to be thickheaded; **faire une ~** (*Football*) to head the ball; **faire la ~** (*fig*) to sulk; **en ~** (*Sport*) in the lead; at the front *ou* head; **de la ~ aux pieds** from head to toe; **~ d'affiche** (*Théât etc*) top of the bill; **~ de bétail** head *inv* of cattle; **~ brûlée** desperado; **~ chercheuse** homing device; **~ d'enregistrement** recording head; **~ d'impression** printhead; **~ de lecture** (playback) head; **~ de ligne** (*Transports*) start of the line; **~ de liste** (*Pol*) chief candidate; **~ de mort** skull and crossbones; **~ de pont** (*Mil*) bridge- *ou* beachhead; **~ de série** (*Tennis*) seeded player, seed; **~ de Turc** (*fig*) whipping boy (*Brit*), butt; **~ de veau** (*Culin*) calf's head

tête-à-queue [tɛtakø] *nm inv*: **faire un ~** to spin round

tête-à-tête [tɛtatɛt] *nm inv* tête-à-tête; (*service*) breakfast set for two; **en ~** in private, alone together

tête-bêche [tɛtbɛʃ] *adv* head to tail

tétée [tete] *nf* (*action*) sucking; (*repas*) feed

téter [tete] *vt*: **~ (sa mère)** to suck at one's mother's breast, feed

tétine [tetin] *nf* teat; (*sucette*) dummy (*Brit*), pacifier (*US*)

téton [tetɔ̃] *nm* breast

têtu, e [tety] *adj* stubborn, pigheaded

texte [tɛkst(ə)] *nm* text; (*Scol: d'un devoir*) subject, topic; **apprendre son ~** (*Théât*) to learn one's lines; **un ~ de loi** the wording of a law

textile [tɛkstil] *adj* textile *cpd* ▷ *nm* textile; (*industrie*) textile industry

Texto® [tɛksto] *nm* text (message)

texto [tɛksto] (*fam*) *adj* word for word

textuel, le [tɛkstɥɛl] *adj* literal, word for word

textuellement [tɛkstɥɛlmɑ̃] *adv* literally

texture [tɛkstyʀ] *nf* texture; (*fig: d'un texte, livre*) feel

TF1 *sigle f* (= *Télévision française 1*) TV channel

TG *sigle f* = **Trésorerie générale**

TGI *sigle m* = **tribunal de grande instance**

TGV *sigle m* = **train à grande vitesse**

thaï, e [taj] *adj* Thai ▷ *nm* (*Ling*) Thai

thaïlandais, e [tailɑ̃dɛ, -ɛz] *adj* Thai

Thaïlande [tailɑ̃d] *nf*: **la ~** Thailand

thalassothérapie [talasɔteʀapi] *nf* sea-water therapy

thé [te] *nm* tea; (*réunion*) tea party; **prendre le ~** to have tea; **~ au lait/citron** tea with milk/lemon

théâtral, e, -aux [teatʀal, -o] *adj* theatrical

théâtre [teatʀ(ə)] *nm* theatre; (*techniques, genre*) drama, theatre; (*activité*) stage, theatre; (*œuvres*) plays *pl*, dramatic works *pl*; (*fig: lieu*): **le ~ de** the scene of; (*péj*) histrionics *pl*, playacting; **faire du ~** (*en professionnel*) to be on the stage; (*en amateur*) to do some acting; **~ filmé** filmed stage productions *pl*

thébain, e [tebɛ̃, -ɛn] *adj* Theban

Thèbes [tɛb] *n* Thebes

théière [tejɛʀ] *nf* teapot

théine [tein] *nf* theine

théisme [teism(ə)] *nm* theism

thématique [tematik] *adj* thematic

thème [tɛm] *nm* theme; (*Scol: traduction*) prose (composition); **~ astral** birth chart

théocratie [teɔkʀasi] *nf* theocracy

théologie [teɔlɔʒi] *nf* theology

théologien, ne [teɔlɔʒjɛ̃, -ɛn] *nm* theologian

théologique [teɔlɔʒik] *adj* theological

théorème [teɔʀɛm] *nm* theorem

théoricien, ne [teɔʀisjɛ̃, -ɛn] *nm/f* theoretician, theorist

théorie [teɔʀi] *nf* theory; **en ~** in theory

théorique [teɔʀik] *adj* theoretical

théoriquement [teɔʀikmɑ̃] *adv* theoretically

théoriser [teɔʀize] *vi* to theorize

thérapeutique [teʀapøtik] *adj* therapeutic ▷ *nf* (*Méd: branche*) therapeutics *nsg*; (: *traitement*) therapy

thérapie [teʀapi] *nf* therapy; **~ de groupe** group therapy

thermal, e, -aux [tɛʀmal, -o] *adj* thermal; **station ~e** spa; **cure ~e** water cure

thermes [tɛʀm(ə)] *nmpl* thermal baths; (*romains*) thermae *pl*

thermique [tɛʀmik] *adj* (*énergie*) thermic; (*unité*) thermal

thermodynamique [tɛʀmɔdinamik] *nf* thermodynamics *nsg*

thermoélectrique [tɛʀmoelɛktʀik] *adj* thermoelectric

thermomètre [tɛʀmɔmɛtʀ(ə)] *nm* thermometer

thermonucléaire [tɛʀmɔnykleɛʀ] *adj* thermonuclear

thermos® [tɛʀmos] *nm ou nf*: **(bouteille) thermos** vacuum *ou* Thermos® flask (*Brit*) *ou* bottle (*US*)

thermostat [tɛʀmɔsta] *nm* thermostat

thésauriser [tezɔʀize] *vi* to hoard money

thèse [tɛz] *nf* thesis

Thessalie [tesali] *nf*: **la ~** Thessaly

thibaude [tibod] *nf* carpet underlay

thon [tɔ̃] *nm* tuna (fish)

thonier [tɔnje] *nm* tuna boat

thoracique [tɔʀasik] *adj* thoracic

t

thorax [tɔRaks] nm thorax
thrombose [tRɔ̃boz] nf thrombosis
thym [tɛ̃] nm thyme
thyroïde [tiRɔid] nf thyroid (gland)
TI sigle m = **tribunal d'instance**
tiare [tjaR] nf tiara
Tibet [tibɛ] nm: **le ~** Tibet
tibétain, e [tibetɛ̃, -ɛn] adj Tibetan
tibia [tibja] nm shin; (os) shinbone, tibia
Tibre [tibR(ə)] nm: **le ~** the Tiber
TIC sigle fpl (= technologies de l'information et de la
  communication) ICT sg
tic [tik] nm tic, (nervous) twitch; (de langage etc)
  mannerism
ticket [tikɛ] nm ticket; **~ de caisse** till receipt; **~**
  modérateur patient's contribution towards medical
  costs; **~ de quai** platform ticket; **~ repas**
  luncheon voucher
tic-tac [tiktak] nm inv tick-tock
tictaquer [tiktake] vi to tick (away)
tiède [tjɛd] adj (bière etc) lukewarm; (thé, café etc)
  tepid; (bain, accueil, sentiment) lukewarm; (vent,
  air) mild, warm ▷ adv: **boire ~** to drink things
  lukewarm
tièdement [tjɛdmɑ̃] adv coolly, half-heartedly
tiédeur [tjedœR] nf lukewarmness; (du vent, de
  l'air) mildness
tiédir [tjediR] vi (se réchauffer) to grow warmer;
  (refroidir) to cool
tien, tienne [tjɛ̃, tjɛn] pron: **le ~ (la ~ne), les ~s**
  (~nes) yours; **à la ~ne!** cheers!
tiendrai etc [tjɛ̃dRe] vb voir **tenir**
tienne [tjɛn] vb voir **tenir** ▷ pron voir **tien**
tiens [tjɛ̃] vb, excl voir **tenir**
tierce [tjɛRs(ə)] adj f, nf voir **tiers**
tiercé [tjɛRse] nm system of forecast betting giving
  first three horses
tiers, tierce [tjɛR, tjɛRs(ə)] adj third ▷ nm (Jur)
  third party; (fraction) third ▷ nf (Mus) third;
  (Cartes) tierce; **une tierce personne** a third
  party; **assurance au ~** third-party insurance;
  le ~ monde the third world; **~ payant** direct
  payment by insurers of medical expenses; **~**
  provisionnel interim payment of tax
tifs [tif] (fam) nmpl hair
TIG sigle m = **travail d'intérêt général**
tige [tiʒ] nf stem; (baguette) rod
tignasse [tiɲas] nf (péj) shock ou mop of hair
Tigre [tigR(ə)] nm: **le ~** the Tigris
tigre [tigR(ə)] nm tiger
tigré, e [tigRe] adj (rayé) striped; (tacheté) spotted
tigresse [tigRɛs] nf tigress
tilleul [tijœl] nm lime (tree), linden (tree);
  (boisson) lime(-blossom) tea
tilt [tilt(ə)] nm: **faire ~** (fig: échouer) to miss the
  target; (: inspirer) to ring a bell
timbale [tɛ̃bal] nf (metal) tumbler; **timbales**
  nfpl (Mus) timpani, kettledrums
timbrage [tɛ̃bRaʒ] nm: **dispensé de ~** post(age)
  paid
timbre [tɛ̃bR(ə)] nm (tampon) stamp; (aussi:
  timbre-poste) (postage) stamp; (cachet de la

poste) postmark; (sonnette) bell; (Mus: de voix,
  instrument) timbre, tone; **~ anti-tabac** nicotine
  patch; **~ dateur** date stamp
timbré, e [tɛ̃bRe] adj (enveloppe) stamped; (voix)
  resonant; (fam: fou) cracked, nuts
timbrer [tɛ̃bRe] vt to stamp
timide [timid] adj (emprunté) shy, timid; (timoré)
  timid, timorous
timidement [timidmɑ̃] adv shyly; timidly
timidité [timidite] nf shyness; timidity
timonerie [timɔnRi] nf wheelhouse
timonier [timɔnje] nm helmsman
timoré, e [timɔRe] adj timorous
tint etc [tɛ̃] vb voir **tenir**
tintamarre [tɛ̃tamaR] nm din, uproar
tintement [tɛ̃tmɑ̃] nm ringing, chiming; **~s**
  d'oreilles ringing in the ears
tinter [tɛ̃te] vi to ring, chime; (argent, clés) to
  jingle
Tipp-Ex® [tipɛks] nm Tipp-Ex®
tique [tik] nf tick (insect)
tiquer [tike] vi (personne) to make a face
TIR sigle mpl (= Transports internationaux routiers) TIR
tir [tiR] nm (sport) shooting; (fait ou manière de tirer)
  firing no pl; (Football) shot; (stand) shooting
  gallery; **~ d'obus/de mitraillette** shell/
  machine gun fire; **~ à l'arc** archery; **~ de**
  barrage barrage fire; **~ au fusil** (rifle)
  shooting; **~ au pigeon** (d'argile) clay pigeon
  shooting
tirade [tiRad] nf tirade
tirage [tiRaʒ] nm (action) printing; (Photo) print;
  (Inform) printout; (de journal) circulation; (de livre)
  (print-)run; edition; (de cheminée) draught (Brit),
  draft (US); (de loterie) draw; (fig: désaccord)
  friction; **~ au sort** drawing lots
tiraillement [tiRajmɑ̃] nm (douleur) sharp pain;
  (fig: doutes) agony no pl of indecision; (conflits)
  friction no pl
tirailler [tiRaje] vt to pull at, tug at; (fig) to gnaw
  at ▷ vi to fire at random
tirailleur [tiRajœR] nm skirmisher
tirant [tiRɑ̃] nm: **~ d'eau** draught (Brit), draft
  (US)
tire [tiR] nf: **vol à la ~** pickpocketing
tiré [tiRe] adj (visage, traits) drawn ▷ nm (Comm)
  drawee; **~ par les cheveux** far-fetched; **~ à**
  part off-print
tire-au-flanc [tiRoflɑ̃] nm inv (péj) skiver
tire-bouchon [tiRbuʃɔ̃] nm corkscrew
tire-bouchonner [tiRbuʃɔne] vt to twirl
tire-d'aile [tiRdɛl]: **à tire-d'aile** adv swiftly
tire-fesses [tiRfɛs] nm inv ski-tow
tire-lait [tiRlɛ] nm inv breast-pump
tire-larigot [tiRlaRigo]: **à ~** adv as much as one
  likes, to one's heart's content
tirelire [tiRliR] nf moneybox
tirer [tiRe] vt (gén) to pull; (extraire): **~ qch de** to
  take ou pull sth out of; to get sth out of; to
  extract sth from; (tracer: ligne, trait) to draw,
  trace; (fermer: volet, porte, trappe) to pull to, close;
  (: rideau) to draw; (choisir: carte, conclusion, aussi

Comm: *chèque*) to draw; (*en faisant feu: balle, coup*) to fire; (: *animal*) to shoot; (*journal, livre, photo*) to print; (*Football: corner etc*) to take ▷ vi (*faire feu*) to fire; (*faire du tir, Football*) to shoot; (*cheminée*) to draw; **se tirer** vi (*fam*) to push off; (*aussi*: **s'en tirer**) to pull through; ~ **sur** (*corde, poignée*) to pull on *ou* at; (*faire feu sur*) to shoot *ou* fire at; (*pipe*) to draw on; (*fig: avoisiner*) to verge *ou* border on; ~ **six mètres** (*Navig*) to draw six metres of water; ~ **son nom de** to take *ou* get its name from; ~ **la langue** to stick out one's tongue; ~ **qn de** (*embarras etc*) to help *ou* get sb out of; ~ **à l'arc/la carabine** to shoot with a bow and arrow/with a rifle; ~ **en longueur** to drag on; ~ **à sa fin** to be drawing to an end; ~ **les cartes** to read *ou* tell the cards

tiret [tiʀɛ] nm dash; (*en fin de ligne*) hyphen

tireur [tiʀœʀ] nm gunman; (*Comm*) drawer; **bon** ~ good shot; ~ **d'élite** marksman; ~ **de cartes** fortuneteller

tiroir [tiʀwaʀ] nm drawer

tiroir-caisse [tiʀwaʀkɛs] nm till

tisane [tizan] nf herb tea

tison [tizɔ̃] nm brand

tisonner [tizɔne] vt to poke

tisonnier [tizɔnje] nm poker

tissage [tisaʒ] nm weaving *no pl*

tisser [tise] vt to weave

tisserand, e [tisʀɑ̃, -ɑ̃d] nm/f weaver

tissu[1] [tisy] nm fabric, material, cloth *no pl*; (*fig*) fabric; (*Anat, Bio*) tissue; ~ **de mensonges** web of lies

tissu[2]**, e** [tisy] adj: ~ **de** woven through with

tissu-éponge [tisyepɔ̃ʒ] nm (terry) towelling *no pl*

titane [titan] nm titanium

titanesque [titanɛsk(ə)] adj titanic

titiller [titile] vt to titillate

titrage [titʀaʒ] nm (*d'un film*) titling; (*d'un alcool*) determination of alcohol content

titre [titʀ(ə)] nm (*gén*) title; (*de journal*) headline; (*diplôme*) qualification; (*Comm*) security; (*Chimie*) titre; **en** ~ (*champion, responsable*) official, recognized; **à juste** ~ with just cause, rightly; **à quel** ~? on what grounds?; **à aucun** ~ on no account; **au même** ~ **(que)** in the same way (as); **au** ~ **de la coopération** *etc* in the name of cooperation *etc*; **à** ~ **d'exemple** as an *ou* by way of an example; **à** ~ **exceptionnel** exceptionally; **à** ~ **d'information** for (your) information; **à** ~ **gracieux** free of charge; **à** ~ **d'essai** on a trial basis; **à** ~ **privé** in a private capacity; ~ **courant** running head; ~ **de propriété** title deed; ~ **de transport** ticket

titré, e [titʀe] adj (*livre, film*) entitled; (*personne*) titled

titrer [titʀe] vt (*Chimie*) to titrate; to assay; (*Presse*) to run as a headline; (*vin*): ~ **10°** to be 10° proof

titubant, e [titybɑ̃, -ɑ̃t] adj staggering, reeling

tituber [titybe] vi to stagger *ou* reel (along)

titulaire [titylɛʀ] adj (*Admin*) appointed, with

tenure ▷ nm (*Admin*) incumbent; **être** ~ **de** to hold

titularisation [titylaʀizasjɔ̃] nf granting of tenure

titulariser [titylaʀize] vt to give tenure to

TNP sigle m = **Théâtre national populaire**

TNT sigle m (= Trinitrotoluène) TNT ▷ sigle f (= Télévision numérique terrestre) digital television

toast [tost] nm slice *ou* piece of toast; (*de bienvenue*) (welcoming) toast; **porter un** ~ **à qn** to propose *ou* drink a toast to sb

toboggan [tɔbɔgɑ̃] nm toboggan; (*jeu*) slide; (*Auto*) flyover (*Brit*), overpass (*US*); ~ **de secours** (*Aviat*) escape chute

toc [tɔk] nm: **en** ~ imitation *cpd*

tocsin [tɔksɛ̃] nm alarm (bell)

toge [tɔʒ] nf toga; (*de juge*) gown

Togo [tɔgo] nm: **le** ~ Togo

togolais, e [tɔgolɛ, -ɛz] adj Togolese

tohu-bohu [tɔybɔy] nm (*désordre*) confusion; (*tumulte*) commotion

toi [twa] pron you; ~, **tu l'as fait?** did YOU do it?

toile [twal] nf (*matériau*) cloth *no pl*; (*bâche*) piece of canvas; (*tableau*) canvas; **grosse** ~ canvas; **tisser sa** ~ (*araignée*) to spin its web; ~ **d'araignée** spider's web; (*au plafond etc: à enlever*) cobweb; ~ **cirée** oilcloth; ~ **émeri** emery cloth; ~ **de fond** (*fig*) backdrop; ~ **de jute** hessian; ~ **de lin** linen; ~ **de tente** canvas

toilettage [twaletaʒ] nm grooming *no pl*; (*d'un texte*) tidying up

toilette [twalɛt] nf wash; (*s'habiller et se préparer*) getting ready, washing and dressing; (*habits*) outfit; dress *no pl*; **toilettes** nfpl toilet nsg; **les** ~**s des dames/messieurs** the ladies'/gents' (toilets) (*Brit*), the ladies'/men's (rest)room (*US*); **faire sa** ~ to have a wash, get washed; **faire la** ~ **de** (*animal*) to groom; (*voiture etc*) to clean, wash; (*texte*) to tidy up; **articles de** ~ toiletries; ~ **intime** personal hygiene

toi-même [twamɛm] pron yourself

toise [twaz] nf: **passer à la** ~ to have one's height measured

toiser [twaze] vt to eye up and down

toison [twazɔ̃] nf (*de mouton*) fleece; (*cheveux*) mane

toit [twa] nm roof; ~ **ouvrant** sun roof

toiture [twatyʀ] nf roof

Tokyo [tɔkjo] n Tokyo

tôle [tol] nf sheet metal *no pl*; (*plaque*) steel (*ou* iron) sheet; **tôles** nfpl (*carrosserie*) bodywork nsg (*Brit*), body nsg; panels; ~ **d'acier** sheet steel *no pl*; ~ **ondulée** corrugated iron

Tolède [tɔlɛd] n Toledo

tolérable [tɔleʀabl(ə)] adj tolerable, bearable

tolérance [tɔleʀɑ̃s] nf tolerance; (*hors taxe*) allowance

tolérant, e [tɔleʀɑ̃, -ɑ̃t] adj tolerant

tolérer [tɔleʀe] vt to tolerate; (*Admin: hors taxe etc*) to allow

tôlerie [tolʀi] nf sheet metal manufacture; (*atelier*) sheet metal workshop; (*ensemble des tôles*) panels *pl*

tollé [tɔle] *nm*: **un ~ (de protestations)** a general outcry

TOM [tɔm] *sigle nm(pl)* = **territoire(s) d'outre-mer**

tomate [tɔmat] *nf* tomato

tombal, e [tɔ̃bal] *adj*: **pierre ~e** tombstone, gravestone

tombant, e [tɔ̃bɑ̃, -ɑ̃t] *adj* (*fig*) drooping, sloping

tombe [tɔ̃b] *nf* (*sépulture*) grave; (*avec monument*) tomb

tombeau, x [tɔ̃bo] *nm* tomb; **à ~ ouvert** at breakneck speed

tombée [tɔ̃be] *nf*: **à la ~ du jour** *ou* **de la nuit** at the close of day, at nightfall

tomber [tɔ̃be] *vi* to fall ▷ *vt*: **~ la veste** to slip off one's jacket; **laisser ~** to drop; **~ sur** *vt* (*rencontrer*) to come across; (*attaquer*) to set about; **~ de fatigue/sommeil** to drop from exhaustion/be falling asleep on one's feet; **~ à l'eau** (*fig: projet etc*) to fall through; **~ en panne** to break down; **~ juste** (*opération, calcul*) to come out right; **~ en ruine** to fall into ruins; **ça tombe bien/mal** (*fig*) that's come at the right/wrong time; **il est bien/mal tombé** (*fig*) he's been lucky/unlucky

tombereau, x [tɔ̃bRo] *nm* tipcart

tombeur [tɔ̃bœR] *nm* (*péj*) Casanova

tombola [tɔ̃bɔla] *nf* tombola

Tombouctou [tɔ̃buktu] *n* Timbuktu

tome [tɔm] *nm* volume

tommette [tɔmɛt] *nf* hexagonal floor tile

ton¹, ta (*pl* **tes**) [tɔ̃, ta, te] *adj poss* your

ton² [tɔ̃] *nm* (*gén*) tone; (*Mus*) key; (*couleur*) shade, tone; (*de la voix: hauteur*) pitch; **donner le ~** to set the tone; **élever** *ou* **hausser le ~** to raise one's voice; **de bon ~** in good taste; **si vous le prenez sur ce ~** if you're going to take it like that; **~ sur ~** in matching shades

tonal, e [tɔnal] *adj* tonal

tonalité [tɔnalite] *nf* (*au téléphone*) dialling tone; (*Mus*) tonality; (: *ton*) key; (*fig*) tone

tondeuse [tɔ̃døz] *nf* (*à gazon*) (lawn)mower; (*du coiffeur*) clippers *pl*; (*pour la tonte*) shears *pl*

tondre [tɔ̃dR(ə)] *vt* (*pelouse, herbe*) to mow; (*haie*) to cut, clip; (*mouton, toison*) to shear; (*cheveux*) to crop

tondu, e [tɔ̃dy] *pp de* **tondre** ▷ *adj* (*cheveux*) cropped; (*mouton, crâne*) shorn

Tonga [tɔ̃ga]: **les îles ~** Tonga

tongs [tɔ̃g] *nfpl* flip-flops (*Brit*), thongs (*US*)

tonicité [tɔnisite] *nf* (*Méd: des tissus*) tone; (*fig: de l'air, la mer*) bracing effect

tonifiant, e [tɔnifjɑ̃, -ɑ̃t] *adj* invigorating, revivifying

tonifier [tɔnifje] *vt* (*air, eau*) to invigorate; (*peau, organisme*) to tone up

tonique [tɔnik] *adj* fortifying; (*personne*) dynamic ▷ *nm, nf* tonic

tonitruant, e [tɔnitRyɑ̃, -ɑ̃t] *adj*: **voix ~e** thundering voice

Tonkin [tɔ̃kɛ̃] *nm*: **le ~** Tonkin, Tongking

tonkinois, e [tɔ̃kinwa, -waz] *adj* Tonkinese

tonnage [tɔnaʒ] *nm* tonnage

tonnant, e [tɔnɑ̃, -ɑ̃t] *adj* thunderous

tonne [tɔn] *nf* metric ton, tonne

tonneau, x [tɔno] *nm* (*à vin, cidre*) barrel; (*Navig*) ton; **faire des ~x** (*voiture, avion*) to roll over

tonnelet [tɔnlɛ] *nm* keg

tonnelier [tɔnəlje] *nm* cooper

tonnelle [tɔnɛl] *nf* bower, arbour (*Brit*), arbor (*US*)

tonner [tɔne] *vi* to thunder; (*parler avec véhémence*): **~ contre qn/qch** to inveigh against sb/sth; **il tonne** it is thundering, there's some thunder

tonnerre [tɔnɛR] *nm* thunder; **coup de ~** (*fig*) thunderbolt, bolt from the blue; **un ~ d'applaudissements** thunderous applause; **du ~** *adj* (*fam*) terrific

tonsure [tɔ̃syR] *nf* bald patch; (*de moine*) tonsure

tonte [tɔ̃t] *nf* shearing

tonton [tɔ̃tɔ̃] *nm* uncle

tonus [tɔnys] *nm* (*des muscles*) tone; (*d'une personne*) dynamism

top [tɔp] *nm*: **au troisième ~** at the third stroke ▷ *adj*: **~ secret** top secret ▷ *excl* go!

topaze [tɔpaz] *nf* topaz

toper [tɔpe] *vi*: **tope-/topez-là** it's a deal!, you're on!

topinambour [tɔpinɑ̃buR] *nm* Jerusalem artichoke

topo [tɔpo] *nm* (*discours, exposé*) talk; (*fam*) spiel

topographie [tɔpɔgRafi] *nf* topography

topographique [tɔpɔgRafik] *adj* topographical

toponymie [tɔpɔnimi] *nf* study of place names, toponymy

toquade [tɔkad] *nf* fad, craze

toque [tɔk] *nf* (*de fourrure*) fur hat; **~ de jockey/juge** jockey's/judge's cap; **~ de cuisinier** chef's hat

toqué, e [tɔke] *adj* (*fam*) touched, cracked

torche [tɔRʃ(ə)] *nf* torch; **se mettre en ~** (*parachute*) to candle

torcher [tɔRʃe] *vt* (*fam*) to wipe

torchère [tɔRʃɛR] *nf* flare

torchon [tɔRʃɔ̃] *nm* cloth, duster; (*à vaisselle*) tea towel *ou* cloth

tordre [tɔRdR(ə)] *vt* (*chiffon*) to wring; (*barre, fig: visage*) to twist; **se tordre** *vi* (*barre*) to bend; (*roue*) to twist, buckle; (*ver, serpent*) to writhe; **se ~ le pied/bras** to twist one's foot/arm; **se ~ de douleur/rire** to writhe in pain/be doubled up with laughter

tordu, e [tɔRdy] *pp de* **tordre** ▷ *adj* (*fig*) warped, twisted

torero [tɔReRo] *nm* bullfighter

tornade [tɔRnad] *nf* tornado

toron [tɔRɔ̃] *nm* strand (of rope)

Toronto [tɔRɔ̃to] *n* Toronto

torontois, e [tɔRɔ̃twa, -waz] *adj* Torontonian ▷ *nm/f*: **Torontois, e** Torontonian

torpeur [tɔRpœR] *nf* torpor, drowsiness

torpille [tɔRpij] *nf* torpedo

torpiller [tɔʀpije] *vt* to torpedo
torpilleur [tɔʀpijœʀ] *nm* torpedo boat
torréfaction [tɔʀefaksjɔ̃] *nf* roasting
torréfier [tɔʀefje] *vt* to roast
torrent [tɔʀɑ̃] *nm* torrent, mountain stream;
(*fig*): **un ~ de** a torrent *ou* flood of; **il pleut à ~s**
the rain is lashing down
torrentiel, le [tɔʀɑ̃sjɛl] *adj* torrential
torride [tɔʀid] *adj* torrid
tors, torse *ou* **torte** [tɔʀ, tɔʀs(ə) ᵉouʰtɔʀt(ə)] *adj*
twisted
torsade [tɔʀsad] *nf* twist; (*Archit*) cable
moulding (*Brit*) *ou* molding (*US*)
torsader [tɔʀsade] *vt* to twist
torse [tɔʀs(ə)] *nm* torso; (*poitrine*) chest
torsion [tɔʀsjɔ̃] *nf* (*action*) twisting; (*Tech,
Physique*) torsion
tort [tɔʀ] *nm* (*défaut*) fault; (*préjudice*) wrong *no pl*;
torts *nmpl* (*Jur*) fault *nsg*; **avoir ~** to be wrong;
être dans son ~ to be in the wrong; **donner ~ à
qn** to lay the blame on sb; (*fig*) to prove sb
wrong; **causer du ~ à** to harm; to be harmful *ou*
detrimental to; **en ~** in the wrong, at fault; **à ~**
wrongly; **à ~ ou à raison** rightly or wrongly; **à
~ et à travers** wildly
torte [tɔʀt(ə)] *adj f voir* **tors**
torticolis [tɔʀtikɔli] *nm* stiff neck
tortiller [tɔʀtije] *vt* (*corde, mouchoir*) to twist;
(*doigts*) to twiddle; **se tortiller** *vi* to wriggle,
squirm
tortionnaire [tɔʀsjɔnɛʀ] *nm* torturer
tortue [tɔʀty] *nf* tortoise; (*fig*) slowcoach (*Brit*),
slowpoke (*US*)
tortueux, -euse [tɔʀtɥø, -øz] *adj* (*rue*) twisting;
(*fig*) tortuous
torture [tɔʀtyʀ] *nf* torture
torturer [tɔʀtyʀe] *vt* to torture; (*fig*) to torment
torve [tɔʀv(ə)] *adj*: **regard ~** menacing *ou* grim
look
toscan, e [tɔskɑ̃, -an] *adj* Tuscan
Toscane [tɔskan] *nf*: **la ~** Tuscany
tôt [to] *adv* early; **~ ou tard** sooner or later; **si ~**
so early; (*déjà*) so soon; **au plus ~** at the earliest,
as soon as possible; **plus ~** earlier; **il eut ~ fait
de faire ...** he soon did ...
total, e, -aux [tɔtal, -o] *adj, nm* total; **au ~** in
total *ou* all; (*fig*) all in all; **faire le ~** to work out
the total
totalement [tɔtalmɑ̃] *adv* totally, completely
totalisateur [tɔtalizatœʀ] *nm* adding machine
totaliser [tɔtalize] *vt* to total (up)
totalitaire [tɔtalitɛʀ] *adj* totalitarian
totalitarisme [tɔtalitarism(ə)] *nm*
totalitarianism
totalité [tɔtalite] *nf*: **la ~ de**: **la ~ des élèves** all
(of) the pupils; **la ~ de la population/classe**
the whole population/class; **en ~** entirely
totem [tɔtɛm] *nm* totem
toubib [tubib] *nm* (*fam*) doctor
touchant, e [tuʃɑ̃, -ɑ̃t] *adj* touching
touche [tuʃ] *nf* (*de piano, de machine à écrire*) key;
(*de violon*) fingerboard; (*de télécommande etc*) key,

button; (*Peinture etc*) stroke, touch; (*fig: de couleur,
nostalgie*) touch, hint; (*Rugby*) line-out; (*Football:
aussi:* **remise en touche**) throw-in; (*aussi:* **ligne
de touche**) touch-line; (*Escrime*) hit; **en ~** in (*ou*
into) touch; **avoir une drôle de ~** to look a
sight; **~ de commande/de fonction/de retour**
(*Inform*) control/function/return key; **~ à
effleurement** *ou* **sensitive** touch-sensitive
control *ou* key
touche-à-tout [tuʃatu] *nm inv* (*péj: gén: enfant*)
meddler; (*: fig: inventeur etc*) dabbler
toucher [tuʃe] *nm* touch ▷ *vt* to touch; (*palper*) to
feel; (*atteindre: d'un coup de feu etc*) to hit; (*affecter*)
to touch, affect; (*concerner*) to concern, affect;
(*contacter*) to reach, contact; (*recevoir: récompense*)
to receive, get; (*: salaire*) to draw, get; (*chèque*) to
cash; (*aborder: problème, sujet*) to touch on; **au ~** to
the touch; by the feel; **se toucher** (*être en contact*)
to touch; **à ~** to touch; (*modifier*) to touch,
tamper *ou* meddle with; (*traiter de, concerner*) to
have to do with, concern; **je vais lui en ~ un
mot** I'll have a word with him about it; **~ au
but** (*fig*) to near one's goal; **~ à sa fin** to be
drawing to a close
touffe [tuf] *nf* tuft
touffu, e [tufy] *adj* thick, dense; (*fig*) complex,
involved
toujours [tuʒuʀ] *adv* always; (*encore*) still;
(*constamment*) forever; **depuis ~** always; **essaie
~** (you can) try anyway; **pour ~** forever; **~ est-il
que** the fact remains that; **~ plus** more and
more
toulonnais, e [tulɔnɛ, -ɛz] *adj* of *ou* from Toulon
toulousain, e [tuluzɛ̃, -ɛn] *adj* of *ou* from
Toulouse
toupet [tupɛ] *nm* quiff (*Brit*), tuft; (*fam*) nerve,
cheek (*Brit*)
toupie [tupi] *nf* (spinning) top
tour [tuʀ] *nf* tower; (*immeuble*) high-rise block
(*Brit*) *ou* building (*US*), tower block (*Brit*); (*Échecs*)
castle, rook ▷ *nm* (*excursion: à pied*) stroll, walk;
(*: en voiture etc*) run, ride; (*: plus long*) trip; (*Sport:
aussi:* **tour de piste**) lap; (*d'être servi ou de jouer etc*,
tournure, de vis ou clef) turn; (*de roue etc*) revolution;
(*circonférence*): **de 3 m de ~** 3 m round, with a
circumference *ou* girth of 3 m; (*Pol: aussi:* **tour de
scrutin**) ballot; (*ruse, de prestidigitation, de cartes*)
trick; (*de potier*) wheel; (*à bois, métaux*) lathe;
faire le ~ de to go (a)round; (*à pied*) to walk
(a)round; (*fig*) to review; **faire le ~ de l'Europe**
to tour Europe; **faire un ~** to go for a walk; (*en
voiture etc*) to go for a ride; **faire 2 ~s** to go
(a)round twice; (*hélice etc*) to turn *ou* revolve
twice; **fermer à double ~** *vi* to double-lock the
door; **c'est au ~ de Renée** it's Renée's turn; **à ~
de rôle, ~ à ~** in turn; **à ~ de bras** with all one's
strength; (*fig*) non-stop, relentlessly; **~ de
taille/tête** waist/head measurement; **~ de
chant** song recital; **~ de contrôle** *nf* control
tower; **le T~ de France** the Tour de France; *see
note*; **~ de garde** spell of duty; **~ d'horizon** (*fig*)
general survey; **~ de lit** valance; **~ de main**

dexterity, knack; **en un ~ de main** (as) quick as a flash; **~ de passe-passe** trick, sleight of hand; **~ de reins** sprained back

tourangeau, elle, x [tuʀãʒo, -ɛl] *adj* (*de la région*) of *ou* from Touraine; (*de la ville*) of *ou* from Tours

tourbe [tuʀb(ə)] *nf* peat

tourbière [tuʀbjɛʀ] *nf* peat-bog

tourbillon [tuʀbijɔ̃] *nm* whirlwind; (*d'eau*) whirlpool; (*fig*) whirl, swirl

tourbillonner [tuʀbijone] *vi* to whirl, swirl; (*objet, personne*) to whirl *ou* twirl round

tourelle [tuʀɛl] *nf* turret

tourisme [tuʀism(ə)] *nm* tourism; **agence de ~** tourist agency; **avion/voiture de ~** private plane/car; **faire du ~** to do some sightseeing, go touring

touriste [tuʀist(ə)] *nm/f* tourist

touristique [tuʀistik] *adj* tourist *cpd*; (*région*) touristic (*péj*), with tourist appeal

tourment [tuʀmã] *nm* torment

tourmente [tuʀmãt] *nf* storm

tourmenté, e [tuʀmãte] *adj* tormented, tortured; (*mer, période*) turbulent

tourmenter [tuʀmãte] *vt* to torment; **se tourmenter** *vi* to fret, worry o.s.

tournage [tuʀnaʒ] *nm* (*d'un film*) shooting

tournant, e [tuʀnã, -ãt] *adj* (*feu, scène*) revolving; (*chemin*) winding; (*escalier*) spiral *cpd*; (*mouvement*) circling ▷ *nm* (*de route*) bend (*Brit*), curve (*US*); (*fig*) turning point; *voir* **plaque; grève**

tourné, e [tuʀne] *adj* (*lait, vin*) sour, off; (*Menuiserie: bois*) turned; (*fig: compliment*) well-phrased; **bien ~** (*femme*) shapely; **mal ~** (*lettre*) badly expressed; **avoir l'esprit mal ~** to have a dirty mind

tournebroche [tuʀnəbʀɔʃ] *nm* roasting spit

tourne-disque [tuʀnədisk(ə)] *nm* record player

tournedos [tuʀnədo] *nm* tournedos

tournée [tuʀne] *nf* (*du facteur etc*) round; (*d'artiste, politicien*) tour; (*au café*) round (of drinks); **faire la ~ de** to go (a)round

tournemain [tuʀnəmɛ̃]: **en un ~** *adv* in a flash

tourner [tuʀne] *vt* to turn; (*sauce, mélange*) to stir; (*contourner*) to get (a)round; (*Ciné*) to shoot; to make ▷ *vi* to turn; (*moteur*) to run; (*compteur*) to tick away; (*lait etc*) to turn (sour); (*fig: chance, vie*) to turn out; **se tourner** *vi* to turn (a)round;

se ~ vers to turn to; to turn towards; **bien ~** to turn out well; **~ autour de** to go (a)round; (*planète*) to revolve (a)round; (*péj*) to hang (a)round; **~ autour du pot** (*fig*) to go (a)round in circles; **~ à/en** to turn into; **~ à la pluie/au rouge** to turn rainy/red; **~ en ridicule** to ridicule; **~ le dos à** (*mouvement*) to turn one's back on; (*position*) to have one's back to; **~ court** to come to a sudden end; **se ~ les pouces** to twiddle one's thumbs; **~ la tête** to look away; **~ la tête à qn** (*fig*) to go to sb's head; **~ de l'œil** to pass out; **~ la page** (*fig*) to turn the page

tournesol [tuʀnəsɔl] *nm* sunflower

tourneur [tuʀnœʀ] *nm* turner; lathe-operator

tournevis [tuʀnəvis] *nm* screwdriver

tourniquer [tuʀnike] *vi* to go (a)round in circles

tourniquet [tuʀnikɛ] *nm* (*pour arroser*) sprinkler; (*portillon*) turnstile; (*présentoir*) revolving stand, spinner; (*Chirurgie*) tourniquet

tournis [tuʀni] *nm*: **avoir/donner le ~** to feel/make dizzy

tournoi [tuʀnwa] *nm* tournament

tournoyer [tuʀnwaje] *vi* (*oiseau*) to wheel (a)round; (*fumée*) to swirl (a)round

tournure [tuʀnyʀ] *nf* (*Ling: syntaxe*) turn of phrase; form; (: *d'une phrase*) phrasing; (*évolution*): **la ~ de qch** the way sth is developing; (*aspect*): **la ~ de** the look of; **la ~ des événements** the turn of events; **prendre ~** to take shape

tour-opérateur [tuʀɔpeʀatœʀ] *nm* tour operator

tourte [tuʀt(ə)] *nf* pie

tourteau, x [tuʀto] *nm* (*Agr*) oilcake, cattle-cake; (*Zool*) edible crab

tourtereaux [tuʀtəʀo] *nmpl* lovebirds

tourterelle [tuʀtəʀɛl] *nf* turtledove

tourtière [tuʀtjɛʀ] *nf* pie dish *ou* plate

tous [tu] *adj* [tus] ▷ *pron voir* **tout**

Toussaint [tusɛ̃] *nf*: **la ~** All Saints' Day

tousser [tuse] *vi* to cough

toussoter [tusɔte] *vi* to have a slight cough; (*pour avertir*) to give a slight cough

○ **MOT-CLÉ**

tout, e [tu, tut] (*mpl* **tous**, *fpl* **toutes**) *adj* **1** (*avec article singulier*) all; **tout le lait** all the milk; **toute la nuit** all night, the whole night; **tout le livre** the whole book; **tout un pain** a whole loaf; **tout le temps** all the time, the whole time; **c'est tout le contraire** it's quite the opposite; **c'est toute une affaire** *ou* **histoire** it's quite a business, it's a whole rigmarole **2** (*avec article pluriel*) every; all; **tous les livres** all the books; **toutes les nuits** every night; **toutes les fois** every time; **toutes les trois/deux semaines** every third/other *ou* second week, every three/two weeks; **tous les deux** both *ou* each of us (*ou* them *ou* you); **toutes les trois** all three of us (*ou* them *ou* you)

3 (sans article): **à tout âge** at any age; **pour toute nourriture, il avait ...** his only food was ...; **de tous côtés, de toutes parts** from everywhere, from every side
▷ pron everything, all; **il a tout fait** he's done everything; **je les vois tous** I can see them all ou all of them; **nous y sommes tous allés** all of us went, we all went; **c'est tout** that's all; **en tout** in all; **en tout et pour tout** all in all; **tout ce qu'il sait** all he knows; **c'était tout ce qu'il y a de chic** it was the last word ou the ultimate in chic
▷ nm whole; **le tout** all of it (ou them); **le tout est de ...** the main thing is to ...; **pas du tout** not at all; **elle a tout d'une mère/d'une intrigante** she's a real ou true mother/ schemer; **du tout au tout** utterly
▷ adv **1** (très, complètement) very; **tout près** ou **à côté** very near; **le tout premier** the very first; **tout seul** all alone; **il était tout rouge** he was really ou all red; **parler tout bas** to speak very quietly; **le livre tout entier** the whole book; **tout en haut** right at the top; **tout droit** straight ahead
2: **tout en** while; **tout en travaillant** while working, as he etc works
3: **tout d'abord** first of all; **tout à coup** suddenly; **tout à fait** absolutely; **tout à fait!** exactly!; **tout à l'heure** a short while ago; (futur) in a short while, shortly; **à tout à l'heure!** see you later!; **il répondit tout court que non** he just answered no (and that was all); **tout de même** all the same; **tout le monde** everybody; **tout ou rien** all or nothing; **tout simplement** quite simply; **tout de suite** immediately, straight away

tout-à-l'égout [tutalegu] nm inv mains drainage
toutefois [tutfwa] adv however
toutou [tutu] nm (fam) doggie
tout-petit [tup(ə)ti] nm toddler
tout-puissant, toute-puissante [tupɥisɑ̃, tutpɥisɑ̃t] adj all-powerful, omnipotent
tout-venant [tuvnɑ̃] nm: **le ~** everyday stuff
toux [tu] nf cough
toxémie [tɔksemi] nf toxaemia (Brit), toxemia (US)
toxicité [tɔksisite] nf toxicity
toxicologie [tɔksikɔlɔʒi] nf toxicology
toxicomane [tɔksikɔman] nm/f drug addict
toxicomanie [tɔksikɔmani] nf drug addiction
toxine [tɔksin] nf toxin
toxique [tɔksik] adj toxic, poisonous
toxoplasmose [tɔksoplasmoz] nf toxoplasmosis
TP sigle mpl = **travaux pratiques; travaux publics**
▷ sigle m = **trésor public**
TPG sigle m = **Trésorier-payeur général**
tps abr = **temps**
trac [tRak] nm nerves pl; (Théât) stage fright; **avoir le ~** to get an attack of nerves; to have

stage fright; **tout à ~** all of a sudden
traçant, e [tRasɑ̃, -ɑ̃t] adj: **table ~e** (Inform) (graph) plotter
tracas [tRaka] nm bother no pl, worry no pl
tracasser [tRakase] vt to worry, bother; (harceler) to harass; **se tracasser** vi to worry o.s., fret
tracasserie [tRakasRi] nf annoyance no pl; harassment no pl
tracassier, -ière [tRakasje, -jɛR] adj irksome
trace [tRas] nf (empreintes) tracks pl; (marques, aussi fig) mark; (restes, vestige) trace; (indice) sign; (aussi: **suivre à la trace**) to track; **~s de pas** footprints
tracé [tRase] nm (contour) line; (plan) layout
tracer [tRase] vt to draw; (mot) to trace; (piste) to open up; (fig: chemin) to show
traceur [tRasœR] nm (Inform) plotter
trachée [tRaʃe], **trachée-artère** [tRaʃeaRtɛR] nf windpipe, trachea
trachéite [tRakeit] nf tracheitis
tract [tRakt] nm tract, pamphlet; (publicitaire) handout
tractations [tRaktɑsjɔ̃] nfpl dealings, bargaining nsg
tracter [tRakte] vt to tow
tracteur [tRaktœR] nm tractor
traction [tRaksjɔ̃] nf traction; (Gym) pull-up; **~ avant/arrière** front-wheel/rear-wheel drive; **~ électrique** electric(al) traction ou haulage
trad. abr (= traduit) translated; (= traduction) translation; (= traducteur) translator
tradition [tRadisjɔ̃] nf tradition
traditionalisme [tRadisjɔnalism(ə)] nm traditionalism
traditionaliste [tRadisjɔnalist(ə)] adj, nm/f traditionalist
traditionnel, le [tRadisjɔnɛl] adj traditional
traditionnellement [tRadisjɔnɛlmɑ̃] adv traditionally
traducteur, -trice [tRadyktœR, -tRis] nm/f translator
traduction [tRadyksjɔ̃] nf translation
traduire [tRadɥiR] vt to translate; (exprimer) to render, convey; **se ~ par** to find expression in; **~ en français** to translate into French; **~ en justice** to bring before the courts
traduis etc [tRadɥi] vb voir **traduire**
traduisible [tRadɥizibl(ə)] adj translatable
traduit, e [tRadɥi, -it] pp de **traduire**
trafic [tRafik] nm traffic; **~ d'armes** arms dealing; **~ de drogue** drug peddling
trafiquant, e [tRafikɑ̃, -ɑ̃t] nm/f trafficker; dealer
trafiquer [tRafike] vt (péj) to doctor, tamper with ▷ vi to traffic, be engaged in trafficking
tragédie [tRaʒedi] nf tragedy
tragédien, ne [tRaʒedjɛ̃, -ɛn] nm/f tragedian/ tragedienne
tragi-comique [tRaʒikɔmik] adj tragi-comic
tragique [tRaʒik] adj tragic ▷ nm: **prendre qch au ~** to make a tragedy out of sth

t

tragiquement [tʀaʒikmɑ̃] *adv* tragically
trahir [tʀaiʀ] *vt* to betray; *(fig)* to give away, reveal; **se trahir** to betray o.s., give o.s. away
trahison [tʀaizɔ̃] *nf* betrayal; *(Jur)* treason
traie *etc* [tʀɛ] *vb voir* **traire**
train [tʀɛ̃] *nm* (Rail) train; *(allure)* pace; *(fig: ensemble)* set; **être en ~ de faire qch** to be doing sth; **mettre qch en ~** to get sth under way; **mettre qn en ~** to put sb in good spirits; **se mettre en ~** *(commencer)* to get started; *(faire de la gymnastique)* to warm up; **se sentir en ~** to feel in good form; **aller bon ~** to make good progress; **~ avant/arrière** front-wheel/rear-wheel axle unit; **~ à grande vitesse (TGV)** high-speed train; **~ d'atterrissage** undercarriage; **~ autos-couchettes** car-sleeper train; **~ électrique** *(jouet)* (electric) train set; **~ de pneus** set of tyres *ou* tires; **~ de vie** style of living
traînailler [tʀɛnaje] *vi* = **traînasser**
traînant, e [tʀɛnɑ̃, -ɑ̃t] *adj (voix, ton)* drawling
traînard, e [tʀɛnaʀ, -aʀd(ə)] *nm/f (péj)* slowcoach *(Brit)*, slowpoke *(US)*
traînasser [tʀɛnase] *vi* to dawdle
traîne [tʀɛn] *nf (de robe)* train; **être à la ~** to be in tow; *(en arrière)* to lag behind; *(en désordre)* to be lying around
traîneau, x [tʀɛno] *nm* sleigh, sledge
traînée [tʀɛne] *nf* streak, trail; *(péj)* slut
traîner [tʀɛne] *vt (remorque)* to pull; *(enfant, chien)* to drag *ou* trail along; *(maladie)*: **il traîne un rhume depuis l'hiver** he has a cold which has been dragging on since winter ▷ *vi (être en désordre)* to lie around; *(marcher lentement)* to dawdle (along); *(vagabonder)* to hang about; *(agir lentement)* to idle about; *(durer)* to drag on; **se traîner** *vi (ramper)* to crawl along; *(marcher avec difficulté)* to drag o.s. along; *(durer)* to drag on; **se ~ par terre** to crawl (on the ground); **~ qn au cinéma** to drag sb to the cinema; **~ les pieds** to drag one's feet; **~ par terre** to trail on the ground; **~ en longueur** to drag out
training [tʀɛniŋ] *nm (pull)* tracksuit top; *(chaussure)* trainer *(Brit)*, sneaker *(US)*
train-train [tʀɛ̃tʀɛ̃] *nm* humdrum routine
traire [tʀɛʀ] *vt* to milk
trait, e [tʀɛ, -ɛt] *pp de* **traire** ▷ *nm (ligne)* line; *(de dessin)* stroke; *(caractéristique)* feature, trait; *(flèche)* dart, arrow; shaft; **traits** *nmpl (du visage)* features; **d'un ~** *(boire)* in one gulp; **de ~** *adj (animal)* draught *(Brit)*, draft *(US)*; **avoir ~ à** to concern; **~ pour ~** line for line; **~ de caractère** characteristic, trait; **~ d'esprit** flash of wit; **~ de génie** brainwave; **~ d'union** hyphen; *(fig)* link
traitable [tʀɛtabl(ə)] *adj (personne)* accommodating; *(sujet)* manageable
traitant, e [tʀɛtɑ̃, -ɑ̃t] *adj*: **votre médecin ~** your usual *ou* family doctor; **shampooing ~** medicated shampoo; **crème ~e** conditioning cream, conditioner
traite [tʀɛt] *nf (Comm)* draft; *(Agr)* milking;

(trajet) stretch; **d'une (seule) ~** without stopping (once); **la ~ des noirs** the slave trade; **la ~ des blanches** the white slave trade
traité [tʀete] *nm* treaty
traitement [tʀɛtmɑ̃] *nm* treatment; processing; *(salaire)* salary; **suivre un ~** to undergo treatment; **mauvais ~** ill-treatment; **~ de données** *ou* **de l'information** *(Inform)* data processing; **~ hormono-supplétif** hormone replacement therapy; **~ par lots** *(Inform)* batch processing; **~ de texte** *(Inform)* word processing
traiter [tʀete] *vt (gén)* to treat; *(Tech: matériaux)* to process, treat; *(Inform)* to process; *(affaire)* to deal with, handle; *(qualifier)*: **~ qn d'idiot** to call sb a fool ▷ *vi* to deal; **~ de** *vt* to deal with; **bien/mal ~** to treat well/ill-treat
traiteur [tʀɛtœʀ] *nm* caterer
traître, -esse [tʀɛtʀ(ə), -tʀɛs] *adj (dangereux)* treacherous ▷ *nm* traitor; **prendre qn en ~** to make an insidious attack on sb
traîtrise [tʀetʀiz] *nf* treachery
trajectoire [tʀaʒɛktwaʀ] *nf* trajectory, path
trajet [tʀaʒɛ] *nm* journey; *(itinéraire)* route; *(fig)* path, course
tralala [tʀalala] *nm (péj)* fuss
tram [tʀam] *nm* tram *(Brit)*, streetcar *(US)*
trame [tʀam] *nf (de tissu)* weft; *(fig)* framework; texture; *(Typo)* screen
tramer [tʀame] *vt* to plot, hatch
trampoline [tʀɑ̃pɔlin], **trampolino** [tʀɑ̃pɔlino] *nm* trampoline; *(Sport)* trampolining
tramway [tʀamwɛ] *nm* tram(way); *(voiture)* tram(car) *(Brit)*, streetcar *(US)*
tranchant, e [tʀɑ̃ʃɑ̃, -ɑ̃t] *adj* sharp; *(fig: personne)* peremptory; *(: couleurs)* striking ▷ *nm (d'un couteau)* cutting edge; *(de la main)* edge; **à double ~** *(argument, procédé)* double-edged
tranche [tʀɑ̃ʃ] *nf (morceau)* slice; *(arête)* edge; *(partie)* section; *(série)* block; *(d'impôts, revenus etc)* bracket; *(loterie)* issue; **~ d'âge** age bracket; **~ (de silicium)** wafer
tranché, e [tʀɑ̃ʃe] *adj (couleurs)* distinct, sharply contrasted; *(opinions)* clear-cut, definite ▷ *nf* trench
trancher [tʀɑ̃ʃe] *vt* to cut, sever; *(fig: résoudre)* to settle ▷ *vi* to be decisive; *(entre deux choses)* to settle the argument; **~ avec** to contrast sharply with
tranchet [tʀɑ̃ʃɛ] *nm* knife
tranchoir [tʀɑ̃ʃwaʀ] *nm* chopper
tranquille [tʀɑ̃kil] *adj* calm, quiet; *(enfant, élève)* quiet; *(rassuré)* easy in one's mind, with one's mind at rest; **se tenir ~** *(enfant)* to be quiet; **avoir la conscience ~** to have an easy conscience; **laisse-moi/laisse-ça ~** leave me/it alone
tranquillement [tʀɑ̃kilmɑ̃] *adv* calmly
tranquillisant, e [tʀɑ̃kilizɑ̃, -ɑ̃t] *adj (nouvelle)* reassuring ▷ *nm* tranquillizer
tranquilliser [tʀɑ̃kilize] *vt* to reassure; **se tranquilliser** to calm (o.s.) down
tranquillité [tʀɑ̃kilite] *nf* quietness, peace (and

quiet); **en toute ~** with complete peace of mind; **~ d'esprit** peace of mind

transaction [tʀɑ̃zaksjɔ̃] nf (Comm) transaction, deal

transafricain, e [tʀɑ̃safʀikɛ̃, -ɛn] adj transafrican

transalpin, e [tʀɑ̃zalpɛ̃, -in] adj transalpine

transaméricain, e [tʀɑ̃zameʀikɛ̃, -ɛn] adj transamerican

transat [tʀɑ̃zat] nm deckchair ▷ nf = **course transatlantique**

transatlantique [tʀɑ̃zatlɑ̃tik] adj transatlantic ▷ nm transatlantic liner

transborder [tʀɑ̃sbɔʀde] vt to tran(s)ship

transcendant, e [tʀɑ̃sɑ̃dɑ̃, -ɑ̃t] adj (Philosophie, Math) transcendental; (supérieur) transcendent

transcodeur [tʀɑ̃skɔdœʀ] nm compiler

transcontinental, e, -aux [tʀɑ̃skɔ̃tinɑtal, -o] adj transcontinental

transcription [tʀɑ̃skʀipsjɔ̃] nf transcription

transcrire [tʀɑ̃skʀiʀ] vt to transcribe

transe [tʀɑ̃s] nf: **entrer en ~** to go into a trance; **transes** nfpl agony nsg

transférable [tʀɑ̃sfeʀabl(ə)] adj transferable

transfèrement [tʀɑ̃sfɛʀmɑ̃] nm transfer

transférer [tʀɑ̃sfeʀe] vt to transfer

transfert [tʀɑ̃sfɛʀ] nm transfer

transfiguration [tʀɑ̃sfigyʀasjɔ̃] nf transformation, transfiguration

transfigurer [tʀɑ̃sfigyʀe] vt to transform

transfo [tʀɑ̃sfo] nm (= transformateur) transformer

transformable [tʀɑ̃sfɔʀmabl(ə)] adj convertible

transformateur [tʀɑ̃sfɔʀmatœʀ] nm transformer

transformation [tʀɑ̃sfɔʀmasjɔ̃] nf transformation; (Rugby) conversion; **industries de ~** processing industries

transformer [tʀɑ̃sfɔʀme] vt to transform, alter ("alter" implique un changement moins radical); (matière première, appartement, Rugby) to convert; **~ en** to transform into; to turn into; to convert into; **se transformer** vi to be transformed; to alter

transfuge [tʀɑ̃sfyʒ] nm renegade

transfuser [tʀɑ̃sfyze] vt to transfuse

transfusion [tʀɑ̃sfyzjɔ̃] nf: **~ sanguine** blood transfusion

transgénique [tʀɑ̃sʒenik] adj transgenic

transgresser [tʀɑ̃sgʀese] vt to contravene, disobey

transhumance [tʀɑ̃zymɑ̃s] nf transhumance, seasonal move to new pastures

transi, e [tʀɑ̃zi] adj numb (with cold), chilled to the bone

transiger [tʀɑ̃ziʒe] vi to compromise, come to an agreement; **~ sur** ou **avec qch** to compromise on sth

transistor [tʀɑ̃zistɔʀ] nm transistor

transistorisé, e [tʀɑ̃zistɔʀize] adj transistorized

transit [tʀɑ̃zit] nm transit; **de ~** transit cpd; **en ~** in transit

transitaire [tʀɑ̃zitɛʀ] nm/f forwarding agent

transiter [tʀɑ̃zite] vi to pass in transit

transitif, -ive [tʀɑ̃zitif, -iv] adj transitive

transition [tʀɑ̃zisjɔ̃] nf transition; **de ~** transitional

transitoire [tʀɑ̃zitwaʀ] adj (mesure, gouvernement) transitional, provisional; (fugitif) transient

translucide [tʀɑ̃slysid] adj translucent

transmet etc [tʀɑ̃smɛ] vb voir **transmettre**

transmettais etc [tʀɑ̃smɛtɛ] vb voir **transmettre**

transmetteur [tʀɑ̃smɛtœʀ] nm transmitter

transmettre [tʀɑ̃smɛtʀ(ə)] vt (passer): **~ qch à qn** to pass sth on to sb; (Tech, Tél, Méd) to transmit; (TV, Radio: retransmettre) to broadcast

transmis, e [tʀɑ̃smi, -iz] pp de **transmettre**

transmissible [tʀɑ̃smisibl(ə)] adj transmissible

transmission [tʀɑ̃smisjɔ̃] nf transmission, passing on; (Auto) transmission; **transmissions** nfpl (Mil) ≈ signals corps nsg; **~ de données** (Inform) data transmission; **~ de pensée** thought transmission

transocéanien, ne [tʀɑ̃zɔseanjɛ̃, -ɛn] **transocéanique** [tʀɑ̃zɔseanik] adj transoceanic

transparaître [tʀɑ̃spaʀɛtʀ(ə)] vi to show (through)

transparence [tʀɑ̃spaʀɑ̃s] nf transparence; **par ~** (regarder) against the light; (voir) showing through

transparent, e [tʀɑ̃spaʀɑ̃, -ɑ̃t] adj transparent

transpercer [tʀɑ̃spɛʀse] vt to go through, pierce

transpiration [tʀɑ̃spiʀasjɔ̃] nf perspiration

transpirer [tʀɑ̃spiʀe] vi to perspire; (information, nouvelle) to come to light

transplant [tʀɑ̃splɑ̃] nm transplant

transplantation [tʀɑ̃splɑ̃tasjɔ̃] nf transplant

transplanter [tʀɑ̃splɑ̃te] vt (Méd, Bot) to transplant; (personne) to uproot, move

transport [tʀɑ̃spɔʀ] nm transport; (émotions): **~ de colère** fit of rage; **~ de joie** transport of delight; **~ de voyageurs/marchandises** passenger/goods transportation; **~s en commun** public transport nsg; **~s routiers** haulage (Brit), trucking (US)

transportable [tʀɑ̃spɔʀtabl(ə)] adj (marchandises) transportable; (malade) fit (enough) to be moved

transporter [tʀɑ̃spɔʀte] vt to carry, move; (Comm) to transport, convey; (fig): **~ qn (de joie)** to send sb into raptures; **se ~ quelque part** (fig) to let one's imagination carry one away (somewhere)

transporteur [tʀɑ̃spɔʀtœʀ] nm haulage contractor (Brit), trucker (US)

transposer [tʀɑ̃spoze] vt to transpose

transposition [tʀɑ̃spozisjɔ̃] nf transposition

transrhénan, e [tʀɑ̃sʀenɑ̃, -an] adj transrhenane

transsaharien, ne [tʀɑ̃ssaaʀjɛ̃, -ɛn] adj trans-Saharan

t

transsexuel, le [tʀɑ̃sɛksɥɛl] *adj*, *nm/f* transsexual

transsibérien, ne [tʀɑ̃ssibeʀjɛ̃, -ɛn] *adj* trans-Siberian

transvaser [tʀɑ̃svaze] *vt* to decant

transversal, e, -aux [tʀɑ̃svɛʀsal, -o] *adj* transverse, cross(-); (*route etc*) cross-country; (*mur, chemin, rue*) running at right angles; (*Auto*): **axe ~** main cross-country road (*Brit*) *ou* highway (*US*)

transversalement [tʀɑ̃svɛʀsalmɑ̃] *adv* crosswise

trapèze [tʀapɛz] *nm* (*Géom*) trapezium; (*au cirque*) trapeze

trapéziste [tʀapezist(ə)] *nm/f* trapeze artist

trappe [tʀap] *nf* (*de cave, grenier*) trap door; (*piège*) trap

trappeur [tʀapœʀ] *nm* trapper, fur trader

trapu, e [tʀapy] *adj* squat, stocky

traquenard [tʀaknaʀ] *nm* trap

traquer [tʀake] *vt* to track down; (*harceler*) to hound

traumatisant, e [tʀomatizɑ̃, -ɑ̃t] *adj* traumatic

traumatiser [tʀomatize] *vt* to traumatize

traumatisme [tʀomatism(ə)] *nm* traumatism

traumatologie [tʀomatɔlɔʒi] *nf* branch of medicine concerned with accidents

travail, -aux [tʀavaj, -o] *nm* (*gén*) work; (*tâche, métier*) work *no pl*, job; (*Écon, Méd*) labour (*Brit*), labor (*US*); (*Inform*) job ▷ *nmpl* (*de réparation, agricoles etc*) work *nsg*; (*sur route*) roadworks; (*de construction*) building (work) *nsg*; **être/entrer en ~** (*Méd*) to be in/go into labour; **être sans ~** (*employé*) to be out of work, be unemployed; **~ d'intérêt général (TIG)** ≈ community service; **~ (au) noir** moonlighting; **~ posté** shiftwork; **travaux des champs** farmwork *nsg*; **travaux dirigés (TD)** (*Scol*) supervised practical work *nsg*; **travaux forcés** hard labour *nsg*; **travaux manuels** (*Scol*) handicrafts; **travaux ménagers** housework *nsg*; **travaux pratiques (TP)** (*gén*) practical work; (*en laboratoire*) lab work (*Brit*), lab (*US*); **travaux publics (TP)** ≈ public works *nsg*

travaillé, e [tʀavaje] *adj* (*style*) polished

travailler [tʀavaje] *vi* to work; (*bois*) to warp ▷ *vt* (*bois, métal*) to work; (*pâte*) to knead; (*objet d'art, discipline, fig: influencer*) to work on; **cela le travaille** it is on his mind; **~ la terre** to work the land; **~ son piano** to do one's piano practice; **~ à** to work on; (*fig: contribuer à*) to work towards; **~ à faire** to endeavour (*Brit*) *ou* endeavor (*US*) to do

travailleur, -euse [tʀavajœʀ, -øz] *adj* hard-working ▷ *nm/f* worker; **~ de force** labourer (*Brit*), laborer (*US*); **~ intellectuel** non-manual worker; **~ social** social worker; **travailleuse familiale** home help

travailliste [tʀavajist(ə)] *adj* ≈ Labour *cpd* ▷ *nm/f* member of the Labour party

travée [tʀave] *nf* row; (*Archit*) bay; span

traveller's [tʀavlœʀs], **traveller's chèque**
[tʀavlœʀsʃɛk] *nm* traveller's cheque

travelling [tʀavliŋ] *nm* (*chariot*) dolly; (*technique*) tracking; **~ optique** zoom shots *pl*

travelo [tʀavlo] *nm* (*fam*) (drag) queen

travers [tʀavɛʀ] *nm* fault, failing; **en ~ (de)** across; **au ~ (de)** through; **de ~** *adj* askew ▷ *adv* sideways; (*fig*) the wrong way; **à ~** through; **regarder de ~** (*fig*) to look askance at

traverse [tʀavɛʀs(ə)] *nf* (*de voie ferrée*) sleeper; **chemin de ~** shortcut

traversée [tʀavɛʀse] *nf* crossing

traverser [tʀavɛʀse] *vt* (*gén*) to cross; (*ville, tunnel, aussi: percer, fig*) to go through; (*ligne, trait*) to run across

traversin [tʀavɛʀsɛ̃] *nm* bolster

travesti [tʀavɛsti] *nm* (*costume*) fancy dress; (*artiste de cabaret*) female impersonator, drag artist; (*comme mode de vie*) transvestite

travestir [tʀavɛstiʀ] *vt* (*vérité*) to misrepresent; **se travestir** (*se costumer*) to dress up; (*artiste*) to put on drag; (*Psych*) to dress as a woman

trayais *etc* [tʀɛjɛ] *vb voir* **traire**

trayeuse [tʀɛjøz] *nf* milking machine

trébucher [tʀebyʃe] *vi*: **~ (sur)** to stumble (over), trip (over)

trèfle [tʀɛfl(ə)] *nm* (*Bot*) clover; (*Cartes: couleur*) clubs *pl*; (*: carte*) club; **~ à quatre feuilles** four-leaf clover

treillage [tʀɛjaʒ] *nm* lattice work

treille [tʀɛj] *nf* (*tonnelle*) vine arbour (*Brit*) *ou* arbor (*US*); (*vigne*) climbing vine

treillis [tʀɛji] *nm* (*métallique*) wire-mesh; (*toile*) canvas; (*Mil: tenue*) combat uniform; (*pantalon*) combat trousers *pl*

treize [tʀɛz] *num* thirteen

treizième [tʀɛzjɛm] *num* thirteenth; *see note*

● TREIZIÈME MOIS

The *treizième mois* is an end-of-year bonus roughly corresponding to one month's salary. For many employees it is a standard part of their salary package.

tréma [tʀema] *nm* diaeresis

tremblant, e [tʀɑ̃blɑ̃, -ɑ̃t] *adj* trembling, shaking

tremble [tʀɑ̃bl(ə)] *nm* (*Bot*) aspen

tremblé, e [tʀɑ̃ble] *adj* shaky

tremblement [tʀɑ̃bləmɑ̃] *nm* trembling *no pl*, shaking *no pl*, shivering *no pl*; **~ de terre** earthquake

trembler [tʀɑ̃ble] *vi* to tremble, shake; **~ de** (*froid, fièvre*) to shiver *ou* tremble with; (*peur*) to shake *ou* tremble with; **~ pour qn** to fear for sb

tremblotant, e [tʀɑ̃blɔtɑ̃, -ɑ̃t] *adj* trembling

trembloter [tʀɑ̃blɔte] *vi* to tremble *ou* shake slightly

trémolo [tʀemɔlo] *nm* (*d'un instrument*) tremolo; (*de la voix*) quaver

trémousser [tʀemuse]: **se trémousser** *vi* to jig about, wriggle about

trempe [tʀɑ̃p] *nf* (*fig*): **de cette/sa ~** of this/his calibre (*Brit*) *ou* caliber (*US*)

trempé, e [tʀɑ̃pe] *adj* soaking (wet), drenched; (*Tech*): **acier ~** tempered steel

tremper [tʀɑ̃pe] *vt* to soak, drench; (*aussi*: **faire tremper, mettre à tremper**) to soak; (*plonger*): **~ qch dans** to dip sth in(to) ▷ *vi* to soak; (*fig*): **~ dans** to be involved *ou* have a hand in; **se tremper** *vi* to have a quick dip; **se faire ~** to get soaked *ou* drenched

trempette [tʀɑ̃pɛt] *nf*: **faire ~** to go paddling

tremplin [tʀɑ̃plɛ̃] *nm* springboard; (*Ski*) ski jump

trentaine [tʀɑ̃tɛn] *nf* (*âge*): **avoir la ~** to be around thirty; **une ~ (de)** thirty or so, about thirty

trente [tʀɑ̃t] *num* thirty; **voir ~-six chandelles** (*fig*) to see stars; **être/se mettre sur son ~ et un** to be/get dressed to kill; **~-trois tours** *nm* long-playing record, LP

trentième [tʀɑ̃tjɛm] *num* thirtieth

trépanation [tʀepanasjɔ̃] *nf* trepan

trépaner [tʀepane] *vt* to trepan, trephine

trépasser [tʀepase] *vi* to pass away

trépidant, e [tʀepidɑ̃, -ɑ̃t] *adj* (*fig*: *rythme*) pulsating; (*: vie*) hectic

trépidation [tʀepidasjɔ̃] *nf* (*d'une machine, d'un moteur*) vibration; (*fig*: *de la vie*) whirl

trépider [tʀepide] *vi* to vibrate

trépied [tʀepje] *nm* (*d'appareil*) tripod; (*meuble*) trivet

trépignement [tʀepiɲmɑ̃] *nm* stamping (of feet)

trépigner [tʀepiɲe] *vi* to stamp (one's feet)

très [tʀɛ] *adv* very; **~ beau/bien** very beautiful/well; **~ critiqué** much criticized; **~ industrialisé** highly industrialized; **j'ai ~ faim** I'm very hungry

trésor [tʀezɔʀ] *nm* treasure; (*Admin*) finances *pl*; (*d'une organisation*) funds *pl*; **~ (public) (TP)** public revenue; (*service*) public revenue office

trésorerie [tʀezɔʀʀi] *nf* (*fonds*) funds *pl*; (*gestion*) accounts *pl*; (*bureaux*) accounts department; (*poste*) treasurership; **difficultés de ~** cash problems, shortage of cash *ou* funds; **~ générale (TG)** *local government finance office*

trésorier, -ière [tʀezɔʀje, -jɛʀ] *nm/f* treasurer

Trésorier-payeur [tʀezɔʀjepɛjœʀ] *nm*: **~ général (TPG)** paymaster

tressaillement [tʀesajmɑ̃] *nm* shiver, shudder; quiver

tressaillir [tʀesajiʀ] *vi* (*de peur etc*) to shiver, shudder; (*de joie*) to quiver

tressauter [tʀesote] *vi* to start, jump

tresse [tʀɛs] *nf* (*de cheveux*) braid, plait; (*cordon, galon*) braid

tresser [tʀese] *vt* (*cheveux*) to braid, plait; (*fil, jonc*) to plait; (*corbeille*) to weave; (*corde*) to twist

tréteau, x [tʀeto] *nm* trestle; **les ~x** (*fig*: *Théât*) the boards

treuil [tʀœj] *nm* winch

trêve [tʀɛv] *nf* (*Mil, Pol*) truce; (*fig*) respite; **sans ~** unremittingly; **~ de ...** enough of this ...; **les États de la T~** the Trucial States

tri [tʀi] *nm* (*voir* **trier**) sorting (out) *no pl*; selection; screening; (*Inform*) sort; (*Postes*: *action*) sorting; (*: bureau*) sorting office

triage [tʀijaʒ] *nm* (*Rail*) shunting; (*gare*) marshalling yard

trial [tʀijal] *nm* (*Sport*) scrambling

triangle [tʀijɑ̃gl(ə)] *nm* triangle; **~ isocèle/équilatéral** isosceles/equilateral triangle; **~ rectangle** right-angled triangle

triangulaire [tʀijɑ̃gylɛʀ] *adj* triangular

triathlon [tʀi(j)atlɔ̃] *nm* triathlon

tribal, e, -aux [tʀibal, -o] *adj* tribal

tribord [tʀibɔʀ] *nm*: **à ~** to starboard, on the starboard side

tribu [tʀiby] *nf* tribe

tribulations [tʀibylɑsjɔ̃] *nfpl* tribulations, trials

tribunal, -aux [tʀibynal, -o] *nm* (*Jur*) court; (*Mil*) tribunal; **~ de police/pour enfants** police/juvenile court; **~ d'instance (TI)** ≈ magistrates' court (*Brit*), ≈ district court (*US*); **~ de grande instance (TGI)** ≈ High Court (*Brit*), ≈ Supreme Court (*US*)

tribune [tʀibyn] *nf* (*estrade*) platform, rostrum; (*débat*) forum; (*d'église, de tribunal*) gallery; (*de stade*) stand; **~ libre** (*Presse*) opinion column

tribut [tʀiby] *nm* tribute

tributaire [tʀibytɛʀ] *adj*: **être ~ de** to be dependent on; (*Géo*) to be a tributary of

tricentenaire [tʀisɑ̃tnɛʀ] *nm* tercentenary, tricentennial

tricher [tʀiʃe] *vi* to cheat

tricherie [tʀiʃʀi] *nf* cheating *no pl*

tricheur, -euse [tʀiʃœʀ, -øz] *nm/f* cheat

trichromie [tʀikʀɔmi] *nf* three-colour (*Brit*) *ou* color (*US*) printing

tricolore [tʀikɔlɔʀ] *adj* three-coloured (*Brit*), three-colored (*US*); (*français*: *drapeau*) red, white and blue; (*: équipe etc*) French

tricot [tʀiko] *nm* (*technique, ouvrage*) knitting *no pl*; (*tissu*) knitted fabric; (*vêtement*) jersey, sweater; **~ de corps** vest (*Brit*), undershirt (*US*)

tricoter [tʀikɔte] *vt* to knit; **machine/aiguille à ~** knitting machine/needle (*Brit*) *ou* pin (*US*)

trictrac [tʀiktʀak] *nm* backgammon

tricycle [tʀisikl(ə)] *nm* tricycle

tridimensionnel, le [tʀidimɑ̃sjɔnɛl] *adj* three-dimensional

triennal, e, -aux [tʀienal, -o] *adj* (*prix, foire, élection*) three-yearly; (*charge, mandat, plan*) three-year

trier [tʀije] *vt* (*classer*) to sort (out); (*choisir*) to select; (*visiteurs*) to screen; (*Postes, Inform*) to sort

trieur, -euse [tʀijœʀ, -øz] *nm/f* sorter

trigonométrie [tʀigɔnɔmetʀi] *nf* trigonometry

trigonométrique [tʀigɔnɔmetʀik] *adj* trigonometric

trilingue [tʀilɛ̃g] *adj* trilingual

trilogie [tʀilɔʒi] *nf* trilogy

trimaran [tʀimaʀɑ̃] *nm* trimaran

trimbaler [tʀɛ̃bale] *vt* to cart around, trail

along

trimer [tʀime] *vi* to slave away

trimestre [tʀimɛstʀ(ə)] *nm* (*Scol*) term; (*Comm*) quarter

trimestriel, le [tʀimɛstʀijɛl] *adj* quarterly; (*Scol*) end-of-term

trimoteur [tʀimɔtœʀ] *nm* three-engined aircraft

tringle [tʀɛ̃gl(ə)] *nf* rod

Trinité [tʀinite] *nf* Trinity

Trinité et Tobago [tʀiniteetɔbago] *nf* Trinidad and Tobago

trinquer [tʀɛ̃ke] *vi* to clink glasses; (*fam*) to cop it; **~ à qch/la santé de qn** to drink to sth/sb

trio [tʀijo] *nm* trio

triolet [tʀijɔlɛ] *nm* (*Mus*) triplet

triomphal, e, -aux [tʀijɔ̃fal, -o] *adj* triumphant, triumphal

triomphalement [tʀijɔ̃falmɑ̃] *adv* triumphantly

triomphant, e [tʀijɔ̃fɑ̃, -ɑ̃t] *adj* triumphant

triomphateur, -trice [tʀijɔ̃fatœʀ, -tʀis] *nm/f* (triumphant) victor

triomphe [tʀijɔ̃f] *nm* triumph; **être reçu/ porté en ~** to be given a triumphant welcome/ be carried shoulder-high in triumph

triompher [tʀijɔ̃fe] *vi* to triumph; **~ de** to triumph over, overcome

triparti, e [tʀipaʀti] *adj* (*aussi*: **tripartite**: *réunion, assemblée*) tripartite, three-party

triperie [tʀipʀi] *nf* tripe shop

tripes [tʀip] *nfpl* (*Culin*) tripe *nsg*; (*fam*) guts

triplace [tʀiplas] *adj* three-seater *cpd*

triple [tʀipl(ə)] *adj* (*à trois éléments*) triple; (*trois fois plus grand*) treble ▷ *nm*: **le ~ (de)** (*comparaison*) three times as much (as); **en ~ exemplaire** in triplicate; **~ saut** (*Sport*) triple jump

triplé [tʀiple] *nm* hat-trick (*Brit*), triple success

triplement [tʀipləmɑ̃] *adv* (*à un degré triple*) three times over; (*de trois façons*) in three ways; (*pour trois raisons*) on three counts ▷ *nm* trebling, threefold increase

tripler [tʀiple] *vi, vt* to triple, treble, increase threefold

triplés, -ées [tʀiple] *nm/fpl* triplets

Tripoli [tʀipoli] *n* Tripoli

triporteur [tʀipɔʀtœʀ] *nm* delivery tricycle

tripot [tʀipo] *nm* (*péj*) dive

tripotage [tʀipotaʒ] *nm* (*péj*) jiggery-pokery

tripoter [tʀipote] *vt* to fiddle with, finger ▷ *vi* (*fam*) to rummage about

trique [tʀik] *nf* cudgel

trisannuel, le [tʀizanɥɛl] *adj* triennial

trisomie [tʀizomi] *nf* Down's syndrome

triste [tʀist(ə)] *adj* sad; (*péj*): **~ personnage/ affaire** sorry individual/affair; **c'est pas ~!** (*fam*) it's something else!

tristement [tʀistəmɑ̃] *adv* sadly

tristesse [tʀistɛs] *nf* sadness

triton [tʀitɔ̃] *nm* triton

triturer [tʀityʀe] *vt* (*pâte*) to knead; (*objets*) to manipulate

trivial, e, -aux [tʀivjal, -o] *adj* coarse, crude; (*commun*) mundane

trivialité [tʀivjalite] *nf* coarseness, crudeness; mundaneness

troc [tʀɔk] *nm* (*Écon*) barter; (*transaction*) exchange, swap

troène [tʀɔɛn] *nm* privet

troglodyte [tʀɔglɔdit] *nm/f* cave dweller, troglodyte

trognon [tʀɔɲɔ̃] *nm* (*de fruit*) core; (*de légume*) stalk

trois [tʀwa] *num* three

trois-huit [tʀwaɥit] *nmpl*: **faire les ~** to work eight-hour shifts (round the clock)

troisième [tʀwazjɛm] *num* third; **le ~ âge** the years of retirement

troisièmement [tʀwazjɛmmɑ̃] *adv* thirdly

trois quarts [tʀwakaʀ] *nmpl*: **les ~ de** three-quarters of

trolleybus [tʀɔlɛbys] *nm* trolley bus

trombe [tʀɔ̃b] *nf* waterspout; **des ~s d'eau** a downpour; **en ~** (*arriver, passer*) like a whirlwind

trombone [tʀɔ̃bɔn] *nm* (*Mus*) trombone; (*de bureau*) paper clip; **~ à coulisse** slide trombone

tromboniste [tʀɔ̃bɔnist(ə)] *nm/f* trombonist

trompe [tʀɔ̃p] *nf* (*d'éléphant*) trunk; (*Mus*) trumpet, horn; **~ d'Eustache** Eustachian tube; **~s utérines** Fallopian tubes

trompe-l'œil [tʀɔ̃plœj] *nm*: **en trompe-l'œil** in trompe-l'œil style

tromper [tʀɔ̃pe] *vt* to deceive; (*fig: espoir, attente*) to disappoint; (*vigilance, poursuivants*) to elude; **se tromper** *vi* to make a mistake, be mistaken; **se tromper de voiture/jour** to take the wrong car/ get the day wrong; **se ~ de 3 cm/20 euros** to be out by 3 cm/20 euros

tromperie [tʀɔ̃pʀi] *nf* deception, trickery *no pl*

trompette [tʀɔ̃pɛt] *nf* trumpet; **en ~** (*nez*) turned-up

trompettiste [tʀɔ̃petist(ə)] *nm/f* trumpet player

trompeur, -euse [tʀɔ̃pœʀ, -øz] *adj* deceptive, misleading

tronc [tʀɔ̃] *nm* (*Bot, Anat*) trunk; (*d'église*) collection box; **~ d'arbre** tree trunk; **~ commun** (*Scol*) common-core syllabus; **~ de cône** truncated cone

tronche [tʀɔ̃ʃ] *nf* (*fam*) mug, face

tronçon [tʀɔ̃sɔ̃] *nm* section

tronçonner [tʀɔ̃sɔne] *vt* (*arbre*) to saw up; (*pierre*) to cut up

tronçonneuse [tʀɔ̃sɔnøz] *nf* chain saw

trône [tʀon] *nm* throne; **monter sur le ~** to ascend the throne

trôner [tʀone] *vi* (*fig*) to have (*ou* take) pride of place (*Brit*), have the place of honour (*Brit*) *ou* honor (*US*)

tronquer [tʀɔ̃ke] *vt* to truncate; (*fig*) to curtail

trop [tʀo] *adv* too; (*avec verbe*) too much; (*aussi*: **trop nombreux**) too many; (*aussi*: **trop souvent**) too often; **~ peu (nombreux)** too few; **~ longtemps** (for) too long; **~ de** (*nombre*) too many; (*quantité*) too much; **de ~, en ~: des livres en ~** a few books too many, a few extra books; **du lait en ~** too much milk; **trois livres/cinq euros de ~** three books too many/five euros too much

trophée [tʀɔfe] *nm* trophy

tropical, e, -aux [tʀɔpikal, -o] *adj* tropical

tropique [tʀɔpik] *nm* tropic; **tropiques** *nmpl* tropics; **~ du Cancer/Capricorne** Tropic of Cancer/Capricorn

trop-plein [tʀɔplɛ̃] *nm* (*tuyau*) overflow *ou* outlet (pipe); (*liquide*) overflow

troquer [tʀɔke] *vt*: **~ qch contre** to barter *ou* trade sth for; (*fig*) to swap sth for

trot [tʀo] *nm* trot; **aller au ~** to trot along; **partir au ~** to set off at a trot

trotter [tʀɔte] *vi* to trot; (*fig*) to scamper along (*ou* about)

trotteuse [tʀɔtøz] *nf* (*de montre*) second hand

trottiner [tʀɔtine] *vi* (*fig*) to scamper along (*ou* about)

trottinette [tʀɔtinɛt] *nf* (child's) scooter

trottoir [tʀɔtwaʀ] *nm* pavement (*Brit*), sidewalk (*US*); **faire le ~** (*péj*) to walk the streets; **~ roulant** moving pavement (*Brit*) *ou* walkway

trou [tʀu] *nm* hole; (*fig*) gap; (*Comm*) deficit; **~ d'aération** (air) vent; **~ d'air** air pocket; **~ de mémoire** blank, lapse of memory; **~ noir** black hole; **~ de la serrure** keyhole

troublant, e [tʀublɑ̃, -ɑ̃t] *adj* disturbing

trouble [tʀubl(ə)] *adj* (*liquide*) cloudy; (*image, mémoire*) indistinct, hazy; (*affaire*) shady, murky ▷ *adv* indistinctly ▷ *nm* (*désarroi*) distress, agitation; (*émoi sensuel*) turmoil, agitation; (*embarras*) confusion; (*zizanie*) unrest, discord; **troubles** *nmpl* (*Pol*) disturbances, troubles, unrest *nsg*; (*Méd*) trouble *nsg*, disorders; **~s de la personnalité** personality problems; **~s de la vision** eye trouble

trouble-fête [tʀubləfɛt] *nm/f inv* spoilsport

troubler [tʀuble] *vt* (*embarrasser*) to confuse, disconcert; (*émouvoir*) to agitate; to disturb; to perturb; (*perturber: ordre etc*) to disrupt, disturb; (*liquide*) to make cloudy; **se troubler** *vi* (*personne*) to become flustered *ou* confused; **~ l'ordre public** to cause a breach of the peace

troué, e [tʀue] *adj* with a hole (*ou* holes) in it ▷ *nf* gap; (*Mil*) breach

trouer [tʀue] *vt* to make a hole (*ou* holes) in; (*fig*) to pierce

trouille [tʀuj] *nf* (*fam*): **avoir la ~** to be scared stiff, be scared out of one's wits

troupe [tʀup] *nf* (*Mil*) troop; (*groupe*) troop, group; **la ~** (*Mil: l'armée*) the army; (*: les simples soldats*) the troops *pl*; **~ (de théâtre)** (theatrical) company; **~s de choc** shock troops

troupeau, x [tʀupo] *nm* (*de moutons*) flock; (*de vaches*) herd

trousse [tʀus] *nf* case, kit; (*d'écolier*) pencil case; (*de docteur*) instrument case; **aux ~s de** (*fig*) on the heels *ou* tail of; **~ à outils** toolkit; **~ de toilette** toilet *ou* sponge (*Brit*) bag

trousseau, x [tʀuso] *nm* (*de mariée*) trousseau; **~ de clefs** bunch of keys

trouvaille [tʀuvaj] *nf* find; (*fig: idée, expression etc*) brainwave

trouvé, e [tʀuve] *adj*: **tout ~** ready-made

trouver [tʀuve] *vt* to find; (*rendre visite*): **aller/venir ~ qn** to go/come and see sb; **je trouve que** I find *ou* think that; **~ à boire/critiquer** to find something to drink/criticize; **~ asile/refuge** to find refuge/shelter; **se trouver** *vi* (*être*) to be; (*être soudain*) to find o.s.; **se ~ être/avoir** to happen to be/have; **il se trouve que** it happens that, it turns out that; **se ~ bien** to feel well; **se ~ mal** to pass out

truand [tʀyɑ̃] *nm* villain, crook

truander [tʀyɑ̃de] *vi* (*fam*) to cheat, do

trublion [tʀyblijɔ̃] *nm* troublemaker

truc [tʀyk] *nm* (*astuce*) way, device; (*de cinéma, prestidigitateur*) trick effect; (*chose*) thing; (*machin*) thingumajig, whatsit (*Brit*); **avoir le ~** to have the knack; **c'est pas son** (*ou* **mon** *etc*) **~** (*fam*) it's not really his (*ou* my *etc*) thing

truchement [tʀyʃmɑ̃] *nm*: **par le ~ de qn** through (the intervention of) sb

trucider [tʀyside] *vt* (*fam*) to do in, bump off

truculence [tʀykylɑ̃s] *nf* colourfulness (*Brit*), colorfulness (*US*)

truculent, e [tʀykylɑ̃, -ɑ̃t] *adj* colourful (*Brit*), colorful (*US*)

truelle [tʀyɛl] *nf* trowel

truffe [tʀyf] *nf* truffle; (*nez*) nose

truffé, e [tʀyfe] *adj*: **~ de** (*fig*) peppered with; (*fautes*) riddled with; (*pièges*) bristling with

truffer [tʀyfe] *vt* (*Culin*) to garnish with truffles; **truffé de** (*fig: citations*) peppered with; (*: pièges*) bristling with

truie [tʀyi] *nf* sow

truite [tʀyit] *nf* trout *inv*

truquage [tʀykaʒ] *nm* fixing; (*Ciné*) special effects *pl*

truquer [tʀyke] *vt* (*élections, serrure, dés*) to fix; (*Ciné*) to use special effects in

trust [tʀœst] *nm* (*Comm*) trust

truster [tʀœste] *vt* (*Comm*) to monopolize

ts *abr* = **tous**

tsar [dzaʀ] *nm* tsar

tsé-tsé [tsetse] *nf*: **mouche ~** tsetse fly

TSF *sigle f* (= *télégraphie sans fil*) wireless

tsigane [tsigan] *adj, nm/f* = **tzigane**

TSVP *abr* (= *tournez s'il vous plaît*) PTO

tt *abr* = **tout**

TT, TTA *sigle m* (= *transit temporaire (autorisé)*) vehicle registration for cars etc bought in France for export tax-free by non-residents

TTC *abr* = **toutes taxes comprises**

ttes *abr* = **toutes**

TU *sigle m* = **temps universel**

tu¹ [ty] *pron* you ▷ *nm*: **employer le tu** to use the "tu" form

tu², e [ty] *pp de* **taire**

tuant, e [tɥɑ̃, -ɑ̃t] *adj* (*épuisant*) killing; (*énervant*) infuriating

tuba [tyba] *nm* (*Mus*) tuba; (*Sport*) snorkel
tubage [tybaʒ] *nm* (*Méd*) intubation
tube [tyb] *nm* tube; (*de canalisation, métallique etc*) pipe; (*chanson, disque*) hit song *ou* record; ~ **digestif** alimentary canal, digestive tract; ~ **à essai** test tube
tuberculeux, -euse [tybɛʀkylø, -øz] *adj* tubercular ▷ *nm/f* tuberculosis *ou* TB patient
tuberculose [tybɛʀkyloz] *nf* tuberculosis, TB
tubulaire [tybylɛʀ] *adj* tubular
tubulure [tybylyʀ] *nf* pipe; piping *no pl*; (*Auto*): ~ **d'échappement/d'admission** exhaust/inlet manifold
TUC [tyk] *sigle m* (= *travail d'utilité collective*) community work scheme for the young unemployed
tuciste [tysist(ə)] *nm/f* young person on a community work scheme
tué, e [tɥe] *nm/f*: **cinq ~s** five killed *ou* dead
tue-mouche [tymuʃ] *adj*: **papier ~(s)** flypaper
tuer [tɥe] *vt* to kill; **se tuer** (*se suicider*) to kill o.s.; (*dans un accident*) to be killed; **se ~ au travail** (*fig*) to work o.s. to death
tuerie [tyʀi] *nf* slaughter *no pl*, massacre
tue-tête [tytɛt]: **à ~** *adv* at the top of one's voice
tueur [tɥœʀ] *nm* killer; ~ **à gages** hired killer
tuile [tɥil] *nf* tile; (*fam*) spot of bad luck, blow
tulipe [tylip] *nf* tulip
tulle [tyl] *nm* tulle
tuméfié, e [tymefje] *adj* puffy, swollen
tumeur [tymœʀ] *nf* growth, tumour (*Brit*), tumor (*US*)
tumulte [tymylt(ə)] *nm* commotion, hubbub
tumultueux, -euse [tymyltɥø, -øz] *adj* stormy, turbulent
tuner [tynɛʀ] *nm* tuner
tungstène [tœ̃kstɛn] *nm* tungsten
tunique [tynik] *nf* tunic; (*de femme*) smock, tunic
Tunis [tynis] *n* Tunis
Tunisie [tynizi] *nf*: **la ~** Tunisia
tunisien, ne [tynizjɛ̃, -ɛn] *adj* Tunisian ▷ *nm/f*: **Tunisien, ne** Tunisian
tunisois, e [tynizwa, -waz] *adj* of *ou* from Tunis
tunnel [tynɛl] *nm* tunnel; **le ~ sous la Manche** the Channel Tunnel, the Chunnel
TUP *sigle m* (= *titre universel de paiement*) ≈ payment slip
turban [tyʀbɑ̃] *nm* turban
turbin [tyʀbɛ̃] *nm* (*fam*) work *no pl*
turbine [tyʀbin] *nf* turbine
turbo [tyʀbo] *nm* turbo; **un moteur ~** a turbo(-charged) engine
turbomoteur [tyʀbɔmɔtœʀ] *nm* turbo(-boosted) engine
turbopropulseur [tyʀbɔpʀɔpylsœʀ] *nm* turboprop
turboréacteur [tyʀbɔʀeaktœʀ] *nm* turbojet
turbot [tyʀbo] *nm* turbot
turbotrain [tyʀbɔtʀɛ̃] *nm* turbotrain
turbulences [tyʀbylɑ̃s] *nfpl* (*Aviat*) turbulence *sg*
turbulent, e [tyʀbylɑ̃, -ɑ̃t] *adj* boisterous, unruly
turc, turque [tyʀk(ə)] *adj* Turkish; (*w.-c.*)

seatless ▷ *nm* (*Ling*) Turkish ▷ *nm/f*: **Turc, Turque** Turk/Turkish woman; **à la turque** *adv* (*assis*) cross-legged
turf [tyʀf] *nm* racing
turfiste [tyʀfist(ə)] *nm/f* racegoer
Turks et Caïques [tyʀkekaik], **Turks et Caicos** [tyʀkekaikɔs] *nfpl* Turks and Caicos Islands
turpitude [tyʀpityd] *nf* base act, baseness *no pl*
turque [tyʀk(ə)] *adj f, nf voir* **turc**
Turquie [tyʀki] *nf*: **la ~** Turkey
turquoise [tyʀkwaz] *nf, adj inv* turquoise
tus *etc* [ty] *vb voir* **taire**
tut *etc* [ty] *vb voir* **taire**
tutelle [tytɛl] *nf* (*Jur*) guardianship; (*Pol*) trusteeship; **sous la ~ de** (*fig*) under the supervision of
tuteur, -trice [tytœʀ, -tʀis] *nm/f* (*Jur*) guardian; (*de plante*) stake, support
tutoiement [tytwamɑ̃] *nm* use of familiar "tu" form
tutoyer [tytwaje] *vt*: ~ **qn** to address sb as "tu"
tutti quanti [tutikwɑ̃ti] *nmpl*: **et ~** and all the rest (of them)
tutu [tyty] *nm* (*Danse*) tutu
tuyau, x [tɥijo] *nm* pipe; (*flexible*) tube; (*fam: conseil*) tip; (*: mise au courant*) gen *no pl*; ~ **d'arrosage** hosepipe; ~ **d'échappement** exhaust pipe; ~ **d'incendie** fire hose
tuyauté, e [tɥijote] *adj* fluted
tuyauterie [tɥijotʀi] *nf* piping *no pl*
tuyère [tɥijɛʀ] *nf* nozzle
TV [teve] *nf* TV, telly (*Brit*)
TVA *sigle f* (= *taxe à*) *ou sur la valeur ajoutée*, VAT
TVHD *abr f* (= *télévision haute-définition*) HDTV
tweed [twid] *nm* tweed
tympan [tɛ̃pɑ̃] *nm* (*Anat*) eardrum
type [tip] *nm* type; (*personne, chose: représentant*) classic example, epitome; (*fam*) chap, guy ▷ *adj* typical, standard; **avoir le ~ nordique** to be Nordic-looking
typé, e [tipe] *adj* ethnic (*euph*)
typhoïde [tifɔid] *nf* typhoid (fever)
typhon [tifɔ̃] *nm* typhoon
typhus [tifys] *nm* typhus (fever)
typique [tipik] *adj* typical
typiquement [tipikmɑ̃] *adv* typically
typographe [tipɔgʀaf] *nm/f* typographer
typographie [tipɔgʀafi] *nf* typography; (*procédé*) letterpress (printing)
typographique [tipɔgʀafik] *adj* typographical; letterpress *cpd*
typologie [tipɔlɔʒi] *nf* typology
tyran [tiʀɑ̃] *nm* tyrant
tyrannie [tiʀani] *nf* tyranny
tyrannique [tiʀanik] *adj* tyrannical
tyranniser [tiʀanize] *vt* to tyrannize
Tyrol [tiʀɔl] *nm*: **le ~** the Tyrol
tyrolien, ne [tiʀɔljɛ̃, -ɛn] *adj* Tyrolean
tzar [dzaʀ] *nm* = **tsar**
tzigane [dzigan] *adj* gipsy, tzigane ▷ *nm/f* (Hungarian) gipsy, Tzigane

Uu

U, u [y] *nm inv* U, u; **U comme Ursule** U for Uncle
ubiquité [ybikɥite] *nf:* **avoir le don d'~** to be everywhere at once, be ubiquitous
UDF *sigle f* (= *Union pour la démocratie française*) political party
UE *sigle f* (= *Union européenne*) EU
UEFA [yefa] *sigle f* (= *Union of European Football Associations*) UEFA
UEM *sigle f* (= *Union économique et monétaire*) EMU
UER *sigle f* (= *unité d'enseignement et de recherche*) old title of UFR; (= *Union européenne de radiodiffusion*) EBU (= *European Broadcasting Union*)
UFC *sigle f* (= *Union fédérale des consommateurs*) national consumer group
UFR *sigle f* (= *unité de formation et de recherche*) ≈ university department
UHF *sigle f* (= *ultra-haute fréquence*) UHF
UHT *sigle* (= *ultra-haute température*) UHT
UIT *sigle f* (= *Union internationale des télécommunications*) ITU (= *International Telecommunications Union*)
Ukraine [ykRɛn] *nf:* **l'~** the Ukraine
ukrainien, ne [ykRɛnjɛ̃, -ɛn] *adj* Ukrainian ▷ *nm* (*Ling*) Ukrainian ▷ *nm/f:* **Ukrainien, ne** Ukrainian
ulcère [ylsɛR] *nm* ulcer; **~ à l'estomac** stomach ulcer
ulcérer [ylseRe] *vt* (*Méd*) to ulcerate; (*fig*) to sicken, appal
ulcéreux, -euse [ylseRø, -øz] *adj* (*plaie, lésion*) ulcerous; (*membre*) ulcerated
ULM *sigle m* (= *ultra léger motorisé*) microlight
ultérieur, e [ylteRjœR] *adj* later, subsequent; **remis à une date ~e** postponed to a later date
ultérieurement [ylteRjœRmɑ̃] *adv* later
ultimatum [yltimatɔm] *nm* ultimatum
ultime [yltim] *adj* final
ultra... [yltRa] *préfixe* ultra...
ultramoderne [yltRamɔdɛRn(ə)] *adj* ultra-modern
ultra-rapide [yltRaRapid] *adj* ultra-fast
ultra-sensible [yltRasɑ̃sibl(ə)] *adj* (*Photo*) high-speed
ultrason, ultra-son [yltRasɔ̃] *nm* ultrasound *no pl*; **ultra(-)sons** *nmpl* ultrasonics
ultraviolet, ultra-violet, te [yltRavjɔlɛ, -ɛt] *adj*

ultraviolet ▷ *nm:* **les ultra(-)violets** ultraviolet rays
ululer [ylyle] *vi* = **hululer**
UME *sigle f* (= *Union monétaire européenne*) EMU
UMP *sigle f* (= *Union pour un mouvement populaire*) political party

 MOT-CLÉ

un, une [œ̃, yn] *art indéf* a; (*devant voyelle*) an; **un garçon/vieillard** a boy/an old man; **une fille** a girl
▷ *pron* one; **l'un des meilleurs** one of the best; **l'un ..., l'autre** (the) one ..., the other; **les uns ..., les autres** some ..., others; **l'un et l'autre** both (of them); **l'un ou l'autre** either (of them); **l'un l'autre, les uns les autres** each other, one another; **pas un seul** not a single one; **un par un** one by one
▷ *num* one; **une pomme seulement** one apple only
▷ *nf:* **la une** (*Presse*) the front page

unanime [ynanim] *adj* unanimous; **ils sont ~s (à penser que)** they are unanimous (in thinking that)
unanimement [ynanimmɑ̃] *adv* (*par tous*) unanimously; (*d'un commun accord*) with one accord
unanimité [ynanimite] *nf* unanimity; **à l'~** unanimously; **faire l'~** to be approved unanimously
UNEF [ynɛf] *sigle f* = **Union nationale des étudiants de France**
UNESCO [ynɛsko] *sigle f* (= *United Nations Educational, Scientific and Cultural Organization*) UNESCO
Unetelle [yntɛl] *nf voir* **Untel**
UNI *sigle f* = **Union nationale interuniversitaire**
uni, e [yni] *adj* (*ton, tissu*) plain; (*surface*) smooth, even; (*famille*) close(-knit); (*pays*) united
UNICEF [ynisɛf] *sigle m ou f* (= *United Nations International Children's Emergency Fund*) UNICEF
unidirectionnel, le [ynidiRɛksjɔnɛl] *adj* unidirectional, one-way
unième [ynjɛm] *num:* **vingt/trente et ~**

u

twenty-/thirty-first; **cent ~** (one) hundred and first

unificateur, -trice [ynifikatœʀ, -tʀis] *adj* unifying

unification [ynifikasjɔ̃] *nf* uniting; unification; standardization

unifier [ynifje] *vt* to unite, unify; (*systèmes*) to standardize, unify; **s'unifier** *vi* to become united

uniforme [ynifɔʀm(ə)] *adj* (*mouvement*) regular, uniform; (*surface, ton*) even; (*objets, maisons*) uniform; (*fig: vie, conduite*) unchanging ▷ *nm* uniform; **être sous l'~** (*Mil*) to be serving

uniformément [ynifɔʀmemɑ̃] *adv* uniformly

uniformisation [ynifɔʀmizasjɔ̃] *nf* standardization

uniformiser [ynifɔʀmize] *vt* to make uniform; (*systèmes*) to standardize

uniformité [ynifɔʀmite] *nf* regularity; uniformity; evenness

unijambiste [yniʒɑ̃bist(ə)] *nm/f* one-legged man/woman

unilatéral, e, -aux [ynilateʀal, -o] *adj* unilateral; **stationnement ~** parking on one side only

unilatéralement [ynilateʀalmɑ̃] *adv* unilaterally

uninominal, e, -aux [yninɔminal, -o] *adj* uncontested

union [ynjɔ̃] *nf* union; **~ conjugale** union of marriage; **~ de consommateurs** consumers' association; **~ libre** free love; **l'U~ des Républiques socialistes soviétiques (URSS)** the Union of Soviet Socialist Republics (USSR); **l'U~ soviétique** the Soviet Union

unique [ynik] *adj* (*seul*) only; (*le même*): **un prix/système ~** a single price/system; (*exceptionnel*) unique; **ménage à salaire ~** one-salary family; **route à voie ~** single-lane road; **fils/fille ~** only son/daughter, only child; **~ en France** the only one of its kind in France

uniquement [ynikmɑ̃] *adv* only, solely; (*juste*) only, merely

unir [yniʀ] *vt* (*nations*) to unite; (*éléments, couleurs*) to combine; (*en mariage*) to unite, join together; **~ qch à** to unite sth with; to combine sth with; **s'unir** *vi* to unite; (*en mariage*) to be joined together; **s'~ à** *ou* **avec** to unite with

unisexe [yniseks] *adj* unisex

unisson [ynisɔ̃]: **à l'~** *adv* in unison

unitaire [yniteʀ] *adj* unitary; (*Pol*) unitarian; **prix ~** unit price

unité [ynite] *nf* (*harmonie, cohésion*) unity; (*Comm, Mil, de mesure, Math*) unit; **~ centrale** central processing unit; **~ de valeur** (university) course, credit

univers [yniveʀ] *nm* universe

universalisation [yniveʀsalizasjɔ̃] *nf* universalization

universaliser [yniveʀsalize] *vt* to universalize

universalité [yniveʀsalite] *nf* universality

universel, le [yniveʀsɛl] *adj* universal; (*esprit*) all-embracing

universellement [yniveʀsɛlmɑ̃] *adv* universally

universitaire [yniveʀsiteʀ] *adj* university *cpd*; (*diplôme, études*) academic, university *cpd* ▷ *nm/f* academic

université [yniveʀsite] *nf* university

univoque [ynivɔk] *adj* unambiguous; (*Math*) one-to-one

UNR *sigle f* (= Union pour la nouvelle république) former political party

UNSS *sigle f* = **Union nationale du sport scolaire**

Untel, Unetelle [œ̃tɛl, yntɛl] *nm/f*: **Monsieur ~** Mr so-and-so

uranium [yʀanjɔm] *nm* uranium

urbain, e [yʀbɛ̃, -ɛn] *adj* urban, city *cpd*, town *cpd*; (*poli*) urbane

urbanisation [yʀbanizasjɔ̃] *nf* urbanization

urbaniser [yʀbanize] *vt* to urbanize

urbanisme [yʀbanism(ə)] *nm* town planning

urbaniste [yʀbanist(ə)] *nm/f* town planner

urbanité [yʀbanite] *nf* urbanity

urée [yʀe] *nf* urea

urémie [yʀemi] *nf* uraemia (*Brit*), uremia (*US*)

urgence [yʀʒɑ̃s] *nf* urgency; (*Méd etc*) emergency; **d'~** *adj* emergency *cpd* ▷ *adv* as a matter of urgency; **en cas d'~** in case of emergency; **service des ~s** emergency service

urgent, e [yʀʒɑ̃, -ɑ̃t] *adj* urgent

urinaire [yʀineʀ] *adj* urinary

urinal, -aux [yʀinal, -o] *nm* (bed) urinal

urine [yʀin] *nf* urine

uriner [yʀine] *vi* to urinate

urinoir [yʀinwaʀ] *nm* (public) urinal

urne [yʀn(ə)] *nf* (*électorale*) ballot box; (*vase*) urn; **aller aux ~s** (*voter*) to go to the polls

urologie [yʀɔlɔʒi] *nf* urology

URSS [parfois : yʀs] *sigle f* (= Union des Républiques Socialistes Soviétiques) USSR

URSSAF [yʀsaf] *sigle f* (= Union pour le recouvrement de la sécurité sociale et des allocations familiales) administrative body responsible for social security funds and payments

urticaire [yʀtikeʀ] *nf* nettle rash, urticaria

Uruguay [yʀygwɛ] *nm*: **l'~** Uruguay

uruguayen, ne [yʀygwajɛ̃, -ɛn] *adj* Uruguayan ▷ *nm/f*: **Uruguayen, ne** Uruguayan

us [ys] *nmpl*: **us et coutumes** (habits and) customs

USA *sigle mpl* (= United States of America) USA

usage [yzaʒ] *nm* (*emploi, utilisation*) use; (*coutume*) custom; (*éducation*) (good) manners *pl*, (good) breeding; (*Ling*): **l'~** usage; **faire ~ de** (*pouvoir, droit*) to exercise; **avoir l'~ de** to have the use of; **à l'~** *adv* with use; **à l'~ de** (*pour*) (for use of); **en ~** in use; **hors d'~** out of service; **à ~ interne** to be taken; **à ~ externe** for external use only

usagé, e [yzaʒe] *adj* (*usé*) worn; (*d'occasion*) used

usager, -ère [yzaʒe, -ɛʀ] *nm/f* user

usé, e [yze] *adj* worn (down *ou* out *ou* away); ruined; (*banal*) hackneyed

user [yze] *vt* (*outil*) to wear down; (*vêtement*) to

wear out; (*matière*) to wear away; (*consommer:
charbon etc*) to use; (*fig: santé*) to ruin; (: *personne*)
to wear out; **s'user** *vi* to wear; to wear out; (*fig*)
to decline; **s'~ à la tâche** to wear o.s. out with
work; **~ de** *vt* (*moyen, procédé*) to use, employ;
(*droit*) to exercise
usine [yzin] *nf* factory; **~ atomique** nuclear
power plant; **~ à gaz** gasworks *sg*; **~
marémotrice** tidal power station
usiner [yzine] *vt* (*Tech*) to machine; (*fabriquer*) to
manufacture
usité, e [yzite] *adj* in common use, common;
peu ~ rarely used
ustensile [ystɑ̃sil] *nm* implement; **~ de cuisine**
kitchen utensil
usuel, le [yzɥɛl] *adj* everyday, common
usufruit [yzyfʀɥi] *nm* usufruct
usuraire [yzyʀɛʀ] *adj* usurious
usure [yzyʀ] *nf* wear; worn state; (*de l'usurier*)
usury; **avoir qn à l'~** to wear sb down; **~
normale** fair wear and tear
usurier, -ière [yzyʀje, -jɛʀ] *nm/f* usurer
usurpateur, -trice [yzyʀpatœʀ, -tʀis] *nm/f*
usurper
usurpation [yzyʀpɑsjɔ̃] *nf* usurpation

usurper [yzyʀpe] *vt* to usurp
ut [yt] *nm* (*Mus*) C
UTA *sigle f* = **Union des transporteurs aériens**
utérin, e [yteʀɛ̃, -in] *adj* uterine
utérus [yteʀys] *nm* uterus, womb
utile [ytil] *adj* useful; **~ à qn/qch** of use to sb/sth
utilement [ytilmɑ̃] *adv* usefully
utilisable [ytilizabl(ə)] *adj* usable
utilisateur, -trice [ytilizatœʀ, -tʀis] *nm/f* user
utilisation [ytilizɑsjɔ̃] *nf* use
utiliser [ytilize] *vt* to use
utilitaire [ytilitɛʀ] *adj* utilitarian; (*objets*)
practical ▷ *nm* (*Inform*) utility
utilité [ytilite] *nf* usefulness *no pl*; use; **jouer les
~s** (*Théât*) to play bit parts; **reconnu d'~
publique** state-approved; **c'est d'une grande
~** it's extremely useful; **il n'y a aucune ~ à ...**
there's no use in ...
utopie [ytɔpi] *nf* (*idée, conception*) utopian idea *ou*
view; (*société etc idéale*) utopia
utopique [ytɔpik] *adj* utopian
utopiste [ytɔpist(ə)] *nm/f* utopian
UV *sigle f* (*Scol*) = **unité de valeur** ▷ *sigle mpl*
(= *ultra-violets*) UV
uvule [yvyl] *nf* uvula

Vv

V, v [ve] *nm inv* V, v ▷ *abr* (= *voir, verset*) v = **vers**; (*de poésie*) l.; (: *en direction de*) toward(s); **V comme Victor** V for Victor; **en V** V-shaped; **encolure en V** V-neck; **décolleté en V** plunging neckline

va [va] *vb voir* **aller**

vacance [vakɑ̃s] *nf* (*Admin*) vacancy; **vacances** *nfpl* holiday(s) *pl* (*Brit*), vacation *sg* (*US*); **les grandes ~s** the summer holidays *ou* vacation; **prendre des/ses ~s** to take a holiday *ou* vacation/one's holiday(s) *ou* vacation; **aller en ~s** to go on holiday *ou* vacation

vacancier, -ière [vakɑ̃sje, -jɛʀ] *nm/f* holidaymaker (*Brit*), vacationer (*US*)

vacant, e [vakɑ̃, -ɑ̃t] *adj* vacant

vacarme [vakaʀm(ə)] *nm* row, din

vacataire [vakatɛʀ] *nm/f* temporary (employee); (*enseignement*) supply (*Brit*) *ou* substitute (*US*) teacher; (*Université*) part-time temporary lecturer

vaccin [vaksɛ̃] *nm* vaccine; (*opération*) vaccination

vaccination [vaksinɑsjɔ̃] *nf* vaccination

vacciner [vaksine] *vt* to vaccinate; (*fig*) to make immune; **être vacciné** (*fig*) to be immune

vache [vaʃ] *nf* (*Zool*) cow; (*cuir*) cowhide ▷ *adj* (*fam*) rotten, mean; **~ à eau** (canvas) water bag; **(manger de la) ~ enragée** (to go through) hard times; **~ à lait** (*péj*) mug, sucker; **~ laitière** dairy cow; **période des ~s maigres** lean times *pl*, lean period

vachement [vaʃmɑ̃] *adv* (*fam*) damned, really

vacher, -ère [vaʃe, -ɛʀ] *nm/f* cowherd

vacherie [vaʃʀi] *nf* (*fam*) meanness *no pl*; (*action*) dirty trick; (*propos*) nasty remark

vacherin [vaʃʀɛ̃] *nm* (*fromage*) vacherin cheese; (*gâteau*): **~ glacé** vacherin (*type of cream gâteau*)

vachette [vaʃɛt] *nf* calfskin

vacillant, e [vasijɑ̃, -ɑ̃t] *adj* wobbly; flickering; failing, faltering

vaciller [vasije] *vi* to sway, wobble; (*bougie, lumière*) to flicker; (*fig*) to be failing, falter; **~ dans ses réponses** to falter in one's replies; **~ dans ses résolutions** to waver in one's resolutions

vacuité [vakɥite] *nf* emptiness, vacuity

vade-mecum [vademekɔm] *nm inv* pocketbook

vadrouille [vadʀuj] *nf*: **être/partir en ~** to be on/go for a wander

vadrouiller [vadʀuje] *vi* to wander around *ou* about

va-et-vient [vaevjɛ̃] *nm inv* (*de pièce mobile*) to and fro (*ou* up and down) movement; (*de personnes, véhicules*) comings and goings *pl*, to-ings and fro-ings *pl*; (*Élec*) two-way switch

vagabond, e [vagabɔ̃, -ɔ̃d] *adj* wandering; (*imagination*) roaming, roving ▷ *nm* (*rôdeur*) tramp, vagrant; (*voyageur*) wanderer

vagabondage [vagabɔ̃daʒ] *nm* roaming, wandering; (*Jur*) vagrancy

vagabonder [vagabɔ̃de] *vi* to roam, wander

vagin [vaʒɛ̃] *nm* vagina

vaginal, e, -aux [vaʒinal, -o] *adj* vaginal

vagissement [vaʒismɑ̃] *nm* cry (*of newborn baby*)

vague [vag] *nf* wave ▷ *adj* vague; (*regard*) faraway; (*manteau, robe*) loose(-fitting); (*quelconque*): **un ~ bureau/cousin** some office/cousin or other ▷ *nm*: **être dans le ~** to be rather in the dark; **rester dans le ~** to keep things rather vague; **regarder dans le ~** to gaze into space; **~ à l'âme** *nm* vague melancholy; **~ d'assaut** *nf* (*Mil*) wave of assault; **~ de chaleur** *nf* heatwave; **~ de fond** *nf* ground swell; **~ de froid** *nf* cold spell

vaguelette [vaglɛt] *nf* ripple

vaguement [vagmɑ̃] *adv* vaguely

vaillamment [vajamɑ̃] *adv* bravely, gallantly

vaillant, e [vajɑ̃, -ɑ̃t] *adj* (*courageux*) brave, gallant; (*robuste*) vigorous, hale and hearty; **n'avoir plus un sou ~** to be penniless

vaille [vaj] *vb voir* **valoir**

vain, e [vɛ̃, vɛn] *adj* vain; **en ~** *adv* in vain

vaincre [vɛ̃kʀ(ə)] *vt* to defeat; (*fig*) to conquer, overcome

vaincu, e [vɛ̃ky] *pp de* **vaincre** ▷ *nm/f* defeated party

vainement [vɛnmɑ̃] *adv* vainly

vainquais *etc* [vɛ̃kɛ] *vb voir* **vaincre**

vainqueur [vɛ̃kœʀ] *nm* victor; (*Sport*) winner ▷ *adj m* victorious

vais [vɛ] *vb voir* **aller**

vaisseau, x [vɛso] *nm* (*Anat*) vessel; (*Navig*) ship, vessel; **~ spatial** spaceship

vaisselier [vɛsəlje] *nm* dresser

vaisselle [vɛsɛl] *nf* (*service*) crockery; (*plats etc à laver*) (dirty) dishes *pl*; **faire la ~** to do the washing-up (*Brit*) *ou* the dishes

val (*pl* **vaux** *ou* **vals**) [val, vo] *nmpl* valley

valable [valabl(ə)] *adj* valid; (*acceptable*) decent, worthwhile

valablement [valabləmã] *adv* legitimately; (*de façon satisfaisante*) satisfactorily

Valence [valãs] *n* (*en Espagne*) Valencia; (*en France*) Valence

valent *etc* [val] *vb voir* **valoir**

valet [valɛ] *nm* valet; (*péj*) lackey; (*Cartes*) jack, knave (*Brit*); **~ de chambre** manservant, valet; **~ de ferme** farmhand; **~ de pied** footman

valeur [valœʀ] *nf* (*gén*) value; (*mérite*) worth, merit; (*Comm: titre*) security; **mettre en ~** (*bien*) to exploit; (*terrain, région*) to develop; (*fig*) to highlight; to show off to advantage; **avoir de la ~** to be valuable; **prendre de la ~** to go up *ou* gain in value; **sans ~** worthless; **~ absolue** absolute value; **~ d'échange** exchange value; **~ nominale** face value; **~s mobilières** transferable securities

valeureux, -euse [valœʀø, -øz] *adj* valorous

validation [validɑsjõ] *nf* validation

valide [valid] *adj* (*en bonne santé*) fit, well; (*indemne*) able-bodied, fit; (*valable*) valid

valider [valide] *vt* to validate

validité [validite] *nf* validity

valions *etc* [valjõ] *vb voir* **valoir**

valise [valiz] *nf* (suit)case; **faire sa ~** to pack one's (suit)case; **la ~ (diplomatique)** the diplomatic bag

vallée [vale] *nf* valley

vallon [valõ] *nm* small valley

vallonné, e [valɔne] *adj* undulating

vallonnement [valɔnmã] *nm* undulation

valoir [valwaʀ] *vi* (*être valable*) to hold, apply ▷ *vt* (*prix, valeur, effort*) to be worth; (*causer*): **~ qch à qn** to earn sb sth; **se valoir** to be of equal merit; (*péj*) to be two of a kind; **faire ~** (*droits, prérogatives*) to assert; (*domaine, capitaux*) to exploit; **faire ~ que** to point out that; **se faire ~** to make the most of o.s.; **à ~ on** account; **à ~ sur** to be deducted from; **vaille que vaille** somehow or other; **cela ne me dit rien qui vaille** I don't like the look of it at all; **ce climat ne me vaut rien** this climate doesn't suit me; **~ la peine** to be worth the trouble, be worth it; **~ mieux: il vaut mieux se taire** it's better to say nothing; **il vaut mieux que je fasse/comme ceci** it's better if I do/like this; **ça ne vaut rien** it's worthless; **que vaut ce candidat?** how good is this applicant?

valorisation [valɔʀizasjõ] *nf* (economic) development; increased standing

valoriser [valɔʀize] *vt* (*Écon*) to develop (the economy of); (*produit*) to increase the value of; (*Psych*) to increase the standing of; (*fig*) to highlight, bring out

valse [vals(ə)] *nf* waltz; **c'est la ~ des étiquettes** the prices don't stay the same from one moment to the next

valser [valse] *vi* to waltz; (*fig*): **aller ~** to go flying

valu, e [valy] *pp de* **valoir**

valve [valv(ə)] *nf* valve

vamp [vãp] *nf* vamp

vampire [vãpiʀ] *nm* vampire

van [vã] *nm* horse box (*Brit*) *ou* trailer (*US*)

vandale [vãdal] *nm/f* vandal

vandalisme [vãdalism(ə)] *nm* vandalism

vanille [vanij] *nf* vanilla; **glace à la ~** vanilla ice cream

vanillé, e [vanije] *adj* vanilla *cpd*

vanité [vanite] *nf* vanity

vaniteux, -euse [vanitø, -øz] *adj* vain, conceited

vanity-case [vaniti(e)kɛz] *nm* vanity case

vanne [van] *nf* gate; (*fam: remarque*) dig, (nasty) crack; **lancer une ~ à qn** to have a go at sb (*Brit*), knock sb

vanneau, x [vano] *nm* lapwing

vanner [vane] *vt* to winnow

vannerie [vanʀi] *nf* basketwork

vantail, -aux [vãtaj, -o] *nm* door, leaf

vantard, e [vãtaʀ, -aʀd(ə)] *adj* boastful

vantardise [vãtaʀdiz] *nf* boastfulness *no pl*; boast

vanter [vãte] *vt* to speak highly of, vaunt; **se vanter** *vi* to boast, brag; **se ~ de** to pride o.s. on; (*péj*) to boast of

va-nu-pieds [vanypje] *nm/f inv* tramp, beggar

vapeur [vapœʀ] *nf* steam; (*émanation*) vapour (*Brit*), vapor (*US*), fumes *pl*; (*brouillard, buée*) haze; **vapeurs** *nfpl* (*bouffées*) vapours, vapors; **à ~** steam-powered, steam *cpd*; **à toute ~** full steam ahead; (*fig*) at full tilt; **renverser la ~** to reverse engines; (*fig*) to backtrack, backpedal; **cuit à la ~** steamed

vapocuiseur [vapokɥizœʀ] *nm* pressure cooker

vaporeux, -euse [vapɔʀø, -øz] *adj* (*flou*) hazy, misty; (*léger*) filmy, gossamer *cpd*

vaporisateur [vapɔʀizatœʀ] *nm* spray

vaporiser [vapɔʀize] *vt* (*Chimie*) to vaporize; (*parfum etc*) to spray

vaquer [vake] *vi* (*Admin*) to be on vacation; **~ à ses occupations** to attend to one's affairs, go about one's business

varappe [vaʀap] *nf* rock climbing

varappeur, -euse [vaʀapœʀ, -øz] *nm/f* (rock) climber

varech [vaʀɛk] *nm* wrack, varec

vareuse [vaʀøz] *nf* (*blouson*) pea jacket; (*d'uniforme*) tunic

variable [vaʀjabl(ə)] *adj* variable; (*temps, humeur*) changeable; (*Tech: à plusieurs positions etc*) adaptable; (*Ling*) inflectional; (*divers: résultats*) varied, various ▷ *nf* (*Inform, Math*) variable

variante [vaʀjãt] *nf* variant

variation [vaʀjɑsjõ] *nf* variation; changing *no pl*, change; (*Mus*) variation

429

varice [vaʀis] *nf* varicose vein
varicelle [vaʀisɛl] *nf* chickenpox
varié, e [vaʀje] *adj* varied; (*divers*) various; **hors-d'œuvre ~s** selection of hors d'œuvres
varier [vaʀje] *vi* to vary; (*temps, humeur*) to change ▷ *vt* to vary
variété [vaʀjete] *nf* variety; **spectacle de ~s** variety show
variole [vaʀjɔl] *nf* smallpox
variqueux, -euse [vaʀikø, -øz] *adj* varicose
Varsovie [vaʀsɔvi] *n* Warsaw
vas [va] *vb voir* **aller**; **~-y!** [vazi] go on!
vasculaire [vaskylɛʀ] *adj* vascular
vase [vaz] *nm* vase ▷ *nf* silt, mud; **en ~ clos** in isolation; **~ de nuit** chamberpot; **~s communicants** communicating vessels
vasectomie [vazɛktɔmi] *nf* vasectomy
vaseline [vazlin] *nf* Vaseline®
vaseux, -euse [vazø, -øz] *adj* silty, muddy; (*fig: confus*) woolly, hazy; (: *fatigué*) peaky; (: *étourdi*) woozy
vasistas [vazistɑs] *nm* fanlight
vasque [vask(ə)] *nf* (*bassin*) basin; (*coupe*) bowl
vassal, e, -aux [vasal, -o] *nm/f* vassal
vaste [vast(ə)] *adj* vast, immense
Vatican [vatikɑ̃] *nm*: **le ~** the Vatican
vaticiner [vatisine] *vi* (*péj*) to make pompous predictions
va-tout [vatu] *nm*: **jouer son ~** to stake one's all
vaudeville [vodvil] *nm* vaudeville, light comedy
vaudrai *etc* [vodʀe] *vb voir* **valoir**
vau-l'eau [volo]: **à vau-l'eau** *adv* with the current; **s'en aller à vau-l'eau** (*fig: projets*) to be adrift
vaurien, ne [voʀjɛ̃, -ɛn] *nm/f* good-for-nothing, guttersnipe
vaut [vo] *vb voir* **valoir**
vautour [votuʀ] *nm* vulture
vautrer [votʀe]: **se vautrer** *vi*: **se ~ dans** to wallow in; **se ~ sur** to sprawl on
vaux [vo] *pl de* **val** ▷ *vb voir* **valoir**
va-vite [vavit]: **à la ~** *adv* in a rush
vd *abr* = **vend**
VDQS *sigle m* (= *vin délimité de qualité supérieure*) label guaranteeing quality of wine
vds *abr* = **vends**
veau, x [vo] *nm* (*Zool*) calf; (*Culin*) veal; (*peau*) calfskin; **tuer le ~ gras** to kill the fatted calf
vecteur [vɛktœʀ] *nm* vector; (*Mil, Bio*) carrier
vécu, e [veky] *pp de* **vivre** ▷ *adj* real(-life)
vedettariat [vədetaʀja] *nm* stardom; (*attitude*) acting like a star
vedette [vədet] *nf* (*artiste etc*) star; (*canot*) patrol boat; launch; **avoir la ~** to top the bill, get star billing; **mettre qn en ~** (*Ciné etc*) to give sb the starring role; (*fig*) to push sb into the limelight; **voler la ~ à qn** to steal the show from sb
végétal, e, -aux [veʒetal, -o] *adj* vegetable ▷ *nm* vegetable, plant
végétalien, ne [veʒetaljɛ̃, -ɛn] *adj, nm/f* vegan
végétalisme [veʒetalism(ə)] *nm* veganism
végétarien, ne [veʒetaʀjɛ̃, -ɛn] *adj, nm/f* vegetarian
végétarisme [veʒetaʀism(ə)] *nm* vegetarianism
végétatif, -ive [veʒetatif, -iv] *adj*: **une vie ~ive** a vegetable existence
végétation [veʒetasjɔ̃] *nf* vegetation; **végétations** *nfpl* (*Méd*) adenoids
végéter [veʒete] *vi* (*fig*) to vegetate
véhémence [veemɑ̃s] *nf* vehemence
véhément, e [veemɑ̃, -ɑ̃t] *adj* vehement
véhicule [veikyl] *nm* vehicle; **~ utilitaire** commercial vehicle
véhiculer [veikyle] *vt* (*personnes, marchandises*) to transport, convey; (*fig: idées, substances*) to convey, serve as a vehicle for
veille [vɛj] *nf* (*garde*) watch; (*Psych*) wakefulness; (*jour*): **la ~** the day before, the previous day; **la ~ au soir** the previous evening; **la ~ de** the day before; **à la ~ de** on the eve of; **l'état de ~** the waking state
veillée [veje] *nf* (*soirée*) evening; (*réunion*) evening gathering; **~ d'armes** night before combat; (*fig*) vigil; **~ (mortuaire)** watch
veiller [veje] *vi* (*rester debout*) to stay *ou* sit up; (*ne pas dormir*) to be awake; (*être de garde*) to be on watch; (*être vigilant*) to be watchful ▷ *vt* (*malade, mort*) to watch over, sit up with; **~ à** *vt* to attend to, see to; **~ à ce que** to make sure that, see to it that; **~ sur** *vt* to keep a watch *ou* an eye on
veilleur [vɛjœʀ] *nm*: **~ de nuit** night watchman
veilleuse [vɛjøz] *nf* (*lampe*) night light; (*Auto*) sidelight; (*flamme*) pilot light; **en ~** *adj* (*lampe*) dimmed; (*fig: affaire*) shelved, set aside
veinard, e [vɛnaʀ, -aʀd(ə)] *nm/f* (*fam*) lucky devil
veine [vɛn] *nf* (*Anat, du bois etc*) vein; (*filon*) vein, seam; (*fam: chance*): **avoir de la ~** to be lucky; (*inspiration*) inspiration
veiné, e [vene] *adj* veined; (*bois*) grained
veineux, -euse [venø, -øz] *adj* venous
Velcro® [vɛlkʀo] *nm* Velcro®
vêler [vele] *vi* to calve
vélin [velɛ̃] *nm*: **(papier) ~** vellum (paper)
véliplanchiste [veliplɑ̃ʃist(ə)] *nm/f* windsurfer
velléitaire [veleitɛʀ] *adj* irresolute, indecisive
velléités [veleite] *nfpl* vague impulses
vélo [velo] *nm* bike, cycle; **faire du ~** to go cycling
véloce [velɔs] *adj* swift
vélocité [velɔsite] *nf* (*Mus*) nimbleness, swiftness; (*vitesse*) velocity
vélodrome [velɔdʀɔm] *nm* velodrome
vélomoteur [velɔmɔtœʀ] *nm* moped
véloski [veloski] *nm* skibob
velours [vəluʀ] *nm* velvet; **~ côtelé** corduroy
velouté, e [vəlute] *adj* (*au toucher*) velvety; (*à la vue*) soft, mellow; (*au goût*) smooth, mellow ▷ *nm*: **~ d'asperges/de tomates** cream of asparagus/tomato soup
velouteux, -euse [vəlutø, -øz] *adj* velvety
velu, e [vəly] *adj* hairy
venais *etc* [vəne] *vb voir* **venir**
venaison [vənɛzɔ̃] *nf* venison

vénal, e, -aux [venal, -o] *adj* venal
vénalité [venalite] *nf* venality
venant [vənã]: **à tout ~** *adv* to all and sundry
vendable [vãdabl(ə)] *adj* saleable, marketable
vendange [vãdãʒ] *nf* (*opération, période: aussi:* **vendanges**) grape harvest; (*raisins*) grape crop, grapes *pl*
vendanger [vãdãʒe] *vi* to harvest the grapes
vendangeur, -euse [vãdãʒœʀ, -øz] *nm/f* grape-picker
vendéen, ne [vãdeɛ̃, -ɛn] *adj* of *ou* from the Vendée
vendeur, -euse [vãdœʀ, -øz] *nm/f* (*de magasin*) shop *ou* sales assistant (*Brit*), sales clerk (*US*); (*Comm*) salesman/woman ▷ *nm* (*Jur*) vendor, seller; **~ de journaux** newspaper seller
vendre [vãdʀ(ə)] *vt* to sell; **~ qch à qn** to sell sb sth; **cela se vend à la douzaine** these are sold by the dozen; **"à ~"** "for sale"
vendredi [vãdʀədi] *nm* Friday; **V~ saint** Good Friday; *voir aussi* **lundi**
vendu, e [vãdy] *pp de* **vendre** ▷ *adj* (*péj*) corrupt
venelle [vənɛl] *nf* alley
vénéneux, -euse [venenø, -øz] *adj* poisonous
vénérable [veneʀabl(ə)] *adj* venerable
vénération [veneʀasjõ] *nf* veneration
vénérer [veneʀe] *vt* to venerate
vénerie [venʀi] *nf* hunting
vénérien, ne [veneʀjɛ̃, -ɛn] *adj* venereal
Venezuela [venezɥɛla] *nm*: **le ~** Venezuela
vénézuélien, ne [venezɥeljɛ̃, -ɛn] *adj* Venezuelan ▷ *nm/f*: **Vénézuélien, ne** Venezuelan
vengeance [vãʒãs] *nf* vengeance *no pl*, revenge *no pl*; (*acte*) act of vengeance *ou* revenge
venger [vãʒe] *vt* to avenge; **se venger** *vi* to avenge o.s.; (*par rancune*) to take revenge; **se ~ de qch** to avenge o.s. for sth; to take one's revenge for sth; **se ~ de qn** to take revenge on sb; **se ~ sur** to wreak vengeance upon; to take revenge on *ou* through; to take it out on
vengeur, -eresse [vãʒœʀ, -ʒʀɛs] *adj* vengeful ▷ *nm/f* avenger
véniel, le [venjɛl] *adj* venial
venimeux, -euse [vənimø, -øz] *adj* poisonous, venomous; (*fig: haineux*) venomous, vicious
venin [vənɛ̃] *nm* venom, poison; (*fig*) venom
venir [vəniʀ] *vi* to come; **~ de** to come from; **~ de faire: je viens d'y aller/de le voir** I've just been there/seen him; **s'il vient à pleuvoir** if it should rain, if it happens to rain; **en ~ à faire: j'en viens à croire que** I am coming to believe that; **où veux-tu en ~?** what are you getting at?; **il en est venu à mendier** he has been reduced to begging; **en ~ aux mains** to come to blows; **les années/générations à ~** the years/generations to come; **il me vient une idée** an idea has just occurred to me; **il me vient des soupçons** I'm beginning to be suspicious; **je te vois ~** I know what you're after; **faire ~** (*docteur, plombier*) to call (out); **d'où vient que ...?** how is it that ...?; **~ au monde** to come into the world
Venise [vəniz] *n* Venice

vénitien, ne [venisjɛ̃, -ɛn] *adj* Venetian
vent [vã] *nm* wind; **il y a du ~** it's windy; **c'est du ~** it's all hot air; **au ~** to windward; **sous le ~** to leeward; **avoir le ~ debout/arrière** to head into the wind/have the wind astern; **dans le ~** (*fam*) trendy; **prendre le ~** (*fig*) to see which way the wind blows; **avoir ~ de** to get wind of; **contre ~s et marées** come hell or high water
vente [vãt] *nf* sale; **la ~** (*activité*) selling; (*secteur*) sales *pl*; **mettre en ~** to put on sale; (*objets personnels*) to put up for sale; **~ de charité** jumble (*Brit*) *ou* rummage (*US*) sale; **~ par correspondance (VPC)** mail-order selling; **~ aux enchères** auction sale
venté, e [vãte] *adj* windswept, windy
venter [vãte] *vb impers*: **il vente** the wind is blowing
venteux, -euse [vãtø, -øz] *adj* windswept, windy
ventilateur [vãtilatœʀ] *nm* fan
ventilation [vãtilasjõ] *nf* ventilation
ventiler [vãtile] *vt* to ventilate; (*total, statistiques*) to break down
ventouse [vãtuz] *nf* (*ampoule*) cupping glass; (*de caoutchouc*) suction pad; (*Zool*) sucker
ventre [vãtʀ(ə)] *nm* (*Anat*) stomach; (*fig*) belly; **prendre du ~** to be getting a paunch; **avoir mal au ~** to have (a) stomach ache
ventricule [vãtʀikyl] *nm* ventricle
ventriloque [vãtʀilɔk] *nm/f* ventriloquist
ventripotent, e [vãtʀipotã, -ãt] *adj* potbellied
ventru, e [vãtʀy] *adj* potbellied
venu, e [vəny] *pp de* **venir** ▷ *adj*: **être mal ~ à** *ou* **de faire** to have no grounds for doing, be in no position to do; **mal ~** ill-timed, unwelcome; **bien ~** timely, welcome ▷ *nf* coming
vêpres [vɛpʀ(ə)] *nfpl* vespers
ver [vɛʀ] *nm* worm; (*des fruits etc*) maggot; (*du bois*) woodworm *no pl*; **~ blanc** May beetle grub; **~ luisant** glow-worm; **~ à soie** silkworm; **~ solitaire** tapeworm; **~ de terre** earthworm
véracité [veʀasite] *nf* veracity
véranda [veʀãda] *nf* veranda(h)
verbal, e, -aux [vɛʀbal, -o] *adj* verbal
verbalement [vɛʀbalmã] *adv* verbally
verbaliser [vɛʀbalize] *vi* (*Police*) to book *ou* report an offender; (*Psych*) to verbalize
verbe [vɛʀb(ə)] *nm* (*Ling*) verb; (*voix*): **avoir le ~ sonore** to have a sonorous tone (of voice); (*expression*): **la magie du ~** the magic of language *ou* the word; (*Rel*): **le V~** the Word
verbeux, -euse [vɛʀbø, -øz] *adj* verbose, wordy
verbiage [vɛʀbjaʒ] *nm* verbiage
verbosité [vɛʀbozite] *nf* verbosity
verdâtre [vɛʀdɑtʀ(ə)] *adj* greenish
verdeur [vɛʀdœʀ] *nf* (*vigueur*) vigour (*Brit*), vigor (*US*), vitality; (*crudité*) forthrightness; (*défaut de maturité*) tartness, sharpness
verdict [vɛʀdik(t)] *nm* verdict
verdir [vɛʀdiʀ] *vi, vt* to turn green
verdoyant, e [vɛʀdwajã, -ãt] *adj* green, verdant
verdure [vɛʀdyʀ] *nf* (*arbres, feuillages*) greenery;

V

431

(*légumes verts*) green vegetables *pl*, greens *pl*

véreux, -euse [veʁø, -øz] *adj* worm-eaten; (*malhonnête*) shady, corrupt

verge [veʁʒ(ə)] *nf* (*Anat*) penis; (*baguette*) stick, cane

verger [veʁʒe] *nm* orchard

vergeture [veʁʒətyʁ] *nf gén pl* stretch mark

verglacé, e [veʁɡlase] *adj* icy, iced-over

verglas [veʁɡla] *nm* (black) ice

vergogne [veʁɡɔɲ]: **sans ~** *adv* shamelessly

véridique [veʁidik] *adj* truthful

vérificateur, -trice [veʁifikatœʁ, -tʁis] *nm/f* controller, checker ▷ *nf* (*machine*) verifier; **~ des comptes** (*Finance*) auditor

vérification [veʁifikasjɔ̃] *nf* checking *no pl*, check; **~ d'identité** identity check

vérifier [veʁifje] *vt* to check; (*corroborer*) to confirm, bear out; **se vérifier** *vi* to be confirmed *ou* verified

vérin [veʁɛ̃] *nm* jack

véritable [veʁitabl(ə)] *adj* real; (*ami, amour*) true; **un ~ désastre** an absolute disaster

véritablement [veʁitabləmɑ̃] *adv* (*effectivement*) really; (*absolument*) absolutely

vérité [veʁite] *nf* truth; (*d'un portrait*) lifelikeness; (*sincérité*) truthfulness, sincerity; **en ~, à la ~** to tell the truth

verlan [veʁlɑ̃] *nm* (back) slang; *see note*

● **VERLAN**

Verlan is a form of slang popularized in the 1950's. It consists of inverting a word's syllables, the term *verlan* itself coming from "l'envers" ("à l'envers" = back to front). Typical examples are "féca" ("café"), "ripou" ("pourri"), "meuf" ("femme"), and "beur" ("Arabe").

vermeil, le [veʁmɛj] *adj* bright red, ruby red ▷ *nm* (*substance*) vermeil

vermicelles [veʁmisɛl] *nmpl* vermicelli *sg*

vermifuge [veʁmifyʒ] *nm*: **poudre ~** worm powder

vermillon [veʁmijɔ̃] *adj inv* vermilion, scarlet

vermine [veʁmin] *nf* vermin *pl*

vermoulu, e [veʁmuly] *adj* worm-eaten, with woodworm

vermout, vermouth [veʁmut] *nm* vermouth

verni, e [veʁni] *adj* varnished; glazed; (*fam*) lucky; **cuir ~** patent leather; **souliers ~s** patent (leather) shoes

vernir [veʁniʁ] *vt* (*bois, tableau, ongles*) to varnish; (*poterie*) to glaze

vernis [veʁni] *nm* (*enduit*) varnish; glaze; (*fig*) veneer; **~ à ongles** nail varnish (*Brit*) *ou* polish

vernissage [veʁnisaʒ] *nm* varnishing; glazing; (*d'une exposition*) preview

vernisser [veʁnise] *vt* to glaze

vérole [veʁɔl] *nf* (*variole*) smallpox; (*fam: syphilis*) pox

Vérone [veʁɔn] *n* Verona

verrai *etc* [veʁe] *vb voir* **voir**

verre [veʁ] *nm* glass; (*de lunettes*) lens *sg*; **verres** *nmpl* (*lunettes*) glasses; **boire** *ou* **prendre un ~** to have a drink; **~ à vin/à liqueur** wine/liqueur glass; **~ à dents** tooth mug; **~ dépoli** frosted glass; **~ de lampe** lamp glass *ou* chimney; **~ de montre** watch glass; **~ à pied** stemmed glass; **~s de contact** contact lenses; **~s fumés** tinted lenses

verrerie [veʁʁi] *nf* (*fabrique*) glassworks *sg*; (*activité*) glass-making, glass-working; (*objets*) glassware

verrier [veʁje] *nm* glass-blower

verrière [veʁjɛʁ] *nf* (*grand vitrage*) window; (*toit vitré*) glass roof

verrons *etc* [veʁɔ̃] *vb voir* **voir**

verroterie [veʁɔtʁi] *nf* glass beads *pl*, glass jewellery (*Brit*) *ou* jewelry (*US*)

verrou [veʁu] *nm* (*targette*) bolt; (*fig*) constriction; **mettre le ~** to bolt the door; **mettre qn sous les ~s** to put sb behind bars

verrouillage [veʁujaʒ] *nm* (*dispositif*) locking mechanism; (*Auto*): **~ central** *ou* **centralisé** central locking

verrouiller [veʁuje] *vt* to bolt; to lock; (*Mil: brèche*) to close

verrue [veʁy] *nf* wart; (*plantaire*) verruca; (*fig*) eyesore

vers [veʁ] *nm* line ▷ *nmpl* (*poésie*) verse *sg* ▷ *prép* (*en direction de*) toward(s); (*près de*) around (about); (*temporel*) about, around

versant [veʁsɑ̃] *nm* slopes *pl*, side

versatile [veʁsatil] *adj* fickle, changeable

verse [veʁs(ə)]: **à ~** *adv*: **il pleut à ~** it's pouring (with rain)

versé, e [veʁse] *adj*: **être ~ dans** (*science*) to be (well-)versed in

Verseau [veʁso] *nm*: **le ~** Aquarius, the water-carrier; **être du ~** to be Aquarius

versement [veʁsəmɑ̃] *nm* payment; (*sur un compte*) deposit, remittance; **en trois ~s** in three instalments

verser [veʁse] *vt* (*liquide, grains*) to pour; (*larmes, sang*) to shed; (*argent*) to pay; (*soldat: affecter*): **~ qn dans** to assign sb to ▷ *vi* (*véhicule*) to overturn; (*fig*): **~ dans** to lapse into; **~ à un compte** to pay into an account

verset [veʁsɛ] *nm* verse; versicle

verseur [veʁsœʁ] *adj m voir* **bec**; **bouchon**

versification [veʁsifikasjɔ̃] *nf* versification

versifier [veʁsifje] *vt* to put into verse ▷ *vi* to versify, write verse

version [veʁsjɔ̃] *nf* version; (*Scol*) translation (*into the mother tongue*); **film en ~ originale** film in the original language

verso [veʁso] *nm* back; **voir au ~** see over(leaf)

vert, e [veʁ, veʁt(ə)] *adj* green; (*vin*) young; (*vigoureux*) sprightly; (*cru*) forthright ▷ *nm* green; **dire des ~es (et des pas mûres)** to say some pretty spicy things; **il en a vu des ~es** he's seen a thing or two; **~ bouteille** *adj inv* bottle-green; **~ d'eau** *adj inv* sea-green; **~**

pomme *adj inv* apple-green
vert-de-gris [vɛʀdəgʀi] *nm* verdigris ▷ *adj inv* grey(ish)-green
vertébral, e, aux [vɛʀtebʀal, -o] *adj* back *cpd*; *voir* **colonne**
vertébré, e [vɛʀtebʀe] *adj, nm* vertebrate
vertèbre [vɛʀtɛbʀ(ə)] *nf* vertebra
vertement [vɛʀtəmɑ̃] *adv* (*réprimander*) sharply
vertical, e, -aux [vɛʀtikal, -o] *adj, nf* vertical; **à la ~e** *adv* vertically
verticalement [vɛʀtikalmɑ̃] *adv* vertically
verticalité [vɛʀtikalite] *nf* verticalness, verticality
vertige [vɛʀtiʒ] *nm* (*peur du vide*) vertigo; (*étourdissement*) dizzy spell; (*fig*) fever; **ça me donne le ~** it makes me dizzy; (*fig*) it makes my head spin *ou* reel
vertigineux, -euse [vɛʀtiʒinø, -øz] *adj* (*hausse, vitesse*) breathtaking; (*altitude, gorge*) breathtakingly high (*ou* deep)
vertu [vɛʀty] *nf* virtue; **une ~** a saint, a paragon of virtue; **avoir la ~ de faire** to have the virtue of doing; **en ~ de** *prép* in accordance with
vertueusement [vɛʀtɥøzmɑ̃] *adv* virtuously
vertueux, -euse [vɛʀtɥø, -øz] *adj* virtuous
verve [vɛʀv(ə)] *nf* witty eloquence; **être en ~** to be in brilliant form
verveine [vɛʀvɛn] *nf* (*Bot*) verbena, vervain; (*infusion*) verbena tea
vésicule [vezikyl] *nf* vesicle; **~ biliaire** gall-bladder
vespasienne [vɛspazjɛn] *nf* urinal
vespéral, e, -aux [vɛspeʀal, -o] *adj* vespertine, evening *cpd*
vessie [vesi] *nf* bladder
veste [vɛst(ə)] *nf* jacket; **~ droite/croisée** single-/double-breasted jacket; **retourner sa ~** (*fig*) to change one's colours
vestiaire [vɛstjɛʀ] *nm* (*au théâtre etc*) cloakroom; (*de stade etc*) changing-room (*Brit*), locker-room (*US*); (*métallique*): (**armoire**) **~** locker
vestibule [vɛstibyl] *nm* hall
vestige [vɛstiʒ] *nm* (*objet*) relic; (*fragment*) trace; (*fig*) remnant, vestige; **vestiges** *nmpl* (*d'une ville*) remains; (*d'une civilisation, du passé*) remnants, relics
vestimentaire [vɛstimɑ̃tɛʀ] *adj* (*dépenses*) clothing; (*détail*) of dress; (*élégance*) sartorial
veston [vɛstɔ̃] *nm* jacket
Vésuve [vezyv] *nm*: **le ~** Vesuvius
vêtais *etc* [vɛtɛ] *vb voir* **vêtir**
vêtement [vɛtmɑ̃] *nm* garment, item of clothing; (*Comm*): **le ~** the clothing industry; **vêtements** *nmpl* clothes; **~s de sport** sportswear *sg*, sports clothes
vétéran [veteʀɑ̃] *nm* veteran
vétérinaire [veteʀinɛʀ] *adj* veterinary ▷ *nm/f* vet, veterinary surgeon (*Brit*), veterinarian (*US*)
vétille [vetij] *nf* trifle, triviality
vétilleux, -euse [vetijø, -øz] *adj* punctilious
vêtir [vetiʀ] *vt* to clothe, dress; **se vêtir** to dress (o.s.)

vêtit *etc* [veti] *vb voir* **vêtir**
vétiver [vetivɛʀ] *nm* (*Bot*) vetiver
veto [veto] *nm* veto; **droit de ~** right of veto; **mettre** *ou* **opposer un ~ à** to veto
vêtu, e [vety] *pp de* **vêtir** ▷ *adj*: **~ de** dressed in, wearing; **chaudement ~** warmly dressed
vétuste [vetyst(ə)] *adj* ancient, timeworn
vétusté [vetyste] *nf* age, delapidation
veuf, veuve [vœf, v v] *adj* widowed ▷ *nm* widower ▷ *nf* widow
veuille [vœj], **veuillez** *etc* [vœje] *vb voir* **vouloir**
veule [vøl] *adj* spineless
veulent *etc* [vœl] *vb voir* **vouloir**
veulerie [vølʀi] *nf* spinelessness
veut [vø] *vb voir* **vouloir**
veuvage [vœvaʒ] *nm* widowhood
veuve [vœv] *adj f, nf voir* **veuf**
veux [vø] *vb voir* **vouloir**
vexant, e [vɛksɑ̃, -ɑ̃t] *adj* (*contrariant*) annoying; (*blessant*) upsetting
vexations [vɛksasjɔ̃] *nfpl* humiliations
vexatoire [vɛksatwaʀ] *adj*: **mesures ~s** harassment *sg*
vexer [vɛkse] *vt* to hurt, upset; **se vexer** *vi* to be hurt, get upset
VF *sigle f* (*Ciné*) = **version française**
VHF *sigle f* (= *Very High Frequency*) VHF
via [vja] *prép* via
viabiliser [vjabilize] *vt* to provide with services (*water etc*)
viabilité [vjabilite] *nf* viability; (*d'un chemin*) practicability
viable [vjabl(ə)] *adj* viable
viaduc [vjadyk] *nm* viaduct
viager, -ère [vjaʒe, -ɛʀ] *adj*: **rente viagère** life annuity ▷ *nm*: **mettre en ~** to sell in return for a life annuity
viande [vjɑ̃d] *nf* meat
viatique [vjatik] *nm* (*Rel*) viaticum; (*fig*) provisions *pl ou* money for the journey
vibrant, e [vibʀɑ̃, -ɑ̃t] *adj* vibrating; (*voix*) vibrant; (*émouvant*) emotive
vibraphone [vibʀafɔn] *nm* vibraphone, vibes *pl*
vibraphoniste [vibʀafɔnist(ə)] *nm/f* vibraphone player
vibration [vibʀasjɔ̃] *nf* vibration
vibratoire [vibʀatwaʀ] *adj* vibratory
vibrer [vibʀe] *vi* to vibrate; (*son, voix*) to be vibrant; (*fig*) to be stirred; **faire ~** to (cause to) vibrate; to stir, thrill
vibromasseur [vibʀomasœʀ] *nm* vibrator
vicaire [vikɛʀ] *nm* curate
vice... [vis] *préfixe* vice-
vice [vis] *nm* vice; (*défaut*) fault; **~ caché** (*Comm*) latent *ou* inherent defect; **~ de forme** legal flaw *ou* irregularity
vice-consul [viskɔ̃syl] *nm* vice-consul
vice-présidence [vispʀezidɑ̃s] *nf* (*d'un pays*) vice-presidency; (*d'une société*) vice-presidency, vice-chairmanship (*Brit*)
vice-président, e [vispʀezidɑ̃, -ɑ̃t] *nm/f* vice-president; vice-chairman

V

vice-roi [visʀwa] *nm* viceroy
vice-versa [viseveʀsa] *adv* vice versa
vichy [viʃi] *nm* (*toile*) gingham; (*eau*) Vichy
water; **carottes V~** boiled carrots
vichyssois, e [viʃiswa, -waz] *adj* of *ou* from
Vichy, Vichy *cpd* ▷ *nf* (*soupe*) vichyssoise (soup),
cream of leek and potato soup ▷ *nm/f*: **Vichyssois, e**
native *ou* inhabitant of Vichy
vicié, e [visje] *adj* (*air*) polluted, tainted; (*Jur*)
invalidated
vicier [visje] *vt* (*Jur*) to invalidate
vicieux, -euse [visjø, -øz] *adj* (*pervers*)
dirty(-minded); (*méchant*) nasty; (*fautif*)
incorrect, wrong
vicinal, e, -aux [visinal, -o] *adj*: **chemin ~**
byroad, byway
vicissitudes [visisityd] *nfpl* (trials and)
tribulations
vicomte [vikɔ̃t] *nm* viscount
vicomtesse [vikɔ̃tɛs] *nf* viscountess
victime [viktim] *nf* victim; (*d'accident*) casualty;
être (la) ~ de to be the victim of; **être ~ d'une
attaque/d'un accident** to suffer a stroke/be
involved in an accident
victoire [viktwaʀ] *nf* victory
victorieusement [viktɔʀjøzmɑ̃] *adv*
triumphantly, victoriously
victorieux, -euse [viktɔʀjø, -øz] *adj* victorious;
(*sourire, attitude*) triumphant
victuailles [viktɥaj] *nfpl* provisions
vidange [vidɑ̃ʒ] *nf* (*d'un fossé, réservoir*) emptying;
(*Auto*) oil change; (*de lavabo: bonde*) waste outlet;
vidanges *nfpl* (*matières*) sewage *sg*; **faire la ~**
(*Auto*) to change the oil, do an oil change;
tuyau de ~ drainage pipe
vidanger [vidɑ̃ʒe] *vt* to empty; **faire ~ la
voiture** to have the oil changed in one's car
vide [vid] *adj* empty ▷ *nm* (*Physique*) vacuum;
(*espace*) (empty) space, gap; (*sous soi: dans une
falaise etc*) drop; (*futilité, néant*) void; **~ de** empty
of; (*de sens etc*) devoid of; **sous ~** *adv* in a
vacuum; **emballé sous ~** vacuum-packed;
regarder dans le ~ to stare into space; **avoir
peur du ~** to be afraid of heights; **parler dans
le ~** to waste one's breath; **faire le ~** (*dans son
esprit*) to make one's mind go blank; **faire le ~
autour de qn** to isolate sb; **à ~** *adv* (*sans
occupants*) empty; (*sans charge*) unladen; (*Tech*)
without gripping *ou* being in gear
vidé, e [vide] *adj* (*épuisé*) done in, all in
vidéo [video] *nf, adj inv* video; **~ inverse** reverse
video
vidéocassette [videokasɛt] *nf* video cassette
vidéoclip [videoklip] *nm* music video
vidéoclub [videoklœb] *nm* video club
vidéoconférence [videokɔ̃feʀɑ̃s] *nf* videoconference
vidéodisque [videodisk] *nm* videodisc
vide-ordures [vidɔʀdyʀ] *nm inv* (rubbish) chute
vidéotex® [videotɛks] *nm* teletext
vidéothèque [videotɛk] *nf* video library
vide-poches [vidpɔʃ] *nm inv* tidy; (*Auto*) glove
compartment

vide-pomme [vidpɔm] *nm inv* apple-corer
vider [vide] *vt* to empty; (*Culin: volaille, poisson*) to
gut, clean out; (*régler: querelle*) to settle; (*fatiguer*)
to wear out; (*fam: expulser*) to throw out, chuck
out; **se vider** *vi* to empty; **~ les lieux** to quit *ou*
vacate the premises
videur [vidœʀ] *nm* (*de boîte de nuit*) bouncer
vie [vi] *nf* life; **être en ~** to be alive; **sans ~**
lifeless; **à ~** for life; **membre à ~** life member;
dans la ~ courante in everyday life; **avoir la ~
dure** to have nine lives; to die hard; **mener la ~
dure à qn** to make life a misery for sb
vieil [vjɛj] *adj m voir* **vieux**
vieillard [vjɛjaʀ] *nm* old man; **les ~s** old people,
the elderly
vieille [vjɛj] *adj f, nf voir* **vieux**
vieilleries [vjɛjʀi] *nfpl* old things *ou* stuff *sg*
vieillesse [vjɛjɛs] *nf* old age; (*vieillards*): **la ~** the
old *pl*, the elderly *pl*
vieilli, e [vjeji] *adj* (*marqué par l'âge*) aged; (*suranné*)
dated
vieillir [vjejiʀ] *vi* (*prendre de l'âge*) to grow old;
(*population, vin*) to age; (*doctrine, auteur*) to become
dated ▷ *vt* to age; **il a beaucoup vieilli** he has
aged a lot; **se vieillir** to make o.s. older
vieillissement [vjejismɑ̃] *nm* growing old;
ageing
vieillot, te [vjejo, -ɔt] *adj* antiquated, quaint
vielle [vjɛl] *nf* hurdy-gurdy
viendrai *etc* [vjɛ̃dʀe] *vb voir* **venir**
Vienne [vjɛn] *n* (*en Autriche*) Vienna
vienne [vjɛn], **viens** *etc* [vjɛ̃] *vb voir* **venir**
viennois, e [vjɛnwa, -waz] *adj* Viennese
viens [vjɛ̃] *vb voir* **venir**
vierge [vjɛʀʒ(ə)] *adj* virgin; (*film*) blank; (*page*)
clean, blank; (*jeune fille*): **être ~** to be a virgin
▷ *nf* virgin; (*signe*): **la V~** Virgo, the Virgin; **être
de la V~** to be Virgo; **~ de** (*sans*) free from,
unsullied by
Viêtnam, Vietnam [vjɛtnam] *nm*: **le ~**
Vietnam; **le ~ du Nord/du Sud** North/South
Vietnam
vietnamien, ne [vjɛtnamjɛ̃, -ɛn] *adj*
Vietnamese ▷ *nm* (*Ling*) Vietnamese ▷ *nm/f*:
Vietnamien, ne Vietnamese; **V~, ne du Nord/
Sud** North/South Vietnamese
vieux, vieil, vieille [vjø, vjɛj] *adj* old ▷ *nm/f* old
man/woman ▷ *nmpl*: **les ~** the old, old people;
(*fam: parents*) the old folk *ou* ones; **un petit ~** a
little old man; **mon ~/ma vieille** (*fam*) old man/
girl; **pauvre ~** poor old soul; **prendre un coup
de ~** to put years on; **se faire ~** to make o.s. look
older; **un ~ de la vieille** one of the old brigade;
~ garçon *nm* bachelor; **~ jeu** *adj inv* old-
fashioned; **~ rose** *adj inv* old rose; **vieil or** *adj
inv* old gold; **vieille fille** *nf* spinster
vif, vive [vif, viv] *adj* (*animé*) lively; (*alerte*) sharp,
quick; (*brusque*) sharp, brusque; (*aigu*) sharp;
(*lumière, couleur*) brilliant; (*air*) crisp; (*vent,
émotion*) keen; (*froid*) bitter; (*fort: regret, déception*)
great, deep; (*vivant*): **brûlé ~** burnt alive; **eau
vive** running water; **de vive voix** personally;

piquer qn au ~ to cut sb to the quick; **tailler dans le ~** to cut into the living flesh; **à ~** (*plaie*) open; **avoir les nerfs à ~** to be on edge; **sur le ~** (*Art*) from life; **entrer dans le ~ du sujet** to get to the very heart of the matter

vif-argent [vifaRʒɑ̃] *nm inv* quicksilver

vigie [viʒi] *nf* (*matelot*) look-out; (*poste*) look-out post, crow's nest

vigilance [viʒilɑ̃s] *nf* vigilance

vigilant, e [viʒilɑ̃, -ɑ̃t] *adj* vigilant

vigile [viʒil] *nm* (*veilleur de nuit*) (night) watchman; (*police privée*) vigilante

vigne [viɲ] *nf* (*plante*) vine; (*plantation*) vineyard; **~ vierge** Virginia creeper

vigneron [viɲRɔ̃] *nm* wine grower

vignette [viɲɛt] *nf* (*motif*) vignette; (*de marque*) manufacturer's label *ou* seal; (*petite illustration*) (small) illustration; (*Admin*) ≈ (road) tax disc (*Brit*), ≈ license plate sticker (*US*); (: *sur médicament*) price label (*on medicines for reimbursement by Social Security*)

vignoble [viɲɔbl(ə)] *nm* (*plantation*) vineyard; (*vignes d'une région*) vineyards *pl*

vigoureusement [viguRøzmɑ̃] *adv* vigorously

vigoureux, -euse [viguRø, -øz] *adj* vigorous, robust

vigueur [vigœR] *nf* vigour (*Brit*), vigor (*US*); **être/entrer en ~** to be in/come into force; **en ~** current

vil, e [vil] *adj* vile, base; **à ~ prix** at a very low price

vilain, e [vilɛ̃, -ɛn] *adj* (*laid*) ugly; (*affaire, blessure*) nasty; (*pas sage: enfant*) naughty ▷ *nm* (*paysan*) villein, villain; **ça va tourner au ~** things are going to turn nasty; **~ mot** bad word

vilainement [vilɛnmɑ̃] *adv* badly

vilebrequin [vilbRəkɛ̃] *nm* (*outil*) (bit-)brace; (*Auto*) crankshaft

vilenie [vilni] *nf* vileness *no pl*, baseness *no pl*

vilipender [vilipɑ̃de] *vt* to revile, vilify

villa [vila] *nf* (detached) house

village [vilaʒ] *nm* village; **~ de toile** tent village; **~ de vacances** holiday village

villageois, e [vilaʒwa, -waz] *adj* village *cpd* ▷ *nm/f* villager

ville [vil] *nf* town; (*importante*) city; (*administration*): **la ~** ≈ the Corporation, ≈ the (town) council; **aller en ~** to go to town; **habiter en ~** to live in town; **~ jumelée** twin town; **~ nouvelle** new town

ville-champignon [vilʃɑ̃piɲɔ̃] (*pl* **villes-champignons**) *nf* boom town

ville-dortoir [vildɔRtwaR] (*pl* **villes-dortoirs**) *nf* dormitory town

villégiature [vileʒjatyR] *nf* (*séjour*) holiday; (*lieu*) (holiday) resort

vin [vɛ̃] *nm* wine; **avoir le ~ gai/triste** to get happy/miserable after a few drinks; **~ blanc/rosé/rouge** white/rosé/red wine; **~ d'honneur** reception; (*with wine and snacks*): **~ de messe** altar wine; **~ ordinaire** *ou* **de table** table wine; **~ de pays** local wine; *voir aussi* **AOC; VDQS**

vinaigre [vinɛgR(ə)] *nm* vinegar; **tourner au ~** (*fig*) to turn sour; **~ de vin/d'alcool** wine/spirit vinegar

vinaigrette [vinɛgRɛt] *nf* vinaigrette, French dressing

vinaigrier [vinɛgRije] *nm* (*fabricant*) vinegar-maker; (*flacon*) vinegar cruet *ou* bottle

vinasse [vinas] *nf* (*péj*) cheap wine, plonk (*Brit*)

vindicatif, -ive [vɛ̃dikatif, -iv] *adj* vindictive

vindicte [vɛ̃dikt(ə)] *nf*: **désigner qn à la ~ publique** to expose sb to public condemnation

vineux, -euse [vinø, -øz] *adj* win(e)y

vingt [vɛ̃, vɛ̃t] (+ *voyelle following 2nd pron*) *num* twenty; **~-quatre heures sur ~-quatre** twenty-four hours a day, round the clock

vingtaine [vɛ̃tɛn] *nf*: **une ~ (de)** around twenty, twenty or so

vingtième [vɛ̃tjɛm] *num* twentieth

vinicole [vinikɔl] *adj* (*production*) wine *cpd*; (*région*) wine-growing

vinification [vinifikasjɔ̃] *nf* wine-making, wine production; (*des sucres*) vinification

vins *etc* [vɛ̃] *vb voir* **venir**

vinyle [vinil] *nm* vinyl

viol [vjɔl] *nm* (*d'une femme*) rape; (*d'un lieu sacré*) violation

violacé, e [vjɔlase] *adj* purplish, mauvish

violation [vjɔlasjɔ̃] *nf* desecration; violation; (*d'un droit*) breach

violemment [vjɔlamɑ̃] *adv* violently

violence [vjɔlɑ̃s] *nf* violence; **violences** *nfpl* acts of violence; **faire ~ à qn** to do violence to sb; **se faire ~** to force o.s

violent, e [vjɔlɑ̃, -ɑ̃t] *adj* violent; (*remède*) drastic; (*besoin, désir*) intense, urgent

violenter [vjɔlɑ̃te] *vt* to assault (sexually)

violer [vjɔle] *vt* (*femme*) to rape; (*sépulture*) to desecrate, violate; (*loi, traité*) to violate

violet, te [vjɔlɛ, -ɛt] *adj, nm* purple, mauve ▷ *nf* (*fleur*) violet

violeur [vjɔlœR] *nm* rapist

violine [vjɔlin] *nf* deep purple

violon [vjɔlɔ̃] *nm* violin; (*dans la musique folklorique etc*) fiddle; (*fam: prison*) lock-up; **premier ~** first violin; **~ d'Ingres** (artistic) hobby

violoncelle [vjɔlɔ̃sɛl] *nm* cello

violoncelliste [vjɔlɔ̃selist(ə)] *nm/f* cellist

violoniste [vjɔlɔnist(ə)] *nm/f* violinist, violin-player; (*folklorique etc*) fiddler

VIP *sigle m* (= *Very Important Person*) VIP

vipère [vipɛR] *nf* viper, adder

virage [viRaʒ] *nm* (*d'un véhicule*) turn; (*d'une route, piste*) bend; (*Chimie*) change in colour (*Brit*) *ou* color (*US*); (*de cuti-réaction*) positive reaction; (*Photo*) toning; (*fig: Pol*) about-turn; **prendre un ~** to go into a bend, take a bend; **~ sans visibilité** blind bend

viral, e, -aux [viRal, -o] *adj* viral

virée [viRe] *nf* (*courte*) run; (: *à pied*) walk; (*longue*) trip; hike, walking tour

virement [viRmɑ̃] *nm* (*Comm*) transfer; **~ bancaire** (bank) credit transfer, ≈ (bank) giro

v

transfer (Brit); **~ postal** Post office credit transfer, ≈ Girobank® transfer (Brit)

virent [viʀ] vb voir **voir**

virer [viʀe] vt (Comm): **~ qch (sur)** to transfer sth (into); (Photo) to tone; (fam: renvoyer) to sack, boot out ▷ vi to turn; (Chimie) to change colour (Brit) ou color (US); (cuti-réaction) to come up positive; (Photo) to tone; **~ au bleu** to turn blue; **~ de bord** to tack; (fig) to change tack; **~ sur l'aile** to bank

virevolte [viʀvɔlt(ə)] nf twirl; (d'avis, d'opinion) about-turn

virevolter [viʀvɔlte] vi to twirl around

virginal, e, -aux [viʀʒinal, -o] adj virginal

virginité [viʀʒinite] nf virginity; (fig) purity

virgule [viʀgyl] nf comma; (Math) point; **quatre ~ deux** four point two; **~ flottante** floating decimal

viril, e [viʀil] adj (propre à l'homme) masculine; (énergique, courageux) manly, virile

viriliser [viʀilize] vt to make (more) manly ou masculine

virilité [viʀilite] nf (attributs masculins) masculinity; (fermeté, courage) manliness; (sexuelle) virility

virologie [viʀɔlɔʒi] nf virology

virtualité [viʀtɥalite] nf virtuality; potentiality

virtuel, le [viʀtɥɛl] adj potential; (théorique) virtual

virtuellement [viʀtɥɛlmɑ̃] adj potentially; (presque) virtually

virtuose [viʀtɥoz] nm/f (Mus) virtuoso; (gén) master

virtuosité [viʀtɥozite] nf virtuosity; masterliness, masterful skills pl

virulence [viʀylɑ̃s] nf virulence

virulent, e [viʀylɑ̃, -ɑ̃t] adj virulent

virus [viʀys] nm virus

vis vb [vi] voir **voir; vivre** ▷ nf [vis] screw; **~ à tête plate/ronde** flat-headed/round-headed screw; **~ platinées** (Auto) (contact) points; **~ sans fin** worm, endless screw

visa [viza] nm (sceau) stamp; (validation de passeport) visa; **~ de censure** (censor's) certificate

visage [vizaʒ] nm face; **à ~ découvert** (franchement) openly

visagiste [vizaʒist(ə)] nm/f beautician

vis-à-vis [vizavi] adv face to face ▷ nm person opposite; house etc opposite; **~ de** prép opposite; (fig) towards, vis-à-vis; **en ~** facing ou opposite each other; **sans ~** (immeuble) with an open outlook

viscéral, e, -aux [viseʀal, -o] adj (fig) deep-seated, deep-rooted

viscères [visɛʀ] nmpl intestines, entrails

viscose [viskoz] nf viscose

viscosité [viskozite] nf viscosity

visée [vize] nf (avec une arme) aiming; (Arpentage) sighting; **visées** nfpl (intentions) designs; **avoir des ~s sur qn/qch** to have designs on sb/sth

viser [vize] vi to aim ▷ vt to aim at; (concerner) to be aimed ou directed at; (apposer un visa sur) to stamp, visa; **~ à qch/faire** to aim at/at doing ou to do

viseur [vizœʀ] nm (d'arme) sights pl; (Photo) viewfinder

visibilité [vizibilite] nf visibility; **sans ~** (pilotage, virage) blind cpd

visible [vizibl(ə)] adj visible; (disponible): **est-il ~?** can he see me?, will he see visitors?

visiblement [vizibləmɑ̃] adv visibly, obviously

visière [vizjɛʀ] nf (de casquette) peak; (qui s'attache) eyeshade

vision [vizjɔ̃] nf vision; (sens) (eye)sight, vision; (fait de voir): **la ~ de** the sight of; **première ~** (Ciné) first showing

visionnaire [vizjɔnɛʀ] adj, nm/f visionary

visionner [vizjɔne] vt to view

visionneuse [vizjɔnøz] nf viewer

visiophone [vizjɔfɔn] nm videophone

visite [vizit] nf visit; (visiteur) visitor; (touristique: d'un musée etc) tour; (Comm: de représentant) call; (expertise, d'inspection) inspection; (médicale, à domicile) visit, call; **la ~** (Méd) medical examination; (Mil: d'entrée) medicals pl; (: quotidienne) sick parade; **faire une ~ à qn** to call on sb, pay sb a visit; **rendre ~ à qn** to visit sb, pay sb a visit; **être en ~ (chez qn)** to be visiting (sb); **heures de ~** (hôpital, prison) visiting hours; **le droit de ~** (Jur: aux enfants) right of access, access; **~ de douane** customs inspection ou examination; **~ guidée** guided tour

visiter [vizite] vt to visit; (musée, ville) to visit, go round

visiteur, -euse [vizitœʀ, -øz] nm/f visitor; **~ des douanes** customs inspector; **~ médical** medical rep(resentative); **~ de prison** prison visitor

vison [vizɔ̃] nm mink

visqueux, -euse [viskø, -øz] adj viscous; (péj) gooey; (: manières) slimy

visser [vise] vt: **~ qch** (fixer, serrer) to screw sth on

visu [vizy]: **de ~** adv with one's own eyes

visualisation [vizɥalizasjɔ̃] nf (Inform) display; **écran de ~** visual display unit (VDU)

visualiser [vizɥalize] vt to visualize; (Inform) to display, bring up on screen

visuel, le [vizɥɛl] adj visual

visuellement [vizɥɛlmɑ̃] adv visually

vit [vi] vb voir **vivre; voir**

vital, e, -aux [vital, -o] adj vital

vitalité [vitalite] nf vitality

vitamine [vitamin] nf vitamin

vitaminé, e [vitamine] adj with (added) vitamins

vitaminique [vitaminik] adj vitamin cpd

vite [vit] adv (rapidement) quickly, fast; (sans délai) quickly; soon; **faire ~** (agir rapidement) to act fast; (se dépêcher) to be quick; **ce sera ~ fini** this will soon be finished; **viens ~** come quick(ly)

vitesse [vitɛs] nf speed; (Auto: dispositif) gear; **faire de la ~** to drive fast ou at speed; **prendre qn de ~** to outstrip sb, get ahead of sb; **prendre**

de la ~ to pick up *ou* gather speed; **à toute** ~ at full *ou* top speed; **en perte de** ~ *(avion)* losing lift; *(fig)* losing momentum; **changer de** ~ *(Auto)* to change gear; ~ **acquise** momentum; ~ **de croisière** cruising speed; ~ **de pointe** top speed; ~ **du son** speed of sound

viticole [vitikɔl] *adj (industrie)* wine *cpd*; *(région)* wine-growing

viticulteur [vitikyltœʀ] *nm* wine grower

viticulture [vitikyltyʀ] *nf* wine growing

vitrage [vitʀaʒ] *nm (cloison)* glass partition; *(toit)* glass roof; *(rideau)* net curtain

vitrail, -aux [vitʀaj, -o] *nm* stained-glass window

vitre [vitʀ(ə)] *nf* (window) pane; *(de portière, voiture)* window

vitré, e [vitʀe] *adj* glass *cpd*

vitrer [vitʀe] *vt* to glaze

vitreux, -euse [vitʀø, -øz] *adj* vitreous; *(terne)* glassy

vitrier [vitʀije] *nm* glazier

vitrifier [vitʀifje] *vt* to vitrify; *(parquet)* to glaze

vitrine [vitʀin] *nf (devanture)* (shop) window; *(étalage)* display; *(petite armoire)* display cabinet; **en** ~ in the window, on display; ~ **publicitaire** display case, showcase

vitriol [vitʀijɔl] *nm* vitriol; **au** ~ *(fig)* vitriolic

vitupérations [vitypeʀɑsjɔ̃] *nfpl* invective *sg*

vitupérer [vitypeʀe] *vi* to rant and rave; ~ **contre** to rail against

vivable [vivabl(ə)] *adj (personne)* livable-with; *(endroit)* fit to live in

vivace *adj* [vivas] *(arbre, plante)* hardy; *(fig)* enduring ▷ *adv* [vivatʃe] *(Mus)* vivace

vivacité [vivasite] *nf (voir vif)* liveliness, vivacity; sharpness; brilliance

vivant, e [vivã, -ãt] *vb voir* **vivre** ▷ *adj (qui vit)* living, alive; *(animé)* lively; *(preuve, exemple)* living; *(langue)* modern ▷ *nm*: **du** ~ **de qn** in sb's lifetime; **les** ~**s et les morts** the living and the dead

vivarium [vivaʀjɔm] *nm* vivarium

vivats [viva] *nmpl* cheers

vive [viv] *adj f voir* **vif** ▷ *vb voir* **vivre** ▷ *excl*: ~ **le roi!** long live the king!; ~ **les vacances!** hurrah for the holidays!

vivement [vivmã] *adv* vivaciously; sharply ▷ *excl*: ~ **les vacances!** I can't wait for the holidays!, roll on the holidays!

viveur [vivœʀ] *nm (péj)* high liver, pleasure-seeker

vivier [vivje] *nm (au restaurant etc)* fish tank; *(étang)* fishpond

vivifiant, e [vivifjã, -ãt] *adj* invigorating

vivifier [vivifje] *vt* to invigorate; *(fig: souvenirs, sentiments)* to liven up, enliven

vivions [vivjɔ̃] *vb voir* **vivre**

vivipare [vivipaʀ] *adj* viviparous

vivisection [vivisɛksjɔ̃] *nf* vivisection

vivoter [vivɔte] *vi (personne)* to scrape a living, get by; *(fig: affaire etc)* to struggle along

vivre [vivʀ(ə)] *vi, vt* to live ▷ *nm*: **le** ~ **et le**

logement board and lodging; **vivres** *nmpl* provisions, food supplies; **il vit encore** he is still alive; **se laisser** ~ to take life as it comes; **ne plus** ~ *(être anxieux)* to live on one's nerves; **il a vécu** *(eu une vie aventureuse)* he has seen life; **ce régime a vécu** this regime has had its day; **être facile à** ~ to be easy to get on with; **faire** ~ **qn** *(pourvoir à sa subsistance)* to provide (a living) for sb; ~ **mal** *(chichement)* to have a meagre existence; ~ **de** *(salaire etc)* to live on

vivrier, -ière [vivʀije, -jɛʀ] *adj* food-producing *cpd*

vlan [vlã] *excl* wham!, bang!

VO *sigle f (Ciné)* = **version originale**; **voir un film en VO** to see a film in its original language

v° *abr* = **verso**

vocable [vɔkabl(ə)] *nm* term

vocabulaire [vɔkabylɛʀ] *nm* vocabulary

vocal, e, -aux [vɔkal, -o] *adj* vocal

vocalique [vɔkalik] *adj* vocalic, vowel *cpd*

vocalise [vɔkaliz] *nf* singing exercise

vocaliser [vɔkalize] *vi (Ling)* to vocalize; *(Mus)* to do one's singing exercises

vocation [vɔkɑsjɔ̃] *nf* vocation, calling; **avoir la** ~ to have a vocation

vociférations [vɔsifeʀɑsjɔ̃] *nfpl* cries of rage, screams

vociférer [vɔsifeʀe] *vi, vt* to scream

vodka [vɔdka] *nf* vodka

vœu, x [vø] *nm* wish; *(à Dieu)* vow; **faire** ~ **de** to take a vow of; **avec tous nos** ~**x** with every good wish *ou* our best wishes; **meilleurs** ~**x** best wishes; *(sur une carte)* "Season's Greetings"; ~**x de bonheur** best wishes for your future happiness; ~**x de bonne année** best wishes for the New Year

vogue [vɔg] *nf* fashion, vogue; **en** ~ in fashion, in vogue

voguer [vɔge] *vi* to sail

voici [vwasi] *prép (pour introduire, désigner)* here is; *(+ sg)* here are; *(+ pl)*: **et** ~ **que ...** and now it *(ou* he) ...; **il est parti** ~ **trois ans** he left three years ago; ~ **une semaine que je l'ai vue** it's a week since I've seen her; **me** ~ here I am; *voir aussi* **voilà**

voie [vwa] *vb voir* **voir** ▷ *nf* way; *(Rail)* track, line; *(Auto)* lane; **par** ~ **buccale** *ou* **orale** orally; **par** ~ **rectale** rectally; **suivre la** ~ **hiérarchique** to go through official channels; **ouvrir/montrer la** ~ to open up/show the way; **être en bonne** ~ to be shaping *ou* going well; **mettre qn sur la** ~ to put sb on the right track; **être en** ~ **d'achèvement/de rénovation** to be nearing completion/in the process of renovation; **à** ~ **étroite** narrow-gauge; **à** ~ **unique** single-track; **route à deux/trois** ~**s** two-/three-lane road; **par la** ~ **aérienne/maritime** by air/sea; ~ **d'eau** *(Navig)* leak; ~ **express** expressway; ~ **de fait** *(Jur)* assault (and battery); ~ **ferrée** track; railway line *(Brit)*, railroad *(US)*; **par** ~ **ferrée** by rail, by railroad; ~ **de garage** *(Rail)* siding; **la** ~ **lactée** the Milky Way; ~ **navigable** waterway;

V

~ **prioritaire** (*Auto*) road with right of way; ~ **privée** private road; **la ~ publique** the public highway

voilà [vwala] *prép* (*en désignant*) there is; (*+sg*) there are; (*+pl*): **les ~ ou voici** here *ou* there they are; **en ~ ou voici un** here's one, there's one; ~ *ou* **voici deux ans** two years ago; ~ *ou* **voici deux ans que** it's two years since; **et ~!** there we are!; ~ **tout** that's all; **"~ ou voici"** (*en offrant etc*) "there *ou* here you are"

voilage [vwalaʒ] *nm* (*rideau*) net curtain; (*tissu*) net

voile [vwal] *nm* veil; (*tissu léger*) net ⊳ *nf* sail; (*sport*) sailing; **prendre le ~** to take the veil; **mettre à la ~** to make way under sail; **~ du palais** *nm* soft palate, velum; **~ au poumon** *nm* shadow on the lung

voiler [vwale] *vt* to veil; (*Photo*) to fog; (*fausser: roue*) to buckle; (: *bois*) to warp; **se voiler** *vi* (*lune, regard*) to mist over; (*ciel*) to grow hazy; (*voix*) to become husky; (*roue, disque*) to buckle; (*planche*) to warp; **se ~ la face** to hide one's face

voilette [vwalɛt] *nf* (*hat*) veil

voilier [vwalje] *nm* sailing ship; (*de plaisance*) sailing boat

voilure [vwalyʀ] *nf* (*de voilier*) sails *pl*; (*d'avion*) aerofoils *pl* (*Brit*), airfoils *pl* (*US*); (*de parachute*) canopy

voir [vwaʀ] *vi, vt* to see; **se voir: se ~ critiquer/transformer** to be criticized/transformed; **cela se voit** (*cela arrive*) it happens; (*c'est visible*) that's obvious, it shows; ~ **à faire qch** to see to it that sth is done; ~ **loin** (*fig*) to be far-sighted; ~ **venir** (*fig*) to wait and see; **faire ~ qch à qn** to show sb sth; **en faire ~ à qn** (*fig*) to give sb a hard time; **ne pas pouvoir ~ qn** (*fig*) not to be able to stand sb; **regardez** ~ just look; **montrez** ~ show (me); **dites** ~ tell me; **voyons!** let's see now; (*indignation etc*) come (along) now!; **c'est à ~!** we'll see!; **c'est ce qu'on va ~!** we'll see about that!; **avoir quelque chose à ~ avec** to have something to do with; **ça n'a rien à ~ avec lui** that has nothing to do with him

voire [vwaʀ] *adv* indeed; nay; or even

voirie [vwaʀi] *nf* highway maintenance; (*administration*) highways department; (*enlèvement des ordures*) refuse (*Brit*) *ou* garbage (*US*) collection

vois [vwa] *vb voir* **voir**

voisin, e [vwazɛ̃, -in] *adj* (*proche*) neighbouring (*Brit*), neighboring (*US*); (*contigu*) next; (*ressemblant*) connected ⊳ *nm/f* neighbo(u)r; (*de table, de dortoir etc*) person next to me (*ou* him *etc*); ~ **de palier** neighbo(u)r across the landing (*Brit*) *ou* hall (*US*)

voisinage [vwazinaʒ] *nm* (*proximité*) proximity; (*environs*) vicinity; (*quartier, voisins*) neighbourhood (*Brit*), neighborhood (*US*); **relations de bon ~** neighbo(u)rly terms

voisiner [vwazine] *vi*: ~ **avec** to be side by side with

voit [vwa] *vb voir* **voir**

voiture [vwatyʀ] *nf* car; (*wagon*) coach, carriage; **en ~!** all aboard!; ~ **à bras** handcart; ~ **d'enfant** pram (*Brit*), baby carriage (*US*); ~ **d'infirme** invalid carriage; ~ **de sport** sports car

voiture-lit [vwatyʀli] (*pl* **voitures-lits**) *nf* sleeper

voiture-restaurant [vwatyʀʀɛstɔʀɑ̃] (*pl* **voitures-restaurants**) *nf* dining car

voix [vwa] *nf* voice; (*Pol*) vote; **la ~ de la conscience/raison** the voice of conscience/reason; **à haute ~** aloud; **à ~ basse** in a low voice; **faire la grosse ~** to speak gruffly; **avoir de la ~** to have a good voice; **rester sans ~** to be speechless; ~ **de basse/ténor** *etc* bass/tenor *etc* voice; **à deux/quatre ~** (*Mus*) in two/four parts; **avoir ~ au chapitre** to have a say in the matter; **mettre aux ~** to put to the vote; ~ **off** voice-over

vol [vɔl] *nm* (*mode de locomotion*) flying; (*trajet, voyage, groupe d'oiseaux*) flight; (*mode d'appropriation*) theft, stealing; (*larcin*) theft; **à d'oiseau** as the crow flies; **au ~: attraper au ~** to catch sth as it flies past; **saisir une remarque au ~** to pick up a passing remark; **prendre son ~** to take flight; **de haut ~** (*fig*) of the highest order; **en ~** in flight; ~ **avec effraction** breaking and entering *no pl*, break-in; **à l'étalage** shoplifting *no pl*; ~ **libre** hang-gliding; ~ **à main armée** armed robbery; ~ **de nuit** night flight; ~ **plané** (*Aviat*) glide, gliding *no pl*; **à la tire** pickpocketing *no pl*; ~ **à voile** gliding

vol. *abr* (= *volume*) vol

volage [vɔlaʒ] *adj* fickle

volaille [vɔlaj] *nf* (*oiseaux*) poultry *pl*; (*viande*) poultry *no pl*; (*oiseau*) fowl

volailler [vɔlaje] *nm* poulterer

volant, e [vɔlɑ̃, -ɑ̃t] *adj voir* **feuille** *etc* ⊳ *nm* (*d'automobile*) (steering) wheel; (*de commande*) wheel; (*objet lancé*) shuttlecock; (*jeu*) battledore and shuttlecock; (*bande de tissu*) flounce; (*feuillet détachable*) tear-off portion; **le personnel ~, les ~s** (*Aviat*) the flight staff; ~ **de sécurité** (*fig*) reserve, margin, safeguard

volatil, e [vɔlatil] *adj* volatile

volatile [vɔlatil] *nm* (*volaille*) bird; (*tout oiseau*) winged creature

volatiliser [vɔlatilize]: **se volatiliser** *vi* (*Chimie*) to volatilize; (*fig*) to vanish into thin air

vol-au-vent [vɔlovɑ̃] *nm inv* vol-au-vent

volcan [vɔlkɑ̃] *nm* volcano; (*fig: personne*) hothead

volcanique [vɔlkanik] *adj* volcanic; (*fig: tempérament*) volatile

volcanologie [vɔlkanɔlɔʒi] *nf* vulcanology

volcanologue [vɔlkanɔlɔg] *nm/f* vulcanologist

volée [vɔle] *nf* (*groupe d'oiseaux*) flight, flock; (*Tennis*) volley; ~ **de coups/de flèches** volley of blows/arrows; **à la ~: rattraper à la ~** to catch in midair; **lancer à la ~** to fling about; **semer à la ~** to (sow) broadcast; **à toute ~** (*sonner les cloches*) vigorously; (*lancer un projectile*) with full force; **de haute ~** (*fig*) of the highest order

voler [vɔle] *vi* (*avion, oiseau, fig*) to fly; (*voleur*) to steal ▷ *vt* (*objet*) to steal; (*personne*) to rob; **~ en éclats** to smash to smithereens; **~ de ses propres ailes** (*fig*) to stand on one's own two feet; **~ au vent** to fly in the wind; **~ qch à qn** to steal sth from sb

volet [vɔlɛ] *nm* (*de fenêtre*) shutter; (*Aviat*) flap; (*de feuillet, document*) section; (*fig: d'un plan*) facet; **trié sur le ~** hand-picked

voleter [vɔlte] *vi* to flutter (about)

voleur, -euse [vɔlœʀ, -øz] *nm/f* thief ▷ *adj* thieving; **"au ~!"** "stop thief!"

volière [vɔljɛʀ] *nf* aviary

volley [vɔlɛ], **volley-ball** [vɔlɛbol] *nm* volleyball

volleyeur, -euse [vɔlɛjœʀ, -øz] *nm/f* volleyball player

volontaire [vɔlɔ̃tɛʀ] *adj* (*acte, activité*) voluntary; (*délibéré*) deliberate; (*caractère, personne: décidé*) self-willed ▷ *nm/f* volunteer

volontairement [vɔlɔ̃tɛʀmɑ̃] *adv* voluntarily; deliberately

volontariat [vɔlɔ̃taʀja] *nm* voluntary service

volontarisme [vɔlɔ̃taʀism(ə)] *nm* voluntarism

volontariste [vɔlɔ̃taʀist(ə)] *adj, nm/f* voluntarist

volonté [vɔlɔ̃te] *nf* (*faculté de vouloir*) will; (*énergie, fermeté*) will(power); (*souhait, désir*) wish; **se servir/boire à ~** to take/drink as much as one likes; **bonne ~** goodwill, willingness; **mauvaise ~** lack of goodwill, unwillingness

volontiers [vɔlɔ̃tje] *adv* (*de bonne grâce*) willingly; (*avec plaisir*) willingly, gladly; (*habituellement, souvent*) readily, willingly; **"~"** "with pleasure", "I'd be glad to"

volt [vɔlt] *nm* volt

voltage [vɔltaʒ] *nm* voltage

volte-face [vɔltəfas] *nf inv* about-turn; (*fig*) about-turn, U-turn; **faire ~** to do an about-turn; to do a U-turn

voltige [vɔltiʒ] *nf* (*Équitation*) trick riding; (*au cirque*) acrobatics *sg*; (*Aviat*) (aerial) acrobatics *sg*; **numéro de haute ~** acrobatic act

voltiger [vɔltiʒe] *vi* to flutter (about)

voltigeur [vɔltiʒœʀ] *nm* (*au cirque*) acrobat; (*Mil*) light infantryman

voltmètre [vɔltmɛtʀ(ə)] *nm* voltmeter

volubile [vɔlybil] *adj* voluble

volubilis [vɔlybilis] *nm* convolvulus

volume [vɔlym] *nm* volume; (*Géom: solide*) solid

volumineux, -euse [vɔlyminø, -øz] *adj* voluminous, bulky

volupté [vɔlypte] *nf* sensual delight *ou* pleasure

voluptueusement [vɔlyptɥøzmɑ̃] *adv* voluptuously

voluptueux, -euse [vɔlyptɥø, -øz] *adj* voluptuous

volute [vɔlyt] *nf* (*Archit*) volute; **~ de fumée** curl of smoke

vomi [vɔmi] *nm* vomit

vomir [vɔmiʀ] *vi* to vomit, be sick ▷ *vt* to vomit, bring up; (*fig*) to belch out, spew out; (*exécrer*) to loathe, abhor

vomissements [vɔmismɑ̃] *nmpl* (*action*) vomiting *no pl*; **des ~** vomit *sg*

vomissure [vɔmisyʀ] *nf* vomit *no pl*

vomitif [vɔmitif] *nm* emetic

vont [vɔ̃] *vb voir* **aller**

vorace [vɔʀas] *adj* voracious

voracement [vɔʀasmɑ̃] *adv* voraciously

voracité [vɔʀasite] *nf* voracity

vos [vo] *adj poss voir* **votre**

Vosges [voʒ] *nfpl*: **les ~** the Vosges

vosgien, ne [voʒjɛ̃, -ɛn] *adj* of *ou* from the Vosges ▷ *nm/f* inhabitant *ou* native of the Vosges

VOST *sigle f* (*Ciné*: = version originale sous-titrée) subtitled version

votant, e [vɔtɑ̃, -ɑ̃t] *nm/f* voter

vote [vɔt] *nm* vote; **~ par correspondance/ procuration** postal/proxy vote; **~ à main levée** vote by show of hands; **~ secret, ~ à bulletins secrets** secret ballot

voter [vɔte] *vi* to vote ▷ *vt* (*loi, décision*) to vote for

votre [vɔtʀ(ə)] (*pl* **vos** [vo]) *adj poss* your

vôtre [vɔtʀ(ə)] *pron*: **le ~, la ~, les ~s** yours; **les ~s** (*fig*) your family *ou* folks; **à la ~** (*toast*) your (good) health!

voudrai *etc* [vudʀe] *vb voir* **vouloir**

voué, e [vwe] *adj*: **~ à** doomed to, destined for

vouer [vwe] *vt*: **~ qch à** (*Dieu/un saint*) to dedicate sth to; **~ sa vie/son temps à** (*étude, cause etc*) to devote one's life/time to; **~ une haine/amitié éternelle à qn** to vow undying hatred/ friendship to sb

---

⬤ **MOT-CLÉ**

vouloir [vulwaʀ] *nm*: **le bon vouloir de qn** sb's goodwill; sb's pleasure

▷ *vt* **1** (*exiger, désirer*) to want; **vouloir faire/que qn fasse** to want to do/sb to do; **voulez-vous du thé?** would you like *ou* do you want some tea?; **vouloir qch à qn** to wish sth for sb; **que me veut-il?** what does he want with me?; **que veux-tu que je te dise?** what do you want me to say?; **sans le vouloir** (*involontairement*) without meaning to, unintentionally; **je voudrais ceci/faire** I would *ou* I'd like this/to do; **le hasard a voulu que ...** as fate would have it, ...; **la tradition veut que ...** tradition demands that ...; **... qui se veut moderne ...** which purports to be modern

2 (*consentir*): **je veux bien** (*bonne volonté*) I'll be happy to; (*concession*) fair enough, that's fine; **oui, si on veut** (*en quelque sorte*) yes, if you like; **comme tu veux** as you wish; (*en quelque sorte*) if you like; **veuillez attendre** please wait; **veuillez agréer ...** (*formule épistolaire*) yours faithfully

3: **en vouloir** (*être ambitieux*) to be out to win; **en vouloir à qn** to bear sb a grudge; **je lui en veux d'avoir fait ça** I resent his having done that; **s'en vouloir (de)** to be annoyed with o.s. (for);

il en veut à mon argent he's after my money 4: **vouloir de** to want; **la compagnie ne veut plus de lui** the firm doesn't want him any more; **elle ne veut pas de son aide** she doesn't want his help 5: **vouloir dire** to mean

voulu, e [vuly] *pp de* **vouloir** ▷ *adj (requis)* required, requisite; *(délibéré)* deliberate, intentional

voulus *etc* [vuly] *vb voir* **vouloir**

vous [vu] *pron* you; *(objet indirect)* (to) you; *(réfléchi)* yourself; *(réciproque)* each other ▷ *nm*: **employer le ~** *(vouvoyer)* to use the "vous" form; **~-même** yourself; **~-mêmes** yourselves

voûte [vut] *nf* vault; **la ~ céleste** the vault of heaven; **~ du palais** *(Anat)* roof of the mouth; **~ plantaire** arch (of the foot)

voûté, e [vute] *adj* vaulted, arched; *(dos, personne)* bent, stooped

voûter [vute] *vt (Archit)* to arch, vault; **se voûter** *vi (dos, personne)* to become stooped

vouvoiement [vuvwamɑ̃] *nm* use of formal "vous" form

vouvoyer [vuvwaje] *vt*: **~ qn** to address sb as "vous"

voyage [vwajaʒ] *nm* journey, trip; *(fait de voyager)*: **le ~** travel(ling); **partir/être en ~** to go off/be away on a journey *ou* trip; **faire un ~** to go on *ou* make a trip *ou* journey; **faire bon ~** to have a good journey; **les gens du ~** travelling people; **~ d'agrément/d'affaires** pleasure/business trip; **~ de noces** honeymoon; **~ organisé** package tour

voyager [vwajaʒe] *vi* to travel

voyageur, -euse [vwajaʒœʀ, -øz] *nm/f* traveller; *(passager)* passenger ▷ *adj (tempérament)* nomadic, wayfaring; **~ (de commerce)** commercial traveller

voyagiste [vwajaʒist(ə)] *nm* tour operator

voyais *etc* [vwajɛ] *vb voir* **voir**

voyance [vwajɑ̃s] *nf* clairvoyance

voyant, e [vwajɑ̃, -ɑ̃t] *adj (couleur)* loud, gaudy ▷ *nm/f (personne qui voit)* sighted person ▷ *nm (signal)* (warning) light ▷ *nf* clairvoyant

voyelle [vwajɛl] *nf* vowel

voyeur, -euse [vwajœʀ, -øz] *nm/f* voyeur; peeping Tom

voyeurisme [vwajœʀism(ə)] *nm* voyeurism

voyons *etc* [vwajɔ̃] *vb voir* **voir**

voyou [vwaju] *nm* lout, hoodlum; *(enfant)* guttersnipe

VPC *sigle f (= vente par correspondance)* mail order selling

vrac [vʀak]: **en ~** *adv* higgledy-piggledy; *(Comm)* in bulk

vrai, e [vʀɛ] *adj (véridique: récit, faits)* true; *(non factice, authentique)* real ▷ *nm*: **le ~** the truth; **à ~ dire** to tell the truth; **il est ~ que** it is true that; **être dans le ~** to be right

vraiment [vʀɛmɑ̃] *adv* really

vraisemblable [vʀɛsɑ̃blabl(ə)] *adj (plausible)* likely, plausible; *(probable)* likely, probable

vraisemblablement [vʀɛsɑ̃blabləmɑ̃] *adv* in all likelihood, very likely

vraisemblance [vʀɛsɑ̃blɑ̃s] *nf* likelihood, plausibility; *(romanesque)* verisimilitude; **selon toute ~** in all likelihood

vraquier [vʀakje] *nm* freighter

vrille [vʀij] *nf (de plante)* tendril; *(outil)* gimlet; *(spirale)* spiral; *(Aviat)* spin

vriller [vʀije] *vt* to bore into, pierce

vrombir [vʀɔ̃biʀ] *vi* to hum

vrombissant, e [vʀɔ̃bisɑ̃, -ɑ̃t] *adj* humming

vrombissement [vʀɔ̃bismɑ̃] *nm* hum(ming)

VRP *sigle m (= voyageur, représentant, placier)* (sales) rep

VTT *sigle m (= vélo tout-terrain)* mountain bike

vu¹ [vy] *prép (en raison de)* in view of; **vu que** in view of the fact that

vu², e¹ [vy] *pp de* **voir** ▷ *adj*: **bien/mal vu** *(personne)* well/poorly thought of; *(conduite)* good/bad form ▷ *nm*: **au vu et au su de tous** openly and publicly; **ni vu ni connu** what the eye doesn't see …!, no one will be any the wiser; **c'est tout vu** it's a foregone conclusion

vue² [vy] *nf (fait de voir)*: **la ~ de** the sight of; *(sens, faculté)* (eye)sight; *(panorama, image, photo)* view; *(spectacle)* sight; **vues** *nfpl (idées)* views; *(dessein)* designs; **perdre la ~** to lose one's (eye)sight; **perdre de ~** to lose sight of; **à la ~ de tous** in full view of everybody; **hors de ~** out of sight; **à première ~** at first sight; **connaître de ~** to know by sight; **à ~** *(Comm)* at sight; **tirer à ~** to shoot on sight; **à ~ d'œil** *adv* visibly; *(à première vue)* at a quick glance; **avoir ~ sur** to have a view of; **en ~** *(visible)* in sight; *(Comm)* in the public eye; **avoir qch en ~** *(intentions)* to have one's sights on sth; **en ~ de faire** with the intention of doing, with a view to doing; **~ d'ensemble** overall view; **~ de l'esprit** theoretical view

vulcanisation [vylkanizasjɔ̃] *nf* vulcanization

vulcaniser [vylkanize] *vt* to vulcanize

vulcanologie [vylkanɔlɔʒi] *nf* = **volcanologie**

vulcanologue [vylkanɔlɔg] *nm/f* = **volcanologue**

vulgaire [vylgɛʀ] *adj (grossier)* vulgar, coarse; *(trivial)* commonplace, mundane; *(péj: quelconque)*: **de ~s touristes/chaises de cuisine** common tourists/kitchen chairs; *(Bot, Zool: non latin)* common

vulgairement [vylgɛʀmɑ̃] *adv* vulgarly, coarsely; *(communément)* commonly

vulgariser [vylgaʀize] *vt* to popularize

vulgarité [vylgaʀite] *nf* vulgarity, coarseness

vulnérabilité [vylneʀabilite] *nf* vulnerability

vulnérable [vylneʀabl(ə)] *adj* vulnerable

vulve [vylv(ə)] *nf* vulva

Vve *abr* = **veuve**

VVF *sigle m (= village vacances famille)* state-subsidized holiday village

vx *abr* = **vieux**

W, w [dubləve] *nm inv* W, w ▷ *abr* (= *watt*) W; **W comme William** W for William

wagon [vagɔ̃] *nm* (*de voyageurs*) carriage; (*de marchandises*) truck, wagon

wagon-citerne [vagɔ̃sitɛrn(ə)] (*pl* **wagons-citernes**) *nm* tanker

wagon-lit [vagɔ̃li] (*pl* **wagons-lits**) *nm* sleeper, sleeping car

wagonnet [vagɔnɛ] *nm* small truck

wagon-poste [vagɔ̃pɔst(ə)] (*pl* **wagons-postes**) *nm* mail van

wagon-restaurant [vagɔ̃rɛstɔrɑ̃] (*pl* **wagons-restaurants**) *nm* restaurant *ou* dining car

Walkman® [wɔkman] *nm* Walkman®, personal stereo

Wallis et Futuna [walisefytyna]: **les îles ~** the Wallis and Futuna Islands

wallon, ne [walɔ̃, -ɔn] *adj* Walloon ▷ *nm* (*Ling*) Walloon ▷ *nm/f*: **Wallon, ne** Walloon

Wallonie [walɔni] *nf*: **la ~** French-speaking (part of) Belgium

water-polo [watɛrpɔlo] *nm* water polo

waters [watɛr] *nmpl* toilet *sg*, loo *sg* (Brit)

watt [wat] *nm* watt

WC [vese] *nmpl* toilet *sg*, lavatory *sg*

Web [wɛb] *nm inv*: **le ~** the (World Wide) Web

webcam [wɛbkam] *nf* webcam

webmaster [-mastœr], **webmestre** [-mɛstr] *nm/f* webmaster

week-end [wikɛnd] *nm* weekend

western [wɛstɛrn] *nm* western

Westphalie [vɛsfali] *nf*: **la ~** Westphalia

whisky [wiski] (*pl* **whiskies**) *nm* whisky

white-spirit [wajtspirit] *nm* white spirit

widget [widʒɛt] *nm* (*Inform*) widget

wifi, Wi-Fi [wifi] *nm inv* (= *wireless fidelity*) wifi, Wi-Fi

wok [wɔk] *nm* wok

WWW *sigle m*: **World Wide Web** WWW

X

Xx

X, x [iks] *nm inv* X, x ▷ *sigle m* = **(École)**
polytechnique; plainte contre X (*Jur*) action
against person or persons unknown; **X comme**
Xavier X for Xmas

xénophobe [gzenɔfɔb] *adj* xenophobic ▷ *nm/f*
xenophobe

xénophobie [gzenɔfɔbi] *nf* xenophobia

xérès [gzeʀɛs] *nm* sherry

xylographie [ksilɔgʀafi] *nf* xylography; (*image*)
xylograph

xylophone [ksilɔfɔn] *nm* xylophone

Yy

Y, y [igʀɛk] *nm inv* Y, y; **Y comme Yvonne** Y for Yellow (*Brit*) *ou* Yoke (*US*)

y [i] *adv* (*à cet endroit*) there; (*dessus*) on it (*ou* them); (*dedans*) in it (*ou* them) ▷ *pron* (*about ou on ou of*) it (*vérifier la syntaxe du verbe employé*); **j'y pense** I'm thinking about it; *voir aussi* **aller**; **avoir**

yacht [jɔt] *nm* yacht

yaourt [jauʀt] *nm* yoghurt

yaourtière [jauʀtjɛʀ] *nf* yoghurt-maker

Yémen [jemɛn] *nm*: **le ~** Yemen

yéménite [jemenit] *adj* Yemeni

yeux [jø] *nmpl de* **œil**

yoga [jɔga] *nm* yoga

yoghourt [jɔguʀt] *nm* = **yaourt**

yole [jɔl] *nf* skiff

yougoslave [jugɔslav] *adj* Yugoslav(ian) ▷ *nm/f*: **Yougoslave** Yugoslav(ian)

Yougoslavie [jugɔslavi] *nf*: **la ~** Yugoslavia

youyou [juju] *nm* dinghy

yo-yo [jojo] *nm inv* yo-yo

yucca [juka] *nm* yucca (tree *ou* plant)

Zz

Z, z [zɛd] *nm inv* Z, z; **Z comme Zoé** Z for Zebra
ZAC [zak] *sigle f* (= *zone d'aménagement concerté*) urban development zone
ZAD [zad] *sigle f* (= *zone d'aménagement différé*) future development zone
Zaïre [zaiʀ] *nm*: **le ~** Zaïre
zaïrois, e [zaiʀwa, -waz] *adj* Zairian
Zambèze [zɑ̃bɛz] *nm*: **le ~** the Zambezi
Zambie [zɑ̃bi] *nf*: **la ~** Zambia
zambien, ne [zɑ̃bjɛ̃, -ɛn] *adj* Zambian
zapper [zape] *vi* to zap
zapping [zapiŋ] *nm*: **faire du ~** to flick through the channels
zébré, e [zebʀe] *adj* striped, streaked
zèbre [zebʀ(ə)] *nm* (*Zool*) zebra
zébrure [zebʀyʀ] *nf* stripe, streak
zélateur, -trice [zelatœʀ, -tʀis] *nm/f* partisan, zealot
zélé, e [zele] *adj* zealous
zèle [zɛl] *nm* diligence, assiduousness; **faire du ~** (*péj*) to be over-zealous
zénith [zenit] *nm* zenith
ZEP [zɛp] *sigle f* (= *zone d'éducation prioritaire*) area targeted for special help in education
zéro [zeʀo] *nm* zero, nought (*Brit*); **au-dessous de ~** below zero (Centigrade), below freezing; **partir de ~** to start from scratch; **réduire à ~** to reduce to nothing; **trois (buts) à ~** three (goals to) nil
zeste [zɛst(ə)] *nm* peel, zest; **un ~ de citron** a piece of lemon peel
zézaiement [zezɛmɑ̃] *nm* lisp
zézayer [zezeje] *vi* to have a lisp
ZI *sigle f* = **zone industrielle**
zibeline [ziblin] *nf* sable
ZIF [zif] *sigle f* (= *zone d'intervention foncière*) intervention zone
zigouiller [ziguje] *vt* (*fam*) to do in

zigzag [zigzag] *nm* zigzag
zigzaguer [zigzage] *vi* to zigzag (along)
Zimbabwe [zimbabwe] *nm*: **le ~** Zimbabwe
zimbabwéen, ne [zimbabweɛ̃, -ɛn] *adj* Zimbabwean
zinc [zɛ̃g] *nm* (*Chimie*) zinc; (*comptoir*) bar, counter
zinguer [zɛ̃ge] *vt* to cover with zinc
zipper [zipe] *vt* (*Inform*) to zip
zircon [ziʀkɔ̃] *nm* zircon
zizanie [zizani] *nf*: **semer la ~** to stir up ill-feeling
zizi [zizi] *nm* (*fam*) willy (*Brit*), peter (*US*)
zodiacal, e, -aux [zɔdjakal, -o] *adj* (*signe*) of the zodiac
zodiaque [zɔdjak] *nm* zodiac
zona [zona] *nm* shingles *sg*
zonage [zonaʒ] *nm* (*Admin*) zoning
zonard, e [zonaʀ, -aʀd] *nm/f* (*fam*) (young) hooligan *ou* thug
zone [zon] *nf* zone, area; (*quartiers*): **la ~** the slum belt; **de seconde ~** (*fig*) second-rate; **~ d'action** (*Mil*) sphere of activity; **~ bleue** ≈ restricted parking area; **~ d'extension** *ou* **d'urbanisation** urban development area; **~ franche** free zone; **~ industrielle (ZI)** industrial estate; **~ piétonne** pedestrian precinct; **~ résidentielle** residential area; **~ tampon** buffer zone
zoner [zone] *vi* (*fam*) to hang around
zoo [zoo] *nm* zoo
zoologie [zɔɔlɔʒi] *nf* zoology
zoologique [zɔɔlɔʒik] *adj* zoological
zoologiste [zɔɔlɔʒist(ə)] *nm/f* zoologist
zoom [zum] *nm* (*Photo*) zoom (lens)
ZUP [zyp] *sigle f* = **zone à urbaniser en priorité**; = **ZAC**
Zurich [zyʀik] *n* Zürich
zut [zyt] *excl* dash (it)! (*Brit*), nuts! (*US*)

Aa

A, aˡ [eɪ] *n* (*letter*) A, a *m*; (*Scol: mark*) A; (*Mus*) la *m*; **A for Andrew, A for Able** (*US*) A comme Anatole; **A shares** *npl* (*Brit Stock Exchange*) actions *fpl* prioritaires

○ **KEYWORD**

a² [eɪ, ə] (*before vowel and silent h* **an**) *indef art* **1** un(e); **a book** un livre; **an apple** une pomme; **she's a doctor** elle est médecin
2 (*instead of the number "one"*) un(e); **a year ago** il y a un an; **a hundred/thousand** *etc* **pounds** cent/mille *etc* livres
3 (*in expressing ratios, prices etc*): **three a day/week** trois par jour/semaine; **10 km an hour** 10 km à l'heure; **£5 a person** 5£ par personne; **30p a kilo** 30p le kilo

a. *abbr* = **acre**
A2 *n* (*Brit: Scol*) *deuxième partie de l'examen équivalent au baccalauréat*
A.A. *n abbr* (*Brit*: = *Automobile Association*) ≈ ACF *m*; (*US*: = *Associate in/of Arts*) *diplôme universitaire*; (= *Alcoholics Anonymous*) AA; (= *anti-aircraft*) AA
A.A.A. *n abbr* (= *American Automobile Association*) ≈ ACF *m*; (*Brit*) = **Amateur Athletics Association**
A & R *n abbr* (*Mus*) = **artists and repertoire**; ~ **man** découvreur *m* de talent
AAUP *n abbr* (= *American Association of University Professors*) *syndicat universitaire*
AB *abbr* (*Brit*) = **able-bodied seaman**; (*Canada*) = **Alberta**
aback [ə'bæk] *adv*: **to be taken ~** être décontenancé(e)
abacus (*pl* **abaci**) ['æbəkəs, -saɪ] *n* boulier *m*
abandon [ə'bændən] *vt* abandonner ▷ *n* abandon *m*; **to ~ ship** évacuer le navire
abandoned [ə'bændənd] *adj* (*child, house etc*) abandonné(e); (*unrestrained*) sans retenue
abase [ə'beɪs] *vt*: **to ~ o.s. (so far as to do)** s'abaisser (à faire)
abashed [ə'bæʃt] *adj* confus(e), embarrassé(e)
abate [ə'beɪt] *vi* s'apaiser, se calmer
abatement [ə'beɪtmənt] *n*: **noise ~** lutte *f* contre le bruit
abattoir ['æbətwɑːʳ] *n* (*Brit*) abattoir *m*

abbey ['æbɪ] *n* abbaye *f*
abbot ['æbət] *n* père supérieur
abbreviate [ə'briːvɪeɪt] *vt* abréger
abbreviation [əbriːvɪ'eɪʃən] *n* abréviation *f*
ABC *n abbr* (= *American Broadcasting Company*) *chaîne de télévision*
abdicate ['æbdɪkeɪt] *vt, vi* abdiquer
abdication [æbdɪ'keɪʃən] *n* abdication *f*
abdomen ['æbdəmən] *n* abdomen *m*
abdominal [æb'dɔmɪnl] *adj* abdominal(e)
abduct [æb'dʌkt] *vt* enlever
abduction [æb'dʌkʃən] *n* enlèvement *m*
Aberdonian [æbə'dəunɪən] *adj* d'Aberdeen ▷ *n* habitant(e) d'Aberdeen, natif(-ive) d'Aberdeen
aberration [æbə'reɪʃən] *n* anomalie *f*; **in a moment of mental ~** dans un moment d'égarement
abet [ə'bɛt] *vt see* **aid**
abeyance [ə'beɪəns] *n*: **in ~** (*law*) en désuétude; (*matter*) en suspens
abhor [əb'hɔːʳ] *vt* abhorrer, exécrer
abhorrent [əb'hɔrənt] *adj* odieux(-euse), exécrable
abide [ə'baɪd] *vt* souffrir, supporter; **I can't ~ it/him** je ne le supporte pas
  ▶ **abide by** *vt fus* observer, respecter
abiding [ə'baɪdɪŋ] *adj* (*memory etc*) durable
ability [ə'bɪlɪtɪ] *n* compétence *f*; capacité *f*; (*skill*) talent *m*; **to the best of my ~** de mon mieux
abject ['æbdʒɛkt] *adj* (*poverty*) sordide; (*coward*) méprisable; **an ~ apology** les excuses les plus plates
ablaze [ə'bleɪz] *adj* en feu, en flammes; **~ with light** resplendissant de lumière
able ['eɪbl] *adj* compétent(e); **to be ~ to do sth** pouvoir faire qch, être capable de faire qch
able-bodied ['eɪbl'bɔdɪd] *adj* robuste; **~ seaman** (*Brit*) matelot breveté
ably ['eɪblɪ] *adv* avec compétence *or* talent, habilement
ABM *n abbr* = **anti-ballistic missile**
abnormal [æb'nɔːməl] *adj* anormal(e)
abnormality [æbnɔː'mælɪtɪ] *n* (*condition*) caractère anormal; (*instance*) anomalie *f*
aboard [ə'bɔːd] *adv* à bord ▷ *prep* à bord de; (*train*) dans

abode [əˈbəud] n (old) demeure f; (Law): **of no fixed ~** sans domicile fixe
abolish [əˈbɒlɪʃ] vt abolir
abolition [æbəˈlɪʃən] n abolition f
abominable [əˈbɒmɪnəbl] adj abominable
aborigine [æbəˈrɪdʒɪnɪ] n aborigène m/f
abort [əˈbɔːt] vt (Med) faire avorter; (Comput, fig) abandonner
abortion [əˈbɔːʃən] n avortement m; **to have an ~** se faire avorter
abortionist [əˈbɔːʃənɪst] n avorteur(-euse)
abortive [əˈbɔːtɪv] adj manqué(e)
abound [əˈbaund] vi abonder; **to ~ in** abonder en, regorger de

○ KEYWORD

about [əˈbaut] adv **1** (approximately) environ, à peu près; **about a hundred/thousand** etc environ cent/mille etc, une centaine (de)/un millier (de) etc; **it takes about 10 hours** ça prend environ or à peu près 10 heures; **at about 2 o'clock** vers 2 heures; **I've just about finished** j'ai presque fini
2 (referring to place) çà et là, de-ci de-là; **to run about** courir çà et là; **to walk about** se promener, aller et venir; **is Paul about?** (Brit) est-ce que Paul est là?; **it's about here** c'est par ici, c'est dans les parages; **they left all their things lying about** ils ont laissé traîner toutes leurs affaires
3: **to be about to do sth** être sur le point de faire qch; **I'm not about to do all that for nothing** (inf) je ne vais quand même pas faire tout ça pour rien
4 (opposite): **it's the other way about** (Brit) c'est l'inverse
▷ prep **1** (relating to) au sujet de, à propos de; **a book about London** un livre sur Londres; **what is it about?** de quoi s'agit-il?; **we talked about it** nous en avons parlé; **do something about it!** faites quelque chose!; **what** or **how about doing this?** et si nous faisions ceci?
2 (referring to place) dans; **to walk about the town** se promener dans la ville

above [əˈbʌv] adv au-dessus ▷ prep au-dessus de; (more than) plus de; **mentioned ~** mentionné ci-dessus; **costing ~ £10** coûtant plus de 10 livres; **~ all** par-dessus tout, surtout
aboveboard [əˈbʌvˈbɔːd] adj franc (franche), loyal(e); honnête
abrasion [əˈbreɪʒən] n frottement m; (on skin) écorchure f
abrasive [əˈbreɪzɪv] adj abrasif(-ive); (fig) caustique, agressif(-ive)
abreast [əˈbrɛst] adv de front; **to keep ~ of** se tenir au courant de
abridge [əˈbrɪdʒ] vt abréger
abroad [əˈbrɔːd] adv à l'étranger; **there is a rumour ~ that ...** (fig) le bruit court que ...
abrupt [əˈbrʌpt] adj (steep, blunt) abrupt(e);

(sudden, gruff) brusque
abruptly [əˈbrʌptlɪ] adv (speak, end) brusquement
abscess [ˈæbsɪs] n abcès m
abscond [əbˈskɒnd] vi disparaître, s'enfuir
absence [ˈæbsəns] n absence f; **in the ~ of** (person) en l'absence de; (thing) faute de
absent [ˈæbsənt] adj absent(e); **~ without leave (AWOL)** (Mil) en absence irrégulière
absentee [æbsənˈtiː] n absent(e)
absenteeism [æbsənˈtiːɪzəm] n absentéisme m
absent-minded [ˈæbsəntˈmaɪndɪd] adj distrait(e)
absent-mindedness [ˈæbsəntˈmaɪndɪdnɪs] n distraction f
absolute [ˈæbsəluːt] adj absolu(e)
absolutely [æbsəˈluːtlɪ] adv absolument
absolve [əbˈzɒlv] vt: **to ~ sb (from)** (sin etc) absoudre qn (de); **to ~ sb from** (oath) délier qn de
absorb [əbˈzɔːb] vt absorber; **to be ~ed in a book** être plongé(e) dans un livre
absorbent [əbˈzɔːbənt] adj absorbant(e)
absorbent cotton [əbˈzɔːbənt-] n (US) coton m hydrophile
absorbing [əbˈzɔːbɪŋ] adj absorbant(e); (book, film etc) captivant(e)
absorption [əbˈzɔːpʃən] n absorption f
abstain [əbˈsteɪn] vi: **to ~ (from)** s'abstenir (de)
abstemious [əbˈstiːmɪəs] adj sobre, frugal(e)
abstention [əbˈstɛnʃən] n abstention f
abstinence [ˈæbstɪnəns] n abstinence f
abstract [ˈæbstrækt] adj abstrait(e) ▷ n (summary) résumé m ▷ vt [æbˈstrækt] extraire
absurd [əbˈsəːd] adj absurde
absurdity [əbˈsəːdɪtɪ] n absurdité f
ABTA [ˈæbtə] n abbr = **Association of British Travel Agents**
Abu Dhabi [ˈæbuːˈdɑːbɪ] n Ab(o)u Dhabî m
abundance [əˈbʌndəns] n abondance f
abundant [əˈbʌndənt] adj abondant(e)
abuse n [əˈbjuːs] (insults) insultes fpl, injures fpl; (ill-treatment) mauvais traitements mpl; (of power etc) abus m ▷ vt [əˈbjuːz] (insult) insulter; (ill-treat) malmener; (power etc) abuser de; **to be open to ~** se prêter à des abus
abusive [əˈbjuːsɪv] adj grossier(-ière), injurieux(-euse)
abysmal [əˈbɪzməl] adj exécrable; (ignorance etc) sans bornes
abyss [əˈbɪs] n abîme m, gouffre m
AC n abbr (US) = **athletic club**
a/c abbr (Banking etc) = **account; account current**
academic [ækəˈdɛmɪk] adj universitaire; (person: scholarly) intellectuel(-le); (pej: issue) oiseux(-euse), purement théorique ▷ n universitaire m/f; **~ freedom** liberté f académique
academic year n (University) année f universitaire; (Scol) année scolaire
academy [əˈkædəmɪ] n (learned body) académie f; (school) collège m; **military/naval ~** école militaire/navale; **~ of music** conservatoire m

ACAS ['eɪkæs] *n abbr* (Brit: = *Advisory, Conciliation and Arbitration Service*) organisme de conciliation et d'arbitrage des conflits du travail

accede [æk'siːd] *vi*: **to ~ to** (*request, throne*) accéder à

accelerate [æk'sɛləreɪt] *vt, vi* accélérer

acceleration [æksɛlə'reɪʃən] *n* accélération *f*

accelerator [æk'sɛləreɪtəʳ] *n* (*Brit*) accélérateur *m*

accent ['æksɛnt] *n* accent *m*

accentuate [æk'sɛntjueɪt] *vt* (*syllable*) accentuer; (*need, difference etc*) souligner

accept [ək'sɛpt] *vt* accepter

acceptable [ək'sɛptəbl] *adj* acceptable

acceptance [ək'sɛptəns] *n* acceptation *f*; **to meet with general ~** être favorablement accueilli par tous

access ['æksɛs] *n* accès *m* ▷ *vt* (*Comput*) accéder à; **to have ~ to** (*information, library etc*) avoir accès à, pouvoir utiliser *or* consulter; (*person*) avoir accès auprès de; **the burglars gained ~ through a window** les cambrioleurs sont entrés par une fenêtre

accessible [æk'sɛsəbl] *adj* accessible

accession [æk'sɛʃən] *n* accession *f*; (*of king*) avènement *m*; (*to library*) acquisition *f*

accessory [æk'sɛsərɪ] *n* accessoire *m*; **toilet accessories** (*Brit*) articles *mpl* de toilette; **~ to** (*Law*) accessoire à

access road *n* voie *f* d'accès; (*to motorway*) bretelle *f* de raccordement

access time *n* (*Comput*) temps *m* d'accès

accident ['æksɪdənt] *n* accident *m*; (*chance*) hasard *m*; **to meet with** *or* **to have an ~** avoir un accident; **I've had an ~** j'ai eu un accident; **~s at work** accidents du travail; **by ~** (*by chance*) par hasard; (*not deliberately*) accidentellement

accidental [æksɪ'dɛntl] *adj* accidentel(le)

accidentally [æksɪ'dɛntəlɪ] *adv* accidentellement

Accident and Emergency Department *n* (*Brit*) service *m* des urgences

accident insurance *n* assurance *f* accident

accident-prone ['æksɪdənt'prəun] *adj* sujet(te) aux accidents

acclaim [ə'kleɪm] *vt* acclamer ▷ *n* acclamations *fpl*

acclamation [æklə'meɪʃən] *n* (*approval*) acclamation *f*; (*applause*) ovation *f*

acclimatize [ə'klaɪmətaɪz] (*US*), **acclimate** [ə'klaɪmət] *vt*: **to become ~d** s'acclimater

accolade ['ækəleɪd] *n* accolade *f*; (*fig*) marque *f* d'honneur

accommodate [ə'kɔmədeɪt] *vt* loger, recevoir; (*oblige, help*) obliger; (*car etc*) contenir; (*adapt*): **to ~ one's plans to** adapter ses projets à

accommodating [ə'kɔmədeɪtɪŋ] *adj* obligeant(e), arrangeant(e)

accommodation, (*US*) **accommodations** [əkɔmə'deɪʃən(z)] *n(pl)* logement *m*; **he's found ~** il a trouvé à se loger; **"~ to let"** (*Brit*) "appartement *or* studio *etc* à louer"; **they have**

~ for 500 ils peuvent recevoir 500 personnes, il y a de la place pour 500 personnes; **the hall has seating ~ for 600** (*Brit*) la salle contient 600 places assises

accompaniment [ə'kʌmpənɪmənt] *n* accompagnement *m*

accompanist [ə'kʌmpənɪst] *n* accompagnateur(-trice)

accompany [ə'kʌmpənɪ] *vt* accompagner

accomplice [ə'kʌmplɪs] *n* complice *m/f*

accomplish [ə'kʌmplɪʃ] *vt* accomplir

accomplished [ə'kʌmplɪʃt] *adj* accompli(e)

accomplishment [ə'kʌmplɪʃmənt] *n* (*skill: gen pl*) talent *m*; (*completion*) accomplissement *m*; (*achievement*) réussite *f*

accord [ə'kɔːd] *n* accord *m* ▷ *vt* accorder; **of his own ~** de son plein gré; **with one ~** d'un commun accord

accordance [ə'kɔːdəns] *n*: **in ~ with** conformément à

according [ə'kɔːdɪŋ]: **~ to** (*prep*) selon; **~ to plan** comme prévu

accordingly [ə'kɔːdɪŋlɪ] *adv* (*appropriately*) en conséquence; (*as a result*) par conséquent

accordion [ə'kɔːdɪən] *n* accordéon *m*

accost [ə'kɔst] *vt* accoster, aborder

account [ə'kaunt] *n* (*Comm*) compte *m*; (*report*) compte rendu, récit *m*; **accounts** *npl* (*Comm: records*) comptabilité *f*, comptes; **"~ payee only"** (*Brit*) "chèque non endossable"; **to keep an ~ of** noter; **to bring sb to ~ for sth/for having done sth** amener qn à rendre compte de qch/ d'avoir fait qch; **by all ~s** au dire de tous; **of little ~** de peu d'importance; **of no ~** sans importance; **on ~** en acompte; **to buy sth on ~** acheter qch à crédit; **on no ~** en aucun cas; **on ~ of** à cause de; **to take into ~, take ~ of** tenir compte de

▷ **account for** *vt fus* (*explain*) expliquer, rendre compte de; (*represent*) représenter; **all the children were ~ed for** aucun enfant ne manquait; **four people are still not ~ed for** on n'a toujours pas retrouvé quatre personnes

accountability [əkauntə'bɪlɪtɪ] *n* responsabilité *f*; (*financial, political*) transparence *f*

accountable [ə'kauntəbl] *adj*: **~ (for/to)** responsable (de/devant)

accountancy [ə'kauntənsɪ] *n* comptabilité *f*

accountant [ə'kauntənt] *n* comptable *m/f*

accounting [ə'kauntɪŋ] *n* comptabilité *f*

accounting period *n* exercice financier, période *f* comptable

account number *n* numéro *m* de compte

account payable *n* compte *m* fournisseurs

account receivable *n* compte *m* clients

accredited [ə'krɛdɪtɪd] *adj* (*person*) accrédité(e)

accretion [ə'kriːʃən] *n* accroissement *m*

accrue [ə'kruː] *vi* s'accroître; (*mount up*) s'accumuler; **to ~ to** s'ajouter à; **~d interest** intérêt couru

accumulate [ə'kjuːmjuleɪt] *vt* accumuler,

amasser ▷ *vi* s'accumuler, s'amasser

accumulation [əkjuːmjuˈleɪʃən] *n* accumulation *f*

accuracy [ˈækjurəsɪ] *n* exactitude *f*, précision *f*

accurate [ˈækjurɪt] *adj* exact(e), précis(e); (*device*) précis

accurately [ˈækjurɪtlɪ] *adv* avec précision

accusation [ækjuˈzeɪʃən] *n* accusation *f*

accusative [əˈkjuːzətɪv] *n* (*Ling*) accusatif *m*

accuse [əˈkjuːz] *vt*: **to ~ sb (of sth)** accuser qn (de qch)

accused [əˈkjuːzd] *n* (*Law*) accusé(e)

accuser [əˈkjuːzəʳ] *n* accusateur(-trice)

accustom [əˈkʌstəm] *vt* accoutumer, habituer; **to ~ o.s. to sth** s'habituer à qch

accustomed [əˈkʌstəmd] *adj* (*usual*) habituel(le); **~ to** habitué(e) *or* accoutumé(e) à

AC/DC *abbr* = **alternating current/direct current**

ACE [eɪs] *n abbr* = **American Council on Education**

ace [eɪs] *n* as *m*; **within an ~ of** (*Brit*) à deux doigts *or* un cheveu de

acerbic [əˈsəːbɪk] *adj* (*also fig*) acerbe

acetate [ˈæsɪteɪt] *n* acétate *m*

ache [eɪk] *n* mal *m*, douleur *f* ▷ *vi* (*be sore*) faire mal, être douloureux(-euse); (*yearn*): **to ~ to do sth** mourir d'envie de faire qch; **I've got stomach ~** *or* (*US*) **a stomach ~** j'ai mal à l'estomac; **my head ~s** j'ai mal à la tête; **I'm aching all over** j'ai mal partout

achieve [əˈtʃiːv] *vt* (*aim*) atteindre; (*victory, success*) remporter, obtenir; (*task*) accomplir

achievement [əˈtʃiːvmənt] *n* exploit *m*, réussite *f*; (*of aims*) réalisation *f*

Achilles heel [əˈkɪliːz-] *n* talon *m* d'Achille

acid [ˈæsɪd] *adj, n* acide (*m*)

acidity [əˈsɪdɪtɪ] *n* acidité *f*

acid rain *n* pluies *fpl* acides

acid test *n* (*fig*) épreuve décisive

acknowledge [əkˈnɔlɪdʒ] *vt* (*also*: **acknowledge receipt of**) accuser réception de; (*fact*) reconnaître

acknowledgement [əkˈnɔlɪdʒmənt] *n* (*of letter*) accusé *m* de réception; **acknowledgements** (*in book*) remerciements *mpl*

ACLU *n abbr* (= *American Civil Liberties Union*) ligue des droits de l'homme

acme [ˈækmɪ] *n* point culminant

acne [ˈæknɪ] *n* acné *m*

acorn [ˈeɪkɔːn] *n* gland *m*

acoustic [əˈkuːstɪk] *adj* acoustique

acoustics [əˈkuːstɪks] *n, npl* acoustique *f*

acquaint [əˈkweɪnt] *vt*: **to ~ sb with sth** mettre qn au courant de qch; **to be ~ed with** (*person*) connaître; (*fact*) savoir

acquaintance [əˈkweɪntəns] *n* connaissance *f*; **to make sb's ~** faire la connaissance de qn

acquiesce [ækwɪˈɛs] *vi* (*agree*): **to ~ (in)** acquiescer (à)

acquire [əˈkwaɪəʳ] *vt* acquérir

acquired [əˈkwaɪəd] *adj* acquis(e); **an ~ taste** un goût acquis

acquisition [ækwɪˈzɪʃən] *n* acquisition *f*

acquisitive [əˈkwɪzɪtɪv] *adj* qui a l'instinct de possession *or* le goût de la propriété

acquit [əˈkwɪt] *vt* acquitter; **to ~ o.s. well** s'en tirer très honorablement

acquittal [əˈkwɪtl] *n* acquittement *m*

acre [ˈeɪkəʳ] *n* acre *f* (= 4047 *m*")

acreage [ˈeɪkərɪdʒ] *n* superficie *f*

acrid [ˈækrɪd] *adj* (*smell*) âcre; (*fig*) mordant(e)

acrimonious [ækrɪˈməunɪəs] *adj* acrimonieux(-euse), aigre

acrobat [ˈækrəbæt] *n* acrobate *m/f*

acrobatic [ækrəˈbætɪk] *adj* acrobatique

acrobatics [ækrəˈbætɪks] *n, npl* acrobatie *f*

acronym [ˈækrənɪm] *n* acronyme *m*

Acropolis [əˈkrɔpəlɪs] *n*: **the ~** l'Acropole *f*

across [əˈkrɔs] *prep* (*on the other side*) de l'autre côté de; (*crosswise*) en travers de ▷ *adv* de l'autre côté; en travers; **to walk ~ (the road)** traverser (la route); **to run/swim ~** traverser en courant/ à la nage; **to take sb ~ the road** faire traverser la route à qn; **a road ~ the wood** une route qui traverse le bois; **the lake is 12 km ~** le lac fait 12 km de large; **~ from** en face de; **to get sth ~ (to sb)** faire comprendre qch (à qn)

acrylic [əˈkrɪlɪk] *adj, n* acrylique (*m*)

ACT *n abbr* (= *American College Test*) examen de fin d'études secondaires

act [ækt] *n* acte *m*, action *f*; (*Theat: part of play*) acte; (: *of performer*) numéro *m*; (*Law*) loi *f* ▷ *vi* agir; (*Theat*) jouer; (*pretend*) jouer la comédie ▷ *vt* (*role*) jouer, tenir; **~ of God** (*Law*) catastrophe naturelle; **to catch sb in the ~** prendre qn sur le fait *or* en flagrant délit; **it's only an ~** c'est du cinéma; **to ~ Hamlet** (*Brit*) tenir *or* jouer le rôle d'Hamlet; **to ~ as** servir de; **it ~s as a deterrent** cela a un effet dissuasif; **~ing in my capacity as chairman, I …** en ma qualité de président, je …

▶ **act on** *vt*: **to ~ on sth** agir sur la base de qch

▶ **act out** *vt* (*event*) raconter en mimant; (*fantasies*) réaliser

▶ **act up** (*inf*) *vi* (*person*) se conduire mal; (*knee, back, injury*) jouer des tours; (*machine*) être capricieux(-ieuse)

acting [ˈæktɪŋ] *adj* suppléant(e), par intérim ▷ *n* (*of actor*) jeu *m*; (*activity*): **to do some ~** faire du théâtre (*or* du cinéma); **he is the ~ manager** il remplace (provisoirement) le directeur

action [ˈækʃən] *n* action *f*; (*Mil*) combat(s) *m(pl)*; (*Law*) procès *m*, action en justice ▷ *vt* (*Comm*) mettre en œuvre; **to bring an ~ against sb** (*Law*) poursuivre qn en justice, intenter un procès contre qn; **killed in ~** (*Mil*) tué au champ d'honneur; **out of ~** hors de combat; (*machine etc*) hors d'usage; **to take ~** agir, prendre des mesures; **to put a plan into ~** mettre un projet à exécution

action replay *n* (*Brit TV*) ralenti *m*

activate [ˈæktɪveɪt] *vt* (*mechanism*) actionner, faire fonctionner; (*Chem, Physics*) activer

active ['æktɪv] *adj* actif(-ive); *(volcano)* en activité; **to play an ~ part in** jouer un rôle actif dans
active duty *n* (US Mil) campagne *f*
actively ['æktɪvlɪ] *adv* activement; *(discourage)* vivement
active partner *n* (Comm) associé(e) *m/f*
active service *n* (Brit Mil) campagne *f*
activist ['æktɪvɪst] *n* activiste *m/f*
activity [æk'tɪvɪtɪ] *n* activité *f*
activity holiday *n* vacances actives
actor ['æktə^r] *n* acteur *m*
actress ['æktrɪs] *n* actrice *f*
actual ['æktjuəl] *adj* réel(le), véritable; *(emphatic use)* lui-même (elle-même)
actually ['æktjuəlɪ] *adv* réellement, véritablement; *(in fact)* en fait
actuary ['æktjuərɪ] *n* actuaire *m*
actuate ['æktjueɪt] *vt* déclencher, actionner
acuity [ə'kjuːɪtɪ] *n* acuité *f*
acumen ['ækjumən] *n* perspicacité *f*; **business ~** sens *m* des affaires
acupuncture ['ækjupʌŋktʃə^r] *n* acuponcture *f*
acute [ə'kjuːt] *adj* aigu(ë); *(mind, observer)* pénétrant(e)
A.D. *adv abbr* (= Anno Domini) ap. J.-C. ▷ *n abbr* (US Mil) = **active duty**
ad [æd] *n abbr* = **advertisement**
adamant ['ædəmənt] *adj* inflexible
Adam's apple ['ædəmz-] *n* pomme *f* d'Adam
adapt [ə'dæpt] *vt* adapter ▷ *vi*: **to ~ (to)** s'adapter (à)
adaptability [ədæptə'bɪlɪtɪ] *n* faculté *f* d'adaptation
adaptable [ə'dæptəbl] *adj (device)* adaptable; *(person)* qui s'adapte facilement
adaptation [ædæp'teɪʃən] *n* adaptation *f*
adapter, adaptor [ə'dæptə^r] *n* (Elec) adaptateur *m*; *(for several plugs)* prise *f* multiple
ADC *n abbr* (Mil) = **aide-de-camp**; (US: = Aid to Dependent Children) aide pour enfants assistés
add [æd] *vt* ajouter; *(figures: also: **to add up**)* additionner ▷ *vi*: **to ~ to** *(increase)* ajouter à, accroître ▷ *n* (Internet) **thanks for the ~** merci pour l'ajout
  ▶ **add on** *vt* ajouter ▷ *vi (fig)*: **it doesn't ~ up** cela ne rime à rien
  ▶ **add up to** *vt fus* (Math) s'élever à; *(fig: mean)* signifier; **it doesn't ~ up to much** ça n'est pas grand'chose
adder ['ædə^r] *n* vipère *f*
addict ['ædɪkt] *n* toxicomane *m/f*; *(fig)* fanatique *m/f*; **heroin ~** héroïnomane *m/f*; **drug ~** drogué(e) *m/f*
addicted [ə'dɪktɪd] *adj*: **to be ~ to** *(drink, drugs)* être adonné(e) à; *(fig: football etc)* être un(e) fanatique de
addiction [ə'dɪkʃən] *n* (Med) dépendance *f*
addictive [ə'dɪktɪv] *adj* qui crée une dépendance
adding machine ['ædɪŋ-] *n* machine *f* à calculer
Addis Ababa ['ædɪs'æbəbə] *n* Addis Abeba, Addis Ababa
addition [ə'dɪʃən] *n* (adding up) addition *f*; *(thing*

added) ajout *m*; **in ~** de plus, de surcroît; **in ~ to** en plus de
additional [ə'dɪʃənl] *adj* supplémentaire
additive ['ædɪtɪv] *n* additif *m*
address [ə'drɛs] *n* adresse *f*; *(talk)* discours *m*, allocution *f* ▷ *vt* adresser; *(speak to)* s'adresser à; **my ~ is ...** mon adresse, c'est ...; **form of ~** titre *m*; **what form of ~ do you use for ...?** comment s'adresse-t-on à ...?; **to ~ (o.s. to) sth** *(problem, issue)* aborder qch; **absolute/relative ~** (Comput) adresse absolue/relative
address book *n* carnet *m* d'adresses
addressee [ædrɛ'siː] *n* destinataire *m/f*
Aden ['eɪdən] *n*: **Gulf of ~** Golfe *m* d'Aden
adenoids ['ædɪnɔɪdz] *npl* végétations *fpl*
adept ['ædɛpt] *adj*: **~ at** expert(e) à *or* en
adequate ['ædɪkwɪt] *adj (enough)* suffisant(e); *(satisfactory)* satisfaisant(e); **to feel ~ to the task** se sentir à la hauteur de la tâche
adequately ['ædɪkwɪtlɪ] *adv* de façon adéquate
adhere [əd'hɪə^r] *vi*: **to ~ to** adhérer à; *(fig: rule, decision)* se tenir à
adhesion [əd'hiːʒən] *n* adhésion *f*
adhesive [əd'hiːzɪv] *adj* adhésif(-ive) ▷ *n* adhésif *m*
adhesive tape *n* (Brit) ruban *m* adhésif; (US Med) sparadrap *m*
ad hoc [æd'hɔk] *adj (decision)* de circonstance; *(committee)* ad hoc
ad infinitum ['ædɪnfɪ'naɪtəm] *adv* à l'infini
adjacent [ə'dʒeɪsənt] *adj* adjacent(e), contigu(ë); **~ to** adjacent à
adjective ['ædʒɛktɪv] *n* adjectif *m*
adjoin [ə'dʒɔɪn] *vt* jouxter
adjoining [ə'dʒɔɪnɪŋ] *adj* voisin(e), adjacent(e), attenant(e) ▷ *prep* voisin de, adjacent à
adjourn [ə'dʒəːn] *vt* ajourner ▷ *vi* suspendre la séance; lever la séance; clore la session; *(go)* se retirer; **to ~ a meeting till the following week** reporter une réunion à la semaine suivante; **they ~ed to the pub** (Brit inf) ils ont filé au pub
adjournment [ə'dʒəːnmənt] *n (period)* ajournement *m*
Adjt *abbr* (Mil: = adjutant) Adj
adjudicate [ə'dʒuːdɪkeɪt] *vt (contest)* juger; *(claim)* statuer (sur) ▷ *vi* se prononcer
adjudication [ədʒuːdɪ'keɪʃən] *n* (Law) jugement *m*
adjust [ə'dʒʌst] *vt (machine)* ajuster, régler; *(prices, wages)* rajuster ▷ *vi*: **to ~ (to)** s'adapter (à)
adjustable [ə'dʒʌstəbl] *adj* réglable
adjuster [ə'dʒʌstə^r] *n see* **loss**
adjustment [ə'dʒʌstmənt] *n (of machine)* ajustage *m*, réglage *m*; *(of prices, wages)* rajustement *m*; *(of person)* adaptation *f*
adjutant ['ædʒətənt] *n* adjudant *m*
ad-lib [æd'lɪb] *vt, vi* improviser ▷ *n* improvisation *f* ▷ *adv*: **ad lib** à volonté, à discrétion
adman ['ædmæn] *(irreg) n (inf)* publicitaire *m*
admin ['ædmɪn] *n abbr (inf)* = **administration**
administer [əd'mɪnɪstə^r] *vt* administrer; *(justice)* rendre

administration [ədmɪnɪsˈtreɪʃən] n
(management) administration f; (government)
gouvernement m
administrative [ədˈmɪnɪstrətɪv] adj
administratif(-ive)
administrator [ədˈmɪnɪstreɪtər] n
administrateur(-trice)
admirable [ˈædmərəbl] adj admirable
admiral [ˈædmərəl] n amiral m
Admiralty [ˈædmərəltɪ] n (Brit: also: **Admiralty
Board**) ministère m de la Marine
admiration [ædməˈreɪʃən] n admiration f
admire [ədˈmaɪər] vt admirer
admirer [ədˈmaɪərər] n (fan) admirateur(-trice)
admiring [ədˈmaɪərɪŋ] adj admiratif(-ive)
admissible [ədˈmɪsəbl] adj acceptable,
admissible; (evidence) recevable
admission [ədˈmɪʃən] n admission f; (to
exhibition, night club etc) entrée f; (confession) aveu
m; **"~ free"**, **"free ~"** "entrée libre"; **by his own
~** de son propre aveu
admission charge n droits mpl d'admission
admit [ədˈmɪt] vt laisser entrer; admettre;
(agree) reconnaître, admettre; (crime)
reconnaître avoir commis; **"children not
~ted"** "entrée interdite aux enfants"; **this
ticket ~s two** ce billet est valable pour deux
personnes; **I must ~ that ...** je dois admettre or
reconnaître que ...
▸ **admit of** vt fus admettre, permettre
▸ **admit to** vt fus reconnaître, avouer
admittance [ədˈmɪtəns] n admission f, (droit m
d')entrée f; **"no ~"** "défense d'entrer"
admittedly [ədˈmɪtɪdlɪ] adv il faut en convenir
admonish [ədˈmɔnɪʃ] vt donner un
avertissement à; réprimander
ad nauseam [ædˈnɔːsɪæm] adv à satiété
ado [əˈduː] n: **without (any) more ~** sans plus
de cérémonies
adolescence [ædəuˈlɛsns] n adolescence f
adolescent [ædəuˈlɛsnt] adj, n adolescent(e)
adopt [əˈdɔpt] vt adopter
adopted [əˈdɔptɪd] adj adoptif(-ive), adopté(e)
adoption [əˈdɔpʃən] n adoption f
adore [əˈdɔːr] vt adorer
adoring [əˈdɔːrɪŋ] adj: **his ~ wife** sa femme qui
est en adoration devant lui
adoringly [əˈdɔːrɪŋlɪ] adv avec adoration
adorn [əˈdɔːn] vt orner
adornment [əˈdɔːnmənt] n ornement m
ADP n abbr = **automatic data processing**
adrenalin [əˈdrɛnəlɪn] n adrénaline f; **to get
the ~ going** faire monter le taux d'adrénaline
Adriatic [eɪdrɪˈætɪk]
Adriatic Sea n: **the Adriatic (Sea)** la mer
Adriatique, l'Adriatique f
adrift [əˈdrɪft] adv à la dérive; **to come ~** (boat)
aller à la dérive; (wire, rope, fastening etc) se défaire
adroit [əˈdrɔɪt] adj adroit(e), habile
ADSL n abbr (asymmetric digital subscriber line)
ADSL m
ADT abbr (US: = Atlantic Daylight Time) heure d'été de

New York
adult [ˈædʌlt] n adulte m/f ▷ adj (grown-up)
adulte; (for adults) pour adultes
adult education n éducation f des adultes
adulterate [əˈdʌltəreɪt] vt frelater, falsifier
adulterer [əˈdʌltərər] n homme m adultère
adulteress [əˈdʌltərɪs] n femme f adultère
adultery [əˈdʌltərɪ] n adultère m
adulthood [ˈædʌlthud] n âge m adulte
advance [ədˈvɑːns] n avance f ▷ vt avancer ▷ vi
s'avancer; **in ~** en avance, d'avance; **to make
~s to sb** (gen) faire des propositions à qn;
(amorously) faire des avances à qn; **~ booking**
location f; **~ notice**, **~ warning** préavis m;
(verbal) avertissement m; **do I need to book in
~?** est-ce qu'il faut réserver à l'avance?
advanced [ədˈvɑːnst] adj avancé(e); (Scol: studies)
supérieur(e); **~ in years** d'un âge avancé
advancement [ədˈvɑːnsmənt] n avancement m
advantage [ədˈvɑːntɪdʒ] n (also Tennis) avantage
m; **to take ~ of** (person) exploiter; (opportunity)
profiter de; **it's to our ~** c'est notre intérêt; **it's
to our ~ to ...** nous avons intérêt à ...
advantageous [ædvənˈteɪdʒəs] adj
avantageux(-euse)
advent [ˈædvənt] n avènement m, venue f; **A~**
(Rel) avent m
Advent calendar n calendrier m de l'avent
adventure [ədˈvɛntʃər] n aventure f
adventure playground n aire f de jeux
adventurous [ədˈvɛntʃərəs] adj
aventureux(-euse)
adverb [ˈædvəːb] n adverbe m
adversary [ˈædvəsərɪ] n adversaire m/f
adverse [ˈædvəːs] adj adverse; (effect)
négatif(-ive); (weather, publicity) mauvais(e);
(wind) contraire; **~ to** hostile à; **in ~
circumstances** dans l'adversité
adversity [ədˈvəːsɪtɪ] n adversité f
advert [ˈædvəːt] n abbr (Brit) = **advertisement**
advertise [ˈædvətaɪz] vi faire de la publicité or
de la réclame; (in classified ads etc) mettre une
annonce ▷ vt faire de la publicité or de la
réclame pour; (in classified ads etc) mettre une
annonce pour vendre; **to ~ for** (staff) recruter
par (voie d')annonce
advertisement [ədˈvəːtɪsmənt] n publicité f,
réclame f; (in classified ads etc) annonce f
advertiser [ˈædvətaɪzər] n annonceur m
advertising [ˈædvətaɪzɪŋ] n publicité f
advertising agency n agence f de publicité
advertising campaign n campagne f de
publicité
advice [ədˈvaɪs] n conseils mpl; (notification) avis
m; **a piece of ~** un conseil; **to ask (sb) for ~**
demander conseil (à qn); **to take legal ~**
consulter un avocat
advice note n (Brit) avis m d'expédition
advisable [ədˈvaɪzəbl] adj recommandable,
indiqué(e)
advise [ədˈvaɪz] vt conseiller; **to ~ sb of sth**
aviser or informer qn de qch; **to ~ against sth/**

doing sth déconseiller qch/conseiller de ne pas faire qch; **you would be well/ill ~d to go** vous feriez mieux d'y aller/de ne pas y aller, vous auriez intérêt à y aller/à ne pas y aller

advisedly [əd'vaɪzɪdlɪ] *adv* (*deliberately*) délibérément

adviser, advisor [əd'vaɪzər] *n* conseiller(-ère)

advisory [əd'vaɪzərɪ] *adj* consultatif(-ive); **in an ~ capacity** à titre consultatif

advocate *n* ['ædvəkɪt] (*lawyer*) avocat (plaidant); (*upholder*) défenseur *m*, avocat(e) ▷ *vt* ['ædvəkeɪt] recommander, prôner; **to be an ~ of** être partisan(e) de

advt. *abbr* = **advertisement**

AEA *n abbr* (*Brit*: = *Atomic Energy Authority*) ≈ AEN *f* (= *Agence pour l'énergie nucléaire*)

AEC *n abbr* (*US*: = *Atomic Energy Commission*) CEA *m* (= *Commissariat à l'énergie atomique*)

AEEU *n abbr* (*Brit*: = *Amalgamated Engineering and Electrical Union*) syndicat de techniciens et d'électriciens

Aegean [iː'dʒiːən] *n, adj*: **the ~ (Sea)** la mer Égée, l'Égée *f*

aegis ['iːdʒɪs] *n*: **under the ~ of** sous l'égide de

aeon ['iːən] *n* éternité *f*

aerial ['ɛərɪəl] *n* antenne *f* ▷ *adj* aérien(ne)

aerobatics ['ɛərəʊ'bætɪks] *npl* acrobaties aériennes

aerobics [ɛə'rəʊbɪks] *n* aérobic *m*

aerodrome ['ɛərədrəʊm] *n* (*Brit*) aérodrome *m*

aerodynamic ['ɛərəʊdaɪ'næmɪk] *adj* aérodynamique

aeronautics [ɛərə'nɔːtɪks] *n* aéronautique *f*

aeroplane ['ɛərəpleɪn] *n* (*Brit*) avion *m*

aerosol ['ɛərəsɔl] *n* aérosol *m*

aerospace industry ['ɛərəʊspeɪs-] *n* (industrie) aérospatiale *f*

aesthetic [ɪs'θɛtɪk] *adj* esthétique

afar [ə'faːr] *adv*: **from ~** de loin

AFB *n abbr* (*US*) = **Air Force Base**

AFDC *n abbr* (*US*: = *Aid to Families with Dependent Children*) aide pour enfants assistés

affable ['æfəbl] *adj* affable

affair [ə'fɛər] *n* affaire *f*; (*also*: **love affair**) liaison *f*; aventure *f*; **affairs** (*business*) affaires

affect [ə'fɛkt] *vt* affecter; (*subj*: *disease*) atteindre

affectation [æfɛk'teɪʃən] *n* affectation *f*

affected [ə'fɛktɪd] *adj* affecté(e)

affection [ə'fɛkʃən] *n* affection *f*

affectionate [ə'fɛkʃənɪt] *adj* affectueux(-euse)

affectionately [ə'fɛkʃənɪtlɪ] *adv* affectueusement

affidavit [æfɪ'deɪvɪt] *n* (*Law*) déclaration écrite sous serment

affiliated [ə'fɪlɪeɪtɪd] *adj* affilié(e); **~ company** filiale *f*

affinity [ə'fɪnɪtɪ] *n* affinité *f*

affirm [ə'fəːm] *vt* affirmer

affirmation [æfə'meɪʃən] *n* affirmation *f*, assertion *f*

affirmative [ə'fəːmətɪv] *adj* affirmatif(-ive) ▷ *n*: **in the ~** dans *or* par l'affirmative

affix [ə'fɪks] *vt* apposer, ajouter

afflict [ə'flɪkt] *vt* affliger

affliction [ə'flɪkʃən] *n* affliction *f*

affluence ['æfluəns] *n* aisance *f*, opulence *f*

affluent ['æfluənt] *adj* opulent(e); (*person, family, surroundings*) aisé(e), riche; **the ~ society** la société d'abondance

afford [ə'fɔːd] *vt* (*goods etc*) avoir les moyens d'acheter *or* d'entretenir; (*behaviour*) se permettre; (*provide*) fournir, procurer; **can we ~ a car?** avons-nous de quoi acheter *or* les moyens d'acheter une voiture?; **I can't ~ the time** je n'ai vraiment pas le temps

affordable [ə'fɔːdəbl] *adj* abordable

affray [ə'freɪ] *n* (*Brit Law*) échauffourée *f*, rixe *f*

affront [ə'frʌnt] *n* affront *m*

affronted [ə'frʌntɪd] *adj* insulté(e)

Afghan ['æfgæn] *adj* afghan(e) ▷ *n* Afghan(e)

Afghanistan [æf'gænɪstæn] *n* Afghanistan *m*

afield [ə'fiːld] *adv*: **far ~** loin

AFL-CIO *n abbr* (= *American Federation of Labor and Congress of Industrial Organizations*) confédération syndicale

afloat [ə'fləʊt] *adj* à flot ▷ *adv*: **to stay ~** surnager; **to keep/get a business ~** maintenir à flot/lancer une affaire

afoot [ə'fut] *adv*: **there is something ~** il se prépare quelque chose

aforementioned [ə'fɔːmɛnʃənd] *adj*, **aforesaid** [ə'fɔːsɛd] ▷ *adj* susdit(e), susmentionné(e)

afraid [ə'freɪd] *adj* effrayé(e); **to be ~ of** *or* **to** avoir peur de; **I am ~ that** je crains que + *sub*; **I'm ~ so/not** oui/non, malheureusement

afresh [ə'frɛʃ] *adv* de nouveau

Africa ['æfrɪkə] *n* Afrique *f*

African ['æfrɪkən] *adj* africain(e) ▷ *n* Africain(e)

African-American ['æfrɪkənə'mɛrɪkən] *adj* afro-américain(e) ▷ *n* Afro-Américain(e)

Afrikaans [æfrɪ'kaːns] *n* afrikaans *m*

Afrikaner [æfrɪ'kaːnər] *n* Afrikaner *m/f*

Afro-American ['æfrəʊə'mɛrɪkən] *adj* afro-américain(e)

AFT *n abbr* (= *American Federation of Teachers*) syndicat enseignant

aft [aːft] *adv* à l'arrière, vers l'arrière

after ['aːftər] *prep*, *adv* après ▷ *conj* après que, après avoir *or* être + *pp*; **~ dinner** après (le) dîner; **the day ~ tomorrow** après demain; **it's quarter ~ two** (*US*) il est deux heures et quart; **~ having done/~ he left** après avoir fait/ après son départ; **to name sb ~ sb** donner à qn le nom de qn; **to ask ~ sb** demander des nouvelles de qn; **what/who are you ~?** que/qui cherchez-vous?; **the police are ~ him** la police est à ses trousses; **~ you!** après vous!; **~ all** après tout

afterbirth ['aːftəbəːθ] *n* placenta *m*

aftercare ['aːftəkɛər] *n* (*Brit Med*) post-cure *f*

after-effects ['aːftərɪfɛkts] *npl* (*of disaster, radiation, drink etc*) répercussions *fpl*; (*of illness*) séquelles *fpl*, suites *fpl*

afterlife ['aːftəlaɪf] *n* vie future

aftermath ['aːftəmaːθ] *n* conséquences *fpl*; **in the ~ of** dans les mois *or* années *etc* qui suivirent, au lendemain de

afternoon ['ɑːftə'nuːn] *n* après-midi *m or f*;
good ~! bonjour!; (*goodbye*) au revoir!

afters ['ɑːftəz] *n* (*Brit inf: dessert*) dessert *m*

after-sales service [ɑːftə'seɪlz-] *n* service *m*
après-vente, SAV *m*

after-shave ['ɑːftəʃeɪv], **after-shave lotion** *n*
lotion *f* après-rasage

aftershock ['ɑːftəʃɔk] *n* réplique *f* (sismique)

aftersun ['ɑːftəsʌn], **aftersun cream,
aftersun lotion** *n* après-soleil *m inv*

aftertaste ['ɑːftəteɪst] *n* arrière-goût *m*

afterthought ['ɑːftəθɔːt] *n*: **I had an ~** il m'est
venu une idée après coup

afterwards ['ɑːftəwədz], (US) **afterward**
['ɑːftəwəd] *adv* après

again [ə'gɛn] *adv* de nouveau, encore (une fois);
to do sth ~ refaire qch; **not ... ~** ne ... plus; **~
and ~** à plusieurs reprises; **he's opened it ~** il
l'a rouvert, il l'a de nouveau *or* l'a encore ouvert;
now and ~ de temps à autre

against [ə'gɛnst] *prep* contre; (*compared to*) par
rapport à; **~ a blue background** sur un fond
bleu; **(as) ~** (*Brit*) contre

age [eɪdʒ] *n* âge *m* ▷ *vt, vi* vieillir; **what ~ is he?**
quel âge a-t-il?; **he is 20 years of ~** il a 20 ans;
under ~ mineur(e); **to come of ~** atteindre sa
majorité; **it's been ~s since I saw you** ça fait
une éternité que je ne t'ai pas vu

aged ['eɪdʒd] *adj* âgé(e); **~ 10** âgé de 10 ans; **the ~**
['eɪdʒɪd] ▷ *npl* les personnes âgées

age group *n* tranche *f* d'âge; **the 40 to 50 ~** la
tranche d'âge des 40 à 50 ans

ageing ['eɪdʒɪŋ] *adj* vieillissant(e)

ageless ['eɪdʒlɪs] *adj* sans âge

age limit *n* limite *f* d'âge

agency ['eɪdʒənsɪ] *n* agence *f*; **through** *or* **by
the ~ of** par l'entremise *or* l'action de

agenda [ə'dʒɛndə] *n* ordre *m* du jour; **on the ~** à
l'ordre du jour

agent ['eɪdʒənt] *n* agent *m*; (*firm*)
concessionnaire *m*

aggravate ['ægrəveɪt] *vt* (*situation*) aggraver;
(*annoy*) exaspérer, agacer

aggravation [ægrə'veɪʃən] *n* agacements *mpl*

aggregate ['ægrɪgɪt] *n* ensemble *m*, total *m*; **on
~** (*Sport*) au total des points

aggression [ə'grɛʃən] *n* agression *f*

aggressive [ə'grɛsɪv] *adj* agressif(-ive)

aggressiveness [ə'grɛsɪvnɪs] *n* agressivité *f*

aggressor [ə'grɛsə'] *n* agresseur *m*

aggrieved [ə'griːvd] *adj* chagriné(e), affligé(e)

aggro ['ægrəu] *n* (*inf: physical*) grabuge *m*;
(*: hassle*) embêtements *mpl*

aghast [ə'gɑːst] *adj* consterné(e), atterré(e)

agile ['ædʒaɪl] *adj* agile

agility [ə'dʒɪlɪtɪ] *n* agilité *f*, souplesse *f*

agitate ['ædʒɪteɪt] *vt* rendre inquiet(-ète) *or*
agité(e) ▷ *vi* faire de l'agitation (politique); **to ~
for** faire campagne pour

agitator ['ædʒɪteɪtə'] *n* agitateur(-trice)
(politique)

AGM *n abbr* (= *annual general meeting*) AG *f*

ago [ə'gəu] *adv*: **two days ~** il y a deux jours; **not
long ~** il n'y a pas longtemps; **as long ~ as 1960**
déjà en 1960; **how long ~?** il y a combien de
temps (de cela)?

agog [ə'gɔg] *adj*: **(all) ~** en émoi

agonize ['ægənaɪz] *vi*: **he ~d over the problem**
ce problème lui a causé bien du tourment

agonizing ['ægənaɪzɪŋ] *adj* angoissant(e); (*cry*)
déchirant(e)

agony ['ægənɪ] *n* (*pain*) douleur *f* atroce; (*distress*)
angoisse *f*; **to be in ~** souffrir le martyre

agony aunt *n* (*Brit inf*) journaliste qui tient la rubrique
du courrier du cœur

agony column *n* courrier *m* du cœur

agree [ə'griː] *vt* (*price*) convenir de ▷ *vi*: **to ~ with**
(*person*) être d'accord avec; (*statements etc*)
concorder avec; (*Ling*) s'accorder avec; **to ~ to
do** accepter *or* consentir à faire; **to ~ to sth**
consentir à qch; **to ~ that** (*admit*) convenir *or*
reconnaître que; **it was ~d that ...** il a été
convenu que ...; **they ~ on this** ils sont d'accord
sur ce point; **they ~d on going/a price** ils se
mirent d'accord pour y aller/sur un prix; **garlic
doesn't ~ with me** je ne supporte pas l'ail

agreeable [ə'griːəbl] *adj* (*pleasant*) agréable;
(*willing*) consentant(e), d'accord; **are you ~ to
this?** est-ce que vous êtes d'accord?

agreed [ə'griːd] *adj* (*time, place*) convenu(e); **to
be ~** être d'accord

agreement [ə'griːmənt] *n* accord *m*; **in ~**
d'accord; **by mutual ~** d'un commun accord

agricultural [ægrɪ'kʌltʃərəl] *adj* agricole

agriculture ['ægrɪkʌltʃə'] *n* agriculture *f*

aground [ə'graund] *adv*: **to run ~** s'échouer

ahead [ə'hɛd] *adv* en avant; devant; **go right** *or*
straight ~ (*direction*) allez tout droit; **go ~!**
(*permission*) allez-y!; **~ of** devant; (*fig: schedule etc*)
en avance sur; **~ of time** en avance; **they were
(right) ~ of us** ils nous précédaient (de peu), ils
étaient (juste) devant nous

AI *n abbr* = **Amnesty International**; (*Comput*) =
artificial intelligence

AIB *n abbr* (*Brit*: = *Accident Investigation Bureau*)
commission d'enquête sur les accidents

AID *n abbr* (= *artificial insemination by donor*) IAD *f*;
(*US*: = *Agency for International Development*) *agence
pour le développement international*

aid [eɪd] *n* aide *f*; (*device*) appareil *m* ▷ *vt* aider;
with the ~ of avec l'aide de; **in ~ of** en faveur
de; **to ~ and abet** (*Law*) se faire le complice de

aide [eɪd] *n* (*person*) assistant(e)

AIDS [eɪdz] *n abbr* (= *acquired immune* (or
immuno-)deficiency syndrome) SIDA *m*

AIH *n abbr* (= *artificial insemination by husband*) IAC *f*

ailing ['eɪlɪŋ] *adj* (*person*) souffreteux(euse);
(*economy*) malade

ailment ['eɪlmənt] *n* affection *f*

aim [eɪm] *vt*: **to ~ sth (at)** (*gun, camera*) braquer *or*
pointer qch (sur); (*missile*) lancer qch (à *or* contre
or en direction de); (*remark, blow*) destiner *or*
adresser qch (à) ▷ *vi* (*also*: **to take aim**) viser ▷ *n*

(objective) but _m_; _(skill)_: **his ~ is bad** il vise mal;
to ~ at viser; _(fig)_ viser (à); avoir pour but or
ambition; **to ~ to do** avoir l'intention de faire
aimless ['eɪmlɪs] _adj_ sans but
aimlessly ['eɪmlɪslɪ] _adv_ sans but
ain't [eɪnt] _(inf)_ = **am not; aren't; isn't**
air [ɛəʳ] _n_ air _m_ ▷ _vt_ aérer; _(idea, grievance, views)_
mettre sur le tapis; _(knowledge)_ faire étalage de
▷ _cpd (currents, attack etc)_ aérien(ne); **to throw
sth into the ~** _(ball etc)_ jeter qch en l'air; **by ~**
par avion; **to be on the ~** _(Radio, TV: programme)_
être diffusé(e); _(: station)_ émettre
airbag ['ɛəbæg] _n_ airbag _m_
air base _n_ base aérienne
airbed ['ɛəbɛd] _n (Brit)_ matelas _m_ pneumatique
airborne ['ɛəbɔːn] _adj (plane)_ en vol; _(troops)_
aéroporté(e); _(particles)_ dans l'air; **as soon as
the plane was ~** dès que l'avion eut décollé
air cargo _n_ fret aérien
air-conditioned ['ɛəkən'dɪʃənd] _adj_
climatisé(e), à air conditionné
air conditioning [-kən'dɪʃnɪŋ] _n_ climatisation _f_
air-cooled ['ɛəkuːld] _adj_ à refroidissement à air
aircraft ['ɛəkrɑːft] _n inv_ avion _m_
aircraft carrier _n_ porte-avions _m inv_
air cushion _n_ coussin _m_ d'air
airdrome ['ɛədrəum] _n (US)_ aérodrome _m_
airfield ['ɛəfiːld] _n_ terrain _m_ d'aviation
Air Force _n_ Armée _f_ de l'air
air freight _n_ fret aérien
air freshener [-'frɛʃnəʳ] _n_ désodorisant _m_
airgun ['ɛəgʌn] _n_ fusil _m_ à air comprimé
air hostess _n (Brit)_ hôtesse _f_ de l'air
airily ['ɛərɪlɪ] _adv_ d'un air dégagé
airing ['ɛərɪŋ] _n_: **to give an ~ to** aérer; _(fig: ideas,
views etc)_ mettre sur le tapis
airing cupboard _n (Brit)_ placard qui contient la
chaudière et dans lequel on met le linge à sécher
air letter _n (Brit)_ aérogramme _m_
airlift ['ɛəlɪft] _n_ pont aérien
airline ['ɛəlaɪn] _n_ ligne aérienne, compagnie
aérienne
airliner ['ɛəlaɪnəʳ] _n_ avion _m_ de ligne
airlock ['ɛəlɔk] _n_ sas _m_
airmail ['ɛəmeɪl] _n_: **by ~** par avion
air mattress _n_ matelas _m_ pneumatique
air mile _n_ air mile _m_
airplane ['ɛəpleɪn] _n (US)_ avion _m_
air pocket _n_ trou _m_ d'air
airport ['ɛəpɔːt] _n_ aéroport _m_
air raid _n_ attaque aérienne
air rifle _n_ carabine _f_ à air comprimé
airsick ['ɛəsɪk] _adj_: **to be ~** avoir le mal de l'air
airspace ['ɛəspeɪs] _n_ espace _m_ aérien
airspeed ['ɛəspiːd] _n_ vitesse relative
airstrip ['ɛəstrɪp] _n_ terrain _m_ d'atterrissage
air terminal _n_ aérogare _f_
airtight ['ɛətaɪt] _adj_ hermétique
air time _n (Radio, TV)_ temps _m_ d'antenne
air traffic control _n_ contrôle _m_ de la navigation
aérienne
air-traffic controller _n_ aiguilleur _m_ du ciel

airway ['ɛəweɪ] _n (Aviat)_ voie aérienne; **airways**
(Anat) voies aériennes
airy ['ɛərɪ] _adj_ bien aéré(e); _(manners)_ dégagé(e)
aisle [aɪl] _n (of church: central)_ allée _f_ centrale;
(: side) nef _f_ latérale, bas-côté _m_; _(in theatre,
supermarket)_ allée; _(on plane)_ couloir _m_
aisle seat _n_ place _f_ côté couloir
ajar [ə'dʒɑːʳ] _adj_ entrouvert(e)
AK _abbr (US)_ = **Alaska**
aka _abbr (= also known as)_ alias
akin [ə'kɪn] _adj_: **~ to** semblable à, du même
ordre que
AL _abbr (US)_ = **Alabama**
ALA _n abbr_ = **American Library Association**
Ala. _abbr (US)_ = **Alabama**
à la carte [ælæ'kɑːt] _adv_ à la carte
alacrity [ə'lækrɪtɪ] _n_: **with ~** avec
empressement, promptement
alarm [ə'lɑːm] _n_ alarme _f_ ▷ _vt_ alarmer
alarm call _n_ coup _m_ de fil pour réveiller; **could I
have an ~ at 7 am, please?** pouvez-vous me
réveiller à 7 heures, s'il vous plaît?
alarm clock _n_ réveille-matin _m inv_, réveil _m_
alarmed [ə'lɑːmd] _adj (frightened)_ alarmé(e);
(protected by an alarm) protégé(e) par un système
d'alarme; **to become ~** prendre peur
alarming [ə'lɑːmɪŋ] _adj_ alarmant(e)
alarmingly [ə'lɑːmɪŋlɪ] _adv_ d'une manière
alarmante; **~ close** dangereusement proche; **~
quickly** à une vitesse inquiétante
alarmist [ə'lɑːmɪst] _n_ alarmiste _m/f_
alas [ə'læs] _excl_ hélas
Alas. _abbr (US)_ = **Alaska**
Alaska [ə'læskə] _n_ Alaska _m_
Albania [æl'beɪnɪə] _n_ Albanie _f_
Albanian [æl'beɪnɪən] _adj_ albanais(e) ▷ _n_
Albanais(e); _(Ling)_ albanais _m_
albatross ['ælbətrɔs] _n_ albatros _m_
albeit [ɔːl'biːɪt] _conj_ bien que + _sub_, encore que +
sub
album ['ælbəm] _n_ album _m_
albumen ['ælbjumɪn] _n_ albumine _f_; _(of egg)_
albumen _m_
alchemy ['ælkɪmɪ] _n_ alchimie _f_
alcohol ['ælkəhɔl] _n_ alcool _m_
alcohol-free ['ælkəhɔlfriː] _adj_ sans alcool
alcoholic [ælkə'hɔlɪk] _adj, n_ alcoolique _(m/f)_
alcoholism ['ælkəhɔlɪzəm] _n_ alcoolisme _m_
alcove ['ælkəuv] _n_ alcôve _f_
Ald. _abbr_ = **alderman**
alderman ['ɔːldəmən] _n_ conseiller municipal
(en Angleterre)
ale [eɪl] _n_ bière _f_
alert [ə'ləːt] _adj_ alerte, vif (vive); _(watchful)_
vigilant(e) ▷ _n_ alerte _f_ ▷ _vt_ alerter; **to ~ sb (to
sth)** attirer l'attention de qn (sur qch); **to ~ sb
to the dangers of sth** avertir qn des dangers de
qch; **on the ~** sur le qui-vive; _(Mil)_ en état
d'alerte
Aleutian Islands [ə'luːʃən-] _npl_ îles
Aléoutiennes
A levels _npl_ ≈ baccalauréat _msg_

Alexandria [ælɪgˈzɑːndrɪə] n Alexandrie
alfresco [ælˈfrɛskəʊ] adj, adv en plein air
algebra [ˈældʒɪbrə] n algèbre m
Algeria [ælˈdʒɪərɪə] n Algérie f
Algerian [ælˈdʒɪərɪən] adj algérien(ne) ▷ n
Algérien(ne)
Algiers [ælˈdʒɪəz] n Alger
algorithm [ˈælgərɪðəm] n algorithme m
alias [ˈeɪlɪəs] adv alias ▷ n faux nom, nom
d'emprunt
alibi [ˈælɪbaɪ] n alibi m
alien [ˈeɪlɪən] n (from abroad) étranger(-ère); (from
outer space) extraterrestre ▷ adj: ~ (to)
étranger(-ère) (à)
alienate [ˈeɪlɪəneɪt] vt aliéner; (subj: person)
s'aliéner
alienation [eɪlɪəˈneɪʃən] n aliénation f
alight [əˈlaɪt] adj, adv en feu ▷ vi mettre pied à
terre; (passenger) descendre; (bird) se poser
align [əˈlaɪn] vt aligner
alignment [əˈlaɪnmənt] n alignement m; it's
out of ~ (with) ce n'est pas aligné (avec)
alike [əˈlaɪk] adj semblable, pareil(le) ▷ adv de
même; to look ~ se ressembler
alimony [ˈælɪmənɪ] n (payment) pension f
alimentaire
alive [əˈlaɪv] adj vivant(e); (active) plein(e) de vie;
~ with grouillant(e) de; ~ to sensible à
alkali [ˈælkəlaɪ] n alcali m

⭘ **KEYWORD**

all [ɔːl] adj (singular) tout(e); (plural) tous (toutes);
all day toute la journée; **all night** toute la nuit;
all men tous les hommes; **all five** tous les cinq;
all the food toute la nourriture; **all the books**
tous les livres; **all the time** tout le temps; **all
his life** toute sa vie
▷ pron **1** tout; **I ate it all, I ate all of it** j'ai tout
mangé; **all of us went** nous y sommes tous
allés; **all of the boys went** tous les garçons y
sont allés; **is that all?** c'est tout?; (in shop) ce
sera tout?
2 (in phrases): **above all** surtout, par-dessus tout;
after all après tout; **at all**: **not at all** (in answer
to question) pas du tout; (in answer to thanks) je
vous en prie!; **I'm not at all tired** je ne suis pas
du tout fatigué(e); **anything at all will do**
n'importe quoi fera l'affaire; **all in all** tout
bien considéré, en fin de compte
▷ adv: **all alone** tout(e) seul(e); **it's not as hard
as all that** ce n'est pas si difficile que ça; **all
the more/the better** d'autant plus/mieux; **all
but** presque, pratiquement; **to be all in** (Brit
inf) être complètement à plat; **the score is 2 all**
le score est de 2 partout

Allah [ˈælə] n Allah m
all-around [ɔːləˈraʊnd] adj (US) = **all-round**
allay [əˈleɪ] vt (fears) apaiser, calmer
all clear n (also fig) fin f d'alerte
allegation [ælɪˈgeɪʃən] n allégation f

allege [əˈlɛdʒ] vt alléguer, prétendre; **he is ~d to
have said** il aurait dit
alleged [əˈlɛdʒd] adj prétendu(e)
allegedly [əˈlɛdʒɪdlɪ] adv à ce que l'on prétend,
paraît-il
allegiance [əˈliːdʒəns] n fidélité f, obéissance f
allegory [ˈælɪgərɪ] n allégorie f
all-embracing [ˈɔːlɪmˈbreɪsɪŋ] adj universel(le)
allergic [əˈləːdʒɪk] adj: ~ **to** allergique à; **I'm ~ to
penicillin** je suis allergique à la pénicilline
allergy [ˈælədʒɪ] n allergie f
alleviate [əˈliːvɪeɪt] vt soulager, adoucir
alley [ˈælɪ] n ruelle f; (in garden) allée f
alleyway [ˈælɪweɪ] n ruelle f
alliance [əˈlaɪəns] n alliance f
allied [ˈælaɪd] adj allié(e)
alligator [ˈælɪgeɪtəʳ] n alligator m
all-important [ˈɔːlɪmˈpɔːtənt] adj capital(e),
crucial(e)
all-in [ˈɔːlɪn] adj, adv (Brit: charge) tout compris
all-in wrestling n (Brit) catch m
alliteration [əlɪtəˈreɪʃən] n allitération f
all-night [ˈɔːlˈnaɪt] adj ouvert(e) or qui dure toute
la nuit
allocate [ˈæləkeɪt] vt (share out) répartir,
distribuer; **to ~ sth to** (duties) assigner or
attribuer qch à; (sum, time) allouer qch à; **to ~
sth for** affecter qch à
allocation [æləʊˈkeɪʃən] n (see vb) répartition f;
attribution f; allocation f; affectation f; (money)
crédit(s) m(pl), somme(s) allouée(s)
allot [əˈlɔt] vt (share out) répartir, distribuer; **to ~
sth to** (time) allouer qch à; (duties) assigner qch
à; **in the ~ted time** dans le temps imparti
allotment [əˈlɔtmənt] n (share) part f; (garden)
lopin m de terre (loué à la municipalité)
all-out [ˈɔːlaʊt] adj (effort etc) total(e)
allow [əˈlaʊ] vt (practice, behaviour) permettre,
autoriser; (sum to spend etc) accorder, allouer;
(sum, time estimated) compter, prévoir; (claim, goal)
admettre; (concede): **to ~ that** convenir que; **to
~ sb to do** permettre à qn de faire, autoriser qn
à faire; **he is ~ed to ...** on lui permet de ...;
smoking is not ~ed il est interdit de fumer; **we
must ~ three days for the journey** il faut
compter trois jours pour le voyage
▶ **allow for** vt fus tenir compte de
allowance [əˈlaʊəns] n (money received) allocation
f; (: from parent etc) subside m; (: for expenses)
indemnité f; (US: pocket money) argent m de
poche; (Tax) somme f déductible du revenu
imposable, abattement m; **to make ~s for**
(person) essayer de comprendre; (thing) tenir
compte de
alloy [ˈælɔɪ] n alliage m
all right adv (feel, work) bien; (as answer) d'accord
all-round [ˈɔːlˈraʊnd] adj compétent(e) dans
tous les domaines; (athlete etc) complet(-ète)
all-rounder [ɔːlˈraʊndəʳ] n (Brit): **to be a good ~**
être doué(e) en tout
allspice [ˈɔːlspaɪs] n poivre m de la Jamaïque
all-time [ˈɔːlˈtaɪm] adj (record) sans précédent,

absolu(e)

allude [əˈluːd] *vi*: **to ~ to** faire allusion à

alluring [əˈljuərɪŋ] *adj* séduisant(e), alléchant(e)

allusion [əˈluːʒən] *n* allusion *f*

alluvium [əˈluːvɪəm] *n* alluvions *fpl*

ally [ˈælaɪ] *n* allié *m* ▷ *vt* [əˈlaɪ]: **to ~ o.s. with** s'allier avec

almighty [ɔːlˈmaɪtɪ] *adj* tout(e)-puissant(e); (*tremendous*) énorme

almond [ˈɑːmənd] *n* amande *f*

almost [ˈɔːlməust] *adv* presque; **he ~ fell** il a failli tomber

alms [ɑːmz] *n* aumône(s) *f(pl)*

aloft [əˈlɔft] *adv* en haut, en l'air; (*Naut*) dans la mâture

alone [əˈləun] *adj, adv* seul(e); **to leave sb ~** laisser qn tranquille; **to leave sth ~** ne pas toucher à qch; **let ~ ...** sans parler de ...; encore moins ...

along [əˈlɔŋ] *prep* le long de ▷ *adv*: **is he coming ~ with us?** vient-il avec nous?; **he was hopping/limping ~** il venait *or* avançait en sautillant/boitant; **~ with** avec, en plus de; (*person*) en compagnie de; **all ~** (*all the time*) depuis le début

alongside [əˈlɔŋˈsaɪd] *prep* (*along*) le long de; (*beside*) à côté de ▷ *adv* bord à bord; côte à côte; **we brought our boat ~** (*of a pier, shore etc*) nous avons accosté

aloof [əˈluːf] *adj* distant(e) ▷ *adv* à distance, à l'écart; **to stand ~** se tenir à l'écart *or* à distance

aloofness [əˈluːfnɪs] *n* réserve (hautaine), attitude distante

aloud [əˈlaud] *adv* à haute voix

alphabet [ˈælfəbɛt] *n* alphabet *m*

alphabetical [ælfəˈbɛtɪkl] *adj* alphabétique; **in ~ order** par ordre alphabétique

alphanumeric [ælfənjuːˈmɛrɪk] *adj* alphanumérique

alpine [ˈælpaɪn] *adj* alpin(e), alpestre; **~ hut** cabane *f or* refuge *m* de montagne; **~ pasture** pâturage *m* (de montagne); **~ skiing** ski alpin

Alps [ælps] *npl*: **the ~** les Alpes *fpl*

already [ɔːlˈrɛdɪ] *adv* déjà

alright [ɔːlˈraɪt] *adv* (*Brit*) = **all right**

Alsace [ælˈsæs] *n* Alsace *f*

Alsatian [ælˈseɪʃən] *adj* alsacien(ne), d'Alsace ▷ *n* Alsacien(ne); (*Brit*: *dog*) berger allemand

also [ˈɔːlsəu] *adv* aussi

Alta. *abbr* (*Canada*) = **Alberta**

altar [ˈɔltər] *n* autel *m*

alter [ˈɔltər] *vt, vi* changer

alteration [ɔltəˈreɪʃən] *n* changement *m*, modification *f*; **alterations** *npl* (*Sewing*) retouches *fpl*; (*Archit*) modifications *fpl*; **timetable subject to ~** horaires sujets à modifications

altercation [ɔltəˈkeɪʃən] *n* altercation *f*

alternate *adj* [ɔlˈtəːnɪt] alterné(e), alternant(e), alternatif(-ive); (*US*) = **alternative** ▷ *vi* [ˈɔltəːneɪt] alterner; **to ~ with** alterner avec; **on**

~ days un jour sur deux, tous les deux jours

alternately [ɔlˈtəːnɪtlɪ] *adv* alternativement, en alternant

alternating [ˈɔltəːneɪtɪŋ] *adj* (*current*) alternatif(-ive)

alternative [ɔlˈtəːnətɪv] *adj* (*solution, plan*) autre, de remplacement; (*energy*) doux (douce); (*lifestyle*) parallèle ▷ *n* (*choice*) alternative *f*; (*other possibility*) autre possibilité *f*; **~ medicine** médecine alternative, médecine douce

alternatively [ɔlˈtəːnətɪvlɪ] *adv*: **~ one could ...** une autre *or* l'autre solution serait de ...

alternative medicine *n* médecines *fpl* parallèles *or* douces

alternator [ˈɔltəːneɪtər] *n* (*Aut*) alternateur *m*

although [ɔːlˈðəu] *conj* bien que + *sub*

altitude [ˈæltɪtjuːd] *n* altitude *f*

alto [ˈæltəu] *n* (*female*) contralto *m*; (*male*) haute-contre *f*

altogether [ɔːltəˈgɛðər] *adv* entièrement, tout à fait; (*on the whole*) tout compte fait; (*in all*) en tout; **how much is that ~?** ça fait combien en tout?

altruism [ˈæltruɪzəm] *n* altruisme *m*

altruistic [æltruˈɪstɪk] *adj* altruiste

aluminium [æljuˈmɪnɪəm] (*US*), **aluminum** [əˈluːmɪnəm] *n* aluminium *m*

alumna (*pl* **-e**) [əˈlʌmnə, -niː] *n* (*US Scol*) ancienne élève; (*University*) ancienne étudiante

alumnus (*pl* **alumni**) [əˈlʌmnəs, -naɪ] *n* (*US Scol*) ancien élève; (*University*) ancien étudiant

always [ˈɔːlweɪz] *adv* toujours

Alzheimer's [ˈæltshaɪməz], **Alzheimer's disease** *n* maladie *f* d'Alzheimer

AM *abbr* = **amplitude modulation** ▷ *n abbr* (= *Assembly Member*) député *m* au Parlement gallois

am [æm] *vb see* **be**

a.m. *adv abbr* (= *ante meridiem*) du matin

AMA *n abbr* = **American Medical Association**

amalgam [əˈmælgəm] *n* amalgame *m*

amalgamate [əˈmælgəmeɪt] *vt, vi* fusionner

amalgamation [əmælgəˈmeɪʃən] *n* fusion *f*; (*Comm*) fusionnement *m*

amass [əˈmæs] *vt* amasser

amateur [ˈæmətər] *n* amateur *m* ▷ *adj* (*Sport*) amateur *inv*; **~ dramatics** le théâtre amateur

amateurish [ˈæmətərɪʃ] *adj* (*pej*) d'amateur, un peu amateur

amaze [əˈmeɪz] *vt* stupéfier; **to be ~d (at)** être stupéfait(e) (de)

amazed [əˈmeɪzd] *adj* stupéfait(e)

amazement [əˈmeɪzmənt] *n* surprise *f*, étonnement *m*

amazing [əˈmeɪzɪŋ] *adj* étonnant(e), incroyable; (*bargain, offer*) exceptionnel(le)

amazingly [əˈmeɪzɪŋlɪ] *adv* incroyablement

Amazon [ˈæməzən] *n* (*Geo, Mythology*) Amazone *f* ▷ *cpd* amazonien(ne), de l'Amazone; **the ~ basin** le bassin de l'Amazone; **the ~ jungle** la forêt amazonienne

Amazonian [æməˈzəunɪən] *adj* amazonien(ne)

ambassador [æm'bæsədə'] *n* ambassadeur *m*

amber ['æmbə'] *n* ambre *m*; **at ~** (*Brit Aut*) à l'orange

ambidextrous [æmbɪ'dɛkstrəs] *adj* ambidextre

ambience ['æmbɪəns] *n* ambiance *f*

ambiguity [æmbɪ'gjuːɪt] *n* ambiguïté *f*

ambiguous [æm'bɪgjuəs] *adj* ambigu(ë)

ambition [æm'bɪʃən] *n* ambition *f*

ambitious [æm'bɪʃəs] *adj* ambitieux(-euse)

ambivalent [æm'bɪvələnt] *adj* (*attitude*) ambivalent(e)

amble ['æmbl] *vi* (*also*: **to amble along**) aller d'un pas tranquille

ambulance ['æmbjuləns] *n* ambulance *f*; **call an ~!** appelez une ambulance!

ambush ['æmbuʃ] *n* embuscade *f* ▷ *vt* tendre une embuscade à

ameba [ə'miːbə] *n* (*US*) = **amoeba**

ameliorate [ə'miːlɪəreɪt] *vt* améliorer

amen ['ɑː'mɛn] *excl* amen

amenable [ə'miːnəbl] *adj*: **~ to** (*advice etc*) disposé(e) à écouter *or* suivre; **~ to the law** responsable devant la loi

amend [ə'mɛnd] *vt* (*law*) amender; (*text*) corriger; (*habits*) réformer ▷ *vi* s'amender, se corriger; **to make ~s** réparer ses torts, faire amende honorable

amendment [ə'mɛndmənt] *n* (*to law*) amendement *m*; (*to text*) correction *f*

amenities [ə'miːnɪtɪz] *npl* aménagements *mpl*, équipements *mpl*

amenity [ə'miːnɪtɪ] *n* charme *m*, agrément *m*

America [ə'mɛrɪkə] *n* Amérique *f*

American [ə'mɛrɪkən] *adj* américain(e) ▷ *n* Américain(e)

American football *n* (*Brit*) football *m* américain

americanize [ə'mɛrɪkənaɪz] *vt* américaniser

amethyst ['æmɪθɪst] *n* améthyste *f*

Amex ['æmɛks] *n abbr* = **American Stock Exchange**

amiable ['eɪmɪəbl] *adj* aimable, affable

amicable ['æmɪkəbl] *adj* amical(e); (*Law*) à l'amiable

amicably ['æmɪkəblɪ] *adv* amicalement

amid [ə'mɪd], **amidst** [ə'mɪdst] *prep* parmi, au milieu de

amiss [ə'mɪs] *adj*, *adv*: **there's something ~** il y a quelque chose qui ne va pas *or* qui cloche; **to take sth ~** prendre qch mal *or* de travers

ammo ['æməu] *n abbr* (*inf*) = **ammunition**

ammonia [ə'məunɪə] *n* (*gas*) ammoniac *m*; (*liquid*) ammoniaque *f*

ammunition [æmju'nɪʃən] *n* munitions *fpl*; (*fig*) arguments *mpl*

ammunition dump *n* dépôt *m* de munitions

amnesia [æm'niːzɪə] *n* amnésie *f*

amnesty ['æmnɪstɪ] *n* amnistie *f*; **to grant an ~ to** accorder une amnistie à

Amnesty International *n* Amnesty International

amoeba, (*US*) **ameba** [ə'miːbə] *n* amibe *f*

amok [ə'mɔk] *adv*: **to run ~** être pris(e) d'un accès de folie furieuse

among [ə'mʌŋ], **amongst** [ə'mʌŋst] *prep* parmi, entre

amoral [æ'mɔrəl] *adj* amoral(e)

amorous ['æmərəs] *adj* amoureux(-euse)

amorphous [ə'mɔːfəs] *adj* amorphe

amortization [əmɔːtaɪ'zeɪʃən] *n* (*Comm*) amortissement *m*

amount [ə'maunt] *n* (*sum of money*) somme *f*; (*total*) montant *m*; (*quantity*) quantité *f*; nombre *m* ▷ *vi*: **to ~ to** (*total*) s'élever à; (*be same as*) équivaloir à, revenir à; **this ~s to a refusal** cela équivaut à un refus; **the total ~** (*of money*) le montant total

amp ['æmp], **ampère** ['æmpeə'] *n* ampère *m*; **a 13 ~ plug** une fiche de 13 A

ampersand ['æmpəsænd] *n* signe &, "et" commercial

amphetamine [æm'fɛtəmiːn] *n* amphétamine *f*

amphibian [æm'fɪbɪən] *n* batracien *m*

amphibious [æm'fɪbɪəs] *adj* amphibie

amphitheatre, (*US*) **amphitheater** ['æmfɪθɪətə'] *n* amphithéâtre *m*

ample ['æmpl] *adj* ample, spacieux(-euse); (*enough*): **this is ~** c'est largement suffisant; **to have ~ time/room** avoir bien assez de temps/place, avoir largement le temps/la place

amplifier ['æmplɪfaɪə'] *n* amplificateur *m*

amplify ['æmplɪfaɪ] *vt* amplifier

amply ['æmplɪ] *adv* amplement, largement

ampoule, (*US*) **ampule** ['æmpuːl] *n* (*Med*) ampoule *f*

amputate ['æmpjuteɪt] *vt* amputer

amputee [æmpju'tiː] *n* amputé(e)

Amsterdam ['æmstədæm] *n* Amsterdam

amt *abbr* = **amount**

Amtrak ['æmtræk] (*US*) *n* société mixte de transports ferroviaires interurbains pour voyageurs

amuck [ə'mʌk] *adv* = **amok**

amuse [ə'mjuːz] *vt* amuser; **to ~ o.s. with sth/by doing sth** se divertir avec qch/à faire qch; **to be ~d at** être amusé par; **he was not ~d** il n'a pas apprécié

amusement [ə'mjuːzmənt] *n* amusement *m*; (*pastime*) distraction *f*

amusement arcade *n* salle *f* de jeu

amusement park *n* parc *m* d'attractions

amusing [ə'mjuːzɪŋ] *adj* amusant(e), divertissant(e)

an [æn, ən, n] *indef art see* **a**

ANA *n abbr* = **American Newspaper Association**; **American Nurses Association**

anachronism [ə'nækrənɪzəm] *n* anachronisme *m*

anaemia, (*US*) **anemia** [ə'niːmɪə] *n* anémie *f*

anaemic, (*US*) **anemic** [ə'niːmɪk] *adj* anémique

anaesthetic, (*US*) **anesthetic** [ænɪs'θɛtɪk] *adj*, *n* anesthésique *m*; **under the ~** sous anesthésie; **local/general ~** anesthésie locale/générale

anaesthetist [æ'niːsθɪtɪst] *n* anesthésiste *m/f*

anagram ['ænəgræm] *n* anagramme *m*

anal ['eɪnl] *adj* anal(e)

analgesic [ænæl'dʒi:sɪk] *adj, n* analgésique (*m*)

analogous [ə'næləgəs] *adj*: ~ **(to** *or* **with)** analogue (à)

analogue, analog ['ænəlɔg] *adj* (*watch, computer*) analogique

analogy [ə'nælədʒɪ] *n* analogie *f*; **to draw an ~ between** établir une analogie entre

analyse, (*US*) **analyze** ['ænəlaɪz] *vt* analyser

analysis (*pl* **analyses**) [ə'næləsɪs, -siːz] *n* analyse *f*; **in the last ~** en dernière analyse

analyst ['ænəlɪst] *n* (*political analyst etc*) analyste *m/f*; (*US*) psychanalyste *m/f*

analytic [ænə'lɪtɪk], **analytical** [ænə'lɪtɪkəl] *adj* analytique

analyze ['ænəlaɪz] *vt* (*US*) = **analyse**

anarchic [æ'nɑ:kɪk] *adj* anarchique

anarchist ['ænəkɪst] *adj, n* anarchiste (*m/f*)

anarchy ['ænəkɪ] *n* anarchie *f*

anathema [ə'næθɪmə] *n*: **it is ~ to him** il a cela en abomination

anatomical [ænə'tɔmɪkəl] *adj* anatomique

anatomy [ə'nætəmɪ] *n* anatomie *f*

ANC *n abbr* (= *African National Congress*) ANC *m*

ancestor ['ænsɪstə'] *n* ancêtre *m*, aïeul *m*

ancestral [æn'sɛstrəl] *adj* ancestral(e)

ancestry ['ænsɪstrɪ] *n* ancêtres *mpl*; ascendance *f*

anchor ['æŋkə'] *n* ancre *f* ▷ *vi* (*also*: **to drop anchor**) jeter l'ancre, mouiller ▷ *vt* mettre à l'ancre; (*fig*): **to ~ sth to** fixer qch à; **to weigh ~** lever l'ancre

anchorage ['æŋkərɪdʒ] *n* mouillage *m*, ancrage *m*

anchor man, anchor woman (*irreg*) *n* (*TV, Radio*) présentateur(-trice)

anchovy ['æntʃəvɪ] *n* anchois *m*

ancient ['eɪnʃənt] *adj* ancien(ne), antique; (*person*) d'un âge vénérable; (*car*) antédiluvien(ne); **~ monument** monument *m* historique

ancillary [æn'sɪlərɪ] *adj* auxiliaire

and [ænd] *conj* et; **~ so on** et ainsi de suite; **try ~ come** tâchez de venir; **come ~ sit here** venez vous asseoir ici; **he talked ~ talked** il a parlé pendant des heures; **better ~ better** de mieux en mieux; **more ~ more** de plus en plus

Andes ['ændi:z] *npl*: **the ~** les Andes *fpl*

Andorra [æn'dɔ:rə] *n* (principauté *f* d')Andorre *f*

anecdote ['ænɪkdəʊt] *n* anecdote *f*

anemia *etc* [ə'ni:mɪə] *n* (*US*) = **anaemia** *etc*

anemic [ə'ni:mɪk] *adj* = **anaemic**

anemone [ə'nɛmənɪ] *n* (*Bot*) anémone *f*; **sea ~** anémone de mer

anesthesiologist [ænɪsθi:zɪ'ɔlədʒɪst] *n* (*US*) anesthésiste *m/f*

anesthetic [ænɪs'θɛtɪk] *n, adj* (*US*) = **anaesthetic**

anesthetist [æ'ni:sθɪtɪst] *n* = **anaesthetist**

anew [ə'nju:] *adv* à nouveau

angel ['eɪndʒəl] *n* ange *m*

angel dust *n* poussière *f* d'ange

anger ['æŋgə'] *n* colère *f* ▷ *vt* mettre en colère, irriter

angina [æn'dʒaɪnə] *n* angine *f* de poitrine

angle ['æŋgl] *n* angle *m* ▷ *vi*: **to ~ for** (*trout*) pêcher; (*compliments*) chercher, quêter; **from their ~** de leur point de vue

angler ['æŋglə'] *n* pêcheur(-euse) à la ligne

Anglican ['æŋglɪkən] *adj, n* anglican(e)

anglicize ['æŋglɪsaɪz] *vt* angliciser

angling ['æŋglɪŋ] *n* pêche *f* à la ligne

Anglo- ['æŋgləʊ] *prefix* anglo(-)

Anglo-French ['æŋgləʊ'frɛntʃ] *adj* anglo-français(e)

Anglo-Saxon ['æŋgləʊ'sæksən] *adj, n* anglo-saxon(ne)

Angola [æŋ'gəʊlə] *n* Angola *m*

Angolan [æŋ'gəʊlən] *adj* angolais(e) ▷ *n* Angolais(e)

angrily ['æŋgrɪlɪ] *adv* avec colère

angry ['æŋgrɪ] *adj* en colère, furieux(-euse); (*wound*) enflammé(e); **to be ~ with sb/at sth** être furieux contre qn/de qch; **to get ~** se fâcher, se mettre en colère; **to make sb ~** mettre qn en colère

anguish ['æŋgwɪʃ] *n* angoisse *f*

anguished ['æŋgwɪʃt] *adj* (*mentally*) angoissé(e); (*physically*) plein(e) de souffrance

angular ['æŋgjʊlə'] *adj* anguleux(-euse)

animal ['ænɪməl] *n* animal *m* ▷ *adj* animal(e)

animal rights *npl* droits *mpl* de l'animal

animate *vt* ['ænɪmeɪt] animer ▷ *adj* ['ænɪmɪt] animé(e), vivant(e)

animated ['ænɪmeɪtɪd] *adj* animé(e)

animation [ænɪ'meɪʃən] *n* (*of person*) entrain *m*; (*of street, Cine*) animation *f*

animosity [ænɪ'mɔsɪtɪ] *n* animosité *f*

aniseed ['ænɪsi:d] *n* anis *m*

Ankara ['æŋkərə] *n* Ankara

ankle ['æŋkl] *n* cheville *f*

ankle socks *npl* socquettes *fpl*

annex ['ænɛks] *n* (*Brit*: *also*: **annexe**) annexe *f* ▷ *vt* [ə'nɛks] annexer

annexation [ænɛks'eɪʃən] *n* annexion *f*

annihilate [ə'naɪəleɪt] *vt* annihiler, anéantir

annihilation [ənaɪə'leɪʃən] *n* anéantissement *m*

anniversary [ænɪ'vəːsərɪ] *n* anniversaire *m*

anniversary dinner *n* dîner commémoratif *or* anniversaire

annotate ['ænəʊteɪt] *vt* annoter

announce [ə'naʊns] *vt* annoncer; (*birth, death*) faire part de; **he ~d that he wasn't going** il a déclaré qu'il n'irait pas

announcement [ə'naʊnsmənt] *n* annonce *f*; (*for births etc*: *in newspaper*) avis *m* de faire-part; (: *letter, card*) faire-part *m*; **I'd like to make an ~** j'ai une communication à faire

announcer [ə'naʊnsə'] *n* (*Radio, TV*: *between programmes*) speaker(ine); (: *in a programme*) présentateur(-trice)

annoy [ə'nɔɪ] *vt* agacer, ennuyer, contrarier; **to be ~ed (at sth/with sb)** être en colère *or* irrité (contre qch/qn); **don't get ~ed!** ne vous fâchez pas!

annoyance [ə'nɔɪəns] n mécontentement m, contrariété f

annoying [ə'nɔɪɪŋ] adj agaçant(e), contrariant(e)

annual ['ænjuəl] adj annuel(le) ▷ n (Bot) plante annuelle; (book) album m

annual general meeting n (Brit) assemblée générale annuelle

annually ['ænjuəlɪ] adv annuellement

annual report n rapport annuel

annuity [ə'nju:ɪtɪ] n rente f; **life** ~ rente viagère

annul [ə'nʌl] vt annuler; (law) abroger

annulment [ə'nʌlmənt] n (see vb) annulation f; abrogation f

annum ['ænəm] n see **per**

Annunciation [ənʌnsɪ'eɪʃən] n Annonciation f

anode ['ænəud] n anode f

anoint [ə'nɔɪnt] vt oindre

anomalous [ə'nɔmələs] adj anormal(e)

anomaly [ə'nɔmælɪ] n anomalie f

anon. [ə'nɔn] abbr = **anonymous**

anonymity [ænə'nɪmɪtɪ] n anonymat m

anonymous [ə'nɔnɪməs] adj anonyme; **to remain** ~ garder l'anonymat

anorak ['ænəræk] n anorak m

anorexia [ænə'rɛksɪə] n (also: **anorexia nervosa**) anorexie f

anorexic [ænə'rɛksɪk] adj, n anorexique (m/f)

another [ə'nʌðə'] adj: ~ **book** (one more) un autre livre, encore un livre, un livre de plus; (a different one) un autre livre ▷ pron un(e) autre, encore un(e), un(e) de plus; ~ **drink?** encore un verre?; **in** ~ **five years** dans cinq ans; see also **one**

ANSI ['ænsɪ] n abbr (= American National Standards Institution) ANSI m (= Institut américain de normalisation)

answer ['ɑ:nsə'] n réponse f; (to problem) solution f ▷ vi répondre ▷ vt (reply to) répondre à; (problem) résoudre; (prayer) exaucer; **in** ~ **to your letter** suite à or en réponse à votre lettre; **to** ~ **the phone** répondre (au téléphone); **to** ~ **the bell** or **the door** aller or venir ouvrir (la porte)
▸ **answer back** vi répondre, répliquer
▸ **answer for** vt fus répondre de, se porter garant de; (crime, one's actions) répondre de
▸ **answer to** vt fus (description) répondre or correspondre à

answerable ['ɑ:nsərəbl] adj: ~ **(to sb/for sth)** responsable (devant qn/de qch); **I am** ~ **to no-one** je n'ai de comptes à rendre à personne

answering machine ['ɑ:nsərɪŋ-] n répondeur m

answerphone ['ɑ:nsərfəun] n (esp Brit) répondeur m (téléphonique)

ant [ænt] n fourmi f

ANTA n abbr = **American National Theater and Academy**

antagonism [æn'tægənɪzəm] n antagonisme m

antagonist [æn'tægənɪst] n antagoniste m/f, adversaire m/f

antagonistic [æntægə'nɪstɪk] adj (attitude, feelings) hostile

antagonize [æn'tægənaɪz] vt éveiller l'hostilité de, contrarier

Antarctic [ænt'ɑ:ktɪk] adj antarctique, austral(e) ▷ n: **the** ~ l'Antarctique m

Antarctica [ænt'ɑ:ktɪkə] n Antarctique m, Terres Australes

Antarctic Circle n cercle m Antarctique

Antarctic Ocean n océan m Antarctique or Austral

ante ['æntɪ] n: **to up the** ~ faire monter les enjeux

ante... ['æntɪ] prefix anté..., anti..., pré...

anteater ['ænti:tə'] n fourmilier m, tamanoir m

antecedent [æntɪ'si:dənt] n antécédent m

antechamber ['æntɪtʃeɪmbə'] n antichambre f

antelope ['æntɪləup] n antilope f

antenatal ['æntɪ'neɪtl] adj prénatal(e)

antenatal clinic n service m de consultation prénatale

antenna (pl **-e**) [æn'tɛnə, -ni:] n antenne f

anthem ['ænθəm] n motet m; **national** ~ hymne national

ant-hill ['ænthɪl] n fourmilière f

anthology [æn'θɔlədʒɪ] n anthologie f

anthrax ['ænθræks] n anthrax m

anthropologist [ænθrə'pɔlədʒɪst] n anthropologue m/f

anthropology [ænθrə'pɔlədʒɪ] n anthropologie f

anti ['æntɪ] prefix anti-

anti-aircraft ['æntɪ'ɛəkrɑ:ft] adj antiaérien(ne)

anti-aircraft defence n défense f contre avions, DCA f

antiballistic ['æntɪbə'lɪstɪk] adj antibalistique

antibiotic ['æntɪbaɪ'ɔtɪk] adj, n antibiotique m

antibody ['æntɪbɔdɪ] n anticorps m

anticipate [æn'tɪsɪpeɪt] vt s'attendre à, prévoir; (wishes, request) aller au devant de, devancer; **this is worse than I** ~**d** c'est pire que je ne pensais; **as** ~**d** comme prévu

anticipation [æntɪsɪ'peɪʃən] n attente f; **thanking you in** ~ en vous remerciant d'avance, avec mes remerciements anticipés

anticlimax ['æntɪ'klaɪmæks] n déception f

anticlockwise ['æntɪ'klɔkwaɪz] (Brit) adv dans le sens inverse des aiguilles d'une montre

antics ['æntɪks] npl singeries fpl

anticyclone ['æntɪ'saɪkləun] n anticyclone m

antidepressant ['æntɪdɪ'prɛsnt] n antidépresseur m

antidote ['æntɪdəut] n antidote m, contrepoison m

antifreeze ['æntɪfri:z] n antigel m

anti-globalization [æntɪgləubəlaɪ'zeɪʃən] n antimondialisation f

antihistamine [æntɪ'hɪstəmɪn] n antihistaminique m

Antilles [æn'tɪli:z] npl: **the** ~ les Antilles fpl

antipathy [æn'tɪpəθɪ] n antipathie f

antiperspirant [æntɪ'pə:spɪrənt] n déodorant m

Antipodean [æntɪpə'di:ən] adj australien(ne) et néozélandais(e), d'Australie et de Nouvelle-Zélande

Antipodes [æn'tɪpədi:z] npl: **the** ~ l'Australie f

et la Nouvelle-Zélande

antiquarian [ˌæntɪˈkwɛərɪən] *adj*: ~ **bookshop** librairie *f* d'ouvrages anciens ▷ *n* expert *m* en objets *or* livres anciens; amateur *m* d'antiquités

antiquated [ˈæntɪkweɪtɪd] *adj* vieilli(e), suranné(e), vieillot(te)

antique [ænˈtiːk] *n* (*ornament*) objet *m* d'art ancien; (*furniture*) meuble ancien ▷ *adj* ancien(ne); (*pre-mediaeval*) antique

antique dealer *n* antiquaire *m/f*

antique shop *n* magasin *m* d'antiquités

antiquity [ænˈtɪkwɪtɪ] *n* antiquité *f*

anti-Semitic [ˈæntɪsɪˈmɪtɪk] *adj* antisémite

anti-Semitism [ˈæntɪˈsɛmɪtɪzəm] *n* antisémitisme *m*

antiseptic [ˌæntɪˈsɛptɪk] *adj, n* antiseptique (*m*)

antisocial [ˈæntɪˈsəʊʃəl] *adj* (*unfriendly*) peu liant(e), insociable; (*against society*) antisocial(e)

antitank [ˈæntɪˈtæŋk] *adj* antichar

antithesis (*pl* **antitheses**) [ænˈtɪθɪsɪs, -siːz] *n* antithèse *f*

antitrust [ˌæntɪˈtrʌst] *adj*: ~ **legislation** loi *f* anti-trust

antiviral [ˌæntɪˈvaɪərəl] *adj* (*Med*) antiviral

antivirus [ˌæntɪˈvaɪərəs] *adj* antivirus *inv*; ~ **software** (logiciel *m*) antivírus *m*

antlers [ˈæntləz] *npl* bois *mpl*, ramure *f*

Antwerp [ˈæntwəːp] *n* Anvers

anus [ˈeɪnəs] *n* anus *m*

anvil [ˈænvɪl] *n* enclume *f*

anxiety [æŋˈzaɪətɪ] *n* anxiété *f*; (*keenness*): ~ **to do** grand désir *or* impatience *f* de faire

anxious [ˈæŋkʃəs] *adj* (*très*) inquiet(-ète), (*always worried*) anxieux(-euse); (*worrying*) angoissant(e); (*keen*): ~ **to do/that** qui tient beaucoup à faire/à ce que + *sub*; impatient(e) de faire/que + *sub*; **I'm very ~ about you** je me fais beaucoup de souci pour toi

anxiously [ˈæŋkʃəslɪ] *adv* anxieusement

○ **KEYWORD**

any [ˈɛnɪ] *adj* **1** (*in questions etc: singular*) du, de l', de la; (: *plural*) des; **do you have any butter/ children/ink?** avez-vous du beurre/des enfants/de l'encre?

2 (*with negative*) de, d'; **I don't have any money/ books** je n'ai pas d'argent/de livres; **without any difficulty** sans la moindre difficulté

3 (*no matter which*) n'importe quel(le); (*each and every*) tout(e), chaque; **choose any book you like** vous pouvez choisir n'importe quel livre; **any teacher you ask will tell you** n'importe quel professeur vous le dira

4 (*in phrases*): **in any case** de toute façon; **any day now** d'un jour à l'autre; **at any moment** à tout moment, d'un instant à l'autre; **at any rate** en tout cas; **any time** n'importe quand; **he might come (at) any time** il pourrait venir n'importe quand; **come (at) any time** venez quand vous voulez

▷ *pron* **1** (*in questions etc*) en; **have you got any?**

est-ce que vous en avez?; **can any of you sing?** est-ce que parmi vous il y en a qui savent chanter?

2 (*with negative*) en; **I don't have any (of them)** je n'en ai pas, je n'en ai aucun

3 (*no matter which one(s)*) n'importe lequel (*or* laquelle); (*anybody*) n'importe qui; **take any of those books (you like)** vous pouvez prendre n'importe lequel de ces livres

▷ *adv* **1** (*in questions etc*): **do you want any more soup/sandwiches?** voulez-vous encore de la soupe/des sandwichs?; **are you feeling any better?** est-ce que vous vous sentez mieux?

2 (*with negative*): **I can't hear him any more** je ne l'entends plus; **don't wait any longer** n'attendez pas plus longtemps

anybody [ˈɛnɪbɔdɪ] *pron* n'importe qui; (*in interrogative sentences*) quelqu'un; (*in negative sentences*): **I don't see ~** je ne vois personne; **if ~ should phone ...** si quelqu'un téléphone ...

anyhow [ˈɛnɪhaʊ] *adv* quoi qu'il en soit; (*haphazardly*) n'importe comment; **she leaves things just ~** elle laisse tout traîner; **I shall go ~** j'irai de toute façon

anyone [ˈɛnɪwʌn] *pron* = **anybody**

anyplace [ˈɛnɪpleɪs] *adv* (*US*) = **anywhere**

anything [ˈɛnɪθɪŋ] *pron* (*no matter what*) n'importe quoi; (*in questions*) quelque chose; (*with negative*) ne ... rien; **I don't want ~** je ne veux rien; **can you see ~?** tu vois quelque chose?; **if ~ happens to me ...** s'il m'arrive quoi que ce soit ...; **you can say ~ you like** vous pouvez dire ce que vous voulez; **~ will do** n'importe quoi fera l'affaire; **he'll eat ~** il mange de tout; **~ else?** (*in shop*) avec ceci?; **it can cost ~ between £15 and £20** (*Brit*) ça peut coûter dans les 15 à 20 livres

anytime [ˈɛnɪtaɪm] *adv* (*at any moment*) d'un moment à l'autre; (*whenever*) n'importe quand

anyway [ˈɛnɪweɪ] *adv* de toute façon; **~, I couldn't come even if I wanted to** de toute façon, je ne pouvais pas venir même si je le voulais; **I shall go ~** j'irai quand même; **why are you phoning, ~?** au fait, pourquoi tu me téléphones?

anywhere [ˈɛnɪwɛər] *adv* n'importe où; (*in interrogative sentences*) quelque part; (*in negative sentences*): **I can't see him ~** je ne le vois nulle part; **can you see him ~?** tu le vois quelque part?; **put the books down ~** pose les livres n'importe où; **~ in the world** (*no matter where*) n'importe où dans le monde

Anzac [ˈænzæk] *n abbr* (= *Australia-New Zealand Army Corps*) *soldat du corps ANZAC*

Anzac Day *n voir article*

● **ANZAC DAY**

Anzac Day est le 25 avril, jour férié en Australie et en Nouvelle-Zélande commémorant le débarquement des soldats

● du corps "ANZAC" à Gallipoli en 1915,
● pendant la Première Guerre mondiale. Ce
● fut la plus célèbre des campagnes du corps
  "ANZAC".

apart [ə'pɑːt] adv (to one side) à part; de côté; à
l'écart; (separately) séparément; **to take/pull ~**
démonter; **10 miles/a long way ~** à 10 miles/
très éloignés l'un de l'autre; **they are living ~**
ils sont séparés; **~ from** (prep) à part, excepté

apartheid [ə'pɑːteɪt] n apartheid m

apartment [ə'pɑːtmənt] n (US) appartement m,
logement m; (room) chambre f

apartment building n (US) immeuble m;
maison divisée en appartements

apathetic [æpə'θɛtɪk] adj apathique,
indifférent(e)

apathy ['æpəθɪ] n apathie f, indifférence f

APB n abbr (US: = all points bulletin) expression de la
police signifiant "découvrir et appréhender le suspect"

ape [eɪp] n (grand) singe ▷ vt singer

Apennines ['æpənaɪnz] npl: **the ~** les Apennins
mpl

aperitif [ə'pɛrɪtɪf] n apéritif m

aperture ['æpətʃuəʳ] n orifice m, ouverture f;
(Phot) ouverture (du diaphragme)

APEX ['eɪpɛks] n abbr (Aviat: = advance purchase
excursion) APEX m

apex ['eɪpɛks] n sommet m

aphid ['eɪfɪd] n puceron m

aphrodisiac [æfrəu'dɪzɪæk] adj, n
aphrodisiaque (m)

API n abbr = **American Press Institute**

apiece [ə'piːs] adv (for each person) chacun(e), par
tête; (for each item) chacun(e), la pièce

aplomb [ə'plɔm] n sang-froid m, assurance f

APO n abbr (US: = Army Post Office) service postal de
l'armée

apocalypse [ə'pɔkəlɪps] n apocalypse f

apolitical [eɪpə'lɪtɪkl] adj apolitique

apologetic [əpɔlə'dʒɛtɪk] adj (tone, letter)
d'excuse; **to be very ~ about** s'excuser
vivement de

apologetically [əpɔlə'dʒɛtɪkəlɪ] adv (say) en
s'excusant

apologize [ə'pɔlədʒaɪz] vi: **to ~ (for sth to sb)**
s'excuser (de qch auprès de qn), présenter des
excuses (à qn pour qch)

apology [ə'pɔlədʒɪ] n excuses fpl; **to send one's
apologies** envoyer une lettre or un mot
d'excuse, s'excuser (de ne pas pouvoir venir);
please accept my apologies vous voudrez bien
m'excuser

apoplectic [æpə'plɛktɪk] adj (Med)
apoplectique; (inf): **~ with rage** fou (folle) de
rage

apoplexy ['æpəplɛksɪ] n apoplexie f

apostle [ə'pɔsl] n apôtre m

apostrophe [ə'pɔstrəfɪ] n apostrophe f

app n abbr (Comput) = application

appal, (US) **appall** [ə'pɔːl] vt consterner,
atterrer; horrifier

Appalachian Mountains [æpə'leɪʃən-] npl: **the
~** les (monts mpl) Appalaches mpl

appalling [ə'pɔːlɪŋ] adj épouvantable; (stupidity)
consternant(e); **she's an ~ cook** c'est une très
mauvaise cuisinière

apparatus [æpə'reɪtəs] n appareil m, dispositif
m; (in gymnasium) agrès mpl

apparel [ə'pærl] n (US) habillement m,
confection f

apparent [ə'pærənt] adj apparent(e); **it is ~
that** il est évident que

apparently [ə'pærəntlɪ] adv apparemment

apparition [æpə'rɪʃən] n apparition f

appeal [ə'piːl] vi (Law) faire or interjeter appel
▷ n (Law) appel m; (request) appel; prière f;
(charm) attrait m, charme m; **to ~ for** demander
(instamment); implorer; **to ~ to** (beg) faire
appel à; (be attractive) plaire à; **to ~ to sb for
mercy** implorer la pitié de qn, prier or adjurer
qn d'avoir pitié; **it doesn't ~ to me** cela ne
m'attire pas; **right of ~** droit m de recours

appealing [ə'piːlɪŋ] adj (attractive) attrayant(e);
(touching) attendrissant(e)

appear [ə'pɪəʳ] vi apparaître, se montrer; (Law)
comparaître; (publication) paraître, sortir, être
publié(e); (seem) paraître, sembler; **it would ~
that** il semble que; **to ~ in Hamlet** jouer dans
Hamlet; **to ~ on TV** passer à la télé

appearance [ə'pɪərəns] n apparition f; parution
f; (look, aspect) apparence f, aspect m; **to put in** or
make an ~ faire acte de présence; (Theat): **by
order of ~** par ordre d'entrée en scène; **to keep
up ~s** sauver les apparences; **to all ~s** selon
toute apparence

appease [ə'piːz] vt apaiser, calmer

appeasement [ə'piːzmənt] n (Pol) apaisement m

append [ə'pɛnd] vt (Comput) ajouter (à la fin
d'un fichier)

appendage [ə'pɛndɪdʒ] n appendice m

appendices [ə'pɛndɪsiːz] npl of **appendix**

appendicitis [əpɛndɪ'saɪtɪs] n appendicite f

appendix (pl **appendices**) [ə'pɛndɪks, -siːz] n
appendice m; **to have one's ~ out** se faire
opérer de l'appendicite

appetite ['æpɪtaɪt] n appétit m; **that walk has
given me an ~** cette promenade m'a ouvert
l'appétit

appetizer ['æpɪtaɪzəʳ] n (food) amuse-gueule m;
(drink) apéritif m

appetizing ['æpɪtaɪzɪŋ] adj appétissant(e)

applaud [ə'plɔːd] vt, vi applaudir

applause [ə'plɔːz] n applaudissements mpl

apple ['æpl] n pomme f; (also: **apple tree**)
pommier m; **it's the ~ of my eye** j'y tiens
comme à la prunelle de mes yeux

apple pie n tarte f aux pommes

apple turnover n chausson m aux pommes

appliance [ə'plaɪəns] n appareil m; **electrical
~s** l'électroménager m

applicable [ə'plɪkəbl] adj applicable; **the law is
~ from January** la loi entre en vigueur au mois
de janvier; **to be ~ to** (relevant) valoir pour

applicant ['æplɪkənt] *n*: ~ **(for)** (*Admin: for benefit etc*) demandeur(-euse) (de); (*for post*) candidat(e) (à)

application [æplɪ'keɪʃən] *n* application *f*; (*for a job, a grant etc*) demande *f*; candidature *f*; (*Comput*) (logiciel *m*) applicatif *m*; **on** ~ sur demande

application form *n* formulaire *m* de demande

application program *n* (*Comput*) (logiciel *m*) applicatif *m*

applications package *n* (*Comput*) progiciel *m* d'application

applied [ə'plaɪd] *adj* appliqué(e); ~ **arts** *npl* arts décoratifs

apply [ə'plaɪ] *vt*: **to** ~ **(to)** (*paint, ointment*) appliquer (sur); (*law, etc*) appliquer (à) ▷ *vi*: **to** ~ **to** (*ask*) s'adresser à; (*be suitable for, relevant to*) s'appliquer à, être valable pour; **to** ~ **(for)** (*permit, grant*) faire une demande (en vue d'obtenir); (*job*) poser sa candidature (pour), faire une demande d'emploi (concernant); **to** ~ **the brakes** actionner les freins, freiner; **to** ~ **o.s. to** s'appliquer à

appoint [ə'pɔɪnt] *vt* (*to post*) nommer, engager; (*date, place*) fixer, désigner

appointee [əpɔɪn'tiː] *n* personne nommée; candidat retenu

appointment [ə'pɔɪntmənt] *n* (*to post*) nomination *f*; (*job*) poste *m*; (*arrangement to meet*) rendez-vous *m*; **to have an** ~ avoir un rendez-vous; **to make an** ~ **(with)** prendre rendez-vous (avec); **I'd like to make an** ~ je voudrais prendre rendez-vous; **"~s (vacant)"** (*Press*) "offres d'emploi"; **by** ~ sur rendez-vous

apportion [ə'pɔːʃən] *vt* (*share out*) répartir, distribuer; **to** ~ **sth to sb** attribuer *or* assigner *or* allouer qch à qn

appraisal [ə'preɪzl] *n* évaluation *f*

appraise [ə'preɪz] *vt* (*value*) estimer; (*situation etc*) évaluer

appreciable [ə'priːʃəbl] *adj* appréciable

appreciably [ə'priːʃəblɪ] *adv* sensiblement, de façon appréciable

appreciate [ə'priːʃɪeɪt] *vt* (*like*) apprécier, faire cas de; (*be grateful for*) être reconnaissant(e) de; (*assess*) évaluer; (*be aware of*) comprendre, se rendre compte de ▷ *vi* (*Finance*) prendre de la valeur; **I** ~ **your help** je vous remercie pour votre aide

appreciation [əpriːʃɪ'eɪʃən] *n* appréciation *f*; (*gratitude*) reconnaissance *f*; (*Finance*) hausse *f*, valorisation *f*

appreciative [ə'priːʃɪətɪv] *adj* (*person*) sensible; (*comment*) élogieux(-euse)

apprehend [æprɪ'hɛnd] *vt* appréhender, arrêter; (*understand*) comprendre

apprehension [æprɪ'hɛnʃən] *n* appréhension *f*, inquiétude *f*

apprehensive [æprɪ'hɛnsɪv] *adj* inquiet(-ète), appréhensif(-ive)

apprentice [ə'prɛntɪs] *n* apprenti *m* ▷ *vt*: **to be** ~**d to** être en apprentissage chez

apprenticeship [ə'prɛntɪsʃɪp] *n* apprentissage

m; **to serve one's** ~ faire son apprentissage

appro. ['æprəu] *abbr* (*Brit Comm: inf*) = **approval**

approach [ə'prəutʃ] *vi* approcher ▷ *vt* (*come near*) approcher de; (*ask, apply to*) s'adresser à; (*subject, passer-by*) aborder ▷ *n* approche *f*; accès *m*, abord *m*; démarche *f* (*auprès de qn*); démarche *f* (*intellectuelle*); **to** ~ **sb about sth** aller *or* venir voir qn pour qch

approachable [ə'prəutʃəbl] *adj* accessible

approach road *n* voie *f* d'accès

approbation [æprə'beɪʃən] *n* approbation *f*

appropriate *adj* [ə'prəuprɪɪt] (*tool etc*) qui convient, approprié(e); (*moment, remark*) opportun(e) ▷ *vt* [ə'prəuprɪeɪt] (*take*) s'approprier; (*allot*): **to** ~ **sth for** affecter qch à; ~ **for** *or* **to** approprié à; **it would not be** ~ **for me to comment** il ne me serait pas approprié de commenter

appropriately [ə'prəuprɪɪtlɪ] *adv* pertinemment, avec à-propos

appropriation [əprəuprɪ'eɪʃən] *n* dotation *f*, affectation *f*

approval [ə'pruːvəl] *n* approbation *f*; **to meet with sb's** ~ (*proposal etc*) recueillir l'assentiment de qn; **on** ~ (*Comm*) à l'examen

approve [ə'pruːv] *vt* approuver
▷ **approve of** *vt fus* (*thing*) approuver; (*person*): **they don't** ~ **of her** ils n'ont pas bonne opinion d'elle

approved school [ə'pruːvd-] *n* (*Brit*) centre *m* d'éducation surveillée

approvingly [ə'pruːvɪŋlɪ] *adv* d'un air approbateur

approx. *abbr* (= *approximately*) env

approximate [ə'prɔksɪmɪt] *adj* approximatif(-ive) ▷ *vt* [ə'prɔksɪmeɪt] se rapprocher de; être proche de

approximately [ə'prɔksɪmətlɪ] *adv* approximativement

approximation [ə'prɔksɪ'meɪʃən] *n* approximation *f*

Apr. *abbr* = **April**

apr *n abbr* (= *annual percentage rate*) taux (d'intérêt) annuel

apricot ['eɪprɪkɔt] *n* abricot *m*

April ['eɪprəl] *n* avril *m*; ~ **fool!** poisson d'avril!; *for phrases see also* **July**

April Fools' Day *n* le premier avril; *voir article*

● **APRIL FOOLS' DAY**
●
● *April Fools' Day* est le 1er avril, à l'occasion
● duquel on fait des farces de toutes sortes. Les
● victimes de ces farces sont les "April fools".
● Traditionnellement, on n'est censé faire des
● farces que jusqu'à midi.

apron ['eɪprən] *n* tablier *m*; (*Aviat*) aire *f* de stationnement

apse [æps] *n* (*Archit*) abside *f*

APT *n abbr* (*Brit*: = *advanced passenger train*) ≈ TGV *m*

Apt. *abbr* (= *apartment*) appt

apt [æpt] *adj* (*suitable*) approprié(e); (*able*): ~ **(at)** doué(e) (pour); apte (à); (*likely*): ~ **to do** susceptible de faire; ayant tendance à faire

aptitude ['æptɪtjuːd] *n* aptitude *f*

aptitude test *n* test *m* d'aptitude

aptly ['æptlɪ] *adv* (*fort*) à propos

aqualung ['ækwəlʌŋ] *n* scaphandre *m* autonome

aquarium [ə'kwɛərɪəm] *n* aquarium *m*

Aquarius [ə'kwɛərɪəs] *n* le Verseau; **to be ~** être du Verseau

aquatic [ə'kwætɪk] *adj* aquatique; (*sport*) nautique

aqueduct ['ækwɪdʌkt] *n* aqueduc *m*

AR *abbr* (*US*) = **Arkansas**

ARA *n abbr* (*Brit*) = **Associate of the Royal Academy**

Arab ['ærəb] *n* Arabe *m/f* ▷ *adj* arabe

Arabia [ə'reɪbɪə] *n* Arabie *f*

Arabian [ə'reɪbɪən] *adj* arabe

Arabian Desert *n* désert *m* d'Arabie

Arabian Sea *n* mer *f* d'Arabie

Arabic ['ærəbɪk] *adj, n* arabe (*m*)

Arabic numerals *npl* chiffres *mpl* arabes

arable ['ærəbl] *adj* arable

ARAM *n abbr* (*Brit*) = **Associate of the Royal Academy of Music**

arbiter ['ɑːbɪtəʳ] *n* arbitre *m*

arbitrary ['ɑːbɪtrərɪ] *adj* arbitraire

arbitrate ['ɑːbɪtreɪt] *vi* arbitrer; trancher

arbitration [ɑːbɪ'treɪʃən] *n* arbitrage *m*; **the dispute went to ~** le litige a été soumis à arbitrage

arbitrator ['ɑːbɪtreɪtəʳ] *n* arbitre *m*, médiateur(-trice)

ARC *n abbr* = **American Red Cross**

arc [ɑːk] *n* arc *m*

arcade [ɑː'keɪd] *n* arcade *f*; (*passage with shops*) passage *m*, galerie *f*; (*with games*) salle *f* de jeu

arch [ɑːtʃ] *n* arche *f*; (*of foot*) cambrure *f*, voûte *f* plantaire ▷ *vt* arquer, cambrer ▷ *adj* malicieux(-euse) ▷ *prefix*: ~(-) achevé(e); par excellence; **pointed ~** ogive *f*

archaeological [ɑːkɪə'lɔdʒɪkl] *adj* archéologique

archaeologist [ɑːkɪ'ɔlədʒɪst] *n* archéologue *m/f*

archaeology, (*US*) **archeology** [ɑːkɪ'ɔlədʒɪ] *n* archéologie *f*

archaic [ɑː'keɪɪk] *adj* archaïque

archangel ['ɑːkeɪndʒəl] *n* archange *m*

archbishop [ɑːtʃ'bɪʃəp] *n* archevêque *m*

archenemy ['ɑːtʃ'ɛnɪmɪ] *n* ennemi *m* de toujours *or* par excellence

archeology [ɑːkɪ'ɔlədʒɪ] (*US*) = **archaeology**

archer ['ɑːtʃəʳ] *n* archer *m*

archery ['ɑːtʃərɪ] *n* tir *m* à l'arc

archetypal ['ɑːkɪtaɪpəl] *adj* archétype

archetype ['ɑːkɪtaɪp] *n* prototype *m*, archétype *m*

archipelago [ɑːkɪ'pɛlɪgəu] *n* archipel *m*

architect ['ɑːkɪtɛkt] *n* architecte *m*

architectural [ɑːkɪ'tɛktʃərəl] *adj*

architectural(e)

architecture ['ɑːkɪtɛktʃəʳ] *n* architecture *f*

archive ['ɑːkaɪv] *n* (*often pl*) archives *fpl*

archive file *n* (*Comput*) fichier *m* d'archives

archives ['ɑːkaɪvz] *npl* archives *fpl*

archivist ['ɑːkɪvɪst] *n* archiviste *m/f*

archway ['ɑːtʃweɪ] *n* voûte *f*, porche voûté *or* cintré

ARCM *n abbr* (*Brit*) = **Associate of the Royal College of Music**

Arctic ['ɑːktɪk] *adj* arctique ▷ *n*: **the ~** l'Arctique *m*

Arctic Circle *n* cercle *m* Arctique

Arctic Ocean *n* océan *m* Arctique

ARD *n abbr* (*US Med*) = **acute respiratory disease**

ardent ['ɑːdənt] *adj* fervent(e)

ardour, (*US*) **ardor** ['ɑːdəʳ] *n* ardeur *f*

arduous ['ɑːdjuəs] *adj* ardu(e)

are [ɑːʳ] *vb see* **be**

area ['ɛərɪə] *n* (*Geom*) superficie *f*; (*zone*) région *f*; (*: smaller*) secteur *m*; (*in room*) coin *m*; (*knowledge, research*) domaine *m*; **the London ~** la région Londonienne

area code (*US*) *n* (*Tel*) indicatif *m* de zone

arena [ə'riːnə] *n* arène *f*

aren't [ɑːnt] = **are not**

Argentina [ɑːdʒən'tiːnə] *n* Argentine *f*

Argentinian [ɑːdʒən'tɪnɪən] *adj* argentin(e) ▷ *n* Argentin(e)

arguable ['ɑːgjuəbl] *adj* discutable, contestable; **it is ~ whether** on peut se demander si

arguably ['ɑːgjuəblɪ] *adv*: **it is ~ ...** on peut soutenir que c'est ...

argue ['ɑːgjuː] *vi* (*quarrel*) se disputer; (*reason*) argumenter ▷ *vt* (*debate: case, matter*) débattre; **to ~ about sth (with sb)** se disputer (avec qn) au sujet de qch; **to ~ that** objecter *or* alléguer que, donner comme argument que

argument ['ɑːgjumənt] *n* (*quarrel*) dispute *f*, discussion *f*; (*reasons*) argument *m*; (*debate*) discussion, controverse *f*; **~ for/against** argument pour/contre

argumentative [ɑːgju'mɛntətɪv] *adj* ergoteur(-euse), raisonneur(-euse)

aria ['ɑːrɪə] *n* aria *f*

ARIBA [ə'riːbə] *n abbr* (*Brit*) = **Associate of the Royal Institute of British Architects**

arid ['ærɪd] *adj* aride

aridity [ə'rɪdɪtɪ] *n* aridité *f*

Aries ['ɛərɪz] *n* le Bélier; **to be ~** être du Bélier

arise (*pt* **arose**, *pp* **-n**) [ə'raɪz, ə'rəuz, ə'rɪzn] *vi* survenir, se présenter; **to ~ from** résulter de; **should the need ~** en cas de besoin

aristocracy [ærɪs'tɔkrəsɪ] *n* aristocratie *f*

aristocrat ['ærɪstəkræt] *n* aristocrate *m/f*

aristocratic [ærɪstə'krætɪk] *adj* aristocratique

arithmetic [ə'rɪθmətɪk] *n* arithmétique *f*

arithmetical [ærɪθ'mɛtɪkl] *adj* arithmétique

Ariz. *abbr* (*US*) = **Arizona**

ark [ɑːk] *n*: **Noah's A~** l'Arche *f* de Noé

Ark. *abbr* (*US*) = **Arkansas**

arm [ɑːm] n bras m ▷ vt armer; **arms** npl
(weapons, Heraldry) armes fpl; ~ **in** ~ bras dessus
bras dessous

armaments ['ɑːməmənts] npl (weapons)
armement m

armband ['ɑːmbænd] n brassard m

armchair ['ɑːmtʃɛəʳ] n fauteuil m

armed [ɑːmd] adj armé(e)

armed forces npl: **the** ~ les forces armées

armed robbery n vol m à main armée

Armenia [ɑːˈmiːnɪə] n Arménie f

Armenian [ɑːˈmiːnɪən] adj arménien(ne) ▷ n
Arménien(ne); (Ling) arménien m

armful ['ɑːmful] n brassée f

armistice ['ɑːmɪstɪs] n armistice m

armour, (US) **armor** ['ɑːməʳ] n armure f; (also:
armour-plating) blindage m; (Mil: tanks)
blindés mpl

armoured car, (US) **armored car** ['ɑːməd-] n
véhicule blindé

armoury, (US) **armory** ['ɑːmərɪ] n arsenal m

armpit ['ɑːmpɪt] n aisselle f

armrest ['ɑːmrɛst] n accoudoir m

arms control n contrôle m des armements

arms race n course f aux armements

army ['ɑːmɪ] n armée f

A road n (Brit) ≈ route nationale

aroma [əˈrəumə] n arôme m

aromatherapy [ərəumə'θɛrəpɪ] n
aromathérapie f

aromatic [ærə'mætɪk] adj aromatique

arose [ə'rəuz] pt of **arise**

around [ə'raund] adv (tout) autour; (nearby)
dans les parages ▷ prep autour de; (near) près de;
(fig: about) environ; (: date, time) vers; **is he ~?** est-
il dans les parages or là?

arousal [ə'rauzəl] n (sexual) excitation sexuelle,
éveil m

arouse [ə'rauz] vt (sleeper) éveiller; (curiosity,
passions) éveiller, susciter; (anger) exciter

arrange [ə'reɪndʒ] vt arranger; (programme)
arrêter, convenir de ▷ vi: **we have ~d for a car
to pick you up** nous avons prévu qu'une
voiture vienne vous prendre; **it was ~d that ...**
il a été convenu que ..., il a été décidé que ...; **to
~ to do sth** prévoir de faire qch

arrangement [ə'reɪndʒmənt] n arrangement
m; **to come to an ~ (with sb)** se mettre d'accord
(avec qn); **home deliveries by ~** livraison à
domicile sur demande; **arrangements** npl
(plans etc) arrangements mpl, dispositions fpl;
I'll make ~s for you to be met je vous enverrai
chercher

arrant ['ærənt] adj: **he's talking ~ nonsense** il
raconte vraiment n'importe quoi

array [ə'reɪ] n (of objects) déploiement m, étalage
m; (Math, Comput) tableau m

arrears [ə'rɪəz] npl arriéré m; **to be in ~ with
one's rent** devoir un arriéré de loyer, être en
retard pour le paiement de son loyer

arrest [ə'rɛst] vt arrêter; (sb's attention) retenir,
attirer ▷ n arrestation f; **under ~** en état

d'arrestation

arresting [ə'rɛstɪŋ] adj (fig: beauty) saisissant(e);
(: charm, candour) désarmant(e)

arrival [ə'raɪvl] n arrivée f; (Comm) arrivage m;
(person) arrivant(e); **new ~** nouveau venu/
nouvelle venue; (baby) nouveau-né(e)

arrive [ə'raɪv] vi arriver

▷ **arrive at** vt fus (decision, solution) parvenir à

arrogance ['ærəgəns] n arrogance f

arrogant ['ærəgənt] adj arrogant(e)

arrow ['ærəu] n flèche f

arse [ɑːs] n (Brit inf!) cul m (!)

arsenal ['ɑːsɪnl] n arsenal m

arsenic ['ɑːsnɪk] n arsenic m

arson ['ɑːsn] n incendie criminel

art [ɑːt] n art m; (craft) métier m; **work of ~**
œuvre f d'art; **Arts** npl (Scol) les lettres fpl

art college n école f des beaux-arts

artefact ['ɑːtɪfækt] n objet fabriqué

arterial [ɑː'tɪərɪəl] adj (Anat) artériel(le); (road
etc) à grande circulation

artery ['ɑːtərɪ] n artère f

artful ['ɑːtful] adj rusé(e)

art gallery n musée m d'art; (saleroom) galerie f
de peinture

arthritis [ɑː'θraɪtɪs] n arthrite f

artichoke ['ɑːtɪtʃəuk] n artichaut m; **Jerusalem
~** topinambour m

article ['ɑːtɪkl] n article m; (Brit Law: training):
articles npl ≈ stage m; **~s of clothing**
vêtements mpl

articles of association npl (Comm) statuts mpl
d'une société

articulate [adj ɑː'tɪkjulɪt, vb ɑː'tɪkjuleɪt] adj
(person) qui s'exprime clairement et aisément;
(speech) bien articulé(e), prononcé(e) clairement
▷ vi articuler, parler distinctement ▷ vt
articuler

articulated lorry [ɑː'tɪkjuleɪtɪd-] n (Brit)
(camion m) semi-remorque m

artifact ['ɑːtɪfækt] n (US) objet fabriqué

artifice ['ɑːtɪfɪs] n ruse f

artificial [ɑːtɪ'fɪʃəl] adj artificiel(le)

artificial insemination [-ɪnsɛmɪ'neɪʃən] n
insémination artificielle

artificial intelligence n intelligence
artificielle

artificial respiration n respiration artificielle

artillery [ɑː'tɪlərɪ] n artillerie f

artisan ['ɑːtɪzæn] n artisan(e)

artist ['ɑːtɪst] n artiste m/f

artistic [ɑː'tɪstɪk] adj artistique

artistry ['ɑːtɪstrɪ] n art m, talent m

artless ['ɑːtlɪs] adj naïf (naïve), simple,
ingénu(e)

arts [ɑːts] npl (Scol) lettres fpl

art school n ≈ école f des beaux-arts

artwork ['ɑːtwəːk] n maquette f (prête pour la
photogravure)

ARV n abbr (= American Revised Version) traduction
américaine de la Bible

AS n abbr (US Scol: = Associate in/of Science) diplôme

universitaire ▷ *abbr* (US) = **American Samoa**

○ KEYWORD

as [æz] *conj* **1** (*time: moment*) comme, alors que; à mesure que; (*: duration*) tandis que; **he came in as I was leaving** il est arrivé comme je partais; **as the years went by** à mesure que les années passaient; **as from tomorrow** à partir de demain
2 (*since, because*) comme, puisque; **he left early as he had to be home by 10** comme il *or* puisqu'il devait être de retour avant 10h, il est parti de bonne heure
3 (*referring to manner, way*) comme; **do as you wish** faites comme vous voudrez; **as she said** comme elle disait
▷ *adv* **1** (*in comparisons*): **as big as** aussi grand que; **twice as big as** deux fois plus grand que; **big as it is** si grand que ce soit; **much as I like them, I ...** je les aime bien, mais je ...; **as much** *or* **many as** autant que; **as much money/many books as** autant d'argent/de livres que; **as soon as** dès que
2 (*concerning*): **as for** *or* **to that** quant à cela, pour ce qui est de cela
3: **as if** *or* **though** comme si; **he looked as if he was ill** il avait l'air d'être malade; *see also* **long**; **such**; **well**
▷ *prep* (*in the capacity of*) en tant que, en qualité de; **he works as a driver** il travaille comme chauffeur; **as chairman of the company, he ...** en tant que président de la société, il ...; **dressed up as a cowboy** déguisé en cowboy; **he gave me it as a present** il me l'a offert, il m'en a fait cadeau

ASA *n abbr* (= *American Standards Association*) *association de normalisation*

a.s.a.p. *abbr* = **as soon as possible**

asbestos [æz'bɛstəs] *n* asbeste *m*, amiante *m*

ascend [ə'sɛnd] *vt* gravir

ascendancy [ə'sɛndənsɪ] *n* ascendant *m*

ascendant [ə'sɛndənt] *n*: **to be in the ~** monter

ascension [ə'sɛnʃən] *n*: **the A~** (*Rel*) l'Ascension *f*

Ascension Island *n* île *f* de l'Ascension

ascent [ə'sɛnt] *n* (*climb*) ascension *f*

ascertain [æsə'teɪn] *vt* s'assurer de, vérifier; établir

ascetic [ə'sɛtɪk] *adj* ascétique

asceticism [ə'sɛtɪsɪzəm] *n* ascétisme *m*

ASCII ['æski:] *n abbr* (= *American Standard Code for Information Interchange*) ASCII

ascribe [ə'skraɪb] *vt*: **to ~ sth to** attribuer qch à; (*blame*) imputer qch à

ASCU *n abbr* (US) = **Association of State Colleges and Universities**

ASE *n abbr* = **American Stock Exchange**

ASH [æʃ] *n abbr* (Brit: = *Action on Smoking and Health*) *ligue anti-tabac*

ash [æʃ] *n* (*dust*) cendre *f*; (*also*: **ash tree**) frêne *m*

ashamed [ə'ʃeɪmd] *adj* honteux(-euse), confus(e); **to be ~ of** avoir honte de; **to be ~ (of o.s.) for having done** avoir honte d'avoir fait

ashen ['æʃən] *adj* (*pale*) cendreux(-euse), blême

ashore [ə'ʃɔːʳ] *adv* à terre; **to go ~** aller à terre, débarquer

ashtray ['æʃtreɪ] *n* cendrier *m*

Ash Wednesday *n* mercredi *m* des Cendres

Asia ['eɪʃə] *n* Asie *f*

Asia Minor *n* Asie Mineure

Asian ['eɪʃən] *n* (*from Asia*) Asiatique *m/f*; (Brit: *from Indian subcontinent*) Indo-Pakistanais(-e) ▷ *adj* asiatique; indo-pakistanais(-e)

Asiatic [eɪsɪ'ætɪk] *adj* asiatique

aside [ə'saɪd] *adv* de côté; à l'écart ▷ *n* aparté *m*; **~ from** *prep* à part, excepté

ask [ɑːsk] *vt* demander; (*invite*) inviter; **to ~ sb sth/to do sth** demander à qn qch/de faire qch; **to ~ sb the time** demander l'heure à qn; **to ~ sb about sth** questionner qn au sujet de qch; se renseigner auprès de qn au sujet de qch; **to ~ about the price** s'informer du prix, se renseigner au sujet du prix; **to ~ (sb) a question** poser une question (à qn); **to ~ sb out to dinner** inviter qn au restaurant
▶ **ask after** *vt fus* demander des nouvelles de
▶ **ask for** *vt fus* demander; **it's just ~ing for trouble** *or* **for it** ce serait chercher des ennuis

askance [ə'skɑːns] *adv*: **to look ~ at sb** regarder qn de travers *or* d'un œil désapprobateur

askew [ə'skjuː] *adv* de travers, de guingois

asking price ['ɑːskɪŋ-] *n* prix demandé

asleep [ə'sliːp] *adj* endormi(e); **to be ~** dormir, être endormi; **to fall ~** s'endormir

ASLEF ['æzlɛf] *n abbr* (Brit: = *Associated Society of Locomotive Engineers and Firemen*) *syndicat de cheminots*

AS level *n abbr* (= *Advanced Subsidiary level*) *première partie de l'examen équivalent au baccalauréat*

asp [æsp] *n* aspic *m*

asparagus [əs'pærəgəs] *n* asperges *fpl*

asparagus tips *npl* pointes *fpl* d'asperges

ASPCA *n abbr* (= *American Society for the Prevention of Cruelty to Animals*) ≈ SPA *f*

aspect ['æspɛkt] *n* aspect *m*; (*direction in which a building etc faces*) orientation *f*, exposition *f*

aspersions [əs'pə:ʃənz] *npl*: **to cast ~ on** dénigrer

asphalt ['æsfælt] *n* asphalte *m*

asphyxiate [æs'fɪksɪeɪt] *vt* asphyxier

asphyxiation [æsfɪksɪ'eɪʃən] *n* asphyxie *f*

aspiration [æspə'reɪʃən] *n* aspiration *f*

aspire [əs'paɪəʳ] *vi*: **to ~ to** aspirer à

aspirin ['æsprɪn] *n* aspirine *f*

aspiring [əs'paɪərɪŋ] *adj* (*artist, writer*) en herbe; (*manager*) potentiel(le)

ass [æs] *n* âne *m*; (*inf*) imbécile *m/f*; (US inf!) cul *m* (!)

assail [ə'seɪl] *vt* assaillir

assailant [ə'seɪlənt] *n* agresseur *m*; assaillant *m*

assassin [ə'sæsɪn] *n* assassin *m*

assassinate [ə'sæsɪneɪt] *vt* assassiner

assassination [əsæsɪ'neɪʃən] n assassinat m

assault [ə'sɔ:lt] n (Mil) assaut m; (gen: attack) agression f; (Law): ~ **(and battery)** voies fpl de fait, coups mpl et blessures fpl ▷ vt attaquer; (sexually) violenter

assemble [ə'sɛmbl] vt assembler ▷ vi s'assembler, se rassembler

assembly [ə'sɛmblɪ] n (meeting) rassemblement m; (parliament) assemblée f; (construction) assemblage m

assembly language n (Comput) langage m d'assemblage

assembly line n chaîne f de montage

assent [ə'sɛnt] n assentiment m, consentement m ▷ vi: **to ~ (to sth)** donner son assentiment (à qch), consentir (à qch)

assert [ə'sə:t] vt affirmer, déclarer; établir; (authority) faire valoir; (innocence) protester de; **to ~ o.s.** s'imposer

assertion [ə'sə:ʃən] n assertion f, affirmation f

assertive [ə'sə:tɪv] adj assuré(e); péremptoire

assess [ə'sɛs] vt évaluer, estimer; (tax, damages) établir or fixer le montant de; (property etc: for tax) calculer la valeur imposable de; (person) juger la valeur de

assessment [ə'sɛsmənt] n évaluation f, estimation f; (of tax) fixation f; (of property) calcul m de la valeur imposable; (judgment): ~ **(of)** jugement m or opinion f (sur)

assessor [ə'sɛsəʳ] n expert m (en matière d'impôt et d'assurance)

asset ['æsɛt] n avantage m, atout m; (person) atout; **assets** npl (Comm) capital m; avoir(s) m(pl); actif m

asset-stripping ['æsɛt'strɪpɪŋ] n (Comm) récupération f (et démantèlement m) d'une entreprise en difficulté

assiduous [ə'sɪdjuəs] adj assidu(e)

assign [ə'saɪn] vt (date) fixer, arrêter; **to ~ sth to** (task) assigner qch à; (resources) affecter qch à; (cause, meaning) attribuer qch à

assignment [ə'saɪnmənt] n (task) mission f; (homework) devoir m

assimilate [ə'sɪmɪleɪt] vt assimiler

assimilation [əsɪmɪ'leɪʃən] n assimilation f

assist [ə'sɪst] vt aider, assister; (injured person etc) secourir

assistance [ə'sɪstəns] n aide f, assistance f; secours mpl

assistant [ə'sɪstənt] n assistant(e), adjoint(e); (Brit: also: **shop assistant**) vendeur(-euse)

assistant manager n sous-directeur m

assizes [ə'saɪzɪz] npl assises fpl

associate [adj, n ə'səʊʃɪɪt, vb ə'səʊʃɪeɪt] adj, n associé(e) ▷ vt associer ▷ vi: **to ~ with sb** fréquenter qn; ~ **director** directeur adjoint; ~**d company** société affiliée

association [əsəʊsɪ'eɪʃən] n association f; **in ~ with** en collaboration avec

association football n (Brit) football m

assorted [ə'sɔ:tɪd] adj assorti(e); **in ~ sizes** en plusieurs tailles

assortment [ə'sɔ:tmənt] n assortiment m; (of people) mélange m

Asst. abbr = **assistant**

assuage [ə'sweɪdʒ] vt (grief, pain) soulager; (thirst, appetite) assouvir

assume [ə'sju:m] vt supposer; (responsibilities etc) assumer; (attitude, name) prendre, adopter

assumed name [ə'sju:md-] n nom m d'emprunt

assumption [ə'sʌmpʃən] n supposition f, hypothèse f; (of power) assomption f, prise f; **on the ~ that** dans l'hypothèse où; (on condition that) à condition que

assurance [ə'ʃuərəns] n assurance f; **I can give you no ~s** je ne peux rien vous garantir

assure [ə'ʃuəʳ] vt assurer

assured [ə'ʃuəd] adj assuré(e)

AST abbr (US: = Atlantic Standard Time) heure d'hiver de New York

asterisk ['æstərɪsk] n astérisque m

astern [ə'stə:n] adv à l'arrière

asteroid ['æstərɔɪd] n astéroïde m

asthma ['æsmə] n asthme m

asthmatic [æs'mætɪk] adj, n asthmatique m/f

astigmatism [ə'stɪgmətɪzəm] n astigmatisme m

astir [ə'stə:ʳ] adv en émoi

astonish [ə'stɒnɪʃ] vt étonner, stupéfier

astonished [ə'stɒnɪʃd] adj étonné(e); **to be ~ at** être étonné(e) de

astonishing [ə'stɒnɪʃɪŋ] adj étonnant(e), stupéfiant(e); **I find it ~ that ...** je trouve incroyable que ... + sub

astonishingly [ə'stɒnɪʃɪŋlɪ] adv incroyablement

astonishment [ə'stɒnɪʃmənt] n (grand) étonnement, stupéfaction f

astound [ə'staund] vt stupéfier, sidérer

astray [ə'streɪ] adv: **to go ~** s'égarer; (fig) quitter le droit chemin; **to lead ~** (morally) détourner du droit chemin; **to go ~ in one's calculations** faire fausse route dans ses calculs

astride [ə'straɪd] adv à cheval ▷ prep à cheval sur

astringent [əs'trɪndʒənt] adj astringent(e) ▷ n astringent m

astrologer [əs'trɒlədʒəʳ] n astrologue m

astrology [əs'trɒlədʒɪ] n astrologie f

astronaut ['æstrənɔ:t] n astronaute m/f

astronomer [əs'trɒnəməʳ] n astronome m

astronomical [æstrə'nɒmɪkl] adj astronomique

astronomy [əs'trɒnəmɪ] n astronomie f

astrophysics ['æstrəʊ'fɪzɪks] n astrophysique f

astute [əs'tju:t] adj astucieux(-euse), malin(-igne)

asunder [ə'sʌndəʳ] adv: **to tear ~** déchirer

ASV n abbr (= American Standard Version) traduction de la Bible

asylum [ə'saɪləm] n asile m; **to seek political ~** demander l'asile politique

asylum seeker [-si:kəʳ] n demandeur(-euse) d'asile

asymmetric [eɪsɪ'mɛtrɪk], **asymmetrical**

[eɪsɪ'mɛtrɪkl] *adj* asymétrique

⭕ **KEYWORD**

at [æt] *prep* **1** (*referring to position, direction*) à; **at the top** au sommet; **at home/school** à la maison *or* chez soi/à l'école; **at the baker's** à la boulangerie, chez le boulanger; **to look at sth** regarder qch
2 (*referring to time*): **at 4 o'clock** à 4 heures; **at Christmas** à Noël; **at night** la nuit; **at times** par moments, parfois
3 (*referring to rates, speed etc*) à; **at £1 a kilo** une livre le kilo; **two at a time** deux à la fois; **at 50 km/h** à 50 km/h; **at full speed** à toute vitesse
4 (*referring to manner*): **at a stroke** d'un seul coup; **at peace** en paix
5 (*referring to activity*): **to be at work** (*in the office etc*) être au travail; (*working*) travailler; **to play at cowboys** jouer aux cowboys; **to be good at sth** être bon en qch
6 (*referring to cause*): **shocked/surprised/annoyed at sth** choqué par/étonné de/agacé par qch; **I went at his suggestion** j'y suis allé sur son conseil
7 (@ *symbol*) arobase *f*

ate [eɪt] *pt of* **eat**
atheism ['eɪθɪɪzəm] *n* athéisme *m*
atheist ['eɪθɪɪst] *n* athée *m/f*
Athenian [ə'θiːnɪən] *adj* athénien(ne) ▷ *n* Athénien(ne)
Athens ['æθɪnz] *n* Athènes
athlete ['æθliːt] *n* athlète *m/f*
athletic [æθ'lɛtɪk] *adj* athlétique
athletics [æθ'lɛtɪks] *n* athlétisme *m*
Atlantic [ət'læntɪk] *adj* atlantique ▷ *n*: **the ~ (Ocean)** l'(océan *m*) Atlantique *m*
atlas ['ætləs] *n* atlas *m*
Atlas Mountains *npl*: **the ~** les monts *mpl* de l'Atlas, l'Atlas *m*
A.T.M. *n abbr* (= *Automated Telling Machine*) guichet *m* automatique
atmosphere ['ætməsfɪər] *n* (*air*) atmosphère *f*; (*fig: of place etc*) atmosphère, ambiance *f*
atmospheric [ætməs'fɛrɪk] *adj* atmosphérique
atmospherics [ætməs'fɛrɪks] *n* (*Radio*) parasites *mpl*
atoll ['ætɔl] *n* atoll *m*
atom ['ætəm] *n* atome *m*
atom bomb *n* bombe *f* atomique
atomic [ə'tɔmɪk] *adj* atomique
atomic bomb *n* bombe *f* atomique
atomizer ['ætəmaɪzər] *n* atomiseur *m*
atone [ə'təun] *vi*: **to ~ for** expier, racheter
atonement [ə'təunmənt] *n* expiation *f*
ATP *n abbr* (= *Association of Tennis Professionals*) ATP *f* (= *Association des tennismen professionnels*)
atrocious [ə'trəuʃəs] *adj* (*very bad*) atroce, exécrable
atrocity [ə'trɔsɪtɪ] *n* atrocité *f*
atrophy ['ætrəfɪ] *n* atrophie *f* ▷ *vt* atrophier ▷ *vi*

s'atrophier

attach [ə'tætʃ] *vt* (*gen*) attacher; (*document, letter, to email*) joindre; (*employee, troops*) affecter; **to be ~ed to sb/sth** (*to like*) être attaché à qn/qch; **the ~ed letter** la lettre ci-jointe
attaché [ə'tæʃeɪ] *n* attaché *m*
attaché case *n* mallette *f*, attaché-case *m*
attachment [ə'tætʃmənt] *n* (*tool*) accessoire *m*; (*Comput*) fichier *m* joint; (*love*): **~ (to)** affection *f* (pour), attachement *m* (à)
attack [ə'tæk] *vt* attaquer; (*task etc*) s'attaquer à ▷ *n* attaque *f*; **heart ~** crise *f* cardiaque
attacker [ə'tækər] *n* attaquant *m*; agresseur *m*
attain [ə'teɪn] *vt* (*also*: **to attain to**) parvenir à, atteindre; (*knowledge*) acquérir
attainments [ə'teɪnmənts] *npl* connaissances *fpl*, résultats *mpl*
attempt [ə'tɛmpt] *n* tentative *f* ▷ *vt* essayer, tenter; **~ed theft** *etc* (*Law*) tentative de vol *etc*; **to make an ~ on sb's life** attenter à la vie de qn; **he made no ~ to help** il n'a rien fait pour m'aider *or* l'aider *etc*
attempted [ə'tɛmptɪd] *adj*: **~ murder/suicide** tentative *f* de meurtre/suicide
attend [ə'tɛnd] *vt* (*course*) suivre; (*meeting, talk*) assister à; (*school, church*) aller à, fréquenter; (*patient*) soigner, s'occuper de; **to ~ (up)on** servir; être au service de
▶ **attend to** *vt fus* (*needs, affairs etc*) s'occuper de; (*customer*) s'occuper de, servir
attendance [ə'tɛndəns] *n* (*being present*) présence *f*; (*people present*) assistance *f*
attendant [ə'tɛndənt] *n* employé(e); gardien(ne) ▷ *adj* concomitant(e), qui accompagne *or* s'ensuit
attention [ə'tɛnʃən] *n* attention *f*; **attentions** attentions *fpl*, prévenances *fpl* ▷ *excl* (*Mil*) garde-à-vous!; **at ~** (*Mil*) au garde-à-vous; **for the ~ of** (*Admin*) à l'attention de; **it has come to my ~ that ...** je constate que ...
attentive [ə'tɛntɪv] *adj* attentif(-ive); (*kind*) prévenant(e)
attentively [ə'tɛntɪvlɪ] *adv* attentivement, avec attention
attenuate [ə'tɛnjueɪt] *vt* atténuer ▷ *vi* s'atténuer
attest [ə'tɛst] *vi*: **to ~ to** témoigner de attester (de)
attic ['ætɪk] *n* grenier *m*, combles *mpl*
attire [ə'taɪər] *n* habit *m*, atours *mpl*
attitude ['ætɪtjuːd] *n* (*behaviour*) attitude *f*, manière *f*; (*posture*) pose *f*, attitude; (*view*): **~ (to)** attitude (envers)
attorney [ə'təːnɪ] *n* (*US: lawyer*) avocat *m*; (*having proxy*) mandataire *m*; **power of ~** procuration *f*
Attorney General *n* (*Brit*) ≈ procureur général; (*US*) ≈ garde *m* des Sceaux, ministre *m* de la Justice
attract [ə'trækt] *vt* attirer
attraction [ə'trækʃən] *n* (*gen pl: pleasant things*) attraction *f*, attrait *m*; (*Physics*) attraction; (*fig: towards sb, sth*) attirance *f*

attractive [ə'træktɪv] *adj* séduisant(e), attrayant(e)

attribute ['ætrɪbjuːt] *n* attribut *m* ▷ *vt* [ə'trɪbjuːt]: **to ~ sth to** attribuer qch à

attrition [ə'trɪʃən] *n*: **war of ~** guerre *f* d'usure

Atty. Gen. *abbr* = **Attorney General**

ATV *n abbr* (= *all terrain vehicle*) véhicule *m* tout-terrain

atypical [eɪ'tɪpɪkl] *adj* atypique

aubergine ['əʊbəʒiːn] *n* aubergine *f*

auburn ['ɔːbən] *adj* auburn *inv*, châtain roux *inv*

auction ['ɔːkʃən] *n* (*also*: **sale by auction**) vente *f* aux enchères *f* ▷ *vt* (*also*: **to sell by auction**) vendre aux enchères; (*also*: **to put up for auction**) mettre aux enchères

auctioneer [ɔːkʃə'nɪə*r*] *n* commissaire-priseur *m*

auction room *n* salle *f* des ventes

audacious [ɔː'deɪʃəs] *adj* impudent(e); audacieux(-euse), intrépide

audacity [ɔː'dæsɪtɪ] *n* impudence *f*; audace *f*

audible ['ɔːdɪbl] *adj* audible

audience ['ɔːdɪəns] *n* (*people*) assistance *f*, public *m*; (*on radio*) auditeurs *mpl*; (*at theatre*) spectateurs *mpl*; (*interview*) audience *f*

audiovisual [ɔːdɪəʊ'vɪzjuəl] *adj* audio-visuel(le); **~ aids** supports *or* moyens audiovisuels

audit ['ɔːdɪt] *n* vérification *f* des comptes, apurement *m* ▷ *vt* vérifier, apurer

audition [ɔː'dɪʃən] *n* audition *f* ▷ *vi* auditionner

auditor ['ɔːdɪtə*r*] *n* vérificateur *m* des comptes

auditorium [ɔːdɪ'tɔːrɪəm] *n* auditorium *m*, salle *f* de concert *or* de spectacle

Aug. *abbr* = **August**

augment [ɔːg'mɛnt] *vt, vi* augmenter

augur ['ɔːgə*r*] *vt* (*be a sign of*) présager, annoncer ▷ *vi*: **it ~s well** c'est bon signe *or* de bon augure, cela s'annonce bien

August ['ɔːgəst] *n* août *m*; *for phrases see also* **July**

august [ɔː'gʌst] *adj* majestueux(-euse), imposant(e)

aunt [ɑːnt] *n* tante *f*

auntie, aunty ['ɑːntɪ] *n diminutive of* **aunt**

au pair ['əʊ'pɛə*r*] *n* (*also*: **au pair girl**) jeune fille *f* au pair

aura ['ɔːrə] *n* atmosphère *f*; (*of person*) aura *f*

auspices ['ɔːspɪsɪz] *npl*: **under the ~ of** sous les auspices de

auspicious [ɔːs'pɪʃəs] *adj* de bon augure, propice

austere [ɔs'tɪə*r*] *adj* austère

austerity [ɔs'tɛrɪtɪ] *n* austérité *f*

Australasia [ɔːstrə'leɪzɪə] *n* Australasie *f*

Australia [ɔs'treɪlɪə] *n* Australie *f*

Australian [ɔs'treɪlɪən] *adj* australien(ne) ▷ *n* Australien(ne)

Austria ['ɔstrɪə] *n* Autriche *f*

Austrian ['ɔstrɪən] *adj* autrichien(ne) ▷ *n* Autrichien(ne)

AUT *n abbr* (Brit: = *Association of University Teachers*) syndicat universitaire

authentic [ɔː'θɛntɪk] *adj* authentique

authenticate [ɔː'θɛntɪkeɪt] *vt* établir l'authenticité de

authenticity [ɔːθɛn'tɪsɪtɪ] *n* authenticité *f*

author ['ɔːθə*r*] *n* auteur *m*

authoritarian [ɔːθɔrɪ'tɛərɪən] *adj* autoritaire

authoritative [ɔː'θɔrɪtətɪv] *adj* (*account*) digne de foi; (*study, treatise*) qui fait autorité; (*manner*) autoritaire

authority [ɔː'θɔrɪtɪ] *n* autorité *f*; (*permission*) autorisation (formelle); **the authorities** les autorités *fpl*, l'administration *f*; **to have ~ to do sth** être habilité à faire qch

authorization [ɔːθəraɪ'zeɪʃən] *n* autorisation *f*

authorize ['ɔːθəraɪz] *vt* autoriser

authorized capital ['ɔːθəraɪzd-] *n* (*Comm*) capital social

authorship ['ɔːθəʃɪp] *n* paternité *f* (*littéraire etc*)

autistic [ɔː'tɪstɪk] *adj* autistique

auto ['ɔːtəʊ] *n* (*US*) auto *f*, voiture *f*

autobiography [ɔːtəbaɪ'ɔgrəfɪ] *n* autobiographie *f*

autocratic [ɔːtə'krætɪk] *adj* autocratique

autograph ['ɔːtəgrɑːf] *n* autographe *m* ▷ *vt* signer, dédicacer

autoimmune [ɔːtəʊɪ'mjuːn] *adj* auto-immune

automat ['ɔːtəmæt] *n* (*vending machine*) distributeur *m* (automatique); (*US: place*) cafétéria *f* avec distributeurs automatiques

automated ['ɔːtəmeɪtɪd] *adj* automatisé(e)

automatic [ɔːtə'mætɪk] *adj* automatique ▷ *n* (*gun*) automatique *m*; (*washing machine*) lave-linge *m* automatique; (*car*) voiture *f* à transmission automatique

automatically [ɔːtə'mætɪklɪ] *adv* automatiquement

automatic data processing *n* traitement *m* automatique des données

automation [ɔːtə'meɪʃən] *n* automatisation *f*

automaton (*pl* **automata**) [ɔː'tɔmətən, -tə] *n* automate *m*

automobile ['ɔːtəməbiːl] *n* (*US*) automobile *f*

autonomous [ɔː'tɔnəməs] *adj* autonome

autonomy [ɔː'tɔnəmɪ] *n* autonomie *f*

autopsy ['ɔːtɔpsɪ] *n* autopsie *f*

autumn ['ɔːtəm] *n* automne *m*

auxiliary [ɔːg'zɪlɪərɪ] *adj, n* auxiliaire (*m/f*)

AV *n abbr* (= *Authorized Version*) traduction anglaise de la Bible ▷ *abbr* = **audiovisual**

Av. *abbr* (= *avenue*) Av

avail [ə'veɪl] *vt*: **to ~ o.s. of** user de; profiter de ▷ *n*: **to no ~** sans résultat, en vain, en pure perte

availability [əveɪlə'bɪlɪtɪ] *n* disponibilité *f*

available [ə'veɪləbl] *adj* disponible; **every ~ means** tous les moyens possibles *or* à sa (*or* notre *etc*) disposition; **is the manager ~?** est-ce que le directeur peut (me) recevoir?; (*on phone*) pourrais-je parler au directeur?; **to make sth ~ to sb** mettre qch à la disposition de qn

avalanche ['ævəlɑːnʃ] *n* avalanche *f*

avant-garde ['ævɑ̃'gɑːd] *adj* d'avant-garde

avaricious [ævə'rɪʃəs] *adj* âpre au gain

avdp. *abbr* = **avoirdupois**

Ave. *abbr* = **avenue**
avenge [ə'vɛndʒ] *vt* venger
avenue ['ævənjuː] *n* avenue *f*; (*fig*) moyen *m*
average ['ævərɪdʒ] *n* moyenne *f* ▷ *adj* moyen(ne) ▷ *vt* (*a certain figure*) atteindre *or* faire *etc* en moyenne; **on** ~ en moyenne; **above/below (the)** ~ au-dessus/en-dessous de la moyenne
  ▶ **average out** *vi*: **to** ~ **out at** représenter en moyenne, donner une moyenne de
averse [ə'vəːs] *adj*: **to be** ~ **to sth/doing** éprouver une forte répugnance envers qch/à faire; **I wouldn't be** ~ **to a drink** un petit verre ne serait pas de refus, je ne dirais pas non à un petit verre
aversion [ə'vəːʃən] *n* aversion *f*, répugnance *f*
avert [ə'vəːt] *vt* (*danger*) prévenir, écarter; (*one's eyes*) détourner
aviary ['eɪvɪərɪ] *n* volière *f*
aviation [eɪvɪ'eɪʃən] *n* aviation *f*
avid ['ævɪd] *adj* avide
avidly ['ævɪdlɪ] *adv* avidement, avec avidité
avocado [ævə'kɑːdəu] *n* (*Brit: also:* **avocado pear**) avocat *m*
avoid [ə'vɔɪd] *vt* éviter
avoidable [ə'vɔɪdəbl] *adj* évitable
avoidance [ə'vɔɪdəns] *n* le fait d'éviter
avowed [ə'vaud] *adj* déclaré(e)
AVP *n abbr* (*US*) = **assistant vice-president**
AWACS ['eɪwæks] *n abbr* (= *airborne warning and control system*) AWACS (*système aéroporté d'alerte et de contrôle*)
await [ə'weɪt] *vt* attendre; **~ing attention/delivery** (*Comm*) en souffrance; **long ~ed** tant attendu(e)
awake [ə'weɪk] (*pt* **awoke**) [ə'wəuk] (*pp* **awoken**) [ə'wəukən] *adj* éveillé(e); (*fig*) en éveil ▷ *vt* éveiller ▷ *vi* s'éveiller; ~ **to** conscient de; **to be** ~ être réveillé(e); **he was still** ~ il ne dormait pas encore
awakening [ə'weɪknɪŋ] *n* réveil *m*
award [ə'wɔːd] *n* (*for bravery*) récompense *f*; (*prize*) prix *m*; (*Law: damages*) dommages-intérêts *mpl* ▷ *vt* (*prize*) décerner; (*Law: damages*) accorder
aware [ə'wɛəʳ] *adj*: ~ **of** (*conscious*) conscient(e) de; (*informed*) au courant de; **to become** ~ **of/that** prendre conscience de/que; se rendre compte de/que; **politically/socially** ~ sensibilisé(e) aux *or* ayant pris conscience des problèmes politiques/sociaux; **I am fully** ~ **that** je me rends parfaitement compte que
awareness [ə'wɛənɪs] *n* conscience *f*, connaissance *f*; **to develop people's** ~ **(of)** sensibiliser le public (à)
awash [ə'wɔʃ] *adj* recouvert(e) (d'eau); ~ **with** inondé(e) de
away [ə'weɪ] *adv* (au) loin; (*movement*): **she went** ~ elle est partie ▷ *adj* (*not in, not here*) absent(e); **far** ~ (au) loin; **two kilometres** ~ à (une distance de) deux kilomètres, à deux kilomètres de distance; **two hours** ~ **by car** à deux heures de voiture *or* de route; **the holiday was two weeks** ~ il restait deux semaines jusqu'aux vacances; ~ **from** loin de; **he's** ~ **for a week** il est parti (pour) une semaine; **he's** ~ **in Milan** il est (parti) à Milan; **to take sth** ~ **from sb** prendre qch à qn; **to take sth** ~ **from sth** (*subtract*) ôter qch de qch; **to work/pedal** ~ travailler/pédaler à cœur joie; **to fade** ~ (*colour*) s'estomper; (*sound*) s'affaiblir
away game *n* (*Sport*) match *m* à l'extérieur
awe [ɔː] *n* respect mêlé de crainte, effroi mêlé d'admiration
awe-inspiring ['ɔːɪnspaɪərɪŋ], **awesome** ['ɔːsəm] *adj* impressionnant(e)
awesome ['ɔːsəm] (*US*) *adj* (*inf: excellent*) génial(e)
awestruck ['ɔːstrʌk] *adj* frappé(e) d'effroi
awful ['ɔːfəl] *adj* affreux(-euse); **an** ~ **lot of** énormément de
awfully ['ɔːfəlɪ] *adv* (*very*) terriblement, vraiment
awhile [ə'waɪl] *adv* un moment, quelque temps
awkward ['ɔːkwəd] *adj* (*clumsy*) gauche, maladroit(e); (*inconvenient*) peu pratique; (*embarrassing*) gênant; **I can't talk just now, it's a bit** ~ je ne peux pas parler tout de suite, c'est un peu difficile
awkwardness ['ɔːkwədnɪs] *n* (*embarrassment*) gêne *f*
awl [ɔːl] *n* alêne *f*
awning ['ɔːnɪŋ] *n* (*of tent*) auvent *m*; (*of shop*) store *m*; (*of hotel etc*) marquise *f* (de toile)
awoke [ə'wəuk] *pt of* **awake**
awoken [ə'wəukən] *pp of* **awake**
AWOL ['eɪwɔl] *abbr* (*Mil*) = **absent without leave**
awry [ə'raɪ] *adv, adj* de travers; **to go** ~ mal tourner
axe, (*US*) **ax** [æks] *n* hache *f* ▷ *vt* (*employee*) renvoyer; (*project etc*) abandonner; (*jobs*) supprimer; **to have an** ~ **to grind** (*fig*) prêcher pour son saint
axes ['æksiːz] *npl of* **axis**
axiom ['æksɪəm] *n* axiome *m*
axiomatic [æksɪəu'mætɪk] *adj* axiomatique
axis (*pl* **axes**) ['æksɪs, -siːz] *n* axe *m*
axle ['æksl] *n* (*also:* **axle-tree**) essieu *m*
ay, aye [aɪ] *excl* (*yes*) oui ▷ *n*: **the ay(e)s** les oui
AYH *n abbr* = **American Youth Hostels**
AZ *abbr* (*US*) = **Arizona**
azalea [ə'zeɪlɪə] *n* azalée *f*
Azerbaijan [æzəbaɪ'dʒɑːn] *n* Azerbaïdjan *m*
Azerbaijani, Azeri [æzəbaɪ'dʒɑːnɪ, ə'zɛərɪ] *adj* azerbaïdjanais(e) ▷ *n* Azerbaïdjanais(e)
Azores [ə'zɔːz] *npl*: **the** ~ les Açores *fpl*
AZT *n abbr* (= *azidothymidine*) AZT *f*
Aztec ['æztɛk] *adj* aztèque ▷ *n* Aztèque *m/f*
azure ['eɪʒəʳ] *adj* azuré(e)

Bb

B, b [bi:] *n* (*letter*) B, b *m*; (*Scol: mark*) B; (*Mus*): **B si**
m; **B for Benjamin**, (US) **B for Baker** B comme
Berthe; **B road** *n* (*Brit Aut*) route
départementale

b. *abbr* = **born**

B.A. *abbr* = **British Academy**; (*Scol*) = **Bachelor of**
Arts

babble ['bæbl] *vi* babiller ▷ *n* babillage *m*

baboon [bə'bu:n] *n* babouin *m*

baby ['beɪbɪ] *n* bébé *m*

baby carriage *n* (US) voiture *f* d'enfant

baby food *n* aliments *mpl* pour bébé(s)

baby grand *n* (*also*: **baby grand piano**) (piano *m*)
demi-queue *m*

babyish ['beɪbɪɪʃ] *adj* enfantin(e), de bébé

baby-minder ['beɪbɪmaɪndə'] *n* (*Brit*)
gardienne *f* (d'enfants)

baby-sit ['beɪbɪsɪt] *vi* garder les enfants

baby-sitter ['beɪbɪsɪtə'] *n* baby-sitter *m/f*

baby wipe *n* lingette *f* (*pour bébé*)

bachelor ['bætʃələ'] *n* célibataire *m*; **B~ of Arts/**
Science (BA/BSc) ≈ licencié(e) ès *or* en lettres/
sciences; **B~ of Arts/Science degree (BA/BSc)**
n ≈ licence *f* ès *or* en lettres/sciences; *voir article*

● BACHELOR'S DEGREE

Un *Bachelor's degree* est un diplôme accordé
après trois ou quatre années d'université.
Les *Bachelor's degrees* les plus courants sont le
"BA" (Bachelor of Arts), le "BSc" (Bachelor of
Science), le "BEd" (Bachelor of Education) et
le "LLB" (Bachelor of Laws).

bachelor party *n* (US) enterrement *m* de vie de
garçon

back [bæk] *n* (*of person, horse*) dos *m*; (*of hand*) dos *m*,
revers *m*; (*of house*) derrière *m*; (*of car, train*)
arrière *m*; (*of chair*) dossier *m*; (*of page*) verso *m*;
(*of crowd*): **can the people at the ~ hear me**
properly? est-ce que les gens du fond peuvent
m'entendre?; (*Football*) arrière *m*; **to have one's**
~ to the wall (*fig*) être au pied du mur; **to break**
the ~ of a job (*Brit*) faire le gros d'un travail; **~**
to front à l'envers ▷ *vt* (*financially*) soutenir
(financièrement); (*candidate: also*: **back up**)

soutenir, appuyer; (*horse: at races*) parier *or* miser
sur; (*car*) (faire) reculer ▷ *vi* reculer; (*car etc*)
faire marche arrière ▷ *adj* (*in compounds*) de
derrière, à l'arrière; **~ seat/wheel** (*Aut*) siège *m*/
roue *f* arrière *inv*; **~ payments/rent** arriéré *m* de
paiements/loyer; **~ garden/room** jardin/pièce
sur l'arrière; **to take a ~ seat** (*fig*) se contenter
d'un second rôle, être relégué(e) au second plan
▷ *adv* (*not forward*) en arrière; (*returned*): **he's ~** il
est rentré, il est de retour; **when will you be ~?**
quand seras-tu de retour?; **he ran ~** il est
revenu en courant; (*restitution*): **throw the ball**
~ renvoie la balle; **can I have it ~?** puis-je le
ravoir?, peux-tu me le rendre?; (*again*): **he**
called ~ il a rappelé

▶ **back down** *vi* rabattre de ses prétentions

▶ **back on to** *vt fus*: **the house ~s on to the golf**
course la maison donne derrière sur le terrain
de golf

▶ **back out** *vi* (*of promise*) se dédire

▶ **back up** *vt* (*person*) soutenir; (*Comput*) faire
une copie de sauvegarde de

backache ['bækeɪk] *n* mal *m* au dos

backbencher [bæk'bentʃə'] (*Brit*) *n membre du*
parlement sans portefeuille

back benches *npl* (*Brit*) *voir article*

● BACK BENCHES

Le terme *back benches* désigne les bancs les
plus éloignés de l'allée centrale de la
Chambre des communes. Les députés qui
occupent ces bancs sont les "backbenchers"
et ils n'ont pas de portefeuille ministériel.

backbiting ['bækbaɪtɪŋ] *n* médisance(s) *f(pl)*

backbone ['bækbəʊn] *n* colonne vertébrale,
épine dorsale; **he's the ~ of the organization**
c'est sur lui que repose l'organisation

backchat ['bæktʃæt] *n* (*Brit inf*) impertinences *fpl*

backcloth ['bækklɔθ] *n* (*Brit*) toile *f* de fond

backcomb ['bækkəʊm] *vt* (*Brit*) crêper

backdate [bæk'deɪt] *vt* (*letter*) antidater; **~d pay**
rise augmentation *f* avec effet rétroactif

back door *n* porte *f* de derrière

backdrop ['bækdrɒp] *n* = **backcloth**

backer ['bækə'] n partisan m; (Comm) commanditaire m

backfire [bæk'faıə'] vi (Aut) pétarader; (plans) mal tourner

backgammon ['bækgæmən] n trictrac m

background ['bækgraund] n arrière-plan m; (of events) situation f, conjoncture f; (basic knowledge) éléments mpl de base; (experience) formation f ▷ cpd (noise, music) de fond; ~ **reading** lecture(s) générale(s) (sur un sujet); **family** ~ milieu familial

backhand ['bækhænd] n (Tennis: also: **backhand stroke**) revers m

backhanded ['bæk'hændɪd] adj (fig) déloyal(e); équivoque

backhander ['bæk'hændə'] n (Brit: bribe) pot-de-vin m

backing ['bækɪŋ] n (fig) soutien m, appui m; (Comm) soutien (financier); (Mus) accompagnement m

backlash ['bæklæʃ] n contre-coup m, répercussion f

backlog ['bæklɔg] n: ~ **of work** travail m en retard

back number n (of magazine etc) vieux numéro

backpack ['bækpæk] n sac m à dos

backpacker ['bækpækə'] n randonneur(-euse)

back pain n mal m de dos

back pay n rappel m de salaire

backpedal ['bækpɛdl] vi (fig) faire marche arrière

backseat driver ['bæksi:t-] n passager qui donne des conseils au conducteur

backside ['bæksaɪd] n (inf) derrière m, postérieur m

backslash ['bækslæʃ] n barre oblique inversée

backslide ['bækslaɪd] vi retomber dans l'erreur

backspace ['bækspeɪs] vi (in typing) appuyer sur la touche retour

backstage [bæk'steɪdʒ] adv dans les coulisses

back-street ['bækstri:t] adj (abortion) clandestin(e); ~ **abortionist** avorteur(-euse) (clandestin)

backstroke ['bækstrəuk] n dos crawlé

backtrack ['bæktræk] vi (fig) = **backpedal**

backup ['bækʌp] adj (train, plane) supplémentaire, de réserve; (Comput) de sauvegarde ▷ n (support) appui m, soutien m; (Comput: also: **backup file**) sauvegarde f

backward ['bækwəd] adj (movement) en arrière; (measure) rétrograde; (person, country) arriéré(e), attardé(e); (shy) hésitant(e); ~ **and forward movement** mouvement de va-et-vient

backwards ['bækwədz] adv (move, go) en arrière; (read a list) à l'envers, à rebours; (fall) à la renverse; (walk) à reculons; (in time) en arrière, vers le passé; **to know sth** ~ or (US) ~ **and forwards** (inf) connaître qch sur le bout des doigts

backwater ['bækwɔ:tə'] n (fig) coin reculé; bled perdu

backyard [bæk'jɑ:d] n arrière-cour f

bacon ['beɪkən] n bacon m, lard m

bacteria [bæk'tɪərɪə] npl bactéries fpl

bacteriology [bæktɪərɪ'ɔlədʒɪ] n bactériologie f

bad [bæd] adj mauvais(e); (child) vilain(e); (mistake, accident) grave; (meat, food) gâté(e), avarié(e); **his** ~ **leg** sa jambe malade; **to go** ~ (meat, food) se gâter; (milk) tourner; **to have a** ~ **time of it** traverser une mauvaise passe; **I feel** ~ **about it** (guilty) j'ai un peu mauvaise conscience; ~ **debt** créance douteuse; **in** ~ **faith** de mauvaise foi

baddie, baddy ['bædɪ] n (inf: Cine etc) méchant m

bade [bæd] pt of **bid**

badge [bædʒ] n insigne m; (of policeman) plaque f; (stick-on, sew-on) badge m

badger ['bædʒə'] n blaireau m ▷ vt harceler

badly ['bædlɪ] adv (work, dress etc) mal; **to reflect** ~ **on sb** donner une mauvaise image de qn; ~ **wounded** grièvement blessé; **he needs it** ~ il en a absolument besoin; **things are going** ~ les choses vont mal; ~ **off** (adj, adv) dans la gêne

bad-mannered ['bæd'mænəd] adj mal élevé(e)

badminton ['bædmɪntən] n badminton m

bad-mouth ['bæd'mauθ] vt (US inf) débiner

bad-tempered ['bæd'tɛmpəd] adj (by nature) ayant mauvais caractère; (on one occasion) de mauvaise humeur

baffle ['bæfl] vt (puzzle) déconcerter

baffling ['bæflɪŋ] adj déroutant(e), déconcertant(e)

bag [bæg] n sac m; (of hunter) gibecière f, chasse f ▷ vt (inf: take) empocher; s'approprier; (Tech) mettre en sacs; ~s **of** (inf: lots of) des tas de; **to pack one's** ~s faire ses valises or bagages; ~s **under the eyes** poches fpl sous les yeux

bagful ['bægful] n plein sac

baggage ['bægɪdʒ] n bagages mpl

baggage allowance n franchise f de bagages

baggage reclaim n (at airport) livraison f des bagages

baggy ['bægɪ] adj avachi(e), qui fait des poches

Baghdad [bæg'dæd] n Baghdâd, Bagdad

bag lady n (inf) clocharde f

bagpipes ['bægpaɪps] npl cornemuse f

bag-snatcher ['bægsnætʃə'] n (Brit) voleur m à l'arraché

bag-snatching ['bægsnætʃɪŋ] n (Brit) vol m à l'arraché

Bahamas [bə'hɑ:məz] npl: **the** ~ les Bahamas fpl

Bahrain [bɑ:'reɪn] n Bahreïn m

bail [beɪl] n caution f ▷ vt (prisoner: also: **grant bail to**) mettre en liberté sous caution; (boat: also: **bail out**) écoper; **to be released on** ~ être libéré(e) sous caution; see **bale**
▶ **bail out** vt (prisoner) payer la caution de

bailiff ['beɪlɪf] n huissier m

bait [beɪt] n appât m ▷ vt appâter; (fig: tease) tourmenter

bake [beɪk] vt (faire) cuire au four ▷ vi (bread etc) cuire (au four); (make cakes etc) faire de la pâtisserie

baked beans [beɪkt-] *npl* haricots blancs à la sauce tomate

baked potato *n* pomme *f* de terre en robe des champs

baker ['beɪkə^r] *n* boulanger *m*

bakery ['beɪkərɪ] *n* boulangerie *f*; boulangerie industrielle

baking ['beɪkɪŋ] *n* (*process*) cuisson *f*

baking powder *n* levure *f* (chimique)

baking tin *n* (*for cake*) moule *m* à gâteaux; (*for meat*) plat *m* pour le four

baking tray *n* plaque *f* à gâteaux

balaclava [bælə'klɑːvə] *n* (*also:* **balaclava helmet**) passe-montagne *m*

balance ['bæləns] *n* équilibre *m*; (*Comm: sum*) solde *m*; (*remainder*) reste *m*; (*scales*) balance *f* ▷ *vt* mettre *or* faire tenir en équilibre; (*pros and cons*) peser; (*budget*) équilibrer; (*account*) balancer; (*compensate*) compenser, contrebalancer; **~ of trade/payments** balance commerciale/des comptes *or* paiements; **~ carried forward** solde *m* à reporter; **~ brought forward** solde reporté; **to ~ the books** arrêter les comptes, dresser le bilan

balanced ['bælənst] *adj* (*personality, diet*) équilibré(e); (*report*) objectif(-ive)

balance sheet *n* bilan *m*

balcony ['bælkənɪ] *n* balcon *m*; **do you have a room with a ~?** avez-vous une chambre avec balcon?

bald [bɔːld] *adj* chauve; (*tyre*) lisse

baldness ['bɔːldnɪs] *n* calvitie *f*

bale [beɪl] *n* balle *f*, ballot *m*
▶ **bale out** *vi* (*of a plane*) sauter en parachute ▷ *vt* (*Naut: water, boat*) écoper

Balearic Islands [bælɪ'ærɪk-] *npl*: **the ~** les (îles *fpl*) Baléares *fpl*

baleful ['beɪlful] *adj* funeste, maléfique

balk [bɔːk] *vi*: **to ~ (at)** (*person*) regimber (contre); (*horse*) se dérober (devant)

Balkan ['bɔːlkən] *adj* balkanique ▷ *n*: **the ~s** les Balkans *mpl*

ball [bɔːl] *n* boule *f*; (*football*) ballon *m*; (*for tennis, golf*) balle *f*; (*dance*) bal *m*; **to play ~** jouer au ballon (*or* à la balle); (*fig*) coopérer; **to be on the ~** (*fig: competent*) être à la hauteur; (: *alert*) être éveillé(e), être vif (vive); **to start the ~ rolling** (*fig*) commencer; **the ~ is in their court** (*fig*) la balle est dans leur camp

ballad ['bæləd] *n* ballade *f*

ballast ['bæləst] *n* lest *m*

ball bearings *n* roulement *m* à billes

ball cock *n* robinet *m* à flotteur

ballerina [bælə'riːnə] *n* ballerine *f*

ballet ['bæleɪ] *n* ballet *m*; (*art*) danse *f* (classique)

ballet dancer *n* danseur(-euse) de ballet

ballet shoe *n* chausson *m* de danse

ballistic [bə'lɪstɪk] *adj* balistique

ballistics [bə'lɪstɪks] *n* balistique *f*

balloon [bə'luːn] *n* ballon *m*; (*in comic strip*) bulle *f* ▷ *vi* gonfler

balloonist [bə'luːnɪst] *n* aéronaute *m/f*

ballot ['bælət] *n* scrutin *m*

ballot box *n* urne (électorale)

ballot paper *n* bulletin *m* de vote

ballpark ['bɔːlpɑːk] *n* (US) stade *m* de base-ball

ballpark figure *n* (*inf*) chiffre approximatif

ballpoint ['bɔːlpɔɪnt], **ballpoint pen** *n* stylo *m* à bille

ballroom ['bɔːlrum] *n* salle *f* de bal

balls [bɔːlz] *npl* (*inf!*) couilles *fpl* (!)

balm [bɑːm] *n* baume *m*

balmy ['bɑːmɪ] *adj* (*breeze, air*) doux (douce); (*Brit inf*) = **barmy**

BALPA ['bælpə] *n abbr* (= *British Airline Pilots' Association*) syndicat des pilotes de ligne

balsa ['bɔːlsə], **balsa wood** *n* balsa *m*

balsam ['bɔːlsəm] *n* baume *m*

Baltic [bɔːltɪk] *adj, n*: **the ~ (Sea)** la (mer) Baltique

balustrade [bæləs'treɪd] *n* balustrade *f*

bamboo [bæm'buː] *n* bambou *m*

bamboozle [bæm'buːzl] *vt* (*inf*) embobiner

ban [bæn] *n* interdiction *f* ▷ *vt* interdire; **he was ~ned from driving** (*Brit*) on lui a retiré le permis (de conduire)

banal [bə'nɑːl] *adj* banal(e)

banana [bə'nɑːnə] *n* banane *f*

band [bænd] *n* bande *f*; (*at a dance*) orchestre *m*; (*Mil*) musique *f*, fanfare *f*
▶ **band together** *vi* se liguer

bandage ['bændɪdʒ] *n* bandage *m*, pansement *m* ▷ *vt* (*wound, leg*) mettre un pansement *or* un bandage sur; (*person*) mettre un pansement *or* un bandage à

Band-Aid® ['bændeɪd] *n* (US) pansement adhésif

B. & B. *n abbr* = **bed and breakfast**

bandit ['bændɪt] *n* bandit *m*

bandstand ['bændstænd] *n* kiosque *m* (à musique)

bandwagon ['bændwægən] *n*: **to jump on the ~** (*fig*) monter dans *or* prendre le train en marche

bandy ['bændɪ] *vt* (*jokes, insults*) échanger
▶ **bandy about** *vt* employer à tout bout de champ *or* à tort et à travers

bandy-legged ['bændɪ'lɛgɪd] *adj* aux jambes arquées

bane [beɪn] *n*: **it** (*or* **he** *etc*) **is the ~ of my life** c'est (*or* il est *etc*) le drame de ma vie

bang [bæŋ] *n* détonation *f*; (*of door*) claquement *m*; (*blow*) coup (violent) ▷ *vt* frapper (violemment); (*door*) claquer ▷ *vi* détoner; claquer ▷ *adv*: **to be ~ on time** (*Brit inf*) être à l'heure pile; **to ~ at the door** cogner à la porte; **to ~ into sth** se cogner contre qch

banger ['bæŋə^r] *n* (*Brit: car: also:* **old banger**) (vieux) tacot; (*Brit inf: sausage*) saucisse *f*; (*firework*) pétard *m*

Bangkok [bæŋ'kɔk] *n* Bangkok

Bangladesh [bæŋglə'dɛʃ] *n* Bangladesh *m*

Bangladeshi [bæŋglə'dɛʃɪ] *adj* du Bangladesh ▷ *n* habitant(e) du Bangladesh

bangle ['bæŋgl] n bracelet m

bangs [bæŋz] npl (US: fringe) frange f

banish ['bænɪʃ] vt bannir

banister ['bænɪstər] n, **banisters** ['bænɪstəz] npl rampe f (d'escalier)

banjo (pl -es or -s) ['bændʒəʊ] n banjo m

bank [bæŋk] n banque f; (of river, lake) bord m, rive f; (of earth) talus m, remblai m ▷ vi (Aviat) virer sur l'aile; (Comm): **they ~ with Pitt's** leur banque or banquier est Pitt's
  ▶ **bank on** vt fus miser or tabler sur

bank account n compte m en banque

bank balance n solde m bancaire

bank card (Brit) n carte f d'identité bancaire

bank charges npl (Brit) frais mpl de banque

bank draft n traite f bancaire

banker ['bæŋkər] n banquier m; **~'s card** (Brit) carte f d'identité bancaire; **~'s order** (Brit) ordre m de virement

bank giro n paiement m par virement

bank holiday n (Brit) jour férié (où les banques sont fermées); voir article

● **BANK HOLIDAY**
●
● Le terme bank holiday s'applique au
● Royaume-Uni aux jours fériés pendant
● lesquels banques et commerces sont fermés.
● Les principaux bank holidays à part Noël et
● Pâques se situent au mois de mai et fin août,
● et contrairement aux pays de tradition
● catholique, ne coïncident pas
● nécessairement avec une fête religieuse.

banking ['bæŋkɪŋ] n opérations fpl bancaires; profession f de banquier

banking hours npl heures fpl d'ouverture des banques

bank loan n prêt m bancaire

bank manager n directeur m d'agence (bancaire)

banknote ['bæŋknəʊt] n billet m de banque

bank rate n taux m de l'escompte

bankrupt ['bæŋkrʌpt] n failli(e) ▷ adj en faillite; **to go ~** faire faillite

bankruptcy ['bæŋkrʌptsɪ] n faillite f

bank statement n relevé m de compte

banner ['bænər] n bannière f

bannister ['bænɪstər] n, **bannisters** ['bænɪstəz] npl = **banister**; **banisters**

banns [bænz] npl bans mpl (de mariage)

banquet ['bæŋkwɪt] n banquet m, festin m

bantam-weight ['bæntəmweɪt] n poids m coq inv

banter ['bæntər] n badinage m

baptism ['bæptɪzəm] n baptême m

Baptist ['bæptɪst] n baptiste m/f

baptize [bæp'taɪz] vt baptiser

bar [ba:r] n (pub) bar m; (counter) comptoir m, bar; (rod: of metal etc) barre f; (of window etc) barreau m; (of chocolate) tablette f, plaque f; (fig: obstacle) obstacle m; (prohibition) mesure f d'exclusion; (Mus) mesure f ▷ vt (road) barrer; (window) munir de barreaux; (person) exclure; (activity) interdire; **~ of soap** savonnette f; **behind ~s** (prisoner) derrière les barreaux; **the B~** (Law) le barreau; **~ none** sans exception

Barbados [ba:'beɪdɔs] n Barbade f

barbaric [ba:'bærɪk] adj barbare

barbarous ['ba:bərəs] adj barbare, cruel(le)

barbecue ['ba:bɪkju:] n barbecue m

barbed wire ['ba:bd-] n fil m de fer barbelé

barber ['ba:bər] n coiffeur m (pour hommes)

barber's ['ba:bəʳz], **barber's shop**, (US) **barber shop** n salon m de coiffure (pour hommes); **to go to the barber's** aller chez le coiffeur

barbiturate [ba:'bɪtjʊrɪt] n barbiturique m

Barcelona [ba:sə'ləʊnə] n Barcelone

bar chart n diagramme m en bâtons

bar code n code m à barres, code-barre m

bare [bɛər] adj nu(e) ▷ vt mettre à nu, dénuder; (teeth) montrer; **the ~ essentials** le strict nécessaire

bareback ['bɛəbæk] adv à cru, sans selle

barefaced ['bɛəfeɪst] adj impudent(e), effronté(e)

barefoot ['bɛəfut] adj, adv nu-pieds, (les) pieds nus

bareheaded [bɛə'hɛdɪd] adj, adv nu-tête, (la) tête nue

barely ['bɛəlɪ] adv à peine

Barents Sea ['bærənts-] n: **the ~** la mer de Barents

bargain ['ba:gɪn] n (transaction) marché m; (good buy) affaire f, occasion f ▷ vi (haggle) marchander; (negotiate) négocier, traiter; **into the ~** par-dessus le marché
  ▶ **bargain for** vt fus (inf): **he got more than he ~ed for!** il en a eu pour son argent!

bargaining ['ba:gənɪŋ] n marchandage m; négociations fpl

bargaining position n: **to be in a weak/strong ~** être en mauvaise/bonne position pour négocier

barge [ba:dʒ] n péniche f
  ▶ **barge in** vi (walk in) faire irruption; (interrupt talk) intervenir mal à propos
  ▶ **barge into** vt fus rentrer dans

baritone ['bærɪtəʊn] n baryton m

barium meal ['bɛərɪəm-] n (bouillie f de) sulfate m de baryum

bark [ba:k] n (of tree) écorce f; (of dog) aboiement m ▷ vi aboyer

barley ['ba:lɪ] n orge f

barley sugar n sucre m d'orge

barmaid ['ba:meɪd] n serveuse f (de bar), barmaid f

barman ['ba:mən] (irreg) n serveur m (de bar), barman m

bar meal n repas m de bistrot; **to go for a ~** aller manger au bistrot

barmy ['ba:mɪ] adj (Brit inf) timbré(e), cinglé(e)

barn [ba:n] n grange f

barnacle ['ba:nəkl] n anatife m, bernache f

barn owl n chouette-effraie f, chat-huant m

barometer [bə'rɔmɪtə^r] *n* baromètre *m*
baron ['bærən] *n* baron *m*; **the press/oil ~s** les magnats *mpl or* barons *mpl* de la presse/du pétrole
baroness ['bærənɪs] *n* baronne *f*
barrack ['bærək] *vt* (*Brit*) chahuter
barracking ['bærəkɪŋ] *n* (*Brit*): **to give sb a ~** chahuter qn
barracks ['bærəks] *npl* caserne *f*
barrage ['bærɑːʒ] *n* (*Mil*) tir *m* de barrage; (*dam*) barrage *m*; (*of criticism*) feu *m*
barrel ['bærəl] *n* tonneau *m*; (*of gun*) canon *m*
barrel organ *n* orgue *m* de Barbarie
barren ['bærən] *adj* stérile; (*hills*) aride
barrette [bə'rɛt] (*US*) *n* barrette *f*
barricade [bærɪ'keɪd] *n* barricade *f* ▷ *vt* barricader
barrier ['bærɪə^r] *n* barrière *f*; (*Brit: also:* **crash barrier**) rail *m* de sécurité
barrier cream *n* (*Brit*) crème protectrice
barring ['bɑːrɪŋ] *prep* sauf
barrister ['bærɪstə^r] *n* (*Brit*) avocat (plaidant); *voir article*

● **BARRISTER**
●
● En Angleterre, un *barrister*, que l'on appelle
● également "barrister-at-law", est un avocat
● qui représente ses clients devant la cour et
● plaide pour eux. Le client doit d'abord passer
● par l'intermédiaire d'un "solicitor". On
● obtient le diplôme de *barrister* après avoir fait
● des études dans l'une des "Inns of Court", les
● quatre écoles de droit londoniennes.

barrow ['bærəu] *n* (*cart*) charrette *f* à bras
barstool ['bɑːstuːl] *n* tabouret *m* de bar
Bart. *abbr* (*Brit*) = **baronet**
bartender ['bɑːtɛndə^r] *n* (*US*) serveur *m* (*de bar*), barman *m*
barter ['bɑːtə^r] *n* échange *m*, troc *m* ▷ *vt*: **to ~ sth for** échanger qch contre
base [beɪs] *n* base *f* ▷ *vt* (*troops*): **to be ~d at** être basé(e) à; (*opinion, belief*): **to ~ sth on** baser *or* fonder qch sur ▷ *adj* vil(e), bas(se); **coffee-~d** à base de café; **a Paris-~d firm** une maison opérant de Paris *or* dont le siège est à Paris; **I'm ~d in London** je suis basé(e) à Londres
baseball ['beɪsbɔːl] *n* base-ball *m*
baseball cap *n* casquette *f* de base-ball
baseboard ['beɪsbɔːd] *n* (*US*) plinthe *f*
base camp *n* camp *m* de base
Basel [bɑːl] *n* = **Basle**
baseline ['beɪslaɪn] *n* (*Tennis*) ligne *f* de fond
basement ['beɪsmənt] *n* sous-sol *m*
base rate *n* taux *m* de base
bases ['beɪsiːz] *npl of* **basis** ['beɪsɪz] ▷ *npl of* **base**
bash [bæʃ] *vt* (*inf*) frapper, cogner ▷ *n*: **I'll have a ~ (at it)** (*Brit inf*) je vais essayer un coup; **~ed in** *adj* enfoncé(e), défoncé(e)
▶ **bash up** *vt* (*inf: car*) bousiller; (: *Brit: person*) tabasser

bashful ['bæʃful] *adj* timide; modeste
bashing ['bæʃɪŋ] *n* (*inf*) raclée *f*; **Paki-~** = ratonnade *f*; **queer-~** chasse *f* aux pédés
BASIC ['beɪsɪk] *n* (*Comput*) BASIC *m*
basic ['beɪsɪk] *adj* (*precautions, rules*) élémentaire; (*principles, research*) fondamental(e); (*vocabulary, salary*) de base; (*minimal*) réduit(e) au minimum, rudimentaire
basically ['beɪsɪklɪ] *adv* (*in fact*) en fait; (*essentially*) fondamentalement
basic rate *n* (*of tax*) première tranche d'imposition
basics ['beɪsɪks] *npl*: **the ~** l'essentiel *m*
basil ['bæzl] *n* basilic *m*
basin ['beɪsn] *n* (*vessel, also Geo*) cuvette *f*, bassin *m*; (*Brit: for food*) bol *m*; (: *bigger*) saladier *m*; (*also:* **washbasin**) lavabo *m*
basis (*pl* **bases**) ['beɪsɪs, -siːz] *n* base *f*; **on a part-time/trial ~** à temps partiel/à l'essai; **on the ~ of what you've said** d'après *or* compte tenu de ce que vous dites
bask [bɑːsk] *vi*: **to ~ in the sun** se chauffer au soleil
basket ['bɑːskɪt] *n* corbeille *f*; (*with handle*) panier *m*
basketball ['bɑːskɪtbɔːl] *n* basket-ball *m*
basketball player *n* basketteur(-euse)
Basle [bɑːl] *n* Bâle
basmati rice [bəz'mɑːtɪ-] *n* riz *m* basmati
Basque [bæsk] *adj* basque ▷ *n* Basque *m/f*; **the ~ Country** le Pays basque
bass [beɪs] *n* (*Mus*) basse *f*
bass clef *n* clé *f* de fa
bass drum *n* grosse caisse *f*
bassoon [bə'suːn] *n* basson *m*
bastard ['bɑːstəd] *n* enfant naturel(le), bâtard(e); (*inf!*) salaud *m* (!)
baste [beɪst] *vt* (*Culin*) arroser; (*Sewing*) bâtir, faufiler
bat [bæt] *n* chauve-souris *f*; (*for baseball etc*) batte *f*; (*Brit: for table tennis*) raquette *f* ▷ *vt*: **he didn't ~ an eyelid** il n'a pas sourcillé *or* bronché; **off one's own ~** de sa propre initiative
batch [bætʃ] *n* (*of bread*) fournée *f*; (*of papers*) liasse *f*; (*of applicants, letters*) paquet *m*; (*of work*) monceau *m*; (*of goods*) lot *m*
bated ['beɪtɪd] *adj*: **with ~ breath** en retenant son souffle
bath (*pl* **-s**) [bɑːθ, bɑːðz] *n* bain *m*; (*bathtub*) baignoire *f* ▷ *vt* baigner, donner un bain à; **to have a ~** prendre un bain; *see also* **baths**
bathe [beɪð] *vi* se baigner ▷ *vt* baigner; (*wound etc*) laver
bather ['beɪðə^r] *n* baigneur(-euse)
bathing ['beɪðɪŋ] *n* baignade *f*
bathing cap *n* bonnet *m* de bain
bathing costume, (*US*) **bathing suit** *n* maillot *m* (de bain)
bathmat ['bɑːθmæt] *n* tapis *m* de bain
bathrobe ['bɑːθrəub] *n* peignoir *m* de bain
bathroom ['bɑːθrum] *n* salle *f* de bains
baths [bɑːðz] *npl* (*Brit: also:* **swimming baths**)

piscine f

bath towel n serviette f de bain

bathtub ['bɑ:θtʌb] n baignoire f

batman ['bætmən] (irreg) n (Brit Mil) ordonnance f

baton ['bætən] n bâton m; (Mus) baguette f; (club) matraque f

battalion [bə'tælɪən] n bataillon m

batten ['bætn] n (Carpentry) latte f; (Naut: on sail) latte de voile

▶ **batten down** vt (Naut): **to ~ down the hatches** fermer les écoutilles

batter ['bætə^r] vt battre ▷ n pâte f à frire

battered ['bætəd] adj (hat, pan) cabossé(e); **~ wife/child** épouse/enfant maltraité(e) or martyr(e)

battering ram ['bætərɪŋ-] n bélier m; (fig)

battery ['bætərɪ] n (for torch, radio) pile f; (Aut, Mil) batterie f

battery charger n chargeur m

battery farming n élevage m en batterie

battle ['bætl] n bataille f, combat m ▷ vi se battre, lutter; **that's half the ~** (fig) c'est déjà bien; **it's a** or **we're fighting a losing ~** (fig) c'est perdu d'avance, c'est peine perdue

battle dress n tenue f de campagne or d'assaut

battlefield ['bætlfi:ld] n champ m de bataille

battlements ['bætlmənts] npl remparts mpl

battleship ['bætlʃɪp] n cuirassé m

batty ['bætɪ] adj (inf: person) toqué(e); (: idea, behaviour) loufoque

bauble ['bɔ:bl] n babiole f

baulk [bɔ:lk] vi = **balk**

bauxite ['bɔ:ksaɪt] n bauxite f

Bavaria [bə'vɛərɪə] n Bavière f

Bavarian [bə'vɛərɪən] adj bavarois(e) ▷ n Bavarois(e)

bawdy ['bɔ:dɪ] adj paillard(e)

bawl [bɔ:l] vi hurler, brailler

bay [beɪ] n (of sea) baie f; (Brit: for parking) place f de stationnement; (: for loading) aire f de chargement; (horse) bai(e) m/f; **B~ of Biscay** golfe m de Gascogne; **to hold sb at ~** tenir qn à distance or en échec

bay leaf n laurier m

bayonet ['beɪənɪt] n baïonnette f

bay tree n laurier m

bay window n baie vitrée

bazaar [bə'zɑ:^{r}] n (shop, market) bazar m; (sale) vente f de charité

bazooka [bə'zu:kə] n bazooka m

BB n abbr (Brit: = Boys' Brigade) mouvement de garçons

BBB n abbr (US: = Better Business Bureau) organisme de défense du consommateur

BBC n abbr (= British Broadcasting Corporation) office de la radiodiffusion et télévision britannique; voir article

● **BBC**
●
●
● La BBC est un organisme centralisé dont les
● membres, nommés par l'État, gèrent les
● chaînes de télévision publiques (BBC1, qui

● présente des émissions d'intérêt général, et
● BBC2, qui est plutôt orientée vers les
● émissions plus culturelles, et les chaînes
● numériques) et les stations de radio
● publiques. Bien que non contrôlée par l'État,
● la BBC est responsable devant le
● "Parliament" quant au contenu des
● émissions qu'elle diffuse. Par ailleurs, la
● BBC offre un service mondial de diffusion
● d'émissions, en anglais et dans 43 autres
● langues, appelé "BBC World Service". La BBC
● est financée par la redevance télévision et
● par l'exportation d'émissions.

B.C. adv abbr (= before Christ) av. J.-C. ▷ abbr (Canada) = **British Columbia**

BCG n abbr (= Bacillus Calmette-Guérin) BCG m

BD n abbr (= Bachelor of Divinity) diplôme universitaire

B/D abbr = **bank draft**

BDS n abbr (= Bachelor of Dental Surgery) diplôme universitaire

 KEYWORD

be [bi:] (pt **was**, **were**, pp **been**) aux vb **1** (with present participle: forming continuous tenses): **what are you doing?** que faites-vous?; **they're coming tomorrow** ils viennent demain; **I've been waiting for you for 2 hours** je t'attends depuis 2 heures

2 (with pp: forming passives) être; **to be killed** être tué(e); **the box had been opened** la boîte avait été ouverte; **he was nowhere to be seen** on ne le voyait nulle part

3 (in tag questions): **it was fun, wasn't it?** c'était drôle, n'est-ce pas?; **he's good-looking, isn't he?** il est beau, n'est-ce pas?; **she's back, is she?** elle est rentrée, n'est-ce pas or alors?

4 (+to +infinitive): **the house is to be sold** (necessity) la maison doit être vendue; (future) la maison va être vendue; **he's not to open it** il ne doit pas l'ouvrir; **am I to understand that ...?** dois-je comprendre que ...?; **he was to have come yesterday** il devait venir hier

5 (possibility, supposition): **if I were you, I ...** à votre place, je ..., si j'étais vous, je ...

▷ vb +complement **1** (gen) être; **I'm English** je suis anglais(e); **I'm tired** je suis fatigué(e); **I'm hot/cold** j'ai chaud/froid; **he's a doctor** il est médecin; **be careful/good/quiet!** faites attention/soyez sages/taisez-vous!; **2 and 2 are 4** 2 et 2 font 4

2 (of health) aller; **how are you?** comment allez-vous?; **I'm better now** je vais mieux maintenant; **he's fine now** il va bien maintenant; **he's very ill** il est très malade

3 (of age) avoir; **how old are you?** quel âge avez-vous?; **I'm sixteen (years old)** j'ai seize ans

4 (cost) coûter; **how much was the meal?** combien a coûté le repas?; **that'll be £5, please** ça fera 5 livres, s'il vous plaît; **this shirt is £17** cette chemise coûte 17 livres

▷ *vi* **1** (*exist, occur etc*) être, exister; **the prettiest girl that ever was** la fille la plus jolie qui ait jamais existé; **is there a God?** y a-t-il un dieu?; **be that as it may** quoi qu'il en soit; **so be it** soit

2 (*referring to place*) être, se trouver; **I won't be here tomorrow** je ne serai pas là demain; **Edinburgh is in Scotland** Édimbourg est *or* se trouve en Écosse

3 (*referring to movement*) aller; **where have you been?** où êtes-vous allé(s)?

▷ *impers vb* **1** (*referring to time*) être; **it's 5 o'clock** il est 5 heures; **it's the 28th of April** c'est le 28 avril

2 (*referring to distance*): **it's 10 km to the village** le village est à 10 km

3 (*referring to the weather*) faire; **it's too hot/cold** il fait trop chaud/froid; **it's windy today** il y a du vent aujourd'hui

4 (*emphatic*): **it's me/the postman** c'est moi/le facteur; **it was Maria who paid the bill** c'est Maria qui a payé la note

B/E *abbr* = **bill of exchange**
beach [biːtʃ] *n* plage *f* ▷ *vt* échouer
beachcomber ['biːtʃkəumə'] *n* ramasseur *m* d'épaves; (*fig*) bon(-ne) *m/f* à rien
beachwear ['biːtʃwɛə'] *n* tenues *fpl* de plage
beacon ['biːkən] *n* (*lighthouse*) fanal *m*; (*marker*) balise *f*; (*also:* **radio beacon**) radiophare *m*
bead [biːd] *n* perle *f*; (*of dew, sweat*) goutte *f*; **beads** *npl* (*necklace*) collier *m*
beady ['biːdɪ] *adj*: ~ **eyes** yeux *mpl* de fouine
beagle [biːgl] *n* beagle *m*
beak [biːk] *n* bec *m*
beaker ['biːkə'] *n* gobelet *m*
beam [biːm] *n* **1** (*Archit*) poutre *f*; (*of light*) rayon *m*; (*Radio*) faisceau *m* radio ▷ *vi* rayonner; **to drive on full** *or* **main** *or* (*US*) **high** ~ rouler en pleins phares
beaming ['biːmɪŋ] *adj* (*sun, smile*) radieux(-euse)
bean [biːn] *n* haricot *m*; (*of coffee*) grain *m*
beanpole ['biːnpəul] *n* (*inf*) perche *f*
beansprouts ['biːnsprauts] *npl* pousses *fpl* *or* germes *mpl* de soja
bear [bɛə'] (*pt* **bore**, *pp* **borne**) [bɔː', bɔːn] *n* ours *m*; (*Stock Exchange*) baissier *m* ▷ *vt* porter; (*endure*) supporter; (*traces, signs*) porter; (*Comm: interest*) rapporter ▷ *vi*: **to ~ right/left** obliquer à droite/gauche, se diriger vers la droite/gauche; **to ~ the responsibility of** assumer la responsabilité de; **to ~ comparison with** soutenir la comparaison avec; **I can't ~ him** je ne peux pas le supporter *or* souffrir; **to bring pressure to ~ on sb** faire pression sur qn
▶ **bear out** *vt* (*theory, suspicion*) confirmer
▶ **bear up** *vi* supporter, tenir le coup; **he bore up well** il a tenu le coup
▶ **bear with** *vt fus* (*sb's moods, temper*) supporter; ~ **with me a minute** un moment, s'il vous plaît
bearable ['bɛərəbl] *adj* supportable
beard [bɪəd] *n* barbe *f*

bearded ['bɪədɪd] *adj* barbu(e)
bearer ['bɛərə'] *n* porteur *m*; (*of passport etc*) titulaire *m/f*
bearing ['bɛərɪŋ] *n* maintien *m*, allure *f*; (*connection*) rapport *m*; (*Tech*): (**ball**) **bearings** *npl* roulement *m* (à billes); **to take a ~** faire le point; **to find one's ~s** s'orienter
beast [biːst] *n* bête *f*; (*inf: person*) brute *f*
beastly ['biːstlɪ] *adj* infect(e)
beat [biːt] *n* battement *m*; (*Mus*) temps *m*, mesure *f*; (*of policeman*) ronde *f* ▷ *vt, vi* (*pt* -, *pp* -en) battre; **off the ~en track** hors des chemins *or* sentiers battus; **to ~ it** (*inf*) ficher le camp; **to ~ about the bush** tourner autour du pot; **that ~s everything!** c'est le comble!
▶ **beat down** *vt* (*door*) enfoncer; (*price*) faire baisser; (*seller*) faire descendre ▷ *vi* (*rain*) tambouriner; (*sun*) taper
▶ **beat off** *vt* repousser
▶ **beat up** *vt* (*eggs*) battre; (*inf: person*) tabasser
beater ['biːtə'] *n* (*for eggs, cream*) fouet *m*, batteur *m*
beating ['biːtɪŋ] *n* raclée *f*
beat-up ['biːt'ʌp] *adj* (*inf*) déglingué(e)
beautician [bjuː'tɪʃən] *n* esthéticien(ne)
beautiful ['bjuːtɪful] *adj* beau (belle)
beautifully ['bjuːtɪflɪ] *adv* admirablement
beautify ['bjuːtɪfaɪ] *vt* embellir
beauty ['bjuːtɪ] *n* beauté *f*; **the ~ of it is that ...** le plus beau, c'est que ...
beauty contest *n* concours *m* de beauté
beauty parlour, (*US*) **beauty parlor** [-'paːlə'] *n* institut *m* de beauté
beauty queen *n* reine *f* de beauté
beauty salon *n* institut *m* de beauté
beauty sleep *n*: **I need my ~** j'ai besoin de faire un gros dodo
beauty spot *n* (*on skin*) grain *m* de beauté; (*Brit Tourism*) site naturel (d'une grande beauté)
beaver ['biːvə'] *n* castor *m*
becalmed [bɪ'kaːmd] *adj* immobilisé(e) par le calme plat
became [bɪ'keɪm] *pt of* **become**
because [bɪ'kɔz] *conj* parce que; ~ **of** (*prep*) à cause de
beck [bɛk] *n*: **to be at sb's ~ and call** être à l'entière disposition de qn
beckon ['bɛkən] *vt* (*also:* **beckon to**) faire signe (de venir) à
become [bɪ'kʌm] *vi* devenir; **to ~ fat/thin** grossir/maigrir; **to ~ angry** se mettre en colère; **it became known that** on apprit que; **what has ~ of him?** qu'est-il devenu?
becoming [bɪ'kʌmɪŋ] *adj* (*behaviour*) convenable, bienséant(e); (*clothes*) seyant(e)
BECTU ['bɛktu] *n abbr* (*Brit*) = **Broadcasting, Entertainment, Cinematographic and Theatre Union**
BEd *n abbr* (= *Bachelor of Education*) diplôme d'aptitude à l'enseignement
bed [bɛd] *n* lit *m*; (*of flowers*) parterre *m*; (*of coal, clay*) couche *f*; (*of sea, lake*) fond *m*; **to go to ~**

aller se coucher
▸ **bed down** vi se coucher
bed and breakfast n (terms) chambre et petit
déjeuner; (place) ≈ chambre f d'hôte; voir article

● **BED AND BREAKFAST**

●
● Un bed and breakfast est une petite pension
● dans une maison particulière ou une ferme
● où l'on peut louer une chambre avec petit
● déjeuner compris pour un prix modique par
● rapport à ce que l'on paierait dans un hôtel.
● Ces établissements sont communément
● appelés "B & B", et sont signalés par une
● pancarte dans le jardin ou au-dessus de la
● porte.

bedbug ['bɛdbʌg] n punaise f
bedclothes ['bɛdkləuðz] npl couvertures fpl et
draps mpl
bedcover ['bɛdkʌvəʳ] n couvre-lit m, dessus-de-
lit m
bedding ['bɛdɪŋ] n literie f
bedevil [bɪ'dɛvl] vt (harass) harceler: **to be ~led
by** être victime de
bedfellow ['bɛdfɛləu] n: **they are strange ~s**
(fig) ça fait un drôle de mélange
bedlam ['bɛdləm] n chahut m, cirque m
bed linen n draps mpl de lit (et taies fpl
d'oreillers), literie f
bedpan ['bɛdpæn] n bassin m (hygiénique)
bedpost ['bɛdpəust] n colonne f de lit
bedraggled [bɪ'drægld] adj dépenaillé(e), les
vêtements en désordre
bedridden ['bɛdrɪdn] adj cloué(e) au lit
bedrock ['bɛdrɔk] n (fig) principes essentiels or
de base, essentiel m; (Geo) roche f en place,
socle m
bedroom ['bɛdrum] n chambre f (à coucher)
Beds abbr (Brit) = **Bedfordshire**
bed settee n canapé-lit m
bedside ['bɛdsaɪd] n: **at sb's ~** au chevet de qn
▸ cpd (book, lamp) de chevet
bedside lamp n lampe f de chevet
bedside table n table f de chevet
bedsit ['bɛdsɪt], **bedsitter** ['bɛdsɪtəʳ] n (Brit)
chambre meublée, studio m
bedspread ['bɛdsprɛd] n couvre-lit m, dessus-
de-lit m
bedtime ['bɛdtaɪm] n: **it's ~** c'est l'heure de se
coucher
bee [biː] n abeille f; **to have a ~ in one's bonnet
(about sth)** être obnubilé(e) (par qch)
beech [biːtʃ] n hêtre m
beef [biːf] n bœuf m; **roast ~** rosbif m
▸ **beef up** vt (inf: support) renforcer; (: essay)
étoffer
beefburger ['biːfbəːgəʳ] n hamburger m
beehive ['biːhaɪv] n ruche f
bee-keeping ['biːkiːpɪŋ] n apiculture f
beeline ['biːlaɪn] n: **to make a ~ for** se diriger
tout droit vers

been [biːn] pp of **be**
beep [biːp] n bip m
beeper ['biːpəʳ] n (pager) bip m
beer [bɪəʳ] n bière f
beer belly n (inf) bedaine f (de buveur de bière)
beer can n canette f de bière
beer garden n (Brit) jardin m d'un pub (où l'on
peut emmener ses consommations)
beet [biːt] n (vegetable) betterave f; (US: also: **red
beet**) betterave (potagère)
beetle ['biːtl] n scarabée m, coléoptère m
beetroot ['biːtruːt] n (Brit) betterave f
befall [bɪ'fɔːl] vi, vt (irreg: like **fall**) advenir (à)
befit [bɪ'fɪt] vt seoir à
before [bɪ'fɔːʳ] prep (of time) avant; (of space)
devant ▷ conj avant que + sub; avant de ▷ adv
avant; **~ going** avant de partir; **~ she goes**
avant qu'elle (ne) parte; **the week ~** la semaine
précédente or d'avant; **I've seen it ~** je l'ai déjà
vu; **I've never seen it ~** c'est la première fois
que je le vois
beforehand [bɪ'fɔːhænd] adv au préalable, à
l'avance
befriend [bɪ'frɛnd] vt venir en aide à; traiter en
ami
befuddled [bɪ'fʌdld] adj: **to be ~** avoir les idées
brouillées
beg [bɛg] vi mendier ▷ vt mendier; (favour)
quémander, solliciter; (forgiveness, mercy etc)
demander; (entreat) supplier; **to ~ sb to do sth**
supplier qn de faire qch; **I ~ your pardon**
(apologising) excusez-moi; (: not hearing) pardon?;
that ~s the question of … cela soulève la
question de …, cela suppose réglée la question
de …; see also **pardon**
began [bɪ'gæn] pt of **begin**
beggar ['bɛgəʳ] n (also: **beggarman,
beggarwoman**) mendiant(e)
begin [bɪ'gɪn] (pt **began**, pp **begun** [bɪ'gɪn, -'gæn,
-'gʌn]) vt, vi commencer; **to ~ doing** or **to do
sth** commencer à faire qch; **~ning (from)
Monday** à partir de lundi; **I can't ~ to thank
you** je ne saurais vous remercier; **to ~ with**
d'abord, pour commencer
beginner [bɪ'gɪnəʳ] n débutant(e)
beginning [bɪ'gɪnɪŋ] n commencement m,
début m; **right from the ~** dès le début
begrudge [bɪ'grʌdʒ] vt: **to ~ sb sth** envier qch à
qn; donner qch à contrecœur or à regret à qn
beguile [bɪ'gaɪl] vt (enchant) enjôler
beguiling [bɪ'gaɪlɪŋ] adj (charming) séduisant(e),
enchanteur(eresse)
begun [bɪ'gʌn] pp of **begin**
behalf [bɪ'hɑːf] n: **on ~ of**, (US) **in ~ of**
(representing) de la part de; au nom de; (for benefit
of) pour le compte de; **on my/his ~** de ma/sa
part
behave [bɪ'heɪv] vi se conduire, se comporter;
(well: also: **behave o.s.**) se conduire bien or
comme il faut
behaviour, (US) **behavior** [bɪ'heɪvjəʳ] n
comportement m, conduite f

behead [bɪ'hɛd] *vt* décapiter

beheld [bɪ'hɛld] *pt, pp of* **behold**

behind [bɪ'haɪnd] *prep* derrière; (*time*) en retard sur; (*supporting*): **to be ~ sb** soutenir qn ▷ *adv* derrière; en retard ▷ *n* derrière *m*; **~ the scenes** dans les coulisses; **to leave sth ~** (*forget*) oublier de prendre qch; **to be ~ (schedule) with sth** être en retard dans qch

behold [bɪ'həʊld] *vt* (*irreg: like* **hold**) apercevoir, voir

beige [beɪʒ] *adj* beige

Beijing ['beɪ'dʒɪŋ] *n* Pékin

being ['biːɪŋ] *n* être *m*; **to come into ~** prendre naissance

Beirut [beɪ'ruːt] *n* Beyrouth

Belarus [bɛlə'rus] *n* Biélorussie *f*, Bélarus *m*

Belarussian [bɛlə'rʌʃən] *adj* biélorusse ▷ *n* Biélorusse *m/f*; (*Ling*) biélorusse *m*

belated [bɪ'leɪtɪd] *adj* tardif(-ive)

belch [bɛltʃ] *vi* avoir un renvoi, roter ▷ *vt* (*also:* **belch out**: *smoke etc*) vomir, cracher

beleaguered [bɪ'liːgɪd] *adj* (*city*) assiégé(e); (*army*) cerné(e); (*fig*) sollicité(e) de toutes parts

Belfast ['bɛlfɑːst] *n* Belfast

belfry ['bɛlfrɪ] *n* beffroi *m*

Belgian ['bɛldʒən] *adj* belge, de Belgique ▷ *n* Belge *m/f*

Belgium ['bɛldʒəm] *n* Belgique *f*

Belgrade [bɛl'greɪd] *n* Belgrade

belie [bɪ'laɪ] *vt* démentir; (*give false impression of*) occulter

belief [bɪ'liːf] *n* (*opinion*) conviction *f*; (*trust, faith*) foi *f*; (*acceptance as true*) croyance *f*; **it's beyond ~** c'est incroyable; **in the ~ that** dans l'idée que

believable [bɪ'liːvəbl] *adj* croyable

believe [bɪ'liːv] *vt, vi* croire, estimer; **to ~ in** (*God*) croire en; (*ghosts, method*) croire à; **I don't ~ in corporal punishment** je ne suis pas partisan des châtiments corporels; **he is ~d to be abroad** il serait à l'étranger

believer [bɪ'liːvər] *n* (*in idea, activity*) partisan(e); **~ in** partisan(e) de; (*Rel*) croyant(e)

belittle [bɪ'lɪtl] *vt* déprécier, rabaisser

Belize [bɛ'liːz] *n* Bélize *m*

bell [bɛl] *n* cloche *f*; (*small*) clochette *f*, grelot *m*; (*on door*) sonnette *f*; (*electric*) sonnerie *f*; **that rings a ~** (*fig*) cela me rappelle qch

bell-bottoms ['bɛlbotəmz] *npl* pantalon *m* à pattes d'éléphant

bellboy ['bɛlbɔɪ], (*US*) **bellhop** ['bɛlhɔp] *n* groom *m*, chasseur *m*

belligerent [bɪ'lɪdʒərənt] *adj* (*at war*) belligérant(e); (*fig*) agressif(-ive)

bellow ['bɛləʊ] *vi* (*bull*) meugler; (*person*) brailler ▷ *vt* (*orders*) hurler

bellows ['bɛləʊz] *npl* soufflet *m*

bell pepper *n* (*esp US*) poivron *m*

bell push *n* (*Brit*) bouton *m* de sonnette

belly ['bɛlɪ] *n* ventre *m*

bellyache ['bɛlɪeɪk] (*inf*) *n* colique *f* ▷ *vi* ronchonner

belly button (*inf*) *n* nombril *m*

bellyful ['bɛlɪful] *n* (*inf*): **I've had a ~** j'en ai ras le bol

belong [bɪ'lɔŋ] *vi*: **to ~ to** appartenir à; (*club etc*) faire partie de; **this book ~s here** ce livre va ici, la place de ce livre est ici

belongings [bɪ'lɔŋɪŋz] *npl* affaires *fpl*, possessions *fpl*; **personal ~** effets personnels

Belorussia [bɛlə'rʌʃə] *n* Biélorussie *f*

Belorussian [bɛlə'rʌʃən] *adj, n* = **Belarussian**

beloved [bɪ'lʌvɪd] *adj* (bien-)aimé(e), chéri(e) ▷ *n* bien-aimé(e)

below [bɪ'ləʊ] *prep* sous, au-dessous de ▷ *adv* en dessous; en contre-bas; **see ~** voir plus bas *or* plus loin *or* ci-dessous; **temperatures ~ normal** températures inférieures à la normale

belt [bɛlt] *n* ceinture *f*; (*Tech*) courroie *f* ▷ *vt* (*thrash*) donner une raclée à ▷ *vi* (*Brit inf*) filer (à toutes jambes); **industrial ~** zone industrielle
  ▶ **belt out** *vt* (*song*) chanter à tue-tête *or* à pleins poumons
  ▶ **belt up** *vi* (*Brit inf*) la boucler

beltway ['bɛltweɪ] *n* (*US Aut*) route *f* de ceinture; (: *motorway*) périphérique *m*

bemoan [bɪ'məʊn] *vt* se lamenter sur

bemused [bɪ'mjuːzd] *adj* médusé(e)

bench [bɛntʃ] *n* banc *m*; (*in workshop*) établi *m*; **the B~** (*Law: judges*) la magistrature, la Cour

bench mark *n* repère *m*

bend [bɛnd] (*pt, pp* **bent** [bɛnt]) *vt* courber; (*leg, arm*) plier ▷ *vi* se courber ▷ *n* (*Brit: in road*) virage *m*, tournant *m*; (*in pipe, river*) coude *m*
  ▶ **bend down** *vi* se baisser
  ▶ **bend over** *vi* se pencher

bends [bɛndz] *npl* (*Med*) maladie *f* des caissons

beneath [bɪ'niːθ] *prep* sous, au-dessous de; (*unworthy of*) indigne de ▷ *adv* dessous, au-dessous, en bas

benefactor ['bɛnɪfæktər] *n* bienfaiteur *m*

benefactress ['bɛnɪfæktrɪs] *n* bienfaitrice *f*

beneficial [bɛnɪ'fɪʃəl] *adj*: **~ (to)** salutaire (pour), bénéfique (à)

beneficiary [bɛnɪ'fɪʃərɪ] *n* (*Law*) bénéficiaire *m/f*

benefit ['bɛnɪfɪt] *n* avantage *m*, profit *m*; (*allowance of money*) allocation *f* ▷ *vt* faire du bien à, profiter à ▷ *vi*: **he'll ~ from it** cela lui fera du bien, il y gagnera *or* s'en trouvera bien

benefit performance *n* représentation *f or* gala *m* de bienfaisance

Benelux ['bɛnɪlʌks] *n* Bénélux *m*

benevolent [bɪ'nɛvələnt] *adj* bienveillant(e)

BEng *n abbr* (= *Bachelor of Engineering*) diplôme universitaire

benign [bɪ'naɪn] *adj* (*person, smile*) bienveillant(e), affable; (*Med*) bénin(-igne)

bent [bɛnt] *pt, pp of* **bend** ▷ *n* inclination *f*, penchant *m* ▷ *adj* (*wire, pipe*) coudé(e); (*inf: dishonest*) véreux(-euse); **to be ~ on** être résolu(e) à

bequeath [bɪ'kwiːð] *vt* léguer

bequest [bɪ'kwɛst] *n* legs *m*

bereaved [bɪ'riːvd] *n*: **the ~** la famille du disparu ▷ *adj* endeuillé(e)

b

bereavement [bɪˈriːvmənt] n deuil m
beret [ˈbɛreɪ] n béret m
Bering Sea [ˈbeɪrɪŋ-] n: **the ~** la mer de Béring
berk [bəːk] n (Brit inf) andouille m/f
Berks abbr (Brit) = **Berkshire**
Berlin [bəːˈlɪn] n Berlin; **East/West ~** Berlin Est/Ouest
berm [bəːm] n (US Aut) accotement m
Bermuda [bəːˈmjuːdə] n Bermudes fpl
Bermuda shorts npl bermuda m
Bern [bəːn] n Berne
berry [ˈbɛrɪ] n baie f
berserk [bəˈsəːk] adj: **to go ~** être pris(e) d'une rage incontrôlable; se déchaîner
berth [bəːθ] n (bed) couchette f; (for ship) poste m d'amarrage, mouillage m ▷ vi (in harbour) venir à quai; (at anchor) mouiller; **to give sb a wide ~** (fig) éviter qn
beseech (pt, pp **besought**) [bɪˈsiːtʃ, -ˈsɔːt] vt implorer, supplier
beset (pt, pp -) [bɪˈsɛt] vt assaillir ▷ adj: **~ with** semé(e) de
besetting [bɪˈsɛtɪŋ] adj: **his ~ sin** son vice, son gros défaut
beside [bɪˈsaɪd] prep à côté de; (compared with) par rapport à; **that's ~ the point** ça n'a rien à voir; **to be ~ o.s. (with anger)** être hors de soi
besides [bɪˈsaɪdz] adv en outre, de plus ▷ prep en plus de; (except) excepté
besiege [bɪˈsiːdʒ] vt (town) assiéger; (fig) assaillir
besotted [bɪˈsɔtɪd] adj (Brit): **~ with** entiché(e) de
besought [bɪˈsɔːt] pt, pp of **beseech**
bespectacled [bɪˈspɛktɪkld] adj à lunettes
bespoke [bɪˈspəuk] adj (Brit: garment) fait(e) sur mesure; **~ tailor** tailleur m à façon
best [bɛst] adj meilleur(e) ▷ adv le mieux; **the ~ part of** (quantity) le plus clair de, la plus grande partie de; **at ~** au mieux; **to make the ~ of sth** s'accommoder de qch (du mieux que l'on peut); **to do one's ~** faire de son mieux; **to the ~ of my knowledge** pour autant que je sache; **to the ~ of my ability** du mieux que je pourrai; **he's not exactly patient at the ~ of times** il n'est jamais spécialement patient; **the ~ thing to do is ...** le mieux, c'est de ...
best-before date n date f de limite d'utilisation or de consommation
best man (irreg) n garçon m d'honneur
bestow [bɪˈstəu] vt accorder; (title) conférer
bestseller [ˈbɛstˈsɛləʳ] n best-seller m, succès m de librairie
bet [bɛt] n pari m ▷ vt, vi (pt, pp - or **-ted**) parier; **it's a safe ~** (fig) il y a de fortes chances; **to ~ sb sth** parier qch à qn
Bethlehem [ˈbɛθlɪhɛm] n Bethléem
betray [bɪˈtreɪ] vt trahir
betrayal [bɪˈtreɪəl] n trahison f
better [ˈbɛtəʳ] adj meilleur(e) ▷ adv mieux ▷ vt améliorer ▷ n: **to get the ~ of** triompher de, l'emporter sur; **a change for the ~** une amélioration; **I had ~ go** il faut que je m'en

aille; **you had ~ do it** vous feriez mieux de le faire; **he thought ~ of it** il s'est ravisé; **to get ~** (Med) aller mieux; (improve) s'améliorer; **that's ~!** c'est mieux!; **~ off** adj plus à l'aise financièrement; (fig): **you'd be ~ off this way** vous vous en trouveriez mieux ainsi, ce serait mieux or plus pratique ainsi
betting [ˈbɛtɪŋ] n paris mpl
betting shop n (Brit) bureau m de paris
between [bɪˈtwiːn] prep entre ▷ adv au milieu, dans l'intervalle; **the road ~ here and London** la route d'ici à Londres; **we only had 5 ~ us** nous n'en avions que 5 en tout
bevel [ˈbɛvəl] n (also: **bevel edge**) biseau m
beverage [ˈbɛvərɪdʒ] n boisson f (gén sans alcool)
bevy [ˈbɛvɪ] n: **a ~ of** un essaim or une volée de
bewail [bɪˈweɪl] vt se lamenter sur
beware [bɪˈwɛəʳ] vt, vi: **to ~ (of)** prendre garde (à); **"~ of the dog"** "(attention) chien méchant"
bewildered [bɪˈwɪldəd] adj dérouté(e), ahuri(e)
bewildering [bɪˈwɪldrɪŋ] adj déroutant(e), ahurissant(e)
bewitching [bɪˈwɪtʃɪŋ] adj enchanteur(-teresse)
beyond [bɪˈjɔnd] prep (in space, time) au-delà de; (exceeding) au-dessus de ▷ adv au-delà; **~ doubt** hors de doute; **~ repair** irréparable
b/f abbr = **brought forward**
BFPO n abbr (= British Forces Post Office) service postal de l'armée
bhp n abbr (Aut: = brake horsepower) puissance f aux freins
bi... [baɪ] prefix bi...
biannual [baɪˈænjuəl] adj semestriel(le)
bias [ˈbaɪəs] n (prejudice) préjugé m, parti pris; (preference) prévention f
biased, biassed [ˈbaɪəst] adj partial(e), montrant un parti pris; **to be bias(s)ed against** avoir un préjugé contre
biathlon [baɪˈæθlən] n biathlon m
bib [bɪb] n bavoir m, bavette f
Bible [ˈbaɪbl] n Bible f
bibliography [bɪblɪˈɔgrəfɪ] n bibliographie f
bicarbonate of soda [baɪˈkɑːbənɪt-] n bicarbonate m de soude
bicentenary [baɪsɛnˈtiːnərɪ] n, **bicentennial** [baɪsɛnˈtɛnɪəl] ▷ n bicentenaire m
biceps [ˈbaɪsɛps] n biceps m
bicker [ˈbɪkəʳ] vi se chamailler
bicycle [ˈbaɪsɪkl] n bicyclette f
bicycle path n, **bicycle track** n piste f cyclable
bicycle pump n pompe f à vélo
bid [bɪd] n offre f; (at auction) enchère f; (attempt) tentative f ▷ vi (pt, pp -) faire une enchère or offre ▷ vt (pt **bade**) [bæd] (pp **-den**) [ˈbɪdn] faire une enchère or offre de; **to ~ sb good day** souhaiter le bonjour à qn
bidden [ˈbɪdn] pp of **bid**
bidder [ˈbɪdəʳ] n: **the highest ~** le plus offrant
bidding [ˈbɪdɪŋ] n enchères fpl
bide [baɪd] vt: **to ~ one's time** attendre son heure

bidet ['biːdeɪ] n bidet m

bidirectional ['baɪdɪ'rɛkʃənl] adj bidirectionnel(le)

biennial [baɪ'ɛnɪəl] adj biennal(e), bisannuel(le) ▷ n biennale f; (plant) plante bisannuelle

bier [bɪəʳ] n bière f (cercueil)

bifocals [baɪ'fəuklz] npl lunettes fpl à double foyer

big [bɪg] adj (in height: person, building, tree) grand(e); (in bulk, amount: person, parcel, book) gros(se); **to do things in a ~ way** faire les choses en grand

bigamy ['bɪgəmɪ] n bigamie f

big dipper [-'dɪpəʳ] n montagnes fpl russes

big end n (Aut) tête f de bielle

biggish ['bɪgɪʃ] adj (see big) assez grand(e), assez gros(se)

bigheaded ['bɪg'hɛdɪd] adj prétentieux(-euse)

big-hearted ['bɪg'hɑːtɪd] adj au grand cœur

bigot ['bɪgət] n fanatique m/f, sectaire m/f

bigoted ['bɪgətɪd] adj fanatique, sectaire

bigotry ['bɪgətrɪ] n fanatisme m, sectarisme m

big toe n gros orteil

big top n grand chapiteau

big wheel n (at fair) grande roue

bigwig ['bɪgwɪg] n (inf) grosse légume, huile f

bike [baɪk] n vélo m, bécane f

bike lane n piste f cyclable

bikini [bɪ'kiːnɪ] n bikini m

bilateral [baɪ'lætərl] adj bilatéral(e)

bile [baɪl] n bile f

bilingual [baɪ'lɪŋgwəl] adj bilingue

bilious ['bɪlɪəs] adj bilieux(-euse); (fig) maussade, irritable

bill [bɪl] n note f, facture f; (in restaurant) addition f, note f; (Pol) projet m de loi; (US: banknote) billet m (de banque); (notice) affiche f; (of bird) bec m; (Theat): **on the ~** à l'affiche ▷ vt (item) facturer; (customer) remettre la facture à; **may I have the ~ please?** (est-ce que je peux avoir) l'addition, s'il vous plaît?; **put it on my ~** mettez-le sur mon compte; **"post no ~s"** "défense d'afficher"; **to fit** or **fill the ~** (fig) faire l'affaire; **~ of exchange** lettre f de change; **~ of lading** connaissement m; **~ of sale** contrat m de vente

billboard ['bɪlbɔːd] (US) n panneau m d'affichage

billet ['bɪlɪt] n cantonnement m (chez l'habitant) ▷ vt (troops) cantonner

billfold ['bɪlfəuld] n (US) portefeuille m

billiards ['bɪljədz] n (jeu m de) billard m

billion ['bɪljən] n (Brit) billion m (million de millions); (US) milliard m

billow ['bɪləu] n nuage m ▷ vi (smoke) s'élever en nuage; (sail) se gonfler

billy goat ['bɪlɪgəut] n bouc m

bimbo ['bɪmbəu] n (inf) ravissante idiote f

bin [bɪn] n boîte f; (Brit: also: **dustbin, litter bin**) poubelle f; (for coal) coffre m

binary ['baɪnərɪ] adj binaire

bind (pt, pp **bound**) [baɪnd, baund] vt attacher; (book) relier; (oblige) obliger, contraindre ▷ n (inf: nuisance) scie f

▶ **bind over** vt (Law) mettre en liberté conditionnelle

▶ **bind up** vt (wound) panser; **to be bound up in** (work, research etc) être complètement absorbé par, être accroché par; **to be bound up with** (person) être accroché à

binder ['baɪndəʳ] n (file) classeur m

binding ['baɪndɪŋ] n (of book) reliure f ▷ adj (contract) qui constitue une obligation

binge [bɪndʒ] n (inf): **to go on a ~** faire la bringue

bingo ['bɪŋgəu] n sorte de jeu de loto pratiqué dans des établissements publics

bin liner n sac m poubelle

binoculars [bɪ'nɔkjuləz] npl jumelles fpl

biochemistry [baɪə'kɛmɪstrɪ] n biochimie f

biodegradable ['baɪəudɪ'greɪdəbl] adj biodégradable

biodiversity ['baɪəudaɪ'vəːsɪtɪ] n biodiversité f

biofuel ['baɪəufjuəl] n combustible m organique

biographer [baɪ'ɔgrəfəʳ] n biographe m/f

biographic [baɪə'græfɪk], **biographical** [baɪə'græfɪkl] adj biographique

biography [baɪ'ɔgrəfɪ] n biographie f

biological [baɪə'lɔdʒɪkl] adj biologique

biological clock n horloge f physiologique

biologist [baɪ'ɔlədʒɪst] n biologiste m/f

biology [baɪ'ɔlədʒɪ] n biologie f

biometric [baɪə'mɛtrɪk] adj biométrique

biophysics ['baɪəu'fɪzɪks] n biophysique f

biopic ['baɪəupɪk] n film m biographique

biopsy ['baɪɔpsɪ] n biopsie f

biosphere ['baɪəsfɪəʳ] n biosphère f

biotechnology ['baɪəutɛk'nɔlədʒɪ] n biotechnologie f

birch [bəːtʃ] n bouleau m

bird [bəːd] n oiseau m; (Brit inf: girl) nana f

bird flu n grippe f aviaire

bird of prey n oiseau m de proie

bird's-eye view ['bəːdzaɪ-] n vue f à vol d'oiseau; (fig) vue d'ensemble or générale

bird watcher [-wɔtʃəʳ] n ornithologue m/f amateur

birdwatching ['bəːdwɔtʃɪŋ] n ornithologie f (d'amateur)

Biro® ['baɪərəu] n stylo m à bille

birth [bəːθ] n naissance f; **to give ~ to** donner naissance à, mettre au monde; (subj: animal) mettre bas

birth certificate n acte m de naissance

birth control n (policy) limitation f des naissances; (methods) méthode(s) contraceptive(s)

birthday ['bəːθdeɪ] n anniversaire m ▷ cpd (cake, card etc) d'anniversaire

birthmark ['bəːθmɑːk] n envie f, tache f de vin

birthplace ['bəːθpleɪs] n lieu m de naissance

birth rate n (taux m de) natalité f

Biscay ['bɪskeɪ] n: **the Bay of ~** le golfe de

Gascogne

biscuit ['bɪskɪt] *n* (*Brit*) biscuit *m*; (*US*) petit pain au lait

bisect [baɪ'sɛkt] *vt* couper *or* diviser en deux

bisexual ['baɪ'sɛksjuəl] *adj, n* bisexuel(le)

bishop ['bɪʃəp] *n* évêque *m*; (*Chess*) fou *m*

bistro ['bi:strəu] *n* petit restaurant *m*, bistrot *m*

bit [bɪt] *pt of* **bite** ▷ *n* morceau *m*; (*Comput*) bit *m*, élément *m* binaire; (*of tool*) mèche *f*; (*of horse*) mors *m*; **a ~ of** un peu de; **a ~ mad/dangerous** un peu fou/risqué; **~ by ~** petit à petit; **to come to ~s** (*break*) tomber en morceaux, se déglinguer; **bring all your ~s and pieces** apporte toutes tes affaires; **to do one's ~** y mettre du sien

bitch [bɪtʃ] *n* (*dog*) chienne *f*; (*inf!*) salope *f* (!), garce *f*

bite [baɪt] *vt, vi* (*pt* **bit**, *pp* **bitten** [bɪt, 'bɪtn]) mordre; (*insect*) piquer ▷ *n* morsure *f*; (*insect bite*) piqûre *f*; (*mouthful*) bouchée *f*; **let's have a ~ (to eat)** mangeons un morceau; **to ~ one's nails** se ronger les ongles

biting ['baɪtɪŋ] *adj* mordant(e)

bit part *n* (*Theat*) petit rôle

bitten ['bɪtn] *pp of* **bite**

bitter ['bɪtə'] *adj* amer(-ère); (*criticism*) cinglant(e); (*icy: weather, wind*) glacial(e) ▷ *n* (*Brit: beer*) bière *f* (*à forte teneur en houblon*); **to the ~ end** jusqu'au bout

bitterly ['bɪtəlɪ] *adv* (*complain, weep*) amèrement; (*oppose, criticise*) durement, âprement; (*jealous, disappointed*) horriblement; **it's ~ cold** il fait un froid de loup

bitterness ['bɪtənɪs] *n* amertume *f*; goût amer

bittersweet ['bɪtəswi:t] *adj* aigre-doux (douce)

bitty ['bɪtɪ] *adj* (*Brit inf*) décousu(e)

bitumen ['bɪtjumɪn] *n* bitume *m*

bivouac ['bɪvuæk] *n* bivouac *m*

bizarre [bɪ'zɑ:'] *adj* bizarre

bk *abbr* = **bank**; **book**

BL *n abbr* (= *Bachelor of Law(s), Bachelor of Letters*) diplôme universitaire; (*US:* = *Bachelor of Literature*) diplôme universitaire

bl *abbr* = **bill of lading**

blab [blæb] *vi* jaser, trop parler ▷ *vt* (*also:* **blab out**) laisser échapper, aller raconter

black [blæk] *adj* noir(e) ▷ *n* (*colour*) noir *m*; (*person*): **B~** noir(e) ▷ *vt* (*shoes*) cirer; (*Brit Industry*) boycotter; **to give sb a ~ eye** pocher l'œil à qn, faire un œil au beurre noir à qn; **there it is in ~ and white** (*fig*) c'est écrit noir sur blanc; **to be in the ~** (*in credit*) avoir un compte créditeur; **~ and blue** (*bruised*) couvert(e) de bleus

▶ **black out** *vi* (*faint*) s'évanouir

black belt *n* (*Judo etc*) ceinture noire; **he's a ~** il est ceinture noire

blackberry ['blækbərɪ] *n* mûre *f*

blackbird ['blækbə:d] *n* merle *m*

blackboard ['blækbɔ:d] *n* tableau noir

black box *n* (*Aviat*) boîte noire

black coffee *n* café noir

Black Country *n* (*Brit*): **the ~** le Pays Noir (*dans les Midlands*)

blackcurrant ['blæk'kʌrənt] *n* cassis *m*

black economy *n* (*Brit*) travail *m* au noir

blacken ['blækn] *vt* noircir

Black Forest *n*: **the ~** la Forêt Noire

blackhead ['blækhɛd] *n* point noir

black hole *n* (*Astronomy*) trou noir

black ice *n* verglas *m*

blackjack ['blækdʒæk] *n* (*Cards*) vingt-et-un *m*; (*US: truncheon*) matraque *f*

blackleg ['blækleg] *n* (*Brit*) briseur *m* de grève, jaune *m*

blacklist ['blæklɪst] *n* liste noire ▷ *vt* mettre sur la liste noire

blackmail ['blækmeɪl] *n* chantage *m* ▷ *vt* faire chanter, soumettre au chantage

blackmailer ['blækmeɪlə'] *n* maître-chanteur *m*

black market *n* marché noir

blackout ['blækaut] *n* panne *f* d'électricité; (*in wartime*) black-out *m*; (*TV*) interruption *f* d'émission; (*fainting*) syncope *f*

black pepper *n* poivre noir

black pudding *n* boudin (noir)

Black Sea *n*: **the ~** la mer Noire

black sheep *n* brebis galeuse

blacksmith ['blæksmɪθ] *n* forgeron *m*

black spot *n* (*Aut*) point noir

bladder ['blædə'] *n* vessie *f*

blade [bleɪd] *n* lame *f*; (*of oar*) plat *m*; (*of propeller*) pale *f*; **a ~ of grass** un brin d'herbe

blame [bleɪm] *n* faute *f*, blâme *m* ▷ *vt*: **to ~ sb/sth for sth** attribuer à qn/qch la responsabilité de qch; reprocher qch à qn/qch; **who's to ~?** qui est le fautif *or* coupable *or* responsable?; **I'm not to ~** ce n'est pas ma faute

blameless ['bleɪmlɪs] *adj* irréprochable

blanch [blɑ:ntʃ] *vi* (*person, face*) blêmir ▷ *vt* (*Culin*) blanchir

bland [blænd] *adj* affable; (*taste, food*) doux (douce), fade

blank [blæŋk] *adj* blanc (blanche); (*look*) sans expression, dénué(e) d'expression ▷ *n* espace *m* vide, blanc *m*; (*cartridge*) cartouche *f* à blanc; **his mind was a ~** il avait la tête vide; **we drew a ~** (*fig*) nous n'avons abouti à rien

blank cheque, (*US*) **blank check** *n* chèque *m* en blanc; **to give sb a ~ to do ...** (*fig*) donner carte blanche à qn pour faire ...

blanket ['blæŋkɪt] *n* couverture *f*; (*of snow, cloud*) couche *f* ▷ *adj* (*statement, agreement*) global(e), de portée générale; **to give ~ cover** (*insurance policy*) couvrir tous les risques

blare [blɛə'] *vi* (*brass band, horns, radio*) beugler

blasé ['blɑ:zeɪ] *adj* blasé(e)

blasphemous ['blæsfɪməs] *adj* (*words*) blasphématoire; (*person*) blasphémateur(-trice)

blasphemy ['blæsfɪmɪ] *n* blasphème *m*

blast [blɑ:st] *n* explosion *f*; (*shock wave*) souffle *m*; (*of air, steam*) bouffée *f* ▷ *vt* faire sauter *or* exploser ▷ *excl* (*Brit inf*) zut!; **(at) full ~** (*play music etc*) à plein volume

▶ **blast off** vi (Space) décoller

blast-off ['blɑːstɔf] n (Space) lancement m

blatant ['bleɪtənt] adj flagrant(e), criant(e)

blatantly ['bleɪtəntlɪ] adv (lie) ouvertement; **it's ~ obvious** c'est l'évidence même

blaze [bleɪz] n (fire) incendie m; (flames: of fire, sun etc) embrasement m; (: in hearth) flamme f, flambée f; (fig) flamboiement m ▷ vi (fire) flamber; (fig) flamboyer, resplendir ▷ vt: **to ~ a trail** (fig) montrer la voie; **in a ~ of publicity** à grand renfort de publicité

blazer ['bleɪzə'] n blazer m

bleach [bliːtʃ] n (also: **household bleach**) eau f de Javel ▷ vt (linen) blanchir

bleached [bliːtʃt] adj (hair) oxygéné(e), décoloré(e)

bleachers ['bliːtʃəz] npl (US Sport) gradins mpl (en plein soleil)

bleak [bliːk] adj morne, désolé(e); (weather) triste, maussade; (smile) lugubre; (prospect, future) morose

bleary-eyed ['blɪərɪ'aɪd] adj aux yeux pleins de sommeil

bleat [bliːt] n bêlement m ▷ vi bêler

bled [bled] pt, pp of **bleed**

bleed (pt, pp **bled**) [bliːd, bled] vt saigner; (brakes, radiator) purger ▷ vi saigner; **my nose is ~ing** je saigne du nez

bleep [bliːp] n (Radio, TV) top m; (of pocket device) bip m ▷ vi émettre des signaux ▷ vt (doctor etc) appeler (au moyen d'un bip)

bleeper ['bliːpə'] n (of doctor etc) bip m

blemish ['blɛmɪʃ] n défaut m; (on reputation) tache f

blend [blend] n mélange m ▷ vt mélanger ▷ vi (colours etc: also: **blend in**) se mélanger, se fondre, s'allier

blender ['blendə'] n (Culin) mixeur m

bless (pt, pp **-ed** or **blest**) [bles, blest] vt bénir; **to be ~ed with** avoir le bonheur de jouir de or d'avoir; **~ you!** (after sneeze) à tes souhaits!

blessed ['blɛsɪd] adj (Rel: holy) béni(e); (happy) bienheureux(-euse); **it rains every ~ day** il ne se passe pas de jour sans qu'il ne pleuve

blessing ['blɛsɪŋ] n bénédiction f; (godsend) bienfait m; **to count one's ~s** s'estimer heureux; **it was a ~ in disguise** c'est un bien pour un mal

blew [bluː] pt of **blow**

blight [blaɪt] n (of plants) rouille f ▷ vt (hopes etc) anéantir, briser

blimey ['blaɪmɪ] excl (Brit inf) mince alors!

blind [blaɪnd] adj aveugle ▷ n (for window) store m ▷ vt aveugler; **to turn a ~ eye (on** or **to)** fermer les yeux (sur); **the blind** npl les aveugles mpl

blind alley n impasse f

blind corner n (Brit) virage m sans visibilité

blind date n rendez-vous galant (avec un(e) inconnu(e))

blindfold ['blaɪndfəuld] n bandeau m ▷ adj, adv les yeux bandés ▷ vt bander les yeux à

blindly ['blaɪndlɪ] adv aveuglément

blindness ['blaɪndnɪs] n cécité f; (fig)

aveuglement m

blind spot n (Aut etc) angle m aveugle; (fig) angle mort

blink [blɪŋk] vi cligner des yeux; (light) clignoter ▷ n: **the TV's on the ~** (inf) la télé ne va pas tarder à nous lâcher

blinkers ['blɪŋkəz] npl œillères fpl

blinking ['blɪŋkɪŋ] adj (Brit inf): **this ~ ...** ce fichu or sacré ...

blip [blɪp] n (on radar etc) spot m; (on graph) petite aberration; (fig) petite anomalie (passagère)

bliss [blɪs] n félicité f, bonheur m sans mélange

blissful ['blɪsful] adj (event, day) merveilleux(-euse); (smile) de bonheur; **a ~ sigh** un soupir d'aise; **in ~ ignorance** dans une ignorance béate

blissfully ['blɪsfulɪ] adv (smile) béatement; (happy) merveilleusement

blister ['blɪstə'] n (on skin) ampoule f, cloque f; (on paintwork) boursouflure f ▷ vi (paint) se boursoufler, se cloquer

BLit, BLitt n abbr (= Bachelor of Literature) diplôme universitaire

blithely ['blaɪðlɪ] adv (unconcernedly) tranquillement; (joyfully) gaiement

blithering ['blɪðərɪŋ] adj (inf): **this ~ idiot** cet espèce d'idiot

blitz [blɪts] n bombardement (aérien); **to have a ~ on sth** (fig) s'attaquer à qch

blizzard ['blɪzəd] n blizzard m, tempête f de neige

BLM n abbr (US: = Bureau of Land Management) ≈ les domaines

bloated ['bləutɪd] adj (face) bouffi(e); (stomach, person) gonflé(e)

blob [blɔb] n (drop) goutte f; (stain, spot) tache f

bloc [blɔk] n (Pol) bloc m

block [blɔk] n bloc m; (in pipes) obstruction f; (toy) cube m; (of buildings) pâté m (de maisons) ▷ vt bloquer; (fig) faire obstacle à; (Comput) grouper; **the sink is ~ed** l'évier est bouché; **~ of flats** (Brit) immeuble (locatif); **3 ~s from here** à trois rues d'ici; **mental ~** blocage m; **~ and tackle** (Tech) palan m

▶ **block up** vt boucher

blockade [blɔ'keɪd] n blocus m ▷ vt faire le blocus de

blockage ['blɔkɪdʒ] n obstruction f

block booking n réservation f en bloc

blockbuster ['blɔkbʌstə'] n (film, book) grand succès

block capitals npl majuscules fpl d'imprimerie

blockhead ['blɔkhɛd] n imbécile m/f

block letters npl majuscules fpl

block release n (Brit) congé m de formation

block vote n (Brit) vote m de délégation

blog [blɔg] n blog m, blogue m ▷ vi bloguer

blogger ['blɔgə'] n (inf) n (person) blogueur(-euse) m/f

blogging ['blɔgɪŋ] n blogging m

bloke [bləuk] n (Brit inf) type m

blond, blonde [blɔnd] adj, n blond(e)

481

blood [blʌd] *n* sang *m*
blood bank *n* banque *f* du sang
blood count *n* numération *f* globulaire
bloodcurdling ['blʌdkə:dlɪŋ] *adj* à vous glacer le sang
blood donor *n* donneur(-euse) de sang
blood group *n* groupe sanguin
bloodhound ['blʌdhaund] *n* limier *m*
bloodless ['blʌdlɪs] *adj* (*victory*) sans effusion de sang; (*pale*) anémié(e)
bloodletting ['blʌdlɛtɪŋ] *n* (*Med*) saignée *f*; (*fig*) effusion *f* de sang, représailles *fpl*
blood poisoning *n* empoisonnement *m* du sang
blood pressure *n* tension (artérielle); **to have high/low ~** faire de l'hypertension/l'hypotension
bloodshed ['blʌdʃɛd] *n* effusion *f* de sang, carnage *m*
bloodshot ['blʌdʃɔt] *adj*: **~ eyes** yeux injectés de sang
blood sports *npl* sports *mpl* sanguinaires
bloodstained ['blʌdsteɪnd] *adj* taché(e) de sang
bloodstream ['blʌdstri:m] *n* sang *m*, système sanguin
blood test *n* analyse *f* de sang
bloodthirsty ['blʌdθə:stɪ] *adj* sanguinaire
blood transfusion *n* transfusion *f* de sang
blood type *n* groupe sanguin
blood vessel *n* vaisseau sanguin
bloody ['blʌdɪ] *adj* sanglant(e); (*Brit inf!*): **this ~ ...** ce foutu ..., ce putain de ... (!) ▷ *adv*: **~ strong/good** (*Brit: inf!*) vachement *or* sacrément fort/bon
bloody-minded ['blʌdɪ'maɪndɪd] *adj* (*Brit inf*) contrariant(e), obstiné(e)
bloom [blu:m] *n* fleur *f*; (*fig*) épanouissement *m* ▷ *vi* être en fleur; (*fig*) s'épanouir; être florissant(e)
blooming ['blu:mɪŋ] *adj* (*inf*): **this ~ ...** ce fichu *or* sacré ...
blossom ['blɔsəm] *n* fleur(s) *f(pl)* ▷ *vi* être en fleurs; (*fig*) s'épanouir; **to ~ into** (*fig*) devenir
blot [blɔt] *n* tache *f* ▷ *vt* tacher; (*ink*) sécher; **to be a ~ on the landscape** gâcher le paysage; **to ~ one's copy book** (*fig*) faire un impair
▶ **blot out** *vt* (*memories*) effacer; (*view*) cacher, masquer; (*nation, city*) annihiler
blotchy ['blɔtʃɪ] *adj* (*complexion*) couvert(e) de marbrures
blotting paper ['blɔtɪŋ-] *n* buvard *m*
blotto ['blɔtəu] *adj* (*inf*) bourré(e)
blouse [blauz] *n* (*feminine garment*) chemisier *m*, corsage *m*
blow [bləu] (*pt* **blew**, *pp* **-n**) [blu:, bləun] *n* coup *m* ▷ *vi* souffler ▷ *vt* (*glass*) souffler; (*instrument*) jouer de; (*fuse*) faire sauter; **to ~ one's nose** se moucher; **to ~ a whistle** siffler; **to come to ~s** en venir aux coups
▶ **blow away** *vi* s'envoler ▷ *vt* chasser, faire s'envoler
▶ **blow down** *vt* faire tomber, renverser
▶ **blow off** *vi* s'envoler ▷ *vt* (*hat*) emporter;

(*ship*): **to ~ off course** faire dévier
▶ **blow out** *vi* (*fire, flame*) s'éteindre; (*tyre*) éclater; (*fuse*) sauter
▶ **blow over** *vi* s'apaiser
▶ **blow up** *vi* exploser, sauter ▷ *vt* faire sauter; (*tyre*) gonfler; (*Phot*) agrandir
blow-dry ['bləudraɪ] *n* (*hairstyle*) brushing *m* ▷ *vt* faire un brushing à
blowlamp ['bləulæmp] *n* (*Brit*) chalumeau *m*
blown [bləun] *pp of* **blow**
blow-out ['bləuaut] *n* (*of tyre*) éclatement *m*; (*Brit: inf: big meal*) gueuleton *m*
blowtorch ['bləutɔ:tʃ] *n* chalumeau *m*
blowzy ['blauzɪ] *adj* (*Brit*) peu soigné(e)
BLS *n abbr* (*US*) = **Bureau of Labor Statistics**
blubber ['blʌbəʳ] *n* blanc *m* de baleine ▷ *vi* (*pej*) pleurer comme un veau
bludgeon ['blʌdʒən] *n* gourdin *m*, trique *f*
blue [blu:] *adj* bleu(e); (*depressed*) triste; **~ film/joke** film *m*/histoire *f* pornographique; (**only**) **once in a ~ moon** tous les trente-six du mois; **out of the ~** (*fig*) à l'improviste, sans qu'on s'y attende
blue baby *n* enfant bleu(e)
bluebell ['blu:bɛl] *n* jacinthe *f* des bois
blueberry ['blu:bərɪ] *n* myrtille *f*, airelle *f*
bluebottle ['blu:bɔtl] *n* mouche *f* à viande
blue cheese *n* (fromage) bleu *m*
blue-chip ['blu:tʃɪp] *adj*: **~ investment** investissement *m* de premier ordre
blue-collar worker ['blu:kɔləʳ-] *n* ouvrier(-ère) col bleu
blue jeans *npl* blue-jeans *mpl*
blueprint ['blu:prɪnt] *n* bleu *m*; (*fig*) projet *m*, plan directeur
blues [blu:z] *npl*: **the ~** (*Mus*) le blues; **to have the ~** (*inf: feeling*) avoir le cafard
bluff [blʌf] *vi* bluffer ▷ *n* bluff *m*; (*cliff*) promontoire *m*, falaise *f* ▷ *adj* (*person*) bourru(e), brusque; **to call sb's ~** mettre qn au défi d'exécuter ses menaces
blunder ['blʌndəʳ] *n* gaffe *f*, bévue *f* ▷ *vi* faire une gaffe *or* une bévue; **to ~ into sb/sth** buter contre qn/qch
blunt [blʌnt] *adj* (*knife*) émoussé(e), peu tranchant(e); (*pencil*) mal taillé(e); (*person*) brusque, ne mâchant pas ses mots ▷ *vt* émousser; **~ instrument** (*Law*) instrument contondant
bluntly ['blʌntlɪ] *adv* carrément, sans prendre de gants
bluntness ['blʌntnɪs] *n* (*of person*) brusquerie *f*, franchise brutale
blur [blə:ʳ] *n* (*shape*): **to become a ~** devenir flou ▷ *vt* brouiller, rendre flou(e)
blurb [blə:b] *n* (*for book*) texte *m* de présentation; (*pej*) baratin *m*
blurred [blə:d] *adj* flou(e)
blurt [blə:t]: **to ~ out** *vt* (*reveal*) lâcher; (*say*) balbutier, dire d'une voix entrecoupée
blush [blʌʃ] *vi* rougir ▷ *n* rougeur *f*
blusher ['blʌʃəʳ] *n* rouge *m* à joues

bluster ['blʌstər] n paroles fpl en l'air; (boasting) fanfaronnades fpl; (threats) menaces fpl en l'air ▷ vi parler en l'air; fanfaronner

blustering ['blʌstərɪŋ] adj fanfaron(ne)

blustery ['blʌstərɪ] adj (weather) à bourrasques

Blvd abbr (= boulevard) Bd

BM n abbr = **British Museum**; (Scol: = Bachelor of Medicine) diplôme universitaire

BMA n abbr = **British Medical Association**

BMJ n abbr = **British Medical Journal**

BMus n abbr (= Bachelor of Music) diplôme universitaire

BMX n abbr (= bicycle motorcross) BMX m

BO n abbr (inf: = body odour) odeurs corporelles; (US) = **box office**

boar [bɔːr] n sanglier m

board [bɔːd] n (wooden) planche f; (on wall) panneau m; (for chess etc) plateau m; (cardboard) carton m; (committee) conseil m, comité m; (in firm) conseil d'administration; (Naut, Aviat): **on ~** à bord ▷ vt (ship) monter à bord de; (train) monter dans; **full ~** (Brit) pension complète; **half ~** (Brit) demi-pension f; **~ and lodging** (n) chambre f avec pension; **with ~ and lodging** logé nourri; **above ~** (fig) régulier(-ère); **across the ~** (fig: adv) systématiquement; (: adj) de portée générale; **to go by the ~** (hopes, principles) être abandonné(e); (be unimportant) compter pour rien, n'avoir aucune importance

▶ **board up** vt (door) condamner (au moyen de planches, de tôle)

boarder ['bɔːdər] n pensionnaire m/f; (Scol) interne m/f, pensionnaire

board game n jeu m de société

boarding card ['bɔːdɪŋ-] n (Aviat, Naut) carte f d'embarquement

boarding house ['bɔːdɪŋ-] n pension f

boarding party ['bɔːdɪŋ-] n section f d'abordage

boarding pass ['bɔːdɪŋ-] n (Brit) = **boarding card**

boarding school ['bɔːdɪŋ-] n internat m, pensionnat m

board meeting n réunion f du conseil d'administration

board room n salle f du conseil d'administration

boardwalk ['bɔːdwɔːk] n (US) cheminement m en planches

boast [bəust] vi: **to ~ (about or of)** se vanter (de) ▷ vt s'enorgueillir de ▷ n vantardise f; sujet m d'orgueil or de fierté

boastful ['bəustful] adj vantard(e)

boastfulness ['bəustfulnɪs] n vantardise f

boat [bəut] n bateau m; (small) canot m; barque f; **to go by ~** aller en bateau; **to be in the same ~** (fig) être logé à la même enseigne

boater ['bəutər] n (hat) canotier m

boating ['bəutɪŋ] n canotage m

boat people npl boat people mpl

boatswain ['bəusn] n maître m d'équipage

bob [bɔb] vi (boat, cork on water: also: **bob up and down**) danser, se balancer ▷ n (Brit inf) = **shilling**

▶ **bob up** vi surgir or apparaître brusquement

bobbin ['bɔbɪn] n bobine f; (of sewing machine) navette f

bobby ['bɔbɪ] n (Brit inf) ≈ agent m (de police)

bobby pin ['bɔbɪ-] n (US) pince f à cheveux

bobsleigh ['bɔbsleɪ] n bob m

bode [bəud] vi: **to ~ well/ill (for)** être de bon/mauvais augure (pour)

bodice ['bɔdɪs] n corsage m

bodily ['bɔdɪlɪ] adj corporel(le); (pain, comfort) physique; (needs) matériel(le) ▷ adv (carry, lift) dans ses bras

body ['bɔdɪ] n corps m; (of car) carrosserie f; (of plane) fuselage m; (also: **body stocking**) body m, justaucorps m; (fig: society) organe m, organisme m; (: quantity) ensemble m, masse f; (of wine) corps; **ruling ~** organe directeur; **in a ~** en masse, ensemble; (speak) comme un seul et même homme

body blow n (fig) coup dur, choc m

body-building ['bɔdɪbɪldɪŋ] n body-building m, culturisme m

bodyguard ['bɔdɪgɑːd] n garde m du corps

body language n langage m du corps

body repairs npl travaux mpl de carrosserie

body search n fouille f (corporelle); **to carry out a ~ on sb** fouiller qn; **to submit to or undergo a ~** se faire fouiller

bodywork ['bɔdɪwəːk] n carrosserie f

boffin ['bɔfɪn] n (Brit) savant m

bog [bɔg] n tourbière f ▷ vt: **to get ~ged down (in)** (fig) s'enliser (dans)

boggle ['bɔgl] vi: **the mind ~s** c'est incroyable, on en reste sidéré

bogie ['bəugɪ] n bogie m

Bogotá [bəugə'tɑː] n Bogotá

bogus ['bəugəs] adj bidon inv; fantôme

Bohemia [bəu'hiːmɪə] n Bohême f

Bohemian [bəu'hiːmɪən] adj bohémien(ne) ▷ n Bohémien(ne); (gipsy: also: **bohemian**) bohémien(ne)

boil [bɔɪl] vt (faire) bouillir ▷ vi bouillir ▷ n (Med) furoncle m; **to come to the or (US) a ~** bouillir; **to bring to the or (US) a ~** porter à ébullition

▶ **boil down** vi (fig): **to ~ down to** se réduire or ramener à

▶ **boil over** vi déborder

boiled egg n œuf m à la coque

boiler ['bɔɪlər] n chaudière f

boiler suit n (Brit) bleu m de travail, combinaison f

boiling ['bɔɪlɪŋ] adj: **I'm ~ (hot)** (inf) je crève de chaud

boiling point n point m d'ébullition

boil-in-the-bag [bɔɪlɪnðə'bæg] adj (rice etc) en sachet cuisson

boisterous ['bɔɪstərəs] adj bruyant(e), tapageur(-euse)

bold [bəuld] adj hardi(e), audacieux(-euse); (pej) effronté(e); (outline, colour) franc (franche), tranché(e), marqué(e)

boldness ['bəʊldnɪs] n hardiesse f, audace f; aplomb m, effronterie f

bold type n (Typ) caractères mpl gras

Bolivia [bə'lɪvɪə] n Bolivie f

Bolivian [bə'lɪvɪən] adj bolivien(ne) ▷ n Bolivien(ne)

bollard ['bɒləd] n (Naut) bitte f d'amarrage; (Brit Aut) borne lumineuse or de signalisation

Bollywood ['bɒlɪwʊd] n Bollywood m

bolshy ['bɒlʃɪ] adj râleur(-euse); **to be in a ~ mood** être peu coopératif(-ive)

bolster ['bəʊlstə^r] n traversin m
▶ **bolster up** vt soutenir

bolt [bəʊlt] n verrou m; (with nut) boulon m ▷ adv: **~ upright** droit(e) comme un piquet ▷ vt (door) verrouiller; (food) engloutir ▷ vi se sauver, filer (comme une flèche); **a ~ from the blue** (horse) s'emballer; (fig) un coup de tonnerre dans un ciel bleu

bomb [bɒm] n bombe f ▷ vt bombarder

bombard [bɒm'bɑːd] vt bombarder

bombardment [bɒm'bɑːdmənt] n bombardement m

bombastic [bɒm'bæstɪk] adj grandiloquent(e), pompeux(-euse)

bomb disposal n: **~ unit** section f de déminage; **~ expert** artificier m

bomber ['bɒmə^r] n caporal m d'artillerie; (Aviat) bombardier m; (terrorist) poseur m de bombes

bombing ['bɒmɪŋ] n bombardement m

bomb scare n alerte f à la bombe

bombshell ['bɒmʃɛl] n obus m; (fig) bombe f

bomb site n zone f de bombardement

bona fide ['bəʊnə'faɪdɪ] adj de bonne foi; (offer) sérieux(-euse)

bonanza [bə'nænzə] n filon m

bond [bɒnd] n lien m; (binding promise) engagement m, obligation f; (Finance) obligation; **bonds** npl (chains) chaînes fpl; **in ~** (of goods) en entrepôt

bondage ['bɒndɪdʒ] n esclavage m

bonded warehouse ['bɒndɪd-] n entrepôt m sous douanes

bone [bəʊn] n os m; (of fish) arête f ▷ vt désosser; ôter les arêtes de

bone china n porcelaine f tendre

bone-dry ['bəʊn'draɪ] adj absolument sec (sèche)

bone idle adj fainéant(e)

bone marrow n moelle osseuse

boner ['bəʊnə^r] n (US) gaffe f, bourde f

bonfire ['bɒnfaɪə^r] n feu m (de joie); (for rubbish) feu

bonk [bɒŋk] (inf!) vt s'envoyer (!), sauter (!) ▷ vi s'envoyer en l'air (!)

bonkers ['bɒŋkəz] adj (Brit inf) cinglé(e), dingue

Bonn [bɒn] n Bonn

bonnet ['bɒnɪt] n bonnet m; (Brit: of car) capot m

bonny ['bɒnɪ] adj (Scottish) joli(e)

bonus ['bəʊnəs] n (money) prime f; (advantage) avantage m

bony ['bəʊnɪ] adj (arm, face: Med: tissue) osseux(-euse); (thin: person) squelettique; (meat) plein(e) d'os; (fish) plein d'arêtes

boo [buː] excl hou!, peuh! ▷ vt huer ▷ n huée f

boob [buːb] n (inf: breast) nichon m; (: Brit: mistake) gaffe f

booby prize ['buːbɪ-] n timbale f (ironique)

booby trap ['buːbɪ-] n guet-apens m

booby-trapped ['buːbɪtræpt] adj piégé(e)

book [buk] n livre m; (of stamps, tickets etc) carnet m; (Comm): **books** npl comptes mpl, comptabilité f ▷ vt (ticket) prendre; (seat, room) réserver; (driver) dresser un procès-verbal à; (football player) prendre le nom de, donner un carton à; **I ~ed a table in the name of ...** j'ai réservé une table au nom de ...; **to keep the ~s** tenir la comptabilité; **by the ~** à la lettre, selon les règles; **to throw the ~ at sb** passer un savon à qn
▶ **book in** vi (Brit: at hotel) prendre sa chambre
▶ **book up** vt réserver; **all seats are ~ed up** tout est pris, c'est complet

bookable ['bukəbl] adj: **seats are ~** on peut réserver ses places

bookcase ['bukkeɪs] n bibliothèque f (meuble)

book ends npl serre-livres m inv

booking ['bukɪŋ] n (Brit) réservation f; **I confirmed my ~ by fax/email** j'ai confirmé ma réservation par fax/e-mail

booking office n (Brit) bureau m de location

book-keeping ['buk'kiːpɪŋ] n comptabilité f

booklet ['buklɪt] n brochure f

bookmaker ['bukmeɪkə^r] n bookmaker m

bookmark ['bukmɑːk] n (for book) marque-page m; (Comput) signet m

bookseller ['buksɛlə^r] n libraire m/f

bookshelf ['bukʃɛlf] n (single) étagère f (à livres); (bookcase) bibliothèque f; **bookshelves** rayons mpl (de bibliothèque)

bookshop ['bukʃɒp], **bookstore** n librairie f

bookstall ['bukstɔːl] n kiosque m à journaux

book store ['bukstɔː^r] n = bookshop

book token n bon-cadeau m (pour un livre)

book value n valeur f comptable

bookworm ['bukwəːm] n dévoreur(-euse) de livres

boom [buːm] n (noise) grondement m; (in prices, population) forte augmentation; (busy period) boom m, vague f de prospérité ▷ vi gronder; prospérer

boomerang ['buːməræŋ] n boomerang m

boom town n ville f en plein essor

boon [buːn] n bénédiction f, grand avantage

boorish ['buərɪʃ] adj grossier(-ère), rustre

boost [buːst] n stimulant m, remontant m ▷ vt stimuler; **to give a ~ to sb's spirits** or **to sb** remonter le moral à qn

booster ['buːstə^r] n (TV) amplificateur m (de signal); (Elec) survolteur m; (also: **booster rocket**) booster m; (Med: vaccine) rappel m

booster seat n (Aut: for children) siège m rehausseur

boot [buːt] n botte f; (for hiking) chaussure f (de

marche); (*ankle boot*) bottine f; (*Brit: of car*) coffre m ▷ vt (*Comput*) lancer, mettre en route; **to ~** (*in addition*) par-dessus le marché, en plus; **to give sb the ~** (*inf*) flanquer qn dehors, virer qn

booth [buːð] n (*at fair*) baraque (foraine); (*of telephone etc*) cabine f; (*also:* **voting booth**) isoloir m

bootleg ['buːtlɛg] adj de contrebande; **~ record** enregistrement m pirate

booty ['buːtɪ] n butin m

booze [buːz] (*inf*) n boissons fpl alcooliques, alcool m ▷ vi boire, picoler

boozer ['buːzə^r] n (*inf: person*): **he's a ~** il picole pas mal; (*Brit inf: pub*) pub m

border ['bɔːdə^r] n bordure f; bord m; (*of a country*) frontière f; **the B~s** la région frontière entre l'Écosse et l'Angleterre

▶ **border on** vt fus être voisin(e) de, toucher à

borderline ['bɔːdəlaɪn] n (*fig*) ligne f de démarcation ▷ adj: **~ case** cas m limite

bore [bɔː^r] pt of **bear** ▷ vt (*person*) ennuyer, raser; (*hole*) percer; (*well, tunnel*) creuser ▷ n (*person*) raseur(-euse); (*boring thing*) barbe f; (*of gun*) calibre m

bored [bɔːd] adj: **to be ~** s'ennuyer; **he's ~ to tears** or **to death** or **stiff** il s'ennuie à mourir

boredom ['bɔːdəm] n ennui m

boring ['bɔːrɪŋ] adj ennuyeux(-euse)

born [bɔːn] adj: **to be ~** naître; **I was ~ in 1960** je suis né en 1960; **~ blind** aveugle de naissance; **a ~ comedian** un comédien-né

born-again [bɔːnə'gɛn] adj: **~ Christian** ≈ évangéliste m/f

borne [bɔːn] pp of **bear**

Borneo ['bɔːnɪəu] n Bornéo f

borough ['bʌrə] n municipalité f

borrow ['bɔrəu] vt: **to ~ sth (from sb)** emprunter qch (à qn); **may I ~ your car?** est-ce que je peux vous emprunter votre voiture?

borrower ['bɔrəuə^r] n emprunteur(-euse)

borrowing ['bɔrəuɪŋ] n emprunt(s) mpl

borstal ['bɔːstl] n (*Brit*) ≈ maison f de correction

Bosnia ['bɔznɪə] n Bosnie f

Bosnia-Herzegovina ['bɔznɪə-hɛrzə'gəuviːnə] n, **Bosnia-Hercegovina** Bosnie-Herzégovine f

Bosnian ['bɔznɪən] adj bosniaque, bosnien(ne) ▷ n Bosniaque m/f, Bosnien(ne)

bosom ['buzəm] n poitrine f; (*fig*) sein m

bosom friend n ami(e) intime

boss [bɔs] n patron(ne) ▷ vt (*also:* **boss about, boss around**) mener à la baguette

bossy ['bɔsɪ] adj autoritaire

bosun ['bəusn] n maître m d'équipage

botanical [bə'tænɪkl] adj botanique

botanist ['bɔtənɪst] n botaniste m/f

botany ['bɔtənɪ] n botanique f

botch [bɔtʃ] vt (*also:* **botch up**) saboter, bâcler

both [bəuθ] adj les deux, l'un(e) et l'autre ▷ pron: **~ (of them)** les deux, tous (toutes) (les) deux, l'un(e) et l'autre; **~ of us went**, **we ~ went** nous y sommes allés tous les deux ▷ adv: **~ A and B** A et B; **they sell ~ the fabric and the finished**

curtains ils vendent (et) le tissu et les rideaux (finis), ils vendent à la fois le tissu et les rideaux (finis)

bother ['bɔðə^r] vt (*worry*) tracasser; (*needle, bait*) importuner, ennuyer; (*disturb*) déranger ▷ vi (*also:* **bother o.s.**) se tracasser, se faire du souci ▷ n (*trouble*) ennuis mpl; **it is a ~ to have to do** c'est vraiment ennuyeux d'avoir à faire ▷ excl zut!; **to ~ doing** prendre la peine de faire; **I'm sorry to ~ you** excusez-moi de vous déranger; **please don't ~** ne vous dérangez pas; **don't ~** ce n'est pas la peine; **it's no ~** aucun problème

Botswana [bɔt'swaːnə] n Botswana m

bottle ['bɔtl] n bouteille f; (*baby's*) biberon m; (*of perfume, medicine*) flacon m ▷ vt mettre en bouteille(s); **~ of wine/milk** bouteille de vin/lait; **wine/milk ~** bouteille à vin/lait

▶ **bottle up** vt refouler, contenir

bottle bank n conteneur m (de bouteilles)

bottleneck ['bɔtlnɛk] n (*in traffic*) bouchon m; (*in production*) goulet m d'étranglement

bottle-opener ['bɔtləupnə^r] n ouvre-bouteille m

bottom ['bɔtəm] n (*of container, sea etc*) fond m; (*buttocks*) derrière m; (*of page, list*) bas m; (*of chair*) siège m; (*of mountain, tree, hill*) pied m ▷ adj (*shelf, step*) du bas; **to get to the ~ of sth** (*fig*) découvrir le fin fond de qch

bottomless ['bɔtəmlɪs] adj sans fond, insondable

bottom line n: **the ~ is that ...** l'essentiel, c'est que ...

botulism ['bɔtjulɪzəm] n botulisme m

bough [bau] n branche f, rameau m

bought [bɔːt] pt, pp of **buy**

boulder ['bəuldə^r] n gros rocher (*gén lisse, arrondi*)

bounce [bauns] vi (*ball*) rebondir; (*cheque*) être refusé (*étant sans provision*); (*also:* **to bounce forward/out etc**) bondir, s'élancer ▷ vt faire rebondir ▷ n (*rebound*) rebond m; **he's got plenty of ~** (*fig*) il est plein d'entrain or d'allant

bouncer ['baunsə^r] n (*inf: at dance, club*) videur m

bound [baund] pt, pp of **bind** ▷ n (*gen pl*) limite f; (*leap*) bond m ▷ vi (*leap*) bondir ▷ vt (*limit*) borner ▷ adj: **to be ~ to do sth** (*obliged*) être obligé(e) or avoir obligation de faire qch; **he's ~ to fail** (*likely*) il est sûr d'échouer, son échec est inévitable or assuré; **~ by** (*law, regulation*) engagé(e) par; **~ for** à destination de; **out of ~s** dont l'accès est interdit

boundary ['baundrɪ] n frontière f

boundless ['baundlɪs] adj illimité(e), sans bornes

bountiful ['bauntɪful] adj (*person*) généreux(-euse); (*God*) bienfaiteur(-trice); (*supply*) ample

bounty ['bauntɪ] n (*generosity*) générosité f

bouquet ['bukeɪ] n bouquet m

bourbon ['buəbən] n (*US: also:* **bourbon whiskey**) bourbon m

bourgeois ['buəʒwɑː] adj, n bourgeois(e)

bout [baut] n période f; (*of malaria etc*) accès m,

crise f, attaque f; (Boxing etc) combat m, match m

boutique [buːˈtiːk] n boutique f

bow¹ [bəu] n nœud m; (weapon) arc m; (Mus) archet m

bow² [bau] n (with body) révérence f, inclination f (du buste or corps); (Naut: also: **bows**) proue f ▷ vi faire une révérence, s'incliner; (yield): **to ~ to** or **before** s'incliner devant, se soumettre à; **to ~ to the inevitable** accepter l'inévitable or l'inéluctable

bowels [bauəlz] npl intestins mpl; (fig) entrailles fpl

bowl [bəul] n (for eating) bol m; (for washing) cuvette f; (ball) boule f; (of pipe) fourneau m ▷ vi (Cricket) lancer (la balle)
  ▶ **bowl over** vt (fig) renverser

bow-legged ['bəuˈlɛgɪd] adj aux jambes arquées

bowler ['bəulər] n joueur m de boules; (Cricket) lanceur m (de la balle); (Brit: also: **bowler hat**) (chapeau m) melon m

bowling ['bəulɪŋ] n (game) jeu m de boules, jeu de quilles

bowling alley n bowling m

bowling green n terrain m de boules (gazonné et carré)

bowls [bəulz] n (jeu m de) boules fpl

bow tie [bəu-] n nœud m papillon

box [bɔks] n boîte f; (also: **cardboard box**) carton m; (crate) caisse f; (Theat) loge f ▷ vt mettre en boîte; (Sport) boxer avec ▷ vi boxer, faire de la boxe

boxer ['bɔksər] n (person) boxeur m; (dog) boxer m

boxer shorts ['bɔksəfɔːts] npl caleçon m

boxing ['bɔksɪŋ] n (sport) boxe f

Boxing Day n (Brit) le lendemain de Noël; voir article

● **BOXING DAY**
●
● Boxing Day est le lendemain de Noël, férié en
● Grande-Bretagne. Ce nom vient d'une
● coutume du XIXe siècle qui consistait à
● donner des cadeaux de Noël (dans des
● boîtes) à ses employés etc le 26 décembre.

boxing gloves npl gants mpl de boxe

boxing ring n ring m

box number n (for advertisements) numéro m d'annonce

box office n bureau m de location

box room n débarras m; chambrette f

boy [bɔɪ] n garçon m

boy band n boys band m

boycott ['bɔɪkɔt] n boycottage m ▷ vt boycotter

boyfriend ['bɔɪfrɛnd] n (petit) ami

boyish ['bɔɪɪʃ] adj d'enfant, de garçon; **to look ~** (man: appear youthful) faire jeune

Bp abbr = **bishop**

BR abbr = **British Rail**

Br. abbr (Rel) = **brother**

bra [braː] n soutien-gorge m

brace [breɪs] n (support) attache f, agrafe f; (Brit: also: **braces**: on teeth) appareil m (dentaire); (tool)

vilebrequin m; (Typ: also: **brace bracket**) accolade f ▷ vt (support) consolider, soutenir; **braces** npl (Brit: for trousers) bretelles fpl; **to ~ o.s.** (fig) se préparer mentalement

bracelet ['breɪslɪt] n bracelet m

bracing ['breɪsɪŋ] adj tonifiant(e), tonique

bracken ['brækən] n fougère f

bracket ['brækɪt] n (Tech) tasseau m, support m; (group) classe f, tranche f; (also: **brace bracket**) accolade f; (also: **round bracket**) parenthèse f; (also: **square bracket**) crochet m ▷ vt mettre entre parenthèses; (fig: also: **bracket together**) regrouper; **income ~** tranche f des revenus; **in ~s** entre parenthèses or crochets

brackish ['brækɪʃ] adj (water) saumâtre

brag [bræg] vi se vanter

braid [breɪd] n (trimming) galon m; (of hair) tresse f, natte f

Braille [breɪl] n braille m

brain [breɪn] n cerveau m; **brains** npl (intellect, food) cervelle f; **he's got ~s** il est intelligent

brainchild ['breɪntʃaɪld] n trouvaille (personnelle), invention f

braindead ['breɪndɛd] adj (Med) dans un coma dépassé; (inf) demeuré(e)

brainless ['breɪnlɪs] adj sans cervelle, stupide

brainstorm ['breɪnstɔːm] n (fig) moment m d'égarement; (US: brainwave) idée f de génie

brainwash ['breɪnwɔʃ] vt faire subir un lavage de cerveau à

brainwave ['breɪnweɪv] n idée f de génie

brainy ['breɪnɪ] adj intelligent(e), doué(e)

braise [breɪz] vt braiser

brake [breɪk] n frein m ▷ vt, vi freiner

brake light n feu m de stop

brake pedal n pédale f de frein

bramble ['bræmbl] n ronces fpl; (fruit) mûre f

bran [bræn] n son m

branch [brɑːntʃ] n branche f; (Comm) succursale f; (: of bank) agence f; (of association) section locale ▷ vi bifurquer
  ▶ **branch off** vi (road) bifurquer
  ▶ **branch out** vi diversifier ses activités; **to ~ out into** étendre ses activités à

branch line n (Rail) bifurcation f, embranchement m

branch manager n directeur(-trice) de succursale (or d'agence)

brand [brænd] n marque (commerciale) ▷ vt (cattle) marquer (au fer rouge); (fig: pej): **to ~ sb a communist** etc traiter or qualifier qn de communiste etc

brandish ['brændɪʃ] vt brandir

brand name n nom m de marque

brand-new ['brænd'njuː] adj tout(e) neuf (neuve), flambant neuf (neuve)

brandy ['brændɪ] n cognac m, fine f

brash [bræʃ] adj effronté(e)

Brasilia [brə'zɪlɪə] n Brasilia

brass [brɑːs] n cuivre m (jaune), laiton m; **the ~** (Mus) les cuivres

brass band n fanfare f

brass tacks *npl*: **to get down to ~** en venir au fait

brat [bræt] *n* (*pej*) mioche *m/f*, môme *m/f*

bravado [brə'vɑːdəu] *n* bravade *f*

brave [breɪv] *adj* courageux(-euse), brave ▷ *n* guerrier indien ▷ *vt* braver, affronter

bravery ['breɪvərɪ] *n* bravoure *f*, courage *m*

brawl [brɔːl] *n* rixe *f*, bagarre *f* ▷ *vi* se bagarrer

brawn [brɔːn] *n* muscle *m*; (*meat*) fromage *m* de tête

brawny ['brɔːnɪ] *adj* musclé(e), costaud(e)

bray [breɪ] *n* braiement *m* ▷ *vi* braire

brazen ['breɪzn] *adj* impudent(e), effronté(e) ▷ *vt*: **to ~ it out** payer d'effronterie, crâner

brazier ['breɪzɪə'] *n* brasero *m*

Brazil [brə'zɪl] *n* Brésil *m*

Brazilian [brə'zɪljən] *adj* brésilien(ne) ▷ *n* Brésilien(ne)

Brazil nut *n* noix *f* du Brésil

breach [briːtʃ] *vt* ouvrir une brèche dans ▷ *n* (*gap*) brèche *f*; (*estrangement*) brouille *f*; (*breaking*): **~ of contract** rupture *f* de contrat; **~ of the peace** attentat *m* à l'ordre public; **~ of trust** abus *m* de confiance

bread [brɛd] *n* pain *m*; (*inf: money*) fric *m*; **~ and butter** (*n*) tartines (beurrées); (*fig*) subsistance *f*; **to earn one's daily ~** gagner son pain; **to know which side one's ~ is buttered (on)** savoir où est son avantage *or* intérêt

breadbin ['brɛdbɪn] *n* (*Brit*) boîte *f or* huche *f* à pain

breadboard ['brɛdbɔːd] *n* planche *f* à pain; (*Comput*) montage expérimental

breadbox ['brɛdbɔks] *n* (*US*) boîte *f or* huche *f* à pain

breadcrumbs ['brɛdkrʌmz] *npl* miettes *fpl* de pain; (*Culin*) chapelure *f*, panure *f*

breadline ['brɛdlaɪn] *n*: **to be on the ~** être sans le sou *or* dans l'indigence

breadth [brɛtθ] *n* largeur *f*

breadwinner ['brɛdwɪnə'] *n* soutien *m* de famille

break [breɪk] (*pt* **broke**, *pp* **broken** [brəuk, 'brəukən]) *vt* casser, briser; (*promise*) rompre; (*law*) violer ▷ *vi* se casser, se briser; (*weather*) tourner; (*storm*) éclater; (*day*) se lever ▷ *n* (*gap*) brèche *f*; (*fracture*) cassure *f*; (*rest*) interruption *f*, arrêt *m*; (*: short*) pause *f*; (*: at school*) récréation *f*; (*chance*) chance *f*, occasion *f* favorable; **to ~ one's leg** *etc* se casser la jambe *etc*; **to ~ a record** battre un record; **to ~ the news to sb** annoncer la nouvelle à qn; **to ~ with sb** rompre avec qn; **to ~ even** *vi* rentrer dans ses frais; **to ~ free** *or* **loose** *vi* se dégager, s'échapper; **to take a ~** (*few minutes*) faire une pause, s'arrêter cinq minutes; (*holiday*) prendre un peu de repos; **without a ~** sans interruption, sans arrêt

▸ **break down** *vt* (*door etc*) enfoncer; (*resistance*) venir à bout de; (*figures, data*) décomposer, analyser ▷ *vi* s'effondrer; (*Med*) faire une dépression (nerveuse); (*Aut*) tomber en panne; **my car has broken down** ma voiture est en

panne

▸ **break in** *vt* (*horse etc*) dresser ▷ *vi* (*burglar*) entrer par effraction; (*interrupt*) interrompre

▸ **break into** *vt fus* (*house*) s'introduire *or* pénétrer par effraction dans

▸ **break off** *vi* (*speaker*) s'interrompre; (*branch*) se rompre ▷ *vt* (*talks, engagement*) rompre

▸ **break open** *vt* (*door etc*) forcer, fracturer

▸ **break out** *vi* éclater, se déclarer; (*prisoner*) s'évader; **to ~ out in spots** se couvrir de boutons

▸ **break through** *vi*: **the sun broke through** le soleil a fait son apparition ▷ *vt fus* (*defences, barrier*) franchir; (*crowd*) se frayer un passage à travers

▸ **break up** *vi* (*partnership*) cesser, prendre fin; (*marriage*) se briser; (*crowd, meeting*) se séparer; (*ship*) se disloquer; (*Scol: pupils*) être en vacances; (*line*) couper; **the line's** *or* **you're ~ing up** ça coupe ▷ *vt* fracasser, casser; (*fight etc*) interrompre, faire cesser; (*marriage*) désunir

breakable ['breɪkəbl] *adj* cassable, fragile ▷ *n*: **~s** objets *mpl* fragiles

breakage ['breɪkɪdʒ] *n* casse *f*; **to pay for ~s** payer la casse

breakaway ['breɪkəweɪ] *adj* (*group etc*) dissident(e)

breakdown ['breɪkdaun] *n* (*Aut*) panne *f*; (*in communications, marriage*) rupture *f*; (*Med: also*: **nervous breakdown**) dépression (nerveuse); (*of figures*) ventilation *f*, répartition *f*

breakdown service *n* (*Brit*) service *m* de dépannage

breakdown truck, (*US*) **breakdown van** *n* dépanneuse *f*

breaker ['breɪkə'] *n* brisant *m*

breakeven ['breɪk'iːvn] *cpd*: **~ chart** graphique *m* de rentabilité; **~ point** seuil *m* de rentabilité

breakfast ['brɛkfəst] *n* petit déjeuner *m*; **what time is ~?** le petit déjeuner est à quelle heure?

breakfast cereal *n* céréales *fpl*

break-in ['breɪkɪn] *n* cambriolage *m*

breaking and entering *n* (*Law*) effraction *f*

breaking point ['breɪkɪŋ-] *n* limites *fpl*

breakthrough ['breɪkθruː] *n* percée *f*

break-up ['breɪkʌp] *n* (*of partnership, marriage*) rupture *f*

break-up value *n* (*Comm*) valeur *f* de liquidation

breakwater ['breɪkwɔːtə'] *n* brise-lames *m inv*, digue *f*

breast [brɛst] *n* (*of woman*) sein *m*; (*chest*) poitrine *f*; (*of chicken, turkey*) blanc *m*

breast-feed ['brɛstfiːd] *vt, vi* (*irreg: like* **feed**) allaiter

breast pocket *n* poche *f* (de) poitrine

breast-stroke ['brɛststrəuk] *n* brasse *f*

breath [brɛθ] *n* haleine *f*, souffle *m*; **to go out for a ~ of air** sortir prendre l'air; **to take a deep ~** respirer à fond; **out of ~** à bout de souffle, essoufflé(e)

breathalyse ['brɛθəlaɪz] *vt* faire subir l'alcootest à

Breathalyser® [ˈbrɛθəlaɪzəʳ] (*Brit*) *n* alcootest *m*
breathe [briːð] *vt, vi* respirer; **I won't ~ a word about it** je n'en soufflerai pas mot, je n'en dirai rien à personne
  ▸ **breathe in** *vi* inspirer ▷ *vt* aspirer
  ▸ **breathe out** *vt, vi* expirer
breather [ˈbriːðəʳ] *n* moment *m* de repos *or* de répit
breathing [ˈbriːðɪŋ] *n* respiration *f*
breathing space *n* (*fig*) (moment *m* de) répit *m*
breathless [ˈbrɛθlɪs] *adj* essoufflé(e), haletant(e), oppressé(e); **~ with excitement** le souffle coupé par l'émotion
breathtaking [ˈbrɛθteɪkɪŋ] *adj* stupéfiant(e), à vous couper le souffle
breath test *n* alcootest *m*
bred [brɛd] *pt, pp of* **breed**
-bred [brɛd] *suffix:* **well/ill~** bien/mal élevé(e)
breed [briːd] (*pt, pp* **bred**) [brɛd] *vt* élever, faire l'élevage de; (*fig: hate, suspicion*) engendrer ▷ *vi* se reproduire ▷ *n* race *f*, variété *f*
breeder [ˈbriːdəʳ] *n* (*person*) éleveur *m*; (*Physics: also:* **breeder reactor**) (réacteur *m*) surrégénérateur *m*
breeding [ˈbriːdɪŋ] *n* reproduction *f*; élevage *m*; (*upbringing*) éducation *f*
breeze [briːz] *n* brise *f*
breeze-block [ˈbriːzblɔk] *n* (*Brit*) parpaing *m*
breezy [ˈbriːzɪ] *adj* (*day, weather*) venteux(-euse); (*manner*) désinvolte; (*person*) jovial(e)
Breton [ˈbrɛtən] *adj* breton(ne) ▷ *n* Breton(ne); (*Ling*) breton *m*
brevity [ˈbrɛvɪtɪ] *n* brièveté *f*
brew [bruː] *vt* (*tea*) faire infuser; (*beer*) brasser; (*plot*) tramer, préparer ▷ *vi* (*tea*) infuser; (*beer*) fermenter; (*fig*) se préparer, couver
brewer [ˈbruːəʳ] *n* brasseur *m*
brewery [ˈbruːərɪ] *n* brasserie *f* (*fabrique*)
briar [ˈbraɪəʳ] *n* (*thorny bush*) ronces *fpl*; (*wild rose*) églantine *f*
bribe [braɪb] *n* pot-de-vin *m* ▷ *vt* acheter; soudoyer; **to ~ sb to do sth** soudoyer qn pour qu'il fasse qch
bribery [ˈbraɪbərɪ] *n* corruption *f*
bric-a-brac [ˈbrɪkəbræk] *n* bric-à-brac *m*
brick [brɪk] *n* brique *f*
bricklayer [ˈbrɪkleɪəʳ] *n* maçon *m*
brickwork [ˈbrɪkwəːk] *n* briquetage *m*, maçonnerie *f*
brickworks [ˈbrɪkwəːks] *n* briqueterie *f*
bridal [ˈbraɪdl] *adj* nuptial(e); **~ party** noce *f*
bride [braɪd] *n* mariée *f*, épouse *f*
bridegroom [ˈbraɪdgruːm] *n* marié *m*, époux *m*
bridesmaid [ˈbraɪdzmeɪd] *n* demoiselle *f* d'honneur
bridge [brɪdʒ] *n* pont *m*; (*Naut*) passerelle *f* (de commandement); (*of nose*) arête *f*; (*Cards, Dentistry*) bridge *m* ▷ *vt* (*river*) construire un pont sur; (*gap*) combler
bridging loan [ˈbrɪdʒɪŋ-] *n* (*Brit*) prêt *m* relais
bridle [ˈbraɪdl] *n* bride *f* ▷ *vt* refréner, mettre la bride à; (*horse*) brider

bridle path *n* piste *or* allée cavalière
brief [briːf] *adj* bref (brève) ▷ *n* (*Law*) dossier *m*, cause *f*; (*gen*) tâche *f* ▷ *vt* mettre au courant; (*Mil*) donner des instructions à; **briefs** *npl* slip *m*; **in ~ ...** (en) bref ...
briefcase [ˈbriːfkeɪs] *n* serviette *f*; porte-documents *m inv*
briefing [ˈbriːfɪŋ] *n* instructions *fpl*; (*Press*) briefing *m*
briefly [ˈbriːflɪ] *adv* brièvement; (*visit*) en coup de vent; **to glimpse ~** entrevoir
briefness [ˈbriːfnɪs] *n* brièveté *f*
Brig. *abbr* = **brigadier**
brigade [brɪˈgeɪd] *n* (*Mil*) brigade *f*
brigadier [brɪgəˈdɪəʳ] *n* brigadier général
bright [braɪt] *adj* brillant(e); (*room, weather*) clair(e); (*person: clever*) intelligent(e), doué(e); (*: cheerful*) gai(e); (*idea*) génial(e); (*colour*) vif (vive); **to look on the ~ side** regarder le bon côté des choses
brighten [ˈbraɪtn] (*also:* **brighten up**) *vt* (*room*) éclaircir; égayer ▷ *vi* s'éclaircir; (*person*) retrouver un peu de sa gaieté
brightly [ˈbraɪtlɪ] *adv* brillamment
brill [brɪl] *adj* (*Brit inf*) super *inv*
brilliance [ˈbrɪljəns] *n* éclat *m*; (*fig: of person*) brio *m*
brilliant [ˈbrɪljənt] *adj* brillant(e); (*light, sunshine*) éclatant(e); (*inf: great*) super
brim [brɪm] *n* bord *m*
brimful [ˈbrɪmˈful] *adj* plein(e) à ras bord; (*fig*) débordant(e)
brine [braɪn] *n* eau salée; (*Culin*) saumure *f*
bring (*pt, pp* **brought**) [brɪŋ, brɔːt] *vt* (*thing*) apporter; (*person*) amener; **to ~ sth to an end** mettre fin à qch; **I can't ~ myself to fire him** je ne peux me résoudre à le mettre à la porte
  ▸ **bring about** *vt* provoquer, entraîner
  ▸ **bring back** *vt* rapporter; (*person*) ramener
  ▸ **bring down** *vt* (*lower*) abaisser; (*shoot down*) abattre; (*government*) faire s'effondrer
  ▸ **bring forward** *vt* avancer; (*Book-Keeping*) reporter
  ▸ **bring in** *vt* (*person*) faire entrer; (*object*) rentrer; (*Pol: legislation*) introduire; (*Law: verdict*) rendre; (*produce: income*) rapporter
  ▸ **bring off** *vt* (*task, plan*) réussir, mener à bien; (*deal*) mener à bien
  ▸ **bring on** *vt* (*illness, attack*) provoquer; (*player, substitute*) amener
  ▸ **bring out** *vt* sortir; (*meaning*) faire ressortir, mettre en relief; (*new product, book*) sortir
  ▸ **bring round, bring to** *vt* (*unconscious person*) ranimer
  ▸ **bring up** *vt* élever; (*carry up*) monter; (*question*) soulever; (*food: vomit*) vomir, rendre
brink [brɪŋk] *n* bord *m*; **on the ~ of doing** sur le point de faire, à deux doigts de faire; **she was on the ~ of tears** elle était au bord des larmes
brisk [brɪsk] *adj* vif (vive); (*abrupt*) brusque; (*trade etc*) actif(-ive); **to go for a ~ walk** se promener d'un bon pas; **business is ~** les

affaires marchent (bien)

bristle ['brɪsl] n poil m ▷ vi se hérisser;
bristling with hérissé(e) de

bristly ['brɪslɪ] adj (beard, hair) hérissé(e); **your
chin's all ~** ton menton gratte

Brit [brɪt] n abbr (inf: = British person) Britannique
m/f

Britain ['brɪtən] n (also: **Great Britain**) la
Grande-Bretagne; **in ~** en Grande-Bretagne

British ['brɪtɪʃ] adj britannique ▷ npl: **the ~** les
Britanniques mpl

British Isles npl: **the ~** les îles fpl Britanniques

British Rail n compagnie ferroviaire britannique,
≈ SNCF f

British Summer Time n heure f d'été
britannique

Briton ['brɪtən] n Britannique m/f

Brittany ['brɪtənɪ] n Bretagne f

brittle ['brɪtl] adj cassant(e), fragile

Bro. abbr (Rel) = **brother**

broach [brəutʃ] vt (subject) aborder

B road n (Brit) ≈ route départementale

broad [brɔ:d] adj large; (distinction) général(e);
(accent) prononcé(e) ▷ n (US inf) nana f; **~ hint**
allusion transparente; **in ~ daylight** en plein
jour; **the ~ outlines** les grandes lignes

broadband ['brɔ:dbænd] n transmission f à
haut débit

broad bean n fève f

broadcast ['brɔ:dkɑ:st] (pt, pp -) n émission f ▷ vt
(Radio) radiodiffuser; (TV) téléviser ▷ vi émettre

broadcaster ['brɔ:dkɑ:stə'] n personnalité f de
la radio or de la télévision

broadcasting ['brɔ:dkɑ:stɪŋ] n radiodiffusion f;
télévision f

broadcasting station n station f de radio (or de
télévision)

broaden ['brɔ:dn] vt élargir; **to ~ one's mind**
élargir ses horizons ▷ vi s'élargir

broadly ['brɔ:dlɪ] adv en gros, généralement

broad-minded ['brɔ:d'maɪndɪd] adj large
d'esprit

broadsheet ['brɔ:dʃi:t] n (Brit) journal m grand
format

broccoli ['brɒkəlɪ] n brocoli m

brochure ['brəuʃjuə'] n prospectus m, dépliant m

brogue [brəug] n (accent) accent régional; (shoe)
(sorte de) chaussure basse de cuir épais

broil [brɔɪl] (US) vt rôtir

broke [brəuk] pt of **break** ▷ adj (inf) fauché(e); **to
go ~** (business) faire faillite

broken ['brəukn] pp of **break** ▷ adj (stick, leg etc)
cassé(e); (machine: also: **broken down**) fichu(e);
(promise, vow) rompu(e); **a ~ marriage** un couple
dissocié; **a ~ home** un foyer désuni; **in ~
French/English** dans un français/anglais
approximatif or hésitant

broken-down ['brəukn'daun] adj (car) en panne;
(machine) fichu(e); (house) en ruines

broken-hearted ['brəukn'hɑ:tɪd] adj (ayant) le
cœur brisé

broker ['brəukə'] n courtier m

brokerage ['brəukrɪdʒ] n courtage m

brolly ['brɒlɪ] n (Brit inf) pépin m, parapluie m

bronchitis [brɒŋ'kaɪtɪs] n bronchite f

bronze [brɒnz] n bronze m

bronzed ['brɒnzd] adj bronzé(e), hâlé(e)

brooch [brəutʃ] n broche f

brood [bru:d] n couvée f ▷ vi (hen, storm) couver;
(person) méditer (sombrement), ruminer

broody ['bru:dɪ] adj (fig) taciturne,
mélancolique

brook [bruk] n ruisseau m

broom [brum] n balai m; (Bot) genêt m

broomstick ['brumstɪk] n manche m à balai

Bros. abbr (Comm: = brothers) Frères

broth [brɒθ] n bouillon m de viande et de
légumes

brothel ['brɒθl] n maison close, bordel m

brother ['brʌðə'] n frère m

brotherhood ['brʌðəhud] n fraternité f

brother-in-law ['brʌðərɪn'lɔ:'] n beau-frère m

brotherly ['brʌðəlɪ] adj fraternel(le)

brought [brɔ:t] pt, pp of **bring**

brow [brau] n front m; (rare: gen: eyebrow) sourcil
m; (of hill) sommet m

browbeat ['braubi:t] vt intimider, brusquer

brown [braun] adj brun(e), marron inv; (hair)
châtain inv; (tanned) bronzé(e); (rice, bread, flour)
complet(-ète) ▷ n (colour) brun m, marron m ▷ vt
brunir; (Culin) faire dorer, faire roussir; **to go ~**
(person) bronzer; (leaves) jaunir

brown bread n pain m bis

Brownie ['braunɪ] n jeannette f éclaireuse
(cadette)

brown paper n papier m d'emballage, papier
kraft

brown rice n riz m complet

brown sugar n cassonade f

browse [brauz] vi (in shop) regarder (sans acheter);
(among books) bouquiner, feuilleter les livres;
(animal) paître; **to ~ through a book** feuilleter
un livre

browser ['brauzə'] n (Comput) navigateur m

bruise [bru:z] n bleu m, ecchymose f, contusion f
▷ vt contusionner, meurtrir ▷ vi (fruit) se taler,
se meurtrir; **to ~ one's arm** se faire un bleu au
bras

Brum [brʌm] n abbr, **Brummagem**
['brʌmədʒəm] n (inf) Birmingham

Brummie ['brʌmɪ] n (inf) habitant(e) de
Birmingham; natif(-ive) de Birmingham

brunch [brʌntʃ] n brunch m

brunette [bru:'nɛt] n (femme) brune

brunt [brʌnt] n: **the ~ of** (attack, criticism etc) le
plus gros de

brush [brʌʃ] n brosse f; (for painting) pinceau m;
(for shaving) blaireau m; (quarrel) accrochage m,
prise f de bec ▷ vt brosser; (also: **brush past,
brush against**) effleurer, frôler; **to have a ~
with sb** s'accrocher avec qn; **to have a ~ with
the police** avoir maille à partir avec la police
▶ **brush aside** vt écarter, balayer
▶ **brush up** vt (knowledge) rafraîchir, réviser

brushed | building society

brushed [brʌʃt] *adj* (Tech: *steel, chrome etc*)
brossé(e); (*nylon, denim etc*) gratté(e)
brush-off ['brʌʃɔf] *n* (*inf*): **to give sb the ~**
envoyer qn promener
brushwood ['brʌʃwud] *n* broussailles *fpl*,
taillis *m*
brusque [bruːsk] *adj* (*person, manner*) brusque,
cassant(e); (*tone*) sec (sèche), cassant(e)
Brussels ['brʌslz] *n* Bruxelles
Brussels sprout [-spraut] *n* chou *m* de
Bruxelles
brutal ['bruːtl] *adj* brutal(e)
brutality [bruː'tælɪtɪ] *n* brutalité *f*
brutalize ['bruːtəlaɪz] *vt* (*harden*) rendre
brutal(e); (*ill-treat*) brutaliser
brute [bruːt] *n* brute *f* ▷ *adj*: **by ~ force** par la
force
brutish ['bruːtɪʃ] *adj* grossier(-ère), brutal(e)
BS *n abbr* (US: = *Bachelor of Science*) diplôme
universitaire
bs *abbr* = **bill of sale**
BSA *n abbr* = **Boy Scouts of America**
B.Sc. *n abbr* = **Bachelor of Science**
BSE *n abbr* (= *bovine spongiform encephalopathy*) ESB *f*,
BSE *f*
BSI *n abbr* (= *British Standards Institution*) association
de normalisation
BST *abbr* (= *British Summer Time*) heure *f* d'été
Bt. *abbr* (*Brit*) = **baronet**
btu *n abbr* (= *British thermal unit*) btu (= 1054,2 joules)
bubble ['bʌbl] *n* bulle *f* ▷ *vi* bouillonner, faire
des bulles; (*sparkle, fig*) pétiller
bubble bath *n* bain moussant
bubble gum *n* chewing-gum *m*
bubblejet printer ['bʌbldʒɛt-] *n* imprimante *f* à
bulle d'encre
bubbly ['bʌblɪ] *adj* (*drink*) pétillant(e); (*person*)
plein(e) de vitalité ▷ *n* (*inf*) champ *m*
Bucharest [buːkə'rɛst] *n* Bucarest
buck [bʌk] *n* mâle *m* (*d'un lapin, lièvre, daim etc*);
(US *inf*) dollar *m* ▷ *vi* ruer, lancer une ruade; **to**
pass the ~ (to sb) se décharger de la
responsabilité (sur qn)
▶ **buck up** *vi* (*cheer up*) reprendre du poil de la
bête, se remonter ▷ *vt*: **to ~ one's ideas up** se
reprendre
bucket ['bʌkɪt] *n* seau *m* ▷ *vi* (*Brit inf*): **the rain**
is ~ing (down) il pleut à verse
Buckingham Palace ['bʌkɪŋhəm-] *n* le palais
de Buckingham; *voir article*

● **BUCKINGHAM PALACE**
●
● Buckingham Palace est la résidence officielle
● londonienne du souverain britannique
● depuis 1762. Construit en 1703, il fut à
● l'origine le palais du duc de Buckingham. Il
● a été partiellement reconstruit au début du
● XXe siècle.

buckle ['bʌkl] *n* boucle *f* ▷ *vt* (*belt etc*) boucler,
attacher ▷ *vi* (*warp*) tordre, gauchir; (: *wheel*) se

voiler
▶ **buckle down** *vi* s'y mettre
Bucks [bʌks] *abbr* (*Brit*) = **Buckinghamshire**
bud [bʌd] *n* bourgeon *m*; (*of flower*) bouton *m* ▷ *vi*
bourgeonner; (*flower*) éclore
Buddha ['budə] *n* Bouddha *m*
Buddhism ['budɪzəm] *n* bouddhisme *m*
Buddhist ['budɪst] *adj* bouddhiste ▷ *n*
Bouddhiste *m/f*
budding ['bʌdɪŋ] *adj* (*flower*) en bouton; (*poet etc*)
en herbe; (*passion etc*) naissant(e)
buddy ['bʌdɪ] *n* (US) copain *m*
budge [bʌdʒ] *vt* faire bouger ▷ *vi* bouger
budgerigar ['bʌdʒərɪgɑːʳ] *n* perruche *f*
budget ['bʌdʒɪt] *n* budget *m* ▷ *vi*: **to ~ for sth**
inscrire qch au budget; **I'm on a tight ~** je dois
faire attention à mon budget
budgie ['bʌdʒɪ] *n* = **budgerigar**
Buenos Aires ['bweɪnɔs'aɪrɪz] *n* Buenos Aires
buff [bʌf] *adj* (couleur *f*) chamois *m* ▷ *n* (*inf*:
enthusiast) mordu(e)
buffalo (*pl - or* **-es**) ['bʌfələu] *n* (*Brit*) buffle *m*;
(US) bison *m*
buffer ['bʌfəʳ] *n* tampon *m*; (Comput) mémoire *f*
tampon ▷ *vi* mettre en mémoire tampon
buffering ['bʌfərɪŋ] *n* (Comput) mise *f* en
mémoire tampon
buffer state *n* état *m* tampon
buffer zone *n* zone *f* tampon
buffet *n* ['bufeɪ] (*food Brit: bar*) buffet *m* ▷ *vt*
['bʌfɪt] gifler, frapper; secouer, ébranler
buffet car *n* (*Brit Rail*) voiture-bar *f*
buffet lunch *n* lunch *m*
buffoon [bə'fuːn] *n* buffon *m*, pitre *m*
bug [bʌg] *n* (*bedbug etc*) punaise *f*; (*esp US: any*
insect) insecte *m*, bestiole *f*; (*fig: germ*) virus *m*,
microbe *m*; (*spy device*) dispositif *m* d'écoute
(électronique), micro clandestin; (Comput: *of*
program) erreur *f*; (: *of equipment*) défaut *m* ▷ *vt*
(*room*) poser des micros dans; (*inf: annoy*)
embêter; **I've got the travel ~** (*fig*) j'ai le virus
du voyage
bugbear ['bʌgbɛəʳ] *n* cauchemar *m*, bête noire
bugger ['bʌgəʳ] (*inf!*) *n* salaud *m* (!), connard *m* (!)
▷ *vb*: **~ off!** tire-toi! (!); **~ (it)!** merde! (!)
buggy ['bʌgɪ] *n* poussette *f*
bugle ['bjuːgl] *n* clairon *m*
build [bɪld] *n* (*of person*) carrure *f*, charpente *f* ▷ *vt*
(*pt, pp* **built**) [bɪlt] construire, bâtir
▶ **build on** *vt fus* (*fig*) tirer parti de, partir de
▶ **build up** *vt* accumuler, amasser; (*business*)
développer; (*reputation*) bâtir
builder ['bɪldəʳ] *n* entrepreneur *m*
building ['bɪldɪŋ] *n* (*trade*) construction *f*;
(*structure*) bâtiment *m*, construction; (: *residential,*
offices) immeuble *m*
building contractor *n* entrepreneur *m* (en
bâtiment)
building industry *n* (industrie *f* du)
bâtiment *m*
building site *n* chantier *m* (de construction)
building society *n* (*Brit*) société *f* de crédit

immobilier; *voir article*

● **BUILDING SOCIETY**

Une *building society* est une mutuelle dont les épargnants et emprunteurs sont les propriétaires. Ces mutuelles offrent deux services principaux: on peut y avoir un compte d'épargne duquel on peut retirer son argent sur demande ou moyennant un court préavis et on peut également y faire des emprunts à long terme, par exemple pour acheter une maison. Les *building societies* ont eu jusqu'en 1985 le quasi-monopole des comptes d'épargne et des prêts immobiliers, mais les banques ont maintenant une part importante de ce marché.

building trade *n* = **building industry**

build-up ['bɪldʌp] *n* (*of gas etc*) accumulation *f*; (*publicity*): **to give sb/sth a good** ~ faire de la pub pour qn/qch

built [bɪlt] *pt, pp of* **build**

built-in ['bɪlt'ɪn] *adj* (*cupboard*) encastré(e); (*device*) incorporé(e); intégré(e)

built-up ['bɪlt'ʌp] *adj:* ~ **area** agglomération (urbaine); zone urbanisée

bulb [bʌlb] *n* (*Bot*) bulbe *m*, oignon *m*; (*Elec*) ampoule *f*

bulbous ['bʌlbəs] *adj* bulbeux(-euse)

Bulgaria [bʌl'gɛərɪə] *n* Bulgarie *f*

Bulgarian [bʌl'gɛərɪən] *adj* bulgare ▷ *n* Bulgare *m/f*; (*Ling*) bulgare *m*

bulge [bʌldʒ] *n* renflement *m*, gonflement *m*; (*in birth rate, sales*) brusque augmentation *f* ▷ *vi* faire saillie; présenter un renflement; (*pocket, file*): **to be bulging with** être plein(e) à craquer de

bulimia [bə'lɪmɪə] *n* boulimie *f*

bulimic [bju:'lɪmɪk] *adj, n* boulimique *m/f*

bulk [bʌlk] *n* masse *f*, volume *m*; **in** ~ (*Comm*) en gros, en vrac; **the** ~ **of** la plus grande *or* grosse partie de

bulk buying [-'baɪɪŋ] *n* achat *m* en gros

bulk carrier *n* cargo *m*

bulkhead ['bʌlkhɛd] *n* cloison *f* (étanche)

bulky ['bʌlkɪ] *adj* volumineux(-euse), encombrant(e)

bull [bul] *n* taureau *m*; (*male elephant, whale*) mâle *m*; (*Stock Exchange*) haussier *m*; (*Rel*) bulle *f*

bulldog ['buldɔg] *n* bouledogue *m*

bulldoze ['buldəuz] *vt* passer *or* raser au bulldozer; **I was ~d into doing it** (*fig: inf*) on m'a forcé la main

bulldozer ['buldəuzəʳ] *n* bulldozer *m*

bullet ['bulɪt] *n* balle *f* (*de fusil etc*)

bulletin ['bulɪtɪn] *n* bulletin *m*, communiqué *m*; (*also:* **news bulletin**) (bulletin d')informations *fpl*

bulletin board *n* (*Comput*) messagerie *f* (électronique)

bulletproof ['bulɪtpru:f] *adj* à l'épreuve des balles; ~ **vest** gilet *m* pare-balles

bullfight ['bulfaɪt] *n* corrida *f*, course *f* de taureaux

bullfighter ['bulfaɪtəʳ] *n* torero *m*

bullfighting ['bulfaɪtɪŋ] *n* tauromachie *f*

bullion ['buljən] *n* or *m* or argent *m* en lingots

bullock ['bulək] *n* bœuf *m*

bullring ['bulrɪŋ] *n* arène *f*

bull's-eye ['bulzaɪ] *n* centre *m* (*de la cible*)

bullshit ['bulʃɪt] (*inf!*) *n* connerie(s) *f(pl)* (!) ▷ *vt* raconter des conneries à (!) ▷ *vi* déconner (!)

bully ['bulɪ] *n* brute *f*, tyran *m* ▷ *vt* tyranniser, rudoyer; (*frighten*) intimider

bullying ['bulɪŋ] *n* brimades *fpl*

bum [bʌm] *n* (*inf: Brit: backside*) derrière *m*; (: *esp US: tramp*) vagabond(e), traîne-savates *m/f inv*; (: *idler*) glandeur *m*
  ▶ **bum around** *vi* (*inf*) vagabonder

bumblebee ['bʌmblbi:] *n* bourdon *m*

bumf [bʌmf] *n* (*inf: forms etc*) paperasses *fpl*

bump [bʌmp] *n* (*blow*) coup *m*, choc *m*; (*jolt*) cahot *m*; (*on road etc, on head*) bosse *f* ▷ *vt* heurter, cogner; (*car*) emboutir
  ▶ **bump along** *vi* avancer en cahotant
  ▶ **bump into** *vt fus* rentrer dans, tamponner; (*inf: meet*) tomber sur

bumper ['bʌmpəʳ] *n* pare-chocs *m inv* ▷ *adj:* ~ **crop/harvest** récolte/moisson exceptionnelle

bumper cars *npl* (*US*) autos tamponneuses

bumph [bʌmf] *n* = **bumf**

bumptious ['bʌmpʃəs] *adj* suffisant(e), prétentieux(-euse)

bumpy ['bʌmpɪ] *adj* (*road*) cahoteux(-euse); **it was a ~ flight/ride** on a été secoués dans l'avion/la voiture

bun [bʌn] *n* (*cake*) petit gâteau; (*bread*) petit pain au lait; (*of hair*) chignon *m*

bunch [bʌntʃ] *n* (*of flowers*) bouquet *m*; (*of keys*) trousseau *m*; (*of bananas*) régime *m*; (*of people*) groupe *m*; **bunches** *npl* (*in hair*) couettes *fpl*; ~ **of grapes** grappe *f* de raisin

bundle ['bʌndl] *n* paquet *m* ▷ *vt* (*also:* **bundle up**) faire un paquet de; (*put*): **to ~ sth/sb into** fourrer *or* enfourner qch/qn dans
  ▶ **bundle off** *vt* (*person*) faire sortir (en toute hâte); expédier
  ▶ **bundle out** *vt* éjecter, sortir (sans ménagements)

bun fight *n* (*Brit inf*) réception *f*; (*tea party*) thé *m*

bung [bʌŋ] *n* bonde *f*, bouchon *m* ▷ *vt* (*Brit: throw: also:* **bung into**) flanquer; (*also:* **bung up**: *pipe, hole*) boucher; **my nose is ~ed up** j'ai le nez bouché

bungalow ['bʌŋgələu] *n* bungalow *m*

bungee jumping ['bʌndʒiː'dʒʌmpɪŋ] *n* saut *m* à l'élastique

bungle ['bʌŋgl] *vt* bâcler, gâcher

bunion ['bʌnjən] *n* oignon *m* (*au pied*)

bunk [bʌŋk] *n* couchette *f*; (*Brit inf*): **to do a** ~ mettre les bouts *or* les voiles
  ▶ **bunk off** *vi* (*Brit inf: Scol*) sécher (les cours); **I'll ~ off at 3 o'clock this afternoon** je vais mettre les bouts *or* les voiles à 3 heures cet après-midi

bunk beds *npl* lits superposés

bunker ['bʌŋkə'] *n* (*coal store*) soute *f* à charbon; (*Mil*, *Golf*) bunker *m*

bunny ['bʌnɪ] *n* (*also:* **bunny rabbit**) lapin *m*

bunny girl *n* (*Brit*) hôtesse de cabaret

bunny hill *n* (*US Ski*) piste *f* pour débutants

bunting ['bʌntɪŋ] *n* pavoisement *m*, drapeaux *mpl*

buoy [bɔɪ] *n* bouée *f*
▶ **buoy up** *vt* faire flotter; (*fig*) soutenir, épauler

buoyancy ['bɔɪənsɪ] *n* (*of ship*) flottabilité *f*

buoyant ['bɔɪənt] *adj* (*ship*) flottable; (*carefree*) gai(e), plein(e) d'entrain; (*Comm: market, economy*) actif(-ive); (: *prices, currency*) soutenu(e)

burden ['bə:dn] *n* fardeau *m*, charge *f* ▷ *vt* charger; (*oppress*) accabler, surcharger; **to be a ~ to sb** être un fardeau pour qn

bureau (*pl* **-x**) ['bjuərəu, -z] *n* (*Brit: writing desk*) bureau *m*, secrétaire *m*; (*US: chest of drawers*) commode *f*; (*office*) bureau, office *m*

bureaucracy [bjuə'rɔkrəsɪ] *n* bureaucratie *f*

bureaucrat ['bjuərəkræt] *n* bureaucrate *m/f*, rond-de-cuir *m*

bureaucratic [bjuərə'krætɪk] *adj* bureaucratique

bureau de change [-də'ʃɑ̃ʒ] (*pl* **bureaux de change**) *n* bureau *m* de change

bureaux ['bjuərəuz] *npl of* **bureau**

burgeon ['bə:dʒən] *vi* (*fig*) être en expansion rapide

burger ['bə:gə'] *n* hamburger *m*

burglar ['bə:glə'] *n* cambrioleur *m*

burglar alarm *n* sonnerie *f* d'alarme

burglarize ['bə:gləraɪz] *vt* (*US*) cambrioler

burglary ['bə:glərɪ] *n* cambriolage *m*

burgle ['bə:gl] *vt* cambrioler

Burgundy ['bə:gəndɪ] *n* Bourgogne *f*

burial ['berɪəl] *n* enterrement *m*

burial ground *n* cimetière *m*

burly ['bə:lɪ] *adj* de forte carrure, costaud(e)

Burma ['bə:mə] *n* Birmanie *f*; *see also* **Myanmar**

Burmese [bə:'mi:z] *adj* birman(e), de Birmanie ▷ *n* (*pl inv*) Birman(e); (*Ling*) birman *m*

burn [bə:n] *vt*, *vi* (*pt*, *pp* **-ed** *or* **-t**) [bə:nt] brûler ▷ *n* brûlure *f*; **the cigarette ~t a hole in her dress** la cigarette a fait un trou dans sa robe; **I've ~t myself!** je me suis brûlé(e)!
▶ **burn down** *vt* incendier, détruire par le feu
▶ **burn out** *vt* (*writer etc*): **to ~ o.s. out** s'user (à force de travailler)

burner ['bə:nə'] *n* brûleur *m*

burning ['bə:nɪŋ] *adj* (*building, forest*) en flammes; (*issue, question*) brûlant(e); (*ambition*) dévorant(e)

burnish ['bə:nɪʃ] *vt* polir

Burns' Night [bə:nz-] *n* fête écossaise à la mémoire du poète Robert Burns; *voir article*

⬤ **BURNS' NIGHT**
⬤
⬤ *Burns' Night* est une fête qui a lieu le 25
⬤ janvier, à la mémoire du poète écossais
⬤ Robert Burns (1759–1796), à l'occasion de
⬤ laquelle les Écossais partout dans le monde
⬤ organisent un souper, en général arrosé de
⬤ whisky. Le plat principal est toujours le
⬤ haggis, servi avec de la purée de pommes de
⬤ terre et de la purée de rutabagas. On apporte
⬤ le haggis au son des cornemuses et au cours
⬤ du repas on lit des poèmes de Burns et on
⬤ chante ses chansons.

burnt [bə:nt] *pt*, *pp of* **burn**

burnt sugar *n* (*Brit*) caramel *m*

burp [bə:p] (*inf*) *n* rot *m* ▷ *vi* roter

burrow ['bʌrəu] *n* terrier *m* ▷ *vt* creuser ▷ *vi* (*rabbit*) creuser un terrier; (*rummage*) fouiller

bursar ['bə:sə'] *n* économe *m/f*; (*Brit: student*) boursier(-ère)

bursary ['bə:sərɪ] *n* (*Brit*) bourse *f* (d'études)

burst [bə:st] (*pt*, *pp* **-**) *vt* faire éclater; (*river: banks etc*) rompre ▷ *vi* éclater; (*tyre*) crever ▷ *n* explosion *f*; (*also:* **burst pipe**) fuite *f* (*due à une rupture*); **a ~ of enthusiasm/energy** un accès d'enthousiasme/d'énergie; **~ of laughter** éclat *m* de rire; **a ~ of applause** une salve d'applaudissement; **a ~ of gunfire** une rafale de tir; **a ~ of speed** une pointe de vitesse; **~ blood vessel** rupture *f* de vaisseau sanguin; **the river has ~ its banks** le cours d'eau est sorti de son lit; **to ~ into flames** s'enflammer soudainement; **to ~ out laughing** éclater de rire; **to ~ into tears** fondre en larmes; **to ~ open** (*vi*) s'ouvrir violemment *or* soudainement; **to be ~ing with** (*container*) être plein(e) (à craquer) de, regorger de; (*fig*) être débordant(e) de
▶ **burst into** *vt fus* (*room etc*) faire irruption dans
▶ **burst out of** *vt fus* sortir précipitamment de

bury ['berɪ] *vt* enterrer; **to ~ one's face in one's hands** se couvrir le visage de ses mains; **to ~ one's head in the sand** (*fig*) pratiquer la politique de l'autruche; **to ~ the hatchet** (*fig*) enterrer la hache de guerre

bus (*pl* **-es**) [bʌs, 'bʌsɪz] *n* autobus *m*

busboy ['bʌsbɔɪ] *n* (*US*) aide-serveur *m*

bus conductor *n* receveur(-euse) *m/f* de bus

bush [buʃ] *n* buisson *m*; (*scrub land*) brousse *f*; **to beat about the ~** tourner autour du pot

bushed [buʃt] *adj* (*inf*) crevé(e), claqué(e)

bushel ['buʃl] *n* boisseau *m*

bushfire ['buʃfaɪə'] *n* feu *m* de brousse

bushy ['buʃɪ] *adj* broussailleux(-euse), touffu(e)

busily ['bɪzɪlɪ] *adv*: **to be ~ doing sth** s'affairer à faire qch

business ['bɪznɪs] *n* (*matter, firm*) affaire *f*; (*trading*) affaires *fpl*; (*job, duty*) travail *m*; **to be away on ~** être en déplacement d'affaires; **I'm here on ~** je suis là pour affaires; **he's in the insurance ~** il est dans les assurances; **to do ~ with sb** traiter avec qn; **it's none of my ~** cela ne me regarde pas, ce ne sont pas mes affaires; **he means ~** il ne plaisante pas, il est sérieux

business address *n* adresse professionnelle *or* au bureau

business card *n* carte *f* de visite
(professionnelle)
business class *n* (*on plane*) classe *f* affaires
businesslike ['bɪznɪslaɪk] *adj* sérieux(-euse),
efficace
businessman ['bɪznɪsmən] (*irreg*) *n* homme *m*
d'affaires
business trip *n* voyage *m* d'affaires
businesswoman ['bɪznɪswumən] (*irreg*) *n*
femme *f* d'affaires
busker ['bʌskə^r] *n* (*Brit*) artiste ambulant(e)
bus lane *n* (*Brit*) voie réservée aux autobus
bus pass *n* carte *f* de bus
bus shelter *n* abribus *m*
bus station *n* gare routière
bus stop *n* arrêt *m* d'autobus
bust [bʌst] *n* buste *m*; (*measurement*) tour *m* de
poitrine ▷ *adj* (*inf: broken*) fichu(e), fini(e) ▷ *vt*
(*inf: Police: arrest*) pincer; **to go ~** faire faillite
bustle ['bʌsl] *n* remue-ménage *m*, affairement
m ▷ *vi* s'affairer, se démener
bustling ['bʌslɪŋ] *adj* (*person*) affairé(e); (*town*)
très animé(e)
bust-up ['bʌstʌp] *n* (*Brit inf*) engueulade *f*
busty ['bʌstɪ] *adj* (*inf*) à la poitrine plantureuse
busy ['bɪzɪ] *adj* occupé(e); (*shop, street*) très
fréquenté(e); (*US: telephone, line*) occupé ▷ *vt*: **to
~ o.s.** s'occuper; **he's a ~ man** (*normally*) c'est un
homme très pris; (*temporarily*) il est très pris
busybody ['bɪzɪbɔdɪ] *n* mouche *f* du coche,
âme *f* charitable
busy signal *n* (*US*) tonalité *f* occupé *inv*

🔵 **KEYWORD**

but [bʌt] *conj* mais; **I'd love to come, but I'm
busy** j'aimerais venir mais je suis occupé; **he's
not English but French** il n'est pas anglais
mais français; **but that's far too expensive!**
mais c'est bien trop cher!
▷ *prep* (*apart from, except*) sauf, excepté; **nothing
but** rien d'autre que; **we've had nothing but
trouble** nous n'avons eu que des ennuis; **no-
one but him can do it** lui seul peut le faire;
who but a lunatic would do such a thing? qui
sinon un fou ferait une chose pareille?; **but for
you/your help** sans toi/ton aide; **anything
but that** tout sauf *or* excepté ça, tout mais pas
ça; **the last but one** (*Brit*) l'avant-dernier(-ère)
▷ *adv* (*just, only*) ne ... que; **she's but a child** elle
n'est qu'une enfant; **had I but known** si
seulement j'avais su; **I can but try** je peux
toujours essayer; **all but finished**
pratiquement terminé; **anything but
finished** tout sauf fini, très loin d'être fini

butane ['bju:teɪn] *n* (*also*: **butane gas**) butane *m*
butch [butʃ] *adj* (*inf: man*) costaud, viril;
(: *woman*) costaude, masculine
butcher ['butʃə^r] *n* boucher *m* ▷ *vt* massacrer;
(*cattle etc for meat*) tuer
butcher's ['butʃə^rz], **butcher's shop** *n*

boucherie *f*
butler ['bʌtlə^r] *n* maître *m* d'hôtel
butt [bʌt] *n* (*cask*) gros tonneau; (*thick end*) (gros)
bout; (*of gun*) crosse *f*; (*of cigarette*) mégot *m*; (*Brit
fig: target*) cible *f* ▷ *vt* donner un coup de tête à
▶ **butt in** *vi* (*interrupt*) interrompre
butter ['bʌtə^r] *n* beurre *m* ▷ *vt* beurrer
buttercup ['bʌtəkʌp] *n* bouton *m* d'or
butter dish *n* beurrier *m*
butterfingers ['bʌtəfɪŋgəz] *n* (*inf*) maladroit(e)
butterfly ['bʌtəflaɪ] *n* papillon *m*; (*Swimming*:
also: **butterfly stroke**) brasse *f* papillon
buttocks ['bʌtəks] *npl* fesses *fpl*
button ['bʌtn] *n* bouton *m*; (*US: badge*) pin *m* ▷ *vt*
(*also*: **button up**) boutonner ▷ *vi* se boutonner
buttonhole ['bʌtnhəul] *n* boutonnière *f* ▷ *vt*
accrocher, arrêter, retenir
buttress ['bʌtrɪs] *n* contrefort *m*
buxom ['bʌksəm] *adj* aux formes avantageuses
or épanouies, bien galbé(e)
buy [baɪ] (*pt, pp* **bought** [bɔ:t]) *vt* acheter; (*Comm*:
company) (r)acheter ▷ *n* achat *m*; **that was a
good/bad ~** c'était un bon/mauvais achat; **to ~
sb sth/sth from sb** acheter qch à qn; **to ~ sb a
drink** offrir un verre *or* à boire à qn; **can I ~ you
a drink?** je vous offre un verre?; **where can I ~
some postcards?** où est-ce que je peux acheter
des cartes postales?
▶ **buy back** *vt* racheter
▶ **buy in** *vt* (*Brit: goods*) acheter, faire venir
▶ **buy into** *vt fus* (*Brit Comm*) acheter des actions
de
▶ **buy off** *vt* (*bribe*) acheter
▶ **buy out** *vt* (*partner*) désintéresser; (*business*)
racheter
▶ **buy up** *vt* acheter en bloc, rafler
buyer ['baɪə^r] *n* acheteur(-euse) *m/f*; **~'s market**
marché *m* favorable aux acheteurs
buy-out ['baɪaut] *n* (*Comm*) rachat *m* (*d'entreprise*)
buzz [bʌz] *n* bourdonnement *m*; (*inf: phone call*):
to give sb a ~ passer un coup de fil à qn ▷ *vi*
bourdonner ▷ *vt* (*call on intercom*) appeler; (*with
buzzer*) sonner; (*Aviat: plane, building*) raser; **my
head is ~ing** j'ai la tête qui bourdonne
▶ **buzz off** *vi* (*inf*) s'en aller, ficher le camp
buzzard ['bʌzəd] *n* buse *f*
buzzer ['bʌzə^r] *n* timbre *m* électrique
buzz word *n* (*inf*) mot *m* à la mode *or* dans
le vent

🔵 **KEYWORD**

by [baɪ] *prep* **1** (*referring to cause, agent*) par, de;
killed by lightning tué par la foudre;
surrounded by a fence entouré d'une barrière;
a painting by Picasso un tableau de Picasso
2 (*referring to method, manner, means*): **by bus/car**
en autobus/voiture; **by train** par le *or* en train;
to pay by cheque payer par chèque; **by
moonlight/candlelight** à la lueur de la lune/
d'une bougie; **by saving hard, he ...** à force
d'économiser, il ...

b

493

3 (*via, through*) par; **we came by Dover** nous sommes venus par Douvres

4 (*close to, past*) à côté de; **the house by the school** la maison à côté de l'école; **a holiday by the sea** des vacances au bord de la mer; **she sat by his bed** elle était assise à son chevet; **she went by me** elle est passée à côté de moi; **I go by the post office every day** je passe devant la poste tous les jours

5 (*with time: not later than*) avant; (: *during*): **by daylight** à la lumière du jour; **by night** la nuit, de nuit; **by 4 o'clock** avant 4 heures; **by this time tomorrow** d'ici demain à la même heure; **by the time I got here it was too late** lorsque je suis arrivé il était déjà trop tard

6 (*amount*) à; **by the kilo/metre** au kilo/au mètre; **paid by the hour** payé à l'heure; **to increase** *etc* **by the hour** augmenter *etc* d'heure en heure

7 (*Math: measure*): **to divide/multiply by 3** diviser/multiplier par 3; **a room 3 metres by 4** une pièce de 3 mètres sur 4; **it's broader by a metre** c'est plus large d'un mètre; **the bullet missed him by inches** la balle est passée à quelques centimètres de lui; **one by one** un à un; **little by little** petit à petit, peu à peu

8 (*according to*) d'après, selon; **it's 3 o'clock by my watch** il est 3 heures à ma montre; **it's all right by me** je n'ai rien contre

9: **(all) by oneself** *etc* tout(e) seul(e)
▷ *adv* **1** *see* **go**; **pass** *etc*
2: **by and by** un peu plus tard, bientôt; **by and large** dans l'ensemble

bye ['baɪ], **bye-bye** ['baɪ'baɪ] *excl* au revoir!, salut!

bye-law ['baɪlɔː] *n* = **by-law**

by-election ['baɪɪlɛkʃən] *n* (*Brit*) élection (législative) partielle

Byelorussia [bjɛləu'rʌʃə] *n* Biélorussie *f*

Byelorussian [bjɛləu'rʌʃən] *adj, n* = **Belorussian**

bygone ['baɪgɔn] *adj* passé(e) ▷ *n*: **let ~s be ~s** passons l'éponge, oublions le passé

by-law ['baɪlɔː] *n* arrêté municipal

bypass ['baɪpɑːs] *n* rocade *f*; (*Med*) pontage *m* ▷ *vt* éviter

by-product ['baɪprɔdʌkt] *n* sous-produit *m*, dérivé *m*; (*fig*) conséquence *f* secondaire, retombée *f*

byre ['baɪər] *n* (*Brit*) étable *f* (à vaches)

bystander ['baɪstændər] *n* spectateur(-trice), badaud(e)

byte [baɪt] *n* (*Comput*) octet *m*

byway ['baɪweɪ] *n* chemin détourné

byword ['baɪwəːd] *n*: **to be a ~ for** être synonyme de (*fig*)

by-your-leave ['baɪjɔː'liːv] *n*: **without so much as a ~** sans même demander la permission

Cc

C¹, c¹ [si:] n (letter) C, c m; (Scol: mark) C; (Mus): **C**
do m; **C for Charlie** C comme Célestin
C² abbr (= Celsius, centigrade) C
c² abbr (= century) s.; (= circa) v.; (US etc) = **cent(s)**
CA n abbr = **Central America**; (Brit) = **chartered
accountant** ▷ abbr (US) = **California**
ca. abbr (= circa) v
c/a abbr = **capital account; credit account;
current account**
CAA n abbr (Brit) = **Civil Aviation Authority**; (US:
= Civil Aeronautics Authority) direction de l'aviation
civile
CAB n abbr (Brit) = **Citizens' Advice Bureau**
cab [kæb] n taxi m; (of train, truck) cabine f; (horse-
drawn) fiacre m
cabaret ['kæbərei] n attractions fpl; (show)
spectacle m de cabaret
cabbage ['kæbɪdʒ] n chou m
cabbie, cabby ['kæbɪ], **cab driver** n (inf) taxi m,
chauffeur m de taxi
cabin ['kæbɪn] n (house) cabane f, hutte f; (on ship)
cabine f; (on plane) compartiment m
cabin crew n (Aviat) équipage m
cabin cruiser n yacht m (à moteur)
cabinet ['kæbɪnɪt] n (Pol) cabinet m; (furniture)
petit meuble à tiroirs et rayons; (also: **display
cabinet**) vitrine f, petite armoire vitrée
cabinet-maker ['kæbɪnɪt'meɪkə'] n ébéniste m
cabinet minister n ministre m (membre du
cabinet)
cable ['keɪbl] n câble m ▷ vt câbler, télégraphier
cable car ['keɪblkɑ:'] n téléphérique m
cablegram ['keɪblgræm] n câblogramme m
cable railway n (Brit) funiculaire m
cable television n télévision f par câble
cache [kæʃ] n cachette f; **a ~ of food** etc un dépôt
secret de provisions etc, une cachette contenant
des provisions etc
cackle ['kækl] vi caqueter
cactus (pl **cacti**) ['kæktəs, -taɪ] n cactus m
CAD n abbr (= computer-aided design) CAO f
caddie ['kædɪ] n caddie m
cadet [kə'dɛt] n (Mil) élève m officier; **police ~**
élève agent de police
cadge [kædʒ] vt (inf) se faire donner; **to ~ a
meal (off sb)** se faire inviter à manger (par qn)

cadre ['kædrɪ] n cadre m
Caesarean, (US) **Cesarean** [si:'zɛərɪən] adj: **~
(section)** césarienne f
CAF abbr (Brit: = cost and freight) C et F
café ['kæfeɪ] n ≈ café(-restaurant) m (sans alcool)
cafeteria [kæfɪ'tɪərɪə] n cafétéria f
caffeine ['kæfi:n] n caféine f
cage [keɪdʒ] n cage f ▷ vt mettre en cage
cagey ['keɪdʒɪ] adj (inf) réticent(e), méfiant(e)
cagoule [kə'gu:l] n K-way® m
cahoots [kə'hu:ts] n: **to be in ~ (with)** être de
mèche (avec)
CAI n abbr (= computer-aided instruction) EAO m
Cairo ['kaɪərəʊ] n le Caire
cajole [kə'dʒəʊl] vt couvrir de flatteries or de
gentillesses
cake [keɪk] n gâteau m; **~ of soap** savonnette f;
it's a piece of ~ (inf) c'est un jeu d'enfant; **he
wants to have his ~ and eat it (too)** (fig) il veut
tout avoir
caked [keɪkt] adj: **~ with** raidi(e) par, couvert(e)
d'une croûte de
cake shop n pâtisserie f
Cal. abbr (US) = **California**
calamitous [kə'læmɪtəs] adj catastrophique,
désastreux(-euse)
calamity [kə'læmɪtɪ] n calamité f, désastre m
calcium ['kælsɪəm] n calcium m
calculate ['kælkjuleɪt] vt calculer; (estimate:
chances, effect) évaluer
▶ **calculate on** vt fus: **to ~ on sth/on doing sth**
compter sur qch/faire qch
calculated ['kælkjuleɪtɪd] adj (insult, action)
délibéré(e); **a ~ risk** un risque pris en toute
connaissance de cause
calculating ['kælkjuleɪtɪŋ] adj
calculateur(-trice)
calculation [kælkju'leɪʃən] n calcul m
calculator ['kælkjuleɪtə'] n machine f à
calculer, calculatrice f
calculus ['kælkjuləs] n analyse f
(mathématique), calcul infinitésimal;
integral/differential ~ calcul intégral/
différentiel
calendar ['kæləndə'] n calendrier m
calendar year n année civile

calf (pl **calves**) [kɑːf, kɑːvz] n (of cow) veau m; (of other animals) petit m; (also: **calfskin**) veau m, vachette f; (Anat) mollet m

caliber ['kælıbəʳ] n (US) = **calibre**

calibrate ['kælıbreıt] vt (gun etc) calibrer; (scale of measuring instrument) étalonner

calibre, (US) **caliber** ['kælıbəʳ] n calibre m

calico ['kælıkəu] n (Brit) calicot m; (US) indienne f

Calif. abbr (US) = **California**

California [kælı'fɔːnıə] n Californie f

calipers ['kælıpəz] npl (US) = **callipers**

call [kɔːl] vt (gen, also Tel) appeler; (announce: flight) annoncer; (meeting) convoquer; (strike) lancer ▷ vi (visit: also: **call in, call round**) passer ▷ n (shout) appel m, cri m; (summons: for flight etc, fig: lure) appel; (visit) visite f; (also: **telephone call**) coup m de téléphone; communication f; **to be on ~** être de permanence; **to be ~ed** s'appeler; **she's ~ed Suzanne** elle s'appelle Suzanne; **who is ~ing?** (Tel) qui est à l'appareil?; **London ~ing** (Radio) ici Londres; **please give me a ~ at 7** appelez-moi à 7 heures; **to make a ~** téléphoner, passer un coup de fil; **can I make a ~ from here?** est-ce que je peux téléphoner d'ici?; **to pay a ~ on sb** rendre visite à qn, passer voir qn; **there's not much ~ for these items** ces articles ne sont pas très demandés

▶ **call at** vt fus (ship) faire escale à; (train) s'arrêter à

▶ **call back** vi (return) repasser; (Tel) rappeler ▷ vt (Tel) rappeler; **can you ~ back later?** pouvez-vous rappeler plus tard?

▶ **call for** vt fus (demand) demander; (fetch) passer prendre

▶ **call in** vt (doctor, expert, police) appeler, faire venir

▶ **call off** vt annuler; **the strike was ~ed off** l'ordre de grève a été rapporté

▶ **call on** vt fus (visit) rendre visite à, passer voir; (request): **to ~ on sb to do** inviter qn à faire

▶ **call out** vi pousser un cri or des cris ▷ vt (doctor, police, troops) appeler

▶ **call up** vt (Mil) appeler, mobiliser; (Tel) appeler

call box ['kɔːlbɔks] n (Brit) cabine f téléphonique

call centre, (US) **call center** n centre m d'appels

caller ['kɔːləʳ] n (Tel) personne f qui appelle; (visitor) visiteur m; **hold the line, ~!** (Tel) ne quittez pas, Monsieur (or Madame)!

call girl n call-girl f

call-in ['kɔːlın] n (US Radio, TV) programme m à ligne ouverte

calling ['kɔːlıŋ] n vocation f; (trade, occupation) état m

calling card n (US) carte f de visite

callipers, (US) **calipers** ['kælıpəz] npl (Math) compas m; (Med) appareil m orthopédique; gouttière f; étrier m

callous ['kæləs] adj dur(e), insensible

callousness ['kæləsnıs] n dureté f, manque m de cœur, insensibilité f

callow ['kæləu] adj sans expérience (de la vie)

calm [kɑːm] adj calme ▷ n calme m ▷ vt calmer, apaiser

▶ **calm down** vi se calmer, s'apaiser ▷ vt calmer, apaiser

calmly ['kɑːmlı] adv calmement, avec calme

calmness ['kɑːmnıs] n calme m

Calor gas® ['kælə⁻] n (Brit) butane m, butagaz® m

calorie ['kælərı] n calorie f; **low ~ product** produit m pauvre en calories

calve [kɑːv] vi vêler, mettre bas

calves [kɑːvz] npl of **calf**

CAM n abbr (= computer-aided manufacturing) FAO f

camber ['kæmbəʳ] n (of road) bombement m

Cambodia [kæm'bəudıə] n Cambodge m

Cambodian [kæm'bəudıən] adj cambodgien(ne) ▷ n Cambodgien(ne)

Cambs abbr (Brit) = **Cambridgeshire**

camcorder ['kæmkɔːdəʳ] n caméscope m

came [keım] pt of **come**

camel ['kæməl] n chameau m

cameo ['kæmıəu] n camée m

camera ['kæmərə] n appareil-photo m; (Cine, TV) caméra f; **digital ~** appareil numérique; **in ~** à huis clos, en privé

cameraman ['kæmərəmæn] (irreg) n caméraman m

camera phone n téléphone m avec appareil photo

Cameroon, Cameroun [kæmə'ruːn] n Cameroun m

camouflage ['kæməflɑːʒ] n camouflage m ▷ vt camoufler

camp [kæmp] n camp m ▷ vi camper ▷ adj (man) efféminé(e)

campaign [kæm'peın] n (Mil, Pol) campagne f ▷ vi (also fig) faire campagne; **to ~ for/against** militer pour/contre

campaigner [kæm'peınəʳ] n: **~ for** partisan(e) de; **~ against** opposant(e) à

camp bed ['kæmp'bɛd] n (Brit) lit m de camp

camper ['kæmpəʳ] n campeur(-euse); (vehicle) camping-car m

camping ['kæmpıŋ] n camping m; **to go ~** faire du camping

camping gas® n butane m

campsite ['kæmpsaıt] n (terrain m de) camping m

campus ['kæmpəs] n campus m

camshaft ['kæmʃɑːft] n arbre m à came

can¹ [kæn] n (of milk, oil, water) bidon m; (tin) boîte f (de conserve) ▷ vt mettre en conserve; **a ~ of beer** une canette de bière; **he had to carry the ~** (Brit inf) on lui a fait porter le chapeau; see also **keyword**

 KEYWORD

can² [kæn] (negative **cannot, can't**, conditional and pt **could**) aux vb **1** (be able to) pouvoir; **you can do**

it if you try vous pouvez le faire si vous essayez;
I can't hear you je ne t'entends pas
2 (know how to) savoir; **I can swim/play tennis/
drive** je sais nager/jouer au tennis/conduire;
can you speak French? parlez-vous français?
3 (may) pouvoir; **can I use your phone?** puis-je
me servir de votre téléphone?
4 (expressing disbelief, puzzlement etc): **it can't be
true!** ce n'est pas possible!; **what CAN he want?**
qu'est-ce qu'il peut bien vouloir?
5 (expressing possibility, suggestion etc): **he could be
in the library** il est peut-être dans la
bibliothèque; **she could have been delayed** il
se peut qu'elle ait été retardée; **they could
have forgotten** ils ont pu oublier

Canada ['kænədə] n Canada m
Canadian [kə'neɪdɪən] adj canadien(ne) ▷ n
Canadien(ne)
canal [kə'næl] n canal m
canary [kə'nɛərɪ] n canari m, serin m
Canary Islands, Canaries [kə'nɛərɪz] npl: **the ~**
les (îles fpl) Canaries fpl
Canberra ['kænbərə] n Canberra
cancel ['kænsəl] vt annuler; (train) supprimer;
(party, appointment) décommander; (cross out)
barrer, rayer; (stamp) oblitérer; (cheque) faire
opposition à; **I would like to ~ my booking** je
voudrais annuler ma réservation
▶ **cancel out** vt annuler; **they ~ each other
out** ils s'annulent
cancellation [kænsə'leɪʃən] n annulation f;
suppression f; oblitération f; (Tourism)
réservation annulée, client etc qui s'est
décommandé
Cancer ['kænsə[r]] n (Astrology) le Cancer; **to be ~**
être du Cancer
cancer ['kænsə[r]] n cancer m
cancerous ['kænsrəs] adj cancéreux(-euse)
cancer patient n cancéreux(-euse)
cancer research n recherche f contre le cancer
C and F abbr (Brit: = cost and freight) C et F
candid ['kændɪd] adj (très) franc (franche),
sincère
candidacy ['kændɪdəsɪ] n candidature f
candidate ['kændɪdeɪt] n candidat(e)
candidature ['kændɪdətʃə[r]] n (Brit) = **candidacy**
candied ['kændɪd] adj confit(e); **~ apple** (US)
pomme caramélisée
candle ['kændl] n bougie f; (of tallow) chandelle
f; (in church) cierge m
candlelight ['kændllaɪt] n: **by ~** à la lumière
d'une bougie; (dinner) aux chandelles
candlestick ['kændlstɪk] n (also: **candle holder**)
bougeoir m; (bigger, ornate) chandelier m
candour, (US) **candor** ['kændə[r]] n (grande)
franchise or sincérité
C & W n abbr = **country and western**
candy ['kændɪ] n sucre candi; (US) bonbon m
candy bar (US) n barre f chocolatée
candyfloss ['kændɪflɔs] n (Brit) barbe f à papa
candy store n (US) confiserie f

cane [keɪn] n canne f; (for baskets, chairs etc)
rotin m ▷ vt (Brit Scol) administrer des coups de
bâton à
canine ['kænaɪn] adj canin(e)
canister ['kænɪstə[r]] n boîte f (gén en métal); (of
gas) bombe f
cannabis ['kænəbɪs] n (drug) cannabis m;
(cannabis plant) chanvre indien
canned ['kænd] adj (food) en boîte, en conserve;
(inf: music) enregistré(e); (Brit inf: drunk)
bourré(e); (US inf: worker) mis(e) à la porte
cannibal ['kænɪbəl] n cannibale m/f,
anthropophage m/f
cannibalism ['kænɪbəlɪzəm] n cannibalisme m,
anthropophagie f
cannon (pl - or **-s**) ['kænən] n (gun) canon m
cannonball ['kænənbɔːl] n boulet m de canon
cannon fodder n chair f à canon
cannot ['kænɔt] = **can not**
canny ['kænɪ] adj madré(e), finaud(e)
canoe [kə'nuː] n pirogue f; (Sport) canoë m
canoeing [kə'nuːɪŋ] n (sport) canoë m
canoeist [kə'nuːɪst] n canoéiste m/f
canon ['kænən] n (clergyman) chanoine m;
(standard) canon m
canonize ['kænənaɪz] vt canoniser
can-opener [-'əupnə[r]] n ouvre-boîte m
canopy ['kænəpɪ] n baldaquin m; dais m
cant [kænt] n jargon m ▷ vt, vi pencher
can't [kɑːnt] = **can not**
Cantab. abbr (Brit: = cantabrigiensis) of Cambridge
cantankerous [kæn'tæŋkərəs] adj
querelleur(-euse), acariâtre
canteen [kæn'tiːn] n (eating place) cantine f;
(Brit: of cutlery) ménagère f
canter ['kæntə[r]] n petit galop ▷ vi aller au petit
galop
cantilever ['kæntɪliːvə[r]] n porte-à-faux m inv
canvas ['kænvəs] n (gen) toile f; **under ~**
(camping) sous la tente; (Naut) toutes voiles
dehors
canvass ['kænvəs] vi (Pol): **to ~ for** faire
campagne pour ▷ vt (Pol: district) faire la tournée
électorale dans; (: person) solliciter le suffrage
de; (Comm: district) prospecter; (citizens, opinions)
sonder
canvasser ['kænvəsə[r]] n (Pol) agent électoral;
(Comm) démarcheur m
canvassing ['kænvəsɪŋ] n (Pol) prospection
électorale, démarchage électoral; (Comm)
démarchage, prospection
canyon ['kænjən] n cañon m, gorge (profonde)
CAP n abbr (= Common Agricultural Policy) PAC f
cap [kæp] n casquette f; (for swimming) bonnet m
de bain; (of pen) capuchon m; (of bottle) capsule f;
(Brit: contraceptive: also: **Dutch cap**) diaphragme
m; (Football) sélection f pour l'équipe nationale
▷ vt capsuler; (outdo) surpasser; (put limit on)
plafonner; **~ped with** coiffé(e) de; **and to ~ it
all, he ...** (Brit) pour couronner le tout, il ...
capability [keɪpə'bɪlɪtɪ] n aptitude f, capacité f
capable ['keɪpəbl] adj capable; **~ of** (interpretation

C

etc) susceptible de

capacious [kə'peɪʃəs] *adj* vaste

capacity [kə'pæsɪtɪ] *n* (*of container*) capacité *f*, contenance *f*; (*ability*) aptitude *f*; **filled to ~** plein(e); **in his ~ as** en sa qualité de; **in an advisory ~** à titre consultatif; **to work at full ~** travailler à plein rendement

cape [keɪp] *n* (*garment*) cape *f*; (*Geo*) cap *m*

Cape of Good Hope *n* cap *m* de Bonne Espérance

caper ['keɪpəʳ] *n* (*Culin: gen pl*) câpre *f*; (*prank*) farce *f*

Cape Town *n* Le Cap

capita ['kæpɪtə] *see* **per capita**

capital ['kæpɪtl] *n* (*also*: **capital city**) capitale *f*; (*money*) capital *m*; (*also*: **capital letter**) majuscule *f*

capital account *n* balance *f* des capitaux; (*of country*) compte capital

capital allowance *n* provision *f* pour amortissement

capital assets *npl* immobilisations *fpl*

capital expenditure *n* dépenses *fpl* d'équipement

capital gains tax *n* impôt *m* sur les plus-values

capital goods *n* biens *mpl* d'équipement

capital-intensive ['kæpɪtlɪn'tɛnsɪv] *adj* à forte proportion de capitaux

capitalism ['kæpɪtəlɪzəm] *n* capitalisme *m*

capitalist ['kæpɪtəlɪst] *adj, n* capitaliste *m/f*

capitalize ['kæpɪtəlaɪz] *vt* (*provide with capital*) financer

▶ **capitalize on** *vt fus* (*fig*) profiter de

capital punishment *n* peine capitale

capital transfer tax *n* (*Brit*) impôt *m* sur le transfert de propriété

Capitol ['kæpɪtl] *n*: **the ~** le Capitole; *voir article*

● **CAPITOL**
●
● Le *Capitol* est le siège du "Congress", à
● Washington. Il est situé sur Capitol Hill.

capitulate [kə'pɪtjuleɪt] *vi* capituler

capitulation [kəpɪtju'leɪʃən] *n* capitulation *f*

capricious [kə'prɪʃəs] *adj* capricieux(-euse), fantasque

Capricorn ['kæprɪkɔːn] *n* le Capricorne; **to be ~** être du Capricorne

caps [kæps] *abbr* = **capital letters**

capsize [kæp'saɪz] *vt* faire chavirer ▷ *vi* chavirer

capsule ['kæpsjuːl] *n* capsule *f*

Capt. *abbr* (= *captain*) Cne

captain ['kæptɪn] *n* capitaine *m* ▷ *vt* commander, être le capitaine de

caption ['kæpʃən] *n* légende *f*

captivate ['kæptɪveɪt] *vt* captiver, fasciner

captive ['kæptɪv] *adj, n* captif(-ive)

captivity [kæp'tɪvɪtɪ] *n* captivité *f*

captor ['kæptəʳ] *n* (*unlawful*) ravisseur *m*; (*lawful*): **his ~s** les gens (*or* ceux *etc*) qui l'ont arrêté

capture ['kæptʃəʳ] *vt* (*prisoner, animal*) capturer; (*town*) prendre; (*attention*) capter; (*Comput*) saisir ▷ *n* capture *f*; (*of data*) saisie *f* de données

car [kɑːʳ] *n* voiture *f*, auto *f*; (*US Rail*) wagon *m*, voiture; **by ~** en voiture

carafe [kə'ræf] *n* carafe *f*

carafe wine *n* (*in restaurant*) ≈ vin ouvert

caramel ['kærəməl] *n* caramel *m*

carat ['kærət] *n* carat *m*; **18 ~ gold** or *m* à 18 carats

caravan ['kærəvæn] *n* caravane *f*

caravan site *n* (*Brit*) camping *m* pour caravanes

caraway ['kærəweɪ] *n*: **~ seed** graine *f* de cumin, cumin *m*

carbohydrate [kɑːbəu'haɪdreɪt] *n* hydrate *m* de carbone; (*food*) féculent *m*

carbolic acid [kɑː'bɔlɪk-] *n* phénol *m*

car bomb *n* voiture piégée

carbon ['kɑːbən] *n* carbone *m*

carbonated ['kɑːbəneɪtɪd] *adj* (*drink*) gazeux(-euse)

carbon copy *n* carbone *m*

carbon dioxide [-daɪ'ɔksaɪd] *n* gaz *m* carbonique, dioxyde *m* de carbone

carbon footprint *n* empreinte *f* carbone

carbon monoxide [-mɔ'nɔksaɪd] *n* oxyde *m* de carbone

carbon paper *n* papier *m* carbone

carbon ribbon *n* ruban *m* carbone

car boot sale *n* marché aux puces où des particuliers vendent des objets entreposés dans le coffre de leur voiture.

carburettor, (*US*) **carburetor** [kɑː'bju'rɛtəʳ] *n* carburateur *m*

carcass ['kɑːkəs] *n* carcasse *f*

carcinogenic [kɑːsɪnə'dʒɛnɪk] *adj* cancérigène

card [kɑːd] *n* carte *f*; (*material*) carton *m*; (*membership card*) carte d'adhérent; **to play ~s** jouer aux cartes

cardamom ['kɑːdəməm] *n* cardamome *f*

cardboard ['kɑːdbɔːd] *n* carton *m*

cardboard box *n* (*boîte f* en) carton *m*

cardboard city *n* endroit de la ville où dorment les SDF dans des boîtes en carton

card-carrying member ['kɑːdkærɪɪŋ-] *n* membre actif

card game *n* jeu *m* de cartes

cardiac ['kɑːdɪæk] *adj* cardiaque

cardigan ['kɑːdɪgən] *n* cardigan *m*

cardinal ['kɑːdɪnl] *adj* cardinal(e); (*importance*) capital(e) ▷ *n* cardinal *m*

card index *n* fichier *m* (alphabétique)

cardphone ['kɑːdfəun] *n* téléphone *m* à carte (magnétique)

cardsharp ['kɑːdʃɑːp] *n* tricheur(-euse) professionnel(le)

card vote *n* (*Brit*) vote *m* de délégués

CARE [kɛəʳ] *n abbr* (= *Cooperative for American Relief Everywhere*) association charitable

care [kɛəʳ] *n* soin *m*, attention *f*; (*worry*) souci *m* ▷ *vi*: **to ~ about** (*feel interest for*) se soucier de, s'intéresser à; (*person: love*) être attaché(e) à; **in sb's ~** à la garde de qn, confié à qn; **~ of** (*on letter*) chez; **"with ~"** "fragile"; **to take ~ (to do)** faire attention (à faire); **to take ~ of** (vt) s'occuper de; **the child has been taken into ~** l'enfant a été placé en institution; **would you ~ to/for ...?** voulez-vous ...?; **I wouldn't ~ to do it** je n'aimerais pas le faire; **I don't ~** ça m'est bien égal, peu m'importe; **I couldn't ~ less** cela m'est complètement égal, je m'en fiche complètement

▸ **care for** vt fus s'occuper de; (like) aimer

careen [kə'ri:n] vi (ship) donner de la bande ▷ vt caréner, mettre en carène

career [kə'rɪə^r] n carrière f ▷ vi (also: **career along**) aller à toute allure

career girl n jeune fille f or femme f qui veut faire carrière

careers officer n conseiller(-ère) d'orientation (professionnelle)

career woman (irreg) n femme ambitieuse

carefree ['kɛəfri:] adj sans souci, insouciant(e)

careful ['kɛəful] adj soigneux(-euse); (cautious) prudent(e); **(be) ~!** (fais) attention!; **to be ~ with one's money** regarder à la dépense

carefully ['kɛəfəlɪ] adv avec soin, soigneusement; prudemment

caregiver ['kɛəgɪvə^r] (US) n (professional) travailleur social; (unpaid) personne qui s'occupe d'un proche qui est malade

careless ['kɛəlɪs] adj négligent(e); (heedless) insouciant(e)

carelessly ['kɛəlɪslɪ] adv négligemment; avec insouciance

carelessness ['kɛəlɪsnɪs] n manque m de soin, négligence f; insouciance f

carer ['kɛərə^r] n (professional) travailleur social; (unpaid) personne qui s'occupe d'un proche qui est malade

caress [kə'rɛs] n caresse f ▷ vt caresser

caretaker ['kɛəteɪkə^r] n gardien(ne), concierge m/f

caretaker government n (Brit) gouvernement m intérimaire

car-ferry ['kɑ:fɛrɪ] n (on sea) ferry(-boat) m; (on river) bac m

cargo (pl **-es**) ['kɑ:gəu] n cargaison f, chargement m

cargo boat n cargo m

cargo plane n avion-cargo m

car hire n (Brit) location f de voitures

Caribbean [kærɪ'bi:ən] adj, n: **the ~ (Sea)** la mer des Antilles or des Caraïbes

caricature ['kærɪkətjuə^r] n caricature f

caring ['kɛərɪŋ] adj (person) bienveillant(e); (society, organization) humanitaire

carnage ['kɑ:nɪdʒ] n carnage m

carnal ['kɑ:nl] adj charnel(le)

carnation [kɑ:'neɪʃən] n œillet m

carnival ['kɑ:nɪvl] n (public celebration) carnaval m; (US: funfair) fête foraine

carnivorous [kɑ:'nɪvərəs] adj carnivore, carnassier(-ière)

carol ['kærəl] n: **(Christmas) ~** chant m de Noël

carouse [kə'rauz] vi faire la bringue

carousel [kærə'sɛl] n (for luggage) carrousel m; (US) manège m

carp [kɑ:p] n (fish) carpe f

▸ **carp at** vt fus critiquer

car park (Brit) n parking m, parc m de stationnement

carpenter ['kɑ:pɪntə^r] n charpentier m; (joiner) menuisier m

carpentry ['kɑ:pɪntrɪ] n charpenterie f, métier m de charpentier; (woodwork: at school etc) menuiserie f

carpet ['kɑ:pɪt] n tapis m ▷ vt recouvrir (d'un tapis); **fitted ~** (Brit) moquette f

carpet bombing n bombardement intensif

carpet slippers npl pantoufles fpl

carpet sweeper [-'swi:pə^r] n balai m mécanique

car phone n téléphone m de voiture

car rental n (US) location f de voitures

carriage ['kærɪdʒ] n (Brit Rail) wagon m; (horse-drawn) voiture f; (of goods) transport m; (: cost) port m; (of typewriter) chariot m; (bearing) maintien m, port m; **~ forward** port dû; **~ free** franco de port; **~ paid** (en) port payé

carriage return n retour m à la ligne

carriageway ['kærɪdʒweɪ] n (Brit: part of road) chaussée f

carrier ['kærɪə^r] n transporteur m, camionneur m; (company) entreprise f de transport; (Med) porteur(-euse); (Naut) porte-avions m inv

carrier bag n (Brit) sac m en papier or en plastique

carrier pigeon n pigeon voyageur

carrion ['kærɪən] n charogne f

carrot ['kærət] n carotte f

carry ['kærɪ] vt (subj: person) porter; (: vehicle) transporter; (a motion, bill) voter, adopter; (Math: figure) retenir; (Comm: interest) rapporter; (involve: responsibilities etc) comporter, impliquer; (Med: disease) être porteur de ▷ vi (sound) porter; **to get carried away** (fig) s'emballer, s'enthousiasmer; **this loan carries 10% interest** ce prêt est à 10% (d'intérêt)

▸ **carry forward** vt (gen, Book-Keeping) reporter

▸ **carry on** vi (continue) continuer; (inf: make a fuss) faire des histoires ▷ vt (conduct: business) diriger; (: conversation) entretenir; (continue: business, conversation) continuer; **to ~ on with sth/doing** continuer qch/à faire

▸ **carry out** vt (orders) exécuter; (investigation) effectuer; (idea, threat) mettre à exécution

carrycot ['kærɪkɔt] n (Brit) porte-bébé m

carry-on ['kærɪ'ɔn] n (inf: fuss) histoires fpl; (: annoying behaviour) cirque m, cinéma m

cart [kɑ:t] n charrette f ▷ vt (inf) transporter

carte blanche ['kɑ:t'blɔnʃ] n: **to give sb ~** donner carte blanche à qn

cartel [kɑ:'tɛl] n (Comm) cartel m

cartilage ['kɑ:tɪlɪdʒ] n cartilage m

cartographer [kɑ:'tɔgrəfə^r] n cartographe m/f

cartography [kɑ:'tɔgrəfɪ] n cartographie f

carton ['kɑ:tən] n (box) carton m; (of yogurt) pot m (en carton); (of cigarettes) cartouche f

cartoon [kɑːˈtuːn] *n* (*Press*) dessin *m* (humoristique); (*satirical*) caricature *f*; (*comic strip*) bande dessinée; (*Cine*) dessin animé

cartoonist [kɑːˈtuːnɪst] *n* dessinateur(-trice) humoristique; caricaturiste *m/f*; auteur *m* de dessins animés; auteur de bandes dessinées

cartridge [ˈkɑːtrɪdʒ] *n* (*for gun, pen*) cartouche *f*; (*for camera*) chargeur *m*; (*music tape*) cassette *f*; (*of record player*) cellule *f*

cartwheel [ˈkɑːtwiːl] *n* roue *f*; **to turn a ~** faire la roue

carve [kɑːv] *vt* (*meat: also:* **carve up**) découper; (*wood, stone*) tailler, sculpter

carving [ˈkɑːvɪŋ] *n* (*in wood etc*) sculpture *f*

carving knife *n* couteau *m* à découper

car wash *n* station *f* de lavage (de voitures)

Casablanca [kæsəˈblæŋkə] *n* Casablanca

cascade [kæsˈkeɪd] *n* cascade *f* ▷ *vi* tomber en cascade

case [keɪs] *n* cas *m*; (*Law*) affaire *f*, procès *m*; (*box*) caisse *f*, boîte *f*; (*for glasses*) étui *m*; (*Brit: also:* **suitcase**) valise *f*; (*Typ*): **lower/upper ~** minuscule *f*/majuscule *f*; **to have a good ~ for reform** il y aurait lieu d'engager une réforme; **in ~ of** en cas de; **in ~ he** au cas où il; **just in ~** à tout hasard; **in any ~** en tout cas, de toute façon

case history *n* (*Med*) dossier médical, antécédents médicaux

case study *n* étude *f* de cas

cash [kæʃ] *n* argent *m*; (*Comm*) (argent *m*) liquide *m*, numéraire *m*; liquidités *fpl*; (: *in payment*) argent comptant, espèces *fpl* ▷ *vt* encaisser; **to pay (in) ~** payer (en argent) comptant *or* en espèces; **~ with order/on delivery** (*Comm*) payable *or* paiement à la commande/livraison; **to be short of ~** être à court d'argent; **I haven't got any ~** je n'ai pas de liquide

▶ **cash in** *vt* (*insurance policy etc*) toucher

▶ **cash in on** *vt fus* profiter de

cash account *n* compte *m* caisse

cash and carry *n* libre-service *m* de gros, cash and carry *m inv*

cashback [ˈkæʃbæk] *n* (*discount*) remise *f*; (*at supermarket etc*) retrait *m* (à la caisse)

cashbook [ˈkæʃbuk] *n* livre *m* de caisse

cash box *n* caisse *f*

cash card *n* carte *f* de retrait

cash desk *n* (*Brit*) caisse *f*

cash discount *n* escompte *m* de caisse (pour paiement au comptant), remise *f* au comptant

cash dispenser *n* distributeur *m* automatique de billets

cashew [kæˈʃuː] *n* (*also:* **cashew nut**) noix *f* de cajou

cash flow *n* cash-flow *m*, marge brute d'autofinancement

cashier [kæˈʃɪər] *n* caissier(-ère) ▷ *vt* (*Mil*) destituer, casser

cashmere [ˈkæʃmɪər] *n* cachemire *m*

cash payment *n* paiement comptant, versement *m* en espèces

cash point *n* distributeur *m* automatique de billets

cash price *n* prix comptant

cash register *n* caisse enregistreuse

cash sale *n* vente *f* au comptant

casing [ˈkeɪsɪŋ] *n* revêtement (protecteur), enveloppe (protectrice)

casino [kəˈsiːnəu] *n* casino *m*

cask [kɑːsk] *n* tonneau *m*

casket [ˈkɑːskɪt] *n* coffret *m*; (*US: coffin*) cercueil *m*

Caspian Sea [ˈkæspɪən-] *n*: **the ~** la mer Caspienne

casserole [ˈkæsərəul] *n* (*pot*) cocotte *f*; (*food*) ragoût *m* (en cocotte)

cassette [kæˈsɛt] *n* cassette *f*

cassette deck *n* platine *f* cassette

cassette player *n* lecteur *m* de cassettes

cassette recorder *n* magnétophone *m* à cassettes

cast [kɑːst] (*vb: pt, pp* ~) *vt* (*throw*) jeter; (*shadow: lit*) projeter; (: *fig*) jeter; (*glance*) jeter; (*shed*) perdre; se dépouiller de; (*metal*) couler, fondre ▷ *n* (*Theat*) distribution *f*; (*mould*) moule *m*; (*also:* **plaster cast**) plâtre *m*; **to ~ sb as Hamlet** attribuer à qn le rôle d'Hamlet; **to ~ one's vote** voter, exprimer son suffrage; **to ~ doubt on** jeter un doute sur

▶ **cast aside** *vt* (*reject*) rejeter

▶ **cast off** *vi* (*Naut*) larguer les amarres; (*Knitting*) arrêter les mailles ▷ *vt* (*Knitting*) arrêter

▶ **cast on** (*Knitting*) *vt* monter ▷ *vi* monter les mailles

castanets [kæstəˈnɛts] *npl* castagnettes *fpl*

castaway [ˈkɑːstəweɪ] *n* naufragé(e)

caste [kɑːst] *n* caste *f*, classe sociale

caster sugar [ˈkɑːstə-] *n* (*Brit*) sucre *m* semoule

casting vote [ˈkɑːstɪŋ-] *n* (*Brit*) voix prépondérante (*pour départager*)

cast-iron [ˈkɑːstaɪən] *adj* (*lit*) de *or* en fonte; (*fig: will*) de fer; (*alibi*) en béton

cast iron *n* fonte *f*

castle [ˈkɑːsl] *n* château *m*; (*fortress*) château-fort *m*; (*Chess*) tour *f*

cast-offs [ˈkɑːstɔfs] *npl* vêtements *mpl* dont on ne veut plus

castor [ˈkɑːstər] *n* (*wheel*) roulette *f*

castor oil *n* huile *f* de ricin

castrate [kæsˈtreɪt] *vt* châtrer

casual [ˈkæʒjul] *adj* (*by chance*) de hasard, fait(e) au hasard, fortuit(e); (*irregular: work etc*) temporaire; (*unconcerned*) désinvolte; **~ wear** vêtements *mpl* sport *inv*

casual labour *n* main-d'œuvre *f* temporaire

casually [ˈkæʒjulɪ] *adv* avec désinvolture, négligemment; (*by chance*) fortuitement

casualty [ˈkæʒjultɪ] *n* accidenté(e), blessé(e); (*dead*) victime *f*, mort(e); (*Brit: Med: department*) urgences *fpl*; **heavy casualties** lourdes pertes

casualty ward *n* (*Brit*) service *m* des urgences

cat [kæt] *n* chat *m*

catacombs ['kætəku:mz] *npl* catacombes *fpl*

Catalan ['kætəlæn] *adj* catalan(e)

catalogue, (US) **catalog** ['kætəlɔg] *n* catalogue *m* ▷ *vt* cataloguer

catalyst ['kætəlɪst] *n* catalyseur *m*

catalytic converter [kætə'lɪtɪkkən'vɜ:tə'] *n* pot *m* catalytique

catapult ['kætəpʌlt] *n* lance-pierres *m inv*, fronde *f*; (History) catapulte *f*

cataract ['kætərækt] *n* (also Med) cataracte *f*

catarrh [kə'tɑ:'] *n* rhume *m* chronique, catarrhe *f*

catastrophe [kə'tæstrəfɪ] *n* catastrophe *f*

catastrophic [kætə'strɔfɪk] *adj* catastrophique

catcall ['kætkɔ:l] *n* (at meeting etc) sifflet *m*

catch [kætʃ] (*pt, pp* **caught** [kɔ:t]) *vt* (ball, train, thief, cold) attraper; (person: by surprise) prendre, surprendre; (understand) saisir; (get entangled) accrocher ▷ *vi* (fire) prendre; (get entangled) s'accrocher ▷ *n* (fish etc) prise *f*; (thief etc) capture *f*; (hidden problem) attrape *f*; (Tech) loquet *m*; cliquet *m*; **to ~ sb's attention** or **eye** attirer l'attention de qn; **to ~ fire** prendre feu; **to ~ sight of** apercevoir; **to play ~** jouer à chat; (with ball) jouer à attraper le ballon
  ▶ **catch on** *vi* (become popular) prendre; (understand): **to ~ on (to sth)** saisir (qch)
  ▶ **catch out** *vt* (Brit: fig: with trick question) prendre en défaut
  ▶ **catch up** *vi* (with work) se rattraper, combler son retard ▷ *vt* (also: **catch up with**) rattraper

catch-22 ['kætʃtwenti'tu:] *n*: **it's a ~ situation** c'est (une situation) sans issue

catching ['kætʃɪŋ] *adj* (Med) contagieux(-euse)

catchment area ['kætʃmənt-] *n* (Brit Scol) aire *f* de recrutement; (Geo) bassin *m* hydrographique

catch phrase *n* slogan *m*, expression toute faite

catchy ['kætʃɪ] *adj* (tune) facile à retenir

catechism ['kætɪkɪzəm] *n* catéchisme *m*

categoric [kætɪ'gɔrɪk], **categorical** [kætɪ'gɔrɪkl] *adj* catégorique

categorize ['kætɪgəraɪz] *vt* classer par catégories

category ['kætɪgərɪ] *n* catégorie *f*

cater ['keɪtə'] *vi*: **to ~ for** (Brit: needs) satisfaire, pourvoir à; (: readers, consumers) s'adresser à, pourvoir aux besoins de; (Comm: parties etc) préparer des repas pour

caterer ['keɪtərə'] *n* traiteur *m*; fournisseur *m*

catering ['keɪtərɪŋ] *n* restauration *f*; approvisionnement *m*, ravitaillement *m*

caterpillar ['kætəpɪlə'] *n* chenille *f* ▷ *cpd* (vehicle) à chenille; **~ track** *n* chenille *f*

cat flap *n* chatière *f*

cathedral [kə'θi:drəl] *n* cathédrale *f*

cathode ['kæθəud] *n* cathode *f*

cathode ray tube *n* tube *m* cathodique

Catholic ['kæθəlɪk] (Rel) *adj* catholique ▷ *n* catholique *m/f*

catholic ['kæθəlɪk] *adj* (wide-ranging) éclectique; universel(le); libéral(e)

catsup ['kætsəp] *n* (US) ketchup *m*

cattle ['kætl] *npl* bétail *m*, bestiaux *mpl*

catty ['kætɪ] *adj* méchant(e)

catwalk ['kætwɔ:k] *n* passerelle *f*; (for models) podium *m* (de défilé de mode)

Caucasian [kɔ:'keɪzɪən] *adj, n* caucasien(ne)

Caucasus ['kɔ:kəsəs] *n* Caucase *m*

caucus ['kɔ:kəs] *n* (US Pol) comité électoral (pour désigner des candidats); *voir article*; (Brit Pol: group) comité local (d'un parti politique)

● **CAUCUS**
●
● Un *caucus* aux États-Unis est une réunion
● restreinte des principaux dirigeants d'un
● parti politique, précédant souvent une
● assemblée générale, dans le but de choisir
● des candidats ou de définir une ligne
● d'action. Par extension, ce terme désigne
● également l'état-major d'un parti politique.

caught [kɔ:t] *pt, pp of* **catch**

cauliflower ['kɔlɪflauə'] *n* chou-fleur *m*

cause [kɔ:z] *n* cause *f* ▷ *vt* causer; **there is no ~ for concern** il n'y a pas lieu de s'inquiéter; **to ~ sth to be done** faire faire qch; **to ~ sb to do sth** faire faire qch à qn

causeway ['kɔ:zweɪ] *n* chaussée (surélevée)

caustic ['kɔ:stɪk] *adj* caustique

caution ['kɔ:ʃən] *n* prudence *f*; (warning) avertissement *m* ▷ *vt* avertir, donner un avertissement à

cautious ['kɔ:ʃəs] *adj* prudent(e)

cautiously ['kɔ:ʃəslɪ] *adv* prudemment, avec prudence

cautiousness ['kɔ:ʃəsnɪs] *n* prudence *f*

cavalier [kævə'lɪə'] *adj* cavalier(-ère), désinvolte ▷ *n* (knight) cavalier *m*

cavalry ['kævəlrɪ] *n* cavalerie *f*

cave [keɪv] *n* caverne *f*, grotte *f* ▷ *vi*: **to go caving** faire de la spéléo(logie)
  ▶ **cave in** *vi* (roof etc) s'effondrer

caveman ['keɪvmæn] (irreg) *n* homme *m* des cavernes

cavern ['kævən] *n* caverne *f*

caviar, caviare ['kævɪɑ:'] *n* caviar *m*

cavity ['kævɪtɪ] *n* cavité *f*; (Med) carie *f*

cavity wall insulation *n* isolation *f* des murs creux

cavort [kə'vɔ:t] *vi* cabrioler, faire des cabrioles

cayenne [keɪ'ɛn] *n* (also: **cayenne pepper**) poivre *m* de cayenne

CB *n abbr* (= Citizens' Band (Radio)) CB *f*; (Brit: = Companion of (the Order of) the Bath) titre honorifique

CBC *n abbr* (= Canadian Broadcasting Corporation) organisme de radiodiffusion

CBE *n abbr* (= Companion of (the Order of) the British Empire) titre honorifique

CBI *n abbr* (= Confederation of British Industry) ≈ MEDEF *m* (= Mouvement des entreprises de France)

CBS *n abbr* (US: = Columbia Broadcasting System) chaîne de télévision

C

CC *abbr* (*Brit*) = **county council**

cc *abbr* (= *cubic centimetre*) cm³; (*on letter etc*) = **carbon copy**

CCA *n abbr* (*US*: = *Circuit Court of Appeals*) cour d'appel itinérante

CCTV *n abbr* = **closed-circuit television**

CCU *n abbr* (*US*: = *coronary care unit*) unité *f* de soins cardiologiques

CD *n abbr* (= *compact disc*) CD *m*; (*Mil: Brit*) = **Civil Defence (Corps)**; (: *US*) = **Civil Defense** ▷ *abbr* (*Brit*: = *Corps Diplomatique*) CD

CD burner *n* graveur *m* de CD

CDC *n abbr* (*US*) = **center for disease control**

CD player *n* platine *f* laser

Cdr. *abbr* (= *commander*) Cdt

CD-ROM [siːdiːˈrɔm] *n abbr* (= *compact disc read-only memory*) CD-ROM *m inv*

CDT *abbr* (*US*: = *Central Daylight Time*) heure d'été du centre

CDW *n abbr* = **collision damage waiver**

CD writer *n* graveur *m* de CD

cease [siːs] *vt, vi* cesser

ceasefire [ˈsiːsfaɪəʳ] *n* cessez-le-feu *m*

ceaseless [ˈsiːslɪs] *adj* incessant(e), continuel(le)

CED *n abbr* (*US*) = **Committee for Economic Development**

cedar [ˈsiːdəʳ] *n* cèdre *m*

cede [siːd] *vt* céder

cedilla [sɪˈdɪlə] *n* cédille *f*

CEEB *n abbr* (*US*: = *College Entrance Examination Board*) commission d'admission dans l'enseignement supérieur

ceilidh [ˈkeɪlɪ] *n* bal *m* folklorique écossais or irlandais

ceiling [ˈsiːlɪŋ] *n* (*also fig*) plafond *m*

celebrate [ˈsɛlɪbreɪt] *vt, vi* célébrer

celebrated [ˈsɛlɪbreɪtɪd] *adj* célèbre

celebration [sɛlɪˈbreɪʃən] *n* célébration *f*

celebrity [sɪˈlɛbrɪtɪ] *n* célébrité *f*

celeriac [səˈlɛrɪæk] *n* céleri(-rave) *m*

celery [ˈsɛlərɪ] *n* céleri *m* (en branches)

celestial [sɪˈlɛstɪəl] *adj* céleste

celibacy [ˈsɛlɪbəsɪ] *n* célibat *m*

cell [sɛl] *n* (*gen*) cellule *f*; (*Elec*) élément *m* (*de pile*)

cellar [ˈsɛləʳ] *n* cave *f*

'cellist [ˈtʃɛlɪst] *n* violoncelliste *m/f*

cello [ˈtʃɛləu] *n* violoncelle *m*

Cellophane® [ˈsɛləfeɪn] *n* cellophane® *f*

cellphone [ˈsɛlfəun] *n* (téléphone *m*) portable *m*, mobile *m*

cellular [ˈsɛljuləʳ] *adj* cellulaire

cellulose [ˈsɛljuləus] *n* cellulose *f*

Celsius [ˈsɛlsɪəs] *adj* Celsius *inv*

Celt [kɛlt, sɛlt] *n* Celte *m/f*

Celtic [ˈkɛltɪk, ˈsɛltɪk] *adj* celte, celtique ▷ *n* (*Ling*) celtique *m*

cement [səˈmɛnt] *n* ciment *m* ▷ *vt* cimenter

cement mixer *n* bétonnière *f*

cemetery [ˈsɛmɪtrɪ] *n* cimetière *m*

cenotaph [ˈsɛnətɑːf] *n* cénotaphe *m*

censor [ˈsɛnsəʳ] *n* censeur *m* ▷ *vt* censurer

censorship [ˈsɛnsəʃɪp] *n* censure *f*

censure [ˈsɛnʃəʳ] *vt* blâmer, critiquer

census [ˈsɛnsəs] *n* recensement *m*

cent [sɛnt] *n* (*unit of dollar, euro*) cent *m* (= *un centième du dollar, de l'euro*); *see also* **per**

centenary [sɛnˈtiːnərɪ], (*US*) **centennial** [sɛnˈtɛnɪəl] *n* centenaire *m*

center [ˈsɛntəʳ] *n, vt* (*US*) = **centre** [sɛntɪ] *prefix*

centigrade [ˈsɛntɪgreɪd] *adj* centigrade

centilitre, (*US*) **centiliter** [ˈsɛntɪliːtəʳ] *n* centilitre *m*

centimetre, (*US*) **centimeter** [ˈsɛntɪmiːtəʳ] *n* centimètre *m*

centipede [ˈsɛntɪpiːd] *n* mille-pattes *m inv*

central [ˈsɛntrəl] *adj* central(e)

Central African Republic *n* République Centrafricaine

Central America *n* Amérique centrale

central heating *n* chauffage central

centralize [ˈsɛntrəlaɪz] *vt* centraliser

central processing unit *n* (*Comput*) unité centrale (de traitement)

central reservation *n* (*Brit Aut*) terre-plein central

centre, (*US*) **center** [ˈsɛntəʳ] *n* centre *m* ▷ *vt* centrer; (*Phot*) cadrer; (*concentrate*): **to ~ (on)** centrer (sur)

centrefold, (*US*) **centerfold** [ˈsɛntəfəuld] *n* (*Press*) pages centrales détachables (*avec photo de pin up*)

centre-forward [ˈsɛntəˈfɔːwəd] *n* (*Sport*) avant-centre *m*

centre-half [ˈsɛntəˈhɑːf] *n* (*Sport*) demi-centre *m*

centrepiece, (*US*) **centerpiece** [ˈsɛntəpiːs] *n* milieu *m* de table; (*fig*) pièce maîtresse

centre spread *n* (*Brit*) publicité *f* en double page

centre-stage [sɛntəˈsteɪdʒ] *n*: **to take ~** occuper le centre de la scène

centrifugal [sɛnˈtrɪfjugl] *adj* centrifuge

centrifuge [ˈsɛntrɪfjuːʒ] *n* centrifugeuse *f*

century [ˈsɛntjurɪ] *n* siècle *m*; **in the twentieth ~** au vingtième siècle

CEO *n abbr* (*US*) = **chief executive officer**

ceramic [sɪˈræmɪk] *adj* céramique

cereal [ˈsiːrɪəl] *n* céréale *f*

cerebral [ˈsɛrɪbrəl] *adj* cérébral(e)

ceremonial [sɛrɪˈməunɪəl] *n* cérémonial *m*; (*rite*) rituel *m*

ceremony [ˈsɛrɪmənɪ] *n* cérémonie *f*; **to stand on ~** faire des façons

cert [səːt] *n* (*Brit inf*): **it's a dead ~** ça ne fait pas un pli

certain [ˈsəːtən] *adj* certain(e); **to make ~ of** s'assurer de; **for ~** certainement, sûrement

certainly [ˈsəːtənlɪ] *adv* certainement

certainty [ˈsəːtəntɪ] *n* certitude *f*

certificate [səˈtɪfɪkɪt] *n* certificat *m*

certified letter [ˈsəːtɪfaɪd-] *n* (*US*) lettre recommandée

certified public accountant [ˈsəːtɪfaɪd-] *n* (*US*) expert-comptable *m*

certify [ˈsəːtɪfaɪ] *vt* certifier; (*award diploma to*)

conférer un diplôme *etc* à; (*declare insane*)
déclarer malade mental(e) ▷ *vi*: **to ~ to** attester
cervical ['sɜːvɪkl] *adj*: **~ cancer** cancer *m* du col
de l'utérus; **~ smear** frottis vaginal
cervix ['sɜːvɪks] *n* col *m* de l'utérus
Cesarean [siːˈzɛərɪən] *adj, n* (*US*) = **Caesarean**
cessation [səˈseɪʃən] *n* cessation *f*, arrêt *m*
cesspit ['sɛspɪt] *n* fosse *f* d'aisance
CET *abbr* (= *Central European Time*) heure d'Europe
centrale
Ceylon [sɪˈlɔn] *n* Ceylan *m*
cf. *abbr* (= *compare*) cf., voir
c/f *abbr* (*Comm*) = **carried forward**
CFC *n abbr* (= *chlorofluorocarbon*) CFC *m*
CG *n abbr* (*US*) = **coastguard**
cg *abbr* (= *centigram*) cg
CH *n abbr* (*Brit*: = *Companion of Honour*) titre
honorifique
ch *abbr* (*Brit*: = *central heating*) cc
ch. *abbr* (= *chapter*) chap
Chad [tʃæd] *n* Tchad *m*
chafe [tʃeɪf] *vt* irriter, frotter contre ▷ *vi* (*fig*): **to
~ against** se rebiffer contre, regimber contre
chaffinch ['tʃæfɪntʃ] *n* pinson *m*
chagrin ['ʃæɡrɪn] *n* contrariété *f*, déception *f*
chain [tʃeɪn] *n* (*gen*) chaîne *f* ▷ *vt* (*also*: **chain up**)
enchaîner, attacher (avec une chaîne)
chain reaction *n* réaction *f* en chaîne
chain-smoke ['tʃeɪnsməuk] *vi* fumer cigarette
sur cigarette
chain store *n* magasin *m* à succursales
multiples
chair [tʃɛəʳ] *n* chaise *f*; (*armchair*) fauteuil *m*; (*of
university*) chaire *f*; (*of meeting*) présidence *f* ▷ *vt*
(*meeting*) présider; **the ~** (*US*: *electric chair*) la
chaise électrique
chairlift ['tʃɛəlɪft] *n* télésiège *m*
chairman ['tʃɛəmən] (*irreg*) *n* président *m*
chairperson ['tʃɛəpɜːsn] (*irreg*) *n* président(e)
chairwoman ['tʃɛəwumən] *n* présidente *f*
chalet ['ʃæleɪ] *n* chalet *m*
chalice ['tʃælɪs] *n* calice *m*
chalk [tʃɔːk] *n* craie *f*
▶ **chalk up** *vt* écrire à la craie; (*fig*: *success etc*)
remporter
challenge ['tʃælɪndʒ] *n* défi *m* ▷ *vt* défier;
(*statement, right*) mettre en question, contester;
to ~ sb to a fight/game inviter qn à se battre/à
jouer (*sous forme d'un défi*); **to ~ sb to do** mettre
qn au défi de faire
challenger ['tʃælɪndʒəʳ] *n* (*Sport*) challenger *m*
challenging ['tʃælɪndʒɪŋ] *adj* (*task, career*) qui
représente un défi *or* une gageure; (*tone, look*) de
défi, provocateur(-trice)
chamber ['tʃeɪmbəʳ] *n* chambre *f*; (*Brit Law: gen
pl*) cabinet *m*; **~ of commerce** chambre de
commerce
chambermaid ['tʃeɪmbəmeɪd] *n* femme *f* de
chambre
chamber music *n* musique *f* de chambre
chamberpot ['tʃeɪmbəpɔt] *n* pot *m* de chambre
chameleon [kəˈmiːlɪən] *n* caméléon *m*

chamois ['ʃæmwɑː] *n* chamois *m*
chamois leather ['ʃæmɪ-] *n* peau *f* de chamois
champagne [ʃæmˈpeɪn] *n* champagne *m*
champers ['ʃæmpəz] *n* (*inf*) champ *m*
champion ['tʃæmpɪən] *n* (*also of cause*)
champion(ne) ▷ *vt* défendre
championship ['tʃæmpɪənʃɪp] *n*
championnat *m*
chance [tʃɑːns] *n* (*luck*) hasard *m*; (*opportunity*)
occasion *f*, possibilité *f*; (*hope, likelihood*) chance
f; (*risk*) risque *m* ▷ *vt* (*risk*) risquer; (*happen*): **to ~
to do** faire par hasard ▷ *adj* fortuit(e), de
hasard; **there is little ~ of his coming** il est
peu probable *or* il y a peu de chances qu'il
vienne; **to take a ~** prendre un risque; **it's the
~ of a lifetime** c'est une occasion unique; **by ~**
par hasard; **to ~ doing sth** se risquer à faire
qch; **to ~ it** risquer le coup, essayer
▶ **chance on, chance upon** *vt fus* (*person*) tomber
sur, rencontrer par hasard; (*thing*) trouver par
hasard
chancel ['tʃɑːnsəl] *n* chœur *m*
chancellor ['tʃɑːnsələʳ] *n* chancelier *m*
Chancellor of the Exchequer [-ɪksˈtʃɛkəʳ] (*Brit*)
n chancelier *m* de l'Échiquier
chandelier [ʃændəˈlɪəʳ] *n* lustre *m*
change [tʃeɪndʒ] *vt* (*alter, replace: Comm: money*)
changer; (*switch, substitute: hands, trains, clothes,
one's name etc*) changer de; (*transform*): **to ~ sb
into** changer *or* transformer qn en ▷ *vi* (*gen*)
changer; (*change clothes*) se changer; (*be
transformed*): **to ~ into** se changer *or* transformer
en ▷ *n* changement *m*; (*money*) monnaie *f*; **to ~
gear** (*Aut*) changer de vitesse; **to ~ one's mind**
changer d'avis; **she ~d into an old skirt** elle
(s'est changée et) a enfilé une vieille jupe; **a ~
of clothes** des vêtements de rechange; **for a ~**
pour changer; **small ~** petite monnaie; **to give
sb ~ for** *or* **of £10** faire à qn la monnaie de 10
livres; **do you have ~ for £10?** vous avez la
monnaie de 10 livres?; **where can I ~ some
money?** où est-ce que je peux changer de
l'argent?; **keep the ~!** gardez la monnaie!
▶ **change over** *vi* (*swap*) échanger; (*change:
drivers etc*) changer; (*change sides: players etc*)
changer de côté; **to ~ over from sth to sth**
passer de qch à qch
changeable ['tʃeɪndʒəbl] *adj* (*weather*) variable;
(*person*) d'humeur changeante
change machine *n* distributeur *m* de monnaie
changeover ['tʃeɪndʒəuvəʳ] *n* (*to new system*)
changement *m*, passage *m*
changing ['tʃeɪndʒɪŋ] *adj* changeant(e)
changing room *n* (*Brit*: *in shop*) salon *m*
d'essayage; (: *Sport*) vestiaire *m*
channel ['tʃænl] *n* (*TV*) chaîne *f*; (*waveband,
groove, fig: medium*) canal *m*; (*of river, sea*) chenal *m*
▷ *vt* canaliser; (*fig: interest, energies*): **to ~ into**
diriger vers; **through the usual ~s** en suivant
la filière habituelle; **green/red ~** (*Customs*)
couloir *m or* sortie *f* "rien à déclarer"/
"marchandises à déclarer"; **the (English) C~** la

Manche

channel-hopping ['tsʃænl'hɔpɪŋ] n (TV) zapping m

Channel Islands npl: **the ~** les îles fpl Anglo-Normandes

Channel Tunnel n: **the ~** le tunnel sous la Manche

chant [tʃɑːnt] n chant m; mélopée f; (Rel) psalmodie f ▷ vt chanter, scander; psalmodier

chaos ['keɪɔs] n chaos m

chaos theory n théorie f du chaos

chaotic [keɪ'ɔtɪk] adj chaotique

chap [tʃæp] n (Brit inf: man) type m; (term of address): **old ~** mon vieux ▷ vt (skin) gercer, crevasser

chapel ['tʃæpl] n chapelle f

chaperon ['ʃæpərəʊn] n chaperon m ▷ vt chaperonner

chaplain ['tʃæplɪn] n aumônier m

chapped [tʃæpt] adj (skin, lips) gercé(e)

chapter ['tʃæptəʳ] n chapitre m

char [tʃɑːʳ] vt (burn) carboniser ▷ vi (Brit: cleaner) faire des ménages ▷ n (Brit) = **charlady**

character ['kærɪktəʳ] n caractère m; (in novel, film) personnage m; (eccentric person) numéro m, phénomène m; **a person of good ~** une personne bien

character code n (Comput) code m de caractère

characteristic ['kærɪktə'rɪstɪk] adj, n caractéristique (f)

characterize ['kærɪktəraɪz] vt caractériser; **to ~ (as)** définir (comme)

charade [ʃə'rɑːd] n charade f

charcoal ['tʃɑːkəʊl] n charbon m de bois; (Art) charbon

charge [tʃɑːdʒ] n (accusation) accusation f; (Law) inculpation f; (cost) prix (demandé); (of gun, battery, Mil: attack) charge f ▷ vt (gun, battery, Mil: enemy) charger; (customer, sum) faire payer ▷ vi (gen with: up, along etc) foncer; **charges** npl (costs) frais mpl; (Brit Tel): **to reverse the ~s** téléphoner en PCV; **bank/labour ~s** frais mpl de banque/main-d'œuvre; **is there a ~?** doit-on payer?; **there's no ~** c'est gratuit, on ne fait pas payer; **extra ~** supplément m; **to take ~ of** se charger de; **to be in ~ of** être responsable de, s'occuper de; **to ~ in/out** entrer/sortir en trombe; **to ~ down/up** dévaler/ grimper à toute allure; **to ~ sb (with)** (Law) inculper qn (de); **to have ~ of sb** avoir la charge de qn; **they ~d us £10 for the meal** ils nous ont fait payer le repas 10 livres, ils nous ont compté 10 livres pour le repas; **how much do you ~ for this repair?** combien demandez-vous pour cette réparation?; **to ~ an expense (up) to sb** mettre une dépense sur le compte de qn; **~ it to my account** facturez-le sur mon compte

charge account n compte m client

charge card n carte f de client (émise par un grand magasin)

chargehand ['tʃɑːdʒhænd] n (Brit) chef m d'équipe

charger ['tʃɑːdʒəʳ] n (also: **battery charger**) chargeur m; (old: warhorse) cheval m de bataille

charismatic [kærɪz'mætɪk] adj charismatique

charitable ['tʃærɪtəbl] adj charitable

charity ['tʃærɪtɪ] n charité f; (organization) institution f charitable or de bienfaisance, œuvre f (de charité)

charity shop n (Brit) boutique vendant des articles d'occasion au profit d'une organisation caritative

charlady ['tʃɑːleɪdɪ] n (Brit) femme f de ménage

charm [tʃɑːm] n charme m; (on bracelet) breloque f ▷ vt charmer, enchanter

charm bracelet n bracelet m à breloques

charming ['tʃɑːmɪŋ] adj charmant(e)

chart [tʃɑːt] n tableau m, diagramme m; graphique m; (map) carte marine; (weather chart) carte f du temps ▷ vt dresser or établir la carte de; (sales, progress) établir la courbe de; **charts** npl (Mus) hit-parade m; **to be in the ~s** (record, pop group) figurer au hit-parade

charter ['tʃɑːtəʳ] vt (plane) affréter ▷ n (document) charte f; **on ~** (plane) affrété(e)

chartered accountant ['tʃɑːtəd-] n (Brit) expert-comptable m

charter flight n charter m

charwoman ['tʃɑːwumən] (irreg) n = **charlady**

chase [tʃeɪs] vt poursuivre, pourchasser; (also: **chase away**) chasser ▷ n poursuite f, chasse f
▶ **chase down** vt (US) = **chase up**
▶ **chase up** vt (Brit: person) relancer; (: information) rechercher

chasm ['kæzəm] n gouffre m, abîme m

chassis ['ʃæsɪ] n châssis m

chastened ['tʃeɪsnd] adj assagi(e), rappelé(e) à la raison

chastening ['tʃeɪsnɪŋ] adj qui fait réfléchir

chastise [tʃæs'taɪz] vt punir, châtier; corriger

chastity ['tʃæstɪtɪ] n chasteté f

chat [tʃæt] vi (also: **have a chat**) bavarder, causer; (on Internet) chatter ▷ n conversation f
▶ **chat up** vt (Brit inf: girl) baratiner

chatline ['tʃætlaɪn] n numéro téléphonique qui permet de bavarder avec plusieurs personnes en même temps

chat room n (Internet) salon m de discussion

chat show n (Brit) talk-show m

chattel ['tʃætl] n see **good**

chatter ['tʃætəʳ] vi (person) bavarder, papoter ▷ n bavardage m, papotage m; **my teeth are ~ing** je claque des dents

chatterbox ['tʃætəbɔks] n moulin m à paroles, babillard(e)

chattering classes ['tʃætərɪŋ-] npl: **the ~** (inf, pej) les intellos mpl

chatty ['tʃætɪ] adj (style) familier(-ière); (person) enclin(e) à bavarder or au papotage

chauffeur ['ʃəʊfəʳ] n chauffeur m (de maître)

chauvinism ['ʃəʊvɪnɪzəm] n (also: **male chauvinism**) phallocratie f, machisme m; (nationalism) chauvinisme m

chauvinist ['ʃəʊvɪnɪst] n (also: **male chauvinist**) phallocrate m, macho m; (nationalist) chauvin(e)

ChE abbr = **chemical engineer**
cheap [tʃiːp] adj bon marché inv, pas cher
(chère); (reduced: ticket) à prix réduit; (: fare)
réduit(e); (joke) facile, d'un goût douteux; (poor
quality) à bon marché, de qualité médiocre ▷ adv
à bon marché, pour pas cher; **~er** adj moins
cher (chère); **can you recommend a ~ hotel/
restaurant, please?** pourriez-vous m'indiquer
un hôtel/restaurant bon marché?
cheap day return n billet m d'aller et retour
réduit (valable pour la journée)
cheapen ['tʃiːpn] vt rabaisser, déprécier
cheaply ['tʃiːplɪ] adv à bon marché, à bon
compte
cheat [tʃiːt] vi tricher; (in exam) copier ▷ vt
tromper, duper; (rob): **to ~ sb out of sth**
escroquer qch à qn ▷ n tricheur(-euse) m/f;
escroc m; (trick) duperie f, tromperie f
▶ **cheat on** vt fus tromper
cheating ['tʃiːtɪŋ] n tricherie f
Chechnya [tʃɪtʃˈnjaː] n Tchétchénie f
check [tʃɛk] vt vérifier; (passport, ticket) contrôler;
(halt) enrayer; (restrain) maîtriser ▷ vi (official etc)
se renseigner ▷ n vérification f; contrôle m;
(curb) frein m; (Brit: bill) addition f; (US) =
cheque; (pattern: gen pl) carreaux mpl ▷ adj (also:
checked: pattern, cloth) à carreaux; **to ~ with sb**
demander à qn; **to keep a ~ on sb/sth**
surveiller qn/qch
▶ **check in** vi (in hotel) remplir sa fiche (d'hôtel);
(at airport) se présenter à l'enregistrement ▷ vt
(luggage) (faire) enregistrer
▶ **check off** vt (tick off) cocher
▶ **check out** vi (in hotel) régler sa note ▷ vt
(luggage) retirer; (investigate: story) vérifier;
(person) prendre des renseignements sur
▶ **check up** vi: **to ~ up (on sth)** vérifier (qch); **to
~ up on sb** se renseigner sur le compte de qn
checkbook ['tʃɛkbuk] n (US) = **chequebook**
checked ['tʃɛkt] adj (pattern, cloth) à carreaux
checkered ['tʃɛkəd] adj (US) = **chequered**
checkers ['tʃɛkəz] n (US) jeu m de dames
check guarantee card n (US) carte f (d'identité)
bancaire
check-in ['tʃɛkin] n (also: **check-in desk**: at airport)
enregistrement m
checking account ['tʃɛkɪŋ-] n (US) compte
courant
checklist ['tʃɛklɪst] n liste f de contrôle
checkmate ['tʃɛkmeɪt] n échec et mat m
checkout ['tʃɛkaut] n (in supermarket) caisse f
checkpoint ['tʃɛkpɔɪnt] n contrôle m
checkroom ['tʃɛkruːm] (US) n consigne f
checkup ['tʃɛkʌp] n (Med) examen médical,
check-up m
cheddar ['tʃɛdər] n (also: **cheddar cheese**)
cheddar m
cheek [tʃiːk] n joue f; (impudence) toupet m, culot
m; **what a ~!** quel toupet!
cheekbone ['tʃiːkbəun] n pommette f
cheeky ['tʃiːkɪ] adj effronté(e), culotté(e)
cheep [tʃiːp] n (of bird) piaulement m ▷ vi piauler

cheer [tʃɪər] vt acclamer, applaudir; (gladden)
réjouir, réconforter ▷ vi applaudir ▷ n (gen pl)
acclamations fpl, applaudissements mpl; bravos
mpl, hourras mpl; **~s!** à la vôtre!
▶ **cheer on** vt encourager (par des cris etc)
▶ **cheer up** vi se dérider, reprendre courage ▷ vt
remonter le moral à or de, dérider, égayer
cheerful ['tʃɪəful] adj gai(e), joyeux(-euse)
cheerfulness ['tʃɪəfulnɪs] n gaieté f, bonne
humeur
cheerio [tʃɪərɪˈəu] excl (Brit) salut!, au revoir!
cheerleader ['tʃɪəliːdər] n membre d'un groupe de
majorettes qui chantent et dansent pour soutenir leur
équipe pendant les matchs de football américain
cheerless ['tʃɪəlɪs] adj sombre, triste
cheese [tʃiːz] n fromage m
cheeseboard ['tʃiːzbɔːd] n plateau m à
fromages; (with cheese on it) plateau m de
fromages
cheeseburger ['tʃiːzbəːgər] n cheeseburger m
cheesecake ['tʃiːzkeɪk] n tarte f au fromage
cheetah ['tʃiːtə] n guépard m
chef [ʃɛf] n chef (cuisinier)
chemical ['kɛmɪkl] adj chimique ▷ n produit m
chimique
chemist ['kɛmɪst] n (Brit: pharmacist)
pharmacien(ne); (scientist) chimiste m/f
chemistry ['kɛmɪstrɪ] n chimie f
chemist's ['kɛmɪsts], **chemist's shop** n (Brit)
pharmacie f
chemotherapy [kiːməuˈθɛrəpɪ] n
chimiothérapie f
cheque, (US) **check** [tʃɛk] n chèque m; **to pay by
~** payer par chèque
chequebook, (US) **checkbook** ['tʃɛkbuk] n
chéquier m, carnet m de chèques
cheque card n (Brit) carte f (d'identité) bancaire
chequered, (US) **checkered** ['tʃɛkəd] adj (fig)
varié(e)
cherish ['tʃɛrɪʃ] vt chérir; (hope etc) entretenir
cheroot [ʃəˈruːt] n cigare m de Manille
cherry ['tʃɛrɪ] n cerise f; (also: **cherry tree**)
cerisier m
Ches abbr (Brit) = **Cheshire**
chess [tʃɛs] n échecs mpl
chessboard ['tʃɛsbɔːd] n échiquier m
chessman ['tʃɛsmən] (irreg) n pièce f (de jeu
d'échecs)
chessplayer ['tʃɛspleɪər] n joueur(-euse)
d'échecs
chest [tʃɛst] n poitrine f; (box) coffre m, caisse f;
to get sth off one's ~ (inf) vider son sac
chest measurement n tour m de poitrine
chestnut ['tʃɛsnʌt] n châtaigne f; (also:
chestnut tree) châtaignier m; (colour) châtain m
▷ adj châtain inv; (hair) châtain inv; (horse) alezan
chest of drawers n commode f
chesty ['tʃɛstɪ] adj (cough) de poitrine
chew [tʃuː] vt mâcher
chewing gum ['tʃuːɪŋ-] n chewing-gum m
chic [ʃiːk] adj chic inv, élégant(e)
chick [tʃɪk] n poussin m; (inf) pépée f

chicken ['tʃɪkɪn] n poulet m; (inf: coward) poule mouillée
▶ **chicken out** vi (inf) se dégonfler
chicken feed n (fig) broutilles fpl, bagatelle f
chickenpox ['tʃɪkɪnpɒks] n varicelle f
chickpea ['tʃɪkpiː] n pois m chiche
chicory ['tʃɪkərɪ] n chicorée f; (salad) endive f
chide [tʃaɪd] vt réprimander, gronder
chief [tʃiːf] n chef m ▷ adj principal(e); **C~ of Staff** (Mil) chef d'État-major
chief constable n (Brit) ≈ préfet m de police
chief executive, (US) **chief executive officer** n directeur(-trice) général(e)
chiefly ['tʃiːflɪ] adv principalement, surtout
chilblain ['tʃɪlbleɪn] n engelure f
child (pl **children**) [tʃaɪld, 'tʃɪldrən] n enfant m/f
child abuse n maltraitance f d'enfants; (sexual) abus mpl sexuels sur des enfants
child benefit n (Brit) ≈ allocations familiales
childbirth ['tʃaɪldbəːθ] n accouchement m
childcare ['tʃaɪldkɛəʳ] n (for working parents) garde f d'enfants (pour les parents qui travaillent)
childhood ['tʃaɪldhud] n enfance f
childish ['tʃaɪldɪʃ] adj puéril(e), enfantin(e)
childless ['tʃaɪldlɪs] adj sans enfants
childlike ['tʃaɪldlaɪk] adj innocent(e), pur(e)
child minder n (Brit) garde f d'enfants
child prodigy n enfant m/f prodige
children ['tʃɪldrən] npl of **child**
children's home ['tʃɪldrənz-] n ≈ foyer m d'accueil (pour enfants)
Chile ['tʃɪlɪ] n Chili m
Chilean ['tʃɪlɪən] adj chilien(ne) ▷ n Chilien(ne)
chill [tʃɪl] n (of water) froid m; (of air) fraîcheur f; (Med) refroidissement m, coup m de froid ▷ adj froid(e), glacial(e) ▷ vt (person) faire frissonner; refroidir; (Culin) mettre au frais, rafraîchir; **"serve ~ed"** "à servir frais"
▶ **chill out** vi (inf: esp US) se relaxer
chilli, **chili** ['tʃɪlɪ] n piment m (rouge)
chilling ['tʃɪlɪŋ] adj (wind) frais (fraîche), froid(e); (look, smile) glacé(e); (thought) qui donne le frisson
chilly ['tʃɪlɪ] adj froid(e), glacé(e); (sensitive to cold) frileux(-euse); **to feel ~** avoir froid
chime [tʃaɪm] n carillon m ▷ vi carillonner, sonner
chimney ['tʃɪmnɪ] n cheminée f
chimney sweep n ramoneur m
chimpanzee [tʃɪmpæn'ziː] n chimpanzé m
chin [tʃɪn] n menton m
China ['tʃaɪnə] n Chine f
china ['tʃaɪnə] n (material) porcelaine f; (crockery) (vaisselle f en) porcelaine
Chinese [tʃaɪ'niːz] adj chinois(e) ▷ n (pl inv) Chinois(e); (Ling) chinois m
chink [tʃɪŋk] n (opening) fente f, fissure f; (noise) tintement m
chinwag ['tʃɪnwæg] n (Brit inf): **to have a ~** tailler une bavette
chip [tʃɪp] n (gen pl: Culin: Brit) frite f; (: US: also: **potato chip**) chip m; (of wood) copeau m; (of glass,

stone) éclat m; (also: **microchip**) puce f; (in gambling) fiche f ▷ vt (cup, plate) ébrécher; **when the ~s are down** (fig) au moment critique
▶ **chip in** vi (inf) mettre son grain de sel
chip and PIN n carte f à puce; **chip and PIN machine** machine f à carte (à puce)
chipboard ['tʃɪpbɔːd] n aggloméré m, panneau m de particules
chipmunk ['tʃɪpmʌŋk] n suisse m (animal)
chippings ['tʃɪpɪŋz] npl: **loose ~** gravillons mpl
chip shop n (Brit) friterie f; voir article

● **CHIP SHOP**

Un chip shop, que l'on appelle également un "fish-and-chip shop", est un magasin où l'on vend des plats à emporter. Les chip shops sont d'ailleurs à l'origine des "takeaways". On y achète en particulier du poisson frit et des frites, mais on y trouve également des plats traditionnels britanniques ("steak pies", saucisses, etc). Tous les plats étaient à l'origine emballés dans du papier journal. Dans certains de ces magasins, on peut s'asseoir pour consommer sur place.

---

chiropodist [kɪ'rɔpədɪst] n (Brit) pédicure m/f
chirp [tʃəːp] n pépiement m, gazouillis m; (of crickets) stridulation f ▷ vi pépier, gazouiller; chanter, striduler
chirpy ['tʃəːpɪ] adj (inf) plein(e) d'entrain, tout guilleret(te)
chisel ['tʃɪzl] n ciseau m
chit [tʃɪt] n mot m, note f
chitchat ['tʃɪttʃæt] n bavardage m, papotage m
chivalrous ['ʃɪvəlrəs] adj chevaleresque
chivalry ['ʃɪvəlrɪ] n chevalerie f; esprit m chevaleresque
chives [tʃaɪvz] npl ciboulette f, civette f
chloride ['klɔːraɪd] n chlorure m
chlorinate ['klɔrɪneɪt] vt chlorer
chlorine ['klɔːriːn] n chlore m
choc-ice ['tʃɔkaɪs] n (Brit) esquimau® m
chock [tʃɔk] n cale f
chock-a-block ['tʃɔkə'blɔk], **chock-full** [tʃɔk'ful] adj plein(e) à craquer
chocolate ['tʃɔklɪt] n chocolat m
choice [tʃɔɪs] n choix m ▷ adj de choix; **by** or **from ~** par choix; **a wide ~** un grand choix
choir ['kwaɪəʳ] n chœur m, chorale f
choirboy ['kwaɪəbɔɪ] n jeune choriste m
choke [tʃəuk] vi étouffer ▷ vt étrangler; étouffer; (block) boucher, obstruer ▷ n (Aut) starter m
cholera ['kɔlərə] n choléra m
cholesterol [kə'lɛstərɔl] n cholestérol m
choose (pt **chose**, pp **chosen**) [tʃuːz, tʃəuz, 'tʃəuzn] vt choisir ▷ vi: **to ~ between** choisir entre; **to ~ from** choisir parmi; **to ~ to do** décider de faire, juger bon de faire
choosy ['tʃuːzɪ] adj: **(to be) ~** (faire le) difficile
chop [tʃɔp] vt (wood) couper (à la hache); (Culin:

also: **chop up**) couper (fin), émincer, hacher (en morceaux) ▷ n coup m (de hache, du tranchant de la main); (Culin) côtelette f; **to get the ~** (Brit inf: project) tomber à l'eau; (: person: be sacked) se faire renvoyer
▶ **chop down** vt (tree) abattre
▶ **chop off** vt trancher
chopper ['tʃɔpəʳ] n (helicopter) hélicoptère m, hélico m
choppy ['tʃɔpɪ] adj (sea) un peu agité(e)
chops [tʃɔps] npl (jaws) mâchoires fpl; babines fpl
chopsticks ['tʃɔpstɪks] npl baguettes fpl
choral ['kɔːrəl] adj choral(e), chanté(e) en chœur
chord [kɔːd] n (Mus) accord m
chore [tʃɔːʳ] n travail m de routine; **household ~s** travaux mpl du ménage
choreographer [kɔrɪ'ɔgrəfəʳ] n chorégraphe m/f
choreography [kɔrɪ'ɔgrəfɪ] n chorégraphie f
chorister ['kɔrɪstəʳ] n choriste m/f
chortle ['tʃɔːtl] vi glousser
chorus ['kɔːrəs] n chœur m; (repeated part of song, also fig) refrain m
chose [tʃəuz] pt of **choose**
chosen ['tʃəuzn] pp of **choose**
chow [tʃau] n (dog) chow-chow m
chowder ['tʃaudəʳ] n soupe f de poisson
Christ [kraɪst] n Christ m
christen ['krɪsn] vt baptiser
christening ['krɪsnɪŋ] n baptême m
Christian ['krɪstɪən] adj, n chrétien(ne)
Christianity [krɪstɪ'ænɪtɪ] n christianisme m
Christian name n prénom m
Christmas ['krɪsməs] n Noël m or f; **happy** or **merry ~!** joyeux Noël!
Christmas card n carte f de Noël
Christmas carol n chant m de Noël
Christmas Day n le jour de Noël
Christmas Eve n la veille de Noël; la nuit de Noël
Christmas Island n île f Christmas
Christmas pudding n (esp Brit) Christmas m pudding
Christmas tree n arbre m de Noël
chrome [krəum] n chrome m
chromium ['krəumɪəm] n chrome m; (also: **chromium plating**) chromage m
chromosome ['krəuməsəum] n chromosome m
chronic ['krɔnɪk] adj chronique; (fig: liar, smoker) invétéré(e)
chronicle ['krɔnɪkl] n chronique f
chronological [krɔnə'lɔdʒɪkl] adj chronologique
chrysanthemum [krɪ'sænθəməm] n chrysanthème m
chubby ['tʃʌbɪ] adj potelé(e), rondelet(te)
chuck [tʃʌk] vt (inf) lancer, jeter; (Brit: also: **chuck up**: job) lâcher; (: person) plaquer
▶ **chuck out** vt (inf: person) flanquer dehors or à la porte; (: rubbish etc) jeter
chuckle ['tʃʌkl] vi glousser
chuffed [tʃʌft] adj (Brit inf): **to be ~ about sth** être content(e) de qch

chug [tʃʌg] vi faire teuf-teuf; souffler
chum [tʃʌm] n copain (copine)
chump ['tʃʌmp] n (inf) imbécile m/f, crétin(e)
chunk [tʃʌŋk] n gros morceau; (of bread) quignon m
chunky ['tʃʌŋkɪ] adj (furniture etc) massif(-ive); (person) trapu(e); (knitwear) en grosse laine
Chunnel ['tʃʌnəl] n = **Channel Tunnel**
church [tʃəːtʃ] n église f; **the C~ of England** l'Église anglicane
churchyard ['tʃəːtʃjɑːd] n cimetière m
churlish ['tʃəːlɪʃ] adj grossier(-ère); hargneux(-euse)
churn [tʃəːn] n (for butter) baratte f; (also: **milk churn**) (grand) bidon à lait
▶ **churn out** vt débiter
chute [ʃuːt] n goulotte f; (also: **rubbish chute**) vide-ordures m inv; (Brit: children's slide) toboggan m
chutney ['tʃʌtnɪ] n chutney m
CIA n abbr (= Central Intelligence Agency) CIA f
CID n abbr (= Criminal Investigation Department) ≈ P.J. f
cider ['saɪdəʳ] n cidre m
CIF abbr (= cost, insurance and freight) CAF
cigar [sɪ'gɑːʳ] n cigare m
cigarette [sɪgə'rɛt] n cigarette f
cigarette case n étui m à cigarettes
cigarette end n mégot m
cigarette holder n fume-cigarettes m inv
cigarette lighter n briquet m
C-in-C abbr = **commander-in-chief**
cinch [sɪntʃ] n (inf): **it's a ~** c'est du gâteau, c'est l'enfance de l'art
Cinderella [sɪndə'rɛlə] n Cendrillon
cine-camera ['sɪnɪ'kæmərə] n (Brit) caméra f
cine-film ['sɪnɪfɪlm] n (Brit) film m
cinema ['sɪnəmə] n cinéma m
cine-projector ['sɪnɪprə'dʒɛktəʳ] n (Brit) projecteur m de cinéma
cinnamon ['sɪnəmən] n cannelle f
cipher ['saɪfəʳ] n code secret; (fig: faceless employee etc) numéro m; **in ~** codé(e)
circa ['səːkə] prep circa, environ
circle ['səːkl] n cercle m; (in cinema) balcon m ▷ vi faire or décrire des cercles ▷ vt (surround) entourer, encercler; (move round) faire le tour de, tourner autour de
circuit ['səːkɪt] n circuit m; (lap) tour m
circuit board n plaquette f
circuitous [səː'kjuɪtəs] adj indirect(e), qui fait un détour
circular ['səːkjuləʳ] adj circulaire ▷ n circulaire f; (as advertisement) prospectus m
circulate ['səːkjuleɪt] vi circuler ▷ vt faire circuler
circulation [səːkju'leɪʃən] n circulation f; (of newspaper) tirage m
circumcise ['səːkəmsaɪz] vt circoncire
circumference [sə'kʌmfərəns] n circonférence f
circumflex ['səːkəmflɛks] n (also: **circumflex accent**) accent m circonflexe

C

circumscribe ['sə:kəmskraɪb] vt circonscrire

circumspect ['sə:kəmspɛkt] adj circonspect(e)

circumstances ['sə:kəmstənsɪz] npl circonstances fpl; (financial condition) moyens mpl, situation financière; **in** or **under the ~** dans ces conditions; **under no ~** en aucun cas, sous aucun prétexte

circumstantial [sə:kəm'stænʃl] adj (report, statement) circonstancié(e); **~ evidence** preuve indirecte

circumvent [sə:kəm'vɛnt] vt (rule etc) tourner

circus ['sə:kəs] n cirque m; (also: **Circus**: in place names) place f

cirrhosis [sɪ'rəusɪs] n (also: **cirrhosis of the liver**) cirrhose f (du foie)

CIS n abbr (= Commonwealth of Independent States) CEI f

cissy ['sɪsɪ] n = **sissy**

cistern ['sɪstən] n réservoir m (d'eau); (in toilet) réservoir de la chasse d'eau

citation [saɪ'teɪʃən] n citation f; (US) P.-V m

cite [saɪt] vt citer

citizen ['sɪtɪzn] n (Pol) citoyen(ne); (resident): **the ~s of this town** les habitants de cette ville

Citizens' Advice Bureau ['sɪtɪznz-] n (Brit) ≈ Bureau m d'aide sociale

citizenship ['sɪtɪznʃɪp] n citoyenneté f; (Brit: Scol) ≈ éducation f civique

citric ['sɪtrɪk] adj: **~ acid** acide m citrique

citrus fruits ['sɪtrəs-] npl agrumes mpl

city ['sɪtɪ] n (grande) ville f; **the C~** la Cité de Londres (centre des affaires)

city centre n centre ville m

City Hall n (US) ≈ hôtel m de ville

city technology college n (Brit) établissement m d'enseignement technologique (situé dans un quartier défavorisé)

civic ['sɪvɪk] adj civique; (authorities) municipal(e)

civic centre n (Brit) centre administratif (municipal)

civil ['sɪvɪl] adj civil(e); (polite) poli(e), civil(e)

civil engineer n ingénieur civil

civil engineering n génie civil, travaux publics

civilian [sɪ'vɪlɪən] adj, n civil(e)

civilization [sɪvɪlaɪ'zeɪʃən] n civilisation f

civilized ['sɪvɪlaɪzd] adj civilisé(e); (fig) où règnent les bonnes manières, empreint(e) d'une courtoisie de bon ton

civil law n code civil; (study) droit civil

civil liberties npl libertés fpl civiques

civil rights npl droits mpl civiques

civil servant n fonctionnaire m/f

Civil Service n fonction publique, administration f

civil war n guerre civile

civvies ['sɪvɪz] npl: **in ~** (inf) en civil

CJD n abbr (= Creutzfeldt-Jakob disease) MCJ f

cl abbr (= centilitre) cl

clad [klæd] adj: **~ (in)** habillé(e) de, vêtu(e) de

claim [kleɪm] vt (rights etc) revendiquer; (compensation) réclamer; (assert) déclarer, prétendre ▷ vi (for insurance) faire une déclaration de sinistre ▷ n revendication f; prétention f; (right) droit m; (for expenses) note f de frais; **(insurance) ~** demande f d'indemnisation, déclaration f de sinistre; **to put in a ~ for** (pay rise etc) demander

claimant ['kleɪmənt] n (Admin, Law) requérant(e)

claim form n (gen) formulaire m de demande

clairvoyant [klɛə'vɔɪənt] n voyant(e), extra-lucide m/f

clam [klæm] n palourde f
  ▷ **clam up** vi (inf) la boucler

clamber ['klæmbəʳ] vi grimper, se hisser

clammy ['klæmɪ] adj humide et froid(e) (au toucher), moite

clamour, (US) **clamor** ['klæməʳ] n (noise) clameurs fpl; (protest) protestations bruyantes ▷ vi: **to ~ for sth** réclamer qch à grands cris

clamp [klæmp] n crampon m; (on workbench) valet m; (on car) sabot m de Denver ▷ vt attacher; (car) mettre un sabot à
  ▷ **clamp down on** vt fus sévir contre, prendre des mesures draconiennes à l'égard de

clampdown ['klæmpdaun] n: **there has been a ~ on ...** des mesures énergiques ont été prises contre ...

clan [klæn] n clan m

clandestine [klæn'dɛstɪn] adj clandestin(e)

clang [klæŋ] n bruit m or fracas m métallique ▷ vi émettre un bruit or fracas métallique

clanger ['klæŋəʳ] n: **to drop a ~** (Brit inf) faire une boulette

clansman ['klænzmən] (irreg) n membre m d'un clan (écossais)

clap [klæp] vi applaudir ▷ vt: **to ~ (one's hands)** battre des mains ▷ n claquement m; tape f; **a ~ of thunder** un coup de tonnerre

clapping ['klæpɪŋ] n applaudissements mpl

claptrap ['klæptræp] n (inf) baratin m

claret ['klærət] n (vin m de) bordeaux m (rouge)

clarification [klærɪfɪ'keɪʃən] n (fig) clarification f, éclaircissement m

clarify ['klærɪfaɪ] vt clarifier

clarinet [klærɪ'nɛt] n clarinette f

clarity ['klærɪtɪ] n clarté f

clash [klæʃ] n (sound) choc m, fracas m; (with police) affrontement m; (fig) conflit m ▷ vi se heurter; être or entrer en conflit; (colours) jurer; (dates, events) tomber en même temps

clasp [klɑ:sp] n (of necklace, bag) fermoir m ▷ vt serrer, étreindre

class [klɑ:s] n (gen) classe f; (group, category) catégorie f ▷ vt classer, classifier

class-conscious ['klɑ:s'kɔnʃəs] adj conscient(e) de son appartenance sociale

class consciousness n conscience f de classe

classic ['klæsɪk] adj classique ▷ n (author, work) classique m; (race etc) classique f

classical ['klæsɪkl] adj classique

classics ['klæsɪks] npl (Scol) lettres fpl classiques

classification [klæsɪfɪ'keɪʃən] n classification f

classified ['klæsɪfaɪd] *adj* (*information*) secret(-ète); ~ **ads** petites annonces

classify ['klæsɪfaɪ] *vt* classifier, classer

classless society ['klɑːslɪs-] *n* société *f* sans classes

classmate ['klɑːsmeɪt] *n* camarade *m/f* de classe

classroom ['klɑːsrum] *n* (salle *f* de) classe *f*

classroom assistant *n* assistant(-e) d'éducation

classy ['klɑːsɪ] (*inf*) *adj* classe (*inf*)

clatter ['klætər] *n* cliquetis *m* ▷ *vi* cliqueter

clause [klɔːz] *n* clause *f*; (*Ling*) proposition *f*

claustrophobia [klɔːstrə'fəubɪə] *n* claustrophobie *f*

claustrophobic [klɔːstrə'fəubɪk] *adj* (*person*) claustrophobe; (*place*) où l'on se sent claustrophobe

claw [klɔː] *n* griffe *f*; (*of bird of prey*) serre *f*; (*of lobster*) pince *f* ▷ *vt* griffer; déchirer

clay [kleɪ] *n* argile *f*

clean [kliːn] *adj* propre; (*clear, smooth*) net(te); (*record, reputation*) sans tache; (*joke, story*) correct(e) ▷ *vt* nettoyer; **he ~ forgot** il a complètement oublié; **to come ~** (*inf: admit guilt*) se mettre à table; **to ~ one's teeth** se laver les dents; **~ driving licence** or (US) **record** *permis où n'est portée aucune indication de contravention*
  ▶ **clean off** *vt* enlever
  ▶ **clean out** *vt* nettoyer (à fond)
  ▶ **clean up** *vt* nettoyer; (*fig*) remettre de l'ordre dans ▷ *vi* (*fig: make profit*): **to ~ up on** faire son beurre avec

clean-cut ['kliːn'kʌt] *adj* (*man*) soigné; (*situation etc*) bien délimité(e), net(te), clair(e)

cleaner ['kliːnər] *n* (*person*) nettoyeur(-euse), femme *f* de ménage; (*also*: **dry cleaner**) teinturier(-ière); (*product*) détachant *m*

cleaner's ['kliːnərz] *n* (*also*: **dry cleaner's**) teinturier *m*

cleaning ['kliːnɪŋ] *n* nettoyage *m*

cleaning lady *n* femme *f* de ménage

cleanliness ['klɛnlɪnɪs] *n* propreté *f*

cleanly ['kliːnlɪ] *adv* proprement; nettement

cleanse [klɛnz] *vt* nettoyer; purifier

cleanser ['klɛnzər] *n* détergent *m*; (*for face*) démaquillant *m*

clean-shaven ['kliːn'ʃeɪvn] *adj* rasé(e) de près

cleansing department ['klɛnzɪŋ-] *n* (*Brit*) service *m* de voirie

clean sweep *n*: **to make a ~** (*Sport*) rafler tous les prix

clean-up ['kliːnʌp] *n* nettoyage *m*

clear [klɪər] *adj* clair(e); (*glass, plastic*) transparent(e); (*road, way*) libre, dégagé(e); (*profit, majority*) net(te); (*conscience*) tranquille; (*skin*) frais (fraîche); (*sky*) dégagé(e) ▷ *vt* (*road*) dégager, déblayer; (*table*) débarrasser; (*room etc: of people*) faire évacuer; (*woodland*) défricher; (*cheque*) compenser; (*Comm: goods*) liquider; (*Law: suspect*) innocenter; (*obstacle*) franchir or sauter sans heurter ▷ *vi* (*weather*) s'éclaircir; (*fog*) se dissiper ▷ *adv*: ~ **of** à distance de, à

l'écart de ▷ *n*: **to be in the ~** (*out of debt*) être dégagé(e) de toute dette; (*out of suspicion*) être lavé(e) de tout soupçon; (*out of danger*) être hors de danger; **to ~ the table** débarrasser la table, desservir; **to ~ one's throat** s'éclaircir la gorge; **to ~ a profit** faire un bénéfice net; **to make o.s. ~** se faire bien comprendre; **to make it ~ to sb that ...** bien faire comprendre à qn que ...; **I have a ~ day tomorrow** (*Brit*) je n'ai rien de prévu demain; **to keep ~ of sb/sth** éviter qn/qch
  ▶ **clear away** *vt* (*things, clothes etc*) enlever, retirer; **to ~ away the dishes** débarrasser la table
  ▶ **clear off** *vi* (*inf: leave*) dégager
  ▶ **clear up** *vi* s'éclaircir, se dissiper ▷ *vt* ranger, mettre en ordre; (*mystery*) éclaircir, résoudre

clearance ['klɪərəns] *n* (*removal*) déblayage *m*; (*free space*) dégagement *m*; (*permission*) autorisation *f*

clearance sale *n* (*Comm*) liquidation *f*

clear-cut ['klɪə'kʌt] *adj* précis(e), nettement défini(e)

clearing ['klɪərɪŋ] *n* (*in forest*) clairière *f*; (*Brit Banking*) compensation *f*, clearing *m*

clearing bank *n* (*Brit*) banque *f* qui appartient à une chambre de compensation

clearly ['klɪəlɪ] *adv* clairement; (*obviously*) de toute évidence

clearway ['klɪəweɪ] *n* (*Brit*) route *f* à stationnement interdit

cleavage ['kliːvɪdʒ] *n* (*of dress*) décolleté *m*

cleaver ['kliːvər] *n* fendoir *m*, couperet *m*

clef [klɛf] *n* (*Mus*) clé *f*

cleft [klɛft] *n* (*in rock*) crevasse *f*, fissure *f*

clemency ['klɛmənsɪ] *n* clémence *f*

clement ['klɛmənt] *adj* (*weather*) clément(e)

clementine ['klɛməntaɪn] *n* clémentine *f*

clench [klɛntʃ] *vt* serrer

clergy ['kləːdʒɪ] *n* clergé *m*

clergyman ['kləːdʒɪmən] (*irreg*) *n* ecclésiastique *m*

clerical ['klɛrɪkl] *adj* de bureau, d'employé de bureau; (*Rel*) clérical(e), du clergé

clerk [klɑːk] (US) [kləːrk] *n* (*Brit*) employé(e) de bureau; (*US: salesman/woman*) vendeur(-euse); **C~ of Court** (*Law*) greffier *m* (du tribunal)

clever ['klɛvər] *adj* (*intelligent*) intelligent(e); (*skilful*) habile, adroit(e); (*device, arrangement*) ingénieux(-euse), astucieux(-euse)

cleverly ['klɛvəlɪ] *adv* (*skilfully*) habilement; (*craftily*) astucieusement

clew [kluː] *n* (US) = **clue**

cliché ['kliːʃeɪ] *n* cliché *m*

click [klɪk] *vi* faire un bruit sec or un déclic; (*Comput*) cliquer ▷ *vt*: **to ~ one's tongue** faire claquer sa langue; **to ~ one's heels** claquer des talons; **to ~ on an icon** cliquer sur une icône

client ['klaɪənt] *n* client(e)

clientele [kliːɑːn'tɛl] *n* clientèle *f*

cliff [klɪf] *n* falaise *f*

cliffhanger ['klɪfhæŋər] *n* (*TV, fig*) histoire

pleine de suspense

climactic [klaɪˈmæktɪk] *adj* à son point culminant, culminant(e)

climate [ˈklaɪmɪt] *n* climat *m*

climate change *n* changement *m* climatique

climax [ˈklaɪmæks] *n* apogée *m*, point culminant; (*sexual*) orgasme *m*

climb [klaɪm] *vi* grimper, monter; (*plane*) prendre de l'altitude ⊳ *vt* (*stairs*) monter; (*mountain*) escalader; (*tree*) grimper à ⊳ *n* montée *f*, escalade *f*; **to ~ over a wall** passer par dessus un mur
▸ **climb down** *vi* (re)descendre; (*Brit fig*) rabattre de ses prétentions

climb-down [ˈklaɪmdaun] *n* (*Brit*) reculade *f*

climber [ˈklaɪmə^r] *n* (*also*: **rock climber**) grimpeur(-euse), varappeur(-euse); (*plant*) plante grimpante

climbing [ˈklaɪmɪŋ] *n* (*also*: **rock climbing**) escalade *f*, varappe *f*

clinch [klɪntʃ] *vt* (*deal*) conclure, sceller

clincher [ˈklɪntʃə^r] *n*: **that was the ~** c'est ce qui a fait pencher la balance

cling (*pt, pp* **clung**) [klɪŋ, klʌŋ] *vi*: **to ~ (to)** se cramponner (à), s'accrocher (à); (*clothes*) coller (à)

Clingfilm® [ˈklɪŋfɪlm] *n* film *m* alimentaire

clinic [ˈklɪnɪk] *n* clinique *f*; centre médical; (*session: Med*) consultation(s) *f(pl)*, séance(s) *f(pl)*; (*Sport*) séance(s) de perfectionnement

clinical [ˈklɪnɪkl] *adj* clinique; (*fig*) froid(e)

clink [klɪŋk] *vi* tinter, cliqueter

clip [klɪp] *n* (*for hair*) barrette *f*; (*also*: **paper clip**) trombone *m*; (*Brit: also*: **bulldog clip**) pince *f* de bureau; (*holding hose etc*) collier *m or* bague *f* (métallique) de serrage; (*TV, Cinema*) clip *m* ⊳ *vt* (*also*: **clip together**: *papers*) attacher; (*hair, nails*) couper; (*hedge*) tailler

clippers [ˈklɪpəz] *npl* tondeuse *f*; (*also*: **nail clippers**) coupe-ongles *m inv*

clipping [ˈklɪpɪŋ] *n* (*from newspaper*) coupure *f* de journal

clique [kliːk] *n* clique *f*, coterie *f*

cloak [kləuk] *n* grande cape ⊳ *vt* (*fig*) masquer, cacher

cloakroom [ˈkləukrum] *n* (*for coats etc*) vestiaire *m*; (*Brit*: W.C.) toilettes *fpl*

clock [klɔk] *n* (*large*) horloge *f*; (*small*) pendule *f*; **round the ~** (*work etc*) vingt-quatre heures sur vingt-quatre; **to sleep round the ~** *or* **the ~ round** faire le tour du cadran; **30,000 on the ~** (*Brit Aut*) 30 000 milles au compteur; **to work against the ~** faire la course contre la montre
▸ **clock in** *or* **on** (*Brit*) *vi* (*with card*) pointer (en arrivant); (*start work*) commencer à travailler
▸ **clock off** *or* **out** (*Brit*) *vi* (*with card*) pointer (en partant); (*leave work*) quitter le travail
▸ **clock up** *vt* (*miles, hours etc*) faire

clockwise [ˈklɔkwaɪz] *adv* dans le sens des aiguilles d'une montre

clockwork [ˈklɔkwəːk] *n* rouages *mpl*, mécanisme *m*; (*of clock*) mouvement *m*

(d'horlogerie) ⊳ *adj* (*toy, train*) mécanique

clog [klɔg] *n* sabot *m* ⊳ *vt* boucher, encrasser ⊳ *vi* (*also*: **clog up**) se boucher, s'encrasser

cloister [ˈklɔɪstə^r] *n* cloître *m*

clone [kləun] *n* clone *m* ⊳ *vt* cloner

close¹ [kləus] *adj* (*near*): **~ (to)** près (de), proche (de); (*writing, texture*) serré(e); (*contact, link, watch*) étroit(e); (*examination*) attentif(-ive), minutieux(-euse); (*contest*) très serré(e); (*weather*) lourd(e), étouffant(e); (*room*) mal aéré(e) ⊳ *adv* près, à proximité; **~ to** (*prep*) près de; **~ by, ~ at hand** (*adj, adv*) tout(e) près; **how ~ is Edinburgh to Glasgow?** combien de kilomètres y-a-t-il entre Édimbourg et Glasgow?; **a ~ friend** un ami intime; **to have a ~ shave** (*fig*) l'échapper belle; **at ~ quarters** tout près, à côté

close² [kləuz] *vt* fermer; (*bargain, deal*) conclure ⊳ *vi* (*shop etc*) fermer; (*lid, door etc*) se fermer; (*end*) se terminer, se conclure ⊳ *n* (*end*) conclusion *f*; **to bring sth to a ~** mettre fin à qch; **what time do you ~?** à quelle heure fermez-vous?
▸ **close down** *vt, vi* fermer (*définitivement*)
▸ **close in** *vi* (*hunters*) approcher; (*night, fog*) tomber; **the days are closing in** les jours raccourcissent; **to ~ in on sb** cerner qn
▸ **close off** *vt* (*area*) boucler

closed [kləuzd] *adj* (*shop etc*) fermé(e); (*road*) fermé à la circulation

closed-circuit [ˈkləuzdˈsəːkɪt] *adj*: **~ television** télévision *f* en circuit fermé

closed shop *n* organisation *f* qui n'admet que des travailleurs syndiqués

close-knit [ˈkləusˈnɪt] *adj* (*family, community*) très uni(e)

closely [ˈkləuslɪ] *adv* (*examine, watch*) de près; **we are ~ related** nous sommes proches parents; **a ~ guarded secret** un secret bien gardé

close season [kləus-] *n* (*Brit: Hunting*) fermeture *f* de la chasse/pêche; (: *Football*) trêve *f*

closet [ˈklɔzɪt] *n* (*cupboard*) placard *m*, réduit *m*

close-up [ˈkləusʌp] *n* gros plan

closing [ˈkləuzɪŋ] *adj* (*stages, remarks*) final(e); **~ price** (*Stock Exchange*) cours *m* de clôture

closing time *n* heure *f* de fermeture

closure [ˈkləuʒə^r] *n* fermeture *f*

clot [klɔt] *n* (*of blood, milk*) caillot *m*; (*inf: person*) ballot *m* ⊳ *vi* (*blood*) former des caillots; (: *external bleeding*) se coaguler

cloth [klɔθ] *n* (*material*) tissu *m*, étoffe *f*; (*Brit: also*: **tea cloth**) torchon *m*; lavette *f*; (*also*: **tablecloth**) nappe *f*

clothe [kləuð] *vt* habiller, vêtir

clothes [kləuðz] *npl* vêtements *mpl*, habits *mpl*; **to put one's ~ on** s'habiller; **to take one's ~ off** enlever ses vêtements

clothes brush *n* brosse *f* à habits

clothes line *n* corde *f* (à linge)

clothes peg, (*US*) **clothes pin** *n* pince *f* à linge

clothing [ˈkləuðɪŋ] *n* = **clothes**

clotted cream [ˈklɔtɪd-] *n* (*Brit*) crème caillée

cloud [klaud] *n* nuage *m* ⊳ *vt* (*liquid*) troubler; **to**

~ **the issue** brouiller les cartes; **every ~ has a silver lining** (*proverb*) à quelque chose malheur est bon (*proverbe*)

▶ **cloud over** *vi* se couvrir; (*fig*) s'assombrir

cloudburst ['klaudbə:st] *n* violente averse

cloud-cuckoo-land ['klaud'kuku:'lænd] *n* (*Brit*) monde *m* imaginaire

cloudy ['klaudı] *adj* nuageux(-euse), couvert(e); (*liquid*) trouble

clout [klaut] *n* (*blow*) taloche *f*; (*fig*) pouvoir *m* ▷ *vt* flanquer une taloche à

clove [kləuv] *n* clou *m* de girofle; **a ~ of garlic** une gousse d'ail

clover ['kləuvə^r] *n* trèfle *m*

cloverleaf ['kləuvəli:f] *n* feuille *f* de trèfle; (*Aut*) croisement *m* en trèfle

clown [klaun] *n* clown *m* ▷ *vi* (*also*: **clown about, clown around**) faire le clown

cloying ['klɔııŋ] *adj* (*taste, smell*) écœurant(e)

club [klʌb] *n* (*society*) club *m*; (*weapon*) massue *f*, matraque *f*; (*also*: **golf club**) club ▷ *vt* matraquer ▷ *vi*: **to ~ together** s'associer; **clubs** *npl* (*Cards*) trèfle *m*

club car *n* (*US Rail*) wagon-restaurant *m*

club class *n* (*Aviat*) classe *f* club

clubhouse ['klʌbhaus] *n* pavillon *m*

club soda *n* (*US*) eau *f* de seltz

cluck [klʌk] *vi* glousser

clue [klu:] *n* indice *m*; (*in crosswords*) définition *f*; **I haven't a ~** je n'en ai pas la moindre idée

clued up, (*US*) **clued in** [klu:d-] *adj* (*inf*) (vachement) calé(e)

clump [klʌmp] *n*: **~ of trees** bouquet *m* d'arbres

clumsy ['klʌmzı] *adj* (*person*) gauche, maladroit(e); (*object*) malcommode, peu maniable

clung [klʌŋ] *pt, pp* of **cling**

cluster ['klʌstə^r] *n* (petit) groupe; (*of flowers*) grappe *f* ▷ *vi* se rassembler

clutch [klʌtʃ] *n* (*Aut*) embrayage *m*; (*grasp*): **~es** étreinte *f*, prise *f* ▷ *vt* (*grasp*) agripper; (*hold tightly*) serrer fort; (*hold on to*) se cramponner à

clutter ['klʌtə^r] *vt* (*also*: **clutter up**) encombrer ▷ *n* désordre *m*, fouillis *m*

cm *abbr* (= *centimetre*) cm

CNAA *n abbr* (*Brit*: = *Council for National Academic Awards*) *organisme non universitaire délivrant des diplômes*

CND *n abbr* = **Campaign for Nuclear Disarmament**

CO *n abbr* (= *commanding officer*) Cdt; (*Brit*) = **Commonwealth Office** ▷ *abbr* (*US*) = **Colorado**

Co. *abbr* = **company, county**

c/o *abbr* (= *care of*) c/o, aux bons soins de

coach [kəutʃ] *n* (*bus*) autocar *m*; (*horse-drawn*) diligence *f*; (*of train*) voiture *f*, wagon *m*; (*Sport*: *trainer*) entraîneur(-euse); (*school*: *tutor*) répétiteur(-trice) ▷ *vt* (*Sport*) entraîner; (*student*) donner des leçons particulières à

coach station (*Brit*) *n* gare routière

coach trip *n* excursion *f* en car

coagulate [kəu'ægjuleɪt] *vt* coaguler ▷ *vi* se coaguler

coal [kəul] *n* charbon *m*

coal face *n* front *m* de taille

coalfield ['kəulfi:ld] *n* bassin houiller

coalition [kəuə'lıʃən] *n* coalition *f*

coalman ['kəulmən] (*irreg*) *n* charbonnier *m*, marchand *m* de charbon

coal mine *n* mine *f* de charbon

coarse [kɔ:s] *adj* grossier(-ère), rude; (*vulgar*) vulgaire

coast [kəust] *n* côte *f* ▷ *vi* (*car, cycle*) descendre en roue libre

coastal ['kəustl] *adj* côtier(-ère)

coaster ['kəustə^r] *n* (*Naut*) caboteur *m*; (*for glass*) dessous *m* de verre

coastguard ['kəustgɑ:d] *n* garde-côte *m*

coastline ['kəustlaın] *n* côte *f*, littoral *m*

coat [kəut] *n* manteau *m*; (*of animal*) pelage *m*, poil *m*; (*of paint*) couche *f* ▷ *vt* couvrir, enduire; **~ of arms** *n* blason *m*, armoiries *fpl*

coat hanger *n* cintre *m*

coating ['kəutıŋ] *n* couche *f*, enduit *m*

co-author ['kəu'ɔ:θə^r] *n* co-auteur *m*

coax [kəuks] *vt* persuader par des cajoleries

cob [kɔb] *n* see **corn**

cobbled ['kɔbld] *adj* pavé(e)

cobbler ['kɔblə^r] *n* cordonnier *m*

cobbles, cobblestones ['kɔblz, 'kɔblstəunz] *npl* pavés (ronds)

COBOL ['kəubɔl] *n* COBOL *m*

cobra ['kəubrə] *n* cobra *m*

cobweb ['kɔbwɛb] *n* toile *f* d'araignée

cocaine [kə'keın] *n* cocaïne *f*

cock [kɔk] *n* (*rooster*) coq *m*; (*male bird*) mâle *m* ▷ *vt* (*gun*) armer; **to ~ one's ears** (*fig*) dresser l'oreille

cock-a-hoop [kɔkə'hu:p] *adj* jubilant(e)

cockerel ['kɔkərl] *n* jeune coq *m*

cock-eyed ['kɔkaıd] *adj* (*fig*) de travers; qui louche; qui ne tient pas debout (*fig*)

cockle ['kɔkl] *n* coque *f*

cockney ['kɔknı] *n* cockney *m/f* (*habitant des quartiers populaires de l'East End de Londres*), ≈ faubourien(ne)

cockpit ['kɔkpıt] *n* (*in aircraft*) poste *m* de pilotage, cockpit *m*

cockroach ['kɔkrəutʃ] *n* cafard *m*, cancrelat *m*

cocktail ['kɔkteıl] *n* cocktail *m*; **prawn ~**, (*US*) **shrimp ~** cocktail de crevettes

cocktail cabinet *n* (meuble-)bar *m*

cocktail party *n* cocktail *m*

cocktail shaker [-'ʃeıkə^r] *n* shaker *m*

cocky ['kɔkı] *adj* trop sûr(e) de soi

cocoa ['kəukəu] *n* cacao *m*

coconut ['kəukənʌt] *n* noix *f* de coco

cocoon [kə'ku:n] *n* cocon *m*

C.O.D. *abbr* = **cash on delivery**; (*US*) = **collect on delivery**

cod [kɔd] *n* morue fraîche, cabillaud *m*

code [kəud] *n* code *m*; (*Tel*: *area code*) indicatif *m*; **~ of behaviour** règles *fpl* de conduite; **~ of practice** déontologie *f*

codeine ['kəʊdiːn] n codéine f
codger ['kɒdʒəʳ] n: **an old ~** (Brit inf) un drôle de vieux bonhomme
codicil ['kɒdɪsɪl] n codicille m
codify ['kəʊdɪfaɪ] vt codifier
cod-liver oil ['kɒdlɪvər-] n huile f de foie de morue
co-driver ['kəʊdraɪvəʳ] n (in race) copilote m; (of lorry) deuxième chauffeur m
co-ed ['kəʊ'ɛd] adj abbr = **coeducational** ▷ n abbr (US: female student) étudiante d'une université mixte; (Brit: school) école f mixte
coeducational ['kəʊɛdju'keɪʃənl] adj mixte
coerce [kəʊ'əːs] vt contraindre
coercion [kəʊ'əːʃən] n contrainte f
coexistence ['kəʊɪg'zɪstəns] n coexistence f
C. of C. n abbr = **chamber of commerce**
C of E n abbr = **Church of England**
coffee ['kɒfɪ] n café m; **white ~**, (US) **~ with cream** (café-)crème m
coffee bar n (Brit) café m
coffee bean n grain m de café
coffee break n pause-café f
coffee cake ['kɒfɪkeɪk] n (US) ≈ petit pain aux raisins
coffee cup n tasse f à café
coffee maker n cafetière f
coffeepot ['kɒfɪpɒt] n cafetière f
coffee shop n café m
coffee table n (petite) table basse
coffin ['kɒfɪn] n cercueil m
C of I n abbr = **Church of Ireland**
C of S n abbr = **Church of Scotland**
cog [kɒg] n (wheel) roue dentée; (tooth) dent f (d'engrenage)
cogent ['kəʊdʒənt] adj puissant(e), convaincant(e)
cognac ['kɒnjæk] n cognac m
cogwheel ['kɒgwiːl] n roue dentée
cohabit [kəʊ'hæbɪt] vi (formal): **to ~ (with sb)** cohabiter (avec qn)
coherent [kəʊ'hɪərənt] adj cohérent(e)
cohesion [kəʊ'hiːʒən] n cohésion f
cohesive [kəʊ'hiːsɪv] adj (fig) cohésif(-ive)
COI n abbr (Brit: = Central Office of Information) service d'information gouvernemental
coil [kɔɪl] n rouleau m, bobine f; (one loop) anneau m, spire f; (of smoke) volute f; (contraceptive) stérilet m ▷ vt enrouler
coin [kɔɪn] n pièce f (de monnaie) ▷ vt (word) inventer
coinage ['kɔɪnɪdʒ] n monnaie f, système m monétaire
coinbox ['kɔɪnbɒks] n (Brit) cabine f téléphonique
coincide [kəʊɪn'saɪd] vi coïncider
coincidence [kəʊ'ɪnsɪdəns] n coïncidence f
coin-operated ['kɔɪn'ɒpəreɪtɪd] adj (machine, launderette) automatique
Coke® [kəʊk] n coca m
coke [kəʊk] n (coal) coke m
Col. abbr (= colonel) Col; (US) = **Colorado**

COLA n abbr (US: = cost-of-living adjustment) réajustement (des salaires, indemnités etc) en fonction du coût de la vie
colander ['kɒləndəʳ] n passoire f (à légumes)
cold [kəʊld] adj froid(e) ▷ n froid m; (Med) rhume m; **it's ~** il fait froid; **to be ~** (person) avoir froid; **to catch ~** prendre or attraper froid; **to catch a ~** s'enrhumer, attraper un rhume; **in ~ blood** de sang-froid; **to have ~ feet** avoir froid aux pieds; (fig) avoir la frousse or la trouille; **to give sb the ~ shoulder** battre froid à qn
cold-blooded ['kəʊld'blʌdɪd] adj (Zool) à sang froid
cold cream n crème f de soins
coldly ['kəʊldlɪ] adv froidement
cold sore n bouton m de fièvre
cold sweat n: **to be in a ~ (about sth)** avoir des sueurs froides (au sujet de qch)
cold turkey n (inf) manque m; **to go ~** être en manque
Cold War n: **the ~** la guerre froide
coleslaw ['kəʊlslɔː] n sorte de salade de chou cru
colic ['kɒlɪk] n colique(s) f(pl)
colicky ['kɒlɪkɪ] adj qui souffre de coliques
collaborate [kə'læbəreɪt] vi collaborer
collaboration [kəlæbə'reɪʃən] n collaboration f
collaborator [kə'læbəreɪtəʳ] n collaborateur(-trice)
collage [kɒ'lɑːʒ] n (Art) collage m
collagen ['kɒlədʒən] n collagène m
collapse [kə'læps] vi s'effondrer, s'écrouler; (Med) avoir un malaise ▷ n effondrement m, écroulement m; (of government) chute f
collapsible [kə'læpsəbl] adj pliant(e), télescopique
collar ['kɒləʳ] n (of coat, shirt) col m; (for dog) collier m; (Tech) collier, bague f ▷ vt (inf: person) pincer
collarbone ['kɒləbəʊn] n clavicule f
collate [kɒ'leɪt] vt collationner
collateral [kə'lætərl] n nantissement m
collation [kə'leɪʃən] n collation f
colleague ['kɒliːg] n collègue m/f
collect [kə'lɛkt] vt rassembler; (pick up) ramasser; (as a hobby) collectionner; (Brit: call for) (passer) prendre; (mail) faire la levée de, ramasser; (money owed) encaisser; (donations, subscriptions) recueillir ▷ vi (people) se rassembler; (dust, dirt) s'amasser; **to ~ one's thoughts** réfléchir, réunir ses idées; **~ on delivery (COD)** (US Comm) payable or paiement à la livraison; **to call ~** (US Tel) téléphoner en PCV
collected [kə'lɛktɪd] adj: **~ works** œuvres complètes
collection [kə'lɛkʃən] n collection f; (of mail) levée f; (for money) collecte f, quête f
collective [kə'lɛktɪv] adj collectif(-ive) ▷ n collectif m
collective bargaining n convention collective
collector [kə'lɛktəʳ] n collectionneur m; (of taxes) percepteur m; (of rent, cash) encaisseur m; **~'s item** or **piece** pièce f de collection
college ['kɒlɪdʒ] n collège m; (of technology,

agriculture etc) institut *m*; **to go to ~** faire des études supérieures; **~ of education** ≈ école normale

collide [kə'laɪd] *vi*: **to ~ (with)** entrer en collision (avec)

collie ['kɔlɪ] *n* (*dog*) colley *m*

colliery ['kɔlɪərɪ] *n* (*Brit*) mine *f* de charbon, houillère *f*

collision [kə'lɪʒən] *n* collision *f*, heurt *m*; **to be on a ~ course** aller droit à la collision; (*fig*) aller vers l'affrontement

collision damage waiver *n* (*Insurance*) rachat *m* de franchise

colloquial [kə'ləukwɪəl] *adj* familier(-ère)

collusion [kə'luːʒən] *n* collusion *f*; **in ~ with** en complicité avec

Colo. *abbr* (*US*) = **Colorado**

cologne [kə'ləun] *n* (*also*: **eau de cologne**) eau *f* de cologne

Colombia [kə'lɔmbɪə] *n* Colombie *f*

Colombian [kə'lɔmbɪən] *adj* colombien(ne) ▷ *n* Colombien(ne)

colon ['kəulən] *n* (*sign*) deux-points *mpl*; (*Med*) côlon *m*

colonel ['kəːnl] *n* colonel *m*

colonial [kə'ləunɪəl] *adj* colonial(e)

colonize ['kɔlənaɪz] *vt* coloniser

colony ['kɔlənɪ] *n* colonie *f*

color ['kʌləʳ] *n* (*US*) = **colour**

Colorado beetle [kɔlə'rɑːdəu-] *n* doryphore *m*

colossal [kə'lɔsl] *adj* colossal(e)

colour, (*US*) **color** ['kʌləʳ] *n* couleur *f* ▷ *vt* colorer; (*dye*) teindre; (*paint*) peindre; (*with crayons*) colorier; (*news*) fausser, exagérer ▷ *vi* (*blush*) rougir ▷ *cpd* (*film, photograph, television*) en couleur; **colours** *npl* (*of party, club*) couleurs *fpl*; **I'd like a different ~** je le voudrais dans un autre coloris

▶ **colour in** *vt* colorier

colour bar, (*US*) **color bar** *n* discrimination raciale (*dans un établissement etc*)

colour-blind, (*US*) **color-blind** ['kʌləblaɪnd] *adj* daltonien(ne)

coloured, (*US*) **colored** ['kʌləd] *adj* coloré(e); (*photo*) en couleur

colour film, (*US*) **color film** *n* (*for camera*) pellicule *f* (en) couleur

colourful, (*US*) **colorful** ['kʌləful] *adj* coloré(e), vif (vive); (*personality*) pittoresque, haut(e) en couleurs

colouring, (*US*) **coloring** ['kʌlərɪŋ] *n* colorant *m*; (*complexion*) teint *m*

colour scheme, (*US*) **color scheme** *n* combinaison *f* de(s) couleur(s)

colour supplement *n* (*Brit Press*) supplément *m* magazine

colour television, (*US*) **color television** *n* télévision *f* (en) couleur

colt [kəult] *n* poulain *m*

column ['kɔləm] *n* colonne *f*; (*fashion column, sports column etc*) rubrique *f*; **the editorial ~** l'éditorial *m*

columnist ['kɔləmnɪst] *n* rédacteur(-trice) d'une rubrique

coma ['kəumə] *n* coma *m*

comb [kəum] *n* peigne *m* ▷ *vt* (*hair*) peigner; (*area*) ratisser, passer au peigne fin

combat ['kɔmbæt] *n* combat *m* ▷ *vt* combattre, lutter contre

combination [kɔmbɪ'neɪʃən] *n* (*gen*) combinaison *f*

combination lock *n* serrure *f* à combinaison

combine [kəm'baɪn] *vt* combiner ▷ *vi* s'associer; (*Chem*) se combiner ▷ *n* ['kɔmbaɪn] association *f*; (*Econ*) trust *m*; (*also*: **combine harvester**) moissonneuse-batteuse(-lieuse) *f*; **to ~ sth with sth** (*one quality with another*) joindre *ou* allier qch à qch; **a ~d effort** un effort conjugué

combine harvester *n* moissonneuse-batteuse(-lieuse) *f*

combo ['kɔmbəu] *n* (*Jazz etc*) groupe *m* de musiciens

combustible [kəm'bʌstɪbl] *adj* combustible

combustion [kəm'bʌstʃən] *n* combustion *f*

 KEYWORD

come (*pt* **came**, *pp* **-**) [kʌm, keɪm] *vi* **1** (*movement towards*) venir; **to ~ running** arriver en courant; **he's ~ here to work** il est venu ici pour travailler; **~ with me** suivez-moi; **to ~ into sight** *or* **view** apparaître

2 (*arrive*) arriver; **to ~ home** rentrer (chez soi *or* à la maison); **we've just ~ from Paris** nous arrivons de Paris; **coming!** j'arrive!

3 (*reach*): **to ~ to** (*decision etc*) parvenir à, arriver à; **the bill came to £40** la note s'est élevée à 40 livres; **if it ~s to it** s'il le faut, dans le pire des cas

4 (*occur*): **an idea came to me** il m'est venu une idée; **what might ~ of it** ce qui pourrait en résulter, ce qui pourrait advenir *or* se produire

5 (*be, become*): **to ~ loose/undone** se défaire/desserrer; **I've ~ to like him** j'ai fini par bien l'aimer

6 (*inf: sexually*) jouir

▶ **come about** *vi* se produire, arriver

▶ **come across** *vt fus* rencontrer par hasard, tomber sur ▷ *vi*: **to ~ across well/badly** faire une bonne/mauvaise impression

▶ **come along** *vi* (*Brit: pupil, work*) faire des progrès, avancer; **~ along!** viens!; allons!, allez!

▶ **come apart** *vi* s'en aller en morceaux; se détacher

▶ **come away** *vi* partir, s'en aller; (*become detached*) se détacher

▶ **come back** *vi* revenir; (*reply*): **can I ~ back to you on that one?** est-ce qu'on peut revenir là-dessus plus tard?

▶ **come by** *vt fus* (*acquire*) obtenir, se procurer

▶ **come down** *vi* descendre; (*prices*) baisser; (*buildings*) s'écrouler; (*: be demolished*) être démoli(e)

▶ **come forward** *vi* s'avancer; (*make o.s. known*) se présenter, s'annoncer

▶ **come from** vt fus (source) venir de; (place) venir de, être originaire de

▶ **come in** vi entrer; (train) arriver; (fashion) entrer en vogue; (on deal etc) participer

▶ **come in for** vt fus (criticism etc) être l'objet de

▶ **come into** vt fus (money) hériter de

▶ **come off** vi (button) se détacher; (attempt) réussir

▶ **come on** vi (lights, electricity) s'allumer; (central heating) se mettre en marche; (pupil, work, project) faire des progrès, avancer; **~ on!** viens!; allons!, allez!

▶ **come out** vi sortir; (sun) se montrer; (book) paraître; (stain) s'enlever; (strike) cesser le travail, se mettre en grève

▶ **come over** vt fus: **I don't know what's ~ over him!** je ne sais pas ce qui lui a pris!

▶ **come round** vi (after faint, operation) revenir à soi, reprendre connaissance

▶ **come through** vi (survive) s'en sortir; (telephone call): **the call came through** l'appel est bien parvenu

▶ **come to** vi revenir à soi ▷ vt (add up to: amount): **how much does it ~ to?** ça fait combien?

▶ **come under** vt fus (heading) se trouver sous; (influence) subir

▶ **come up** vi monter; (sun) se lever; (problem) se poser; (event) survenir; (in conversation) être soulevé

▶ **come up against** vt fus (resistance, difficulties) rencontrer

▶ **come up to** vt fus arriver à; **the film didn't ~ up to our expectations** le film nous a déçu

▶ **come up with** vt fus (money) fournir; **he came up with an idea** il a eu une idée, il a proposé quelque chose

▶ **come upon** vt fus tomber sur

comeback ['kʌmbæk] n (Theat) rentrée f; (reaction) réaction f; (response) réponse f

Comecon ['kɔmɪkɔn] n abbr (= Council for Mutual Economic Aid) COMECON m

comedian [kə'miːdɪən] n (comic) comique m; (Theat) comédien m

comedienne [kəmiːdɪ'ɛn] n comique f

comedown ['kʌmdaun] n déchéance f

comedy ['kɔmɪdɪ] n comédie f; (humour) comique m

comet ['kɔmɪt] n comète f

comeuppance [kʌm'ʌpəns] n: **to get one's ~** recevoir ce qu'on mérite

comfort ['kʌmfət] n confort m, bien-être m; (solace) consolation f, réconfort m ▷ vt consoler, réconforter

comfortable ['kʌmfətəbl] adj confortable; (person) à l'aise; (financially) aisé(e); (patient) dont l'état est stationnaire; **I don't feel very ~ about it** cela m'inquiète un peu

comfortably ['kʌmfətəblɪ] adv (sit) confortablement; (live) à l'aise

comforter ['kʌmfətər] n (US) édredon m

comforts ['kʌmfəts] npl aises fpl

comfort station n (US) toilettes fpl

comic ['kɔmɪk] adj (also: **comical**) comique ▷ n (person) comique m; (Brit: magazine: for children) magazine m de bandes dessinées or de BD; (: for adults) illustré m

comical ['kɔmɪkl] adj amusant(e)

comic book (US) n (for children) magazine m de bandes dessinées or de BD; (for adults) illustré m

comic strip n bande dessinée

coming ['kʌmɪŋ] n arrivée f ▷ adj (next) prochain(e); (future) à venir; **in the ~ weeks** dans les prochaines semaines

Comintern ['kɔmɪntəːn] n Comintern m

comma ['kɔmə] n virgule f

command [kə'mɑːnd] n ordre m, commandement m; (Mil: authority) commandement; (mastery) maîtrise f; (Comput) commande f ▷ vt (troops) commander; (be able to get) (pouvoir) disposer de, avoir à sa disposition; (deserve) avoir droit à; **to ~ sb to do** donner l'ordre or commander à qn de faire; **to have/ take ~ of** avoir/prendre le commandement de; **to have at one's ~** (money, resources etc) disposer de

command economy n économie planifiée

commandeer [kɔmən'dɪər] vt réquisitionner (par la force)

commander [kə'mɑːndər] n chef m; (Mil) commandant m

commander-in-chief [kə'mɑːndərɪn'tʃiːf] n (Mil) commandant m en chef

commanding [kə'mɑːndɪŋ] adj (appearance) imposant(e); (voice, tone) autoritaire; (lead, position) dominant(e)

commanding officer n commandant m

commandment [kə'mɑːndmənt] n (Rel) commandement m

command module n (Space) module m de commande

commando [kə'mɑːndəu] n commando m; membre m d'un commando

commemorate [kə'mɛməreɪt] vt commémorer

commemoration [kəmɛmə'reɪʃən] n commémoration f

commemorative [kə'mɛmərətɪv] adj commémoratif(-ive)

commence [kə'mɛns] vt, vi commencer

commend [kə'mɛnd] vt louer; (recommend) recommander

commendable [kə'mɛndəbl] adj louable

commendation [kɔmɛn'deɪʃən] n éloge m; recommandation f

commensurate [kə'mɛnʃərɪt] adj: **~ with/to** en rapport avec/selon

comment ['kɔmɛnt] n commentaire m ▷ vi faire des remarques or commentaires; **to ~ on** faire des remarques sur; **to ~ that** faire remarquer que; **"no ~"** "je n'ai rien à déclarer"

commentary ['kɔməntərɪ] n commentaire m; (Sport) reportage m (en direct)

commentator ['kɔmənteɪtər] n commentateur m; (Sport) reporter m

commerce ['kɔməːs] n commerce m

commercial [kə'məːʃəl] adj commercial(e) ▷ n

(*Radio, TV*) annonce f publicitaire, spot m
(publicitaire)
commercial bank n banque f d'affaires
commercial break n (*Radio, TV*) spot m
(publicitaire)
commercial college n école f de commerce
commercialism [kə'mə:ʃəlɪzəm] n
mercantilisme m
commercial television n publicité f à la
télévision, chaînes privées (financées par la
publicité)
commercial traveller n voyageur m de
commerce
commercial vehicle n véhicule m utilitaire
commiserate [kə'mɪzəreɪt] vi: **to ~ with sb**
témoigner de la sympathie pour qn
commission [kə'mɪʃən] n (*committee, fee*)
commission f; (*order for work of art etc*) commande
f ▷ vt (*Mil*) nommer (à un commandement);
(*work of art*) commander, charger un artiste de
l'exécution de; **out of ~** (*Naut*) hors de service;
(*machine*) hors service; **I get 10% ~** je reçois une
commission de 10%; **~ of inquiry** (*Brit*)
commission d'enquête
commissionaire [kəmɪʃə'nɛəʳ] n (*Brit: at shop,
cinema etc*) portier m (en uniforme)
commissioner [kə'mɪʃənəʳ] n membre m d'une
commission; (*Police*) préfet m (de police)
commit [kə'mɪt] vt (*act*) commettre; (*resources*)
consacrer; (*to sb's care*) confier (à); **to ~ o.s. (to
do)** s'engager (à faire); **to ~ suicide** se suicider;
to ~ to writing coucher par écrit; **to ~ sb for
trial** traduire qn en justice
commitment [kə'mɪtmənt] n engagement m;
(*obligation*) responsabilité(s) (fpl)
committed [kə'mɪtɪd] adj (*writer, politician etc*)
engagé(e)
committee [kə'mɪtɪ] n comité m; commission f;
to be on a ~ siéger dans un comité or une
commission)
committee meeting n réunion f de comité or
commission
commodity [kə'mɔdɪtɪ] n produit m,
marchandise f, article m; (*food*) denrée f
commodity exchange n bourse f de
marchandises
common ['kɔmən] adj (*gen*) commun(e); (*usual*)
courant(e) ▷ n terrain communal; **in ~** en
commun; **in ~ use** d'un usage courant; **it's ~
knowledge that** il est bien connu or notoire
que; **to the ~ good** pour le bien de tous, dans
l'intérêt général
common cold n: **the ~** le rhume
common denominator n dénominateur
commun
commoner ['kɔmənəʳ] n roturier(-ière)
common ground n (*fig*) terrain m d'entente
common land n terrain communal
common law n droit coutumier
common-law ['kɔmənlɔ:] adj: **~ wife** épouse f
de facto
commonly ['kɔmənlɪ] adv communément,

généralement; couramment
Common Market n Marché commun
commonplace ['kɔmənpleɪs] adj banal(e),
ordinaire
commonroom ['kɔmənrum] n salle commune;
(*Scol*) salle des professeurs
Commons ['kɔmənz] npl (*Brit Pol*): **the (House
of) ~** la chambre des Communes
common sense n bon sens
Commonwealth ['kɔmənwɛlθ] n: **the ~** le
Commonwealth; *voir article*

● **COMMONWEALTH**
●
● Le *Commonwealth* regroupe 50 États
● indépendants et plusieurs territoires qui
● reconnaissent tous le souverain britannique
● comme chef de cette association.

commotion [kə'məuʃən] n désordre m,
tumulte m
communal ['kɔmju:nl] adj (*life*)
communautaire; (*for common use*) commun(e)
commune ['kɔmju:n] n (*group*) communauté f
▷ vi [kə'mju:n]: **to ~ with** (*nature*) converser
intimement avec; communier avec
communicate [kə'mju:nɪkeɪt] vt
communiquer, transmettre ▷ vi: **to ~ (with)**
communiquer (avec)
communication [kəmju:nɪ'keɪʃən] n
communication f
communication cord n (*Brit*) sonnette f
d'alarme
communications network n réseau m de
communications
communications satellite n satellite m de
télécommunications
communicative [kə'mju:nɪkətɪv] adj
communicatif(-ive)
communion [kə'mju:nɪən] n (*also:* **Holy
Communion**) communion f
communism ['kɔmjunɪzəm] n communisme m
communist ['kɔmjunɪst] adj, n communiste m/f
community [kə'mju:nɪtɪ] n communauté f
community centre, (*US*) **community center** n
foyer socio-éducatif, centre m de loisirs
community chest n (US) fonds commun
community health centre n centre médico-
social
community service n ≈ travail m d'intérêt
général, TIG m
community spirit n solidarité f
commutation ticket [kɔmju'teɪʃən-] n (US)
carte f d'abonnement
commute [kə'mju:t] vi faire le trajet journalier
(*de son domicile à un lieu de travail assez éloigné*) ▷ vt
(*Law*) commuer; (*Math: terms etc*) opérer la
commutation de
commuter [kə'mju:təʳ] n banlieusard(e) (*qui fait
un trajet journalier pour se rendre à son travail*)
compact adj [kəm'pækt] compact(e) ▷ n
['kɔmpækt] contrat m, entente f; (*also:* **powder**

compact) poudrier *m*
compact disc *n* disque compact
compact disc player *n* lecteur *m* de disques compacts
companion [kəm'pænjən] *n* compagnon (compagne)
companionship [kəm'pænjənʃɪp] *n* camaraderie *f*
companionway [kəm'pænjənweɪ] *n* (*Naut*) escalier *m* des cabines
company ['kʌmpənɪ] *n* (*also Comm, Mil, Theat*) compagnie *f*; **he's good ~** il est d'une compagnie agréable; **we have ~** nous avons de la visite; **to keep sb ~** tenir compagnie à qn; **to part ~ with** se séparer de; **Smith and C~** Smith et Compagnie
company car *n* voiture *f* de fonction
company director *n* administrateur(-trice)
company secretary *n* (*Brit Comm*) secrétaire général (*d'une société*)
comparable ['kɔmpərəbl] *adj* comparable
comparative [kəm'pærətɪv] *adj* (*study*) comparatif(-ive); (*relative*) relatif(-ive)
comparatively [kəm'pærətɪvlɪ] *adv* (*relatively*) relativement
compare [kəm'pɛəʳ] *vt*: **to ~ sth/sb with** *or* **to** comparer qch/qn avec *or* à ▷ *vi*: **to ~ (with)** se comparer (à); être comparable (à); **how do the prices ~?** comment sont les prix?, est-ce que les prix sont comparables?; **~d with** *or* **to** par rapport à
comparison [kəm'pærɪsn] *n* comparaison *f*; **in ~ (with)** en comparaison (de)
compartment [kəm'pɑːtmənt] *n* (*also Rail*) compartiment *m*; **a non-smoking ~** un compartiment non-fumeurs
compass ['kʌmpəs] *n* boussole *f*; **compasses** *npl* (*Math*) compas *m*; **within the ~ of** dans les limites de
compassion [kəm'pæʃən] *n* compassion *f*, humanité *f*
compassionate [kəm'pæʃənɪt] *adj* accessible à la compassion, au cœur charitable et bienveillant; **on ~ grounds** pour raisons personnelles *or* de famille
compassionate leave *n* congé exceptionnel (*pour raisons de famille*)
compatibility [kəmpætɪ'bɪlɪtɪ] *n* compatibilité *f*
compatible [kəm'pætɪbl] *adj* compatible
compel [kəm'pɛl] *vt* contraindre, obliger
compelling [kəm'pɛlɪŋ] *adj* (*fig: argument*) irrésistible
compendium [kəm'pɛndɪəm] *n* (*summary*) abrégé *m*
compensate ['kɔmpənseɪt] *vt* indemniser, dédommager ▷ *vi*: **to ~ for** compenser
compensation [kɔmpən'seɪʃən] *n* compensation *f*; (*money*) dédommagement *m*, indemnité *f*
compere ['kɔmpɛəʳ] *n* présentateur(-trice), animateur(-trice)
compete [kəm'piːt] *vi* (*take part*) concourir; (*vie*):

to ~ (with) rivaliser (avec), faire concurrence (à)
competence ['kɔmpɪtəns] *n* compétence *f*, aptitude *f*
competent ['kɔmpɪtənt] *adj* compétent(e), capable
competing [kəm'piːtɪŋ] *adj* (*ideas, theories*) opposé(e); (*companies*) concurrent(e)
competition [kɔmpɪ'tɪʃən] *n* (*contest*) compétition *f*, concours *m*; (*Econ*) concurrence *f*; **in ~ with** en concurrence avec
competitive [kəm'pɛtɪtɪv] *adj* (*Econ*) concurrentiel(le); (*sports*) de compétition; (*person*) qui a l'esprit de compétition
competitive examination *n* concours *m*
competitor [kəm'pɛtɪtəʳ] *n* concurrent(e)
compile [kəm'paɪl] *vt* compiler
complacency [kəm'pleɪsnsɪ] *n* contentement *m* de soi, autosatisfaction *f*
complacent [kəm'pleɪsnt] *adj* (*trop*) content(e) de soi
complain [kəm'pleɪn] *vi*: **to ~ (about)** se plaindre (de); (*in shop etc*) réclamer (au sujet de)
▶ **complain of** *vt fus* (*Med*) se plaindre de
complaint [kəm'pleɪnt] *n* plainte *f*; (*in shop etc*) réclamation *f*; (*Med*) affection *f*
complement ['kɔmplɪmənt] *n* complément *m*; (*esp of ship's crew etc*) effectif complet ▷ *vt* (*enhance*) compléter
complementary [kɔmplɪ'mɛntərɪ] *adj* complémentaire
complete [kəm'pliːt] *adj* complet(-ète); (*finished*) achevé(e) ▷ *vt* achever, parachever; (*set, group*) compléter; (*a form*) remplir
completely [kəm'pliːtlɪ] *adv* complètement
completion [kəm'pliːʃən] *n* achèvement *m*; (*of contract*) exécution *f*; **to be nearing ~** être presque terminé
complex ['kɔmplɛks] *adj* complexe ▷ *n* (*Psych, buildings etc*) complexe *m*
complexion [kəm'plɛkʃən] *n* (*of face*) teint *m*; (*of event etc*) aspect *m*, caractère *m*
complexity [kəm'plɛksɪtɪ] *n* complexité *f*
compliance [kəm'plaɪəns] *n* (*submission*) docilité *f*; (*agreement*): **~ with** le fait de se conformer à; **in ~ with** en conformité avec, conformément à
compliant [kəm'plaɪənt] *adj* docile, très accommodant(e)
complicate ['kɔmplɪkeɪt] *vt* compliquer
complicated ['kɔmplɪkeɪtɪd] *adj* compliqué(e)
complication [kɔmplɪ'keɪʃən] *n* complication *f*
compliment *n* ['kɔmplɪmənt] compliment *m* ▷ *vt* ['kɔmplɪmɛnt] complimenter; **compliments** *npl* compliments *mpl*, hommages *mpl*; vœux *mpl*; **to pay sb a ~** faire *or* adresser un compliment à qn; **to ~ sb (on sth/on doing sth)** féliciter qn (pour qch/de faire qch)
complimentary [kɔmplɪ'mɛntərɪ] *adj* flatteur(-euse); (*free*) à titre gracieux
complimentary ticket *n* billet *m* de faveur
compliments slip *n* fiche *f* de transmission
comply [kəm'plaɪ] *vi*: **to ~ with** se soumettre à, se conformer à

component [kəm'pəunənt] *adj* composant(e),
constituant(e) ▷ *n* composant *m*, élément *m*
compose [kəm'pəuz] *vt* composer; (*form*): **to be
~d of** se composer de; **to ~ o.s.** se calmer, se
maîtriser; **to ~ one's features** prendre une
contenance
composed [kəm'pəuzd] *adj* calme, posé(e)
composer [kəm'pəuzər] *n* (*Mus*) compositeur *m*
composite ['kɔmpəzɪt] *adj* composite; (*Bot,
Math*) composé(e)
composition [kɔmpə'zɪʃən] *n* composition *f*
compost ['kɔmpɔst] *n* compost *m*
composure [kəm'pəuʒər] *n* calme *m*, maîtrise *f*
de soi
compound ['kɔmpaund] *n* (*Chem, Ling*) composé
m; (*enclosure*) enclos *m*, enceinte *f* ▷ *adj*
composé(e); (*fracture*) compliqué(e) ▷ *vt*
[kəm'paund] (*fig: problem etc*) aggraver
compound fracture *n* fracture compliquée
compound interest *n* intérêt composé
comprehend [kɔmprɪ'hɛnd] *vt* comprendre
comprehension [kɔmprɪ'hɛnʃən] *n*
compréhension *f*
comprehensive [kɔmprɪ'hɛnsɪv] *adj* (très)
complet(-ète); **~ policy** (*Insurance*) assurance *f*
tous risques
comprehensive [kɔmprɪ'hɛnsɪv],
comprehensive school *n* (Brit) *école secondaire
non sélective avec libre circulation d'une section à l'autre*,
≈ CES *m*
compress *vt* [kəm'prɛs] comprimer; (*text,
information*) condenser ▷ *n* ['kɔmprɛs] (*Med*)
compresse *f*
compression [kəm'prɛʃən] *n* compression *f*
comprise [kəm'praɪz] *vt* (*also*: **be comprised of**)
comprendre; (*constitute*) constituer, représenter
compromise ['kɔmprəmaɪz] *n* compromis *m*
▷ *vt* compromettre ▷ *vi* transiger, accepter un
compromis ▷ *cpd* (*decision, solution*) de
compromis
compulsion [kəm'pʌlʃən] *n* contrainte *f*, force *f*;
under ~ sous la contrainte
compulsive [kəm'pʌlsɪv] *adj* (*Psych*)
compulsif(-ive); (*book, film etc*) captivant(e);
he's a ~ smoker c'est un fumeur invétéré
compulsory [kəm'pʌlsərɪ] *adj* obligatoire
compulsory purchase *n* expropriation *f*
compunction [kəm'pʌŋkʃən] *n* scrupule *m*; **to
have no ~ about doing sth** n'avoir aucun
scrupule à faire qch
computer [kəm'pjuːtər] *n* ordinateur *m*;
(*mechanical*) calculatrice *f*
computer game *n* jeu *m* vidéo
computer-generated [kəm'pjuːtər'dʒɛnəreɪtɪd]
adj de synthèse
computerize [kəm'pjuːtəraɪz] *vt* (*data*) traiter
par ordinateur; (*system, office*) informatiser
computer language *n* langage *m* machine *or*
informatique
computer literate *adj* initié(e) à l'informatique
computer peripheral *n* périphérique *m*
computer program *n* programme *m*

informatique
computer programmer *n*
programmeur(-euse)
computer programming *n* programmation *f*
computer science *n* informatique *f*
computer scientist *n* informaticien(ne)
computer studies *npl* informatique *f*
computing [kəm'pjuːtɪŋ] *n* informatique *f*
comrade ['kɔmrɪd] *n* camarade *m/f*
comradeship ['kɔmrɪdʃɪp] *n* camaraderie *f*
Comsat ['kɔmsæt] *n abbr* = **communications
satellite**
con [kɔn] *vt* duper; (*cheat*) escroquer ▷ *n*
escroquerie *f*; **to ~ sb into doing sth** tromper
qn pour lui faire faire qch
concave ['kɔn'keɪv] *adj* concave
conceal [kən'siːl] *vt* cacher, dissimuler
concede [kən'siːd] *vt* concéder ▷ *vi* céder
conceit [kən'siːt] *n* vanité *f*, suffisance *f*,
prétention *f*
conceited [kən'siːtɪd] *adj* vaniteux(-euse),
suffisant(e)
conceivable [kən'siːvəbl] *adj* concevable,
imaginable; **it is ~ that** il est concevable que
conceivably [kən'siːvəblɪ] *adv*: **he may ~ be
right** il n'est pas impossible qu'il ait raison
conceive [kən'siːv] *vt, vi* concevoir; **to ~ of sth/
of doing sth** imaginer qch/de faire qch
concentrate ['kɔnsəntreɪt] *vi* se concentrer ▷ *vt*
concentrer
concentration [kɔnsən'treɪʃən] *n*
concentration *f*
concentration camp *n* camp *m* de
concentration
concentric [kɔn'sɛntrɪk] *adj* concentrique
concept ['kɔnsɛpt] *n* concept *m*
conception [kən'sɛpʃən] *n* conception *f*; (*idea*)
idée *f*
concern [kən'səːn] *n* affaire *f*; (*Comm*) entreprise
f, firme *f*; (*anxiety*) inquiétude *f*, souci *m* ▷ *vt*
(*worry*) inquiéter; (*involve*) concerner; (*relate to*) se
rapporter à; **to be ~ed (about)** s'inquiéter (de),
être inquiet(-ète) (au sujet de); **"to whom it
may ~"** "à qui de droit"; **as far as I am ~ed** en
ce qui me concerne; **to be ~ed with** (*person:
involved with*) s'occuper de; **the department ~ed**
(*under discussion*) le service en question; (*involved*)
le service concerné
concerning [kən'səːnɪŋ] *prep* en ce qui
concerne, à propos de
concert ['kɔnsət] *n* concert *m*; **in ~** à l'unisson,
en chœur; ensemble
concerted [kən'səːtɪd] *adj* concerté(e)
concert hall *n* salle *f* de concert
concertina [kɔnsə'tiːnə] *n* concertina *m* ▷ *vi* se
télescoper, se caramboler
concerto [kən'tʃəːtəu] *n* concerto *m*
concession [kən'sɛʃən] *n* (*compromise*)
concession *f*; (*reduced price*) réduction *f*; **tax ~**
dégrèvement fiscal; **"~s"** tarif réduit
concessionaire [kənsɛʃə'nɛər] *n*
concessionnaire *m/f*

concessionary [kən'sɛʃənrɪ] *adj* (*ticket, fare*) à tarif réduit

conciliation [kənsɪlɪ'eɪʃən] *n* conciliation *f*, apaisement *m*

conciliatory [kən'sɪlɪətrɪ] *adj* conciliateur(-trice); conciliant(e)

concise [kən'saɪs] *adj* concis(e)

conclave ['kɔnkleɪv] *n* assemblée secrète; (*Rel*) conclave *m*

conclude [kən'kluːd] *vt* conclure ▷ *vi* (*speaker*) conclure; (*events*): **to ~ (with)** se terminer (par)

concluding [kən'kluːdɪŋ] *adj* (*remarks etc*) final(e)

conclusion [kən'kluːʒən] *n* conclusion *f*; **to come to the ~ that** (en) conclure que

conclusive [kən'kluːsɪv] *adj* concluant(e), définitif(-ive)

concoct [kən'kɔkt] *vt* confectionner, composer

concoction [kən'kɔkʃən] *n* (*food, drink*) mélange *m*

concord ['kɔŋkɔːd] *n* (*harmony*) harmonie *f*; (*treaty*) accord *m*

concourse ['kɔŋkɔːs] *n* (*hall*) hall *m*, salle *f* des pas perdus; (*crowd*) affluence *f*; multitude *f*

concrete ['kɔŋkriːt] *n* béton *m* ▷ *adj* concret(-ète); (*Constr*) en béton

concrete mixer *n* bétonnière *f*

concur [kən'kəːʳ] *vi* être d'accord

concurrently [kən'kʌrntlɪ] *adv* simultanément

concussion [kən'kʌʃən] *n* (*Med*) commotion (cérébrale)

condemn [kən'dɛm] *vt* condamner

condemnation [kɔndɛm'neɪʃən] *n* condamnation *f*

condensation [kɔndɛn'seɪʃən] *n* condensation *f*

condense [kən'dɛns] *vi* se condenser ▷ *vt* condenser

condensed milk [kən'dɛnst-] *n* lait concentré (sucré)

condescend [kɔndɪ'sɛnd] *vi* condescendre, s'abaisser; **to ~ to do sth** daigner faire qch

condescending [kɔndɪ'sɛndɪŋ] *adj* condescendant(e)

condition [kən'dɪʃən] *n* condition *f*; (*disease*) maladie *f* ▷ *vt* déterminer, conditionner; **in good/poor ~** en bon/mauvais état; **a heart ~** une maladie cardiaque; **weather ~s** conditions *fpl* météorologiques; **on ~ that** à condition que + *sub*, à condition de

conditional [kən'dɪʃənl] *adj* conditionnel(le); **to be ~ upon** dépendre de

conditioner [kən'dɪʃənəʳ] *n* (*for hair*) baume démêlant; (*for fabrics*) assouplissant *m*

condo ['kɔndəu] *n* (*US inf*) = **condominium**

condolences [kən'dəulənsɪz] *npl* condoléances *fpl*

condom ['kɔndəm] *n* préservatif *m*

condominium [kɔndə'mɪnɪəm] *n* (*US: building*) immeuble *m* (en copropriété); (: *rooms*) appartement *m* (dans un immeuble en copropriété)

condone [kən'dəun] *vt* fermer les yeux sur, approuver (tacitement)

conducive [kən'djuːsɪv] *adj*: **~ to** favorable à, qui contribue à

conduct *n* ['kɔndʌkt] conduite *f* ▷ *vt* [kən'dʌkt] conduire; (*manage*) mener, diriger; (*Mus*) diriger; **to ~ o.s.** se conduire, se comporter

conductor [kən'dʌktəʳ] *n* (*of orchestra*) chef *m* d'orchestre; (*on bus*) receveur *m*; (*US: on train*) chef *m* de train; (*Elec*) conducteur *m*

conductress [kən'dʌktrɪs] *n* (*on bus*) receveuse *f*

conduit ['kɔndɪt] *n* conduit *m*, tuyau *m*; tube *m*

cone [kəun] *n* cône *m*; (*for ice-cream*) cornet *m*; (*Bot*) pomme *f* de pin, cône

confectioner [kən'fɛkʃənəʳ] *n* (*of cakes*) pâtissier(-ière); (*of sweets*) confiseur(-euse); **~'s (shop)** confiserie(-pâtisserie) *f*

confectionery [kən'fɛkʃənrɪ] *n* (*sweets*) confiserie *f*; (*cakes*) pâtisserie *f*

confederate [kən'fɛdrɪt] *adj* confédéré(e) ▷ *n* (*pej*) acolyte *m*; (*US History*) confédéré(e)

confederation [kənfɛdə'reɪʃən] *n* confédération *f*

confer [kən'fəːʳ] *vt*: **to ~ sth on** conférer qch à ▷ *vi* conférer, s'entretenir; **to ~ (with sb about sth)** s'entretenir (de qch avec qn)

conference ['kɔnfərns] *n* conférence *f*; **to be in ~** être en réunion *or* en conférence

conference room *n* salle *f* de conférence

confess [kən'fɛs] *vt* confesser, avouer ▷ *vi* (*admit sth*) avouer; (*Rel*) se confesser

confession [kən'fɛʃən] *n* confession *f*

confessional [kən'fɛʃənl] *n* confessional *m*

confessor [kən'fɛsəʳ] *n* confesseur *m*

confetti [kən'fɛtɪ] *n* confettis *mpl*

confide [kən'faɪd] *vi*: **to ~ in** s'ouvrir à, se confier à

confidence ['kɔnfɪdns] *n* confiance *f*; (*also*: **self-confidence**) assurance *f*, confiance en soi; (*secret*) confidence *f*; **to have (every) ~ that** être certain que; **motion of no ~** motion *f* de censure; **in ~** (*speak, write*) en confidence, confidentiellement; **to tell sb sth in strict ~** dire qch à qn en toute confidence

confidence trick *n* escroquerie *f*

confident ['kɔnfɪdənt] *adj* (*self-assured*) sûr(e) de soi; (*sure*) sûr

confidential [kɔnfɪ'dɛnʃəl] *adj* confidentiel(le); (*secretary*) particulier(-ère)

confidentiality ['kɔnfɪdɛnʃɪ'ælɪtɪ] *n* confidentialité *f*

configuration [kən'fɪgju'reɪʃən] *n* (*also Comput*) configuration *f*

confine [kən'faɪn] *vt* limiter, borner; (*shut up*) confiner, enfermer; **to ~ o.s. to doing sth/to sth** se contenter de faire qch/se limiter à qch

confined [kən'faɪnd] *adj* (*space*) restreint(e), réduit(e)

confinement [kən'faɪnmənt] *n* emprisonnement *m*, détention *f*; (*Mil*) consigne *f* (au quartier); (*Med*) accouchement *m*

confines ['kɔnfaɪnz] *npl* confins *mpl*, bornes *fpl*

confirm [kən'fəːm] *vt* (*report, Rel*) confirmer; (*appointment*) ratifier

confirmation [kɔnfə'meɪʃən] n confirmation f; ratification f

confirmed [kən'fə:md] adj invétéré(e), incorrigible

confiscate ['kɔnfɪskeɪt] vt confisquer

confiscation [kɔnfɪs'keɪʃən] n confiscation f

conflagration [kɔnflə'greɪʃən] n incendie m; (fig) conflagration f

conflict n ['kɔnflɪkt] conflit m, lutte f ▷ vi [kən'flɪkt] être or entrer en conflit; (opinions) s'opposer, se heurter

conflicting [kən'flɪktɪŋ] adj contradictoire

conform [kən'fɔ:m] vi: **to ~ (to)** se conformer (à)

conformist [kən'fɔ:mɪst] n (gen, Rel) conformiste m/f

confound [kən'faund] vt confondre; (amaze) rendre perplexe

confounded [kən'faundɪd] adj maudit(e), sacré(e)

confront [kən'frʌnt] vt (two people) confronter; (enemy, danger) affronter, faire face à; (problem) faire face à

confrontation [kɔnfrən'teɪʃən] n confrontation f

confrontational [kɔnfrən'teɪʃənl] adj conflictuel(le)

confuse [kən'fju:z] vt (person) troubler; (situation) embrouiller; (one thing with another) confondre

confused [kən'fju:zd] adj (person) dérouté(e), désorienté(e); (situation) embrouillé(e)

confusing [kən'fju:zɪŋ] adj peu clair(e), déroutant(e)

confusion [kən'fju:ʒən] n confusion f

congeal [kən'dʒi:l] vi (oil) se figer; (blood) se coaguler

congenial [kən'dʒi:nɪəl] adj sympathique, agréable

congenital [kən'dʒenɪtl] adj congénital(e)

conger eel ['kɔŋgər-] n congre m, anguille f de roche

congested [kən'dʒestɪd] adj (Med) congestionné(e); (fig) surpeuplé(e); congestionné; bloqué(e); (telephone lines) encombré(e)

congestion [kən'dʒestʃən] n (Med) congestion f; (fig: traffic) encombrement m

conglomerate [kən'glɔmərɪt] n (Comm) conglomérat m

conglomeration [kənglɔmə'reɪʃən] n groupement m; agglomération f

Congo ['kɔŋgəu] n (state) (république f du) Congo

congratulate [kən'grætjuleɪt] vt: **to ~ sb (on)** féliciter qn (de)

congratulations [kəngrætju'leɪʃənz] npl: **~ (on)** félicitations fpl (pour) ▷ excl: **~!** (toutes mes) félicitations!

congregate ['kɔŋgrɪgeɪt] vi se rassembler, se réunir

congregation [kɔŋgrɪ'geɪʃən] n assemblée f (des fidèles)

congress ['kɔŋgres] n congrès m; (Pol): **C~**

Congrès m; voir article

● **CONGRESS**

Le Congress est le parlement des États-Unis. Il comprend la "House of Representatives" et le "Senate". Représentants et sénateurs sont élus au suffrage universel direct. Le Congrès se réunit au "Capitol", à Washington.

congressman ['kɔŋgresmən] (irreg) n membre m du Congrès

congresswoman ['kɔŋgreswumən] (irreg) n membre m du Congrès

conical ['kɔnɪkl] adj (de forme) conique

conifer ['kɔnɪfər] n conifère m

coniferous [kə'nɪfərəs] adj (forest) de conifères

conjecture [kən'dʒektʃər] n conjecture f ▷ vt, vi conjecturer

conjugal ['kɔndʒugl] adj conjugal(e)

conjugate ['kɔndʒugeɪt] vt conjuguer

conjugation [kɔndʒə'geɪʃən] n conjugaison f

conjunction [kən'dʒʌŋkʃən] n conjonction f; **in ~ with** (conjointement) avec

conjunctivitis [kəndʒʌŋktɪ'vaɪtɪs] n conjonctivite f

conjure ['kʌndʒər] vt faire apparaître (par la prestidigitation) [kən'dʒuər] conjurer, supplier ▷ vi faire des tours de passe-passe
 ▸ **conjure up** vt (ghost, spirit) faire apparaître; (memories) évoquer

conjurer ['kʌndʒərər] n prestidigitateur m, illusionniste m/f

conjuring trick ['kʌndʒərɪŋ-] n tour m de prestidigitation

conker ['kɔŋkər] n (Brit) marron m (d'Inde)

conk out [kɔŋk-] vi (inf) tomber or rester en panne

conman ['kɔnmæn] (irreg) n escroc m

Conn. abbr (US) = **Connecticut**

connect [kə'nekt] vt joindre, relier; (Elec) connecter; (Tel: caller) mettre en connexion; (: subscriber) brancher; (fig) établir un rapport entre, faire un rapprochement entre ▷ vi (train): **to ~ with** assurer la correspondance avec; **to be ~ed with** avoir un rapport avec; (have dealings with) avoir des rapports avec, être en relation avec; **I am trying to ~ you** (Tel) j'essaie d'obtenir votre communication

connecting flight n (vol m de) correspondance f

connection [kə'nekʃən] n relation f, lien m; (Elec) connexion f; (Tel) communication f; (train etc) correspondance f; **in ~ with** à propos de; **what is the ~ between them?** quel est le lien entre eux?; **business ~s** relations d'affaires; **to miss/get one's ~** (train etc) rater/avoir sa correspondance

connexion [kə'nekʃən] n (Brit) = **connection**

conning tower ['kɔnɪŋ-] n kiosque m (de sous-marin)

connive [kə'naɪv] vi: **to ~ at** se faire le complice de

connoisseur [kɔnɪ'səːʳ] n connaisseur m
connotation [kɔnə'teɪʃən] n connotation f, implication f
connubial [kə'njuːbɪəl] adj conjugal(e)
conquer ['kɔŋkəʳ] vt conquérir; (feelings) vaincre, surmonter
conqueror ['kɔŋkərəʳ] n conquérant m, vainqueur m
conquest ['kɔŋkwɛst] n conquête f
cons [kɔnz] npl see convenience; pro
conscience ['kɔnʃəns] n conscience f; in all ~ en conscience
conscientious [kɔnʃɪ'ɛnʃəs] adj consciencieux(-euse); (scruple, objection) de conscience
conscientious objector n objecteur m de conscience
conscious ['kɔnʃəs] adj conscient(e); (deliberate: insult, error) délibéré(e); to become ~ of sth/ that prendre conscience de qch/que
consciousness ['kɔnʃəsnɪs] n conscience f; (Med) connaissance f; to lose/regain ~ perdre/ reprendre connaissance
conscript ['kɔnskrɪpt] n conscrit m
conscription [kən'skrɪpʃən] n conscription f
consecrate ['kɔnsɪkreɪt] vt consacrer
consecutive [kən'sɛkjutɪv] adj consécutif(-ive); on three ~ occasions trois fois de suite
consensus [kən'sɛnsəs] n consensus m; the ~ (of opinion) le consensus (d'opinion)
consent [kən'sɛnt] n consentement m ▷ vi: to ~ (to) consentir (à); age of ~ âge nubile (légal); by common ~ d'un commun accord
consenting adults [kən'sɛntɪŋ-] npl personnes consentantes
consequence ['kɔnsɪkwəns] n suites fpl, conséquence f; (significance) importance f; in ~ en conséquence, par conséquent
consequently ['kɔnsɪkwəntlɪ] adv par conséquent, donc
conservation [kɔnsə'veɪʃən] n préservation f, protection f; (also: nature conservation) défense f de l'environnement; energy ~ économies fpl d'énergie
conservationist [kɔnsə'veɪʃnɪst] n protecteur(-trice) de la nature
conservative [kən'səːvətɪv] adj conservateur(-trice); (cautious) prudent(e)
Conservative [kən'səːvətɪv] adj, n (Brit Pol) conservateur(-trice); the ~ Party le parti conservateur
conservatory [kən'səːvətrɪ] n (room) jardin m d'hiver; (Mus) conservatoire m
conserve [kən'səːv] vt conserver, préserver; (supplies, energy) économiser ▷ n confiture f, conserve f (de fruits)
consider [kən'sɪdəʳ] vt (study) considérer, réfléchir à; (take into account) penser à, prendre en considération; (regard, judge) considérer, estimer; to ~ doing sth envisager de faire qch; ~ yourself lucky estimez-vous heureux; all things ~ed (toute) réflexion faite

considerable [kən'sɪdərəbl] adj considérable
considerably [kən'sɪdərəblɪ] adv nettement
considerate [kən'sɪdərɪt] adj prévenant(e), plein(e) d'égards
consideration [kənsɪdə'reɪʃən] n considération f; (reward) rétribution f, rémunération f; out of ~ for par égard pour; under ~ à l'étude; my first ~ is my family ma famille passe avant tout le reste
considered [kən'sɪdəd] adj: it is my ~ opinion that ... après avoir mûrement réfléchi, je pense que ...
considering [kən'sɪdərɪŋ] prep: ~ (that) étant donné (que)
consign [kən'saɪn] vt expédier, livrer
consignee [kɔnsaɪ'niː] n destinataire m/f
consignment [kən'saɪnmənt] n arrivage m, envoi m
consignment note n (Comm) bordereau m d'expédition
consignor [kən'saɪnəʳ] n expéditeur(-trice)
consist [kən'sɪst] vi: to ~ of consister en, se composer de
consistency [kən'sɪstənsɪ] n (thickness) consistance f; (fig) cohérence f
consistent [kən'sɪstənt] adj logique, cohérent(e); ~ with compatible avec, en accord avec
consolation [kɔnsə'leɪʃən] n consolation f
console[1] [kən'səul] vt consoler
console[2] ['kɔnsəul] n console f
consolidate [kən'sɔlɪdeɪt] vt consolider
consols ['kɔnsɔlz] npl (Brit Stock Exchange) rente f d'État
consommé [kən'sɔmeɪ] n consommé m
consonant ['kɔnsənənt] n consonne f
consort ['kɔnsɔːt] n époux (épouse); prince ~ prince m consort ▷ vi [kən'sɔːt] (often pej): to ~ with sb frayer avec qn
consortium [kən'sɔːtɪəm] n consortium m, comptoir m
conspicuous [kən'spɪkjuəs] adj voyant(e), qui attire l'attention; to make o.s. ~ se faire remarquer
conspiracy [kən'spɪrəsɪ] n conspiration f, complot m
conspiratorial [kən'spɪrə'tɔːrɪəl] adj (behaviour) de conspirateur; (glance) conspirateur(-trice)
conspire [kən'spaɪəʳ] vi conspirer, comploter
constable ['kʌnstəbl] n (Brit) ≈ agent m de police, gendarme m; chief ~ ≈ préfet m de police
constabulary [kən'stæbjulərɪ] n ≈ police f, gendarmerie f
constant ['kɔnstənt] adj constant(e); incessant(e)
constantly ['kɔnstəntlɪ] adv constamment, sans cesse
constellation [kɔnstə'leɪʃən] n constellation f
consternation [kɔnstə'neɪʃən] n consternation f
constipated ['kɔnstɪpeɪtɪd] adj constipé(e)
constipation [kɔnstɪ'peɪʃən] n constipation f

constituency [kən'stɪtjuənsɪ] n (Pol: area) circonscription électorale; (: electors) électorat m; voir article

● **CONSTITUENCY**
●
● Une constituency est à la fois une région qui
● élit un député au parlement et l'ensemble
● des électeurs dans cette région. En Grande-
● Bretagne, les députés font régulièrement
● des "permanences" dans leur
● circonscription électorale lors desquelles les
● électeurs peuvent venir les voir pour parler
● de leurs problèmes de logement etc.

constituency party n section locale (d'un parti)
constituent [kən'stɪtjuənt] n électeur(-trice); (part) élément constitutif, composant m
constitute ['kɔnstɪtjuːt] vt constituer
constitution [kɔnstɪ'tjuːʃən] n constitution f
constitutional [kɔnstɪ'tjuːʃənl] adj constitutionnel(le)
constitutional monarchy n monarchie constitutionnelle
constrain [kən'streɪn] vt contraindre, forcer
constrained [kən'streɪnd] adj contraint(e), gêné(e)
constraint [kən'streɪnt] n contrainte f; (embarrassment) gêne f
constrict [kən'strɪkt] vt rétrécir, resserrer; gêner, limiter
construct [kən'strʌkt] vt construire
construction [kən'strʌkʃən] n construction f; (fig: interpretation) interprétation f; **under ~** (building etc) en construction
construction industry n (industrie f du) bâtiment
constructive [kən'strʌktɪv] adj constructif(-ive)
construe [kən'struː] vt analyser, expliquer
consul ['kɔnsl] n consul m
consulate ['kɔnsjulɪt] n consulat m
consult [kən'sʌlt] vt consulter; **to ~ sb (about sth)** consulter qn (à propos de qch)
consultancy [kən'sʌltənsɪ] n service m de conseils
consultancy fee n honoraires mpl d'expert
consultant [kən'sʌltənt] n (Med) médecin consultant; (other specialist) consultant m, (expert-)conseil m ▷ cpd: **~ engineer** n ingénieur-conseil m; **~ paediatrician** n pédiatre m; **legal/management ~** conseiller m juridique/en gestion
consultation [kɔnsəl'teɪʃən] n consultation f; **in ~ with** en consultation avec
consultative [kən'sʌltətɪv] adj consultatif(-ive)
consulting room [kən'sʌltɪŋ-] n (Brit) cabinet m de consultation
consume [kən'sjuːm] vt consommer; (subj: flames, hatred, desire) consumer; **to be ~d with hatred** être dévoré par la haine; **to be ~d with desire** brûler de désir

consumer [kən'sjuːmə^r] n consommateur(-trice); (of electricity, gas etc) usager m
consumer credit n crédit m aux consommateurs
consumer durables npl biens mpl de consommation durables
consumer goods npl biens mpl de consommation
consumerism [kən'sjuːmərɪzəm] n (consumer protection) défense f du consommateur; (Econ) consumérisme m
consumer society n société f de consommation
consumer watchdog n organisme m pour la défense des consommateurs
consummate ['kɔnsʌmeɪt] vt consommer
consumption [kən'sʌmpʃən] n consommation f; **not fit for human ~** non comestible
cont. abbr (= continued) suite
contact ['kɔntækt] n contact m; (person) connaissance f, relation f ▷ vt se mettre en contact or en rapport avec; **to be in ~ with sb/sth** être en contact avec qn/qch; **business ~s** relations fpl d'affaires, contacts mpl
contact lenses npl verres mpl de contact
contagious [kən'teɪdʒəs] adj contagieux(-euse)
contain [kən'teɪn] vt contenir; **to ~ o.s.** se contenir, se maîtriser
container [kən'teɪnə^r] n récipient m; (for shipping etc) conteneur m
containerize [kən'teɪnəraɪz] vt conteneuriser
container ship n porte-conteneurs m inv
contaminate [kən'tæmɪneɪt] vt contaminer
contamination [kəntæmɪ'neɪʃən] n contamination f
cont'd abbr (= continued) suite
contemplate ['kɔntəmpleɪt] vt contempler; (consider) envisager
contemplation [kɔntəm'pleɪʃən] n contemplation f
contemporary [kən'tɛmpərərɪ] adj contemporain(e); (design, wallpaper) moderne ▷ n contemporain(e)
contempt [kən'tɛmpt] n mépris m, dédain m; **~ of court** (Law) outrage m à l'autorité de la justice
contemptible [kən'tɛmptəbl] adj méprisable, vil(e)
contemptuous [kən'tɛmptjuəs] adj dédaigneux(-euse), méprisant(e)
contend [kən'tɛnd] vt: **to ~ that** soutenir or prétendre que ▷ vi: **to ~ with** (compete) rivaliser avec; (struggle) lutter avec; **to have to ~ with** (be faced with) avoir affaire à, être aux prises avec
contender [kən'tɛndə^r] n prétendant(e); candidat(e)
content [kən'tɛnt] adj content(e), satisfait(e) ▷ vt contenter, satisfaire ▷ n ['kɔntɛnt] contenu m; (of fat, moisture) teneur f; **contents** npl (of container etc) contenu m; **(table of) ~s** table f des matières; **to be ~ with** se contenter de; **to ~ o.s. with sth/with doing sth** se contenter de

521

qch/de faire qch

contented [kən'tɛntɪd] *adj* content(e), satisfait(e)

contentedly [kən'tɛntɪdlɪ] *adv* avec un sentiment de (profonde) satisfaction

contention [kən'tɛnʃən] *n* dispute *f*, contestation *f*; (*argument*) assertion *f*, affirmation *f*; **bone of ~** sujet *m* de discorde

contentious [kən'tɛnʃəs] *adj* querelleur(-euse); litigieux(-euse)

contentment [kən'tɛntmənt] *n* contentement *m*, satisfaction *f*

contest *n* ['kɔntɛst] combat *m*, lutte *f*; (*competition*) concours *m* ▷ *vt* [kən'tɛst] contester, discuter; (*compete for*) disputer; (*Law*) attaquer

contestant [kən'tɛstənt] *n* concurrent(e); (*in fight*) adversaire *m/f*

context ['kɔntɛkst] *n* contexte *m*; **in/out of ~** dans le/hors contexte

continent ['kɔntɪnənt] *n* continent *m*; **the C~** (*Brit*) l'Europe continentale; **on the C~** en Europe (continentale)

continental [kɔntɪ'nɛntl] *adj* continental(e) ▷ *n* (*Brit*) Européen(ne) (continental(e))

continental breakfast *n* café (*or* thé) complet

continental quilt *n* (*Brit*) couette *f*

contingency [kən'tɪndʒənsɪ] *n* éventualité *f*, événement imprévu

contingency plan *n* plan *m* d'urgence

contingent [kən'tɪndʒənt] *adj* contingent(e) ▷ *n* contingent *m*; **to be ~ upon** dépendre de

continual [kən'tɪnjuəl] *adj* continuel(le)

continually [kən'tɪnjuəlɪ] *adv* continuellement, sans cesse

continuation [kəntɪnju'eɪʃən] *n* continuation *f*; (*after interruption*) reprise *f*; (*of story*) suite *f*

continue [kən'tɪnju:] *vi* continuer ▷ *vt* continuer; (*start again*) reprendre; **to be ~d** (*story*) à suivre; **~d on page 10** suite page 10

continuing education [kən'tɪnjuɪŋ-] *n* formation permanente *or* continue

continuity [kɔntɪ'njuːɪtɪ] *n* continuité *f*; (*TV*) enchaînement *m*; (*Cine*) script *m*

continuity girl *n* (*Cine*) script-girl *f*

continuous [kən'tɪnjuəs] *adj* continu(e), permanent(e); (*Ling*) progressif(-ive); **~ performance** (*Cine*) séance permanente; **~ stationery** (*Comput*) papier *m* en continu

continuous assessment (*Brit*) *n* contrôle continu

continuously [kən'tɪnjuəslɪ] *adv* (*repeatedly*) continuellement; (*uninterruptedly*) sans interruption

contort [kən'tɔ:t] *vt* tordre, crisper

contortion [kən'tɔ:ʃən] *n* crispation *f*, torsion *f*; (*of acrobat*) contorsion *f*

contortionist [kən'tɔ:ʃənɪst] *n* contorsionniste *m/f*

contour ['kɔntuər] *n* contour *m*, profil *m*; (*also:* **contour line**) courbe *f* de niveau

contraband ['kɔntrəbænd] *n* contrebande *f*

▷ *adj* de contrebande

contraception [kɔntrə'sɛpʃən] *n* contraception *f*

contraceptive [kɔntrə'sɛptɪv] *adj* contraceptif(-ive), anticonceptionnel(le) ▷ *n* contraceptif *m*

contract [*n, cpd* 'kɔntrækt, *vb* kən'trækt] *n* contrat *m* ▷ *cpd* (*price, date*) contractuel(le); (*work*) à forfait ▷ *vi* (*become smaller*) se contracter, se resserrer ▷ *vt* contracter; (*Comm*): **to ~ to do sth** s'engager (par contrat) à faire qch; **~ of employment/service** contrat de travail/de service

▷ **contract in** *vi* s'engager (par contrat); (*Brit Admin*) s'affilier au régime de retraite complémentaire

▷ **contract out** *vi* se dégager; (*Brit Admin*) opter pour la non-affiliation au régime de retraite complémentaire

contraction [kən'trækʃən] *n* contraction *f*; (*Ling*) forme contractée

contractor [kən'træktər] *n* entrepreneur *m*

contractual [kən'træktʃuəl] *adj* contractuel(le)

contradict [kɔntrə'dɪkt] *vt* contredire; (*be contrary to*) démentir, être en contradiction avec

contradiction [kɔntrə'dɪkʃən] *n* contradiction *f*; **to be in ~ with** contredire, être en contradiction avec

contradictory [kɔntrə'dɪktərɪ] *adj* contradictoire

contraflow ['kɔntrəfləu] *n* (*Aut*): **~ lane** voie *f* à contresens; **there's a ~ system in operation on ...** une voie a été mise en sens inverse sur ...

contralto [kən'træltəu] *n* contralto *m*

contraption [kən'træpʃən] *n* (*pej*) machin *m*, truc *m*

contrary¹ ['kɔntrərɪ] *adj* contraire, opposé(e) ▷ *n* contraire *m*; **on the ~** au contraire; **unless you hear to the ~** sauf avis contraire; **~ to what we thought** contrairement à ce que nous pensions

contrary² [kən'trɛərɪ] *adj* (*perverse*) contrariant(e), entêté(e)

contrast *n* ['kɔntrɑ:st] contraste *m* ▷ *vt* [kən'trɑ:st] mettre en contraste, contraster; **in ~ to** *or* **with** contrairement à, par opposition à

contrasting [kən'trɑ:stɪŋ] *adj* opposé(e), contrasté(e)

contravene [kɔntrə'vi:n] *vt* enfreindre, violer, contrevenir à

contravention [kɔntrə'vɛnʃən] *n*: **~ (of)** infraction *f* (à)

contribute [kən'trɪbju:t] *vi* contribuer ▷ *vt*: **to ~ £10/an article to** donner 10 livres/un article à; **to ~ to** (*gen*) contribuer à; (*newspaper*) collaborer à; (*discussion*) prendre part à

contribution [kɔntrɪ'bju:ʃən] *n* contribution *f*; (*Brit: for social security*) cotisation *f*; (*to publication*) article *m*

contributor [kən'trɪbjutər] *n* (*to newspaper*) collaborateur(-trice); (*of money, goods*) donateur(-trice)

contributory [kən'trɪbjutərɪ] *adj* (*cause*) annexe;

it was a ~ factor in ... ce facteur a contribué à ...
contributory pension scheme *n* (*Brit*) régime *m* de retraite salariale
contrite ['kɔntraɪt] *adj* contrit(e)
contrivance [kən'traɪvəns] *n* (*scheme*) machination *f*, combinaison *f*; (*device*) appareil *m*, dispositif *m*
contrive [kən'traɪv] *vt* combiner, inventer ▷ *vi*: **to ~ to do** s'arranger pour faire, trouver le moyen de faire
control [kən'trəul] *vt* (*process, machinery*) commander; (*temper*) maîtriser; (*disease*) enrayer; (*check*) contrôler ▷ *n* maîtrise *f*; (*power*) autorité *f*; **controls** *npl* (*of machine etc*) commandes *fpl*; (*on radio*) boutons *mpl* de réglage; **to take ~ of** se rendre maître de; (*Comm*) acquérir une participation majoritaire dans; **to be in ~ of** être maître de, maîtriser; (*in charge of*) être responsable de; **to ~ o.s.** se contrôler; **everything is under ~** j'ai (*or* il a *etc*) la situation en main; **the car went out of ~** j'ai (*or* il a *etc*) perdu le contrôle du véhicule; **beyond our ~** indépendant(e) de notre volonté
control key *n* (*Comput*) touche *f* de commande
controller [kən'trəulə^r] *n* contrôleur *m*
controlling interest [kən'trəulɪŋ-] *n* (*Comm*) participation *f* majoritaire
control panel *n* (*on aircraft, ship, TV etc*) tableau *m* de commandes
control point *n* (*poste m de*) contrôle *m*
control room *n* (*Naut Mil*) salle *f* des commandes; (*Radio, TV*) régie *f*
control tower *n* (*Aviat*) tour *f* de contrôle
control unit *n* (*Comput*) unité *f* de contrôle
controversial [kɔntrə'və:ʃl] *adj* discutable, controversé(e)
controversy ['kɔntrəvə:sɪ] *n* controverse *f*, polémique *f*
conurbation [kɔnə'beɪʃən] *n* conurbation *f*
convalesce [kɔnvə'lɛs] *vi* relever de maladie, se remettre (d'une maladie)
convalescence [kɔnvə'lɛsns] *n* convalescence *f*
convalescent [kɔnvə'lɛsnt] *adj, n* convalescent(e)
convector [kən'vɛktə^r] *n* radiateur *m* à convection, appareil *m* de chauffage par convection
convene [kən'vi:n] *vt* convoquer, assembler ▷ *vi* se réunir, s'assembler
convener [kən'vi:nə^r] *n* organisateur *m*
convenience [kən'vi:nɪəns] *n* commodité *f*; **at your ~** quand *or* comme cela vous convient; **at your earliest ~** (*Comm*) dans les meilleurs délais, le plus tôt possible; **all modern ~s, all mod cons** (*Brit*) avec tout le confort moderne, tout confort
convenience foods *npl* plats cuisinés
convenient [kən'vi:nɪənt] *adj* commode; **if it is ~ to you** si cela vous convient, si cela ne vous dérange pas
conveniently [kən'vi:nɪəntlɪ] *adv* (*happen*) à pic; (*situated*) commodément

convent ['kɔnvənt] *n* couvent *m*
convention [kən'vɛnʃən] *n* convention *f*; (*custom*) usage *m*
conventional [kən'vɛnʃnl] *adj* conventionnel(le)
convent school *n* couvent *m*
converge [kən'və:dʒ] *vi* converger
conversant [kən'və:snt] *adj*: **to be ~ with** s'y connaître en; être au courant de
conversation [kɔnvə'seɪʃən] *n* conversation *f*
conversational [kɔnvə'seɪʃnl] *adj* de la conversation; (*Comput*) conversationnel(le)
conversationalist [kɔnvə'seɪʃnəlɪst] *n* brillant(e) causeur(-euse)
converse ['kɔnvə:s] *n* contraire *m*, inverse *m* ▷ *vi* [kən'və:s]: **to ~ (with sb about sth)** s'entretenir (avec qn de qch)
conversely [kɔn'və:slɪ] *adv* inversement, réciproquement
conversion [kən'və:ʃən] *n* conversion *f*; (*Brit: of house*) transformation *f*, aménagement *m*; (*Rugby*) transformation *f*
conversion table *n* table *f* de conversion
convert *vt* [kən'və:t] (*Rel, Comm*) convertir; (*alter*) transformer; (*house*) aménager; (*Rugby*) transformer ▷ *n* ['kɔnvə:t] converti(e)
convertible [kən'və:təbl] *adj* convertible ▷ *n* (*voiture f*) décapotable *f*
convex ['kɔn'vɛks] *adj* convexe
convey [kən'veɪ] *vt* transporter; (*thanks*) transmettre; (*idea*) communiquer
conveyance [kən'veɪəns] *n* (*of goods*) transport *m* de marchandises; (*vehicle*) moyen *m* de transport
conveyancing [kən'veɪənsɪŋ] *n* (*Law*) rédaction *f* des actes de cession de propriété
conveyor belt [kən'veɪə^r-] *n* convoyeur *m* tapis roulant
convict *vt* [kən'vɪkt] déclarer (*or* reconnaître) coupable ▷ *n* ['kɔnvɪkt] forçat *m*, convict *m*
conviction [kən'vɪkʃən] *n* (*Law*) condamnation *f*; (*belief*) conviction *f*
convince [kən'vɪns] *vt* convaincre, persuader; **to ~ sb (of sth/that)** persuader qn (de qch/que)
convinced [kən'vɪnst] *adj*: **~ of/that** convaincu(e) de/que
convincing [kən'vɪnsɪŋ] *adj* persuasif(-ive), convaincant(e)
convincingly [kən'vɪnsɪŋlɪ] *adv* de façon convaincante
convivial [kən'vɪvɪəl] *adj* joyeux(-euse), plein(e) d'entrain
convoluted ['kɔnvəlu:tɪd] *adj* (*shape*) tarabiscoté(e); (*argument*) compliqué(e)
convoy ['kɔnvɔɪ] *n* convoi *m*
convulse [kən'vʌls] *vt* ébranler; **to be ~d with laughter** se tordre de rire
convulsion [kən'vʌlʃən] *n* convulsion *f*
coo [ku:] *vi* roucouler
cook [kuk] *vt* (faire) cuire ▷ *vi* cuire; (*person*) faire la cuisine ▷ *n* cuisinier(-ière)
▶ **cook up** *vt* (*inf: excuse, story*) inventer

cookbook ['kukbuk] n livre m de cuisine
cooker ['kukəʳ] n cuisinière f
cookery ['kukərɪ] n cuisine f
cookery book n (Brit) = **cookbook**
cookie ['kukɪ] n (US) biscuit m, petit gâteau sec; (Comput) cookie m, témoin m de connexion
cooking ['kukɪŋ] n cuisine f ▷ cpd (apples, chocolate) à cuire; (utensils, salt) de cuisine
cookout ['kukaut] n (US) barbecue m
cool [ku:l] adj frais (fraîche); (not afraid) calme; (unfriendly) froid(e); (impertinent) effronté(e); (inf: trendy) cool inv (inf); (: great) super inv (inf) ▷ vt, vi rafraîchir, refroidir; **it's ~** (weather) il fait frais; **to keep sth ~** or **in a ~ place** garder or conserver qch au frais
   ▶ **cool down** vi refroidir; (fig: person, situation) se calmer
   ▶ **cool off** vi (become calmer) se calmer; (lose enthusiasm) perdre son enthousiasme
coolant ['ku:lənt] n liquide m de refroidissement
cool box, (US) **cooler** ['ku:ləʳ] n boîte f isotherme
cooling ['ku:lɪŋ] adj (breeze) rafraîchissant(e)
cooling tower n refroidisseur m
coolly ['ku:lɪ] adv (calmly) calmement; (audaciously) sans se gêner; (unenthusiastically) froidement
coolness ['ku:lnɪs] n fraîcheur f; sang-froid m, calme m; froideur f
coop [ku:p] n poulailler m ▷ vt: **to ~ up** (fig) cloîtrer, enfermer
co-op ['kəuɔp] n abbr (= cooperative (society)) coop f
cooperate [kəu'ɔpəreɪt] vi coopérer, collaborer
cooperation [kəuɔpə'reɪʃən] n coopération f, collaboration f
cooperative [kəu'ɔpərətɪv] adj coopératif(-ive) ▷ n coopérative f
coopt [kəu'ɔpt] vt: **to ~ sb onto a committee** coopter qn pour faire partie d'un comité
coordinate vt [kəu'ɔːdɪneɪt] coordonner ▷ n [kəu'ɔdɪnət] (Math) coordonnée f; **coordinates** npl (clothes) ensemble m, coordonnés mpl
coordination [kəuɔːdɪ'neɪʃən] n coordination f
coot [ku:t] n foulque f
co-ownership ['kəu'əunəʃɪp] n copropriété f
cop [kɔp] n (inf) flic m
cope [kəup] vi s'en sortir, tenir le coup; **to ~ with** (problem) faire face à; (take care of) s'occuper de
Copenhagen ['kəupn'heɪgən] n Copenhague
copier ['kɔpɪəʳ] n (also: **photocopier**) copieur m
co-pilot ['kəu'paɪlət] n copilote m
copious ['kəupɪəs] adj copieux(-euse), abondant(e)
copper ['kɔpəʳ] n cuivre m; (Brit: inf: policeman) flic m; **coppers** npl petite monnaie
coppice ['kɔpɪs], **copse** [kɔps] n taillis m
copulate ['kɔpjuleɪt] vi copuler
copy ['kɔpɪ] n copie f; (book etc) exemplaire m; (material: for printing) copie ▷ vt copier; (imitate) imiter; **rough ~** (gen) premier jet; (Scol) brouillon m; **fair ~** version définitive; propre m;

to make good ~ (Press) faire un bon sujet d'article
   ▶ **copy out** vt copier
copycat ['kɔpɪkæt] n (pej) copieur(-euse)
copyright ['kɔpɪraɪt] n droit m d'auteur, copyright m; **~ reserved** tous droits (de reproduction) réservés
copy typist n dactylo m/f
copywriter ['kɔpɪraɪtəʳ] n rédacteur(-trice) publicitaire
coral ['kɔrəl] n corail m
coral reef n récif m de corail
Coral Sea n: **the ~** la mer de Corail
cord [kɔːd] n corde f; (fabric) velours côtelé; whipcord m; corde f; (Elec) cordon m (d'alimentation), fil m (électrique); **cords** npl (trousers) pantalon m de velours côtelé
cordial ['kɔːdɪəl] adj cordial(e), chaleureux(-euse) ▷ n sirop m; cordial m
cordless ['kɔːdlɪs] adj sans fil
cordon ['kɔːdn] n cordon m
   ▶ **cordon off** vt (area) interdire l'accès à; (crowd) tenir à l'écart
corduroy ['kɔːdərɔɪ] n velours côtelé
CORE [kɔːʳ] n abbr (US) = **Congress of Racial Equality**
core [kɔːʳ] n (of fruit) trognon m, cœur m; (Tech: also of earth) noyau m; cœur ▷ vt enlever le trognon or le cœur de; **rotten to the ~** complètement pourri
Corfu [kɔː'fuː] n Corfou
coriander [kɔrɪ'ændəʳ] n coriandre f
cork [kɔːk] n (material) liège m; (of bottle) bouchon m
corkage ['kɔːkɪdʒ] n droit payé par le client qui apporte sa propre bouteille de vin
corked [kɔːkt], (US) **corky** ['kɔːkɪ] adj (wine) qui sent le bouchon
corkscrew ['kɔːkskruː] n tire-bouchon m
cormorant ['kɔːmərnt] n cormoran m
corn [kɔːn] n (Brit: wheat) blé m; (US: maize) maïs m; (on foot) cor m; **~ on the cob** (Culin) épi m de maïs au naturel
cornea ['kɔːnɪə] n cornée f
corned beef ['kɔːnd-] n corned-beef m
corner ['kɔːnəʳ] n coin m; (in road) tournant m, virage m; (Football: also: **corner kick**) corner m ▷ vt (trap: prey) acculer; (fig) coincer; (Comm: market) accaparer ▷ vi prendre un virage; **to cut ~s** (fig) prendre des raccourcis
corner flag n (Football) piquet m de coin
corner kick n (Football) corner m
corner shop (Brit) n magasin m du coin
cornerstone ['kɔːnəstəun] n pierre f angulaire
cornet ['kɔːnɪt] n (Mus) cornet m à pistons; (Brit: of ice-cream) cornet (de glace)
cornflakes ['kɔːnfleɪks] npl cornflakes mpl
cornflour ['kɔːnflauəʳ] n (Brit) farine f de maïs, maïzena® f
cornice ['kɔːnɪs] n corniche f
Cornish ['kɔːnɪʃ] adj de Cornouailles, cornouaillais(e)

corn oil n huile f de maïs
cornstarch ['kɔːnstɑːtʃ] n (US) farine f de maïs, maïzena® f
cornucopia [kɔːnjuːˈkəʊpɪə] n corne f d'abondance
Cornwall ['kɔːnwəl] n Cornouailles f
corny ['kɔːnɪ] adj (inf) rebattu(e), galvaudé(e)
corollary [kəˈrɒlərɪ] n corollaire m
coronary ['kɒrənərɪ] n: **~ (thrombosis)** infarctus m (du myocarde), thrombose f coronaire
coronation [kɒrəˈneɪʃən] n couronnement m
coroner ['kɒrənər] n coroner m, officier de police judiciaire chargé de déterminer les causes d'un décès
coronet ['kɒrənɪt] n couronne f
Corp. abbr = **corporation**
corporal ['kɔːpərl] n caporal m, brigadier m ▷ adj: **~ punishment** châtiment corporel
corporate ['kɔːpərɪt] adj (action, ownership) en commun; (Comm) de la société
corporate hospitality n arrangement selon lequel une société offre des places de théâtre, concert etc à ses clients
corporate identity, corporate image n (of organization) image f de la société
corporation [kɔːpəˈreɪʃən] n (of town) municipalité f, conseil municipal; (Comm) société f
corporation tax n ≈ impôt m sur les bénéfices
corps [kɔːr] (pl - [kɔːz]) n corps m; **the diplomatic ~** le corps diplomatique; **the press ~** la presse
corpse [kɔːps] n cadavre m
corpuscle ['kɔːpʌsl] n corpuscule m
corral [kəˈrɑːl] n corral m
correct [kəˈrɛkt] adj (accurate) correct(e), exact(e); (proper) correct, convenable ▷ vt corriger; **you are ~** vous avez raison
correction [kəˈrɛkʃən] n correction f
correlate ['kɒrɪleɪt] vt mettre en corrélation ▷ vi: **to ~ with** correspondre à
correlation [kɒrɪˈleɪʃən] n corrélation f
correspond [kɒrɪsˈpɒnd] vi correspondre; **to ~ to sth** (be equivalent to) correspondre à qch
correspondence [kɒrɪsˈpɒndəns] n correspondance f
correspondence course n cours m par correspondance
correspondent [kɒrɪsˈpɒndənt] n correspondant(e)
corresponding [kɒrɪsˈpɒndɪŋ] adj correspondant(e)
corridor ['kɒrɪdɔːr] n couloir m, corridor m
corroborate [kəˈrɒbəreɪt] vt corroborer, confirmer
corrode [kəˈrəʊd] vt corroder, ronger ▷ vi se corroder
corrosion [kəˈrəʊʒən] n corrosion f
corrosive [kəˈrəʊzɪv] adj corrosif(-ive)
corrugated ['kɒrəgeɪtɪd] adj plissé(e); ondulé(e)
corrugated iron n tôle ondulée
corrupt [kəˈrʌpt] adj corrompu(e); (Comput)

altéré(e) ▷ vt corrompre; (Comput) altérer; **~ practices** (dishonesty, bribery) malversation f
corruption [kəˈrʌpʃən] n corruption f; (Comput) altération f (de données)
corset ['kɔːsɪt] n corset m
Corsica ['kɔːsɪkə] n Corse f
Corsican ['kɔːsɪkən] adj corse ▷ n Corse m/f
cortège [kɔːˈteɪʒ] n cortège m (gén funèbre)
cortisone ['kɔːtɪzəʊn] n cortisone f
coruscating ['kɒrəskeɪtɪŋ] adj scintillant(e)
cosh [kɒʃ] n (Brit) matraque f
cosignatory ['kəʊˈsɪgnətərɪ] n cosignataire m/f
cosiness ['kəʊzɪnɪs] n atmosphère douillette, confort m
cos lettuce ['kɒs-] n (laitue f) romaine f
cosmetic [kɒzˈmɛtɪk] n produit m de beauté, cosmétique m ▷ adj (preparation) cosmétique; (fig: reforms) symbolique, superficiel(le)
cosmetic surgery n chirurgie f esthétique
cosmic ['kɒzmɪk] adj cosmique
cosmonaut ['kɒzmənɔːt] n cosmonaute m/f
cosmopolitan [kɒzməˈpɒlɪtn] adj cosmopolite
cosmos ['kɒzmɒs] n cosmos m
cosset ['kɒsɪt] vt choyer, dorloter
cost [kɒst] (pt, pp -) n coût m ▷ vi coûter ▷ vt établir or calculer le prix de revient de; **costs** npl (Comm) frais mpl; (Law) dépens mpl; **how much does it ~?** combien ça coûte?; **it ~s £5/too much** cela coûte 5 livres/trop cher; **what will it ~ to have it repaired?** combien cela coûtera de le faire réparer?; **to ~ sb time/effort** demander du temps/un effort à qn; **it ~ him his life/job** ça lui a coûté la vie/son emploi; **at all ~s** coûte que coûte, à tout prix
cost accountant n analyste m/f de coûts
co-star ['kəʊstɑːr] n partenaire m/f
Costa Rica ['kɒstə'riːkə] n Costa Rica m
cost centre n centre m de coût
cost control n contrôle m des coûts
cost-effective ['kɒstɪˈfɛktɪv] adj rentable
cost-effectiveness ['kɒstɪˈfɛktɪvnɪs] n rentabilité f
costing ['kɒstɪŋ] n calcul m du prix de revient
costly ['kɒstlɪ] adj coûteux(-euse)
cost of living ['kɒstəv'lɪvɪŋ] n coût m de la vie ▷ adj: **~ allowance** indemnité f de vie chère; **~ index** indice m du coût de la vie
cost price n (Brit) prix coûtant or de revient
costume ['kɒstjuːm] n costume m; (lady's suit) tailleur m; (Brit: also: **swimming costume**) maillot m (de bain)
costume jewellery n bijoux mpl de fantaisie
cosy, (US) **cozy** ['kəʊzɪ] adj (room, bed) douillet(te); (scarf, gloves) bien chaud(e); (atmosphere) chaleureux(-euse); **to be ~** (person) être bien (au chaud)
cot [kɒt] n (Brit: child's) lit m d'enfant, petit lit; (US: campbed) lit de camp
cot death n mort subite du nourrisson
Cotswolds ['kɒtswəʊldz] npl: **the ~** région de collines du Gloucestershire
cottage ['kɒtɪdʒ] n petite maison (à la

C

campagne), cottage *m*

cottage cheese *n* fromage blanc (*maigre*)

cottage industry *n* industrie familiale *or* artisanale

cottage pie *n* ≈ hachis *m* Parmentier

cotton ['kɔtn] *n* coton *m*; (*thread*) fil *m* (de coton); ~ **dress** *etc* robe *etc* en *or* de coton

▶ **cotton on** *vi* (*inf*): **to ~ on (to sth)** piger (qch)

cotton bud (*Brit*) *n* coton-tige ® *m*

cotton candy (*US*) *n* barbe *f* à papa

cotton wool *n* (*Brit*) ouate *f*, coton *m* hydrophile

couch [kautʃ] *n* canapé *m*; divan *m*; (*doctor's*) table *f* d'examen; (*psychiatrist's*) divan ▷ *vt* formuler, exprimer

couchette [ku:'ʃɛt] *n* couchette *f*

couch potato *n* (*inf*) mollasson(ne) (*qui passe son temps devant la télé*)

cough [kɔf] *vi* tousser ▷ *n* toux *f*; **I've got a ~** j'ai la toux

cough drop *n* pastille *f* pour *or* contre la toux

cough mixture, cough syrup *n* sirop *m* pour la toux

cough sweet *n* pastille *f* pour *or* contre la toux

could [kud] *pt of* **can²**

couldn't ['kudnt] = **could not**

council ['kaunsl] *n* conseil *m*; **city** *or* **town ~** conseil municipal; **C~ of Europe** Conseil de l'Europe

council estate *n* (*Brit*) (quartier *m or* zone *f* de) logements loués à/par la municipalité

council house *n* (*Brit*) maison *f* (à loyer modéré) louée par la municipalité

councillor, (*US*) **councilor** ['kaunslə^r] *n* conseiller(-ère)

council tax *n* (*Brit*) impôts locaux

counsel ['kaunsl] *n* conseil *m*; (*lawyer*) avocat(e) ▷ *vt*: **to ~ (sb to do sth)** conseiller (à qn de faire qch); **~ for the defence/the prosecution** (avocat de la) défense/ avocat du ministère public

counselling, (*US*) **counseling** ['kaunslɪŋ] *n* (*Psych*) aide psychosociale

counsellor, (*US*) **counselor** ['kaunslə^r] *n* conseiller(-ère); (*US Law*) avocat *m*

count [kaunt] *vt, vi* compter ▷ *n* compte *m*; (*nobleman*) comte *m*; **to ~ (up) to 10** compter jusqu'à 10; **to keep ~ of sth** tenir le compte de qch; **not ~ing the children** sans compter les enfants; **10 ~ing him** 10 avec lui, 10 en le comptant; **to ~ the cost of** établir le coût de; **it ~s for very little** cela n'a pas beaucoup d'importance; **~ yourself lucky** estimez-vous heureux

▶ **count in** *vt* (*inf*): **to ~ sb in on sth** inclure qn dans qch

▶ **count on** *vt fus* compter sur; **to ~ on doing sth** compter faire qch

▶ **count up** *vt* compter, additionner

countdown ['kauntdaun] *n* compte *m* à rebours

countenance ['kauntɪnəns] *n* expression *f* ▷ *vt* approuver

counter ['kauntə^r] *n* comptoir *m*; (*in post office,* bank) guichet *m*; (*in game*) jeton *m* ▷ *vt* aller à l'encontre de, opposer; (*blow*) parer ▷ *adv*: ~ **to** à l'encontre de; contrairement à; **to buy under the ~** (*fig*) acheter sous le manteau *or* en sous-main; **to ~ sth with sth/by doing sth** contrer *or* riposter à qch par qch/en faisant qch

counteract ['kauntər'ækt] *vt* neutraliser, contrebalancer

counterattack ['kauntərə'tæk] *n* contre-attaque *f* ▷ *vi* contre-attaquer

counterbalance ['kauntə'bæləns] *vt* contrebalancer, faire contrepoids à

counterclockwise ['kauntə'klɔkwaɪz] (*US*) *adv* en sens inverse des aiguilles d'une montre

counter-espionage ['kauntər'ɛspɪənɑ:ʒ] *n* contre-espionnage *m*

counterfeit ['kauntəfɪt] *n* faux *m*, contrefaçon *f* ▷ *vt* contrefaire ▷ *adj* faux (fausse)

counterfoil ['kauntəfɔɪl] *n* talon *m*, souche *f*

counterintelligence ['kauntərɪn'tɛlɪdʒəns] *n* contre-espionnage *m*

countermand ['kauntəmɑ:nd] *vt* annuler

countermeasure ['kauntəmɛʒə^r] *n* contre-mesure *f*

counteroffensive ['kauntərə'fɛnsɪv] *n* contre-offensive *f*

counterpane ['kauntəpeɪn] *n* dessus-de-lit *m*

counterpart ['kauntəpɑ:t] *n* (*of document etc*) double *m*; (*of person*) homologue *m/f*

counterproductive ['kauntəprə'dʌktɪv] *adj* contre-productif(-ive)

counterproposal ['kauntəprə'pəuzl] *n* contre-proposition *f*

countersign ['kauntəsaɪn] *vt* contresigner

countersink ['kauntəsɪŋk] *vt* (*hole*) fraiser

countess ['kauntɪs] *n* comtesse *f*

countless ['kauntlɪs] *adj* innombrable

countrified ['kʌntrɪfaɪd] *adj* rustique, à l'air campagnard

country ['kʌntrɪ] *n* pays *m*; (*native land*) patrie *f*; (*as opposed to town*) campagne *f*; (*region*) région *f*, pays; **in the ~** à la campagne; **mountainous ~** pays de montagne, région montagneuse

country and western, country and western music *n* musique *f* country

country dancing *n* (*Brit*) danse *f* folklorique

country house *n* manoir *m*, (petit) château

countryman ['kʌntrɪmən] (*irreg*) *n* (*national*) compatriote *m*; (*rural*) habitant *m* de la campagne, campagnard *m*

countryside ['kʌntrɪsaɪd] *n* campagne *f*

countrywide ['kʌntrɪ'waɪd] *adj* s'étendant à l'ensemble du pays; (*problem*) à l'échelle nationale ▷ *adv* à travers *or* dans tout le pays

county ['kauntɪ] *n* comté *m*

county council *n* (*Brit*) ≈ conseil régional

county town *n* (*Brit*) chef-lieu *m*

coup [ku:^r] (*pl* **-s**) [ku:z] *n* (*achievement*) beau coup; (*also:* **coup d'état**) coup d'État

coupé [ku:'peɪ] *n* (*Aut*) coupé *m*

couple ['kʌpl] *n* couple *m* ▷ *vt* (*carriages*) atteler; (*Tech*) coupler; (*ideas, names*) associer; **a ~ of** (*two*) deux; (*a few*) deux ou trois

couplet ['kʌplɪt] *n* distique *m*

coupling ['kʌplɪŋ] *n* (*Rail*) attelage *m*

coupon ['kuːpɔn] *n* (*voucher*) bon *m* de réduction; (*detachable form*) coupon *m* détachable, coupon-réponse *m*; (*Finance*) coupon

courage ['kʌrɪdʒ] *n* courage *m*

courageous [kə'reɪdʒəs] *adj* courageux(-euse)

courgette [kuə'ʒɛt] *n* (*Brit*) courgette *f*

courier ['kurɪəʳ] *n* messager *m*, courrier *m*; (*for tourists*) accompagnateur(-trice)

course [kɔːs] *n* cours *m*; (*of ship*) route *f*; (*for golf*) terrain *m*; (*part of meal*) plat *m*; **first ~** entrée *f*; **of ~** (*adv*) bien sûr; **(no,) of ~ not!** bien sûr que non!, évidemment que non!; **in the ~ of** au cours de; **in the ~ of the next few days** au cours des prochains jours; **in due ~** en temps utile *or* voulu; **~ (of action)** parti *m*, ligne *f* de conduite; **the best ~ would be to ...** le mieux serait de ...; **we have no other ~ but to ...** nous n'avons pas d'autre solution que de ...; **~ of lectures** série *f* de conférences; **~ of treatment** (*Med*) traitement *m*

court [kɔːt] *n* cour *f*; (*Law*) cour, tribunal *m*; (*Tennis*) court *m* ▷ *vt* (*woman*) courtiser, faire la cour à; (*fig: favour, popularity*) rechercher; (: *death, disaster*) courir après, flirter avec; **out of ~** (*Law: settle*) à l'amiable; **to take to ~** actionner *or* poursuivre en justice; **~ of appeal** cour d'appel

courteous ['kəːtɪəs] *adj* courtois(e), poli(e)

courtesan [kɔːtɪ'zæn] *n* courtisane *f*

courtesy ['kəːtəsɪ] *n* courtoisie *f*, politesse *f*; **(by) ~ of** avec l'aimable autorisation de

courtesy bus, courtesy coach *n* navette gratuite

courtesy light *n* (*Aut*) plafonnier *m*

court-house ['kɔːthaus] *n* (*US*) palais *m* de justice

courtier ['kɔːtɪəʳ] *n* courtisan *m*, dame *f* de cour

court martial (*pl* **courts martial**) *n* cour martiale, conseil *m* de guerre

courtroom ['kɔːtrum] *n* salle *f* de tribunal

court shoe *n* escarpin *m*

courtyard ['kɔːtjɑːd] *n* cour *f*

cousin ['kʌzn] *n* cousin(e); **first ~** cousin(e) germain(e)

cove [kəuv] *n* petite baie, anse *f*

covenant ['kʌvənənt] *n* contrat *m*, engagement *m* ▷ *vt*: **to ~ £200 per year to a charity** s'engager à verser 200 livres par an à une œuvre de bienfaisance

Coventry ['kɔvəntrɪ] *n*: **to send sb to ~** (*fig*) mettre qn en quarantaine

cover ['kʌvəʳ] *vt* couvrir; (*Press: report on*) faire un reportage sur; (*feelings, mistake*) cacher; (*include*) englober; (*discuss*) traiter ▷ *n* (*of book, Comm*) couverture *f*; (*of pan*) couvercle *m*; (*over furniture*) housse *f*; (*shelter*) abri *m*; **covers** *npl* (*on bed*) couvertures; **to take ~** se mettre à l'abri; **under ~** à l'abri; **under ~ of darkness** à la faveur de la nuit; **under separate ~** (*Comm*) sous pli séparé; **£10 will ~ everything** 10 livres suffiront (pour tout payer)

▶ **cover up** *vt* (*person, object*): **to ~ up (with)** couvrir (de); (*fig: truth, facts*) occulter ▷ *vi*: **to ~ up for sb** (*fig*) couvrir qn

coverage ['kʌvərɪdʒ] *n* (*in media*) reportage *m*; (*Insurance*) couverture *f*

cover charge *n* couvert *m* (*supplément à payer*)

covering ['kʌvərɪŋ] *n* couverture *f*, enveloppe *f*

covering letter, (*US*) **cover letter** *n* lettre explicative

cover note *n* (*Insurance*) police *f* provisoire

cover price *n* prix *m* de l'exemplaire

covert ['kʌvət] *adj* (*threat*) voilé(e), caché(e); (*attack*) indirect(e); (*glance*) furtif(-ive)

cover-up ['kʌvərʌp] *n* tentative *f* pour étouffer une affaire

covet ['kʌvɪt] *vt* convoiter

cow [kau] *n* vache *f* ▷ *cpd* femelle ▷ *vt* effrayer, intimider

coward ['kauəd] *n* lâche *m/f*

cowardice ['kauədɪs] *n* lâcheté *f*

cowardly ['kauədlɪ] *adj* lâche

cowboy ['kaubɔɪ] *n* cow-boy *m*

cower ['kauəʳ] *vi* se recroqueviller; trembler

cowshed ['kauʃɛd] *n* étable *f*

cowslip ['kauslɪp] *n* (*Bot*) (fleur *f* de) coucou *m*

coy [kɔɪ] *adj* faussement effarouché(e) *or* timide

coyote [kɔɪ'əutɪ] *n* coyote *m*

cozy ['kəuzɪ] *adj* (*US*) = **cosy**

CP *n abbr* (= *Communist Party*) PC *m*

cp. *abbr* (= *compare*) cf

CPA *n abbr* (*US*) = **certified public accountant**

CPI *n abbr* (= *Consumer Price Index*) IPC *m*

Cpl. *abbr* (= *corporal*) C/C

CP/M *n abbr* (= *Central Program for Microprocessors*) CP/M *m*

c.p.s. *abbr* (= *characters per second*) caractères/seconde

CPSA *n abbr* (*Brit*: = *Civil and Public Services Association*) syndicat de la fonction publique

CPU *n abbr* = **central processing unit**

cr. *abbr* = **credit; creditor**

crab [kræb] *n* crabe *m*

crab apple *n* pomme *f* sauvage

crack [kræk] *n* (*split*) fente *f*, fissure *f*; (*in cup, bone*) fêlure *f*; (*in wall*) lézarde *f*; (*noise*) craquement *m*, coup (sec); (*joke*) plaisanterie *f*; (*inf: attempt*): **to have a ~ (at sth)** essayer (qch); (*Drugs*) crack *m* ▷ *vt* fendre, fissurer; fêler; lézarder; (*whip*) faire claquer; (*nut*) casser; (*problem*) résoudre, trouver la clef de; (*code*) déchiffrer ▷ *cpd* (*athlete*) de première classe, d'élite; **to ~ jokes** (*inf*) raconter des blagues; **to get ~ing** (*inf*) s'y mettre, se magner

▶ **crack down on** *vt fus* (*crime*) sévir contre, réprimer; (*spending*) mettre un frein à

▶ **crack up** *vi* être au bout de son rouleau, flancher

crackdown ['krækdaun] *n*: **~ (on)** (*on crime*) répression *f* (de); (*on spending*) restrictions *fpl* (de)

cracked [krækt] *adj* (*cup, bone*) fêlé(e); (*broken*) cassé(e); (*wall*) lézardé(e); (*surface*) craquelé(e);

C

(inf) toqué(e), timbré(e)

cracker ['krækə'] n (also: **Christmas cracker**) pétard m; (biscuit) biscuit (salé), craquelin m; **a ~ of a ...** (Brit inf) un(e) ... formidable; **he's ~s** (Brit inf) il est cinglé

crackle ['krækl] vi crépiter, grésiller

crackling ['kræklɪŋ] n crépitement m, grésillement m; (on radio, telephone) grésillement m; friture f; (of pork) couenne f

crackpot ['krækpɔt] n (inf) tordu(e)

cradle ['kreɪdl] n berceau m ▷ vt (child) bercer; (object) tenir dans ses bras

craft [krɑ:ft] n métier (artisanal); (cunning) ruse f, astuce f; (boat: pl inv) embarcation f, barque f; (plane: pl inv) appareil m

craftsman (irreg) ['krɑ:ftsmən] (irreg) n artisan m ouvrier (qualifié)

craftsmanship ['krɑ:ftsmənʃɪp] n métier m, habileté f

crafty ['krɑ:ftɪ] adj rusé(e), malin(-igne), astucieux(-euse)

crag [kræg] n rocher escarpé

cram [kræm] vt (fill): **to ~ sth with** bourrer qch de; (put): **to ~ sth into** fourrer qch dans ▷ vi (for exams) bachoter

cramming ['kræmɪŋ] n (for exams) bachotage m

cramp [kræmp] n crampe f ▷ vt gêner, entraver; **I've got ~ in my leg** j'ai une crampe à la jambe

cramped [kræmpt] adj à l'étroit, très serré(e)

crampon ['kræmpən] n crampon m

cranberry ['krænbərɪ] n canneberge f

crane [kreɪn] n grue f ▷ vt, vi: **to ~ forward, to ~ one's neck** allonger le cou

cranium (pl **crania**) ['kreɪnɪəm, 'kreɪnɪə] n boîte crânienne

crank [kræŋk] n manivelle f; (person) excentrique m/f

crankshaft ['kræŋkʃɑ:ft] n vilebrequin m

cranky ['kræŋkɪ] adj excentrique, loufoque; (bad-tempered) grincheux(-euse), revêche

cranny ['krænɪ] n see **nook**

crap [kræp] n (inf!: nonsense) conneries fpl (!); (: excrement) merde f (!); **the party was ~** la fête était merdique (!); **to have a ~** chier (!)

crappy ['kræpɪ] adj (inf) merdique (!)

crash [kræʃ] n (noise) fracas m; (of car, plane) collision f; (of business) faillite f; (Stock Exchange) krach m ▷ vt (plane) écraser ▷ vi (plane) s'écraser; (two cars) se percuter, s'emboutir; (business) s'effondrer; **to ~ into** se jeter or se fracasser contre; **he ~ed the car into a wall** il s'est écrasé contre un mur avec sa voiture

crash barrier n (Brit Aut) rail m de sécurité

crash course n cours intensif

crash helmet n casque (protecteur)

crash landing n atterrissage forcé or en catastrophe

crass [kræs] adj grossier(-ière), crasse

crate [kreɪt] n cageot m; (for bottles) caisse f

crater ['kreɪtə'] n cratère m

cravat [krə'væt] n foulard (noué autour du cou)

crave [kreɪv] vt, vi: **to ~ (for)** désirer

violemment, avoir un besoin physiologique de, avoir une envie irrésistible de

craving ['kreɪvɪŋ] n: **~ (for)** (for food, cigarettes etc) envie f irrésistible (de)

crawl [krɔ:l] vi ramper; (vehicle) avancer au pas ▷ n (Swimming) crawl m; **to ~ on one's hands and knees** aller à quatre pattes; **to ~ to sb** (inf) faire de la lèche à qn

crawler lane ['krɔ:lə-] n (Brit Aut) file f or voie f pour véhicules lents

crayfish ['kreɪfɪʃ] n (pl inv: freshwater) écrevisse f; (saltwater) langoustine f

crayon ['kreɪən] n crayon m (de couleur)

craze [kreɪz] n engouement m

crazed [kreɪzd] adj (look, person) affolé(e); (pottery, glaze) craquelé(e)

crazy ['kreɪzɪ] adj fou (folle); **to go ~** devenir fou; **to be ~ about sb/sth** (inf) être fou de qn/qch

crazy paving n (Brit) dallage irrégulier (en pierres plates)

creak [kri:k] vi (hinge) grincer; (floor, shoes) craquer

cream [kri:m] n crème f ▷ adj (colour) crème inv; **whipped ~** crème fouettée
   ▶ **cream off** vt (fig) prélever

cream cake n (petit) gâteau à la crème

cream cheese n fromage m à la crème, fromage blanc

creamery ['kri:mərɪ] n (shop) crémerie f; (factory) laiterie f

creamy ['kri:mɪ] adj crémeux(-euse)

crease [kri:s] n pli m ▷ vt froisser, chiffonner ▷ vi se froisser, se chiffonner

crease-resistant ['kri:srɪzɪstənt] adj infroissable

create [kri:'eɪt] vt créer; (impression, fuss) faire

creation [kri:'eɪʃən] n création f

creative [kri:'eɪtɪv] adj créatif(-ive)

creativity [kri:eɪ'tɪvɪtɪ] n créativité f

creator [kri:'eɪtə'] n créateur(-trice)

creature ['kri:tʃə'] n créature f

creature comforts npl petit confort

crèche [krɛʃ] n garderie f, crèche f

credence ['kri:dns] n croyance f, foi f

credentials [krɪ'dɛnʃlz] npl (references) références fpl; (identity papers) pièce f d'identité; (letters of reference) pièces justificatives

credibility [krɛdɪ'bɪlɪtɪ] n crédibilité f

credible ['krɛdɪbl] adj digne de foi, crédible

credit ['krɛdɪt] n crédit m; (recognition) honneur m; (Scol) unité f de valeur ▷ vt (Comm) créditer; (believe: also: **give credit to**) ajouter foi à, croire; **credits** npl (Cine) générique m; **to be in ~** (person, bank account) être créditeur(-trice); **on ~** à crédit; **to one's ~** à son honneur; à son actif; **to take the ~ for** s'attribuer le mérite de; **it does him ~** cela lui fait honneur; **to ~ sb with** (fig) prêter or attribuer à qn; **to ~ £5 to sb** créditer (le compte de) qn de 5 livres

creditable ['krɛdɪtəbl] adj honorable, estimable

credit account n compte m client

credit agency n (Brit) agence f de

renseignements commerciaux
credit balance n solde créditeur
credit bureau n (US) agence f de
renseignements commerciaux
credit card n carte f de crédit; **do you take ~s?**
acceptez-vous les cartes de crédit?
credit control n suivi m des factures
credit crunch n crise f du crédit
credit facilities npl facilités fpl de paiement
credit limit n limite f de crédit
credit note n (Brit) avoir m
creditor ['krɛdɪtər] n créancier(-ière)
credit transfer n virement m
creditworthy ['krɛdɪtwəːðɪ] adj solvable
credulity [krɪ'djuːlɪtɪ] n crédulité f
creed [kriːd] n croyance f; credo m, principes mpl
creek [kriːk] n (inlet) crique f, anse f; (US: stream)
ruisseau m, petit cours d'eau
creel ['kriːl] n panier m de pêche; (also: **lobster
creel**) panier à homards
creep (pt, pp **crept**) [kriːp, krɛpt] vi ramper;
(silently) se faufiler, se glisser; (plant) grimper
▷ n (inf: flatterer) lèche-botte m; **he's a ~** c'est un
type puant; **it gives me the ~s** cela me fait
froid dans le dos; **to ~ up on sb** s'approcher
furtivement de qn
creeper ['kriːpər] n plante grimpante
creepers ['kriːpəz] npl (US: for baby) barboteuse f
creepy ['kriːpɪ] adj (frightening) qui fait
frissonner, qui donne la chair de poule
creepy-crawly ['kriːpɪ'krɔːlɪ] n (inf) bestiole f
cremate [krɪ'meɪt] vt incinérer
cremation [krɪ'meɪʃən] n incinération f
crematorium (pl **crematoria**) [krɛmə'tɔːrɪəm,
-'tɔːrɪə] n four m crématoire
creosote ['krɪəsəut] n créosote f
crepe [kreɪp] n crêpe m
crepe bandage n (Brit) bande f Velpeau®
crepe paper n papier m crépon
crept [krɛpt] pt, pp of **creep**
crescendo [krɪ'ʃɛndəu] n crescendo m
crescent ['krɛsnt] n croissant m; (street) rue f (en
arc de cercle)
cress [krɛs] n cresson m
crest [krɛst] n crête f; (of helmet) cimier m; (of coat
of arms) timbre m
crestfallen ['krɛstfɔːlən] adj déconfit(e),
découragé(e)
Crete ['kriːt] n Crète f
crevasse [krɪ'væs] n crevasse f
crevice ['krɛvɪs] n fissure f, lézarde f, fente f
crew [kruː] n équipage m; (Cine) équipe f (de
tournage); (gang) bande f
crew-cut ['kruːkʌt] n: **to have a ~** avoir les
cheveux en brosse
crew-neck ['kruːnɛk] n col ras
crib [krɪb] n lit m d'enfant; (for baby) berceau m
▷ vt (inf) copier
cribbage ['krɪbɪdʒ] n sorte de jeu de cartes
crick [krɪk] n crampe f; **~ in the neck** torticolis m
cricket ['krɪkɪt] n (insect) grillon m, cri-cri m inv;
(game) cricket m

cricketer ['krɪkɪtər] n joueur m de cricket
crime [kraɪm] n crime m; **minor ~** délit mineur,
infraction mineure
crime wave n poussée f de la criminalité
criminal ['krɪmɪnl] adj, n criminel(le)
crimp [krɪmp] vt friser, frisotter
crimson ['krɪmzn] adj cramoisi(e)
cringe [krɪndʒ] vi avoir un mouvement de recul;
(fig) s'humilier, ramper
crinkle ['krɪŋkl] vt froisser, chiffonner
cripple ['krɪpl] n boiteux(-euse), infirme m/f ▷ vt
(person) estropier, paralyser; (ship, plane)
immobiliser; (production, exports) paralyser; **~d
with rheumatism** perclus(e) de rhumatismes
crippling ['krɪplɪŋ] adj (disease) handicapant(e);
(taxation, debts) écrasant(e)
crisis (pl **crises**) ['kraɪsɪs, -siːz] n crise f
crisp [krɪsp] adj croquant(e); (weather) vif (vive);
(manner etc) brusque
crisps [krɪsps] (Brit) npl (pommes fpl) chips fpl
crispy ['krɪspɪ] adj croustillant(e)
crisscross ['krɪskrɔs] adj entrecroisé(e), en
croisillons ▷ vt sillonner; **~ pattern** croisillons
mpl
criterion (pl **criteria**) [kraɪ'tɪərɪən, -'tɪərɪə] n
critère m
critic ['krɪtɪk] n critique m/f
critical ['krɪtɪkl] adj critique; **to be ~ of sb/sth**
critiquer qn/qch
critically ['krɪtɪklɪ] adv (examine) d'un œil
critique; (speak) sévèrement; **~ ill** gravement
malade
criticism ['krɪtɪsɪzəm] n critique f
criticize ['krɪtɪsaɪz] vt critiquer
croak [krəuk] vi (frog) coasser; (raven) croasser
Croat ['krəuæt] adj, n = **Croatian**
Croatia [krəu'eɪʃə] n Croatie f
Croatian [krəu'eɪʃən] adj croate ▷ n Croate m/f;
(Ling) croate m
crochet ['krəuʃeɪ] n travail m au crochet
crock [krɔk] n cruche f; (inf: also: **old crock**)
épave f
crockery ['krɔkərɪ] n vaisselle f
crocodile ['krɔkədaɪl] n crocodile m
crocus ['krəukəs] n crocus m
croft [krɔft] n (Brit) petite ferme
crofter ['krɔftər] n (Brit) fermier m
croissant ['krwasã] n croissant m
crone [krəun] n vieille bique, (vieille) sorcière
crony ['krəunɪ] n copain (copine)
crook [kruk] n escroc m; (of shepherd) houlette f
crooked ['krukɪd] adj courbé(e), tordu(e);
(action) malhonnête
crop [krɔp] n (produce) culture f; (amount produced)
récolte f; (riding crop) cravache f; (of bird) jabot m
▷ vt (hair) tondre; (animals: grass) brouter
▶ **crop up** vi surgir, se présenter, survenir
cropper ['krɔpər] n: **to come a ~** (inf) faire la
culbute, s'étaler
crop spraying [-spreɪɪŋ] n pulvérisation f des
cultures
croquet ['krəukeɪ] n croquet m

cross [krɔs] n croix f; (Biol) croisement m ▷ vt
(street etc) traverser; (arms, legs, Biol) croiser;
(cheque) barrer; (thwart: person, plan) contrarier
▷ vi: **the boat ~es from ... to ...** le bateau fait la
traversée de ... à ... ▷ adj en colère, fâché(e); **to ~
o.s.** se signer, faire le signe de (la) croix; **we
have a ~ed line** (Brit: on telephone) il y a des
interférences; **they've got their lines ~ed** (fig)
il y a un malentendu entre eux; **to be/get ~
with sb (about sth)** être en colère/(se) fâcher
contre qn (à propos de qch)
▶ **cross off** or **out** vt barrer, rayer
▶ **cross over** vi traverser
crossbar ['krɔsbɑːʳ] n barre transversale
crossbow ['krɔsbəu] n arbalète f
crossbreed ['krɔsbriːd] n hybride m, métis(se)
cross-Channel ferry ['krɔs'tʃænl-] n ferry m qui
fait la traversée de la Manche
cross-check ['krɔstʃɛk] n recoupement m ▷ vi
vérifier par recoupement
cross-country ['krɔs'kʌntrɪ], **cross-country
race** n cross(-country) m
cross-dressing [krɔs'drɛsɪŋ] n travestisme m
cross-examination ['krɔsɪɡzæmɪ'neɪʃən] n
(Law) examen m contradictoire (d'un témoin)
cross-examine ['krɔsɪɡ'zæmɪn] vt (Law) faire
subir un examen contradictoire à
cross-eyed ['krɔsaɪd] adj qui louche
crossfire ['krɔsfaɪəʳ] n feux croisés
crossing ['krɔsɪŋ] n croisement m, carrefour m;
(sea passage) traversée f; (also: **pedestrian
crossing**) passage clouté; **how long does the ~
take?** combien de temps dura la traversée?
crossing guard (US) n contractuel qui fait traverser
la rue aux enfants
crossing point n poste frontalier
cross-purposes ['krɔs'pə:pəsɪz] npl: **to be at ~
with sb** comprendre qn de travers; **we're
(talking) at ~** on ne parle pas de la même chose
cross-question ['krɔs'kwɛstʃən] vt faire subir
un interrogatoire à
cross-reference ['krɔs'rɛfrəns] n renvoi m,
référence f
crossroads ['krɔsrəudz] n carrefour m
cross section n (Biol) coupe transversale; (in
population) échantillon m
crosswalk ['krɔswɔːk] n (US) passage clouté
crosswind ['krɔswɪnd] n vent m de travers
crosswise ['krɔswaɪz] adv en travers
crossword ['krɔswəːd] n mots mpl croisés
crotch [krɔtʃ] n (of garment) entrejambe m; (Anat)
entrecuisse m
crotchet ['krɔtʃɪt] n (Mus) noire f
crotchety ['krɔtʃɪtɪ] adj (person) grognon(ne),
grincheux(-euse)
crouch [krautʃ] vi s'accroupir; (hide) se tapir;
(before springing) se ramasser
croup [kruːp] n (Med) croup m
crouton ['kruːtɔn] n croûton m
crow [krəu] n (bird) corneille f; (of cock) chant m
du coq, cocorico m ▷ vi (cock) chanter; (fig)
pavoiser, chanter victoire

crowbar ['krəubɑːʳ] n levier m
crowd [kraud] n foule f ▷ vt bourrer, remplir
▷ vi affluer, s'attrouper, s'entasser; **~s of
people** une foule de gens
crowded ['kraudɪd] adj bondé(e), plein(e); **~
with** plein de
crowd scene n (Cine, Theat) scène f de foule
crown [kraun] n couronne f; (of head) sommet m
de la tête, calotte crânienne; (of hat) fond m; (of
hill) sommet m ▷ vt (also tooth) couronner
crown court n (Brit) ≈ Cour f d'assises; voir article

● **CROWN COURT**
●
● En Angleterre et au pays de Galles, une crown
● court est une cour de justice où sont jugées
● les affaires très graves, telles que le meurtre,
● l'homicide, le viol et le vol, en présence d'un
● jury. Tous les crimes et délits, quel que soit
● leur degré de gravité, doivent d'abord passer
● devant une "magistrates' court". Il existe
● environ 90 crown courts.

crowning ['kraunɪŋ] adj (achievement, glory)
suprême
crown jewels npl joyaux mpl de la Couronne
crown prince n prince héritier
crow's-feet ['krəuzfiːt] npl pattes fpl d'oie (fig)
crow's-nest ['krəuznɛst] n (on sailing-ship) nid m
de pie
crucial ['kruːʃl] adj crucial(e), décisif(-ive); (also:
crucial to) essentiel(le) à
crucifix ['kruːsɪfɪks] n crucifix m
crucifixion [kruːsɪ'fɪkʃən] n crucifiement m,
crucifixion f
crucify ['kruːsɪfaɪ] vt crucifier, mettre en croix;
(fig) crucifier
crude [kruːd] adj (materials) brut(e); non
raffiné(e); (basic) rudimentaire, sommaire;
(vulgar) cru(e), grossier(-ière) ▷ n (also: **crude oil**)
(pétrole m) brut m
cruel ['kruəl] adj cruel(le)
cruelty ['kruəltɪ] n cruauté f
cruet ['kruːɪt] n huilier m; vinaigrier m
cruise [kruːz] n croisière f ▷ vi (ship) croiser; (car)
rouler; (aircraft) voler; (taxi) être en maraude
cruise missile n missile m de croisière
cruiser ['kruːzəʳ] n croiseur m
cruising speed ['kruːzɪŋ-] n vitesse f de croisière
crumb [krʌm] n miette f
crumble ['krʌmbl] vt émietter ▷ vi s'émietter;
(plaster etc) s'effriter; (land, earth) s'ébouler;
(building) s'écrouler, crouler; (fig) s'effondrer
crumbly ['krʌmblɪ] adj friable
crummy ['krʌmɪ] adj (inf) minable; (: unwell) mal
fichu(e), patraque
crumpet ['krʌmpɪt] n petite crêpe (épaisse)
crumple ['krʌmpl] vt froisser, friper
crunch [krʌntʃ] vt croquer; (underfoot) faire
craquer, écraser; faire crisser ▷ n (fig) instant m
or moment m critique, moment de vérité
crunchy ['krʌntʃɪ] adj croquant(e),

croustillant(e)

crusade [kruːˈseɪd] *n* croisade *f* ▷ *vi* (*fig*): **to ~ for/against** partir en croisade pour/contre

crusader [kruːˈseɪdə^r] *n* croisé *m*; (*fig*): ~ **(for)** champion *m* (de)

crush [krʌʃ] *n* (*crowd*) foule *f*, cohue *f*; (*love*): **to have a ~ on sb** avoir le béguin pour qn; (*drink*): **lemon ~** citron pressé ▷ *vt* écraser; (*crumple*) froisser; (*grind, break up: garlic, ice*) piler; (: *grapes*) presser; (*hopes*) anéantir

crush barrier *n* (*Brit*) barrière *f* de sécurité

crushing [ˈkrʌʃɪŋ] *adj* écrasant(e)

crust [krʌst] *n* croûte *f*

crustacean [krʌsˈteɪʃən] *n* crustacé *m*

crusty [ˈkrʌstɪ] *adj* (*bread*) croustillant(e); (*inf: person*) revêche, bourru(e); (: *remark*) irrité(e)

crutch [krʌtʃ] *n* béquille *f*; (*Tech*) support *m*; (*also*: **crotch**) entrejambe *m*

crux [krʌks] *n* point crucial

cry [kraɪ] *vi* pleurer; (*shout: also*: **cry out**) crier ▷ *n* cri *m*; **why are you ~ing?** pourquoi pleures-tu?; **to ~ for help** appeler à l'aide; **she had a good ~** elle a pleuré un bon coup; **it's a far ~ from ...** (*fig*) on est loin de ...
▶ **cry off** *vi* se dédire; se décommander
▶ **cry out** *vi* (*call out, shout*) pousser un cri ▷ *vt* crier

crying [ˈkraɪɪŋ] *adj* (*fig*) criant(e), flagrant(e)

crypt [krɪpt] *n* crypte *f*

cryptic [ˈkrɪptɪk] *adj* énigmatique

crystal [ˈkrɪstl] *n* cristal *m*

crystal-clear [ˈkrɪstlˈklɪə^r] *adj* clair(e) comme de l'eau de roche

crystallize [ˈkrɪstəlaɪz] *vt* cristalliser ▷ *vi* (se) cristalliser; **~d fruits** (*Brit*) fruits confits

CSA *n abbr* = **Confederate States of America**; (*Brit*: = *Child Support Agency*) organisme pour la protection des enfants de parents séparés, qui contrôle le versement des pensions alimentaires.

CSC *n abbr* (= *Civil Service Commission*) commission de recrutement des fonctionnaires

CS gas *n* (*Brit*) gaz *m* C.S.

CST *abbr* (*US*: = *Central Standard Time*) fuseau horaire

CT *abbr* (*US*) = **Connecticut**

ct *abbr* = **carat**

CTC *n abbr* (*Brit*) = **city technology college**

CT scanner *n abbr* (*Med*: = *computerized tomography scanner*) scanner *m*, tomodensitomètre *m*

cu. *abbr* = **cubic**

cub [kʌb] *n* petit *m* (*d'un animal*); (*also*: **cub scout**) louveteau *m*

Cuba [ˈkjuːbə] *n* Cuba *m*

Cuban [ˈkjuːbən] *adj* cubain(e) ▷ *n* Cubain(e)

cubbyhole [ˈkʌbɪhəul] *n* cagibi *m*

cube [kjuːb] *n* cube *m* ▷ *vt* (*Math*) élever au cube

cube root *n* racine *f* cubique

cubic [ˈkjuːbɪk] *adj* cubique; ~ **metre** *etc* mètre *m* *etc* cube; ~ **capacity** (*Aut*) cylindrée *f*

cubicle [ˈkjuːbɪkl] *n* (*in hospital*) box *m*; (*at pool*) cabine *f*

cuckoo [ˈkuku:] *n* coucou *m*

cuckoo clock *n* (*pendule f à*) coucou *m*

cucumber [ˈkjuːkʌmbə^r] *n* concombre *m*

cud [kʌd] *n*: **to chew the ~** ruminer

cuddle [ˈkʌdl] *vt* câliner, caresser ▷ *vi* se blottir l'un contre l'autre

cuddly [ˈkʌdlɪ] *adj* câlin(e)

cudgel [ˈkʌdʒl] *n* gourdin *m* ▷ *vt*: **to ~ one's brains** se creuser la tête

cue [kjuː] *n* queue *f* de billard; (*Theat etc*) signal *m*

cuff [kʌf] *n* (*Brit: of shirt, coat etc*) poignet *m*, manchette *f*; (*US: on trousers*) revers *m*; (*blow*) gifle *f* ▷ *vt* gifler; **off the ~** (*adv*) à l'improviste

cufflinks [ˈkʌflɪŋks] *n* boutons *m* de manchette

cu. in. *abbr* = **cubic inches**

cuisine [kwɪˈziːn] *n* cuisine *f*, art *m* culinaire

cul-de-sac [ˈkʌldəsæk] *n* cul-de-sac *m*, impasse *f*

culinary [ˈkʌlɪnərɪ] *adj* culinaire

cull [kʌl] *vt* sélectionner; (*kill selectively*) pratiquer l'abattage sélectif de ▷ *n* (*of animals*) abattage sélectif

culminate [ˈkʌlmɪneɪt] *vi*: **to ~ in** finir *or* se terminer par; (*lead to*) mener à

culmination [kʌlmɪˈneɪʃən] *n* point culminant

culottes [kjuːˈlɔts] *npl* jupe-culotte *f*

culpable [ˈkʌlpəbl] *adj* coupable

culprit [ˈkʌlprɪt] *n* coupable *m/f*

cult [kʌlt] *n* culte *m*

cult figure *n* idole *f*

cultivate [ˈkʌltɪveɪt] *vt* (*also fig*) cultiver

cultivation [kʌltɪˈveɪʃən] *n* culture *f*

cultural [ˈkʌltʃərəl] *adj* culturel(le)

culture [ˈkʌltʃə^r] *n* (*also fig*) culture *f*

cultured [ˈkʌltʃəd] *adj* cultivé(e) (*fig*)

cumbersome [ˈkʌmbəsəm] *adj* encombrant(e), embarrassant(e)

cumin [ˈkʌmɪn] *n* (*spice*) cumin *m*

cumulative [ˈkjuːmjʊlətɪv] *adj* cumulatif(-ive)

cunning [ˈkʌnɪŋ] *n* ruse *f*, astuce *f* ▷ *adj* rusé(e), malin(-igne); (*clever: device, idea*) astucieux(-euse)

cunt [kʌnt] *n* (*inf!*) chatte *f* (!); (*insult*) salaud *m* (!), salope *f* (!)

cup [kʌp] *n* tasse *f*; (*prize, event*) coupe *f*; (*of bra*) bonnet *m*; **a ~ of tea** une tasse de thé

cupboard [ˈkʌbəd] *n* placard *m*

cup final *n* (*Brit Football*) finale *f* de la coupe

Cupid [ˈkjuːpɪd] *n* Cupidon *m*; (*figurine*) amour *m*

cupidity [kjuːˈpɪdɪtɪ] *n* cupidité *f*

cupola [ˈkjuːpələ] *n* coupole *f*

cuppa [ˈkʌpə] *n* (*Brit inf*) tasse *f* de thé

cup tie [ˈkʌptaɪ] *n* (*Brit Football*) match *m* de coupe

curable [ˈkjuərəbl] *adj* guérissable, curable

curate [ˈkjuərɪt] *n* vicaire *m*

curator [kjuəˈreɪtə^r] *n* conservateur *m* (*d'un musée etc*)

curb [kəːb] *vt* refréner, mettre un frein à; (*expenditure*) limiter, juguler ▷ *n* (*fig*) frein *m*; (*US*) bord *m* du trottoir

curd cheese *n* ≈ fromage blanc

curdle [ˈkəːdl] *vi* (se) cailler

curds [kəːdz] *npl* lait caillé

cure [kjuəʳ] vt guérir; (Culin: salt) saler; (: smoke) fumer; (: dry) sécher ▷ n remède m; **to be ~d of sth** être guéri de qch

cure-all ['kjuərɔːl] n (also fig) panacée f

curfew ['kəːfjuː] n couvre-feu m

curio ['kjuərɪəu] n bibelot m, curiosité f

curiosity [kjuərɪ'ɔsɪtɪ] n curiosité f

curious ['kjuərɪəs] adj curieux(-euse); **I'm ~ about him** il m'intrigue

curiously ['kjuərɪəslɪ] adv curieusement; (inquisitively) avec curiosité; **~ enough, ...** bizarrement, ...

curl [kəːl] n boucle f (de cheveux); (of smoke etc) volute f ▷ vt, vi boucler; (tightly) friser
▶ **curl up** vi s'enrouler; (person) se pelotonner

curler ['kəːləʳ] n bigoudi m, rouleau m; (Sport) joueur(-euse) de curling

curlew ['kəːluː] n courlis m

curling ['kəːlɪŋ] n (sport) curling m

curling tongs, (US) **curling irons** npl fer m à friser

curly ['kəːlɪ] adj bouclé(e); (tightly curled) frisé(e)

currant ['kʌrnt] n raisin m de Corinthe, raisin sec; (fruit) groseille f

currency ['kʌrnsɪ] n monnaie f; **foreign ~** devises étrangères, monnaie étrangère; **to gain ~** (fig) s'accréditer

current ['kʌrnt] n courant m ▷ adj (common) courant(e); (tendency, price, event) actuel(le); **direct/alternating ~** (Elec) courant continu/alternatif; **the ~ issue of a magazine** le dernier numéro d'un magazine; **in ~ use** d'usage courant

current account n (Brit) compte courant

current affairs npl (questions fpl d')actualité f

current assets npl (Comm) actif m disponible

current liabilities npl (Comm) passif m exigible

currently ['kʌrntlɪ] adv actuellement

curriculum (pl -s or **curricula**) [kə'rɪkjuləm, -lə] n programme m d'études

curriculum vitae [-'viːtaɪ] n curriculum vitae (CV) m

curry ['kʌrɪ] n curry m ▷ vt: **to ~ favour with** chercher à gagner la faveur or à s'attirer les bonnes grâces de; **chicken ~** curry de poulet, poulet m au curry

curry powder n poudre f de curry

curse [kəːs] vi jurer, blasphémer ▷ vt maudire ▷ n (spell) malédiction f; (problem, scourge) fléau m; (swearword) juron m

cursor ['kəːsəʳ] n (Comput) curseur m

cursory ['kəːsərɪ] adj superficiel(le), hâtif(-ive)

curt [kəːt] adj brusque, sec(-sèche)

curtail [kəː'teɪl] vt (visit etc) écourter; (expenses etc) réduire

curtain ['kəːtn] n rideau m; **to draw the ~s** (together) fermer or tirer les rideaux; (apart) ouvrir les rideaux

curtain call n (Theat) rappel m

curtsey, curtsy ['kəːtsɪ] n révérence f ▷ vi faire une révérence

curvature ['kəːvətʃəʳ] n courbure f

curve [kəːv] n courbe f; (in the road) tournant m, virage m ▷ vt courber ▷ vi se courber; (road) faire une courbe

curved [kəːvd] adj courbe

cushion ['kuʃən] n coussin m ▷ vt (seat) rembourrer; (fall, shock) amortir

cushy ['kuʃɪ] adj (inf): **a ~ job** un boulot de tout repos; **to have a ~ time** se la couler douce

custard ['kʌstəd] n (for pouring) crème anglaise

custard powder n (Brit) ≈ crème pâtissière instantanée

custodial sentence [kʌs'təudɪəl-] n peine f de prison

custodian [kʌs'təudɪən] n gardien(ne); (of collection etc) conservateur(-trice)

custody ['kʌstədɪ] n (of child) garde f; (for offenders) détention préventive; **to take sb into ~** placer qn en détention préventive; **in the ~ of** sous la garde de

custom ['kʌstəm] n coutume f, usage m; (Law) droit coutumier, coutume; (Comm) clientèle f

customary ['kʌstəmərɪ] adj habituel(le); **it is ~ to do it** l'usage veut qu'on le fasse

custom-built ['kʌstəm'bɪlt] adj see **custom-made**

customer ['kʌstəməʳ] n client(e); **he's an awkward ~** (inf) ce n'est pas quelqu'un de facile

customer profile n profil m du client

customized ['kʌstəmaɪzd] adj personnalisé(e); (car etc) construit(e) sur commande

custom-made ['kʌstəm'meɪd] adj (clothes) fait(e) sur mesure; (other goods: also: **custom-built**) hors série, fait(e) sur commande

customs ['kʌstəmz] npl douane f; **to go through (the) ~** passer la douane

Customs and Excise n (Brit) administration f des douanes

customs officer n douanier m

cut [kʌt] (pt, pp -) vt couper; (meat) découper; (shape, make) tailler; couper; creuser; graver; (reduce) réduire; (inf: lecture, appointment) manquer ▷ vi couper; (intersect) se couper ▷ n (gen) coupure f; (of clothes) coupe f; (of jewel) taille f; (in salary etc) réduction f; (of meat) morceau m; **to ~ teeth** (baby) faire ses dents; **to ~ a tooth** percer une dent; **to ~ one's finger** se couper le doigt; **to get one's hair ~** se faire couper les cheveux; **I've ~ myself** je me suis coupé; **to ~ sth short** couper court à qch; **to ~ sb dead** ignorer (complètement) qn
▶ **cut back** vt (plants) tailler; (production, expenditure) réduire
▶ **cut down** vt (tree) abattre; (reduce) réduire; **to ~ sb down to size** (fig) remettre qn à sa place
▶ **cut down on** vt fus réduire
▶ **cut in** vi (interrupt: conversation): **to ~ in (on)** couper la parole (à); (Aut) faire une queue de poisson
▶ **cut off** vt couper; (fig) isoler; **we've been ~ off** (Tel) nous avons été coupés
▶ **cut out** vt (picture etc) découper; (remove) supprimer

▶ **cut up** vt découper
cut-and-dried ['kʌtən'draɪd] adj (also: **cut-and-dry**) tout(e) fait(e), tout(e) décidé(e)
cutaway ['kʌtəweɪ] adj, n: ~ **(drawing)** écorché m
cutback ['kʌtbæk] n réduction f
cute [kjuːt] adj mignon(ne), adorable; (clever) rusé(e), astucieux(-euse)
cut glass n cristal taillé
cuticle ['kjuːtɪkl] n (on nail): ~ **remover** repousse-peaux m inv
cutlery ['kʌtlərɪ] n couverts mpl; (trade) coutellerie f
cutlet ['kʌtlɪt] n côtelette f
cutoff ['kʌtɔf] n (also: **cutoff point**) seuil-limite m
cutoff switch n interrupteur m
cutout ['kʌtaut] n coupe-circuit m inv; (paper figure) découpage m
cut-price ['kʌt'praɪs], (US) **cut-rate** ['kʌt'reɪt] adj au rabais, à prix réduit
cut-throat ['kʌtθrəut] n assassin m ▷ adj: ~ **competition** concurrence f sauvage
cutting ['kʌtɪŋ] adj tranchant(e), coupant(e); (fig) cinglant(e) ▷ n (Brit: from newspaper) coupure f (de journal); (from plant) bouture f; (Rail) tranchée f; (Cine) montage m
cutting edge n (of knife) tranchant m; **on** or **at the ~ of** à la pointe de
cuttlefish ['kʌtlfɪʃ] n seiche f
cut-up ['kʌtʌp] adj affecté(e), démoralisé(e)
CV n abbr = **curriculum vitae**
cwo abbr (Comm) = **cash with order**
cwt abbr = **hundredweight**
cyanide ['saɪənaɪd] n cyanure m
cybernetics [saɪbə'nɛtɪks] n cybernétique f
cyberspace ['saɪbəspeɪs] n cyberespace m

cyclamen ['sɪkləmən] n cyclamen m
cycle ['saɪkl] n cycle m; (bicycle) bicyclette f, vélo m ▷ vi faire de la bicyclette
cycle hire n location f de vélos
cycle lane, cycle path n piste f cyclable
cycle race n course f cycliste
cycle rack n râtelier m à bicyclette
cycling ['saɪklɪŋ] n cyclisme m; **to go on a ~ holiday** (Brit) faire du cyclotourisme
cyclist ['saɪklɪst] n cycliste m/f
cyclone ['saɪkləun] n cyclone m
cygnet ['sɪgnɪt] n jeune cygne m
cylinder ['sɪlɪndəʳ] n cylindre m
cylinder capacity n cylindrée f
cylinder head n culasse f
cymbals ['sɪmblz] npl cymbales fpl
cynic ['sɪnɪk] n cynique m/f
cynical ['sɪnɪkl] adj cynique
cynicism ['sɪnɪsɪzəm] n cynisme m
CYO n abbr (US: = Catholic Youth Organization) ≈ JC f
cypress ['saɪprɪs] n cyprès m
Cypriot ['sɪprɪət] adj cypriote, chypriote ▷ n Cypriote m/f, Chypriote m/f
Cyprus ['saɪprəs] n Chypre f
cyst [sɪst] n kyste m
cystitis [sɪs'taɪtɪs] n cystite f
CZ n abbr (US: = Central Zone) zone du canal de Panama
czar [zɑːʳ] n tsar m
Czech [tʃɛk] adj tchèque ▷ n Tchèque m/f; (Ling) tchèque m
Czechoslovak [tʃɛkə'sləuvæk] adj, n = **Czechoslovakian**
Czechoslovakia [tʃɛkəslə'vækɪə] n Tchécoslovaquie f
Czechoslovakian [tʃɛkəslə'vækɪən] adj tchécoslovaque ▷ n Tchécoslovaque m/f
Czech Republic n: **the ~** la République tchèque

Dd

D¹, d¹ [diː] *n* (*letter*) D, d *m*; (*Mus*): **D** ré *m*; **D for David**, (*US*) **D for Dog** D comme Désirée

D² *abbr* (*US Pol*) = **democrat**; **democratic**

d² *abbr* (*Brit: old*) = **penny**

d. *abbr* = **died**

DA *n abbr* (*US*) = **district attorney**

dab [dæb] *vt* (*eyes, wound*) tamponner; (*paint, cream*) appliquer (par petites touches *or* rapidement); **a ~ of paint** un petit coup de peinture

dabble ['dæbl] *vi*: **to ~ in** faire *or* se mêler *or* s'occuper un peu de

Dacca ['dækə] *n* Dacca

dachshund ['dækshund] *n* teckel *m*

dad, daddy [dæd, 'dædɪ] *n* papa *m*

daddy-long-legs [dædɪ'lɒŋlegz] *n* tipule *f*; faucheux *m*

daffodil ['dæfədɪl] *n* jonquille *f*

daft [dɑːft] *adj* (*inf*) idiot(e), stupide; **to be ~ about** être toqué(e) *or* mordu(e) de

dagger ['dægə'] *n* poignard *m*; **to be at ~s drawn with sb** être à couteaux tirés avec qn; **to look ~s at sb** foudroyer qn du regard

dahlia ['deɪljə] *n* dahlia *m*

daily ['deɪlɪ] *adj* quotidien(ne), journalier(-ière) ▷ *n* quotidien *m*; (*Brit: servant*) femme *f* de ménage (à la journée) ▷ *adv* tous les jours; **twice ~** deux fois par jour

dainty ['deɪntɪ] *adj* délicat(e), mignon(ne)

dairy ['dɛərɪ] *n* (*shop*) crémerie *f*, laiterie *f*; (*on farm*) laiterie ▷ *adj* laitier(-ière)

dairy cow *n* vache laitière

dairy farm *n* exploitation *f* pratiquant l'élevage laitier

dairy produce *n* produits laitiers

dairy products *npl* produits laitier

dais ['deɪɪs] *n* estrade *f*

daisy ['deɪzɪ] *n* pâquerette *f*

daisy wheel *n* (*on printer*) marguerite *f*

daisy-wheel printer ['deɪzɪwiːl-] *n* imprimante *f* à marguerite

Dakar ['dækə] *n* Dakar

dale [deɪl] *n* vallon *m*

dally ['dælɪ] *vi* musarder, flâner

dalmatian [dæl'meɪʃən] *n* (*dog*) dalmatien(ne)

dam [dæm] *n* (*wall*) barrage *m*; (*water*) réservoir *m*, lac *m* de retenue ▷ *vt* endiguer

damage ['dæmɪdʒ] *n* dégâts *mpl*, dommages *mpl*; (*fig*) tort *m* ▷ *vt* endommager, abîmer; (*fig*) faire du tort à; **damages** *npl* (*Law*) dommages-intérêts *mpl*; **to pay £5000 in ~s** payer 5000 livres de dommages-intérêts; **~ to property** dégâts matériels

damaging ['dæmɪdʒɪŋ] *adj*: **~ (to)** préjudiciable (à), nuisible (à)

Damascus [də'mɑːskəs] *n* Damas

dame [deɪm] *n* (*title*) titre porté par une femme décorée de l'ordre de l'Empire Britannique ou d'un ordre de chevalerie, titre porté par la femme ou la veuve d'un chevalier ou baronnet; (*US inf*) nana *f*; (*Theat*) vieille dame (*rôle comique joué par un homme*)

damn [dæm] *vt* condamner; (*curse*) maudire ▷ *n* (*inf*): **I don't give a ~** je m'en fous ▷ *adj* (*inf: also*: **damned**): **this ~ ...** ce sacré *or* foutu ...; **~ (it)!** zut!

damnable ['dæmnəbl] *adj* (*inf: behaviour*) odieux(-euse), détestable; (: *weather*) épouvantable, abominable

damnation [dæm'neɪʃən] *n* (*Rel*) damnation *f* ▷ *excl* (*inf*) malédiction!, merde!

damning ['dæmɪŋ] *adj* (*evidence*) accablant(e)

damp [dæmp] *adj* humide ▷ *n* humidité *f* ▷ *vt* (*also*: **dampen**: *cloth, rag*) humecter; (: *enthusiasm etc*) refroidir

dampcourse ['dæmpkɔːs] *n* couche isolante (contre l'humidité)

damper ['dæmpə'] *n* (*Mus*) étouffoir *m*; (*of fire*) registre *m*; **to put a ~ on** (*fig: atmosphere, enthusiasm*) refroidir

dampness ['dæmpnɪs] *n* humidité *f*

damson ['dæmzən] *n* prune *f* de Damas

dance [dɑːns] *n* danse *f*; (*ball*) bal *m* ▷ *vi* danser; **to ~ about** sautiller, gambader

dance floor *n* piste *f* de danse

dance hall *n* salle *f* de bal, dancing *m*

dancer ['dɑːnsə'] *n* danseur(-euse)

dancing ['dɑːnsɪŋ] *n* danse *f*

D and C *n abbr* (*Med*: = *dilation and curettage*) curetage *m*

dandelion ['dændɪlaɪən] *n* pissenlit *m*

dandruff ['dændrəf] *n* pellicules *fpl*

D & T *n abbr* (*Brit: Scol*) = **design and technology**

dandy ['dændɪ] *n* dandy *m*, élégant *m* ▷ *adj* (*US inf*) fantastique, super
Dane [deɪn] *n* Danois(e)
danger ['deɪndʒəʳ] *n* danger *m*; ~! (*on sign*) danger!; **there is a ~ of fire** il y a (un) risque d'incendie; **in ~** en danger; **he was in ~ of falling** il risquait de tomber; **out of ~** hors de danger
danger list *n* (*Med*): **on the ~** dans un état critique
danger money *n* (*Brit*) prime *f* de risque
dangerous ['deɪndʒrəs] *adj* dangereux(-euse)
dangerously ['deɪndʒrəslɪ] *adv* dangereusement; **~ ill** très gravement malade, en danger de mort
danger zone *n* zone dangereuse
dangle ['dæŋgl] *vt* balancer; (*fig*) faire miroiter ▷ *vi* pendre, se balancer
Danish ['deɪnɪʃ] *adj* danois(e) ▷ *n* (*Ling*) danois *m*
Danish pastry *n* feuilleté *m* (*recouvert d'un glaçage et fourré aux fruits etc*)
dank [dæŋk] *adj* froid(e) et humide
Danube ['dænju:b] *n*: **the ~** le Danube
dapper ['dæpəʳ] *adj* pimpant(e)
Dardanelles [dɑ:də'nɛlz] *npl* Dardanelles *fpl*
dare [dɛəʳ] *vt*: **to ~ sb to do** défier qn *or* mettre qn au défi de faire ▷ *vi*: **to ~ (to) do sth** oser faire qch; **I ~n't tell him** (*Brit*) je n'ose pas le lui dire; **I ~ say he'll turn up** il est probable qu'il viendra
daredevil ['dɛədɛvl] *n* casse-cou *m inv*
Dar-es-Salaam ['dɑ:rɛssə'lɑ:m] *n* Dar-es-Salaam, Dar-es-Salam
daring ['dɛərɪŋ] *adj* hardi(e), audacieux(-euse) ▷ *n* audace *f*, hardiesse *f*
dark [dɑ:k] *adj* (*night, room*) obscur(e), sombre; (*colour, complexion*) foncé(e), sombre; (*fig*) sombre ▷ *n*: **in the ~** dans le noir; **to be in the ~ about** (*fig*) ignorer tout de; **after ~** après la tombée de la nuit; **it is/is getting ~** il fait nuit/commence à faire nuit
darken [dɑ:kn] *vt* obscurcir, assombrir ▷ *vi* s'obscurcir, s'assombrir
dark glasses *npl* lunettes noires
dark horse *n* (*fig*): **he's a ~** on ne sait pas grand-chose de lui
darkly ['dɑ:klɪ] *adv* (*gloomily*) mélancoliquement; (*in a sinister way*) lugubrement
darkness ['dɑ:knɪs] *n* obscurité *f*
darkroom ['dɑ:krʊm] *n* chambre noire
darling ['dɑ:lɪŋ] *adj*, *n* chéri(e)
darn [dɑ:n] *vt* repriser
dart [dɑ:t] *n* fléchette *f*; (*in sewing*) pince *f* ▷ *vi*: **to ~ towards** (*also*: **make a dart towards**) se précipiter *or* s'élancer vers; **to ~ away/along** partir/passer comme une flèche
dartboard ['dɑ:tbɔ:d] *n* cible *f* (de jeu de fléchettes)
darts [dɑ:ts] *n* jeu *m* de fléchettes
dash [dæʃ] *n* (*sign*) tiret *m*; (*small quantity*) goutte *f*, larme *f* ▷ *vt* (*throw*) jeter *or* lancer violemment; (*hopes*) anéantir ▷ *vi*: **to ~ towards** (*also*: **make a**

dash towards) se précipiter *or* se ruer vers; **a ~ of soda** un peu d'eau gazeuse
  ▶ **dash away** *vi* partir à toute allure
  ▶ **dash off** *vi* = **dash away**
dashboard ['dæʃbɔ:d] *n* (*Aut*) tableau *m* de bord
dashing ['dæʃɪŋ] *adj* fringant(e)
dastardly ['dæstədlɪ] *adj* lâche
DAT *n abbr* (= *digital audio tape*) cassette *f* audio digitale
data ['deɪtə] *npl* données *fpl*
database ['deɪtəbeɪs] *n* base *f* de données
data capture *n* saisie *f* de données
data processing *n* traitement *m* (électronique) de l'information
data transmission *n* transmission *f* de données
date [deɪt] *n* date *f*; (*with sb*) rendez-vous *m*; (*fruit*) datte *f* ▷ *vt* dater; (*person*) sortir avec; **what's the ~ today?** quelle date sommes-nous aujourd'hui?; **~ of birth** date de naissance; **closing ~** date de clôture; **to ~** (*adv*) à ce jour; **out of ~** périmé(e); **up to ~** à la page, mis(e) à jour, moderne; **to bring up to ~** (*correspondence, information*) mettre à jour; (*method*) moderniser; (*person*) mettre au courant; **letter ~d 5th July** *or* (*US*) **July 5th** lettre (datée) du 5 juillet
dated ['deɪtɪd] *adj* démodé(e)
dateline ['deɪtlaɪn] *n* ligne *f* de changement de date
date rape *n* viol *m* (à l'issue d'un rendez-vous galant)
date stamp *n* timbre-dateur *m*
daub [dɔ:b] *vt* barbouiller
daughter ['dɔ:təʳ] *n* fille *f*
daughter-in-law ['dɔ:tərɪnlɔ:] *n* belle-fille *f*, bru *f*
daunt [dɔ:nt] *vt* intimider, décourager
daunting ['dɔ:ntɪŋ] *adj* décourageant(e), intimidant(e)
dauntless ['dɔ:ntlɪs] *adj* intrépide
dawdle ['dɔ:dl] *vi* traîner, lambiner; **to ~ over one's work** traînasser *or* lambiner sur son travail
dawn [dɔ:n] *n* aube *f*, aurore *f* ▷ *vi* (*day*) se lever, poindre; (*fig*) naître, se faire jour; **at ~** à l'aube; **from ~ to dusk** du matin au soir; **it ~ed on him that ...** il lui vint à l'esprit que ...
dawn chorus *n* (*Brit*) chant *m* des oiseaux à l'aube
day [deɪ] *n* jour *m*; (*as duration*) journée *f*; (*period of time, age*) époque *f*, temps *m*; **the ~ before** la veille, le jour précédent; **the ~ after, the following ~** le lendemain, le jour suivant; **the ~ before yesterday** avant-hier; **the ~ after tomorrow** après-demain; **(on) the ~ that ...** le jour où ...; **~ by ~** jour après jour; **by ~** de jour; **paid by the ~** payé(e) à la journée; **these ~s, in the present** de nos jours, à l'heure actuelle
daybook ['deɪbuk] *n* (*Brit*) main courante, brouillard *m*, journal *m*
day boy *n* (*Scol*) externe *m*
daybreak ['deɪbreɪk] *n* point *m* du jour
day-care centre ['deɪkɛə-] *n* (*for elderly etc*)

centre *m* d'accueil de jour; (*for children*) garderie *f*

daydream ['deɪdriːm] *n* rêverie *f* ▷ *vi* rêver (tout éveillé)

day girl *n* (*Scol*) externe *f*

daylight ['deɪlaɪt] *n* (lumière *f* du) jour *m*

daylight robbery *n*: **it's ~** (*fig: inf*) c'est du vol caractérisé *or* manifeste

daylight saving time *n* (*US*) heure *f* d'été

day release *n*: **to be on ~** avoir une journée de congé pour formation professionnelle

day return *n* (*Brit*) billet *m* d'aller-retour (*valable pour la journée*)

day shift *n* équipe *f* de jour

daytime ['deɪtaɪm] *n* jour *m*, journée *f*

day-to-day ['deɪtə'deɪ] *adj* (*routine, expenses*) journalier(-ière); **on a ~ basis** au jour le jour

day trip *n* excursion *f* (d'une journée)

day tripper *n* excursionniste *m/f*

daze [deɪz] *vt* (*drug*) hébéter; (*blow*) étourdir ▷ *n*: **in a ~** hébété(e), étourdi(e)

dazed [deɪzd] *adj* abruti(e)

dazzle ['dæzl] *vt* éblouir, aveugler

dazzling ['dæzlɪŋ] *adj* (*light*) aveuglant(e), éblouissant(e); (*fig*) éblouissant(e)

DC *abbr* (*Elec*) = **direct current**; (*US*) = **District of Columbia**

DD *n abbr* (= *Doctor of Divinity*) *titre universitaire*

dd. *abbr* (*Comm*) = **delivered**

D/D *abbr* = **direct debit**

D-day ['diːdeɪ] *n* le jour J

DDS *n abbr* (*US*: = *Doctor of Dental Science*; *Brit*: = *Doctor of Dental Surgery*) *titres universitaires*

DDT *n abbr* (= *dichlorodiphenyl trichloroethane*) DDT *m*

DE *abbr* (*US*) = **Delaware**

DEA *n abbr* (*US*: = *Drug Enforcement Administration*) ≈ brigade *f* des stupéfiants

deacon ['diːkən] *n* diacre *m*

dead [dɛd] *adj* mort(e); (*numb*) engourdi(e), insensible; (*battery*) à plat ▷ *adv* (*completely*) absolument, complètement; (*exactly*) juste; **the dead** *npl* les morts; **he was shot ~** il a été tué d'un coup de revolver; **~ on time** à l'heure pile; **~ tired** éreinté(e), complètement fourbu(e); **to stop ~** s'arrêter pile *or* net; **the line is ~** (*Tel*) la ligne est coupée

dead beat *adj* (*inf*) claqué(e), crevé(e)

deaden [dɛdn] *vt* (*blow, sound*) amortir; (*make numb*) endormir, rendre insensible

dead end *n* impasse *f*

dead-end ['dɛdɛnd] *adj*: **a ~ job** un emploi *or* poste sans avenir

dead heat *n* (*Sport*): **to finish in a ~** terminer ex aequo

dead-letter office [dɛd'lɛtər-] *n* ≈ centre *m* de recherche du courrier

deadline ['dɛdlaɪn] *n* date *f* or heure *f* limite; **to work to a ~** avoir des délais stricts à respecter

deadlock ['dɛdlɔk] *n* impasse *f*; (*fig*)

dead loss *n* (*inf*): **to be a ~** (*person*) n'être bon (bonne à rien); (*thing*) ne rien valoir

deadly ['dɛdlɪ] *adj* mortel(le); (*weapon*) meurtrier(-ière); **~ dull** ennuyeux(-euse) à

mourir, mortellement ennuyeux

deadpan ['dɛdpæn] *adj* impassible; (*humour*) pince-sans-rire *inv*

Dead Sea *n*: **the ~** la mer Morte

deaf [dɛf] *adj* sourd(e); **to turn a ~ ear to sth** faire la sourde oreille à qch

deaf-aid ['dɛfeɪd] *n* (*Brit*) appareil auditif

deaf-and-dumb ['dɛfən'dʌm] *adj* sourd(e)-muet(te); **~ alphabet** alphabet *m* des sourds-muets

deafen ['dɛfn] *vt* rendre sourd(e); (*fig*) assourdir

deafening ['dɛfnɪŋ] *adj* assourdissant(e)

deaf-mute ['dɛfmjuːt] *n* sourd/e-muet/te

deafness ['dɛfnɪs] *n* surdité *f*

deal [diːl] *n* affaire *f*, marché *m* ▷ *vt* (*pt, pp* **-t**) [dɛlt] (*blow*) porter; (*cards*) donner, distribuer; **to strike a ~ with sb** faire *or* conclure un marché avec qn; **it's a ~!** (*inf*) marché conclu!, tope-là!, topez-là!; **he got a bad ~ from them** ils ont mal agi envers lui; **he got a fair ~ from them** ils ont agi loyalement envers lui; **a good ~** (*a lot*) beaucoup; **a good ~ of, a great ~ of** beaucoup de, énormément de

▶ **deal in** *vt fus* (*Comm*) faire le commerce de, être dans le commerce de

▶ **deal with** *vt fus* (*Comm*) traiter avec; (*handle*) s'occuper *or* se charger de; (*be about: book etc*) traiter de

dealer ['diːlər] *n* (*Comm*) marchand *m*; (*Cards*) donneur *m*

dealership ['diːləʃɪp] *n* concession *f*

dealings ['diːlɪŋz] *npl* (*in goods, shares*) opérations *fpl*, transactions *fpl*; (*relations*) relations *fpl*, rapports *mpl*

dealt [dɛlt] *pt, pp of* **deal**

dean [diːn] *n* (*Rel, Brit Scol*) doyen *m*; (*US Scol*) conseiller principal (conseillère principale) d'éducation

dear [dɪər] *adj* cher (chère); (*expensive*) cher, coûteux(-euse) ▷ *n*: **my ~** mon cher (ma chère) ▷ *excl*: **~ me!** mon Dieu!; **D~ Sir/Madam** (*in letter*) Monsieur/Madame; **D~ Mr/Mrs X** Cher Monsieur/Chère Madame X

dearly ['dɪəlɪ] *adv* (*love*) tendrement; (*pay*) cher

dearth [dəːθ] *n* disette *f*, pénurie *f*

death [dɛθ] *n* mort *f*; (*Admin*) décès *m*

deathbed ['dɛθbɛd] *n* lit *m* de mort

death certificate *n* acte *m* de décès

deathly ['dɛθlɪ] *adj* de mort ▷ *adv* comme la mort

death penalty *n* peine *f* de mort

death rate *n* taux *m* de mortalité

death row [-'rəu] *n* (*US*) quartier *m* des condamnés à mort; **to be on ~** être condamné à la peine de mort

death sentence *n* condamnation *f* à mort

death squad *n* escadron *m* de la mort

death toll *n* nombre *m* de morts

deathtrap ['dɛθtræp] *n* endroit *or* véhicule *etc* dangereux

deb [dɛb] *n abbr* (*inf*) = **debutante**

debar [dɪ'bɑːr] *vt*: **to ~ sb from a club** *etc* exclure qn d'un club *etc*; **to ~ sb from doing** interdire à qn de faire

debase [dɪ'beɪs] *vt* (*currency*) déprécier, dévaloriser; (*person*) abaisser, avilir

debatable [dɪ'beɪtəbl] *adj* discutable, contestable; **it is ~ whether ...** il est douteux que ...

debate [dɪ'beɪt] *n* discussion *f*, débat *m* ▷ *vt* discuter, débattre ▷ *vi* (*consider*): **to ~ whether** se demander si

debauchery [dɪ'bɔ:tʃərɪ] *n* débauche *f*

debenture [dɪ'bɛntʃər] *n* (*Comm*) obligation *f*

debilitate [dɪ'bɪlɪteɪt] *vt* débiliter

debit ['dɛbɪt] *n* débit *m* ▷ *vt*: **to ~ a sum to sb** or **to sb's account** porter une somme au débit de qn, débiter qn d'une somme

debit balance *n* solde débiteur

debit card *n* carte *f* de paiement

debit note *n* note *f* de débit

debrief [di:'bri:f] *vt* demander un compte rendu de fin de mission à

debriefing [di:'bri:fɪŋ] *n* compte rendu *m*

debris ['dɛbri:] *n* débris *mpl*, décombres *mpl*

debt [dɛt] *n* dette *f*; **to be in ~** avoir des dettes, être endetté(e); **bad ~** créance *f* irrécouvrable

debt collector *n* agent *m* de recouvrements

debtor ['dɛtər] *n* débiteur(-trice)

debug ['di:'bʌg] *vt* (*Comput*) déboguer

debunk [di:'bʌŋk] *vt* (*theory, claim*) montrer le ridicule de

debut ['deɪbju:] *n* début(s) *m(pl)*

debutante ['dɛbjutænt] *n* débutante *f*

Dec. *abbr* (= *December*) déc

decade ['dɛkeɪd] *n* décennie *f*, décade *f*

decadence ['dɛkədəns] *n* décadence *f*

decadent ['dɛkədənt] *adj* décadent(e)

decaf ['di:kæf] *n* (*inf*) déca *m*

decaffeinated [dɪ'kæfɪneɪtɪd] *adj* décaféiné(e)

decamp [dɪ'kæmp] *vi* (*inf*) décamper, filer

decant [dɪ'kænt] *vt* (*wine*) décanter

decanter [dɪ'kæntər] *n* carafe *f*

decarbonize [di:'kɑ:bənaɪz] *vt* (*Aut*) décalaminer

decathlon [dɪ'kæθlən] *n* décathlon *m*

decay [dɪ'keɪ] *n* (*of food, wood etc*) décomposition *f*, pourriture *f*; (*of building*) délabrement *m*; (*fig*) déclin *m*; (*also*: **tooth decay**) carie *f* (dentaire) ▷ *vi* (*rot*) se décomposer, pourrir; (: *teeth*) se carier; (*fig: city, district, building*) se délabrer; (: *civilization*) décliner; (: *system*) tomber en ruine

decease [dɪ'si:s] *n* décès *m*

deceased [dɪ'si:st] *n*: **the ~** le (la) défunt(e)

deceit [dɪ'si:t] *n* tromperie *f*, supercherie *f*

deceitful [dɪ'si:tful] *adj* trompeur(-euse)

deceive [dɪ'si:v] *vt* tromper; **to ~ o.s.** s'abuser

decelerate [di:'sɛləreɪt] *vt, vi* ralentir

December [dɪ'sɛmbər] *n* décembre *m*; *for phrases see also* **July**

decency ['di:sənsɪ] *n* décence *f*

decent ['di:sənt] *adj* (*proper*) décent(e), convenable; **they were very ~ about it** ils se sont montrés très chics

decently ['di:səntlɪ] *adv* (*respectably*) décemment, convenablement; (*kindly*) décemment

decentralization [di:sɛntrəlaɪ'zeɪʃən] *n* décentralisation *f*

decentralize [di:'sɛntrəlaɪz] *vt* décentraliser

deception [dɪ'sɛpʃən] *n* tromperie *f*

deceptive [dɪ'sɛptɪv] *adj* trompeur(-euse)

decibel ['dɛsɪbɛl] *n* décibel *m*

decide [dɪ'saɪd] *vt* (*subj: person*) décider; (*question, argument*) trancher, régler ▷ *vi* se décider, décider; **to ~ to do/that** décider de faire/que; **to ~ on** décider, se décider pour; **to ~ on doing** décider de faire; **to ~ against doing** décider de ne pas faire

decided [dɪ'saɪdɪd] *adj* (*resolute*) résolu(e), décidé(e); (*clear, definite*) net(te), marqué(e)

decidedly [dɪ'saɪdɪdlɪ] *adv* résolument; incontestablement, nettement

deciding [dɪ'saɪdɪŋ] *adj* décisif(-ive)

deciduous [dɪ'sɪdjuəs] *adj* à feuilles caduques

decimal ['dɛsɪməl] *adj* décimal(e) ▷ *n* décimale *f*; **to three ~ places** (jusqu')à la troisième décimale

decimalize ['dɛsɪməlaɪz] *vt* (*Brit*) décimaliser

decimal point *n* ≈ virgule *f*

decimate ['dɛsɪmeɪt] *vt* décimer

decipher [dɪ'saɪfər] *vt* déchiffrer

decision [dɪ'sɪʒən] *n* décision *f*; **to make a ~** prendre une décision

decisive [dɪ'saɪsɪv] *adj* décisif(-ive); (*influence*) décisif, déterminant(e); (*manner, person*) décidé(e), catégorique; (*reply*) ferme, catégorique

deck [dɛk] *n* (*Naut*) pont *m*; (*of cards*) jeu *m*; (*record deck*) platine *f*; (*of bus*): **top ~** impériale *f*; **to go up on ~** monter sur le pont; **below ~** dans l'entrepont

deckchair ['dɛktʃɛər] *n* chaise longue

deck hand *n* matelot *m*

declaration [dɛklə'reɪʃən] *n* déclaration *f*

declare [dɪ'klɛər] *vt* déclarer

declassify [di:'klæsɪfaɪ] *vt* rendre accessible au public *or* à tous

decline [dɪ'klaɪn] *n* (*decay*) déclin *m*; (*lessening*) baisse *f* ▷ *vt* refuser, décliner ▷ *vi* décliner; (*business*) baisser; **~ in living standards** baisse du niveau de vie; **to ~ to do sth** refuser (poliment) de faire qch

declutch ['di:'klʌtʃ] *vi* (*Brit*) débrayer

decode ['di:'kəud] *vt* décoder

decoder [di:'kəudər] *n* (*Comput, TV*) décodeur *m*

decompose [di:kəm'pəuz] *vi* se décomposer

decomposition [di:kɔmpə'zɪʃən] *n* décomposition *f*

decompression [di:kəm'prɛʃən] *n* décompression *f*

decompression chamber *n* caisson *m* de décompression

decongestant [di:kən'dʒɛstənt] *n* décongestif *m*

decontaminate [di:kən'tæmɪneɪt] *vt*

décontaminer

decontrol [di:kən'trəul] vt (prices etc) libérer

décor ['deɪkɔːʳ] n décor m

decorate ['dɛkəreɪt] vt (adorn, give a medal to) décorer; (paint and paper) peindre et tapisser

decoration [dɛkə'reɪʃən] n (medal etc, adornment) décoration f

decorative ['dɛkərətɪv] adj décoratif(-ive)

decorator ['dɛkəreɪtəʳ] n peintre m en bâtiment

decorum [dɪ'kɔːrəm] n décorum m, bienséance f

decoy ['di:kɔɪ] n piège m; **they used him as a ~ for the enemy** ils se sont servis de lui pour attirer l'ennemi

decrease n ['di:kri:s] diminution f ▷ vt, vi [di:'kri:s] diminuer; **to be on the ~** diminuer, être en diminution

decreasing [di:'kri:sɪŋ] adj en voie de diminution

decree [dɪ'kri:] n (Pol, Rel) décret m; (Law) arrêt m, jugement m ▷ vt: **to ~ (that)** décréter (que), ordonner (que); **~ absolute** jugement définitif (de divorce); **~ nisi** jugement provisoire de divorce

decrepit [dɪ'krɛpɪt] adj (person) décrépit(e); (building) délabré(e)

decry [dɪ'kraɪ] vt condamner ouvertement, déplorer; (disparage) dénigrer, décrier

dedicate ['dɛdɪkeɪt] vt consacrer; (book etc) dédier

dedicated ['dɛdɪkeɪtɪd] adj (person) dévoué(e); (Comput) spécialisé(e), dédié(e); **~ word processor** station f de traitement de texte

dedication [dɛdɪ'keɪʃən] n (devotion) dévouement m; (in book) dédicace f

deduce [dɪ'dju:s] vt déduire, conclure

deduct [dɪ'dʌkt] vt: **to ~ sth (from)** déduire qch (de), retrancher qch (de); (from wage etc) prélever qch (sur), retenir qch (sur)

deduction [dɪ'dʌkʃən] n (deducting, deducing) déduction f; (from wage etc) prélèvement m, retenue f

deed [di:d] n action f, acte m; (Law) acte notarié, contrat m; **~ of covenant** (acte m de) donation f

deem [di:m] vt (formal) juger, estimer; **to ~ it wise to do** juger bon de faire

deep [di:p] adj (water, sigh, sorrow, thoughts) profond(e); (voice) grave ▷ adv: **~ in snow** recouvert(e) d'une épaisse couche de neige; **spectators stood 20 ~** il y avait 20 rangs de spectateurs; **knee-~ in water** dans l'eau jusqu'aux genoux; **4 metres ~** de 4 mètres de profondeur; **how ~ is the water?** l'eau a quelle profondeur?; **he took a ~ breath** il inspira profondément, il prit son souffle

deepen [di:pn] vt (hole) approfondir ▷ vi s'approfondir; (darkness) s'épaissir

deepfreeze ['di:p'fri:z] n congélateur m ▷ vt surgeler

deep-fry ['di:p'fraɪ] vt faire frire (dans une friteuse)

deeply ['di:plɪ] adv profondément; (dig) en profondeur; (regret, interested) vivement

deep-rooted ['di:p'ru:tɪd] adj (prejudice) profondément enraciné(e); (affection) profond(e); (habit) invétéré(e)

deep-sea ['di:p'si:] adj: **~ diver** plongeur sous-marin; **~ diving** plongée sous-marine; **~ fishing** pêche hauturière

deep-seated ['di:p'si:tɪd] adj (belief) profondément enraciné(e)

deep-set ['di:psɛt] adj (eyes) enfoncé(e)

deep vein thrombosis n thrombose f veineuse profonde

deer [dɪəʳ] n (pl inv): **the ~** les cervidés mpl; (Zool): **(red) ~** cerf m; **(fallow) ~** daim m; **(roe) ~** chevreuil m

deerskin ['dɪəskɪn] n peau f de daim

deerstalker ['dɪəstɔ:kəʳ] n (person) chasseur m de cerf; (hat) casquette f à la Sherlock Holmes

deface [dɪ'feɪs] vt dégrader; barbouiller rendre illisible

defamation [dɛfə'meɪʃən] n diffamation f

defamatory [dɪ'fæmətrɪ] adj diffamatoire, diffamant(e)

default [dɪ'fɔ:lt] vi (Law) faire défaut; (gen) manquer à ses engagements ▷ n (Comput: also: **default value**) valeur f par défaut; **by ~** (Law) par défaut, par contumace; (Sport) par forfait; **to ~ on a debt** ne pas s'acquitter d'une dette

defaulter [dɪ'fɔ:ltəʳ] n (on debt) débiteur défaillant

default option n (Comput) option f par défaut

defeat [dɪ'fi:t] n défaite f ▷ vt (team, opponents) battre; (fig: plans, efforts) faire échouer

defeatism [dɪ'fi:tɪzəm] n défaitisme m

defeatist [dɪ'fi:tɪst] adj, n défaitiste m/f

defecate ['dɛfəkeɪt] vi déféquer

defect ['di:fɛkt] n défaut m ▷ vi [dɪ'fɛkt]: **to ~ to the enemy/the West** passer à l'ennemi/ l'Ouest; **physical ~** malformation f, vice m de conformation; **mental ~** anomalie or déficience mentale

defective [dɪ'fɛktɪv] adj défectueux(-euse)

defector [dɪ'fɛktəʳ] n transfuge m/f

defence, (US) defense [dɪ'fɛns] n défense f; **in ~ of** pour défendre; **witness for the ~** témoin m à décharge; **the Ministry of D~, (US) the Department of Defense** le ministère de la Défense nationale

defenceless [dɪ'fɛnslɪs] adj sans défense

defend [dɪ'fɛnd] vt défendre; (decision, action, opinion) justifier, défendre

defendant [dɪ'fɛndənt] n défendeur(-deresse); (in criminal case) accusé(e), prévenu(e)

defender [dɪ'fɛndəʳ] n défenseur m

defending champion [dɪ'fɛndɪŋ-] n (Sport) champion(ne) en titre

defending counsel [dɪ'fɛndɪŋ-] n (Law) avocat m de la défense

defense [dɪ'fɛns] n (US) = **defence**

defensive [dɪ'fɛnsɪv] adj défensif(-ive) ▷ n défensive f; **on the ~** sur la défensive

defer [dɪ'fə:ʳ] vt (postpone) différer, ajourner ▷ vi (submit): **to ~ to sb/sth** déférer à qn/qch, s'en remettre à qn/qch

deference ['dɛfərəns] n déférence f, égards mpl;
out of or **in ~ to** par déférence or égards pour

defiance [dɪ'faɪəns] n défi m; **in ~ of** au mépris
de

defiant [dɪ'faɪənt] adj provocant(e), de défi;
(person) rebelle, intraitable

defiantly [dɪ'faɪəntlɪ] adv d'un air (or d'un ton)
de défi

deficiency [dɪ'fɪʃənsɪ] n (lack) insuffisance f;
(: Med) carence f; (flaw) faiblesse f; (Comm)
déficit m, découvert m

deficiency disease n maladie f de carence

deficient [dɪ'fɪʃənt] adj (inadequate)
insuffisant(e); (defective) défectueux(-euse); **to
be ~ in** manquer de

deficit ['dɛfɪsɪt] n déficit m

defile [dɪ'faɪl] vt souiller ▷ vi défiler ▷ n ['diːfaɪl]
défilé m

define [dɪ'faɪn] vt définir

definite ['dɛfɪnɪt] adj (fixed) défini(e), (bien)
déterminé(e); (clear, obvious) net(te), manifeste;
(Ling) défini(e); (certain) sûr(e); **he was ~ about
it** il a été catégorique; il était sûr de son fait

definitely ['dɛfɪnɪtlɪ] adv sans aucun doute

definition [dɛfɪ'nɪʃən] n définition f; (clearness)
netteté f

definitive [dɪ'fɪnɪtɪv] adj définitif(-ive)

deflate [diː'fleɪt] vt dégonfler; (pompous person)
rabattre le caquet à; (Econ) provoquer la
déflation de; (: prices) faire tomber or baisser

deflation [diː'fleɪʃən] n (Econ) déflation f

deflationary [diː'fleɪʃənrɪ] adj (Econ)
déflationniste

deflect [dɪ'flɛkt] vt détourner, faire dévier

defog ['diː'fɔg] vt (US Aut) désembuer

defogger ['diː'fɔgər] n (US Aut) dispositif m anti-
buée inv

deform [dɪ'fɔːm] vt déformer

deformed [dɪ'fɔːmd] adj difforme

deformity [dɪ'fɔːmɪtɪ] n difformité f

defraud [dɪ'frɔːd] vt frauder; **to ~ sb of sth**
soutirer qch malhonnêtement à qn; escroquer
qch à qn; frustrer qn de qch

defray [dɪ'freɪ] vt: **to ~ sb's expenses** défrayer
qn (de ses frais), rembourser or payer à qn ses
frais

defrost [diː'frɔst] vt (fridge) dégivrer; (frozen food)
décongeler

deft [dɛft] adj adroit(e), preste

defunct [dɪ'fʌŋkt] adj défunt(e)

defuse [diː'fjuːz] vt désamorcer

defy [dɪ'faɪ] vt défier; (efforts etc) résister à; **it
defies description** cela défie toute description

degenerate vi [dɪ'dʒɛnəreɪt] dégénérer ▷ adj
[dɪ'dʒɛnərɪt] dégénéré(e)

degradation [dɛgrə'deɪʃən] n dégradation f

degrade [dɪ'greɪd] vt dégrader

degrading [dɪ'greɪdɪŋ] adj dégradant(e)

degree [dɪ'griː] n degré m; (Scol) diplôme m
(universitaire); **10 ~s below (zero)** 10 degrés
au-dessous de zéro; **a (first) ~ in maths** (Brit)

une licence en maths; **a considerable ~ of risk**
un considérable facteur or élément de risque;
by ~s (gradually) par degrés; **to some ~, to a
certain ~** jusqu'à un certain point, dans une
certaine mesure

dehydrated [diːhaɪ'dreɪtɪd] adj déshydraté(e);
(milk, eggs) en poudre

dehydration [diːhaɪ'dreɪʃən] n déshydratation f

de-ice ['diː'aɪs] vt (windscreen) dégivrer

de-icer ['diː'aɪsər] n dégivreur m

deign [deɪn] vi: **to ~ to do** daigner faire

deity ['diːɪtɪ] n divinité f; dieu m, déesse f

déjà vu [deɪʒɑː'vuː] n: **I had a sense of ~** j'ai eu
une impression de déjà-vu

dejected [dɪ'dʒɛktɪd] adj abattu(e), déprimé(e)

dejection [dɪ'dʒɛkʃən] n abattement m,
découragement m

Del. abbr (US) = **Delaware**

del. abbr = **delete**

delay [dɪ'leɪ] vt (journey, operation) retarder,
différer; (traveller, train) retarder; (payment)
différer ▷ vi s'attarder ▷ n délai m, retard m; **to
be ~ed** être en retard; **without ~** sans délai,
sans tarder

delayed-action [dɪ'leɪd'ækʃən] adj à
retardement

delectable [dɪ'lɛktəbl] adj délicieux(-euse)

delegate n ['dɛlɪgɪt] délégué(e) ▷ vt ['dɛlɪgeɪt]
déléguer; **to ~ sth to sb/sb to do sth** déléguer
qch à qn/qn pour faire qch

delegation [dɛlɪ'geɪʃən] n délégation f

delete [dɪ'liːt] vt rayer, supprimer; (Comput)
effacer

Delhi ['dɛlɪ] n Delhi

deli ['dɛlɪ] n épicerie fine

deliberate adj [dɪ'lɪbərɪt] (intentional) délibéré(e);
(slow) mesuré(e) ▷ vi [dɪ'lɪbəreɪt] délibérer,
réfléchir

deliberately [dɪ'lɪbərɪtlɪ] adv (on purpose) exprès,
délibérément

deliberation [dɪlɪbə'reɪʃən] n délibération f,
réflexion f; (gen pl: discussion) délibérations,
débats mpl

delicacy ['dɛlɪkəsɪ] n délicatesse f; (choice food)
mets fin or délicat, friandise f

delicate ['dɛlɪkɪt] adj délicat(e)

delicately ['dɛlɪkɪtlɪ] adv délicatement; (act,
express) avec délicatesse, avec tact

delicatessen [dɛlɪkə'tɛsn] n épicerie fine

delicious [dɪ'lɪʃəs] adj délicieux(-euse), exquis(e)

delight [dɪ'laɪt] n (grande) joie, grand plaisir
▷ vt enchanter; **she's a ~ to work with** c'est un
plaisir de travailler avec elle; **a ~ to the eyes** un
régal or plaisir pour les yeux; **to take ~ in**
prendre grand plaisir à; **to be the ~ of** faire les
délices or la joie de

delighted [dɪ'laɪtɪd] adj: **~ (at** or **with sth)**
ravi(e) (de qch); **to be ~ to do sth/that** être
enchanté(e) or ravi(e) de faire qch/que; **I'd be ~**
j'en serais enchanté or ravi

delightful [dɪ'laɪtful] adj (person) absolument
charmant(e), adorable; (meal, evening)

merveilleux(-euse)

delimit [diː'lɪmɪt] vt délimiter

delineate [dɪ'lɪnɪeɪt] vt tracer, esquisser; (fig) dépeindre, décrire

delinquency [dɪ'lɪŋkwənsɪ] n délinquance f

delinquent [dɪ'lɪŋkwənt] adj, n délinquant(e)

delirious [dɪ'lɪrɪəs] adj (Med: fig) délirant(e); **to be ~** délirer

delirium [dɪ'lɪrɪəm] n délire m

deliver [dɪ'lɪvə*] vt (mail) distribuer; (goods) livrer; (message) remettre; (speech) prononcer; (warning, ultimatum) lancer; (free) délivrer; (Med: baby) mettre au monde; (: woman) accoucher; **to ~ the goods** (fig) tenir ses promesses

deliverance [dɪ'lɪvrəns] n délivrance f, libération f

delivery [dɪ'lɪvərɪ] n (of mail) distribution f; (of goods) livraison f; (of speaker) élocution f; (Med) accouchement m; **to take ~ of** prendre livraison de

delivery note n bon m de livraison

delivery van, (US) **delivery truck** n fourgonnette f or camionnette f de livraison

delta ['dɛltə] n delta m

delude [dɪ'luːd] vt tromper, leurrer; **to ~ o.s.** se leurrer, se faire des illusions

deluge ['dɛljuːdʒ] n déluge m ▷ vt (fig): **to ~ (with)** inonder (de)

delusion [dɪ'luːʒən] n illusion f; **to have ~s of grandeur** être un peu mégalomane

de luxe [də'lʌks] adj de luxe

delve [dɛlv] vi: **to ~ into** fouiller dans

Dem. abbr (US Pol) = **democrat; democratic**

demagogue ['dɛməgɔg] n démagogue m/f

demand [dɪ'mɑːnd] vt réclamer, exiger; (need) exiger, requérir ▷ n exigence f; (claim) revendication f; (Econ) demande f; **to ~ sth (from** or **of sb)** exiger qch (de qn), réclamer qch (à qn); **in ~** demandé(e), recherché(e); **on ~** sur demande

demanding [dɪ'mɑːndɪŋ] adj (person) exigeant(e); (work) astreignant(e)

demarcation [diːmɑː'keɪʃən] n démarcation f

demarcation dispute n (Industry) conflit m d'attributions

demean [dɪ'miːn] vt: **to ~ o.s.** s'abaisser

demeanour, (US) **demeanor** [dɪ'miːnə*] n comportement m; maintien m

demented [dɪ'mɛntɪd] adj dément(e), fou (folle)

demilitarized zone [diː'mɪlɪtəraɪzd-] n zone démilitarisée

demise [dɪ'maɪz] n décès m

demist [diː'mɪst] vt (Brit Aut) désembuer

demister [diː'mɪstə*] n (Brit Aut) dispositif m anti-buée inv

demo ['dɛməu] n abbr (inf) = **demonstration**; (protest) manif f; (Comput) démonstration f

demobilize [diː'məubɪlaɪz] vt démobiliser

democracy [dɪ'mɔkrəsɪ] n démocratie f

democrat ['dɛməkræt] n démocrate m/f

democratic [dɛmə'krætɪk] adj démocratique; **the D~ Party** (US) le parti démocrate

demography [dɪ'mɔgrəfɪ] n démographie f

demolish [dɪ'mɔlɪʃ] vt démolir

demolition [dɛmə'lɪʃən] n démolition f

demon ['diːmən] n démon m ▷ cpd: **a ~ squash player** un crack en squash; **a ~ driver** un fou du volant

demonstrate ['dɛmənstreɪt] vt démontrer, prouver; (show) faire une démonstration de ▷ vi: **to ~ (for/against)** manifester (en faveur de/ contre)

demonstration [dɛmən'streɪʃən] n démonstration f; (Pol etc) manifestation f; **to hold a ~** (Pol etc) organiser une manifestation, manifester

demonstrative [dɪ'mɔnstrətɪv] adj démonstratif(-ive)

demonstrator ['dɛmənstreɪtə*] n (Pol etc) manifestant(e); (Comm: sales person) vendeur(-euse); (: car, computer etc) modèle m de démonstration

demoralize [dɪ'mɔrəlaɪz] vt démoraliser

demote [dɪ'məut] vt rétrograder

demotion [dɪ'məuʃən] n rétrogradation f

demur [dɪ'məː*] vi: **to ~ (at sth)** hésiter (devant qch); (object) élever des objections (contre qch) ▷ n: **without ~** sans hésiter; sans faire de difficultés

demure [dɪ'mjuə*] adj sage, réservé(e), d'une modestie affectée

demurrage [dɪ'mʌrɪdʒ] n droits mpl de magasinage; surestarie f

den [dɛn] n (of lion) tanière f; (room) repaire m

denationalization [diːnæfnəlaɪ'zeɪʃən] n dénationalisation f

denationalize [diː'næfnəlaɪz] vt dénationaliser

denial [dɪ'naɪəl] n (of accusation) démenti m; (of rights, guilt, truth) dénégation f

denier ['dɛnɪə*] n denier m; **15 ~ stockings** bas de 15 deniers

denigrate ['dɛnɪgreɪt] vt dénigrer

denim ['dɛnɪm] n jean m; **denims** npl (blue-)jeans mpl

denim jacket n veste f en jean

denizen ['dɛnɪzn] n (inhabitant) habitant(e); (foreigner) étranger(-ère)

Denmark ['dɛnmɑːk] n Danemark m

denomination [dɪnɔmɪ'neɪʃən] n (money) valeur f; (Rel) confession f; culte m

denominator [dɪ'nɔmɪneɪtə*] n dénominateur m

denote [dɪ'nəut] vt dénoter

denounce [dɪ'nauns] vt dénoncer

dense [dɛns] adj dense; (inf: stupid) obtus(e), dur(e) or lent(e) à la comprenette

densely ['dɛnslɪ] adv: **~ wooded** couvert(e) d'épaisses forêts; **~ populated** à forte densité (de population), très peuplé(e)

density ['dɛnsɪtɪ] n densité f

dent [dɛnt] n bosse f ▷ vt (also: **make a dent in**) cabosser; **to make a ~ in** (fig) entamer

dental ['dɛntl] adj dentaire

dental floss [-flɔs] n fil m dentaire

dental surgeon n (chirurgien(ne)) dentiste
dental surgery n cabinet m de dentiste
dentist ['dɛntɪst] n dentiste m/f; **~'s surgery**
(Brit) cabinet m de dentiste
dentistry ['dɛntɪstrɪ] n art m dentaire
dentures ['dɛntʃəz] npl dentier msg
denunciation [dɪnʌnsɪ'eɪʃən] n dénonciation f
deny [dɪ'naɪ] vt nier; (refuse) refuser; (disown)
renier; **he denies having said it** il nie l'avoir
dit
deodorant [di:'əudərənt] n désodorisant m,
déodorant m
depart [dɪ'pɑːt] vi partir; **to ~ from** (leave)
quitter, partir de; (fig: differ from) s'écarter de
departed [dɪ'pɑːtɪd] adj (dead) défunt(e); **the
(dear) ~** le défunt/la défunte/les défunts
department [dɪ'pɑːtmənt] n (Comm) rayon m;
(Scol) section f; (Pol) ministère m, département
m; **that's not my ~** (fig) ce n'est pas mon
domaine or ma compétence, ce n'est pas mon
rayon; **D~ of State** (US) Département d'État
departmental [di:pɑːt'mɛntl] adj d'une or de la
section; d'un or du ministère, d'un or du
département; **~ manager** chef m de service; (in
shop) chef de rayon
department store n grand magasin
departure [dɪ'pɑːtʃə'] n départ m; (fig): **~ from**
écart m par rapport à; **a new ~** une nouvelle voie
departure lounge n salle f de départ
depend [dɪ'pɛnd] vi: **to ~ (up)on** dépendre de;
(rely on) compter sur; (financially) dépendre
(financièrement) de, être à la charge de; **it ~s**
cela dépend; **~ing on the result ...** selon le
résultat ...
dependable [dɪ'pɛndəbl] adj sûr(e), digne de
confiance
dependant [dɪ'pɛndənt] n personne f à charge
dependence [dɪ'pɛndəns] n dépendance f
dependent [dɪ'pɛndənt] adj: **to be ~ (on)**
dépendre (de) ▷ n = **dependant**
depict [dɪ'pɪkt] vt (in picture) représenter; (in
words) (dé)peindre, décrire
depilatory [dɪ'pɪlətrɪ] n (also: **depilatory cream**)
dépilatoire m, crème f à épiler
depleted [dɪ'pliːtɪd] adj (considérablement)
réduit(e) or diminué(e)
deplorable [dɪ'plɔːrəbl] adj déplorable,
lamentable
deplore [dɪ'plɔː'] vt déplorer
deploy [dɪ'plɔɪ] vt déployer
depopulate [di:'pɔpjuleɪt] vt dépeupler
depopulation ['di:pɔpju'leɪʃən] n dépopulation
f, dépeuplement m
deport [dɪ'pɔːt] vt déporter, expulser
deportation [di:pɔ'teɪʃən] n déportation f,
expulsion f
deportation order n arrêté m d'expulsion
deportee [di:pɔ'tiː] n déporté(e)
deportment [dɪ'pɔːtmənt] n maintien m,
tenue f
depose [dɪ'pəuz] vt déposer
deposit [dɪ'pɔzɪt] n (Chem, Comm, Geo) dépôt m;

(of ore, oil) gisement m; (part payment) arrhes fpl,
acompte m; (on bottle etc) consigne f; (for hired
goods etc) cautionnement m, garantie f ▷ vt
déposer; (valuables) mettre or laisser en dépôt;
to put down a ~ of £50 verser 50 livres d'arrhes
or d'acompte; laisser 50 livres en garantie
deposit account n compte m sur livret
depositor [dɪ'pɔzɪtə'] n déposant(e)
depository [dɪ'pɔzɪtərɪ] n (person) dépositaire m/
f; (place) dépôt m
depot ['dɛpəu] n dépôt m; (US: Rail) gare f
depraved [dɪ'preɪvd] adj dépravé(e), perverti(e)
depravity [dɪ'prævɪtɪ] n dépravation f
deprecate ['dɛprɪkeɪt] vt désapprouver
deprecating ['dɛprɪkeɪtɪŋ] adj (disapproving)
désapprobateur(-trice); (apologetic): **a ~ smile**
un sourire d'excuse
depreciate [dɪ'priːʃɪeɪt] vt déprécier ▷ vi se
déprécier, se dévaloriser
depreciation [dɪpriːʃɪ'eɪʃən] n dépréciation f
depress [dɪ'prɛs] vt déprimer; (press down)
appuyer sur, abaisser; (wages etc) faire baisser
depressant [dɪ'prɛsnt] n (Med) dépresseur m
depressed [dɪ'prɛst] adj (person) déprimé(e),
abattu(e); (area) en déclin, touché(e) par le sous-
emploi; (Comm: market, trade) maussade; **to get
~** se démoraliser, se laisser abattre
depressing [dɪ'prɛsɪŋ] adj déprimant(e)
depression [dɪ'prɛʃən] n (Econ) dépression f
deprivation [dɛprɪ'veɪʃən] n privation f; (loss)
perte f
deprive [dɪ'praɪv] vt: **to ~ sb of** priver qn de
deprived [dɪ'praɪvd] adj déshérité(e)
dept. abbr (= department) dép, dépt
depth [dɛpθ] n profondeur f; **in the ~s of** au
fond de; au cœur de; au plus profond de; **to be
in the ~s of despair** être au plus profond du
désespoir; **at a ~ of 3 metres** à 3 mètres de
profondeur; **to be out of one's ~** (Brit: swimmer)
ne plus avoir pied; (fig) être dépassé(e), nager;
to study sth in ~ étudier qch en profondeur
depth charge n grenade sous-marine
deputation [dɛpju'teɪʃən] n députation f,
délégation f
deputize ['dɛpjutaɪz] vi: **to ~ for** assurer
l'intérim de
deputy ['dɛpjutɪ] n (replacement) suppléant(e),
intérimaire m/f; (second in command) adjoint(e);
(Pol) député m; (US: also: **deputy sheriff**) shérif
adjoint ▷ adj: **~ chairman** vice-président m; **~
head** (Scol) directeur(-trice) adjoint(e), sous-
directeur(-trice); **~ leader** (Brit Pol) vice-
président(e), secrétaire adjoint(e)
derail [dɪ'reɪl] vt faire dérailler; **to be ~ed**
dérailler
derailment [dɪ'reɪlmənt] n déraillement m
deranged [dɪ'reɪndʒd] adj: **to be (mentally) ~**
avoir le cerveau dérangé
derby ['dəːrbɪ] n (US) (chapeau m) melon m
deregulate [dɪ'rɛgjuleɪt] vt libérer, dérégler
deregulation [dɪrɛgju'leɪʃən] n libération f,
dérèglement m

derelict ['dɛrɪlɪkt] *adj* abandonné(e), à l'abandon

deride [dɪ'raɪd] *vt* railler

derision [dɪ'rɪʒən] *n* dérision *f*

derisive [dɪ'raɪsɪv] *adj* moqueur(-euse), railleur(-euse)

derisory [dɪ'raɪsərɪ] *adj* (*sum*) dérisoire; (*smile, person*) moqueur(-euse), railleur(-euse)

derivation [dɛrɪ'veɪʃən] *n* dérivation *f*

derivative [dɪ'rɪvətɪv] *n* dérivé *m* ▷ *adj* dérivé(e)

derive [dɪ'raɪv] *vt*: **to ~ sth from** tirer qch de; trouver qch dans ▷ *vi*: **to ~ from** provenir de, dériver de

dermatitis [də:mə'taɪtɪs] *n* dermatite *f*

dermatology [də:mə'tɔlədʒɪ] *n* dermatologie *f*

derogatory [dɪ'rɔgətərɪ] *adj* désobligeant(e), péjoratif(-ive)

derrick ['dɛrɪk] *n* mât *m* de charge, derrick *m*

derv [də:v] *n* (*Brit*) gas-oil *m*, diesel *m*

DES *n abbr* (*Brit*: = *Department of Education and Science*) ministère de l'éducation nationale et des sciences

desalination [di:sælɪ'neɪʃən] *n* dessalement *m*, dessalage *m*

descend [dɪ'sɛnd] *vt, vi* descendre; **to ~ from** descendre de, être issu(e) de; **to ~ to** s'abaisser à; **in ~ing order of importance** par ordre d'importance décroissante

▸ **descend on** *vt fus* (*enemy, angry person*) tomber *or* sauter sur; (*misfortune*) s'abattre sur; (*gloom, silence*) envahir; **visitors ~ed (up)on us** des gens sont arrivés chez nous à l'improviste

descendant [dɪ'sɛndənt] *n* descendant(e)

descent [dɪ'sɛnt] *n* descente *f*; (*origin*) origine *f*

describe [dɪs'kraɪb] *vt* décrire

description [dɪs'krɪpʃən] *n* description *f*; (*sort*) sorte *f*, espèce *f*; **of every ~** de toutes sortes

descriptive [dɪs'krɪptɪv] *adj* descriptif(-ive)

desecrate ['dɛsɪkreɪt] *vt* profaner

desert [*n* 'dɛzət, *vb* dɪ'zə:t] *n* désert *m* ▷ *vt* déserter, abandonner ▷ *vi* (*Mil*) déserter

deserted [dɪ'zə:tɪd] *adj* désert(e)

deserter [dɪ'zə:tər] *n* déserteur *m*

desertion [dɪ'zə:ʃən] *n* désertion *f*

desert island *n* île déserte

deserts [dɪ'zə:ts] *npl*: **to get one's just ~** n'avoir que ce qu'on mérite

deserve [dɪ'zə:v] *vt* mériter

deservedly [dɪ'zə:vɪdlɪ] *adv* à juste titre, à bon droit

deserving [dɪ'zə:vɪŋ] *adj* (*person*) méritant(e); (*action, cause*) méritoire

desiccated ['dɛsɪkeɪtɪd] *adj* séché(e)

design [dɪ'zaɪn] *n* (*sketch*) plan *m*, dessin *m*; (*layout, shape*) conception *f*, ligne *f*; (*pattern*) dessin, motif(s) *m(pl)*; (*of dress, car*) modèle *m*; (*art*) design *m*, stylisme *m*; (*intention*) dessein *m* ▷ *vt* dessiner; (*plan*) concevoir; **to have ~s on** avoir des visées sur; **well-~ed** *adj* bien conçu(e); **industrial ~** esthétique industrielle

design and technology *n* (*Brit: Scol*) technologie *f*

designate *vt* ['dɛzɪgneɪt] désigner ▷ *adj* ['dɛzɪgnɪt] désigné(e)

designation [dɛzɪg'neɪʃən] *n* désignation *f*

designer [dɪ'zaɪnər] *n* (*Archit, Art*) dessinateur(-trice); (*Industry*) concepteur *m*, designer *m*; (*Fashion*) styliste *m/f*

desirability [dɪzaɪərə'bɪlɪtɪ] *n* avantage *m*; attrait *m*

desirable [dɪ'zaɪərəbl] *adj* (*property, location, purchase*) attrayant(e); **it is ~ that** il est souhaitable que

desire [dɪ'zaɪər] *n* désir *m* ▷ *vt* désirer, vouloir; **to ~ to do sth/that** désirer faire qch/que

desirous [dɪ'zaɪərəs] *adj*: **~ of** désireux(-euse) de

desk [dɛsk] *n* (*in office*) bureau *m*; (*for pupil*) pupitre *m*; (*Brit: in shop, restaurant*) caisse *f*; (*in hotel, at airport*) réception *f*

desktop computer ['dɛsktɔp-] *n* ordinateur *m* de bureau *or* de table

desk-top publishing ['dɛsktɔp-] *n* publication assistée par ordinateur, PAO *f*

desolate ['dɛsəlɪt] *adj* désolé(e)

desolation [dɛsə'leɪʃən] *n* désolation *f*

despair [dɪs'pɛər] *n* désespoir *m* ▷ *vi*: **to ~ of** désespérer de; **to be in ~** être au désespoir

despatch [dɪs'pætʃ] *n, vt* = **dispatch**

desperate ['dɛspərɪt] *adj* désespéré(e); (*fugitive*) prêt(e) à tout; (*measures*) désespéré, extrême; **to be ~ for sth/to do sth** avoir désespérément besoin de qch/de faire qch; **we are getting ~** nous commençons à désespérer

desperately ['dɛspərɪtlɪ] *adv* désespérément; (*very*) terriblement, extrêmement; **~ ill** très gravement malade

desperation [dɛspə'reɪʃən] *n* désespoir *m*; **in (sheer) ~** en désespoir de cause

despicable [dɪs'pɪkəbl] *adj* méprisable

despise [dɪs'paɪz] *vt* mépriser, dédaigner

despite [dɪs'paɪt] *prep* malgré, en dépit de

despondent [dɪs'pɔndənt] *adj* découragé(e), abattu(e)

despot ['dɛspɔt] *n* despote *m/f*

dessert [dɪ'zə:t] *n* dessert *m*

dessertspoon [dɪ'zə:tspu:n] *n* cuiller *f* à dessert

destabilize [di:'steɪbɪlaɪz] *vt* déstabiliser

destination [dɛstɪ'neɪʃən] *n* destination *f*

destine ['dɛstɪn] *vt* destiner

destined ['dɛstɪnd] *adj*: **to be ~ to do sth** être destiné(e) à faire qch; **~ for London** à destination de Londres

destiny ['dɛstɪnɪ] *n* destinée *f*, destin *m*

destitute ['dɛstɪtju:t] *adj* indigent(e), dans le dénuement; **~ of** dépourvu(e) *or* dénué(e) de

destroy [dɪs'trɔɪ] *vt* détruire; (*injured horse*) abattre; (*dog*) faire piquer

destroyer [dɪs'trɔɪər] *n* (*Naut*) contre-torpilleur *m*

destruction [dɪs'trʌkʃən] *n* destruction *f*

destructive [dɪs'trʌktɪv] *adj* destructeur(-trice)

desultory ['dɛsəltərɪ] *adj* (*reading, conversation*) décousu(e); (*contact*) irrégulier(-ière)

detach [dɪ'tætʃ] *vt* détacher

detachable [dɪ'tætʃəbl] *adj* amovible,

détachable

detached [dɪ'tætʃt] *adj* (*attitude*) détaché(e)

detached house *n* pavillon *m* maison(nette) (individuelle)

detachment [dɪ'tætʃmənt] *n* (*Mil*) détachement *m*; (*fig*) détachement, indifférence *f*

detail ['di:teɪl] *n* détail *m*; (*Mil*) détachement *m* ▷ *vt* raconter en détail, énumérer; (*Mil*): **to ~ sb (for)** affecter qn (à), détacher qn (pour); **in ~** en détail; **to go into ~(s)** entrer dans les détails

detailed ['di:teɪld] *adj* détaillé(e)

detain [dɪ'teɪn] *vt* retenir; (*in captivity*) détenir; (*in hospital*) hospitaliser

detainee [di:teɪ'ni:] *n* détenu(e)

detect [dɪ'tɛkt] *vt* déceler, percevoir; (*Med, Police*) dépister; (*Mil, Radar, Tech*) détecter

detection [dɪ'tɛkʃən] *n* découverte *f*; (*Med, Police*) dépistage *m*; (*Mil, Radar, Tech*) détection *f*; **to escape ~** échapper aux recherches, éviter d'être découvert(e); (*mistake*) passer inaperçu(e); **crime ~** le dépistage des criminels

detective [dɪ'tɛktɪv] *n* agent *m* de la sûreté, policier *m*; **private ~** détective privé

detective story *n* roman policier

detector [dɪ'tɛktə^r] *n* détecteur *m*

détente [deɪ'tɑ:nt] *n* détente *f*

detention [dɪ'tɛnʃən] *n* détention *f*; (*Scol*) retenue *f*, consigne *f*

deter [dɪ'tə:^r] *vt* dissuader

detergent [dɪ'tə:dʒənt] *n* détersif *m*, détergent *m*

deteriorate [dɪ'tɪərɪəreɪt] *vi* se détériorer, se dégrader

deterioration [dɪtɪərɪə'reɪʃən] *n* détérioration *f*

determination [dɪtə:mɪ'neɪʃən] *n* détermination *f*

determine [dɪ'tə:mɪn] *vt* déterminer; **to ~ to do** résoudre de faire, se déterminer à faire

determined [dɪ'tə:mɪnd] *adj* (*person*) déterminé(e), décidé(e); (*quantity*) déterminé, établi(e); (*effort*) très gros(se); **~ to do** bien décidé à faire

deterrence [dɪ'tɛrns] *n* dissuasion *f*

deterrent [dɪ'tɛrənt] *n* effet *m* de dissuasion; force *f* de dissuasion; **to act as a ~** avoir un effet dissuasif

detest [dɪ'tɛst] *vt* détester, avoir horreur de

detestable [dɪ'tɛstəbl] *adj* détestable, odieux(-euse)

detonate ['dɛtəneɪt] *vi* exploser ▷ *vt* faire exploser *or* détoner

detonator ['dɛtəneɪtə^r] *n* détonateur *m*

detour ['di:tuə^r] *n* détour *m*; (*US Aut: diversion*) déviation *f*

detract [dɪ'trækt] *vt*: **to ~ from** (*quality, pleasure*) diminuer; (*reputation*) porter atteinte à

detractor [dɪ'træktə^r] *n* détracteur(-trice)

detriment ['dɛtrɪmənt] *n*: **to the ~ of** au détriment de, au préjudice de; **without ~ to** sans porter atteinte *or* préjudice à, sans conséquences fâcheuses pour

detrimental [dɛtrɪ'mɛntl] *adj*: **~ to**

préjudiciable *or* nuisible à

deuce [dju:s] *n* (*Tennis*) égalité *f*

devaluation [dɪvælju'eɪʃən] *n* dévaluation *f*

devalue ['di:'vælju:] *vt* dévaluer

devastate ['dɛvəsteɪt] *vt* dévaster; **he was ~d by the news** cette nouvelle lui a porté un coup terrible

devastating ['dɛvəsteɪtɪŋ] *adj* dévastateur(-trice); (*news*) accablant(e)

devastation [dɛvəs'teɪʃən] *n* dévastation *f*

develop [dɪ'vɛləp] *vt* (*gen*) développer; (*disease*) commencer à souffrir de; (*habit*) contracter; (*resources*) mettre en valeur, exploiter; (*land*) aménager ▷ *vi* se développer; (*situation, disease: evolve*) évoluer; (*facts, symptoms: appear*) se manifester, se produire; **can you ~ this film?** pouvez-vous développer cette pellicule?; **to ~ a taste for sth** prendre goût à qch; **to ~ into** devenir

developer [dɪ'vɛləpə^r] *n* (*Phot*) révélateur *m*; (*of land*) promoteur *m*; (*also: **property developer***) promoteur immobilier

developing country [dɪ'vɛləpɪŋ-] *n* pays *m* en voie de développement

development [dɪ'vɛləpmənt] *n* développement *m*; (*of land*) exploitation *f*; (*new fact, event*) rebondissement *m*, fait(s) nouveau(x)

development area *n* zone *f* à urbaniser

deviate ['di:vɪeɪt] *vi*: **to ~ (from)** dévier (de)

deviation [di:vɪ'eɪʃən] *n* déviation *f*

device [dɪ'vaɪs] *n* (*scheme*) moyen *m*, expédient *m*; (*apparatus*) appareil *m*, dispositif *m*; **explosive ~** engin explosif

devil ['dɛvl] *n* diable *m*; démon *m*

devilish ['dɛvlɪʃ] *adj* diabolique

devil-may-care ['dɛvlmeɪ'kɛə^r] *adj* je-m'en-foutiste

devil's advocate *n*: **to play devil's advocate** se faire avocat du diable

devious ['di:vɪəs] *adj* (*means*) détourné(e); (*person*) sournois(e), dissimulé(e)

devise [dɪ'vaɪz] *vt* imaginer, concevoir

devoid [dɪ'vɔɪd] *adj*: **~ of** dépourvu(e) de, dénué(e) de

devolution [di:və'lu:ʃən] *n* (*Pol*) décentralisation *f*

devolve [dɪ'vɔlv] *vi*: **to ~ (up)on** retomber sur

devote [dɪ'vəut] *vt*: **to ~ sth to** consacrer qch à

devoted [dɪ'vəutɪd] *adj* dévoué(e); **to be ~ to** être dévoué(e) *or* très attaché(e) à; (*book etc*) être consacré(e) à

devotee [dɛvəu'ti:] *n* (*Rel*) adepte *m/f*; (*Mus, Sport*) fervent(e)

devotion [dɪ'vəuʃən] *n* dévouement *m*, attachement *m*; (*Rel*) dévotion *f*, piété *f*

devour [dɪ'vauə^r] *vt* dévorer

devout [dɪ'vaut] *adj* pieux(-euse), dévot(e)

dew [dju:] *n* rosée *f*

dexterity [dɛks'tɛrɪtɪ] *n* dextérité *f*, adresse *f*

DfEE *n abbr* (*Brit*: = *Department for Education and Employment*) Ministère de l'éducation et de l'emploi

d

dg *abbr* (= *decigram*) dg
diabetes [daɪə'biːtiːz] *n* diabète *m*
diabetic [daɪə'bɛtɪk] *n* diabétique *m/f* ▷ *adj*
(*person*) diabétique; (*chocolate, jam*) pour
diabétiques
diabolical [daɪə'bɔlɪkl] *adj* diabolique; (*inf:
dreadful*) infernal(e), atroce
diagnose [daɪəg'nəuz] *vt* diagnostiquer
diagnosis (*pl* **diagnoses**) [daɪəg'nəusɪs, -siːz] *n*
diagnostic *m*
diagonal [daɪ'ægənl] *adj* diagonal(e) ▷ *n*
diagonale *f*
diagram ['daɪəgræm] *n* diagramme *m*,
schéma *m*
dial ['daɪəl] *n* cadran *m* ▷ *vt* (*number*) faire,
composer; **to ~ a wrong number** faire un faux
numéro; **can I ~ London direct?** puis-je *or* est-
ce-que je peux avoir Londres par
l'automatique?
dial. *abbr* = **dialect**
dialect ['daɪəlɛkt] *n* dialecte *m*
dialling code ['daɪəlɪŋ-], (*US*) **dial code** *n*
indicatif *m* (téléphonique); **what's the ~ for
Paris?** quel est l'indicatif de Paris?
dialling tone ['daɪəlɪŋ-], (*US*) **dial tone** *n*
tonalité *f*
dialogue, (*US*) **dialog** ['daɪəlɔg] *n* dialogue *m*
dialysis [daɪ'ælɪsɪs] *n* dialyse *f*
diameter [daɪ'æmɪtər] *n* diamètre *m*
diametrically [daɪə'mɛtrɪklɪ] *adv*: **~ opposed
(to)** diamétralement opposé(e) (à)
diamond ['daɪəmənd] *n* diamant *m*; (*shape*)
losange *m*; **diamonds** *npl* (*Cards*) carreau *m*
diamond ring *n* bague *f* de diamant(s)
diaper ['daɪəpər] *n* (*US*) couche *f*
diaphragm ['daɪəfræm] *n* diaphragme *m*
diarrhoea, (*US*) **diarrhea** [daɪə'riːə] *n*
diarrhée *f*
diary ['daɪərɪ] *n* (*daily account*) journal *m*; (*book*)
agenda *m*; **to keep a ~** tenir un journal
diatribe ['daɪətraɪb] *n* diatribe *f*
dice [daɪs] *n* (*pl inv*) dé *m* ▷ *vt* (*Culin*) couper en
dés *or* en cubes
dicey ['daɪsɪ] *adj* (*inf*): **it's a bit ~** c'est un peu
risqué
dichotomy [daɪ'kɔtəmɪ] *n* dichotomie *f*
dickhead ['dɪkhɛd] *n* (*Brit inf!*) tête *f* de nœud (!)
Dictaphone® ['dɪktəfəun] *n* Dictaphone®
dictate [*vb* dɪk'teɪt, *n* 'dɪkteɪt] *vt* dicter ▷ *vi*: **to ~
to** (*person*) imposer sa volonté à, régenter; **I
won't be ~d to** je n'ai d'ordres à recevoir de
personne ▷ *n* injonction *f*
dictation [dɪk'teɪʃən] *n* dictée *f*; **at ~ speed** à
une vitesse de dictée
dictator [dɪk'teɪtər] *n* dictateur *m*
dictatorship [dɪk'teɪtəʃɪp] *n* dictature *f*
diction ['dɪkʃən] *n* diction *f*, élocution *f*
dictionary ['dɪkʃənrɪ] *n* dictionnaire *m*
did [dɪd] *pt of* **do**
didactic [daɪ'dæktɪk] *adj* didactique
didn't [dɪdnt] = **did not**
die [daɪ] *n* (*pl* **dice**) dé *m*; (*pl* **-s**) coin *m*; matrice *f*;

étampe *f* ▷ *vi* mourir; **to ~ of** *or* **from** mourir de;
to be dying être mourant(e); **to be dying for
sth** avoir une envie folle de qch; **to be dying to
do sth** mourir d'envie de faire qch
▸ **die away** *vi* s'éteindre
▸ **die down** *vi* se calmer, s'apaiser
▸ **die out** *vi* disparaître, s'éteindre
diehard ['daɪhɑːd] *n* réactionnaire *m/f*,
jusqu'au-boutiste *m/f*
diesel ['diːzl] *n* (*vehicle*) diesel *m*; (*also*: **diesel oil**)
carburant *m* diesel, gas-oil *m*
diesel engine *n* moteur *m* diesel
diesel fuel, diesel oil *n* carburant *m* diesel
diet ['daɪət] *n* alimentation *f*; (*restricted food*)
régime *m* ▷ *vi* (*also*: **be on a diet**) suivre un
régime; **to live on a ~ of** se nourrir de
dietician [daɪə'tɪʃən] *n* diététicien(ne)
differ ['dɪfər] *vi*: **to ~ from sth** (*be different*) être
différent(e) de qch, différer de qch; **to ~ from
sb over sth** ne pas être d'accord avec qn au
sujet de qch
difference ['dɪfrəns] *n* différence *f*; (*quarrel*)
différend *m*, désaccord *m*; **it makes no ~ to me**
cela m'est égal, cela m'est indifférent; **to
settle one's ~s** résoudre la situation
different ['dɪfrənt] *adj* différent(e)
differential [dɪfə'rɛnʃəl] *n* (*Aut, wages*)
différentiel *m*
differentiate [dɪfə'rɛnʃɪeɪt] *vt* différencier ▷ *vi*
se différencier; **to ~ between** faire une
différence entre
differently ['dɪfrəntlɪ] *adv* différemment
difficult ['dɪfɪkəlt] *adj* difficile; **~ to
understand** difficile à comprendre
difficulty ['dɪfɪkəltɪ] *n* difficulté *f*; **to have
difficulties with** avoir des ennuis *or* problèmes
avec; **to be in ~** avoir des difficultés, avoir des
problèmes
diffidence ['dɪfɪdəns] *n* manque *m* de confiance
en soi, manque d'assurance
diffident ['dɪfɪdənt] *adj* qui manque de
confiance *or* d'assurance, peu sûr(e) de soi
diffuse *adj* [dɪ'fjuːs] diffus(e) ▷ *vt* [dɪ'fjuːz]
diffuser, répandre
dig [dɪg] *vt* (*pt, pp* **dug** [dʌg]) (*hole*) creuser;
(*garden*) bêcher ▷ *n* (*prod*) coup *m* de coude; (*fig:
remark*) coup de griffe *or* de patte; (*Archaeology*)
fouille *f*; **to ~ into** (*snow, soil*) creuser; **to ~ into
one's pockets for sth** fouiller dans ses poches
pour chercher *or* prendre qch; **to ~ one's nails
into** enfoncer ses ongles dans
▸ **dig in** *vi* (*also*: **dig o.s. in**: *Mil*) se retrancher;
(*: fig*) tenir bon, se braquer; (*inf: eat*) attaquer (un
repas *or* un plat *etc*) ▷ *vt* (*compost*) bien mélanger
à la bêche; (*knife, claw*) enfoncer; **to ~ in one's
heels** (*fig*) se braquer, se buter
▸ **dig out** *vt* (*survivors, car from snow*) sortir *or*
dégager (à coups de pelles *or* pioches)
▸ **dig up** *vt* déterrer
digest *vt* [daɪ'dʒɛst] digérer ▷ *n* ['daɪdʒɛst]
sommaire *m*, résumé *m*
digestible [dɪ'dʒɛstəbl] *adj* digestible

digestion [dɪ'dʒɛstʃən] n digestion f
digestive [dɪ'dʒɛstɪv] adj digestif(-ive)
digit ['dɪdʒɪt] n (number) chiffre m (de o à 9); (finger) doigt m
digital ['dɪdʒɪtl] adj (system, recording, radio) numérique, digital(e); (watch) à affichage numérique or digital
digital camera n appareil m photo numérique
digital compact cassette n cassette f numérique
digital TV n télévision f numérique
dignified ['dɪgnɪfaɪd] adj digne
dignitary ['dɪgnɪtərɪ] n dignitaire m
dignity ['dɪgnɪtɪ] n dignité f
digress [daɪ'grɛs] vi: **to ~ from** s'écarter de, s'éloigner de
digression [daɪ'grɛʃən] n digression f
digs [dɪgz] npl (Brit inf) piaule f, chambre meublée
dilapidated [dɪ'læpɪdeɪtɪd] adj délabré(e)
dilate [daɪ'leɪt] vt dilater ▷ vi se dilater
dilatory ['dɪlətərɪ] adj dilatoire
dilemma [daɪ'lɛmə] n dilemme m; **to be in a ~** être pris dans un dilemme
diligent ['dɪlɪdʒənt] adj appliqué(e), assidu(e)
dill [dɪl] n aneth m
dilly-dally ['dɪlɪ'dælɪ] vi hésiter, tergiverser; traînasser, lambiner
dilute [daɪ'luːt] vt diluer ▷ adj dilué(e)
dim [dɪm] adj (light, eyesight) faible; (memory, outline) vague, indécis(e); (room) sombre; (inf: stupid) borné(e), obtus(e) ▷ vt (light) réduire, baisser; (US Aut) mettre en code, baisser; **to take a ~ view of sth** voir qch d'un mauvais œil
dime [daɪm] n (US) pièce f de 10 cents
dimension [daɪ'mɛnʃən] n dimension f
-dimensional [dɪ'mɛnʃənl] adj suffix: **two-** à deux dimensions
diminish [dɪ'mɪnɪʃ] vt, vi diminuer
diminished [dɪ'mɪnɪʃt] adj: **~ responsibility** (Law) responsabilité atténuée
diminutive [dɪ'mɪnjutɪv] adj minuscule, tout(e) petit(e) ▷ n (Ling) diminutif m
dimly ['dɪmlɪ] adv faiblement; vaguement
dimmer ['dɪmər] n (also: **dimmer switch**) variateur m; **dimmers** npl (US Aut: dipped headlights) phares mpl, code inv; (parking lights) feux mpl de position
dimple ['dɪmpl] n fossette f
dim-witted ['dɪm'wɪtɪd] adj (inf) stupide, borné(e)
din [dɪn] n vacarme m ▷ vt: **to ~ sth into sb** (inf) enfoncer qch dans la tête or la caboche de qn
dine [daɪn] vi dîner
diner ['daɪnər] n (person) dîneur(-euse); (Rail) = **dining car**; (US: eating place) petit restaurant
dinghy ['dɪŋgɪ] n youyou m; (inflatable) canot m pneumatique; (also: **sailing dinghy**) voilier m, dériveur m
dingy ['dɪndʒɪ] adj miteux(-euse), minable
dining car ['daɪnɪŋ-] n (Brit) voiture-restaurant f, wagon-restaurant m

dining room ['daɪnɪŋ-] n salle f à manger
dining table [daɪnɪŋ-] n table f de (la) salle à manger
dinner ['dɪnər] n (evening meal) dîner m; (lunch) déjeuner m; (public) banquet m; **~'s ready!** à table!
dinner jacket n smoking m
dinner party n dîner m
dinner time n (evening) heure f du dîner; (midday) heure du déjeuner
dinosaur ['daɪnəsɔːr] n dinosaure m
dint [dɪnt] n: **by ~ of (doing) sth** à force de (faire) qch
diocese ['daɪəsɪs] n diocèse m
dioxide [daɪ'ɔksaɪd] n dioxyde m
Dip. abbr (Brit) = **diploma**
dip [dɪp] n (slope) déclivité f; (in sea) baignade f, bain m; (Culin) ≈ sauce f ▷ vt tremper, plonger; (Brit Aut: lights) mettre en code, baisser ▷ vi plonger
diphtheria [dɪf'θɪərɪə] n diphtérie f
diphthong ['dɪfθɔŋ] n diphtongue f
diploma [dɪ'pləumə] n diplôme m
diplomacy [dɪ'pləuməsɪ] n diplomatie f
diplomat ['dɪpləmæt] n diplomate m
diplomatic [dɪplə'mætɪk] adj diplomatique; **to break off ~ relations (with)** rompre les relations diplomatiques (avec)
diplomatic corps n corps m diplomatique
diplomatic immunity n immunité f diplomatique
dipstick ['dɪpstɪk] n (Brit Aut) jauge f de niveau d'huile
dipswitch ['dɪpswɪtʃ] n (Brit Aut) commutateur m de code
dire [daɪər] adj (poverty) extrême; (awful) affreux(-euse)
direct [daɪ'rɛkt] adj direct(e); (manner, person) direct, franc (franche) ▷ vt (tell way) diriger, orienter; (letter, remark) adresser; (Cine, TV) réaliser; (Theat) mettre en scène; (order): **to ~ sb to do sth** ordonner à qn de faire qch ▷ adv directement; **can you ~ me to ...?** pouvez-vous m'indiquer le chemin de ...?
direct cost n (Comm) coût m variable
direct current n (Elec) courant continu
direct debit n (Brit Banking) prélèvement m automatique
direct dialling n (Tel) automatique m
direct hit n (Mil) coup m au but, touché m
direction [dɪ'rɛkʃən] n direction f; (Theat) mise f en scène; (Cine, TV) réalisation f; **directions** npl (to a place) indications fpl; **~s for use** mode m d'emploi; **to ask for ~s** demander sa route or son chemin; **sense of ~** sens m de l'orientation; **in the ~ of** dans la direction de, vers
directive [dɪ'rɛktɪv] n directive f; **a government ~** une directive du gouvernement
direct labour n main-d'œuvre directe; employés municipaux
directly [dɪ'rɛktlɪ] adv (in straight line) directement, tout droit; (at once) tout de suite,

immédiatement

direct mail n vente f par publicité directe

direct mailshot n (Brit) publicité postale

directness [daɪ'rɛktnɪs] n (of person, speech) franchise f

director [dɪ'rɛktər] n directeur m; (board member) administrateur m; (Theat) metteur m en scène; (Cine, TV) réalisateur(-trice); **D~ of Public Prosecutions** (Brit) ≈ procureur général

directory [dɪ'rɛktərɪ] n annuaire m; (also: **street directory**) indicateur m de rues; (also: **trade directory**) annuaire du commerce; (Comput) répertoire m

directory enquiries, (US) **directory assistance** n (Tel: service) renseignements mpl

dirt [dəːt] n saleté f; (mud) boue f; **to treat sb like ~** traiter qn comme un chien

dirt-cheap ['dəːt'tʃiːp] adj (ne) coûtant presque rien

dirt road n chemin non macadamisé or non revêtu

dirty ['dəːtɪ] adj sale; (joke) cochon(ne) ▷ vt salir; **~ story** histoire cochonne; **~ trick** coup tordu

disability [dɪsə'bɪlɪtɪ] n invalidité f, infirmité f

disability allowance n allocation f d'invalidité or d'infirmité

disable [dɪs'eɪbl] vt (illness, accident) rendre or laisser infirme; (tank, gun) mettre hors d'action

disabled [dɪs'eɪbld] adj handicapé(e); (maimed) mutilé(e); (through illness, old age) impotent(e)

disadvantage [dɪsəd'vɑːntɪdʒ] n désavantage m, inconvénient m

disadvantaged [dɪsəd'vɑːntɪdʒd] adj (person) désavantagé(e)

disadvantageous [dɪsædvɑːn'teɪdʒəs] adj désavantageux(-euse)

disaffected [dɪsə'fɛktɪd] adj: **~ (to or towards)** mécontent(e) (de)

disaffection [dɪsə'fɛkʃən] n désaffection f, mécontentement m

disagree [dɪsə'griː] vi (differ) ne pas concorder; (be against, think otherwise): **to ~ (with)** ne pas être d'accord (avec); **garlic ~s with me** l'ail ne me convient pas, je ne supporte pas l'ail

disagreeable [dɪsə'griːəbl] adj désagréable

disagreement [dɪsə'griːmənt] n désaccord m, différend m

disallow ['dɪsə'lau] vt rejeter, désavouer; (Brit Football: goal) refuser

disappear [dɪsə'pɪər] vi disparaître

disappearance [dɪsə'pɪərəns] n disparition f

disappoint [dɪsə'pɔɪnt] vt décevoir

disappointed [dɪsə'pɔɪntɪd] adj déçu(e)

disappointing [dɪsə'pɔɪntɪŋ] adj décevant(e)

disappointment [dɪsə'pɔɪntmənt] n déception f

disapproval [dɪsə'pruːvəl] n désapprobation f

disapprove [dɪsə'pruːv] vi: **to ~ of** désapprouver

disapproving [dɪsə'pruːvɪŋ] adj désapprobateur(-trice), de désapprobation

disarm [dɪs'ɑːm] vt désarmer

disarmament [dɪs'ɑːməmənt] n

disarming [dɪs'ɑːmɪŋ] adj (smile) désarmant(e)

disarray [dɪsə'reɪ] n désordre m, confusion f; **in ~** (troops) en déroute; (thoughts) embrouillé(e); (clothes) en désordre; **to throw into ~** semer la confusion or le désordre dans (or parmi)

disaster [dɪ'zɑːstər] n catastrophe f, désastre m

disastrous [dɪ'zɑːstrəs] adj désastreux(-euse)

disband [dɪs'bænd] vt démobiliser; disperser ▷ vi se séparer; se disperser

disbelief ['dɪsbə'liːf] n incrédulité f; **in ~** avec incrédulité

disbelieve ['dɪsbə'liːv] vt (person) ne pas croire; (story) mettre en doute; **I don't ~ you** je veux bien vous croire

disc [dɪsk] n disque m; (Comput) = **disk**

disc. abbr (Comm) = **discount**

discard [dɪs'kɑːd] vt (old things) se débarrasser de, mettre au rencart or au rebut; (fig) écarter, renoncer à

disc brake n frein m à disque

discern [dɪ'səːn] vt discerner, distinguer

discernible [dɪ'səːnəbl] adj discernable, perceptible; (object) visible

discerning [dɪ'səːnɪŋ] adj judicieux(-euse), perspicace

discharge vt [dɪs'tʃɑːdʒ] (duties) s'acquitter de; (settle: debt) s'acquitter de, régler; (waste etc) déverser; décharger; (Elec, Med) émettre; (patient) renvoyer (chez lui); (employee, soldier) congédier, licencier; (defendant) relaxer, élargir ▷ n ['dɪstʃɑːdʒ] (Elec, Med) émission f; (also: **vaginal discharge**) pertes blanches; (dismissal) renvoi m; licenciement m; élargissement m; **to ~ one's gun** faire feu; **~d bankrupt** failli(e), réhabilité(e)

disciple [dɪ'saɪpl] n disciple m

disciplinary ['dɪsɪplɪnərɪ] adj disciplinaire; **to take ~ action against sb** prendre des mesures disciplinaires à l'encontre de qn

discipline ['dɪsɪplɪn] n discipline f ▷ vt discipliner; (punish) punir; **to ~ o.s. to do sth** s'imposer or s'astreindre à une discipline pour faire qch

disc jockey n disque-jockey m (DJ)

disclaim [dɪs'kleɪm] vt désavouer, dénier

disclaimer [dɪs'kleɪmər] n démenti m, dénégation f; **to issue a ~** publier un démenti

disclose [dɪs'kləuz] vt révéler, divulguer

disclosure [dɪs'kləuʒər] n révélation f, divulgation f

disco ['dɪskəu] n abbr discothèque f

discolour, (US) **discolor** [dɪs'kʌlər] vt décolorer; (sth white) jaunir ▷ vi se décolorer; jaunir

discolouration, (US) **discoloration** [dɪskʌlə'reɪʃən] n décoloration f; jaunissement m

discoloured, (US) **discolored** [dɪs'kʌləd] adj décoloré(e), jauni(e)

discomfort [dɪs'kʌmfət] n malaise m, gêne f; (lack of comfort) manque m de confort

disconcert [dɪskən'səːt] vt déconcerter,

décontenancer

disconnect [dɪskə'nɛkt] *vt* détacher; (*Elec, Radio*) débrancher; (*gas, water*) couper

disconnected [dɪskə'nɛktɪd] *adj* (*speech, thoughts*) décousu(e), peu cohérent(e)

disconsolate [dɪs'kɔnsəlɪt] *adj* inconsolable

discontent [dɪskən'tɛnt] *n* mécontentement *m*

discontented [dɪskən'tɛntɪd] *adj* mécontent(e)

discontinue [dɪskən'tɪnjuː] *vt* cesser, interrompre; "**~d**" (*Comm*) "fin de série"

discord ['dɪskɔːd] *n* discorde *f*, dissension *f*; (*Mus*) dissonance *f*

discordant [dɪs'kɔːdənt] *adj* discordant(e), dissonant(e)

discount *n* ['dɪskaunt] remise *f*, rabais *m* ▷ *vt* [dɪs'kaunt] (*report etc*) ne pas tenir compte de; **to give sb a ~ on sth** faire une remise *or* un rabais à qn sur qch; **~ for cash** escompte *f* au comptant; **at a ~** avec une remise *or* réduction, au rabais

discount house *n* (*Finance*) banque *f* d'escompte; (*Comm: also*: **discount store**) magasin *m* de discount

discount rate *n* taux *m* de remise

discourage [dɪs'kʌrɪdʒ] *vt* décourager; (*dissuade, deter*) dissuader, décourager

discouragement [dɪs'kʌrɪdʒmənt] *n* (*depression*) découragement *m*; **to act as a ~ to sb** dissuader qn

discouraging [dɪs'kʌrɪdʒɪŋ] *adj* décourageant(e)

discourteous [dɪs'kəːtɪəs] *adj* incivil(e), discourtois(e)

discover [dɪs'kʌvər] *vt* découvrir

discovery [dɪs'kʌvərɪ] *n* découverte *f*

discredit [dɪs'krɛdɪt] *vt* (*idea*) mettre en doute; (*person*) discréditer ▷ *n* discrédit *m*

discreet [dɪ'skriːt] *adj* discret(-ète)

discreetly [dɪ'skriːtlɪ] *adv* discrètement

discrepancy [dɪ'skrɛpənsɪ] *n* divergence *f*, contradiction *f*

discretion [dɪ'skrɛʃən] *n* discrétion *f*; **at the ~ of** à la discrétion de; **use your own ~** à vous de juger

discretionary [dɪ'skrɛʃənrɪ] *adj* (*powers*) discrétionnaire

discriminate [dɪ'skrɪmɪneɪt] *vi*: **to ~ between** établir une distinction entre, faire la différence entre; **to ~ against** pratiquer une discrimination contre

discriminating [dɪ'skrɪmɪneɪtɪŋ] *adj* qui a du discernement

discrimination [dɪskrɪmɪ'neɪʃən] *n* discrimination *f*; (*judgment*) discernement *m*; **racial/sexual ~** discrimination raciale/sexuelle

discus ['dɪskəs] *n* disque *m*

discuss [dɪ'skʌs] *vt* discuter de; (*debate*) discuter

discussion [dɪ'skʌʃən] *n* discussion *f*; **under ~** en discussion

disdain [dɪs'deɪn] *n* dédain *m*

disease [dɪ'ziːz] *n* maladie *f*

diseased [dɪ'ziːzd] *adj* malade

disembark [dɪsɪm'baːk] *vt, vi* débarquer

disembarkation [dɪsɛmbaː'keɪʃən] *n* débarquement *m*

disembodied ['dɪsɪm'bɔdɪd] *adj* désincarné(e)

disembowel ['dɪsɪm'bauəl] *vt* éviscérer, étriper

disenchanted ['dɪsɪn'tʃaːntɪd] *adj*: **~ (with)** désenchanté(e) (de), désabusé(e) (de)

disenfranchise ['dɪsɪn'fræntʃaɪz] *vt* priver du droit de vote; (*Comm*) retirer la franchise à

disengage [dɪsɪn'geɪdʒ] *vt* dégager; (*Tech*) déclencher; **to ~ the clutch** (*Aut*) débrayer

disentangle [dɪsɪn'tæŋgl] *vt* démêler

disfavour, (*US*) **disfavor** [dɪs'feɪvər] *n* défaveur *f*; disgrâce *f*

disfigure [dɪs'fɪgər] *vt* défigurer

disgorge [dɪs'gɔːdʒ] *vt* déverser

disgrace [dɪs'greɪs] *n* honte *f*; (*disfavour*) disgrâce *f* ▷ *vt* déshonorer, couvrir de honte

disgraceful [dɪs'greɪsful] *adj* scandaleux(-euse), honteux(-euse)

disgruntled [dɪs'grʌntld] *adj* mécontent(e)

disguise [dɪs'gaɪz] *n* déguisement *m* ▷ *vt* déguiser; (*voice*) déguiser, contrefaire; (*feelings etc*) masquer, dissimuler; **in ~** déguisé(e); **to ~ o.s. as** se déguiser en; **there's no disguising the fact that ...** on ne peut pas se dissimuler que ...

disgust [dɪs'gʌst] *n* dégoût *m*, aversion *f* ▷ *vt* dégoûter, écœurer

disgusted [dɪs'gʌstɪd] *adj* dégoûté(e), écœuré(e)

disgusting [dɪs'gʌstɪŋ] *adj* dégoûtant(e), révoltant(e)

dish [dɪʃ] *n* plat *m*; **to do** *or* **wash the ~es** faire la vaisselle
  ▶ **dish out** *vt* distribuer
  ▶ **dish up** *vt* servir; (*facts, statistics*) sortir, débiter

dishcloth ['dɪʃklɔθ] *n* (*for drying*) torchon *m*; (*for washing*) lavette *f*

dishearten [dɪs'haːtn] *vt* décourager

dishevelled, (*US*) **disheveled** [dɪ'ʃɛvəld] *adj* ébouriffé(e), décoiffé(e), débraillé(e)

dishonest [dɪs'ɔnɪst] *adj* malhonnête

dishonesty [dɪs'ɔnɪstɪ] *n* malhonnêteté *f*

dishonour, (*US*) **dishonor** [dɪs'ɔnər] *n* déshonneur *m*

dishonourable, (*US*) **dishonorable** [dɪs'ɔnərəbl] *adj* déshonorant(e)

dish soap *n* (*US*) produit *m* pour la vaisselle

dishtowel ['dɪʃtauəl] *n* (*US*) torchon *m* (à vaisselle)

dishwasher ['dɪʃwɔʃər] *n* lave-vaisselle *m*; (*person*) plongeur(-euse)

dishy ['dɪʃɪ] *adj* (*Brit inf*) séduisant(e), sexy *inv*

disillusion [dɪsɪ'luːʒən] *vt* désabuser, désenchanter ▷ *n* désenchantement *m*; **to become ~ed (with)** perdre ses illusions (en ce qui concerne)

disillusionment [dɪsɪ'luːʒənmənt] *n* désillusionnement *m*, désillusion *f*

disincentive [dɪsɪn'sɛntɪv] *n*: **it's a ~** c'est démotivant; **to be a ~ to sb** démotiver qn

disinclined ['dɪsɪn'klaɪnd] *adj*: **to be ~ to do sth**

être peu disposé(e) or peu enclin(e) à faire qch

disinfect [dɪsɪn'fɛkt] vt désinfecter

disinfectant [dɪsɪn'fɛktənt] n désinfectant m

disinflation [dɪsɪn'fleɪʃən] n désinflation f

disinformation [dɪsɪnfə'meɪʃən] n désinformation f

disinherit [dɪsɪn'hɛrɪt] vt déshériter

disintegrate [dɪs'ɪntɪgreɪt] vi se désintégrer

disinterested [dɪs'ɪntrəstɪd] adj désintéressé(e)

disjointed [dɪs'dʒɔɪntɪd] adj décousu(e), incohérent(e)

disk [dɪsk] n (Comput) disquette f; **single-/double-sided ~** disquette une face/double face

disk drive n lecteur m de disquette

diskette [dɪs'kɛt] n (Comput) disquette f

disk operating system n système m d'exploitation à disques

dislike [dɪs'laɪk] n aversion f, antipathie f ▷ vt ne pas aimer; **to take a ~ to sb/sth** prendre qn/qch en grippe; **I ~ the idea** l'idée me déplaît

dislocate ['dɪsləkeɪt] vt disloquer, déboîter; (services etc) désorganiser; **he has ~d his shoulder** il s'est disloqué l'épaule

dislodge [dɪs'lɔdʒ] vt déplacer, faire bouger; (enemy) déloger

disloyal [dɪs'lɔɪəl] adj déloyal(e)

dismal ['dɪzml] adj (gloomy) lugubre, maussade; (very bad) lamentable

dismantle [dɪs'mæntl] vt démonter; (fort, warship) démanteler

dismast [dɪs'mɑːst] vt démâter

dismay [dɪs'meɪ] n consternation f ▷ vt consterner; **much to my ~** à ma grande consternation, à ma grande inquiétude

dismiss [dɪs'mɪs] vt congédier, renvoyer; (idea) écarter; (Law) rejeter ▷ vi (Mil) rompre les rangs

dismissal [dɪs'mɪsl] n renvoi m

dismount [dɪs'maunt] vi mettre pied à terre

disobedience [dɪsə'biːdɪəns] n désobéissance f

disobedient [dɪsə'biːdɪənt] adj désobéissant(e), indiscipliné(e)

disobey [dɪsə'beɪ] vt désobéir à; (rule) transgresser, enfreindre

disorder [dɪs'ɔːdə^r] n désordre m; (rioting) désordres mpl; (Med) troubles mpl

disorderly [dɪs'ɔːdəlɪ] adj (room) en désordre; (behaviour, retreat, crowd) désordonné(e)

disorderly conduct n (Law) conduite f contraire aux bonnes mœurs

disorganized [dɪs'ɔːɡənaɪzd] adj désorganisé(e)

disorientated [dɪs'ɔːrɪenteɪtɪd] adj désorienté(e)

disown [dɪs'əun] vt renier

disparaging [dɪs'pærɪdʒɪŋ] adj désobligeant(e); **to be ~ about sb/sth** faire des remarques désobligeantes sur qn/qch

disparate ['dɪspərɪt] adj disparate

disparity [dɪs'pærɪtɪ] n disparité f

dispassionate [dɪs'pæʃənət] adj calme, froid(e), impartial(e), objectif(-ive)

dispatch [dɪs'pætʃ] vt expédier, envoyer; (deal with: business) régler, en finir avec ▷ n envoi m,

expédition f; (Mil, Press) dépêche f

dispatch department n service m des expéditions

dispatch rider n (Mil) estafette f

dispel [dɪs'pɛl] vt dissiper, chasser

dispensary [dɪs'pɛnsərɪ] n pharmacie f; (in chemist's) officine f

dispense [dɪs'pɛns] vt distribuer, administrer; (medicine) préparer (et vendre); **to ~ sb from** dispenser qn de
▶ **dispense with** vt fus se passer de; (make unnecessary) rendre superflu(e)

dispenser [dɪs'pɛnsə^r] n (device) distributeur m

dispensing chemist [dɪs'pɛnsɪŋ-] n (Brit) pharmacie f

dispersal [dɪs'pəːsl] n dispersion f; (Admin) déconcentration f

disperse [dɪs'pəːs] vt disperser; (knowledge) disséminer ▷ vi se disperser

dispirited [dɪs'pɪrɪtɪd] adj découragé(e), déprimé(e)

displace [dɪs'pleɪs] vt déplacer

displaced person [dɪs'pleɪst-] n (Pol) personne déplacée

displacement [dɪs'pleɪsmənt] n déplacement m

display [dɪs'pleɪ] n (of goods) étalage m; affichage m; (Comput: information) visualisation f; (: device) visuel m; (of feeling) manifestation f; (pej) ostentation f; (show, spectacle) spectacle m; (military display) parade f militaire ▷ vt montrer; (goods) mettre à l'étalage, exposer; (results, departure times) afficher; (pej) faire étalage de; **on ~** (exhibits) exposé(e), exhibé(e); (goods) à l'étalage

display advertising n publicité rédactionnelle

displease [dɪs'pliːz] vt mécontenter, contrarier; **~d with** mécontent(e) de

displeasure [dɪs'plɛʒə^r] n mécontentement m

disposable [dɪs'pəuzəbl] adj (pack etc) jetable; (income) disponible; **~ nappy** (Brit) couche f à jeter, couche-culotte f

disposal [dɪs'pəuzl] n (of rubbish) évacuation f, destruction f; (of property etc: by selling) vente f; (: by giving away) cession f; (availability, arrangement) disposition f; **at one's ~** à sa disposition; **to put sth at sb's ~** mettre qch à la disposition de qn

dispose [dɪs'pəuz] vt disposer ▷ vi: **to ~ of** (time, money) disposer de; (unwanted goods) se débarrasser de, se défaire de; (Comm: stock) écouler, vendre; (problem) expédier

disposed [dɪs'pəuzd] adj: **~ to do** disposé(e) à faire

disposition [dɪspə'zɪʃən] n disposition f; (temperament) naturel m

dispossess ['dɪspə'zɛs] vt: **to ~ sb (of)** déposséder qn (de)

disproportion [dɪsprə'pɔːʃən] n disproportion f

disproportionate [dɪsprə'pɔːʃənət] adj disproportionné(e)

disprove [dɪs'pruːv] *vt* réfuter
dispute [dɪs'pjuːt] *n* discussion *f*; (*also*:
industrial dispute) conflit *m* ▷ *vt* (*question*)
contester; (*matter*) discuter; (*victory*) disputer;
to be in *or* **under ~** (*matter*) être en discussion;
(*territory*) être contesté(e)
disqualification [dɪskwɔlɪfɪ'keɪʃən] *n*
disqualification *f*; **~ (from driving)** (*Brit*)
retrait *m* du permis (de conduire)
disqualify [dɪs'kwɔlɪfaɪ] *vt* (*Sport*) disqualifier;
to ~ sb for sth/from doing (*status, situation*)
rendre qn inapte à qch/à faire; (*authority*)
signifier à qn l'interdiction de faire; **to ~ sb**
(from driving) (*Brit*) retirer à qn son permis (de
conduire)
disquiet [dɪs'kwaɪət] *n* inquiétude *f*, trouble *m*
disquieting [dɪs'kwaɪətɪŋ] *adj* inquiétant(e),
alarmant(e)
disregard [dɪsrɪ'gɑːd] *vt* ne pas tenir compte de
▷ *n* (*indifference*): **~ (for)** (*feelings*) indifférence *f*
(pour), insensibilité *f* (à); (*danger, money*)
mépris *m* (pour)
disrepair ['dɪsrɪ'pɛər] *n* mauvais état; **to fall**
into ~ (*building*) tomber en ruine; (*street*) se
dégrader
disreputable [dɪs'rɛpjutəbl] *adj* (*person*) de
mauvaise réputation, peu recommandable;
(*behaviour*) déshonorant(e); (*area*) mal famé(e),
louche
disrepute ['dɪsrɪ'pjuːt] *n* déshonneur *m*,
discrédit *m*; **to bring into ~** faire tomber dans
le discrédit
disrespectful [dɪsrɪ'spɛktful] *adj*
irrespectueux(-euse)
disrupt [dɪs'rʌpt] *vt* (*plans, meeting, lesson*)
perturber, déranger
disruption [dɪs'rʌpʃən] *n* perturbation *f*,
dérangement *m*
disruptive [dɪs'rʌptɪv] *adj* perturbateur(-trice)
dissatisfaction [dɪssætɪs'fækʃən] *n*
mécontentement *m*, insatisfaction *f*
dissatisfied [dɪs'sætɪsfaɪd] *adj*: **~ (with)**
insatisfait(e) (de)
dissect [dɪ'sɛkt] *vt* disséquer; (*fig*) disséquer,
éplucher
disseminate [dɪ'sɛmɪneɪt] *vt* disséminer
dissent [dɪ'sɛnt] *n* dissentiment *m*, différence *f*
d'opinion
dissenter [dɪ'sɛntər] *n* (*Rel, Pol etc*) dissident(e)
dissertation [dɪsə'teɪʃən] *n* (*Scol*) mémoire *m*
disservice [dɪs'sə:vɪs] *n*: **to do sb a ~** rendre un
mauvais service à qn; desservir qn
dissident ['dɪsɪdnt] *adj, n* dissident(e)
dissimilar [dɪ'sɪmɪlər] *adj*: **~ (to)** dissemblable
(à), différent(e) (de)
dissipate ['dɪsɪpeɪt] *vt* dissiper; (*energy, efforts*)
disperser
dissipated ['dɪsɪpeɪtɪd] *adj* dissolu(e),
débauché(e)
dissociate [dɪ'səʊʃɪeɪt] *vt* dissocier; **to ~ o.s.**
from se désolidariser de
dissolute ['dɪsəluːt] *adj* débauché(e), dissolu(e)

dissolve [dɪ'zɔlv] *vt* dissoudre ▷ *vi* se dissoudre,
fondre; (*fig*) disparaître; **to ~ in(to) tears**
fondre en larmes
dissuade [dɪ'sweɪd] *vt*: **to ~ sb (from)** dissuader
qn (de)
distance ['dɪstns] *n* distance *f*; **what's the ~ to**
London? à quelle distance se trouve Londres?;
it's within walking ~ on peut y aller à pied; **in**
the ~ au loin
distant ['dɪstnt] *adj* lointain(e), éloigné(e);
(*manner*) distant(e), froid(e)
distaste [dɪs'teɪst] *n* dégoût *m*
distasteful [dɪs'teɪstful] *adj* déplaisant(e),
désagréable
Dist. Atty. *abbr* (*US*) = **district attorney**
distemper [dɪs'tɛmpər] *n* (*paint*) détrempe *f*,
badigeon *m*; (*of dogs*) maladie *f* de Carré
distended [dɪs'tɛndɪd] *adj* (*stomach*) dilaté(e)
distil, (*US*) **distill** [dɪs'tɪl] *vt* distiller
distillery [dɪs'tɪlərɪ] *n* distillerie *f*
distinct [dɪs'tɪŋkt] *adj* distinct(e); (*clear*)
marqué(e); **as ~ from** par opposition à, en
contraste avec
distinction [dɪs'tɪŋkʃən] *n* distinction *f*; (*in*
exam) mention *f* très bien; **to draw a ~ between**
faire une distinction entre; **a writer of ~** un
écrivain réputé
distinctive [dɪs'tɪŋktɪv] *adj* distinctif(-ive)
distinctly [dɪs'tɪŋktlɪ] *adv* distinctement;
(*specify*) expressément
distinguish [dɪs'tɪŋgwɪʃ] *vt* distinguer ▷ *vi*: **to ~**
between (*concepts*) distinguer entre, faire une
distinction entre; **to ~ o.s.** se distinguer
distinguished [dɪs'tɪŋgwɪʃt] *adj* (*eminent,*
refined) distingué(e); (*career*) remarquable,
brillant(e)
distinguishing [dɪs'tɪŋgwɪʃɪŋ] *adj* (*feature*)
distinctif(-ive), caractéristique
distort [dɪs'tɔːt] *vt* déformer
distortion [dɪs'tɔːʃən] *n* déformation *f*
distract [dɪs'trækt] *vt* distraire, déranger
distracted [dɪs'træktɪd] *adj* (*not concentrating*)
distrait(e); (*worried*) affolé(e)
distraction [dɪs'trækʃən] *n* distraction *f*,
dérangement *m*; **to drive sb to ~** rendre qn fou
(folle)
distraught [dɪs'trɔːt] *adj* éperdu(e)
distress [dɪs'trɛs] *n* détresse *f*; (*pain*) douleur *f*
▷ *vt* affliger; **in ~** (*ship*) en perdition; (*plane*) en
détresse; **~ed area** (*Brit*) zone sinistrée
distressing [dɪs'trɛsɪŋ] *adj* douloureux(-euse),
pénible, affligeant(e)
distress signal *n* signal *m* de détresse
distribute [dɪs'trɪbjuːt] *vt* distribuer
distribution [dɪstrɪ'bjuːʃən] *n* distribution *f*
distribution cost *n* coût *m* de distribution
distributor [dɪs'trɪbjutər] *n* (*gen: Tech*)
distributeur *m*; (*Comm*) concessionnaire *m/f*
district ['dɪstrɪkt] *n* (*of country*) région *f*; (*of town*)
quartier *m*; (*Admin*) district *m*
district attorney *n* (*US*) ≈ procureur *m* de la
République

district council n (Brit) ≈ conseil municipal; *voir article*

● **DISTRICT COUNCIL**

● En Grande-Bretagne, un *district council* est
● une administration locale qui gère un
● "district". Les conseillers ("councillors")
● sont élus au niveau local, en général tous les
● 4 ans. Le *district council* est financé par des
● impôts locaux et par des subventions du
● gouvernement.

district nurse n (Brit) infirmière visiteuse

distrust [dɪs'trʌst] n méfiance f, doute m ▷ vt se
méfier de

distrustful [dɪs'trʌstful] adj méfiant(e)

disturb [dɪs'təːb] vt troubler; (*inconvenience*)
déranger; **sorry to ~ you** excusez-moi de vous
déranger

disturbance [dɪs'təːbəns] n dérangement m;
(*political etc*) troubles mpl; (*by drunks etc*) tapage m;
to cause a ~ troubler l'ordre public; **~ of the
peace** (*Law*) tapage m injurieux or nocturne

disturbed [dɪs'təːbd] adj (*worried, upset*) agité(e),
troublé(e); **to be emotionally ~** avoir des
problèmes affectifs

disturbing [dɪs'təːbɪŋ] adj troublant(e),
inquiétant(e)

disuse [dɪs'juːs] n: **to fall into ~** tomber en
désuétude

disused [dɪs'juːzd] adj désaffecté(e)

ditch [dɪtʃ] n fossé m; (*for irrigation*) rigole f ▷ vt
(*inf*) abandonner; (*person*) plaquer

dither ['dɪðəʳ] vi hésiter

ditto ['dɪtəu] adv idem

divan [dɪ'væn] n divan m

divan bed n divan-lit m

dive [daɪv] n plongeon m; (*of submarine*) plongée
f; (*Aviat*) piqué m; (*pej: café, bar etc*) bouge m ▷ vi
plonger; **to ~ into** (*bag etc*) plonger la main
dans; (*place*) se précipiter dans

diver ['daɪvəʳ] n plongeur m

diverge [daɪ'vəːdʒ] vi diverger

diverse [daɪ'vəːs] adj divers(e)

diversification [daɪvəːsɪfɪ'keɪʃən] n
diversification f

diversify [daɪ'vəːsɪfaɪ] vt diversifier

diversion [daɪ'vəːʃən] n (*Brit Aut*) déviation f;
(*distraction, Mil*) diversion f

diversionary tactics [daɪ'vəːʃənrɪ-] npl tactique
fsg de diversion

diversity [daɪ'vəːsɪtɪ] n diversité f, variété f

divert [daɪ'vəːt] vt (*Brit: traffic*) dévier; (*plane*)
dérouter; (*train, river*) détourner; (*amuse*) divertir

divest [daɪ'vɛst] vt: **to ~ sb of** dépouiller qn de

divide [dɪ'vaɪd] vt diviser; (*separate*) séparer ▷ vi
se diviser; **to ~ (between** or **among)** répartir or
diviser (entre); **40 ~d by 5** 40 divisé par 5
▶ **divide out** vt: **to ~ out (between** or **among)**
distribuer or répartir (entre)

divided [dɪ'vaɪdɪd] adj (*fig: country, couple*)

désuni(e); (*opinions*) partagé(e)

divided highway (US) n route f à quatre voies

divided skirt n jupe-culotte f

dividend ['dɪvɪdɛnd] n dividende m

dividend cover n rapport m dividendes-résultat

dividers [dɪ'vaɪdəz] npl compas m à pointes
sèches; (*between pages*) feuillets mpl intercalaires

divine [dɪ'vaɪn] adj divin(e) ▷ vt (*future*) prédire;
(*truth*) deviner, entrevoir; (*water, metal*) détecter
la présence de (*par l'intermédiaire de la radiesthésie*)

diving ['daɪvɪŋ] n plongée (sous-marine)

diving board n plongeoir m

diving suit n scaphandre m

divinity [dɪ'vɪnɪtɪ] n divinité f; (*as study*)
théologie f

division [dɪ'vɪʒən] n division f; (*Brit: Football*)
division f; (*separation*) séparation f; (*Comm*)
service m; (*Brit: Pol*) vote m; (*also:* **division of
labour**) division du travail

divisive [dɪ'vaɪsɪv] adj qui entraîne la division,
qui crée des dissensions

divorce [dɪ'vɔːs] n divorce m ▷ vt divorcer d'avec

divorced [dɪ'vɔːst] adj divorcé(e)

divorcee [dɪvɔː'siː] n divorcé(e)

divot ['dɪvət] n (*Golf*) motte f de gazon

divulge [daɪ'vʌldʒ] vt divulguer, révéler

DIY adj, n abbr (*Brit*) = **do-it-yourself**

dizziness ['dɪzɪnɪs] n vertige m,
étourdissement m

dizzy ['dɪzɪ] adj (*height*) vertigineux(-euse); **to
make sb ~** donner le vertige à qn; **I feel ~** la tête
me tourne, j'ai la tête qui tourne

DJ n abbr = **disc jockey**

d.j. n abbr = **dinner jacket**

Djakarta [dʒə'kɑːtə] n Djakarta

DJIA n abbr (*US Stock Exchange*) = **Dow-Jones
Industrial Average**

dl abbr (= *decilitre*) dl

DLit, DLitt n abbr (= *Doctor of Literature, Doctor of
Letters*) titre universitaire

DMus n abbr (= *Doctor of Music*) titre universitaire

DMZ n abbr = **demilitarized zone**

DNA n abbr (= *deoxyribonucleic acid*) ADN m

DNA fingerprinting [-'fɪŋgəprɪntɪŋ] n
technique f des empreintes génétiques

do abbr (= *ditto*) d

 KEYWORD

do [duː] (*pt* **did**, *pp* **done**) n (*inf: party etc*) soirée f,
fête f; (: *formal gathering*) réception f
▷ vb **1** (*in negative constructions*) non traduit; **I don't
understand** je ne comprends pas
2 (*to form questions*) non traduit; **didn't you know?**
vous ne le saviez pas?; **what do you think?**
qu'en pensez-vous?; **why didn't you come?**
pourquoi n'êtes-vous pas venu?
3 (*for emphasis, in polite expressions*): **people do
make mistakes sometimes** on peut toujours
se tromper; **she does seem rather late** je
trouve qu'elle est bien en retard; **do sit down/
help yourself** asseyez-vous/servez-vous je vous

en prie; **do take care!** faites bien attention à vous!; **I DO wish I could go** j'aimerais tant y aller; **but I DO like it!** mais si, je l'aime!
4 (*used to avoid repeating vb*): **she swims better than I do** elle nage mieux que moi; **do you agree? — yes, I do/no I don't** vous êtes d'accord? — oui/non; **she lives in Glasgow — so do I** elle habite Glasgow — moi aussi; **he didn't like it and neither did we** il n'a pas aimé ça, et nous non plus; **who broke it? — I did** qui l'a cassé? — c'est moi; **he asked me to help him and I did** il m'a demandé de l'aider, et c'est que j'ai fait
5 (*in question tags*): **you like him, don't you?** vous l'aimez bien, n'est-ce pas?; **he laughed, didn't he?** il a ri, n'est-ce pas?; **I don't know him, do I?** je ne crois pas le connaître
▷ *vt* **1** (*gen: carry out, perform etc*) faire; (*visit: city, museum*) faire, visiter; **what are you doing tonight?** qu'est-ce que vous faites ce soir?; **what do you do?** (*job*) que faites-vous dans la vie?; **what did he do with the cat?** qu'a-t-il fait du chat?; **what can I do for you?** que puis-je faire pour vous?; **to do the cooking/washing-up** faire la cuisine/la vaisselle; **to do one's teeth/hair/nails** se brosser les dents/se coiffer/se faire les ongles
2 (*Aut etc: distance*) faire; (*: speed*) faire du; **we've done 200 km already** nous avons déjà fait 200 km; **the car was doing 100** la voiture faisait du 100 (à l'heure); **he can do 100 in that car** il peut faire du 100 (à l'heure) dans cette voiture-là
▷ *vi* **1** (*act, behave*) faire; **do as I do** faites comme moi
2 (*get on, fare*) marcher; **the firm is doing well** l'entreprise marche bien; **he's doing well/badly at school** ça marche bien/mal pour lui à l'école; **how do you do?** comment allez-vous?; (*on being introduced*) enchanté(e)!
3 (*suit*) aller; **will it do?** est-ce que ça ira?
4 (*be sufficient*) suffire, aller; **will £10 do?** est-ce que 10 livres suffiront?; **that'll do** ça suffit, ça ira; **that'll do!** (*in annoyance*) ça va *or* suffit comme ça!; **to make do (with)** se contenter (de)
▶ **do away with** *vt fus* abolir; (*kill*) supprimer
▶ **do for** *vt fus* (*Brit inf: clean for*) faire le ménage chez
▶ **do up** *vt* (*laces, dress*) attacher; (*buttons*) boutonner; (*zip*) fermer; (*renovate: room*) refaire; (*: house*) remettre à neuf; **to do o.s. up** se faire beau (belle)
▶ **do with** *vt fus* (*need*): **I could do with a drink/some help** quelque chose à boire/un peu d'aide ne serait pas de refus; **it could do with a wash** ça ne lui ferait pas de mal d'être lavé; (*be connected with*): **that has nothing to do with you** cela ne vous concerne pas; **I won't have anything to do with it** je ne veux pas m'en mêler; **what has that got to do with it?** quel est le rapport?, qu'est-ce que cela vient faire là-

dedans?
▶ **do without** *vi* s'en passer; **if you're late for tea then you'll do without** si vous êtes en retard pour le dîner il faudra vous en passer ▷ *vt fus* se passer de; **I can do without a car** je peux me passer de voiture

DOA *abbr* (= *dead on arrival*) décédé(e) à l'admission
d.o.b. *abbr* = **date of birth**
doc [dɔk] *n* (*inf*) toubib *m*
docile ['dəusaɪl] *adj* docile
dock [dɔk] *n* dock *m*; (*wharf*) quai *m*; (*Law*) banc *m* des accusés ▷ *vi* se mettre à quai; (*Space*) s'arrimer ▷ *vt*: **they ~ed a third of his wages** ils lui ont retenu *or* décompté un tiers de son salaire; **docks** *npl* (*Naut*) docks
dock dues *npl* droits *mpl* de bassin
docker ['dɔkər] *n* docker *m*
docket ['dɔkɪt] *n* bordereau *m*; (*on parcel etc*) étiquette *f or* fiche *f* (*décrivant le contenu d'un paquet etc*)
dockyard ['dɔkjɑːd] *n* chantier *m* de construction navale
doctor ['dɔktər] *n* médecin *m*, docteur *m*; (*PhD etc*) docteur ▷ *vt* (*cat*) couper; (*interfere with: food*) altérer; (*: drink*) frelater; (*: text, document*) arranger; **~'s office** (*US*) cabinet *m* de consultation; **call a ~!** appelez un docteur *or* un médecin!
doctorate ['dɔktərɪt] *n* doctorat *m*; *voir article*

● **DOCTORATE**
●
● Le *doctorate* est le diplôme universitaire le
● plus prestigieux. Il est le résultat d'au
● minimum trois années de recherche et est
● accordé après soutenance d'une thèse
● devant un jury. Le "doctorat" le plus courant
● est le "PhD" (Doctor of Philosophy), accordé
● en lettres, en sciences et en ingénierie, bien
● qu'il existe également d'autres doctorats
● spécialisés (en musique, en droit, etc); voir
● "Bachelor's degree", "Master's degree"

Doctor of Philosophy *n* (*degree*) doctorat *m*; (*person*) titulaire *m/f* d'un doctorat
docudrama ['dɔkjudrɑːmə] *n* (*TV*) docudrame *m*
document ['dɔkjumənt] *n* document *m* ▷ *vt* ['dɔkjumɛnt] documenter
documentary [dɔkju'mɛntərɪ] *adj, n* documentaire (*m*)
documentation [dɔkjumən'teɪʃən] *n* documentation *f*
DOD *n abbr* (*US*) = **Department of Defense**
doddering ['dɔdərɪŋ] *adj* (*senile*) gâteux(-euse)
doddery ['dɔdərɪ] *adj* branlant(e)
doddle ['dɔdl] *n*: **it's a ~** (*inf*) c'est simple comme bonjour, c'est du gâteau
Dodecanese [dəudɪkə'niːz] *n*, **Dodecanese Islands** *npl* Dodécanèse *m*
dodge [dɔdʒ] *n* truc *m*; combine *f* ▷ *vt* esquiver,

éviter ▷ vi faire un saut de côté; (Sport) faire une esquive; **to ~ out of the way** s'esquiver; **to ~ through the traffic** se faufiler or faire de savantes manœuvres entre les voitures

dodgems ['dɔdʒəmz] npl (Brit) autos tamponneuses

dodgy ['dɔdʒɪ] adj (inf: uncertain) douteux(-euse); (: shady) louche

DOE n abbr (Brit) = **Department of the Environment**; (US) = **Department of Energy**

doe [dəu] n (deer) biche f; (rabbit) lapine f

does [dʌz] vb see **do**

doesn't ['dʌznt] = **does not**

dog [dɔg] n chien(ne) ▷ vt (follow closely) suivre de près, ne pas lâcher d'une semelle; (fig: memory etc) poursuivre, harceler; **to go to the ~s** (nation etc) aller à vau-l'eau

dog biscuits npl biscuits mpl pour chien

dog collar n collier m de chien; (fig) faux-col m d'ecclésiastique

dog-eared ['dɔgɪəd] adj corné(e)

dog food n nourriture f pour les chiens or le chien

dogged ['dɔgɪd] adj obstiné(e), opiniâtre

doggy ['dɔgɪ] n (inf) toutou m

doggy bag ['dɔgɪ-] n petit sac pour emporter les restes

dogma ['dɔgmə] n dogme m

dogmatic [dɔg'mætɪk] adj dogmatique

do-gooder [duː'gudər] n (pej) faiseur(-euse) de bonnes œuvres

dogsbody ['dɔgzbɔdɪ] n (Brit) bonne f à tout faire, tâcheron m

doily ['dɔɪlɪ] n dessus m d'assiette

doing ['duːɪŋ] n: **this is your ~** c'est votre travail, c'est vous qui avez fait ça

doings ['duːɪŋz] npl activités fpl

do-it-yourself ['duːɪtjɔː'sɛlf] n bricolage m

doldrums ['dɔldrəmz] npl: **to be in the ~** avoir le cafard; être dans le marasme

dole [dəul] n (Brit: payment) allocation f de chômage; **on the ~** au chômage

▶ **dole out** vt donner au compte-goutte

doleful ['dəulful] adj triste, lugubre

doll [dɔl] n poupée f

▶ **doll up** vt: **to ~ o.s. up** se faire beau (belle)

dollar ['dɔlər] n dollar m

dollop ['dɔləp] n (of butter, cheese) bon morceau; (of cream) bonne cuillerée

dolly ['dɔlɪ] n poupée f

dolphin ['dɔlfɪn] n dauphin m

domain [də'meɪn] n (also fig) domaine m

dome [dəum] n dôme m

domestic [də'mɛstɪk] adj (duty, happiness) familial(e); (policy, affairs, flight) intérieur(e); (news) national(e); (animal) domestique

domesticated [də'mɛstɪkeɪtɪd] adj domestiqué(e); (pej) d'intérieur; **he's very ~** il participe volontiers aux tâches ménagères; question ménage, il est très organisé

domesticity [dəumɛs'tɪsɪtɪ] n vie f de famille

domestic servant n domestique m/f

domicile ['dɔmɪsaɪl] n domicile m

dominant ['dɔmɪnənt] adj dominant(e)

dominate ['dɔmɪneɪt] vt dominer

domination [dɔmɪ'neɪʃən] n domination f

domineering [dɔmɪ'nɪərɪŋ] adj dominateur(-trice), autoritaire

Dominican Republic [də'mɪnɪkən-] n République Dominicaine

dominion [də'mɪnɪən] n domination f; territoire m; dominion m

domino ['dɔmɪnəu] (pl **-es**) n domino m

dominoes ['dɔmɪnəuz] n (game) dominos mpl

don [dɔn] n (Brit) professeur m d'université ▷ vt revêtir

donate [də'neɪt] vt faire don de, donner

donation [də'neɪʃən] n donation f, don m

done [dʌn] pp of **do**

donkey ['dɔŋkɪ] n âne m

donkey-work ['dɔŋkɪwəːk] n (Brit inf) le gros du travail, le plus dur (du travail)

donor ['dəunər] n (of blood etc) donneur(-euse); (to charity) donateur(-trice)

donor card n carte f de don d'organes

don't [dəunt] = **do not**

donut ['dəunʌt] (US) n = **doughnut**

doodle ['duːdl] n griffonnage m, gribouillage m ▷ vi griffonner, gribouiller

doom [duːm] n (fate) destin m; (ruin) ruine f ▷ vt: **to be ~ed to failure** être voué(e) à l'échec

doomsday ['duːmzdeɪ] n le Jugement dernier

door [dɔːr] n porte f; (Rail, car) portière f; **to go from ~ to ~** aller de porte en porte

doorbell ['dɔːbɛl] n sonnette f

door handle n poignée f de porte; (of car) poignée de portière

doorknob ['dɔːnɔb] n poignée f or bouton m de porte

doorman ['dɔːmən] (irreg) n (in hotel) portier m; (in block of flats) concierge m

doormat ['dɔːmæt] n paillasson m

doorpost ['dɔːpəust] n montant m de porte

doorstep ['dɔːstɛp] n pas m de (la) porte, seuil m

door-to-door ['dɔːtə'dɔːr] adj: **~ selling** vente f à domicile

doorway ['dɔːweɪ] n (embrasure f de) porte f

dope [dəup] n (inf: drug) drogue f; (: person) andouille f; (: information) tuyaux mpl, rancards mpl ▷ vt (horse etc) doper

dopey ['dəupɪ] adj (inf) à moitié endormi(e)

dormant ['dɔːmənt] adj assoupi(e), en veilleuse; (rule, law) inappliqué(e)

dormer ['dɔːmər] n (also: **dormer window**) lucarne f

dormice ['dɔːmaɪs] npl of **dormouse**

dormitory ['dɔːmɪtrɪ] n (Brit) dortoir m; (US: hall of residence) résidence f universitaire

dormouse (pl **dormice**) ['dɔːmaus, -maɪs] n loir m

DOS [dɔs] n abbr (= disk operating system) DOS m

dosage ['dəusɪdʒ] n dose f; dosage m; (on label) posologie f

dose [dəus] n dose f; (Brit: bout) attaque f ▷ vt: **to ~ o.s.** se bourrer de médicaments; **a ~ of flu** une belle or bonne grippe

dosh [dɔʃ] (inf) n fric m
dosser ['dɔsə^r] n (Brit inf) clochard(e)
doss house ['dɔs-] n (Brit) asile m de nuit
DOT n abbr (US) = **Department of Transportation**
dot [dɔt] n point m; (on material) pois m ▷ vt: **~ted with** parsemé(e) de; **on the ~** à l'heure tapante
dotcom [dɔt'kɔm] n point com m, pointcom m
dot command n (Comput) commande précédée d'un point
dote [dəut]: **to ~ on** vt fus être fou (folle de)
dot-matrix printer [dɔt'meɪtrɪks-] n imprimante matricielle
dotted line ['dɔtɪd-] n ligne pointillée; (Aut) ligne discontinue; **to sign on the ~** signer à l'endroit indiqué or sur la ligne pointillée; (fig) donner son consentement
dotty ['dɔtɪ] adj (inf) loufoque, farfelu(e)
double ['dʌbl] adj double ▷ adv (fold) en deux; (twice): **to cost ~ (sth)** coûter le double (de qch) or deux fois plus (que qch) ▷ n double m; (Cine) doublure f ▷ vt doubler; (fold) plier en deux ▷ vi doubler; (have two uses): **to ~ as** servir aussi de; **~ five two six (5526)** (Brit Tel) cinquante-cinq – vingt-six; **it's spelt with a ~ "l"** ça s'écrit avec deux "l"; **on the ~, at the ~** au pas de course
  ▶ **double back** vi (person) revenir sur ses pas
  ▶ **double up** vi (bend over) se courber, se plier; (share room) partager la chambre
double bass n contrebasse f
double bed n grand lit
double-breasted ['dʌbl'brestɪd] adj croisé(e)
double-check ['dʌbl'tʃek] vt, vi revérifier
double-click ['dʌbl'klɪk] vi (Comput) double-cliquer
double-clutch ['dʌbl'klʌtʃ] vi (US) faire un double débrayage
double cream n (Brit) crème fraîche épaisse
double-cross ['dʌbl'krɔs] vt doubler, trahir
double-decker ['dʌbl'dekə^r] n autobus m à impériale
double declutch vi (Brit) faire un double débrayage
double exposure n (Phot) surimpression f
double glazing n (Brit) double vitrage m
double-page ['dʌblpeɪdʒ] adj: **~ spread** publicité f en double page
double parking n stationnement m en double file
double room n chambre f pour deux
doubles ['dʌblz] n (Tennis) double m
double whammy [-'wæmɪ] n (inf) double contretemps m
double yellow lines npl (Brit: Aut) double bande jaune marquant l'interdiction de stationner
doubly ['dʌblɪ] adv doublement, deux fois plus
doubt [daut] n doute m ▷ vt douter de; **no ~** sans doute; **without (a) ~** sans aucun doute; **beyond ~** adv indubitablement ▷ adj indubitable; **to ~ that** douter que + sub; **I ~ it very much** j'en doute fort
doubtful ['dautful] adj douteux(-euse); (person)

incertain(e); **to be ~ about sth** avoir des doutes sur qch, ne pas être convaincu de qch; **I'm a bit ~** je n'en suis pas certain or sûr
doubtless ['dautlɪs] adv sans doute, sûrement
dough [dəu] n pâte f; (inf: money) fric m, pognon m
doughnut ['dəunʌt], (US) **donut** n beignet m
dour [duə^r] adj austère
douse [dauz] vt (with water) tremper, inonder; (flames) éteindre
dove [dʌv] n colombe f
Dover ['dəuvə^r] n Douvres
dovetail ['dʌvteɪl] n: **~ joint** assemblage m à queue d'aronde ▷ vi (fig) concorder
dowager ['dauədʒə^r] n douairière f
dowdy ['daudɪ] adj démodé(e), mal fagoté(e)
Dow-Jones average ['dau'dʒəunz-] n (US) indice m Dow-Jones
down [daun] n (fluff) duvet m; (hill) colline (dénudée) ▷ adv en bas, vers le bas; (on the ground) par terre ▷ prep en bas de; (along) le long de ▷ vt (enemy) abattre; (inf: drink) siffler; **to fall ~** tomber; **she's going ~ to Bristol** elle descend à Bristol; **to write sth ~** écrire qch; **~ there** là-bas (en bas), là au fond; **~ here** ici en bas; **the price of meat is ~** le prix de la viande a baissé; **I've got it ~ in my diary** c'est inscrit dans mon agenda; **to pay £2 ~** verser 2 livres d'arrhes or en acompte; **England is two goals ~** l'Angleterre a deux buts de retard; **to walk ~ a hill** descendre une colline; **to run ~ the street** descendre la rue en courant; **to ~ tools** (Brit) cesser le travail; **~ with X!** à bas X!
down-and-out ['daunəndaut] n (tramp) clochard(e)
down-at-heel ['daunət'hiːl] adj (fig) miteux(-euse)
downbeat ['daunbiːt] n (Mus) temps frappé ▷ adj sombre, négatif(-ive)
downcast ['daunkɑːst] adj démoralisé(e)
downer ['daunə^r] n (inf: drug) tranquillisant m; **to be on a ~** (depressed) flipper
downfall ['daunfɔːl] n chute f; ruine f
downgrade ['daungreɪd] vt déclasser
downhearted ['daun'hɑːtɪd] adj découragé(e)
downhill ['daun'hɪl] adv (face, look) en aval, vers l'aval; (roll, go) vers le bas, en bas ▷ n (Ski: also: **downhill race**) descente f; **to go ~** descendre; (business) péricliter, aller à vau-l'eau
Downing Street ['daunɪŋ-] n (Brit): **10 ~** résidence du Premier ministre; voir article

● **DOWNING STREET**
●
● Downing Street est une rue de Westminster (à
● Londres) où se trouvent la résidence
● officielle du Premier ministre et celle du
● ministre des Finances. Le nom Downing Street
● est souvent utilisé pour désigner le
● gouvernement britannique.

download ['daunləud] n téléchargement m ▷ vt

(*Comput*) télécharger

downloadable [daun'ləudəbl] *adj*
téléchargeable

down-market ['daun'mɑːkɪt] *adj* (*product*) bas de
gamme *inv*

down payment *n* acompte *m*

downplay ['daunpleɪ] *vt* (*US*) minimiser
(l'importance de)

downpour ['daunpɔː'] *n* pluie torrentielle,
déluge *m*

downright ['daunraɪt] *adj* (*lie etc*) effronté(e);
(*refusal*) catégorique

Downs [daunz] *npl* (*Brit*): **the ~** collines crayeuses
du sud-est de l'Angleterre

downsize [daun'saɪz] *vt* réduire l'effectif de

Down's syndrome [daunz-] *n* mongolisme *m*,
trisomie *f*; **a ~ baby** un bébé mongolien *or*
trisomique

downstairs ['daun'stɛəz] *adv* (*on or to ground floor*)
au rez-de-chaussée; (*on or to floor below*) à l'étage
inférieur; **to come ~, to go ~** descendre
(l'escalier)

downstream ['daunstriːm] *adv* en aval

downtime ['dauntaɪm] *n* (*of machine etc*) temps
mort; (*of person*) temps d'arrêt

down-to-earth ['dauntuˈəːθ] *adj* terre à terre *inv*

downtown ['daun'taun] *adv* en ville ▷ *adj* (*US*):
~ Chicago le centre commerçant de Chicago

downtrodden ['dauntrɔdn] *adj* opprimé(e)

down under *adv* en Australie *or* Nouvelle
Zélande

downward ['daunwəd] *adj, adv* vers le bas; **a ~
trend** une tendance à la baisse, une
diminution progressive

downwards ['daunwədz] *adv* vers le bas

dowry ['dauri] *n* dot *f*

doz. *abbr* = **dozen**

doze [dəuz] *vi* sommeiller
  ▶ **doze off** *vi* s'assoupir

dozen ['dʌzn] *n* douzaine *f*; **a ~ books** une
douzaine de livres; **80p a ~** 80p la douzaine; **~s
of** des centaines de

DPh, DPhil *n abbr* (= *Doctor of Philosophy*) titre
universitaire

DPP *n abbr* (*Brit*) = **Director of Public
Prosecutions**

DPT *n abbr* (*Med*: = *diphtheria, pertussis, tetanus*)
DCT *m*

DPW *n abbr* (*US*) = **Department of Public Works**

Dr. *abbr* (= *doctor*) Dr; (*in street names*) = **drive**

drab [dræb] *adj* terne, morne

draft [drɑːft] *n* (*of letter, school work*) brouillon *m*;
(*of literary work*) ébauche *f*; (*of contract, document*)
version *f* préliminaire; (*Comm*) traite *f*; (*US Mil*)
contingent *m*; (: *call-up*) conscription *f* ▷ *vt* faire
le brouillon de; (*document, report*) rédiger une
version préliminaire de; (*Mil: send*) détacher; *see
also* **draught**

drag [dræg] *vt* traîner; (*river*) draguer ▷ *vi*
traîner ▷ *n* (*Aviat, Naut*) résistance *f*; (*inf*) casse-
pieds *m/f*; (*women's clothing*): **in ~** (en) travesti; **to
~ and drop** (*Comput*) glisser-poser

▶ **drag away** *vt*: **to ~ away (from)** arracher *or*
emmener de force (de)
  ▶ **drag on** *vi* s'éterniser

dragnet ['drægnɛt] *n* drège *f*; (*fig*) piège *m*,
filets *mpl*

dragon ['drægn] *n* dragon *m*

dragonfly ['drægənflaɪ] *n* libellule *f*

dragoon [drəˈguːn] *n* (*cavalryman*) dragon *m* ▷ *vt*:
to ~ sb into doing sth (*Brit*) forcer qn à faire qch

drain [dreɪn] *n* égout *m*; (*on resources*) saignée *f*
▷ *vt* (*land, marshes*) drainer, assécher; (*vegetables*)
égoutter; (*reservoir etc*) vider ▷ *vi* (*water*)
s'écouler; **to feel ~ed (of energy** *or* **emotion)**
être miné(e)

drainage ['dreɪnɪdʒ] *n* (*system*) système *m*
d'égouts; (*act*) drainage *m*

draining board ['dreɪnɪŋ-] (*US*), **drainboard**
['dreɪnbɔːd] *n* égouttoir *m*

drainpipe ['dreɪnpaɪp] *n* tuyau *m* d'écoulement

drake [dreɪk] *n* canard *m* (mâle)

dram [dræm] *n* petit verre

drama ['drɑːmə] *n* (*art*) théâtre *m*, art *m*
dramatique; (*play*) pièce *f*; (*event*) drame *m*

dramatic [drəˈmætɪk] *adj* (*Theat*) dramatique;
(*impressive*) spectaculaire

dramatically [drəˈmætɪklɪ] *adv* de façon
spectaculaire

dramatist ['dræmətɪst] *n* auteur *m* dramatique

dramatize ['dræmətaɪz] *vt* (*events etc*)
dramatiser; (*adapt*) adapter pour la télévision
(*or* pour l'écran)

drank [dræŋk] *pt of* **drink**

drape [dreɪp] *vt* draper; **drapes** *npl* (*US*)
rideaux *mpl*

draper ['dreɪpə'] *n* (*Brit*) marchand(e) de
nouveautés

drastic ['dræstɪk] *adj* (*measures*) d'urgence,
énergique; (*change*) radical(e)

drastically ['dræstɪklɪ] *adv* radicalement

draught, (*US*) **draft** [drɑːft] *n* courant *m* d'air;
(*of chimney*) tirage *m*; (*Naut*) tirant *m* d'eau; **on ~**
(*beer*) à la pression

draught beer *n* bière *f* (à la) pression

draughtboard ['drɑːftbɔːd] *n* (*Brit*) damier *m*

draughts [drɑːfts] *n* (*Brit: game*) (jeu *m* de)
dames *fpl*

draughtsman, (*US*) **draftsman** ['drɑːftsmən]
(*irreg*) *n* dessinateur(-trice) (industriel(le))

draughtsmanship, (*US*) **draftsmanship** ['drɑː
ftsmənʃɪp] *n* (*technique*) dessin industriel; (*art*)
graphisme *m*

draw [drɔː] (*vb: pt* **drew**, *pp* **-n**) [druː, drɔːn] *vt*
tirer; (*picture*) dessiner; (*attract*) attirer; (*line,
circle*) tracer; (*money*) retirer; (*wages*) toucher;
(*comparison, distinction*): **to ~ (between)** faire
(entre) ▷ *vi* (*Sport*) faire match nul ▷ *n* match
nul; (*lottery*) loterie *f*; (: *picking of ticket*) tirage *m*
au sort; **to ~ to a close** toucher à *or* tirer à sa fin;
to ~ near *vi* s'approcher; approcher

▶ **draw back** *vi* (*move back*): **to ~ back (from)**
reculer (de)
  ▶ **draw in** *vi* (*Brit: car*) s'arrêter le long du

trottoir; (: *train*) entrer en gare *or* dans la station
▶ **draw on** *vt* (*resources*) faire appel à;
(*imagination, person*) avoir recours à, faire appel à
▶ **draw out** *vi* (*lengthen*) s'allonger ▷ *vt* (*money*)
retirer
▶ **draw up** *vi* (*stop*) s'arrêter ▷ *vt* (*document*)
établir, dresser; (*plan*) formuler, dessiner; (*chair*)
approcher

drawback ['drɔːbæk] *n* inconvénient *m*,
désavantage *m*

drawbridge ['drɔːbrɪdʒ] *n* pont-levis *m*

drawee [drɔːˈiː] *n* tiré *m*

drawer [drɔːˈ] *n* tiroir *m* ['drɔːəʳ] (*of cheque*)
tireur *m*

drawing ['drɔːɪŋ] *n* dessin *m*

drawing board *n* planche *f* à dessin

drawing pin *n* (*Brit*) punaise *f*

drawing room *n* salon *m*

drawl [drɔːl] *n* accent traînant

drawn [drɔːn] *pp of* **draw** ▷ *adj* (*haggard*) tiré(e),
crispé(e)

drawstring ['drɔːstrɪŋ] *n* cordon *m*

dread [drɛd] *n* épouvante *f*, effroi *m* ▷ *vt*
redouter, appréhender

dreadful ['drɛdful] *adj* épouvantable,
affreux(-euse)

dream [driːm] *n* rêve *m* ▷ *vt, vi* (*pt, pp* **-ed** *or* **-t**)
[drɛmt] rêver; **to have a ~ about sb/sth** rêver à
qn/qch; **sweet ~s!** faites de beaux rêves!
▶ **dream up** *vt* inventer

dreamer ['driːməʳ] *n* rêveur(-euse)

dreamt [drɛmt] *pt, pp of* **dream**

dreamy ['driːmɪ] *adj* (*absent-minded*)
rêveur(-euse)

dreary ['drɪərɪ] *adj* triste; monotone

dredge [drɛdʒ] *vt* draguer
▶ **dredge up** *vt* draguer; (*fig: unpleasant facts*)
(faire) ressortir

dredger ['drɛdʒəʳ] *n* (*ship*) dragueur *m*; (*machine*)
drague *f*; (*Brit: also*: **sugar dredger**)
saupoudreuse *f*

dregs [drɛgz] *npl* lie *f*

drench [drɛntʃ] *vt* tremper; **~ed to the skin**
trempé(e) jusqu'aux os

dress [drɛs] *n* robe *f*; (*clothing*) habillement *m*,
tenue *f* ▷ *vt* habiller; (*wound*) panser; (*food*)
préparer ▷ *vi*: **she ~es very well** elle s'habille
très bien; **to ~ o.s., to get ~ed** s'habiller; **to ~ a
shop window** faire l'étalage *or* la vitrine
▶ **dress up** *vi* s'habiller; (*in fancy dress*) se
déguiser

dress circle *n* (*Brit*) premier balcon

dress designer *n* modéliste *m/f*,
dessinateur(-trice) de mode

dresser ['drɛsəʳ] *n* (*Theat*) habilleur(-euse); (*also*:
window dresser) étalagiste *m/f*; (*furniture*)
vaisselier *m*; (: *US*) coiffeuse *f*, commode *f*

dressing ['drɛsɪŋ] *n* (*Med*) pansement *m*; (*Culin*)
sauce *f*, assaisonnement *m*

dressing gown *n* (*Brit*) robe *f* de chambre

dressing room *n* (*Theat*) loge *f*; (*Sport*)
vestiaire *m*

dressing table *n* coiffeuse *f*

dressmaker ['drɛsmeɪkəʳ] *n* couturière *f*

dressmaking ['drɛsmeɪkɪŋ] *n* couture *f*; travaux
mpl de couture

dress rehearsal *n* (répétition *f*) générale *f*

dress shirt *n* chemise *f* à plastron

dressy ['drɛsɪ] *adj* (*inf: clothes*) (qui fait) habillé(e)

drew [druː] *pt of* **draw**

dribble ['drɪbl] *vi* tomber goutte à goutte; (*baby*)
baver ▷ *vt* (*ball*) dribbler

dried [draɪd] *adj* (*fruit, beans*) sec (sèche); (*eggs,
milk*) en poudre

drier ['draɪəʳ] *n* = **dryer**

drift [drɪft] *n* (*of current etc*) force *f*; direction *f*; (*of
sand etc*) amoncellement *m*; (*of snow*) rafale *f*;
coulée *f*; (: *on ground*) congère *f*; (*general meaning*)
sens général ▷ *vi* (*boat*) aller à la dérive, dériver;
(*sand, snow*) s'amonceler, s'entasser; **to let
things ~** laisser les choses aller à la dérive; **to ~
apart** (*friends, lovers*) s'éloigner l'un de l'autre; **I
get** *or* **catch your ~** je vois en gros ce que vous
voulez dire

drifter ['drɪftəʳ] *n* personne *f* sans but dans la vie

driftwood ['drɪftwud] *n* bois flotté

drill [drɪl] *n* perceuse *f*; (*bit*) foret *m*; (*of dentist*)
roulette *f*, fraise *f*; (*Mil*) exercice *m* ▷ *vt* percer;
(*troops*) entraîner; (*pupils: in grammar*) faire faire
des exercices à ▷ *vi* (*for oil*) faire un *or* des
forage(s)

drilling ['drɪlɪŋ] *n* (*for oil*) forage *m*

drilling rig *n* (*on land*) tour *f* (de forage), derrick
m; (*at sea*) plate-forme *f* de forage

drily ['draɪlɪ] *adv* = **dryly**

drink [drɪŋk] *n* boisson *f*; (*alcoholic*) verre *m* ▷ *vt,
vi* (*pt* **drank**, *pp* **drunk** [dræŋk, drʌŋk]) boire; **to
have a ~** boire quelque chose, boire un verre; **a ~
of water** un verre d'eau; **would you like a ~?** tu
veux boire quelque chose?; **we had ~s before
lunch** on a pris l'apéritif
▶ **drink in** *vt* (*fresh air*) inspirer profondément;
(*story*) avaler, ne pas perdre une miette de;
(*sight*) se remplir la vue de

drinkable ['drɪŋkəbl] *adj* (*not dangerous*) potable;
(*palatable*) buvable

drink-driving ['drɪŋk'draɪvɪŋ] *n* conduite *f* en
état d'ivresse

drinker ['drɪŋkəʳ] *n* buveur(-euse)

drinking ['drɪŋkɪŋ] *n* (*drunkenness*) boisson *f*,
alcoolisme *m*

drinking fountain *n* (*in park etc*) fontaine
publique; (*in building*) jet *m* d'eau potable

drinking water *n* eau *f* potable

drip [drɪp] *n* (*drop*) goutte *f*; (*sound: of water etc*)
bruit *m* de l'eau qui tombe goutte à goutte;
(*Med: device*) goutte-à-goutte *m inv*; (: *liquid*)
perfusion *f*; (*inf: person*) lavette *f*, nouille *f* ▷ *vi*
tomber goutte à goutte; (*tap*) goutter; (*washing*)
s'égoutter; (*wall*) suinter

drip-dry ['drɪp'draɪ] *adj* (*shirt*) sans repassage

drip-feed ['drɪpfiːd] *vt* alimenter au goutte-à-
goutte *or* par perfusion

dripping ['drɪpɪŋ] *n* graisse *f* de rôti ▷ *adj*: **~ wet**

trempé(e)

drive [draɪv] (pt **drove**, pp **driven** [drəuv, 'drɪvn])
n promenade f or trajet m en voiture; (also:
driveway) allée f; (energy) dynamisme m,
énergie f; (Psych) besoin m; pulsion f; (push)
effort (concerté); campagne f; (Sport) drive m;
(Tech) entraînement m; traction f; transmission
f; (Comput: also: **disk drive**) lecteur m de
disquette ▷ vt conduire; (nail) enfoncer; (push)
chasser, pousser; (Tech: motor) actionner;
entraîner ▷ vi (be at the wheel) conduire; (travel by
car) aller en voiture; **to go for a ~** aller faire une
promenade en voiture; **it's 3 hours' ~ from
London** Londres est à 3 heures de route; **left-/
right-hand ~** (Aut) conduite f à gauche/droite;
front-/rear-wheel ~ (Aut) traction f avant/
arrière; **to ~ sb to (do) sth** pousser or conduire
qn à (faire) qch; **to ~ sb mad** rendre qn fou
(folle)
  ▶ **drive at** vt fus (fig: intend, mean) vouloir dire, en
  venir à
  ▶ **drive on** vi poursuivre sa route, continuer;
  (after stopping) reprendre sa route, repartir ▷ vt
  (incite, encourage) inciter
  ▶ **drive out** vt (force out) chasser
drive-by ['draɪvbaɪ] n (also: **drive-by shooting**)
tentative d'assassinat par coups de feu tirés d'une voiture
drive-in ['draɪvɪn] adj, n (esp US) drive-in m
drive-in window n (US) guichet-auto m
drivel ['drɪvl] n (inf) idioties fpl, imbécillités fpl
driven ['drɪvn] pp of **drive**
driver ['draɪvər] n conducteur(-trice); (of taxi,
bus) chauffeur m
driver's license n (US) permis m de conduire
driveway ['draɪvweɪ] n allée f
driving ['draɪvɪŋ] adj: **~ rain** n pluie battante
▷ n conduite f
driving force n locomotive f, élément m
dynamique
driving instructor n moniteur m d'auto-école
driving lesson n leçon f de conduite
driving licence n (Brit) permis m de conduire
driving school n auto-école f
driving test n examen m du permis de conduire
drizzle ['drɪzl] n bruine f, crachin m ▷ vi bruiner
droll [drəul] adj drôle
dromedary ['drɒmədərɪ] n dromadaire m
drone [drəun] vi (bee) bourdonner; (engine etc)
ronronner; (also: **drone on**) parler d'une voix
monocorde ▷ n bourdonnement m;
ronronnement m; (male bee) faux-bourdon m
drool [druːl] vi baver; **to ~ over sb/sth** (fig) baver
d'admiration or être en extase devant qn/qch
droop [druːp] vi (flower) commencer à se faner;
(shoulders, head) tomber
drop [drɒp] n (of liquid) goutte f; (fall) baisse f; (: in
salary) réduction f; (also: **parachute drop**) saut
m; (of cliff) dénivellation f; à-pic m ▷ vt laisser
tomber; (voice, eyes, price) baisser; (passenger)
déposer ▷ vi (wind, temperature, price, voice)
tomber; (numbers, attendance) diminuer; **drops**
npl (Med) gouttes fpl; **cough ~s** pastilles fpl pour la

toux; **a ~ of 10%** une baisse or réduction) de 10%;
to ~ anchor jeter l'ancre; **to ~ sb a line** mettre
un mot à qn
  ▶ **drop in** vi (inf: visit): **to ~ in (on)** faire un saut
  (chez), passer (chez)
  ▶ **drop off** vi (sleep) s'assoupir ▷ vt (passenger)
  déposer; **to ~ sb off** déposer qn
  ▶ **drop out** vi (withdraw) se retirer; (student etc)
  abandonner, décrocher
droplet ['drɒplɪt] n gouttelette f
dropout ['drɒpaut] n (from society) marginal(e);
(from university) drop-out m/f, dropé(e)
dropper ['drɒpər] n (Med etc) compte-gouttes
m inv
droppings ['drɒpɪŋz] npl crottes fpl
dross [drɒs] n déchets mpl; rebut m
drought [draut] n sécheresse f
drove [drəuv] pt of **drive** ▷ n: **~s of people** une
foule de gens
drown [draun] vt noyer; (also: **drown out**: sound)
couvrir, étouffer ▷ vi se noyer
drowse [drauz] vi somnoler
drowsy ['drauzɪ] adj somnolent(e)
drudge [drʌdʒ] n bête f de somme (fig)
drudgery ['drʌdʒərɪ] n corvée f
drug [drʌg] n médicament m; (narcotic) drogue f
▷ vt droguer; **to be on ~s** se droguer; **he's on ~s**
il se drogue; (Med) il est sous médication
drug addict n toxicomane m/f
drug dealer n revendeur(-euse) de drogue
druggist ['drʌgɪst] n (US) pharmacien(ne)-
droguiste
drug peddler n revendeur(-euse) de drogue
drugstore ['drʌgstɔːr] n (US) pharmacie-
droguerie f, drugstore m
drum [drʌm] n tambour m; (for oil, petrol) bidon m
▷ vt: **to ~ one's fingers on the table** pianoter or
tambouriner sur la table; **drums** npl (Mus)
batterie f
  ▶ **drum up** vt (enthusiasm, support) susciter,
  rallier
drummer ['drʌmər] n (joueur m de) tambour m
drum roll n roulement m de tambour
drumstick ['drʌmstɪk] n (Mus) baguette f de
tambour; (of chicken) pilon m
drunk [drʌŋk] pp of **drink** ▷ adj ivre, soûl(e) ▷ n
(also: **drunkard**) ivrogne m/f; **to get ~** s'enivrer,
se soûler
drunkard ['drʌŋkəd] n ivrogne m/f
drunken ['drʌŋkən] adj ivre, soûl(e); (rage, stupor)
ivrogne, d'ivrogne; **~ driving** conduite f en état
d'ivresse
drunkenness ['drʌŋkənnɪs] n ivresse f;
ivrognerie f
dry [draɪ] adj sec (sèche); (day) sans pluie;
(humour) pince-sans-rire; (uninteresting) aride,
rébarbatif(-ive) ▷ vt sécher; (clothes) faire
sécher ▷ vi sécher; **on ~ land** sur la terre ferme;
to ~ one's hands/hair/eyes se sécher les
mains/les cheveux/les yeux
  ▶ **dry off** vi, vt sécher
  ▶ **dry up** vi (river, supplies) se tarir; (: speaker)

sécher, rester sec

dry-clean ['draɪˈkliːn] vt nettoyer à sec

dry-cleaner ['draɪˈkliːnəʳ] n teinturier m

dry-cleaner's ['draɪˈkliːnəz] n teinturerie f

dry-cleaning ['draɪˈkliːnɪŋ] n (process) nettoyage m à sec

dry dock n (Naut) cale sèche, bassin m de radoub

dryer ['draɪəʳ] n (tumble-dryer) sèche-linge m inv; (for hair) sèche-cheveux m inv

dry goods npl (Comm) textiles mpl, mercerie f

dry goods store n (US) magasin m de nouveautés

dry ice n neige f carbonique

dryly ['draɪlɪ] adv sèchement, d'un ton sec

dryness ['draɪnɪs] n sécheresse f

dry rot n pourriture sèche (du bois)

dry run n (fig) essai m

dry ski slope n piste (de ski) artificielle

DSc n abbr (= Doctor of Science) titre universitaire

DSS n abbr (Brit) = **Department of Social Security**

DST abbr (US: = Daylight Saving Time) heure d'été

DT n abbr (Comput) = **data transmission**

DTI n abbr (Brit) = **Department of Trade and Industry**

DTP n abbr (= desktop publishing) PAO f

DT's [diːˈtiːz] n abbr (inf: = delirium tremens) delirium tremens m

dual ['djuəl] adj double

dual carriageway n (Brit) route f à quatre voies

dual-control ['djuəlkənˈtrəul] adj à doubles commandes

dual nationality n double nationalité f

dual-purpose ['djuəlˈpəːpəs] adj à double emploi

dubbed [dʌbd] adj (Cine) doublé(e); (nicknamed) surnommé(e)

dubious ['djuːbɪəs] adj hésitant(e), incertain(e); (reputation, company) douteux(-euse); (also: **I'm very dubious about it**) j'ai des doutes sur la question, je n'en suis pas sûr du tout

Dublin ['dʌblɪn] n Dublin

Dubliner ['dʌblɪnəʳ] n habitant(e) de Dublin, originaire m/f de Dublin

duchess ['dʌtʃɪs] n duchesse f

duck [dʌk] n canard m ▷ vi se baisser vivement, baisser subitement la tête ▷ vt plonger dans l'eau

duckling ['dʌklɪŋ] n caneton m

duct [dʌkt] n conduite f, canalisation f; (Anat) conduit m

dud [dʌd] n (shell) obus non éclaté; (object, tool): **it's a** ~ c'est de la camelote, ça ne marche pas ▷ adj (Brit: cheque) sans provision; (: note, coin) faux (fausse)

due [djuː] adj (money, payment) dû (due); (expected) attendu(e); (fitting) qui convient ▷ n dû m ▷ adv: ~ **north** droit vers le nord; **dues** npl (for club, union) cotisation f; (in harbour) droits mpl (de port); ~ **to** (because of) en raison de; (caused by) dû à; **in** ~ **course** en temps utile or voulu; (in the end) finalement; **the rent is** ~ **on the 30th** il faut payer le loyer le 30; **the train is** ~ **at 8 a.m.**

le train est attendu à 8 h; **she is** ~ **back tomorrow** elle doit rentrer demain; **he is** ~ **£10** on lui doit 10 livres; **I am** ~ **6 days' leave** j'ai droit à 6 jours de congé; **to give sb his** or **her** ~ être juste envers qn

due date n date f d'échéance

duel ['djuəl] n duel m

duet [djuːˈɛt] n duo m

duff [dʌf] adj (Brit inf) nullard(e), nul(le)

duffel bag, duffle bag ['dʌfl-] n sac marin

duffel coat, duffle coat ['dʌfl-] n duffel-coat m

duffer ['dʌfəʳ] n (inf) nullard(e)

dug [dʌg] pt, pp of **dig**

dugout ['dʌgaut] n (Sport) banc m de touche

duke [djuːk] n duc m

dull [dʌl] adj (boring) ennuyeux(-euse); (slow) borné(e); (not bright) morne, terne; (sound, pain) sourd(e); (weather, day) gris(e), maussade; (blade) émoussé(e) ▷ vt (pain, grief) atténuer; (mind, senses) engourdir

duly ['djuːlɪ] adv (on time) en temps voulu; (as expected) comme il se doit

dumb [dʌm] adj muet(te); (stupid) bête; **to be struck** ~ (fig) rester abasourdi(e), être sidéré(e)

dumbbell ['dʌmbɛl] n (Sport) haltère m

dumbfounded [dʌmˈfaundɪd] adj sidéré(e)

dummy ['dʌmɪ] n (tailor's model) mannequin m; (mock-up) factice m, maquette f; (Sport) feinte f; (Brit: for baby) tétine f ▷ adj faux (fausse), factice

dummy run n essai m

dump [dʌmp] n tas m d'ordures; (also: **rubbish dump**) décharge (publique); (Mil) dépôt m; (Comput) listage m (de la mémoire); (inf: place) trou m ▷ vt (put down) déposer; déverser; (get rid of) se débarrasser de; (Comput) lister; (Comm: goods) vendre à perte (sur le marché extérieur); **to be (down) in the** ~**s** (inf) avoir le cafard, broyer du noir

dumping ['dʌmpɪŋ] n (Econ) dumping m; (of rubbish): **"no** ~**"** "décharge interdite"

dumpling ['dʌmplɪŋ] n boulette f (de pâte)

dumpy ['dʌmpɪ] adj courtaud(e), boulot(te)

dunce [dʌns] n âne m, cancre m

dune [djuːn] n dune f

dung [dʌŋ] n fumier m

dungarees [dʌŋɡəˈriːz] npl bleu(s) m(pl); (for child, woman) salopette f

dungeon ['dʌndʒən] n cachot m

dunk [dʌŋk] vt tremper

Dunkirk [dʌnˈkəːk] n Dunkerque

duo ['djuːəu] n (gen: Mus) duo m

duodenal [djuːəuˈdiːnl] adj duodénal(e); ~ **ulcer** ulcère m du duodénum

dupe [djuːp] n dupe f ▷ vt duper, tromper

duplex ['djuːplɛks] n (US: also: **duplex apartment**) duplex m

duplicate n ['djuːplɪkət] double m, copie exacte; (copy of letter etc) duplicata m ▷ adj (copy) en double ▷ vt ['djuːplɪkeɪt] faire un double de; (on machine) polycopier; **in** ~ en deux exemplaires, en double; ~ **key** double m de la (or d'une) clé

duplicating machine ['djuːplɪkeɪtɪŋ-],

d

duplicator ['dju:plɪkeɪtəʳ] n duplicateur m
duplicity [dju:'plɪsɪtɪ] n duplicité f, fausseté f
durability [djuərə'bɪlɪtɪ] n solidité f; durabilité f
durable ['djuərəbl] adj durable; (clothes, metal) résistant(e), solide
duration [djuə'reɪʃən] n durée f
duress [djuə'rɛs] n: **under ~** sous la contrainte
Durex® ['djuərɛks] n (Brit) préservatif (masculin)
during ['djuərɪŋ] prep pendant, au cours de
dusk [dʌsk] n crépuscule m
dusky ['dʌskɪ] adj sombre
dust [dʌst] n poussière f ▷ vt (furniture) essuyer, épousseter; (cake etc): **to ~ with** saupoudrer de
 ▶ **dust off** vt (also fig) dépoussiérer
dustbin ['dʌstbɪn] n (Brit) poubelle f
duster ['dʌstəʳ] n chiffon m
dust jacket n jaquette f
dustman ['dʌstmən] (irreg) n (Brit) boueux m, éboueur m
dustpan ['dʌstpæn] n pelle f à poussière
dusty ['dʌstɪ] adj poussiéreux(-euse)
Dutch [dʌtʃ] adj hollandais(e), néerlandais(e) ▷ n (Ling) hollandais m, néerlandais m ▷ adv: **to go ~** or **dutch** (inf) partager les frais; **the Dutch** npl les Hollandais, les Néerlandais
Dutch auction n enchères fpl à la baisse
Dutchman ['dʌtʃmən] (irreg) n Hollandais m
Dutchwoman ['dʌtʃwumən] (irreg) n Hollandaise f
dutiable ['dju:tɪəbl] adj taxable, soumis(e) à des droits de douane
dutiful ['dju:tɪful] adj (child) respectueux(-euse); (husband, wife) plein(e) d'égards, prévenant(e); (employee) consciencieux(-euse)
duty ['dju:tɪ] n devoir m; (tax) droit m, taxe f; **duties** npl fonctions fpl; **to make it one's ~ to do sth** se faire un devoir de faire qch; **to pay ~ on sth** payer un droit or une taxe sur qch; **on ~** de service; (at night etc) de garde; **off ~** libre, pas de service or de garde
duty-free ['dju:tɪ'fri:] adj exempté(e) de douane,

hors-taxe; **~ shop** boutique f hors-taxe
duty officer n (Mil etc) officier m de permanence
duvet ['du:veɪ] n (Brit) couette f
DV abbr (= Deo volente) si Dieu le veut
DVD n abbr (= digital versatile or video disc) DVD m
DVD burner n graveur m de DVD
DVD player n lecteur m de DVD
DVD writer n graveur m de DVD
DVLA n abbr (Brit: = Driver and Vehicle Licensing Agency) service qui délivre les cartes grises et les permis de conduire
DVM n abbr (US: = Doctor of Veterinary Medicine) titre universitaire
DVT n abbr = **deep vein thrombosis**
dwarf (pl **dwarves**) [dwɔːf, dwɔːvz] n nain(e) ▷ vt écraser
dwell (pt, pp **dwelt**) [dwɛl, dwɛlt] vi demeurer
 ▶ **dwell on** vt fus s'étendre sur
dweller ['dwɛləʳ] n habitant(e)
dwelling ['dwɛlɪŋ] n habitation f, demeure f
dwelt [dwɛlt] pt, pp of **dwell**
dwindle ['dwɪndl] vi diminuer, décroître
dwindling ['dwɪndlɪŋ] adj décroissant(e), en diminution
dye [daɪ] n teinture f ▷ vt teindre; **hair ~** teinture pour les cheveux
dyestuffs ['daɪstʌfs] npl colorants mpl
dying ['daɪɪŋ] adj mourant(e), agonisant(e)
dyke [daɪk] n (embankment) digue f
dynamic [daɪ'næmɪk] adj dynamique
dynamics [daɪ'næmɪks] n or npl dynamique f
dynamite ['daɪnəmaɪt] n dynamite f ▷ vt dynamiter, faire sauter à la dynamite
dynamo ['daɪnəməu] n dynamo f
dynasty ['dɪnəstɪ] n dynastie f
dysentery ['dɪsntrɪ] n dysenterie f
dyslexia [dɪs'lɛksɪə] n dyslexie f
dyslexic [dɪs'lɛksɪk] adj, n dyslexique m/f
dyspepsia [dɪs'pɛpsɪə] n dyspepsie f
dystrophy ['dɪstrəfɪ] n dystrophie f; **muscular ~** dystrophie musculaire

Ee

e

E¹, e [i:] *n* (*letter*) E, e *m*; (*Mus*): **E** mi *m*; **E for Edward**, (*US*) **E for Easy** E comme Eugène
E² *abbr* (= *east*) E ▷ *n abbr* (*Drugs*) = **ecstasy**
ea. *abbr* = **each**
E.A. *n abbr* (*US*: = *educational age*) niveau scolaire
each [i:tʃ] *adj* chaque ▷ *pron* chacun(e); **~ one** chacun(e); **~ other** l'un l'autre; **they hate ~ other** ils se détestent (mutuellement); **you are jealous of ~ other** vous êtes jaloux l'un de l'autre; **~ day** chaque jour, tous les jours; **they have 2 books ~** ils ont 2 livres chacun; **they cost £5 ~** ils coûtent 5 livres (la) pièce; **~ of us** chacun(e) de nous
eager ['i:gə^r] *adj* (*person, buyer*) empressé(e); (*lover*) ardent(e), passionné(e); (*keen: pupil, worker*) enthousiaste; **to be ~ to do sth** (*impatient*) brûler de faire qch; (*keen*) désirer vivement faire qch; **to be ~ for** (*event*) désirer vivement; (*vengeance, affection, information*) être avide de
eagle ['i:gl] *n* aigle *m*
E and OE *abbr* = **errors and omissions excepted**
ear [ɪə^r] *n* oreille *f*; (*of corn*) épi *m*; **up to one's ~s in debt** endetté(e) jusqu'au cou
earache ['ɪəreɪk] *n* mal *m* aux oreilles
eardrum ['ɪədrʌm] *n* tympan *m*
earful ['ɪəful] *n* (*inf*): **to give sb an ~** passer un savon à qn
earl [ə:l] *n* comte *m*
earlier ['ə:lɪə^r] *adj* (*date etc*) plus rapproché(e); (*edition etc*) plus ancien(ne), antérieur(e) ▷ *adv* plus tôt
early ['ə:lɪ] *adv* tôt, de bonne heure; (*ahead of time*) en avance; (*near the beginning*) au début ▷ *adj* précoce, qui se manifeste (*or* se fait) tôt *or* de bonne heure; (*Christians, settlers*) premier(-ière); (*reply*) rapide; (*death*) prématuré(e); (*work*) de jeunesse; **to have an ~ night/start** se coucher/partir tôt *or* de bonne heure; **take the ~ train** prenez le premier train; **in the ~** *or* **in the spring/19th century** au début *or* commencement du printemps/19ème siècle; **you're ~!** tu es en avance!; **~ in the morning** tôt le matin; **she's in her ~ forties** elle a un peu plus de quarante ans *or* de la quarantaine; **at your earliest convenience** (*Comm*) dans les meilleurs délais

early retirement *n* retraite anticipée
early warning system *n* système *m* de première alerte
earmark ['ɪəmɑ:k] *vt*: **to ~ sth for** réserver *or* destiner qch à
earn [ə:n] *vt* gagner; (*Comm: yield*) rapporter; **to ~ one's living** gagner sa vie; **this ~ed him much praise, he ~ed much praise for this** ceci lui a valu de nombreux éloges; **he's ~ed his rest/reward** il mérite *or* a bien mérité *or* a bien gagné son repos/sa récompense
earned income [ə:nd-] *n* revenu *m* du travail
earnest ['ə:nɪst] *adj* sérieux(-euse) ▷ *n* (*also*: **earnest money**) acompte *m*, arrhes *fpl*; **in ~** (*adv*) sérieusement, pour de bon
earnings ['ə:nɪŋz] *npl* salaire *m*; gains *mpl*; (*of company etc*) profits *mpl*, bénéfices *mpl*
ear, nose and throat specialist *n* oto-rhino-laryngologiste *m/f*
earphones ['ɪəfəunz] *npl* écouteurs *mpl*
earplugs ['ɪəplʌgz] *npl* boules *fpl* Quiès®; (*to keep out water*) protège-tympans *mpl*
earring ['ɪərɪŋ] *n* boucle *f* d'oreille
earshot ['ɪəʃɔt] *n*: **out of/within ~** hors de portée/à portée de voix
earth [ə:θ] *n* (*gen, also Brit Elec*) terre *f*; (*of fox etc*) terrier *m* ▷ *vt* (*Brit Elec*) relier à la terre
earthenware ['ə:θnwɛə^r] *n* poterie *f*; faïence *f* ▷ *adj* de *or* en faïence
earthly ['ə:θlɪ] *adj* terrestre; (*also*: **earthly paradise**) paradis *m* terrestre; **there is no ~ reason to think that ...** il n'y a absolument aucune raison *or* pas la moindre raison de penser que ...
earthquake ['ə:θkweɪk] *n* tremblement *m* de terre, séisme *m*
earth-shattering ['ə:θʃætərɪŋ] *adj* stupéfiant(e)
earth tremor *n* secousse *f* sismique
earthworks ['ə:θwə:ks] *npl* travaux *mpl* de terrassement
earthy ['ə:θɪ] *adj* (*fig*) terre à terre *inv*, truculent(e)
earwax ['ɪəwæks] *n* cérumen *m*
earwig ['ɪəwɪg] *n* perce-oreille *m*
ease [i:z] *n* facilité *f*, aisance *f*; (*comfort*) bien-être *m* ▷ *vt* (*soothe: mind*) tranquilliser; (*reduce*:

pain, problem) atténuer; (: *tension*) réduire; (*loosen*) relâcher, détendre; (*help pass*): **to ~ sth in/out** faire pénétrer/sortir qch délicatement or avec douceur, faciliter la pénétration/la sortie de qch ▷ *vi* (*situation*) se détendre; **with ~** sans difficulté, aisément; **life of ~** vie oisive; **at ~** à l'aise; (*Mil*) au repos
▶ **ease off, ease up** *vi* diminuer; (*slow down*) ralentir; (*relax*) se détendre

easel ['i:zl] *n* chevalet *m*

easily ['i:zɪlɪ] *adv* facilement; (*by far*) de loin

easiness ['i:sɪnɪs] *n* facilité *f*; (*of manner*) aisance *f*; nonchalance *f*

east [i:st] *n* est *m* ▷ *adj* (*wind*) d'est; (*side*) est *inv* ▷ *adv* à l'est, vers l'est; **the E~** l'Orient *m*; (*Pol*) les pays *mpl* de l'Est

eastbound ['i:stbaund] *adj* en direction de l'est; (*carriageway*) est *inv*

Easter ['i:stə^r] *n* Pâques *fpl* ▷ *adj* (*holidays*) de Pâques, pascal(e)

Easter egg *n* œuf *m* de Pâques

Easter Island *n* île *f* de Pâques

easterly ['i:stəlɪ] *adj* d'est

Easter Monday *n* le lundi de Pâques

eastern ['i:stən] *adj* de l'est, oriental(e); **E~ Europe** l'Europe de l'Est; **the E~ bloc** (*Pol*) les pays *mpl* de l'est

Easter Sunday *n* le dimanche de Pâques

East Germany *n* (*formerly*) Allemagne *f* de l'Est

eastward ['i:stwəd], **eastwards** ['i:stwədz] *adv* vers l'est, à l'est

easy ['i:zɪ] *adj* facile; (*manner*) aisé(e) ▷ *adv*: **to take it** or **things ~** (*rest*) ne pas se fatiguer; (*not worry*) ne pas (trop) s'en faire; **to have an ~ life** avoir la vie facile; **payment on ~ terms** (*Comm*) facilités *fpl* de paiement; **that's easier said than done** c'est plus facile à dire qu'à faire, c'est vite dit; **I'm ~** (*inf*) ça m'est égal

easy chair *n* fauteuil *m*

easy-going ['i:zɪ'gəuɪŋ] *adj* accommodant(e), facile à vivre

easy touch *n* (*inf*): **he's an ~** c'est une bonne poire

eat (*pt* **ate**, *pp* **-en**) [i:t, eɪt, 'i:tn] *vt*, *vi* manger; **can we have something to ~?** est-ce qu'on peut manger quelque chose?
▶ **eat away** *vt* (*sea*) saper, éroder; (*acid*) ronger, corroder
▶ **eat away at, eat into** *vt fus* ronger, attaquer
▶ **eat out** *vi* manger au restaurant
▶ **eat up** *vt* (*food*) finir (de manger); **it ~s up electricity** ça bouffe du courant, ça consomme beaucoup d'électricité

eatable ['i:təbl] *adj* mangeable; (*safe to eat*) comestible

eaten ['i:tn] *pp of* **eat**

eau de Cologne ['əudəkə'ləun] *n* eau *f* de Cologne

eaves [i:vz] *npl* avant-toit *m*

eavesdrop ['i:vzdrɔp] *vi*: **to ~ (on)** écouter de façon indiscrète

ebb [ɛb] *n* reflux *m* ▷ *vi* refluer; (*fig: also*: **ebb away**) décliner; **the ~ and flow** le flux et le reflux; **to be at a low ~** (*fig*) être bien bas(se), ne pas aller bien fort

ebb tide *n* marée descendante, reflux *m*

ebony ['ɛbənɪ] *n* ébène *f*

e-book ['i:buk] *n* livre *m* électronique

ebullient [ɪ'bʌlɪənt] *adj* exubérant(e)

e-business ['i:bɪznɪs] *n* (*company*) entreprise *f* électronique; (*commerce*) commerce *m* électronique

ECB *n abbr* (= *European Central Bank*) BCE *f* (= *Banque centrale européenne*)

eccentric [ɪk'sɛntrɪk] *adj*, *n* excentrique *m/f*

ecclesiastic [ɪkli:zɪ'æstɪk], **ecclesiastical** [ɪkli:zɪ'æstɪkl] *adj* ecclésiastique

ECG *n abbr* = **electrocardiogram**

echo ['ɛkəu] (*pl* **-es**) *n* écho *m* ▷ *vt* répéter; faire chorus avec ▷ *vi* résonner; faire écho

éclair ['eɪklɛə^r] *n* éclair *m* (*Culin*)

eclipse [ɪ'klɪps] *n* éclipse *f* ▷ *vt* éclipser

eco- ['i:kəu] *prefix* éco-

eco-friendly [i:kəu'frɛndlɪ] *adj* non nuisible à or qui ne nuit pas à l'environnement

ecological [i:kə'lɔdʒɪkəl] *adj* écologique

ecologist [ɪ'kɔlədʒɪst] *n* écologiste *m/f*

ecology [ɪ'kɔlədʒɪ] *n* écologie *f*

e-commerce [i:kɔmə:s] *n* commerce *m* électronique

economic [i:kə'nɔmɪk] *adj* économique; (*profitable*) rentable

economical [i:kə'nɔmɪkl] *adj* économique; (*person*) économe

economically [i:kə'nɔmɪklɪ] *adv* économiquement

economics [i:kə'nɔmɪks] *n* (*Scol*) économie *f* politique ▷ *npl* (*of project etc*) côté *m* or aspect *m* économique

economist [ɪ'kɔnəmɪst] *n* économiste *m/f*

economize [ɪ'kɔnəmaɪz] *vi* économiser, faire des économies

economy [ɪ'kɔnəmɪ] *n* économie *f*; **economies of scale** économies d'échelle

economy class *n* (*Aviat*) classe *f* touriste

economy class syndrome *n* syndrome *m* de la classe économique

economy size *n* taille *f* économique

ecosystem ['i:kəusɪstəm] *n* écosystème *m*

eco-tourism [i:kəu'tuərɪzəm] *n* écotourisme *m*

ECSC *n abbr* (= *European Coal & Steel Community*) CECA *f* (= *Communauté européenne du charbon et de l'acier*)

ecstasy ['ɛkstəsɪ] *n* extase *f*; (*Drugs*) ecstasy *m*; **to go into ecstasies over** s'extasier sur

ecstatic [ɛks'tætɪk] *adj* extatique, en extase

ECT *n abbr* = **electroconvulsive therapy**

Ecuador ['ɛkwədɔ:^r] *n* Équateur *m*

ecumenical [i:kju'mɛnɪkl] *adj* œcuménique

eczema ['ɛksɪmə] *n* eczéma *m*

eddy ['ɛdɪ] *n* tourbillon *m*

edge [ɛdʒ] *n* bord *m*; (*of knife etc*) tranchant *m*, fil *m* ▷ *vt* border ▷ *vi*: **to ~ forward** avancer petit à petit; **to ~ away from** s'éloigner furtivement de; **on** ~ (*fig*) crispé(e), tendu(e); **to have the** ~ **on** (*fig*) l'emporter (de justesse) sur, être légèrement meilleur que

edgeways ['ɛdʒweɪz] *adv* latéralement; **he couldn't get a word in** ~ il ne pouvait pas placer un mot

edging ['ɛdʒɪŋ] *n* bordure *f*

edgy ['ɛdʒɪ] *adj* crispé(e), tendu(e)

edible ['ɛdɪbl] *adj* comestible; (*meal*) mangeable

edict ['iːdɪkt] *n* décret *m*

edifice ['ɛdɪfɪs] *n* édifice *m*

edifying ['ɛdɪfaɪɪŋ] *adj* édifiant(e)

Edinburgh ['ɛdɪnbərə] *n* Édimbourg

edit ['ɛdɪt] *vt* (*text, book*) éditer; (*report*) préparer; (*film*) monter; (*broadcast*) réaliser; (*magazine*) diriger; (*newspaper*) être le rédacteur *or* la rédactrice en chef de

edition [ɪ'dɪʃən] *n* édition *f*

editor ['ɛdɪtər] *n* (*of newspaper*) rédacteur(-trice), rédacteur(-trice) en chef; (*of sb's work*) éditeur(-trice); (*also:* **film editor**) monteur(-euse); **political/ foreign** ~ rédacteur politique/au service étranger

editorial [ɛdɪ'tɔːrɪəl] *adj* de la rédaction, éditorial(e) ▷ *n* éditorial *m*; **the** ~ **staff** la rédaction

EDP *n abbr* = **electronic data processing**

EDT *abbr* (*US:* = *Eastern Daylight Time*) *heure d'été de New York*

educate ['ɛdjukeɪt] *vt* (*teach*) instruire; (*bring up*) éduquer; ~**d at** ... qui a fait ses études à ...

educated ['ɛdjukeɪtɪd] *adj* (*person*) cultivé(e)

educated guess *n* supposition éclairée

education [ɛdju'keɪʃən] *n* éducation *f*; (*studies*) études *fpl*; (*teaching*) enseignement *m*, instruction *f*; (*at university: subject etc*) pédagogie *f*; **primary** *or* (*US*) **elementary/secondary** ~ instruction *f* primaire/secondaire

educational [ɛdju'keɪʃənl] *adj* pédagogique; (*institution*) scolaire; (*useful*) instructif(-ive); (*game, toy*) éducatif(-ive); ~ **technology** technologie *f* de l'enseignement

Edwardian [ɛd'wɔːdɪən] *adj* de l'époque du roi Édouard VII, des années 1900

EE *abbr* = **electrical engineer**

EEG *n abbr* = **electroencephalogram**

eel [iːl] *n* anguille *f*

EENT *n abbr* (*US Med*) = **eye, ear, nose and throat**

EEOC *n abbr* (*US*) = **Equal Employment Opportunity Commission**

eerie ['ɪərɪ] *adj* inquiétant(e), spectral(e), surnaturel(le)

EET *abbr* (= *Eastern European Time*) HEO (= *heure d'Europe orientale*)

effect [ɪ'fɛkt] *n* effet *m* ▷ *vt* effectuer; **effects** *npl* (*Theat*) effets *mpl*; (*property*) effets, affaires *fpl*; **to take** ~ (*Law*) entrer en vigueur, prendre effet; (*drug*) agir, faire son effet; **to put into** ~ (*plan*) mettre en application *or* à exécution; **to have an** ~ **on sb/sth** avoir *or* produire un effet sur qn/ qch; **in** ~ en fait; **his letter is to the** ~ **that** ... sa lettre nous apprend que ...

effective [ɪ'fɛktɪv] *adj* efficace; (*striking: display, outfit*) frappant(e), qui produit *or* fait de l'effet; (*actual*) véritable; **to become** ~ (*Law*) entrer en vigueur, prendre effet; ~ **date** date *f* d'effet *or* d'entrée en vigueur

effectively [ɪ'fɛktɪvlɪ] *adv* efficacement; (*strikingly*) d'une manière frappante, avec beaucoup d'effet; (*in reality*) effectivement, en fait

effectiveness [ɪ'fɛktɪvnɪs] *n* efficacité *f*

effeminate [ɪ'fɛmɪnɪt] *adj* efféminé(e)

effervescent [ɛfə'vɛsnt] *adj* effervescent(e)

efficacy ['ɛfɪkəsɪ] *n* efficacité *f*

efficiency [ɪ'fɪʃənsɪ] *n* efficacité *f*; (*of machine, car*) rendement *m*

efficiency apartment *n* (*US*) studio *m* avec coin cuisine

efficient [ɪ'fɪʃənt] *adj* efficace; (*machine, car*) d'un bon rendement

efficiently [ɪ'fɪʃəntlɪ] *adv* efficacement

effigy ['ɛfɪdʒɪ] *n* effigie *f*

effluent ['ɛfluənt] *n* effluent *m*

effort ['ɛfət] *n* effort *m*; **to make an** ~ **to do sth** faire *or* fournir un effort pour faire qch

effortless ['ɛfətlɪs] *adj* sans effort, aisé(e); (*achievement*) facile

effrontery [ɪ'frʌntərɪ] *n* effronterie *f*

effusive [ɪ'fjuːsɪv] *adj* (*person*) expansif(-ive); (*welcome*) chaleureux(-euse)

EFL *n abbr* (*Scol*) = **English as a Foreign Language**

EFTA ['ɛftə] *n abbr* (= *European Free Trade Association*) AELE *f* (= *Association européenne de libre-échange*)

e.g. *adv abbr* (= *exempli gratia*) par exemple, p. ex.

egalitarian [ɪgælɪ'tɛərɪən] *adj* égalitaire

egg [ɛg] *n* œuf *m*; **hard-boiled/soft-boiled** ~ œuf dur/à la coque

▶ **egg on** *vt* pousser

eggcup ['ɛgkʌp] *n* coquetier *m*

egg plant ['ɛgplɑːnt] (*US*) *n* aubergine *f*

eggshell ['ɛgʃɛl] *n* coquille *f* d'œuf ▷ *adj* (*colour*) blanc cassé *inv*

egg-timer ['ɛgtaɪmər] *n* sablier *m*

egg white *n* blanc *m* d'œuf

egg yolk *n* jaune *m* d'œuf

ego ['iːgəu] *n* (*self-esteem*) amour-propre *m*; (*Psych*) moi *m*

egoism ['ɛgəuɪzəm] *n* égoïsme *m*

egoist ['ɛgəuɪst] *n* égoïste *m/f*

egotism ['ɛgəutɪzəm] *n* égotisme *m*

egotist ['ɛgəutɪst] *n* égocentrique *m/f*

ego trip *n*: **to be on an** ~ être en plein délire d'autosatisfaction

Egypt ['iːdʒɪpt] *n* Égypte *f*

Egyptian [ɪ'dʒɪpʃən] *adj* égyptien(ne) ▷ *n* Égyptien(ne)

EHIC *n abbr* (= *European Health Insurance Card*) CEAM *f*

eiderdown ['aɪdədaun] *n* édredon *m*

Eiffel Tower ['aɪfəl-] *n* tour *f* Eiffel

eight [eɪt] *num* huit

eighteen [eɪ'tiːn] *num* dix-huit

eighteenth [eɪ'tiːnθ] *num* dix-huitième

eighth [eɪtθ] *num* huitième
eightieth ['eɪtɪɪθ] *num* quatre-vingtième
eighty ['eɪtɪ] *num* quatre-vingt(s)
Eire ['ɛərə] *n* République *f* d'Irlande
EIS *n abbr* (= *Educational Institute of Scotland*) syndicat enseignant
either ['aɪðə^r] *adj* l'un ou l'autre; (*both, each*) chaque ▷ *pron*: ~ (of them) l'un ou l'autre ▷ *adv* non plus ▷ *conj*: ~ good or bad ou bon ou mauvais, soit bon soit mauvais; I haven't seen ~ one or the other je n'ai vu ni l'un ni l'autre; on ~ side de chaque côté; I don't like ~ je n'aime ni l'un ni l'autre; no, I don't ~ moi non plus; which bike do you want? — ~ will do quel vélo voulez-vous? — n'importe lequel; answer with ~ yes or no répondez par oui ou par non
ejaculation [ɪdʒækju'leɪʃən] *n* (Physiol) éjaculation *f*
eject [ɪ'dʒɛkt] *vt* (*tenant etc*) expulser; (*object*) éjecter ▷ *vi* (*pilot*) s'éjecter
ejector seat [ɪ'dʒɛktə-] *n* siège *m* éjectable
eke [iːk]: to ~ out *vt* faire durer; augmenter
EKG *n abbr* (US) = **electrocardiogram**
el [ɛl] *n abbr* (US inf) = **elevated railroad**
elaborate [*adj* ɪ'læbərɪt, *vb* ɪ'læbəreɪt] *adj* compliqué(e), recherché(e), minutieux(-euse) ▷ *vt* élaborer ▷ *vi* entrer dans les détails
elapse [ɪ'læps] *vi* s'écouler, passer
elastic [ɪ'læstɪk] *adj, n* élastique (*m*)
elastic band *n* (Brit) élastique *m*
elasticity [ɪlæs'tɪsɪtɪ] *n* élasticité *f*
elated [ɪ'leɪtɪd] *adj* transporté(e) de joie
elation [ɪ'leɪʃən] *n* (grande) joie, allégresse *f*
elbow ['ɛlbəu] *n* coude *m* ▷ *vt*: to ~ one's way through the crowd se frayer un passage à travers la foule (en jouant des coudes)
elbow grease *n*: to use a bit of ~ mettre de l'huile de coude
elder ['ɛldə^r] *adj* aîné(e) ▷ *n* (*tree*) sureau *m*; one's ~s ses aînés
elderly ['ɛldəlɪ] *adj* âgé(e) ▷ *npl*: the ~ les personnes âgées
elder statesman (*irreg*) *n* vétéran *m* de la politique
eldest ['ɛldɪst] *adj, n*: the ~ (child) l'aîné(e) (des enfants)
elect [ɪ'lɛkt] *vt* élire; (*choose*): to ~ to do choisir de faire ▷ *adj*: the president ~ le président désigné
election [ɪ'lɛkʃən] *n* élection *f*; to hold an ~ procéder à une élection
election campaign *n* campagne électorale
electioneering [ɪlɛkʃə'nɪərɪŋ] *n* propagande électorale, manœuvres électorales
elector [ɪ'lɛktə^r] *n* électeur(-trice)
electoral [ɪ'lɛktərəl] *adj* électoral(e)
electoral college *n* collège électoral
electoral roll *n* (Brit) liste électorale
electorate [ɪ'lɛktərɪt] *n* électorat *m*
electric [ɪ'lɛktrɪk] *adj* électrique
electrical [ɪ'lɛktrɪkl] *adj* électrique

electrical engineer *n* ingénieur électricien
electrical failure *n* panne *f* d'électricité *or* de courant
electric blanket *n* couverture chauffante
electric chair *n* chaise *f* électrique
electric cooker *n* cuisinière *f* électrique
electric current *n* courant *m* électrique
electric fire *n* (Brit) radiateur *m* électrique
electrician [ɪlɛk'trɪʃən] *n* électricien *m*
electricity [ɪlɛk'trɪsɪtɪ] *n* électricité *f*; to switch on/off the ~ rétablir/couper le courant
electricity board *n* (Brit) ≈ agence régionale de l'E.D.F.
electric light *n* lumière *f* électrique
electric shock *n* choc *m* *or* décharge *f* électrique
electrify [ɪ'lɛktrɪfaɪ] *vt* (Rail) électrifier; (*audience*) électriser
electro... [ɪ'lɛktrəu] *prefix* électro...
electrocardiogram [ɪ'lɛktrə] *n* électrocardiogramme *m*
electro-convulsive therapy [ɪ'lɛktrə] *n* électrochocs *mpl*
electrocute [ɪ'lɛktrəkjuːt] *vt* électrocuter
electrode [ɪ'lɛktrəud] *n* électrode *f*
electroencephalogram [ɪ'lɛktrəu] *n* électroencéphalogramme *m*
electrolysis [ɪlɛk'trɔlɪsɪs] *n* électrolyse *f*
electromagnetic [ɪ'lɛktrəmæg'nɛtɪk] *adj* électromagnétique
electron [ɪ'lɛktrɔn] *n* électron *m*
electronic [ɪlɛk'trɔnɪk] *adj* électronique
electronic data processing *n* traitement *m* électronique des données
electronic mail *n* courrier *m* électronique
electronics [ɪlɛk'trɔnɪks] *n* électronique *f*
electron microscope *n* microscope *m* électronique
electroplated [ɪ'lɛktrə'pleɪtɪd] *adj* plaqué(e) *or* doré(e) *or* argenté(e) par galvanoplastie
electrotherapy [ɪ'lɛktrə'θɛrəpɪ] *n* électrothérapie *f*
elegance ['ɛlɪgəns] *n* élégance *f*
elegant ['ɛlɪgənt] *adj* élégant(e)
element ['ɛlɪmənt] *n* (*gen*) élément *m*; (*of heater, kettle etc*) résistance *f*
elementary [ɛlɪ'mɛntərɪ] *adj* élémentaire; (*school, education*) primaire
elementary school *n* (US) école *f* primaire; *voir article*

● ELEMENTARY SCHOOL

Aux États-Unis et au Canada, une *elementary school* (également appelée "grade school" ou "grammar school" aux États-Unis) est une école publique où les enfants passent les six à huit premières années de leur scolarité.

elephant ['ɛlɪfənt] *n* éléphant *m*
elevate ['ɛlɪveɪt] *vt* élever
elevated railroad ['ɛlɪveɪtɪd-] *n* (US) métro *m* aérien

elevation [ɛlɪ'veɪʃən] n élévation f; (height) altitude f
elevator ['ɛliveɪtər] n (in warehouse etc) élévateur m, monte-charge m inv; (US: lift) ascenseur m
eleven [ɪ'lɛvn] num onze
elevenses [ɪ'lɛvnzɪz] npl (Brit) ≈ pause-café f
eleventh [ɪ'lɛvnθ] num onzième; **at the ~ hour** (fig) à la dernière minute
elf (pl **elves**) [ɛlf, ɛlvz] n lutin m
elicit [ɪ'lɪsɪt] vt: **to ~ (from)** obtenir (de); tirer (de)
eligible ['ɛlɪdʒəbl] adj éligible; (for membership) admissible; **an ~ young man** un beau parti; **to be ~ for sth** remplir les conditions requises pour qch; **~ for a pension** ayant droit à la retraite
eliminate [ɪ'lɪmɪneɪt] vt éliminer
elimination [ɪlɪmɪ'neɪʃən] n élimination f; **by process of ~** par élimination
elitist [eɪ'liːtɪst] adj (pej) élitiste
Elizabethan [ɪlɪzə'biːθən] adj élisabéthain(e)
ellipse [ɪ'lɪps] n ellipse f
elliptical [ɪ'lɪptɪkl] adj elliptique
elm [ɛlm] n orme m
elocution [ɛlə'kjuːʃən] n élocution f
elongated ['iːlɔŋgeɪtɪd] adj étiré(e), allongé(e)
elope [ɪ'ləup] vi (lovers) s'enfuir (ensemble)
elopement [ɪ'ləupmənt] n fugue amoureuse
eloquence ['ɛləkwəns] n éloquence f
eloquent ['ɛləkwənt] adj éloquent(e)
else [ɛls] adv d'autre; **something ~** quelque chose d'autre, autre chose; **somewhere ~** ailleurs, autre part; **everywhere ~** partout ailleurs; **everyone ~** tous les autres; **nothing ~** rien d'autre; **is there anything ~ I can do?** est-ce que je peux faire quelque chose d'autre?; **where ~?** à quel autre endroit?; **little ~** pas grand-chose d'autre
elsewhere [ɛls'wɛər] adv ailleurs, autre part
ELT n abbr (Scol) = **English Language Teaching**
elucidate [ɪ'luːsɪdeɪt] vt élucider
elude [ɪ'luːd] vt échapper à; (question) éluder
elusive [ɪ'luːsɪv] adj insaisissable; (answer) évasif(-ive)
elves [ɛlvz] npl of **elf**
emaciated [ɪ'meɪsɪeɪtɪd] adj émacié(e), décharné(e)
email ['iːmeɪl] n abbr (= electronic mail) (e-)mail m, courriel m ▷ vt: **to ~ sb** envoyer un (e-)mail or un courriel à qn
email account n compte m (e-)mail
email address n adresse f (e-)mail or électronique
emanate ['ɛməneɪt] vi: **to ~ from** émaner de
emancipate [ɪ'mænsɪpeɪt] vt émanciper
emancipation [ɪmænsɪ'peɪʃən] n émancipation f
emasculate [ɪ'mæskjuleɪt] vt émasculer
embalm [ɪm'baːm] vt embaumer
embankment [ɪm'bæŋkmənt] n (of road, railway) remblai m, talus m; (of river) berge f, quai m; (dyke) digue f

embargo [ɪm'baːgəu] (pl **-es**) n (Comm, Naut) embargo m; (prohibition) interdiction f ▷ vt frapper d'embargo, mettre l'embargo sur; **to put an ~ on sth** mettre l'embargo sur qch
embark [ɪm'baːk] vi embarquer; **to ~ on** (s')embarquer à bord de or sur ▷ vt embarquer; **to ~ on** (journey etc) commencer, entreprendre; (fig) se lancer or s'embarquer dans
embarkation [ɛmbaː'keɪʃən] n embarquement m
embarkation card n carte f d'embarquement
embarrass [ɪm'bærəs] vt embarrasser, gêner
embarrassed [ɪm'bærəst] adj gêné(e); **to be ~** être gêné(e)
embarrassing [ɪm'bærəsɪŋ] adj gênant(e), embarrassant(e)
embarrassment [ɪm'bærəsmənt] n embarras m, gêne f; (embarrassing thing, person) source f d'embarras
embassy ['ɛmbəsɪ] n ambassade f; **the French E~** l'ambassade de France
embed [ɪm'bɛd] vt enfoncer; sceller
embellish [ɪm'bɛlɪʃ] vt embellir; enjoliver
embers ['ɛmbəz] npl braise f
embezzle [ɪm'bɛzl] vt détourner
embezzlement [ɪm'bɛzlmənt] n détournement m (de fonds)
embezzler [ɪm'bɛzlər] n escroc m
embitter [ɪm'bɪtər] vt aigrir; envenimer
emblem ['ɛmbləm] n emblème m
embodiment [ɪm'bɔdɪmənt] n personnification f, incarnation f
embody [ɪm'bɔdɪ] vt (features) réunir, comprendre; (ideas) formuler, exprimer
embolden [ɪm'bəuldn] vt enhardir
embolism ['ɛmbəlɪzəm] n embolie f
embossed [ɪm'bɔst] adj repoussé(e), gaufré(e); **~ with** où figure(nt) en relief
embrace [ɪm'breɪs] vt embrasser, étreindre; (include) embrasser, couvrir, comprendre ▷ vi s'embrasser, s'étreindre ▷ n étreinte f
embroider [ɪm'brɔɪdər] vt broder; (fig: story) enjoliver
embroidery [ɪm'brɔɪdərɪ] n broderie f
embroil [ɪm'brɔɪl] vt: **to become ~ed (in sth)** se retrouver mêlé(e) (à qch), se laisser entraîner (dans qch)
embryo ['ɛmbrɪəu] n (also fig) embryon m
emcee [ɛm'siː] n maître m de cérémonie
emend [ɪ'mɛnd] vt (text) corriger
emerald ['ɛmərəld] n émeraude f
emerge [ɪ'məːdʒ] vi apparaître; (from room, car) surgir; (from sleep, imprisonment) sortir; **it ~s that** (Brit) il ressort que
emergence [ɪ'məːdʒəns] n apparition f; (of nation) naissance f
emergency [ɪ'məːdʒənsɪ] n (crisis) cas m d'urgence; (Med) urgence f; **in an ~** en cas d'urgence; **state of ~** état m d'urgence
emergency brake (US) n frein m à main
emergency exit n sortie f de secours
emergency landing n atterrissage forcé

emergency lane n (US Aut) accotement stabilisé

emergency road service n (US) service m de dépannage

emergency room n (US: Med) urgences fpl

emergency services npl: **the ~** (fire, police, ambulance) les services mpl d'urgence

emergency stop n (Brit Aut) arrêt m d'urgence

emergent [ɪ'məːdʒənt] adj: **~ nation** pays m en voie de développement

emery board ['ɛməri-] n lime f à ongles (en carton émerisé)

emery paper ['ɛməri-] n papier m (d')émeri

emetic [ɪ'mɛtɪk] n vomitif m, émétique m

emigrant ['ɛmɪgrənt] n émigrant(e)

emigrate ['ɛmɪgreɪt] vi émigrer

emigration [ɛmɪ'greɪʃən] n émigration f

émigré ['ɛmɪgreɪ] n émigré(e)

eminence ['ɛmɪnəns] n éminence f

eminent ['ɛmɪnənt] adj éminent(e)

eminently ['ɛmɪnəntlɪ] adv éminemment, admirablement

emissions [ɪ'mɪʃənz] npl émissions fpl

emit [ɪ'mɪt] vt émettre

emolument [ɪ'mɔljumənt] n (often pl: formal) émoluments mpl; (fee) honoraires mpl; (salary) traitement m

emoticon [ɪ'məʊtɪkɔn] n (Comput) émoticone m

emotion [ɪ'məʊʃən] n sentiment m; (as opposed to reason) émotion f, sentiments

emotional [ɪ'məʊʃənl] adj (person) émotif(-ive), très sensible; (needs) affectif(-ive); (scene) émouvant(e); (tone, speech) qui fait appel aux sentiments

emotionally [ɪ'məʊʃnəlɪ] adv (behave) émotivement; (be involved) affectivement; (speak) avec émotion; **~ disturbed** qui souffre de troubles de l'affectivité

emotive [ɪ'məʊtɪv] adj émotif(-ive); **~ power** capacité f d'émouvoir or de toucher

empathy ['ɛmpəθɪ] n communion f d'idées or de sentiments, empathie f; **to feel ~ with sb** se mettre à la place de qn

emperor ['ɛmpərər] n empereur m

emphasis (pl **-ases**) ['ɛmfəsɪs, -siːz] n accent m; **to lay** or **place ~ on sth** (fig) mettre l'accent sur, insister sur; **the ~ is on reading** la lecture tient une place primordiale, on accorde une importance particulière à la lecture

emphasize ['ɛmfəsaɪz] vt (syllable, word, point) appuyer or insister sur; (feature) souligner, accentuer

emphatic [ɛm'fætɪk] adj (strong) énergique, vigoureux(-euse); (unambiguous, clear) catégorique

emphatically [ɛm'fætɪklɪ] adv avec vigueur or énergie; catégoriquement

empire ['ɛmpaɪər] n empire m

empirical [ɛm'pɪrɪkl] adj empirique

employ [ɪm'plɔɪ] vt employer; **he's ~ed in a bank** il est employé de banque, il travaille dans une banque

employee [ɪmplɔɪ'iː] n employé(e)

employer [ɪm'plɔɪər] n employeur(-euse)

employment [ɪm'plɔɪmənt] n emploi m; **to find ~** trouver un emploi or du travail; **without ~** au chômage, sans emploi; **place of ~** lieu m de travail

employment agency n agence f or bureau m de placement

employment exchange n (Brit) agence f pour l'emploi

empower [ɪm'paʊər] vt: **to ~ sb to do** autoriser or habiliter qn à faire

empress ['ɛmprɪs] n impératrice f

emptiness ['ɛmptɪnɪs] n vide m; (of area) aspect m désertique

empty ['ɛmptɪ] adj vide; (street, area) désert(e); (threat, promise) en l'air, vain(e) ▷ n (bottle) bouteille f vide ▷ vt vider ▷ vi se vider; (liquid) s'écouler; **on an ~ stomach** à jeun; **to ~ into** (river) se jeter dans, se déverser dans

empty-handed ['ɛmptɪ'hændɪd] adj les mains vides

empty-headed ['ɛmptɪ'hɛdɪd] adj écervelé(e), qui n'a rien dans la tête

EMS n abbr (= European Monetary System) SME m

EMT n abbr = **emergency medical technician**

EMU n abbr (= European Monetary Union) UME f

emulate ['ɛmjuleɪt] vt rivaliser avec, imiter

emulsion [ɪ'mʌlʃən] n émulsion f; (also: **emulsion paint**) peinture mate

enable [ɪ'neɪbl] vt: **to ~ sb to do** permettre à qn de faire, donner à qn la possibilité de faire

enact [ɪ'nækt] vt (Law) promulguer; (play, scene) jouer, représenter

enamel [ɪ'næməl] n émail m; (also: **enamel paint**) (peinture f) laque f

enamoured [ɪ'næməd] adj: **~ of** amoureux(-euse) de; (idea) enchanté(e) par

encampment [ɪn'kæmpmənt] n campement m

encased [ɪn'keɪst] adj: **~ in** enfermé(e) dans, recouvert(e) de

enchant [ɪn'tʃɑːnt] vt enchanter

enchanting [ɪn'tʃɑːntɪŋ] adj ravissant(e), enchanteur(-eresse)

encircle [ɪn'səːkl] vt entourer, encercler

encl. abbr (on letters etc: = enclosed) ci-joint(e); (= enclosure) PJ f

enclose [ɪn'kləʊz] vt (land) clôturer; (space, object) entourer; (letter etc): **to ~ (with)** joindre (à); **please find ~d** veuillez trouver ci-joint

enclosure [ɪn'kləʊʒər] n enceinte f; (in letter etc) annexe f

encoder [ɪn'kəʊdər] n (Comput) encodeur m

encompass [ɪn'kʌmpəs] vt encercler, entourer; (include) contenir, inclure

encore [ɔŋ'kɔːr] excl, n bis (m)

encounter [ɪn'kauntər] n rencontre f ▷ vt rencontrer

encourage [ɪn'kʌrɪdʒ] vt encourager; (industry, growth) favoriser; **to ~ sb to do sth** encourager qn à faire qch

encouragement [ɪn'kʌrɪdʒmənt] n encouragement m

encouraging [ɪnˈkʌrɪdʒɪŋ] *adj* encourageant(e)
encroach [ɪnˈkrəʊtʃ] *vi*: **to ~ (up)on** empiéter sur
encrusted [ɪnˈkrʌstɪd] *adj*: ~ **(with)** incrusté(e) (de)
encyclopaedia, encyclopedia [ɛnsaɪkləʊˈpiːdɪə] *n* encyclopédie *f*
end [ɛnd] *n* fin *f*; (*of table, street, rope etc*) bout *m*, extrémité *f*; (*of pointed object*) pointe *f*; (*of town*) bout; (*Sport*) côté *m* ▷ *vt* terminer; (*also*: **bring to an end, put an end to**) mettre fin à ▷ *vi* se terminer, finir; **from ~ to ~** d'un bout à l'autre; **to come to an ~** prendre fin; **to be at an ~** être fini(e), être terminé(e); **in the ~** finalement; **on ~** (*object*) debout, dressé(e); **to stand on ~** (*hair*) se dresser sur la tête; **for 5 hours on ~** durant 5 heures d'affilée *or* de suite; **for hours on ~** pendant des heures (et des heures); **at the ~ of the day** (*Brit fig*) en fin de compte; **to this ~, with this ~ in view** à cette fin, dans ce but
▶ **end up** *vi*: **to ~ up in** (*condition*) finir *or* se terminer par; (*place*) finir *or* aboutir à
endanger [ɪnˈdeɪndʒər] *vt* mettre en danger; **an ~ed species** une espèce en voie de disparition
endear [ɪnˈdɪər] *vt*: **to ~ o.s. to sb** se faire aimer de qn
endearing [ɪnˈdɪərɪŋ] *adj* attachant(e)
endearment [ɪnˈdɪəmənt] *n*: **to whisper ~s** murmurer des mots *or* choses tendres; **term of ~** terme *m* d'affection
endeavour, (*US*) **endeavor** [ɪnˈdɛvər] *n* effort *m*; (*attempt*) tentative *f* ▷ *vt*: **to ~ to do** tenter *or* s'efforcer de faire
endemic [ɛnˈdɛmɪk] *adj* endémique
ending [ˈɛndɪŋ] *n* dénouement *m*, conclusion *f*; (*Ling*) terminaison *f*
endive [ˈɛndaɪv] *n* (*curly*) chicorée *f*; (*smooth, flat*) endive *f*
endless [ˈɛndlɪs] *adj* sans fin, interminable; (*patience, resources*) inépuisable, sans limites; (*possibilities*) illimité(e)
endorse [ɪnˈdɔːs] *vt* (*cheque*) endosser; (*approve*) appuyer, approuver, sanctionner
endorsee [ɪndɔːˈsiː] *n* bénéficiaire *m/f*, endossataire *m/f*
endorsement [ɪnˈdɔːsmənt] *n* (*approval*) appui *m*, aval *m*; (*signature*) endossement *m*; (*Brit: on driving licence*) contravention *f* (*portée au permis de conduire*)
endorser [ɪnˈdɔːsər] *n* avaliste *m*, endosseur *m*
endow [ɪnˈdaʊ] *vt* (*provide with money*) faire une donation à, doter; (*equip*): **to ~ with** gratifier de, doter de
endowment [ɪnˈdaʊmənt] *n* dotation *f*
endowment mortgage *n* hypothèque liée à une assurance-vie
endowment policy *n* assurance *f* à capital différé
end product *n* (*Industry*) produit fini; (*fig*) résultat *m*, aboutissement *m*
end result *n* résultat final
endurable [ɪnˈdjuərəbl] *adj* supportable

endurance [ɪnˈdjuərəns] *n* endurance *f*
endurance test *n* test *m* d'endurance
endure [ɪnˈdjuər] *vt* (*bear*) supporter, endurer ▷ *vi* (*last*) durer
end user *n* (*Comput*) utilisateur final
enema [ˈɛnɪmə] *n* (*Med*) lavement *m*
enemy [ˈɛnəmɪ] *adj, n* ennemi(e); **to make an ~ of sb** se faire un(e) ennemi(e) de qn, se mettre qn à dos
energetic [ɛnəˈdʒɛtɪk] *adj* énergique; (*activity*) très actif(-ive), qui fait se dépenser (physiquement)
energy [ˈɛnədʒɪ] *n* énergie *f*; **Department of E~** ministère *m* de l'Énergie
energy crisis *n* crise *f* de l'énergie
energy-saving [ˈɛnədʒɪˈseɪvɪŋ] *adj* (*policy*) d'économie d'énergie; (*device*) qui permet de réaliser des économies d'énergie
enervating [ˈɛnəveɪtɪŋ] *adj* débilitant(e), affaiblissant(e)
enforce [ɪnˈfɔːs] *vt* (*law*) appliquer, faire respecter
enforced [ɪnˈfɔːst] *adj* forcé(e)
enfranchise [ɪnˈfræntʃaɪz] *vt* accorder le droit de vote à; (*set free*) affranchir
engage [ɪnˈgeɪdʒ] *vt* engager; (*Mil*) engager le combat avec; (*lawyer*) prendre ▷ *vi* (*Tech*) s'enclencher, s'engrener; **to ~ in** se lancer dans; **to ~ sb in conversation** engager la conversation avec qn
engaged [ɪnˈgeɪdʒd] *adj* (*Brit: busy, in use*) occupé(e); (*betrothed*) fiancé(e); **to get ~** se fiancer; **the line's ~** la ligne est occupée; **he is ~ in research/a survey** il fait de la recherche/une enquête
engaged tone *n* (*Brit Tel*) tonalité *f* occupé *inv*
engagement [ɪnˈgeɪdʒmənt] *n* (*undertaking*) obligation *f*, engagement *m*; (*appointment*) rendez-vous *m*; (*to marry*) fiançailles *fpl*; (*Mil*) combat *m*; **I have a previous ~** j'ai déjà un rendez-vous, je suis déjà pris(e)
engagement ring *n* bague *f* de fiançailles
engaging [ɪnˈgeɪdʒɪŋ] *adj* engageant(e), attirant(e)
engender [ɪnˈdʒɛndər] *vt* produire, causer
engine [ˈɛndʒɪn] *n* (*Aut*) moteur *m*; (*Rail*) locomotive *f*
engine driver *n* (*Brit: of train*) mécanicien *m*
engineer [ɛndʒɪˈnɪər] *n* ingénieur *m*; (*Brit: repairer*) dépanneur *m*; (*Navy, US Rail*) mécanicien *m*; **civil/mechanical ~** ingénieur des Travaux Publics *or* des Ponts et Chaussées/mécanicien
engineering [ɛndʒɪˈnɪərɪŋ] *n* engineering *m*, ingénierie *f*; (*of bridges, ships*) génie *m*; (*of machine*) mécanique *f* ▷ *cpd*: ~ **works** *or* **factory** atelier *m* de construction mécanique
engine failure *n* panne *f*
engine trouble *n* ennuis *mpl* mécaniques
England [ˈɪŋglənd] *n* Angleterre *f*
English [ˈɪŋglɪʃ] *adj* anglais(e) ▷ *n* (*Ling*) anglais *m*; **the ~** (*npl*) les Anglais; **an ~ speaker** un

e

anglophone
English Channel *n*: **the ~** la Manche
Englishman ['ɪŋglɪʃmən] (*irreg*) *n* Anglais *m*
English-speaking ['ɪŋglɪʃ'spiːkɪŋ] *adj* qui parle anglais; anglophone
Englishwoman ['ɪŋglɪʃwumən] (*irreg*) *n* Anglaise *f*
engrave [ɪn'greɪv] *vt* graver
engraving [ɪn'greɪvɪŋ] *n* gravure *f*
engrossed [ɪn'grəust] *adj*: **~ in** absorbé(e) par, plongé(e) dans
engulf [ɪn'gʌlf] *vt* engloutir
enhance [ɪn'hɑːns] *vt* rehausser, mettre en valeur; (*position*) améliorer; (*reputation*) accroître
enigma [ɪ'nɪgmə] *n* énigme *f*
enigmatic [ɛnɪg'mætɪk] *adj* énigmatique
enjoy [ɪn'dʒɔɪ] *vt* aimer, prendre plaisir à; (*have benefit of: health, fortune*) jouir de; (: *success*) connaître; **to ~ o.s.** s'amuser
enjoyable [ɪn'dʒɔɪəbl] *adj* agréable
enjoyment [ɪn'dʒɔɪmənt] *n* plaisir *m*
enlarge [ɪn'lɑːdʒ] *vt* accroître; (*Phot*) agrandir ▷ *vi*: **to ~ on** (*subject*) s'étendre sur
enlarged [ɪn'lɑːdʒd] *adj* (*edition*) augmenté(e); (*Med: organ, gland*) anormalement gros(se), hypertrophié(e)
enlargement [ɪn'lɑːdʒmənt] *n* (*Phot*) agrandissement *m*
enlighten [ɪn'laɪtn] *vt* éclairer
enlightened [ɪn'laɪtnd] *adj* éclairé(e)
enlightening [ɪn'laɪtnɪŋ] *adj* instructif(-ive), révélateur(-trice)
enlightenment [ɪn'laɪtnmənt] *n* édification *f*; éclaircissements *mpl*; (*History*): **the E~** ≈ le Siècle des lumières
enlist [ɪn'lɪst] *vt* recruter; (*support*) s'assurer ▷ *vi* s'engager; **~ed man** (*US Mil*) simple soldat *m*
enliven [ɪn'laɪvn] *vt* animer, égayer
enmity ['ɛnmɪtɪ] *n* inimitié *f*
ennoble [ɪ'nəubl] *vt* (*with title*) anoblir
enormity [ɪ'nɔːmɪtɪ] *n* énormité *f*
enormous [ɪ'nɔːməs] *adj* énorme
enormously [ɪ'nɔːməslɪ] *adv* (*increase*) dans des proportions énormes; (*rich*) extrêmement
enough [ɪ'nʌf] *adj*: **~ time/books** assez or suffisamment de temps/livres ▷ *adv*: **big ~** assez or suffisamment grand ▷ *pron*: **have you got ~?** (en) avez-vous assez?; **will five be ~?** est-ce que cinq suffiront?, est-ce qu'il y en aura assez avec cinq?; **~ to eat** assez à manger; **that's ~!** ça suffit!, assez!; **that's ~, thanks** cela suffit or c'est assez, merci; **I've had ~** je n'en peux plus!; **I've had ~ of him** j'en ai assez de lui; **he has not worked ~** il n'a pas assez or suffisamment travaillé, il n'a pas travaillé assez or suffisamment; **~! assez!**, ça suffit!; **it's hot ~ (as it is)!** il fait assez chaud comme ça!; **he was kind ~ to lend me the money** il a eu la gentillesse de me prêter l'argent; **... which, funnily** or **oddly ~ ...** qui, chose curieuse, ...
enquire [ɪn'kwaɪə'] *vt, vi* = **inquire**
enquiry [ɪn'kwaɪərɪ] *n* = **inquiry**

enrage [ɪn'reɪdʒ] *vt* mettre en fureur or en rage, rendre furieux(-euse)
enrich [ɪn'rɪtʃ] *vt* enrichir
enrol, (*US*) **enroll** [ɪn'rəul] *vt* inscrire ▷ *vi* s'inscrire
enrolment, (*US*) **enrollment** [ɪn'rəulmənt] *n* inscription *f*
en route [ɔn'ruːt] *adv* en route, en chemin; **~ for** or **to** en route vers, à destination de
ensconced [ɪn'skɔnst] *adj*: **~ in** bien calé(e) dans
enshrine [ɪn'ʃraɪn] *vt* (*fig*) préserver
ensign *n* (*Naut*) ['ɛnsən] enseigne *f*, pavillon *m*; (*Mil*) ['ɛnsaɪn] porte-étendard *m*
enslave [ɪn'sleɪv] *vt* asservir
ensue [ɪn'sjuː] *vi* s'ensuivre, résulter
en suite ['ɔnswiːt] *adj*: **with ~ bathroom** avec salle de bains en attenante
ensure [ɪn'ʃuə'] *vt* assurer, garantir; **to ~ that** s'assurer que
ENT *n abbr* (= *Ear, Nose and Throat*) ORL *f*
entail [ɪn'teɪl] *vt* entraîner, nécessiter
entangle [ɪn'tæŋgl] *vt* emmêler, embrouiller; **to become ~d in sth** (*fig*) se laisser entraîner or empêtrer dans qch
enter ['ɛntə'] *vt* (*room*) entrer dans, pénétrer dans; (*club, army*) entrer à; (*profession*) embrasser; (*competition*) s'inscrire à or pour; (*sb for a competition*) (faire) inscrire; (*write down*) inscrire, noter; (*Comput*) entrer, introduire ▷ *vi* entrer
  ▶ **enter for** *vt fus* s'inscrire à, se présenter pour or à
  ▶ **enter into** *vt fus* (*explanation*) se lancer dans; (*negotiations*) entamer; (*debate*) prendre part à; (*agreement*) conclure
  ▶ **enter on** *vt fus* commencer
  ▶ **enter up** *vt* inscrire
  ▶ **enter upon** *vt fus* = **enter on**
enteritis [ɛntə'raɪtɪs] *n* entérite *f*
enterprise ['ɛntəpraɪz] *n* (*company, undertaking*) entreprise *f*; (*initiative*) (esprit *m* d')initiative *f*; **free ~** libre entreprise; **private ~** entreprise privée
enterprising ['ɛntəpraɪzɪŋ] *adj* entreprenant(e), dynamique; (*scheme*) audacieux(-euse)
entertain [ɛntə'teɪn] *vt* amuser, distraire; (*invite*) recevoir (à dîner); (*idea, plan*) envisager
entertainer [ɛntə'teɪnə'] *n* artiste *m/f* de variétés
entertaining [ɛntə'teɪnɪŋ] *adj* amusant(e), distrayant(e) ▷ *n*: **to do a lot of ~** beaucoup recevoir
entertainment [ɛntə'teɪnmənt] *n* (*amusement*) distraction *f*, divertissement *m*, amusement *m*; (*show*) spectacle *m*
entertainment allowance *n* frais *mpl* de représentation
enthralled [ɪn'θrɔːld] *adj* captivé(e)
enthralling [ɪn'θrɔːlɪŋ] *adj* captivant(e), enchanteur(-eresse)
enthuse [ɪn'θuːz] *vi*: **to ~ about** or **over** parler avec enthousiasme de
enthusiasm [ɪn'θuːzɪæzəm] *n* enthousiasme *m*

enthusiast [ɪn'θu:zɪæst] n enthousiaste m/f; **a jazz** etc ~ un fervent or passionné du jazz etc

enthusiastic [ɪnθu:zɪ'æstɪk] adj enthousiaste; **to be ~ about** être enthousiasmé(e) par

entice [ɪn'taɪs] vt attirer, séduire

enticing [ɪn'taɪsɪŋ] adj (person, offer) séduisant(e); (food) alléchant(e)

entire [ɪn'taɪər] adj (tout) entier(-ère)

entirely [ɪn'taɪəlɪ] adv entièrement, complètement

entirety [ɪn'taɪərətɪ] n: **in its ~** dans sa totalité

entitle [ɪn'taɪtl] vt (allow): **to ~ sb to do** donner (le) droit à qn de faire; **to ~ sb to sth** donner droit à qch à qn

entitled [ɪn'taɪtld] adj (book) intitulé(e); **to be ~ to do** avoir le droit de faire

entity ['ɛntɪtɪ] n entité f

entrails ['ɛntreɪlz] npl entrailles fpl

entrance n ['ɛntrns] entrée f ⊳ vt [ɪn'trɑ:ns] enchanter, ravir; **where's the ~?** où est l'entrée?; **to gain ~ to** (university etc) être admis à

entrance examination n examen m d'entrée or d'admission

entrance fee n (to museum etc) prix m d'entrée; (to join club etc) droit m d'inscription

entrance ramp n (US Aut) bretelle f d'accès

entrancing [ɪn'trɑ:nsɪŋ] adj enchanteur(-eresse), ravissant(e)

entrant ['ɛntrnt] n (in race etc) participant(e), concurrent(e); (Brit: in exam) candidat(e)

entreat [ɛn'tri:t] vt supplier

entreaty [ɛn'tri:tɪ] n supplication f, prière f

entrée ['ɔntreɪ] n (Culin) entrée f

entrenched [ɛn'trɛntʃt] adj retranché(e)

entrepreneur ['ɔntrəprə'nə:ʳ] n entrepreneur m

entrepreneurial ['ɔntrəprə'nə:rɪəl] adj animé(e) d'un esprit d'entreprise

entrust [ɪn'trʌst] vt: **to ~ sth to** confier qch à

entry ['ɛntrɪ] n entrée f; (in register, diary) inscription f; (in ledger) écriture f; **"no ~"** "défense d'entrer", "entrée interdite"; (Aut) "sens interdit"; **single/double ~ book-keeping** comptabilité f en partie simple/double

entry form n feuille f d'inscription

entry phone n (Brit) interphone m (à l'entrée d'un immeuble)

entwine [ɪn'twaɪn] vt entrelacer

E-number ['i:nʌmbəʳ] n additif m (alimentaire)

enumerate [ɪ'nju:məreɪt] vt énumérer

enunciate [ɪ'nʌnsɪeɪt] vt énoncer; prononcer

envelop [ɪn'vɛləp] vt envelopper

envelope ['ɛnvələup] n enveloppe f

enviable ['ɛnvɪəbl] adj enviable

envious ['ɛnvɪəs] adj envieux(-euse)

environment [ɪn'vaɪərnmənt] n (social, moral) milieu m; (natural world): **the ~** l'environnement m; **Department of the E~** (Brit) ministère de l'Équipement et de l'Aménagement du territoire

environmental [ɪnvaɪərn'mɛntl] adj (of surroundings) du milieu; (issue, disaster) écologique; **~ studies** (in school etc) écologie f

environmentalist [ɪnvaɪərn'mɛntlɪst] n écologiste m/f

environmentally [ɪnvaɪərn'mɛntlɪ] adv: **~ sound/friendly** qui ne nuit pas à l'environnement

Environmental Protection Agency n (US) ≈ ministère m de l'Environnement

envisage [ɪn'vɪzɪdʒ] vt (imagine) envisager; (foresee) prévoir

envision [ɪn'vɪʒən] vt envisager, concevoir

envoy ['ɛnvɔɪ] n envoyé(e); (diplomat) ministre m plénipotentiaire

envy ['ɛnvɪ] n envie f ⊳ vt envier; **to ~ sb sth** envier qch à qn

enzyme ['ɛnzaɪm] n enzyme m

EPA n abbr (US) = **Environmental Protection Agency**

ephemeral [ɪ'fɛmərl] adj éphémère

epic ['ɛpɪk] n épopée f ⊳ adj épique

epicentre, (US) **epicenter** ['ɛpɪsɛntəʳ] n épicentre m

epidemic [ɛpɪ'dɛmɪk] n épidémie f

epilepsy ['ɛpɪlɛpsɪ] n épilepsie f

epileptic [ɛpɪ'lɛptɪk] adj, n épileptique m/f

epileptic fit [ɛpɪ'lɛptɪk-] n crise f d'épilepsie

epilogue ['ɛpɪlɔg] n épilogue m

episcopal [ɪ'pɪskəpl] adj épiscopal(e)

episode ['ɛpɪsəud] n épisode m

epistle [ɪ'pɪsl] n épître f

epitaph ['ɛpɪtɑ:f] n épitaphe f

epithet ['ɛpɪθɛt] n épithète f

epitome [ɪ'pɪtəmɪ] n (fig) quintessence f, type m

epitomize [ɪ'pɪtəmaɪz] vt (fig) illustrer, incarner

epoch ['i:pɔk] n époque f, ère f

epoch-making ['i:pɔkmeɪkɪŋ] adj qui fait époque

eponymous [ɪ'pɔnɪməs] adj de ce or du même nom, éponyme

equable ['ɛkwəbl] adj égal(e), de tempérament égal

equal ['i:kwl] adj égal(e) ⊳ n égal(e) ⊳ vt égaler; **~ to** (task) à la hauteur de; **~ to doing** de taille à or capable de faire

equality [i:'kwɔlɪtɪ] n égalité f

equalize ['i:kwəlaɪz] vt, vi (Sport) égaliser

equalizer ['i:kwəlaɪzəʳ] n but égalisateur

equally ['i:kwəlɪ] adv également; (share) en parts égales; (treat) de la même façon; (pay) autant; (just as) tout aussi; **they are ~ clever** ils sont tout aussi intelligents

Equal Opportunities Commission, (US) **Equal Employment Opportunity Commission** n commission pour la non discrimination dans l'emploi

equal sign, equals sign n signe m d'égalité

equanimity [ɛkwə'nɪmɪtɪ] n égalité f d'humeur

equate [ɪ'kweɪt] vt: **to ~ sth with** comparer qch à; assimiler qch à; **to ~ sth to** mettre qch en équation avec; égaler qch à

equation [ɪ'kweɪʃən] n (Math) équation f

equator [ɪ'kweɪtəʳ] n équateur m

Equatorial Guinea [ɛkwə'tɔ:rɪəl 'gɪnɪ] n Guinée équatoriale

equestrian [ɪ'kwɛstrɪən] adj équestre ⊳ n

écuyer(-ère), cavalier(-ère)

equilibrium [iːkwɪˈlɪbrɪəm] *n* équilibre *m*

equinox [ˈiːkwɪnɒks] *n* équinoxe *m*

equip [ɪˈkwɪp] *vt* équiper; **to ~ sb/sth with** équiper *or* munir qn/qch de; **he is well ~ped for the job** il a les compétences *or* les qualités requises pour ce travail

equipment [ɪˈkwɪpmənt] *n* équipement *m*; (*electrical etc*) appareillage *m*, installation *f*

equitable [ˈɛkwɪtəbl] *adj* équitable

equities [ˈɛkwɪtɪz] *npl* (*Brit Comm*) actions cotées en Bourse

equity [ˈɛkwɪtɪ] *n* équité *f*

equity capital *n* capitaux *mpl* propres

equivalent [ɪˈkwɪvəlnt] *adj* équivalent(e) ▷ *n* équivalent *m*; **to be ~ to** équivaloir à, être équivalent(e) à

equivocal [ɪˈkwɪvəkl] *adj* équivoque; (*open to suspicion*) douteux(-euse)

equivocate [ɪˈkwɪvəkeɪt] *vi* user de faux-fuyants; éviter de répondre

equivocation [ɪkwɪvəˈkeɪʃən] *n* équivoque *f*

ER *abbr* (*Brit*: = *Elizabeth Regina*) la reine Élisabeth; (*US*: *Med*: = *emergency room*) urgences *fpl*

ERA *n abbr* (*US Pol*: = *Equal Rights Amendment*) amendement sur l'égalité des droits des femmes

era [ˈɪərə] *n* ère *f*, époque *f*

eradicate [ɪˈrædɪkeɪt] *vt* éliminer

erase [ɪˈreɪz] *vt* effacer

eraser [ɪˈreɪzər] *n* gomme *f*

erect [ɪˈrɛkt] *adj* droit(e) ▷ *vt* construire; (*monument*) ériger, élever; (*tent etc*) dresser

erection [ɪˈrɛkʃən] *n* (*Physiol*) érection *f*; (*of building*) construction *f*; (*of machinery etc*) installation *f*

ergonomics [əːgəˈnɒmɪks] *n* ergonomie *f*

ERISA *n abbr* (*US*: = *Employee Retirement Income Security Act*) loi sur les pensions de retraite

Eritrea [ɛrɪˈtreɪə] *n* Érythrée *f*

ERM *n abbr* (= *Exchange Rate Mechanism*) mécanisme *m* des taux de change

ermine [ˈəːmɪn] *n* hermine *f*

ERNIE [ˈəːnɪ] *n abbr* (*Brit*: = *Electronic Random Number Indicator Equipment*) ordinateur servant au tirage des bons à lots gagnants

erode [ɪˈrəud] *vt* éroder; (*metal*) ronger

erogenous zone [ɪˈrɒdʒənəs-] *n* zone *f* érogène

erosion [ɪˈrəuʒən] *n* érosion *f*

erotic [ɪˈrɒtɪk] *adj* érotique

eroticism [ɪˈrɒtɪsɪzəm] *n* érotisme *m*

err [əːr] *vi* se tromper; (*Rel*) pécher

errand [ˈɛrnd] *n* course *f*, commission *f*; **to run ~s** faire des courses; **~ of mercy** mission *f* de charité, acte *m* charitable

errand boy *n* garçon *m* de courses

erratic [ɪˈrætɪk] *adj* irrégulier(-ière), inconstant(e)

erroneous [ɪˈrəunɪəs] *adj* erroné(e)

error [ˈɛrər] *n* erreur *f*; **typing/spelling ~** faute *f* de frappe/d'orthographe; **in ~** par erreur, par méprise; **~s and omissions excepted** sauf erreur ou omission

error message *n* (*Comput*) message *m* d'erreur

erstwhile [ˈəːstwaɪl] *adj* précédent(e), d'autrefois

erudite [ˈɛrjudaɪt] *adj* savant(e)

erupt [ɪˈrʌpt] *vi* entrer en éruption; (*fig*) éclater, exploser

eruption [ɪˈrʌpʃən] *n* éruption *f*; (*of anger, violence*) explosion *f*

ESA *n abbr* (= *European Space Agency*) ASE *f* (= *Agence spatiale européenne*)

escalate [ˈɛskəleɪt] *vi* s'intensifier; (*costs*) monter en flèche

escalation [ɛskəˈleɪʃən] *n* escalade *f*

escalation clause *n* clause *f* d'indexation

escalator [ˈɛskəleɪtər] *n* escalier roulant

escapade [ɛskəˈpeɪd] *n* fredaine *f*; équipée *f*

escape [ɪˈskeɪp] *n* évasion *f*, fuite *f*; (*of gas etc*) fuite; (*Tech*) échappement *m* ▷ *vi* s'échapper, fuir; (*from jail*) s'évader; (*fig*) s'en tirer, en réchapper; (*leak*) fuir; s'échapper ▷ *vt* échapper à; **to ~ from** (*person*) échapper à; (*place*) s'échapper de; (*fig*) fuir; **to ~ to** (*another place*) fuir à, s'enfuir à; **to ~ to safety** se réfugier dans *or* gagner un endroit sûr; **to ~ notice** passer inaperçu(e); **his name ~s me** son nom m'échappe

escape artist *n* virtuose *m/f* de l'évasion

escape clause *n* clause *f* dérogatoire

escapee [ɪskerˈpiː] *n* évadé(e)

escape key *n* (*Comput*) touche *f* d'échappement

escape route *n* (*from fire*) issue *f* de secours; (*of prisoners etc*) voie empruntée pour s'échapper

escapism [ɪˈskeɪpɪzəm] *n* évasion *f* (*fig*)

escapist [ɪˈskeɪpɪst] *adj* (*literature*) d'évasion ▷ *n* personne *f* qui se réfugie hors de la réalité

escapologist [ɛskəˈpɔlədʒɪst] *n* (*Brit*) = **escape artist**

escarpment [ɪsˈkɑːpmənt] *n* escarpement *m*

eschew [ɪsˈtʃuː] *vt* éviter

escort *vt* [ɪˈskɔːt] escorter ▷ *n* [ˈɛskɔːt] (*Mil*) escorte *f*; (*to dance etc*): **her ~** son compagnon *or* cavalier; **his ~** sa compagne

escort agency *n* bureau *m* d'hôtesses

Eskimo [ˈɛskɪməu] *adj* esquimau(de), eskimo ▷ *n* Esquimau(de); (*Ling*) esquimau *m*

ESL *n abbr* (*Scol*) = **English as a Second Language**

esophagus [iːˈsɔfəgəs] *n* (*US*) = **oesophagus**

esoteric [ɛsəˈtɛrɪk] *adj* ésotérique

ESP *n abbr* = **extrasensory perception**; (*Scol*) = **English for Special Purposes**

esp. *abbr* = **especially**

especially [ɪˈspɛʃlɪ] *adv* (*particularly*) particulièrement; (*above all*) surtout

espionage [ˈɛspɪənɑːʒ] *n* espionnage *m*

esplanade [ɛspləˈneɪd] *n* esplanade *f*

espouse [ɪˈspauz] *vt* épouser, embrasser

Esquire [ɪˈskwaɪər] *n* (*Brit*: *abbr* **Esq.**): **J. Brown, ~** Monsieur J. Brown

essay [ˈɛseɪ] *n* (*Scol*) dissertation *f*; (*Literature*) essai *m*; (*attempt*) tentative *f*

essence [ˈɛsns] *n* essence *f*; (*Culin*) extrait *m*; **in ~** en substance; **speed is of the ~** l'essentiel,

c'est la rapidité
essential [ɪ'sɛnʃl] *adj* essentiel(le); (*basic*)
fondamental(e); **essentials** *npl* éléments
essentiels; **it is ~ that** il est essentiel *or*
primordial que
essentially [ɪ'sɛnʃlɪ] *adv* essentiellement
EST *abbr* (*US= Eastern Standard Time*) heure d'hiver de
New York
est. *abbr* = **established, estimate(d)**
establish [ɪ'stæblɪʃ] *vt* établir; (*business*) fonder,
créer; (*one's power etc*) asseoir, affermir
established [ɪ'stæblɪʃt] *adj* bien établi(e)
establishment [ɪ'stæblɪʃmənt] *n* établissement
m; (*founding*) création *f*; (*institution*)
établissement; **the E~** les pouvoirs établis;
l'ordre établi
estate [ɪ'steɪt] *n* (*land*) domaine *m*, propriété *f*;
(*Law*) biens *mpl*, succession *f*; (*Brit: also:* **housing
estate**) lotissement *m*
estate agency *n* (*Brit*) agence immobilière
estate agent *n* (*Brit*) agent immobilier
estate car *n* (*Brit*) break *m*
esteem [ɪ'sti:m] *n* estime *f* ▷ *vt* estimer;
apprécier; **to hold sb in high ~** tenir qn en
haute estime
esthetic [ɪs'θɛtɪk] *adj* (*US*) = **aesthetic**
estimate [*n* 'ɛstɪmət, *vb* 'ɛstɪmeɪt] *n* estimation
f; (*Comm*) devis *m* ▷ *vt* estimer ▷ *vi* (*Brit Comm*):
to ~ for estimer, faire une estimation de; (*bid
for*) faire un devis pour; **to give sb an ~ of** faire
or donner un devis à qn pour; **at a rough ~**
approximativement
estimation [ɛstɪ'meɪʃən] *n* opinion *f*; estime *f*;
in my ~ à mon avis, selon moi
Estonia [ɛ'stəʊnɪə] *n* Estonie *f*
Estonian [ɛ'stəʊnɪən] *adj* estonien(ne) ▷ *n*
Estonien(ne); (*Ling*) estonien *m*
estranged [ɪs'treɪndʒd] *adj* (*couple*) séparé(e);
(*husband, wife*) dont on s'est séparé(e)
estrangement [ɪs'treɪndʒmənt] *n* (*from wife,
family*) séparation *f*
estrogen ['i:strəudʒən] *n* (*US*) = **oestrogen**
estuary ['ɛstjuərɪ] *n* estuaire *m*
ET *n abbr* (*Brit: = Employment Training*) formation
professionnelle pour les demandeurs d'emploi ▷ *abbr*
(*US: = Eastern Time*) heure de New York
ETA *n abbr* (*= estimated time of arrival*) HPA *f* (*=* heure
probable d'arrivée)
et al. *abbr* (*= et alii: and others*) et coll
etc *abbr* (*= et cetera*) etc
etch [ɛtʃ] *vt* graver à l'eau forte
etching ['ɛtʃɪŋ] *n* eau-forte *f*
ETD *n abbr* (*= estimated time of departure*) HPD *f*
(*= heure probable de départ*)
eternal [ɪ'tə:nl] *adj* éternel(le)
eternity [ɪ'tə:nɪtɪ] *n* éternité *f*
ether ['i:θər] *n* éther *m*
ethereal [ɪ'θɪərɪəl] *adj* éthéré(e)
ethical ['ɛθɪkl] *adj* moral(e)
ethics ['ɛθɪks] *n* éthique *f* ▷ *npl* moralité *f*
Ethiopia [i:θɪ'əʊpɪə] *n* Éthiopie *f*
Ethiopian [i:θɪ'əʊpɪən] *adj* éthiopien(ne) ▷ *n*

Éthiopien(ne)
ethnic ['ɛθnɪk] *adj* ethnique; (*clothes, food*)
folklorique, exotique, *propre aux minorités ethniques
non-occidentales*
ethnic cleansing [-'klɛnzɪŋ] *n* purification *f*
ethnique
ethnic minority *n* minorité *f* ethnique
ethnology [ɛθ'nɔlədʒɪ] *n* ethnologie *f*
ethos ['i:θɔs] *n* (*système m de*) valeurs *fpl*
e-ticket ['i:tɪkɪt] *n* billet *m* électronique
etiquette ['ɛtɪkɛt] *n* convenances *fpl*,
étiquette *f*
ETV *n abbr* (*US: = Educational Television*) télévision
scolaire
etymology [ɛtɪ'mɔlədʒɪ] *n* étymologie *f*
EU *n abbr* (*= European Union*) UE *f*
eucalyptus [ju:kə'lɪptəs] *n* eucalyptus *m*
eulogy ['ju:lədʒɪ] *n* éloge *m*
euphemism ['ju:fəmɪzəm] *n* euphémisme *m*
euphemistic [ju:fə'mɪstɪk] *adj* euphémique
euphoria [ju:'fɔ:rɪə] *n* euphorie *f*
Eurasia [juə'reɪʃə] *n* Eurasie *f*
Eurasian [juə'reɪʃən] *adj* eurasien(ne);
(*continent*) eurasiatique ▷ *n* Eurasien(ne)
Euratom [juə'rætəm] *n abbr* (*= European Atomic
Energy Community*) EURATOM *f*
euro ['juərəu] *n* (*currency*) euro *m*
Euro- ['juərəu] *prefix* euro-
Eurocrat ['juərəukræt] *n* eurocrate *m/f*
Euroland ['juərəulænd] *n* Euroland *m*
Europe ['juərəp] *n* Europe *f*
European [juərə'pi:ən] *adj* européen(ne) ▷ *n*
Européen(ne)
European Community *n* Communauté
européenne
European Court of Justice *n* Cour *f* de Justice
de la CEE
European Union *n* Union européenne
Euro-sceptic ['juərəuskɛptɪk] *n* eurosceptique
m/f
Eurostar® ['juərəustɑ:r] *n* Eurostar® *m*
euthanasia [ju:θə'neɪzɪə] *n* euthanasie *f*
evacuate [ɪ'vækjueɪt] *vt* évacuer
evacuation [ɪvækju'eɪʃən] *n* évacuation *f*
evacuee [ɪvækju'i:] *n* évacué(e)
evade [ɪ'veɪd] *vt* échapper à; (*question etc*) éluder;
(*duties*) se dérober à
evaluate [ɪ'væljueɪt] *vt* évaluer
evangelist [ɪ'vændʒəlɪst] *n* évangéliste *m*
evangelize [ɪ'vændʒəlaɪz] *vt* évangéliser,
prêcher l'Évangile à
evaporate [ɪ'væpəreɪt] *vi* s'évaporer; (*fig: hopes,
fear*) s'envoler; (*anger*) se dissiper ▷ *vt* faire
évaporer
evaporated milk [ɪ'væpəreɪtɪd-] *n* lait
condensé (non sucré)
evaporation [ɪvæpə'reɪʃən] *n* évaporation *f*
evasion [ɪ'veɪʒən] *n* dérobade *f*; (*excuse*) faux-
fuyant *m*
evasive [ɪ'veɪsɪv] *adj* évasif(-ive)
eve [i:v] *n*: **on the ~ of** à la veille de
even ['i:vn] *adj* (*level, smooth*) régulier(-ière);

e

(*equal*) égal(e); (*number*) pair(e) ▷ *adv* même; **~ if** même si + *indic*; **~ though** quand (bien) même + *cond*, alors même que + *cond*; **~ more** encore plus; **~ faster** encore plus vite; **~ so** quand même; **not ~** pas même; **~ he was there** même lui était là; **~ on Sundays** même le dimanche; **to break ~** s'y retrouver, équilibrer ses comptes; **to get ~ with sb** prendre sa revanche sur qn
▶ **even out** *vi* s'égaliser

even-handed [iːvnˈhændɪd] *adj* équitable

evening [ˈiːvnɪŋ] *n* soir *m*; (*as duration, event*) soirée *f*; **in the ~** le soir; **this ~** ce soir; **tomorrow/yesterday ~** demain/hier soir

evening class *n* cours *m* du soir

evening dress *n* (*man's*) tenue *f* de soirée, smoking *m*; (*woman's*) robe *f* de soirée

evenly [ˈiːvnlɪ] *adv* uniformément, également; (*space*) régulièrement

evensong [ˈiːvnsɔŋ] *n* office *m* du soir

event [ɪˈvɛnt] *n* événement *m*; (*Sport*) épreuve *f*; **in the course of ~s** par la suite; **in the ~ of** en cas de; **in the ~** en réalité, en fait; **at all ~s** (*Brit*): **in any ~** en tout cas, de toute manière

eventful [ɪˈvɛntfʊl] *adj* mouvementé(e)

eventing [ɪˈvɛntɪŋ] *n* (*Horse-Riding*) concours complet (*équitation*)

eventual [ɪˈvɛntʃʊəl] *adj* final(e)

eventuality [ɪvɛntʃʊˈælɪtɪ] *n* possibilité *f*, éventualité *f*

eventually [ɪˈvɛntʃʊəlɪ] *adv* finalement

ever [ˈɛvəʳ] *adv* jamais; (*at all times*) toujours; (*in questions*): **why ~ not?** mais enfin, pourquoi pas?; **the best ~** le meilleur qu'on ait jamais vu; **have you ~ seen it?** l'as-tu déjà vu?, as-tu eu l'occasion *or* t'est-il arrivé de le voir?; **did you ~ meet him?** est-ce qu'il vous est arrivé de le rencontrer?; **have you ~ been there?** y êtes-vous déjà allé?; **for ~** pour toujours; **hardly ~** ne ... presque jamais; **~ since** (*as adv*) depuis; (*as conj*) depuis que; **~ so pretty** si joli; **thank you ~ so much** merci mille fois

Everest [ˈɛvərɪst] *n* (*also*: **Mount Everest**) le mont Everest, l'Everest *m*

evergreen [ˈɛvəgriːn] *n* arbre *m* à feuilles persistantes

everlasting [ɛvəˈlɑːstɪŋ] *adj* éternel(le)

KEYWORD

every [ˈɛvrɪ] *adj* **1** (*each*) chaque; **every one of them** tous (sans exception); **every shop in town was closed** tous les magasins en ville étaient fermés
2 (*all possible*) tous (toutes) les; **I gave you every assistance** j'ai fait tout mon possible pour vous aider; **I have every confidence in him** j'ai entièrement *or* pleinement confiance en lui; **we wish you every success** nous vous souhaitons beaucoup de succès
3 (*showing recurrence*) tous les; **every day** tous les jours, chaque jour; **every other car** une

voiture sur deux; **every other/third day** tous les deux/trois jours; **every now and then** de temps en temps

everybody [ˈɛvrɪbɔdɪ] *pron* = **everyone**

everyday [ˈɛvrɪdeɪ] *adj* (*expression*) courant(e), d'usage courant; (*use*) courant; (*clothes, life*) de tous les jours; (*occurrence, problem*) quotidien(ne)

everyone [ˈɛvrɪwʌn] *pron* tout le monde, tous *pl*; **~ knows about it** tout le monde le sait; **~ else** tous les autres

everything [ˈɛvrɪθɪŋ] *pron* tout; **~ is ready** tout est prêt; **he did ~ possible** il a fait tout son possible

everywhere [ˈɛvrɪwɛəʳ] *adv* partout; **~ you go you meet ...** où qu'on aille on rencontre ...

evict [ɪˈvɪkt] *vt* expulser

eviction [ɪˈvɪkʃən] *n* expulsion *f*

eviction notice *n* préavis *m* d'expulsion

evidence [ˈɛvɪdns] *n* (*proof*) preuve(s) *f(pl)*; (*of witness*) témoignage *m*; (*sign*): **to show ~ of** donner des signes de; **to give ~** témoigner, déposer; **in ~** (*obvious*) en évidence; en vue

evident [ˈɛvɪdnt] *adj* évident(e)

evidently [ˈɛvɪdntlɪ] *adv* de toute évidence; (*apparently*) apparemment

evil [ˈiːvl] *adj* mauvais(e) ▷ *n* mal *m*

evince [ɪˈvɪns] *vt* manifester

evocative [ɪˈvɔkətɪv] *adj* évocateur(-trice)

evoke [ɪˈvəʊk] *vt* évoquer; (*admiration*) susciter

evolution [iːvəˈluːʃən] *n* évolution *f*

evolve [ɪˈvɔlv] *vt* élaborer ▷ *vi* évoluer, se transformer

ewe [juː] *n* brebis *f*

ex [ɛks] *n* (*inf*): **my ex** mon ex

ex- [ɛks] *prefix* (*former: husband, president etc*) ex-; (*out of*): **the price ~works** le prix départ usine

exacerbate [ɛksˈæsəbeɪt] *vt* (*pain*) exacerber, accentuer; (*fig*) aggraver

exact [ɪgˈzækt] *adj* exact(e) ▷ *vt*: **to ~ sth (from)** (*signature, confession*) extorquer qch (à); (*apology*) exiger qch (de)

exacting [ɪgˈzæktɪŋ] *adj* exigeant(e); (*work*) fatigant(e)

exactitude [ɪgˈzæktɪtjuːd] *n* exactitude *f*, précision *f*

exactly [ɪgˈzæktlɪ] *adv* exactement; **~!** parfaitement!, précisément!

exaggerate [ɪgˈzædʒəreɪt] *vt*, *vi* exagérer

exaggeration [ɪgzædʒəˈreɪʃən] *n* exagération *f*

exalted [ɪgˈzɔːltɪd] *adj* (*rank*) élevé(e); (*person*) haut placé(e); (*elated*) exalté(e)

exam [ɪgˈzæm] *n abbr* (*Scol*) = **examination**

examination [ɪgzæmɪˈneɪʃən] *n* (*Scol, Med*) examen *m*; **to take** *or* **sit an ~** (*Brit*) passer un examen; **the matter is under ~** la question est à l'examen

examine [ɪgˈzæmɪn] *vt* (*gen*) examiner; (*Scol, Law: person*) interroger; (*inspect: machine, premises*) inspecter; (*passport*) contrôler; (*luggage*) fouiller

examiner [ɪgˈzæmɪnəʳ] *n* examinateur(-trice)

example [ɪgˈzɑːmpl] *n* exemple *m*; **for ~** par

exemple; **to set a good/bad** ~ donner le bon/mauvais exemple

exasperate [ɪgˈzɑːspəreɪt] vt exaspérer, agacer

exasperated [ɪgˈzɑːspəreɪtɪd] adj exaspéré(e)

exasperation [ɪgzɑːspəˈreɪʃən] n exaspération f, irritation f

excavate [ˈɛkskəveɪt] vt (site) fouiller, excaver; (object) mettre au jour

excavation [ɛkskəˈveɪʃən] n excavation f

excavator [ˈɛkskəveɪtəʳ] n excavateur m, excavatrice f

exceed [ɪkˈsiːd] vt dépasser; (one's powers) outrepasser

exceedingly [ɪkˈsiːdɪŋlɪ] adv extrêmement

excel [ɪkˈsɛl] vi exceller ▷ vt surpasser; **to ~ o.s.** se surpasser

excellence [ˈɛksələns] n excellence f

Excellency [ˈɛksələnsɪ] n: **His** ~ son Excellence f

excellent [ˈɛksələnt] adj excellent(e)

except [ɪkˈsɛpt] prep (also: **except for, excepting**) sauf, excepté, à l'exception de ▷ vt excepter; ~ **if/when** sauf si/quand; ~ **that** excepté que, si ce n'est que

exception [ɪkˈsɛpʃən] n exception f; **to take ~ to** s'offusquer de; **with the ~ of** à l'exception de

exceptional [ɪkˈsɛpʃənl] adj exceptionnel(le)

exceptionally [ɪkˈsɛpʃənəlɪ] adv exceptionnellement

excerpt [ˈɛksəːpt] n extrait m

excess [ɪkˈsɛs] n excès m; **in ~ of** plus de

excess baggage n excédent m de bagages

excess fare n supplément m

excessive [ɪkˈsɛsɪv] adj excessif(-ive)

excess supply n suroffre f, offre f excédentaire

exchange [ɪksˈtʃeɪndʒ] n échange m; (also: **telephone exchange**) central m ▷ vt: **to ~ (for)** échanger (contre); **could I ~ this, please?** est-ce que je peux échanger ceci, s'il vous plaît?; **in ~ for** en échange de; **foreign ~** (Comm) change m

exchange control n contrôle m des changes

exchange market n marché m des changes

exchange rate n taux m de change

excisable [ɪkˈsaɪzəbl] adj taxable

excise n [ˈɛksaɪz] taxe f ▷ vt [ɛkˈsaɪz] exciser

excise duties npl impôts indirects

excitable [ɪkˈsaɪtəbl] adj excitable, nerveux(-euse)

excite [ɪkˈsaɪt] vt exciter

excited [ɪkˈsaɪtəd] adj (tout (toute)) excité(e); **to get ~** s'exciter

excitement [ɪkˈsaɪtmənt] n excitation f

exciting [ɪkˈsaɪtɪŋ] adj passionnant(e)

excl. abbr = **excluding**; **exclusive (of)**

exclaim [ɪkˈskleɪm] vi s'exclamer

exclamation [ɛksklə'meɪʃən] n exclamation f

exclamation mark, (US) **exclamation point** n point m d'exclamation

exclude [ɪkˈskluːd] vt exclure

excluding [ɪkˈskluːdɪŋ] prep: ~ **VAT** la TVA non comprise

exclusion [ɪkˈskluːʒən] n exclusion f; **to the ~ of** à l'exclusion de

exclusion clause n clause f d'exclusion

exclusion zone n zone interdite

exclusive [ɪkˈskluːsɪv] adj exclusif(-ive); (club, district) sélect(e); (item of news) en exclusivité ▷ adv (Comm) exclusivement, non inclus; ~ **of** VAT TVA non comprise; ~ **of postage** (les) frais de poste non compris; **from 1st to 15th March** ~ du 1er au 15 mars exclusivement or exclu; ~ **rights** (Comm) exclusivité f

exclusively [ɪkˈskluːsɪvlɪ] adv exclusivement

excommunicate [ɛkskəˈmjuːnɪkeɪt] vt excommunier

excrement [ˈɛkskrəmənt] n excrément m

excruciating [ɪkˈskruːʃɪeɪtɪŋ] adj (pain) atroce, déchirant(e); (embarrassing) pénible

excursion [ɪkˈskəːʃən] n excursion f

excursion ticket n billet m tarif excursion

excusable [ɪkˈskjuːzəbl] adj excusable

excuse n [ɪkˈskjuːs] excuse f ▷ vt [ɪkˈskjuːz] (forgive) excuser; (justify) excuser, justifier; **to ~ sb from** (activity) dispenser qn de; ~ **me!** excusez-moi!, pardon!; **now if you will ~ me, ...** maintenant, si vous (le) permettez ...; **to make ~s for sb** trouver des excuses à qn; **to ~ o.s. for sth/for doing sth** s'excuser de/d'avoir fait qch

ex-directory [ˈɛksdɪˈrɛktərɪ] adj (Brit) sur la liste rouge

execute [ˈɛksɪkjuːt] vt exécuter

execution [ɛksɪˈkjuːʃən] n exécution f

executioner [ɛksɪˈkjuːʃnəʳ] n bourreau m

executive [ɪgˈzɛkjutɪv] n (person) cadre m; (managing group) bureau m; (Pol) exécutif m ▷ adj exécutif(-ive); (position, job) de cadre; (secretary) de direction; (offices) de la direction; (car, plane) de fonction

executive director n administrateur(-trice)

executor [ɪgˈzɛkjutəʳ] n exécuteur(-trice) testamentaire

exemplary [ɪgˈzɛmplərɪ] adj exemplaire

exemplify [ɪgˈzɛmplɪfaɪ] vt illustrer

exempt [ɪgˈzɛmpt] adj: ~ **from** exempté(e) or dispensé(e) de ▷ vt: **to ~ sb from** exempter or dispenser qn de

exemption [ɪgˈzɛmpʃən] n exemption f, dispense f

exercise [ˈɛksəsaɪz] n exercice m ▷ vt exercer; (patience etc) faire preuve de; (dog) promener ▷ vi (also: **to take exercise**) prendre de l'exercice

exercise bike n vélo m d'appartement

exercise book n cahier m

exert [ɪgˈzəːt] vt exercer, employer; (strength, force) employer; **to ~ o.s.** se dépenser

exertion [ɪgˈzəːʃən] n effort m

ex gratia [ˈɛksˈɡreɪʃə] adj: ~ **payment** gratification f

exhale [ɛksˈheɪl] vt (breathe out) expirer; exhaler ▷ vi expirer

exhaust [ɪgˈzɔːst] n (also: **exhaust fumes**) gaz mpl d'échappement; (also: **exhaust pipe**) tuyau m d'échappement ▷ vt épuiser; **to ~ o.s.** s'épuiser

e

exhausted [ɪɡˈzɔːstɪd] *adj* épuisé(e)
exhausting [ɪɡˈzɔːstɪŋ] *adj* épuisant(e)
exhaustion [ɪɡˈzɔːstʃən] *n* épuisement *m*;
nervous ~ fatigue nerveuse
exhaustive [ɪɡˈzɔːstɪv] *adj* très complet(-ète)
exhibit [ɪɡˈzɪbɪt] *n* (*Art*) objet exposé, pièce
exposée; (*Law*) pièce à conviction ▷ *vt* (*Art*)
exposer; (*courage, skill*) faire preuve de
exhibition [ɛksɪˈbɪʃən] *n* exposition *f*; **~ of**
temper manifestation *f* de colère
exhibitionist [ɛksɪˈbɪʃənɪst] *n*
exhibitionniste *m/f*
exhibitor [ɪɡˈzɪbɪtəʳ] *n* exposant(e)
exhilarating [ɪɡˈzɪləreɪtɪŋ] *adj* grisant(e),
stimulant(e)
exhilaration [ɪɡzɪləˈreɪʃən] *n* euphorie *f*,
ivresse *f*
exhort [ɪɡˈzɔːt] *vt* exhorter
ex-husband [ˈɛksˈhʌzbənd] *n* ex-mari *m*
exile [ˈɛksaɪl] *n* exil *m*; (*person*) exilé(e) ▷ *vt*
exiler; **in ~** en exil
exist [ɪɡˈzɪst] *vi* exister
existence [ɪɡˈzɪstəns] *n* existence *f*; **to be in ~**
exister
existentialism [ɛɡzɪsˈtɛnʃlɪzəm] *n*
existentialisme *m*
existing [ɪɡˈzɪstɪŋ] *adj* (*laws*) existant(e); (*system,
regime*) actuel(le)
exit [ˈɛksɪt] *n* sortie *f* ▷ *vi* (*Comput, Theat*) sortir;
where's the ~? où est la sortie?
exit poll *n* sondage *m* (*fait à la sortie de l'isoloir*)
exit ramp *n* (*US Aut*) bretelle *f* d'accès
exit visa *n* visa *m* de sortie
exodus [ˈɛksədəs] *n* exode *m*
ex officio [ˈɛksəˈfɪʃɪəu] *adj, adv* d'office, de droit
exonerate [ɪɡˈzɔnəreɪt] *vt*: **to ~ from**
disculper de
exorbitant [ɪɡˈzɔːbɪtnt] *adj* (*price*) exorbitant(e),
excessif(-ive); (*demands*) exorbitant,
démesuré(e)
exorcize [ˈɛksɔːsaɪz] *vt* exorciser
exotic [ɪɡˈzɔtɪk] *adj* exotique
expand [ɪkˈspænd] *vt* (*area*) agrandir; (*quantity*)
accroître; (*influence etc*) étendre ▷ *vi* (*population,
production*) s'accroître; (*trade, etc*) se développer,
s'accroître; (*gas, metal*) se dilater, dilater; **to ~**
on (*notes, story etc*) développer
expanse [ɪkˈspæns] *n* étendue *f*
expansion [ɪkˈspænʃən] *n* (*territorial, economic*)
expansion *f*; (*of trade, influence etc*)
développement *m*; (*of production*) accroissement
m; (*of population*) croissance *f*; (*of gas, metal*)
expansion, dilatation *f*
expansionism [ɪkˈspænʃənɪzəm] *n*
expansionnisme *m*
expansionist [ɪkˈspænʃənɪst] *adj*
expansionniste
expatriate *n* [ɛksˈpætrɪət] expatrié(e) ▷ *vt*
[ɛksˈpætrɪeɪt] expatrier, exiler
expect [ɪkˈspɛkt] *vt* (*anticipate*) s'attendre à,
s'attendre à ce que + *sub*; (*count on*) compter sur,
escompter; (*hope for*) espérer; (*require*) demander,

exiger; (*suppose*) supposer; (*await: also baby*)
attendre ▷ *vi*: **to be ~ing** (*pregnant woman*) être
enceinte; **to ~ sb to do** (*anticipate*) s'attendre à
ce que qn fasse; (*demand*) attendre de qn qu'il
fasse; **to ~ to do sth** penser *or* compter faire
qch, s'attendre à faire qch; **as ~ed** comme
prévu; **I ~ so** je crois que oui, je crois bien
expectancy [ɪksˈpɛktənsɪ] *n* attente *f*; **life ~**
espérance *f* de vie
expectant [ɪkˈspɛktənt] *adj* qui attend (quelque
chose); **~ mother** future maman
expectantly [ɪkˈspɛktəntlɪ] *adv* (*look, listen*) avec
l'air d'attendre quelque chose
expectation [ɛkspɛkˈteɪʃən] *n* (*hope*) attente *f*,
espérance(s) *f(pl)*; (*belief*) attente; **in ~ of** dans
l'attente de, en prévision de; **against** *or*
contrary to all ~(s) contre toute attente,
contrairement à ce qu'on attendait; **to come** *or*
live up to sb's ~s répondre à l'attente *or* aux
espérances de qn
expedience, expediency [ɪkˈspiːdɪəns,
ɪkˈspiːdɪənsɪ] *n* opportunité *f*; convenance *f* (du
moment); **for the sake of ~** parce que c'est (*or*
c'était) plus simple *or* plus commode
expedient [ɪkˈspiːdɪənt] *adj* indiqué(e),
opportun(e), commode ▷ *n* expédient *m*
expedite [ˈɛkspədaɪt] *vt* hâter; expédier
expedition [ɛkspəˈdɪʃən] *n* expédition *f*
expeditionary force [ɛkspəˈdɪʃənrɪ-] *n* corps *m*
expéditionnaire
expeditious [ɛkspəˈdɪʃəs] *adj* expéditif(-ive),
prompt(e)
expel [ɪkˈspɛl] *vt* chasser, expulser; (*Scol*)
renvoyer, exclure
expend [ɪkˈspɛnd] *vt* consacrer; (*use up*)
dépenser
expendable [ɪkˈspɛndəbl] *adj* remplaçable
expenditure [ɪkˈspɛndɪtʃəʳ] *n* (*act of spending*)
dépense *f*; (*money spent*) dépenses *fpl*
expense [ɪkˈspɛns] *n* (*high cost*) coût *m*; (*spending*)
dépense *f*, frais *mpl*; **expenses** *npl* frais *mpl*;
dépenses; **to go to the ~ of** faire la dépense de;
at great/little ~ à grands/peu de frais; **at the ~**
of aux frais de; (*fig*) aux dépens de
expense account *n* (*note f de*) frais *mpl*
expensive [ɪkˈspɛnsɪv] *adj* cher (chère),
coûteux(-euse); **to be ~** coûter cher; **it's too ~**
ça coûte trop cher; **~ tastes** goûts *mpl* de luxe
experience [ɪkˈspɪərɪəns] *n* expérience *f* ▷ *vt*
connaître; (*feeling*) éprouver; **to know by ~**
savoir par expérience
experienced [ɪkˈspɪərɪənst] *adj* expérimenté(e)
experiment [ɪkˈspɛrɪmənt] *n* expérience *f* ▷ *vi*
faire une expérience; **to ~ with** expérimenter;
to perform *or* **carry out an ~** faire une
expérience; **as an ~** à titre d'expérience
experimental [ɪksperɪˈmɛntl] *adj*
expérimental(e)
expert [ˈɛkspəːt] *adj* expert(e) ▷ *n* expert *m*; **~ in**
or **at doing sth** spécialiste de qch; **an ~ on sth**
un spécialiste de qch; **~ witness** (*Law*) expert *m*
expertise [ɛkspəːˈtiːz] *n* (grande) compétence

expire [ɪkˈspaɪə^r] *vi* expirer
expiry [ɪkˈspaɪərɪ] *n* expiration *f*
expiry date *n* date *f* d'expiration; *(on label)* à utiliser avant ...
explain [ɪkˈspleɪn] *vt* expliquer
▸ **explain away** *vt* justifier, excuser
explanation [ɛksplə'neɪʃən] *n* explication *f*; **to find an ~ for sth** trouver une explication à qch
explanatory [ɪkˈsplænətrɪ] *adj* explicatif(-ive)
expletive [ɪkˈspliːtɪv] *n* juron *m*
explicit [ɪkˈsplɪsɪt] *adj* explicite; *(definite)* formel(le)
explode [ɪkˈspləud] *vi* exploser ▷ *vt* faire exploser; *(fig: theory)* démolir; **to ~ a myth** détruire un mythe
exploit *n* [ˈɛksplɔɪt] exploit *m* ▷ *vt* [ɪkˈsplɔɪt] exploiter
exploitation [ɛksplɔɪ'teɪʃən] *n* exploitation *f*
exploration [ɛksplə'reɪʃən] *n* exploration *f*
exploratory [ɪkˈsplɔrətrɪ] *adj* *(fig: talks)* préliminaire; **~ operation** *(Med)* intervention *f* (à visée) exploratrice
explore [ɪkˈsplɔː^r] *vt* explorer; *(possibilities)* étudier, examiner
explorer [ɪkˈsplɔːrə^r] *n* explorateur(-trice)
explosion [ɪkˈspləuʒən] *n* explosion *f*
explosive [ɪkˈspləusɪv] *adj* explosif(-ive) ▷ *n* explosif *m*
exponent [ɪkˈspəunənt] *n* *(of school of thought etc)* interprète *m*, représentant *m*; *(Math)* exposant *m*
export *vt* [ɛkˈspɔːt] exporter ▷ *n* [ˈɛkspɔːt] exportation *f* ▷ *cpd* [ˈɛkspɔːt] d'exportation
exportation [ɛkspɔː'teɪʃən] *n* exportation *f*
exporter [ɛkˈspɔːtə^r] *n* exportateur *m*
export licence *n* licence *f* d'exportation
expose [ɪkˈspəuz] *vt* exposer; *(unmask)* démasquer, dévoiler; **to ~ o.s.** *(Law)* commettre un outrage à la pudeur
exposed [ɪkˈspəuzd] *adj* *(land, house)* exposé(e); *(Elec: wire)* à nu; *(pipe, beam)* apparent(e)
exposition [ɛkspə'zɪʃən] *n* exposition *f*
exposure [ɪkˈspəuʒə^r] *n* exposition *f*; *(publicity)* couverture *f*; *(Phot: speed)* (temps *m* de) pose *f*; *(: shot)* pose; **suffering from ~** *(Med)* souffrant des effets du froid et de l'épuisement; **to die of ~** *(Med)* mourir de froid
exposure meter *n* posemètre *m*
expound [ɪkˈspaund] *vt* exposer, expliquer
express [ɪkˈsprɛs] *adj* *(definite)* formel(le), exprès(-esse); *(Brit: letter etc)* exprès *inv* ▷ *n* *(train)* rapide *m* ▷ *adv* *(send)* exprès ▷ *vt* exprimer; **to ~ o.s.** s'exprimer
expression [ɪkˈsprɛʃən] *n* expression *f*
expressionism [ɪkˈsprɛʃənɪzəm] *n* expressionnisme *m*
expressive [ɪkˈsprɛsɪv] *adj* expressif(-ive)
expressly [ɪkˈsprɛslɪ] *adv* expressément, formellement
expressway [ɪkˈsprɛsweɪ] *n* *(US)* voie *f* express (à plusieurs files)
expropriate [ɛksˈprəuprɪeɪt] *vt* exproprier

expulsion [ɪkˈspʌlʃən] *n* expulsion *f*; renvoi *m*
exquisite [ɛkˈskwɪzɪt] *adj* exquis(e)
ex-serviceman [ˈɛksˈsəːvɪsmən] *(irreg)* *n* ancien combattant
ext. *abbr* *(Tel)* = **extension**
extemporize [ɪkˈstɛmpəraɪz] *vi* improviser
extend [ɪkˈstɛnd] *vt* *(visit, street)* prolonger; *(deadline)* reporter, remettre; *(building)* agrandir; *(offer)* présenter, offrir; *(Comm: credit)* accorder; *(hand, arm)* tendre ▷ *vi* *(land)* s'étendre
extension [ɪkˈstɛnʃən] *n* *(of visit, street)* prolongation *f*; *(of building)* agrandissement *m*; *(building)* annexe *f*; *(to wire, table)* rallonge *f*; *(telephone: in offices)* poste *m*; *(: in private house)* téléphone *m* supplémentaire; **~ 3718** *(Tel)* poste 3718
extension cable, extension lead *n* *(Elec)* rallonge *f*
extensive [ɪkˈstɛnsɪv] *adj* étendu(e), vaste; *(damage, alterations)* considérable; *(inquiries)* approfondi(e); *(use)* largement répandu(e)
extensively [ɪkˈstɛnsɪvlɪ] *adv* *(altered, damaged etc)* considérablement; **he's travelled ~** il a beaucoup voyagé
extent [ɪkˈstɛnt] *n* étendue *f*; *(degree: of damage, loss)* importance *f*; **to some ~** dans une certaine mesure; **to a certain ~** dans une certaine mesure, jusqu'à un certain point; **to a large ~** en grande partie; **to the ~ of ...** au point de ...; **to what ~?** dans quelle mesure?, jusqu'à quel point?; **to such an ~ that ...** à tel point que ...
extenuating [ɪkˈstɛnjueɪtɪŋ] *adj*: **~ circumstances** circonstances atténuantes
exterior [ɛkˈstɪərɪə^r] *adj* extérieur(e) ▷ *n* extérieur *m*
exterminate [ɪkˈstəːmɪneɪt] *vt* exterminer
extermination [ɪkstəːmɪ'neɪʃən] *n* extermination *f*
external [ɛkˈstəːnl] *adj* externe ▷ *n*: **the ~s** les apparences *fpl*; **for ~ use only** *(Med)* à usage externe
externally [ɛkˈstəːnəlɪ] *adv* extérieurement
extinct [ɪkˈstɪŋkt] *adj* *(volcano)* éteint(e); *(species)* disparu(e)
extinction [ɪkˈstɪŋkʃən] *n* extinction *f*
extinguish [ɪkˈstɪŋgwɪʃ] *vt* éteindre
extinguisher [ɪkˈstɪŋgwɪʃə^r] *n* extincteur *m*
extol, *(US)* **extoll** [ɪkˈstəul] *vt* *(merits)* chanter, prôner; *(person)* chanter les louanges de
extort [ɪkˈstɔːt] *vt*: **to ~ sth (from)** extorquer qch (à)
extortion [ɪkˈstɔːʃən] *n* extorsion *f*
extortionate [ɪkˈstɔːʃnɪt] *adj* exorbitant(e)
extra [ˈɛkstrə] *adj* supplémentaire, de plus ▷ *adv* *(in addition)* en plus ▷ *n* supplément *m*; *(perk)* à-coté *m*; *(Cine, Theat)* figurant(e); **wine will cost ~** le vin sera en supplément; **~ large sizes** très grandes tailles
extra... [ˈɛkstrə] *prefix* extra...
extract *vt* [ɪkˈstrækt] extraire; *(tooth)* arracher; *(money, promise)* soutirer ▷ *n* [ˈɛkstrækt] extrait *m*
extraction [ɪkˈstrækʃən] *n* extraction *f*

extractor fan [ɪk'stræktə-] n exhausteur m, ventilateur m extracteur

extracurricular ['ɛkstrəkə'rɪkjuləʳ] adj (Scol) parascolaire

extradite ['ɛkstrədaɪt] vt extrader

extradition [ɛkstrə'dɪʃən] n extradition f

extramarital ['ɛkstrə'mærɪtl] adj extraconjugal(e)

extramural ['ɛkstrə'mjuərl] adj hors-faculté inv

extraneous [ɛk'streɪnɪəs] adj: ~ **to** étranger(-ère) à

extraordinary [ɪk'strɔ:dnrɪ] adj extraordinaire; **the ~ thing is that ...** le plus étrange or étonnant c'est que ...

extraordinary general meeting n assemblée f générale extraordinaire

extrapolation [ɛkstræpə'leɪʃən] n extrapolation f

extrasensory perception ['ɛkstrə'sɛnsərɪ-] n perception f extrasensorielle

extra time n (Football) prolongations fpl

extravagance [ɪk'strævəgəns] n (excessive spending) prodigalités fpl; (thing bought) folie f, dépense excessive

extravagant [ɪk'strævəgənt] adj extravagant(e); (in spending: person) prodigue, dépensier(-ière); (: tastes) dispendieux(-euse)

extreme [ɪk'stri:m] adj, n extrême (m); **the ~ left/right** (Pol) l'extrême gauche f/droite f; **~s of temperature** différences fpl extrêmes de température

extremely [ɪk'stri:mlɪ] adv extrêmement

extremist [ɪk'stri:mɪst] adj, n extrémiste m/f

extremity [ɪk'strɛmɪtɪ] n extrémité f

extricate ['ɛkstrɪkeɪt] vt: **to ~ sth (from)** dégager qch (de)

extrovert ['ɛkstrəvə:t] n extraverti(e)

exuberance [ɪg'zju:bərns] n exubérance f

exuberant [ɪg'zju:bərnt] adj exubérant(e)

exude [ɪg'zju:d] vt exsuder; (fig) respirer; **the**

charm etc **he ~s** le charme etc qui émane de lui

exult [ɪg'zʌlt] vi exulter, jubiler

exultant [ɪg'zʌltənt] adj (shout, expression) de triomphe; **to be ~** jubiler, triompher

exultation [ɛgzʌl'teɪʃən] n exultation f, jubilation f

ex-wife ['ɛkswaɪf] n ex-femme f

eye [aɪ] n œil m; (of needle) trou m, chas m ▷ vt examiner; **as far as the ~ can see** à perte de vue; **to keep an ~ on** surveiller; **to have an ~ for sth** avoir l'œil pour qch; **in the public ~** en vue; **with an ~ to doing sth** (Brit) en vue de faire qch; **there's more to this than meets the ~** ce n'est pas aussi simple que cela paraît

eyeball ['aɪbɔ:l] n globe m oculaire

eyebath ['aɪbɑ:θ] n (Brit) œillère f (pour bains d'œil)

eyebrow ['aɪbrau] n sourcil m

eyebrow pencil n crayon m à sourcils

eye-catching ['aɪkætʃɪŋ] adj voyant(e), accrocheur(-euse)

eye cup n (US) = **eyebath**

eye drops ['aɪdrɔps] npl gouttes fpl pour les yeux

eyeful ['aɪful] n: **to get an ~ (of sth)** se rincer l'œil (en voyant qch)

eyeglass ['aɪglɑ:s] n monocle m

eyelash ['aɪlæʃ] n cil m

eyelet ['aɪlɪt] n œillet m

eye-level ['aɪlɛvl] adj en hauteur

eyelid ['aɪlɪd] n paupière f

eyeliner ['aɪlaɪnəʳ] n eye-liner m

eye-opener ['aɪəupnəʳ] n révélation f

eye shadow ['aɪʃædəu] n ombre f à paupières

eyesight ['aɪsaɪt] n vue f

eyesore ['aɪsɔ:ʳ] n horreur f, chose f qui dépare or enlaidit

eyestrain ['aɪstreɪn] adj: **to get ~** se fatiguer la vue or les yeux

eyewash ['aɪwɔʃ] n bain m d'œil; (fig) frime f

eye witness n témoin m oculaire

eyrie ['ɪərɪ] n aire f

Ff

F¹, f [εf] *n* (*letter*) F, f *m*; (*Mus*): **F** fa *m*; **F for Frederick**, (*US*) **F for Fox** F comme François
F² *abbr* (= *Fahrenheit*) F
FA *n abbr* (*Brit*: = *Football Association*) *fédération de football*
FAA *n abbr* (*US*) = **Federal Aviation Administration**
fable ['feɪbl] *n* fable *f*
fabric ['fæbrɪk] *n* tissu *m* ▷ *cpd*: **~ ribbon** (*for typewriter*) ruban *m* (en) tissu
fabricate ['fæbrɪkeɪt] *vt* fabriquer, inventer
fabrication [fæbrɪ'keɪʃən] *n* fabrication *f*, invention *f*
fabulous ['fæbjʊləs] *adj* fabuleux(-euse); (*inf*: *super*) formidable, sensationnel(le)
façade [fə'sɑːd] *n* façade *f*
face [feɪs] *n* visage *m*, figure *f*; (*expression*) air *m*; grimace *f*; (*of clock*) cadran *m*; (*of cliff*) paroi *f*; (*of mountain*) face *f*; (*of building*) façade *f*; (*side, surface*) face *f* ▷ *vt* faire face à; (*facts etc*) accepter; **~ down** (*person*) à plat ventre; (*card*) face en dessous; **to lose/save ~** perdre/sauver la face; **to pull a ~** faire une grimace; **in the ~ of** (*difficulties etc*) face à, devant; **on the ~ of it** à première vue; **~ to ~** face à face
▶ **face up to** *vt fus* faire face à, affronter
face cloth *n* (*Brit*) gant *m* de toilette
face cream *n* crème *f* pour le visage
face lift *n* lifting *m*; (*of façade etc*) ravalement *m*, retapage *m*
face pack *n* (*Brit*) masque *m* (de beauté)
face powder *n* poudre *f* (pour le visage)
face-saving ['feɪsseɪvɪŋ] *adj* qui sauve la face
facet ['fæsɪt] *n* facette *f*
facetious [fə'siːʃəs] *adj* facétieux(-euse)
face-to-face ['feɪstə'feɪs] *adv* face à face
face value ['feɪs'væljuː] *n* (*of coin*) valeur nominale; **to take sth at ~** (*fig*) prendre qch pour argent comptant
facia ['feɪʃə] *n* = **fascia**
facial ['feɪʃl] *adj* facial(e) ▷ *n* soin complet du visage
facile ['fæsaɪl] *adj* facile
facilitate [fə'sɪlɪteɪt] *vt* faciliter
facilities [fə'sɪlɪtɪz] *npl* installations *fpl*, équipement *m*; **credit ~** facilités de paiement

facility [fə'sɪlɪtɪ] *n* facilité *f*
facing ['feɪsɪŋ] *prep* face à, en face de ▷ *n* (*of wall etc*) revêtement *m*; (*Sewing*) revers *m*
facsimile [fæk'sɪmɪlɪ] *n* (*exact replica*) facsimilé *m*; (*also*: **facsimile machine**) télécopieur *m*; (*transmitted document*) télécopie *f*
fact [fækt] *n* fait *m*; **in ~** en fait; **to know for a ~ that** ... savoir pertinemment que ...
fact-finding ['fæktfaɪndɪŋ] *adj*: **a ~ tour** *or* **mission** une mission d'enquête
faction ['fækʃən] *n* faction *f*
factional ['fækʃənl] *adj* de factions
factor ['fæktə'] *n* facteur *m*; (*of sun cream*) indice *m* (de protection); (*Comm*) factor *m*, société *f* d'affacturage; (: *agent*) dépositaire *m/f* ▷ *vi* faire du factoring; **safety ~** facteur de sécurité; **I'd like a ~ 15 suntan lotion** je voudrais une crème solaire d'indice 15
factory ['fæktərɪ] *n* usine *f*, fabrique *f*
factory farming *n* (*Brit*) élevage industriel
factory floor *n*: **the ~** (*workers*) les ouvriers *mpl*; (*workshop*) l'usine *f*; **on the ~** dans les ateliers
factory ship *n* navire-usine *m*
factual ['fæktjʊəl] *adj* basé(e) sur les faits
faculty ['fækəltɪ] *n* faculté *f*; (*US*: *teaching staff*) corps enseignant
fad [fæd] *n* (*personal*) manie *f*; (*craze*) engouement *m*
fade [feɪd] *vi* se décolorer, passer; (*light, sound*) s'affaiblir, disparaître; (*flower*) se faner
▶ **fade away** *vi* (*sound*) s'affaiblir
▶ **fade in** *vt* (*picture*) ouvrir en fondu; (*sound*) monter progressivement
▶ **fade out** *vt* (*picture*) fermer en fondu; (*sound*) baisser progressivement
faeces, (*US*) **feces** ['fiːsiːz] *npl* fèces *fpl*
fag [fæg] *n* (*Brit inf*: *cigarette*) clope *f*; (: *chore*): **what a ~!** quelle corvée!; (*US inf*: *homosexual*) pédé *m*
fag end *n* (*Brit inf*) mégot *m*
fagged out ['fægd-] *adj* (*Brit inf*) crevé(e)
Fahrenheit ['fɑːrənhaɪt] *n* Fahrenheit *m inv*
fail [feɪl] *vt* (*exam*) échouer à; (*candidate*) recaler; (*subj*: *courage, memory*) faire défaut à ▷ *vi* échouer; (*supplies*) manquer; (*eyesight, health, light*: *also*: **be failing**) baisser, s'affaiblir; (*brakes*) lâcher; **to ~**

to do sth (*neglect*) négliger de *or* ne pas faire qch; (*be unable*) ne pas arriver *or* parvenir à faire qch; **without ~** à coup sûr; sans faute

failing ['feɪlɪŋ] *n* défaut *m* ▷ *prep* faute de; **~ that** à défaut, sinon

failsafe ['feɪlseɪf] *adj* (*device etc*) à sûreté intégrée

failure ['feɪljə'] *n* échec *m*; (*person*) raté(e); (*mechanical etc*) défaillance *f*; **his ~ to turn up** le fait de n'être pas venu *or* qu'il ne soit pas venu

faint [feɪnt] *adj* faible; (*recollection*) vague; (*mark*) à peine visible; (*smell, breeze, trace*) léger(-ère) ▷ *n* évanouissement *m* ▷ *vi* s'évanouir; **to feel ~** défaillir

faintest ['feɪntɪst] *adj*: **I haven't the ~ idea** je n'en ai pas la moindre idée

faint-hearted ['feɪnt'hɑːtɪd] *adj* pusillanime

faintly ['feɪntlɪ] *adv* faiblement; (*vaguely*) vaguement

faintness ['feɪntnɪs] *n* faiblesse *f*

fair [fɛə'] *adj* équitable, juste; (*reasonable*) correct(e), honnête; (*hair*) blond(e); (*skin, complexion*) pâle, blanc (blanche); (*weather*) beau (belle); (*good enough*) assez bon(ne); (*sizeable*) considérable ▷ *adv*: **to play ~** jouer franc jeu ▷ *n* foire *f*; (*Brit: funfair*) fête (foraine); (*also*: **trade fair**) foire(-exposition) commerciale; **it's not ~!** ce n'est pas juste!; **a ~ amount of** une quantité considérable de

fair copy *n* copie *f* au propre, corrigé *m*

fair game *n*: **to be ~ (for)** être une cible légitime (pour)

fairground ['fɛəgraund] *n* champ *m* de foire

fair-haired [fɛə'hɛəd] *adj* (*person*) aux cheveux clairs, blond(e)

fairly ['fɛəlɪ] *adv* (*justly*) équitablement; (*quite*) assez; **I'm ~ sure** j'en suis quasiment *or* presque sûr

fairness ['fɛənɪs] *n* (*of trial etc*) justice *f*, équité *f*; (*of person*) sens *m* de la justice; **in all ~** en toute justice

fair play *n* fair play *m*

fair trade *n* commerce *m* équitable

fairway ['fɛəweɪ] *n* (*Golf*) fairway *m*

fairy ['fɛərɪ] *n* fée *f*

fairy godmother *n* bonne fée

fairy lights *npl* (*Brit*) guirlande *f* électrique

fairy tale *n* conte *m* de fées

faith [feɪθ] *n* foi *f*; (*trust*) confiance *f*; (*sect*) culte *m*, religion *f*; **to have ~ in sb/sth** avoir confiance en qn/qch

faithful ['feɪθful] *adj* fidèle

faithfully ['feɪθfəlɪ] *adv* fidèlement; **yours ~** (*Brit: in letters*) veuillez agréer l'expression de mes salutations les plus distinguées

faith healer [-hiːlə'] *n* guérisseur(-euse)

fake [feɪk] *n* (*painting etc*) faux *m*; (*photo*) trucage *m*; (*person*) imposteur *m* ▷ *adj* faux (fausse) ▷ *vt* (*emotions*) simuler; (*painting*) faire un faux de; (*photo*) truquer; (*story*) fabriquer; **his illness is a ~** sa maladie est une comédie *or* de la simulation

falcon ['fɔːlkən] *n* faucon *m*

Falkland Islands ['fɔːlklənd-] *npl*: **the ~** les Malouines *fpl*, les îles *fpl* Falkland

fall [fɔːl] *n* chute *f*; (*decrease*) baisse *f*; (*US: autumn*) automne *m* ▷ *vi* (*pt* **fell**, *pp* **-en** [fɛl, 'fɔːlən]) tomber; (*price, temperature, dollar*) baisser; **falls** *npl* (*waterfall*) chute *f* d'eau, cascade *f*; **to ~ flat** (*vi: on one's face*) tomber de tout son long, s'étaler; (*joke*) tomber à plat; (*plan*) échouer; **to ~ short of** (*sb's expectations*) ne pas répondre à; **a ~ of snow** (*Brit*) une chute de neige

▶ **fall apart** *vi* (*object*) tomber en morceaux; (*inf: emotionally*) craquer

▶ **fall back** *vi* reculer, se retirer

▶ **fall back on** *vt fus* se rabattre sur; **to have something to ~ back on** (*money etc*) avoir quelque chose en réserve; (*job etc*) avoir une solution de rechange

▶ **fall behind** *vi* prendre du retard

▶ **fall down** *vi* (*person*) tomber; (*building*) s'effondrer, s'écrouler

▶ **fall for** *vt fus* (*trick*) se laisser prendre à; (*person*) tomber amoureux(-euse) de

▶ **fall in** *vi* s'effondrer; (*Mil*) se mettre en rangs

▶ **fall in with** *vt fus* (*sb's plans etc*) accepter

▶ **fall off** *vi* tomber; (*diminish*) baisser, diminuer

▶ **fall out** *vi* (*friends etc*) se brouiller; (*hair, teeth*) tomber

▶ **fall over** *vi* tomber (par terre)

▶ **fall through** *vi* (*plan, project*) tomber à l'eau

fallacy ['fæləsɪ] *n* erreur *f*, illusion *f*

fallback ['fɔːlbæk] *adj*: **~ position** position *f* de repli

fallen ['fɔːlən] *pp of* **fall**

fallible ['fæləbl] *adj* faillible

fallopian tube [fə'ləupɪən-] *n* (*Anat*) trompe *f* de Fallope

fallout ['fɔːlaut] *n* retombées (radioactives)

fallout shelter *n* abri *m* anti-atomique

fallow ['fæləu] *adj* en jachère; en friche

false [fɔːls] *adj* faux (fausse); **under ~ pretences** sous un faux prétexte

false alarm *n* fausse alerte

falsehood ['fɔːlshud] *n* mensonge *m*

falsely ['fɔːlslɪ] *adv* (*accuse*) à tort

false teeth *npl* (*Brit*) fausses dents, dentier *m*

falsify ['fɔːlsɪfaɪ] *vt* falsifier; (*accounts*) maquiller

falter ['fɔːltə'] *vi* chanceler, vaciller

fame [feɪm] *n* renommée *f*, renom *m*

familiar [fə'mɪlɪə'] *adj* familier(-ière); **to be ~ with sth** connaître qch; **to make o.s. ~ with sth** se familiariser avec qch; **to be on ~ terms with sb** bien connaître qn

familiarity [fəmɪlɪ'ærɪtɪ] *n* familiarité *f*

familiarize [fə'mɪlɪəraɪz] *vt* familiariser; **to ~ o.s. with** se familiariser avec

family ['fæmɪlɪ] *n* famille *f*

family allowance *n* (*Brit*) allocations familiales

family business *n* entreprise familiale

family credit *n* (*Brit*) complément familial

family doctor *n* médecin *m* de famille

family life *n* vie *f* de famille

family man (*irreg*) *n* père *m* de famille
family planning *n* planning familial
family planning clinic *n* centre *m* de planning familial
family tree *n* arbre *m* généalogique
famine ['fæmɪn] *n* famine *f*
famished ['fæmɪʃt] *adj* affamé(e); **I'm ~!** (*inf*) je meurs de faim!
famous ['feɪməs] *adj* célèbre
famously ['feɪməslɪ] *adv* (*get on*) fameusement, à merveille
fan [fæn] *n* (*folding*) éventail *m*; (*Elec*) ventilateur *m*; (*person*) fan *m*, admirateur(-trice); (*Sport*) supporter *m/f* ▷ *vt* éventer; (*fire, quarrel*) attiser
  ▶ **fan out** *vi* se déployer (en éventail)
fanatic [fə'nætɪk] *n* fanatique *m/f*
fanatical [fə'nætɪkl] *adj* fanatique
fan belt *n* courroie *f* de ventilateur
fancied ['fænsɪd] *adj* imaginaire
fanciful ['fænsɪful] *adj* fantaisiste
fan club *n* fan-club *m*
fancy ['fænsɪ] *n* (*whim*) fantaisie *f*, envie *f*; (*imagination*) imagination *f* ▷ *adj* (*luxury*) de luxe; (*elaborate: jewellery, packaging*) fantaisie *inv*; (*showy*) tape-à-l'œil *inv*; (*pretentious: words*) recherché(e) ▷ *vt* (*feel like, want*) avoir envie de; (*imagine*) imaginer; **to take a ~ to** se prendre d'affection pour; s'enticher de; **it took** *or* **caught my ~** ça m'a plu; **when the ~ takes him** quand ça lui prend; **to ~ that ...** se figurer *or* s'imaginer que ...; **he fancies her** elle lui plaît
fancy dress *n* déguisement *m*, travesti *m*
fancy-dress ball [fænsɪ'drɛs-] *n* bal masqué *or* costumé
fancy goods *npl* articles *mpl* (de) fantaisie
fanfare ['fænfɛəʳ] *n* fanfare *f* (*musique*)
fanfold paper ['fænfəuld-] *n* papier *m* à pliage accordéon
fang [fæŋ] *n* croc *m*; (*of snake*) crochet *m*
fan heater *n* (*Brit*) radiateur soufflant
fanlight ['fænlaɪt] *n* imposte *f*
fanny ['fænɪ] *n* (*Brit inf!*) chatte *f* (!); (*US inf*) cul *m* (!)
fantasize ['fæntəsaɪz] *vi* fantasmer
fantastic [fæn'tæstɪk] *adj* fantastique
fantasy ['fæntəsɪ] *n* imagination *f*, fantaisie *f*; (*unreality*) fantasme *m*
fanzine ['fænziːn] *n* fanzine *m*
FAO *n abbr* (= *Food and Agriculture Organization*) FAO *f*
FAQ *n abbr* (= *frequently asked question*) FAQ *f inv*, faq *f inv* ▷ *abbr* (= *free alongside quay*) FLQ
far [fɑːʳ] *adj* (*distant*) lointain(e), éloigné(e) ▷ *adv* loin; **the ~ side/end** l'autre côté/bout; **the ~ left/right** (*Pol*) l'extrême gauche *f*/droite *f*; **is it ~ to London?** est-ce qu'on est loin de Londres?; **it's not ~ (from here)** ce n'est pas loin (d'ici); **~ away, ~ off** au loin, dans le lointain; **~ better** beaucoup mieux; **~ from** loin de; **by ~** de loin, de beaucoup; **as ~ back as the 13th century** dès le 13e siècle; **go as ~ as the bridge** allez jusqu'au pont; **as ~ as I know** pour autant que

je sache; **how ~ is it to ...?** combien y a-t-il jusqu'à ...?; **as ~ as possible** dans la mesure du possible; **how ~ have you got with your work?** où en êtes-vous dans votre travail?
faraway ['fɑːrəweɪ] *adj* lointain(e); (*look*) absent(e)
farce [fɑːs] *n* farce *f*
farcical ['fɑːsɪkl] *adj* grotesque
fare [fɛəʳ] *n* (*on trains, buses*) prix *m* du billet; (*in taxi*) prix de la course; (*passenger in taxi*) client *m*; (*food*) table *f*, chère *f* ▷ *vi* se débrouiller; **half ~** demi-tarif; **full ~** plein tarif
Far East *n*: **the ~** l'Extrême-Orient *m*
farewell [fɛə'wɛl] *excl, n* adieu *m* ▷ *cpd* (*party etc*) d'adieux
far-fetched ['fɑː'fɛtʃt] *adj* exagéré(e), poussé(e)
farm [fɑːm] *n* ferme *f* ▷ *vt* cultiver
  ▶ **farm out** *vt* (*work etc*) distribuer
farmer ['fɑːməʳ] *n* fermier(-ière), cultivateur(-trice)
farmhand ['fɑːmhænd] *n* ouvrier(-ière) agricole
farmhouse ['fɑːmhaus] *n* (maison *f* de) ferme *f*
farming ['fɑːmɪŋ] *n* agriculture *f*; (*of animals*) élevage *m*; **intensive ~** culture intensive
farm labourer *n* = **farmhand**
farmland ['fɑːmlænd] *n* terres cultivées *or* arables
farm produce *n* produits *mpl* agricoles
farm worker *n* = **farmhand**
farmyard ['fɑːmjɑːd] *n* cour *f* de ferme
Faroe Islands ['fɛərəu-] *npl*, **Faroes** ['fɛərəuz] *npl*: **the ~** les îles *fpl* Féroé *or* Faeroe
far-reaching ['fɑː'riːtʃɪŋ] *adj* d'une grande portée
far-sighted ['fɑː'saɪtɪd] *adj* presbyte; (*fig*) prévoyant(e), qui voit loin
fart [fɑːt] (*inf!*) *n* pet *m* ▷ *vi* péter
farther ['fɑːðəʳ] *adv* plus loin ▷ *adj* plus éloigné(e), plus lointain(e)
farthest ['fɑːðɪst] *superlative of* **far**
FAS *abbr* (*Brit*: = *free alongside ship*) FLB
fascia ['feɪʃə] *n* (*Aut*) (garniture *f* du) tableau *m* de bord
fascinate ['fæsɪneɪt] *vt* fasciner, captiver
fascinating ['fæsɪneɪtɪŋ] *adj* fascinant(e)
fascination [fæsɪ'neɪʃən] *n* fascination *f*
fascism ['fæʃɪzəm] *n* fascisme *m*
fascist ['fæʃɪst] *adj, n* fasciste *m/f*
fashion ['fæʃən] *n* mode *f*; (*manner*) façon *f*, manière *f* ▷ *vt* façonner; **in ~** à la mode; **out of ~** démodé(e); **in the Greek ~** à la grecque; **after a ~** (*finish, manage etc*) tant bien que mal
fashionable ['fæʃnəbl] *adj* à la mode
fashion designer *n* (grand(e)) couturier(-ière)
fashionista [fœʃə'nɪstə] *n* fashionista *mf*
fashion show *n* défilé *m* de mannequins *or* de mode
fast [fɑːst] *adj* rapide; (*clock*): **to be ~** avancer; (*dye, colour*) grand *or* bon teint *inv* ▷ *adv* vite, rapidement; (*stuck, held*) solidement ▷ *n* jeûne *m* ▷ *vi* jeûner; **my watch is 5 minutes ~** ma montre avance de 5 minutes; **~ asleep**

profondément endormi; **as ~ as I can** aussi vite que je peux; **to make a boat ~** (Brit) amarrer un bateau

fasten ['fɑ:sn] vt attacher, fixer; (coat) attacher, fermer ▷ vi se fermer, s'attacher

▶ **fasten on, fasten upon** vt fus (idea) se cramponner à

fastener ['fɑ:snə'], **fastening** ['fɑ:snɪŋ] n fermeture f, attache f; (Brit: zip fastener) fermeture éclair® inv or à glissière

fast food n fast food m, restauration f rapide

fastidious [fæs'tɪdɪəs] adj exigeant(e), difficile

fast lane n (Aut: in Britain) voie f de droite

fat [fæt] adj gros(se) ▷ n graisse f; (on meat) gras m; (for cooking) matière grasse; **to live off the ~ of the land** vivre grassement

fatal ['feɪtl] adj (mistake) fatal(e); (injury) mortel(le)

fatalism ['feɪtlɪzəm] n fatalisme m

fatality [fə'tælɪtɪ] n (road death etc) victime f, décès m

fatally ['feɪtəlɪ] adv fatalement; (injured) mortellement

fate [feɪt] n destin m; (of person) sort m; **to meet one's ~** trouver la mort

fated ['feɪtɪd] adj (person) condamné(e); (project) voué(e) à l'échec

fateful ['feɪtful] adj fatidique

fat-free ['fæt'fri:] adj sans matières grasses

father ['fɑ:ðə'] n père m

Father Christmas n le Père Noël

fatherhood ['fɑ:ðəhud] n paternité f

father-in-law ['fɑ:ðərənlɔ:] n beau-père m

fatherland ['fɑ:ðəlænd] n (mère f) patrie f

fatherly ['fɑ:ðəlɪ] adj paternel(le)

fathom ['fæðəm] n brasse f (= 1828 mm) ▷ vt (mystery) sonder, pénétrer

fatigue [fə'ti:g] n fatigue f; (Mil) corvée f; **metal ~** fatigue du métal

fatness ['fætnɪs] n corpulence f, grosseur f

fatten ['fætn] vt, vi engraisser

fattening ['fætnɪŋ] adj (food) qui fait grossir; **chocolate is ~** le chocolat fait grossir

fatty ['fætɪ] adj (food) gras(se) ▷ n (inf) gros (grosse)

fatuous ['fætjuəs] adj stupide

faucet ['fɔ:sɪt] n (US) robinet m

fault [fɔ:lt] n faute f; (defect) défaut m; (Geo) faille f ▷ vt trouver des défauts à, prendre en défaut; **it's my ~** c'est de ma faute; **to find ~ with** trouver à redire or à critiquer à; **at ~** fautif(-ive), coupable; **to a ~** à l'excès

faultless ['fɔ:ltlɪs] adj impeccable; irréprochable

faulty ['fɔ:ltɪ] adj défectueux(-euse)

fauna ['fɔ:nə] n faune f

faux pas ['fəu'pɑ:] n impair m, bévue f, gaffe f

favour, (US) **favor** ['feɪvə'] n faveur f; (help) service m ▷ vt (proposition) être en faveur de; (pupil etc) favoriser; (team, horse) donner gagnant; **to do sb a ~** rendre un service à qn; **in ~ of** en faveur de; **to be in ~ of sth/of doing sth** être partisan de qch/de faire qch; **to find ~**

with sb trouver grâce aux yeux de qn

favourable, (US) **favorable** ['feɪvrəbl] adj favorable; (price) avantageux(-euse)

favourably, (US) **favorably** ['feɪvrəblɪ] adv favorablement

favourite, (US) **favorite** ['feɪvrɪt] adj, n favori(te)

favouritism, (US) **favoritism** ['feɪvrɪtɪzəm] n favoritisme m

fawn [fɔ:n] n (deer) faon m ▷ adj (also: **fawn-coloured**) fauve ▷ vi: **to ~ (up)on** flatter servilement

fax [fæks] n (document) télécopie f; (machine) télécopieur m ▷ vt envoyer par télécopie

FBI n abbr (US: = Federal Bureau of Investigation) FBI m

FCC n abbr (US) = **Federal Communications Commission**

FCO n abbr (Brit: = Foreign and Commonwealth Office) ministère des Affaires étrangères et du Commonwealth

FD n abbr (US) = **fire department**

FDA n abbr (US: = Food and Drug Administration) office de contrôle des produits pharmaceutiques et alimentaires

FE n abbr = **further education**

fear [fɪə'] n crainte f, peur f ▷ vt craindre ▷ vi: **to ~ for** craindre pour; **to ~ that** craindre que; **~ of heights** vertige m; **for ~ of** de peur que + sub or de + infinitive

fearful ['fɪəful] adj craintif(-ive); (sight, noise) affreux(-euse), épouvantable; **to be ~ of** avoir peur de, craindre

fearfully ['fɪəfəlɪ] adv (timidly) craintivement; (inf: very) affreusement

fearless ['fɪəlɪs] adj intrépide, sans peur

fearsome ['fɪəsəm] adj (opponent) redoutable; (sight) épouvantable

feasibility [fi:zə'bɪlɪtɪ] n (of plan) possibilité f de réalisation, faisabilité f

feasibility study n étude f de faisabilité

feasible ['fi:zəbl] adj faisable, réalisable

feast [fi:st] n festin m, banquet m; (Rel: also: **feast day**) fête f ▷ vi festoyer; **to ~ on** se régaler de

feat [fi:t] n exploit m, prouesse f

feather ['fɛðə'] n plume f ▷ vt: **to ~ one's nest** (fig) faire sa pelote ▷ cpd (bed etc) de plumes

feather-weight ['fɛðəweɪt] n poids m plume inv

feature ['fi:tʃə'] n caractéristique f; (article) chronique f, rubrique f ▷ vt (film) avoir pour vedette(s) ▷ vi figurer (en bonne place); **features** npl (of face) traits mpl; **a (special) ~ on sth/sb** un reportage sur qch/qn; **it ~d prominently in ...** cela a figuré en bonne place sur or dans ...

feature film n long métrage

featureless ['fi:tʃəlɪs] adj anonyme, sans traits distinctifs

Feb. abbr (= February) fév

February ['fɛbruərɪ] n février m; for phrases see also **July**

feces ['fi:si:z] npl (US) = **faeces**

feckless ['fɛklɪs] adj inepte

Fed abbr (US) = **federal; federation**

fed [fɛd] *pt, pp of* **feed**

Fed. [fɛd] *n abbr* (*US inf*) = **Federal Reserve Board**

federal ['fɛdərəl] *adj* fédéral(e)

Federal Reserve Board *n* (*US*) *organe de contrôle de la banque centrale américaine*

Federal Trade Commission *n* (*US*) *organisme de protection contre les pratiques commerciales abusives*

federation [fɛdə'reɪʃən] *n* fédération *f*

fed up [fɛd'ʌp] *adj*: **to be ~ (with)** en avoir marre *or* plein le dos (de)

fee [fiː] *n* rémunération *f*; (*of doctor, lawyer*) honoraires *mpl*; (*of school, college etc*) frais *mpl* de scolarité; (*for examination*) droits *mpl*; **entrance/membership ~** droit d'entrée/d'inscription; **for a small ~** pour une somme modique

feeble ['fiːbl] *adj* faible; (*attempt, excuse*) pauvre; (*joke*) piteux(-euse)

feeble-minded ['fiːbl'maɪndɪd] *adj* faible d'esprit

feed [fiːd] *n* (*of baby*) tétée *f*; (*of animal*) nourriture *f*, pâture *f*; (*on printer*) mécanisme *m* d'alimentation ▷ *vt* (*pt, pp* **fed** [fɛd]) (*person*) nourrir; (*Brit: baby: breastfeed*) allaiter; (: *with bottle*) donner le biberon à; (*horse etc*) donner à manger à; (*machine*) alimenter; (*data etc*): **to ~ sth into** enregistrer qch dans

▸ **feed back** *vt* (*results*) donner en retour

▸ **feed on** *vt fus* se nourrir de

feedback ['fiːdbæk] *n* (*Elec*) effet *m* Larsen; (*from person*) réactions *fpl*

feeder ['fiːdə^r] *n* (*bib*) bavette *f*

feeding bottle ['fiːdɪŋ-] *n* (*Brit*) biberon *m*

feel [fiːl] *n* (*sensation*) sensation *f*; (*impression*) impression *f* ▷ *vt* (*pt, pp* **felt** [fɛlt]) (*touch*) toucher; (*explore*) tâter, palper; (*cold, pain*) sentir; (*grief, anger*) ressentir, éprouver; (*think, believe*): **to ~ (that)** trouver que; **I ~ that you ought to do it** il me semble que vous devriez le faire; **to ~ hungry/cold** avoir faim/froid; **to ~ lonely/better** se sentir seul/mieux; **I don't ~ well** je ne me sens pas bien; **to ~ sorry for** avoir pitié de; **it ~s soft** c'est doux au toucher; **it ~s colder here** je trouve qu'il fait plus froid ici; **it ~s like velvet** on dirait du velours, ça ressemble au velours; **to ~ like** (*want*) avoir envie de; **to ~ about** *or* **around** fouiller, tâtonner; **to get the ~ of sth** (*fig*) s'habituer à qch

feeler ['fiːlə^r] *n* (*of insect*) antenne *f*; (*fig*): **to put out a ~** *or* **~s** tâter le terrain

feeling ['fiːlɪŋ] *n* (*physical*) sensation *f*; (*emotion, impression*) sentiment *m*; **to hurt sb's ~s** froisser qn; **~s ran high about it** cela a déchaîné les passions; **what are your ~s about the matter?** quel est votre sentiment sur cette question?; **my ~ is that ...** j'estime que ...; **I have a ~ that ...** j'ai l'impression que ...

fee-paying school ['fiːpeɪɪŋ-] *n* établissement (d'enseignement) privé

feet [fiːt] *npl of* **foot**

feign [feɪn] *vt* feindre, simuler

felicitous [fɪ'lɪsɪtəs] *adj* heureux(-euse)

fell [fɛl] *pt of* **fall** ▷ *vt* (*tree*) abattre ▷ *n* (*Brit: mountain*) montagne *f*; (: *moorland*): **the ~s** la lande ▷ *adj*: **with one ~ blow** d'un seul coup

fellow ['fɛləu] *n* type *m*; (*comrade*) compagnon *m*; (*of learned society*) membre *m*; (*of university*) universitaire *m/f* (*membre du conseil*) ▷ *cpd*: **their ~ prisoners/students** leurs camarades prisonniers/étudiants; **his ~ workers** ses collègues *mpl* (de travail)

fellow citizen *n* concitoyen(ne)

fellow countryman (*irreg*) *n* compatriote *m*

fellow feeling *n* sympathie *f*

fellow men *npl* semblables *mpl*

fellowship ['fɛləuʃɪp] *n* (*society*) association *f*; (*comradeship*) amitié *f*, camaraderie *f*; (*Scol*) sorte de bourse universitaire

fellow traveller *n* compagnon (compagne) de route; (*Pol*) communisant(e)

fell-walking ['fɛlwɔːkɪŋ] *n* (*Brit*) randonnée *f* en montagne

felon ['fɛlən] *n* (*Law*) criminel(le)

felony ['fɛlənɪ] *n* crime *m*, forfait *m*

felt [fɛlt] *pt, pp of* **feel** ▷ *n* feutre *m*

felt-tip ['fɛltɪp-] *n* (*also:* **felt-tip pen**) stylo-feutre *m*

female ['fiːmeɪl] *n* (*Zool*) femelle *f*; (*pej: woman*) bonne femme ▷ *adj* (*Biol, Elec*) femelle; (*sex, character*) féminin(e); (*vote etc*) des femmes; (*child etc*) du sexe féminin; **male and ~ students** étudiants et étudiantes

female impersonator *n* (*Theat*) travesti *m*

feminine ['fɛmɪnɪn] *adj* féminin(e) ▷ *n* féminin *m*

femininity [fɛmɪ'nɪnɪtɪ] *n* féminité *f*

feminism ['fɛmɪnɪzəm] *n* féminisme *m*

feminist ['fɛmɪnɪst] *n* féministe *m/f*

fen [fɛn] *n* (*Brit*): **the F~s** les plaines *fpl* du Norfolk (*anciennement marécageuses*)

fence [fɛns] *n* barrière *f*; (*Sport*) obstacle *m*; (*inf: person*) receleur(-euse) ▷ *vt* (*also:* **fence in**) clôturer ▷ *vi* faire de l'escrime; **to sit on the ~** (*fig*) ne pas se mouiller

fencing ['fɛnsɪŋ] *n* (*sport*) escrime *m*

fend [fɛnd] *vi*: **to ~ for o.s.** se débrouiller (tout seul)

▸ **fend off** *vt* (*attack etc*) parer; (*questions*) éluder

fender ['fɛndə^r] *n* garde-feu *m inv*; (*on boat*) défense *f*; (*US: of car*) aile *f*

fennel ['fɛnl] *n* fenouil *m*

ferment *vi* [fə'mɛnt] fermenter ▷ *n* ['fəːmɛnt] (*fig*) agitation *f*, effervescence *f*

fermentation [fəːmɛn'teɪʃən] *n* fermentation *f*

fern [fəːn] *n* fougère *f*

ferocious [fə'rəuʃəs] *adj* féroce

ferocity [fə'rɔsɪtɪ] *n* férocité *f*

ferret ['fɛrɪt] *n* furet *m*

▸ **ferret about, ferret around** *vi* fureter

▸ **ferret out** *vt* dénicher

ferry ['fɛrɪ] *n* (*small*) bac *m*; (*large: also:* **ferryboat**) ferry(-boat *m*) *m* ▷ *vt* transporter; **to ~ sth/sb across** *or* **over** faire traverser qch/qn

ferryman ['fɛrɪmən] (*irreg*) *n* passeur *m*

fertile ['fə:taɪl] *adj* fertile; (*Biol*) fécond(e); **~ period** période *f* de fécondité
fertility [fə'tɪlɪtɪ] *n* fertilité *f*; fécondité *f*
fertility drug *n* médicament *m* contre la stérilité
fertilize ['fə:tɪlaɪz] *vt* fertiliser; (*Biol*) féconder
fertilizer ['fə:tɪlaɪzə'] *n* engrais *m*
fervent ['fə:vənt] *adj* fervent(e), ardent(e)
fervour, (*US*) **fervor** ['fə:və'] *n* ferveur *f*
fester ['fɛstə'] *vi* suppurer
festival ['fɛstɪvəl] *n* (*Rel*) fête *f*; (*Art, Mus*) festival *m*
festive ['fɛstɪv] *adj* de fête; **the ~ season** (*Brit: Christmas*) la période des fêtes
festivities [fɛs'tɪvɪtɪz] *npl* réjouissances *fpl*
festoon [fɛs'tu:n] *vt*: **to ~ with** orner de
fetch [fɛtʃ] *vt* aller chercher; (*Brit: sell for*) rapporter; **how much did it ~?** ça a atteint quel prix?
  ▶ **fetch up** *vi* (*Brit*) se retrouver
fetching ['fɛtʃɪŋ] *adj* charmant(e)
fête [feɪt] *n* fête *f*, kermesse *f*
fetid ['fɛtɪd] *adj* fétide
fetish ['fɛtɪʃ] *n* fétiche *m*
fetter ['fɛtə'] *vt* entraver
fetters ['fɛtəz] *npl* chaînes *fpl*
fettle ['fɛtl] *n* (*Brit*): **in fine ~** en bonne forme
fetus ['fi:təs] *n* (*US*) = **foetus**
feud [fju:d] *n* querelle *f*, dispute *f* ▷ *vi* se quereller, se disputer; **a family ~** une querelle de famille
feudal ['fju:dl] *adj* féodal(e)
feudalism ['fju:dlɪzəm] *n* féodalité *f*
fever ['fi:və'] *n* fièvre *f*; **he has a ~** il a de la fièvre
feverish ['fi:vərɪʃ] *adj* fiévreux(-euse), fébrile
few [fju:] *adj* (*not many*) peu de ▷ *pron* peu; **~ succeed** il y en a peu qui réussissent, (bien) peu réussissent; **they were ~** ils étaient peu (nombreux), il y en avait peu; **a ~** (*as adj*) quelques; (*as pron*) quelques-uns(-unes); **I know a ~** j'en connais quelques-uns; **quite a ~ ...** (*adj*) un certain nombre de ..., pas mal de ...; **in the next ~ days** dans les jours qui viennent; **in the past ~ days** ces derniers jours; **every ~ days/ months** tous les deux ou trois jours/mois; **a ~ more ...** encore quelques ..., quelques ... de plus
fewer ['fju:ə'] *adj* moins de ▷ *pron* moins; **they are ~ now** il y a moins maintenant, ils sont moins (nombreux) maintenant
fewest ['fju:ɪst] *adj* le moins nombreux
FFA *n abbr* = **Future Farmers of America**
FH *abbr* (*Brit*) = **fire hydrant**
FHA *n abbr* (*US*: = *Federal Housing Administration*) office fédéral du logement
fiancé [fɪ'ā:ŋseɪ] *n* fiancé *m*
fiancée [fɪ'ā:ŋseɪ] *n* fiancée *f*
fiasco [fɪ'æskəu] *n* fiasco *m*
fib [fɪb] *n* bobard *m*
fibre, (*US*) **fiber** ['faɪbə'] *n* fibre *f*
fibreboard, (*US*) **fiberboard** ['faɪbəbɔ:d] *n* panneau *m* de fibres
fibreglass, (*US*) **Fiberglass**® ['faɪbəglɑ:s] *n* fibre *f* de verre
fibrositis [faɪbrə'saɪtɪs] *n* aponévrosite *f*
FICA *n abbr* (*US*) = **Federal Insurance Contributions Act**
fickle ['fɪkl] *adj* inconstant(e), volage, capricieux(-euse)
fiction ['fɪkʃən] *n* romans *mpl*, littérature *f* romanesque; (*invention*) fiction *f*
fictional ['fɪkʃənl] *adj* fictif(-ive)
fictionalize ['fɪkʃnəlaɪz] *vt* romancer
fictitious [fɪk'tɪʃəs] *adj* fictif(-ive), imaginaire
fiddle ['fɪdl] *n* (*Mus*) violon *m*; (*cheating*) combine *f*; escroquerie *f* ▷ *vt* (*Brit: accounts*) falsifier, maquiller; **tax ~** fraude fiscale, combine *f* pour échapper au fisc; **to work a ~** traficoter
  ▶ **fiddle with** *vt fus* tripoter
fiddler ['fɪdlə'] *n* violoniste *m/f*
fiddly ['fɪdlɪ] *adj* (*task*) minutieux(-euse)
fidelity [fɪ'dɛlɪtɪ] *n* fidélité *f*
fidget ['fɪdʒɪt] *vi* se trémousser, remuer
fidgety ['fɪdʒɪtɪ] *adj* agité(e), qui a la bougeotte
fiduciary [fɪ'dju:ʃɪərɪ] *n* agent *m* fiduciaire
field [fi:ld] *n* champ *m*; (*fig*) domaine *m*, champ; (*Sport: ground*) terrain *m*; (*Comput*) champ, zone *f*; **to lead the ~** (*Sport, Comm*) dominer; **the children had a ~ day** (*fig*) c'était un grand jour pour les enfants
field glasses *npl* jumelles *fpl*
field hospital *n* antenne chirurgicale
field marshal *n* maréchal *m*
fieldwork ['fi:ldwə:k] *n* travaux *mpl* pratiques (*or* recherches *fpl*) sur le terrain
fiend [fi:nd] *n* démon *m*
fiendish ['fi:ndɪʃ] *adj* diabolique
fierce [fɪəs] *adj* (*look, animal*) féroce, sauvage; (*wind, attack, person*) (très) violent(e); (*fighting, enemy*) acharné(e)
fiery ['faɪərɪ] *adj* ardent(e), brûlant(e), fougueux(-euse)
FIFA ['fi:fə] *n abbr* (= *Fédération Internationale de Football Association*) FIFA *f*
fifteen [fɪf'ti:n] *num* quinze
fifteenth [fɪf'ti:nθ] *num* quinzième
fifth [fɪfθ] *num* cinquième
fiftieth ['fɪftɪɪθ] *num* cinquantième
fifty ['fɪftɪ] *num* cinquante
fifty-fifty ['fɪftɪ'fɪftɪ] *adv* moitié-moitié; **to share ~ with sb** partager moitié-moitié avec qn ▷ *adj*: **to have a ~ chance (of success)** avoir une chance sur deux (de réussir)
fig [fɪg] *n* figue *f*
fight [faɪt] (*pt, pp* **fought** [fɔ:t]) *n* (*between persons*) bagarre *f*; (*argument*) dispute *f*; (*Mil*) combat *m*; (*against cancer etc*) lutte *f* ▷ *vt* se battre contre; (*cancer, alcoholism, emotion*) combattre, lutter contre; (*election*) se présenter à; (*Law: case*) défendre ▷ *vi* se battre; (*argue*) se disputer; (*fig*): **to ~ (for/against)** lutter (pour/contre)
  ▶ **fight back** *vi* rendre les coups; (*after illness*) reprendre le dessus ▷ *vt* (*tears*) réprimer
  ▶ **fight off** *vt* repousser; (*disease, sleep, urge*) lutter contre

fighter ['faɪtə'] *n* lutteur *m*; (*fig: plane*) chasseur *m*

fighter pilot *n* pilote *m* de chasse

fighting ['faɪtɪŋ] *n* combats *mpl*; (*brawls*) bagarres *fpl*

figment ['fɪgmənt] *n*: **a ~ of the imagination** une invention

figurative ['fɪgjʊrətɪv] *adj* figuré(e)

figure ['fɪgə'] *n* (*Drawing, Geom*) figure *f*; (*number*) chiffre *m*; (*body, outline*) silhouette *f*; (*person's shape*) ligne *f*, formes *fpl*; (*person*) personnage *m* ▷ *vt* (*US: think*) supposer ▷ *vi* (*appear*) figurer; (*US: make sense*) s'expliquer; **public ~** personnalité *f*; **~ of speech** figure *f* de rhétorique
▶ **figure on** *vt fus* (*US*): **to ~ on doing** compter faire
▶ **figure out** *vt* (*understand*) arriver à comprendre; (*plan*) calculer

figurehead ['fɪgəhɛd] *n* (*Naut*) figure *f* de proue; (*pej*) prête-nom *m*

figure skating *n* figures imposées (*en patinage*), patinage *m* artistique

Fiji ['fi:dʒi:] *n*, **Fiji Islands** *npl* (îles *fpl*) Fi(d)ji *fpl*

filament ['fɪləmənt] *n* filament *m*

filch [fɪltʃ] *vt* (*inf: steal*) voler, chiper

file [faɪl] *n* (*tool*) lime *f*; (*dossier*) dossier *m*; (*folder*) dossier, chemise *f*; (*: binder*) classeur *m*; (*Comput*) fichier *m*; (*row*) file *f* ▷ *vt* (*nails, wood*) limer; (*papers*) classer; (*Law: claim*) faire enregistrer; déposer ▷ *vi*: **to ~ in/out** entrer/sortir l'un derrière l'autre; **to ~ past** défiler devant; **to ~ a suit against sb** (*Law*) intenter un procès à qn

file name *n* (*Comput*) nom *m* de fichier

filibuster ['fɪlɪbʌstə'] (*esp US Pol*) *n* (*also*: **filibusterer**) obstructionniste *m/f* ▷ *vi* faire de l'obstructionnisme

filing ['faɪlɪŋ] *n* (*travaux mpl de*) classement *m*; **filings** *npl* limaille *f*

filing cabinet *n* classeur *m* (*meuble*)

filing clerk *n* documentaliste *m/f*

Filipino [fɪlɪ'pi:nəʊ] *adj* philippin(e) ▷ *n* (*person*) Philippin(e); (*Ling*) tagalog *m*

fill [fɪl] *vt* remplir; (*vacancy*) pourvoir à ▷ *n*: **to eat one's ~** manger à sa faim; **to ~ with** remplir de
▶ **fill in** *vt* (*hole*) boucher; (*form*) remplir; (*details, report*) compléter
▶ **fill out** *vt* (*form, receipt*) remplir
▶ **fill up** *vt* remplir ▷ *vi* (*Aut*) faire le plein; **~ it up, please** (*Aut*) le plein, s'il vous plaît

fillet ['fɪlɪt] *n* filet *m* ▷ *vt* préparer en filets

fillet steak *n* filet *m* de bœuf, tournedos *m*

filling ['fɪlɪŋ] *n* (*Culin*) garniture *f*, farce *f*; (*for tooth*) plombage *m*

filling station *n* station-service *f*, station *f* d'essence

fillip ['fɪlɪp] *n* coup *m* de fouet (*fig*)

filly ['fɪlɪ] *n* pouliche *f*

film [fɪlm] *n* film *m*; (*Phot*) pellicule *f*, film; (*of powder, liquid*) couche *f*, pellicule ▷ *vt* (*scene*) filmer ▷ *vi* tourner; **I'd like a 36-exposure ~** je voudrais une pellicule de 36 poses

film star *n* vedette *f* de cinéma

filmstrip ['fɪlmstrɪp] *n* (film *m* pour) projection *f* fixe

film studio *n* studio *m* (de cinéma)

Filofax® ['faɪləʊfæks] *n* Filofax® *m*

filter ['fɪltə'] *n* filtre *m* ▷ *vt* filtrer

filter coffee *n* café *m* filtre

filter lane *n* (*Brit Aut: at traffic lights*) voie *f* de dégagement; (*: on motorway*) voie *f* de sortie

filter tip *n* bout *m* filtre

filth [fɪlθ] *n* saleté *f*

filthy ['fɪlθɪ] *adj* sale, dégoûtant(e); (*language*) ordurier(-ière), grossier(-ière)

fin [fɪn] *n* (*of fish*) nageoire *f*; (*of shark*) aileron *m*; (*of diver*) palme *f*

final ['faɪnl] *adj* final(e), dernier(-ière); (*decision, answer*) définitif(-ive) ▷ *n* (*Brit Sport*) finale *f*; **finals** *npl* (*Scol*) examens *mpl* de dernière année; (*US Sport*) finale *f*; **~ demand** (*on invoice etc*) dernier rappel

finale [fɪ'nɑ:lɪ] *n* finale *m*

finalist ['faɪnəlɪst] *n* (*Sport*) finaliste *m/f*

finalize ['faɪnəlaɪz] *vt* mettre au point

finally ['faɪnəlɪ] *adv* (*eventually*) enfin, finalement; (*lastly*) en dernier lieu; (*irrevocably*) définitivement

finance [faɪ'næns] *n* finance *f* ▷ *vt* financer; **finances** *npl* finances *fpl*

financial [faɪ'nænʃəl] *adj* financier(-ière); **~ statement** bilan *m*, exercice financier

financially [faɪ'nænʃəlɪ] *adv* financièrement

financial year *n* année *f* budgétaire

financier [faɪ'nænsɪə'] *n* financier *m*

find [faɪnd] *vt* (*pt, pp* **found** [faʊnd]) trouver; (*lost object*) retrouver ▷ *n* trouvaille *f*, découverte *f*; **to ~ sb guilty** (*Law*) déclarer qn coupable; **to ~ (some) difficulty in doing sth** avoir du mal à faire qch
▶ **find out** *vt* se renseigner sur; (*truth, secret*) découvrir; (*person*) démasquer ▷ *vi*: **to ~ out about** (*make enquiries*) se renseigner sur; (*by chance*) apprendre

findings ['faɪndɪŋz] *npl* (*Law*) conclusions *fpl*, verdict *m*; (*of report*) constatations *fpl*

fine [faɪn] *adj* (*weather*) beau (belle); (*excellent*) excellent(e); (*thin, subtle, not coarse*) fin(e); (*acceptable*) bien *inv* ▷ *adv* (*well*) très bien; (*small*) fin, finement ▷ *n* (*Law*) amende *f*; contravention *f* ▷ *vt* (*Law*) condamner à une amende; donner une contravention à; **he's ~** il va bien; **the weather is ~** il fait beau; **you're doing ~** c'est bien, vous vous débrouillez bien; **to cut it ~** calculer un peu juste

fine arts *npl* beaux-arts *mpl*

fine print *n*: **the ~** ce qui est imprimé en tout petit

finery ['faɪnərɪ] *n* parure *f*

finesse [fɪ'nɛs] *n* finesse *f*, élégance *f*

fine-tooth comb ['faɪntu:θ-] *n*: **to go through sth with a ~** (*fig*) passer qch au peigne fin *or* au crible

finger ['fɪŋgə'] *n* doigt *m* ▷ *vt* palper, toucher;
index ~ index *m*

fingernail ['fɪŋgəneɪl] *n* ongle *m* (de la main)

fingerprint ['fɪŋgəprɪnt] *n* empreinte digitale
▷ *vt* (*person*) prendre les empreintes digitales de

fingerstall ['fɪŋgəstɔːl] *n* doigtier *m*

fingertip ['fɪŋgətɪp] *n* bout *m* du doigt; (*fig*): **to
have sth at one's ~s** avoir qch à sa disposition;
(*knowledge*) savoir qch sur le bout du doigt

finicky ['fɪnɪkɪ] *adj* tatillon(ne),
méticuleux(-euse), minutieux(-euse)

finish ['fɪnɪʃ] *n* fin *f*; (*Sport*) arrivée *f*; (*polish etc*)
finition *f* ▷ *vt* finir, terminer ▷ *vi* finir, se
terminer; (*session*) s'achever; **to ~ doing sth**
finir de faire qch; **to ~ third** arriver *or* terminer
troisième; **when does the show ~?** quand est-
ce que le spectacle se termine?
 ▸ **finish off** *vt* finir, terminer; (*kill*) achever
 ▸ **finish up** *vi*, *vt* finir

finishing line ['fɪnɪʃɪŋ-] *n* ligne *f* d'arrivée

finishing school ['fɪnɪʃɪŋ-] *n* institution privée
(*pour jeunes filles*)

finite ['faɪnaɪt] *adj* fini(e); (*verb*) conjugué(e)

Finland ['fɪnlənd] *n* Finlande *f*

Finn [fɪn] *n* Finnois(e), Finlandais(e)

Finnish ['fɪnɪʃ] *adj* finnois(e), finlandais(e) ▷ *n*
(*Ling*) finnois *m*

fiord [fjɔːd] *n* fjord *m*

fir [fəːʳ] *n* sapin *m*

fire ['faɪəʳ] *n* feu *m*; (*accidental*) incendie *m*;
(*heater*) radiateur *m* ▷ *vt* (*discharge*): **to ~ a gun**
tirer un coup de feu; (*fig: interest*) enflammer,
animer; (*inf: dismiss*) mettre à la porte, renvoyer
▷ *vi* (*shoot*) tirer, faire feu ▷ *cpd*: **~ hazard, ~
risk: that's a ~ hazard** *or* **risk** cela présente un
risque d'incendie; **~! au feu!**; **on ~** en feu; **to
set ~ to sth, set sth on ~** mettre le feu à qch;
insured against ~ assuré contre l'incendie

fire alarm *n* avertisseur *m* d'incendie

firearm ['faɪərɑːm] *n* arme *f* à feu

fire brigade *n* (régiment *m* de sapeurs-)
pompiers *mpl*

fire chief *n* (US) = **fire master**

fire department *n* (US) = **fire brigade**

fire door *n* porte *f* coupe-feu

fire engine *n* (Brit) pompe *f* à incendie

fire escape *n* escalier *m* de secours

fire exit *n* issue *f* or sortie *f* de secours

fire extinguisher *n* extincteur *m*

fireguard ['faɪəgɑːd] *n* (Brit) garde-feu *m inv*

fire insurance *n* assurance *f* incendie

fireman (*irreg*) ['faɪəmən] *n* pompier *m*

fire master *n* (Brit) capitaine *m* des pompiers

fireplace ['faɪəpleɪs] *n* cheminée *f*

fireproof ['faɪəpruːf] *adj* ignifuge

fire regulations *npl* consignes *fpl* en cas
d'incendie

fire screen *n* (*decorative*) écran *m* de cheminée;
(*for protection*) garde-feu *m inv*

fireside ['faɪəsaɪd] *n* foyer *m*, coin *m* du feu

fire station *n* caserne *f* de pompiers

fire truck *n* (US) = **fire engine**

firewall ['faɪəwɔːl] *n* (*Internet*) pare-feu *m*

firewood ['faɪəwud] *n* bois *m* de chauffage

fireworks ['faɪəwəːks] *npl* (*display*) feu(x) *m(pl)*
d'artifice

firing ['faɪərɪŋ] *n* (*Mil*) feu *m*, tir *m*

firing squad *n* peloton *m* d'exécution

firm [fəːm] *adj* ferme ▷ *n* compagnie *f*, firme *f*;
it is my ~ belief that ... je crois fermement
que ...

firmly ['fəːmlɪ] *adv* fermement

firmness ['fəːmnɪs] *n* fermeté *f*

first [fəːst] *adj* premier(-ière) ▷ *adv* (*before other
people*) le premier, la première; (*before other things*)
en premier, d'abord; (*when listing reasons etc*) en
premier lieu, premièrement; (*in the beginning*) au
début ▷ *n* (*person: in race*) premier(-ière); (*Brit
Scol*) mention *f* très bien; (*Aut*) première *f*; **the ~
of January** le premier janvier; **at ~** au
commencement, au début; **~ of all** tout
d'abord, pour commencer; **in the ~ instance**
en premier lieu; **I'll do it ~ thing tomorrow** je
le ferai tout de suite demain matin

first aid *n* premiers secours *or* soins

first-aid kit [fəːst'eɪd-] *n* trousse *f* à pharmacie

first-class ['fəːst'klɑːs] *adj* (*ticket etc*) de première
classe; (*excellent*) excellent(e), exceptionnel(le);
(*post*) en tarif prioritaire

first-class mail *n* courrier *m* rapide

first-hand ['fəːst'hænd] *adj* de première main

first lady *n* (US) femme *f* du président

firstly ['fəːstlɪ] *adv* premièrement, en premier
lieu

first name *n* prénom *m*

first night *n* (*Theat*) première *f*

first-rate ['fəːst'reɪt] *adj* excellent(e)

first-time buyer ['fəːstaɪm-] *n* personne achetant
une maison ou un appartement pour la première fois

fir tree *n* sapin *m*

fiscal ['fɪskl] *adj* fiscal(e)

fiscal year *n* exercice financier

fish [fɪʃ] *n* (*pl inv*) poisson *m*; poissons *mpl* ▷ *vt*, *vi*
pêcher; **to ~ a river** pêcher dans une rivière; **~
and chips** poisson frit et frites

fisherman (*irreg*) ['fɪʃəmən] *n* pêcheur *m*

fishery ['fɪʃərɪ] *n* pêcherie *f*

fish factory *n* (Brit) conserverie *f* de poissons

fish farm *n* établissement *m* piscicole

fish fingers *npl* (Brit) bâtonnets *mpl* de poisson
(congelés)

fish hook *n* hameçon *m*

fishing ['fɪʃɪŋ] *n* pêche *f*; **to go ~** aller à la pêche

fishing boat ['fɪʃɪŋ-] *n* barque *f* de pêche

fishing industry ['fɪʃɪŋ-] *n* industrie *f* de la
pêche

fishing line ['fɪʃɪŋ-] *n* ligne *f* (de pêche)

fishing rod ['fɪʃɪŋ-] *n* canne *f* à pêche

fishing tackle ['fɪʃɪŋ-] *n* attirail *m* de pêche

fish market *n* marché *m* au poisson

fishmonger ['fɪʃmʌŋgəʳ] *n* (Brit) marchand *m* de
poisson

fishmonger's ['fɪʃmʌŋgəz], **fishmonger's
shop** *n* (Brit) poissonnerie *f*

fish slice n (Brit) pelle f à poisson
fish sticks npl (US) = **fish fingers**
fishy ['fɪʃɪ] adj (inf) suspect(e), louche
fission ['fɪʃən] n fission f; **atomic** or **nuclear** ~ fission nucléaire
fissure ['fɪʃər] n fissure f
fist [fɪst] n poing m
fistfight ['fɪstfaɪt] n pugilat m, bagarre f (à coups de poing)
fit [fɪt] adj (Med, Sport) en (bonne) forme; (proper) convenable; approprié(e) ▷ vt (subj: clothes) aller à; (adjust) ajuster; (put in, attach) installer, poser; adapter; (equip) équiper, garnir, munir; (suit) convenir à ▷ vi (clothes) aller; (parts) s'adapter; (in space, gap) entrer, s'adapter ▷ n (Med) accès m, crise f; (of anger) accès; (of hysterics, jealousy) crise; ~ **to** (ready to) en état de; ~ **for** (worthy) digne de; (capable) apte à; **to keep** ~ se maintenir en forme; **this dress is a tight/good** ~ cette robe est un peu juste/(me) va très bien; **a** ~ **of coughing** une quinte de toux; **to have a** ~ (Med) faire or avoir une crise; (inf) piquer une crise; **by** ~**s and starts** par à-coups
  ▶ **fit in** vi (add up) cadrer; (integrate) s'intégrer; (to new situation) s'adapter
  ▶ **fit out** vt (Brit: also: **fit up**) équiper
fitful ['fɪtful] adj intermittent(e)
fitment ['fɪtmənt] n meuble encastré, élément m
fitness ['fɪtnɪs] n (Med) forme f physique; (of remark) à-propos m, justesse f
fitted ['fɪtɪd] adj (jacket, shirt) ajusté(e)
fitted carpet ['fɪtɪd-] n moquette f
fitted kitchen ['fɪtɪd-] n (Brit) cuisine équipée
fitted sheet ['fɪtɪd-] n drap-housse m
fitter ['fɪtər] n monteur m; (Dressmaking) essayeur(-euse)
fitting ['fɪtɪŋ] adj approprié(e) ▷ n (of dress) essayage m; (of piece of equipment) pose f, installation f
fitting room n (in shop) cabine f d'essayage
fittings ['fɪtɪŋz] npl installations fpl
five [faɪv] num cinq
five-day week ['faɪvdeɪ-] n semaine f de cinq jours
fiver ['faɪvər] n (inf: Brit) billet m de cinq livres; (: US) billet de cinq dollars
fix [fɪks] vt (date, amount etc) fixer; (sort out) arranger; (mend) réparer; (make ready: meal, drink) préparer; (inf: game etc) truquer ▷ n: **to be in a** ~ être dans le pétrin
  ▶ **fix up** vt (meeting) arranger; **to** ~ **sb up with sth** faire avoir qch à qn
fixation [fɪk'seɪʃən] n (Psych) fixation f; (fig) obsession f
fixed [fɪkst] adj (prices etc) fixe; **there's a** ~ **charge** il y a un prix forfaitaire; **how are you** ~ **for money?** (inf) question fric, ça va?
fixed assets npl immobilisations fpl
fixture ['fɪkstʃər] n installation f (fixe); (Sport) rencontre f (au programme)
fizz [fɪz] vi pétiller

fizzle ['fɪzl] vi pétiller
  ▶ **fizzle out** vi rater
fizzy ['fɪzɪ] adj pétillant(e), gazeux(-euse)
fjord [fjɔːd] n = **fiord**
FL, Fla. abbr (US) = **Florida**
flabbergasted ['flæbəgɑːstɪd] adj sidéré(e), ahuri(e)
flabby ['flæbɪ] adj mou (molle)
flag [flæg] n drapeau m; (also: **flagstone**) dalle f ▷ vi faiblir; fléchir; ~ **of convenience** pavillon m de complaisance
  ▶ **flag down** vt héler, faire signe (de s'arrêter) à
flagon ['flægən] n bonbonne f
flagpole ['flægpəul] n mât m
flagrant ['fleɪgrənt] adj flagrant(e)
flagship ['flægʃɪp] n vaisseau m amiral; (fig) produit m vedette
flag stop n (US: for bus) arrêt facultatif
flair [flɛər] n flair m
flak [flæk] n (Mil) tir antiaérien; (inf: criticism) critiques fpl
flake [fleɪk] n (of rust, paint) écaille f; (of snow, soap powder) flocon m ▷ vi (also: **flake off**) s'écailler
flaky ['fleɪkɪ] adj (paintwork) écaillé(e); (skin) desquamé(e); (pastry) feuilleté(e)
flamboyant [flæm'bɔɪənt] adj flamboyant(e), éclatant(e); (person) haut(e) en couleur
flame [fleɪm] n flamme f
flamingo [flə'mɪŋgəu] n flamant m (rose)
flammable ['flæməbl] adj inflammable
flan [flæn] n (Brit) tarte f
Flanders ['flɑːndəz] n Flandre(s) f(pl)
flange [flændʒ] n boudin m; collerette f
flank [flæŋk] n flanc m ▷ vt flanquer
flannel ['flænl] n (Brit: also: **face flannel**) gant m de toilette; (fabric) flanelle f; (Brit inf) baratin m; **flannels** npl pantalon m de flanelle
flap [flæp] n (of pocket, envelope) rabat m ▷ vt (wings) battre (de) ▷ vi (sail, flag) claquer; (inf: also: **be in a flap**) paniquer
flapjack ['flæpdʒæk] n (US: pancake) ≈ crêpe f; (Brit: biscuit) galette f
flare [flɛər] n (signal) signal lumineux; (Mil) fusée éclairante; (in skirt etc) évasement m; **flares** npl (trousers) pantalon m à pattes d'éléphant
  ▶ **flare up** vi s'embraser; (fig: person) se mettre en colère, s'emporter; (: revolt) éclater
flared ['flɛəd] adj (trousers) à jambes évasées; (skirt) évasé(e)
flash [flæʃ] n éclair m; (also: **news flash**) flash m (d'information); (Phot) flash ▷ vt (switch on) allumer (brièvement); (direct): **to** ~ **sth at** braquer qch sur; (flaunt) étaler, exhiber; (send: message) câbler; (smile) lancer ▷ vi briller; jeter des éclairs; (light on ambulance etc) clignoter; **a** ~ **of lightning** un éclair; **in a** ~ en un clin d'œil; **to** ~ **one's headlights** faire un appel de phares; **he** ~**ed by** or **past** il passa (devant nous) comme un éclair
flashback ['flæʃbæk] n flashback m, retour m en arrière

flashbulb ['flæʃbʌlb] n ampoule f de flash
flash card n (Scol) carte f (support visuel)
flashcube ['flæʃkju:b] n cube-flash m
flasher ['flæʃəʳ] n (Aut) clignotant m
flashlight ['flæʃlaɪt] n lampe f de poche
flashpoint ['flæʃpɔɪnt] n point m d'ignition;
(fig): **to be at ~** être sur le point d'exploser
flashy ['flæʃɪ] adj (pej) tape-à-l'œil inv,
tapageur(-euse)
flask [flɑ:sk] n flacon m, bouteille f; (Chem)
ballon m; (also: **vacuum flask**) bouteille f
thermos®
flat [flæt] adj plat(e); (tyre) dégonflé(e), à plat;
(beer) éventé(e); (battery) à plat; (denial)
catégorique; (Mus) bémol inv; (: voice) faux
(fausse) ▷ n (Brit: apartment) appartement m;
(Aut) crevaison f, pneu crevé; (Mus) bémol m; ~
out (work) sans relâche; (race) à fond; **~ rate of
pay** (Comm) salaire m fixe
flat-footed ['flæt'futɪd] adj: **to be ~** avoir les
pieds plats
flatly ['flætlɪ] adv catégoriquement
flatmate ['flætmeɪt] n (Brit): **he's my ~** il
partage l'appartement avec moi
flatness ['flætnɪs] n (of land) absence f de relief,
aspect plat
flat-screen ['flætskri:n] adj à écran plat
flatten ['flætn] vt (also: **flatten out**) aplatir;
(crop) coucher; (house, city) raser
flatter ['flætəʳ] vt flatter
flatterer ['flætərəʳ] n flatteur m
flattering ['flætərɪŋ] adj flatteur(-euse); (clothes
etc) seyant(e)
flattery ['flætərɪ] n flatterie f
flatulence ['flætjuləns] n flatulence f
flaunt [flɔ:nt] vt faire étalage de
flavour, (US) **flavor** ['fleɪvəʳ] n goût m, saveur f;
(of ice cream etc) parfum m ▷ vt parfumer,
aromatiser; **vanilla--ed** à l'arôme de vanille,
vanillé(e); **what ~s do you have?** quels
parfums avez-vous?; **to give** or **add ~ to** donner
du goût à, relever
flavouring, (US) **flavoring** ['fleɪvərɪŋ] n
arôme m (synthétique)
flaw [flɔ:] n défaut m
flawless ['flɔ:lɪs] adj sans défaut
flax [flæks] n lin m
flaxen ['flæksən] adj blond(e)
flea [fli:] n puce f
flea market n marché m aux puces
fleck [flɛk] n (of dust) particule f; (of mud, paint,
colour) tacheture f, moucheture f ▷ vt tacher,
éclabousser; **brown ~ed with white** brun
moucheté de blanc
fled [flɛd] pt, pp of **flee**
fledgeling, fledgling ['flɛdʒlɪŋ] n oisillon m
flee (pt, pp **fled**) [fli:, flɛd] vt fuir, s'enfuir de ▷ vi
fuir, s'enfuir
fleece [fli:s] n (of sheep) toison f; (top) (laine f)
polaire f ▷ vt (inf) voler, filouter
fleecy ['fli:sɪ] adj (blanket) moelleux(-euse);
(cloud) floconneux(-euse)

fleet [fli:t] n flotte f; (of lorries, cars etc) parc m;
convoi m
fleeting ['fli:tɪŋ] adj fugace, fugitif(-ive); (visit)
très bref (brève)
Flemish ['flɛmɪʃ] adj flamand(e) ▷ n (Ling)
flamand m; **the ~** (npl) les Flamands
flesh [flɛʃ] n chair f
flesh wound [-wu:nd] n blessure superficielle
flew [flu:] pt of **fly**
flex [flɛks] n fil m or câble m électrique (souple)
▷ vt (knee) fléchir; (muscles) tendre
flexibility [flɛksɪ'bɪlɪtɪ] n flexibilité f
flexible ['flɛksəbl] adj flexible; (person, schedule)
souple
flexitime ['flɛksɪtaɪm], (US) **flextime**
['flɛkstaɪm] n horaire m variable or à la carte
flick [flɪk] n petit coup m; (with finger) chiquenaude
f ▷ vt donner un petit coup à; (switch) appuyer
sur
▶ **flick through** vt fus feuilleter
flicker ['flɪkəʳ] vi (light, flame) vaciller ▷ n
vacillement m; **a ~ of light** une brève lueur
flick knife n (Brit) couteau m à cran d'arrêt
flicks [flɪks] npl (inf) ciné m
flier ['flaɪəʳ] n aviateur m
flies [flaɪz] npl of **fly**
flight [flaɪt] n vol m; (escape) fuite f; (also: **flight
of steps**) escalier m; **to take ~** prendre la fuite;
to put to ~ mettre en fuite
flight attendant n steward m, hôtesse f de l'air
flight crew n équipage m
flight deck n (Aviat) poste m de pilotage; (Naut)
pont m d'envol
flight path n trajectoire f (de vol)
flight recorder n enregistreur m de vol
flimsy ['flɪmzɪ] adj peu solide; (clothes) trop
léger(-ère); (excuse) pauvre, mince
flinch [flɪntʃ] vi tressaillir; **to ~ from** se dérober
à, reculer devant
fling [flɪŋ] vt (pt, pp **flung** [flʌŋ]) jeter, lancer ▷ n
(love affair) brève liaison, passade f
flint [flɪnt] n silex m; (in lighter) pierre f (à
briquet)
flip [flɪp] n chiquenaude f ▷ vt (throw) donner
une chiquenaude à; (switch) appuyer sur; (US:
pancake) faire sauter; **to ~ sth over** retourner
qch ▷ vi: **to ~ for sth** (US) jouer qch à pile ou
face
▶ **flip through** vt fus feuilleter
flip-flops ['flɪpflɔps] npl (esp Brit) tongs fpl
flippant ['flɪpənt] adj désinvolte,
irrévérencieux(-euse)
flipper ['flɪpəʳ] n (of animal) nageoire f; (for
swimmer) palme f
flip side n (of record) deuxième face f
flirt [flə:t] vi flirter ▷ n flirteur(-euse)
flirtation [flə:'teɪʃən] n flirt m
flit [flɪt] vi voleter
float [fləut] n flotteur m; (in procession) char m;
(sum of money) réserve f ▷ vi flotter; (bather)
flotter, faire la planche ▷ vt faire flotter; (loan,
business, idea) lancer

floating ['fləutɪŋ] *adj* flottant(e); ~ **vote** voix flottante; ~ **voter** électeur indécis

flock [flɔk] *n* (*of sheep*) troupeau *m*; (*of birds*) vol *m*; (*of people*) foule *f*

floe [fləu] *n* (*also*: **ice floe**) iceberg *m*

flog [flɔg] *vt* fouetter

flood [flʌd] *n* inondation *f*; (*of letters, refugees etc*) flot *m* ▷ *vt* inonder; (*Aut: carburettor*) noyer ▷ *vi* (*place*) être inondé; (*people*): **to ~ into** envahir; **to ~ the market** (*Comm*) inonder le marché; **in ~** en crue

flooding ['flʌdɪŋ] *n* inondation *f*

floodlight ['flʌdlaɪt] *n* projecteur *m* ▷ *vt* éclairer aux projecteurs, illuminer

floodlit ['flʌdlɪt] *pt, pp of* **floodlight** ▷ *adj* illuminé(e)

flood tide *n* marée montante

floodwater ['flʌdwɔːtər] *n* eau *f* de la crue

floor [flɔːr] *n* sol *m*; (*storey*) étage *m*; (*of sea, valley*) fond *m*; (*fig: at meeting*): **the ~** l'assemblée *f*, les membres *mpl* de l'assemblée ▷ *vt* (*knock down*) terrasser; (*baffle*) désorienter; **on the ~** par terre; (*baffle*) désorienter; **on the ~** par terre; **ground ~**, (*US*) **first ~** rez-de-chaussée *m*; **first ~**, (*US*) **second ~** premier étage; **top ~** dernier étage; **what ~ is it on?** c'est à quel étage?; **to have the ~** (*speaker*) avoir la parole

floorboard ['flɔːbɔːd] *n* planche *f* (*du plancher*)

flooring ['flɔːrɪŋ] *n* sol *m*; (*wooden*) plancher *m*; (*material to make floor*) matériau(x) *m(pl)* pour planchers; (*covering*) revêtement *m* de sol

floor lamp *n* (*US*) lampadaire *m*

floor show *n* spectacle *m* de variétés

floorwalker ['flɔːwɔːkər] *n* (*esp US*) surveillant *m* (de grand magasin)

flop [flɔp] *n* fiasco *m* ▷ *vi* (*fail*) faire fiasco; (*fall*) s'affaler, s'effondrer

floppy ['flɔpɪ] *adj* lâche, flottant(e) ▷ *n* (*Comput: also*: **floppy disk**) disquette *f*; ~ **hat** chapeau *m* à bords flottants

floppy disk *n* disquette *f*, disque *m* souple

flora ['flɔːrə] *n* flore *f*

floral ['flɔːrl] *adj* floral(e); (*dress*) à fleurs

Florence ['flɔrəns] *n* Florence

florid ['flɔrɪd] *adj* (*complexion*) fleuri(e); (*style*) plein(e) de fioritures

florist ['flɔrɪst] *n* fleuriste *m/f*

florist's ['flɔrɪsts], **florist's shop** *n* magasin *m* or boutique *f* de fleuriste

flotation [fləu'teɪʃən] *n* (*of shares*) émission *f*; (*of company*) lancement *m* (en Bourse)

flounce [flauns] *n* volant *m*
▸ **flounce out** *vi* sortir dans un mouvement d'humeur

flounder ['flaundər] *n* (*Zool*) flet *m* ▷ *vi* patauger

flour ['flauər] *n* farine *f*

flourish ['flʌrɪʃ] *vi* prospérer ▷ *vt* brandir ▷ *n* (*gesture*) moulinet *m*; (*decoration*) fioriture *f*; (*of trumpets*) fanfare *f*

flourishing ['flʌrɪʃɪŋ] *adj* prospère, florissant(e)

flout [flaut] *vt* se moquer de, faire fi de

flow [fləu] *n* (*of water, traffic etc*) écoulement *m*; (*tide, influx*) flux *m*; (*of orders, letters etc*) flot *m*; (*of blood, Elec*) circulation *f*; (*of river*) courant *m* ▷ *vi* couler; (*traffic*) s'écouler; (*robes, hair*) flotter

flow chart, flow diagram *n* organigramme *m*

flower ['flauər] *n* fleur *f* ▷ *vi* fleurir; **in ~** en fleur

flower bed *n* plate-bande *f*

flowerpot ['flauəpɔt] *n* pot *m* (à fleurs)

flowery ['flauərɪ] *adj* fleuri(e)

flown [fləun] *pp of* **fly**

fl. oz. *abbr* = **fluid ounce**

flu [fluː] *n* grippe *f*

fluctuate ['flʌktjueɪt] *vi* varier, fluctuer

fluctuation [flʌktju'eɪʃən] *n* fluctuation *f*, variation *f*

flue [fluː] *n* conduit *m*

fluency ['fluːənsɪ] *n* facilité *f*, aisance *f*

fluent ['fluːənt] *adj* (*speech, style*) coulant(e), aisé(e); **he's a ~ speaker/reader** il s'exprime/lit avec aisance or facilité; **he speaks ~ French**, **he's ~ in French** il parle le français couramment

fluently ['fluːəntlɪ] *adv* couramment; avec aisance or facilité

fluff [flʌf] *n* duvet *m*; (*on jacket, carpet*) peluche *f*

fluffy ['flʌfɪ] *adj* duveteux(-euse); (*jacket, carpet*) pelucheux(-euse); (*toy*) en peluche

fluid ['fluːɪd] *n* fluide *m*; (*in diet*) liquide *m* ▷ *adj* fluide

fluid ounce *n* (*Brit*) = 0.028 l; 0.05 pints

fluke [fluːk] *n* coup *m* de veine

flummox ['flʌməks] *vt* dérouter, déconcerter

flung [flʌŋ] *pt, pp of* **fling**

flunky ['flʌŋkɪ] *n* larbin *m*

fluorescent [fluə'resnt] *adj* fluorescent(e)

fluoride ['fluəraɪd] *n* fluor *m*

fluorine ['fluəriːn] *n* fluor *m*

flurry ['flʌrɪ] *n* (*of snow*) rafale *f*, bourrasque *f*; **a ~ of activity** un affairement soudain; **a ~ of excitement** une excitation soudaine

flush [flʌʃ] *n* (*on face*) rougeur *f*; (*fig: of youth etc*) éclat *m*; (*of blood*) afflux *m* ▷ *vt* nettoyer à grande eau; (*also*: **flush out**) débusquer ▷ *vi* rougir ▷ *adj* (*inf*) en fonds; (*level*): **~ with** au ras de, de niveau avec; **to ~ the toilet** tirer la chasse (d'eau); **hot ~es** (*Med*) bouffées *fpl* de chaleur

flushed ['flʌʃt] *adj* (tout(e)) rouge

fluster ['flʌstər] *n* agitation *f*, trouble *m*

flustered ['flʌstəd] *adj* énervé(e)

flute [fluːt] *n* flûte *f*

flutter ['flʌtər] *n* (*of panic, excitement*) agitation *f*; (*of wings*) battement *m* ▷ *vi* (*bird*) battre des ailes, voleter; (*person*) aller et venir dans une grande agitation

flux [flʌks] *n*: **in a state of ~** fluctuant sans cesse

fly [flaɪ] (*pt* **flew**, *pp* **flown** [fluː, fləun]) *n* (*insect*) mouche *f*; (*on trousers: also*: **flies**) braguette *f* ▷ *vt* (*plane*) piloter; (*passengers, cargo*) transporter (par avion); (*distance*) parcourir ▷ *vi* voler; (*passengers*) aller en avion; (*escape*) s'enfuir, fuir; (*flag*) se déployer; **to ~ open** s'ouvrir brusquement; **to ~ off the handle** s'énerver, s'emporter
▸ **fly away, fly off** *vi* s'envoler

▶ **fly in** vi (plane) atterrir; **he flew in yesterday** il est arrivé hier (par avion)

▶ **fly out** vi partir (par avion)

fly-drive ['flaɪdraɪv] n formule f avion plus voiture

fly-fishing ['flaɪfɪʃɪŋ] n pêche f à la mouche

flying ['flaɪɪŋ] n (activity) aviation f; (action) vol m ▷ adj: ~ **visit** visite f éclair inv; **with ~ colours** haut la main; **he doesn't like ~** il n'aime pas voyager en avion

flying buttress n arc-boutant m

flying picket n piquet m de grève volant

flying saucer n soucoupe volante

flying squad n (Police) brigade volante

flying start n: **to get off to a ~** faire un excellent départ

flyleaf ['flaɪliːf] n page f de garde

flyover ['flaɪəʊvəʳ] n (Brit: overpass) pont routier, saut-de-mouton m (Canada)

flypast ['flaɪpɑːst] n défilé aérien

flysheet ['flaɪʃiːt] n (for tent) double toit m

flyweight ['flaɪweɪt] n (Sport) poids m mouche

flywheel ['flaɪwiːl] n volant m (de commande)

FM abbr (Brit Mil) = **field marshal**; (Radio: = frequency modulation) FM

FMB n abbr (US) = **Federal Maritime Board**

FMCS n abbr (US: = Federal Mediation and Conciliation Services) organisme de conciliation en cas de conflits du travail

FO n abbr (Brit) = **Foreign Office**

foal [fəʊl] n poulain m

foam [fəʊm] n écume f; (on beer) mousse f; (also: **foam rubber**) caoutchouc m mousse; (also: **plastic foam**) mousse cellulaire or de plastique ▷ vi (liquid) écumer; (soapy water) mousser

foam rubber n caoutchouc m mousse

FOB abbr (= free on board) fob

fob [fɔb] n (also: **watch fob**) chaîne f, ruban m ▷ vt: **to ~ sb off with sth** refiler qch à qn

foc abbr (Brit) = **free of charge**

focal ['fəʊkl] adj (also fig) focal(e)

focal point n foyer m; (fig) centre m de l'attention, point focal

focus ['fəʊkəs] n (pl **-es**) foyer m; (of interest) centre m ▷ vt (field glasses etc) mettre au point; (light rays) faire converger ▷ vi: **to ~ (on)** (with camera) régler la mise au point (sur); (with eyes) fixer son regard (sur); (fig: concentrate) se concentrer; **out of/in ~** (picture) flou(e)/net(te); (camera) pas au point/au point

fodder ['fɔdəʳ] n fourrage m

FOE n abbr (= Friends of the Earth) AT mpl (= Amis de la Terre); (US: = Fraternal Order of Eagles) organisation charitable

foe [fəʊ] n ennemi m

foetus, (US) **fetus** ['fiːtəs] n fœtus m

fog [fɔg] n brouillard m

fogbound ['fɔgbaʊnd] adj bloqué(e) par le brouillard

foggy ['fɔgɪ] adj: **it's ~** il y a du brouillard

fog lamp, (US) **fog light** n (Aut) phare m anti-brouillard

foible ['fɔɪbl] n faiblesse f

foil [fɔɪl] vt déjouer, contrecarrer ▷ n feuille f de métal; (kitchen foil) papier m d'alu(minium); (Fencing) fleuret m; **to act as a ~ to** (fig) servir de repoussoir or de faire-valoir à

foist [fɔɪst] vt: **to ~ sth on sb** imposer qch à qn

fold [fəʊld] n (bend, crease) pli m; (Agr) parc m à moutons; (fig) bercail m ▷ vt plier; **to ~ one's arms** croiser les bras

▶ **fold up** vi (map etc) se plier, se replier; (business) fermer boutique ▷ vt (map etc) plier, replier

folder ['fəʊldəʳ] n (for papers) chemise f; (: binder) classeur m; (brochure) dépliant m; (Comput) dossier m

folding ['fəʊldɪŋ] adj (chair, bed) pliant(e)

foliage ['fəʊliːɪdʒ] n feuillage m

folk [fəʊk] npl gens mpl ▷ cpd folklorique; **folks** npl (inf: parents) famille f, parents mpl

folklore ['fəʊklɔːʳ] n folklore m

folk music n musique f folklorique; (contemporary) musique folk, folk m

folk song ['fəʊksɔŋ] n chanson f folklorique; (contemporary) chanson folk inv

follow ['fɔləʊ] vt suivre ▷ vi suivre; (result) s'ensuivre; **to ~ sb's advice** suivre les conseils de qn; **I don't quite ~ you** je ne vous suis plus; **to ~ in sb's footsteps** emboîter le pas à qn; (fig) suivre les traces de qn; **it ~s that ...** de ce fait, il s'ensuit que ...; **to ~ suit** (fig) faire de même

▶ **follow out** vt (idea, plan) poursuivre, mener à terme

▶ **follow through** vt = **follow out**

▶ **follow up** vt (victory) tirer parti de; (letter, offer) donner suite à; (case) suivre

follower ['fɔləʊəʳ] n disciple m/f, partisan(e)

following ['fɔləʊɪŋ] adj suivant(e) ▷ n partisans mpl, disciples mpl

follow-up ['fɔləʊʌp] n suite f; (on file, case) suivi m

folly ['fɔlɪ] n inconscience f; sottise f; (building) folie f

fond [fɔnd] adj (memory, look) tendre, affectueux(-euse); (hopes, dreams) un peu fou (folle); **to be ~ of** aimer beaucoup

fondle ['fɔndl] vt caresser

fondly ['fɔndlɪ] adv (lovingly) tendrement; (naïvely) naïvement

fondness ['fɔndnɪs] n (for things) attachement m; (for people) sentiments affectueux; **a special ~ for** une prédilection pour

font [fɔnt] n (Rel) fonts baptismaux; (Typ) police f de caractères

food [fuːd] n nourriture f

food chain n chaîne f alimentaire

food mixer n mixeur m

food poisoning n intoxication f alimentaire

food processor n robot m de cuisine

food stamp n (US) bon m de nourriture (pour indigents)

foodstuffs ['fuːdstʌfs] npl denrées fpl alimentaires

fool [fuːl] n idiot(e); (History: of king) bouffon m,

fou *m*; (*Culin*) mousse *f* de fruits ▷ *vt* berner, duper ▷ *vi* (*also*: **fool around**) faire l'idiot *or* l'imbécile; **to make a ~ of sb** (*ridicule*) ridiculiser qn; (*trick*) avoir *or* duper qn; **to make a ~ of o.s.** se couvrir de ridicule; **you can't ~ me** vous (ne) me la ferez pas, on (ne) me la fait pas

▸ **fool about, fool around** *vi* (*pej*: *waste time*) traînailler, glandouiller; (: *behave foolishly*) faire l'idiot *or* l'imbécile

foolhardy ['fuːlhɑːdɪ] *adj* téméraire, imprudent(e)

foolish ['fuːlɪʃ] *adj* idiot(e), stupide; (*rash*) imprudent(e)

foolishly ['fuːlɪʃlɪ] *adv* stupidement

foolishness ['fuːlɪʃnɪs] *n* idiotie *f*, stupidité *f*

foolproof ['fuːlpruːf] *adj* (*plan etc*) infaillible

foolscap ['fuːlskæp] *n* ≈ papier *m* ministre

foot (*pl* **feet**) [fut, fiːt] *n* pied *m*; (*of animal*) patte *f*; (*measure*) pied (= 30.48 cm; 12 *inches*) ▷ *vt* (*bill*) casquer, payer; **on ~** à pied; **to find one's feet** (*fig*) s'acclimater; **to put one's ~ down** (*Aut*) appuyer sur le champignon; (*say no*) s'imposer

footage ['futɪdʒ] *n* (*Cine*: *length*) ≈ métrage *m*; (: *material*) séquences *fpl*

foot-and-mouth [futənd'mauθ], **foot-and-mouth disease** *n* fièvre aphteuse

football ['futbɔːl] *n* (*ball*) ballon *m* (de football); (*sport*: *Brit*) football *m*; (: *US*) football américain

footballer ['futbɔːləʳ] *n* (*Brit*) = **football player**

football ground *n* terrain *m* de football

football match *n* (*Brit*) match *m* de foot(ball)

football player *n* footballeur(-euse), joueur(-euse) de football; (*US*) joueur(-euse) de football américain

football pools *npl* (*US*) ≈ loto *m* sportif, ≈ pronostics *mpl* (sur les matchs de football)

footbrake ['futbreɪk] *n* frein *m* à pédale

footbridge ['futbrɪdʒ] *n* passerelle *f*

foothills ['futhɪlz] *npl* contreforts *mpl*

foothold ['futhəuld] *n* prise *f* (de pied)

footing ['futɪŋ] *n* (*fig*) position *f*; **to lose one's ~** perdre pied; **on an equal ~** sur pied d'égalité

footlights ['futlaɪts] *npl* rampe *f*

footman ['futmən] (*irreg*) *n* laquais *m*

footnote ['futnəut] *n* note *f* (en bas de page)

footpath ['futpɑːθ] *n* sentier *m*; (*in street*) trottoir *m*

footprint ['futprɪnt] *n* trace *f* (de pied)

footrest ['futrest] *n* marchepied *m*

footsie ['futsɪ] *n* (*inf*): **to play ~ with sb** faire du pied à qn

footsore ['futsɔːʳ] *adj*: **to be ~** avoir mal aux pieds

footstep ['futstep] *n* pas *m*

footwear ['futwɛəʳ] *n* chaussures *fpl*

FOR *abbr* (= *free on rail*) franco wagon

 KEYWORD

for [fɔːʳ] *prep* **1** (*indicating destination, intention, purpose*) pour; **the train for London** le train pour (*or* à destination de) Londres; **he left for** Rome il est parti pour Rome; **he went for the paper** il est allé chercher le journal; **is this for me?** c'est pour moi?; **it's time for lunch** c'est l'heure du déjeuner; **what's it for?** ça sert à quoi?; **what for?** (*why*) pourquoi?; (*to what end*) pour quoi faire?, à quoi bon?; **for sale** à vendre; **to pray for peace** prier pour la paix

2 (*on behalf of, representing*) pour; **the MP for Hove** le député de Hove; **to work for sb/sth** travailler pour qn/qch; **I'll ask him for you** je vais lui demander pour toi; **G for George** G comme Georges

3 (*because of*) pour; **for this reason** pour cette raison; **for fear of being criticized** de peur d'être critiqué

4 (*with regard to*) pour; **it's cold for July** il fait froid pour juillet; **a gift for languages** un don pour les langues

5 (*in exchange for*): **I sold it for £5** je l'ai vendu 5 livres; **to pay 50 pence for a ticket** payer un billet 50 pence

6 (*in favour of*) pour; **are you for or against us?** êtes-vous pour ou contre nous?; **I'm all for it** je suis tout à fait pour; **vote for X** votez pour X

7 (*referring to distance*) pendant, sur; **there are roadworks for 5 km** il y a des travaux sur *or* pendant 5 km; **we walked for miles** nous avons marché pendant des kilomètres

8 (*referring to time*) pendant; depuis; pour; **he was away for 2 years** il a été absent pendant 2 ans; **she will be away for a month** elle sera absente (pendant) un mois; **it hasn't rained for 3 weeks** ça fait 3 semaines qu'il ne pleut pas, il ne pleut pas depuis 3 semaines; **I have known her for years** je la connais depuis des années; **can you do it for tomorrow?** est-ce que tu peux le faire pour demain?

9 (*with infinitive clauses*): **it is not for me to decide** ce n'est pas à moi de décider; **it would be best for you to leave** le mieux serait que vous partiez; **there is still time for you to do it** vous avez encore le temps de le faire; **for this to be possible** ... pour que cela soit possible ..

10 (*in spite of*): **for all that** malgré cela, néanmoins; **for all his work/efforts** malgré tout son travail/tous ses efforts; **for all his complaints, he's very fond of her** il a beau se plaindre, il l'aime beaucoup

▷ *conj* (*since, as*: *formal*) car

forage ['fɔrɪdʒ] *n* fourrage *m* ▷ *vi* fourrager, fouiller

forage cap *n* calot *m*

foray ['fɔreɪ] *n* incursion *f*

forbad, forbade [fə'bæd] *pt of* **forbid**

forbearing [fɔː'bɛərɪŋ] *adj* patient(e), tolérant(e)

forbid (*pt* **forbad(e)**, *pp* **-den**) [fə'bɪd, -'bæd, -'bɪdn] *vt* défendre, interdire; **to ~ sb to do** défendre *or* interdire à qn de faire

forbidden [fə'bɪdn] *adj* défendu(e)

forbidding [fə'bɪdɪŋ] *adj* d'aspect *or* d'allure

sévère *or* sombre

force [fɔːs] *n* force *f* ▷ *vt* forcer; (*push*) pousser (de force); **Forces** *npl*: **the F~s** (*Brit Mil*) les forces armées; **to ~ o.s. to do** se forcer à faire; **to ~ sb to do sth** forcer qn à faire qch; **in ~** (*being used: rule, law, prices*) en vigueur; (*in large numbers*) en force; **to come into ~** entrer en vigueur; **a ~ 5 wind** un vent de force 5; **the sales ~** (*Comm*) la force de vente; **to join ~s** unir ses forces
▶ **force back** *vt* (*crowd, enemy*) repousser; (*tears*) refouler
▶ **force down** *vt* (*food*) se forcer à manger
forced [fɔːst] *adj* forcé(e)
force-feed ['fɔːsfiːd] *vt* nourrir de force
forceful ['fɔːsful] *adj* énergique
forcemeat ['fɔːsmiːt] *n* (*Brit Culin*) farce *f*
forceps ['fɔːsɛps] *npl* forceps *m*
forcibly ['fɔːsəblɪ] *adv* par la force, de force; (*vigorously*) énergiquement
ford [fɔːd] *n* gué *m* ▷ *vt* passer à gué
fore [fɔːʳ] *n*: **to the ~** en évidence; **to come to the ~** se faire remarquer
forearm ['fɔːrɑːm] *n* avant-bras *m inv*
forebear ['fɔːbɛəʳ] *n* ancêtre *m*
foreboding [fɔː'bəudɪŋ] *n* pressentiment *m* (néfaste)
forecast ['fɔːkɑːst] *n* prévision *f*; (*also:* **weather forecast**) prévisions *fpl* météorologiques, météo *f* ▷ *vt* (*irreg: like* **cast**) prévoir
foreclose [fɔː'kləuz] *vt* (*Law: also:* **foreclose on**) saisir
foreclosure [fɔː'kləuʒəʳ] *n* saisie *f* du bien hypothéqué
forecourt ['fɔːkɔːt] *n* (*of garage*) devant *m*
forefathers ['fɔːfɑːðəz] *npl* ancêtres *mpl*
forefinger ['fɔːfɪŋgəʳ] *n* index *m*
forefront ['fɔːfrʌnt] *n*: **in the ~ of** au premier rang *or* plan de
forego (*pt* **forewent**, *pp* **foregone**) [fɔː'gəu, -'wɛnt, -'gɔn] *vt* renoncer à
foregoing ['fɔːgəuɪŋ] *adj* susmentionné(e) ▷ *n*: **the ~** ce qui précède
foregone ['fɔːgɔn] *adj*: **it's a ~ conclusion** c'est à prévoir, c'est couru d'avance
foreground ['fɔːgraund] *n* premier plan ▷ *cpd* (*Comput*) prioritaire
forehand ['fɔːhænd] *n* (*Tennis*) coup droit
forehead ['fɔrɪd] *n* front *m*
foreign ['fɔrɪn] *adj* étranger(-ère); (*trade*) extérieur(e); (*travel*) à l'étranger
foreign body *n* corps étranger
foreign currency *n* devises étrangères
foreigner ['fɔrɪnəʳ] *n* étranger(-ère)
foreign exchange *n* (*system*) change *m*; (*money*) devises *fpl*
foreign exchange market *n* marché *m* des devises
foreign exchange rate *n* cours *m* des devises
foreign investment *n* investissement *m* à l'étranger
Foreign Office *n* (*Brit*) ministère *m* des Affaires étrangères

Foreign Secretary *n* (*Brit*) ministre *m* des Affaires étrangères
foreleg ['fɔːlɛg] *n* patte *f* de devant, jambe antérieure
foreman (*irreg*) ['fɔːmən] *n* (*in construction*) contremaître *m*; (*Law: of jury*) président *m* (du jury)
foremost ['fɔːməust] *adj* le (la) plus en vue, premier(-ière) ▷ *adv*: **first and ~** avant tout, tout d'abord
forename ['fɔːneɪm] *n* prénom *m*
forensic [fə'rɛnsɪk] *adj*: **~ medicine** médecine légale; **~ expert** expert *m* de la police, expert légiste
foreplay ['fɔːpleɪ] *n* stimulation *f* érotique, prélude *m*
forerunner ['fɔːrʌnəʳ] *n* précurseur *m*
foresee (*pt* **foresaw**, *pp* **foreseen**) [fɔː'siː, -'sɔː, -'siːn] *vt* prévoir
foreseeable [fɔː'siːəbl] *adj* prévisible
foreseen [fɔː'siːn] *pp of* **foresee**
foreshadow [fɔː'ʃædəu] *vt* présager, annoncer, laisser prévoir
foreshorten [fɔː'ʃɔːtn] *vt* (*figure, scene*) réduire, faire en raccourci
foresight ['fɔːsaɪt] *n* prévoyance *f*
foreskin ['fɔːskɪn] *n* (*Anat*) prépuce *m*
forest ['fɔrɪst] *n* forêt *f*
forestall [fɔː'stɔːl] *vt* devancer
forestry ['fɔrɪstrɪ] *n* sylviculture *f*
foretaste ['fɔːteɪst] *n* avant-goût *m*
foretell (*pt, pp* **foretold**) [fɔː'tɛl, -'təuld] *vt* prédire
forethought ['fɔːθɔːt] *n* prévoyance *f*
foretold [fɔː'təuld] *pt, pp of* **foretell**
forever [fə'rɛvəʳ] *adv* pour toujours; (*fig: endlessly*) continuellement
forewarn [fɔː'wɔːn] *vt* avertir
forewent [fɔː'wɛnt] *pt of* **forego**
foreword ['fɔːwəːd] *n* avant-propos *m inv*
forfeit ['fɔːfɪt] *n* prix *m*, rançon *f* ▷ *vt* perdre; (*one's life, health*) payer de
forgave [fə'geɪv] *pt of* **forgive**
forge [fɔːdʒ] *n* forge *f* ▷ *vt* (*signature*) contrefaire; (*wrought iron*) forger; **to ~ documents/a will** fabriquer de faux papiers/un faux testament; **to ~ money** (*Brit*) fabriquer de la fausse monnaie
▶ **forge ahead** *vi* pousser de l'avant, prendre de l'avance
forged [fɔːdʒd] *adj* faux (fausse)
forger ['fɔːdʒəʳ] *n* faussaire *m*
forgery ['fɔːdʒərɪ] *n* faux *m*, contrefaçon *f*
forget (*pt* **forgot**, *pp* **forgotten**) [fə'gɛt, -'gɔt, -'gɔtn] *vt, vi* oublier; **to ~ to do sth** oublier de faire qch; **to ~ about sth** (*accidentally*) oublier qch; (*on purpose*) ne plus penser à qch; **I've forgotten my key/passport** j'ai oublié ma clé/ mon passeport
forgetful [fə'gɛtful] *adj* distrait(e), étourdi(e); **~ of** oublieux(-euse) de
forgetfulness [fə'gɛtfulnɪs] *n* tendance *f* aux

oublis; (*oblivion*) oubli *m*

forget-me-not [fə'gɛtmɪnɔt] *n* myosotis *m*

forgive (*pt* **forgave**, *pp* **forgiven**) [fə'gɪv, -'geɪv, -'gɪvn] *vt* pardonner; **to ~ sb for sth/for doing sth** pardonner qch à qn/à qn de faire qch

forgiveness [fə'gɪvnɪs] *n* pardon *m*

forgiving [fə'gɪvɪŋ] *adj* indulgent(e)

forgo (*pt* **forwent**, *pp* **forgone**) [fɔː'gəu, -'wɛnt, -'gɔn] *vt* = **forego**

forgot [fə'gɔt] *pt of* **forget**

forgotten [fə'gɔtn] *pp of* **forget**

fork [fɔːk] *n* (*for eating*) fourchette *f*; (*for gardening*) fourche *f*; (*of roads*) bifurcation *f*; (*of railways*) embranchement *m* ▷ *vi* (*road*) bifurquer
  ▶ **fork out** (*inf: pay*) *vt* allonger, se fendre de ▷ *vi* casquer

forked [fɔːkt] *adj* (*lightning*) en zigzags, ramifié(e)

fork-lift truck ['fɔːklɪft-] *n* chariot élévateur

forlorn [fə'lɔːn] *adj* (*person*) délaissé(e); (*deserted*) abandonné(e); (*hope, attempt*) désespéré(e)

form [fɔːm] *n* forme *f*; (*Scol*) classe *f*; (*questionnaire*) formulaire *m* ▷ *vt* former; (*habit*) contracter; **in the ~ of** sous forme de; **to ~ part of sth** faire partie de qch; **to be on good ~** (*Sport: fig*) être en forme; **on top ~** en pleine forme

formal ['fɔːməl] *adj* (*offer, receipt*) en bonne et due forme; (*person*) cérémonieux(-euse), à cheval sur les convenances; (*occasion, dinner*) officiel(le); (*garden*) à la française; (*Art, Philosophy*) formel(le); (*clothes*) de soirée

formality [fɔː'mælɪtɪ] *n* formalité *f*, cérémonie(s) *f(pl)*

formalize ['fɔːməlaɪz] *vt* officialiser

formally ['fɔːməlɪ] *adv* officiellement; formellement; cérémonieusement

format ['fɔːmæt] *n* format *m* ▷ *vt* (*Comput*) formater

formation [fɔː'meɪʃən] *n* formation *f*

formative ['fɔːmətɪv] *adj*: ~ **years** années *fpl* d'apprentissage (*fig*) or de formation (*d'un enfant, d'un adolescent*)

former ['fɔːmər] *adj* ancien(ne); (*before n*) précédent(e); **the ~ ... the latter** le premier ... le second, celui-là ... celui-ci; **the ~ president** l'ex-président; **the ~ Yugoslavia/Soviet Union** l'ex Yougoslavie/Union Soviétique

formerly ['fɔːməlɪ] *adv* autrefois

form feed *n* (*on printer*) alimentation *f* en feuilles

formidable ['fɔːmɪdəbl] *adj* redoutable

formula ['fɔːmjulə] *n* formule *f*; **F~ One** (*Aut*) Formule un

formulate ['fɔːmjuleɪt] *vt* formuler

fornicate ['fɔːnɪkeɪt] *vi* forniquer

forsake (*pt* **forsook**, *pp* **forsaken**) [fə'seɪk, -'suk, -'seɪkən] *vt* abandonner

fort [fɔːt] *n* fort *m*; **to hold the ~** (*fig*) assurer la permanence

forte ['fɔːtɪ] *n* (point) fort *m*

forth [fɔːθ] *adv* en avant; **to go back and ~** aller et venir; **and so ~** et ainsi de suite

forthcoming [fɔːθ'kʌmɪŋ] *adj* qui va paraître or avoir lieu prochainement; (*character*) ouvert(e), communicatif(-ive); (*available*) disponible

forthright ['fɔːθraɪt] *adj* franc (franche), direct(e)

forthwith ['fɔːθ'wɪθ] *adv* sur le champ

fortieth ['fɔːtɪɪθ] *num* quarantième

fortification [fɔːtɪfɪ'keɪʃən] *n* fortification *f*

fortified wine ['fɔːtɪfaɪd-] *n* vin liquoreux or de liqueur

fortify ['fɔːtɪfaɪ] *vt* (*city*) fortifier; (*person*) remonter

fortitude ['fɔːtɪtjuːd] *n* courage *m*, force *f* d'âme

fortnight ['fɔːtnaɪt] *n* (*Brit*) quinzaine *f*, quinze jours *mpl*; **it's a ~ since ...** il y a quinze jours que ...

fortnightly ['fɔːtnaɪtlɪ] *adj* bimensuel(le) ▷ *adv* tous les quinze jours

FORTRAN ['fɔːtræn] *n* FORTRAN *m*

fortress ['fɔːtrɪs] *n* forteresse *f*

fortuitous [fɔː'tjuːɪtəs] *adj* fortuit(e)

fortunate ['fɔːtʃənɪt] *adj* heureux(-euse); (*person*) chanceux(-euse); **to be ~** avoir de la chance; **it is ~ that** c'est une chance que, il est heureux que

fortunately ['fɔːtʃənɪtlɪ] *adv* heureusement, par bonheur

fortune ['fɔːtʃən] *n* chance *f*; (*wealth*) fortune *f*; **to make a ~** faire fortune

fortune-teller ['fɔːtʃəntɛlər] *n* diseuse *f* de bonne aventure

forty ['fɔːtɪ] *num* quarante

forum ['fɔːrəm] *n* forum *m*, tribune *f*

forward ['fɔːwəd] *adj* (*movement, position*) en avant, vers l'avant; (*not shy*) effronté(e); (*in time*) en avance; (*Comm: delivery, sales, exchange*) à terme ▷ *adv* (*also:* **forwards**) en avant ▷ *n* (*Sport*) avant *m* ▷ *vt* (*letter*) faire suivre; (*parcel, goods*) expédier; (*fig*) promouvoir, favoriser; **to look ~ to sth** attendre qch avec impatience; **to move ~** avancer; **"please ~"** "prière de faire suivre"; **~ planning** planification *f* à long terme

forwarding address *n* adresse *f* de réexpédition

forward slash *n* barre *f* oblique

forwent [fɔː'wɛnt] *pt of* **forgo**

fossil ['fɔsl] *adj, n* fossile *m*; **~ fuel** combustible *m* fossile

foster ['fɔstər] *vt* (*encourage*) encourager, favoriser; (*child*) élever (*sans adopter*)

foster brother *n* frère adoptif; frère de lait

foster child *n* enfant élevé dans une famille d'accueil

foster mother *n* mère adoptive; mère nourricière

foster parent *n* parent qui élève un enfant sans l'adopter

fought [fɔːt] *pt, pp of* **fight**

foul [faul] *adj* (*weather, smell, food*) infect(e); (*language*) ordurier(-ière); (*deed*) infâme ▷ *n* (*Football*) faute *f* ▷ *vt* (*dirty*) salir, encrasser; (*football player*) commettre une faute sur; (*entangle: anchor, propeller*) emmêler; **he's got a ~ temper** il a un caractère de chien

foul play n (Sport) jeu déloyal; (Law) acte criminel; ~ **is not suspected** la mort (or l'incendie etc) n'a pas de causes suspectes, on écarte l'hypothèse d'un meurtre (or d'un acte criminel)

found [faund] pt, pp of **find** ▷ vt (establish) fonder

foundation [faun'deɪʃən] n (act) fondation f; (base) fondement m; (also: **foundation cream**) fond m de teint; **foundations** npl (of building) fondations fpl; **to lay the ~s** (fig) poser les fondements

foundation stone n première pierre

founder ['faundəʳ] n fondateur m ▷ vi couler, sombrer

founding ['faundɪŋ] adj: ~ **fathers** (esp US) pères mpl fondateurs; ~ **member** membre m fondateur

foundry ['faundrɪ] n fonderie f

fount [faunt] n source f; (Typ) fonte f

fountain ['fauntɪn] n fontaine f

fountain pen n stylo m (à encre)

four [fɔːʳ] num quatre; **on all ~s** à quatre pattes

four-letter word ['fɔːlɛtə-] n obscénité f, gros mot

four-poster ['fɔː'pəustəʳ] n (also: **four-poster bed**) lit m à baldaquin

foursome ['fɔːsəm] n partie f à quatre; sortie f à quatre

fourteen ['fɔː'tiːn] num quatorze

fourteenth ['fɔː'tiːnθ] num quatorzième

fourth ['fɔːθ] num quatrième ▷ n (Aut: also: **fourth gear**) quatrième f

four-wheel drive ['fɔːwiːl-] n (Aut: car) voiture f à quatre roues motrices; **with ~** à quatre roues motrices

fowl [faul] n volaille f

fox [fɔks] n renard m ▷ vt mystifier

fox fur n renard m

foxglove ['fɔksglʌv] n (Bot) digitale f

fox-hunting ['fɔkshʌntɪŋ] n chasse f au renard

foyer ['fɔɪeɪ] n (in hotel) vestibule m; (Theat) foyer m

FP n abbr (Brit) = **former pupil**; (US) = **fireplug**

FPA n abbr (Brit) = **Family Planning Association**

Fr. abbr (Rel = father) P; (= friar) F

fr. abbr (= franc) F

fracas ['fræka:] n bagarre f

fraction ['frækʃən] n fraction f

fractionally ['frækʃnəlɪ] adv: ~ **smaller** etc un poil plus petit etc

fractious ['frækʃəs] adj grincheux(-euse)

fracture ['fræktʃəʳ] n fracture f ▷ vt fracturer

fragile ['frædʒaɪl] adj fragile

fragment ['frægmənt] n fragment m

fragmentary ['frægməntərɪ] adj fragmentaire

fragrance ['freɪgrəns] n parfum m

fragrant ['freɪgrənt] adj parfumé(e), odorant(e)

frail [freɪl] adj fragile, délicat(e); (person) frêle

frame [freɪm] n (of building) charpente f; (of human, animal) charpente, ossature f; (of picture) cadre m; (of door, window) encadrement m, chambranle m; (of spectacles: also: **frames**) monture f ▷ vt (picture) encadrer; (theory, plan) construire, élaborer; **to ~ sb** (inf) monter un coup contre qn; ~ **of mind** disposition f d'esprit

framework ['freɪmwəːk] n structure f

France [frɑːns] n la France; **in ~** en France

franchise ['fræntʃaɪz] n (Pol) droit m de vote; (Comm) franchise f

franchisee [fræntʃaɪˈziː] n franchisé m

franchiser ['fræntʃaɪzəʳ] n franchiseur m

frank [fræŋk] adj franc (franche) ▷ vt (letter) affranchir

Frankfurt ['fræŋkfəːt] n Francfort

franking machine ['fræŋkɪŋ-] n machine f à affranchir

frankly ['fræŋklɪ] adv franchement

frankness ['fræŋknɪs] n franchise f

frantic ['fræntɪk] adj (hectic) frénétique; (need, desire) effréné(e); (distraught) hors de soi

frantically ['fræntɪklɪ] adv frénétiquement

fraternal [frəˈtəːnl] adj fraternel(le)

fraternity [frəˈtəːnɪtɪ] n (club) communauté f, confrérie f; (spirit) fraternité f

fraternize ['frætənaɪz] vi fraterniser

fraud [frɔːd] n supercherie f, fraude f, tromperie f; (person) imposteur m

fraudulent ['frɔːdjulənt] adj frauduleux(-euse)

fraught [frɔːt] adj (tense: person) très tendu(e); (: situation) pénible; ~ **with** (difficulties etc) chargé(e) de, plein(e) de

fray [freɪ] n bagarre f; (Mil) combat m ▷ vt effilocher ▷ vi s'effilocher; **tempers were ~ed** les gens commençaient à s'énerver; **her nerves were ~ed** elle était à bout de nerfs

FRB n abbr (US) = **Federal Reserve Board**

FRCM n abbr (Brit) = **Fellow of the Royal College of Music**

FRCO n abbr (Brit) = **Fellow of the Royal College of Organists**

FRCP n abbr (Brit) = **Fellow of the Royal College of Physicians**

FRCS n abbr (Brit) = **Fellow of the Royal College of Surgeons**

freak [friːk] n (eccentric person) phénomène m; (unusual event) hasard m extraordinaire; (pej: fanatic): **health food ~** fana m/f or obsédé(e) de l'alimentation saine ▷ adj (storm) exceptionnel(le); (accident) bizarre

▶ **freak out** vi (inf: drop out) se marginaliser; (: on drugs) se défoncer

freakish ['friːkɪʃ] adj insolite, anormal(e)

freckle ['frɛkl] n tache f de rousseur

free [friː] adj libre; (gratis) gratuit(e); (liberal) généreux(-euse), large ▷ vt (prisoner etc) libérer; (jammed object or person) dégager; **is this seat ~?** la place est libre?; **to give sb a ~ hand** donner carte blanche à qn; ~ **and easy** sans façon, décontracté(e); **admission ~** entrée libre; ~ **(of charge)** gratuitement

freebie ['friːbɪ] n (inf): **it's a ~** c'est gratuit

freedom ['friːdəm] n liberté f

freedom fighter n combattant m de la liberté

free enterprise n libre entreprise f

Freefone® ['friːfəun] n numéro vert

free-for-all ['friːfərɔːl] n mêlée générale
free gift n prime f
freehold ['friːhəuld] n propriété foncière libre
free kick n (Sport) coup franc
freelance ['friːlɑːns] adj (journalist etc) indépendant(e), free-lance inv; (work) en free-lance ▷ adv en free-lance
freeloader ['friːləudər] n (pej) parasite m
freely ['friːlɪ] adv librement; (liberally) libéralement
free-market economy [friː'mɑːkɪt-] n économie f de marché
freemason ['friːmeɪsn] n franc-maçon m
freemasonry ['friːmeɪsnrɪ] n franc-maçonnerie f
Freepost® ['friːpəust] n (Brit) port payé
free-range ['friː'reɪndʒ] adj (egg) de ferme; (chicken) fermier
free sample n échantillon gratuit
free speech n liberté f d'expression
free trade n libre-échange m
freeway ['friːweɪ] n (US) autoroute f
freewheel [friː'wiːl] vi descendre en roue libre
freewheeling [friː'wiːlɪŋ] adj indépendant(e), libre
free will n libre arbitre m; **of one's own ~** de son plein gré
freeze [friːz] (pt **froze**, pp **frozen** [frəuz, 'frəuzn]) vi geler ▷ vt geler; (food) congeler; (prices, salaries) bloquer, geler ▷ n gel m; (of prices, salaries) blocage m
▸ **freeze over** vi (river) geler; (windscreen) se couvrir de givre or de glace
▸ **freeze up** vi geler
freeze-dried ['friːzdraɪd] adj lyophilisé(e)
freezer ['friːzər] n congélateur m
freezing ['friːzɪŋ] adj: **~ (cold)** (room etc) glacial(e); (person, hands) gelé(e), glacé(e) ▷ n: **3 degrees below ~** 3 degrés au-dessous de zéro; **it's ~** il fait un froid glacial
freezing point n point m de congélation
freight [freɪt] n (goods) fret m, cargaison f; (money charged) fret, prix m du transport; **~ forward** port dû; **~ inward** port payé par le destinataire
freighter ['freɪtər] n (Naut) cargo m
freight forwarder [-fɔːwədər] n transitaire m
freight train n (US) train m de marchandises
French [frɛntʃ] adj français(e) ▷ n (Ling) français m; **the ~** (npl) les Français; **what's the ~ (word) for ...?** comment dit-on ... en français?
French bean n (Brit) haricot vert
French bread n pain m français
French Canadian adj canadien(ne) français(e) ▷ n Canadien(ne) français(e)
French dressing n (Culin) vinaigrette f
French fried potatoes, (US) **French fries** npl (pommes de terre fpl) frites fpl
French Guiana [-gaɪ'ænə] n Guyane française
French horn n (Mus) cor m (d'harmonie)
French kiss n baiser profond
French loaf n ≈ pain m, ≈ parisien m
Frenchman ['frɛntʃmən] (irreg) n Français m

French Riviera n: **the ~** la Côte d'Azur
French stick n ≈ baguette f
French window n porte-fenêtre f
Frenchwoman ['frɛntʃwumən] (irreg) n Française f
frenetic [frə'nɛtɪk] adj frénétique
frenzy ['frɛnzɪ] n frénésie f
frequency ['friːkwənsɪ] n fréquence f
frequency modulation n modulation f de fréquence
frequent adj ['friːkwənt] fréquent(e) ▷ vt [frɪ'kwɛnt] fréquenter
frequently ['friːkwəntlɪ] adv fréquemment
fresco ['frɛskəu] n fresque f
fresh [frɛʃ] adj frais (fraîche); (new) nouveau (nouvelle); (cheeky) familier(-ière), culotté(e); **to make a ~ start** prendre un nouveau départ
freshen ['frɛʃən] vi (wind, air) fraîchir
▸ **freshen up** vi faire un brin de toilette
freshener ['frɛʃnər] n: **skin ~** astringent m; **air ~** désodorisant m
fresher ['frɛʃər] n (Brit University: inf) bizuth m, étudiant(e) de première année
freshly ['frɛʃlɪ] adv nouvellement, récemment
freshman (US: irreg) ['frɛʃmən] n = **fresher**
freshness ['frɛʃnɪs] n fraîcheur f
freshwater ['frɛʃwɔːtər] adj (fish) d'eau douce
fret [frɛt] vi s'agiter, se tracasser
fretful ['frɛtful] adj (child) grincheux(-euse)
Freudian ['frɔɪdɪən] adj freudien(ne); **~ slip** lapsus m
FRG n abbr (= Federal Republic of Germany) RFA f
friar ['fraɪər] n moine m, frère m
friction ['frɪkʃən] n friction f, frottement m
friction feed n (on printer) entraînement m par friction
Friday ['fraɪdɪ] n vendredi m; for phrases see also **Tuesday**
fridge [frɪdʒ] n (Brit) frigo m, frigidaire® m
fridge-freezer ['frɪdʒ'friːzər] n réfrigérateur-congélateur m
fried [fraɪd] pt, pp of **fry** ▷ adj frit(e); **~ egg** œuf m sur le plat
friend [frɛnd] n ami(e) ▷ vt (Internet) ajouter comme ami(e); **to make ~s with** se lier (d'amitié) avec
friendliness ['frɛndlɪnɪs] n attitude amicale
friendly ['frɛndlɪ] adj amical(e); (kind) sympathique, gentil(le); (place) accueillant(e); (Pol: country) ami(e) ▷ n (also: **friendly match**) match amical; **to be ~ with** être ami(e) avec; **to be ~ to** être bien disposé(e) à l'égard de
friendly fire n: **they were killed by ~** ils sont morts sous les tirs de leur propre camp
friendly society n société f mutualiste
friendship ['frɛndʃɪp] n amitié f
fries [fraɪz] (esp US) npl = **French fried potatoes**
frieze [friːz] n frise f, bordure f
frigate ['frɪgɪt] n (Naut: modern) frégate f
fright [fraɪt] n peur f, effroi m; **to give sb a ~** faire peur à qn; **to take ~** prendre peur, s'effrayer; **she looks a ~** elle a l'air d'un

épouvantail

frighten ['fraɪtn] *vt* effrayer, faire peur à
▸ **frighten away**, **frighten off** *vt* (*birds, children etc*) faire fuir, effaroucher

frightened ['fraɪtnd] *adj*: **to be ~ (of)** avoir peur (de)

frightening ['fraɪtnɪŋ] *adj* effrayant(e)

frightful ['fraɪtful] *adj* affreux(-euse)

frightfully ['fraɪtfəlɪ] *adv* affreusement

frigid ['frɪdʒɪd] *adj* frigide

frigidity [frɪ'dʒɪdɪtɪ] *n* frigidité *f*

frill [frɪl] *n* (*of dress*) volant *m*; (*of shirt*) jabot *m*; **without ~s** (*fig*) sans manières

frilly ['frɪlɪ] *adj* à fanfreluches

fringe [frɪndʒ] *n* (*Brit: of hair*) frange *f*; (*edge: of forest etc*) bordure *f*; (*fig*): **on the ~** en marge

fringe benefits *npl* avantages sociaux *or* en nature

fringe theatre *n* théâtre *m* d'avant-garde

Frisbee® ['frɪzbɪ] *n* Frisbee® *m*

frisk [frɪsk] *vt* fouiller

frisky ['frɪskɪ] *adj* vif (vive), sémillant(e)

fritter ['frɪtəʳ] *n* beignet *m*
▸ **fritter away** *vt* gaspiller

frivolity [frɪ'vɔlɪtɪ] *n* frivolité *f*

frivolous ['frɪvələs] *adj* frivole

frizzy ['frɪzɪ] *adj* crépu(e)

fro [frəu] *adv see* **to**

frock [frɔk] *n* robe *f*

frog [frɔg] *n* grenouille *f*; **to have a ~ in one's throat** avoir un chat dans la gorge

frogman (*irreg*) ['frɔgmən] *n* homme-grenouille *m*

frogmarch ['frɔgmɑːtʃ] *vt* (*Brit*): **to ~ sb in/out** faire entrer/sortir qn de force

frolic ['frɔlɪk] *n* ébats *mpl* ▸ *vi* folâtrer, batifoler

⬤ KEYWORD

from [frɔm] *prep* **1** (*indicating starting place, origin etc*) de; **where do you come from?**, **where are you from?** d'où venez-vous?; **where has he come from?** d'où arrive-t-il?; **from London to Paris** de Londres à Paris; **to escape from sb/sth** échapper à qn/qch; **a letter/telephone call from my sister** une lettre/un appel de ma sœur; **to drink from the bottle** boire à (même) la bouteille; **tell him from me that ...** dites-lui de ma part que ...

2 (*indicating time*) (à partir) de; **from one o'clock to** *or* **until** *or* **till two** d'une heure à deux heures; **from January (on)** à partir de janvier

3 (*indicating distance*) de; **the hotel is one kilometre from the beach** l'hôtel est à un kilomètre de la plage

4 (*indicating price, number etc*) de; **prices range from £10 to £50** les prix varient entre 10 livres et 50 livres; **the interest rate was increased from 9% to 10%** le taux d'intérêt est passé de 9% à 10%

5 (*indicating difference*) de; **he can't tell red from green** il ne peut pas distinguer le rouge du vert;

to be different from sb/sth être différent de qn/qch

6 (*because of, on the basis of*): **from what he says** d'après ce qu'il dit; **weak from hunger** affaibli par la faim

frond [frɔnd] *n* fronde *f*

front [frʌnt] *n* (*of house, dress*) devant *m*; (*of coach, train*) avant *m*; (*of book*) couverture *f*; (*promenade: also*: **sea front**) bord *m* de mer; (*Mil, Pol, Meteorology*) front *m*; (*fig: appearances*) contenance *f*, façade *f* ▸ *adj* de devant; (*page, row*) premier(-ière); (*seat, wheel*) avant *inv* ▸ *vi*: **to ~ onto sth** donner sur qch; **in ~ (of)** devant

frontage ['frʌntɪdʒ] *n* façade *f*; (*of shop*) devanture *f*

frontal ['frʌntl] *adj* frontal(e)

front bench *n* (*Brit: Pol*) *voir article*

⬤ **FRONT BENCH**

Le *front bench* est le banc du gouvernement, placé à la droite du "Speaker", ou celui du cabinet fantôme, placé à sa gauche. Ils se font face dans l'enceinte de la Chambre des communes. Par extension, *front bench* désigne les dirigeants des groupes parlementaires de la majorité et de l'opposition, qui sont appelés "frontbenchers" par opposition aux autres députés qui sont appelés "backbenchers".

front desk *n* (*US: in hotel, at doctor's*) réception *f*

front door *n* porte *f* d'entrée; (*of car*) portière *f* avant

frontier ['frʌntɪəʳ] *n* frontière *f*

frontispiece ['frʌntɪspiːs] *n* frontispice *m*

front page *n* première page

front room *n* (*Brit*) pièce *f* de devant, salon *m*

front runner *n* (*fig*) favori(te)

front-wheel drive ['frʌntwiːl-] *n* traction *f* avant

frost [frɔst] *n* gel *m*, gelée *f*; (*also*: **hoarfrost**) givre *m*

frostbite ['frɔstbaɪt] *n* gelures *fpl*

frosted ['frɔstɪd] *adj* (*glass*) dépoli(e); (*esp US: cake*) glacé(e)

frosting ['frɔstɪŋ] *n* (*esp US: on cake*) glaçage *m*

frosty ['frɔstɪ] *adj* (*window*) couvert(e) de givre; (*weather, welcome*) glacial(e)

froth [frɔθ] *n* mousse *f*; écume *f*

frown [fraun] *n* froncement *m* de sourcils ▸ *vi* froncer les sourcils
▸ **frown on** *vt* (*fig*) désapprouver

froze [frəuz] *pt of* **freeze**

frozen ['frəuzn] *pp of* **freeze** ▸ *adj* (*food*) congelé(e); (*very cold: person; Comm: assets*) gelé(e)

FRS *n abbr* (*Brit*: = *Fellow of the Royal Society*) membre de l'Académie des sciences; (*US*: = *Federal Reserve System*) banque centrale américaine

frugal ['fruːgl] *adj* frugal(e)

fruit [fruːt] *n* (*pl inv*) fruit *m*

fruiterer ['fru:tərəʳ] n fruitier m, marchand(e) de fruits; **~'s (shop)** fruiterie f

fruit fly n mouche f du vinaigre, drosophile f

fruitful ['fru:tful] adj fructueux(-euse); (plant, soil) fécond(e)

fruition [fru:'ɪʃən] n: **to come to ~** se réaliser

fruit juice n jus m de fruit

fruitless ['fru:tlɪs] adj (fig) vain(e), infructueux(-euse)

fruit machine n (Brit) machine f à sous

fruit salad n salade f de fruits

frump [frʌmp] n mocheté f

frustrate [frʌs'treɪt] vt frustrer; (plot, plans) faire échouer

frustrated [frʌs'treɪtɪd] adj frustré(e)

frustrating [frʌs'treɪtɪŋ] adj (job) frustrant(e); (day) démoralisant(e)

frustration [frʌs'treɪʃən] n frustration f

fry (pt, pp **fried**) [fraɪ, -d] vt (faire) frire ▷ n: **small ~** le menu fretin

frying pan ['fraɪɪŋ-] n poêle f (à frire)

FT n abbr (Brit: = Financial Times) journal financier

ft. abbr = **foot**; **feet**

FTC n abbr (US) = **Federal Trade Commission**

FTSE 100 (Share) Index n abbr (= Financial Times Stock Exchange 100 (Share) Index) indice m Footsie des cent grandes valeurs

fuchsia ['fju:ʃə] n fuchsia m

fuck [fʌk] vt, vi (inf!) baiser (!); **~ off!** fous le camp! (!)

fuddled ['fʌdld] adj (muddled) embrouillé(e), confus(e)

fuddy-duddy ['fʌdɪdʌdɪ] adj (pej) vieux jeu inv, ringard(e)

fudge [fʌdʒ] n (Culin) sorte de confiserie à base de sucre, de beurre et de lait ▷ vt (issue, problem) esquiver

fuel [fjuəl] n (for heating) combustible m; (for engine) carburant m

fuel oil n mazout m

fuel poverty n pauvreté f énergétique

fuel pump n (Aut) pompe f d'alimentation

fuel tank n cuve f à mazout, citerne f; (in vehicle) réservoir m de or à carburant

fug [fʌg] n (Brit) puanteur f, odeur f de renfermé

fugitive ['fju:dʒɪtɪv] n fugitif(-ive)

fulfil, (US) **fulfill** [ful'fɪl] vt (function, condition) remplir; (order) exécuter; (wish, desire) satisfaire, réaliser

fulfilled [ful'fɪld] adj (person) comblé(e), épanoui(e)

fulfilment, (US) **fulfillment** [ful'fɪlmənt] n (of wishes) réalisation f

full [ful] adj plein(e); (details, hotel, bus) complet(-ète); (price) fort(e), normal(e); (busy: day) chargé(e); (skirt) ample, large ▷ adv: **to know ~ well that** savoir fort bien que; **~ (up)** (hotel etc) complet(-ète); **I'm ~ (up)** j'ai bien mangé; **~ employment/fare** plein emploi/tarif; **a ~ two hours** deux bonnes heures; **at ~ speed** à toute vitesse; **in ~** (reproduce, quote, pay) intégralement; (write name etc) en toutes lettres

fullback ['fulbæk] n (Rugby, Football) arrière m

full-blooded ['ful'blʌdɪd] adj (vigorous) vigoureux(-euse)

full-cream ['ful'kri:m] adj: **~ milk** (Brit) lait entier

full-grown ['ful'grəun] adj arrivé(e) à maturité, adulte

full-length ['ful'leŋθ] adj (portrait) en pied; (coat) long(ue); **~ film** long métrage

full moon n pleine lune

full-scale ['fulskeɪl] adj (model) grandeur nature inv; (search, retreat) complet(-ète), total(e)

full-sized ['ful'saɪzd] adj (portrait etc) grandeur nature inv

full stop n point m

full-time ['ful'taɪm] adj, adv (work) à plein temps ▷ n (Sport) fin f du match

fully ['fulɪ] adv entièrement, complètement; (at least): **~ as big** au moins aussi grand

fully-fledged ['fulɪ'flɛdʒd] adj (teacher, barrister) diplômé(e); (citizen, member) à part entière

fulsome ['fulsəm] adj (pej: praise) excessif(-ive); (: manner) exagéré(e)

fumble ['fʌmbl] vi fouiller, tâtonner ▷ vt (ball) mal réceptionner, cafouiller

▶ **fumble with** vt fus tripoter

fume [fju:m] vi (rage) rager

fumes [fju:mz] npl vapeurs fpl, émanations fpl, gaz mpl

fumigate ['fju:mɪgeɪt] vt désinfecter (par fumigation)

fun [fʌn] n amusement m, divertissement m; **to have ~** s'amuser; **for ~** pour rire; **it's not much ~** ce n'est pas très drôle or amusant; **to make ~ of** se moquer de

function ['fʌŋkʃən] n fonction f; (reception, dinner) cérémonie f, soirée officielle ▷ vi fonctionner; **to ~ as** faire office de

functional ['fʌŋkʃənl] adj fonctionnel(le)

function key n (Comput) touche f de fonction

fund [fʌnd] n caisse f, fonds m; (source, store) source f, mine f; **funds** npl (money) fonds mpl

fundamental [fʌndə'mɛntl] adj fondamental(e); **fundamentals** npl principes mpl de base

fundamentalism [fʌndə'mɛntəlɪzəm] n intégrisme m

fundamentalist [fʌndə'mɛntəlɪst] n intégriste m/f

fundamentally [fʌndə'mɛntəlɪ] adv fondamentalement

funding ['fʌndɪŋ] n financement m

fund-raising ['fʌndreɪzɪŋ] n collecte f de fonds

funeral ['fju:nərəl] n enterrement m, obsèques fpl (more formal occasion)

funeral director n entrepreneur m des pompes funèbres

funeral parlour n (Brit) dépôt m mortuaire

funeral service n service m funèbre

funereal [fju:'nɪərɪəl] adj lugubre, funèbre

funfair ['fʌnfɛəʳ] n (Brit) fête (foraine)

fungus (pl **fungi**) ['fʌŋgəs, -gaɪ] n champignon m; (mould) moisissure f

funicular [fjuːˈnɪkjuləʳ] n (also: **funicular railway**) funiculaire m
funky [ˈfʌŋkɪ] adj (music) funky inv; (inf: excellent) super inv
funnel [ˈfʌnl] n entonnoir m; (of ship) cheminée f
funnily [ˈfʌnɪlɪ] adv drôlement; (strangely) curieusement
funny [ˈfʌnɪ] adj amusant(e), drôle; (strange) curieux(-euse), bizarre
funny bone n endroit sensible du coude
fun run n course f de fond (pour amateurs)
fur [fəːʳ] n fourrure f; (Brit: in kettle etc) (dépôt m de) tartre m
fur coat n manteau m de fourrure
furious [ˈfjuərɪəs] adj furieux(-euse); (effort) acharné(e); **to be ~ with sb** être dans une fureur noire contre qn
furiously [ˈfjuərɪəslɪ] adv furieusement; avec acharnement
furl [fəːl] vt rouler; (Naut) ferler
furlong [ˈfəːlɔŋ] n = 201.17 m (terme d'hippisme)
furlough [ˈfəːləu] n permission f, congé m
furnace [ˈfəːnɪs] n fourneau m
furnish [ˈfəːnɪʃ] vt meubler; (supply) fournir; **~ed flat** or (US) **apartment** meublé m
furnishings [ˈfəːnɪʃɪŋz] npl mobilier m, articles mpl d'ameublement
furniture [ˈfəːnɪtʃəʳ] n meubles mpl, mobilier m; **piece of ~** meuble m
furniture polish n encaustique f
furore [fjuəˈrɔːrɪ] n (protests) protestations fpl
furrier [ˈfʌrɪəʳ] n fourreur m
furrow [ˈfʌrəu] n sillon m
furry [ˈfəːrɪ] adj (animal) à fourrure; (toy) en peluche
further [ˈfəːðəʳ] adj supplémentaire, autre; nouveau (nouvelle) ▷ adv plus loin; (more) davantage; (moreover) de plus ▷ vt faire avancer or progresser, promouvoir; **how much ~ is it?** quelle distance or combien reste-t-il à parcourir?; **until ~ notice** jusqu'à nouvel ordre or avis; **~ to your letter of …** (Comm) suite à votre lettre du …
further education n enseignement m postscolaire (recyclage, formation professionnelle)

furthermore [fəːðəˈmɔːʳ] adv de plus, en outre
furthermost [ˈfəːðəməust] adj le (la) plus éloigné(e)
furthest [ˈfəːðɪst] superlative of **far**
furtive [ˈfəːtɪv] adj furtif(-ive)
fury [ˈfjuərɪ] n fureur f
fuse, (US) **fuze** [fjuːz] n fusible m; (for bomb etc) amorce f, détonateur m ▷ vt, vi (metal) fondre; (fig) fusionner; (Brit: Elec): **to ~ the lights** faire sauter les fusibles or les plombs; **a ~ has blown** un fusible a sauté
fuse box n boîte f à fusibles
fuselage [ˈfjuːzəlɑːʒ] n fuselage m
fuse wire n fusible m
fusillade [fjuːzɪˈleɪd] n fusillade f; (fig) feu roulant
fusion [ˈfjuːʒən] n fusion f
fuss [fʌs] n (anxiety, excitement) chichis mpl, façons fpl; (commotion) tapage m; (complaining, trouble) histoire(s) f(pl) ▷ vi faire des histoires ▷ vt (person) embêter; **to make a ~** faire des façons (or des histoires); **to make a ~ of sb** dorloter qn
▶ **fuss over** vt fus (person) dorloter
fusspot [ˈfʌspɔt] n (inf): **don't be such a ~!** ne fais pas tant d'histoires!
fussy [ˈfʌsɪ] adj (person) tatillon(ne), difficile, chichiteux(-euse); (dress, style) tarabiscoté(e); **I'm not ~** (inf) ça m'est égal
fusty [ˈfʌstɪ] adj (old-fashioned) vieillot(te); (smell) de renfermé or moisi
futile [ˈfjuːtaɪl] adj futile
futility [fjuːˈtɪlɪtɪ] n futilité f
futon [ˈfuːtɔn] n futon m
future [ˈfjuːtʃəʳ] adj futur(e) ▷ n avenir m; (Ling) futur m; **futures** npl (Comm) opérations fpl à terme; **in (the) ~** à l'avenir; **in the near/immediate ~** dans un avenir proche/immédiat
futuristic [fjuːtʃəˈrɪstɪk] adj futuriste
fuze [fjuːz] n, vt, vi (US) = **fuse**
fuzzy [ˈfʌzɪ] adj (Phot) flou(e); (hair) crépu(e)
fwd. abbr = **forward**
fwy abbr (US) = **freeway**
FY abbr = **fiscal year**
FYI abbr = **for your information**

Gg

G¹, g [dʒi:] *n* (*letter*) G, g *m*; (*Mus*): **G** sol *m*; **G for George** G comme Gaston

G² *n abbr* (*Brit Scol*: = *good*) b (= *bien*); (*US Cine*: = *general* (*audience*)) ≈ tous publics; (*Pol*: = G8) G8 *m*

g. *abbr* (= *gram*) g; (= *gravity*) g

G8 *abbr* (*Pol*): **the G8 nations** le G8

G20 *n abbr* (*Pol*) G20 *m*

GA *abbr* (*US*) = **Georgia**

gab [gæb] *n* (*inf*): **to have the gift of the ~** avoir la langue bien pendue

gabble ['gæbl] *vi* bredouiller; jacasser

gaberdine [gæbə'di:n] *n* gabardine *f*

gable ['geɪbl] *n* pignon *m*

Gabon [gə'bɒn] *n* Gabon *m*

gad about ['gædə'baut] *vi* (*inf*) se balader

gadget ['gædʒɪt] *n* gadget *m*

Gaelic ['geɪlɪk] *adj, n* (*Ling*) gaélique (*m*)

gaffe [gæf] *n* gaffe *f*

gaffer ['gæfəʳ] *n* (*Brit: foreman*) contremaître *m*; (*Brit inf: boss*) patron *m*

gag [gæg] *n* (*on mouth*) bâillon *m*; (*joke*) gag *m* ▷ *vt* (*prisoner etc*) bâillonner ▷ *vi* (*choke*) étouffer

gaga ['gɑːgɑː] *adj*: **to go ~** devenir gaga *or* gâteux(-euse)

gaiety ['geɪɪtɪ] *n* gaieté *f*

gaily ['geɪlɪ] *adv* gaiement

gain [geɪn] *n* (*improvement*) gain *m*; (*profit*) gain, profit *m* ▷ *vt* gagner ▷ *vi* (*watch*) avancer; **to ~ from/by** gagner de/à; **to ~ on sb** (*catch up*) rattraper qn; **to ~ 3lbs (in weight)** prendre 3 livres; **to ~ ground** gagner du terrain

gainful ['geɪnful] *adj* profitable, lucratif(-ive)

gainfully ['geɪnfəlɪ] *adv*: **to be ~ employed** avoir un emploi rémunéré

gainsay [geɪn'seɪ] *vt* (*irreg: like* **say**) contredire; nier

gait [geɪt] *n* démarche *f*

gal. *abbr* = **gallon**

gala ['gɑːlə] *n* gala *m*; **swimming ~** grand concours de natation

Galápagos [gə'læpəgəs], **Galápagos Islands** *npl*: **the ~ (Islands)** les (îles *fpl*) Galapagos *fpl*

galaxy ['gæləksɪ] *n* galaxie *f*

gale [geɪl] *n* coup *m* de vent; **~ force 10** vent *m* de force 10

gall [gɔːl] *n* (*Anat*) bile *f*; (*fig*) effronterie *f* ▷ *vt* ulcérer, irriter

gall. *abbr* = **gallon**

gallant ['gælənt] *adj* vaillant(e), brave; (*towards ladies*) empressé(e), galant(e)

gallantry ['gæləntrɪ] *n* bravoure *f*, vaillance *f*; empressement *m*, galanterie *f*

gall bladder ['gɔːl-] *n* vésicule *f* biliaire

galleon ['gælɪən] *n* galion *m*

gallery ['gælərɪ] *n* galerie *f*; (*also:* **art gallery**) musée *m*; (*: private*) galerie; (*for spectators*) tribune *f*; (*: in theatre*) dernier balcon

galley ['gælɪ] *n* (*ship's kitchen*) cambuse *f*; (*ship*) galère *f*; (*also:* **galley proof**) placard *m*, galée *f*

Gallic ['gælɪk] *adj* (*of Gaul*) gaulois(e); (*French*) français(e)

galling ['gɔːlɪŋ] *adj* irritant(e)

gallon ['gæln] *n* gallon *m* (*Brit* = 4.543 l; *US* = 3.785 l), = 8 *pints*

gallop ['gæləp] *n* galop *m* ▷ *vi* galoper; **~ing inflation** inflation galopante

gallows ['gæləuz] *n* potence *f*

gallstone ['gɔːlstəun] *n* calcul *m* (biliaire)

Gallup Poll ['gæləp-] *n* sondage *m* Gallup

galore [gə'lɔːʳ] *adv* en abondance, à gogo

galvanize ['gælvənaɪz] *vt* galvaniser; (*fig*): **to ~ sb into action** galvaniser qn

Gambia ['gæmbɪə] *n* Gambie *f*

gambit ['gæmbɪt] *n* (*fig*): (**opening**) **~** manœuvre *f* stratégique

gamble ['gæmbl] *n* pari *m*, risque calculé ▷ *vt, vi* jouer; **to ~ on the Stock Exchange** jouer en *or* à la Bourse; **to ~ on** (*fig*) miser sur

gambler ['gæmbləʳ] *n* joueur *m*

gambling ['gæmblɪŋ] *n* jeu *m*

gambol ['gæmbl] *vi* gambader

game [geɪm] *n* jeu *m*; (*event*) match *m*; (*of tennis, chess, cards*) partie *f*; (*Hunting*) gibier *m* ▷ *adj* brave; (*willing*): **to be ~ (for)** être prêt(e) (à *or* pour); **a ~ of football/tennis** une partie de football/tennis; **big ~** gros gibier; **games** *npl* (*Scol*) sport *m*; (*sport event*) jeux

game bird *n* gibier *m* à plume

gamekeeper ['geɪmkiːpəʳ] *n* garde-chasse *m*

gamely ['geɪmlɪ] *adv* vaillamment

gamer ['geɪməʳ] *n* jouer(-euse) de jeux vidéos

game reserve *n* réserve animalière

games console ['geɪmz-] n console f de jeux vidéo

game show ['geɪmʃəu] n jeu télévisé

gamesmanship ['geɪmzmənʃip] n roublardise f

gaming ['geɪmɪŋ] n jeu m, jeux mpl d'argent; (video games) jeux mpl vidéos

gammon ['gæmən] n (bacon) quartier m de lard fumé; (ham) jambon fumé or salé

gamut ['gæmət] n gamme f

gang [gæŋ] n bande f, groupe m; (of workmen) équipe f

▸ **gang up** vi: **to ~ up on sb** se liguer contre qn

Ganges ['gændʒiːz] n: **the ~** le Gange

gangland ['gæŋlænd] adj: **~ killer** tueur professionnel du milieu; **~ boss** chef m de gang

gangling ['gæŋglɪŋ], **gangly** ['gæŋglɪ] adj dégingandé(e)

gangplank ['gæŋplæŋk] n passerelle f

gangrene ['gæŋgriːn] n gangrène f

gangster ['gæŋstər] n gangster m, bandit m

gangway ['gæŋweɪ] n passerelle f; (Brit: of bus) couloir central

gantry ['gæntrɪ] n portique m; (for rocket) tour f de lancement

GAO n abbr (US: = General Accounting Office) ≈ Cour f des comptes

gaol [dʒeɪl] n, vt (Brit) = **jail**

gap [gæp] n trou m; (in time) intervalle m; (fig) lacune f; vide m; (difference): **~ (between)** écart m (entre)

gape [geɪp] vi (person) être or rester bouche bée; (hole, shirt) être ouvert(e)

gaping ['geɪpɪŋ] adj (hole) béant(e)

gap year n année que certains étudiants prennent pour voyager ou pour travailler avant d'entrer à l'université

garage ['gærɑːʒ] n garage m

garage sale n vide-grenier m

garb [gɑːb] n tenue f, costume m

garbage ['gɑːbɪdʒ] n (US: rubbish) ordures fpl, détritus mpl; (inf: nonsense) âneries fpl

garbage can n (US) poubelle f, boîte f à ordures

garbage collector n (US) éboueur m

garbage disposal unit n broyeur m d'ordures

garbage truck n (US) camion m (de ramassage des ordures), benne f à ordures

garbled ['gɑːbld] adj déformé(e), faussé(e)

garden ['gɑːdn] n jardin m ▸ vi jardiner; **gardens** npl (public) jardin public; (private) parc m

garden centre (Brit) n pépinière f, jardinerie f

garden city n (Brit) cité-jardin f

gardener ['gɑːdnər] n jardinier m

gardening ['gɑːdnɪŋ] n jardinage m

gargle ['gɑːgl] vi se gargariser ▸ n gargarisme m

gargoyle ['gɑːgɔɪl] n gargouille f

garish ['gɛərɪʃ] adj criard(e), voyant(e)

garland ['gɑːlənd] n guirlande f; couronne f

garlic ['gɑːlɪk] n ail m

garment ['gɑːmənt] n vêtement m

garner ['gɑːnər] vt engranger, amasser

garnish ['gɑːnɪʃ] (Culin) vt garnir ▸ n décoration f

garret ['gærɪt] n mansarde f

garrison ['gærɪsn] n garnison f ▸ vt mettre en garnison, stationner

garrulous ['gærjuləs] adj volubile, loquace

garter ['gɑːtər] n jarretière f; (US: suspender) jarretelle f

garter belt n (US) porte-jarretelles m inv

gas [gæs] n gaz m; (used as anaesthetic): **to be given ~** se faire endormir; (US: gasoline) essence f ▸ vt asphyxier; (Mil) gazer; **I can smell ~** ça sent le gaz

Gascony ['gæskənɪ] n Gascogne f

gas cooker n (Brit) cuisinière f à gaz

gas cylinder n bouteille f de gaz

gaseous ['gæsɪəs] adj gazeux(-euse)

gas fire n (Brit) radiateur m à gaz

gas-fired ['gæsfaɪəd] adj au gaz

gash [gæʃ] n entaille f; (on face) balafre f ▸ vt taillader; balafrer

gasket ['gæskɪt] n (Aut) joint m de culasse

gas mask n masque m à gaz

gas meter n compteur m à gaz

gasoline ['gæsəliːn] n (US) essence f

gasp [gɑːsp] n halètement m; (of shock etc): **she gave a small ~ of pain** la douleur lui coupa le souffle ▸ vi haleter; (fig) avoir le souffle coupé

▸ **gasp out** vt (say) dire dans un souffle or d'une voix entrecoupée

gas pedal n (US) accélérateur m

gas ring n brûleur m

gas station n (US) station-service f

gas stove n réchaud m à gaz; (cooker) cuisinière f à gaz

gassy ['gæsɪ] adj gazeux(-euse)

gas tank n (US Aut) réservoir m d'essence

gas tap n bouton m (de cuisinière à gaz); (on pipe) robinet m à gaz

gastric ['gæstrɪk] adj gastrique

gastric ulcer n ulcère m de l'estomac

gastroenteritis ['gæstrəuentə'raɪtɪs] n gastroentérite f

gastronomy [gæs'trɔnəmɪ] n gastronomie f

gasworks ['gæswɜːks] n, npl usine f à gaz

gate [geɪt] n (of garden) portail m; (of field, at level crossing) barrière f; (of building, town, at airport) porte f; (of lock) vanne f

gateau (pl **-x**) ['gætəu, -z] n gros gâteau à la crème

gatecrash ['geɪtkræʃ] vt s'introduire sans invitation dans

gatecrasher ['geɪtkræʃər] n intrus(e)

gatehouse ['geɪthaus] n loge f

gateway ['geɪtweɪ] n porte f

gather ['gæðər] vt (flowers, fruit) cueillir; (pick up) ramasser; (assemble: objects) rassembler; (: people) réunir; (: information) recueillir; (understand) comprendre ▸ vi (assemble) se rassembler; (dust) s'amasser; (clouds) s'amonceler; **to ~ (from/that)** conclure or déduire (de/que); **as far as I can ~** d'après ce que je comprends; **to ~ speed** prendre de la vitesse

gathering ['gæðərɪŋ] n rassemblement m

GATT [gæt] n abbr (= General Agreement on Tariffs and

Trade) GATT *m*
gauche [gəuʃ] *adj* gauche, maladroit(e)
gaudy ['gɔːdɪ] *adj* voyant(e)
gauge [geɪdʒ] *n (standard measure)* calibre *m*; *(Rail)* écartement *m*; *(instrument)* jauge *f* ▷ *vt* jauger; *(fig: sb's capabilities, character)* juger de; **to ~ the right moment** calculer le moment propice; **petrol ~**, *(US)* **gas ~** jauge d'essence
Gaul [gɔːl] *n (country)* Gaule *f*; *(person)* Gaulois(e)
gaunt [gɔːnt] *adj* décharné(e); *(grim, desolate)* désolé(e)
gauntlet ['gɔːntlɪt] *n (fig)*: **to throw down the ~** jeter le gant; **to run the ~ through an angry crowd** se frayer un passage à travers une foule hostile *or* entre deux haies de manifestants *etc* hostiles
gauze [gɔːz] *n* gaze *f*
gave [geɪv] *pt of* **give**
gawky ['gɔːkɪ] *adj* dégingandé(e), godiche
gawp [gɔːp] *vi*: **to ~ at** regarder bouche bée
gay [geɪ] *adj (homosexual)* homosexuel(le); *(slightly old-fashioned: cheerful)* gai(e), réjoui(e); *(colour)* gai, vif (vive)
gaze [geɪz] *n* regard *m* fixe ▷ *vi*: **to ~ at** *(vt)* fixer du regard
gazelle [gə'zɛl] *n* gazelle *f*
gazette [gə'zɛt] *n (newspaper)* gazette *f*; *(official publication)* journal officiel
gazetteer [gæzə'tɪər] *n* dictionnaire *m* géographique
gazump [gə'zʌmp] *vi* *(Brit) revenir sur une promesse de vente pour accepter un prix plus élevé*
GB *abbr* = **Great Britain**
GBH *n abbr (Brit Law: inf)* = **grievous bodily harm**
GC *n abbr (Brit: = George Cross) distinction honorifique*
GCE *n abbr (Brit)* = **General Certificate of Education**
GCHQ *n abbr (Brit: = Government Communications Headquarters) centre d'interception des télécommunications étrangères*
GCSE *n abbr (Brit: = General Certificate of Secondary Education) examen passé à l'âge de 16 ans sanctionnant les connaissances de l'élève;* **she's got eight ~s** elle a réussi dans huit matières aux épreuves du GCSE
Gdns. *abbr* = **gardens**
GDP *n abbr* = **gross domestic product**
GDR *n abbr (old: = German Democratic Republic)* RDA *f*
gear [gɪər] *n* matériel *m*, équipement *m*; *(Tech)* engrenage *m*; *(Aut)* vitesse *f* ▷ *vt (fig: adapt)* adapter; **top** *or (US)* **high/low ~** quatrième *(or* cinquième)/première vitesse; **in ~** en prise; **out of ~** au point mort; **our service is ~ed to meet the needs of the disabled** notre service répond de façon spécifique aux besoins des handicapés
▶ **gear up** *vi*: **to ~ up (to do)** se préparer (à faire)
gear box *n* boîte *f* de vitesse
gear lever *n* levier *m* de vitesse
gear shift *(US)* *n* = **gear lever**
gear stick *(Brit)* *n* = **gear lever**
GED *n abbr (US Scol)* = **general educational development**

geese [giːs] *npl of* **goose**
geezer ['giːzər] *n (Brit inf)* mec *m*
Geiger counter ['gaɪgə-] *n* compteur *m* Geiger
gel [dʒɛl] *n* gelée *f*; *(Chem)* colloïde *m*
gelatin, gelatine ['dʒɛlətiːn] *n* gélatine *f*
gelignite ['dʒɛlɪgnaɪt] *n* plastic *m*
gem [dʒɛm] *n* pierre précieuse
Gemini ['dʒɛmɪnaɪ] *n* les Gémeaux *mpl*; **to be ~** être des Gémeaux
gen [dʒɛn] *n (Brit inf)*: **to give sb the ~ on sth** mettre qn au courant de qch
Gen. *abbr (Mil: = general)* Gal
gen. *abbr (= general, generally)* gén
gender ['dʒɛndər] *n* genre *m*; *(person's sex)* sexe *m*
gene [dʒiːn] *n (Biol)* gène *m*
genealogy [dʒiːnɪ'ælədʒɪ] *n* généalogie *f*
general ['dʒɛnərl] *n* général *m* ▷ *adj* général(e); **in ~** en général; **the ~ public** le grand public; **~ audit** *(Comm)* vérification annuelle
general anaesthetic, *(US)* **general anesthetic** *n* anesthésie générale
general delivery *n* poste restante
general election *n* élection(s) législative(s)
generalization ['dʒɛnrəlaɪ'zeɪʃən] *n* généralisation *f*
generalize ['dʒɛnrəlaɪz] *vi* généraliser
general knowledge *n* connaissances générales
generally ['dʒɛnrəlɪ] *adv* généralement
general manager *n* directeur général
general practitioner *n* généraliste *m/f*
general store *n* épicerie *f*
general strike *n* grève générale
generate ['dʒɛnəreɪt] *vt* engendrer; *(electricity)* produire
generation [dʒɛnə'reɪʃən] *n* génération *f*; *(of electricity etc)* production *f*
generator ['dʒɛnəreɪtər] *n* générateur *m*
generic [dʒɪ'nɛrɪk] *adj* générique
generosity [dʒɛnə'rɔsɪtɪ] *n* générosité *f*
generous ['dʒɛnərəs] *adj* généreux(-euse); *(copious)* copieux(-euse)
genesis ['dʒɛnɪsɪs] *n* genèse *f*
genetic [dʒɪ'nɛtɪk] *adj* génétique; **~ engineering** ingénierie *m* génétique; **~ fingerprinting** système *m* d'empreinte génétique
genetically modified *adj (food etc)* génétiquement modifié(e)
genetics [dʒɪ'nɛtɪks] *n* génétique *f*
Geneva [dʒɪ'niːvə] *n* Genève; **Lake ~** le lac Léman
genial ['dʒiːnɪəl] *adj* cordial(e), chaleureux(-euse); *(climate)* clément(e)
genitals ['dʒɛnɪtlz] *npl* organes génitaux
genitive ['dʒɛnɪtɪv] *n* génitif *m*
genius ['dʒiːnɪəs] *n* génie *m*
Genoa ['dʒɛnəuə] *n* Gênes
genocide ['dʒɛnəusaɪd] *n* génocide *m*
gent [dʒɛnt] *n abbr (Brit inf)* = **gentleman**
genteel [dʒɛn'tiːl] *adj* de bon ton, distingué(e)
gentle ['dʒɛntl] *adj* doux (douce); *(breeze, touch)*

léger(-ère)

gentleman (irreg) ['dʒɛntlmən] n monsieur m;
(well-bred man) gentleman m; **~'s agreement**
gentleman's agreement m

gentlemanly ['dʒɛntlmənlɪ] adj bien élevé(e)

gentleness ['dʒɛntlnɪs] n douceur f

gently ['dʒɛntlɪ] adv doucement

gentry ['dʒɛntrɪ] n petite noblesse

gents [dʒɛnts] n W.-C. mpl (pour hommes)

genuine ['dʒɛnjuɪn] adj véritable, authentique;
(person, emotion) sincère

genuinely ['dʒɛnjuɪnlɪ] adv sincèrement,
vraiment

geographer [dʒɪˈɔgrəfəʳ] n géographe m/f

geographic [dʒɪəˈgræfɪk], **geographical**
[dʒɪəˈgræfɪkl] adj géographique

geography [dʒɪˈɔgrəfɪ] n géographie f

geological [dʒɪəˈlɔdʒɪkl] adj géologique

geologist [dʒɪˈɔlədʒɪst] n géologue m/f

geology [dʒɪˈɔlədʒɪ] n géologie f

geometric [dʒɪəˈmɛtrɪk], **geometrical**
[dʒɪəˈmɛtrɪkl] adj géométrique

geometry [dʒɪˈɔmətrɪ] n géométrie f

Geordie ['dʒɔːdɪ] n (inf) habitant(e) de Tyneside,
originaire m/f de Tyneside.

Georgia ['dʒɔːdʒə] n Géorgie f

Georgian ['dʒɔːdʒən] adj (Geo) géorgien(ne) ▷ n
Géorgien(ne); (Ling) géorgien m

geranium [dʒɪˈreɪnɪəm] n géranium m

geriatric [dʒɛrɪˈætrɪk] adj gériatrique ▷ n
patient(e) gériatrique

germ [dʒəːm] n (Med) microbe m; (Biol: fig)
germe m

German ['dʒəːmən] adj allemand(e) ▷ n
Allemand(e); (Ling) allemand m

germane [dʒəːˈmeɪn] adj (formal): ~ (to) se
rapportant (à)

German measles n rubéole f

Germany ['dʒəːmənɪ] n Allemagne f

germination [dʒəːmɪˈneɪʃən] n germination f

germ warfare n guerre f bactériologique

gerrymandering ['dʒɛrɪmændərɪŋ] n
tripotage m du découpage électoral

gestation [dʒɛsˈteɪʃən] n gestation f

gesticulate [dʒɛsˈtɪkjuleɪt] vi gesticuler

gesture ['dʒɛstjəʳ] n geste m; **as a ~ of
friendship** en témoignage d'amitié

⊙ KEYWORD

get [gɛt] (pt, pp **got**, pp **gotten**) (US) vi **1** (become,
be) devenir; **to get old/tired** devenir vieux/
fatigué, vieillir/se fatiguer; **to get drunk**
s'enivrer; **to get ready/washed/shaved** etc se
préparer/laver/raser etc; **to get killed** se faire
tuer; **to get dirty** se salir; **to get married** se
marier; **when do I get paid?** quand est-ce que
je serai payé?; **it's getting late** il se fait tard
2 (go): **to get to/from** aller à/de; **to get home**
rentrer chez soi; **how did you get here?**
comment es-tu arrivé ici?; **he got across the
bridge/under the fence** il a traversé le pont/

est passé au-dessous de la barrière
3 (begin) commencer or se mettre à; **to get to
know sb** apprendre à connaître qn; **I'm
getting to like him** je commence à l'apprécier;
let's get going or **started** allons-y
4 (modal aux vb): **you've got to do it** il faut que
vous le fassiez; **I've got to tell the police** je
dois le dire à la police
▷ vt **1**: **to get sth done** (do) faire qch; (have done)
faire faire qch; **to get sth/sb ready** préparer
qch/qn; **to get one's hair cut** se faire couper
les cheveux; **to get the car going** or **to go**
(faire) démarrer la voiture; **to get sb to do sth**
faire faire qch à qn; **to get sb drunk** enivrer qn
2 (obtain: money, permission, results) obtenir, avoir;
(buy) acheter; (find: job, flat) trouver; (fetch: person,
doctor, object) aller chercher; **to get sth for sb**
procurer qch à qn; **get me Mr Jones, please** (on
phone) passez-moi Mr Jones, s'il vous plaît; **can I
get you a drink?** est-ce que je peux vous servir
à boire?
3 (receive: present, letter) recevoir, avoir; (acquire:
reputation) avoir; (prize) obtenir; **what did you
get for your birthday?** qu'est-ce que tu as eu
pour ton anniversaire?; **how much did you
get for the painting?** combien avez-vous
vendu le tableau?
4 (catch) prendre, saisir, attraper; (hit: target etc)
atteindre; **to get sb by the arm/throat**
prendre or saisir or attraper qn par le bras/à la
gorge; **get him!** arrête-le!; **the bullet got him
in the leg** il a pris la balle dans la jambe; **he
really gets me!** il me porte sur les nerfs!
5 (take, move): **to get sth to sb** faire parvenir
qch à qn; **do you think we'll get it through
the door?** on arrivera à le faire passer par la
porte?; **I'll get you there somehow** je me
débrouillerai pour t'y emmener
6 (catch, take: plane, bus etc) prendre; **where do I
get the train for Birmingham?** où prend-on
le train pour Birmingham?
7 (understand) comprendre, saisir; (hear)
entendre; **I've got it!** j'ai compris!; **I don't get
your meaning** je ne vois or comprends pas ce
que vous voulez dire; **I didn't get your name** je
n'ai pas entendu votre nom
8 (have, possess): **to have got** avoir; **how many
have you got?** vous en avez combien?
9 (illness) avoir; **I've got a cold** j'ai le rhume;
she got pneumonia and died elle a fait une
pneumonie et elle en est morte

▸ **get about** vi se déplacer; (news) se répandre

▸ **get across** vt: **to get across (to)** (message,
meaning) faire passer (à) ▷ vi: **to get across (to)**
(speaker) se faire comprendre (par)

▸ **get along** vi (agree) s'entendre; (depart) s'en
aller; (manage) = **get by**

▸ **get at** vt fus (attack) s'en prendre à; (reach)
attraper, atteindre; **what are you getting at?** à
quoi voulez-vous en venir?

▸ **get away** vi partir, s'en aller; (escape)
s'échapper

▶ **get away with** *vt fus* (*punishment*) en être quitte pour; (*crime etc*) se faire pardonner

▶ **get back** *vi* (*return*) rentrer ▷ *vt* récupérer, recouvrer; **to get back to** (*start again*) retourner *or* revenir à; (*contact again*) recontacter; **when do we get back?** quand serons-nous de retour?

▶ **get back at** *vt fus* (*inf*): **to get back at sb** rendre la monnaie de sa pièce à qn

▶ **get by** *vi* (*pass*) passer; (*manage*) se débrouiller; **I can get by in Dutch** je me débrouille en hollandais

▶ **get down** *vi, vt fus* descendre ▷ *vt* descendre; (*depress*) déprimer

▶ **get down to** *vt fus* (*work*) se mettre à (faire); **to get down to business** passer aux choses sérieuses

▶ **get in** *vi* entrer; (*arrive home*) rentrer; (*train*) arriver ▷ *vt* (*bring in: harvest*) rentrer; (: *coal*) faire rentrer; (: *supplies*) faire des provisions de

▶ **get into** *vt fus* entrer dans; (*car, train etc*) monter dans; (*clothes*) mettre, enfiler, endosser; **to get into bed/a rage** se mettre au lit/en colère

▶ **get off** *vi* (*from train etc*) descendre; (*depart: person, car*) s'en aller; (*escape*) s'en tirer ▷ *vt* (*remove: clothes, stain*) enlever; (*send off*) expédier; (*have as leave: day, time*): **we got 2 days off** nous avons eu 2 jours de congé ▷ *vt fus* (*train, bus*) descendre de; **where do I get off?** où est-ce que je dois descendre?; **to get off to a good start** (*fig*) prendre un bon départ

▶ **get on** *vi* (*at exam etc*) se débrouiller; (*agree*): **to get on (with)** s'entendre (avec); **how are you getting on?** comment ça va? ▷ *vt fus* monter dans; (*horse*) monter sur

▶ **get on to** *vt fus* (*Brit: deal with: problem*) s'occuper de; (*contact: person*) contacter

▶ **get out** *vi* sortir; (*of vehicle*) descendre; (*news etc*) s'ébruiter ▷ *vt* sortir

▶ **get out of** *vt fus* sortir de; (*duty etc*) échapper à, se soustraire à

▶ **get over** *vt fus* (*illness*) se remettre de ▷ *vt* (*communicate: idea etc*) communiquer; (*finish*): **let's get it over (with)** finissons-en

▶ **get round** *vi*: **to get round to doing sth** se mettre (finalement) à faire qch ▷ *vt fus* contourner; (*fig: person*) entortiller

▶ **get through** *vi* (*Tel*) avoir la communication; **to get through to sb** atteindre qn ▷ *vt fus* (*finish: work, book*) finir, terminer

▶ **get together** *vi* se réunir ▷ *vt* rassembler

▶ **get up** *vi* (*rise*) se lever ▷ *vt fus* monter

▶ **get up to** *vt fus* (*reach*) arriver à; (*prank etc*) faire

getaway ['gɛtəweɪ] *n* fuite *f*

getaway car *n* voiture prévue pour prendre la fuite

get-together ['gɛttəgɛðəʳ] *n* petite réunion, petite fête

get-up ['gɛtʌp] *n* (*inf: outfit*) accoutrement *m*

get-well card [gɛt'wɛl-] *n* carte *f* de vœux de bon rétablissement

geyser ['giːzəʳ] *n* chauffe-eau *m inv*; (*Geo*) geyser *m*

Ghana ['gɑːnə] *n* Ghana *m*

Ghanaian [gɑːˈneɪən] *adj* ghanéen(ne) ▷ *n* Ghanéen(ne)

ghastly ['gɑːstlɪ] *adj* atroce, horrible; (*pale*) livide, blême

gherkin ['gəːkɪn] *n* cornichon *m*

ghetto ['gɛtəu] *n* ghetto *m*

ghetto blaster [-blɑːstəʳ] *n* (*inf*) gros radiocassette

ghost [gəust] *n* fantôme *m*, revenant *m* ▷ *vt* (*sb else's book*) écrire

ghostly ['gəustlɪ] *adj* fantomatique

ghostwriter ['gəustraɪtəʳ] *n* nègre *m* (*fig*)

ghoul [guːl] *n* (*ghost*) vampire *m*

ghoulish ['guːlɪʃ] *adj* (*tastes etc*) morbide

GHQ *n abbr* (*Mil: = general headquarters*) GQG *m*

GI *n abbr* (*US inf: = government issue*) soldat de l'armée américaine, GI *m*

giant ['dʒaɪənt] *n* géant(e) ▷ *adj* géant(e), énorme; ~ **(size) packet** paquet géant

giant killer *n* (*Sport*) équipe inconnue qui remporte un match contre une équipe renommée

gibber ['dʒɪbəʳ] *vi* émettre des sons inintelligibles

gibberish ['dʒɪbərɪʃ] *n* charabia *m*

gibe [dʒaɪb] *n* sarcasme *m* ▷ *vi*: **to ~ at** railler

giblets ['dʒɪblɪts] *npl* abats *mpl*

Gibraltar [dʒɪˈbrɔːltəʳ] *n* Gibraltar *m*

giddiness ['gɪdɪnɪs] *n* vertige *m*

giddy ['gɪdɪ] *adj* (*dizzy*): **to be** (*or* **feel**) ~ avoir le vertige; (*height*) vertigineux(-euse); (*thoughtless*) sot(te), étourdi(e)

gift [gɪft] *n* cadeau *m*, présent *m*; (*donation, talent*) don *m*; (*Comm: also:* **free gift**) cadeau(-réclame) *m*; **to have a ~ for sth** avoir des dons pour *or* le don de qch

gifted ['gɪftɪd] *adj* doué(e)

gift shop, (*US*) **gift store** *n* boutique *f* de cadeaux

gift token, **gift voucher** *n* chèque-cadeau *m*

gig [gɪg] *n* (*inf: concert*) concert *m*

gigabyte ['dʒɪgəbaɪt] *n* gigaoctet *m*

gigantic [dʒaɪˈgæntɪk] *adj* gigantesque

giggle ['gɪgl] *vi* pouffer, ricaner sottement ▷ *n* petit rire sot, ricanement *m*

GIGO ['gaɪgəu] *abbr* (*Comput: inf: = garbage in, garbage out*) qualité d'entrée = qualité de sortie

gild [gɪld] *vt* dorer

gill [dʒɪl] *n* (*measure*) = 0.25 pints (*Brit* = 0.148 l; *US* = 0.118 l)

gills [gɪlz] *npl* (*of fish*) ouïes *fpl*, branchies *fpl*

gilt [gɪlt] *n* dorure *f* ▷ *adj* doré(e)

gilt-edged ['gɪltɛdʒd] *adj* (*stocks, securities*) de premier ordre

gimlet ['gɪmlɪt] *n* vrille *f*

gimmick ['gɪmɪk] *n* truc *m*; **sales** ~ offre promotionnelle

gin [dʒɪn] *n* gin *m*

ginger ['dʒɪndʒəʳ] *n* gingembre *m*

▶ **ginger up** *vt* secouer; animer

ginger ale, ginger beer n boisson gazeuse au gingembre

gingerbread ['dʒɪndʒəbrɛd] n pain m d'épices

ginger group n (Brit) groupe m de pression

ginger-haired ['dʒɪndʒə'hɛəd] adj roux (rousse)

gingerly ['dʒɪndʒəlɪ] adv avec précaution

gingham ['gɪŋəm] n vichy m

ginseng ['dʒɪnsɛŋ] n ginseng m

gipsy ['dʒɪpsɪ] n = **gypsy**

giraffe [dʒɪ'rɑːf] n girafe f

girder ['gəːdə'] n poutrelle f

girdle ['gəːdl] n (corset) gaine f ▷ vt ceindre

girl [gəːl] n fille f, fillette f; (young unmarried woman) jeune fille; (daughter) fille; **an English ~** une jeune Anglaise; **a little English ~** une petite Anglaise

girl band n girls band m

girlfriend ['gəːlfrɛnd] n (of girl) amie f; (of boy) petite amie

Girl Guide n (Brit) éclaireuse f; (Roman Catholic) guide f

girlish ['gəːlɪʃ] adj de jeune fille

Girl Scout n (US) = **Girl Guide**

Giro ['dʒaɪrəu] n: **the National ~** (Brit) ≈ les comptes chèques postaux

giro ['dʒaɪrəu] n (bank giro) virement m bancaire; (post office giro) mandat m

girth [gəːθ] n circonférence f; (of horse) sangle f

gist [dʒɪst] n essentiel m

give [gɪv] (pt **gave**, pp **given** [geɪv, 'gɪvn]) n (of fabric) élasticité f ▷ vt donner ▷ vi (break) céder; (stretch: fabric) se prêter; **to ~ sb sth, ~ sth to sb** donner qch à qn; (gift) offrir qch à qn; (message) transmettre qch à qn; **to ~ sb a call/kiss** appeler/embrasser qn; **to ~ a cry/sigh** pousser un cri/un soupir; **how much did you ~ for it?** combien (l')avez-vous payé?; **12 o'clock, ~ or take a few minutes** midi, à quelques minutes près; **to ~ way** céder; (Brit Aut) donner la priorité
  ▶ **give away** vt donner; (give free) faire cadeau de; (betray) donner, trahir; (disclose) révéler; (bride) conduire à l'autel
  ▶ **give back** vt rendre
  ▶ **give in** vi céder ▷ vt donner
  ▶ **give off** vt dégager
  ▶ **give out** vt (food etc) distribuer; (news) annoncer ▷ vi (be exhausted: supplies) s'épuiser; (fail) lâcher
  ▶ **give up** vi renoncer ▷ vt renoncer à; **to ~ up smoking** arrêter de fumer; **to ~ o.s. up** se rendre

give-and-take ['gɪvənd'teɪk] n concessions mutuelles

giveaway ['gɪvəweɪ] n (inf): **her expression was a ~** son expression la trahissait; **the exam was a ~!** cet examen, c'était du gâteau! ▷ cpd: **~ prices** prix sacrifiés

given ['gɪvn] pp of **give** ▷ adj (fixed: time, amount) donné(e), déterminé(e) ▷ conj: **~ the circumstances ...** étant donné les circonstances ..., vu les circonstances ...; **~**

that ... étant donné que ...

glacial ['gleɪsɪəl] adj (Geo) glaciaire; (wind, weather) glacial(e)

glacier ['glæsɪə'] n glacier m

glad [glæd] adj content(e); **to be ~ about sth/ that** être heureux(-euse) or bien content de qch/que; **I was ~ of his help** j'étais bien content de (pouvoir compter sur) son aide or qu'il m'aide

gladden ['glædn] vt réjouir

glade [gleɪd] n clairière f

gladioli [glædɪ'əulaɪ] npl glaïeuls mpl

gladly ['glædlɪ] adv volontiers

glamorous ['glæmərəs] adj (person) séduisant(e); (job) prestigieux(-euse)

glamour, (US) **glamor** ['glæmə'] n éclat m, prestige m

glance [glɑːns] n coup m d'œil ▷ vi: **to ~ at** jeter un coup d'œil à
  ▶ **glance off** vt fus (bullet) ricocher sur

glancing ['glɑːnsɪŋ] adj (blow) oblique

gland [glænd] n glande f

glandular ['glændjulə'] adj: **~ fever** (Brit) mononucléose infectieuse

glare [glɛə'] n (of anger) regard furieux; (of light) lumière éblouissante; (of publicity) feux mpl ▷ vi briller d'un éclat aveuglant; **to ~ at** lancer un regard or des regards furieux à

glaring ['glɛərɪŋ] adj (mistake) criant(e), qui saute aux yeux

glasnost ['glæznɔst] n glasnost f

glass [glɑːs] n verre m; (also: **looking glass**) miroir m; **glasses** npl (spectacles) lunettes fpl

glass-blowing ['glɑːsbləuɪŋ] n soufflage m (du verre)

glass ceiling n (fig) plafond dans l'échelle hiérarchique au-dessus duquel les femmes ou les membres d'une minorité ethnique ne semblent pouvoir s'élever

glass fibre n fibre f de verre

glasshouse ['glɑːshaus] n serre f

glassware ['glɑːswɛə'] n verrerie f

glassy ['glɑːsɪ] adj (eyes) vitreux(-euse)

Glaswegian [glæs'wiːdʒən] adj de Glasgow ▷ n habitant(e) de Glasgow, natif(-ive) de Glasgow

glaze [gleɪz] vt (door) vitrer; (pottery) vernir; (Culin) glacer ▷ n vernis m; (Culin) glaçage m

glazed [gleɪzd] adj (eye) vitreux(-euse); (pottery) verni(e); (tiles) vitrifié(e)

glazier ['gleɪzɪə'] n vitrier m

gleam [gliːm] n lueur f ▷ vi luire, briller; **a ~ of hope** une lueur d'espoir

gleaming ['gliːmɪŋ] adj luisant(e)

glean [gliːn] vt (information) recueillir

glee [gliː] n joie f

gleeful ['gliːful] adj joyeux(-euse)

glen [glɛn] n vallée f

glib [glɪb] adj qui a du bagou; facile

glide [glaɪd] vi glisser; (Aviat, bird) planer ▷ n glissement m; vol plané

glider ['glaɪdə'] n (Aviat) planeur m

gliding ['glaɪdɪŋ] n (Aviat) vol m à voile

glimmer ['glɪmə'] vi luire ▷ n lueur f

glimpse [glɪmps] *n* vision passagère, aperçu *m* ▷ *vt* entrevoir, apercevoir; **to catch a ~ of** entrevoir

glint [glɪnt] *n* éclair *m* ▷ *vi* étinceler

glisten ['glɪsn] *vi* briller, luire

glitter ['glɪtər] *vi* scintiller, briller ▷ *n* scintillement *m*

glitz [glɪts] *n* (*inf*) clinquant *m*

gloat [gləʊt] *vi*: **to ~ (over)** jubiler (à propos de)

global ['gləʊbl] *adj* (*world-wide*) mondial(e); (*overall*) global(e)

globalization [gləʊblaɪz'eɪʃən] *n* mondialisation *f*

global warming [-'wɔːmɪŋ] *n* réchauffement *m* de la planète

globe [gləʊb] *n* globe *m*

globe-trotter ['gləʊbtrɔtər] *n* globe-trotter *m*

globule ['glɔbjuːl] *n* (*Anat*) globule *m*; (*of water etc*) gouttelette *f*

gloom [gluːm] *n* obscurité *f*; (*sadness*) tristesse *f*, mélancolie *f*

gloomy ['gluːmɪ] *adj* (*person*) morose; (*place, outlook*) sombre; **to feel ~** avoir *or* se faire des idées noires

glorification [glɔːrɪfɪ'keɪʃən] *n* glorification *f*

glorify ['glɔːrɪfaɪ] *vt* glorifier

glorious ['glɔːrɪəs] *adj* glorieux(-euse); (*beautiful*) splendide

glory ['glɔːrɪ] *n* gloire *f*; splendeur *f* ▷ *vi*: **to ~ in** se glorifier de

glory hole *n* (*inf*) capharnaüm *m*

Glos *abbr* (*Brit*) = **Gloucestershire**

gloss [glɔs] *n* (*shine*) brillant *m*, vernis *m*; (*also:* **gloss paint**) peinture brillante *or* laquée
▸ **gloss over** *vt fus* glisser sur

glossary ['glɔsərɪ] *n* glossaire *m*, lexique *m*

glossy ['glɔsɪ] *adj* brillant(e), luisant(e) ▷ *n* (*also:* **glossy magazine**) revue *f* de luxe

glove [glʌv] *n* gant *m*

glove compartment *n* (*Aut*) boîte *f* à gants, vide-poches *m inv*

glow [gləʊ] *vi* rougeoyer; (*face*) rayonner; (*eyes*) briller ▷ *n* rougeoiement *m*

glower ['glaʊər] *vi* lancer des regards mauvais

glowing ['gləʊɪŋ] *adj* (*fire*) rougeoyant(e); (*complexion*) éclatant(e); (*report, description etc*) dithyrambique

glow-worm ['gləʊwəːm] *n* ver luisant

glucose ['gluːkəʊs] *n* glucose *m*

glue [gluː] *n* colle *f* ▷ *vt* coller

glue-sniffing ['gluːsnɪfɪŋ] *n* inhalation *f* de colle

glum [glʌm] *adj* maussade, morose

glut [glʌt] *n* surabondance *f* ▷ *vt* rassasier; (*market*) encombrer

glutinous ['gluːtɪnəs] *adj* visqueux(-euse)

glutton ['glʌtn] *n* glouton(ne); **a ~ for work** un bourreau de travail

gluttonous ['glʌtənəs] *adj* glouton(ne)

gluttony ['glʌtənɪ] *n* gloutonnerie *f*; (*sin*) gourmandise *f*

glycerin, glycerine ['glɪsəriːn] *n* glycérine *f*

GM *abbr* (= *genetically modified*) génétiquement modifié(e)

gm *abbr* (= *gram*) g

GMAT *n abbr* (*US:* = *Graduate Management Admissions Test*) examen d'admission dans le 2e cycle de l'enseignement supérieur

GMO *n abbr* (= *genetically modified organism*) OGM *m*

GMT *abbr* (= *Greenwich Mean Time*) GMT

gnarled [nɑːld] *adj* noueux(-euse)

gnash [næʃ] *vt*: **to ~ one's teeth** grincer des dents

gnat [næt] *n* moucheron *m*

gnaw [nɔː] *vt* ronger

gnome [nəʊm] *n* gnome *m*, lutin *m*

GNP *n abbr* = **gross national product**

go [gəʊ] (*pt* **went**, *pp* **gone** [wɛnt, gɔn]) *vi* aller; (*depart*) partir, s'en aller; (*work*) marcher; (*break*) céder; (*time*) passer; (*be sold*): **to go for £10** se vendre 10 livres; (*become*): **to go pale/mouldy** pâlir/moisir ▷ *n* (*pl* **goes**): **to have a go (at)** essayer (de faire); **to be on the go** être en mouvement; **whose go is it?** à qui est-ce de jouer?; **to go by car/on foot** aller en voiture/à pied; **he's going to do it** il va le faire, il est sur le point de le faire; **to go for a walk** aller se promener; **to go dancing/shopping** aller danser/faire les courses; **to go looking for sb/sth** aller *or* partir à la recherche de qn/qch; **to go to sleep** s'endormir; **to go and see sb, go to see sb** aller voir qn; **how is it going?** comment ça marche?; **how did it go?** comment est-ce que ça s'est passé?; **to go round the back/by the shop** passer par derrière/devant le magasin; **my voice has gone** j'ai une extinction de voix; **the cake is all gone** il n'y a plus de gâteau; **I'll take whatever is going** (*Brit*) je prendrai ce qu'il y a (*or* ce que vous avez); **... to go** (*US: food*) ... à emporter
▸ **go about** *vi* (*also:* **go around**) aller çà et là; (*rumour*) se répandre ▷ *vt fus*: **how do I go about this?** comment dois-je m'y prendre (pour faire ceci)?; **to go about one's business** s'occuper de ses affaires
▸ **go after** *vt fus* (*pursue*) poursuivre, courir après; (*job, record etc*) essayer d'obtenir
▸ **go against** *vt fus* (*be unfavourable to*) être défavorable à; (*be contrary to*) être contraire à
▸ **go ahead** *vi* (*make progress*) avancer; (*take place*) avoir lieu; (*get going*) y aller
▸ **go along** *vi* aller, avancer ▷ *vt fus* longer, parcourir; **as you go along (with your work)** au fur et à mesure (de votre travail); **to go along with** (*accompany*) accompagner; (*agree with: idea*) être d'accord sur; (*: person*) suivre
▸ **go away** *vi* partir, s'en aller
▸ **go back** *vi* rentrer; revenir; (*go again*) retourner
▸ **go back on** *vt fus* (*promise*) revenir sur
▸ **go by** *vi* (*years, time*) passer, s'écouler ▷ *vt fus* s'en tenir à; (*believe*) en croire
▸ **go down** *vi* descendre; (*number, price, amount*) baisser; (*ship*) couler; (*sun*) se coucher ▷ *vt fus*

g

descendre; **that should go down well with him** (*fig*) ça devrait lui plaire

▶ **go for** *vt fus* (*fetch*) aller chercher; (*like*) aimer; (*attack*) s'en prendre à; attaquer

▶ **go in** *vi* entrer

▶ **go in for** *vt fus* (*competition*) se présenter à; (*like*) aimer

▶ **go into** *vt fus* entrer dans; (*investigate*) étudier, examiner; (*embark on*) se lancer dans

▶ **go off** *vi* partir, s'en aller; (*food*) se gâter; (*milk*) tourner; (*bomb*) sauter; (*alarm clock*) sonner; (*alarm*) se déclencher; (*lights etc*) s'éteindre; (*event*) se dérouler ▷ *vt fus* ne plus aimer, ne plus avoir envie de; **the gun went off** le coup est parti; **to go off to sleep** s'endormir; **the party went off well** la fête s'est bien passée *or* était très réussie

▶ **go on** *vi* continuer; (*happen*) se passer; (*lights*) s'allumer ▷ *vt fus* (*be guided by: evidence etc*) se fonder sur; **to go on doing** continuer à faire; **what's going on here?** qu'est-ce qui se passe ici?

▶ **go on at** *vt fus* (*nag*) tomber sur le dos de

▶ **go on with** *vt fus* poursuivre, continuer

▶ **go out** *vi* sortir; (*fire, light*) s'éteindre; (*tide*) descendre; **to go out with sb** sortir avec qn

▶ **go over** *vi* (*ship*) chavirer ▷ *vt fus* (*check*) revoir, vérifier; **to go over sth in one's mind** repasser qch dans son esprit

▶ **go past** *vt fus*: **to go past sth** passer devant qch

▶ **go round** *vi* (*circulate: news, rumour*) circuler; (*revolve*) tourner; (*suffice*) suffire (pour tout le monde); (*visit*): **to go round to sb's** passer chez qn; aller chez qn; (*make a detour*): **to go round (by)** faire un détour (par)

▶ **go through** *vt fus* (*town etc*) traverser; (*search through*) fouiller; (*suffer*) subir; (*examine: list, book*) lire *or* regarder en détail, éplucher; (*perform: lesson*) réciter; (: *formalities*) remplir; (: *programme*) exécuter

▶ **go through with** *vt fus* (*plan, crime*) aller jusqu'au bout de

▶ **go under** *vi* (*sink: also fig*) couler; (: *person*) succomber

▶ **go up** *vi* monter; (*price*) augmenter ▷ *vt fus* gravir; (*also:* **go up in flames**) flamber, s'enflammer brusquement

▶ **go with** *vt fus* aller avec

▶ **go without** *vt fus* se passer de

goad [gəud] *vt* aiguillonner

go-ahead ['gəuəhɛd] *adj* dynamique, entreprenant(e) ▷ *n* feu vert

goal [gəul] *n* but *m*

goal difference *n* différence *f* de buts

goalie ['gəulɪ] *n* (*inf*) goal *m*

goalkeeper ['gəulkiːpər] *n* gardien *m* de but

goal-post ['gəulpəust] *n* poteau *m* de but

goat [gəut] *n* chèvre *f*

gobble ['gɔbl] *vt* (*also:* **gobble down**, **gobble up**) engloutir

go-between ['gəubɪtwiːn] *n* médiateur *m*

Gobi Desert ['gəubɪ-] *n* désert *m* de Gobi

goblet ['gɔblɪt] *n* coupe *f*

goblin ['gɔblɪn] *n* lutin *m*

go-cart ['gəukɑːt] *n* kart *m* ▷ *cpd*: ~ **racing** karting *m*

god [gɔd] *n* dieu *m*; **G~** Dieu

god-awful [gɔd'ɔːfəl] *adj* (*inf*) franchement atroce

godchild ['gɔdtʃaɪld] *n* filleul(e)

goddamn ['gɔddæm], **goddamned** ['gɔddæmd] *excl* (*esp US inf*): ~ **(it)!** nom de Dieu! ▷ *adj* satané(e), sacré(e) ▷ *adv* sacrément

goddaughter ['gɔddɔːtər] *n* filleule *f*

goddess ['gɔdɪs] *n* déesse *f*

godfather ['gɔdfɑːðər] *n* parrain *m*

god-fearing ['gɔdfɪərɪŋ] *adj* croyant(e)

god-forsaken ['gɔdfəseɪkən] *adj* maudit(e)

godmother ['gɔdmʌðər] *n* marraine *f*

godparents ['gɔdpɛərənts] *npl*: **the ~** le parrain et la marraine

godsend ['gɔdsɛnd] *n* aubaine *f*

godson ['gɔdsʌn] *n* filleul *m*

goes [gəuz] *vb see* **go**

gofer ['gəufər] *n* coursier(-ière)

go-getter ['gəugɛtər] *n* arriviste *m/f*

goggle ['gɔgl] *vi*: **to ~ at** regarder avec des yeux ronds

goggles ['gɔglz] *npl* (*for skiing etc*) lunettes (protectrices); (*for swimming*) lunettes de piscine

going ['gəuɪŋ] *n* (*conditions*) état *m* du terrain ▷ *adj*: **the ~ rate** le tarif (en vigueur); **a ~ concern** une affaire prospère; **it was slow ~** les progrès étaient lents, ça n'avançait pas vite

going-over [gəuɪŋ'əuvər] *n* vérification *f*, révision *f*; (*inf: beating*) passage *m* à tabac

goings-on ['gəuɪŋz'ɔn] *npl* (*inf*) manigances *fpl*

go-kart ['gəukɑːt] *n* = **go-cart**

gold [gəuld] *n or m* ▷ *adj* en or; (*reserves*) d'or

golden ['gəuldən] *adj* (*made of gold*) en or; (*gold in colour*) doré(e)

golden age *n* âge *m* d'or

golden handshake *n* (*Brit*) prime *f* de départ

golden rule *n* règle *f* d'or

goldfish ['gəuldfɪʃ] *n* poisson *m* rouge

gold leaf *n or m* en feuille

gold medal *n* (*Sport*) médaille *f* d'or

goldmine ['gəuldmaɪn] *n* mine *f* d'or

gold-plated ['gəuld'pleɪtɪd] *adj* plaqué(e) or *inv*

goldsmith ['gəuldsmɪθ] *n* orfèvre *m*

gold standard *n* étalon-or *m*

golf [gɔlf] *n* golf *m*

golf ball *n* balle *f* de golf; (*on typewriter*) boule *f*

golf club *n* club *m* de golf; (*stick*) club *m*, crosse *f* de golf

golf course *n* terrain *m* de golf

golfer ['gɔlfər] *n* joueur(-euse) de golf

golfing ['gɔlfɪŋ] *n* golf *m*

gondola ['gɔndələ] *n* gondole *f*

gondolier [gɔndə'lɪər] *n* gondolier *m*

gone [gɔn] *pp of* **go** ▷ *adj* parti(e)

goner ['gɔnər] *n* (*inf*): **to be a ~** être fichu(e) *or* foutu(e)

gong [gɒŋ] *n* gong *m*
good [gud] *adj* bon(ne); (*kind*) gentil(le); (*child*) sage; (*weather*) beau (belle) ▷ *n* bien *m*; **goods** *npl* marchandise *f*, articles *mpl*; (*Comm etc*) marchandises; **~!** bon!, très bien!; **to be ~ at** être bon en; **to be ~ for** être bon pour; **it's ~ for you** c'est bon pour vous; **it's a ~ thing you were there** heureusement que vous étiez là; **she is ~ with children/her hands** elle sait bien s'occuper des enfants/sait se servir de ses mains; **to feel ~** se sentir bien; **it's ~ to see you** ça me fait plaisir de vous voir, je suis content de vous voir; **he's up to no ~** il prépare quelque mauvais coup; **it's no ~ complaining** cela ne sert à rien de se plaindre; **to make ~** (*deficit*) combler; (*losses*) compenser; **for the common ~** dans l'intérêt commun; **for ~** (*for ever*) pour de bon, une fois pour toutes; **would you be ~ enough to ...?** auriez-vous la bonté *or* l'amabilité de ...?; **that's very ~ of you** c'est très gentil de votre part; **is this any ~?** (*will it do?*) est-ce que ceci fera l'affaire?, est-ce que cela peut vous rendre service?; (*what's it like?*) qu'est-ce que ça vaut?; **~s and chattels** biens *mpl* et effets *mpl*; **a ~ deal (of)** beaucoup (de); **a ~ many** beaucoup (de); **~ morning/afternoon!** bonjour!; **~ evening!** bonsoir!; **~ night!** bonsoir!; (*on going to bed*) bonne nuit!
goodbye [gud'baɪ] *excl* au revoir!; **to say ~ to sb** dire au revoir à qn
good faith *n* bonne foi
good-for-nothing ['gudfənʌθɪŋ] *adj* bon(ne) *or* propre à rien
Good Friday *n* Vendredi saint
good-humoured ['gud'hjuːməd] *adj* (*person*) jovial(e); (*remark, joke*) sans malice
good-looking ['gud'lukɪŋ] *adj* beau (belle), bien *inv*
good-natured ['gud'neɪtʃəd] *adj* (*person*) qui a un bon naturel; (*discussion*) enjoué(e)
goodness ['gudnɪs] *n* (*of person*) bonté *f*; **for ~ sake!** je vous en prie!; **~ gracious!** mon Dieu!
goods train *n* (*Brit*) train *m* de marchandises
goodwill [gud'wɪl] *n* bonne volonté; (*Comm*) réputation *f* (auprès de la clientèle)
goody-goody ['gudɪgudɪ] *n* (*pej*) petit saint, sainte nitouche
gooey ['guːɪ] *adj* (*Brit inf*) gluant(e)
Google® ['gugl] *vi, vt* googler®
goose (*pl* **geese**) [guːs, giːs] *n* oie *f*
gooseberry ['guzbərɪ] *n* groseille *f* à maquereau; **to play ~** (*Brit*) tenir la chandelle
goose bumps, goose pimples *npl* chair *f* de poule
gooseflesh ['guːsfleʃ] *n*, **goosepimples** ['guːspɪmplz] ▷ *npl* chair *f* de poule
goose step *n* (*Mil*) pas *m* de l'oie
GOP *n abbr* (*US Pol: inf: = Grand Old Party*) parti républicain
gopher ['gəufəʳ] *n* = **gofer**
gore [gɔːʳ] *vt* encorner ▷ *n* sang *m*
gorge [gɔːdʒ] *n* gorge *f* ▷ *vt*: **to ~ o.s. (on)** se

gorger (de)
gorgeous ['gɔːdʒəs] *adj* splendide, superbe
gorilla [gə'rɪlə] *n* gorille *m*
gormless ['gɔːmlɪs] *adj* (*Brit inf*) lourdaud(e)
gorse [gɔːs] *n* ajoncs *mpl*
gory ['gɔːrɪ] *adj* sanglant(e)
gosh [gɒʃ] (*inf*) *excl* mince alors!
go-slow ['gəu'sləu] *n* (*Brit*) grève perlée
gospel ['gɒspl] *n* évangile *m*
gossamer ['gɒsəməʳ] *n* (*cobweb*) fils *mpl* de la vierge; (*light fabric*) étoffe très légère
gossip ['gɒsɪp] *n* (*chat*) bavardages *mpl*; (*malicious*) commérage *m*, cancans *mpl*; (*person*) commère *f* ▷ *vi* bavarder; cancaner, faire des commérages; **a piece of ~** un ragot, un racontar
gossip column *n* (*Press*) échos *mpl*
got [gɒt] *pt, pp of* **get**
Gothic ['gɒθɪk] *adj* gothique
gotten ['gɒtn] (*US*) *pp of* **get**
gouge [gaudʒ] *vt* (*also:* **gouge out**: *hole etc*) évider; (: *initials*) tailler; **to ~ sb's eyes out** crever les yeux à qn
gourd [guəd] *n* calebasse *f*, gourde *f*
gourmet ['guəmeɪ] *n* gourmet *m*, gastronome *m/f*
gout [gaut] *n* goutte *f*
govern ['gʌvən] *vt* (*gen: Ling*) gouverner; (*influence*) déterminer
governess ['gʌvənɪs] *n* gouvernante *f*
governing ['gʌvənɪŋ] *adj* (*Pol*) au pouvoir, au gouvernement; **~ body** conseil *m* d'administration
government ['gʌvnmənt] *n* gouvernement *m*; (*Brit: ministers*) ministère *m* ▷ *cpd* de l'État
governmental [gʌvn'mɛntl] *adj* gouvernemental(e)
government housing *n* (*US*) logements sociaux
government stock *n* titres *mpl* d'État
governor ['gʌvənəʳ] *n* (*of colony, state, bank*) gouverneur *m*; (*of school, hospital etc*) administrateur(-trice); (*Brit: of prison*) directeur(-trice)
Govt *abbr* (*= government*) gvt
gown [gaun] *n* robe *f*; (*of teacher, Brit: of judge*) toge *f*
GP *n abbr* (*Med*) = **general practitioner; who's your GP?** qui est votre médecin traitant?
GPMU *n abbr* (*Brit*) = **Graphical, Paper and Media Union**
GPO *n abbr* (*Brit: old*) = **General Post Office**; (*US*) = **Government Printing Office**
GPS *n abbr* (*= global positioning system*) GPS *m*
gr. *abbr* (*Comm*) = **gross**
grab [græb] *vt* saisir, empoigner; (*property, power*) se saisir de ▷ *vi*: **to ~ at** essayer de saisir
grace [greɪs] *n* grâce *f* ▷ *vt* (*honour*) honorer; (*adorn*) orner; **5 days' ~** un répit de 5 jours; **to say ~** dire le bénédicité; (*after meal*) dire les grâces; **with a good/bad ~** de bonne/mauvaise grâce; **his sense of humour is his saving ~** il

g

se rachète par son sens de l'humour

graceful ['greɪsful] *adj* gracieux(-euse), élégant(e)

gracious ['greɪʃəs] *adj* (*kind*) charmant(e), bienveillant(e); (*elegant*) plein(e) d'élégance, d'une grande élégance; (*formal: pardon etc*) miséricordieux(-euse) ▷ *excl*: (**good**) ~! mon Dieu!

gradation [grə'deɪʃən] *n* gradation *f*

grade [greɪd] *n* (*Comm: quality*) qualité *f*; (*size*) calibre *m*; (*type*) catégorie *f*; (*in hierarchy*) grade *m*, échelon *m*; (*Scol*) note *f*; (*US: school class*) classe *f*; (: *gradient*) pente *f* ▷ *vt* classer; (*by size*) calibrer; graduer; **to make the** ~ (*fig*) réussir

grade crossing *n* (*US*) passage *m* à niveau

grade school *n* (*US*) école *f* primaire

gradient ['greɪdɪənt] *n* inclinaison *f*, pente *f*; (*Geom*) gradient *m*

gradual ['grædjʊəl] *adj* graduel(le), progressif(-ive)

gradually ['grædjʊəlɪ] *adv* peu à peu, graduellement

graduate *n* ['grædjuɪt] diplômé(e) d'université; (*US: of high school*) diplômé(e) de fin d'études ▷ *vi* ['grædjueɪt] obtenir un diplôme d'université (*or* de fin d'études)

graduated pension ['grædjueɪtɪd-] *n* retraite calculée en fonction des derniers salaires

graduation [grædju'eɪʃən] *n* cérémonie *f* de remise des diplômes

graffiti [grə'fi:tɪ] *npl* graffiti *mpl*

graft [grɑ:ft] *n* (*Agr, Med*) greffe *f*; (*bribery*) corruption *f* ▷ *vt* greffer; **hard ~** (*Brit: inf*) boulot acharné

grain [greɪn] *n* (*single piece*) grain *m*; (*no pl: cereals*) céréales *fpl*; (*US: corn*) blé *m*; (*of wood*) fibre *f*; **it goes against the ~** cela va à l'encontre de sa (*or* ma *etc*) nature

gram [græm] *n* gramme *m*

grammar ['græmə'] *n* grammaire *f*

grammar school *n* (*Brit*) ≈ lycée *m*

grammatical [grə'mætɪkl] *adj* grammatical(e)

gramme [græm] *n* = **gram**

gramophone ['græməfəʊn] *n* (*Brit*) gramophone *m*

gran [græn] (*inf*) *n* (*Brit*) mamie *f* (*inf*), mémé *f* (*inf*); **my ~** (*young child speaking*) ma mamie *or* mémé; (*older child or adult speaking*) ma grand-mère

granary ['grænərɪ] *n* grenier *m*

grand [grænd] *adj* magnifique, splendide; (*terrific*) magnifique, formidable; (*gesture etc*) noble ▷ *n* (*inf: thousand*) mille livres *fpl* (*or* dollars *mpl*)

grandad ['grændæd] (*inf*) *n* = **granddad**

grandchild (*pl* **grandchildren**) ['græntʃaɪld, 'græntʃɪldrən] *n* petit-fils *m*, petite-fille *f*; **grandchildren** *npl* petits-enfants

granddad ['grændæd] *n* (*inf*) papy *m* (*inf*), papi *m* (*inf*), pépé *m* (*inf*); **my ~** (*young child speaking*) mon papy *or* papi *or* pépé; (*older child or adult speaking*) mon grand-père

granddaughter ['grændɔ:tə'] *n* petite-fille *f*

grandeur ['grændjə'] *n* magnificence *f*, splendeur *f*; (*of position etc*) éminence *f*

grandfather ['grændfɑ:ðə'] *n* grand-père *m*

grandiose ['grændɪəʊs] *adj* grandiose; (*pej*) pompeux(-euse)

grand jury *n* (*US*) jury *m* d'accusation (*formé de 12 à 23 jurés*)

grandma ['grænmɑ:] *n* (*inf*) = **gran**

grandmother ['grænmʌðə'] *n* grand-mère *f*

grandpa ['grænpɑ:] *n* (*inf*) = **granddad**

grandparents ['grændpɛərənts] *npl* grands-parents *mpl*

grand piano *n* piano *m* à queue

Grand Prix ['grɑ̃:'pri:] *n* (*Aut*) grand prix automobile

grandson ['grænsʌn] *n* petit-fils *m*

grandstand ['grændstænd] *n* (*Sport*) tribune *f*

grand total *n* total général

granite ['grænɪt] *n* granit *m*

granny ['grænɪ] *n* (*inf*) = **gran**

grant [grɑ:nt] *vt* accorder; (*a request*) accéder à; (*admit*) concéder ▷ *n* (*Scol*) bourse *f*; (*Admin*) subside *m*, subvention *f*; **to take sth for ~ed** considérer qch comme acquis; **to take sb for ~ed** considérer qn comme faisant partie du décor; **to ~ that** admettre que

granulated ['grænjuleɪtɪd] *adj*: ~ **sugar** sucre *m* en poudre

granule ['grænju:l] *n* granule *m*

grape [greɪp] *n* raisin *m*; **a bunch of ~s** une grappe de raisin

grapefruit ['greɪpfru:t] *n* pamplemousse *m*

grapevine ['greɪpvaɪn] *n* vigne *f*; **I heard it on the ~** (*fig*) je l'ai appris par le téléphone arabe

graph [grɑ:f] *n* graphique *m*, courbe *f*

graphic ['græfɪk] *adj* graphique; (*vivid*) vivant(e)

graphic designer *n* graphiste *m/f*

graphic equalizer *n* égaliseur *m* graphique

graphics ['græfɪks] *n* (*art*) arts *mpl* graphiques; (*process*) graphisme *m* ▷ *npl* (*drawings*) illustrations *fpl*

graphite ['græfaɪt] *n* graphite *m*

graph paper *n* papier millimétré

grapple ['græpl] *vi*: **to ~ with** être aux prises avec

grappling iron ['græplɪŋ-] *n* (*Naut*) grappin *m*

grasp [grɑ:sp] *vt* saisir, empoigner; (*understand*) saisir, comprendre ▷ *n* (*grip*) prise *f*; (*fig*) compréhension *f*, connaissance *f*; **to have sth within one's ~** avoir qch à sa portée; **to have a good ~ of sth** (*fig*) bien comprendre qch

▶ **grasp at** *vt fus* (*rope etc*) essayer de saisir; (*fig: opportunity*) sauter sur

grasping ['grɑ:spɪŋ] *adj* avide

grass [grɑ:s] *n* herbe *f*; (*lawn*) gazon *m*; (*Brit inf: informer*) mouchard(e); (: *ex-terrorist*) balanceur(-euse)

grasshopper ['grɑ:shɔpə'] *n* sauterelle *f*

grassland ['grɑ:slænd] *n* prairie *f*

grass roots *npl* (*fig*) base *f*

grass snake *n* couleuvre *f*

grassy ['grɑːsɪ] *adj* herbeux(-euse)
grate [greɪt] *n* grille *f* de cheminée ▷ *vi* grincer
▷ *vt* (*Culin*) râper
grateful ['greɪtful] *adj* reconnaissant(e)
gratefully ['greɪtfəlɪ] *adv* avec reconnaissance
grater ['greɪtə'] *n* râpe *f*
gratification [grætɪfɪ'keɪʃən] *n* satisfaction *f*
gratify ['grætɪfaɪ] *vt* faire plaisir à; (*whim*)
satisfaire
gratifying ['grætɪfaɪɪŋ] *adj* agréable,
satisfaisant(e)
grating ['greɪtɪŋ] *n* (*iron bars*) grille *f* ▷ *adj* (*noise*)
grinçant(e)
gratitude ['grætɪtjuːd] *n* gratitude *f*
gratuitous [grə'tjuːɪtəs] *adj* gratuit(e)
gratuity [grə'tjuːɪtɪ] *n* pourboire *m*
grave [greɪv] *n* tombe *f* ▷ *adj* grave,
sérieux(-euse)
gravedigger ['greɪvdɪgə'] *n* fossoyeur *m*
gravel ['grævl] *n* gravier *m*
gravely ['greɪvlɪ] *adv* gravement, sérieusement;
~ **ill** gravement malade
gravestone ['greɪvstəun] *n* pierre tombale
graveyard ['greɪvjɑːd] *n* cimetière *m*
gravitate ['grævɪteɪt] *vi* graviter
gravity ['grævɪtɪ] *n* (*Physics*) gravité *f*; pesanteur
f; (*seriousness*) gravité, sérieux *m*
gravy ['greɪvɪ] *n* jus *m* (de viande), sauce *f* (au jus
de viande)
gravy boat *n* saucière *f*
gravy train *n* (*inf*): **to ride the** ~ avoir une
bonne planque
gray [greɪ] *adj* (*US*) = **grey**
graze [greɪz] *vi* paître, brouter ▷ *vt* (*touch lightly*)
frôler, effleurer; (*scrape*) écorcher ▷ *n*
écorchure *f*
grazing ['greɪzɪŋ] *n* (*pasture*) pâturage *m*
grease [griːs] *n* (*fat*) graisse *f*; (*lubricant*)
lubrifiant *m* ▷ *vt* graisser; lubrifier; **to ~ the
skids** (*US: fig*) huiler les rouages
grease gun *n* graisseur *m*
greasepaint ['griːspeɪnt] *n* produits *mpl* de
maquillage
greaseproof paper ['griːspruː-] *n* (*Brit*) papier
sulfurisé
greasy ['griːsɪ] *adj* gras(se), graisseux(-euse);
(*hands, clothes*) graisseux; (*Brit: road, surface*)
glissant(e)
great [greɪt] *adj* grand(e); (*heat, pain etc*) très
fort(e), intense; (*inf*) formidable; **they're ~
friends** ils sont très amis, ce sont de grands
amis; **we had a ~ time** nous nous sommes bien
amusés; **it was ~!** c'était fantastique *or* super!;
the ~ thing is that ... ce qu'il y a de vraiment
bien c'est que ...
Great Barrier Reef *n*: **the** ~ la Grande Barrière
Great Britain *n* Grande-Bretagne *f*
great-grandchild (*pl* **-children**)
[greɪt'græntʃaɪld, -tʃɪldrən] *n* arrière-petit(e)-
enfant
great-grandfather [greɪt'grænfɑːðə'] *n* arrière-
grand-père *m*

great-grandmother [greɪt'grænmʌðə'] *n*
arrière-grand-mère *f*
Great Lakes *npl*: **the** ~ les Grands Lacs
greatly ['greɪtlɪ] *adv* très, grandement; (*with
verbs*) beaucoup
greatness ['greɪtnɪs] *n* grandeur *f*
Grecian ['griːʃən] *adj* grec (grecque)
Greece [griːs] *n* Grèce *f*
greed [griːd] *n* (*also*: **greediness**) avidité *f*; (*for
food*) gourmandise *f*
greedily ['griːdɪlɪ] *adv* avidement; avec
gourmandise
greedy ['griːdɪ] *adj* avide; (*for food*) gourmand(e)
Greek [griːk] *adj* grec (grecque) ▷ *n* Grec
(Grecque); (*Ling*) grec *m*; **ancient/modern** ~
grec classique/moderne
green [griːn] *adj* vert(e); (*inexperienced*) (bien)
jeune, naïf(-ïve); (*ecological: product etc*)
écologique ▷ *n* (*colour*) vert *m*; (*on golf course*)
green *m*; (*stretch of grass*) pelouse *f*; (*also*: **village
green**) ≈ place *f* du village; **greens** *npl*
(*vegetables*) légumes verts; **to have ~ fingers** *or*
(*US*) **a ~ thumb** (*fig*) avoir le pouce vert; **G~** (*Pol*)
écologiste *m/f*; **the G~ Party** le parti écologiste
green belt *n* (*round town*) ceinture verte
green card *n* (*Aut*) carte verte; (*US: work permit*)
permis *m* de travail
greenery ['griːnərɪ] *n* verdure *f*
greenfly ['griːnflaɪ] *n* (*Brit*) puceron *m*
greengage ['griːngeɪdʒ] *n* reine-claude *f*
greengrocer ['griːngrəusə'] *n* (*Brit*) marchand *m*
de fruits et légumes
greengrocer's ['griːngrəusə' z], **greengrocer's
shop** *n* magasin *m* de fruits et légumes
greenhouse ['griːnhaus] *n* serre *f*
greenhouse effect *n*: **the** ~ l'effet *m* de serre
greenhouse gas *n* gaz *m* contribuant à l'effet
de serre
greenish ['griːnɪʃ] *adj* verdâtre
Greenland ['griːnlənd] *n* Groenland *m*
Greenlander ['griːnləndə'] *n* Groenlandais(e)
green light *n*: **to give sb/sth the** ~ donner le feu
vert à qn/qch
green pepper *n* poivron (vert)
green pound *n* (*Econ*) livre verte
green salad *n* salade verte
greet [griːt] *vt* accueillir
greeting ['griːtɪŋ] *n* salutation *f*; **Christmas/
birthday ~s** souhaits *mpl* de Noël/de bon
anniversaire
greeting card, greetings card *n* carte *f* de
vœux
gregarious [grə'gɛərɪəs] *adj* grégaire; sociable
grenade [grə'neɪd] *n* (*also*: **hand grenade**)
grenade *f*
grew [gruː] *pt of* **grow**
grey, (*US*) **gray** [greɪ] *adj* gris(e); (*dismal*)
sombre; **to go** ~ (commencer à) grisonner
grey-haired, (*US*) **gray-haired** [greɪ'hɛəd] *adj*
aux cheveux gris
greyhound ['greɪhaund] *n* lévrier *m*
grid [grɪd] *n* grille *f*; (*Elec*) réseau *m*; (*US Aut*)

intersection f (*matérialisée par des marques au sol*)

griddle [grɪdl] n (*on cooker*) plaque chauffante

gridiron ['grɪdaɪən] n gril m

gridlock ['grɪdlɔk] n (*traffic jam*) embouteillage m

gridlocked ['grɪdlɔk t] adj: **to be ~** (*roads*) être bloqué par un embouteillage; (*talks etc*) être suspendu

grief [gri:f] n chagrin m, douleur f; **to come to ~** (*plan*) échouer; (*person*) avoir un malheur

grievance ['gri:vəns] n doléance f, grief m; (*cause for complaint*) grief

grieve [gri:v] vi avoir du chagrin; se désoler ▷ vt faire de la peine à, affliger; **to ~ for sb** pleurer qn; **to ~ at** se désoler de; pleurer

grievous ['gri:vəs] adj grave, cruel(le); **~ bodily harm** (*Law*) coups mpl et blessures fpl

grill [grɪl] n (*on cooker*) gril m; (*also:* **mixed grill**) grillade(s) f(pl); (*also:* **grillroom**) rôtisserie f ▷ vt (*Brit*) griller; (*inf: question*) interroger longuement, cuisiner

grille [grɪl] n grillage m; (*Aut*) calandre f

grillroom ['grɪlrum] n rôtisserie f

grim [grɪm] adj sinistre, lugubre; (*serious, stern*) sévère

grimace [grɪ'meɪs] n grimace f ▷ vi grimacer, faire une grimace

grime [graɪm] n crasse f

grimy ['graɪmɪ] adj crasseux(-euse)

grin [grɪn] n large sourire m ▷ vi sourire; **to ~ (at)** faire un grand sourire (à)

grind [graɪnd] (pt, pp **ground** [graund]) vt écraser; (*coffee, pepper etc*) moudre; (*US: meat*) hacher; (*make sharp*) aiguiser; (*polish: gem, lens*) polir ▷ vi (*car gears*) grincer ▷ n (*work*) corvée f; **to ~ one's teeth** grincer des dents; **to ~ to a halt** (*vehicle*) s'arrêter dans un grincement de freins; (*fig*) s'arrêter, s'immobiliser; **the daily ~** (*inf*) le train-train quotidien

grinder ['graɪndə'] n (*machine: for coffee*) moulin m (à café); (: *for waste disposal etc*) broyeur m

grindstone ['graɪndstəun] n: **to keep one's nose to the ~** travailler sans relâche

grip [grɪp] n (*handclasp*) poigne f; (*control*) prise f; (*handle*) poignée f; (*holdall*) sac m de voyage ▷ vt saisir, empoigner; (*viewer, reader*) captiver; **to come to ~s with** se colleter avec, en venir aux prises avec; **to ~ the road** (*Aut*) adhérer à la route; **to lose one's ~** lâcher prise; (*fig*) perdre les pédales, être dépassé(e)

gripe [graɪp] n (*Med*) coliques fpl; (*inf: complaint*) ronchonnement m, rouspétance f ▷ vi (*inf*) râler

gripping ['grɪpɪŋ] adj prenant(e), palpitant(e)

grisly ['grɪzlɪ] adj sinistre, macabre

grist [grɪst] n (*fig*): **it's (all) ~ to his mill** ça l'arrange, ça apporte de l'eau à son moulin

gristle ['grɪsl] n cartilage m (*de poulet etc*)

grit [grɪt] n gravillon m; (*courage*) cran m ▷ vt (*road*) sabler; **to ~ one's teeth** serrer les dents; **to have a piece of ~ in one's eye** avoir une poussière or saleté dans l'œil

grits [grɪts] npl (*US*) gruau m de maïs

grizzle ['grɪzl] vi (*Brit*) pleurnicher

grizzly ['grɪzlɪ] n (*also:* **grizzly bear**) grizzli m, ours gris

groan [grəun] n (*of pain*) gémissement m; (*of disapproval, dismay*) grognement m ▷ vi gémir; grogner

grocer ['grəusə'] n épicier m

groceries ['grəusərɪz] npl provisions fpl

grocer's ['grəusə'z], **grocer's shop, grocery** ['grəusərɪ] n épicerie f

grog [grɔg] n grog m

groggy ['grɔgɪ] adj groggy inv

groin [grɔɪn] n aine f

groom [gru:m] n (*for horses*) palefrenier m; (*also:* **bridegroom**) marié m ▷ vt (*horse*) panser; (*fig*): **to ~ sb for** former qn pour

groove [gru:v] n sillon m, rainure f

grope [grəup] vi tâtonner; **to ~ for** chercher à tâtons

gross [grəus] adj grossier(-ière); (*Comm*) brut(e) ▷ n (pl inv: twelve dozen) grosse f ▷ vt (*Comm*): **to ~ £500,000** gagner 500 000 livres avant impôt

gross domestic product n produit brut intérieur

grossly ['grəuslɪ] adv (*greatly*) très, grandement

gross national product n produit national brut

grotesque [grə'tɛsk] adj grotesque

grotto ['grɔtəu] n grotte f

grotty ['grɔtɪ] adj (*Brit inf*) minable

grouch [grautʃ] (*inf*) vi rouspéter ▷ n (*person*) rouspéteur(-euse)

ground [graund] pt, pp of **grind** ▷ n sol m, terre f; (*land*) terrain m, terres fpl; (*Sport*) terrain m; (*reason: gen pl*) raison f; (*US: also:* **ground wire**) terre f ▷ vt (*plane*) empêcher de décoller, retenir au sol; (*US Elec*) équiper d'une prise de terre, mettre à la terre ▷ vi (*ship*) s'échouer ▷ adj (*coffee etc*) moulu(e); (*US: meat*) haché(e); **grounds** npl (*gardens etc*) parc m, domaine m; (*of coffee*) marc m; **on the ~, to the ~** par terre; **below ~** sous terre; **to gain/lose ~** gagner/perdre du terrain; **common ~** terrain d'entente; **he covered a lot of ~ in his lecture** sa conférence a traité un grand nombre de questions or la question en profondeur

ground cloth n (*US*) = **groundsheet**

ground control n (*Aviat, Space*) centre m de contrôle (au sol)

ground floor n (*Brit*) rez-de-chaussée m

grounding ['graundɪŋ] n (*in education*) connaissances fpl de base

groundless ['graundlɪs] adj sans fondement

groundnut ['graundnʌt] n arachide f

ground rent n (*Brit*) fermage m

ground rules npl: **the ~** les principes mpl de base

groundsheet ['graundʃi:t] n (*Brit*) tapis m de sol

groundsman ['graundzmən] (*irreg*), (*US*) **groundskeeper** ['graundzki:pə'] n (*Sport*) gardien m de stade

ground staff n équipage m au sol

groundswell ['graundswɛl] n lame f or vague f de fond

ground-to-air ['grauntu'εər] adj (Mil) sol-air inv

ground-to-ground ['graunta'graund] adj (Mil) sol-sol inv

groundwork ['graundwə:k] n préparation f

group [gru:p] n groupe m ▷ vt (also: **group together**) grouper ▷ vi (also: **group together**) se grouper

groupie ['gru:pɪ] n groupie f

group therapy n thérapie f de groupe

grouse [graus] n (pl inv: bird) grouse f (sorte de coq de bruyère) ▷ vi (complain) rouspéter, râler

grove [grəuv] n bosquet m

grovel ['grɔvl] vi (fig): **to ~ (before)** ramper (devant)

grow (pt **grew**, pp **-n**) [grəu, gru:, grəun] vi (plant) pousser, croître; (person) grandir; (increase) augmenter, se développer; (become) devenir; **to ~ rich/weak** s'enrichir/s'affaiblir ▷ vt cultiver, faire pousser; (hair, beard) laisser pousser
  ▶ **grow apart** vi (fig) se détacher (l'un de l'autre)
  ▶ **grow away from** vt fus (fig) s'éloigner de
  ▶ **grow on** vt fus: **that painting is ~ing on me** je finirai par aimer ce tableau
  ▶ **grow out of** vt fus (clothes) devenir trop grand pour; (habit) perdre (avec le temps); **he'll ~ out of it** ça lui passera
  ▶ **grow up** vi grandir

grower ['grəuər] n producteur m; (Agr) cultivateur(-trice)

growing ['grəuɪŋ] adj (fear, amount) croissant(e), grandissant(e); **~ pains** (Med) fièvre f de croissance; (fig) difficultés fpl de croissance

growl [graul] vi grogner

grown [grəun] pp of **grow** ▷ adj adulte

grown-up [grəun'ʌp] n adulte m/f, grande personne

growth [grəuθ] n croissance f, développement m; (what has grown) pousse f; poussée f; (Med) grosseur f, tumeur f

growth rate n taux m de croissance

GRSM n abbr (Brit) = **Graduate of the Royal Schools of Music**

grub [grʌb] n larve f; (inf: food) bouffe f

grubby ['grʌbɪ] adj crasseux(-euse)

grudge [grʌdʒ] n rancune f ▷ vt: **to ~ sb sth** (in giving) donner qch à qn à contre-cœur; (resent) reprocher qch à qn; **to bear sb a ~ (for)** garder rancune or en vouloir à qn (de); **he ~s spending** il rechigne à dépenser

grudgingly ['grʌdʒɪŋlɪ] adv à contre-cœur, de mauvaise grâce

gruelling, (US) **grueling** ['gruəlɪŋ] adj exténuant(e)

gruesome ['gru:səm] adj horrible

gruff [grʌf] adj bourru(e)

grumble ['grʌmbl] vi rouspéter, ronchonner

grumpy ['grʌmpɪ] adj grincheux(-euse)

grunge [grʌndʒ] n (Mus: style) grunge m

grunt [grʌnt] vi grogner ▷ n grognement m

G-string ['dʒi:strɪŋ] n (garment) cache-sexe m inv

GSUSA n abbr = **Girl Scouts of the United States**

of America

GU abbr (US) = **Guam**

guarantee [gærən'ti:] n garantie f ▷ vt garantir; **he can't ~ (that) he'll come** il n'est pas absolument certain de pouvoir venir

guarantor [gærən'tɔ:ʳ] n garant(e)

guard [gɑ:d] n garde f, surveillance f; (squad: Boxing, Fencing) garde f; (one man) garde m; (Brit Rail) chef m de train; (safety device: on machine) dispositif m de sûreté; (also: **fireguard**) garde-feu m inv ▷ vt garder, surveiller; (protect): **to ~ sb/sth (against** or **from)** protéger qn/qch (contre); **to be on one's ~** (fig) être sur ses gardes
  ▶ **guard against** vi: **to ~ against doing sth** se garder de faire qch

guard dog n chien m de garde

guarded ['gɑ:dɪd] adj (fig) prudent(e)

guardian ['gɑ:dɪən] n gardien(ne); (of minor) tuteur(-trice)

guard's van ['gɑ:dz-] n (Brit Rail) fourgon m

Guatemala [gwɑ:tɪ'mɑ:lə] n Guatémala m

Guernsey ['gə:nzɪ] n Guernesey m or f

guerrilla [gə'rɪlə] n guérillero m

guerrilla warfare n guérilla f

guess [gɛs] vi deviner ▷ vt deviner; (estimate) évaluer; (US) croire, penser ▷ n supposition f, hypothèse f; **to take** or **have a ~** essayer de deviner; **to keep sb ~ing** laisser qn dans le doute or l'incertitude, tenir qn en haleine

guesstimate ['gɛstɪmɪt] n (inf) estimation f

guesswork ['gɛswə:k] n hypothèse f; **I got the answer by ~** j'ai deviné la réponse

guest [gɛst] n invité(e); (in hotel) client(e); **be my ~** faites comme chez vous

guest house ['gɛsthaus] n pension f

guest room n chambre f d'amis

guff [gʌf] n (inf) bêtises fpl

guffaw [gʌ'fɔ:] n gros rire ▷ vi pouffer de rire

guidance ['gaɪdəns] n (advice) conseils mpl; **under the ~ of** conseillé(e) or encadré(e) par, sous la conduite de; **vocational ~** orientation professionnelle; **marriage ~** conseils conjugaux

guide [gaɪd] n (person) guide m/f; (book) guide m; (also: **Girl Guide**) éclaireuse f; (Roman Catholic) guide f ▷ vt guider; **to be ~d by sb/sth** se laisser guider par qn/qch; **is there an English-speaking ~?** est-ce que l'un des guides parle anglais?

guidebook ['gaɪdbuk] n guide m; **do you have a ~ in English?** est-ce que vous avez un guide en anglais?

guided missile ['gaɪdɪd-] n missile téléguidé

guide dog n chien m d'aveugle

guided tour n visite guidée; **what time does the ~ start?** la visite guidée commence à quelle heure?

guidelines ['gaɪdlaɪnz] npl (advice) instructions générales, conseils mpl

guild [gɪld] n (History) corporation f; (sharing interests) cercle m, association f

g

guildhall ['gɪldhɔːl] *n* (*Brit*) hôtel *m* de ville
guile [gaɪl] *n* astuce *f*
guileless ['gaɪllɪs] *adj* candide
guillotine ['gɪlətiːn] *n* guillotine *f*; (*for paper*) massicot *m*
guilt [gɪlt] *n* culpabilité *f*
guilty ['gɪltɪ] *adj* coupable; **to plead ~/not ~** plaider coupable/non coupable; **to feel ~ about doing sth** avoir mauvaise conscience à faire qch
Guinea ['gɪnɪ] *n*: **Republic of ~** (République *f* de) Guinée *f*
guinea ['gɪnɪ] *n* (*Brit: formerly*) guinée *f* (= 21 shillings)
guinea pig ['gɪnɪ-] *n* cobaye *m*
guise [gaɪz] *n* aspect *m*, apparence *f*
guitar [gɪ'tɑːʳ] *n* guitare *f*
guitarist [gɪ'tɑːrɪst] *n* guitariste *m/f*
gulch [gʌltʃ] *n* (*US*) ravin *m*
gulf [gʌlf] *n* golfe *m*; (*abyss*) gouffre *m*; **the (Persian) G-** le golfe Persique
Gulf States *npl*: **the ~** (*in Middle East*) les pays *mpl* du Golfe
Gulf Stream *n*: **the ~** le Gulf Stream
gull [gʌl] *n* mouette *f*
gullet ['gʌlɪt] *n* gosier *m*
gullibility [gʌlɪ'bɪlɪtɪ] *n* crédulité *f*
gullible ['gʌlɪbl] *adj* crédule
gully ['gʌlɪ] *n* ravin *m*; ravine *f*; couloir *m*
gulp [gʌlp] *vi* avaler sa salive; (*from emotion*) avoir la gorge serrée, s'étrangler ▷ *vt* (*also:* **gulp down**) avaler ▷ *n* (*of drink*) gorgée *f*; **at one ~** d'un seul coup
gum [gʌm] *n* (*Anat*) gencive *f*; (*glue*) colle *f*; (*sweet*) boule *f* de gomme; (*also:* **chewing-gum**) chewing-gum *m* ▷ *vt* coller
  gumboil ['gʌmbɔɪl] *n* abcès *m* dentaire
gumboots ['gʌmbuːts] *npl* (*Brit*) bottes *fpl* en caoutchouc
gumption ['gʌmpʃən] *n* bon sens, jugeote *f*
gun [gʌn] *n* (*small*) revolver *m*, pistolet *m*; (*rifle*) fusil *m*, carabine *f*; (*cannon*) canon *m* ▷ *vt* (*also:* **gun down**) abattre; **to stick to one's ~s** (*fig*) ne pas en démordre
gunboat ['gʌnbəut] *n* canonnière *f*
gun dog *n* chien *m* de chasse
gunfire ['gʌnfaɪəʳ] *n* fusillade *f*
gunk [gʌŋk] *n* (*inf*) saleté *f*
gunman (*irreg*) ['gʌnmən] *n* bandit armé
gunner ['gʌnəʳ] *n* artilleur *m*
gunpoint ['gʌnpɔɪnt] *n*: **at ~** sous la menace du pistolet (*or* fusil)
gunpowder ['gʌnpaudəʳ] *n* poudre *f* à canon
gunrunner ['gʌnrʌnəʳ] *n* trafiquant *m* d'armes
gunrunning ['gʌnrʌnɪŋ] *n* trafic *m* d'armes
gunshot ['gʌnʃɔt] *n* coup *m* de feu; **within ~** à portée de fusil
gunsmith ['gʌnsmɪθ] *n* armurier *m*
gurgle ['gəːgl] *n* gargouillis *m* ▷ *vi* gargouiller
guru ['guruː] *n* gourou *m*
gush [gʌʃ] *n* jaillissement *m*, jet *m* ▷ *vi* jaillir; (*fig*) se répandre en effusions
gushing ['gʌʃɪŋ] *adj* (*person*) trop exubérant(e) or

expansif(-ive); (*compliments*) exagéré(e)
gusset ['gʌsɪt] *n* gousset *m*, soufflet *m*; (*in tights, pants*) entre-jambes *m*
gust [gʌst] *n* (*of wind*) rafale *f*; (*of smoke*) bouffée *f*
gusto ['gʌstəu] *n* enthousiasme *m*
gusty ['gʌstɪ] *adj* venteux(-euse); **~ winds** des rafales de vent
gut [gʌt] *n* intestin *m*, boyau *m*; (*Mus etc*) boyau ▷ *vt* (*poultry, fish*) vider; (*building*) ne laisser que les murs de; **guts** *npl* (*Anat*) boyaux *mpl*; (*inf: courage*) cran *m*; **to hate sb's ~s** ne pas pouvoir voir qn en peinture *or* sentir qn
gut reaction *n* réaction instinctive
gutsy ['gʌtsɪ] *adj* (*person*) qui a du cran; (*style*) qui a du punch
gutted ['gʌtɪd] *adj*: **I was ~** (*inf: disappointed*) j'étais carrément dégoûté
gutter ['gʌtəʳ] *n* (*of roof*) gouttière *f*; (*in street*) caniveau *m*; (*fig*) ruisseau *m*
gutter press *n*: **the ~** la presse de bas étage *or* à scandale
guttural ['gʌtərl] *adj* guttural(e)
guy [gaɪ] *n* (*inf: man*) type *m*; (*also:* **guyrope**) corde *f*; (*figure*) *effigie de Guy Fawkes*
Guyana [gaɪ'ænə] *n* Guyane *f*
Guy Fawkes' Night [gaɪ'fɔːks-] *n voir article*

● GUY FAWKES' NIGHT
●
● *Guy Fawkes' Night*, que l'on appelle
● également "bonfire night", commémore
● l'échec du complot (le "Gunpowder Plot")
● contre James Ist et son parlement le 5
● novembre 1605. L'un des conspirateurs,
● Guy Fawkes, avait été surpris dans les caves
● du parlement alors qu'il s'apprêtait à y
● mettre le feu. Chaque année pour le 5
● novembre, les enfants préparent à l'avance
● une effigie de Guy Fawkes et ils demandent
● aux passants "un penny pour le guy" avec
● lequel ils pourront s'acheter des fusées de
● feu d'artifice. Beaucoup de gens font
● encore un feu dans leur jardin sur lequel ils
● brûlent le "guy".

guzzle ['gʌzl] *vi* s'empiffrer ▷ *vt* avaler gloutonnement
gym [dʒɪm] *n* (*also:* **gymnasium**) gymnase *m*; (*also:* **gymnastics**) gym *f*
gymkhana [dʒɪm'kɑːnə] *n* gymkhana *m*
gymnasium [dʒɪm'neɪzɪəm] *n* gymnase *m*
gymnast ['dʒɪmnæst] *n* gymnaste *m/f*
gymnastics [dʒɪm'næstɪks] *n*, *npl* gymnastique *f*
gym shoes *npl* chaussures *fpl* de gym(nastique)
gynaecologist, (*US*) **gynecologist** [gaɪnɪ'kɔlədʒɪst] *n* gynécologue *m/f*
gynaecology, (*US*) **gynecology** [gaɪnə'kɔlədʒɪ] *n* gynécologie *f*
gypsy ['dʒɪpsɪ] *n* gitan(e), bohémien(ne) ▷ *cpd*: **~ caravan** *n* roulotte *f*
gyrate [dʒaɪ'reɪt] *vi* tournoyer

Hh

H, h [eɪtʃ] *n* (*letter*) H, h *m*; **H for Harry**, (US) **H for How** H comme Henri

habeas corpus ['heɪbɪəs'kɔ:pəs] *n* (*Law*) habeas corpus *m*

haberdashery [hæbə'dæʃərɪ] *n* (*Brit*) mercerie *f*

habit ['hæbɪt] *n* habitude *f*; (*costume: Rel*) habit *m*; (*for riding*) tenue *f* d'équitation; **to get out of/ into the ~ of doing sth** perdre/prendre l'habitude de faire qch

habitable ['hæbɪtəbl] *adj* habitable

habitat ['hæbɪtæt] *n* habitat *m*

habitation [hæbɪ'teɪʃən] *n* habitation *f*

habitual [hə'bɪtjuəl] *adj* habituel(le); (*drinker, liar*) invétéré(e)

habitually [hə'bɪtjuəlɪ] *adv* habituellement, d'habitude

hack [hæk] *vt* hacher, tailler ▷ *n* (*cut*) entaille *f*; (*blow*) coup *m*; (*pej: writer*) nègre *m*; (*old horse*) canasson *m*

hacker ['hækər] *n* (*Comput*) pirate *m* (informatique); (: *enthusiast*) passionné(e) *m/f* des ordinateurs

hackles ['hæklz] *npl*: **to make sb's ~ rise** (*fig*) mettre qn hors de soi

hackney cab ['hæknɪ-] *n* fiacre *m*

hackneyed ['hæknɪd] *adj* usé(e), rebattu(e)

hacksaw ['hæksɔ:] *n* scie *f* à métaux

had [hæd] *pt, pp of* **have**

haddock (*pl* - *or* **-s**) ['hædək] *n* églefin *m*; **smoked ~** haddock *m*

hadn't ['hædnt] = **had not**

haematology, (US) **hematology** ['hi:mə'tɔlədʒɪ] *n* hématologie *f*

haemoglobin, (US) **hemoglobin** ['hi:mə'gləubɪn] *n* hémoglobine *f*

haemophilia, (US) **hemophilia** ['hi:mə'fɪlɪə] *n* hémophilie *f*

haemorrhage, (US) **hemorrhage** ['hɛmərɪdʒ] *n* hémorragie *f*

haemorrhoids, (US) **hemorrhoids** ['hɛmərɔɪdz] *npl* hémorroïdes *fpl*

hag [hæg] *n* (*ugly*) vieille sorcière; (*nasty*) chameau *m*, harpie *f*; (*witch*) sorcière

haggard ['hægəd] *adj* hagard(e), égaré(e)

haggis ['hægɪs] *n* haggis *m*

haggle ['hægl] *vi* marchander; **to ~ over**

chicaner sur

haggling ['hæglɪŋ] *n* marchandage *m*

Hague [heɪg] *n*: **The ~** La Haye

hail [heɪl] *n* grêle *f* ▷ *vt* (*call*) héler; (*greet*) acclamer ▷ *vi* grêler; (*originate*): **he ~s from Scotland** il est originaire d'Écosse

hailstone ['heɪlstəun] *n* grêlon *m*

hailstorm ['heɪlstɔ:m] *n* averse *f* de grêle

hair [hɛər] *n* cheveux *mpl*; (*on body*) poils *mpl*, pilosité *f*; (*of animal*) pelage *m*; (*single hair: on head*) cheveu *m*; (: *on body, of animal*) poil *m*; **to do one's ~** se coiffer

hairband ['hɛəbænd] *n* (*elasticated*) bandeau *m*; (*plastic*) serre-tête *m*

hairbrush ['hɛəbrʌʃ] *n* brosse *f* à cheveux

haircut ['hɛəkʌt] *n* coupe *f* (de cheveux)

hairdo ['hɛədu:] *n* coiffure *f*

hairdresser ['hɛədrɛsər] *n* coiffeur(-euse)

hairdresser's ['hɛədrɛsəz] *n* salon *m* de coiffure, coiffeur *m*

hair dryer ['hɛədraɪər] *n* sèche-cheveux *m*, séchoir *m*

-haired [hɛəd] *suffix*: **fair/long~** aux cheveux blonds/longs

hair gel *n* gel *m* pour cheveux

hairgrip ['hɛəgrɪp] *n* pince *f* à cheveux

hairline ['hɛəlaɪn] *n* naissance *f* des cheveux

hairline fracture *n* fêlure *f*

hairnet ['hɛənɛt] *n* résille *f*

hair oil *n* huile *f* capillaire

hairpiece ['hɛəpi:s] *n* postiche *m*

hairpin ['hɛəpɪn] *n* épingle *f* à cheveux

hairpin bend, (US) **hairpin curve** *n* virage *m* en épingle à cheveux

hair-raising ['hɛəreɪzɪŋ] *adj* à (vous) faire dresser les cheveux sur la tête

hair remover *n* dépilateur *m*

hair removing cream *n* crème *f* dépilatoire

hair spray *n* laque *f* (pour les cheveux)

hairstyle ['hɛəstaɪl] *n* coiffure *f*

hairy ['hɛərɪ] *adj* poilu(e), chevelu(e); (*inf: frightening*) effrayant(e)

Haiti ['heɪtɪ] *n* Haïti *m*

hake (*pl* - *or* **-s**) [heɪk] *n* colin *m*, merlu *m*

halcyon ['hælsɪən] *adj* merveilleux(-euse)

hale [heɪl] *adj*: **~ and hearty** robuste, en

pleine santé

half [hɑ:f] n (pl **halves** [hɑ:vz]) moitié f; (of beer: also: **half pint**) ≈ demi m; (Rail, bus: also: **half fare**) demi-tarif m; (Sport: of match) mi-temps f; (: of ground) moitié (du terrain) ▷ adj demi(e) ▷ adv (à) moitié, à demi; ~ **an hour** une demi-heure; ~ **a dozen** une demi-douzaine; ~ **a pound** une demi-livre, ≈ 250 g; **two and a** ~ deux et demi; **a week and a** ~ une semaine et demie; ~ **(of it)** la moitié; ~ **(of)** la moitié de; ~ **the amount of** la moitié de; **to cut sth in** ~ couper qch en deux; ~ **past three** trois heures et demie; ~ **empty/ closed** à moitié vide/fermé; **to go halves (with sb)** se mettre de moitié avec qn

half-back ['hɑ:fbæk] n (Sport) demi m

half-baked ['hɑ:f'beɪkt] adj (inf: idea, scheme) qui ne tient pas debout

half board n (Brit: in hotel) demi-pension f

half-breed ['hɑ:fbri:d] n (pej) = **half-caste**

half-brother ['hɑ:fbrʌðər] n demi-frère m

half-caste ['hɑ:fkɑ:st] n (pej) métis(se)

half day n demi-journée f

half fare n demi-tarif m

half-hearted ['hɑ:f'hɑ:tɪd] adj tiède, sans enthousiasme

half-hour [hɑ:f'auər] n demi-heure f

half-mast ['hɑ:f'mɑ:st] n: **at** ~ (flag) en berne, à mi-mât

halfpenny ['heɪpnɪ] n demi-penny m

half-price ['hɑ:f'praɪs] adj à moitié prix ▷ adv (also: **at half-price**) à moitié prix

half term n (Brit Scol) vacances fpl (de demi-trimestre)

half-time [hɑ:f'taɪm] n mi-temps f

halfway ['hɑ:f'weɪ] adv à mi-chemin; **to meet sb** ~ (fig) parvenir à un compromis avec qn; ~ **through sth** au milieu de qch

halfway house n (hostel) centre m de réadaptation (pour anciens prisonniers, malades mentaux etc); (fig): **a** ~ **(between)** une étape intermédiaire (entre)

half-wit ['hɑ:fwɪt] n (inf) idiot(e), imbécile m/f

half-yearly [hɑ:f'jɪəlɪ] adv deux fois par an ▷ adj semestriel(le)

halibut ['hælɪbət] n (pl inv) flétan m

halitosis [hælɪ'təusɪs] n mauvaise haleine

hall [hɔ:l] n salle f; (entrance way: big) hall m; (small) entrée f; (US: corridor) couloir m; (mansion) château m, manoir m

hallmark ['hɔ:lmɑ:k] n poinçon m; (fig) marque f

hallo [hə'ləu] excl = **hello**

hall of residence n (Brit) pavillon m or résidence f universitaire

Hallowe'en, Halloween ['hæləu'i:n] n veille f de la Toussaint; voir article

● **HALLOWE'EN**
●
●
● Selon la tradition, Hallowe'en est la nuit des
● fantômes et des sorcières. En Écosse et aux
● États-Unis surtout (et de plus en plus en
● Angleterre) les enfants, pour fêter

● Hallowe'en, se déguisent ce soir-là et ils vont
● ainsi de porte en porte en demandant de
● petits cadeaux (du chocolat, etc).

hallucination [həlu:sɪ'neɪʃən] n hallucination f

hallucinogenic [həlu:sɪnəu'dʒɛnɪk] adj hallucinogène

hallway ['hɔ:lweɪ] n (entrance) vestibule m; (corridor) couloir m

halo ['heɪləu] n (of saint etc) auréole f; (of sun) halo m

halt [hɔ:lt] n halte f, arrêt m ▷ vt faire arrêter; (progress etc) interrompre ▷ vi faire halte, s'arrêter; **to call a** ~ **to sth** (fig) mettre fin à qch

halter ['hɔ:ltər] n (for horse) licou m

halterneck ['hɔ:ltənɛk] adj (dress) (avec) dos nu inv

halve [hɑ:v] vt (apple etc) partager or diviser en deux; (reduce by half) réduire de moitié

halves [hɑ:vz] npl of **half**

ham [hæm] n jambon m; (inf: also: **radio ham**) radio-amateur m; (also: **ham actor**) cabotin(e)

Hamburg ['hæmbə:g] n Hambourg

hamburger ['hæmbə:gər] n hamburger m

ham-fisted ['hæm'fɪstɪd], (US) **ham-handed** ['hæm'hændɪd] adj maladroit(e)

hamlet ['hæmlɪt] n hameau m

hammer ['hæmər] n marteau m ▷ vt (nail) enfoncer; (fig) éreinter, démolir ▷ vi (at door) frapper à coups redoublés; **to** ~ **a point home to sb** faire rentrer qch dans la tête de qn
▶ **hammer out** vt (metal) étendre au marteau; (fig: solution) élaborer

hammock ['hæmək] n hamac m

hamper ['hæmpər] vt gêner ▷ n panier m (d'osier)

hamster ['hæmstər] n hamster m

hamstring ['hæmstrɪŋ] n (Anat) tendon m du jarret

hand [hænd] n main f; (of clock) aiguille f; (handwriting) écriture f; (at cards) jeu m; (measurement: of horse) paume f; (worker) ouvrier(-ière) ▷ vt passer, donner; **to give sb a** ~ donner un coup de main à qn; **at** ~ à portée de la main; **in** ~ (situation) en main; (work) en cours; **we have the situation in** ~ nous avons la situation bien en main; **to be on** ~ (person) être disponible; (emergency services) se tenir prêt(e) (à intervenir); **to** ~ (information etc) sous la main, à portée de la main; **to force sb's** ~ forcer la main à qn; **to have a free** ~ avoir carte blanche; **to have sth in one's** ~ tenir qch à la main; **on the one** ~ ..., **on the other** ~ d'une part ..., d'autre part
▶ **hand down** vt passer; (tradition, heirloom) transmettre; (US: sentence, verdict) prononcer
▶ **hand in** vt remettre
▶ **hand out** vt distribuer
▶ **hand over** vt remettre; (powers etc) transmettre
▶ **hand round** vt (Brit: information) faire circuler; (: chocolates etc) faire passer

handbag ['hændbæg] *n* sac *m* à main
hand baggage *n* = **hand luggage**
handball ['hændbɔːl] *n* handball *m*
handbasin ['hændbeɪsn] *n* lavabo *m*
handbook ['hændbuk] *n* manuel *m*
handbrake ['hændbreɪk] *n* frein *m* à main
h & c *abbr* (*Brit*) = **hot and cold (water)**
hand cream *n* crème *f* pour les mains
handcuffs ['hændkʌfs] *npl* menottes *fpl*
handful ['hændful] *n* poignée *f*
hand-held ['hænd'held] *adj* à main
handicap ['hændɪkæp] *n* handicap *m* ▷ *vt*
handicaper; **mentally/physically ~ped**
handicapé(e) mentalement/physiquement
handicraft ['hændɪkrɑːft] *n* travail *m*
d'artisanat, technique artisanale
handiwork ['hændɪwəːk] *n* ouvrage *m*; **this
looks like his ~** (*pej*) ça a tout l'air d'être son
œuvre
handkerchief ['hæŋkətʃɪf] *n* mouchoir *m*
handle ['hændl] *n* (*of door etc*) poignée *f*; (*of cup
etc*) anse *f*; (*of knife etc*) manche *m*; (*of saucepan*)
queue *f*; (*for winding*) manivelle *f* ▷ *vt* toucher,
manier; (*deal with*) s'occuper de; (*treat: people*)
prendre; **"~ with care"** "fragile"; **to fly off the
~** s'énerver
handlebar ['hændlbɑːʳ] *n*, **handlebars**
['hændlbɑːz] *npl* guidon *m*
handling ['hændlɪŋ] *n* (*Aut*) maniement *m*;
(*treatment*): **his ~ of the matter** la façon dont il
a traité l'affaire
handling charges *npl* frais *mpl* de
manutention; (*Banking*) agios *mpl*
hand luggage ['hændlʌgɪdʒ] *n* bagages *mpl* à
main; **one item of ~** un bagage à main
handmade ['hænd'meɪd] *adj* fait(e) à la main
handout ['hændaut] *n* (*money*) aide *f*, don *m*;
(*leaflet*) prospectus *m*; (*press handout*)
communiqué *m* de presse; (*at lecture*)
polycopié *m*
hand-picked ['hænd'pɪkt] *adj* (*produce*) cueilli(e)
à la main; (*staff etc*) trié(e) sur le volet
handrail ['hændreɪl] *n* (*on staircase etc*) rampe *f*,
main courante
handset ['hændset] *n* (*Tel*) combiné *m*
hands-free [hændz'friː] *adj* mains libres *inv* ▷ *n*
(*also*: **hands-free kit**) kit *m* mains libres *inv*
handshake ['hændʃeɪk] *n* poignée *f* de main;
(*Comput*) établissement *m* de la liaison
handsome ['hænsəm] *adj* beau (belle); (*gift*)
généreux(-euse); (*profit*) considérable
hands-on [hændz'ɔn] *adj* (*training, experience*) sur
le tas; **she has a very ~ approach** sa politique
est de mettre la main à la pâte
handstand ['hændstænd] *n*: **to do a ~** faire
l'arbre droit
hand-to-mouth ['hændtə'mauθ] *adj* (*existence*)
au jour le jour
handwriting ['hændraɪtɪŋ] *n* écriture *f*
handwritten ['hændrɪtn] *adj* manuscrit(e),
écrit(e) à la main
handy ['hændɪ] *adj* (*person*) adroit(e); (*close at*

hand) sous la main; (*convenient*) pratique; **to
come in ~** être (*or* s'avérer) utile
handyman ['hændɪmæn] (*irreg*) *n* bricoleur *m*;
(*servant*) homme *m* à tout faire
hang (*pt, pp* **hung**) [hæŋ, hʌŋ] *vt* accrocher;
(*criminal: pt, pp* **-ed**) pendre ▷ *vi* pendre; (*hair,
drapery*) tomber ▷ *n*: **to get the ~ of (doing) sth**
(*inf*) attraper le coup pour faire qch
▶ **hang about, hang around** *vi* flâner, traîner
▶ **hang back** *vi* (*hesitate*): **to ~ back (from
doing)** être réticent(e) (pour faire)
▶ **hang down** *vi* pendre
▶ **hang on** *vi* (*wait*) attendre ▷ *vt fus* (*depend on*)
dépendre de; **to ~ on to** (*keep hold of*) ne pas
lâcher; (*keep*) garder
▶ **hang out** *vt* (*washing*) étendre (dehors) ▷ *vi*
pendre; (*inf: live*) habiter, percher; (*: spend time*)
traîner
▶ **hang round** *vi* = **hang around**
▶ **hang together** *vi* (*argument etc*) se tenir, être
cohérent(e)
▶ **hang up** *vi* (*Tel*) raccrocher ▷ *vt* (*coat, painting
etc*) accrocher, suspendre; **to ~ up on sb** (*Tel*)
raccrocher au nez de qn
hangar ['hæŋəʳ] *n* hangar *m*
hangdog ['hæŋdɔg] *adj* (*look, expression*) de chien
battu
hanger ['hæŋəʳ] *n* cintre *m*, portemanteau *m*
hanger-on [hæŋər'ɔn] *n* parasite *m*
hang-glider ['hæŋglaɪdəʳ] *n* deltaplane *m*
hang-gliding ['hæŋglaɪdɪŋ] *n* vol *m* libre *or* sur
aile delta
hanging ['hæŋɪŋ] *n* (*execution*) pendaison *f*
hangman ['hæŋmən] (*irreg*) *n* bourreau *m*
hangover ['hæŋəuvəʳ] *n* (*after drinking*) gueule *f*
de bois
hang-up ['hæŋʌp] *n* complexe *m*
hank [hæŋk] *n* écheveau *m*
hanker ['hæŋkəʳ] *vi*: **to ~ after** avoir envie de
hankering ['hæŋkərɪŋ] *n*: **to have a ~ for/to do
sth** avoir une grande envie de/de faire qch
hankie, hanky ['hæŋkɪ] *n abbr* = **handkerchief**
Hants *abbr* (*Brit*) = **Hampshire**
haphazard [hæp'hæzəd] *adj* fait(e) au hasard,
fait(e) au petit bonheur
hapless ['hæplɪs] *adj* malheureux(-euse)
happen ['hæpən] *vi* arriver, se passer, se
produire; **what's ~ing?** que se passe-t-il?; **she
~ed to be free** il s'est trouvé (*or* se trouvait)
qu'elle était libre; **if anything ~ed to him** s'il
lui arrivait quoi que ce soit; **as it ~s** justement
▶ **happen on, happen upon** *vt fus* tomber sur
happening ['hæpnɪŋ] *n* événement *m*
happily ['hæpɪlɪ] *adv* heureusement; (*cheerfully*)
joyeusement
happiness ['hæpɪnɪs] *n* bonheur *m*
happy ['hæpɪ] *adj* heureux(-euse); **~ with**
(*arrangements etc*) satisfait(e) de; **to be ~ to do**
faire volontiers; **yes, I'd be ~ to** oui, avec plaisir
or (bien) volontiers; **~ birthday!** bon
anniversaire!; **~ Christmas/New Year!** joyeux
Noël/bonne année!

happy-go-lucky ['hæpɪgəu'lʌkɪ] *adj* insouciant(e)

happy hour *n* l'heure *f* de l'apéritif, *heure pendant laquelle les consommations sont à prix réduit*

harangue [hə'ræŋ] *vt* haranguer

harass ['hærəs] *vt* accabler, tourmenter

harassed ['hærəst] *adj* tracassé(e)

harassment ['hærəsmənt] *n* tracasseries *fpl*; **sexual** ~ harcèlement sexuel

harbour, (US) **harbor** ['hɑ:bə^r] *n* port *m* ▷ *vt* héberger, abriter; (*hopes, suspicions*) entretenir; **to** ~ **a grudge against sb** en vouloir à qn

harbour dues, (US) **harbor dues** *npl* droits *mpl* de port

harbour master, (US) **harbor master** *n* capitaine *m* du port

hard [hɑ:d] *adj* dur(e); (*question, problem*) difficile; (*facts, evidence*) concret(-ète) ▷ *adv* (*work*) dur; (*think, try*) sérieusement; **to look** ~ **at** regarder fixement; (*thing*) regarder de près; **to drink** ~ boire sec; ~ **luck!** pas de veine!; **no** ~ **feelings!** sans rancune!; **to be** ~ **of hearing** être dur(e) d'oreille; **to be** ~ **done by** être traité(e) injustement; **to be** ~ **on sb** être dur(e) avec qn; **I find it** ~ **to believe that ...** je n'arrive pas à croire que ...

hard-and-fast ['hɑ:dən'fɑ:st] *adj* strict(e), absolu(e)

hardback ['hɑ:dbæk] *n* livre relié

hardboard ['hɑ:dbɔ:d] *n* Isorel® *m*

hard-boiled egg ['hɑ:d'bɔɪld-] *n* œuf dur

hard cash *n* espèces *fpl*

hard copy *n* (*Comput*) sortie *f* or copie *f* papier

hard-core ['hɑ:d'kɔ:^{r}] *adj* (*pornography*) (dit(e)) dur(e); (*supporters*) inconditionnel(le)

hard court *n* (*Tennis*) court *m* en dur

hard disk *n* (*Comput*) disque dur

harden ['hɑ:dn] *vt* durcir; (*steel*) tremper; (*fig*) endurcir ▷ *vi* (*substance*) durcir

hardened ['hɑ:dnd] *adj* (*criminal*) endurci(e); **to be** ~ **to sth** s'être endurci(e) à qch, être (devenu(e)) insensible à qch

hard-headed ['hɑ:d'hɛdɪd] *adj* réaliste; décidé(e)

hard-hearted ['hɑ:d'hɑ:tɪd] *adj* dur(e), impitoyable

hard-hitting ['hɑ:d'hɪtɪŋ] *adj* (*speech, article*) sans complaisances

hard labour *n* travaux forcés

hardliner [hɑ:d'laɪnə^r] *n* intransigeant(e), dur(e)

hard-luck story [hɑ:d'lʌk-] *n* histoire larmoyante

hardly ['hɑ:dlɪ] *adv* (*scarcely*) à peine; (*harshly*) durement; **it's** ~ **the case** ce n'est guère le cas; ~ **anywhere/ever** presque nulle part/jamais; **I can** ~ **believe it** j'ai du mal à le croire

hardness ['hɑ:dnɪs] *n* dureté *f*

hard-nosed ['hɑ:d'nəuzd] *adj* impitoyable, dur(e)

hard-pressed ['hɑ:d'prɛst] *adj* sous pression

hard sell *n* vente agressive

hardship ['hɑ:dʃɪp] *n* (*difficulties*) épreuves *fpl*; (*deprivation*) privations *fpl*

hard shoulder *n* (*Brit Aut*) accotement stabilisé

hard-up [hɑ:d'ʌp] *adj* (*inf*) fauché(e)

hardware ['hɑ:dwɛə^r] *n* quincaillerie *f*; (*Comput, Mil*) matériel *m*

hardware shop, (US) **hardware store** *n* quincaillerie *f*

hard-wearing [hɑ:d'wɛərɪŋ] *adj* solide

hard-won ['hɑ:d'wʌn] *adj* (si) durement gagné(e)

hard-working [hɑ:d'wə:kɪŋ] *adj* travailleur(-euse), consciencieux(-euse)

hardy ['hɑ:dɪ] *adj* robuste; (*plant*) résistant(e) au gel

hare [hɛə^r] *n* lièvre *m*

hare-brained ['hɛəbreɪnd] *adj* farfelu(e), écervelé(e)

harelip ['hɛəlɪp] *n* (*Med*) bec-de-lièvre *m*

harem [hɑ:'ri:m] *n* harem *m*

hark back [hɑ:k-] *vi*: **to** ~ **to** (en) revenir toujours à

harm [hɑ:m] *n* mal *m*; (*wrong*) tort *m* ▷ *vt* (*person*) faire du mal or du tort à; (*thing*) endommager; **to mean no** ~ ne pas avoir de mauvaises intentions; **there's no** ~ **in trying** on peut toujours essayer; **out of** ~'s **way** à l'abri du danger, en lieu sûr

harmful ['hɑ:mful] *adj* nuisible

harmless [hɑ:mlɪs] *adj* inoffensif(-ive)

harmonic [hɑ:'mɔnɪk] *adj* harmonique

harmonica [hɑ:'mɔnɪkə] *n* harmonica *m*

harmonics [hɑ:'mɔnɪks] *npl* harmoniques *mpl* or *fpl*

harmonious [hɑ:'məunɪəs] *adj* harmonieux(-euse)

harmonium [hɑ:'məunɪəm] *n* harmonium *m*

harmonize ['hɑ:mənaɪz] *vt* harmoniser ▷ *vi* s'harmoniser

harmony ['hɑ:mənɪ] *n* harmonie *f*

harness ['hɑ:nɪs] *n* harnais *m* ▷ *vt* (*horse*) harnacher; (*resources*) exploiter

harp [hɑ:p] *n* harpe *f* ▷ *vi*: **to** ~ **on about** revenir toujours sur

harpist ['hɑ:pɪst] *n* harpiste *m/f*

harpoon [hɑ:'pu:n] *n* harpon *m*

harpsichord ['hɑ:psɪkɔ:d] *n* clavecin *m*

harrowing ['hærəuɪŋ] *adj* déchirant(e)

harsh [hɑ:ʃ] *adj* (*hard*) dur(e); (*severe*) sévère; (*rough: surface*) rugueux(-euse); (*unpleasant: sound*) discordant(e); (*: light*) cru(e); (*: taste*) âpre

harshly ['hɑ:ʃlɪ] *adv* durement, sévèrement

harshness ['hɑ:ʃnɪs] *n* dureté *f*, sévérité *f*

harvest ['hɑ:vɪst] *n* (*of corn*) moisson *f*; (*of fruit*) récolte *f*; (*of grapes*) vendange *f* ▷ *vi, vt* moissonner; récolter; vendanger

harvester ['hɑ:vɪstə^r] *n* (*machine*) moissonneuse *f*; (*also*: **combine harvester**) moissonneuse-batteuse(-lieuse *f*) *f*

has [hæz] *vb see* **have**

has-been ['hæzbi:n] *n* (*inf*: *person*): **he/she's a** ~ il/elle a fait son temps or est fini(e)

hash [hæʃ] n (Culin) hachis m; (fig: mess) gâchis m
  ▷ n abbr (inf) = **hashish**
hashish ['hæʃiʃ] n haschisch m
hasn't ['hæznt] = **has not**
hassle ['hæsl] n (inf: fuss) histoire(s) f(pl)
haste [heist] n hâte f, précipitation f; **in ~** à la
  hâte, précipitamment
hasten ['heisn] vt hâter, accélérer ▷ vi se hâter,
  s'empresser
hastily ['heistili] adv à la hâte; (leave)
  précipitamment
hasty ['heisti] adj (decision, action) hâtif(-ive);
  (departure, escape) précipité(e)
hat [hæt] n chapeau m
hatbox ['hætbɔks] n carton m à chapeau
hatch [hætʃ] n (Naut: also: **hatchway**) écoutille f;
  (Brit: also: **service hatch**) passe-plats m inv ▷ vi
  éclore ▷ vt faire éclore; (fig: scheme) tramer,
  ourdir
hatchback ['hætʃbæk] n (Aut) modèle m avec
  hayon arrière
hatchet ['hætʃit] n hachette f
hatchet job n (inf) démolissage m
hatchet man (irreg) n (inf) homme m de main
hate [heit] vt haïr, détester ▷ n haine f; **to ~ to
  do** or **doing** détester faire; **I ~ to trouble you,
  but ...** désolé de vous déranger, mais ...
hateful ['heitful] adj odieux(-euse), détestable
hater ['heitəʳ] n: cop-hater anti-flic mf; woman-
  hater misogyne m/f (haineux(-euse))
hatred ['heitrid] n haine f
hat trick n (Brit Sport, also fig): **to get a ~** réussir
  trois coups (or gagner trois matchs etc)
  consécutifs
haughty ['hɔ:ti] adj hautain(e), arrogant(e)
haul [hɔ:l] vt traîner, tirer; (by lorry) camionner;
  (Naut) haler ▷ n (of fish) prise f; (of stolen goods etc)
  butin m
haulage ['hɔ:lidʒ] n transport routier
haulage contractor n (Brit: firm) entreprise f de
  transport (routier); (: person) transporteur
  routier
haulier ['hɔ:liəʳ], (US) **hauler** ['hɔ:ləʳ] n
  transporteur (routier), camionneur m
haunch [hɔ:ntʃ] n hanche f; **~ of venison**
  cuissot m de chevreuil
haunt [hɔ:nt] vt (subj: ghost, fear) hanter; (: person)
  fréquenter ▷ n repaire m
haunted ['hɔ:ntid] adj (castle etc) hanté(e); (look)
  égaré(e), hagard(e)
haunting ['hɔ:ntiŋ] adj (sight, music) obsédant(e)
Havana [hə'vænə] n La Havane

⊙ KEYWORD

have [hæv] (pt, pp **had**) aux vb **1** (gen) avoir; être;
  to have eaten/slept avoir mangé/dormi; **to
  have arrived/gone** être arrivé(e)/allé(e); **he
  has been promoted** il a eu une promotion;
  having finished or **when he had finished, he
  left** quand il a eu fini, il est parti; **we'd already
  eaten** nous avions déjà mangé

2 (in tag questions): **you've done it, haven't you?**
vous l'avez fait, n'est-ce pas?

3 (in short answers and questions): **no I haven't!/yes
we have!** mais non!/mais si!; **so I have!** ah oui!,
oui c'est vrai!; **I've been there before, have
you?** j'y suis déjà allé, et vous?
  ▷ modal aux vb (be obliged): **to have (got) to do
  sth** devoir faire qch, être obligé(e) de faire qch;
  she has (got) to do it elle doit le faire, il faut
  qu'elle le fasse; **you haven't to tell her** vous
  n'êtes pas obligé de le lui dire; (must not) ne le
  lui dites surtout pas; **do you have to book?** il
  faut réserver?
  ▷ vt **1** (possess) avoir; **he has (got) blue eyes/
  dark hair** il a les yeux bleus/les cheveux bruns
  2 (referring to meals etc): **to have breakfast**
  prendre le petit déjeuner; **to have dinner/
  lunch** dîner/déjeuner; **to have a drink**
  prendre un verre; **to have a cigarette** fumer
  une cigarette
  3 (receive) avoir, recevoir; (obtain) avoir; **may I
  have your address?** puis-je avoir votre
  adresse?; **you can have it for £5** vous pouvez
  l'avoir pour 5 livres; **I must have it for
  tomorrow** il me le faut pour demain; **to have a
  baby** avoir un bébé
  4 (maintain, allow): **I won't have it!** ça ne se
  passera pas comme ça!; **we can't have that**
  nous ne tolérerons pas ça
  5 (by sb else): **to have sth done** faire faire qch;
  to have one's hair cut se faire couper les
  cheveux; **to have sb do sth** faire faire qch à qn
  6 (experience, suffer) avoir; **to have a cold/flu**
  avoir un rhume/la grippe; **to have an
  operation** se faire opérer; **she had her bag
  stolen** elle s'est fait voler son sac
  7 (+noun): **to have a swim/walk** nager/se
  promener; **to have a bath/shower** prendre un
  bain/une douche; **let's have a look** regardons;
  to have a meeting se réunir; **to have a party**
  organiser une fête; **let me have a try** laissez-
  moi essayer
  8 (inf: dupe) avoir; **he's been had** il s'est fait
  avoir or rouler
  ▶ **have out** vt: **to have it out with sb** (settle a
  problem etc) s'expliquer (franchement) avec qn

haven ['heivn] n port m; (fig) havre m
haven't ['hævnt] = **have not**
haversack ['hævəsæk] n sac m à dos
haves [hævz] npl (inf): **the ~ and have-nots** les
  riches et les pauvres
havoc ['hævək] n ravages mpl, dégâts mpl; **to
  play ~ with** (fig) désorganiser complètement;
  détraquer
Hawaii [hə'wai:] n (îles fpl) Hawaï m
Hawaiian [hə'waijən] adj hawaïen(ne) ▷ n
  Hawaïen(ne); (Ling) hawaïen m
hawk [hɔ:k] n faucon m ▷ vt (goods) colporter
hawker ['hɔ:kəʳ] n colporteur m
hawkish ['hɔ:kiʃ] adj belliciste
hawthorn ['hɔ:θɔ:n] n aubépine f

hay [heɪ] *n* foin *m*
hay fever *n* rhume *m* des foins
haystack ['heɪstæk] *n* meule *f* de foin
haywire ['heɪwaɪəʳ] *adj* (*inf*): **to go** ~ perdre la tête; mal tourner
hazard ['hæzəd] *n* (*risk*) danger *m*, risque *m*; (*chance*) hasard *m*, chance *f* ▷ *vt* risquer, hasarder; **to be a health/fire** ~ présenter un risque pour la santé/d'incendie; **to** ~ **a guess** émettre *or* hasarder une hypothèse
hazardous ['hæzədəs] *adj* hasardeux(-euse), risqué(e)
hazard pay *n* (*US*) prime *f* de risque
hazard warning lights *npl* (*Aut*) feux *mpl* de détresse
haze [heɪz] *n* brume *f*
hazel [heɪzl] *n* (*tree*) noisetier *m* ▷ *adj* (*eyes*) noisette *inv*
hazelnut ['heɪzlnʌt] *n* noisette *f*
hazy ['heɪzɪ] *adj* brumeux(-euse); (*idea*) vague; (*photograph*) flou(e)
H-bomb ['eɪtʃbɔm] *n* bombe *f* H
HD *abbr* (= *high definition*) HD (= *haute définition*)
HE *abbr* = **high explosive**; (*Rel, Diplomacy*) = **His (or Her) Excellency**
he [hi:] *pron* il; **it is he who ...** c'est lui qui ...; **here he is** le voici; **he-bear** *etc* ours *etc* mâle
head [hɛd] *n* tête *f*; (*leader*) chef *m*; (*of school*) directeur(-trice); (*of secondary school*) proviseur *m* ▷ *vt* (*list*) être en tête de; (*group, company*) être à la tête de; **heads** *pl* (*on coin*) (le côté) face; **~s or tails** pile ou face; **~ first** la tête la première; **~ over heels in love** follement *or* éperdument amoureux(-euse); **to ~ the ball** faire une tête; **10 euros a** *or* **per** ~ 10 euros par personne; **to sit at the ~ of the table** présider la tablée; **to have a ~ for business** avoir des dispositions pour les affaires; **to have no ~ for heights** être sujet(te) au vertige; **to come to a ~** (*fig: situation etc*) devenir critique
  ▶ **head for** *vt fus* se diriger vers; (*disaster*) aller à
  ▶ **head off** *vt* (*threat, danger*) détourner
headache ['hɛdeɪk] *n* mal *m* de tête; **to have a ~** avoir mal à la tête
headband ['hɛdbænd] *n* bandeau *m*
headboard ['hɛdbɔːd] *n* dosseret *m*
head cold *n* rhume *m* de cerveau
headdress ['hɛddrɛs] *n* coiffure *f*
headed notepaper ['hɛdɪd-] *n* papier *m* à lettres à en-tête
header ['hɛdəʳ] *n* (*Brit inf: Football*) (coup *m* de) tête *f*; (: *fall*) chute *f* (*or* plongeon *m*) la tête la première
head-first ['hɛd'fəːst] *adv* (*lit*) la tête la première
headhunt ['hɛdhʌnt] *vt*: **she was ~ed** elle a été recrutée par un chasseur de têtes
headhunter ['hɛdhʌntəʳ] *n* chasseur *m* de têtes
heading ['hɛdɪŋ] *n* titre *m*; (*subject title*) rubrique *f*
headlamp ['hɛdlæmp] (*Brit*) *n* = **headlight**
headland ['hɛdlənd] *n* promontoire *m*, cap *m*
headlight ['hɛdlaɪt] *n* phare *m*

headline ['hɛdlaɪn] *n* titre *m*
headlong ['hɛdlɔŋ] *adv* (*fall*) la tête la première; (*rush*) tête baissée
headmaster [hɛd'mɑːstəʳ] *n* directeur *m*
headmistress [hɛd'mɪstrɪs] *n* directrice *f*
head office *n* siège *m*, bureau *m* central
head-on [hɛd'ɔn] *adj* (*collision*) de plein fouet
headphones ['hɛdfəunz] *npl* casque *m* (à écouteurs)
headquarters ['hɛdkwɔːtəz] *npl* (*of business*) bureau *or* siège central; (*Mil*) quartier général
headrest ['hɛdrɛst] *n* appui-tête *m*
headroom ['hɛdrum] *n* (*in car*) hauteur *f* de plafond; (*under bridge*) hauteur limite; dégagement *m*
headscarf ['hɛdskɑːf] (*pl* **headscarves** [-skɑːvz]) *n* foulard *m*
headset ['hɛdsɛt] *n* = **headphones**
headstone ['hɛdstəun] *n* pierre tombale
headstrong ['hɛdstrɔŋ] *adj* têtu(e), entêté(e)
headteacher [hɛd'tiːtʃəʳ] *n* directeur(-trice); (*of secondary school*) proviseur *m*
head waiter *n* maître *m* d'hôtel
headway ['hɛdweɪ] *n*: **to make** ~ avancer, faire des progrès
headwind ['hɛdwɪnd] *n* vent *m* contraire
heady ['hɛdɪ] *adj* capiteux(-euse), enivrant(e)
heal [hiːl] *vt, vi* guérir
health [hɛlθ] *n* santé *f*; **Department of H~** (*Brit, US*) ≈ ministère *m* de la Santé
health care *n* services médicaux
health centre *n* (*Brit*) centre *m* de santé
health food *n* aliment(s) naturel(s)
health food shop *n* magasin *m* diététique
health hazard *n* risque *m* pour la santé
Health Service *n*: **the ~** (*Brit*) ≈ la Sécurité Sociale
healthy ['hɛlθɪ] *adj* (*person*) en bonne santé; (*climate, food, attitude etc*) sain(e)
heap [hiːp] *n* tas *m*, monceau *m* ▷ *vt* (*also*: **heap up**) entasser, amonceler; **she ~ed her plate with cakes** elle a chargé son assiette de gâteaux; **~s (of)** (*inf: lots*) des tas (de); **to ~ favours/praise/gifts** *etc* **on sb** combler qn de faveurs/d'éloges/de cadeaux *etc*
hear (*pt, pp* **heard**) [hɪəʳ, həːd] *vt* entendre; (*news*) apprendre; (*lecture*) assister à, écouter ▷ *vi* entendre; **to ~ about** entendre parler de; (*have news of*) avoir des nouvelles de; **did you ~ about the move?** tu es au courant du déménagement?; **to ~ from sb** recevoir des nouvelles de qn; **I've never ~d of that book** je n'ai jamais entendu parler de ce livre
  ▶ **hear out** *vt* écouter jusqu'au bout
heard [həːd] *pt, pp of* **hear**
hearing ['hɪərɪŋ] *n* (*sense*) ouïe *f*; (*of witnesses*) audition *f*; (*of a case*) audience *f*; (*of committee*) séance *f*; **to give sb a ~** (*Brit*) écouter ce que qn a à dire
hearing aid *n* appareil *m* acoustique
hearsay ['hɪəseɪ] *n* on-dit *mpl*, rumeurs *fpl*; **by ~** *adv* par ouï-dire

hearse [hə:s] *n* corbillard *m*

heart [hɑ:t] *n* cœur *m*; **hearts** *npl* (*Cards*) cœur; **at ~** au fond; **by ~** (*learn, know*) par cœur; **to have a weak ~** avoir le cœur malade, avoir des problèmes de cœur; **to lose/take ~** perdre/prendre courage; **to set one's ~ on sth/on doing sth** vouloir absolument qch/faire qch; **the ~ of the matter** le fond du problème

heartache ['hɑ:teɪk] *n* chagrin *m*, douleur *f*

heart attack *n* crise *f* cardiaque

heartbeat ['hɑ:tbi:t] *n* battement *m* de cœur

heartbreak ['hɑ:tbreɪk] *n* immense chagrin *m*

heartbreaking ['hɑ:tbreɪkɪŋ] *adj* navrant(e), déchirant(e)

heartbroken ['hɑ:tbrəukən] *adj*: **to be ~** avoir beaucoup de chagrin

heartburn ['hɑ:tbə:n] *n* brûlures *fpl* d'estomac

heart disease *n* maladie *f* cardiaque

-hearted ['hɑ:tɪd] *suffix*: **kind~** généreux(-euse), qui a bon cœur

heartening ['hɑ:tnɪŋ] *adj* encourageant(e), réconfortant(e)

heart failure *n* (*Med*) arrêt *m* du cœur

heartfelt ['hɑ:tfelt] *adj* sincère

hearth [hɑ:θ] *n* foyer *m*, cheminée *f*

heartily ['hɑ:tɪlɪ] *adv* chaleureusement; (*laugh*) de bon cœur; (*eat*) de bon appétit; **to agree ~** être entièrement d'accord; **to be ~ sick of** (*Brit*) en avoir ras le bol de

heartland ['hɑ:tlænd] *n* centre *m*, cœur *m*; **France's ~s** la France profonde

heartless ['hɑ:tlɪs] *adj* (*person*) sans cœur, insensible; (*treatment*) cruel(le)

heartstrings ['hɑ:tstrɪŋz] *npl*: **to tug (at) sb's ~** toucher *or* faire vibrer les cordes sensibles de qn

heartthrob ['hɑ:tθrɔb] *n* idole *f*

heart-to-heart ['hɑ:t'tə'hɑ:t] *adj, adv* à cœur ouvert

heart transplant *n* greffe *f* du cœur

heartwarming ['hɑ:twɔ:mɪŋ] *adj* réconfortant(e)

hearty ['hɑ:tɪ] *adj* chaleureux(-euse); (*appetite*) solide; (*dislike*) cordial(e); (*meal*) copieux(-euse)

heat [hi:t] *n* chaleur *f*; (*fig*) ardeur *f*; feu *m*; (*Sport: also*: **qualifying heat**) éliminatoire *f*; (*Zool*): **in** *or* **on ~** (*Brit*) en chaleur ▷ *vt* chauffer
▶ **heat up** *vi* (*liquid*) chauffer; (*room*) se réchauffer ▷ *vt* réchauffer

heated ['hi:tɪd] *adj* chauffé(e); (*fig*) passionné(e), échauffé(e), excité(e)

heater ['hi:tə^r] *n* appareil *m* de chauffage; radiateur *m*; (*in car*) chauffage *m*; (*water heater*) chauffe-eau *m*

heath [hi:θ] *n* (*Brit*) lande *f*

heathen ['hi:ðn] *adj, n* païen(ne)

heather ['heðə^r] *n* bruyère *f*

heating ['hi:tɪŋ] *n* chauffage *m*

heat-resistant ['hi:trɪzɪstənt] *adj* résistant(e) à la chaleur

heat-seeking ['hi:tsi:kɪŋ] *adj* guidé(e) par infrarouge

heatstroke ['hi:tstrəuk] *n* coup *m* de chaleur

heatwave ['hi:tweɪv] *n* vague *f* de chaleur

heave [hi:v] *vt* soulever (avec effort) ▷ *vi* se soulever; (*retch*) avoir des haut-le-cœur ▷ *n* (*push*) poussée *f*; **to ~ a sigh** pousser un gros soupir

heaven ['hevn] *n* ciel *m*, paradis *m*; (*fig*) paradis; **~ forbid!** surtout pas!; **thank ~!** Dieu merci!; **for ~`s sake!** (*pleading*) je vous en prie!; (*protesting*) mince alors!

heavenly ['hevnlɪ] *adj* céleste, divin(e)

heavily ['hevɪlɪ] *adv* lourdement; (*drink, smoke*) beaucoup; (*sleep, sigh*) profondément

heavy ['hevɪ] *adj* lourd(e); (*work, rain, user, eater*) gros(se); (*drinker, smoker*) grand(e); (*schedule, week*) chargé(e); **it's too ~** c'est trop lourd; **it's ~ going** ça ne va pas tout seul, c'est pénible

heavy cream *n* (*US*) crème fraîche épaisse

heavy-duty ['hevɪ'dju:tɪ] *adj* à usage intensif

heavy goods vehicle *n* (*Brit*) poids lourd *m*

heavy-handed ['hevɪ'hændɪd] *adj* (*fig*) maladroit(e), qui manque de tact

heavy metal *n* (*Mus*) heavy metal *m*

heavy-set ['hevɪ'set] *adj* (*esp US*) costaud(e)

heavyweight ['hevɪweɪt] *n* (*Sport*) poids lourd

Hebrew ['hi:bru:] *adj* hébraïque ▷ *n* (*Ling*) hébreu *m*

Hebrides ['hebrɪdi:z] *npl*: **the ~** les Hébrides *fpl*

heck [hek] *n* (*inf*): **why the ~ ...?** pourquoi diable ...?; **a ~ of a lot** une sacrée quantité; **he has done a ~ of a lot for us** il a vraiment beaucoup fait pour nous

heckle ['hekl] *vt* interpeller (*un orateur*)

heckler ['heklə^r] *n* interrupteur *m*; élément perturbateur

hectare ['hektɑ:^r] *n* (*Brit*) hectare *m*

hectic ['hektɪk] *adj* (*schedule*) très chargé(e); (*day*) mouvementé(e); (*activity*) fiévreux(-euse); (*lifestyle*) trépidant(e)

he'd [hi:d] = **he would**; **he had**

hedge [hedʒ] *n* haie *f* ▷ *vi* se dérober ▷ *vt*: **to ~ one's bets** (*fig*) se couvrir; **as a ~ against inflation** pour se prémunir contre l'inflation
▶ **hedge in** *vt* entourer d'une haie

hedgehog ['hedʒhɔg] *n* hérisson *m*

hedgerow ['hedʒrəu] *n* haie(s) *f(pl)*

hedonism ['hi:dənɪzəm] *n* hédonisme *m*

heed [hi:d] *vt* (*also*: **take heed of**) tenir compte de, prendre garde à

heedless ['hi:dlɪs] *adj* insouciant(e)

heel [hi:l] *n* talon *m* ▷ *vt* (*shoe*) retalonner; **to bring to ~** (*dog*) faire venir à ses pieds; (*fig: person*) rappeler à l'ordre; **to take to one's ~s** prendre ses jambes à son cou

hefty ['heftɪ] *adj* (*person*) costaud(e); (*parcel*) lourd(e); (*piece, price*) gros(se)

heifer ['hefə^r] *n* génisse *f*

height [haɪt] *n* (*of person*) taille *f*, grandeur *f*; (*of object*) hauteur *f*; (*of plane, mountain*) altitude *f*; (*high ground*) hauteur, éminence *f*; (*fig: of glory, fame, power*) sommet *m*; (: *of luxury, stupidity*) comble *m*; **at the ~ of summer** au cœur de l'été; **what ~ are you?** combien mesurez-vous?, quelle est votre taille?; **of average ~** de taille moyenne; **to be afraid of ~s** être sujet(te) au vertige; **it's the ~ of fashion** c'est le dernier cri

heighten ['haɪtn] *vt* hausser, surélever; (*fig*) augmenter

heinous ['heɪnəs] *adj* odieux(-euse), atroce

heir [ɛəʳ] *n* héritier *m*

heir apparent *n* héritier présomptif

heiress ['ɛərɛs] *n* héritière *f*

heirloom ['ɛəluːm] *n* meuble *m* (or bijou *m* or tableau *m*) de famille

heist [haɪst] *n* (*US inf: hold-up*) casse *m*

held [hɛld] *pt, pp of* **hold**

helicopter ['hɛlɪkɔptəʳ] *n* hélicoptère *m*

heliport ['hɛlɪpɔːt] *n* (*Aviat*) héliport *m*

helium ['hiːlɪəm] *n* hélium *m*

hell [hɛl] *n* enfer *m*; **a ~ of a ...** (*inf*) un(e) sacré(e) ...; **oh ~!** (*inf*) merde!

he'll [hiːl] = **he will; he shall**

hell-bent [hɛl'bɛnt] *adj* (*inf*): **to be ~ on doing sth** vouloir à tout prix faire qch

hellish ['hɛlɪʃ] *adj* infernal(e)

hello [hə'ləu] *excl* bonjour!; (*to attract attention*) hé!; (*surprise*) tiens!

helm [hɛlm] *n* (*Naut*) barre *f*

helmet ['hɛlmɪt] *n* casque *m*

helmsman ['hɛlmzmən] (*irreg*) *n* timonier *m*

help [hɛlp] *n* aide *f*; (*cleaner etc*) femme *f* de ménage; (*assistant etc*) employé(e) ▷ *vt, vi* aider; **~!** au secours!; **~ yourself** servez-vous; **can you ~ me?** pouvez-vous m'aider?; **can I ~ you?** (*in shop*) vous désirez?; **with the ~ of** (*person*) avec l'aide de; (*tool etc*) à l'aide de; **to be of ~ to sb** être utile à qn; **to ~ sb (to) do sth** aider qn à faire qch; **I can't ~ saying** je ne peux pas m'empêcher de dire; **he can't ~ it** il n'y peut rien

▶ **help out** *vi* aider ▷ *vt*: **to ~ sb out** aider qn

helper ['hɛlpəʳ] *n* aide *m/f*, assistant(e)

helpful ['hɛlpful] *adj* serviable, obligeant(e); (*useful*) utile

helping ['hɛlpɪŋ] *n* portion *f*

helping hand *n* coup *m* de main; **to give sb a ~** prêter main-forte à qn

helpless ['hɛlplɪs] *adj* impuissant(e); (*baby*) sans défense

helplessly ['hɛlplɪslɪ] *adv* (*watch*) sans pouvoir rien faire

helpline ['hɛlplaɪn] *n* service *m* d'assistance téléphonique; (*free*) ≈ numéro vert

Helsinki ['hɛlsɪŋkɪ] *n* Helsinki

helter-skelter ['hɛltə'skɛltəʳ] *n* (*Brit: at amusement park*) toboggan *m*

hem [hɛm] *n* ourlet *m* ▷ *vt* ourler

▶ **hem in** *vt* cerner; **to feel ~med in** (*fig*) avoir l'impression d'étouffer, se sentir oppressé(e) or écrasé(e)

he-man ['hiːmæn] (*irreg*) *n* (*inf*) macho *m*

hematology ['hiːmə'tɔlədʒɪ] *n* (*US*) = **haematology**

hemisphere ['hɛmɪsfɪəʳ] *n* hémisphère *m*

hemlock ['hɛmlɔk] *n* cigüe *f*

hemoglobin ['hiːmə'gləubɪn] *n* (*US*) = **haemoglobin**

hemophilia ['hiːmə'fɪlɪə] *n* (*US*) = **haemophilia**

hemorrhage ['hɛmərɪdʒ] *n* (*US*) = **haemorrhage**

hemorrhoids ['hɛmərɔɪdz] *npl* (*US*) = **haemorrhoids**

hemp [hɛmp] *n* chanvre *m*

hen [hɛn] *n* poule *f*; (*female bird*) femelle *f*

hence [hɛns] *adv* (*therefore*) d'où, de là; **2 years ~** d'ici 2 ans

henceforth [hɛns'fɔːθ] *adv* dorénavant

henchman ['hɛntʃmən] (*irreg*) *n* (*pej*) acolyte *m*, séide *m*

henna ['hɛnə] *n* henné *m*

hen night, hen party *n* soirée *f* entre filles (*avant le mariage de l'une d'elles*)

henpecked ['hɛnpɛkt] *adj* dominé par sa femme

hepatitis [hɛpə'taɪtɪs] *n* hépatite *f*

her [həːʳ] *pron* (*direct*) la, l' + *vowel or h mute*; (*indirect*) lui; (*stressed, after prep*) elle ▷ *adj* son (sa), ses *pl*; **I see ~** je la vois; **give ~ a book** donne-lui un livre; **after ~** après elle; *see also* **me; my**

herald ['hɛrəld] *n* héraut *m* ▷ *vt* annoncer

heraldic [hɛ'rældɪk] *adj* héraldique

heraldry ['hɛrəldrɪ] *n* héraldique *f*; (*coat of arms*) blason *m*

herb [həːb] *n* herbe *f*; **herbs** *npl* fines herbes

herbaceous [həː'beɪʃəs] *adj* herbacé(e)

herbal ['həːbl] *adj* à base de plantes

herbal tea *n* tisane *f*

herbicide ['həːbɪsaɪd] *n* herbicide *m*

herd [həːd] *n* troupeau *m*; (*of wild animals, swine*) troupeau, troupe *f* ▷ *vt* (*drive: animals, people*) mener, conduire; (*gather*) rassembler; **~ed together** parqués (comme du bétail)

here [hɪəʳ] *adv* ici; (*time*) alors ▷ *excl* tiens!, tenez!; **~!** (*present*) présent!; **~ is, ~ are** voici; **~'s my sister** voici ma sœur; **~ he/she is** le (la) voici; **~ she comes** la voici qui vient; **come ~!** viens ici!; **~ and there** ici et là

hereabouts ['hɪərə'bauts] *adv* par ici, dans les parages

hereafter [hɪər'aːftəʳ] *adv* après, plus tard; ci-après ▷ *n*: **the ~** l'au-delà *m*

hereby [hɪə'baɪ] *adv* (*in letter*) par la présente

hereditary [hɪ'rɛdɪtrɪ] *adj* héréditaire

heredity [hɪ'rɛdɪtɪ] *n* hérédité *f*

heresy ['hɛrəsɪ] *n* hérésie *f*

heretic ['hɛrətɪk] *n* hérétique *m/f*

heretical [hɪ'rɛtɪkl] *adj* hérétique

herewith [hɪə'wɪð] *adv* avec ceci, ci-joint

heritage ['hɛrɪtɪdʒ] *n* héritage *m*, patrimoine *m*; **our national ~** notre patrimoine national

hermetically [həː'mɛtɪklɪ] *adv* hermétique

hermit ['həːmɪt] *n* ermite *m*

hernia ['həːnɪə] *n* hernie *f*

hero ['hɪərəu] (*pl* **-es**) *n* héros *m*

heroic [hɪ'rəuɪk] *adj* héroïque

heroin ['hɛrəuɪn] *n* héroïne *f* (*drogue*)

heroin addict *n* héroïnomane *m/f*

heroine ['hɛrəuɪn] *n* héroïne *f* (*femme*)
heroism ['hɛrəuɪzəm] *n* héroïsme *m*
heron ['hɛrən] *n* héron *m*
hero worship *n* culte *m* (du héros)
herring ['hɛrɪŋ] *n* hareng *m*
hers [hə:z] *pron* le (la) sien(ne), les siens
(siennes); **a friend of ~** un(e) ami(e) à elle,
un(e) de ses ami(e)s; *see also* **mine¹**
herself [hə:'sɛlf] *pron* (*reflexive*) se; (*emphatic*) elle-
même; (*after prep*) elle; *see also* **oneself**
Herts [hɑ:ts] *abbr* (*Brit*) = **Hertfordshire**
he's [hi:z] = **he is; he has**
hesitant ['hɛzɪtənt] *adj* hésitant(e), indécis(e);
to be ~ about doing sth hésiter à faire qch
hesitate ['hɛzɪteɪt] *vi*: **to ~ (about/to do)**
hésiter (sur/à faire)
hesitation [hɛzɪ'teɪʃən] *n* hésitation *f*; **I have
no ~ in saying (that) ...** je n'hésiterais pas à
dire (que) ...
hessian ['hɛsɪən] *n* (toile *f* de) jute *m*
heterogeneous ['hɛtərə'dʒi:nɪəs] *adj*
hétérogène
heterosexual ['hɛtərəu'sɛksjuəl] *adj, n*
hétérosexuel(le)
het up [hɛt'ʌp] *adj* (*inf*) agité(e), excité(e)
HEW *n abbr* (*US*: = *Department of Health, Education
and Welfare*) *ministère de la santé publique, de
l'enseignement et du bien-être*
hew [hju:] *vt* tailler (*à la hache*)
hex [hɛks] (*US*) *n* sort *m* ▷ *vt* jeter un sort sur
hexagon ['hɛksəgən] *n* hexagone *m*
hexagonal [hɛk'sægənl] *adj* hexagonal(e)
hey [heɪ] *excl* hé!
heyday ['heɪdeɪ] *n*: **the ~ of** l'âge *m* d'or de, les
beaux jours de
HF *n abbr* (= *high frequency*) HF *f*
HGV *n abbr* = **heavy goods vehicle**
HI *abbr* (*US*) = **Hawaii**
hi [haɪ] *excl* salut!; (*to attract attention*) hé!
hiatus [haɪ'eɪtəs] *n* trou *m*, lacune *f*; (*Ling*)
hiatus *m*
hibernate ['haɪbəneɪt] *vi* hiberner
hibernation [haɪbə'neɪʃən] *n* hibernation *f*
hiccough, hiccup ['hɪkʌp] *vi* hoqueter ▷ *n*
hoquet *m*; **to have (the) ~s** avoir le hoquet
hick [hɪk] *n* (*US inf*) plouc *m*, péquenaud(e)
hid [hɪd] *pt of* **hide**
hidden ['hɪdn] *pp of* **hide** ▷ *adj*: **there are no ~
extras** absolument tout est compris dans le
prix; **~ agenda** intentions non déclarées
hide [haɪd] (*pt* **hid**, *pp* **hidden** [hɪd, 'hɪdn]) *n* (*skin*)
peau *f* ▷ *vt* cacher; (*feelings, truth*) dissimuler; **to
~ sth from sb** cacher qch à qn ▷ *vi*: **to ~ (from
sb)** se cacher (de qn)
hide-and-seek ['haɪdən'si:k] *n* cache-cache *m*
hideaway ['haɪdəweɪ] *n* cachette *f*
hideous ['hɪdɪəs] *adj* hideux(-euse), atroce
hide-out ['haɪdaut] *n* cachette *f*
hiding ['haɪdɪŋ] *n* (*beating*) correction *f*, volée *f* de
coups; **to be in ~** (*concealed*) se tenir caché(e)
hiding place *n* cachette *f*
hierarchy ['haɪərɑ:kɪ] *n* hiérarchie *f*

hieroglyphic [haɪərə'glɪfɪk] *adj* hiéroglyphique;
hieroglyphics *npl* hiéroglyphes *mpl*
hi-fi ['haɪfaɪ] *adj, n abbr* (= *high fidelity*) hi-fi *f inv*
higgledy-piggledy ['hɪgldɪ'pɪgldɪ] *adv* pêle-
mêle, dans le plus grand désordre
high [haɪ] *adj* haut(e); (*speed, respect, number*)
grand(e); (*price*) élevé(e); (*wind*) fort(e),
violent(e); (*voice*) aigu(ë); (*inf: person: on drugs*)
défoncé(e), fait(e); (: *on drink*) soûl(e), bourré(e);
(*Brit Culin: meat, game*) faisandé(e); (: *spoilt*)
avarié(e) ▷ *adv* haut, en haut ▷ *n* (*weather*) zone
f de haute pression; **exports have reached a
new ~** les exportations ont atteint un nouveau
record; **20 m ~** haut(e) de 20 m; **to pay a ~ price
for sth** payer cher pour qch; **~ in the air** haut
dans le ciel
highball ['haɪbɔ:l] *n* (*US*) whisky *m* à l'eau avec
des glaçons
highboy ['haɪbɔɪ] *n* (*US*) grande commode
highbrow ['haɪbrau] *adj, n* intellectuel(le)
highchair ['haɪtʃɛəʳ] *n* (*child's*) chaise haute
high-class ['haɪ'klɑ:s] *adj* (*neighbourhood, hotel*)
chic *inv*, de grand standing; (*performance etc*) de
haut niveau
High Court *n* (*Law*) cour *f* suprême; *voir article*

● **HIGH COURT**
●
● Dans le système juridique anglais et gallois,
● la High Court est une cour de droit civil
● chargée des affaires plus importantes et
● complexes que celles traitées par les "county
● courts". En Écosse en revanche, la High Court
● (*of Justiciary*) est la plus haute cour de justice
● à laquelle les affaires les plus graves telles
● que le meurtre et le viol sont soumises et où
● elles sont jugées devant un jury.

higher ['haɪəʳ] *adj* (*form of life, study etc*)
supérieur(e) ▷ *adv* plus haut
higher education *n* études supérieures
highfalutin [haɪfə'lu:tɪn] *adj* (*inf*) affecté(e)
high finance *n* la haute finance
high-flier, high-flyer [haɪ'flaɪəʳ] *n* (*fig:
ambitious*) ambitieux(-euse); (: *gifted*) personne
particulièrement douée et promise à un avenir brillant
high-flying [haɪ'flaɪɪŋ] *adj* (*fig*)
ambitieux(-euse), de haut niveau
high-handed [haɪ'hændɪd] *adj* très autoritaire;
très cavalier(-ière)
high-heeled [haɪ'hi:ld] *adj* à hauts talons
high heels *npl* talons hauts, hauts talons
high jump *n* (*Sport*) saut *m* en hauteur
highlands ['haɪləndz] *npl* région montagneuse;
the H~ (*in Scotland*) les Highlands *mpl*
high-level ['haɪlɛvl] *adj* (*talks etc*) à un haut
niveau; **~ language** (*Comput*) langage évolué
highlight ['haɪlaɪt] *n* (*fig: of event*) point
culminant ▷ *vt* (*emphasize*) faire ressortir,
souligner; **highlights** *npl* (*in hair*) reflets *mpl*
highlighter ['haɪlaɪtəʳ] *n* (*pen*) surligneur
(lumineux)

h

highly ['haɪlɪ] *adv* extrêmement, très; (*unlikely*) fort; (*recommended, skilled, qualified*) hautement; ~ **paid** très bien payé(e); **to speak ~ of** dire beaucoup de bien de

highly strung *adj* nerveux(-euse), toujours tendu(e)

High Mass *n* grand-messe *f*

highness ['haɪnɪs] *n* hauteur *f*; **His/Her H~** son Altesse *f*

high-pitched [haɪ'pɪtʃt] *adj* aigu(ë)

high point *n*: **the ~ (of)** le clou (de), le point culminant (de)

high-powered ['haɪ'pauəd] *adj* (*engine*) performant(e); (*fig: person*) dynamique; (:*job, businessman*) très important(e)

high-pressure ['haɪprɛʃə'] *adj* à haute pression

high-rise ['haɪraɪz] *n* (*also*: **high-rise block, high-rise building**) tour *f* (d'habitation)

high school *n* lycée *m*; (US) établissement *m* d'enseignement supérieur; *voir article*

● **HIGH SCHOOL**

● Une *high school* est un établissement
● d'enseignement secondaire. Aux États-
● Unis, il y a la "Junior High School", qui
● correspond au collège, et la "Senior High
● School", qui correspond au lycée. En Grande-
● Bretagne, c'est un nom que l'on donne
● parfois aux écoles secondaires; voir
● "elementary school".

high season *n* (*Brit*) haute saison

high spirits *npl* pétulance *f*; **to be in ~** être plein(e) d'entrain

high street *n* (*Brit*) grand-rue *f*

high-tech ['haɪ'tɛk] (*inf*) *adj* de pointe

highway ['haɪweɪ] *n* (*Brit*) route *f*; (US) route nationale; **the information ~** l'autoroute *f* de l'information

Highway Code *n* (*Brit*) code *m* de la route

highwayman ['haɪweɪmən] (*irreg*) *n* voleur *m* de grand chemin

hijack ['haɪdʒæk] *vt* détourner (*par la force*) ▷ *n* (*also*: **hijacking**) détournement *m* (d'avion)

hijacker ['haɪdʒækə'] *n* auteur *m* d'un détournement d'avion, pirate *m* de l'air

hike [haɪk] *vi* faire des excursions à pied ▷ *n* excursion *f* à pied, randonnée *f*; (*inf: in prices etc*) augmentation *f* ▷ *vt* (*inf*) augmenter

hiker ['haɪkə'] *n* promeneur(-euse), excursionniste *m/f*

hiking ['haɪkɪŋ] *n* excursions *fpl* à pied, randonnée *f*

hilarious [hɪ'lɛərɪəs] *adj* (*behaviour, event*) désopilant(e)

hilarity [hɪ'lærɪtɪ] *n* hilarité *f*

hill [hɪl] *n* colline *f*; (*fairly high*) montagne *f*; (*on road*) côte *f*

hillbilly ['hɪlbɪlɪ] *n* (US) montagnard(e) du sud des USA; (*pej*) péquenaud *m*

hillock ['hɪlək] *n* petite colline, butte *f*

hillside ['hɪlsaɪd] *n* (*flanc m de*) coteau *m*

hill start *n* (*Aut*) démarrage *m* en côte

hill walking ['hɪl'wɔːkɪŋ] *n* randonnée *f* de basse montagne

hilly ['hɪlɪ] *adj* vallonné(e), montagneux(-euse); (*road*) à fortes côtes

hilt [hɪlt] *n* (*of sword*) garde *f*; **to the ~** (*fig: support*) à fond

him [hɪm] *pron* (*direct*) le, l' + *vowel or h mute*; (*stressed, indirect, after prep*) lui; **I see ~** je le vois; **give ~ a book** donne-lui un livre; **after ~** après lui; *see also* **me**

Himalayas [hɪmə'leɪəz] *npl*: **the ~** l'Himalaya *m*

himself [hɪm'sɛlf] *pron* (*reflexive*) se; (*emphatic*) lui-même; (*after prep*) lui; *see also* **oneself**

hind [haɪnd] *adj* de derrière ▷ *n* biche *f*

hinder ['hɪndə'] *vt* gêner; (*delay*) retarder; (*prevent*): **to ~ sb from doing** empêcher qn de faire

hindquarters ['haɪnd'kwɔːtəz] *npl* (*Zool*) arrière-train *m*

hindrance ['hɪndrəns] *n* gêne *f*, obstacle *m*

hindsight ['haɪndsaɪt] *n* bon sens après coup; **with (the benefit of) ~** avec du recul, rétrospectivement

Hindu ['hɪnduː] *n* Hindou(e)

Hinduism ['hɪnduɪzəm] *n* (*Rel*) hindouisme *m*

hinge [hɪndʒ] *n* charnière *f* ▷ *vi* (*fig*): **to ~ on** dépendre de

hint [hɪnt] *n* allusion *f*; (*advice*) conseil *m*; (*clue*) indication *f* ▷ *vt*: **to ~ that** insinuer que ▷ *vi*: **to ~ at** faire une allusion à; **to drop a ~** faire une allusion *or* insinuation; **give me a ~** (*clue*) mettez-moi sur la voie, donnez-moi une indication

hip [hɪp] *n* hanche *f*; (*Bot*) fruit *m* de l'églantier *or* du rosier

hip flask *n* flacon *m* (pour la poche)

hip hop *n* hip hop *m*

hippie, hippy ['hɪpɪ] *n* hippie *m/f*

hippo ['hɪpəu] (*pl* **-s**) *n* hippopotame *m*

hippopotamus [hɪpə'pɔtəməs] (*pl* **-es** *or* **hippopotami** [hɪpə'pɔtəmɪ]) *n* hippopotame *m*

hippy ['hɪpɪ] *n* = **hippie**

hire ['haɪə'] *vt* (*Brit: car, equipment*) louer; (*worker*) embaucher, engager ▷ *n* location *f*; **for ~** à louer; (*taxi*) libre; **on ~** en location; **I'd like to ~ a car** je voudrais louer une voiture
▶ **hire out** *vt* louer

hire car, hired car ['haɪəd-] *n* (*Brit*) voiture *f* de location

hire purchase *n* (*Brit*) achat *m* (*or* vente *f*) à tempérament *or* crédit; **to buy sth on ~** acheter qch en location-vente

his [hɪz] *pron* le (la) sien(ne), les siens (siennes) ▷ *adj* son (sa), ses *pl*; **this is ~** c'est à lui, c'est le sien; **a friend of ~** un(e) de ses ami(e)s, un(e) ami(e) à lui; *see also* **mine**¹; *see also* **my**

Hispanic [hɪs'pænɪk] *adj* (*in US*) hispano-américain(e) ▷ *n* Hispano-Américain(e)

hiss [hɪs] *vi* siffler ▷ *n* sifflement *m*

histogram ['hɪstəgræm] *n* histogramme *m*

historian [hɪˈstɔːrɪən] *n* historien(ne)
historic [hɪˈstɔrɪk], **historical** [hɪˈstɔrɪkl] *adj*
historique
history [ˈhɪstərɪ] *n* histoire *f*; **medical ~** (*of patient*) passé médical
histrionics [hɪstrɪˈɔnɪks] *n* gestes *mpl*
dramatiques, cinéma *m* (*fig*)
hit [hɪt] *vt* (*pt, pp* **-**) frapper; (*knock against*) cogner;
(*reach: target*) atteindre, toucher; (*collide with: car*)
entrer en collision avec, heurter; (*fig: affect*)
toucher; (*find*) tomber sur ▷ *n* coup *m*; (*success*)
coup réussi; succès *m*; (*song*) chanson *f* à succès,
tube *m*; (*to website*) visite *f*; (*on search engine*)
résultat *m* de recherche; **to ~ it off with sb** bien
s'entendre avec qn; **to ~ the headlines** être à la
une des journaux; **to ~ the road** (*inf*) se mettre
en route
  ▶ **hit back** *vi*: **to ~ back at sb** prendre sa
revanche sur qn
  ▶ **hit on** *vt fus* (*answer*) trouver (par hasard);
(*solution*) tomber sur (par hasard)
  ▶ **hit out at** *vt fus* envoyer un coup à; (*fig*)
attaquer
  ▶ **hit upon** *vt fus* = **hit on**
hit-and-miss [ˈhɪtændˈmɪs] *adj* au petit
bonheur (la chance)
hit-and-run driver [ˈhɪtændˈrʌn-] *n*
chauffard *m*
hitch [hɪtʃ] *vt* (*fasten*) accrocher, attacher; (*also:*
hitch up) remonter d'une saccade ▷ *vi* faire de
l'autostop ▷ *n* (*knot*) nœud *m*; (*difficulty*)
anicroche *f*, contretemps *m*; **to ~ a lift** faire du
stop; **technical ~** incident *m* technique
  ▶ **hitch up** *vt* (*horse, cart*) atteler; *see also* **hitch**
hitch-hike [ˈhɪtʃhaɪk] *vi* faire de l'auto-stop
hitch-hiker [ˈhɪtʃhaɪkə^r] *n* auto-stoppeur(-euse)
hitch-hiking [ˈhɪtʃhaɪkɪŋ] *n* auto-stop *m*, stop *m*
(*inf*)
hi-tech [ˈhaɪtɛk] *adj* de pointe ▷ *n* high-tech *m*
hitherto [hɪðəˈtuː] *adv* jusqu'ici, jusqu'à
présent
hit list *n* liste noire
hitman [ˈhɪtmæn] (*irreg*) *n* (*inf*) tueur *m* à gages
hit-or-miss [ˈhɪtəˈmɪs] *adj* au petit bonheur (la
chance); **it's ~ whether ...** il est loin d'être
certain que ... + *sub*
hit parade *n* hit parade *m*
HIV *n abbr* (= *human immunodeficiency virus*) HIV *m*,
VIH *m*; **~-negative/positive** séronégatif(-ive)/
positif(-ive)
hive [haɪv] *n* ruche *f*; **the shop was a ~ of
activity** (*fig*) le magasin était une véritable
ruche
  ▶ **hive off** *vt* (*inf*) mettre à part, séparer
hl *abbr* (= *hectolitre*) hl
HM *abbr* (= *His (or Her) Majesty*) SM
HMG *abbr* (*Brit*) = **His (or Her) Majesty's
Government**
HMI *n abbr* (*Brit Scol*) = **His (or Her) Majesty's
Inspector**
HMO *n abbr* (*US*: = *health maintenance organization*)
organisme médical assurant un forfait entretien de santé

HMS *abbr* (*Brit*) = **His (or Her) Majesty's Ship**
HMSO *n abbr* (*Brit*: = *His (or Her) Majesty's Stationery
Office*) ≈ Imprimerie nationale
HNC *n abbr* (*Brit*: = *Higher National Certificate*)
≈ DUT *m*
HND *n abbr* (*Brit*: = *Higher National Diploma*)
≈ licence *f* de sciences et techniques
hoard [hɔːd] *n* (*of food*) provisions *fpl*, réserves *fpl*;
(*of money*) trésor *m* ▷ *vt* amasser
hoarding [ˈhɔːdɪŋ] *n* (*Brit*) panneau *m*
d'affichage *or* publicitaire
hoarfrost [ˈhɔːfrɔst] *n* givre *m*
hoarse [hɔːs] *adj* enroué(e)
hoax [həuks] *n* canular *m*
hob [hɔb] *n* plaque chauffante
hobble [ˈhɔbl] *vi* boitiller
hobby [ˈhɔbɪ] *n* passe-temps favori
hobby-horse [ˈhɔbɪhɔːs] *n* cheval *m* à bascule;
(*fig*) dada *m*
hobnob [ˈhɔbnɔb] *vi*: **to ~ with** frayer avec,
fréquenter
hobo [ˈhəubəu] *n* (*US*) vagabond *m*
hock [hɔk] *n* (*Brit: wine*) vin *m* du Rhin; (*of animal:
Culin*) jarret *m*
hockey [ˈhɔkɪ] *n* hockey *m*
hockey stick *n* crosse *f* de hockey
hocus-pocus [ˈhəukəsˈpəukəs] *n* (*trickery*)
supercherie *f*; (*words: of magician*) formules *fpl*
magiques; (: *jargon*) galimatias *m*
hod [hɔd] *n* oiseau *m*, hotte *f*
hodgepodge [ˈhɔdʒpɔdʒ] *n* = **hotchpotch**
hoe [həu] *n* houe *f*, binette *f* ▷ *vt* (*ground*) biner;
(*plants etc*) sarcler
hog [hɔg] *n* porc (châtré) ▷ *vt* (*fig*) accaparer; **to
go the whole ~** aller jusqu'au bout
Hogmanay [hɔgməˈneɪ] *n* réveillon *m* du jour
de l'An, Saint-Sylvestre *f*; *voir article*

● **HOGMANAY**
●
● La Saint-Sylvestre ou "New Year's Eve" se
● nomme *Hogmanay* en Écosse. En cette
● occasion, la famille et les amis se réunissent
● pour entendre sonner les douze coups de
● minuit et pour fêter le "first-footing", une
● coutume qui veut qu'on se rende chez ses
● amis et voisins en apportant quelque chose
● à boire (du whisky en général) et un
● morceau de charbon en gage de prospérité
● pour la nouvelle année.

hogwash [ˈhɔgwɔʃ] *n* (*inf*) foutaises *fpl*
hoist [hɔɪst] *n* palan *m* ▷ *vt* hisser
hoity-toity [ˈhɔɪtɪˈtɔɪtɪ] *adj* (*inf*)
prétentieux(-euse), qui se donne
hold [həuld] (*pt, pp* **held** [hɛld]) *vt* tenir; (*contain*)
contenir; (*meeting*) tenir; (*keep back*) retenir;
(*believe*) maintenir; considérer; (*possess*) avoir;
détenir ▷ *vi* (*withstand pressure*) tenir (bon); (*be
valid*) valoir; (*on telephone*) attendre ▷ *n* prise *f*;
(*find*) influence *f*; (*Naut*) cale *f*; **to catch** *or* **get
(a) ~ of** saisir; **to get ~ of** (*find*) trouver; **to get ~**

of o.s. se contrôler; **~ the line!** (*Tel*) ne quittez pas!; **to ~ one's own** (*fig*) (bien) se défendre; **to ~ office** (*Pol*) avoir un portefeuille; **to ~ firm** or **fast** tenir bon; **he ~s the view that ...** il pense que ..., d'après lui ...; **to ~ sb responsible for sth** tenir qn pour responsable de qch

▶ **hold back** *vt* retenir; (*secret*) cacher; **to ~ sb back from doing sth** empêcher qn de faire qch

▶ **hold down** *vt* (*person*) maintenir à terre; (*job*) occuper

▶ **hold forth** *vi* pérorer

▶ **hold off** *vt* tenir à distance ▷ *vi*: **if the rain ~s off** s'il ne pleut pas, s'il ne se met pas à pleuvoir

▶ **hold on** *vi* tenir bon; (*wait*) attendre; **~ on!** (*Tel*) ne quittez pas!; **to ~ on to sth** (*grasp*) se cramponner à qch; (*keep*) conserver or garder qch

▶ **hold out** *vt* offrir ▷ *vi* (*resist*): **to ~ out (against)** résister (devant), tenir bon (devant)

▶ **hold over** *vt* (*meeting etc*) ajourner, reporter

▶ **hold up** *vt* (*raise*) lever; (*support*) soutenir; (*delay*) retarder; (*: traffic*) ralentir; (*rob*) braquer

holdall ['həʊldɔːl] *n* (*Brit*) fourre-tout *m inv*

holder ['həʊldə'] *n* (*container*) support *m*; (*of ticket, record*) détenteur(-trice); (*of office, title, passport etc*) titulaire *m/f*

holding ['həʊldɪŋ] *n* (*share*) intérêts *mpl*; (*farm*) ferme *f*

holding company *n* holding *m*

hold-up ['həʊldʌp] *n* (*robbery*) hold-up *m*; (*delay*) retard *m*; (*Brit: in traffic*) embouteillage *m*

hole [həʊl] *n* trou *m* ▷ *vt* trouer, faire un trou dans; **~ in the heart** (*Med*) communication *f* interventriculaire; **to pick ~s (in)** (*fig*) chercher des poux (dans)

▶ **hole up** *vi* se terrer

holiday ['hɔlədɪ] *n* (*Brit: vacation*) vacances *fpl*; (*day off*) jour *m* de congé; (*public*) jour férié; **to be on ~** être en vacances; **I'm here on ~** je suis ici en vacances; **tomorrow is a ~** demain c'est fête, on a un congé demain

holiday camp *n* (*Brit: for children*) colonie *f* de vacances; (*also*: **holiday centre**) camp *m* de vacances

holiday home *n* (*rented*) location *f* de vacances; (*owned*) résidence *f* secondaire

holiday job *n* (*Brit*) boulot *m* (*inf*) de vacances

holiday-maker ['hɔlədɪmeɪkə'] *n* (*Brit*) vacancier(-ière)

holiday pay *n* paie *f* des vacances

holiday resort *n* centre *m* de villégiature or de vacances

holiday season *n* période *f* des vacances

holiness ['həʊlɪnɪs] *n* sainteté *f*

holistic [həʊ'lɪstɪk] *adj* holiste, holistique

Holland ['hɔlənd] *n* Hollande *f*

holler ['hɔlə'] *vi* (*inf*) brailler

hollow ['hɔləʊ] *adj* creux(-euse); (*fig*) faux (fausse) ▷ *n* creux *m*; (*in land*) dépression *f* (de terrain), cuvette *f* ▷ *vt*: **to ~ out** creuser, évider

holly ['hɔlɪ] *n* houx *m*

hollyhock ['hɔlɪhɔk] *n* rose trémière

Hollywood ['hɔlɪwʊd] *n* Hollywood

holocaust ['hɔləkɔːst] *n* holocauste *m*

hologram ['hɔləɡræm] *n* hologramme *m*

hols [hɔlz] *npl* (*inf*) vacances *fpl*

holster ['həʊlstə'] *n* étui *m* de revolver

holy ['həʊlɪ] *adj* saint(e); (*bread, water*) bénit(e); (*ground*) sacré(e)

Holy Communion *n* la (sainte) communion

Holy Ghost, Holy Spirit *n* Saint-Esprit *m*

Holy Land *n*: **the ~** la Terre Sainte

holy orders *npl* ordres (majeurs)

homage ['hɔmɪdʒ] *n* hommage *m*; **to pay ~ to** rendre hommage à

home [həʊm] *n* foyer *m*, maison *f*; (*country*) pays natal, patrie *f*; (*institution*) maison ▷ *adj* de famille; (*Econ, Pol*) national(e), intérieur(e); (*Sport: team*) qui reçoit; (*: match, win*) sur leur (or notre) terrain ▷ *adv* chez soi, à la maison; au pays natal; (*right in: nail etc*) à fond; **at ~** chez soi, à la maison; **to go (or come) ~** rentrer (chez soi), rentrer à la maison (or au pays); **I'm going ~ on Tuesday** je rentre mardi; **make yourself at ~** faites comme chez vous; **near my ~** près de chez moi

▶ **home in on** *vt fus* (*missile*) se diriger automatiquement vers or sur

home address *n* domicile permanent

home-brew [həʊm'bruː] *n* vin *m* (or bière *f*) maison

homecoming ['həʊmkʌmɪŋ] *n* retour *m* (au bercail)

home computer *n* ordinateur *m* domestique

Home Counties *npl* les comtés autour de Londres

home economics *n* économie *f* domestique

home ground *n*: **to be on ~** être sur son terrain

home-grown ['həʊmɡrəʊn] *adj* (*not foreign*) du pays; (*from garden*) du jardin

home help *n* (*Brit*) aide-ménagère *f*

homeland ['həʊmlænd] *n* patrie *f*

homeless ['həʊmlɪs] *adj* sans foyer, sans abri; **the homeless** *npl* les sans-abri *mpl*

home loan *n* prêt *m* sur hypothèque

homely ['həʊmlɪ] *adj* (*plain*) simple, sans prétention; (*welcoming*) accueillant(e)

home-made [həʊm'meɪd] *adj* fait(e) à la maison

home match *n* match *m* à domicile

Home Office *n* (*Brit*) ministère *m* de l'Intérieur

homeopathy *etc* [həʊmɪ'ɔpəθɪ] (*US*) = **homoeopathy** *etc*

home owner ['həʊməʊnə'] *n* propriétaire occupant

home page *n* (*Comput*) page *f* d'accueil

home rule *n* autonomie *f*

Home Secretary *n* (*Brit*) ministre *m* de l'Intérieur

homesick ['həʊmsɪk] *adj*: **to be ~** avoir le mal du pays; (*missing one's family*) s'ennuyer de sa famille

homestead ['həʊmstɛd] *n* propriété *f*; (*farm*) ferme *f*

home town *n* ville natale

home truth *n*: **to tell sb a few ~s** dire ses quatre vérités à qn

homeward ['həumwəd] *adj* (*journey*) du retour
▷ *adv* = **homewards**
homewards ['həumwədz] *adv* vers la maison
homework ['həumwə:k] *n* devoirs *mpl*
homicidal [hɔmɪ'saɪdl] *adj* homicide
homicide ['hɔmɪsaɪd] *n* (*US*) homicide *m*
homily ['hɔmɪlɪ] *n* homélie *f*
homing ['həumɪŋ] *adj* (*device, missile*) à tête
chercheuse; ~ **pigeon** pigeon voyageur
homoeopath ['həumɪəupæθ], (*US*) **homeopath**
n homéopathe *m/f*
homoeopathic, (*US*) **homeopathic**
[həumɪə'pæθɪk] *adj* (*medicine*) homéopathique;
(*doctor*) homéopathe
homoeopathy, (*US*) **homeopathy**
[həumɪ'ɔpəθɪ] *n* homéopathie *f*
homogeneous [hɔməu'dʒi:nɪəs] *adj* homogène
homogenize [hə'mɔdʒənaɪz] *vt* homogénéiser
homosexual [hɔməu'sɛksjuəl] *adj, n*
homosexuel(le)
Hon. *abbr* (= *honourable, honorary*) *dans un titre*
Honduras [hɔn'djuərəs] *n* Honduras *m*
hone [həun] *n* pierre *f* à aiguiser ▷ *vt* affûter,
aiguiser
honest ['ɔnɪst] *adj* honnête; (*sincere*) franc
(franche); **to be quite ~ with you ...** à dire
vrai ...
honestly ['ɔnɪstlɪ] *adv* honnêtement;
franchement
honesty ['ɔnɪstɪ] *n* honnêteté *f*
honey ['hʌnɪ] *n* miel *m*; (*inf: darling*) chéri(e)
honeycomb ['hʌnɪkəum] *n* rayon *m* de miel;
(*pattern*) nid *m* d'abeilles, motif alvéolé ▷ *vt* (*fig*):
to ~ with cribler de
honeymoon ['hʌnɪmu:n] *n* lune *f* de miel,
voyage *m* de noces; **we're on ~** nous sommes en
voyage de noces
honeysuckle ['hʌnɪsʌkl] *n* chèvrefeuille *m*
Hong Kong ['hɔŋ'kɔŋ] *n* Hong Kong
honk [hɔŋk] *n* (*Aut*) coup *m* de klaxon ▷ *vi*
klaxonner
Honolulu [hɔnə'lu:lu:] *n* Honolulu
honorary ['ɔnərərɪ] *adj* honoraire; (*duty, title*)
honorifique; ~ **degree** diplôme *m* honoris
causa
honour, (*US*) **honor** ['ɔnə'] *vt* honorer ▷ *n*
honneur *m*; **in ~ of** en l'honneur de; **to
graduate with ~s** obtenir sa licence avec
mention
honourable, (*US*) **honorable** ['ɔnərəbl] *adj*
honorable
honour-bound, (*US*) **honor-bound** ['ɔnə'baund]
adj: **to be ~ to do** se devoir de faire
honours degree ['ɔnəz-] *n* (*Scol*) ≈ licence *f* avec
mention; *voir article*

● **HONOURS DEGREE**
●
● Un *honours degree* est un diplôme
● universitaire que l'on reçoit après trois
● années d'études en Angleterre et quatre
● années en Écosse. Les mentions qui

● l'accompagnent sont, par ordre décroissant:
● "first class" (très bien/bien), "upper second
● class" (assez bien), "lower second class"
● (passable), et "third class" (diplôme sans
● mention). Le titulaire d'un *honours degree* a
● un titre qu'il peut mettre à la suite de son
● nom, par exemple: Peter Jones BA Hons; voir
● "ordinary degree".

honours list *n* (*Brit*): *voir article*

● **HONOURS LIST**
●
● L' *honours list* est la liste des citoyens du
● Royaume-Uni et du Commonwealth
● auxquels le souverain confère un titre ou
● une décoration. Cette liste est préparée par
● le Premier ministre et paraît deux fois par
● an, au Nouvel An et lors de l'anniversaire
● officiel du règne du souverain. Des
● personnes qui se sont distinguées dans le
● monde des affaires, des sports et des médias,
● ainsi que dans les forces armées, mais
● également des citoyens "ordinaires" qui se
● consacrent à des œuvres de charité sont
● ainsi récompensées.

Hons. *abbr* (*Scol*) = **honours degree**
hood [hud] *n* capuchon *m*; (*of cooker*) hotte *f*; (*Brit
Aut*) capote *f*; (*US Aut*) capot *m*; (*inf*) truand *m*
hoodie ['hudɪ] *n* (*top*) sweat *m* à capuche; (*youth*)
jeune *m* à capuche
hoodlum ['hu:dləm] *n* truand *m*
hoodwink ['hudwɪŋk] *vt* tromper
hoof (*pl* **-s** *or* **hooves**) [hu:f, hu:vz] *n* sabot *m*
hook [huk] *n* crochet *m*; (*on dress*) agrafe *f*; (*for
fishing*) hameçon *m* ▷ *vt* accrocher; (*dress*)
agrafer; **off the ~** (*Tel*) décroché; **~ and eye**
agrafe; **by ~ or by crook** de gré ou de force,
coûte que coûte; **to be ~ed (on)** (*inf*) être
accroché(e) (par); (*person*) être dingue (de)
▶ **hook up** *vt* (*Radio, TV etc*) faire un duplex entre
hooligan ['hu:lɪgən] *n* voyou *m*
hoop [hu:p] *n* cerceau *m*; (*of barrel*) cercle *m*
hoot [hu:t] *vi* (*Brit: Aut*) klaxonner; (*siren*) mugir;
(*owl*) hululer ▷ *vt* (*jeer at*) huer ▷ *n* huée *f*; coup
m de klaxon; mugissement *m*; hululement *m*;
to ~ with laughter rire aux éclats
hooter ['hu:tə'] *n* (*Brit Aut*) klaxon *m*; (*Naut,
factory*) sirène *f*
Hoover® ['hu:və'] *n* (*Brit*) aspirateur *m* ▷ *vt*: **to
hoover** (*room*) passer l'aspirateur dans; (*carpet*)
passer l'aspirateur sur
hooves [hu:vz] *npl of* **hoof**
hop [hɔp] *vi* sauter; (*on one foot*) sauter à cloche-
pied; (*bird*) sautiller ▷ *n* saut *m*
hope [həup] *vt, vi* espérer ▷ *n* espoir *m*; **I ~ so** je
l'espère; **I ~ not** j'espère que non
hopeful ['həupful] *adj* (*person*) plein(e) d'espoir;
(*situation*) prometteur(-euse), encourageant(e);
I'm ~ that she'll manage to come j'ai bon
espoir qu'elle pourra venir

621

hopefully ['həupfulɪ] *adv* (*expectantly*) avec espoir, avec optimisme; (*one hopes*) avec un peu de chance; **~, they'll come back** espérons bien qu'ils reviendront

hopeless ['həuplɪs] *adj* désespéré(e), sans espoir; (*useless*) nul(le)

hopelessly ['həuplɪslɪ] *adv* (*live etc*) sans espoir; **~ confused** *etc* complètement désorienté *etc*

hops [hɔps] *npl* houblon *m*

horizon [hə'raɪzn] *n* horizon *m*

horizontal [hɔrɪ'zɔntl] *adj* horizontal(e)

hormone ['hɔːməun] *n* hormone *f*

hormone replacement therapy *n* hormonothérapie substitutive, traitement hormono-supplétif

horn [hɔːn] *n* corne *f*; (*Mus*) cor *m*; (*Aut*) klaxon *m*

horned [hɔːnd] *adj* (*animal*) à cornes

hornet ['hɔːnɪt] *n* frelon *m*

horny ['hɔːnɪ] *adj* corné(e); (*hands*) calleux(-euse); (*inf: aroused*) excité(e)

horoscope ['hɔrəskəup] *n* horoscope *m*

horrendous [hə'rɛndəs] *adj* horrible, affreux(-euse)

horrible ['hɔrɪbl] *adj* horrible, affreux(-euse)

horrid ['hɔrɪd] *adj* (*person*) détestable; (*weather, place, smell*) épouvantable

horrific [hɔ'rɪfɪk] *adj* horrible

horrify ['hɔrɪfaɪ] *vt* horrifier

horrifying ['hɔrɪfaɪɪŋ] *adj* horrifiant(e)

horror ['hɔrə'] *n* horreur *f*

horror film *n* film *m* d'épouvante

horror-struck ['hɔrəstrʌk], **horror-stricken** ['hɔrəstrɪkn] *adj* horrifié(e)

hors d'œuvre [ɔː'də:vrə] *n* hors d'œuvre *m*

horse [hɔːs] *n* cheval *m*

horseback ['hɔːsbæk]: **on ~** (*adj, adv*) à cheval

horsebox ['hɔːsbɔks] *n* van *m*

horse chestnut *n* (*nut*) marron *m* (d'Inde); (*tree*) marronnier *m* (d'Inde)

horse-drawn ['hɔːsdrɔːn] *adj* tiré(e) par des chevaux

horsefly ['hɔːsflaɪ] *n* taon *m*

horseman ['hɔːsmən] (*irreg*) *n* cavalier *m*

horsemanship ['hɔːsmənʃɪp] *n* talents *mpl* de cavalier

horseplay ['hɔːspleɪ] *n* chahut *m* (*blagues etc*)

horsepower ['hɔːspauə'] *n* puissance *f* (en chevaux); (*unit*) cheval-vapeur *m* (CV)

horse-racing ['hɔːsreɪsɪŋ] *n* courses *fpl* de chevaux

horseradish ['hɔːsrædɪʃ] *n* raifort *m*

horse riding *n* (*Brit*) équitation *f*

horseshoe ['hɔːsʃuː] *n* fer *m* à cheval

horse show *n* concours *m* hippique

horse-trading ['hɔːstreɪdɪŋ] *n* maquignonnage *m*

horse trials *npl* = **horse show**

horsewhip ['hɔːswɪp] *vt* cravacher

horsewoman ['hɔːswumən] (*irreg*) *n* cavalière *f*

horsey ['hɔːsɪ] *adj* féru(e) d'équitation *or* de cheval; (*appearance*) chevalin(e)

horticulture ['hɔːtɪkʌltʃə'] *n* horticulture *f*

hose [həuz] *n* (*also*: **hosepipe**) tuyau *m*; (*also*: **garden hose**) tuyau d'arrosage
  ▸ **hose down** *vt* laver au jet

hosepipe ['həuzpaɪp] *n* tuyau *m*; (*in garden*) tuyau d'arrosage; (*for fire*) tuyau d'incendie

hosiery ['həuzɪərɪ] *n* (rayon *m* des) bas *mpl*

hospice ['hɔspɪs] *n* hospice *m*

hospitable ['hɔspɪtəbl] *adj* hospitalier(-ière)

hospital ['hɔspɪtl] *n* hôpital *m*; **in ~**, (US) **in the ~** à l'hôpital; **where's the nearest ~?** où est l'hôpital le plus proche?

hospitality [hɔspɪ'tælɪtɪ] *n* hospitalité *f*

hospitalize ['hɔspɪtəlaɪz] *vt* hospitaliser

host [həust] *n* hôte *m*; (*in hotel etc*) patron *m*; (*TV, Radio*) présentateur(-trice), animateur(-trice); (*large number*): **a ~ of** une foule de; (*Rel*) hostie *f*
  ▸ *vt* (*TV programme*) présenter, animer

hostage ['hɔstɪdʒ] *n* otage *m*

host country *n* pays *m* d'accueil, pays-hôte *m*

hostel ['hɔstl] *n* foyer *m*; (*also*: **youth hostel**) auberge *f* de jeunesse

hostelling ['hɔstlɪŋ] *n*: **to go (youth) ~** faire une virée *or* randonnée en séjournant dans des auberges de jeunesse

hostess ['həustɪs] *n* hôtesse *f*; (*Brit: also*: **air hostess**) hôtesse de l'air; (*TV, Radio*) animatrice *f*; (*in nightclub*) entraîneuse *f*

hostile ['hɔstaɪl] *adj* hostile

hostility [hɔ'stɪlɪtɪ] *n* hostilité *f*

hot [hɔt] *adj* chaud(e); (*as opposed to only warm*) très chaud; (*spicy*) fort(e); (*fig: contest*) acharné(e); (*topic*) brûlant(e); (*temper*) violent(e), passionné(e); **to be ~** (*person*) avoir chaud; (*thing*) être (très) chaud; (*weather*) faire chaud
  ▸ **hot up** (*Brit inf*) *vi* (*situation*) devenir tendu(e); (*party*) s'animer ▸ *vt* (*pace*) accélérer, forcer; (*engine*) gonfler

hot-air balloon [hɔt'ɛə-] *n* montgolfière *f*, ballon *m*

hotbed ['hɔtbɛd] *n* (*fig*) foyer *m*, pépinière *f*

hotchpotch ['hɔtʃpɔtʃ] *n* (*Brit*) mélange *m* hétéroclite

hot dog *n* hot-dog *m*

hotel [həu'tɛl] *n* hôtel *m*

hotelier [həu'tɛlɪə'] *n* hôtelier(-ière)

hotel industry *n* industrie hôtelière

hotel room *n* chambre *f* d'hôtel

hot flush *n* (*Brit*) bouffée *f* de chaleur

hotfoot ['hɔtfut] *adv* à toute vitesse

hothead ['hɔthɛd] *n* (*fig*) tête brûlée

hotheaded [hɔt'hɛdɪd] *adj* impétueux(-euse)

hothouse ['hɔthaus] *n* serre chaude

hotline ['hɔtlaɪn] *n* (*Pol*) téléphone *m* rouge, ligne directe

hotly ['hɔtlɪ] *adv* passionnément, violemment

hotplate ['hɔtpleɪt] *n* (*on cooker*) plaque chauffante

hotpot ['hɔtpɔt] *n* (*Brit Culin*) ragoût *m*

hot potato *n* (*Brit inf*) sujet brûlant; **to drop sb/ sth like a ~** laisser tomber qn/qch brusquement

hot seat *n* (*fig*) poste chaud

hotspot ['hɔtspɔt] *n* (*Comput: also:* **wireless hotspot**) borne *f* wifi, hotspot *m*

hot spot *n* point chaud

hot spring *n* source thermale

hot-tempered ['hɔt'tɛmpəd] *adj* emporté(e)

hot-water bottle ['hɔt'wɔːtə-] *n* bouillotte *f*

hot-wire ['hɔtwaɪəʳ] *vt* (*inf: car*) démarrer en faisant se toucher les fils de contact

hound [haund] *vt* poursuivre avec acharnement ▷ *n* chien courant; **the ~s** la meute

hour ['auəʳ] *n* heure *f*; **at 30 miles an ~** ≈ à 50 km à l'heure; **lunch ~** heure du déjeuner; **to pay sb by the ~** payer qn à l'heure

hourly ['auəlɪ] *adj* toutes les heures; (*rate*) horaire; **~ paid** *adj* payé(e) à l'heure

house *n* [haus] (*pl* **-s** ['hauzɪz]) maison *f*; (*Pol*) chambre *f*; (*Theat*) salle *f*; auditoire *m* ▷ *vt* [hauz] (*person*) loger, héberger; **at** (*or* **to**) **my ~** chez moi; **the H~ of Commons/of Lords** (*Brit*) la Chambre des communes/des lords; *voir article*; **the H~ (of Representatives)** (*US*) la Chambre des représentants; *voir article*; **on the ~** (*fig*) aux frais de la maison

● HOUSE OF COMMONS/OF LORDS

Le parlement en Grande-Bretagne est constitué de deux assemblées: la *House of Commons*, présidée par le "Speaker" et composée de plus de 600 députés (les "MP") élus au suffrage universel direct. Ceux-ci reçoivent tous un salaire. La Chambre des communes siège environ 175 jours par an. La *House of Lords*, présidée par le "Lord Chancellor" est composée de lords dont le titre est attribué par le souverain à vie; elle peut amender certains projets de loi votés par la *House of Commons*, mais elle n'est pas habilitée à débattre des projets de lois de finances. La *House of Lords* fait également office de juridiction suprême en Angleterre et au pays de Galles.

● HOUSE OF REPRESENTATIVES

Aux États-Unis, le parlement, appelé le "Congress", est constitué du "Senate" et de la *House of Representatives*. Cette dernière comprend 435 membres, le nombre de ces représentants par État étant proportionnel à la densité de population de cet État. Ils sont élus pour deux ans au suffrage universel direct et siègent au "Capitol", à Washington D.C.

house arrest *n* assignation *f* à domicile

houseboat ['hausbəut] *n* bateau (aménagé en habitation)

housebound ['hausbaund] *adj* confiné(e) chez soi

housebreaking ['hausbreɪkɪŋ] *n* cambriolage *m* (avec effraction)

house-broken ['hausbrəukn] *adj* (*US*) = **house-trained**

housecoat ['hauskəut] *n* peignoir *m*

household ['haushəuld] *n* (*Admin etc*) ménage *m*; (*people*) famille *f*, maisonnée *f*; **~ name** nom connu de tout le monde

householder ['haushəuldəʳ] *n* propriétaire *m/f*; (*head of house*) chef *m* de famille

househunting ['haushʌntɪŋ] *n*: **to go ~** se mettre en quête d'une maison (*or* d'un appartement)

housekeeper ['hauskiːpəʳ] *n* gouvernante *f*

housekeeping ['hauskiːpɪŋ] *n* (*work*) ménage *m*; (*also:* **housekeeping money**) argent *m* du ménage; (*Comput*) gestion *f* (des disques)

houseman ['hausmən] (*irreg*) *n* (*Brit Med*) ≈ interne *m*

house-owner ['hausəunəʳ] *n* propriétaire *m/f* (*de maison ou d'appartement*)

house-proud ['hauspraud] *adj* qui tient à avoir une maison impeccable

house-to-house ['haustə'haus] *adj* (*enquiries etc*) chez tous les habitants (du quartier *etc*)

house-train ['haustreɪn] *vt* (*pet*) apprendre à être propre à

house-trained ['haustreɪnd] *adj* (*pet*) propre

house-warming ['hauswɔːmɪŋ] *n* (*also:* **house-warming party**) pendaison *f* de crémaillère

housewife ['hauswaɪf] (*irreg*) *n* ménagère *f*; femme *f* au foyer

house wine *n* cuvée *f* maison *or* du patron

housework ['hauswəːk] *n* (travaux *mpl* du) ménage *m*

housing ['hauzɪŋ] *n* logement *m* ▷ *cpd* (*problem, shortage*) de *or* du logement

housing association *n* fondation *f* charitable fournissant des logements

housing benefit *n* (*Brit*) ≈ allocations *fpl* logement

housing development, (*Brit*) **housing estate** *n* (*blocks of flats*) cité *f*; (*houses*) lotissement *m*

hovel ['hɔvl] *n* taudis *m*

hover ['hɔvəʳ] *vi* planer; **to ~ round sb** rôder *or* tourner autour de qn

hovercraft ['hɔvəkrɑːft] *n* aéroglisseur *m*, hovercraft *m*

hoverport ['hɔvəpɔːt] *n* hoverport *m*

how [hau] *adv* comment; **~ are you?** comment allez-vous?; **~ do you do?** bonjour; (*on being introduced*) enchanté(e); **~ far is it to ...?** combien y a-t-il jusqu'à ...?; **~ long have you been here?** depuis combien de temps êtes-vous là?; **~ lovely/awful!** que *or* comme c'est joli/affreux!; **~ many/much?** combien?; **~ much does it cost?** ça coûte combien?; **~ old are you?** quel âge avez-vous?; **~ tall is he?** combien mesure-t-il?; **~ is school?** ça va à l'école?; **~ was the film?** comment était le film?; **~'s life?** (*inf*) comment ça va?; **~ about a drink?** si on buvait quelque chose?; **~ is it that ...?** comment se fait-il que ... + *sub*?

however [hau'ɛvəʳ] *conj* pourtant, cependant ▷ *adv* de quelque façon *or* manière que + *sub*; (+ *adjective*) quelque *or* si ... que + *sub*; (*in questions*) comment; **~ I do it** de quelque manière que je m'y prenne; **~ cold it is** même s'il fait très froid; **~ did you do it?** comment y êtes-vous donc arrivé?

howitzer ['hauɪtsəʳ] *n* (*Mil*) obusier *m*

howl [haul] *n* hurlement *m* ▷ *vi* hurler; (*wind*) mugir

howler ['haulǝʳ] *n* gaffe *f*, bourde *f*

howling ['haulɪŋ] *adj*: **a ~ wind** *or* **gale** un vent à décorner les bœufs

H.P. *n abbr* (*Brit*) = **hire purchase**

h.p. *abbr* (*Aut*) = **horsepower**

HQ *n abbr* (= *headquarters*) QG *m*

HR *n abbr* (*US*) = **House of Representatives**

hr *abbr* (= *hour*) h

HRH *abbr* (= *His* (*or Her*) *Royal Highness*) SAR

hrs *abbr* (= *hours*) h

HRT *n abbr* = **hormone replacement therapy**

HS *abbr* (*US*) = **high school**

HST *abbr* (*US*: = *Hawaiian Standard Time*) heure de Hawaii

HTML *n abbr* (= *hypertext markup language*) HTML *m*

hub [hʌb] *n* (*of wheel*) moyeu *m*; (*fig*) centre *m*, foyer *m*

hubbub ['hʌbʌb] *n* brouhaha *m*

hubcap [hʌbkæp] *n* (*Aut*) enjoliveur *m*

HUD *n abbr* (*US*: = *Department of Housing and Urban Development*) ministère de l'urbanisme et du logement

huddle ['hʌdl] *vi*: **to ~ together** se blottir les uns contre les autres

hue [hju:] *n* teinte *f*, nuance *f*; **~ and cry** *n* tollé (général), clameur *f*

huff [hʌf] *n*: **in a ~** fâché(e); **to take the ~** prendre la mouche

huffy ['hʌfɪ] *adj* (*inf*) froissé(e)

hug [hʌg] *vt* serrer dans ses bras; (*shore, kerb*) serrer ▷ *n* étreinte *f*; **to give sb a ~** serrer qn dans ses bras

huge [hju:dʒ] *adj* énorme, immense

hulk [hʌlk] *n* (*ship*) vieux rafiot; (*car, building*) carcasse *f*; (*person*) mastodonte *m*, malabar *m*

hulking ['hʌlkɪŋ] *adj* balourd(e)

hull [hʌl] *n* (*of ship*) coque *f*; (*of nuts*) coque *f*; (*of peas*) cosse *f*

hullabaloo ['hʌləbə'lu:] *n* (*inf: noise*) tapage *m*, raffut *m*

hullo [hə'ləu] *excl* = **hello**

hum [hʌm] *vt* (*tune*) fredonner ▷ *vi* fredonner; (*insect*) bourdonner; (*plane, tool*) vrombir ▷ *n* fredonnement *m*; bourdonnement *m*; vrombissement *m*

human ['hju:mən] *adj* humain(e) ▷ *n* (*also:* **human being**) être humain

humane [hju:'meɪn] *adj* humain(e), humanitaire

humanism ['hju:mənɪzəm] *n* humanisme *m*

humanitarian [hju:mænɪ'tɛərɪən] *adj* humanitaire

humanity [hju:'mænɪtɪ] *n* humanité *f*

humanly ['hju:mənlɪ] *adv* humainement

humanoid ['hju:mənɔɪd] *adj, n* humanoïde *m/f*

human rights *npl* droits *mpl* de l'homme

humble ['hʌmbl] *adj* humble, modeste ▷ *vt* humilier

humbly ['hʌmblɪ] *adv* humblement, modestement

humbug ['hʌmbʌg] *n* fumisterie *f*; (*Brit: sweet*) bonbon *m* à la menthe

humdrum ['hʌmdrʌm] *adj* monotone, routinier(-ière)

humid ['hju:mɪd] *adj* humide

humidifier [hju:'mɪdɪfaɪəʳ] *n* humidificateur *m*

humidity [hju:'mɪdɪtɪ] *n* humidité *f*

humiliate [hju:'mɪlɪeɪt] *vt* humilier

humiliating [hju:'mɪlɪeɪtɪŋ] *adj* humiliant(e)

humiliation [hju:mɪlɪ'eɪʃən] *n* humiliation *f*

humility [hju:'mɪlɪtɪ] *n* humilité *f*

hummus ['huməs] *n* houm(m)ous *m*

humorist ['hju:mərɪst] *n* humoriste *m/f*

humorous ['hju:mərəs] *adj* humoristique; (*person*) plein(e) d'humour

humour, (*US*) **humor** ['hju:məʳ] *n* humour *m*; (*mood*) humeur *f* ▷ *vt* (*person*) faire plaisir à; se prêter aux caprices de; **sense of ~** sens *m* de l'humour; **to be in a good/bad ~** être de bonne/mauvaise humeur

humourless, (*US*) **humorless** ['hu:məlɪs] *adj* dépourvu(e) d'humour

hump [hʌmp] *n* bosse *f*

humpback ['hʌmpbæk] *n* bossu(e); (*Brit: also:* **humpback bridge**) dos-d'âne *m*

humus ['hju:məs] *n* humus *m*

hunch [hʌntʃ] *n* bosse *f*; (*premonition*) intuition *f*; **I have a ~ that** j'ai (comme une vague) idée que

hunchback ['hʌntʃbæk] *n* bossu(e)

hunched [hʌntʃt] *adj* arrondi(e), voûté(e)

hundred ['hʌndrəd] *num* cent; **about a ~ people** une centaine de personnes; **~s of** des centaines de; **I'm a ~ per cent sure** j'en suis absolument certain

hundredth [-ɪdθ] *num* centième

hundredweight ['hʌndrɪdweɪt] *n* (*Brit*) = 50.8 kg; 112 lb; (*US*) = 45.3 kg; 100 lb

hung [hʌŋ] *pt, pp of* **hang**

Hungarian [hʌŋ'gɛərɪən] *adj* hongrois(e) ▷ *n* Hongrois(e); (*Ling*) hongrois *m*

Hungary ['hʌŋgərɪ] *n* Hongrie *f*

hunger ['hʌŋgəʳ] *n* faim *f* ▷ *vi*: **to ~ for** avoir faim de, désirer ardemment

hunger strike *n* grève *f* de la faim

hungover [hʌŋ'əuvəʳ] *adj* (*inf*): **to be ~** avoir la gueule de bois

hungrily ['hʌŋgrəlɪ] *adv* voracement; (*fig*) avidement

hungry ['hʌŋgrɪ] *adj* affamé(e); **to be ~** avoir faim; **~ for** (*fig*) avide de

hung up *adj* (*inf*) complexé(e), bourré(e) de complexes

hunk [hʌŋk] n gros morceau; (inf: man) beau mec

hunt [hʌnt] vt (seek) chercher; (criminal) pourchasser; (Sport) chasser ▷ vi (search): **to ~ for** chercher (partout); (Sport) chasser ▷ n (Sport) chasse f
▶ **hunt down** vt pourchasser

hunter [ˈhʌntəʳ] n chasseur m; (Brit: horse) cheval m de chasse

hunting [ˈhʌntɪŋ] n chasse f

hurdle [ˈhəːdl] n (for fences) claie f; (Sport) haie f; (fig) obstacle m

hurl [həːl] vt lancer (avec violence); (abuse, insults) lancer

hurling [ˈhəːlɪŋ] n (Sport) genre de hockey joué en Irlande

hurly-burly [ˈhəːlɪˈbəːlɪ] n tohu-bohu m inv; brouhaha m

hurrah, hurray [huˈrɑː, huˈreɪ] excl hourra!

hurricane [ˈhʌrɪkən] n ouragan m

hurried [ˈhʌrɪd] adj pressé(e), précipité(e); (work) fait(e) à la hâte

hurriedly [ˈhʌrɪdlɪ] adv précipitamment, à la hâte

hurry [ˈhʌrɪ] n hâte f, précipitation f ▷ vi se presser, se dépêcher ▷ vt (person) faire presser, faire se dépêcher; (work) presser; **to be in a ~** être pressé(e); **to do sth in a ~** faire qch en vitesse; **to ~ in/out** entrer/sortir précipitamment; **to ~ home** se dépêcher de rentrer
▶ **hurry along** vi marcher d'un pas pressé
▶ **hurry away, hurry off** vi partir précipitamment
▶ **hurry up** vi se dépêcher

hurt [həːt] (pt, pp **-**) vt (cause pain to) faire mal à; (injure, fig) blesser; (damage: business, interests etc) nuire à; faire du tort à ▷ vi faire mal ▷ adj blessé(e); **my arm ~s** j'ai mal au bras; **I ~ my arm** je me suis fait mal au bras; **to ~ o.s.** se faire mal; **where does it ~?** où avez-vous mal?, où est-ce que ça vous fait mal?

hurtful [ˈhəːtful] adj (remark) blessant(e)

hurtle [ˈhəːtl] vt lancer (de toutes ses forces) ▷ vi: **to ~ past** passer en trombe; **to ~ down** dégringoler

husband [ˈhʌzbənd] n mari m

hush [hʌʃ] n calme m, silence m ▷ vt faire taire; **~!** chut!
▶ **hush up** vt (fact) étouffer

hush-hush [hʌʃˈhʌʃ] adj (inf) ultra-secret(-ète)

husk [hʌsk] n (of wheat) balle f; (of rice, maize) enveloppe f; (of peas) cosse f

husky [ˈhʌskɪ] adj (voice) rauque; (burly) costaud(e) ▷ n chien m esquimau or de traîneau

hustings [ˈhʌstɪŋz] npl (Brit Pol) plate-forme électorale

hustle [ˈhʌsl] vt pousser, bousculer ▷ n bousculade f; **~ and bustle** n tourbillon m (d'activité)

hut [hʌt] n hutte f; (shed) cabane f

hutch [hʌtʃ] n clapier m

hyacinth [ˈhaɪəsɪnθ] n jacinthe f

hybrid [ˈhaɪbrɪd] adj, n hybride (m)

hydrant [ˈhaɪdrənt] n prise f d'eau; (also: **fire hydrant**) bouche f d'incendie

hydraulic [haɪˈdrɔːlɪk] adj hydraulique

hydraulics [haɪˈdrɔːlɪks] n hydraulique f

hydrochloric [ˈhaɪdrəuˈklɔrɪk] adj: **~ acid** acide m chlorhydrique

hydroelectric [ˈhaɪdrəuɪˈlɛktrɪk] adj hydro-électrique

hydrofoil [ˈhaɪdrəfɔɪl] n hydrofoil m

hydrogen [ˈhaɪdrədʒən] n hydrogène m

hydrogen bomb n bombe f à hydrogène

hydrophobia [ˈhaɪdrəˈfəubɪə] n hydrophobie f

hydroplane [ˈhaɪdrəpleɪn] n (seaplane) hydravion m; (jetfoil) hydroglisseur m

hyena [haɪˈiːnə] n hyène f

hygiene [ˈhaɪdʒiːn] n hygiène f

hygienic [haɪˈdʒiːnɪk] adj hygiénique

hymn [hɪm] n hymne m; cantique m

hype [haɪp] n (inf) matraquage m publicitaire or médiatique

hyperactive [ˈhaɪpərˈæktɪv] adj hyperactif(-ive)

hyperlink [ˈhaɪpəlɪŋk] n hyperlien m

hypermarket [ˈhaɪpəmɑːkɪt] (Brit) n hypermarché m

hypertension [ˈhaɪpəˈtɛnʃən] n (Med) hypertension f

hypertext [ˈhaɪpətɛkst] n (Comput) hypertexte m

hyphen [ˈhaɪfn] n trait m d'union

hypnosis [hɪpˈnəusɪs] n hypnose f

hypnotic [hɪpˈnɔtɪk] adj hypnotique

hypnotism [ˈhɪpnətɪzəm] n hypnotisme m

hypnotist [ˈhɪpnətɪst] n hypnotiseur(-euse)

hypnotize [ˈhɪpnətaɪz] vt hypnotiser

hypoallergenic [ˈhaɪpəuæləˈdʒɛnɪk] adj hypoallergénique

hypochondriac [haɪpəˈkɔndriæk] n hypocondriaque m/f

hypocrisy [hɪˈpɔkrɪsɪ] n hypocrisie f

hypocrite [ˈhɪpəkrɪt] n hypocrite m/f

hypocritical [hɪpəˈkrɪtɪkl] adj hypocrite

hypodermic [haɪpəˈdəːmɪk] adj hypodermique ▷ n (syringe) seringue f hypodermique

hypotenuse [haɪˈpɔtɪnjuːz] n hypoténuse f

hypothermia [haɪpəˈθəːmɪə] n hypothermie f

hypothesis (pl **hypotheses**) [haɪˈpɔθɪsɪs, -siːz] n hypothèse f

hysterectomy [hɪstəˈrɛktəmɪ] n hystérectomie f

hysteria [hɪˈstɪərɪə] n hystérie f

hysterical [hɪˈstɛrɪkl] adj hystérique; (funny) hilarant(e); **to become ~** avoir une crise de nerfs

hysterics [hɪˈstɛrɪks] npl (violente) crise de nerfs; (laughter) crise de rire; **to be in/have ~** (anger, panic) avoir une crise de nerfs; (laughter) attraper un fou rire

Hz abbr (= hertz) Hz

I i

I¹, i [aɪ] *n* (*letter*) I, i *m*; **I for Isaac,** (US) **I for Item** I comme Irma

I² [aɪ] *pron* je; (*before vowel*) j'; (*stressed*) moi ▷ *abbr* (= *island, isle*) I

IA, Ia. *abbr* (US) = **Iowa**

IAEA *n abbr* = **International Atomic Energy Agency**

IBA *n abbr* (Brit: = *Independent Broadcasting Authority*) ≈ CNCL *f* (= *Commission nationale de la communication audio-visuelle*)

Iberian [aɪˈbɪərɪən] *adj* ibérique, ibérien(ne)

Iberian Peninsula *n*: **the ~** la péninsule Ibérique

IBEW *n abbr* (US: = *International Brotherhood of Electrical Workers*) syndicat international des électriciens

i/c *abbr* (Brit) = **in charge**

ICBM *n abbr* (= *intercontinental ballistic missile*) ICBM *m*, engin *m* balistique à portée intercontinentale

ICC *n abbr* (= *International Chamber of Commerce*) CCI *f*; (US) = **Interstate Commerce Commission**

ice [aɪs] *n* glace *f*; (*on road*) verglas *m* ▷ *vt* (*cake*) glacer; (*drink*) faire rafraîchir ▷ *vi* (*also*: **ice over**) geler; (*also*: **ice up**) se givrer; **to put sth on ~** (*fig*) mettre qch en attente

Ice Age *n* ère *f* glaciaire

ice axe, (US) **ice ax** *n* piolet *m*

iceberg [ˈaɪsbəːg] *n* iceberg *m*; **the tip of the ~** (*also fig*) la partie émergée de l'iceberg

icebox [ˈaɪsbɒks] *n* (US) réfrigérateur *m*; (Brit) compartiment *m* à glace; (*insulated box*) glacière *f*

icebreaker [ˈaɪsbreɪkəʳ] *n* brise-glace *m*

ice bucket *n* seau *m* à glace

ice-cap [ˈaɪskæp] *n* calotte *f* glaciaire

ice-cold [aɪsˈkəuld] *adj* glacé(e)

ice cream *n* glace *f*

ice cube *n* glaçon *m*

iced [aɪst] *adj* (*drink*) frappé(e); (*coffee, tea, also cake*) glacé(e)

ice hockey *n* hockey *m* sur glace

Iceland [ˈaɪslənd] *n* Islande *f*

Icelander [ˈaɪsləndəʳ] *n* Islandais(e)

Icelandic [aɪsˈlændɪk] *adj* islandais(e) ▷ *n* (Ling) islandais *m*

ice lolly *n* (Brit) esquimau *m*

ice pick *n* pic *m* à glace

ice rink *n* patinoire *f*

ice-skate [ˈaɪsskeɪt] *n* patin *m* à glace ▷ *vi* faire du patin à glace

ice skating [ˈaɪsskeɪtɪŋ] *n* patinage *m* (sur glace)

icicle [ˈaɪsɪkl] *n* glaçon *m* (*naturel*)

icing [ˈaɪsɪŋ] *n* (*Aviat etc*) givrage *m*; (*Culin*) glaçage *m*

icing sugar *n* (Brit) sucre *m* glace

ICJ *n abbr* = **International Court of Justice**

icon [ˈaɪkɒn] *n* icône *f*

ICR *n abbr* (US) = **Institute for Cancer Research**

ICRC *n abbr* (= *International Committee of the Red Cross*) CICR *m*

ICT *n abbr* (Brit: Scol: = *information and communications technology*) TIC *fpl*

ICU *n abbr* = **intensive care unit**

icy [ˈaɪsɪ] *adj* glacé(e); (*road*) verglacé(e); (*weather, temperature*) glacial(e)

ID *abbr* (US) = **Idaho**

I'd [aɪd] = **I would**; **I had**

Ida. *abbr* (US) = **Idaho**

ID card *n* carte *f* d'identité

IDD *n abbr* (Brit Tel: = *international direct dialling*) automatique international

idea [aɪˈdɪə] *n* idée *f*; **good ~!** bonne idée!; **to have an ~ that ...** avoir idée que ...; **I have no ~** je n'ai pas la moindre idée

ideal [aɪˈdɪəl] *n* idéal *m* ▷ *adj* idéal(e)

idealist [aɪˈdɪəlɪst] *n* idéaliste *m/f*

ideally [aɪˈdɪəlɪ] *adv* (*preferably*) dans l'idéal; (*perfectly*): **he is ~ suited to the job** il est parfait pour ce poste; **~ the book should have ...** l'idéal serait que le livre ait ...

identical [aɪˈdɛntɪkl] *adj* identique

identification [aɪdɛntɪfɪˈkeɪʃən] *n* identification *f*; **means of ~** pièce *f* d'identité

identify [aɪˈdɛntɪfaɪ] *vt* identifier ▷ *vi*: **to ~ with** s'identifier à

Identikit® [aɪˈdɛntɪkɪt] *n*: **~ (picture)** portrait-robot *m*

identity [aɪˈdɛntɪtɪ] *n* identité *f*

identity card *n* carte *f* d'identité

identity parade *n* (Brit) parade *f* d'identification

identity theft *n* usurpation *f* d'identité

ideological [aɪdɪə'lɒdʒɪkl] *adj* idéologique
ideology [aɪdɪ'ɔlədʒɪ] *n* idéologie *f*
idiocy ['ɪdɪəsɪ] *n* idiotie *f*, stupidité *f*
idiom ['ɪdɪəm] *n* (*language*) langue *f*, idiome *m*;
(*phrase*) expression *f* idiomatique; (*style*) style *m*
idiomatic [ɪdɪə'mætɪk] *adj* idiomatique
idiosyncrasy [ɪdɪəu'sɪŋkrəsɪ] *n* particularité *f*,
caractéristique *f*
idiot ['ɪdɪət] *n* idiot(e), imbécile *m/f*
idiotic [ɪdɪ'ɔtɪk] *adj* idiot(e), bête, stupide
idle ['aɪdl] *adj* (*doing nothing*) sans occupation,
désœuvré(e); (*lazy*) oisif(-ive), paresseux(-euse);
(*unemployed*) au chômage; (*machinery*) au repos;
(*question, pleasures*) vain(e), futile ▷ *vi* (*engine*)
tourner au ralenti; **to lie ~** être arrêté, ne pas
fonctionner
  ▶ **idle away** *vt*: **to ~ away one's time** passer son
  temps à ne rien faire
idleness ['aɪdlnɪs] *n* désœuvrement *m*; oisiveté *f*
idler ['aɪdlə'] *n* désœuvré(e), oisif(-ive)
idle time *n* (*Comm*) temps mort
idol ['aɪdl] *n* idole *f*
idolize ['aɪdəlaɪz] *vt* idolâtrer, adorer
idyllic [ɪ'dɪlɪk] *adj* idyllique
i.e. *abbr* (= *id est: that is*) c. à d., c'est-à-dire
if [ɪf] *conj* si ▷ *n*: **there are a lot of ifs and buts**
il y a beaucoup de si *mpl* et de mais *mpl*; **I'd be
pleased if you could do it** je serais très
heureux si vous pouviez le faire; **if necessary** si
nécessaire, le cas échéant; **if so** si c'est le cas; **if
not** sinon; **if only I could!** si seulement je
pouvais!; **if only he were here** si seulement il
était là; **if only to show him my gratitude** ne
serait-ce que pour lui témoigner ma gratitude;
see also **as; even**
iffy ['ɪfɪ] *adj* (*inf*) douteux(-euse)
igloo ['ɪgluː] *n* igloo *m*
ignite [ɪg'naɪt] *vt* mettre le feu à, enflammer
▷ *vi* s'enflammer
ignition [ɪg'nɪʃən] *n* (*Aut*) allumage *m*; **to
switch on/off the ~** mettre/couper le contact
ignition key *n* (*Aut*) clé *f* de contact
ignoble [ɪg'nəubl] *adj* ignoble, indigne
ignominious [ɪgnə'mɪnɪəs] *adj* honteux(-euse),
ignominieux(-euse)
ignoramus [ɪgnə'reɪməs] *n* personne *f* ignare
ignorance ['ɪgnərəns] *n* ignorance *f*; **to keep sb
in ~ of sth** tenir qn dans l'ignorance de qch
ignorant ['ɪgnərənt] *adj* ignorant(e); **to be ~ of**
(*subject*) ne rien connaître en; (*events*) ne pas être
au courant de
ignore [ɪg'nɔː'] *vt* ne tenir aucun compte de;
(*mistake*) ne pas relever; (*person: pretend to not see*)
faire semblant de ne pas reconnaître; (: *pay no
attention to*) ignorer
ikon ['aɪkɔn] *n* = **icon**
IL *abbr* (*US*) = **Illinois**
ill [ɪl] *adj* (*sick*) malade; (*bad*) mauvais(e) ▷ *n* mal
m ▷ *adv*: **to speak/think ~ of sb** dire/penser du
mal de qn; **to be taken ~** tomber malade
Ill. *abbr* (*US*) = **Illinois**
I'll [aɪl] = **I will; I shall**

ill-advised [ɪləd'vaɪzd] *adj* (*decision*) peu
judicieux(-euse); (*person*) malavisé(e)
ill-at-ease [ɪlət'iːz] *adj* mal à l'aise
ill-considered [ɪlkən'sɪdəd] *adj* (*plan*)
inconsidéré(e), irréfléchi(e)
ill-disposed [ɪldɪs'pəuzd] *adj*: **to be ~ towards
sb/sth** être mal disposé(e) envers qn/qch
illegal [ɪ'liːgl] *adj* illégal(e)
illegally [ɪ'liːgəlɪ] *adv* illégalement
illegible [ɪ'lɛdʒɪbl] *adj* illisible
illegitimate [ɪlɪ'dʒɪtɪmət] *adj* illégitime
ill-fated [ɪl'feɪtɪd] *adj* malheureux(-euse); (*day*)
néfaste
ill-favoured, (*US*) **ill-favored** [ɪl'feɪvəd] *adj*
déplaisant(e)
ill feeling *n* ressentiment *m*, rancune *f*
ill-gotten ['ɪlgɔtn] *adj* (*gains etc*) mal acquis(e)
ill health *n* mauvaise santé
illicit [ɪ'lɪsɪt] *adj* illicite
ill-informed [ɪlɪn'fɔːmd] *adj* (*judgment*) erroné(e);
(*person*) mal renseigné(e)
illiterate [ɪ'lɪtərət] *adj* illettré(e); (*letter*) plein(e)
de fautes
ill-mannered [ɪl'mænəd] *adj* impoli(e),
grossier(-ière)
illness ['ɪlnɪs] *n* maladie *f*
illogical [ɪ'lɔdʒɪkl] *adj* illogique
ill-suited [ɪl'suːtɪd] *adj* (*couple*) mal assorti(e); **he
is ~ to the job** il n'est pas vraiment fait pour ce
travail
ill-timed [ɪl'taɪmd] *adj* inopportun(e)
ill-treat [ɪl'triːt] *vt* maltraiter
ill-treatment [ɪl'triːtmənt] *n* mauvais
traitement
illuminate [ɪ'luːmɪneɪt] *vt* (*room, street*) éclairer;
(*for special effect*) illuminer; **~d sign** enseigne
lumineuse
illuminating [ɪ'luːmɪneɪtɪŋ] *adj* éclairant(e)
illumination [ɪluːmɪ'neɪʃən] *n* éclairage *m*;
illumination *f*
illusion [ɪ'luːʒən] *n* illusion *f*; **to be under the ~
that** avoir l'illusion que
illusive [ɪ'luːsɪv], **illusory** [ɪ'luːsərɪ] *adj* illusoire
illustrate ['ɪləstreɪt] *vt* illustrer
illustration [ɪlə'streɪʃən] *n* illustration *f*
illustrator ['ɪləstreɪtə'] *n* illustrateur(-trice)
illustrious [ɪ'lʌstrɪəs] *adj* illustre
ill will *n* malveillance *f*
ILO *n abbr* (= *International Labour Organization*) OIT *f*
ILWU *n abbr* (*US*: = *International Longshoremen's and
Warehousemen's Union*) syndicat international des
dockers et des magasiniers
IM *n abbr* (= *instant message*) messagerie *f* instantée
▷ *vt* envoyer un message instantané à
I'm [aɪm] = **I am**
image ['ɪmɪdʒ] *n* image *f*; (*public face*) image de
marque
imagery ['ɪmɪdʒərɪ] *n* images *fpl*
imaginable [ɪ'mædʒɪnəbl] *adj* imaginable
imaginary [ɪ'mædʒɪnərɪ] *adj* imaginaire
imagination [ɪmædʒɪ'neɪʃən] *n* imagination *f*
imaginative [ɪ'mædʒɪnətɪv] *adj*

imaginatif(-ive); (*person*) plein(e)
d'imagination
imagine [ɪ'mædʒɪn] *vt* s'imaginer; (*suppose*)
imaginer, supposer
imbalance [ɪm'bæləns] *n* déséquilibre *m*
imbecile ['ɪmbəsi:l] *n* imbécile *m/f*
imbue [ɪm'bju:] *vt*: **to ~ sth with** imprégner qch
de
IMF *n abbr* = **International Monetary Fund**
imitate ['ɪmɪteɪt] *vt* imiter
imitation [ɪmɪ'teɪʃən] *n* imitation *f*
imitator ['ɪmɪteɪtəʳ] *n* imitateur(-trice)
immaculate [ɪ'mækjulət] *adj* impeccable; (*Rel*)
immaculé(e)
immaterial [ɪmə'tɪərɪəl] *adj* sans importance,
insignifiant(e)
immature [ɪmə'tjuəʳ] *adj* (*fruit*) qui n'est pas
mûr(e); (*person*) qui manque de maturité
immaturity [ɪmə'tjuərɪtɪ] *n* immaturité *f*
immeasurable [ɪ'mɛʒrəbl] *adj*
incommensurable
immediacy [ɪ'mi:dɪəsɪ] *n* (*of events etc*) caractère
or rapport immédiat; (*of needs*) urgence *f*
immediate [ɪ'mi:dɪət] *adj* immédiat(e)
immediately [ɪ'mi:dɪətlɪ] *adv* (*at once*)
immédiatement; **~ next to** juste à côté de
immense [ɪ'mɛns] *adj* immense, énorme
immensity [ɪ'mɛnsɪtɪ] *n* immensité *f*
immerse [ɪ'mə:s] *vt* immerger, plonger; **to ~
sth in** plonger qch dans; **to be ~d in** (*fig*) être
plongé dans
immersion heater [ɪ'mə:ʃən-] *n* (*Brit*) chauffe-
eau *m* électrique
immigrant ['ɪmɪgrənt] *n* immigrant(e); (*already
established*) immigré(e)
immigration [ɪmɪ'greɪʃən] *n* immigration *f*
immigration authorities *npl* service *m* de
l'immigration
immigration laws *npl* lois *fpl* sur l'immigration
imminent ['ɪmɪnənt] *adj* imminent(e)
immobile [ɪ'məubaɪl] *adj* immobile
immobilize [ɪ'məubɪlaɪz] *vt* immobiliser
immoderate [ɪ'mɔdərət] *adj* immodéré(e),
démesuré(e)
immodest [ɪ'mɔdɪst] *adj* (*indecent*) indécent(e);
(*boasting*) pas modeste, présomptueux(-euse)
immoral [ɪ'mɔrl] *adj* immoral(e)
immorality [ɪmɔ'rælɪtɪ] *n* immoralité *f*
immortal [ɪ'mɔ:tl] *adj, n* immortel(le)
immortalize [ɪ'mɔ:tlaɪz] *vt* immortaliser
immovable [ɪ'mu:vəbl] *adj* (*object*) fixe;
immobilier(-ière); (*person*) inflexible; (*opinion*)
immuable
immune [ɪ'mju:n] *adj*: **~ (to)** immunisé(e)
(contre)
immune system *n* système *m* immunitaire
immunity [ɪ'mju:nɪtɪ] *n* immunité *f*;
diplomatic ~ immunité diplomatique
immunization [ɪmjunaɪ'zeɪʃən] *n*
immunisation *f*
immunize ['ɪmjunaɪz] *vt* immuniser
imp [ɪmp] *n* (*small devil*) lutin *m*; (*child*) petit

diable
impact ['ɪmpækt] *n* choc *m*, impact *m*; (*fig*)
impact
impair [ɪm'pɛəʳ] *vt* détériorer, diminuer
impaired [ɪm'pɛəd] *adj* (*organ, vision*) abimé(e),
détérioré(e); **his memory/circulation is ~** il a
des problèmes de mémoire/circulation;
visually ~ malvoyant(e); **hearing ~**
malentendant(e); **mentally/physically ~**
intellectuellement/physiquement diminué(e)
impale [ɪm'peɪl] *vt* empaler
impart [ɪm'pɑ:t] *vt* (*make known*) communiquer,
transmettre; (*bestow*) confier, donner
impartial [ɪm'pɑ:ʃl] *adj* impartial(e)
impartiality [ɪmpɑ:ʃɪ'ælɪtɪ] *n* impartialité *f*
impassable [ɪm'pɑ:səbl] *adj* infranchissable;
(*road*) impraticable
impasse [æm'pɑ:s] *n* (*fig*) impasse *f*
impassioned [ɪm'pæʃənd] *adj* passionné(e)
impassive [ɪm'pæsɪv] *adj* impassible
impatience [ɪm'peɪʃəns] *n* impatience *f*
impatient [ɪm'peɪʃənt] *adj* impatient(e); **to get**
or **grow ~** s'impatienter
impatiently [ɪm'peɪʃəntlɪ] *adv* avec impatience
impeach [ɪm'pi:tʃ] *vt* accuser, attaquer; (*public
official*) mettre en accusation
impeachment [ɪm'pi:tʃmənt] *n* (*Law*) (mise *f*
en) accusation *f*
impeccable [ɪm'pɛkəbl] *adj* impeccable,
parfait(e)
impecunious [ɪmpɪ'kju:nɪəs] *adj* sans
ressources
impede [ɪm'pi:d] *vt* gêner
impediment [ɪm'pɛdɪmənt] *n* obstacle *m*; (*also:*
speech impediment) défaut *m* d'élocution
impel [ɪm'pɛl] *vt* (*force*): **to ~ sb (to do sth)**
forcer qn (à faire qch)
impending [ɪm'pɛndɪŋ] *adj* imminent(e)
impenetrable [ɪm'pɛnɪtrəbl] *adj* impénétrable
imperative [ɪm'pɛrətɪv] *adj* nécessaire; (*need*)
urgent(e), pressant(e); (*tone*) impérieux(-euse)
▷ *n* (*Ling*) impératif *m*
imperceptible [ɪmpə'sɛptɪbl] *adj* imperceptible
imperfect [ɪm'pə:fɪkt] *adj* imparfait(e); (*goods
etc*) défectueux(-euse) ▷ *n* (*Ling: also:* **imperfect
tense**) imparfait *m*
imperfection [ɪmpə'fɛkʃən] *n* imperfection *f*;
défectuosité *f*
imperial [ɪm'pɪərɪəl] *adj* impérial(e); (*Brit:
measure*) légal(e)
imperialism [ɪm'pɪərɪəlɪzəm] *n* impérialisme *m*
imperil [ɪm'pɛrɪl] *vt* mettre en péril
imperious [ɪm'pɪərɪəs] *adj* impérieux(-euse)
impersonal [ɪm'pə:sənl] *adj* impersonnel(le)
impersonate [ɪm'pə:səneɪt] *vt* se faire passer
pour; (*Theat*) imiter
impersonation [ɪmpə:sə'neɪʃən] *n* (*Law*)
usurpation *f* d'identité; (*Theat*) imitation *f*
impersonator [ɪm'pə:səneɪtəʳ] *n* imposteur *m*;
(*Theat*) imitateur(-trice)
impertinence [ɪm'pə:tɪnəns] *n* impertinence *f*,
insolence *f*

impertinent [ɪm'pəːtɪnənt] *adj* impertinent(e), insolent(e)

imperturbable [ɪmpə'təːbəbl] *adj* imperturbable

impervious [ɪm'pəːvɪəs] *adj* imperméable; (*fig*): ~ **to** insensible à; inaccessible à

impetuous [ɪm'pɛtjuəs] *adj* impétueux(-euse), fougueux(-euse)

impetus ['ɪmpətəs] *n* impulsion *f*; (*of runner*) élan *m*

impinge [ɪm'pɪndʒ]: **to ~ on** *vt fus* (*person*) affecter, toucher; (*rights*) empiéter sur

impish ['ɪmpɪʃ] *adj* espiègle

implacable [ɪm'plækəbl] *adj* implacable

implant [ɪm'plɑːnt] *vt* (*Med*) implanter; (*fig: idea, principle*) inculquer

implausible [ɪm'plɔːzɪbl] *adj* peu plausible

implement *n* ['ɪmplɪmənt] outil *m*, instrument *m*; (*for cooking*) ustensile *m* ▷ *vt* ['ɪmplɪmənt] exécuter, mettre à effet

implicate ['ɪmplɪkeɪt] *vt* impliquer, compromettre

implication [ɪmplɪ'keɪʃən] *n* implication *f*; **by ~** indirectement

implicit [ɪm'plɪsɪt] *adj* implicite; (*complete*) absolu(e), sans réserve

implicitly [ɪm'plɪsɪtlɪ] *adv* implicitement; absolument, sans réserve

implore [ɪm'plɔː'] *vt* implorer, supplier

imply [ɪm'plaɪ] *vt* (*hint*) suggérer, laisser entendre; (*mean*) indiquer, supposer

impolite [ɪmpə'laɪt] *adj* impoli(e)

imponderable [ɪm'pɔndərəbl] *adj* impondérable

import *vt* [ɪm'pɔːt] importer ▷ *n* ['ɪmpɔːt] (*Comm*) importation *f*; (*meaning*) portée *f*, signification *f* ▷ *cpd* ['ɪmpɔːt] (*duty, licence etc*) d'importation

importance [ɪm'pɔːtns] *n* importance *f*; **to be of great/little ~** avoir beaucoup/peu d'importance

important [ɪm'pɔːtnt] *adj* important(e); **it is ~ that** il importe que, il est important que; **it's not ~** c'est sans importance, ce n'est pas important

importantly [ɪm'pɔːtntlɪ] *adv* (*with an air of importance*) d'un air important; (*essentially*): **but, more ~ ...** mais, (ce qui est) plus important encore ...

importation [ɪmpɔː'teɪʃən] *n* importation *f*

imported [ɪm'pɔːtɪd] *adj* importé(e), d'importation

importer [ɪm'pɔːtə'] *n* importateur(-trice)

impose [ɪm'pəuz] *vt* imposer ▷ *vi*: **to ~ on sb** abuser de la gentillesse de qn

imposing [ɪm'pəuzɪŋ] *adj* imposant(e), impressionnant(e)

imposition [ɪmpə'zɪʃən] *n* (*of tax etc*) imposition *f*; **to be an ~ on** (*person*) abuser de la gentillesse *ou* la bonté de

impossibility [ɪmpɔsə'bɪlɪtɪ] *n* impossibilité *f*

impossible [ɪm'pɔsɪbl] *adj* impossible; **it is ~**

for me to leave il m'est impossible de partir

impostor [ɪm'pɔstə'] *n* imposteur *m*

impotence ['ɪmpətns] *n* impuissance *f*

impotent ['ɪmpətnt] *adj* impuissant(e)

impound [ɪm'paund] *vt* confisquer, saisir

impoverished [ɪm'pɔvərɪʃt] *adj* pauvre, appauvri(e)

impracticable [ɪm'præktɪkəbl] *adj* impraticable

impractical [ɪm'præktɪkl] *adj* pas pratique; (*person*) qui manque d'esprit pratique

imprecise [ɪmprɪ'saɪs] *adj* imprécis(e)

impregnable [ɪm'prɛgnəbl] *adj* (*fortress*) imprenable; (*fig*) inattaquable, irréfutable

impregnate ['ɪmprɛgneɪt] *vt* imprégner; (*fertilize*) féconder

impresario [ɪmprɪ'sɑːrɪəu] *n* impresario *m*

impress [ɪm'prɛs] *vt* impressionner, faire impression sur; (*mark*) imprimer, marquer; **to ~ sth on sb** faire bien comprendre qch à qn

impressed [ɪm'prɛst] *adj* impressionné(e)

impression [ɪm'prɛʃən] *n* impression *f*; (*of stamp, seal*) empreinte *f*; (*imitation*) imitation *f*; **to make a good/bad ~ on sb** faire bonne/mauvaise impression sur qn; **to be under the ~ that** avoir l'impression que

impressionable [ɪm'prɛʃnəbl] *adj* impressionnable, sensible

impressionist [ɪm'prɛʃənɪst] *n* impressionniste *m/f*

impressive [ɪm'prɛsɪv] *adj* impressionnant(e)

imprint ['ɪmprɪnt] *n* empreinte *f*; (*Publishing*) notice *f*; (: *label*) nom *m* (de collection or d'éditeur)

imprinted [ɪm'prɪntɪd] *adj*: **~ on** imprimé(e) sur; (*fig*) imprimé(e) *or* gravé(e) dans

imprison [ɪm'prɪzn] *vt* emprisonner, mettre en prison

imprisonment [ɪm'prɪznmənt] *n* emprisonnement *m*; (*period*): **to sentence sb to 10 years' ~** condamner qn à 10 ans de prison

improbable [ɪm'prɔbəbl] *adj* improbable; (*excuse*) peu plausible

impromptu [ɪm'prɔmptjuː] *adj* impromptu(e) ▷ *adv* impromptu

improper [ɪm'prɔpə'] *adj* (*wrong*) incorrect(e); (*unsuitable*) déplacé(e), de mauvais goût; (*indecent*) indécent(e); (*dishonest*) malhonnête

impropriety [ɪmprə'praɪətɪ] *n* inconvenance *f*; (*of expression*) impropriété *f*

improve [ɪm'pruːv] *vt* améliorer ▷ *vi* s'améliorer; (*pupil etc*) faire des progrès
  ▶ **improve on, improve upon** *vt fus* (*offer*) enchérir sur

improvement [ɪm'pruːvmənt] *n* amélioration *f*; (*of pupil etc*) progrès *m*; **to make ~s to** apporter des améliorations à

improvisation [ɪmprəvaɪ'zeɪʃən] *n* improvisation *f*

improvise ['ɪmprəvaɪz] *vt, vi* improviser

imprudence [ɪm'pruːdns] *n* imprudence *f*

imprudent [ɪm'pruːdnt] *adj* imprudent(e)

impudent ['ɪmpjudnt] *adj* impudent(e)

impugn [ɪmˈpjuːn] *vt* contester, attaquer
impulse [ˈɪmpʌls] *n* impulsion *f*; **on ~**
impulsivement, sur un coup de tête
impulse buy *n* achat *m* d'impulsion
impulsive [ɪmˈpʌlsɪv] *adj* impulsif(-ive)
impunity [ɪmˈpjuːnɪtɪ] *n*: **with ~** impunément
impure [ɪmˈpjuəʳ] *adj* impur(e)
impurity [ɪmˈpjuərɪtɪ] *n* impureté *f*
IN *abbr* (US) = **Indiana**

 KEYWORD

in [ɪn] *prep* **1** (*indicating place, position*) dans; **in the house/the fridge** dans la maison/le frigo; **in the garden** dans le *or* au jardin; **in town** en ville; **in the country** à la campagne; **in school** à l'école; **in here/there** ici/là
2 (*with place names: of town, region, country*): **in London** à Londres; **in England** en Angleterre; **in Japan** au Japon; **in the United States** aux États-Unis
3 (*indicating time: during*): **in spring** au printemps; **in summer** en été; **in May/2005** en mai/2005; **in the afternoon** (dans) l'après-midi; **at 4 o'clock in the afternoon** à 4 heures de l'après-midi
4 (*indicating time: in the space of*) en; (: *future*) dans; **I did it in 3 hours/days** je l'ai fait en 3 heures/jours; **I'll see you in 2 weeks** *or* **in 2 weeks' time** je te verrai dans 2 semaines; **once in a hundred years** une fois tous les cent ans
5 (*indicating manner etc*) à; **in a loud/soft voice** à voix haute/basse; **in pencil** au crayon; **in writing** par écrit; **in French** en français; **to pay in dollars** payer en dollars; **the boy in the blue shirt** le garçon à *or* avec la chemise bleue
6 (*indicating circumstances*): **in the sun** au soleil; **in the shade** à l'ombre; **in the rain** sous la pluie; **a change in policy** un changement de politique
7 (*indicating mood, state*): **in tears** en larmes; **in anger** sous le coup de la colère; **in despair** au désespoir; **in good condition** en bon état; **to live in luxury** vivre dans le luxe
8 (*with ratios, numbers*): **1 in 10 households, 1 household in 10** 1 ménage sur 10; **20 pence in the pound** 20 pence par livre sterling; **they lined up in twos** ils se mirent en rangs (deux) par deux; **in hundreds** par centaines
9 (*referring to people, works*) chez; **the disease is common in children** c'est une maladie courante chez les enfants; **in (the works of) Dickens** chez Dickens, dans (l'œuvre de) Dickens
10 (*indicating profession etc*) dans; **to be in teaching** être dans l'enseignement
11 (*after superlative*) de; **the best pupil in the class** le meilleur élève de la classe
12 (*with present participle*): **in saying this** en disant ceci
▷ *adv*: **to be in** (*person: at home, work*) être là; (*train, ship, plane*) être arrivé(e); (*in fashion*) être à

la mode; **to ask sb in** inviter qn à entrer; **to run/limp** *etc* **in** entrer en courant/boitant *etc*; **their party is in** leur parti est au pouvoir
▷ *n*: **the ins and outs (of)** (*of proposal, situation etc*) les tenants et aboutissants (de)

in. *abbr* = **inch; inches**
inability [ɪnəˈbɪlɪtɪ] *n* incapacité *f*; **~ to pay** incapacité de payer
inaccessible [ɪnəkˈsɛsɪbl] *adj* inaccessible
inaccuracy [ɪnˈækjurəsɪ] *n* inexactitude *f*; manque *m* de précision
inaccurate [ɪnˈækjurət] *adj* inexact(e); (*person*) qui manque de précision
inaction [ɪnˈækʃən] *n* inaction *f*, inactivité *f*
inactivity [ɪnækˈtɪvɪtɪ] *n* inactivité *f*
inadequacy [ɪnˈædɪkwəsɪ] *n* insuffisance *f*
inadequate [ɪnˈædɪkwət] *adj* insuffisant(e), inadéquat(e)
inadmissible [ɪnədˈmɪsəbl] *adj* (*behaviour*) inadmissible; (*Law: evidence*) irrecevable
inadvertent [ɪnədˈvəːtnt] *adj* (*mistake*) commis(e) par inadvertance
inadvertently [ɪnədˈvəːtntlɪ] *adv* par mégarde
inadvisable [ɪnədˈvaɪzəbl] *adj* à déconseiller; **it is ~ to** il est déconseillé de
inane [ɪˈneɪn] *adj* inepte, stupide
inanimate [ɪnˈænɪmət] *adj* inanimé(e)
inapplicable [ɪnˈæplɪkəbl] *adj* inapplicable
inappropriate [ɪnəˈprəuprɪət] *adj* inopportun(e), mal à propos; (*word, expression*) impropre
inapt [ɪnˈæpt] *adj* inapte; peu approprié(e)
inaptitude [ɪnˈæptɪtjuːd] *n* inaptitude *f*
inarticulate [ɪnɑːˈtɪkjulət] *adj* (*person*) qui s'exprime mal; (*speech*) indistinct(e)
inasmuch [ɪnəzˈmʌtʃ] *adv*: **~ as** vu que, en ce sens que
inattention [ɪnəˈtɛnʃən] *n* manque *m* d'attention
inattentive [ɪnəˈtɛntɪv] *adj* inattentif(-ive), distrait(e); négligent(e)
inaudible [ɪnˈɔːdɪbl] *adj* inaudible
inaugural [ɪˈnɔːgjurəl] *adj* inaugural(e)
inaugurate [ɪˈnɔːgjureɪt] *vt* inaugurer; (*president, official*) investir de ses fonctions
inauguration [ɪnɔːgjuˈreɪʃən] *n* inauguration *f*; investiture *f*
inauspicious [ɪnɔːsˈpɪʃəs] *adj* peu propice
in-between [ɪnbɪˈtwiːn] *adj* entre les deux
inborn [ɪnˈbɔːn] *adj* (*feeling*) inné(e); (*defect*) congénital(e)
inbred [ɪnˈbrɛd] *adj* inné(e), naturel(le); (*family*) consanguin(e)
inbreeding [ɪnˈbriːdɪŋ] *n* croisement *m* d'animaux de même souche; unions consanguines
Inc. *abbr* = **incorporated**
Inca [ˈɪŋkə] *adj* (*also*: **Incan**) inca *inv* ▷ *n* Inca *m/f*
incalculable [ɪnˈkælkjulǝbl] *adj* incalculable
incapability [ɪnkeɪpəˈbɪlɪtɪ] *n* incapacité *f*
incapable [ɪnˈkeɪpəbl] *adj*: **~ (of)** incapable (de)

incapacitate [ɪnkə'pæsɪteɪt] vt: **to ~ sb from doing** rendre qn incapable de faire

incapacitated [ɪnkə'pæsɪteɪtɪd] adj (Law) frappé(e) d'incapacité

incapacity [ɪnkə'pæsɪtɪ] n incapacité f

incarcerate [ɪn'kɑ:səreɪt] vt incarcérer

incarnate adj [ɪn'kɑ:nɪt] incarné(e) ▷ vt ['ɪnkɑ:neɪt] incarner

incarnation [ɪnkɑ:'neɪʃən] n incarnation f

incendiary [ɪn'sɛndɪərɪ] adj incendiaire ▷ n (bomb) bombe f incendiaire

incense n ['ɪnsɛns] encens m ▷ vt [ɪn'sɛns] (anger) mettre en colère

incense burner n encensoir m

incentive [ɪn'sɛntɪv] n encouragement m, raison f de se donner de la peine

incentive scheme n système m de primes d'encouragement

inception [ɪn'sɛpʃən] n commencement m, début m

incessant [ɪn'sɛsnt] adj incessant(e)

incessantly [ɪn'sɛsntlɪ] adv sans cesse, constamment

incest ['ɪnsɛst] n inceste m

inch [ɪntʃ] n pouce m (=25 mm; 12 in a foot); **within an ~ of** à deux doigts de; **he wouldn't give an ~** (fig) il n'a pas voulu céder d'un pouce
▶ **inch forward** vi avancer petit à petit

inch tape n (Brit) centimètre m (de couturière)

incidence ['ɪnsɪdns] n (of crime, disease) fréquence f

incident ['ɪnsɪdnt] n incident m; (in book) péripétie f

incidental [ɪnsɪ'dɛntl] adj accessoire; (unplanned) accidentel(le); **~ to** qui accompagne; **~ expenses** faux frais mpl

incidentally [ɪnsɪ'dɛntəlɪ] adv (by the way) à propos

incidental music n musique f de fond

incident room n (Police) salle f d'opérations

incinerate [ɪn'sɪnəreɪt] vt incinérer

incinerator [ɪn'sɪnəreɪtə'] n incinérateur m

incipient [ɪn'sɪpɪənt] adj naissant(e)

incision [ɪn'sɪʒən] n incision f

incisive [ɪn'saɪsɪv] adj incisif(-ive), mordant(e)

incisor [ɪn'saɪzə'] n incisive f

incite [ɪn'saɪt] vt inciter, pousser

incl. abbr = **including**; **inclusive (of)**

inclement [ɪn'klɛmənt] adj inclément(e), rigoureux(-euse)

inclination [ɪnklɪ'neɪʃən] n inclination f; (desire) envie f

incline [n 'ɪnklaɪn, vb ɪn'klaɪn] n pente f, plan incliné ▷ vt incliner ▷ vi (surface) s'incliner; **to ~ to** avoir tendance à; **to be ~d to do** (want to) être enclin(e) à faire; (have a tendency to do) avoir tendance à faire; **to be well ~d towards sb** être bien disposé(e) à l'égard de qn

include [ɪn'klu:d] vt inclure, comprendre; **service is/is not ~d** le service est compris/n'est pas compris

including [ɪn'klu:dɪŋ] prep y compris; **~ service**

service compris

inclusion [ɪn'klu:ʒən] n inclusion f

inclusive [ɪn'klu:sɪv] adj inclus(e), compris(e); **~ of tax** taxes comprises; **£50 ~ of all surcharges** 50 livres tous frais compris

inclusive terms npl (Brit) prix tout compris

incognito [ɪnkɔg'ni:təu] adv incognito

incoherent [ɪnkəu'hɪərənt] adj incohérent(e)

income ['ɪnkʌm] n revenu m; (from property etc) rentes fpl; **gross/net ~** revenu brut/net; **~ and expenditure account** compte m de recettes et de dépenses

income support n (Brit) ≈ revenu m minimum d'insertion, RMI m

income tax n impôt m sur le revenu

income tax inspector n inspecteur m des contributions directes

income tax return n déclaration f des revenus

incoming ['ɪnkʌmɪŋ] adj (passengers, mail) à l'arrivée; (government, tenant) nouveau (nouvelle); **~ tide** marée montante

incommunicado ['ɪnkəmjuni'kɑ:dəu] adj: **to hold sb ~** tenir qn au secret

incomparable [ɪn'kɔmpərəbl] adj incomparable

incompatible [ɪnkəm'pætɪbl] adj incompatible

incompetence [ɪn'kɔmpɪtns] n incompétence f, incapacité f

incompetent [ɪn'kɔmpɪtnt] adj incompétent(e), incapable

incomplete [ɪnkəm'pli:t] adj incomplet(-ète)

incomprehensible [ɪnkɔmprɪ'hɛnsɪbl] adj incompréhensible

inconceivable [ɪnkən'si:vəbl] adj inconcevable

inconclusive [ɪnkən'klu:sɪv] adj peu concluant(e); (argument) peu convaincant(e)

incongruous [ɪn'kɔŋgruəs] adj peu approprié(e); (remark, act) incongru(e), déplacé(e)

inconsequential [ɪnkɔnsɪ'kwɛnʃl] adj sans importance

inconsiderable [ɪnkən'sɪdərəbl] adj: **not ~** non négligeable

inconsiderate [ɪnkən'sɪdərət] adj (action) inconsidéré(e); (person) qui manque d'égards

inconsistency [ɪnkən'sɪstənsɪ] n (of actions etc) inconséquence f; (of work) irrégularité f; (of statement etc) incohérence f

inconsistent [ɪnkən'sɪstnt] adj qui manque de constance; (work) irrégulier(-ière); (statement) peu cohérent(e); **~ with** en contradiction avec

inconsolable [ɪnkən'səuləbl] adj inconsolable

inconspicuous [ɪnkən'spɪkjuəs] adj qui passe inaperçu(e); (colour, dress) discret(-ète); **to make o.s. ~** ne pas se faire remarquer

inconstant [ɪn'kɔnstnt] adj inconstant(e), variable

incontinence [ɪn'kɔntɪnəns] n incontinence f

incontinent [ɪn'kɔntɪnənt] adj incontinent(e)

incontrovertible [ɪnkɔntrə'və:təbl] adj irréfutable

inconvenience [ɪnkən'vi:njəns] n inconvénient

m; (*trouble*) dérangement *m* ▷ *vt* déranger;
don't ~ yourself ne vous dérangez pas
inconvenient [ɪnkən'viːnjənt] *adj*
malcommode; (*time, place*) mal choisi(e), qui ne
convient pas; (*visitor*) importun(e); **that time is
very ~ for me** c'est un moment qui ne me
convient pas du tout
incorporate [ɪn'kɔːpəreɪt] *vt* incorporer;
(*contain*) contenir ▷ *vi* fusionner; (*two firms*) se
constituer en société
incorporated [ɪn'kɔːpəreɪtɪd] *adj*: **~ company**
(US) ≈ société *f* anonyme
incorrect [ɪnkə'rɛkt] *adj* incorrect(e); (*opinion,
statement*) inexact(e)
incorrigible [ɪn'kɔrɪdʒɪbl] *adj* incorrigible
incorruptible [ɪnkə'rʌptɪbl] *adj* incorruptible
increase *n* ['ɪnkriːs] augmentation *f* ▷ *vi, vt*
[ɪn'kriːs] augmenter; **an ~ of 5%** une
augmentation de 5%; **to be on the ~** être en
augmentation
increasing [ɪn'kriːsɪŋ] *adj* croissant(e)
increasingly [ɪn'kriːsɪŋlɪ] *adv* de plus en plus
incredible [ɪn'krɛdɪbl] *adj* incroyable
incredibly [ɪn'krɛdɪblɪ] *adv* incroyablement
incredulous [ɪn'krɛdjuləs] *adj* incrédule
increment ['ɪnkrɪmənt] *n* augmentation *f*
incriminate [ɪn'krɪmɪneɪt] *vt* incriminer,
compromettre
incriminating [ɪn'krɪmɪneɪtɪŋ] *adj*
compromettant(e)
incubate ['ɪnkjubeɪt] *vt* (*egg*) couver, incuber
▷ *vi* (*eggs*) couver; (*disease*) couver
incubation [ɪnkju'beɪʃən] *n* incubation *f*
incubation period *n* période *f* d'incubation
incubator ['ɪnkjubeɪtər] *n* incubateur *m*; (*for
babies*) couveuse *f*
inculcate ['ɪnkʌlkeɪt] *vt*: **to ~ sth in sb**
inculquer qch à qn
incumbent [ɪn'kʌmbənt] *adj*: **it is ~ on him
to ...** il lui appartient de ... ▷ *n* titulaire *m/f*
incur [ɪn'kəːr] *vt* (*expenses*) encourir; (*anger, risk*)
s'exposer à; (*debt*) contracter; (*loss*) subir
incurable [ɪn'kjuərəbl] *adj* incurable
incursion [ɪn'kəːʃən] *n* incursion *f*
Ind. *abbr* (US) = **Indiana**
indebted [ɪn'dɛtɪd] *adj*: **to be ~ to sb (for)** être
redevable à qn (de)
indecency [ɪn'diːsnsɪ] *n* indécence *f*
indecent [ɪn'diːsnt] *adj* indécent(e),
inconvenant(e)
indecent assault *n* (*Brit*) attentat *m* à la pudeur
indecent exposure *n* outrage *m* public à la
pudeur
indecipherable [ɪndɪ'saɪfərəbl] *adj*
indéchiffrable
indecision [ɪndɪ'sɪʒən] *n* indécision *f*
indecisive [ɪndɪ'saɪsɪv] *adj* indécis(e); (*discussion*)
peu concluant(e)
indeed [ɪn'diːd] *adv* (*confirming, agreeing*) en effet,
effectivement; (*for emphasis*) vraiment;
(*furthermore*) d'ailleurs; **yes ~!** certainement!
indefatigable [ɪndɪ'fætɪgəbl] *adj* infatigable

indefensible [ɪndɪ'fɛnsɪbl] *adj* (*conduct*)
indéfendable
indefinable [ɪndɪ'faɪnəbl] *adj* indéfinissable
indefinite [ɪn'dɛfɪnɪt] *adj* indéfini(e); (*answer*)
vague; (*period, number*) indéterminé(e)
indefinitely [ɪn'dɛfɪnɪtlɪ] *adv* (*wait*)
indéfiniment; (*speak*) vaguement, avec
imprécision
indelible [ɪn'dɛlɪbl] *adj* indélébile
indelicate [ɪn'dɛlɪkɪt] *adj* (*tactless*) indélicat(e),
grossier(-ière); (*not polite*) inconvenant(e),
malséant(e)
indemnify [ɪn'dɛmnɪfaɪ] *vt* indemniser,
dédommager
indemnity [ɪn'dɛmnɪtɪ] *n* (*insurance*) assurance *f*,
garantie *f*; (*compensation*) indemnité *f*
indent [ɪn'dɛnt] *vt* (*text*) commencer en retrait
indentation [ɪndɛn'teɪʃən] *n* découpure *f*; (*Typ*)
alinéa *m*; (*on metal*) bosse *f*
indenture [ɪn'dɛntʃər] *n* contrat *m* d'emploi-
formation
independence [ɪndɪ'pɛndns] *n* indépendance *f*
Independence Day *n* (US) *fête de l'Indépendance
américaine*; *voir article*

● **INDEPENDENCE DAY**
●
● L'*Independence Day* est la fête nationale aux
● États-Unis, le 4 juillet. Il commémore
● l'adoption de la déclaration
● d'Indépendance, en 1776, écrite par Thomas
● Jefferson et proclamant la séparation des 13
● colonies américaines de la Grande-
● Bretagne.

independent [ɪndɪ'pɛndnt] *adj* indépendant(e);
(*radio*) libre; **to become ~** s'affranchir
independently [ɪndɪ'pɛndntlɪ] *adv* de façon
indépendante; **~ of** indépendamment de
independent school *n* (*Brit*) école privée
in-depth ['ɪndɛpθ] *adj* approfondi(e)
indescribable [ɪndɪ'skraɪbəbl] *adj*
indescriptible
indeterminate [ɪndɪ'təːmɪnɪt] *adj*
indéterminé(e)
index ['ɪndɛks] *n* (*pl* **-es**) (*in book*) index *m*; (: *in
library etc*) catalogue *m* (*pl* **indices** ['ɪndɪsiːz])
(*ratio, sign*) indice *m*
index card *n* fiche *f*
index finger *n* index *m*
index-linked ['ɪndɛks'lɪŋkt], (US) **indexed**
['ɪndɛkst] *adj* indexé(e) (sur le coût de la vie *etc*)
India ['ɪndɪə] *n* Inde *f*
Indian ['ɪndɪən] *adj* indien(ne) ▷ *n* Indien(ne);
(American) ~ Indien(ne) (d'Amérique)
Indian ink *n* encre *f* de Chine
Indian Ocean *n*: **the ~** l'océan Indien
Indian summer *n* (*fig*) été indien, beaux jours
en automne
India paper *n* papier *m* bible
India rubber *n* gomme *f*
indicate ['ɪndɪkeɪt] *vt* indiquer ▷ *vi* (*Brit Aut*): **to**

~ left/right mettre son clignotant à gauche/à droite

indication [ɪndɪˈkeɪʃən] *n* indication *f*, signe *m*

indicative [ɪnˈdɪkətɪv] *adj* indicatif(-ive); **to be ~ of sth** être symptomatique de qch ▷ *n* (*Ling*) indicatif *m*

indicator [ˈɪndɪkeɪtə^r] *n* (*sign*) indicateur *m*; (*Aut*) clignotant *m*

indices [ˈɪndɪsiːz] *npl of* **index**

indict [ɪnˈdaɪt] *vt* accuser

indictable [ɪnˈdaɪtəbl] *adj* (*person*) passible de poursuites; **~ offence** délit *m* tombant sous le coup de la loi

indictment [ɪnˈdaɪtmənt] *n* accusation *f*

indifference [ɪnˈdɪfrəns] *n* indifférence *f*

indifferent [ɪnˈdɪfrənt] *adj* indifférent(e); (*poor*) médiocre, quelconque

indigenous [ɪnˈdɪdʒɪnəs] *adj* indigène

indigestible [ɪndɪˈdʒɛstɪbl] *adj* indigeste

indigestion [ɪndɪˈdʒɛstʃən] *n* indigestion *f*, mauvaise digestion

indignant [ɪnˈdɪgnənt] *adj*: **~ (at sth/with sb)** indigné (e) (de qch/contre qn)

indignation [ɪndɪgˈneɪʃən] *n* indignation *f*

indignity [ɪnˈdɪgnɪtɪ] *n* indignité *f*, affront *m*

indigo [ˈɪndɪgəu] *adj* indigo *inv* ▷ *n* indigo *m*

indirect [ɪndɪˈrɛkt] *adj* indirect(e)

indirectly [ɪndɪˈrɛktlɪ] *adv* indirectement

indiscreet [ɪndɪˈskriːt] *adj* indiscret(-ète); (*rash*) imprudent(e)

indiscretion [ɪndɪˈskrɛʃən] *n* indiscrétion *f*; (*rashness*) imprudence *f*

indiscriminate [ɪndɪˈskrɪmɪnət] *adj* (*person*) qui manque de discernement; (*admiration*) aveugle; (*killings*) commis(e) au hasard

indispensable [ɪndɪˈspɛnsəbl] *adj* indispensable

indisposed [ɪndɪˈspəuzd] *adj* (*unwell*) indisposé(e), souffrant(e)

indisposition [ɪndɪspəˈzɪʃən] *n* (*illness*) indisposition *f*, malaise *m*

indisputable [ɪndɪˈspjuːtəbl] *adj* incontestable, indiscutable

indistinct [ɪndɪˈstɪŋkt] *adj* indistinct(e); (*memory, noise*) vague

indistinguishable [ɪndɪˈstɪŋgwɪʃəbl] *adj* impossible à distinguer

individual [ɪndɪˈvɪdjuəl] *n* individu *m* ▷ *adj* individuel(le); (*characteristic*) particulier(-ière), original(e)

individualist [ɪndɪˈvɪdjuəlɪst] *n* individualiste *m/f*

individuality [ɪndɪvɪdjuˈælɪtɪ] *n* individualité *f*

individually [ɪndɪˈvɪdjuəlɪ] *adv* individuellement

indivisible [ɪndɪˈvɪzɪbl] *adj* indivisible; (*Math*) insécable

Indo-China [ˈɪndəuˈtʃaɪnə] *n* Indochine *f*

indoctrinate [ɪnˈdɔktrɪneɪt] *vt* endoctriner

indoctrination [ɪndɔktrɪˈneɪʃən] *n* endoctrinement *m*

indolent [ˈɪndələnt] *adj* indolent(e), nonchalant(e)

Indonesia [ɪndəˈniːzɪə] *n* Indonésie *f*

Indonesian [ɪndəˈniːzɪən] *adj* indonésien(ne) ▷ *n* Indonésien(ne); (*Ling*) indonésien *m*

indoor [ˈɪndɔː^r] *adj* d'intérieur; (*plant*) d'appartement; (*swimming pool*) couvert(e); (*sport, games*) pratiqué(e) en salle

indoors [ɪnˈdɔːz] *adv* à l'intérieur; (*at home*) à la maison

indubitable [ɪnˈdjuːbɪtəbl] *adj* indubitable, incontestable

induce [ɪnˈdjuːs] *vt* (*persuade*) persuader; (*bring about*) provoquer; (*labour*) déclencher; **to ~ sb to do sth** inciter *or* pousser qn à faire qch

inducement [ɪnˈdjuːsmənt] *n* incitation *f*; (*incentive*) but *m*; (*pej: bribe*) pot-de-vin *m*

induct [ɪnˈdʌkt] *vt* établir dans ses fonctions; (*fig*) initier

induction [ɪnˈdʌkʃən] *n* (*Med: of birth*) accouchement provoqué

induction course *n* (*Brit*) stage *m* de mise au courant

indulge [ɪnˈdʌldʒ] *vt* (*whim*) céder à, satisfaire; (*child*) gâter ▷ *vi*: **to ~ in sth** (*luxury*) s'offrir qch, se permettre qch; (*fantasies etc*) se livrer à qch

indulgence [ɪnˈdʌldʒəns] *n* fantaisie *f* (que l'on s'offre); (*leniency*) indulgence *f*

indulgent [ɪnˈdʌldʒənt] *adj* indulgent(e)

industrial [ɪnˈdʌstrɪəl] *adj* industriel(le); (*injury*) du travail; (*dispute*) ouvrier(-ière)

industrial action *n* action revendicative

industrial estate *n* (*Brit*) zone industrielle

industrialist [ɪnˈdʌstrɪəlɪst] *n* industriel *m*

industrialize [ɪnˈdʌstrɪəlaɪz] *vt* industrialiser

industrial park *n* (*US*) zone industrielle

industrial relations *npl* relations *fpl* dans l'entreprise

industrial tribunal *n* (*Brit*) ≈ conseil *m* de prud'hommes

industrious [ɪnˈdʌstrɪəs] *adj* travailleur(-euse)

industry [ˈɪndəstrɪ] *n* industrie *f*; (*diligence*) zèle *m*, application *f*

inebriated [ɪˈniːbrɪeɪtɪd] *adj* ivre

inedible [ɪnˈɛdɪbl] *adj* immangeable; (*plant etc*) non comestible

ineffective [ɪnɪˈfɛktɪv], **ineffectual** [ɪnɪˈfɛktʃuəl] *adj* inefficace; incompétent(e)

inefficiency [ɪnɪˈfɪʃənsɪ] *n* inefficacité *f*

inefficient [ɪnɪˈfɪʃənt] *adj* inefficace

inelegant [ɪnˈɛlɪgənt] *adj* peu élégant(e), inélégant(e)

ineligible [ɪnˈɛlɪdʒɪbl] *adj* (*candidate*) inéligible; **to be ~ for sth** ne pas avoir droit à qch

inept [ɪˈnɛpt] *adj* inepte

ineptitude [ɪˈnɛptɪtjuːd] *n* ineptie *f*

inequality [ɪnɪˈkwɔlɪtɪ] *n* inégalité *f*

inequitable [ɪnˈɛkwɪtəbl] *adj* inéquitable, inique

ineradicable [ɪnɪˈrædɪkəbl] *adj* indéracinable, tenace

inert [ɪˈnəːt] *adj* inerte

inertia [ɪˈnəːʃə] *n* inertie *f*

inertia-reel seat belt [ɪ'nə:ʃə'ri:l-] *n* ceinture *f* de sécurité à enrouleur

inescapable [ɪnɪ'skeɪpəbl] *adj* inéluctable, inévitable

inessential [ɪnɪ'sɛnʃl] *adj* superflu(e)

inestimable [ɪn'ɛstɪməbl] *adj* inestimable, incalculable

inevitable [ɪn'ɛvɪtəbl] *adj* inévitable

inevitably [ɪn'ɛvɪtəblɪ] *adv* inévitablement, fatalement

inexact [ɪnɪg'zækt] *adj* inexact(e)

inexcusable [ɪnɪks'kju:zəbl] *adj* inexcusable

inexhaustible [ɪnɪg'zɔ:stɪbl] *adj* inépuisable

inexorable [ɪn'ɛksərəbl] *adj* inexorable

inexpensive [ɪnɪk'spɛnsɪv] *adj* bon marché *inv*

inexperience [ɪnɪk'spɪərɪəns] *n* inexpérience *f*, manque *m* d'expérience

inexperienced [ɪnɪk'spɪərɪənst] *adj* inexpérimenté(e); **to be ~ in sth** manquer d'expérience dans qch

inexplicable [ɪnɪk'splɪkəbl] *adj* inexplicable

inexpressible [ɪnɪk'sprɛsɪbl] *adj* inexprimable; indicible

inextricable [ɪnɪk'strɪkəbl] *adj* inextricable

infallibility [ɪnfælə'bɪlɪtɪ] *n* infaillibilité *f*

infallible [ɪn'fælɪbl] *adj* infaillible

infamous ['ɪnfəməs] *adj* infâme, abominable

infamy ['ɪnfəmɪ] *n* infamie *f*

infancy ['ɪnfənsɪ] *n* petite enfance, bas âge; (*fig*) enfance, débuts *mpl*

infant ['ɪnfənt] *n* (*baby*) nourrisson *m*; (*young child*) petit(e) enfant

infantile ['ɪnfəntaɪl] *adj* infantile

infant mortality *n* mortalité *f* infantile

infantry ['ɪnfəntrɪ] *n* infanterie *f*

infantryman ['ɪnfəntrɪmən] (*irreg*) *n* fantassin *m*

infant school *n* (*Brit*) classes *fpl* préparatoires (*entre 5 et 7 ans*)

infatuated [ɪn'fætjueɪtɪd] *adj*: **~ with** entiché(e) de; **to become ~ (with sb)** s'enticher (de qn)

infatuation [ɪnfætju'eɪʃən] *n* toquade *f*; engouement *m*

infect [ɪn'fɛkt] *vt* (*wound*) infecter; (*person, blood*) contaminer; (*fig pej*) corrompre; **~ed with** (*illness*) atteint(e) de; **to become ~ed** (*wound*) s'infecter

infection [ɪn'fɛkʃən] *n* infection *f*; (*contagion*) contagion *f*

infectious [ɪn'fɛkʃəs] *adj* infectieux(-euse); (*also fig*) contagieux(-euse)

infer [ɪn'fə:ʳ] *vt*: **to ~ (from)** conclure (de), déduire (de)

inference ['ɪnfərəns] *n* conclusion *f*, déduction *f*

inferior [ɪn'fɪərɪəʳ] *adj* inférieur(e); (*goods*) de qualité inférieure ▷ *n* inférieur(e); (*in rank*) subalterne *m/f*; **to feel ~** avoir un sentiment d'infériorité

inferiority [ɪnfɪərɪ'ɔrətɪ] *n* infériorité *f*

inferiority complex *n* complexe *m* d'infériorité

infernal [ɪn'fə:nl] *adj* infernal(e)

inferno [ɪn'fə:nəu] *n* enfer *m*; brasier *m*

infertile [ɪn'fə:taɪl] *adj* stérile

infertility [ɪnfə'tɪlɪtɪ] *n* infertilité *f*, stérilité *f*

infested [ɪn'fɛstɪd] *adj*: **~ (with)** infesté(e) (de)

infidelity [ɪnfɪ'dɛlɪtɪ] *n* infidélité *f*

in-fighting ['ɪnfaɪtɪŋ] *n* querelles *fpl* internes

infiltrate ['ɪnfɪltreɪt] *vt* (*troops etc*) faire s'infiltrer; (*enemy line etc*) s'infiltrer dans ▷ *vi* s'infiltrer

infinite ['ɪnfɪnɪt] *adj* infini(e); (*time, money*) illimité(e)

infinitely ['ɪnfɪnɪtlɪ] *adv* infiniment

infinitesimal [ɪnfɪnɪ'tɛsɪməl] *adj* infinitésimal(e)

infinitive [ɪn'fɪnɪtɪv] *n* infinitif *m*

infinity [ɪn'fɪnɪtɪ] *n* infinité *f*; (*also Math*) infini *m*

infirm [ɪn'fə:m] *adj* infirme

infirmary [ɪn'fə:mərɪ] *n* hôpital *m*; (*in school, factory*) infirmerie *f*

infirmity [ɪn'fə:mɪtɪ] *n* infirmité *f*

inflamed [ɪn'fleɪmd] *adj* enflammé(e)

inflammable [ɪn'flæməbl] *adj* (*Brit*) inflammable

inflammation [ɪnflə'meɪʃən] *n* inflammation *f*

inflammatory [ɪn'flæmətərɪ] *adj* (*speech*) incendiaire

inflatable [ɪn'fleɪtəbl] *adj* gonflable

inflate [ɪn'fleɪt] *vt* (*tyre, balloon*) gonfler; (*fig: exaggerate*) grossir, gonfler; (: *increase*) gonfler

inflated [ɪn'fleɪtɪd] *adj* (*style*) enflé(e); (*value*) exagéré(e)

inflation [ɪn'fleɪʃən] *n* (*Econ*) inflation *f*

inflationary [ɪn'fleɪʃənərɪ] *adj* inflationniste

inflexible [ɪn'flɛksɪbl] *adj* inflexible, rigide

inflict [ɪn'flɪkt] *vt*: **to ~ on** infliger à

infliction [ɪn'flɪkʃən] *n*: **without the ~ of pain** sans infliger de douleurs

in-flight ['ɪnflaɪt] *adj* (*refuelling*) en vol; (*service etc*) à bord

inflow ['ɪnfləu] *n* afflux *m*

influence ['ɪnfluəns] *n* influence *f* ▷ *vt* influencer; **under the ~ of** sous l'effet de; **under the ~ of alcohol** en état d'ébriété

influential [ɪnflu'ɛnʃl] *adj* influent(e)

influenza [ɪnflu'ɛnzə] *n* grippe *f*

influx ['ɪnflʌks] *n* afflux *m*

info (*inf*) ['ɪnfəu] *n* (= *information*) renseignements *mpl*

infomercial ['ɪnfəumə:ʃl] (*US*) *n* (*for product*) publi-information *f*; (*Pol*) émission où un candidat présente son programme électoral

inform [ɪn'fɔ:m] *vt*: **to ~ sb (of)** informer *or* avertir qn (de) ▷ *vi*: **to ~ on sb** dénoncer qn, informer contre qn; **to ~ sb about** renseigner qn sur, mettre qn au courant de

informal [ɪn'fɔ:ml] *adj* (*person, manner, party*) simple, sans cérémonie; (*visit, discussion*) dénué(e) de formalités; (*announcement, invitation*) non officiel(le); (*colloquial*) familier(-ère); **"dress ~"** "tenue de ville"

informality [ɪnfɔ:'mælɪtɪ] *n* simplicité *f*, absence *f* de cérémonie; caractère non officiel

informally [ɪnˈfɔːməlɪ] *adv* sans cérémonie, en toute simplicité; non officiellement
informant [ɪnˈfɔːmənt] *n* informateur(-trice)
information [ɪnfəˈmeɪʃən] *n* information(s) *f(pl)*; renseignements *mpl*; (*knowledge*) connaissances *fpl*; **to get ~ on** se renseigner sur; **a piece of ~** un renseignement; **for your ~** à titre d'information
information bureau *n* bureau *m* de renseignements
information desk *n* accueil *m*
information office *n* bureau *m* de renseignements
information processing *n* traitement *m* de l'information
information technology *n* informatique *f*
informative [ɪnˈfɔːmətɪv] *adj* instructif(-ive)
informed [ɪnˈfɔːmd] *adj* (bien) informé(e); **an ~ guess** une hypothèse fondée sur la connaissance des faits
informer [ɪnˈfɔːməʳ] *n* dénonciateur(-trice); (*also*: **police informer**) indicateur(-trice)
infra dig [ˈɪnfrəˈdɪg] *adj abbr* (*inf*: = *infra dignitatem*) au-dessous de ma (*or* sa *etc*) dignité
infra-red [ɪnfrəˈrɛd] *adj* infrarouge
infrastructure [ˈɪnfrəstrʌktʃəʳ] *n* infrastructure *f*
infrequent [ɪnˈfriːkwənt] *adj* peu fréquent(e), rare
infringe [ɪnˈfrɪndʒ] *vt* enfreindre ▷ *vi*: **to ~ on** empiéter sur
infringement [ɪnˈfrɪndʒmənt] *n*: **~ (of)** infraction *f* (à)
infuriate [ɪnˈfjuərɪeɪt] *vt* mettre en fureur
infuriating [ɪnˈfjuərɪeɪtɪŋ] *adj* exaspérant(e)
infuse [ɪnˈfjuːz] *vt*: **to ~ sb with sth** (*fig*) insuffler qch à qn
infusion [ɪnˈfjuːʒən] *n* (*tea etc*) infusion *f*
ingenious [ɪnˈdʒiːnjəs] *adj* ingénieux(-euse)
ingenuity [ɪndʒɪˈnjuːɪtɪ] *n* ingéniosité *f*
ingenuous [ɪnˈdʒɛnjuəs] *adj* franc (franche), ouvert(e)
ingot [ˈɪŋgət] *n* lingot *m*
ingrained [ɪnˈgreɪnd] *adj* enraciné(e)
ingratiate [ɪnˈgreɪʃɪeɪt] *vt*: **to ~ o.s. with** s'insinuer dans les bonnes grâces de, se faire bien voir de
ingratiating [ɪnˈgreɪʃɪeɪtɪŋ] *adj* (*smile, speech*) insinuant(e); (*person*) patelin(e)
ingratitude [ɪnˈgrætɪtjuːd] *n* ingratitude *f*
ingredient [ɪnˈgriːdɪənt] *n* ingrédient *m*; (*fig*) élément *m*
ingrowing [ˈɪngrəʊɪŋ], **ingrown** [ˈɪngrəʊn] *adj*: **~ toenail** ongle incarné
inhabit [ɪnˈhæbɪt] *vt* habiter
inhabitable [ɪnˈhæbɪtəbl] *adj* habitable
inhabitant [ɪnˈhæbɪtnt] *n* habitant(e)
inhale [ɪnˈheɪl] *vt* inhaler; (*perfume*) respirer; (*smoke*) avaler ▷ *vi* (*breathe in*) aspirer; (*in smoking*) avaler la fumée
inhaler [ɪnˈheɪləʳ] *n* inhalateur *m*
inherent [ɪnˈhɪərənt] *adj*: **~ (in *or* to)**

inhérent(e) (à)
inherently [ɪnˈhɪərəntlɪ] *adv* (*easy, difficult*) en soi; (*lazy*) fondamentalement
inherit [ɪnˈhɛrɪt] *vt* hériter (de)
inheritance [ɪnˈhɛrɪtəns] *n* héritage *m*; (*fig*): **the situation that was his ~ as president** la situation dont il a hérité en tant que président; **law of ~** droit *m* de la succession
inhibit [ɪnˈhɪbɪt] *vt* (*Psych*) inhiber; (*growth*) freiner; **to ~ sb from doing** empêcher *or* retenir qn de faire
inhibited [ɪnˈhɪbɪtɪd] *adj* (*person*) inhibé(e)
inhibiting [ɪnˈhɪbɪtɪŋ] *adj* gênant(e)
inhibition [ɪnhɪˈbɪʃən] *n* inhibition *f*
inhospitable [ɪnhɒsˈpɪtəbl] *adj* inhospitalier(-ière)
in-house [ˈɪnˈhaʊs] *adj* (*system*) interne; (*training*) effectué(e) sur place *or* dans le cadre de la compagnie ▷ *adv* (*train, produce*) sur place
inhuman [ɪnˈhjuːmən] *adj* inhumain(e)
inhumane [ɪnhjuːˈmeɪn] *adj* inhumain(e)
inimitable [ɪˈnɪmɪtəbl] *adj* inimitable
iniquity [ɪˈnɪkwɪtɪ] *n* iniquité *f*
initial [ɪˈnɪʃl] *adj* initial(e) ▷ *n* initiale *f* ▷ *vt* parafer; **initials** *npl* initiales *fpl*; (*as signature*) parafe *m*
initialize [ɪˈnɪʃəlaɪz] *vt* (*Comput*) initialiser
initially [ɪˈnɪʃəlɪ] *adv* initialement, au début
initiate [ɪˈnɪʃɪeɪt] *vt* (*start*) entreprendre; amorcer; (*enterprise*) lancer; (*person*) initier; **to ~ sb into a secret** initier qn à un secret; **to ~ proceedings against sb** (*Law*) intenter une action à qn, engager des poursuites contre qn
initiation [ɪnɪʃɪˈeɪʃən] *n* (*into secret etc*) initiation *f*
initiative [ɪˈnɪʃətɪv] *n* initiative *f*; **to take the ~** prendre l'initiative
inject [ɪnˈdʒɛkt] *vt* (*liquid, fig: money*) injecter; (*person*): **to ~ sb with sth** faire une piqûre de qch à qn
injection [ɪnˈdʒɛkʃən] *n* injection *f*, piqûre *f*; **to have an ~** se faire faire une piqûre
injudicious [ɪndʒuˈdɪʃəs] *adj* peu judicieux(-euse)
injunction [ɪnˈdʒʌŋkʃən] *n* (*Law*) injonction *f*, ordre *m*
injure [ˈɪndʒəʳ] *vt* blesser; (*wrong*) faire du tort à; (*damage: reputation etc*) compromettre; (*feelings*) heurter; **to ~ o.s.** se blesser
injured [ˈɪndʒəd] *adj* (*person, leg etc*) blessé(e); (*tone, feelings*) offensé(e); **~ party** (*Law*) partie lésée
injurious [ɪnˈdʒuərɪəs] *adj*: **~ (to)** préjudiciable (à)
injury [ˈɪndʒərɪ] *n* blessure *f*; (*wrong*) tort *m*; **to escape without ~** s'en sortir sain et sauf
injury time *n* (*Sport*) arrêts *mpl* de jeu
injustice [ɪnˈdʒʌstɪs] *n* injustice *f*; **you do me an ~** vous êtes injuste envers moi
ink [ɪŋk] *n* encre *f*
ink-jet printer [ˈɪŋkdʒɛt-] *n* imprimante *f* à jet d'encre
inkling [ˈɪŋklɪŋ] *n* soupçon *m*, vague idée *f*

inkpad ['ɪŋkpæd] *n* tampon *m* encreur

inky ['ɪŋkɪ] *adj* taché(e) d'encre

inlaid ['ɪnleɪd] *adj* incrusté(e); (*table etc*) marqueté(e)

inland *adj* ['ɪnlənd] intérieur(e) ▷ *adv* [ɪn'lænd] à l'intérieur, dans les terres; ~ **waterways** canaux *mpl* et rivières *fpl*

Inland Revenue *n* (*Brit*) fisc *m*

in-laws ['ɪnlɔːz] *npl* beaux-parents *mpl*; belle famille

inlet ['ɪnlɛt] *n* (*Geo*) crique *f*

inlet pipe *n* (*Tech*) tuyau *m* d'arrivée

inmate ['ɪnmeɪt] *n* (*in prison*) détenu(e); (*in asylum*) interné(e)

inmost ['ɪnməʊst] *adj* le (la) plus profond(e)

inn [ɪn] *n* auberge *f*

innards ['ɪnədz] *npl* (*inf*) entrailles *fpl*

innate [ɪ'neɪt] *adj* inné(e)

inner ['ɪnəʳ] *adj* intérieur(e)

inner city *n* centre *m* urbain (*souffrant souvent de délabrement, d'embouteillages etc*)

inner-city ['ɪnə'sɪtɪ] *adj* (*schools, problems*) de quartiers déshérités

innermost ['ɪnəməʊst] *adj* le (la) plus profond(e)

inner tube *n* (*of tyre*) chambre *f* à air

inning ['ɪnɪŋ] *n* (*US: Baseball*) tour *m* de batte; **innings** *npl* (*Cricket*) tour de batte; (*Brit fig*): **he has had a good ~s** il (en) a bien profité

innocence ['ɪnəsns] *n* innocence *f*

innocent ['ɪnəsnt] *adj* innocent(e)

innocuous [ɪ'nɔkjuəs] *adj* inoffensif(-ive)

innovation [ɪnəu'veɪʃən] *n* innovation *f*

innovative ['ɪnəu'veɪtɪv] *adj* novateur(-trice); (*product*) innovant(e)

innuendo (*pl* -es [ɪnju'ɛndəu]) *n* insinuation *f*, allusion (malveillante)

innumerable [ɪ'njuːmrəbl] *adj* innombrable

inoculate [ɪ'nɔkjuleɪt] *vt*: **to ~ sb with sth** inoculer qch à qn; **to ~ sb against sth** vacciner qn contre qch

inoculation [ɪnɔkju'leɪʃən] *n* inoculation *f*

inoffensive [ɪnə'fɛnsɪv] *adj* inoffensif(-ive)

inopportune [ɪn'ɔpətjuːn] *adj* inopportun(e)

inordinate [ɪ'nɔːdɪnət] *adj* démesuré(e)

inordinately [ɪ'nɔːdɪnətlɪ] *adv* démesurément

inorganic [ɪnɔː'gænɪk] *adj* inorganique

in-patient ['ɪnpeɪʃənt] *n* malade hospitalisé(e)

input ['ɪnput] *n* (*contribution*) contribution *f*; (*resources*) ressources *fpl*; (*Elec*) énergie *f*, puissance *f*; (*of machine*) consommation *f*; (*Comput*) entrée *f* (de données); (: *data*) données *fpl* ▷ *vt* (*Comput*) introduire, entrer

inquest ['ɪnkwɛst] *n* enquête (criminelle); (*coroner's*) enquête judiciaire

inquire [ɪn'kwaɪəʳ] *vi* demander ▷ *vt* demander, s'informer de; **to ~ about** s'informer de, se renseigner sur; **to ~ when/where/whether** demander quand/où/si

▶ **inquire after** *vt fus* demander des nouvelles de

▶ **inquire into** *vt fus* faire une enquête sur

inquiring [ɪn'kwaɪərɪŋ] *adj* (*mind*) curieux(-euse), investigateur(-trice)

inquiry [ɪn'kwaɪərɪ] *n* demande *f* de renseignements; (*Law*) enquête *f*, investigation *f*; **"inquiries"** "renseignements"; **to hold an ~ into sth** enquêter sur qch

inquiry desk *n* (*Brit*) guichet *m* de renseignements

inquiry office *n* (*Brit*) bureau *m* de renseignements

inquisition [ɪnkwɪ'zɪʃən] *n* enquête *f*, investigation *f*; (*Rel*): **the I~** l'Inquisition *f*

inquisitive [ɪn'kwɪzɪtɪv] *adj* curieux(-euse)

inroads ['ɪnrəudz] *npl*: **to make ~ into** (*savings, supplies*) entamer

ins. *abbr* = **inches**

insane [ɪn'seɪn] *adj* fou (folle); (*Med*) aliéné(e)

insanitary [ɪn'sænɪtərɪ] *adj* insalubre

insanity [ɪn'sænɪtɪ] *n* folie *f*; (*Med*) aliénation (mentale)

insatiable [ɪn'seɪʃəbl] *adj* insatiable

inscribe [ɪn'skraɪb] *vt* inscrire; (*book etc*): **to ~ (to sb)** dédicacer (à qn)

inscription [ɪn'skrɪpʃən] *n* inscription *f*; (*in book*) dédicace *f*

inscrutable [ɪn'skruːtəbl] *adj* impénétrable

inseam ['ɪnsiːm] *n* (*US*): ~ **measurement** hauteur *f* d'entre-jambe

insect ['ɪnsɛkt] *n* insecte *m*

insect bite *n* piqûre *f* d'insecte

insecticide [ɪn'sɛktɪsaɪd] *n* insecticide *m*

insect repellent *n* crème *f* anti-insectes

insecure [ɪnsɪ'kjuəʳ] *adj* (*person*) anxieux(-euse); (*job*) précaire; (*building etc*) peu sûr(e)

insecurity [ɪnsɪ'kjuərɪtɪ] *n* insécurité *f*

insensible [ɪn'sɛnsɪbl] *adj* insensible; (*unconscious*) sans connaissance

insensitive [ɪn'sɛnsɪtɪv] *adj* insensible

insensitivity [ɪnsɛnsɪ'tɪvɪtɪ] *n* insensibilité *f*

inseparable [ɪn'sɛprəbl] *adj* inséparable

insert *vt* [ɪn'səːt] insérer ▷ *n* ['ɪnsəːt] insertion *f*

insertion [ɪn'səːʃən] *n* insertion *f*

in-service ['ɪn'səːvɪs] *adj* (*training*) continu(e); (*course*) d'initiation; de perfectionnement; de recyclage

inshore [ɪn'ʃɔːʳ] *adj* côtier(-ière) ▷ *adv* près de la côte; vers la côte

inside ['ɪn'saɪd] *n* intérieur *m*; (*of road: Brit*) côté *m* gauche (*de la route*); (: *US, Europe etc*) côté droit (*de la route*) ▷ *adj* intérieur(e) ▷ *adv* à l'intérieur, dedans ▷ *prep* à l'intérieur de; (*of time*): ~ **10 minutes** en moins de 10 minutes; **insides** *npl* (*inf*) intestins *mpl*; ~ **information** renseignements *mpl* à la source; ~ **story** histoire racontée par un témoin; **to go ~** rentrer

inside forward *n* (*Sport*) intérieur *m*

inside lane *n* (*Aut: in Britain*) voie *f* de gauche; (: *in US, Europe*) voie *f* de droite

inside leg measurement *n* (*Brit*) hauteur *f* d'entre-jambe

inside out *adv* à l'envers; (*know*) à fond; **to turn**

sth ~ retourner qch
insider [ɪn'saɪdər] *n* initié(e)
insider dealing, insider trading *n* (*Stock Exchange*) délit *m* d'initiés
insidious [ɪn'sɪdɪəs] *adj* insidieux(-euse)
insight ['ɪnsaɪt] *n* perspicacité *f*; (*glimpse, idea*) aperçu *m*; **to gain (an) ~ into** parvenir à comprendre
insignia [ɪn'sɪgnɪə] *npl* insignes *mpl*
insignificant [ɪnsɪg'nɪfɪkənt] *adj* insignifiant(e)
insincere [ɪnsɪn'sɪər] *adj* hypocrite
insincerity [ɪnsɪn'sɛrɪtɪ] *n* manque *m* de sincérité, hypocrisie *f*
insinuate [ɪn'sɪnjueɪt] *vt* insinuer
insinuation [ɪnsɪnju'eɪʃən] *n* insinuation *f*
insipid [ɪn'sɪpɪd] *adj* insipide, fade
insist [ɪn'sɪst] *vi* insister; **to ~ on doing** insister pour faire; **to ~ on sth** exiger qch; **to ~ that** insister pour que + *sub*; (*claim*) maintenir *or* soutenir que
insistence [ɪn'sɪstəns] *n* insistance *f*
insistent [ɪn'sɪstənt] *adj* insistant(e), pressant(e); (*noise, action*) ininterrompu(e)
insofar [ɪnsəu'fɑːr]: **~ as** *conj* dans la mesure où
insole ['ɪnsəul] *n* semelle intérieure; (*fixed part of shoe*) première *f*
insolence ['ɪnsələns] *n* insolence *f*
insolent ['ɪnsələnt] *adj* insolent(e)
insoluble [ɪn'sɔljubl] *adj* insoluble
insolvency [ɪn'sɔlvənsɪ] *n* insolvabilité *f*; faillite *f*
insolvent [ɪn'sɔlvənt] *adj* insolvable; (*bankrupt*) en faillite
insomnia [ɪn'sɔmnɪə] *n* insomnie *f*
insomniac [ɪn'sɔmnɪæk] *n* insomniaque *m/f*
inspect [ɪn'spɛkt] *vt* inspecter; (*Brit: ticket*) contrôler
inspection [ɪn'spɛkʃən] *n* inspection *f*; (*Brit: of tickets*) contrôle *m*
inspector [ɪn'spɛktər] *n* inspecteur(-trice); (*Brit: on buses, trains*) contrôleur(-euse)
inspiration [ɪnspə'reɪʃən] *n* inspiration *f*
inspire [ɪn'spaɪər] *vt* inspirer
inspired [ɪn'spaɪəd] *adj* (*writer, book etc*) inspiré(e); **in an ~ moment** dans un moment d'inspiration
inspiring [ɪn'spaɪərɪŋ] *adj* inspirant(e)
inst. *abbr* (*Brit Comm*) = **instant**; **of the 16th ~** du 16 courant
instability [ɪnstə'bɪlɪtɪ] *n* instabilité *f*
install, (*US*) **instal** [ɪn'stɔːl] *vt* installer
installation [ɪnstə'leɪʃən] *n* installation *f*
installment plan *n* (*US*) achat *m* (*or* vente *f*) à tempérament *or* crédit
instalment, (*US*) **installment** [ɪn'stɔːlmənt] *n* (*payment*) acompte *m*, versement partiel; (*of TV serial etc*) épisode *m*; **in ~s** (*pay*) à tempérament; (*receive*) en plusieurs fois
instance ['ɪnstəns] *n* exemple *m*; **for ~** par exemple; **in many ~s** dans bien des cas; **in that ~** dans ce cas; **in the first ~** tout d'abord, en premier lieu

instant ['ɪnstənt] *n* instant *m* ▷ *adj* immédiat(e), urgent(e); (*coffee, food*) instantané(e), en poudre; **the 10th ~** le 10 courant
instantaneous [ɪnstən'teɪnɪəs] *adj* instantané(e)
instantly ['ɪnstəntlɪ] *adv* immédiatement, tout de suite
instant messaging *n* messagerie *f* instantanée
instant replay *n* (*US TV*) retour *m* sur une séquence
instead [ɪn'stɛd] *adv* au lieu de cela; **~ of** au lieu de; **~ of sb** à la place de qn
instep ['ɪnstɛp] *n* cou-de-pied *m*; (*of shoe*) cambrure *f*
instigate ['ɪnstɪgeɪt] *vt* (*rebellion, strike, crime*) inciter à; (*new ideas etc*) susciter
instigation [ɪnstɪ'geɪʃən] *n* instigation *f*; **at sb's ~** à l'instigation de qn
instil [ɪn'stɪl] *vt*: **to ~ (into)** inculquer (à); (*courage*) insuffler (à)
instinct ['ɪnstɪŋkt] *n* instinct *m*
instinctive [ɪn'stɪŋktɪv] *adj* instinctif(-ive)
instinctively [ɪn'stɪŋktɪvlɪ] *adv* instinctivement
institute ['ɪnstɪtjuːt] *n* institut *m* ▷ *vt* instituer, établir; (*inquiry*) ouvrir; (*proceedings*) entamer
institution [ɪnstɪ'tjuːʃən] *n* institution *f*; (*school*) établissement *m* (scolaire); (*for care*) établissement (psychiatrique *etc*)
institutional [ɪnstɪ'tjuːʃənl] *adj* institutionnel(le); **~ care** soins fournis par un établissement médico-social
instruct [ɪn'strʌkt] *vt* instruire, former; **to ~ sb in sth** enseigner qch à qn; **to ~ sb to do** charger qn *or* ordonner à qn de faire
instruction [ɪn'strʌkʃən] *n* instruction *f*; **instructions** *npl* (*orders*) directives *fpl*; **~s for use** mode *m* d'emploi
instruction book *n* manuel *m* d'instructions
instructive [ɪn'strʌktɪv] *adj* instructif(-ive)
instructor [ɪn'strʌktər] *n* professeur *m*; (*for skiing, driving*) moniteur *m*
instrument ['ɪnstrumənt] *n* instrument *m*
instrumental [ɪnstru'mɛntl] *adj* (*Mus*) instrumental(e); **to be ~ in sth/in doing sth** contribuer à qch/à faire qch
instrumentalist [ɪnstru'mɛntəlɪst] *n* instrumentiste *m/f*
instrument panel *n* tableau *m* de bord
insubordinate [ɪnsə'bɔːdənɪt] *adj* insubordonné(e)
insubordination [ɪnsəbɔːdə'neɪʃən] *n* insubordination *f*
insufferable [ɪn'sʌfrəbl] *adj* insupportable
insufficient [ɪnsə'fɪʃənt] *adj* insuffisant(e)
insufficiently [ɪnsə'fɪʃəntlɪ] *adv* insuffisamment
insular ['ɪnsjulər] *adj* insulaire; (*outlook*) étroit(e); (*person*) aux vues étroites
insulate ['ɪnsjuleɪt] *vt* isoler; (*against sound*) insonoriser

insulating tape ['ɪnsjuleɪtɪŋ-] n ruban isolant
insulation [ɪnsjuˈleɪʃən] n isolation f; (against sound) insonorisation f
insulin ['ɪnsjulɪn] n insuline f
insult n ['ɪnsʌlt] insulte f, affront m ▷ vt [ɪnˈsʌlt] insulter, faire un affront à
insulting [ɪnˈsʌltɪŋ] adj insultant(e), injurieux(-euse)
insuperable [ɪnˈsjuːprəbl] adj insurmontable
insurance [ɪnˈʃuərəns] n assurance f; **fire/life ~** assurance-incendie/-vie; **to take out ~ (against)** s'assurer (contre)
insurance agent n agent m d'assurances
insurance broker n courtier m en assurances
insurance company n compagnie f or société f d'assurances
insurance policy n police f d'assurance
insurance premium n prime f d'assurance
insure [ɪnˈʃuəʳ] vt assurer; **to ~ (o.s.) against** (fig) parer à; **to ~ sb/sb's life** assurer qn/la vie de qn; **to be ~d for £5000** être assuré(e) pour 5000 livres
insured [ɪnˈʃuəd] n: **the ~** l'assuré(e)
insurer [ɪnˈʃuərəʳ] n assureur m
insurgent [ɪnˈsəːdʒənt] adj, n insurgé(e)
insurmountable [ɪnsəˈmauntəbl] adj insurmontable
insurrection [ɪnsəˈrɛkʃən] n insurrection f
intact [ɪnˈtækt] adj intact(e)
intake ['ɪnteɪk] n (Tech) admission f; (consumption) consommation f; (Brit Scol): **an ~ of 200 a year** 200 admissions par an
intangible [ɪnˈtændʒɪbl] adj intangible; (assets) immatériel(le)
integral ['ɪntɪɡrəl] adj (whole) intégral(e); (part) intégrant(e)
integrate ['ɪntɪɡreɪt] vt intégrer ▷ vi s'intégrer
integrated circuit ['ɪntɪɡreɪtɪd-] n (Comput) circuit intégré
integration [ɪntɪˈɡreɪʃən] n intégration f; **racial ~** intégration raciale
integrity [ɪnˈtɛɡrɪtɪ] n intégrité f
intellect ['ɪntəlɛkt] n intelligence f
intellectual [ɪntəˈlɛktjuəl] adj, n intellectuel(le)
intelligence [ɪnˈtɛlɪdʒəns] n intelligence f; (Mil) informations fpl, renseignements mpl
intelligence quotient n quotient intellectuel
Intelligence Service n services mpl de renseignements
intelligence test n test m d'intelligence
intelligent [ɪnˈtɛlɪdʒənt] adj intelligent(e)
intelligently [ɪnˈtɛlɪdʒəntlɪ] adv intelligemment
intelligible [ɪnˈtɛlɪdʒɪbl] adj intelligible
intemperate [ɪnˈtɛmpərət] adj immodéré(e); (drinking too much) adonné(e) à la boisson
intend [ɪnˈtɛnd] vt (gift etc): **to ~ sth for** destiner qch à; **to ~ to do** avoir l'intention de faire
intended [ɪnˈtɛndɪd] adj (insult) intentionnel(le); (journey) projeté(e); (effect) voulu(e)
intense [ɪnˈtɛns] adj intense; (person) véhément(e)

intensely [ɪnˈtɛnslɪ] adv intensément; (moving) profondément
intensify [ɪnˈtɛnsɪfaɪ] vt intensifier
intensity [ɪnˈtɛnsɪtɪ] n intensité f
intensive [ɪnˈtɛnsɪv] adj intensif(-ive)
intensive care n: **to be in ~** être en réanimation
intensive care unit n service m de réanimation
intent [ɪnˈtɛnt] n intention f ▷ adj attentif(-ive), absorbé(e); **to all ~s and purposes** en fait, pratiquement; **to be ~ on doing sth** être (bien) décidé à faire qch
intention [ɪnˈtɛnʃən] n intention f
intentional [ɪnˈtɛnʃənl] adj intentionnel(le), délibéré(e)
intently [ɪnˈtɛntlɪ] adv attentivement
inter [ɪnˈtəːʳ] vt enterrer
interact [ɪntərˈækt] vi avoir une action réciproque; (people) communiquer
interaction [ɪntərˈækʃən] n interaction f
interactive [ɪntərˈæktɪv] adj (group) interactif(-ive); (Comput) interactif, conversationnel(le)
intercede [ɪntəˈsiːd] vi: **to ~ with sb/on behalf of sb** intercéder auprès de qn/en faveur de qn
intercept [ɪntəˈsɛpt] vt intercepter; (person) arrêter au passage
interception [ɪntəˈsɛpʃən] n interception f
interchange n ['ɪntətʃeɪndʒ] (exchange) échange m; (on motorway) échangeur m ▷ vt [ɪntəˈtʃeɪndʒ] échanger; mettre à la place l'un(e) de l'autre
interchangeable [ɪntəˈtʃeɪndʒəbl] adj interchangeable
intercity [ɪntəˈsɪtɪ] adj: **~ (train)** train m rapide
intercom ['ɪntəkɔm] n interphone m
interconnect [ɪntəkəˈnɛkt] vi (rooms) communiquer
intercontinental ['ɪntəkɔntɪˈnɛntl] adj intercontinental(e)
intercourse ['ɪntəkɔːs] n rapports mpl; **sexual ~** rapports sexuels
interdependent [ɪntədɪˈpɛndənt] adj interdépendant(e)
interest ['ɪntrɪst] n intérêt m; (Comm: stake, share) participation f, intérêts mpl ▷ vt intéresser; **compound/simple ~** intérêt composé/simple; **British ~s in the Middle East** les intérêts britanniques au Moyen-Orient; **his main ~ is ...** ce qui l'intéresse le plus est ...
interested ['ɪntrɪstɪd] adj intéressé(e); **to be ~ in sth** s'intéresser à qch; **I'm ~ in going** ça m'intéresse d'y aller
interest-free ['ɪntrɪstˈfriː] adj sans intérêt
interesting ['ɪntrɪstɪŋ] adj intéressant(e)
interest rate n taux m d'intérêt
interface ['ɪntəfeɪs] n (Comput) interface f
interfere [ɪntəˈfɪəʳ] vi: **to ~ in** (quarrel) s'immiscer dans; (other people's business) se mêler de; **to ~ with** (object) tripoter, toucher à; (plans) contrecarrer; (duty) être en conflit avec; **don't ~** mêlez-vous de vos affaires
interference [ɪntəˈfɪərəns] n (gen) ingérence f; (Physics) interférence f; (Radio, TV) parasites mpl

interfering [ɪntəˈfɪərɪŋ] adj importun(e)
interim [ˈɪntərɪm] adj provisoire; (post)
intérimaire ▷ n: **in the ~** dans l'intérim
interior [ɪnˈtɪərɪər] n intérieur m ▷ adj
intérieur(e); (minister, department) de l'intérieur
interior decorator, interior designer n
décorateur(-trice) d'intérieur
interior design n architecture f d'intérieur
interjection [ɪntəˈdʒɛkʃən] n interjection f
interlock [ɪntəˈlɔk] vi s'enclencher ▷ vt
enclencher
interloper [ˈɪntələupər] n intrus(e)
interlude [ˈɪntəluːd] n intervalle m; (Theat)
intermède m
intermarry [ɪntəˈmærɪ] vi former des alliances
entre familles (or tribus); former des unions
consanguines
intermediary [ɪntəˈmiːdɪərɪ] n intermédiaire
m/f
intermediate [ɪntəˈmiːdɪət] adj intermédiaire;
(Scol: course, level) moyen(ne)
interment [ɪnˈtəːmənt] n inhumation f,
enterrement m
interminable [ɪnˈtəːmɪnəbl] adj sans fin,
interminable
intermission [ɪntəˈmɪʃən] n pause f; (Theat, Cine)
entracte m
intermittent [ɪntəˈmɪtnt] adj intermittent(e)
intermittently [ɪntəˈmɪtntlɪ] adv par
intermittence, par intervalles
intern vt [ɪnˈtəːn] interner ▷ n [ˈɪntəːn] (US)
interne m/f
internal [ɪnˈtəːnl] adj interne; (dispute, reform etc)
intérieur(e); **~ injuries** lésions fpl internes
internally [ɪnˈtəːnəlɪ] adv intérieurement; **"not
to be taken ~"** "pour usage externe"
Internal Revenue Service n (US) fisc m
international [ɪntəˈnæʃənl] adj international(e)
▷ n (Brit Sport) international m
International Atomic Energy Agency n
Agence Internationale de l'Énergie Atomique
International Court of Justice n Cour
internationale de justice
international date line n ligne f de
changement de date
internationally [ɪntəˈnæʃnəlɪ] adv dans le
monde entier
International Monetary Fund n Fonds
monétaire international
international relations npl relations
internationales
internecine [ɪntəˈniːsaɪn] adj mutuellement
destructeur(-trice)
internee [ɪntəːˈniː] n interné(e)
Internet [ɪntəˈnɛt] n: **the ~** l'Internet m
Internet café n cybercafé m
Internet Service Provider n fournisseur m
d'accès à Internet
Internet user n internaute m/f
internment [ɪnˈtəːnmənt] n internement m
interplay [ˈɪntəpleɪ] n effet m réciproque, jeu m
Interpol [ˈɪntəpɔl] n Interpol m

interpret [ɪnˈtəːprɪt] vt interpréter ▷ vi servir
d'interprète
interpretation [ɪntəːprɪˈteɪʃən] n
interprétation f
interpreter [ɪnˈtəːprɪtər] n interprète m/f; **could
you act as an ~ for us?** pourriez-vous nous
servir d'interprète?
interpreting [ɪnˈtəːprɪtɪŋ] n (profession)
interprétariat m
interrelated [ɪntərɪˈleɪtɪd] adj en corrélation, en
rapport étroit
interrogate [ɪnˈtɛrəugeɪt] vt interroger; (suspect
etc) soumettre à un interrogatoire
interrogation [ɪntɛrəuˈgeɪʃən] n interrogation
f; (by police) interrogatoire m
interrogative [ɪntəˈrɔgətɪv] adj
interrogateur(-trice) ▷ n (Ling) interrogatif m
interrogator [ɪnˈtɛrəgeɪtər] n
interrogateur(-trice)
interrupt [ɪntəˈrʌpt] vt, vi interrompre
interruption [ɪntəˈrʌpʃən] n interruption f
intersect [ɪntəˈsɛkt] vt couper, croiser; (Math)
intersecter ▷ vi se croiser, se couper;
s'intersecter
intersection [ɪntəˈsɛkʃən] n intersection f; (of
roads) croisement m
intersperse [ɪntəˈspəːs] vt: **to ~ with** parsemer
de
interstate [ˈɪntərsteɪt] (US) n autoroute f (qui
relie plusieurs États)
intertwine [ɪntəˈtwaɪn] vt entrelacer ▷ vi
s'entrelacer
interval [ˈɪntəvl] n intervalle m; (Brit: Theat)
entracte m; (: Sport) mi-temps f; **bright ~s** (in
weather) éclaircies fpl; **at ~s** par intervalles
intervene [ɪntəˈviːn] vi (time) s'écouler (entre-
temps); (event) survenir; (person) intervenir
intervention [ɪntəˈvɛnʃən] n intervention f
interview [ˈɪntəvjuː] n (Radio, TV) interview f;
(for job) entrevue f ▷ vt interviewer, avoir une
entrevue avec
interviewee [ɪntəvjuˈiː] n (for job) candidat m (qui
passe un entretien); (TV etc) invité(e), personne
interviewée
interviewer [ˈɪntəvjuər] n (Radio, TV)
interviewer m
intestate [ɪnˈtɛsteɪt] adj intestat f inv
intestinal [ɪnˈtɛstɪnl] adj intestinal(e)
intestine [ɪnˈtɛstɪn] n intestin m; **large ~** gros
intestin; **small ~** intestin grêle
intimacy [ˈɪntɪməsɪ] n intimité f
intimate adj [ˈɪntɪmət] intime; (friendship)
profond(e); (knowledge) approfondi(e) ▷ vt
[ˈɪntɪmeɪt] suggérer, laisser entendre;
(announce) faire savoir
intimately [ˈɪntɪmətlɪ] adv intimement
intimation [ɪntɪˈmeɪʃən] n annonce f
intimidate [ɪnˈtɪmɪdeɪt] vt intimider
intimidating [ɪnˈtɪmɪdeɪtɪŋ] adj intimidant(e)
intimidation [ɪntɪmɪˈdeɪʃən] n intimidation f
into [ˈɪntu] prep dans; **~ pieces/French** en
morceaux/français; **to change pounds ~**

dollars changer des livres en dollars; **3 ~ 9 goes 3** 9 divisé par 3 donne 3; **she's ~ opera** c'est une passionnée d'opéra

intolerable [ɪn'tɔlərəbl] *adj* intolérable

intolerance [ɪn'tɔlərns] *n* intolérance *f*

intolerant [ɪn'tɔlərnt] *adj*: **~ (of)** intolérant(e) (de); (*Med*) intolérant (à)

intonation [ɪntəu'neɪʃən] *n* intonation *f*

intoxicate [ɪn'tɔksɪkeɪt] *vt* enivrer

intoxicated [ɪn'tɔksɪkeɪtɪd] *adj* ivre

intoxication [ɪntɔksɪ'keɪʃən] *n* ivresse *f*

intractable [ɪn'træktəbl] *adj* (*child, temper*) indocile, insoumis(e); (*problem*) insoluble; (*illness*) incurable

intranet [ɪn'trənet] *n* intranet *m*

intransigent [ɪn'trænsɪdʒənt] *adj* intransigeant(e)

intransitive [ɪn'trænsɪtɪv] *adj* intransitif(-ive)

intra-uterine device ['ɪntrə'juːtəraɪn-] *n* dispositif intra-utérin, stérilet *m*

intravenous [ɪntrə'viːnəs] *adj* intraveineux(-euse)

in-tray ['ɪntreɪ] *n* courrier *m* "arrivée"

intrepid [ɪn'trepɪd] *adj* intrépide

intricacy ['ɪntrɪkəsɪ] *n* complexité *f*

intricate ['ɪntrɪkət] *adj* complexe, compliqué(e)

intrigue [ɪn'triːg] *n* intrigue *f* ▷ *vt* intriguer ▷ *vi* intriguer, comploter

intriguing [ɪn'triːgɪŋ] *adj* fascinant(e)

intrinsic [ɪn'trɪnsɪk] *adj* intrinsèque

introduce [ɪntrə'djuːs] *vt* introduire; (*TV show etc*) présenter; **to ~ sb (to sb)** présenter qn (à qn); **to ~ sb to** (*pastime, technique*) initier qn à; **may I ~ ...?** je vous présente ...

introduction [ɪntrə'dʌkʃən] *n* introduction *f*; (*of person*) présentation *f*; (*to new experience*) initiation *f*; **a letter of ~** une lettre de recommandation

introductory [ɪntrə'dʌktərɪ] *adj* préliminaire, introductif(-ive); **~ remarks** remarques *fpl* liminaires; **an ~ offer** une offre de lancement

introspection [ɪntrəu'spɛkʃən] *n* introspection *f*

introspective [ɪntrəu'spɛktɪv] *adj* introspectif(-ive)

introvert ['ɪntrəuvəːt] *adj, n* introverti(e)

intrude [ɪn'truːd] *vi* (*person*) être importun(e); **to ~ on** or **into** (*conversation etc*) s'immiscer dans; **am I intruding?** est-ce que je vous dérange?

intruder [ɪn'truːdər] *n* intrus(e)

intrusion [ɪn'truːʒən] *n* intrusion *f*

intrusive [ɪn'truːsɪv] *adj* importun(e), gênant(e)

intuition [ɪntjuː'ɪʃən] *n* intuition *f*

intuitive [ɪn'tjuːɪtɪv] *adj* intuitif(-ive)

inundate ['ɪnʌndeɪt] *vt*: **to ~ with** inonder de

inure [ɪn'juər] *vt*: **to ~ (to)** habituer (à)

invade [ɪn'veɪd] *vt* envahir

invader [ɪn'veɪdər] *n* envahisseur *m*

invalid *n* ['ɪnvəlɪd] malade *m/f*; (*with disability*) invalide *m/f* ▷ *adj* [ɪn'vælɪd] (*not valid*) invalide, non valide

invalidate [ɪn'vælɪdeɪt] *vt* invalider, annuler

invalid chair ['ɪnvəlɪd-] *n* (*Brit*) fauteuil *m* d'infirme

invaluable [ɪn'væljuəbl] *adj* inestimable, inappréciable

invariable [ɪn'vɛərɪəbl] *adj* invariable; (*fig*) immanquable

invariably [ɪn'vɛərɪəblɪ] *adv* invariablement; **she is ~ late** elle est toujours en retard

invasion [ɪn'veɪʒən] *n* invasion *f*

invective [ɪn'vɛktɪv] *n* invective *f*

inveigle [ɪn'viːgl] *vt*: **to ~ sb into (doing) sth** amener qn à (faire) qch (par la ruse *or* la flatterie)

invent [ɪn'vɛnt] *vt* inventer

invention [ɪn'vɛnʃən] *n* invention *f*

inventive [ɪn'vɛntɪv] *adj* inventif(-ive)

inventiveness [ɪn'vɛntɪvnɪs] *n* esprit inventif *or* d'invention

inventor [ɪn'vɛntər] *n* inventeur(-trice)

inventory ['ɪnvəntrɪ] *n* inventaire *m*

inventory control *n* (*Comm*) contrôle *m* des stocks

inverse [ɪn'vəːs] *adj* inverse ▷ *n* inverse *m*, contraire *m*; **in ~ proportion (to)** inversement proportionnel(le) (à)

inversely [ɪn'vəːslɪ] *adv* inversement

invert [ɪn'vəːt] *vt* intervertir; (*cup, object*) retourner

invertebrate [ɪn'vəːtɪbrət] *n* invertébré *m*

inverted commas [ɪn'vəːtɪd-] *npl* (*Brit*) guillemets *mpl*

invest [ɪn'vɛst] *vt* investir; (*endow*): **to ~ sb with sth** conférer qch à qn ▷ *vi* faire un investissement, investir; **to ~ in** placer de l'argent *or* investir dans; (*fig: acquire*) s'offrir, faire l'acquisition de

investigate [ɪn'vɛstɪgeɪt] *vt* étudier, examiner; (*crime*) faire une enquête sur

investigation [ɪnvɛstɪ'geɪʃən] *n* examen *m*; (*of crime*) enquête *f*, investigation *f*

investigative [ɪn'vɛstɪgeɪtɪv] *adj*: **~ journalism** enquête-reportage *f*, journalisme *m* d'enquête

investigator [ɪn'vɛstɪgeɪtər] *n* investigateur(-trice); **private ~** détective privé

investiture [ɪn'vɛstɪtʃər] *n* investiture *f*

investment [ɪn'vɛstmənt] *n* investissement *m*, placement *m*

investment income *n* revenu *m* de placement

investment trust *n* société *f* d'investissements

investor [ɪn'vɛstər] *n* épargnant(e); (*shareholder*) actionnaire *m/f*

inveterate [ɪn'vɛtərət] *adj* invétéré(e)

invidious [ɪn'vɪdɪəs] *adj* injuste; (*task*) déplaisant(e)

invigilate [ɪn'vɪdʒɪleɪt] (*Brit*) *vt* surveiller ▷ *vi* être de surveillance

invigilator [ɪn'vɪdʒɪleɪtər] *n* (*Brit*) surveillant *m* (d'examen)

invigorating [ɪn'vɪgəreɪtɪŋ] *adj* vivifiant(e), stimulant(e)

invincible [ɪn'vɪnsɪbl] *adj* invincible

inviolate [ɪn'vaɪələt] *adj* inviolé(e)

invisible [ɪnˈvɪzɪbl] *adj* invisible
invisible assets *npl* (*Brit*) actif incorporel
invisible ink *n* encre *f* sympathique
invisible mending *n* stoppage *m*
invitation [ɪnvɪˈteɪʃən] *n* invitation *f*; **by ~ only**
sur invitation; **at sb's ~** à la demande de qn
invite [ɪnˈvaɪt] *vt* inviter; (*opinions etc*)
demander; (*trouble*) chercher; **to ~ sb (to do)**
inviter qn (à faire); **to ~ sb to dinner** inviter qn
à dîner
▸ **invite out** *vt* inviter (à sortir)
▸ **invite over** *vt* inviter (chez soi)
inviting [ɪnˈvaɪtɪŋ] *adj* engageant(e),
attrayant(e); (*gesture*) encourageant(e)
invoice [ˈɪnvɔɪs] *n* facture *f* ▹ *vt* facturer; **to ~ sb**
for goods facturer des marchandises à qn
invoke [ɪnˈvəuk] *vt* invoquer
involuntary [ɪnˈvɔləntrɪ] *adj* involontaire
involve [ɪnˈvɔlv] *vt* (*entail*) impliquer; (*concern*)
concerner; (*require*) nécessiter; **to ~ sb in** (*theft
etc*) impliquer qn dans; (*activity, meeting*) faire
participer qn à
involved [ɪnˈvɔlvd] *adj* (*complicated*) complexe;
to be ~ in (*take part*) participer à; (*be engrossed*)
être plongé(e) dans; **to feel ~** se sentir
concerné(e); **to become ~** (*in love etc*) s'engager
involvement [ɪnˈvɔlvmənt] *n* (*personal role*) rôle
m; (*participation*) participation *f*; (*enthusiasm*)
enthousiasme *m*; (*of resources, funds*) mise *f* en jeu
invulnerable [ɪnˈvʌlnərəbl] *adj* invulnérable
inward [ˈɪnwəd] *adj* (*movement*) vers l'intérieur;
(*thought*) profond(e), intime ▹ *adv* = **inwards**
inwardly [ˈɪnwədlɪ] *adv* (*feel, think etc*)
secrètement, en son for intérieur
inwards [ˈɪnwədz] *adv* vers l'intérieur
I/O *abbr* (*Comput*: = *input/output*) E/S
IOC *n abbr* (= *International Olympic Committee*) CIO *m*
(= *Comité international olympique*)
iodine [ˈaɪəudiːn] *n* iode *m*
IOM *abbr* = **Isle of Man**
ion [ˈaɪən] *n* ion *m*
Ionian Sea [aɪˈəunɪən-] *n*: **the ~** la mer Ionienne
ioniser [ˈaɪənaɪzər] *n* ioniseur *m*
iota [aɪˈəutə] *n* (*fig*) brin *m*, grain *m*
IOU *n abbr* (= *I owe you*) reconnaissance *f* de dette
IOW *abbr* (*Brit*) = **Isle of Wight**
IPA *n abbr* (= *International Phonetic Alphabet*) A.P.I *m*
iPod® [ˈaɪpɔd] *n* iPod® *m*
IQ *n abbr* (= *intelligence quotient*) Q.I. *m*
IRA *n abbr* (= *Irish Republican Army*) IRA *f*; (*US*)
= **individual retirement account**
Iran [ɪˈrɑːn] *n* Iran *m*
Iranian [ɪˈreɪnɪən] *adj* iranien(ne) ▹ *n*
Iranien(ne); (*Ling*) iranien *m*
Iraq [ɪˈrɑːk] *n* Irak *m*
Iraqi [ɪˈrɑːkɪ] *adj* irakien(ne) ▹ *n* Irakien(ne)
irascible [ɪˈræsɪbl] *adj* irascible
irate [aɪˈreɪt] *adj* courroucé(e)
Ireland [ˈaɪələnd] *n* Irlande *f*; **Republic of ~**
République *f* d'Irlande
iris, irises [ˈaɪrɪs, -ɪz] *n* iris *m*
Irish [ˈaɪrɪʃ] *adj* irlandais(e) ▹ *npl*: **the ~** les

Irlandais ▹ *n* (*Ling*) irlandais *m*; **the Irish** *npl* les
Irlandais
Irishman [ˈaɪrɪʃmən] (*irreg*) *n* Irlandais *m*
Irish Sea *n*: **the ~** la mer d'Irlande
Irishwoman [ˈaɪrɪʃwumən] (*irreg*) *n* Irlandaise *f*
irk [əːk] *vt* ennuyer
irksome [ˈəːksəm] *adj* ennuyeux(-euse)
IRN *n abbr* (= *Independent Radio News*) agence de presse
radiophonique
IRO *n abbr* (*US*) = **International Refugee
Organization**
iron [ˈaɪən] *n* fer *m*; (*for clothes*) fer *m* à repasser
▹ *adj* de or en fer ▹ *vt* (*clothes*) repasser; **irons** *npl*
(*chains*) fers *mpl*, chaînes *fpl*
▸ **iron out** *vt* (*crease*) faire disparaître au fer;
(*fig*) aplanir; faire disparaître
Iron Curtain *n*: **the ~** le rideau de fer
iron foundry *n* fonderie *f* de fonte
ironic [aɪˈrɔnɪk], **ironical** [aɪˈrɔnɪkl] *adj*
ironique
ironically [aɪˈrɔnɪklɪ] *adv* ironiquement
ironing [ˈaɪənɪŋ] *n* (*activity*) repassage *m*; (*clothes:
ironed*) linge repassé; (*: to be ironed*) linge à
repasser
ironing board *n* planche *f* à repasser
ironmonger [ˈaɪənmʌŋgər] *n* (*Brit*) quincaillier
m; **~'s (shop)** quincaillerie *f*
iron ore *n* minerai *m* de fer
ironworks [ˈaɪənwəːks] *n* usine *f* sidérurgique
irony [ˈaɪrənɪ] *n* ironie *f*
irrational [ɪˈræʃənl] *adj* irrationnel(le); (*person*)
qui n'est pas rationnel
irreconcilable [ɪrɛkənˈsaɪləbl] *adj*
irréconciliable; (*opinion*): **~ with** inconciliable
avec
irredeemable [ɪrɪˈdiːməbl] *adj* (*Comm*) non
remboursable
irrefutable [ɪrɪˈfjuːtəbl] *adj* irréfutable
irregular [ɪˈrɛgjulər] *adj* irrégulier(-ière);
(*surface*) inégal(e); (*action, event*) peu orthodoxe
irregularity [ɪrɛgjuˈlærɪtɪ] *n* irrégularité *f*
irrelevance [ɪˈrɛləvəns] *n* manque *m* de rapport
or d'à-propos
irrelevant [ɪˈrɛləvənt] *adj* sans rapport, hors de
propos
irreligious [ɪrɪˈlɪdʒəs] *adj* irréligieux(-euse)
irreparable [ɪˈrɛprəbl] *adj* irréparable
irreplaceable [ɪrɪˈpleɪsəbl] *adj* irremplaçable
irrepressible [ɪrɪˈprɛsɪbl] *adj* irrépressible
irreproachable [ɪrɪˈprəutʃəbl] *adj* irréprochable
irresistible [ɪrɪˈzɪstɪbl] *adj* irrésistible
irresolute [ɪˈrɛzəluːt] *adj* irrésolu(e), indécis(e)
irrespective [ɪrɪˈspɛktɪv]: **~ of** *prep* sans tenir
compte de
irresponsible [ɪrɪˈspɔnsɪbl] *adj* (*act*)
irréfléchi(e); (*person*) qui n'a pas le sens des
responsabilités
irretrievable [ɪrɪˈtriːvəbl] *adj* irréparable,
irrémédiable; (*object*) introuvable
irreverent [ɪˈrɛvərnt] *adj* irrévérencieux(-euse)
irrevocable [ɪˈrɛvəkəbl] *adj* irrévocable
irrigate [ˈɪrɪgeɪt] *vt* irriguer

irrigation [ɪrɪˈɡeɪʃən] *n* irrigation *f*
irritable [ˈɪrɪtəbl] *adj* irritable
irritate [ˈɪrɪteɪt] *vt* irriter
irritating [ˈɪrɪteɪtɪŋ] *adj* irritant(e)
irritation [ɪrɪˈteɪʃən] *n* irritation *f*
IRS *n abbr* (*US*) = **Internal Revenue Service**
is [ɪz] *vb see* **be**
ISA *n abbr* (Brit: = *Individual Savings Account*) plan *m* d'épargne défiscalisé
ISBN *n abbr* (= *International Standard Book Number*) ISBN *m*
ISDN *n abbr* (= *Integrated Services Digital Network*) RNIS *m*
Islam [ˈɪzlɑːm] *n* Islam *m*
Islamic [ɪzˈlɑːmɪk] *adj* islamique; **~ fundamentalists** intégristes *mpl* musulmans
island [ˈaɪlənd] *n* île *f*; (*also:* **traffic island**) refuge *m* (pour piétons)
islander [ˈaɪləndəʳ] *n* habitant(e) d'une île, insulaire *m/f*
isle [aɪl] *n* île *f*
isn't [ˈɪznt] = **is not**
isolate [ˈaɪsəleɪt] *vt* isoler
isolated [ˈaɪsəleɪtɪd] *adj* isolé(e)
isolation [aɪsəˈleɪʃən] *n* isolement *m*
ISP *n abbr* = **Internet Service Provider**
Israel [ˈɪzreɪl] *n* Israël *m*
Israeli [ɪzˈreɪlɪ] *adj* israélien(ne) ▷ *n* Israélien(ne)
issue [ˈɪʃuː] *n* question *f*, problème *m*; (*outcome*) résultat *m*, issue *f*; (*of banknotes*) émission *f*; (*of newspaper*) numéro *m*; (*of book*) publication *f*, parution *f*; (*offspring*) descendance *f* ▷ *vt* (*rations, equipment*) distribuer; (*orders*) donner; (*statement*) publier, faire; (*certificate, passport*) délivrer; (*book*) faire paraître; publier; (*banknotes, cheques, stamps*) émettre, mettre en circulation ▷ *vi*: **to ~ from** provenir de; **at ~** en jeu, en cause; **to avoid the ~** éluder le problème; **to take ~ with sb (over sth)** exprimer son désaccord avec qn (sur qch); **to make an ~ of sth** faire de qch un problème; **to confuse** *or* **obscure the ~** embrouiller la question
Istanbul [ɪstænˈbuːl] *n* Istamboul, Istanbul
isthmus [ˈɪsməs] *n* isthme *m*
IT *n abbr* = **information technology**

 KEYWORD

it [ɪt] *pron* **1** (*specific: subject*) il (elle); (: *direct object*) le (la, l'); (: *indirect object*) lui; **it's on the table** c'est *or* il (*or* elle) est sur la table; **I can't find it** je n'arrive pas à le trouver; **give it to me** donne-le-moi
2 (*after prep*): **about/from/of it** en; **I spoke to him about it** je lui en ai parlé; **what did you learn from it?** qu'est-ce que vous en avez retiré?; **I'm proud of it** j'en suis fier; **I've come from it** j'en viens; **in/to it** y; **put the book in it** mettez-y le livre; **it's on it** c'est dessus; **he agreed to it** il y a consenti; **did you go to it?** (*party, concert etc*) est-ce que vous y êtes

allé(s)?; **above it, over it** (au-)dessus; **below it, under it** (en-)dessous; **in front of/behind it** devant/derrière
3 (*impersonal*) il; ce, cela, ça; **it's raining** il pleut; **it's Friday tomorrow** demain, c'est vendredi *or* nous sommes, vendredi; **it's 6 o'clock** il est 6 heures; **how far is it? — it's 10 miles** c'est loin? — c'est à 10 miles; **it's 2 hours by train** c'est à 2 heures de train; **who is it? — it's me** qui est-ce? — c'est moi

ITA *n abbr* (Brit: = *initial teaching alphabet*) alphabet en partie phonétique utilisé pour l'enseignement de la lecture
Italian [ɪˈtæljən] *adj* italien(ne) ▷ *n* Italien(ne); (*Ling*) italien *m*
italic [ɪˈtælɪk] *adj* italique
italics [ɪˈtælɪks] *npl* italique *m*
Italy [ˈɪtəlɪ] *n* Italie *f*
itch [ɪtʃ] *n* démangeaison *f* ▷ *vi* (*person*) éprouver des démangeaisons; (*part of body*) démanger; **I'm ~ing to do** l'envie me démange de faire
itchy [ˈɪtʃɪ] *adj* qui démange; **my back is ~** j'ai le dos qui me démange
it'd [ˈɪtd] = **it would; it had**
item [ˈaɪtəm] *n* (*gen*) article *m*; (*on agenda*) question *f*, point *m*; (*in programme*) numéro *m*; (*also:* **news item**) nouvelle *f*; **~s of clothing** articles vestimentaires
itemize [ˈaɪtəmaɪz] *vt* détailler, spécifier
itemized bill [ˈaɪtəmaɪzd-] *n* facture détaillée
itinerant [ɪˈtɪnərənt] *adj* itinérant(e); (*musician*) ambulant(e)
itinerary [aɪˈtɪnərərɪ] *n* itinéraire *m*
it'll [ˈɪtl] = **it will; it shall**
ITN *n abbr* (Brit: = *Independent Television News*) chaîne de télévision commerciale
its [ɪts] *adj* son (sa), ses *pl* ▷ *pron* le (la) sien(ne), les siens (siennes)
it's [ɪts] = **it is; it has**
itself [ɪtˈsɛlf] *pron* (*reflexive*) se; (*emphatic*) lui-même (elle-même)
ITV *n abbr* (Brit: = *Independent Television*) chaîne de télévision commerciale
IUD *n abbr* = **intra-uterine device**
I've [aɪv] = **I have**
ivory [ˈaɪvərɪ] *n* ivoire *m*
Ivory Coast *n* Côte *f* d'Ivoire
ivy [ˈaɪvɪ] *n* lierre *m*
Ivy League *n* (*US*) *voir article*

IVY LEAGUE

L'*Ivy League* regroupe les huit universités les plus prestigieuses du nord-est des États-Unis, ainsi surnommées à cause de leurs murs recouverts de lierre. Elles organisent des compétitions sportives entre elles. Ces universités sont: Brown, Columbia, Cornell, Dartmouth College, Harvard, Princeton, l'université de Pennsylvanie et Yale.

Jj

J, j [dʒeɪ] n (letter) J, j m; **J for Jack**, (US) **J for Jig** J comme Joseph

JA n abbr = **judge advocate**

J/A n abbr = **joint account**

jab [dʒæb] vt: **to ~ sth into** enfoncer or planter qch dans ▷ n coup m; (Med: inf) piqûre f

jabber ['dʒæbəʳ] vt, vi bredouiller, baragouiner

jack [dʒæk] n (Aut) cric m; (Bowls) cochonnet m; (Cards) valet m

▸ **jack in** vt (inf) laisser tomber

▸ **jack up** vt soulever (au cric)

jackal ['dʒækl] n chacal m

jackass ['dʒækæs] n (also fig) âne m

jackdaw ['dʒækdɔ:] n choucas m

jacket ['dʒækɪt] n veste f, veston m; (of boiler etc) enveloppe f; (of book) couverture f, jaquette f

jacket potato n pomme f de terre en robe des champs

jack-in-the-box ['dʒækɪnðəbɔks] n diable m à ressort

jackknife ['dʒæknaɪf] n couteau m de poche ▷ vi: **the lorry ~d** la remorque (du camion) s'est mise en travers

jack-of-all-trades ['dʒækəv'ɔ:ltreɪdz] n bricoleur m

jack plug n (Brit) jack m

jackpot ['dʒækpɔt] n gros lot

Jacuzzi® [dʒə'ku:zɪ] n jacuzzi® m

jaded ['dʒeɪdɪd] adj éreinté(e), fatigué(e)

JAG n abbr = **Judge Advocate General**

jagged ['dʒægɪd] adj dentelé(e)

jaguar ['dʒægjuəʳ] n jaguar m

jail [dʒeɪl] n prison f ▷ vt emprisonner, mettre en prison

jailbird ['dʒeɪlbə:d] n récidiviste m/f

jailbreak ['dʒeɪlbreɪk] n évasion f

jailer ['dʒeɪləʳ] n geôlier(-ière)

jail sentence n peine f de prison

jalopy [dʒə'lɔpɪ] n (inf) vieux clou

jam [dʒæm] n confiture f; (of shoppers etc) cohue f; (also: **traffic jam**) embouteillage m ▷ vt (passage etc) encombrer, obstruer; (mechanism, drawer etc) bloquer, coincer; (Radio) brouiller ▷ vi (mechanism, sliding part) se coincer, se bloquer; (gun) s'enrayer; **to be in a ~** (inf) être dans le pétrin; **to get sb out of a ~** (inf) sortir qn du pétrin; **to ~ sth into** (stuff) entasser or comprimer qch dans; (thrust) enfoncer qch dans; **the telephone lines are ~med** les lignes (téléphoniques) sont encombrées

Jamaica [dʒə'meɪkə] n Jamaïque f

Jamaican [dʒə'meɪkən] adj jamaïquain(e) ▷ n Jamaïquain(e)

jamb [dʒæm] n jambage m

jam jar n pot m à confiture

jammed [dʒæmd] adj (window etc) coincé(e)

jam-packed [dʒæm'pækt] adj: ~ **(with)** bourré(e) (de)

jam session n jam session f

jangle ['dʒæŋgl] vi cliqueter

janitor ['dʒænɪtəʳ] n (caretaker) concierge m

January ['dʒænjuərɪ] n janvier m; for phrases see also **July**

Japan [dʒə'pæn] n Japon m

Japanese [dʒæpə'ni:z] adj japonais(e) ▷ n (pl inv) Japonais(e); (Ling) japonais m

jar [dʒɑ:ʳ] n (stone, earthenware) pot m; (glass) bocal m ▷ vi (sound) produire un son grinçant or discordant; (colours etc) détonner, jurer ▷ vt (shake) ébranler, secouer

jargon ['dʒɑ:gən] n jargon m

jarring ['dʒɑ:rɪŋ] adj (sound, colour) discordant(e)

Jas. abbr = **James**

jasmin, jasmine ['dʒæzmɪn] n jasmin m

jaundice ['dʒɔ:ndɪs] n jaunisse f

jaundiced ['dʒɔ:ndɪst] adj (fig) envieux(-euse), désapprobateur(-trice)

jaunt [dʒɔ:nt] n balade f

jaunty ['dʒɔ:ntɪ] adj enjoué(e), désinvolte

Java ['dʒɑ:və] n Java f

javelin ['dʒævlɪn] n javelot m

jaw [dʒɔ:] n mâchoire f

jawbone ['dʒɔ:bəun] n maxillaire m

jay [dʒeɪ] n geai m

jaywalker ['dʒeɪwɔ:kəʳ] n piéton indiscipliné

jazz [dʒæz] n jazz m

▸ **jazz up** vt animer, égayer

jazz band n orchestre m or groupe m de jazz

jazzy ['dʒæzɪ] adj bariolé(e), tapageur(-euse); (beat) de jazz

JCB® n excavatrice f

JCS n abbr (US) = **Joint Chiefs of Staff**

JD *n abbr* (US: = *Doctor of Laws*) titre universitaire; (= *Justice Department*) ministère de la Justice
jealous ['dʒɛləs] *adj* jaloux(-ouse)
jealously ['dʒɛləslɪ] *adv* jalousement
jealousy ['dʒɛləsɪ] *n* jalousie *f*
jeans [dʒiːnz] *npl* jean *m*
Jeep® [dʒiːp] *n* jeep *f*
jeer [dʒɪə'] *vi*: **to ~ (at)** huer; se moquer cruellement (de), railler
jeering ['dʒɪərɪŋ] *adj* railleur(-euse), moqueur(-euse) ▷ *n* huées *fpl*
jeers ['dʒɪəz] *npl* huées *fpl*; sarcasmes *mpl*
Jehovah's Witness [dʒɪ'həʊvəz-] *n* témoin *m* de Jéhovah
Jello® ['dʒɛləʊ] (US) *n* gelée *f*
jelly ['dʒɛlɪ] *n* (*dessert*) gelée *f*; (US: *jam*) confiture *f*
jellyfish ['dʒɛlɪfɪʃ] *n* méduse *f*
jeopardize ['dʒɛpədaɪz] *vt* mettre en danger *or* péril
jeopardy ['dʒɛpədɪ] *n*: **in ~** en danger *or* péril
jerk [dʒəːk] *n* secousse *f*, saccade *f*; (*of muscle*) spasme *m*; (*inf*) pauvre type *m* ▷ *vt* (*shake*) donner une secousse à; (*pull*) tirer brusquement ▷ *vi* (*vehicles*) cahoter
jerkin ['dʒəːkɪn] *n* blouson *m*
jerky ['dʒəːkɪ] *adj* saccadé(e), cahotant(e)
jerry-built ['dʒɛrɪbɪlt] *adj* de mauvaise qualité
jerry can ['dʒɛrɪ-] *n* bidon *m*
Jersey ['dʒəːzɪ] *n* Jersey *f*
jersey ['dʒəːzɪ] *n* tricot *m*; (*fabric*) jersey *m*
Jerusalem [dʒə'ruːsləm] *n* Jérusalem
jest [dʒɛst] *n* plaisanterie *f*; **in ~** en plaisantant
jester ['dʒɛstə'] *n* (*History*) plaisantin *m*
Jesus ['dʒiːzəs] *n* Jésus; **~ Christ** Jésus-Christ
jet [dʒɛt] *n* (*of gas, liquid*) jet *m*; (*Aut*) gicleur *m*; (*Aviat*) avion *m* à réaction, jet *m*
jet-black ['dʒɛt'blæk] *adj* (d'un noir) de jais
jet engine *n* moteur *m* à réaction
jet lag *n* décalage *m* horaire
jetsam ['dʒɛtsəm] *n* objets jetés à la mer (et rejetés sur la côte)
jet-setter ['dʒɛtsɛtə'] *n* membre *m* du *or* de la jet set
jet-ski *vi* faire du jet-ski *or* scooter des mers
jettison ['dʒɛtɪsn] *vt* jeter par-dessus bord
jetty ['dʒɛtɪ] *n* jetée *f*, digue *f*
Jew [dʒuː] *n* Juif *m*
jewel ['dʒuːəl] *n* bijou *m*, joyau *m*; (*in watch*) rubis *m*
jeweller, (US) **jeweler** ['dʒuːələ'] *n* bijoutier(-ière), joaillier *m*
jeweller's, jeweller's shop *n* (*Brit*) bijouterie *f*, joaillerie *f*
jewellery, (US) **jewelry** ['dʒuːəlrɪ] *n* bijoux *mpl*
Jewess ['dʒuːɪs] *n* Juive *f*
Jewish ['dʒuːɪʃ] *adj* juif (juive)
JFK *n abbr* (US) = **John Fitzgerald Kennedy International Airport**
jib [dʒɪb] *n* (*Naut*) foc *m*; (*of crane*) flèche *f* ▷ *vi* (*horse*) regimber; **to ~ at doing sth** rechigner à faire qch
jibe [dʒaɪb] *n* sarcasme *m*

jiffy ['dʒɪfɪ] *n* (*inf*): **in a ~** en un clin d'œil
jig [dʒɪg] *n* (*dance, tune*) gigue *m*
jigsaw ['dʒɪgsɔː] *n* (*also*: **jigsaw puzzle**) puzzle *m*; (*tool*) scie sauteuse
jilt [dʒɪlt] *vt* laisser tomber, plaquer
jingle ['dʒɪŋgl] *n* (*advertising jingle*) couplet *m* publicitaire ▷ *vi* cliqueter, tinter
jingoism ['dʒɪŋgəʊɪzəm] *n* chauvinisme *m*
jinx [dʒɪŋks] *n* (*inf*) (mauvais) sort
jitters ['dʒɪtəz] *npl* (*inf*): **to get the ~** avoir la trouille *or* la frousse
jittery ['dʒɪtərɪ] *adj* (*inf*) nerveux(-euse); **to be ~** avoir les nerfs en pelote
jiujitsu [dʒuː'dʒɪtsuː] *n* jiu-jitsu *m*
job [dʒɔb] *n* (*chore, task*) travail *m*, tâche *f*; (*employment*) emploi *m*, poste *m*, place *f*; **a part-time/full-time ~** un emploi à temps partiel/à plein temps; **he's only doing his ~** il fait son boulot; **it's a good ~ that ...** c'est heureux *or* c'est une chance que ... + *sub*; **just the ~!** (c'est) juste *or* exactement ce qu'il faut!
jobber ['dʒɔbə'] *n* (*Brit Stock Exchange*) négociant *m* en titres
jobbing ['dʒɔbɪŋ] *adj* (*Brit: workman*) à la tâche, à la journée
job centre ['dʒɔbsɛntə'] (*Brit*) *n* ≈ ANPE *f*, ≈ Agence nationale pour l'emploi
job creation scheme *n* plan *m* pour la création d'emplois
job description *n* description *f* du poste
jobless ['dʒɔblɪs] *adj* sans travail, au chômage ▷ *npl*: **the ~** les sans-emploi *m inv*, les chômeurs *mpl*
job lot *n* lot *m* (d'articles divers)
job satisfaction *n* satisfaction professionnelle
job security *n* sécurité *f* de l'emploi
job specification *n* caractéristiques *fpl* du poste
Jock [dʒɔk] *n* (*inf: Scotsman*) Écossais *m*
jockey ['dʒɔkɪ] *n* jockey *m* ▷ *vi*: **to ~ for position** manœuvrer pour être bien placé
jockey box *n* (*US Aut*) boîte *f* à gants, vide-poches *m inv*
jockstrap ['dʒɔkstræp] *n* slip *m* de sport
jocular ['dʒɔkjulə'] *adj* jovial(e), enjoué(e); facétieux(-euse)
jog [dʒɔg] *vt* secouer ▷ *vi* (*Sport*) faire du jogging; **to ~ along** cahoter; trotter; **to ~ sb's memory** rafraîchir la mémoire de qn
jogger ['dʒɔgə'] *n* jogger *m/f*
jogging ['dʒɔgɪŋ] *n* jogging *m*
john [dʒɔn] *n* (*US inf*): **the ~** (*toilet*) les cabinets *mpl*
join [dʒɔɪn] *vt* (*put together*) unir, assembler; (*become member of*) s'inscrire à; (*meet*) rejoindre, retrouver; (*queue*) se joindre à ▷ *vi* (*roads, rivers*) se rejoindre, se rencontrer ▷ *n* raccord *m*; **will you ~ us for dinner?** vous dînerez bien avec nous?; **I'll ~ you later** je vous rejoindrai plus tard; **to ~ forces (with)** s'associer (à)
  ▶ **join in** *vi* se mettre de la partie ▷ *vt fus* se mêler à
  ▶ **join up** *vi* (*meet*) se rejoindre; (*Mil*) s'engager

joiner ['dʒɔɪnə^r] (*Brit*) *n* menuisier *m*
joinery ['dʒɔɪnərɪ] *n* menuiserie *f*
joint [dʒɔɪnt] *n* (*Tech*) jointure *f*; joint *m*; (*Anat*) articulation *f*, jointure; (*Brit Culin*) rôti *m*; (*inf: place*) boîte *f*; (*of cannabis*) joint ▷ *adj* commun(e); (*committee*) mixte, paritaire; (*winner*) ex aequo; **~ responsibility** coresponsabilité *f*
joint account *n* compte joint
jointly ['dʒɔɪntlɪ] *adv* ensemble, en commun
joint ownership *n* copropriété *f*
joint-stock company ['dʒɔɪntstɔk-] *n* société *f* par actions
joint venture *n* entreprise commune
joist [dʒɔɪst] *n* solive *f*
joke [dʒəuk] *n* plaisanterie *f*; (*also:* **practical joke**) farce *f* ▷ *vi* plaisanter; **to play a ~ on** jouer un tour à, faire une farce à
joker ['dʒəukə^r] *n* plaisantin *m*, blagueur(-euse); (*Cards*) joker *m*
joking ['dʒəukɪŋ] *n* plaisanterie *f*
jollity ['dʒɔlɪtɪ] *n* réjouissances *fpl*, gaieté *f*
jolly ['dʒɔlɪ] *adj* gai(e), enjoué(e); (*enjoyable*) amusant(e), plaisant(e) ▷ *adv* (*Brit inf*) rudement, drôlement ▷ *vt* (*Brit*): **to ~ sb along** amadouer qn, convaincre *or* entraîner qn à force d'encouragements; **~ good!** (*Brit*) formidable!
jolt [dʒəult] *n* cahot *m*, secousse *f*; (*shock*) choc *m* ▷ *vt* cahoter, secouer
Jordan ['dʒɔː.dən] *n* (*country*) Jordanie *f*; (*river*) Jourdain *m*
Jordanian [dʒɔː'deɪnɪən] *adj* jordanien(ne) ▷ *n* Jordanien(ne)
joss stick ['dʒɔsstɪk] *n* bâton *m* d'encens
jostle ['dʒɔsl] *vt* bousculer, pousser ▷ *vi* jouer des coudes
jot [dʒɔt] *n*: **not one ~** pas un brin
▶ **jot down** *vt* inscrire rapidement, noter
jotter ['dʒɔtə^r] *n* (*Brit*) cahier *m* (de brouillon); bloc-notes *m*
journal ['dʒəː.nl] *n* journal *m*
journalese [dʒəː.nə'liːz] *n* (*pej*) style *m* journalistique
journalism ['dʒəː.nəlɪzəm] *n* journalisme *m*
journalist ['dʒəː.nəlɪst] *n* journaliste *m/f*
journey ['dʒəː.nɪ] *n* voyage *m*; (*distance covered*) trajet *m* ▷ *vi* voyager; **the ~ takes two hours** le trajet dure deux heures; **a 5-hour ~** un voyage de 5 heures; **how was your ~?** votre voyage s'est bien passé?
jovial ['dʒəuvɪəl] *adj* jovial(e)
jowl [dʒaul] *n* mâchoire *f* (*inférieure*); bajoue *f*
joy [dʒɔɪ] *n* joie *f*
joyful ['dʒɔɪful], **joyous** ['dʒɔɪəs] *adj* joyeux(-euse)
joyride ['dʒɔɪraɪd] *vi*: **to go joyriding** *faire une virée dans une voiture volée*
joyrider ['dʒɔɪraɪdə^r] *n* voleur(-euse) de voiture (*qui fait une virée dans le véhicule volé*)
joy stick ['dʒɔɪstɪk] *n* (*Aviat*) manche *m* à balai; (*Comput*) manche à balai, manette *f* (de jeu)
JP *n abbr* = **Justice of the Peace**

Jr *abbr* = **junior**
JTPA *n abbr* (*US*: = *Job Training Partnership Act*) programme gouvernemental *de formation*
jubilant ['dʒuː.bɪlnt] *adj* triomphant(e), réjoui(e)
jubilation [dʒuː.bɪ'leɪʃən] *n* jubilation *f*
jubilee ['dʒuː.bɪliː] *n* jubilé *m*; **silver ~** (jubilé du) vingt-cinquième anniversaire
judge [dʒʌdʒ] *n* juge *m* ▷ *vt* juger; (*estimate: weight, size etc*) apprécier; (*consider*) estimer ▷ *vi*: **judging** *or* **to ~ by his expression** d'après son expression; **as far as I can ~** autant que je puisse en juger
judge advocate *n* (*Mil*) magistrat *m* militaire
judgment, judgement ['dʒʌdʒmənt] *n* jugement *m*; (*punishment*) châtiment *m*; **in my ~** à mon avis; **to pass ~ on** (*Law*) prononcer un jugement (sur)
judicial [dʒuː'dɪʃl] *adj* judiciaire; (*fair*) impartial(e)
judiciary [dʒuː'dɪʃɪərɪ] *n* (pouvoir *m*) judiciaire *m*
judicious [dʒuː'dɪʃəs] *adj* judicieux(-euse)
judo ['dʒuː.dəu] *n* judo *m*
jug ['dʒʌg] *n* pot *m*, cruche *f*
jugged hare ['dʒʌgd-] *n* (*Brit*) civet *m* de lièvre
juggernaut ['dʒʌgənɔːt] *n* (*Brit: huge truck*) mastodonte *m*
juggle ['dʒʌgl] *vi* jongler
juggler ['dʒʌglə^r] *n* jongleur *m*
Jugoslav ['juː.gəu'slɑː.v] *adj*, *n* = **Yugoslav**
jugular ['dʒʌgjulə^r] *adj*: **~ (vein)** veine *f* jugulaire
juice [dʒuːs] *n* jus *m*; (*inf: petrol*): **we've run out of ~** c'est la panne sèche
juicy ['dʒuː.sɪ] *adj* juteux(-euse)
jukebox ['dʒuː.kbɔks] *n* juke-box *m*
July [dʒuː'laɪ] *n* juillet *m*; **the first of ~** le premier juillet; **(on) the eleventh of ~** le onze juillet; **in the month of ~** au mois de juillet; **at the beginning/end of ~** au début/à la fin (du mois) de juillet, début/fin juillet; **in the middle of ~** au milieu (du mois) de juillet, à la mi-juillet; **during ~** pendant le mois de juillet; **in ~ of next year** en juillet de l'année prochaine; **each** *or* **every ~** tous les ans *or* chaque année en juillet; **~ was wet this year** il a beaucoup plu cette année en juillet
jumble ['dʒʌmbl] *n* fouillis *m* ▷ *vt* (*also:* **jumble up, jumble together**) mélanger, brouiller
jumble sale *n* (*Brit*) vente *f* de charité
jumbo ['dʒʌmbəu] *adj* (*also:* **jumbo jet**) (avion) gros porteur (à réaction); **~ size** format maxi *or* extra-grand
jump [dʒʌmp] *vi* sauter, bondir; (*with fear etc*) sursauter; (*increase*) monter en flèche ▷ *vt* sauter, franchir ▷ *n* saut *m*, bond *m*; (*with fear etc*) sursaut *m*; (*fence*) obstacle *m*; **to ~ the queue** (*Brit*) passer avant son tour
▶ **jump about** *vi* sautiller
▶ **jump at** *vt fus* (*fig*) sauter sur; **he ~ed at the offer** il s'est empressé d'accepter la proposition
▶ **jump down** *vi* sauter (pour descendre)
▶ **jump up** *vi* se lever (d'un bond)
jumped-up ['dʒʌmptʌp] *adj* (*Brit pej*) parvenu(e)

jumper ['dʒʌmpə^r] n (Brit: pullover) pull-over m; (US: pinafore dress) robe-chasuble f; (Sport) sauteur(-euse)

jump leads, (US) **jumper cables** npl câbles mpl de démarrage

jump-start ['dʒʌmpstɑːt] vt (car: push) démarrer en poussant; (: with jump leads) démarrer avec des câbles (de démarrage); (fig: project, situation) faire redémarrer promptement

jumpy ['dʒʌmpɪ] adj nerveux(-euse), agité(e)

Jun. abbr = **June; junior**

junction ['dʒʌŋkʃən] n (Brit: of roads) carrefour m; (of rails) embranchement m

juncture ['dʒʌŋktʃə^r] n: **at this** ~ à ce moment-là, sur ces entrefaites

June [dʒuːn] n juin m; for phrases see also **July**

jungle ['dʒʌŋgl] n jungle f

junior ['dʒuːnɪə^r] adj, n: **he's ~ to me (by two years), he's my ~ (by two years)** il est mon cadet (de deux ans), il est plus jeune que moi (de deux ans); **he's ~ to me** (seniority) il est en dessous de moi (dans la hiérarchie), j'ai plus d'ancienneté que lui

junior executive n cadre moyen

junior high school n (US) ≈ collège m d'enseignement secondaire; see also **high school**

junior minister n (Brit) ministre m sous tutelle

junior partner n associé(-adjoint) m

junior school n (Brit) école f primaire

junior sizes npl (Comm) tailles fpl fillettes/garçonnets

juniper ['dʒuːnɪpə^r] n: ~ **berry** baie f de genièvre

junk [dʒʌŋk] n (rubbish) camelote f; (cheap goods) bric-à-brac m inv; (ship) jonque f ▷ vt (inf) abandonner, mettre au rancart

junk bond n (Comm) obligation hautement spéculative utilisée dans les OPA agressives

junk dealer n brocanteur(-euse)

junket ['dʒʌŋkɪt] n (Culin) lait caillé; (Brit inf): **to go on a ~, go ~ing** voyager aux frais de la princesse

junk food n snacks vite prêts (sans valeur nutritive)

junkie ['dʒʌŋkɪ] n (inf) junkie m, drogué(e)

junk mail n prospectus mpl; (Comput) messages mpl publicitaires

junk room n (US) débarras m

junk shop n (boutique f de) brocanteur m

Junr abbr = **junior**

junta ['dʒʌntə] n junte f

Jupiter ['dʒuːpɪtə^r] n (planet) Jupiter f

jurisdiction [dʒuərɪs'dɪkʃən] n juridiction f; **it falls** or **comes within/outside our** ~ cela est/n'est pas de notre compétence or ressort

jurisprudence [dʒuərɪs'pruːdəns] n jurisprudence f

juror ['dʒuərə^r] n juré m

jury ['dʒuərɪ] n jury m

jury box n banc m des jurés

juryman ['dʒuərɪmən] (irreg) n = **juror**

just [dʒʌst] adj juste ▷ adv: **he's ~ done it/left** il vient de le faire/partir; **~ as I expected** exactement or précisément comme je m'y attendais; ~ **right/two o'clock** exactement or juste ce qu'il faut/deux heures; **we were ~ going** nous partions; **I was ~ about to phone** j'allais téléphoner; **~ as he was leaving** au moment or à l'instant précis où il partait; ~ **before/enough/here** juste avant/assez/là; **it's ~ me/a mistake** ce n'est que moi/(rien) qu'une erreur; ~ **missed/caught** manqué/attrapé de justesse; ~ **listen to this!** écoutez un peu ça!; ~ **ask someone the way** vous n'avez qu'à demander votre chemin à quelqu'un; **it's ~ as good** c'est (vraiment) aussi bon; **she's ~ as clever as you** elle est tout aussi intelligente que vous; **it's ~ as well that you ...** heureusement que vous ...; **not ~ now** pas tout de suite; ~ **a minute!**, ~ **one moment!** un instant (s'il vous plaît)!

justice ['dʒʌstɪs] n justice f; (US: judge) juge m de la Cour suprême; **Lord Chief J~** (Brit) premier président de la cour d'appel; **this photo doesn't do you ~** cette photo ne vous avantage pas

Justice of the Peace n juge m de paix

justifiable [dʒʌstɪ'faɪəbl] adj justifiable

justifiably [dʒʌstɪ'faɪəblɪ] adv légitimement, à juste titre

justification [dʒʌstɪfɪ'keɪʃən] n justification f

justify ['dʒʌstɪfaɪ] vt justifier; **to be justified in doing sth** être en droit de faire qch

justly ['dʒʌstlɪ] adv avec raison, justement

justness ['dʒʌstnɪs] n justesse f

jut [dʒʌt] vi (also: **jut out**) dépasser, faire saillie

jute [dʒuːt] n jute m

juvenile ['dʒuːvənaɪl] adj juvénile; (court, books) pour enfants ▷ n adolescent(e)

juvenile delinquency n délinquance f juvénile

juxtapose ['dʒʌkstəpəuz] vt juxtaposer

juxtaposition [dʒʌkstəpə'zɪʃən] n juxtaposition f

Kk

K, k [keɪ] n (letter) K, k m; **K for King** K comme
Kléber ▷ abbr (= one thousand) K; (Brit: = Knight)
titre honorifique

kaftan ['kæftæn] n cafetan m

Kalahari Desert [kælə'hɑːrɪ-] n désert m de
Kalahari

kale [keɪl] n chou frisé

kaleidoscope [kə'laɪdəskəup] n kaléidoscope m

kamikaze [kæmɪ'kɑːzɪ] adj kamikaze

Kampala [kæm'pɑːlə] n Kampala

Kampuchea [kæmpu'tʃɪə] n Kampuchéa m

kangaroo [kæŋgə'ruː] n kangourou m

Kans. abbr (US) = **Kansas**

kaput [kə'put] adj (inf) kaput

karaoke [kɑːrə'əukɪ] n karaoké m

karate [kə'rɑːtɪ] n karaté m

Kashmir [kæʃ'mɪəʳ] n Cachemire m

Kazakhstan [kɑːzɑː'kstæn] n Kazakhstan m

kB n abbr (= kilobyte) Ko m

KC n abbr (Brit Law: = King's Counsel) titre donné à
certains avocats; see also **QC**

kd abbr (US: = knocked down) en pièces détachées

kebab [kə'bæb] n kebab m

keel [kiːl] n quille f; **on an even ~** (fig) à flot
▶ **keel over** vi (Naut) chavirer, dessaler; (person)
tomber dans les pommes

keen [kiːn] adj (eager) plein(e) d'enthousiasme;
(interest, desire, competition) vif (vive); (eye,
intelligence) pénétrant(e); (edge) effilé(e); **to be ~
to do** or **on doing sth** désirer vivement faire
qch, tenir beaucoup à faire qch; **to be ~ on sth/
sb** aimer beaucoup qch/qn; **I'm not ~ on going**
je ne suis pas chaud pour y aller, je n'ai pas très
envie d'y aller

keenly ['kiːnlɪ] adv (enthusiastically) avec
enthousiasme; (feel) vivement, profondément;
(look) intensément

keenness ['kiːnnɪs] n (eagerness) enthousiasme
m; ~ **to do** vif désir de faire

keep [kiːp] (pt, pp **kept** [kɛpt]) vt (retain, preserve)
garder; (hold back) retenir; (shop, accounts, promise,
diary) tenir; (support) entretenir, assurer la
subsistance de; (a promise) tenir; (chickens, bees,
pigs etc) élever ▷ vi (food) se conserver; (remain: in
a certain state or place) rester ▷ n (of castle) donjon
m; (food etc): **enough for his ~** assez pour

(assurer) sa subsistance; **to ~ doing sth**
(continue) continuer à faire qch; (repeatedly) ne
pas arrêter de faire qch; **to ~ sb from doing/
sth from happening** empêcher qn de faire or
que qn (ne) fasse/que qch (n')arrive; **to ~ sb
happy/a place tidy** faire que qn soit content/
qu'un endroit reste propre; **to ~ sb waiting**
faire attendre qn; **to ~ an appointment** ne pas
manquer un rendez-vous; **to ~ a record of sth**
prendre note de qch; **to ~ sth to o.s.** garder qch
pour soi, tenir qch secret; **to ~ sth from sb**
cacher qch à qn; **to ~ time** (clock) être à l'heure,
ne pas retarder; **for ~s** (inf) pour de bon, pour
toujours
▶ **keep away** vt: **to ~ sth/sb away from sb**
tenir qch/qn éloigné de qn ▷ vi: **to ~ away
(from)** ne pas s'approcher (de)
▶ **keep back** vt (crowds, tears, money) retenir;
(conceal: information): **to ~ sth back from sb**
cacher qch à qn ▷ vi rester en arrière
▶ **keep down** vt (control: prices, spending)
empêcher d'augmenter, limiter; (retain: food)
garder ▷ vi (person) rester assis(e); rester par
terre
▶ **keep in** vt (invalid, child) garder à la maison;
(Scol) consigner ▷ vi (inf): **to ~ in with sb** rester
en bons termes avec qn
▶ **keep off** vt (dog, person) éloigner ▷ vi ne pas
s'approcher; **if the rain ~s off** s'il ne pleut pas;
~ your hands off! pas touche! (inf); **"~ off the
grass"** "pelouse interdite"
▶ **keep on** vi continuer; **to ~ on doing**
continuer à faire; **don't ~ on about it!** arrête
(d'en parler)!
▶ **keep out** vt empêcher d'entrer ▷ vi (stay out)
rester en dehors; **"~ out"** "défense d'entrer"
▶ **keep up** vi (fig: in comprehension) suivre ▷ vt
continuer, maintenir; **to ~ up with sb** (in work
etc) se maintenir au même niveau que qn; (in
race etc) aller aussi vite que qn

keeper ['kiːpəʳ] n gardien(ne)

keep-fit [kiːp'fɪt] n gymnastique f (d'entretien)

keeping ['kiːpɪŋ] n (care) garde f; **in ~ with** en
harmonie avec

keeps [kiːps] n: **for ~** (inf) pour de bon, pour
toujours

keepsake ['ki:pseɪk] *n* souvenir *m*

keg [kɛg] *n* barrique *f*, tonnelet *m*

Ken. *abbr* (US) = **Kentucky**

kennel ['kɛnl] *n* niche *f*; **kennels** *npl* (*for boarding*) chenil *m*

Kenya ['kɛnjə] *n* Kenya *m*

Kenyan ['kɛnjən] *adj* kényan(ne) ▷ *n* Kényan(ne)

kept [kɛpt] *pt, pp of* **keep**

kerb [kə:b] *n* (*Brit*) bordure *f* du trottoir

kerb crawler [-krɔ:lə^r] *n* personne qui accoste les prostitué(e)s en voiture

kernel ['kə:nl] *n* amande *f*; (*fig*) noyau *m*

kerosene ['kɛrəsi:n] *n* kérosène *m*

ketchup ['kɛtʃəp] *n* ketchup *m*

kettle ['kɛtl] *n* bouilloire *f*

key [ki:] *n*; clé *f*; (*of piano, typewriter*) touche *f*; (*on map*) légende *f* ▷ *adj* (*factor, role, area*) clé *inv* ▷ *cpd* (-)clé ▷ *vt* (*also*: **key in**: *text*) saisir; **can I have my ~?** je peux avoir ma clé?; **a ~ issue** un problème fondamental

keyboard ['ki:bɔ:d] *n* clavier *m* ▷ *vt* (*text*) saisir

keyboarder ['ki:bɔ:də^r] *n* claviste *m/f*

keyed up [ki:d'ʌp] *adj*: **to be (all) ~** être surexcité(e)

keyhole ['ki:həul] *n* trou *m* de la serrure

keyhole surgery *n* chirurgie très minutieuse où l'incision est minimale

keynote ['ki:nəut] *n* (*Mus*) tonique *f*; (*fig*) note dominante

keypad ['ki:pæd] *n* pavé *m* numérique

keyring ['ki:rɪŋ] *n* porte-clés *m*

keystroke ['ki:strəuk] *n* frappe *f*

kg *abbr* (= *kilogram*) K

KGB *n abbr* KGB *m*

khaki ['kɑ:kɪ] *adj, n* kaki *m*

kibbutz [kɪ'buts] *n* kibboutz *m*

kick [kɪk] *vt* donner un coup de pied à ▷ *vi* (*horse*) ruer ▷ *n* coup *m* de pied; (*of rifle*) recul *m*; (*inf*: *thrill*): **he does it for ~s** il le fait parce que ça l'excite, il le fait pour le plaisir; **to ~ the habit** (*inf*) arrêter
  ▶ **kick around** *vi* (*inf*) traîner
  ▶ **kick off** *vi* (*Sport*) donner le coup d'envoi

kick-off ['kɪkɔf] *n* (*Sport*) coup *m* d'envoi

kick-start ['kɪkstɑ:t] *n* (*also*: **kick-starter**) lanceur *m* au pied

kid [kɪd] *n* (*inf*: *child*) gamin(e), gosse *m/f*; (*animal, leather*) chevreau *m* ▷ *vi* (*inf*) plaisanter, blaguer

kid gloves *npl*: **to treat sb with ~** traiter qn avec ménagement

kidnap ['kɪdnæp] *vt* enlever, kidnapper

kidnapper ['kɪdnæpə^r] *n* ravisseur(-euse)

kidnapping ['kɪdnæpɪŋ] *n* enlèvement *m*

kidney ['kɪdnɪ] *n* (*Anat*) rein *m*; (*Culin*) rognon *m*

kidney bean *n* haricot *m* rouge

kidney machine *n* (*Med*) rein artificiel

Kilimanjaro [kɪlɪmən'dʒɑ:rəu] *n*: **Mount ~** Kilimandjaro *m*

kill [kɪl] *vt* tuer; (*fig*) faire échouer; détruire; supprimer ▷ *n* mise *f* à mort; **to ~ time** tuer le temps

▶ **kill off** *vt* exterminer; (*fig*) éliminer

killer ['kɪlə^r] *n* tueur(-euse); (*murderer*) meurtrier(-ière)

killer instinct *n* combativité *f*; **to have the ~** avoir un tempérament de battant

killing ['kɪlɪŋ] *n* meurtre *m*; (*of group of people*) tuerie *f*, massacre *m*; (*inf*): **to make a ~** se remplir les poches, réussir un beau coup ▷ *adj* (*inf*) tordant(e)

killjoy ['kɪldʒɔɪ] *n* rabat-joie *m inv*

kiln [kɪln] *n* four *m*

kilo ['ki:ləu] *n* kilo *m*

kilobyte ['ki:ləubaɪt] *n* (*Comput*) kilo-octet *m*

kilogram, kilogramme ['kɪləugræm] *n* kilogramme *m*

kilometre, (US) **kilometer** ['kɪləmi:tə^r] *n* kilomètre *m*

kilowatt ['kɪləuwɔt] *n* kilowatt *m*

kilt [kɪlt] *n* kilt *m*

kilter ['kɪltə^r] *n*: **out of ~** déréglé(e), détraqué(e)

kimono [kɪ'məunəu] *n* kimono *m*

kin [kɪn] *n see* **next-of-kin**; **kith**

kind [kaɪnd] *adj* gentil(le), aimable ▷ *n* sorte *f*, espèce *f*; (*species*) genre *m*; **would you be ~ enough to ...?**, **would you be so ~ as to ...?** auriez-vous la gentillesse *or* l'obligeance de ...?; **it's very ~ of you (to do)** c'est très aimable à vous (de faire); **to be two of a ~** se ressembler; **in ~** (*Comm*) en nature; (*fig*): **to repay sb in ~** rendre la pareille à qn; **~ of** (*inf*: *rather*) plutôt; **a ~ of** une sorte de; **what ~ of ...?** quelle sorte de ...?

kindergarten ['kɪndəgɑ:tn] *n* jardin *m* d'enfants

kind-hearted [kaɪnd'hɑ:tɪd] *adj* bon (bonne)

kindle ['kɪndl] *vt* allumer, enflammer

kindling ['kɪndlɪŋ] *n* petit bois

kindly ['kaɪndlɪ] *adj* bienveillant(e), plein(e) de gentillesse ▷ *adv* avec bonté; **will you ~ ...** auriez-vous la bonté *or* l'obligeance de ...; **he didn't take it ~** il l'a mal pris

kindness ['kaɪndnɪs] *n* (*quality*) bonté *f*, gentillesse *f*

kindred ['kɪndrɪd] *adj* apparenté(e); **~ spirit** âme *f* sœur

kinetic [kɪ'nɛtɪk] *adj* cinétique

king [kɪŋ] *n* roi *m*

kingdom ['kɪŋdəm] *n* royaume *m*

kingfisher ['kɪŋfɪʃə^r] *n* martin-pêcheur *m*

kingpin ['kɪŋpɪn] *n* (*Tech*) pivot *m*; (*fig*) cheville ouvrière

king-size ['kɪŋsaɪz], **king-sized** ['kɪŋsaɪzd] *adj* (*cigarette*) (format) extra-long (longue)

king-size bed, king-sized bed *n* grand lit (*de* 1,95 *m de large*)

kink [kɪŋk] *n* (*of rope*) entortillement *m*; (*in hair*) ondulation *f*; (*inf*: *fig*) aberration *f*

kinky ['kɪŋkɪ] *adj* (*fig*) excentrique; (*pej*) aux goûts spéciaux

kinship ['kɪnʃɪp] *n* parenté *f*

kinsman ['kɪnzmən] (*irreg*) *n* parent *m*

kinswoman ['kɪnzwumən] (*irreg*) *n* parente *f*

kiosk ['kiːɔsk] *n* kiosque *m*; (*Brit: also:* **telephone kiosk**) cabine *f* (téléphonique); (*also:* **newspaper kiosk**) kiosque à journaux

kipper ['kɪpəʳ] *n* hareng fumé et salé

Kirghizia [kəːˈgɪzɪə] *n* Kirghizistan *m*

kiss [kɪs] *n* baiser *m* ▷ *vt* embrasser; **to ~ (each other)** s'embrasser; **to ~ sb goodbye** dire au revoir à qn en l'embrassant

kissagram ['kɪsəgræm] *n* baiser envoyé à l'occasion d'une célébration par l'intermédiaire d'une personne employée à cet effet

kiss of life *n* (*Brit*) bouche à bouche *m*

kit [kɪt] *n* équipement *m*, matériel *m*; (*set of tools etc*) trousse *f*; (*for assembly*) kit *m*; **tool ~** nécessaire *m* à outils
▸ **kit out** *vt* (*Brit*) équiper

kitbag ['kɪtbæg] *n* sac *m* de voyage *or* de marin

kitchen ['kɪtʃɪn] *n* cuisine *f*

kitchen garden *n* jardin *m* potager

kitchen sink *n* évier *m*

kitchen unit *n* (*Brit*) élément *m* de cuisine

kitchenware ['kɪtʃɪnwɛəʳ] *n* vaisselle *f*; ustensiles *mpl* de cuisine

kite [kaɪt] *n* (*toy*) cerf-volant *m*; (*Zool*) milan *m*

kith [kɪθ] *n*: **~ and kin** parents et amis *mpl*

kitten ['kɪtn] *n* petit chat, chaton *m*

kitty ['kɪtɪ] *n* (*money*) cagnotte *f*

kiwi ['kiːwiː] *n* (*also:* **kiwi fruit**) kiwi *m*

KKK *n abbr* (*US*) = **Ku Klux Klan**

Kleenex® ['kliːnɛks] *n* Kleenex® *m*

kleptomaniac [klɛptəuˈmeɪnɪæk] *n* kleptomane *m/f*

km *abbr* (= *kilometre*) km

km/h *abbr* (= *kilometres per hour*) km/h

knack [næk] *n*: **to have the ~ (of doing)** avoir le coup (pour faire); **there's a ~** il y a un coup à prendre *or* une combine

knackered ['nækəd] *adj* (*inf*) crevé(e), nase

knapsack ['næpsæk] *n* musette *f*

knave [neɪv] *n* (*Cards*) valet *m*

knead [niːd] *vt* pétrir

knee [niː] *n* genou *m*

kneecap ['niːkæp] *n* rotule *f* ▷ *vt* tirer un coup de feu dans la rotule de

knee-deep ['niːˈdiːp] *adj*: **the water was ~** l'eau arrivait aux genoux

kneel (*pt, pp* **knelt**) [niːl, nɛlt] *vi* (*also:* **kneel down**) s'agenouiller

kneepad ['niːpæd] *n* genouillère *f*

knell [nɛl] *n* glas *m*

knelt [nɛlt] *pt, pp of* **kneel**

knew [njuː] *pt of* **know**

knickers ['nɪkəz] *npl* (*Brit*) culotte *f* (de femme)

knick-knack ['nɪknæk] *n* colifichet *m*

knife [naɪf] *n* (*pl* **knives** [naɪvz]) couteau *m* ▷ *vt* poignarder, frapper d'un coup de couteau; **~, fork and spoon** couvert *m*

knife-edge ['naɪfɛdʒ] *n*: **to be on a ~** être sur le fil du rasoir

knight [naɪt] *n* chevalier *m*; (*Chess*) cavalier *m*

knighthood ['naɪthud] *n* chevalerie *f*; (*title*): **to get a ~** être fait chevalier

knit [nɪt] *vt* tricoter; (*fig*): **to ~ together** unir ▷ *vi* tricoter; (*broken bones*) se ressouder; **to ~ one's brows** froncer les sourcils

knitted ['nɪtɪd] *adj* en tricot

knitting ['nɪtɪŋ] *n* tricot *m*

knitting machine *n* machine *f* à tricoter

knitting needle *n* aiguille *f* à tricoter

knitting pattern *n* modèle *m* (pour tricot)

knitwear ['nɪtwɛəʳ] *n* tricots *mpl*, lainages *mpl*

knives [naɪvz] *npl of* **knife**

knob [nɔb] *n* bouton *m*; (*Brit*): **a ~ of butter** une noix de beurre

knobbly ['nɔblɪ], (*US*) **knobby** ['nɔbɪ] *adj* (*wood, surface*) noueux(-euse); (*knees*) noueux

knock [nɔk] *vt* frapper; (*bump into*) heurter; (*make: hole etc*): **to ~ a hole in** faire un trou dans, trouer; (*force: nail etc*): **to ~ a nail into** enfoncer un clou dans; (*fig: col*) dénigrer ▷ *vi* (*engine*) cogner; (*at door etc*): **to ~ at/on** frapper à/sur ▷ *n* coup *m*; **he ~ed at the door** il frappa à la porte
▸ **knock down** *vt* renverser; (*price*) réduire
▸ **knock off** *vi* (*inf: finish*) s'arrêter (de travailler) ▷ *vt* (*vase, object*) faire tomber; (*inf: steal*) piquer; (*fig: from price etc*): **to ~ off £10** faire une remise de 10 livres
▸ **knock out** *vt* assommer; (*Boxing*) mettre k.-o.; (*in competition*) éliminer
▸ **knock over** *vt* (*object*) faire tomber; (*pedestrian*) renverser

knockdown ['nɔkdaun] *adj* (*price*) sacrifié(e)

knocker ['nɔkəʳ] *n* (*on door*) heurtoir *m*

knocking ['nɔkɪŋ] *n* coups *mpl*

knock-kneed [nɔk'niːd] *adj* aux genoux cagneux

knockout ['nɔkaut] *n* (*Boxing*) knock-out *m*, K.-O. *m*; **~ competition** (*Brit*) compétition *f* avec épreuves éliminatoires

knock-up ['nɔkʌp] *n* (*Tennis*): **to have a ~** faire des balles

knot [nɔt] *n* (*gen*) nœud *m* ▷ *vt* nouer; **to tie a ~** faire un nœud

knotty ['nɔtɪ] *adj* (*fig*) épineux(-euse)

know [nəu] *vt* (*pt* **knew**, *pp* **known** [njuː, nəun]) savoir; (*person, place*) connaître; **to ~ that** savoir que; **to ~ how to do** savoir faire; **to ~ how to swim** savoir nager; **to ~ about/of sth** (*event*) être au courant de qch; (*subject*) connaître qch; **to get to ~ sth** (*fact*) apprendre qch; (*place*) apprendre à connaître qch; **I don't ~** je ne sais pas; **I don't ~ him** je ne le connais pas; **do you ~ where I can ...?** savez-vous où je peux ...?; **to ~ right from wrong** savoir distinguer le bon du mauvais; **as far as I ~ ...** à ma connaissance ..., autant que je sache ...

know-all ['nəuɔːl] *n* (*Brit pej*) je-sais-tout *m/f*

know-how ['nəuhau] *n* savoir-faire *m*, technique *f*, compétence *f*

knowing ['nəuɪŋ] *adj* (*look etc*) entendu(e)

knowingly ['nəuɪŋlɪ] *adv* (*on purpose*) sciemment; (*smile, look*) d'un air entendu

know-it-all ['nəuɪtɔːl] *n* (*US*) = **know-all**

knowledge ['nɔlɪdʒ] *n* connaissance *f*; (*learning*)

connaissances, savoir *m*; **to have no ~ of** ignorer; **not to my ~** pas à ma connaissance; **without my ~** à mon insu; **to have a working ~ of French** se débrouiller en français; **it is common ~ that ...** chacun sait que ...; **it has come to my ~ that ...** j'ai appris que ...

knowledgeable ['nɔlɪdʒəbl] *adj* bien informé(e)

known [nəun] *pp of* **know** ▷ *adj* (*thief, facts*) notoire; (*expert*) célèbre

knuckle ['nʌkl] *n* articulation *f* (des phalanges), jointure *f*
  ▶ **knuckle down** *vi* (*inf*) s'y mettre
  ▶ **knuckle under** *vi* (*inf*) céder

knuckleduster ['nʌkldʌstəʳ] *n* coup-de-poing américain

KO *abbr* = **knock out** ▷ *n* K.-O. *m* ▷ *vt* mettre K.-O.

koala [kəu'ɑːlə] *n* (*also*: **koala bear**) koala *m*

kook [kuːk] *n* (US *inf*) loufoque *m/f*

Koran [kɔ'rɑːn] *n* Coran *m*

Korea [kə'rɪə] *n* Corée *f*; **North/South ~** Corée du Nord/Sud

Korean [kə'rɪən] *adj* coréen(ne) ▷ *n* Coréen(ne)

kosher ['kəuʃəʳ] *adj* kascher *inv*

Kosovar, Kosovan ['kɔsəvɑːʳ, 'kɔsəvən] *adj* kosovar(e)

Kosovo ['kɔsɔvəu] *n* Kosovo *m*

kowtow ['kau'tau] *vi*: **to ~ to sb** s'aplatir devant qn

Kremlin ['krɛmlɪn] *n*: **the ~** le Kremlin

KS *abbr* (US) = **Kansas**

Kt *abbr* (*Brit*: = *Knight*) *titre honorifique*

Kuala Lumpur ['kwɑːlə'lumpuəʳ] *n* Kuala Lumpur

kudos ['kjuːdɔs] *n* gloire *f*, lauriers *mpl*

Kurd [kəːd] *n* Kurde *m/f*

Kuwait [ku'weɪt] *n* Koweït *m*

Kuwaiti [ku'weɪtɪ] *adj* koweïtien(ne) ▷ *n* Koweïtien(ne)

kW *abbr* (= *kilowatt*) kW

KY, Ky. *abbr* (US) = **Kentucky**

L

L¹, l [ɛl] *n* (*letter*) L, l *m*; **L for Lucy**, (US) **L for Love** L comme Louis

L² *abbr* (= *lake, large*) L; (= *left*) g; (*Brit Aut*: = *learner*) signale un conducteur débutant

l. *abbr* (= *litre*) l

LA *n abbr* (US) = **Los Angeles** ▷ *abbr* (US) = **Louisiana**

La. *abbr* (US) = **Louisiana**

lab [læb] *n abbr* (= *laboratory*) labo *m*

Lab. *abbr* (*Canada*) = **Labrador**

label ['leɪbl] *n* étiquette *f*; (*brand: of record*) marque *f* ▷ *vt* étiqueter; **to ~ sb a ...** qualifier qn de ...

labor *etc* ['leɪbəʳ] (US) = **labour** *etc*

laboratory [lə'bɒrətəri] *n* laboratoire *m*

Labor Day *n* (*US, Canada*) fête *f* du travail (*le premier lundi de septembre*); *voir article*

● LABOR DAY

Labor Day aux États-Unis et au Canada est fixée au premier lundi de septembre. Instituée par le Congrès en 1894 après avoir été réclamée par les mouvements ouvriers pendant douze ans, elle a perdu une grande partie de son caractère politique pour devenir un jour férié assez ordinaire et l'occasion de partir pour un long week-end avant la rentrée des classes.

laborious [lə'bɔːrɪəs] *adj* laborieux(-euse)

labor union *n* (US) syndicat *m*

Labour ['leɪbəʳ] *n* (*Brit Pol: also:* **the Labour Party**) le parti travailliste, les travaillistes *mpl*

labour, (US) **labor** ['leɪbəʳ] *n* (*work*) travail *m*; (*workforce*) main-d'œuvre *f*; (*Med*) travail, accouchement *m* ▷ *vi*: **to ~ (at)** travailler dur (à), peiner (sur) ▷ *vt*: **to ~ a point** insister sur un point; **in ~** (*Med*) en travail

labour camp, (US) **labor camp** *n* camp *m* de travaux forcés

labour cost, (US) **labor cost** *n* coût *m* de la main-d'œuvre; coût de la façon

laboured, (US) **labored** ['leɪbəd] *adj* lourd(e), laborieux(-euse); (*breathing*) difficile, pénible; (*style*) lourd, embarrassé(e)

labourer, (US) **laborer** ['leɪbərəʳ] *n* manœuvre *m*; **farm ~** ouvrier *m* agricole

labour force, (US) **labor force** *n* main-d'œuvre *f*

labour-intensive, (US) **labor-intensive** [leɪbərɪn'tɛnsɪv] *adj* intensif(-ive) en main-d'œuvre

labour market, (US) **labor market** *n* marché *m* du travail

labour pains, (US) **labor pains** *npl* douleurs *fpl* de l'accouchement

labour relations, (US) **labor relations** *npl* relations *fpl* dans l'entreprise

labour-saving, (US) **labor-saving** ['leɪbəseɪvɪŋ] *adj* qui simplifie le travail

labour unrest, (US) **labor unrest** *n* agitation sociale

labyrinth ['læbɪrɪnθ] *n* labyrinthe *m*, dédale *m*

lace [leɪs] *n* dentelle *f*; (*of shoe etc*) lacet *m* ▷ *vt* (*shoe: also:* **lace up**) lacer; (*drink*) arroser, corser

lacemaking ['leɪsmeɪkɪŋ] *n* fabrication *f* de dentelle

laceration [læsə'reɪʃən] *n* lacération *f*

lace-up ['leɪsʌp] *adj* (*shoes etc*) à lacets

lack [læk] *n* manque *m* ▷ *vt* manquer de; **through** *or* **for ~ of** faute de, par manque de; **to be ~ing** manquer, faire défaut; **to be ~ing in** manquer de

lackadaisical [lækə'deɪzɪkl] *adj* nonchalant(e), indolent(e)

lackey ['lækɪ] *n* (*also fig*) laquais *m*

lacklustre ['læklʌstəʳ] *adj* terne

laconic [lə'kɒnɪk] *adj* laconique

lacquer ['lækəʳ] *n* laque *f*

lacy ['leɪsɪ] *adj* (*made of lace*) en dentelle; (*like lace*) comme de la dentelle, qui ressemble à de la dentelle

lad [læd] *n* garçon *m*, gars *m*; (*Brit: in stable etc*) lad *m*

ladder ['lædəʳ] *n* échelle *f*; (*Brit: in tights*) maille filée ▷ *vt, vi* (*Brit: tights*) filer

laden ['leɪdn] *adj*: **~ (with)** chargé(e) (de); **fully ~** (*truck, ship*) en pleine charge

ladle ['leɪdl] *n* louche *f*

lady ['leɪdɪ] *n* dame *f*; **"ladies and gentlemen ..."** "Mesdames (et) Messieurs ..."; **young ~** jeune fille *f*; (*married*) jeune femme *f*;

L~ Smith lady Smith; **the ladies' (room)** les toilettes *fpl* des dames; **a ~ doctor** une doctoresse, une femme médecin

ladybird ['leɪdɪbəːd], (US) **ladybug** ['leɪdɪbʌg] *n* coccinelle *f*

lady-in-waiting ['leɪdɪɪn'weɪtɪŋ] *n* dame *f* d'honneur

lady-killer ['leɪdɪkɪlə'] *n* don Juan *m*

ladylike ['leɪdɪlaɪk] *adj* distingué(e)

ladyship ['leɪdɪʃɪp] *n*: **your L~** Madame la comtesse (*or* la baronne *etc*)

lag [læg] *n* retard *m* ▷ *vi* (*also*: **lag behind**) rester en arrière, traîner; (*fig*) rester à la traîne ▷ *vt* (*pipes*) calorifuger

lager ['lɑːgə'] *n* bière blonde

lager lout *n* (*Brit inf*) jeune voyou *m* (*porté sur la boisson*)

lagging ['lægɪŋ] *n* enveloppe isolante, calorifuge *m*

lagoon [lə'guːn] *n* lagune *f*

Lagos ['leɪgɔs] *n* Lagos

laid [leɪd] *pt, pp of* **lay**

laid back *adj* (*inf*) relaxe, décontracté(e)

laid up *adj* alité(e)

lain [leɪn] *pp of* **lie**

lair [lɛə'] *n* tanière *f*, gîte *m*

laissez-faire [lɛseɪ'fɛə'] *n* libéralisme *m*

laity ['leɪətɪ] *n* laïques *mpl*

lake [leɪk] *n* lac *m*

Lake District *n*: **the ~** (*Brit*) la région des lacs

lamb [læm] *n* agneau *m*

lamb chop *n* côtelette *f* d'agneau

lambskin ['læmskɪn] *n* (peau *f* d')agneau *m*

lambswool ['læmzwul] *n* laine *f* d'agneau

lame [leɪm] *adj* (*also fig*) boiteux(-euse); **~ duck** (*fig*) canard boiteux

lamely ['leɪmlɪ] *adv* (*fig*) sans conviction

lament [lə'mɛnt] *n* lamentation *f* ▷ *vt* pleurer, se lamenter sur

lamentable ['læməntəbl] *adj* déplorable, lamentable

laminated ['læmɪneɪtɪd] *adj* laminé(e); (*windscreen*) (en verre) feuilleté

lamp [læmp] *n* lampe *f*

lamplight ['læmplaɪt] *n*: **by ~** à la lumière de la (*or* d'une) lampe

lampoon [læm'puːn] *n* pamphlet *m*

lamppost ['læmppəust] *n* (*Brit*) réverbère *m*

lampshade ['læmpʃeɪd] *n* abat-jour *m inv*

lance [lɑːns] *n* lance *f* ▷ *vt* (*Med*) inciser

lance corporal *n* (*Brit*) (soldat *m* de) première classe *m*

lancet ['lɑːnsɪt] *n* (*Med*) bistouri *m*

Lancs [læŋks] *abbr* (*Brit*) = **Lancashire**

land [lænd] *n* (*as opposed to sea*) terre *f* (ferme); (*country*) pays *m*; (*soil*) terre; (*piece of land*) terrain *m*; (*estate*) terre(s), domaine(s) *m(pl)* ▷ *vi* (*from ship*) débarquer; (*Aviat*) atterrir; (*fig: fall*) (re)tomber ▷ *vt* (*passengers, goods*) débarquer; (*obtain*) décrocher; **to go/travel by ~** se déplacer par voie de terre; **to own ~** être propriétaire foncier; **to ~ on one's feet** (*also fig*)

retomber sur ses pieds; **to ~ sb with sth** (*inf*) coller qch à qn

▶ **land up** *vi* atterrir, (finir par) se retrouver

landed gentry ['lændɪd-] *n* (*Brit*) propriétaires terriens *or* fonciers

landfill site ['lændfɪl-] *n* centre *m* d'enfouissement des déchets

landing ['lændɪŋ] *n* (*from ship*) débarquement *m*; (*Aviat*) atterrissage *m*; (*of staircase*) palier *m*

landing card *n* carte *f* de débarquement

landing craft *n* péniche *f* de débarquement

landing gear *n* train *m* d'atterrissage

landing stage *n* (*Brit*) débarcadère *m*, embarcadère *m*

landing strip *n* piste *f* d'atterrissage

landlady ['lændleɪdɪ] *n* propriétaire *f*, logeuse *f*; (*of pub*) patronne *f*

landlocked ['lændlɔkt] *adj* entouré(e) de terre(s), sans accès à la mer

landlord ['lændlɔːd] *n* propriétaire *m*, logeur *m*; (*of pub etc*) patron *m*

landlubber ['lændlʌbə'] *n* terrien(ne)

landmark ['lændmɑːk] *n* (point *m* de) repère *m*; **to be a ~** (*fig*) faire date *or* époque

landowner ['lændəunə'] *n* propriétaire foncier *or* terrien

landscape ['lænskeɪp] *n* paysage *m*

landscape architect, landscape gardener *n* paysagiste *m/f*

landscape painting *n* (*Art*) paysage *m*

landslide ['lændslaɪd] *n* (*Geo*) glissement *m* (de terrain); (*fig: Pol*) raz-de-marée (électoral)

lane [leɪn] *n* (*in country*) chemin *m*; (*in town*) ruelle *f*; (*Aut: of road*) voie *f*; (: *line of traffic*) file *f*; (*in race*) couloir *m*; **shipping ~** route *f* maritime *or* de navigation

language ['læŋgwɪdʒ] *n* langue *f*; (*way one speaks*) langage *m*; **what ~s do you speak?** quelles langues parlez-vous?; **bad ~** grossièretés *fpl*, langage grossier

language laboratory *n* laboratoire *m* de langues

language school *n* école *f* de langue

languid ['læŋgwɪd] *adj* languissant(e), langoureux(-euse)

languish ['læŋgwɪʃ] *vi* languir

lank [læŋk] *adj* (*hair*) raide et terne

lanky ['læŋkɪ] *adj* grand(e) et maigre, efflanqué(e)

lanolin, lanoline ['lænəlɪn] *n* lanoline *f*

lantern ['læntn] *n* lanterne *f*

Laos [laus] *n* Laos *m*

lap [læp] *n* (*of track*) tour *m* (de piste); (*of body*): **in** *or* **on one's ~** sur les genoux ▷ *vt* (*also*: **lap up**) laper ▷ *vi* (*waves*) clapoter

▶ **lap up** *vt* (*fig*) boire comme du petit-lait, se gargariser de; (: *lies etc*) gober

La Paz [læ'pæz] *n* La Paz

lapdog ['læpdɔg] *n* chien *m* d'appartement

lapel [lə'pɛl] *n* revers *m*

Lapland ['læplænd] *n* Laponie *f*

lapse [læps] *n* défaillance *f*; (*in behaviour*) écart *m* (de conduite) ▷ vi (*Law*) cesser d'être en vigueur; (*contract*) expirer; (*pass*) être périmé; (*subscription*) prendre fin; **to ~ into bad habits** prendre de mauvaises habitudes; **~ of time** laps *m* de temps, intervalle *m*; **a ~ of memory** un trou de mémoire

laptop ['læptɔp], **laptop computer** *n* (ordinateur *m*) portable *m*

larceny ['lɑːsənɪ] *n* vol *m*

larch [lɑːtʃ] *n* mélèze *m*

lard [lɑːd] *n* saindoux *m*

larder ['lɑːdəʳ] *n* garde-manger *m inv*

large [lɑːdʒ] *adj* grand(e); (*person, animal*) gros (grosse); **to make ~r** agrandir; **a ~ number of people** beaucoup de gens; **by and ~** en général; **on a ~ scale** sur une grande échelle; **at ~** (*free*) en liberté; (*generally*) en général; pour la plupart; *see also* **by**

largely ['lɑːdʒlɪ] *adv* en grande partie; (*principally*) surtout

large-scale ['lɑːdʒ'skeɪl] *adj* (*map, drawing etc*) à grande échelle; (*fig*) important(e)

lark [lɑːk] *n* (*bird*) alouette *f*; (*joke*) blague *f*, farce *f*

▶ **lark about** *vi* faire l'idiot, rigoler

larva (*pl* **-e**) ['lɑːvə, -iː] *n* larve *f*

laryngitis [lærɪn'dʒaɪtɪs] *n* laryngite *f*

larynx ['lærɪŋks] *n* larynx *m*

lasagne [lə'zænjə] *n* lasagne *f*

lascivious [lə'sɪvɪəs] *adj* lascif(-ive)

laser ['leɪzəʳ] *n* laser *m*

laser beam *n* rayon *m* laser

laser printer *n* imprimante *f* laser

lash [læʃ] *n* coup *m* de fouet; (*also:* **eyelash**) cil *m* ▷ vt fouetter; (*tie*) attacher

▶ **lash down** *vt* attacher; amarrer; arrimer ▷ vi (*rain*) tomber avec violence

▶ **lash out** *vi:* **to ~ out (at** *or* **against sb/sth)** attaquer violemment (qn/qch); **to ~ out (on sth)** (*inf: spend*) se fendre (de qch)

lashing ['læʃɪŋ] *n:* **~s of** (*Brit inf: cream etc*) des masses de

lass [læs] (*Brit*) *n* (jeune) fille *f*

lasso [læ'suː] *n* lasso *m* ▷ vt prendre au lasso

last [lɑːst] *adj* dernier(-ière) ▷ adv en dernier; (*most recently*) la dernière fois; (*finally*) finalement ▷ vi durer; **~ week** la semaine dernière; **~ night** (*evening*) hier soir; (*night*) la nuit dernière; **at ~** enfin; **~ but one** avant-dernier(-ière); **the ~ time** la dernière fois; **it ~s (for) 2 hours** ça dure 2 heures

last-ditch ['lɑːst'dɪtʃ] *adj* ultime, désespéré(e)

lasting ['lɑːstɪŋ] *adj* durable

lastly ['lɑːstlɪ] *adv* en dernier lieu, pour finir

last-minute ['lɑːstmɪnɪt] *adj* de dernière minute

latch [lætʃ] *n* loquet *m*

▶ **latch onto** *vt fus* (*cling to: person, group*) s'accrocher à; (*idea*) se mettre en tête

latchkey ['lætʃkiː] *n* clé *f* (de la porte d'entrée)

late [leɪt] *adj* (*not on time*) en retard; (*far on in day etc*) tardif(-ive); (: *edition, delivery*) dernier(-ière);

(*recent*) récent(e), dernier; (*former*) ancien(ne); (*dead*) défunt(e) ▷ adv tard; (*behind time, schedule*) en retard; **to be ~** avoir du retard; **to be 10 minutes ~** avoir 10 minutes de retard; **sorry I'm ~** désolé d'être en retard; **it's too ~** il est trop tard; **to work ~** travailler tard; **~ in life** sur le tard, à un âge avancé; **of ~** dernièrement; **in ~ May** vers la fin (du mois) de mai, fin mai; **the ~ Mr X** feu M. X

latecomer ['leɪtkʌməʳ] *n* retardataire *m/f*

lately ['leɪtlɪ] *adv* récemment

lateness ['leɪtnɪs] *n* (*of person*) retard *m*; (*of event*) heure tardive

latent ['leɪtnt] *adj* latent(e); **~ defect** vice caché

later ['leɪtəʳ] *adj* (*date etc*) ultérieur(e); (*version etc*) plus récent(e) ▷ adv plus tard; **~ on today** plus tard dans la journée

lateral ['lætərl] *adj* latéral(e)

latest ['leɪtɪst] *adj* tout(e) dernier(-ière); **the ~ news** les dernières nouvelles; **at the ~** au plus tard

latex ['leɪtɛks] *n* latex *m*

lath (*pl* **-s**) [læθ, læðz] *n* latte *f*

lathe [leɪð] *n* tour *m*

lather ['lɑːðəʳ] *n* mousse *f* (de savon) ▷ vt savonner ▷ vi mousser

Latin ['lætɪn] *n* latin *m* ▷ adj latin(e)

Latin America *n* Amérique latine

Latin American *adj* latino-américain(e), d'Amérique latine ▷ *n* Latino-Américain(e)

latitude ['lætɪtjuːd] *n* (*also fig*) latitude *f*

latrine [lə'triːn] *n* latrines *fpl*

latter ['lætəʳ] *adj* deuxième, dernier(-ière) ▷ *n:* **the ~** ce dernier, celui-ci

latterly ['lætəlɪ] *adv* dernièrement, récemment

lattice ['lætɪs] *n* treillis *m*; treillage *m*

lattice window *n* fenêtre treillissée, fenêtre à croisillons

Latvia ['lætvɪə] *n* Lettonie *f*

Latvian ['lætvɪən] *adj* letton(ne) ▷ *n* Letton(ne); (*Ling*) letton *m*

laudable ['lɔːdəbl] *adj* louable

laudatory ['lɔːdətrɪ] *adj* élogieux(-euse)

laugh [lɑːf] *n* rire *m* ▷ vi rire; (**to do sth) for a ~** (faire qch) pour rire

▶ **laugh at** *vt fus* se moquer de; (*joke*) rire de

▶ **laugh off** *vt* écarter *or* rejeter par une plaisanterie *or* par une boutade

laughable ['lɑːfəbl] *adj* risible, ridicule

laughing ['lɑːfɪŋ] *adj* rieur(-euse); **this is no ~ matter** il n'y a pas de quoi rire, ça n'a rien d'amusant

laughing gas *n* gaz hilarant

laughing stock *n:* **the ~ of** la risée de

laughter ['lɑːftəʳ] *n* rire *m*; (*of several people*) rires *mpl*

launch [lɔːntʃ] *n* lancement *m*; (*boat*) chaloupe *f*; (*also:* **motor launch**) vedette *f* ▷ vt (*ship, rocket, plan*) lancer

▶ **launch into** *vt fus* se lancer dans

▶ **launch out** *vi:* **to ~ out (into)** se lancer (dans)

launching ['lɔːntʃɪŋ] *n* lancement *m*

launder ['lɔ:ndə^r] vt laver; (fig: money) blanchir

Launderette® [lɔ:n'drɛt], (US) **Laundromat**® ['lɔ:ndrəmæt] n laverie f (automatique)

laundry ['lɔ:ndrɪ] n (clothes) linge m; (business) blanchisserie f; (room) buanderie f; **to do the ~** faire la lessive

laureate ['lɔ:rɪət] adj see **poet laureate**

laurel ['lɔrl] n laurier m; **to rest on one's ~s** se reposer sur ses lauriers

lava ['lɑ:və] n lave f

lavatory ['lævətərɪ] n toilettes fpl

lavatory paper n (Brit) papier m hygiénique

lavender ['lævəndə^r] n lavande f

lavish ['lævɪʃ] adj (amount) copieux(-euse); (meal) somptueux(-euse); (hospitality) généreux(-euse); (person: giving freely): **~ with** prodigue de ▷ vt: **to ~ sth on sb** prodiguer qch à qn; (money) dépenser qch sans compter pour qn

lavishly ['lævɪʃlɪ] adv (give, spend) sans compter; (furnished) luxueusement

law [lɔ:] n loi f; (science) droit m; **against the ~** contraire à la loi; **to study ~** faire du droit; **to go to ~** (Brit) avoir recours à la justice; **~ and order** (n) l'ordre public

law-abiding ['lɔ:əbaɪdɪŋ] adj respectueux(-euse) des lois

lawbreaker ['lɔ:breɪkə^r] n personne f qui transgresse la loi

law court n tribunal m, cour f de justice

lawful ['lɔ:ful] adj légal(e), permis(e)

lawfully ['lɔ:fəlɪ] adv légalement

lawless ['lɔ:lɪs] adj (action) illégal(e); (place) sans loi

Law Lord n (Brit) juge siégeant à la Chambre des Lords

lawmaker ['lɔ:meɪkə^r] n législateur(-trice)

lawn [lɔ:n] n pelouse f

lawnmower ['lɔ:nməuə^r] n tondeuse f à gazon

lawn tennis n tennis m

law school n faculté f de droit

law student n étudiant(e) en droit

lawsuit ['lɔ:su:t] n procès m; **to bring a ~ against** engager des poursuites contre

lawyer ['lɔ:jə^r] n (consultant, with company) juriste m; (for sales, wills etc) ≈ notaire m; (partner, in court) ≈ avocat m

lax [læks] adj relâché(e)

laxative ['læksətɪv] n laxatif m

laxity ['læksɪtɪ] n relâchement m

lay [leɪ] pt of **lie** ▷ adj laïque; (not expert) profane ▷ vt (pt, pp **laid** [leɪd]) poser, mettre; (eggs) pondre; (trap) tendre; (plans) élaborer; **to ~ the table** mettre la table; **to ~ the facts/one's proposals before sb** présenter les faits/ses propositions à qn; **to get laid** (inf!) baiser (!), se faire baiser (!)

▶ **lay aside, lay by** vt mettre de côté

▶ **lay down** vt poser; (rules etc) établir; **to ~ down the law** (fig) faire la loi

▶ **lay in** vt accumuler, s'approvisionner en

▶ **lay into** vi (inf: attack) tomber sur; (: scold) passer une engueulade à

▶ **lay off** vt (workers) licencier

▶ **lay on** vt (water, gas) mettre, installer; (provide: meal etc) fournir; (paint) étaler

▶ **lay out** vt (design) dessiner, concevoir; (display) disposer; (spend) dépenser

▶ **lay up** vt (store) amasser; (car) remiser; (ship) désarmer; (illness) forcer à s'aliter

layabout ['leɪəbaut] n fainéant(e)

lay-by ['leɪbaɪ] n (Brit) aire f de stationnement (sur le bas-côté)

lay days npl (Naut) estarie f

layer ['leɪə^r] n couche f

layette [leɪ'ɛt] n layette f

layman ['leɪmən] (irreg) n (Rel) laïque m; (non-expert) profane m

lay-off ['leɪɔf] n licenciement m

layout ['leɪaut] n disposition f, plan m, agencement m; (Press) mise f en page

laze [leɪz] vi paresser

laziness ['leɪzɪnɪs] n paresse f

lazy ['leɪzɪ] adj paresseux(-euse)

LB abbr (Canada) = **Labrador**

lb. abbr (weight) = **pound**

lbw abbr (Cricket: = leg before wicket) faute dans laquelle le joueur a la jambe devant le guichet

LC n abbr (US) = **Library of Congress**

lc abbr (Typ: = lower case) b.d.c.

L/C abbr = **letter of credit**

LCD n abbr = **liquid crystal display**

Ld abbr (Brit: = lord) titre honorifique

LDS n abbr (= Licentiate in Dental Surgery) diplôme universitaire; (= Latter-day Saints) Église de Jésus-Christ des Saints du dernier jour

LEA n abbr (Brit: = local education authority) services locaux de l'enseignement

lead¹ [li:d] (pt, pp **led** [lɛd]) n (front position) tête f; (distance, time ahead) avance f; (clue) piste f; (to battery) raccord m; (Elec) fil m; (for dog) laisse f; (Theat) rôle principal ▷ vt (guide) mener, conduire; (induce) amener; (be leader of) être à la tête de; (Sport) être en tête de; (orchestra: Brit) être le premier violon de; (: US) diriger ▷ vi (Sport) mener, être en tête; **to ~ to** (road, pipe) mener à, conduire à; (result in) conduire à; aboutir à; **to ~ sb astray** détourner qn du droit chemin; **to be in the ~** (Sport: in race) mener, être en tête; (: in match) mener (à la marque); **to take the ~** (Sport) passer en tête, prendre la tête; mener; (fig) prendre l'initiative; **to ~ sb to believe that ...** amener qn à croire que ...; **to ~ sb to do sth** amener qn à faire qch; **to ~ the way** montrer le chemin

▶ **lead away** vt emmener

▶ **lead back** vt ramener

▶ **lead off** vi (in game etc) commencer

▶ **lead on** vt (tease) faire marcher; **to ~ sb on to** (induce) amener qn à

▶ **lead up to** vt conduire à; (in conversation) en venir à

lead² [lɛd] n (metal) plomb m; (in pencil) mine f

leaded ['lɛdɪd] adj (windows) à petits carreaux

leaded petrol n essence f au plomb

leaden ['lɛdn] adj de or en plomb

leader ['li:dəʳ] n (of team) chef m; (of party etc)
dirigeant(e), leader m; (Sport: in league) leader;
(: in race) coureur m de tête; (in newspaper)
éditorial m; **they are ~s in their field** (fig) ils
sont à la pointe du progrès dans leur domaine;
the L~ of the House (Brit) le chef de la majorité
ministérielle

leadership ['li:dəʃɪp] n (position) direction f;
under the ~ of … sous la direction de …;
qualities of ~ qualités fpl de chef or de meneur

lead-free ['lɛdfri:] adj sans plomb

leading ['li:dɪŋ] adj de premier plan; (main)
principal(e); (in race) de tête; **a ~ question** une
question tendancieuse; **~ role** rôle
prépondérant or de premier plan

leading lady n (Theat) vedette (féminine)

leading light n (person) sommité f, personnalité f
de premier plan

leading man (irreg) n (Theat) vedette
(masculine)

lead pencil [lɛd-] n crayon noir or à papier

lead poisoning [lɛd-] n saturnisme m

lead singer [li:d-] n (in pop group) (chanteur m)
vedette f

lead time [li:d-] n (Comm) délai m de livraison

lead weight [lɛd-] n plomb m

leaf (pl **leaves**) [li:f, li:vz] n feuille f; (of table)
rallonge f; **to turn over a new ~** (fig) changer de
conduite or d'existence; **to take a ~ out of sb's
book** (fig) prendre exemple sur qn
▶ **leaf through** vt (book) feuilleter

leaflet ['li:flɪt] n prospectus m, brochure f; (Pol,
Rel) tract m

leafy ['li:fɪ] adj feuillu(e)

league [li:g] n ligue f; (Football) championnat m;
(measure) lieue f; **to be in ~ with** avoir partie liée
avec, être de mèche avec

league table n classement m

leak [li:k] n (out: also fig) fuite f; (in) infiltration f
▷ vi (pipe, liquid etc) fuir; (shoes) prendre l'eau;
(ship) faire eau ▷ vt (liquid) répandre;
(information) divulguer
▶ **leak out** vi fuir; (information) être divulgué(e)

leakage ['li:kɪdʒ] n (also fig) fuite f

leaky ['li:kɪ] adj (pipe, bucket) qui fuit, percé(e);
(roof) qui coule; (shoe) qui prend l'eau; (boat) qui
fait eau

lean [li:n] (pt, pp **-ed** or **leant** [lɛnt]) adj maigre
▷ n (of meat) maigre m ▷ vt: **to ~ sth on** appuyer
qch sur ▷ vi (slope) pencher; (rest): **to ~ against**
s'appuyer contre; être appuyé(e) contre; **to ~ on**
s'appuyer sur
▶ **lean back** vi se pencher en arrière
▶ **lean forward** vi se pencher en avant
▶ **lean out** vi: **to ~ out (of)** se pencher au
dehors (de)
▶ **lean over** vi se pencher

leaning ['li:nɪŋ] adj penché(e) ▷ n: **~ (towards)**
penchant m (pour); **the L~ Tower of Pisa** la
tour penchée de Pise

leant [lɛnt] pt, pp of **lean**

lean-to ['li:ntu:] n appentis m

leap [li:p] n bond m, saut m ▷ vi (pt, pp **-ed** or
leapt [lɛpt]) bondir, sauter; **to ~ at an offer**
saisir une offre
▶ **leap up** vi (person) faire un bond; se lever d'un
bond

leapfrog ['li:pfrɔg] n jeu m de saute-mouton

leapt [lɛpt] pt, pp of **leap**

leap year n année f bissextile

learn (pt, pp **-ed** or **-t**) [lə:n, -t] vt, vi apprendre; **to
~ (how) to do sth** apprendre à faire qch; **we
were sorry to ~ that …** nous avons appris avec
regret que …; **to ~ about sth** (Scol) étudier qch;
(hear, read) apprendre qch

learned ['lə:nɪd] adj érudit(e), savant(e)

learner ['lə:nəʳ] n débutant(e); (Brit: also: **learner
driver**) (conducteur(-trice)) débutant(e)

learning ['lə:nɪŋ] n savoir m

learnt [lə:nt] pp of **learn**

lease [li:s] n bail m ▷ vt louer à bail; **on ~** en
location
▶ **lease back** vt vendre en cession-bail

leaseback ['li:sbæk] n cession-bail f

leasehold ['li:shəuld] n (contract) bail m ▷ adj
loué(e) à bail

leash [li:ʃ] n laisse f

least [li:st] adj: **the ~** (+ noun) le (la) plus petit(e),
le (la) moindre; (smallest amount of) le moins de
▷ pron: **(the) ~** le moins ▷ adv (+ verb) le moins;
(+ adj): **the ~** le (la) moins; **the ~ money** le
moins d'argent; **the ~ expensive** le (la) moins
cher (chère); **the ~ possible effort** le moins
d'effort possible; **at ~** au moins; (or rather) du
moins; **you could at ~ have written** tu aurais
au moins pu écrire; **not in the ~** pas le moins
du monde

leather ['lɛðəʳ] n cuir m ▷ cpd en or de cuir; **~
goods** maroquinerie f

leave [li:v] (vb: pt, pp **left** [lɛft]) vt laisser; (go away
from) quitter; (forget) oublier ▷ vi partir, s'en
aller ▷ n (time off) congé m; (Mil, also: consent)
permission f; **what time does the train/bus
~?** le train/le bus part à quelle heure?; **to ~ sth
to sb** (money etc) laisser qch à qn; **to be left**
rester; **there's some milk left over** il reste du
lait; **to ~ school** quitter l'école, terminer sa
scolarité; **~ it to me!** laissez-moi faire!, je m'en
occupe!; **on ~** en permission; **to take one's ~ of**
prendre congé de; **~ of absence** n congé
exceptionnel; (Mil) permission spéciale
▶ **leave behind** vt (also fig) laisser; (opponent in
race) distancer; (forget) laisser, oublier
▶ **leave off** vt (cover, lid, heating) ne pas
(re)mettre; (light) ne pas (r)allumer, laisser
éteint(e); (Brit inf: stop): **to ~ off (doing sth)**
s'arrêter (de faire qch)
▶ **leave on** vt (coat etc) garder, ne pas enlever;
(lid) laisser dessus; (light, fire, cooker) laisser
allumé(e)
▶ **leave out** vt oublier, omettre

leaves [li:vz] npl of **leaf**

leavetaking ['li:vteɪkɪŋ] n adieux mpl

Lebanese [lɛbə'ni:z] adj libanais(e) ▷ n (pl inv)

Libanais(e)

Lebanon ['lɛbənən] n Liban m

lecherous ['lɛtʃərəs] adj lubrique

lectern ['lɛktə:n] n lutrin m, pupitre m

lecture ['lɛktʃəʳ] n conférence f; (Scol) cours (magistral) ▷ vi donner des cours; enseigner ▷ vt (scold) sermonner, réprimander; **to ~ on** faire un cours (or son cours) sur; **to give a ~ (on)** faire une conférence (sur), faire un cours (sur)

lecture hall n amphithéâtre m

lecturer ['lɛktʃərəʳ] n (speaker) conférencier(-ière); (Brit: at university) professeur m (d'université), prof m/f de fac (inf); **assistant ~** (Brit) ≈ assistant(e); **senior ~** (Brit) ≈ chargé(e) d'enseignement

lecture theatre n = **lecture hall**

LED n abbr (= light-emitting diode) LED f, diode électroluminescente

led [lɛd] pt, pp of **lead**¹

ledge [lɛdʒ] n (of window, on wall) rebord m; (of mountain) saillie f, corniche f

ledger ['lɛdʒəʳ] n registre m, grand livre

lee [li:] n côté m sous le vent; **in the ~ of** à l'abri de

leech [li:tʃ] n sangsue f

leek [li:k] n poireau m

leer [lɪəʳ] vi: **to ~ at sb** regarder qn d'un air mauvais or concupiscent, lorgner qn

leeward ['li:wəd] adj, adv sous le vent ▷ n côté m sous le vent; **to ~** sous le vent

leeway ['li:weɪ] n (fig): **to make up ~** rattraper son retard; **to have some ~** avoir une certaine liberté d'action

left [lɛft] pt, pp of **leave** ▷ adj gauche ▷ adv à gauche ▷ n gauche f; **there are two ~** il en reste deux; **on the ~, to the ~** à gauche; **the L~** (Pol) la gauche

left-hand ['lɛfthænd] adj: **the ~ side** la gauche, le côté gauche

left-hand drive ['lɛfthænd-] n (Brit) conduite f à gauche; (vehicle) véhicule m avec la conduite à gauche

left-handed [lɛft'hændɪd] adj gaucher(-ère); (scissors etc) pour gauchers

leftie ['lɛftɪ] n (inf) gaucho m/f, gauchiste m/f

leftist ['lɛftɪst] adj (Pol) gauchiste, de gauche

left-luggage [lɛft'lʌgɪdʒ], **left-luggage office** n (Brit) consigne f

left-luggage locker [lɛft'lʌgɪdʒ-] n (Brit) (casier m à) consigne f automatique

left-overs ['lɛftəuvəz] npl restes mpl

left wing n (Mil, Sport) aile f gauche; (Pol) gauche f

left-wing ['lɛft'wɪŋ] adj (Pol) de gauche

left-winger ['lɛft'wɪŋgəʳ] n (Pol) membre m de la gauche; (Sport) ailier m gauche

lefty ['lɛftɪ] n (inf) = **leftie**

leg [lɛg] n jambe f; (of animal) patte f; (of furniture) pied m; (Culin: of chicken) cuisse f; (of journey) étape f; **1st/2nd ~** (Sport) match m aller/retour; (of journey) 1ère/2ème étape; **~ of lamb** (Culin) gigot m d'agneau; **to stretch one's ~s** se

dégourdir les jambes

legacy ['lɛgəsɪ] n (also fig) héritage m, legs m

legal ['li:gl] adj (permitted by law) légal(e); (relating to law) juridique; **to take ~ action** or **proceedings against sb** poursuivre qn en justice

legal adviser n conseiller(-ère) juridique

legal holiday (US) n jour férié

legality [lɪ'gælɪtɪ] n légalité f

legalize ['li:gəlaɪz] vt légaliser

legally ['li:gəlɪ] adv légalement; **~ binding** juridiquement contraignant(e)

legal tender n monnaie légale

legation [lɪ'geɪʃən] n légation f

legend ['lɛdʒənd] n légende f

legendary ['lɛdʒəndərɪ] adj légendaire

-legged ['lɛgɪd] suffix: **two~** à deux pattes (or jambes or pieds)

leggings ['lɛgɪŋz] npl caleçon m

leggy ['lɛgɪ] adj aux longues jambes

legibility [lɛdʒɪ'bɪlɪtɪ] n lisibilité f

legible ['lɛdʒəbl] adj lisible

legibly ['lɛdʒəblɪ] adv lisiblement

legion ['li:dʒən] n légion f

legionnaire [li:dʒə'nɛəʳ] n légionnaire m; **~'s disease** maladie f du légionnaire

legislate ['lɛdʒɪsleɪt] vi légiférer

legislation [lɛdʒɪs'leɪʃən] n législation f; **a piece of ~** un texte de loi

legislative ['lɛdʒɪslətɪv] adj législatif(-ive)

legislator ['lɛdʒɪsleɪtəʳ] n législateur(-trice)

legislature ['lɛdʒɪslətʃəʳ] n corps législatif

legitimacy [lɪ'dʒɪtɪməsɪ] n légitimité f

legitimate [lɪ'dʒɪtɪmət] adj légitime

legitimize [lɪ'dʒɪtɪmaɪz] vt légitimer

legless ['lɛglɪs] adj (Brit inf) bourré(e)

leg-room ['lɛgru:m] n place f pour les jambes

Leics abbr (Brit) = **Leicestershire**

leisure ['lɛʒəʳ] n (free time) temps libre, loisirs mpl; **at ~** (tout) à loisir; **at your ~** (later) à tête reposée

leisure centre n (Brit) centre m de loisirs

leisurely ['lɛʒəlɪ] adj tranquille, fait(e) sans se presser

leisure suit n (Brit) survêtement m (mode)

lemon ['lɛmən] n citron m

lemonade [lɛmə'neɪd] n (fizzy) limonade f

lemon cheese, lemon curd n crème f de citron

lemon juice n jus m de citron

lemon squeezer [-skwi:zəʳ] n presse-citron m inv

lemon tea n thé m au citron

lend (pt, pp **lent**) [lɛnd, lɛnt] vt: **to ~ sth (to sb)** prêter qch (à qn); **could you ~ me some money?** pourriez-vous me prêter de l'argent?; **to ~ a hand** donner un coup de main

lender ['lɛndəʳ] n prêteur(-euse)

lending library ['lɛndɪŋ-] n bibliothèque f de prêt

length [lɛŋθ] n longueur f; (section: of road, pipe etc) morceau m, bout m; **~ of time** durée f; **what ~ is it?** quelle longueur fait-il?; **it is 2 metres**

in ~ cela fait 2 mètres de long; **to fall full ~** tomber de tout son long; **at ~** (*at last*) enfin, à la fin; (*lengthily*) longuement; **to go to any ~(s) to do sth** faire n'importe quoi pour faire qch, ne reculer devant rien pour faire qch

lengthen ['lɛŋθn] *vt* allonger, prolonger ▷ *vi* s'allonger

lengthways ['lɛŋθweɪz] *adv* dans le sens de la longueur, en long

lengthy ['lɛŋθɪ] *adj* (très) long (longue)

leniency ['liːnɪənsɪ] *n* indulgence *f*, clémence *f*

lenient ['liːnɪənt] *adj* indulgent(e), clément(e)

leniently ['liːnɪəntlɪ] *adv* avec indulgence or clémence

lens [lɛnz] *n* lentille *f*; (*of spectacles*) verre *m*; (*of camera*) objectif *m*

Lent [lɛnt] *n* carême *m*

lent [lɛnt] *pt, pp of* **lend**

lentil ['lɛntl] *n* lentille *f*

Leo ['liːəu] *n* le Lion; **to be ~** être du Lion

leopard ['lɛpəd] *n* léopard *m*

leotard ['liːətɑːd] *n* justaucorps *m*

leper ['lɛpəʳ] *n* lépreux(-euse)

leper colony *n* léproserie *f*

leprosy ['lɛprəsɪ] *n* lèpre *f*

lesbian ['lɛzbɪən] *n* lesbienne *f* ▷ *adj* lesbien(ne)

lesion ['liːʒən] *n* (*Med*) lésion *f*

Lesotho [lɪ'suːtuː] *n* Lesotho *m*

less [lɛs] *adj* moins de ▷ *pron, adv* moins ▷ *prep*: **~ tax/10% discount** avant impôt/moins 10% de remise; **~ than that/you** moins que cela/vous; **~ than half** moins de la moitié; **~ than one/a kilo/3 metres** moins de un/d'un kilo/de 3 mètres; **~ than ever** moins que jamais; **~ and ~** de moins en moins; **the ~ he works ...** moins il travaille ...

lessee [lɛ'siː] *n* locataire *m/f* (à bail), preneur(-euse) du bail

lessen ['lɛsn] *vi* diminuer, s'amoindrir, s'atténuer ▷ *vt* diminuer, réduire, atténuer

lesser ['lɛsəʳ] *adj* moindre; **to a ~ extent** or **degree** à un degré moindre

lesson ['lɛsn] *n* leçon *f*; **a maths ~** une leçon or un cours de maths; **to give ~s in** donner des cours de; **to teach sb a ~** (*fig*) donner une bonne leçon à qn; **it taught him a ~** (*fig*) cela lui a servi de leçon

lessor ['lɛsɔːʳ, lɛ'sɔːʳ] *n* bailleur(-eresse)

lest [lɛst] *conj* de peur de + *infinitive*, de peur que + *sub*

let (*pt, pp ~*) [lɛt] *vt* laisser; (*Brit: lease*) louer; **to ~ sb do sth** laisser qn faire qch; **to ~ sb know sth** faire savoir qch à qn, prévenir qn de qch; **he ~ me go** il m'a laissé partir; **~ the water boil and ...** faites bouillir l'eau et ...; **to ~ go** lâcher prise; **to ~ go of sth, to ~ sth go** lâcher qch; **~'s go** allons-y; **~ him come** qu'il vienne; **"to ~"** (*Brit*) "à louer"

▸ **let down** *vt* (*lower*) baisser; (*dress*) rallonger; (*hair*) défaire; (*Brit: tyre*) dégonfler; (*disappoint*) décevoir

▸ **let go** *vi* lâcher prise ▷ *vt* lâcher

▸ **let in** *vt* laisser entrer; (*visitor etc*) faire entrer; **what have you ~ yourself in for?** à quoi t'es-tu engagé?

▸ **let off** *vt* (*allow to leave*) laisser partir; (*not punish*) ne pas punir; (*taxi driver, bus driver*) déposer; (*firework etc*) faire partir; (*bomb*) faire exploser; (*smell etc*) dégager; **to ~ off steam** (*fig: inf*) se défouler, décharger sa rate or bile

▸ **let on** *vi* (*inf*): **to ~ on that ....** révéler que ..., dire que ...

▸ **let out** *vt* laisser sortir; (*dress*) élargir; (*scream*) laisser échapper; (*Brit: rent out*) louer

▸ **let up** *vi* diminuer, s'arrêter

let-down ['lɛtdaun] *n* (*disappointment*) déception *f*

lethal ['liːθl] *adj* mortel(le), fatal(e); (*weapon*) meurtrier(-ère)

lethargic [lɛ'θɑːdʒɪk] *adj* léthargique

lethargy ['lɛθədʒɪ] *n* léthargie *f*

letter ['lɛtəʳ] *n* lettre *f*; **letters** *npl* (*Literature*) lettres; **small/capital ~** minuscule *f*/majuscule *f*; **~ of credit** lettre *f* de crédit

letter bomb *n* lettre piégée

letterbox ['lɛtəbɔks] *n* (*Brit*) boîte *f* aux or à lettres

letterhead ['lɛtəhɛd] *n* en-tête *m*

lettering ['lɛtərɪŋ] *n* lettres *fpl*; caractères *mpl*

letter opener *n* coupe-papier *m*

letterpress ['lɛtəprɛs] *n* (*method*) typographie *f*

letter quality *n* qualité *f* "courrier"

letters patent *npl* brevet *m* d'invention

lettuce ['lɛtɪs] *n* laitue *f*, salade *f*

let-up ['lɛtʌp] *n* répit *m*, détente *f*

leukaemia, (*US*) **leukemia** [luː'kiːmɪə] *n* leucémie *f*

level ['lɛvl] *adj* (*flat*) plat(e), plan(e), uni(e); (*horizontal*) horizontal(e) ▷ *n* niveau *m*; (*flat place*) terrain plat; (*also*: **spirit level**) niveau à bulle ▷ *vt* niveler, aplanir; (*gun*) pointer, braquer; (*accusation*): **to ~ (against)** lancer or porter (contre) ▷ *vi* (*inf*): **to ~ with sb** être franc (franche) avec qn; **"A" ~s** (*npl: Brit*) ≈ baccalauréat *m*; **"O" ~s** *npl* (*Brit: formerly*) *examens passés à l'âge de 16 ans sanctionnant les connaissances de l'élève*, ≈ brevet *m* des collèges; **a ~ spoonful** (*Culin*) une cuillerée rase; **to be ~ with** être au même niveau que; **to draw ~ with** (*team*) arriver à égalité de points avec, égaliser avec; arriver au même classement que; (*runner, car*) arriver à la hauteur de, rattraper; **on the ~** à l'horizontale; (*fig: honest*) régulier(-ière)

▸ **level off, level out** *vi* (*prices etc*) se stabiliser ▷ *vt* (*ground*) aplanir, niveler

level crossing *n* (*Brit*) passage *m* à niveau

level-headed [lɛvl'hɛdɪd] *adj* équilibré(e)

levelling, (*US*) **leveling** ['lɛvlɪŋ] *adj* (*process, effect*) de nivellement

level playing field *n*: **to compete on a ~** jouer sur un terrain d'égalité

lever ['liːvəʳ] *n* levier *m* ▷ *vt*: **to ~ up/out** soulever/extraire au moyen d'un levier

leverage ['liːvərɪdʒ] *n* (*influence*): **~ (on** or **with)**

prise f (sur)

levity ['lɛvɪtɪ] n manque m de sérieux, légèreté f

levy ['lɛvɪ] n taxe f, impôt m ▷ vt (tax) lever; (fine) infliger

lewd [luːd] adj obscène, lubrique

lexicographer [lɛksɪ'kɔgrəfəʳ] n lexicographe m/f

lexicography [lɛksɪ'kɔgrəfɪ] n lexicographie f

LGV n abbr (= Large Goods Vehicle) poids lourd

LI abbr (US) = **Long Island**

liabilities [laɪə'bɪlətɪz] npl (Comm) obligations fpl, engagements mpl; (on balance sheet) passif m

liability [laɪə'bɪlətɪ] n responsabilité f; (handicap) handicap m

liable ['laɪəbl] adj (subject): ~ **to** sujet(te) à, passible de; (responsible): ~ **(for)** responsable (de); (likely): ~ **to do** susceptible de faire; **to be ~ to a fine** être passible d'une amende

liaise [liː'eɪz] vi: **to ~ with** assurer la liaison avec

liaison [liː'eɪzɔn] n liaison f

liar ['laɪəʳ] n menteur(-euse)

libel ['laɪbl] n diffamation f; (document) écrit m diffamatoire ▷ vt diffamer

libellous ['laɪbləs] adj diffamatoire

liberal ['lɪbərl] adj libéral(e); (generous): ~ **with** prodigue de, généreux(-euse) avec ▷ n: **L~** (Pol) libéral(e)

Liberal Democrat n (Brit) libéral(e)-démocrate m/f

liberality [lɪbə'rælɪtɪ] n (generosity) générosité f, libéralité f

liberalize ['lɪbərəlaɪz] vt libéraliser

liberal-minded ['lɪbərl'maɪndɪd] adj libéral(e), tolérant(e)

liberate ['lɪbəreɪt] vt libérer

liberation [lɪbə'reɪʃən] n libération f

liberation theology n théologie f de libération

Liberia [laɪ'bɪərɪə] n Libéria m, Liberia m

Liberian [laɪ'bɪərɪən] adj libérien(ne) ▷ n Libérien(ne)

liberty ['lɪbətɪ] n liberté f; **to be at ~** (criminal) être en liberté; **at ~ to do** libre de faire; **to take the ~ of** prendre la liberté de, se permettre de

libido [lɪ'biːdəu] n libido f

Libra ['liːbrə] n la Balance; **to be ~** être de la Balance

librarian [laɪ'brɛərɪən] n bibliothécaire m/f

library ['laɪbrərɪ] n bibliothèque f

library book n livre m de bibliothèque

libretto [lɪ'brɛtəu] n livret m

Libya ['lɪbɪə] n Libye f

Libyan ['lɪbɪən] adj libyen(ne), de Libye ▷ n Libyen(ne)

lice [laɪs] npl of **louse**

licence, (US) **license** ['laɪsns] n autorisation f, permis m; (Comm) licence f; (Radio, TV) redevance f; (also: **driving licence**; US: also: **driver's license**) permis m (de conduire); (excessive freedom) licence; **import ~** licence d'importation; **produced under ~** fabriqué(e) sous licence

licence number n (Brit Aut) numéro m

d'immatriculation

license ['laɪsns] n (US) = **licence** ▷ vt donner une licence à; (car) acheter la vignette de; délivrer la vignette de

licensed ['laɪsnst] adj (for alcohol) patenté(e) pour la vente des spiritueux, qui a une patente de débit de boissons; (car) muni(e) de la vignette

licensee [laɪsən'siː] n (Brit: of pub) patron(ne), gérant(e)

license plate n (US Aut) plaque f minéralogique

licensing hours (Brit) npl heures fpl d'ouvertures (des pubs)

licentious [laɪ'sɛnʃəs] adj licencieux(-euse)

lichen ['laɪkən] n lichen m

lick [lɪk] vt lécher; (inf: defeat) écraser, flanquer une piquette or raclée à ▷ n coup m de langue; **a ~ of paint** un petit coup de peinture; **to ~ one's lips** (fig) se frotter les mains

licorice ['lɪkərɪs] n = **liquorice**

lid [lɪd] n couvercle m; (eyelid) paupière f; **to take the ~ off sth** (fig) exposer or étaler qch au grand jour

lido ['laɪdəu] n piscine f en plein air, complexe m balnéaire

lie [laɪ] n mensonge m ▷ vi (pt, pp **-d**) (tell lies) mentir; (pt **lay**, pp **lain** [leɪ, leɪn]) (rest) être étendu(e) or allongé(e) or couché(e); (in grave) être enterré(e), reposer; (object: be situated) se trouver, être; **to ~ low** (fig) se cacher, rester caché(e); **to tell ~s** mentir

▶ **lie about, lie around** vi (things) traîner; (Brit: person) traînasser, flemmarder

▶ **lie back** vi se renverser en arrière

▶ **lie down** vi se coucher, s'étendre

▶ **lie up** vi (hide) se cacher

Liechtenstein ['lɪktənstaɪn] n Liechtenstein m

lie detector n détecteur m de mensonges

lie-down ['laɪdaun] n (Brit): **to have a ~** s'allonger, se reposer

lie-in ['laɪɪn] n (Brit): **to have a ~** faire la grasse matinée

lieu [luː]: **in ~ of** prep au lieu de, à la place de

Lieut. abbr (= lieutenant) Lt

lieutenant [lɛf'tɛnənt, (US) luː'tɛnənt] n lieutenant m

lieutenant-colonel [lɛf'tɛnənt'kəːnl, (US) luː'tɛnənt'kəːnl] n lieutenant-colonel m

life (pl **lives**) [laɪf, laɪvz] n vie f; **to come to ~** (fig) s'animer ▷ cpd de vie; de la vie; à vie; **true to ~** réaliste, fidèle à la réalité; **to paint from ~** peindre d'après nature; **to be sent to prison for ~** être condamné(e) (à la réclusion criminelle) à perpétuité; **country/city ~** la vie à la campagne/à la ville

life annuity n pension f, rente viagère

life assurance n (Brit) = **life insurance**

lifebelt ['laɪfbɛlt] n (Brit) bouée f de sauvetage

lifeblood ['laɪfblʌd] n (fig) élément moteur

lifeboat ['laɪfbəut] n canot m or chaloupe f de sauvetage

lifebuoy ['laɪfbɔɪ] n bouée f de sauvetage

life expectancy n espérance f de vie

lifeguard ['laɪfgɑːd] n surveillant m de baignade
life imprisonment n prison f à vie; (Law) réclusion f à perpétuité
life insurance n assurance-vie f
life jacket n gilet m or ceinture f de sauvetage
lifeless ['laɪflɪs] adj sans vie, inanimé(e); (dull) qui manque de vie or de vigueur
lifelike ['laɪflaɪk] adj qui semble vrai(e) or vivant(e), ressemblant(e); (painting) réaliste
lifeline ['laɪflaɪn] n corde f de sauvetage
lifelong ['laɪflɔŋ] adj de toute une vie, de toujours
life preserver [-prɪˈzəːvəʳ] n (US) gilet m or ceinture f de sauvetage
lifer ['laɪfəʳ] n (inf) condamné(e) à perpète
life-raft ['laɪfrɑːft] n radeau m de sauvetage
life-saver ['laɪfseɪvəʳ] n surveillant m de baignade
life-saving ['laɪfseɪvɪŋ] n sauvetage m
life sentence n condamnation f à vie or à perpétuité
life-size ['laɪfsaɪz], **life-sized** ['laɪfsaɪzd] adj grandeur nature inv
life span n (durée f de) vie f
lifestyle ['laɪfstaɪl] n style m de vie
life-support system n (Med) respirateur artificiel
lifetime ['laɪftaɪm] n: **in his ~** de son vivant; **the chance of a ~** la chance de ma (or sa etc) vie), une occasion unique
lift [lɪft] vt soulever, lever; (end) supprimer, lever; (steal) prendre, voler ▷ vi (fog) se lever ▷ n (Brit: elevator) ascenseur m; **to give sb a ~** (Brit) emmener or prendre qn en voiture; **can you give me a ~ to the station?** pouvez-vous m'emmener à la gare?
 ▶ **lift off** vi (rocket, helicopter) décoller
 ▶ **lift out** vt sortir; (troops, evacuees etc) évacuer par avion or hélicoptère
 ▶ **lift up** vt soulever
lift-off ['lɪftɔf] n décollage m
ligament ['lɪgəmənt] n ligament m
light [laɪt] n lumière f; (daylight) lumière, jour m; (lamp) lampe f; (Aut: rear light) feu m; (: headlamp) phare m; (for cigarette etc): **have you got a ~?** avez-vous du feu? ▷ vt (pt, pp **-ed**, pt, pp lit [lɪt]) (candle, cigarette, fire) allumer; (room) éclairer ▷ adj (room, colour) clair(e); (not heavy, also fig) léger(-ère); (not strenuous) peu fatigant(e) ▷ adv (travel) avec peu de bagages; **lights** npl (traffic lights) feux mpl; **to turn the ~ on/off** allumer/ éteindre; **to cast** or **shed** or **throw ~ on** éclaircir; **to come to ~** être dévoilé(e) or découvert(e); **in the ~ of** à la lumière de; étant donné; **to make ~ of sth** (fig) prendre qch à la légère, faire peu de cas de qch
 ▶ **light up** vi s'allumer; (face) s'éclairer; (smoke) allumer une cigarette or une pipe etc ▷ vt (illuminate) éclairer, illuminer
light bulb n ampoule f
lighten ['laɪtn] vi s'éclairer ▷ vt (light up) éclairer; (make lighter) éclaircir; (make less heavy)

alléger
lighter ['laɪtəʳ] n (also: **cigarette lighter**) briquet m; (: in car) allume-cigare m inv; (boat) péniche f
light-fingered [laɪtˈfɪŋgəd] adj chapardeur(-euse)
light-headed [laɪtˈhɛdɪd] adj étourdi(e), écervelé(e)
light-hearted [laɪtˈhɑːtɪd] adj gai(e), joyeux(-euse), enjoué(e)
lighthouse ['laɪthaus] n phare m
lighting ['laɪtɪŋ] n éclairage m; (in theatre) éclairages
lighting-up time [laɪtɪŋˈʌp-] n (Brit) heure officielle de la tombée du jour
lightly ['laɪtlɪ] adv légèrement; **to get off ~** s'en tirer à bon compte
light meter n (Phot) photomètre m, cellule f
lightness ['laɪtnɪs] n clarté f; (in weight) légèreté f
lightning ['laɪtnɪŋ] n foudre f; (flash) éclair m
lightning conductor, (US) **lightning rod** n paratonnerre m
lightning strike n (Brit) grève f surprise
light pen n crayon m optique
lightship ['laɪtʃɪp] n bateau-phare m
lightweight ['laɪtweɪt] adj (suit) léger(-ère) ▷ n (Boxing) poids léger
light year ['laɪtjɪəʳ] n année-lumière f
like [laɪk] vt aimer (bien) ▷ prep comme ▷ adj semblable, pareil(le) ▷ n: **the ~** un(e) pareil(e) or semblable; **le (la) pareil(le)**; (pej) (d')autres du même genre or acabit; **his ~s and dislikes** ses goûts mpl or préférences fpl; **I would ~**, **I'd ~** je voudrais, j'aimerais; **would you ~ a coffee?** voulez-vous du café?; **to be/look ~ sb/sth** ressembler à qn/qch; **what's he ~?** comment est-il?; **what's the weather ~?** quel temps fait-il?; **what does it look ~?** de quoi est-ce que ça a l'air?; **what does it taste ~?** quel goût est-ce que ça a?; **that's just ~ him** c'est bien de lui, ça lui ressemble; **something ~ that** quelque chose comme ça; **do it ~ this** fais-le comme ceci; **I feel ~ a drink** je boirais bien quelque chose; **if you ~** si vous voulez; **it's nothing ~ ...** ce n'est pas du tout comme ...; **there's nothing ~ ...** il n'y a rien de tel que ...
likeable ['laɪkəbl] adj sympathique, agréable
likelihood ['laɪklɪhud] n probabilité f; **in all ~** selon toute vraisemblance
likely ['laɪklɪ] adj (result, outcome) probable; (excuse) plausible; **he's ~ to leave** il va sûrement partir, il risque fort de partir; **not ~!** (inf) pas de danger!
like-minded ['laɪkˈmaɪndɪd] adj de même opinion
liken ['laɪkən] vt: **to ~ sth to** comparer qch à
likeness ['laɪknɪs] n ressemblance f
likewise ['laɪkwaɪz] adv de même, pareillement
liking ['laɪkɪŋ] n (for person) affection f; (for thing) penchant m, goût m; **to take a ~ to sb** se prendre d'amitié pour qn; **to be to sb's ~** être au goût de qn, plaire à qn
lilac ['laɪlək] n lilas m ▷ adj lilas inv

Lilo® ['laɪləu] n matelas m pneumatique
lilt [lɪlt] n rythme m, cadence f
lilting ['lɪltɪŋ] adj aux cadences mélodieuses; chantant(e)
lily ['lɪlɪ] n lis m; ~ **of the valley** muguet m
Lima ['li:mə] n Lima
limb [lɪm] n membre m; **to be out on a ~** (fig) être isolé(e)
limber ['lɪmbə^r]: **to ~ up** vi se dégourdir, se mettre en train
limbo ['lɪmbəu] n: **to be in ~** (fig) être tombé(e) dans l'oubli
lime [laɪm] n (tree) tilleul m; (fruit) citron vert, lime f; (Geo) chaux f
lime juice n jus m de citron vert
limelight ['laɪmlaɪt] n: **in the ~** (fig) en vedette, au premier plan
limerick ['lɪmərɪk] n petit poème humoristique
limestone ['laɪmstəun] n pierre f à chaux; (Geo) calcaire m
limit ['lɪmɪt] n limite f ▷ vt limiter; **weight/speed ~** limite de poids/de vitesse
limitation [lɪmɪ'teɪʃən] n limitation f, restriction f
limited ['lɪmɪtɪd] adj limité(e), restreint(e); **~ edition** édition f à tirage limité; **to be ~ to** se limiter à, ne concerner que
limited company, limited liability company n (Brit) ≈ société f anonyme
limitless ['lɪmɪtlɪs] adj illimité(e)
limousine ['lɪməzi:n] n limousine f
limp [lɪmp] n: **to have a ~** boiter ▷ vi boiter ▷ adj mou (molle)
limpet ['lɪmpɪt] n patelle f; **like a ~** (fig) comme une ventouse
limpid ['lɪmpɪd] adj limpide
linchpin ['lɪntʃpɪn] n esse f; (fig) pivot m
Lincs [lɪŋks] abbr (Brit) = **Lincolnshire**
line [laɪn] n (gen) ligne f; (stroke) trait m; (wrinkle) ride f; (rope) corde f; (wire) fil m; (of poem) vers m; (row, series) rangée f; (of people) file f, queue f; (railway track) voie f; (Comm: series of goods) article(s) m(pl), ligne de produits; (work) métier m ▷ vt: **to ~ (with)** (clothes) doubler (de); (box) garnir or tapisser (de); (subj: trees, crowd) border; **to stand in ~** (US) faire la queue; **to cut in ~** (US) passer avant son tour; **in his ~ of business** dans sa partie, dans son rayon; **on the right ~s** sur la bonne voie; **a new ~ in cosmetics** une nouvelle ligne de produits de beauté; **hold the ~ please** (Brit Tel) ne quittez pas; **to be in ~ for sth** (fig) être en lice pour qch; **in ~ with** en accord avec, en conformité avec; **in a ~** aligné(e); **to bring sth into ~ with sth** aligner qch sur qch; **to draw the ~ at (doing) sth** (fig) se refuser à (faire) qch; ne pas tolérer or admettre (qu'on fasse) qch; **to take the ~ that ...** être d'avis or de l'opinion que ...
  ▶ **line up** vi s'aligner, se mettre en rang(s); (in queue) faire la queue ▷ vt aligner; (event) prévoir; (find) trouver; **to have sb/sth ~d up** avoir qn/qch en vue or de prévu(e)

linear ['lɪnɪə^r] adj linéaire
lined [laɪnd] adj (paper) réglé(e); (face) marqué(e), ridé(e); (clothes) doublé(e)
lineman ['laɪnmən] (irreg) n (US: Rail) poseur m de rails; (: Tel) ouvrier m de ligne; (: Football) avant m
linen ['lɪnɪn] n linge m (de corps or de maison); (cloth) lin m
line printer n imprimante f (ligne par) ligne
liner ['laɪnə^r] n (ship) paquebot m de ligne; (for bin) sac-poubelle m
linesman ['laɪnzmən] (irreg) n (Tennis) juge m de ligne; (Football) juge de touche
line-up ['laɪnʌp] n (US: queue) file f; (also: **police line-up**) parade f d'identification; (Sport) (composition f de l')équipe f
linger ['lɪŋgə^r] vi s'attarder; traîner; (smell, tradition) persister
lingerie ['lænʒəri:] n lingerie f
lingering ['lɪŋgərɪŋ] adj persistant(e); qui subsiste; (death) lent(e)
lingo ['lɪŋgəu] (pl -es) n (pej) jargon m
linguist ['lɪŋgwɪst] n linguiste m/f; **to be a good ~** être doué(e) pour les langues
linguistic [lɪŋ'gwɪstɪk] adj linguistique
linguistics [lɪŋ'gwɪstɪks] n linguistique f
lining ['laɪnɪŋ] n doublure f; (Tech) revêtement m; (: of brakes) garniture f
link [lɪŋk] n (connection) lien m, rapport m; (Internet) lien; (of a chain) maillon m ▷ vt relier, lier, unir; **links** npl (Golf) (terrain m de) golf m; **rail ~** liaison f ferroviaire
  ▶ **link up** vt relier ▷ vi (people) se rejoindre; (companies etc) s'associer
link-up ['lɪŋkʌp] n lien m, rapport m; (of roads) jonction f, raccordement m; (of spaceships) arrimage m; (Radio, TV) liaison f; (: programme) duplex m
lino ['laɪnəu] n = **linoleum**
linoleum [lɪ'nəulɪəm] n linoléum m
linseed oil ['lɪnsi:d-] n huile f de lin
lint [lɪnt] n tissu ouaté (pour pansements)
lintel ['lɪntl] n linteau m
lion ['laɪən] n lion m
lion cub n lionceau m
lioness ['laɪənɪs] n lionne f
lip [lɪp] n lèvre f; (of cup etc) rebord m; (insolence) insolences fpl
liposuction ['lɪpəusʌkʃən] n liposuccion f
lipread ['lɪpri:d] vi (irreg: like **read**) lire sur les lèvres
lip salve [-sælv] n pommade f pour les lèvres, pommade rosat
lip service n: **to pay ~ to sth** ne reconnaître le mérite de qch que pour la forme or qu'en paroles
lipstick ['lɪpstɪk] n rouge m à lèvres
liquefy ['lɪkwɪfaɪ] vt liquéfier ▷ vi se liquéfier
liqueur [lɪ'kjuə^r] n liqueur f
liquid ['lɪkwɪd] n liquide m ▷ adj liquide
liquid assets npl liquidités fpl, disponibilités fpl
liquidate ['lɪkwɪdeɪt] vt liquider
liquidation [lɪkwɪ'deɪʃən] n liquidation f; **to go**

into ~ déposer son bilan
liquidator ['lɪkwɪdeɪtəʳ] *n* liquidateur *m*
liquid crystal display *n* affichage *m* à cristaux liquides
liquidize ['lɪkwɪdaɪz] *vt* (*Brit Culin*) passer au mixer
liquidizer ['lɪkwɪdaɪzəʳ] *n* (*Brit Culin*) mixer *m*
liquor ['lɪkəʳ] *n* spiritueux *m*, alcool *m*
liquorice ['lɪkərɪs] *n* (*Brit*) réglisse *m*
liquor store (*US*) *n* magasin *m* de vins et spiritueux
Lisbon ['lɪzbən] *n* Lisbonne
lisp [lɪsp] *n* zézaiement *m* ▷ *vi* zézayer
lissom ['lɪsəm] *adj* souple, agile
list [lɪst] *n* liste *f*; (*of ship*) inclinaison *f* ▷ *vt* (*write down*) inscrire; (*make list of*) faire la liste de; (*enumerate*) énumérer; (*Comput*) lister ▷ *vi* (*ship*) gîter, donner de la bande; **shopping ~** liste des courses
listed building ['lɪstɪd-] *n* (*Archit*) monument classé
listed company ['lɪstɪd-] *n* société cotée en Bourse
listen ['lɪsn] *vi* écouter; **to ~ to** écouter
listener ['lɪsnəʳ] *n* auditeur(-trice)
listeria [lɪs'tɪərɪə] *n* listéria *f*
listing ['lɪstɪŋ] *n* (*Comput*) listage *m*; (: *hard copy*) liste *f*, listing *m*
listless ['lɪstlɪs] *adj* indolent(e), apathique
listlessly ['lɪstlɪslɪ] *adv* avec indolence *or* apathie
list price *n* prix *m* de catalogue
lit [lɪt] *pt, pp of* **light**
litany ['lɪtənɪ] *n* litanie *f*
liter ['liːtəʳ] *n* (*US*) = **litre**
literacy ['lɪtərəsɪ] *n* degré *m* d'alphabétisation, fait *m* de savoir lire et écrire; (*Brit: Scol*) enseignement *m* de la lecture et de l'écriture
literal ['lɪtərl] *adj* littéral(e)
literally ['lɪtrəlɪ] *adv* littéralement; (*really*) réellement
literary ['lɪtərərɪ] *adj* littéraire
literate ['lɪtərət] *adj* qui sait lire et écrire; (*educated*) instruit(e)
literature ['lɪtrɪtʃəʳ] *n* littérature *f*; (*brochures etc*) copie *f* publicitaire, prospectus *mpl*
lithe [laɪð] *adj* agile, souple
lithography [lɪ'θɒgrəfɪ] *n* lithographie *f*
Lithuania [lɪθju'eɪnɪə] *n* Lituanie *f*
Lithuanian [lɪθju'eɪnɪən] *adj* lituanien(ne) ▷ *n* Lituanien(ne); (*Ling*) lituanien *m*
litigate ['lɪtɪgeɪt] *vt* mettre en litige ▷ *vi* plaider
litigation [lɪtɪ'geɪʃən] *n* litige *m*; contentieux *m*
litmus ['lɪtməs] *n*: ~ **paper** papier *m* de tournesol
litre, (*US*) **liter** ['liːtəʳ] *n* litre *m*
litter ['lɪtəʳ] *n* (*rubbish*) détritus *mpl*; (*dirtier*) ordures *fpl*; (*young animals*) portée *f* ▷ *vt* éparpiller; laisser des détritus dans; **~ed with** jonché(e) de, couvert(e) de
litter bin *n* (*Brit*) poubelle *f*
litter lout, (*US*) **litterbug** ['lɪtəbʌg] *n* *personne qui jette des détritus par terre*
little ['lɪtl] *adj* (*small*) petit(e); (*not much*): ~ **milk**

peu de lait ▷ *adv* peu; **a ~** un peu (de); **a ~ milk** un peu de lait; **a ~ bit** un peu; **for a ~ while** pendant un petit moment; **with ~ difficulty** sans trop de difficulté; **as ~ as possible** le moins possible; **~ by ~** petit à petit, peu à peu; **to make ~ of** faire peu de cas de
little finger *n* auriculaire *m*, petit doigt
little-known ['lɪtl'nəun] *adj* peu connu(e)
liturgy ['lɪtədʒɪ] *n* liturgie *f*
live¹ [laɪv] *adj* (*animal*) vivant(e), en vie; (*wire*) sous tension; (*broadcast*) (transmis(e)) en direct; (*issue*) d'actualité, brûlant(e); (*unexploded*) non explosé(e); ~ **ammunition** munitions *fpl* de combat
live² [lɪv] *vi* vivre; (*reside*) vivre, habiter; **to ~ in London** habiter (à) Londres; **where do you ~?** où habitez-vous?
▶ **live down** *vt* faire oublier (avec le temps)
▶ **live in** *vi* être logé(e) et nourri(e); être interne
▶ **live off** *vt* (*land, fish etc*) vivre de; (*pej: parents etc*) vivre aux crochets de
▶ **live on** *vt fus* (*food*) vivre de ▷ *vi* survivre; **to ~ on £50 a week** vivre avec 50 livres par semaine
▶ **live out** *vi* (*Brit: students*) être externe ▷ *vt*: **to ~ out one's days** *or* **life** passer sa vie
▶ **live together** *vi* vivre ensemble, cohabiter
▶ **live up** *vt*: **to ~ it up** (*inf*) faire la fête; mener la grande vie
▶ **live up to** *vt fus* se montrer à la hauteur de
live-in ['lɪvɪn] *adj* (*nanny*) à demeure; ~ **partner** concubin(e)
livelihood ['laɪvlɪhud] *n* moyens *mpl* d'existence
liveliness ['laɪvlɪnəs] *n* vivacité *f*, entrain *m*
lively ['laɪvlɪ] *adj* vif (vive), plein(e) d'entrain; (*place, book*) vivant(e)
liven up ['laɪvn-] *vt* (*room etc*) égayer; (*discussion, evening*) animer ▷ *vi* s'animer
liver ['lɪvəʳ] *n* foie *m*
liverish ['lɪvərɪʃ] *adj* qui a mal au foie; (*fig*) grincheux(-euse)
Liverpudlian [lɪvə'pʌdlɪən] *adj* de Liverpool ▷ *n* habitant(e) de Liverpool, natif(-ive) de Liverpool
livery ['lɪvərɪ] *n* livrée *f*
lives [laɪvz] *npl of* **life**
livestock ['laɪvstɒk] *n* cheptel *m*, bétail *m*
live wire [laɪv-] *n* (*inf, fig*): **to be a (real) ~** péter le feu
livid ['lɪvɪd] *adj* livide, blafard(e); (*furious*) furieux(-euse), furibond(e)
living ['lɪvɪŋ] *adj* vivant(e), en vie ▷ *n*: **to earn** *or* **make a ~** gagner sa vie; **within ~ memory** de mémoire d'homme
living conditions *npl* conditions *fpl* de vie
living expenses *npl* dépenses courantes
living room *n* salle *f* de séjour
living standards *npl* niveau *m* de vie
living wage *n* salaire *m* permettant de vivre (décemment)
lizard ['lɪzəd] *n* lézard *m*
llama ['lɑːmə] *n* lama *m*
LLB *n abbr* (= *Bachelor of Laws*) *titre universitaire*

LLD *n abbr* (= *Doctor of Laws*) *titre universitaire*
LMT *abbr* (*US*: = *Local Mean Time*) *heure locale*
load [ləʊd] *n* (*weight*) poids *m*; (*thing carried*) chargement *m*, charge *f*; (*Elec, Tech*) charge ▷ *vt*: **to ~ (with)** (*also*: **load up**: *lorry, ship*) charger (de); (*gun, camera*) charger (avec); (*Comput*) charger; **a ~ of, ~s of** (*fig*) un or des tas de, des masses de; **to talk a ~ of rubbish** (*inf*) dire des bêtises
loaded [ˈləʊdɪd] *adj* (*dice*) pipé(e); (*question*) insidieux(-euse); (*inf: rich*) bourré(e) de fric; (: *drunk*) bourré
loading bay [ˈləʊdɪŋ-] *n* aire *f* de chargement
loaf (*pl* **loaves**) [ləʊf, ləʊvz] *n* pain *m*, miche *f* ▷ *vi* (*also*: **loaf about, loaf around**) fainéanter, traîner
loam [ləʊm] *n* terreau *m*
loan [ləʊn] *n* prêt *m* ▷ *vt* prêter; **on ~** prêté(e), en prêt; **public ~** emprunt public
loan account *n* compte *m* de prêt
loan capital *n* capital *m* d'emprunt
loan shark *n* (*inf, pej*) usurier *m*
loath [ləʊθ] *adj*: **to be ~ to do** répugner à faire
loathe [ləʊð] *vt* détester, avoir en horreur
loathing [ˈləʊðɪŋ] *n* dégoût *m*, répugnance *f*
loathsome [ˈləʊðsəm] *adj* répugnant(e), détestable
loaves [ləʊvz] *npl of* **loaf**
lob [lɒb] *vt* (*ball*) lober
lobby [ˈlɒbɪ] *n* hall *m*, entrée *f*; (*Pol*) groupe *m* de pression, lobby *m* ▷ *vt* faire pression sur
lobbyist [ˈlɒbɪɪst] *n* membre *m/f* d'un groupe de pression
lobe [ləʊb] *n* lobe *m*
lobster [ˈlɒbstəʳ] *n* homard *m*
lobster pot *n* casier *m* à homards
local [ˈləʊkl] *adj* local(e) ▷ *n* (*Brit: pub*) pub *m* or café *m* du coin; **the locals** *npl* les gens *mpl* du pays or du coin
local anaesthetic, (*US*) **local anesthetic** *n* anesthésie locale
local authority *n* collectivité locale, municipalité *f*
local call *n* (*Tel*) communication urbaine
local government *n* administration locale or municipale
locality [ləʊˈkælɪtɪ] *n* région *f*, environs *mpl*; (*position*) lieu *m*
localize [ˈləʊkəlaɪz] *vt* localiser
locally [ˈləʊkəlɪ] *adv* localement; dans les environs or la région
locate [ləʊˈkeɪt] *vt* (*find*) trouver, repérer; (*situate*) situer; **to be ~d in** être situé à or en
location [ləʊˈkeɪʃən] *n* emplacement *m*; **on ~** (*Cine*) en extérieur
loch [lɒx] *n* lac *m*, loch *m*
lock [lɒk] *n* (*of door, box*) serrure *f*; (*of canal*) écluse *f*; (*of hair*) mèche *f*, boucle *f* ▷ *vt* (*with key*) fermer à clé; (*immobilize*) bloquer ▷ *vi* (*door etc*) fermer à clé; (*wheels*) se bloquer; **~ stock and barrel** (*fig*) en bloc; **on full ~** (*Brit Aut*) le volant tourné à fond
▶ **lock away** *vt* (*valuables*) mettre sous clé;

(*criminal*) mettre sous les verrous, enfermer
▶ **lock in** *vt* enfermer
▶ **lock out** *vt* enfermer dehors; (*on purpose*) mettre à la porte; (: *workers*) lock-outer
▶ **lock up** *vt* (*person*) enfermer; (*house*) fermer à clé ▷ *vi* tout fermer (à clé)
locker [ˈlɒkəʳ] *n* casier *m*; (*in station*) consigne *f* automatique
locker-room [ˈlɒkəˈruːm] (*US*) *n* (*Sport*) vestiaire *m*
locket [ˈlɒkɪt] *n* médaillon *m*
lockjaw [ˈlɒkdʒɔː] *n* tétanos *m*
lockout [ˈlɒkaut] *n* (*Industry*) lock-out *m*, grève patronale
locksmith [ˈlɒksmɪθ] *n* serrurier *m*
lock-up [ˈlɒkʌp] *n* (*prison*) prison *f*; (*cell*) cellule *f* provisoire; (*also*: **lock-up garage**) box *m*
locomotive [ləʊkəˈməʊtɪv] *n* locomotive *f*
locum [ˈləʊkəm] *n* (*Med*) suppléant(e) de médecin *etc*
locust [ˈləʊkəst] *n* locuste *f*, sauterelle *f*
lodge [lɒdʒ] *n* pavillon *m* (de gardien); (*also*: **hunting lodge**) pavillon de chasse; (*Freemasonry*) loge *f* ▷ *vi* (*person*): **to ~ with** être logé(e) chez, être en pension chez; (*bullet*) se loger ▷ *vt* (*appeal etc*) présenter; déposer; **to ~ a complaint** porter plainte; **to ~ (itself) in/between** se loger dans/ entre
lodger [ˈlɒdʒəʳ] *n* locataire *m/f*; (*with room and meals*) pensionnaire *m/f*
lodging [ˈlɒdʒɪŋ] *n* logement *m*; *see also* **board**
lodging house *n* (*Brit*) pension *f* de famille
lodgings [ˈlɒdʒɪŋz] *npl* chambre *f*, meublé *m*
loft [lɒft] *n* grenier *m*; (*apartment*) grenier aménagé (en appartement) (*gén dans ancien entrepôt ou fabrique*)
lofty [ˈlɒftɪ] *adj* élevé(e); (*haughty*) hautain(e); (*sentiments, aims*) noble
log [lɒg] *n* (*of wood*) bûche *f*; (*Naut*) livre *m* or journal *m* de bord; (*of car*) ≈ carte grise ▷ *n abbr* (= *logarithm*) log *m* ▷ *vt* enregistrer
▶ **log in, log on** *vi* (*Comput*) ouvrir une session, entrer dans le système
▶ **log off, log out** *vi* (*Comput*) clore une session, sortir du système
logarithm [ˈlɒgərɪðm] *n* logarithme *m*
logbook [ˈlɒgbuk] *n* (*Naut*) livre *m* or journal *m* de bord; (*Aviat*) carnet *m* de vol; (*of lorry driver*) carnet de route; (*of movement of goods etc*) registre *m*; (*of car*) ≈ carte grise
log cabin *n* cabane *f* en rondins
log fire *n* feu *m* de bois
logger [ˈlɒgəʳ] *n* bûcheron *m*
loggerheads [ˈlɒgəhɛdz] *npl*: **at ~ (with)** à couteaux tirés (avec)
logic [ˈlɒdʒɪk] *n* logique *f*
logical [ˈlɒdʒɪkl] *adj* logique
logically [ˈlɒdʒɪkəlɪ] *adv* logiquement
login [ˈlɒgɪn] *n* (*Comput*) identifiant *m*
logistics [lɒˈdʒɪstɪks] *n* logistique *f*
logjam [ˈlɒgdʒæm] *n*: **to break the ~** créer une ouverture dans l'impasse
logo [ˈləʊgəʊ] *n* logo *m*

loin [lɔɪn] n (Culin) filet m, longe f; **loins** npl
reins mpl
loin cloth n pagne m
Loire [lwa:] n: **the (River)** ~ la Loire
loiter ['lɔɪtər] vi s'attarder; **to ~ (about)** traîner,
musarder; (pej) rôder
lol abbr (Internet, Tel: = laugh out loud) MDR
(= mort(e) de vive)
loll [lɔl] vi (also: **loll about**) se prélasser,
fainéanter
lollipop ['lɔlɪpɔp] n sucette f
lollipop man/lady (Brit: irreg) n contractuel(le) qui
fait traverser la rue aux enfants; voir article

⬤ LOLLIPOP MEN/LADIES

Les lollipop men/ladies sont employés pour
aider les enfants à traverser la rue à
proximité des écoles à l'heure où ils entrent
en classe et à la sortie. On les repère
facilement à cause de leur long ciré jaune et
ils portent une pancarte ronde pour faire
signe aux automobilistes de s'arrêter. On les
appelle ainsi car la forme circulaire de cette
pancarte rappelle une sucette.

lollop ['lɔləp] vi (Brit) avancer (or courir)
maladroitement
lolly ['lɔli] n (inf: ice) esquimau m; (: lollipop)
sucette f; (: money) fric m
Lombardy ['lɔmbədɪ] n Lombardie f
London ['lʌndən] n Londres
Londoner ['lʌndənər] n Londonien(ne)
lone [ləun] adj solitaire
loneliness ['ləunlɪnɪs] n solitude f, isolement m
lonely ['ləunlɪ] adj seul(e); (childhood etc)
solitaire; (place) solitaire, isolé(e)
lonely hearts adj: ~ **ad** petite annonce
(personnelle); ~ **club** club m de rencontres (pour
personnes seules)
lone parent n parent m unique
loner ['ləunər] n solitaire m/f
lonesome ['ləunsəm] adj seul(e), solitaire
long [lɔŋ] adj long (longue) ▷ adv longtemps
▷ n: **the ~ and the short of it is that ...** (fig) le
fin mot de l'histoire c'est que ... ▷ vi: **to ~ for
sth/to do sth** avoir très envie de qch/de faire
qch, attendre qch avec impatience/attendre
avec impatience de faire qch; **he had ~
understood that ...** il avait compris depuis
longtemps que ...; **how ~ is this river/course?**
quelle est la longueur de ce fleuve/la durée de ce
cours?; **6 metres ~** (long) de 6 mètres; **6
months ~** qui dure 6 mois, de 6 mois; **all night
~** toute la nuit; **he no ~er comes** il ne vient
plus; **I can't stand it any ~er** je ne peux plus le
supporter; ~ **before** longtemps avant; **before ~**
(+ future) avant peu, dans peu de temps; (+ past)
peu de temps après; ~ **ago** il y a longtemps;
don't be ~! fais vite!, dépêche-toi!; **I shan't be
~** je n'en ai pas pour longtemps; **at ~ last** enfin;
in the ~ run à la longue; finalement; **so** or **as ~**

as à condition que + sub
long-distance [lɔŋ'dɪstəns] adj (race) de fond;
(call) interurbain(e)
longer ['lɔŋgər] adv see **long**
long-haired ['lɔŋ'hɛəd] adj (person) aux cheveux
longs; (animal) aux longs poils
longhand ['lɔŋhænd] n écriture normale or
courante
long-haul ['lɔŋhɔ:l] adj (flight) long-courrier
longing ['lɔŋɪŋ] n désir m, envie f; (nostalgia)
nostalgie f ▷ adj plein(e) d'envie or de nostalgie
longingly ['lɔŋɪŋlɪ] adv avec désir or nostalgie
longitude ['lɔŋgɪtju:d] n longitude f
long johns [-dʒɔnz] npl caleçons longs
long jump n saut m en longueur
long-life [lɔŋ'laɪf] adj (batteries etc) longue durée
inv; (milk) longue conservation
long-lost ['lɔŋlɔst] adj perdu(e) depuis
longtemps
long-range ['lɔŋ'reɪndʒ] adj à longue portée;
(weather forecast) à long terme
longshoreman ['lɔŋʃɔ:mən] (irreg) n (US) docker
m, débardeur m
long-sighted ['lɔŋ'saɪtɪd] adj (Brit) presbyte; (fig)
prévoyant(e)
long-standing ['lɔŋ'stændɪŋ] adj de longue date
long-suffering [lɔŋ'sʌfərɪŋ] adj empreint(e)
d'une patience résignée; extrêmement
patient(e)
long-term ['lɔŋtə:m] adj à long terme
long wave n (Radio) grandes ondes, ondes
longues
long-winded [lɔŋ'wɪndɪd] adj intarissable,
interminable
loo [lu:] n (Brit inf) w.-c mpl, petit coin
loofah ['lu:fə] n sorte d'éponge végétale
look [luk] vi regarder; (seem) sembler, paraître,
avoir l'air; (building etc): **to ~ south/on to the
sea** donner au sud/sur la mer ▷ n regard m;
(appearance) air m, allure f, aspect m; **looks** npl
(good looks) physique m, beauté f; **to ~ like**
ressembler à; **it ~s like him** on dirait que c'est
lui; **it ~s about 4 metres long** je dirais que ça
fait 4 mètres de long; **it ~s all right to me** ça
me paraît bien; **to have a ~** regarder; **to have a
~ at sth** jeter un coup d'œil à qch; **to have a ~
for sth** chercher qch; **to ~ ahead** regarder
devant soi; (fig) envisager l'avenir; ~ **(here)!**
(annoyance) écoutez!
▶ **look after** vt fus s'occuper de, prendre soin de;
(luggage etc: watch over) garder, surveiller
▶ **look around** vi regarder autour de soi
▶ **look at** vt fus regarder; (problem etc) examiner
▶ **look back** vi: **to ~ back at sth/sb** se retourner
pour regarder qch/qn; **to ~ back on** (event, period)
évoquer, repenser à
▶ **look down on** vt fus (fig) regarder de haut,
dédaigner
▶ **look for** vt fus chercher; **we're ~ing for a
hotel/restaurant** nous cherchons un hôtel/
restaurant
▶ **look forward to** vt fus attendre avec

impatience; **I'm not ~ing forward to it** cette perspective ne me réjouit guère; **~ing forward to hearing from you** (in letter) dans l'attente de vous lire

▸ **look in** vi: **to ~ in on sb** passer voir qn

▸ **look into** vt fus (matter, possibility) examiner, étudier

▸ **look on** vi regarder (en spectateur)

▸ **look out** vi (beware): **to ~ out (for)** prendre garde (à), faire attention (à); **~ out!** attention!

▸ **look out for** vt fus (seek) être à la recherche de; (try to spot) guetter

▸ **look over** vt (essay) jeter un coup d'œil à; (town, building) visiter (rapidement); (person) jeter un coup d'œil à; examiner de la tête aux pieds

▸ **look round** vt fus (house, shop) faire le tour de ▹ vi (turn) regarder derrière soi, se retourner; **to ~ round for sth** chercher qch

▸ **look through** vt fus (papers, book) examiner; (: briefly) parcourir; (telescope) regarder à travers

▸ **look to** vt fus veiller à; (rely on) compter sur

▸ **look up** vi lever les yeux; (improve) s'améliorer ▹ vt (word) chercher; (friend) passer voir

▸ **look up to** vt fus avoir du respect pour

lookout ['lukaut] n (tower etc) poste m de guet; (person) guetteur m; **to be on the ~ (for)** guetter

look-up table ['lukʌp-] n (Comput) table f à consulter

loom [luːm] n métier m à tisser ▹ vi (also: **loom up**) surgir; (event) paraître imminent(e); (threaten) menacer

loony ['luːnɪ] adj, n (inf) timbré(e), cinglé(e) m/f

loop [luːp] n boucle f; (contraceptive) stérilet m ▹ vt: **to ~ sth round sth** passer qch autour de qch

loophole ['luːpfəul] n (fig) porte f de sortie; échappatoire f

loose [luːs] adj (knot, screw) desserré(e); (stone) branlant(e); (clothes) vague, ample, lâche; (hair) dénoué(e), épars(e); (not firmly fixed) pas solide; (animal) en liberté, échappé(e); (life) dissolu(e); (morals, discipline) relâché(e); (thinking) peu rigoureux(-euse), vague; (translation) approximatif(-ive) ▹ n: **to be on the ~** être en liberté ▹ vt (free: animal) lâcher; (: prisoner) relâcher, libérer; (slacken) détendre, relâcher; desserrer; défaire; donner du mou à; donner du ballant à; (Brit: arrow) tirer; **~ connection** (Elec) mauvais contact; **to be at a ~ end** or (US) **at ~ ends** (fig) ne pas trop savoir quoi faire; **to tie up ~ ends** (fig) mettre au point or régler les derniers détails

loose change n petite monnaie

loose chippings [-'tʃɪpɪŋz] npl (on road) gravillons mpl

loose-fitting ['luːsfɪtɪŋ] adj (clothes) ample

loose-leaf ['luːsliːf] adj: **~ binder** or **folder** classeur m à feuilles or feuillets mobiles

loose-limbed [luːs'lɪmd] adj agile, souple

loosely ['luːslɪ] adv sans serrer; (imprecisely) approximativement

loosely-knit ['luːslɪ'nɪt] adj élastique

loosen ['luːsn] vt desserrer, relâcher, défaire

▸ **loosen up** vi (before game) s'échauffer; (inf: relax) se détendre, se laisser aller

loot [luːt] n butin m ▹ vt piller

looter ['luːtər] n pillard m, casseur m

looting ['luːtɪŋ] n pillage m

lop [lɔp] : **to ~ off** vt couper, trancher

lop-sided ['lɔp'saɪdɪd] adj de travers, asymétrique

lord [lɔːd] n seigneur m; **L~ Smith** lord Smith; **the L~** (Rel) le Seigneur; **my L~** (to noble) Monsieur le comte/le baron; (to judge) Monsieur le juge; (to bishop) Monseigneur; **good L~!** mon Dieu!

lordly ['lɔːdlɪ] adj noble, majestueux(-euse); (arrogant) hautain(e)

Lords ['lɔːdz] npl (Brit: Pol): **the (House of) ~** (Brit) la Chambre des Lords

lordship ['lɔːdʃɪp] n (Brit): **your L~** Monsieur le comte (or le baron or le Juge)

lore [lɔːr] n tradition(s) f(pl)

lorry ['lɔrɪ] n (Brit) camion m

lorry driver n (Brit) camionneur m, routier m

lose (pt, pp **lost**) [luːz, lɔst] vt perdre; (opportunity) manquer, perdre; (pursuers) distancer, semer ▹ vi perdre; **I've lost my wallet/passport** j'ai perdu mon portefeuille/passeport; **to ~ (time)** (clock) retarder; **to ~ no time (in doing sth)** ne pas perdre de temps (à faire qch); **to get lost** (vi: person) se perdre; **my watch has got lost** ma montre est perdue

▸ **lose out** vi être perdant(e)

loser ['luːzər] n perdant(e); **to be a good/bad ~** être beau/mauvais joueur

loss [lɔs] n perte f; **to cut one's ~es** limiter les dégâts; **to make a ~** enregistrer une perte; **to sell sth at a ~** vendre qch à perte; **to be at a ~** être perplexe or embarrassé(e); **to be at a ~ to do** se trouver incapable de faire

loss adjuster n (Insurance) responsable m/f de l'évaluation des dommages

loss leader n (Comm) article sacrifié

lost [lɔst] pt, pp of **lose** ▹ adj perdu(e); **to get ~** (vi) se perdre; **I'm ~** je me suis perdu(e); **~ in thought** perdu dans ses pensées; **~ and found property** (n: US) objets trouvés; **~ and found** (n: US) bureau m des objets trouvés

lost property n (Brit) objets trouvés; **~ office** or **department** (bureau m des) objets trouvés

lot [lɔt] n (at auctions, set) lot m; (destiny) sort m, destinée f; **the ~** (everything) le tout; (everyone) tous mpl, toutes fpl; **a ~** beaucoup; **a ~ of** beaucoup de; **~s of** des tas de; **to draw ~s (for sth)** tirer (qch) au sort

lotion ['ləuʃən] n lotion f

lottery ['lɔtərɪ] n loterie f

loud [laud] adj bruyant(e), sonore; (voice) fort(e); (condemnation etc) vigoureux(-euse); (gaudy) voyant(e), tapageur(-euse) ▹ adv (speak etc) fort; **out ~** tout haut

loud-hailer [laud'heɪlər] n porte-voix m inv

loudly ['laudlı] *adv* fort, bruyamment
loudspeaker [laud'spi:kə^r] *n* haut-parleur *m*
lounge [laundʒ] *n* salon *m*; (*of airport*) salle *f*;
  (*Brit: also*: **lounge bar**) (salle de) café *m or* bar *m*
  ▷ *vi* (*also*: **lounge about, lounge around**) se
  prélasser, paresser
lounge-bar *n* (salle *f* de) bar *m*
lounge suit *n* (*Brit*) complet *m*; (: *on invitation*)
  "tenue de ville"
louse (*pl* **lice**) [laus, laɪs] *n* pou *m*
  ▸ **louse up** [lauz-] *vt* (*inf*) gâcher
lousy ['lauzı] (*inf*) *adj* (*bad quality*) infect(e),
  moche; **I feel ~** je suis mal fichu(e)
lout [laut] *n* rustre *m*, butor *m*
louvre, (*US*) **louver** ['lu:və^r] *adj* (*door, window*) à
  claire-voie
lovable ['lʌvəbl] *adj* très sympathique; adorable
love [lʌv] *n* amour *m* ▷ *vt* aimer; (*caringly, kindly*)
  aimer beaucoup; **I ~ chocolate** j'adore le
  chocolat; **to ~ to do** aimer beaucoup *or* adorer
  faire; **I'd ~ to come** cela me ferait très plaisir
  (de venir); **"15 ~"** (*Tennis*) "15 à rien *or* zéro"; **to
  be/fall in ~ with** être/tomber amoureux(-euse)
  de; **to make ~** faire l'amour; **~ at first sight** le
  coup de foudre; **to send one's ~ to sb** adresser
  ses amitiés à qn; **~ from Anne**, **~, Anne**
  affectueusement, Anne; **I ~ you** je t'aime
love affair *n* liaison (amoureuse)
love child *n* (*irreg*) enfant *m/f* illégitime *or*
  naturel(le)
loved ones ['lʌvdwʌnz] *npl* proches *mpl* et amis
  chers
love-hate relationship [lʌv'heıt-] *n* rapport
  ambigu; **they have a ~** ils s'aiment et se
  détestent à la fois
love life *n* vie sentimentale
lovely ['lʌvlı] *adj* (*pretty*) ravissant(e); (*friend, wife*)
  charmant(e); (*holiday, surprise*) très agréable,
  merveilleux(-euse); **we had a ~ time** c'était
  vraiment très bien, nous avons eu beaucoup de
  plaisir
lover ['lʌvə^r] *n* amant *m*; (*person in love*)
  amoureux(-euse); (*amateur*): **a ~ of** un(e) ami(e)
  de, un(e) amoureux(-euse) de
lovesick ['lʌvsık] *adj* qui se languit d'amour
love song ['lʌvsɔŋ] *n* chanson *f* d'amour
loving ['lʌvıŋ] *adj* affectueux(-euse), tendre,
  aimant(e)
low [ləu] *adj* bas (basse); (*quality*) mauvais(e),
  inférieur(e) ▷ *adv* bas ▷ *n* (*Meteorology*)
  dépression *f* ▷ *vi* (*cow*) mugir; **to feel ~** se sentir
  déprimé(e); **he's very ~** (*ill*) il est bien bas *or* très
  affaibli; **to turn (down) ~** (*vt*) baisser; **to be ~
  on** (*supplies etc*) être à court de; **to reach a new *or*
  an all-time ~** tomber au niveau le plus bas
low-alcohol [ləu'ælkəhɔl] *adj* à faible teneur en
  alcool, peu alcoolisé(e)
lowbrow ['ləubrau] *adj* sans prétentions
  intellectuelles
low-calorie ['ləu'kælərı] *adj* hypocalorique
low-cut ['ləukʌt] *adj* (*dress*) décolleté(e)
low-down ['ləudaun] *n* (*inf*): **he gave me the ~**

(on it) il m'a mis au courant ▷ *adj* (*mean*)
  méprisable
lower *adj* ['ləuə^r] inférieur(e) ▷ *vt* ['lauə^r]
  baisser; (*resistance*) diminuer ▷ *vi* ['lauə^r]
  (*person*): **to ~ at sb** jeter un regard mauvais *or*
  noir à qn; (*sky, clouds*) être menaçant; **to ~ o.s.
  to** s'abaisser à
lower sixth (*Brit*) *n* (*Scol*) première *f*
low-fat ['ləu'fæt] *adj* maigre
low-key ['ləu'ki:] *adj* modéré(e), discret(-ète)
lowland, lowlands ['ləulənd(z)] *n(pl)*
  plaine(s) *f(pl)*
low-level ['ləulɛvl] *adj* bas (basse); (*flying*) à
  basse altitude
low-loader ['ləuləudə^r] *n* semi-remorque *f* à
  plate-forme surbaissée
lowly ['ləulı] *adj* humble, modeste
low-lying [ləu'laııŋ] *adj* à faible altitude
low-paid [ləu'peıd] *adj* mal payé(e), aux salaires
  bas
low-rise ['ləuraız] *adj* bas(se), de faible hauteur
low-tech ['ləutɛk] *adj* sommaire
loyal ['lɔıəl] *adj* loyal(e), fidèle
loyalist ['lɔıəlıst] *n* loyaliste *m/f*
loyalty ['lɔıəltı] *n* loyauté *f*, fidélité *f*
loyalty card *n* carte *f* de fidélité
lozenge ['lɔzındʒ] *n* (*Med*) pastille *f*; (*Geom*)
  losange *m*
LP *n abbr* = **long-playing record**
LPG *n abbr* (= *liquid petroleum gas*) GPL *m*
L-plates ['ɛlpleıts] *npl* (*Brit*) plaques *fpl*
  (obligatoires) d'apprenti conducteur
LPN *n abbr* (*US*: = *Licensed Practical Nurse*)
  infirmier(-ière) diplômé(e)
LRAM *n abbr* (*Brit*) = **Licentiate of the Royal
  Academy of Music**
LSAT *n abbr* (*US*) = **Law School Admissions Test**
LSD *n abbr* (= *lysergic acid diethylamide*) LSD *m*; (*Brit*:
  = *pounds, shillings and pence*) *système monétaire en
  usage en GB jusqu'en 1971*
LSE *n abbr* = **London School of Economics**
LT *abbr* (*Elec*: = *low tension*) BT
Lt *abbr* (= *lieutenant*) Lt.
Ltd *abbr* (*Comm: company*: = *limited*) ≈ S.A.
lubricant ['lu:brıkənt] *n* lubrifiant *m*
lubricate ['lu:brıkeıt] *vt* lubrifier, graisser
lucid ['lu:sıd] *adj* lucide
lucidity [lu:'sıdıtı] *n* lucidité *f*
luck [lʌk] *n* chance *f*; **bad ~** malchance *f*,
  malheur *m*; **to be in ~** avoir de la chance; **to be
  out of ~** ne pas avoir de chance; **good ~!** bonne
  chance!; **bad *or* hard *or* tough ~!** pas de chance!
luckily ['lʌkılı] *adv* heureusement, par bonheur
luckless ['lʌklıs] *adj* (*person*)
  malchanceux(-euse); (*trip*) marqué(e) par la
  malchance
lucky ['lʌkı] *adj* (*person*) qui a de la chance;
  (*coincidence*) heureux(-euse); (*number etc*) qui
  porte bonheur
lucrative ['lu:krətıv] *adj* lucratif(-ive), rentable,
  qui rapporte
ludicrous ['lu:dıkrəs] *adj* ridicule, absurde

ludo ['luːdəu] n jeu m des petits chevaux

lug [lʌg] vt traîner, tirer

luggage ['lʌgɪdʒ] n bagages mpl; **our ~ hasn't arrived** nos bagages ne sont pas arrivés; **could you send someone to collect our ~?** pourriez-vous envoyer quelqu'un chercher nos bagages?

luggage lockers npl consigne f automatique

luggage rack n (in train) porte-bagages m inv; (: made of string) filet m à bagages; (on car) galerie f

luggage van, (US) **luggage car** n (Rail) fourgon m (à bagages)

lugubrious [lu'guːbrɪəs] adj lugubre

lukewarm ['luːkwɔːm] adj tiède

lull [lʌl] n accalmie f; (in conversation) pause f ▷ vt: **to ~ sb to sleep** bercer qn pour qu'il s'endorme; **to be ~ed into a false sense of security** s'endormir dans une fausse sécurité

lullaby ['lʌləbaɪ] n berceuse f

lumbago [lʌm'beɪgəu] n lumbago m

lumber ['lʌmbəʳ] n (wood) bois m de charpente; (junk) bric-à-brac m inv ▷ vt (Brit inf): **to ~ sb with sth/sb** coller or refiler qch/qn à qn ▷ vi (also: **lumber about, lumber along**) marcher pesamment

lumberjack ['lʌmbədʒæk] n bûcheron m

lumber room n (Brit) débarras m

lumber yard n entrepôt m de bois

luminous ['luːmɪnəs] adj lumineux(-euse)

lump [lʌmp] n morceau m; (in sauce) grumeau m; (swelling) grosseur f ▷ vt (also: **lump together**) réunir, mettre en tas

lump sum n somme globale or forfaitaire

lumpy ['lʌmpɪ] adj (sauce) qui a des grumeaux; (bed) défoncé(e), peu confortable

lunacy ['luːnəsɪ] n démence f, folie f

lunar ['luːnəʳ] adj lunaire

lunatic ['luːnətɪk] n fou (folle), dément(e) ▷ adj fou (folle), dément(e)

lunatic asylum n asile m d'aliénés

lunch [lʌntʃ] n déjeuner m ▷ vi déjeuner; **it is his ~ hour** c'est l'heure où il déjeune; **to invite sb to** or **for ~** inviter qn à déjeuner

lunch break, lunch hour n pause f de midi, heure f du déjeuner

luncheon ['lʌntʃən] n déjeuner m

luncheon meat n sorte de saucisson

luncheon voucher n chèque-repas m, ticket-repas m

lunchtime ['lʌntʃtaɪm] n: **it's ~** c'est l'heure du déjeuner

lung [lʌŋ] n poumon m

lung cancer n cancer m du poumon

lunge [lʌndʒ] vi (also: **lunge forward**) faire un mouvement brusque en avant; **to ~ at sb** envoyer or assener un coup à qn

lupin ['luːpɪn] n lupin m

lurch [ləːtʃ] vi vaciller, tituber ▷ n écart m brusque, embardée f; **to leave sb in the ~** laisser qn se débrouiller or se dépêtrer tout(e) seul(e)

lure [luəʳ] n (attraction) attrait m, charme m; (in hunting) appât m, leurre m ▷ vt attirer or persuader par la ruse

lurid ['luərɪd] adj affreux(-euse), atroce

lurk [ləːk] vi se tapir, se cacher

luscious ['lʌʃəs] adj succulent(e), appétissant(e)

lush [lʌʃ] adj luxuriant(e)

lust [lʌst] n (sexual) désir (sexuel); (Rel) luxure f; (fig): **~ for** soif f de
▶ **lust after** vt fus convoiter, désirer

luster ['lʌstəʳ] n (US) = **lustre**

lustful ['lʌstful] adj lascif(-ive)

lustre, (US) **luster** ['lʌstəʳ] n lustre m, brillant m

lusty ['lʌstɪ] adj vigoureux(-euse), robuste

lute [luːt] n luth m

Luxembourg ['lʌksəmbəːg] n Luxembourg m

luxuriant [lʌg'zjuərɪənt] adj luxuriant(e)

luxurious [lʌg'zjuərɪəs] adj luxueux(-euse)

luxury ['lʌkʃərɪ] n luxe m ▷ cpd de luxe

LV n abbr (Brit) = **luncheon voucher**

LW abbr (Radio: = long wave) GO

Lycra® ['laɪkrə] n Lycra® m

lying ['laɪɪŋ] n mensonge(s) m(pl) ▷ adj (statement, story) mensonger(-ère), faux (fausse); (person) menteur(-euse)

lynch [lɪntʃ] vt lyncher

lynx [lɪŋks] n lynx m inv

Lyons ['ljɔ̃] n Lyon

lyre ['laɪəʳ] n lyre f

lyric ['lɪrɪk] adj lyrique

lyrical ['lɪrɪkl] adj lyrique

lyricism ['lɪrɪsɪzəm] n lyrisme m

lyrics ['lɪrɪks] npl (of song) paroles fpl

Mm

M, m [ɛm] *n* (*letter*) M, m *m*; **M for Mary**, (US) **M for Mike** M comme Marcel

M *n abbr* (*Brit*) = **motorway**; (= *the M8*) ≈ l'A8
▷ *abbr* (= *medium*) M

m. *abbr* (= *metre*) m; (= *million*) M; (= *mile*) mi

M.A. *n abbr* (*Scol*) = **Master of Arts** ▷ *abbr* (*US*) = **military academy**; (*US*) = **Massachusetts**

ma [mɑː] (*inf*) *n* maman *f*

mac [mæk] *n* (*Brit*) imper(méable *m*) *m*

macabre [mə'kɑːbrə] *adj* macabre

macaroni [mækə'rəʊnɪ] *n* macaronis *mpl*

macaroon [mækə'ruːn] *n* macaron *m*

mace [meɪs] *n* masse *f*; (*spice*) macis *m*

Macedonia [mæsɪ'dəʊnɪə] *n* Macédoine *f*

Macedonian [mæsɪ'dəʊnɪən] *adj* macédonien(ne) ▷ *n* Macédonien(ne); (*Ling*) macédonien *m*

machinations [mækɪ'neɪʃənz] *npl* machinations *fpl*, intrigues *fpl*

machine [mə'ʃiːn] *n* machine *f* ▷ *vt* (*dress etc*) coudre à la machine; (*Tech*) usiner

machine code *n* (*Comput*) code *m* machine

machine gun *n* mitrailleuse *f*

machine language *n* (*Comput*) langage *m* machine

machine-readable [mə'ʃiːnriːdəbl] *adj* (*Comput*) exploitable par une machine

machinery [mə'ʃiːnərɪ] *n* machinerie *f*, machines *fpl*; (*fig*) mécanisme(s) *m(pl)*

machine shop *n* atelier *m* d'usinage

machine tool *n* machine-outil *f*

machine washable *adj* (*garment*) lavable en machine

machinist [mə'ʃiːnɪst] *n* machiniste *m/f*

macho ['mætʃəʊ] *adj* macho *inv*

mackerel ['mækrl] *n* (*pl inv*) maquereau *m*

mackintosh ['mækɪntɔʃ] *n* (*Brit*) imperméable *m*

macro... ['mækrəʊ] *prefix* macro...

macro-economics ['mækrəʊiːkə'nɔmɪks] *n* macro-économie *f*

mad [mæd] *adj* fou (folle); (*foolish*) insensé(e); (*angry*) furieux(-euse); **to go ~** devenir fou; **to be ~ (keen) about** *or* **on sth** (*inf*) être follement passionné de qch, être fou de qch

Madagascar [mædə'gæskər] *n* Madagascar *m*

madam ['mædəm] *n* madame *f*; **yes ~** oui

Madame; **M~ Chairman** Madame la Présidente

madcap ['mædkæp] *adj* (*inf*) écervelé(e)

mad cow disease *n* maladie *f* des vaches folles

madden ['mædn] *vt* exaspérer

maddening ['mædnɪŋ] *adj* exaspérant(e)

made [meɪd] *pt, pp of* **make**

Madeira [mə'dɪərə] *n* (*Geo*) Madère *f*; (*wine*) madère *m*

made-to-measure ['meɪdtə'mɛʒər] *adj* (*Brit*) fait(e) sur mesure

made-up ['meɪdʌp] *adj* (*story*) inventé(e), fabriqué(e)

madhouse ['mædhaʊs] *n* (*also fig*) maison *f* de fous

madly ['mædlɪ] *adv* follement; **~ in love** éperdument amoureux(-euse)

madman ['mædmən] (*irreg*) *n* fou *m*, aliéné *m*

madness ['mædnɪs] *n* folie *f*

Madrid [mə'drɪd] *n* Madrid

Mafia ['mæfɪə] *n* maf(f)ia *f*

mag [mæg] *n abbr* (*Brit inf*: = *magazine*) magazine *m*

magazine [mægə'ziːn] *n* (*Press*) magazine *m*, revue *f*; (*Radio, TV*) magazine; (*Mil: store*) dépôt *m*, arsenal *m*; (*of firearm*) magasin *m*

maggot ['mægət] *n* ver *m*, asticot *m*

magic ['mædʒɪk] *n* magie *f* ▷ *adj* magique

magical ['mædʒɪkl] *adj* magique; (*experience, evening*) merveilleux(-euse)

magician [mə'dʒɪʃən] *n* magicien(ne)

magistrate ['mædʒɪstreɪt] *n* magistrat *m*; juge *m*; **~s' court** (*Brit*) ≈ tribunal *m* d'instance

magnanimous [mæg'nænɪməs] *adj* magnanime

magnate ['mægneɪt] *n* magnat *m*

magnesium [mæg'niːzɪəm] *n* magnésium *m*

magnet ['mægnɪt] *n* aimant *m*

magnetic [mæg'nɛtɪk] *adj* magnétique

magnetic disk *n* (*Comput*) disque *m* magnétique

magnetic tape *n* bande *f* magnétique

magnetism ['mægnɪtɪzəm] *n* magnétisme *m*

magnification [mægnɪfɪ'keɪʃən] *n* grossissement *m*

magnificence [mæg'nɪfɪsns] *n* magnificence *f*

magnificent [mæg'nɪfɪsnt] *adj* superbe,

magnifique; (*splendid: robe, building*) somptueux(-euse), magnifique

magnify ['mægnɪfaɪ] *vt* grossir; (*sound*) amplifier

magnifying glass ['mægnɪfaɪɪŋ-] *n* loupe *f*

magnitude ['mægnɪtjuːd] *n* ampleur *f*

magnolia [mæg'nəʊlɪə] *n* magnolia *m*

magpie ['mægpaɪ] *n* pie *f*

mahogany [mə'hɒgənɪ] *n* acajou *m* ▷ *cpd* en (bois d')acajou

maid [meɪd] *n* bonne *f*; (*in hotel*) femme *f* de chambre; **old ~** (*pej*) vieille fille

maiden ['meɪdn] *n* jeune fille *f* ▷ *adj* (*aunt etc*) non mariée; (*speech, voyage*) inaugural(e)

maiden name *n* nom *m* de jeune fille

mail [meɪl] *n* poste *f*; (*letters*) courrier *m* ▷ *vt* envoyer (par la poste); **by ~** par la poste

mailbag ['meɪlbæg] *n* (*US*) sac postal; (*postman's*) sacoche *f*

mailbox ['meɪlbɒks] *n* (*US: also Comput*) boîte *f* aux lettres

mailing list ['meɪlɪŋ-] *n* liste *f* d'adresses

mailman ['meɪlmæn] (*irreg*) *n* (*US*) facteur *m*

mail-order ['meɪlɔːdəʳ] *n* vente *f* or achat *m* par correspondance ▷ *cpd*: **~ firm** or **house** maison *f* de vente par correspondance

mailshot ['meɪlʃɒt] *n* (*Brit*) mailing *m*

mail train *n* train postal

mail truck *n* (*US Aut*) = **mail van**

mail van *n* (*Brit Aut*) voiture *f* or fourgonnette *f* des postes; (: *Rail*) wagon-poste *m*

maim [meɪm] *vt* mutiler

main [meɪn] *adj* principal(e) ▷ *n* (*pipe*) conduite principale, canalisation *f*; **the ~s** (*Elec*) le secteur; **the ~ thing** l'essentiel *m*; **in the ~** dans l'ensemble

main course *n* (*Culin*) plat *m* de résistance

mainframe ['meɪnfreɪm] *n* (*also*: **mainframe computer**) (gros) ordinateur, unité centrale

mainland ['meɪnlənd] *n* continent *m*

mainline ['meɪnlaɪn] *adj* (*Rail*) de grande ligne ▷ *vt* (*drugs slang*) se shooter à ▷ *vi* (*drugs slang*) se shooter

main line *n* (*Rail*) grande ligne

mainly ['meɪnlɪ] *adv* principalement, surtout

main road *n* grand axe, route nationale

mainstay ['meɪnsteɪ] *n* (*fig*) pilier *m*

mainstream ['meɪnstriːm] *n* (*fig*) courant principal

main street *n* rue *f* principale

maintain [meɪn'teɪn] *vt* entretenir; (*continue*) maintenir, préserver; (*affirm*) soutenir; **to ~ that ...** soutenir que ...

maintenance ['meɪntənəns] *n* entretien *m*; (*Law: alimony*) pension *f* alimentaire

maintenance contract *n* contrat *m* d'entretien

maintenance order *n* (*Law*) obligation *f* alimentaire

maisonette [meɪzə'nɛt] *n* (*Brit*) appartement *m* en duplex

maize [meɪz] *n* (*Brit*) maïs *m*

Maj. *abbr* (*Mil*) = **major**

majestic [mə'dʒɛstɪk] *adj* majestueux(-euse)

majesty ['mædʒɪstɪ] *n* majesté *f*; (*title*): **Your M~** Votre Majesté

major ['meɪdʒəʳ] *n* (*Mil*) commandant *m* ▷ *adj* (*important*) important(e); (*most important*) principal(e); (*Mus*) majeur(e) ▷ *vi* (*US Scol*): **to ~ (in)** se spécialiser (en); **a ~ operation** (*Med*) une grosse opération

Majorca [mə'jɔːkə] *n* Majorque *f*

major general *n* (*Mil*) général *m* de division

majority [mə'dʒɔrɪtɪ] *n* majorité *f* ▷ *cpd* (*verdict, holding*) majoritaire

make [meɪk] *vt* (*pt, pp* **made**) [meɪd] faire; (*manufacture*) faire, fabriquer; (*earn*) gagner; (*decision*) prendre; (*friend*) se faire; (*speech*) faire, prononcer; (*cause to be*): **to ~ sb sad** *etc* rendre qn triste *etc*; (*force*): **to ~ sb do sth** obliger qn à faire qch, faire faire qch à qn; (*equal*): **2 and 2 ~ 4** 2 et 2 font 4 ▷ *n* (*manufacture*) fabrication *f*; (*brand*) marque *f*; **to ~ the bed** faire le lit; **to ~ a fool of sb** (*ridicule*) ridiculiser qn; (*trick*) avoir or duper qn; **to ~ a profit** faire un or des bénéfice(s); **to ~ a loss** essuyer une perte; **to ~ it** (*in time etc*) y arriver; (*succeed*) réussir; **what time do you ~ it?** quelle heure avez-vous?; **I ~ it £249** d'après mes calculs ça fait 249 livres; **to be made of** être en; **to ~ good** *vi* (*succeed*) faire son chemin, réussir ▷ *vt* (*deficit*) combler; (*losses*) compenser; **to ~ do with** se contenter de; se débrouiller avec

▶ **make for** *vt fus* (*place*) se diriger vers

▶ **make off** *vi* filer

▶ **make out** *vt* (*write out: cheque*) faire; (*decipher*) déchiffrer; (*understand*) comprendre; (*see*) distinguer; (*claim, imply*) prétendre, vouloir faire croire; **to ~ out a case for sth** présenter des arguments solides en faveur de qch

▶ **make over** *vt* (*assign*): **to ~ over (to)** céder (à), transférer (au nom de)

▶ **make up** *vt* (*invent*) inventer, imaginer; (*constitute*) constituer; (*parcel, bed*) faire ▷ *vi* se réconcilier; (*with cosmetics*) se maquiller, se farder; **to be made up of** se composer de

▶ **make up for** *vt fus* compenser; (*lost time*) rattraper

make-believe ['meɪkbɪliːv] *n*: **a world of ~** un monde de chimères or d'illusions; **it's just ~** c'est de la fantaisie; c'est une illusion

makeover ['meɪkəʊvəʳ] *n* (*by beautician*) soins *mpl* de maquillage; (*change of image*) changement *m* d'image; **to give sb a ~** relooker qn

maker ['meɪkəʳ] *n* fabricant *m*; (*of film, programme*) réalisateur(-trice)

makeshift ['meɪkʃɪft] *adj* provisoire, improvisé(e)

make-up ['meɪkʌp] *n* maquillage *m*

make-up bag *n* trousse *f* de maquillage

make-up remover *n* démaquillant *m*

making ['meɪkɪŋ] *n* (*fig*): **in the ~** en formation or gestation; **to have the ~s of** (*actor, athlete*) avoir l'étoffe de

maladjusted [mælə'dʒʌstɪd] *adj* inadapté(e)

malaise [mæˈleɪz] n malaise m
malaria [məˈlɛərɪə] n malaria f, paludisme m
Malawi [məˈlɑːwɪ] n Malawi m
Malay [məˈleɪ] adj malais(e) ▷ n (person) Malais(e); (language) malais m
Malaya [məˈleɪə] n Malaisie f
Malayan [məˈleɪən] adj, n = **Malay**
Malaysia [məˈleɪzɪə] n Malaisie f
Malaysian [məˈleɪzɪən] adj malaisien(ne) ▷ n Malaisien(ne)
Maldives [ˈmɔːldaɪvz] npl: **the ~** les Maldives fpl
male [meɪl] n (Biol, Elec) mâle m ▷ adj (sex, attitude) masculin(e); (animal) mâle; (child etc) du sexe masculin; **~ and female students** étudiants et étudiantes
male chauvinist n phallocrate m
male nurse n infirmier m
malevolence [məˈlevələns] n malveillance f
malevolent [məˈlevələnt] adj malveillant(e)
malfunction [mælˈfʌŋkʃən] n fonctionnement défectueux
malice [ˈmælɪs] n méchanceté f, malveillance f
malicious [məˈlɪʃəs] adj méchant(e), malveillant(e); (Law) avec intention criminelle
malign [məˈlaɪn] vt diffamer, calomnier
malignant [məˈlɪɡnənt] adj (Med) malin(-igne)
malingerer [məˈlɪŋɡərər] n simulateur(-trice)
mall [mɔːl] n (also: **shopping mall**) centre commercial
malleable [ˈmælɪəbl] adj malléable
mallet [ˈmælɪt] n maillet m
malnutrition [mælnjuːˈtrɪʃən] n malnutrition f
malpractice [mælˈpræktɪs] n faute professionnelle; négligence f
malt [mɔːlt] n malt m ▷ cpd (whisky) pur malt
Malta [ˈmɔːltə] n Malte f
Maltese [mɔːlˈtiːz] adj maltais(e) ▷ n (pl inv) Maltais(e); (Ling) maltais m
maltreat [mælˈtriːt] vt maltraiter
mammal [ˈmæml] n mammifère m
mammoth [ˈmæməθ] n mammouth m ▷ adj géant(e), monstre
man (pl men) [mæn, mɛn] n homme m; (Sport) joueur m; (Chess) pièce f; (Draughts) pion m ▷ vt (Naut: ship) garnir d'hommes; (machine) assurer le fonctionnement de; (Mil: gun) servir; (: post) être de service à; **an old ~** un vieillard; **~ and wife** mari et femme
Man. abbr (Canada) = **Manitoba**
manacles [ˈmænəklz] npl menottes fpl
manage [ˈmænɪdʒ] vi se débrouiller; (succeed) y arriver, réussir ▷ vt (business) gérer; (team, operation) diriger; (control: ship) manier, manœuvrer; (: person) savoir s'y prendre avec; (device, things to do, carry etc) arriver à se débrouiller avec, s'en tirer avec; **to ~ to do** se débrouiller pour faire; (succeed) réussir à faire
manageable [ˈmænɪdʒəbl] adj maniable; (task etc) faisable; (number) raisonnable
management [ˈmænɪdʒmənt] n (running) administration f, direction f; (people in charge: of business, firm) dirigeants mpl, cadres mpl; (: of

hotel, shop, theatre) direction; **"under new ~"** "changement de gérant", "changement de propriétaire"
management accounting n comptabilité f de gestion
management consultant n conseiller(-ère) de direction
manager [ˈmænɪdʒər] n (of business) directeur m; (of institution etc) administrateur m; (of department, unit) responsable m/f, chef m; (of hotel etc) gérant m; (Sport) manager m; (of artist) impresario m; **sales ~** responsable or chef des ventes
manageress [mænɪdʒəˈrɛs] n directrice f; (of hotel etc) gérante f
managerial [mænɪˈdʒɪərɪəl] adj directorial(e); (skills) de cadre, de gestion; **~ staff** cadres mpl
managing director [ˈmænɪdʒɪŋ-] n directeur général
Mancunian [mænˈkjuːnɪən] adj de Manchester ▷ n habitant(e) de Manchester; natif(-ive) de Manchester
mandarin [ˈmændərɪn] n (also: **mandarin orange**) mandarine f; (person) mandarin m
mandate [ˈmændeɪt] n mandat m
mandatory [ˈmændətərɪ] adj obligatoire; (powers etc) mandataire
mandolin, mandoline [ˈmændəlɪn] n mandoline f
mane [meɪn] n crinière f
maneuver [məˈnuːvər] (US) = **manoeuvre**
manfully [ˈmænfəlɪ] adv vaillamment
manganese [mæŋɡəˈniːz] n manganèse m
mangetout [ˈmɒnʒˈtuː] n mange-tout m inv
mangle [ˈmæŋɡl] vt déchiqueter; mutiler ▷ n essoreuse f; calandre f
mango (pl **-es**) [ˈmæŋɡəʊ] n mangue f
mangrove [ˈmæŋɡrəʊv] n palétuvier m
mangy [ˈmeɪndʒɪ] adj galeux(-euse)
manhandle [ˈmænhændl] vt (mistreat) maltraiter, malmener; (move by hand) manutentionner
manhole [ˈmænhəʊl] n trou m d'homme
manhood [ˈmænhʊd] n (age) âge m d'homme; (manliness) virilité f
man-hour [ˈmænaʊər] n heure-homme f, heure f de main-d'œuvre
manhunt [ˈmænhʌnt] n chasse f à l'homme
mania [ˈmeɪnɪə] n manie f
maniac [ˈmeɪnɪæk] n maniaque m/f; (fig) fou (folle)
manic [ˈmænɪk] adj maniaque
manic-depressive [ˈmænɪkdɪˈpresɪv] adj, n (Psych) maniaco-dépressif(-ive)
manicure [ˈmænɪkjʊər] n manucure f ▷ vt (person) faire les mains à
manicure set n trousse f à ongles
manifest [ˈmænɪfest] vt manifester ▷ adj manifeste, évident(e) ▷ n (Aviat, Naut) manifeste m
manifestation [mænɪfesˈteɪʃən] n manifestation f

manifesto [mænɪˈfɛstəu] *n* (*Pol*) manifeste *m*

manifold [ˈmænɪfəuld] *adj* multiple, varié(e)
▷ *n* (*Aut etc*): **exhaust ~** collecteur *m*
d'échappement

Manila [məˈnɪlə] *n* Manille, Manila

manila [məˈnɪlə] *adj*: **~ paper** papier *m* bulle

manipulate [məˈnɪpjuleɪt] *vt* manipuler;
(*system, situation*) exploiter

manipulation [mənɪpjuˈleɪʃən] *n*
manipulation *f*

mankind [mænˈkaɪnd] *n* humanité *f*, genre
humain

manliness [ˈmænlɪnɪs] *n* virilité *f*

manly [ˈmænlɪ] *adj* viril(e)

man-made [ˈmænˈmeɪd] *adj* artificiel(le); (*fibre*)
synthétique

manna [ˈmænə] *n* manne *f*

mannequin [ˈmænɪkɪn] *n* mannequin *m*

manner [ˈmænəʳ] *n* manière *f*, façon *f*;
(*behaviour*) attitude *f*, comportement *m*;
manners *npl*: (**good**) **~s** (bonnes) manières;
bad ~s mauvaises manières; **all ~ of** toutes
sortes de

mannerism [ˈmænərɪzəm] *n* particularité *f* de
langage (*or* de comportement), tic *m*

mannerly [ˈmænəlɪ] *adj* poli(e), courtois(e)

manoeuvrable, (*US*) **maneuverable** [məˈnu:
vrəbl] *adj* facile à manœuvrer

manoeuvre, (*US*) **maneuver** [məˈnu:vəʳ] *vt*
(*move*) manœuvrer; (*manipulate: person*)
manipuler; (: *situation*) exploiter ▷ *n* manœuvre
f; **to ~ sb into doing sth** manipuler qn pour lui
faire faire qch

manor [ˈmænəʳ] *n* (*also*: **manor house**) manoir *m*

manpower [ˈmænpauəʳ] *n* main-d'œuvre *f*

manservant (*pl* **menservants**) [ˈmænsə:vənt,
ˈmɛn-] *n* domestique *m*

mansion [ˈmænʃən] *n* château *m*, manoir *m*

manslaughter [ˈmænslɔ:təʳ] *n* homicide *m*
involontaire

mantelpiece [ˈmæntlpi:s] *n* cheminée *f*

mantle [ˈmæntl] *n* cape *f*; (*fig*) manteau *m*

man-to-man [ˈmæntəˈmæn] *adj*, *adv* d'homme
à homme

manual [ˈmænjuəl] *adj* manuel(le) ▷ *n*
manuel *m*

manual worker *n* travailleur manuel

manufacture [mænjuˈfæktʃəʳ] *vt* fabriquer ▷ *n*
fabrication *f*

manufactured goods [mænjuˈfæktʃəd-] *npl*
produits manufacturés

manufacturer [mænjuˈfæktʃərəʳ] *n* fabricant *m*

manufacturing industries [mænju] *npl*
industries *fpl* de transformation

manure [məˈnjuəʳ] *n* fumier *m*; (*artificial*)
engrais *m*

manuscript [ˈmænjuskrɪpt] *n* manuscrit *m*

many [ˈmɛnɪ] *adj* beaucoup de, de
nombreux(-euses) ▷ *pron* beaucoup, un grand
nombre; **how ~?** combien?; **a great ~** un grand
nombre (de); **too ~ difficulties** trop de
difficultés; **twice as ~** deux fois plus; **~ a ...**

bien des ..., plus d'un(e) ...

Maori [ˈmaurɪ] *n* Maori(e) ▷ *adj* maori(e)

map [mæp] *n* carte *f*; (*of town*) plan *m* ▷ *vt*
dresser la carte de; **can you show it to me on
the ~?** pouvez-vous me l'indiquer sur la carte?
▶ **map out** *vt* tracer; (*fig: task*) planifier; (*career,
holiday*) organiser, préparer (à l'avance); (: *essay*)
faire le plan de

maple [ˈmeɪpl] *n* érable *m*

mar [mɑ:ʳ] *vt* gâcher, gâter

marathon [ˈmærəθən] *n* marathon *m* ▷ *adj*: **a ~
session** une séance-marathon

marathon runner *n* coureur(-euse) de
marathon, marathonien(ne)

marauder [məˈrɔ:dəʳ] *n* maraudeur(-euse)

marble [ˈmɑ:bl] *n* marbre *m*; (*toy*) bille *f*;
marbles *npl* (*game*) billes

March [mɑ:tʃ] *n* mars *m*

march [mɑ:tʃ] *vi* marcher au pas; (*demonstrators*)
défiler ▷ *n* marche *f*; (*demonstration*)
manifestation *f*; **to ~ out of/into** *etc* sortir de/
entrer dans *etc* (*de manière décidée ou impulsive*)

marcher [ˈmɑ:tʃəʳ] *n* (*demonstrator*)
manifestant(e), marcheur(-euse)

marching [ˈmɑ:tʃɪŋ] *n*: **to give sb his ~ orders**
(*fig*) renvoyer qn; envoyer promener qn

march-past [ˈmɑ:tʃpɑ:st] *n* défilé *m*

mare [mɛəʳ] *n* jument *f*

marg. [mɑ:dʒ] *n abbr* (*inf*) = **margarine**

margarine [mɑ:dʒəˈri:n] *n* margarine *f*

margin [ˈmɑ:dʒɪn] *n* marge *f*

marginal [ˈmɑ:dʒɪnl] *adj* marginal(e); **~ seat**
(*Pol*) siège disputé

marginally [ˈmɑ:dʒɪnəlɪ] *adv* très légèrement,
sensiblement

marigold [ˈmærɪɡəuld] *n* souci *m*

marijuana [mærɪˈwɑ:nə] *n* marijuana *f*

marina [məˈri:nə] *n* marina *f*

marinade *n* [mærɪˈneɪd] marinade *f* ▷ *vt*
[ˈmærɪneɪd] = **marinate**

marinate [ˈmærɪneɪt] *vt* (faire) mariner

marine [məˈri:n] *adj* marin(e) ▷ *n* fusilier
marin; (*US*) marine *m*

marine insurance *n* assurance *f* maritime

marital [ˈmærɪtl] *adj* matrimonial(e)

marital status *n* situation *f* de famille

maritime [ˈmærɪtaɪm] *adj* maritime

maritime law *n* droit *m* maritime

marjoram [ˈmɑ:dʒərəm] *n* marjolaine *f*

mark [mɑ:k] *n* marque *f*; (*of skid etc*) trace *f*; (*Brit
Scol*) note *f*; (*Sport*) cible *f*; (*currency*) mark *m*; (*Brit
Tech*): **M~ 2/3** 2ème/3ème série *f* or version *f*;
(*oven temperature*): (**gas**) **~ 4** thermostat *m* 4 ▷ *vt*
(*also Sport: player*) marquer; (*stain*) tacher; (*Brit
Scol*) corriger, noter; (*also*: **punctuation marks**)
signes *mpl* de ponctuation; **to ~ time** marquer
le pas; **to be quick off the ~ (in doing)** (*fig*) ne
pas perdre de temps (pour faire); **up to the ~** (*in
efficiency*) à la hauteur
▶ **mark down** *vt* (*prices, goods*) démarquer,
réduire le prix de
▶ **mark off** *vt* (*tick off*) cocher, pointer

▶ **mark out** vt désigner
▶ **mark up** vt (price) majorer
marked [mɑːkt] adj (obvious) marqué(e), net(te)
markedly ['mɑːkɪdlɪ] adv visiblement, manifestement
marker ['mɑːkə'] n (sign) jalon m; (bookmark) signet m
market ['mɑːkɪt] n marché m ▷ vt (Comm) commercialiser; **to be on the ~** être sur le marché; **on the open ~** en vente libre; **to play the ~** jouer à la or spéculer en Bourse
marketable ['mɑːkɪtəbl] adj commercialisable
market analysis n analyse f de marché
market day n jour m de marché
market demand n besoins mpl du marché
market economy n économie f de marché
market forces npl tendances fpl du marché
market garden n (Brit) jardin maraîcher
marketing ['mɑːkɪtɪŋ] n marketing m
marketplace ['mɑːkɪtpleɪs] n place f du marché; (Comm) marché m
market price n prix marchand
market research n étude f de marché
market value n valeur marchande; valeur du marché
marking ['mɑːkɪŋ] n (on animal) marque f, tache f; (on road) signalisation f
marksman ['mɑːksmən] (irreg) n tireur m d'élite
marksmanship ['mɑːksmənʃɪp] n adresse f au tir
mark-up ['mɑːkʌp] n (Comm: margin) marge f (bénéficiaire); (: increase) majoration f
marmalade ['mɑːməleɪd] n confiture f d'oranges
maroon [mə'ruːn] vt: **to be ~ed** être abandonné(e); (fig) être bloqué(e) ▷ adj (colour) bordeaux inv
marquee [mɑː'kiː] n chapiteau m
marquess, marquis ['mɑːkwɪs] n marquis m
Marrakech, Marrakesh [mærə'kɛʃ] n Marrakech
marriage ['mærɪdʒ] n mariage m
marriage bureau n agence matrimoniale
marriage certificate n extrait m d'acte de mariage
marriage guidance, (US) **marriage counseling** n conseils conjugaux
marriage of convenience n mariage m de convenance
married ['mærɪd] adj marié(e); (life, love) conjugal(e)
marrow ['mærəu] n (of bone) moelle f; (vegetable) courge f
marry ['mærɪ] vt épouser, se marier avec; (subj: father, priest etc) marier ▷ vi (also: **get married**) se marier
Mars [mɑːz] n (planet) Mars f
Marseilles [mɑː'seɪ] n Marseille
marsh [mɑːʃ] n marais m, marécage m
marshal ['mɑːʃl] n maréchal m; (US: fire, police) ≈ capitaine m; (for demonstration, meeting) membre m du service d'ordre ▷ vt rassembler

marshalling yard ['mɑːʃlɪŋ-] n (Rail) gare f de triage
marshmallow [mɑːʃ'mæləu] n (Bot) guimauve f; (sweet) (pâte f de) guimauve
marshy ['mɑːʃɪ] adj marécageux(-euse)
marsupial [mɑː'suːpɪəl] adj marsupial(e) ▷ n marsupial m
martial ['mɑːʃl] adj martial(e)
martial arts npl arts martiaux
martial law n loi martiale
Martian ['mɑːʃən] n Martien(ne)
martin ['mɑːtɪn] n (also: **house martin**) martinet m
martyr ['mɑːtə'] n martyr(e) ▷ vt martyriser
martyrdom ['mɑːtədəm] n martyre m
marvel ['mɑːvl] n merveille f ▷ vi: **to ~ (at)** s'émerveiller (de)
marvellous, (US) **marvelous** ['mɑːvləs] adj merveilleux(-euse)
Marxism ['mɑːksɪzəm] n marxisme m
Marxist ['mɑːksɪst] adj, n marxiste (m/f)
marzipan ['mɑːzɪpæn] n pâte f d'amandes
mascara [mæs'kɑːrə] n mascara m
mascot ['mæskət] n mascotte f
masculine ['mæskjulɪn] adj masculin(e) ▷ n masculin m
masculinity [mæskju'lɪnɪtɪ] n masculinité f
MASH [mæʃ] n abbr (US Mil) = **mobile army surgical hospital**
mash [mæʃ] vt (Culin) faire une purée de
mashed potato n, **mashed potatoes** npl purée f de pommes de terre
mask [mɑːsk] n masque m ▷ vt masquer
masochism ['mæsəukɪzəm] n masochisme m
masochist ['mæsəukɪst] n masochiste m/f
mason ['meɪsn] n (also: **stonemason**) maçon m; (also: **freemason**) franc-maçon m
masonic [mə'sɔnɪk] adj maçonnique
masonry ['meɪsnrɪ] n maçonnerie f
masquerade [mæskə'reɪd] n bal masqué; (fig) mascarade f ▷ vi: **to ~ as** se faire passer pour
mass [mæs] n multitude f, masse f; (Physics) masse; (Rel) messe f ▷ cpd (communication) de masse; (unemployment) massif(-ive) ▷ vi se masser; **masses** npl: **the ~es** les masses; **~es of** (inf) des tas de; **to go to ~** aller à la messe
Mass. abbr (US) = **Massachusetts.**
massacre ['mæsəkə'] n massacre m ▷ vt massacrer
massage ['mæsɑːʒ] n massage m ▷ vt masser
massive ['mæsɪv] adj énorme, massif(-ive)
mass market n marché m grand public
mass media npl mass-media mpl
mass meeting n rassemblement m de masse
mass-produce ['mæsprə'djuːs] vt fabriquer en série
mass production n fabrication f en série
mast [mɑːst] n mât m; (Radio, TV) pylône m
mastectomy [mæs'tɛktəmɪ] n mastectomie f
master ['mɑːstə'] n maître m; (in secondary school) professeur m; (in primary school) instituteur m; (title for boys): **M~ X** Monsieur X ▷ vt maîtriser;

m

(*learn*) apprendre à fond; (*understand*) posséder parfaitement *or* à fond; ~ **of ceremonies (MC)** *n* maître des cérémonies; **M~ of Arts/Science (MA/MSc)** (*n*) ≈ titulaire *m/f* d'une maîtrise (en lettres/science); **M~ of Arts/Science degree (MA/MSc)** (*n*) ≈ maîtrise *f*; **M~'s degree** (*n*) ≈ maîtrise; *voir article*

⬤ **MASTER'S DEGREE**
⬤
⬤ Le *Master's degree* est un diplôme que l'on
⬤ prépare en général après le "Bachelor's
⬤ degree", bien que certaines universités
⬤ décernent un *Master's* au lieu d'un
⬤ "Bachelor's". Il consiste soit à suivre des
⬤ cours, soit à rédiger un mémoire à partir
⬤ d'une recherche personnelle, soit encore les
⬤ deux. Les principaux masters sont le "MA"
⬤ (Master of Arts), et le "MSc" (Master of
⬤ Science), qui comprennent cours et
⬤ mémoire, et le "MLitt "(Master of Letters) et
⬤ le "MPhil" (Master of Philosophy), qui
⬤ reposent uniquement sur le mémoire; voir
⬤ "doctorate".

master disk *n* (*Comput*) disque original
masterful ['mɑːstəful] *adj* autoritaire, impérieux(-euse)
master key *n* passe-partout *m inv*
masterly ['mɑːstəlɪ] *adj* magistral(e)
mastermind ['mɑːstəmaɪnd] *n* esprit supérieur ▷ *vt* diriger, être le cerveau de
masterpiece ['mɑːstəpiːs] *n* chef-d'œuvre *m*
master plan *n* stratégie *f* d'ensemble
master stroke *n* coup *m* de maître
mastery ['mɑːstərɪ] *n* maîtrise *f*; connaissance parfaite
mastiff ['mæstɪf] *n* mastiff *m*
masturbate ['mæstəbeɪt] *vi* se masturber
masturbation [mæstə'beɪʃən] *n* masturbation *f*
mat [mæt] *n* petit tapis; (*also*: **doormat**) paillasson *m*; (*also*: **tablemat**) set *m* de table ▷ *adj* = **matt**
match [mætʃ] *n* allumette *f*; (*game*) match *m*, partie *f*; (*fig*) égal(e); mariage *m*; parti *m* ▷ *vt* (*also*: **match up**) assortir; (*go well with*) aller bien avec, s'assortir à; (*equal*) égaler, valoir ▷ *vi* être assorti(e); **to be a good ~** être bien assorti(e)
▶ **match up** *vt* assortir
matchbox ['mætʃbɒks] *n* boîte *f* d'allumettes
matching ['mætʃɪŋ] *adj* assorti(e)
matchless ['mætʃlɪs] *adj* sans égal
mate [meɪt] *n* camarade *m/f* de travail; (*inf*) copain (copine); (*animal*) partenaire *m/f*, mâle (femelle); (*in merchant navy*) second *m* ▷ *vi* s'accoupler ▷ *vt* accoupler
material [mə'tɪərɪəl] *n* (*substance*) matière *f*, matériau *m*; (*cloth*) tissu *m*, étoffe *f*; (*information, data*) données *fpl* ▷ *adj* matériel(le); (*relevant: evidence*) pertinent(e); (*important*) essentiel(le); **materials** *npl* (*equipment*) matériaux *mpl*; **reading ~** de quoi lire, de la lecture

materialistic [mətɪərɪə'lɪstɪk] *adj* matérialiste
materialize [mə'tɪərɪəlaɪz] *vi* se matérialiser, se réaliser
materially [mə'tɪərɪəlɪ] *adv* matériellement; essentiellement
maternal [mə'təːnl] *adj* maternel(le)
maternity [mə'təːnɪtɪ] *n* maternité *f* ▷ *cpd* de maternité, de grossesse
maternity benefit *n* prestation *f* de maternité
maternity dress *n* robe *f* de grossesse
maternity hospital *n* maternité *f*
maternity leave *n* congé *m* de maternité
matey ['meɪtɪ] *adj* (*Brit inf*) copain-copain *inv*
math [mæθ] *n* (*US*: = *mathematics*) maths *fpl*
mathematical [mæθə'mætɪkl] *adj* mathématique
mathematician [mæθəmə'tɪʃən] *n* mathématicien(ne)
mathematics [mæθə'mætɪks] *n* mathématiques *fpl*
maths [mæθs] *n abbr* (*Brit*: = *mathematics*) maths *fpl*
matinée ['mætɪneɪ] *n* matinée *f*
mating ['meɪtɪŋ] *n* accouplement *m*
mating call *n* appel *m* du mâle
mating season *n* saison *f* des amours
matriarchal [meɪtrɪ'ɑːkl] *adj* matriarcal(e)
matrices ['meɪtrɪsiːz] *npl of* **matrix**
matriculation [mətrɪkju'leɪʃn] *n* inscription *f*
matrimonial [mætrɪ'məunɪəl] *adj* matrimonial(e), conjugal(e)
matrimony ['mætrɪmənɪ] *n* mariage *m*
matrix (*pl* **matrices**) ['meɪtrɪks, 'meɪtrɪsiːz] *n* matrice *f*
matron ['meɪtrən] *n* (*in hospital*) infirmière-chef *f*; (*in school*) infirmière *f*
matronly ['meɪtrənlɪ] *adj* de matrone; imposant(e)
matt [mæt] *adj* mat(e)
matted ['mætɪd] *adj* emmêlé(e)
matter ['mætə'] *n* question *f*; (*Physics*) matière *f*, substance *f*; (*content*) contenu *m*, fond *m*; (*Med: pus*) pus *m* ▷ *vi* importer; **matters** *npl* (*affairs, situation*) la situation; **it doesn't ~** cela n'a pas d'importance; (*I don't mind*) cela ne fait rien; **what's the ~?** qu'est-ce qu'il y a?, qu'est-ce qui ne va pas?; **no ~ what** quoi qu'il arrive; **that's another ~** c'est une autre affaire; **as a ~ of course** tout naturellement; **as a ~ of fact** en fait; **it's a ~ of habit** c'est une question d'habitude; **printed ~** imprimés *mpl*; **reading ~** (*Brit*) de quoi lire, de la lecture
matter-of-fact ['mætərəv'fækt] *adj* terre à terre, neutre
matting ['mætɪŋ] *n* natte *f*
mattress ['mætrɪs] *n* matelas *m*
mature [mə'tjuə'] *adj* mûr(e); (*cheese*) fait(e); (*wine*) arrive(e) à maturité ▷ *vi* mûrir; (*cheese, wine*) se faire
mature student *n* étudiant(e) plus âgé(e) que la moyenne
maturity [mə'tjuərɪtɪ] *n* maturité *f*

maudlin ['mɔːdlɪn] *adj* larmoyant(e)

maul [mɔːl] *vt* lacérer

Mauritania [mɔːrɪ'teɪnɪə] *n* Mauritanie *f*

Mauritius [mə'rɪʃəs] *n* l'île *f* Maurice

mausoleum [mɔːsə'lɪəm] *n* mausolée *m*

mauve [məuv] *adj* mauve

maverick ['mævrɪk] *n* (*fig*) franc-tireur *m*, non-conformiste *m/f*

mawkish ['mɔːkɪʃ] *adj* mièvre; fade

max *abbr* = **maximum**

maxim ['mæksɪm] *n* maxime *f*

maxima ['mæksɪmə] *npl of* **maximum**

maximize ['mæksɪmaɪz] *vt* (*profits etc, chances*) maximiser

maximum ['mæksɪməm] (*pl* **maxima**) ['mæksɪmə] *adj* maximum ▷ *n* maximum *m*

May [meɪ] *n* mai *m*; *for phrases see also* **July**

may [meɪ] (*conditional* **might**) *vi* (*indicating possibility*): **he ~ come** il se peut qu'il vienne; (*be allowed to*): **~ I smoke?** puis-je fumer?; (*wishes*): **~ God bless you!** (que) Dieu vous bénisse!; **~ I sit here?** vous permettez que je m'assoie ici?; **he might be there** il pourrait bien y être, il se pourrait qu'il y soit; **you ~ as well go** vous feriez aussi bien d'y aller; **I might as well go** je ferais aussi bien d'y aller, autant y aller; **you might like to try** vous pourriez (peut-être) essayer

maybe ['meɪbiː] *adv* peut-être; **~ he'll ...** peut-être qu'il ...; **~ not** peut-être pas

May Day *n* le Premier mai

mayday ['meɪdeɪ] *n* S.O.S *m*

mayhem ['meɪhɛm] *n* grabuge *m*

mayonnaise [meɪə'neɪz] *n* mayonnaise *f*

mayor [mɛəʳ] *n* maire *m*

mayoress ['mɛərɛs] *n* (*female mayor*) maire *m*; (*wife of mayor*) épouse *f* du maire

maypole ['meɪpəul] *n* mât enrubanné (*autour duquel on danse*)

maze [meɪz] *n* labyrinthe *m*, dédale *m*

MB *abbr* (*Comput*) = **megabyte**; (*Canada*) = **Manitoba**

MBA *n abbr* (= *Master of Business Administration*) titre universitaire

MBBS, MBChB *n abbr* (*Brit*: = *Bachelor of Medicine and Surgery*) titre universitaire

MBE *n abbr* (*Brit*: = *Member of the Order of the British Empire*) titre honorifique

MBO *n abbr* (*Brit*) = **management buyout**

MC *n abbr* = **master of ceremonies**

MCAT *n abbr* (*US*) = **Medical College Admissions Test**

MD *n abbr* (= *Doctor of Medicine*) titre universitaire; (*Comm*) = **managing director** ▷ *abbr* (*US*) = **Maryland**

Md. *abbr* (*US*) = **Maryland**

MDT *abbr* (*US*: = *Mountain Daylight Time*) heure d'été des Montagnes Rocheuses

ME *n abbr* (*US*: = *medical examiner*) médecin légiste *m/f*; (*Med*: = *myalgic encephalomyelitis*) encéphalomyélite *f* myalgique ▷ *abbr* (*US*) = **Maine**

me [miː] *pron* me, m' + *vowel or h mute*; (*stressed, after prep*) moi; **it's me** c'est moi; **he heard me** il m'a entendu; **give me a book** donnez-moi un livre; **it's for me** c'est pour moi

meadow ['mɛdəu] *n* prairie *f*, pré *m*

meagre, (*US*) **meager** ['miːgəʳ] *adj* maigre

meal [miːl] *n* repas *m*; (*flour*) farine *f*; **to go out for a ~** sortir manger

meals on wheels *npl* (*Brit*) repas livrés à domicile aux personnes âgées ou handicapées

mealtime ['miːltaɪm] *n* heure *f* du repas

mealy-mouthed ['miːlɪmauðd] *adj* mielleux(-euse)

mean [miːn] *adj* (*with money*) avare, radin(e); (*unkind*) mesquin(e), méchant(e); (*shabby*) misérable; (*US inf*: *animal*) méchant, vicieux(-euse); (: *person*) vache; (*average*) moyen(ne) ▷ *vt* (*pt, pp* **-t**) [mɛnt] (*signify*) signifier, vouloir dire; (*refer to*) faire allusion à, parler de; (*intend*): **to ~ to do** avoir l'intention de faire ▷ *n* moyenne *f*; **means** *npl* (*way, money*) moyens *mpl*; **by ~s of** (*instrument*) au moyen de; **by all ~s** je vous en prie; **to be ~t for** être destiné(e) à; **do you ~ it?** vous êtes sérieux?; **what do you ~?** que voulez-vous dire?

meander [mɪ'ændəʳ] *vi* faire des méandres; (*fig*) flâner

meaning ['miːnɪŋ] *n* signification *f*, sens *m*

meaningful ['miːnɪŋful] *adj* significatif(-ive); (*relationship*) valable

meaningless ['miːnɪŋlɪs] *adj* dénué(e) de sens

meanness ['miːnnɪs] *n* avarice *f*; mesquinerie *f*

means test *n* (*Admin*) contrôle *m* des conditions de ressources

meant [mɛnt] *pt, pp of* **mean**

meantime ['miːntaɪm] *adv* (*also*: **in the meantime**) pendant ce temps

meanwhile ['miːnwaɪl] *adv* = **meantime**

measles ['miːzlz] *n* rougeole *f*

measly ['miːzlɪ] *adj* (*inf*) minable

measurable ['mɛʒərəbl] *adj* mesurable

measure ['mɛʒəʳ] *vt, vi* mesurer ▷ *n* mesure *f*; (*ruler*) règle (graduée); **a litre ~** un litre; **some ~ of success** un certain succès; **to take ~s to do sth** prendre des mesures pour faire qch

▶ **measure up** *vi*: **to ~ up (to)** être à la hauteur (de)

measured ['mɛʒəd] *adj* mesuré(e)

measurements ['mɛʒəmənts] *npl* mesures *fpl*; **chest/hip ~** tour *m* de poitrine/hanches; **to take sb's ~** prendre les mesures de qn

meat [miːt] *n* viande *f*; **I don't eat ~** je ne mange pas de viande; **cold ~s** (*Brit*) viandes froides; **crab ~** crabe *f*

meatball ['miːtbɔːl] *n* boulette *f* de viande

meat pie *n* pâté *m* en croûte

meaty ['miːtɪ] *adj* (*flavour*) de viande; (*fig*: *argument, book*) étoffé(e), substantiel(le)

Mecca ['mɛkə] *n* la Mecque; (*fig*): **a ~ (for)** la Mecque (de)

mechanic [mɪ'kænɪk] *n* mécanicien *m*; **can you send a ~?** pouvez-vous nous envoyer un

m

mécanicien?

mechanical [mɪ'kænɪkl] *adj* mécanique
mechanical engineering *n* (*science*) mécanique *f*; (*industry*) construction *f* mécanique
mechanics [mə'kænɪks] *n* mécanique *f* ▷ *npl* mécanisme *m*
mechanism ['mɛkənɪzəm] *n* mécanisme *m*
mechanization [mɛkənaɪ'zeɪʃən] *n* mécanisation *f*
MEd *n abbr* (= *Master of Education*) *titre universitaire*
medal ['mɛdl] *n* médaille *f*
medallion [mɪ'dælɪən] *n* médaillon *m*
medallist ['mɛdlɪst] *n* (*Sport*) médaillé(e)
meddle ['mɛdl] *vi*: **to ~ in** se mêler de, s'occuper de; **to ~ with** toucher à
meddlesome ['mɛdlsəm], **meddling** ['mɛdlɪŋ] *adj* indiscret(-ète), qui se mêle de ce qui ne le (*or* la) regarde pas; touche-à-tout *inv*
media ['mi:dɪə] *npl* media *mpl* ▷ *npl of* **medium**
media circus *n* (*event*) battage *m* médiatique; (*group of journalists*) cortège *m* médiatique
mediaeval [mɛdɪ'i:vl] *adj* = **medieval**
median ['mi:dɪən] *n* (*US: also*: **median strip**) bande médiane
media research *n* étude *f* de l'audience
mediate ['mi:dɪeɪt] *vi* servir d'intermédiaire
mediation [mi:dɪ'eɪʃən] *n* médiation *f*
mediator ['mi:dɪeɪtə'] *n* médiateur(-trice)
Medicaid ['mɛdɪkeɪd] *n* (*US*) *assistance médicale aux indigents*
medical ['mɛdɪkl] *adj* médical(e) ▷ *n* (*also*: **medical examination**) visite médicale; (*private*) examen médical
medical certificate *n* certificat médical
medical student *n* étudiant(e) en médecine
Medicare ['mɛdɪkɛə'] *n* (*US*) *régime d'assurance maladie*
medicated ['mɛdɪkeɪtɪd] *adj* traitant(e), médicamenteux(-euse)
medication [mɛdɪ'keɪʃən] *n* (*drugs etc*) médication *f*
medicinal [mɛ'dɪsɪnl] *adj* médicinal(e)
medicine ['mɛdsɪn] *n* médecine *f*; (*drug*) médicament *m*
medicine chest *n* pharmacie *f* (*murale ou portative*)
medicine man (*irreg*) *n* sorcier *m*
medieval [mɛdɪ'i:vl] *adj* médiéval(e)
mediocre [mi:dɪ'əukə'] *adj* médiocre
mediocrity [mi:dɪ'ɔkrɪtɪ] *n* médiocrité *f*
meditate ['mɛdɪteɪt] *vi*: **to ~ (on)** méditer (sur)
meditation [mɛdɪ'teɪʃən] *n* méditation *f*
Mediterranean [mɛdɪtə'reɪnɪən] *adj* méditerranéen(ne); **the ~ (Sea)** la (mer) Méditerranée
medium ['mi:dɪəm] *adj* moyen(ne) ▷ *n* (*pl* **media**) (*means*) moyen *m*; (*pl* **-s**) (*person*) médium *m*; **the happy ~** le juste milieu
medium-dry ['mi:dɪəm'draɪ] *adj* demi-sec
medium-sized ['mi:dɪəm'saɪzd] *adj* de taille moyenne
medium wave *n* (*Radio*) ondes moyennes, petites ondes
medley ['mɛdlɪ] *n* mélange *m*
meek [mi:k] *adj* doux (douce), humble
meet (*pt, pp* **met**) [mi:t, mɛt] *vt* rencontrer; (*by arrangement*) retrouver, rejoindre; (*for the first time*) faire la connaissance de; (*go and fetch*): **I'll ~ you at the station** j'irai te chercher à la gare; (*opponent, danger, problem*) faire face à; (*requirements*) satisfaire à, répondre à; (*bill, expenses*) régler, honorer ▷ *vi* (*friends*) se rencontrer; se retrouver; (*in session*) se réunir; (*join: lines, roads*) se joindre ▷ *n* (*Brit Hunting*) rendez-vous *m* de chasse; (*US Sport*) rencontre *f*, meeting *m*; **pleased to ~ you!** enchanté!; **nice ~ing you** ravi d'avoir fait votre connaissance
  ▸ **meet up** *vi*: **to ~ up with sb** rencontrer qn
  ▸ **meet with** *vt fus* (*difficulty*) rencontrer; **to ~ with success** être couronné(e) de succès
meeting ['mi:tɪŋ] *n* (*of group of people*) réunion *f*; (*between individuals*) rendez-vous *m*; (*formal*) assemblée *f*; (*Sport: rally*) rencontre, meeting *m*; (*interview*) entrevue *f*; **she's at** *or* **in a ~** (*Comm*) elle est en réunion; **to call a ~** convoquer une réunion
meeting place *n* lieu *m* de (la) réunion; (*for appointment*) lieu de rendez-vous
mega ['mɛgə] (*inf*) *adv*: **he's ~ rich** il est hyper-riche
megabyte ['mɛgəbaɪt] *n* (*Comput*) méga-octet *m*
megaphone ['mɛgəfəun] *n* porte-voix *m inv*
megapixel ['mɛgəpɪksl] *n* mégapixel *m*
meh [mɛ] *excl* bof
melancholy ['mɛlənkəlɪ] *n* mélancolie *f* ▷ *adj* mélancolique
mellow ['mɛləu] *adj* velouté(e), doux (douce); (*colour*) riche et profond(e); (*fruit*) mûr(e) ▷ *vi* (*person*) s'adoucir
melodious [mɪ'ləudɪəs] *adj* mélodieux(-euse)
melodrama ['mɛləudrɑːmə] *n* mélodrame *m*
melodramatic [mɛlədrə'mætɪk] *adj* mélodramatique
melody ['mɛlədɪ] *n* mélodie *f*
melon ['mɛlən] *n* melon *m*
melt [mɛlt] *vi* fondre; (*become soft*) s'amollir; (*fig*) s'attendrir ▷ *vt* faire fondre
  ▸ **melt away** *vi* fondre complètement
  ▸ **melt down** *vt* fondre
meltdown ['mɛltdaun] *n* fusion *f* (du cœur d'un réacteur nucléaire)
melting point ['mɛltɪŋ-] *n* point *m* de fusion
melting pot ['mɛltɪŋ-] *n* (*fig*) creuset *m*; **to be in the ~** être encore en discussion
member ['mɛmbə'] *n* membre *m*; (*of club, political party*) membre, adhérent(e) ▷ *cpd*: **~ country/ state** *n* pays *m*/état *m* membre
membership ['mɛmbəʃɪp] *n* (*becoming a member*) adhésion *f*; admission *f*; (*being a member*) qualité *f* de membre, fait *m* d'être membre; (*members*) membres *mpl*, adhérents *mpl*; (*number of members*) nombre *m* des membres *or* adhérents
membership card *n* carte *f* de membre
membrane ['mɛmbreɪn] *n* membrane *f*

memento [mə'mɛntəʊ] n souvenir m
memo ['mɛməʊ] n note f (de service)
memoir ['mɛmwɑ:ʳ] n mémoire m, étude f;
  memoirs npl mémoires
memo pad n bloc-notes m
memorable ['mɛmərəbl] adj mémorable
memorandum (pl **memoranda**)
  [mɛmə'rændəm, -də] n note f (de service);
  (Diplomacy) mémorandum m
memorial [mɪ'mɔ:rɪəl] n mémorial m ▷ adj
  commémoratif(-ive)
Memorial Day n (US) voir article

● **MEMORIAL DAY**
●
● Memorial Day est un jour férié aux États-Unis,
● le dernier lundi de mai dans la plupart des
● États, à la mémoire des soldats américains
● morts au combat.

memorize ['mɛməraɪz] vt apprendre or retenir
  par cœur
memory ['mɛmərɪ] n (also Comput) mémoire f;
  (recollection) souvenir m; **to have a good/bad ~**
  avoir une bonne/mauvaise mémoire; **loss of ~**
  perte f de mémoire; **in ~ of** à la mémoire de
memory card n (for digital camera) carte f
  mémoire
memory stick n (Comput: flash pen) clé f USB
  (: card) carte f mémoire
men [mɛn] npl of **man**
menace ['mɛnɪs] n menace f; (inf: nuisance) peste f,
  plaie f ▷ vt menacer; **a public ~** un danger public
menacing ['mɛnɪsɪŋ] adj menaçant(e)
menagerie [mɪ'nædʒərɪ] n ménagerie f
mend [mɛnd] vt réparer; (darn) raccommoder,
  repriser ▷ n reprise f; **on the ~** en voie de
  guérison; **to ~ one's ways** s'amender
mending ['mɛndɪŋ] n raccommodages mpl
menial ['mi:nɪəl] adj de domestique,
  inférieur(e); subalterne
meningitis [mɛnɪn'dʒaɪtɪs] n méningite f
menopause ['mɛnəʊpɔ:z] n ménopause f
menservants ['mɛnsə:vənts] npl of **manservant**
men's room (US) n: **the men's room** les
  toilettes fpl pour hommes
menstruate ['mɛnstrueɪt] vi avoir ses règles
menstruation [mɛnstru'eɪʃən] n menstruation f
menswear ['mɛnzwɛəʳ] n vêtements mpl
  d'hommes
mental ['mɛntl] adj mental(e); **~ illness**
  maladie mentale
mental hospital n hôpital m psychiatrique
mentality [mɛn'tælɪtɪ] n mentalité f
mentally ['mɛntlɪ] adv: **to be ~ handicapped**
  être handicapé(e) mental(e); **the ~ ill** les
  malades mentaux
menthol ['mɛnθɔl] n menthol m
mention ['mɛnʃən] n mention f ▷ vt
  mentionner, faire mention de; **don't ~ it!** je
  vous en prie, il n'y a pas de quoi!; **I need hardly
  ~ that ...** est-il besoin de rappeler que ...?; **not**

to ~ ..., **without ~ing ...** sans parler de ..., sans
  compter ...
mentor ['mɛntɔ:ʳ] n mentor m
menu ['mɛnju:] n (set menu, Comput) menu m; (list
  of dishes) carte f; **could we see the ~?** est-ce
  qu'on peut voir la carte?
menu-driven ['mɛnju:drɪvn] adj (Comput)
  piloté(e) par menu
MEP n abbr = **Member of the European
  Parliament**
mercantile ['mə:kəntaɪl] adj marchand(e);
  (law) commercial(e)
mercenary ['mə:sɪnərɪ] adj (person) intéressé(e),
  mercenaire ▷ n mercenaire m
merchandise ['mə:tʃəndaɪz] n marchandises fpl
  ▷ vt commercialiser
merchandiser ['mə:tʃəndaɪzəʳ] n
  marchandiseur m
merchant ['mə:tʃənt] n négociant m, marchand
  m; **timber/wine ~** négociant en bois/vins,
  marchand de bois/vins
merchant bank n (Brit) banque f d'affaires
merchantman ['mə:tʃəntmən] (irreg) n navire
  marchand
merchant navy, (US) **merchant marine** n
  marine marchande
merciful ['mə:sɪful] adj miséricordieux(-euse),
  clément(e)
mercifully ['mə:sɪflɪ] adv avec clémence;
  (fortunately) par bonheur, Dieu merci
merciless ['mə:sɪlɪs] adj impitoyable, sans pitié
mercurial [mə:'kjʊərɪəl] adj changeant(e);
  (lively) vif (vive)
mercury ['mə:kjʊrɪ] n mercure m
mercy ['mə:sɪ] n pitié f, merci f; (Rel)
  miséricorde f; **to have ~ on sb** avoir pitié de qn;
  at the ~ of à la merci de
mercy killing n euthanasie f
mere [mɪəʳ] adj simple; (chance) pur(e); **a ~ two
  hours** seulement deux heures
merely ['mɪəlɪ] adv simplement, purement
merge [mə:dʒ] vt unir; (Comput) fusionner,
  interclasser ▷ vi (colours, shapes, sounds) se mêler;
  (roads) se joindre; (Comm) fusionner
merger ['mə:dʒəʳ] n (Comm) fusion f
meridian [mə'rɪdɪən] n méridien m
meringue [mə'ræŋ] n meringue f
merit ['mɛrɪt] n mérite m, valeur f ▷ vt mériter
meritocracy [mɛrɪ'tɔkrəsɪ] n méritocratie f
mermaid ['mə:meɪd] n sirène f
merriment ['mɛrɪmənt] n gaieté f
merry ['mɛrɪ] adj gai(e); **M~ Christmas!** joyeux
  Noël!
merry-go-round ['mɛrɪgəʊraund] n manège m
mesh [mɛʃ] n mailles fpl ▷ vi (gears) s'engrener;
  wire ~ grillage m (métallique), treillis m
  (métallique)
mesmerize ['mɛzməraɪz] vt hypnotiser;
  fasciner
mess [mɛs] n désordre m, fouillis m, pagaille f;
  (muddle: of life) gâchis m; (: of economy) pagaille f;
  (dirt) saleté f; (Mil) mess m, cantine f; **to be (in)**

m

a ~ être en désordre; **to be/get o.s. in a** ~ (fig) être/se mettre dans le pétrin
▶ **mess about** or **around** (inf) vi perdre son temps
▶ **mess about** or **around with** vt fus (inf) chambarder, tripoter
▶ **mess up** vt (dirty) salir; (spoil) gâcher
▶ **mess with** (inf) vt fus (challenge, confront) se frotter à; (interfere with) toucher à

message ['mɛsɪdʒ] n message m; **can I leave a** ~? est-ce que je peux laisser un message?; **are there any ~s for me?** est-ce que j'ai des messages?; **to get the** ~ (fig: inf) saisir, piger

message switching [-swɪtʃɪŋ] n (Comput) commutation f de messages

messenger ['mɛsɪndʒəʳ] n messager m

Messiah [mɪ'saɪə] n Messie m

Messrs, Messrs. ['mɛsəz] abbr (on letters: = messieurs) MM

messy ['mɛsɪ] adj (dirty) sale; (untidy) en désordre

Met [mɛt] n abbr (US) = **Metropolitan Opera**

met [mɛt] pt, pp of **meet** ▷ adj abbr (= meteorological) météo inv

metabolism [mɛ'tæbəlɪzəm] n métabolisme m

metal ['mɛtl] n métal m ▷ cpd en métal ▷ vt empierrer

metallic [mɛ'tælɪk] adj métallique

metallurgy [mɛ'tælədʒɪ] n métallurgie f

metalwork ['mɛtlwəːk] n (craft) ferronnerie f

metamorphosis (pl -ses) [mɛtə'mɔːfəsɪs, -siːz] n métamorphose f

metaphor ['mɛtəfəʳ] n métaphore f

metaphysics [mɛtə'fɪzɪks] n métaphysique f

mete [miːt] **to ~ out** vt fus infliger

meteor ['miːtɪəʳ] n météore m

meteoric [miːtɪ'ɔrɪk] adj (fig) fulgurant(e)

meteorite ['miːtɪəraɪt] n météorite m or f

meteorological [miːtɪərə'lɔdʒɪkl] adj météorologique

meteorology [miːtɪə'rɔlədʒɪ] n météorologie f

meter ['miːtəʳ] n (instrument) compteur m; (also: **parking meter**) parc(o)mètre m; (US: unit) = **metre** ▷ vt (US Post) affranchir à la machine

methane ['miːθeɪn] n méthane m

method ['mɛθəd] n méthode f; ~ **of payment** mode m or modalité f de paiement

methodical [mɪ'θɔdɪkl] adj méthodique

Methodist ['mɛθədɪst] adj, n méthodiste (m/f)

methylated spirit ['mɛθɪleɪtɪd-] n (Brit: also: **meths**) alcool m à brûler

meticulous [mɛ'tɪkjuləs] adj méticuleux(-euse)

Met Office ['mɛt'ɔfɪs] n (Brit): **the** ~ ≈ la Météorologie nationale

metre, (US) **meter** ['miːtəʳ] n mètre m

metric ['mɛtrɪk] adj métrique; **to go** ~ adopter le système métrique

metrical ['mɛtrɪkl] adj métrique

metrication [mɛtrɪ'keɪʃən] n conversion f au système métrique

metric system n système m métrique

metric ton n tonne f

metro ['mɛtrəu] n métro m

metronome ['mɛtrənəum] n métronome m

metropolis [mɪ'trɔpəlɪs] n métropole f

metropolitan [mɛtrə'pɔlɪtən] adj métropolitain(e); **the M~ Police** (Brit) la police londonienne

mettle ['mɛtl] n courage m

mew [mjuː] vi (cat) miauler

mews [mjuːz] n (Brit): ~ **cottage** maisonnette aménagée dans une ancienne écurie ou remise

Mexican ['mɛksɪkən] adj mexicain(e) ▷ n Mexicain(e)

Mexico ['mɛksɪkəu] n Mexique m

Mexico City n Mexico

mezzanine ['mɛtsəniːn] n mezzanine f; (of shops, offices) entresol m

MFA n abbr (US: = Master of Fine Arts) titre universitaire

mfr abbr = **manufacture; manufacturer**

mg abbr (= milligram) mg

Mgr abbr (= Monseigneur, Monsignor) Mgr; (= manager) dir

MHR n abbr (US) = **Member of the House of Representatives**

MHz abbr (= megahertz) MHz

Mi abbr (US) = **Michigan**

MI5 n abbr (Brit: = Military Intelligence 5) ≈ DST f

MI6 n abbr (Brit: = Military Intelligence 6) ≈ DGSE f

MIA abbr (= missing in action) disparu au combat

miaow [miː'au] vi miauler

mice [maɪs] npl of **mouse**

Mich. abbr (US) = **Michigan**

micro ['maɪkrəu] n (also: **microcomputer**) micro(-ordinateur m) m

micro... [maɪkrəu] prefix

microbe ['maɪkrəub] n microbe m

microbiology [maɪkrəbaɪ'ɔlədʒɪ] n microbiologie f

microchip ['maɪkrəutʃɪp] n (Elec) puce f

microcomputer ['maɪkrəukəm'pjuːtəʳ] n micro-ordinateur m

microcosm ['maɪkrəukɔzəm] n microcosme m

microeconomics ['maɪkrəuiːkə'nɔmɪks] n micro-économie f

microfiche ['maɪkrəufiːʃ] n microfiche f

microfilm ['maɪkrəufɪlm] n microfilm m ▷ vt microfilmer

microlight ['maɪkrəulaɪt] n ULM m

micrometer [maɪ'krɔmɪtəʳ] n palmer m, micromètre m

microphone ['maɪkrəfəun] n microphone m

microprocessor ['maɪkrəu'prəusɛsəʳ] n microprocesseur m

microscope ['maɪkrəskəup] n microscope m; **under the** ~ au microscope

microscopic [maɪkrə'skɔpɪk] adj microscopique ▷ n

mid [mɪd] adj: ~ **May** la mi-mai; ~ **afternoon** le milieu de l'après-midi; **in** ~ **air** en plein ciel; **he's in his** ~ **thirties** il a dans les trente-cinq ans

midday [mɪd'deɪ] n midi m

middle ['mɪdl] n milieu m; (waist) ceinture f,

taille f ▷ adj du milieu; (average) moyen(ne); **in the ~ of the night** au milieu de la nuit; **I'm in the ~ of reading it** je suis (justement) en train de le lire

middle age n tranche d'âge aux limites floues, entre la quarantaine et le début du troisième âge

middle-aged ['mɪdl'eɪdʒd] adj d'un certain âge, ni vieux ni jeune; (pej: values, outlook) conventionnel(le), rassis(e)

Middle Ages npl: **the ~** le moyen âge

middle-class [mɪdl'klɑ:s] adj bourgeois(e)

middle class n, **middle classes** npl: **the ~(es)** ≈ les classes moyennes

Middle East n: **the ~** le Proche-Orient, le Moyen-Orient

middleman ['mɪdlmæn] (irreg) n intermédiaire m

middle management n cadres moyens

middle name n second prénom

middle-of-the-road ['mɪdləvðə'rəud] adj (policy) modéré(e), du juste milieu; (music etc) plutôt classique, assez traditionnel(le)

middle school n (US) école pour les enfants de 12 à 14 ans, ≈ collège m; (Brit) école pour les enfants de 8 à 14 ans

middleweight ['mɪdlweɪt] n (Boxing) poids moyen

middling ['mɪdlɪŋ] adj moyen(ne)

midge [mɪdʒ] n moucheron m

midget ['mɪdʒɪt] n nain(e) ▷ adj minuscule

midi system ['mɪdɪ-] n chaîne f midi

Midlands ['mɪdləndz] npl comtés du centre de l'Angleterre

midnight ['mɪdnaɪt] n minuit m; **at ~** à minuit

midriff ['mɪdrɪf] n estomac m, taille f

midst [mɪdst] n: **in the ~ of** au milieu de

midsummer [mɪd'sʌmər] n milieu m de l'été

midway [mɪd'weɪ] adj, adv: **~ (between)** à mi-chemin (entre); **~ through ...** au milieu de ..., en plein(e) ...

midweek [mɪd'wi:k] adj du milieu de la semaine ▷ adv au milieu de la semaine, en pleine semaine

midwife (pl **midwives**) ['mɪdwaɪf, -vz] n sage-femme f

midwifery ['mɪdwɪfərɪ] n obstétrique f

midwinter [mɪd'wɪntər] n milieu m de l'hiver

miffed [mɪft] adj (inf) fâché(e), vexé(e)

might [maɪt] vb see **may** ▷ n puissance f, force f

mighty ['maɪtɪ] adj puissant(e) ▷ adv (inf) rudement

migraine ['mi:greɪn] n migraine f

migrant ['maɪgrənt] n (bird, animal) migrateur m; (person) migrant(e); nomade m/f ▷ adj migrateur(-trice); migrant(e); nomade; (worker) saisonnier(-ière)

migrate [maɪ'greɪt] vi migrer

migration [maɪ'greɪʃən] n migration f

mike [maɪk] n abbr (= microphone) micro m

Milan [mɪ'læn] n Milan

mild [maɪld] adj doux (douce); (reproach, infection) léger(-ère); (illness) bénin(-igne); (interest) modéré(e); (taste) peu relevé(e) ▷ n bière légère

mildew ['mɪldju:] n mildiou m

mildly ['maɪldlɪ] adv doucement; légèrement; **to put it ~** (inf) c'est le moins qu'on puisse dire

mildness ['maɪldnɪs] n douceur f

mile [maɪl] n mil(l)e m (= 1609 m); **to do 30 ~s per gallon** ≈ faire 9, 4 litres aux cent

mileage ['maɪlɪdʒ] n distance f en milles, ≈ kilométrage m

mileage allowance n ≈ indemnité f kilométrique

mileometer [maɪ'lɔmɪtər] n compteur m kilométrique

milestone ['maɪlstəun] n borne f; (fig) jalon m

milieu ['mi:ljə:] n milieu m

militant ['mɪlɪtnt] adj, n militant(e)

militarism ['mɪlɪtərɪzəm] n militarisme m

militaristic [mɪlɪtə'rɪstɪk] adj militariste

military ['mɪlɪtərɪ] adj militaire ▷ n: **the ~** l'armée f, les militaires mpl

military service n service m (militaire ou national)

militate ['mɪlɪteɪt] vi: **to ~ against** militer contre

militia [mɪ'lɪʃə] n milice f

milk [mɪlk] n lait m ▷ vt (cow) traire; (fig: person) dépouiller, plumer; (: situation) exploiter à fond

milk chocolate n chocolat m au lait

milk float n (Brit) voiture f or camionnette f du or de laitier

milking ['mɪlkɪŋ] n traite f

milkman ['mɪlkmən] (irreg) n laitier m

milk shake n milk-shake m

milk tooth n dent f de lait

milk truck n (US) = **milk float**

milky ['mɪlkɪ] adj (drink) au lait; (colour) laiteux(-euse)

Milky Way n Voie lactée

mill [mɪl] n moulin m; (factory) usine f, fabrique f; (spinning mill) filature f; (flour mill) minoterie f; (steel mill) aciérie f ▷ vt moudre, broyer ▷ vi (also: **mill about**) grouiller

millennium (pl **-s** or **millennia**) [mɪ'lɛnɪəm, -'lɛnɪə] n millénaire m

millennium bug [mɪ'lɛnɪəm-] n bogue m or bug m de l'an 2000

miller ['mɪlər] n meunier m

millet ['mɪlɪt] n millet m

milli... ['mɪlɪ] prefix milli...

milligram, milligramme ['mɪlɪgræm] n milligramme m

millilitre, (US) **milliliter** ['mɪlɪli:tər] n millilitre m

millimetre, (US) **millimeter** ['mɪlɪmi:tər] n millimètre m

milliner ['mɪlɪnər] n modiste f

millinery ['mɪlɪnərɪ] n modes fpl

million ['mɪljən] n million m; **a ~ pounds** un million de livres sterling

millionaire [mɪljə'nɛər] n millionnaire m

millionth [-θ] num millionième

millipede ['mɪlɪpi:d] n mille-pattes m inv

millstone ['mɪlstəun] n meule f
millwheel ['mɪlwiːl] n roue f de moulin
milometer [maɪ'lɒmɪtər] n = **mileometer**
mime [maɪm] n mime m ▷ vt, vi mimer
mimic ['mɪmɪk] n imitateur(-trice) ▷ vt, vi
imiter, contrefaire
mimicry ['mɪmɪkrɪ] n imitation f; (Zool)
mimétisme m
Min. abbr (Brit Pol) = **ministry**
min. abbr (= minute(s)) mn.; (= minimum) min.
minaret [mɪnə'rɛt] n minaret m
mince [mɪns] vt hacher ▷ vi (attend to, look after)
à petits pas maniérés ▷ n (Brit Culin) viande
hachée, hachis m; **he does not ~ (his) words** il
ne mâche pas ses mots
mincemeat ['mɪnsmiːt] n hachis de fruits secs
utilisés en pâtisserie; (US) viande hachée, hachis m
mince pie n sorte de tarte aux fruits secs
mincer ['mɪnsər] n hachoir m
mincing ['mɪnsɪŋ] adj affecté(e)
mind [maɪnd] n esprit m ▷ vt (attend to, look after)
s'occuper de; (be careful) faire attention à; (object
to): **I don't ~ the noise** je ne crains pas le bruit,
le bruit ne me dérange pas; **it is on my ~** cela
me préoccupe; **to change one's ~** changer
d'avis; **to be in two ~s about sth** (Brit) être
indécis(e) or irrésolu(e) en ce qui concerne qch;
to my ~ à mon avis, selon moi; **to be out of
one's ~** ne plus avoir toute sa raison; **to keep
sth in ~** ne pas oublier qch; **to bear sth in ~**
tenir compte de qch; **to have sb/sth in ~** avoir
qn/qch en tête; **to have in ~ to do** avoir
l'intention de faire; **it went right out of my ~**
ça m'est complètement sorti de la tête; **to
bring** or **call sth to ~** se rappeler qch; **to make
up one's ~** se décider; **do you ~ if ...?** est-ce que
cela vous gêne si ...?; **I don't ~** cela ne me
dérange pas; (don't care) ça m'est égal; **~ you, ...**
remarquez, ...; **never ~** peu importe, ça ne fait
rien; (don't worry) ne vous en faîtes pas; **"~ the
step"** "attention à la marche"
mind-boggling ['maɪndbɒglɪŋ] adj (inf)
époustouflant(e), ahurissant(e)
-minded ['maɪndɪd] adj: **fair~** impartial(e); **an
industrially~ nation** une nation orientée vers
l'industrie
minder ['maɪndər] n (child minder) gardienne f;
(bodyguard) ange gardien (fig)
mindful ['maɪndful] adj: **~ of** attentif(-ive) à,
soucieux(-euse) de
mindless ['maɪndlɪs] adj irréfléchi(e); (violence,
crime) insensé(e); (boring: job) idiot(e)
mine¹ [maɪn] pron le (la) mien(ne), les miens
(miennes); **a friend of ~** un de mes amis, un
ami à moi; **this book is ~** ce livre est à moi
mine² [maɪn] n mine f ▷ vt (coal) extraire; (ship,
beach) miner
mine detector n détecteur m de mines
minefield ['maɪnfiːld] n champ m de mines
miner ['maɪnər] n mineur m
mineral ['mɪnərəl] adj minéral(e) ▷ n minéral
m; **minerals** npl (Brit: soft drinks) boissons

gazeuses (sucrées)
mineralogy [mɪnə'rælədʒɪ] n minéralogie f
mineral water n eau minérale
minesweeper ['maɪnswiːpər] n dragueur m de
mines
mingle ['mɪŋgl] vt mêler, mélanger ▷ vi: **to ~
with** se mêler à
mingy ['mɪndʒɪ] adj (inf) radin(e)
miniature ['mɪnətʃər] adj (en) miniature ▷ n
miniature f
minibar ['mɪnɪbɑːr] n minibar m
minibus ['mɪnɪbʌs] n minibus m
minicab ['mɪnɪkæb] n (Brit) taxi m indépendant
minicomputer ['mɪnɪkəm'pjuːtər] n mini-
ordinateur m
minim ['mɪnɪm] n (Mus) blanche f
minima ['mɪnɪmə] npl of **minimum**
minimal ['mɪnɪml] adj minimal(e)
minimalist ['mɪnɪməlɪst] adj, n minimaliste
(m/f)
minimize ['mɪnɪmaɪz] vt (reduce) réduire au
minimum; (play down) minimiser
minimum ['mɪnɪməm] n (pl **minima**) [-mə]
minimum m ▷ adj minimum; **to reduce to a ~**
réduire au minimum
minimum lending rate n (Econ) taux m de
crédit minimum
mining ['maɪnɪŋ] n exploitation minière ▷ adj
minier(-ière); de mineurs
minion ['mɪnjən] n (pej) laquais m; favori(te)
mini-series ['mɪnɪsɪəriːz] n téléfilm m en
plusieurs parties
miniskirt ['mɪnɪskəːt] n mini-jupe f
minister ['mɪnɪstər] n (Brit Pol) ministre m; (Rel)
pasteur m ▷ vi: **to ~ to sb** donner ses soins à qn;
to ~ to sb's needs pourvoir aux besoins de qn
ministerial [mɪnɪs'tɪərɪəl] adj (Brit Pol)
ministériel(le)
ministry ['mɪnɪstrɪ] n (Brit Pol) ministère m;
(Rel): **to go into the ~** devenir pasteur
mink [mɪŋk] n vison m
mink coat n manteau m de vison
Minn. abbr (US) = **Minnesota**
minnow ['mɪnəu] n vairon m
minor ['maɪnər] adj petit(e), de peu
d'importance; (Mus, poet, problem) mineur(e) ▷ n
(Law) mineur(e)
Minorca [mɪ'nɔːkə] n Minorque f
minority [maɪ'nɔrɪtɪ] n minorité f; **to be in a ~**
être en minorité
minster ['mɪnstər] n église abbatiale
minstrel ['mɪnstrəl] n trouvère m, ménestrel m
mint [mɪnt] n (plant) menthe f; (sweet) bonbon m
à la menthe ▷ vt (coins) battre; **the (Royal) M~,
the (US) M~** ≈ l'hôtel m de la Monnaie; **in ~
condition** à l'état de neuf
mint sauce n sauce f à la menthe
minuet [mɪnju'ɛt] n menuet m
minus ['maɪnəs] n (also: **minus sign**) signe m
moins ▷ prep moins; **12 ~ 6 equals 6** 12 moins 6
égal 6; **~ 24°C** moins 24°C
minuscule ['mɪnəskjuːl] adj minuscule

minute¹ n ['mɪnɪt] minute f; (official record) procès-verbal m, compte rendu; **minutes** npl (of meeting) procès-verbal m, compte rendu; **it is 5 ~s past 3** il est 3 heures 5; **wait a ~!** (attendez) un instant!; **at the last ~** à la dernière minute; **up to the ~** (fashion) dernier cri; (news) de dernière minute; (machine, technology) de pointe

minute² adj [maɪ'nju:t] minuscule; (detailed) minutieux(-euse); **in ~ detail** par le menu

minute book n registre m des procès-verbaux

minute hand n aiguille f des minutes

minutely [maɪ'nju:tlɪ] adv (by a small amount) de peu, de manière infime; (in detail) minutieusement, dans les moindres détails

minutiae [mɪ'nju:ʃɪː] npl menus détails

miracle ['mɪrəkl] n miracle m

miraculous [mɪ'rækjuləs] adj miraculeux(-euse)

mirage ['mɪrɑːʒ] n mirage m

mire ['maɪəʳ] n bourbe f, boue f

mirror ['mɪrəʳ] n miroir m, glace f; (in car) rétroviseur m ▷ vt reflétér

mirror image n image inversée

mirth [mɜː:θ] n gaieté f

misadventure [mɪsəd'vɛntʃəʳ] n mésaventure f; **death by ~** (Brit) décès accidentel

misanthropist [mɪ'zænθrəpɪst] n misanthrope m/f

misapply [mɪsə'plaɪ] vt mal employer

misapprehension ['mɪsæprɪ'hɛnʃən] n malentendu m, méprise f

misappropriate [mɪsə'prəuprɪeɪt] vt détourner

misappropriation ['mɪsəprəuprɪ'eɪʃən] n escroquerie f, détournement m

misbehave [mɪsbɪ'heɪv] vi mal se conduire

misbehaviour, (US) **misbehavior** [mɪsbɪ'heɪvjəʳ] n mauvaise conduite

misc. abbr = **miscellaneous**

miscalculate [mɪs'kælkjuleɪt] vt mal calculer

miscalculation ['mɪskælkju'leɪʃən] n erreur f de calcul

miscarriage ['mɪskærɪdʒ] n (Med) fausse couche; **~ of justice** erreur f judiciaire

miscarry [mɪs'kærɪ] vi (Med) faire une fausse couche; (fail: plans) échouer, mal tourner

miscellaneous [mɪsɪ'leɪnɪəs] adj (items, expenses) divers(es); (selection) varié(e)

miscellany [mɪ'sɛlənɪ] n recueil m

mischance [mɪs'tʃɑːns] n malchance f; **by (some) ~** par malheur

mischief ['mɪstʃɪf] n (naughtiness) sottises fpl; (fun) farce f; (playfulness) espièglerie f; (harm) mal m, dommage m; (maliciousness) méchanceté f

mischievous ['mɪstʃɪvəs] adj (playful, naughty) coquin(e), espiègle; (harmful) méchant(e)

misconception ['mɪskən'sɛpʃən] n idée fausse

misconduct [mɪs'kɔndʌkt] n inconduite f; **professional ~** faute professionnelle

misconstrue [mɪskən'struː] vt mal interpréter

miscount [mɪs'kaunt] vt, vi mal compter

misdeed ['mɪs'diːd] n méfait m

misdemeanour, (US) **misdemeanor** [mɪsdɪ'miː-nəʳ] n écart m de conduite; infraction f

misdirect [mɪsdɪ'rɛkt] vt (person) mal renseigner; (letter) mal adresser

miser ['maɪzəʳ] n avare m/f

miserable ['mɪzərəbl] adj (person, expression) malheureux(-euse); (conditions) misérable; (weather) maussade; (offer, donation) minable; (failure) pitoyable; **to feel ~** avoir le cafard

miserably ['mɪzərəblɪ] adv (smile, answer) tristement; (live, pay) misérablement; (fail) lamentablement

miserly ['maɪzəlɪ] adj avare

misery ['mɪzərɪ] n (unhappiness) tristesse f; (pain) souffrances fpl; (wretchedness) misère f

misfire [mɪs'faɪəʳ] vi rater; (car engine) avoir des ratés

misfit ['mɪsfɪt] n (person) inadapté(e)

misfortune [mɪs'fɔːtʃən] n malchance f, malheur m

misgiving [mɪs'gɪvɪŋ] n (apprehension) craintes fpl; **to have ~s about sth** avoir des doutes quant à qch

misguided [mɪs'gaɪdɪd] adj malavisé(e)

mishandle [mɪs'hændl] vt (treat roughly) malmener; (mismanage) mal s'y prendre pour faire or résoudre etc

mishap ['mɪshæp] n mésaventure f

mishear [mɪs'hɪəʳ] vt, vi (irreg: like **hear**) mal entendre

mishmash ['mɪʃmæʃ] n (inf) fatras m, méli-mélo m

misinform [mɪsɪn'fɔːm] vt mal renseigner

misinterpret [mɪsɪn'təːprɪt] vt mal interpréter

misinterpretation ['mɪsɪntə:prɪ'teɪʃən] n interprétation erronée, contresens m

misjudge [mɪs'dʒʌdʒ] vt méjuger, se méprendre sur le compte de

mislay [mɪs'leɪ] vt (irreg: like **lay**) égarer

mislead [mɪs'liːd] vt (irreg: like **lead**) induire en erreur

misleading [mɪs'liːdɪŋ] adj trompeur(-euse)

misled [mɪs'lɛd] pt, pp of **mislead**

mismanage [mɪs'mænɪdʒ] vt mal gérer; mal s'y prendre pour faire or résoudre etc

mismanagement [mɪs'mænɪdʒmənt] n mauvaise gestion

misnomer [mɪs'nəuməʳ] n terme or qualificatif trompeur or peu approprié

misogynist [mɪ'sɔdʒɪnɪst] n misogyne m/f

misplace [mɪs'pleɪs] vt égarer; **to be ~d** (trust etc) être mal placé(e)

misprint ['mɪsprɪnt] n faute f d'impression

mispronounce [mɪsprə'nauns] vt mal prononcer

misquote ['mɪs'kwəut] vt citer erronément or inexactement

misread [mɪs'riːd] vt (irreg: like **read**) mal lire

misrepresent [mɪsrɛprɪ'zɛnt] vt présenter sous un faux jour

Miss [mɪs] n Mademoiselle; **Dear ~ Smith** Chère Mademoiselle Smith

miss [mɪs] vt (fail to get, attend, see) manquer,

rater; (*appointment, class*) manquer; (*escape, avoid*) échapper à, éviter; (*notice loss of: money etc*) s'apercevoir de l'absence de; (*regret the absence of*): **I ~ him/it** il/cela me manque ▷ *vi* manquer ▷ *n* (*shot*) coup manqué; **we ~ed our train** nous avons raté notre train; **the bus just ~ed the wall** le bus a évité le mur de justesse; **you're ~ing the point** vous êtes à côté de la question; **you can't ~ it** vous ne pouvez pas vous tromper
▶ **miss out** *vt* (*Brit*) oublier
▶ **miss out on** *vt fus* (*fun, party*) rater, manquer; (*chance, bargain*) laisser passer

Miss. *abbr* (*US*) = **Mississippi**

missal ['mɪsl] *n* missel *m*

misshapen [mɪs'ʃeɪpən] *adj* difforme

missile ['mɪsaɪl] *n* (*Aviat*) missile *m*; (*object thrown*) projectile *m*

missile base *n* base *f* de missiles

missile launcher [-lɔːntʃəʳ] *n* lance-missiles *m*

missing ['mɪsɪŋ] *adj* manquant(e); (*after escape, disaster: person*) disparu(e); **to go ~** disparaître; **~ person** personne disparue, disparu(e); **~ in action** (*Mil*) porté(e) disparu(e)

mission ['mɪʃən] *n* mission *f*; **on a ~ to sb** en mission auprès de qn

missionary ['mɪʃənrɪ] *n* missionnaire *m/f*

mission statement *n* déclaration *f* d'intention

missive ['mɪsɪv] *n* missive *f*

misspell ['mɪs'spɛl] *vt* (*irreg: like* **spell**) mal orthographier

misspent ['mɪs'spɛnt] *adj*: **his ~ youth** sa folle jeunesse

mist [mɪst] *n* brume *f* ▷ *vi* (*also:* **mist over, mist up**) devenir brumeux(-euse); (*Brit: windows*) s'embuer

mistake [mɪs'teɪk] *n* erreur *f*, faute *f* ▷ *vt* (*irreg: like* **take**); (*meaning*) mal comprendre; (*intentions*) se méprendre sur; **to ~ for** prendre pour; **by ~** par erreur, par inadvertance; **to make a ~** (*in writing*) faire une faute; (*in calculating etc*) faire une erreur; **there must be some ~** il doit y avoir une erreur, se tromper; **to make a ~ about sb/sth** se tromper sur le compte de qn/sur qch

mistaken [mɪs'teɪkən] *pp of* **mistake** ▷ *adj* (*idea etc*) erroné(e); **to be ~** faire erreur, se tromper

mistaken identity *n* erreur *f* d'identité

mistakenly [mɪs'teɪkənlɪ] *adv* par erreur, par mégarde

mister ['mɪstəʳ] *n* (*inf*) Monsieur *m*; *see* **Mr**

mistletoe ['mɪsltəu] *n* gui *m*

mistook [mɪs'tuk] *pt of* **mistake**

mistranslation [mɪstræns'leɪʃən] *n* erreur *f* de traduction, contresens *m*

mistreat [mɪs'triːt] *vt* maltraiter

mistress ['mɪstrɪs] *n* maîtresse *f*; (*Brit: in primary school*) institutrice *f*; (*: in secondary school*) professeur *m*

mistrust [mɪs'trʌst] *vt* se méfier de ▷ *n*: **~ (of)** méfiance *f* (à l'égard de)

mistrustful [mɪs'trʌstful] *adj*: **~ (of)** méfiant(e) (à l'égard de)

misty ['mɪstɪ] *adj* brumeux(-euse); (*glasses, window*) embué(e)

misty-eyed ['mɪstɪ'aɪd] *adj* les yeux embués de larmes; (*fig*) sentimental(e)

misunderstand [mɪsʌndə'stænd] *vt, vi* (*irreg: like* **stand**) mal comprendre

misunderstanding ['mɪsʌndə'stændɪŋ] *n* méprise *f*, malentendu *m*; **there's been a ~** il y a eu un malentendu

misunderstood [mɪsʌndə'stud] *pt, pp of* **misunderstand** ▷ *adj* (*person*) incompris(e)

misuse *n* [mɪs'juːs] mauvais emploi; (*of power*) abus *m* ▷ *vt* [mɪs'juːz] mal employer; abuser de

MIT *n abbr* (*US*) = **Massachusetts Institute of Technology**

mite [maɪt] *n* (*small quantity*) grain *m*, miette *f*; (*Brit: small child*) petit(e)

mitigate ['mɪtɪgeɪt] *vt* atténuer; **mitigating circumstances** circonstances atténuantes

mitigation [mɪtɪ'geɪʃən] *n* atténuation *f*

mitre, (*US*) **miter** ['maɪtəʳ] *n* mitre *f*; (*Carpentry*) onglet *m*

mitt ['mɪt], **mitten** ['mɪtn] *n* moufle *f*; (*fingerless*) mitaine *f*

mix [mɪks] *vt* mélanger; (*sauce, drink etc*) préparer ▷ *vi* se mélanger; (*socialize*): **he doesn't ~ well** il est peu sociable ▷ *n* mélange *m*; **to ~ sth with sth** mélanger qch à qch; **to ~ business with pleasure** unir l'utile à l'agréable; **cake ~** préparation *f* pour gâteau
▶ **mix in** *vt* incorporer, mélanger
▶ **mix up** *vt* mélanger; (*confuse*) confondre; **to be ~ed up in sth** être mêlé(e) à qch *or* impliqué(e) dans qch

mixed [mɪkst] *adj* (*feelings, reactions*) contradictoire; (*school, marriage*) mixte

mixed-ability ['mɪkstə'bɪlɪtɪ] *adj* (*class etc*) sans groupes de niveaux

mixed bag *n*: **it's a (bit of a) ~** il y a (un peu) de tout

mixed blessing *n*: **it's a ~** cela a du bon et du mauvais

mixed doubles *npl* (*Sport*) double *m* mixte

mixed economy *n* économie *f* mixte

mixed grill *n* (*Brit*) assortiment *m* de grillades

mixed marriage *n* mariage *m* mixte

mixed salad *n* salade *f* de crudités

mixed-up [mɪkst'ʌp] *adj* (*person*) désorienté(e), embrouillé(e)

mixer ['mɪksəʳ] *n* (*for food*) batteur *m*, mixeur *m*; (*drink*) boisson gazeuse (*servant à couper un alcool*); (*person*): **he is a good ~** il est très sociable

mixer tap *n* (*robinet m*) mélangeur *m*

mixture ['mɪkstʃəʳ] *n* assortiment *m*, mélange *m*; (*Med*) préparation *f*

mix-up ['mɪksʌp] *n*: **there was a ~** il y a eu confusion

MK *abbr* (*Brit Tech*) = **mark**

mk *abbr* = **mark**

mkt *abbr* = **market**

ml *abbr* (= *millilitre(s)*) ml

MLitt *n abbr* (= *Master of Literature, Master of Letters*) *titre universitaire*

MLR *n abbr* (Brit) = **minimum lending rate**

mm *abbr* (= millimetre) mm

MN *abbr* (Brit) = **Merchant Navy**; (US) = **Minnesota**

MO *n abbr* (Med) = **medical officer**; (US inf: = *modus operandi*) méthode *f* ▷ *abbr* (US) = **Missouri**

m.o. *abbr* = **money order**

moan [məʊn] *n* gémissement *m* ▷ *vi* gémir; (inf: *complain*): **to ~ (about)** se plaindre (de)

moaner ['məʊnəʳ] *n* (inf) rouspéteur(-euse), râleur(-euse)

moaning ['məʊnɪŋ] *n* gémissements *mpl*

moat [məʊt] *n* fossé *m*, douves *fpl*

mob [mɔb] *n* foule *f*; (disorderly) cohue *f*; (pej): **the ~** la populace ▷ *vt* assaillir

mobile ['məʊbaɪl] *adj* mobile ▷ *n* (Art) mobile *m*; (Brit inf: mobile phone) (téléphone *m*) portable *m*, mobile *m*; **applicants must be ~** (Brit) les candidats devront être prêts à accepter tout déplacement

mobile home *n* caravane *f*

mobile phone *n* (téléphone *m*) portable *m*, mobile *m*

mobile shop *n* (Brit) camion *m* magasin

mobility [məʊ'bɪlɪtɪ] *n* mobilité *f*

mobilize ['məʊbɪlaɪz] *vt, vi* mobiliser

moccasin ['mɔkəsɪn] *n* mocassin *m*

mock [mɔk] *vt* ridiculiser; (laugh at) se moquer de ▷ *adj* faux (fausse); **mocks** *npl* (Brit: Scol) examens blancs

mockery ['mɔkərɪ] *n* moquerie *f*, raillerie *f*; **to make a ~ of** ridiculiser, tourner en dérision

mocking ['mɔkɪŋ] *adj* moqueur(-euse)

mockingbird ['mɔkɪŋbəːd] *n* moqueur *m*

mock-up ['mɔkʌp] *n* maquette *f*

MOD *n abbr* (Brit) = **Ministry of Defence**; *see* **defence**

mod [mɔd] *adj see* **convenience**

mod cons ['mɔd'kɔnz] *npl abbr* (Brit) = **modern conveniences**; *see* **convenience**

mode [məʊd] *n* mode *m*; (of transport) moyen *m*

model ['mɔdl] *n* modèle *m*; (person: for fashion) mannequin *m*; (: for artist) modèle ▷ *vt* (with clay etc) modeler ▷ *vi* travailler comme mannequin ▷ *adj* (railway: toy) modèle réduit *inv*; (child, factory) modèle; **to ~ clothes** présenter des vêtements; **to ~ o.s. on** imiter; **to ~ sb/sth on** modeler qn/qch sur

modem ['məʊdɛm] *n* modem *m*

moderate [adj, n 'mɔdərət, vb 'mɔdəreɪt] *adj* modéré(e); (amount, change) peu important(e) ▷ *n* (Pol) modéré(e) ▷ *vi* se modérer, se calmer ▷ *vt* modérer

moderately ['mɔdərətlɪ] *adv* (act) avec modération *or* mesure; (expensive, difficult) moyennement; (pleased, happy) raisonnablement, assez; **~ priced** à un prix raisonnable

moderation [mɔdə'reɪʃən] *n* modération *f*, mesure *f*; **in ~** à dose raisonnable, pris(e) *or*

pratiqué(e) modérément

moderator ['mɔdəreɪtəʳ] *n* (Rel): **M~** président *m* (de l'Assemblée générale de l'Église presbytérienne); (Pol) modérateur *m*

modern ['mɔdən] *adj* moderne

modernization [mɔdənaɪ'zeɪʃən] *n* modernisation *f*

modernize ['mɔdənaɪz] *vt* moderniser

modern languages *npl* langues vivantes

modest ['mɔdɪst] *adj* modeste

modesty ['mɔdɪstɪ] *n* modestie *f*

modicum ['mɔdɪkəm] *n*: **a ~ of** un minimum de

modification [mɔdɪfɪ'keɪʃən] *n* modification *f*; **to make ~s** faire *or* apporter des modifications

modify ['mɔdɪfaɪ] *vt* modifier

modish ['məʊdɪʃ] *adj* à la mode

Mods [mɔdz] *n abbr* (Brit: = (Honour) Moderations) premier examen universitaire (à Oxford)

modular ['mɔdjulə] *adj* (filing, unit) modulaire

modulate ['mɔdjuleɪt] *vt* moduler

modulation [mɔdju'leɪʃən] *n* modulation *f*

module ['mɔdju:l] *n* module *m*

mogul ['məʊgl] *n* (fig) nabab *m*; (Ski) bosse *f*

MOH *n abbr* (Brit) = **Medical Officer of Health**

mohair ['məʊhɛəʳ] *n* mohair *m*

Mohammed [mə'hæmɛd] *n* Mahomet *m*

moist [mɔɪst] *adj* humide, moite

moisten ['mɔɪsn] *vt* humecter, mouiller légèrement

moisture ['mɔɪstʃəʳ] *n* humidité *f*; (on glass) buée *f*

moisturize ['mɔɪstʃəraɪz] *vt* (skin) hydrater

moisturizer ['mɔɪstʃəraɪzəʳ] *n* crème hydratante

molar ['məʊləʳ] *n* molaire *f*

molasses [məʊ'læsɪz] *n* mélasse *f*

mold *etc* [məʊld] (US) = **mould** *etc*

Moldavia [mɔl'deɪvɪə], **Moldova** [mɔl'dəʊvə] *n* Moldavie *f*

Moldavian [mɔl'deɪvɪən], **Moldovan** [mɔl'dəʊvən] *adj* moldave

mole [məʊl] *n* (animal, spy) taupe *f*; (spot) grain *m* de beauté

molecule ['mɔlɪkju:l] *n* molécule *f*

molehill ['məʊlhɪl] *n* taupinière *f*

molest [məʊ'lɛst] *vt* (assault sexually) attenter à la pudeur de; (attack) molester; (harass) tracasser

mollusc ['mɔləsk] *n* mollusque *m*

mollycoddle ['mɔlɪkɔdl] *vt* chouchouter, couver

Molotov cocktail ['mɔlətɔf-] *n* cocktail *m* Molotov

molt [məʊlt] *vi* (US) = **moult**

molten ['məʊltən] *adj* fondu(e); (rock) en fusion

mom [mɔm] *n* (US) = **mum**

moment ['məʊmənt] *n* moment *m*, instant *m*; (importance) importance *f*; **at the ~** en ce moment; **for the ~** pour l'instant; **in a ~** dans un instant; **"one ~ please"** (Tel) "ne quittez pas"

momentarily ['məʊməntrɪlɪ] *adv* momentanément; (US: soon) bientôt

momentary ['məʊməntərɪ] *adj* momentané(e), passager(-ère)

m

momentous [məu'mɛntəs] *adj* important(e), capital(e)

momentum [məu'mɛntəm] *n* élan *m*, vitesse acquise; (*fig*) dynamique *f*; **to gather ~** prendre de la vitesse; (*fig*) gagner du terrain

mommy ['mɔmɪ] *n* (*US: mother*) maman *f*

Monaco ['mɔnəkəu] *n* Monaco *f*

monarch ['mɔnək] *n* monarque *m*

monarchist ['mɔnəkɪst] *n* monarchiste *m/f*

monarchy ['mɔnəkɪ] *n* monarchie *f*

monastery ['mɔnəstərɪ] *n* monastère *m*

monastic [mə'næstɪk] *adj* monastique

Monday ['mʌndɪ] *n* lundi *m*; *for phrases see also* **Tuesday**

monetarist ['mʌnɪtərɪst] *n* monétariste *m/f*

monetary ['mʌnɪtərɪ] *adj* monétaire

money ['mʌnɪ] *n* argent *m*; **to make ~** (*person*) gagner de l'argent; (*business*) rapporter; **I've got no ~ left** je n'ai plus d'argent, je n'ai plus un sou

money belt *n* ceinture-portefeuille *f*

moneyed ['mʌnɪd] *adj* riche

moneylender ['mʌnɪlɛndə'] *n* prêteur(-euse)

moneymaker ['mʌnɪmeɪkə'] *n* (*Brit: col: business*) affaire lucrative

moneymaking ['mʌnɪmeɪkɪŋ] *adj* lucratif(-ive), qui rapporte (de l'argent)

money market *n* marché financier

money order *n* mandat *m*

money-spinner ['mʌnɪspɪnə'] *n* (*inf*) mine *f* d'or (*fig*)

money supply *n* masse *f* monétaire

Mongol ['mɔŋgəl] *n* Mongol(e); (*Ling*) mongol *m*

mongol ['mɔŋgəl] *adj, n* (*Med*) mongolien(ne)

Mongolia [mɔŋ'gəulɪə] *n* Mongolie *f*

Mongolian [mɔŋ'gəulɪən] *adj* mongol(e) ▷ *n* Mongol(e); (*Ling*) mongol *m*

mongoose ['mɔŋguːs] *n* mangouste *f*

mongrel ['mʌŋgrəl] *n* (*dog*) bâtard *m*

monitor ['mɔnɪtə'] *n* (*TV, Comput*) écran *m*, moniteur *m*; (*Brit Scol*) chef *m* de classe; (*US Scol*) surveillant *m* (d'examen) ▷ *vt* contrôler; (*foreign station*) être à l'écoute de; (*progress*) suivre de près

monk [mʌŋk] *n* moine *m*

monkey ['mʌŋkɪ] *n* singe *m*

monkey nut *n* (*Brit*) cacahuète *f*

monkey wrench *n* clé *f* à molette

mono ['mɔnəu] *adj* mono *inv*

mono... ['mɔnəu] *prefix* mono...

monochrome ['mɔnəkrəum] *adj* monochrome

monocle ['mɔnəkl] *n* monocle *m*

monogamous [mɔ'nɔgəməs] *adj* monogame

monogamy [mɔ'nɔgəmɪ] *n* monogamie *f*

monogram ['mɔnəgræm] *n* monogramme *m*

monolith ['mɔnəlɪθ] *n* monolithe *m*

monologue ['mɔnəlɔg] *n* monologue *m*

monoplane ['mɔnəpleɪn] *n* monoplan *m*

monopolize [mə'nɔpəlaɪz] *vt* monopoliser

monopoly [mə'nɔpəlɪ] *n* monopole *m*;
Monopolies and Mergers Commission (*Brit*) *commission britannique d'enquête sur les monopoles*

monorail ['mɔnəureɪl] *n* monorail *m*

monosodium glutamate [mɔnə'səudɪəm 'gluːtəmeɪt] *n* glutamate *m* de sodium

monosyllabic [mɔnəsɪ'læbɪk] *adj* monosyllabique; (*person*) laconique

monosyllable ['mɔnəsɪləbl] *n* monosyllabe *m*

monotone ['mɔnətəun] *n* ton *m* (*or* voix *f*) monocorde; **to speak in a ~** parler sur un ton monocorde

monotonous [mə'nɔtənəs] *adj* monotone

monotony [mə'nɔtənɪ] *n* monotonie *f*

monoxide [mɔ'nɔksaɪd] *n*: **carbon ~** oxyde *m* de carbone

monsoon [mɔn'suːn] *n* mousson *f*

monster ['mɔnstə'] *n* monstre *m*

monstrosity [mɔns'trɔsɪtɪ] *n* monstruosité *f*, atrocité *f*

monstrous ['mɔnstrəs] *adj* (*huge*) gigantesque; (*atrocious*) monstrueux(-euse), atroce

Mont. *abbr* (*US*) = **Montana**

montage [mɔn'tɑːʒ] *n* montage *m*

Mont Blanc [mɔ̃blɑ̃] *n* Mont Blanc *m*

month [mʌnθ] *n* mois *m*; **every ~** tous les mois; **300 dollars a ~** 300 dollars par mois

monthly ['mʌnθlɪ] *adj* mensuel(le) ▷ *adv* mensuellement ▷ *n* (*magazine*) mensuel *m*, publication mensuelle; **twice ~** deux fois par mois

Montreal [mɔntrɪ'ɔːl] *n* Montréal

monument ['mɔnjumənt] *n* monument *m*

monumental [mɔnju'mɛntl] *adj* monumental(e)

monumental mason *n* marbrier *m*

moo [muː] *vi* meugler, beugler

mood [muːd] *n* humeur *f*, disposition *f*; **to be in a good/bad ~** être de bonne/mauvaise humeur; **to be in the ~ for** être d'humeur à, avoir envie de

moody ['muːdɪ] *adj* (*variable*) d'humeur changeante, lunatique; (*sullen*) morose, maussade

moon [muːn] *n* lune *f*

moonbeam ['muːnbiːm] *n* rayon *m* de lune

moon landing *n* alunissage *m*

moonlight ['muːnlaɪt] *n* clair *m* de lune ▷ *vi* travailler au noir

moonlighting ['muːnlaɪtɪŋ] *n* travail *m* au noir

moonlit ['muːnlɪt] *adj* éclairé(e) par la lune; **a ~ night** une nuit de lune

moonshot ['muːnʃɔt] *n* (*Space*) tir *m* lunaire

moonstruck ['muːnstrʌk] *adj* fou (folle), dérangé(e)

moony ['muːnɪ] *adj*: **to have ~ eyes** avoir l'air dans la lune *or* rêveur

Moor [muə'] *n* Maure (Mauresque)

moor [muə'] *n* lande *f* ▷ *vt* (*ship*) amarrer ▷ *vi* mouiller

moorings ['muərɪŋz] *npl* (*chains*) amarres *fpl*; (*place*) mouillage *m*

Moorish ['muərɪʃ] *adj* maure, mauresque

moorland ['muələnd] *n* lande *f*

moose [muːs] *n* (*pl inv*) élan *m*

moot [muːt] *vt* soulever ▷ *adj*: **~ point** point *m* discutable

mop [mɔp] *n* balai *m* à laver; (*for dishes*) lavette *f* à vaisselle ▷ *vt* éponger, essuyer; **~ of hair** tignasse *f*
▶ **mop up** *vt* éponger

mope [məup] *vi* avoir le cafard, se morfondre
▶ **mope about, mope around** *vi* broyer du noir, se morfondre

moped ['məupɛd] *n* cyclomoteur *m*

MOR *adj abbr* (*Mus*: = *middle-of-the-road*) tous publics

moral ['mɔrl] *adj* moral(e) ▷ *n* morale *f*; **morals** *npl* moralité *f*

morale [mɔ'rɑːl] *n* moral *m*

morality [mə'ræliti] *n* moralité *f*

moralize ['mɔrəlaiz] *vi*: **to ~ (about)** moraliser (sur)

morally ['mɔrəli] *adv* moralement

moral victory *n* victoire morale

morass [mə'ræs] *n* marais *m*, marécage *m*

moratorium [mɔrə'tɔːriəm] *n* moratoire *m*

morbid ['mɔːbid] *adj* morbide

○ KEYWORD

more [mɔːʳ] *adj* **1** (*greater in number etc*) plus (de), davantage (de); **more people/work (than)** plus de gens/de travail (que)
2 (*additional*) encore (de); **do you want (some) more tea?** voulez-vous encore du thé?; **is there any more wine?** reste-t-il du vin?; **I have no** *or* **I don't have any more money** je n'ai plus d'argent; **it'll take a few more weeks** ça prendra encore quelques semaines
▷ *pron* plus, davantage; **more than 10** plus de 10; **it cost more than we expected** cela a coûté plus que prévu; **I want more** j'en veux plus *or* davantage; **is there any more?** est-ce qu'il en reste?; **there's no more** il n'y en a plus; **a little more** un peu plus; **many/much more** beaucoup plus, bien davantage
▷ *adv* plus; **more dangerous/easily (than)** plus dangereux/facilement (que); **more and more expensive** de plus en plus cher; **more or less** plus ou moins; **more than ever** plus que jamais; **once more** encore une fois, une fois de plus; **and what's more ...** et de plus ..., et qui plus est ...

moreover [mɔː'rəuvəʳ] *adv* de plus

morgue [mɔːg] *n* morgue *f*

MORI ['mɔːri] *n abbr* (*Brit*: = *Market & Opinion Research Institute*) institut de sondage

moribund ['mɔribʌnd] *adj* moribond(e)

morning ['mɔːniŋ] *n* matin *m*; (*as duration*) matinée *f* ▷ *cpd* matinal(e); (*paper*) du matin; **in the ~** le matin; **7 o'clock in the ~** 7 heures du matin; **this ~** ce matin

morning-after pill ['mɔːniŋ'ɑːftə-] *n* pilule *f* du lendemain

morning sickness *n* nausées matinales

Moroccan [mə'rɔkən] *adj* marocain(e) ▷ *n*

Marocain(e)

Morocco [mə'rɔkəu] *n* Maroc *m*

moron ['mɔːrɔn] *n* idiot(e), minus *m/f*

moronic [mə'rɔnik] *adj* idiot(e), imbécile

morose [mə'rəus] *adj* morose, maussade

morphine ['mɔːfiːn] *n* morphine *f*

morris dancing ['mɔris-] *n* (*Brit*) danses folkloriques anglaises

Morse [mɔːs] *n* (*also*: **Morse code**) morse *m*

morsel ['mɔːsl] *n* bouchée *f*

mortal ['mɔːtl] *adj, n* mortel(le)

mortality [mɔː'tæliti] *n* mortalité *f*

mortality rate *n* (taux *m* de) mortalité *f*

mortar ['mɔːtəʳ] *n* mortier *m*

mortgage ['mɔːgidʒ] *n* hypothèque *f*; (*loan*) prêt *m* (*or* crédit *m*) hypothécaire ▷ *vt* hypothéquer; **to take out a ~** prendre une hypothèque, faire un emprunt

mortgage company *n* (*US*) société *f* de crédit immobilier

mortgagee [mɔːgə'dʒiː] *n* prêteur(-euse) (sur hypothèque)

mortgagor ['mɔːgədʒəʳ] *n* emprunteur(-euse) (sur hypothèque)

mortician [mɔː'tiʃən] *n* (*US*) entrepreneur *m* de pompes funèbres

mortified ['mɔːtifaid] *adj* mort(e) de honte

mortise lock ['mɔːtis-] *n* serrure encastrée

mortuary ['mɔːtjuəri] *n* morgue *f*

mosaic [məu'zeiik] *n* mosaïque *f*

Moscow ['mɔskəu] *n* Moscou

Moslem ['mɔzləm] *adj, n* = **Muslim**

mosque [mɔsk] *n* mosquée *f*

mosquito (*pl* **-es**) [mɔs'kiːtəu] *n* moustique *m*

mosquito net *n* moustiquaire *f*

moss [mɔs] *n* mousse *f*

mossy ['mɔsi] *adj* moussu(e)

most [məust] *adj* (*majority of*) la plupart de; (*greatest amount of*) le plus de ▷ *pron* la plupart ▷ *adv* le plus; (*very*) très, extrêmement; **the ~** plus; **~ fish** la plupart des poissons; **the ~ beautiful woman in the world** la plus belle femme du monde; **~ of** (*with plural*) la plupart de; (*with singular*) la plus grande partie de; **~ of them** la plupart d'entre eux; **~ of the time** la plupart du temps; **I saw ~** (*a lot but not all*) j'en ai vu la plupart; (*more than anyone else*) c'est moi qui en ai vu le plus; **at the (very)** ~ au plus; **to make the ~ of** profiter au maximum de

mostly ['məustli] *adv* (*chiefly*) surtout, principalement; (*usually*) généralement

MOT *n abbr* (*Brit*) = **Ministry of Transport**; **the ~ (test)** visite technique (annuelle) obligatoire des véhicules à moteur

motel [məu'tɛl] *n* motel *m*

moth [mɔθ] *n* papillon *m* de nuit; (*in clothes*) mite *f*

mothball ['mɔθbɔːl] *n* boule *f* de naphtaline

moth-eaten ['mɔθiːtn] *adj* mité(e)

mother ['mʌðəʳ] *n* mère *f* ▷ *vt* (*pamper, protect*) dorloter

mother board *n* (*Comput*) carte-mère *f*

motherhood ['mʌðəhud] *n* maternité *f*
mother-in-law ['mʌðərɪnlɔ:] *n* belle-mère *f*
motherly ['mʌðəlɪ] *adj* maternel(le)
mother-of-pearl ['mʌðərəv'pə:l] *n* nacre *f*
Mother's Day *n* fête *f* des Mères
mother's help *n* aide *f* or auxiliaire *f* familiale
mother-to-be ['mʌðətə'bi:] *n* future maman
mother tongue *n* langue maternelle
mothproof ['mɔθpru:f] *adj* traité(e) à l'antimite
motif [məu'ti:f] *n* motif *m*
motion ['məuʃən] *n* mouvement *m*; (*gesture*)
geste *m*; (*at meeting*) motion *f*; (*Brit: also:* **bowel
motion**) selles *fpl* ▷ *vt, vi:* **to ~ (to) sb to do** faire
signe à qn de faire; **to be in ~** (*vehicle*) être en
marche; **to set in ~** mettre en marche; **to go
through the ~s of doing sth** (*fig*) faire qch
machinalement or sans conviction
motionless ['məuʃənlɪs] *adj* immobile, sans
mouvement
motion picture *n* film *m*
motivate ['məutɪveɪt] *vt* motiver
motivated ['məutɪveɪtɪd] *adj* motivé(e)
motivation [məutɪ'veɪʃən] *n* motivation *f*
motive ['məutɪv] *n* motif *m*, mobile *m* ▷ *adj*
moteur(-trice); **from the best (of) ~s** avec les
meilleures intentions (du monde)
motley ['mɔtlɪ] *adj* hétéroclite; bigarré(e),
bariolé(e)
motor ['məutə'] *n* moteur *m*; (*Brit inf: vehicle*)
auto *f* ▷ *adj* moteur(-trice)
motorbike ['məutəbaɪk] *n* moto *f*
motorboat ['məutəbəut] *n* bateau *m* à moteur
motorcade ['məutəkeɪd] *n* cortège *m*
d'automobiles or de voitures
motorcar ['məutəka:] *n* (*Brit*) automobile *f*
motorcoach ['məutəkəutʃ] *n* (*Brit*) car *m*
motorcycle ['məutəsaɪkl] *n* moto *f*
motorcycle racing *n* course *f* de motos
motorcyclist ['məutəsaɪklɪst] *n* motocycliste
m/f
motoring ['məutərɪŋ] (*Brit*) *n* tourisme *m*
automobile ▷ *adj* (*accident*) de voiture, de la
route; **~ holiday** vacances *fpl* en voiture; **~
offence** infraction *f* au code de la route
motorist ['məutərɪst] *n* automobiliste *m/f*
motorize ['məutəraɪz] *vt* motoriser
motor mechanic *n* mécanicien *m* garagiste
motor oil *n* huile *f* de graissage
motor racing *n* (*Brit*) course *f* automobile
motor scooter *n* scooter *m*
motor trade *n* secteur *m* de l'automobile
motor vehicle *n* véhicule *m* automobile
motorway ['məutəweɪ] *n* (*Brit*) autoroute *f*
mottled ['mɔtld] *adj* tacheté(e), marbré(e)
motto (*pl* **-es**) ['mɔtəu] *n* devise *f*
mould, (*US*) **mold** [məuld] *n* moule *m*; (*mildew*)
moisissure *f* ▷ *vt* mouler, modeler; (*fig*)
façonner
moulder, (*US*) **molder** ['məuldə'] *vi* (*decay*)
moisir
moulding, (*US*) **mold** ['məuldɪŋ] *n* (*Archit*)
moulure *f*

mouldy, (*US*) **moldy** ['məuldɪ] *adj* moisi(e);
(*smell*) de moisi
moult, (*US*) **molt** [məult] *vi* muer
mound [maund] *n* monticule *m*, tertre *m*
mount [maunt] *n* (*hill*) mont *m*, montagne *f*;
(*horse*) monture *f*; (*for picture*) carton *m* de
montage; (*for jewel etc*) monture ▷ *vt* monter;
(*horse*) monter à; (*bike*) monter sur; (*exhibition*)
organiser, monter; (*picture*) monter sur carton;
(*stamp*) coller dans un album ▷ *vi* (*inflation,
tension*) augmenter
  ▸ **mount up** *vi* s'élever, monter; (*bills, problems,
  savings*) s'accumuler
mountain ['mauntɪn] *n* montagne *f* ▷ *cpd* de
(la) montagne; **to make a ~ out of a molehill**
(*fig*) se faire une montagne d'un rien
mountain bike *n* VTT *m*, vélo *m* tout terrain
mountaineer [mauntɪ'nɪə'] *n* alpiniste *m/f*
mountaineering [mauntɪ'nɪərɪŋ] *n* alpinisme
m; **to go ~** faire de l'alpinisme
mountainous ['mauntɪnəs] *adj*
montagneux(-euse)
mountain range *n* chaîne *f* de montagnes
mountain rescue team *n* colonne *f* de secours
mountainside ['mauntɪnsaɪd] *n* flanc *m* or
versant *m* de la montagne
mounted ['mauntɪd] *adj* monté(e)
mourn [mɔ:n] *vt* pleurer ▷ *vi:* **to ~ for sb** pleurer
qn; **to ~ for sth** se lamenter sur qch
mourner ['mɔ:nə'] *n* parent(e) or ami(e) du
défunt; personne *f* en deuil or venue rendre
hommage au défunt
mourning ['mɔ:nɪŋ] *n* deuil *m* ▷ *cpd* (*dress*) de
deuil; **in ~** en deuil
mouse (*pl* **mice**) [maus, maɪs] *n* (*also Comput*)
souris *f*
mouse mat *n* (*Comput*) tapis *m* de souris
mousetrap ['maustræp] *n* souricière *f*
moussaka [mu'sɑ:kə] *n* moussaka *f*
mousse [mu:s] *n* mousse *f*
moustache, (*US*) **mustache** [məs'tɑ:ʃ] *n*
moustache(s) *f(pl)*
mousy ['mausɪ] *adj* (*person*) effacé(e); (*hair*) d'un
châtain terne
mouth [mauθ, *pl* mauðz] *n* bouche *f*; (*of dog, cat*)
gueule *f*; (*of river*) embouchure *f*; (*of hole, cave*)
ouverture *f*; (*of bottle*) goulot *m*; (*opening*)
orifice *m*
mouthful ['mauθful] *n* bouchée *f*
mouth organ *n* harmonica *m*
mouthpiece ['mauθpi:s] *n* (*of musical instrument*)
bec *m*, embouchure *f*; (*spokesperson*) porte-parole
m inv
mouth-to-mouth ['mauθtə'mauθ] *adj:* **~
resuscitation** bouche à bouche *m*
mouthwash ['mauθwɔʃ] *n* eau *f* dentifrice
mouth-watering ['mauθwɔ:tərɪŋ] *adj* qui met
l'eau à la bouche
movable ['mu:vəbl] *adj* mobile
move [mu:v] *n* (*movement*) mouvement *m*; (*in
game*) coup *m*; (*: turn to play*) tour *m*; (*change of
house*) déménagement *m*; (*change of job*)

changement *m* d'emploi ▷ *vt* déplacer, bouger; (*emotionally*) émouvoir; (*Pol: resolution etc*) proposer ▷ *vi* (*gen*) bouger, remuer; (*traffic*) circuler; (*also:* **move house**) déménager; (*in game*) jouer; **can you ~ your car, please?** pouvez-vous déplacer votre voiture, s'il vous plaît?; **to ~ towards** se diriger vers; **to ~ sb to do sth** pousser *or* inciter qn à faire qch; **to get a ~ on** se dépêcher, se remuer

▸ **move about, move around** *vi* (*fidget*) remuer; (*travel*) voyager, se déplacer

▸ **move along** *vi* se pousser

▸ **move away** *vi* s'en aller, s'éloigner

▸ **move back** *vi* revenir, retourner

▸ **move forward** *vi* avancer ▷ *vt* avancer; (*people*) faire avancer

▸ **move in** *vi* (*to a house*) emménager; (*police, soldiers*) intervenir

▸ **move off** *vi* s'éloigner, s'en aller

▸ **move on** *vi* se remettre en route ▷ *vt* (*onlookers*) faire circuler

▸ **move out** *vi* (*of house*) déménager

▸ **move over** *vi* se pousser, se déplacer

▸ **move up** *vi* avancer; (*employee*) avoir de l'avancement; (*pupil*) passer dans la classe supérieure

moveable [muːvəbl] *adj* = **movable**

movement ['muːvmənt] *n* mouvement *m*; **~ (of the bowels)** (*Med*) selles *fpl*

mover ['muːvəʳ] *n* auteur *m* d'une proposition

movie ['muːvɪ] *n* film *m*; **movies** *npl*: **the ~s** le cinéma

movie camera *n* caméra *f*

moviegoer ['muːvɪɡəuəʳ] *n* (*US*) cinéphile *m/f*

movie theater (*US*) *n* cinéma *m*

moving ['muːvɪŋ] *adj* en mouvement; (*touching*) émouvant(e) ▷ *n* (*US*) déménagement *m*

mow (*pt* **-ed**, *pp* **-ed** *or* **-n**) [məu, -d, -n] *vt* faucher; (*lawn*) tondre

▸ **mow down** *vt* faucher

mower ['məuəʳ] *n* (*also:* **lawnmower**) tondeuse *f* à gazon

mown [məun] *pp of* **mow**

Mozambique [məuzəm'biːk] *n* Mozambique *m*

MP *n abbr* (= *Military Police*) PM; (*Brit*) = **Member of Parliament**; (*Canada*) = **Mounted Police**

MP3 *n* mp3 *m*

MP3 player *n* baladeur *m* numérique, lecteur *m* mp3

mpg *n abbr* (= *miles per gallon*) (*30 mpg = 9,4 l. aux 100 km*)

m.p.h. *abbr* (= *miles per hour*) (*60 mph = 96 km/h*)

MPhil *n abbr* (*US*: = *Master of Philosophy*) *titre universitaire*

MPS *n abbr* (*Brit*) = **Member of the Pharmaceutical Society**

Mr, (*US*) **Mr.** ['mɪstəʳ] *n*: **Mr X** Monsieur X, M. X

MRC *n abbr* (*Brit*: = *Medical Research Council*) *conseil de la recherche médicale*

MRCP *n abbr* (*Brit*) = **Member of the Royal College of Physicians**

MRCS *n abbr* (*Brit*) = **Member of the Royal College of Surgeons**

MRCVS *n abbr* (*Brit*) = **Member of the Royal College of Veterinary Surgeons**

Mrs, (*US*) **Mrs.** ['mɪsɪz] *n*: **~ X** Madame X, Mme X

MS *n abbr* (= *manuscript*) ms; (= *multiple sclerosis*) SEP *f*; (*US*: = *Master of Science*) *titre universitaire* ▷ *abbr* (*US*) = **Mississippi**

Ms, (*US*) **Ms.** [mɪz] *n* (*Miss or Mrs*): **Ms X** Madame X, Mme X; *voir article*

● **M s**

Ms est un titre utilisé à la place de "Mrs" (Mme) ou de "Miss" (Mlle) pour éviter la distinction traditionnelle entre femmes mariées et femmes non mariées.

MSA *n abbr* (*US*: = *Master of Science in Agriculture*) *titre universitaire*

MSc *n abbr* = **Master of Science**

MSG *n abbr* = **monosodium glutamate**

MSP *n abbr* (= *Member of the Scottish Parliament*) député *m* au Parlement écossais

MST *abbr* (*US*: = *Mountain Standard Time*) *heure d'hiver des Montagnes Rocheuses*

MT *n abbr* (= *machine translation*) TM ▷ *abbr* (*US*) = **Montana**

Mt *abbr* (*Geo*: = *mount*) Mt

mth *abbr* (= *month*) m

MTV *n abbr* = **music television**

much [mʌtʃ] *adj* beaucoup de ▷ *adv, n or pron* beaucoup; **~ milk** beaucoup de lait; **we don't have ~ time** nous n'avons pas beaucoup de temps; **how ~ is it?** combien est-ce que ça coûte?; **it's not ~** ce n'est pas beaucoup; **too ~** trop (de); **so ~** tant (de); **I like it very/so ~** j'aime beaucoup/tellement ça; **as ~ as** autant de; **thank you very ~** merci beaucoup; **that's ~ better** c'est beaucoup mieux; **~ to my amazement ...** à mon grand étonnement ...

muck [mʌk] *n* (*mud*) boue *f*; (*dirt*) ordures *fpl*

▸ **muck about** *vi* (*inf*) faire l'imbécile; (: *waste time*) traînasser; (: *tinker*) bricoler; tripoter

▸ **muck in** *vi* (*Brit inf*) donner un coup de main

▸ **muck out** *vt* (*stable*) nettoyer

▸ **muck up** *vt* (*inf: ruin*) gâcher, esquinter; (: *dirty*) salir; (: *exam, interview*) se planter à

muckraking ['mʌkreɪkɪŋ] *n* (*fig: inf*) déterrement *m* d'ordures

mucky ['mʌkɪ] *adj* (*dirty*) boueux(-euse), sale

mucus ['mjuːkəs] *n* mucus *m*

mud [mʌd] *n* boue *f*

muddle ['mʌdl] *n* (*mess*) pagaille *f*, fouillis *m*; (*mix-up*) confusion *f* ▷ *vt* (*also:* **muddle up**) brouiller, embrouiller; **to be in a ~** (*person*) ne plus savoir où l'on en est; **to get in a ~** (*while explaining etc*) s'embrouiller

▸ **muddle along** *vi* aller son chemin tant bien que mal

▸ **muddle through** *vi* se débrouiller

muddle-headed [mʌdl'hɛdɪd] *adj* (*person*) à l'esprit embrouillé *or* confus, dans le brouillard

m

muddy ['mʌdɪ] *adj* boueux(-euse)

mud flats *npl* plage *f* de vase

mudguard ['mʌdgɑːd] *n* garde-boue *m inv*

mudpack ['mʌdpæk] *n* masque *m* de beauté

mud-slinging ['mʌdslɪŋɪŋ] *n* médisance *f*, dénigrement *m*

muesli ['mjuːzlɪ] *n* muesli *m*

muff [mʌf] *n* manchon *m* ▷ *vt* (*inf: shot, catch etc*) rater, louper; **to ~ it** rater *or* louper son coup

muffin ['mʌfɪn] *n* (*roll*) petit pain rond et plat; (*cake*) petit gâteau au chocolat ou aux fruits

muffle ['mʌfl] *vt* (*sound*) assourdir, étouffer; (*against cold*) emmitoufler

muffled ['mʌfld] *adj* étouffé(e), voilé(e)

muffler ['mʌflə^r] *n* (*scarf*) cache-nez *m inv*; (*US Aut*) silencieux *m*

mufti ['mʌftɪ] *n*: **in ~** en civil

mug [mʌg] *n* (*cup*) tasse *f* (*sans soucoupe*); (*: for beer*) chope *f*; (*inf: face*) bouille *f*; (*: fool*) poire *f* ▷ *vt* (*assault*) agresser; **it's a ~'s game** (*Brit*) c'est bon pour les imbéciles

▶ **mug up** *vt* (*Brit inf: also*: **mug up on**) bosser, bûcher

mugger ['mʌgə^r] *n* agresseur *m*

mugging ['mʌgɪŋ] *n* agression *f*

muggins ['mʌgɪnz] *n* (*inf*) ma pomme

muggy ['mʌgɪ] *adj* lourd(e), moite

mug shot *n* (*inf: Police*) photo *f* de criminel; (*: gen: photo*) photo d'identité

mulatto (*pl* -**es**) [mjuː'lætəu] *n* mulâtre(-esse)

mulberry ['mʌlbrɪ] *n* (*fruit*) mûre *f*; (*tree*) mûrier *m*

mule [mjuːl] *n* mule *f*

mull [mʌl]: **to ~ over** *vt* réfléchir à, ruminer

mulled [mʌld] *adj*: **~ wine** vin chaud

multi... ['mʌltɪ] *prefix* multi...

multi-access ['mʌltɪ'ækses] *adj* (*Comput*) à accès multiple

multicoloured, (*US*) **multicolored** ['mʌltɪkʌləd] *adj* multicolore

multifarious [mʌltɪ'fɛərɪəs] *adj* divers(es), varié(e)

multilateral [mʌltɪ'lætərl] *adj* (*Pol*) multilatéral(e)

multi-level ['mʌltɪlɛvl] *adj* (*US*) = **multistorey**

multimedia ['mʌltɪ'miːdɪə] *adj* multimédia *inv*

multimillionaire [mʌltɪmɪljə'nɛə^r] *n* milliardaire *m/f*

multinational [mʌltɪ'næʃənl] *n* multinationale *f* ▷ *adj* multinational(e)

multiple ['mʌltɪpl] *adj* multiple ▷ *n* multiple *m*; (*Brit: also*: **multiple store**) magasin *m* à succursales (multiples)

multiple choice, multiple choice test *n* QCM *m*, questionnaire *m* à choix multiple

multiple crash *n* carambolage *m*

multiple sclerosis [-sklɪ'rəusɪs] *n* sclérose *f* en plaques

multiplex ['mʌltɪplɛks], **multiplex cinema** *n* (cinéma *m*) multisalles *m*

multiplication [mʌltɪplɪ'keɪʃən] *n* multiplication *f*

multiplication table *n* table *f* de multiplication

multiplicity [mʌltɪ'plɪsɪtɪ] *n* multiplicité *f*

multiply ['mʌltɪplaɪ] *vt* multiplier ▷ *vi* se multiplier

multiracial [mʌltɪ'reɪʃl] *adj* multiracial(e)

multistorey ['mʌltɪ'stɔːrɪ] *adj* (*Brit: building*) à étages; (*: car park*) à étages *or* niveaux multiples

multitude ['mʌltɪtjuːd] *n* multitude *f*

mum [mʌm] *n* (*Brit*) maman *f* ▷ *adj*: **to keep ~** ne pas souffler mot; **~'s the word!** motus et bouche cousue!

mumble ['mʌmbl] *vt, vi* marmotter, marmonner

mumbo jumbo ['mʌmbəu-] *n* (*inf*) baragouin *m*, charabia *m*

mummify ['mʌmɪfaɪ] *vt* momifier

mummy ['mʌmɪ] *n* (*Brit: mother*) maman *f*; (*embalmed*) momie *f*

mumps [mʌmps] *n* oreillons *mpl*

munch [mʌntʃ] *vt, vi* mâcher

mundane [mʌn'deɪn] *adj* banal(e), terre à terre *inv*

municipal [mjuː'nɪsɪpl] *adj* municipal(e)

municipality [mjuːnɪsɪ'pælɪtɪ] *n* municipalité *f*

munitions [mjuː'nɪʃənz] *npl* munitions *fpl*

mural ['mjuərl] *n* peinture murale

murder ['məːdə^r] *n* meurtre *m*, assassinat *m* ▷ *vt* assassiner; **to commit ~** commettre un meurtre

murderer ['məːdərə^r] *n* meurtrier *m*, assassin *m*

murderess ['məːdərɪs] *n* meurtrière *f*

murderous ['məːdərəs] *adj* meurtrier(-ière)

murk [məːk] *n* obscurité *f*

murky ['məːkɪ] *adj* sombre, ténébreux(-euse); (*water*) trouble

murmur ['məːmə^r] *n* murmure *m* ▷ *vt, vi* murmurer; **heart ~** (*Med*) souffle *m* au cœur

MusB, MusBac *n abbr* (= *Bachelor of Music*) titre universitaire

muscle ['mʌsl] *n* muscle *m*; (*fig*) force *f*

▶ **muscle in** *vi* s'imposer, s'immiscer

muscular ['mʌskjulə^r] *adj* musculaire; (*person, arm*) musclé(e)

muscular dystrophy *n* dystrophie *f* musculaire

MusD, MusDoc *n abbr* (= *Doctor of Music*) titre universitaire

muse [mjuːz] *vi* méditer, songer ▷ *n* muse *f*

museum [mjuː'zɪəm] *n* musée *m*

mush [mʌʃ] *n* bouillie *f*; (*pej*) sentimentalité *f* à l'eau de rose

mushroom ['mʌʃrum] *n* champignon *m* ▷ *vi* (*fig*) pousser comme un (*or* des) champignon(s)

mushy ['mʌʃɪ] *adj* (*vegetables, fruit*) en bouillie; (*movie etc*) à l'eau de rose

music ['mjuːzɪk] *n* musique *f*

musical ['mjuːzɪkl] *adj* musical(e); (*person*) musicien(ne) ▷ *n* (*show*) comédie musicale

musical box *n* = **music box**

musical chairs *npl* chaises musicales; (*fig*): **to play ~** faire des permutations

musical instrument *n* instrument *m* de musique

music box n boîte f à musique
music centre n chaîne compacte
music hall n music-hall m
musician [mjuːˈzɪʃən] n musicien(ne)
music stand n pupitre m à musique
musk [mʌsk] n musc m
musket [ˈmʌskɪt] n mousquet m
muskrat [ˈmʌskræt] n rat musqué
musk rose n (Bot) rose f muscade
Muslim [ˈmʌzlɪm] adj, n musulman(e)
muslin [ˈmʌzlɪn] n mousseline f
musquash [ˈmʌskwɔʃ] n loutre f; (fur) rat m
d'Amérique, ondatra m
mussel [ˈmʌsl] n moule f
must [mʌst] aux vb (obligation): **I ~ do it** je dois le
faire, il faut que je le fasse; (probability): **he ~ be
there by now** il doit y être maintenant, il y est
probablement maintenant; (suggestion,
invitation): **you ~ come and see me** il faut que
vous veniez me voir ▷ n nécessité f, impératif
m; **it's a ~** c'est indispensable; **I ~ have made a
mistake** j'ai dû me tromper
mustache [ˈmʌstæʃ] n (US) = **moustache**
mustard [ˈmʌstəd] n moutarde f
mustard gas n ypérite f, gaz m moutarde
muster [ˈmʌstəʳ] vt rassembler; (also: **muster
up**: strength, courage) rassembler
mustiness [ˈmʌstɪnɪs] n goût m de moisi;
odeur f de moisi or de renfermé
mustn't [ˈmʌsnt] = **must not**
musty [ˈmʌstɪ] adj qui sent le moisi or le
renfermé
mutant [ˈmjuːtənt] adj mutant(e) ▷ n mutant m
mutate [mjuːˈteɪt] vi subir une mutation
mutation [mjuːˈteɪʃən] n mutation f
mute [mjuːt] adj, n muet(te)
muted [ˈmjuːtɪd] adj (noise) sourd(e), assourdi(e);
(criticism) voilé(e); (Mus) en sourdine; (: trumpet)
bouché(e)
mutilate [ˈmjuːtɪleɪt] vt mutiler

mutilation [mjuːtɪˈleɪʃən] n mutilation f
mutinous [ˈmjuːtɪnəs] adj (troops) mutiné(e);
(attitude) rebelle
mutiny [ˈmjuːtɪnɪ] n mutinerie f ▷ vi se
mutiner
mutter [ˈmʌtəʳ] vt, vi marmonner, marmotter
mutton [ˈmʌtn] n mouton m
mutual [ˈmjuːtʃuəl] adj mutuel(le), réciproque;
(benefit, interest) commun(e)
mutually [ˈmjuːtʃuəlɪ] adv mutuellement,
réciproquement
Muzak® [ˈmjuːzæk] n (often pej) musique f
d'ambiance
muzzle [ˈmʌzl] n museau m; (protective device)
muselière f; (of gun) gueule f ▷ vt museler
MVP n abbr (US Sport) = **most valuable player**
MW abbr (= medium wave) PO
my [maɪ] adj mon (ma), mes pl; **my house/car/
gloves** ma maison/ma voiture/mes gants; **I've
washed my hair/cut my finger** je me suis lavé
les cheveux/coupé le doigt; **is this my pen or
yours?** c'est mon stylo ou c'est le vôtre?
Myanmar [ˈmaɪænmɑːʳ] n Myanmar m
myopic [maɪˈɔpɪk] adj myope
myriad [ˈmɪrɪəd] n myriade f
myself [maɪˈself] pron (reflexive) me; (emphatic)
moi-même; (after prep) moi; see also **oneself**
mysterious [mɪsˈtɪərɪəs] adj mystérieux(-euse)
mystery [ˈmɪstərɪ] n mystère m
mystery story n roman m à suspense
mystic [ˈmɪstɪk] n mystique m/f ▷ adj (mysterious)
ésotérique
mystical [ˈmɪstɪkl] adj mystique
mystify [ˈmɪstɪfaɪ] vt (deliberately) mystifier;
(puzzle) ébahir
mystique [mɪsˈtiːk] n mystique f
myth [mɪθ] n mythe m
mythical [ˈmɪθɪkl] adj mythique
mythological [mɪθəˈlɔdʒɪkl] adj mythologique
mythology [mɪˈθɔlədʒɪ] n mythologie f

m

Nn

N, n [ɛn] *n* (*letter*) N, n *m*; **N for Nellie**, (US) **N for Nan** N comme Nicolas

N *abbr* (= *north*) N

NA *n abbr* (US: = *Narcotics Anonymous*) association d'aide aux drogués; (US) = **National Academy**

n/a *abbr* (= *not applicable*) n.a.; (*Comm etc*) = **no account**

NAACP *n abbr* (US) = **National Association for the Advancement of Colored People**

NAAFI ['næfɪ] *n abbr* (Brit: = *Navy, Army & Air Force Institute*) *organisme responsable des magasins et cantines de l'armée*

nab [næb] *vt* (*inf*) pincer, attraper

NACU *n abbr* (US) = **National Association of Colleges and Universities**

nadir ['neɪdɪər] *n* (*Astronomy*) nadir *m*; (*fig*) fond *m*, point *m* extrême

naff [næf] (Brit: *inf*) *adj* nul(le)

nag [næg] *vt* (*scold*) être toujours après, reprendre sans arrêt ▷ *n* (*pej: horse*) canasson *m*; (*person*): **she's an awful ~** elle est constamment après lui (*or eux etc*), elle est très casse-pieds

nagging ['nægɪŋ] *adj* (*doubt, pain*) persistant(e) ▷ *n* remarques continuelles

nail [neɪl] *n* (*human*) ongle *m*; (*metal*) clou *m* ▷ *vt* clouer; **to ~ sth to sth** clouer qch à qch; **to ~ sb down to a date/price** contraindre qn à accepter *or* donner une date/un prix; **to pay cash on the ~** (Brit) payer rubis sur l'ongle

nailbrush ['neɪlbrʌʃ] *n* brosse *f* à ongles

nailfile ['neɪlfaɪl] *n* lime *f* à ongles

nail polish *n* vernis *m* à ongles

nail polish remover *n* dissolvant *m*

nail scissors *npl* ciseaux *mpl* à ongles

nail varnish *n* (Brit) = **nail polish**

Nairobi [naɪ'rəubɪ] *n* Nairobi

naïve [naɪ'iːv] *adj* naïf(-ïve)

naïveté [naɪ'iːvteɪ], **naivety** [naɪ'iːvɪtɪ] *n* naïveté *f*

naked ['neɪkɪd] *adj* nu(e); **with the ~ eye** à l'œil nu

nakedness ['neɪkɪdnɪs] *n* nudité *f*

NAM *n abbr* (US) = **National Association of Manufacturers**

name [neɪm] *n* nom *m*; (*reputation*) réputation *f* ▷ *vt* nommer; (*identify: accomplice etc*) citer; (*price,*

date) fixer, donner; **by ~** par son nom; de nom; **in the ~ of** au nom de; **what's your ~?** comment vous appelez-vous?, quel est votre nom?; **my ~ is Peter** je m'appelle Peter; **to take sb's ~ and address** relever l'identité de qn *or* les nom et adresse de qn; **to make a ~ for o.s.** se faire un nom; **to get (o.s.) a bad ~** se faire une mauvaise réputation; **to call sb ~s** traiter qn de tous les noms

name dropping *n* mention (*pour se faire valoir*) *du nom de personnalités qu'on connaît (ou prétend connaître*)

nameless ['neɪmlɪs] *adj* sans nom; (*witness, contributor*) anonyme

namely ['neɪmlɪ] *adv* à savoir

nameplate ['neɪmpleɪt] *n* (*on door etc*) plaque *f*

namesake ['neɪmseɪk] *n* homonyme *m*

nan bread [nɑːn-] *n* nan *m*

nanny ['nænɪ] *n* bonne *f* d'enfants

nanny goat *n* chèvre *f*

nap [næp] *n* (*sleep*) (petit) somme ▷ *vi*: **to be caught ~ping** être pris(e) à l'improviste *or* en défaut

NAPA *n abbr* (US: = *National Association of Performing Artists*) *syndicat des gens du spectacle*

napalm ['neɪpɑːm] *n* napalm *m*

nape [neɪp] *n*: **~ of the neck** nuque *f*

napkin ['næpkɪn] *n* serviette *f* (de table)

Naples ['neɪplz] *n* Naples

Napoleonic [nəpəulɪ'ɔnɪk] *adj* napoléonien(ne)

nappy ['næpɪ] *n* (Brit) couche *f*

nappy liner *n* (Brit) protège-couche *m*

nappy rash *n*: **to have ~** avoir les fesses rouges

narcissistic [nɑːsɪ'sɪstɪk] *adj* narcissique

narcissus (*pl* **narcissi**) [nɑː'sɪsəs, -saɪ] *n* narcisse *m*

narcotic [nɑː'kɔtɪk] *n* (*Med*) narcotique *m*

narcotics [nɑː'kɔtɪkz] *npl* (*illegal drugs*) stupéfiants *mpl*

nark [nɑːk] *vt* (Brit *inf*) mettre en rogne

narrate [nə'reɪt] *vt* raconter, narrer

narration [nə'reɪʃən] *n* narration *f*

narrative ['nærətɪv] *n* récit *m* ▷ *adj* narratif(-ive)

narrator [nə'reɪtər] *n* narrateur(-trice)

narrow ['nærəu] *adj* étroit(e); (*fig*) restreint(e),

limité(e) ▷ *vi* (*road*) devenir plus étroit, se
rétrécir; (*gap, difference*) se réduire; **to have a ~**
escape l'échapper belle
▶ **narrow down** *vt* restreindre
narrow gauge *adj* (*Rail*) à voie étroite
narrowly ['nærəʊlɪ] *adv*: **he ~ missed injury/**
the tree il a failli se blesser/rentrer dans
l'arbre; **he only ~ missed the target** il a
manqué la cible de peu *or* de justesse
narrow-minded [nærəʊ'maɪndɪd] *adj* à l'esprit
étroit, borné(e); (*attitude*) borné(e)
NAS *n abbr* (*US*) = **National Academy of Sciences**
NASA ['næsə] *n abbr* (*US*: = *National Aeronautics and
Space Administration*) NASA *f*
nasal ['neɪzl] *adj* nasal(e)
Nassau ['næsɔ:] *n* (*in Bahamas*) Nassau
nastily ['nɑ:stɪlɪ] *adv* (*say, act*) méchamment
nastiness ['nɑ:stɪnɪs] *n* (*of person, remark*)
méchanceté *f*
nasturtium [nəs'tə:ʃəm] *n* capucine *f*
nasty ['nɑ:stɪ] *adj* (*person: malicious*) méchant(e);
(: *rude*) très désagréable; (*smell*) dégoûtant(e);
(*wound, situation*) mauvais(e), vilain(e); (*weather*)
affreux(-euse); **to turn ~** (*situation*) mal tourner;
(*weather*) se gâter; (*person*) devenir méchant; **it's**
a ~ business c'est une sale affaire
NAS/UWT *n abbr* (*Brit*: = *National Association of
Schoolmasters/Union of Women Teachers*) *syndicat
enseignant*
nation ['neɪʃən] *n* nation *f*
national ['næʃənl] *adj* national(e) ▷ *n* (*abroad*)
ressortissant(e); (*when home*) national(e)
national anthem *n* hymne national
National Curriculum *n* (*Brit*) *programme scolaire
commun à toutes les écoles publiques en Angleterre et au
Pays de Galles comprenant dix disciplines*
national debt *n* dette publique
national dress *n* costume national
National Guard *n* (*US*) milice *f* (*de volontaires*)
National Health Service *n* (*Brit*) *service national
de santé*, ≈ Sécurité Sociale
National Insurance *n* (*Brit*) ≈ Sécurité Sociale
nationalism ['næʃnəlɪzəm] *n* nationalisme *m*
nationalist ['næʃnəlɪst] *adj, n* nationaliste *m/f*
nationality [næʃə'nælɪtɪ] *n* nationalité *f*
nationalization [næʃnəlaɪ'zeɪʃən] *n*
nationalisation *f*
nationalize ['næʃnəlaɪz] *vt* nationaliser
nationally ['næʃnəlɪ] *adv* du point de vue
national; dans le pays entier
national park *n* parc national
national press *n* presse nationale
National Security Council *n* (*US*) conseil
national de sécurité
national service *n* (*Mil*) service *m* militaire
National Trust *n* (*Brit*) ≈ Caisse *f* nationale des
monuments historiques et des sites; *voir article*

nationwide ['neɪʃənwaɪd] *adj* s'étendant à
l'ensemble du pays; (*problem*) à l'échelle du pays
entier ▷ *adv* à travers *or* dans tout le pays
native ['neɪtɪv] *n* habitant(e) du pays,
autochtone *m/f*; (*in colonies*) indigène *m/f* ▷ *adj*
du pays, indigène; (*country*) natal(e); (*language*)
maternel(le); (*ability*) inné(e); **a ~ of Russia** une
personne originaire de Russie; **a ~ speaker of**
French une personne de langue maternelle
française
Native American *n* Indien(ne) d'Amérique
▷ *adj* amérindien(ne)
native speaker *n* locuteur natif
Nativity [nə'tɪvɪtɪ] *n* (*Rel*): **the ~** la Nativité
nativity play *n* mystère *m* or miracle *m* de la
Nativité
NATO ['neɪtəʊ] *n abbr* (= *North Atlantic Treaty
Organization*) OTAN *f*
natter ['nætə'] *vi* (*Brit*) bavarder
natural ['nætʃrəl] *adj* naturel(le); **to die of ~**
causes mourir d'une mort naturelle
natural childbirth *n* accouchement *m* sans
douleur
natural gas *n* gaz naturel
natural history *n* histoire naturelle
naturalist ['nætʃrəlɪst] *n* naturaliste *m/f*
naturalization ['nætʃrəlaɪ'zeɪʃən] *n*
naturalisation *f*; acclimatation *f*
naturalize ['nætʃrəlaɪz] *vt* naturaliser; (*plant*)
acclimater; **to become ~d** (*person*) se faire
naturaliser
naturally ['nætʃrəlɪ] *adv* naturellement
natural resources *npl* ressources naturelles
natural selection *n* sélection naturelle
natural wastage *n* (*Industry*) départs naturels et
volontaires
nature ['neɪtʃə'] *n* nature *f*; **by ~** par
tempérament, de nature; **documents of a**
confidential ~ documents à caractère
confidentiel
-natured ['neɪtʃəd] *suffix*: **ill~** qui a mauvais
caractère
nature reserve *n* (*Brit*) réserve naturelle
nature trail *n* *sentier de découverte de la nature*
naturist ['neɪtʃərɪst] *n* naturiste *m/f*
naught [nɔ:t] *n* = **nought**
naughtiness ['nɔ:tɪnɪs] *n* (*of child*)
désobéissance *f*; (*of story etc*) grivoiserie *f*
naughty ['nɔ:tɪ] *adj* (*child*) vilain(e), pas sage;
(*story, film*) grivois(e)
nausea ['nɔ:sɪə] *n* nausée *f*
nauseate ['nɔ:sɪeɪt] *vt* écœurer, donner la
nausée à
nauseating ['nɔ:sɪeɪtɪŋ] *adj* écœurant(e),
dégoûtant(e)
nauseous ['nɔ:sɪəs] *adj* nauséabond(e),
écœurant(e); (*feeling sick*): **to be ~** avoir des

nausées

nautical ['nɔ:tɪkl] *adj* nautique

nautical mile *n* mille marin (= 1853 m)

naval ['neɪvl] *adj* naval(e)

naval officer *n* officier *m* de marine

nave [neɪv] *n* nef *f*

navel ['neɪvl] *n* nombril *m*

navigable ['nævɪgəbl] *adj* navigable

navigate ['nævɪgeɪt] *vt* (*steer*) diriger, piloter ▷ *vi* naviguer; (*Aut*) indiquer la route à suivre

navigation [nævɪ'geɪʃən] *n* navigation *f*

navigator ['nævɪgeɪtər] *n* navigateur *m*

navvy ['nævɪ] *n* (*Brit*) terrassier *m*

navy ['neɪvɪ] *n* marine *f*; **Department of the N~** (*US*) ministère *m* de la Marine

navy-blue ['neɪvɪ'blu:] *adj* bleu marine *inv*

Nazi ['nɑ:tsɪ] *adj* nazi(e) ▷ *n* Nazi(e)

NB *abbr* (= *nota bene*) NB; (*Canada*) = **New Brunswick**

NBA *n abbr* (*US*) = **National Basketball Association; National Boxing Association**

NBC *n abbr* (*US*: = *National Broadcasting Company*) *chaîne de télévision*

NBS *n abbr* (*US*: = *National Bureau of Standards*) *office de normalisation*

NC *abbr* (*Comm etc*) = **no charge**; (*US*) = **North Carolina**

NCC *n abbr* (*Brit*: = *Nature Conservancy Council*) *organisme de protection de la nature*; (*US*) = **National Council of Churches**

NCO *n abbr* = **non-commissioned officer**

ND, N. Dak. *abbr* (*US*) = **North Dakota**

NE *abbr* (*US*) = **Nebraska; New England**

NEA *n abbr* (*US*) = **National Education Association**

neap [ni:p] *n* (*also*: **neaptide**) mortes-eaux *fpl*

near [nɪər] *adj* proche ▷ *adv* près ▷ *prep* (*also*: **near to**) près de ▷ *vt* approcher de; **~ here/ there** près d'ici/non loin de là; **£25,000 or ~est offer** (*Brit*) 25 000 livres à débattre; **in the ~ future** dans un proche avenir; **to come ~** *vi* s'approcher

nearby [nɪə'baɪ] *adj* proche ▷ *adv* tout près, à proximité

Near East *n*: **the ~** le Proche-Orient

nearer ['nɪərər] *adj* plus proche ▷ *adv* plus près

nearly ['nɪəlɪ] *adv* presque; **I ~ fell** j'ai failli tomber; **it's not ~ big enough** ce n'est vraiment pas assez grand, c'est loin d'être assez grand

near miss *n* collision évitée de justesse; (*when aiming*) coup manqué de peu *or* de justesse

nearness ['nɪənɪs] *n* proximité *f*

nearside ['nɪəsaɪd] (*Aut*) *n* (*right-hand drive*) côté *m* gauche; (*left-hand drive*) côté droit ▷ *adj* de gauche; de droite

near-sighted [nɪə'saɪtɪd] *adj* myope

neat [ni:t] *adj* (*person, work*) soigné(e); (*room etc*) bien tenu(e) *or* rangé(e); (*solution, plan*) habile; (*spirits*) pur(e); **I drink it ~** je le bois sec *or* sans eau

neatly ['ni:tlɪ] *adv* avec soin *or* ordre; (*skilfully*)

habilement

neatness ['ni:tnɪs] *n* (*tidiness*) netteté *f*; (*skilfulness*) habileté *f*

Nebr. *abbr* (*US*) = **Nebraska**

nebulous ['nɛbjʊləs] *adj* nébuleux(-euse)

necessarily ['nɛsɪsrɪlɪ] *adv* nécessairement; **not ~** pas nécessairement *or* forcément

necessary ['nɛsɪsrɪ] *adj* nécessaire; **if ~** si besoin est, le cas échéant

necessitate [nɪ'sɛsɪteɪt] *vt* nécessiter

necessity [nɪ'sɛsɪtɪ] *n* nécessité *f*; chose nécessaire *or* essentielle; **in case of ~** en cas d'urgence

neck [nɛk] *n* cou *m*; (*of horse, garment*) encolure *f*; (*of bottle*) goulot *m* ▷ *vi* (*inf*) se peloter; **~ and ~** à égalité; **to stick one's ~ out** (*inf*) se mouiller

necklace ['nɛklɪs] *n* collier *m*

neckline ['nɛklaɪn] *n* encolure *f*

necktie ['nɛktaɪ] *n* (*esp US*) cravate *f*

nectar ['nɛktər] *n* nectar *m*

nectarine ['nɛktərɪn] *n* brugnon *m*, nectarine *f*

née [neɪ] *adj*: **~ Scott** née Scott

need [ni:d] *n* besoin *m* ▷ *vt* avoir besoin de; **to ~ to do** devoir faire; avoir besoin de faire; **you don't ~ to go** vous n'avez pas besoin *or* vous n'êtes pas obligé de partir; **a signature is ~ed** il faut une signature; **to be in ~ of** *or* **have ~ of** avoir besoin de; **£10 will meet my immediate ~s** 10 livres suffiront pour mes besoins immédiats; **in case of ~** en cas de besoin, au besoin; **there's no ~ to do** .... il n'y a pas lieu de faire ..., il n'est pas nécessaire de faire ...; **there's no ~ for that** ce n'est pas la peine, cela n'est pas nécessaire

needle ['ni:dl] *n* aiguille *f*; (*on record player*) saphir *m* ▷ *vt* (*inf*) asticoter, tourmenter

needlecord ['ni:dlkɔ:d] *n* (*Brit*) velours *m* milleraies

needless ['ni:dlɪs] *adj* inutile; **~ to say, ...** inutile de dire que ...

needlessly ['ni:dlɪslɪ] *adv* inutilement

needlework ['ni:dlwə:k] *n* (*activity*) travaux *mpl* d'aiguille; (*object*) ouvrage *m*

needn't ['ni:dnt] = **need not**

needy ['ni:dɪ] *adj* nécessiteux(-euse)

negation [nɪ'geɪʃən] *n* négation *f*

negative ['nɛgətɪv] *n* (*Phot, Elec*) négatif *m*; (*Ling*) terme *m* de négation ▷ *adj* négatif(-ive); **to answer in the ~** répondre par la négative

negative equity *n* situation dans laquelle la valeur d'une maison est inférieure à celle du prêt immobilier contracté pour la payer

neglect [nɪ'glɛkt] *vt* négliger; (*garden*) ne pas entretenir; (*duty*) manquer à ▷ *n* (*of person, duty, garden*) le fait de négliger; (**state of**) **~** abandon *m*; **to ~ to do sth** négliger *or* omettre de faire qch; **to ~ one's appearance** se négliger

neglected [nɪ'glɛktɪd] *adj* négligé(e), à l'abandon

neglectful [nɪ'glɛktful] *adj* (*gen*) négligent(e); **to be ~ of sb/sth** négliger qn/qch

negligee ['nɛglɪʒeɪ] *n* déshabillé *m*

negligence ['nɛɡlɪdʒəns] *n* négligence *f*

negligent ['nɛɡlɪdʒənt] *adj* négligent(e)

negligently ['nɛɡlɪdʒəntlɪ] *adv* par négligence; (*offhandedly*) négligemment

negligible ['nɛɡlɪdʒɪbl] *adj* négligeable

negotiable [nɪ'ɡəʊʃɪəbl] *adj* négociable; **not ~** (*cheque*) non négociable

negotiate [nɪ'ɡəʊʃɪeɪt] *vi* négocier ▷ *vt* négocier; (*Comm*) négocier; (*obstacle*) franchir, négocier; (*bend in road*) négocier; **to ~ with sb for sth** négocier avec qn en vue d'obtenir qch

negotiating table [nɪ'ɡəʊʃɪeɪtɪŋ-] *n* table *f* des négociations

negotiation [nɪɡəʊʃɪ'eɪʃən] *n* négociation *f*, pourparlers *mpl*; **to enter into ~s with sb** engager des négociations avec qn

negotiator [nɪ'ɡəʊʃɪeɪtə^r] *n* négociateur(-trice)

Negress ['niːɡrɪs] *n* négresse *f*

Negro ['niːɡrəʊ] *adj* (*gen*) noir(e); (*music, arts*) nègre, noir ▷ *n* (*pl* **-es**) Noir(e)

neigh [neɪ] *vi* hennir

neighbour, (US) **neighbor** ['neɪbə^r] *n* voisin(e)

neighbourhood, (US) **neighborhood** ['neɪbəhʊd] *n* (*place*) quartier *m*; (*people*) voisinage *m*

neighbourhood watch *n* *système de surveillance, assuré par les habitants d'un même quartier*

neighbouring, (US) **neighboring** ['neɪbərɪŋ] *adj* voisin(e), avoisinant(e)

neighbourly, (US) **neighborly** ['neɪbəlɪ] *adj* obligeant(e); (*relations*) de bon voisinage

neither ['naɪðə^r] *adj, pron* aucun(e) (des deux), ni l'un(e) ni l'autre ▷ *conj*: **~ do I** moi non plus; **I didn't move and ~ did Claude** je n'ai pas bougé, (et) Claude non plus ▷ *adv*: **~ good nor bad** ni bon ni mauvais; **~ did I refuse** (et *or* mais) je n'ai pas non plus refusé; **~ of them** ni l'un ni l'autre

neo... ['niːəʊ] *prefix* néo-

neolithic [niːəʊ'lɪθɪk] *adj* néolithique

neologism [nɪ'ɔlədʒɪzəm] *n* néologisme *m*

neon ['niːɔn] *n* néon *m*

neon light *n* lampe *f* au néon

neon sign *n* enseigne *f* (lumineuse) au néon

Nepal [nɪ'pɔːl] *n* Népal *m*

nephew ['nɛvjuː] *n* neveu *m*

nepotism ['nɛpətɪzəm] *n* népotisme *m*

nerd [nəːd] *n* (*inf*) pauvre mec *m*, ballot *m*

nerve [nəːv] *n* nerf *m*; (*bravery*) sang-froid *m*, courage *m*; (*cheek*) aplomb *m*, toupet *m*; **nerves** *npl* nervosité *f*; **he gets on my ~s** il m'énerve; **to have a fit of ~s** avoir le trac; **to lose one's ~** (*self-confidence*) perdre son sang-froid

nerve centre *n* (*Anat*) centre nerveux; (*fig*) centre névralgique

nerve gas *n* gaz *m* neuroplégique

nerve-racking ['nəːvrækɪŋ] *adj* angoissant(e)

nervous ['nəːvəs] *adj* nerveux(-euse); (*anxious*) inquiet(-ète), plein(e) d'appréhension; (*timid*) intimidé(e)

nervous breakdown *n* dépression nerveuse

nervously ['nəːvəslɪ] *adv* nerveusement

nervousness ['nəːvəsnɪs] *n* nervosité *f*; inquiétude *f*, appréhension *f*

nervous wreck *n*: **to be a ~** être une boule de nerfs

nervy ['nəːvɪ] *adj*: **he's very ~** il a les nerfs à fleur de peau *or* à vif

nest [nɛst] *n* nid *m* ▷ *vi* (se) nicher, faire son nid; **~ of tables** table *f* gigogne

nest egg *n* (*fig*) bas *m* de laine, magot *m*

nestle ['nɛsl] *vi* se blottir

nestling ['nɛstlɪŋ] *n* oisillon *m*

Net [nɛt] *n* (*Comput*): **the ~** (*Internet*) le Net

net [nɛt] *n* filet *m*; (*fabric*) tulle *f* ▷ *adj* net(te) ▷ *vt* (*fish etc*) prendre au filet; (*money: person*) toucher; (: *deal, sale*) rapporter; **~ of tax** net d'impôt; **he earns £10,000 ~ per year** il gagne 10 000 livres net par an

netball ['nɛtbɔːl] *n* netball *m*

net curtains *npl* voilages *mpl*

Netherlands ['nɛðələndz] *npl*: **the ~** les Pays-Bas *mpl*

netiquette ['nɛtɪkɛt] *n* netiquette *f*

net profit *n* bénéfice net

nett [nɛt] *adj* = **net**

netting ['nɛtɪŋ] *n* (*for fence etc*) treillis *m*, grillage *m*; (*fabric*) voile *m*

nettle ['nɛtl] *n* ortie *f*

network ['nɛtwəːk] *n* réseau *m* ▷ *vt* (*Radio, TV*) diffuser sur l'ensemble du réseau; (*computers*) interconnecter; **there's no ~ coverage here** (*Tel*) il n'y a pas de réseau ici

neuralgia [njuə'rældʒə] *n* névralgie *f*

neurological [njuərə'lɔdʒɪkl] *adj* neurologique

neurosis (*pl* **neuroses**) [njuə'rəʊsɪs, -siːz] *n* névrose *f*

neurotic [njuə'rɔtɪk] *adj, n* névrosé(e)

neuter ['njuːtə^r] *adj* neutre ▷ *n* neutre *m* ▷ *vt* (*cat etc*) châtrer, couper

neutral ['njuːtrəl] *adj* neutre ▷ *n* (*Aut*) point mort

neutrality [njuː'trælɪtɪ] *n* neutralité *f*

neutralize ['njuːtrəlaɪz] *vt* neutraliser

neutron bomb ['njuːtrɔn-] *n* bombe *f* à neutrons

Nev. *abbr* (US) = **Nevada**

never ['nɛvə^r] *adv* (ne ...) jamais; **I ~ went** je n'y suis pas allé; **I've ~ been to Spain** je ne suis jamais allé en Espagne; **~ again** plus jamais; **~ in my life** jamais de ma vie; *see also* **mind**

never-ending [nɛvər'ɛndɪŋ] *adj* interminable

nevertheless [nɛvəðə'lɛs] *adv* néanmoins, malgré tout

new [njuː] *adj* nouveau (nouvelle); (*brand new*) neuf (neuve); **as good as ~** comme neuf

New Age *n* New Age *m*

newbie ['njuːbɪ] *n* (*beginner*) newbie *m/f*; (*on forum*) nouveau(-elle)

newborn ['njuːbɔːn] *adj* nouveau-né(e)

newcomer ['njuːkʌmə^r] *n* nouveau venu (nouvelle venue)

new-fangled ['njuːfæŋɡld] *adj* (*pej*) ultramoderne (et farfelu(e))

new-found ['njuːfaʊnd] *adj* de fraîche date;

n

691

(*friend*) nouveau (nouvelle)

Newfoundland ['nju:fənlənd] *n* Terre-Neuve *f*

New Guinea *n* Nouvelle-Guinée *f*

newly ['nju:lɪ] *adv* nouvellement, récemment

newly-weds ['nju:lɪwɛdz] *npl* jeunes mariés *mpl*

new moon *n* nouvelle lune

newness ['nju:nɪs] *n* nouveauté *f*; (*of fabric, clothes etc*) état neuf

New Orleans [-'ɔ:li:ənz] *n* la Nouvelle-Orléans

news [nju:z] *n* nouvelle(s) *f(pl)*; (*Radio, TV*) informations *fpl*, actualités *fpl*; **a piece of** ~ une nouvelle; **good/bad** ~ bonne/mauvaise nouvelle; **financial** ~ (*Press, Radio, TV*) page financière

news agency *n* agence *f* de presse

newsagent ['nju:zeɪdʒənt] *n* (*Brit*) marchand *m* de journaux

news bulletin *n* (*Radio TV*) bulletin *m* d'informations

newscaster ['nju:zkɑ:stə^r] *n* (*Radio, TV*) présentateur(-trice)

news flash *n* flash *m* d'information

newsletter ['nju:zlɛtə^r] *n* bulletin *m*

newspaper ['nju:zpeɪpə^r] *n* journal *m*; **daily** ~ quotidien *m*; **weekly** ~ hebdomadaire *m*

newsprint ['nju:zprɪnt] *n* papier *m* (de) journal

newsreader ['nju:zri:də^r] *n* = **newscaster**

newsreel ['nju:zri:l] *n* actualités (filmées)

newsroom ['nju:zru:m] *n* (*Press*) salle *f* de rédaction; (*Radio, TV*) studio *m*

news stand *n* kiosque *m* à journaux

newsworthy ['nju:zwə:ðɪ] *adj*: **to be** ~ valoir la peine d'être publié

newt [nju:t] *n* triton *m*

new town *n* (*Brit*) ville nouvelle

New Year *n* Nouvel An; **Happy** ~! Bonne Année!; **to wish sb a happy** ~ souhaiter la Bonne Année à qn

New Year's Day *n* le jour de l'An

New Year's Eve *n* la Saint-Sylvestre

New York [-'jɔ:k] *n* New York; (*also*: **New York State**) New York *m*

New Zealand [-'zi:lənd] *n* Nouvelle-Zélande *f* ▷ *adj* néo-zélandais(e)

New Zealander [-'zi:ləndə^r] *n* Néo-Zélandais(e)

next [nɛkst] *adj* (*in time*) prochain(e); (*seat, room*) voisin(e), d'à côté; (*meeting, bus stop*) suivant(e) ▷ *adv* la fois suivante; la prochaine fois; (*afterwards*) ensuite; ~ **to** (*prep*) à côté de; ~ **to nothing** presque rien; ~ **time** (*adv*) la prochaine fois; **the** ~ **day** le lendemain, le jour suivant *or* d'après; ~ **week** la semaine prochaine; **the** ~ **week** la semaine suivante; ~ **year** l'année prochaine; **"turn to the** ~ **page"** "voir page suivante"; ~ **please!** (*at doctor's etc*) au suivant!; **who's** ~? c'est à qui?; **the week after** ~ dans deux semaines; **when do we meet** ~? quand nous revoyons-nous?

next door *adv* à côté ▷ *adj* (*neighbour*) d'à côté

next-of-kin ['nɛkstəv'kɪn] *n* parent *m* le plus proche

NF *n abbr* (*Brit Pol*: = *National Front*) ≈ FN ▷ *abbr*

(*Canada*) = **Newfoundland**

NFL *n abbr* (*US*) = **National Football League**

Nfld. *abbr* (*Canada*) = **Newfoundland**

NG *abbr* (*US*) = **National Guard**

NGO *n abbr* (*US*: = *non-governmental organization*) ONG *f*

NH *abbr* (*US*) = **New Hampshire**

NHL *n abbr* (*US*) = **National Hockey League**

NHS *n abbr* (*Brit*) = **National Health Service**

NI *abbr* = **Northern Ireland**; (*Brit*) = **National Insurance**

Niagara Falls [naɪ'ægərə-] *npl*: **the** ~ les chutes *fpl* du Niagara

nib [nɪb] *n* (*of pen*) (bec *m* de) plume *f*

nibble ['nɪbl] *vt* grignoter

Nicaragua [nɪkə'rægjuə] *n* Nicaragua *m*

Nicaraguan [nɪkə'rægjuən] *adj* nicaraguayen(ne) ▷ *n* Nicaraguayen(ne)

nice [naɪs] *adj* (*holiday, trip, taste*) agréable; (*flat, picture*) joli(e); (*person*) gentil(le); (*distinction, point*) subtil(e)

nice-looking ['naɪslukɪŋ] *adj* joli(e)

nicely ['naɪslɪ] *adv* agréablement; joliment; gentiment; subtilement; **that will do** ~ cé sera parfait

niceties ['naɪsɪtɪz] *npl* subtilités *fpl*

niche [ni:ʃ] *n* (*Archit*) niche *f*

nick [nɪk] *n* (*indentation*) encoche *f*; (*wound*) entaille *f*; (*Brit inf*): **in good** ~ en bon état ▷ *vt* (*cut*): **to** ~ **o.s.** se couper; (*inf: steal*) faucher, piquer; (: *Brit: arrest*) choper, pincer; **in the** ~ **of time** juste à temps

nickel ['nɪkl] *n* nickel *m*; (*US*) pièce *f* de 5 cents

nickname ['nɪkneɪm] *n* surnom *m* ▷ *vt* surnommer

Nicosia [nɪkə'si:ə] *n* Nicosie

nicotine ['nɪkəti:n] *n* nicotine *f*

nicotine patch *n* timbre *m* anti-tabac, patch *m*

niece [ni:s] *n* nièce *f*

nifty ['nɪftɪ] *adj* (*inf: car, jacket*) qui a du chic *or* de la classe; (: *gadget, tool*) astucieux(-euse)

Niger ['naɪdʒə^r] *n* (*country, river*) Niger *m*

Nigeria [naɪ'dʒɪərɪə] *n* Nigéria *m or f*

Nigerian [naɪ'dʒɪərɪən] *adj* nigérien(ne) ▷ *n* Nigérien(ne)

niggardly ['nɪgədlɪ] *adj* (*person*) parcimonieux(-euse), pingre; (*allowance, amount*) misérable

nigger ['nɪgə^r] *n* (*inf!: highly offensive*) nègre (négresse)

niggle ['nɪgl] *vt* tracasser ▷ *vi* (*find fault*) trouver toujours à redire; (*fuss*) n'être jamais content(e)

niggling ['nɪglɪŋ] *adj* tatillon(ne); (*detail*) insignifiant(e); (*doubt, pain*) persistant(e)

night [naɪt] *n* nuit *f*; (*evening*) soir *m*; **at** ~ la nuit; **by** ~ de nuit; **in the** ~, **during the** ~ pendant la nuit; **last** ~ (*evening*) hier soir; (*night-time*) la nuit dernière; **the** ~ **before last** avant-hier soir

night-bird ['naɪtbə:d] *n* oiseau *m* nocturne; (*fig*) couche-tard *m inv*, noctambule *m/f*

nightcap ['naɪtkæp] *n* boisson prise avant le coucher

nightclub *n* boîte *f* de nuit

nightdress ['naɪtdrɛs] n chemise f de nuit
nightfall ['naɪtfɔːl] n tombée f de la nuit
nightie ['naɪtɪ] n chemise f de nuit
nightingale ['naɪtɪŋgeɪl] n rossignol m
nightlife ['naɪtlaɪf] n vie f nocturne
nightly ['naɪtlɪ] adj (news) du soir; (by night) nocturne ▷ adv (every evening) tous les soirs; (every night) toutes les nuits
nightmare ['naɪtmɛəʳ] n cauchemar m
night porter n gardien m de nuit, concierge m de service la nuit
night safe n coffre m de nuit
night school n cours mpl du soir
nightshade ['naɪtʃeɪd] n: **deadly ~** (Bot) belladone f
night shift ['naɪtʃɪft] n équipe f de nuit
night-time ['naɪttaɪm] n nuit f
night watchman (irreg) n veilleur m de nuit; poste m de nuit
nihilism ['naɪɪlɪzəm] n nihilisme m
nil [nɪl] n rien m; (Brit Sport) zéro m
Nile [naɪl] n: **the ~** le Nil
nimble ['nɪmbl] adj agile
nine [naɪn] num neuf
nineteen ['naɪn'tiːn] num dix-neuf
nineteenth [naɪn'tiːnθ] num dix-neuvième
ninetieth ['naɪntɪɪθ] num quatre-vingt-dixième
ninety ['naɪntɪ] num quatre-vingt-dix
ninth [naɪnθ] num neuvième
nip [nɪp] vt pincer ▷ vi (Brit inf): **to ~ out/down/ up** sortir/descendre/monter en vitesse ▷ n pincement m; (drink) petit verre; **to ~ into a shop** faire un saut dans un magasin
nipple ['nɪpl] n (Anat) mamelon m, bout m du sein
nippy ['nɪpɪ] adj (Brit: person) alerte, leste; (: car) nerveux(-euse)
nit [nɪt] n (in hair) lente f; (inf: idiot) imbécile m/f, crétin m
nit-pick ['nɪtpɪk] vi (inf) être tatillon(ne)
nitrogen ['naɪtrədʒən] n azote m
nitroglycerin, nitroglycerine ['naɪtrəu'glɪsəriːn] n nitroglycérine f
nitty-gritty ['nɪtɪ'grɪtɪ] n (fam): **to get down to the ~** en venir au fond du problème
nitwit ['nɪtwɪt] n (inf) nigaud(e)
NJ abbr (US) = **New Jersey**
NLF n abbr (= National Liberation Front) FLN m
NLQ abbr (= near letter quality) qualité f courrier
NLRB n abbr (US: = National Labor Relations Board) organisme de protection des travailleurs
NM, N. Mex. abbr (US) = **New Mexico**

⊙ KEYWORD

no [nəu] (pl **noes**) adv (opposite of "yes") non; **are you coming? — no (I'm not)** est-ce que vous venez? — non; **would you like some more? — no thank you** vous en voulez encore? — non merci
▷ adj (not any) (ne ...) pas de, (ne ...) aucun(e); **I have no money/books** je n'ai pas d'argent/de

livres; **no student would have done it** aucun étudiant ne l'aurait fait; **"no smoking"** "défense de fumer"; **"no dogs"** "les chiens ne sont pas admis"
▷ n non m; **I won't take no for an answer** il n'est pas question de refuser

no. abbr (= number) n°
nobble ['nɔbl] vt (Brit inf: bribe: person) soudoyer, acheter; (: person: to speak to) mettre le grappin sur; (Racing: horse, dog) droguer (pour l'empêcher de gagner)
Nobel prize [nəu'bɛl-] n prix m Nobel
nobility [nəu'bɪlɪtɪ] n noblesse f
noble ['nəubl] adj noble
nobleman ['nəublmən] (irreg) n noble m
nobly ['nəublɪ] adv noblement
nobody ['nəubədɪ] pron (ne ...) personne
no-claims bonus ['nəukleɪmz-] n bonus m
nocturnal [nɔk'təːnl] adj nocturne
nod [nɔd] vi faire un signe de (la) tête (affirmatif ou amical); (sleep) somnoler ▷ vt: **to ~ one's head** faire un signe de (la) tête; (in agreement) faire signe que oui ▷ n signe m de (la) tête; **they ~ded their agreement** ils ont acquiescé d'un signe de la tête
▶ **nod off** vi s'assoupir
no-fly zone [nəu'flaɪ-] n zone interdite (aux avions et hélicoptères)
noise [nɔɪz] n bruit m; **I can't sleep for the ~** je n'arrive pas à dormir à cause du bruit
noiseless ['nɔɪzlɪs] adj silencieux(-euse)
noisily ['nɔɪzɪlɪ] adv bruyamment
noisy ['nɔɪzɪ] adj bruyant(e)
nomad ['nəumæd] n nomade m/f
nomadic [nəu'mædɪk] adj nomade
no man's land n no man's land m
nominal ['nɔmɪnl] adj (rent, fee) symbolique; (value) nominal(e)
nominate ['nɔmɪneɪt] vt (propose) proposer; (appoint) nommer
nomination [nɔmɪ'neɪʃən] n nomination f
nominee [nɔmɪ'niː] n candidat agréé; personne nommée
non- [nɔn] prefix non-
nonalcoholic [nɔnælkə'hɔlɪk] adj non alcoolisé(e)
nonbreakable [nɔn'breɪkəbl] adj incassable
nonce word ['nɔns-] n mot créé pour l'occasion
nonchalant ['nɔnʃələnt] adj nonchalant(e)
non-commissioned [nɔnkə'mɪʃənd] adj: **~ officer** sous-officier m
noncommittal [nɔnkə'mɪtl] adj évasif(-ive)
nonconformist [nɔnkən'fɔːmɪst] n non-conformiste m/f ▷ adj non-conformiste, dissident(e)
noncooperation ['nɔnkəuɔpə'reɪʃən] n refus m de coopérer, non-coopération f
nondescript ['nɔndɪskrɪpt] adj quelconque, indéfinissable
none [nʌn] pron aucun(e); **~ of you** aucun d'entre vous, personne parmi vous; **I have ~** je

n'en ai pas; **I have ~ left** je n'en ai plus; **~ at all** (*not one*) aucun(e); **how much milk? — ~ at all** combien de lait? — pas du tout; **he's ~ the worse for it** il ne s'en porte pas plus mal

nonentity [nɔˈnɛntɪtɪ] *n* personne insignifiante

nonessential [nɔnɪˈsɛnʃl] *adj* accessoire, superflu(e) ▷ *n*: **~s** le superflu

nonetheless [ˈnʌnðəˈlɛs] *adv* néanmoins

nonevent [nɔnɪˈvɛnt] *n* événement manqué

nonexecutive [nɔnɪgˈzɛkjutɪv] *adj*: **~ director** administrateur(-trice), conseiller(-ère) de direction

nonexistent [nɔnɪgˈzɪstənt] *adj* inexistant(e)

non-fiction [nɔnˈfɪkʃən] *n* littérature *f* non romanesque

nonintervention [ˈnɔnɪntəˈvɛnʃən] *n* non-intervention *f*

no-no [ˈnəunəu] *n* (*inf*): **it's a ~** il n'en est pas question

non obst. *abbr* (= *non obstante: notwithstanding*) nonobstant

no-nonsense [nəuˈnɔnsəns] *adj* (*manner, person*) plein(e) de bon sens

nonpayment [nɔnˈpeɪmənt] *n* non-paiement *m*

nonplussed [nɔnˈplʌst] *adj* perplexe

non-profit-making [nɔnˈprɔfɪtmeɪkɪŋ] *adj* à but non lucratif

nonsense [ˈnɔnsəns] *n* absurdités *fpl*, idioties *fpl*; **~!** ne dites pas d'idioties!; **it is ~ to say that** ... il est absurde de dire que ....

nonsensical [nɔnˈsɛnsɪkl] *adj* absurde, qui n'a pas de sens

non-smoker [ˈnɔnˈsməukəʳ] *n* non-fumeur *m*

non-smoking [ˈnɔnˈsməukɪŋ] *adj* non-fumeur

nonstarter [nɔnˈstɑːtəʳ] *n*: **it's a ~** c'est voué à l'échec

non-stick [ˈnɔnˈstɪk] *adj* qui n'attache pas

nonstop [ˈnɔnˈstɔp] *adj* direct(e), sans arrêt (*or* escale) ▷ *adv* sans arrêt

nontaxable [nɔnˈtæksəbl] *adj*: **~ income** revenu *m* non imposable

non-U [ˈnɔnjuː] *adj abbr* (*Brit inf*: = *non-upper class*) qui ne se dit (*or* se fait) pas

nonvolatile [nɔnˈvɔlətaɪl] *adj*: **~ memory** (*Comput*) mémoire rémanente *or* non volatile

nonvoting [nɔnˈvəutɪŋ] *adj*: **~ shares** actions *fpl* sans droit de vote

non-white [ˈnɔnˈwaɪt] *adj* de couleur ▷ *n* personne *f* de couleur

noodles [ˈnuːdlz] *npl* nouilles *fpl*

nook [nuk] *n*: **~s and crannies** recoins *mpl*

noon [nuːn] *n* midi *m*

no-one [ˈnəuwʌn] *pron* = **nobody**

noose [nuːs] *n* nœud coulant; (*hangman's*) corde *f*

nor [nɔːʳ] *conj* = **neither** ▷ *adv see* **neither**

norm [nɔːm] *n* norme *f*

normal [ˈnɔːml] *adj* normal(e) ▷ *n*: **to return to ~** redevenir normal(e)

normality [nɔːˈmælɪtɪ] *n* normalité *f*

normally [ˈnɔːməlɪ] *adv* normalement

Normandy [ˈnɔːməndɪ] *n* Normandie *f*

north [nɔːθ] *n* nord *m* ▷ *adj* nord *inv*; (*wind*) du nord ▷ *adv* au *or* vers le nord

North Africa *n* Afrique *f* du Nord

North African *adj* nord-africain(e), d'Afrique du Nord ▷ *n* Nord-Africain(e)

North America *n* Amérique *f* du Nord

North American *n* Nord-Américain(e) ▷ *adj* nord-américain(e), d'Amérique du Nord

Northants [nɔːˈθænts] *abbr* (*Brit*) = **Northamptonshire**

northbound [ˈnɔːθbaund] *adj* (*traffic*) en direction du nord; (*carriageway*) nord *inv*

north-east [nɔːθˈiːst] *n* nord-est *m*

northerly [ˈnɔːðəlɪ] *adj* (*wind, direction*) du nord

northern [ˈnɔːðən] *adj* du nord, septentrional(e)

Northern Ireland *n* Irlande *f* du Nord

North Korea *n* Corée *f* du Nord

North Pole *n*: **the ~** le pôle Nord

North Sea *n*: **the ~** la mer du Nord

North Sea oil *n* pétrole *m* de la mer du Nord

northward [ˈnɔːθwəd], **northwards** [ˈnɔːθwədz] *adv* vers le nord

north-west [nɔːθˈwɛst] *n* nord-ouest *m*

Norway [ˈnɔːweɪ] *n* Norvège *f*

Norwegian [nɔːˈwiːdʒən] *adj* norvégien(ne) ▷ *n* Norvégien(ne); (*Ling*) norvégien *m*

nos. *abbr* (= *numbers*) n^{os}

nose [nəuz] *n* nez *m*; (*of dog, cat*) museau *m*; (*fig*) flair *m* ▷ *vi* (*also*: **nose one's way**) avancer précautionneusement; **to pay through the ~ (for sth)** (*inf*) payer un prix excessif (pour qch)
▶ **nose about, nose around** *vi* fouiner *or* fureter (partout)

nosebleed [ˈnəuzbliːd] *n* saignement *m* de nez

nose-dive [ˈnəuzdaɪv] *n* (descente *f* en) piqué *m*

nose drops *npl* gouttes *fpl* pour le nez

nosey [ˈnəuzɪ] *adj* (*inf*) curieux(-euse)

nostalgia [nɔsˈtældʒɪə] *n* nostalgie *f*

nostalgic [nɔsˈtældʒɪk] *adj* nostalgique

nostril [ˈnɔstrɪl] *n* narine *f*; (*of horse*) naseau *m*

nosy [ˈnəuzɪ] (*inf*) *adj* = **nosey**

not [nɔt] *adv* (ne ...) pas; **he is ~** *or* **isn't here** il n'est pas ici; **you must ~** *or* **mustn't do that** tu ne dois pas faire ça; **I hope ~** j'espère que non; **~ at all** pas du tout; (*after thanks*) de rien; **it's too late, isn't it?** c'est trop tard, n'est-ce pas?; **~ yet/now** pas encore/maintenant; *see also* **only**

notable [ˈnəutəbl] *adj* notable

notably [ˈnəutəblɪ] *adv* (*particularly*) en particulier; (*markedly*) spécialement

notary [ˈnəutərɪ] *n* (*also*: **notary public**) notaire *m*

notation [nəuˈteɪʃən] *n* notation *f*

notch [nɔtʃ] *n* encoche *f*
▶ **notch up** *vt* (*score*) marquer; (*victory*) remporter

note [nəut] *n* note *f*; (*letter*) mot *m*; (*banknote*) billet *m* ▷ *vt* (*also*: **note down**) noter; (*notice*) constater; **just a quick ~ to let you know ...** juste un mot pour vous dire ...; **to take ~s** prendre des notes; **to compare ~s** (*fig*) échanger des (or leurs etc) impressions; **to take ~ of** prendre note de; **a person of ~** une personne éminente

notebook ['nəʊtbʊk] n carnet m; (for shorthand etc) bloc-notes m

note-case ['nəʊtkeɪs] n (Brit) porte-feuille m

noted ['nəʊtɪd] adj réputé(e)

notepad ['nəʊtpæd] n bloc-notes m

notepaper ['nəʊtpeɪpəʳ] n papier m à lettres

noteworthy ['nəʊtwɜːðɪ] adj remarquable

nothing ['nʌθɪŋ] n rien m; **he does ~** il ne fait rien; **~ new** rien de nouveau; **for ~** (free) pour rien, gratuitement; (in vain) pour rien; **~ at all** rien du tout; **~ much** pas grand-chose

notice ['nəʊtɪs] n (announcement, warning) avis m; (of leaving) congé m; (Brit: review: of play etc) critique f, compte rendu m ▷ vt remarquer, s'apercevoir de; **without ~** sans préavis; **advance ~** préavis m; **to give sb ~ of sth** notifier qn de qch; **at short ~** dans un délai très court; **until further ~** jusqu'à nouvel ordre; **to give ~, hand in one's ~** (employee) donner sa démission, démissionner; **to take ~ of** prêter attention à; **to bring sth to sb's ~** porter qch à la connaissance de qn; **it has come to my ~ that** ... on m'a signalé que ...; **to escape** or **avoid ~** (essayer de) passer inaperçu or ne pas se faire remarquer

noticeable ['nəʊtɪsəbl] adj visible

notice board n (Brit) panneau m d'affichage

notification [nəʊtɪfɪ'keɪʃən] n notification f

notify ['nəʊtɪfaɪ] vt: **to ~ sth to sb** notifier qch à qn; **to ~ sb of sth** avertir qn de qch

notion ['nəʊʃən] n idée f; (concept) notion f; **notions** npl (US: haberdashery) mercerie f

notoriety [nəʊtə'raɪətɪ] n notoriété f

notorious [nəʊ'tɔːrɪəs] adj notoire (souvent en mal)

notoriously [nəʊ'tɔːrɪəslɪ] adj notoirement

Notts [nɒts] abbr (Brit) = **Nottinghamshire**

notwithstanding [nɒtwɪθ'stændɪŋ] adv néanmoins ▷ prep en dépit de

nougat ['nuːɡaː] n nougat m

nought [nɔːt] n zéro m

noun [naʊn] n nom m

nourish ['nʌrɪʃ] vt nourrir

nourishing ['nʌrɪʃɪŋ] adj nourrissant(e)

nourishment ['nʌrɪʃmənt] n nourriture f

Nov. abbr (= November) nov

Nova Scotia ['nəʊvə'skəʊʃə] n Nouvelle-Écosse f

novel ['nɒvl] n roman m ▷ adj nouveau (nouvelle), original(e)

novelist ['nɒvəlɪst] n romancier m

novelty ['nɒvəltɪ] n nouveauté f

November [nəʊ'vɛmbəʳ] n novembre m; for phrases see also **July**

novice ['nɒvɪs] n novice m/f

NOW [naʊ] n abbr (US) = **National Organization for Women**

now [naʊ] adv maintenant ▷ conj: **~ (that)** maintenant (que); **right ~** tout de suite; **by ~** à l'heure qu'il est; **just ~** (:): **that's the fashion**

just ~ c'est la mode en ce moment or maintenant; **I saw her just ~** je viens de la voir, je l'ai vue à l'instant; **I'll read it just ~** je vais le lire à l'instant or dès maintenant; **~ and then, ~ and again** de temps en temps; **from ~ on** dorénavant; **in 3 days from ~** dans or d'ici trois jours; **between ~ and Monday** d'ici (à) lundi; **that's all for ~** c'est tout pour l'instant

nowadays ['naʊədeɪz] adv de nos jours

nowhere ['nəʊwɛəʳ] adv (ne ...) nulle part; **~ else** nulle part ailleurs

no-win situation [nəʊ'wɪn-] n impasse f; **we're in a ~** nous sommes dans l'impasse

noxious ['nɒkʃəs] adj toxique

nozzle ['nɒzl] n (of hose) jet m, lance f; (of vacuum cleaner) suceur m

NP n abbr = **notary public**

nr abbr (Brit) = **near**

NS abbr (Canada) = **Nova Scotia**

NSC n abbr (US) = **National Security Council**

NSF n abbr (US) = **National Science Foundation**

NSPCC n abbr (Brit) = **National Society for the Prevention of Cruelty to Children**

NSW abbr (Australia) = **New South Wales**

NT n abbr (= New Testament) NT m ▷ abbr (Canada) = **Northwest Territories**

nth [ɛnθ] adj: **for the ~ time** (inf) pour la énième fois

nuance ['njuːɑːns] n nuance f

nubile ['njuːbaɪl] adj nubile; (attractive) jeune et désirable

nuclear ['njuːklɪəʳ] adj nucléaire

nuclear disarmament n désarmement m nucléaire

nuclear family n famille f nucléaire

nuclear-free zone ['njuːklɪə'friː-] n zone f où le nucléaire est interdit

nucleus (pl **nuclei**) ['njuːklɪəs, 'njuːklɪaɪ] n noyau m

NUCPS n abbr (Brit: = National Union of Civil and Public Servants) syndicat des fonctionnaires

nude [njuːd] adj nu(e) ▷ n (Art) nu m; **in the ~** (tout(e)) nu(e)

nudge [nʌdʒ] vt donner un (petit) coup de coude à

nudist ['njuːdɪst] n nudiste m/f

nudist colony n colonie f de nudistes

nudity ['njuːdɪtɪ] n nudité f

nugget ['nʌɡɪt] n pépite f

nuisance ['njuːsns] n: **it's a ~** c'est (très) ennuyeux or gênant; **he's a ~** il est assommant or casse-pieds; **what a ~!** quelle barbe!

NUJ n abbr (Brit: = National Union of Journalists) syndicat des journalistes

nuke [njuːk] n (inf) bombe f atomique

null [nʌl] adj: **~ and void** nul(le) et non avenu(e)

nullify ['nʌlɪfaɪ] vt invalider

NUM n abbr (Brit: = National Union of Mineworkers) syndicat des mineurs

numb [nʌm] adj engourdi(e); (with fear) paralysé(e) ▷ vt engourdir; **~ with cold** engourdi(e) par le froid, transi(e) (de froid); **~**

n

with fear transi de peur, paralysé(e) par la peur

number ['nʌmbəʳ] *n* nombre *m*; (*numeral*) chiffre *m*; (*of house, car, telephone, newspaper*) numéro *m* ▷ *vt* numéroter; (*amount to*) compter; **a ~ of** un certain nombre de; **they were seven in ~** ils étaient (au nombre de) sept; **to be ~ed among** compter parmi; **the staff ~s 20** le nombre d'employés s'élève à *or* est de 20; **wrong ~** (Tel) mauvais numéro

numbered account ['nʌmbəd-] *n* (*in bank*) compte numéroté

number plate *n* (*Brit Aut*) plaque *f* minéralogique *or* d'immatriculation

Number Ten *n* (*Brit: 10 Downing Street*) résidence du Premier ministre

numbness ['nʌmnɪs] *n* torpeur *f*; (*due to cold*) engourdissement *m*

numbskull ['nʌmskʌl] *n* (*inf*) gourde *f*

numeral ['njuːmərəl] *n* chiffre *m*

numerate ['njuːmərɪt] *adj* (*Brit*): **to be ~** avoir des notions d'arithmétique

numerical [njuːˈmɛrɪkl] *adj* numérique

numerous ['njuːmərəs] *adj* nombreux(-euse)

nun [nʌn] *n* religieuse *f*, sœur *f*

nunnery ['nʌnərɪ] *n* couvent *m*

nuptial ['nʌpʃəl] *adj* nuptial(e)

nurse [nəːs] *n* infirmière *f*; (*also:* **nursemaid**) bonne *f* d'enfants ▷ *vt* (*patient, cold*) soigner; (*baby: Brit*) bercer (dans ses bras); (*: US*) allaiter, nourrir; (*hope*) nourrir

nursery ['nəːsərɪ] *n* (*room*) nursery *f*; (*institution*) crèche *f*, garderie *f*; (*for plants*) pépinière *f*

nursery rhyme *n* comptine *f*, chansonnette *f* pour enfants

nursery school *n* école maternelle

nursery slope *n* (*Brit Ski*) piste *f* pour débutants

nursing ['nəːsɪŋ] *n* (*profession*) profession *f* d'infirmière; (*care*) soins *mpl* ▷ *adj* (*mother*) qui allaite

nursing home *n* clinique *f*; (*for convalescence*) maison *f* de convalescence *or* de repos; (*for old people*) maison de retraite

nurture ['nəːtʃəʳ] *vt* élever

NUS *n abbr* (*Brit:* = *National Union of Students*) syndicat des étudiants

NUT *n abbr* (*Brit:* = *National Union of Teachers*) syndicat enseignant

nut [nʌt] *n* (*of metal*) écrou *m*; (*fruit: walnut*) noix *f*; (*: hazelnut*) noisette *f*; (*: peanut*) cacahuète *f* (*terme générique en anglais*) ▷ *adj* (*chocolate etc*) aux noisettes; **he's ~s** (*inf*) il est dingue

nutcase ['nʌtkeɪs] *n* (*inf*) dingue *m/f*

nutcrackers ['nʌtkrækəz] *npl* casse-noix *m inv*, casse-noisette(s) *m*

nutmeg ['nʌtmɛg] *n* (*noix f*) muscade *f*

nutrient ['njuːtrɪənt] *adj* nutritif(-ive) ▷ *n* substance nutritive

nutrition [njuːˈtrɪʃən] *n* nutrition *f*, alimentation *f*

nutritionist [njuːˈtrɪʃənɪst] *n* nutritionniste *m/f*

nutritious [njuːˈtrɪʃəs] *adj* nutritif(-ive), nourrissant(e)

nuts [nʌts] (*inf*) *adj* dingue

nutshell ['nʌtʃɛl] *n* coquille *f* de noix; **in a ~** en un mot

nutter ['nʌtəʳ] (*Brit: inf*) *n*: **he's a complete ~** il est complètement cinglé

nutty ['nʌtɪ] *adj* (*flavour*) à la noisette; (*inf: person*) cinglé(e), dingue

nuzzle ['nʌzl] *vi*: **to ~ up to** fourrer son nez contre

NV *abbr* (*US*) = **Nevada**

NVQ *n abbr* (*Brit*) = **National Vocational Qualification**

NWT *abbr* (*Canada*) = **Northwest Territories**

NY *abbr* (*US*) = **New York**

NYC *abbr* (*US*) = **New York City**

nylon ['naɪlɔn] *n* nylon *m* ▷ *adj* de *or* en nylon; **nylons** *npl* bas *mpl* nylon

nymph [nɪmf] *n* nymphe *f*

nymphomaniac ['nɪmfəuˈmeɪnɪæk] *adj, n* nymphomane *f*

NYSE *n abbr* (*US*) = **New York Stock Exchange**

NZ *abbr* = **New Zealand**

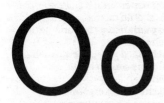

Oo

O, o [əu] *n* (*letter*) O, o *m*; (*US Scol*: = *outstanding*) tb (= *très bien*); **O for Oliver**, (*US*) **O for Oboe** O comme Oscar

oaf [əuf] *n* balourd *m*

oak [əuk] *n* chêne *m* ▷ *cpd* de *or* en (bois de) chêne

O&M *n abbr* = **organization and method**

O.A.P. *n abbr* (*Brit*) = **old age pensioner**

oar [ɔːʳ] *n* aviron *m*, rame *f*; **to put** *or* **shove one's ~ in** (*fig*: *inf*) mettre son grain de sel

oarsman [ˈɔːzmən], **oarswoman** [ˈɔːzwumən] (*irreg*) *n* rameur(-euse); (*Naut*, *Sport*) nageur(-euse)

OAS *n abbr* (= *Organization of American States*) OEA *f* (= *Organisation des États américains*)

oasis (*pl* **oases**) [əuˈeɪsɪs, əuˈeɪsiːz] *n* oasis *f*

oath [əuθ] *n* serment *m*; (*swear word*) juron *m*; **to take the ~** prêter serment; **on** (*Brit*) *or* **under ~** sous serment; assermenté(e)

oatmeal [ˈəutmiːl] *n* flocons *mpl* d'avoine

oats [əuts] *n* avoine *f*

OAU *n abbr* (= *Organization of African Unity*) OUA *f* (= *Organisation de l'unité africaine*)

obdurate [ˈɔbdjurɪt] *adj* obstiné(e), impénitent(e); intraitable

OBE *n abbr* (*Brit*: = *Order of the British Empire*) *distinction honorifique*

obedience [əˈbiːdɪəns] *n* obéissance *f*; **in ~ to** conformément à

obedient [əˈbiːdɪənt] *adj* obéissant(e); **to be ~ to sb/sth** obéir à qn/qch

obelisk [ˈɔbɪlɪsk] *n* obélisque *m*

obese [əuˈbiːs] *adj* obèse

obesity [əuˈbiːsɪti] *n* obésité *f*

obey [əˈbeɪ] *vt* obéir à; (*instructions*, *regulations*) se conformer à ▷ *vi* obéir

obituary [əˈbɪtjuərɪ] *n* nécrologie *f*

object *n* [ˈɔbdʒɪkt] objet *m*; (*purpose*) but *m*, objet; (*Ling*) complément *m* d'objet ▷ *vi* [əbˈdʒɛkt]: **to ~ to** (*attitude*) désapprouver; (*proposal*) protester contre, élever une objection contre; **I ~!** je proteste!; **he ~ed that ...** il a fait valoir *or* a objecté que ...; **do you ~ to my smoking?** est-ce que cela vous gêne si je fume?; **what's the ~ of doing that?** quel est l'intérêt de faire cela?; **money is no ~** l'argent n'est pas un problème

objection [əbˈdʒɛkʃən] *n* objection *f*; (*drawback*) inconvénient *m*; **if you have no ~** si vous n'y voyez pas d'inconvénient; **to make** *or* **raise an ~** élever une objection

objectionable [əbˈdʒɛkʃənəbl] *adj* très désagréable; choquant(e)

objective [əbˈdʒɛktɪv] *n* objectif *m* ▷ *adj* objectif(-ive)

objectivity [ɔbdʒɪkˈtɪvɪtɪ] *n* objectivité *f*

object lesson *n* (*fig*) (bonne) illustration

objector [əbˈdʒɛktə] *n* opposant(e)

obligation [ɔblɪˈgeɪʃən] *n* obligation *f*, devoir *m*; (*debt*) dette *f* (de reconnaissance); **"without ~"** "sans engagement"

obligatory [əˈblɪgətərɪ] *adj* obligatoire

oblige [əˈblaɪdʒ] *vt* (*force*): **to ~ sb to do** obliger *or* forcer qn à faire; (*do a favour*) rendre service à, obliger; **to be ~d to sb for sth** être obligé(e) à qn de qch; **anything to ~!** (*inf*) (toujours prêt à rendre) service!

obliging [əˈblaɪdʒɪŋ] *adj* obligeant(e), serviable

oblique [əˈbliːk] *adj* oblique; (*allusion*) indirect(e) ▷ *n* (*Brit Typ*): **~ (stroke)** barre *f* oblique

obliterate [əˈblɪtəreɪt] *vt* effacer

oblivion [əˈblɪvɪən] *n* oubli *m*

oblivious [əˈblɪvɪəs] *adj*: **~ of** oublieux(-euse) de

oblong [ˈɔblɔŋ] *adj* oblong(ue) ▷ *n* rectangle *m*

obnoxious [əbˈnɔkʃəs] *adj* odieux(-euse); (*smell*) nauséabond(e)

o.b.o. *abbr* (*US*) = **or best offer**; (*in classified ads*) ≈ à débattre

oboe [ˈəubəu] *n* hautbois *m*

obscene [əbˈsiːn] *adj* obscène

obscenity [əbˈsɛnɪti] *n* obscénité *f*

obscure [əbˈskjuəʳ] *adj* obscur(e) ▷ *vt* obscurcir; (*hide: sun*) cacher

obscurity [əbˈskjuərɪti] *n* obscurité *f*

obsequious [əbˈsiːkwɪəs] *adj* obséquieux(-euse)

observable [əbˈzəːvəbl] *adj* observable; (*appreciable*) notable

observance [əbˈzəːvns] *n* observance *f*, observation *f*; **religious ~s** observances religieuses

observant [əbˈzəːvnt] *adj* observateur(-trice)

observation [ɔbzəˈveɪʃən] *n* observation *f*; (*by police etc*) surveillance *f*

observation post n (Mil) poste m d'observation
observatory [əb'zə:vətrɪ] n observatoire m
observe [əb'zə:v] vt observer; (remark) faire observer or remarquer
observer [əb'zə:vəʳ] n observateur(-trice)
obsess [əb'sɛs] vt obséder; **to be ~ed by** or **with sb/sth** être obsédé(e) par qn/qch
obsession [əb'sɛʃən] n obsession f
obsessive [əb'sɛsɪv] adj obsédant(e)
obsolescence [ɔbsə'lɛsns] n vieillissement m; obsolescence f; **built-in** or **planned ~** (Comm) désuétude calculée
obsolescent [ɔbsə'lɛsnt] adj obsolescent(e), en voie d'être périmé(e)
obsolete ['ɔbsəli:t] adj dépassé(e), périmé(e)
obstacle ['ɔbstəkl] n obstacle m
obstacle race n course f d'obstacles
obstetrician [ɔbstə'trɪʃən] n obstétricien(ne)
obstetrics [ɔb'stɛtrɪks] n obstétrique f
obstinacy ['ɔbstɪnəsɪ] n obstination f
obstinate ['ɔbstɪnɪt] adj obstiné(e); (pain, cold) persistant(e)
obstreperous [əb'strɛpərəs] adj turbulent(e)
obstruct [əb'strʌkt] vt (block) boucher, obstruer; (halt) arrêter; (hinder) entraver
obstruction [əb'strʌkʃən] n obstruction f; (to plan, progress) obstacle m
obstructive [əb'strʌktɪv] adj obstructionniste
obtain [əb'teɪn] vt obtenir ▷ vi avoir cours
obtainable [əb'teɪnəbl] adj qu'on peut obtenir
obtrusive [əb'tru:sɪv] adj (person) importun(e); (smell) pénétrant(e); (building etc) trop en évidence
obtuse [əb'tju:s] adj obtus(e)
obverse ['ɔbvə:s] n (of medal, coin) côté m face; (fig) contrepartie f
obviate ['ɔbvɪeɪt] vt parer à, obvier à
obvious ['ɔbvɪəs] adj évident(e), manifeste
obviously ['ɔbvɪəslɪ] adv manifestement; (of course): **~, he ...** or **he ~ ...** il est bien évident qu'il ...; **~!** bien sûr!; **~ not!** évidemment pas!, bien sûr que non!
OCAS n abbr (= Organization of Central American States) ODEAC f (= Organisation des États d'Amérique centrale)
occasion [ə'keɪʒən] n occasion f; (event) événement m ▷ vt occasionner, causer; **on that ~** à cette occasion; **to rise to the ~** se montrer à la hauteur de la situation
occasional [ə'keɪʒənl] adj pris(e) (or fait(e) etc) de temps en temps; (worker, spending) occasionnel(le)
occasionally [ə'keɪʒənəlɪ] adv de temps en temps, quelquefois; **very ~** (assez) rarement
occasional table n table décorative
occult [ɔ'kʌlt] adj occulte ▷ n: **the ~** le surnaturel
occupancy ['ɔkjupənsɪ] n occupation f
occupant ['ɔkjupənt] n occupant m
occupation [ɔkju'peɪʃən] n occupation f; (job) métier m, profession f; **unfit for ~** (house) impropre à l'habitation

occupational [ɔkju'peɪʃnl] adj (accident, disease) du travail; (hazard) du métier
occupational guidance n (Brit) orientation professionnelle
occupational hazard n risque m du métier
occupational pension n retraite professionnelle
occupational therapy n ergothérapie f
occupier ['ɔkjupaɪəʳ] n occupant(e)
occupy ['ɔkjupaɪ] vt occuper; **to ~ o.s. with** or **by doing** s'occuper à faire; **to be occupied with sth** être occupé avec qch
occur [ə'kə:ʳ] vi se produire; (difficulty, opportunity) se présenter; (phenomenon, error) se rencontrer; **to ~ to sb** venir à l'esprit de qn
occurrence [ə'kʌrəns] n (existence) présence f, existence f; (event) cas m, fait m
ocean ['əuʃən] n océan m; **~s of** (inf) des masses de
ocean bed n fond (sous-)marin
ocean-going ['əuʃəngəuɪŋ] adj de haute mer
Oceania [əuʃɪ'eɪnɪə] n Océanie f
ocean liner n paquebot m
ochre ['əukəʳ] adj ocre
o'clock [ə'klɔk] adv: **it is 5 o'clock** il est 5 heures
OCR n abbr = **optical character reader; optical character recognition**
Oct. abbr (= October) oct
octagonal [ɔk'tægənl] adj octogonal(e)
octane ['ɔkteɪn] n octane m; **high-~ petrol** or (US) **gas** essence f à indice d'octane élevé
octave ['ɔktɪv] n octave f
October [ɔk'təubəʳ] n octobre m; for phrases see also **July**
octogenarian ['ɔktəudʒɪ'nɛərɪən] n octogénaire m/f
octopus ['ɔktəpəs] n pieuvre f
odd [ɔd] adj (strange) bizarre, curieux(-euse); (number) impair(e); (left over) qui reste, en plus; (not of a set) dépareillé(e); **60-~** 60 et quelques; **at ~ times** de temps en temps; **the ~ one out** l'exception f
oddball ['ɔdbɔ:l] n (inf) excentrique m/f
oddity ['ɔdɪtɪ] n bizarrerie f; (person) excentrique m/f
odd-job man [ɔd'dʒɔb-] (irreg) n homme m à tout faire
odd jobs npl petits travaux divers
oddly ['ɔdlɪ] adv bizarrement, curieusement
oddments ['ɔdmənts] npl (Brit Comm) fins fpl de série
odds [ɔdz] npl (in betting) cote f; **the ~ are against his coming** il y a peu de chances qu'il vienne; **it makes no ~** cela n'a pas d'importance; **to succeed against all the ~** réussir contre toute attente; **~ and ends** de petites choses; **at ~** en désaccord
odds-on [ɔdz'ɔn] adj: **the ~ favourite** le grand favori; **it's ~ that he'll come** il y a toutes les chances or gros à parier qu'il vienne
ode [əud] n ode f
odious ['əudɪəs] adj odieux(-euse), détestable

odometer [ɔ'dɒmɪtə^r] n (US) odomètre m

odour, (US) **odor** ['əʊdə^r] n odeur f

odourless, (US) **odorless** ['əʊdəlɪs] adj inodore

OECD n abbr (= Organization for Economic Cooperation and Development) OCDE f (= Organisation de coopération et de développement économique)

oesophagus, (US) **esophagus** [iː'sɒfəɡəs] n œsophage m

oestrogen, (US) **estrogen** ['iːstrəʊdʒən] n œstrogène m

⬤ KEYWORD

of [ɒv, əv] prep **1** (gen) de; **a friend of ours** un de nos amis; **a boy of 10** un garçon de 10 ans; **that was kind of you** c'était gentil de votre part **2** (expressing quantity, amount, dates etc) de; **a kilo of flour** un kilo de farine; **how much of this do you need?** combien vous en faut-il?; **there were three of them** (people) ils étaient 3; (objects) il y en avait 3; **three of us went** 3 d'entre nous y sont allé(e)s; **the 5th of July** le 5 juillet; **a quarter of 4** (US) 4 heures moins le quart **3** (from, out of) en, de; **a statue of marble** une statue de or en marbre; **made of wood** (fait) en bois

Ofcom ['ɒfkɒm] n abbr (Brit: = Office of Communications Regulation) organe de régulation de télécommunications

off [ɒf] adj, adv (engine) coupé(e); (light, TV) éteint(e); (tap) fermé(e); (Brit: food) mauvais(e), avancé(e); (: milk) tourné(e); (absent) absent(e); (cancelled) annulé(e); (removed): **the lid was ~** le couvercle était retiré or n'était pas mis; (away): **to run/drive ~** partir en courant/en voiture ▷ prep de; **to be ~** (to leave) partir, s'en aller; **I must be ~** il faut que je file; **to be ~ sick** être absent pour cause de maladie; **a day ~** un jour de congé; **to have an ~ day** n'être pas en forme; **he had his coat ~** il avait enlevé son manteau; **the hook is ~** le crochet s'est détaché; le crochet n'est pas mis; **10% ~** (Comm) 10% de rabais; **5 km ~ (the road)** à 5 km (de la route); **~ the coast** au large de la côte; **a house ~ the main road** une maison à l'écart de la grand-route; **it's a long way ~** c'est loin (d'ici); **I'm ~ meat** je ne mange plus de viande; je n'aime plus la viande; **on the ~ chance** à tout hasard; **to be well/badly ~** être bien/mal loti; (financially) être aisé/dans la gêne; **~ and on, on and ~** de temps à autre; **I'm afraid the chicken is ~** (Brit: not available) je regrette, il n'y a plus de poulet; **that's a bit ~** (fig: inf) c'est un peu fort

offal ['ɒfl] n (Culin) abats mpl

offbeat ['ɒfbiːt] adj excentrique

off-centre [ɒf'sɛntə^r] adj décentré(e), excentré(e)

off-colour ['ɒf'kʌlə^r] adj (Brit: ill) malade, mal fichu(e); **to feel ~** être mal fichu

offence, (US) **offense** [ə'fɛns] n (crime) délit m,

infraction f; **to give ~ to** blesser, offenser; **to take ~ at** se vexer de, s'offenser de; **to commit an ~** commettre une infraction

offend [ə'fɛnd] vt (person) offenser, blesser ▷ vi: **to ~ against** (law, rule) contrevenir à, enfreindre

offender [ə'fɛndə^r] n délinquant(e); (against regulations) contrevenant(e)

offending [ə'fɛndɪŋ] adj incriminé(e)

offense [ə'fɛns] n (US) = **offence**

offensive [ə'fɛnsɪv] adj offensant(e), choquant(e); (smell etc) très déplaisant(e); (weapon) offensif(-ive) ▷ n (Mil) offensive f

offer ['ɒfə^r] n offre f, proposition f ▷ vt offrir, proposer; **to make an ~ for sth** faire une offre pour qch; **to ~ sth to sb, ~ sb sth** offrir qch à qn; **to ~ to do sth** proposer de faire qch; **"on ~"** (Comm) "en promotion"

offering ['ɒfərɪŋ] n offrande f

offhand [ɒf'hænd] adj désinvolte ▷ adv spontanément; **I can't tell you ~** je ne peux pas vous le dire comme ça

office ['ɒfɪs] n (place) bureau m; (position) charge f, fonction f; **doctor's ~** (US) cabinet (médical); **to take ~** entrer en fonctions; **through his good ~s** (fig) grâce à ses bons offices; **O~ of Fair Trading** (Brit) organisme de protection contre les pratiques commerciales abusives

office automation n bureautique f

office bearer n (of club etc) membre m du bureau

office block, (US) **office building** n immeuble m de bureaux

office boy n garçon m de bureau

office hours npl heures fpl de bureau; (US Med) heures de consultation

office manager n responsable administratif(-ive)

officer ['ɒfɪsə^r] n (Mil etc) officier m; (also: **police officer**) agent m (de police); (of organization) membre m du bureau directeur

office work n travail m de bureau

office worker n employé(e) de bureau

official [ə'fɪʃl] adj (authorized) officiel(le) ▷ n officiel m; (civil servant) fonctionnaire m/f; (of railways, post office, town hall) employé(e)

officialdom [ə'fɪʃldəm] n bureaucratie f

officially [ə'fɪʃəlɪ] adv officiellement

official receiver n administrateur m judiciaire, syndic m de faillite

officiate [ə'fɪʃɪeɪt] vi (Rel) officier; **to ~ as Mayor** exercer les fonctions de maire; **to ~ at a marriage** célébrer un mariage

officious [ə'fɪʃəs] adj trop empressé(e)

offing ['ɒfɪŋ] n: **in the ~** (fig) en perspective

off-key [ɒf'kiː] adj faux (fausse) ▷ adv faux

off-licence ['ɒflaɪsns] n (Brit: shop) débit m de vins et de spiritueux

off-limits [ɒf'lɪmɪts] adj (esp US) dont l'accès est interdit

off-line [ɒf'laɪn] adj (Comput) (en mode) autonome; (: switched off) non connecté(e)

off-load ['ɒfləʊd] vt: **to ~ sth (onto)** (goods) décharger qch (sur); (job) se décharger de qch

(sur)

off-peak [ɔfˈpiːk] adj aux heures creuses; (electricity, ticket) au tarif heures creuses

off-putting [ˈɔfputɪŋ] adj (Brit: remark) rébarbatif(-ive); (person) rebutant(e), peu engageant(e)

off-road vehicle [ˈɔfrəud-] n véhicule m tout-terrain

off-season [ˈɔfsiːzn] adj, adv hors-saison inv

offset [ˈɔfsɛt] vt (irreg: like set); (counteract) contrebalancer, compenser ▷ n (also: **offset printing**) offset m

offshoot [ˈɔfʃuːt] n (fig) ramification f, antenne f; (: of discussion etc) conséquence f

offshore [ɔfˈʃɔːʳ] adj (breeze) de terre; (island) proche du littoral; (fishing) côtier(-ière); **~ oilfield** gisement m pétrolifère en mer

offside [ˈɔfˈsaɪd] n (Aut: with right-hand drive) côté droit; (: with left-hand drive) côté gauche ▷ adj (Sport) hors jeu; (Aut: in Britain) de droite; (: in US, Europe) de gauche

offspring [ˈɔfsprɪŋ] n progéniture f

offstage [ɔfˈsteɪdʒ] adv dans les coulisses

off-the-cuff [ɔfðəˈkʌf] adv au pied levé; de chic

off-the-job [ˈɔfðəˈdʒɔb] adj: **~ training** formation professionnelle extérieure

off-the-peg [ˈɔfðəˈpɛg], (US) **off-the-rack** [ˈɔfðəˈræk] adv en prêt-à-porter

off-the-record [ˈɔfðəˈrɛkɔːd] adj (remark) confidentiel(le), sans caractère officiel ▷ adv officieusement

off-white [ˈɔfwaɪt] adj blanc cassé inv

often [ˈɔfn] adv souvent; **how ~ do you go?** vous y allez tous les combien?; **every so ~** de temps en temps, de temps à autre; **as ~ as not** la plupart du temps

Ofwat [ˈɔfwɔt] n abbr (Brit: = Office of Water Services) organisme qui surveille les activités des compagnies des eaux

ogle [ˈəugl] vt lorgner

ogre [ˈəugəʳ] n ogre m

OH abbr (US) = Ohio

oh [əu] excl ô!, oh!, ah!

OHMS abbr (Brit) = **On His (or Her) Majesty's Service**

oil [ɔɪl] n huile f; (petroleum) pétrole m; (for central heating) mazout m ▷ vt (machine) graisser

oilcan [ˈɔɪlkæn] n burette f de graissage; (for storing) bidon m à huile

oil change n vidange f

oilfield [ˈɔɪlfiːld] n gisement m de pétrole

oil filter n (Aut) filtre m à huile

oil-fired [ˈɔɪlfaɪəd] adj au mazout

oil gauge n jauge f de niveau d'huile

oil industry n industrie pétrolière

oil level n niveau m d'huile

oil painting n peinture f à l'huile

oil refinery n raffinerie f de pétrole

oil rig n derrick m; (at sea) plate-forme pétrolière

oilskins [ˈɔɪlskɪnz] npl ciré m

oil slick n nappe f de mazout

oil tanker n (ship) pétrolier m; (truck) camion-

citerne m

oil well n puits m de pétrole

oily [ˈɔɪlɪ] adj huileux(-euse); (food) gras(se)

ointment [ˈɔɪntmənt] n onguent m

OK abbr (US) = **Oklahoma**

O.K., okay [ˈəuˈkeɪ] (inf) excl d'accord! ▷ vt approuver, donner son accord à ▷ n: **to give sth one's O.K.** donner son accord à qch ▷ adj (not bad) pas mal, en règle; en bon état; sain et sauf; acceptable; **is it O.K.?, are you O.K.?** ça va?; **are you O.K. for money?** ça va or ira question argent?; **it's O.K. with** or **by me** ça me va, c'est d'accord en ce qui me concerne

Okla. abbr (US) = **Oklahoma**

old [əuld] adj vieux (vieille); (person) vieux, âgé(e); (former) ancien(ne), vieux; **how ~ are you?** quel âge avez-vous?; **he's 10 years ~** il a 10 ans, il est âgé de 10 ans; **~er brother/sister** frère/sœur aîné(e); **any ~ thing will do** n'importe quoi fera l'affaire

old age n vieillesse f

old-age pensioner n (Brit) retraité(e)

old-fashioned [ˈəuldˈfæʃnd] adj démodé(e); (person) vieux jeu inv

old maid n vieille fille

old people's home n (esp Brit) maison f de retraite

old-style [ˈəuldstaɪl] adj à l'ancienne (mode)

old-time [ˈəuldˈtaɪm] adj du temps jadis, d'autrefois

old-timer [əuldˈtaɪməʳ] n ancien m

old wives' tale n conte m de bonne femme

O-level [ˈəulɛvl] n (in England and Wales: formerly) examen passé à l'âge de 16 ans sanctionnant les connaissances de l'élève, ≈ brevet m des collèges

olive [ˈɔlɪv] n (fruit) olive f; (tree) olivier m ▷ adj (also: **olive-green**) (vert) olive inv

olive oil n huile f d'olive

Olympic [əuˈlɪmpɪk] adj olympique; **the ~ Games, the ~s** les Jeux mpl olympiques

OM n abbr (Brit: = Order of Merit) titre honorifique

Oman [əuˈmɑːn] n Oman m

OMB n abbr (US: = Office of Management and Budget) service conseillant le président en matière budgétaire

omelette, omelet [ˈɔmlɪt] n omelette f; **ham/cheese omelet(te)** omelette au jambon/fromage

omen [ˈəumən] n présage m

ominous [ˈɔmɪnəs] adj menaçant(e), inquiétant(e); (event) de mauvais augure

omission [əuˈmɪʃən] n omission f

omit [əuˈmɪt] vt omettre; **to ~ to do sth** négliger de faire qch

omnivorous [ɔmˈnɪvrəs] adj omnivore

ON abbr (Canada) = **Ontario**

 KEYWORD

on [ɔn] prep **1** (indicating position) sur; **on the table** sur la table; **on the wall** sur le or au mur; **on the left** à gauche; **I haven't any money on me** je n'ai pas d'argent sur moi

2 (*indicating means, method, condition etc*): **on foot** à pied; **on the train/plane** (*be*) dans le train/l'avion; (*go*) en train/avion; **on the telephone/radio/television** au téléphone/à la radio/à la télévision; **to be on drugs** se droguer; **on holiday** (*Brit*): **on vacation** (*US*) en vacances; **on the continent** sur le continent

3 (*referring to time*): **on Friday** vendredi; **on Fridays** le vendredi; **on June 20th** le 20 juin; **a week on Friday** vendredi en huit; **on arrival** à l'arrivée; **on seeing this** en voyant cela

4 (*about, concerning*) sur, de; **a book on Balzac/physics** un livre sur Balzac/de physique

5 (*at the expense of*): **this round is on me** c'est ma tournée

▷ *adv* **1** (*referring to dress*): **to have one's coat on** avoir (mis) son manteau; **to put one's coat on** mettre son manteau; **what's she got on?** qu'est-ce qu'elle porte?

2 (*referring to covering*): **screw the lid on tightly** vissez bien le couvercle

3 (*further, continuously*): **to walk** *etc* **on** continuer à marcher *etc*; **on and off** de temps à autre; **from that day on** depuis ce jour

▷ *adj* **1** (*in operation: machine*) en marche; (: *radio, TV, light*) allumé(e); (: *tap, gas*) ouvert(e); (: *brakes*) mis(e); **is the meeting still on?** (*not cancelled*) est-ce que la réunion a bien lieu?; **it was well on in the evening** c'était tard dans la soirée; **when is this film on?** quand passe ce film?

2 (*inf*): **that's not on!** (*not acceptable*) cela ne se fait pas!; (*not possible*) pas question!

ONC *n abbr* (*Brit*: = *Ordinary National Certificate*) ≈ BT *m*

once [wʌns] *adv* une fois; (*formerly*) autrefois ▷ *conj* une fois que + *sub*; ~ **he had left/it was done** une fois qu'il fut parti/ que ce fut terminé; **at** ~ tout de suite, immédiatement; (*simultaneously*) à la fois; **all at** ~ (*adv*) tout d'un coup; ~ **a week** une fois par semaine; ~ **more** encore une fois; **I knew him** ~ je l'ai connu autrefois; ~ **and for all** une fois pour toutes; ~ **upon a time there was ...** il y avait une fois ..., il était une fois ...

oncoming [ˈɒnkʌmɪŋ] *adj* (*traffic*) venant en sens inverse

OND *n abbr* (*Brit*: = *Ordinary National Diploma*) ≈ BTS *m*

 KEYWORD

one [wʌn] *num* un(e); **one hundred and fifty** cent cinquante; **one by one** un(e) à *or* par un(e); **one day** un jour

▷ *adj* **1** (*sole*) seul(e), unique; **the one book which** l'unique *or* le seul livre qui; **the one man who** le seul (homme) qui

2 (*same*) même; **they came in the one car** ils sont venus dans la même voiture

▷ *pron* **1**: **this one** celui-ci (celle-ci); **that one** celui-là (celle-là); **I've already got one/a red one** j'en ai déjà un(e)/un(e) rouge; **which one do you want?** lequel voulez-vous?

2: **one another** l'un(e) l'autre; **to look at one another** se regarder

3 (*impersonal*) on; **one never knows** on ne sait jamais; **to cut one's finger** se couper le doigt; **one needs to eat** il faut manger

4 (*phrases*): **to be one up on sb** avoir l'avantage sur qn; **to be at one (with sb)** être d'accord (avec qn)

one-armed bandit [ˈwʌnɑːmd-] *n* machine *f* à sous

one-day excursion [ˈwʌndeɪ-] *n* (*US*) billet *m* d'aller-retour (valable pour la journée)

One-hundred share index [ˈwʌnhʌndrəd-] *n* indice *m* Footsie des cent grandes valeurs

one-man [ˈwʌnˈmæn] *adj* (*business*) dirigé(e) *etc* par un seul homme

one-man band *n* homme-orchestre *m*

one-off [wʌnˈɒf] *n* (*Brit inf*) exemplaire *m* unique ▷ *adj* unique

one-parent family [ˈwʌnpɛərənt-] *n* famille monoparentale

one-piece [ˈwʌnpiːs] *adj*: ~ **bathing suit** maillot *m* une pièce

onerous [ˈɒnərəs] *adj* (*task, duty*) pénible; (*responsibility*) lourd(e)

oneself [wʌnˈsɛlf] *pron* se; (*after prep, also emphatic*) soi-même; **to hurt** ~ se faire mal; **to keep sth for** ~ garder qch pour soi; **to talk to** ~ se parler à soi-même; **by** ~ tout seul

one-shot [wʌnˈʃɒt] (*US*) *n* = **one-off**

one-sided [wʌnˈsaɪdɪd] *adj* (*argument, decision*) unilatéral(e); (*judgment, account*) partial(e); (*contest*) inégal(e)

one-time [ˈwʌntaɪm] *adj* d'autrefois

one-to-one [ˈwʌntəwʌn] *adj* (*relationship*) univoque

one-upmanship [wʌnˈʌpmənʃɪp] *n*: **the art of** ~ l'art de faire mieux que les autres

one-way [ˈwʌnweɪ] *adj* (*street, traffic*) à sens unique

ongoing [ˈɒŋgəʊɪŋ] *adj* en cours; (*relationship*) suivi(e)

onion [ˈʌnjən] *n* oignon *m*

on-line [ˈɒnlaɪn] *adj* (*Comput*) en ligne; (: *switched on*) connecté(e)

onlooker [ˈɒnlukəʳ] *n* spectateur(-trice)

only [ˈəʊnlɪ] *adv* seulement ▷ *adj* seul(e), unique ▷ *conj* seulement, mais; **an** ~ **child** un enfant unique; **not** ~ **... but also** non seulement ... mais aussi; **I** ~ **took one** j'en ai seulement pris un, je n'en ai pris qu'un; **I saw her** ~ **yesterday** je l'ai vue hier encore; **I'd be** ~ **too pleased to help** je ne serais que trop content de vous aider; **I would come,** ~ **I'm very busy** je viendrais bien mais j'ai beaucoup à faire

ono *abbr* (*Brit*) = **or nearest offer**; (*in classified ads*) ≈ à débattre

on-screen [ɒnˈskriːn] *adj* à l'écran

onset [ˈɒnsɛt] *n* début *m*; (*of winter, old age*)

approche f

onshore ['ɔnʃɔːʳ] adj (wind) du large

onslaught ['ɔnslɔːt] n attaque f, assaut m

Ont. abbr (Canada) = **Ontario**

on-the-job ['ɔnðə'dʒɔb] adj: ~ **training** formation f sur place

onto ['ɔntu] prep = **on to**

onus ['əunəs] n responsabilité f; **the ~ is upon him to prove it** c'est à lui de le prouver

onward ['ɔnwəd], **onwards** ['ɔnwədz] adv (move) en avant; **from that time ~s** à partir de ce moment

oops [ups] excl houp!; **~-a-daisy!** houp-là!

ooze [uːz] vi suinter

opacity [əu'pæsɪtɪ] n opacité f

opal ['əupl] n opale f

opaque [əu'peɪk] adj opaque

OPEC ['əupɛk] n abbr (= Organization of Petroleum-Exporting Countries) OPEP f

open ['əupn] adj ouvert(e); (car) découvert(e); (road, view) dégagé(e); (meeting) public(-ique); (admiration) manifeste; (question) non résolu(e); (enemy) déclaré(e) ▷ vt ouvrir ▷ vi (flower, eyes, door, debate) s'ouvrir; (shop, bank, museum) ouvrir; (book etc: commence) commencer, débuter; **is it ~ to public?** est-ce ouvert au public?; **what time do you ~?** à quelle heure ouvrez-vous?; **in the ~ (air)** en plein air; **the ~ sea** le large; **~ ground** (among trees) clairière f; (waste ground) terrain m vague; **to have an ~ mind (on sth)** avoir l'esprit ouvert (sur qch)
  ▶ **open on to** vt fus (room, door) donner sur
  ▶ **open out** vt ouvrir ▷ vi s'ouvrir
  ▶ **open up** vt ouvrir; (blocked road) dégager ▷ vi s'ouvrir

open-air [əupn'ɛəʳ] adj en plein air

open-and-shut ['əupnən'ʃʌt] adj: ~ **case** cas m limpide

open day n journée f portes ouvertes

open-ended [əupn'ɛndɪd] adj (fig) non limité(e)

opener ['əupnəʳ] n (also: **can opener, tin opener**) ouvre-boîtes m

open-heart surgery [əupn'hɑːt-] n chirurgie f à cœur ouvert

opening ['əupnɪŋ] n ouverture f; (opportunity) occasion f; (work) débouché m; (job) poste vacant

opening hours npl heures fpl d'ouverture

opening night n (Theat) première f

open learning n enseignement universitaire à la carte, notamment par correspondance; (distance learning) télé-enseignement m

open learning centre n centre ouvert à tous où l'on dispense un enseignement général à temps partiel

openly ['əupnlɪ] adv ouvertement

open-minded [əupn'maɪndɪd] adj à l'esprit ouvert

open-necked ['əupnnɛkt] adj à col ouvert

openness ['əupnnɪs] n (frankness) franchise f

open-plan ['əupn'plæn] adj sans cloisons

open prison n prison ouverte

open sandwich n canapé m

open shop n entreprise qui admet les travailleurs non syndiqués

Open University n (Brit) cours universitaires par correspondance

opera ['ɔpərə] n opéra m

opera glasses npl jumelles fpl de théâtre

opera house n opéra m

opera singer n chanteur(-euse) d'opéra

operate ['ɔpəreɪt] vt (machine) faire marcher, faire fonctionner; (system) pratiquer ▷ vi fonctionner; (drug) faire effet; **to ~ on sb (for)** (Med) opérer qn (de)

operatic [ɔpə'rætɪk] adj d'opéra

operating ['ɔpəreɪtɪŋ] adj (Comm: costs, profit) d'exploitation; (Med): ~ **table** table f d'opération

operating room n (US: Med) salle f d'opération

operating system n (Comput) système m d'exploitation

operating theatre n (Brit: Med) salle f d'opération

operation [ɔpə'reɪʃən] n opération f; (of machine) fonctionnement m; **to have an ~ (for)** se faire opérer (de); **to be in ~** (machine) être en service; (system) être en vigueur

operational [ɔpə'reɪʃnl] adj opérationnel(le); (ready for use) en état de marche; **when the service is fully ~** lorsque le service fonctionnera pleinement

operative ['ɔpərətɪv] adj (measure) en vigueur ▷ n (in factory) ouvrier(-ière); **the ~ word** le mot clef

operator ['ɔpəreɪtəʳ] n (of machine) opérateur(-trice); (Tel) téléphoniste m/f

operetta [ɔpə'rɛtə] n opérette f

ophthalmologist [ɔfθæl'mɔlədʒɪst] n ophtalmologiste m/f, ophtalmologue m/f

opinion [ə'pɪnjən] n opinion f, avis m; **in my ~** à mon avis; **to seek a second ~** demander un deuxième avis

opinionated [ə'pɪnjəneɪtɪd] adj aux idées bien arrêtées

opinion poll n sondage m d'opinion

opium ['əupɪəm] n opium m

opponent [ə'pəunənt] n adversaire m/f

opportune ['ɔpətjuːn] adj opportun(e)

opportunist [ɔpə'tjuːnɪst] n opportuniste m/f

opportunity [ɔpə'tjuːnɪtɪ] n occasion f; **to take the ~ to do** or **of doing** profiter de l'occasion pour faire

oppose [ə'pəuz] vt s'opposer à; **to be ~d to sth** être opposé(e) à qch; **as ~d to** par opposition à

opposing [ə'pəuzɪŋ] adj (side) opposé(e)

opposite ['ɔpəzɪt] adj opposé(e); (house etc) d'en face ▷ adv en face ▷ prep en face de ▷ n opposé m, contraire m; (of word) contraire m; **"see ~ page"** "voir ci-contre"

opposite number n (Brit) homologue m/f

opposite sex n: **the ~** l'autre sexe

opposition [ɔpə'zɪʃən] n opposition f

oppress [ə'prɛs] vt opprimer

oppression [ə'prɛʃən] n oppression f

oppressive [ə'prɛsɪv] *adj* oppressif(-ive)
opprobrium [ə'prəubrɪəm] *n* (*formal*) opprobre *m*
opt [ɔpt] *vi*: **to ~ for** opter pour; **to ~ to do** choisir de faire
▸ **opt out** *vi* (*school, hospital*) devenir autonome; (*health service*) devenir privé(e); **to ~ out of** choisir de ne pas participer à *or* de ne pas faire
optical ['ɔptɪkl] *adj* optique; (*instrument*) d'optique
optical character reader *n* lecteur *m* optique
optical character recognition *n* lecture *f* optique
optical fibre *n* fibre *f* optique
optician [ɔp'tɪʃən] *n* opticien(ne)
optics ['ɔptɪks] *n* optique *f*
optimism ['ɔptɪmɪzəm] *n* optimisme *m*
optimist ['ɔptɪmɪst] *n* optimiste *m/f*
optimistic [ɔptɪ'mɪstɪk] *adj* optimiste
optimum ['ɔptɪməm] *adj* optimum
option ['ɔpʃən] *n* choix *m*, option *f*; (*Scol*) matière *f* à option; (*Comm*) option; **to keep one's ~s open** (*fig*) ne pas s'engager; **I have no ~** je n'ai pas le choix
optional ['ɔpʃənl] *adj* facultatif(-ive); (*Comm*) en option; **~ extras** accessoires *mpl* en option, options *fpl*
opulence ['ɔpjuləns] *n* opulence *f*; abondance *f*
opulent ['ɔpjulənt] *adj* opulent(e); abondant(e)
OR *abbr* (*US*) = **Oregon**
or [ɔːʳ] *conj* ou; (*with negative*): **he hasn't seen or heard anything** il n'a rien vu ni entendu; **or else** sinon; ou bien
oracle ['ɔrəkl] *n* oracle *m*
oral ['ɔːrəl] *adj* oral(e) ▷ *n* oral *m*
orange ['ɔrɪndʒ] *n* (*fruit*) orange *f* ▷ *adj* orange *inv*
orangeade [ɔrɪndʒ'eɪd] *n* orangeade *f*
orange juice *n* jus *m* d'orange
oration [ɔː'reɪʃən] *n* discours solennel
orator ['ɔrətəʳ] *n* orateur(-trice)
oratorio [ɔrə'tɔːrɪəu] *n* oratorio *m*
orb [ɔːb] *n* orbe *m*
orbit ['ɔːbɪt] *n* orbite *f* ▷ *vt* graviter autour de; **to be in/go into ~ (round)** être/entrer en orbite (autour de)
orbital ['ɔːbɪtl] *n* (*also*: **orbital motorway**) périphérique *f*
orchard ['ɔːtʃəd] *n* verger *m*; **apple ~** verger de pommiers
orchestra ['ɔːkɪstrə] *n* orchestre *m*; (*US: seating*) (fauteils *mpl* d')orchestre
orchestral [ɔː'kɛstrəl] *adj* orchestral(e); (*concert*) symphonique
orchestrate ['ɔːkɪstreɪt] *vt* (*Mus, fig*) orchestrer
orchid ['ɔːkɪd] *n* orchidée *f*
ordain [ɔː'deɪn] *vt* (*Rel*) ordonner; (*decide*) décréter
ordeal [ɔː'diːl] *n* épreuve *f*
order ['ɔːdəʳ] *n* ordre *m*; (*Comm*) commande *f* ▷ *vt* ordonner; (*Comm*) commander; **in ~** en ordre; (*of document*) en règle; **out of ~** (*not in correct order*) en désordre; (*machine*) hors service; (*telephone*)

en dérangement; **a machine in working ~** une machine en état de marche; **in ~ of size** par ordre de grandeur; **in ~ to do/that** pour faire/que + *sub*; **to place an ~ for sth with sb** commander qch auprès de qn, passer commande de qch à qn; **could I ~ now, please?** je peux commander, s'il vous plaît?; **to be on ~** être en commande; **made to ~** fait sur commande; **to be under ~s to do sth** avoir ordre de faire qch; **a point of ~** un point de procédure; **to the ~ of** (*Banking*) à l'ordre de; **to ~ sb to do** ordonner à qn de faire
order book *n* carnet *m* de commandes
order form *n* bon *m* de commande
orderly ['ɔːdəlɪ] *n* (*Mil*) ordonnance *f*; (*Med*) garçon *m* de salle ▷ *adj* (*room*) en ordre; (*mind*) méthodique; (*person*) qui a de l'ordre
order number *n* (*Comm*) numéro *m* de commande
ordinal ['ɔːdɪnl] *adj* (*number*) ordinal(e)
ordinary ['ɔːdnrɪ] *adj* ordinaire, normal(e); (*pej*) ordinaire, quelconque; **out of the ~** exceptionnel(le)
ordinary degree *n* (*Scol*) ≈ licence *f* libre; *voir article*

● **ORDINARY DEGREE**

Un *ordinary degree* est un diplôme inférieur à l'"honours degree" que l'on obtient en général après trois années d'études universitaires. Il peut aussi être décerné en cas d'échec à l'"honours degree".

ordinary seaman *n* (*Brit*) matelot *m*
ordinary shares *npl* actions *fpl* ordinaires
ordination [ɔːdɪ'neɪʃən] *n* ordination *f*
ordnance ['ɔːdnəns] *n* (*Mil: unit*) service *m* du matériel
Ordnance Survey map *n* (*Brit*) ≈ carte *f* d'État-major
ore [ɔːʳ] *n* minerai *m*
Ore., Oreg. *abbr* (*US*) = **Oregon**
oregano [ɔrɪ'gaːnəu] *n* origan *m*
organ ['ɔːgən] *n* organe *m*; (*Mus*) orgue *m*, orgues *fpl*
organic [ɔː'gænɪk] *adj* organique; (*crops etc*) biologique, naturel(le)
organism ['ɔːgənɪzəm] *n* organisme *m*
organist ['ɔːgənɪst] *n* organiste *m/f*
organization [ɔːgənaɪ'zeɪʃən] *n* organisation *f*
organization chart *n* organigramme *m*
organize ['ɔːgənaɪz] *vt* organiser; **to get ~d** s'organiser
organized ['ɔːgənaɪzd] *adj* (*planned*) organisé(e); (*efficient*) bien organisé
organized crime ['ɔːgənaɪzd-] *n* crime organisé, grand banditisme
organized labour ['ɔːgənaɪzd-] *n* main-d'œuvre syndiquée
organizer ['ɔːgənaɪzəʳ] *n* organisateur(-trice)
orgasm ['ɔːgæzəm] *n* orgasme *m*

orgy ['ɔ:dʒɪ] n orgie f
Orient ['ɔ:rɪənt] n: **the ~** l'Orient m
oriental [ɔ:rɪ'ɛntl] adj oriental(e) ▷ n
Oriental(e)
orientate ['ɔ:rɪənteɪt] vt orienter
orientation [ɔ:rɪen'teɪʃən] n (attitudes) tendance
f; (in job) orientation f; (of building) orientation,
exposition f
orifice ['ɔrɪfɪs] n orifice m
origin ['ɔrɪdʒɪn] n origine f; **country of ~** pays m
d'origine
original [ə'rɪdʒɪnl] adj original(e); (earliest)
originel(le) ▷ n original m
originality [ərɪdʒɪ'nælɪtɪ] n originalité f
originally [ə'rɪdʒɪnəlɪ] adv (at first) à l'origine
originate [ə'rɪdʒɪneɪt] vi: **to ~ from** être
originaire de; (suggestion) provenir de; **to ~ in**
(custom) prendre naissance dans, avoir son
origine dans
originator [ə'rɪdʒɪneɪtər] n auteur m
Orkney ['ɔ:knɪ] n (also: **the Orkneys, the Orkney
Islands**) les Orcades fpl
ornament ['ɔ:nəmənt] n ornement m; (trinket)
bibelot m
ornamental [ɔ:nə'mɛntl] adj décoratif(-ive);
(garden) d'agrément
ornamentation [ɔ:nəmɛn'teɪʃən] n
ornementation f
ornate [ɔ:'neɪt] adj très orné(e)
ornithologist [ɔ:nɪ'θɔlədʒɪst] n ornithologue
m/f
ornithology [ɔ:nɪ'θɔlədʒɪ] n ornithologie f
orphan ['ɔ:fn] n orphelin(e) ▷ vt: **to be ~ed**
devenir orphelin
orphanage ['ɔ:fənɪdʒ] n orphelinat m
orthodox ['ɔ:θədɔks] adj orthodoxe
orthopaedic, (US) **orthopedic** [ɔ:θə'pi:dɪk] adj
orthopédique
OS abbr (Brit: = Ordnance Survey) ≈ IGN m (= Institut
géographique national); (: Naut) = **ordinary
seaman**; (: Dress) = **outsize**
O/S abbr = **out of stock**
Oscar ['ɔskər] n oscar m
oscillate ['ɔsɪleɪt] vi osciller
OSHA n abbr (US: = Occupational Safety and Health
Administration) office de l'hygiène et de la sécurité au
travail
Oslo ['ɔzləu] n Oslo
ostensible [ɔs'tɛnsɪbl] adj prétendu(e);
apparent(e)
ostensibly [ɔs'tɛnsɪblɪ] adv en apparence
ostentation [ɔstɛn'teɪʃən] n ostentation f
ostentatious [ɔstɛn'teɪʃəs] adj
prétentieux(-euse); ostentatoire
osteopath ['ɔstɪəpæθ] n ostéopathe m/f
ostracize ['ɔstrəsaɪz] vt frapper d'ostracisme
ostrich ['ɔstrɪtʃ] n autruche f
OT n abbr (= Old Testament) AT m
OTB n abbr (US: = off-track betting) paris pris en dehors
du champ de course
O.T.E. abbr (= on-target earnings) primes fpl sur
objectifs inclus

other ['ʌðər] adj autre ▷ pron: **the ~ (one)** l'autre;
~s (other people) d'autres ▷ adv: **~ than**
autrement que; à part; **some actor or ~** un
certain acteur, je ne sais quel acteur;
somebody or ~ quelqu'un; **some ~ people
have still to arrive** on attend encore quelques
personnes; **the ~ day** l'autre jour; **the car was
none ~ than John's** la voiture n'était autre que
celle de John
otherwise ['ʌðəwaɪz] adv, conj autrement; **an ~
good piece of work** par ailleurs, un beau
travail
OTT abbr (inf) = **over the top**; see **top**
Ottawa ['ɔtəwə] n Ottawa
otter ['ɔtər] n loutre f
OU n abbr (Brit) = **Open University**
ouch [autʃ] excl aïe!
ought (pt ~) [ɔ:t] aux vb: **I ~ to do it** je devrais le
faire, il faudrait que je le fasse; **this ~ to have
been corrected** cela aurait dû être corrigé; **he
~ to win** (probability) il devrait gagner; **you ~ to
go and see it** vous devriez aller le voir
ounce [auns] n once f (28.35g; 16 in a pound)
our ['auər] adj notre, nos pl; see also **my**
ours [auəz] pron le (la) nôtre, les nôtres; see also
mine¹
ourselves [auə'sɛlvz] pron pl (reflexive, after
preposition) nous; (emphatic) nous-mêmes; **we
did it (all) by ~** nous avons fait ça tout seuls; see
also **oneself**
oust [aust] vt évincer
out [aut] adv dehors; (published, not at home etc)
sorti(e); (light, fire) éteint(e); (on strike) en grève
▷ vt: **to ~ sb** révéler l'homosexualité de qn; **~
here** ici; **~ there** là-bas; **he's ~** (absent) il est
sorti; (unconscious) il est sans connaissance; **to
be ~ in one's calculations** s'être trompé dans
ses calculs; **to run/back** etc **~** sortir en courant/
en reculant etc; **to be ~ and about** or (US)
around again être de nouveau sur pied; **before
the week was ~** avant la fin de la semaine; **the
journey ~** l'aller m; **the boat was 10 km ~** le
bateau était à 10 km du rivage; **~ loud** (adv) à
haute voix; **~ of** (prep: outside) en dehors de;
(because of: anger etc) par; (from among): **10 ~ of 10**
10 sur 10; (without): **~ of petrol** sans essence, à
court d'essence; **made ~ of wood** en or de bois;
~ of order (machine) en panne; (Tel: line) en
dérangement; **~ of stock** (Comm: article)
épuisé(e); (: shop) en rupture de stock
outage ['autɪdʒ] n (esp US: power failure) panne f or
coupure f de courant
out-and-out ['autəndaut] adj véritable
outback ['autbæk] n campagne isolée; (in
Australia) intérieur m
outbid [aut'bɪd] vt (irreg: like **bid**) surenchérir
outboard ['autbɔ:d] n: **~ (motor)** (moteur m)
hors-bord m
outbound ['autbaund] adj: **~ (from/for)** en
partance (de/pour)
outbreak ['autbreɪk] n (of violence) éruption f,
explosion f; (of disease) de nombreux cas; **the ~**

of war south of the border la guerre qui s'est déclarée au sud de la frontière

outbuilding ['autbɪldɪŋ] n dépendance f

outburst ['autbə:st] n explosion f, accès m

outcast ['autkɑ:st] n exilé(e); (socially) paria m

outclass [aut'klɑ:s] vt surclasser

outcome ['autkʌm] n issue f, résultat m

outcrop ['autkrɔp] n affleurement m

outcry ['autkraɪ] n tollé (général)

outdated [aut'deɪtɪd] adj démodé(e)

outdistance [aut'dɪstəns] vt distancer

outdo [aut'du:] vt (irreg: like **do**) surpasser

outdoor [aut'dɔ:'] adj de or en plein air

outdoors [aut'dɔ:z] adv dehors; au grand air

outer ['autə'] adj extérieur(e); **~ suburbs** grande banlieue

outer space n espace m cosmique

outfit ['autfɪt] n équipement m; (clothes) tenue f; (inf: Comm) organisation f, boîte f

outfitter ['autfɪtə'] n (Brit): **"(gent's) ~'s"** "confection pour hommes"

outgoing ['autgəuɪŋ] adj (president, tenant) sortant(e); (character) ouvert(e), extraverti(e)

outgoings ['autgəuɪŋz] npl (Brit: expenses) dépenses fpl

outgrow [aut'grəu] vt (irreg: like **grow**); (clothes) devenir trop grand(e) pour

outhouse ['authaus] n appentis m, remise f

outing ['autɪŋ] n sortie f; excursion f

outlandish [aut'lændɪʃ] adj étrange

outlast [aut'lɑ:st] vt survivre à

outlaw ['autlɔ:] n hors-la-loi m inv ▷ vt (person) mettre hors la loi; (practice) proscrire

outlay ['autleɪ] n dépenses fpl; (investment) mise f de fonds

outlet ['autlɛt] n (for liquid etc) issue f, sortie f; (for emotion) exutoire m; (for goods) débouché m; (also: **retail outlet**) point m de vente; (US: Elec) prise f de courant

outline ['autlaɪn] n (shape) contour m; (summary) esquisse f, grandes lignes ▷ vt (fig: theory, plan) exposer à grands traits

outlive [aut'lɪv] vt survivre à

outlook ['autluk] n perspective f; (point of view) attitude f

outlying ['autlaɪɪŋ] adj écarté(e)

outmanoeuvre [autmə'nu:və'] vt (rival etc) avoir au tournant

outmoded [aut'məudɪd] adj démodé(e); dépassé(e)

outnumber [aut'nʌmbə'] vt surpasser en nombre

out-of-court [autəv'kɔ:t] adj, adv à l'aimable

out-of-date [autəv'deɪt] adj (passport, ticket) périmé(e); (theory, idea) dépassé(e); (custom) désuet(-ète); (clothes) démodé(e)

out-of-doors [autəv'dɔ:z] adv = **outdoors**

out-of-the-way ['autəvðə'weɪ] adj loin de tout; (fig) insolite

out-of-town [autəv'taun] adj (shopping centre etc) en périphérie

outpatient ['autpeɪʃənt] n malade m/f en consultation externe

outpost ['autpəust] n avant-poste m

outpouring ['autpɔ:rɪŋ] n (fig) épanchement(s) m(pl)

output ['autput] n rendement m, production f; (Comput) sortie f ▷ vt (Comput) sortir

outrage ['autreɪdʒ] n (anger) indignation f; (violent act) atrocité f, acte m de violence; (scandal) scandale m ▷ vt outrager

outrageous [aut'reɪdʒəs] adj atroce; (scandalous) scandaleux(-euse)

outrider ['autraɪdə'] n (on motorcycle) motard m

outright adv [aut'raɪt] complètement; (deny, refuse) catégoriquement; (ask) carrément; (kill) sur le coup ▷ adj ['autraɪt] complet(-ète); catégorique

outrun [aut'rʌn] vt (irreg: like **run**) dépasser

outset ['autset] n début m

outshine [aut'ʃaɪn] vt (irreg: like **shine**); (fig) éclipser

outside [aut'saɪd] n extérieur m ▷ adj extérieur(e); (remote, unlikely): **an ~ chance** une (très) faible chance ▷ adv (au) dehors, à l'extérieur ▷ prep hors de, à l'extérieur de; (in front of) devant; **at the ~** (fig) au plus or maximum; **~ left/right** n (Football) ailier gauche/droit

outside broadcast n (Radio, TV) reportage m

outside lane n (Aut: in Britain) voie f de droite; (: in US, Europe) voie de gauche

outside line n (Tel) ligne extérieure

outsider [aut'saɪdə'] n (in race etc) outsider m; (stranger) étranger(-ère)

outsize ['autsaɪz] adj énorme; (clothes) grande taille inv

outskirts ['autskə:ts] npl faubourgs mpl

outsmart [aut'smɑ:t] vt se montrer plus malin(-igne) or futé(e) que

outspoken [aut'spəukən] adj très franc (franche)

outspread [aut'sprɛd] adj (wings) déployé(e)

outstanding [aut'stændɪŋ] adj remarquable, exceptionnel(le); (unfinished: work, business) en suspens, en souffrance; (debt) impayé(e); (problem) non réglé(e); **your account is still ~** vous n'avez pas encore tout remboursé

outstay [aut'steɪ] vt: **to ~ one's welcome** abuser de l'hospitalité de son hôte

outstretched [aut'strɛtʃt] adj (hand) tendu(e); (body) étendu(e)

outstrip [aut'strɪp] vt (also fig) dépasser

out-tray ['auttreɪ] n courrier m "départ"

outvote [aut'vəut] vt: **to ~ sb (by)** mettre qn en minorité (par); **to ~ sth (by)** rejeter qch (par)

outward ['autwəd] adj (sign, appearances) extérieur(e); (journey) (d')aller

outwardly ['autwədlɪ] adv extérieurement; en apparence

outwards ['autwədz] adv (esp Brit) = **outward**

outweigh [aut'weɪ] vt l'emporter sur

outwit [aut'wɪt] vt se montrer plus malin que

oval ['əuvl] adj, n ovale m

Oval Office *n* (US: Pol) *voir article*

● **OVAL OFFICE**
●
● L'*Oval Office* est le bureau personnel du
● président des États-Unis à la Maison-
● Blanche, ainsi appelé du fait de sa forme
● ovale. Par extension, ce terme désigne la
● présidence elle-même.

ovarian [əu'vɛərɪən] *adj* ovarien(ne); (*cancer*) des
ovaires
ovary ['əuvərɪ] *n* ovaire *m*
ovation [əu'veɪʃən] *n* ovation *f*
oven ['ʌvn] *n* four *m*
oven glove *n* gant *m* de cuisine
ovenproof ['ʌvnpruːf] *adj* allant au four
oven-ready ['ʌvnrɛdɪ] *adj* prêt(e) à cuire
ovenware ['ʌvnwɛər] *n* plats *mpl* allant au four
over ['əuvər] *adv* (par-)dessus; (*excessively*) trop
▷ *adj* (*or adv*) (*finished*) fini(e), terminé(e); (*too
much*) en plus ▷ *prep* sur; par-dessus; (*above*) au-
dessus de; (*on the other side of*) de l'autre côté de;
(*more than*) plus de; (*during*) pendant; (*about,
concerning*): **they fell out ~ money/her** ils se
sont brouillés pour des questions d'argent/à
cause d'elle; **~ here** ici; **~ there** là-bas; **all ~**
(*everywhere*) partout; (*finished*) fini(e); **~ and ~**
(*again*) à plusieurs reprises; **~ and above** en
plus de; **to ask sb ~** inviter qn (à passer); **to go
~ to sb's** passer chez qn; **to fall ~** tomber; **to
turn sth ~** retourner qch; **now ~ to our Paris
correspondent** nous passons l'antenne à
notre correspondant à Paris; **the world ~** dans
le monde entier; **she's not ~ intelligent** (*Brit*)
elle n'est pas particulièrement intelligente
over... ['əuvər] *prefix*: **overabundant**
surabondant(e)
overact [əuvər'ækt] *vi* (*Theat*) outrer son rôle
overall ['əuvərɔːl] *adj* (*length*) total(e); (*study,
impression*) d'ensemble ▷ *n* (*Brit*) blouse *f* ▷ *adv*
[əuvər'ɔːl] dans l'ensemble, en général;
overalls *npl* (*boiler suit*) bleus *mpl* (de travail)
overall majority *n* majorité absolue
overanxious [əuvər'æŋkʃəs] *adj* trop
anxieux(-euse)
overawe [əuvər'ɔː] *vt* impressionner
overbalance [əuvə'bæləns] *vi* basculer
overbearing [əuvə'bɛərɪŋ] *adj*
impérieux(-euse), autoritaire
overboard ['əuvəbɔːd] *adv* (*Naut*) par-dessus
bord; **to go ~ for sth** (*fig*) s'emballer (pour qch)
overbook [əuvə'buk] *vi* faire du surbooking
overcame [əuvə'keɪm] *pt of* **overcome**
overcapitalize [əuvə'kæpɪtəlaɪz] *vt*
surcapitaliser
overcast ['əuvəkɑːst] *adj* couvert(e)
overcharge [əuvə'tʃɑːdʒ] *vt*: **to ~ sb for sth** faire
payer qch trop cher à qn
overcoat ['əuvəkəut] *n* pardessus *m*
overcome [əuvə'kʌm] *vt* (*irreg: like* **come**);
(*defeat*) triompher de; (*difficulty*) surmonter ▷ *adj*

(*emotionally*) bouleversé(e); **~ with grief**
accablé(e) de douleur
overconfident [əuvə'kɔnfɪdənt] *adj* trop sûr(e)
de soi
overcrowded [əuvə'kraudɪd] *adj* bondé(e); (*city,
country*) surpeuplé(e)
overcrowding [əuvə'kraudɪŋ] *n*
surpeuplement *m*; (*in bus*) encombrement *m*
overdo [əuvə'duː] *vt* (*irreg: like* **do**) exagérer;
(*overcook*) trop cuire; **to ~ it, to ~ things** (*work too
hard*) en faire trop, se surmener
overdone [əuvə'dʌn] *adj* (*vegetables, steak*) trop
cuit(e)
overdose ['əuvədəus] *n* dose excessive
overdraft ['əuvədrɑːft] *n* découvert *m*
overdrawn [əuvə'drɔːn] *adj* (*account*) à découvert
overdrive ['əuvədraɪv] *n* (*Aut*) (vitesse *f*)
surmultipliée *f*
overdue [əuvə'djuː] *adj* en retard; (*bill*)
impayé(e); (*change*) qui tarde; **that change was
long ~** ce changement n'avait que trop tardé
overemphasis [əuvər'ɛmfəsɪs] *n*: **to put an ~
on** accorder trop d'importance à
overestimate [əuvər'ɛstɪmeɪt] *vt* surestimer
overexcited [əuvərɪk'saɪtɪd] *adj* surexcité(e)
overexertion [əuvərɪg'zəːʃən] *n* surmenage *m*
(physique)
overexpose [əuvərɪk'spəuz] *vt* (*Phot*) surexposer
overflow *vi* [əuvə'fləu] déborder ▷ *n* ['əuvəfləu]
trop-plein *m*; (*also:* **overflow pipe**) tuyau *m*
d'écoulement, trop-plein *m*
overfly [əuvə'flaɪ] *vt* (*irreg: like* **fly**) survoler
overgenerous [əuvə'dʒɛnərəs] *adj* (*person*)
prodigue; (*offer*) excessif(-ive)
overgrown [əuvə'grəun] *adj* (*garden*) envahi(e)
par la végétation; **he's just an ~ schoolboy** (*fig*)
c'est un écolier attardé
overhang ['əuvə'hæŋ] *vt* (*irreg: like* **hang**)
surplomber ▷ *vi* faire saillie
overhaul *vt* [əuvə'hɔːl] réviser ▷ *n* ['əuvəhɔːl]
révision *f*
overhead *adv* [əuvə'hɛd] au-dessus ▷ *adj, n*
['əuvəhɛd] ▷ *adj* aérien(ne); (*lighting*) vertical(e)
▷ *n* (US) = **overheads**
overhead projector *n* rétroprojecteur *m*
overheads ['əuvəhɛdz] *npl* (*Brit*) frais généraux
overhear [əuvə'hɪər] *vt* (*irreg: like* **hear**) entendre
(par hasard)
overheat [əuvə'hiːt] *vi* devenir surchauffé(e);
(*engine*) chauffer
overjoyed [əuvə'dʒɔɪd] *adj* ravi(e), enchanté(e)
overkill ['əuvəkɪl] *n* (*fig*): **it would be ~** ce serait
de trop
overland ['əuvəlænd] *adj, adv* par voie de terre
overlap *vi* [əuvə'læp] se chevaucher ▷ *n*
['əuvəlæp] chevauchement *m*
overleaf [əuvə'liːf] *adv* au verso
overload [əuvə'ləud] *vt* surcharger
overlook [əuvə'luk] *vt* (*have view of*) donner sur;
(*miss*) oublier, négliger; (*forgive*) fermer les yeux
sur
overlord ['əuvəlɔːd] *n* chef *m* suprême

overmanning [əuvəˈmænɪŋ] n sureffectif m, main-d'œuvre f pléthorique

overnight adv [əuvəˈnaɪt] (happen) durant la nuit; (fig) soudain ▷ adj [ˈəuvənaɪt] d'une (or de) nuit; soudain(e); **to stay ~ (with sb)** passer la nuit (chez qn); **he stayed there ~** il y a passé la nuit; **if you travel ~ ...** si tu fais le voyage de nuit ...; **he'll be away ~** il ne rentrera pas ce soir

overnight bag n nécessaire m de voyage

overpass [ˈəuvəpɑːs] n (US: for cars) pont autoroutier; (: for pedestrians) passerelle f, pont m

overpay [əuvəˈpeɪ] vt (irreg: like **pay**); **to ~ sb by £50** donner à qn 50 livres de trop

overplay [əuvəˈpleɪ] vt exagérer; **to ~ one's hand** trop présumer de sa situation

overpower [əuvəˈpauəʳ] vt vaincre; (fig) accabler

overpowering [əuvəˈpauərɪŋ] adj irrésistible; (heat, stench) suffocant(e)

overproduction [ˈəuvəprəˈdʌkʃən] n surproduction f

overrate [əuvəˈreɪt] vt surestimer

overreact [əuvəriˈækt] vi réagir de façon excessive

override [əuvəˈraɪd] vt (irreg: like **ride**); (order, objection) passer outre à; (decision) annuler

overriding [əuvəˈraɪdɪŋ] adj prépondérant(e)

overrule [əuvəˈruːl] vt (decision) annuler; (claim) rejeter; (person) rejeter l'avis de

overrun [əuvəˈrʌn] vt (irreg: like **run**); (Mil: country etc) occuper; (time limit etc) dépasser ▷ vi dépasser le temps imparti; **the town is ~ with tourists** la ville est envahie de touristes

overseas [əuvəˈsiːz] adv outre-mer; (abroad) à l'étranger ▷ adj (trade) extérieur(e); (visitor) étranger(-ère)

oversee [əuvəˈsiː] vt (irreg: like **see**) surveiller

overseer [ˈəuvəsɪəʳ] n (in factory) contremaître m

overshadow [əuvəˈʃædəu] vt (fig) éclipser

overshoot [əuvəˈʃuːt] vt (irreg: like **shoot**) dépasser

oversight [ˈəuvəsaɪt] n omission f, oubli m; **due to an ~** par suite d'une inadvertance

oversimplify [əuvəˈsɪmplɪfaɪ] vt simplifier à l'excès

oversleep [əuvəˈsliːp] vi (irreg: like **sleep**) se réveiller (trop) tard

overspend [əuvəˈspɛnd] vi (irreg: like **spend**) dépenser de trop; **we have overspent by 5,000 dollars** nous avons dépassé notre budget de 5 000 dollars, nous avons dépensé 5 000 dollars de trop

overspill [ˈəuvəspɪl] n excédent m de population

overstaffed [əuvəˈstɑːft] adj: **to be ~** avoir trop de personnel, être en surnombre

overstate [əuvəˈsteɪt] vt exagérer

overstatement [əuvəˈsteɪtmənt] n exagération f

overstay [əuvəˈsteɪ] vt: **to ~ one's welcome (at sb's)** abuser de l'hospitalité de qn

overstep [əuvəˈstɛp] vt: **to ~ the mark** dépasser la mesure

overstock [əuvəˈstɔk] vt stocker en surabondance

overstretched [əuvəˈstrɛtʃt] adj (person) débordé(e); **my budget is ~** j'ai atteint les limites de mon budget

overstrike n [ˈəuvəstraɪk] (on printer) superposition f, double frappe f ▷ vt (irreg: like **strike**) [əuvəˈstraɪk] surimprimer

overt [əuˈvəːt] adj non dissimulé(e)

overtake [əuvəˈteɪk] vt (irreg: like **take**) dépasser; (Brit: Aut) dépasser, doubler

overtaking [əuvəˈteɪkɪŋ] n (Aut) dépassement m

overtax [əuvəˈtæks] vt (Econ) surimposer; (fig: strength, patience) abuser de; **to ~ o.s.** se surmener

overthrow [əuvəˈθrəu] vt (irreg: like **throw**); (government) renverser

overtime [ˈəuvətaɪm] n heures fpl supplémentaires; **to do** or **work ~** faire des heures supplémentaires

overtime ban n refus m de faire des heures supplémentaires

overtone [ˈəuvətəun] n (also: **overtones**) note f, sous-entendus mpl

overtook [əuvəˈtuk] pt of **overtake**

overture [ˈəuvətʃuəʳ] n (Mus, fig) ouverture f

overturn [əuvəˈtəːn] vt renverser; (decision, plan) annuler ▷ vi se retourner

overview [ˈəuvəvjuː] n vue f d'ensemble

overweight [əuvəˈweɪt] adj (person) trop gros(se); (luggage) trop lourd(e)

overwhelm [əuvəˈwɛlm] vt (subj: emotion) accabler, submerger; (enemy, opponent) écraser

overwhelming [əuvəˈwɛlmɪŋ] adj (victory, defeat) écrasant(e); (desire) irrésistible; **one's ~ impression is of heat** on a une impression dominante de chaleur

overwhelmingly [əuvəˈwɛlmɪŋlɪ] adv (vote) en masse; (win) d'une manière écrasante

overwork [əuvəˈwəːk] n surmenage m ▷ vt surmener ▷ vi se surmener

overwrite [əuvəˈraɪt] vt (irreg: like **write**); (Comput) écraser

overwrought [əuvəˈrɔːt] adj excédé(e)

ovulation [ɔvjuˈleɪʃən] n ovulation f

owe [əu] vt devoir; **to ~ sb sth, to ~ sth to sb** devoir qch à qn; **how much do I ~ you?** combien est-ce que je vous dois?

owing to [ˈəuɪŋtuː] prep à cause de, en raison de

owl [aul] n hibou m

own [əun] vt posséder ▷ vi (Brit): **to ~ to sth** reconnaître or avouer qch; **to ~ to having done sth** avouer avoir fait qch ▷ adj propre; **a room of my ~** une chambre à moi, ma propre chambre; **can I have it for my (very) ~?** puis-je l'avoir pour moi (tout) seul?; **to get one's ~ back** prendre sa revanche; **on one's ~** tout(e) seul(e); **to come into one's ~** trouver sa voie; trouver sa justification

o

▶ **own up** *vi* avouer

own brand *n* (*Comm*) marque *f* de distributeur

owner ['əunə^r] *n* propriétaire *m/f*

owner-occupier ['əunər'ɔkjupaɪə^r] *n* propriétaire occupant

ownership ['əunəʃɪp] *n* possession *f*; **it's under new ~** (*shop etc*) il y a eu un changement de propriétaire

own goal *n*: **he scored an ~** (*Sport*) il a marqué un but contre son camp; (*fig*) cela s'est retourné contre lui

ox (*pl* **oxen**) [ɔks, 'ɔksn] *n* bœuf *m*

Oxbridge ['ɔksbrɪdʒ] *n* (*Brit*) *les universités d'Oxford et de Cambridge; voir article*

● **OXBRIDGE**
●
● Oxbridge, nom formé à partir des mots
● Ox(ford) et (Cam)bridge, s'utilise pour
● parler de ces deux universités comme
● formant un tout, dans la mesure où elles

● sont toutes deux les universités
● britanniques les plus prestigieuses et
● mondialement connues.

oxen ['ɔksən] *npl of* **ox**

Oxfam ['ɔksfæm] *n abbr* (*Brit: = Oxford Committee for Famine Relief*) *association humanitaire*

oxide ['ɔksaɪd] *n* oxyde *m*

Oxon. ['ɔksn] *abbr* (*Brit: Oxoniensis*) = **of Oxford**

oxtail ['ɔksteɪl] *n*: **~ soup** soupe *f* à la queue de bœuf

oxygen ['ɔksɪdʒən] *n* oxygène *m*

oxygen mask *n* masque *m* à oxygène

oxygen tent *n* tente *f* à oxygène

oyster ['ɔɪstə^r] *n* huître *f*

oz. *abbr* = **ounce; ounces**

ozone ['əuzəun] *n* ozone *m*

ozone friendly ['əuzəunfrendlɪ] *adj* qui n'attaque pas *or* qui préserve la couche d'ozone

ozone hole *n* trou *m* d'ozone

ozone layer *n* couche *f* d'ozone

Pp

P, p [piː] n (letter) P, p m; **P for Peter** P comme Pierre

P abbr = **president; prince**

p abbr (= page) p; (Brit) = **penny; pence**

P.A. n abbr = **personal assistant; public address system** ▷ abbr (US) = **Pennsylvania**

pa [pɑː] n (inf) papa m

Pa. abbr (US) = **Pennsylvania**

p.a. abbr = **per annum**

PAC n abbr (US) = **political action committee**

pace [peɪs] n pas m; (speed) allure f; vitesse f ▷ vi: **to ~ up and down** faire les cent pas; **to keep ~ with** aller à la même vitesse que; (events) se tenir au courant de; **to set the ~** (running) donner l'allure; (fig) donner le ton; **to put sb through his ~s** (fig) mettre qn à l'épreuve

pacemaker ['peɪsmeɪkə'] n (Med) stimulateur m cardiaque; (Sport: also: **pacesetter**) meneur(-euse) de train

Pacific [pə'sɪfɪk] n: **the ~ (Ocean)** le Pacifique, l'océan m Pacifique

pacific [pə'sɪfɪk] adj pacifique

pacification [pæsɪfɪ'keɪʃən] n pacification f

pacifier ['pæsɪfaɪə'] n (US: dummy) tétine f

pacifist ['pæsɪfɪst] n pacifiste m/f

pacify ['pæsɪfaɪ] vt pacifier; (soothe) calmer

pack [pæk] n paquet m; (bundle) ballot m; (of hounds) meute f; (of thieves, wolves etc) bande f; (of cards) jeu m; (US: of cigarettes) paquet; (back pack) sac m à dos ▷ vt (goods) empaqueter, emballer; (in suitcase etc) emballer; (box) remplir; (cram) entasser; (press down) tasser; damer; (Comput) grouper, tasser ▷ vi: **to ~ (one's bags)** faire ses bagages; **to ~ into** (room, stadium) s'entasser dans; **to send sb ~ing** (inf) envoyer promener qn

▶ **pack in** (Brit inf) vi (machine) tomber en panne ▷ vt (boyfriend) plaquer; **~ it in!** laisse tomber!

▶ **pack off** vt: **to ~ sb off to** expédier qn à

▶ **pack up** vi (Brit inf: machine) tomber en panne; (: person) se tirer ▷ vt (belongings) ranger; (goods, presents) empaqueter, emballer

package ['pækɪdʒ] n paquet m; (of goods) emballage m, conditionnement m; (also: **package deal**: agreement) marché global; (: purchase) forfait m; (Comput) progiciel m ▷ vt

(goods) conditionner

package holiday n (Brit) vacances organisées

package tour n voyage organisé

packaging ['pækɪdʒɪŋ] n (wrapping materials) emballage m; (of goods) conditionnement m

packed [pækt] adj (crowded) bondé(e)

packed lunch (Brit) n repas froid

packer ['pækə'] n (person) emballeur(-euse); conditionneur(-euse)

packet ['pækɪt] n paquet m

packet switching [-swɪtʃɪŋ] n (Comput) commutation f de paquets

pack ice ['pækaɪs] n banquise f

packing ['pækɪŋ] n emballage m

packing case n caisse f (d'emballage)

pact [pækt] n pacte m, traité m

pad [pæd] n bloc(-notes m) m; (to prevent friction) tampon m; (for inking) tampon m encreur; (inf: flat) piaule f ▷ vt rembourrer ▷ vi: **to ~ in/about** etc entrer/aller et venir etc à pas feutrés

padded ['pædɪd] adj (jacket) matelassé(e); (bra) rembourré(e); **~ cell** cellule capitonnée

padding ['pædɪŋ] n rembourrage m; (fig) délayage m

paddle ['pædl] n (oar) pagaie f; (US: for table tennis) raquette f de ping-pong ▷ vi (with feet) barboter, faire trempette ▷ vt: **to ~ a canoe** etc pagayer

paddle steamer n bateau m à aubes

paddling pool ['pædlɪŋ-] n petit bassin

paddock ['pædək] n enclos m; (Racing) paddock m

paddy ['pædɪ] n (also: **paddy field**) rizière f

padlock ['pædlɔk] n cadenas m ▷ vt cadenasser

padre ['pɑːdrɪ] n aumônier m

paediatrician, (US) **pediatrician** [piːdɪə'trɪʃən] n pédiatre m/f

paediatrics, (US) **pediatrics** [piːdɪ'ætrɪks] n pédiatrie f

paedophile, (US) **pedophile** ['piːdəufaɪl] n pédophile m

pagan ['peɪɡən] adj, n païen(ne)

page [peɪdʒ] n (of book) page f; (also: **page boy**) groom m, chasseur m; (at wedding) garçon m d'honneur ▷ vt (in hotel etc) (faire) appeler

pageant ['pædʒənt] n spectacle m historique; grande cérémonie

pageantry ['pædʒəntrɪ] n apparat m, pompe f
page break n fin f or saut m de page
pager ['peɪdʒəʳ] n bip m (inf), Alphapage® m
paginate ['pædʒɪneɪt] vt paginer
pagination [pædʒɪ'neɪʃən] n pagination f
pagoda [pə'gəudə] n pagode f
paid [peɪd] pt, pp of **pay** ▷ adj (work, official) rémunéré(e); (holiday) payé(e); **to put ~ to** (Brit) mettre fin à, mettre par terre
paid-up ['peɪdʌp], (US) **paid-in** ['peɪdɪn] adj (member) à jour de sa cotisation; (shares) libéré(e); **~ capital** capital versé
pail [peɪl] n seau m
pain [peɪn] n douleur f; (inf: nuisance) plaie f; **to be in ~** souffrir, avoir mal; **to have a ~ in** avoir mal à or une douleur à or dans; **to take ~s to do** se donner du mal pour faire; **on ~ of death** sous peine de mort
pained ['peɪnd] adj peiné(e), chagrin(e)
painful ['peɪnful] adj douloureux(-euse); (difficult) difficile, pénible
painfully ['peɪnfəlɪ] adv (fig: very) terriblement
painkiller ['peɪnkɪləʳ] n calmant m, analgésique m
painless ['peɪnlɪs] adj indolore
painstaking ['peɪnzteɪkɪŋ] adj (person) soigneux(-euse); (work) soigné(e)
paint [peɪnt] n peinture f ▷ vt peindre; (fig) dépeindre; **to ~ the door blue** peindre la porte en bleu; **to ~ in oils** faire de la peinture à l'huile
paintbox ['peɪntbɔks] n boîte f de couleurs
paintbrush ['peɪntbrʌʃ] n pinceau m
painter ['peɪntəʳ] n peintre m
painting ['peɪntɪŋ] n peinture f; (picture) tableau m
paint-stripper ['peɪntstrɪpəʳ] n décapant m
paintwork ['peɪntwəːk] n (Brit) peintures fpl; (: of car) peinture f
pair [pɛəʳ] n (of shoes, gloves etc) paire f; (of people) couple m; (twosome) duo m; **~ of scissors** (paire de) ciseaux mpl; **~ of trousers** pantalon m
▶ **pair off** vi se mettre par deux
pajamas [pə'dʒɑːməz] npl (US) pyjama(s) m(pl)
Pakistan [pɑːkɪ'stɑːn] n Pakistan m
Pakistani [pɑːkɪ'stɑːnɪ] adj pakistanais(e) ▷ n Pakistanais(e)
PAL [pæl] n abbr (TV: = phase alternation line) PAL m
pal [pæl] n (inf) copain (copine)
palace ['pæləs] n palais m
palatable ['pælɪtəbl] adj bon (bonne), agréable au goût
palate ['pælɪt] n palais m (Anat)
palatial [pə'leɪʃəl] adj grandiose, magnifique
palaver [pə'lɑːvəʳ] n palabres fpl or mpl; histoire(s) f(pl)
pale [peɪl] adj pâle ▷ vi pâlir ▷ n: **to be beyond the ~** être au ban de la société; **to grow** or **turn ~** (person) pâlir; **~ blue** (adj) bleu pâle inv; **to ~ into insignificance (beside)** perdre beaucoup d'importance (par rapport à)
paleness ['peɪlnɪs] n pâleur f

Palestine ['pælɪstaɪn] n Palestine f
Palestinian [pælɪs'tɪnɪən] adj palestinien(ne) ▷ n Palestinien(ne)
palette ['pælɪt] n palette f
paling ['peɪlɪŋ] n (stake) palis m; (fence) palissade f
palisade [pælɪ'seɪd] n palissade f
pall [pɔːl] n (of smoke) voile m ▷ vi: **to ~ (on)** devenir lassant (pour)
pallet ['pælɪt] n (for goods) palette f
pallid ['pælɪd] adj blême
pallor ['pæləʳ] n pâleur f
pally ['pælɪ] adj (inf) copain (copine)
palm [pɑːm] n (Anat) paume f; (also: **palm tree**) palmier m; (leaf, symbol) palme f ▷ vt: **to ~ sth off on sb** (inf) refiler qch à qn
palmist ['pɑːmɪst] n chiromancien(ne)
Palm Sunday n le dimanche des Rameaux
palpable ['pælpəbl] adj évident(e), manifeste
palpitation [pælpɪ'teɪʃən] n palpitation f
paltry ['pɔːltrɪ] adj dérisoire; piètre
pamper ['pæmpəʳ] vt gâter, dorloter
pamphlet ['pæmflət] n brochure f; (political etc) tract m
pan [pæn] n (also: **saucepan**) casserole f; (also: **frying pan**) poêle f; (of lavatory) cuvette f ▷ vi (Cine) faire un panoramique ▷ vt (inf: book, film) éreinter; **to ~ for gold** laver du sable aurifère
panacea [pænə'sɪə] n panacée f
Panama ['pænəmɑː] n Panama m
Panama Canal n canal m de Panama
pancake ['pænkeɪk] n crêpe f
Pancake Day n (Brit) mardi gras
pancake roll n rouleau m de printemps
pancreas ['pæŋkrɪəs] n pancréas m
panda ['pændə] n panda m
panda car n (Brit) ≈ voiture f pie inv
pandemic [pæn'dɛmɪk] n pandémie f
pandemonium [pændɪ'məunɪəm] n tohu-bohu m
pander ['pændəʳ] vi: **to ~ to** flatter bassement; obéir servilement à
p&h abbr (US: = postage and handling) frais mpl de port
P&L abbr = **profit and loss**
p&p abbr (Brit: = postage and packing) frais mpl de port
pane [peɪn] n carreau m (de fenêtre), vitre f
panel ['pænl] n (of wood, cloth etc) panneau m; (Radio, TV) panel m, invités mpl; (for interview, exams) jury m; (official: of experts) table ronde, comité m
panel game n (Brit) jeu m (radiophonique/ télévisé)
panelling, (US) **paneling** ['pænəlɪŋ] n boiseries fpl
panellist, (US) **panelist** ['pænəlɪst] n invité(e) (d'un panel), membre d'un panel
pang [pæŋ] n: **~s of remorse** pincements mpl de remords; **~s of hunger/conscience** tiraillements mpl d'estomac/de la conscience
panhandler ['pænhændləʳ] n (US inf) mendiant(e)

panic ['pænɪk] n panique f, affolement m ▷ vi s'affoler, paniquer
panic buying [-baɪɪŋ] n achats mpl de précaution
panicky ['pænɪkɪ] adj (person) qui panique or s'affole facilement
panic-stricken ['pænɪkstrɪkən] adj affolé(e)
pannier ['pænɪə'] n (on animal) bât m; (on bicycle) sacoche f
panorama [pænə'rɑːmə] n panorama m
panoramic [pænə'ræmɪk] adj panoramique
pansy ['pænzɪ] n (Bot) pensée f; (inf) tapette f, pédé m
pant [pænt] vi haleter
pantechnicon [pæn'tɛknɪkən] n (Brit) (grand) camion de déménagement
panther ['pænθə'] n panthère f
panties ['pæntɪz] npl slip m, culotte f
pantihose ['pæntɪhəuz] n (US) collant m
panto ['pæntəu] n = **pantomime**
pantomime ['pæntəmaɪm] n (Brit) spectacle m de Noël
pantry ['pæntrɪ] n garde-manger m inv; (room) office m
pants [pænts] n (Brit: woman's) culotte f, slip m; (: man's) slip, caleçon m; (US: trousers) pantalon m
pantsuit ['pæntsuːt] n (US) tailleur-pantalon m
pantyhose ['pæntɪhəuz] (US) npl collant m
papacy ['peɪpəsɪ] n papauté f
papal ['peɪpəl] adj papal(e), pontifical(e)
paparazzi [pæpə'rætsiː] npl paparazzi mpl
paper ['peɪpə'] n papier m; (also: **wallpaper**) papier peint; (also: **newspaper**) journal m; (academic essay) article m; (exam) épreuve écrite ▷ adj en or de papier ▷ vt tapisser (de papier peint); **papers** npl (also: **identity papers**) papiers mpl (d'identité); **a piece of** ~ (odd bit) un bout de papier; (sheet) une feuille de papier; **to put sth down on** ~ mettre qch par écrit
paper advance n (on printer) avance f (du) papier
paperback ['peɪpəbæk] n livre broché or non relié; (small) livre m de poche ▷ adj: ~ **edition** édition brochée
paper bag n sac m en papier
paperboy ['peɪpəbɔɪ] n (selling) vendeur m de journaux; (delivering) livreur m de journaux
paper clip n trombone m
paper handkerchief n, **paper hankie** n (inf) mouchoir m en papier
paper mill n papeterie f
paper money n papier-monnaie m
paper profit n profit m théorique
paper shop n (Brit) marchand m de journaux
paperweight ['peɪpəweɪt] n presse-papiers m inv
paperwork ['peɪpəwəːk] n papiers mpl; (pej) paperasserie f
papier-mâché ['pæpɪeɪ'mæʃeɪ] n papier mâché m
paprika ['pæprɪkə] n paprika m
Pap test, Pap smear ['pæp-] n (Med) frottis m
par [pɑː'] n pair m; (Golf) normale f du parcours; **on a** ~ **with** à égalité avec, au même niveau que;

at ~ au pair; **above/below** ~ au-dessus/au-dessous du pair; **to feel below** or **under** or **not up to** ~ ne pas se sentir en forme
parable ['pærəbl] n parabole f (Rel)
parabola [pə'ræbələ] n parabole f (Math)
paracetamol [pærə'siːtəmɔl] (Brit) n paracétamol m
parachute ['pærəʃuːt] n parachute m ▷ vi sauter en parachute
parachute jump n saut m en parachute
parachutist ['pærəʃuːtɪst] n parachutiste m/f
parade [pə'reɪd] n défilé m; (inspection) revue f; (street) boulevard m ▷ vt (fig) faire étalage de ▷ vi défiler; **a fashion** ~ (Brit) un défilé de mode
parade ground n terrain m de manœuvre
paradise ['pærədaɪs] n paradis m
paradox ['pærədɔks] n paradoxe m
paradoxical [pærə'dɔksɪkl] adj paradoxal(e)
paradoxically [pærə'dɔksɪklɪ] adv paradoxalement
paraffin ['pærəfɪn] n (Brit): ~ **(oil)** pétrole (lampant); **liquid** ~ huile f de paraffine
paraffin heater n (Brit) poêle m à mazout
paraffin lamp n (Brit) lampe f à pétrole
paragon ['pærəgən] n parangon m
paragraph ['pærəgrɑːf] n paragraphe m; **to begin a new** ~ aller à la ligne
Paraguay ['pærəgwaɪ] n Paraguay m
Paraguayan [pærə'gwaɪən] adj paraguayen(ne) ▷ n Paraguayen(ne)
parallel ['pærəlɛl] adj: ~ **(with** or **to)** parallèle (à); (fig) analogue (à) ▷ n (line) parallèle f; (fig, Geo) parallèle m
paralysed ['pærəlaɪzd] adj paralysé(e)
paralysis (pl **paralyses**) [pə'rælɪsɪs, -siːz] n paralysie f
paralytic [pærə'lɪtɪk] adj paralytique; (Brit inf: drunk) ivre mort(e)
paralyze ['pærəlaɪz] vt paralyser
paramedic [pærə'mɛdɪk] n auxiliaire m/f médical(e)
parameter [pə'ræmɪtə'] n paramètre m
paramilitary [pærə'mɪlɪtərɪ] adj paramilitaire
paramount ['pærəmaunt] adj: **of** ~ **importance** de la plus haute or grande importance
paranoia [pærə'nɔɪə] n paranoïa f
paranoid ['pærənɔɪd] adj (Psych) paranoïaque; (neurotic) paranoïde
paranormal [pærə'nɔːml] adj paranormal(e)
paraphernalia [pærəfə'neɪlɪə] n attirail m, affaires fpl
paraphrase ['pærəfreɪz] vt paraphraser
paraplegic [pærə'pliːdʒɪk] n paraplégique m/f
parapsychology [pærəsaɪ'kɔlədʒɪ] n parapsychologie f
parasite ['pærəsaɪt] n parasite m
parasol ['pærəsɔl] n ombrelle f; (at café etc) parasol m
paratrooper ['pærətruːpə'] n parachutiste m (soldat)
parcel ['pɑːsl] n paquet m, colis m ▷ vt (also: **parcel up**) empaqueter

P

▶**parcel out** *vt* répartir
parcel bomb *n* (*Brit*) colis piégé
parcel post *n* service *m* de colis postaux
parch [pɑːtʃ] *vt* dessécher
parched [pɑːtʃt] *adj* (*person*) assoiffé(e)
parchment ['pɑːtʃmənt] *n* parchemin *m*
pardon ['pɑːdn] *n* pardon *m*; (*Law*) grâce *f* ▷ *vt* pardonner à; (*Law*) gracier; **~! pardon!**; **~ me!** (*after burping etc*) excusez-moi!; **I beg your ~!** (*I'm sorry*) pardon!, je suis désolé!; **(I beg your) ~?**, (*US*) **~ me?** (*what did you say?*) pardon?
pare [pɛəʳ] *vt* (*Brit*: *nails*) couper; (*fruit etc*) peler; (*fig*: *costs etc*) réduire
parent ['pɛərənt] *n* (*father*) père *m*; (*mother*) mère *f*; **parents** *npl* parents *mpl*
parentage ['pɛərəntɪdʒ] *n* naissance *f*; **of unknown ~** de parents inconnus
parental [pəˈrɛntl] *adj* parental(e), des parents
parent company *n* société *f* mère
parenthesis (*pl* **parentheses**) [pəˈrɛnθɪsɪs, -siːz] *n* parenthèse *f*; **in parentheses** entre parenthèses
parenthood ['pɛərənthud] *n* paternité *f* or maternité *f*
parenting ['pɛərəntɪŋ] *n* le métier de parent, le travail d'un parent
Paris ['pærɪs] *n* Paris
parish ['pærɪʃ] *n* paroisse *f*; (*Brit*: *civil*) ≈ commune *f* ▷ *adj* paroissial(e)
parish council *n* (*Brit*) ≈ conseil municipal
parishioner [pəˈrɪʃənəʳ] *n* paroissien(ne)
Parisian [pəˈrɪzɪən] *adj* parisien(ne), de Paris ▷ *n* Parisien(ne)
parity ['pærɪtɪ] *n* parité *f*
park [pɑːk] *n* parc *m*, jardin public ▷ *vt* garer ▷ *vi* se garer; **can I ~ here?** est-ce que je peux me garer ici?
parka ['pɑːkə] *n* parka *m*
parking ['pɑːkɪŋ] *n* stationnement *m*; **"no ~"** "stationnement interdit"
parking lights *npl* feux *mpl* de stationnement
parking lot *n* (*US*) parking *m*, parc *m* de stationnement
parking meter *n* parc(o)mètre *m*
parking offence, (*US*) **parking violation** *n* infraction *f* au stationnement
parking place *n* place *f* de stationnement
parking ticket *n* P.-V. *m*
Parkinson's ['pɑːkɪnsənz] *n* (*also*: **Parkinson's disease**) maladie *f* de Parkinson, parkinson *m*
parkway ['pɑːkweɪ] *n* (*US*) route *f* express (*en site vert ou aménagé*)
parlance ['pɑːləns] *n*: **in common/modern ~** dans le langage courant/actuel
parliament ['pɑːləmənt] *n* parlement *m*; *voir article*

● **PARLIAMENT**
●
● Le *Parliament* est l'assemblée législative
● britannique; elle est composée de deux
● chambres: la "House of Commons" et la

● "House of Lords". Ses bureaux sont les
● "Houses of Parliament" au palais de
● Westminster à Londres. Chaque *Parliament*
● est en général élu pour cinq ans. Les débats
● du *Parliament* sont maintenant retransmis à
● la télévision.

parliamentary [pɑːləˈmɛntərɪ] *adj* parlementaire
parlour, (*US*) **parlor** ['pɑːləʳ] *n* salon *m*
parlous ['pɑːləs] *adj* (*formal*) précaire
Parmesan [pɑːmɪˈzæn] *n* (*also*: **Parmesan cheese**) Parmesan *m*
parochial [pəˈrəukɪəl] *adj* paroissial(e); (*pej*) à l'esprit de clocher
parody ['pærədɪ] *n* parodie *f*
parole [pəˈrəul] *n*: **on ~** en liberté conditionnelle
paroxysm ['pærəksɪzəm] *n* (*Med*, *of grief*) paroxysme *m*; (*of anger*) accès *m*
parquet ['pɑːkeɪ] *n*: **~ floor(ing)** parquet *m*
parrot ['pærət] *n* perroquet *m*
parrot fashion *adv* comme un perroquet
parry ['pærɪ] *vt* esquiver, parer à
parsimonious [pɑːsɪˈməunɪəs] *adj* parcimonieux(-euse)
parsley ['pɑːslɪ] *n* persil *m*
parsnip ['pɑːsnɪp] *n* panais *m*
parson ['pɑːsn] *n* ecclésiastique *m*; (*Church of England*) pasteur *m*
part [pɑːt] *n* partie *f*; (*of machine*) pièce *f*; (*Theat*) rôle *m*; (*Mus*) voix *f*; partie; (*of serial*) épisode *m*; (*US*: *in hair*) raie *f* ▷ *adj* partiel(le) ▷ *adv* = **partly** ▷ *vt* séparer ▷ *vi* (*people*) se séparer; (*crowd*) s'ouvrir; (*roads*) se diviser; **to take ~ in** participer à, prendre part à; **to take sb's ~** prendre le parti de qn, prendre parti pour qn; **on his ~** de sa part; **for my ~** en ce qui me concerne; **for the most ~** en grande partie; dans la plupart des cas; **for the better ~ of the day** pendant la plus grande partie de la journée; **to be ~ and parcel of** faire partie de; **in ~** en partie; **to take sth in good/bad ~** prendre qch du bon/mauvais côté
▶**part with** *vt fus* (*person*) se séparer de; (*possessions*) se défaire de
partake [pɑːˈteɪk] *vi* (*irreg*: *like* **take**); (*formal*): **to ~ of sth** prendre part à qch, partager qch
part exchange *n* (*Brit*): **in ~** en reprise
partial ['pɑːʃl] *adj* (*incomplete*) partiel(le); (*unjust*) partial(e); **to be ~ to** aimer, avoir un faible pour
partially ['pɑːʃəlɪ] *adv* en partie, partiellement; partialement
participant [pɑːˈtɪsɪpənt] *n* (*in competition, campaign*) participant(e)
participate [pɑːˈtɪsɪpeɪt] *vi*: **to ~ (in)** participer (à), prendre part (à)
participation [pɑːtɪsɪˈpeɪʃən] *n* participation *f*
participle ['pɑːtɪsɪpl] *n* participe *m*
particle ['pɑːtɪkl] *n* particule *f*; (*of dust*) grain *m*
particular [pəˈtɪkjuləʳ] *adj* (*specific*) particulier(-ière); (*special*) particulier, spécial(e); (*fussy*) difficile, exigeant(e); (*careful*)

méticuleux(-euse); **in ~** en particulier, surtout

particularly [pə'tɪkjuləlɪ] *adv* particulièrement; (*in particular*) en particulier

particulars [pə'tɪkjuləz] *npl* détails *mpl*; (*information*) renseignements *mpl*

parting ['pɑːtɪŋ] *n* séparation *f*; (*Brit: in hair*) raie *f* ▷ *adj* d'adieu; **his ~ shot was ...** il lança en partant ....

partisan [pɑːtɪ'zæn] *n* partisan(e) ▷ *adj* partisan(e); de parti

partition [pɑːˈtɪʃən] *n* (*Pol*) partition *f*, division *f*; (*wall*) cloison *f*

partly ['pɑːtlɪ] *adv* en partie, partiellement

partner ['pɑːtnəʳ] *n* (*Comm*) associé(e); (*Sport*) partenaire *m/f*; (*spouse*) conjoint(e); (*lover*) ami(e); (*at dance*) cavalier(-ière) ▷ *vt* être l'associé *or* le partenaire *or* le cavalier de

partnership ['pɑːtnəʃɪp] *n* association *f*; **to go into ~ (with), form a ~ (with)** s'associer (avec)

part payment *n* acompte *m*

partridge ['pɑːtrɪdʒ] *n* perdrix *f*

part-time ['pɑːt'taɪm] *adj, adv* à mi-temps, à temps partiel

part-timer ['pɑːt'taɪməʳ] *n* (*also:* **part-time worker**) travailleur(-euse) à temps partiel

party ['pɑːtɪ] *n* (*Pol*) parti *m*; (*celebration*) fête *f*; (*: formal*) réception *f*; (*: in evening*) soirée *f*; (*team*) équipe *f*; (*group*) groupe *m*; (*Law*) partie *f*; **dinner ~** dîner *m*; **to give** *or* **throw a ~** donner une réception; **we're having a ~ next Saturday** nous organisons une soirée *or* réunion entre amis samedi prochain; **it's for our son's birthday ~** c'est pour la fête (*or* le goûter) d'anniversaire de notre garçon; **to be a ~ to a crime** être impliqué(e) dans un crime

party dress *n* robe habillée

party line *n* (*Pol*) ligne *f* politique; (*Tel*) ligne partagée

party piece *n* numéro habituel

party political broadcast *n* émission réservée à un parti politique.

pass [pɑːs] *vt* (*time, object*) passer; (*place*) passer devant; (*friend*) croiser; (*exam*) être reçu(e) à, réussir; (*candidate*) admettre; (*overtake*) dépasser; (*approve*) approuver, accepter; (*law*) promulguer ▷ *vi* passer; (*Scol*) être reçu(e) *or* admis(e), réussir ▷ *n* (*permit*) laissez-passer *m inv*; (*membership card*) carte *f* d'accès *or* d'abonnement; (*in mountains*) col *m*; (*Sport*) passe *f*; (*Scol: also:* **pass mark**): **to get a ~** être reçu(e) (sans mention); **to ~ sb sth** passer qch à qn; **could you ~ the salt/oil, please?** pouvez-vous me passer le sel/l'huile, s'il vous plaît?; **she could ~ for 25** on lui donnerait 25 ans; **to ~ sth through a ring** *etc* (faire) passer qch dans un anneau *etc*; **could you ~ the vegetables round?** pourriez-vous faire passer les légumes?; **things have come to a pretty ~** (*Brit*) voilà où on en est!; **to make a ~ at sb** (*inf*) faire des avances à qn

▸ **pass away** *vi* mourir

▸ **pass by** *vi* passer ▷ *vt* (*ignore*) négliger

▸ **pass down** *vt* (*customs, inheritance*) transmettre

▸ **pass on** *vi* (*die*) s'éteindre, décéder ▷ *vt* (*hand on*): **to ~ on (to)** transmettre (à); (*: illness*) passer (à); (*: price rises*) répercuter (sur)

▸ **pass out** *vi* s'évanouir; (*Brit Mil*) sortir (*d'une école militaire*)

▸ **pass over** *vt* (*ignore*) passer sous silence

▸ **pass up** *vt* (*opportunity*) laisser passer

passable ['pɑːsəbl] *adj* (*road*) praticable; (*work*) acceptable

passage ['pæsɪdʒ] *n* (*also:* **passageway**) couloir *m*; (*gen, in book*) passage *m*; (*by boat*) traversée *f*

passbook ['pɑːsbuk] *n* livret *m*

passenger ['pæsɪndʒəʳ] *n* passager(-ère)

passer-by [pɑːsə'baɪ] *n* passant(e)

passing ['pɑːsɪŋ] *adj* (*fig*) passager(-ère); **in ~** en passant

passing place *n* (*Aut*) aire *f* de croisement

passion ['pæʃən] *n* passion *f*; **to have a ~ for sth** avoir la passion de qch

passionate ['pæʃənɪt] *adj* passionné(e)

passion fruit *n* fruit *m* de la passion

passion play *n* mystère *m* de la Passion

passive ['pæsɪv] *adj* (*also Ling*) passif(-ive)

passive smoking *n* tabagisme passif

passkey ['pɑːskiː] *n* passe *m*

Passover ['pɑːsəuvəʳ] *n* Pâque juive

passport ['pɑːspɔːt] *n* passeport *m*

passport control *n* contrôle *m* des passeports

passport office *n* bureau *m* de délivrance des passeports

password ['pɑːswəːd] *n* mot *m* de passe

past [pɑːst] *prep* (*in front of*) devant; (*further than*) au delà de, plus loin que; après; (*later than*) après ▷ *adv*: **to run ~** passer en courant ▷ *adj* passé(e); (*president etc*) ancien(ne) ▷ *n* passé *m*; **he's ~ forty** il a dépassé la quarantaine, il a plus de *or* passé quarante ans; **ten/quarter ~ eight** huit heures dix/un *or* et quart; **it's ~ midnight** il est plus de minuit, il est passé minuit; **he ran ~ me** il m'a dépassé en courant, il a passé devant moi en courant; **for the ~ few/3 days** depuis quelques/3 jours; ces derniers/3 derniers jours; **in the ~** (*gen*) dans le temps, autrefois; (*Ling*) au passé; **I'm ~ caring** je ne m'en fais plus; **to be ~ it** (*Brit inf: person*) avoir passé l'âge

pasta ['pæstə] *n* pâtes *fpl*

paste [peɪst] *n* pâte *f*; (*Culin: meat*) pâté *m* (à tartiner); (*: tomato*) purée *f*, concentré *m*; (*glue*) colle *f* (de pâte); (*jewellery*) strass *m* ▷ *vt* coller

pastel ['pæstl] *adj* pastel *inv* ▷ *n* (*Art: pencil*) (crayon *m*) pastel *m*; (*: drawing*) (dessin *m* au) pastel; (*colour*) ton *m* pastel *inv*

pasteurized ['pæstəraɪzd] *adj* pasteurisé(e)

pastille ['pæstl] *n* pastille *f*

pastime ['pɑːstaɪm] *n* passe-temps *m inv*, distraction *f*

past master *n* (*Brit*): **to be a ~ at** être expert en

pastor ['pɑːstəʳ] *n* pasteur *m*

pastoral ['pɑːstərl] *adj* pastoral(e)

pastry ['peɪstrɪ] *n* pâte *f*; (*cake*) pâtisserie *f*

pasture ['pɑːstʃəʳ] *n* pâturage *m*

p

pasty¹ n ['pæstɪ] petit pâté (en croûte)

pasty² ['peɪstɪ] adj pâteux(-euse); (complexion) terreux(-euse)

pat [pæt] vt donner une petite tape à; (dog) caresser ▷ n: **a ~ of butter** une noisette de beurre; **to give sb/o.s. a ~ on the back** (fig) congratuler qn/se congratuler; **he knows it (off) ~**, (US) **he has it down ~** il sait cela sur le bout des doigts

patch [pætʃ] n (of material) pièce f; (eye patch) cache m; (spot) tache f; (of land) parcelle f; (on tyre) rustine f ▷ vt (clothes) rapiécer; **a bad ~** (Brit) une période difficile
▶ **patch up** vt réparer

patchwork ['pætʃwəːk] n patchwork m

patchy ['pætʃɪ] adj inégal(e); (incomplete) fragmentaire

pate [peɪt] n: **a bald ~** un crâne chauve or dégarni

pâté ['pæteɪ] n pâté m, terrine f

patent ['peɪtnt] (US) ['pætnt] n brevet m (d'invention) ▷ vt faire breveter ▷ adj patent(e), manifeste

patent leather n cuir verni

patently ['peɪtntlɪ] adv manifestement

patent medicine n spécialité f pharmaceutique

patent office n bureau m des brevets

paternal [pə'təːnl] adj paternel(le)

paternity [pə'təːnɪtɪ] n paternité f

paternity leave [pə'təːnɪtɪ-] n congé m de paternité

paternity suit n (Law) action f en recherche de paternité

path [pɑːθ] n chemin m, sentier m; (in garden) allée f; (of planet) course f; (of missile) trajectoire f

pathetic [pə'θetɪk] adj (pitiful) pitoyable; (very bad) lamentable, minable; (moving) pathétique

pathological [pæθə'lɔdʒɪkl] adj pathologique

pathologist [pə'θɔlədʒɪst] n pathologiste m/f

pathology [pə'θɔlədʒɪ] n pathologie f

pathos ['peɪθɔs] n pathétique m

pathway ['pɑːθweɪ] n chemin m, sentier m; (in garden) allée f

patience ['peɪʃns] n patience f; (Brit: Cards) réussite f; **to lose (one's) ~** perdre patience

patient ['peɪʃnt] n malade m/f; (of dentist etc) patient(e) ▷ adj patient(e)

patiently ['peɪʃntlɪ] adv patiemment

patio ['pætɪəu] n patio m

patriot ['peɪtrɪət] n patriote m/f

patriotic [pætrɪ'ɔtɪk] adj patriotique; (person) patriote

patriotism ['pætrɪətɪzəm] n patriotisme m

patrol [pə'trəul] n patrouille f ▷ vt patrouiller dans; **to be on ~** être de patrouille

patrol boat n patrouilleur m

patrol car n voiture f de police

patrolman [pə'trəulmən] (irreg) n (US) agent m de police

patron ['peɪtrən] n (in shop) client(e); (of charity) patron(ne); **~ of the arts** mécène m

patronage ['pætrənɪdʒ] n patronage m, appui m

patronize ['pætrənaɪz] vt être (un) client or un habitué de; (fig) traiter avec condescendance

patronizing ['pætrənaɪzɪŋ] adj condescendant(e)

patron saint n saint(e) patron(ne)

patter ['pætər] n crépitement m, tapotement m; (sales talk) boniment m ▷ vi crépiter, tapoter

pattern ['pætən] n modèle m; (Sewing) patron m; (design) motif m; (sample) échantillon m; **behaviour ~** mode m de comportement

patterned ['pætənd] adj à motifs

paucity ['pɔːsɪtɪ] n pénurie f, carence f

paunch [pɔːntʃ] n gros ventre, bedaine f

pauper ['pɔːpər] n indigent(e); **~'s grave** fosse commune

pause [pɔːz] n pause f, arrêt m; (Mus) silence m ▷ vi faire une pause, s'arrêter; **to ~ for breath** reprendre son souffle; (fig) faire une pause

pave [peɪv] vt paver, daller; **to ~ the way for** ouvrir la voie à

pavement ['peɪvmənt] n (Brit) trottoir m; (US) chaussée f

pavilion [pə'vɪlɪən] n pavillon m; tente f; (Sport) stand m

paving ['peɪvɪŋ] n (material) pavé m, dalle f; (area) pavage m, dallage m

paving stone n pavé m

paw [pɔː] n patte f ▷ vt donner un coup de patte à; (person: pej) tripoter

pawn [pɔːn] n gage m; (Chess, also fig) pion m ▷ vt mettre en gage

pawnbroker ['pɔːnbrəukər] n prêteur m sur gages

pawnshop ['pɔːnʃɔp] n mont-de-piété m

pay [peɪ] (pt, pp **paid**) [peɪd] n salaire m; (of manual worker) paie f ▷ vt payer; (be profitable to: also fig) rapporter à ▷ vi payer; (be profitable) être rentable; **how much did you ~ for it?** combien l'avez-vous payé?, vous l'avez payé combien?; **I paid £5 for that ticket** j'ai payé ce billet 5 livres; **can I ~ by credit card?** est-ce que je peux payer par carte de crédit?; **to ~ one's way** payer sa part; (company) couvrir ses frais; **to ~ dividends** (fig) porter ses fruits, s'avérer rentable; **it won't ~ you to do that** vous ne gagnerez rien à faire cela; **to ~ attention (to)** prêter attention (à); **to ~ sb a visit** rendre visite à qn; **to ~ one's respects to sb** présenter ses respects à qn
▶ **pay back** vt rembourser
▶ **pay for** vt fus payer
▶ **pay in** vt verser
▶ **pay off** vt (debts) régler, acquitter; (person) rembourser; (workers) licencier ▷ vi (scheme, decision) se révéler payant(e); **to ~ sth off in instalments** payer qch à tempérament
▶ **pay out** vt (money) payer, sortir de sa poche; (rope) laisser filer
▶ **pay up** vt (debts) régler; (amount) payer

payable ['peɪəbl] adj payable; **to make a cheque ~ to sb** établir un chèque à l'ordre de qn

pay-as-you-go [ˌpeɪəzjə'gəu] adj (mobile phone) à

carte prépayée
pay award n augmentation f
payday n jour m de paie
PAYE n abbr (Brit: = pay as you earn) système de retenue des impôts à la source
payee [peɪ'iː] n bénéficiaire m/f
pay envelope n (US) paie f
paying ['peɪɪŋ] adj payant(e); ~ **guest** hôte payant
payload ['peɪləʊd] n charge f utile
payment ['peɪmənt] n paiement m; (of bill) règlement m; (of deposit, cheque) versement m; **advance** ~ (part sum) acompte m; (total sum) paiement anticipé; **deferred** ~, ~ **by instalments** paiement par versements échelonnés; **monthly** ~ mensualité f; **in** ~ **for**, **in** ~ **of** en règlement de; **on** ~ **of £5** pour 5 livres
payout ['peɪaʊt] n (from insurance) dédommagement m; (in competition) prix m
pay packet n (Brit) paie f
pay phone n cabine f téléphonique, téléphone public
pay raise n (US) = **pay rise**
pay rise n (Brit) augmentation f (de salaire)
payroll ['peɪrəʊl] n registre m du personnel; **to be on a firm's** ~ être employé par une entreprise
pay slip n (Brit) bulletin m de paie, feuille f de paie
pay station n (US) cabine f téléphonique
pay television n chaînes fpl payantes
PBS n abbr (US: = Public Broadcasting Service) groupement d'aide à la réalisation d'émissions pour la TV publique
PBX n abbr (Brit: = private branch exchange) PBX m, commutateur m privé
PC n abbr = **personal computer**; (Brit) = **police constable** ▷ adj abbr = **politically correct** ▷ abbr (Brit) = **Privy Councillor**
p.c. abbr = **per cent**; **postcard**
p/c abbr = **petty cash**
PCB n abbr = **printed circuit board**
pcm n abbr (= per calender month) par mois
PD n abbr (US) = **police department**
pd abbr = **paid**
PDA n abbr (= personal digital assistant) agenda m électronique
PDQ n abbr = **pretty damn quick**
PDSA n abbr (Brit) = **People's Dispensary for Sick Animals**
PDT abbr (US: = Pacific Daylight Time) heure d'été du Pacifique
PE n abbr (= physical education) EPS f ▷ abbr (Canada) = **Prince Edward Island**
pea [piː] n (petit) pois
peace [piːs] n paix f; (calm) calme m, tranquillité f; **to be at** ~ **with sb/sth** être en paix avec qn/ qch; **to keep the** ~ (policeman) assurer le maintien de l'ordre; (citizen) ne pas troubler l'ordre
peaceable ['piːsəbl] adj paisible, pacifique
peaceful ['piːsful] adj paisible, calme

peacekeeper ['piːskiːpəʳ] n (force) force gardienne de la paix
peacekeeping ['piːskiːpɪŋ] n maintien m de la paix
peacekeeping force n forces fpl qui assurent le maintien de la paix
peace offering n gage m de réconciliation; (humorous) gage de paix
peach [piːtʃ] n pêche f
peacock ['piːkɔk] n paon m
peak [piːk] n (mountain) pic m, cime f; (of cap) visière f; (fig: highest level) maximum m; (: of career, fame) apogée m
peak-hour ['piːkaʊəʳ] adj (traffic etc) de pointe
peak hours npl heures fpl d'affluence or de pointe
peak period n période f de pointe
peak rate n plein tarif
peaky ['piːkɪ] adj (Brit inf) fatigué(e)
peal [piːl] n (of bells) carillon m; ~**s of laughter** éclats mpl de rire
peanut ['piːnʌt] n arachide f, cacahuète f
peanut butter n beurre m de cacahuète
pear [pɛəʳ] n poire f
pearl [pəːl] n perle f
peasant ['pɛznt] n paysan(ne)
peat [piːt] n tourbe f
pebble ['pɛbl] n galet m, caillou m
peck [pɛk] vt (also: **peck at**) donner un coup de bec à; (food) picorer ▷ n coup m de bec; (kiss) bécot m
pecking order ['pɛkɪŋ-] n ordre m hiérarchique
peckish ['pɛkɪʃ] adj (Brit inf): **I feel** ~ je mangerais bien quelque chose, j'ai la dent
peculiar [pɪ'kjuːlɪəʳ] adj (odd) étrange, bizarre, curieux(-euse); (particular) particulier(-ière); ~ **to** particulier à
peculiarity [pɪkjuːlɪ'ærɪtɪ] n bizarrerie f; particularité f
pecuniary [pɪ'kjuːnɪərɪ] adj pécuniaire
pedal ['pɛdl] n pédale f ▷ vi pédaler
pedal bin n (Brit) poubelle f à pédale
pedantic [pɪ'dæntɪk] adj pédant(e)
peddle ['pɛdl] vt colporter; (drugs) faire le trafic de
peddler ['pɛdləʳ] n colporteur m; camelot m
pedestal ['pɛdəstl] n piédestal m
pedestrian [pɪ'dɛstrɪən] n piéton m ▷ adj piétonnier(-ière); (fig) prosaïque, terre à terre inv
pedestrian crossing n (Brit) passage clouté
pedestrianized [pɪ'dɛstrɪənaɪzd] adj: **a** ~ **street** une rue piétonne
pedestrian precinct, (US) **pedestrian zone** n (Brit) zone piétonne
pediatrics [piːdɪ'ætrɪks] n (US) = **paediatrics**
pedigree ['pɛdɪgriː] n ascendance f; (of animal) pedigree m ▷ cpd (animal) de race
pedlar ['pɛdləʳ] n = **peddler**
pedophile ['piːdəʊfaɪl] (US) n = **paedophile**
pee [piː] vi (inf) faire pipi, pisser
peek [piːk] vi jeter un coup d'œil (furtif)

peel [pi:l] n pelure f, épluchure f; (of orange, lemon) écorce f ▷ vt peler, éplucher ▷ vi (paint etc) s'écailler; (wallpaper) se décoller; (skin) peler
▶ **peel back** vt décoller

peeler ['pi:lə'] n (potato etc peeler) éplucheur m

peelings ['pi:lɪŋz] npl pelures fpl, épluchures fpl

peep [pi:p] n (Brit: look) coup d'œil furtif; (sound) pépiement m ▷ vi (Brit) jeter un coup d'œil (furtif)
▶ **peep out** vi (Brit) se montrer (furtivement)

peephole ['pi:phəul] n judas m

peer [pɪə'] vi: **to ~ at** regarder attentivement, scruter ▷ n (noble) pair m; (equal) pair, égal(e)

peerage ['pɪərɪdʒ] n pairie f

peerless ['pɪəlɪs] adj incomparable, sans égal

peeved [pi:vd] adj irrité(e), ennuyé(e)

peevish ['pi:vɪʃ] adj grincheux(-euse), maussade

peg [pɛg] n cheville f; (for coat etc) patère f; (Brit: also: **clothes peg**) pince f à linge ▷ vt (clothes) accrocher; (Brit: groundsheet) fixer (avec des piquets); (fig: prices, wages) contrôler, stabiliser

pejorative [pɪ'dʒɔrətɪv] adj péjoratif(-ive)

Pekin [pi:'kɪn] n, **Peking** [pi:'kɪŋ] n Pékin

Pekinese, Pekingese [pi:kɪ'ni:z] n pékinois m

pelican ['pɛlɪkən] n pélican m

pelican crossing n (Brit Aut) feu m à commande manuelle

pellet ['pɛlɪt] n boulette f; (of lead) plomb m

pell-mell ['pɛl'mɛl] adv pêle-mêle

pelmet ['pɛlmɪt] n cantonnière f; lambrequin m

pelt [pɛlt] vt: **to ~ sb (with)** bombarder qn (de) ▷ vi (rain) tomber à seaux; (inf: run) courir à toutes jambes ▷ n peau f

pelvis ['pɛlvɪs] n bassin m

pen [pɛn] n (for writing) stylo m; (for sheep) parc m; (US inf: prison) taule f; **to put ~ to paper** prendre la plume

penal ['pi:nl] adj pénal(e)

penalize ['pi:nəlaɪz] vt pénaliser; (fig) désavantager

penal servitude [-'sə:vɪtjuːd] n travaux forcés

penalty ['pɛnltɪ] n pénalité f; sanction f; (fine) amende f; (Sport) pénalisation f; (also: **penalty kick**: Football) penalty m; (: Rugby) pénalité f; **to pay the ~ for** être pénalisé(e) pour

penalty area n (Brit Sport) surface f de réparation

penalty clause n clause pénale

penalty kick n (Football) penalty m

penalty shoot-out [-'ʃuːtaut] n (Football) épreuve f des penalties

penance ['pɛnəns] n pénitence f

pence [pɛns] npl of **penny**

penchant ['pɑ̃:ʃɑ̃:ŋ] n penchant m

pencil ['pɛnsl] n crayon m
▶ **pencil in** vt noter provisoirement

pencil case n trousse f (d'écolier)

pencil sharpener n taille-crayon(s) m inv

pendant ['pɛndnt] n pendentif m

pending ['pɛndɪŋ] prep en attendant ▷ adj en suspens

pendulum ['pɛndjuləm] n pendule m; (of clock) balancier m

penetrate ['pɛnɪtreɪt] vt pénétrer dans; (enemy territory) entrer en; (sexually) pénétrer

penetrating ['pɛnɪtreɪtɪŋ] adj pénétrant(e)

penetration [pɛnɪ'treɪʃən] n pénétration f

penfriend ['pɛnfrɛnd] n (Brit) correspondant(e)

penguin ['pɛŋgwɪn] n pingouin m

penicillin [pɛnɪ'sɪlɪn] n pénicilline f

peninsula [pə'nɪnsjulə] n péninsule f

penis ['pi:nɪs] n pénis m, verge f

penitence ['pɛnɪtns] n repentir m

penitent ['pɛnɪtnt] adj repentant(e)

penitentiary [pɛnɪ'tɛnʃərɪ] n (US) prison f

penknife ['pɛnnaɪf] n canif m

Penn., Penna. abbr (US) = **Pennsylvania**

pen name n nom m de plume, pseudonyme m

pennant ['pɛnənt] n flamme f, banderole f

penniless ['pɛnɪlɪs] adj sans le sou

Pennines ['pɛnaɪnz] npl: **the ~** les Pennines fpl

penny (pl **pennies** or **pence**) ['pɛnɪ, 'pɛnɪz, pɛns] n (Brit) penny m; (US) cent m

penpal ['pɛnpæl] n correspondant(e)

penpusher ['pɛnpuʃə'] n (pej) gratte-papier m inv

pension ['pɛnʃən] n (from company) retraite f; (Mil) pension f
▶ **pension off** vt mettre à la retraite

pensionable ['pɛnʃnəbl] adj qui a droit à une retraite

pensioner ['pɛnʃənə'] n (Brit) retraité(e)

pension fund n caisse f de retraite

pension plan n plan m de retraite

pensive ['pɛnsɪv] adj pensif(-ive)

pentagon ['pɛntəgən] n pentagone m; **the P~** (US Pol) le Pentagone; voir article

● **PENTAGON**

○
○ Le Pentagon est le nom donné aux bureaux du
● ministère de la Défense américain, situés à
● Arlington en Virginie, à cause de la forme
● pentagonale du bâtiment dans lequel ils se
● trouvent. Par extension, ce terme est
● également utilisé en parlant du ministère
● lui-même.

pentathlon [pɛn'tæθlən] n pentathlon m

Pentecost ['pɛntɪkɔst] n Pentecôte f

penthouse ['pɛnthaus] n appartement m (de luxe) en attique

pent-up ['pɛntʌp] adj (feelings) refoulé(e)

penultimate [pɪ'nʌltɪmət] adj pénultième, avant-dernier(-ière)

penury ['pɛnjurɪ] n misère f

people ['pi:pl] npl gens mpl; personnes fpl; (inhabitants) population f; (Pol) peuple m ▷ n (nation, race) peuple m ▷ vt peupler; **I know ~ who ...** je connais des gens qui ...; **the room was full of ~** la salle était pleine de monde or de gens; **several ~ came** plusieurs personnes sont venues; **~ say that ...** on dit or les gens disent que ...; **old ~** les personnes âgées; **young ~** les jeunes; **a man of the ~** un homme du peuple

PEP [pɛp] n (= personal equity plan) ≈ CEA m

(= compte d'épargne en actions)

pep [pɛp] *n* (*inf*) entrain *m*, dynamisme *m*
▶ **pep up** *vt* (*inf*) remonter

pepper ['pɛpəʳ] *n* poivre *m*; (*vegetable*) poivron *m*
▷ *vt* (*Culin*) poivrer

pepper mill *n* moulin *m* à poivre

peppermint ['pɛpəmɪnt] *n* (*plant*) menthe
poivrée; (*sweet*) pastille *f* de menthe

pepperoni [pɛpə'rəʊnɪ] *n* saucisson sec de porc et de
bœuf très poivré.

pepperpot ['pɛpəpɔt] *n* poivrière *f*

pep talk ['pɛptɔːk] *n* (*inf*) (petit) discours
d'encouragement

per [pəːʳ] *prep* par; ~ **hour** (*miles etc*) à l'heure;
(*fee*) (de) l'heure; ~ **kilo** *etc* le kilo *etc*; ~ **day/
person** par jour/personne; ~ **annum** per an; **as
~ your instructions** conformément à vos
instructions

per annum *adv* par an

per capita *adj*, *adv* par habitant, par personne

perceive [pə'siːv] *vt* percevoir; (*notice*)
remarquer, s'apercevoir de

per cent *adv* pour cent; **a 20 ~ discount** une
réduction de 20 pour cent

percentage [pə'sɛntɪdʒ] *n* pourcentage *m*; **on a
~ basis** au pourcentage

percentage point *n*: **ten ~s** dix pour cent

perceptible [pə'sɛptɪbl] *adj* perceptible

perception [pə'sɛpʃən] *n* perception *f*; (*insight*)
sensibilité *f*

perceptive [pə'sɛptɪv] *adj* (*remark*, *person*)
perspicace

perch [pəːtʃ] *n* (*fish*) perche *f*; (*for bird*) perchoir *m*
▷ *vi* (se) percher

percolate ['pəːkəleɪt] *vt*, *vi* passer

percolator ['pəːkəleɪtəʳ] *n* percolateur *m*;
cafetière *f* électrique

percussion [pə'kʌʃən] *n* percussion *f*

peremptory [pə'rɛmptərɪ] *adj* péremptoire

perennial [pə'rɛnɪəl] *adj* perpétuel(le); (*Bot*)
vivace ▷ *n* (*Bot*) (plante *f*) vivace *f*, plante
pluriannuelle

perfect ['pəːfɪkt] *adj* parfait(e) ▷ *n* (*also*: **perfect
tense**) parfait *m* ▷ *vt* [pə'fɛkt] (*technique*, *skill*,
work of art) parfaire; (*method*, *plan*) mettre au
point; **he's a ~ stranger to me** il m'est
totalement inconnu

perfection [pə'fɛkʃən] *n* perfection *f*

perfectionist [pə'fɛkʃənɪst] *n* perfectionniste
m/f

perfectly ['pəːfɪktlɪ] *adv* parfaitement; **I'm ~
happy with the situation** cette situation me
convient parfaitement; **you know ~ well** vous
le savez très bien

perforate ['pəːfəreɪt] *vt* perforer, percer

perforated ulcer ['pəːfəreɪtɪd-] *n* (*Med*) ulcère
perforé

perforation [pəːfə'reɪʃən] *n* perforation *f*; (*line of
holes*) pointillé *m*

perform [pə'fɔːm] *vt* (*carry out*) exécuter,
remplir; (*concert etc*) jouer, donner ▷ *vi* (*actor*,
musician) jouer; (*machine*, *car*) marcher,

fonctionner; (*company*, *economy*): **to ~ well/
badly** produire de bons/mauvais résultats

performance [pə'fɔːməns] *n* représentation *f*,
spectacle *m*; (*of an artist*) interprétation *f*; (*Sport:
of car*, *engine*) performance *f*; (*of company*, *economy*)
résultats *mpl*; **the team put up a good ~**
l'équipe a bien joué

performer [pə'fɔːməʳ] *n* artiste *m/f*

performing [pə'fɔːmɪŋ] *adj* (*animal*) savant(e)

performing arts *npl*: **the ~** les arts *mpl* du
spectacle

perfume ['pəːfjuːm] *n* parfum *m* ▷ *vt* parfumer

perfunctory [pə'fʌŋktərɪ] *adj* négligent(e), pour
la forme

perhaps [pə'hæps] *adv* peut-être; ~ **he'll ...**
peut-être qu'il ...; ~ **so/not** peut-être que oui/
que non

peril ['pɛrɪl] *n* péril *m*

perilous ['pɛrɪləs] *adj* périlleux(-euse)

perilously ['pɛrɪləslɪ] *adv*: **they came ~ close to
being caught** ils ont été à deux doigts de se
faire prendre

perimeter [pə'rɪmɪtəʳ] *n* périmètre *m*

perimeter wall *n* mur *m* d'enceinte

period ['pɪərɪəd] *n* période *f*; (*History*) époque *f*;
(*Scol*) cours *m*; (*full stop*) point *m*; (*Med*) règles *fpl*
▷ *adj* (*costume*, *furniture*) d'époque; **for a ~ of
three weeks** pour (une période de) trois
semaines; **the holiday ~** (*Brit*) la période des
vacances

periodic [pɪərɪ'ɔdɪk] *adj* périodique

periodical [pɪərɪ'ɔdɪkl] *adj* périodique ▷ *n*
périodique *m*

periodically [pɪərɪ'ɔdɪklɪ] *adv* périodiquement

period pains *npl* (*Brit*) douleurs menstruelles

peripatetic [pɛrɪpə'tɛtɪk] *adj* (*salesman*)
ambulant; (*Brit: teacher*) qui travaille dans
plusieurs établissements

peripheral [pə'rɪfərəl] *adj* périphérique ▷ *n*
(*Comput*) périphérique *m*

periphery [pə'rɪfərɪ] *n* périphérie *f*

periscope ['pɛrɪskəʊp] *n* périscope *m*

perish ['pɛrɪʃ] *vi* périr, mourir; (*decay*) se
détériorer

perishable ['pɛrɪʃəbl] *adj* périssable

perishables ['pɛrɪʃəblz] *npl* denrées *fpl*
périssables

perishing ['pɛrɪʃɪŋ] *adj* (*Brit inf: cold*) glacial(e)

peritonitis [pɛrɪtə'naɪtɪs] *n* péritonite *f*

perjure ['pəːdʒəʳ] *vt*: **to ~ o.s.** se parjurer

perjury ['pəːdʒərɪ] *n* (*Law: in court*) faux
témoignage; (*breach of oath*) parjure *m*

perk [pəːk] *n* (*inf*) avantage *m*, à-côté *m*
▶ **perk up** *vi* (*inf: cheer up*) se ragaillardir

perky ['pəːkɪ] *adj* (*cheerful*) guilleret(te), gai(e)

perm [pəːm] *n* (*for hair*) permanente *f* ▷ *vt*: **to
have one's hair ~ed** se faire faire une
permanente

permanence ['pəːmənəns] *n* permanence *f*

permanent ['pəːmənənt] *adj* permanent(e);
(*job*, *position*) permanent, fixe; (*dye*, *ink*)
indélébile; **I'm not ~ here** je ne suis pas ici à

titre définitif; **~ address** adresse habituelle
permanently ['pə:mənəntlı] *adv* de façon permanente; (*move abroad*) définitivement; (*open, closed*) en permanence; (*tired, unhappy*) constamment
permeable ['pə:mıəbl] *adj* perméable
permeate ['pə:mıeıt] *vi* s'infiltrer ▷ *vt* s'infiltrer dans; pénétrer
permissible [pə'mısıbl] *adj* permis(e), acceptable
permission [pə'mıʃən] *n* permission *f*, autorisation *f*; **to give sb ~ to do sth** donner à qn la permission de faire qch
permissive [pə'mısıv] *adj* tolérant(e); **the ~ society** la société de tolérance
permit *n* ['pə:mıt] permis *m*; (*entrance pass*) autorisation *f*, laissez-passer *m*; (*for goods*) licence *f* ▷ *vt* [pə'mıt] permettre; **to ~ sb to do** autoriser qn à faire, permettre à qn de faire; **weather ~ting** si le temps le permet
permutation [pə:mju'teıʃən] *n* permutation *f*
pernicious [pə:'nıʃəs] *adj* pernicieux(-euse), nocif(-ive)
pernickety [pə'nıkıtı] *adj* (*inf*) pointilleux(-euse), tatillon(ne); (*task*) minutieux(-euse)
perpendicular [pə:pən'dıkjuləʳ] *adj, n* perpendiculaire *f*
perpetrate ['pə:pıtreıt] *vt* perpétrer, commettre
perpetual [pə'pɛtjuəl] *adj* perpétuel(le)
perpetuate [pə'pɛtjueıt] *vt* perpétuer
perpetuity [pə:pı'tju:ıtı] *n*: **in ~** à perpétuité
perplex [pə'plɛks] *vt* (*person*) rendre perplexe; (*complicate*) embrouiller
perplexing [pə'plɛksıŋ] *adj* embarrassant(e)
perquisites ['pə:kwızıts] *npl* (*also*: **perks**) avantages *mpl* annexes
persecute ['pə:sıkju:t] *vt* persécuter
persecution [pə:sı'kju:ʃən] *n* persécution *f*
perseverance [pə:sı'vıərns] *n* persévérance *f*, ténacité *f*
persevere [pə:sı'vıəʳ] *vi* persévérer
Persia ['pə:ʃə] *n* Perse *f*
Persian ['pə:ʃən] *adj* persan(e) ▷ *n* (*Ling*) persan *m*; **the ~ Gulf** le golfe Persique
Persian cat *n* chat persan
persist [pə'sıst] *vi*: **to ~ (in doing)** persister (à faire), s'obstiner (à faire)
persistence [pə'sıstəns] *n* persistance *f*, obstination *f*; opiniâtreté *f*
persistent [pə'sıstənt] *adj* persistant(e), tenace; (*lateness, rain*) persistant; **~ offender** (*Law*) multirécidiviste *m/f*
persnickety [pə'snıkıtı] *adj* (*US inf*) = **pernickety**
person ['pə:sn] *n* personne *f*; **in ~** en personne; **on** *or* **about one's ~** sur soi; **~ to ~ call** (*Tel*) appel *m* avec préavis
personable ['pə:snəbl] *adj* de belle prestance, au physique attrayant
personal ['pə:snl] *adj* personnel(le); **~ belongings, ~ effects** effets personnels; **~**

hygiene hygiène *f* intime; **a ~ interview** un entretien
personal allowance *n* (*Tax*) part *f* du revenu non imposable
personal assistant *n* secrétaire personnel(le)
personal call *n* (*Tel*) communication *f* avec préavis
personal column *n* annonces personnelles
personal computer *n* ordinateur individuel, PC *m*
personal details *npl* (*on form etc*) coordonnées *fpl*
personal identification number *n* (*Comput, Banking*) numéro *m* d'identification personnel
personality [pə:sə'nælıtı] *n* personnalité *f*
personally ['pə:snəlı] *adv* personnellement; **to take sth ~** se sentir visé(e) par qch
personal organizer *n* agenda (personnel); (*electronic*) agenda électronique
personal property *n* biens personnels
personal stereo *n* Walkman® *m*, baladeur *m*
personify [pə:'sonıfaı] *vt* personnifier
personnel [pə:sə'nel] *n* personnel *m*
personnel department *n* service *m* du personnel
personnel manager *n* chef *m* du personnel
perspective [pə'spɛktıv] *n* perspective *f*; **to get sth into ~** ramener qch à sa juste mesure
perspex® ['pə:spɛks] *n* (*Brit*) Plexiglas® *m*
perspicacity [pə:spı'kæsıtı] *n* perspicacité *f*
perspiration [pə:spı'reıʃən] *n* transpiration *f*
perspire [pə'spaıəʳ] *vi* transpirer
persuade [pə'sweıd] *vt*: **to ~ sb to do sth** persuader qn de faire qch, amener *or* décider qn à faire qch; **to ~ sb of sth/that** persuader qn de qch/que
persuasion [pə'sweıʒən] *n* persuasion *f*; (*creed*) conviction *f*
persuasive [pə'sweısıv] *adj* persuasif(-ive)
pert [pə:t] *adj* coquin(e), mutin(e)
pertaining [pə:'teınıŋ]: **~ to** *prep* relatif(-ive) à
pertinent ['pə:tınənt] *adj* pertinent(e)
perturb [pə'tə:b] *vt* troubler, inquiéter
perturbing [pə'tə:bıŋ] *adj* troublant(e)
Peru [pə'ru:] *n* Pérou *m*
perusal [pə'ru:zl] *n* lecture (attentive)
Peruvian [pə'ru:vjən] *adj* péruvien(ne) ▷ *n* Péruvien(ne)
pervade [pə'veıd] *vt* se répandre dans, envahir
pervasive [pə'veısıv] *adj* (*smell*) pénétrant(e); (*influence*) insidieux(-euse); (*gloom, ideas*) diffus(e)
perverse [pə'və:s] *adj* pervers(e); (*contrary*) entêté(e), contrariant(e)
perversion [pə'və:ʃən] *n* perversion *f*
perversity [pə'və:sıtı] *n* perversité *f*
pervert *n* ['pə:və:t] perverti(e) ▷ *vt* [pə'və:t] pervertir; (*words*) déformer
pessimism ['pɛsımızəm] *n* pessimisme *m*
pessimist ['pɛsımıst] *n* pessimiste *m/f*
pessimistic [pɛsı'mıstık] *adj* pessimiste
pest [pɛst] *n* animal *m* (*or* insecte *m*) nuisible; (*fig*) fléau *m*

pest control n lutte f contre les nuisibles
pester ['pɛstər] vt importuner, harceler
pesticide ['pɛstısaıd] n pesticide m
pestilence ['pɛstıləns] n peste f
pestle ['pɛsl] n pilon m
pet [pɛt] n animal familier; (favourite) chouchou m ▷ cpd (favourite) favori(e) ▷ vt choyer; (stroke) caresser, câliner ▷ vi (inf) se peloter; ~ **lion** etc lion etc apprivoisé; **teacher's** ~ chouchou m du professeur; ~ **hate** bête noire
petal ['pɛtl] n pétale m
peter ['pi:tər]: **to ~ out** vi s'épuiser; s'affaiblir
petite [pə'ti:t] adj menu(e)
petition [pə'tıʃən] n pétition f ▷ vt adresser une pétition à ▷ vi: **to ~ for divorce** demander le divorce
pet name n (Brit) petit nom
petrified ['pɛtrıfaıd] adj (fig) mort(e) de peur
petrify ['pɛtrıfaı] vt pétrifier
petrochemical [pɛtrə'kɛmıkl] adj pétrochimique
petrodollars ['pɛtrəudɔləz] npl pétrodollars mpl
petrol ['pɛtrəl] n (Brit) essence f; **I've run out of ~** je suis en panne d'essence
petrol bomb n cocktail m Molotov
petrol can n (Brit) bidon m à essence
petrol engine n (Brit) moteur m à essence
petroleum [pə'trəulıəm] n pétrole m
petroleum jelly n vaseline f
petrol pump n (Brit: in car, at garage) pompe f à essence
petrol station n (Brit) station-service f
petrol tank n (Brit) réservoir m d'essence
petticoat ['pɛtıkəut] n jupon m
pettifogging ['pɛtıfɔgıŋ] adj chicanier(-ière)
pettiness ['pɛtınıs] n mesquinerie f
petty ['pɛtı] adj (mean) mesquin(e); (unimportant) insignifiant(e), sans importance
petty cash n caisse f des dépenses courantes, petite caisse
petty officer n second-maître m
petulant ['pɛtjulənt] adj irritable
pew [pju:] n banc m (d'église)
pewter ['pju:tər] n étain m
Pfc abbr (US Mil) = **private first class**
PG n abbr (Cine: = parental guidance) avis des parents recommandé
PGA n abbr = **Professional Golfers Association**
PH n abbr (US Mil: = Purple Heart) décoration accordée aux blessés de guerre
PHA n abbr (US: = Public Housing Administration) organisme d'aide à la construction
phallic ['fælık] adj phallique
phantom ['fæntəm] n fantôme m; (vision) fantasme m
Pharaoh ['fɛərəu] n pharaon m
pharmaceutical [fa:mə'sju:tıkl] adj pharmaceutique ▷ n: ~s produits mpl pharmaceutiques
pharmacist ['fa:məsıst] n pharmacien(ne)
pharmacy ['fa:məsı] n pharmacie f
phase [feız] n phase f, période f

▶ **phase in** vt introduire progressivement
▶ **phase out** vt supprimer progressivement
Ph.D. abbr = **Doctor of Philosophy**
pheasant ['fɛznt] n faisan m
phenomena [fə'nɔmınə] npl of **phenomenon**
phenomenal [fı'nɔmınl] adj phénoménal(e)
phenomenon (pl **phenomena**) [fə'nɔmınən, -nə] n phénomène m
phew [fju:] excl ouf!
phial ['faıəl] n fiole f
philanderer [fı'lændərər] n don Juan m
philanthropic [fılən'θrɔpık] adj philanthropique
philanthropist [fı'lænθrəpıst] n philanthrope m/f
philatelist [fı'lætəlıst] n philatéliste m/f
philately [fı'lætəlı] n philatélie f
Philippines ['fılıpi:nz] npl (also: **Philippine Islands**): **the** ~ les Philippines fpl
philosopher [fı'lɔsəfər] n philosophe m
philosophical [fılə'sɔfıkl] adj philosophique
philosophy [fı'lɔsəfı] n philosophie f
phishing ['fıʃıŋ] n phishing m
phlegm [flɛm] n flegme m
phlegmatic [flɛg'mætık] adj flegmatique
phobia ['fəubjə] n phobie f
phone [fəun] n téléphone m ▷ vt téléphoner à ▷ vi téléphoner; **to be on the** ~ avoir le téléphone; (be calling) être au téléphone
▶ **phone back** vt, vi rappeler
▶ **phone up** vt téléphoner à ▷ vi téléphoner
phone bill n facture f de téléphone
phone book n annuaire m
phone box, (US) **phone booth** n cabine f téléphonique
phone call n coup m de fil or de téléphone
phonecard ['fəunka:d] n télécarte f
phone-in ['fəunın] n (Brit Radio, TV) programme m à ligne ouverte
phone number n numéro m de téléphone
phone tapping [-tæpıŋ] n mise f sur écoutes téléphoniques
phonetics [fə'nɛtıks] n phonétique f
phoney ['fəunı] adj faux (fausse), factice; (person) pas franc (franche) ▷ n (person) charlatan m; fumiste m/f
phonograph ['fəunəgra:f] n (US) électrophone m
phony ['fəunı] adj, n = **phoney**
phosphate ['fɔsfeıt] n phosphate m
phosphorus ['fɔsfərəs] n phosphore m
photo ['fəutəu] n photo f; **to take a ~ of** prendre en photo
photo... ['fəutəu] prefix photo...
photo album n album m de photos
photocall ['fəutəukɔ:l] n séance f de photos pour la presse
photocopier ['fəutəukɔpıər] n copieur m
photocopy ['fəutəukɔpı] n photocopie f ▷ vt photocopier
photoelectric [fəutəuı'lɛktrık] adj photoélectrique; ~ **cell** cellule f photoélectrique

P

719

Photofit® ['fəutəufɪt] n portrait-robot m
photogenic [fəutəu'dʒɛnɪk] adj photogénique
photograph ['fəutəgræf] n photographie f ▷ vt
photographier; **to take a ~ of sb** prendre qn en
photo
photographer [fə'tɔgrəfəʳ] n photographe m/f
photographic [fəutə'græfɪk] adj
photographique
photography [fə'tɔgrəfɪ] n photographie f
photo opportunity n occasion, souvent arrangée,
pour prendre des photos d'une personnalité.
Photostat® ['fəutəustæt] n photocopie f,
photostat m
photosynthesis [fəutəu'sɪnθəsɪs] n
photosynthèse f
phrase [freɪz] n expression f; (Ling) locution f
▷ vt exprimer; (letter) rédiger
phrase book n recueil m d'expressions (pour
touristes)
physical ['fɪzɪkl] adj physique; **~ examination**
examen médical; **~ exercises** gymnastique f
physical education n éducation f physique
physically ['fɪzɪklɪ] adv physiquement
physician [fɪ'zɪʃən] n médecin m
physicist ['fɪzɪsɪst] n physicien(ne)
physics ['fɪzɪks] n physique f
physiological [fɪzɪə'lɔdʒɪkl] adj physiologique
physiology [fɪzɪ'ɔlədʒɪ] n physiologie f
physiotherapist [fɪzɪəu'θɛrəpɪst] n
kinésithérapeute m/f
physiotherapy [fɪzɪəu'θɛrəpɪ] n
kinésithérapie f
physique [fɪ'ziːk] n (appearance) physique m;
(health etc) constitution f
pianist ['piːənɪst] n pianiste m/f
piano [pɪ'ænəu] n piano m
piano accordion n (Brit) accordéon m à touches
Picardy ['pɪkədɪ] n Picardie f
piccolo ['pɪkələu] n piccolo m
pick [pɪk] n (tool: also: **pick-axe**) pic m, pioche f
▷ vt choisir; (gather) cueillir; (remove) prendre;
(lock) forcer; (scab, spot) gratter, écorcher; **take
your ~** faites votre choix; **the ~ of** le (la)
meilleur(e) de; **to ~ a bone** ronger un os; **to ~
one's nose** se mettre les doigts dans le nez; **to ~
one's teeth** se curer les dents; **to ~ sb's brains**
faire appel aux lumières de qn; **to ~ pockets**
pratiquer le vol à la tire; **to ~ a quarrel with sb**
chercher noise à qn
  ▸ **pick at** vt fus: **to ~ at one's food** manger du
  bout des dents, chipoter
  ▸ **pick off** vt (kill) (viser soigneusement et)
  abattre
  ▸ **pick on** vt fus (person) harceler
  ▸ **pick out** vt choisir; (distinguish) distinguer
  ▸ **pick up** vi (improve) remonter, s'améliorer ▷ vt
  ramasser; (telephone) décrocher; (collect) passer
  prendre; (Aut: give lift to) prendre; (learn)
  apprendre; (Radio) capter; **to ~ up speed**
  prendre de la vitesse; **to ~ o.s. up** se relever; **to
  ~ up where one left off** reprendre là où l'on
  s'est arrêté

pickaxe, (US) **pickax** ['pɪkæks] n pioche f
picket ['pɪkɪt] n (in strike) gréviste m/f participant
à un piquet de grève; piquet m de grève ▷ vt
mettre un piquet de grève devant
picket line n piquet m de grève
pickings ['pɪkɪŋz] npl: **there are rich ~ to be
had in ...** il y a gros à gagner dans ...
pickle ['pɪkl] n (also: **pickles**: as condiment) pickles
mpl ▷ vt conserver dans du vinaigre or dans de
la saumure; **in a ~** (fig) dans le pétrin
pick-me-up ['pɪkmiːʌp] n remontant m
pickpocket ['pɪkpɔkɪt] n pickpocket m
pick-up ['pɪkʌp] n (also: **pick-up truck**) pick-up m
inv; (Brit: on record player) bras m pick-up
picnic ['pɪknɪk] n pique-nique m ▷ vi pique-
niquer
picnic area n aire f de pique-nique
picnicker ['pɪknɪkəʳ] n pique-niqueur(-euse)
pictorial [pɪk'tɔːrɪəl] adj illustré(e)
picture ['pɪktʃəʳ] n (also TV) image f; (painting)
peinture f, tableau m; (photograph)
photo(graphie) f; (drawing) dessin m; (film) film
m; (fig: description) description f ▷ vt (imagine) se
représenter; (describe) dépeindre, représenter;
pictures npl: **the ~s** (Brit) le cinéma; **to take a ~
of sb/sth** prendre qn/qch en photo; **would you
take a ~ of us, please?** pourriez-vous nous
prendre en photo, s'il vous plaît?; **the overall ~**
le tableau d'ensemble; **to put sb in the ~**
mettre qn au courant
picture book n livre m d'images
picture frame n cadre m
picture messaging n picture messaging m,
messagerie f d'images
picturesque [pɪktʃə'rɛsk] adj pittoresque
picture window n baie vitrée, fenêtre f
panoramique
piddling ['pɪdlɪŋ] adj (inf) insignifiant(e)
pie [paɪ] n tourte f; (of fruit) tarte f; (of meat)
pâté m en croûte
piebald ['paɪbɔːld] adj pie inv
piece [piːs] n morceau m; (of land) parcelle f;
(item): **a ~ of furniture/advice** un meuble/
conseil; (Draughts) pion m ▷ vt: **to ~ together**
rassembler; **in ~s** (broken) en morceaux, en
miettes; (not yet assembled) en pièces détachées;
to take to ~s démonter; **in one ~** (object)
intact(e); **to get back all in one ~** (person)
rentrer sain et sauf; **a 10p ~** (Brit) une pièce de
10p; **~ by ~** morceau par morceau; **a six-~ band**
un orchestre de six musiciens; **to say one's ~**
réciter son morceau
piecemeal ['piːsmiːl] adv par bouts
piece rate n taux m or tarif m à la pièce
piecework ['piːswəːk] n travail m aux pièces or à
la pièce
pie chart n graphique m à secteurs,
camembert m
Piedmont ['piːdmɔnt] n Piémont m
pier [pɪəʳ] n jetée f; (of bridge etc) pile f
pierce [pɪəs] vt percer, transpercer; **to have
one's ears ~d** se faire percer les oreilles

pierced [pɪəst] *adj* (*ears*) percé(e)
piercing ['pɪəsɪŋ] *adj* (*cry*) perçant(e)
piety ['paɪətɪ] *n* piété *f*
piffling ['pɪflɪŋ] *adj* insignifiant(e)
pig [pɪg] *n* cochon *m*, porc *m*; (*pej: unkind person*) mufle *m*; (: *greedy person*) goinfre *m*
pigeon ['pɪdʒən] *n* pigeon *m*
pigeonhole ['pɪdʒənhəul] *n* casier *m*
pigeon-toed ['pɪdʒəntəud] *adj* marchant les pieds en dedans
piggy bank ['pɪgɪ-] *n* tirelire *f*
pigheaded ['pɪg'hɛdɪd] *adj* entêté(e), têtu(e)
piglet ['pɪglɪt] *n* petit cochon, porcelet *m*
pigment ['pɪgmənt] *n* pigment *m*
pigmentation [pɪgmən'teɪʃən] *n* pigmentation *f*
pigmy ['pɪgmɪ] *n* = **pygmy**
pigskin ['pɪgskɪn] *n* (peau *f* de) porc *m*
pigsty ['pɪgstaɪ] *n* porcherie *f*
pigtail ['pɪgteɪl] *n* natte *f*, tresse *f*
pike [paɪk] *n* (*spear*) pique *f*; (*fish*) brochet *m*
pilchard ['pɪltʃəd] *n* pilchard *m* (*sorte de sardine*)
pile [paɪl] *n* (*pillar, of books*) pile *f*; (*heap*) tas *m*; (*of carpet*) épaisseur *f*; **in a ~** en tas
  ▶ **pile on** *vt*: **to ~ it on** (*inf*) exagérer
  ▶ **pile up** *vi* (*accumulate*) s'entasser, s'accumuler ▷ *vt* (*put in heap*) empiler, entasser; (*accumulate*) accumuler
piles [paɪlz] *npl* hémorroïdes *fpl*
pile-up ['paɪlʌp] *n* (*Aut*) télescopage *m*, collision *f* en série
pilfer ['pɪlfə^r] *vt* chaparder ▷ *vi* commettre des larcins
pilfering ['pɪlfərɪŋ] *n* chapardage *m*
pilgrim ['pɪlgrɪm] *n* pèlerin *m*; *voir article*

◉ **PILGRIM FATHERS**

Les *Pilgrim Fathers* ("Pères pèlerins") sont un groupe de puritains qui quittèrent l'Angleterre en 1620 pour fuir les persécutions religieuses. Ayant traversé l'Atlantique à bord du "Mayflower", ils fondèrent New Plymouth en Nouvelle-Angleterre, dans ce qui est aujourd'hui le Massachusetts. Ces Pères pèlerins sont considérés comme les fondateurs des États-Unis, et l'on commémore chaque année, le jour de "Thanksgiving", la réussite de leur première récolte.

pilgrimage ['pɪlgrɪmɪdʒ] *n* pèlerinage *m*
pill [pɪl] *n* pilule *f*; **the ~** la pilule; **to be on the ~** prendre la pilule
pillage ['pɪlɪdʒ] *vt* piller
pillar ['pɪlə^r] *n* pilier *m*
pillar box *n* (*Brit*) boîte *f* aux lettres (*publique*)
pillion ['pɪljən] *n* (*of motor cycle*) siège *m* arrière; **to ride ~** être derrière; (*on horse*) être en croupe
pillory ['pɪlərɪ] *n* pilori *m* ▷ *vt* mettre au pilori
pillow ['pɪləu] *n* oreiller *m*
pillowcase ['pɪləukeɪs], **pillowslip** ['pɪləuslɪp]

n taie *f* d'oreiller
pilot ['paɪlət] *n* pilote *m* ▷ *cpd* (*scheme etc*) pilote, expérimental(e) ▷ *vt* piloter
pilot boat *n* bateau-pilote *m*
pilot light *n* veilleuse *f*
pimento [pɪ'mɛntəu] *n* piment *m*
pimp [pɪmp] *n* souteneur *m*, maquereau *m*
pimple ['pɪmpl] *n* bouton *m*
pimply ['pɪmplɪ] *adj* boutonneux(-euse)
PIN *n abbr* (= *personal identification number*) code *m* confidentiel
pin [pɪn] *n* épingle *f*; (*Tech*) cheville *f*; (*Brit: drawing pin*) punaise *f*; (*in grenade*) goupille *f*; (*Brit Elec: of plug*) broche *f* ▷ *vt* épingler; **~s and needles** fourmis *fpl*; **to ~ sb against/to** clouer qn contre/à; **to ~ sb down** (*fig*) coincer qn; **to ~ sth on sb** (*fig*) mettre qch sur le dos de qn
  ▶ **pin down** *vt* (*fig*): **to ~ sb down** obliger qn à répondre; **there's something strange here but I can't quite ~ it down** il y a quelque chose d'étrange ici, mais je n'arrive pas exactement à savoir quoi
pinafore ['pɪnəfɔː^r] *n* tablier *m*
pinafore dress *n* robe-chasuble *f*
pinball ['pɪnbɔːl] *n* flipper *m*
pincers ['pɪnsəz] *npl* tenailles *fpl*
pinch [pɪntʃ] *n* pincement *m*; (*of salt etc*) pincée *f* ▷ *vt* pincer; (*inf: steal*) piquer, chiper ▷ *vi* (*shoe*) serrer; **at a ~** à la rigueur; **to feel the ~** (*fig*) se ressentir des restrictions (*or de la récession etc*)
pinched [pɪntʃt] *adj* (*drawn*) tiré(e); **~ with cold** transi(e) de froid; **~ for** (*short of*): **~ for money** à court d'argent; **~ for space** à l'étroit
pincushion ['pɪnkuʃən] *n* pelote *f* à épingles
pine [paɪn] *n* (*also*: **pine tree**) pin *m* ▷ *vi*: **to ~ for** aspirer à, désirer ardemment
  ▶ **pine away** *vi* dépérir
pineapple ['paɪnæpl] *n* ananas *m*
pine cone *n* pomme *f* de pin
ping [pɪŋ] *n* (*noise*) tintement *m*
ping-pong® ['pɪŋpɔŋ] *n* ping-pong® *m*
pink [pɪŋk] *adj* rose ▷ *n* (*colour*) rose *m*; (*Bot*) œillet *m*, mignardise *f*
pinking shears ['pɪŋkɪŋ-] *npl* ciseaux *mpl* à denteler
pin money *n* (*Brit*) argent *m* de poche
pinnacle ['pɪnəkl] *n* pinacle *m*
pinpoint ['pɪnpɔɪnt] *vt* indiquer (avec précision)
pinstripe ['pɪnstraɪp] *n* rayure très fine
pint [paɪnt] *n* pinte *f* (*Brit* = 0,57 l; *US* = 0,47 l); (*Brit inf*) ≈ demi *m*, ≈ pot *m*
pinup ['pɪnʌp] *n* pin-up *f inv*
pioneer [paɪə'nɪə^r] *n* explorateur(-trice); (*early settler*) pionnier *m*; (*fig*) pionnier, précurseur *m* ▷ *vt* être un pionnier de
pious ['paɪəs] *adj* pieux(-euse)
pip [pɪp] *n* (*seed*) pépin *m*; **pips** *npl*: **the ~s** (*Brit: time signal on radio*) le top
pipe [paɪp] *n* tuyau *m*, conduite *f*; (*for smoking*) pipe *f*; (*Mus*) pipeau *m* ▷ *vt* amener par tuyau; **pipes** *npl* (*also*: **bagpipes**) cornemuse *f*
  ▶ **pipe down** *vi* (*inf*) se taire

P

pipe cleaner n cure-pipe m
piped music [paɪpt-] n musique f de fond
pipe dream n chimère f, utopie f
pipeline ['paɪplaɪn] n (for gas) gazoduc m, pipeline m; (for oil) oléoduc m, pipeline; **it is in the ~** (fig) c'est en route, ça va se faire
piper ['paɪpə'] n (flautist) joueur(-euse) de pipeau; (of bagpipes) joueur(-euse) de cornemuse
pipe tobacco n tabac m pour la pipe
piping ['paɪpɪŋ] adv: **~ hot** très chaud(e)
piquant ['pi:kənt] adj piquant(e)
pique [pi:k] n dépit m
piracy ['paɪərəsi] n piraterie f
pirate ['paɪərət] n pirate m ▷ vt (CD, video, book) pirater
pirated ['paɪərətɪd] adj pirate
pirate radio n (Brit) radio f pirate
pirouette [pɪru'ɛt] n pirouette f ▷ vi faire une or des pirouette(s)
Pisces ['paɪsi:z] n les Poissons mpl; **to be ~** être des Poissons
piss [pɪs] vi (inf!) pisser (!); **~ off!** tire-toi! (!)
pissed [pɪst] (inf!) adj (Brit: drunk) bourré(e); (US: angry) furieux(-euse)
pistol ['pɪstl] n pistolet m
piston ['pɪstən] n piston m
pit [pɪt] n trou m, fosse f; (also: **coal pit**) puits m de mine; (also: **orchestra pit**) fosse d'orchestre; (US: fruit stone) noyau m ▷ vt: **to ~ sb against sb** opposer qn à qn; **to ~ o.s.** or **one's wits against** se mesurer à; **pits** npl (in motor racing) aire f de service
pitapat ['pɪtə'pæt] adv (Brit): **to go ~** (heart) battre la chamade; (rain) tambouriner
pitch [pɪtʃ] n (Brit Sport) terrain m; (throw) lancement m; (Mus) ton m; (of voice) hauteur f; (fig: degree) degré m; (also: **sales pitch**) baratin m, boniment m; (Naut) tangage m; (tar) poix f ▷ vt (throw) lancer; (tent) dresser; (set: price, message) adapter, positionner ▷ vi (Naut) tanguer; (fall): **to ~ into/off** tomber dans/de; **to be ~ed forward** être projeté(e) en avant; **at this ~** à ce rythme
pitch-black ['pɪtʃ'blæk] adj noir(e) comme poix
pitched battle [pɪtʃt-] n bataille rangée
pitcher ['pɪtʃə'] n cruche f
pitchfork ['pɪtʃfɔ:k] n fourche f
piteous ['pɪtɪəs] adj pitoyable
pitfall ['pɪtfɔ:l] n trappe f, piège m
pith [pɪθ] n (of plant) moelle f; (of orange etc) intérieur m de l'écorce; (fig) essence f; vigueur f
pithead ['pɪthɛd] n (Brit) bouche f de puits
pithy ['pɪθɪ] adj piquant(e); vigoureux(-euse)
pitiable ['pɪtɪəbl] adj pitoyable
pitiful ['pɪtɪful] adj (touching) pitoyable; (contemptible) lamentable
pitifully ['pɪtɪfəli] adv pitoyablement; lamentablement
pitiless ['pɪtɪlɪs] adj impitoyable
pittance ['pɪtns] n salaire m de misère
pitted ['pɪtɪd] adj: **~ with** (chickenpox) grêlé(e) par; (rust) piqué(e) de

pity ['pɪtɪ] n pitié f ▷ vt plaindre; **what a ~!** quel dommage!; **it is a ~ that you can't come** c'est dommage que vous ne puissiez venir; **to have** or **take ~ on sb** avoir pitié de qn
pitying ['pɪtɪɪŋ] adj compatissant(e)
pivot ['pɪvət] n pivot m ▷ vi pivoter
pixel ['pɪksl] n (Comput) pixel m
pixie ['pɪksɪ] n lutin m
pizza ['pi:tsə] n pizza f
placard ['plækɑ:d] n affiche f; (in march) pancarte f
placate [plə'keɪt] vt apaiser, calmer
placatory [plə'keɪtəri] adj d'apaisement, lénifiant(e)
place [pleɪs] n endroit m, lieu m; (proper position, job, rank, seat) place f; (house) maison f, logement m; (in street names): **Laurel ~** = rue des Lauriers; (home): **at/to his ~** chez lui ▷ vt (position) placer, mettre; (identify) situer; reconnaître; **to take ~** avoir lieu; (occur) se produire; **to take sb's ~** remplacer qn; **to change ~s with sb** changer de place avec qn; **from ~ to ~** d'un endroit à l'autre; **all over the ~** partout; **out of ~** (not suitable) déplacé(e), inopportun(e); **I feel out of ~ here** je ne me sens pas à ma place ici; **in the first ~** d'abord, en premier; **to put sb in his ~** (fig) remettre qn à sa place; **he's going ~s** (fig: inf) il fait son chemin; **it is not my ~ to do it** ce n'est pas à moi de le faire; **to ~ an order with sb (for)** (Comm) passer commande à qn (de); **to be ~d** (in race, exam) se placer; **how are you ~d next week?** comment ça se présente pour la semaine prochaine?
placebo [plə'si:bəu] n placebo m
place mat n set m de table; (in linen etc) napperon m
placement ['pleɪsmənt] n placement m; (during studies) stage m
place name n nom m de lieu
placenta [plə'sɛntə] n placenta m
placid ['plæsɪd] adj placide
placidity [plə'sɪdɪtɪ] n placidité f
plagiarism ['pleɪdʒərɪzəm] n plagiat m
plagiarist ['pleɪdʒərɪst] n plagiaire m/f
plagiarize ['pleɪdʒəraɪz] vt plagier
plague [pleɪg] n fléau m; (Med) peste f ▷ vt (fig) tourmenter; **to ~ sb with questions** harceler qn de questions
plaice [pleɪs] n (pl inv) carrelet m
plaid [plæd] n tissu écossais
plain [pleɪn] adj (in one colour) uni(e); (clear) clair(e), évident(e); (simple) simple, ordinaire; (frank) franc (franche); (not handsome) quelconque, ordinaire; (cigarette) sans filtre; (without seasoning etc) nature inv ▷ adv franchement, carrément ▷ n plaine f; **in ~ clothes** (police) en civil; **to make sth ~ to sb** faire clairement comprendre qch à qn
plain chocolate n chocolat m à croquer
plainly ['pleɪnlɪ] adv clairement; (frankly) carrément, sans détours
plainness ['pleɪnnɪs] n simplicité f

plain speaking n propos mpl sans équivoque;
she has a reputation for ~ elle est bien connue
pour son franc parler or sa franchise
plaintiff ['pleɪntɪf] n plaignant(e)
plaintive ['pleɪntɪv] adj plaintif(-ive)
plait [plæt] n tresse f, natte f ▷ vt tresser, natter
plan [plæn] n plan m; (scheme) projet m ▷ vt
(think in advance) projeter; (prepare) organiser ▷ vi
faire des projets; **to ~ to do** projeter de faire;
how long do you ~ to stay? combien de temps
comptez-vous rester?
plane [pleɪn] n (Aviat) avion m; (also: **plane tree**)
platane m; (tool) rabot m; (Art, Math etc) plan m;
(fig) niveau m, plan ▷ adj plan(e); plat(e) ▷ vt
(with tool) raboter
planet ['plænɪt] n planète f
planetarium [plænɪ'tɛərɪəm] n planétarium m
plank [plæŋk] n planche f; (Pol) point m d'un
programme
plankton ['plæŋktən] n plancton m
planned economy [plænd-] n économie
planifiée
planner ['plænə^r] n planificateur(-trice); (chart)
planning m; **town** or (US) **city ~** urbaniste m/f
planning ['plænɪŋ] n planification f; **family ~**
planning familial
planning permission n (Brit) permis m de
construire
plant [plɑːnt] n plante f; (machinery) matériel m;
(factory) usine f ▷ vt planter; (bomb) déposer,
poser; (microphone, evidence) cacher
plantation [plæn'teɪʃən] n plantation f
plant pot n (Brit) pot m de fleurs
plaque [plæk] n plaque f
plasma ['plæzmə] n plasma m
plaster ['plɑːstə^r] n plâtre m; (also: **plaster of
Paris**) plâtre à mouler; (Brit: also: **sticking
plaster**) pansement adhésif ▷ vt plâtrer; (cover):
to ~ with couvrir de; **in ~** (Brit: leg etc) dans le
plâtre
plasterboard ['plɑːstəbɔːd] n Placoplâtre® m
plaster cast n (Med) plâtre m; (model, statue)
moule m
plastered ['plɑːstəd] adj (inf) soûl(e)
plasterer ['plɑːstərə^r] n plâtrier m
plastic ['plæstɪk] n plastique m ▷ adj (made of
plastic) en plastique; (flexible) plastique,
malléable; (art) plastique
plastic bag n sac m en plastique
plastic bullet n balle f de plastique
plastic explosive n plastic m
plasticine® ['plæstɪsiːn] n pâte f à modeler
plastic surgery n chirurgie f esthétique
plate [pleɪt] n (dish) assiette f; (sheet of metal, on
door: Phot) plaque f; (Typ) cliché m; (in book)
gravure f; (dental) dentier m; (Aut: number plate)
plaque minéralogique; **gold/silver ~** (dishes)
vaisselle f d'or/d'argent
plateau (pl **-s** or **-x**) ['plætəu, -z] n plateau m
plateful ['pleɪtful] n assiette f, assiettée f
plate glass n verre m à vitre, vitre f
platen ['plætən] n (on typewriter, printer) rouleau m

plate rack n égouttoir m
platform ['plætfɔːm] n (at meeting) tribune f;
(Brit: of bus) plate-forme f; (stage) estrade f; (Rail)
quai m; (Pol) plateforme f; **the train leaves
from ~ 7** le train part de la voie 7
platform ticket n (Brit) billet m de quai
platinum ['plætɪnəm] n platine m
platitude ['plætɪtjuːd] n platitude f, lieu
commun
platoon [plə'tuːn] n peloton m
platter ['plætə^r] n plat m
plaudits ['plɔːdɪts] npl applaudissements mpl
plausible ['plɔːzɪbl] adj plausible; (person)
convaincant(e)
play [pleɪ] n jeu m; (Theat) pièce f (de théâtre)
▷ vt (game) jouer à; (team, opponent) jouer contre;
(instrument) jouer de; (part, piece of music, note)
jouer; (CD etc) passer ▷ vi jouer; **to bring** or **call
into ~** faire entrer en jeu; **~ on words** jeu de
mots; **to ~ safe** ne prendre aucun risque; **to ~ a
trick on sb** jouer un tour à qn; **they're ~ing at
soldiers** ils jouent aux soldats; **to ~ for time**
(fig) chercher à gagner du temps; **to ~ into sb's
hands** (fig) faire le jeu de qn
▶ **play about, play around** vi (person) s'amuser
▶ **play along** vi (fig): **to ~ along with** (person)
entrer dans le jeu de ▷ vt (fig): **to ~ sb along**
faire marcher qn
▶ **play back** vt repasser, réécouter
▶ **play down** vt minimiser
▶ **play on** vt fus (sb's feelings, credulity) jouer sur;
to ~ on sb's nerves porter sur les nerfs de qn
▶ **play up** vi (cause trouble) faire des siennes
playact ['pleɪækt] vi jouer la comédie
playboy ['pleɪbɔɪ] n playboy m
played-out ['pleɪd'aut] adj épuisé(e)
player ['pleɪə^r] n joueur(-euse); (Theat)
acteur(-trice); (Mus) musicien(ne)
playful ['pleɪful] adj enjoué(e)
playgoer ['pleɪgəuə^r] n amateur(-trice) de
théâtre, habitué(e) des théâtres
playground ['pleɪgraund] n cour f de récréation;
(in park) aire f de jeux
playgroup ['pleɪgruːp] n garderie f
playing card ['pleɪɪŋ-] n carte f à jouer
playing field ['pleɪɪŋ-] n terrain m de sport
playmaker ['pleɪmeɪkə^r] n (Sport) joueur qui crée des
occasions de marquer des buts pour ses coéquipiers.
playmate ['pleɪmeɪt] n camarade m/f, copain
(copine)
play-off ['pleɪɔf] n (Sport) belle f
playpen ['pleɪpɛn] n parc m (pour bébé)
playroom ['pleɪruːm] n salle f de jeux
playschool ['pleɪskuːl] n = **playgroup**
plaything ['pleɪθɪŋ] n jouet m
playtime ['pleɪtaɪm] n (Scol) récréation f
playwright ['pleɪraɪt] n dramaturge m
plc abbr (Brit: = public limited company) ≈ SARL f
plea [pliː] n (request) appel m; (excuse) excuse f;
(Law) défense f
plea bargaining n (Law) négociations entre le
procureur, l'avocat de la défense et parfois le juge, pour

P

réduire la gravité des charges.

plead [pli:d] *vt* plaider; (*give as excuse*) invoquer ▷ *vi* (*Law*) plaider; (*beg*): **to ~ with sb (for sth)** implorer qn (d'accorder qch); **to ~ for sth** implorer qch; **to ~ guilty/not guilty** plaider coupable/non coupable

pleasant ['plɛznt] *adj* agréable

pleasantly ['plɛzntlı] *adv* agréablement

pleasantry ['plɛzntrı] *n* (*joke*) plaisanterie *f*; **pleasantries** *npl* (*polite remarks*) civilités *fpl*

please [pli:z] *excl* s'il te (*or* vous) plaît ▷ *vt* plaire à ▷ *vi* (*think fit*): **do as you ~** faites comme il vous plaira; **my bill, ~** l'addition, s'il vous plaît; **~ don't cry!** je t'en prie, ne pleure pas!; **~ yourself!** (*inf*) (faites) comme vous voulez!

pleased [pli:zd] *adj*: **~ (with)** content(e) (de); **~ to meet you** enchanté (de faire votre connaissance); **we are ~ to inform you that ...** nous sommes heureux de vous annoncer que ...

pleasing ['pli:zıŋ] *adj* plaisant(e), qui fait plaisir

pleasurable ['plɛʒərəbl] *adj* très agréable

pleasure ['plɛʒəʳ] *n* plaisir *m*; **"it's a ~"** "je vous en prie"; **with ~** avec plaisir; **is this trip for business or ~?** est-ce un voyage d'affaires ou d'agrément?

pleasure cruise *n* croisière *f*

pleat [pli:t] *n* pli *m*

plebiscite ['plɛbısıt] *n* plébiscite *m*

plebs [plɛbz] *npl* (*pej*) bas peuple

plectrum ['plɛktrəm] *n* plectre *m*

pledge [plɛdʒ] *n* gage *m*; (*promise*) promesse *f* ▷ *vt* engager; promettre; **to ~ support for sb** s'engager à soutenir qn; **to ~ sb to secrecy** faire promettre à qn de garder le secret

plenary ['pli:nərı] *adj*: **in ~ session** en séance plénière

plentiful ['plɛntıful] *adj* abondant(e), copieux(-euse)

plenty ['plɛntı] *n* abondance *f*; **~ of** beaucoup de; (*sufficient*) (bien) assez de; **we've got ~ of time** nous avons largement le temps

pleurisy ['pluərısı] *n* pleurésie *f*

pliable ['plaıəbl] *adj* flexible; (*person*) malléable

pliers ['plaıəz] *npl* pinces *fpl*

plight [plaıt] *n* situation *f* critique

plimsolls ['plımsəlz] *npl* (*Brit*) (chaussures *fpl*) tennis *fpl*

plinth [plınθ] *n* socle *m*

PLO *n abbr* (= *Palestine Liberation Organization*) OLP *f*

plod [plɔd] *vi* avancer péniblement; (*fig*) peiner

plodder ['plɔdəʳ] *n* bûcheur(-euse)

plodding ['plɔdıŋ] *adj* pesant(e)

plonk [plɔŋk] (*inf*) *n* (*Brit*: *wine*) pinard *m*, piquette *f* ▷ *vt*: **to ~ sth down** poser brusquement qch

plot [plɔt] *n* complot *m*, conspiration *f*; (*of story, play*) intrigue *f*; (*of land*) lot *m* de terrain, lopin *m* ▷ *vt* (*mark out*) tracer point par point; (*Naut*) pointer; (*make graph of*) faire le graphique de; (*conspire*) comploter ▷ *vi* comploter; **a vegetable ~** (*Brit*) un carré de légumes

plotter ['plɔtəʳ] *n* conspirateur(-trice); (*Comput*)

traceur *m*

plough, (*US*) **plow** [plau] *n* charrue *f* ▷ *vt* (*earth*) labourer; **to ~ money into** investir dans
  ▶ **plough back** *vt* (*Comm*) réinvestir
  ▶ **plough through** *vt fus* (*snow etc*) avancer péniblement dans

ploughing, (*US*) **plowing** ['plauıŋ] *n* labourage *m*

ploughman, (*US*) **plowman** ['plaumən] (*irreg*) *n* laboureur *m*

plow [plau] (*US*) = **plough**

ploy [plɔı] *n* stratagème *m*

pls *abbr* (= *please*) SVP *m*

pluck [plʌk] *vt* (*fruit*) cueillir; (*musical instrument*) pincer; (*bird*) plumer ▷ *n* courage *m*, cran *m*; **to ~ one's eyebrows** s'épiler les sourcils; **to ~ up courage** prendre son courage à deux mains

plucky ['plʌkı] *adj* courageux(-euse)

plug [plʌg] *n* (*stopper*) bouchon *m*, bonde *f*; (*Elec*) prise *f* de courant; (*Aut*: *also*: **spark(ing) plug**) bougie *f* ▷ *vt* (*hole*) boucher; (*inf*: *advertise*) faire du battage pour, matraquer; **to give sb/sth a ~** (*inf*) faire de la pub pour qn/qch
  ▶ **plug in** *vt* (*Elec*) brancher ▷ *vi* (*Elec*) se brancher

plughole ['plʌghəul] *n* (*Brit*) trou *m* (d'écoulement)

plum [plʌm] *n* (*fruit*) prune *f* ▷ *adj*: **~ job** (*inf*) travail *m* en or

plumb [plʌm] *adj* vertical(e) ▷ *n* plomb *m* ▷ *adv* (*exactly*) en plein ▷ *vt* sonder
  ▶ **plumb in** *vt* (*washing machine*) faire le raccordement de

plumber ['plʌməʳ] *n* plombier *m*

plumbing ['plʌmıŋ] *n* (*trade*) plomberie *f*; (*piping*) tuyauterie *f*

plumbline ['plʌmlaın] *n* fil *m* à plomb

plume [plu:m] *n* plume *f*, plumet *m*

plummet ['plʌmıt] *vi* (*person, object*) plonger; (*sales, prices*) dégringoler

plump [plʌmp] *adj* rondelet(te), dodu(e), bien en chair ▷ *vt*: **to ~ sth (down) on** laisser tomber qch lourdement sur
  ▶ **plump for** *vt fus* (*inf*: *choose*) se décider pour
  ▶ **plump up** *vt* (*cushion*) battre (pour lui redonner forme)

plunder ['plʌndəʳ] *n* pillage *m* ▷ *vt* piller

plunge [plʌndʒ] *n* plongeon *m*; (*fig*) chute *f* ▷ *vt* plonger ▷ *vi* (*fall*) tomber, dégringoler; (*dive*) plonger; **to take the ~** se jeter à l'eau

plunger ['plʌndʒəʳ] *n* piston *m*; (*for blocked sink*) (débouchoir *m* à) ventouse *f*

plunging ['plʌndʒıŋ] *adj* (*neckline*) plongeant(e)

pluperfect [plu:'pə:fıkt] *n* (*Ling*) plus-que-parfait *m*

plural ['pluərl] *adj* pluriel(le) ▷ *n* pluriel *m*

plus [plʌs] *n* (*also*: **plus sign**) signe *m* plus; (*advantage*) atout *m* ▷ *prep* plus; **ten/twenty ~** plus de dix/vingt; **it's a ~** c'est un atout

plus fours *npl* pantalon *m* (de) golf

plush [plʌʃ] *adj* somptueux(-euse) ▷ *n* peluche *f*

ply [plaı] *n* (*of wool*) fil *m*; (*of wood*) feuille *f*, épaisseur f ▷ vt (tool) manier; (a trade) exercer ▷ vi (ship) faire la navette; **three ~ (wool)** n laine f trois fils; **to ~ sb with drink** donner continuellement à boire à qn

plywood ['plaɪwʊd] n contreplaqué m

P.M. n abbr (Brit) = **prime minister**

p.m. adv abbr (= post meridiem) de l'après-midi

PMS n abbr (= premenstrual syndrome) syndrome prémenstruel

PMT n abbr (= premenstrual tension) syndrome prémenstruel

pneumatic [njuː'mætɪk] adj pneumatique

pneumatic drill [njuː'mætɪk-] n marteau-piqueur m

pneumonia [njuː'məʊnɪə] n pneumonie f

PO n abbr (= Post Office) PTT fpl; (Mil) = **petty officer**

po abbr = **postal order**

POA n abbr (Brit) = **Prison Officers' Association**

poach [pəʊtʃ] vt (cook) pocher; (steal) pêcher (or chasser) sans permis ▷ vi braconner

poached [pəʊtʃt] adj (egg) poché(e)

poacher ['pəʊtʃər] n braconnier m

poaching ['pəʊtʃɪŋ] n braconnage m

P.O. Box n abbr = **post office box**

pocket ['pɔkɪt] n poche f ▷ vt empocher; **to be (£5) out of ~** (Brit) en être de sa poche (pour 5 livres)

pocketbook ['pɔkɪtbʊk] n (notebook) carnet m; (US: wallet) portefeuille m; (: handbag) sac m à main

pocket knife n canif m

pocket money n argent m de poche

pockmarked ['pɔkmɑːkt] adj (face) grêlé(e)

pod [pɔd] n cosse f ▷ vt écosser

podcast n podcast m ▷ vi podcaster

podcasting ['pɔdkɑːstɪŋ] n podcasting m, baladodiffusion f

podgy ['pɔdʒɪ] adj rondelet(te)

podiatrist [pɔ'diːətrɪst] n (US) pédicure m/f

podiatry [pɔ'diːətrɪ] n (US) pédicurie f

podium ['pəʊdɪəm] n podium m

POE n abbr = **port of embarkation; port of entry**

poem ['pəʊɪm] n poème m

poet ['pəʊɪt] n poète m

poetic [pəʊ'ɛtɪk] adj poétique

poet laureate n poète lauréat; voir article

◉ **POET LAUREATE**
◉
◉ En Grande-Bretagne, le poet laureate est un
◉ poète qui reçoit un traitement en tant que
◉ poète de la cour et qui est officier de la
◉ maison royale à vie. Le premier d'entre eux
◉ fut Ben Jonson, en 1616. Jadis, le "poète
◉ lauréat" écrivait des poèmes lors des
◉ grandes occasions, mais cette tradition
◉ n'est plus guère observée.

poetry ['pəʊɪtrɪ] n poésie f

poignant ['pɔɪnjənt] adj poignant(e); (sharp) vif (vive)

point [pɔɪnt] n (Geom, Scol, Sport, on scale) point m; (tip) pointe f; (in time) moment m; (in space) endroit m; (subject, idea) point, sujet m; (purpose) but m; (also: **decimal point**): **2 ~ 3 (2.3)** 2 virgule 3 (2,3); (Brit Elec: also: **power point**) prise f (de courant) ▷ vt (show) indiquer; (wall, window) jointoyer; (gun etc): **to ~ sth at** braquer or diriger qch sur ▷ vi: **to ~ at** montrer du doigt; **points** npl (Aut) vis platinées; (Rail) aiguillage m; **good ~s** qualités fpl; **the train stops at Carlisle and all ~s south** le train dessert Carlisle et toutes les gares vers le sud; **to make a ~** faire une remarque; **to make a ~ of doing sth** ne pas manquer de faire qch; **to make one's ~** se faire comprendre; **to get/miss the ~** comprendre/ne pas comprendre; **to come to the ~** en venir au fait; **when it comes to the ~** le moment venu; **there's no ~ (in doing)** cela ne sert à rien (de faire); **what's the ~?** à quoi ça sert?; **to be on the ~ of doing sth** être sur le point de faire qch; **that's the whole ~!** précisément!; **to be beside the ~** être à côté de la question; **you've got a ~ there!** (c'est) juste!; **in ~ of fact** en fait, en réalité; **~ of departure** (also fig) point de départ; **~ of order** point de procédure; **~ of sale** (Comm) point de vente; **to ~ to sth** (fig) signaler
  ▶ **point out** vt (show) montrer, indiquer; (mention) faire remarquer, souligner

point-blank ['pɔɪnt'blæŋk] adv (fig) catégoriquement; (also: **at point-blank range**) à bout portant ▷ adj (fig) catégorique

point duty n (Brit): **to be on ~** diriger la circulation

pointed ['pɔɪntɪd] adj (shape) pointu(e); (remark) plein(e) de sous-entendus

pointedly ['pɔɪntɪdlɪ] adv d'une manière significative

pointer ['pɔɪntər] n (stick) baguette f; (needle) aiguille f; (dog) chien m d'arrêt; (clue) indication f; (advice) tuyau m

pointless ['pɔɪntlɪs] adj inutile, vain(e)

point of view n point m de vue

poise [pɔɪz] n (balance) équilibre m; (of head, body) port m; (calmness) calme m ▷ vt placer en équilibre; **to be ~d for** (fig) être prêt à

poison ['pɔɪzn] n poison m ▷ vt empoisonner

poisoning ['pɔɪznɪŋ] n empoisonnement m

poisonous ['pɔɪznəs] adj (snake) venimeux(-euse); (substance, plant) vénéneux(-euse); (fumes) toxique; (fig) pernicieux(-euse)

poke [pəʊk] vt (fire) tisonner; (jab with finger, stick etc) piquer; pousser du doigt; (put): **to ~ sth in(to)** fourrer or enfoncer qch dans ▷ n (jab) (petit) coup; (to fire) coup m de tisonnier; **to ~ fun at sb** se moquer de qn
  ▶ **poke about** vi fureter
  ▶ **poke out** vi (stick out) sortir ▷ vt: **to ~ one's head out of the window** passer la tête par la fenêtre

poker ['pəʊkər] n tisonnier m; (Cards) poker m

poker-faced ['pəukə'feɪst] *adj* au visage impassible
poky ['pəukɪ] *adj* exigu(ë)
Poland ['pəulənd] *n* Pologne *f*
polar ['pəulə^r] *adj* polaire
polar bear *n* ours blanc
polarize ['pəuləraɪz] *vt* polariser
Pole [pəul] *n* Polonais(e)
pole [pəul] *n* (*of wood*) mât *m*, perche *f*; (*Elec*) poteau *m*; (*Geo*) pôle *m*
poleaxe ['pəulæks] *vt* (*fig*) terrasser
pole bean *n* (*US*) haricot *m* (à rames)
polecat ['pəulkæt] *n* putois *m*
Pol. Econ. ['pɒlɪkɒn] *n abbr* = **political economy**
polemic [pɒ'lɛmɪk] *n* polémique *f*
pole star ['pəulstɑ:^r] *n* étoile *f* polaire
pole vault ['pəulvɔ:lt] *n* saut *m* à la perche
police [pə'li:s] *npl* police *f* ▷ *vt* maintenir l'ordre dans; **a large number of ~ were hurt** de nombreux policiers ont été blessés
police car *n* voiture *f* de police
police constable *n* (*Brit*) agent *m* de police
police department *n* (*US*) services *mpl* de police
police force *n* police *f*, forces *fpl* de l'ordre
policeman [pə'li:smən] (*irreg*) *n* agent *m* de police, policier *m*
police officer *n* agent *m* de police
police record *n* casier *m* judiciaire
police state *n* état policier
police station *n* commissariat *m* de police
policewoman [pə'li:swumən] (*irreg*) *n* femme-agent *f*
policy ['pɒlɪsɪ] *n* politique *f*; (*also*: **insurance policy**) police *f* (d'assurance); (*of newspaper, company*) politique générale; **to take out a ~** (*Insurance*) souscrire une police d'assurance
policy holder *n* assuré(e)
policy-making ['pɒlɪsɪmeɪkɪŋ] *n* élaboration *f* de nouvelles lignes d'action
polio ['pəulɪəu] *n* polio *f*
Polish ['pəulɪʃ] *adj* polonais(e) ▷ *n* (*Ling*) polonais *m*
polish ['pɒlɪʃ] *n* (*for shoes*) cirage *m*; (*for floor*) cire *f*, encaustique *f*; (*for nails*) vernis *m*; (*shine*) éclat *m*, poli *m*; (*fig: refinement*) raffinement *m* ▷ *vt* (*put polish on: shoes, wood*) cirer; (*make shiny*) astiquer, faire briller; (*fig: improve*) perfectionner
▶ **polish off** *vt* (*work*) expédier; (*food*) liquider
polished ['pɒlɪʃt] *adj* (*fig*) raffiné(e)
polite [pə'laɪt] *adj* poli(e); **it's not ~ to do that** ça ne se fait pas
politely [pə'laɪtlɪ] *adv* poliment
politeness [pə'laɪtnɪs] *n* politesse *f*
politic ['pɒlɪtɪk] *adj* diplomatique
political [pə'lɪtɪkl] *adj* politique
political asylum *n* asile *m* politique
politically [pə'lɪtɪklɪ] *adv* politiquement; **~ correct** politiquement correct(e)
politician [pɒlɪ'tɪʃən] *n* homme/femme politique, politicien(ne)
politics ['pɒlɪtɪks] *n* politique *f*
polka ['pɒlkə] *n* polka *f*

polka dot *n* pois *m*
poll [pəul] *n* scrutin *m*, vote *m*; (*also*: **opinion poll**) sondage *m* (d'opinion) ▷ *vt* (*votes*) obtenir; **to go to the ~s** (*voters*) aller aux urnes; (*government*) tenir des élections
pollen ['pɒlən] *n* pollen *m*
pollen count *n* taux *m* de pollen
pollination [pɒlɪ'neɪʃən] *n* pollinisation *f*
polling ['pəulɪŋ] *n* (*Brit Pol*) élections *fpl*; (*Tel*) invitation *f* à émettre
polling booth *n* (*Brit*) isoloir *m*
polling day *n* (*Brit*) jour *m* des élections
polling station *n* (*Brit*) bureau *m* de vote
pollster ['pəulstə^r] *n* sondeur *m*, enquêteur(-euse)
poll tax *n* (*Brit: formerly*) ≈ impôts locaux.
pollutant [pə'lu:tənt] *n* polluant *m*
pollute [pə'lu:t] *vt* polluer
pollution [pə'lu:ʃən] *n* pollution *f*
polo ['pəuləu] *n* polo *m*
polo-neck ['pəuləunɛk] *adj* à col roulé ▷ *n* (*sweater*) pull *m* à col roulé
polo shirt *n* polo *m*
poly ['pɒlɪ] *n abbr* (*Brit*) = **polytechnic**
poly bag *n* (*Brit inf*) sac *m* en plastique
polyester [pɒlɪ'ɛstə^r] *n* polyester *m*
polygamy [pə'lɪgəmɪ] *n* polygamie *f*
polygraph ['pɒlɪgrɑ:f] *n* détecteur *m* de mensonges
Polynesia [pɒlɪ'ni:zɪə] *n* Polynésie *f*
Polynesian [pɒlɪ'ni:zɪən] *adj* polynésien(ne) ▷ *n* Polynésien(ne)
polyp ['pɒlɪp] *n* (*Med*) polype *m*
polystyrene [pɒlɪ'staɪri:n] *n* polystyrène *m*
polytechnic [pɒlɪ'tɛknɪk] *n* (*college*) IUT *m*, Institut *m* universitaire de technologie
polythene ['pɒlɪθi:n] *n* (*Brit*) polyéthylène *m*
polythene bag *n* sac *m* en plastique
polyurethane [pɒlɪ'juərɪθeɪn] *n* polyuréthane *m*
pomegranate ['pɒmɪgrænɪt] *n* grenade *f*
pommel ['pɒml] *n* pommeau *m* ▷ *vt* = **pummel**
pomp [pɒmp] *n* pompe *f*, faste *f*, apparat *m*
pompom ['pɒmpɒm] *n* pompon *m*
pompous ['pɒmpəs] *adj* pompeux(-euse)
pond [pɒnd] *n* étang *m*; (*stagnant*) mare *f*
ponder ['pɒndə^r] *vi* réfléchir ▷ *vt* considérer, peser
ponderous ['pɒndərəs] *adj* pesant(e), lourd(e)
pong [pɒŋ] (*Brit inf*) *n* puanteur *f* ▷ *vi* schlinguer
pontiff ['pɒntɪf] *n* pontife *m*
pontificate [pɒn'tɪfɪkeɪt] *vi* (*fig*): **to ~ (about)** pontifier (sur)
pontoon [pɒn'tu:n] *n* ponton *m*; (*Brit Cards*) vingt-et-un *m*
pony ['pəunɪ] *n* poney *m*
ponytail ['pəunɪteɪl] *n* queue *f* de cheval
pony trekking [-trɛkɪŋ] *n* (*Brit*) randonnée *f* équestre *or* à cheval
poodle ['pu:dl] *n* caniche *m*
pooh-pooh ['pu:'pu:] *vt* dédaigner
pool [pu:l] *n* (*of rain*) flaque *f*; (*pond*) mare *f*;

(*artificial*) bassin *m*; (*also*: **swimming pool**) piscine *f*; (*sth shared*) fonds commun; (*money at cards*) cagnotte *f*; (*billiards*) poule *f*; (*Comm: consortium*) pool *m*; (*US: monopoly trust*) trust *m* ▷ *vt* mettre en commun; **pools** *npl* (*football*) ≈ loto sportif; **typing ~**, (*US*) **secretary ~** pool *m* dactylographique; **to do the (football) ~s** (*Brit*) ≈ jouer au loto sportif; *see also* **football pools**

poor [puə^r] *adj* pauvre; (*mediocre*) médiocre, faible, mauvais(e) ▷ *npl*: **the ~** les pauvres *mpl*

poorly ['puəlɪ] *adv* pauvrement; (*badly*) mal, médiocrement ▷ *adj* souffrant(e), malade

pop [pɒp] *n* (*noise*) bruit sec; (*Mus*) musique *f* pop; (*inf: drink*) soda *m*; (*US inf: father*) papa *m* ▷ *vt* (*put*) fourrer, mettre (rapidement) ▷ *vi* éclater; (*cork*) sauter; **she ~ped her head out of the window** elle passa la tête par la fenêtre
  ▶ **pop in** *vi* entrer en passant
  ▶ **pop out** *vi* sortir
  ▶ **pop up** *vi* apparaître, surgir

pop concert *n* concert *m* pop

popcorn ['pɒpkɔːn] *n* pop-corn *m*

pope [pəup] *n* pape *m*

poplar ['pɒplə^r] *n* peuplier *m*

poplin ['pɒplɪn] *n* popeline *f*

popper ['pɒpə^r] *n* (*Brit*) bouton-pression *m*

poppy ['pɒpɪ] *n* (*wild*) coquelicot *m*; (*cultivated*) pavot *m*

poppycock ['pɒpɪkɒk] *n* (*inf*) balivernes *fpl*

Popsicle® ['pɒpsɪkl] *n* (*US*) esquimau *m* (*glace*)

pop star *n* pop star *f*

populace ['pɒpjuləs] *n* peuple *m*

popular ['pɒpjulə^r] *adj* populaire; (*fashionable*) à la mode; **to be ~ (with)** (*person*) avoir du succès (auprès de); (*decision*) être bien accueilli(e) (par)

popularity [pɒpju'lærɪtɪ] *n* popularité *f*

popularize ['pɒpjuləraɪz] *vt* populariser; (*science*) vulgariser

populate ['pɒpjuleɪt] *vt* peupler

population [pɒpju'leɪʃən] *n* population *f*

population explosion *n* explosion *f* démographique

populous ['pɒpjuləs] *adj* populeux(-euse)

pop-up *adj* (*Comput: menu, window*) pop up *inv* ▷ *n* pop up *m inv*, fenêtre *f* pop up

porcelain ['pɔːslɪn] *n* porcelaine *f*

porch [pɔːtʃ] *n* porche *m*; (*US*) véranda *f*

porcupine ['pɔːkjupaɪn] *n* porc-épic *m*

pore [pɔː^r] *n* pore *m* ▷ *vi*: **to ~ over** s'absorber dans, être plongé(e) dans

pork [pɔːk] *n* porc *m*

pork chop *n* côte *f* de porc

pork pie *n* pâté *m* de porc en croûte

porn [pɔːn] *adj* (*inf*) porno ▷ *n* (*inf*) porno *m*

pornographic [pɔːnə'græfɪk] *adj* pornographique

pornography [pɔː'nɒgrəfɪ] *n* pornographie *f*

porous ['pɔːrəs] *adj* poreux(-euse)

porpoise ['pɔːpəs] *n* marsouin *m*

porridge ['pɒrɪdʒ] *n* porridge *m*

port [pɔːt] *n* (*harbour*) port *m*; (*opening in ship*) sabord *m*; (*Naut: left side*) bâbord *m*; (*wine*) porto

m; (*Comput*) port *m*, accès *m* ▷ *cpd* portuaire, du port; **to ~** (*Naut*) à bâbord; **~ of call** (port d')escale *f*

portable ['pɔːtəbl] *adj* portatif(-ive)

portal ['pɔːtl] *n* portail *m*

portcullis [pɔːt'kʌlɪs] *n* herse *f*

portent ['pɔːtɛnt] *n* présage *m*

porter ['pɔːtə^r] *n* (*for luggage*) porteur *m*; (*doorkeeper*) gardien(ne); portier *m*

portfolio [pɔːt'fəulɪəu] *n* portefeuille *m*; (*of artist*) portfolio *m*

porthole ['pɔːthəul] *n* hublot *m*

portico ['pɔːtɪkəu] *n* portique *m*

portion ['pɔːʃən] *n* portion *f*, part *f*

portly ['pɔːtlɪ] *adj* corpulent(e)

portrait ['pɔːtreɪt] *n* portrait *m*

portray [pɔː'treɪ] *vt* faire le portrait de; (*in writing*) dépeindre, représenter; (*subj: actor*) jouer

portrayal [pɔː'treɪəl] *n* portrait *m*, représentation *f*

Portugal ['pɔːtjugl] *n* Portugal *m*

Portuguese [pɔːtju'giːz] *adj* portugais(e) ▷ *n* (*pl inv*) Portugais(e); (*Ling*) portugais *m*

Portuguese man-of-war [-mænəv'wɔː^r] *n* (*jellyfish*) galère *f*

pose [pəuz] *n* pose *f*; (*pej*) affectation *f* ▷ *vi* poser; (*pretend*): **to ~ as** se faire passer pour ▷ *vt* poser; (*problem*) créer; **to strike a ~** poser (pour la galerie)

poser ['pəuzə^r] *n* question difficile *or* embarrassante; (*person*) = **poseur**

poseur [pəu'zə:^r] *n* (*pej*) poseur(-euse)

posh [pɒʃ] *adj* (*inf*) chic *inv*; **to talk ~** parler d'une manière affectée

position [pə'zɪʃən] *n* position *f*; (*job, situation*) situation *f* ▷ *vt* mettre en place *or* en position; **to be in a ~ to do sth** être en mesure de faire qch

positive ['pɒzɪtɪv] *adj* positif(-ive); (*certain*) sûr(e), certain(e); (*definite*) formel(le), catégorique; (*clear*) indéniable, réel(le)

positively ['pɒzɪtɪvlɪ] *adv* (*affirmatively, enthusiastically*) de façon positive; (*inf: really*) carrément; **to think ~** être positif(-ive)

posse ['pɒsɪ] *n* (*US*) détachement *m*

possess [pə'zɛs] *vt* posséder; **like one ~ed** comme un fou; **whatever can have ~ed you?** qu'est-ce qui vous a pris?

possession [pə'zɛʃən] *n* possession *f*; **possessions** *npl* (*belongings*) affaires *fpl*; **to take ~ of sth** prendre possession de qch

possessive [pə'zɛsɪv] *adj* possessif(-ive)

possessiveness [pə'zɛsɪvnɪs] *n* possessivité *f*

possessor [pə'zɛsə^r] *n* possesseur *m*

possibility [pɒsɪ'bɪlɪtɪ] *n* possibilité *f*; (*event*) éventualité *f*; **he's a ~ for the part** c'est un candidat possible pour le rôle

possible ['pɒsɪbl] *adj* possible; (*solution*) envisageable, éventuel(le); **it is ~ to do it** il est possible de le faire; **as far as ~** dans la mesure du possible, autant que possible; **if ~** si possible; **as big as ~** aussi gros que possible

possibly ['pɒsɪblɪ] *adv* (*perhaps*) peut-être; **if you ~ can** si cela vous est possible; **I cannot ~ come** il m'est impossible de venir

post [pəust] *n* (*Brit: mail*) poste *f*; (: *collection*) levée *f*; (: *letters, delivery*) courrier *m*; (*job, situation*) poste *m*; (*pole*) poteau *m*; (*trading post*) comptoir (commercial); (*on internet forum*) billet *m*, post *m* ▷ *vt* (*Brit: send by post, Mil, to internet*) poster; (: *appoint*): **to ~ to** affecter à; (*notice*) afficher; **by ~** (*Brit*) par la poste; **by return of ~** (*Brit*) par retour du courrier; **to keep sb ~ed** tenir qn au courant

post... [pəust] *prefix* post...; **post 1990** *adj* d'après 1990 ▷ *adv* après 1990

postage ['pəustɪdʒ] *n* tarifs *mpl* d'affranchissement; **~ paid** port payé; **~ prepaid** (*US*) franco (de port)

postage stamp *n* timbre-poste *m*

postal ['pəustl] *adj* postal(e)

postal order *n* mandat(-poste *m*) *m*

postbag ['pəustbæg] *n* (*Brit*) sac postal; (*postman's*) sacoche *f*

postbox ['pəustbɒks] *n* (*Brit*) boîte *f* aux lettres (*publique*)

postcard ['pəustkɑːd] *n* carte postale

postcode ['pəustkəud] *n* (*Brit*) code postal

postdate ['pəust'deɪt] *vt* (*cheque*) postdater

poster ['pəustər] *n* affiche *f*

poste restante [pəust'rɛstɑ̃ːnt] *n* (*Brit*) poste restante

posterior [pɒs'tɪərɪər] *n* (*inf*) postérieur *m*, derrière *m*

posterity [pɒs'tɛrɪtɪ] *n* postérité *f*

poster paint *n* gouache *f*

post exchange *n* (*US Mil*) magasin *m* de l'armée

post-free ['pəust'friː] *adj* (*Brit*) franco (de port)

postgraduate ['pəust'grædjuət] *n* ≈ étudiant(e) de troisième cycle

posthumous ['pɒstjuməs] *adj* posthume

posthumously ['pɒstjuməslɪ] *adv* après la mort de l'auteur, à titre posthume

posting ['pəustɪŋ] *n* (*Brit*) affectation *f*

postman ['pəustmən] (*Brit: irreg*) *n* facteur *m*

postmark ['pəustmɑːk] *n* cachet *m* (de la poste)

postmaster ['pəustmɑːstər] *n* receveur *m* des postes

Postmaster General *n* ≈ ministre *m* des Postes et Télécommunications

postmistress ['pəustmɪstrɪs] *n* receveuse *f* des postes

post-mortem [pəust'mɔːtəm] *n* autopsie *f*

postnatal ['pəust'neɪtl] *adj* postnatal(e)

post office *n* (*building*) poste *f*; (*organization*): **the Post Office** les postes *fpl*

post office box *n* boîte postale

post-paid ['pəust'peɪd] *adj* (*Brit*) port payé

postpone [pəs'pəun] *vt* remettre (à plus tard), reculer

postponement [pəs'pəunmənt] *n* ajournement *m*, renvoi *m*

postscript ['pəustskrɪpt] *n* post-scriptum *m*

postulate ['pɒstjuleɪt] *vt* postuler

posture ['pɒstʃər] *n* posture *f*; (*fig*) attitude *f* ▷ *vi* poser

postwar [pəust'wɔːr] *adj* d'après-guerre

postwoman [pəust'wumən] (*Brit: irreg*) *n* factrice *f*

posy ['pəuzɪ] *n* petit bouquet

pot [pɒt] *n* (*for cooking*) marmite *f*; casserole *f*; (*teapot*) théière *f*; (*for coffee*) cafetière *f*; (*for plants, jam*) pot *m*; (*piece of pottery*) poterie *f*; (*inf: marijuana*) herbe *f* ▷ *vt* (*plant*) mettre en pot; **to go to ~** (*inf*) aller à vau-l'eau; **~s of** (*Brit inf*) beaucoup de, plein de

potash ['pɒtæʃ] *n* potasse *f*

potassium [pə'tæsɪəm] *n* potassium *m*

potato (*pl* **-es**) [pə'teɪtəu] *n* pomme *f* de terre

potato crisps, (*US*) **potato chips** *npl* chips *mpl*

potato flour *n* fécule *f*

potato peeler *n* épluche-légumes *m*

potbellied ['pɒtbɛlɪd] *adj* (*from overeating*) bedonnant(e); (*from malnutrition*) au ventre ballonné

potency ['pəutnsɪ] *n* puissance *f*, force *f*; (*of drink*) degré *m* d'alcool

potent ['pəutnt] *adj* puissant(e); (*drink*) fort(e), très alcoolisé(e); (*man*) viril

potentate ['pəutnteɪt] *n* potentat *m*

potential [pə'tɛnʃl] *adj* potentiel(le) ▷ *n* potentiel *m*; **to have ~** être prometteur(-euse); ouvrir des possibilités

potentially [pə'tɛnʃəlɪ] *adv* potentiellement; **it's ~ dangerous** ça pourrait se révéler dangereux, il y a une possibilité de danger

pothole ['pɒthəul] *n* (*in road*) nid *m* de poule; (*Brit: underground*) gouffre *m*, caverne *f*

potholer ['pɒthəulər] *n* (*Brit*) spéléologue *m/f*

potholing ['pɒthəulɪŋ] *n* (*Brit*): **to go ~** faire de la spéléologie

potion ['pəuʃən] *n* potion *f*

potluck [pɒt'lʌk] *n*: **to take ~** tenter sa chance

pot plant *n* plante *f* d'appartement

potpourri [pəu'puriː] *n* pot-pourri *m*

pot roast *n* rôti *m* à la cocotte

pot shot ['pɒtʃɒt] *n*: **to take ~s at** canarder

potted ['pɒtɪd] *adj* (*food*) en conserve; (*plant*) en pot; (*fig: shortened*) abrégé(e)

potter ['pɒtər] *n* potier *m* ▷ *vi* (*Brit*): **to ~ around** *or* **about** bricoler; **~'s wheel** tour *m* de potier

pottery ['pɒtərɪ] *n* poterie *f*; **a piece of ~** une poterie

potty ['pɒtɪ] *adj* (*Brit inf: mad*) dingue ▷ *n* (*child's*) pot *m*

potty-training ['pɒtɪtreɪnɪŋ] *n* apprentissage *m* de la propreté

pouch [pautʃ] *n* (*Zool*) poche *f*; (*for tobacco*) blague *f*; (*for money*) bourse *f*

pouf, pouffe [puːf] *n* (*stool*) pouf *m*

poultice ['pəultɪs] *n* cataplasme *m*

poultry ['pəultrɪ] *n* volaille *f*

poultry farm *n* élevage *m* de volaille

poultry farmer *n* aviculteur *m*

pounce [pauns] *vi*: **to ~ (on)** bondir (sur), fondre (sur) ▷ *n* bond *m*, attaque *f*

pound [paund] n livre f (weight = 453g, 16 ounces; money = 100 pence); (for dogs, cars) fourrière f ▷ vt (beat) bourrer de coups, marteler; (crush) piler, pulvériser; (with guns) pilonner ▷ vi (heart) battre violemment, taper; **half a ~ (of)** une demi-livre (de); **a five-~ note** un billet de cinq livres

pounding ['paundɪŋ] n: **to take a ~** (fig) prendre une râclée

pound sterling n livre f sterling

pour [pɔː'] vt verser ▷ vi couler à flots; (rain) pleuvoir à verse; **to ~ sb a drink** verser or servir à boire à qn; **to come ~ing in** (water) entrer à flots; (letters) arriver par milliers; (cars, people) affluer

▶ **pour away, pour off** vt vider
▶ **pour in** vi (people) affluer, se précipiter; (news, letters) arriver en masse
▶ **pour out** vi (people) sortir en masse ▷ vt vider; (fig) déverser; (serve: a drink) verser

pouring ['pɔːrɪŋ] adj: **~ rain** pluie torrentielle
pout [paut] n moue f ▷ vi faire la moue
poverty ['pɔvətɪ] n pauvreté f, misère f
poverty line n seuil m de pauvreté
poverty-stricken ['pɔvətɪstrɪkn] adj pauvre, déshérité(e)
poverty trap n (Brit) piège m de la pauvreté
POW n abbr = **prisoner of war**
powder ['paudə'] n poudre f ▷ vt poudrer; **to ~ one's nose** se poudrer; (euphemism) aller à la salle de bain
powder compact n poudrier m
powdered milk n lait m en poudre
powder keg n (fig) poudrière f
powder puff n houppette f
powder room n toilettes fpl (pour dames)
powdery ['paudərɪ] adj poudreux(-euse)
power ['pauə'] n (strength, nation) puissance f, force f; (ability, Pol: of party, leader) pouvoir m; (Math) puissance; (of speech, thought) faculté f; (Elec) courant m ▷ vt faire marcher, actionner; **to do all in one's ~ to help sb** faire tout ce qui est en son pouvoir pour aider qn; **the world ~s** les grandes puissances; **to be in ~** être au pouvoir
powerboat ['pauəbəut] n (Brit) hors-bord m
power cut n (Brit) coupure f de courant
powered ['pauəd] adj: **~ by** actionné(e) par, fonctionnant à; **nuclear-~ submarine** sous-marin m (à propulsion) nucléaire
power failure n panne f de courant
powerful ['pauəful] adj puissant(e); (performance etc) très fort(e)
powerhouse ['pauəhaus] n (fig: person) fonceur m; **a ~ of ideas** une mine d'idées
powerless ['pauəlɪs] adj impuissant(e)
power line n ligne f électrique
power of attorney n procuration f
power point n (Brit) prise f de courant
power station n centrale f électrique
power steering n direction assistée
power struggle n lutte f pour le pouvoir

powwow ['pauwau] n conciliabule m
p.p. abbr (= per procurationem: by proxy) p.p.
PPE n abbr (Brit Scol) = **philosophy, politics and economics**
PPS n abbr (= post postscriptum) PPS; (Brit: = parliamentary private secretary) parlementaire chargé de mission auprès d'un ministre
PQ abbr (Canada: = Province of Quebec) PQ
PR n abbr = **proportional representation; public relations** ▷ abbr (US) = **Puerto Rico**
Pr. abbr (= prince) Pce
practicability [præktɪkə'bɪlɪtɪ] n possibilité f de réalisation
practicable ['præktɪkəbl] adj (scheme) réalisable
practical ['præktɪkl] adj pratique
practicality [præktɪ'kælɪtɪ] n (of plan) aspect m pratique; (of person) sens m pratique; **practicalities** npl détails mpl pratiques
practical joke n farce f
practically ['præktɪklɪ] adv (almost) pratiquement
practice ['præktɪs] n pratique f; (of profession) exercice m; (at football etc) entraînement m; (business) cabinet m; clientèle f ▷ vt, vi (US) = **practise**; **in ~** (in reality) en pratique; **out of ~** rouillé(e); **2 hours' piano ~** 2 heures de travail or d'exercices au piano; **target ~** exercices de tir; **it's common ~** c'est courant, ça se fait couramment; **to put sth into ~** mettre qch en pratique
practice match n match m d'entraînement
practise, (US) **practice** ['præktɪs] vt (work at: piano, backhand etc) s'exercer à, travailler; (train for: sport) s'entraîner à; (a sport, religion, method) pratiquer; (profession) exercer ▷ vi s'exercer, travailler; (train) s'entraîner; (lawyer, doctor) exercer; **to ~ for a match** s'entraîner pour un match
practised, (US) **practiced** ['præktɪst] adj (person) expérimenté(e); (performance) impeccable; (liar) invétéré(e); **with a ~ eye** d'un œil exercé
practising, (US) **practicing** ['præktɪsɪŋ] adj (Christian etc) pratiquant(e); (lawyer) en exercice; (homosexual) déclaré
practitioner [præk'tɪʃənə'] n praticien(ne)
pragmatic [præg'mætɪk] adj pragmatique
Prague [prɑːg] n Prague
prairie ['prɛərɪ] n savane f; (US): **the ~s** la Prairie
praise [preɪz] n éloge(s) m(pl), louange(s) f(pl) ▷ vt louer, faire l'éloge de
praiseworthy ['preɪzwə:ðɪ] adj digne de louanges
pram [præm] n (Brit) landau m, voiture f d'enfant
prance [prɑːns] vi (horse) caracoler
prank [præŋk] n farce f
prat [præt] n (Brit inf) imbécile m, andouille f
prattle ['prætl] vi jacasser
prawn [prɔːn] n crevette f (rose)
prawn cocktail n cocktail m de crevettes
pray [preɪ] vi prier
prayer [prɛə'] n prière f

p

prayer book *n* livre *m* de prières

pre... ['pri:] *prefix* pré...; **pre-1970** *adj* d'avant 1970 ▷ *adv* avant 1970

preach [pri:tʃ] *vt, vi* prêcher; **to ~ at sb** faire la morale à qn

preacher ['pri:tʃə'] *n* prédicateur *m*; (*US: clergyman*) pasteur *m*

preamble [prɪ'æmbl] *n* préambule *m*

prearranged [pri:ə'reɪndʒd] *adj* organisé(e) *or* fixé(e) à l'avance

precarious [prɪ'kɛərɪəs] *adj* précaire

precaution [prɪ'kɔ:ʃən] *n* précaution *f*

precautionary [prɪ'kɔ:ʃənrɪ] *adj* (*measure*) de précaution

precede [prɪ'si:d] *vt, vi* précéder

precedence ['prɛsɪdəns] *n* préséance *f*

precedent ['prɛsɪdənt] *n* précédent *m*; **to establish** *or* **set a ~** créer un précédent

preceding [prɪ'si:dɪŋ] *adj* qui précède (*or* précédait)

precept ['pri:sɛpt] *n* précepte *m*

precinct ['pri:sɪŋkt] *n* (*round cathedral*) pourtour *m*, enceinte *f*; (*US: district*) circonscription *f*, arrondissement *m*; **precincts** *npl* (*neighbourhood*) alentours *mpl*, environs *mpl*; **pedestrian ~** (*Brit*) zone piétonnière; **shopping ~** (*Brit*) centre commercial

precious ['prɛʃəs] *adj* précieux(-euse) ▷ *adv* (*inf*): **~ little** *or* **few** fort peu; **your ~ dog** (*ironic*) ton chien chéri, ton chéri chien

precipice ['prɛsɪpɪs] *n* précipice *m*

precipitate [prɪ'sɪpɪtɪt] *adj* (*hasty*) précipité(e) ▷ *vt* [prɪ'sɪpɪteɪt] précipiter

precipitation [prɪsɪpɪ'teɪʃən] *n* précipitation *f*

precipitous [prɪ'sɪpɪtəs] *adj* (*steep*) abrupt(e), à pic

précis (*pl* -) ['preɪsi:, -z] *n* résumé *m*

precise [prɪ'saɪs] *adj* précis(e)

precisely [prɪ'saɪslɪ] *adv* précisément

precision [prɪ'sɪʒən] *n* précision *f*

preclude [prɪ'klu:d] *vt* exclure, empêcher; **to ~ sb from doing** empêcher qn de faire

precocious [prɪ'kəuʃəs] *adj* précoce

preconceived [pri:kən'si:vd] *adj* (*idea*) préconçu(e)

preconception [pri:kən'sɛpʃən] *n* idée préconçue

precondition ['pri:kən'dɪʃən] *n* condition *f* nécessaire

precursor [pri:'kə:sə'] *n* précurseur *m*

predate ['pri:'deɪt] *vt* (*precede*) antidater

predator ['prɛdətə'] *n* prédateur *m*, rapace *m*

predatory ['prɛdətərɪ] *adj* rapace

predecessor ['pri:dɪsɛsə'] *n* prédécesseur *m*

predestination [pri:dɛstɪ'neɪʃən] *n* prédestination *f*

predetermine [pri:dɪ'tə:mɪn] *vt* déterminer à l'avance

predicament [prɪ'dɪkəmənt] *n* situation *f* difficile

predicate ['prɛdɪkɪt] *n* (*Ling*) prédicat *m*

predict [prɪ'dɪkt] *vt* prédire

predictable [prɪ'dɪktəbl] *adj* prévisible

predictably [prɪ'dɪktəblɪ] *adv* (*behave, react*) de façon prévisible; **~ she didn't arrive** comme on pouvait s'y attendre, elle n'est pas venue

prediction [prɪ'dɪkʃən] *n* prédiction *f*

predispose [pri:dɪs'pəuz] *vt* prédisposer

predominance [prɪ'dɔmɪnəns] *n* prédominance *f*

predominant [prɪ'dɔmɪnənt] *adj* prédominant(e)

predominantly [prɪ'dɔmɪnəntlɪ] *adv* en majeure partie; (*especially*) surtout

predominate [prɪ'dɔmɪneɪt] *vi* prédominer

pre-eminent [pri:'ɛmɪnənt] *adj* prééminent(e)

pre-empt [pri:'ɛmt] *vt* (*Brit*) acquérir par droit de préemption; (*fig*) anticiper sur; **to ~ the issue** conclure avant même d'ouvrir les débats

pre-emptive [prɪ'ɛmtɪv] *adj*: **~ strike** attaque (*or* action) préventive

preen [pri:n] *vt*: **to ~ itself** (*bird*) se lisser les plumes; **to ~ o.s.** s'admirer

prefab ['pri:fæb] *n abbr* (= *prefabricated building*) bâtiment préfabriqué

prefabricated [pri:'fæbrɪkeɪtɪd] *adj* préfabriqué(e)

preface ['prɛfəs] *n* préface *f*

prefect ['pri:fɛkt] *n* (*Brit: in school*) élève chargé de certaines fonctions de discipline; (*in France*) préfet *m*

prefer [prɪ'fə:'] *vt* préférer; (*Law*): **to ~ charges** procéder à une inculpation; **to ~ coffee to tea** préférer le café au thé; **to ~ doing** *or* **to do sth** préférer faire qch

preferable ['prɛfrəbl] *adj* préférable

preferably ['prɛfrəblɪ] *adv* de préférence

preference ['prɛfrəns] *n* préférence *f*; **in ~ to sth** plutôt que qch, de préférence à qch

preference shares *npl* (*Brit*) actions privilégiées

preferential [prɛfə'rɛnʃəl] *adj* préférentiel(le); **~ treatment** traitement *m* de faveur

preferred stock [prɪ'fə:d-] *npl* (*US*) = **preference shares**

prefix ['pri:fɪks] *n* préfixe *m*

pregnancy ['prɛgnənsɪ] *n* grossesse *f*

pregnancy test *n* test *m* de grossesse

pregnant ['prɛgnənt] *adj* enceinte *adj f*; (*animal*) pleine; **3 months ~** enceinte de 3 mois

prehistoric ['pri:hɪs'tɔrɪk] *adj* préhistorique

prehistory [pri:'hɪstərɪ] *n* préhistoire *f*

prejudge [pri:'dʒʌdʒ] *vt* préjuger de

prejudice ['prɛdʒudɪs] *n* préjugé *m*; (*harm*) tort *m*, préjudice *m* ▷ *vt* porter préjudice à; (*bias*): **to ~ sb in favour of/against** prévenir qn en faveur de/contre; **racial ~** préjugés raciaux

prejudiced ['prɛdʒudɪst] *adj* (*person*) plein(e) de préjugés; (*in a matter*) partial(e); (*view*) préconçu(e), partial(e); **to be ~ against sb/sth** avoir un parti-pris contre qn/qch; **to be racially ~** avoir des préjugés raciaux

prelate ['prɛlət] *n* prélat *m*

preliminaries [prɪ'lɪmɪnərɪz] *npl* préliminaires *mpl*

preliminary [prɪ'lɪmɪnərɪ] *adj* préliminaire

prelude ['prɛljuːd] n prélude m
premarital ['priːˈmærɪtl] adj avant le mariage; ~
contract contrat m de mariage
premature ['prɛmətʃuəʳ] adj prématuré(e); **to
be ~ (in doing sth)** aller un peu (trop) vite (en
faisant qch)
premeditated [priːˈmɛdɪteɪtɪd] adj prémédité(e)
premeditation [priːmɛdɪˈteɪʃən] n
préméditation f
premenstrual [priːˈmɛnstruəl] adj
prémenstruel(le)
premenstrual tension n irritabilité f avant les
règles
premier ['prɛmɪəʳ] adj premier(-ière),
principal(e) ▷ n (Pol: Prime Minister) premier
ministre; (Pol: President) chef m de l'État
premiere ['prɛmɪɛəʳ] n première f
Premier League n première division
premise ['prɛmɪs] n prémisse f
premises ['prɛmɪsɪz] npl locaux mpl; **on the ~**
sur les lieux; sur place; **business ~** locaux
commerciaux
premium ['priːmɪəm] n prime f; **to be at a ~** (fig:
housing etc) être très demandé(e), être rarissime;
to sell at a ~ (shares) vendre au-dessus du pair
premium bond n (Brit) obligation f à prime,
bon m à lots
premium deal n (Comm) offre spéciale
premium fuel, (US) **premium gasoline** n
super m
premonition [prɛməˈnɪʃən] n prémonition f
preoccupation [priːɔkjuˈpeɪʃən] n
préoccupation f
preoccupied [priːˈɔkjupaɪd] adj préoccupé(e)
prep [prɛp] adj abbr: ~ **school**; = **preparatory
school** ▷ n abbr (Scol: = preparation) étude f
prepackaged [priːˈpækɪdʒd] adj
préempaqueté(e)
prepaid [priːˈpeɪd] adj payé(e) d'avance
preparation [prɛpəˈreɪʃən] n préparation f;
preparations npl (for trip, war) préparatifs mpl;
in ~ for en vue de
preparatory [prɪˈpærətərɪ] adj préparatoire; ~
to sth/to doing sth en prévision de qch/avant
de faire qch
preparatory school n (Brit) école primaire
privée; (US) lycée privé; voir article

● **PREPARATORY SCHOOL**
●
● En Grande-Bretagne, une preparatory school –
● ou, plus familièrement, une prep school – est
● une école payante qui prépare les enfants de
● 7 à 13 ans aux "public schools".

prepare [prɪˈpɛəʳ] vt préparer ▷ vi: **to ~ for** se
préparer à
prepared [prɪˈpɛəd] adj: ~ **for** préparé(e) à; ~ **to**
prêt(e) à
preponderance [prɪˈpɔndərns] n
prépondérance f
preposition [prɛpəˈzɪʃən] n préposition f

prepossessing [priːpəˈzɛsɪŋ] adj avenant(e),
engageant(e)
preposterous [prɪˈpɔstərəs] adj ridicule,
absurde
prep school n = **preparatory school**
prerecord ['priːrɪˈkɔːd] vt: ~**ed broadcast**
émission f en différé; ~**ed cassette** cassette
enregistrée
prerequisite [priːˈrɛkwɪzɪt] n condition f
préalable
prerogative [prɪˈrɔgətɪv] n prérogative f
presbyterian [prɛzbɪˈtɪərɪən] adj, n
presbytérien(ne)
presbytery ['prɛzbɪtərɪ] n presbytère m
preschool ['priːˈskuːl] adj préscolaire; (child)
d'âge préscolaire
prescribe [prɪˈskraɪb] vt prescrire; ~**d books**
(Brit Scol) œuvres fpl au programme
prescription [prɪˈskrɪpʃən] n prescription f;
(Med) ordonnance f; (: medicine) médicament m
(obtenu sur ordonnance); **to make up** or (US)
fill a ~ faire une ordonnance; **could you write
me a ~?** pouvez-vous me faire une ordonnance?;
"only available on ~" "uniquement sur
ordonnance"
prescription charges npl (Brit) participation f
fixe au coût de l'ordonnance
prescriptive [prɪˈskrɪptɪv] adj normatif(-ive)
presence ['prɛzns] n présence f; **in sb's ~** en
présence de qn; ~ **of mind** présence d'esprit
present ['prɛznt] adj présent(e); (current)
présent, actuel(le) ▷ n cadeau m; (actuality, also:
present tense) présent m ▷ vt [prɪˈzɛnt]
présenter; (prize, medal) remettre; (give): **to ~ sb
with sth** offrir qch à qn; **to be ~ at** assister à;
those ~ les présents; **at ~** en ce moment; **to
give sb a ~** offrir un cadeau à qn; **to ~ sb (to sb)**
présenter qn (à qn)
presentable [prɪˈzɛntəbl] adj présentable
presentation [prɛznˈteɪʃən] n présentation f;
(gift) cadeau m, présent m; (ceremony) remise f du
cadeau (or de la médaille etc); **on ~ of** (voucher etc)
sur présentation de
present-day ['prɛzntdeɪ] adj contemporain(e),
actuel(le)
presenter [prɪˈzɛntəʳ] n (Brit Radio, TV)
présentateur(-trice)
presently ['prɛzntlɪ] adv (soon) tout à l'heure,
bientôt; (with verb in past) peu après; (at present)
en ce moment; (US: now) maintenant
preservation [prɛzəˈveɪʃən] n préservation f,
conservation f
preservative [prɪˈzəːvətɪv] n agent m de
conservation
preserve [prɪˈzəːv] vt (keep safe) préserver,
protéger; (maintain) conserver, garder; (food)
mettre en conserve ▷ n (for game, fish) réserve f;
(often pl: jam) confiture f; (: fruit) fruits mpl en
conserve
preshrunk [priːˈʃrʌŋk] adj irrétrécissable
preside [prɪˈzaɪd] vi présider
presidency ['prɛzɪdənsɪ] n présidence f

P

president ['prɛzɪdənt] n président(e); (US: of company) président-directeur général, PDG m

presidential [prɛzɪ'dɛnʃl] adj présidentiel(le)

press [prɛs] n (tool, machine, newspapers) presse f; (for wine) pressoir m; (crowd) cohue f, foule f ▷ vt (push) appuyer sur; (squeeze) presser, serrer; (clothes: iron) repasser; (pursue) talonner; (insist): **to ~ sth on sb** presser qn d'accepter qch; (urge, entreat): **to ~ sb to do** or **into doing sth** pousser qn à faire qch ▷ vi appuyer, peser; se presser; **we are ~ed for time** le temps nous manque; **to ~ for sth** faire pression pour obtenir qch; **to ~ sb for an answer** presser qn de répondre; **to ~ charges against sb** (Law) engager des poursuites contre qn; **to go to ~** (newspaper) aller à l'impression; **to be in the ~** (being printed) être sous presse; (in the newspapers) être dans le journal

▶ **press ahead** vi = **press on**
▶ **press on** vi continuer

press agency n agence f de presse

press clipping n coupure f de presse

press conference n conférence f de presse

press cutting n = **press clipping**

press-gang ['prɛsgæŋ] vt (fig): **to ~ sb into doing sth** faire pression sur qn pour qu'il fasse qch

pressing ['prɛsɪŋ] adj urgent(e), pressant(e) ▷ n repassage m

press officer n attaché(e) de presse

press release n communiqué m de presse

press stud n (Brit) bouton-pression m

press-up ['prɛsʌp] n (Brit) traction f

pressure ['prɛʃər] n pression f; (stress) tension f ▷ vt = **to put pressure on**; **to put ~ on sb (to do sth)** faire pression sur qn (pour qu'il fasse qch)

pressure cooker n cocotte-minute f

pressure gauge n manomètre m

pressure group n groupe m de pression

pressurize ['prɛʃəraɪz] vt pressuriser; (Brit fig): **to ~ sb (into doing sth)** faire pression sur qn (pour qu'il fasse qch)

pressurized ['prɛʃəraɪzd] adj pressurisé(e)

prestige [prɛs'tiːʒ] n prestige m

prestigious [prɛs'tɪdʒəs] adj prestigieux(-euse)

presumably [prɪ'zjuːməblɪ] adv vraisemblablement; **~ he did it** c'est sans doute lui (qui a fait cela)

presume [prɪ'zjuːm] vt présumer, supposer; **to ~ to do** (dare) se permettre de faire

presumption [prɪ'zʌmpʃən] n supposition f, présomption f; (boldness) audace f

presumptuous [prɪ'zʌmpʃəs] adj présomptueux(-euse)

presuppose [priːsə'pəʊz] vt présupposer

pre-tax [priː'tæks] adj avant impôt(s)

pretence, (US) **pretense** [prɪ'tɛns] n (claim) prétention f; (pretext) prétexte m; **she is devoid of all ~** elle n'est pas du tout prétentieuse; **to make a ~ of doing** faire semblant de faire; **on** or **under the ~ of doing sth** sous prétexte de faire qch; **under false ~s** sous des prétextes fallacieux

pretend [prɪ'tɛnd] vt (feign) feindre, simuler ▷ vi (feign) faire semblant; (claim): **to ~ to sth** prétendre à qch; **to ~ to do** faire semblant de faire

pretense [prɪ'tɛns] n (US) = **pretence**

pretension [prɪ'tɛnʃən] n (claim) prétention f; **have no ~s to sth/to being sth** n'avoir aucune prétention à qch/à être qch

pretentious [prɪ'tɛnʃəs] adj prétentieux(-euse)

preterite ['prɛtərɪt] n prétérit m

pretext ['priːtɛkst] n prétexte m; **on** or **under the ~ of doing sth** sous prétexte de faire qch

pretty ['prɪtɪ] adj joli(e) ▷ adv assez

prevail [prɪ'veɪl] vi (win) l'emporter, prévaloir; (be usual) avoir cours; (persuade): **to ~ (up)on sb to do** persuader qn de faire

prevailing [prɪ'veɪlɪŋ] adj (widespread) courant(e), répandu(e); (wind) dominant(e)

prevalent ['prɛvələnt] adj répandu(e), courant(e); (fashion) en vogue

prevarication [prɪværɪ'keɪʃən] n (usage m de) faux-fuyants mpl

prevent [prɪ'vɛnt] vt: **to ~ (from doing)** empêcher (de faire)

preventable [prɪ'vɛntəbl] adj évitable

preventative [prɪ'vɛntətɪv] adj préventif(-ive)

prevention [prɪ'vɛnʃən] n prévention f

preventive [prɪ'vɛntɪv] adj préventif(-ive)

preview ['priːvjuː] n (of film) avant-première f; (fig) aperçu m

previous ['priːvɪəs] adj (last) précédent(e); (earlier) antérieur(e); (question, experience) préalable; **I have a ~ engagement** je suis déjà pris(e); **~ to doing** avant de faire

previously ['priːvɪəslɪ] adv précédemment, auparavant

prewar [priː'wɔːr] adj d'avant-guerre

prey [preɪ] n proie f ▷ vi: **to ~ on** s'attaquer à; **it was ~ing on his mind** ça le rongeait or minait

price [praɪs] n prix m; (Betting: odds) cote f ▷ vt (goods) fixer le prix de; tarifer; **what is the ~ of ...?** combien coûte ...?, quel est le prix de ...?; **to go up** or **rise in ~** augmenter; **to put a ~ on sth** chiffrer qch; **to be ~d out of the market** (article) être trop cher pour soutenir la concurrence; (producer, nation) ne pas pouvoir soutenir la concurrence; **what ~ his promises now?** (Brit) que valent maintenant toutes ses promesses?; **he regained his freedom, but at a ~** il a retrouvé sa liberté, mais cela lui a coûté cher

price control n contrôle m des prix

price-cutting ['praɪskʌtɪŋ] n réductions fpl de prix

priceless ['praɪslɪs] adj sans prix, inestimable; (inf: amusing) impayable

price list n tarif m

price range n gamme f de prix; **it's within my ~** c'est dans mes prix

price tag n étiquette f

price war n guerre f des prix

pricey ['praɪsɪ] *adj* (*inf*) chérot *inv*
prick [prɪk] *n* (*sting*) piqûre *f*; (*inf!*) bitte *f* (!);
connard *m* (!) ▷ *vt* piquer; **to ~ up one's ears**
dresser *or* tendre l'oreille
prickle ['prɪkl] *n* (*of plant*) épine *f*; (*sensation*)
picotement *m*
prickly ['prɪklɪ] *adj* piquant(e), épineux(-euse);
(*fig: person*) irritable
prickly heat *n* fièvre *f* miliaire
prickly pear *n* figue *f* de Barbarie
pride [praɪd] *n* (*feeling proud*) fierté *f*; (*pej*) orgueil
m; (*self-esteem*) amour-propre *m* ▷ *vt*: **to ~ o.s.
on** se flatter de; s'enorgueillir de; **to take (a) ~
in** être (très) fier(-ère) de; **to take a ~ in doing**
mettre sa fierté à faire; **to have ~ of place** (*Brit*)
avoir la place d'honneur
priest [priːst] *n* prêtre *m*
priestess ['priːstɪs] *n* prêtresse *f*
priesthood ['priːsthud] *n* prêtrise *f*, sacerdoce *m*
prig [prɪg] *n* poseur(-euse), fat *m*
prim [prɪm] *adj* collet monté *inv*, guindé(e)
prima facie ['praɪmə'feɪʃɪ] *adj*: **to have a ~ case**
(*Law*) avoir une affaire recevable
primal ['praɪməl] *adj* (*first in time*) primitif(-ive);
(*first in importance*) primordial(e)
primarily ['praɪmərɪlɪ] *adv* principalement,
essentiellement
primary ['praɪmərɪ] *adj* primaire; (*first in
importance*) premier(-ière), primordial(e) ▷ *n*
(*US: election*) (élection *f*) primaire *f*; *voir article*

● **PRIMARIES**
●
● Aux États-Unis, les *primaries* constituent un
● processus de sélection préliminaire des
● candidats qui seront choisis par les
● principaux partis lors de la campagne
● électorale pour l'élection présidentielle.
● Elles ont lieu dans 35 États, de février à juin,
● l'année de l'élection. Chaque État envoie en
● juillet–août des "delegates" aux
● conventions démocrate et républicaine
● chargées de désigner leur candidat à la
● présidence. Ces "delegates" sont
● généralement choisis en fonction du
● nombre de voix obtenu par les candidats lors
● des *primaries*.

primary colour *n* couleur fondamentale
primary school *n* (*Brit*) école *f* primaire; *voir article*

● **PRIMARY SCHOOL**
●
● Les *primary schools* en Grande-Bretagne
● accueillent les enfants de 5 à 11 ans. Elles
● marquent le début du cycle scolaire
● obligatoire et elles comprennent deux
● sections: la section des petits ("infant
● school") et la section des grands ("junior
● school"); voir "secondary school".

primate *n* (*Rel*) ['praɪmɪt] primat *m*; (*Zool*)
['praɪmeɪt] primate *m*
prime [praɪm] *adj* primordial(e),
fondamental(e); (*excellent*) excellent(e) ▷ *vt*
(*gun, pump*) amorcer; (*fig*) mettre au courant ▷ *n*:
in the ~ of life dans la fleur de l'âge
Prime Minister *n* Premier ministre
primer ['praɪmə'] *n* (*book*) premier livre, manuel
m élémentaire; (*paint*) apprêt *m*
prime time *n* (*Radio, TV*) heure(s) *f(pl)* de grande
écoute
primeval [praɪ'miːvl] *adj* primitif(-ive)
primitive ['prɪmɪtɪv] *adj* primitif(-ive)
primrose ['prɪmrəuz] *n* primevère *f*
primus® ['praɪməs], **primus**® **stove** *n* (*Brit*)
réchaud *m* de camping
prince [prɪns] *n* prince *m*
princess [prɪn'sɛs] *n* princesse *f*
principal ['prɪnsɪpl] *adj* principal(e) ▷ *n* (*head
teacher*) directeur *m*, principal *m*; (*in play*) rôle
principal; (*money*) principal *m*
principality [prɪnsɪ'pælɪtɪ] *n* principauté *f*
principally ['prɪnsɪplɪ] *adv* principalement
principle ['prɪnsɪpl] *n* principe *m*; **in ~** en
principe; **on ~** par principe
print [prɪnt] *n* (*mark*) empreinte *f*; (*letters*)
caractères *mpl*; (*fabric*) imprimé *m*; (*Art*) gravure
f, estampe *f*; (*Phot*) épreuve *f* ▷ *vt* imprimer;
(*publish*) publier; (*write in capitals*) écrire en
majuscules; **out of ~** épuisé(e)
▶ **print out** *vt* (*Comput*) imprimer
printed circuit board ['prɪntɪd-] *n* carte *f* à
circuit imprimé
printed matter ['prɪntɪd-] *n* imprimés *mpl*
printer ['prɪntə'] *n* (*machine*) imprimante *f*;
(*person*) imprimeur *m*
printhead ['prɪnthɛd] *n* tête *f* d'impression
printing ['prɪntɪŋ] *n* impression *f*
printing press *n* presse *f* typographique
printout ['prɪntaut] *n* (*Comput*) sortie *f*
imprimante
print wheel *n* marguerite *f*
prior ['praɪə'] *adj* antérieur(e), précédent(e);
(*more important*) prioritaire ▷ *n* (*Rel*) prieur *m*
▷ *adv*: **~ to doing** avant de faire; **without ~
notice** sans préavis; **to have a ~ claim to sth**
avoir priorité pour qch
priority [praɪ'ɔrɪtɪ] *n* priorité *f*; **to have** *or* **take ~
over sth/sb** avoir la priorité sur qch/qn
priory ['praɪərɪ] *n* prieuré *m*
prise [praɪz] *vt*: **to ~ open** forcer
prism ['prɪzəm] *n* prisme *m*
prison ['prɪzn] *n* prison *f* ▷ *cpd* pénitentiaire
prison camp *n* camp *m* de prisonniers
prisoner ['prɪznə'] *n* prisonnier(-ière); **the ~ at
the bar** l'accusé(e); **to take sb ~** faire qn
prisonnier
prisoner of war *n* prisonnier(-ière) de guerre
prissy ['prɪsɪ] *adj* bégueule
pristine ['prɪstiːn] *adj* virginal(e)
privacy ['prɪvəsɪ] *n* intimité *f*, solitude *f*
private ['praɪvɪt] *adj* (*not public*) privé(e);
(*personal*) personnel(le); (*house, car, lesson*)

particulier(-ière); (*quiet: place*) tranquille ▷ *n* soldat *m* de deuxième classe; **"~"** (*on envelope*) "personnelle"; (*on door*) "privé"; **in ~** en privé; **in** (**his**) **~ life** dans sa vie privée; **he is a very ~ person** il est très secret; **to be in ~ practice** être médecin (*or* dentiste *etc*) non conventionné; **~ hearing** (*Law*) audience *f* à huis-clos

private detective *n* détective privé

private enterprise *n* entreprise privée

private eye *n* détective privé

private limited company *n* (*Brit*) société *f* à participation restreinte (*non cotée en Bourse*)

privately ['praɪvɪtlɪ] *adv* en privé; (*within oneself*) intérieurement

private parts *npl* parties (génitales)

private property *n* propriété privée

private school *n* école privée

privatize ['praɪvɪtaɪz] *vt* privatiser

privet ['prɪvɪt] *n* troène *m*

privilege ['prɪvɪlɪdʒ] *n* privilège *m*

privileged ['prɪvɪlɪdʒd] *adj* privilégié(e); **to be ~ to do sth** avoir le privilège de faire qch

privy ['prɪvɪ] *adj*: **to be ~ to** être au courant de

privy council *n* conseil privé; *voir article*

● **PRIVY COUNCIL**

● Le *privy council* existe en Angleterre depuis
● l'avènement des Normands. À l'époque, ses
● membres étaient les conseillers privés du
● roi, mais en 1688 le cabinet les a supplantés.
● Les ministres du cabinet sont aujourd'hui
● automatiquement conseillers du roi, et ce
● titre est également accordé aux personnes
● qui ont occupé de hautes fonctions en
● politique, dans le clergé ou dans les milieux
● juridiques. Les pouvoirs de ces conseillers en
● tant que tels sont maintenant limités.

prize [praɪz] *n* prix *m* ▷ *adj* (*example, idiot*) parfait(e); (*bull, novel*) primé(e) ▷ *vt* priser, faire grand cas de

prize-fighter ['praɪzfaɪtə*r*] *n* boxeur professionnel

prize-giving ['praɪzgɪvɪŋ] *n* distribution *f* des prix

prize money *n* argent *m* du prix

prizewinner ['praɪzwɪnə*r*] *n* gagnant(e)

prizewinning ['praɪzwɪnɪŋ] *adj* gagnant(e); (*novel, essay etc*) primé(e)

PRO *n abbr* = **public relations officer**

pro [prəu] *n* (*inf: Sport*) professionnel(le) ▷ *prep* pro; **pros** *npl*: **the ~s and cons** le pour et le contre

pro- [prəu] *prefix* (*in favour of*) pro-

pro-active [prəu'æktɪv] *adj* dynamique

probability [prɔbə'bɪlɪtɪ] *n* probabilité *f*; **in all ~** très probablement

probable ['prɔbəbl] *adj* probable; **it is ~/hardly ~ that ...** il est probable/peu probable que ...

probably ['prɔbəblɪ] *adv* probablement

probate ['prəubɪt] *n* (*Law*) validation *f*, homologation *f*

probation [prə'beɪʃən] *n* (*in employment*) (période *f* d')essai *m*; (*Law*) liberté surveillée; (*Rel*) noviciat *m*, probation *f*; **on ~** (*employee*) à l'essai; (*Law*) en liberté surveillée

probationary [prə'beɪʃənrɪ] *adj* (*period*) d'essai

probe [prəub] *n* (*Med, Space*) sonde *f*; (*enquiry*) enquête *f*, investigation *f* ▷ *vt* sonder, explorer

probity ['prəubɪtɪ] *n* probité *f*

problem ['prɔbləm] *n* problème *m*; **to have ~s with the car** avoir des ennuis avec la voiture; **what's the ~?** qu'y a-t-il?, quel est le problème?; **I had no ~ in finding her** je n'ai pas eu de mal à la trouver; **no ~!** pas de problème!

problematic [prɔblə'mætɪk] *adj* problématique

problem-solving ['prɔbləmsɔlvɪŋ] *n* résolution *f* de problèmes; **an approach to ~** une approche en matière de résolution de problèmes

procedure [prə'si:dʒə*r*] *n* (*Admin, Law*) procédure *f*; (*method*) marche *f* à suivre, façon *f* de procéder

proceed [prə'si:d] *vi* (*go forward*) avancer; (*act*) procéder; (*continue*): **to ~ (with)** continuer, poursuivre; **to ~ to** aller à; passer à; **to ~ to do** se mettre à faire; **I am not sure how to ~** je ne sais pas exactement comment m'y prendre; **to ~ against sb** (*Law*) intenter des poursuites contre qn

proceedings [prə'si:dɪŋz] *npl* (*measures*) mesures *fpl*; (*Law: against sb*) poursuites *fpl*; (*meeting*) réunion *f*, séance *f*; (*records*) compte rendu; actes *mpl*

proceeds ['prəusi:dz] *npl* produit *m*, recette *f*

process ['prəuses] *n* processus *m*; (*method*) procédé *m* ▷ *vt* traiter ▷ *vi* [prə'ses] (*Brit formal: go in procession*) défiler; **in ~** en cours; **we are in the ~ of doing** nous sommes en train de faire

processed cheese ['prəuses*t*-] *n* ≈ fromage fondu

processing ['prəusesɪŋ] *n* traitement *m*

procession [prə'seʃən] *n* défilé *m*, cortège *m*; **funeral ~** (*on foot*) cortège funèbre; (*in cars*) convoi *m* mortuaire

pro-choice [prəu'tʃɔɪs] *adj* en faveur de l'avortement

proclaim [prə'kleɪm] *vt* déclarer, proclamer

proclamation [prɔklə'meɪʃən] *n* proclamation *f*

proclivity [prə'klɪvɪtɪ] *n* inclination *f*

procrastinate [prəu'kræstɪneɪt] *vi* faire traîner les choses, vouloir tout remettre au lendemain

procrastination [prəukræstɪ'neɪʃən] *n* procrastination *f*

procreation [prəukrɪ'eɪʃən] *n* procréation *f*

Procurator Fiscal ['prɔkjureɪtə-] *n* (*Scottish*) ≈ procureur *m* (*de la République*)

procure [prə'kjuə*r*] *vt* (*for o.s.*) se procurer; (*for sb*) procurer

procurement [prə'kjuəmənt] *n* achat *m*, approvisionnement *m*

prod [prɔd] *vt* pousser ▷ *n* (*push, jab*) petit coup, poussée *f*

prodigal ['prɔdɪgl] *adj* prodigue

prodigious [prə'dɪdʒəs] *adj* prodigieux(-euse)
prodigy ['prɒdɪdʒɪ] *n* prodige *m*
produce *n* ['prɒdjuːs] (*Agr*) produits *mpl* ▷ *vt*
[prə'djuːs] produire; (*show*) présenter; (*cause*)
provoquer, causer; (*Theat*) monter, mettre en
scène; (*TV: programme*) réaliser; (: *play, film*)
mettre en scène; (*Radio: programme*) réaliser;
(: *play*) mettre en ondes
producer [prə'djuːsə^r] *n* (*Theat*) metteur *m* en
scène; (*Agr, Comm, Cine*) producteur *m*; (*TV: of
programme*) réalisateur *m*; (: *of play, film*) metteur
en scène; (*Radio: of programme*) réalisateur; (: *of
play*) metteur en ondes
product ['prɒdʌkt] *n* produit *m*
production [prə'dʌkʃən] *n* production *f*; (*Theat*)
mise *f* en scène; **to put into ~** (*goods*)
entreprendre la fabrication de
production agreement *n* (*US*) accord *m* de
productivité
production line *n* chaîne *f* (de fabrication)
production manager *n* directeur(-trice) de la
production
productive [prə'dʌktɪv] *adj* productif(-ive)
productivity [prɒdʌk'tɪvɪtɪ] *n* productivité *f*
productivity agreement *n* (*Brit*) accord *m* de
productivité
productivity bonus *n* prime *f* de rendement
Prof. [prɒf] *abbr* (= *professor*) Prof
profane [prə'feɪn] *adj* sacrilège; (*lay*) profane
profess [prə'fɛs] *vt* professer; **I do not ~ to be
an expert** je ne prétends pas être spécialiste
professed [prə'fɛst] *adj* (*self-declared*) déclaré(e)
profession [prə'fɛʃən] *n* profession *f*; **the ~s** les
professions libérales
professional [prə'fɛʃənl] *n* professionnel(le)
▷ *adj* professionnel(le); (*work*) de professionnel;
he's a ~ man il exerce une profession libérale;
to take ~ advice consulter un spécialiste
professionalism [prə'fɛʃnəlɪzəm] *n*
professionnalisme *m*
professionally [prə'fɛʃnəlɪ] *adv*
professionnellement; (*Sport: play*) en
professionnel; **I only know him ~** je n'ai avec
lui que des relations de travail
professor [prə'fɛsə^r] *n* professeur *m* (*titulaire
d'une chaire*); (*US: teacher*) professeur *m*
professorship [prə'fɛsəʃɪp] *n* chaire *f*
proffer ['prɒfə^r] *vt* (*hand*) tendre; (*remark*) faire;
(*apologies*) présenter
proficiency [prə'fɪʃənsɪ] *n* compétence *f*,
aptitude *f*
proficient [prə'fɪʃənt] *adj* compétent(e), capable
profile ['prəufaɪl] *n* profil *m*; **to keep a high/
low ~** (*fig*) rester *or* être très en évidence/
discret(-ète)
profit ['prɒfɪt] *n* (*from trading*) bénéfice *m*;
(*advantage*) profit *m* ▷ *vi*: **to ~ (by or from)**
profiter (de); **~ and loss account** compte *m* de
profits et pertes; **to make a ~** faire un *or* des
bénéfice(s); **to sell sth at a ~** vendre qch à
profit
profitability [prɒfɪtə'bɪlɪtɪ] *n* rentabilité *f*

profitable ['prɒfɪtəbl] *adj* lucratif(-ive),
rentable; (*fig: beneficial*) avantageux(-euse);
(: *meeting*) fructueux(-euse)
profit centre *n* centre *m* de profit
profiteering [prɒfɪ'tɪərɪŋ] *n* (*pej*)
mercantilisme *m*
profit-making ['prɒfɪtmeɪkɪŋ] *adj* à but lucratif
profit margin *n* marge *f* bénéficiaire
profit-sharing ['prɒfɪtʃɛərɪŋ] *n* intéressement *m*
aux bénéfices
profits tax *n* (*Brit*) impôt *m* sur les bénéfices
profligate ['prɒflɪgɪt] *adj* (*behaviour, act*)
dissolu(e); (*person*) débauché(e); (*extravagant*): ~
(with) prodigue (de)
pro forma ['prəu'fɔːmə] *adj*: ~ **invoice** facture *f*
pro-forma
profound [prə'faund] *adj* profond(e)
profuse [prə'fjuːs] *adj* abondant(e)
profusely [prə'fjuːslɪ] *adv* abondamment;
(*thank etc*) avec effusion
profusion [prə'fjuːʒən] *n* profusion *f*,
abondance *f*
progeny ['prɒdʒɪnɪ] *n* progéniture *f*;
descendants *mpl*
prognosis [prɒg'nəusɪs] (*pl* **prognoses**) *n*
pronostic *m*
programme, (*US*) **program** ['prəugræm] *n*
(*Comput: also Brit*) programme *m*; (*Radio, TV*)
émission *f* ▷ *vt* programmer
programmer ['prəugræmə^r] *n*
programmeur(-euse)
programming, (*US*) **programing**
['prəugræmɪŋ] *n* programmation *f*
programming language, (*US*) **programing
language** *n* langage *m* de programmation
progress *n* ['prəugrɛs] progrès *m(pl)* ▷ *vi*
[prə'grɛs] progresser, avancer; **in ~** en cours; **to
make ~** progresser, faire des progrès, être en
progrès; **as the match ~ed** au fur et à mesure
que la partie avançait
progression [prə'grɛʃən] *n* progression *f*
progressive [prə'grɛsɪv] *adj* progressif(-ive);
(*person*) progressiste
progressively [prə'grɛsɪvlɪ] *adv*
progressivement
progress report *n* (*Med*) bulletin *m* de santé;
(*Admin*) rapport *m* d'activité; rapport sur l'état
(d'avancement) des travaux
prohibit [prə'hɪbɪt] *vt* interdire, défendre; **to ~
sb from doing sth** défendre *or* interdire à qn de
faire qch; **"smoking ~ed"** "défense de fumer"
prohibition [prəuɪ'bɪʃən] *n* prohibition *f*
prohibitive [prə'hɪbɪtɪv] *adj* (*price etc*)
prohibitif(-ive)
project [*n* 'prɒdʒɛkt, *vb* prə'dʒɛkt] *n* (*plan*) projet
m, plan *m*; (*venture*) opération *f*, entreprise *f*;
(*Scol: research*) étude *f*, dossier *m* ▷ *vt* projeter ▷ *vi*
(*stick out*) faire saillie, s'avancer
projectile [prə'dʒɛktaɪl] *n* projectile *m*
projection [prə'dʒɛkʃən] *n* projection *f*;
(*overhang*) saillie *f*
projectionist [prə'dʒɛkʃənɪst] *n* (*Cine*)

P

735

projectionniste *m/f*

projection room *n* (*Cine*) cabine *f* de projection

projector [prə'dʒɛktə^r] *n* (*Cine etc*) projecteur *m*

proletarian [prəʊlɪ'tɛərɪən] *adj* prolétarien(ne)
▷ *n* prolétaire *m/f*

proletariat [prəʊlɪ'tɛərɪət] *n* prolétariat *m*

pro-life [prəʊ'laɪf] *adj* contre l'avortement

proliferate [prə'lɪfəreɪt] *vi* proliférer

proliferation [prəlɪfə'reɪʃən] *n* prolifération *f*

prolific [prə'lɪfɪk] *adj* prolifique

prologue ['prəʊlɒg] *n* prologue *m*

prolong [prə'lɒŋ] *vt* prolonger

prom [prɒm] *n abbr* = **promenade**; **promenade concert**; (*US: ball*) bal *m* d'étudiants; **the P~s** *série de concerts de musique classique*; *voir article*

PROM

En Grande-Bretagne, un *promenade concert* ou *prom* est un concert de musique classique, ainsi appelé car, à l'origine, le public restait debout et se promenait au lieu de rester assis. De nos jours, une partie du public reste debout, mais il y a également des places assises (plus chères). Les *Proms* les plus connus sont les Proms londoniens. La dernière séance (the "Last Night of the Proms") est un grand événement médiatique où se jouent des airs traditionnels et patriotiques.
Aux États-Unis et au Canada, le *prom* ou *promenade* est un bal organisé par le lycée.

---

promenade [prɒmə'nɑːd] *n* (*by sea*) esplanade *f*, promenade *f*

promenade concert *n* concert *m* (de musique classique)

promenade deck *n* (*Naut*) pont *m* promenade

prominence ['prɒmɪnəns] *n* proéminence *f*; importance *f*

prominent ['prɒmɪnənt] *adj* (*standing out*) proéminent(e); (*important*) important(e); **he is ~ in the field of** ... il est très connu dans le domaine de ...

prominently ['prɒmɪnəntlɪ] *adv* (*display, set*) bien en évidence; **he figured ~ in the case** il a joué un rôle important dans l'affaire

promiscuity [prɒmɪs'kjuːɪtɪ] *n* (*sexual*) légèreté *f* de mœurs

promiscuous [prə'mɪskjuəs] *adj* (*sexually*) de mœurs légères

promise ['prɒmɪs] *n* promesse *f* ▷ *vt, vi* promettre; **to make sb a ~** faire une promesse à qn; **a young man of ~** un jeune homme plein d'avenir; **to ~ well** *vi* promettre

promising ['prɒmɪsɪŋ] *adj* prometteur(-euse)

promissory note ['prɒmɪsərɪ-] *n* billet *m* à ordre

promontory ['prɒməntrɪ] *n* promontoire *m*

promote [prə'məʊt] *vt* promouvoir; (*venture, event*) organiser, mettre sur pied; (*new product*) lancer; **the team was ~d to the second division** (*Brit Football*) l'équipe est montée en 2e division

promoter [prə'məʊtə^r] *n* (*of event*) organisateur(-trice)

promotion [prə'məʊʃən] *n* promotion *f*

prompt [prɒmpt] *adj* rapide ▷ *n* (*Comput*) message *m* (de guidage) ▷ *vt* inciter; (*cause*) entraîner, provoquer; (*Theat*) souffler (son rôle *or* ses répliques) à; **they're very ~** (*punctual*) ils sont ponctuels; **at 8 o'clock ~** à 8 heures précises; **he was ~ to accept** il a tout de suite accepté; **to ~ sb to do** inciter *or* pousser qn à faire

prompter ['prɒmptə^r] *n* (*Theat*) souffleur *m*

promptly ['prɒmptlɪ] *adv* (*quickly*) rapidement, sans délai; (*on time*) ponctuellement

promptness ['prɒmptnɪs] *n* rapidité *f*; promptitude *f*; ponctualité *f*

prone [prəʊn] *adj* (*lying*) couché(e) (face contre terre); (*liable*): **~ to** enclin(e) à; **to be ~ to illness** être facilement malade; **to be ~ to an illness** être sujet à une maladie; **she is ~ to burst into tears if ...** elle a tendance à tomber en larmes si ...

prong [prɒŋ] *n* pointe *f*; (*of fork*) dent *f*

pronoun ['prəʊnaʊn] *n* pronom *m*

pronounce [prə'naʊns] *vt* prononcer ▷ *vi*: **to ~ (up)on** se prononcer sur; **how do you ~ it?** comment est-ce que ça se prononce?; **they ~d him unfit to drive** ils l'ont déclaré inapte à la conduite

pronounced [prə'naʊnst] *adj* (*marked*) prononcé(e)

pronouncement [prə'naʊnsmənt] *n* déclaration *f*

pronunciation [prənʌnsɪ'eɪʃən] *n* prononciation *f*

proof [pruːf] *n* preuve *f*; (*test, of book, Phot*) épreuve *f*; (*of alcohol*) degré *m* ▷ *adj*: **~ against** à l'épreuve de ▷ *vt* (*Brit: tent, anorak*) imperméabiliser; **to be 70° ~** ≈ titrer 40 degrés

proofreader ['pruːfriːdə^r] *n* correcteur(-trice) (d'épreuves)

prop [prɒp] *n* support *m*, étai *m*; (*fig*) soutien *m* ▷ *vt* (*also*: **prop up**) étayer, soutenir; **props** *npl* accessoires *mpl*; (*lean*): **to ~ sth against** appuyer qch contre *or* à

Prop. *abbr* (*Comm*) = **proprietor**

propaganda [prɒpə'gændə] *n* propagande *f*

propagation [prɒpə'geɪʃən] *n* propagation *f*

propel [prə'pɛl] *vt* propulser, faire avancer

propeller [prə'pɛlə^r] *n* hélice *f*

propelling pencil [prə'pɛlɪŋ-] *n* (*Brit*) porte-mine *m inv*

propensity [prə'pɛnsɪtɪ] *n* propension *f*

proper ['prɒpə^r] *adj* (*suited, right*) approprié(e), bon (bonne); (*seemly*) correct(e), convenable; (*authentic*) vrai(e), véritable; (*inf: real*) fini(e), vrai(e); (*referring to place*): **the village ~** le village proprement dit; **to go through the ~ channels** (*Admin*) passer par la voie officielle

properly ['prɒpəlɪ] *adv* correctement, convenablement; (*really*) bel et bien

proper noun *n* nom *m* propre
property ['prɔpətɪ] *n* (*possessions*) biens *mpl*;
(*house etc*) propriété *f*; (*land*) terres *fpl*, domaine
m; (*Chem etc: quality*) propriété *f*; **it's their** ~ cela
leur appartient, c'est leur propriété
property developer *n* (*Brit*) promoteur
immobilier
property owner *n* propriétaire *m*
property tax *n* impôt foncier
prophecy ['prɔfɪsɪ] *n* prophétie *f*
prophesy ['prɔfɪsaɪ] *vt* prédire ▷ *vi* prophétiser
prophet ['prɔfɪt] *n* prophète *m*
prophetic [prə'fɛtɪk] *adj* prophétique
proportion [prə'pɔːʃən] *n* proportion *f*; (*share*)
part *f*; partie *f* ▷ *vt* proportionner; **proportions**
npl (*size*) dimensions *fpl*; **to be in/out of** ~ **to** *or*
with sth être à la mesure de/hors de proportion
avec qch; **to see sth in** ~ (*fig*) ramener qch à de
justes proportions
proportional [prə'pɔːʃnl], **proportionate**
[prə'pɔːʃnɪt] *adj* proportionnel(le)
proportional representation *n* (*Pol*)
représentation proportionnelle
proposal [prə'pəʊzl] *n* proposition *f*, offre *f*;
(*plan*) projet *m*; (*of marriage*) demande *f* en
mariage
propose [prə'pəʊz] *vt* proposer, suggérer; (*have
in mind*): **to** ~ **sth/to do** *or* **doing sth** envisager
qch/de faire qch ▷ *vi* faire sa demande en
mariage; **to** ~ **to do** avoir l'intention de faire
proposer [prə'pəʊzə'] *n* (*Brit: of motion etc*)
auteur *m*
proposition [prɔpə'zɪʃən] *n* proposition *f*; **to
make sb a** ~ faire une proposition à qn
propound [prə'paʊnd] *vt* proposer, soumettre
proprietary [prə'praɪətərɪ] *adj* de marque
déposée; ~ **article** article *m* *or* produit *m* de
marque; ~ **brand** marque déposée
proprietor [prə'praɪətə'] *n* propriétaire *m/f*
propriety [prə'praɪətɪ] *n* (*seemliness*) bienséance
f, convenance *f*
propulsion [prə'pʌlʃən] *n* propulsion *f*
pro rata [prəʊ'rɑːtə] *adv* au prorata
prosaic [prəʊ'zeɪɪk] *adj* prosaïque
Pros. Atty. *abbr* (*US*) = **prosecuting attorney**
proscribe [prə'skraɪb] *vt* proscrire
prose [prəʊz] *n* prose *f*; (*Scol: translation*) thème *m*
prosecute ['prɔsɪkjuːt] *vt* poursuivre
prosecuting attorney ['prɔsɪkjuːtɪŋ-] *n* (*US*)
procureur *m*
prosecution [prɔsɪ'kjuːʃən] *n* poursuites *fpl*
judiciaires; (*accusing side: in criminal case*)
accusation *f*; (: *in civil case*) la partie plaignante
prosecutor ['prɔsɪkjuːtə'] *n* (*lawyer*) procureur
m; (*also*: **public prosecutor**) ministère public;
(*US: plaintiff*) plaignant(e)
prospect *n* ['prɔspɛkt] perspective *f*; (*hope*)
espoir *m*, chances *fpl* ▷ *vt,vi* [prə'spɛkt]
prospecter; **prospects** *npl* (*for work etc*)
possibilités *fpl* d'avenir, débouchés *mpl*; **we are
faced with the** ~ **of leaving** nous risquons de
devoir partir; **there is every** ~ **of an early**

victory tout laisse prévoir une victoire rapide
prospecting [prə'spɛktɪŋ] *n* prospection *f*
prospective [prə'spɛktɪv] *adj* (*possible*)
éventuel(le); (*future*) futur(e)
prospector [prə'spɛktə'] *n* prospecteur *m*; **gold**
~ chercheur *m* d'or
prospectus [prə'spɛktəs] *n* prospectus *m*
prosper ['prɔspə'] *vi* prospérer
prosperity [prɔ'spɛrɪtɪ] *n* prospérité *f*
prosperous ['prɔspərəs] *adj* prospère
prostate ['prɔsteɪt] *n* (*also*: **prostate gland**)
prostate *f*
prostitute ['prɔstɪtjuːt] *n* prostituée *f*; **male** ~
prostitué *m*
prostitution [prɔstɪ'tjuːʃən] *n* prostitution *f*
prostrate *adj* ['prɔstreɪt] prosterné(e); (*fig*)
prostré(e) ▷ *vt* [prɔ'streɪt]: **to** ~ **o.s. (before sb)**
se prosterner (devant qn)
protagonist [prə'tægənɪst] *n* protagoniste *m*
protect [prə'tɛkt] *vt* protéger
protection [prə'tɛkʃən] *n* protection *f*; **to be
under sb's** ~ être sous la protection de qn
protectionism [prə'tɛkʃənɪzəm] *n*
protectionnisme *m*
protection racket *n* racket *m*
protective [prə'tɛktɪv] *adj* protecteur(-trice);
(*clothing*) de protection; ~ **custody** (*Law*)
détention préventive
protector [prə'tɛktə'] *n* protecteur(-trice)
protégé ['prəʊtɛʒeɪ] *n* protégé *m*
protégée ['prəʊtɛʒeɪ] *n* protégée *f*
protein ['prəʊtiːn] *n* protéine *f*
pro tem [prəʊ'tɛm] *adv abbr* (= *pro tempore: for the
time being*) provisoirement
protest [*n* 'prəʊtɛst, *vb* prə'tɛst] *n* protestation *f*
▷ *vi*: **to** ~ **against/about** protester contre/à
propos de ▷ *vt* protester de; **to** ~ **(that)**
protester que
Protestant ['prɔtɪstənt] *adj, n* protestant(e)
protester, protestor [prə'tɛstə'] *n* (*in
demonstration*) manifestant(e)
protest march *n* manifestation *f*
protocol ['prəʊtəkɔl] *n* protocole *m*
prototype ['prəʊtətaɪp] *n* prototype *m*
protracted [prə'træktɪd] *adj* prolongé(e)
protractor [prə'træktə'] *n* (*Geom*) rapporteur *m*
protrude [prə'truːd] *vi* avancer, dépasser
protuberance [prə'tjuːbərəns] *n* protubérance *f*
proud [praʊd] *adj* fier(-ère); (*pej*)
orgueilleux(-euse); **to be** ~ **to do sth** être fier
de faire qch; **to do sb** ~ (*inf*) faire honneur à qn;
to do o.s. ~ (*inf*) ne se priver de rien
proudly ['praʊdlɪ] *adv* fièrement
prove [pruːv] *vt* prouver, démontrer ▷ *vi*: **to** ~
correct *etc* s'avérer juste *etc*; **to** ~ **o.s.** montrer
ce dont on est capable; **to** ~ **o.s./itself (to be)**
useful *etc* se montrer *or* se révéler utile *etc*; **he
was** ~**d right in the end** il s'est avéré qu'il avait
raison
proverb ['prɔvəːb] *n* proverbe *m*
proverbial [prə'vəːbɪəl] *adj* proverbial(e)
provide [prə'vaɪd] *vt* fournir; **to** ~ **sb with sth**

fournir qch à qn; **to be ~d with** (*person*) disposer de; (*thing*) être équipé(e) *or* muni(e) de
▶ **provide for** *vt fus* (*person*) subvenir aux besoins de; (*future event*) prévoir
provided [prə'vaɪdɪd] *conj:* ~ **(that)** à condition que + *sub*
Providence ['prɔvɪdəns] *n* la Providence
providing [prə'vaɪdɪŋ] *conj* à condition que + *sub*
province ['prɔvɪns] *n* province *f*; (*fig*) domaine *m*
provincial [prə'vɪnʃəl] *adj* provincial(e)
provision [prə'vɪʒən] *n* (*supply*) provision *f*; (*supplying*) fourniture *f*; approvisionnement *m*; (*stipulation*) disposition *f*; **provisions** *npl* (*food*) provisions *fpl*; **to make ~ for** (*one's future*) assurer; (*one's family*) assurer l'avenir de; **there's no ~ for this in the contract** le contrat ne prévoit pas cela
provisional [prə'vɪʒənl] *adj* provisoire ▷ *n*: **P~** (*Irish Pol*) Provisional *m* (*membre de la tendance activiste de l'IRA*)
provisional licence *n* (*Brit Aut*) permis *m* provisoire
provisionally [prə'vɪʒnəlɪ] *adv* provisoirement
proviso [prə'vaɪzəu] *n* condition *f*; **with the ~ that** à la condition (expresse) que
Provo ['prɔvəu] *n abbr* (*inf*) = **Provisional**
provocation [prɔvə'keɪʃən] *n* provocation *f*
provocative [prə'vɔkətɪv] *adj* provocateur(-trice), provocant(e)
provoke [prə'vəuk] *vt* provoquer; **to ~ sb to sth/ to do** *or* **into doing sth** pousser qn à qch/à faire qch
provoking [prə'vəukɪŋ] *adj* énervant(e), exaspérant(e)
provost ['prɔvəst] *n* (*Brit*: *of university*) principal *m*; (*Scottish*) maire *m*
prow [prau] *n* proue *f*
prowess ['prauɪs] *n* prouesse *f*
prowl [praul] *vi* (*also*: **prowl about, prowl around**) rôder ▷ *n*: **to be on the ~** rôder
prowler ['praulə'] *n* rôdeur(-euse)
proximity [prɔk'sɪmɪtɪ] *n* proximité *f*
proxy ['prɔksɪ] *n* procuration *f*; **by ~** par procuration
PRP *n abbr* (= *performance related pay*) salaire *m* au rendement
prude [pru:d] *n* prude *f*
prudence ['pru:dns] *n* prudence *f*
prudent ['pru:dnt] *adj* prudent(e)
prudish ['pru:dɪʃ] *adj* prude, pudibond(e)
prune [pru:n] *n* pruneau *m* ▷ *vt* élaguer
pry [praɪ] *vi*: **to ~ into** fourrer son nez dans
PS *n abbr* (= *postscript*) PS *m*
psalm [sɑ:m] *n* psaume *m*
PSAT *n abbr* (*US*) = **Preliminary Scholastic Aptitude Test**
PSBR *n abbr* (*Brit*: = *public sector borrowing requirement*) besoins *mpl* d'emprunts des pouvoirs publics
pseud [sju:d] *n* (*Brit inf*: *intellectually*) pseudo-intello *m*; (: *socially*) snob *m/f*
pseudo- ['sju:dəu] *prefix* pseudo-

pseudonym ['sju:dənɪm] *n* pseudonyme *m*
PSHE *n abbr* (*Brit: Scol:* = *personal, social and health education*) *cours d'éducation personnelle, sanitaire et sociale préparant à la vie adulte*
PST *abbr* (*US:* = *Pacific Standard Time*) *heure d'hiver du Pacifique*
PSV *n abbr* (*Brit*) = **public service vehicle**
psyche ['saɪkɪ] *n* psychisme *m*
psychiatric [saɪkɪ'ætrɪk] *adj* psychiatrique
psychiatrist [saɪ'kaɪətrɪst] *n* psychiatre *m/f*
psychiatry [saɪ'kaɪətrɪ] *n* psychiatrie *f*
psychic ['saɪkɪk] *adj* (*also*: **psychical**) (méta)psychique; (*person*) doué(e) de télépathie *or* d'un sixième sens
psycho ['saɪkəu] *n* (*inf*) psychopathe *m/f*
psychoanalysis (*pl* **-ses**) [saɪkəuə'nælɪsɪs, -si:z] *n* psychanalyse *f*
psychoanalyst [saɪkəu'ænəlɪst] *n* psychanalyste *m/f*
psychological [saɪkə'lɔdʒɪkl] *adj* psychologique
psychologist [saɪ'kɔlədʒɪst] *n* psychologue *m/f*
psychology [saɪ'kɔlədʒɪ] *n* psychologie *f*
psychopath ['saɪkəupæθ] *n* psychopathe *m/f*
psychosis (*pl* **psychoses**) [saɪ'kəusɪs, -si:z] *n* psychose *f*
psychosomatic [saɪkəusə'mætɪk] *adj* psychosomatique
psychotherapy [saɪkəu'θɛrəpɪ] *n* psychothérapie *f*
psychotic [saɪ'kɔtɪk] *adj, n* psychotique *m/f*
PT *n abbr* (*Brit*: = *physical training*) EPS *f*
Pt. *abbr* (*in place names*: = *Point*) Pte
pt *abbr* = **pint; pints; point; points**
PTA *n abbr* = **Parent-Teacher Association**
Pte. *abbr* (*Brit Mil*) = **private**
PTO *abbr* (= *please turn over*) TSVP
PTV *abbr* (*US*) = **pay television**
pub [pʌb] *n abbr* (= *public house*) pub *m*
pub crawl *n* (*Brit inf*): **to go on a ~** faire la tournée des bars
puberty ['pju:bətɪ] *n* puberté *f*
pubic ['pju:bɪk] *adj* pubien(ne), du pubis
public ['pʌblɪk] *adj* public(-ique) ▷ *n* public *m*; **in ~** en public; **the general ~** le grand public; **to be ~ knowledge** être de notoriété publique; **to go ~** (*Comm*) être coté(e) en Bourse; **to make ~** rendre public
public address system *n* (système *m* de) sonorisation *f*, sono *f* (*col*)
publican ['pʌblɪkən] *n* patron *m or* gérant *m* de pub
publication [pʌblɪ'keɪʃən] *n* publication *f*
public company *n* société *f* anonyme
public convenience *n* (*Brit*) toilettes *fpl*
public holiday *n* (*Brit*) jour férié
public house *n* (*Brit*) pub *m*
publicity [pʌb'lɪsɪtɪ] *n* publicité *f*
publicize ['pʌblɪsaɪz] *vt* (*make known*) faire connaître, rendre public; (*advertise*) faire de la publicité pour
public limited company *n* ≈ société *f* anonyme (SA) (*cotée en Bourse*)

publicly ['pʌblɪklɪ] *adv* publiquement, en public
public opinion *n* opinion publique
public ownership *n*: **to be taken into ~** être nationalisé(e), devenir propriété de l'État
public prosecutor *n* ≈ procureur *m* (*de la République*); **~'s office** parquet *m*
public relations *n or npl* relations publiques (RP)
public relations officer *n* responsable *m/f* des relations publiques
public school *n* (*Brit*) école privée; (*US*) école publique; *voir article*

● **PUBLIC SCHOOL**
●
● Une *public school* est un établissement
● d'enseignement secondaire privé. Bon
● nombre d'entre elles sont des pensionnats.
● Beaucoup ont également une école primaire
● qui leur est rattachée (une "prep" ou
● "preparatory school") pour préparer les
● élèves au cycle secondaire. Ces écoles sont
● en général prestigieuses, et les frais de
● scolarité sont très élevés dans les plus
● connues (Westminster, Eton, Harrow).
● Beaucoup d'élèves vont ensuite à
● l'université, et un grand nombre entre à
● Oxford ou à Cambridge. Les grands
● industriels, les députés et les hauts
● fonctionnaires sortent souvent de ces
● écoles. Aux États-Unis, le terme "public
● school" désigne tout simplement une école
● publique gratuite.

public sector *n* secteur public
public service vehicle *n* (*Brit*) véhicule affecté au transport de personnes
public-spirited [pʌblɪk'spɪrɪtɪd] *adj* qui fait preuve de civisme
public transport, (*US*) **public transportation** *n* transports *mpl* en commun
public utility *n* service public
public works *npl* travaux publics
publish ['pʌblɪʃ] *vt* publier
publisher ['pʌblɪʃər] *n* éditeur *m*
publishing ['pʌblɪʃɪŋ] *n* (*industry*) édition *f*; (*of a book*) publication *f*
publishing company *n* maison *f* d'édition
pub lunch *n* repas *m* de bistrot
puce [pjuːs] *adj* puce
puck [pʌk] *n* (*elf*) lutin *m*; (*Ice Hockey*) palet *m*
pucker ['pʌkər] *vt* plisser
pudding ['pudɪŋ] *n* (*Brit*: *dessert*) dessert *m*, entremets *m*; (*sweet dish*) pudding *m*, gâteau *m*; (*sausage*) boudin *m*; **rice ~** ≈ riz *m* au lait; **black ~**, (*US*) **blood ~** boudin (noir)
puddle ['pʌdl] *n* flaque *f* d'eau
puerile ['pjuəraɪl] *adj* puéril(e)
Puerto Rico ['pwəːtəu'riːkəu] *n* Porto Rico *f*
puff [pʌf] *n* bouffée *f* ▷ *vt*: **to ~ one's pipe** tirer sur sa pipe; (*also*: **puff out**: *sails, cheeks*) gonfler ▷ *vi* sortir par bouffées; (*pant*) haleter; **to ~ out smoke** envoyer des bouffées de fumée

puffed [pʌft] *adj* (*inf*: *out of breath*) tout(e) essoufflé(e)
puffin ['pʌfɪn] *n* macareux *m*
puff pastry, (*US*) **puff paste** *n* pâte feuilletée
puffy ['pʌfɪ] *adj* bouffi(e), boursouflé(e)
pugnacious [pʌg'neɪʃəs] *adj* pugnace, batailleur(-euse)
pull [pul] *n* (*tug*): **to give sth a ~** tirer sur qch; (*of moon, magnet, the sea etc*) attraction *f*; (*fig*) influence *f* ▷ *vt* tirer; (*trigger*) presser; (*strain*: *muscle, tendon*) se claquer ▷ *vi* tirer; **to ~ a face** faire une grimace; **to ~ to pieces** mettre en morceaux; **to ~ one's punches** (*also fig*) ménager son adversaire; **to ~ one's weight** y mettre du sien; **to ~ o.s. together** se ressaisir; **to ~ sb's leg** (*fig*) faire marcher qn; **to ~ strings (for sb)** intervenir (en faveur de qn)
▶ **pull about** *vt* (*Brit*: *handle roughly*: *object*) maltraiter; (*: person*) malmener
▶ **pull apart** *vt* séparer; (*break*) mettre en pièces, démantibuler
▶ **pull away** *vi* (*vehicle*: *move off*) partir; (*draw back*) s'éloigner
▶ **pull back** *vt* (*lever etc*) tirer sur; (*curtains*) ouvrir ▷ *vi* (*refrain*) s'abstenir; (*Mil*: *withdraw*) se retirer
▶ **pull down** *vt* baisser, abaisser; (*house*) démolir; (*tree*) abattre
▶ **pull in** *vi* (*Aut*) se ranger; (*Rail*) entrer en gare
▶ **pull off** *vt* enlever, ôter; (*deal etc*) conclure
▶ **pull out** *vi* démarrer, partir; (*withdraw*) se retirer; (*Aut*: *come out of line*) déboîter ▷ *vt* (*from bag, pocket*) sortir; (*remove*) arracher; (*withdraw*) retirer
▶ **pull over** *vi* (*Aut*) se ranger
▶ **pull round** *vi* (*unconscious person*) revenir à soi; (*sick person*) se rétablir
▶ **pull through** *vi* s'en sortir
▶ **pull up** *vi* (*stop*) s'arrêter ▷ *vt* remonter; (*uproot*) déraciner, arracher; (*stop*) arrêter
pulley ['pulɪ] *n* poulie *f*
pull-out ['pulaut] *n* (*of forces etc*) retrait *m* ▷ *cpd* (*magazine, pages*) détachable
pullover ['puləuvər] *n* pull-over *m*, tricot *m*
pulp [pʌlp] *n* (*of fruit*) pulpe *f*; (*for paper*) pâte *f* à papier; (*pej*: *also*: **pulp magazines** *etc*) presse *f* à sensation or de bas étage; **to reduce sth to (a) ~** réduire qch en purée
pulpit ['pulpɪt] *n* chaire *f*
pulsate [pʌl'seɪt] *vi* battre, palpiter; (*music*) vibrer
pulse [pʌls] *n* (*of blood*) pouls *m*; (*of heart*) battement *m*; (*of music, engine*) vibrations *fpl*; **pulses** *npl* (*Culin*) légumineuses *fpl*; **to feel or take sb's ~** prendre le pouls à qn
pulverize ['pʌlvəraɪz] *vt* pulvériser
puma ['pjuːmə] *n* puma *m*
pumice ['pʌmɪs] *n* (*also*: **pumice stone**) pierre *f* ponce
pummel ['pʌml] *vt* rouer de coups
pump [pʌmp] *n* pompe *f*; (*shoe*) escarpin *m* ▷ *vt* pomper; (*fig*: *inf*) faire parler; **to ~ sb for information** essayer de soutirer des

P

renseignements à qn
▶ **pump up** vt gonfler

pumpkin ['pʌmpkɪn] n potiron m, citrouille f

pun [pʌn] n jeu m de mots, calembour m

punch [pʌntʃ] n (blow) coup m de poing; (fig: force) vivacité f, mordant m; (tool) poinçon m; (drink) punch m ▷ vt (make a hole in) poinçonner, perforer; (hit): **to ~ sb/sth** donner un coup de poing à qn/sur qch; **to ~ a hole (in)** faire un trou (dans)
▶ **punch in** vi (US) pointer (en arrivant)
▶ **punch out** vi (US) pointer (en partant)

punch card, punched card [pʌntʃt-] n carte perforée

punch-drunk ['pʌntʃdrʌŋk] adj (Brit) sonné(e)

punch line n (of joke) conclusion f

punch-up ['pʌntʃʌp] n (Brit inf) bagarre f

punctual ['pʌŋktjuəl] adj ponctuel(le)

punctuality [pʌŋktju'ælɪtɪ] n ponctualité f

punctually ['pʌŋktjuəlɪ] adv ponctuellement; **it will start ~ at 6** cela commencera à 6 heures précises

punctuate ['pʌŋktjueɪt] vt ponctuer

punctuation [pʌŋktju'eɪʃən] n ponctuation f

punctuation mark n signe m de ponctuation

puncture ['pʌŋktʃəʳ] n (Brit) crevaison f ▷ vt crever; **I have a ~** (Aut) j'ai (un pneu) crevé

pundit ['pʌndɪt] n individu m qui pontifie, pontife m

pungent ['pʌndʒənt] adj piquant(e); (fig) mordant(e), caustique

punish ['pʌnɪʃ] vt punir; **to ~ sb for sth/for doing sth** punir qn de qch/d'avoir fait qch

punishable ['pʌnɪʃəbl] adj punissable

punishing ['pʌnɪʃɪŋ] adj (fig: exhausting) épuisant(e) ▷ n punition f

punishment ['pʌnɪʃmənt] n punition f, châtiment m; (fig: inf): **to take a lot of ~** (boxer) encaisser; (car, person etc) être mis(e) à dure épreuve

punk [pʌŋk] n (person: also: **punk rocker**) punk m/f; (music: also: **punk rock**) le punk; (US inf: hoodlum) voyou m

punt [pʌnt] n (boat) bachot m; (Irish) livre irlandaise ▷ vi (Brit: bet) parier

punter ['pʌntəʳ] n (Brit: gambler) parieur(-euse); (: inf) Monsieur m tout le monde; type m

puny ['pjuːnɪ] adj chétif(-ive)

pup [pʌp] n chiot m

pupil ['pjuːpl] n élève m/f; (of eye) pupille f

puppet ['pʌpɪt] n marionnette f, pantin m

puppet government n gouvernement m fantoche

puppy ['pʌpɪ] n chiot m, petit chien

purchase ['pəːtʃɪs] n achat m; (grip) prise f ▷ vt acheter; **to get a ~ on** trouver appui sur

purchase order n ordre m d'achat

purchase price n prix m d'achat

purchaser ['pəːtʃɪsəʳ] n acheteur(-euse)

purchase tax n (Brit) taxe f à l'achat

purchasing power ['pəːtʃɪsɪŋ-] n pouvoir m d'achat

pure [pjuəʳ] adj pur(e); **a ~ wool jumper** un pull en pure laine; **~ and simple** pur(e) et simple

purebred ['pjuəbrɛd] adj de race

purée ['pjuəreɪ] n purée f

purely ['pjuəlɪ] adv purement

purge [pəːdʒ] n (Med) purge f; (Pol) épuration f, purge ▷ vt purger; (fig) épurer, purger

purification [pjuərɪfɪ'keɪʃən] n purification f

purify ['pjuərɪfaɪ] vt purifier, épurer

purist ['pjuərɪst] n puriste m/f

puritan ['pjuərɪtən] n puritain(e)

puritanical [pjuərɪ'tænɪkl] adj puritain(e)

purity ['pjuərɪtɪ] n pureté f

purl [pəːl] n maille f à l'envers ▷ vt tricoter à l'envers

purloin [pəː'lɔɪn] vt dérober

purple ['pəːpl] adj violet(te); (face) cramoisi(e)

purport [pəː'pɔːt] vi: **to ~ to be/do** prétendre être/faire

purpose ['pəːpəs] n intention f, but m; **on ~** exprès; **for illustrative ~s** à titre d'illustration; **for teaching ~s** dans un but pédagogique; **for the ~s of this meeting** pour cette réunion; **to no ~** en pure perte

purpose-built ['pəːpəs'bɪlt] adj (Brit) fait(e) sur mesure

purposeful ['pəːpəsful] adj déterminé(e), résolu(e)

purposely ['pəːpəslɪ] adv exprès

purr [pəːʳ] n ronronnement m ▷ vi ronronner

purse [pəːs] n (Brit: for money) porte-monnaie m inv, bourse f; (US: handbag) sac m (à main) ▷ vt serrer, pincer

purser ['pəːsəʳ] n (Naut) commissaire m du bord

purse snatcher [-'snætʃəʳ] n (US) voleur m à l'arraché

pursue [pə'sjuː] vt poursuivre; (pleasures) rechercher; (inquiry, matter) approfondir

pursuer [pə'sjuːəʳ] n poursuivant(e)

pursuit [pə'sjuːt] n poursuite f; (occupation) occupation f, activité f; **scientific ~s** recherches fpl scientifiques; **in (the) ~ of sth** à la recherche de qch

purveyor [pə'veɪəʳ] n fournisseur m

pus [pʌs] n pus m

push [puʃ] n poussée f; (effort) gros effort; (drive) énergie f ▷ vt pousser; (button) appuyer sur; (thrust): **to ~ sth (into)** enfoncer qch (dans); (fig: product) mettre en avant, faire de la publicité pour ▷ vi pousser; appuyer; **to ~ a door open/shut** pousser une porte (pour l'ouvrir/pour la fermer); **"~"** (on door) "pousser"; (on bell) "appuyer"; **to ~ for** (better pay, conditions) réclamer; **to be ~ed for time/money** être à court de temps/d'argent; **she is ~ing fifty** (inf) elle frise la cinquantaine; **at a ~** (Brit inf) à la limite, à la rigueur
▶ **push aside** vt écarter
▶ **push in** vi s'introduire de force
▶ **push off** vi (inf) filer, ficher le camp
▶ **push on** vi (continue) continuer
▶ **push over** vt renverser

▶ **push through** vt (*measure*) faire voter ▷ vi (*in crowd*) se frayer un chemin

▶ **push up** vt (*total, prices*) faire monter

push-bike ['puʃbaɪk] n (*Brit*) vélo m

push-button ['puʃbʌtn] n bouton(-poussoir m) m

pushchair ['puʃtʃɛəʳ] n (*Brit*) poussette f

pusher ['puʃəʳ] n (*also*: **drug pusher**) revendeur(-euse) (de drogue), ravitailleur(-euse) (en drogue)

pushover ['puʃəuvəʳ] n (*inf*): **it's a ~** c'est un jeu d'enfant

push-up ['puʃʌp] n (*US*) traction f

pushy ['puʃi] adj (*pej*) arriviste

pussy ['pusi], **pussy-cat** n (*inf*) minet m

put (*pt, pp* -) [put] vt mettre; (*place*) poser, placer; (*say*) dire, exprimer; (*a question*) poser; (*case, view*) exposer, présenter; (*estimate*) estimer; **to ~ sb in a good/bad mood** mettre qn de bonne/ mauvaise humeur; **to ~ sb to bed** mettre qn au lit, coucher qn; **to ~ sb to a lot of trouble** déranger qn; **how shall I ~ it?** comment dirais-je?, comment dire?; **to ~ a lot of time into sth** passer beaucoup de temps à qch; **to ~ money on a horse** miser sur un cheval; **I ~ it to you that ...** (*Brit*) je (vous) suggère que ..., je suis d'avis que ...; **to stay ~** ne pas bouger

▶ **put about** vi (*Naut*) virer de bord ▷ vt (*rumour*) faire courir

▶ **put across** vt (*ideas etc*) communiquer; faire comprendre

▶ **put aside** vt mettre de côté

▶ **put away** vt (*store*) ranger

▶ **put back** vt (*replace*) remettre, replacer; (*postpone*) remettre; (*delay, watch, clock*) retarder; **this will ~ us back ten years** cela nous ramènera dix ans en arrière

▶ **put by** vt (*money*) mettre de côté, économiser

▶ **put down** vt (*parcel etc*) poser, déposer; (*pay*) verser; (*in writing*) mettre par écrit, inscrire; (*suppress: revolt etc*) réprimer, écraser; (*attribute*) attribuer; (*animal*) abattre; (*cat, dog*) faire piquer

▶ **put forward** vt (*ideas*) avancer, proposer; (*date, watch, clock*) avancer

▶ **put in** vt (*gas, electricity*) installer; (*complaint*) soumettre; (*time, effort*) consacrer

▶ **put in for** vt fus (*job*) poser sa candidature pour; (*promotion*) solliciter

▶ **put off** vt (*light etc*) éteindre; (*postpone*) remettre à plus tard, ajourner; (*discourage*) dissuader

▶ **put on** vt (*clothes, lipstick, CD*) mettre; (*light etc*) allumer; (*play etc*) monter; (*extra bus, train etc*) mettre en service; (*food, meal: provide*) servir; (*: cook*) mettre à cuire or à chauffer; (*weight*) prendre; (*assume: accent, manner*) prendre; (*: airs*)

se donner, prendre; (*inf: tease*) faire marcher; (*inform, indicate*): **to ~ sb on to sb/sth** indiquer qn/qch à qn; **to ~ the brakes on** freiner

▶ **put out** vt (*take outside*) mettre dehors; (*one's hand*) tendre; (*news, rumour*) faire courir, répandre; (*light etc*) éteindre; (*person: inconvenience*) déranger, gêner; (*Brit: dislocate*) se démettre ▷ vi (*Naut*): **to ~ out to sea** prendre le large; **to ~ out from Plymouth** quitter Plymouth

▶ **put through** vt (*Tel: caller*) mettre en communication; (*: call*) passer; (*plan*) faire accepter; **~ me through to Miss Blair** passez-moi Miss Blair

▶ **put together** vt mettre ensemble; (*assemble: furniture*) monter, assembler; (*meal*) préparer

▶ **put up** vt (*raise*) lever, relever, remonter; (*pin up*) afficher; (*hang*) accrocher; (*build*) construire, ériger; (*tent*) monter; (*umbrella*) ouvrir; (*increase*) augmenter; (*accommodate*) loger; (*incite*): **to ~ sb up to doing sth** pousser qn à faire qch; **to ~ sth up for sale** mettre qch en vente

▶ **put upon** vt fus: **to be ~ upon** (*imposed on*) se laisser faire

▶ **put up with** vt fus supporter

putrid ['pju:trɪd] adj putride

putt [pʌt] vt, vi putter ▷ n putt m

putter ['pʌtəʳ] n (*Golf*) putter m

putting green ['pʌtɪŋ-] n green m

putty ['pʌti] n mastic m

put-up ['putʌp] adj: **~ job** coup monté

puzzle ['pʌzl] n énigme f, mystère m; (*game*) jeu m, casse-tête m; (*jigsaw*) puzzle m; (*also:* **crossword puzzle**) mots croisés ▷ vt intriguer, rendre perplexe ▷ vi se creuser la tête; **to ~ over** chercher à comprendre

puzzled ['pʌzld] adj perplexe; **to be ~ about sth** être perplexe au sujet de qch

puzzling ['pʌzlɪŋ] adj déconcertant(e), inexplicable

PVC n abbr (= *polyvinyl chloride*) PVC m

Pvt. abbr (*US Mil*) = **private**

pw abbr (= *per week*) p. sem.

PX n abbr (*US Mil*) = **post exchange**

pygmy ['pɪɡmɪ] n pygmée m/f

pyjamas [pɪ'dʒɑːməz] npl (*Brit*) pyjama m; **a pair of ~** un pyjama

pylon ['paɪlən] n pylône m

pyramid ['pɪrəmɪd] n pyramide f

Pyrenean [pɪrə'niːən] adj pyrénéen(ne), des Pyrénées

Pyrenees [pɪrə'niːz] npl Pyrénées fpl

Pyrex® ['paɪrɛks] n Pyrex® m ▷ cpd: **Pyrex dish** plat m en Pyrex

python ['paɪθən] n python m

Qq

Q, q [kjuː] n (letter) Q, q m; **Q for Queen** Q
comme Quintal
Qatar [kæ'tɑːʳ] n Qatar m, Katar m
QC n abbr = **Queen's Counsel**; voir article

● QC
●
● En Angleterre, un QC ou *Queen's Counsel* (ou
● "KC" pour "King's Counsel", sous le règne
● d'un roi) est un avocat qui reçoit un poste de
● haut fonctionnaire sur recommandation du
● "Lord Chancellor". Il fait alors souvent
● suivre son nom des lettres QC, et lorsqu'il va
● au tribunal, il est toujours accompagné par
● un autre avocat (un "junior barrister").

QED abbr (= quod erat demonstrandum) CQFD
q.t. n abbr (inf) = **quiet**; **on the q.t.** discrètement
qty abbr (= quantity) qté
quack [kwæk] n (of duck) coin-coin m inv; (pej:
doctor) charlatan m ▷ vi faire coin-coin
quad [kwɔd] n abbr = **quadruplet**; **quadrangle**
quadrangle ['kwɔdræŋgl] n (Math) quadrilatère
m; (courtyard: abbr: quad) cour f
quadruped ['kwɔdrupɛd] n quadrupède m
quadruple [kwɔ'druːpl] adj, n quadruple m ▷ vt,
vi quadrupler
quadruplet [kwɔ'druːplɪt] n quadruplé(e)
quagmire ['kwægmaɪəʳ] n bourbier m
quail [kweɪl] n (Zool) caille f ▷ vi: **to ~ at** or
before reculer devant
quaint [kweɪnt] adj bizarre; (old-fashioned)
désuet(-ète); (picturesque) au charme vieillot,
pittoresque
quake [kweɪk] vi trembler ▷ n abbr = **earthquake**
Quaker ['kweɪkəʳ] n quaker(esse)
qualification [kwɔlɪfɪ'keɪʃən] n (often pl: degree
etc) diplôme m; (training) qualification(s) f(pl);
(ability) compétence(s) f(pl); (limitation) réserve f,
restriction f; **what are your ~s?** qu'avez-vous
comme diplômes?; quelles sont vos
qualifications?
qualified ['kwɔlɪfaɪd] adj (trained) qualifié(e);
(professionally) diplômé(e); (fit, competent)
compétent(e), qualifié(e); (limited)
conditionnel(le); **it was a ~ success** ce fut un

succès mitigé; **~ for/to do** qui a les diplômes
requis pour/pour faire; qualifié pour/pour faire
qualify ['kwɔlɪfaɪ] vt qualifier; (modify) atténuer,
nuancer; (limit: statement) apporter des réserves
à ▷ vi: **to ~ (as)** obtenir son diplôme (de); **to ~
(for)** remplir les conditions requises (pour);
(Sport) se qualifier (pour)
qualifying ['kwɔlɪfaɪɪŋ] adj: **~ exam** examen m
d'entrée; **~ round** éliminatoires fpl
qualitative ['kwɔlɪtətɪv] adj qualitatif(-ive)
quality ['kwɔlɪtɪ] n qualité f ▷ cpd de qualité; **of
good/poor ~** de bonne/mauvaise qualité
quality control n contrôle m de qualité

● QUALITY PRESS
●
● La *quality press* ou les "quality (news)papers"
● englobent les journaux sérieux, quotidiens
● ou hebdomadaires, par opposition aux
● journaux populaires ("tabloid press"). Ces
● journaux visent un public qui souhaite des
● informations détaillées sur un éventail très
● vaste de sujets et qui est prêt à consacrer
● beaucoup de temps à leur lecture. Les
● "quality newspapers" sont en général de
● grand format.

quality time n moments privilégiés
qualm [kwɑːm] n doute m; scrupule m; **to have
~s about sth** avoir des doutes sur qch; éprouver
des scrupules à propos de qch
quandary ['kwɔndrɪ] n: **in a ~** devant un
dilemme, dans l'embarras
quango ['kwæŋgəu] n abbr (Brit: = quasi-
autonomous non-governmental organization)
commission nommée par le gouvernement
quantify ['kwɔntɪfaɪ] vt quantifier
quantitative ['kwɔntɪtətɪv] adj
quantitatif(-ive)
quantity ['kwɔntɪtɪ] n quantité f; **in ~** en
grande quantité
quantity surveyor n (Brit) métreur vérificateur
quantum leap ['kwɔntəm-] n (fig) bond m en
avant
quarantine ['kwɔrntiːn] n quarantaine f
quark [kwɑːk] n quark m

quarrel ['kwɔrl] n querelle f, dispute f ▷ vi se disputer, se quereller; **to have a ~ with sb** se quereller avec qn; **I've no ~ with him** je n'ai rien contre lui; **I can't ~ with that** je ne vois rien à redire à cela

quarrelsome ['kwɔrəlsəm] adj querelleur(-euse)

quarry ['kwɔrɪ] n (for stone) carrière f; (animal) proie f, gibier m ▷ vt (marble etc) extraire

quart [kwɔ:t] n ≈ litre m

quarter ['kwɔ:tər] n quart m; (of year) trimestre m; (district) quartier m; (US, Canada: 25 cents) (pièce f de) vingt-cinq cents mpl ▷ vt partager en quartiers or en quatre; (Mil) caserner, cantonner; **quarters** npl logement m; (Mil) quartiers mpl, cantonnement m; **a ~ of an hour** un quart d'heure; **it's a ~ to 3**, (US) **it's a ~ of 3** il est 3 heures moins le quart; **it's a ~ past 3**, (US) **it's a ~ after 3** il est 3 heures et quart; **from all ~s** de tous côtés

quarterback ['kwɔ:təbæk] n (US Football) quarterback m/f

quarter-deck ['kwɔ:tədɛk] n (Naut) plage f arrière

quarter final n quart m de finale

quarterly ['kwɔ:təlɪ] adj trimestriel(le) ▷ adv tous les trois mois ▷ n (Press) revue trimestrielle

quartermaster ['kwɔ:təmɑːstər] n (Mil) intendant m militaire de troisième classe; (Naut) maître m de manœuvre

quartet, quartette [kwɔ:'tɛt] n quatuor m; (jazz players) quartette m

quarto ['kwɔ:təu] adj, n in-quarto m inv

quartz [kwɔ:ts] n quartz m ▷ cpd de or en quartz; (watch, clock) à quartz

quash [kwɔʃ] vt (verdict) annuler, casser

quasi- ['kweɪzaɪ] prefix quasi-+noun; quasi, presque + adjective

quaver ['kweɪvər] n (Brit Mus) croche f ▷ vi trembler

quay [ki:] n (also: **quayside**) quai m

Que. abbr (Canada) = **Quebec**

queasy ['kwi:zɪ] adj (stomach) délicat(e); **to feel ~** avoir mal au cœur

Quebec [kwɪ'bɛk] n (city) Québec; (province) Québec m

queen [kwi:n] n (gen) reine f; (Cards etc) dame f

queen mother n reine mère f

Queen's speech n (Brit) discours m de la reine; voir article

● **QUEEN'S SPEECH**

● Le Queen's speech (ou "King's speech") est le discours lu par le souverain à l'ouverture du "Parliament", dans la "House of Lords", en présence des lords et des députés. Il contient le programme de politique générale que propose le gouvernement pour la session, et il est préparé par le Premier ministre en consultation avec le cabinet.

queer [kwɪər] adj étrange, curieux(-euse);

(suspicious) louche; (Brit: sick): **I feel ~** je ne me sens pas bien ▷ n (inf: highly offensive) homosexuel m

quell [kwɛl] vt réprimer, étouffer

quench [kwɛntʃ] vt (flames) éteindre; **to ~ one's thirst** se désaltérer

querulous ['kwɛrʊləs] adj (person) récriminateur(-trice); (voice) plaintif(-ive)

query ['kwɪərɪ] n question f; (doubt) doute m; (question mark) point m d'interrogation ▷ vt (disagree with, dispute) mettre en doute, questionner

quest [kwɛst] n recherche f, quête f

question ['kwɛstʃən] n question f ▷ vt (person) interroger; (plan, idea) mettre en question or en doute; **to ask sb a ~**, **to put a ~ to sb** poser une question à qn; **to bring** or **call sth into ~** remettre qch en question; **the ~ is ...** la question est de savoir ...; **it's a ~ of doing** il s'agit de faire; **there's some ~ of doing** il est question de faire; **beyond ~** sans aucun doute; **out of the ~** hors de question

questionable ['kwɛstʃənəbl] adj discutable

questioner ['kwɛstʃənər] n personne f qui pose une question (or qui a posé la question etc)

questioning ['kwɛstʃənɪŋ] adj interrogateur(-trice) ▷ n interrogatoire m

question mark n point m d'interrogation

questionnaire [kwɛstʃə'nɛər] n questionnaire m

queue [kju:] (Brit) n queue f, file f ▷ vi (also: **queue up**) faire la queue; **to jump the ~** passer avant son tour

quibble ['kwɪbl] vi ergoter, chicaner

quiche [ki:ʃ] n quiche f

quick [kwɪk] adj rapide; (reply) prompt(e), rapide; (mind) vif (vive); (agile) agile, vif (vive) ▷ adv vite, rapidement ▷ n: **cut to the ~** (fig) touché(e) au vif; **be ~!** dépêche-toi!; **to be ~ to act** agir tout de suite

quicken ['kwɪkən] vt accélérer, presser; (rouse) stimuler ▷ vi s'accélérer, devenir plus rapide

quick fix n solution f de fortune

quicklime ['kwɪklaɪm] n chaux vive

quickly ['kwɪklɪ] adv (fast) vite, rapidement; (immediately) tout de suite

quickness ['kwɪknɪs] n rapidité f, promptitude f; (of mind) vivacité f

quicksand ['kwɪksænd] n sables mouvants

quickstep ['kwɪkstɛp] n fox-trot m

quick-tempered [kwɪk'tɛmpəd] adj emporté(e)

quick-witted [kwɪk'wɪtɪd] adj à l'esprit vif

quid [kwɪd] n (pl inv: Brit inf) livre f

quid pro quo ['kwɪdprəu'kwəu] n contrepartie f

quiet ['kwaɪət] adj tranquille, calme; (not noisy: engine) silencieux(-euse); (reserved) réservé(e); (voice) bas(se); (not busy: day, business) calme; (ceremony, colour) discret(-ète) ▷ n tranquillité f, calme m; (silence) silence m ▷ vt, vi (US) = **quieten**; **keep ~!** tais-toi!; **on the ~** en secret, discrètement; **I'll have a ~ word with him** je lui en parlerai discrètement

quieten ['kwaɪətn] (also: **quieten down**) vi se

q

calmer, s'apaiser ▷ *vt* calmer, apaiser

quietly ['kwaɪətlɪ] *adv* tranquillement; (*silently*) silencieusement; (*discreetly*) discrètement

quietness ['kwaɪətnɪs] *n* tranquillité *f*, calme *m*; silence *m*

quill [kwɪl] *n* plume *f* (d'oie)

quilt [kwɪlt] *n* édredon *m*; (*continental quilt*) couette *f*

quin [kwɪn] *n abbr* = **quintuplet**

quince [kwɪns] *n* coing *m*; (*tree*) cognassier *m*

quinine [kwɪ'niːn] *n* quinine *f*

quintet, quintette [kwɪn'tet] *n* quintette *m*

quintuplet [kwɪn'tjuːplɪt] *n* quintuplé(e)

quip [kwɪp] *n* remarque piquante *or* spirituelle, pointe *f* ▷ *vt*: ... he ~**ped** ... lança-t-il

quire ['kwaɪə'] *n* ≈ main *f* (*de papier*)

quirk [kwəːk] *n* bizarrerie *f*; **by some ~ of fate** par un caprice du hasard

quirky ['kwɜːkɪ] *adj* singulier(-ère)

quit [kwɪt] (*pt, pp* - *or* -**ted**) *vt* quitter ▷ *vi* (*give up*) abandonner, renoncer; (*resign*) démissionner; **to ~ doing** arrêter de faire; **~ stalling!** (*US inf*) arrête de te dérober!; **notice to ~** (*Brit*) congé *m* (*signifié au locataire*)

quite [kwaɪt] *adv* (*rather*) assez, plutôt; (*entirely*) complètement, tout à fait; ~ **new** plutôt neuf; tout à fait neuf; **she's ~ pretty** elle est plutôt jolie; **I ~ understand** je comprends très bien; ~ **a few of them** un assez grand nombre d'entre eux; **that's not ~ right** ce n'est pas tout à fait juste; **not ~ as many as last time** pas tout à fait autant que la dernière fois; ~ **(so)!** exactement!

Quito ['kiːtəu] *n* Quito

quits [kwɪts] *adj*: ~ **(with)** quitte (envers); **let's call it ~** restons-en là

quiver ['kwɪvə'] *vi* trembler, frémir ▷ *n* (*for arrows*) carquois *m*

quiz [kwɪz] *n* (*on TV*) jeu-concours *m* (télévisé); (*in magazine etc*) test *m* de connaissances ▷ *vt* interroger

quizzical ['kwɪzɪkl] *adj* narquois(e)

quoits [kwɔɪts] *npl* jeu *m* du palet

quorum ['kwɔːrəm] *n* quorum *m*

quota ['kwəutə] *n* quota *m*

quotation [kwəu'teɪʃən] *n* citation *f*; (*of shares etc*) cote *f*, cours *m*; (*estimate*) devis *m*

quotation marks *npl* guillemets *mpl*

quote [kwəut] *n* citation *f*; (*estimate*) devis *m* ▷ *vt* (*sentence, author*) citer; (*price*) donner, soumettre; (*shares*) coter ▷ *vi*: **to ~ from** citer; **to ~ for a job** établir un devis pour des travaux; **quotes** *npl* (*inverted commas*) guillemets *mpl*; **in ~s** entre guillemets; ~ ... **unquote** (*in dictation*) ouvrez les guillemets ... fermez les guillemets

quotient ['kwəuʃənt] *n* quotient *m*

qv *abbr* (= *quod vide: which see*) voir

qwerty keyboard ['kwəːtɪ-] *n* clavier *m* QWERTY

Rr

R, r [ɑːʳ] *n* (*letter*) R, r *m*; **R for Robert**, (US) **R for Roger** R comme Raoul

R *abbr* (= *right*) dr; (= *river*) riv., fl.; (= *Réaumur* (*scale*)) R; (*US Cine*: = *restricted*) *interdit aux moins de* 17 *ans*; (*US Pol*) = **republican**; (*Brit*) *Rex, Regina*

RA *abbr* = **rear admiral** ▷ *n abbr* (Brit) = **Royal Academy** = **Royal Academician**

RAAF *n abbr* = **Royal Australian Air Force**

Rabat [rə'bɑːt] *n* Rabat

rabbi ['ræbaɪ] *n* rabbin *m*

rabbit ['ræbɪt] *n* lapin *m* ▷ *vi*: **to ~ (on)** (Brit) parler à n'en plus finir

rabbit hole *n* terrier *m* (de lapin)

rabbit hutch *n* clapier *m*

rabble ['ræbl] *n* (*pej*) populace *f*

rabid ['ræbɪd] *adj* enragé(e)

rabies ['reɪbiːz] *n* rage *f*

RAC *n abbr* (Brit: = *Royal Automobile Club*) ≈ ACF *m*

raccoon, racoon [rə'kuːn] *n* raton *m* laveur

race [reɪs] *n* (*species*) race *f*; (*competition, rush*) course *f* ▷ *vt* (*person*) faire la course avec; (*horse*) faire courir; (*engine*) emballer ▷ *vi* (*compete*) faire la course, courir; (*hurry*) aller à toute vitesse, courir; (*engine*) s'emballer; (*pulse*) battre très vite; **the human ~** la race humaine; **to ~ in/out** *etc* entrer/sortir *etc* à toute vitesse

race car *n* (US) = **racing car**

race car driver *n* (US) = **racing driver**

racecourse ['reɪskɔːs] *n* champ *m* de courses

racehorse ['reɪshɔːs] *n* cheval *m* de course

racer ['reɪsəʳ] *n* (*bike*) vélo *m* de course

race relations *npl* rapports *mpl* entre les races

racetrack ['reɪstræk] *n* piste *f*

racial ['reɪʃl] *adj* racial(e)

racialism ['reɪʃlɪzəm] *n* racisme *m*

racialist ['reɪʃlɪst] *adj, n* raciste (*m/f*)

racing ['reɪsɪŋ] *n* courses *fpl*

racing car *n* (Brit) voiture *f* de course

racing driver *n* (Brit) pilote *m* de course

racism ['reɪsɪzəm] *n* racisme *m*

racist ['reɪsɪst] *adj, n* raciste *m/f*

rack [ræk] *n* (*for guns, tools*) râtelier *m*; (*for clothes*) portant *m*; (*for bottles*) casier *m*; (*also*: **luggage rack**) filet *m* à bagages; (*also*: **roof rack**) galerie *f*; (*also*: **dish rack**) égouttoir *m* ▷ *vt* tourmenter; **magazine ~** porte-revues *m inv*; **shoe ~** étagère *f* à chaussures; **toast ~** porte-toast *m*; **to ~ one's brains** se creuser la cervelle; **to go to ~ and ruin** (*building*) tomber en ruine; (*business*) péricliter

▶ **rack up** *vt* accumuler

racket ['rækɪt] *n* (*for tennis*) raquette *f*; (*noise*) tapage *m*, vacarme *m*; (*swindle*) escroquerie *f*; (*organized crime*) racket *m*

racketeer [rækɪ'tɪəʳ] *n* (*esp US*) racketteur *m*

racquet ['rækɪt] *n* raquette *f*

racy ['reɪsɪ] *adj* plein(e) de verve, osé(e)

RADA [rɑːdə] *n abbr* (Brit) = **Royal Academy of Dramatic Art**

radar ['reɪdɑːʳ] *n* radar *m* ▷ *cpd* radar *inv*

radar trap *n* (Aut: *police*) contrôle *m* radar

radial ['reɪdɪəl] *adj* (*also*: **radial-ply**) à carcasse radiale

radiance ['reɪdɪəns] *n* éclat *m*, rayonnement *m*

radiant ['reɪdɪənt] *adj* rayonnant(e); (*Physics*) radiant(e)

radiate ['reɪdɪeɪt] *vt* (*heat*) émettre, dégager ▷ *vi* (*lines*) rayonner

radiation [reɪdɪ'eɪʃən] *n* rayonnement *m*; (*radioactive*) radiation *f*

radiation sickness *n* mal *m* des rayons

radiator ['reɪdɪeɪtəʳ] *n* radiateur *m*

radiator cap *n* bouchon *m* de radiateur

radiator grill *n* (Aut) calandre *f*

radical ['rædɪkl] *adj* radical(e)

radii ['reɪdɪaɪ] *npl of* **radius**

radio ['reɪdɪəu] *n* radio *f* ▷ *vi*: **to ~ to sb** envoyer un message radio à qn ▷ *vt* (*information*) transmettre par radio; (*one's position*) signaler par radio; (*person*) appeler par radio; **on the ~** à la radio

radioactive ['reɪdɪəu'æktɪv] *adj* radioactif(-ive)

radioactivity ['reɪdɪəuæk'tɪvɪtɪ] *n* radioactivité *f*

radio announcer *n* annonceur *m*

radio cassette *n* radiocassette *m*

radio-controlled ['reɪdɪəukən'trəuld] *adj* radioguidé(e)

radiographer [reɪdɪ'ɔgrəfəʳ] *n* radiologue *m/f* (*technicien*)

radiography [reɪdɪ'ɔgrəfɪ] *n* radiographie *f*

radiologist [reɪdɪ'ɔlədʒɪst] *n* radiologue *m/f*

(*médecin*)

radiology [reɪdɪˈɔlədʒɪ] *n* radiologie *f*

radio station *n* station *f* de radio

radio taxi *n* radio-taxi *m*

radiotelephone [ˈreɪdɪəʊˈtɛlɪfəʊn] *n* radiotéléphone *m*

radiotherapist [ˈreɪdɪəʊˈθɛrəpɪst] *n* radiothérapeute *m/f*

radiotherapy [ˈreɪdɪəʊˈθɛrəpɪ] *n* radiothérapie *f*

radish [ˈrædɪʃ] *n* radis *m*

radium [ˈreɪdɪəm] *n* radium *m*

radius (*pl* **radii**) [ˈreɪdɪəs, -ɪaɪ] *n* rayon *m*; (*Anat*) radius *m*; **within a ~ of 50 miles** dans un rayon de 50 milles

RAF *n abbr* (*Brit*) = **Royal Air Force**

raffia [ˈræfɪə] *n* raphia *m*

raffish [ˈræfɪʃ] *adj* dissolu(e), canaille

raffle [ˈræfl] *n* tombola *f* ⊳ *vt* mettre comme lot dans une tombola

raft [rɑːft] *n* (*craft: also:* **life raft**) radeau *m*; (*logs*) train *m* de flottage

rafter [ˈrɑːftər] *n* chevron *m*

rag [ræg] *n* chiffon *m*; (*pej: newspaper*) feuille *f*, torchon *m*; (*for charity*) *attractions organisées par les étudiants au profit d'œuvres de charité* ⊳ *vt* (*Brit*) chahuter, mettre en boîte; **rags** *npl* haillons *mpl*; **in ~s** (*person*) en haillons; (*clothes*) en lambeaux

rag-and-bone man [rægənˈbəʊnmæn] (*irreg*) *n* chiffonnier *m*

ragbag [ˈrægbæg] *n* (*fig*) ramassis *m*

rag doll *n* poupée *f* de chiffon

rage [reɪdʒ] *n* (*fury*) rage *f*, fureur *f* ⊳ *vi* (*person*) être fou (folle) de rage; (*storm*) faire rage, être déchaîné(e); **to fly into a ~** se mettre en rage; **it's all the ~** cela fait fureur

ragged [ˈrægɪd] *adj* (*edge*) inégal(e), qui accroche; (*clothes*) en loques; (*cuff*) effiloché(e); (*appearance*) déguenillé(e)

raging [ˈreɪdʒɪŋ] *adj* (*sea, storm*) en furie; (*fever, pain*) violent(e); **~ toothache** rage *f* de dents; **in a ~ temper** dans une rage folle

rag trade *n* (*inf*): **the ~** la confection

◉ RAG WEEK

Rag Week, est une semaine où les étudiants se déguisent et collectent de l'argent pour les œuvres de charité. Toutes sortes d'animations sont organisées à cette occasion (marches sponsorisées, spectacles de rue etc). Des magazines (les "rag mags") contenant des plaisanteries osées sont vendus dans les rues, également au profit des œuvres. Enfin, la plupart des universités organisent un bal (le "rag ball").

raid [reɪd] *n* (*Mil*) raid *m*; (*criminal*) hold-up *m inv*; (*by police*) descente *f*, rafle *f* ⊳ *vt* faire un raid sur *or* un hold-up dans *or* une descente dans

raider [ˈreɪdər] *n* malfaiteur *m*

rail [reɪl] *n* (*on stair*) rampe *f*; (*on bridge, balcony*)

balustrade *f*; (*of ship*) bastingage *m*; (*for train*) rail *m*; **rails** *npl* rails *mpl*, voie ferrée; **by ~** en train, par le train

railcard [ˈreɪlkɑːd] *n* (*Brit*) carte *f* de chemin de fer; **young person's ~** carte *f* jeune

railing [ˈreɪlɪŋ] *n*, **railings** [ˈreɪlɪŋz] ⊳ *npl* grille *f*

railway [ˈreɪlweɪ], (*US*) **railroad** [ˈreɪlrəʊd] *n* chemin *m* de fer; (*track*) voie *f* ferrée

railway engine *n* locomotive *f*

railway line *n* (*Brit*) ligne *f* de chemin de fer; (*track*) voie ferrée

railwayman [ˈreɪlweɪmən] (*irreg*) *n* cheminot *m*

railway station *n* (*Brit*) gare *f*

rain [reɪn] *n* pluie *f* ⊳ *vi* pleuvoir; **in the ~** sous la pluie; **it's ~ing** il pleut; **it's ~ing cats and dogs** il pleut à torrents

rainbow [ˈreɪnbəʊ] *n* arc-en-ciel *m*

raincoat [ˈreɪnkəʊt] *n* imperméable *m*

raindrop [ˈreɪndrɔp] *n* goutte *f* de pluie

rainfall [ˈreɪnfɔːl] *n* chute *f* de pluie; (*measurement*) hauteur *f* des précipitations

rainforest [ˈreɪnfɔrɪst] *n* forêt tropicale

rainproof [ˈreɪnpruːf] *adj* imperméable

rainstorm [ˈreɪnstɔːm] *n* pluie torrentielle

rainwater [ˈreɪnwɔːtər] *n* eau *f* de pluie

rainy [ˈreɪnɪ] *adj* pluvieux(-euse)

raise [reɪz] *n* augmentation *f* ⊳ *vt* (*lift*) lever; hausser; (*end: siege, embargo*) lever; (*build*) ériger; (*increase*) augmenter; (*morale*) remonter; (*standards*) améliorer; (*a protest, doubt*) provoquer, causer; (*a question*) soulever; (*cattle, family*) élever; (*crop*) faire pousser; (*army, funds*) rassembler; (*loan*) obtenir; **to ~ one's glass to sb/sth** porter un toast en l'honneur de qn/qch; **to ~ one's voice** élever la voix; **to ~ sb's hopes** donner de l'espoir à qn; **to ~ a laugh/a smile** faire rire/sourire

raisin [ˈreɪzn] *n* raisin sec

Raj [rɑːdʒ] *n*: **the ~** l'empire *m* (*aux Indes*)

rajah [ˈrɑːdʒə] *n* radja(h) *m*

rake [reɪk] *n* (*tool*) râteau *m*; (*person*) débauché *m* ⊳ *vt* (*garden*) ratisser; (*fire*) tisonner; (*with machine gun*) balayer ⊳ *vi*: **to ~ through** (*fig: search*) fouiller (dans)

rake-off [ˈreɪkɔf] *n* (*inf*) pourcentage *m*

rakish [ˈreɪkɪʃ] *adj* dissolu(e); cavalier(-ière)

rally [ˈrælɪ] *n* (*Pol etc*) meeting *m*, rassemblement *m*; (*Aut*) rallye *m*; (*Tennis*) échange *m* ⊳ *vt* rassembler, rallier; (*support*) gagner ⊳ *vi* se rallier; (*sick person*) aller mieux; (*Stock Exchange*) reprendre

▶ **rally round** *vi* venir en aide ⊳ *vt fus* se rallier à; venir en aide à

rallying point [ˈrælɪɪŋ-] *n* (*Mil*) point *m* de ralliement

RAM [ræm] *n abbr* (*Comput: = random access memory*) mémoire vive

ram [ræm] *n* bélier *m* ⊳ *vt* (*push*) enfoncer; (*soil*) tasser; (*crash into: vehicle*) emboutir; (*: lamppost etc*) percuter; (*in battle*) éperonner

Ramadan [ræməˈdæn] *n* Ramadan *m*

ramble [ˈræmbl] *n* randonnée *f* ⊳ *vi* (*walk*) se

promener, faire une randonnée; (*pej: also:*
ramble on) discourir, pérorer
rambler ['ræmblə^r] n promeneur(-euse),
randonneur(-euse); (*Bot*) rosier grimpant
rambling ['ræmblɪŋ] adj (*speech*) décousu(e);
(*house*) plein(e) de coins et de recoins; (*Bot*)
grimpant(e)
RAMC n abbr (*Brit*) = **Royal Army Medical Corps**
ramification [ræmɪfɪ'keɪʃən] n ramification f
ramp [ræmp] n (*incline*) rampe f; (*Aut*)
dénivellation f; (*in garage*) pont m; **on/off** ~ (*US
Aut*) bretelle f d'accès
rampage [ræm'peɪdʒ] n: **to be on the** ~ se
déchaîner ▷ vi: **they went rampaging
through the town** ils ont envahi les rues et ont
tout saccagé sur leur passage
rampant ['ræmpənt] adj (*disease etc*) qui sévit
rampart ['ræmpɑ:t] n rempart m
ram raiding [-reɪdɪŋ] n pillage d'un magasin en
enfonçant la vitrine avec une voiture volée
ramshackle ['ræmʃækl] adj (*house*) délabré(e);
(*car etc*) déglingué(e)
RAN n abbr = **Royal Australian Navy**
ran [ræn] pt of **run**
ranch [rɑ:ntʃ] n ranch m
rancher ['rɑ:ntʃə^r] n (*owner*) propriétaire m de
ranch; (*ranch hand*) cowboy m
rancid ['rænsɪd] adj rance
rancour, (*US*) **rancor** ['ræŋkə^r] n rancune f,
rancœur f
R&B n abbr = **rhythm and blues**
R&D n abbr (= *research and development*) R-D f
random ['rændəm] adj fait(e) or établi(e) au
hasard; (*Comput, Math*) aléatoire ▷ n: **at** ~ au
hasard
random access memory n (*Comput*) mémoire
vive, RAM f
R&R n abbr (*US Mil*) = **rest and recreation**
randy ['rændɪ] adj (*Brit inf*) excité(e); lubrique
rang [ræŋ] pt of **ring**
range [reɪndʒ] n (*of mountains*) chaîne f; (*of missile,
voice*) portée f; (*of products*) choix m, gamme f;
(*also:* **shooting range**) champ m de tir; (: *indoor*)
stand m de tir; (*also:* **kitchen range**) fourneau m
(de cuisine) ▷ vt (*place*) mettre en rang, placer;
(*roam*) parcourir ▷ vi: **to** ~ **over** couvrir; **to** ~
from ... to aller de ... à; **price** ~ éventail m des
prix; **do you have anything else in this price
~?** avez-vous autre chose dans ces prix?; **within
(firing)** ~ à portée (de tir); ~**d left/right** (*text*)
justifié à gauche/à droite
ranger ['reɪndʒə^r] n garde m forestier
Rangoon [ræŋ'gu:n] n Rangoon
rank [ræŋk] n rang m; (*Mil*) grade m; (*Brit: also:*
taxi rank) station f de taxis ▷ vi: **to** ~ **among**
compter or se classer parmi ▷ vt: **I** ~ **him sixth**
je le place sixième ▷ adj (*smell*) nauséabond(e);
(*hypocrisy, injustice etc*) flagrant(e); **he's a** ~
outsider il n'est vraiment pas dans la course;
the ~**s** (*Mil*) la troupe; **the** ~ **and file** (*fig*) la
masse, la base; **to close** ~**s** (*Mil: fig*) serrer les
rangs

rankle ['ræŋkl] vi (*insult*) rester sur le cœur
ransack ['rænsæk] vt fouiller (à fond); (*plunder*)
piller
ransom ['rænsəm] n rançon f; **to hold sb to** ~
(*fig*) exercer un chantage sur qn
rant [rænt] vi fulminer
ranting ['ræntɪŋ] n invectives fpl
rap [ræp] n petit coup sec; tape f; (*music*) rap m
▷ vt (*door*) frapper sur or à; (*table etc*) taper sur
rape [reɪp] n viol m; (*Bot*) colza m ▷ vt violer
rape oil, rapeseed oil ['reɪp(si:d)] n huile f de
colza
rapid ['ræpɪd] adj rapide
rapidity [rə'pɪdɪtɪ] n rapidité f
rapidly ['ræpɪdlɪ] adv rapidement
rapids ['ræpɪdz] npl (*Geo*) rapides mpl
rapist ['reɪpɪst] n auteur m d'un viol
rapport [ræ'pɔ:^r] n entente f
rapt [ræpt] adj (*attention*) extrême; **to be** ~ **in
contemplation** être perdu(e) dans la
contemplation
rapture ['ræptʃə^r] n extase f, ravissement m; **to
go into** ~**s over** s'extasier sur
rapturous ['ræptʃərəs] adj extasié(e); frénétique
rare [reə^r] adj rare; (*Culin: steak*) saignant(e)
rarebit ['reəbit] n see **Welsh rarebit**
rarefied ['reərɪfaɪd] adj (*air, atmosphere*) raréfié(e)
rarely ['reəlɪ] adv rarement
raring ['reərɪŋ] adj: **to be** ~ **to go** (*inf*) être très
impatient(e) de commencer
rarity ['reərɪtɪ] n rareté f
rascal ['rɑ:skl] n vaurien m
rash [ræʃ] adj imprudent(e), irréfléchi(e) ▷ n
(*Med*) rougeur f, éruption f; (*of events*) série f
(noire); **to come out in a** ~ avoir une éruption
rasher ['ræʃə^r] n fine tranche (de lard)
rasp [rɑ:sp] n (*tool*) lime f ▷ vt (*speak: also:* **rasp
out**) dire d'une voix grinçante
raspberry ['rɑ:zbərɪ] n framboise f
raspberry bush n framboisier m
rasping ['rɑ:spɪŋ] adj: ~ **noise** grincement m
Rastafarian [ræstə'feərɪən] adj, n rastafari (m/f)
rat [ræt] n rat m
ratable ['reɪtəbl] adj see **rateable value**
ratchet ['rætʃɪt] n: ~ **wheel** roue f à rochet
rate [reɪt] n (*ratio*) taux m, pourcentage m; (*speed*)
vitesse f, rythme m; (*price*) tarif m ▷ vt (*price*)
évaluer, estimer; (*people*) classer; (*deserve*)
mériter; **rates** npl (*Brit: property tax*) impôts
locaux; **to** ~ **sb/sth as** considérer qn/qch
comme; **to** ~ **sb/sth among** classer qn/qch
parmi; **to** ~ **sb/sth highly** avoir une haute
opinion de qn/qch; **at a** ~ **of 60 kph** à une
vitesse de 60 km/h; **at any** ~ en tout cas; ~ **of
exchange** taux or cours m du change; ~ **of flow**
débit m; ~ **of return** (taux de) rendement m;
pulse ~ fréquence f des pulsations
rateable value ['reɪtəbl-] n (*Brit*) valeur locative
imposable
ratepayer ['reɪtpeɪə^r] n (*Brit*) contribuable m/f
(*payant les impôts locaux*)
rather ['rɑ:ðə^r] adv (*somewhat*) assez, plutôt; (*to

r

some extent) un peu; **it's ~ expensive** c'est assez cher; (*too much*) c'est un peu cher; **there's ~ a lot** il y en a beaucoup; **I would** or **I'd ~ go** j'aimerais mieux or je préférerais partir; **I had ~ go** il vaudrait mieux que je parte; **I'd ~ not leave** j'aimerais mieux ne pas partir; **or ~** (*more accurately*) ou plutôt; **I ~ think he won't come** je crois bien qu'il ne viendra pas

ratification [rætɪfɪ'keɪʃən] *n* ratification *f*

ratify ['rætɪfaɪ] *vt* ratifier

rating ['reɪtɪŋ] *n* (*assessment*) évaluation *f*; (*score*) classement *m*; (*Finance*) cote *f*; (*Naut: category*) classe *f*; (*: sailor: Brit*) matelot *m*; **ratings** *npl* (*Radio*) indice(s) *m(pl)* d'écoute; (*TV*) Audimat® *m*

ratio ['reɪʃɪəu] *n* proportion *f*; **in the ~ of 100 to 1** dans la proportion de 100 contre 1

ration ['ræʃən] *n* ration *f* ▷ *vt* rationner; **rations** *npl* (*food*) vivres *mpl*

rational ['ræʃənl] *adj* raisonnable, sensé(e); (*solution, reasoning*) logique; (*Med: person*) lucide

rationale [ræʃə'nɑːl] *n* raisonnement *m*; justification *f*

rationalization [ræʃnəlaɪ'zeɪʃən] *n* rationalisation *f*

rationalize ['ræʃnəlaɪz] *vt* rationaliser; (*conduct*) essayer d'expliquer or de motiver

rationally ['ræʃnəlɪ] *adv* raisonnablement; logiquement

rationing ['ræʃnɪŋ] *n* rationnement *m*

rat pack ['rætpæk] *n* (*Brit inf*) journalistes *mpl* de la presse à sensation

rat poison *n* mort-aux-rats *f inv*

rat race *n* foire *f* d'empoigne

rattan [ræ'tæn] *n* rotin *m*

rattle ['rætl] *n* (*of door, window*) battement *m*; (*of coins, chain*) cliquetis *m*; (*of train, engine*) bruit *m* de ferraille; (*for baby*) hochet *m*; (*of sports fan*) crécelle *f* ▷ *vi* cliqueter; (*car, bus*): **to ~ along** rouler en faisant un bruit de ferraille ▷ *vt* agiter (bruyamment); (*inf: disconcert*) décontenancer; (*: annoy*) embêter

rattlesnake ['rætlsneɪk] *n* serpent *m* à sonnettes

ratty ['rætɪ] *adj* (*inf*) en rogne

raucous ['rɔːkəs] *adj* rauque

raucously ['rɔːkəslɪ] *adv* d'une voix rauque

raunchy ['rɔːntʃɪ] *adj* (*inf: voice, image, act*) sexy; (*scenes, film*) lubrique

ravage ['rævɪdʒ] *vt* ravager

ravages ['rævɪdʒɪz] *npl* ravages *mpl*

rave [reɪv] *vi* (*in anger*) s'emporter; (*with enthusiasm*) s'extasier; (*Med*) délirer ▷ *n* (*inf: party*) rave *f*, soirée *f* techno ▷ *adj* (*scene, culture, music*) rave, techno ▷ *cpd*: **~ review** (*inf*) critique *f* dithyrambique

raven ['reɪvən] *n* grand corbeau

ravenous ['rævənəs] *adj* affamé(e)

ravine [rə'viːn] *n* ravin *m*

raving ['reɪvɪŋ] *adj*: **he's ~ mad** il est complètement cinglé

ravings ['reɪvɪŋz] *npl* divagations *fpl*

ravioli [rævɪ'əulɪ] *n* ravioli *mpl*

ravish ['rævɪʃ] *vt* ravir

ravishing ['rævɪʃɪŋ] *adj* enchanteur(-eresse)

raw [rɔː] *adj* (*uncooked*) cru(e); (*not processed*) brut(e); (*sore*) à vif, irrité(e); (*inexperienced*) inexpérimenté(e); (*weather, day*) froid(e) et humide; **~ deal** (*inf: bad bargain*) sale coup *m*; (*: unfair treatment*): **to get a ~ deal** être traité(e) injustement; **~ materials** matières premières

Rawalpindi [rɔːl'pɪndɪ] *n* Rawalpindi

raw material *n* matière première

ray [reɪ] *n* rayon *m*; **~ of hope** lueur *f* d'espoir

rayon ['reɪɔn] *n* rayonne *f*

raze [reɪz] *vt* (*also*: **raze to the ground**) raser

razor ['reɪzə^r] *n* rasoir *m*

razor blade *n* lame *f* de rasoir

razzle ['ræzl], **razzle-dazzle** ['ræzl'dæzl] *n* (*Brit inf*): **to go on the ~(-dazzle)** faire la bringue

razzmatazz ['ræzmə'tæz] *n* (*inf*) tralala *m*, tapage *m*

RC *abbr* = **Roman Catholic**

RCAF *n abbr* = **Royal Canadian Air Force**

RCMP *n abbr* = **Royal Canadian Mounted Police**

RCN *n abbr* = **Royal Canadian Navy**

RD *abbr* (*US*) = **rural delivery**

Rd *abbr* = **road**

RDC *n abbr* (*Brit*) = **rural district council**

RE *n abbr* (*Brit*) = **religious education**; (*Brit Mil*) = **Royal Engineers**

re [riː] *prep* concernant

reach [riːtʃ] *n* portée *f*, atteinte *f*; (*of river etc*) étendue *f* ▷ *vt* atteindre, arriver à; (*conclusion, decision*) parvenir à ▷ *vi* s'étendre; (*stretch out hand*): **to ~ up/down** *etc* (**for sth**) lever/baisser *etc* le bras (pour prendre qch); **to ~ sb by phone** joindre qn par téléphone; **out of/within ~** (*object*) hors de/à portée; **within easy ~ (of)** (*place*) à proximité (de), proche (de)

▶ **reach out** *vt* tendre ▷ *vi*: **to ~ out (for)** allonger le bras (pour prendre)

react [riː'ækt] *vi* réagir

reaction [riː'ækʃən] *n* réaction *f*

reactionary [riː'ækʃənrɪ] *adj, n* réactionnaire (*m/f*)

reactor [riː'æktə^r] *n* réacteur *m*

read (*pt, pp ~*) [riːd, rɛd] *vi* lire ▷ *vt* lire; (*understand*) comprendre, interpréter; (*study*) étudier; (*meter*) relever; (*subj: instrument etc*) indiquer, marquer; **to take sth as ~** (*fig*) considérer qch comme accepté; **do you ~ me?** (*Tel*) est-ce que vous me recevez?

▶ **read out** *vt* lire à haute voix

▶ **read over** *vt* relire

▶ **read through** *vt* (*quickly*) parcourir; (*thoroughly*) lire jusqu'au bout

▶ **read up** *vt*, **read up on** *vt fus* étudier

readable ['riːdəbl] *adj* facile or agréable à lire

reader ['riːdə^r] *n* lecteur(-trice); (*book*) livre *m* de lecture; (*Brit: at university*) maître *m* de conférences

readership ['riːdəʃɪp] *n* (*of paper etc*) (nombre *m* de) lecteurs *mpl*

readily ['rɛdɪlɪ] *adv* volontiers, avec empressement; *(easily)* facilement

readiness ['rɛdɪnɪs] *n* empressement *m*; **in ~** *(prepared)* prêt(e)

reading ['riːdɪŋ] *n* lecture *f*; *(understanding)* interprétation *f*; *(on instrument)* indications *fpl*

reading lamp *n* lampe *f* de bureau

reading room *n* salle *f* de lecture

readjust [riːə'dʒʌst] *vt* rajuster; *(instrument)* régler de nouveau ▷ *vi (person)*: **to ~ (to)** se réadapter (à)

ready ['rɛdɪ] *adj* prêt(e); *(willing)* prêt, disposé(e); *(quick)* prompt(e); *(available)* disponible ▷ *n*: **at the ~** *(Mil)* prêt à faire feu; *(fig)* tout(e) prêt(e); **~ for use** prêt à l'emploi; **to be ~ to do sth** être prêt à faire qch; **when will my photos be ~?** quand est-ce que mes photos seront prêtes?; **to get ~** *(as vi)* se préparer; *(as vt)* préparer

ready cash *n* (argent *m*) liquide *m*

ready-cooked ['rɛdɪ'kukd] *adj* précuit(e)

ready-made ['rɛdɪ'meɪd] *adj* tout(e) faite(e)

ready-mix ['rɛdɪmɪks] *n* *(for cakes etc)* préparation *f* en sachet

ready reckoner [-'rɛknər] *n* *(Brit)* barème *m*

ready-to-wear ['rɛdɪtə'wɛər] *adj* (en) prêt-à-porter

reagent [riː'eɪdʒənt] *n* réactif *m*

real [rɪəl] *adj (world, life)* réel(le); *(genuine)* véritable; *(proper)* vrai(e) ▷ *adv (US inf: very)* vraiment; **in ~ life** dans la réalité

real ale *n* bière traditionnelle

real estate *n* biens fonciers *or* immobiliers

realism ['rɪəlɪzəm] *n* réalisme *m*

realist ['rɪəlɪst] *n* réaliste *m/f*

realistic [rɪə'lɪstɪk] *adj* réaliste

reality [riː'ælɪtɪ] *n* réalité *f*; **in ~** en réalité, en fait

reality TV *n* téléréalité *f*

realization [rɪəlaɪ'zeɪʃən] *n* *(awareness)* prise *f* de conscience; *(fulfilment: also: of asset)* réalisation *f*

realize ['rɪəlaɪz] *vt (understand)* se rendre compte de, prendre conscience de; *(a project, Comm: asset)* réaliser

really ['rɪəlɪ] *adv* vraiment; **~?** vraiment?, c'est vrai?

realm [rɛlm] *n* royaume *m*; *(fig)* domaine *m*

real-time ['riːltaɪm] *adj (Comput)* en temps réel

realtor ['rɪəltɔːr] *n* *(US)* agent immobilier

ream [riːm] *n* rame *f* (*de papier*); **reams** *npl (fig: inf)* des pages et des pages

reap [riːp] *vt* moissonner; *(fig)* récolter

reaper ['riːpər] *n* *(machine)* moissonneuse *f*

reappear [riːə'pɪər] *vi* réapparaître, reparaître

reappearance [riːə'pɪərəns] *n* réapparition *f*

reapply [riːə'plaɪ] *vi*: **to ~ for** *(job)* faire une nouvelle demande d'emploi concernant; reposer sa candidature à; *(loan, grant)* faire une nouvelle demande de

reappraisal [riːə'preɪzl] *n* réévaluation *f*

rear [rɪər] *adj* de derrière, arrière *inv*; *(Aut: wheel etc)* arrière ▷ *n* arrière *m*, derrière *m* ▷ *vt (cattle, family)* élever ▷ *vi (also: rear up: animal)* se cabrer

rear admiral *n* vice-amiral *m*

rear-engined ['rɪər'ɛndʒɪnd] *adj (Aut)* avec moteur à l'arrière

rearguard ['rɪəɡɑːd] *n* arrière-garde *f*

rearmament [riː'ɑːməmənt] *n* réarmement *m*

rearrange [riːə'reɪndʒ] *vt* réarranger

rear-view mirror *n* *(Aut)* rétroviseur *m*

rear-wheel drive *n* *(Aut)* traction *f* arrière

reason ['riːzn] *n* raison *f* ▷ *vi*: **to ~ with sb** raisonner qn, faire entendre raison à qn; **the ~ for/why** la raison de/pour laquelle; **to have ~ to think** avoir lieu de penser; **it stands to ~ that** il va sans dire que; **she claims with good ~ that ...** elle affirme à juste titre que ...; **all the more ~ why** raison de plus pour + *infinitive or* pour que + *sub*; **within ~** dans les limites du raisonnable

reasonable ['riːznəbl] *adj* raisonnable; *(not bad)* acceptable

reasonably ['riːznəblɪ] *adv (behave)* raisonnablement; *(fairly)* assez; **one can ~ assume that ...** on est fondé à *or* il est permis de supposer que ...

reasoned ['riːznd] *adj (argument)* raisonné(e)

reasoning ['riːznɪŋ] *n* raisonnement *m*

reassemble [riːə'sɛmbl] *vt* rassembler; *(machine)* remonter

reassert [riːə'səːt] *vt* réaffirmer

reassurance [riːə'ʃuərəns] *n* *(factual)* assurance *f*, garantie *f*; *(emotional)* réconfort *m*

reassure [riːə'ʃuər] *vt* rassurer; **to ~ sb of** donner à qn l'assurance répétée de

reassuring [riːə'ʃuərɪŋ] *adj* rassurant(e)

reawakening [riːə'weɪknɪŋ] *n* réveil *m*

rebate ['riːbeɪt] *n* *(on product)* rabais *m*; *(on tax etc)* dégrèvement *m*; *(repayment)* remboursement *m*

rebel *n* ['rɛbl] rebelle *m/f* ▷ *vi* [rɪ'bɛl] se rebeller, se révolter

rebellion [rɪ'bɛljən] *n* rébellion *f*, révolte *f*

rebellious [rɪ'bɛljəs] *adj* rebelle

rebirth [riː'bəːθ] *n* renaissance *f*

rebound *vi* [rɪ'baund] *(ball)* rebondir ▷ *n* ['riːbaund] rebond *m*

rebuff [rɪ'bʌf] *n* rebuffade *f* ▷ *vt* repousser

rebuild [riː'bɪld] *vt (irreg: like* **build***)* reconstruire

rebuke [rɪ'bjuːk] *n* réprimande *f*, reproche *m* ▷ *vt* réprimander

rebut [rɪ'bʌt] *vt* réfuter

rebuttal [rɪ'bʌtl] *n* réfutation *f*

recalcitrant [rɪ'kælsɪtrənt] *adj* récalcitrant(e)

recall *vt* [rɪ'kɔːl] rappeler; *(remember)* se rappeler, se souvenir de ▷ *n* ['riːkɔl] rappel *m*; *(ability to remember)* mémoire *f*; **beyond ~** *adj* irrévocable

recant [rɪ'kænt] *vi* se rétracter; *(Rel)* abjurer

recap ['riːkæp] *n* récapitulation *f* ▷ *vt, vi* récapituler

recapture [riː'kæptʃər] *vt* reprendre; *(atmosphere)* recréer

recede [rɪ'siːd] *vi* s'éloigner; reculer

receding [rɪ'siːdɪŋ] *adj (forehead, chin)* fuyant(e); **~ hairline** front dégarni

receipt [rɪ'siːt] *n* *(document)* reçu *m*; *(for parcel etc)* accusé *m* de réception; (*act of receiving*) réception *f*; **receipts** *npl* (*Comm*) recettes *fpl*; **to acknowledge ~ of** accuser réception de; **we are in ~ of ...** nous avons reçu ...; **can I have a ~, please?** je peux avoir un reçu, s'il vous plaît?

receivable [rɪˈsiːvəbl] *adj* (*Comm*) recevable; (: *owing*) à recevoir

receive [rɪˈsiːv] *vt* recevoir; (*guest*) recevoir, accueillir; **"~d with thanks"** (*Comm*) "pour acquit"; **R~d Pronunciation**: *voir article*

● RECEIVED PRONUNCIATION

En Grande-Bretagne, la *Received Pronunciation* ou "RP" est une prononciation de la langue anglaise qui, récemment encore, était surtout associée à l'aristocratie et à la bourgeoisie, mais qui maintenant est en général considérée comme la prononciation correcte.

receiver [rɪˈsiːvəʳ] *n* (*Tel*) récepteur *m*, combiné *m*; (*Radio*) récepteur; (*of stolen goods*) receleur *m*; (*for bankruptcies*) administrateur *m* judiciaire

receivership [rɪˈsiːvəʃɪp] *n*: **to go into ~** être placé sous administration judiciaire

recent [ˈriːsnt] *adj* récent(e); **in ~ years** au cours de ces dernières années

recently [ˈriːsntlɪ] *adv* récemment; **as ~ as** pas plus tard que; **until ~** jusqu'à il y a peu de temps encore

receptacle [rɪˈsɛptɪkl] *n* récipient *m*

reception [rɪˈsɛpʃən] *n* réception *f*; (*welcome*) accueil *m*, réception

reception centre *n* (*Brit*) centre *m* d'accueil

reception desk *n* réception *f*

receptionist [rɪˈsɛpʃənɪst] *n* réceptionniste *m/f*

receptive [rɪˈsɛptɪv] *adj* réceptif(-ive)

recess [rɪˈsɛs] *n* (*in room*) renfoncement *m*; (*for bed*) alcôve *f*; (*secret place*) recoin *m*; (*Pol etc: holiday*) vacances *fpl*; (*US Law: short break*) suspension *f* d'audience; (*Scol: esp US*) récréation *f*

recession [rɪˈsɛʃən] *n* (*Econ*) récession *f*

recessionista [rɪsɛʃəˈnɪstə] *n* recessionista *m/f*

recharge [riːˈtʃɑːdʒ] *vt* (*battery*) recharger

rechargeable [riːˈtʃɑːdʒəbl] *adj* rechargeable

recipe [ˈrɛsɪpɪ] *n* recette *f*

recipient [rɪˈsɪpɪənt] *n* (*of payment*) bénéficiaire *m/f*; (*of letter*) destinataire *m/f*

reciprocal [rɪˈsɪprəkl] *adj* réciproque

reciprocate [rɪˈsɪprəkeɪt] *vt* retourner, offrir en retour ▷ *vi* en faire autant

recital [rɪˈsaɪtl] *n* récital *m*

recite [rɪˈsaɪt] *vt* (*poem*) réciter; (*complaints etc*) énumérer

reckless [ˈrɛkləs] *adj* (*driver etc*) imprudent(e); (*spender etc*) insouciant(e)

recklessly [ˈrɛkləslɪ] *adv* imprudemment; avec insouciance

reckon [ˈrɛkən] *vt* (*count*) calculer, compter; (*consider*) considérer, estimer; (*think*): **I ~ (that)**

... je pense (que) ..., j'estime (que) ... ▷ *vi*: **he is somebody to be ~ed with** il ne faut pas le sous-estimer; **to ~ without sb/sth** ne pas tenir compte de qn/qch

▸ **reckon on** *vt fus* compter sur, s'attendre à

reckoning [ˈrɛknɪŋ] *n* compte *m*, calcul *m*; estimation *f*; **the day of ~** le jour du Jugement

reclaim [rɪˈkleɪm] *vt* (*land: from sea*) assécher; (: *from forest*) défricher; (: *with fertilizer*) amender; (*demand back*) réclamer (le remboursement *or* la restitution de); (*waste materials*) récupérer

reclamation [rɛkləˈmeɪʃən] *n* (*of land*) amendement *m*; assèchement *m*; défrichement *m*

recline [rɪˈklaɪn] *vi* être allongé(e) *or* étendu(e)

reclining [rɪˈklaɪnɪŋ] *adj* (*seat*) à dossier réglable

recluse [rɪˈkluːs] *n* reclus(e), ermite *m*

recognition [rɛkəgˈnɪʃən] *n* reconnaissance *f*; **in ~ of** en reconnaissance de; **to gain ~** être reconnu(e); **transformed beyond ~** méconnaissable

recognizable [ˈrɛkəgnaɪzəbl] *adj*: **~ (by)** reconnaissable (à)

recognize [ˈrɛkəgnaɪz] *vt*: **to ~ (by/as)** reconnaître (à/comme étant)

recoil [rɪˈkɔɪl] *vi* (*person*): **to ~ (from)** reculer (devant) ▷ *n* (*of gun*) recul *m*

recollect [rɛkəˈlɛkt] *vt* se rappeler, se souvenir de

recollection [rɛkəˈlɛkʃən] *n* souvenir *m*; **to the best of my ~** autant que je m'en souvienne

recommend [rɛkəˈmɛnd] *vt* recommander; **can you ~ a good restaurant?** pouvez-vous me conseiller un bon restaurant?; **she has a lot to ~ her** elle a beaucoup de choses en sa faveur

recommendation [rɛkəmɛnˈdeɪʃən] *n* recommandation *f*

recommended retail price [rɛkəˈmɛndɪd-] *n* (*Brit*) prix conseillé

recompense [ˈrɛkəmpɛns] *vt* récompenser; (*compensate*) dédommager ▷ *n* récompense *f*; dédommagement *m*

reconcilable [ˈrɛkənsaɪləbl] *adj* (*ideas*) conciliable

reconcile [ˈrɛkənsaɪl] *vt* (*two people*) réconcilier; (*two facts*) concilier, accorder; **to ~ o.s. to** se résigner à

reconciliation [rɛkənsɪlɪˈeɪʃən] *n* réconciliation *f*; conciliation *f*

recondite [rɪˈkɔndaɪt] *adj* abstrus(e), obscur(e)

recondition [riːkənˈdɪʃən] *vt* remettre à neuf; réviser entièrement

reconnaissance [rɪˈkɔnɪsns] *n* (*Mil*) reconnaissance *f*

reconnoitre, (*US*) **reconnoiter** [rɛkəˈnɔɪtəʳ] (*Mil*) *vt* reconnaître ▷ *vi* faire une reconnaissance

reconsider [riːkənˈsɪdəʳ] *vt* reconsidérer

reconstitute [riːˈkɔnstɪtjuːt] *vt* reconstituer

reconstruct [riːkənˈstrʌkt] *vt* (*building*) reconstruire; (*crime, system*) reconstituer

reconstruction [riːkənˈstrʌkʃən] *n* reconstruction *f*; reconstitution *f*

reconvene [riːkən'viːn] *vt* reconvoquer ▷ *vi* se réunir *or* s'assembler de nouveau

record *n* ['rɛkɔːd] rapport *m*, récit *m*; (*of meeting etc*) procès-verbal *m*; (*register*) registre *m*; (*file*) dossier *m*; (*Comput*) article *m*; (*also:* **police record**) casier *m* judiciaire; (*Mus: disc*) disque *m*; (*Sport*) record *m* ▷ *adj* record *inv* ▷ *vt* [ri'kɔːd] (*set down*) noter; (*relate*) rapporter; (*Mus: song etc*) enregistrer; **public ~s** archives *fpl*; **to keep a ~ of** noter; **to keep the ~ straight** (*fig*) mettre les choses au point; **he is on ~ as saying that ...** il a déclaré en public que ...; **Italy's excellent ~** les excellents résultats obtenus par l'Italie; **off the ~** *adj* officieux(-euse) ▷ *adv* officieusement; **in ~ time** dans un temps record

record card *n* (*in file*) fiche *f*

recorded delivery [ri'kɔːdɪd-] *n* (*Brit Post*): **to send sth ~** ≈ envoyer qch en recommandé

recorded delivery letter [ri'kɔːdɪd-] *n* (*Brit Post*) ≈ lettre recommandée

recorder [ri'kɔːdər] *n* (*Law*) avocat nommé à la fonction de juge; (*Mus*) flûte *f* à bec

record holder *n* (*Sport*) détenteur(-trice) du record

recording [ri'kɔːdɪŋ] *n* (*Mus*) enregistrement *m*

recording studio *n* studio *m* d'enregistrement

record library *n* discothèque *f*

record player *n* tourne-disque *m*

recount [ri'kaunt] *vt* raconter

re-count *n* ['riːkaunt] (*Pol: of votes*) nouveau décompte (des suffrages) ▷ *vt* [riː'kaunt] recompter

recoup [ri'kuːp] *vt*: **to ~ one's losses** récupérer ce qu'on a perdu, se refaire

recourse [ri'kɔːs] *n* recours *m*; expédient *m*; **to have ~ to** recourir à, avoir recours à

recover [ri'kʌvər] *vt* récupérer ▷ *vi* (*from illness*) se rétablir; (*from shock*) se remettre; (*country*) se redresser

re-cover [riː'kʌvər] *vt* (*chair etc*) recouvrir

recovery [ri'kʌvəri] *n* récupération *f*; rétablissement *m*; (*Econ*) redressement *m*

recreate [riːkri'eɪt] *vt* recréer

recreation [rɛkri'eɪʃən] *n* (*leisure*) récréation *f*, détente *f*

recreational [rɛkri'eɪʃənl] *adj* pour la détente, récréatif(-ive)

recreational drug [rɛkri'eɪʃnl-] *n* drogue récréative

recreational vehicle [rɛkri'eɪʃnl-] *n* (*US*) camping-car *m*

recrimination [rɪkrɪmɪ'neɪʃən] *n* récrimination *f*

recruit [ri'kruːt] *n* recrue *f* ▷ *vt* recruter

recruiting office [ri'kruːtɪŋ-] *n* bureau *m* de recrutement

recruitment [ri'kruːtmənt] *n* recrutement *m*

rectangle ['rɛktæŋgl] *n* rectangle *m*

rectangular [rɛk'tæŋgjulər] *adj* rectangulaire

rectify ['rɛktɪfaɪ] *vt* (*error*) rectifier, corriger; (*omission*) réparer

rector ['rɛktər] *n* (*Rel*) pasteur *m*; (*in Scottish*

universities) personnalité élue par les étudiants pour les représenter

rectory ['rɛktəri] *n* presbytère *m*

rectum ['rɛktəm] *n* (*Anat*) rectum *m*

recuperate [ri'kjuːpəreɪt] *vi* (*from illness*) se rétablir

recur [ri'kəːr] *vi* se reproduire; (*idea, opportunity*) se retrouver; (*symptoms*) réapparaître

recurrence [ri'kərns] *n* répétition *f*; réapparition *f*

recurrent [ri'kərnt] *adj* périodique, fréquent(e)

recurring [ri'kərɪŋ] *adj* (*problem*) périodique, fréquent(e); (*Math*) périodique

recyclable [riː'saɪkləbl] *adj* recyclable

recycle [riː'saɪkl] *vt, vi* recycler

recycling [riː'saɪklɪŋ] *n* recyclage *m*

red [rɛd] *n* rouge *m*; (*Pol: pej*) rouge *m/f* ▷ *adj* rouge; (*hair*) roux (rousse); **in the ~** (*account*) à découvert; (*business*) en déficit

red alert *n* alerte *f* rouge

red-blooded [rɛd'blʌdɪd] *adj* (*inf*) viril(e), vigoureux(-euse)

● REDBRICK UNIVERSITY

Une *redbrick university*, ainsi nommée à cause du matériau de construction répandu à l'époque (la brique), est une université britannique provinciale construite assez récemment, en particulier fin XIXe-début XXe siècle. Il y en a notamment une à Manchester, une à Liverpool et une à Bristol. Ce terme est utilisé pour établir une distinction avec les universités les plus anciennes et traditionnelles.

red carpet treatment *n* réception *f* en grande pompe

Red Cross *n* Croix-Rouge *f*

redcurrant ['rɛdkʌrənt] *n* groseille *f* (rouge)

redden ['rɛdn] *vt, vi* rougir

reddish ['rɛdɪʃ] *adj* rougeâtre; (*hair*) plutôt roux (rousse)

redecorate [riː'dɛkəreɪt] *vt* refaire à neuf, repeindre et retapisser

redeem [ri'diːm] *vt* (*debt*) rembourser; (*sth in pawn*) dégager; (*fig, also Rel*) racheter

redeemable [ri'diːməbl] *adj* rachetable; remboursable, amortissable

redeeming [ri'diːmɪŋ] *adj* (*feature*) qui sauve, qui rachète (le reste)

redefine [riːdɪ'faɪn] *vt* redéfinir

redemption [ri'dɛmʃən] *n* (*Rel*) rédemption *f*; **past** *or* **beyond ~** (*situation*) irrémédiable; (*place*) qui ne peut plus être sauvé(e); (*person*) irrécupérable

redeploy [riːdɪ'plɔɪ] *vt* (*Mil*) redéployer; (*staff, resources*) reconvertir

redeployment [riːdɪ'plɔɪmənt] *n* redéploiement *m*; reconversion *f*

redevelop [riːdɪ'vɛləp] *vt* rénover

redevelopment [riːdɪ'vɛləpmənt] *n*

rénovation f

red-haired [rɛdˈhɛəʳd] adj roux (rousse)

red-handed [rɛdˈhændɪd] adj: **to be caught ~** être pris(e) en flagrant délit or la main dans le sac

redhead [ˈrɛdhɛd] n roux (rousse)

red herring n (fig) diversion f, fausse piste

red-hot [rɛdˈhɔt] adj chauffé(e) au rouge, brûlant(e)

redirect [riːdaɪˈrɛkt] vt (mail) faire suivre

redistribute [riːdɪˈstrɪbjuːt] vt redistribuer

red-letter day [ˈrɛdlɛtə-] n grand jour, jour mémorable

red light n: **to go through a ~** (Aut) brûler un feu rouge

red-light district [ˈrɛdlaɪt-] n quartier mal famé

red meat n viande f rouge

redness [ˈrɛdnɪs] n rougeur f; (of hair) rousseur f

redo [riːˈduː] vt (irreg: like **do**) refaire

redolent [ˈrɛdələnt] adj: **~ of** qui sent; (fig) qui évoque

redouble [riːˈdʌbl] vt: **to ~ one's efforts** redoubler d'efforts

redraft [riːˈdrɑːft] vt remanier

redress [rɪˈdrɛs] n réparation f ▷ vt redresser; **to ~ the balance** rétablir l'équilibre

Red Sea n: **the ~** la mer Rouge

redskin [ˈrɛdskɪn] n Peau-Rouge m/f

red tape n (fig) paperasserie (administrative)

reduce [rɪˈdjuːs] vt réduire; (lower) abaisser; "**~ speed now**" (Aut) "ralentir"; **to ~ sth by/to** réduire qch de/à; **to ~ sb to tears** faire pleurer qn

reduced [rɪˈdjuːst] adj réduit(e); "**greatly ~ prices**" "gros rabais"; **at a ~ price** (goods) au rabais; (ticket etc) à prix réduit

reduction [rɪˈdʌkʃən] n réduction f; (of price) baisse f; (discount) rabais m; réduction; **is there a ~ for children/students?** y a-t-il une réduction pour les enfants/les étudiants?

redundancy [rɪˈdʌndənsɪ] n (Brit) licenciement m, mise f au chômage; **compulsory ~** licenciement; **voluntary ~** départ m volontaire

redundancy payment n (Brit) indemnité f de licenciement

redundant [rɪˈdʌndnt] adj (Brit: worker) licencié(e), mis(e) au chômage; (detail, object) superflu(e); **to be made ~** (worker) être licencié, être mis au chômage

reed [riːd] n (Bot) roseau m; (Mus: of clarinet etc) anche f

re-educate [riːˈɛdjukeɪt] vt rééduquer

reedy [ˈriːdɪ] adj (voice, instrument) ténu(e)

reef [riːf] n (at sea) récif m, écueil m

reek [riːk] vi: **to ~ (of)** puer, empester

reel [riːl] n bobine f; (Tech) dévidoir m; (Fishing) moulinet m; (Cine) bande f; (dance) quadrille écossais ▷ vt (Tech) bobiner; (also: **reel up**) enrouler ▷ vi (sway) chanceler; **my head is ~ing** j'ai la tête qui tourne

▸ **reel in** vt (fish, line) ramener

▸ **reel off** vt (say) énumérer, débiter

re-election [riːɪˈlɛkʃən] n réélection f

re-enter [riːˈɛntəʳ] vt (also Space) rentrer dans

re-entry [riːˈɛntrɪ] n (also Space) rentrée f

re-export vt [ˈriːˈɪksˈpɔːt] réexporter ▷ n [riːˈɛkspɔːt] marchandise réexportée; (act) réexportation f

ref [rɛf] n abbr (inf: = referee) arbitre m

ref. abbr (Comm: = with reference to) réf

refectory [rɪˈfɛktərɪ] n réfectoire m

refer [rɪˈfəːʳ] vt: **to ~ sth to** (dispute, decision) soumettre qch à; **to ~ sb to** (inquirer, patient) adresser qn à; (reader: to text) renvoyer qn à ▷ vi: **to ~ to** (allude to) parler de, faire allusion à; (consult) se reporter à; (apply to) s'appliquer à; **~ring to your letter** (Comm) en réponse à votre lettre; **he ~red me to the manager** il m'a dit de m'adresser au directeur

referee [rɛfəˈriː] n arbitre m; (Tennis) juge-arbitre m; (Brit: for job application) répondant(e) ▷ vt arbitrer

reference [ˈrɛfrəns] n référence f, renvoi m; (mention) allusion f, mention f; (for job application: letter) références; lettre f de recommandation; (: person) répondant(e); **with ~ to** en ce qui concerne; (Comm: in letter) me référant à; "**please quote this ~**" (Comm) "prière de rappeler cette référence"

reference book n ouvrage m de référence

reference library n bibliothèque f d'ouvrages à consulter

reference number n (Comm) numéro m de référence

referendum (pl **referenda**) [rɛfəˈrɛndəm, -də] n référendum m

referral [rɪˈfəːrəl] n soumission f; **she got a ~ to a specialist** elle a été adressée à un spécialiste

refill vt [riːˈfɪl] remplir à nouveau; (pen, lighter etc) recharger ▷ n [ˈriːfɪl] (for pen etc) recharge f

refine [rɪˈfaɪn] vt (sugar, oil) raffiner; (taste) affiner; (idea, theory) peaufiner

refined [rɪˈfaɪnd] adj (person, taste) raffiné(e)

refinement [rɪˈfaɪnmənt] n (of person) raffinement m

refinery [rɪˈfaɪnərɪ] n raffinerie f

refit (Naut) n [ˈriːfɪt] remise f en état ▷ vt [riːˈfɪt] remettre en état

reflate [riːˈfleɪt] vt (economy) relancer

reflation [riːˈfleɪʃən] n relance f

reflationary [riːˈfleɪʃənrɪ] adj de relance

reflect [rɪˈflɛkt] vt (light, image) réfléchir, refléter; (fig) refléter ▷ vi (think) réfléchir, méditer; **it ~s badly on him** cela le discrédite; **it ~s well on him** c'est tout à son honneur

reflection [rɪˈflɛkʃən] n réflexion f; (image) reflet m; (criticism): **~ on** critique f de; atteinte f à; **on ~** réflexion faite

reflector [rɪˈflɛktəʳ] n (also Aut) réflecteur m

reflex [ˈriːflɛks] adj, n réflexe (m)

reflexive [rɪˈflɛksɪv] adj (Ling) réfléchi(e)

reform [rɪˈfɔːm] n réforme f ▷ vt réformer

reformat [riːˈfɔːmæt] vt (Comput) reformater

Reformation [rɛfə'meɪʃən] *n*: **the ~** la Réforme
reformatory [rɪ'fɔːmətərɪ] *n* (US) centre *m* d'éducation surveillée
reformed [rɪ'fɔːmd] *adj* amendé(e), assagi(e)
reformer [rɪ'fɔːmə^r] *n* réformateur(-trice)
refrain [rɪ'freɪn] *vi*: **to ~ from doing** s'abstenir de faire ▷ *n* refrain *m*
refresh [rɪ'frɛʃ] *vt* rafraîchir; (*subj: food, sleep etc*) redonner des forces à
refresher course [rɪ'frɛʃə-] *n* (Brit) cours *m* de recyclage
refreshing [rɪ'frɛʃɪŋ] *adj* (*drink*) rafraîchissant(e); (*sleep*) réparateur(-trice); (*fact, idea etc*) qui réjouit par son originalité *or* sa rareté
refreshment [rɪ'frɛʃmənt] *n*: **for some ~** (*eating*) pour se restaurer *or* sustenter; **in need of ~** (*resting etc*) ayant besoin de refaire ses forces
refreshments [rɪ'frɛʃmənts] *npl* rafraîchissements *mpl*
refrigeration [rɪfrɪdʒə'reɪʃən] *n* réfrigération *f*
refrigerator [rɪ'frɪdʒəreɪtə^r] *n* réfrigérateur *m*, frigidaire *m*
refuel [riː'fjuəl] *vt* ravitailler en carburant ▷ *vi* se ravitailler en carburant
refuge ['rɛfjuːdʒ] *n* refuge *m*; **to take ~ in** se réfugier dans
refugee [rɛfju'dʒiː] *n* réfugié(e)
refugee camp *n* camp *m* de réfugiés
refund *n* ['riːfʌnd] remboursement *m* ▷ *vt* [rɪ'fʌnd] rembourser
refurbish [riː'fəːbɪʃ] *vt* remettre à neuf
refurnish [riː'fəːnɪʃ] *vt* remeubler
refusal [rɪ'fjuːzəl] *n* refus *m*; **to have first ~ on sth** avoir droit de préemption sur qch
refuse¹ ['rɛfjuːs] *n* ordures *fpl*, détritus *mpl*
refuse² [rɪ'fjuːz] *vt*, *vi* refuser; **to ~ to do sth** refuser de faire qch
refuse collection *n* ramassage *m* d'ordures
refuse disposal *n* élimination *f* des ordures
refusenik [rɪ'fjuːznɪk] *n* refuznik *m/f*
refute [rɪ'fjuːt] *vt* réfuter
regain [rɪ'geɪn] *vt* (*lost ground*) regagner; (*strength*) retrouver
regal ['riːgl] *adj* royal(e)
regale [rɪ'geɪl] *vt*: **to ~ sb with sth** régaler qn de qch
regalia [rɪ'geɪlɪə] *n* insignes *mpl* de la royauté
regard [rɪ'gɑːd] *n* respect *m*, estime *f*, considération *f* ▷ *vt* considérer; **to give one's ~s to** faire ses amitiés à; **"with kindest ~s"** "bien amicalement"; **as ~s, with ~ to** en ce qui concerne
regarding [rɪ'gɑːdɪŋ] *prep* en ce qui concerne
regardless [rɪ'gɑːdlɪs] *adv* quand même; **~ of** sans se soucier de
regatta [rɪ'gætə] *n* régate *f*
regency ['riːdʒənsɪ] *n* régence *f*
regenerate [rɪ'dʒɛnəreɪt] *vt* régénérer ▷ *vi* se régénérer
regent ['riːdʒənt] *n* régent(e)
reggae ['rɛgeɪ] *n* reggae *m*
régime [reɪ'ʒiːm] *n* régime *m*

regiment *n* ['rɛdʒɪmənt] *n* régiment *m* ▷ *vt* ['rɛdʒɪmɛnt] imposer une discipline trop stricte à
regimental [rɛdʒɪ'mɛntl] *adj* d'un régiment
regimentation [rɛdʒɪmɛn'teɪʃən] *n* réglementation excessive
region ['riːdʒən] *n* région *f*; **in the ~ of** (*fig*) aux alentours de
regional ['riːdʒənl] *adj* régional(e)
regional development *n* aménagement *m* du territoire
register ['rɛdʒɪstə^r] *n* registre *m*; (*also*: **electoral register**) liste électorale ▷ *vt* enregistrer, inscrire; (*birth*) déclarer; (*vehicle*) immatriculer; (*luggage*) enregistrer; (*letter*) envoyer en recommandé; (*subj: instrument*) marquer ▷ *vi* s'inscrire; (*at hotel*) signer le registre; (*make impression*) être (bien) compris(e); **to ~ for a course** s'inscrire à un cours; **to ~ a protest** protester
registered ['rɛdʒɪstəd] *adj* (*design*) déposé(e); (*Brit: letter*) recommandé(e); (*student, voter*) inscrit(e)
registered company *n* société immatriculée
registered nurse *n* (US) infirmier(-ière) diplômé(e) d'État
registered office *n* siège social
registered trademark *n* marque déposée
registrar ['rɛdʒɪstrɑː^r] *n* officier *m* de l'état civil; secrétaire *m/f* général
registration [rɛdʒɪs'treɪʃən] *n* (*act*) enregistrement *m*; (*of student*) inscription *f*; (*Brit Aut: also*: **registration number**) numéro *m* d'immatriculation
registry ['rɛdʒɪstrɪ] *n* bureau *m* de l'enregistrement
registry office ['rɛdʒɪstrɪ-] *n* (Brit) bureau *m* de l'état civil; **to get married in a ~** ≈ se marier à la mairie
regret [rɪ'grɛt] *n* regret *m* ▷ *vt* regretter; **to ~ that** regretter que + *sub*; **we ~ to inform you that ...** nous sommes au regret de vous informer que ...
regretfully [rɪ'grɛtfəlɪ] *adv* à *or* avec regret
regrettable [rɪ'grɛtəbl] *adj* regrettable, fâcheux(-euse)
regrettably [rɪ'grɛtəblɪ] *adv* (*drunk, late*) fâcheusement; **~, he ...** malheureusement, il ...
regroup [riː'gruːp] *vt* regrouper ▷ *vi* se regrouper
regt *abbr* = **regiment**
regular ['rɛgjulə^r] *adj* régulier(-ière); (*usual*) habituel(le), normal(e); (*listener, reader*) fidèle; (*soldier*) de métier; (*Comm: size*) ordinaire ▷ *n* (*client etc*) habitué(e)
regularity [rɛgju'lærɪtɪ] *n* régularité *f*
regularly ['rɛgjuləlɪ] *adv* régulièrement
regulate ['rɛgjuleɪt] *vt* régler
regulation [rɛgju'leɪʃən] *n* (*rule*) règlement *m*; (*adjustment*) réglage *m* ▷ *cpd* réglementaire
rehabilitate [riːə'bɪlɪteɪt] *vt* (*criminal*) réinsérer; (*drug addict*) désintoxiquer; (*invalid*) rééduquer

r

rehabilitation ['ri:əbɪlɪ'teɪʃən] *n* (*of offender*) réhabilitation *f*; (*of addict*) réadaptation *f*; (*of disabled*) rééducation *f*, réadaptation *f*
rehash [ri:'hæʃ] *vt* (*inf*) remanier
rehearsal [rɪ'hə:səl] *n* répétition *f*; **dress ~** (*répétition*) générale *f*
rehearse [rɪ'hə:s] *vt* répéter
rehouse [ri:'hauz] *vt* reloger
reign [reɪn] *n* règne *m* ▷ *vi* régner
reigning ['reɪnɪŋ] *adj* (*monarch*) régnant(e); (*champion*) actuel(le)
reimburse [ri:ɪm'bə:s] *vt* rembourser
rein [reɪn] *n* (*for horse*) rêne *f*; **to give sb free ~** (*fig*) donner carte blanche à qn
reincarnation [ri:ɪnkɑ:'neɪʃən] *n* réincarnation *f*
reindeer ['reɪndɪə'] *n* (*pl inv*) renne *m*
reinforce [ri:ɪn'fɔ:s] *vt* renforcer
reinforced concrete [ri:ɪn'fɔst-] *n* béton armé
reinforcement [ri:ɪn'fɔ:smənt] *n* (*action*) renforcement *m*
reinforcements [ri:ɪn'fɔ:smənts] *npl* (*Mil*) renfort(s) *m(pl)*
reinstate [ri:ɪn'steɪt] *vt* rétablir, réintégrer
reinstatement [ri:ɪn'steɪtmənt] *n* réintégration *f*
reissue [ri:'ɪʃju:] *vt* (*book*) rééditer; (*film*) ressortir
reiterate [ri:'ɪtəreɪt] *vt* réitérer, répéter
reject *n* ['ri:dʒɛkt] (*Comm*) article *m* de rebut ▷ *vt* [rɪ'dʒɛkt] refuser; (*Comm: goods*) mettre au rebut; (*idea*) rejeter
rejection [rɪ'dʒɛkʃən] *n* rejet *m*, refus *m*
rejoice [rɪ'dʒɔɪs] *vi*: **to ~ (at** or **over)** se réjouir (de)
rejoinder [rɪ'dʒɔɪndə'] *n* (*retort*) réplique *f*
rejuvenate [rɪ'dʒu:vəneɪt] *vt* rajeunir
rekindle [ri:'kɪndl] *vt* rallumer; (*fig*) raviver
relapse [rɪ'læps] *n* (*Med*) rechute *f*
relate [rɪ'leɪt] *vt* (*tell*) raconter; (*connect*) établir un rapport entre ▷ *vi*: **to ~ to** (*connect*) se rapporter à; **to ~ to sb** (*interact*) entretenir des rapports avec qn
related [rɪ'leɪtɪd] *adj* apparenté(e); **~ to** (*subject*) lié(e) à
relating to [rɪ'leɪtɪŋ-] *prep* concernant
relation [rɪ'leɪʃən] *n* (*person*) parent(e); (*link*) rapport *m*, lien *m*; **relations** *npl* (*relatives*) famille *f*; **diplomatic/international ~s** relations diplomatiques/internationales; **in ~ to** en ce qui concerne; par rapport à; **to bear no ~ to** être sans rapport avec
relationship [rɪ'leɪʃənʃɪp] *n* rapport *m*, lien *m*; (*personal ties*) relations *fpl*, rapports; (*also:* **family relationship**) lien de parenté; (*affair*) liaison *f*; **they have a good ~** ils s'entendent bien
relative ['rɛlətɪv] *n* parent(e) ▷ *adj* relatif(-ive); (*respective*) respectif(-ive); **all her ~s** toute sa famille
relatively ['rɛlətɪvlɪ] *adv* relativement
relax [rɪ'læks] *vi* (*muscle*) se relâcher; (*person: unwind*) se détendre; (*calm down*) se calmer ▷ *vt* relâcher; (*mind, person*) détendre

relaxation [ri:læk'seɪʃən] *n* relâchement *m*; (*of mind*) détente *f*; (*recreation*) détente, délassement *m*; (*entertainment*) distraction *f*
relaxed [rɪ'lækst] *adj* relâché(e); détendu(e)
relaxing [rɪ'læksɪŋ] *adj* délassant(e)
relay ['ri:leɪ] *n* (*Sport*) course *f* de relais ▷ *vt* (*message*) retransmettre, relayer
release [rɪ'li:s] *n* (*from prison, obligation*) libération *f*; (*of gas etc*) émission *f*; (*of film etc*) sortie *f*; (*new recording*) disque *m*; (*device*) déclencheur *m* ▷ *vt* (*prisoner*) libérer; (*book, film*) sortir; (*report, news*) rendre public, publier; (*gas etc*) émettre, dégager; (*free: from wreckage etc*) dégager; (*Tech: catch, spring etc*) déclencher; (*let go: person, animal*) relâcher; (: *hand, object*) lâcher; (: *grip, brake*) desserrer; **to ~ one's grip** or **hold** lâcher prise; **to ~ the clutch** (*Aut*) débrayer
relegate ['rɛləgeɪt] *vt* reléguer; (*Brit Sport*): **to be ~d** descendre dans une division inférieure
relent [rɪ'lɛnt] *vi* se laisser fléchir
relentless [rɪ'lɛntlɪs] *adj* implacable; (*non-stop*) continuel(le)
relevance ['rɛləvəns] *n* pertinence *f*; **~ of sth to sth** rapport *m* entre qch et qch
relevant ['rɛləvənt] *adj* (*question*) pertinent(e); (*corresponding*) approprié(e); (*fact*) significatif(-ive); (*information*) utile; **~ to** ayant rapport à, approprié à
reliability [rɪlaɪə'bɪlɪtɪ] *n* sérieux *m*; fiabilité *f*
reliable [rɪ'laɪəbl] *adj* (*person, firm*) sérieux(-euse), fiable; (*method, machine*) fiable; (*news, information*) sûr(e)
reliably [rɪ'laɪəblɪ] *adv*: **to be ~ informed** savoir de source sûre
reliance [rɪ'laɪəns] *n*: **~ (on)** (*trust*) confiance *f* (en); (*dependence*) besoin *m* (de), dépendance *f* (de)
reliant [rɪ'laɪənt] *adj*: **to be ~ on sth/sb** dépendre de qch/qn
relic ['rɛlɪk] *n* (*Rel*) relique *f*; (*of the past*) vestige *m*
relief [rɪ'li:f] *n* (*from pain, anxiety*) soulagement *m*; (*help, supplies*) secours *m(pl)*; (*of guard*) relève *f*; (*Art, Geo*) relief *m*; **by way of light ~** pour faire diversion
relief map *n* carte *f* en relief
relief road *n* (*Brit*) route *f* de délestage
relieve [rɪ'li:v] *vt* (*pain, patient*) soulager; (*fear, worry*) dissiper; (*bring help*) secourir; (*take over from: gen*) relayer; (: *guard*) relever; **to ~ sb of sth** débarrasser qn de qch; **to ~ sb of his command** (*Mil*) relever qn de ses fonctions; **to ~ o.s.** (*euphemism*) se soulager, faire ses besoins
relieved [rɪ'li:vd] *adj* soulagé(e); **to be ~ that ...** être soulagé que ...; **I'm ~ to hear it** je suis soulagé de l'entendre
religion [rɪ'lɪdʒən] *n* religion *f*
religious [rɪ'lɪdʒəs] *adj* religieux(-euse); (*book*) de piété
religious education *n* instruction religieuse
relinquish [rɪ'lɪŋkwɪʃ] *vt* abandonner; (*plan, habit*) renoncer à
relish ['rɛlɪʃ] *n* (*Culin*) condiment *m*; (*enjoyment*)

délectation f ▷ vt (food etc) savourer; **to ~ doing** se délecter à faire

relive [ri:'lɪv] vt revivre

reload [ri:'ləʊd] vt recharger

relocate [ri:ləʊ'keɪt] vt (business) transférer ▷ vi se transférer, s'installer or s'établir ailleurs; **to ~ in** (déménager et) s'installer or s'établir à, se transférer à

reluctance [rɪ'lʌktəns] n répugnance f

reluctant [rɪ'lʌktənt] adj peu disposé(e), qui hésite; **to be ~ to do sth** hésiter à faire qch

reluctantly [rɪ'lʌktəntlɪ] adv à contrecœur, sans enthousiasme

rely on [rɪ'laɪ-] vt fus (be dependent on) dépendre de; (trust) compter sur

remain [rɪ'meɪn] vi rester; **to ~ silent** garder le silence; **I ~, yours faithfully** (Brit: in letters) je vous prie d'agréer, Monsieur etc l'assurance de mes sentiments distingués

remainder [rɪ'meɪndər] n reste m; (Comm) fin f de série

remaining [rɪ'meɪnɪŋ] adj qui reste

remains [rɪ'meɪnz] npl restes mpl

remake ['ri:meɪk] n (Cine) remake m

remand [rɪ'mɑːnd] n: **on ~** en détention préventive ▷ vt: **to be ~ed in custody** être placé(e) en détention préventive

remand home n (Brit) centre m d'éducation surveillée

remark [rɪ'mɑːk] n remarque f, observation f ▷ vt (faire) remarquer, dire; (notice) remarquer; **to ~ on sth** faire une or des remarque(s) sur qch

remarkable [rɪ'mɑːkəbl] adj remarquable

remarkably [rɪ'mɑːkəblɪ] adv remarquablement

remarry [ri:'mærɪ] vi se remarier

remedial [rɪ'miːdɪəl] adj (tuition, classes) de rattrapage

remedy ['rɛmədɪ] n: **~ (for)** remède m (contre or à) ▷ vt remédier à

remember [rɪ'mɛmbər] vt se rappeler, se souvenir de; (send greetings): **~ me to him** saluez-le de ma part; **I ~ seeing it, I ~ having seen it** je me rappelle l'avoir vu or que je l'ai vu; **she ~ed to do it** elle a pensé à le faire; **~ me to your wife** rappelez-moi au bon souvenir de votre femme

remembrance [rɪ'mɛmbrəns] n souvenir m; mémoire f

Remembrance Day [rɪ'mɛmbrəns-] n (Brit) ≈ (le jour de) l'Armistice m, ≈ le 11 novembre; voir article

REMEMBRANCE DAY

Remembrance Day ou Remembrance Sunday est le dimanche le plus proche du 11 novembre, jour où la Première Guerre mondiale a officiellement pris fin. Il rend hommage aux victimes des deux guerres mondiales. À cette occasion, on observe deux minutes de silence à 11h, heure de la signature de l'armistice avec l'Allemagne en 1918; certaines membres de la famille royale et du gouvernement déposent des gerbes de coquelicots au cénotaphe de Whitehall, et des couronnes sont placées sur les monuments aux morts dans toute la Grande-Bretagne; par ailleurs, les gens portent des coquelicots artificiels fabriqués et vendus par des membres de la légion britannique blessés au combat, au profit des blessés de guerre et de leur famille.

remind [rɪ'maɪnd] vt: **to ~ sb of sth** rappeler qch à qn; **to ~ sb to do** faire penser à qn à faire, rappeler à qn qu'il doit faire; **that ~s me!** j'y pense!

reminder [rɪ'maɪndər] n (Comm: letter) rappel m; (note etc) pense-bête m; (souvenir) souvenir m

reminisce [rɛmɪ'nɪs] vi: **to ~ (about)** évoquer ses souvenirs (de)

reminiscences [rɛmɪ'nɪsnsɪz] npl réminiscences fpl, souvenirs mpl

reminiscent [rɛmɪ'nɪsnt] adj: **~ of** qui rappelle, qui fait penser à

remiss [rɪ'mɪs] adj négligent(e); **it was ~ of me** c'était une négligence de ma part

remission [rɪ'mɪʃən] n rémission f; (of debt, sentence) remise f; (of fee) exemption f

remit [rɪ'mɪt] vt (send: money) envoyer

remittance [rɪ'mɪtns] n envoi m, paiement m

remnant [rɛmnənt] n reste m, restant m; (of cloth) coupon m; **remnants** npl (Comm) fins fpl de série

remonstrate ['rɛmənstreɪt] vi: **to ~ (with sb about sth)** se plaindre (à qn de qch)

remorse [rɪ'mɔːs] n remords m

remorseful [rɪ'mɔːsful] adj plein(e) de remords

remorseless [rɪ'mɔːslɪs] adj (fig) impitoyable

remote [rɪ'məʊt] adj éloigné(e), lointain(e); (person) distant(e); (possibility) vague; **there is a ~ possibility that ...** il est tout juste possible que ...

remote control n télécommande f

remote-controlled [rɪ'məʊtkən'trəʊld] adj téléguidé(e)

remotely [rɪ'məʊtlɪ] adv au loin; (slightly) très vaguement

remould ['ri:məʊld] n (Brit: tyre) pneu m rechapé

removable [rɪ'muːvəbl] adj (detachable) amovible

removal [rɪ'muːvəl] n (taking away) enlèvement m; suppression f; (Brit: from house) déménagement m; (from office: dismissal) renvoi m; (of stain) nettoyage m; (Med) ablation f

removal man (irreg) n (Brit) déménageur m

removal van n (Brit) camion m de déménagement

remove [rɪ'muːv] vt enlever, retirer; (employee) renvoyer; (stain) faire partir; (abuse) supprimer; (doubt) chasser; **first cousin once ~d** cousin(e) au deuxième degré

remover [rɪ'muːvər] n (for paint) décapant m; (for

r

varnish) dissolvant *m*; **make-up ~** démaquillant *m*

remunerate [rɪ'mjuːnəreɪt] *vt* rémunérer

remuneration [rɪmjuːnə'reɪʃən] *n* rémunération *f*

Renaissance [rɪ'neɪsãns] *n*: **the ~** la Renaissance

rename [riː'neɪm] *vt* rebaptiser

rend (*pt, pp* **rent**) [rɛnd, rɛnt] *vt* déchirer

render ['rɛndər] *vt* rendre; (*Culin: fat*) clarifier

rendering ['rɛndərɪŋ] *n* (*Mus etc*) interprétation *f*

rendezvous ['rɔndɪvuː] *n* rendez-vous *m inv* ▷ *vi* opérer une jonction, se rejoindre; **to ~ with sb** rejoindre qn

renegade ['rɛnɪgeɪd] *n* renégat(e)

renew [rɪ'njuː] *vt* renouveler; (*negotiations*) reprendre; (*acquaintance*) renouer

renewable [rɪ'njuːəbl] *adj* renouvelable; **~ energy, ~s** énergies renouvelables

renewal [rɪ'njuːəl] *n* renouvellement *m*; reprise *f*

renounce [rɪ'nauns] *vt* renoncer à; (*disown*) renier

renovate ['rɛnəveɪt] *vt* rénover; (*work of art*) restaurer

renovation [rɛnə'veɪʃən] *n* rénovation *f*; restauration *f*

renown [rɪ'naun] *n* renommée *f*

renowned [rɪ'naund] *adj* renommé(e)

rent [rɛnt] *pt, pp of* **rend** ▷ *n* loyer *m* ▷ *vt* louer; (*car, TV*) louer, prendre en location; (*also*: **rent out**: *car, TV*) louer, donner en location

rental ['rɛntl] *n* (*for television, car*) (prix *m* de) location *f*

rent boy *n* (*Brit inf*) jeune prostitué

renunciation [rɪnʌnsɪ'eɪʃən] *n* renonciation *f*; (*self-denial*) renoncement *m*

reopen [riː'əupən] *vt* rouvrir

reorder [riː'ɔːdər] *vt* commander de nouveau; (*rearrange*) réorganiser

reorganize [riː'ɔːgənaɪz] *vt* réorganiser

rep [rɛp] *n abbr* (*Comm*) = **representative**; (*Theat*) = **repertory**

Rep. *abbr* (*US Pol*) = **representative**; **republican**

repair [rɪ'pɛər] *n* réparation *f* ▷ *vt* réparer; **in good/bad ~** en bon/mauvais état; **under ~** en réparation; **where can I get this ~ed?** où est-ce que je peux faire réparer ceci?

repair kit *n* trousse *f* de réparations

repair man (*irreg*) *n* réparateur *m*

repair shop *n* (*Aut etc*) atelier *m* de réparations

repartee [rɛpɑː'tiː] *n* repartie *f*

repast [rɪ'pɑːst] *n* (*formal*) repas *m*

repatriate [riː'pætrɪeɪt] *vt* rapatrier

repay [riː'peɪ] *vt* (*irreg: like* **pay**); (*money, creditor*) rembourser; (*sb's efforts*) récompenser

repayment [riː'peɪmənt] *n* remboursement *m*; récompense *f*

repeal [rɪ'piːl] *n* (*of law*) abrogation *f*; (*of sentence*) annulation *f* ▷ *vt* abroger; annuler

repeat [rɪ'piːt] *n* (*Radio, TV*) reprise *f* ▷ *vt* répéter; (*pattern*) reproduire; (*promise, attack, also Comm*:

order) renouveler; (*Scol: a class*) redoubler ▷ *vi* répéter; **can you ~ that, please?** pouvez-vous répéter, s'il vous plaît?

repeatedly [rɪ'piːtɪdlɪ] *adv* souvent, à plusieurs reprises

repeat prescription *n* (*Brit*): **I'd like a ~** je voudrais renouveler mon ordonnance

repel [rɪ'pɛl] *vt* repousser

repellent [rɪ'pɛlənt] *adj* repoussant(e) ▷ *n*: **insect ~** insectifuge *m*; **moth ~** produit *m* antimite(s)

repent [rɪ'pɛnt] *vi*: **to ~ (of)** se repentir (de)

repentance [rɪ'pɛntəns] *n* repentir *m*

repercussions [riːpə'kʌʃənz] *npl* répercussions *fpl*

repertoire ['rɛpətwaːr] *n* répertoire *m*

repertory ['rɛpətərɪ] *n* (*also*: **repertory theatre**) théâtre *m* de répertoire

repertory company *n* troupe théâtrale permanente

repetition [rɛpɪ'tɪʃən] *n* répétition *f*

repetitious [rɛpɪ'tɪʃəs] *adj* (*speech*) plein(e) de redites

repetitive [rɪ'pɛtɪtɪv] *adj* (*movement, work*) répétitif(-ive); (*speech*) plein(e) de redites

replace [rɪ'pleɪs] *vt* (*put back*) remettre, replacer; (*take the place of*) remplacer; (*Tel*): **"~ the receiver"** "raccrochez"

replacement [rɪ'pleɪsmənt] *n* replacement *m*; (*substitution*) remplacement *m*; (*person*) remplaçant(e)

replacement part *n* pièce *f* de rechange

replay ['riːpleɪ] *n* (*of match*) match rejoué; (*of tape, film*) répétition *f*

replenish [rɪ'plɛnɪʃ] *vt* (*glass*) remplir (de nouveau); (*stock etc*) réapprovisionner

replete [rɪ'pliːt] *adj* rempli(e); (*well-fed*): **~ (with)** rassasié(e) (de)

replica ['rɛplɪkə] *n* réplique *f*, copie exacte

reply [rɪ'plaɪ] *n* réponse *f* ▷ *vi* répondre; **in ~ (to)** en réponse (à); **there's no ~** (*Tel*) ça ne répond pas

reply coupon *n* coupon-réponse *m*

report [rɪ'pɔːt] *n* rapport *m*; (*Press etc*) reportage *m*; (*Brit: also*: **school report**) bulletin *m* (scolaire); (*of gun*) détonation *f* ▷ *vt* rapporter, faire un compte rendu de; (*Press etc*) faire un reportage sur; (*notify: accident*) signaler; (: *culprit*) dénoncer ▷ *vi* (*make a report*) faire un rapport; (*for newspaper*) faire un reportage (sur); **I'd like to ~ a theft** je voudrais signaler un vol; (*present o.s.*): **to ~ (to sb)** se présenter (chez qn); **it is ~ed that** on dit *or* annonce que; **it is ~ed from Berlin that** on nous apprend de Berlin que

report card *n* (*US, Scottish*) bulletin *m* (scolaire)

reportedly [rɪ'pɔːtɪdlɪ] *adv*: **she is ~ living in Spain** elle habiterait en Espagne; **he ~ told them to ...** il leur aurait dit de ...

reported speech *n* (*Ling*) discours indirect

reporter [rɪ'pɔːtər] *n* reporter *m*

repose [rɪ'pəuz] *n*: **in ~** en *or* au repos

repossess [riːpə'zɛs] *vt* saisir

repossession order [ri:pə'zɛʃən-] n ordre m de reprise de possession

reprehensible [rɛprɪ'hɛnsɪbl] adj répréhensible

represent [rɛprɪ'zɛnt] vt représenter; (view, belief) présenter, expliquer; (describe): **to ~ sth as** présenter or décrire qch comme; **to ~ to sb that** expliquer à qn que

representation [rɛprɪzɛn'teɪʃən] n représentation f; **representations** npl (protest) démarche f

representative [rɛprɪ'zɛntətɪv] n représentant(e); (Comm) représentant(e) (de commerce); (US Pol) député m ▷ adj représentatif(-ive), caractéristique

repress [rɪ'prɛs] vt réprimer

repression [rɪ'prɛʃən] n répression f

repressive [rɪ'prɛsɪv] adj répressif(-ive)

reprieve [rɪ'pri:v] n (Law) grâce f; (fig) sursis m, délai m ▷ vt gracier; accorder un sursis or un délai à

reprimand ['rɛprɪmɑ:nd] n réprimande f ▷ vt réprimander

reprint n ['ri:prɪnt] réimpression f ▷ vt [ri:'prɪnt] réimprimer

reprisal [rɪ'praɪzl] n représailles fpl; **to take ~s** user de représailles

reproach [rɪ'prəʊtʃ] n reproche m ▷ vt: **to ~ sb with sth** reprocher qch à qn; **beyond ~** irréprochable

reproachful [rɪ'prəʊtʃful] adj de reproche

reproduce [ri:prə'dju:s] vt reproduire ▷ vi se reproduire

reproduction [ri:prə'dʌkʃən] n reproduction f

reproductive [ri:prə'dʌktɪv] adj reproducteur(-trice)

reproof [rɪ'pru:f] n reproche m

reprove [rɪ'pru:v] vt (action) réprouver; (person): **to ~ (for)** blâmer (de)

reproving [rɪ'pru:vɪŋ] adj réprobateur(-trice)

reptile ['rɛptaɪl] n reptile m

Repub. abbr (US Pol) = **republican**

republic [rɪ'pʌblɪk] n république f

republican [rɪ'pʌblɪkən] adj, n républicain(e)

repudiate [rɪ'pju:dɪeɪt] vt (ally, behaviour) désavouer; (accusation) rejeter; (wife) répudier

repugnant [rɪ'pʌgnənt] adj répugnant(e)

repulse [rɪ'pʌls] vt repousser

repulsion [rɪ'pʌlʃən] n répulsion f

repulsive [rɪ'pʌlsɪv] adj repoussant(e), répulsif(-ive)

reputable ['rɛpjutəbl] adj de bonne réputation; (occupation) honorable

reputation [rɛpju'teɪʃən] n réputation f; **to have a ~ for** être réputé(e) pour; **he has a ~ for being awkward** il a la réputation de ne pas être commode

repute [rɪ'pju:t] n (bonne) réputation

reputed [rɪ'pju:tɪd] adj réputé(e); **he is ~ to be rich/intelligent** etc on dit qu'il est riche/ intelligent etc

reputedly [rɪ'pju:tɪdlɪ] adv d'après ce qu'on dit

request [rɪ'kwɛst] n demande f; (formal) requête f ▷ vt: **to ~ (of or from sb)** demander (à qn); **at the ~ of** à la demande de

request stop n (Brit: for bus) arrêt facultatif

requiem ['rɛkwɪəm] n requiem m

require [rɪ'kwaɪəʳ] vt (need: subj: person) avoir besoin de; (: thing, situation) nécessiter, demander; (want) exiger; (order): **to ~ sb to do sth/sth of sb** exiger que qn fasse qch/qch de qn; **if ~d** s'il le faut; **what qualifications are ~d?** quelles sont les qualifications requises?; **~d by law** requis par la loi

required [rɪ'kwaɪəd] adj requis(e), voulu(e)

requirement [rɪ'kwaɪəmənt] n (need) exigence f; besoin m; (condition) condition f (requise)

requisite ['rɛkwɪzɪt] n chose f nécessaire ▷ adj requis(e), nécessaire; **toilet ~s** accessoires mpl de toilette

requisition [rɛkwɪ'zɪʃən] n: **~ (for)** demande f (de) ▷ vt (Mil) réquisitionner

reroute [ri:'ru:t] vt (train etc) dérouter

resale ['ri:'seɪl] n revente f

resale price maintenance n vente au détail à prix imposé

resat [ri:'sæt] pt, pp of **resit**

rescind [rɪ'sɪnd] vt annuler; (law) abroger; (judgment) rescinder

rescue ['rɛskju:] n (from accident) sauvetage m; (help) secours mpl ▷ vt sauver; **to come to sb's ~** venir au secours de qn

rescue party n équipe f de sauvetage

rescuer ['rɛskjuəʳ] n sauveteur m

research [rɪ'sə:tʃ] n recherche(s) f(pl) ▷ vt faire des recherches sur ▷ vi: **to ~ (into sth)** faire des recherches (sur qch); **a piece of ~** un travail de recherche; **~ and development (R & D)** recherche-développement (R-D)

researcher [rɪ'sə:tʃəʳ] n chercheur(-euse)

research work n recherches fpl

resell [ri:'sɛl] vt (irreg: like **sell**) revendre

resemblance [rɪ'zɛmbləns] n ressemblance f; **to bear a strong ~ to** ressembler beaucoup à

resemble [rɪ'zɛmbl] vt ressembler à

resent [rɪ'zɛnt] vt éprouver du ressentiment de, être contrarié(e) par

resentful [rɪ'zɛntful] adj irrité(e), plein(e) de ressentiment

resentment [rɪ'zɛntmənt] n ressentiment m

reservation [rɛzə'veɪʃən] n (booking) réservation f; (doubt, protected area) réserve f; (Brit Aut: also: **central reservation**) bande médiane; **to make a ~ (in an hotel/a restaurant/on a plane)** réserver or retenir une chambre/une table/une place; **with ~s** (doubts) avec certaines réserves

reservation desk n (US: in hotel) réception f

reserve [rɪ'zə:v] n réserve f; (Sport) remplaçant(e) ▷ vt (seats etc) réserver, retenir; **reserves** npl (Mil) réservistes mpl; **in ~** en réserve

reserve currency n monnaie f de réserve

reserved [rɪ'zə:vd] adj réservé(e)

reserve price n (Brit) mise f à prix, prix m de départ

r

reserve team n (Brit Sport) deuxième équipe f
reservist [rɪ'zə:vɪst] n (Mil) réserviste m
reservoir ['rezəvwɑ:ʳ] n réservoir m
reset [ri:'set] vt (irreg: like **set**) remettre; (clock, watch) mettre à l'heure; (Comput) remettre à zéro
reshape [ri:'ʃeɪp] vt (policy) réorganiser
reshuffle [ri:'ʃʌfl] n: **Cabinet ~** (Pol) remaniement ministériel
reside [rɪ'zaɪd] vi résider
residence ['rezɪdəns] n résidence f; **to take up ~** s'installer; **in ~** (queen etc) en résidence; (doctor) résidant(e)
residence permit n (Brit) permis m de séjour
resident ['rezɪdənt] n (of country) résident(e); (of area, house) habitant(e); (in hotel) pensionnaire ▷ adj résidant(e)
residential [rezɪ'denʃəl] adj de résidence; (area) résidentiel(le); (course) avec hébergement sur place
residential school n internat m
residue ['rezɪdju:] n reste m; (Chem, Physics) résidu m
resign [rɪ'zaɪn] vt (one's post) se démettre de ▷ vi démissionner; **to ~ o.s. to** (endure) se résigner à
resignation [rezɪg'neɪʃən] n (from post) démission f; (state of mind) résignation f; **to tender one's ~** donner sa démission
resigned [rɪ'zaɪnd] adj résigné(e)
resilience [rɪ'zɪlɪəns] n (of material) élasticité f; (of person) ressort m
resilient [rɪ'zɪlɪənt] adj (person) qui réagit, qui a du ressort
resin ['rezɪn] n résine f
resist [rɪ'zɪst] vt résister à
resistance [rɪ'zɪstəns] n résistance f
resistant [rɪ'zɪstənt] adj: **~ (to)** résistant(e) (à)
resit vt [ri:'sɪt] (Brit: pt, pp **resat**) (exam) repasser ▷ n ['ri:sɪt] deuxième session f (d'un examen)
resolute ['rezəlu:t] adj résolu(e)
resolution [rezə'lu:ʃən] n résolution f; **to make a ~** prendre une résolution
resolve [rɪ'zɔlv] n résolution f ▷ vt (decide): **to ~ to do** résoudre or décider de faire; (problem) résoudre
resolved [rɪ'zɔlvd] adj résolu(e)
resonance ['rezənəns] n résonance f
resonant ['rezənənt] adj résonnant(e)
resort [rɪ'zɔ:t] n (seaside town) station f balnéaire; (for skiing) station de ski; (recourse) recours m ▷ vi: **to ~ to** avoir recours à; **in the last ~** en dernier ressort
resound [rɪ'zaund] vi: **to ~ (with)** retentir (de)
resounding [rɪ'zaundɪŋ] adj retentissant(e)
resource [rɪ'sɔ:s] n ressource f; **resources** npl ressources; **natural ~s** ressources naturelles; **to leave sb to his** (or **her**) **own ~s** (fig) livrer qn à lui-même (or elle-même)
resourceful [rɪ'sɔ:sful] adj ingénieux(-euse), débrouillard(e)
resourcefulness [rɪ'sɔ:sfəlnɪs] n ressource f
respect [rɪs'pekt] n respect m; (point, detail): **in**
some **~s** à certains égards ▷ vt respecter; **respects** npl respects, hommages mpl; **to have** or **show ~ for sb/sth** respecter qn/qch; **out of ~ for** par respect pour; **with ~ to** en ce qui concerne; **in ~ of** sous le rapport de, quant à; **in this ~** sous ce rapport, à cet égard; **with due ~ I** ... malgré le respect que je vous dois, je ...
respectability [rɪspektə'bɪlɪtɪ] n respectabilité f
respectable [rɪs'pektəbl] adj respectable; (quite good: result etc) honorable; (player) assez bon (bonne)
respectful [rɪs'pektful] adj respectueux(-euse)
respective [rɪs'pektɪv] adj respectif(-ive)
respectively [rɪs'pektɪvlɪ] adv respectivement
respiration [respɪ'reɪʃən] n respiration f
respirator ['respɪreɪtəʳ] n respirateur m
respiratory ['respərətərɪ] adj respiratoire
respite ['respaɪt] n répit m
resplendent [rɪs'plendənt] adj resplendissant(e)
respond [rɪs'pɔnd] vi répondre; (react) réagir
respondent [rɪs'pɔndənt] n (Law) défendeur(-deresse)
response [rɪs'pɔns] n réponse f; (reaction) réaction f; **in ~ to** en réponse à
responsibility [rɪspɔnsɪ'bɪlɪtɪ] n responsabilité f; **to take ~ for sth/sb** accepter la responsabilité de qch/d'être responsable de qn
responsible [rɪs'pɔnsɪbl] adj (liable): **~ (for)** responsable (de); (person) digne de confiance; (job) qui comporte des responsabilités; **to be ~ to sb (for sth)** être responsable devant qn (de qch)
responsibly [rɪs'pɔnsɪblɪ] adv avec sérieux
responsive [rɪs'pɔnsɪv] adj (student, audience) réceptif(-ive); (brakes, steering) sensible
rest [rest] n repos m; (stop) arrêt m, pause f; (Mus) silence m; (support) support m, appui m; (remainder) reste m, restant m ▷ vi se reposer; (be supported): **to ~ on** appuyer or reposer sur; (remain) rester ▷ vt (lean): **to ~ sth on/against** appuyer qch sur/contre; **the ~ of them** les autres; **to set sb's mind at ~** tranquilliser qn; **it ~s with him to** c'est à lui de; **~ assured that** ... soyez assuré que ...
restart [ri:'stɑ:t] vt (engine) remettre en marche; (work) reprendre
restaurant ['restərɔŋ] n restaurant m
restaurant car n (Brit Rail) wagon-restaurant m
rest cure n cure f de repos
restful ['restful] adj reposant(e)
rest home n maison f de repos
restitution [restɪ'tju:ʃən] n (act) restitution f; (reparation) réparation f
restive ['restɪv] adj agité(e), impatient(e); (horse) rétif(-ive)
restless ['restlɪs] adj agité(e); **to get ~** s'impatienter
restlessly ['restlɪslɪ] adv avec agitation
restock [ri:'stɔk] vt réapprovisionner
restoration [restə'reɪʃən] n (of building) restauration f; (of stolen goods) restitution f

restorative [rɪˈstɔrətɪv] *adj* reconstituant(e) ▷ *n* reconstituant *m*

restore [rɪˈstɔːʳ] *vt* (*building*) restaurer; (*sth stolen*) restituer; (*peace, health*) rétablir; **to ~ to** (*former state*) ramener à

restorer [rɪˈstɔːrəʳ] *n* (*Art etc*) restaurateur(-trice) (d'œuvres d'art)

restrain [rɪsˈtreɪn] *vt* (*feeling*) contenir; (*person*): **to ~ (from doing)** retenir (de faire)

restrained [rɪsˈtreɪnd] *adj* (*style*) sobre; (*manner*) mesuré(e)

restraint [rɪsˈtreɪnt] *n* (*restriction*) contrainte *f*; (*moderation*) retenue *f*; (*of style*) sobriété *f*; **wage ~** limitations salariales

restrict [rɪsˈtrɪkt] *vt* restreindre, limiter

restricted area [rɪsˈtrɪktɪd-] *n* (*Aut*) zone *f* à vitesse limitée

restriction [rɪsˈtrɪkʃən] *n* restriction *f*, limitation *f*

restrictive [rɪsˈtrɪktɪv] *adj* restrictif(-ive)

restrictive practices *npl* (*Industry*) pratiques *fpl* entravant la libre concurrence

rest room *n* (*US*) toilettes *fpl*

restructure [riːˈstrʌktʃəʳ] *vt* restructurer

result [rɪˈzʌlt] *n* résultat *m* ▷ *vi*: **to ~ (from)** résulter (de); **to ~ in** aboutir à, se terminer par; **as a ~ it is too expensive** il en résulte que c'est trop cher; **as a ~ of** à la suite de

resultant [rɪˈzʌltənt] *adj* résultant(e)

resume [rɪˈzjuːm] *vt* (*work, journey*) reprendre; (*sum up*) résumer ▷ *vi* (*work etc*) reprendre

résumé [ˈreɪzjuːmeɪ] *n* (*summary*) résumé *m*; (*US: curriculum vitae*) curriculum vitae *m inv*

resumption [rɪˈzʌmpʃən] *n* reprise *f*

resurgence [rɪˈsəːdʒəns] *n* réapparition *f*

resurrection [rɛzəˈrɛkʃən] *n* résurrection *f*

resuscitate [rɪˈsʌsɪteɪt] *vt* (*Med*) réanimer

resuscitation [rɪsʌsɪˈteɪʃən] *n* réanimation *f*

retail [ˈriːteɪl] *n* (*vente f au*) détail *m* ▷ *adj* de or au détail ▷ *adv* au détail ▷ *vt* vendre au détail ▷ *vi*: **to ~ at 10 euros** se vendre au détail à 10 euros

retailer [ˈriːteɪləʳ] *n* détaillant(e)

retail outlet *n* point *m* de vente

retail price *n* prix *m* de détail

retail price index *n* ≈ indice *m* des prix

retain [rɪˈteɪn] *vt* (*keep*) garder, conserver; (*employ*) engager

retainer [rɪˈteɪnəʳ] *n* (*servant*) serviteur *m*; (*fee*) acompte *m*, provision *f*

retaliate [rɪˈtælɪeɪt] *vi*: **to ~ (against)** se venger (de); **to ~ (on sb)** rendre la pareille (à qn)

retaliation [rɪtælɪˈeɪʃən] *n* représailles *fpl*, vengeance *f*; **in ~ for** par représailles pour

retaliatory [rɪˈtælɪətərɪ] *adj* de représailles

retarded [rɪˈtɑːdɪd] *adj* retardé(e)

retch [rɛtʃ] *vi* avoir des haut-le-cœur

retentive [rɪˈtɛntɪv] *adj*: **~ memory** excellente mémoire

rethink [ˈriːˈθɪŋk] *vt* repenser

reticence [ˈrɛtɪsns] *n* réticence *f*

reticent [ˈrɛtɪsnt] *adj* réticent(e)

retina [ˈrɛtɪnə] *n* rétine *f*

retinue [ˈrɛtɪnjuː] *n* suite *f*, cortège *m*

retire [rɪˈtaɪəʳ] *vi* (*give up work*) prendre sa retraite; (*withdraw*) se retirer, partir; (*go to bed*) (aller) se coucher

retired [rɪˈtaɪəd] *adj* (*person*) retraité(e)

retirement [rɪˈtaɪəmənt] *n* retraite *f*

retirement age *n* âge *m* de la retraite

retiring [rɪˈtaɪərɪŋ] *adj* (*person*) réservé(e); (*chairman etc*) sortant(e)

retort [rɪˈtɔːt] *n* (*reply*) riposte *f*; (*container*) cornue *f* ▷ *vi* riposter

retrace [riːˈtreɪs] *vt* reconstituer; **to ~ one's steps** revenir sur ses pas

retract [rɪˈtrækt] *vt* (*statement, claws*) rétracter; (*undercarriage, aerial*) rentrer, escamoter ▷ *vi* se rétracter; rentrer

retractable [rɪˈtræktəbl] *adj* escamotable

retrain [riːˈtreɪn] *vt* recycler ▷ *vi* se recycler

retraining [riːˈtreɪnɪŋ] *n* recyclage *m*

retread *vt* [riːˈtrɛd] (*Aut: tyre*) rechaper ▷ *n* [ˈriːtrɛd] pneu rechapé

retreat [rɪˈtriːt] *n* retraite *f* ▷ *vi* battre en retraite; (*flood*) reculer; **to beat a hasty ~** (*fig*) partir avec précipitation

retrial [riːˈtraɪəl] *n* nouveau procès

retribution [rɛtrɪˈbjuːʃən] *n* châtiment *m*

retrieval [rɪˈtriːvəl] *n* récupération *f*; réparation *f*; recherche *f* et extraction *f*

retrieve [rɪˈtriːv] *vt* (*sth lost*) récupérer; (*situation, honour*) sauver; (*error, loss*) réparer; (*Comput*) rechercher

retriever [rɪˈtriːvəʳ] *n* chien *m* d'arrêt

retroactive [rɛtrəuˈæktɪv] *adj* rétroactif(-ive)

retrograde [ˈrɛtrəgreɪd] *adj* rétrograde

retrospect [ˈrɛtrəspɛkt] *n*: **in ~** rétrospectivement, après coup

retrospective [rɛtrəˈspɛktɪv] *adj* rétrospectif(-ive); (*law*) rétroactif(-ive) ▷ *n* (*Art*) rétrospective *f*

return [rɪˈtəːn] *n* (*going or coming back*) retour *m*; (*of sth stolen etc*) restitution *f*; (*recompense*) récompense *f*; (*Finance: from land, shares*) rapport *m*; (*report*) relevé *m*, rapport ▷ *cpd* (*journey*) de retour; (*Brit: ticket*) aller et retour; (*match*) retour ▷ *vi* (*person etc: come back*) revenir; (: *go back*) retourner ▷ *vt* rendre; (*bring back*) rapporter; (*send back*) renvoyer; (*put back*) remettre; (*Pol: candidate*) élire; **returns** *npl* (*Comm*) recettes *fpl*; (*Finance*) bénéfices *mpl*; (: *returned goods*) marchandises renvoyées; **many happy ~s (of the day)!** bon anniversaire!; **by ~ (of post)** par retour (du courrier); **in ~ (for)** en échange (de); **a ~ (ticket) for ...** un billet aller et retour pour ...

returnable [rɪˈtəːnəbl] *adj* (*bottle etc*) consigné(e)

returner [rɪˈtəːnəʳ] *n femme qui reprend un travail après avoir élevé ses enfants*

returning officer [rɪˈtəːnɪŋ-] *n* (*Brit Pol*) président *m* de bureau de vote

return key *n* (*Comput*) touche *f* de retour

return ticket *n* (*esp Brit*) billet *m* aller-retour

r

reunion [riːˈjuːnɪən] n réunion f
reunite [riːjuːˈnaɪt] vt réunir
reuse [riːˈjuːz] vt réutiliser
rev [rɛv] n abbr = **revolution**; (Aut) tour m ▷ vt (also: **rev up**) emballer ▷ vi (also: **rev up**) s'emballer
Rev. abbr = **reverend**
revaluation [riːvæljuˈeɪʃən] n réévaluation f
revamp [riːˈvæmp] vt (house) retaper; (firm) réorganiser
rev counter n (Brit) compte-tours m inv
Revd. abbr = **reverend**
reveal [rɪˈviːl] vt (make known) révéler; (display) laisser voir
revealing [rɪˈviːlɪŋ] adj révélateur(-trice); (dress) au décolleté généreux or suggestif
reveille [rɪˈvælɪ] n (Mil) réveil m
revel [ˈrɛvl] vi: **to ~ in sth/in doing** se délecter de qch/à faire
revelation [rɛvəˈleɪʃən] n révélation f
reveller [ˈrɛvləʳ] n fêtard m
revelry [ˈrɛvlrɪ] n festivités fpl
revenge [rɪˈvɛndʒ] n vengeance f; (in game etc) revanche f ▷ vt venger; **to take ~ (on)** se venger (sur)
revengeful [rɪˈvɛndʒful] adj vengeur(-eresse), vindicatif(-ive)
revenue [ˈrɛvənjuː] n revenu m
reverberate [rɪˈvəːbəreɪt] vi (sound) retentir, se répercuter; (light) se réverbérer
reverberation [rɪvəːbəˈreɪʃən] n répercussion f; réverbération f
revere [rɪˈvɪəʳ] vt vénérer, révérer
reverence [ˈrɛvərəns] n vénération f, révérence f
Reverend [ˈrɛvərənd] adj vénérable; (in titles): **the ~ John Smith** (Anglican) le révérend John Smith; (Catholic) l'abbé (John) Smith; (Protestant) le pasteur (John) Smith
reverent [ˈrɛvərənt] adj respectueux(-euse)
reverie [ˈrɛvərɪ] n rêverie f
reversal [rɪˈvəːsl] n (of opinion) revirement m; (of order) renversement m; (of direction) changement m
reverse [rɪˈvəːs] n contraire m, opposé m; (back) dos m, envers m; (of paper) verso m; (of coin) revers m; (Aut: also: **reverse gear**) marche f arrière ▷ adj (order, direction) opposé(e), inverse ▷ vt (order, position) changer, inverser; (direction, policy) changer complètement de; (decision) annuler; (roles) renverser; (car) faire marche arrière avec; (Law: judgment) réformer ▷ vi (Brit Aut) faire marche arrière; **to go into ~** faire marche arrière; **in ~ order** en ordre inverse
reverse video n vidéo m inverse
reversible [rɪˈvəːsəbl] adj (garment) réversible; (procedure) révocable
reversing lights [rɪˈvəːsɪŋ-] npl (Brit Aut) feux mpl de marche arrière or de recul
reversion [rɪˈvəːʃən] n retour m
revert [rɪˈvəːt] vi: **to ~ to** revenir à, retourner à
review [rɪˈvjuː] n revue f; (of book, film) critique f; (of situation, policy) examen m, bilan m; (US:

examination) examen ▷ vt passer en revue; faire la critique de; examiner; **to come under ~** être révisé(e)
reviewer [rɪˈvjuːəʳ] n critique m
revile [rɪˈvaɪl] vt injurier
revise [rɪˈvaɪz] vt réviser, modifier; (manuscript) revoir, corriger ▷ vi (study) réviser; **~d edition** édition revue et corrigée
revision [rɪˈvɪʒən] n révision f; (revised version) version corrigée
revitalize [riːˈvaɪtəlaɪz] vt revitaliser
revival [rɪˈvaɪvəl] n reprise f; (recovery) rétablissement m; (of faith) renouveau m
revive [rɪˈvaɪv] vt (person) ranimer; (custom) rétablir; (economy) relancer; (hope, courage) raviver, faire renaître; (play, fashion) reprendre ▷ vi (person) reprendre connaissance; (: from ill health) se rétablir; (hope etc) renaître; (activity) reprendre
revoke [rɪˈvəuk] vt révoquer; (promise, decision) revenir sur
revolt [rɪˈvəult] n révolte f ▷ vi se révolter, se rebeller ▷ vt révolter, dégoûter
revolting [rɪˈvəultɪŋ] adj dégoûtant(e)
revolution [rɛvəˈluːʃən] n révolution f; (of wheel etc) tour m, révolution
revolutionary [rɛvəˈluːʃənrɪ] adj, n révolutionnaire (m/f)
revolutionize [rɛvəˈluːʃənaɪz] vt révolutionner
revolve [rɪˈvɔlv] vi tourner
revolver [rɪˈvɔlvəʳ] n revolver m
revolving [rɪˈvɔlvɪŋ] adj (chair) pivotant(e); (light) tournant(e)
revolving door n (porte f à) tambour m
revue [rɪˈvjuː] n (Theat) revue f
revulsion [rɪˈvʌlʃən] n dégoût m, répugnance f
reward [rɪˈwɔːd] n récompense f ▷ vt: **to ~ (for)** récompenser (de)
rewarding [rɪˈwɔːdɪŋ] adj (fig) qui (en) vaut la peine, gratifiant(e); **financially ~** financièrement intéressant(e)
rewind [riːˈwaɪnd] vt (irreg: like **wind**); (watch) remonter; (tape) réembobiner
rewire [riːˈwaɪəʳ] vt (house) refaire l'installation électrique de
reword [riːˈwəːd] vt formuler or exprimer différemment
rewritable [riːˈraɪtəbl] adj (CD, DVD) réinscriptible
rewrite [riːˈraɪt] (pt **rewrote**, pp **rewritten**) vt récrire
Reykjavik [ˈreɪkjəviːk] n Reykjavik
RFD abbr (US Post) = **rural free delivery**
Rh abbr (= rhesus) Rh
rhapsody [ˈræpsədɪ] n (Mus) rhapsodie f; (fig) éloge délirant
rhesus negative [ˈriːsəs-] adj (Med) de rhésus négatif
rhesus positive [ˈriːsəs-] adj (Med) de rhésus positif
rhetoric [ˈrɛtərɪk] n rhétorique f
rhetorical [rɪˈtɔrɪkl] adj rhétorique

rheumatic [ruːˈmætɪk] *adj* rhumatismal(e)
rheumatism [ˈruːmətɪzəm] *n* rhumatisme *m*
rheumatoid arthritis [ˈruːmətɔɪd-] *n* polyarthrite *f* chronique
Rhine [raɪn] *n*: **the (River) ~** le Rhin
rhinestone [ˈraɪnstəun] *n* faux diamant
rhinoceros [raɪˈnɔsərəs] *n* rhinocéros *m*
Rhodes [rəudz] *n* Rhodes *f*
Rhodesia [rəuˈdiːʒə] *n* Rhodésie *f*
Rhodesian [rəuˈdiːʒən] *adj* rhodésien(ne) ▷ *n* Rhodésien(ne)
rhododendron [rəudəˈdɛndrn] *n* rhododendron *m*
rhubarb [ˈruːbɑːb] *n* rhubarbe *f*
rhyme [raɪm] *n* rime *f*; (*verse*) vers *mpl* ▷ *vi*: **to ~ (with)** rimer (avec); **without ~ or reason** sans rime ni raison
rhythm [ˈrɪðm] *n* rythme *m*
rhythmic [ˈrɪðmɪk], **rhythmical** [ˈrɪðmɪkl] *adj* rythmique
rhythmically [ˈrɪðmɪklɪ] *adv* avec rythme
rhythm method *n* méthode *f* des températures
RI *n abbr* (*Brit*) = **religious instruction** ▷ *abbr* (*US*) = **Rhode Island**
rib [rɪb] *n* (*Anat*) côte *f* ▷ *vt* (*mock*) taquiner
ribald [ˈrɪbəld] *adj* paillard(e)
ribbed [rɪbd] *adj* (*knitting*) à côtes; (*shell*) strié(e)
ribbon [ˈrɪbən] *n* ruban *m*; **in ~s** (*torn*) en lambeaux
rice [raɪs] *n* riz *m*
rice field [ˈraɪsfiːld] *n* rizière *f*
rice pudding *n* riz *m* au lait
rich [rɪtʃ] *adj* riche; (*gift, clothes*) somptueux(-euse); **the ~** (*npl*) les riches *mpl*; **riches** *npl* richesses *fpl*; **to be ~ in sth** être riche en qch
richly [ˈrɪtʃlɪ] *adv* richement; (*deserved, earned*) largement, grandement
rickets [ˈrɪkɪts] *n* rachitisme *m*
rickety [ˈrɪkɪtɪ] *adj* branlant(e)
rickshaw [ˈrɪkʃɔː] *n* pousse(-pousse) *m inv*
ricochet [ˈrɪkəʃeɪ] *n* ricochet *m* ▷ *vi* ricocher
rid [rɪd] (*pt, pp* -) *vt*: **to ~ sb of** débarrasser qn de; **to get ~ of** se débarrasser de
riddance [ˈrɪdns] *n*: **good ~!** bon débarras!
ridden [ˈrɪdn] *pp of* **ride**
riddle [ˈrɪdl] *n* (*puzzle*) énigme *f* ▷ *vt*: **to be ~d with** être criblé(e) de; (*fig*) être en proie à
ride [raɪd] (*pt* **rode**, *pp* **ridden**) [rəud, ˈrɪdn] *n* promenade *f*, tour *m*; (*distance covered*) trajet *m* ▷ *vi* (*as sport*) monter (à cheval), faire du cheval; (*go somewhere: on horse, bicycle*) aller (à cheval *or* bicyclette *etc*); (*travel: on bicycle, motor cycle, bus*) rouler ▷ *vt* (*a horse*) monter; (*distance*) parcourir, faire; **we rode all day/all the way** nous sommes restés toute la journée en selle/avons fait tout le chemin en selle *or* à cheval; **to ~ a horse/bicycle** monter à cheval/à bicyclette; **can you ~ a bike?** est-ce que tu sais monter à bicyclette?; **to ~ at anchor** (*Naut*) être à l'ancre; **horse/car ~** promenade *or* tour à cheval/en voiture; **to go for a ~** faire une promenade (en voiture *or* à bicyclette *etc*); **to take sb for a ~** (*fig*) faire marcher qn; (*cheat*) rouler qn
▶ **ride out** *vt*: **to ~ out the storm** (*fig*) surmonter les difficultés
rider [ˈraɪdəʳ] *n* cavalier(-ière); (*in race*) jockey *m*; (*on bicycle*) cycliste *m/f*; (*on motorcycle*) motocycliste *m/f*; (*in document*) annexe *f*, clause additionnelle
ridge [rɪdʒ] *n* (*of hill*) faîte *m*; (*of roof, mountain*) arête *f*; (*on object*) strie *f*
ridicule [ˈrɪdɪkjuːl] *n* ridicule *m*; dérision *f* ▷ *vt* ridiculiser, tourner en dérision; **to hold sb/sth up to ~** tourner qn/qch en ridicule
ridiculous [rɪˈdɪkjuləs] *adj* ridicule
riding [ˈraɪdɪŋ] *n* équitation *f*
riding school *n* manège *m*, école *f* d'équitation
rife [raɪf] *adj* répandu(e); **~ with** abondant(e) en
riffraff [ˈrɪfræf] *n* racaille *f*
rifle [ˈraɪfl] *n* fusil *m* (à canon rayé) ▷ *vt* vider, dévaliser
▶ **rifle through** *vt fus* fouiller dans
rifle range *n* champ *m* de tir; (*indoor*) stand *m* de tir
rift [rɪft] *n* fente *f*, fissure *f*; (*fig: disagreement*) désaccord *m*
rig [rɪg] *n* (*also*: **oil rig**: *on land*) derrick *m*; (*: at sea*) plate-forme pétrolière ▷ *vt* (*election etc*) truquer
▶ **rig out** *vt* (*Brit*) habiller; (*: pej*) fringuer, attifer
▶ **rig up** *vt* arranger, faire avec des moyens de fortune
rigging [ˈrɪgɪŋ] *n* (*Naut*) gréement *m*
right [raɪt] *adj* (*true*) juste, exact(e); (*correct*) bon (bonne); (*suitable*) approprié(e), convenable; (*just*) juste, équitable; (*morally good*) bien *inv*; (*not left*) droit(e) ▷ *n* (*moral good*) bien *m*; (*title, claim*) droit *m*; (*not left*) droite *f* ▷ *adv* (*answer*) correctement; (*treat*) bien, comme il faut; (*not on the left*) à droite ▷ *vt* redresser ▷ *excl* bon!; **rights** *npl* (*Comm*) droits *mpl*; **the ~ time** (*precise*) l'heure exacte; (*not wrong*) la bonne heure; **do you have the ~ time?** avez-vous l'heure juste *or* exacte?; **to be ~** (*person*) avoir raison; (*answer*) être juste *or* correct(e); **to get sth ~** ne pas se tromper sur qch; **let's get it ~ this time!** essayons de ne pas nous tromper cette fois-ci!; **you did the ~ thing** vous avez bien fait; **to put a mistake ~** (*Brit*) rectifier une erreur; **by ~s** en toute justice; **on the ~** à droite; **~ and wrong** le bien et le mal; **to be in the ~** avoir raison; **film ~s** droits d'adaptation cinématographique; **~ now** en ce moment même; (*immediately*) tout de suite; **~ before/after** juste avant/après; **~ against the wall** tout contre le mur; **~ ahead** tout droit; droit devant; **~ in the middle** en plein milieu; **~ away** immédiatement; **to go ~ to the end of sth** aller jusqu'au bout de qch
right angle *n* (*Math*) angle droit
righteous [ˈraɪtʃəs] *adj* droit(e), vertueux(-euse); (*anger*) justifié(e)
righteousness [ˈraɪtʃəsnɪs] *n* droiture *f*, vertu *f*
rightful [ˈraɪtful] *adj* (*heir*) légitime
rightfully [ˈraɪtfəlɪ] *adv* à juste titre,

r

légitimement

right-hand ['raɪthænd] *adj*: **the ~ side** la droite

right-hand drive *n* (*Brit*) conduite *f* à droite; (*vehicle*) véhicule *m* avec la conduite à droite

right-handed [raɪt'hændɪd] *adj* (*person*) droitier(-ière)

right-hand man ['raɪthænd-] (*irreg*) *n* bras droit (*fig*)

rightly ['raɪtlɪ] *adv* bien, correctement; (*with reason*) à juste titre; **if I remember ~** (*Brit*) si je me souviens bien

right-minded ['raɪt'maɪndɪd] *adj* sensé(e), sain(e) d'esprit

right of way *n* (*on path etc*) droit *m* de passage; (*Aut*) priorité *f*

rights issue *n* (*Stock Exchange*) émission préférentielle *or* de droit de souscription

right wing *n* (*Mil, Sport*) aile droite; (*Pol*) droite *f*

right-wing [raɪt'wɪŋ] *adj* (*Pol*) de droite

right-winger [raɪt'wɪŋəʳ] *n* (*Pol*) membre *m* de la droite; (*Sport*) ailier droit

rigid ['rɪdʒɪd] *adj* rigide; (*principle, control*) strict(e)

rigidity [rɪ'dʒɪdɪtɪ] *n* rigidité *f*

rigidly ['rɪdʒɪdlɪ] *adv* rigidement; (*behave*) inflexiblement

rigmarole ['rɪgmərəul] *n* galimatias *m*, comédie *f*

rigor ['rɪgəʳ] *n* (*US*) = **rigour**

rigor mortis ['rɪgə'mɔːtɪs] *n* rigidité *f* cadavérique

rigorous ['rɪgərəs] *adj* rigoureux(-euse)

rigorously ['rɪgərəslɪ] *adv* rigoureusement

rigour, (*US*) **rigor** ['rɪgəʳ] *n* rigueur *f*

rig-out ['rɪgaut] *n* (*Brit inf*) tenue *f*

rile [raɪl] *vt* agacer

rim [rɪm] *n* bord *m*; (*of spectacles*) monture *f*; (*of wheel*) jante *f*

rimless ['rɪmlɪs] *adj* (*spectacles*) à monture invisible

rind [raɪnd] *n* (*of bacon*) couenne *f*; (*of lemon etc*) écorce *f*, zeste *m*; (*of cheese*) croûte *f*

ring [rɪŋ] (*pt* **rang**, *pp* **rung**) [ræŋ, rʌŋ] *n* anneau *m*; (*on finger*) bague *f*; (*also*: **wedding ring**) alliance *f*; (*for napkin*) rond *m*; (*of people, objects*) cercle *m*; (*of spies*) réseau *m*; (*of smoke etc*) rond *m*; (*arena*) piste *f*, arène *f*; (*for boxing*) ring *m*; (*sound of bell*) sonnerie *f*; (*telephone call*) coup *m* de téléphone ▷ *vi* (*telephone, bell*) sonner; (*person: by telephone*) téléphoner; (*ears*) bourdonner; (*also*: **ring out**: *voice, words*) retentir ▷ *vt* (*Brit Tel*: *also*: **ring up**) téléphoner à, appeler; **to ~ the bell** sonner; **to give sb a ~** (*Tel*) passer un coup de téléphone *or* de fil à qn; **that has the ~ of truth about it** cela sonne vrai; **the name doesn't ~ a bell (with me)** ce nom ne me dit rien

▶ **ring back** *vt, vi* (*Brit Tel*) rappeler

▶ **ring off** *vi* (*Brit Tel*) raccrocher

▶ **ring up** (*Brit*) *vt* (*Tel*) téléphoner à, appeler

ring binder *n* classeur *m* à anneaux

ring finger *n* annulaire *m*

ringing ['rɪŋɪŋ] *n* (*of bell*) tintement *m*; (*louder: also*: **of telephone**) sonnerie *f*; (*in ears*)

bourdonnement *m*

ringing tone *n* (*Brit Tel*) tonalité *f* d'appel

ringleader ['rɪŋliːdəʳ] *n* (*of gang*) chef *m*, meneur *m*

ringlets ['rɪŋlɪts] *npl* anglaises *fpl*

ring road *n* (*Brit*) rocade *f*; (*motorway*) périphérique *m*

ring tone ['rɪŋtəun] *n* (*on mobile*) sonnerie *f* (*de téléphone portable*)

rink [rɪŋk] *n* (*also*: **ice rink**) patinoire *f*; (*for roller-skating*) skating *m*

rinse [rɪns] *n* rinçage *m* ▷ *vt* rincer

Rio ['riːəu], **Rio de Janeiro** ['riːəudədʒə'nɪərəu] *n* Rio de Janeiro

riot ['raɪət] *n* émeute *f*, bagarres *fpl* ▷ *vi* (*demonstrators*) manifester avec violence; (*population*) se soulever, se révolter; **a ~ of colours** une débauche *or* orgie de couleurs; **to run ~** se déchaîner

rioter ['raɪətəʳ] *n* émeutier(-ière), manifestant(e)

riot gear *n*: **in ~** casqué et portant un bouclier

riotous ['raɪətəs] *adj* tapageur(-euse); tordant(e)

riotously ['raɪətəslɪ] *adv*: **~ funny** tordant(e)

riot police *n* forces *fpl* de police intervenant en cas d'émeute; **hundreds of ~** des centaines de policiers casqués et armés

RIP *abbr* (= *rest in peace*) RIP

rip [rɪp] *n* déchirure *f* ▷ *vt* déchirer ▷ *vi* se déchirer

▶ **rip off** *vt* (*inf*: *cheat*) arnaquer

▶ **rip up** *vt* déchirer

ripcord ['rɪpkɔːd] *n* poignée *f* d'ouverture

ripe [raɪp] *adj* (*fruit*) mûr(e); (*cheese*) fait(e)

ripen ['raɪpn] *vt* mûrir ▷ *vi* mûrir; se faire

ripeness ['raɪpnɪs] *n* maturité *f*

rip-off ['rɪpɔf] *n* (*inf*): **it's a ~!** c'est du vol manifeste!, c'est de l'arnaque!

riposte [rɪ'pɔst] *n* riposte *f*

ripple ['rɪpl] *n* ride *f*, ondulation *f*; (*of applause, laughter*) cascade *f* ▷ *vi* se rider, onduler ▷ *vt* rider, faire onduler

rise [raɪz] *n* (*slope*) côte *f*, pente *f*; (*hill*) élévation *f*; (*increase: in wages: Brit*) augmentation *f*; (: *in prices, temperature*) hausse *f*, augmentation; (*fig: to power etc*) ascension *f* ▷ *vi* (*pt* **rose**, *pp* **-n**) [rəuz, rɪzn] s'élever, monter; (*prices, numbers*) augmenter, monter; (*waters, river*) monter; (*sun, wind, person: from chair, bed*) se lever; (*also*: **rise up**: *tower, building*) s'élever; (: *rebel*) se révolter; se rebeller; (*in rank*) s'élever; **~ to power** montée *f* au pouvoir; **to give ~ to** donner lieu à; **to ~ to the occasion** se montrer à la hauteur

risen ['rɪzn] *pp of* **rise**

rising ['raɪzɪŋ] *adj* (*increasing: number, prices*) en hausse; (*tide*) montant(e); (*sun, moon*) levant(e) ▷ *n* (*uprising*) soulèvement *m*, insurrection *f*

rising damp *n* humidité *f* (montant des fondations)

rising star *n* (*also fig*) étoile montante

risk [rɪsk] *n* risque *m*, danger *m*; (*deliberate*) risque ▷ *vt* risquer; **to take** *or* **run the ~ of**

doing courir le risque de faire; **at ~** en danger; **at one's own ~** à ses risques et périls; **it's a fire/health ~** cela présente un risque d'incendie/pour la santé; **I'll ~ it** je vais risquer le coup

risk capital n capital-risque m

risky ['rɪskɪ] adj risqué(e)

risqué ['riːskeɪ] adj (joke) risqué(e)

rissole ['rɪsəul] n croquette f

rite [raɪt] n rite m; **the last ~s** les derniers sacrements

ritual ['rɪtjuəl] adj rituel(le) ▷ n rituel m

rival ['raɪvl] n rival(e); (in business) concurrent(e) ▷ adj rival(e); qui fait concurrence ▷ vt (match) égaler; (compete with) être en concurrence avec; **to ~ sb/sth in** rivaliser avec qn/qch de

rivalry ['raɪvlrɪ] n rivalité f; (in business) concurrence f

river ['rɪvər] n rivière f; (major: also fig) fleuve m ▷ cpd (port, traffic) fluvial(e); **up/down ~** en amont/aval

riverbank ['rɪvəbæŋk] n rive f, berge f

riverbed ['rɪvəbed] n lit m (de rivière or de fleuve)

riverside ['rɪvəsaɪd] n bord m de la rivière or du fleuve

rivet ['rɪvɪt] n rivet m ▷ vt riveter; (fig) river, fixer

riveting ['rɪvɪtɪŋ] adj (fig) fascinant(e)

Riviera [rɪvɪ'ɛərə] n: **the (French) ~** la Côte d'Azur; **the Italian ~** la Riviera (italienne)

Riyadh [rɪ'jɑːd] n Riyad

RMT n abbr (= Rail, Maritime and Transport) syndicat des transports

RN n abbr = **registered nurse**; (Brit) = **Royal Navy**

RNA n abbr (= ribonucleic acid) ARN m

RNLI n abbr (Brit: = Royal National Lifeboat Institution) ≈ SNSM f

RNZAF n abbr = **Royal New Zealand Air Force**

RNZN n abbr = **Royal New Zealand Navy**

road [rəud] n route f; (in town) rue f; (fig) chemin, voie f ▷ cpd (accident) de la route; **main ~** grande route; **major/minor ~** route principale or à priorité/voie secondaire; **it takes four hours by ~** il y a quatre heures de route; **which ~ do I take for ...?** quelle route dois-je prendre pour aller à ...?; **"~ up"** (Brit) "attention travaux"

road accident n accident m de la circulation

roadblock ['rəudblɔk] n barrage routier

road haulage n transports routiers

roadhog ['rəudhɔg] n chauffard m

road map n carte routière

road rage n comportement très agressif de certains usagers de la route

road safety n sécurité routière

roadside ['rəudsaɪd] n bord m de la route, bas-côté m ▷ cpd (situé(e) etc) au bord de la route; **by the ~** au bord de la route

road sign ['rəudsaɪn] n panneau m de signalisation

road sweeper ['rəudswiːpər] n (Brit: person) balayeur(-euse)

road tax n (Brit Aut) taxe f sur les automobiles

road user n usager m de la route

roadway ['rəudweɪ] n chaussée f

roadworks ['rəudwəːks] npl travaux mpl (de réfection des routes)

roadworthy ['rəudwəːðɪ] adj en bon état de marche

roam [rəum] vi errer, vagabonder ▷ vt parcourir, errer par

roar [rɔːr] n rugissement m; (of crowd) hurlements mpl; (of vehicle, thunder, storm) grondement m ▷ vi rugir; hurler; gronder; **to ~ with laughter** rire à gorge déployée

roaring ['rɔːrɪŋ] adj: **a ~ fire** une belle flambée; **a ~ success** un succès fou; **to do a ~ trade** faire des affaires en or

roast [rəust] n rôti m ▷ vt (meat) (faire) rôtir; (coffee) griller, torréfier

roast beef n rôti m de bœuf, rosbif m

roasting ['rəustɪŋ] n (inf): **to give sb a ~** sonner les cloches à qn

rob [rɔb] vt (person) voler; (bank) dévaliser; **to ~ sb of sth** voler or dérober qch à qn; (fig: deprive) priver qn de qch

robber ['rɔbər] n bandit m, voleur m

robbery ['rɔbərɪ] n vol m

robe [rəub] n (for ceremony etc) robe f; (also: **bathrobe**) peignoir m; (US: rug) couverture f ▷ vt revêtir (d'une robe)

robin ['rɔbɪn] n rouge-gorge m

robot ['rəubɔt] n robot m

robotics [rə'bɔtɪks] n robotique m

robust [rəu'bʌst] adj robuste; (material, appetite) solide

rock [rɔk] n (substance) roche f, roc m; (boulder) rocher m, roche; (US: small stone) caillou m; (Brit: sweet) ≈ sucre m d'orge ▷ vt (swing gently: cradle) balancer; (: child) bercer; (shake) ébranler, secouer ▷ vi se balancer, être ébranlé(e) or secoué(e); **on the ~s** (drink) avec des glaçons; (ship) sur les écueils; (marriage etc) en train de craquer; **to ~ the boat** (fig) jouer les trouble-fête

rock and roll n rock (and roll) m, rock'n'roll m

rock-bottom ['rɔk'bɔtəm] n (fig) niveau le plus bas ▷ adj (fig: prices) sacrifié(e); **to reach** or **touch ~** (price, person) tomber au plus bas

rock climber n varappeur(-euse)

rock climbing n varappe f

rockery ['rɔkərɪ] n (jardin m de) rocaille f

rocket ['rɔkɪt] n fusée f; (Mil) fusée, roquette f; (Culin) roquette ▷ vi (prices) monter en flèche

rocket launcher [-lɔːnfər] n lance-roquettes m inv

rock face n paroi rocheuse

rock fall n chute f de pierres

rocking chair ['rɔkɪŋ-] n fauteuil m à bascule

rocking horse ['rɔkɪŋ-] n cheval m à bascule

rocky ['rɔkɪ] adj (hill) rocheux(-euse); (path) rocailleux(-euse); (unsteady: table) branlant(e)

Rocky Mountains npl: **the ~** les (montagnes fpl) Rocheuses fpl

rod [rɔd] n (metallic) tringle f; (Tech) tige f;

r

(*wooden*) baguette *f*; (*also*: **fishing rod**) canne *f* à pêche

rode [rəʊd] *pt of* **ride**

rodent ['rəʊdnt] *n* rongeur *m*

rodeo ['rəʊdɪəʊ] *n* rodéo *m*

roe [rəʊ] *n* (*species: also*: **roe deer**) chevreuil *m*; (*of fish: also*: **hard roe**) œufs *mpl* de poisson; **soft ~** laitance *f*

roe deer *n* chevreuil *m*; chevreuil femelle

rogue [rəʊg] *n* coquin(e)

roguish ['rəʊgɪʃ] *adj* coquin(e)

role [rəʊl] *n* rôle *m*

role-model ['rəʊlmɔdl] *n* modèle *m* à émuler

role play, role playing *n* jeu *m* de rôle

roll [rəʊl] *n* rouleau *m*; (*of banknotes*) liasse *f*; (*also*: **bread roll**) petit pain; (*register*) liste *f*; (*sound: of drums etc*) roulement *m*; (*movement: of ship*) roulis *m* ▷ *vt* rouler; (*also*: **roll up**: *string*) enrouler; (*also*: **roll out**: *pastry*) étendre au rouleau, abaisser ▷ *vi* rouler; (*wheel*) tourner; **cheese ~** = sandwich *m* au fromage (*dans un petit pain*)

▸ **roll about, roll around** *vi* rouler çà et là; (*person*) se rouler par terre

▸ **roll by** *vi* (*time*) s'écouler, passer

▸ **roll in** *vi* (*mail, cash*) affluer

▸ **roll over** *vi* se retourner

▸ **roll up** *vi* (*inf: arrive*) arriver, s'amener ▷ *vt* (*carpet, cloth, map*) rouler; (*sleeves*) retrousser; **to ~ o.s. up into a ball** se rouler en boule

roll call *n* appel *m*

roller ['rəʊlə'] *n* rouleau *m*; (*wheel*) roulette *f*; (*for road*) rouleau compresseur; (*for hair*) bigoudi *m*

Rollerblades® ['rəʊlə'bleɪdz] *npl* patins *mpl* en ligne

roller blind *n* (*Brit*) store *m*

roller coaster *n* montagnes *fpl* russes

roller skates *npl* patins *mpl* à roulettes

roller-skating ['rəʊlə'skeɪtɪŋ] *n* patin *m* à roulettes; **to go ~** faire du patin à roulettes

rollicking ['rɔlɪkɪŋ] *adj* bruyant(e) et joyeux(-euse); (*play*) bouffon(ne); **to have a ~ time** s'amuser follement

rolling ['rəʊlɪŋ] *adj* (*landscape*) onduleux(-euse)

rolling mill *n* laminoir *m*

rolling pin *n* rouleau *m* à pâtisserie

rolling stock *n* (*Rail*) matériel roulant

roll-on-roll-off ['rəʊlɔn'rəʊlɔf] *adj* (*Brit: ferry*) roulier(-ière)

roly-poly ['rəʊlɪ'pəʊlɪ] *n* (*Brit Culin*) roulé *m* à la confiture

ROM [rɔm] *n abbr* (*Comput*: = *read-only memory*) mémoire morte, ROM *f*

Roman ['rəʊmən] *adj* romain(e) ▷ *n* Romain(e)

Roman Catholic *adj, n* catholique (*m/f*)

romance [rə'mæns] *n* (*love affair*) idylle *f*; (*charm*) poésie *f*; (*novel*) roman *m* à l'eau de rose

Romanesque [rəʊmə'nɛsk] *adj* roman(e)

Romania [rəʊ'meɪnɪə] = **Rumania**

Romanian [rəʊ'meɪnɪən] *adj, n see* **Rumanian**

Roman numeral *n* chiffre romain

romantic [rə'mæntɪk] *adj* romantique; (*novel,*

attachment) sentimental(e)

romanticism [rə'mæntɪsɪzəm] *n* romantisme *m*

Romany ['rɔmənɪ] *adj* de bohémien ▷ *n* bohémien(ne); (*Ling*) romani *m*

Rome [rəʊm] *n* Rome

romp [rɔmp] *n* jeux bruyants ▷ *vi* (*also*: **romp about**) s'ébattre, jouer bruyamment; **to ~ home** (*horse*) arriver bon premier

rompers ['rɔmpəz] *npl* barboteuse *f*

rondo ['rɔndəʊ] *n* (*Mus*) rondeau *m*

roof [ru:f] *n* toit *m*; (*of tunnel, cave*) plafond *m* ▷ *vt* couvrir (d'un toit); **the ~ of the mouth** la voûte du palais

roof garden *n* toit-terrasse *m*

roofing ['ru:fɪŋ] *n* toiture *f*

roof rack *n* (*Aut*) galerie *f*

rook [ruk] *n* (*bird*) freux *m*; (*Chess*) tour *f* ▷ *vt* (*inf: cheat*) rouler, escroquer

rookie ['rukɪ] *n* (*inf: esp Mil*) bleu *m*

room [ru:m] *n* (*in house*) pièce *f*; (*also*: **bedroom**) chambre *f* (à coucher); (*in school etc*) salle *f*; (*space*) place *f*; **rooms** *npl* (*lodging*) meublé *m*; "**~s to let**", (*US*) "**~s for rent**" "chambres à louer"; **is there ~ for this?** est-ce qu'il y a de la place pour ceci?; **to make ~ for sb** faire de la place à qn; **there is ~ for improvement** on peut faire mieux

rooming house ['ru:mɪŋ-] *n* (*US*) maison *f* de rapport

roommate ['ru:mmeɪt] *n* camarade *m/f* de chambre

room service *n* service *m* des chambres (*dans un hôtel*)

room temperature *n* température ambiante; "**serve at ~**" (*wine*) "servir chambré"

roomy ['ru:mɪ] *adj* spacieux(-euse); (*garment*) ample

roost [ru:st] *n* juchoir *m* ▷ *vi* se jucher

rooster ['ru:stə'] *n* coq *m*

root [ru:t] *n* (*Bot, Math*) racine *f*; (*fig: of problem*) origine *f*, fond *m* ▷ *vi* (*plant*) s'enraciner; **to take ~** (*plant, idea*) prendre racine

▸ **root about** *vi* (*fig*) fouiller

▸ **root for** *vt fus* (*inf*) applaudir

▸ **root out** *vt* extirper

root beer *n* (*US*) *sorte de limonade à base d'extraits végétaux*

rope [rəʊp] *n* corde *f*; (*Naut*) cordage *m* ▷ *vt* (*box*) corder; (*tie up or together*) attacher; (*climbers: also*: **rope together**) encorder; (*area: also*: **rope off**) interdire l'accès de; (: *divide off*) séparer; **to ~ sb in** (*fig*) embringuer qn; **to know the ~s** (*fig*) être au courant, connaître les ficelles

rope ladder *n* échelle *f* de corde

ropey ['rəʊpɪ] *adj* (*inf*) pas fameux(-euse) *or* brillant(e); **I feel a bit ~ today** c'est pas la forme aujourd'hui

rosary ['rəʊzərɪ] *n* chapelet *m*

rose [rəʊz] *pt of* **rise** ▷ *n* rose *f*; (*also*: **rosebush**) rosier *m*; (*on watering can*) pomme *f* ▷ *adj* rose

rosé ['rəʊzeɪ] *n* rosé *m*

rosebed ['rəʊzbɛd] *n* massif *m* de rosiers

rosebud ['rəuzbʌd] *n* bouton *m* de rose
rosebush ['rəuzbuʃ] *n* rosier *m*
rosemary ['rəuzmərɪ] *n* romarin *m*
rosette [rəu'zɛt] *n* rosette *f*; (*larger*) cocarde *f*
ROSPA ['rɒspə] *n abbr* (*Brit*) = **Royal Society for the Prevention of Accidents**
roster ['rɒstə^r] *n*: **duty ~** tableau *m* de service
rostrum ['rɒstrəm] *n* tribune *f* (*pour un orateur etc*)
rosy ['rəuzɪ] *adj* rose; **a ~ future** un bel avenir
rot [rɒt] *n* (*decay*) pourriture *f*; (*fig: pej: nonsense*) idioties *fpl*, balivernes *fpl* ▷ *vt, vi* pourrir; **to stop the ~** (*Brit fig*) rétablir la situation; **dry ~** pourriture sèche (*du bois*); **wet ~** pourriture (*du bois*)
rota ['rəutə] *n* liste *f*, tableau *m* de service; **on a ~ basis** par roulement
rotary ['rəutərɪ] *adj* rotatif(-ive)
rotate [rəu'teɪt] *vt* (*revolve*) faire tourner; (*change round: crops*) alterner; (: *jobs*) faire à tour de rôle ▷ *vi* (*revolve*) tourner
rotating [rəu'teɪtɪŋ] *adj* (*movement*) tournant(e)
rotation [rəu'teɪʃən] *n* rotation *f*; **in ~** à tour de rôle
rote [rəut] *n*: **by ~** machinalement, par cœur
rotor ['rəutə^r] *n* rotor *m*
rotten ['rɒtn] *adj* (*decayed*) pourri(e); (*dishonest*) corrompu(e); (*inf: bad*) mauvais(e), moche; **to feel ~** (*ill*) être mal fichu(e)
rotting ['rɒtɪŋ] *adj* pourrissant(e)
rotund [rəu'tʌnd] *adj* rondelet(te); arrondi(e)
rouble, (*US*) **ruble** ['ru:bl] *n* rouble *m*
rouge [ru:ʒ] *n* rouge *m* (à joues)
rough [rʌf] *adj* (*cloth, skin*) rêche, rugueux(-euse); (*terrain*) accidenté(e); (*path*) rocailleux(-euse); (*voice*) rauque, rude; (*person, manner: coarse*) rude, fruste; (: *violent*) brutal(e); (*district, weather*) mauvais(e); (*sea*) houleux(-euse); (*plan*) ébauché(e); (*guess*) approximatif(-ive) ▷ *n* (*Golf*) rough *m* ▷ *vt*: **to ~ it** vivre à la dure; **the sea is ~ today** la mer est agitée aujourd'hui; **to have a ~ time (of it)** en voir de dures; **~ estimate** approximation *f*; **to play ~** jouer avec brutalité; **to sleep ~** (*Brit*) coucher à la dure; **to feel ~** (*Brit*) être mal fichu(e)
▶ **rough out** *vt* (*draft*) ébaucher
roughage ['rʌfɪdʒ] *n* fibres *fpl* diététiques
rough-and-ready ['rʌfən'rɛdɪ] *adj* (*accommodation, method*) rudimentaire
rough-and-tumble ['rʌfən'tʌmbl] *n* agitation *f*
roughcast ['rʌfkɑ:st] *n* crépi *m*
rough copy, rough draft *n* brouillon *m*
roughen ['rʌfn] *vt* (*a surface*) rendre rude or rugueux(-euse)
rough justice *n* justice *f* sommaire
roughly ['rʌflɪ] *adv* (*handle*) rudement, brutalement; (*speak*) avec brusquerie; (*make*) grossièrement; (*approximately*) à peu près, en gros; **~ speaking** en gros
roughness ['rʌfnɪs] *n* (*of cloth, skin*) rugosité *f*; (*of person*) rudesse *f*; brutalité *f*
roughshod ['rʌfʃɒd] *adv*: **to ride ~ over** ne tenir aucun compte de

rough work *n* (*at school etc*) brouillon *m*
roulette [ru:'lɛt] *n* roulette *f*
Roumania *etc* [ru:'meɪnɪə] = **Romania** *etc*
round [raund] *adj* rond(e) ▷ *n* rond *m*, cercle *m*; (*Brit: of toast*) tranche *f*; (*duty: of policeman, milkman etc*) tournée *f*; (: *of doctor*) visites *fpl*; (*game: of cards, in competition*) partie *f*; (*Boxing*) round *m*; (*of talks*) série *f* ▷ *vt* (*corner*) tourner; (*bend*) prendre; (*cape*) doubler ▷ *prep* autour de ▷ *adv*: **right ~, all ~** tout autour; **in ~ figures** en chiffres ronds; **to go the ~s** (*disease, story*) circuler; **the daily ~** (*fig*) la routine quotidienne; **~ of ammunition** cartouche *f*; **~ of applause** applaudissements *mpl*; **~ of drinks** tournée *f*; **~ of sandwiches** (*Brit*) sandwich *m*; **the long way ~** (par) le chemin le plus long; **all (the) year ~** toute l'année; **it's just ~ the corner** c'est juste après le coin; (*fig*) c'est tout près; **to ask sb ~** inviter qn (chez soi); **I'll be ~ at 6 o'clock** je serai là à 6 heures; **to go ~** faire le tour or un détour; **to go ~ to sb's (house)** aller chez qn; **to go ~ an obstacle** contourner un obstacle; **go ~ the back** passez par derrière; **to go ~ a house** visiter une maison, faire le tour d'une maison; **enough to go ~** assez pour tout le monde; **she arrived ~ (about) noon** (*Brit*) elle est arrivée vers midi; **~ the clock** 24 heures sur 24
▶ **round off** *vt* (*speech etc*) terminer
▶ **round up** *vt* rassembler; (*criminals*) effectuer une rafle de; (*prices*) arrondir (au chiffre supérieur)
roundabout ['raundəbaut] *n* (*Brit Aut*) rond-point *m* (à sens giratoire); (*at fair*) manège *m* (de chevaux de bois) ▷ *adj* (*route, means*) détourné(e)
rounded ['raundɪd] *adj* arrondi(e); (*style*) harmonieux(-euse)
rounders ['raundəz] *npl* (*game*) ≈ balle *f* au camp
roundly ['raundlɪ] *adv* (*fig*) tout net, carrément
round-shouldered ['raund'ʃəuldəd] *adj* au dos rond
round trip *n* (voyage *m*) aller et retour *m*
roundup ['raundʌp] *n* rassemblement *m*; (*of criminals*) rafle *f*; **a ~ of the latest news** un rappel des derniers événements
rouse [rauz] *vt* (*wake up*) réveiller; (*stir up*) susciter, provoquer; (*interest*) éveiller; (*suspicions*) susciter, éveiller
rousing ['rauzɪŋ] *adj* (*welcome*) enthousiaste
rout [raut] *n* (*Mil*) déroute *f* ▷ *vt* mettre en déroute
route [ru:t] *n* itinéraire *m*; (*of bus*) parcours *m*; (*of trade, shipping*) route *f*; **"all ~s"** (*Aut*) "toutes directions"; **the best ~ to London** le meilleur itinéraire pour aller à Londres
route map *n* (*Brit: for journey*) croquis *m* d'itinéraire; (*for trains etc*) carte *f* du réseau
routine [ru:'ti:n] *adj* (*work*) ordinaire, courant(e); (*procedure*) d'usage ▷ *n* (*habits*) habitudes *fpl*; (*pej*) train-train *m*; (*Theat*) numéro *m*; **daily ~** occupations journalières
roving ['rəuvɪŋ] *adj* (*life*) vagabond(e)
roving reporter *n* reporter volant

r

row¹ [rəu] n (line) rangée f; (of people, seats, Knitting) rang m; (behind one another: of cars, people) file f ▷ vi (in boat) ramer; (as sport) faire de l'aviron ▷ vt (boat) faire aller à la rame or à l'aviron; **in a ~** (fig) d'affilée

row² [rau] n (noise) vacarme m; (dispute) dispute f, querelle f; (scolding) réprimande f, savon m ▷ vi (also: **to have a row**) se disputer, se quereller

rowboat ['rəubəut] n (US) canot m (à rames)

rowdiness ['raudɪnɪs] n tapage m, chahut m; (fighting) bagarre f

rowdy ['raudɪ] adj chahuteur(-euse); bagarreur(-euse) ▷ n voyou m

rowdyism ['raudɪɪzəm] n tapage m, chahut m

rowing ['rəuɪŋ] n canotage m; (as sport) aviron m

rowing boat n (Brit) canot m (à rames)

rowlock ['rɔlək] n (Brit) dame f de nage, tolet m

royal ['rɔɪəl] adj royal(e)

Royal Academy, Royal Academy of Arts n (Brit) l'Académie f royale des Beaux-Arts; voir article

● ROYAL ACADEMY (OF ARTS)

● La Royal Academy ou Royal Academy of Arts,
● fondée en 1768 par George III pour
● encourager la peinture, la sculpture et
● l'architecture, est située à Burlington
● House, sur Piccadilly. Une exposition des
● œuvres d'artistes contemporains a lieu tous
● les étés. L'Académie dispense également des
● cours en peinture, sculpture et architecture.

Royal Air Force n (Brit) armée de l'air britannique

royal blue adj bleu roi inv

royalist ['rɔɪəlɪst] adj, n royaliste m/f

Royal Navy n (Brit) marine de guerre britannique

royalty ['rɔɪəltɪ] n (royal persons) (membres mpl de la) famille royale; (payment: to author) droits mpl d'auteur; (: to inventor) royalties fpl

RP n abbr (Brit: = received pronunciation) prononciation f standard

RPI n abbr = **retail price index**

rpm abbr (= revolutions per minute) t/mn (= = tours/minute)

RR abbr (US) = **railroad**

RRP abbr = **recommended retail price**

RSA n abbr (Brit) = **Royal Society of Arts; Royal Scottish Academy**

RSI n abbr (Med: = repetitive strain injury) microtraumatisme permanent

RSPB n abbr (Brit: = Royal Society for the Protection of Birds) ≈ LPO f

RSPCA n abbr (Brit: = Royal Society for the Prevention of Cruelty to Animals) ≈ SPA f

R.S.V.P. abbr (= répondez s'il vous plaît) RSVP

RTA n abbr (= road traffic accident) accident m de la route

Rt. Hon. abbr (Brit: = Right Honourable) titre donné aux députés de la Chambre des communes

Rt Rev. abbr (= Right Reverend) très révérend

rub [rʌb] n (with cloth) coup m de chiffon or de torchon; (on person) friction f; **to give sth a ~** donner un coup de chiffon or de torchon à qch ▷ vt frotter; (person) frictionner; (hands) se frotter; **to ~ sb up** (Brit) or **to ~ sb** (US) **the wrong way** prendre qn à rebrousse-poil

▶ **rub down** vt (body) frictionner; (horse) bouchonner

▶ **rub in** vt (ointment) faire pénétrer

▶ **rub off** vi partir; **to ~ off on** déteindre sur

▶ **rub out** vt effacer ▷ vi s'effacer

rubber ['rʌbəʳ] n caoutchouc m; (Brit: eraser) gomme f (à effacer)

rubber band n élastique m

rubber bullet n balle f en caoutchouc

rubber gloves npl gants mpl en caoutchouc

rubber plant n caoutchouc m (plante verte)

rubber ring n (for swimming) bouée f (de natation)

rubber stamp n tampon m

rubber-stamp [rʌbə'stæmp] vt (fig) approuver sans discussion

rubbery ['rʌbərɪ] adj caoutchouteux(-euse)

rubbish ['rʌbɪʃ] n (from household) ordures fpl; (fig: pej) choses fpl sans valeur; camelote f; (nonsense) bêtises fpl, idioties fpl ▷ vt (Brit inf) dénigrer, rabaisser; **what you've just said is ~** tu viens de dire une bêtise

rubbish bin n (Brit) boîte f à ordures, poubelle f

rubbish dump n (Brit: in town) décharge publique, dépotoir m

rubbishy ['rʌbɪʃɪ] adj (Brit inf) qui ne vaut rien, moche

rubble ['rʌbl] n décombres mpl; (smaller) gravats mpl; (Constr) blocage m

ruble ['ru:bl] n (US) = **rouble**

ruby ['ru:bɪ] n rubis m

RUC n abbr (Brit) = **Royal Ulster Constabulary**

rucksack ['rʌksæk] n sac m à dos

ructions ['rʌkʃənz] npl grabuge m

rudder ['rʌdəʳ] n gouvernail m

ruddy ['rʌdɪ] adj (face) coloré(e); (inf: damned) sacré(e), fichu(e)

rude [ru:d] adj (impolite: person) impoli(e); (: word, manners) grossier(-ière); (shocking) indécent(e), inconvenant(e); **to be ~ to sb** être grossier envers qn

rudely ['ru:dlɪ] adv impoliment; grossièrement

rudeness ['ru:dnɪs] n impolitesse f; grossièreté f

rudiment ['ru:dɪmənt] n rudiment m

rudimentary [ru:dɪ'mɛntərɪ] adj rudimentaire

rue [ru:] vt se repentir de, regretter amèrement

rueful ['ru:ful] adj triste

ruff [rʌf] n fraise f, collerette f

ruffian ['rʌfɪən] n brute f, voyou m

ruffle ['rʌfl] vt (hair) ébouriffer; (clothes) chiffonner; (water) agiter; (fig: person) émouvoir, faire perdre son flegme à; **to get ~d** s'énerver

rug [rʌg] n petit tapis; (Brit: blanket) couverture f

rugby ['rʌgbɪ] n (also: **rugby football**) rugby m

rugged ['rʌgɪd] adj (landscape) accidenté(e); (features, character) rude; (determination) farouche

rugger ['rʌgəʳ] n (Brit inf) rugby m

ruin ['ru:ɪn] n ruine f ▷ vt ruiner; (spoil: clothes)

abîmer; (: *event*) gâcher; **ruins** *npl* (*of building*) ruine(s); **in ~s** en ruine
ruination [ruːɪˈneɪʃən] *n* ruine *f*
ruinous [ˈruːɪnəs] *adj* ruineux(-euse)
rule [ruːl] *n* règle *f*; (*regulation*) règlement *m*; (*government*) autorité *f*, gouvernement *m*; (*dominion etc*): **under British ~** sous l'autorité britannique ▷ *vt* (*country*) gouverner; (*person*) dominer; (*decide*) décider ▷ *vi* commander; décider; (*Law*): **to ~ against/in favour of/on** statuer contre/en faveur de/sur; **to ~ that** (*umpire, judge etc*) décider que; **it's against the ~s** c'est contraire au règlement; **by ~ of thumb** à vue de nez; **as a ~** normalement, en règle générale
▸ **rule out** *vt* exclure; **murder cannot be ~d out** l'hypothèse d'un meurtre ne peut être exclue
ruled [ruːld] *adj* (*paper*) réglé(e)
ruler [ˈruːləʳ] *n* (*sovereign*) souverain(e); (*leader*) chef *m* (d'État); (*for measuring*) règle *f*
ruling [ˈruːlɪŋ] *adj* (*party*) au pouvoir; (*class*) dirigeant(e) ▷ *n* (*Law*) décision *f*
rum [rʌm] *n* rhum *m* ▷ *adj* (*Brit inf*) bizarre
Rumania [ruːˈmeɪnɪə] *n* Roumanie *f*
Rumanian [ruːˈmeɪnɪən] *adj* roumain(e) ▷ *n* Roumain(e); (*Ling*) roumain *m*
rumble [ˈrʌmbl] *n* grondement *m*; (*of stomach, pipe*) gargouillement *m* ▷ *vi* gronder; (*stomach, pipe*) gargouiller
rumbustious [rʌmˈbʌstʃəs], **rumbunctious** [rʌmˈbʌŋkʃəs] *adj* (*US: person*) exubérant(e)
rummage [ˈrʌmɪdʒ] *vi* fouiller
rumour, (*US*) **rumor** [ˈruːməʳ] *n* rumeur *f*, bruit *m* (qui court) ▷ *vt*: **it is ~ed that** le bruit court que
rump [rʌmp] *n* (*of animal*) croupe *f*
rumple [ˈrʌmpl] *vt* (*hair*) ébouriffer; (*clothes*) chiffonner, friper
rump steak *n* romsteck *m*
rumpus [ˈrʌmpəs] *n* (*inf*) tapage *m*, chahut *m*; (*quarrel*) prise *f* de bec; **to kick up a ~** faire toute une histoire
run [rʌn] (*pt* **ran**, *pp* ~) [ræn, rʌn] *n* (*race*) course *f*; (*outing*) tour *m* or promenade *f* (en voiture); (*distance travelled*) parcours *m*, trajet *m*; (*series*) suite *f*, série *f*; (*Theat*) série de représentations; (*Ski*) piste *f*; (*Cricket, Baseball*) point *m*; (*in tights, stockings*) maille filée, échelle *f* ▷ *vt* (*business*) diriger; (*competition, course*) organiser; (*hotel, house*) tenir; (*race*) participer à; (*Comput: program*) exécuter; (*force through: rope, pipe*): **to ~ sth through** faire passer qch à travers; (*to pass: hand, finger*): **to ~ sth over** promener or passer qch sur; (*water, bath*) faire couler; (*Press: feature*) publier ▷ *vi* courir; (*pass: road etc*) passer; (*work: machine, factory*) marcher; (*bus, train*) circuler; (*continue: play*) se jouer, être à l'affiche; (: *contract*) être valide or en vigueur; (*slide: drawer etc*) glisser; (*flow: river, bath, nose*) couler; (*colours, washing*) déteindre; (*in election*) être candidat, se présenter; **at a ~** au pas de course; **to go for a ~**

aller courir or faire un peu de course à pied; (*in car*) faire un tour or une promenade (en voiture); **to break into a ~** se mettre à courir; **a ~ of luck** une série de coups de chance; **to have the ~ of sb's house** avoir la maison de qn à sa disposition; **there was a ~ on** (*meat, tickets*) les gens se sont rués sur; **in the long ~** à la longue, à longue échéance; **in the short ~** à brève échéance, à court terme; **on the ~** en fuite; **to make a ~ for it** s'enfuir; **I'll ~ you to the station** je vais vous emmener or conduire à la gare; **to ~ errands** faire des commissions; **the train ~s between Gatwick and Victoria** le train assure le service entre Gatwick et Victoria; **the bus ~s every 20 minutes** il y a un autobus toutes les 20 minutes; **it's very cheap to ~** (*car, machine*) c'est très économique; **to ~ on petrol** or (*US*) **gas/on diesel/off batteries** marcher à l'essence/au diesel/sur piles; **to ~ for president** être candidat à la présidence; **to ~ a risk** courir un risque; **their losses ran into millions** leurs pertes se sont élevées à plusieurs millions; **to be ~ off one's feet** (*Brit*) ne plus savoir où donner de la tête
▸ **run about** *vi* (*children*) courir çà et là
▸ **run across** *vt fus* (*find*) trouver par hasard
▸ **run after** *vt fus* (*to catch up*) courir après; (*chase*) poursuivre
▸ **run around** *vi* = **run about**
▸ **run away** *vi* s'enfuir
▸ **run down** *vi* (*clock*) s'arrêter (faute d'avoir été remonté) ▷ *vt* (*Aut: knock over*) renverser; (*Brit: reduce: production*) réduire progressivement; (: *factory/shop*) réduire progressivement la production/l'activité de; (*criticize*) critiquer, dénigrer; **to be ~ down** (*tired*) être fatigué(e) or à plat
▸ **run in** *vt* (*Brit: car*) roder
▸ **run into** *vt fus* (*meet: person*) rencontrer par hasard; (: *trouble*) se heurter à; (*collide with*) heurter; **to ~ into debt** contracter des dettes
▸ **run off** *vi* s'enfuir ▷ *vt* (*water*) laisser s'écouler; (*copies*) tirer
▸ **run out** *vi* (*person*) sortir en courant; (*liquid*) couler; (*lease*) expirer; (*money*) être épuisé(e)
▸ **run out of** *vt fus* se trouver à court de; **I've ~ out of petrol** or (*US*) **gas** je suis en panne d'essence
▸ **run over** *vt* (*Aut*) écraser ▷ *vt fus* (*revise*) revoir, reprendre
▸ **run through** *vt fus* (*recap*) reprendre, revoir; (*play*) répéter
▸ **run up** *vi*: **to ~ up against** (*difficulties*) se heurter à ▷ *vt*: **to ~ up a debt** s'endetter
runaround [ˈrʌnəraund] *n* (*inf*): **to give sb the ~** rester très évasif
runaway [ˈrʌnəweɪ] *adj* (*horse*) emballé(e); (*truck*) fou (folle); (*person*) fugitif(-ive); (*child*) fugueur(-euse); (*inflation*) galopant(e)
rundown [ˈrʌndaun] *n* (*Brit: of industry etc*) réduction progressive
rung [rʌŋ] *pp of* **ring** ▷ *n* (*of ladder*) barreau *m*

r

run-in ['rʌnɪn] *n (inf)* accrochage *m*, prise *f* de bec
runner ['rʌnəʳ] *n (in race: person)* coureur(-euse); (*: horse*) partant *m*; *(on sledge)* patin *m*; *(for drawer etc)* coulisseau *m*; *(carpet: in hall etc)* chemin *m*
runner bean *n (Brit)* haricot *m* (à rames)
runner-up [rʌnər'ʌp] *n* second(e)
running ['rʌnɪŋ] *n (in race etc)* course *f*; *(of business, organization)* direction *f*, gestion *f*; *(of event)* organisation *f*; *(of machine etc)* marche *f*, fonctionnement *m* ▷ *adj (water)* courant(e); *(commentary)* suivi(e); **6 days ~** 6 jours de suite; **to be in/out of the ~ for sth** être/ne pas être sur les rangs pour qch
running commentary *n* commentaire détaillé
running costs *npl (of business)* frais *mpl* de gestion; *(of car)*: **the ~ are high** elle revient cher
running head *n (Typ, Comput)* titre courant
running mate *n (US Pol)* candidat à la vice-présidence
runny ['rʌnɪ] *adj* qui coule
run-off ['rʌnɔf] *n (in contest, election)* deuxième tour *m*; *(extra race etc)* épreuve *f* supplémentaire
run-of-the-mill ['rʌnəvðə'mɪl] *adj* ordinaire, banal(e)
runt [rʌnt] *n* avorton *m*
run-through ['rʌnθruː] *n* répétition *f*, essai *m*
run-up ['rʌnʌp] *n (Brit)*: **~ to sth** période *f* précédant qch
runway ['rʌnweɪ] *n (Aviat)* piste *f* (d'envol or d'atterrissage)
rupee [ruː'piː] *n* roupie *f*
rupture ['rʌptʃəʳ] *n (Med)* hernie *f* ▷ *vt*: **to ~ o.s.** se donner une hernie
rural ['ruərl] *adj* rural(e)
ruse [ruːz] *n* ruse *f*
rush [rʌʃ] *n* course précipitée; *(of crowd, Comm: sudden demand)* ruée *f*; *(hurry)* hâte *f*; *(of anger, joy)*

accès *m*; *(current)* flot *m*; *(Bot)* jonc *m*; *(for chair)* paille *f* ▷ *vt (hurry)* transporter or envoyer d'urgence; *(attack: town etc)* prendre d'assaut; *(Brit inf: overcharge)* estamper; faire payer ▷ *vi* se précipiter; **don't ~ me!** laissez-moi le temps de souffler!; **to ~ sth off** *(do quickly)* faire qch à la hâte; *(send)* envoyer qch d'urgence; **is there any ~ for this?** est-ce urgent?; **we've had a ~ of orders** nous avons reçu une avalanche de commandes; **I'm in a ~ (to do)** je suis vraiment pressé (de faire); **gold ~** ruée vers l'or
▶ **rush through** *vt fus (work)* exécuter à la hâte ▷ *vt (Comm: order)* exécuter d'urgence
rush hour *n* heures *fpl* de pointe or d'affluence
rush job *n* travail urgent
rush matting *n* natte *f* de paille
rusk [rʌsk] *n* biscotte *f*
Russia ['rʌʃə] *n* Russie *f*
Russian ['rʌʃən] *adj* russe ▷ *n* Russe *m/f*; *(Ling)* russe *m*
rust [rʌst] *n* rouille *f* ▷ *vi* rouiller
rustic ['rʌstɪk] *adj* rustique ▷ *n (pej)* rustaud(e)
rustle ['rʌsl] *vi* bruire, produire un bruissement ▷ *vt (paper)* froisser; *(US: cattle)* voler
rustproof ['rʌstpruːf] *adj* inoxydable
rustproofing ['rʌstpruːfɪŋ] *n* traitement *m* antirouille
rusty ['rʌstɪ] *adj* rouillé(e)
rut [rʌt] *n* ornière *f*; *(Zool)* rut *m*; **to be in a ~** *(fig)* suivre l'ornière, s'encroûter
rutabaga [ruːtə'beɪgə] *n (US)* rutabaga *m*
ruthless ['ruːθlɪs] *adj* sans pitié, impitoyable
ruthlessness ['ruːθlɪsnɪs] *n* dureté *f*, cruauté *f*
RV *abbr (= revised version)* traduction anglaise de la Bible de 1885 ▷ *n abbr (US)* = **recreational vehicle**
rye [raɪ] *n* seigle *m*
rye bread *n* pain *m* de seigle

Ss

S, s [ɛs] n (letter) S, s m; (US Scol: satisfactory)
≈ assez bien; **S for Sugar** S comme Suzanne
S abbr (= south, small) S; (= saint) St
SA n abbr = **South Africa**; **South America**
Sabbath ['sæbəθ] n (Jewish) sabbat m; (Christian)
dimanche m
sabbatical [sə'bætɪkl] adj: **~ year** année f
sabbatique
sabotage ['sæbətɑːʒ] n sabotage m ▷ vt saboter
saccharin, saccharine ['sækərɪn] n
saccharine f
sachet ['sæʃeɪ] n sachet m
sack [sæk] n (bag) sac m ▷ vt (dismiss) renvoyer,
mettre à la porte; (plunder) piller, mettre à sac;
to give sb the ~ renvoyer qn, mettre qn à la
porte; **to get the ~** être renvoyé(e) or mis(e) à la
porte
sackful ['sækful] n: **a ~ of** un (plein) sac de
sacking ['sækɪŋ] n toile f à sac; (dismissal)
renvoi m
sacrament ['sækrəmənt] n sacrement m
sacred ['seɪkrɪd] adj sacré(e)
sacred cow n (fig) chose sacro-sainte
sacrifice ['sækrɪfaɪs] n sacrifice m ▷ vt sacrifier;
to make ~s (for sb) se sacrifier or faire des
sacrifices (pour qn)
sacrilege ['sækrɪlɪdʒ] n sacrilège m
sacrosanct ['sækrəusæŋkt] adj sacro-saint(e)
sad [sæd] adj (unhappy) triste; (deplorable) triste,
fâcheux(-euse); (inf: pathetic: thing) triste,
lamentable; (: person) minable
sadden ['sædn] vt attrister, affliger
saddle ['sædl] n selle f ▷ vt (horse) seller; **to be
~d with sth** (inf) avoir qch sur les bras
saddlebag ['sædlbæg] n sacoche f
sadism ['seɪdɪzəm] n sadisme m
sadist ['seɪdɪst] n sadique m/f
sadistic [sə'dɪstɪk] adj sadique
sadly ['sædlɪ] adv tristement; (unfortunately)
malheureusement; (seriously) fort
sadness ['sædnɪs] n tristesse f
sado-masochism [seɪdəu'mæsəkɪzəm] n
sadomasochisme m
s.a.e. n abbr (Brit: = stamped addressed envelope)
enveloppe affranchie pour la réponse
safari [sə'fɑːrɪ] n safari m

safari park n réserve f
safe [seɪf] adj (out of danger) hors de danger, en
sécurité; (not dangerous) sans danger; (cautious)
prudent(e); (sure: bet) assuré(e) ▷ n coffre-fort
m; **~ from** à l'abri de; **~ and sound** sain(e) et
sauf (sauve); **(just) to be on the ~ side** pour
plus de sûreté, par précaution; **to play ~** ne
prendre aucun risque; **it is ~ to say that ...** on
peut dire sans crainte que ...; **~ journey!** bon
voyage!
safe bet n: **it was a ~** ça ne comportait pas trop
de risques; **it's a ~ that he'll be late** il y a
toutes les chances pour qu'il soit en retard
safe-breaker ['seɪfbreɪkəʳ] n (Brit) perceur m de
coffre-fort
safe-conduct [seɪf'kɔndʌkt] n sauf-conduit m
safe-cracker ['seɪfkrækəʳ] n = **safe-breaker**
safe-deposit ['seɪfdɪpɔzɪt] n (vault) dépôt m de
coffres-forts; (box) coffre-fort m
safeguard ['seɪfgɑːd] n sauvegarde f, protection
f ▷ vt sauvegarder, protéger
safe haven n zone f de sécurité
safekeeping ['seɪf'kiːpɪŋ] n bonne garde
safely ['seɪflɪ] adv (assume, say) sans risque
d'erreur; (drive, arrive) sans accident; **I can ~
say ...** je peux dire à coup sûr ...
safe passage n: **to grant sb ~** accorder un
laissez-passer à qn
safe sex n rapports sexuels protégés
safety ['seɪftɪ] n sécurité f; **~ first!** la sécurité
d'abord!
safety belt n ceinture f de sécurité
safety catch n cran m de sûreté or sécurité
safety net n filet m de sécurité
safety pin n épingle f de sûreté or de nourrice
safety valve n soupape f de sûreté
saffron ['sæfrən] n safran m
sag [sæg] vi s'affaisser, fléchir; (hem, breasts)
pendre
saga ['sɑːgə] n saga f; (fig) épopée f
sage [seɪdʒ] n (herb) sauge f; (person) sage m
Sagittarius [sædʒɪ'tɛərɪəs] n le Sagittaire; **to be
~** être du Sagittaire
sago ['seɪgəu] n sagou m
Sahara [sə'hɑːrə] n: **the ~ (Desert)** le (désert du)
Sahara m

Sahel [sæ'hɛl] n Sahel m
said [sɛd] pt, pp of **say**
Saigon [saɪ'gɔn] n Saigon
sail [seɪl] n (on boat) voile f; (trip): **to go for a ~**
faire un tour en bateau ▷ vt (boat) manœuvrer,
piloter ▷ vi (travel: ship) avancer, naviguer;
(: passenger) aller or se rendre (en bateau); (set off)
partir, prendre la mer; (Sport) faire de la voile;
they ~ed into Le Havre ils sont entrés dans le
port du Havre
  ▶ **sail through** vi, vt fus (fig) réussir haut la main
sailboat ['seɪlbəut] n (US) bateau m à voiles,
voilier m
sailing ['seɪlɪŋ] n (Sport) voile f; **to go ~** faire de la
voile
sailing boat n bateau m à voiles, voilier m
sailing ship n grand voilier
sailor ['seɪləʳ] n marin m, matelot m
saint [seɪnt] n saint(e)
saintly ['seɪntlɪ] adj saint(e), plein(e) de bonté
sake [seɪk] n: **for the ~ of** (out of concern for) pour
(l'amour de), dans l'intérêt de; (out of
consideration for) par égard pour; (in order to achieve)
pour plus de, par souci de; **arguing for
arguing's ~** discuter pour (le plaisir de)
discuter; **for heaven's ~!** pour l'amour du ciel!;
for the ~ of argument à titre d'exemple
salad ['sæləd] n salade f; **tomato ~** salade de
tomates
salad bowl n saladier m
salad cream n (Brit) (sorte f de) mayonnaise f
salad dressing n vinaigrette f
salad oil n huile f de table
salami [sə'lɑːmɪ] n salami m
salaried ['sælərɪd] adj (staff) salarié(e), qui
touche un traitement
salary ['sælərɪ] n salaire m, traitement m
salary scale n échelle f des traitements
sale [seɪl] n vente f; (at reduced prices) soldes mpl;
sales npl (total amount sold) chiffre m de ventes;
"for ~" "à vendre"; **on ~** en vente; **on ~ or
return** vendu(e) avec faculté de retour;
closing-down or **liquidation ~** (US) liquidation
f (avant fermeture); **~ and lease back** n cession-
bail f
saleroom ['seɪlruːm] n salle f des ventes
sales assistant, (US) **sales clerk** n
vendeur(-euse)
sales conference n réunion f de vente
sales drive n campagne commerciale,
animation f des ventes
sales force n (ensemble m du) service des ventes
salesman ['seɪlzmən] (irreg) n (in shop) vendeur
m; (representative) représentant m de commerce
sales manager n directeur commercial
salesmanship ['seɪlzmənʃɪp] n art m de la vente
salesperson ['seɪlzpəːsn] (irreg) n (in shop)
vendeur(-euse)
sales rep n (Comm) représentant(e) m/f
sales tax n (US) taxe f à l'achat
saleswoman ['seɪlzwumən] (irreg) n (in shop)
vendeuse f

salient ['seɪlɪənt] adj saillant(e)
saline ['seɪlaɪn] adj salin(e)
saliva [sə'laɪvə] n salive f
sallow ['sæləu] adj cireux(-euse)
sally forth, sally out ['sælɪ-] vi partir plein(e)
d'entrain
salmon ['sæmən] n (pl inv) saumon m
salmon trout n truite saumonée
salon ['sælɔn] n salon m
saloon [sə'luːn] n (US) bar m; (Brit Aut) berline f;
(ship's lounge) salon m
SALT [sɔːlt] n abbr (= Strategic Arms Limitation Talks/
Treaty) SALT m
salt [sɔːlt] n sel m ▷ vt saler ▷ cpd de sel; (Culin)
salé(e); **an old ~** un vieux loup de mer
  ▶ **salt away** vt mettre de côté
salt cellar n salière f
salt-free ['sɔːlt'friː] adj sans sel
saltwater ['sɔːlt'wɔːtəʳ] adj (fish etc) (d'eau) de
mer
salty ['sɔːltɪ] adj salé(e)
salubrious [sə'luːbrɪəs] adj salubre
salutary ['sæljutərɪ] adj salutaire
salute [sə'luːt] n salut m; (of guns) salve f ▷ vt
saluer
salvage ['sælvɪdʒ] n (saving) sauvetage m; (things
saved) biens sauvés or récupérés ▷ vt sauver,
récupérer
salvage vessel n bateau m de sauvetage
salvation [sæl'veɪʃən] n salut m
Salvation Army [sæl'veɪʃən-] n Armée f du
Salut
salver ['sælvəʳ] n plateau m de métal
salvo ['sælvəu] n salve f
Samaritan [sə'mærɪtən] n: **the ~s** (organization)
≈ S.O.S. Amitié
same [seɪm] adj même ▷ pron: **the ~** le (la)
même, les mêmes; **the ~ book as** le même livre
que; **on the ~ day** le même jour; **at the ~ time**
en même temps; (yet) néanmoins; **all** or **just
the ~** tout de même, quand même; **they're one
and the ~** (person/thing) c'est une seule et même
personne/chose; **to do the ~** faire de même, en
faire autant; **to do the ~ as sb** faire comme qn;
and the ~ to you! et à vous de même!; (after
insult) toi-même!; **~ here!** moi aussi!; **the ~
again!** (in bar etc) la même chose!
sample ['sɑːmpl] n échantillon m; (Med)
prélèvement m ▷ vt (food, wine) goûter; **to take a
~** prélever un échantillon; **free ~** échantillon
gratuit
sanatorium (pl **sanatoria**) [sænə'tɔːrɪəm, -rɪə] n
sanatorium m
sanctify ['sæŋktɪfaɪ] vt sanctifier
sanctimonious [sæŋktɪ'məunɪəs] adj
moralisateur(-trice)
sanction ['sæŋkʃən] n approbation f, sanction f
▷ vt cautionner, sanctionner; **sanctions** npl
(Pol) sanctions; **to impose economic ~s on** or
against prendre des sanctions économiques
contre
sanctity ['sæŋktɪtɪ] n sainteté f, caractère sacré

sanctuary ['sæŋktjuərɪ] n (holy place) sanctuaire m; (refuge) asile m; (for wildlife) réserve f

sand [sænd] n sable m ▷ vt sabler; (also: **sand down**: wood etc) poncer

sandal ['sændl] n sandale f

sandbag ['sændbæg] n sac m de sable

sandblast ['sændblɑːst] vt décaper à la sableuse

sandbox ['sændbɔks] n (US: for children) tas m de sable

sand castle ['sændkɑːsl] n château m de sable

sand dune n dune f de sable

sander ['sændər] n ponceuse f

S&M n abbr (= sadomasochism) sadomasochisme m

sandpaper ['sændpeɪpər] n papier m de verre

sandpit ['sændpɪt] n (Brit: for children) tas m de sable

sands [sændz] npl plage f (de sable)

sandstone ['sændstəun] n grès m

sandstorm ['sændstɔːm] n tempête f de sable

sandwich ['sændwɪtʃ] n sandwich m ▷ vt (also: **sandwich in**) intercaler; **~ed between** pris en sandwich entre; **cheese/ham ~** sandwich au fromage/jambon

sandwich board n panneau m publicitaire (porté par un homme-sandwich)

sandwich course n (Brit) cours m de formation professionnelle

sandy ['sændɪ] adj sablonneux(-euse); couvert(e) de sable; (colour) sable inv, blond roux inv

sane [seɪn] adj (person) sain(e) d'esprit; (outlook) sensé(e), sain(e)

sang [sæŋ] pt of **sing**

sanguine ['sæŋgwɪn] adj optimiste

sanitarium (pl **sanitaria**) [sænɪˈtɛərɪəm, -rɪə] n (US) = **sanatorium**

sanitary ['sænɪtərɪ] adj (system, arrangements) sanitaire; (clean) hygiénique

sanitary towel, (US) **sanitary napkin** ['sænɪtərɪ-] n serviette f hygiénique

sanitation [sænɪˈteɪʃən] n (in house) installations fpl sanitaires; (in town) système m sanitaire

sanitation department n (US) service m de voirie

sanity ['sænɪtɪ] n santé mentale; (common sense) bon sens

sank [sæŋk] pt of **sink**

San Marino ['sænməˈriːnəu] n Saint-Marin m

Santa Claus [sæntəˈklɔːz] n le Père Noël

Santiago [sæntɪˈɑːgəu] n (also: **Santiago de Chile**) Santiago (du Chili)

sap [sæp] n (of plants) sève f ▷ vt (strength) saper, miner

sapling ['sæplɪŋ] n jeune arbre m

sapphire ['sæfaɪər] n saphir m

sarcasm ['sɑːkæzm] n sarcasme m, raillerie f

sarcastic [sɑːˈkæstɪk] adj sarcastique

sarcophagus (pl **sarcophagi**) [sɑːˈkɔfəgəs, -gaɪ] n sarcophage m

sardine [sɑːˈdiːn] n sardine f

Sardinia [sɑːˈdɪnɪə] n Sardaigne f

Sardinian [sɑːˈdɪnɪən] adj sarde ▷ n Sarde m/f;

(Ling) sarde m

sardonic [sɑːˈdɔnɪk] adj sardonique

sari ['sɑːrɪ] n sari m

SARS ['sɑːrz] n abbr = severe acute respiratory syndrome

sartorial [sɑːˈtɔːrɪəl] adj vestimentaire

SAS n abbr (Brit Mil: = Special Air Service) ≈ GIGN m

SASE n abbr (US: = self-addressed stamped envelope) enveloppe affranchie pour la réponse

sash [sæʃ] n écharpe f

sash window n fenêtre f à guillotine

Sask. abbr (Canada) = **Saskatchewan**

sat [sæt] pt, pp of **sit**

Sat. abbr (= Saturday) sa

Satan ['seɪtn] n Satan m

satanic [səˈtænɪk] adj satanique, démoniaque

satchel ['sætʃl] n cartable m

sated ['seɪtɪd] adj repu(e); blasé(e)

satellite ['sætəlaɪt] adj, n satellite m

satellite dish n antenne f parabolique

satellite navigation system n système m de navigation par satellite

satellite television n télévision f par satellite

satiate ['seɪʃɪeɪt] vt rassasier

satin ['sætɪn] n satin m ▷ adj en or de satin, satiné(e); **with a ~ finish** satiné(e)

satire ['sætaɪər] n satire f

satirical [səˈtɪrɪkl] adj satirique

satirist ['sætɪrɪst] n (writer) auteur m satirique; (cartoonist) caricaturiste m/f

satirize ['sætɪraɪz] vt faire la satire de, satiriser

satisfaction [sætɪsˈfækʃən] n satisfaction f

satisfactory [sætɪsˈfæktərɪ] adj satisfaisant(e)

satisfied ['sætɪsfaɪd] adj satisfait(e); **to be ~ with sth** être satisfait de qch

satisfy ['sætɪsfaɪ] vt satisfaire, contenter; (convince) convaincre, persuader; **to ~ the requirements** remplir les conditions; **to ~ sb (that)** convaincre qn (que); **to ~ o.s. of sth** vérifier qch, s'assurer de qch

satisfying ['sætɪsfaɪɪŋ] adj satisfaisant(e)

SAT(s) n abbr (US) = **Scholastic Aptitude Test(s)**

satsuma [sæt'suːmə] n satsuma f

saturate ['sætʃəreɪt] vt: **to ~ (with)** saturer (de)

saturated fat ['sætʃəreɪtɪd-] n graisse saturée

saturation [sætʃəˈreɪʃən] n saturation f

Saturday ['sætədɪ] n samedi m; for phrases see also **Tuesday**

sauce [sɔːs] n sauce f

saucepan ['sɔːspən] n casserole f

saucer ['sɔːsər] n soucoupe f

saucy ['sɔːsɪ] adj impertinent(e)

Saudi Arabia n Arabie f Saoudite

Saudi (Arabian) ['saudi] adj saoudien(ne) ▷ n Saoudien(ne)

sauna ['sɔːnə] n sauna m

saunter ['sɔːntər] vi: **to ~ to** aller en flânant or se balader jusqu'à

sausage ['sɔsɪdʒ] n saucisse f; (salami etc) saucisson m

sausage roll n friand m

sauté ['səuteɪ] adj (Culin: potatoes) sauté(e);

S

(: *onions*) revenu(e) ▷ *vt* faire sauter; faire revenir

sautéed ['səuteɪd] *adj* sauté(e)

savage ['sævɪdʒ] *adj* (*cruel, fierce*) brutal(e), féroce; (*primitive*) primitif(-ive), sauvage ▷ *n* sauvage *m/f* ▷ *vt* attaquer férocement

savagery ['sævɪdʒrɪ] *n* sauvagerie *f*, brutalité *f*, férocité *f*

save [seɪv] *vt* (*person, belongings*) sauver; (*money*) mettre de côté, économiser; (*time*) (faire) gagner; (*keep*) garder; (*Comput*) sauvegarder; (*Sport: stop*) arrêter; (*avoid: trouble*) éviter ▷ *vi* (*also:* **save up**) mettre de l'argent de côté ▷ *n* (*Sport*) arrêt *m* (du ballon) ▷ *prep* sauf, à l'exception de; **it will ~ me an hour** ça me fera gagner une heure; **to ~ face** sauver la face; **God ~ the Queen!** vive la Reine!

saving ['seɪvɪŋ] *n* économie *f* ▷ *adj*: **the ~ grace of** ce qui rachète; **savings** *npl* économies *fpl*; **to make ~s** faire des économies

savings account *n* compte *m* d'épargne

savings and loan association (*US*) *n* ≈ société *f* de crédit immobilier

savings bank *n* caisse *f* d'épargne

saviour, (*US*) **savior** ['seɪvjə^r] *n* sauveur *m*

savour, (*US*) **savor** ['seɪvə^r] *n* saveur *f*, goût *m* ▷ *vt* savourer

savoury, (*US*) **savory** ['seɪvərɪ] *adj* savoureux(-euse); (*dish: not sweet*) salé(e)

savvy ['sævɪ] *n* (*inf*) jugeote *f*

saw [sɔː] *pt of* **see** ▷ *n* (*tool*) scie *f* ▷ *vt* (*pt* **-ed**, *pp* **-ed** *or* **-n** [sɔːn]) scier; **to ~ sth up** débiter qch à la scie

sawdust ['sɔːdʌst] *n* sciure *f*

sawmill ['sɔːmɪl] *n* scierie *f*

sawn [sɔːn] *pp of* **saw**

sawn-off ['sɔːnɔf], **sawed-off** ['sɔːdɔf] (*US*) *adj*: **~ shotgun** carabine *f* à canon scié

sax [sæks] (*inf*) *n* saxo *m*

saxophone ['sæksəfəun] *n* saxophone *m*

say [seɪ] *n*: **to have one's ~** dire ce qu'on a à dire ▷ *vt* (*pt, pp* **said**) [sɛd] dire; **to have a ~** avoir voix au chapitre; **could you ~ that again?** pourriez-vous répéter ce que vous venez de dire?; **to ~ yes/no** dire oui/non; **she said (that) I was to give you this** elle m'a chargé de vous remettre ceci; **my watch ~s 3 o'clock** ma montre indique 3 heures, il est 3 heures à ma montre; **shall we ~ Tuesday?** disons mardi?; **that doesn't ~ much for him** ce n'est pas vraiment à son honneur; **when all is said and done** en fin de compte, en définitive; **there is something** *or* **a lot to be said for it** cela a des avantages; **that is to ~** c'est-à-dire; **to ~ nothing of** sans compter; **~ that ...** mettons *or* disons que ...; **that goes without ~ing** cela va sans dire, cela va de soi

saying ['seɪɪŋ] *n* dicton *m*, proverbe *m*

SBA *n abbr* (*US*: = *Small Business Administration*) organisme d'aide aux PME

SC *n abbr* (*US*) = **supreme court** ▷ *abbr* (*US*) = **South Carolina**

s/c *abbr* = **self-contained**

scab [skæb] *n* croûte *f*; (*pej*) jaune *m*

scabby ['skæbɪ] *adj* croûteux(-euse)

scaffold ['skæfəld] *n* échafaud *m*

scaffolding ['skæfəldɪŋ] *n* échafaudage *m*

scald [skɔːld] *n* brûlure *f* ▷ *vt* ébouillanter

scalding ['skɔːldɪŋ] *adj* (*also:* **scalding hot**) brûlant(e), bouillant(e)

scale [skeɪl] *n* (*of fish*) écaille *f*; (*Mus*) gamme *f*; (*of ruler, thermometer etc*) graduation *f*, échelle (graduée); (*of salaries, fees etc*) barème *m*; (*of map, also size, extent*) échelle ▷ *vt* (*mountain*) escalader; (*fish*) écailler; **scales** *npl* balance *f*; (*larger*) bascule *f*; (*also:* **bathroom scales**) pèse-personne *m inv*; **pay ~** échelle des salaires; **~ of charges** tableau *m* des tarifs; **on a large ~** sur une grande échelle, en grand; **to draw sth to ~** dessiner qch à l'échelle; **small-~ model** modèle réduit

▶ **scale down** *vt* réduire

scaled-down [skeɪld'daun] *adj* à échelle réduite

scale drawing *n* dessin *m* à l'échelle

scale model *n* modèle *m* à l'échelle

scallion ['skæljən] *n* oignon *m*; (*US: salad onion*) ciboule *f*; (: *shallot*) échalote *f*; (: *leek*) poireau *m*

scallop ['skɔləp] *n* coquille *f* Saint-Jacques; (*Sewing*) feston *m*

scalp [skælp] *n* cuir chevelu ▷ *vt* scalper

scalpel ['skælpl] *n* scalpel *m*

scalper ['skælpə^r] *n* (*US inf: of tickets*) revendeur *m* de billets

scam [skæm] *n* (*inf*) arnaque *f*

scamp [skæmp] *vt* bâcler

scamper ['skæmpə^r] *vi*: **to ~ away**, **~ off** détaler

scampi ['skæmpɪ] *npl* langoustines (frites), scampi *mpl*

scan [skæn] *vt* (*examine*) scruter, examiner; (*glance at quickly*) parcourir; (*poetry*) scander; (*TV, Radar*) balayer ▷ *n* (*Med*) scanographie *f*

scandal ['skændl] *n* scandale *m*; (*gossip*) ragots *mpl*

scandalize ['skændəlaɪz] *vt* scandaliser, indigner

scandalous ['skændələs] *adj* scandaleux(-euse).

Scandinavia [skændɪ'neɪvɪə] *n* Scandinavie *f*

Scandinavian [skændɪ'neɪvɪən] *adj* scandinave ▷ *n* Scandinave *m/f*

scanner ['skænə^r] *n* (*Radar, Med*) scanner *m*, scanographe *m*; (*Comput*) scanner

scant [skænt] *adj* insuffisant(e)

scantily ['skæntɪlɪ] *adv*: **~ clad** *or* **dressed** vêtu(e) du strict minimum

scanty ['skæntɪ] *adj* peu abondant(e), insuffisant(e), maigre

scapegoat ['skeɪpgəut] *n* bouc *m* émissaire

scar [skɑː^r] *n* cicatrice *f* ▷ *vt* laisser une cicatrice *or* une marque à

scarce [skɛəs] *adj* rare, peu abondant(e); **to make o.s. ~** (*inf*) se sauver

scarcely ['skɛəslɪ] *adv* à peine, presque pas; **~ anybody** pratiquement personne; **I can ~ believe it** j'ai du mal à le croire

scarcity ['skɛəsɪtɪ] n rareté f, manque m, pénurie f

scarcity value n valeur f de rareté

scare [skɛə^r] n peur f, panique f ▷ vt effrayer, faire peur à; **to ~ sb stiff** faire une peur bleue à qn; **bomb ~** alerte f à la bombe
▶ **scare away, scare off** vt faire fuir

scarecrow ['skɛəkrəu] n épouvantail m

scared ['skɛəd] adj: **to be ~** avoir peur

scaremonger ['skɛəmʌŋgə^r] n alarmiste m/f

scarf (pl **scarves**) [skɑ:f, skɑ:vz] n (long) écharpe f; (square) foulard m

scarlet ['skɑ:lɪt] adj écarlate

scarlet fever n scarlatine f

scarper ['skɑ:pə^r] vi (Brit inf) ficher le camp

scarves [skɑ:vz] npl of **scarf**

scary ['skɛərɪ] adj (inf) effrayant(e); (film) qui fait peur

scathing ['skeɪðɪŋ] adj cinglant(e), acerbe; **to be ~ about sth** être très critique vis-à-vis de qch

scatter ['skætə^r] vt éparpiller, répandre; (crowd) disperser ▷ vi se disperser

scatterbrained ['skætəbreɪnd] adj écervelé(e), étourdi(e)

scattered ['skætəd] adj épars(e), dispersé(e)

scatty ['skætɪ] adj (Brit inf) loufoque

scavenge ['skævəndʒ] vi (person): **to ~ (for)** faire les poubelles (pour trouver); **to ~ for food** (hyenas etc) se nourrir de charognes

scavenger ['skævəndʒə^r] n éboueur m

SCE n abbr = **Scottish Certificate of Education**

scenario [sɪ'nɑ:rɪəu] n scénario m

scene [si:n] n (Theat, fig etc) scène f; (of crime, accident) lieu(x) m(pl), endroit m; (sight, view) spectacle m, vue f; **behind the ~s** (also fig) dans les coulisses; **to make a ~** (inf: fuss) faire une scène or toute une histoire; **to appear on the ~** (also fig) faire son apparition, arriver; **the political ~** la situation politique

scenery ['si:nərɪ] n (Theat) décor(s) m(pl); (landscape) paysage m

scenic ['si:nɪk] adj scénique; offrant de beaux paysages or panoramas

scent [sɛnt] n parfum m, odeur f; (fig: track) piste f; (sense of smell) odorat m ▷ vt parfumer; (smell: also fig) flairer; (also: **to put** or **throw sb off the scent**: fig) mettre qn sur une mauvaise piste

sceptic, (US) **skeptic** ['skɛptɪk] n sceptique m/f

sceptical, (US) **skeptical** ['skɛptɪkl] adj sceptique

scepticism, (US) **skepticism** ['skɛptɪsɪzəm] n scepticisme m

sceptre, (US) **scepter** ['sɛptə^r] n sceptre m

schedule ['ʃɛdju:l] (US) ['skɛdju:l] n programme m, plan m; (of trains) horaire m; (of prices etc) barème m, tarif m ▷ vt prévoir; **as ~d** comme prévu; **on ~** à l'heure (prévue); à la date prévue; **to be ahead of/behind ~** avoir de l'avance/du retard; **we are working to a very tight ~** notre programme de travail est très serré or intense; **everything went according to ~** tout s'est passé comme prévu

scheduled ['ʃɛdju:ld, (US) 'skɛdju:ld] adj (date, time) prévu(e), indiqué(e); (visit, event) programmé(e), prévu; (train, bus, stop, flight) régulier(-ière)

scheduled flight n vol régulier

schematic [skɪ'mætɪk] adj schématique

scheme [ski:m] n plan m, projet m; (method) procédé m; (plot) complot m, combine f; (arrangement) arrangement m, classification f; (pension scheme etc) régime m ▷ vt, vi comploter, manigancer; **colour ~** combinaison f de(s) couleurs

scheming ['ski:mɪŋ] adj rusé(e), intrigant(e) ▷ n manigances fpl, intrigues fpl

schism ['skɪzəm] n schisme m

schizophrenia [skɪtsə'fri:nɪə] n schizophrénie f

schizophrenic [skɪtsə'frɛnɪk] adj schizophrène

scholar ['skɔlə^r] n érudit(e); (pupil) boursier(-ère)

scholarly ['skɔləlɪ] adj érudit(e), savant(e)

scholarship ['skɔləʃɪp] n érudition f; (grant) bourse f (d'études)

school [sku:l] n (gen) école f; (secondary school) collège m; lycée m; (in university) faculté f; (US: university) université f; (of fish) banc m ▷ cpd scolaire ▷ vt (animal) dresser

school age n âge m scolaire

schoolbook ['sku:lbuk] n livre m scolaire or de classe

schoolboy ['sku:lbɔɪ] n écolier m; (at secondary school) collégien m; lycéen m

schoolchildren ['sku:ltʃɪldrən] npl écoliers mpl; (at secondary school) collégiens mpl; lycéens mpl

schooldays ['sku:ldeɪz] npl années fpl de scolarité

schoolgirl ['sku:lgə:l] n écolière f; (at secondary school) collégienne f; lycéenne f

schooling ['sku:lɪŋ] n instruction f, études fpl

school-leaver ['sku:lli:və^r] n (Brit) jeune qui vient de terminer ses études secondaires

schoolmaster ['sku:lmɑ:stə^r] n (primary) instituteur m; (secondary) professeur m

schoolmistress ['sku:lmɪstrɪs] n (primary) institutrice f; (secondary) professeur m

school report n (Brit) bulletin m (scolaire)

schoolroom ['sku:lru:m] n (salle f de) classe f

schoolteacher ['sku:lti:tʃə^r] n (primary) instituteur(-trice); (secondary) professeur m

schoolyard ['sku:ljɑ:d] n (US) cour f de récréation

schooner ['sku:nə^r] n (ship) schooner m, goélette f; (glass) grand verre (à xérès)

sciatica [saɪ'ætɪkə] n sciatique f

science ['saɪəns] n science f; **the ~s** les sciences; (Scol) les matières fpl scientifiques

science fiction n science-fiction f

scientific [saɪən'tɪfɪk] adj scientifique

scientist ['saɪəntɪst] n scientifique m/f; (eminent) savant m

sci-fi ['saɪfaɪ] n abbr (inf: = science fiction) SF f

Scilly Isles ['sɪlɪ'aɪlz], **Scillies** ['sɪlɪz] npl: **the ~** les Sorlingues fpl, les îles fpl Scilly

S

773

scintillating ['sıntıleıtıŋ] *adj* scintillant(e), étincelant(e); (*wit etc*) brillant(e)

scissors ['sızəz] *npl* ciseaux *mpl*; **a pair of** ~ une paire de ciseaux

sclerosis [sklı'rəusıs] *n* sclérose *f*

scoff [skɔf] *vt* (*Brit inf: eat*) avaler, bouffer ▷ *vi*: **to** ~ **(at)** (*mock*) se moquer (de)

scold [skəuld] *vt* gronder, attraper, réprimander

scolding ['skəuldıŋ] *n* réprimande *f*

scone [skɔn] *n sorte de petit pain rond au lait*

scoop [sku:p] *n* pelle *f* (à main); (*for ice cream*) boule *f* à glace; (*Press*) reportage exclusif *or* à sensation
  ▶ **scoop out** *vt* évider, creuser
  ▶ **scoop up** *vt* ramasser

scooter ['sku:tə^r] *n* (*motor cycle*) scooter *m*; (*toy*) trottinette *f*

scope [skəup] *n* (*capacity: of plan, undertaking*) portée *f*, envergure *f*; (*: of person*) compétence *f*, capacités *fpl*; (*opportunity*) possibilités *fpl*; **within the** ~ **of** dans les limites de; **there is plenty of** ~ **for improvement** (*Brit*) cela pourrait être beaucoup mieux

scorch [skɔ:tʃ] *vt* (*clothes*) brûler (légèrement), roussir; (*earth, grass*) dessécher, brûler

scorched earth policy ['skɔ:tʃt-] *n* politique *f* de la terre brûlée

scorcher ['skɔ:tʃə^r] *n* (*inf: hot day*) journée *f* torride

scorching ['skɔ:tʃıŋ] *adj* torride, brûlant(e)

score [skɔ:^r] *n* score *m*, décompte *m* des points; (*Mus*) partition *f* ▷ *vt* (*goal, point*) marquer; (*success*) remporter; (*cut: leather, wood, card*) entailler, inciser ▷ *vi* marquer des points; (*Football*) marquer un but; (*keep score*) compter les points; **on that** ~ sur ce chapitre, à cet égard; **to have an old** ~ **to settle with sb** (*fig*) avoir un (vieux) compte à régler avec qn; **a** ~ **of** (*twenty*) vingt; ~**s of** (*fig*) des tas de; **to** ~ **6 out of 10** obtenir 6 sur 10
  ▶ **score out** *vt* rayer, barrer, biffer

scoreboard ['skɔ:bɔ:d] *n* tableau *m*

scorecard ['skɔ:kɑ:d] *n* (*Sport*) carton *m*, feuille *f* de marque

scoreline ['skɔ:laın] *n* (*Sport*) score *m*

scorer ['skɔ:rə^r] *n* (*Football*) auteur *m* du but; buteur *m*; (*keeping score*) marqueur *m*

scorn [skɔ:n] *n* mépris *m*, dédain *m* ▷ *vt* mépriser, dédaigner

scornful ['skɔ:nful] *adj* méprisant(e), dédaigneux(-euse)

Scorpio ['skɔ:pıəu] *n* le Scorpion; **to be** ~ être du Scorpion

scorpion ['skɔ:pıən] *n* scorpion *m*

Scot [skɔt] *n* Écossais(e)

Scotch [skɔtʃ] *n* whisky *m*, scotch *m*

scotch [skɔtʃ] *vt* faire échouer; enrayer; étouffer

Scotch tape® (*US*) *n* scotch® *m*, ruban adhésif

scot-free ['skɔt'fri:] *adj*: **to get off** ~ s'en tirer sans être puni(e); s'en sortir indemne

Scotland ['skɔtlənd] *n* Écosse *f*

Scots [skɔts] *adj* écossais(e)

Scotsman ['skɔtsmən] (*irreg*) *n* Écossais *m*

Scotswoman ['skɔtswumən] (*irreg*) *n* Écossaise *f*

Scottish ['skɔtıʃ] *adj* écossais(e); **the** ~ **National Party** le parti national écossais; **the** ~ **Parliament** le Parlement écossais

scoundrel ['skaundrl] *n* vaurien *m*

scour ['skauə^r] *vt* (*clean*) récurer; frotter; décaper; (*search*) battre, parcourir

scourer ['skauərə^r] *n* tampon abrasif *or* à récurer; (*powder*) poudre *f* à récurer

scourge [skə:dʒ] *n* fléau *m*

scout [skaut] *n* (*Mil*) éclaireur *m*; (*also:* **boy scout**) scout *m*; **girl** ~ (*US*) guide *f*
  ▶ **scout around** *vi* chercher

scowl [skaul] *vi* se renfrogner, avoir l'air maussade; **to** ~ **at** regarder de travers

scrabble ['skræbl] *vi* (*claw*): **to** ~ **(at)** gratter; **to** ~ **about** *or* **around for sth** chercher qch à tâtons ▷ *n*: **S**~® Scrabble® *m*

scraggy ['skrægı] *adj* décharné(e), efflanqué(e), famélique

scram [skræm] *vi* (*inf*) ficher le camp

scramble ['skræmbl] *n* (*rush*) bousculade *f*, ruée *f* ▷ *vi* grimper/descendre tant bien que mal; **to** ~ **for** se bousculer *or* se disputer pour (avoir); **to go scrambling** (*Sport*) faire du trial

scrambled eggs ['skræmbld-] *npl* œufs brouillés

scrap [skræp] *n* bout *m*, morceau *m*; (*fight*) bagarre *f*; (*also:* **scrap iron**) ferraille *f* ▷ *vt* jeter, mettre au rebut; (*fig*) abandonner, laisser tomber ▷ *vi* se bagarrer; **scraps** *npl* (*waste*) déchets *mpl*; **to sell sth for** ~ vendre qch à la casse *or* à la ferraille

scrapbook ['skræpbuk] *n* album *m*

scrap dealer *n* marchand *m* de ferraille

scrape [skreıp] *vt, vi* gratter, racler ▷ *n*: **to get into a** ~ s'attirer des ennuis
  ▶ **scrape through** *vi* (*exam etc*) réussir de justesse
  ▶ **scrape together** *vt* (*money*) racler ses fonds de tiroir pour réunir

scraper ['skreıpə^r] *n* grattoir *m*, racloir *m*

scrap heap *n* tas *m* de ferraille; (*fig*): **on the** ~ au rancart *or* rebut

scrap merchant *n* (*Brit*) marchand *m* de ferraille

scrap metal *n* ferraille *f*

scrap paper *n* papier *m* brouillon

scrappy ['skræpı] *adj* fragmentaire, décousu(e)

scrap yard *n* parc *m* à ferrailles; (*for cars*) cimetière *m* de voitures

scratch [skrætʃ] *n* égratignure *f*, rayure *f*; (*on paint*) éraflure *f*; (*from claw*) coup *m* de griffe ▷ *adj*: ~ **team** équipe de fortune *or* improvisée ▷ *vt* (*rub*) (se) gratter; (*record*) rayer; (*paint etc*) érafler; (*with claw, nail*) griffer; (*Comput*) effacer ▷ *vi* (se) gratter; **to start from** ~ partir de zéro; **to be up to** ~ être à la hauteur

scratch card *n* carte *f* à gratter

scrawl [skrɔ:l] *n* gribouillage *m* ▷ *vi* gribouiller

scrawny ['skrɔ:nı] *adj* décharné(e)

scream [skri:m] *n* cri perçant, hurlement *m* ▷ *vi* crier, hurler; **to be a ~** (*inf*) être impayable; **to ~ at sb to do sth** crier *or* hurler à qn de faire qch
scree [skri:] *n* éboulis *m*
screech [skri:tʃ] *n* cri strident, hurlement *m*; (*of tyres, brakes*) crissement *m*, grincement *m* ▷ *vi* hurler; crisser, grincer
screen [skri:n] *n* écran *m*; (*in room*) paravent *m*; (*Cine, TV*) écran; (*fig*) écran, rideau *m* ▷ *vt* masquer, cacher; (*from the wind etc*) abriter, protéger; (*film*) projeter; (*candidates etc*) filtrer; (*for illness*): **to ~ sb for sth** faire subir un test de dépistage de qch à qn
screen editing [-'edɪtɪŋ] *n* (*Comput*) édition *f or* correction *f* sur écran
screening ['skri:nɪŋ] *n* (*of film*) projection *f*; (*Med*) test *m* (*or* tests) de dépistage; (*for security*) filtrage *m*
screen memory *n* (*Comput*) mémoire *f* écran
screenplay ['skri:npleɪ] *n* scénario *m*
screen saver *n* (*Comput*) économiseur *m* d'écran
screen test *n* bout *m* d'essai
screw [skru:] *n* vis *f*; (*propeller*) hélice *f* ▷ *vt* (*also*: **screw in**) visser; (*inf!*: *woman*) baiser (*!*); **to ~ sth to the wall** visser qch au mur; **to have one's head ~ed on** (*fig*) avoir la tête sur les épaules
▶ **screw up** *vt* (*paper etc*) froisser; (*inf*: *ruin*) bousiller; **to ~ up one's eyes** se plisser les yeux; **to ~ up one's face** faire la grimace
screwdriver ['skru:draɪvə^r] *n* tournevis *m*
screwed-up ['skru:d'ʌp] *adj* (*inf*): **to be ~** être paumé(e)
screwy ['skru:ɪ] *adj* (*inf*) dingue, cinglé(e)
scribble ['skrɪbl] *n* gribouillage *m* ▷ *vt* gribouiller, griffonner; **to ~ sth down** griffonner qch
scribe [skraɪb] *n* scribe *m*
script [skrɪpt] *n* (*Cine etc*) scénario *m*, texte *m*; (*in exam*) copie *f*; (*writing*) (écriture *f*) script *m*
scripted ['skrɪptɪd] *adj* (*Radio, TV*) préparé(e) à l'avance
Scripture ['skrɪptʃər] *n* Écriture sainte
scriptwriter ['skrɪptraɪtər] *n* scénariste *m/f*, dialoguiste *m/f*
scroll [skrəul] *n* rouleau *m* ▷ *vt* (*Comput*) faire défiler (sur l'écran)
scrotum ['skrəutəm] *n* scrotum *m*
scrounge [skraundʒ] (*inf*) *vt*: **to ~ sth (off** *or* **from sb)** se faire payer qch (par qn), emprunter qch (à qn) ▷ *vi*: **to ~ on sb** vivre aux crochets de qn
scrounger ['skraundʒə^r] *n* parasite *m*
scrub [skrʌb] *n* (*clean*) nettoyage *m* (à la brosse); (*land*) broussailles *fpl* ▷ *vt* (*floor*) nettoyer à la brosse; (*pan*) récurer; (*washing*) frotter; (*reject*) annuler
scrubbing brush ['skrʌbɪŋ-] *n* brosse dure
scruff [skrʌf] *n*: **by the ~ of the neck** par la peau du cou
scruffy ['skrʌfɪ] *adj* débraillé(e)
scrum ['skrʌm], **scrummage** ['skrʌmɪdʒ] *n* mêlée *f*

scruple ['skru:pl] *n* scrupule *m*; **to have no ~s about doing sth** n'avoir aucun scrupule à faire qch
scrupulous ['skru:pjuləs] *adj* scrupuleux(-euse)
scrupulously ['skru:pjuləslɪ] *adv* scrupuleusement; **to be ~ honest** être d'une honnêteté scrupuleuse
scrutinize ['skru:tɪnaɪz] *vt* scruter, examiner minutieusement
scrutiny ['skru:tɪnɪ] *n* examen minutieux; **under the ~ of sb** sous la surveillance de qn
scuba ['sku:bə] *n* scaphandre *m* (autonome)
scuba diving ['sku:bə-] *n* plongée sous-marine
scuff [skʌf] *vt* érafler
scuffle ['skʌfl] *n* échauffourée *f*, rixe *f*
scullery ['skʌlərɪ] *n* arrière-cuisine *f*
sculptor ['skʌlptər] *n* sculpteur *m*
sculpture ['skʌlptʃər] *n* sculpture *f*
scum [skʌm] *n* écume *f*, mousse *f*; (*pej*: *people*) rebut *m*, lie *f*
scupper ['skʌpər] *vt* (*Brit*) saborder
scurrilous ['skʌrɪləs] *adj* haineux(-euse), virulent(e); calomnieux(-euse)
scurry ['skʌrɪ] *vi* filer à toute allure; **to ~ off** détaler, se sauver
scurvy ['skə:vɪ] *n* scorbut *m*
scuttle ['skʌtl] *n* (*Naut*) écoutille *f*; (*also*: **coal scuttle**) seau *m* (à charbon) ▷ *vt* (*ship*) saborder ▷ *vi* (*scamper*): **to ~ away, ~ off** détaler
scythe [saɪð] *n* faux *f*
SD, S. Dak. *abbr* (*US*) = **South Dakota**
SDI *n abbr* (= *Strategic Defense Initiative*) IDS *f*
SDLP *n abbr* (*Brit Pol*) = **Social Democratic and Labour Party**
sea [si:] *n* mer *f* ▷ *cpd* marin(e), de (la) mer, maritime; **on the ~** (*boat*) en mer; (*town*) au bord de la mer; **by** *or* **beside the ~** (*holiday, town*) au bord de la mer; **by ~** par mer, en bateau; **out to ~** au large; (**out**) **at ~** en mer; **heavy** *or* **rough ~(s)** grosse mer, mer agitée; **a ~ of faces** (*fig*) une multitude de visages; **to be all at ~** (*fig*) nager complètement
sea bed *n* fond *m* de la mer
sea bird *n* oiseau *m* de mer
seaboard ['si:bɔ:d] *n* côte *f*
sea breeze *n* brise *f* de mer
seafarer ['si:fɛərə^r] *n* marin *m*
seafaring ['si:fɛərɪŋ] *adj* (*life*) de marin; **~ people** les gens *mpl* de mer
seafood ['si:fu:d] *n* fruits *mpl* de mer
sea front ['si:frʌnt] *n* bord *m* de mer
seagoing ['si:gəuɪŋ] *adj* (*ship*) de haute mer
seagull ['si:gʌl] *n* mouette *f*
seal [si:l] *n* (*animal*) phoque *m*; (*stamp*) sceau *m*, cachet *m*; (*impression*) cachet, estampille *f* ▷ *vt* sceller; (*envelope*) coller; (*: with seal*) cacheter; (*decide: sb's fate*) décider (de); (*: bargain*) conclure; **~ of approval** approbation *f*
▶ **seal off** *vt* (*close*) condamner; (*forbid entry to*) interdire l'accès de
sea level *n* niveau *m* de la mer
sealing wax ['si:lɪŋ-] *n* cire *f* à cacheter

sea lion n lion m de mer
sealskin ['si:lskɪn] n peau f de phoque
seam [si:m] n couture f; (of coal) veine f, filon m;
 the hall was bursting at the ~s la salle était
 pleine à craquer
seaman ['si:mən] (irreg) n marin m
seamanship ['si:mənʃɪp] n qualités fpl de marin
seamless ['si:mlɪs] adj sans couture(s)
seamy ['si:mɪ] adj louche, mal famé(e)
seance ['seɪɒns] n séance f de spiritisme
seaplane ['si:pleɪn] n hydravion m
seaport ['si:pɔ:t] n port m de mer
search [sə:tʃ] n (for person, thing, Comput)
 recherche(s) f(pl); (of drawer, pockets) fouille f;
 (Law: at sb's home) perquisition f ▷ vt fouiller;
 (examine) examiner minutieusement; scruter
 ▷ vi: **to ~ for** chercher; **in ~ of** à la recherche de
 ▶ **search through** vt fus fouiller
search engine n (Comput) moteur m de
 recherche
searcher ['sə:tʃər] n chercheur(-euse)
searching ['sə:tʃɪŋ] adj (look, question)
 pénétrant(e); (examination) minutieux(-euse)
searchlight ['sə:tʃlaɪt] n projecteur m
search party n expédition f de secours
search warrant n mandat m de perquisition
searing ['sɪərɪŋ] adj (heat) brûlant(e); (pain)
 aigu(ë)
seashore ['si:ʃɔ:ʳ] n rivage m, plage f, bord m de
 (la) mer; **on the ~** sur le rivage
seasick ['si:sɪk] adj: **to be ~** avoir le mal de mer
seaside ['si:saɪd] n bord m de mer
seaside resort n station f balnéaire
season ['si:zn] n saison f ▷ vt assaisonner,
 relever; **to be in/out of ~** être/ne pas être de
 saison; **the busy ~** (for shops) la période de
 pointe; (for hotels etc) la pleine saison; **the open
 ~** (Hunting) la saison de la chasse
seasonal ['si:znl] adj saisonnier(-ière)
seasoned ['si:znd] adj (wood) séché(e); (fig:
 worker, actor, troops) expérimenté(e); **a ~
 campaigner** un vieux militant, un vétéran
seasoning ['si:znɪŋ] n assaisonnement m
season ticket n carte f d'abonnement
seat [si:t] n siège m; (in bus, train: place) place f;
 (Parliament) siège; (buttocks) postérieur m; (of
 trousers) fond m ▷ vt faire asseoir, placer; (have
 room for) avoir des places assises pour, pouvoir
 accueillir; **are there any ~s left?** est-ce qu'il
 reste des places?; **to take one's ~** prendre place;
 to be ~ed être assis; **please be ~ed** veuillez
 vous asseoir
seat belt n ceinture f de sécurité
seating ['si:tɪŋ] n sièges fpl, places assises
seating capacity ['si:tɪŋ-] n nombre m de
 places assises
sea urchin n oursin m
sea water n eau f de mer
seaweed ['si:wi:d] n algues fpl
seaworthy ['si:wə:ðɪ] adj en état de naviguer
SEC n abbr (US: = Securities and Exchange Commission)
 ≈ COB f (= Commission des opérations de Bourse)

sec. abbr (= second) sec
secateurs [sɛkə'tə:z] npl sécateur m
secede [sɪ'si:d] vi faire sécession
secluded [sɪ'klu:dɪd] adj retiré(e), à l'écart
seclusion [sɪ'klu:ʒən] n solitude f
second[1] ['sɛkənd] num deuxième, second(e)
 ▷ adv (in race etc) en seconde position ▷ n (unit of
 time) seconde f; (Aut: also: **second gear**) seconde;
 (in series, position) deuxième m/f, second(e);
 (Comm: imperfect) article m de second choix; (Brit
 Scol) ≈ licence f avec mention ▷ vt (motion)
 appuyer; **seconds** npl (inf: food) rab m (inf);
 Charles the S~ Charles II; **just a ~!** une
 seconde!, un instant!; (stopping sb) pas si vite!; ~
 floor (Brit) deuxième (étage) m; (US) premier
 (étage) m; **to ask for a ~ opinion** (Med)
 demander l'avis d'un autre médecin
second[2] [sɪ'kɒnd] vt (employee) détacher, mettre
 en détachement
secondary ['sɛkəndərɪ] adj secondaire
secondary school n (age 11 to 15) collège m; (age 15
 to 18) lycée m
second-best [sɛkənd'bɛst] n deuxième choix m;
 as a ~ faute de mieux
second-class ['sɛkənd'klɑ:s] adj de deuxième
 classe; (Rail) de seconde (classe); (Post) au tarif
 réduit; (pej) de qualité inférieure ▷ adv (Rail) en
 seconde; (Post) au tarif réduit; **~ citizen**
 citoyen(ne) de deuxième classe
second cousin n cousin(e) issu(e) de germains
seconder ['sɛkəndəʳ] n personne f qui appuie
 une motion
second-guess ['sɛkənd'gɛs] vt (predict) (essayer
 d')anticiper; **they're still trying to ~ his
 motives** ils essaient toujours de comprendre
 ses raisons
second hand n (on clock) trotteuse f
secondhand ['sɛkənd'hænd] adj d'occasion;
 (information) de seconde main ▷ adv (buy)
 d'occasion; **to hear sth ~** apprendre qch
 indirectement
second-in-command ['sɛkəndɪnkə'mɑ:nd] n
 (Mil) commandant m en second; (Admin)
 adjoint(e), sous-chef m
secondly ['sɛkəndlɪ] adv deuxièmement;
 firstly ... ~ ... d'abord ... ensuite ... or de plus ...
secondment [sɪ'kɒndmənt] n (Brit)
 détachement m
second-rate ['sɛkənd'reɪt] adj de deuxième
 ordre, de qualité inférieure
second thoughts npl: **to have ~** changer d'avis;
 on ~ or **thought** (US) à la réflexion
secrecy ['si:krəsɪ] n secret m; **in ~** en secret
secret ['si:krɪt] adj secret(-ète) ▷ n secret m; **in ~**
 (adv) en secret, secrètement, en cachette; **to
 keep sth ~ from sb** cacher qch à qn, ne pas
 révéler qch à qn; **to make no ~ of sth** ne pas
 cacher qch; **keep it ~** n'en parle à personne
secret agent n agent secret
secretarial [sɛkrɪ'tɛərɪəl] adj de secrétaire, de
 secrétariat
secretariat [sɛkrɪ'tɛərɪət] n secrétariat m

secretary ['sɛkrətrɪ] n secrétaire m/f; (Comm) secrétaire général; **S~ of State** (US Pol) ≈ ministre m des Affaires étrangères; **S~ of State (for)** (Brit Pol) ministre m (de)

secretary-general ['sɛkrətrɪ'dʒɛnərl] n secrétaire général

secrete [sɪ'kriːt] vt (Anat, Biol, Med) sécréter; (hide) cacher

secretion [sɪ'kriːʃən] n sécrétion f

secretive ['siːkrətɪv] adj réservé(e); (pej) cachottier(-ière), dissimulé(e)

secretly ['siːkrɪtlɪ] adv en secret, secrètement, en cachette

secret police n police secrète

secret service n services secrets

sect [sɛkt] n secte f

sectarian [sɛk'tɛərɪən] adj sectaire

section ['sɛkʃən] n section f; (department) section; (Comm) rayon m; (of document) section, article m, paragraphe m; (cut) coupe f ▷ vt sectionner; **the business** etc ~ (Press) la page des affaires etc

sector ['sɛktəʳ] n secteur m

secular ['sɛkjuləʳ] adj laïque

secure [sɪ'kjuəʳ] adj (free from anxiety) sans inquiétude, sécurisé(e); (firmly fixed) solide, bien attaché(e) (or fermé(e) etc); (in safe place) en lieu sûr, en sûreté ▷ vt (fix) fixer, attacher; (get) obtenir, se procurer; (Comm: loan) garantir; **to make sth ~** bien fixer or attacher qch; **to ~ sth for sb** obtenir qch pour qn, procurer qch à qn

secured creditor [sɪ'kjuəd-] n créancier(-ière), privilégié(e)

security [sɪ'kjuərɪtɪ] n sécurité f, mesures fpl de sécurité; (for loan) caution f, garantie f; **securities** npl (Stock Exchange) valeurs fpl, titres mpl; **to increase** or **tighten** ~ renforcer les mesures de sécurité; **~ of tenure** stabilité f d'un emploi, titularisation f

Security Council n: **the** ~ le Conseil de sécurité

security forces npl forces fpl de sécurité

security guard n garde chargé de la sécurité; (transporting money) convoyeur m de fonds

security risk n menace f pour la sécurité de l'état (or d'une entreprise etc)

sedan [sə'dæn] n (US Aut) berline f

sedate [sɪ'deɪt] adj calme; posé(e) ▷ vt donner des sédatifs à

sedation [sɪ'deɪʃən] n (Med) sédation f; **to be under** ~ être sous calmants

sedative ['sɛdɪtɪv] n calmant m, sédatif m

sedentary ['sɛdntrɪ] adj sédentaire

sediment ['sɛdɪmənt] n sédiment m, dépôt m

sedition [sɪ'dɪʃən] n sédition f

seduce [sɪ'djuːs] vt séduire

seduction [sɪ'dʌkʃən] n séduction f

seductive [sɪ'dʌktɪv] adj séduisant(e); (smile) séducteur(-trice); (fig: offer) alléchant(e)

see [siː] (pt **saw**, pp **seen** [sɔː, siːn]) vt (gen) voir; (accompany): **to ~ sb to the door** reconduire or raccompagner qn jusqu'à la porte ▷ vi voir ▷ n évêché m; **to ~ that** (ensure) veiller à ce que+sub,

faire en sorte que+sub, s'assurer que; **there was nobody to be ~n** il n'y avait pas un chat; **let me ~** (show me) fais(-moi) voir; (let me think) voyons (un peu); **to go and ~ sb** aller voir qn; ~ **for yourself** voyez vous-même; **I don't know what she ~s in him** je ne sais pas ce qu'elle lui trouve; **as far as I can** ~ pour autant que je puisse en juger; ~ **you!** au revoir!, à bientôt!; ~ **you soon/later/tomorrow!** à bientôt/plus tard/demain!

▸ **see about** vt fus (deal with) s'occuper de

▸ **see off** vt accompagner (à l'aéroport etc)

▸ **see out** vt (take to door) raccompagner à la porte

▸ **see through** vt mener à bonne fin ▷ vt fus voir clair dans

▸ **see to** vt fus s'occuper de, se charger de

seed [siːd] n graine f; (fig) germe m; (Tennis etc) tête f de série; **to go to** ~ (plant) monter en graine; (fig) se laisser aller

seedless ['siːdlɪs] adj sans pépins

seedling ['siːdlɪŋ] n jeune plant m, semis m

seedy ['siːdɪ] adj (shabby) minable, miteux(-euse)

seeing ['siːɪŋ] conj: ~ **(that)** vu que, étant donné que

seek [siːk] (pt, pp **sought** [sɔːt]) vt chercher, rechercher; **to ~ advice/help from sb** demander conseil/de l'aide à qn

▸ **seek out** vt (person) chercher

seem [siːm] vi sembler, paraître; **there ~s to be …** il semble qu'il y a …, on dirait qu'il y a …; **it ~s (that) …** il semble que …; **what ~s to be the trouble?** qu'est-ce qui ne va pas?

seemingly ['siːmɪŋlɪ] adv apparemment

seen [siːn] pp of **see**

seep [siːp] vi suinter, filtrer

seer [sɪəʳ] n prophète (prophétesse) voyant(e)

seersucker ['sɪəsʌkəʳ] n cloqué m, étoffe cloquée

seesaw ['siːsɔː] n (jeu m de) bascule f

seethe [siːð] vi être en effervescence; **to ~ with anger** bouillir de colère

see-through ['siːθruː] adj transparent(e)

segment ['sɛgmənt] n segment m; (of orange) quartier m

segregate ['sɛgrɪgeɪt] vt séparer, isoler

segregation [sɛgrɪ'geɪʃən] n ségrégation f

Seine [seɪn] n: **the (River)** ~ la Seine

seismic ['saɪzmɪk] adj sismique

seize [siːz] vt (grasp) saisir, attraper; (take possession of) s'emparer de; (opportunity) saisir; (Law) saisir

▸ **seize on** vt fus saisir, sauter sur

▸ **seize up** vi (Tech) se gripper

▸ **seize upon** vt fus = **seize on**

seizure ['siːʒəʳ] n (Med) crise f, attaque f; (of power) prise f; (Law) saisie f

seldom ['sɛldəm] adv rarement

select [sɪ'lɛkt] adj choisi(e), d'élite; (hotel, restaurant, club) chic inv, sélect inv ▷ vt sélectionner, choisir; **a ~ few** quelques privilégiés

selection [sɪ'lɛkʃən] n sélection f, choix m

S

selection committee n comité m de sélection
selective [sɪ'lɛktɪv] adj sélectif(-ive); (school) à recrutement sélectif
selector [sɪ'lɛktəʳ] n (person) sélectionneur(-euse); (Tech) sélecteur m
self [sɛlf] n (pl **selves**) [sɛlvz]: **the ~** le moi inv ▷ prefix auto-
self-addressed ['sɛlfə'drɛst] adj: **~ envelope** enveloppe f à mon (or votre etc) nom
self-adhesive [sɛlfəd'hi:zɪv] adj autocollant(e)
self-assertive [sɛlfə'sə:tɪv] adj autoritaire
self-assurance [sɛlfə'ʃuərəns] n assurance f
self-assured [sɛlfə'ʃuəd] adj sûr(e) de soi, plein(e) d'assurance
self-catering [sɛlf'keɪtərɪŋ] adj (Brit: flat) avec cuisine, où l'on peut faire sa cuisine; (: holiday) en appartement (or chalet etc) loué
self-centred, (US) **self-centered** [sɛlf'sɛntəd] adj égocentrique
self-cleaning [sɛlf'kli:nɪŋ] adj autonettoyant(e).
self-confessed [sɛlfkən'fɛst] adj (alcoholic etc) déclaré(e), qui ne s'en cache pas
self-confidence [sɛlf'kɒnfɪdns] n confiance f en soi
self-confident [sɛlf'kɒnfɪdnt] adj sûr(e) de soi, plein(e) d'assurance
self-conscious [sɛlf'kɒnʃəs] adj timide, qui manque d'assurance
self-contained [sɛlfkən'teɪnd] adj (Brit: flat) avec entrée particulière, indépendant(e)
self-control [sɛlfkən'trəul] n maîtrise f de soi
self-defeating [sɛlfdɪ'fi:tɪŋ] adj qui a un effet contraire à l'effet recherché
self-defence, (US) **self-defense** [sɛlfdɪ'fɛns] n autodéfense f; (Law) légitime défense f
self-discipline [sɛlf'dɪsɪplɪn] n discipline personnelle
self-drive [sɛlf'draɪv] adj (Brit): **~ car** voiture f de location
self-employed [sɛlfɪm'plɔɪd] adj qui travaille à son compte
self-esteem [sɛlfɪ'sti:m] n amour-propre m
self-evident [sɛlf'ɛvɪdnt] adj évident(e), qui va de soi
self-explanatory [sɛlfɪk'splænətrɪ] adj qui se passe d'explication
self-governing [sɛlf'gʌvənɪŋ] adj autonome
self-help ['sɛlf'hɛlp] n initiative personnelle, efforts personnels
self-importance [sɛlfɪm'pɔ:tns] n suffisance f
self-indulgent [sɛlfɪn'dʌldʒənt] adj qui ne se refuse rien
self-inflicted [sɛlfɪn'flɪktɪd] adj volontaire
self-interest [sɛlf'ɪntrɪst] n intérêt personnel
selfish ['sɛlfɪʃ] adj égoïste
selfishness ['sɛlfɪʃnɪs] n égoïsme m
selfless ['sɛlflɪs] adj désintéressé(e)
selflessly ['sɛlflɪslɪ] adv sans penser à soi
self-made man ['sɛlfmeɪd-] n self-made man m
self-pity [sɛlf'pɪtɪ] n apitoiement m sur soi-même

self-portrait [sɛlf'pɔ:treɪt] n autoportrait m
self-possessed [sɛlfpə'zɛst] adj assuré(e)
self-preservation ['sɛlfprɛzə'veɪʃən] n instinct m de conservation
self-raising [sɛlf'reɪzɪŋ], (US) **self-rising** [sɛlf'raɪzɪŋ] adj: **~ flour** farine f pour gâteaux (avec levure incorporée)
self-reliant [sɛlfrɪ'laɪənt] adj indépendant(e)
self-respect [sɛlfrɪs'pɛkt] n respect m de soi, amour-propre m
self-respecting [sɛlfrɪs'pɛktɪŋ] adj qui se respecte
self-righteous [sɛlf'raɪtʃəs] adj satisfait(e) de soi, pharisaïque
self-rising [sɛlf'raɪzɪŋ] adj (US) = **self-raising**
self-sacrifice [sɛlf'sækrɪfaɪs] n abnégation f
self-same ['sɛlfseɪm] adj même
self-satisfied [sɛlf'sætɪsfaɪd] adj content(e) de soi, suffisant(e)
self-sealing [sɛlf'si:lɪŋ] adj (envelope) autocollant(e)
self-service [sɛlf'sə:vɪs] adj, n libre-service (m), self-service (m)
self-styled ['sɛlfstaɪld] adj soi-disant inv
self-sufficient [sɛlfsə'fɪʃənt] adj indépendant(e)
self-supporting [sɛlfsə'pɔ:tɪŋ] adj financièrement indépendant(e)
self-tanning ['sɛlf'tænɪŋ] adj: **~ cream** or **lotion** etc autobronzant m
self-taught [sɛlf'tɔ:t] adj autodidacte
sell (pt, pp **sold**) [sɛl, səuld] vt vendre ▷ vi se vendre; **to ~ at** or **for 10 euros** se vendre 10 euros; **to ~ sb an idea** (fig) faire accepter une idée à qn
  ▶ **sell off** vt liquider
  ▶ **sell out** vi: **to ~ out (of sth)** (use up stock) vendre tout son stock (de qch); **to ~ out (to)** (Comm) vendre son fonds or son affaire (à) ▷ vt vendre tout son stock de; **the tickets are all sold out** il ne reste plus de billets
  ▶ **sell up** vi vendre son fonds or son affaire
sell-by date ['sɛlbaɪ-] n date f limite de vente
seller ['sɛləʳ] n vendeur(-euse), marchand(e); **~'s market** marché m à la hausse
selling price ['sɛlɪŋ-] n prix m de vente
Sellotape® ['sɛləuteɪp] n (Brit) scotch® m
sellout ['sɛlaut] n trahison f, capitulation f; (of tickets): **it was a ~** tous les billets ont été vendus
selves [sɛlvz] npl of **self**
semantic [sɪ'mæntɪk] adj sémantique
semantics [sɪ'mæntɪks] n sémantique f
semaphore ['sɛməfɔ:ʳ] n signaux mpl à bras; (Rail) sémaphore m
semblance ['sɛmblns] n semblant m
semen ['si:mən] n sperme m
semester [sɪ'mɛstəʳ] n (esp US) semestre m
semi... ['sɛmɪ] prefix semi-, demi-; à demi, à moitié ▷ n: **semi** = **semidetached house**
semi-breve ['sɛmɪbri:v] n (Brit) ronde f
semicircle ['sɛmɪsə:kl] n demi-cercle m
semicircular ['sɛmɪ'sə:kjuləʳ] adj en demi-cercle, semi-circulaire

semicolon [ˈsɛmɪˈkəulən] n point-virgule m
semiconductor [sɛmɪkənˈdʌktər] n semi-conducteur m
semiconscious [sɛmɪˈkɔnʃəs] adj à demi conscient(e)
semidetached [sɛmɪdɪˈtætʃt], **semidetached house** n (Brit) maison jumelée or jumelle
semi-final [sɛmɪˈfaɪnl] n demi-finale f
seminar [ˈsɛmɪnɑːr] n séminaire m
seminary [ˈsɛmɪnərɪ] n (Rel: for priests) séminaire m
semiprecious [sɛmɪˈprɛʃəs] adj semi-précieux(-euse)
semiquaver [ˈsɛmɪkweɪvər] n (Brit) double croche f
semiskilled [sɛmɪˈskɪld] adj: ~ **worker** ouvrier(-ière) spécialisé(e)
semi-skimmed [ˈsɛmɪˈskɪmd] adj demi-écrémé(e)
semitone [ˈsɛmɪtəun] n (Mus) demi-ton m
semolina [sɛməˈliːnə] n semoule f
SEN n abbr (Brit) = **State Enrolled Nurse**
Sen., sen. abbr = **senator; senior**
senate [ˈsɛnɪt] n sénat m; (US): **the S~** le Sénat; voir article

SENATE

Le Senate est la chambre haute du "Congress", le parlement des États-Unis. Il est composé de 100 sénateurs, 2 par État, élus au suffrage universel direct tous les 6 ans, un tiers d'entre eux étant renouvelé tous les 2 ans.

senator [ˈsɛnɪtər] n sénateur m
send (pt, pp **sent**) [sɛnd, sɛnt] vt envoyer; **to ~ by post** or (US) **mail** envoyer or expédier par la poste; **to ~ sb for sth** envoyer qn chercher qch; **to ~ word that ...** faire dire que ...; **she ~s (you) her love** elle vous adresse ses amitiés; **to ~ sb to Coventry** (Brit) mettre qn en quarantaine; **to ~ sb to sleep** endormir qn; **to ~ sb into fits of laughter** faire rire qn aux éclats; **to ~ sth flying** envoyer valser qch
▶ **send away** vt (letter, goods) envoyer, expédier
▶ **send away for** vt fus commander par correspondance, se faire envoyer
▶ **send back** vt renvoyer
▶ **send for** vt fus envoyer chercher; faire venir; (by post) se faire envoyer, commander par correspondance
▶ **send in** vt (report, application, resignation) remettre
▶ **send off** vt (goods) envoyer, expédier; (Brit Sport: player) expulser or renvoyer du terrain
▶ **send on** vt (Brit: letter) faire suivre; (luggage etc: in advance) (faire) expédier à l'avance
▶ **send out** vt (invitation) envoyer (par la poste); (emit: light, heat, signal) émettre
▶ **send round** vt (letter, document etc) faire circuler

▶ **send up** vt (person, price) faire monter; (Brit: parody) mettre en boîte, parodier
sender [ˈsɛndər] n expéditeur(-trice)
send-off [ˈsɛndɔf] n: **a good ~** des adieux chaleureux
Senegal [sɛnɪˈgɔːl] n Sénégal m
Senegalese [sɛnɪgəˈliːz] adj sénégalais(e) ⊳ n (pl inv) Sénégalais(e)
senile [ˈsiːnaɪl] adj sénile
senility [sɪˈnɪlɪtɪ] n sénilité f
senior [ˈsiːnɪər] adj (older) aîné(e), plus âgé(e); (high-ranking) de haut niveau; (of higher rank): **to be ~ to sb** être le supérieur de qn ⊳ n (older): **she is 15 years his ~** elle est son aînée de 15 ans, elle est plus âgée que lui de 15 ans; (in service) personne f qui a plus d'ancienneté; **P. Jones ~** P. Jones père
senior citizen n personne f du troisième âge
senior high school n (US) ≈ lycée m
seniority [siːnɪˈɔrɪtɪ] n priorité f d'âge, ancienneté f; (in rank) supériorité f (hiérarchique)
sensation [sɛnˈseɪʃən] n sensation f; **to create a ~** faire sensation
sensational [sɛnˈseɪʃənl] adj qui fait sensation; (marvellous) sensationnel(le)
sense [sɛns] n sens m; (feeling) sentiment m; (meaning) sens, signification f; (wisdom) bon sens ⊳ vt sentir, pressentir; **senses** npl raison f; **it makes ~** c'est logique; **there is no ~ in (doing) that** cela n'a pas de sens; **to come to one's ~s** (regain consciousness) reprendre conscience; (become reasonable) revenir à la raison; **to take leave of one's ~s** perdre la tête
senseless [ˈsɛnslɪs] adj insensé(e), stupide; (unconscious) sans connaissance
sense of humour, (US) **sense of humor** n sens m de l'humour
sensibility [sɛnsɪˈbɪlɪtɪ] n sensibilité f; **sensibilities** npl susceptibilité f
sensible [ˈsɛnsɪbl] adj sensé(e), raisonnable; (shoes etc) pratique
sensitive [ˈsɛnsɪtɪv] adj: ~ **(to)** sensible (à); **he is very ~ about it** c'est un point très sensible (chez lui)
sensitivity [sɛnsɪˈtɪvɪtɪ] n sensibilité f
sensual [ˈsɛnsjuəl] adj sensuel(le)
sensuous [ˈsɛnsjuəs] adj voluptueux(-euse), sensuel(le)
sent [sɛnt] pt, pp of **send**
sentence [ˈsɛntns] n (Ling) phrase f; (Law: judgment) condamnation f, sentence f; (: punishment) peine f ⊳ vt: **to ~ sb to death/to 5 years** condamner qn à mort/à 5 ans; **to pass ~ on sb** prononcer une peine contre qn
sentiment [ˈsɛntɪmənt] n sentiment m; (opinion) opinion f, avis m
sentimental [sɛntɪˈmɛntl] adj sentimental(e)
sentimentality [sɛntɪmɛnˈtælɪtɪ] n sentimentalité f, sensiblerie f
sentry [ˈsɛntrɪ] n sentinelle f, factionnaire m
sentry duty n: **to be on ~** être de faction

S

Seoul [səul] n Séoul

separable ['sɛprəbl] adj séparable

separate [adj 'sɛprɪt, vb 'sɛpəreɪt] adj séparé(e); (organization) indépendant(e); (day, occasion, issue) différent(e) ▷ vt séparer; (distinguish) distinguer ▷ vi se séparer; **~ from** distinct(e) de; **under ~ cover** (Comm) sous pli séparé; **to ~ into** diviser en

separately ['sɛprɪtlɪ] adv séparément

separates ['sɛprɪts] npl (clothes) coordonnés mpl

separation [sɛpə'reɪʃən] n séparation f

Sept. abbr (= September) sept

September [sɛp'tɛmbər] n septembre m; for phrases see also **July**

septic ['sɛptɪk] adj septique; (wound) infecté(e); **to go ~** s'infecter

septicaemia [sɛptɪ'si:mɪə] n septicémie f

septic tank n fosse f septique

sequel ['si:kwl] n conséquence f; séquelles fpl; (of story) suite f

sequence ['si:kwəns] n ordre m, suite f; (in film) séquence f; (dance) numéro m; **in ~** par ordre, dans l'ordre, les uns après les autres; **~ of tenses** concordance f des temps

sequential [sɪ'kwɛnʃəl] adj: **~ access** (Comput) accès séquentiel

sequin ['si:kwɪn] n paillette f

Serb [sə:b] adj, n = **Serbian**

Serbia ['sə:bɪə] n Serbie f

Serbian ['sə:bɪən] adj serbe ▷ n Serbe m/f; (Ling) serbe m

Serbo-Croat ['sə:bəu'krəuæt] n (Ling) serbo-croate m

serenade [sɛrə'neɪd] n sérénade f ▷ vt donner une sérénade à

serene [sɪ'ri:n] adj serein(e), calme, paisible

serenity [sə'rɛnɪtɪ] n sérénité f, calme m

sergeant ['sɑ:dʒənt] n sergent m; (Police) brigadier m

sergeant major n sergent-major m

serial ['sɪərɪəl] n feuilleton m ▷ adj (Comput: interface, printer) série inv; (: access) séquentiel(le)

serialize ['sɪərɪəlaɪz] vt publier (or adapter) en feuilleton

serial killer n meurtrier m tuant en série

serial number n numéro m de série

series ['sɪərɪz] n série f; (Publishing) collection f

serious ['sɪərɪəs] adj sérieux(-euse); (accident etc) grave; **are you ~ (about it)?** parlez-vous sérieusement?

seriously ['sɪərɪəslɪ] adv sérieusement; (hurt) gravement; **~ rich/difficult** (inf: extremely) drôlement riche/difficile; **to take sth/sb ~** prendre qch/qn au sérieux

seriousness ['sɪərɪəsnɪs] n sérieux m, gravité f

sermon ['sə:mən] n sermon m

serrated [sɪ'reɪtɪd] adj en dents de scie

serum ['sɪərəm] n sérum m

servant ['sə:vənt] n domestique m/f; (fig) serviteur (servante)

serve [sə:v] vt (employer etc) servir, être au service de; (purpose) servir à; (customer, food, meal) servir; (subj: train) desservir; (apprenticeship) faire, accomplir; (prison term) faire; purger ▷ vi (Tennis) servir; (be useful): **to ~ as/for/to do** servir de/à/à faire ▷ n (Tennis) service m; **are you being ~d?** est-ce qu'on s'occupe de vous?; **to ~ on a committee/jury** faire partie d'un comité/ jury; **it ~s him right** c'est bien fait pour lui; **it ~s my purpose** cela fait mon affaire

▶ **serve out, serve up** vt (food) servir

server [sə:vər] n (Comput) serveur m

service ['sə:vɪs] n (gen) service m; (Aut) révision f; (Rel) office m ▷ vt (car etc) réviser; **services** npl (Econ: tertiary sector) (secteur m) tertiaire m, secteur des services; (Brit: on motorway) station-service f; (Mil): **the S~s** (npl) les forces armées; **to be of ~ to sb, to do sb a ~** rendre service à qn; **~ included/not included** service compris/non compris; **to put one's car in for ~** donner sa voiture à réviser; **dinner ~** service de table

serviceable ['sə:vɪsəbl] adj pratique, commode

service area n (on motorway) aire f de services

service charge n (Brit) service m

service industries npl les industries fpl de service, les services mpl

serviceman ['sə:vɪsmən] (irreg) n militaire m

service station n station-service f

serviette [sə:vɪ'ɛt] n (Brit) serviette f (de table)

servile ['sə:vaɪl] adj servile

session ['sɛʃən] n (sitting) séance f; (Scol) année f scolaire (or universitaire); **to be in ~** siéger, être en session or en séance

session musician n musicien(ne) de studio

set [sɛt] (pt, pp set) n série f, assortiment m; (of tools etc) jeu m; (Radio, TV) poste m; (Tennis) set m; (group of people) cercle m, milieu m; (Cine) plateau m; (Theat: stage) scène f; (: scenery) décor m; (Math) ensemble m; (Hairdressing) mise f en plis ▷ adj (fixed) fixe, déterminé(e); (ready) prêt(e) ▷ vt (place) mettre, poser, placer; (fix, establish) fixer; (: record) établir; (assign: task, homework) donner; (exam) composer; (adjust) régler; (decide: rules etc) fixer, choisir; (Typ) composer ▷ vi (sun) se coucher; (jam, jelly, concrete) prendre; (bone) se ressouder; **to be ~ on doing** être résolu(e) à faire; **to be all ~ to do** être (fin) prêt(e) pour faire; **to be (dead) ~ against** être (totalement) opposé à; **he's ~ in his ways** il n'est pas très souple, il tient à ses habitudes; **to ~ to music** mettre en musique; **to ~ on fire** mettre le feu à; **to ~ free** libérer; **to ~ sth going** déclencher qch; **to ~ the alarm clock for seven o'clock** mettre le réveil à sonner à sept heures; **to ~ sail** partir, prendre la mer; **a ~ phrase** une expression toute faite, une locution; **a ~ of false teeth** un dentier; **a ~ of dining-room furniture** une salle à manger

▶ **set about** vt fus (task) entreprendre, se mettre à; **to ~ about doing sth** se mettre à faire qch

▶ **set aside** vt mettre de côté; (time) garder

▶ **set back** vt (in time): **to ~ back (by)** retarder (de); (place): **a house ~ back from the road** une maison située en retrait de la route

▶ **set down** vt (subj: bus, train) déposer
▶ **set in** vi (infection, bad weather) s'installer; (complications) survenir, surgir; **the rain has ~ in for the day** c'est parti pour qu'il pleuve toute la journée
▶ **set off** vi se mettre en route, partir ▷ vt (bomb) faire exploser; (cause to start) déclencher; (show up well) mettre en valeur, faire valoir
▶ **set out** vi: **to ~ out (from)** partir (de) ▷ vt (arrange) disposer; (state) présenter, exposer; **to ~ out to do** entreprendre de faire; avoir pour but or intention de faire
▶ **set up** vt (organization) fonder, créer; (monument) ériger; **to ~ up shop** (fig) s'établir, s'installer

setback ['sɛtbæk] n (hitch) revers m, contretemps m; (in health) rechute f
set menu n menu m
set square n équerre f
settee [sɛ'tiː] n canapé m
setting ['sɛtɪŋ] n cadre m; (of jewel) monture f; (position: of controls) réglage m
setting lotion n lotion f pour mise en plis
settle ['sɛtl] vt (argument, matter, account) régler; (problem) résoudre; (Med: calm) calmer; (colonize: land) coloniser ▷ vi (bird, dust etc) se poser; (sediment) se déposer; **to ~ to sth** se mettre sérieusement à qch; **to ~ for sth** accepter qch, se contenter de qch; **to ~ on sth** opter or se décider pour qch; **that's ~d then** alors, c'est d'accord!; **to ~ one's stomach** calmer des maux d'estomac
▶ **settle down** vi (get comfortable) s'installer; (become calmer) se calmer; se ranger
▶ **settle in** vi s'installer
▶ **settle up** vi: **to ~ up with sb** régler (ce que l'on doit à) qn
settlement ['sɛtlmənt] n (payment) règlement m; (agreement) accord m; (colony) colonie f; (village etc) village m, hameau m; **in ~ of our account** (Comm) en règlement de notre compte
settler ['sɛtlər] n colon m
setup ['sɛtʌp] n (arrangement) manière f dont les choses sont organisées; (situation) situation f, allure f des choses
seven ['sɛvn] num sept
seventeen [sɛvn'tiːn] num dix-sept
seventeenth [sɛvn'tiːnθ] num dix-septième
seventh ['sɛvnθ] num septième
seventieth ['sɛvntɪɪθ] num soixante-dixième
seventy ['sɛvntɪ] num soixante-dix
sever ['sɛvər] vt couper, trancher; (relations) rompre
several ['sɛvərl] adj, pron plusieurs pl; **~ of us** plusieurs d'entre nous; **~ times** plusieurs fois
severance ['sɛvərəns] n (of relations) rupture f
severance pay n indemnité f de licenciement
severe [sɪ'vɪər] adj (stern) sévère, strict(e); (serious) grave, sérieux(-euse); (hard) rigoureux(-euse), dur(e); (plain) sévère, austère
severely [sɪ'vɪəlɪ] adv sévèrement; (wounded, ill) gravement

severity [sɪ'vɛrɪtɪ] n sévérité f; gravité f; rigueur f
sew (pt **-ed**, pp **-n**) [səu, səud, səun] vt, vi coudre
▶ **sew up** vt (re)coudre; **it is all ~n up** (fig) c'est dans le sac or dans la poche
sewage ['suːɪdʒ] n vidange(s) f(pl)
sewage works n champ m d'épandage
sewer ['suːər] n égout m
sewing ['səuɪŋ] n couture f; (item(s)) ouvrage m
sewing machine n machine f à coudre
sewn [səun] pp of **sew**
sex [sɛks] n sexe m; **to have ~ with** avoir des rapports (sexuels) avec
sex act n acte sexuel
sex appeal n sex-appeal m
sex education n éducation sexuelle
sexism ['sɛksɪzəm] n sexisme m
sexist ['sɛksɪst] adj sexiste
sex life n vie sexuelle
sex object n femme-objet f, objet sexuel
sextet [sɛks'tɛt] n sextuor m
sexual ['sɛksjuəl] adj sexuel(le); **~ assault** attentat m à la pudeur; **~ harassment** harcèlement sexuel
sexual intercourse n rapports sexuels
sexuality [sɛksju'ælɪtɪ] n sexualité f
sexy ['sɛksɪ] adj sexy inv
Seychelles [seɪ'ʃɛl(z)] npl: **the ~** les Seychelles fpl
SF n abbr (= science fiction) SF f
SG n abbr (US) = **Surgeon General**
Sgt abbr (= sergeant) Sgt
shabbiness ['ʃæbɪnɪs] n aspect miteux; mesquinerie f
shabby ['ʃæbɪ] adj miteux(-euse); (behaviour) mesquin(e), méprisable
shack [ʃæk] n cabane f, hutte f
shackles ['ʃæklz] npl chaînes fpl, entraves fpl
shade [ʃeɪd] n ombre f; (for lamp) abat-jour m inv; (of colour) nuance f, ton m; (US: window shade) store m; (small quantity): **a ~ of** un soupçon de ▷ vt abriter du soleil, ombrager; **shades** npl (US: sunglasses) lunettes fpl de soleil; **in the ~** à l'ombre; **a ~ smaller** un tout petit peu plus petit
shadow ['ʃædəu] n ombre f ▷ vt (follow) filer; **without** or **beyond a ~ of doubt** sans l'ombre d'un doute
shadow cabinet n (Brit Pol) cabinet parallèle formé par le parti qui n'est pas au pouvoir
shadowy ['ʃædəuɪ] adj ombragé(e); (dim) vague, indistinct(e)
shady ['ʃeɪdɪ] adj ombragé(e); (fig: dishonest) louche, véreux(-euse)
shaft [ʃɑːft] n (of arrow, spear) hampe f; (Aut, Tech) arbre m; (of mine) puits m; (of lift) cage f; (of light) rayon m, trait m; **ventilator ~** conduit m d'aération or de ventilation
shaggy ['ʃægɪ] adj hirsute; en broussaille
shake [ʃeɪk] (pt **shook**, pp **shaken** [ʃuk, 'ʃeɪkn]) vt secouer; (bottle, cocktail) agiter; (house, confidence) ébranler ▷ vi trembler ▷ n secousse f; **to ~ one's head** (in refusal etc) dire or faire non de la

tête; (in dismay) secouer la tête; **to ~ hands with sb** serrer la main à qn
▶ **shake off** vt secouer; (pursuer) se débarrasser de
▶ **shake up** vt secouer

shake-up ['ʃeɪkʌp] n grand remaniement

shakily ['ʃeɪkɪlɪ] adv (reply) d'une voix tremblante; (walk) d'un pas mal assuré; (write) d'une main tremblante

shaky ['ʃeɪkɪ] adj (hand, voice) tremblant(e); (building) branlant(e), peu solide; (memory) chancelant(e); (knowledge) incertain(e)

shale [ʃeɪl] n schiste argileux

shall [ʃæl] aux vb: **I ~ go** j'irai; **~ I open the door?** j'ouvre la porte?; **I'll get the coffee, ~ I?** je vais chercher le café, d'accord?

shallot [ʃə'lɒt] n (Brit) échalote f

shallow ['ʃæləu] adj peu profond(e); (fig) superficiel(le), qui manque de profondeur

sham [ʃæm] n frime f; (jewellery, furniture) imitation f ▷ adj feint(e), simulé(e) ▷ vt feindre, simuler

shambles ['ʃæmblz] n confusion f, pagaïe f, fouillis m; **the economy is (in) a complete ~** l'économie est dans la confusion la plus totale

shambolic [ʃæm'bɒlɪk] adj (inf) bordélique

shame [ʃeɪm] n honte f ▷ vt faire honte à; **it is a ~ (that/to do)** c'est dommage (que+sub/de faire); **what a ~!** quel dommage!; **to put sb/sth to ~** (fig) faire honte à qn/qch

shamefaced ['ʃeɪmfeɪst] adj honteux(-euse), penaud(e)

shameful ['ʃeɪmful] adj honteux(-euse), scandaleux(-euse)

shameless ['ʃeɪmlɪs] adj éhonté(e), effronté(e); (immodest) impudique

shampoo [ʃæm'puː] n shampooing m ▷ vt faire un shampooing à; **~ and set** shampooing et mise f en plis

shamrock ['ʃæmrɒk] n trèfle m (emblème national de l'Irlande)

shandy ['ʃændɪ] n bière panachée

shan't [ʃɑːnt] = **shall not**

shantytown ['ʃæntɪtaun] n bidonville m

SHAPE [ʃeɪp] n abbr (= Supreme Headquarters Allied Powers, Europe) quartier général des forces alliées en Europe

shape [ʃeɪp] n forme f ▷ vt façonner, modeler; (clay, stone) donner forme à; (statement) formuler; (sb's ideas, character) former; (sb's life) déterminer; (course of events) influer sur le cours de ▷ vi (also: **shape up**: events) prendre tournure; (: person) faire des progrès, s'en sortir; **to take ~** prendre forme or tournure; **in the ~ of a heart** en forme de cœur; **I can't bear gardening in any ~ or form** je déteste le jardinage sous quelque forme que ce soit; **to get o.s. into ~** (re)trouver la forme

-shaped [ʃeɪpt] suffix: **heart~** en forme de cœur

shapeless ['ʃeɪplɪs] adj informe, sans forme

shapely ['ʃeɪplɪ] adj bien proportionné(e), beau (belle)

share [ʃɛəʳ] n (thing received, contribution) part f; (Comm) action f ▷ vt partager; (have in common) avoir en commun; **to ~ out (among or between)** partager (entre); **to ~ in** (joy, sorrow) prendre part à; (profits) participer à, avoir part à; (work) partager

share capital n capital social

share certificate n certificat m or titre m d'action

shareholder ['ʃɛəhəuldəʳ] n (Brit) actionnaire m/f

share index n indice m de la Bourse

shark [ʃɑːk] n requin m

sharp [ʃɑːp] adj (razor, knife) tranchant(e), bien aiguisé(e); (point, voice) aigu(ë); (nose, chin) pointu(e); (outline, increase) net(te); (curve, bend) brusque; (cold, pain) vif (vive); (taste) piquant(e), âcre; (Mus) dièse; (person: quick-witted) vif (vive), éveillé(e); (: unscrupulous) malhonnête ▷ n (Mus) dièse m ▷ adv: **at 2 o'clock ~** à 2 heures pile or tapantes; **turn ~ left** tournez immédiatement à gauche; **to be ~ with sb** être brusque avec qn; **look ~!** dépêche-toi!

sharpen ['ʃɑːpn] vt aiguiser; (pencil) tailler; (fig) aviver

sharpener ['ʃɑːpnəʳ] n (also: **pencil sharpener**) taille-crayon(s) m inv; (also: **knife sharpener**) aiguisoir m

sharp-eyed [ʃɑːp'aɪd] adj à qui rien n'échappe

sharpish ['ʃɑːpɪʃ] adv (Brit inf: quickly) en vitesse

sharply ['ʃɑːplɪ] adv (turn, stop) brusquement; (stand out) nettement; (criticize, retort) sèchement, vertement

sharp-tempered [ʃɑːp'tɛmpəd] adj prompt(e) à se mettre en colère

sharp-witted [ʃɑːp'wɪtɪd] adj à l'esprit vif, malin(-igne)

shatter ['ʃætəʳ] vt fracasser, briser, faire voler en éclats; (fig: upset) bouleverser; (: ruin) briser, ruiner ▷ vi voler en éclats, se briser, se fracasser

shattered ['ʃætəd] adj (overwhelmed, grief-stricken) bouleversé(e); (inf: exhausted) éreinté(e)

shatterproof ['ʃætəpruːf] adj incassable

shave [ʃeɪv] vt raser ▷ vi se raser ▷ n: **to have a ~** se raser

shaven ['ʃeɪvn] adj (head) rasé(e)

shaver ['ʃeɪvəʳ] n (also: **electric shaver**) rasoir m électrique

shaving ['ʃeɪvɪŋ] n (action) rasage m

shaving brush n blaireau m

shaving cream n crème f à raser

shaving foam n mousse f à raser

shavings ['ʃeɪvɪŋz] npl (of wood etc) copeaux mpl

shaving soap n savon m à barbe

shawl [ʃɔːl] n châle m

she [ʃiː] pron elle; **there ~ is** la voilà; **~-elephant** etc éléphant m etc femelle

sheaf (pl **sheaves**) [ʃiːf, ʃiːvz] n gerbe f

shear [ʃɪəʳ] vt (pt **-ed**, pp **-ed** or **shorn** [ʃɔːn]) (sheep) tondre
▶ **shear off** vt tondre; (branch) élaguer

shears ['ʃɪəz] npl (for hedge) cisaille(s) f(pl)

sheath [ʃi:θ] *n* gaine *f*, fourreau *m*, étui *m*; (*contraceptive*) préservatif *m*
sheathe [ʃi:ð] *vt* gainer; (*sword*) rengainer
sheath knife *n* couteau *m* à gaine
sheaves [ʃi:vz] *npl of* **sheaf**
shed [ʃɛd] *n* remise *f*, resserre *f*; (*Industry, Rail*) hangar *m* ▷ *vt* (*pt, pp* -) (*leaves, fur etc*) perdre; (*tears*) verser, répandre; (*workers*) congédier; **to ~ light on** (*problem, mystery*) faire la lumière sur
she'd [ʃi:d] = **she had; she would**
sheen [ʃi:n] *n* lustre *m*
sheep [ʃi:p] *n* (*pl inv*) mouton *m*
sheepdog [ʃi:pdɔg] *n* chien *m* de berger
sheep farmer *n* éleveur *m* de moutons
sheepish [ʃi:pɪʃ] *adj* penaud(e), timide
sheepskin [ʃi:pskɪn] *n* peau *f* de mouton
sheepskin jacket *n* canadienne *f*
sheer [ʃɪər] *adj* (*utter*) pur(e), pur et simple; (*steep*) à pic, abrupt(e); (*almost transparent*) extrêmement fin(e) ▷ *adv* à pic, abruptement; **by ~ chance** par pur hasard
sheet [ʃi:t] *n* (*on bed*) drap *m*; (*of paper*) feuille *f*; (*of glass, metal etc*) feuille, plaque *f*
sheet feed *n* (*on printer*) alimentation *f* en papier (feuille à feuille)
sheet lightning *n* éclair *m* en nappe(s)
sheet metal *n* tôle *f*
sheet music *n* partition(s) *f(pl)*
sheik, sheikh [ʃeɪk] *n* cheik *m*
shelf (*pl* **shelves**) [ʃɛlf, ʃɛlvz] *n* étagère *f*, rayon *m*; **set of shelves** rayonnage *m*
shelf life *n* (*Comm*) durée *f* de conservation (avant la vente)
shell [ʃɛl] *n* (*on beach*) coquillage *m*; (*of egg, nut etc*) coquille *f*; (*explosive*) obus *m*; (*of building*) carcasse *f* ▷ *vt* (*crab, prawn etc*) décortiquer; (*peas*) écosser; (*Mil*) bombarder (d'obus)
▶ **shell out** *vi* (*inf*): **to ~ out (for)** casquer (pour)
she'll [ʃi:l] = **she will; she shall**
shellfish [ʃɛlfɪʃ] *n* (*pl inv*: *crab etc*) crustacé *m*; (: *scallop etc*) coquillage *m* ▷ *npl* (*as food*) fruits *mpl* de mer
shell suit *n* survêtement *m*
shelter [ʃɛltər] *n* abri *m*, refuge *m* ▷ *vt* abriter, protéger; (*give lodging to*) donner asile à ▷ *vi* s'abriter, se mettre à l'abri; **to take ~ (from)** s'abriter (de)
sheltered [ʃɛltəd] *adj* (*life*) retiré(e), à l'abri des soucis; (*spot*) abrité(e)
sheltered housing *n* foyers *mpl* (*pour personnes âgées ou handicapées*)
shelve [ʃɛlv] *vt* (*fig*) mettre en suspens *or* en sommeil
shelves [ʃɛlvz] *npl of* **shelf**
shelving [ʃɛlvɪŋ] *n* (*shelves*) rayonnage(s) *m(pl)*
shepherd [ʃɛpəd] *n* berger *m* ▷ *vt* (*guide*) guider, escorter
shepherdess [ʃɛpədɪs] *n* bergère *f*
shepherd's pie [ʃɛpədz-] *n* ≈ hachis *m* Parmentier
sherbet [ʃə:bət] *n* (*Brit*: *powder*) poudre acidulée; (*US*: *water ice*) sorbet *m*

sheriff [ʃɛrɪf] (*US*) *n* shérif *m*
sherry [ʃɛrɪ] *n* xérès *m*, sherry *m*
she's [ʃi:z] = **she is; she has**
Shetland [ʃɛtlənd] *n* (*also*: **the Shetlands, the Shetland Isles** *or* **Islands**) les îles *fpl* Shetland
Shetland pony *n* poney *m* des îles Shetland
shield [ʃi:ld] *n* bouclier *m*; (*protection*) écran *m* de protection ▷ *vt*: **to ~ (from)** protéger (de *or* contre)
shift [ʃɪft] *n* (*change*) changement *m*; (*work period*) période *f* de travail; (*of workers*) équipe *f*, poste *m* ▷ *vt* déplacer, changer de place; (*remove*) enlever ▷ *vi* changer de place, bouger; **the wind has ~ed to the south** le vent a tourné au sud; **a ~ in demand** (*Comm*) un déplacement de la demande
shift key *n* (*on typewriter*) touche *f* de majuscule
shiftless [ʃɪftlɪs] *adj* fainéant(e)
shift work *n* travail *m* par roulement; **to do ~** travailler par roulement
shifty [ʃɪftɪ] *adj* sournois(e); (*eyes*) fuyant(e)
Shiite [ʃi:aɪt] *n* Chiite *m/f* ▷ *adj* chiite
shilling [ʃɪlɪŋ] *n* (*Brit*) shilling *m* (= 12 old pence; 20 in a pound)
shilly-shally [ʃɪlɪʃælɪ] *vi* tergiverser, atermoyer
shimmer [ʃɪmər] *n* miroitement *m*, chatoiement *m* ▷ *vi* miroiter, chatoyer
shin [ʃɪn] *n* tibia *m* ▷ *vi*: **to ~ up/down a tree** grimper dans un/descendre d'un arbre
shindig [ʃɪndɪg] *n* (*inf*) bamboula *f*
shine [ʃaɪn] (*pt, pp* **shone**) [ʃɔn] *n* éclat *m*, brillant *m* ▷ *vi* briller ▷ *vt* (*torch*): **to ~ on** braquer sur; (*polish*) (*pt, pp* -**d**) faire briller *or* reluire
shingle [ʃɪŋgl] *n* (*on beach*) galets *mpl*; (*on roof*) bardeau *m*
shingles [ʃɪŋglz] *n* (*Med*) zona *m*
shining [ʃaɪnɪŋ] *adj* brillant(e)
shiny [ʃaɪnɪ] *adj* brillant(e)
ship [ʃɪp] *n* bateau *m*; (*large*) navire *m* ▷ *vt* transporter (par mer); (*send*) expédier (par mer); (*load*) charger, embarquer; **on board ~** à bord
shipbuilder [ʃɪpbɪldər] *n* constructeur *m* de navires
shipbuilding [ʃɪpbɪldɪŋ] *n* construction navale
ship chandler [-ˈtʃɑ:ndlər] *n* fournisseur *m* maritime, shipchandler *m*
shipment [ʃɪpmənt] *n* cargaison *f*
shipowner [ʃɪpəunər] *n* armateur *m*
shipper [ʃɪpər] *n* affréteur *m*, expéditeur *m*
shipping [ʃɪpɪŋ] *n* (*ships*) navires *mpl*; (*traffic*) navigation *f*; (*the industry*) industrie navale; (*transport*) transport *m*
shipping agent *n* agent *m* maritime
shipping company *n* compagnie *f* de navigation
shipping lane *n* couloir *m* de navigation
shipping line *n* = **shipping company**
shipshape [ʃɪpʃeɪp] *adj* en ordre impeccable
shipwreck [ʃɪprɛk] *n* épave *f*; (*event*) naufrage *m* ▷ *vt*: **to be ~ed** faire naufrage
shipyard [ʃɪpjɑ:d] *n* chantier naval
shire [ʃaɪər] *n* (*Brit*) comté *m*

shirk [ʃəːk] vt esquiver, se dérober à
shirt [ʃəːt] n chemise f; (woman's) chemisier m; **in ~ sleeves** en bras de chemise
shirty ['ʃəːtɪ] adj (Brit inf) de mauvais poil
shit [ʃɪt] excl (inf!) merde (!)
shiver ['ʃɪvəʳ] n frisson m ▷ vi frissonner
shoal [ʃəʊl] n (of fish) banc m
shock [ʃɔk] n (impact) choc m, heurt m; (Elec) secousse f, décharge f; (emotional) choc; (Med) commotion f, choc ▷ vt (scandalize) choquer, scandaliser; (upset) bouleverser; **suffering from ~** (Med) commotionné(e); **it gave us a ~** ça nous a fait un choc; **it came as a ~ to hear that ...** nous avons appris avec stupeur que ...
shock absorber [-əbzɔːbəʳ] n amortisseur m
shocker ['ʃɔkəʳ] n (inf): **the news was a real ~ to him** il a vraiment été choqué par cette nouvelle
shocking ['ʃɔkɪŋ] adj (outrageous) choquant(e), scandaleux(-euse); (awful) épouvantable
shockproof ['ʃɔkpruːf] adj anti-choc inv
shock therapy, shock treatment n (Med) (traitement m par) électrochoc(s) m(pl)
shock wave n (also fig) onde f de choc
shod [ʃɔd] pt, pp of **shoe**; **well-~** bien chaussé(e)
shoddy ['ʃɔdɪ] adj de mauvaise qualité, mal fait(e)
shoe [ʃuː] n chaussure f, soulier m; (also: **horseshoe**) fer m à cheval; (also: **brake shoe**) mâchoire f de frein ▷ vt (pt, pp **shod**) [ʃɔd] (horse) ferrer
shoebrush ['ʃuːbrʌʃ] n brosse f à chaussures
shoehorn ['ʃuːhɔːn] n chausse-pied m
shoelace ['ʃuːleɪs] n lacet m (de soulier)
shoemaker ['ʃuːmeɪkəʳ] n cordonnier m, fabricant m de chaussures
shoe polish n cirage m
shoeshop ['ʃuːʃɔp] n magasin m de chaussures
shoestring ['ʃuːstrɪŋ] n: **on a ~** (fig) avec un budget dérisoire; avec des moyens très restreints
shoetree ['ʃuːtriː] n embauchoir m
shone [ʃɔn] pt, pp of **shine**
shoo [ʃuː] excl allez, ouste! ▷ vt (also: **shoo away, shoo off**) chasser
shook [ʃuk] pt of **shake**
shoot [ʃuːt] (pt, pp **shot**) [ʃɔt] n (on branch, seedling) pousse f; (shooting party) partie f de chasse ▷ vt (game: hunt) chasser; (: aim at) tirer; (: kill) abattre; (person) blesser/tuer d'un coup de fusil (or de revolver); (execute) fusiller; (arrow) tirer; (gun) tirer un coup de; (Cine) tourner ▷ vi (with gun, bow): **to ~ (at)** tirer (sur); (Football) shooter, tirer; **to ~ past sb** passer en flèche devant qn; **to ~ in/out** entrer/sortir comme une flèche
▶ **shoot down** vt (plane) abattre
▶ **shoot up** vi (fig: prices etc) monter en flèche
shooting ['ʃuːtɪŋ] n (shots) coups mpl de feu; (attack) fusillade f; (murder) homicide m (à l'aide d'une arme à feu); (Hunting) chasse f; (Cine) tournage m
shooting range n stand m de tir
shooting star n étoile filante

shop [ʃɔp] n magasin m; (workshop) atelier m ▷ vi (also: **go shopping**) faire ses courses or ses achats; **repair ~** atelier de réparations; **to talk ~** (fig) parler boutique
▶ **shop around** vi faire le tour des magasins (pour comparer les prix); (fig) se renseigner avant de choisir or décider
shopaholic [ʃɔpə'hɔlɪk] n (inf) personne qui achète sans pouvoir s'arrêter
shop assistant n (Brit) vendeur(-euse)
shop floor n (Brit: fig) ouvriers mpl
shopkeeper ['ʃɔpkiːpəʳ] n marchand(e), commerçant(e)
shoplift ['ʃɔplɪft] vi voler à l'étalage
shoplifter ['ʃɔplɪftəʳ] n voleur(-euse) à l'étalage
shoplifting ['ʃɔplɪftɪŋ] n vol m à l'étalage
shopper ['ʃɔpəʳ] n personne f qui fait ses courses, acheteur(-euse)
shopping ['ʃɔpɪŋ] n (goods) achats mpl, provisions fpl
shopping bag n sac m (à provisions)
shopping centre, (US) **shopping center** n centre commercial
shopping mall n centre commercial
shopping trolley n (Brit) Caddie® m
shop-soiled ['ʃɔpsɔɪld] adj défraîchi(e), qui a fait la vitrine
shop window n vitrine f
shore [ʃɔːʳ] n (of sea, lake) rivage m, rive f ▷ vt: **to ~ (up)** étayer; **on ~** à terre
shore leave n (Naut) permission f à terre
shorn [ʃɔːn] pp of **shear** ▷ adj: **~ of** dépouillé(e) de
short [ʃɔːt] adj (not long) court(e); (soon finished) court, bref (brève); (person, step) petit(e); (curt) brusque, sec (sèche); (insufficient) insuffisant(e) ▷ n (also: **short film**) court métrage; (Elec) court-circuit m; **to be ~ of sth** être à court de or manquer de qch; **to be in ~ supply** manquer, être difficile à trouver; **I'm 3 ~** il m'en manque 3; **in ~** bref; en bref; **~ of doing** à moins de faire; **everything ~ of** tout sauf; **it is ~ for** c'est l'abréviation or le diminutif de; **a ~ time ago** il y a peu de temps; **in the ~ term** à court terme; **to cut ~** (speech, visit) abréger, écourter; (person) couper la parole à; **to fall ~ of** ne pas être à la hauteur de; **to run ~ of** arriver à court de, venir à manquer de; **to stop ~** s'arrêter net; **to stop ~ of** ne pas aller jusqu'à
shortage ['ʃɔːtɪdʒ] n manque m, pénurie f
shortbread ['ʃɔːtbrɛd] n ≈ sablé m
short-change [ʃɔːt'tʃeɪndʒ] vt: **to ~ sb** ne pas rendre assez à qn
short-circuit [ʃɔːt'səːkɪt] n court-circuit m ▷ vt court-circuiter ▷ vi se mettre en court-circuit
shortcoming ['ʃɔːtkʌmɪŋ] n défaut m
shortcrust pastry ['ʃɔːtkrʌst-], **short pastry** n (Brit) pâte brisée
shortcut ['ʃɔːtkʌt] n raccourci m
shorten ['ʃɔːtn] vt raccourcir; (text, visit) abréger
shortening ['ʃɔːtnɪŋ] n (Culin) matière grasse
shortfall ['ʃɔːtfɔːl] n déficit m

shorthand ['ʃɔːthænd] n (Brit) sténo(graphie) f;
to take sth down in ~ prendre qch en sténo
shorthand notebook n bloc m sténo
shorthand typist n (Brit) sténodactylo m/f
shortlist ['ʃɔːtlɪst] n (Brit: for job) liste f des
candidats sélectionnés
short-lived ['ʃɔːt'lɪvd] adj de courte durée
shortly ['ʃɔːtlɪ] adv bientôt, sous peu
shortness ['ʃɔːtnɪs] n brièveté f
short notice n: **at ~** au dernier moment
shorts [ʃɔːts] npl: **(a pair of) ~** un short
short-sighted [ʃɔːt'saɪtɪd] adj (Brit) myope; (fig)
qui manque de clairvoyance
short-sleeved [ʃɔːt'sliːvd] adj à manches
courtes
short-staffed [ʃɔːt'stɑːft] adj à court de
personnel
short-stay [ʃɔːt'steɪ] adj (car park) de courte
durée
short story n nouvelle f
short-tempered [ʃɔːt'tɛmpəd] adj qui
s'emporte facilement
short-term ['ʃɔːttəːm] adj (effect) à court terme
short time n: **to work ~, to be on ~** (Industry) être
en chômage partiel, travailler à horaire réduit
short wave n (Radio) ondes courtes
shot [ʃɔt] pt, pp of **shoot** ▷ n coup m (de feu);
(shotgun pellets) plombs mpl; (try) coup, essai m;
(injection) piqûre f; (Phot) photo f; **to be a good/
poor ~** (person) tirer bien/mal; **to fire a ~ at sb/
sth** tirer sur qn/qch; **to have a ~ at (doing) sth**
essayer de faire qch; **like a ~** comme une flèche;
(very readily) sans hésiter; **to get ~ of sb/sth** (inf)
se débarrasser de qn/qch; **a big ~** (inf) un gros
bonnet
shotgun ['ʃɔtɡʌn] n fusil m de chasse
should [ʃud] aux vb: **I ~ go now** je devrais partir
maintenant; **he ~ be there now** il devrait être
arrivé maintenant; **I ~ go if I were you** si j'étais
vous j'irais; **I ~ like to** volontiers, j'aimerais
bien; **~ he phone ...** si jamais il téléphone ...
shoulder ['ʃəuldəʳ] n épaule f; (Brit: of road): **hard
~** accotement m ▷ vt (fig) endosser, se charger
de; **to look over one's ~** regarder derrière soi
(en tournant la tête); **to rub ~s with sb** (fig)
côtoyer qn; **to give sb the cold ~** (fig) battre
froid à qn
shoulder bag n sac m à bandoulière
shoulder blade n omoplate f
shoulder strap n bretelle f
shouldn't ['ʃudnt] = **should not**
shout [ʃaut] n cri m ▷ vt crier ▷ vi crier, pousser
des cris; **to give sb a ~** appeler qn
▶ **shout down** vt huer
shouting ['ʃautɪŋ] n cris mpl
shouting match n (inf) engueulade f,
empoignade f
shove [ʃʌv] vt pousser; (inf: put): **to ~ sth in**
fourrer or ficher qch dans ▷ n poussée f; **he ~d
me out of the way** il m'a écarté en me
poussant
▶ **shove off** vi (Naut) pousser au large; (fig: col)

ficher le camp
shovel ['ʃʌvl] n pelle f ▷ vt pelleter, enlever (or
enfourner) à la pelle
show [ʃəu] (pt **-ed**, pp **-n**) [ʃəun] n (of emotion)
manifestation f, démonstration f; (semblance)
semblant m, apparence f; (exhibition) exposition
f, salon m; (Theat, TV) spectacle m; (Cine) séance f
▷ vt montrer; (film) passer; (courage etc) faire
preuve de, manifester; (exhibit) exposer ▷ vi se
voir, être visible; **can you ~ me where it is,
please?** pouvez-vous me montrer où c'est?; **to
ask for a ~ of hands** demander que l'on vote à
main levée; **to be on ~** être exposé(e); **it's just
for ~** c'est juste pour l'effet; **who's running
the ~ here?** (inf) qui est-ce qui commande ici?;
to ~ sb to his seat/to the door accompagner
qn jusqu'à sa place/la porte; **to ~ a profit/loss**
(Comm) indiquer un bénéfice/une perte; **it just
goes to ~ that ...** ça prouve bien que ...
▶ **show in** vt faire entrer
▶ **show off** vi (pej) crâner ▷ vt (display) faire
valoir; (pej) faire étalage de
▶ **show out** vt reconduire à la porte
▶ **show up** vi (stand out) ressortir; (inf: turn up) se
montrer ▷ vt démontrer; (unmask) démasquer,
dénoncer; (flaw) faire ressortir
showbiz ['ʃəubɪz] n (inf) showbiz m
show business n le monde du spectacle
showcase ['ʃəukeɪs] n vitrine f
showdown ['ʃəudaun] n épreuve f de force
shower ['ʃauəʳ] n (for washing) douche f; (rain)
averse f; (of stones etc) pluie f, grêle f; (US: party)
réunion organisée pour la remise de cadeaux ▷ vi
prendre une douche, se doucher ▷ vt: **to ~ sb
with** (gifts etc) combler qn de; (abuse etc) accabler
qn de; (missiles) bombarder qn de; **to have** or
take a ~ prendre une douche, se doucher
shower cap n bonnet m de douche
shower gel n gel m douche
showerproof ['ʃauəpruːf] adj imperméable
showery ['ʃauərɪ] adj (weather) pluvieux(-euse)
showground ['ʃəuɡraund] n champ m de foire
showing ['ʃəuɪŋ] n (of film) projection f
show jumping [-dʒʌmpɪŋ] n concours m
hippique
showman ['ʃəumən] n (irreg) n (at fair, circus) forain
m; (fig) comédien m
showmanship ['ʃəumənʃɪp] n art m de la mise
en scène
shown [ʃəun] pp of **show**
show-off ['ʃəuɔf] n (inf: person) crâneur(-euse),
m'as-tu-vu(e)
showpiece ['ʃəupiːs] n (of exhibition etc) joyau m,
clou m; **that hospital is a ~** cet hôpital est un
modèle du genre
showroom ['ʃəurum] n magasin m or salle f
d'exposition
show trial n grand procès m médiatique (qui fait
un exemple)
showy ['ʃəuɪ] adj tapageur(-euse)
shrank [ʃræŋk] pt of **shrink**
shrapnel ['ʃræpnl] n éclats mpl d'obus

785

shred [ʃrɛd] *n* (*gen pl*) lambeau *m*, petit morceau; (*fig: of truth, evidence*) parcelle *f* ▷ *vt* mettre en lambeaux, déchirer; (*documents*) détruire; (*Culin: grate*) râper; (: *lettuce etc*) couper en lanières

shredder [ʃrɛdəʳ] *n* (*for vegetables*) râpeur *m*; (*for documents, papers*) déchiqueteuse *f*

shrewd [ʃruːd] *adj* astucieux(-euse), perspicace; (*business person*) habile

shrewdness [ʃruːdnɪs] *n* perspicacité *f*

shriek [ʃriːk] *n* cri perçant *or* aigu, hurlement *m* ▷ *vt, vi* hurler, crier

shrift [ʃrɪft] *n*: **to give sb short ~** expédier qn sans ménagements

shrill [ʃrɪl] *adj* perçant(e), aigu(ë), strident(e)

shrimp [ʃrɪmp] *n* crevette grise

shrine [ʃraɪn] *n* châsse *f*; (*place*) lieu *m* de pèlerinage

shrink (*pt* **shrank**, *pp* **shrunk**) [ʃrɪŋk, ʃræŋk, ʃrʌŋk] *vi* rétrécir; (*fig*) diminuer; (*also:* **shrink away**) reculer ▷ *vt* (*wool*) (faire) rétrécir ▷ *n* (*inf: pej*) psychanalyste *m/f*; **to ~ from (doing) sth** reculer devant (la pensée de faire) qch

shrinkage [ʃrɪŋkɪdʒ] *n* (*of clothes*) rétrécissement *m*

shrink-wrap [ʃrɪŋkræp] *vt* emballer sous film plastique

shrivel [ʃrɪvl] (*also:* **shrivel up**) *vt* ratatiner, flétrir ▷ *vi* se ratatiner, se flétrir

shroud [ʃraud] *n* linceul *m* ▷ *vt*: **~ed in mystery** enveloppé(e) de mystère

Shrove Tuesday [ʃrəuv-] *n* (le) Mardi gras

shrub [ʃrʌb] *n* arbuste *m*

shrubbery [ʃrʌbərɪ] *n* massif *m* d'arbustes

shrug [ʃrʌg] *n* haussement *m* d'épaules ▷ *vt, vi*: **to ~ (one's shoulders)** hausser les épaules
  ▶ **shrug off** *vt* faire fi de; (*cold, illness*) se débarrasser de

shrunk [ʃrʌŋk] *pp of* **shrink**

shrunken [ʃrʌŋkn] *adj* ratatiné(e)

shudder [ʃʌdəʳ] *n* frisson *m*, frémissement *m* ▷ *vi* frissonner, frémir

shuffle [ʃʌfl] *vt* (*cards*) battre; **to ~ (one's feet)** traîner les pieds

shun [ʃʌn] *vt* éviter, fuir

shunt [ʃʌnt] *vt* (*Rail: direct*) aiguiller; (: *divert*) détourner ▷ *vi*: **to ~ (to and fro)** faire la navette

shunting yard [ʃʌntɪŋ-] *n* voies *fpl* de garage *or* de triage

shush [ʃuʃ] *excl* chut!

shut (*pt, pp ~*) [ʃʌt] *vt* fermer ▷ *vi* (se) fermer
  ▶ **shut down** *vt* fermer définitivement; (*machine*) arrêter ▷ *vi* fermer définitivement
  ▶ **shut off** *vt* couper, arrêter
  ▶ **shut out** *vt* (*person, cold*) empêcher d'entrer; (*noise*) éviter d'entendre; (*block: view*) boucher; (: *memory of sth*) chasser de son esprit
  ▶ **shut up** *vi* (*inf: keep quiet*) se taire ▷ *vt* (*close*) fermer; (*silence*) faire taire

shutdown [ʃʌtdaun] *n* fermeture *f*

shutter [ʃʌtəʳ] *n* volet *m*; (*Phot*) obturateur *m*

shuttle [ʃʌtl] *n* navette *f*; (*also:* **shuttle service**) (service *m* de) navette *f* ▷ *vi* (*vehicle, person*) faire la navette ▷ *vt* (*passengers*) transporter par un système de navette

shuttlecock [ʃʌtlkɔk] *n* volant *m* (*de badminton*)

shuttle diplomacy *n* navettes *fpl* diplomatiques

shy [ʃaɪ] *adj* timide; **to fight ~ of** se dérober devant; **to be ~ of doing sth** hésiter à faire qch, ne pas oser faire qch ▷ *vi*: **to ~ away from doing sth** (*fig*) craindre de faire qch

shyness [ʃaɪnɪs] *n* timidité *f*

Siam [saɪæm] *n* Siam *m*

Siamese [saɪəmiːz] *adj*: **~ cat** chat siamois *mpl*; **~ twins** (frères *mpl*) siamois *mpl*, (sœurs *fpl*) siamoises *fpl*

Siberia [saɪbɪərɪə] *n* Sibérie *f*

siblings [sɪblɪŋz] *npl* (*formal*) frères et sœurs *mpl* (*de mêmes parents*)

Sicilian [sɪsɪlɪən] *adj* sicilien(ne) ▷ *n* Sicilien(ne)

Sicily [sɪsɪlɪ] *n* Sicile *f*

sick [sɪk] *adj* (*ill*) malade; (*Brit: vomiting*): **to be ~** vomir; (*humour*) noir(e), macabre; **to feel ~** avoir envie de vomir, avoir mal au cœur; **to fall ~** tomber malade; **to be (off) ~** être absent(e) pour cause de maladie; **a ~ person** un(e) malade; **to be ~ of** (*fig*) en avoir assez de

sick bag *n* sac *m* vomitoire

sick bay *n* infirmerie *f*

sick building syndrome *n* maladie dûe à la climatisation, l'éclairage artificiel etc des bureaux

sicken [sɪkn] *vt* écœurer ▷ *vi*: **to be ~ing for sth** (*cold, flu etc*) couver qch

sickening [sɪknɪŋ] *adj* (*fig*) écœurant(e), révoltant(e), répugnant(e)

sickle [sɪkl] *n* faucille *f*

sick leave *n* congé *m* de maladie

sickle-cell anaemia [sɪklsɛl-] *n* anémie *f* à hématies falciformes, drépanocytose *f*

sickly [sɪklɪ] *adj* maladif(-ive), souffreteux(-euse); (*causing nausea*) écœurant(e)

sickness [sɪknɪs] *n* maladie *f*; (*vomiting*) vomissement(s) *m(pl)*

sickness benefit *n* (prestations *fpl* de l')assurance-maladie *f*

sick note *n* (*from parents*) mot *m* d'absence; (*from doctor*) certificat médical

sick pay *n* indemnité *f* de maladie (*versée par l'employeur*)

sickroom [sɪkruːm] *n* infirmerie *f*

side [saɪd] *n* côté *m*; (*of animal*) flanc *m*; (*of lake, road*) bord *m*; (*of mountain*) versant *m*; (*fig: aspect*) côté, aspect *m*; (*team: Sport*) équipe *f*; (*TV: channel*) chaîne *f* ▷ *adj* (*door, entrance*) latéral(e) ▷ *vi*: **to ~ with sb** prendre le parti de qn, se ranger du côté de qn; **by the ~ of** au bord de; **~ by ~** côte à côte; **the right/wrong ~** le bon/mauvais côté, l'endroit/l'envers *m*; **they are on our ~** ils sont avec nous; **from all ~s** de tous côtés; **to rock from ~ to ~** se balancer; **to take ~s (with)** prendre parti (pour); **a ~ of beef** ≈ un quartier de bœuf

sideboard [saɪdbɔːd] *n* buffet *m*

sideboards [saɪdbɔːdz] (*Brit*), **sideburns**

['saɪdbə:nz] *npl* (*whiskers*) pattes *fpl*

sidecar ['saɪdkɑ:ʳ] *n* side-car *m*

side dish *n* (plat *m* d')accompagnement *m*

side drum *n* (*Mus*) tambour plat, caisse claire

side effect *n* effet *m* secondaire

sidekick ['saɪdkɪk] *n* (*inf*) sous-fifre *m*

sidelight ['saɪdlaɪt] *n* (*Aut*) veilleuse *f*

sideline ['saɪdlaɪn] *n* (*Sport*) (ligne *f* de) touche *f*; (*fig*) activité *f* secondaire

sidelong ['saɪdlɔŋ] *adj*: **to give sb a ~ glance** regarder qn du coin de l'œil

side order *n* garniture *f*

side plate *n* petite assiette

side road *n* petite route, route transversale

sidesaddle ['saɪdsædl] *adv* en amazone

sideshow ['saɪdʃəu] *n* attraction *f*

sidestep ['saɪdstɛp] *vt* (*question*) éluder; (*problem*) éviter ▷ *vi* (*Boxing etc*) esquiver

side street *n* rue transversale

sidetrack ['saɪdtræk] *vt* (*fig*) faire dévier de son sujet

sidewalk ['saɪdwɔ:k] *n* (*US*) trottoir *m*

sideways ['saɪdweɪz] *adv* de côté

siding ['saɪdɪŋ] *n* (*Rail*) voie *f* de garage

sidle ['saɪdl] *vi*: **to ~ up (to)** s'approcher furtivement (de)

SIDS [sɪdz] *n abbr* (= *sudden infant death syndrome*) mort subite du nourrisson, mort *f* au berceau

siege [si:dʒ] *n* siège *m*; **to lay ~ to** assiéger

siege economy *n* économie *f* de (temps de) siège

Sierra Leone [sɪˈɛrəlɪˈəun] *n* Sierra Leone *f*

sieve [sɪv] *n* tamis *m*, passoire *f* ▷ *vt* tamiser, passer (au tamis)

sift [sɪft] *vt* passer au tamis *or* au crible; (*fig*) passer au crible ▷ *vi* (*fig*): **to ~ through** passer en revue

sigh [saɪ] *n* soupir *m* ▷ *vi* soupirer, pousser un soupir

sight [saɪt] *n* (*faculty*) vue *f*; (*spectacle*) spectacle *m*; (*on gun*) mire *f* ▷ *vt* apercevoir; **in ~** visible; (*fig*) en vue; **out of ~** hors de vue; **at ~** (*Comm*) à vue; **at first ~** à première vue, au premier abord; **I know her by ~** je la connais de vue; **to catch ~ of sb/sth** apercevoir qn/qch; **to lose ~ of sb/sth** perdre qn/qch de vue; **to set one's ~s on sth** jeter son dévolu sur qch

sighted ['saɪtɪd] *adj* qui voit; **partially ~** qui a un certain degré de vision

sightseeing ['saɪtsi:ɪŋ] *n* tourisme *m*; **to go ~** faire du tourisme

sightseer ['saɪtsi:əʳ] *n* touriste *m/f*

sign [saɪn] *n* (*gen*) signe *m*; (*with hand etc*) signe, geste *m*; (*notice*) panneau *m*, écriteau *m*; (*also*: **road sign**) panneau de signalisation ▷ *vt* signer; **as a ~ of** en signe de; **it's a good/bad ~** c'est bon/mauvais signe; **plus/minus ~** signe plus/moins; **there's no ~ of a change of mind** rien ne laisse présager un revirement; **he was showing ~s of improvement** il commençait visiblement à faire des progrès; **to ~ one's name** signer; **where do I ~?** où dois-je signer?

▶ **sign away** *vt* (*rights etc*) renoncer officiellement à

▶ **sign for** *vt fus* (*item*) signer le reçu pour

▶ **sign in** *vi* signer le registre (en arrivant)

▶ **sign off** *vi* (*Radio, TV*) terminer l'émission

▶ **sign on** *vi* (*Mil*) s'engager; (*Brit: as unemployed*) s'inscrire au chômage; (*enrol*) s'inscrire ▷ *vt* (*Mil*) engager; (*employee*) embaucher; **to ~ on for a course** s'inscrire pour un cours

▶ **sign out** *vi* signer le registre (en partant)

▶ **sign over** *vt*: **to ~ sth over to sb** céder qch par écrit à qn

▶ **sign up** *vt* (*Mil*) engager ▷ *vi* (*Mil*) s'engager; (*for course*) s'inscrire

signal ['sɪgnl] *n* signal *m* ▷ *vi* (*Aut*) mettre son clignotant ▷ *vt* (*person*) faire signe à; (*message*) communiquer par signaux; **to ~ a left/right turn** (*Aut*) indiquer *or* signaler que l'on tourne à gauche/droite; **to ~ to sb (to do sth)** faire signe à qn (de faire qch)

signal box *n* (*Rail*) poste *m* d'aiguillage

signalman [sɪgnlmən] *n* (*Rail*) aiguilleur *m*

signatory ['sɪgnətərɪ] *n* signataire *m/f*

signature ['sɪgnətʃəʳ] *n* signature *f*

signature tune *n* indicatif musical

signet ring ['sɪgnət-] *n* chevalière *f*

significance [sɪg'nɪfɪkəns] *n* signification *f*; importance *f*; **that is of no ~** ceci n'a pas d'importance

significant [sɪg'nɪfɪkənt] *adj* significatif(-ive); (*important*) important(e), considérable

significantly [sɪg'nɪfɪkəntlɪ] *adv* (*improve, increase*) sensiblement; (*smile*) d'un air entendu, éloquemment; **~, ...** fait significatif, ...

signify ['sɪgnɪfaɪ] *vt* signifier

sign language *n* langage *m* par signes

signpost ['saɪnpəust] *n* poteau indicateur

Sikh [si:k] *adj, n* Sikh *m/f*

silage ['saɪlɪdʒ] *n* (*fodder*) fourrage vert; (*method*) ensilage *m*

silence ['saɪlns] *n* silence *m* ▷ *vt* faire taire, réduire au silence

silencer ['saɪlənsəʳ] *n* (*Brit: on gun, Aut*) silencieux *m*

silent ['saɪlnt] *adj* silencieux(-euse); (*film*) muet(te); **to keep** *or* **remain ~** garder le silence, ne rien dire

silently ['saɪlntlɪ] *adv* silencieusement

silent partner *n* (*Comm*) bailleur *m* de fonds, commanditaire *m*

silhouette [sɪlu:'ɛt] *n* silhouette *f* ▷ *vt*: **~d against** se profilant sur, se découpant contre

silicon ['sɪlɪkən] *n* silicium *m*

silicon chip ['sɪlɪkən-] *n* puce *f* électronique

silicone ['sɪlɪkəun] *n* silicone *f*

silk [sɪlk] *n* soie *f* ▷ *cpd* de *or* en soie

silky ['sɪlkɪ] *adj* soyeux(-euse)

sill [sɪl] *n* (*also*: **windowsill**) rebord *m* (de la fenêtre); (*of door*) seuil *m*; (*Aut*) bas *m* de marche

silly ['sɪlɪ] *adj* stupide, sot(te), bête; **to do something ~** faire une bêtise

silo ['saɪləu] *n* silo *m*

S

silt [sɪlt] n vase f; limon m
silver ['sɪlvəʳ] n argent m; (money) monnaie f (en
pièces d'argent); (also: **silverware**) argenterie f
▷ adj (made of silver) d'argent, en argent; (in
colour) argenté(e); (car) gris métallisé inv
silver-plated [sɪlvə'pleɪtɪd] adj plaqué(e) argent
silversmith ['sɪlvəsmɪθ] n orfèvre m/f
silverware ['sɪlvəwɛəʳ] n argenterie f
silver wedding, silver wedding anniversary
n noces fpl d'argent
silvery ['sɪlvrɪ] adj argenté(e)
SIM card abbr (= subscriber identity module card)
carte f SIM
similar ['sɪmɪləʳ] adj: ~ (**to**) semblable (à)
similarity [sɪmɪ'lærɪtɪ] n ressemblance f,
similarité f
similarly ['sɪmɪləlɪ] adv de la même façon, de
même
simile ['sɪmɪlɪ] n comparaison f
simmer ['sɪməʳ] vi cuire à feu doux, mijoter
▶ **simmer down** vi (fig: inf) se calmer
simper ['sɪmpəʳ] vi minauder
simpering ['sɪmpɪrɪŋ] adj stupide
simple [sɪmpl] adj simple; **the ~ truth** la vérité
pure et simple
simple interest n (Math, Comm) intérêts mpl
simples
simple-minded [sɪmpl'maɪndɪd] adj
simplet(te), simple d'esprit
simpleton ['sɪmpltən] n nigaud(e), niais(e)
simplicity [sɪm'plɪsɪtɪ] n simplicité f
simplification [sɪmplɪfɪ'keɪʃən] n
simplification f
simplify ['sɪmplɪfaɪ] vt simplifier
simply ['sɪmplɪ] adv simplement; (without fuss)
avec simplicité; (absolutely) absolument
simulate ['sɪmjuleɪt] vt simuler, feindre
simulation [sɪmju'leɪʃən] n simulation f
simultaneous [sɪməl'teɪnɪəs] adj simultané(e)
simultaneously [sɪməl'teɪnɪəslɪ] adv
simultanément
sin [sɪn] n péché m ▷ vi pécher
Sinai ['saɪneɪaɪ] n Sinaï m
since [sɪns] adv, prep depuis ▷ conj (time) depuis
que; (because) puisque, étant donné que,
comme; ~ **then, ever ~** depuis ce moment-là; ~
Monday depuis lundi; (**ever**) ~ **I arrived**
depuis mon arrivée, depuis que je suis arrivé
sincere [sɪn'sɪəʳ] adj sincère
sincerely [sɪn'sɪəlɪ] adv sincèrement; **Yours ~**
(at end of letter) veuillez agréer, Monsieur (or
Madame) l'expression de mes sentiments
distingués or les meilleurs
sincerity [sɪn'sɛrɪtɪ] n sincérité f
sine [saɪn] n (Math) sinus m
sinew ['sɪnju:] n tendon m; **sinews** npl muscles
mpl
sinful ['sɪnful] adj coupable
sing (pt **sang**, pp **sung**) [sɪŋ, sæŋ, sʌŋ] vt, vi
chanter
Singapore [sɪŋgə'pɔːʳ] n Singapour m
singe [sɪndʒ] vt brûler légèrement; (clothes)
roussir
singer ['sɪŋəʳ] n chanteur(-euse)
Singhalese [sɪŋə'liːz] adj = **Sinhalese**
singing ['sɪŋɪŋ] n (of person, bird) chant m; façon f
de chanter; (of kettle, bullet, in ears) sifflement m
single ['sɪŋgl] adj seul(e), unique; (unmarried)
célibataire; (not double) simple ▷ n (Brit: also:
single ticket) aller m (simple); (record) 45 tours
m; **singles** npl (Tennis) simple m; (US: single
people) célibataires m/fpl; **not a ~ one was left** il
n'en est pas resté un(e), seul(e); **every ~ day**
chaque jour sans exception
▶ **single out** vt choisir; (distinguish) distinguer
single bed n lit m d'une personne or à une place
single-breasted ['sɪŋglbrɛstɪd] adj droit(e)
Single European Market n: **the ~** le marché
unique européen
single file n: **in ~** en file indienne
single-handed [sɪŋgl'hændɪd] adv tout(e)
seul(e), sans (aucune) aide
single-minded [sɪŋgl'maɪndɪd] adj résolu(e),
tenace
single parent n parent unique (or célibataire);
single-parent family famille monoparentale
single room n chambre f à un lit or pour une
personne
singles bar n (esp US) bar m de rencontres pour
célibataires
single-sex school [sɪŋgl'sɛks-] n école f non
mixte
singlet ['sɪŋglɪt] n tricot m de corps
single-track road [sɪŋgl'træk-] n route f à voie
unique
singly ['sɪŋglɪ] adv séparément
singsong ['sɪŋsɔŋ] adj (tone) chantant(e) ▷ n
(songs): **to have a ~** chanter quelque chose
(ensemble)
singular ['sɪŋgjuləʳ] adj singulier(-ière); (odd)
singulier, étrange; (outstanding) remarquable;
(Ling) (au) singulier, du singulier ▷ n (Ling)
singulier m; **in the feminine ~** au féminin
singulier
singularly ['sɪŋgjuləlɪ] adv singulièrement;
étrangement
Sinhalese [sɪnhə'liːz] adj cingalais(e)
sinister ['sɪnɪstəʳ] adj sinistre
sink [sɪŋk] (pt **sank**, pp **sunk**) [sæŋk, sʌŋk] n
évier m; (washbasin) lavabo m ▷ vt (ship) (faire)
couler, faire sombrer; (foundations) creuser; (piles
etc): **to ~ sth into** enfoncer qch dans ▷ vi
couler, sombrer; (ground etc) s'affaisser; **to ~**
into sth (chair) s'enfoncer dans qch; **he sank**
into a chair/the mud il s'est enfoncé dans un
fauteuil/la boue; **a ~ing feeling** un serrement
de cœur
▶ **sink in** vi s'enfoncer, pénétrer; (explanation)
rentrer (inf), être compris; **it took a long time**
to ~ in il a fallu longtemps pour que ça rentre
sinking fund n fonds mpl d'amortissement
sink unit n bloc-évier m
sinner ['sɪnəʳ] n pécheur(-eresse)
Sinn Féin [ʃɪn'feɪn] n Sinn Féin m (parti politique

irlandais qui soutient l'IRA)
Sino- ['saɪnəʊ] _prefix_ sino-
sinuous ['sɪnjuəs] _adj_ sinueux(-euse)
sinus ['saɪnəs] _n_ (_Anat_) sinus _m inv_
sip [sɪp] _n_ petite gorgée ▷ _vt_ boire à petites gorgées
siphon ['saɪfən] _n_ siphon _m_ ▷ _vt_ (_also:_ **siphon off**) siphonner; (: _fig: funds_) transférer; (: _illegally_) détourner
sir [səʳ] _n_ monsieur _m_; **S~ John Smith** sir John Smith; **yes ~** oui Monsieur; **Dear S~** (_in letter_) Monsieur
siren ['saɪərn] _n_ sirène _f_
sirloin ['səːlɔɪn] _n_ (_also:_ **sirloin steak**) aloyau _m_
sirloin steak _n_ bifteck _m_ dans l'aloyau
sirocco [sɪ'rɔkəʊ] _n_ sirocco _m_
sisal ['saɪsəl] _n_ sisal _m_
sissy ['sɪsɪ] _n_ (_inf: coward_) poule mouillée
sister ['sɪstəʳ] _n_ sœur _f_; (_nun_) religieuse _f_, (bonne) sœur; (_Brit: nurse_) infirmière _f_ en chef ▷ _cpd_: **~ organization** organisation _f_ sœur; **~ ship** sister(-)ship _m_
sister-in-law ['sɪstərɪnlɔː] _n_ belle-sœur _f_
sit (_pt, pp_ **sat**) [sɪt, sæt] _vi_ s'asseoir; (_be sitting_) être assis(e); (_assembly_) être en séance, siéger; (_for painter_) poser; (_dress etc_) tomber ▷ _vt_ (_exam_) passer, se présenter à; **to ~ tight** ne pas bouger
▶ **sit about, sit around** _vi_ être assis(e) _or_ rester à ne rien faire
▶ **sit back** _vi_ (_in seat_) bien s'installer, se carrer
▶ **sit down** _vi_ s'asseoir; **to be ~ting down** être assis(e)
▶ **sit in** _vi_: **to ~ in on a discussion** assister à une discussion
▶ **sit on** _vt fus_ (_jury, committee_) faire partie de
▶ **sit up** _vi_ s'asseoir; (_straight_) se redresser; (_not go to bed_) rester debout, ne pas se coucher
sitcom ['sɪtkɔm] _n abbr_ (_TV_: = _situation comedy_) sitcom _f_, comédie _f_ de situation
sit-down ['sɪtdaʊn] _adj_: **a ~ strike** une grève sur le tas; **a ~ meal** un repas assis
site [saɪt] _n_ emplacement _m_, site _m_; (_also:_ **building site**) chantier _m_ ▷ _vt_ placer
sit-in ['sɪtɪn] _n_ (_demonstration_) sit-in _m inv_, occupation _f_ de locaux
siting ['saɪtɪŋ] _n_ (_location_) emplacement _m_
sitter ['sɪtəʳ] _n_ (_for painter_) modèle _m_; (_also:_ **babysitter**) baby-sitter _m/f_
sitting ['sɪtɪŋ] _n_ (_of assembly etc_) séance _f_; (_in canteen_) service _m_
sitting member _n_ (_Pol_) parlementaire _m/f_ en exercice
sitting room _n_ salon _m_
sitting tenant _n_ (_Brit_) locataire occupant(e)
situate ['sɪtjueɪt] _vt_ situer
situated ['sɪtjueɪtɪd] _adj_ situé(e)
situation [sɪtju'eɪʃən] _n_ situation _f_; **"~s vacant/ wanted"** (_Brit_) "offres/demandes d'emploi"
situation comedy _n_ (_Theat_) comédie _f_ de situation
six [sɪks] _num_ six
six-pack ['sɪkspæk] _n_ (_esp US_) pack _m_ de six

canettes
sixteen [sɪks'tiːn] _num_ seize
sixteenth [sɪks'tiːnθ] _num_ seizième
sixth ['sɪksθ] _num_ sixième ▷ _n_: **the upper/ lower ~** (_Brit Scol_) la terminale/la première
sixth form _n_ (_Brit_) ≈ classes _fpl_ de première et de terminale
sixth-form college _n_ lycée n'ayant que des classes de première et de terminale
sixtieth ['sɪkstɪɪθ] _num_ soixantième
sixty ['sɪkstɪ] _num_ soixante
size [saɪz] _n_ dimensions _fpl_; (_of person_) taille _f_; (_of clothing_) taille; (_of shoes_) pointure _f_; (_of estate, area_) étendue _f_; (_of problem_) ampleur _f_; (_of company_) importance _f_; (_glue_) colle _f_; **I take ~ 14** (_of dress etc_) ≈ je prends du 42 _or_ la taille 42; **the small/ large ~** (_of soap powder etc_) le petit/grand modèle; **it's the ~ of ...** c'est de la taille (_or_ grosseur) de ..., c'est grand (_or_ gros) comme ...; **cut to ~** découpé(e) aux dimensions voulues
▶ **size up** _vt_ juger, jauger
sizeable ['saɪzəbl] _adj_ (_object, building, estate_) assez grand(e); (_amount, problem, majority_) assez important(e)
sizzle ['sɪzl] _vi_ grésiller
SK _abbr_ (_Canada_) = **Saskatchewan**
skate [skeɪt] _n_ patin _m_; (_fish: pl inv_) raie _f_ ▷ _vi_ patiner
▶ **skate over, skate around** _vt_ (_problem, issue_) éluder
skateboard ['skeɪtbɔːd] _n_ skateboard _m_, planche _f_ à roulettes
skateboarding ['skeɪtbɔːdɪŋ] _n_ skateboard _m_
skater ['skeɪtəʳ] _n_ patineur(-euse)
skating ['skeɪtɪŋ] _n_ patinage _m_
skating rink _n_ patinoire _f_
skeleton ['skɛlɪtn] _n_ squelette _m_; (_outline_) schéma _m_
skeleton key _n_ passe-partout _m_
skeleton staff _n_ effectifs réduits
skeptic ['skɛptɪk] (_US_) = **sceptic**
skeptical ['skɛptɪkl] (_US_) = **sceptical**
sketch [skɛtʃ] _n_ (_drawing_) croquis _m_, esquisse _f_; (_outline plan_) aperçu _m_; (_Theat_) sketch _m_, saynète _f_ ▷ _vt_ esquisser, faire un croquis _or_ une esquisse de; (_plan etc_) esquisser
sketch book _n_ carnet _m_ à dessin
sketch pad _n_ bloc _m_ à dessin
sketchy ['skɛtʃɪ] _adj_ incomplet(-ète), fragmentaire
skew [skjuː] _n_ (_Brit_): **on the ~** de travers, en biais
skewer ['skjuːəʳ] _n_ brochette _f_
ski [skiː] _n_ ski _m_ ▷ _vi_ skier, faire du ski
ski boot _n_ chaussure _f_ de ski
skid [skɪd] _n_ dérapage _m_ ▷ _vi_ déraper; **to go into a ~** déraper
skid mark _n_ trace _f_ de dérapage
skier ['skiːəʳ] _n_ skieur(-euse)
skiing ['skiːɪŋ] _n_ ski _m_; **to go ~** (aller) faire du ski
ski instructor _n_ moniteur(-trice) de ski
ski jump _n_ (_ramp_) tremplin _m_; (_event_) saut _m_ à skis

S

skilful, (US) **skillful** ['skɪlful] *adj* habile, adroit(e)

skilfully, (US) **skillfully** ['skɪlfəlɪ] *adv* habilement, adroitement

ski lift *n* remonte-pente *m inv*

skill [skɪl] *n* (*ability*) habileté *f*, adresse *f*, talent *m*; (*requiring training*) compétences *fpl*

skilled [skɪld] *adj* habile, adroit(e); (*worker*) qualifié(e)

skillet ['skɪlɪt] *n* poêlon *m*

skillful *etc* ['skɪlful] (US) = **skilful** *etc*

skim [skɪm] *vt* (*milk*) écrémer; (*soup*) écumer; (*glide over*) raser, effleurer ▷ *vi*: **to ~ through** (*fig*) parcourir

skimmed milk [skɪmd-], (US) **skim milk** *n* lait écrémé

skimp [skɪmp] *vt* (*work*) bâcler, faire à la va-vite; (*cloth etc*) lésiner sur

skimpy ['skɪmpɪ] *adj* étriqué(e); maigre

skin [skɪn] *n* peau *f* ▷ *vt* (*fruit etc*) éplucher; (*animal*) écorcher; **wet** *or* **soaked to the ~** trempé(e) jusqu'aux os

skin-deep ['skɪn'diːp] *adj* superficiel(le)

skin diver *n* plongeur(-euse) sous-marin(e)

skin diving *n* plongée sous-marine

skinflint ['skɪnflɪnt] *n* grippe-sou *m*

skin graft *n* greffe *f* de peau

skinhead ['skɪnhed] *n* skinhead *m*

skinny ['skɪnɪ] *adj* maigre, maigrichon(ne)

skin test *n* cuti *f* (-réaction) *f*

skintight ['skɪntaɪt] *adj* (*dress etc*) collant(e), ajusté(e)

skip [skɪp] *n* petit bond *or* saut; (*Brit: container*) benne *f* ▷ *vi* gambader, sautiller; (*with rope*) sauter à la corde ▷ *vt* (*pass over*) sauter; **to ~ school** (*esp US*) faire l'école buissonnière

ski pants *npl* pantalon *m* de ski

ski pass *n* forfait-skieur(s) *m*

ski pole *n* bâton *m* de ski

skipper ['skɪpəʳ] *n* (*Naut, Sport*) capitaine *m*; (*in race*) skipper *m* ▷ *vt* (*boat*) commander; (*team*) être le chef de

skipping rope ['skɪpɪŋ-], (US) **skip rope** *n* corde *f* à sauter

ski resort *n* station *f* de sports d'hiver

skirmish ['skəːmɪʃ] *n* escarmouche *f*, accrochage *m*

skirt [skəːt] *n* jupe *f* ▷ *vt* longer, contourner

skirting board ['skəːtɪŋ-] *n* (*Brit*) plinthe *f*

ski run *n* piste *f* de ski

ski slope *n* piste *f* de ski

ski suit *n* combinaison *f* de ski

skit [skɪt] *n* sketch *m* satirique

ski tow *n* = **ski lift**

skittle ['skɪtl] *n* quille *f*; **skittles** (*game*) (jeu *m* de) quilles *fpl*

skive [skaɪv] *vi* (*Brit inf*) tirer au flanc

skulk [skʌlk] *vi* rôder furtivement

skull [skʌl] *n* crâne *m*

skullcap ['skʌlkæp] *n* calotte *f*

skunk [skʌŋk] *n* mouffette *f*; (*fur*) sconse *m*

sky [skaɪ] *n* ciel *m*; **to praise sb to the skies** porter qn aux nues

sky-blue [skaɪ'bluː] *adj* bleu ciel *inv*

skydiving ['skaɪdaɪvɪŋ] *n* parachutisme *m* (*en chute libre*)

sky-high ['skaɪ'haɪ] *adv* très haut ▷ *adj* exorbitant(e); **prices are ~** les prix sont exorbitants

skylark ['skaɪlɑːk] *n* (*bird*) alouette *f* (des champs)

skylight ['skaɪlaɪt] *n* lucarne *f*

skyline ['skaɪlaɪn] *n* (*horizon*) (ligne *f* d')horizon *m*; (*of city*) ligne des toits

Skype® [skaɪ'] (*Internet, Tel*) *n* Skype® ▷ *vt* contacter via Skype®

skyscraper ['skaɪskreɪpəʳ] *n* gratte-ciel *m inv*

slab [slæb] *n* plaque *f*; (*of stone*) dalle *f*; (*of wood*) bloc *m*; (*of meat, cheese*) tranche épaisse

slack [slæk] *adj* (*loose*) lâche, desserré(e); (*slow*) stagnant(e); (*careless*) négligent(e), peu sérieux(-euse) *or* consciencieux(-euse); (*Comm: market*) peu actif(-ive); (: *demand*) faible; (*period*) creux(-euse) ▷ *n* (*in rope etc*) mou *m*; **business is ~** les affaires vont mal

slacken ['slækn] (*also*: **slacken off**) *vi* ralentir, diminuer ▷ *vt* relâcher

slacks [slæks] *npl* pantalon *m*

slag [slæg] *n* scories *fpl*

slag heap *n* crassier *m*

slag off (*Brit: inf*) *vt* dire du mal de

slain [sleɪn] *pp of* **slay**

slake [sleɪk] *vt* (*one's thirst*) étancher

slalom ['slɑːləm] *n* slalom *m*

slam [slæm] *vt* (*door*) (faire) claquer; (*throw*) jeter violemment, flanquer; (*inf: criticize*) éreinter, démolir ▷ *vi* claquer

slammer ['slæməʳ] *n* (*inf*): **the ~** la taule

slander ['slɑːndəʳ] *n* calomnie *f*; (*Law*) diffamation *f* ▷ *vt* calomnier; diffamer

slanderous ['slɑːndrəs] *adj* calomnieux(-euse); diffamatoire

slang [slæŋ] *n* argot *m*

slanging match ['slæŋɪŋ-] *n* (*Brit inf*) engueulade *f*, empoignade *f*

slant [slɑːnt] *n* inclinaison *f*; (*fig*) angle *m*, point *m* de vue

slanted ['slɑːntɪd] *adj* tendancieux(-euse)

slanting ['slɑːntɪŋ] *adj* en pente, incliné(e); couché(e)

slap [slæp] *n* claque *f*, gifle *f*; (*on the back*) tape *f* ▷ *vt* donner une claque *or* une gifle (*or* une tape) à; **to ~ on** (*paint*) appliquer rapidement ▷ *adv* (*directly*) tout droit, en plein

slapdash ['slæpdæʃ] *adj* (*work*) fait(e) sans soin *or* à la va-vite; (*person*) insouciant(e), négligent(e)

slaphead ['slæphed] *n* (*Brit inf*) chauve

slapstick ['slæpstɪk] *n* (*comedy*) grosse farce (*style tarte à la crème*)

slap-up ['slæpʌp] *adj* (*Brit*): **a ~ meal** un repas extra *or* fameux

slash [slæʃ] *vt* entailler, taillader; (*fig: prices*) casser

slat [slæt] *n* (*of wood*) latte *f*, lame *f*

slate [sleɪt] *n* ardoise *f* ▷ *vt* (*fig: criticize*) éreinter, démolir

slaughter ['slɔːtəʳ] n carnage m, massacre m; (of animals) abattage m ▷ vt (animal) abattre; (people) massacrer
slaughterhouse ['slɔːtəhaus] n abattoir m
Slav [slɑːv] adj slave
slave [sleɪv] n esclave m/f ▷ vi (also: **slave away**) trimer, travailler comme un forçat; **to ~ (away) at sth/at doing sth** se tuer à qch/à faire qch
slave driver n (inf: pej) négrier(-ière)
slave labour n travail m d'esclave; **it's just ~** (fig) c'est de l'esclavage
slaver ['slævəʳ] vi (dribble) baver
slavery ['sleɪvərɪ] n esclavage m
Slavic ['slævɪk] adj slave
slavish ['sleɪvɪʃ] adj servile
slavishly ['sleɪvɪʃlɪ] adv (copy) servilement
Slavonic [slə'vɔnɪk] adj slave
slay (pt **slew**, pp **slain**) [sleɪ, sluː, sleɪn] vt (literary) tuer
sleazy ['sliːzɪ] adj miteux(-euse), minable
sled [slɛd] (US) = **sledge**
sledge [slɛdʒ] n luge f
sledgehammer ['slɛdʒhæməʳ] n marteau m de forgeron
sleek [sliːk] adj (hair, fur) brillant(e), luisant(e); (car, boat) aux lignes pures or élégantes
sleep [sliːp] n sommeil m ▷ vi (pt, pp **slept**) [slɛpt] dormir; (spend night) dormir, coucher ▷ vt: **we can ~ 4** on peut coucher or loger 4 personnes; **to go to ~** s'endormir; **to have a good night's ~** passer une bonne nuit; **to put to ~** (patient) endormir; (animal: euphemism: kill) piquer; **to ~ lightly** avoir le sommeil léger; **to ~ with sb** (have sex) coucher avec qn
▶ **sleep around** vi coucher à droite et à gauche
▶ **sleep in** vi (oversleep) se réveiller trop tard; (on purpose) faire la grasse matinée
▶ **sleep together** vi (have sex) coucher ensemble
sleeper ['sliːpəʳ] n (person) dormeur(-euse); (Brit Rail: on track) traverse f; (: train) train-couchettes m; (: carriage) wagon-lits m, voiture-lits f; (: berth) couchette f
sleepily ['sliːpɪlɪ] adv d'un air endormi
sleeping ['sliːpɪŋ] adj qui dort, endormi(e)
sleeping bag n sac m de couchage
sleeping car n wagon-lits m, voiture-lits f
sleeping partner n (Brit Comm) = **silent partner**
sleeping pill n somnifère m
sleeping sickness n maladie f du sommeil
sleepless ['sliːplɪs] adj: **a ~ night** une nuit blanche
sleeplessness ['sliːplɪsnɪs] n insomnie f
sleepover ['sliːpəuvəʳ] n nuit f chez un copain or une copine; **we're having a ~ at Jo's** nous allons passer la nuit chez Jo
sleepwalk ['sliːpwɔːk] vi marcher en dormant
sleepwalker ['sliːpwɔːkəʳ] n somnambule m/f
sleepy ['sliːpɪ] adj qui a envie de dormir; (fig) endormi(e); **to be** or **feel ~** avoir sommeil, avoir envie de dormir
sleet [sliːt] n neige fondue
sleeve [sliːv] n manche f; (of record) pochette f

sleeveless ['sliːvlɪs] adj (garment) sans manches
sleigh [sleɪ] n traîneau m
sleight [slaɪt] n: **~ of hand** tour m de passe-passe
slender ['slɛndəʳ] adj svelte, mince; (fig) faible, ténu(e)
slept [slɛpt] pt, pp of **sleep**
sleuth [sluːθ] n (inf) détective (privé)
slew [sluː] vi (also: **slew round**) virer, pivoter ▷ pt of **slay**
slice [slaɪs] n tranche f; (round) rondelle f; (utensil) spatule f; (also: **fish slice**) pelle f à poisson ▷ vt couper en tranches (or en rondelles); **~d bread** pain m en tranches
slick [slɪk] adj (skilful) bien ficelé(e); (salesperson) qui a du bagout, mielleux(-euse) ▷ n (also: **oil slick**) nappe f de pétrole, marée noire
slid [slɪd] pt, pp of **slide**
slide [slaɪd] (pt, pp **slid**) [slɪd] n (in playground) toboggan m; (Phot) diapositive f; (Brit: also: **hair slide**) barrette f; (microscope slide) (lame f) porte-objet m; (in prices) chute f, baisse f ▷ vt (faire) glisser ▷ vi glisser; **to let things ~** (fig) laisser les choses aller à la dérive
slide projector n (Phot) projecteur m de diapositives
slide rule n règle f à calcul
sliding ['slaɪdɪŋ] adj (door) coulissant(e); **~ roof** (Aut) toit ouvrant
sliding scale n échelle f mobile
slight [slaɪt] adj (slim) mince, menu(e); (frail) frêle; (trivial) faible, insignifiant(e); (small) petit(e), léger(-ère) (before n) ▷ n offense f, affront m ▷ vt (offend) blesser, offenser; **the ~est** le (or la) moindre; **not in the ~est** pas le moins du monde, pas du tout
slightly ['slaɪtlɪ] adv légèrement, un peu; **~ built** fluet(te)
slim [slɪm] adj mince ▷ vi maigrir; (diet) suivre un régime amaigrissant
slime [slaɪm] n vase f; substance visqueuse
slimming ['slɪmɪŋ] n amaigrissement m ▷ adj (diet, pills) amaigrissant(e), pour maigrir; (food) qui ne fait pas grossir
slimy ['slaɪmɪ] adj visqueux(-euse), gluant(e); (covered with mud) vaseux(-euse)
sling [slɪŋ] n (Med) écharpe f; (for baby) porte-bébé m; (weapon) fronde f, lance-pierre m ▷ vt (pt, pp **slung**) [slʌŋ] lancer, jeter; **to have one's arm in a ~** avoir le bras en écharpe
slink (pt, pp **slunk**) [slɪŋk, slʌŋk] vi: **to ~ away** or **off** s'en aller furtivement
slinky ['slɪŋkɪ] adj (clothes) moulant(e)
slip [slɪp] n faux pas; (mistake) erreur f, bévue f; (underskirt) combinaison f; (of paper) petite feuille, fiche f ▷ vt (slide) glisser ▷ vi (slide) glisser; (decline) baisser; (move smoothly): **to ~ into/out of** se glisser or se faufiler dans/hors de; **to let a chance ~ by** laisser passer une occasion; **to ~ sth on/off** enfiler/enlever qch; **it ~ped from her hand** cela lui a glissé des mains; **to give sb the ~** fausser compagnie à

S

qn; **a ~ of the tongue** un lapsus
▶ **slip away** *vi* s'esquiver
▶ **slip in** *vt* glisser
▶ **slip out** *vi* sortir
▶ **slip up** *vi* faire une erreur, gaffer
slip-on ['slɪpɒn] *adj* facile à enfiler; **~ shoes** mocassins *mpl*
slipped disc [slɪpt-] *n* déplacement *m* de vertèbre
slipper ['slɪpəʳ] *n* pantoufle *f*
slippery ['slɪpərɪ] *adj* glissant(e); (*fig: person*) insaisissable
slip road *n* (*Brit: to motorway*) bretelle *f* d'accès
slipshod ['slɪpʃɒd] *adj* négligé(e), peu soigné(e)
slip-up ['slɪpʌp] *n* bévue *f*
slipway ['slɪpweɪ] *n* cale *f* (de construction *or* de lancement)
slit [slɪt] *n* fente *f*; (*cut*) incision *f*; (*tear*) déchirure *f* ▷ *vt* (*pt, pp* -) fendre; couper, inciser; déchirer; **to ~ sb's throat** trancher la gorge à qn
slither ['slɪðəʳ] *vi* glisser, déraper
sliver ['slɪvəʳ] *n* (*of glass, wood*) éclat *m*; (*of cheese, sausage*) petit morceau
slob [slɒb] *n* (*inf*) rustaud(e)
slog [slɒg] *n* (*Brit: effort*) gros effort; (: *work*) tâche fastidieuse ▷ *vi* travailler très dur
slogan ['sləugən] *n* slogan *m*
slop [slɒp] *vi* (*also:* **slop over**) se renverser; déborder ▷ *vt* répandre; renverser
slope [sləup] *n* pente *f*, côte *f*; (*side of mountain*) versant *m*; (*slant*) inclinaison *f* ▷ *vi*: **to ~ down** être *or* descendre en pente; **to ~ up** monter
sloping ['sləupɪŋ] *adj* en pente, incliné(e); (*handwriting*) penché(e)
sloppy ['slɒpɪ] *adj* (*work*) peu soigné(e), bâclé(e); (*appearance*) négligé(e), débraillé(e); (*film etc*) sentimental(e)
slosh [slɒʃ] *vi* (*inf*): **to ~ about** *or* **around** (*children*) patauger; (*liquid*) clapoter
sloshed [slɒʃt] *adj* (*inf: drunk*) bourré(e)
slot [slɒt] *n* fente *f*; (*fig: in timetable, Radio, TV*) créneau *m*, plage *f* ▷ *vt*: **to ~ sth into** encastrer *or* insérer qch dans ▷ *vi*: **to ~ into** s'encastrer *or* s'insérer dans
sloth [sləuθ] *n* (*vice*) paresse *f*; (*Zool*) paresseux *m*
slot machine *n* (*Brit: vending machine*) distributeur *m* (automatique), machine *f* à sous; (*for gambling*) appareil *m* *or* machine à sous
slot meter *n* (*Brit*) compteur *m* à pièces
slouch [slautʃ] *vi* avoir le dos rond, être voûté(e)
▶ **slouch about, slouch around** *vi* traîner à ne rien faire
Slovak ['sləuvæk] *adj* slovaque ▷ *n* Slovaque *m/f*; (*Ling*) slovaque *m*; **the ~ Republic** la République slovaque
Slovakia [sləu'vækɪə] *n* Slovaquie *f*
Slovakian [sləu'vækɪən] *adj, n* = **Slovak**
Slovene [sləu'viːn] *adj* slovène ▷ *n* Slovène *m/f*; (*Ling*) slovène *m*
Slovenia [sləu'viːnɪə] *n* Slovénie *f*
Slovenian [sləu'viːnɪən] *adj, n* = **Slovene**

slovenly ['slʌvənlɪ] *adj* sale, débraillé(e), négligé(e)
slow [sləu] *adj* lent(e); (*watch*): **to be ~** retarder ▷ *adv* lentement ▷ *vt, vi* ralentir; **"~"** (*road sign*) "ralentir"; **at a ~ speed** à petite vitesse; **to be ~ to act/decide** être lent à agir/décider; **my watch is 20 minutes ~** ma montre retarde de 20 minutes; **business is ~** les affaires marchent au ralenti; **to go ~** (*driver*) rouler lentement; (*in industrial dispute*) faire la grève perlée
▶ **slow down** *vi* ralentir
slow-acting [sləu'æktɪŋ] *adj* qui agit lentement, à action lente
slowcoach ['sləukəutʃ] *n* (*Brit inf*) lambin(e)
slowly ['sləulɪ] *adv* lentement
slow motion *n*: **in ~** au ralenti
slowness ['sləunɪs] *n* lenteur *f*
slowpoke ['sləupəuk] *n* (*US inf*) = **slowcoach**
sludge [slʌdʒ] *n* boue *f*
slug [slʌg] *n* limace *f*; (*bullet*) balle *f*
sluggish ['slʌgɪʃ] *adj* (*person*) mou (molle), lent(e); (*stream, engine, trading*) lent(e); (*business, sales*) stagnant(e)
sluice [sluːs] *n* écluse *f*; (*also:* **sluice gate**) vanne *f* ▷ *vt*: **to ~ down** *or* **out** laver à grande eau
slum [slʌm] *n* (*house*) taudis *m*; **slums** *npl* (*area*) quartiers *mpl* pauvres
slumber ['slʌmbəʳ] *n* sommeil *m*
slump [slʌmp] *n* baisse soudaine, effondrement *m*; (*Econ*) crise *f* ▷ *vi* s'effondrer, s'affaisser
slung [slʌŋ] *pt, pp of* **sling**
slunk [slʌŋk] *pt, pp of* **slink**
slur [sləːʳ] *n* bredouillement *m*; (*smear*): **~ (on)** atteinte *f* (à); insinuation *f* (contre) ▷ *vt* mal articuler; **to be a ~ on** porter atteinte à
slurp [sləːp] *vt, vi* boire à grand bruit
slurred [sləːd] *adj* (*pronunciation*) inarticulé(e), indistinct(e)
slush [slʌʃ] *n* neige fondue
slush fund *n* caisse noire, fonds secrets
slushy ['slʌʃɪ] *adj* (*snow*) fondu(e); (*street*) couvert(e) de neige fondue; (*Brit: fig*) à l'eau de rose
slut [slʌt] *n* souillon *f*
sly [slaɪ] *adj* (*person*) rusé(e); (*smile, expression, remark*) sournois(e); **on the ~** en cachette
smack [smæk] *n* (*slap*) tape *f*; (*on face*) gifle *f* ▷ *vt* donner une tape à; (*on face*) gifler; (*on bottom*) donner la fessée à ▷ *vi*: **to ~ of** avoir des relents de, sentir ▷ *adv* (*inf*): **it fell ~ in the middle** c'est tombé en plein milieu *or* en plein dedans; **to ~ one's lips** se lécher les babines
smacker ['smækəʳ] *n* (*inf: kiss*) bisou *m* *or* bise *f* sonore; (: *Brit: pound note*) livre *f*; (: *US: dollar bill*) dollar *m*
small [smɔːl] *adj* petit(e); (*letter*) minuscule ▷ *n*: **the ~ of the back** le creux des reins; **to get** *or* **grow ~er** diminuer; **to make ~er** (*amount, income*) diminuer; (*object, garment*) rapetisser; **a ~ shopkeeper** un petit commerçant
small ads *npl* (*Brit*) petites annonces

small arms *npl* armes individuelles
small business *n* petit commerce, petite affaire
small change *n* petite *or* menue monnaie
smallholder ['smɔ:lhəuldəʳ] *n* (*Brit*) petit cultivateur
smallholding ['smɔ:lhəuldɪŋ] *n* (*Brit*) petite ferme
small hours *npl*: **in the ~** au petit matin
smallish ['smɔ:lɪʃ] *adj* plutôt *or* assez petit(e)
small-minded [smɔ:l'maɪndɪd] *adj* mesquin(e)
smallpox ['smɔ:lpɔks] *n* variole *f*
small print *n* (*in contract etc*) clause(s) imprimée(s) en petits caractères
small-scale ['smɔ:lskeɪl] *adj* (*map, model*) à échelle réduite, à petite échelle; (*business, farming*) peu important(e), modeste
small talk *n* menus propos
small-time ['smɔ:ltaɪm] *adj* (*farmer etc*) petit(e); **a ~ thief** un voleur à la petite semaine
small-town ['smɔ:ltaun] *adj* provincial(e)
smarmy ['smɑ:mɪ] *adj* (*Brit pej*) flagorneur(-euse), lécheur(-euse)
smart [smɑ:t] *adj* élégant(e), chic *inv*; (*clever*) intelligent(e); (*pej*) futé(e); (*quick*) vif (vive), prompt(e) ▷ *vi* faire mal, brûler; **the ~ set** le beau monde; **to look ~** être élégant(e); **my eyes are ~ing** j'ai les yeux irrités *or* qui me piquent
smart card ['smɑ:t'kɑ:d] *n* carte *f* à puce
smart phone *n* smartphone *m*
smarten up ['smɑ:tn-] *vi* devenir plus élégant(e), se faire beau (belle) ▷ *vt* rendre plus élégant(e)
smash [smæʃ] *n* (*also:* **smash-up**) collision *f*, accident *m*; (*Mus*) succès foudroyant; (*sound*) fracas *m* ▷ *vt* casser, briser, fracasser; (*opponent*) écraser; (*hopes*) ruiner, détruire; (*Sport: record*) pulvériser ▷ *vi* se briser, se fracasser; s'écraser
▶ **smash up** *vt* (*car*) bousiller; (*room*) tout casser dans
smashing ['smæʃɪŋ] *adj* (*inf*) formidable
smattering ['smætərɪŋ] *n*: **a ~ of** quelques notions de
smear [smɪəʳ] *n* (*stain*) tache *f*; (*mark*) trace *f*; (*Med*) frottis *m*; (*insult*) calomnie *f* ▷ *vt* enduire; (*make dirty*) salir; (*fig*) porter atteinte à; **his hands were ~ed with oil/ink** il avait les mains maculées de cambouis/d'encre
smear campaign *n* campagne *f* de dénigrement
smear test *n* (*Brit Med*) frottis *m*
smell [smɛl] (*pt, pp* **smelt** *or* **-ed**) [smɛlt, smɛld] *n* odeur *f*; (*sense*) odorat *m* ▷ *vt* sentir ▷ *vi* (*pej*) sentir mauvais; (*food etc*): **to ~ (of)** sentir; **it ~s good** ça sent bon
smelly ['smɛlɪ] *adj* qui sent mauvais, malodorant(e)
smelt [smɛlt] *pt, pp of* **smell** ▷ *vt* (*ore*) fondre
smile [smaɪl] *n* sourire *m* ▷ *vi* sourire
smiling ['smaɪlɪŋ] *adj* souriant(e)
smirk [smə:k] *n* petit sourire suffisant *or* affecté
smith [smɪθ] *n* maréchal-ferrant *m*; forgeron *m*
smithy ['smɪðɪ] *n* forge *f*
smitten ['smɪtn] *adj*: **~ with** pris(e) de;

frappé(e) de
smock [smɔk] *n* blouse *f*, sarrau *m*
smog [smɔg] *n* brouillard mêlé de fumée
smoke [sməuk] *n* fumée *f* ▷ *vt, vi* fumer; **to have a ~** fumer une cigarette; **do you ~?** est-ce que vous fumez?; **do you mind if I ~?** ça ne vous dérange pas que je fume?; **to go up in ~** (*house etc*) brûler; (*fig*) partir en fumée
smoke alarm *n* détecteur *m* de fumée
smoked ['sməukt] *adj* (*bacon, glass*) fumé(e)
smokeless fuel ['sməuklɪs-] *n* combustible non polluant
smokeless zone ['sməuklɪs-] *n* (*Brit*) zone *f* où l'usage du charbon est réglementé
smoker ['sməukəʳ] *n* (*person*) fumeur(-euse); (*Rail*) wagon *m* fumeurs
smoke screen *n* rideau *m* *or* écran *m* de fumée; (*fig*) paravent *m*
smoke shop *n* (*US*) (bureau *m* de) tabac *m*
smoking ['sməukɪŋ] *n*: **"no ~"** (*sign*) "défense de fumer"; **to give up ~** arrêter de fumer
smoking compartment, (*US*) **smoking car** *n* wagon *m* fumeurs
smoky ['sməukɪ] *adj* enfumé(e); (*taste*) fumé(e)
smolder ['sməuldəʳ] *vi* (*US*) = **smoulder**
smoochy ['smu:tʃɪ] *adj* (*inf*) langoureux(-euse)
smooth [smu:ð] *adj* lisse; (*sauce*) onctueux(-euse); (*flavour, whisky*) moelleux(-euse); (*cigarette*) doux (douce); (*movement*) régulier(-ière), sans à-coups *or* heurts; (*landing, takeoff*) en douceur; (*flight*) sans secousses; (*pej: person*) doucereux(-euse), mielleux(-euse) ▷ *vt* (*also:* **smooth out**) lisser, défroisser; (*creases, difficulties*) faire disparaître
▶ **smooth over** *vt*: **to ~ things over** (*fig*) arranger les choses
smoothly ['smu:ðlɪ] *adv* (*easily*) facilement, sans difficulté(s); **everything went ~** tout s'est bien passé
smother ['smʌðəʳ] *vt* étouffer
smoulder, (*US*) **smolder** ['sməuldəʳ] *vi* couver
SMS *n abbr* (= *short message service*) SMS *m*
SMS message *n* (message *m*) SMS *m*
smudge [smʌdʒ] *n* tache *f*, bavure *f* ▷ *vt* salir, maculer
smug [smʌg] *adj* suffisant(e), content(e) de soi
smuggle ['smʌgl] *vt* passer en contrebande *or* en fraude; **to ~ in/out** (*goods etc*) faire entrer/sortir clandestinement *or* en fraude
smuggler ['smʌgləʳ] *n* contrebandier(-ière)
smuggling ['smʌglɪŋ] *n* contrebande *f*
smut [smʌt] *n* (*grain of soot*) grain *m* de suie; (*mark*) tache *f* de suie; (*in conversation etc*) obscénités *fpl*
smutty ['smʌtɪ] *adj* (*fig*) grossier(-ière), obscène
snack [snæk] *n* casse-croûte *m inv*; **to have a ~** prendre un en-cas, manger quelque chose (de léger)
snack bar *n* snack(-bar) *m*
snag [snæg] *n* inconvénient *m*, difficulté *f*
snail [sneɪl] *n* escargot *m*
snake [sneɪk] *n* serpent *m*

S

snap [snæp] n (sound) claquement m, bruit sec; (photograph) photo f, instantané m; (game) sorte de jeu de bataille ▷ adj subit(e), fait(e) sans réfléchir ▷ vt (fingers) faire claquer; (break) casser net; (photograph) prendre un instantané de ▷ vi se casser net or avec un bruit sec; (fig: person) craquer; (speak sharply) parler d'un ton brusque; **to ~ open/shut** s'ouvrir/se refermer brusquement; **to ~ one's fingers at** (fig) se moquer de; **a cold ~** (of weather) un refroidissement soudain de la température
  ▶ **snap at** vt fus (subj: dog) essayer de mordre
  ▶ **snap off** vt (break) casser net
  ▶ **snap up** vt sauter sur, saisir
snap fastener n bouton-pression m
snappy ['snæpɪ] adj prompt(e); (slogan) qui a du punch; **make it ~!** (inf: hurry up) grouille-toi!, magne-toi!
snapshot ['snæpʃɒt] n photo f, instantané m
snare [snɛəʳ] n piège m ▷ vt attraper, prendre au piège
snarl [snɑːl] n grondement m or grognement m féroce ▷ vi gronder ▷ vt: **to get ~ed up** (wool, plans) s'emmêler; (traffic) se bloquer
snatch [snætʃ] n (fig) vol m; (small amount): **~es of** des fragments mpl or bribes fpl de ▷ vt saisir (d'un geste vif); (steal) voler ▷ vi: **don't ~!** doucement!; **to ~ a sandwich** manger or avaler un sandwich à la hâte; **to ~ some sleep** arriver à dormir un peu
  ▶ **snatch up** vt saisir, s'emparer de
snazzy ['snæzɪ] adj (inf: clothes) classe inv, chouette
sneak [sniːk] (US: pt **snuck**) vi: **to ~ in/out** entrer/sortir furtivement or à la dérobée ▷ vt: **to ~ a look at sth** regarder furtivement qch ▷ n (inf: pej: informer) faux jeton; **to ~ up on sb** s'approcher de qn sans faire de bruit
sneakers ['sniːkəz] npl tennis mpl, baskets fpl
sneaking ['sniːkɪŋ] adj: **to have a ~ feeling** or **suspicion that ...** avoir la vague impression que ...
sneaky ['sniːkɪ] adj sournois(e)
sneer [snɪəʳ] n ricanement m ▷ vi ricaner, sourire d'un air sarcastique; **to ~ at sb/sth** se moquer de qn/qch avec mépris
sneeze [sniːz] n éternuement m ▷ vi éternuer
snide [snaɪd] adj sarcastique, narquois(e)
sniff [snɪf] n reniflement m ▷ vi renifler ▷ vt renifler, flairer; (glue, drug) sniffer, respirer
  ▶ **sniff at** vt fus: **it's not to be ~ed at** il ne faut pas cracher dessus, ce n'est pas à dédaigner
sniffer dog ['snɪfə-] n (Police) chien dressé pour la recherche d'explosifs et de stupéfiants
snigger ['snɪgəʳ] n ricanement m; rire moqueur ▷ vi ricaner
snip [snɪp] n (cut) entaille f; (piece) petit bout; (Brit: inf: bargain) (bonne) occasion or affaire ▷ vt couper
sniper ['snaɪpəʳ] n (marksman) tireur embusqué
snippet ['snɪpɪt] n bribes fpl
snivelling ['snɪvlɪŋ] adj larmoyant(e),

pleurnicheur(-euse)
snob [snɒb] n snob m/f
snobbery ['snɒbərɪ] n snobisme m
snobbish ['snɒbɪʃ] adj snob inv
snog [snɒg] vi (inf) se bécoter
snooker ['snuːkəʳ] n sorte de jeu de billard
snoop [snuːp] vi: **to ~ on sb** espionner qn; **to ~ about** fureter
snooper ['snuːpəʳ] n fureteur(-euse)
snooty ['snuːtɪ] adj snob inv, prétentieux(-euse)
snooze [snuːz] n petit somme ▷ vi faire un petit somme
snore [snɔːʳ] vi ronfler ▷ n ronflement m
snoring ['snɔːrɪŋ] n ronflement(s) m(pl)
snorkel ['snɔːkl] n (of swimmer) tuba m
snort [snɔːt] n grognement m ▷ vi grogner; (horse) renâcler ▷ vt (inf: drugs) sniffer
snotty ['snɒtɪ] adj morveux(-euse)
snout [snaut] n museau m
snow [snəu] n neige f ▷ vi neiger ▷ vt: **to be ~ed under with work** être débordé(e) de travail
snowball ['snəubɔːl] n boule f de neige
snowbound ['snəubaund] adj enneigé(e), bloqué(e) par la neige
snow-capped ['snəukæpt] adj (peak, mountain) couvert(e) de neige
snowdrift ['snəudrɪft] n congère f
snowdrop ['snəudrɒp] n perce-neige m
snowfall ['snəufɔːl] n chute f de neige
snowflake ['snəufleɪk] n flocon m de neige
snowman ['snəumæn] (irreg) n bonhomme m de neige
snowplough, (US) **snowplow** ['snəuplau] n chasse-neige m inv
snowshoe ['snəuʃuː] n raquette f (pour la neige)
snowstorm ['snəustɔːm] n tempête f de neige
snowy ['snəuɪ] adj neigeux(-euse); (covered with snow) enneigé(e)
SNP n abbr (Brit Pol) = **Scottish National Party**
snub [snʌb] vt repousser, snober ▷ n rebuffade f
snub-nosed [snʌb'nəuzd] adj au nez retroussé
snuck [snʌk] (US) pt, pp of **sneak**
snuff [snʌf] n tabac m à priser ▷ vt (also: **snuff out**: candle) moucher
snuff movie n (inf) film pornographique qui se termine par le meurtre réel de l'un des acteurs
snug [snʌg] adj douillet(te), confortable; (person) bien au chaud; **it's a ~ fit** c'est bien ajusté(e)
snuggle ['snʌgl] vi: **to ~ down in bed/up to sb** se pelotonner dans son lit/contre qn
SO abbr (Banking) = **standing order**

 KEYWORD

so [səu] adv 1 (thus, likewise) ainsi, de cette façon; **if so** si oui; **so do** or **have I** moi aussi; **it's 5 o'clock — so it is!** il est 5 heures — en effet! or c'est vrai!; **I hope/think so** je l'espère/le crois; **so far** jusqu'ici, jusqu'à maintenant; (in past) jusque-là; **quite so!** exactement!, c'est bien ça!; **even so** quand même, tout de même
2 (in comparisons etc: to such a degree) si, tellement;

so big (that) si or tellement grand (que); **she's not so clever as her brother** elle n'est pas aussi intelligente que son frère

3: **so much** (adj, adv) tant (de); **I've got so much work** j'ai tant de travail; **I love you so much** je vous aime tant; **so many** tant (de)

4 (phrases): **10 or so** à peu près or environ 10; **so long!** (inf: goodbye) au revoir!, à un de ces jours!; **so to speak** pour ainsi dire; **so (what)?** (inf) (bon) et alors?, et après?

▷ conj **1** (expressing purpose): **so as to do** pour faire, afin de faire; **so (that)** pour que or afin que + sub

2 (expressing result) donc, par conséquent; **so that** si bien que, de (telle) sorte que; **so that's the reason!** c'est donc (pour) ça!; **so you see, I could have gone** alors tu vois, j'aurais pu y aller

soak [səuk] vt faire or laisser tremper; (drench) tremper ▷ vi tremper; **to be ~ed through** être trempé jusqu'aux os
  ▸ **soak in** vi pénétrer, être absorbé(e)
  ▸ **soak up** vt absorber
soaking ['səukɪŋ] adj (also: **soaking wet**) trempé(e)
so-and-so ['səuənsəu] n (somebody) un(e) tel(le)
soap [səup] n savon m
soapflakes ['səupfleɪks] npl paillettes fpl de savon
soap opera n feuilleton télévisé (quotidienneté réaliste ou embellie)
soap powder n lessive f, détergent m
soapsuds ['səupsʌds] npl mousse f de savon
soapy ['səupɪ] adj savonneux(-euse)
soar [sɔːʳ] vi monter (en flèche), s'élancer; (building) s'élancer; **~ing prices** prix qui grimpent
sob [sɔb] n sanglot m ▷ vi sangloter
s.o.b. n abbr (US inf!: = son of a bitch) salaud m (!)
sober ['səubəʳ] adj qui n'est pas (or plus) ivre; (serious) sérieux(-euse), sensé(e); (moderate) mesuré(e); (colour, style) sobre, discret(-ète)
  ▸ **sober up** vt dégriser ▷ vi se dégriser
sobriety [sə'braɪətɪ] n (not being drunk) sobriété f; (seriousness, sedateness) sérieux m
sob story n (inf: pej) histoire larmoyante
Soc. abbr (= society) Soc
so-called ['səu'kɔːld] adj soi-disant inv
soccer ['sɔkəʳ] n football m
soccer pitch n terrain m de football
soccer player n footballeur m
sociable ['səuʃəbl] adj sociable
social ['səuʃl] adj social(e); (sociable) sociable ▷ n (petite) fête
social climber n arriviste m/f
social club n amicale f, foyer m
Social Democrat n social-démocrate m/f
social insurance n (US) sécurité sociale
socialism ['səuʃəlɪzəm] n socialisme m
socialist ['səuʃəlɪst] adj, n socialiste (m/f)
socialite ['səuʃəlaɪt] n personnalité mondaine

socialize ['səuʃəlaɪz] vi voir or rencontrer des gens, se faire des amis; **to ~ with** (meet often) fréquenter; (get to know) lier connaissance or parler avec
social life n vie sociale; **how's your ~?** est-ce que tu sors beaucoup?
socially ['səuʃəlɪ] adv socialement, en société
social networking [-'nɛtwə:kɪŋ] n réseaux mpl sociaux
social science n sciences humaines
social security n aide sociale
social services npl services sociaux
social welfare n sécurité sociale
social work n assistance sociale
social worker n assistant(e) sociale(e)
society [sə'saɪətɪ] n société f; (club) société, association f; (also: **high society**) (haute) société, grand monde ▷ cpd (party) mondain(e)
socio-economic ['səusɪəuɪ:kə'nɔmɪk] adj socioéconomique
sociological [səusɪə'lɔdʒɪkl] adj sociologique
sociologist [səusɪ'ɔledʒɪst] n sociologue m/f
sociology [səusɪ'ɔledʒɪ] n sociologie f
sock [sɔk] n chaussette f ▷ vt (inf: hit) flanquer un coup à; **to pull one's ~s up** (fig) se secouer (les puces)
socket ['sɔkɪt] n cavité f; (Elec: also: **wall socket**) prise f de courant; (: for light bulb) douille f
sod [sɔd] n (of earth) motte f; (Brit inf!) con m (!), salaud m (!)
  ▸ **sod off** vi: **~ off!** (Brit inf!) fous le camp!, va te faire foutre! (!)
soda ['səudə] n (Chem) soude f; (also: **soda water**) eau f de Seltz; (US: also: **soda pop**) soda m
sodden ['sɔdn] adj trempé(e), détrempé(e)
sodium ['səudɪəm] n sodium m
sodium chloride n chlorure m de sodium
sofa ['səufə] n sofa m, canapé m
sofa bed n canapé-lit m
Sofia ['səufɪə] n Sofia
soft [sɔft] adj (not rough) doux (douce); (not hard) doux, mou (molle); (not loud) doux, léger(-ère); (kind) doux, gentil(le); (weak) indulgent(e); (stupid) stupide, débile
soft-boiled ['sɔftbɔɪld] adj (egg) à la coque
soft drink n boisson non alcoolisée
soft drugs npl drogues douces
soften ['sɔfn] vt (r)amollir; (fig) adoucir ▷ vi se ramollir; (fig) s'adoucir
softener ['sɔfnəʳ] n (water softener) adoucisseur m; (fabric softener) produit assouplissant
soft fruit n (Brit) baies fpl
soft furnishings npl tissus mpl d'ameublement
soft-hearted [sɔft'hɑːtɪd] adj au cœur tendre
softly ['sɔftlɪ] adv doucement; (touch) légèrement; (kiss) tendrement
softness ['sɔftnɪs] n douceur f
soft option n solution f de facilité
soft sell n promotion f de vente discrète
soft target n cible f facile
soft toy n jouet m en peluche
software ['sɔftwɛəʳ] n (Comput) logiciel m,

S

795

software *m*

software package *n* (*Comput*) progiciel *m*

soggy ['sɔgɪ] *adj* (*clothes*) trempé(e); (*ground*) détrempé(e)

soil [sɔɪl] *n* (*earth*) sol *m*, terre *f* ▷ *vt* salir; (*fig*) souiller

soiled [sɔɪld] *adj* sale; (*Comm*) défraîchi(e)

sojourn ['sɔdʒəːn] *n* (*formal*) séjour *m*

solace ['sɔlɪs] *n* consolation *f*, réconfort *m*

solar ['səʊləʳ] *adj* solaire

solarium (*pl* **solaria**) [sə'lɛərɪəm, -rɪə] *n* solarium *m*

solar panel *n* panneau *m* solaire

solar plexus [-'plɛksəs] *n* (*Anat*) plexus *m* solaire

solar power *n* énergie *f* solaire

solar system *n* système *m* solaire

sold [səʊld] *pt, pp of* **sell**

solder ['səʊldəʳ] *vt* souder (*au fil à souder*) ▷ *n* soudure *f*

soldier ['səʊldʒəʳ] *n* soldat *m*, militaire *m* ▷ *vi*: **to ~ on** persévérer, s'accrocher; **toy ~** petit soldat

sold out *adj* (*Comm*) épuisé(e)

sole [səʊl] *n* (*of foot*) plante *f*; (*of shoe*) semelle *f*; (*fish: pl inv*) sole *f* ▷ *adj* seul(e), unique; **the ~ reason** la seule et unique raison

solely ['səʊllɪ] *adv* seulement, uniquement; **I will hold you ~ responsible** je vous en tiendrai pour seul responsable

solemn ['sɔləm] *adj* solennel(le); (*person*) sérieux(-euse), grave

sole trader *n* (*Comm*) chef *m* d'entreprise individuelle

solicit [sə'lɪsɪt] *vt* (*request*) solliciter ▷ *vi* (*prostitute*) racoler

solicitor [sə'lɪsɪtəʳ] *n* (*Brit: for wills etc*) ≈ notaire *m*; (: *in court*) ≈ avocat *m*

solid ['sɔlɪd] *adj* (*strong, sound, reliable: not liquid*) solide; (*not hollow: mass*) compact(e); (: *metal, rock, wood*) massif(-ive); (*meal*) consistant(e), substantiel(le); (*vote*) unanime ▷ *n* solide *m*; **to be on ~ ground** être sur la terre ferme; (*fig*) être en terrain sûr; **we waited two ~ hours** nous avons attendu deux heures entières

solidarity [sɔlɪ'dærɪtɪ] *n* solidarité *f*

solid fuel *n* combustible *m* solide

solidify [sə'lɪdɪfaɪ] *vi* se solidifier ▷ *vt* solidifier

solidity [sə'lɪdɪtɪ] *n* solidité *f*

solid-state ['sɔlɪdsteɪt] *adj* (*Elec*) à circuits intégrés

soliloquy [sə'lɪləkwɪ] *n* monologue *m*

solitaire [sɔlɪ'tɛəʳ] *n* (*gem, Brit: game*) solitaire *m*; (*US: card game*) réussite *f*

solitary ['sɔlɪtərɪ] *adj* solitaire

solitary confinement *n* (*Law*) isolement *m* (cellulaire)

solitude ['sɔlɪtjuːd] *n* solitude *f*

solo ['səʊləʊ] *n* solo *m* ▷ *adv* (*fly*) en solitaire

soloist ['səʊləʊɪst] *n* soliste *m/f*

Solomon Islands ['sɔləmən-] *npl*: **the ~** les (îles *fpl*) Salomon *fpl*

solstice ['sɔlstɪs] *n* solstice *m*

soluble ['sɔljubl] *adj* soluble

solution [sə'luːʃən] *n* solution *f*

solve [sɔlv] *vt* résoudre

solvency ['sɔlvənsɪ] *n* (*Comm*) solvabilité *f*

solvent ['sɔlvənt] *adj* (*Comm*) solvable ▷ *n* (*Chem*) (dis)solvant *m*

solvent abuse *n* usage *m* de solvants hallucinogènes

Somali [səʊ'mɑːlɪ] *adj* somali(e), somalien(ne) ▷ *n* Somali(e), Somalien(ne)

Somalia [səʊ'mɑːlɪə] *n* (République *f* de) Somalie *f*

Somaliland [səʊ'mɑːlɪlænd] *n* Somaliland *m*

sombre, (*US*) **somber** ['sɔmbəʳ] *adj* sombre, morne

 KEYWORD

some [sʌm] *adj* **1** (*a certain amount or number of*): **some tea/water/ice cream** du thé/de l'eau/de la glace; **some children/apples** des enfants/pommes; **I've got some money but not much** j'ai de l'argent mais pas beaucoup

2 (*certain: in contrasts*): **some people say that ...** il y a des gens qui disent que ...; **some films were excellent, but most were mediocre** certains films étaient excellents, mais la plupart étaient médiocres

3 (*unspecified*): **some woman was asking for you** il y avait une dame qui vous demandait; **he was asking for some book (or other)** il demandait un livre quelconque; **some day** un de ces jours; **some day next week** un jour la semaine prochaine; **after some time** après un certain temps; **at some length** assez longuement; **in some form or other** sous une forme ou une autre, sous une forme quelconque

▷ *pron* **1** (*a certain number*) quelques-un(e)s, certain(e)s; **I've got some** (*books etc*) j'en ai (quelques-uns); **some (of them) have been sold** certains ont été vendus

2 (*a certain amount*) un peu; **I've got some** (*money, milk*) j'en ai (un peu); **would you like some?** est-ce que vous en voulez?, en voulez-vous?; **could I have some of that cheese?** pourrais-je avoir un peu de ce fromage?; **I've read some of the book** j'ai lu une partie du livre

▷ *adv*: **some 10 people** quelque 10 personnes, 10 personnes environ

somebody ['sʌmbədɪ] *pron* = **someone**

someday ['sʌmdeɪ] *adv* un de ces jours, un jour ou l'autre

somehow ['sʌmhaʊ] *adv* d'une façon ou d'une autre; (*for some reason*) pour une raison ou une autre

someone ['sʌmwʌn] *pron* quelqu'un; **~ or other** quelqu'un, je ne sais qui

someplace ['sʌmpleɪs] *adv* (*US*) = **somewhere**

somersault ['sʌməsɔːlt] *n* culbute *f*, saut périlleux ▷ *vi* faire la culbute *or* un saut périlleux; (*car*) faire un tonneau

something ['sʌmθɪŋ] *pron* quelque chose *m*; ~ **interesting** quelque chose d'intéressant; ~ **to do** quelque chose à faire; **he's ~ like me** il est un peu comme moi; **it's ~ of a problem** il y a là un problème

sometime ['sʌmtaɪm] *adv* (*in future*) un de ces jours, un jour ou l'autre; (*in past*): ~ **last month** au cours du mois dernier

sometimes ['sʌmtaɪmz] *adv* quelquefois, parfois

somewhat ['sʌmwɔt] *adv* quelque peu, un peu

somewhere ['sʌmwɛər] *adv* quelque part; ~ **else** ailleurs, autre part

son [sʌn] *n* fils *m*

sonar ['səunɑːr] *n* sonar *m*

sonata [sə'nɑːtə] *n* sonate *f*

song [sɔŋ] *n* chanson *f*; (*of bird*) chant *m*

songbook ['sɔŋbuk] *n* chansonnier *m*

songwriter ['sɔŋraɪtər] *n* auteur-compositeur *m*

sonic ['sɔnɪk] *adj* (*boom*) supersonique

son-in-law ['sʌnɪnlɔː] *n* gendre *m*, beau-fils *m*

sonnet ['sɔnɪt] *n* sonnet *m*

sonny ['sʌnɪ] *n* (*inf*) fiston *m*

soon [suːn] *adv* bientôt; (*early*) tôt; ~ **afterwards** peu après; **quite ~** sous peu; **how ~ can you do it?** combien de temps vous faut-il pour le faire, au plus pressé?; **how ~ can you come back?** quand *or* dans combien de temps pouvez-vous revenir, au plus tôt?; **see you ~!** à bientôt!; *see also* **as**

sooner ['suːnər] *adv* (*time*) plus tôt; (*preference*): **I would ~ do that** j'aimerais autant *or* je préférerais faire ça; ~ **or later** tôt ou tard; **no ~ said than done** sitôt dit, sitôt fait; **the ~ the better** le plus tôt sera le mieux; **no ~ had we left than …** à peine étions-nous partis que …

soot [sut] *n* suie *f*

soothe [suːð] *vt* calmer, apaiser

soothing ['suːðɪŋ] *adj* (*ointment etc*) lénitif(-ive), lénifiant(e); (*tone, words etc*) apaisant(e); (*drink, bath*) relaxant(e)

SOP *n abbr* = **standard operating procedure**

sop [sɔp] *n*: **that's only a ~** c'est pour nous (*or les etc*) amadouer

sophisticated [sə'fɪstɪkeɪtɪd] *adj* raffiné(e), sophistiqué(e); (*machinery*) hautement perfectionné(e), très complexe; (*system etc*) très perfectionné(e), sophistiqué

sophistication [səfɪstɪ'keɪʃən] *n* raffinement *m*, niveau *m* (de) perfectionnement *m*

sophomore ['sɔfəmɔːr] *n* (*US*) étudiant(e) de seconde année

soporific [sɔpə'rɪfɪk] *adj* soporifique ▷ *n* somnifère *m*

sopping ['sɔpɪŋ] *adj* (*also*: **sopping wet**) tout(e) trempé(e)

soppy ['sɔpɪ] *adj* (*pej*) sentimental(e)

soprano [sə'prɑːnəu] *n* (*voice*) soprano *m*; (*singer*) soprano *m/f*

sorbet ['sɔːbeɪ] *n* sorbet *m*

sorcerer ['sɔːsərər] *n* sorcier *m*

sordid ['sɔːdɪd] *adj* sordide

sore [sɔːr] *adj* (*painful*) douloureux(-euse), sensible; (*offended*) contrarié(e), vexé(e) ▷ *n* plaie *f*; **to have a ~ throat** avoir mal à la gorge; **it's a ~ point** (*fig*) c'est un point délicat

sorely ['sɔːlɪ] *adv* (*tempted*) fortement

sorrel ['sɔrəl] *n* oseille *f*

sorrow ['sɔrəu] *n* peine *f*, chagrin *m*

sorrowful ['sɔrəuful] *adj* triste

sorry ['sɔrɪ] *adj* désolé(e); (*condition, excuse, tale*) triste, déplorable; (*sight*) désolant(e); ~! pardon!, excusez-moi!; ~? pardon?; **to feel ~ for sb** plaindre qn; **I'm ~ to hear that …** je suis désolé(e) *or* navré(e) d'apprendre que …; **to be ~ about sth** regretter qch

sort [sɔːt] *n* genre *m*, espèce *f*, sorte *f*; (*make: of coffee, car etc*) marque *f* ▷ *vt* (*also*: **sort out**: *select which to keep*) trier; (*classify*) classer; (*tidy*) ranger; (*letters etc*) trier; (*Comput*) trier; **what ~ do you want?** quelle sorte *or* quel genre voulez-vous?; **what ~ of car?** quelle marque de voiture?; **I'll do nothing of the ~!** je ne ferai rien de tel!; **it's ~ of awkward** (*inf*) c'est plutôt gênant
▶ **sort out** *vt* (*problem*) résoudre, régler

sortie ['sɔːtɪ] *n* sortie *f*

sorting office ['sɔːtɪŋ-] *n* (*Post*) bureau *m* de tri

SOS *n* SOS *m*

so-so ['səusəu] *adv* comme ci comme ça

soufflé ['suːfleɪ] *n* soufflé *m*

sought [sɔːt] *pt, pp of* **seek**

sought-after ['sɔːtɑːftər] *adj* recherché(e)

soul [səul] *n* âme *f*; **the poor ~ had nowhere to sleep** le pauvre n'avait nulle part où dormir; **I didn't see a ~** je n'ai vu (absolument) personne

soul-destroying ['səuldɪstrɔɪɪŋ] *adj* démoralisant(e)

soulful ['səulful] *adj* plein(e) de sentiment

soulless ['səullɪs] *adj* sans cœur, inhumain(e)

soul mate *n* âme *f* sœur

soul-searching ['səulsəːtʃɪŋ] *n*: **after much ~, I decided …** j'ai longuement réfléchi avant de décider …

sound [saund] *adj* (*healthy*) en bonne santé, sain(e); (*safe, not damaged*) solide, en bon état; (*reliable, not superficial*) sérieux(-euse), solide; (*sensible*) sensé(e) ▷ *adv*: ~ **asleep** profondément endormi(e) ▷ *n* (*noise, volume*) son *m*; (*louder*) bruit *m*; (*Geo*) détroit *m*, bras *m* de mer ▷ *vt* (*alarm*) sonner; (*also*: **sound out**: *opinions*) sonder ▷ *vi* sonner, retentir; (*fig: seem*) sembler (être); **to be of ~ mind** être sain(e) d'esprit; **I don't like the ~ of it** ça ne me dit rien qui vaille; **to ~ one's horn** (*Aut*) klaxonner, actionner son avertisseur; **to ~ like** ressembler à; **it ~s as if …** il semblerait que …, j'ai l'impression que …
▶ **sound off** *vi* (*inf*): **to ~ off (about)** la ramener (sur)

sound barrier *n* mur *m* du son

sound bite *n* phrase toute faite (*pour être citée dans les médias*)

sound effects *npl* bruitage *m*

sound engineer *n* ingénieur *m* du son

sounding ['saundɪŋ] *n* (*Naut etc*) sondage *m*

S

sounding board n (Mus) table f d'harmonie; (fig): **to use sb as a ~ for one's ideas** essayer ses idées sur qn

soundly ['saundlɪ] adv (sleep) profondément; (beat) complètement, à plate couture

soundproof ['saundpruːf] vt insonoriser ▷ adj insonorisé(e)

sound system n sono(risation) f

soundtrack ['saundtræk] n (of film) bande f sonore

sound wave n (Physics) onde f sonore

soup [suːp] n soupe f, potage m; **in the ~** (fig) dans le pétrin

soup course n potage m

soup kitchen n soupe f populaire

soup plate n assiette creuse or à soupe

soupspoon ['suːpspuːn] n cuiller f à soupe

sour ['sauəʳ] adj aigre, acide; (milk) tourné(e), aigre; (fig) acerbe, aigre; revêche; **to go** or **turn ~** (milk, wine) tourner; (fig: relationship, plans) mal tourner; **it's ~ grapes** c'est du dépit

source [sɔːs] n source f; **I have it from a reliable ~ that** je sais de source sûre que

south [sauθ] n sud m ▷ adj sud inv; (wind) du sud ▷ adv au sud, vers le sud; **(to the) ~ of** au sud de; **to travel ~** aller en direction du sud

South Africa n Afrique f du Sud

South African adj sud-africain(e) ▷ n Sud-Africain(e)

South America n Amérique f du Sud

South American adj sud-américain(e) ▷ n Sud-Américain(e)

southbound ['sauθbaund] adj en direction du sud; (carriageway) sud inv

south-east [sauθ'iːst] n sud-est m

South-East Asia n le Sud-Est asiatique

southerly ['sʌðəlɪ] adj du sud; au sud

southern ['sʌðən] adj (du) sud; méridional(e); **with a ~ aspect** orienté(e) or exposé(e) au sud; **the ~ hemisphere** l'hémisphère sud or austral

South Korea n Corée f du Sud

South of France n: **the ~** le Sud de la France, le Midi

South Pole n Pôle m Sud

South Sea Islands npl: **the ~** l'Océanie f

South Seas npl: **the ~** les mers fpl du Sud

South Vietnam n Viêt-Nam m du Sud

South Wales n sud m du Pays de Galles

southward ['sauθwəd], **southwards** ['sauθwədz] adv vers le sud

south-west [sauθ'wɛst] n sud-ouest m

souvenir [suːvə'nɪəʳ] n souvenir m (objet)

sovereign ['sɔvrɪn] adj, n souverain(e)

sovereignty ['sɔvrɪntɪ] n souveraineté f

soviet ['səuvɪət] adj soviétique

Soviet Union n: **the ~** l'Union f soviétique

sow¹ [səu] (pt **-ed**, pp **-n**) [səun] vt semer

sow² [sau] n truie f

soya ['sɔɪə], (US) **soy** [sɔɪ] n: **~ bean** graine f de soja; **~ sauce** sauce f au soja

sozzled ['sɔzld] adj (Brit inf) paf inv

spa [spaː] n (town) station thermale; (US: also:

health spa) établissement m de cure de rajeunissement

space [speɪs] n (gen) espace m; (room) place f; espace; (length of time) laps m de temps ▷ cpd spatial(e) ▷ vt (also: **space out**) espacer; **to clear a ~ for sth** faire de la place pour qch; **in a confined ~** dans un espace réduit or restreint; **in a short ~ of time** dans peu de temps; **(with)in the ~ of an hour** en l'espace d'une heure

space bar n (on typewriter) barre f d'espacement

spacecraft ['speɪskrɑːft] n engin or vaisseau spatial

spaceman ['speɪsmæn] (irreg) n astronaute m, cosmonaute m

spaceship ['speɪsʃɪp] n = **spacecraft**

space shuttle n navette spatiale

spacesuit ['speɪssuːt] n combinaison spatiale

spacewoman ['speɪswumən] (irreg) n astronaute f, cosmonaute f

spacing ['speɪsɪŋ] n espacement m; **single/ double ~** (Typ etc) interligne m simple/double

spacious ['speɪʃəs] adj spacieux(-euse), grand(e)

spade [speɪd] n (tool) bêche f, pelle f; (child's) pelle; **spades** npl (Cards) pique m

spadework ['speɪdwəːk] n (fig) gros m du travail

spaghetti [spə'gɛtɪ] n spaghetti mpl

Spain [speɪn] n Espagne f

spam [spæm] n (Comput) spam m

span [spæn] n (of bird, plane) envergure f; (of arch) portée f; (in time) espace m de temps, durée f ▷ vt enjamber, franchir; (fig) couvrir, embrasser

Spaniard ['spænjəd] n Espagnol(e)

spaniel ['spænjəl] n épagneul m

Spanish ['spænɪʃ] adj espagnol(e), d'Espagne ▷ n (Ling) espagnol m; **the Spanish** npl les Espagnols; **~ omelette** omelette f à l'espagnole

spank [spæŋk] vt donner une fessée à

spanner ['spænəʳ] n (Brit) clé f (de mécanicien)

spar [spaːʳ] n espar m ▷ vi (Boxing) s'entraîner

spare [spɛəʳ] adj de réserve, de rechange; (surplus) de or en trop, de reste ▷ n (part) pièce f de rechange, pièce détachée ▷ vt (do without) se passer de; (afford to give) donner, accorder, passer; (not hurt) épargner; (not use) ménager; **to ~** (surplus) en surplus, de trop; **there are 2 going ~** (Brit) il y en a 2 de disponible; **to ~ no expense** ne pas reculer devant la dépense; **can you ~ the time?** est-ce que vous avez le temps?; **there is no time to ~** il n'y a pas de temps à perdre; **I've a few minutes to ~** je dispose de quelques minutes

spare part n pièce f de rechange, pièce détachée

spare room n chambre f d'ami

spare time n moments mpl de loisir

spare tyre, (US) **spare tire** n (Aut) pneu m de rechange

spare wheel n (Aut) roue f de secours

sparing ['spɛərɪŋ] adj: **to be ~ with** ménager

sparingly ['spɛərɪŋlɪ] adv avec modération

spark [spaːk] n étincelle f; (fig) étincelle, lueur f

sparkle ['spaːkl] n scintillement m,

étincellement *m*, éclat *m* ▷ *vi* étinceler, scintiller; (*bubble*) pétiller

sparkler ['spɑːklə^r] *n* cierge *m* magique

sparkling ['spɑːklɪŋ] *adj* étincelant(e), scintillant(e); (*wine*) mousseux(-euse), pétillant(e); (*water*) pétillant(e), gazeux(-euse)

spark plug *n* bougie *f*

sparring partner ['spɑːrɪŋ-] *n* sparring-partner *m*; (*fig*) vieil(le) ennemi(e)

sparrow ['spærəu] *n* moineau *m*

sparse [spɑːs] *adj* clairsemé(e)

spartan ['spɑːtən] *adj* (*fig*) spartiate

spasm ['spæzəm] *n* (*Med*) spasme *m*; (*fig*) accès *m*

spasmodic [spæz'mɔdɪk] *adj* (*fig*) intermittent(e)

spastic ['spæstɪk] *n* handicapé(e) moteur

spat [spæt] *pt, pp of* **spit** ▷ *n* (*US*) prise *f* de bec

spate [speɪt] *n* (*fig*): ~ **of** avalanche *f or* torrent *m* de; **in** ~ (*river*) en crue

spatial ['speɪʃl] *adj* spatial(e)

spatter ['spætə^r] *n* éclaboussure(s) *f(pl)* ▷ *vt* éclabousser ▷ *vi* gicler

spatula ['spætjulə] *n* spatule *f*

spawn [spɔːn] *vt* pondre; (*pej*) engendrer ▷ *vi* frayer ▷ *n* frai *m*

SPCA *n abbr* (*US*: = *Society for the Prevention of Cruelty to Animals*) ≈ SPA *f*

SPCC *n abbr* (*US*) = **Society for the Prevention of Cruelty to Children**

speak (*pt* **spoke**, *pp* **spoken**) [spiːk, spəuk, 'spəukn] *vt* (*language*) parler; (*truth*) dire ▷ *vi* parler; (*make a speech*) prendre la parole; **to** ~ **to sb/of** *or* **about sth** parler à qn/de qch; **I don't** ~ **French** je ne parle pas français; **do you** ~ **English?** parlez-vous anglais?; **can I** ~ **to ...?** est-ce que je peux parler à ...?; ~**ing!** (*on telephone*) c'est moi-même!; **to** ~ **one's mind** dire ce que l'on pense; **it** ~**s for itself** c'est évident; ~ **up!** parle plus fort!; **he has no money to** ~ **of** il n'a pas d'argent
▶ **speak for** *vt fus*: **to** ~ **for sb** parler pour qn; **that picture is already spoken for** (*in shop*) ce tableau est déjà réservé

speaker ['spiːkə^r] *n* (*in public*) orateur *m*; (*also:* **loudspeaker**) haut-parleur *m*; (*for stereo etc*) baffle *m*, enceinte *f*; (*Pol*): **the S~** (*Brit*) le président de la Chambre des communes *or* des représentants; (*US*) le président de la Chambre; **are you a Welsh ~?** parlez-vous gallois?

speaking ['spiːkɪŋ] *adj* parlant(e); **French-~ people** les francophones; **to be on ~ terms** se parler

spear [spɪə^r] *n* lance *f* ▷ *vt* transpercer

spearhead ['spɪəhɛd] *n* fer *m* de lance; (*Mil*) colonne *f* d'attaque ▷ *vt* (*attack etc*) mener

spearmint ['spɪəmɪnt] *n* (*Bot etc*) menthe verte

spec [spɛk] *n* (*Brit inf*): **on** ~ à tout hasard; **to buy on** ~ acheter avec l'espoir de faire une bonne affaire

special ['spɛʃl] *adj* spécial(e) ▷ *n* (*train*) train spécial; **take** ~ **care** soyez particulièrement prudents; **nothing** ~ rien de spécial; **today's** ~ (*at restaurant*) le plat du jour

special agent *n* agent secret

special correspondent *n* envoyé spécial

special delivery *n* (*Post*): **by** ~ en express

special effects *npl* (*Cine*) effets spéciaux

specialist ['spɛʃlɪst] *n* spécialiste *m/f*; **heart** ~ cardiologue *m/f*

speciality [spɛʃɪ'ælɪtɪ] *n* (*Brit*) spécialité *f*

specialize ['spɛʃəlaɪz] *vi*: **to** ~ **(in)** se spécialiser (dans)

specially ['spɛʃlɪ] *adv* spécialement, particulièrement

special needs *npl* (*Brit*) difficultés *fpl* d'apprentissage scolaire

special offer *n* (*Comm*) réclame *f*

special school *n* (*Brit*) établissement *m* d'enseignement spécialisé

specialty ['spɛʃəltɪ] *n* (*US*) = **speciality**

species ['spiːʃiːz] *n* (*pl inv*) espèce *f*

specific [spə'sɪfɪk] *adj* (*not vague*) précis(e), explicite; (*particular*) particulier(-ière); (*Bot, Chem etc*) spécifique; **to be** ~ **to** être particulier à, être le *or* un caractère (*or* les caractères) spécifique(s) de

specifically [spə'sɪfɪklɪ] *adv* explicitement, précisément; (*intend, ask, design*) expressément, spécialement; (*exclusively*) exclusivement, spécifiquement

specification [spɛsɪfɪ'keɪʃən] *n* spécification *f*; stipulation *f*; **specifications** *npl* (*of car, building etc*) spécification

specify ['spɛsɪfaɪ] *vt* spécifier, préciser; **unless otherwise specified** sauf indication contraire

specimen ['spɛsɪmən] *n* spécimen *m*, échantillon *m*; (*Med: of blood*) prélèvement *m*; (: *of urine*) échantillon *m*

specimen copy *n* spécimen *m*

specimen signature *n* spécimen *m* de signature

speck [spɛk] *n* petite tache, petit point; (*particle*) grain *m*

speckled ['spɛkld] *adj* tacheté(e), moucheté(e)

specs [spɛks] *npl* (*inf*) lunettes *fpl*

spectacle ['spɛktəkl] *n* spectacle *m*; **spectacles** *npl* (*Brit*) lunettes *fpl*

spectacle case *n* (*Brit*) étui *m* à lunettes

spectacular [spɛk'tækjulə^r] *adj* spectaculaire ▷ *n* (*Cine etc*) superproduction *f*

spectator [spɛk'teɪtə^r] *n* spectateur(-trice)

spectator sport *n*: **football is a great** ~ le football est un sport qui passionne les foules

spectra ['spɛktrə] *npl of* **spectrum**

spectre, (*US*) **specter** ['spɛktə^r] *n* spectre *m*, fantôme *m*

spectrum (*pl* **spectra**) ['spɛktrəm, -rə] *n* spectre *m*; (*fig*) gamme *f*

speculate ['spɛkjuleɪt] *vi* spéculer; (*try to guess*): **to** ~ **about** s'interroger sur

speculation [spɛkju'leɪʃən] *n* spéculation *f*; conjectures *fpl*

speculative ['spɛkjulətɪv] *adj* spéculatif(-ive)

speculator ['spɛkjuleɪtə^r] *n* spéculateur(-trice)

S

sped [spɛd] *pt, pp of* **speed**

speech [spi:tʃ] *n* (*faculty*) parole *f*; (*talk*) discours *m*, allocution *f*; (*manner of speaking*) façon *f* de parler, langage *m*; (*language*) langage *m*; (*enunciation*) élocution *f*

speech day *n* (*Brit Scol*) distribution *f* des prix

speech impediment *n* défaut *m* d'élocution

speechless ['spi:tʃlɪs] *adj* muet(te)

speech therapy *n* orthophonie *f*

speed [spi:d] *n* vitesse *f*; (*promptness*) rapidité *f* ▷ *vi* (*pt, pp* **sped**) [spɛd] (*Aut: exceed speed limit*) faire un excès de vitesse; **to ~ along/by** *etc* aller/ passer *etc* à toute vitesse; **at ~** (*Brit*) rapidement; **at full** *or* **top ~** à toute vitesse *or* allure; **at a ~ of 70 km/h** à une vitesse de 70 km/h; **shorthand/ typing ~s** nombre *m* de mots à la minute en sténographie/dactylographie; **a five-~ gearbox** une boîte cinq vitesses
  ▶ **speed up** (*pt, pp* **-ed up**) *vi* aller plus vite, accélérer ▷ *vt* accélérer

speedboat ['spi:dbəut] *n* vedette *f*, hors-bord *m inv*

speedily ['spi:dɪlɪ] *adv* rapidement, promptement

speeding ['spi:dɪŋ] *n* (*Aut*) excès *m* de vitesse

speed limit *n* limitation *f* de vitesse, vitesse maximale permise

speedometer [spɪ'dɔmɪtər] *n* compteur *m* (de vitesse)

speed trap *n* (*Aut*) piège *m* de police pour contrôle de vitesse

speedway *n* (*Sport*) piste *f* de vitesse pour motos; (*also:* **speedway racing**) épreuve(s) *f(pl)* de vitesse de motos

speedy ['spi:dɪ] *adj* rapide, prompt(e)

speleologist [spɛlɪ'ɔlədʒɪst] *n* spéléologue *m/f*

spell [spɛl] *n* (*also:* **magic spell**) sortilège *m*, charme *m*; (*period of time*) (courte) période ▷ *vt* (*pt, pp* **spelt** *or* **-ed**) [spɛlt, spɛld] (*in writing*) écrire, orthographier; (*aloud*) épeler; (*fig*) signifier; **to cast a ~ on sb** jeter un sort à qn; **he can't ~** il fait des fautes d'orthographe; **how do you ~ your name?** comment écrivez-vous votre nom?; **can you ~ it for me?** pouvez-vous me l'épeler?
  ▶ **spell out** *vt* (*explain*): **to ~ sth out for sb** expliquer qch clairement à qn

spellbound ['spɛlbaund] *adj* envoûté(e), subjugué(e)

spellchecker ['spɛltʃɛkər] *n* (*Comput*) correcteur *m or* vérificateur *m* orthographique

spelling ['spɛlɪŋ] *n* orthographe *f*

spelt [spɛlt] *pt, pp of* **spell**

spend (*pt, pp* **spent**) [spɛnd, spɛnt] *vt* (*money*) dépenser; (*time, life*) passer; (*devote*) consacrer; **to ~ time/money/effort on sth** consacrer du temps/de l'argent/de l'énergie à qch

spending ['spɛndɪŋ] *n* dépenses *fpl*; **government ~** les dépenses publiques

spending money *n* argent *m* de poche

spending power *n* pouvoir *m* d'achat

spendthrift ['spɛndθrɪft] *n* dépensier(-ière)

spent [spɛnt] *pt, pp of* **spend** ▷ *adj* (*patience*) épuisé(e), à bout; (*cartridge, bullets*) vide; **~ matches** vieilles allumettes

sperm [spə:m] *n* spermatozoïde *m*; (*semen*) sperme *m*

sperm bank *n* banque *f* du sperme

sperm whale *n* cachalot *m*

spew [spju:] *vt* vomir

sphere [sfɪər] *n* sphère *f*; (*fig*) sphère, domaine *m*

spherical ['sfɛrɪkl] *adj* sphérique

sphinx [sfɪŋks] *n* sphinx *m*

spice [spaɪs] *n* épice *f* ▷ *vt* épicer

spick-and-span ['spɪkən'spæn] *adj* impeccable

spicy ['spaɪsɪ] *adj* épicé(e), relevé(e); (*fig*) piquant(e)

spider ['spaɪdər] *n* araignée *f*; **~'s web** toile *f* d'araignée

spiel [spi:l] *n* laïus *m inv*

spike [spaɪk] *n* pointe *f*; (*Elec*) pointe de tension; (*Bot*) épi *m*; **spikes** *npl* (*Sport*) chaussures *fpl* à pointes

spike heel *n* (*US*) talon *m* aiguille

spiky ['spaɪkɪ] *adj* (*bush, branch*) épineux(-euse); (*animal*) plein(e) de piquants

spill (*pt, pp* **spilt** *or* **-ed**) [spɪl, -t, -d] *vt* renverser; répandre ▷ *vi* se répandre; **to ~ the beans** (*inf*) vendre la mèche; (*: confess*) lâcher le morceau
  ▶ **spill out** *vi* sortir à flots, se répandre
  ▶ **spill over** *vi* déborder

spillage ['spɪlɪdʒ] *n* (*of oil*) déversement *m* (accidentel)

spilt [spɪlt] *pt, pp of* **spill**

spin [spɪn] (*pt, pp* **spun**) [spʌn] *n* (*revolution of wheel*) tour *m*; (*Aviat*) (chute *f* en) vrille *f*; (*trip in car*) petit tour, balade *f*; (*on ball*) effet *m* ▷ *vt* (*wool etc*) filer; (*wheel*) faire tourner; (*Brit: clothes*) essorer ▷ *vi* (*turn*) tourner, tournoyer; **to ~ a yarn** débiter une longue histoire; **to ~ a coin** (*Brit*) jouer à pile ou face
  ▶ **spin out** *vt* faire durer

spina bifida ['spaɪnə'bɪfɪdə] *n* spina-bifida *m inv*

spinach ['spɪnɪtʃ] *n* épinard *m*; (*as food*) épinards *mpl*

spinal ['spaɪnl] *adj* vertébral(e), spinal(e)

spinal column *n* colonne vertébrale

spinal cord *n* moelle épinière

spindly ['spɪndlɪ] *adj* grêle, filiforme

spin doctor *n* (*inf*) personne employée pour présenter un parti politique sous un jour favorable

spin-dry ['spɪn'draɪ] *vt* essorer

spin-dryer [spɪn'draɪər] *n* (*Brit*) essoreuse *f*

spine [spaɪn] *n* colonne vertébrale; (*thorn*) épine *f*, piquant *m*

spine-chilling ['spaɪntʃɪlɪŋ] *adj* terrifiant(e)

spineless ['spaɪnlɪs] *adj* invertébré(e); (*fig*) mou (molle), sans caractère

spinner ['spɪnər] *n* (*of thread*) fileur(-euse)

spinning ['spɪnɪŋ] *n* (*of thread*) filage *m*; (*by machine*) filature *f*

spinning top *n* toupie *f*

spinning wheel *n* rouet *m*

spin-off ['spɪnɔf] *n* sous-produit *m*; avantage

inattendu

spinster ['spɪnstər] n célibataire f; vieille fille

spiral ['spaɪərl] n spirale f ▷ adj en spirale ▷ vi (fig: prices etc) monter en flèche; **the inflationary ~** la spirale inflationniste

spiral staircase n escalier m en colimaçon

spire ['spaɪər] n flèche f, aiguille f

spirit ['spɪrɪt] n (soul) esprit m, âme f; (ghost) esprit, revenant m; (mood) esprit, état m d'esprit; (courage) courage m, énergie f; **spirits** npl (drink) spiritueux mpl, alcool m; **in good ~s** de bonne humeur; **in low ~s** démoralisé(e); **community ~** solidarité f; **public ~** civisme m

spirit duplicator n duplicateur m à alcool

spirited ['spɪrɪtɪd] adj vif (vive), fougueux(-euse), plein(e) d'allant

spirit level n niveau m à bulle

spiritual ['spɪrɪtjuəl] adj spirituel(le); (religious) religieux(-euse) ▷ n (also: **Negro spiritual**) spiritual m

spiritualism ['spɪrɪtjuəlɪzəm] n spiritisme m

spit [spɪt] n (for roasting) broche f; (spittle) crachat m; (saliva) salive f ▷ vi (pt, pp **spat**) [spæt] cracher; (sound) crépiter; (rain) crachiner

spite [spaɪt] n rancune f, dépit m ▷ vt contrarier, vexer; **in ~ of** en dépit de, malgré

spiteful ['spaɪtful] adj malveillant(e), rancunier(-ière)

spitroast ['spɪt'rəust] vt faire rôtir à la broche

spitting ['spɪtɪŋ] n: **"~ prohibited"** "défense de cracher" ▷ adj: **to be the ~ image of sb** être le portrait tout craché de qn

spittle ['spɪtl] n salive f; bave f; crachat m

spiv [spɪv] n (Brit inf) chevalier m d'industrie, aigrefin m

splash [splæʃ] n (sound) plouf m; (of colour) tache f ▷ vt éclabousser ▷ vi (also: **splash about**) barboter, patauger
  ▸ **splash out** vi (Brit) faire une folie

splashdown ['splæʃdaun] n amerrissage m

splay [spleɪ] adj: **~footed** marchant les pieds en dehors

spleen [spli:n] n (Anat) rate f

splendid ['splendɪd] adj splendide, superbe, magnifique

splendour, (US) **splendor** ['splendər] n splendeur f, magnificence f

splice [splaɪs] vt épisser

splint [splɪnt] n attelle f, éclisse f

splinter ['splɪntər] n (wood) écharde f; (metal) éclat m ▷ vi (wood) se fendre; (glass) se briser

splinter group n groupe dissident

split [splɪt] (pt, pp **split**) n fente f, déchirure f; (fig: Pol) scission f ▷ vt fendre, déchirer; (party) diviser; (work, profits) partager, répartir ▷ vi (break) se fendre, se briser; (divide) se diviser; **let's ~ the difference** coupons la poire en deux; **to do the ~s** faire le grand écart
  ▸ **split up** vi (couple) se séparer, rompre; (meeting) se disperser

split-level ['splɪtlevl] adj (house) à deux or plusieurs niveaux

split peas npl pois cassés

split personality n double personnalité f

split second n fraction f de seconde

splitting ['splɪtɪŋ] adj: **a ~ headache** un mal de tête atroce

splutter ['splʌtər] vi bafouiller; postillonner

spoil (pt, pp **-ed** or **spoilt**) [spɔɪl, -d, -t] vt (damage) abîmer; (mar) gâcher; (child) gâter; (ballot paper) rendre nul ▷ vi: **to be ~ing for a fight** chercher la bagarre

spoils [spɔɪlz] npl butin m

spoilsport ['spɔɪlspɔ:t] n trouble-fête m/f inv, rabat-joie m inv

spoilt [spɔɪlt] pt, pp of **spoil** ▷ adj (child) gâté(e); (ballot paper) nul(le)

spoke [spəuk] pt of **speak** ▷ n rayon m

spoken ['spəukn] pp of **speak**

spokesman ['spəuksmən] (irreg) n porte-parole m inv

spokesperson ['spəukspə:sn] (irreg) n porte-parole m inv

spokeswoman ['spəukswumən] (irreg) n porte-parole m inv

sponge [spʌndʒ] n éponge f; (Culin: also: **sponge cake**) ≈ biscuit m de Savoie ▷ vt éponger ▷ vi: **to ~ off** or **on** vivre aux crochets de

sponge bag n (Brit) trousse f de toilette

sponge cake n ≈ biscuit m de Savoie

sponger ['spʌndʒər] n (pej) parasite m

spongy ['spʌndʒɪ] adj spongieux(-euse)

sponsor ['spɔnsər] n (Radio, TV, Sport) sponsor m; (for application) parrain m, marraine f; (Brit: for fund-raising event) donateur(-trice) ▷ vt (programme, competition etc) parrainer, patronner, sponsoriser; (Pol: bill) présenter; (new member) parrainer; (fund-raiser) faire un don à; **I ~ed him at 3p a mile** (in fund-raising race) je me suis engagé à lui donner 3p par mile

sponsorship ['spɔnsəʃɪp] n sponsoring m; patronage m, parrainage m; dons mpl

spontaneity [spɔntə'neɪɪtɪ] n spontanéité f

spontaneous [spɔn'teɪnɪəs] adj spontané(e)

spoof [spu:f] n (parody) parodie f; (trick) canular m

spooky ['spu:kɪ] adj (inf) qui donne la chair de poule

spool [spu:l] n bobine f

spoon [spu:n] n cuiller f

spoon-feed ['spu:nfi:d] vt nourrir à la cuiller; (fig) mâcher le travail à

spoonful ['spu:nful] n cuillerée f

sporadic [spə'rædɪk] adj sporadique

sport [spɔ:t] n sport m; (amusement) divertissement m; (person) chic type m/chic fille f ▷ vt (wear) arborer; **indoor/outdoor ~s** sports en salle/de plein air; **to say sth in ~** dire qch pour rire

sporting ['spɔ:tɪŋ] adj sportif(-ive); **to give sb a ~ chance** donner sa chance à qn

sport jacket n (US) = **sports jacket**

sports car n voiture f de sport

sports centre (Brit) n centre sportif

sports ground n terrain m de sport
sports jacket n (Brit) veste f de sport
sportsman ['spɔːtsmən] (irreg) n sportif m
sportsmanship ['spɔːtsmənʃɪp] n esprit sportif, sportivité f
sports page n page f des sports
sports utility vehicle n véhicule m de loisirs (de type SUV)
sportswear ['spɔːtswɛəʳ] n vêtements mpl de sport
sportswoman ['spɔːtswumən] (irreg) n sportive f
sporty ['spɔːtɪ] adj sportif(-ive)
spot [spɔt] n tache f; (dot: on pattern) pois m; (pimple) bouton m; (place) endroit m, coin m; (also: **spot advertisement**) message m publicitaire; (small amount): **a ~ of** un peu de ▷ vt (notice) apercevoir, repérer; **on the ~** sur place, sur les lieux; (immediately) sur le champ; **to put sb on the ~** (fig) mettre qn dans l'embarras; **to come out in ~s** se couvrir de boutons, avoir une éruption de boutons
spot check n contrôle intermittent
spotless ['spɔtlɪs] adj immaculé(e)
spotlight ['spɔtlaɪt] n projecteur m; (Aut) phare m auxiliaire
spot-on [spɔt'ɔn] adj (Brit inf) en plein dans le mille
spot price n prix m sur place
spotted ['spɔtɪd] adj tacheté(e), moucheté(e); à pois; **~ with** tacheté(e) de
spotty ['spɔtɪ] adj (face) boutonneux(-euse)
spouse [spauz] n époux (épouse)
spout [spaut] n (of jug) bec m; (of liquid) jet m ▷ vi jaillir
sprain [spreɪn] n entorse f, foulure f ▷ vt: **to ~ one's ankle** se fouler or se tordre la cheville
sprang [spræŋ] pt of **spring**
sprawl [sprɔːl] vi s'étaler ▷ n: **urban ~** expansion urbaine; **to send sb ~ing** envoyer qn rouler par terre
spray [spreɪ] n jet m (en fines gouttelettes); (from sea) embruns mpl; (aerosol) vaporisateur m, bombe f; (for garden) pulvérisateur m; (of flowers) petit bouquet ▷ vt vaporiser, pulvériser; (crops) traiter ▷ cpd (deodorant etc) en bombe or atomiseur
spread [sprɛd] (pt, pp **spread**) n (distribution) répartition f; (Culin) pâte f à tartiner; (inf: meal) festin m; (Press, Typ: two pages) double page f ▷ vt (paste, contents) étendre, étaler; (rumour, disease) répandre, propager; (repayments) échelonner, étaler; (wealth) répartir ▷ vi s'étendre; se répandre; se propager; (stain) s'étaler; **middle-age ~** embonpoint m (pris avec l'âge)
▶ **spread out** vi (people) se disperser
spread-eagled ['sprɛdiːgld] adj: **to be** or **lie ~** être étendu(e) bras et jambes écartés
spreadsheet ['sprɛdʃiːt] n (Comput) tableur m
spree [spriː] n: **to go on a ~** faire la fête
sprig [sprɪg] n rameau m
sprightly ['spraɪtlɪ] adj alerte

spring [sprɪŋ] (pt **sprang**, pp **sprung** [spræŋ, sprʌŋ]) n (season) printemps m; (leap) bond m, saut m; (coiled metal) ressort m; (bounciness) élasticité f; (of water) source f ▷ vi bondir, sauter ▷ vt: **to ~ a leak** (pipe etc) se mettre à fuir; **he sprang the news on me** il m'a annoncé la nouvelle de but en blanc; **in ~, in the ~** au printemps; **to ~ from** provenir de; **to ~ into action** passer à l'action; **to walk with a ~ in one's step** marcher d'un pas souple
▶ **spring up** vi (problem) se présenter, surgir; (plant, buildings) surgir de terre
springboard ['sprɪŋbɔːd] n tremplin m
spring-clean [sprɪŋ'kliːn] n (also: **spring-cleaning**) grand nettoyage de printemps
spring onion n (Brit) ciboule f, cive f
spring roll n rouleau m de printemps
springtime ['sprɪŋtaɪm] n printemps m
springy ['sprɪŋɪ] adj élastique, souple
sprinkle ['sprɪŋkl] vt (pour) répandre; verser; **to ~ water etc on, ~ with water etc** asperger d'eau etc; **to ~ sugar etc on, ~ with sugar etc** saupoudrer de sucre etc; **~d with** (fig) parsemé(e) de
sprinkler ['sprɪŋkləʳ] n (for lawn etc) arroseur m; (to put out fire) diffuseur m d'extincteur automatique d'incendie
sprinkling ['sprɪŋklɪŋ] n (of water) quelques gouttes fpl; (of salt) pincée f; (of sugar) légère couche
sprint [sprɪnt] n sprint m ▷ vi courir à toute vitesse; (Sport) sprinter
sprinter ['sprɪntəʳ] n sprinteur(-euse)
sprite [spraɪt] n lutin m
spritzer ['sprɪtsəʳ] n boisson à base de vin blanc et d'eau de Seltz
sprocket ['sprɔkɪt] n (on printer etc) picot m
sprout [spraut] vi germer, pousser
sprouts [sprauts] npl (also: **Brussels sprouts**) choux mpl de Bruxelles
spruce [spruːs] n épicéa m ▷ adj net(te), pimpant(e)
▶ **spruce up** vt (smarten up: room etc) apprêter; **to ~ o.s. up** se faire beau (belle)
sprung [sprʌŋ] pp of **spring**
spry [spraɪ] adj alerte, vif (vive)
SPUC n abbr = **Society for the Protection of Unborn Children**
spud [spʌd] n (inf: potato) patate f
spun [spʌn] pt, pp of **spin**
spur [spəːʳ] n éperon m; (fig) aiguillon m ▷ vt (also: **spur on**) éperonner; aiguillonner; **on the ~ of the moment** sous l'impulsion du moment
spurious ['spjuərɪəs] adj faux (fausse)
spurn [spəːn] vt repousser avec mépris
spurt [spəːt] n jet m; (of blood) jaillissement m; (of energy) regain m, sursaut m ▷ vi jaillir, gicler; **to put in** or **on a ~** (runner) piquer un sprint; (fig: in work etc) donner un coup de collier
sputter ['spʌtəʳ] vi = **splutter**
spy [spaɪ] n espion(ne) ▷ vi: **to ~ on** espionner, épier ▷ vt (see) apercevoir ▷ cpd (film, story)

d'espionnage

spying ['spaɪɪŋ] *n* espionnage *m*

Sq. *abbr* (*in address*) = **square**

sq. *abbr* (*Math etc*) = **square**

squabble ['skwɔbl] *n* querelle *f*, chamaillerie *f* ▷ *vi* se chamailler

squad [skwɔd] *n* (*Mil*, *Police*) escouade *f*, groupe *m*; (*Football*) contingent *m*; **flying ~** (*Police*) brigade volante

squad car *n* (*Brit Police*) voiture *f* de police

squaddie ['skwɔdɪ] *n* (*Mil: inf*) troufion *m*, bidasse *m*

squadron ['skwɔdrn] *n* (*Mil*) escadron *m*; (*Aviat*, *Naut*) escadrille *f*

squalid ['skwɔlɪd] *adj* sordide, ignoble

squall [skwɔːl] *n* rafale *f*, bourrasque *f*

squalor ['skwɔlər] *n* conditions *fpl* sordides

squander ['skwɔndər] *vt* gaspiller, dilapider

square [skwɛər] *n* carré *m*; (*in town*) place *f*; (*US: block of houses*) îlot *m*, pâté *m* de maisons; (*instrument*) équerre *f* ▷ *adj* carré(e); (*honest*) honnête, régulier(-ière); (*inf: ideas, tastes*) vieux jeu *inv*, qui retarde ▷ *vt* (*arrange*) régler; arranger; (*Math*) élever au carré; (*reconcile*) concilier ▷ *vi* (*agree*) cadrer, s'accorder; **all ~** quitte; à égalité; **a ~ meal** un repas convenable; **2 metres ~** (de) 2 mètres sur 2; **1 ~ metre** 1 mètre carré; **we're back to ~ one** (*fig*) on se retrouve à la case départ

▸ **square up** *vi* (*Brit: settle*) régler; **to ~ up with sb** régler ses comptes avec qn

square bracket *n* (*Typ*) crochet *m*

squarely ['skwɛəlɪ] *adv* carrément; (*honestly, fairly*) honnêtement, équitablement

square root *n* racine carrée

squash [skwɔʃ] *n* (*Brit: drink*): **lemon/orange ~** citronnade *f*/orangeade *f*; (*Sport*) squash *m*; (*US: vegetable*) courge *f* ▷ *vt* écraser

squat [skwɔt] *adj* petit(e) et épais(se), ramassé(e) ▷ *vi* (*also:* **squat down**) s'accroupir; (*on property*) squatter, squattériser

squatter ['skwɔtər] *n* squatter *m*

squawk [skwɔːk] *vi* pousser un *or* des gloussement(s)

squeak [skwiːk] *n* (*of hinge, wheel etc*) grincement *m*; (*of shoes*) craquement *m*; (*of mouse etc*) petit cri aigu ▷ *vi* (*hinge, wheel*) grincer; (*mouse*) pousser un petit cri

squeaky ['skwiːkɪ] *adj* grinçant(e); **to be ~ clean** (*fig*) être au-dessus de tout soupçon

squeal [skwiːl] *vi* pousser un *or* des cri(s) aigu(s) *or* perçant(s); (*brakes*) grincer

squeamish ['skwiːmɪʃ] *adj* facilement dégoûté(e); facilement scandalisé(e)

squeeze [skwiːz] *n* pression *f*; (*also:* **credit squeeze**) encadrement *m* du crédit, restrictions *fpl* de crédit ▷ *vt* presser; (*hand, arm*) serrer ▷ *vi:* **to ~ past/under sth** se glisser avec (beaucoup de) difficulté devant/sous qch; **a ~ of lemon** quelques gouttes de citron

▸ **squeeze out** *vt* exprimer; (*fig*) soutirer

squelch [skwɛltʃ] *vi* faire un bruit de succion;

patauger

squib [skwɪb] *n* pétard *m*

squid [skwɪd] *n* calmar *m*

squiggle ['skwɪgl] *n* gribouillis *m*

squint [skwɪnt] *vi* loucher ▷ *n*: **he has a ~** il louche, il souffre de strabisme; **to ~ at sth** regarder qch du coin de l'œil; (*quickly*) jeter un coup d'œil à qch

squire ['skwaɪər] *n* (*Brit*) propriétaire terrien

squirm [skwəːm] *vi* se tortiller

squirrel ['skwɪrəl] *n* écureuil *m*

squirt [skwəːt] *n* jet *m* ▷ *vi* jaillir, gicler ▷ *vt* faire gicler

Sr *abbr* = **senior**; = **sister**

SRC *n abbr* (*Brit*: = *Students' Representative Council*) ≈ CROUS *m*

Sri Lanka [srɪ'læŋkə] *n* Sri Lanka *m*

SRN *n abbr* (*Brit*) = **State Registered Nurse**

SRO *abbr* (*US*) = **standing room only**

SS *abbr* (= *steamship*) S/S

SSA *n abbr* (*US*: = *Social Security Administration*) organisme de sécurité sociale

SST *n abbr* (*US*) = **supersonic transport**

ST *abbr* (*US*: = *Standard Time*) heure officielle

St *abbr* = **saint**; **street**

stab [stæb] *n* (*with knife etc*) coup *m* (de couteau *etc*); (*of pain*) lancée *f*; (*inf: try*): **to have a ~ at (doing) sth** s'essayer à (faire) qch ▷ *vt* poignarder; **to ~ sb to death** tuer qn à coups de couteau

stabbing ['stæbɪŋ] *n*: **there's been a ~** quelqu'un a été attaqué à coups de couteau ▷ *adj* (*pain, ache*) lancinant(e)

stability [stə'bɪlɪtɪ] *n* stabilité *f*

stabilization [steɪbəlaɪ'zeɪʃən] *n* stabilisation *f*

stabilize ['steɪbəlaɪz] *vt* stabiliser ▷ *vi* se stabiliser

stabilizer ['steɪbəlaɪzər] *n* stabilisateur *m*

stable ['steɪbl] *n* écurie *f* ▷ *adj* stable; **riding ~s** centre *m* d'équitation

staccato [stə'kɑːtəu] *adv* staccato ▷ *adj* (*Mus*) piqué(e); (*noise, voice*) saccadé(e)

stack [stæk] *n* tas *m*, pile *f* ▷ *vt* empiler, entasser; **there's ~s of time** (*Brit inf*) on a tout le temps

stadium ['steɪdɪəm] *n* stade *m*

staff [stɑːf] *n* (*work force*) personnel *m*; (*Brit Scol: also:* **teaching staff**) professeurs *mpl*, enseignants *mpl*, personnel enseignant; (*servants*) domestiques *mpl*; (*Mil*) état-major *m*; (*stick*) perche *f*, bâton *m* ▷ *vt* pourvoir en personnel

staffroom ['stɑːfruːm] *n* salle *f* des professeurs

Staffs *abbr* (*Brit*) = **Staffordshire**

stag [stæg] *n* cerf *m*; (*Brit Stock Exchange*) loup *m*

stage [steɪdʒ] *n* scène *f*; (*platform*) estrade *f*; (*point*) étape *f*, stade *m*; (*profession*): **the ~** le théâtre ▷ *vt* (*play*) monter, mettre en scène; (*demonstration*) organiser; (*fig: recovery etc*) effectuer; **in ~s** par étapes, par degrés; **to go through a difficult ~** traverser une période difficile; **in the early ~s** au début; **in the final**

~**s** à la fin

stagecoach ['steɪdʒkəʊtʃ] n diligence f

stage door n entrée f des artistes

stage fright n trac m

stagehand ['steɪdʒhænd] n machiniste m

stage-manage ['steɪdʒmænɪdʒ] vt (fig) orchestrer

stage manager n régisseur m

stagger ['stægər] vi chanceler, tituber ▷ vt (person: amaze) stupéfier; bouleverser; (hours, holidays) étaler, échelonner

staggering ['stægərɪŋ] adj (amazing) stupéfiant(e), renversant(e)

staging post ['steɪdʒɪŋ-] n relais m

stagnant ['stægnənt] adj stagnant(e)

stagnate [stæg'neɪt] vi stagner, croupir

stagnation [stæg'neɪʃən] n stagnation f

stag night, stag party n enterrement m de vie de garçon

staid [steɪd] adj posé(e), rassis(e)

stain [steɪn] n tache f; (colouring) colorant m ▷ vt tacher; (wood) teindre

stained glass [steɪnd-] n (decorative) verre coloré; (in church) vitraux mpl; ~ **window** vitrail m

stainless ['steɪnlɪs] adj (steel) inoxydable

stainless steel n inox m, acier m inoxydable

stain remover n détachant m

stair [steər] n (step) marche f

staircase ['steəkeɪs] n = **stairway**

stairs [steəz] npl escalier m; **on the** ~ dans l'escalier

stairway ['steəweɪ] n escalier m

stairwell ['steəwɛl] n cage f d'escalier

stake [steɪk] n pieu m, poteau m; (Comm: interest) intérêts mpl; (Betting) enjeu m ▷ vt risquer, jouer; (also: **stake out**: area) marquer, délimiter; **to be at** ~ être en jeu; **to have a ~ in sth** avoir des intérêts (en jeu) dans qch; **to ~ a claim (to sth)** revendiquer (qch)

stakeout ['steɪkaʊt] n surveillance f; **to be on a** ~ effectuer une surveillance

stalactite ['stæləktaɪt] n stalactite f

stalagmite ['stæləgmaɪt] n stalagmite f

stale [steɪl] adj (bread) rassis(e); (food) pas frais (fraîche); (beer) éventé(e); (smell) de renfermé; (air) confiné(e)

stalemate ['steɪlmeɪt] n pat m; (fig) impasse f

stalk [stɔːk] n tige f ▷ vt traquer ▷ vi: **to ~ out/off** sortir/partir d'un air digne

stall [stɔːl] n (Brit: in street, market etc) éventaire m, étal m; (in stable) stalle f ▷ vt (Aut) caler; (fig: delay) retarder ▷ vi (Aut) caler; (fig) essayer de gagner du temps; **stalls** npl (Brit: in cinema, theatre) orchestre m; **a newspaper/flower** ~ un kiosque à journaux/de fleuriste

stallholder ['stɔːlhəʊldər] n (Brit) marchand(e) en plein air

stallion ['stæljən] n étalon m (cheval)

stalwart ['stɔːlwət] n partisan m fidèle

stamen ['steɪmɛn] n étamine f

stamina ['stæmɪnə] n vigueur f, endurance f

stammer ['stæmər] n bégaiement m ▷ vi bégayer

stamp [stæmp] n timbre m; (also: **rubber stamp**) tampon m; (mark, also fig) empreinte f; (on document) cachet m ▷ vi (also: **stamp one's foot**) taper du pied ▷ vt (letter) timbrer; (with rubber stamp) tamponner

▶ **stamp out** vt (fire) piétiner; (crime) éradiquer; (opposition) éliminer

stamp album n album m de timbres(-poste)

stamp collecting [-kəlɛktɪŋ] n philatélie f

stamp duty n (Brit) droit m de timbre

stamped addressed envelope n (Brit) enveloppe affranchie pour la réponse

stampede [stæm'piːd] n ruée f; (of cattle) débandade f

stamp machine n distributeur m de timbres

stance [stæns] n position f

stand [stænd] (pt, pp **stood**) [stʊd] n (position) position f; (for taxis) station f (de taxis); (Mil) résistance f; (structure) guéridon m; support m; (Comm) étalage m, stand m; (Sport: also: **stands**) tribune f; (also: **music stand**) pupitre m ▷ vi être or se tenir (debout); (rise) se lever, se mettre debout; (be placed) se trouver; (remain: offer etc) rester valable ▷ vt (place) mettre, poser; (tolerate, withstand) supporter; (treat, invite) offrir, payer; **to make a** ~ prendre position; **to take a ~ on an issue** prendre position sur un problème; **to ~ for parliament** (Brit) se présenter aux élections (comme candidat à la députation); **to ~ guard** or **watch** (Mil) monter la garde; **it ~s to reason** c'est logique; cela va de soi; **as things ~** dans l'état actuel des choses; **to ~ sb a drink/meal** payer à boire/à manger à qn; **I can't ~ him** je ne peux pas le voir

▶ **stand aside** vi s'écarter

▶ **stand back** vi (move back) reculer, s'écarter

▶ **stand by** vi (be ready) se tenir prêt(e) ▷ vt fus (opinion) s'en tenir à; (person) ne pas abandonner, soutenir

▶ **stand down** vi (withdraw) se retirer; (Law) renoncer à ses droits

▶ **stand for** vt fus (signify) représenter, signifier; (tolerate) supporter, tolérer

▶ **stand in for** vt fus remplacer

▶ **stand out** vi (be prominent) ressortir

▶ **stand up** vi (rise) se lever, se mettre debout

▶ **stand up for** vt fus défendre

▶ **stand up to** vt fus tenir tête à, résister à

stand-alone ['stændələun] adj (Comput) autonome

standard ['stændəd] n (norm) norme f, étalon m; (level) niveau m (voulu); (criterion) critère m; (flag) étendard m ▷ adj (size etc) ordinaire, normal(e); (model, feature) standard inv; (practice) courant(e); (text) de base; **standards** npl (morals) morale f, principes mpl; **to be** or **come up to ~** être du niveau voulu or à la hauteur; **to apply a double** ~ avoir or appliquer deux poids deux mesures

standardization [stændədaɪ'zeɪʃən] n standardisation f

standardize ['stændədaɪz] vt standardiser

standard lamp n (Brit) lampadaire m
standard of living n niveau m de vie
standard time n heure légale
stand-by ['stændbaɪ] n remplaçant(e) ▷ adj (provisions) de réserve; **to be on ~** se tenir prêt(e) (à intervenir); (doctor) être de garde
stand-by generator n générateur m de secours
stand-by passenger n passager(-ère) en stand-by or en attente
stand-by ticket n (Aviat) billet m stand-by
stand-in ['stændɪn] n remplaçant(e); (Cine) doublure f
standing ['stændɪŋ] adj debout inv; (permanent) permanent(e); (rule) immuable; (army) de métier; (grievance) constant(e), de longue date ▷ n réputation f, rang m, standing m; (duration): **of 6 months'** ~ qui dure depuis 6 mois; **of many years'** ~ qui dure or existe depuis longtemps; **he was given a ~ ovation** on s'est levé pour l'acclamer; **it's a ~ joke** c'est un vieux sujet de plaisanterie; **a man of some** ~ un homme estimé
standing committee n commission permanente
standing order n (Brit: at bank) virement m automatique, prélèvement m bancaire; **standing orders** npl (Mil) règlement m
standing room n places fpl debout
stand-off ['stændɔf] n (esp US: stalemate) impasse f
stand-offish [stænd'ɔfɪʃ] adj distant(e), froid(e)
standpat ['stændpæt] adj (US) inflexible, rigide
standpipe ['stændpaɪp] n colonne f d'alimentation
standpoint ['stændpɔɪnt] n point m de vue
standstill ['stændstɪl] n: **at a** ~ à l'arrêt; (fig) au point mort; **to come to a** ~ s'immobiliser, s'arrêter
stank [stæŋk] pt of **stink**
stanza ['stænzə] n strophe f; couplet m
staple ['steɪpl] n (for papers) agrafe f; (chief product) produit m de base ▷ adj (food, crop, industry etc) de base principal(e) ▷ vt agrafer
stapler ['steɪplə'] n agrafeuse f
star [stɑː'] n étoile f; (celebrity) vedette f ▷ vi: **to** ~ **(in)** être la vedette (de) ▷ vt (Cine) avoir pour vedette; **4-~ hotel** hôtel m 4 étoiles; **2-~ petrol** (Brit) essence f ordinaire; **4-~ petrol** (Brit) super m; **stars** npl: **the ~s** (Astrology) l'horoscope m
star attraction n grande attraction
starboard ['stɑːbəd] n tribord m; **to** ~ à tribord
starch [stɑːtʃ] n amidon m; (in food) fécule f
starched ['stɑːtʃt] adj (collar) amidonné(e), empesé(e)
starchy ['stɑːtʃɪ] adj riche en féculents; (person) guindé(e)
stardom ['stɑːdəm] n célébrité f
stare [stɛə'] n regard m fixe ▷ vi: **to** ~ **at** regarder fixement
starfish ['stɑːfɪʃ] n étoile f de mer
stark [stɑːk] adj (bleak) désolé(e), morne; (simplicity, colour) austère; (reality, poverty) nu(e)

▷ adv: ~ **naked** complètement nu(e)
starkers ['stɑːkəz] adj: **to be** ~ (Brit inf) être à poil
starlet ['stɑːlɪt] n (Cine) starlette f
starlight ['stɑːlaɪt] n: **by** ~ à la lumière des étoiles
starling ['stɑːlɪŋ] n étourneau m
starlit ['stɑːlɪt] adj étoilé(e); illuminé(e) par les étoiles
starry ['stɑːrɪ] adj étoilé(e)
starry-eyed [stɑːrɪ'aɪd] adj (innocent) ingénu(e)
Stars and Stripes npl: **the** ~ la bannière étoilée
star sign n signe zodiacal or du zodiaque
star-studded ['stɑːstʌdɪd] adj: **a ~ cast** une distribution prestigieuse
start [stɑːt] n commencement m, début m; (of race) départ m; (sudden movement) sursaut m; (advantage) avance f, avantage m ▷ vt commencer; (cause: fight) déclencher; (rumour) donner naissance à; (fashion) lancer; (found: business, newspaper) lancer, créer; (engine) mettre en marche ▷ vi (begin) commencer; (begin journey) partir, se mettre en route; (jump) sursauter; **when does the film ~?** à quelle heure est-ce que le film commence?; **at the** ~ au début; **for a** ~ d'abord, pour commencer; **to make an early** ~ partir or commencer de bonne heure; **to** ~ **doing** or **to do sth** se mettre à faire qch; **to** ~ **(off) with ...** (firstly) d'abord ...; (at the beginning) au commencement ...
  ▶ **start off** vi commencer; (leave) partir
  ▶ **start out** vi (begin) commencer; (set out) partir
  ▶ **start over** vi (US) recommencer
  ▶ **start up** vi commencer; (car) démarrer ▷ vt (fight) déclencher; (business) créer; (car) mettre en marche
starter ['stɑːtə'] n (Aut) démarreur m; (Sport: official) starter m; (: runner, horse) partant m; (Brit Culin) entrée f
starting handle ['stɑːtɪŋ-] n (Brit) manivelle f
starting point ['stɑːtɪŋ-] n point m de départ
starting price ['stɑːtɪŋ-] n prix initial
startle ['stɑːtl] vt faire sursauter; donner un choc à
startling ['stɑːtlɪŋ] adj surprenant(e), saisissant(e)
star turn n (Brit) vedette f
starvation [stɑː'veɪʃən] n faim f, famine f; **to die of** ~ mourir de faim or d'inanition
starve [stɑːv] vi mourir de faim ▷ vt laisser mourir de faim; **I'm starving** je meurs de faim
stash [stæʃ] vt (inf): **to** ~ **sth away** planquer qch
state [steɪt] n état m; (Pol) État; (pomp): **in** ~ en grande pompe ▷ vt (declare) déclarer, affirmer; (specify) indiquer, spécifier; **States** npl: **the S~s** les États-Unis; **to be in a** ~ être dans tous ses états; ~ **of emergency** état d'urgence; ~ **of mind** état d'esprit; **the ~ of the art** l'état actuel de la technologie (or des connaissances)
state control n contrôle m de l'État
stated ['steɪtɪd] adj fixé(e), prescrit(e)
State Department n (US) Département m d'État, ≈ ministère m des Affaires étrangères

state education n (Brit) enseignement public
stateless ['steɪtlɪs] adj apatride
stately ['steɪtlɪ] adj majestueux(-euse),
imposant(e)
stately home ['steɪtlɪ-] n manoir m or château m
(ouvert au public)
statement ['steɪtmənt] n déclaration f; (Law)
déposition f; (Econ) relevé m; **official ~**
communiqué officiel; **~ of account**, **bank ~**
relevé de compte
state-owned ['steɪtəund] adj étatisé(e)
States [steɪts] npl: **the ~** les États-Unis mpl
state school n école publique
statesman ['steɪtsmən] (irreg) n homme m
d'État
statesmanship ['steɪtsmənʃɪp] n qualités fpl
d'homme d'État
static ['stætɪk] n (Radio) parasites mpl; (also:
static electricity) électricité f statique ▷ adj
statique
station ['steɪʃən] n gare f; (also: **police station**)
poste m or commissariat m (de police); (Mil)
poste m (militaire); (rank) condition f, rang m
▷ vt placer, poster; **action ~s** postes de combat;
to be ~ed in (Mil) être en garnison à
stationary ['steɪʃnərɪ] adj à l'arrêt, immobile
stationer ['steɪʃənə'] n papetier(-ière)
stationer's, stationer's shop n (Brit)
papeterie f
stationery ['steɪʃnərɪ] n papier m à lettres, petit
matériel de bureau
station wagon n (US) break m
statistic [stə'tɪstɪk] n statistique f
statistical [stə'tɪstɪkl] adj statistique
statistics [stə'tɪstɪks] n (science) statistique f
statue ['stætjuː] n statue f
statuesque [stætju'ɛsk] adj sculptural(e)
statuette [stætju'ɛt] n statuette f
stature ['stætʃə'] n stature f; (fig) envergure f
status ['steɪtəs] n position f, situation f;
(prestige) prestige m; (Admin, official position)
statut m
status quo [-'kwəu] n: **the ~** le statu quo
status symbol n marque f de standing, signe
extérieur de richesse
statute ['stætjuːt] n loi f; **statutes** npl (of club
etc) statuts mpl
statute book n ≈ code m, textes mpl de loi
statutory ['stætjutrɪ] adj statutaire, prévu(e)
par un article de loi; **~ meeting** assemblée
constitutive or statutaire
staunch [stɔːntʃ] adj sûr(e), loyal(e) ▷ vt
étancher
stave [steɪv] n (Mus) portée f ▷ vt: **to ~ off**
(attack) parer; (threat) conjurer
stay [steɪ] n (period of time) séjour m; (Law): **~ of
execution** sursis m à statuer ▷ vi rester; (reside)
loger; (spend some time) séjourner; **to ~ put** ne
pas bouger; **to ~ with friends** loger chez des
amis; **to ~ the night** passer la nuit
 ▶ **stay away** vi (from person, building) ne pas
s'approcher; (from event) ne pas venir

 ▶ **stay behind** vi rester en arrière
 ▶ **stay in** vi (at home) rester à la maison
 ▶ **stay on** vi rester
 ▶ **stay out** vi (of house) ne pas rentrer; (strikers)
rester en grève
 ▶ **stay up** vi (at night) ne pas se coucher
staying power ['steɪɪŋ-] n endurance f
STD n abbr (= sexually transmitted disease) MST f;
(Brit: = subscriber trunk dialling) l'automatique m
stead [stɛd] n (Brit): **in sb's ~** à la place de qn; **to
stand sb in good ~** être très utile or servir
beaucoup à qn
steadfast ['stɛdfɑːst] adj ferme, résolu(e)
steadily ['stɛdɪlɪ] adv (regularly)
progressivement; (firmly) fermement; (walk)
d'un pas ferme; (fixedly: look) sans détourner les
yeux
steady ['stɛdɪ] adj stable, solide, ferme; (regular)
constant(e), régulier(-ière); (person) calme,
pondéré(e) ▷ vt assurer, stabiliser; (nerves)
calmer; (voice) assurer; **a ~ boyfriend** un petit
ami; **to ~ oneself** reprendre son aplomb
steak [steɪk] n (meat) bifteck m, steak m; (fish,
pork) tranche f
steakhouse ['steɪkhaus] n ≈ grill-room m
steal (pt stole, pp stolen) [stiːl, stəul, 'stəuln] vt,
vi voler; (move) se faufiler, se déplacer
furtivement; **my wallet has been stolen** on
m'a volé mon portefeuille
 ▶ **steal away, steal off** vi s'esquiver
stealth [stɛlθ] n: **by ~** furtivement
stealthy ['stɛlθɪ] adj furtif(-ive)
steam [stiːm] n vapeur f ▷ vt passer à la vapeur;
(Culin) cuire à la vapeur ▷ vi fumer; (ship): **to ~
along** filer; **under one's own ~** (fig) par ses
propres moyens; **to run out of ~** (fig: person)
caler; être à bout; **to let off ~** (fig: inf) se défouler
 ▶ **steam up** vi (window) se couvrir de buée; **to
get ~ed up about sth** (fig: inf) s'exciter à propos
de qch
steam engine n locomotive f à vapeur
steamer ['stiːmə'] n (bateau m à) vapeur m;
(Culin) ≈ couscoussier m
steam iron n fer m à repasser à vapeur
steamroller ['stiːmrəulə'] n rouleau
compresseur
steamship ['stiːmʃɪp] n = **steamer**
steamy ['stiːmɪ] adj humide; (window)
embué(e); (sexy) torride
steed [stiːd] n (literary) coursier m
steel [stiːl] n acier m ▷ cpd d'acier
steel band n steel band m
steel industry n sidérurgie f
steel mill n aciérie f, usine f sidérurgique
steelworks ['stiːlwəːks] n aciérie f
steely ['stiːlɪ] adj (determination) inflexible; (eyes,
gaze) d'acier
steep [stiːp] adj raide, escarpé(e); (price) très
élevé(e), excessif(-ive) ▷ vt (faire) tremper
steeple ['stiːpl] n clocher m
steeplechase ['stiːpltʃeɪs] n steeple(-chase) m
steeplejack ['stiːpldʒæk] n réparateur m de

clochers et de hautes cheminées
steeply ['stiːplɪ] *adv* en pente raide
steer [stɪə^r] *n* bœuf *m* ▷ *vt* diriger; (*boat*)
gouverner; (*lead: person*) guider, conduire ▷ *vi*
tenir le gouvernail; **to ~ clear of sb/sth** (*fig*)
éviter qn/qch
steering ['stɪərɪŋ] *n* (*Aut*) conduite *f*
steering column *n* (*Aut*) colonne *f* de direction
steering committee *n* comité *m* d'organisation
steering wheel *n* volant *m*
stellar ['stɛlə^r] *adj* stellaire
stem [stɛm] *n* (*of plant*) tige *f*; (*of leaf, fruit*) queue
f; (*of glass*) pied *m* ▷ *vt* contenir, endiguer;
(*attack, spread of disease*) juguler
▶ **stem from** *vt fus* provenir de, découler de
stem cell *n* cellule *f* souche
stench [stɛntʃ] *n* puanteur *f*
stencil ['stɛnsl] *n* stencil *m*; pochoir *m* ▷ *vt*
polycopier
stenographer [stɛ'nɔɡrəfə^r] *n* (*US*) sténographe
m/f
stenography [stɛ'nɔɡrəfɪ] *n* (*US*)
sténo(graphie) *f*
step [stɛp] *n* pas *m*; (*stair*) marche *f*; (*action*)
mesure *f*, disposition *f* ▷ *vi*: **to ~ forward/back**
faire un pas en avant/arrière, avancer/reculer;
steps *npl* (*Brit*) = **stepladder**; **~ by ~** pas à pas;
(*fig*) petit à petit; **to be in/out of ~ (with)** (*fig*)
aller dans le sens (de)/être déphasé(e) (par
rapport à)
▶ **step down** *vi* (*fig*) se retirer, se désister
▶ **step in** *vi* (*fig*) intervenir
▶ **step off** *vt fus* descendre de
▶ **step over** *vt fus* enjamber
▶ **step up** *vt* (*production, sales*) augmenter;
(*campaign, efforts*) intensifier
step aerobics® *npl* step® *m*
stepbrother ['stɛpbrʌðə^r] *n* demi-frère *m*
stepchild ['stɛptʃaɪld] (*pl* **-ren**) *n* beau-fils *m*,
belle-fille *f*
stepdaughter ['stɛpdɔːtə^r] *n* belle-fille *f*
stepfather ['stɛpfɑːðə^r] *n* beau-père *m*
stepladder ['stɛplædə^r] *n* (*Brit*) escabeau *m*
stepmother ['stɛpmʌðə^r] *n* belle-mère *f*
stepping stone ['stɛpɪŋ-] *n* pierre *f* de gué; (*fig*)
tremplin *m*
stepsister ['stɛpsɪstə^r] *n* demi-sœur *f*
stepson ['stɛpsʌn] *n* beau-fils *m*
stereo ['stɛrɪəu] *n* (*sound*) stéréo *f*; (*hi-fi*) chaîne *f*
stéréo ▷ *adj* (*also*: **stereophonic**)
stéréo(phonique); **in ~** en stéréo
stereotype ['stɪərɪətaɪp] *n* stéréotype *m* ▷ *vt*
stéréotyper
sterile ['stɛraɪl] *adj* stérile
sterility [stɛ'rɪlɪtɪ] *n* stérilité *f*
sterilization [stɛrɪlaɪ'zeɪʃən] *n* stérilisation *f*
sterilize ['stɛrɪlaɪz] *vt* stériliser
sterling ['stəːlɪŋ] *adj* sterling *inv*; (*silver*) de bon
aloi, fin(e); (*fig*) à toute épreuve, excellent(e) ▷ *n*
(*currency*) livre *f* sterling *inv*; **a pound ~** une livre
sterling
sterling area *n* zone *f* sterling *inv*

stern [stəːn] *adj* sévère ▷ *n* (*Naut*) arrière *m*,
poupe *f*
sternum ['stəːnəm] *n* sternum *m*
steroid ['stɪərɔɪd] *n* stéroïde *m*
stethoscope ['stɛθəskəup] *n* stéthoscope *m*
stevedore ['stiːvədɔː^r] *n* docker *m*, débardeur *m*
stew [stjuː] *n* ragoût *m* ▷ *vt, vi* cuire à la
casserole; **~ed tea** thé trop infusé; **~ed fruit**
fruits cuits *or* en compote
steward ['stjuəd] *n* (*Aviat, Naut, Rail*) steward *m*;
(*in club etc*) intendant *m*; (*also*: **shop steward**)
délégué syndical
stewardess ['stjuədɛs] *n* hôtesse *f*
stewardship ['stjuədʃɪp] *n* intendance *f*
stewing steak ['stjuːɪŋ-], (*US*) **stew meat** *n*
bœuf *m* à braiser
St. Ex. *abbr* = **stock exchange**
stg *abbr* = **sterling**
stick [stɪk] (*pt, pp* **stuck**) [stʌk] *n* bâton *m*; (*for
walking*) canne *f*; (*of chalk etc*) morceau *m* ▷ *vt*
(*glue*) coller; (*thrust*): **to ~ sth into** piquer *or*
planter *or* enfoncer qch dans; (*inf: put*) mettre,
fourrer; (: *tolerate*) supporter ▷ *vi* (*adhere*) tenir,
coller; (*remain*) rester; (*get jammed: door, lift*) se
bloquer; **to get hold of the wrong end of the ~**
(*Brit fig*) comprendre de travers; **to ~ to** (*one's
promise*) s'en tenir à; (*principles*) rester fidèle à
▶ **stick around** *vi* (*inf*) rester (dans les parages)
▶ **stick out** *vi* dépasser, sortir ▷ *vt*: **to ~ it out**
(*inf*) tenir le coup
▶ **stick up** *vi* dépasser, sortir
▶ **stick up for** *vt fus* défendre
sticker ['stɪkə^r] *n* auto-collant *m*
sticking plaster ['stɪkɪŋ-] *n* sparadrap *m*,
pansement adhésif
sticking point ['stɪkɪŋ-] *n* (*fig*) point *m* de
friction
stick insect *n* phasme *m*
stickleback ['stɪklbæk] *n* épinoche *f*
stickler ['stɪklə^r] *n*: **to be a ~ for** être
pointilleux(-euse) sur
stick shift *n* (*US Aut*) levier *m* de vitesses
stick-up ['stɪkʌp] *n* (*inf*) braquage *m*, hold-up *m*
sticky ['stɪkɪ] *adj* poisseux(-euse); (*label*)
adhésif(-ive); (*fig: situation*) délicat(e)
stiff [stɪf] *adj* (*gen*) raide, rigide; (*door, brush*)
dur(e); (*difficult*) difficile, ardu(e); (*cold*) froid(e),
distant(e); (*strong, high*) fort(e), élevé(e) ▷ *adv*: **to
be bored/scared/frozen ~** s'ennuyer à mourir/
être mort(e) de peur/froid; **to be** *or* **feel ~**
(*person*) avoir des courbatures; **to have a ~ back**
avoir mal au dos; **~ upper lip** (*Brit: fig*) flegme *m*
(*typiquement britannique*)
stiffen ['stɪfn] *vt* raidir, renforcer ▷ *vi* se raidir;
se durcir
stiff neck *n* torticolis *m*
stiffness ['stɪfnɪs] *n* raideur *f*
stifle ['staɪfl] *vt* étouffer, réprimer
stifling ['staɪflɪŋ] *adj* (*heat*) suffocant(e)
stigma ['stɪɡmə] (*Bot, Med, Rel*) (*pl* **-ta**) [stɪɡ'mɑː
tə] (*fig*), **stigmas** *n* stigmate *m*
stile [staɪl] *n* échalier *m*

stiletto [stɪ'lɛtəu] *n* (*Brit: also:* **stiletto heel**) talon *m* aiguille

still [stɪl] *adj* (*motionless*) immobile; (*calm*) calme, tranquille; (*Brit: mineral water etc*) non gazeux(-euse) ▷ *adv* (*up to this time*) encore, toujours; (*even*) encore; (*nonetheless*) quand même, tout de même ▷ *n* (*Cine*) photo *f*; **to stand ~** rester immobile, ne pas bouger; **keep ~!** ne bouge pas!; **he ~ hasn't arrived** il n'est pas encore arrivé, il n'est toujours pas arrivé

stillborn ['stɪlbɔːn] *adj* mort-né(e)

still life *n* nature morte

stilt [stɪlt] *n* échasse *f*; (*pile*) pilotis *m*

stilted ['stɪltɪd] *adj* guindé(e), emprunté(e)

stimulant ['stɪmjulənt] *n* stimulant *m*

stimulate ['stɪmjuleɪt] *vt* stimuler

stimulating ['stɪmjuleɪtɪŋ] *adj* stimulant(e)

stimulation [stɪmju'leɪʃən] *n* stimulation *f*

stimulus (*pl* **stimuli**) ['stɪmjuləs, 'stɪmjulaɪ] *n* stimulant *m*; (*Biol, Psych*) stimulus *m*

sting [stɪŋ] *n* piqûre *f*; (*organ*) dard *m*; (*inf: confidence trick*) arnaque *m* ▷ *vt, vi* (*pt, pp* **stung**) [stʌŋ] piquer; **my eyes are ~ing** j'ai les yeux qui piquent

stingy ['stɪndʒɪ] *adj* avare, pingre, chiche

stink [stɪŋk] *n* puanteur *f* ▷ *vi* (*pt* **stank**, *pp* **stunk**) [stæŋk, stʌŋk] puer, empester

stinker ['stɪŋkə'] *n* (*inf: problem, exam*) vacherie *f*; (*person*) dégueulasse *m/f*

stinking ['stɪŋkɪŋ] *adj* (*fig: inf*) infect(e); **~ rich** bourré(e) de pognon

stint [stɪnt] *n* part *f* de travail ▷ *vi*: **to ~ on** lésiner sur, être chiche de

stipend ['staɪpɛnd] *n* (*of vicar etc*) traitement *m*

stipendiary [staɪ'pɛndɪərɪ] *adj*: **~ magistrate** juge *m* de tribunal d'instance

stipulate ['stɪpjuleɪt] *vt* stipuler

stipulation [stɪpju'leɪʃən] *n* stipulation *f*, condition *f*

stir [stəː'] *n* agitation *f*, sensation *f* ▷ *vt* remuer ▷ *vi* remuer, bouger; **to give sth a ~** remuer qch; **to cause a ~** faire sensation

▶ **stir up** *vt* exciter; (*trouble*) fomenter, provoquer

stir-fry ['stəːfraɪ] *vt* faire sauter ▷ *n*: **vegetable ~** légumes sautés à la poêle

stirring ['stəːrɪŋ] *adj* excitant(e); émouvant(e)

stirrup ['stɪrəp] *n* étrier *m*

stitch [stɪtʃ] *n* (*Sewing*) point *m*; (*Knitting*) maille *f*; (*Med*) point de suture; (*pain*) point de côté ▷ *vt* coudre, piquer; (*Med*) suturer

stoat [stəut] *n* hermine *f* (*avec son pelage d'été*)

stock [stɔk] *n* réserve *f*, provision *f*; (*Comm*) stock *m*; (*Agr*) cheptel *m*, bétail *m*; (*Culin*) bouillon *m*; (*Finance*) valeurs *fpl*, titres *mpl*; (*Rail: also:* **rolling stock**) matériel roulant; (*descent, origin*) souche *f* ▷ *adj* (*fig: reply etc*) courant(e); classique ▷ *vt* (*have in stock*) avoir, vendre; **well-~ed** bien approvisionné(e) *or* fourni(e); **in ~** en stock, en magasin; **out of ~** épuisé(e); **to take ~** (*fig*) faire le point; **~s and shares** valeurs (mobilières), titres; **government ~** fonds publics

▶ **stock up** *vi*: **to ~ up (with)** s'approvisionner (en)

stockade [stɔ'keɪd] *n* palissade *f*

stockbroker ['stɔkbrəukə'] *n* agent *m* de change

stock control *n* (*Comm*) gestion *f* des stocks

stock cube *n* (*Brit Culin*) bouillon-cube *m*

stock exchange *n* Bourse *f* (des valeurs)

stockholder ['stɔkhəuldə'] *n* (*US*) actionnaire *m/f*

Stockholm ['stɔkhəum] *n* Stockholm

stocking ['stɔkɪŋ] *n* bas *m*

stock-in-trade ['stɔkɪn'treɪd] *n* (*fig*): **it's his ~** c'est sa spécialité

stockist ['stɔkɪst] *n* (*Brit*) stockiste *m*

stock market *n* Bourse *f*, marché financier

stock phrase *n* cliché *m*

stockpile ['stɔkpaɪl] *n* stock *m*, réserve *f* ▷ *vt* stocker, accumuler

stockroom ['stɔkruːm] *n* réserve *f*, magasin *m*

stocktaking ['stɔkteɪkɪŋ] *n* (*Brit Comm*) inventaire *m*

stocky ['stɔkɪ] *adj* trapu(e), râblé(e)

stodgy ['stɔdʒɪ] *adj* bourratif(-ive), lourd(e)

stoic ['stəuɪk] *n* stoïque *m/f*

stoical ['stəuɪkl] *adj* stoïque

stoke [stəuk] *vt* garnir, entretenir; chauffer

stoker ['stəukə'] *n* (*Rail, Naut etc*) chauffeur *m*

stole [stəul] *pt of* **steal** ▷ *n* étole *f*

stolen ['stəuln] *pp of* **steal**

stolid ['stɔlɪd] *adj* impassible, flegmatique

stomach ['stʌmək] *n* estomac *m*; (*abdomen*) ventre *m* ▷ *vt* supporter, digérer

stomachache ['stʌməkeɪk] *n* mal *m* à l'estomac *or* au ventre

stomach pump *n* pompe stomacale

stomach ulcer *n* ulcère *m* à l'estomac

stomp [stɔmp] *vi*: **to ~ in/out** entrer/sortir d'un pas bruyant

stone [stəun] *n* pierre *f*; (*pebble*) caillou *m*, galet *m*; (*in fruit*) noyau *m*; (*Med*) calcul *m*; (*Brit: weight*) = 6.348 kg; 14 pounds ▷ *cpd* de pierre ▷ *vt* (*person*) lancer des pierres sur, lapider; (*fruit*) dénoyauter; **within a ~'s throw of the station** à deux pas de la gare

Stone Age *n*: **the ~** l'âge *m* de pierre

stone-cold ['stəun'kəuld] *adj* complètement froid(e)

stoned [stəund] *adj* (*inf: drunk*) bourré(e); (: *on drugs*) défoncé(e)

stone-deaf ['stəun'dɛf] *adj* sourd(e) comme un pot

stonemason ['stəunmeɪsn] *n* tailleur *m* de pierre(s)

stonewall [stəun'wɔːl] *vi* faire de l'obstruction ▷ *vt* faire obstruction à

stonework ['stəunwəːk] *n* maçonnerie *f*

stony ['stəunɪ] *adj* pierreux(-euse), rocailleux(-euse)

stood [stud] *pt, pp of* **stand**

stooge [stuːdʒ] *n* (*inf*) larbin *m*

stool [stuːl] *n* tabouret *m*

stoop [stuːp] *vi* (*also:* **have a stoop**) être voûté(e);

(also: **stoop down**: bend) se baisser, se courber;
(fig): **to ~ to sth/doing sth** s'abaisser jusqu'à
qch/jusqu'à faire qch

stop [stɒp] n arrêt m; (short stay) halte f; (in
punctuation) point m ▷ vt arrêter; (break off)
interrompre; (also: **put a stop to**) mettre fin à;
(prevent) empêcher ▷ vi s'arrêter; (rain, noise etc)
cesser, s'arrêter; **could you ~ here/at the
corner?** arrêtez-vous ici/au coin, s'il vous plaît;
to ~ doing sth cesser or arrêter de faire qch; **to ~
sb (from) doing sth** empêcher qn de faire qch;
to ~ dead vi s'arrêter net; **~ it!** arrête!
  ▶ **stop by** vi s'arrêter (au passage)
  ▶ **stop off** vi faire une courte halte
  ▶ **stop up** vt (hole) boucher

stopcock ['stɒpkɒk] n robinet m d'arrêt

stopgap ['stɒpgæp] n (person) bouche-trou m;
(also: **stopgap measure**) mesure f intérimaire

stoplights ['stɒplaɪts] npl (Aut) signaux mpl de
stop, feux mpl arrière

stopover ['stɒpəʊvəʳ] n halte f; (Aviat) escale f

stoppage ['stɒpɪdʒ] n arrêt m; (of pay) retenue f;
(strike) arrêt m de travail; (obstruction) obstruction f

stopper ['stɒpəʳ] n bouchon m

stop press n nouvelles fpl de dernière heure

stopwatch ['stɒpwɒtʃ] n chronomètre m

storage ['stɔːrɪdʒ] n emmagasinage m; (of
nuclear waste etc) stockage m; (in house) rangement
m; (Comput) mise f en mémoire or réserve

storage heater n (Brit) radiateur m électrique
par accumulation

store [stɔːʳ] n (stock) provision f, réserve f; (depot)
entrepôt m; (Brit: large shop) grand magasin; (US:
shop) magasin m ▷ vt emmagasiner; (nuclear
waste etc) stocker; (information) enregistrer; (in
filing system) classer, ranger; (Comput) mettre en
mémoire; **stores** npl (food) provisions; **who
knows what is in ~ for us?** qui sait ce que
l'avenir nous réserve or ce qui nous attend?; **to
set great/little ~ by sth** faire grand cas/peu de
cas de qch
  ▶ **store up** vt mettre en réserve, emmagasiner

storehouse ['stɔːhaus] n entrepôt m

storekeeper ['stɔːkiːpəʳ] n (US) commerçant(e)

storeroom ['stɔːruːm] n réserve f, magasin m

storey, (US) **story** ['stɔːrɪ] n étage m

stork [stɔːk] n cigogne f

storm [stɔːm] n tempête f; (thunderstorm) orage
m ▷ vi (fig) fulminer ▷ vt prendre d'assaut

storm cloud n nuage m d'orage

storm door n double-porte (extérieure)

stormy ['stɔːmɪ] adj orageux(-euse)

story ['stɔːrɪ] n histoire f; récit m; (Press: article)
article m; (: subject) affaire f; (US) = **storey**

storybook ['stɔːrɪbuk] n livre m d'histoires or de
contes

storyteller ['stɔːrɪtɛləʳ] n conteur(-euse)

stout [staut] adj (strong) solide; (brave) intrépide;
(fat) gros(se), corpulent(e) ▷ n bière brune

stove [stəuv] n (for cooking) fourneau m; (: small)
réchaud m; (for heating) poêle m; **gas/electric ~**
(cooker) cuisinière f à gaz/électrique

stow [stəu] vt ranger; cacher

stowaway ['stəuəwei] n passager(-ère)
clandestin(e)

straddle ['strædl] vt enjamber, être à cheval sur

strafe [strɑːf] vt mitrailler

straggle ['strægl] vi être (or marcher) en
désordre; **~d along the coast** disséminé(e) tout
au long de la côte

straggler ['strægləʳ] n traînard(e)

straggling ['stræglɪŋ], **straggly** ['stræglɪ] adj
(hair) en désordre

straight [streit] adj droit(e); (hair) raide; (frank)
honnête, franc (franche); (simple) simple;
(Theat: part, play) sérieux(-euse); (inf: heterosexual)
hétéro inv ▷ adv (tout) droit; (drink) sec, sans eau
▷ n: **the ~** (Sport) la ligne droite; **to put** or **get ~**
mettre en ordre, mettre de l'ordre dans; (fig)
mettre au clair; **let's get this ~** mettons les
choses au point; **10 ~ wins** 10 victoires d'affilée;
to go ~ home rentrer directement à la maison;
~ away, ~ off (at once) tout de suite; **~ off, ~ out**
sans hésiter

straighten ['streitn] vt ajuster; (bed) arranger
  ▶ **straighten out** vt (fig) débrouiller; **to ~
things out** arranger les choses
  ▶ **straighten up** vi (stand up) se redresser; (tidy)
ranger

straighteners ['streitnəz] npl (for hair) lisseur m

straight-faced [streit'feist] adj impassible
▷ adv en gardant son sérieux

straightforward [streit'fɔːwəd] adj simple;
(frank) honnête, direct(e)

strain [strein] n (Tech) tension f; pression f;
(physical) effort m; (mental) tension (nerveuse);
(Med) entorse f; (streak, trace) tendance f;
élément m; (breed: of plants) variété f; (: of animals)
race f; (of virus) souche f ▷ vt (stretch) tendre
fortement; (fig: resources etc) mettre à rude
épreuve, grever; (hurt: back etc) se faire mal à;
(filter) passer, filtrer; (vegetables) égoutter ▷ vi
peiner, fournir un gros effort; **strains** npl (Mus)
accords mpl, accents mpl; **he's been under a lot
of ~** il a traversé des moments difficiles, il est
très éprouvé nerveusement

strained [streind] adj (muscle) froissé(e); (laugh
etc) forcé(e), contraint(e); (relations) tendu(e)

strainer ['streinəʳ] n passoire f

strait [streit] n (Geo) détroit m; **straits** npl: **to be
in dire ~s** (fig) avoir de sérieux ennuis

straitjacket ['streitdʒækit] n camisole f de
force

strait-laced [streit'leist] adj collet monté inv

strand [strænd] n (of thread) fil m, brin m; (of rope)
toron m; (of hair) mèche f ▷ vt (boat) échouer

stranded ['strændid] adj en rade, en plan

strange [streindʒ] adj (not known) inconnu(e);
(odd) étrange, bizarre

strangely ['streindʒli] adv étrangement,
bizarrement; see also **enough**

stranger ['streindʒəʳ] n (unknown) inconnu(e);
(from somewhere else) étranger(-ère); **I'm a ~ here**
je ne suis pas d'ici

S

strangle ['stræŋgl] vt étrangler

stranglehold ['stræŋglhəʊld] n (fig) emprise totale, mainmise f

strangulation [stræŋgju'leɪʃən] n strangulation f

strap [stræp] n lanière f, courroie f, sangle f; (of slip, dress) bretelle f ▷ vt attacher (avec une courroie etc)

straphanging ['stræphæŋɪŋ] n (fait m de) voyager debout (dans le métro etc)

strapless ['stræplɪs] adj (bra, dress) sans bretelles

strapped [stræpt] adj: **to be ~ for cash** (inf) être à court d'argent

strapping ['stræpɪŋ] adj bien découplé(e), costaud(e)

strappy ['stræpɪ] adj (dress) à bretelles; (sandals) à lanières

Strasbourg ['stræzbə:g] n Strasbourg

strata ['strɑ:tə] npl of **stratum**

stratagem ['strætɪdʒəm] n stratagème m

strategic [strə'ti:dʒɪk] adj stratégique

strategist ['strætɪdʒɪst] n stratège m

strategy ['strætɪdʒɪ] n stratégie f

stratosphere ['strætəsfɪə'] n stratosphère f

stratum (pl **strata**) ['strɑ:təm, 'strɑ:tə] n strate f, couche f

straw [strɔ:] n paille f; **that's the last ~!** ça c'est le comble!

strawberry ['strɔ:bərɪ] n fraise f; (plant) fraisier m

stray [streɪ] adj (animal) perdu(e), errant(e); (scattered) isolé(e) ▷ vi s'égarer; **~ bullet** balle perdue

streak [stri:k] n bande f, filet m; (in hair) raie f; (fig: of madness etc): **a ~ of** une or des tendance(s) à ▷ vt zébrer, strier ▷ vi: **to ~ past** passer à toute allure; **to have ~s in one's hair** s'être fait faire des mèches; **a winning/losing ~** une bonne/ mauvaise série or période

streaker ['stri:kə'] n streaker(-euse)

streaky ['stri:kɪ] adj zébré(e), strié(e)

streaky bacon n (Brit) ≈ lard m (maigre)

stream [stri:m] n (brook) ruisseau m; (current) courant m, flot m; (of people) défilé ininterrompu, flot ▷ vt (Scol) répartir par niveau ▷ vi ruisseler; **to ~ in/out** entrer/sortir à flots; **against the ~** à contre courant; **on ~** (new power plant etc) en service

streamer ['stri:mə'] n serpentin m, banderole f

stream feed n (on photocopier etc) alimentation f en continu

streamline ['stri:mlaɪn] vt donner un profil aérodynamique à; (fig) rationaliser

streamlined ['stri:mlaɪnd] adj (Aviat) fuselé(e), profilé(e); (Aut) aérodynamique; (fig) rationalisé(e)

street [stri:t] n rue f; **the back ~s** les quartiers pauvres; **to be on the ~s** (homeless) être à la rue or sans abri

streetcar ['stri:tkɑ:'] n (US) tramway m

street cred [-krɛd] n (inf): **to have ~** être branché(e)

street lamp n réverbère m

street light n réverbère m

street lighting n éclairage public

street map, street plan n plan m des rues

street market n marché m à ciel ouvert

streetwise ['stri:twaɪz] adj (inf) futé(e), réaliste

strength [strɛŋθ] n force f; (of girder, knot etc) solidité f; (of chemical solution) titre m; (of wine) degré m d'alcool; **on the ~ of** en vertu de; **at full ~** au grand complet; **below ~** à effectifs réduits

strengthen ['strɛŋθn] vt renforcer; (muscle) fortifier; (building, Econ) consolider

strenuous ['strɛnjuəs] adj vigoureux(-euse), énergique; (tiring) ardu(e), fatigant(e)

stress [strɛs] n (force, pressure) pression f; (mental strain) tension (nerveuse), stress m; (accent) accent m; (emphasis) insistance f ▷ vt insister sur, souligner; (syllable) accentuer; **to lay great ~ on sth** insister beaucoup sur qch; **to be under ~** être stressé(e)

stressed [strɛst] adj (tense) stressé(e); (syllable) accentué(e)

stressful ['strɛsful] adj (job) stressant(e)

stretch [strɛtʃ] n (of sand etc) étendue f; (of time) période f ▷ vi s'étirer; (extend): **to ~ to** or **as far as** s'étendre jusqu'à; (be enough: money, food): **to ~ to** aller pour ▷ vt tendre, étirer; (spread) étendre; (fig) pousser (au maximum); **at a ~** d'affilée; **to ~ a muscle** se distendre un muscle; **to ~ one's legs** se dégourdir les jambes ▶ **stretch out** vi s'étendre ▷ vt (arm etc) allonger, tendre; (to spread) étendre; **to ~ out for sth** allonger la main pour prendre qch

stretcher ['strɛtʃə'] n brancard m, civière f

stretcher-bearer ['strɛtʃəbɛərə'] n brancardier m

stretch marks npl (on skin) vergetures fpl

stretchy ['strɛtʃɪ] adj élastique

strewn [stru:n] adj: **~ with** jonché(e) de

stricken ['strɪkən] adj très éprouvé(e); dévasté(e); (ship) très endommagé(e); **~ with** frappé(e) or atteint(e) de

strict [strɪkt] adj strict(e); **in ~ confidence** tout à fait confidentiellement

strictly ['strɪktlɪ] adv strictement; **~ confidential** strictement confidentiel(le); **~ speaking** à strictement parler

stride [straɪd] n grand pas, enjambée f ▷ vi (pt **strode**) [strəʊd] marcher à grands pas; **to take in one's ~** (fig: changes etc) accepter sans sourciller

strident ['straɪdnt] adj strident(e)

strife [straɪf] n conflit m, dissensions fpl

strike [straɪk] (pt, pp **struck**) [strʌk] n grève f; (of oil etc) découverte f; (attack) raid m ▷ vt frapper; (oil etc) trouver, découvrir; (make: agreement, deal) conclure ▷ vi faire grève; (attack) attaquer; (clock) sonner; **to go on** or **come out on ~** se mettre en grève, faire grève; **to ~ a match** frotter une allumette; **to ~ a balance** (fig) trouver un juste milieu

▶ **strike back** vi (Mil, fig) contre-attaquer

▶ **strike down** vt (fig) terrasser

▶ **strike off** vt (from list) rayer; (: doctor etc) radier

▶ **strike out** vt rayer

▶ **strike up** vt (Mus) se mettre à jouer; **to ~ up a friendship with** se lier d'amitié avec

strikebreaker ['straɪkbreɪkə^r] n briseur m de grève

striker ['straɪkə^r] n gréviste m/f; (Sport) buteur m

striking ['straɪkɪŋ] adj frappant(e), saisissant(e); (attractive) éblouissant(e)

strimmer® ['strɪmə^r] n (Brit) coupe-bordures m

string [strɪŋ] n ficelle f, fil m; (row: of beads) rang m; (: of onions, excuses) chapelet m; (: of people, cars) file f; (Mus) corde f; (Comput) chaîne f ▷ vt (pt, pp **strung**) [strʌŋ]: **to ~ out** échelonner; **to ~ together** enchaîner; **the strings** npl (Mus) les instruments mpl à cordes; **to pull ~s** (fig) faire jouer le piston; **to get a job by pulling ~s** obtenir un emploi en faisant jouer le piston; **with no ~s attached** (fig) sans conditions

string bean n haricot vert

stringed instrument [strɪŋ(d)-], **string instrument** n (Mus) instrument m à cordes

stringent ['strɪndʒənt] adj rigoureux(-euse); (need) impérieux(-euse)

string quartet n quatuor m à cordes

strip [strɪp] n bande f; (Sport) tenue f ▷ vt (undress) déshabiller; (paint) décaper; (fig) dégarnir, dépouiller; (also: **strip down**: machine) démonter ▷ vi se déshabiller; **wearing the Celtic ~** en tenue du Celtic

▶ **strip off** vt (paint etc) décaper ▷ vi (person) se déshabiller

strip cartoon n bande dessinée

stripe [straɪp] n raie f, rayure f; (Mil) galon m

striped ['straɪpt] adj rayé(e), à rayures

strip light n (Brit) (tube m au) néon m

stripper ['strɪpə^r] n strip-teaseuse f

strip-search ['strɪpsə:tʃ] n fouille corporelle (en faisant se déshabiller la personne) ▷ vt: **to ~ sb** fouiller qn (en le faisant se déshabiller)

striptease ['strɪptiːz] n strip-tease m

stripy ['straɪpɪ] adj rayé(e)

strive (pt **strove**, pp **striven**) [straɪv, strəuv, 'strɪvn] vi: **to ~ to do/for sth** s'efforcer de faire/ d'obtenir qch

strobe [strəub] n (also: **strobe light**) stroboscope m

strode [strəud] pt of **stride**

stroke [strəuk] n coup m; (Med) attaque f; (caress) caresse f; (Swimming: style) (sorte f de) nage f; (of piston) course f ▷ vt caresser; **at a ~** d'un (seul) coup; **on the ~ of 5** à 5 heures sonnantes; **a ~ of luck** un coup de chance; **a 2-~ engine** un moteur à 2 temps

stroll [strəul] n petite promenade ▷ vi flâner, se promener nonchalamment; **to go for a ~** aller se promener or faire un tour

stroller ['strəulə^r] n (US: for child) poussette f

strong [strɔŋ] adj (gen) fort(e); (healthy) vigoureux(-euse); (heart, nerves) solide; (distaste,

desire) vif (vive); (drugs, chemicals) puissant(e) ▷ adv: **to be going ~** (company) marcher bien; (person) être toujours solide; **they are 50 ~** ils sont au nombre de 50

strong-arm ['strɔŋɑ:m] adj (tactics, methods) musclé(e)

strongbox ['strɔŋbɔks] n coffre-fort m

stronghold ['strɔŋhəuld] n forteresse f, fort m; (fig) bastion m

strongly ['strɔŋlɪ] adv fortement, avec force; vigoureusement; solidement; **I feel ~ about it** c'est une question qui me tient particulièrement à cœur; (negatively) j'y suis profondément opposé(e)

strongman ['strɔŋmæn] (irreg) n hercule m, colosse m; (fig) homme m à poigne

strongroom ['strɔŋruːm] n chambre forte

stroppy ['strɔpɪ] adj (Brit inf) contrariant(e), difficile

strove [strəuv] pt of **strive**

struck [strʌk] pt, pp of **strike**

structural ['strʌktʃrəl] adj structural(e); (Constr) de construction; affectant les parties portantes

structurally ['strʌktʃrəlɪ] adv du point de vue de la construction

structure ['strʌktʃə^r] n structure f; (building) construction f

struggle ['strʌgl] n lutte f ▷ vi lutter, se battre; **to have a ~ to do sth** avoir beaucoup de mal à faire qch

strum [strʌm] vt (guitar) gratter de

strung [strʌŋ] pt, pp of **string**

strut [strʌt] n étai m, support m ▷ vi se pavaner

strychnine ['strɪkniːn] n strychnine f

stub [stʌb] n (of cigarette) bout m, mégot m; (of ticket etc) talon m ▷ vt: **to ~ one's toe (on sth)** se heurter le doigt de pied (contre qch)

▶ **stub out** vt écraser

stubble ['stʌbl] n chaume m; (on chin) barbe f de plusieurs jours

stubborn ['stʌbən] adj têtu(e), obstiné(e), opiniâtre

stubby ['stʌbɪ] adj trapu(e); gros(se) et court(e)

stucco ['stʌkəu] n stuc m

stuck [stʌk] pt, pp of **stick** ▷ adj (jammed) bloqué(e), coincé(e); **to get ~** se bloquer or coincer

stuck-up [stʌk'ʌp] adj prétentieux(-euse)

stud [stʌd] n (on boots etc) clou m; (collar stud) bouton m de col; (earring) petite boucle d'oreille; (of horses: also: **stud farm**) écurie f, haras m; (also: **stud horse**) étalon m ▷ vt (fig): **~ded with** parsemé(e) or criblé(e) de

student ['stjuːdənt] n étudiant(e) ▷ adj (life) estudiantin(e), étudiant(e), d'étudiant; (residence, restaurant) universitaire; (loan, movement) étudiant, universitaire d'étudiant); **law/medical ~** étudiant en droit/ médecine

student driver n (US) (conducteur(-trice)) débutant(e)

students' union n (Brit: association) ≈ union f des étudiants; (: building) ≈ foyer m des étudiants

studied ['stʌdɪd] *adj* étudié(e), calculé(e)

studio ['stju:dɪəu] *n* studio *m*, atelier *m*; (*TV etc*) studio

studio flat, (US) **studio apartment** *n* studio *m*

studious ['stju:dɪəs] *adj* studieux(-euse), appliqué(e); (*studied*) étudié(e)

studiously ['stju:dɪəslɪ] *adv* (*carefully*) soigneusement

study ['stʌdɪ] *n* étude *f*; (*room*) bureau *m* ▷ *vt* étudier; (*examine*) examiner ▷ *vi* étudier, faire ses études; **to make a ~ of sth** étudier qch, faire une étude de qch; **to ~ for an exam** préparer un examen

stuff [stʌf] *n* (*gen*) chose(s) *f*(*pl*), truc *m*; (*belongings*) affaires *fpl*, trucs; (*substance*) substance *f* ▷ *vt* rembourrer; (*Culin*) farcir; (*inf: push*) fourrer; (*animal: for exhibition*) empailler; **my nose is ~ed up** j'ai le nez bouché; **get ~ed!** (*inf!*) va te faire foutre! (*!*); **~ed toy** jouet *m* en peluche

stuffing ['stʌfɪŋ] *n* bourre *f*, rembourrage *m*; (*Culin*) farce *f*

stuffy ['stʌfɪ] *adj* (*room*) mal ventilé(e) *or* aéré(e); (*ideas*) vieux jeu *inv*

stumble ['stʌmbl] *vi* trébucher; **to ~ across** *or* **on** (*fig*) tomber sur

stumbling block ['stʌmblɪŋ-] *n* pierre *f* d'achoppement

stump [stʌmp] *n* souche *f*; (*of limb*) moignon *m* ▷ *vt*: **to be ~ed** sécher, ne pas savoir que répondre

stun [stʌn] *vt* (*blow*) étourdir; (*news*) abasourdir, stupéfier

stung [stʌŋ] *pt, pp of* **sting**

stunk [stʌŋk] *pp of* **stink**

stunned [stʌnd] *adj* assommé(e); (*fig*) sidéré(e)

stunning ['stʌnɪŋ] *adj* (*beautiful*) étourdissant(e); (*news etc*) stupéfiant(e)

stunt [stʌnt] *n* tour *m* de force; (*in film*) cascade *f*, acrobatie *f*; (*publicity*) truc *m* publicitaire; (*Aviat*) acrobatie *f* ▷ *vt* retarder, arrêter

stunted ['stʌntɪd] *adj* rabougri(e)

stuntman ['stʌntmæn] (*irreg*) *n* cascadeur *m*

stupefaction [stju:pɪ'fækʃən] *n* stupéfaction *f*, stupeur *f*

stupefy ['stju:pɪfaɪ] *vt* étourdir; abrutir; (*fig*) stupéfier

stupendous [stju:'pɛndəs] *adj* prodigieux(-euse), fantastique

stupid ['stju:pɪd] *adj* stupide, bête

stupidity [stju:'pɪdɪtɪ] *n* stupidité *f*, bêtise *f*

stupidly ['stju:pɪdlɪ] *adv* stupidement, bêtement

stupor ['stju:pəʳ] *n* stupeur *f*

sturdy ['stə:dɪ] *adj* (*person, plant*) robuste, vigoureux(-euse); (*object*) solide

sturgeon ['stə:dʒən] *n* esturgeon *m*

stutter ['stʌtəʳ] *n* bégaiement *m* ▷ *vi* bégayer

sty [staɪ] *n* (*of pigs*) porcherie *f*

stye [staɪ] *n* (*Med*) orgelet *m*

style [staɪl] *n* style *m*; (*of dress etc*) genre *m*; (*distinction*) allure *f*, cachet *m*, style; (*design*) modèle *m*; **in the latest ~** à la dernière mode; **hair ~** coiffure *f*

stylish ['staɪlɪʃ] *adj* élégant(e), chic *inv*

stylist ['staɪlɪst] *n* (*hair stylist*) coiffeur(-euse); (*literary stylist*) styliste *m/f*

stylized ['staɪlaɪzd] *adj* stylisé(e)

stylus (*pl* **styli** *or* **-es**) ['staɪləs, -laɪ] *n* (*of record player*) pointe *f* de lecture

Styrofoam® ['staɪrəfəum] *n* (US) polystyrène expansé ▷ *adj* en polystyrène

suave [swɑ:v] *adj* doucereux(-euse), onctueux(-euse)

sub [sʌb] *n abbr* = **submarine**; **subscription**

sub... [sʌb] *prefix* sub..., sous-

subcommittee ['sʌbkəmɪtɪ] *n* sous-comité *m*

subconscious [sʌb'kɔnʃəs] *adj* subconscient(e) ▷ *n* subconscient *m*

subcontinent [sʌb'kɔntɪnənt] *n*: **the (Indian) ~** le sous-continent indien

subcontract *n* ['sʌb'kɔntrækt] contrat *m* de sous-traitance ▷ *vt* [sʌbkən'trækt] sous-traiter

subcontractor ['sʌbkən'træktəʳ] *n* sous-traitant *m*

subdivide [sʌbdɪ'vaɪd] *vt* subdiviser

subdivision ['sʌbdɪvɪʒən] *n* subdivision *f*

subdue [səb'dju:] *vt* subjuguer, soumettre

subdued [səb'dju:d] *adj* contenu(e), atténué(e); (*light*) tamisé(e); (*person*) qui a perdu de son entrain

sub-editor ['sʌb'ɛdɪtəʳ] *n* (*Brit*) secrétaire *m/f* de (la) rédaction

subject *n* ['sʌbdʒɪkt] sujet *m*; (*Scol*) matière *f* ▷ *vt* [səb'dʒɛkt]: **to ~ to** soumettre à; exposer à; **to be ~ to** (*law*) être soumis(e) à; (*disease*) être sujet(te) à; **~ to confirmation in writing** sous réserve de confirmation écrite; **to change the ~** changer de conversation

subjection [səb'dʒɛkʃən] *n* soumission *f*, sujétion *f*

subjective [səb'dʒɛktɪv] *adj* subjectif(-ive)

subject matter *n* sujet *m*; (*content*) contenu *m*

sub judice [sʌb'dju:dɪsɪ] *adj* (*Law*) devant les tribunaux

subjugate ['sʌbdʒugeɪt] *vt* subjuguer

subjunctive [səb'dʒʌŋktɪv] *adj* subjonctif(-ive) ▷ *n* subjonctif *m*

sublet [sʌb'lɛt] *vt* sous-louer

sublime [sə'blaɪm] *adj* sublime

subliminal [sʌb'lɪmɪnl] *adj* subliminal(e)

submachine gun ['sʌbmə'ʃi:n-] *n* mitraillette *f*

submarine [sʌbmə'ri:n] *n* sous-marin *m*

submerge [səb'mə:dʒ] *vt* submerger; immerger ▷ *vi* plonger

submersion [səb'mə:ʃən] *n* submersion *f*; immersion *f*

submission [səb'mɪʃən] *n* soumission *f*; (*to committee etc*) présentation *f*

submissive [səb'mɪsɪv] *adj* soumis(e)

submit [səb'mɪt] *vt* soumettre ▷ *vi* se soumettre

subnormal [sʌb'nɔ:ml] *adj* au-dessous de la normale; (*person*) arriéré(e)

subordinate [sə'bɔ:dɪnət] *adj* (*junior*) subalterne;

(*Grammar*) subordonné(e) ▷ *n* subordonné(e)

subpoena [səb'pi:nə] (*Law*) *n* citation *f*, assignation *f* ▷ *vt* citer *or* assigner (à comparaître)

subroutine [sʌbru:'ti:n] *n* (*Comput*) sous-programme *m*

subscribe [səb'skraɪb] *vi* cotiser; **to ~ to** (*opinion, fund*) souscrire à; (*newspaper*) s'abonner à; être abonné(e) à

subscriber [səb'skraɪbəʳ] *n* (*to periodical, telephone*) abonné(e)

subscript ['sʌbskrɪpt] *n* (*Typ*) indice inférieur

subscription [səb'skrɪpʃən] *n* (*to fund*) souscription *f*; (*to magazine etc*) abonnement *m*; (*membership dues*) cotisation *f*; **to take out a ~ to** s'abonner à

subsequent ['sʌbsɪkwənt] *adj* ultérieur(e), suivant(e); **~ to** *prep* à la suite de

subsequently ['sʌbsɪkwəntlɪ] *adv.* par la suite

subservient [səb'sə:vɪənt] *adj* obséquieux(-euse)

subside [səb'saɪd] *vi* (*land*) s'affaisser; (*flood*) baisser; (*wind, feelings*) tomber

subsidence [səb'saɪdns] *n* affaissement *m*

subsidiarity [səbsɪdɪ'ærɪtɪ] *n* (*Pol*) subsidiarité *f*

subsidiary [səb'sɪdɪərɪ] *adj* subsidiaire; accessoire; (*Brit Scol: subject*) complémentaire ▷ *n* filiale *f*

subsidize ['sʌbsɪdaɪz] *vt* subventionner

subsidy ['sʌbsɪdɪ] *n* subvention *f*

subsist [səb'sɪst] *vi:* **to ~ on sth** (arriver à) vivre avec *or* subsister avec qch

subsistence [səb'sɪstəns] *n* existence *f*, subsistance *f*

subsistence allowance *n* indemnité *f* de séjour

subsistence level *n* niveau *m* de vie minimum

substance ['sʌbstəns] *n* substance *f*; (*fig*) essentiel *m*; **a man of ~** un homme jouissant d'une certaine fortune; **to lack ~** être plutôt mince (*fig*)

substance abuse *n* abus *m* de substances toxiques

substandard [sʌb'stændəd] *adj* (*goods*) de qualité inférieure, qui laisse à désirer; (*housing*) inférieur(e) aux normes requises

substantial [səb'stænʃl] *adj* substantiel(le); (*fig*) important(e)

substantially [səb'stænʃəlɪ] *adv* considérablement; en grande partie

substantiate [səb'stænʃɪeɪt] *vt* étayer, fournir des preuves à l'appui de

substitute ['sʌbstɪtju:t] *n* (*person*) remplaçant(e); (*thing*) succédané *m* ▷ *vt:* **to ~ sth/sb for** substituer qch/qn à, remplacer par qch/qn

substitute teacher *n* (*US*) suppléant(e)

substitution [sʌbstɪ'tju:ʃən] *n* substitution *f*

subterfuge ['sʌbtəfju:dʒ] *n* subterfuge *m*

subterranean [sʌbtə'reɪnɪən] *adj* souterrain(e)

subtitled ['sʌbtaɪtld] *adj* sous-titré(e)

subtitles ['sʌbtaɪtlz] *npl* (*Cine*) sous-titres *mpl*

subtle ['sʌtl] *adj* subtil(e)

subtlety ['sʌtltɪ] *n* subtilité *f*

subtly ['sʌtlɪ] *adv* subtilement

subtotal [sʌb'təutl] *n* total partiel

subtract [səb'trækt] *vt* soustraire, retrancher

subtraction [səb'trækʃən] *n* soustraction *f*

subtropical [sʌb'trɔpɪkl] *adj* subtropical(e)

suburb ['sʌbə:b] *n* faubourg *m*; **the ~s** la banlieue

suburban [sə'bə:bən] *adj* de banlieue, suburbain(e)

suburbia [sə'bə:bɪə] *n* la banlieue

subvention [səb'vɛnʃən] *n* (*subsidy*) subvention *f*

subversion [səb'və:ʃən] *n* subversion *f*

subversive [səb'və:sɪv] *adj* subversif(-ive)

subway ['sʌbweɪ] *n* (*Brit: underpass*) passage souterrain; (*US: railway*) métro *m*

sub-zero [sʌb'zɪərəu] *adj* au-dessous de zéro

succeed [sək'si:d] *vi* réussir ▷ *vt* succéder à; **to ~ in doing** réussir à faire

succeeding [sək'si:dɪŋ] *adj* suivant(e), qui suit (*or* suivent *or* suivront *etc*)

success [sək'sɛs] *n* succès *m*; réussite *f*

successful [sək'sɛsful] *adj* qui a du succès; (*candidate*) choisi(e), agréé(e); (*business*) prospère, qui réussit; (*attempt*) couronné(e) de succès; **to be ~ (in doing)** réussir (à faire)

successfully [sək'sɛsfəlɪ] *adv* avec succès

succession [sək'sɛʃən] *n* succession *f*; **in ~** successivement; **3 years in ~** 3 ans de suite

successive [sək'sɛsɪv] *adj* successif(-ive); **on 3 ~ days** 3 jours de suite *or* consécutifs

successor [sək'sɛsəʳ] *n* successeur *m*

succinct [sək'sɪŋkt] *adj* succinct(e), bref (brève)

succulent ['sʌkjulənt] *adj* succulent(e) ▷ *n* (*Bot*): **~s** plantes grasses

succumb [sə'kʌm] *vi* succomber

such [sʌtʃ] *adj* tel (telle); (*of that kind*): **~ a book** un livre de ce genre *or* pareil, un tel livre; (*so much*): **~ courage** un tel courage ▷ *adv* si; **~ books** des livres de ce genre *or* pareils, de tels livres; **~ a long trip** un si long voyage; **~ good books** de si bons livres; **~ a long trip that** un voyage si *or* tellement long que; **~ a lot of** tellement *or* tant de; **making ~ a noise that** faisant un tel bruit que *or* tellement de bruit que; **~ a long time ago** il y a si *or* tellement longtemps; **~ as** (*like*) tel (telle) que, comme; **a noise ~ as to** un bruit de nature à; **~ books as I have** les quelques livres que j'ai; **as ~** (*adv*) en tant que tel (telle), à proprement parler

such-and-such ['sʌtʃənsʌtʃ] *adj* tel ou tel (telle ou telle)

suchlike ['sʌtʃlaɪk] *pron* (*inf*): **and ~** et le reste

suck [sʌk] *vt* sucer; (*breast, bottle*) téter; (*pump, machine*) aspirer

sucker ['sʌkəʳ] *n* (*Bot, Zool, Tech*) ventouse *f*; (*inf*) naïf(-ïve), poire *f*

suckle ['sʌkl] *vt* allaiter

sucrose ['su:krəuz] *n* saccharose *m*

suction ['sʌkʃən] *n* succion *f*

suction pump *n* pompe aspirante

Sudan [su'dɑ:n] *n* Soudan *m*

S

Sudanese [suːdəˈniːz] *adj* soudanais(e) ▷ *n* Soudanais(e)

sudden [ˈsʌdn] *adj* soudain(e), subit(e); **all of a ~** soudain, tout à coup

sudden-death [sʌdnˈdeθ] *n*: **~ play-off** partie supplémentaire pour départager les adversaires

suddenly [ˈsʌdnlɪ] *adv* brusquement, tout à coup, soudain

sudoku [sʊˈdəʊkuː] *n* sudoku *m*

suds [sʌdz] *npl* eau savonneuse

sue [suː] *vt* poursuivre en justice, intenter un procès à ▷ *vi*: **to ~ (for)** intenter un procès (pour); **to ~ for divorce** engager une procédure de divorce; **to ~ sb for damages** poursuivre qn en dommages-intérêts

suede [sweɪd] *n* daim *m*, cuir suédé ▷ *cpd* de daim

suet [ˈsuɪt] *n* graisse *f* de rognon or de bœuf

Suez Canal [ˈsuːɪz-] *n* canal *m* de Suez

suffer [ˈsʌfə^r] *vt* souffrir, subir; (*bear*) tolérer, supporter, subir ▷ *vi* souffrir; **to ~ from** (*illness*) souffrir de, avoir; **to ~ from the effects of alcohol/a fall** se ressentir des effets de l'alcool/des conséquences d'une chute

sufferance [ˈsʌfərns] *n*: **he was only there on ~** sa présence était seulement tolérée

sufferer [ˈsʌfərə^r] *n* malade *m/f*; victime *m/f*

suffering [ˈsʌfərɪŋ] *n* souffrance(s) *f(pl)*

suffice [səˈfaɪs] *vi* suffire

sufficient [səˈfɪʃənt] *adj* suffisant(e); **~ money** suffisamment d'argent

sufficiently [səˈfɪʃəntlɪ] *adv* suffisamment, assez

suffix [ˈsʌfɪks] *n* suffixe *m*

suffocate [ˈsʌfəkeɪt] *vi* suffoquer; étouffer

suffocation [sʌfəˈkeɪʃən] *n* suffocation *f*; (*Med*) asphyxie *f*

suffrage [ˈsʌfrɪdʒ] *n* suffrage *m*; droit *m* de suffrage or de vote

suffuse [səˈfjuːz] *vt* baigner, imprégner; **the room was ~d with light** la pièce baignait dans la lumière or était imprégnée de lumière

sugar [ˈʃʊɡə^r] *n* sucre *m* ▷ *vt* sucrer

sugar beet *n* betterave sucrière

sugar bowl *n* sucrier *m*

sugar cane *n* canne *f* à sucre

sugar-coated [ˈʃʊɡəˈkəʊtɪd] *adj* dragéifié(e)

sugar lump *n* morceau *m* de sucre

sugar refinery *n* raffinerie *f* de sucre

sugary [ˈʃʊɡərɪ] *adj* sucré(e)

suggest [səˈdʒɛst] *vt* suggérer, proposer; (*indicate*) sembler indiquer; **what do you ~ I do?** que vous me suggérez de faire?

suggestion [səˈdʒɛstʃən] *n* suggestion *f*

suggestive [səˈdʒɛstɪv] *adj* suggestif(-ive)

suicidal [suɪˈsaɪdl] *adj* suicidaire

suicide [ˈsuɪsaɪd] *n* suicide *m*; **to commit ~** se suicider; **~ bombing** attentat *m* suicide; *see also* **commit**

suicide bomber *n* kamikaze *m/f*

suit [suːt] *n* (*man's*) costume *m*, complet *m*; (*woman's*) tailleur *m*, ensemble *m*; (*Cards*) couleur *f*; (*lawsuit*) procès *m* ▷ *vt* (*subj: clothes, hairstyle*) aller à; (*be convenient for*) convenir à; (*adapt*): **to ~ sth to** adapter or approprier qch à; **to be ~ed to sth** (*suitable for*) être adapté(e) or approprié(e) à qch; **well ~ed** (*couple*) faits l'un pour l'autre, très bien assortis; **to bring a ~ against sb** intenter un procès contre qn; **to follow ~** (*fig*) faire de même

suitable [ˈsuːtəbl] *adj* qui convient; approprié(e), adéquat(e); **would tomorrow be ~?** est-ce que demain vous conviendrait?; **we found somebody ~** nous avons trouvé la personne qu'il nous faut

suitably [ˈsuːtəblɪ] *adv* comme il se doit (*or* se devait *etc*), convenablement

suitcase [ˈsuːtkeɪs] *n* valise *f*

suite [swiːt] *n* (*of rooms, also Mus*) suite *f*; (*furniture*): **bedroom/dining room ~** (ensemble *m* de) chambre *f* à coucher/salle *f* à manger; **a three-piece ~** un salon (canapé et deux fauteuils)

suitor [ˈsuːtə^r] *n* soupirant *m*, prétendant *m*

sulfate [ˈsʌlfeɪt] *n* (*US*) = **sulphate**

sulfur [ˈsʌlfə^r] (*US*) *n* = **sulphur**

sulk [sʌlk] *vi* bouder

sulky [ˈsʌlkɪ] *adj* boudeur(-euse), maussade

sullen [ˈsʌlən] *adj* renfrogné(e), maussade; morne

sulphate, (*US*) **sulfate** [ˈsʌlfeɪt] *n* sulfate *m*; **copper ~** sulfate de cuivre

sulphur, (*US*) **sulfur** [ˈsʌlfə^r] *n* soufre *m*

sulphur dioxide *n* anhydride sulfureux

sulphuric, (*US*) **sulfuric** [sʌlˈfjʊərɪk] *adj*: **~ acid** acide *m* sulfurique

sultan [ˈsʌltən] *n* sultan *m*

sultana [sʌlˈtɑːnə] *n* (*fruit*) raisin (sec) de Smyrne

sultry [ˈsʌltrɪ] *adj* étouffant(e)

sum [sʌm] *n* somme *f*; (*Scol etc*) calcul *m*
▶ **sum up** *vt* résumer; (*evaluate rapidly*) récapituler ▷ *vi* résumer

Sumatra [suˈmɑːtrə] *n* Sumatra

summarize [ˈsʌməraɪz] *vt* résumer

summary [ˈsʌmərɪ] *n* résumé *m* ▷ *adj* (*justice*) sommaire

summer [ˈsʌmə^r] *n* été *m* ▷ *cpd* d'été, estival(e); **in (the) ~** en été, pendant l'été

summer camp *n* (*US*) colonie *f* de vacances

summer holidays *npl* grandes vacances

summerhouse [ˈsʌməhaus] *n* (*in garden*) pavillon *m*

summertime [ˈsʌmətaɪm] *n* (*season*) été *m*

summer time *n* (*by clock*) heure *f* d'été

summery [ˈsʌmərɪ] *adj* estival(e); d'été

summing-up [sʌmɪŋˈʌp] *n* résumé *m*, récapitulation *f*

summit [ˈsʌmɪt] *n* sommet *m*; (*also:* **summit conference**) (conférence *f* au) sommet *m*

summon [ˈsʌmən] *vt* appeler, convoquer; **to ~ a witness** citer or assigner un témoin
▶ **summon up** *vt* rassembler, faire appel à

summons [ˈsʌmənz] *n* citation *f*, assignation *f*

▷ *vt* citer, assigner; **to serve a ~ on sb** remettre une assignation à qn

sumo ['su:məʊ] *n*: **~ wrestling** sumo *m*

sump [sʌmp] *n* (*Brit Aut*) carter *m*

sumptuous ['sʌmptjʊəs] *adj* somptueux(-euse)

Sun. *abbr* (= *Sunday*) dim

sun [sʌn] *n* soleil *m*; **in the ~** au soleil; **to catch the ~** prendre le soleil; **everything under the ~** absolument tout

sunbathe ['sʌnbeɪð] *vi* prendre un bain de soleil

sunbeam ['sʌnbi:m] *n* rayon *m* de soleil

sunbed ['sʌnbɛd] *n* lit pliant; (*with sun lamp*) lit à ultra-violets

sunblock ['sʌnblɒk] *n* écran *m* total

sunburn ['sʌnbə:n] *n* coup *m* de soleil

sunburned ['sʌnbə:nd], **sunburnt** ['sʌnbə:nt] *adj* bronzé(e), hâlé(e); (*painfully*) brûlé(e) par le soleil

sun cream *n* crème *f* (anti-)solaire

sundae ['sʌndeɪ] *n* sundae *m*, coupe glacée

Sunday ['sʌndɪ] *n* dimanche *m*; *for phrases see also* **Tuesday**

Sunday paper *n* journal *m* du dimanche; *voir article*

● **SUNDAY PAPER**

Les *Sunday papers* sont une véritable institution en Grande-Bretagne. Il y a des "quality Sunday papers" et des "popular Sunday papers", et la plupart des quotidiens ont un journal du dimanche qui leur est associé, bien que leurs équipes de rédacteurs soient différentes. Les quality Sunday papers ont plusieurs suppléments et magazines; voir "quality press" et "tabloid press".

Sunday school *n* ≈ catéchisme *m*

sundial ['sʌndaɪəl] *n* cadran *m* solaire

sundown ['sʌndaʊn] *n* coucher *m* du soleil

sundries ['sʌndrɪz] *npl* articles divers

sundry ['sʌndrɪ] *adj* divers(e), différent(e); **all and ~** tout le monde, n'importe qui

sunflower ['sʌnflaʊər] *n* tournesol *m*

sung [sʌŋ] *pp of* **sing**

sunglasses ['sʌngla:sɪz] *npl* lunettes *fpl* de soleil

sunk [sʌŋk] *pp of* **sink**

sunken ['sʌŋkn] *adj* (*rock, ship*) submergé(e); (*cheeks*) creux(-euse); (*bath*) encastré(e)

sunlamp ['sʌnlæmp] *n* lampe *f* à rayons ultra-violets

sunlight ['sʌnlaɪt] *n* (lumière *f* du) soleil *m*

sunlit ['sʌnlɪt] *adj* ensoleillé(e)

sun lounger *n* chaise longue

sunny ['sʌnɪ] *adj* ensoleillé(e); (*fig*) épanoui(e), radieux(-euse); **it is ~** il fait (du) soleil, il y a du soleil

sunrise ['sʌnraɪz] *n* lever *m* du soleil

sun roof *n* (*Aut*) toit ouvrant

sunscreen ['sʌnskri:n] *n* crème *f* solaire

sunset ['sʌnsɛt] *n* coucher *m* du soleil

sunshade ['sʌnʃeɪd] *n* (*lady's*) ombrelle *f*; (*over table*) parasol *m*

sunshine ['sʌnʃaɪn] *n* (lumière *f* du) soleil *m*

sunspot ['sʌnspɒt] *n* tache *f* solaire

sunstroke ['sʌnstrəʊk] *n* insolation *f*, coup *m* de soleil

suntan ['sʌntæn] *n* bronzage *m*

suntan lotion *n* lotion *f* or lait *m* solaire

suntanned ['sʌntænd] *adj* bronzé(e)

suntan oil *n* huile *f* solaire

suntrap ['sʌntræp] *n* coin très ensoleillé

super ['su:pər] *adj* (*inf*) formidable

superannuation [su:pərænju'eɪʃən] *n* cotisations *fpl* pour la pension

superb [su:'pə:b] *adj* superbe, magnifique

Super Bowl *n* (*US Sport*) Super Bowl *m*

supercilious [su:pə'sɪlɪəs] *adj* hautain(e), dédaigneux(-euse)

superconductor [su:pəkən'dʌktər] *n* supraconducteur *m*

superficial [su:pə'fɪʃəl] *adj* superficiel(le)

superficially [su:pə'fɪʃəlɪ] *adv* superficiellement

superfluous [su:'pə:flʊəs] *adj* superflu(e)

superglue ['su:pəglu:] *n* colle forte

superhighway ['su:pəhaɪweɪ] *n* (*US*) voie *f* express (à plusieurs files); **the information ~** la super-autoroute de l'information

superhuman [su:pə'hju:mən] *adj* surhumain(e)

superimpose ['su:pərɪm'pəʊz] *vt* superposer

superintend [su:pərɪn'tɛnd] *vt* surveiller

superintendent [su:pərɪn'tɛndənt] *n* directeur(-trice); (*Police*) ≈ commissaire *m*

superior [su'pɪərɪər] *adj* supérieur(e); (*Comm: goods, quality*) de qualité supérieure; (*smug*) condescendant(e), méprisant(e) ▷ *n* supérieur(e); **Mother S~** (*Rel*) Mère supérieure

superiority [supɪərɪ'ɔrɪtɪ] *n* supériorité *f*

superlative [su'pə:lətɪv] *adj* sans pareil(le), suprême ▷ *n* (*Ling*) superlatif *m*

superman ['su:pəmæn] (*irreg*) *n* surhomme *m*

supermarket ['su:pəma:kɪt] *n* supermarché *m*

supermodel ['su:pəmɔdl] *n* top model *m*

supernatural [su:pə'nætʃərəl] *adj* surnaturel(le) ▷ *n*: **the ~** le surnaturel

supernova [su:pə'nəʊvə] *n* supernova *f*

superpower ['su:pəpaʊər] *n* (*Pol*) superpuissance *f*

supersede [su:pə'si:d] *vt* remplacer, supplanter

supersonic ['su:pə'sɒnɪk] *adj* supersonique

superstar ['su:pəsta:r] *n* (*Cine etc*) superstar *f*; (*Sport*) superchampion(ne) ▷ *adj* (*status, lifestyle*) de superstar

superstition [su:pə'stɪʃən] *n* superstition *f*

superstitious [su:pə'stɪʃəs] *adj* superstitieux(-euse)

superstore ['su:pəstɔ:r] *n* (*Brit*) hypermarché *m*, grande surface

supertanker ['su:pətæŋkər] *n* pétrolier géant, superpétrolier *m*

supertax ['su:pətæks] *n* tranche supérieure de l'impôt

S

supervise ['su:pəvaɪz] *vt* (*children etc*) surveiller; (*organization, work*) diriger

supervision [su:pə'vɪʒən] *n* surveillance *f*; (*monitoring*) contrôle *m*; (*management*) direction *f*; **under medical ~** sous contrôle du médecin

supervisor ['su:pəvaɪzəʳ] *n* surveillant(e); (*in shop*) chef *m* de rayon; (*Scol*) directeur(-trice) de thèse

supervisory ['su:pəvaɪzərɪ] *adj* de surveillance

supine ['su:paɪn] *adj* couché(e) or étendu(e) sur le dos

supper ['sʌpəʳ] *n* dîner *m*; (*late*) souper *m*; **to have ~** dîner; souper

supplant [sə'plɑ:nt] *vt* supplanter

supple ['sʌpl] *adj* souple

supplement *n* ['sʌplɪmənt] supplément *m* ▷ *vt* [sʌplɪ'mɛnt] ajouter à, compléter

supplementary [sʌplɪ'mɛntərɪ] *adj* supplémentaire

supplementary benefit *n* (*Brit*) allocation *f* supplémentaire d'aide sociale

supplier [sə'plaɪəʳ] *n* fournisseur *m*

supply [sə'plaɪ] *vt* (*provide*) fournir; (*equip*): **to ~ (with)** approvisionner or ravitailler (en); fournir (en); (*system, machine*): **to ~ sth (with sth)** alimenter qch (en qch); (*a need*) répondre à ▷ *n* provision *f*, réserve *f*; (*supplying*) approvisionnement *m*; (*Tech*) alimentation *f*; **supplies** *npl* (*food*) vivres *mpl*; (*Mil*) subsistances *fpl*; **office supplies** fournitures *fpl* de bureau; **to be in short ~** être rare, manquer; **the electricity/water/gas ~** l'alimentation *f* en électricité/eau/gaz; **~ and demand** l'offre *f* et la demande; **it comes supplied with an adaptor** il (*or* elle) est pourvu(e) d'un adaptateur

supply teacher *n* (*Brit*) suppléant(e)

support [sə'pɔ:t] *n* (*moral, financial etc*) soutien *m*, appui *m*; (*Tech*) support *m*, soutien ▷ *vt* soutenir, supporter; (*financially*) subvenir aux besoins de; (*uphold*) être pour, être partisan de, appuyer; (*Sport: team*) être pour; **to ~ o.s.** (*financially*) gagner sa vie

supporter [sə'pɔ:təʳ] *n* (*Pol etc*) partisan(e); (*Sport*) supporter *m*

supporting [sə'pɔ:tɪŋ] *adj* (*wall*) d'appui

supporting role *n* second rôle *m*

supportive [sə'pɔ:tɪv] *adj*: **my family were very ~** ma famille m'a été d'un grand soutien

suppose [sə'pəuz] *vt, vi* supposer; imaginer; **to be ~d to do/be** être censé(e) faire/être; **I don't ~ she'll come** je suppose qu'elle ne viendra pas, cela m'étonnerait qu'elle vienne

supposedly [sə'pəuzɪdlɪ] *adv* soi-disant

supposing [sə'pəuzɪŋ] *conj* si, à supposer que + *sub*

supposition [sʌpə'zɪʃən] *n* supposition *f*, hypothèse *f*

suppository [sə'pɔzɪtrɪ] *n* suppositoire *m*

suppress [sə'prɛs] *vt* (*revolt, feeling*) réprimer; (*information*) faire disparaître; (*scandal, yawn*) étouffer

suppression [sə'prɛʃən] *n* suppression *f*, répression *f*

suppressor [sə'prɛsəʳ] *n* (*Elec etc*) dispositif *m* antiparasite

supremacy [su'prɛməsɪ] *n* suprématie *f*

supreme [su'pri:m] *adj* suprême

Supreme Court *n* (*US*) Cour *f* suprême

supremo [su'pri:məu] *n* grand chef

Supt. *abbr* (*Police*) = **superintendent**

surcharge ['sə:tʃɑ:dʒ] *n* surcharge *f*; (*extra tax*) surtaxe *f*

sure [ʃuəʳ] *adj* (*gen*) sûr(e); (*definite, convinced*) sûr, certain(e) ▷ *adv* (*inf: US*): **that ~ is pretty, that's ~ pretty** c'est drôlement joli(e); **~!** (*of course*) bien sûr!; **~ enough** effectivement; **I'm not ~ how/why/when** je ne sais pas très bien comment/pourquoi/quand; **to be ~ of o.s.** être sûr de soi; **to make ~ of sth/that** s'assurer de qch/que, vérifier qch/que

sure-fire ['ʃuəfaɪəʳ] *adj* (*inf*) certain(e), infaillible

sure-footed [ʃuə'futɪd] *adj* au pied sûr

surely ['ʃuəlɪ] *adv* sûrement; certainement; **~ you don't mean that!** vous ne parlez pas sérieusement!

surety ['ʃuərətɪ] *n* caution *f*; **to go** or **stand ~ for sb** se porter caution pour qn

surf [sə:f] *n* (*waves*) ressac *m* ▷ *vt*: **to ~ the Net** surfer sur Internet, surfer sur le net

surface ['sə:fɪs] *n* surface *f* ▷ *vt* (*road*) poser un revêtement sur ▷ *vi* remonter à la surface; (*fig*) faire surface; **on the ~** (*fig*) au premier abord; **by ~ mail** par voie de terre; (*by sea*) par voie maritime

surface area *n* superficie *f*, aire *f*

surface mail *n* courrier *m* par voie de terre (*or* maritime)

surface-to-surface ['sə:fɪstə'sə:fɪs] *adj* (*Mil*) sol-sol *inv*

surfboard ['sə:fbɔ:d] *n* planche *f* de surf

surfeit ['sə:fɪt] *n*: **a ~ of** un excès de; une indigestion de

surfer ['sə:fəʳ] *n* (*in sea*) surfeur(-euse); **web** or **net ~** internaute *m/f*

surfing ['sə:fɪŋ] *n* surf *m*

surge [sə:dʒ] *n* (*of emotion*) vague *f*; (*Elec*) pointe *f* de courant ▷ *vi* déferler; **to ~ forward** se précipiter (en avant)

surgeon ['sə:dʒən] *n* chirurgien *m*

Surgeon General *n* (*US*) chef *m* du service fédéral de la santé publique

surgery ['sə:dʒərɪ] *n* chirurgie *f*; (*Brit: room*) cabinet *m* (de consultation); (*also:* **surgery hours**) heures *fpl* de consultation; (*of MP etc*) permanence *f* (*où le député etc reçoit les électeurs etc*); **to undergo ~** être opéré(e)

surgery hours *npl* (*Brit*) heures *fpl* de consultation

surgical ['sə:dʒɪkl] *adj* chirurgical(e)

surgical spirit *n* (*Brit*) alcool *m* à 90°

surly ['sə:lɪ] *adj* revêche, maussade

surmise [sə:'maɪz] *vt* présumer, conjecturer

surmount [sə:'maunt] *vt* surmonter

surname ['sə:neɪm] *n* nom *m* de famille

surpass [sə'pɑːs] vt surpasser, dépasser
surplus ['sə:pləs] n surplus m, excédent m ▷ adj
en surplus, de trop; (Comm) excédentaire; **it is ~
to our requirements** cela dépasse nos besoins;
~ stock surplus m
surprise [sə'praɪz] n (gen) surprise f;
(astonishment) étonnement m ▷ vt surprendre,
étonner; **to take by ~** (person) prendre au
dépourvu; (Mil: town, fort) prendre par surprise
surprised [sə'praɪzd] adj (look, smile) surpris(e),
étonné(e); **to be ~** être surpris
surprising [sə'praɪzɪŋ] adj surprenant(e),
étonnant(e)
surprisingly [sə'praɪzɪŋlɪ] adv (easy, helpful)
étonnamment, étrangement; **(somewhat) ~,
he agreed** curieusement, il a accepté
surrealism [sə'rɪəlɪzəm] n surréalisme m
surrealist [sə'rɪəlɪst] adj, n surréaliste (m/f)
surrender [sə'rɛndə'] n reddition f, capitulation
f ▷ vi se rendre, capituler ▷ vt (claim, right)
renoncer à
surrender value n valeur f de rachat
surreptitious [sʌrəp'tɪʃəs] adj subreptice,
furtif(-ive)
surrogate ['sʌrəgɪt] n (Brit: substitute) substitut m
▷ adj de substitution, de remplacement; **a food
~** un succédané alimentaire; **~ coffee** ersatz m
or succédané m de café
surrogate mother n mère porteuse or de
substitution
surround [sə'raund] vt entourer; (Mil etc)
encercler
surrounding [sə'raundɪŋ] adj environnant(e)
surroundings [sə'raundɪŋz] npl environs mpl,
alentours mpl
surtax ['sə:tæks] n surtaxe f
surveillance [sə:'veɪləns] n surveillance f
survey n ['sə:veɪ] enquête f, étude f; (in house
buying etc) inspection f, (rapport m d')expertise f;
(of land) levé m; (comprehensive view: of situation etc)
vue f d'ensemble ▷ vt [sə:'veɪ] (situation) passer
en revue; (examine carefully) inspecter; (building)
expertiser; (land) faire le levé de; (look at)
embrasser du regard
surveying [sə'veɪɪŋ] n arpentage m
surveyor [sə'veɪə'] n (of building) expert m; (of
land) (arpenteur m) géomètre m
survival [sə'vaɪvl] n survie f; (relic) vestige m
▷ cpd (course, kit) de survie
survive [sə'vaɪv] vi survivre; (custom etc)
subsister ▷ vt (accident etc) survivre à, réchapper
de; (person) survivre à
survivor [sə'vaɪvə'] n survivant(e)
susceptible [sə'sɛptəbl] adj: **~ (to)** sensible (à);
(disease) prédisposé(e) (à)
suspect adj, n ['sʌspɛkt] suspect(e) ▷ vt [səs'pɛkt]
soupçonner, suspecter
suspected [səs'pɛktɪd] adj: **a ~ terrorist** une
personne soupçonnée de terrorisme; **he had a
~ broken arm** il avait une supposée fracture du
bras
suspend [səs'pɛnd] vt suspendre

suspended animation [səs'pɛndɪd-] n: **in a
state of ~** en hibernation
suspended sentence [səs'pɛndɪd-] n (Law)
condamnation f avec sursis
suspender belt [səs'pɛndə-] n (Brit) porte-
jarretelles m inv
suspenders [səs'pɛndəz] npl (Brit) jarretelles fpl;
(US) bretelles fpl
suspense [səs'pɛns] n attente f, incertitude f; (in
film etc) suspense m; **to keep sb in ~** tenir qn en
suspens, laisser qn dans l'incertitude
suspension [səs'pɛnʃən] n (gen, Aut) suspension
f; (of driving licence) retrait m provisoire
suspension bridge n pont suspendu
suspicion [səs'pɪʃən] n soupçon(s) m(pl); **to be
under ~** être considéré(e) comme suspect(e),
être suspecté(e); **arrested on ~ of murder**
arrêté sur présomption de meurtre
suspicious [səs'pɪʃəs] adj (suspecting)
soupçonneux(-euse), méfiant(e); (causing
suspicion) suspect(e); **to be ~ of or about sb/sth**
avoir des doutes à propos de qn/sur qch, trouver
qn/qch suspect(e)
suss out ['sʌs'aut] vt (Brit inf: discover) supputer
(: understand) piger
sustain [səs'teɪn] vt soutenir; supporter;
corroborer; (subj: food) nourrir, donner des forces
à; (damage) subir; (injury) recevoir
sustainable [səs'teɪnəbl] adj (rate, growth) qui
peut être maintenu(e); (development) durable
sustained [səs'teɪnd] adj (effort) soutenu(e),
prolongé(e)
sustenance ['sʌstɪnəns] n nourriture f; moyens
mpl de subsistance
suture ['suːtʃə'] n suture f
SUV n abbr (esp US: = sports utility vehicle) SUV m,
véhicule m de loisirs
SW abbr (= short wave) OC
swab [swɔb] n (Med) tampon m; prélèvement m
▷ vt (Naut: also: **swab down**) nettoyer
swagger ['swægə'] vi plastronner, parader
swallow ['swɔləu] n (bird) hirondelle f; (of food
etc) gorgée f ▷ vt avaler; (fig: story) gober
▶ **swallow up** vt engloutir
swam [swæm] pt of **swim**
swamp [swɔmp] n marais m, marécage m ▷ vt
submerger
swampy ['swɔmpɪ] adj marécageux(-euse)
swan [swɔn] n cygne m
swank [swæŋk] vi (inf) faire de l'épate
swan song n (fig) chant m du cygne
swap [swɔp] n échange m, troc m ▷ vt: **to ~ (for)**
échanger (contre), troquer (contre)
SWAPO ['swɑ:pəu] n abbr (= South-West Africa
People's Organization) SWAPO f
swarm [swɔ:m] n essaim m ▷ vi (bees) essaimer;
(people) grouiller; **to be ~ing with** grouiller de
swarthy ['swɔ:ðɪ] adj basané(e), bistré(e)
swashbuckling ['swɔʃbʌklɪŋ] adj (film) de cape
et d'épée
swastika ['swɔstɪkə] n croix gammée
SWAT n abbr (US: = Special Weapons and Tactics)

S

≈ CRS f

swat [swɔt] vt écraser ▷ n (Brit: also: **fly swat**) tapette f

swathe [sweɪð] vt: **to ~ in** (bandages, blankets) embobiner de

swatter ['swɔtər] n (also: **fly swatter**) tapette f

sway [sweɪ] vi se balancer, osciller; tanguer ▷ vt (influence) influencer ▷ n (rule, power): ~ **(over)** emprise f (sur); **to hold ~ over sb** avoir de l'emprise sur qn

Swaziland ['swɑ:zɪlænd] n Swaziland m

swear [swɛər] (pt **swore**, pp **sworn**) [swɔːr, swɔːn] vt, vi jurer; **to ~ to sth** jurer de qch; **to ~ an oath** prêter serment
▶ **swear in** vt assermenter

swearword ['swɛəwəːd] n gros mot, juron m

sweat [swɛt] n sueur f, transpiration f ▷ vi suer; **in a ~** en sueur

sweatband ['swɛtbænd] n (Sport) bandeau m

sweater ['swɛtər] n tricot m, pull m

sweatshirt ['swɛtʃəːt] n sweat-shirt m

sweatshop ['swɛtʃɔp] n atelier m où les ouvriers sont exploités

sweaty ['swɛtɪ] adj en sueur, moite or mouillé(e) de sueur

Swede [swiːd] n Suédois(e)

swede [swiːd] n (Brit) rutabaga m

Sweden ['swiːdn] n Suède f

Swedish ['swiːdɪʃ] adj suédois(e) ▷ n (Ling) suédois m

sweep [swiːp] (pt, pp **swept**) [swɛpt] n coup m de balai; (curve) grande courbe; (range) champ m; (also: **chimney sweep**) ramoneur m ▷ vt balayer; (subj: current) emporter; (subj: fashion, craze) se répandre dans ▷ vi avancer majestueusement or rapidement; s'élancer; s'étendre
▶ **sweep away** vt balayer; entraîner; emporter
▶ **sweep past** vi passer majestueusement or rapidement
▶ **sweep up** vt, vi balayer

sweeper ['swiːpər] n (person) balayeur m; (machine) balayeuse f; (Football) libéro m

sweeping ['swiːpɪŋ] adj (gesture) large; circulaire; (changes, reforms) radical(e); **a ~ statement** une généralisation hâtive

sweepstake ['swiːpsteɪk] n sweepstake m

sweet [swiːt] n (Brit: pudding) dessert m; (candy) bonbon m ▷ adj doux (douce); (not savoury) sucré(e); (fresh) frais (fraîche), pur(e); (kind) gentil(le); (baby) mignon(ne) ▷ adv: **to smell ~** sentir bon; **to taste ~** avoir un goût sucré; ~ **and sour** adj aigre-doux (douce)

sweetbread ['swiːtbrɛd] n ris m de veau

sweetcorn ['swiːtkɔːn] n maïs doux

sweeten ['swiːtn] vt sucrer; (fig) adoucir

sweetener ['swiːtnər] n (Culin) édulcorant m

sweetheart ['swiːthɑːt] n amoureux(-euse)

sweetly ['swiːtlɪ] adv (smile) gentiment; (sing, play) mélodieusement

sweetness ['swiːtnɪs] n douceur f; (of taste) goût sucré

sweet pea n pois m de senteur

sweet potato n patate douce

sweetshop ['swiːtʃɔp] n (Brit) confiserie f

sweet tooth n: **to have a ~** aimer les sucreries

swell [swɛl] (pt **-ed**, pp **swollen** or **-ed**) ['swəulən] n (of sea) houle f ▷ adj (US: inf: excellent) chouette ▷ vt (increase) grossir, augmenter ▷ vi (increase) grossir, augmenter; (sound) s'enfler; (Med: also: **swell up**) enfler

swelling ['swɛlɪŋ] n (Med) enflure f; (: lump) grosseur f

sweltering ['swɛltərɪŋ] adj étouffant(e), oppressant(e)

swept [swɛpt] pt, pp of **sweep**

swerve [swəːv] vi (to avoid obstacle) faire une embardée or un écart; (off the road) dévier

swift [swɪft] n (bird) martinet m ▷ adj rapide, prompt(e)

swiftly ['swɪftlɪ] adv rapidement, vite

swig [swɪg] n (inf: drink) lampée f

swill [swɪl] n pâtée f ▷ vt (also: **swill out, swill down**) laver à grande eau

swim [swɪm] (pt **swam**, pp **swum**) [swæm, swʌm] n: **to go for a ~** aller nager or se baigner ▷ vi nager; (Sport) faire de la natation; (fig: head, room) tourner ▷ vt traverser (à la nage); (distance) faire (à la nage); **to ~ a length** nager une longueur; **to go ~ming** aller nager

swimmer ['swɪmər] n nageur(-euse)

swimming ['swɪmɪŋ] n nage f, natation f

swimming baths npl (Brit) piscine f

swimming cap n bonnet m de bain

swimming costume n (Brit) maillot m (de bain)

swimmingly ['swɪmɪŋlɪ] adv: **to go ~** (wonderfully) se dérouler à merveille

swimming pool n piscine f

swimming trunks npl maillot m de bain

swimsuit ['swɪmsuːt] n maillot m (de bain)

swindle ['swɪndl] n escroquerie f ▷ vt escroquer

swindler ['swɪndlər] n escroc m

swine [swaɪn] n (pl inv) pourceau m, porc m; (inf!) salaud m (!)

swine flu n grippe f porcine

swing [swɪŋ] (pt, pp **swung**) [swʌŋ] n (in playground) balançoire f; (movement) balancement m, oscillations fpl; (change in opinion etc) revirement m; (Mus) swing m; rythme m ▷ vt balancer, faire osciller; (also: **swing round**) tourner, faire virer ▷ vi se balancer, osciller; (also: **swing round**) virer, tourner; **a ~ to the left** (Pol) un revirement en faveur de la gauche; **to be in full ~** battre son plein; **to get into the ~ of things** se mettre dans le bain; **the road ~s south** la route prend la direction sud

swing bridge n pont tournant

swing door n (Brit) porte battante

swingeing ['swɪndʒɪŋ] adj (Brit) écrasant(e); considérable

swinging ['swɪŋɪŋ] adj rythmé(e); entraînant(e); (fig) dans le vent; ~ **door** (US) porte battante

swipe [swaɪp] n grand coup; gifle f ▷ vt (hit) frapper à toute volée; gifler; (inf: steal) piquer;

(*credit card etc*) faire passer (dans la machine)

swipe card *n* carte *f* magnétique

swirl [swəːl] *n* tourbillon *m* ▷ *vi* tourbillonner, tournoyer

swish [swɪʃ] *adj* (*Brit inf: smart*) rupin(e) ▷ *vi* (*whip*) siffler; (*skirt, long grass*) bruire

Swiss [swɪs] *adj* suisse ▷ *n* (*pl inv*) Suisse(-esse)

Swiss French *adj* suisse romand(e)

Swiss German *adj* suisse-allemand(e)

Swiss roll *n* gâteau roulé

switch [swɪtʃ] *n* (*for light, radio etc*) bouton *m*; (*change*) changement *m*, revirement *m* ▷ *vt* (*change*) changer; (*exchange*) intervertir; (*invert*): **to ~** (**round** *or* **over**) changer de place
▶ **switch off** *vt* éteindre; (*engine, machine*) arrêter; **could you ~ off the light?** pouvez-vous éteindre la lumière?
▶ **switch on** *vt* allumer; (*engine, machine*) mettre en marche; (*Brit: water supply*) ouvrir

switchback ['swɪtʃbæk] *n* (*Brit*) montagnes *fpl* russes

switchblade ['swɪtʃbleɪd] *n* (*also:* **switchblade knife**) couteau *m* à cran d'arrêt

switchboard ['swɪtʃbɔːd] *n* (*Tel*) standard *m*

switchboard operator *n* (*Tel*) standardiste *m/f*

Switzerland ['swɪtsələnd] *n* Suisse *f*

swivel ['swɪvl] *vi* (*also:* **swivel round**) pivoter, tourner

swollen ['swəulən] *pp of* **swell** ▷ *adj* (*ankle etc*) enflé(e)

swoon [swuːn] *vi* se pâmer

swoop [swuːp] *n* (*by police etc*) rafle *f*, descente *f*; (*of bird etc*) descente *f* en piqué ▷ *vi* (*bird: also:* **swoop down**) descendre en piqué, piquer

swop [swɔp] *n, vt* = **swap**

sword [sɔːd] *n* épée *f*

swordfish ['sɔːdfɪʃ] *n* espadon *m*

swore [swɔːr] *pt of* **swear**

sworn [swɔːn] *pp of* **swear** ▷ *adj* (*statement, evidence*) donné(e) sous serment; (*enemy*) juré(e)

swot [swɔt] *vt, vi* bûcher, potasser

swum [swʌm] *pp of* **swim**

swung [swʌŋ] *pt, pp of* **swing**

sycamore ['sɪkəmɔːr] *n* sycomore *m*

sycophant ['sɪkəfænt] *n* flagorneur(-euse)

sycophantic [sɪkə'fæntɪk] *adj* flagorneur(-euse)

Sydney ['sɪdnɪ] *n* Sydney

syllable ['sɪləbl] *n* syllabe *f*

syllabus ['sɪləbəs] *n* programme *m*; **on the ~** au programme

symbol ['sɪmbl] *n* symbole *m*

symbolic [sɪm'bɔlɪk], **symbolical** [sɪm'bɔlɪkl] *adj* symbolique

symbolism ['sɪmbəlɪzəm] *n* symbolisme *m*

symbolize ['sɪmbəlaɪz] *vt* symboliser

symmetrical [sɪ'mɛtrɪkl] *adj* symétrique

symmetry ['sɪmɪtrɪ] *n* symétrie *f*

sympathetic [sɪmpə'θɛtɪk] *adj* (*showing pity*) compatissant(e); (*understanding*) bienveillant(e), compréhensif(-ive); **~ towards** bien disposé(e) envers

sympathetically [sɪmpə'θɛtɪklɪ] *adv* avec compassion (*or* bienveillance)

sympathize ['sɪmpəθaɪz] *vi*: **to ~ with sb** plaindre qn; (*in grief*) s'associer à la douleur de qn; **to ~ with sth** comprendre qch

sympathizer ['sɪmpəθaɪzər] *n* (*Pol*) sympathisant(e)

sympathy ['sɪmpəθɪ] *n* (*pity*) compassion *f*; **sympathies** *npl* (*support*) soutien *m*; **in ~ with** en accord avec; (*strike*) en *or* par solidarité avec; **with our deepest ~** en vous priant d'accepter nos sincères condoléances

symphonic [sɪm'fɔnɪk] *adj* symphonique

symphony ['sɪmfənɪ] *n* symphonie *f*

symphony orchestra *n* orchestre *m* symphonique

symposium [sɪm'pəuzɪəm] *n* symposium *m*

symptom ['sɪmptəm] *n* symptôme *m*; indice *m*

symptomatic [sɪmptə'mætɪk] *adj* symptomatique

synagogue ['sɪnəgɔg] *n* synagogue *f*

sync [sɪŋk] *n* (*inf*): **in/out of ~** bien/mal synchronisé(e); **they're in ~ with each other** (*fig*) le courant passe bien entre eux

synchromesh [sɪŋkrəu'mɛʃ] *n* (*Aut*) synchronisation *f*

synchronize ['sɪŋkrənaɪz] *vt* synchroniser ▷ *vi*: **to ~ with** se produire en même temps que

synchronized swimming ['sɪŋkrənaɪzd-] *n* natation synchronisée

syncopated ['sɪŋkəpeɪtɪd] *adj* syncopé(e)

syndicate ['sɪndɪkɪt] *n* syndicat *m*, coopérative *f*; (*Press*) agence *f* de presse

syndrome ['sɪndrəum] *n* syndrome *m*

synonym ['sɪnənɪm] *n* synonyme *m*

synonymous [sɪ'nɔnɪməs] *adj*: **~ (with)** synonyme (de)

synopsis (*pl* **synopses**) [sɪ'nɔpsɪs, -siːz] *n* résumé *m*, synopsis *m* or *f*

syntax ['sɪntæks] *n* syntaxe *f*

synthesis (*pl* **syntheses**) ['sɪnθəsɪs, -siːz] *n* synthèse *f*

synthesizer ['sɪnθəsaɪzər] *n* (*Mus*) synthétiseur *m*

synthetic [sɪn'θɛtɪk] *adj* synthétique ▷ *n* matière *f* synthétique; **synthetics** *npl* textiles artificiels

syphilis ['sɪfɪlɪs] *n* syphilis *f*

syphon ['saɪfən] *n, vb* = **siphon**

Syria ['sɪrɪə] *n* Syrie *f*

Syrian ['sɪrɪən] *adj* syrien(ne) ▷ *n* Syrien(ne)

syringe [sɪ'rɪndʒ] *n* seringue *f*

syrup ['sɪrəp] *n* sirop *m*; (*Brit: also:* **golden syrup**) mélasse raffinée

syrupy ['sɪrəpɪ] *adj* sirupeux(-euse)

system ['sɪstəm] *n* système *m*; (*order*) méthode *f*; (*Anat*) organisme *m*

systematic [sɪstə'mætɪk] *adj* systématique; méthodique

system disk *n* (*Comput*) disque *m* système

systems analyst *n* analyste-programmeur *m/f*

S

Tt

T, t [tiː] *n* (*letter*) T, t *m*; **T for Tommy** T comme Thérèse

TA *n abbr* (*Brit*) = **Territorial Army**

ta [taː] *excl* (*Brit inf*) merci!

tab [tæb] *n abbr* = **tabulator** ▷ *n* (*loop on coat etc*) attache *f*; (*label*) étiquette *f*; (*on drinks can etc*) languette *f*; **to keep ~s on** (*fig*) surveiller

tabby ['tæbɪ] *n* (*also*: **tabby cat**) chat(te) tigré(e)

table ['teɪbl] *n* table *f* ▷ *vt* (*Brit: motion etc*) présenter; **to lay** *or* **set the ~** mettre le couvert *or* la table; **to clear the ~** débarrasser la table; **league ~** (*Brit Football, Rugby*) classement *m* (du championnat); **~ of contents** table des matières

tablecloth ['teɪblklɔθ] *n* nappe *f*

table d'hôte [taːblˈdəut] *adj* (*meal*) à prix fixe

table football *n* baby-foot *m*

table lamp *n* lampe décorative *or* de table

tablemat ['teɪblmæt] *n* (*for plate*) napperon *m*, set *m*; (*for hot dish*) dessous-de-plat *m inv*

table salt *n* sel fin *or* de table

tablespoon ['teɪblspuːn] *n* cuiller *f* de service; (*also*: **tablespoonful**: *as measurement*) cuillerée *f* à soupe

tablet ['tæblɪt] *n* (*Med*) comprimé *m*; (: *for sucking*) pastille *f*; (*of stone*) plaque *f*; **~ of soap** (*Brit*) savonnette *f*

table tennis *n* ping-pong *m*, tennis *m* de table

table wine *n* vin *m* de table

tabloid ['tæblɔɪd] *n* (*newspaper*) quotidien *m* populaire; *voir article*

● TABLOID PRESS

Le terme *tabloid press* désigne les journaux populaires de demi-format où l'on trouve beaucoup de photos et qui adoptent un style très concis. Ce type de journaux vise des lecteurs s'intéressant aux faits divers ayant un parfum de scandale; voir "quality press"

taboo [təˈbuː] *adj, n* tabou (*m*)

tabulate ['tæbjuleɪt] *vt* (*data, figures*) mettre sous forme de table(s)

tabulator ['tæbjuleɪtəʳ] *n* tabulateur *m*

tachograph ['tækəgraːf] *n* tachygraphe *m*

tachometer [tæˈkɔmɪtəʳ] *n* tachymètre *m*

tacit ['tæsɪt] *adj* tacite

taciturn ['tæsɪtəːn] *adj* taciturne

tack [tæk] *n* (*nail*) petit clou; (*stitch*) point *m* de bâti; (*Naut*) bord *m*, bordée *f*; (*fig*) direction *f* ▷ *vt* (*nail*) clouer; (*sew*) bâtir ▷ *vi* (*Naut*) tirer un *or* des bord(s); **to change ~** virer de bord; **on the wrong ~** (*fig*) sur la mauvaise voie; **to ~ sth on to (the end of) sth** (*of letter, book*) rajouter qch à la fin de qch

tackle ['tækl] *n* matériel *m*, équipement *m*; (*for lifting*) appareil *m* de levage; (*Football, Rugby*) plaquage *m* ▷ *vt* (*difficulty, animal, burglar*) s'attaquer à; (*person: challenge*) s'expliquer avec; (*Football, Rugby*) plaquer

tacky ['tækɪ] *adj* collant(e); (*paint*) pas sec (sèche); (*inf: shabby*) moche; (*pej: poor-quality*) minable; (: *showing bad taste*) ringard(e)

tact [tækt] *n* tact *m*

tactful ['tæktful] *adj* plein(e) de tact

tactfully ['tæktfəlɪ] *adv* avec tact

tactical ['tæktɪkl] *adj* tactique; **~ error** erreur *f* de tactique

tactician [tækˈtɪʃən] *n* tacticien(ne)

tactics ['tæktɪks] *n, npl* tactique *f*

tactless ['tæktlɪs] *adj* qui manque de tact

tactlessly ['tæktlɪslɪ] *adv* sans tact

tadpole ['tædpəul] *n* têtard *m*

Tadzhikistan [tædʒɪkɪˈstaːn] *n* = **Tajikistan**

taffy ['tæfɪ] *n* (*US*) (bonbon *m* au) caramel *m*

tag [tæg] *n* étiquette *f*; **price/name ~** étiquette (portant le prix/le nom)

▶ **tag along** *vi* suivre

Tahiti [taːˈhiːtɪ] *n* Tahiti *m*

tail [teɪl] *n* queue *f*; (*of shirt*) pan *m* ▷ *vt* (*follow*) suivre, filer; **tails** *npl* (*suit*) habit *m*; **to turn ~** se sauver à toutes jambes; *see also* **head**

▶ **tail away, tail off** *vi* (*in size, quality etc*) baisser peu à peu

tailback ['teɪlbæk] *n* (*Brit*) bouchon *m*

tail coat *n* habit *m*

tail end *n* bout *m*, fin *f*

tailgate ['teɪlgeɪt] *n* (*Aut*) hayon *m* arrière

tail light *n* (*Aut*) feu *m* arrière

tailor ['teɪləʳ] *n* tailleur *m* (*artisan*) ▷ *vt*: **to ~ sth (to)** adapter qch exactement (à); **~'s (shop)**

(boutique *f* de) tailleur *m*
tailoring ['teɪlərɪŋ] *n* (*cut*) coupe *f*
tailor-made ['teɪlə'meɪd] *adj* fait(e) sur mesure; (*fig*) conçu(e) spécialement
tailwind ['teɪlwɪnd] *n* vent *m* arrière *inv*
taint [teɪnt] *vt* (*meat, food*) gâter; (*fig: reputation*) salir
tainted ['teɪntɪd] *adj* (*food*) gâté(e); (*water, air*) infecté(e); (*fig*) souillé(e)
Taiwan ['taɪ'wɑːn] *n* Taïwan (*no article*)
Taiwanese [taɪwə'niːz] *adj* taïwanais(e) ▷ *n inv* Taïwanais(e)
Tajikistan [tædʒɪkɪ'stɑːn] *n* Tadjikistan *m/f*
take [teɪk] (*pt* **took**, *pp* **-n**) [tuk, 'teɪkn] *vt* prendre; (*gain: prize*) remporter; (*require: effort, courage*) demander; (*tolerate*) accepter; supporter; (*hold: passengers etc*) contenir; (*accompany*) emmener, accompagner; (*bring, carry*) apporter, emporter; (*exam*) passer, se présenter à; (*conduct: meeting*) présider ▷ *vi* (*dye, fire etc*) prendre ▷ *n* (*Cine*) prise *f* de vues; **to ~ sth from** (*drawer etc*) prendre qch dans; (*person*) prendre qch à; **I ~ it that** je suppose que; **I took him for a doctor** je l'ai pris pour un docteur; **to ~ sb's hand** prendre qn par la main; **to ~ for a walk** (*child, dog*) emmener promener; **to be ~n ill** tomber malade; **to ~ it upon o.s. to do sth** prendre sur soi de faire qch; **~ the first (street) on the left** prenez la première à gauche; **it won't ~ long** ça ne prendra pas longtemps; **I was quite ~n with her/it** elle/cela m'a beaucoup plu
▸ **take after** *vt fus* ressembler à
▸ **take apart** *vt* démonter
▸ **take away** *vt* (*carry off*) emporter; (*remove*) enlever; (*subtract*) soustraire ▷ *vi*: **to ~ away from** diminuer
▸ **take back** *vt* (*return*) rendre, rapporter; (*one's words*) retirer
▸ **take down** *vt* (*building*) démolir; (*dismantle: scaffolding*) démonter; (*letter etc*) prendre, écrire
▸ **take in** *vt* (*deceive*) tromper, rouler; (*understand*) comprendre, saisir; (*include*) couvrir, inclure; (*lodger*) prendre; (*orphan, stray dog*) recueillir; (*dress, waistband*) reprendre
▸ **take off** *vi* (*Aviat*) décoller ▷ *vt* (*remove*) enlever; (*imitate*) imiter, pasticher
▸ **take on** *vt* (*work*) accepter, se charger de; (*employee*) prendre, embaucher; (*opponent*) accepter de se battre contre
▸ **take out** *vt* sortir; (*remove*) enlever; (*invite*) sortir avec; (*licence*) prendre, se procurer; **to ~ sth out of** enlever qch de; (*out of drawer etc*) prendre qch dans; **don't ~ it out on me!** ne t'en prends pas à moi!; **to ~ sb out to a restaurant** emmener qn au restaurant
▸ **take over** *vt* (*business*) reprendre ▷ *vi*: **to ~ over from sb** prendre la relève de qn
▸ **take to** *vt fus* (*person*) se prendre d'amitié pour; (*activity*) prendre goût à; **to ~ to doing sth** prendre l'habitude de faire qch
▸ **take up** *vt* (*one's story*) reprendre; (*dress*)

raccourcir; (*occupy: time, space*) prendre, occuper; (*engage in: hobby etc*) se mettre à; (*accept: offer, challenge*) accepter; (*absorb: liquids*) absorber ▷ *vi*: **to ~ up with sb** se lier d'amitié avec qn
takeaway ['teɪkəweɪ] (*Brit*) *adj* (*food*) à emporter ▷ *n* (*shop, restaurant*) ≈ magasin *m* qui vend des plats à emporter
take-home pay ['teɪkhəum-] *n* salaire net
taken ['teɪkən] *pp of* **take**
takeoff ['teɪkɔf] *n* (*Aviat*) décollage *m*
takeout ['teɪkaut] *adj, n* (*US*) = **takeaway**
takeover ['teɪkəuvər] *n* (*Comm*) rachat *m*
takeover bid *n* offre publique d'achat, OPA *f*
takings ['teɪkɪŋz] *npl* (*Comm*) recette *f*
talc [tælk] *n* (*also*: **talcum powder**) talc *m*
tale [teɪl] *n* (*story*) conte *m*, histoire *f*; (*account*) récit *m*; (*pej*) histoire; **to tell ~s** (*fig*) rapporter
talent ['tælnt] *n* talent *m*, don *m*
talented ['tæləntɪd] *adj* doué(e), plein(e) de talent
talent scout *n* découvreur *m* de vedettes (*or* joueurs *etc*)
talisman ['tælɪzmən] *n* talisman *m*
talk [tɔːk] *n* (*a speech*) causerie *f*, exposé *m*; (*conversation*) discussion *f*; (*interview*) entretien *m*, propos *mpl*; (*gossip*) racontars *mpl* (*pej*) ▷ *vi* parler; (*chatter*) bavarder; **talks** *npl* (*Pol etc*) entretiens *mpl*; conférence *f*; **to give a ~** faire un exposé; **to ~ about** parler de; (*converse*) s'entretenir *or* parler de; **~ing of films, have you seen ...?** à propos de films, as-tu vu ...?; **to ~ sb out of/into doing** persuader qn de ne pas faire/de faire; **to ~ shop** parler métier *or* affaires
▸ **talk over** *vt* discuter (de)
talkative ['tɔːkətɪv] *adj* bavard(e)
talking point ['tɔːkɪŋ-] *n* sujet *m* de conversation
talking-to ['tɔːkɪŋtu] *n*: **to give sb a good ~** passer un savon à qn
talk show *n* (*TV, Radio*) émission-débat *f*
tall [tɔːl] *adj* (*person*) grand(e); (*building, tree*) haut(e); **to be 6 feet ~** ≈ mesurer 1 mètre 80; **how ~ are you?** combien mesurez-vous?
tallboy ['tɔːlbɔɪ] *n* (*Brit*) grande commode
tallness ['tɔːlnɪs] *n* grande taille; hauteur *f*
tall story *n* histoire *f* invraisemblable
tally ['tælɪ] *n* compte *m* ▷ *vi*: **to ~ (with)** correspondre (à); **to keep a ~ of sth** tenir le compte de qch
talon ['tælən] *n* griffe *f*; (*of eagle*) serre *f*
tambourine [tæmbə'riːn] *n* tambourin *m*
tame [teɪm] *adj* apprivoisé(e); (*fig: story, style*) insipide
Tamil ['tæmɪl] *adj* tamoul(e) *or* tamil(e) ▷ *n* Tamoul(e) *or* Tamil(e); (*Ling*) tamoul *m or* tamil *m*
tamper ['tæmpər] *vi*: **to ~ with** toucher à (*en cachette ou sans permission*)
tampon ['tæmpən] *n* tampon *m* hygiénique *or* périodique
tan [tæn] *n* (*also*: **suntan**) bronzage *m* ▷ *vt*, *vi*

t

bronzer, brunir ▷ *adj* (*colour*) marron clair *inv*; **to get a ~** bronzer

tandem ['tændəm] *n* tandem *m*

tandoori [tæn'duərı] *adj* tandouri

tang [tæŋ] *n* odeur (*or* saveur) piquante

tangent ['tændʒənt] *n* (*Math*) tangente *f*; **to go off at a ~** (*fig*) partir dans une digression

tangerine [tændʒə'ri:n] *n* mandarine *f*

tangible ['tændʒəbl] *adj* tangible; **~ assets** biens réels

Tangier [tæn'dʒıər] *n* Tanger

tangle ['tæŋgl] *n* enchevêtrement *m* ▷ *vt* enchevêtrer; **to get in(to) a ~** s'emmêler

tango ['tæŋgəu] *n* tango *m*

tank [tæŋk] *n* réservoir *m*; (*for processing*) cuve *f*; (*for fish*) aquarium *m*; (*Mil*) char *m* d'assaut, tank *m*

tankard ['tæŋkəd] *n* chope *f*

tanker ['tæŋkər] *n* (*ship*) pétrolier *m*, tanker *m*; (*truck*) camion-citerne *m*; (*Rail*) wagon-citerne *m*

tankini [tæn'kını] *n* tankini *m*

tanned [tænd] *adj* bronzé(e)

tannin ['tænın] *n* tanin *m*

tanning ['tænıŋ] *n* (*of leather*) tannage *m*

tannoy® ['tænɔı] *n* (*Brit*) haut-parleur *m*; **over the tannoy** par haut-parleur

tantalizing ['tæntəlaızıŋ] *adj* (*smell*) extrêmement appétissant(e); (*offer*) terriblement tentant(e)

tantamount ['tæntəmaunt] *adj*: **~ to** qui équivaut à

tantrum ['tæntrəm] *n* accès *m* de colère; **to throw a ~** piquer une colère

Tanzania [tænzə'nıə] *n* Tanzanie *f*

Tanzanian [tænzə'nıən] *adj* tanzanien(ne) ▷ *n* Tanzanien(ne)

tap [tæp] *n* (*on sink etc*) robinet *m*; (*gentle blow*) petite tape ▷ *vt* frapper *or* taper légèrement; (*resources*) exploiter, utiliser; (*telephone*) mettre sur écoute; **on ~** (*beer*) en tonneau; (*fig: resources*) disponible

tap dancing ['tæpdɑ:nsıŋ] *n* claquettes *fpl*

tape [teıp] *n* (*for tying*) ruban *m*; (*also:* **magnetic tape**) bande *f* (magnétique); (*cassette*) cassette *f*; (*sticky*) Scotch® *m* ▷ *vt* (*record*) enregistrer (au magnétoscope *or* sur cassette); (*stick*) coller avec du Scotch®; **on ~** (*song etc*) enregistré(e)

tape measure *n* mètre *m* à ruban

taper ['teıpər] *n* cierge *m* ▷ *vi* s'effiler

tape recorder *n* magnétophone *m*

tapered ['teıpəd], **tapering** ['teıpərıŋ] *adj* fuselé(e), effilé(e)

tapestry ['tæpıstrı] *n* tapisserie *f*

tape-worm ['teıpwə:m] *n* ver *m* solitaire, ténia *m*

tapioca [tæpı'əukə] *n* tapioca *m*

tappet ['tæpıt] *n* (*Aut*) poussoir *m* (de soupape)

tar [tɑ:] *n* goudron *m*; **low-/middle-~ cigarettes** *fpl* à faible/moyenne teneur en goudron

tarantula [tə'ræntjulə] *n* tarentule *f*

tardy ['tɑ:dı] *adj* tardif(-ive)

target ['tɑ:gıt] *n* cible *f*; (*fig: objective*) objectif *m*; **to be on ~** (*project*) progresser comme prévu

target practice *n* exercices *mpl* de tir (à la cible)

tariff ['tærıf] *n* (*Comm*) tarif *m*; (*taxes*) tarif douanier

tarmac ['tɑ:mæk] *n* (*Brit: on road*) macadam *m*; (*Aviat*) aire *f* d'envol ▷ *vt* (*Brit*) goudronner

tarnish ['tɑ:nıʃ] *vt* ternir

tarot ['tærəu] *n* tarot *m*

tarpaulin [tɑ:'pɔ:lın] *n* bâche goudronnée

tarragon ['tærəgən] *n* estragon *m*

tart [tɑ:t] *n* (*Culin*) tarte *f*; (*Brit inf: pej: prostitute*) poule *f* ▷ *adj* (*flavour*) âpre, aigrelet(te)

▶ **tart up** *vt* (*inf*): **to ~ o.s. up** se faire beau (belle); (*: pej*) s'attifer

tartan ['tɑ:tn] *n* tartan *m* ▷ *adj* écossais(e)

tartar ['tɑ:tər] *n* (*on teeth*) tartre *m*

tartar sauce, tartare sauce *n* sauce *f* tartare

task [tɑ:sk] *n* tâche *f*; **to take to ~** prendre à partie

task force *n* (*Mil, Police*) détachement spécial

taskmaster ['tɑ:skmɑ:stər] *n*: **he's a hard ~** il est très exigeant dans le travail

Tasmania [tæz'meınıə] *n* Tasmanie *f*

tassel ['tæsl] *n* gland *m*; pompon *m*

taste [teıst] *n* goût *m*; (*fig: glimpse, idea*) idée *f*, aperçu *m* ▷ *vt* goûter ▷ *vi*: **to ~ of** (*fish etc*) avoir le *or* un goût de; **it ~s like fish** ça a un *or* le goût de poisson, on dirait du poisson; **what does it ~ like?** quel goût ça a?; **you can ~ the garlic (in it)** on sent bien l'ail; **to have a ~ of sth** goûter (à) qch; **can I have a ~?** je peux goûter?; **to have a ~ for sth** aimer qch, avoir un penchant pour qch; **to be in good/bad** *or* **poor ~** être de bon/mauvais goût

taste bud *n* papille *f*

tasteful ['teıstful] *adj* de bon goût

tastefully ['teıstfəlı] *adv* avec goût

tasteless ['teıstlıs] *adj* (*food*) insipide; (*remark*) de mauvais goût

tasty ['teıstı] *adj* savoureux(-euse), délicieux(-euse)

tattered ['tætəd] *adj see* **tatters**

tatters ['tætəz] *npl*: **in ~** (*also:* **tattered**) en lambeaux

tattoo [tə'tu:] *n* tatouage *m*; (*spectacle*) parade *f* militaire ▷ *vt* tatouer

tatty ['tætı] *adj* (*Brit inf*) défraîchi(e), en piteux état

taught [tɔ:t] *pt*, *pp of* **teach**

taunt [tɔ:nt] *n* raillerie *f* ▷ *vt* railler

Taurus ['tɔ:rəs] *n* le Taureau; **to be ~** être du Taureau

taut [tɔ:t] *adj* tendu(e)

tavern ['tævən] *n* taverne *f*

tawdry ['tɔ:drı] *adj* (d'un mauvais goût) criard

tawny ['tɔ:nı] *adj* fauve (couleur)

tax [tæks] *n* (*on goods etc*) taxe *f*; (*on income*) impôts *mpl*, contributions *fpl* ▷ *vt* taxer; imposer; (*fig: patience etc*) mettre à l'épreuve; **before/after ~** avant/après l'impôt; **free of ~** exonéré(e) d'impôt

taxable ['tæksəbl] *adj* (*income*) imposable

tax allowance *n* part *f* du revenu non imposable, abattement *m* à la base

taxation [tæk'seɪʃən] *n* taxation *f*; impôts *mpl*, contributions *fpl*; **system of** ~ système fiscal

tax avoidance *n* évasion fiscale

tax collector *n* percepteur *m*

tax disc *n* (*Brit Aut*) vignette *f* (automobile)

tax evasion *n* fraude fiscale

tax exemption *n* exonération fiscale, exemption *f* d'impôts

tax exile *n* personne qui s'expatrie pour raisons fiscales

tax-free ['tæksfriː] *adj* exempt(e) d'impôts

tax haven *n* paradis fiscal

taxi ['tæksɪ] *n* taxi *m* ▷ *vi* (*Aviat*) rouler (lentement) au sol

taxidermist ['tæksɪdəːmɪst] *n* empailleur(-euse) (*d'animaux*)

taxi driver *n* chauffeur *m* de taxi

tax inspector *n* (*Brit*) percepteur *m*

taxi rank, (*Brit*) **taxi stand** *n* station *f* de taxis

tax payer [-peɪəʳ] *n* contribuable *m/f*

tax rebate *n* ristourne *f* d'impôt

tax relief *n* dégrèvement *or* allègement fiscal, réduction *f* d'impôt

tax return *n* déclaration *f* d'impôts *or* de revenus

tax year *n* année fiscale

TB *n abbr* = **tuberculosis**

tbc *abbr* = **to be confirmed**

TD *n abbr* (*US*) = **Treasury Department**; (: *Football*) = **touchdown**

tea [tiː] *n* thé *m*; (*Brit: snack: for children*) goûter *m*; **high** ~ (*Brit*) collation combinant goûter et dîner

tea bag *n* sachet *m* de thé

tea break *n* (*Brit*) pause-thé *f*

teacake ['tiːkeɪk] *n* (*Brit*) ≈ petit pain aux raisins

teach (*pt, pp* **taught**) [tiːtʃ, tɔːt] *vt*: **to ~ sb sth, to ~ sth to sb** apprendre qch à qn; (*in school etc*) enseigner qch à qn ▷ *vi* enseigner; **it taught him a lesson** (*fig*) ça lui a servi de leçon

teacher ['tiːtʃəʳ] *n* (*in secondary school*) professeur *m*; (*in primary school*) instituteur(-trice); **French** ~ professeur de français

teacher training college *n* (*for primary schools*) ≈ école normale d'instituteurs; (*for secondary schools*) collège *m* de formation pédagogique (*pour l'enseignement secondaire*)

teaching ['tiːtʃɪŋ] *n* enseignement *m*

teaching aids *npl* supports *mpl* pédagogiques

teaching hospital *n* (*Brit*) C.H.U. *m*, centre *m* hospitalo-universitaire

teaching staff *n* (*Brit*) enseignants *mpl*

tea cosy *n* couvre-théière *m*

teacup ['tiːkʌp] *n* tasse *f* à thé

teak [tiːk] *n* teck *m* ▷ *adj* en or de teck

tea leaves *npl* feuilles *fpl* de thé

team [tiːm] *n* équipe *f*; (*of animals*) attelage *m*
▶ **team up** *vi*: **to ~ up (with)** faire équipe (avec)

team games *npl* jeux *mpl* d'équipe

teamwork ['tiːmwəːk] *n* travail *m* d'équipe

tea party *n* thé *m* (*réception*)

teapot ['tiːpɔt] *n* théière *f*

tear¹ ['tɪəʳ] *n* larme *f*; **in** ~**s** en larmes; **to burst into** ~**s** fondre en larmes

tear² [tɛəʳ] (*pt* **tore**, *pp* **torn**) [tɔːʳ, tɔːn] *n* déchirure *f* ▷ *vt* déchirer ▷ *vi* se déchirer; **to** ~ **to pieces** *or* **to bits** *or* **to shreds** mettre en pièces; (*fig*) démolir
▶ **tear along** *vi* (*rush*) aller à toute vitesse
▶ **tear apart** *vt* (*also fig*) déchirer
▶ **tear away** *vt*: **to** ~ **o.s. away (from sth)** (*fig*) s'arracher (de qch)
▶ **tear down** *vt* (*building, statue*) démolir; (*poster, flag*) arracher
▶ **tear off** *vt* (*sheet of paper etc*) arracher; (*one's clothes*) enlever à toute vitesse
▶ **tear out** *vt* (*sheet of paper, cheque*) arracher
▶ **tear up** *vt* (*sheet of paper etc*) déchirer, mettre en morceaux *or* pièces

tearaway ['tɛərəweɪ] *n* (*inf*) casse-cou *m inv*

teardrop ['tɪədrɔp] *n* larme *f*

tearful ['tɪəful] *adj* larmoyant(e)

tear gas ['tɪə-] *n* gaz *m* lacrymogène

tearoom ['tiːruːm] *n* salon *m* de thé

tease [tiːz] *n* taquin(e) ▷ *vt* taquiner; (*unkindly*) tourmenter

tea set *n* service *m* à thé

teashop ['tiːʃɔp] *n* (*Brit*) salon *m* de thé

teaspoon ['tiːspuːn] *n* petite cuiller; (*also:* **teaspoonful**: *as measurement*) ≈ cuillerée *f* à café

tea strainer *n* passoire *f* (à thé)

teat [tiːt] *n* tétine *f*

teatime ['tiːtaɪm] *n* l'heure *f* du thé

tea towel *n* (*Brit*) torchon *m* (à vaisselle)

tea urn *n* fontaine *f* à thé

tech [tɛk] *n abbr* (*inf*) = **technology; technical college**

technical ['tɛknɪkl] *adj* technique

technical college *n* C.E.T. *m*, collège *m* d'enseignement technique

technicality [tɛknɪ'kælɪtɪ] *n* technicité *f*; (*detail*) détail *m* technique; **on a legal** ~ à cause de (*or* grâce à) l'application à la lettre d'une subtilité juridique; pour vice de forme

technically ['tɛknɪklɪ] *adv* techniquement; (*strictly speaking*) en théorie, en principe

technician [tɛk'nɪʃən] *n* technicien(ne)

technique [tɛk'niːk] *n* technique *f*

techno ['tɛknəu] *n* (*Mus*) techno *f*

technocrat ['tɛknəkræt] *n* technocrate *m/f*

technological [tɛknə'lɔdʒɪkl] *adj* technologique

technologist [tɛk'nɔlədʒɪst] *n* technologue *m/f*

technology [tɛk'nɔlədʒɪ] *n* technologie *f*

teddy ['tɛdɪ], **teddy bear** *n* ours *m* (en peluche)

tedious ['tiːdɪəs] *adj* fastidieux(-euse)

tedium ['tiːdɪəm] *n* ennui *m*

tee [tiː] *n* (*Golf*) tee *m*

teem [tiːm] *vi*: **to** ~ **(with)** grouiller (de); **it is** ~**ing (with rain)** il pleut à torrents

teen [tiːn] *adj* = **teenage** ▷ *n* (*US*) = **teenager**

teenage ['tiːneɪdʒ] *adj* (*fashions etc*) pour jeunes, pour adolescents; (*child*) qui est adolescent(e)

teenager ['tiːneɪdʒəʳ] *n* adolescent(e)

teens [ti:nz] *npl*: **to be in one's ~** être adolescent(e)

tee-shirt ['ti:ʃə:t] *n* = **T-shirt**

teeter ['ti:təʳ] *vi* chanceler, vaciller

teeth [ti:θ] *npl of* **tooth**

teethe [ti:ð] *vi* percer ses dents

teething ring ['ti:ðɪŋ-] *n* anneau *m* (*pour bébé qui perce ses dents*)

teething troubles ['ti:ðɪŋ-] *npl* (*fig*) difficultés initiales

teetotal ['ti:'təutl] *adj* (*person*) qui ne boit jamais d'alcool

teetotaller, (US) **teetotaler** ['ti:'təutləʳ] *n* personne *f* qui ne boit jamais d'alcool

TEFL ['tɛfl] *n abbr* = **Teaching of English as a Foreign Language**

Teflon® ['tɛflɔn] *n* Téflon® *m*

Teheran [tɛə'rɑ:n] *n* Téhéran

tel. *abbr* (= *telephone*) tél

Tel Aviv ['tɛlə'vi:v] *n* Tel Aviv

telecast ['tɛlɪkɑ:st] *vt* télédiffuser, téléviser

telecommunications ['tɛlɪkəmju:nɪ'keɪʃənz] *n* télécommunications *fpl*

teleconferencing [tɛlɪ'kɔnfərənsɪŋ] *n* téléconférence(s) *f(pl)*

telegram ['tɛlɪgræm] *n* télégramme *m*

telegraph ['tɛlɪgrɑ:f] *n* télégraphe *m*

telegraphic [tɛlɪ'græfɪk] *adj* télégraphique

telegraph pole ['tɛlɪgrɑ:f-] *n* poteau *m* télégraphique

telegraph wire *n* fil *m* télégraphique

telepathic [tɛlɪ'pæθɪk] *adj* télépathique

telepathy [tə'lɛpəθɪ] *n* télépathie *f*

telephone ['tɛlɪfəun] *n* téléphone *m* ▷ *vt* (*person*) téléphoner à; (*message*) téléphoner; **to have a ~** (*Brit*): **to be on the ~** (*subscriber*) être abonné(e) au téléphone; **to be on the ~** (*be speaking*) être au téléphone

telephone book *n* = **telephone directory**

telephone booth, (*Brit*) **telephone box** *n* cabine *f* téléphonique

telephone call *n* appel *m* téléphonique

telephone directory *n* annuaire *m* (du téléphone)

telephone exchange *n* central *m* (téléphonique)

telephone number *n* numéro *m* de téléphone

telephone operator *n* téléphoniste *m/f*, standardiste *m/f*

telephone tapping [-tæpɪŋ] *n* mise *f* sur écoute

telephonist [tə'lɛfənɪst] *n* (*Brit*) téléphoniste *m/f*

telephoto [tɛlɪ'fəutəu] *adj*: **~ lens** téléobjectif *m*

teleprinter ['tɛlɪprɪntəʳ] *n* téléscripteur *m*

telesales ['tɛlɪseɪlz] *npl* télévente *f*

telescope ['tɛlɪskəup] *n* télescope *m* ▷ *vi* se télescoper ▷ *vt* télescoper

telescopic [tɛlɪ'skɔpɪk] *adj* télescopique; (*umbrella*) à manche télescopique

Teletext® ['tɛlɪtɛkst] *n* télétexte *m*

telethon ['tɛlɪθɔn] *n* téléthon *m*

televise ['tɛlɪvaɪz] *vt* téléviser

television ['tɛlɪvɪʒən] *n* télévision *f*; **on ~** à la télévision

television licence *n* (*Brit*) redevance *f* (de l'audio-visuel)

television programme *n* émission *f* de télévision

television set *n* poste *m* de télévision, téléviseur *m*

telex ['tɛlɛks] *n* télex *m* ▷ *vt* (*message*) envoyer par télex; (*person*) envoyer un télex à ▷ *vi* envoyer un télex

tell (*pt, pp* told) [tɛl, təuld] *vt* dire; (*relate: story*) raconter; (*distinguish*): **to ~ sth from** distinguer qch de ▷ *vi* (*talk*): **to ~ of** parler de; (*have effect*) se faire sentir, se voir; **to ~ sb to do** dire à qn de faire; **to ~ sb about sth** (*place, object etc*) parler de qch à qn; (*what happened etc*) raconter qch à qn; **to ~ the time** (*know how to*) savoir lire l'heure; **can you ~ me the time?** pourriez-vous me dire l'heure?; **(I) ~ you what,** ... écoute, ...; **I can't ~ them apart** je n'arrive pas à les distinguer

▶ **tell off** *vt* réprimander, gronder

▶ **tell on** *vt fus* (*inform against*) dénoncer, rapporter contre

teller ['tɛləʳ] *n* (*in bank*) caissier(-ière)

telling ['tɛlɪŋ] *adj* (*remark, detail*) révélateur(-trice)

telltale ['tɛlteɪl] *n* rapporteur(-euse) ▷ *adj* (*sign*) éloquent(e), révélateur(-trice)

telly ['tɛlɪ] *n abbr* (Brit inf: = *television*) télé *f*

temerity [tə'mɛrɪtɪ] *n* témérité *f*

temp [tɛmp] *n* (*Brit*: = *temporary worker*) intérimaire *m/f* ▷ *vi* travailler comme intérimaire

temper ['tɛmpəʳ] *n* (*nature*) caractère *m*; (*mood*) humeur *f*; (*fit of anger*) colère *f* ▷ *vt* (*moderate*) tempérer, adoucir; **to be in a ~** être en colère; **to lose one's ~** se mettre en colère; **to keep one's ~** rester calme

temperament ['tɛmprəmənt] *n* (*nature*) tempérament *m*

temperamental [tɛmprə'mɛntl] *adj* capricieux(-euse)

temperance ['tɛmpərns] *n* modération *f*; (*in drinking*) tempérance *f*

temperate ['tɛmprət] *adj* modéré(e); (*climate*) tempéré(e)

temperature ['tɛmprətʃəʳ] *n* température *f*; **to have** *or* **run a ~** avoir de la fièvre

temperature chart *n* (*Med*) feuille *f* de température

tempered ['tɛmpəd] *adj* (*steel*) trempé(e)

tempest ['tɛmpɪst] *n* tempête *f*

tempestuous [tɛm'pɛstjuəs] *adj* (*fig*) orageux(-euse); (: *person*) passionné(e)

tempi ['tɛmpɪ] *npl of* **tempo**

template ['tɛmplɪt] *n* patron *m*

temple ['tɛmpl] *n* (*building*) temple *m*; (*Anat*) tempe *f*

templet ['tɛmplɪt] *n* = **template**

tempo (*pl* **-s** *or* **tempi**) ['tɛmpəu, 'tɛmpi:] *n*

tempo m; (fig: of life etc) rythme m
temporal ['tempərl] adj temporel(le)
temporarily ['tempərərılı] adv
temporairement; provisoirement
temporary ['tempərərı] adj temporaire,
provisoire; (job, worker) temporaire; **~ secretary**
(secrétaire f) intérimaire f; **a ~ teacher** un
professeur remplaçant or suppléant
temporize ['tempəraız] vi atermoyer; transiger
tempt [tempt] vt tenter; **to ~ sb into doing**
induire qn à faire; **to be ~ed to do sth** être
tenté(e) de faire qch
temptation [temp'teıʃən] n tentation f
tempting ['temptıŋ] adj tentant(e); (food)
appétissant(e)
ten [ten] num dix ▷ n: **~s of thousands** des
dizaines fpl de milliers
tenable ['tenəbl] adj défendable
tenacious [tə'neıʃəs] adj tenace
tenacity [tə'næsıtı] n ténacité f
tenancy ['tenənsı] n location f; état m de
locataire
tenant ['tenənt] n locataire m/f
tend [tend] vt s'occuper de; (sick etc) soigner ▷ vi:
to ~ to do avoir tendance à faire; (colour): **to ~
to** tirer sur
tendency ['tendənsı] n tendance f
tender ['tendər] adj tendre; (delicate) délicat(e);
(sore) sensible; (affectionate) tendre, doux (douce)
▷ n (Comm: offer) soumission f; (money): **legal ~**
cours légal ▷ vt offrir; **to ~ one's resignation**
donner sa démission; **to put in a ~ (for)** faire
une soumission (pour); **to put work out to ~**
(Brit) mettre un contrat en adjudication
tenderize ['tendəraız] vt (Culin) attendrir
tenderly ['tendəlı] adv tendrement
tenderness ['tendənıs] n tendresse f; (of meat)
tendreté f
tendon ['tendən] n tendon m
tenement ['tenəmənt] n immeuble m (de
rapport)
Tenerife [tenə'ri:f] n Ténérife f
tenet ['tenət] n principe m
Tenn. abbr (US) = **Tennessee**
tenner ['tenər] n (Brit inf) billet m de dix livres
tennis ['tenıs] n tennis m ▷ cpd (club, match,
racket, player) de tennis
tennis ball n balle f de tennis
tennis court n (court m de) tennis m
tennis elbow n (Med) synovite f du coude
tennis match n match m de tennis
tennis player n joueur(-euse) de tennis
tennis racket n raquette f de tennis
tennis shoes npl (chaussures fpl de) tennis mpl
tenor ['tenər] n (Mus) ténor m; (of speech etc) sens
général
tenpin bowling ['tenpın-] n (Brit) bowling m (à
10 quilles)
tense [tens] adj tendu(e); (person) tendu,
crispé(e) ▷ n (Ling) temps m ▷ vt (tighten: muscles)
tendre
tenseness ['tensnıs] n tension f

tension ['tenʃən] n tension f
tent [tent] n tente f
tentacle ['tentəkl] n tentacule m
tentative ['tentətıv] adj timide, hésitant(e);
(conclusion) provisoire
tenterhooks ['tentəhuks] npl: **on ~** sur des
charbons ardents
tenth [tenθ] num dixième
tent peg n piquet m de tente
tent pole n montant m de tente
tenuous ['tenjuəs] adj ténu(e)
tenure ['tenjuər] n (of property) bail m; (of job)
période f de jouissance; statut m de titulaire
tepid ['tepıd] adj tiède
Ter. abbr = **terrace**
term [tə:m] n (limit) terme m; (word) terme, mot
m; (Scol) trimestre m; (Law) session f ▷ vt
appeler; **terms** npl (conditions) conditions fpl;
(Comm) tarif m; **~ of imprisonment** peine f de
prison; **his ~ of office** la période où il était en
fonction; **in the short/long ~** à court/long
terme; **"easy ~s"** (Comm) "facilités de
paiement"; **to come to ~s with** (problem) faire
face à; **to be on good ~s with** bien s'entendre
avec, être en bons termes avec
terminal ['tə:mınl] adj terminal(e); (disease)
dans sa phase terminale; (patient) incurable ▷ n
(Elec) borne f; (for oil, ore etc, also Comput) terminal
m; (also: **air terminal**) aérogare f; (Brit: also:
coach terminal) gare routière
terminally ['tə:mınlı] adv: **to be ~ ill** être
condamné(e)
terminate ['tə:mıneıt] vt mettre fin à;
(pregnancy) interrompre ▷ vi: **to ~ in** finir en or
par
termination [tə:mı'neıʃən] n fin f; cessation f;
(of contract) résiliation f; **~ of pregnancy** (Med)
interruption f de grossesse
termini ['tə:mınaı] npl of **terminus**
terminology [tə:mı'nɔlədʒı] n terminologie f
terminus (pl **termini**) ['tə:mınəs, 'tə:mınaı] n
terminus m inv
termite ['tə:maıt] n termite m
term paper n (US University) dissertation
trimestrielle
terrace ['terəs] n terrasse f; (Brit: row of houses)
rangée f de maisons (attenantes les unes aux autres);
the ~s (Brit Sport) les gradins mpl
terraced ['terəst] adj (garden) en terrasses; (in a
row: house) attenant(e) aux maisons voisines
terracotta ['terə'kɔtə] n terre cuite
terrain [te'reın] n terrain m (sol)
terrestrial [tı'restrıəl] adj terrestre
terrible ['terıbl] adj terrible, atroce; (weather,
work) affreux(-euse), épouvantable
terribly ['terıblı] adv terriblement; (very badly)
affreusement mal
terrier ['terıər] n terrier m (chien)
terrific [tə'rıfık] adj (very great) fantastique,
incroyable, terrible; (wonderful) formidable,
sensationnel(le)
terrified ['terıfaıd] adj terrifié(e); **to be ~ of sth**

avoir très peur de qch

terrify ['tɛrɪfaɪ] vt terrifier

terrifying ['tɛrɪfaɪɪŋ] adj terrifiant(e)

territorial [tɛrɪ'tɔːrɪəl] adj territorial(e)

territorial waters npl eaux territoriales

territory ['tɛrɪtərɪ] n territoire m

terror ['tɛrə'] n terreur f

terrorism ['tɛrərɪzəm] n terrorisme m

terrorist ['tɛrərɪst] n terroriste m/f

terrorist attack n attentat m terroriste

terrorize ['tɛrəraɪz] vt terroriser

terse [tɜːs] adj (style) concis(e); (reply) laconique

tertiary ['tɜːʃərɪ] adj tertiaire; ~ **education** (Brit) enseignement m postscolaire

TESL ['tɛsl] n abbr = **Teaching of English as a Second Language**

test [tɛst] n (trial, check) essai m; (: of goods in factory) contrôle m; (of courage etc) épreuve f; (Med) examen m; (Chem) analyse f; (exam: of intelligence etc) test m (d'aptitude); (Scol) interrogation f de contrôle; (also: **driving test**) (examen du) permis m de conduire ▷ vt essayer; contrôler; mettre à l'épreuve; examiner; analyser; tester; faire subir une interrogation à; **to put sth to the ~** mettre qch à l'épreuve

testament ['tɛstəmənt] n testament m; **the Old/New T~** l'Ancien/le Nouveau Testament

test ban n (also: **nuclear test ban**) interdiction f des essais nucléaires

test case n (Law) affaire f qui fait jurisprudence

testes ['tɛstiːz] npl testicules mpl

test flight n vol m d'essai

testicle ['tɛstɪkl] n testicule m

testify ['tɛstɪfaɪ] vi (Law) témoigner, déposer; **to ~ to sth** (Law) attester qch; (gen) témoigner de qch

testimonial [tɛstɪ'məunɪəl] n (Brit: reference) recommandation f; (gift) témoignage m d'estime

testimony ['tɛstɪmənɪ] n (Law) témoignage m, déposition f

testing ['tɛstɪŋ] adj (situation, period) difficile

test match n (Cricket, Rugby) match international

testosterone [tɛs'tɔstərəun] n testostérone f

test paper n (Scol) interrogation écrite

test pilot n pilote m d'essai

test tube n éprouvette f

test-tube baby ['tɛsttjuːb-] n bébé-éprouvette m

testy ['tɛstɪ] adj irritable

tetanus ['tɛtənəs] n tétanos m

tetchy ['tɛtʃɪ] adj hargneux(-euse)

tether ['tɛðə'] vt attacher ▷ n: **at the end of one's ~** à bout (de patience)

Tex. abbr (US) = **Texas**

text [tɛkst] n texte m; (on mobile phone) texto m, SMS m inv ▷ vt (inf) envoyer un texto or SMS à

textbook ['tɛkstbuk] n manuel m

textile ['tɛkstaɪl] n textile m

text message n texto m, SMS m inv

text messaging [-'mɛsɪdʒɪŋ] n messagerie textuelle

textual ['tɛkstjuəl] adj textuel(le)

texture ['tɛkstʃə'] n texture f; (of skin, paper etc) grain m

TGIF abbr (inf) = **thank God it's Friday**

TGWU n abbr (Brit: = Transport and General Workers' Union) syndicat de transporteurs

Thai [taɪ] adj thaïlandais(e) ▷ n Thaïlandais(e); (Ling) thaï m

Thailand ['taɪlænd] n Thaïlande f

Thames [tɛmz] n: **the (River)** ~ la Tamise

than [ðæn, ðən] conj que; (with numerals): **more ~ 10/once** plus de 10/d'une fois; **I have more/less ~ you** j'en ai plus/moins que toi; **she has more apples ~ pears** elle a plus de pommes que de poires; **it is better to phone ~ to write** il vaut mieux téléphoner (plutôt) qu'écrire; **she is older ~ you think** elle est plus âgée que tu le crois; **no sooner did he leave ~ the phone rang** il venait de partir quand le téléphone a sonné

thank [θæŋk] vt remercier, dire merci à; **thanks** npl remerciements mpl ▷ excl merci!; **~ you (very much)** merci (beaucoup); **~ heavens, ~ God** Dieu merci; **~s to** (prep) grâce à

thankful ['θæŋkful] adj: **~ (for)** reconnaissant(e) (de); **~ for/that** (relieved) soulagé(e) de/que

thankfully ['θæŋkfəlɪ] adv avec reconnaissance; avec soulagement; (fortunately) heureusement; **~ there were few victims** il y eut fort heureusement peu de victimes

thankless ['θæŋklɪs] adj ingrat(e)

Thanksgiving ['θæŋksgɪvɪŋ], **Thanksgiving Day** n jour m d'action de grâce

 KEYWORD

that [ðæt] adj (demonstrative: pl **those**) ce, cet + vowel or h mute, cette f; **that man/woman/book** cet homme/cette femme/ce livre; (not this) cet homme-là/cette femme-là/ce livre-là; **that one** celui-là (celle-là)

▷ pron **1** (demonstrative: pl **those**) ce; (not this one) cela, ça; (that one) celui (celle); **who's that?** qui est-ce?; **what's that?** qu'est-ce que c'est?; **is that you?** c'est toi?; **I prefer this to that** je préfère ceci à cela or ça; **that's what he said** c'est or voilà ce qu'il a dit; **will you eat all that?** tu vas manger tout ça?; **that is (to say)** c'est-à-dire, à savoir; **at or with that, he ...** là-dessus, il ...; **do it like that** fais-le comme ça

2 (relative: subject) qui; (: object) que; (: after prep) lequel (laquelle), lesquels (lesquelles) pl; **the book that I read** le livre que j'ai lu; **the books that are in the library** les livres qui sont dans la bibliothèque; **all that I have** tout ce que j'ai; **the box that I put it in** la boîte dans laquelle je l'ai mis; **the people that I spoke to** les gens auxquels or à qui j'ai parlé; **not that I know of** pas à ma connaissance

3 (*relative: of time*) où; **the day that he came** le jour où il est venu

▷ *conj* que; **he thought that I was ill** il pensait que j'étais malade

▷ *adv* (*demonstrative*): **I don't like it that much** ça ne me plaît pas tant que ça; **I didn't know it was that bad** je ne savais pas que c'était si *or* aussi mauvais; **that high** aussi haut; si haut; **it's about that high** c'est à peu près de cette hauteur

thatched [θætʃt] *adj* (*roof*) de chaume; **~ cottage** chaumière *f*

Thatcherism ['θætʃərɪzəm] *n* thatchérisme *m*

thaw [θɔː] *n* dégel *m* ▷ *vi* (*ice*) fondre; (*food*) dégeler ▷ *vt* (*food*) (faire) dégeler; **it's ~ing** (*weather*) il dégèle

 KEYWORD

the [ðiː, ðə] *def art* **1** (*gen*) le, la *f*, l' + *vowel or h mute*, les *pl* (NB: *à* + *le(s)* = **au(x)**; *de* + *le* = **du**; *de* + *les* = **des**); **the boy/girl/ink** le garçon/la fille/l'encre; **the children** les enfants; **the history of the world** l'histoire du monde; **give it to the postman** donne-le au facteur; **to play the piano/flute** jouer du piano/de la flûte

2 (+ *adj to form n*) le, la *f*, l' + *vowel or* h *mute*, les *pl*; **the rich and the poor** les riches et les pauvres; **to attempt the impossible** tenter l'impossible

3 (*in titles*): **Elizabeth the First** Elisabeth première; **Peter the Great** Pierre le Grand

4 (*in comparisons*): **the more he works, the more he earns** plus il travaille, plus il gagne de l'argent; **the sooner the better** le plus tôt sera le mieux

theatre, (*US*) **theater** ['θɪətə^r] *n* théâtre *m*; (*also:* **lecture theatre**) amphithéâtre *m*, amphi *m* (*inf*); (*Med: also:* **operating theatre**) salle *f* d'opération

theatre-goer, (*US*) **theater-goer** ['θɪətəɡəʊə^r] *n* habitué(e) du théâtre

theatrical [θɪ'ætrɪkl] *adj* théâtral(e); **~ company** troupe *f* de théâtre

theft [θɛft] *n* vol *m* (*larcin*)

their [ðɛə^r] *adj* leur, leurs *pl*; *see also* **my**

theirs [ðɛəz] *pron* le (la) leur, les leurs; **it is ~** c'est à eux; **a friend of ~** un de leurs amis; *see also* **mine**¹

them [ðɛm, ðəm] *pron* (*direct*) les; (*indirect*) leur; (*stressed, after prep*) eux (elles); **I see ~** je les vois; **give ~ the book** donne-leur le livre; **give me a few of ~** donnez m'en quelques uns (*or* quelques unes); *see also* **me**

theme [θiːm] *n* thème *m*

theme park *n* parc *m* à thème

theme song *n* chanson principale

themselves [ðəm'sɛlvz] *pl pron* (*reflexive*) se; (*emphatic, after prep*) eux-mêmes (elles-mêmes); **between ~** entre eux (elles); *see also* **oneself**

then [ðɛn] *adv* (*at that time*) alors, à ce moment-là; (*next*) puis, ensuite; (*and also*) et puis ▷ *conj* (*therefore*) alors, dans ce cas ▷ *adj*: **the ~ president** le président d'alors *or* de l'époque; **by ~** (*past*) à ce moment-là; (*future*) d'ici là; **from ~ on** dès lors; **before ~** avant; **until ~** jusqu'à ce moment-là, jusque-là; **and ~ what?** et puis après?; **what do you want me to do ~?** (*afterwards*) que veux-tu que je fasse ensuite?; (*in that case*) bon alors, qu'est-ce que je fais?

theologian [θɪə'ləudʒən] *n* théologien(ne)

theological [θɪə'lɔdʒɪkl] *adj* théologique

theology [θɪ'ɔlədʒɪ] *n* théologie *f*

theorem ['θɪərəm] *n* théorème *m*

theoretical [θɪə'rɛtɪkl] *adj* théorique

theorize ['θɪəraɪz] *vi* élaborer une théorie, (*pej*) faire des théories

theory ['θɪərɪ] *n* théorie *f*

therapeutic [θɛrə'pjuːtɪk] *adj* thérapeutique

therapist ['θɛrəpɪst] *n* thérapeute *m/f*

therapy ['θɛrəpɪ] *n* thérapie *f*

 KEYWORD

there [ðɛə^r] *adv* **1**: **there is**, **there are** il y a; **there are 3 of them** (*people, things*) il y en a 3; **there is no-one here/no bread left** il n'y a personne/il n'y a plus de pain; **there has been an accident** il y a eu un accident

2 (*referring to place*) là, là-bas; **it's there** c'est là(-bas); **in/on/up/down there** là-dedans/là-dessus/là-haut/en bas; **he went there on Friday** il y est allé vendredi; **to go there and back** faire l'aller-retour; **I want that book there** je veux ce livre-là; **there he is!** le voilà!

3: **there, there** (*esp to child*) allons, allons!

thereabouts ['ðɛərə'bauts] *adv* (*place*) par là, près de là; (*amount*) environ, à peu près

thereafter [ðɛər'ɑːftə^r] *adv* par la suite

thereby ['ðɛəbaɪ] *adv* ainsi

therefore ['ðɛəfɔː^r] *adv* donc, par conséquent

there's ['ðɛəz] = **there is; there has**

thereupon [ðɛərə'pɔn] *adv* (*at that point*) sur ce; (*formal: on that subject*) à ce sujet

thermal ['θəːml] *adj* thermique; **~ paper/ printer** papier *m*/imprimante *f* thermique; **~ underwear** sous-vêtements *mpl* en Thermolactyl®

thermodynamics ['θəːmədaɪ'næmɪks] *n* thermodynamique *f*

thermometer [θə'mɔmɪtə^r] *n* thermomètre *m*

thermonuclear ['θəːməu'njuːklɪə^r] *adj* thermonucléaire

Thermos® ['θəːməs] *n* (*also:* **Thermos flask**) thermos® *m or f inv*

thermostat ['θəːməustæt] *n* thermostat *m*

thesaurus [θɪ'sɔːrəs] *n* dictionnaire *m* synonymique

these [ðiːz] *pl pron* ceux-ci (celles-ci) ▷ *pl adj* ces; (*not those*): **~ books** ces livres-ci

thesis (*pl* **theses**) ['θiːsɪs, 'θiːsiːz] *n* thèse *f*

they [ðeɪ] *pl pron* ils (elles); (*stressed*) eux (elles); **~**

t

say that ... (it is said that) on dit que ...

they'd [ðeɪd] = **they had; they would**

they'll [ðeɪl] = **they shall; they will**

they're [ðɛəʳ] = **they are**

they've [ðeɪv] = **they have**

thick [θɪk] adj épais(se); (crowd) dense; (stupid) bête, borné(e) ▷ n: **in the ~ of** au beau milieu de, en plein cœur de; **it's 20 cm ~** ça a 20 cm d'épaisseur

thicken ['θɪkn] vi s'épaissir ▷ vt (sauce etc) épaissir

thicket ['θɪkɪt] n fourré m, hallier m

thickly ['θɪklɪ] adv (spread) en couche épaisse; (cut) en tranches épaisses; **~ populated** à forte densité de population

thickness ['θɪknɪs] n épaisseur f

thickset [θɪk'sɛt] adj trapu(e), costaud(e)

thick-skinned [θɪk'skɪnd] adj (fig) peu sensible

thief (pl **thieves**) [θi:f, θi:vz] n voleur(-euse)

thieving ['θi:vɪŋ] n vol m (larcin)

thigh [θaɪ] n cuisse f

thighbone ['θaɪbəun] n fémur m

thimble ['θɪmbl] n dé m (à coudre)

thin [θɪn] adj mince; (skinny) maigre; (soup) peu épais(se); (hair, crowd) clairsemé(e); (fog) léger(-ère) ▷ vt (hair) éclaircir; (also: **thin down**: sauce, paint) délayer ▷ vi (fog) s'éclaircir; (also: **thin out**: crowd) se disperser; **his hair is ~ning** il se dégarnit

thing [θɪŋ] n chose f; (object) objet m; (contraption) truc m; **things** npl (belongings) affaires fpl; **first ~ (in the morning)** à la première heure, tout de suite (le matin); **last ~ (at night), he ...** juste avant de se coucher, il ...; **the ~ is ...** c'est que ...; **for one ~** d'abord; **the best ~ would be to** le mieux serait de; **how are ~s?** comment ça va?; **to have a ~ about** (be obsessed by) être obsédé(e) par; (hate) détester; **poor ~!** le (or la) pauvre!

think (pt, pp **thought**) [θɪŋk, θɔ:t] vi penser, réfléchir ▷ vt penser, croire; (imagine) s'imaginer; **to ~ of** penser à; **what do you ~ of it?** qu'en pensez-vous?; **what did you ~ of them?** qu'avez-vous pensé d'eux?; **to ~ about sth/sb** penser à qch/qn; **I'll ~ about it** je vais y réfléchir; **to ~ of doing** avoir l'idée de faire; **I ~ so/not** je crois or pense que oui/non; **to ~ well of** avoir une haute opinion de; **~ again!** attention, réfléchis bien!; **to ~ aloud** penser tout haut

▶ **think out** vt (plan) bien réfléchir à; (solution) trouver

▶ **think over** vt bien réfléchir à; **I'd like to ~ things over** (offer, suggestion) j'aimerais bien y réfléchir un peu

▶ **think through** vt étudier dans tous les détails

▶ **think up** vt inventer, trouver

thinking ['θɪŋkɪŋ] n: **to my (way of) ~** selon moi

think tank n groupe m de réflexion

thinly ['θɪnlɪ] adv (cut) en tranches fines; (spread) en couche mince

thinness ['θɪnnɪs] n minceur f; maigreur f

third [θə:d] num troisième ▷ n troisième m/f; (fraction) tiers m; (Aut) troisième (vitesse) f; (Brit Scol: degree) ≈ licence f avec mention passable; **a ~ of** le tiers de

third-degree burns ['θə:ddɪgri:-] npl brûlures fpl au troisième degré

thirdly ['θə:dlɪ] adv troisièmement

third party insurance n (Brit) assurance f au tiers

third-rate ['θə:d'reɪt] adj de qualité médiocre

Third World n: **the ~** le Tiers-Monde

thirst [θə:st] n soif f

thirsty ['θə:stɪ] adj qui a soif, assoiffé(e); (work) qui donne soif; **to be ~** avoir soif

thirteen [θə:'ti:n] num treize

thirteenth [-'ti:nθ] num treizième

thirtieth ['θə:tɪɪθ] num trentième

thirty ['θə:tɪ] num trente

○ **KEYWORD**

this [ðɪs] adj (demonstrative: pl **these**) ce, cet + vowel or h mute, cette f; **this man/woman/book** cet homme/cette femme/ce livre; (not that) cet homme-ci/cette femme-ci/ce livre-ci; **this one** celui-ci (celle-ci); **this time** cette fois-ci; **this time last year** l'année dernière à la même époque; **this way** (in this direction) par ici; (in this fashion) de cette façon, ainsi

▷ pron (demonstrative: pl **these**) ce; (not that one) celui-ci (celle-ci), ceci; **who's this?** qui est-ce?; **what's this?** qu'est-ce que c'est?; **I prefer this to that** je préfère ceci à cela; **they were talking of this and that** ils parlaient de choses et d'autres; **this is where I live** c'est ici que j'habite; **this is what he said** voici ce qu'il a dit; **this is Mr Brown** (in introductions) je vous présente Mr Brown; (in photo) c'est Mr Brown; (on telephone) ici Mr Brown

▷ adv (demonstrative): **it was about this big** c'était à peu près de cette grandeur or grand comme ça; **I didn't know it was this bad** je ne savais pas que c'était si or aussi mauvais

thistle ['θɪsl] n chardon m

thong [θɔŋ] n lanière f

thorn [θɔ:n] n épine f

thorny ['θɔ:nɪ] adj épineux(-euse)

thorough ['θʌrə] adj (search) minutieux(-euse); (knowledge, research) approfondi(e); (work, person) consciencieux(-euse); (cleaning) à fond

thoroughbred ['θʌrəbrɛd] n (horse) pur-sang m inv

thoroughfare ['θʌrəfɛəʳ] n rue f; **"no ~"** (Brit) "passage interdit"

thoroughgoing ['θʌrəgəuɪŋ] adj (analysis) approfondi(e); (reform) profond(e)

thoroughly ['θʌrəlɪ] adv (search) minutieusement; (study) en profondeur; (clean) à fond; (very) tout à fait; **he ~ agreed** il était tout à fait d'accord

thoroughness ['θʌrənɪs] n soin (méticuleux)

those [ðəuz] pl pron ceux-là (celles-là) ▷ pl adj

ces; (not these): ~ **books** ces livres-là

though [ðəu] conj bien que + sub, quoique + sub ▷ adv pourtant; **even** ~ quand bien même + conditional; **it's not easy,** ~ pourtant, ce n'est pas facile

thought [θɔ:t] pt, pp of **think** ▷ n pensée f; (idea) idée f; (opinion) avis m; (intention) intention f; **after much** ~ après mûre réflexion; **I've just had a** ~ je viens de penser à quelque chose; **to give sth some** ~ réfléchir à qch

thoughtful ['θɔ:tful] adj (deep in thought) pensif(-ive); (serious) réfléchi(e); (considerate) prévenant(e)

thoughtfully ['θɔ:tfəli] adv pensivement; avec prévenance

thoughtless ['θɔ:tlɪs] adj qui manque de considération

thoughtlessly ['θɔ:tlɪsli] adv inconsidérément

thought-provoking ['θɔ:tprəvəukɪŋ] adj stimulant(e)

thousand ['θauzənd] num mille; **one** ~ mille; **two** ~ deux mille; **~s of** des milliers de

thousandth ['θauzəntθ] num millième

thrash [θræʃ] vt rouer de coups; (as punishment) donner une correction à; (inf: defeat) battre à plate(s) couture(s)
  ▶ **thrash about** vi se débattre
  ▶ **thrash out** vt débattre de

thrashing ['θræʃɪŋ] n: **to give sb a** ~; = **to thrash sb**

thread [θrɛd] n fil m; (of screw) pas m, filetage m ▷ vt (needle) enfiler; **to** ~ **one's way between** se faufiler entre

threadbare ['θrɛdbɛəʳ] adj râpé(e), élimé(e)

threat [θrɛt] n menace f; **to be under** ~ **of** être menacé(e) de

threaten ['θrɛtn] vi (storm) menacer ▷ vt: **to** ~ **sb with sth/to do** menacer qn de qch/de faire

threatening ['θrɛtnɪŋ] adj menaçant(e)

three [θri:] num trois

three-dimensional [θri:dɪ'mɛnʃənl] adj à trois dimensions; (film) en relief

threefold ['θri:fəuld] adv: **to increase** ~ tripler

three-piece suit ['θri:pi:s-] n complet m (avec gilet)

three-piece suite n salon m (canapé et deux fauteuils)

three-ply [θri:'plaɪ] adj (wood) à trois épaisseurs; (wool) trois fils inv

three-quarters [θri:'kwɔ:təz] npl trois-quarts mpl; ~ **full** aux trois-quarts plein

three-wheeler [θri:'wi:ləʳ] n (car) voiture f à trois roues

thresh [θrɛʃ] vt (Agr) battre

threshing machine ['θrɛʃɪŋ-] n batteuse f

threshold ['θrɛʃhəuld] n seuil m; **to be on the** ~ **of** (fig) être au seuil de

threshold agreement n (Econ) accord m d'indexation des salaires

threw [θru:] pt of **throw**

thrift [θrɪft] n économie f

thrifty ['θrɪfti] adj économe

thrill [θrɪl] n (excitement) émotion f, sensation forte; (shudder) frisson m ▷ vi tressaillir, frissonner ▷ vt (audience) électriser

thrilled [θrɪld] adj: ~ **(with)** ravi(e) de

thriller ['θrɪləʳ] n film m (or roman m or pièce f) à suspense

thrilling ['θrɪlɪŋ] adj (book, play etc) saisissant(e); (news, discovery) excitant(e)

thrive (pt **-d** or **throve**, pp **-d** or **thriven**) [θraɪv, θrəuv, 'θrɪvn] vi pousser or se développer bien; (business) prospérer; **he ~s on it** cela lui réussit

thriving ['θraɪvɪŋ] adj vigoureux(-euse); (business, community) prospère

throat [θrəut] n gorge f; **to have a sore** ~ avoir mal à la gorge

throb [θrɔb] n (of heart) pulsation f; (of engine) vibration f; (of pain) élancement m ▷ vi (heart) palpiter; (engine) vibrer; (pain) lanciner; (wound) causer des élancements; **my head is ~bing** j'ai des élancements dans la tête

throes [θrəuz] npl: **in the** ~ **of** au beau milieu de; en proie à; **in the** ~ **of death** à l'agonie

thrombosis [θrɔm'bəusɪs] n thrombose f

throne [θrəun] n trône m

throng ['θrɔŋ] n foule f ▷ vt se presser dans

throttle ['θrɔtl] n (Aut) accélérateur m ▷ vt étrangler

through [θru:] prep à travers; (time) pendant, durant; (by means of) par, par l'intermédiaire de; (owing to) à cause de ▷ adj (ticket, train, passage) direct(e) ▷ adv à travers; **(from) Monday ~ Friday** (US) de lundi à vendredi; **to let sb** ~ laisser passer qn; **to put sb** ~ **to sb** (Tel) passer qn à qn; **to be** ~ (Brit; Tel) avoir la communication; (esp US: have finished) avoir fini; **"no ~ traffic"** (US) "passage interdit"; **"no ~ road"** (Brit) "impasse"

throughout [θru:'aut] prep (place) partout dans; (time) durant tout(e) le (la) ▷ adv partout

throughput ['θru:put] n (of goods, materials) quantité de matières premières utilisée; (Comput) débit m

throve [θrəuv] pt of **thrive**

throw [θrəu] n jet m; (Sport) lancer m ▷ vt (pt **threw**, pp **-n**) [θru:, θrəun] lancer, jeter; (Sport) lancer; (rider) désarçonner; (fig) décontenancer; (pottery) tourner; **to** ~ **a party** donner une réception
  ▶ **throw about, throw around** vt (litter etc) éparpiller
  ▶ **throw away** vt jeter; (money) gaspiller
  ▶ **throw in** vt (Sport: ball) remettre en jeu; (include) ajouter
  ▶ **throw off** vt se débarrasser de
  ▶ **throw out** vt jeter; (reject) rejeter; (person) mettre à la porte
  ▶ **throw together** vt (clothes, meal etc) assembler à la hâte; (essay) bâcler
  ▶ **throw up** vi vomir

throwaway ['θrəuəweɪ] adj à jeter

throwback ['θrəubæk] n: **it's a** ~ **to** ça nous etc ramène à

t

throw-in ['θrəʊɪn] n (Sport) remise f en jeu
thrown [θrəʊn] pp of **throw**
thru [θruː] (US) = **through**
thrush [θrʌʃ] n (Zool) grive f; (Med: esp in children) muguet m; (: in women: Brit) muguet vaginal
thrust [θrʌst] n (Tech) poussée f ▷ vt (pt, pp **thrust**) pousser brusquement; (push in) enfoncer
thrusting ['θrʌstɪŋ] adj dynamique; qui se met trop en avant
thud [θʌd] n bruit sourd
thug [θʌg] n voyou m
thumb [θʌm] n (Anat) pouce m ▷ vt (book) feuilleter; **to ~ a lift** faire de l'auto-stop, arrêter une voiture; **to give sb/sth the ~s up/~s down** donner/refuser de donner le feu vert à qn/qch
  ▸ **thumb through** vt (book) feuilleter
thumb index n répertoire m (à onglets)
thumbnail ['θʌmneɪl] n ongle m du pouce
thumbnail sketch n croquis m
thumbtack ['θʌmtæk] n (US) punaise f (clou)
thump [θʌmp] n grand coup; (sound) bruit sourd ▷ vt cogner sur ▷ vi cogner, frapper
thunder ['θʌndəʳ] n tonnerre m ▷ vi tonner; (train etc): **to ~ past** passer dans un grondement or un bruit de tonnerre
thunderbolt ['θʌndəbəʊlt] n foudre f
thunderclap ['θʌndəklæp] n coup m de tonnerre
thunderous ['θʌndrəs] adj étourdissant(e)
thunderstorm ['θʌndəstɔːm] n orage m
thunderstruck ['θʌndəstrʌk] adj (fig) abasourdi(e)
thundery ['θʌndərɪ] adj orageux(-euse)
Thursday ['θəːzdɪ] n jeudi m; see also **Tuesday**
thus [ðʌs] adv ainsi
thwart [θwɔːt] vt contrecarrer
thyme [taɪm] n thym m
thyroid ['θaɪrɔɪd] n thyroïde f
tiara [tɪ'ɑːrə] n (woman's) diadème m
Tibet [tɪ'bɛt] n Tibet m
Tibetan [tɪ'bɛtən] adj tibétain(e) ▷ n Tibétain(e); (Ling) tibétain m
tibia ['tɪbɪə] n tibia m
tic [tɪk] n tic (nerveux)
tick [tɪk] n (sound: of clock) tic-tac m; (mark) coche f; (Zool) tique f; (Brit inf): **in a ~** dans un instant; (Brit inf: credit): **to buy sth on ~** acheter qch à crédit ▷ vi faire tic-tac ▷ vt (item on list) cocher; **to put a ~ against sth** cocher qch
  ▸ **tick off** vt (item on list) cocher; (person) réprimander, attraper
  ▸ **tick over** vi (Brit: engine) tourner au ralenti; (: fig) aller or marcher doucement
ticker tape ['tɪkə-] n bande f de téléscripteur; (US: in celebrations) ≈ serpentin m
ticket ['tɪkɪt] n billet m; (for bus, tube) ticket m; (in shop: on goods) étiquette f; (: from cash register) reçu m, ticket; (for library) carte f; (also: **parking ticket**) contravention f, p.-v. m; (US Pol) liste électorale (soutenue par un parti); **to get a (parking) ~** (Aut) attraper une contravention (pour stationnement illégal)
ticket agency n (Theat) agence f de spectacles

ticket barrier n (Brit: Rail) portillon m automatique
ticket collector n contrôleur(-euse)
ticket holder n personne munie d'un billet
ticket inspector n contrôleur(-euse)
ticket machine n billetterie f automatique
ticket office n guichet m, bureau m de vente des billets
tickle ['tɪkl] n chatouillement m ▷ vi chatouiller ▷ vt chatouiller; (fig) plaire à; faire rire
ticklish ['tɪklɪʃ] adj (person) chatouilleux(-euse); (which tickles: blanket) qui chatouille; (: cough) qui irrite; (problem) épineux(-euse)
tidal ['taɪdl] adj à marée
tidal wave n raz-de-marée m inv
tidbit ['tɪdbɪt] n (esp US) = **titbit**
tiddlywinks ['tɪdlɪwɪŋks] n jeu m de puce
tide [taɪd] n marée f; (fig: of events) cours m ▷ vt: **to ~ sb over** dépanner qn; **high/low ~** marée haute/basse
tidily ['taɪdɪlɪ] adv avec soin, soigneusement
tidiness ['taɪdɪnɪs] n bon ordre; goût m de l'ordre
tidy ['taɪdɪ] adj (room) bien rangé(e); (dress, work) net (nette), soigné(e); (person) ordonné(e), qui a de l'ordre; (: in character) soigneux(-euse); (mind) méthodique ▷ vt (also: **tidy up**) ranger; **to ~ o.s. up** s'arranger
tie [taɪ] n (string etc) cordon m; (Brit: also: **necktie**) cravate f; (fig: link) lien m; (Sport: draw) égalité f de points; match nul; (: match) rencontre f; (US Rail) traverse f ▷ vt (parcel) attacher; (ribbon) nouer ▷ vi (Sport) faire match nul; finir à égalité de points; **"black/white ~"** "smoking/habit de rigueur"; **family ~s** liens de famille; **to ~ sth in a bow** faire un nœud à or avec qch; **to ~ a knot in sth** faire un nœud à qch
  ▸ **tie down** vt attacher; (fig): **to ~ sb down to** contraindre qn à accepter; **to feel ~d down** (by relationship) se sentir coincé(e)
  ▸ **tie in** vi: **to ~ in (with)** (correspond) correspondre (à)
  ▸ **tie on** vt (Brit: label etc) attacher (avec une ficelle)
  ▸ **tie up** vt (parcel) ficeler; (dog, boat) attacher; (prisoner) ligoter; (arrangements) conclure; **to be ~d up** (busy) être pris(e) or occupé(e)
tie-break ['taɪbreɪk], **tie-breaker** ['taɪbreɪkəʳ] n (Tennis) tie-break m; (in quiz) question f subsidiaire
tie-on ['taɪɔn] adj (Brit: label) qui s'attache
tie-pin ['taɪpɪn] n (Brit) épingle f de cravate
tier [tɪəʳ] n gradin m; (of cake) étage m
Tierra del Fuego [tɪ'ɛrədɛl'fweɪgəu] n Terre f de Feu
tie tack n (US) épingle f de cravate
tiff [tɪf] n petite querelle
tiger ['taɪgəʳ] n tigre m
tight [taɪt] adj (rope) tendu(e), raide; (clothes) étroit(e), très juste; (budget, programme, bend) serré(e); (control) strict(e), sévère; (inf: drunk) ivre, rond(e) ▷ adv (squeeze) très fort; (shut) à bloc, hermétiquement; **to be packed ~** (suitcase)

être bourré(e); (*people*) être serré(e); **hold ~!** accrochez-vous bien!

tighten ['taɪtn] *vt* (*rope*) tendre; (*screw*) resserrer; (*control*) renforcer ▷ *vi* se tendre; se resserrer

tightfisted [taɪt'fɪstɪd] *adj* avare

tight-lipped ['taɪt'lɪpt] *adj*: **to be ~ (about sth)** (*silent*) ne pas desserrer les lèvres *or* les dents (au sujet de qch); **she was ~ with anger** elle pinçait les lèvres de colère

tightly ['taɪtlɪ] *adv* (*grasp*) bien, très fort

tightrope ['taɪtrəʊp] *n* corde *f* raide

tights [taɪts] *npl* (*Brit*) collant *m*

tigress ['taɪgrɪs] *n* tigresse *f*

tilde ['tɪldə] *n* tilde *m*

tile [taɪl] *n* (*on roof*) tuile *f*; (*on wall or floor*) carreau *m* ▷ *vt* (*floor, bathroom etc*) carreler

tiled [taɪld] *adj* en tuiles; carrelé(e)

till [tɪl] *n* caisse (enregistreuse) ▷ *vt* (*land*) cultiver ▷ *prep, conj* = **until**

tiller ['tɪlə^r] *n* (*Naut*) barre *f* (du gouvernail)

tilt [tɪlt] *vt* pencher, incliner ▷ *vi* pencher, être incliné(e) ▷ *n* (*slope*) inclinaison *f*; **to wear one's hat at a ~** porter son chapeau incliné sur le côté; **(at) full ~** à toute vitesse

timber ['tɪmbə^r] *n* (*material*) bois *m* de construction; (*trees*) arbres *mpl*

time [taɪm] *n* temps *m*; (*epoch: often pl*) époque *f*, temps; (*by clock*) heure *f*; (*moment*) moment *m*; (*occasion, also Math*) fois *f*; (*Mus*) mesure *f* ▷ *vt* (*race*) chronométrer; (*programme*) minuter; (*visit*) fixer; (*remark etc*) choisir le moment de; **a long ~** un long moment, longtemps; **four at a ~** quatre à la fois; **for the ~ being** pour le moment; **from ~ to ~** de temps en temps; **~ after ~, ~ and again** bien des fois; **at ~s** parfois; **in ~** (*soon enough*) à temps; (*after some time*) avec le temps, à la longue; (*Mus*) en mesure; **in a week's ~** dans une semaine; **in no ~** en un rien de temps; **any ~** n'importe quand; **on ~** à l'heure; **to be 30 minutes behind/ahead of ~** avoir 30 minutes de retard/d'avance; **by the ~ he arrived** quand il est arrivé, le temps qu'il arrive + *sub*; **5 ~s 5** 5 fois 5; **what ~ is it?** quelle heure est-il?; **what ~ do you make it?** quelle heure avez-vous?; **what ~ is the museum/ shop open?** à quelle heure ouvre le musée/ magasin?; **to have a good ~** bien s'amuser; **we** (*or* **they** *etc*) **had a hard ~** ça a été difficile *or* pénible; **~'s up!** c'est l'heure!; **I've no ~ for it** (*fig*) cela m'agace; **he'll do it in his own (good) ~** (*without being hurried*) il le fera quand il en aura le temps; **he'll do it in** *or* (*US*) **on his own ~** (*out of working hours*) il le fera à ses heures perdues; **to be behind the ~s** retarder (sur son temps)

time-and-motion study ['taɪmənd'məʊʃən-] *n* étude *f* des cadences

time bomb *n* bombe *f* à retardement

time clock *n* horloge pointeuse

time-consuming ['taɪmkənsjuːmɪŋ] *adj* qui prend beaucoup de temps

time difference *n* décalage *m* horaire

time frame *n* délais *mpl*

time-honoured, (US) **time-honored** ['taɪmɔnəd] *adj* consacré(e)

timekeeper ['taɪmkiːpə^r] *n* (*Sport*) chronomètre *m*

time lag *n* (*Brit*) décalage *m*; (: *in travel*) décalage horaire

timeless ['taɪmlɪs] *adj* éternel(le)

time limit *n* limite *f* de temps, délai *m*

timely ['taɪmlɪ] *adj* opportun(e)

time off *n* temps *m* libre

timer ['taɪmə^r] *n* (*in kitchen*) compte-minutes *m inv*; (*Tech*) minuteur *m*

time-saving ['taɪmseɪvɪŋ] *adj* qui fait gagner du temps

timescale ['taɪmskeɪl] *n* délais *mpl*

time-share ['taɪmʃɛə^r] *n* maison *f*/ appartement *m* en multipropriété

time-sharing ['taɪmʃɛərɪŋ] *n* (*Comput*) temps partagé

time sheet *n* feuille *f* de présence

time signal *n* signal *m* horaire

time switch *n* (*Brit*) minuteur *m*; (: *for lighting*) minuterie *f*

timetable ['taɪmteɪbl] *n* (*Rail*) (indicateur *m*) horaire *m*; (*Scol*) emploi *m* du temps; (*programme of events etc*) programme *m*

time zone *n* fuseau *m* horaire

timid ['tɪmɪd] *adj* timide; (*easily scared*) peureux(-euse)

timidity [tɪ'mɪdɪtɪ] *n* timidité *f*

timing ['taɪmɪŋ] *n* minutage *m*; (*Sport*) chronométrage *m*; **the ~ of his resignation** le moment choisi pour sa démission

timing device *n* (*on bomb*) mécanisme *m* de retardement

timpani ['tɪmpənɪ] *npl* timbales *fpl*

tin [tɪn] *n* étain *m*; (*also:* **tin plate**) fer-blanc *m*; (*Brit: can*) boîte *f* (de conserve); (: *for baking*) moule *m* (à gâteau); (*for storage*) boîte *f*; **a ~ of paint** un pot de peinture

tinfoil ['tɪnfɔɪl] *n* papier *m* d'étain *or* d'aluminium

tinge [tɪndʒ] *n* nuance *f* ▷ *vt*: **~d with** teinté(e) de

tingle ['tɪŋgl] *n* picotement *m*; frisson *m* ▷ *vi* picoter; (*person*) avoir des picotements

tinker ['tɪŋkə^r] *n* rétameur ambulant; (*gipsy*) romanichel *m*

▷ **tinker with** *vt fus* bricoler, rafistoler

tinkle ['tɪŋkl] *vi* tinter ▷ *n* (*inf*): **to give sb a ~** passer un coup de fil à qn

tin mine *n* mine *f* d'étain

tinned [tɪnd] *adj* (*Brit: food*) en boîte, en conserve

tinnitus ['tɪnɪtəs] *n* (*Med*) acouphène *m*

tinny ['tɪnɪ] *adj* métallique

tin opener [-'əʊpnə^r] *n* (*Brit*) ouvre-boîte(s) *m*

tinsel ['tɪnsl] *n* guirlandes *fpl* de Noël (*argentées*)

tint [tɪnt] *n* teinte *f*; (*for hair*) shampooing colorant ▷ *vt* (*hair*) faire un shampooing colorant à

tinted ['tɪntɪd] *adj* (*hair*) teint(e); (*spectacles, glass*) teinté(e)

tiny ['taɪnɪ] *adj* minuscule

tip [tɪp] *n* (*end*) bout *m*; (*protective: on umbrella etc*)

t

embout *m*; (*gratuity*) pourboire *m*; (*Brit: for coal*)
terril *m*; (*Brit: for rubbish*) décharge *f*; (*advice*)
tuyau *m* ▷ *vt* (*waiter*) donner un pourboire à;
(*tilt*) incliner; (*overturn: also:* **tip over**) renverser;
(*empty: also:* **tip out**) déverser; (*predict: winner etc*)
pronostiquer; **he ~ped out the contents of
the box** il a vidé le contenu de la boîte; **how
much should I ~?** combien de pourboire est-ce
qu'il faut laisser?
  ▶ **tip off** *vt* prévenir, avertir
tip-off ['tɪpɒf] *n* (*hint*) tuyau *m*
tipped ['tɪpt] *adj* (*Brit: cigarette*) (à bout) filtre *inv*;
  steel-~ à bout métallique, à embout de métal
Tipp-Ex® ['tɪpɛks] *n* (*Brit*) Tipp-Ex® *m*
tipple ['tɪpl] (*Brit*) *vi* picoler ▷ *n*: **to have a ~**
  boire un petit coup
tipster ['tɪpstə^r] *n* (*Racing*) pronostiqueur *m*
tipsy ['tɪpsɪ] *adj* un peu ivre, éméché(e)
tiptoe ['tɪptəʊ] *n*: **on ~** sur la pointe des pieds
tiptop ['tɪptɒp] *adj*: **in ~ condition** en excellent
  état
tirade [taɪ'reɪd] *n* diatribe *f*
tire ['taɪə^r] *n* (*US*) = **tyre** ▷ *vt* fatiguer ▷ *vi* se
  fatiguer
  ▶ **tire out** *vt* épuiser
tired ['taɪəd] *adj* fatigué(e); **to be/feel/look ~**
  être/se sentir/avoir l'air fatigué; **to be ~ of** en
  avoir assez de, être las (lasse) de
tiredness ['taɪədnɪs] *n* fatigue *f*
tireless ['taɪəlɪs] *adj* infatigable, inlassable
tire pressure (*US*) = **tyre pressure**
tiresome ['taɪəsəm] *adj* ennuyeux(-euse)
tiring ['taɪərɪŋ] *adj* fatigant(e)
tissue ['tɪʃuː] *n* tissu *m*; (*paper handkerchief*)
  mouchoir *m* en papier, kleenex® *m*
tissue paper *n* papier *m* de soie
tit [tɪt] *n* (*bird*) mésange *f*; (*inf: breast*) nichon *m*;
  to give ~ for tat rendre coup pour coup
titanium [tɪ'teɪnɪəm] *n* titane *m*
titbit ['tɪtbɪt] *n* (*food*) friandise *f*; (*before meal*)
  amuse-gueule *m inv*; (*news*) potin *m*
titillate ['tɪtɪleɪt] *vt* titiller, exciter
titivate ['tɪtɪveɪt] *vt* pomponner
title ['taɪtl] *n* titre *m*; (*Law: right*): **~ (to)** droit *m* (à)
title deed *n* (*Law*) titre (constitutif) de propriété
title page *n* page *f* de titre
title role *n* rôle principal
titter ['tɪtə^r] *vi* rire (bêtement)
tittle-tattle ['tɪtltætl] *n* bavardages *mpl*
titular ['tɪtjulə^r] *adj* (*in name only*) nominal(e)
tizzy ['tɪzɪ] *n*: **to be in a ~** être dans tous ses états
T-junction ['tiː'dʒʌŋkʃən] *n* croisement *m* en T
TM *n abbr* = **trademark; transcendental
  meditation**
TN *abbr* (*US*) = **Tennessee**
TNT *n abbr* (= *trinitrotoluene*) TNT *m*

 KEYWORD

to [tuː, tə] *prep* (*with noun/pronoun*) **1** (*direction*) à;
  (*towards*) vers; envers; **to go to France/
  Portugal/London/school** aller en France/au

Portugal/à Londres/à l'école; **to go to
Claude's/the doctor's** aller chez Claude/le
docteur; **the road to Edinburgh** la route
d'Édimbourg

2 (*as far as*) (jusqu')à; **to count to 10** compter
jusqu'à 10; **from 40 to 50 people** de 40 à 50
personnes

3 (*with expressions of time*): **a quarter to 5** 5
heures moins le quart; **it's twenty to 3** il est 3
heures moins vingt

4 (*for, of*) de; **the key to the front door** la clé de
la porte d'entrée; **a letter to his wife** une lettre
(adressée) à sa femme

5 (*expressing indirect object*) à; **to give sth to sb**
donner qch à qn; **to talk to sb** parler à qn; **it
belongs to him** cela lui appartient, c'est à lui;
to be a danger to sb être dangereux(-euse)
pour qn

6 (*in relation to*) à; **3 goals to 2** 3 (buts) à 2; **30
miles to the gallon** ≈ 9,4 litres aux cent (km)

7 (*purpose, result*): **to come to sb's aid** venir au
secours de qn, porter secours à qn; **to sentence
sb to death** condamner qn à mort; **to my
surprise** à ma grande surprise
  ▷ *prep* (*with vb*) **1** (*simple infinitive*): **to go/eat**
aller/manger

2 (*following another vb*): **to want/try/start to do**
vouloir/essayer de/commencer à faire

3 (*with vb omitted*): **I don't want to** je ne veux
pas

4 (*purpose, result*) pour; **I did it to help you** je l'ai
fait pour vous aider

5 (*equivalent to relative clause*): **I have things to do**
j'ai des choses à faire; **the main thing is to try**
l'important est d'essayer

6 (*after adjective etc*): **ready to go** prêt(e) à partir;
too old/young to ... trop vieux/jeune pour ...
  ▷ *adv*: **push/pull the door to** tirez/poussez la
porte; **to go to and fro** aller et venir

toad [təʊd] *n* crapaud *m*
toadstool ['təʊdstuːl] *n* champignon
  (vénéneux)
toady ['təʊdɪ] *vi* flatter bassement
toast [təʊst] *n* (*Culin*) pain grillé, toast *m*; (*drink,
  speech*) toast ▷ *vt* (*Culin*) faire griller; (*drink to*)
  porter un toast à; **a piece** *or* **slice of ~** un toast
toaster ['təʊstə^r] *n* grille-pain *m inv*
toastmaster ['təʊstmaːstə^r] *n* animateur *m*
  pour réceptions
toast rack *n* porte-toast *m inv*
tobacco [tə'bækəʊ] *n* tabac *m*; **pipe ~** tabac à
  pipe
tobacconist [tə'bækənɪst] *n* marchand(e) de
  tabac; **~'s (shop)** (bureau *m* de) tabac *m*
Tobago [tə'beɪɡəʊ] *n see* **Trinidad and Tobago**
toboggan [tə'bɒɡən] *n* toboggan *m*; (*child's*)
  luge *f*
today [tə'deɪ] *adv, n* (*also fig*) aujourd'hui (*m*);
  what day is it ~? quel jour sommes-nous
  aujourd'hui?; **what date is it ~?** quelle est la
  date aujourd'hui?; **~ is the 4th of March**

aujourd'hui nous sommes le 4 mars; **a week ago ~** il y a huit jours aujourd'hui

toddler ['tɔdlə'] n enfant m/f qui commence à marcher, bambin m

toddy ['tɔdɪ] n grog m

to-do [tə'du:] n (fuss) histoire f, affaire f

toe [təu] n doigt m de pied, orteil m; (of shoe) bout m ▷ vt: **to ~ the line** (fig) obéir, se conformer; **big ~** gros orteil; **little ~** petit orteil

TOEFL n abbr = **Test(ing) of English as a Foreign Language**

toehold ['təuhəuld] n prise f

toenail ['təuneɪl] n ongle m de l'orteil

toffee ['tɔfɪ] n caramel m

toffee apple n (Brit) pomme caramélisée

tofu ['təufu:] n fromage m de soja

toga ['təugə] n toge f

together [tə'gɛðə'] adv ensemble; (at same time) en même temps; **~ with** (prep) avec

togetherness [tə'gɛðənɪs] n camaraderie f; intimité f

toggle switch ['tɔgl-] n (Comput) interrupteur m à bascule

Togo ['təugəu] n Togo m

togs [tɔgz] npl (inf: clothes) fringues fpl

toil [tɔɪl] n dur travail, labeur m ▷ vi travailler dur; peiner

toilet ['tɔɪlət] n (Brit: lavatory) toilettes fpl, cabinets mpl ▷ cpd (bag, soap etc) de toilette; **to go to the ~** aller aux toilettes; **where's the ~?** où sont les toilettes?

toilet bag n (Brit) nécessaire m de toilette

toilet bowl n cuvette f des W.-C.

toilet paper n papier m hygiénique

toiletries ['tɔɪlətrɪz] npl articles mpl de toilette

toilet roll n rouleau m de papier hygiénique

toilet water n eau f de toilette

to-ing and fro-ing ['tu:ɪŋən'frəuɪŋ] n (Brit) allées et venues fpl

token ['təukən] n (sign) marque f, témoignage m; (metal disc) jeton m; (voucher) bon m, coupon m ▷ adj (fee, strike) symbolique; **by the same ~** (fig) de même; **book/record ~** (Brit) chèque-livre/-disque m

tokenism ['təukənɪzəm] n (Pol): **it's just ~** c'est une politique de pure forme

Tokyo ['təukjəu] n Tokyo

told [təuld] pt, pp of **tell**

tolerable ['tɔlərəbl] adj (bearable) tolérable; (fairly good) passable

tolerably ['tɔlərəblɪ] adv: **~ good** tolérable

tolerance ['tɔlərns] n (also Tech) tolérance f

tolerant ['tɔlərnt] adj: **~ (of)** tolérant(e) (à l'égard de)

tolerate ['tɔləreɪt] vt supporter; (Med,: Tech) tolérer

toleration [tɔlə'reɪʃən] n tolérance f

toll [təul] n (tax, charge) péage m ▷ vi (bell) sonner; **the accident ~ on the roads** le nombre des victimes de la route

tollbridge ['təulbrɪdʒ] n pont m à péage

toll call n (US Tel) appel m (à) longue distance

toll-free ['təul'fri:] adj (US) gratuit(e) ▷ adv gratuitement

tomato [tə'mɑ:təu] (pl **-es**) n tomate f

tomato sauce n sauce f tomate

tomb [tu:m] n tombe f

tombola [tɔm'bəulə] n tombola f

tomboy ['tɔmbɔɪ] n garçon manqué

tombstone ['tu:mstəun] n pierre tombale

tomcat ['tɔmkæt] n matou m

tomorrow [tə'mɔrəu] adv, n (also fig) demain (m); **the day after ~** après-demain; **a week ~** demain en huit; **~ morning** demain matin

ton [tʌn] n tonne f (Brit: = 1016 kg; US = 907 kg; metric = 1000 kg); (Naut: also: **register ton**) tonneau m (= 2.83 cu.m); **~s of** (inf) des tas de

tonal ['təunl] adj tonal(e)

tone [təun] n ton m; (of radio, Brit Tel) tonalité f ▷ vi (also: **tone in**) s'harmoniser
  ▶ **tone down** vt (colour, criticism) adoucir; (sound) baisser
  ▶ **tone up** vt (muscles) tonifier

tone-deaf [təun'dɛf] adj qui n'a pas d'oreille

toner ['təunə'] n (for photocopier) encre f

Tonga [tɔŋə] n îles fpl Tonga

tongs [tɔŋz] npl pinces fpl; (for coal) pincettes fpl; (for hair) fer m à friser

tongue [tʌŋ] n langue f; **~ in cheek** (adv) ironiquement

tongue-tied ['tʌŋtaɪd] adj (fig) muet(te)

tonic ['tɔnɪk] n (Med) tonique m; (Mus) tonique f; (also: **tonic water**) Schweppes® m

tonight [tə'naɪt] adv, n cette nuit; (this evening) ce soir; **(I'll) see you ~!** à ce soir!

tonnage ['tʌnɪdʒ] n (Naut) tonnage m

tonne [tʌn] n (Brit: metric ton) tonne f

tonsil ['tɔnsl] n amygdale f; **to have one's ~s out** se faire opérer des amygdales

tonsillitis [tɔnsɪ'laɪtɪs] n amygdalite f; **to have ~** avoir une angine or une amygdalite

too [tu:] adv (excessively) trop; (also) aussi; **it's ~ sweet** c'est trop sucré; **I went ~** moi aussi, j'y suis allé; **~ much** (as adv) trop; (as adj) trop de; **~ many** (adj) trop de; **~ bad!** tant pis!

took [tuk] pt of **take**

tool [tu:l] n outil m; (fig) instrument m ▷ vt travailler, ouvrager

tool box n boîte f à outils

tool kit n trousse f à outils

toot [tu:t] n coup m de sifflet (or de klaxon) ▷ vi siffler; (with car-horn) klaxonner

tooth (pl **teeth**) [tu:θ, ti:θ] n (Anat, Tech) dent f; **to have a ~ out** or (US) **pulled** se faire arracher une dent; **to brush one's teeth** se laver les dents; **by the skin of one's teeth** (fig) de justesse

toothache ['tu:θeɪk] n mal m de dents; **to have ~** avoir mal aux dents

toothbrush ['tu:θbrʌʃ] n brosse f à dents

toothpaste ['tu:θpeɪst] n (pâte f) dentifrice m

toothpick ['tu:θpɪk] n cure-dent m

tooth powder n poudre f dentifrice

top [tɔp] n (of mountain, head) sommet m; (of page, ladder) haut m; (of list, queue) commencement m;

t

(*of box, cupboard, table*) dessus *m*; (*lid: of box, jar*) couvercle *m*; (: *of bottle*) bouchon *m*; (*toy*) toupie *f*; (*Dress: blouse etc*) haut; (: *of pyjamas*) veste *f* ▷ *adj* du haut; (*in rank*) premier(-ière); (*best*) meilleur(e) ▷ *vt* (*exceed*) dépasser; (*be first in*) être en tête de; **at the ~ of the stairs/page/street** en haut de l'escalier/de la page/de la rue; **from ~ to bottom** de fond en comble; **on ~ of** sur; (*in addition to*) en plus de; **from ~ to toe** (*Brit*) de la tête aux pieds; **at the ~ of the list** en tête de liste; **at the ~ of one's voice** à tue-tête; **at ~ speed** à toute vitesse; **over the ~** (*inf: behaviour etc*) qui dépasse les limites

▶ **top up** (*Brit*), **top off** *vt* (*bottle*) remplir; (*salary*) compléter; **to ~ up one's mobile (phone)** recharger son compte

topaz ['təupæz] *n* topaze *f*

top-class ['tɔp'klɑːs] *adj* de première classe; (*Sport*) de haute compétition

topcoat ['tɔpkəut] *n* pardessus *m*

topflight ['tɔpflaɪt] *adj* excellent(e)

top floor *n* dernier étage

top hat *n* haut-de-forme *m*

top-heavy [tɔp'hɛvɪ] *adj* (*object*) trop lourd(e) du haut

topic ['tɔpɪk] *n* sujet *m*, thème *m*

topical ['tɔpɪkl] *adj* d'actualité

topless ['tɔplɪs] *adj* (*bather etc*) aux seins nus; **~ swimsuit** monokini *m*

top-level ['tɔplɛvl] *adj* (*talks*) à l'échelon le plus élevé

topmost ['tɔpməust] *adj* le (la) plus haut(e)

top-notch ['tɔp'nɔtʃ] *adj* (*inf*) de premier ordre

topography [tə'pɔgrəfɪ] *n* topographie *f*

topping ['tɔpɪŋ] *n* (*Culin*) *couche de crème, fromage etc qui recouvre un plat*

topple ['tɔpl] *vt* renverser, faire tomber ▷ *vi* basculer; tomber

top-ranking ['tɔpræŋkɪŋ] *adj* très haut placé(e)

top-secret ['tɔp'siːkrɪt] *adj* ultra-secret(-ète)

top-security ['tɔpsə'kjuərɪtɪ] *adj* (*Brit*) de haute sécurité

topsy-turvy ['tɔpsɪ'təːvɪ] *adj, adv* sens dessus-dessous

top-up ['tɔpʌp] *n* (*for mobile phone*) recharge *f*, minutes *fpl*; **would you like a ~?** je vous en remets *or* rajoute?

top-up card *n* (*for mobile phone*) recharge *f*

top-up loan *n* (*Brit*) prêt *m* complémentaire

torch [tɔːtʃ] *n* torche *f*; (*Brit: electric*) lampe *f* de poche

tore [tɔːʳ] *pt of* **tear²**

torment *n* ['tɔːmɛnt] tourment *m* ▷ *vt* [tɔː'mɛnt] tourmenter; (*fig: annoy*) agacer

torn [tɔːn] *pp of* **tear²** ▷ *adj*: **~ between** (*fig*) tiraillé(e) entre

tornado [tɔː'neɪdəu] (*pl* **-es**) *n* tornade *f*

torpedo [tɔː'piːdəu] (*pl* **-es**) *n* torpille *f*

torpedo boat *n* torpilleur *m*

torpor ['tɔːpəʳ] *n* torpeur *f*

torrent ['tɔrnt] *n* torrent *m*

torrential [tɔ'rɛnʃl] *adj* torrentiel(le)

torrid ['tɔrɪd] *adj* torride; (*fig*) ardent(e)

torso ['tɔːsəu] *n* torse *m*

tortoise ['tɔːtəs] *n* tortue *f*

tortoiseshell ['tɔːtəʃɛl] *adj* en écaille

tortuous ['tɔːtjuəs] *adj* tortueux(-euse)

torture ['tɔːtʃəʳ] *n* torture *f* ▷ *vt* torturer

torturer ['tɔːtʃərəʳ] *n* tortionnaire *m*

Tory ['tɔːrɪ] *adj, n* (*Brit Pol*) tory *m/f*, conservateur(-trice)

toss [tɔs] *vt* lancer, jeter; (*Brit: pancake*) faire sauter; (*head*) rejeter en arrière ▷ *vi*: **to ~ up for sth** (*Brit*) jouer qch à pile ou face ▷ *n* (*movement: of head etc*) mouvement soudain; (*of coin*) tirage *m* à pile ou face; **to ~ a coin** jouer à pile ou face; **to ~ and turn** (*in bed*) se tourner et se retourner; **to win/lose the ~** gagner/perdre à pile ou face; (*Sport*) gagner/perdre le tirage au sort

tot [tɔt] *n* (*Brit: drink*) petit verre; (*child*) bambin *m*

▶ **tot up** *vt* (*Brit: figures*) additionner

total ['təutl] *adj* total(e) ▷ *n* total *m* ▷ *vt* (*add up*) faire le total de, additionner; (*amount to*) s'élever à; **in ~** au total

totalitarian [təutælɪ'tɛərɪən] *adj* totalitaire

totality [təu'tælɪtɪ] *n* totalité *f*

totally ['təutəlɪ] *adv* totalement

tote bag [təut-] *n* fourre-tout *m inv*

totem pole ['təutəm-] *n* mât *m* totémique

totter ['tɔtəʳ] *vi* chanceler; (*object, government*) être chancelant(e)

touch [tʌtʃ] *n* contact *m*, toucher *m*; (*sense, skill: of pianist etc*) toucher; (*fig: note, also Football*) touche *f* ▷ *vt* (*gen*) toucher; (*tamper with*) toucher à; **the personal ~** la petite note personnelle; **to put the finishing ~es to sth** mettre la dernière main à qch; **a ~ of** (*fig*) un petit peu de; une touche de; **in ~ with** en contact *or* rapport avec; **to get in ~ with** prendre contact avec; **I'll be in ~** je resterai en contact; **to lose ~** (*friends*) se perdre de vue; **to be out of ~ with events** ne pas être au courant de ce qui se passe

▶ **touch down** *vi* (*Aviat*) atterrir; (*on sea*) amerrir

▶ **touch on** *vt fus* (*topic*) effleurer, toucher

▶ **touch up** *vt* (*paint*) retoucher

touch-and-go ['tʌtʃən'gəu] *adj* incertain(e); **it was ~ whether we did it** nous avons failli ne pas le faire

touchdown ['tʌtʃdaun] *n* (*Aviat*) atterrissage *m*; (*on sea*) amerrissage *m*; (*US Football*) essai *m*

touched [tʌtʃt] *adj* (*moved*) touché(e); (*inf*) cinglé(e)

touching ['tʌtʃɪŋ] *adj* touchant(e), attendrissant(e)

touchline ['tʌtʃlaɪn] *n* (*Sport*) (ligne *f* de) touche *f*

touch screen *n* (*Tech*) écran tactile; **~ mobile** (*téléphone*) portable *m* à écran tactile; **~ technology** technologie *f* à écran tactile

touch-sensitive ['tʌtʃsɛnsɪtɪv] *adj* (*keypad*) à effleurement; (*screen*) tactile

touch-type ['tʌtʃtaɪp] *vi* taper au toucher

touchy ['tʌtʃɪ] *adj* (*person*) susceptible

tough [tʌf] *adj* dur(e); (*resistant*) résistant(e), solide; (*meat*) dur, coriace; (*firm*) inflexible; (*journey*) pénible; (*task, problem, situation*) difficile; (*rough*) dur ▷ *n* (*gangster etc*) dur *m*; **~ luck!** pas de chance!; tant pis!

toughen ['tʌfn] *vt* rendre plus dur(e) (*or* plus résistant(e) *or* plus solide)

toughness ['tʌfnɪs] *n* dureté *f*; résistance *f*; solidité *f*

toupee ['tu:peɪ] *n* postiche *m*

tour ['tuər] *n* voyage *m*; (*also*: **package tour**) voyage organisé; (*of town, museum*) tour *m*, visite *f*; (*by band*) tournée *f* ▷ *vt* visiter; **to go on a ~ of** (*museum, region*) visiter; **to go on ~** partir en tournée

tour guide *n* (*person*) guide *m/f*

touring ['tuərɪŋ] *n* voyages *mpl* touristiques, tourisme *m*

tourism ['tuərɪzm] *n* tourisme *m*

tourist ['tuərɪst] *n* touriste *m/f* ▷ *adv* (*travel*) en classe touriste ▷ *cpd* touristique; **the ~ trade** le tourisme

tourist class *n* (*Aviat*) classe *f* touriste

tourist office *n* syndicat *m* d'initiative

tournament ['tuənəmənt] *n* tournoi *m*

tourniquet ['tuənɪkeɪ] *n* (*Med*) garrot *m*

tour operator *n* (*Brit*) organisateur *m* de voyages, tour-opérateur *m*

tousled ['tauzld] *adj* (*hair*) ébouriffé(e)

tout [taut] *vi*: **to ~ for** essayer de raccrocher, racoler; **to ~ sth (around)** (*Brit*) essayer de placer *or* (re)vendre qch ▷ *n* (*Brit: ticket tout*) revendeur *m* de billets

tow [təu] *n*: **to give sb a ~** (*Aut*) remorquer qn ▷ *vt* remorquer; (*caravan, trailer*) tracter; **"on ~"**, (*US*) **"in ~"** (*Aut*) "véhicule en remorque"
  ▶ **tow away** *vt* (*subj: police*) emmener à la fourrière; (*: breakdown service*) remorquer

toward [tə'wɔːd], **towards** [tə'wɔːdz] *prep* vers; (*of attitude*) envers, à l'égard de; (*of purpose*) pour; **~(s) noon/the end of the year** vers midi/la fin de l'année; **to feel friendly ~(s) sb** être bien disposé envers qn

towel ['tauəl] *n* serviette *f* (de toilette); (*also*: **tea towel**) torchon *m*; **to throw in the ~** (*fig*) jeter l'éponge

towelling ['tauəlɪŋ] *n* (*fabric*) tissu-éponge *m*

towel rail, (*US*) **towel rack** *n* porte-serviettes *m inv*

tower ['tauər] *n* tour *f* ▷ *vi* (*building, mountain*) se dresser (majestueusement); **to ~ above** *or* **over sb/sth** dominer qn/qch

tower block *n* (*Brit*) tour *f* (d'habitation)

towering ['tauərɪŋ] *adj* très haut(e), imposant(e)

towline ['təulaɪn] *n* (câble *m* de) remorque *f*

town [taun] *n* ville *f*; **to go to ~** aller en ville; (*fig*) y mettre le paquet; **in the ~** dans la ville, en ville; **to be out of ~** (*person*) être en déplacement

town centre *n* (*Brit*) centre *m* de la ville, centre-ville *m*

town clerk *n* ≈ secrétaire *m/f* de mairie

town council *n* conseil municipal

town crier [-'kraɪər] *n* (*Brit*) crieur public

town hall *n* ≈ mairie *f*

townie ['taunɪ] *n* (*Brit inf*) citadin(e)

town plan *n* plan *m* de ville

town planner *n* urbaniste *m/f*

town planning *n* urbanisme *m*

township ['taunʃɪp] *n* banlieue noire (*établie sous le régime de l'apartheid*)

townspeople ['taunzpi:pl] *npl* citadins *mpl*

towpath ['təupɑ:θ] *n* (chemin *m* de) halage *m*

towrope ['təurəup] *n* (câble *m* de) remorque *f*

tow truck *n* (*US*) dépanneuse *f*

toxic ['tɔksɪk] *adj* toxique

toxic asset *n* (*Econ*) actif *m* toxique

toxic bank *n* (*Econ*) bad bank *f*, banque *f* toxique

toxin ['tɔksɪn] *n* toxine *f*

toy [tɔɪ] *n* jouet *m*
  ▶ **toy with** *vt fus* jouer avec; (*idea*) caresser

toyshop ['tɔɪʃɔp] *n* magasin *m* de jouets

trace [treɪs] *n* trace *f* ▷ *vt* (*draw*) tracer, dessiner; (*follow*) suivre la trace de; (*locate*) retrouver; **without ~** (*disappear*) sans laisser de traces; **there was no ~ of it** il n'y en avait pas trace

trace element *n* oligo-élément *m*

trachea [trə'kɪə] *n* (*Anat*) trachée *f*

tracing paper ['treɪsɪŋ-] *n* papier-calque *m*

track [træk] *n* (*mark*) trace *f*; (*path: gen*) chemin *m*, piste *f*; (*: of bullet etc*) trajectoire *f*; (*: of suspect, animal*) piste *f*; (*Rail*) voie ferrée, rails *mpl*; (*on tape, Comput, Sport*) piste *f*; (*on CD*) piste *f*; (*on record*) plage *f* ▷ *vt* suivre la trace *or* la piste de; **to keep ~ of** suivre; **to be on the right ~** (*fig*) être sur la bonne voie
  ▶ **track down** *vt* (*prey*) trouver et capturer; (*sth lost*) finir par retrouver

tracker dog ['trækə-] *n* (*Brit*) chien *dressé pour suivre une piste*

track events *npl* (*Sport*) épreuves *fpl* sur piste

tracking station ['trækɪŋ-] *n* (*Space*) centre *m* d'observation de satellites

track meet *n* (*US*) réunion sportive sur piste

track record *n*: **to have a good ~** (*fig*) avoir fait ses preuves

tracksuit ['træksu:t] *n* survêtement *m*

tract [trækt] *n* (*Geo*) étendue *f*, zone *f*; (*pamphlet*) tract *m*; **respiratory ~** (*Anat*) système *m* respiratoire

traction ['trækʃən] *n* traction *f*

tractor ['træktər] *n* tracteur *m*

trade [treɪd] *n* commerce *m*; (*skill, job*) métier *m* ▷ *vi* faire du commerce ▷ *vt* (*exchange*): **to ~ sth (for sth)** échanger qch (contre qch); **to ~ with/in** faire du commerce avec/le commerce de; **foreign ~** commerce extérieur
  ▶ **trade in** *vt* (*old car etc*) faire reprendre

trade barrier *n* barrière commerciale

trade deficit *n* déficit extérieur

Trade Descriptions Act *n* (*Brit*) *loi contre les appellations et la publicité mensongères*

trade discount *n* remise *f* au détaillant

trade fair *n* foire(-exposition) commerciale

trade-in ['treɪdɪn] *n* reprise *f*

trade-in price n prix m à la reprise
trademark ['treɪdmɑːk] n marque f de fabrique
trade mission n mission commerciale
trade name n marque déposée
trade-off ['treɪdɔf] n (exchange) échange f;
(balancing) équilibre m
trader ['treɪdə'] n commerçant(e),
négociant(e)
trade secret n secret m de fabrication
tradesman ['treɪdzmən] (irreg) n (shopkeeper)
commerçant m; (skilled worker) ouvrier qualifié
trade union n syndicat m
trade unionist [-'juːnjənɪst] n syndicaliste m/f
trade wind n alizé m
trading ['treɪdɪŋ] n affaires fpl, commerce m
trading estate n (Brit) zone industrielle
trading stamp n timbre-prime m
tradition [trə'dɪʃən] n tradition f; **traditions** npl
coutumes fpl, traditions
traditional [trə'dɪʃənl] adj traditionnel(le)
traffic ['træfɪk] n trafic m; (cars) circulation f
▷ vi: **to ~ in** (pej: liquor, drugs) faire le trafic de
traffic calming [-'kɑːmɪŋ] n ralentissement m
de la circulation
traffic circle n (US) rond-point m
traffic island n refuge m (pour piétons)
traffic jam n embouteillage m
trafficker ['træfɪkə'] n trafiquant(e)
traffic lights npl feux mpl (de signalisation)
traffic offence n (Brit) infraction f au code de la
route
traffic sign n panneau m de signalisation
traffic violation n (US) = **traffic offence**
traffic warden n contractuel(le)
tragedy ['trædʒədɪ] n tragédie f
tragic ['trædʒɪk] adj tragique
trail [treɪl] n (tracks) trace f, piste f; (path) chemin
m, piste f; (of smoke etc) traînée f ▷ vt (drag) traîner,
tirer; (follow) suivre ▷ vi traîner; (in game, contest)
être en retard; **to be on sb's ~** être sur la piste
de qn
▶ **trail away, trail off** vi (sound, voice) s'évanouir;
(interest) disparaître
▶ **trail behind** vi traîner, être à la traîne
trailer ['treɪlə'] n (Aut) remorque f; (US) caravane
f; (Cine) bande-annonce f
trailer truck n (US) (camion m) semi-remorque m
train [treɪn] n train m; (in underground) rame f; (of
dress) traîne f; (Brit: series): **~ of events** série f
d'événements ▷ vt (apprentice, doctor etc) former;
(Sport) entraîner; (dog) dresser; (memory) exercer;
(point: gun etc): **to ~ sth on** braquer qch sur ▷ vi
recevoir sa formation; (Sport) s'entraîner; **one's
~ of thought** le fil de sa pensée; **to go by ~**
voyager par le train or en train; **what time
does the ~ from Paris get in?** à quelle heure
arrive le train de Paris?; **is this the ~ for ...?**
c'est bien le train pour ...?; **to ~ sb to do sth**
apprendre à qn à faire qch; (employee) former qn
à faire qch
train attendant n (US) employé(e) des
wagons-lits

trained [treɪnd] adj qualifié(e), qui a reçu une
formation; dressé(e)
trainee [treɪ'niː] n stagiaire m/f; (in trade)
apprenti(e)
trainer ['treɪnə'] n (Sport) entraîneur(-euse); (of
dogs etc) dresseur(-euse); **trainers** npl (shoes)
chaussures fpl de sport
training ['treɪnɪŋ] n formation f; (Sport)
entraînement m; (of dog etc) dressage m; **in ~**
(Sport) à l'entraînement; (fit) en forme
training college n école professionnelle; (for
teachers) ≈ école normale
training course n cours m de formation
professionnelle
training shoes npl chaussures fpl de sport
train wreck n (fig) épave f; **he's a complete ~**
c'est une épave
traipse [treɪps] vi (se) traîner, déambuler
trait [treɪt] n trait m (de caractère)
traitor ['treɪtə'] n traître m
trajectory [trə'dʒɛktərɪ] n trajectoire f
tram [træm] n (Brit: also: **tramcar**) tram(way) m
tramline ['træmlaɪn] n ligne f de tram(way)
tramp [træmp] n (person) vagabond(e),
clochard(e), (inf: pej: woman): **to be a ~** être
coureuse ▷ vi marcher d'un pas lourd ▷ vt (walk
through: town, streets) parcourir à pied
trample ['træmpl] vt: **to ~ (underfoot)** piétiner;
(fig) bafouer
trampoline ['træmpəliːn] n trampoline m
trance [trɑːns] n transe f; (Med) catalepsie f; **to
go into a ~** entrer en transe
tranquil ['træŋkwɪl] adj tranquille
tranquillity [træŋ'kwɪlɪtɪ] n tranquillité f
tranquillizer, (US) **tranquilizer** ['træŋkwɪlaɪzə']
n (Med) tranquillisant m
transact [træn'zækt] vt (business) traiter
transaction [træn'zækʃən] n transaction f;
transactions npl (minutes) actes mpl; **cash ~**
transaction au comptant
transatlantic ['trænzət'læntɪk] adj
transatlantique
transcend [træn'sɛnd] vt transcender; (excel
over) surpasser
transcendental [trænsɛn'dɛntl] adj: **~
meditation** méditation transcendantale
transcribe [træn'skraɪb] vt transcrire
transcript ['trænskrɪpt] n transcription f (texte)
transcription [træn'skrɪpʃən] n transcription f
transept ['trænsɛpt] n transept m
transfer n ['trænsfə'] (gen, also Sport) transfert m;
(Pol: of power) passation f; (of money) virement m;
(picture, design) décalcomanie f; (: stick-on)
autocollant m ▷ vt [træns'fəː'] transférer;
passer; virer; décalquer; **to ~ the charges** (Brit
Tel) téléphoner en P.C.V.; **by bank ~** par
virement bancaire
transferable [træns'fəːrəbl] adj transmissible,
transférable; **"not ~"** "personnel"
transfer desk n (Aviat) guichet m de transit
transfix [træns'fɪks] vt transpercer; (fig): **~ed
with fear** paralysé(e) par la peur

transform [træns'fɔ:m] *vt* transformer
transformation [trænsfə'meɪʃən] *n*
transformation *f*
transformer [træns'fɔ:məʳ] *n* (*Elec*)
transformateur *m*
transfusion [træns'fju:ʒən] *n* transfusion *f*
transgress [træns'grɛs] *vt* transgresser
transient ['trænzɪənt] *adj* transitoire,
éphémère
transistor [træn'zɪstəʳ] *n* (*Elec: also:* **transistor
radio**) transistor *m*
transit ['trænzɪt] *n*: **in ~** en transit
transit camp *n* camp *m* de transit
transition [træn'zɪʃən] *n* transition *f*
transitional [træn'zɪʃənl] *adj* transitoire
transitive ['trænzɪtɪv] *adj* (*Ling*) transitif(-ive)
transit lounge *n* (*Aviat*) salle *f* de transit
transitory ['trænzɪtərɪ] *adj* transitoire
translate [trænz'leɪt] *vt*: **to ~ (from/into)**
traduire (du/en); **can you ~ this for me?**
pouvez-vous me traduire ceci?
translation [trænz'leɪʃən] *n* traduction *f*; (*Scol:
as opposed to prose*) version *f*
translator [trænz'leɪtəʳ] *n* traducteur(-trice)
translucent [trænz'lu:snt] *adj* translucide
transmission [trænz'mɪʃən] *n* transmission *f*
transmit [trænz'mɪt] *vt* transmettre; (*Radio, TV*)
émettre
transmitter [trænz'mɪtəʳ] *n* émetteur *m*
transparency [træns'pɛərnsɪ] *n* (*Brit Phot*)
diapositive *f*
transparent [træns'pærnt] *adj* transparent(e)
transpire [træns'paɪəʳ] *vi* (*become known*): **it
finally ~d that ...** on a finalement appris que
...; (*happen*) arriver
transplant *vt* [træns'plɑ:nt] transplanter;
(*seedlings*) repiquer ▷ *n* ['trænsplɑ:nt] (*Med*)
transplantation *f*; **to have a heart ~** subir une
greffe du cœur
transport *n* ['trænspɔ:t] transport *m* ▷ *vt*
[træns'pɔ:t] transporter; **public ~** transports en
commun; **Department of T~** (*Brit*) ministère *m*
des Transports
transportation [trænspɔ:'teɪʃən] *n* (moyen *m*
de) transport *m*; (*of prisoners*) transportation *f*;
Department of T~ (*US*) ministère *m* des
Transports
transport café *n* (*Brit*) ≈ routier *m*
transpose [træns'pəuz] *vt* transposer
transsexual [trænz'sɛksjuəl] *adj, n*
transsexuel(le)
transverse ['trænzvə:s] *adj* transversal(e)
transvestite [trænz'vɛstaɪt] *n* travesti(e)
trap [træp] *n* (*snare, trick*) piège *m*; (*carriage*)
cabriolet *m* ▷ *vt* prendre au piège; (*immobilize*)
bloquer; (*confine*) coincer; **to set** *or* **lay a ~ (for
sb)** tendre un piège (à qn); **to shut one's ~** (*inf*)
la fermer
trap door *n* trappe *f*
trapeze [trə'pi:z] *n* trapèze *m*
trapper ['træpəʳ] *n* trappeur *m*
trappings ['træpɪŋz] *npl* ornements *mpl*;

attributs *mpl*
trash [træʃ] *n* (*pej: goods*) camelote *f*; (*: nonsense*)
sottises *fpl*; (*US: rubbish*) ordures *fpl*
trash can *n* (*US*) poubelle *f*
trashy ['træʃɪ] *adj* (*inf*) de camelote, qui ne vaut
rien
trauma ['trɔ:mə] *n* traumatisme *m*
traumatic [trɔ:'mætɪk] *adj* traumatisant(e)
travel ['trævl] *n* voyage(s) *m(pl)* ▷ *vi* voyager;
(*move*) aller, se déplacer; (*news, sound*) se
propager ▷ *vt* (*distance*) parcourir; **this wine
doesn't ~ well** ce vin voyage mal
travel agency *n* agence *f* de voyages
travel agent *n* agent *m* de voyages
travel brochure *n* brochure *f* touristique
travel insurance *n* assurance-voyage *f*
traveller, (*US*) **traveler** ['trævləʳ] *n*
voyageur(-euse); (*Comm*) représentant *m* de
commerce
traveller's cheque, (*US*) **traveler's check** *n*
chèque *m* de voyage
travelling, (*US*) **traveling** ['trævlɪŋ] *n* voyage(s)
m(pl) ▷ *adj* (*circus, exhibition*) ambulant(e) ▷ *cpd*
(*bag, clock*) de voyage; (*expenses*) de déplacement
travelling salesman, (*US*) **traveling salesman**
(*irreg*) *n* voyageur *m* de commerce
travelogue ['trævəlɔg] *n* (*book, talk*) récit *m* de
voyage; (*film*) documentaire *m* de voyage
travel-sick ['trævlsɪk] *adj*: **to get ~** avoir le mal
de la route (*or* de mer *or* de l'air)
travel sickness *n* mal *m* de la route (*or* de mer *or*
de l'air)
traverse ['trævəs] *vt* traverser
travesty ['trævəstɪ] *n* parodie *f*
trawler ['trɔ:ləʳ] *n* chalutier *m*
tray [treɪ] *n* (*for carrying*) plateau *m*; (*on desk*)
corbeille *f*
treacherous ['trɛtʃərəs] *adj* traître(sse); (*ground,
tide*) dont il faut se méfier; **road conditions
are ~** l'état des routes est dangereux
treachery ['trɛtʃərɪ] *n* traîtrise *f*
treacle ['tri:kl] *n* mélasse *f*
tread [trɛd] *n* (*step*) pas *m*; (*sound*) bruit *m* de pas;
(*of tyre*) chape *f*, bande *f* de roulement ▷ *vi* (*pt
trod, pp trodden*) [trɔd, 'trɔdn] marcher
▶ **tread on** *vt fus* marcher sur
treadle ['trɛdl] *n* pédale *f* (*de machine*)
treas. *abbr* = **treasurer**
treason ['tri:zn] *n* trahison *f*
treasure ['trɛʒəʳ] *n* trésor *m* ▷ *vt* (*value*) tenir
beaucoup à; (*store*) conserver précieusement
treasure hunt *n* chasse *f* au trésor
treasurer ['trɛʒərəʳ] *n* trésorier(-ière)
treasury ['trɛʒərɪ] *n* trésorerie *f*; **the T~**, (*US*) **the
T~ Department** ≈ le ministère des Finances
treasury bill *n* bon *m* du Trésor
treat [tri:t] *n* petit cadeau, petite surprise ▷ *vt*
traiter; **it was a ~** ça m'a (*or* nous a *etc*) vraiment
fait plaisir; **to ~ sb to sth** offrir qch à qn; **to ~
sth as a joke** prendre qch à la plaisanterie
treatise ['tri:tɪz] *n* traité *m* (*ouvrage*)
treatment ['tri:tmənt] *n* traitement *m*; **to have**

837

~ for sth (*Med*) suivre un traitement pour qch
treaty ['tri:tɪ] *n* traité *m*
treble ['trɛbl] *adj* triple ▷ *n* (*Mus*) soprano *m* ▷ *vt*, *vi* tripler
treble clef *n* clé *f* de sol
tree [tri:] *n* arbre *m*
tree-lined ['tri:laɪnd] *adj* bordé(e) d'arbres
treetop ['tri:tɔp] *n* cime *f* d'un arbre
tree trunk *n* tronc *m* d'arbre
trek [trɛk] *n* (*long walk*) randonnée *f*; (*tiring walk*) longue marche, trotte *f* ▷ *vi* (*as holiday*) faire de la randonnée
trellis ['trɛlɪs] *n* treillis *m*, treillage *m*
tremble ['trɛmbl] *vi* trembler
trembling ['trɛmblɪŋ] *n* tremblement *m* ▷ *adj* tremblant(e)
tremendous [trɪ'mɛndəs] *adj* (*enormous*) énorme; (*excellent*) formidable, fantastique
tremendously [trɪ'mɛndəslɪ] *adv* énormément, extrêmement + *adjective*; formidablement
tremor ['trɛməʳ] *n* tremblement *m*; (*also*: **earth tremor**) secousse *f* sismique
trench [trɛntʃ] *n* tranchée *f*
trench coat *n* trench-coat *m*
trench warfare *n* guerre *f* de tranchées
trend [trɛnd] *n* (*tendency*) tendance *f*; (*of events*) cours *m*; (*fashion*) mode *f*; **~ towards/away from doing** tendance à faire/à ne pas faire; **to set the ~** donner le ton; **to set a ~** lancer une mode
trendy ['trɛndɪ] *adj* (*idea, person*) dans le vent; (*clothes*) dernier cri *inv*
trepidation [trɛpɪ'deɪʃən] *n* vive agitation
trespass ['trɛspəs] *vi*: **to ~ on** s'introduire sans permission dans; (*fig*) empiéter sur; **"no ~ing"** "propriété privée", "défense d'entrer"
trespasser ['trɛspəsəʳ] *n* intrus(e); **"~s will be prosecuted"** "interdiction d'entrer sous peine de poursuites"
trestle ['trɛsl] *n* tréteau *m*
trestle table *n* table *f* à tréteaux
trial ['traɪəl] *n* (*Law*) procès *m*, jugement *m*; (*test: of machine etc*) essai *m*; (*worry*) souci *m*; **trials** *npl* (*unpleasant experiences*) épreuves *fpl*; (*Sport*) épreuves éliminatoires; **horse ~s** concours *m* hippique; **~ by jury** jugement par jury; **to be sent for ~** être traduit(e) en justice; **to be on ~** passer en jugement; **by ~ and error** par tâtonnements
trial balance *n* (*Comm*) balance *f* de vérification
trial basis *n*: **on a ~** pour une période d'essai
trial period *n* période *f* d'essai
trial run *n* essai *m*
triangle ['traɪæŋgl] *n* (*Math, Mus*) triangle *m*
triangular [traɪ'æŋgjuləʳ] *adj* triangulaire
triathlon [traɪ'æθlən] *n* triathlon *m*
tribal ['traɪbl] *adj* tribal(e)
tribe [traɪb] *n* tribu *f*
tribesman ['traɪbzmən] *n* membre *m* de la tribu
tribulation [trɪbju'leɪʃən] *n* tribulation *f*, malheur *m*
tribunal [traɪ'bju:nl] *n* tribunal *m*
tributary ['trɪbjutərɪ] *n* (*river*) affluent *m*

tribute ['trɪbju:t] *n* tribut *m*, hommage *m*; **to pay ~ to** rendre hommage à
trice [traɪs] *n*: **in a ~** en un clin d'œil
trick [trɪk] *n* (*magic*) tour *m*; (*joke, prank*) tour, farce *f*; (*skill, knack*) astuce *f*; (*Cards*) levée *f* ▷ *vt* attraper, rouler; **to play a ~ on sb** jouer un tour à qn; **to ~ sb into doing sth** persuader qn par la ruse de faire qch; **to ~ sb out of sth** obtenir qch de qn par la ruse; **it's a ~ of the light** c'est une illusion d'optique causée par la lumière; **that should do the ~** (*fam*) ça devrait faire l'affaire
trickery ['trɪkərɪ] *n* ruse *f*
trickle ['trɪkl] *n* (*of water etc*) filet *m* ▷ *vi* couler en un filet *or* goutte à goutte; **to ~ in/out** (*people*) entrer/sortir par petits groupes
trick question *n* question-piège *f*
trickster ['trɪkstəʳ] *n* arnaqueur(-euse), filou *m*
tricky ['trɪkɪ] *adj* difficile, délicat(e)
tricycle ['traɪsɪkl] *n* tricycle *m*
trifle ['traɪfl] *n* bagatelle *f*; (*Culin*) ≈ diplomate *m* ▷ *adv*: **a ~ long** un peu long ▷ *vi*: **to ~ with** traiter à la légère
trifling ['traɪflɪŋ] *adj* insignifiant(e)
trigger ['trɪgəʳ] *n* (*of gun*) gâchette *f*
  ▶ **trigger off** *vt* déclencher
trigonometry [trɪgə'nɔmətrɪ] *n* trigonométrie *f*
trilby ['trɪlbɪ] *n* (*Brit: also*: **trilby hat**) chapeau mou, feutre *m*
trill [trɪl] *n* (*of bird, Mus*) trille *m*
trilogy ['trɪlədʒɪ] *n* trilogie *f*
trim [trɪm] *adj* net(te); (*house, garden*) bien tenu(e); (*figure*) svelte ▷ *n* (*haircut etc*) légère coupe; (*embellishment*) finitions *fpl*; (*on car*) garnitures *fpl* ▷ *vt* (*cut*) couper légèrement; (*decorate*): **to ~ (with)** décorer (de); (*Naut: a sail*) gréer; **to keep in (good) ~** maintenir en (bon) état
trimmings ['trɪmɪŋz] *npl* décorations *fpl*; (*extras: gen Culin*) garniture *f*
Trinidad and Tobago ['trɪnɪdæd-] *n* Trinité et Tobago *f*
Trinity ['trɪnɪtɪ] *n*: **the ~** la Trinité
trinket ['trɪŋkɪt] *n* bibelot *m*; (*piece of jewellery*) colifichet *m*
trio ['tri:əu] *n* trio *m*
trip [trɪp] *n* voyage *m*; (*excursion*) excursion *f*; (*stumble*) faux pas ▷ *vi* faire un faux pas, trébucher; (*go lightly*) marcher d'un pas léger; **on a ~** en voyage
  ▶ **trip up** *vi* trébucher ▷ *vt* faire un croc-en-jambe à
tripartite [traɪ'pɑ:taɪt] *adj* triparti(e)
tripe [traɪp] *n* (*Culin*) tripes *fpl*; (*pej: rubbish*) idioties *fpl*
triple ['trɪpl] *adj* triple ▷ *adv*: **~ the distance/the speed** trois fois la distance/la vitesse
triple jump *n* triple saut *m*
triplets ['trɪplɪts] *npl* triplés(-ées)
triplicate ['trɪplɪkət] *n*: **in ~** en trois exemplaires
tripod ['traɪpɔd] *n* trépied *m*
Tripoli ['trɪpəlɪ] *n* Tripoli

tripper ['trɪpəʳ] n (Brit) touriste m/f; excursionniste m/f

tripwire ['trɪpwaɪəʳ] n fil m de déclenchement

trite [traɪt] adj banal(e)

triumph ['traɪʌmf] n triomphe m ▷ vi: **to ~ (over)** triompher (de)

triumphal [traɪ'ʌmfl] adj triomphal(e)

triumphant [traɪ'ʌmfənt] adj triomphant(e)

trivia ['trɪvɪə] npl futilités fpl

trivial ['trɪvɪəl] adj insignifiant(e); (commonplace) banal(e)

triviality [trɪvɪ'ælɪtɪ] n caractère insignifiant; banalité f

trivialize ['trɪvɪəlaɪz] vt rendre banal(e)

trod [trɒd] pt of **tread**

trodden [trɒdn] pp of **tread**

trolley ['trɒlɪ] n chariot m

trolley bus n trolleybus m

trollop ['trɒləp] n prostituée f

trombone [trɒm'bəun] n trombone m

troop [tru:p] n bande f, groupe m ▷ vi: **to ~ in/ out** entrer/sortir en groupe; **troops** npl (Mil) troupes fpl; (: men) hommes mpl, soldats mpl; **~ing the colour** (Brit: ceremony) le salut au drapeau

troop carrier n (plane) avion m de transport de troupes; (Naut: also: **troopship**) transport m (navire)

trooper ['tru:pəʳ] n (Mil) soldat m de cavalerie; (US: policeman) ≈ gendarme m

troopship ['tru:pʃɪp] n transport m (navire)

trophy ['trəufɪ] n trophée m

tropic ['trɒpɪk] n tropique m; **in the ~s** sous les tropiques; **T~ of Cancer/Capricorn** tropique du Cancer/Capricorne

tropical ['trɒpɪkl] adj tropical(e)

trot [trɒt] n trot m ▷ vi trotter; **on the ~** (Brit: fig) d'affilée
   ▶ **trot out** vt (excuse, reason) débiter; (names, facts) réciter les uns après les autres

trouble ['trʌbl] n difficulté(s) f(pl), problème(s) m(pl); (worry) ennuis mpl, soucis mpl; (bother, effort) peine f; (Pol) conflit(s) m(pl), troubles mpl; (Med): **stomach** etc **~** troubles gastriques etc ▷ vt (disturb) déranger, gêner; (worry) inquiéter ▷ vi: **to ~ to do** prendre la peine de faire; **troubles** npl (Pol etc) troubles; (personal) ennuis, soucis; **to be in ~** avoir des ennuis; (ship, climber etc) être en difficulté; **to have ~ doing sth** avoir du mal à faire qch; **to go to the ~ of doing** se donner le mal de faire; **it's no ~!** je vous en prie!; **please don't ~ yourself** je vous en prie, ne vous dérangez pas!; **the ~ is ...** le problème, c'est que ...; **what's the ~?** qu'est-ce qui ne va pas?

troubled [trʌbld] adj (person) inquiet(-ète); (times, life) agité(e)

trouble-free ['trʌblfri:] adj sans problèmes or ennuis

troublemaker ['trʌblmeɪkəʳ] n élément perturbateur, fauteur m de troubles

troubleshooter ['trʌblʃu:təʳ] n (in conflict) conciliateur m

troublesome ['trʌblsəm] adj (child) fatigant(e), difficile; (cough) gênant(e)

trouble spot n point chaud (fig)

troubling ['trʌblɪŋ] adj (times, thought) inquiétant(e)

trough [trɒf] n (also: **drinking trough**) abreuvoir m; (also: **feeding trough**) auge f; (depression) creux m; (channel) chenal m; **~ of low pressure** (Meteorology) dépression f

trounce [trauns] vt (defeat) battre à plates coutures

troupe [tru:p] n troupe f

trouser press n presse-pantalon m inv

trousers ['trauzəz] npl pantalon m; **short ~** (Brit) culottes courtes

trouser suit n (Brit) tailleur-pantalon m

trousseau (pl **-x** or **-s**) ['tru:səu, -z] n trousseau m

trout [traut] n (pl inv) truite f

trowel ['trauəl] n truelle f; (garden tool) déplantoir m

truant ['truənt] n: **to play ~** (Brit) faire l'école buissonnière

truce [tru:s] n trêve f

truck [trʌk] n camion m; (Rail) wagon m à plate-forme; (for luggage) chariot m (à bagages)

truck driver n camionneur m

trucker ['trʌkəʳ] n (esp US) camionneur m

truck farm n (US) jardin maraîcher

trucking ['trʌkɪŋ] n (esp US) transport routier

trucking company n (US) entreprise f de transport (routier)

truck stop (US) n routier m, restaurant m de routiers

truculent ['trʌkjulənt] adj agressif(-ive)

trudge [trʌdʒ] vi marcher lourdement, se traîner

true [tru:] adj vrai(e); (accurate) exact(e); (genuine) vrai, véritable; (faithful) fidèle; (wall) d'aplomb; (beam) droit(e); (wheel) dans l'axe; **to come ~** se réaliser; **~ to life** réaliste

truffle ['trʌfl] n truffe f

truly ['tru:lɪ] adv vraiment, réellement; (truthfully) sans mentir; (faithfully) fidèlement; **yours ~** (in letter) je vous prie d'agréer, Monsieur (or Madame etc), l'expression de mes sentiments respectueux

trump [trʌmp] n atout m; **to turn up ~s** (fig) faire des miracles

trump card n atout m; (fig) carte maîtresse f

trumped-up [trʌmpt'ʌp] adj inventé(e) (de toutes pièces)

trumpet ['trʌmpɪt] n trompette f

truncated [trʌŋ'keɪtɪd] adj tronqué(e)

truncheon ['trʌntʃən] n bâton m (d'agent de police); matraque f

trundle ['trʌndl] vt, vi: **to ~ along** rouler bruyamment

trunk [trʌŋk] n (of tree, person) tronc m; (of elephant) trompe f; (case) malle f; (US Aut) coffre m; **trunks** npl (also: **swimming trunks**) maillot m or slip m de bain

trunk call n (Brit Tel) communication

interurbaine

trunk road n (Brit) ≈ (route f) nationale f

truss [trʌs] n (Med) bandage m herniaire ▷ vt: **to ~ (up)** (Culin) brider

trust [trʌst] n confiance f; (responsibility): **to place sth in sb's ~** confier la responsabilité de qch à qn; (Law) fidéicommis m; (Comm) trust m ▷ vt (rely on) avoir confiance en; (entrust): **to ~ sth to sb** confier qch à qn; (hope): **to ~ (that)** espérer (que); **to take sth on ~** accepter qch les yeux fermés; **in ~** (Law) par fidéicommis

trust company n société f fiduciaire

trusted ['trʌstɪd] adj en qui l'on a confiance

trustee [trʌs'tiː] n (Law) fidéicommissaire m/f; (of school etc) administrateur(-trice)

trustful ['trʌstful] adj confiant(e)

trust fund n fonds m en fidéicommis

trusting ['trʌstɪŋ] adj confiant(e)

trustworthy ['trʌstwəːðɪ] adj digne de confiance

trusty ['trʌstɪ] adj fidèle

truth [truːθ, pl truːðz] n vérité f

truthful ['truːθful] adj (person) qui dit la vérité; (answer) sincère; (description) exact(e), vrai(e)

truthfully ['truːθfəlɪ] adv sincèrement, sans mentir

truthfulness ['truːθfəlnɪs] n véracité f

try [traɪ] n essai m, tentative f; (Rugby) essai ▷ vt (attempt) essayer, tenter; (test: sth new: also: **try out**) essayer, tester; (Law: person) juger; (strain) éprouver ▷ vi essayer; **to ~ to do** essayer de faire; (seek) chercher à faire; **to ~ one's (very) best** or **one's (very) hardest** faire de son mieux; **to give sth a ~** essayer qch
  ▶ **try on** vt (clothes) essayer; **to ~ it on** (fig) tenter le coup, bluffer
  ▶ **try out** vt essayer, mettre à l'essai

trying ['traɪɪŋ] adj pénible

tsar [zɑːʳ] n tsar m

T-shirt ['tiːʃəːt] n tee-shirt m

T-square ['tiːskwɛəʳ] n équerre f en T

tsunami [tsʊ'nɑːmɪ] n tsunami m

TT adj abbr (Brit inf) = **teetotal** ▷ abbr (US) = **Trust Territory**

tub [tʌb] n cuve f; (for washing clothes) baquet m; (bath) baignoire f

tuba ['tjuːbə] n tuba m

tubby ['tʌbɪ] adj rondelet(te)

tube [tjuːb] n tube m; (Brit: underground) métro m; (for tyre) chambre f à air; (inf: television): **the ~** la télé

tubeless ['tjuːblɪs] adj (tyre) sans chambre à air

tuber ['tjuːbəʳ] n (Bot) tubercule m

tuberculosis [tjubəːkju'ləusɪs] n tuberculose f

tube station n (Brit) station f de métro

tubing ['tjuːbɪŋ] n tubes mpl; **a piece of ~** un tube

tubular ['tjuːbjuləʳ] adj tubulaire

TUC n abbr (Brit: = Trades Union Congress) confédération f des syndicats britanniques

tuck [tʌk] n (Sewing) pli m, rempli m ▷ vt (put) mettre

  ▶ **tuck away** vt cacher, ranger; (money) mettre de côté; (building): **to be ~ed away** être caché(e)
  ▶ **tuck in** vt rentrer; (child) border ▷ vi (eat) manger de bon appétit; attaquer le repas
  ▶ **tuck up** vt (child) border

tuck shop n (Brit Scol) boutique f à provisions

Tuesday ['tjuːzdɪ] n mardi m; **(the date) today is ~ 23rd March** nous sommes aujourd'hui le mardi 23 mars; **on ~** mardi; **on ~s** le mardi; **every ~** tous les mardis, chaque mardi; **every other ~** un mardi sur deux; **last/next ~** mardi dernier/prochain; **~ next** mardi qui vient; **the following ~** le mardi suivant; **a week/fortnight on ~**, **~ week/fortnight** mardi en huit/quinze; **the ~ before last** l'autre mardi; **the ~ after next** mardi en huit; **~ morning/lunchtime/afternoon/evening** mardi matin/midi/après-midi/soir; **~ night** mardi soir; (overnight) la nuit de mardi (à mercredi); **~'s newspaper** le journal de mardi

tuft [tʌft] n touffe f

tug [tʌg] n (ship) remorqueur m ▷ vt tirer (sur)

tug-of-love [tʌgəv'lʌv] n lutte acharnée entre parents divorcés pour avoir la garde d'un enfant

tug-of-war [tʌgəv'wɔːʳ] n lutte f à la corde

tuition [tjuː'ɪʃən] n (Brit: lessons) leçons fpl; (: private) cours particuliers; (US: fees) frais mpl de scolarité

tulip ['tjuːlɪp] n tulipe f

tumble ['tʌmbl] n (fall) chute f, culbute f ▷ vi tomber, dégringoler; (somersault) faire une or des culbute(s) ▷ vt renverser, faire tomber; **to ~ to sth** (inf) réaliser qch

tumbledown ['tʌmbldaun] adj délabré(e)

tumble dryer n (Brit) séchoir m (à linge) à air chaud

tumbler ['tʌmbləʳ] n verre (droit), gobelet m

tummy ['tʌmɪ] n (inf) ventre m

tumour, (US) **tumor** ['tjuːməʳ] n tumeur f

tumult ['tjuːmʌlt] n tumulte m

tumultuous [tjuː'mʌltjuəs] adj tumultueux(-euse)

tuna ['tjuːnə] n (pl inv: also: **tuna fish**) thon m

tune [tjuːn] n (melody) air m ▷ vt (Mus) accorder; (Radio, TV, Aut) régler, mettre au point; **to be in/out of ~** (instrument) être accordé/désaccordé; (singer) chanter juste/faux; **to be in/out of ~ with** (fig) être en accord/désaccord avec; **she was robbed to the ~ of £30,000** (fig) on lui a volé la jolie somme de 10 000 livres
  ▶ **tune in** vi (Radio, TV): **to ~ in (to)** se mettre à l'écoute (de)
  ▶ **tune up** vi (musician) accorder son instrument

tuneful ['tjuːnful] adj mélodieux(-euse)

tuner ['tjuːnəʳ] n (radio set) tuner m; **piano ~** accordeur m de pianos

tuner amplifier n ampli-tuner m

tungsten ['tʌŋstn] n tungstène m

tunic ['tjuːnɪk] n tunique f

tuning ['tjuːnɪŋ] n réglage m

tuning fork n diapason m

Tunis ['tjuːnɪs] n Tunis

Tunisia [tjuːˈnɪzɪə] *n* Tunisie *f*
Tunisian [tjuːˈnɪzɪən] *adj* tunisien(ne) ▷ *n*
Tunisien(ne)
tunnel [ˈtʌnl] *n* tunnel *m*; (*in mine*) galerie *f* ▷ *vi*
creuser un tunnel (*or* une galerie)
tunnel vision *n* (*Med*) rétrécissement *m* du
champ visuel; (*fig*) vision étroite des choses
tunny [ˈtʌnɪ] *n* thon *m*
turban [ˈtəːbən] *n* turban *m*
turbid [ˈtəːbɪd] *adj* boueux(-euse)
turbine [ˈtəːbaɪn] *n* turbine *f*
turbo [ˈtəːbəʊ] *n* turbo *m*
turbojet [təːbəʊˈdʒɛt] *n* turboréacteur *m*
turboprop [təːbəʊˈprɔp] *n* (*engine*)
turbopropulseur *m*
turbot [ˈtəːbət] *n* (*pl inv*) turbot *m*
turbulence [ˈtəːbjʊləns] *n* (*Aviat*) turbulence *f*
turbulent [ˈtəːbjʊlənt] *adj* turbulent(e); (*sea*)
agité(e)
tureen [təˈriːn] *n* soupière *f*
turf [təːf] *n* gazon *m*; (*clod*) motte *f* (de gazon)
▷ *vt* gazonner; **the T~** le turf, les courses *fpl*
▶ **turf out** *vt* (*inf*) jeter; jeter dehors
turf accountant *n* (*Brit*) bookmaker *m*
turgid [ˈtəːdʒɪd] *adj* (*speech*) pompeux(-euse)
Turin [tjʊəˈrɪn] *n* Turin
Turk [təːk] *n* Turc (Turque)
Turkey [ˈtəːkɪ] *n* Turquie *f*
turkey [ˈtəːkɪ] *n* dindon *m*, dinde *f*
Turkish [ˈtəːkɪʃ] *adj* turc (turque) ▷ *n* (*Ling*)
turc *m*
Turkish bath *n* bain turc
Turkish delight *n* loukoum *m*
turmeric [ˈtəːmərɪk] *n* curcuma *m*
turmoil [ˈtəːmɔɪl] *n* trouble *m*,
bouleversement *m*
turn [təːn] *n* tour *m*; (*in road*) tournant *m*;
(*tendency: of mind, events*) tournure *f*; (*performance*)
numéro *m*; (*Med*) crise *f*, attaque *f* ▷ *vt* tourner;
(*collar, steak*) retourner; (*age*) atteindre; (*shape:
wood, metal*) tourner; (*milk*) faire tourner;
(*change*): **to ~ sth into** changer qch en ▷ *vi*
(*object, wind, milk*) tourner; (*person: look back*) se
(re)tourner; (*reverse direction*) faire demi-tour;
(*change*) changer; (*become*) devenir; **to ~ into** se
changer en, se transformer en; **a good ~** un
service; **a bad ~** un mauvais tour; **it gave me
quite a ~** ça m'a fait un coup; **"no left ~"** (*Aut*)
"défense de tourner à gauche"; **~ left/right at
the next junction** tournez à gauche/droite au
prochain carrefour; **it's your ~** c'est (à) votre
tour; **in ~** à son tour; à tour de rôle; **to take ~s**
se relayer; **to take ~s at** faire à tour de rôle; **at
the ~ of the year/century** à la fin de l'année/
du siècle; **to take a ~ for the worse** (*situation,
events*) empirer; **his health** *or* **he has taken a ~
for the worse** son état s'est aggravé
▶ **turn about** *vi* faire demi-tour; faire un demi-
tour
▶ **turn around** *vi* (*person*) se retourner ▷ *vt*
(*object*) tourner
▶ **turn away** *vi* se détourner, tourner la tête ▷ *vt*

(*reject: person*) renvoyer; (: *business*) refuser
▶ **turn back** *vi* revenir, faire demi-tour
▶ **turn down** *vt* (*refuse*) rejeter, refuser; (*reduce*)
baisser; (*fold*) rabattre
▶ **turn in** *vi* (*inf: go to bed*) aller se coucher ▷ *vt*
(*fold*) rentrer
▶ **turn off** *vi* (*from road*) tourner ▷ *vt* (*light, radio
etc*) éteindre; (*tap*) fermer; (*engine*) arrêter; **I
can't ~ the heating off** je n'arrive pas à
éteindre le chauffage
▶ **turn on** *vt* (*light, radio etc*) allumer; (*tap*) ouvrir;
(*engine*) mettre en marche; **I can't ~ the
heating on** je n'arrive pas à allumer le
chauffage
▶ **turn out** *vt* (*light, gas*) éteindre; (*produce: goods,
novel, good pupils*) produire ▷ *vi* (*voters, troops*) se
présenter; **to ~ out to be ...** s'avérer ..., se
révéler ...
▶ **turn over** *vi* (*person*) se retourner ▷ *vt* (*object*)
retourner; (*page*) tourner
▶ **turn round** *vi* faire demi-tour; (*rotate*) tourner
▶ **turn to** *vt fus*: **to ~ to sb** s'adresser à qn
▶ **turn up** *vi* (*person*) arriver, se pointer (*inf*); (*lost
object*) être retrouvé(e) ▷ *vt* (*collar*) remonter;
(*radio, heater*) mettre plus fort
turnabout [ˈtəːnəbaʊt], **turnaround**
[ˈtəːnəraʊnd] *n* volte-face *f inv*
turncoat [ˈtəːnkəʊt] *n* renégat(e)
turned-up [ˈtəːndʌp] *adj* (*nose*) retroussé(e)
turning [ˈtəːnɪŋ] *n* (*in road*) tournant *m*; **the
first ~ on the right** la première (rue *or* route) à
droite
turning circle *n* (*Brit*) rayon *m* de braquage
turning point *n* (*fig*) tournant *m*, moment
décisif
turning radius *n* (*US*) = **turning circle**
turnip [ˈtəːnɪp] *n* navet *m*
turnout [ˈtəːnaʊt] *n* (nombre *m* de personnes
dans l')assistance *f*; (*of voters*) taux *m* de
participation
turnover [ˈtəːnəʊvəʳ] *n* (*Comm: amount of money*)
chiffre *m* d'affaires; (: *of goods*) roulement *m*; (*of
staff*) renouvellement *m*, changement *m*; (*Culin*)
sorte de chausson; **there is a rapid ~ in staff** le
personnel change souvent
turnpike [ˈtəːnpaɪk] *n* (*US*) autoroute *f* à péage
turnstile [ˈtəːnstaɪl] *n* tourniquet *m* (*d'entrée*)
turntable [ˈtəːnteɪbl] *n* (*on record player*) platine *f*
turn-up [ˈtəːnʌp] *n* (*Brit: on trousers*) revers *m*
turpentine [ˈtəːpəntaɪn] *n* (*also*: **turps**) (essence
f de) térébenthine *f*
turquoise [ˈtəːkwɔɪz] *n* (*stone*) turquoise *f* ▷ *adj*
turquoise *inv*
turret [ˈtʌrɪt] *n* tourelle *f*
turtle [ˈtəːtl] *n* tortue marine
turtleneck [ˈtəːtlnɛk], **turtleneck sweater** *n*
pullover *m* à col montant
Tuscany [ˈtʌskənɪ] *n* Toscane *f*
tusk [tʌsk] *n* défense *f* (d'éléphant)
tussle [ˈtʌsl] *n* bagarre *f*, mêlée *f*
tutor [ˈtjuːtəʳ] *n* (*Brit Scol: in college*)
directeur(-trice) d'études; (*private teacher*)

t

précepteur(-trice)

tutorial [tjuːˈtɔːrɪəl] *n* (*Scol*) (séance *f* de) travaux *mpl* pratiques

tuxedo [tʌkˈsiːdəu] *n* (*US*) smoking *m*

TV [tiːˈviː] *n abbr* (= television) télé *f*, TV *f*

TV dinner *n* plateau-repas surgelé

twaddle [ˈtwɔdl] *n* balivernes *fpl*

twang [twæŋ] *n* (*of instrument*) son vibrant; (*of voice*) ton nasillard ▷ *vi* vibrer ▷ *vt* (*guitar*) pincer les cordes de

tweak [twiːk] *vt* (*nose*) tordre; (*ear, hair*) tirer

tweed [twiːd] *n* tweed *m*

tweezers [ˈtwiːzəz] *npl* pince *f* à épiler

twelfth [twelfθ] *num* douzième

Twelfth Night *n* la fête des Rois

twelve [twɛlv] *num* douze; **at ~ (o'clock)** à midi; (*midnight*) à minuit

twentieth [ˈtwɛntɪɪθ] *num* vingtième

twenty [ˈtwɛntɪ] *num* vingt

twerp [twəːp] *n* (*inf*) imbécile *m/f*

twice [twaɪs] *adv* deux fois; **~ as much** deux fois plus; **~ a week** deux fois par semaine; **she is ~ your age** elle a deux fois ton âge

twiddle [ˈtwɪdl] *vt, vi*: **to ~ (with) sth** tripoter qch; **to ~ one's thumbs** (*fig*) se tourner les pouces

twig [twɪg] *n* brindille *f* ▷ *vt, vi* (*inf*) piger

twilight [ˈtwaɪlaɪt] *n* crépuscule *m*; (*morning*) aube *f*; **in the ~** dans la pénombre

twill [twɪl] *n* sergé *m*

twin [twɪn] *adj, n* jumeau(-elle) ▷ *vt* jumeler

twin-bedded room [ˈtwɪnˈbɛdɪd-] *n* = **twin room**

twin beds *npl* lits *mpl* jumeaux

twin-carburettor [ˈtwɪnkɑːbjuˈrɛtəʳ] *adj* à double carburateur

twine [twaɪn] *n* ficelle *f* ▷ *vi* (*plant*) s'enrouler

twin-engined [twɪnˈɛndʒɪnd] *adj* bimoteur; **~ aircraft** bimoteur *m*

twinge [twɪndʒ] *n* (*of pain*) élancement *m*; (*of conscience*) remords *m*

twinkle [ˈtwɪŋkl] *n* scintillement *m*; pétillement *m* ▷ *vi* scintiller; (*eyes*) pétiller

twin room *n* chambre *f* à deux lits

twin town *n* ville jumelée

twirl [twəːl] *n* tournoiement *m* ▷ *vt* faire tournoyer ▷ *vi* tournoyer

twist [twɪst] *n* torsion *f*, tour *m*; (*in wire, flex*) tortillon *m*; (*bend: in road*) tournant *m*; (*in story*) coup *m* de théâtre ▷ *vt* tordre; (*weave*) entortiller; (*roll around*) enrouler; (*fig*) déformer ▷ *vi* s'entortiller; s'enrouler; (*road, river*) serpenter; **to ~ one's ankle/wrist** (*Med*) se tordre la cheville/le poignet

twisted [ˈtwɪstɪd] *adj* (*wire, rope*) entortillé(e); (*ankle, wrist*) tordu(e), foulé(e); (*fig: logic, mind*) tordu

twit [twɪt] *n* (*inf*) crétin(e)

twitch [twɪtʃ] *n* (*pull*) coup sec, saccade *f*; (*nervous*) tic *m* ▷ *vi* se convulser; avoir un tic

Twitter® [ˈtwɪtəʳ] *n* Twitter® ▷ *vi* twitter

two [tuː] *num* deux; **~ by ~, in ~s** par deux; **to put ~ and ~ together** (*fig*) faire le rapprochement

two-bit [tuːˈbɪt] *adj* (*esp US inf, pej*) de pacotille

two-door [tuːˈdɔːʳ] *adj* (*Aut*) à deux portes

two-faced [tuːˈfeɪst] *adj* (*pej: person*) faux (fausse)

twofold [ˈtuːfəuld] *adv*: **to increase ~** doubler ▷ *adj* (*increase*) de cent pour cent; (*reply*) en deux parties

two-piece [ˈtuːpiːs] *n* (*also*: **two-piece suit**) (costume *m*) deux-pièces *m inv*; (*also*: **two-piece swimsuit**) (maillot *m* de bain) deux-pièces

two-seater [tuːˈsiːtəʳ] *n* (*plane*) (avion *m*) biplace *m*; (*car*) voiture *f* à deux places

twosome [ˈtuːsəm] *n* (*people*) couple *m*

two-stroke [ˈtuːstrəuk] *n* (*also*: **two-stroke engine**) moteur *m* à deux temps ▷ *adj* à deux temps

two-tone [ˈtuːtəun] *adj* (*in colour*) à deux tons

two-way [ˈtuːweɪ] *adj* (*traffic*) dans les deux sens; **~ radio** émetteur-récepteur *m*

TX *abbr* (*US*) = **Texas**

tycoon [taɪˈkuːn] *n*: **(business) ~** gros homme d'affaires

type [taɪp] *n* (*category*) genre *m*, espèce *f*; (*model*) modèle *m*; (*example*) type *m*; (*Typ*) type, caractère *m* ▷ *vt* (*letter etc*) taper (à la machine); **what ~ do you want?** quel genre voulez-vous?; **in bold/ italic ~** en caractères gras/en italiques

typecast [ˈtaɪpkɑːst] *adj* condamné(e) à toujours jouer le même rôle

typeface [ˈtaɪpfeɪs] *n* police *f* (de caractères)

typescript [ˈtaɪpskrɪpt] *n* texte dactylographié

typeset [ˈtaɪpsɛt] *vt* composer (*en imprimerie*)

typesetter [ˈtaɪpsɛtəʳ] *n* compositeur *m*

typewriter [ˈtaɪpraɪtəʳ] *n* machine *f* à écrire

typewritten [ˈtaɪprɪtn] *adj* dactylographié(e)

typhoid [ˈtaɪfɔɪd] *n* typhoïde *f*

typhoon [taɪˈfuːn] *n* typhon *m*

typhus [ˈtaɪfəs] *n* typhus *m*

typical [ˈtɪpɪkl] *adj* typique, caractéristique

typically [ˈtɪpɪklɪ] *adv* (*as usual*) comme d'habitude; (*characteristically*) typiquement

typify [ˈtɪpɪfaɪ] *vt* être caractéristique de

typing [ˈtaɪpɪŋ] *n* dactylo(graphie) *f*

typing error *n* faute *f* de frappe

typing pool *n* pool *m* de dactylos

typist [ˈtaɪpɪst] *n* dactylo *m/f*

typo [ˈtaɪpəu] *n abbr* (*inf*: = typographical error) coquille *f*

typography [taɪˈpɔgrəfɪ] *n* typographie *f*

tyranny [ˈtɪrənɪ] *n* tyrannie *f*

tyrant [ˈtaɪrənt] *n* tyran *m*

tyre, (*US*) **tire** [ˈtaɪəʳ] *n* pneu *m*

tyre pressure *n* (*Brit*) pression *f* (de gonflage)

Tyrol [tɪˈrəul] *n* Tyrol *m*

Tyrrhenian Sea [tɪˈriːnɪən-] *n*: **the ~** la mer Tyrrhénienne

tzar [zɑːʳ] *n* = **tsar**

Uu

U, u [juː] n (letter) U, u m; **U for Uncle** U comme
Ursule

U n abbr (Brit Cine: = universal) ≈ tous publics

UAW n abbr (US: = United Automobile Workers)
syndicat des ouvriers de l'automobile

UB40 n abbr (Brit: = unemployment benefit form 40)
numéro de référence d'un formulaire d'inscription au
chômage: par extension, le bénéficiaire

U-bend ['juːbɛnd] n (Brit Aut) coude m, virage m
en épingle à cheveux; (in pipe) coude

ubiquitous [juːˈbɪkwɪtəs] adj doué(e)
d'ubiquité, omniprésent(e)

UCAS ['juːkæs] n abbr (Brit) = **Universities and
Colleges Admissions Service**

UDA n abbr (Brit) = **Ulster Defence Association**

UDC n abbr (Brit) = **Urban District Council**

udder ['ʌdəʳ] n pis m, mamelle f

UDI n abbr (Brit Pol) = **unilateral declaration of
independence**

UDR n abbr (Brit) = **Ulster Defence Regiment**

UEFA [juːˈeɪfə] n abbr (= Union of European Football
Associations) UEFA f

UFO ['juːfəu] n abbr (= unidentified flying object)
ovni m

Uganda [juːˈgændə] n Ouganda m

Ugandan [juːˈgændən] adj ougandais(e) ▷ n
Ougandais(e)

UGC n abbr (Brit: = University Grants Committee)
commission d'attribution des dotations aux universités

ugh [əːh] excl pouah!

ugliness ['ʌglɪnɪs] n laideur f

ugly ['ʌglɪ] adj laid(e), vilain(e); (fig)
répugnant(e)

UHF abbr (= ultra-high frequency) UHF

UHT adj abbr = **ultra-heat treated**; **~ milk** lait m
UHT or longue conservation

UK n abbr = **United Kingdom**

Ukraine [juːˈkreɪn] n Ukraine f

Ukrainian [juːˈkreɪnɪən] adj ukrainien(ne) ▷ n
Ukrainien(ne); (Ling) ukrainien m

ulcer ['ʌlsəʳ] n ulcère m; **mouth ~** aphte f

Ulster ['ʌlstəʳ] n Ulster m

ulterior [ʌlˈtɪərɪəʳ] adj ultérieur(e); **~ motive**
arrière-pensée f

ultimate ['ʌltɪmət] adj ultime, final(e);
(authority) suprême ▷ n: **the ~ in luxury** le

summum du luxe

ultimately ['ʌltɪmətlɪ] adv (at last) en fin de
compte; (fundamentally) finalement; (eventually)
par la suite

ultimatum (pl **-s** or **ultimata**) [ʌltɪˈmeɪtəm, -tə]
n ultimatum m

ultrasonic [ʌltrəˈsɒnɪk] adj ultrasonique

ultrasound ['ʌltrəsaund] n (Med) ultrason m

ultraviolet ['ʌltrəˈvaɪəlɪt] adj ultraviolet(te)

umbilical [ʌmbɪˈlaɪkl] adj: **~ cord** cordon
ombilical

umbrage ['ʌmbrɪdʒ] n: **to take ~** prendre
ombrage, se froisser

umbrella [ʌmˈbrɛlə] n parapluie m; (for sun)
parasol m; (fig): **under the ~ of** sous les
auspices de; chapeauté(e) par

umlaut ['umlaut] n tréma m

umpire ['ʌmpaɪəʳ] n arbitre m; (Tennis) juge m de
chaise ▷ vt arbitrer

umpteen [ʌmpˈtiːn] adj je ne sais combien de;
for the ~th time pour la nième fois

UMW n abbr (= United Mineworkers of America)
syndicat des mineurs

UN n abbr = **United Nations**

unabashed [ʌnəˈbæʃt] adj nullement
intimidé(e)

unabated [ʌnəˈbeɪtɪd] adj non diminué(e)

unable [ʌnˈeɪbl] adj: **to be ~ to** ne (pas) pouvoir,
être dans l'impossibilité de; (not capable) être
incapable de

unabridged [ʌnəˈbrɪdʒd] adj complet(-ète),
intégral(e)

unacceptable [ʌnəkˈsɛptəbl] adj (behaviour)
inadmissible; (price, proposal) inacceptable

unaccompanied [ʌnəˈkʌmpənɪd] adj (child, lady)
non accompagné(e); (singing, song) sans
accompagnement

unaccountably [ʌnəˈkauntəblɪ] adv
inexplicablement

unaccounted [ʌnəˈkauntɪd] adj: **two
passengers are ~ for** on est sans nouvelles de
deux passagers

unaccustomed [ʌnəˈkʌstəmd] adj
inaccoutumé(e), inhabituel(le); **to be ~ to sth**
ne pas avoir l'habitude de qch

unacquainted [ʌnəˈkweɪntɪd] adj: **to be ~ with**

u

ne pas connaître

unadulterated [ʌnə'dʌltəreɪtɪd] *adj* pur(e), naturel(le)

unaffected [ʌnə'fɛktɪd] *adj* (*person, behaviour*) naturel(le); (*emotionally*): **to be ~ by** ne pas être touché(e) par

unafraid [ʌnə'freɪd] *adj*: **to be ~** ne pas avoir peur

unaided [ʌn'eɪdɪd] *adj* sans aide, tout(e) seul(e)

unanimity [juːnə'nɪmɪtɪ] *n* unanimité *f*

unanimous [juː'nænɪməs] *adj* unanime

unanimously [juː'nænɪməslɪ] *adv* à l'unanimité

unanswered [ʌn'ɑːnsəd] *adj* (*question, letter*) sans réponse

unappetizing [ʌn'æpɪtaɪzɪŋ] *adj* peu appétissant(e)

unappreciative [ʌnə'priːʃɪətɪv] *adj* indifférent(e)

unarmed [ʌn'ɑːmd] *adj* (*person*) non armé(e); (*combat*) sans armes

unashamed [ʌnə'ʃeɪmd] *adj* sans honte; impudent(e)

unassisted [ʌnə'sɪstɪd] *adj* non assisté(e) ▷ *adv* sans aide, tout(e) seul(e)

unassuming [ʌnə'sjuːmɪŋ] *adj* modeste, sans prétentions

unattached [ʌnə'tætʃt] *adj* libre, sans attaches

unattended [ʌnə'tɛndɪd] *adj* (*car, child, luggage*) sans surveillance

unattractive [ʌnə'træktɪv] *adj* peu attrayant(e); (*character*) peu sympathique

unauthorized [ʌn'ɔːθəraɪzd] *adj* non autorisé(e), sans autorisation

unavailable [ʌnə'veɪləbl] *adj* (*article, room, book*) (qui n'est) pas disponible; (*person*) (qui n'est) pas libre

unavoidable [ʌnə'vɔɪdəbl] *adj* inévitable

unavoidably [ʌnə'vɔɪdəblɪ] *adv* inévitablement

unaware [ʌnə'wɛəʳ] *adj*: **to be ~ of** ignorer, ne pas savoir, être inconscient(e) de

unawares [ʌnə'wɛəz] *adv* à l'improviste, au dépourvu

unbalanced [ʌn'bælənst] *adj* déséquilibré(e)

unbearable [ʌn'bɛərəbl] *adj* insupportable

unbeatable [ʌn'biːtəbl] *adj* imbattable

unbeaten [ʌn'biːtn] *adj* invaincu(e); (*record*) non battu(e)

unbecoming [ʌnbɪ'kʌmɪŋ] *adj* (*unseemly: language, behaviour*) malséant(e), inconvenant(e); (*unflattering: garment*) peu seyant(e)

unbeknown [ʌnbɪ'nəun], **unbeknownst** [ʌnbɪ'nəunst] *adv*: **~ to** à l'insu de

unbelief [ʌnbɪ'liːf] *n* incrédulité *f*

unbelievable [ʌnbɪ'liːvəbl] *adj* incroyable

unbelievingly [ʌnbɪ'liːvɪŋlɪ] *adv* avec incrédulité

unbend [ʌn'bɛnd] (*irreg: like* bend) *vi* se détendre ▷ *vt* (*wire*) redresser, détordre

unbending [ʌn'bɛndɪŋ] *adj* (*fig*) inflexible

unbiased, unbiassed [ʌn'baɪəst] *adj* impartial(e)

unblemished [ʌn'blɛmɪʃt] *adj* impeccable

unblock [ʌn'blɔk] *vt* (*pipe*) déboucher; (*road*) dégager

unborn [ʌn'bɔːn] *adj* à naître

unbounded [ʌn'baundɪd] *adj* sans bornes, illimité(e)

unbreakable [ʌn'breɪkəbl] *adj* incassable

unbridled [ʌn'braɪdld] *adj* débridé(e), déchaîné(e)

unbroken [ʌn'brəukn] *adj* intact(e); (*line*) continu(e); (*record*) non battu(e)

unbuckle [ʌn'bʌkl] *vt* déboucler

unburden [ʌn'bəːdn] *vt*: **to ~ o.s.** s'épancher, se livrer

unbutton [ʌn'bʌtn] *vt* déboutonner

uncalled-for [ʌn'kɔːldfɔːʳ] *adj* déplacé(e), injustifié(e)

uncanny [ʌn'kænɪ] *adj* étrange, troublant(e)

unceasing [ʌn'siːsɪŋ] *adj* incessant(e), continu(e)

unceremonious [ʌnsɛrɪ'məunɪəs] *adj* (*abrupt, rude*) brusque

uncertain [ʌn'səːtn] *adj* incertain(e); (*hesitant*) hésitant(e); **we were ~ whether ...** nous ne savions pas vraiment si ...; **in no ~ terms** sans équivoque possible

uncertainty [ʌn'səːtntɪ] *n* incertitude *f*, doutes *mpl*

unchallenged [ʌn'tʃælɪndʒd] *adj* (*gen*) incontesté(e); (*information*) non contesté(e); **to go ~** ne pas être contesté

unchanged [ʌn'tʃeɪndʒd] *adj* inchangé(e)

uncharitable [ʌn'tʃærɪtəbl] *adj* peu charitable

uncharted [ʌn'tʃɑːtɪd] *adj* inexploré(e)

unchecked [ʌn'tʃɛkt] *adj* non réprimé(e)

uncivilized [ʌn'sɪvɪlaɪzd] *adj* non civilisé(e); (*fig*) barbare

uncle ['ʌŋkl] *n* oncle *m*

unclear [ʌn'klɪəʳ] *adj* (qui n'est) pas clair(e) *or* évident(e); **I'm still ~ about what I'm supposed to do** je ne sais pas encore exactement ce que je dois faire

uncoil [ʌn'kɔɪl] *vt* dérouler ▷ *vi* se dérouler

uncomfortable [ʌn'kʌmfətəbl] *adj* inconfortable, peu confortable; (*uneasy*) mal à l'aise, gêné(e); (*situation*) désagréable

uncomfortably [ʌn'kʌmfətəblɪ] *adv* inconfortablement; d'un ton *etc* gêné *or* embarrassé; désagréablement

uncommitted [ʌnkə'mɪtɪd] *adj* (*attitude, country*) non engagé(e)

uncommon [ʌn'kɔmən] *adj* rare, singulier(-ière), peu commun(e)

uncommunicative [ʌnkə'mjuːnɪkətɪv] *adj* réservé(e)

uncomplicated [ʌn'kɔmplɪkeɪtɪd] *adj* simple, peu compliqué(e)

uncompromising [ʌn'kɔmprəmaɪzɪŋ] *adj* intransigeant(e), inflexible

unconcerned [ʌnkən'səːnd] *adj* (*unworried*): **to be ~ (about)** ne pas s'inquiéter (de)

unconditional [ʌnkən'dɪʃənl] *adj* sans

conditions

uncongenial [ʌnkən'dʒi:nɪəl] *adj* peu agréable

unconnected [ʌnkə'nɛktɪd] *adj* (*unrelated*): ~ **(with)** sans rapport (avec)

unconscious [ʌn'kɒnʃəs] *adj* sans connaissance, évanoui(e); (*unaware*): ~ **(of)** inconscient(e) (de) ▷ *n*: **the** ~ l'inconscient *m*; **to knock sb** ~ assommer qn

unconsciously [ʌn'kɒnʃəslɪ] *adv* inconsciemment

unconstitutional [ʌnkɒnstɪ'tju:ʃənl] *adj* anticonstitutionnel(le)

uncontested [ʌnkən'tɛstɪd] *adj* (*champion*) incontesté(e); (*Pol: seat*) non disputé(e)

uncontrollable [ʌnkən'trəuləbl] *adj* (*child, dog*) indiscipliné(e); (*temper, laughter*) irrépressible

uncontrolled [ʌnkən'trəuld] *adj* (*laughter, price rises*) incontrôlé(e)

unconventional [ʌnkən'vɛnʃənl] *adj* peu conventionnel(le)

unconvinced [ʌnkən'vɪnst] *adj*: **to be** ~ ne pas être convaincu(e)

unconvincing [ʌnkən'vɪnsɪŋ] *adj* peu convaincant(e)

uncork [ʌn'kɔ:k] *vt* déboucher

uncorroborated [ʌnkə'rɒbəreɪtɪd] *adj* non confirmé(e)

uncouth [ʌn'ku:θ] *adj* grossier(-ière), fruste

uncover [ʌn'kʌvər] *vt* découvrir

unctuous ['ʌŋktjuəs] *adj* onctueux(-euse), mielleux(-euse)

undamaged [ʌn'dæmɪdʒd] *adj* (*goods*) intact(e), en bon état; (*fig: reputation*) intact

undaunted [ʌn'dɔ:ntɪd] *adj* non intimidé(e), inébranlable

undecided [ʌndɪ'saɪdɪd] *adj* indécis(e), irrésolu(e)

undelivered [ʌndɪ'lɪvəd] *adj* non remis(e), non livré(e)

undeniable [ʌndɪ'naɪəbl] *adj* indéniable, incontestable

under ['ʌndər] *prep* sous; (*less than*) (de) moins de; au-dessous de; (*according to*) selon, en vertu de ▷ *adv* au-dessous; en dessous; **from** ~ **sth** de dessous *or* de sous qch; ~ **there** là-dessous; **in** ~ **2 hours** en moins de 2 heures; ~ **anaesthetic** sous anesthésie; ~ **discussion** en discussion; ~ **the circumstances** étant donné les circonstances; ~ **repair** en (cours de) réparation

under... ['ʌndər] *prefix* sous-

underage [ʌndər'eɪdʒ] *adj* qui n'a pas l'âge réglementaire

underarm ['ʌndəra:m] *adv* par en-dessous ▷ *adj* (*throw*) par en-dessous; (*deodorant*) pour les aisselles

undercapitalized [ʌndə'kæpɪtəlaɪzd] *adj* sous-capitalisé(e)

undercarriage ['ʌndəkærɪdʒ] *n* (*Brit Aviat*) train *m* d'atterrissage

undercharge [ʌndə'tʃa:dʒ] *vt* ne pas faire payer assez à

underclass ['ʌndəkla:s] *n* ≈ quart-monde *m*

underclothes ['ʌndəkləuðz] *npl* sous-vêtements *mpl*; (*women's only*) dessous *mpl*

undercoat ['ʌndəkəut] *n* (*paint*) couche *f* de fond

undercover [ʌndə'kʌvər] *adj* secret(-ète), clandestin(e)

undercurrent ['ʌndəkʌrnt] *n* courant sous-jacent

undercut [ʌndə'kʌt] *vt* (*irreg: like* **cut**) vendre moins cher que

underdeveloped ['ʌndədɪ'vɛləpt] *adj* sous-développé(e)

underdog ['ʌndədɒg] *n* opprimé *m*

underdone [ʌndə'dʌn] *adj* (*Culin*) saignant(e); (: *pej*) pas assez cuit(e)

underestimate ['ʌndər'ɛstɪmeɪt] *vt* sous-estimer, mésestimer

underexposed ['ʌndəriks'pəuzd] *adj* (*Phot*) sous-exposé(e)

underfed [ʌndə'fɛd] *adj* sous-alimenté(e)

underfoot [ʌndə'fut] *adv* sous les pieds

under-funded ['ʌndə'fʌndɪd] *adj*: **to be** ~ (*organization*) ne pas être doté(e) de fonds suffisants

undergo [ʌndə'gəu] *vt* (*irreg: like* **go**) subir; (*treatment*) suivre; **the car is** ~**ing repairs** la voiture est en réparation

undergraduate [ʌndə'grædjuət] *n* étudiant(e) (qui prépare la licence) ▷ *cpd*: ~ **courses** cours *mpl* préparant à la licence

underground ['ʌndəgraund] *adj* souterrain(e); (*fig*) clandestin(e) ▷ *n* (*Brit: railway*) métro *m*; (*Pol*) clandestinité *f*

undergrowth ['ʌndəgrəuθ] *n* broussailles *fpl*, sous-bois *m*

underhand [ʌndə'hænd], **underhanded** [ʌndə'hændɪd] *adj* (*fig*) sournois(e), en dessous

underinsured [ʌndərɪn'ʃuəd] *adj* sous-assuré(e)

underlie [ʌndə'laɪ] *vt* (*irreg: like* **lie**) être à la base de; **the underlying cause** la cause sous-jacente

underline [ʌndə'laɪn] *vt* souligner

underling ['ʌndəlɪŋ] *n* (*pej*) sous-fifre *m*, subalterne *m*

undermanning [ʌndə'mænɪŋ] *n* pénurie *f* de main-d'œuvre

undermentioned [ʌndə'mɛnʃənd] *adj* mentionné(e) ci-dessous

undermine [ʌndə'maɪn] *vt* saper, miner

underneath [ʌndə'ni:θ] *adv* (en) dessous ▷ *prep* sous, au-dessous de

undernourished [ʌndə'nʌrɪʃt] *adj* sous-alimenté(e)

underpaid [ʌndə'peɪd] *adj* sous-payé(e)

underpants ['ʌndəpænts] *npl* caleçon *m*, slip *m*

underpass ['ʌndəpa:s] *n* (*Brit: for pedestrians*) passage souterrain; (: *for cars*) passage inférieur

underpin [ʌndə'pɪn] *vt* (*argument, case*) étayer

underplay [ʌndə'pleɪ] *vt* (*Brit*) minimiser

underpopulated [ʌndə'pɒpjuleɪtɪd] *adj* sous-peuplé(e)

underprice [ʌndə'praɪs] *vt* vendre à un prix trop bas

u

underprivileged [ˌʌndəˈprɪvɪlɪdʒd] *adj* défavorisé(e)

underrate [ˌʌndəˈreɪt] *vt* sous-estimer, mésestimer

underscore [ˌʌndəˈskɔːʳ] *vt* souligner

underseal [ˌʌndəˈsiːl] *vt* (*Brit*) traiter contre la rouille

undersecretary [ˈʌndəˈsɛkrətrɪ] *n* sous-secrétaire *m*

undersell [ˌʌndəˈsɛl] *vt* (*irreg*: *like* **sell**: *competitors*) vendre moins cher que

undershirt [ˈʌndəʃəːt] *n* (*US*) tricot *m* de corps

undershorts [ˈʌndəʃɔːts] *npl* (*US*) caleçon *m*, slip *m*

underside [ˈʌndəsaɪd] *n* dessous *m*

undersigned [ˈʌndəˈsaɪnd] *adj*, *n* soussigné(e) *m/f*

underskirt [ˈʌndəskəːt] *n* (*Brit*) jupon *m*

understaffed [ˌʌndəˈstɑːft] *adj* qui manque de personnel

understand [ˌʌndəˈstænd] *vt*, *vi* (*irreg*: *like* **stand**) comprendre; **I don't ~** je ne comprends pas; **I ~ that** ... je me suis laissé dire que ..., je crois comprendre que ...; **to make o.s. understood** se faire comprendre

understandable [ˌʌndəˈstændəbl] *adj* compréhensible

understanding [ˌʌndəˈstændɪŋ] *adj* compréhensif(-ive) ▷ *n* compréhension *f*; (*agreement*) accord *m*; **to come to an ~ with sb** s'entendre avec qn; **on the ~ that** ... à condition que ...

understate [ˌʌndəˈsteɪt] *vt* minimiser

understatement [ˈʌndəsteɪtmənt] *n*: **that's an ~** c'est (bien) peu dire, le terme est faible

understood [ˌʌndəˈstud] *pt*, *pp of* **understand** ▷ *adj* entendu(e); (*implied*) sous-entendu(e)

understudy [ˈʌndəstʌdɪ] *n* doublure *f*

undertake [ˌʌndəˈteɪk] *vt* (*irreg*: *like* **take**: *job*, *task*) entreprendre; (*duty*) se charger de; **to ~ to do sth** s'engager à faire qch

undertaker [ˈʌndəteɪkəʳ] *n* (*Brit*) entrepreneur *m* des pompes funèbres, croque-mort *m*

undertaking [ˈʌndəteɪkɪŋ] *n* entreprise *f*; (*promise*) promesse *f*

undertone [ˈʌndətəun] *n* (*low voice*): **in an ~** à mi-voix; (*of criticism etc*) nuance cachée

undervalue [ˌʌndəˈvælju:] *vt* sous-estimer

underwater [ˌʌndəˈwɔːtəʳ] *adv* sous l'eau ▷ *adj* sous-marin(e)

underway [ˌʌndəˈweɪ] *adj*: **to be ~** (*meeting*, *investigation*) être en cours

underwear [ˈʌndəwɛəʳ] *n* sous-vêtements *mpl*; (*women's only*) dessous *mpl*

underweight [ˌʌndəˈweɪt] *adj* d'un poids insuffisant; (*person*) (trop) maigre

underwent [ˌʌndəˈwɛnt] *pt of* **undergo**

underworld [ˈʌndəwəːld] *n* (*of crime*) milieu *m*, pègre *f*

underwrite [ˌʌndəˈraɪt] *vt* (*Finance*) garantir; (*Insurance*) souscrire

underwriter [ˈʌndəraɪtəʳ] *n* (*Insurance*) souscripteur *m*

undeserving [ˌʌndɪˈzəːvɪŋ] *adj*: **to be ~ of** ne pas mériter

undesirable [ˌʌndɪˈzaɪərəbl] *adj* peu souhaitable; (*person*, *effect*) indésirable

undeveloped [ˌʌndɪˈvɛləpt] *adj* (*land*, *resources*) non exploité(e)

undies [ˈʌndɪz] *npl* (*inf*) dessous *mpl*, lingerie *f*

undiluted [ˈʌndaɪˈluːtɪd] *adj* pur(e), non dilué(e)

undiplomatic [ˈʌndɪpləˈmætɪk] *adj* peu diplomatique, maladroit(e)

undischarged [ˈʌndɪsˈtʃɑːdʒd] *adj*: **~ bankrupt** failli(e) non réhabilité(e)

undisciplined [ʌnˈdɪsɪplɪnd] *adj* indiscipliné(e)

undisguised [ˈʌndɪsˈgaɪzd] *adj* (*dislike*, *amusement etc*) franc (franche)

undisputed [ˈʌndɪsˈpjuːtɪd] *adj* incontesté(e)

undistinguished [ˈʌndɪsˈtɪŋgwɪʃt] *adj* médiocre, quelconque

undisturbed [ˈʌndɪsˈtəːbd] *adj* (*sleep*) tranquille, paisible; **to leave ~** ne pas déranger

undivided [ˈʌndɪˈvaɪdɪd] *adj*: **can I have your ~ attention?** puis-je avoir toute votre attention?

undo [ʌnˈduː] *vt* (*irreg*: *like* **do**) défaire

undoing [ʌnˈduːɪŋ] *n* ruine *f*, perte *f*

undone [ʌnˈdʌn] *pp of* **undo** ▷ *adj*: **to come ~** se défaire

undoubted [ʌnˈdautɪd] *adj* indubitable, certain(e)

undoubtedly [ʌnˈdautɪdlɪ] *adv* sans aucun doute

undress [ʌnˈdrɛs] *vi* se déshabiller ▷ *vt* déshabiller

undrinkable [ʌnˈdrɪŋkəbl] *adj* (*unpalatable*) imbuvable; (*poisonous*) non potable

undue [ʌnˈdjuː] *adj* indu(e), excessif(-ive)

undulating [ˈʌndjuleɪtɪŋ] *adj* ondoyant(e), onduleux(-euse)

unduly [ʌnˈdjuːlɪ] *adv* trop, excessivement

undying [ʌnˈdaɪɪŋ] *adj* éternel(le)

unearned [ʌnˈəːnd] *adj* (*praise*, *respect*) immérité(e); **~ income** rentes *fpl*

unearth [ʌnˈəːθ] *vt* déterrer; (*fig*) dénicher

unearthly [ʌnˈəːθlɪ] *adj* surnaturel(le); (*hour*) indu(e), impossible

uneasy [ʌnˈiːzɪ] *adj* mal à l'aise, gêné(e); (*worried*) inquiet(-ète); (*feeling*) désagréable; (*peace*, *truce*) fragile; **to feel ~ about doing sth** se sentir mal à l'aise à l'idée de faire qch

uneconomic [ˈʌniːkəˈnɔmɪk], **uneconomical** [ˈʌniːkəˈnɔmɪkl] *adj* peu économique; peu rentable

uneducated [ʌnˈɛdjukeɪtɪd] *adj* sans éducation

unemployed [ʌnɪmˈplɔɪd] *adj* sans travail, au chômage ▷ *n*: **the ~** les chômeurs *mpl*

unemployment [ʌnɪmˈplɔɪmənt] *n* chômage *m*

unemployment benefit, (*US*) **unemployment compensation** *n* allocation *f* de chômage

unending [ʌnˈɛndɪŋ] *adj* interminable

unenviable [ʌnˈɛnvɪəbl] *adj* peu enviable

unequal [ʌnˈiːkwəl] *adj* inégal(e)

unequalled, (*US*) **unequaled** [ʌnˈiːkwəld] *adj*

inégalé(e)

unequivocal [ʌnɪ'kwɪvəkl] *adj* (*answer*) sans équivoque; (*person*) catégorique

unerring [ʌn'əːrɪŋ] *adj* infaillible, sûr(e)

UNESCO [juːˈnɛskəu] *n abbr* (= *United Nations Educational, Scientific and Cultural Organization*) UNESCO *f*

unethical [ʌn'ɛθɪkl] *adj* (*methods*) immoral(e); (*doctor's behaviour*) qui ne respecte pas l'éthique

uneven [ʌn'iːvn] *adj* inégal(e); (*quality, work*) irrégulier(-ière)

uneventful [ʌnɪ'vɛntful] *adj* tranquille, sans histoires

unexceptional [ʌnɪk'sɛpʃənl] *adj* banal(e), quelconque

unexciting [ʌnɪk'saɪtɪŋ] *adj* pas passionnant(e)

unexpected [ʌnɪk'spɛktɪd] *adj* inattendu(e), imprévu(e)

unexpectedly [ʌnɪk'spɛktɪdlɪ] *adv* (*succeed*) contre toute attente; (*arrive*) à l'improviste

unexplained [ʌnɪk'spleɪnd] *adj* inexpliqué(e)

unexploded [ʌnɪk'spləudɪd] *adj* non explosé(e) *or* éclaté(e)

unfailing [ʌn'feɪlɪŋ] *adj* inépuisable; infaillible

unfair [ʌn'fɛəʳ] *adj*: ~ (**to**) injuste (envers); **it's ~ that** ... il n'est pas juste que ...

unfair dismissal *n* licenciement abusif

unfairly [ʌn'fɛəlɪ] *adv* injustement

unfaithful [ʌn'feɪθful] *adj* infidèle

unfamiliar [ʌnfə'mɪlɪəʳ] *adj* étrange, inconnu(e); **to be ~ with sth** mal connaître qch

unfashionable [ʌn'fæʃnəbl] *adj* (*clothes*) démodé(e); (*place*) peu chic *inv*; (*district*) déshérité(e), pas à la mode

unfasten [ʌn'fɑːsn] *vt* défaire; (*belt, necklace*) détacher; (*open*) ouvrir

unfathomable [ʌn'fæðəməbl] *adj* insondable

unfavourable, (US) **unfavorable** [ʌn'feɪvrəbl] *adj* défavorable

unfavourably, (US) **unfavorably** [ʌn'feɪvrəblɪ] *adv*: **to look ~ upon** ne pas être favorable à

unfeeling [ʌn'fiːlɪŋ] *adj* insensible, dur(e)

unfinished [ʌn'fɪnɪʃt] *adj* inachevé(e)

unfit [ʌn'fɪt] *adj* (*physically: ill*) en mauvaise santé; (: *out of condition*) pas en forme; (*incompetent*): ~ (**for**) impropre (à); (*work, service*) inapte (à)

unflagging [ʌn'flægɪŋ] *adj* infatigable, inlassable

unflappable [ʌn'flæpəbl] *adj* imperturbable

unflattering [ʌn'flætərɪŋ] *adj* (*dress, hairstyle*) qui n'avantage pas; (*remark*) peu flatteur(-euse)

unflinching [ʌn'flɪntʃɪŋ] *adj* stoïque

unfold [ʌn'fəuld] *vt* déplier; (*fig*) révéler, exposer ▷ *vi* se dérouler

unforeseeable [ʌnfɔː'siːəbl] *adj* imprévisible

unforeseen ['ʌnfɔː'siːn] *adj* imprévu(e)

unforgettable [ʌnfə'gɛtəbl] *adj* inoubliable

unforgivable [ʌnfə'gɪvəbl] *adj* impardonnable

unformatted [ʌn'fɔːmætɪd] *adj* (*disk, text*) non formaté(e)

unfortunate [ʌn'fɔːtʃnət] *adj* malheureux(-euse); (*event, remark*) malencontreux(-euse)

unfortunately [ʌn'fɔːtʃnətlɪ] *adv* malheureusement

unfounded [ʌn'faundɪd] *adj* sans fondement

unfriendly [ʌn'frɛndlɪ] *adj* peu aimable, froid(e), inamical(e)

unfulfilled [ʌnful'fɪld] *adj* (*ambition, prophecy*) non réalisé(e); (*desire*) insatisfait(e); (*promise*) non tenu(e); (*terms of contract*) non rempli(e); (*person*) qui n'a pas su se réaliser

unfurl [ʌn'fəːl] *vt* déployer

unfurnished [ʌn'fəːnɪʃt] *adj* non meublé(e)

ungainly [ʌn'geɪnlɪ] *adj* gauche, dégingandé(e)

ungodly [ʌn'gɔdlɪ] *adj* impie; **at an ~ hour** à une heure indue

ungrateful [ʌn'greɪtful] *adj* qui manque de reconnaissance, ingrat(e)

unguarded [ʌn'gɑːdɪd] *adj*: ~ **moment** moment *m* d'inattention

unhappily [ʌn'hæpɪlɪ] *adv* tristement; (*unfortunately*) malheureusement

unhappiness [ʌn'hæpɪnɪs] *n* tristesse *f*, peine *f*

unhappy [ʌn'hæpɪ] *adj* triste, malheureux(-euse); (*unfortunate: remark etc*) malheureux(-euse); (*not pleased*): ~ **with** mécontent(e) de, peu satisfait(e) de

unharmed [ʌn'hɑːmd] *adj* indemne, sain(e) et sauf (sauve)

UNHCR *n abbr* (= *United Nations High Commission for Refugees*) HCR *m*

unhealthy [ʌn'hɛlθɪ] *adj* (*gen*) malsain(e); (*person*) maladif(-ive)

unheard-of [ʌn'həːdɔv] *adj* inouï(e), sans précédent

unhelpful [ʌn'hɛlpful] *adj* (*person*) peu serviable; (*advice*) peu utile

unhesitating [ʌn'hɛzɪteɪtɪŋ] *adj* (*loyalty*) spontané(e); (*reply, offer*) immédiat(e)

unholy [ʌn'həulɪ] *adj*: **an ~ alliance** une alliance contre nature; **he got home at an ~ hour** il est rentré à une heure impossible

unhook [ʌn'huk] *vt* décrocher; dégrafer

unhurt [ʌn'həːt] *adj* indemne, sain(e) et sauf (sauve)

unhygienic ['ʌnhaɪ'dʒiːnɪk] *adj* antihygiénique

UNICEF ['juːnɪsɛf] *n abbr* (= *United Nations International Children's Emergency Fund*) UNICEF *m*, FISE *m*

unicorn ['juːnɪkɔːn] *n* licorne *f*

unidentified [ʌnaɪ'dɛntɪfaɪd] *adj* non identifié(e); *see also* **UFO**

uniform ['juːnɪfɔːm] *n* uniforme *m* ▷ *adj* uniforme

uniformity [juːnɪ'fɔːmɪtɪ] *n* uniformité *f*

unify ['juːnɪfaɪ] *vt* unifier

unilateral [juːnɪ'lætərəl] *adj* unilatéral(e)

unimaginable [ʌnɪ'mædʒɪnəbl] *adj* inimaginable, inconcevable

unimaginative [ʌnɪ'mædʒɪnətɪv] *adj* sans imagination

u

unimpaired [ʌnɪmˈpɛəd] *adj* intact(e)

unimportant [ʌnɪmˈpɔːtənt] *adj* sans importance

unimpressed [ʌnɪmˈprɛst] *adj* pas impressionné(e)

uninhabited [ʌnɪnˈhæbɪtɪd] *adj* inhabité(e)

uninhibited [ʌnɪnˈhɪbɪtɪd] *adj* sans inhibitions; sans retenue

uninjured [ʌnˈɪndʒəd] *adj* indemne

uninspiring [ʌnɪnˈspaɪərɪŋ] *adj* peu inspirant(e)

unintelligent [ʌnɪnˈtɛlɪdʒənt] *adj* inintelligent(e)

unintentional [ʌnɪnˈtɛnʃənəl] *adj* involontaire

unintentionally [ʌnɪnˈtɛnʃnəlɪ] *adv* sans le vouloir

uninvited [ʌnɪnˈvaɪtɪd] *adj* (*guest*) qui n'a pas été invité(e)

uninviting [ʌnɪnˈvaɪtɪŋ] *adj* (*place*) peu attirant(e); (*food*) peu appétissant(e)

union [ˈjuːnjən] *n* union *f*; (*also*: **trade union**) syndicat *m* ▷ *cpd* du syndicat, syndical(e)

unionize [ˈjuːnjənaɪz] *vt* syndiquer

Union Jack *n* drapeau du Royaume-Uni

Union of Soviet Socialist Republics *n* (formerly) Union *f* des républiques socialistes soviétiques

union shop *n* entreprise où tous les travailleurs doivent être syndiqués

unique [juːˈniːk] *adj* unique

unisex [ˈjuːnɪsɛks] *adj* unisexe

Unison [ˈjuːnɪsn] *n* (trade union) grand syndicat des services publics en Grande-Bretagne

unison [ˈjuːnɪsn] *n*: **in ~** à l'unisson, en chœur

unit [ˈjuːnɪt] *n* unité *f*; (*section: of furniture etc*) élément *m*, bloc *m*; (*team, squad*) groupe *m*, service *m*; **production ~** atelier *m* de fabrication; **kitchen ~** élément de cuisine; **sink ~** bloc-évier *m*

unit cost *n* coût *m* unitaire

unite [juːˈnaɪt] *vt* unir ▷ *vi* s'unir

united [juːˈnaɪtɪd] *adj* uni(e); (*country, party*) unifié(e); (*efforts*) conjugué(e)

United Arab Emirates *npl* Émirats Arabes Unis

United Kingdom *n* Royaume-Uni *m*

United Nations, United Nations Organization *n* (Organisation *f* des) Nations unies

United States, United States of America *n* États-Unis *mpl*

unit price *n* prix *m* unitaire

unit trust *n* (Brit Comm) fonds commun de placement, FCP *m*

unity [ˈjuːnɪtɪ] *n* unité *f*

Univ. *abbr* = **university**

universal [juːnɪˈvɜːsl] *adj* universel(le)

universe [ˈjuːnɪvɜːs] *n* univers *m*

university [juːnɪˈvɜːsɪtɪ] *n* université *f* ▷ *cpd* (*student, professor*) d'université; (*education, year, degree*) universitaire

unjust [ʌnˈdʒʌst] *adj* injuste

unjustifiable [ˈʌndʒʌstɪˈfaɪəbl] *adj* injustifiable

unjustified [ʌnˈdʒʌstɪfaɪd] *adj* injustifié(e);

(*text*) non justifié(e)

unkempt [ʌnˈkɛmpt] *adj* mal tenu(e), débraillé(e); mal peigné(e)

unkind [ʌnˈkaɪnd] *adj* peu gentil(le), méchant(e)

unkindly [ʌnˈkaɪndlɪ] *adv* (*treat, speak*) avec méchanceté

unknown [ʌnˈnəun] *adj* inconnu(e); **~ to me** sans que je le sache; **~ quantity** (*Math, fig*) inconnue *f*

unladen [ʌnˈleɪdn] *adj* (*ship, weight*) à vide

unlawful [ʌnˈlɔːful] *adj* illégal(e)

unleaded [ʌnˈlɛdɪd] *n* (*also*: **unleaded petrol**) essence *f* sans plomb

unleash [ʌnˈliːʃ] *vt* détacher; (*fig*) déchaîner, déclencher

unleavened [ʌnˈlɛvnd] *adj* sans levain

unless [ʌnˈlɛs] *conj*: **~ he leaves** à moins qu'il (ne) parte; **~ we leave** à moins de partir, à moins que nous (ne) partions; **~ otherwise stated** sauf indication contraire; **~ I am mistaken** si je ne me trompe

unlicensed [ʌnˈlaɪsnst] *adj* (*Brit*) non patenté(e) pour la vente des spiritueux

unlike [ʌnˈlaɪk] *adj* dissemblable, différent(e) ▷ *prep* à la différence de, contrairement à

unlikelihood [ʌnˈlaɪklɪhud] *adj* improbabilité *f*

unlikely [ʌnˈlaɪklɪ] *adj* (*result, event*) improbable; (*explanation*) invraisemblable

unlimited [ʌnˈlɪmɪtɪd] *adj* illimité(e)

unlisted [ˈʌnˈlɪstɪd] *adj* (*US Tel*) sur la liste rouge; (*Stock Exchange*) non coté(e) en Bourse

unlit [ʌnˈlɪt] *adj* (*room*) non éclairé(e)

unload [ʌnˈləud] *vt* décharger

unlock [ʌnˈlɔk] *vt* ouvrir

unlucky [ʌnˈlʌkɪ] *adj* (*person*) malchanceux(-euse); (*object, number*) qui porte malheur; **to be ~** (*person*) ne pas avoir de chance

unmanageable [ʌnˈmænɪdʒəbl] *adj* (*unwieldy: tool, vehicle*) peu maniable; (: *situation*) inextricable

unmanned [ʌnˈmænd] *adj* sans équipage

unmannerly [ʌnˈmænəlɪ] *adj* mal élevé(e), impoli(e)

unmarked [ʌnˈmɑːkt] *adj* (*unstained*) sans marque; **~ police car** voiture de police banalisée

unmarried [ʌnˈmærɪd] *adj* célibataire

unmask [ʌnˈmɑːsk] *vt* démasquer

unmatched [ʌnˈmætʃt] *adj* sans égal(e)

unmentionable [ʌnˈmɛnʃnəbl] *adj* (*topic*) dont on ne parle pas; (*word*) qui ne se dit pas

unmerciful [ʌnˈmɜːsɪful] *adj* sans pitié

unmistakable, unmistakeable [ʌnmɪsˈteɪkəbl] *adj* indubitable; qu'on ne peut pas ne pas reconnaître

unmitigated [ʌnˈmɪtɪgeɪtɪd] *adj* non mitigé(e), absolu(e), pur(e)

unnamed [ʌnˈneɪmd] *adj* (*nameless*) sans nom; (*anonymous*) anonyme

unnatural [ʌnˈnætʃrəl] *adj* non naturel(le); (*perversion*) contre nature

unnecessary [ʌn'nɛsəsərɪ] *adj* inutile, superflu(e)

unnerve [ʌn'nə:v] *vt* faire perdre son sang-froid à

unnoticed [ʌn'nəʊtɪst] *adj* inaperçu(e); **to go ~** passer inaperçu

UNO ['juːnəʊ] *n abbr* = **United Nations Organization**

unobservant [ʌnəb'zə:vnt] *adj* pas observateur(-trice)

unobtainable [ʌnəb'teɪnəbl] *adj* (*Tel*) impossible à obtenir

unobtrusive [ʌnəb'tru:sɪv] *adj* discret(-ète)

unoccupied [ʌn'ɔkjupaɪd] *adj* (*seat, table, Mil*) libre; (*house*) inoccupé(e)

unofficial [ʌnə'fɪʃl] *adj* (*news*) officieux(-euse), non officiel(le); (*strike*) ≈ sauvage

unopposed [ʌnə'pəʊzd] *adj* sans opposition

unorthodox [ʌn'ɔ:θədɔks] *adj* peu orthodoxe

unpack [ʌn'pæk] *vi* défaire sa valise, déballer ses affaires ▷ *vt* (*suitcase*) défaire; (*belongings*) déballer

unpaid [ʌn'peɪd] *adj* (*bill*) impayé(e); (*holiday*) non-payé(e), sans salaire; (*work*) non rétribué(e); (*worker*) bénévole

unpalatable [ʌn'pælətəbl] *adj* (*truth*) désagréable (à entendre)

unparalleled [ʌn'pærəlɛld] *adj* incomparable, sans égal

unpatriotic ['ʌnpætrɪ'ɔtɪk] *adj* (*person*) manquant de patriotisme; (*speech, attitude*) antipatriotique

unplanned [ʌn'plænd] *adj* (*visit*) imprévu(e); (*baby*) non prévu(e)

unpleasant [ʌn'plɛznt] *adj* déplaisant(e), désagréable

unplug [ʌn'plʌg] *vt* débrancher

unpolluted [ʌnpə'lu:tɪd] *adj* non pollué(e)

unpopular [ʌn'pɔpjulə^r] *adj* impopulaire; **to make o.s. ~ (with)** se rendre impopulaire (auprès de)

unprecedented [ʌn'prɛsɪdɛntɪd] *adj* sans précédent

unpredictable [ʌnprɪ'dɪktəbl] *adj* imprévisible

unprejudiced [ʌn'prɛdʒudɪst] *adj* (*not biased*) impartial(e); (*having no prejudices*) qui n'a pas de préjugés

unprepared [ʌnprɪ'pɛəd] *adj* (*person*) qui n'est pas suffisamment préparé(e); (*speech*) improvisé(e)

unprepossessing ['ʌnpri:pə'zɛsɪŋ] *adj* peu avenant(e)

unpretentious [ʌnprɪ'tɛnʃəs] *adj* sans prétention(s)

unprincipled [ʌn'prɪnsɪpld] *adj* sans principes

unproductive [ʌnprə'dʌktɪv] *adj* improductif(-ive); (*discussion*) stérile

unprofessional [ʌnprə'fɛʃənl] *adj* (*conduct*) contraire à la déontologie

unprofitable [ʌn'prɔfɪtəbl] *adj* non rentable

UNPROFOR [ʌn'prəʊfɔ:^r] *n abbr* (= *United Nations Protection Force*) FORPRONU f

unprotected ['ʌnprə'tɛktɪd] *adj* (*sex*) non protégé(e)

unprovoked [ʌnprə'vəʊkt] *adj* (*attack*) sans provocation

unpunished [ʌn'pʌnɪʃt] *adj* impuni(e); **to go ~** rester impuni

unqualified [ʌn'kwɔlɪfaɪd] *adj* (*teacher*) non diplômé(e), sans titres; (*success*) sans réserve, total(e); (*disaster*) total(e)

unquestionably [ʌn'kwɛstʃənəblɪ] *adv* incontestablement

unquestioning [ʌn'kwɛstʃənɪŋ] *adj* (*obedience, acceptance*) inconditionnel(le)

unravel [ʌn'rævl] *vt* démêler

unreal [ʌn'rɪəl] *adj* irréel(le); (*extraordinary*) incroyable

unrealistic ['ʌnrɪə'lɪstɪk] *adj* (*idea*) irréaliste; (*estimate*) peu réaliste

unreasonable [ʌn'ri:znəbl] *adj* qui n'est pas raisonnable; **to make ~ demands on sb** exiger trop de qn

unrecognizable [ʌn'rɛkəgnaɪzəbl] *adj* pas reconnaissable

unrecognized [ʌn'rɛkəgnaɪzd] *adj* (*talent, genius*) méconnu(e); (*Pol: régime*) non reconnu(e)

unrecorded [ʌnrɪ'kɔ:dɪd] *adj* non enregistré(e)

unrefined [ʌnrɪ'faɪnd] *adj* (*sugar, petroleum*) non raffiné(e)

unrehearsed [ʌnrɪ'hə:st] *adj* (*Theat etc*) qui n'a pas été répété(e); (*spontaneous*) spontané(e)

unrelated [ʌnrɪ'leɪtɪd] *adj* sans rapport; (*people*) sans lien de parenté

unrelenting [ʌnrɪ'lɛntɪŋ] *adj* implacable; acharné(e)

unreliable [ʌnrɪ'laɪəbl] *adj* sur qui (*or* quoi) on ne peut pas compter, peu fiable

unrelieved [ʌnrɪ'li:vd] *adj* (*monotony*) constant(e), uniforme

unremitting [ʌnrɪ'mɪtɪŋ] *adj* inlassable, infatigable, acharné(e)

unrepeatable [ʌnrɪ'pi:təbl] *adj* (*offer*) unique, exceptionnel(le)

unrepentant [ʌnrɪ'pɛntənt] *adj* impénitent(e)

unrepresentative ['ʌnrɛprɪ'zɛntətɪv] *adj:* **~ (of)** peu représentatif(-ive) (de)

unreserved [ʌnrɪ'zə:vd] *adj* (*seat*) non réservé(e); (*approval, admiration*) sans réserve

unreservedly [ʌnrɪ'zə:vɪdlɪ] *adv* sans réserve

unresponsive [ʌnrɪs'pɔnsɪv] *adj* insensible

unrest [ʌn'rɛst] *n* agitation f, troubles mpl

unrestricted [ʌnrɪ'strɪktɪd] *adj* illimité(e); **to have ~ access to** avoir librement accès *or* accès en tout temps à

unrewarded [ʌnrɪ'wɔ:dɪd] *adj* pas récompensé(e)

unripe [ʌn'raɪp] *adj* pas mûr(e)

unrivalled, (*US*) **unrivaled** [ʌn'raɪvəld] *adj* sans égal, incomparable

unroll [ʌn'rəʊl] *vt* dérouler

unruffled [ʌn'rʌfld] *adj* (*person*) imperturbable; (*hair*) qui n'est pas ébouriffé(e)

unruly [ʌn'ru:lɪ] *adj* indiscipliné(e)

u

unsafe [ʌn'seɪf] *adj* (*in danger*) en danger; (*journey, car*) dangereux(-euse); (*method*) hasardeux(-euse); ~ **to drink/eat** non potable/comestible

unsaid [ʌn'sɛd] *adj*: **to leave sth** ~ passer qch sous silence

unsaleable, (*US*) **unsalable** [ʌn'seɪləbl] *adj* invendable

unsatisfactory ['ʌnsætɪs'fæktərɪ] *adj* peu satisfaisant(e), qui laisse à désirer

unsavory, (*US*) **unsavory** [ʌn'seɪvərɪ] *adj* (*fig*) peu recommandable, répugnant(e)

unscathed [ʌn'skeɪðd] *adj* indemne

unscientific ['ʌnsaɪən'tɪfɪk] *adj* non scientifique

unscrew [ʌn'skruː] *vt* dévisser

unscrupulous [ʌn'skruːpjuləs] *adj* sans scrupules

unseat [ʌn'siːt] *vt* (*rider*) désarçonner; (*fig: official*) faire perdre son siège à

unsecured ['ʌnsɪ'kjuəd] *adj*: ~ **creditor** créancier(-ière) sans garantie

unseeded [ʌn'siːdɪd] *adj* (*Sport*) non classé(e)

unseemly [ʌn'siːmlɪ] *adj* inconvenant(e)

unseen [ʌn'siːn] *adj* (*person*) invisible; (*danger*) imprévu(e)

unselfish [ʌn'sɛlfɪʃ] *adj* désintéressé(e)

unsettled [ʌn'sɛtld] *adj* (*restless*) perturbé(e); (*unpredictable*) instable; incertain(e); (*not finalized*) non résolu(e)

unsettling [ʌn'sɛtlɪŋ] *adj* qui a un effet perturbateur

unshakable, unshakeable [ʌn'ʃeɪkəbl] *adj* inébranlable

unshaven [ʌn'ʃeɪvn] *adj* non *or* mal rasé(e)

unsightly [ʌn'saɪtlɪ] *adj* disgracieux(-euse), laid(e)

unskilled [ʌn'skɪld] *adj*: ~ **worker** manœuvre *m*

unsociable [ʌn'səuʃəbl] *adj* (*person*) peu sociable; (*behaviour*) qui manque de sociabilité

unsocial [ʌn'səuʃl] *adj* (*hours*) en dehors de l'horaire normal

unsold [ʌn'səuld] *adj* invendu(e), non vendu(e)

unsolicited [ʌnsə'lɪsɪtɪd] *adj* non sollicité(e)

unsophisticated [ʌnsə'fɪstɪkeɪtɪd] *adj* simple, naturel(le)

unsound [ʌn'saund] *adj* (*health*) chancelant(e); (*floor, foundations*) peu solide; (*policy, advice*) peu judicieux(-euse)

unspeakable [ʌn'spiːkəbl] *adj* indicible; (*awful*) innommable

unspoiled ['ʌn'spɔɪld], **unspoilt** ['ʌn'spɔɪlt] *adj* (*place*) non dégradé(e)

unspoken [ʌn'spəukn] *adj* (*word*) qui n'est pas prononcé(e); (*agreement, approval*) tacite

unstable [ʌn'steɪbl] *adj* instable

unsteady [ʌn'stɛdɪ] *adj* mal assuré(e), chancelant(e), instable

unstinting [ʌn'stɪntɪŋ] *adj* (*support*) total(e), sans réserve; (*generosity*) sans limites

unstuck [ʌn'stʌk] *adj*: **to come** ~ se décoller; (*fig*) faire fiasco

unsubstantiated ['ʌnsəb'stænʃɪeɪtɪd] *adj* (*rumour*) qui n'est pas confirmé(e); (*accusation*) sans preuve

unsuccessful [ʌnsək'sɛsful] *adj* (*attempt*) infructueux(-euse); (*writer, proposal*) qui n'a pas de succès; (*marriage*) malheureux(-euse), qui ne réussit pas; **to be** ~ (*in attempting sth*) ne pas réussir; ne pas avoir de succès; (*application*) ne pas être retenu(e)

unsuccessfully [ʌnsək'sɛsfəlɪ] *adv* en vain

unsuitable [ʌn'suːtəbl] *adj* qui ne convient pas, peu approprié(e); (*time*) inopportun(e)

unsuited [ʌn'suːtɪd] *adj*: **to be** ~ **for** *or* **to** être inapte *or* impropre à

unsung ['ʌnsʌŋ] *adj*: **an** ~ **hero** un héros méconnu

unsupported [ʌnsə'pɔːtɪd] *adj* (*claim*) non soutenu(e); (*theory*) qui n'est pas corroboré(e)

unsure [ʌn'ʃuər] *adj* pas sûr(e); **to be** ~ **of o.s.** ne pas être sûr de soi, manquer de confiance en soi

unsuspecting [ʌnsə'spɛktɪŋ] *adj* qui ne se méfie pas

unsweetened [ʌn'swiːtnd] *adj* non sucré(e)

unswerving [ʌn'swəːvɪŋ] *adj* inébranlable

unsympathetic ['ʌnsɪmpə'θɛtɪk] *adj* hostile; (*unpleasant*) antipathique; ~ **to** indifférent(e) à

untangle [ʌn'tæŋgl] *vt* démêler, débrouiller

untapped [ʌn'tæpt] *adj* (*resources*) inexploité(e)

untaxed [ʌn'tækst] *adj* (*goods*) non taxé(e); (*income*) non imposé(e)

unthinkable [ʌn'θɪŋkəbl] *adj* impensable, inconcevable

unthinkingly [ʌn'θɪŋkɪŋlɪ] *adv* sans réfléchir

untidy [ʌn'taɪdɪ] *adj* (*room*) en désordre; (*appearance, person*) débraillé(e); (*person: in character*) sans ordre, désordonné; débraillé; (*work*) peu soigné(e)

untie [ʌn'taɪ] *vt* (*knot, parcel*) défaire; (*prisoner, dog*) détacher

until [ən'tɪl] *prep* jusqu'à; (*after negative*) avant ▷ *conj* jusqu'à ce que + *sub*, en attendant que + *sub*; (*in past, after negative*) avant que + *sub*; ~ **he comes** jusqu'à ce qu'il vienne, jusqu'à son arrivée; ~ **now** jusqu'à présent, jusqu'ici; ~ **then** jusque-là; **from morning** ~ **night** du matin au soir *or* jusqu'au soir

untimely [ʌn'taɪmlɪ] *adj* inopportun(e); (*death*) prématuré(e)

untold [ʌn'təuld] *adj* incalculable; indescriptible

untouched [ʌn'tʌtʃt] *adj* (*not used etc*) tel(le) quel(le), intact(e); (*safe: person*) indemne; (*unaffected*): ~ **by** indifférent(e) à

untoward [ʌntə'wɔːd] *adj* fâcheux(-euse), malencontreux(-euse)

untrained ['ʌn'treɪnd] *adj* (*worker*) sans formation; (*troops*) sans entraînement; **to the** ~ **eye** à l'œil non exercé

untrammelled [ʌn'træmld] *adj* sans entraves

untranslatable [ʌntrænz'leɪtəbl] *adj* intraduisible

untrue [ʌn'truː] *adj* (*statement*) faux (fausse)

untrustworthy [ʌn'trʌstwəːðɪ] *adj* (*person*) pas digne de confiance, peu sûr(e)

unusable [ʌn'juːzəbl] *adj* inutilisable

unused¹ [ʌn'juːzd] *adj* (*new*) neuf (neuve)

unused² [ʌn'juːst] *adj*: **to be ~ to sth/to doing sth** ne pas avoir l'habitude de qch/de faire qch

unusual [ʌn'juːʒuəl] *adj* insolite, exceptionnel(le), rare

unusually [ʌn'juːʒuəlɪ] *adv* exceptionnellement, particulièrement

unveil [ʌn'veɪl] *vt* dévoiler

unwanted [ʌn'wɒntɪd] *adj* (*child, pregnancy*) non désiré(e); (*clothes etc*) à donner

unwarranted [ʌn'wɒrəntɪd] *adj* injustifié(e)

unwary [ʌn'wɛərɪ] *adj* imprudent(e)

unwavering [ʌn'weɪvərɪŋ] *adj* inébranlable

unwelcome [ʌn'wɛlkəm] *adj* importun(e); **to feel ~** se sentir de trop

unwell [ʌn'wɛl] *adj* indisposé(e), souffrant(e); **to feel ~** ne pas se sentir bien

unwieldy [ʌn'wiːldɪ] *adj* difficile à manier

unwilling [ʌn'wɪlɪŋ] *adj*: **to be ~ to do** ne pas vouloir faire

unwillingly [ʌn'wɪlɪŋlɪ] *adv* à contrecœur, contre son gré

unwind [ʌn'waɪnd] (*irreg: like* **wind**) *vt* dérouler ▷ *vi* (*relax*) se détendre

unwise [ʌn'waɪz] *adj* imprudent(e), peu judicieux(-euse)

unwitting [ʌn'wɪtɪŋ] *adj* involontaire

unwittingly [ʌn'wɪtɪŋlɪ] *adv* involontairement

unworkable [ʌn'wəːkəbl] *adj* (*plan etc*) inexploitable

unworthy [ʌn'wəːðɪ] *adj* indigne

unwrap [ʌn'ræp] *vt* défaire; ouvrir

unwritten [ʌn'rɪtn] *adj* (*agreement*) tacite

unzip [ʌn'zɪp] *vt* ouvrir (la fermeture éclair de); (*Comput*) dézipper

◯ **KEYWORD**

up [ʌp] *prep*: **he went up the stairs/the hill** il a monté l'escalier/la colline; **the cat was up a tree** le chat était dans un arbre; **they live further up the street** ils habitent plus haut dans la rue; **go up that road and turn left** remontez la rue et tournez à gauche
▷ *vi* (*inf*): **she upped and left** elle a fichu le camp sans plus attendre
▷ *adv* **1** en haut; en l'air; (*upwards, higher*): **up in the sky/the mountains** (là-haut) dans le ciel/les montagnes; **put it a bit higher up** mettez-le un peu plus haut; **to stand up** (*get up*) se lever, se mettre debout; (*be standing*) être debout; **up there** là-haut; **up above** au-dessus; **"this side up"** "haut"
2: **to be up** (*out of bed*) être levé(e); (*prices*) avoir augmenté *or* monté; (*finished*): **when the year was up** à la fin de l'année; **time's up** c'est l'heure
3: **up to** (*as far as*) jusqu'à; **up to now** jusqu'à présent

4: **to be up to** (*depending on*): **it's up to you** c'est à vous de décider; (*equal to*): **he's not up to it** (*job, task etc*) il n'en est pas capable; (*inf: be doing*): **what is he up to?** qu'est-ce qu'il peut bien faire?
5 (*phrases*): **he's well up in** *or* **on ...** (*Brit: knowledgeable*) il s'y connaît en ...; **up with Leeds United!** vive Leeds United!; **what's up?** (*inf*) qu'est-ce qui ne va pas?; **what's up with him?** (*inf*) qu'est-ce qui lui arrive?
▷ *n*: **ups and downs** hauts et bas *mpl*

up-and-coming [ʌpənd'kʌmɪŋ] *adj* plein(e) d'avenir *or* de promesses

upbeat ['ʌpbiːt] *n* (*Mus*) levé *m*; (*in economy, prosperity*) amélioration *f* ▷ *adj* (*optimistic*) optimiste

upbraid [ʌp'breɪd] *vt* morigéner

upbringing ['ʌpbrɪŋɪŋ] *n* éducation *f*

upcoming ['ʌpkʌmɪŋ] *adj* tout(e) prochain(e)

update [ʌp'deɪt] *vt* mettre à jour

upend [ʌp'ɛnd] *vt* mettre debout

upfront [ʌp'frʌnt] *adj* (*open*) franc (franche) ▷ *adv* (*pay*) d'avance; **to be ~ about sth** ne rien cacher de qch

upgrade [ʌp'greɪd] *vt* (*person*) promouvoir; (*job*) revaloriser; (*property, equipment*) moderniser

upheaval [ʌp'hiːvl] *n* bouleversement *m*; (*in room*) branle-bas *m*; (*event*) crise *f*

uphill [ʌp'hɪl] *adj* qui monte; (*fig: task*) difficile, pénible ▷ *adv* (*face, look*) en amont, vers l'amont; (*go, move*) vers le haut, en haut; **to go ~** monter

uphold [ʌp'həuld] *vt* (*irreg: like* **hold**) maintenir; soutenir

upholstery [ʌp'həulstərɪ] *n* rembourrage *m*; (*cover*) tissu *m* d'ameublement; (*of car*) garniture *f*

upkeep ['ʌpkiːp] *n* entretien *m*

upmarket [ʌp'mɑːkɪt] *adj* (*product*) haut de gamme *inv*; (*area*) chic *inv*

upon [ə'pɒn] *prep* sur

upper ['ʌpəʳ] *adj* supérieur(e); du dessus ▷ *n* (*of shoe*) empeigne *f*

upper class *n*: **the ~** = la haute bourgeoisie

upper-class [ʌpə'klɑːs] *adj* de la haute société, aristocratique; (*district*) élégant(e), huppé(e); (*accent, attitude*) caractéristique des classes supérieures

uppercut ['ʌpəkʌt] *n* uppercut *m*

upper hand *n*: **to have the ~** avoir le dessus

Upper House *n*: **the ~** (*in Britain*) la Chambre des Lords, la Chambre haute; (*in France, in the US etc*) le Sénat

uppermost ['ʌpəməust] *adj* le (la) plus haut(e), en dessus; **it was ~ in my mind** j'y pensais avant tout autre chose

upper sixth *n* terminale *f*

Upper Volta [-'vɒltə] *n* Haute Volta

upright ['ʌpraɪt] *adj* droit(e); (*fig*) droit, honnête ▷ *n* montant *m*

uprising ['ʌpraɪzɪŋ] *n* soulèvement *m*, insurrection *f*

u

uproar ['ʌprɔːʳ] *n* tumulte *m*, vacarme *m*; (*protests*) protestations *fpl*

uproarious [ʌp'rɔːrɪəs] *adj* (*event etc*) désopilant(e); ~ **laughter** un brouhaha de rires

uproot [ʌp'ruːt] *vt* déraciner

upset *n* ['ʌpsɛt] dérangement *m* ▷ *vt* [ʌp'sɛt] (*irreg: like* set: *glass etc*) renverser; (*plan*) déranger; (*person: offend*) contrarier; (: *grieve*) faire de la peine à; bouleverser ▷ *adj* [ʌp'sɛt] contrarié(e); peiné(e); (*stomach*) détraqué(e), dérangé(e); **to get** ~ (*sad*) devenir triste; (*offended*) se vexer; **to have a stomach** ~ (*Brit*) avoir une indigestion

upset price *n* (*US, Scottish*) mise *f* à prix, prix *m* de départ

upsetting [ʌp'sɛtɪŋ] *adj* (*offending*) vexant(e); (*annoying*) ennuyeux(-euse)

upshot ['ʌpʃɔt] *n* résultat *m*; **the ~ of it all was that …** il a résulté de tout cela que …

upside down ['ʌpsaɪd-] *adv* à l'envers; **to turn sth ~** (*fig: place*) mettre sens dessus dessous

upstage ['ʌp'steɪdʒ] *vt*: **to ~ sb** souffler la vedette à qn

upstairs [ʌp'stɛəz] *adv* en haut ▷ *adj* (*room*) du dessus, d'en haut ▷ *n*: **the ~** l'étage *m*; **there's no ~** il n'y a pas d'étage

upstart ['ʌpstɑːt] *n* parvenu(e)

upstream [ʌp'striːm] *adv* en amont

upsurge ['ʌpsəːdʒ] *n* (*of enthusiasm etc*) vague *f*

uptake ['ʌpteɪk] *n*: **he is quick/slow on the ~** il comprend vite/est lent à comprendre

uptight [ʌp'taɪt] *adj* (*inf*) très tendu(e), crispé(e)

up-to-date ['ʌptə'deɪt] *adj* moderne; (*information*) très récent(e)

upturn ['ʌptəːn] *n* (*in economy*) reprise *f*

upturned ['ʌptəːnd] *adj* (*nose*) retroussé(e)

upward ['ʌpwəd] *adj* ascendant(e); vers le haut ▷ *adv* vers le haut; (*more than*): ~ **of** plus de; **and ~** et plus, et au-dessus

upwardly-mobile ['ʌpwədlɪ'məubaɪl] *adj* à mobilité sociale ascendante

upwards ['ʌpwədz] *adv* vers le haut; (*more than*): ~ **of** plus de; **and ~** et plus, et au-dessus

URA *n abbr* (*US*) = **Urban Renewal Administration**

Ural Mountains ['juərəl-] *npl*: **the ~** (*also*: **the Urals**) les monts *mpl* Oural, l'Oural *m*

uranium [juə'reɪnɪəm] *n* uranium *m*

Uranus [juə'reɪnəs] *n* Uranus *f*

urban ['əːbən] *adj* urbain(e)

urban clearway *n* rue *f* à stationnement interdit

urbane [əː'beɪn] *adj* urbain(e), courtois(e)

urbanization [əːbənaɪ'zeɪʃən] *n* urbanisation *f*

urchin ['əːtʃɪn] *n* gosse *m*, garnement *m*

Urdu ['uəduː] *n* ourdou *m*

urge [əːdʒ] *n* besoin (impératif), envie (pressante) ▷ *vt* (*caution etc*) recommander avec insistance; (*person*): **to ~ sb to do** exhorter qn à faire, pousser qn à faire, recommander vivement à qn de faire

▶ **urge on** *vt* pousser, presser

urgency ['əːdʒənsɪ] *n* urgence *f*; (*of tone*) insistance *f*

urgent ['əːdʒənt] *adj* urgent(e); (*plea, tone*) pressant(e)

urgently ['əːdʒəntlɪ] *adv* d'urgence, de toute urgence; (*need*) sans délai

urinal ['juərɪnl] *n* (*Brit: place*) urinoir *m*

urinate ['juərɪneɪt] *vi* uriner

urine ['juərɪn] *n* urine *f*

URL *abbr* (= *uniform resource locator*) URL *f*

urn [əːn] *n* urne *f*; (*also:* **tea urn**) fontaine *f* à thé

Uruguay ['juərəgwaɪ] *n* Uruguay *m*

Uruguayan [juərə'gwaɪən] *adj* uruguayen(ne) ▷ *n* Uruguayen(ne)

US *n abbr* = **United States**

us [ʌs] *pron* nous; *see also* **me**

USA *n abbr* = **United States of America**; (*Mil*) = **United States Army**

usable ['juːzəbl] *adj* utilisable

USAF *n abbr* = **United States Air Force**

usage ['juːzɪdʒ] *n* usage *m*

USCG *n abbr* = **United States Coast Guard**

USDA *n abbr* = **United States Department of Agriculture**

USDAW ['ʌzdɔː] *n abbr* (*Brit*: = *Union of Shop, Distributive and Allied Workers*) syndicat du commerce de détail et de la distribution

USDI *n abbr* = **United States Department of the Interior**

use *n* [juːs] emploi *m*, utilisation *f*; usage *m*; (*usefulness*) utilité *f* ▷ *vt* [juːz] se servir de, utiliser, employer; **in ~** en usage; **out of ~** hors d'usage; **to be of ~** servir, être utile; **to make ~ of sth** utiliser qch; **ready for ~** prêt à l'emploi; **it's no ~** ça ne sert à rien; **to have the ~ of** avoir l'usage de; **what's this ~d for?** à quoi est-ce que ça sert?; **she ~d to do it** elle le faisait (autrefois), elle avait coutume de le faire; **to be ~d to** avoir l'habitude de, être habitué(e) à; **to get ~d to** s'habituer à

▶ **use up** *vt* finir, épuiser; (*food*) consommer

used [juːzd] *adj* (*car*) d'occasion

useful ['juːsful] *adj* utile; **to come in ~** être utile

usefulness ['juːsfəlnɪs] *n* utilité *f*

useless ['juːslɪs] *adj* inutile; (*inf: person*) nul(le)

user ['juːzəʳ] *n* utilisateur(-trice), usager *m*

user-friendly ['juːzə'frɛndlɪ] *adj* convivial(e), facile d'emploi

username ['juːzəneɪm] nom *m* d'utilisateur

USES *n abbr* = **United States Employment Service**

usher ['ʌʃəʳ] *n* placeur *m* ▷ *vt*: **to ~ sb in** faire entrer qn

usherette [ʌʃə'rɛt] *n* (*in cinema*) ouvreuse *f*

USIA *n abbr* = **United States Information Agency**

USM *n abbr* = **United States Mail**; **United States Mint**

USN *n abbr* = **United States Navy**

USP *n abbr* = **unique selling proposition**

USPHS *n abbr* = **United States Public Health Service**

USPO *n abbr* = **United States Post Office**
USS *abbr* = **United States Ship (or Steamer)**
USSR *n abbr* = **Union of Soviet Socialist Republics**
usu. *abbr* = **usually**
usual ['juːʒuəl] *adj* habituel(le); **as ~** comme d'habitude
usually ['juːʒuəlɪ] *adv* d'habitude, d'ordinaire
usurer ['juːʒərəʳ] *n* usurier(-ière)
usurp [juːˈzəːp] *vt* usurper
UT *abbr* (*US*) = **Utah**
utensil [juːˈtɛnsl] *n* ustensile *m*; **kitchen ~s** batterie *f* de cuisine
uterus ['juːtərəs] *n* utérus *m*
utilitarian [juːtɪlɪˈtɛərɪən] *adj* utilitaire
utility [juːˈtɪlɪtɪ] *n* utilité *f*; (*also*: **public utility**) service public

utility room *n* buanderie *f*
utilization [juːtɪlaɪˈzeɪʃən] *n* utilisation *f*
utilize ['juːtɪlaɪz] *vt* utiliser; (*make good use of*) exploiter
utmost ['ʌtməust] *adj* extrême, le (la) plus grand(e) ▷ *n*: **to do one's ~** faire tout son possible; **of the ~ importance** d'une importance capitale, de la plus haute importance
utter ['ʌtəʳ] *adj* total(e), complet(-ète) ▷ *vt* prononcer, proférer; (*sounds*) émettre
utterance ['ʌtrns] *n* paroles *fpl*
utterly ['ʌtəlɪ] *adv* complètement, totalement
U-turn ['juːˈtəːn] *n* demi-tour *m*; (*fig*) volte-face *f inv*
Uzbekistan [ʌzbɛkɪˈstɑːn] *n* Ouzbékistan *m*

u

Vv

V, v [viː] *n* (*letter*) V, v *m*; **V for Victor** V comme Victor

v. *abbr* = **verse**; (= *vide*) v.; (= *versus*) vs; (= *volt*) V

VA, Va. *abbr* (*US*) = **Virginia**

vac [væk] *n abbr* (*Brit inf*) = **vacation**

vacancy ['veɪkənsɪ] *n* (*Brit: job*) poste vacant; (*room*) chambre *f* disponible; **"no vacancies"** "complet"

vacant ['veɪkənt] *adj* (*post*) vacant(e); (*seat etc*) libre, disponible; (*expression*) distrait(e)

vacant lot *n* terrain inoccupé; (*for sale*) terrain à vendre

vacate [və'keɪt] *vt* quitter

vacation [və'keɪʃən] *n* (*esp US*) vacances *fpl*; **to take a ~** prendre des vacances; **on ~** en vacances

vacation course *n* cours *mpl* de vacances

vacationer [və'keɪʃənə^r], (*US*) **vacationist** [və'keɪʃənɪst] *n* vacancier(-ière)

vaccinate ['væksɪneɪt] *vt* vacciner

vaccination [væksɪ'neɪʃən] *n* vaccination *f*

vaccine ['væksiːn] *n* vaccin *m*

vacuum ['vækjum] *n* vide *m*

vacuum bottle *n* (*US*) = **vacuum flask**

vacuum cleaner *n* aspirateur *m*

vacuum flask *n* (*Brit*) bouteille *f* thermos®

vacuum-packed ['vækjumpækt] *adj* emballé(e) sous vide

vagabond ['vægəbɔnd] *n* vagabond(e); (*tramp*) chemineau *m*, clochard(e)

vagary ['veɪgərɪ] *n* caprice *m*

vagina [və'dʒaɪnə] *n* vagin *m*

vagrancy ['veɪgrənsɪ] *n* vagabondage *m*

vagrant ['veɪgrənt] *n* vagabond(e), mendiant(e)

vague [veɪg] *adj* vague, imprécis(e); (*blurred: photo, memory*) flou(e); **I haven't the ~st idea** je n'en ai pas la moindre idée

vaguely ['veɪglɪ] *adv* vaguement

vain [veɪn] *adj* (*useless*) vain(e); (*conceited*) vaniteux(-euse); **in ~** en vain

valance ['væləns] *n* (*of bed*) tour *m* de lit

valedictory [vælɪ'dɪktərɪ] *adj* d'adieu

valentine ['væləntaɪn] *n* (*also:* **valentine card**) carte *f* de la Saint-Valentin

Valentine's Day ['væləntaɪnz-] *n* Saint-Valentin *f*

valet ['væleɪ] *n* valet *m* de chambre

valet parking *n* parcage *m* par les soins du personnel (de l'hôtel *etc*)

valet service *n* (*for clothes*) pressing *m*; (*for car*) nettoyage complet

valiant ['vælɪənt] *adj* vaillant(e), courageux(-euse)

valid ['vælɪd] *adj* (*document*) valide, valable; (*excuse*) valable

validate ['vælɪdeɪt] *vt* (*contract, document*) valider; (*argument, claim*) prouver la justesse de, confirmer

validity [və'lɪdɪtɪ] *n* validité *f*

valise [və'liːz] *n* sac *m* de voyage

valley ['vælɪ] *n* vallée *f*

valour, (*US*) **valor** ['vælə^r] *n* courage *m*

valuable ['væljuəbl] *adj* (*jewel*) de grande valeur; (*time, help*) précieux(-euse)

valuables ['væljuəblz] *npl* objets *mpl* de valeur

valuation [vælju'eɪʃən] *n* évaluation *f*, expertise *f*

value ['væljuː] *n* valeur *f* ▷ *vt* (*fix price*) évaluer, expertiser; (*appreciate*) apprécier; (*cherish*) tenir à; **values** *npl* (*principles*) valeurs *fpl*; **you get good ~ (for money) in that shop** vous en avez pour votre argent dans ce magasin; **to lose (in) ~** (*currency*) baisser; (*property*) se déprécier; **to gain (in) ~** (*currency*) monter; (*property*) prendre de la valeur; **to be of great ~ to sb** (*fig*) être très utile à qn

value added tax [-'ædɪd-] *n* (*Brit*) taxe *f* à la valeur ajoutée

valued ['væljuːd] *adj* (*appreciated*) estimé(e)

valuer ['væljuə^r] *n* expert *m* (en estimations)

valve [vælv] *n* (*in machine*) soupape *f*; (*on tyre*) valve *f*; (*in radio*) lampe *f*; (*Med*) valve, valvule *f*

vampire ['væmpaɪə^r] *n* vampire *m*

van [væn] *n* (*Aut*) camionnette *f*; (*Brit Rail*) fourgon *m*

V and A *n abbr* (*Brit*) = **Victoria and Albert Museum**

vandal ['vændl] *n* vandale *m/f*

vandalism ['vændəlɪzəm] *n* vandalisme *m*

vandalize ['vændəlaɪz] *vt* saccager

vanguard ['vængɑːd] *n* avant-garde *m*

vanilla [və'nɪlə] *n* vanille *f* ▷ *cpd* (*ice cream*) à la vanille

vanish ['vænɪʃ] *vi* disparaître

vanity ['vænɪtɪ] *n* vanité *f*

vanity case *n* sac *m* de toilette

vantage ['vɑːntɪdʒ] *n*: ~ **point** bonne position

vaporize ['veɪpəraɪz] *vt* vaporiser ▷ *vi* se vaporiser

vapour, (*US*) **vapor** ['veɪpər] *n* vapeur *f*; (*on window*) buée *f*

variable ['vɛərɪəbl] *adj* variable; (*mood*) changeant(e) ▷ *n* variable *f*

variance ['vɛərɪəns] *n*: **to be at ~ (with)** être en désaccord (avec); (*facts*) être en contradiction (avec)

variant ['vɛərɪənt] *n* variante *f*

variation [vɛərɪ'eɪʃən] *n* variation *f*; (*in opinion*) changement *m*

varicose ['værɪkəus] *adj*: ~ **veins** varices *fpl*

varied ['vɛərɪd] *adj* varié(e), divers(e)

variety [və'raɪətɪ] *n* variété *f*; (*quantity*) nombre *m*, quantité *f*; **a wide ~ of ...** une quantité *or* un grand nombre de ... (différent(e)s *or* divers(es)); **for a ~ of reasons** pour diverses raisons

variety show *n* (spectacle *m* de) variétés *fpl*

various ['vɛərɪəs] *adj* divers(e), différent(e); (*several*) divers, plusieurs; **at ~ times** (*different*) en diverses occasions; (*several*) à plusieurs reprises

varnish ['vɑːnɪʃ] *n* vernis *m*; (*for nails*) vernis (à ongles) ▷ *vt* vernir; **to ~ one's nails** se vernir les ongles

vary ['vɛərɪ] *vt, vi* varier, changer; **to ~ with** *or* **according to** varier selon

varying ['vɛərɪɪŋ] *adj* variable

vase [vɑːz] *n* vase *m*

vasectomy [væ'sɛktəmɪ] *n* vasectomie *f*

Vaseline® ['væsɪliːn] *n* vaseline *f*

vast [vɑːst] *adj* vaste, immense; (*amount, success*) énorme

vastly ['vɑːstlɪ] *adv* infiniment, extrêmement

vastness ['vɑːstnɪs] *n* immensité *f*

VAT [væt] *n abbr* (*Brit*: = *value added tax*) TVA *f*

vat [væt] *n* cuve *f*

Vatican ['vætɪkən] *n*: **the ~** le Vatican

vatman ['vætmæn] (*irreg*) *n* (*Brit inf*) contrôleur *m* de la T.V.A.

vault [vɔːlt] *n* (*of roof*) voûte *f*; (*tomb*) caveau *m*; (*in bank*) salle *f* des coffres; chambre forte; (*jump*) saut *m* ▷ *vt* (*also*: **vault over**) sauter (d'un bond)

vaunted ['vɔːntɪd] *adj*: **much-~** tant célébré(e)

VC *n abbr* = **vice-chairman**; (*Brit*: = *Victoria Cross*) *distinction militaire*

VCR *n abbr* = **video cassette recorder**

VD *n abbr* = **venereal disease**

VDU *n abbr* = **visual display unit**

veal [viːl] *n* veau *m*

veer [vɪər] *vi* tourner; (*car, ship*) virer

veg. [vɛdʒ] *n abbr* (*Brit inf*) = **vegetable**; **vegetables**

vegan ['viːgən] *n* végétalien(ne)

vegeburger ['vɛdʒɪbəːgər] *n* burger végétarien

vegetable ['vɛdʒtəbl] *n* légume *m* ▷ *adj* végétal(e)

vegetable garden *n* (jardin *m*) potager *m*

vegetarian [vɛdʒɪ'tɛərɪən] *adj, n* végétarien(ne); **do you have any ~ dishes?** avez-vous des plats végétariens?

vegetate ['vɛdʒɪteɪt] *vi* végéter

vegetation [vɛdʒɪ'teɪʃən] *n* végétation *f*

vegetative ['vɛdʒɪtətɪv] *adj* (*lit*) végétal(e); (*fig*) végétatif(-ive)

veggieburger ['vɛdʒɪbəːgər] *n* = **vegeburger**

vehemence ['viːɪməns] *n* véhémence *f*, violence *f*

vehement ['viːɪmənt] *adj* violent(e), impétueux(-euse); (*impassioned*) ardent(e)

vehicle ['viːɪkl] *n* véhicule *m*

vehicular [vɪ'hɪkjulər] *adj*: **"no ~ traffic"** "interdit à tout véhicule"

veil [veɪl] *n* voile *m* ▷ *vt* voiler; **under a ~ of secrecy** (*fig*) dans le plus grand secret

veiled [veɪld] *adj* voilé(e)

vein [veɪn] *n* veine *f*; (*on leaf*) nervure *f*; (*fig: mood*) esprit *m*

Velcro® ['vɛlkrəu] *n* velcro® *m*

vellum ['vɛləm] *n* (*writing paper*) vélin *m*

velocity [vɪ'lɔsɪtɪ] *n* vitesse *f*, vélocité *f*

velour, velours [və'luər] *n* velours *m*

velvet ['vɛlvɪt] *n* velours *m*

vending machine ['vɛndɪŋ-] *n* distributeur *m* automatique

vendor ['vɛndər] *n* vendeur(-euse); **street ~** marchand ambulant

veneer [və'nɪər] *n* placage *m* de bois; (*fig*) vernis *m*

venerable ['vɛnərəbl] *adj* vénérable

venereal [vɪ'nɪərɪəl] *adj*: ~ **disease** maladie vénérienne

Venetian blind [vɪ'niːʃən-] *n* store vénitien

Venezuela [vɛnɛ'zweɪlə] *n* Venezuela *m*

Venezuelan [vɛnɛ'zweɪlən] *adj* vénézuélien(ne) ▷ *n* Vénézuélien(ne)

vengeance ['vɛndʒəns] *n* vengeance *f*; **with a ~** (*fig*) vraiment, pour de bon

vengeful ['vɛndʒful] *adj* vengeur(-geresse)

Venice ['vɛnɪs] *n* Venise

venison ['vɛnɪsn] *n* venaison *f*

venom ['vɛnəm] *n* venin *m*

venomous ['vɛnəməs] *adj* venimeux(-euse)

vent [vɛnt] *n* conduit *m* d'aération; (*in dress, jacket*) fente *f* ▷ *vt* (*fig: one's feelings*) donner libre cours à

ventilate ['vɛntɪleɪt] *vt* (*room*) ventiler, aérer

ventilation [vɛntɪ'leɪʃən] *n* ventilation *f*, aération *f*

ventilation shaft *n* conduit *m* de ventilation *or* d'aération

ventilator ['vɛntɪleɪtər] *n* ventilateur *m*

ventriloquist [vɛn'trɪləkwɪst] *n* ventriloque *m/f*

venture ['vɛntʃər] *n* entreprise *f* ▷ *vt* risquer, hasarder ▷ *vi* s'aventurer, se risquer; **a business ~** une entreprise commerciale; **to ~ to do sth** se risquer à faire qch

venture capital *n* capital-risque *m*

venue ['vɛnjuː] *n* lieu *m*; (*of conference etc*) lieu de

V

la réunion (or manifestation etc); (of match) lieu de la rencontre

Venus ['viːnəs] n (planet) Vénus f

veracity [və'ræsɪtɪ] n véracité f

veranda, verandah [və'rændə] n véranda f

verb [vəːb] n verbe m

verbal ['vəːbl] adj verbal(e); (translation) littéral(e)

verbally ['vəːbəlɪ] adv verbalement

verbatim [vəː'beɪtɪm] adj, adv mot pour mot

verbose [vəː'bəʊs] adj verbeux(-euse)

verdict ['vəːdɪkt] n verdict m; ~ **of guilty/not guilty** verdict de culpabilité/de non-culpabilité

verge [vəːdʒ] n bord m; **"soft ~s"** (Brit) "accotements non stabilisés"; **on the ~ of doing** sur le point de faire
  ▸ **verge on** vt fus approcher de

verger ['vəːdʒəʳ] n (Rel) bedeau m

verification [vɛrɪfɪ'keɪʃən] n vérification f

verify ['vɛrɪfaɪ] vt vérifier

veritable ['vɛrɪtəbl] adj véritable

vermin ['vəːmɪn] npl animaux mpl nuisibles; (insects) vermine f

vermouth ['vəːməθ] n vermouth m

vernacular [və'nækjʊləʳ] n langue f vernaculaire, dialecte m

versatile ['vəːsətaɪl] adj polyvalent(e)

verse [vəːs] n vers mpl; (stanza) strophe f; (in Bible) verset m; **in ~** en vers

versed [vəːst] adj: **(well-)~ in** versé(e) dans

version ['vəːʃən] n version f

versus ['vəːsəs] prep contre

vertebra (pl **-e**) ['vəːtɪbrə, -briː] n vertèbre f

vertebrate ['vəːtɪbrɪt] n vertébré m

vertical ['vəːtɪkl] adj vertical(e) ▸ n verticale f

vertically ['vəːtɪklɪ] adv verticalement

vertigo ['vəːtɪgəʊ] n vertige m; **to suffer from ~** avoir des vertiges

verve [vəːv] n brio m; enthousiasme m

very ['vɛrɪ] adv très ▸ adj: **the ~ book which** le livre même que; **the ~ thought (of it)** ... rien que d'y penser ...; **at the ~ end** tout à la fin; **the ~ last** le tout dernier; **at the ~ least** au moins; **~ well** très bien; **~ little** très peu; **~ much** beaucoup

vespers ['vɛspəz] npl vêpres fpl

vessel ['vɛsl] n (Anat, Naut) vaisseau m; (container) récipient m; see also **blood**

vest [vɛst] n (Brit: underwear) tricot m de corps; (US: waistcoat) gilet m ▸ vt: **to ~ sb with sth, to ~ sth in sb** investir qn de qch

vested interest n: **to have a ~ in doing** avoir tout intérêt à faire; **vested interests** npl (Comm) droits acquis

vestibule ['vɛstɪbjuːl] n vestibule m

vestige ['vɛstɪdʒ] n vestige m

vestry ['vɛstrɪ] n sacristie f

Vesuvius [vɪ'suːvɪəs] n Vésuve m

vet [vɛt] n abbr (Brit: = veterinary surgeon) vétérinaire m/f; (US: = veteran) ancien(ne) combattant(e) ▸ vt examiner minutieusement; (text) revoir; (candidate) se renseigner

soigneusement sur, soumettre à une enquête approfondie

veteran ['vɛtərn] n vétéran m; (also: **war veteran**) ancien combattant ▸ adj: **she's a ~ campaigner for ...** cela fait très longtemps qu'elle lutte pour ...

veteran car n voiture f d'époque

veterinarian [vɛtrɪ'nɛərɪən] n (US) = **veterinary surgeon**

veterinary ['vɛtrɪnərɪ] adj vétérinaire

veterinary surgeon ['vɛtrɪnərɪ-] (Brit) n vétérinaire m/f

veto ['viːtəʊ] n (pl **-es**) veto m ▸ vt opposer son veto à; **to put a ~ on** mettre (or opposer) son veto à

vetting ['vɛtɪŋ] n: **positive ~** enquête f de sécurité

vex [vɛks] vt fâcher, contrarier

vexed [vɛkst] adj (question) controversé(e)

VFD n abbr (US) = **voluntary fire department**

VG n abbr (Brit: Scol etc: = very good) tb (= très bien)

VHF abbr (= very high frequency) VHF

VI abbr (US) = **Virgin Islands**

via ['vaɪə] prep par, via

viability [vaɪə'bɪlɪtɪ] n viabilité f

viable ['vaɪəbl] adj viable

viaduct ['vaɪədʌkt] n viaduc m

vial ['vaɪəl] n fiole f

vibes [vaɪbz] npl (inf): **I get good/bad ~ about it** je le sens bien/ne le sens pas; **there are good/ bad ~ between us** entre nous le courant passe bien/ne passe pas

vibrant ['vaɪbrnt] adj (sound, colour) vibrant(e)

vibraphone ['vaɪbrəfəʊn] n vibraphone m

vibrate [vaɪ'breɪt] vi: **to ~ (with)** vibrer (de); (resound) retentir (de)

vibration [vaɪ'breɪʃən] n vibration f

vibrator [vaɪ'breɪtəʳ] n vibromasseur m

vicar ['vɪkəʳ] n pasteur m (de l'Église anglicane)

vicarage ['vɪkərɪdʒ] n presbytère m

vicarious [vɪ'kɛərɪəs] adj (pleasure, experience) indirect(e)

vice [vaɪs] n (evil) vice m; (Tech) étau m

vice- [vaɪs] prefix vice-

vice-chairman [vaɪs'tʃɛəmən] (irreg) n vice-président(e)

vice-chancellor [vaɪs'tʃɑːnsələʳ] n (Brit) ≈ président(e) d'université

vice-president [vaɪs'prɛzɪdənt] n vice-président(e)

viceroy ['vaɪsrɔɪ] n vice-roi m

vice squad n ≈ brigade mondaine

vice versa ['vaɪsɪ'vəːsə] adv vice versa

vicinity [vɪ'sɪnɪtɪ] n environs mpl, alentours mpl

vicious ['vɪʃəs] adj (remark) cruel(le), méchant(e); (blow) brutal(e); (dog) méchant(e), dangereux(-euse); **a ~ circle** un cercle vicieux

viciousness ['vɪʃəsnɪs] n méchanceté f, cruauté f; brutalité f

vicissitudes [vɪ'sɪsɪtjuːdz] npl vicissitudes fpl

victim ['vɪktɪm] n victime f; **to be the ~ of** être victime de

victimization [vɪktɪmaɪˈzeɪʃən] n brimades fpl;
représailles fpl
victimize [ˈvɪktɪmaɪz] vt brimer; exercer des
représailles sur
victor [ˈvɪktə^r] n vainqueur m
Victorian [vɪkˈtɔːrɪən] adj victorien(ne)
victorious [vɪkˈtɔːrɪəs] adj victorieux(-euse)
victory [ˈvɪktərɪ] n victoire f; **to win a ~ over sb**
remporter une victoire sur qn
video [ˈvɪdɪəʊ] n (video film) vidéo f; (also: **video**
cassette) vidéocassette f; (also: **video cassette**
recorder) magnétoscope m ▷ vt (with recorder)
enregistrer; (with camera) filmer ▷ cpd vidéo inv
video camera n caméra f vidéo inv
video cassette n vidéocassette f
video cassette recorder n = **video recorder**
videodisc [ˈvɪdɪəʊdɪsk] n vidéodisque m
video game n jeu m vidéo inv
video nasty n vidéo à caractère violent ou
pornographique
videophone [ˈvɪdɪəʊfəʊn] n visiophone m,
vidéophone m
video recorder n magnétoscope m
video recording n enregistrement m (en) vidéo
inv
video shop n vidéoclub m
video tape n bande f vidéo inv; (cassette)
vidéocassette f
video wall n mur m d'images vidéo
vie [vaɪ] vi: **to ~ with** lutter avec, rivaliser avec
Vienna [vɪˈɛnə] n Vienne
Vietnam, Viet Nam [ˈvjɛtˈnæm] n Viêt-nam or
Vietnam m
Vietnamese [vjɛtnəˈmiːz] adj vietnamien(ne)
▷ n (pl inv) Vietnamien(ne); (Ling) vietnamien m
view [vjuː] n vue f; (opinion) avis m, vue ▷ vt voir,
regarder; (situation) considérer; (house) visiter;
on ~ (in museum etc) exposé(e); **in full ~ of sb**
sous les yeux de qn; **to be within ~ (of sth)** être
à portée de vue (de qch); **an overall ~ of the**
situation une vue d'ensemble de la situation;
in my ~ à mon avis; **in ~ of the fact that** étant
donné que; **with a ~ to doing sth** dans
l'intention de faire qch
viewdata [ˈvjuːdeɪtə] n (Brit) télétexte m (version
téléphonique)
viewer [ˈvjuːə^r] n (viewfinder) viseur m; (small
projector) visionneuse f; (TV)
téléspectateur(-trice)
viewfinder [ˈvjuːfaɪndə^r] n viseur m
viewpoint [ˈvjuːpɔɪnt] n point m de vue
vigil [ˈvɪdʒɪl] n veille f; **to keep ~** veiller
vigilance [ˈvɪdʒɪləns] n vigilance f
vigilant [ˈvɪdʒɪlənt] adj vigilant(e)
vigilante [vɪdʒɪˈlæntɪ] n justicier ou membre d'un
groupe d'autodéfense
vigorous [ˈvɪgərəs] adj vigoureux(-euse)
vigour, (US) **vigor** [ˈvɪgə^r] n vigueur f
vile [vaɪl] adj (action) vil(e); (smell, food)
abominable; (temper) massacrant(e)
vilify [ˈvɪlɪfaɪ] vt calomnier, vilipender
villa [ˈvɪlə] n villa f

village [ˈvɪlɪdʒ] n village m
villager [ˈvɪlɪdʒə^r] n villageois(e)
villain [ˈvɪlən] n (scoundrel) scélérat m; (Brit:
criminal) bandit m; (in novel etc) traître m
VIN n abbr (US) = **vehicle identification number**
vinaigrette [vɪneɪˈgrɛt] n vinaigrette f
vindicate [ˈvɪndɪkeɪt] vt défendre avec succès;
justifier
vindication [vɪndɪˈkeɪʃən] n: **in ~ of** pour
justifier
vindictive [vɪnˈdɪktɪv] adj vindicatif(-ive),
rancunier(-ière)
vine [vaɪn] n vigne f; (climbing plant) plante
grimpante
vinegar [ˈvɪnɪgə^r] n vinaigre m
vine grower n viticulteur m
vine-growing [ˈvaɪngrəʊɪŋ] adj viticole ▷ n
viticulture f
vineyard [ˈvɪnjaːd] n vignoble m
vintage [ˈvɪntɪdʒ] n (year) année f, millésime m
▷ cpd (car) d'époque; (wine) de grand cru; **the**
1970 ~ le millésime 1970
vinyl [ˈvaɪnl] n vinyle m
viola [vɪˈəʊlə] n alto m
violate [ˈvaɪəleɪt] vt violer
violation [vaɪəˈleɪʃən] n violation f; **in ~ of** (rule,
law) en infraction à, en violation de
violence [ˈvaɪələns] n violence f; (Pol etc)
incidents violents
violent [ˈvaɪələnt] adj violent(e); **a ~ dislike of**
sb/sth une aversion profonde pour qn/qch
violently [ˈvaɪələntlɪ] adv violemment; (ill,
angry) terriblement
violet [ˈvaɪələt] adj (colour) violet(te) ▷ n (plant)
violette f
violin [vaɪəˈlɪn] n violon m
violinist [vaɪəˈlɪnɪst] n violoniste m/f
VIP n abbr (= very important person) VIP m
viper [ˈvaɪpə^r] n vipère f
viral [ˈvaɪərəl] adj viral(e)
virgin [ˈvəːdʒɪn] n vierge f ▷ adj vierge; **she is a ~**
elle est vierge; **the Blessed V~** la Sainte Vierge
virginity [vəːˈdʒɪnɪtɪ] n virginité f
Virgo [ˈvəːgəʊ] n la Vierge; **to be ~** être de la
Vierge
virile [ˈvɪraɪl] adj viril(e)
virility [vɪˈrɪlɪtɪ] n virilité f
virtual [ˈvəːtjuəl] adj (Comput, Physics) virtuel(le);
(in effect): **it's a ~ impossibility** c'est quasiment
impossible; **the ~ leader** le chef dans la
pratique
virtually [ˈvəːtjuəlɪ] adv (almost) pratiquement;
it is ~ impossible c'est quasiment impossible
virtual reality n (Comput) réalité virtuelle
virtue [ˈvəːtjuː] n vertu f; (advantage) mérite m,
avantage m; **by ~ of** en vertu or raison de
virtuosity [vəːtjuˈɒsɪtɪ] n virtuosité f
virtuoso [vəːtjuˈəʊzəʊ] n virtuose m/f
virtuous [ˈvəːtjuəs] adj vertueux(-euse)
virulent [ˈvɪrulənt] adj virulent(e)
virus [ˈvaɪərəs] n (Med, Comput) virus m
visa [ˈviːzə] n visa m

V

vis-à-vis [viːzəˈviː] *prep* vis-à-vis de

viscount [ˈvaɪkaunt] *n* vicomte *m*

viscous [ˈvɪskəs] *adj* visqueux(-euse), gluant(e)

vise [vaɪs] *n* (US Tech) = **vice**

visibility [vɪzɪˈbɪlɪtɪ] *n* visibilité *f*

visible [ˈvɪzəbl] *adj* visible; **~ exports/imports** exportations/importations *fpl* visibles

visibly [ˈvɪzəblɪ] *adv* visiblement

vision [ˈvɪʒən] *n* (sight) vue *f*, vision *f*; (foresight, in dream) vision

visionary [ˈvɪʒənrɪ] *n* visionnaire *m/f*

visit [ˈvɪzɪt] *n* visite *f*; (stay) séjour *m* ▷ *vt* (person: US: also: **visit with**) rendre visite à; (place) visiter; **on a private/official ~** en visite privée/officielle

visiting [ˈvɪzɪtɪŋ] *adj* (speaker, team) invité(e), de l'extérieur

visiting card *n* carte *f* de visite

visiting hours *npl* heures *fpl* de visite

visitor [ˈvɪzɪtəʳ] *n* visiteur(-euse); (to one's house) invité(e); (in hotel) client(e)

visitor centre, (US) **visitor center** *n* hall *m* or centre *m* d'accueil

visitors' book *n* livre *m* d'or; (in hotel) registre *m*

visor [ˈvaɪzəʳ] *n* visière *f*

VISTA [ˈvɪstə] *n abbr* (= Volunteers in Service to America) programme d'assistance bénévole aux régions pauvres

vista [ˈvɪstə] *n* vue *f*, perspective *f*

visual [ˈvɪzjuəl] *adj* visuel(le)

visual aid *n* support visuel (pour l'enseignement)

visual arts *npl* arts *mpl* plastiques

visual display unit *n* console *f* de visualisation, visuel *m*

visualize [ˈvɪzjuəlaɪz] *vt* se représenter; (foresee) prévoir

visually [ˈvɪzjuəlɪ] *adv* visuellement; **~ handicapped** handicapé(e) visuel(le)

visually-impaired [ˈvɪzjuəliːmˈpɛəʳd] *adj* malvoyant(e)

vital [ˈvaɪtl] *adj* vital(e); **of ~ importance (to sb/sth)** d'une importance capitale (pour qn/qch)

vitality [vaɪˈtælɪtɪ] *n* vitalité *f*

vitally [ˈvaɪtəlɪ] *adv* extrêmement

vital statistics *npl* (of population) statistiques *fpl* démographiques; (inf: woman's) mensurations *fpl*

vitamin [ˈvɪtəmɪn] *n* vitamine *f*

vitiate [ˈvɪʃɪeɪt] *vt* vicier

vitreous [ˈvɪtrɪəs] *adj* (china) vitreux(-euse); (enamel) vitrifié(e)

vitriolic [vɪtrɪˈɔlɪk] *adj* (fig) venimeux(-euse)

viva [ˈvaɪvə] *n* (also: **viva voce**) (examen) oral

vivacious [vɪˈveɪʃəs] *adj* animé(e), qui a de la vivacité

vivacity [vɪˈvæsɪtɪ] *n* vivacité *f*

vivid [ˈvɪvɪd] *adj* (account) frappant(e), vivant(e); (light, imagination) vif (vive)

vividly [ˈvɪvɪdlɪ] *adv* (describe) d'une manière vivante; (remember) de façon précise

vivisection [vɪvɪˈsɛkʃən] *n* vivisection *f*

vixen [ˈvɪksn] *n* renarde *f*; (pej: woman) mégère *f*

viz [vɪz] *abbr* (= vide licet: namely) à savoir, c. à d.

VLF *abbr* = **very low frequency**

V-neck [ˈviːnɛk] *n* décolleté *m* en V

VOA *n abbr* (= Voice of America) voix *f* de l'Amérique (émissions de radio à destination de l'étranger)

vocabulary [vəuˈkæbjulərɪ] *n* vocabulaire *m*

vocal [ˈvəukl] *adj* vocal(e); (articulate) qui n'hésite pas à s'exprimer, qui sait faire entendre ses opinions; **vocals** *npl* voix *fpl*

vocal cords *npl* cordes vocales

vocalist [ˈvəukəlɪst] *n* chanteur(-euse)

vocation [vəuˈkeɪʃən] *n* vocation *f*

vocational [vəuˈkeɪʃənl] *adj* professionnel(le); **~ guidance/training** orientation/formation professionnelle

vociferous [vəˈsɪfərəs] *adj* bruyant(e)

vodka [ˈvɔdkə] *n* vodka *f*

vogue [vəug] *n* mode *f*; (popularity) vogue *f*; **to be in ~** être en vogue or à la mode

voice [vɔɪs] *n* voix *f*; (opinion) avis *m* ▷ *vt* (opinion) exprimer, formuler; **in a loud/soft ~** à voix haute/basse; **to give ~ to** exprimer

voice mail *n* (system) messagerie *f* vocale, boîte *f* vocale; (device) répondeur *m*

voice-over [ˈvɔɪsəuvəʳ] *n* voix off *f*

void [vɔɪd] *n* vide *m* ▷ *adj* (invalid) nul(le); (empty): **~ of** vide de, dépourvu(e) de

voile [vɔɪl] *n* voile *m* (tissu)

vol. *abbr* (= volume) vol

volatile [ˈvɔlətaɪl] *adj* volatil(e); (fig: person) versatile; (: situation) explosif(-ive)

volcanic [vɔlˈkænɪk] *adj* volcanique

volcano (*pl* **-es**) [vɔlˈkeɪnəu] *n* volcan *m*

volition [vəˈlɪʃən] *n*: **of one's own ~** de son propre gré

volley [ˈvɔlɪ] *n* (of gunfire) salve *f*; (of stones etc) pluie *f*, volée *f*; (Tennis etc) volée

volleyball [ˈvɔlɪbɔːl] *n* volley(-ball) *m*

volt [vəult] *n* volt *m*

voltage [ˈvəultɪdʒ] *n* tension *f*, voltage *m*; **high/low ~** haute/basse tension

voluble [ˈvɔljubl] *adj* volubile

volume [ˈvɔljuːm] *n* volume *m*; (of tank) capacité *f*; **~ one/two** (of book) tome un/deux; **his expression spoke ~s** son expression en disait long

volume control *n* (Radio, TV) bouton *m* de réglage du volume

volume discount *n* (Comm) remise *f* sur la quantité

voluminous [vəˈluːmɪnəs] *adj* volumineux(-euse)

voluntarily [ˈvɔləntrɪlɪ] *adv* volontairement; bénévolement

voluntary [ˈvɔləntərɪ] *adj* volontaire; (unpaid) bénévole

voluntary liquidation *n* (Comm) dépôt *m* de bilan

voluntary redundancy *n* (Brit) départ *m* volontaire (en cas de licenciements)

volunteer [vɔlən'tɪəʳ] n volontaire m/f ▷ vt (information) donner spontanément ▷ vi (Mil) s'engager comme volontaire; **to ~ to do** se proposer pour faire

voluptuous [və'lʌptjuəs] adj voluptueux(-euse)

vomit ['vɔmɪt] n vomissure f ▷ vt, vi vomir

voracious [və'reɪʃəs] adj vorace; (reader) avide

vote [vəut] n vote m, suffrage m; (votes cast) voix f, vote; (franchise) droit m de vote ▷ vt (bill) voter; (chairman) élire; (propose): **to ~ that** proposer que +sub ▷ vi voter; **to put sth to the ~, to take a ~ on sth** mettre qch aux voix, procéder à un vote sur qch; **~ for** or **in favour of/against** vote pour/contre; **to ~ to do sth** voter en faveur de faire qch; **~ of censure** motion f de censure; **~ of thanks** discours m de remerciement

voter ['vəutəʳ] n électeur(-trice)

voting ['vəutɪŋ] n scrutin m, vote m

voting paper n (Brit) bulletin m de vote

voting right n droit m de vote

vouch [vautʃ]: **to ~ for** vt fus se porter garant de

voucher ['vautʃəʳ] n (for meal, petrol, gift) bon m; (receipt) reçu m; **travel ~** bon m de transport

vow [vau] n vœu m, serment m ▷ vi jurer; **to take** or **make a ~ to do sth** faire le vœu de faire qch

vowel ['vauəl] n voyelle f

voyage ['vɔiɪdʒ] n voyage m par mer, traversée f; (by spacecraft) voyage

voyeur [vwa:'jə:ʳ] n voyeur m

VP n abbr = **vice-president**

vs abbr (= versus) vs

VSO n abbr (Brit: = Voluntary Service Overseas) ≈ coopération civile

VT, Vt. abbr (US) = **Vermont**

vulgar ['vʌlgəʳ] adj vulgaire

vulgarity [vʌl'gærɪtɪ] n vulgarité f

vulnerability [vʌlnərə'bɪlɪtɪ] n vulnérabilité f

vulnerable ['vʌlnərəbl] adj vulnérable

vulture ['vʌltʃəʳ] n vautour m

V

Ww

W, w ['dʌblju:] *n* (*letter*) W, w *m*; **W for William** W comme William

W *abbr* (= *west*) O; (*Elec*: = *watt*) W

WA *abbr* (US) = **Washington**

wad [wɔd] *n* (*of cotton wool, paper*) tampon *m*; (*of banknotes etc*) liasse *f*

wadding ['wɔdɪŋ] *n* rembourrage *m*

waddle ['wɔdl] *vi* se dandiner

wade [weɪd] *vi*: **to ~ through** marcher dans, patauger dans; (*fig*: *book*) venir à bout de ▷ *vt* passer à gué

wafer ['weɪfə'] *n* (*Culin*) gaufrette *f*; (*Rel*) pain *m* d'hostie; (*Comput*) tranche *f* (de silicium)

wafer-thin ['weɪfə'θɪn] *adj* ultra-mince, mince comme du papier à cigarette

waffle ['wɔfl] *n* (*Culin*) gaufre *f*; (*inf*) rabâchage *m*; remplissage *m* ▷ *vi* parler pour ne rien dire; faire du remplissage

waffle iron *n* gaufrier *m*

waft [wɔft] *vt* porter ▷ *vi* flotter

wag [wæg] *vt* agiter, remuer ▷ *vi* remuer; **the dog ~ged its tail** le chien a remué la queue

wage [weɪdʒ] *n* (*also*: **wages**) salaire *m*, paye *f* ▷ *vt*: **to ~ war** faire la guerre; **a day's ~s** un jour de salaire

wage claim *n* demande *f* d'augmentation de salaire

wage differential *n* éventail *m* des salaires

wage earner [-əːnə'] *n* salarié(e); (*breadwinner*) soutien *m* de famille

wage freeze *n* blocage *m* des salaires

wage packet *n* (Brit) (enveloppe *f* de) paye *f*

wager ['weɪdʒə'] *n* pari *m* ▷ *vt* parier

waggle ['wægl] *vt, vi* remuer

wagon, waggon ['wægən] *n* (*horse-drawn*) chariot *m*; (Brit Rail) wagon *m* (de marchandises)

wail [weɪl] *n* gémissement *m*; (*of siren*) hurlement *m* ▷ *vi* gémir; (*siren*) hurler

waist [weɪst] *n* taille *f*, ceinture *f*

waistcoat ['weɪskəut] *n* (Brit) gilet *m*

waistline ['weɪstlaɪn] *n* (tour *m* de) taille *f*

wait [weɪt] *n* attente *f* ▷ *vi* attendre; **to ~ for sb/ sth** attendre qn/qch; **to keep sb ~ing** faire attendre qn; **~ for me, please** attendez-moi, s'il vous plaît; **~ a minute!** un instant!;

"**repairs while you ~**" "réparations minute"; **I can't ~ to …** (*fig*) je meurs d'envie de …; **to lie in ~ for** guetter

▶ **wait behind** *vi* rester (à attendre)

▶ **wait on** *vt fus* servir

▶ **wait up** *vi* attendre, ne pas se coucher; **don't ~ up for me** ne m'attendez pas pour aller vous coucher

waiter ['weɪtə'] *n* garçon *m* (de café), serveur *m*

waiting ['weɪtɪŋ] *n*: "**no ~**" (Brit Aut) "stationnement interdit"

waiting list *n* liste *f* d'attente

waiting room *n* salle *f* d'attente

waitress ['weɪtrɪs] *n* serveuse *f*

waive [weɪv] *vt* renoncer à, abandonner

waiver ['weɪvə'] *n* dispense *f*

wake [weɪk] (*pt* **woke** *or* **-d**, *pp* **woken** *or* **waked** [wəuk, 'wəukn]) *vt* (*also*: **wake up**) réveiller ▷ *vi* (*also*: **wake up**) se réveiller ▷ *n* (*for dead person*) veillée *f* mortuaire; (*Naut*) sillage *m*; **to ~ up to sth** (*fig*) se rendre compte de qch; **in the ~ of** (*fig*) à la suite de; **to follow in sb's ~** (*fig*) marcher sur les traces de qn

waken ['weɪkn] *vt, vi* = **wake**

Wales [weɪlz] *n* pays *m* de Galles; **the Prince of ~** le prince de Galles

walk [wɔːk] *n* promenade *f*; (*short*) petit tour; (*gait*) démarche *f*; (*path*) chemin *m*; (*in park etc*) allée *f*; (*pace*): **at a quick ~** d'un pas rapide ▷ *vi* marcher; (*for pleasure, exercise*) se promener ▷ *vt* (*distance*) faire à pied; (*dog*) promener; **10 minutes' ~ from** à 10 minutes de marche de; **to go for a ~** se promener; faire un tour; **from all ~s of life** de toutes conditions sociales; **I'll ~ you home** je vais vous raccompagner chez vous

▶ **walk out** *vi* (*go out*) sortir; (*as protest*) partir (en signe de protestation); (*strike*) se mettre en grève; **to ~ out on sb** quitter qn

walkabout ['wɔːkəbaut] *n*: **to go (on a) ~** (VIP) prendre un bain de foule

walker ['wɔːkə'] *n* (*person*) marcheur(-euse)

walkie-talkie ['wɔːkɪ'tɔːkɪ] *n* talkie-walkie *m*

walking ['wɔːkɪŋ] *n* marche *f* à pied; **it's within ~ distance** on peut y aller à pied

walking holiday *n* vacances passées à faire de

la randonnée

walking shoes npl chaussures fpl de marche

walking stick n canne f

Walkman® ['wɔ:kmən] n Walkman® m

walk-on ['wɔ:kɔn] adj (Theat: part) de figurant(e)

walkout ['wɔ:kaut] n (of workers) grève-surprise f

walkover ['wɔ:kəuvəʳ] n (inf) victoire f or examen m etc facile

walkway ['wɔ:kweɪ] n promenade f, cheminement piéton

wall [wɔ:l] n mur m; (of tunnel, cave) paroi f; **to go to the ~** (fig: firm etc) faire faillite
  ▶ **wall in** vt (garden etc) entourer d'un mur

wall cupboard n placard mural

walled [wɔ:ld] adj (city) fortifié(e)

wallet ['wɔlɪt] n portefeuille m; **I can't find my ~** je ne retrouve plus mon portefeuille

wallflower ['wɔ:lflauəʳ] n giroflée f; **to be a ~** (fig) faire tapisserie

wall hanging n tenture (murale), tapisserie f

wallop ['wɔləp] vt (Brit inf) taper sur, cogner

wallow ['wɔləu] vi se vautrer; **to ~ in one's grief** se complaire à sa douleur

wallpaper ['wɔ:lpeɪpəʳ] n papier peint ▷ vt tapisser

wall-to-wall ['wɔ:ltə'wɔ:l] adj: **~ carpeting** moquette f

walnut ['wɔ:lnʌt] n noix f; (tree, wood) noyer m

walrus (pl **walrus** or **-es**) ['wɔ:lrəs] n morse m

waltz [wɔ:lts] n valse f ▷ vi valser

wan [wɔn] adj pâle; triste

wand [wɔnd] n (also: **magic wand**) baguette f (magique)

wander ['wɔndəʳ] vi (person) errer, aller sans but; (thoughts) vagabonder; (river) serpenter ▷ vt errer dans

wanderer ['wɔndərəʳ] n vagabond(e)

wandering ['wɔndrɪŋ] adj (tribe) nomade; (minstrel, actor) ambulant(e)

wane [weɪn] vi (moon) décroître; (reputation) décliner

wangle ['wæŋgl] (Brit inf) vt se débrouiller pour avoir; carotter ▷ n combine f, magouille f

wanker ['wæŋkəʳ] n (inf!) branleur m (!)

want [wɔnt] vt vouloir; (need) avoir besoin de; (lack) manquer de ▷ n (poverty) pauvreté f, besoin m; **wants** npl (needs) besoins mpl; **to ~ to do** vouloir faire; **to ~ sb to do** vouloir que qn fasse; **you're ~ed on the phone** on vous demande au téléphone; **"cook ~ed"** "on demande un cuisinier"; **for ~ of** par manque de, faute de

want ads npl (US) petites annonces

wanted ['wɔntɪd] adj (criminal) recherché(e) par la police

wanting ['wɔntɪŋ] adj: **to be ~ (in)** manquer (de); **to be found ~** ne pas être à la hauteur

wanton ['wɔntn] adj capricieux(-euse), dévergondé(e)

war [wɔːʳ] n guerre f; **to go to ~** se mettre en

guerre; **to make ~ (on)** faire la guerre (à)

warble ['wɔ:bl] n (of bird) gazouillis m ▷ vi gazouiller

war cry n cri m de guerre

ward [wɔ:d] n (in hospital) salle f; (Pol) section électorale; (Law: child: also: **ward of court**) pupille m/f
  ▶ **ward off** vt parer, éviter

warden ['wɔ:dn] n (Brit: of institution) directeur(-trice); (of park, game reserve) gardien(ne); (Brit: also: **traffic warden**) contractuel(le); (of youth hostel) responsable m/f

warder ['wɔ:dəʳ] n (Brit) gardien m de prison

wardrobe ['wɔ:drəub] n (cupboard) armoire f; (clothes) garde-robe f; (Theat) costumes mpl

warehouse ['wɛəhaus] n entrepôt m

wares [wɛəz] npl marchandises fpl

warfare ['wɔ:fɛəʳ] n guerre f

war game n jeu m de stratégie militaire

warhead ['wɔ:hɛd] n (Mil) ogive f

warily ['wɛərɪlɪ] adv avec prudence, avec précaution

warlike ['wɔ:laɪk] adj guerrier(-ière)

warm [wɔ:m] adj chaud(e); (person, thanks, welcome, applause) chaleureux(-euse); (supporter) ardent(e), enthousiaste; **it's ~** il fait chaud; **I'm ~** j'ai chaud; **to keep sth ~** tenir qch au chaud; **with my ~est thanks/congratulations** avec mes remerciements/mes félicitations les plus sincères
  ▶ **warm up** vi (person, room) se réchauffer; (water) chauffer; (athlete, discussion) s'échauffer ▷ vt (food) (faire) réchauffer; (water) (faire) chauffer; (engine) faire chauffer

warm-blooded ['wɔ:m'blʌdɪd] adj (Zool) à sang chaud

war memorial n monument m aux morts

warm-hearted [wɔ:m'hɑ:tɪd] adj affectueux(-euse)

warmly ['wɔ:mlɪ] adv (dress) chaudement; (thank, welcome) chaleureusement

warmonger ['wɔ:mʌŋgəʳ] n belliciste m/f

warmongering ['wɔ:mʌŋgrɪŋ] n propagande f belliciste, bellicisme m

warmth [wɔ:mθ] n chaleur f

warm-up ['wɔ:mʌp] n (Sport) période f d'échauffement

warn [wɔ:n] vt avertir, prévenir; **to ~ sb (not) to do** conseiller à qn de (ne pas) faire

warning ['wɔ:nɪŋ] n avertissement m; (notice) avis m; (signal) avertisseur m; **without (any) ~** (suddenly) inopinément; (without notifying) sans prévenir; **gale ~** (Meteorology) avis de grand vent

warning light n avertisseur lumineux

warning triangle n (Aut) triangle m de présignalisation

warp [wɔ:p] n (Textiles) chaîne f ▷ vi (wood) travailler, se voiler or gauchir ▷ vt voiler; (fig) pervertir

warpath ['wɔ:pɑ:θ] n: **to be on the ~** (fig) être sur le sentier de la guerre

W

warped [wɔːpt] *adj* (*wood*) gauchi(e); (*fig*) perverti(e)

warrant ['wɔrnt] *n* (*guarantee*) garantie *f*; (*Law:* *to arrest*) mandat *m* d'arrêt; (: *to search*) mandat de perquisition ▷ *vt* (*justify, merit*) justifier

warrant officer *n* (*Mil*) adjudant *m*; (*Naut*) premier-maître *m*

warranty ['wɔrəntɪ] *n* garantie *f*; **under ~** (*Comm*) sous garantie

warren ['wɔrən] *n* (*of rabbits*) terriers *mpl*, garenne *f*

warring ['wɔrɪŋ] *adj* (*nations*) en guerre; (*interests etc*) contradictoire, opposé(e)

warrior ['wɔrɪəʳ] *n* guerrier(-ière)

Warsaw ['wɔːsɔː] *n* Varsovie

warship ['wɔːʃɪp] *n* navire *m* de guerre

wart [wɔːt] *n* verrue *f*

wartime ['wɔːtaɪm] *n*: **in ~** en temps de guerre

wary ['wɛərɪ] *adj* prudent(e); **to be ~ about** *or* **of doing sth** hésiter beaucoup à faire qch

was [wɔz] *pt of* **be**

wash [wɔʃ] *vt* laver; (*sweep, carry: sea etc*) emporter, entraîner; (: *ashore*) rejeter ▷ *vi* se laver; (*sea*): **to ~ over/against sth** inonder/baigner qch ▷ *n* (*paint*) badigeon *m*; (*clothes*) lessive *f*; (*washing programme*) lavage *m*; (*of ship*) sillage *m*; **to give sth a ~** laver qch; **to have a ~** se laver, faire sa toilette; **he was ~ed overboard** il a été emporté par une vague

▶ **wash away** *vt* (*stain*) enlever au lavage; (*subj: river etc*) emporter

▶ **wash down** *vt* laver; laver à grande eau

▶ **wash off** *vi* partir au lavage

▶ **wash up** *vi* (*Brit*) faire la vaisselle; (*US: have a wash*) se débarbouiller

Wash. *abbr* (*US*) = **Washington**

washable ['wɔʃəbl] *adj* lavable

washbasin ['wɔʃbeɪsn] *n* lavabo *m*

washer ['wɔʃəʳ] *n* (*Tech*) rondelle *f*, joint *m*

washing ['wɔʃɪŋ] *n* (*Brit: linen etc: dirty*) linge *m*; (: *clean*) lessive *f*

washing line *n* (*Brit*) corde *f* à linge

washing machine *n* machine *f* à laver

washing powder *n* (*Brit*) lessive *f* (en poudre)

Washington ['wɔʃɪŋtən] *n* (*city, state*) Washington *m*

washing-up [wɔʃɪŋ'ʌp] *n* (*Brit*) vaisselle *f*

washing-up liquid *n* (*Brit*) produit *m* pour la vaisselle

wash-out ['wɔʃaut] *n* (*inf*) désastre *m*

washroom ['wɔʃrum] *n* (*US*) toilettes *fpl*

wasn't ['wɔznt] = **was not**

Wasp, WASP [wɔsp] *n abbr* (*US inf*: = *White Anglo-Saxon Protestant*) surnom, souvent péjoratif, donné à l'américain de souche anglo-saxonne, aisé et de tendance conservatrice

wasp [wɔsp] *n* guêpe *f*

waspish ['wɔspɪʃ] *adj* irritable

wastage ['weɪstɪdʒ] *n* gaspillage *m*; (*in manufacturing, transport etc*) déchet *m*

waste [weɪst] *n* gaspillage *m*; (*of time*) perte *f*; (*rubbish*) déchets *mpl*; (*also:* **household waste**)

ordures *fpl* ▷ *adj* (*energy, heat*) perdu(e); (*food*) inutilisé(e); (*land, ground: in city*) à l'abandon; (: *in country*) inculte, en friche; (*leftover*): **~ material** déchets ▷ *vt* gaspiller; (*time, opportunity*) perdre; **wastes** *npl* étendue *f* désertique; **it's a ~ of money** c'est de l'argent jeté en l'air; **to go to ~** être gaspillé(e); **to lay ~** (*destroy*) dévaster

▶ **waste away** *vi* dépérir

wastebasket ['weɪstbɑːskɪt] *n* = **wastepaper basket**

waste disposal, waste disposal unit *n* (*Brit*) broyeur *m* d'ordures

wasteful ['weɪstful] *adj* gaspilleur(-euse); (*process*) peu économique

waste ground *n* (*Brit*) terrain *m* vague

wasteland ['weɪstlənd] *n* terres *fpl* à l'abandon; (*in town*) terrain(s) *m(pl)* vague(s)

wastepaper basket ['weɪstpeɪpə-] *n* corbeille *f* à papier

waste pipe *n* (tuyau *m* de) vidange *f*

waste products *npl* (*Industry*) déchets *mpl* (de fabrication)

waster ['weɪstəʳ] *n* (*inf*) bon(ne) à rien

watch [wɔtʃ] *n* montre *f*; (*act of watching*) surveillance *f*; (*guard: Mil*) sentinelle *f*; (: *Naut*) homme *m* de quart; (*Naut: spell of duty*) quart *m* ▷ *vt* (*look at*) observer; (: *match, programme*) regarder; (*spy on, guard*) surveiller; (*be careful of*) faire attention à ▷ *vi* regarder; (*keep guard*) monter la garde; **to keep a close ~ on sb/sth** surveiller qn/qch de près; **to keep ~** faire le guet; **~ what you're doing** fais attention à ce que tu fais

▶ **watch out** *vi* faire attention

watchband ['wɔtʃbænd] *n* (*US*) bracelet *m* de montre

watchdog ['wɔtʃdɔg] *n* chien *m* de garde; (*fig*) gardien(ne)

watchful ['wɔtʃful] *adj* attentif(-ive), vigilant(e)

watchmaker ['wɔtʃmeɪkəʳ] *n* horloger(-ère)

watchman ['wɔtʃmən] (*irreg*) *n* gardien *m*; (*also:* **night watchman**) veilleur *m* de nuit

watch stem *n* (*US*) remontoir *m*

watch strap ['wɔtʃstræp] *n* bracelet *m* de montre

watchword ['wɔtʃwəːd] *n* mot *m* de passe

water ['wɔːtəʳ] *n* eau *f* ▷ *vt* (*plant, garden*) arroser ▷ *vi* (*eyes*) larmoyer; **a drink of ~** un verre d'eau; **in British ~s** dans les eaux territoriales Britanniques; **to pass ~** uriner; **to make sb's mouth ~** mettre l'eau à la bouche de qn

▶ **water down** *vt* (*milk etc*) couper avec de l'eau; (*fig: story*) édulcorer

water closet *n* (*Brit*) w.-c. *mpl*, waters *mpl*

watercolour, (*US*) **watercolor** ['wɔːtəkʌləʳ] *n* aquarelle *f*; **watercolours** *npl* couleurs *fpl* pour aquarelle

water-cooled ['wɔːtəkuːld] *adj* à refroidissement par eau

watercress ['wɔːtəkrɛs] *n* cresson *m* (de

fontaine)

waterfall ['wɔ:təfɔ:l] *n* chute *f* d'eau

waterfront ['wɔ:təfrʌnt] *n* (*seafront*) front *m* de mer; (*at docks*) quais *mpl*

water heater *n* chauffe-eau *m*

water hole *n* mare *f*

water ice *n* (*Brit*) sorbet *m*

watering can ['wɔ:tərɪŋ-] *n* arrosoir *m*

water level *n* niveau *m* de l'eau; (*of flood*) niveau des eaux

water lily *n* nénuphar *m*

waterline ['wɔ:təlaɪn] *n* (*Naut*) ligne *f* de flottaison

waterlogged ['wɔ:təlɒgd] *adj* détrempé(e); imbibé(e) d'eau

water main *n* canalisation *f* d'eau

watermark ['wɔ:təmɑ:k] *n* (*on paper*) filigrane *m*

watermelon ['wɔ:təmɛlən] *n* pastèque *f*

water polo *n* water-polo *m*

waterproof ['wɔ:təpru:f] *adj* imperméable

water-repellent ['wɔ:tərɪ'pɛlnt] *adj* hydrofuge

watershed ['wɔ:təʃɛd] *n* (*Geo*) ligne *f* de partage des eaux; (*fig*) moment *m* critique, point décisif

water-skiing ['wɔ:təski:ɪŋ] *n* ski *m* nautique

water softener *n* adoucisseur *m* d'eau

water tank *n* réservoir *m* d'eau

watertight ['wɔ:tətaɪt] *adj* étanche

water vapour *n* vapeur *f* d'eau

waterway ['wɔ:təweɪ] *n* cours *m* d'eau navigable

waterworks ['wɔ:təwə:ks] *npl* station *f* hydraulique

watery ['wɔ:tərɪ] *adj* (*colour*) délavé(e); (*coffee*) trop faible

watt [wɒt] *n* watt *m*

wattage ['wɒtɪdʒ] *n* puissance *f* or consommation *f* en watts

wattle ['wɒtl] *n* clayonnage *m*

wave [weɪv] *n* vague *f*; (*of hand*) geste *m*, signe *m*; (*Radio*) onde *f*; (*in hair*) ondulation *f*; (*fig: of enthusiasm, strikes etc*) vague ▷ *vi* faire signe de la main; (*flag*) flotter au vent; (*grass*) ondoyer ▷ *vt* (*handkerchief*) agiter; (*stick*) brandir; (*hair*) onduler; **short/medium ~** (*Radio*) ondes courtes/moyennes; **long ~** (*Radio*) grandes ondes; **the new ~** (*Cine, Mus*) la nouvelle vague; **to ~ goodbye to sb** dire au revoir de la main à qn

  ▸ **wave aside**

  ▸ **wave away** *vt* (*fig: suggestion, objection*) rejeter, repousser; (: *doubts*) chasser; (*person*): **to ~ sb aside** faire signe à qn de s'écarter

waveband ['weɪvbænd] *n* bande *f* de fréquences

wavelength ['weɪvlɛŋθ] *n* longueur *f* d'ondes

waver ['weɪvə*] *vi* vaciller; (*voice*) trembler; (*person*) hésiter

wavy ['weɪvɪ] *adj* (*hair, surface*) ondulé(e); (*line*) onduleux(-euse)

wax [wæks] *n* cire *f*; (*for skis*) fart *m* ▷ *vt* cirer; (*car*) lustrer; (*skis*) farter ▷ *vi* (*moon*) croître

waxworks ['wækswə:ks] *npl* personnages *mpl*

de cire; musée *m* de cire

way [weɪ] *n* chemin *m*, voie *f*; (*path, access*) passage *m*; (*distance*) distance *f*; (*direction*) chemin, direction *f*; (*manner*) façon *f*, manière *f*; (*habit*) habitude *f*, façon; (*condition*) état *m*; **which ~? — this ~/that ~** par où *or* de quel côté? — par ici/par là; **to crawl one's ~ to ...** ramper jusqu'à ...; **to lie one's ~ out of it** s'en sortir par un mensonge; **to lose one's ~** perdre son chemin; **on the ~ (to)** en route (pour); **to be on one's ~** être en route; **to be in the ~** bloquer le passage; (*fig*) gêner; **to keep out of sb's ~** éviter qn; **it's a long ~ away** c'est loin d'ici; **the village is rather out of the ~** le village est plutôt à l'écart *or* isolé; **to go out of one's ~ to do** (*fig*) se donner beaucoup de mal pour faire; **to be under ~** (*work, project*) être en cours; **to make ~ (for sb/sth)** faire place (à qn/qch), s'écarter pour laisser passer (qn/qch); **to get one's own ~** arriver à ses fins; **put it the right ~ up** (*Brit*) mettez-le dans le bon sens; **to be the wrong ~ round** être à l'envers, ne pas être dans le bon sens; **he's in a bad ~** il va mal; **in a ~** dans un sens; **by the ~** à propos; **in some ~s** à certains égards; d'un côté; **in the ~ of** en fait de, comme; **by ~ of** (*through*) en passant par, via; (*as a sort of*) en guise de; **"~ in"** (*Brit*) "entrée"; **"~ out"** (*Brit*) "sortie"; **the ~ back** le chemin du retour; **this ~ and that** par-ci par-là; **"give ~"** (*Brit Aut*) "cédez la priorité"; **no ~!** (*inf*) pas question!

waybill ['weɪbɪl] *n* (*Comm*) récépissé *m*

waylay [weɪ'leɪ] *vt* (*irreg: like* lay) attaquer; (*fig*): **I got waylaid** quelqu'un m'a accroché

wayside ['weɪsaɪd] *n* bord *m* de la route; **to fall by the ~** (*fig*) abandonner; (*morally*) quitter le droit chemin

way station *n* (*US Rail*) petite gare; (: *fig*) étape *f*

wayward ['weɪwəd] *adj* capricieux(-euse), entêté(e)

W.C. *n abbr* (*Brit*: = *water closet*) w.-c. *mpl*, waters *mpl*

WCC *n abbr* (= *World Council of Churches*) COE *m* (*Conseil œcuménique des Églises*)

we [wi:] *pl pron* nous

weak [wi:k] *adj* faible; (*health*) fragile; (*beam etc*) peu solide; (*tea, coffee*) léger(-ère); **to grow ~(er)** s'affaiblir, faiblir

weaken ['wi:kn] *vi* faiblir ▷ *vt* affaiblir

weak-kneed ['wi:k'ni:d] *adj* (*fig*) lâche, faible

weakling ['wi:klɪŋ] *n* gringalet *m*; faible *m/f*

weakly ['wi:klɪ] *adj* chétif(-ive) ▷ *adv* faiblement

weakness ['wi:knɪs] *n* faiblesse *f*; (*fault*) point *m* faible

wealth [wɛlθ] *n* (*money, resources*) richesse(s) *f(pl)*; (*of details*) profusion *f*

wealth tax *n* impôt *m* sur la fortune

wealthy ['wɛlθɪ] *adj* riche

wean [wi:n] *vt* sevrer

weapon ['wɛpən] *n* arme *f*; **~s of mass destruction** armes *fpl* de destruction massive

W

863

wear [wεəʳ] (*pt* **wore**, *pp* **worn**) [wɔːʳ, wɔːn] *n*
(*use*) usage *m*; (*deterioration through use*) usure *f*
▷ *vt* (*clothes*) porter; (*put on*) mettre; (*beard etc*)
avoir; (*damage: through use*) user ▷ *vi* (*last*) faire de
l'usage; (*rub etc through*) s'user; **sports/baby~**
vêtements *mpl* de sport/pour bébés; **evening ~**
tenue *f* de soirée; **~ and tear** usure *f*; **to ~ a hole
in sth** faire (à la longue) un trou dans qch
  ▶ **wear away** *vt* user, ronger ▷ *vi* s'user, être
rongé(e)
  ▶ **wear down** *vt* user; (*strength*) épuiser
  ▶ **wear off** *vi* disparaître
  ▶ **wear on** *vi* se poursuivre; passer
  ▶ **wear out** *vt* user; (*person, strength*) épuiser
wearable ['wεərəbl] *adj* mettable
wearily ['wɪərɪlɪ] *adv* avec lassitude
weariness ['wɪərɪnɪs] *n* épuisement *m*,
lassitude *f*
wearisome ['wɪərɪsəm] *adj* (*tiring*) fatigant(e);
(*boring*) ennuyeux(-euse)
weary ['wɪərɪ] *adj* (*tired*) épuisé(e); (*dispirited*) las
(lasse); abattu(e) ▷ *vt* lasser ▷ *vi*: **to ~ of** se
lasser de
weasel ['wiːzl] *n* (*Zool*) belette *f*
weather ['wεðəʳ] *n* temps *m* ▷ *vt* (*wood*) faire
mûrir; (*storm: lit, fig*) essuyer; (*crisis*) survivre à;
what's the ~ like? quel temps fait-il?; **under
the ~** (*fig: ill*) mal fichu(e)
weather-beaten ['wεðəbiːtn] *adj* (*person*)
hâlé(e); (*building*) dégradé(e) par les intempéries
weather forecast *n* prévisions *fpl*
météorologiques, météo *f*
weatherman ['wεðəmæn] (*irreg*) *n*
météorologue *m*
weatherproof ['wεðəpruːf] *adj* (*garment*)
imperméable; (*building*) étanche
weather report *n* bulletin *m* météo, météo *f*
weather vane [-veɪn] *n* = **weather cock**
weave (*pt* **wove**, *pp* **woven**) [wiːv, wəuv, 'wəuvn]
vt (*cloth*) tisser; (*basket*) tresser ▷ *vi* (*fig: pt, pp*
weaved) (*move in and out*) se faufiler
weaver ['wiːvəʳ] *n* tisserand(e)
weaving ['wiːvɪŋ] *n* tissage *m*
web [wεb] *n* (*of spider*) toile *f*; (*on duck's foot*)
palmure *f*; (*fig*) tissu *m*; (*Comput*): **the (World-
Wide) W~** le Web
web address *n* adresse *f* Web
webbed ['wεbd] *adj* (*foot*) palmé(e)
webbing ['wεbɪŋ] *n* (*on chair*) sangles *fpl*
webcam ['wεbkæm] *n* webcam *f*
weblog ['wεblɔg] *n* blog *m*, blogue *m*
web page *n* (*Comput*) page *f* Web
website ['wεbsaɪt] *n* (*Comput*) site *m* web
wed [wεd] (*pt, pp* **-ded**) *vt* épouser ▷ *vi* se marier
▷ *n*: **the newly-~s** les jeunes mariés
we'd [wiːd] = **we had**; **we would**
wedded ['wεdɪd] *pt, pp of* **wed**
wedding ['wεdɪŋ] *n* mariage *m*
wedding anniversary *n* anniversaire *m* de
mariage; **silver/golden ~** noces *fpl* d'argent/
d'or
wedding day *n* jour *m* du mariage

wedding dress *n* robe *f* de mariée
wedding present *n* cadeau *m* de mariage
wedding ring *n* alliance *f*
wedge [wεdʒ] *n* (*of wood etc*) coin *m*; (*under door
etc*) cale *f*; (*of cake*) part *f* ▷ *vt* (*fix*) caler; (*push*)
enfoncer, coincer
wedge-heeled shoes ['wεdʒhiːld-] *npl*
chaussures *fpl* à semelles compensées
wedlock ['wεdlɔk] *n* (union *f* du) mariage *m*
Wednesday ['wεdnzdɪ] *n* mercredi *m*; *for phrases
see also* **Tuesday**
wee [wiː] *adj* (*Scottish*) petit(e); tout(e) petit(e)
weed [wiːd] *n* mauvaise herbe ▷ *vt* désherber
  ▶ **weed out** *vt* éliminer
weedkiller ['wiːdkɪləʳ] *n* désherbant *m*
weedy ['wiːdɪ] *adj* (*man*) gringalet
week [wiːk] *n* semaine *f*; **once/twice a ~** une
fois/deux fois par semaine; **in two ~s' time**
dans quinze jours; **a ~ today/on Tuesday**
aujourd'hui/mardi en huit
weekday ['wiːkdeɪ] *n* jour *m* de semaine;
(*Comm*) jour ouvrable; **on ~s** en semaine
weekend [wiːk'εnd] *n* week-end *m*
weekend case *n* sac *m* de voyage
weekly ['wiːklɪ] *adv* une fois par semaine,
chaque semaine ▷ *adj*, *n* hebdomadaire (*m*)
weep [wiːp] (*pt, pp* **wept**) [wεpt] *vi* (*person*)
pleurer; (*Med: wound etc*) suinter
weeping willow ['wiːpɪŋ-] *n* saule pleureur
weepy ['wiːpɪ] *n* (*inf: film*) mélo *m*
weft [wεft] *n* (*Textiles*) trame *f*
weigh [weɪ] *vt*, *vi* peser; **to ~ anchor** lever
l'ancre; **to ~ the pros and cons** peser le pour et
le contre
  ▶ **weigh down** *vt* (*branch*) faire plier; (*fig: with
worry*) accabler
  ▶ **weigh out** *vt* (*goods*) peser
  ▶ **weigh up** *vt* examiner
weighbridge ['weɪbrɪdʒ] *n* pont-bascule *m*
weighing machine ['weɪɪŋ-] *n* balance *f*,
bascule *f*
weight [weɪt] *n* poids *m* ▷ *vt* alourdir; (*fig: factor*)
pondérer; **sold by ~** vendu au poids; **to put on/
lose ~** grossir/maigrir; **~s and measures** poids
et mesures
weighting ['weɪtɪŋ] *n*: **~ allowance** indemnité *f*
de résidence
weightlessness ['weɪtlɪsnɪs] *n* apesanteur *f*
weightlifter ['weɪtlɪftəʳ] *n* haltérophile *m*
weightlifting ['weɪtlɪftɪŋ] *n* haltérophilie *f*
weight training *n* musculation *f*
weighty ['weɪtɪ] *adj* lourd(e)
weir [wɪəʳ] *n* barrage *m*
weird [wɪəd] *adj* bizarre; (*eerie*) surnaturel(le)
weirdo ['wɪədəu] *n* (*inf*) type *m* bizarre
welcome ['wεlkəm] *adj* bienvenu(e) ▷ *n* accueil
m ▷ *vt* accueillir; (*also*: **bid welcome**) souhaiter
la bienvenue à; (*be glad of*) se réjouir de; **to be ~**
être le (la) bienvenu(e); **to make sb ~** faire bon
accueil à qn; **you're ~ to try** vous pouvez
essayer si vous voulez; **you're ~!** (*after thanks*) de
rien, il n'y a pas de quoi

welcoming ['wɛlkəmɪŋ] *adj* accueillant(e); (*speech*) d'accueil

weld [wɛld] *n* soudure *f* ▷ *vt* souder

welder ['wɛldəʳ] *n* (*person*) soudeur *m*

welding ['wɛldɪŋ] *n* soudure *f* (autogène)

welfare ['wɛlfɛəʳ] *n* (*wellbeing*) bien-être *m*; (*social aid*) assistance sociale

welfare state *n* État-providence *m*

welfare work *n* travail social

well [wɛl] *n* puits *m* ▷ *adv* bien ▷ *adj*: **to be ~** aller bien ▷ *excl* eh bien!; (*relief also*) bon!; (*resignation*) enfin!; **~ done!** bravo!; **I don't feel ~** je ne me sens pas bien; **get ~ soon!** remets-toi vite!; **to do ~** bien réussir; (*business*) prospérer; **to think ~ of sb** penser du bien de qn; **as ~** (*in addition*) aussi, également; **you might as ~ tell me** tu ferais aussi bien de me le dire; **as ~ as** aussi bien que *or* de; en plus de; **~, as I was saying …** donc, comme je disais …
  ▶ **well up** *vi* (*tears, emotions*) monter

we'll [wiːl] = **we will; we shall**

well-behaved ['wɛlbɪ'heɪvd] *adj* sage, obéissant(e)

well-being ['wɛl'biːɪŋ] *n* bien-être *m*

well-bred ['wɛl'brɛd] *adj* bien élevé(e)

well-built ['wɛl'bɪlt] *adj* (*house*) bien construit(e); (*person*) bien bâti(e)

well-chosen ['wɛl'tʃəuzn] *adj* (*remarks, words*) bien choisi(e), pertinent(e)

well-deserved ['wɛldɪ'zəːvd] *adj* (bien) mérité(e)

well-developed ['wɛldɪ'vɛləpt] *adj* (*girl*) bien fait(e)

well-disposed ['wɛldɪs'pəuzd] *adj*: **~ to(wards)** bien disposé(e) envers

well-dressed ['wɛl'drɛst] *adj* bien habillé(e), bien vêtu(e)

well-earned ['wɛl'əːnd] *adj* (*rest*) bien mérité(e)

well-groomed [-'gruːmd] *adj* très soigné(e)

well-heeled ['wɛl'hiːld] *adj* (*inf: wealthy*) fortuné(e), riche

wellies ['wɛlɪz] (*inf*) *npl* (*Brit*) = **wellingtons**

well-informed ['wɛlɪn'fɔːmd] *adj* (*having knowledge of sth*) bien renseigné(e); (*having general knowledge*) cultivé(e)

Wellington ['wɛlɪŋtən] *n* Wellington

wellingtons ['wɛlɪŋtənz] *npl* (*also:* **wellington boots**) bottes *fpl* en caoutchouc

well-kept ['wɛl'kɛpt] *adj* (*house, grounds*) bien tenu(e), bien entretenu(e); (*secret*) bien gardé(e); (*hair, hands*) soigné(e)

well-known ['wɛl'nəun] *adj* (*person*) bien connu(e)

well-mannered ['wɛl'mænəd] *adj* bien élevé(e)

well-meaning ['wɛl'miːnɪŋ] *adj* bien intentionné(e)

well-nigh ['wɛl'naɪ] *adv*: **~ impossible** pratiquement impossible

well-off ['wɛl'ɔf] *adj* aisé(e), assez riche

well-paid [wɛl'peɪd] *adj* bien payé(e)

well-read ['wɛl'rɛd] *adj* cultivé(e)

well-spoken ['wɛl'spəukn] *adj* (*person*) qui parle bien; (*words*) bien choisi(e)

well-stocked ['wɛl'stɔkt] *adj* bien approvisionné(e)

well-timed ['wɛl'taɪmd] *adj* opportun(e)

well-to-do ['wɛltə'duː] *adj* aisé(e), assez riche

well-wisher ['wɛlwɪʃəʳ] *n* ami(e), admirateur(-trice); **scores of ~s had gathered** de nombreux amis et admirateurs s'étaient rassemblés; **letters from ~s** des lettres d'encouragement

well-woman clinic ['wɛlwumən-] *n* centre prophylactique et thérapeutique pour femmes

Welsh [wɛlʃ] *adj* gallois(e) ▷ *n* (*Ling*) gallois *m*; **the Welsh** *npl* (*people*) les Gallois

Welsh Assembly *n* Parlement gallois

Welshman ['wɛlʃmən] (*irreg*) *n* Gallois *m*

Welsh rarebit *n* croûte *f* au fromage

Welshwoman ['wɛlʃwumən] (*irreg*) *n* Galloise *f*

welter ['wɛltəʳ] *n* fatras *m*

went [wɛnt] *pt of* **go**

wept [wɛpt] *pt, pp of* **weep**

were [wəːʳ] *pt of* **be**

we're [wɪəʳ] = **we are**

weren't [wəːnt] = **were not**

werewolf (*pl* **-wolves**) ['wɪəwulf, -wulvz] *n* loup-garou *m*

west [wɛst] *n* ouest *m* ▷ *adj* (*wind*) d'ouest; (*side*) ouest *inv* ▷ *adv* à *or* vers l'ouest; **the W~** l'Occident *m*, l'Ouest

westbound ['wɛstbaund] *adj* en direction de l'ouest; (*carriageway*) ouest *inv*

West Country *n*: **the ~** le sud-ouest de l'Angleterre

westerly ['wɛstəlɪ] *adj* (*situation*) à l'ouest; (*wind*) d'ouest

western ['wɛstən] *adj* occidental(e), de *or* à l'ouest ▷ *n* (*Cine*) western *m*

westerner ['wɛstənəʳ] *n* occidental(e)

westernized ['wɛstənaɪzd] *adj* occidentalisé(e)

West German (*formerly*) *adj* ouest-allemand(e) ▷ *n* Allemand(e) de l'Ouest

West Germany *n* (*formerly*) Allemagne *f* de l'Ouest

West Indian *adj* antillais(e) ▷ *n* Antillais(e)

West Indies [-'ɪndɪz] *npl* Antilles *fpl*

Westminster ['wɛstmɪnstəʳ] *n* (*Brit Parliament*) Westminster *m*

westward ['wɛstwəd], **westwards** ['wɛstwədz] *adv* vers l'ouest

wet [wɛt] *adj* mouillé(e); (*damp*) humide; (*soaked: also:* **wet through**) trempé(e); (*rainy*) pluvieux(-euse) ▷ *vt*: **to ~ one's pants** *or* **o.s.** mouiller sa culotte, faire pipi dans sa culotte; **to get ~** se mouiller; **"~ paint"** "attention peinture fraîche"

wet blanket *n* (*fig*) rabat-joie *m inv*

wetness ['wɛtnɪs] *n* humidité *f*

wetsuit ['wɛtsuːt] *n* combinaison *f* de plongée

we've [wiːv] = **we have**

whack [wæk] *vt* donner un grand coup à

whacked [wækt] *adj* (*Brit inf: tired*) crevé(e)

whale [weɪl] *n* (*Zool*) baleine *f*

W

KEYWORD

whaler ['weɪlə^r] *n* (*ship*) baleinier *m*
whaling ['weɪlɪŋ] *n* pêche *f* à la baleine
wharf (*pl* **wharves**) [wɔːf, wɔːvz] *n* quai *m*

 KEYWORD

what [wɔt] *adj* **1** (*in questions*) quel(le); **what size is he?** quelle taille fait-il?; **what colour is it?** de quelle couleur est-ce?; **what books do you need?** quels livres vous faut-il?
2 (*in exclamations*): **what a mess!** quel désordre!; **what a fool I am!** que je suis bête!
▷ *pron* **1** (*interrogative*) que; de/à/en *etc* quoi; **what are you doing?** que faites-vous?, qu'est-ce que vous faites?; **what is happening?** qu'est-ce qui se passe?, que se passe-t-il?; **what are you talking about?** de quoi parlez-vous?; **what are you thinking about?** à quoi pensez-vous?; **what is it called?** comment est-ce que ça s'appelle?; **what about me?** et moi?; **what about doing …?** et si on faisait …?
2 (*relative: subject*) ce qui; (*: direct object*) ce que; (*: indirect object*) ce à quoi, ce dont; **I saw what you did/was on the table** j'ai vu ce que vous avez fait/ce qui était sur la table; **tell me what you remember** dites-moi ce dont vous vous souvenez; **what I want is a cup of tea** ce que je veux, c'est une tasse de thé
▷ *excl* (*disbelieving*) quoi!, comment!

whatever [wɔt'ɛvə^r] *adj*: **take ~ book you prefer** prenez le livre que vous préférez, peu importe lequel; **~ book you take** quel que soit le livre que vous preniez ▷ *pron*: **do ~ is necessary** faites (tout) ce qui est nécessaire; **~ happens** quoi qu'il arrive; **no reason ~** or **whatsoever** pas la moindre raison; **nothing ~** or **whatsoever** rien du tout
whatsoever [wɔtsəu'ɛvə^r] *adj see* **whatever**
wheat [wiːt] *n* blé *m*, froment *m*
wheatgerm ['wiːtdʒɜːm] *n* germe *m* de blé
wheatmeal ['wiːtmiːl] *n* farine bise
wheedle ['wiːdl] *vt*: **to ~ sb into doing sth** cajoler *or* enjôler qn pour qu'il fasse qch; **to ~ sth out of sb** obtenir qch de qn par des cajoleries
wheel [wiːl] *n* roue *f*; (*Aut: also:* **steering wheel**) volant *m*; (*Naut*) gouvernail *m* ▷ *vt* (*pram etc*) pousser, rouler ▷ *vi* (*birds*) tournoyer; (*also:* **wheel round**: *person*) se retourner, faire volte-face
wheelbarrow ['wiːlbærəu] *n* brouette *f*
wheelbase ['wiːlbeɪs] *n* empattement *m*
wheelchair ['wiːltʃɛə^r] *n* fauteuil roulant
wheel clamp *n* (*Aut*) sabot *m* (de Denver)
wheeler-dealer ['wiːlə'diːlə^r] *n* (*pej*) combinard(e), affairiste *m/f*
wheelie-bin ['wiːlɪbɪn] *n* (*Brit*) poubelle *f* à roulettes
wheeling ['wiːlɪŋ] *n*: **~ and dealing** (*pej*) manigances *fpl*, magouilles *fpl*
wheeze [wiːz] *n* respiration bruyante

(*d'asthmatique*) ▷ *vi* respirer bruyamment
wheezy ['wiːzɪ] *adj* sifflant(e)

 KEYWORD

when [wen] *adv* quand; **when did he go?** quand est-ce qu'il est parti?
▷ *conj* **1** (*at, during, after the time that*) quand, lorsque; **she was reading when I came in** elle lisait quand *or* lorsque je suis entré
2 (*on, at which*): **on the day when I met him** le jour où je l'ai rencontré
3 (*whereas*) alors que; **I thought I was wrong when in fact I was right** j'ai cru que j'avais tort alors qu'en fait j'avais raison

whenever [wɛn'ɛvə^r] *adv* quand donc ▷ *conj* quand; (*every time that*) chaque fois que; **I go ~ I can** j'y vais quand *or* chaque fois que je le peux
where [wɛə^r] *adv, conj* où; **this is ~** c'est là que; **~ are you from?** d'où venez vous?
whereabouts ['wɛərəbauts] *adv* où donc ▷ *n*: **nobody knows his ~** personne ne sait où il se trouve
whereas [wɛər'æz] *conj* alors que
whereby [wɛə'baɪ] *adv* (*formal*) par lequel (*or* laquelle *etc*)
whereupon [wɛərə'pɔn] *adv* sur quoi, et sur ce
wherever [wɛər'ɛvə^r] *adv* où donc ▷ *conj* où que + *sub*; **sit ~ you like** asseyez-vous (là) où vous voulez
wherewithal ['wɛəwɪðɔːl] *n*: **the ~ (to do sth)** les moyens *mpl* (de faire qch)
whet [wɛt] *vt* aiguiser
whether ['wɛðə^r] *conj* si; **I don't know ~ to accept or not** je ne sais pas si je dois accepter ou non; **it's doubtful ~** il est peu probable que + *sub*; **~ you go or not** que vous y alliez ou non
whey [weɪ] *n* petit-lait *m*

 KEYWORD

which [wɪtʃ] *adj* **1** (*interrogative: direct, indirect*) quel(le); **which picture do you want?** quel tableau voulez-vous?; **which one?** lequel (laquelle)?
2: **in which case** auquel cas; **we got there at 8pm, by which time the cinema was full** quand nous sommes arrivés à 20h, le cinéma était complet
▷ *pron* **1** (*interrogative*) lequel (laquelle), lesquels (lesquelles) *pl*; **I don't mind which** peu importe lequel; **which (of these) are yours?** lesquels sont à vous?; **tell me which you want** dites-moi lesquels *or* ceux que vous voulez
2 (*relative: subject*) qui; (*: object*) que; sur/vers *etc* lequel (laquelle) (NB: *à + lequel* = **auquel**; *de + lequel* = **duquel**); **the apple which you ate/which is on the table** la pomme que vous avez mangée/qui est sur la table; **the chair on which you are sitting** la chaise sur laquelle vous êtes assis; **the book of which you spoke** le livre

dont vous avez parlé; **he said he knew, which is true/I was afraid of** il a dit qu'il le savait, ce qui est vrai/ce que je craignais; **after which** après quoi

whichever [wɪtʃˈɛvəʳ] *adj*: **take ~ book you prefer** prenez le livre que vous préférez, peu importe lequel; **~ book you take** quel que soit le livre que vous preniez; **~ way you** de quelque façon que vous + *sub*

whiff [wɪf] *n* bouffée *f*; **to catch a ~ of sth** sentir l'odeur de qch

while [waɪl] *n* moment *m* ▷ *conj* pendant que; (*as long as*) tant que; (*as, whereas*) alors que; (*though*) bien que + *sub*, quoique + *sub*; **for a ~** pendant quelque temps; **in a ~** dans un moment; **all the ~** pendant tout ce temps-là; **we'll make it worth your ~** nous vous récompenserons de votre peine
▶ **while away** *vt* (*time*) (faire) passer

whilst [waɪlst] *conj* = **while**

whim [wɪm] *n* caprice *m*

whimper ['wɪmpəʳ] *n* geignement *m* ▷ *vi* geindre

whimsical ['wɪmzɪkl] *adj* (*person*) capricieux(-euse); (*look*) étrange

whine [waɪn] *n* gémissement *m*; (*of engine, siren*) plainte stridente ▷ *vi* gémir, geindre, pleurnicher; (*dog, engine, siren*) gémir

whip [wɪp] *n* fouet *m*; (*for riding*) cravache *f*; (*Pol: person*) chef *m* de file (*assurant la discipline dans son groupe parlementaire*) ▷ *vt* fouetter; (*snatch*) enlever (*or sortir*) brusquement
▶ **whip up** *vt* (*cream*) fouetter; (*inf: meal*) préparer en vitesse; (*stir up: support*) stimuler; (*: feeling*) attiser, aviver; *voir article*

○ **WHIP**
○
○
○ Un *whip* est un député dont le rôle est, entre
○ autres, de s'assurer que les membres de son
○ parti sont régulièrement présents à la
○ "House of Commons", surtout lorsque les
○ votes ont lieu. Les convocations que les *whips*
○ envoient se distinguent, selon leur degré
○ d'importance, par le fait qu'elles sont
○ soulignées 1, 2 ou 3 fois (les "1-, 2-, ou 3-line
○ whips").

whiplash ['wɪplæʃ] *n* (*Med: also:* **whiplash injury**) coup *m* du lapin

whipped cream [wɪpt-] *n* crème fouettée

whipping boy ['wɪpɪŋ-] *n* (*fig*) bouc *m* émissaire

whip-round ['wɪpraund] *n* (*Brit*) collecte *f*

whirl [wəːl] *n* tourbillon *m* ▷ *vi* tourbillonner; (*dancers*) tournoyer ▷ *vt* faire tourbillonner; faire tournoyer

whirlpool ['wəːlpuːl] *n* tourbillon *m*

whirlwind ['wəːlwɪnd] *n* tornade *f*

whirr [wəːʳ] *vi* bruire; ronronner; vrombir

whisk [wɪsk] *n* (*Culin*) fouet *m* ▷ *vt* (*eggs*) fouetter, battre; **to ~ sb away** *or* **off** emmener

qn rapidement

whiskers ['wɪskəz] *npl* (*of animal*) moustaches *fpl*; (*of man*) favoris *mpl*

whisky, (*Irish, US*) **whiskey** ['wɪskɪ] *n* whisky *m*

whisper ['wɪspəʳ] *n* chuchotement *m*; (*fig: of leaves*) bruissement *m*; (*rumour*) rumeur *f* ▷ *vt, vi* chuchoter

whispering ['wɪspərɪŋ] *n* chuchotement(s) *m(pl)*

whist [wɪst] *n* (*Brit*) whist *m*

whistle ['wɪsl] *n* (*sound*) sifflement *m*; (*object*) sifflet *m* ▷ *vi* siffler ▷ *vt* siffler, siffloter

whistle-stop ['wɪslstɔp] *adj*: **to make a ~ tour of** (*Pol*) faire la tournée électorale des petits patelins de

Whit [wɪt] *n* la Pentecôte

white [waɪt] *adj* blanc (blanche); (*with fear*) blême ▷ *n* blanc *m*; (*person*) blanc (blanche); **to turn** *or* **go ~** (*person*) pâlir, blêmir; (*hair*) blanchir; **the ~s** (*washing*) le linge blanc; **tennis ~s** tenue *f* de tennis

whitebait ['waɪtbeɪt] *n* blanchaille *f*

whiteboard ['waɪtbɔːd] *n* tableau *m* blanc; **interactive ~** tableau *m* (blanc) interactif

white coffee *n* (*Brit*) café *m* au lait, (café) crème *m*

white-collar worker ['waɪtkɔlə-] *n* employé(e) de bureau

white elephant *n* (*fig*) objet dispendieux et superflu

white goods *npl* (*appliances*) (gros) électroménager *m*; (*linen etc*) linge *m* de maison

white-hot [waɪt'hɔt] *adj* (*metal*) incandescent(e)

White House *n* (*US*): **the ~** la Maison-Blanche; *voir article*

○ **WHITE HOUSE**
○
○ La *White House* est un grand bâtiment blanc
○ situé à Washington D.C. où réside le
○ Président des États-Unis. Par extension, ce
○ terme désigne l'exécutif américain.

white lie *n* pieux mensonge

whiteness ['waɪtnɪs] *n* blancheur *f*

white noise *n* son *m* blanc

whiteout ['waɪtaut] *n* jour blanc

white paper *n* (*Pol*) livre blanc

whitewash ['waɪtwɔʃ] *n* (*paint*) lait *m* de chaux ▷ *vt* blanchir à la chaux; (*fig*) blanchir

whiting ['waɪtɪŋ] *n* (*pl inv: fish*) merlan *m*

Whit Monday *n* le lundi de Pentecôte

Whitsun ['wɪtsn] *n* la Pentecôte

whittle ['wɪtl] *vt*: **to ~ away, to ~ down** (*costs*) réduire, rogner

whizz [wɪz] *vi* aller (*or* passer) à toute vitesse

whizz kid *n* (*inf*) petit prodige

WHO *n abbr* (= *World Health Organization*) OMS *f* (*Organisation mondiale de la Santé*)

who [huː] *pron* qui

whodunit [huːˈdʌnɪt] *n* (*inf*) roman policier

W

whoever [huː'ɛvəʳ] *pron*: ~ **finds it** celui (celle) qui le trouve (, qui que ce soit), quiconque le trouve; **ask ~ you like** demandez à qui vous voulez; **~ he marries** qui que ce soit *or* quelle que soit la personne qu'il épouse; **~ told you that?** qui a bien pu vous dire ça?, qui donc vous a dit ça?

whole [həul] *adj* (*complete*) entier(-ière), tout(e); (*not broken*) intact(e), complet(-ète) ▷ *n* (*entire unit*) tout *m*; (*all*): **the ~ of** la totalité de, tout(e) le (la); **the ~ lot** (**of it**) tout; **the ~ lot** (**of them**) tous (sans exception); **the ~ of the time** tout le temps; **the ~ of the town** la ville tout entière; **on the ~, as a ~** dans l'ensemble

wholefood ['həulfuːd] *n*, **wholefoods** ['həulfuːdz] *npl* aliments complets

wholehearted [həul'hɑːtɪd] *adj* sans réserve(s), sincère

wholeheartedly [həul'hɑːtɪdlɪ] *adv* sans réserve; **to agree ~** être entièrement d'accord

wholemeal ['həulmiːl] *adj* (Brit: *flour, bread*) complet(-ète)

wholesale ['həulseɪl] *n* (vente *f* en) gros *m* ▷ *adj* (*price*) de gros; (*destruction*) systématique

wholesaler ['həulseɪləʳ] *n* grossiste *m/f*

wholesome ['həulsəm] *adj* sain(e); (*advice*) salutaire

wholewheat ['həulwiːt] *adj* = **wholemeal**

wholly ['həulɪ] *adv* entièrement, tout à fait

○ KEYWORD

whom [huːm] *pron* **1** (*interrogative*) qui; **whom did you see?** qui avez-vous vu?; **to whom did you give it?** à qui l'avez-vous donné?
2 (*relative*) que; à/de *etc* qui; **the man whom I saw/to whom I spoke** l'homme que j'ai vu/à qui j'ai parlé

whooping cough ['huːpɪŋ-] *n* coqueluche *f*

whoops [wuːps] *excl* (*also:* **whoops-a-daisy**) oups!, houp-là!

whoosh [wuːʃ] *vi*: **the skiers ~ed past** les skieurs passèrent dans un glissement rapide

whopper ['wɔpəʳ] *n* (inf: *lie*) gros bobard; (: *large thing*) monstre *m*, phénomène *m*

whopping ['wɔpɪŋ] *adj* (inf: *big*) énorme

whore [hɔːʳ] *n* (inf: *pej*) putain *f*

○ KEYWORD

whose [huːz] *adj* **1** (*possessive: interrogative*): **whose book is this?, whose is this book?** à qui est ce livre?; **whose pencil have you taken?** à qui est le crayon que vous avez pris?, c'est le crayon de qui que vous avez pris?; **whose daughter are you?** de qui êtes-vous la fille?
2 (*possessive: relative*): **the man whose son you rescued** l'homme dont *or* de qui vous avez sauvé le fils; **the girl whose sister you were speaking to** la fille à la sœur de qui *or* de laquelle vous parliez; **the woman whose car**

was stolen la femme dont la voiture a été volée
▷ *pron* à qui; **whose is this?** à qui est ceci?; **I know whose it is** je sais à qui c'est

Who's Who ['huːz'huː] *n* ≈ Bottin Mondain

 KEYWORD

why [waɪ] *adv* pourquoi; **why is he late?** pourquoi est-il en retard?; **why not?** pourquoi pas?
▷ *conj*: **I wonder why he said that** je me demande pourquoi il a dit ça; **that's not why I'm here** ce n'est pas pour ça que je suis là; **the reason why** la raison pour laquelle
▷ *excl* eh bien!, tiens!; **why, it's you!** tiens, c'est vous!; **why, that's impossible!** voyons, c'est impossible!

whyever [waɪ'ɛvəʳ] *adv* pourquoi donc, mais pourquoi

WI *n abbr* (Brit: = *Women's Institute*) amicale de femmes au foyer ▷ *abbr* (Geo) = **West Indies**; (US) = **Wisconsin**

wick [wɪk] *n* mèche *f* (*de bougie*)

wicked ['wɪkɪd] *adj* méchant(e); (*mischievous: grin, look*) espiègle, malicieux(-euse); (*crime*) pervers(e); (*terrible: prices, weather*) épouvantable; (inf: *very good*) génial(e) (inf)

wicker ['wɪkəʳ] *n* osier *m*; (*also:* **wickerwork**) vannerie *f*

wicket ['wɪkɪt] *n* (Cricket: *stumps*) guichet *m*; (: *grass area*) espace compris entre les deux guichets

wicket keeper *n* (Cricket) gardien *m* de guichet

wide [waɪd] *adj* large; (*area, knowledge*) vaste, très étendu(e); (*choice*) grand(e) ▷ *adv*: **to open ~** ouvrir tout grand; **to shoot ~** tirer à côté; **it is 3 metres ~** cela fait 3 mètres de large

wide-angle lens ['waɪdæŋgl-] *n* objectif *m* grand-angulaire

wide-awake [waɪdə'weɪk] *adj* bien éveillé(e)

wide-eyed [waɪd'aɪd] *adj* aux yeux écarquillés; (fig) naïf(-ïve), crédule

widely ['waɪdlɪ] *adv* (*different*) radicalement; (*spaced*) sur une grande étendue; (*believed*) généralement; (*travel*) beaucoup; **to be ~ read** (*author*) être beaucoup lu(e); (*reader*) avoir beaucoup lu, être cultivé(e)

widen ['waɪdn] *vt* élargir ▷ *vi* s'élargir

wideness ['waɪdnɪs] *n* largeur *f*

wide open *adj* grand(e) ouvert(e)

wide-ranging [waɪd'reɪndʒɪŋ] *adj* (*survey, report*) vaste; (*interests*) divers(e)

widespread ['waɪdsprɛd] *adj* (*belief etc*) très répandu(e)

widget ['wɪdʒɪt] *n* (Comput) widget *m*

widow ['wɪdəu] *n* veuve *f*

widowed ['wɪdəud] *adj* (qui est devenu(e)) veuf (veuve)

widower ['wɪdəuəʳ] *n* veuf *m*

width [wɪdθ] n largeur f; **it's 7 metres in** ~ cela fait 7 mètres de large

widthways ['wɪdθweɪz] adv en largeur

wield [wi:ld] vt (sword) manier; (power) exercer

wife (pl **wives**) [waɪf, waɪvz] n femme f, épouse f

WiFi ['waɪfaɪ] n abbr (= wireless fidelity) WiFi m ▷ adj (hot spot, network) WiFi inv

wig [wɪg] n perruque f

wigging ['wɪgɪŋ] n (Brit inf) savon m, engueulade f

wiggle ['wɪgl] vt agiter, remuer ▷ vi (loose screw etc) branler; (worm) se tortiller

wiggly ['wɪglɪ] adj (line) ondulé(e)

wild [waɪld] adj sauvage; (sea) déchaîné(e); (idea, life) fou (folle); (behaviour) déchaîné(e), extravagant(e); (inf: angry) hors de soi, furieux(-euse); (: enthusiastic): **to be** ~ **about** être fou (folle) or dingue de ▷ n: **the** ~ la nature; **wilds** npl régions fpl sauvages

wild card n (Comput) caractère m de remplacement

wildcat ['waɪldkæt] n chat m sauvage

wildcat strike n grève f sauvage

wilderness ['wɪldənɪs] n désert m, région f sauvage

wildfire ['waɪldfaɪə^r] n: **to spread like** ~ se répandre comme une traînée de poudre

wild-goose chase [waɪld'gu:s-] n (fig) fausse piste

wildlife ['waɪldlaɪf] n faune f (et flore f)

wildly ['waɪldlɪ] adv (behave) de manière déchaînée; (applaud) frénétiquement; (hit, guess) au hasard; (happy) follement

wiles [waɪlz] npl ruses fpl, artifices mpl

wilful, (US) **willful** ['wɪlful] adj (person) obstiné(e); (action) délibéré(e); (crime) prémédité(e)

⬤ KEYWORD

will [wɪl] aux vb **1** (forming future tense): **I will finish it tomorrow** je le finirai demain; **I will have finished it by tomorrow** je l'aurai fini d'ici demain; **will you do it? — yes I will/no I won't** le ferez-vous? — oui/non; **you won't lose it, will you?** vous ne le perdrez pas, n'est-ce pas?

2 (in conjectures, predictions): **he will** or **he'll be there by now** il doit être arrivé à l'heure qu'il est; **that will be the postman** ça doit être le facteur

3 (in commands, requests, offers): **will you be quiet!** voulez-vous bien vous taire!; **will you help me?** est-ce que vous pouvez m'aider?; **will you have a cup of tea?** voulez-vous une tasse de thé?; **I won't put up with it!** je ne le tolérerai pas!

▷ vt (pt, pp **willed**): **to will sb to do** souhaiter ardemment que qn fasse; **he willed himself to go on** par un suprême effort de volonté, il continua

▷ n volonté f; (document) testament m; **to do sth**

of one's own free will faire qch de son propre gré; **against one's will** à contre-cœur

willful ['wɪlful] adj (US) = **wilful**

willing ['wɪlɪŋ] adj de bonne volonté, serviable ▷ n: **to show** ~ faire preuve de bonne volonté; **he's** ~ **to do it** il est disposé à le faire, il veut bien le faire

willingly ['wɪlɪŋlɪ] adv volontiers

willingness ['wɪlɪŋnɪs] n bonne volonté

will-o'-the-wisp ['wɪlədə'wɪsp] n (also fig) feu follet m

willow ['wɪləu] n saule m

willpower ['wɪl'pauə^r] n volonté f

willy-nilly ['wɪlɪ'nɪlɪ] adv bon gré mal gré

wilt [wɪlt] vi dépérir

Wilts [wɪlts] abbr (Brit) = **Wiltshire**

wily ['waɪlɪ] adj rusé(e)

wimp [wɪmp] n (inf) mauviette f

win [wɪn] (pt, pp **won**) [wʌn] n (in sports etc) victoire f ▷ vt (battle, money) gagner; (prize, contract) remporter; (popularity) acquérir ▷ vi gagner

▶ **win over** vt convaincre

▶ **win round** vt gagner, se concilier

wince [wɪns] n tressaillement m ▷ vi tressaillir

winch [wɪntʃ] n treuil m

Winchester disk ['wɪntʃɪstə-] n (Comput) disque m Winchester

wind[1] [wɪnd] n (also Med) vent m; (breath) souffle m ▷ vt (take breath away) couper le souffle à; **the ~(s)** (Mus) les instruments mpl à vent; **into** or **against the** ~ contre le vent; **to get** ~ **of sth** (fig) avoir vent de qch; **to break** ~ avoir des gaz

wind[2] (pt, pp **wound**) [waɪnd, waund] vt enrouler; (wrap) envelopper; (clock, toy) remonter ▷ vi (road, river) serpenter

▶ **wind down** vt (car window) baisser; (fig: production, business) réduire progressivement

▶ **wind up** vt (clock) remonter; (debate) terminer, clôturer

windbreak ['wɪndbreɪk] n brise-vent m inv

windcheater ['wɪndtʃi:tə^r], (US) **windbreaker** ['wɪndbreɪkə^r] n anorak m

winder ['waɪndə^r] n (Brit: on watch) remontoir m

windfall ['wɪndfɔ:l] n coup m de chance

wind farm n ferme f éolienne

winding ['waɪndɪŋ] adj (road) sinueux(-euse); (staircase) tournant(e)

wind instrument n (Mus) instrument m à vent

windmill ['wɪndmɪl] n moulin m à vent

window ['wɪndəu] n fenêtre f; (in car, train: also: **windowpane**) vitre f; (in shop etc) vitrine f

window box n jardinière f

window cleaner n (person) laveur(-euse) de vitres

window dressing n arrangement m de la vitrine

window envelope n enveloppe f à fenêtre

window frame n châssis m de fenêtre

window ledge n rebord m de la fenêtre

window pane n vitre f, carreau m

W

window seat n (in vehicle) place f côté fenêtre
window-shopping ['wɪndəʊʃɔpɪŋ] n: **to go ~**
faire du lèche-vitrines
windowsill ['wɪndəʊsɪl] n (inside) appui m de la
fenêtre; (outside) rebord m de la fenêtre
windpipe ['wɪndpaɪp] n gosier m
wind power n énergie éolienne
windscreen ['wɪndskriːn] n pare-brise m inv
windscreen washer n lave-glace m inv
windscreen wiper, (US) **windshield wiper**
[-waɪpəʳ] n essuie-glace m inv
windshield ['wɪndʃiːld] (US) n = **windscreen**
windsurfing ['wɪndsəːfɪŋ] n planche f à voile
windswept ['wɪndswɛpt] adj balayé(e) par le
vent
wind tunnel n soufflerie f
windy ['wɪndɪ] adj (day) de vent, venteux(-euse);
(place, weather) venteux; **it's ~** il y a du vent
wine [waɪn] n vin m ▷ vt: **to ~ and dine sb** offrir
un dîner bien arrosé à qn
wine bar n bar m à vin
wine cellar n cave f à vins
wine glass n verre m à vin
wine list n carte f des vins
wine merchant n marchand(e) de vins
~~**wine tasting**~~ [-teɪstɪŋ] n dégustation f (de vins)
wine waiter n sommelier m
wing [wɪŋ] n aile f; (in air force) groupe m
d'escadrilles; **wings** npl (Theat) coulisses fpl
winger ['wɪŋəʳ] n (Sport) ailier m
wing mirror n (Brit) rétroviseur latéral
wing nut n papillon m, écrou m à ailettes
wingspan ['wɪŋspæn], **wingspread**
['wɪŋsprɛd] n envergure f
wink [wɪŋk] n clin m d'œil ▷ vi faire un clin
d'œil; (blink) cligner des yeux
winkle [wɪŋkl] n bigorneau m
winner ['wɪnəʳ] n gagnant(e)
winning ['wɪnɪŋ] adj (team) gagnant(e); (goal)
décisif(-ive); (charming) charmeur(-euse)
winning post n poteau m d'arrivée
winnings ['wɪnɪŋz] npl gains mpl
winsome ['wɪnsəm] adj avenant(e),
engageant(e)
winter ['wɪntəʳ] n hiver m ▷ vi hiverner; **in ~** en
hiver
winter sports npl sports mpl d'hiver
wintertime ['wɪntəˈtaɪm] n hiver m
wintry ['wɪntrɪ] adj hivernal(e)
wipe [waɪp] n coup m de torchon (or de chiffon or
d'éponge); **to give sth a ~** donner un coup de
torchon/de chiffon/d'éponge à qch ▷ vt
essuyer; (erase: tape) effacer; **to ~ one's nose** se
moucher
▶ **wipe off** vt essuyer
▶ **wipe out** vt (debt) éteindre, amortir; (memory)
effacer; (destroy) anéantir
▶ **wipe up** vt essuyer
wire ['waɪəʳ] n fil m (de fer); (Elec) fil électrique;
(Tel) télégramme m ▷ vt (fence) grillager; (house)
faire l'installation électrique de; (also: **wire up**)
brancher; (person: send telegram to) télégraphier à

wire brush n brosse f métallique
wire cutters [-kʌtəz] npl cisaille f
wireless ['waɪəlɪs] n (Brit) télégraphie f sans fil;
(set) T.S.F. f
wire netting n treillis m métallique, grillage m
wire service n (US) revue f de presse (par
téléscripteur)
wire-tapping ['waɪə'tæpɪŋ] n écoute f
téléphonique
wiring ['waɪərɪŋ] n (Elec) installation f
électrique
wiry ['waɪərɪ] adj noueux(-euse), nerveux(-euse)
Wis. abbr (US) = **Wisconsin**
wisdom ['wɪzdəm] n sagesse f; (of action)
prudence f
wisdom tooth n dent f de sagesse
wise [waɪz] adj sage, prudent(e); (remark)
judicieux(-euse); **I'm none the ~r** je ne suis
pas plus avancé(e) pour autant
▶ **wise up** vi (inf): **to ~ up to** commencer à se
rendre compte de
...wise [waɪz] suffix: **time~** en ce qui concerne le
temps, question temps
wisecrack ['waɪzkræk] n sarcasme m
wish [wɪʃ] n (desire) désir m; (specific desire)
souhait m, vœu m ▷ vt souhaiter, désirer,
vouloir; **best ~es** (on birthday etc) meilleurs
vœux; **with best ~es** (in letter) bien
amicalement; **give her my best ~es** faites-lui
mes amitiés; **to ~ sb goodbye** dire au revoir à
qn; **he ~ed me well** il m'a souhaité bonne
chance; **to ~ to do/sb to do** désirer or vouloir
faire/que qn fasse; **to ~ for** souhaiter; **to ~ sth
on sb** souhaiter qch à qn
wishbone ['wɪʃbəun] n fourchette f
wishful ['wɪʃful] adj: **it's ~ thinking** c'est
prendre ses désirs pour des réalités
wishy-washy ['wɪʃɪ'wɔʃɪ] adj (inf: person) qui
manque de caractère falot(e); (: ideas, thinking)
faiblard(e)
wisp [wɪsp] n fine mèche (de cheveux); (of smoke)
mince volute f; **a ~ of straw** un fétu de paille
wistful ['wɪstful] adj mélancolique
wit [wɪt] n (also: **wits**: intelligence) intelligence f,
esprit m; (presence of mind) présence f d'esprit;
(wittiness) esprit; (person) homme/femme
d'esprit; **to be at one's ~s' end** (fig) ne plus
savoir que faire; **to have one's ~s about one**
avoir toute sa présence d'esprit, ne pas perdre la
tête; **to ~** adv à savoir
witch [wɪtʃ] n sorcière f
witchcraft ['wɪtʃkrɑːft] n sorcellerie f
witch doctor n sorcier m
witch-hunt ['wɪtʃhʌnt] n chasse f aux sorcières

 KEYWORD

with [wɪð, wɪθ] prep **1** (in the company of) avec; (at
the home of) chez; **we stayed with friends** nous
avons logé chez des amis; **I'll be with you in a
minute** je suis à vous dans un instant
2 (descriptive): **a room with a view** une chambre

avec vue; **the man with the grey hat/blue eyes** l'homme au chapeau gris/aux yeux bleus **3** (*indicating manner, means, cause*): **with tears in her eyes** les larmes aux yeux; **to walk with a stick** marcher avec une canne; **red with anger** rouge de colère; **to shake with fear** trembler de peur; **to fill sth with water** remplir qch d'eau

4 (*in phrases*): **I'm with you** (*I understand*) je vous suis; **to be with it** (*inf: up-to-date*) être dans le vent

withdraw [wɪθˈdrɔː] *vt* (*irreg: like* **draw**) retirer ▷ *vi* se retirer; (*go back on promise*) se rétracter; **to ~ into o.s.** se replier sur soi-même

withdrawal [wɪθˈdrɔːəl] *n* retrait *m*; (*Med*) état *m* de manque

withdrawal symptoms *npl*: **to have ~** être en état de manque, présenter les symptômes *mpl* de sevrage

withdrawn [wɪθˈdrɔːn] *pp of* **withdraw** ▷ *adj* (*person*) renfermé(e)

withdrew [wɪθˈdruː] *pt of* **withdraw**

wither [ˈwɪðəʳ] *vi* se faner

withered [ˈwɪðəd] *adj* fané(e), flétri(e); (*limb*) atrophié(e)

withhold [wɪθˈhəuld] *vt* (*irreg: like* **hold**: *money*) retenir; (*decision*) remettre; **to ~ (from)** (*permission*) refuser (à); (*information*) cacher (à)

within [wɪðˈɪn] *prep* à l'intérieur de ▷ *adv* à l'intérieur; **~ his reach** à sa portée; **~ sight of** en vue de; **~ a mile of** à moins d'un mille de; **~ the week** avant la fin de la semaine; **~ an hour from now** d'ici une heure; **to be ~ the law** être légal(e) or dans les limites de la légalité

without [wɪðˈaut] *prep* sans; **~ a coat** sans manteau; **~ speaking** sans parler; **~ anybody knowing** sans que personne le sache; **to go** or **do ~ sth** se passer de qch

withstand [wɪθˈstænd] *vt* (*irreg: like* **stand**) résister à

witness [ˈwɪtnɪs] *n* (*person*) témoin *m*; (*evidence*) témoignage *m* ▷ *vt* (*event*) être témoin de; (*document*) attester l'authenticité de; **to bear ~ to sth** témoigner de qch; **~ for the prosecution/defence** témoin à charge/à décharge; **to ~ to sth/having seen sth** témoigner de qch/d'avoir vu qch

witness box, (*US*) **witness stand** *n* barre *f* des témoins

witticism [ˈwɪtɪsɪzəm] *n* mot *m* d'esprit

witty [ˈwɪtɪ] *adj* spirituel(le), plein(e) d'esprit

wives [waɪvz] *npl of* **wife**

wizard [ˈwɪzəd] *n* magicien *m*

wizened [ˈwɪznd] *adj* ratatiné(e)

wk *abbr* = **week**

Wm. *abbr* = **William**

WMD. *abbr* = **weapons of mass destruction**

WO *n abbr* = **warrant officer**

wobble [ˈwɔbl] *vi* trembler; (*chair*) branler

wobbly [ˈwɔblɪ] *adj* tremblant(e), branlant(e)

woe [wəu] *n* malheur *m*

woeful [ˈwəuful] *adj* (*sad*) malheureux(-euse); (*terrible*) affligeant(e)

wok [wɔk] *n* wok *m*

woke [wəuk] *pt of* **wake**

woken [ˈwəukn] *pp of* **wake**

wolf (*pl* **wolves**) [wulf, wulvz] *n* loup *m*

woman (*pl* **women**) [ˈwumən, ˈwɪmɪn] *n* femme *f* ▷ *cpd*: **~ doctor** femme *f* médecin; **~ friend** amie *f*; **~ teacher** professeur *m* femme; **young ~** jeune femme; **women's page** (*Press*) page *f* des lectrices

womanize [ˈwumənaɪz] *vi* jouer les séducteurs

womanly [ˈwumənlɪ] *adj* féminin(e)

womb [wuːm] *n* (*Anat*) utérus *m*

women [ˈwɪmɪn] *npl of* **woman**

won [wʌn] *pt, pp of* **win**

wonder [ˈwʌndəʳ] *n* merveille *f*, miracle *m*; (*feeling*) émerveillement *m* ▷ *vi*: **to ~ whether/why** se demander si/pourquoi; **to ~ at** (*surprise*) s'étonner de; (*admiration*) s'émerveiller de; **to ~ about** songer à; **it's no ~ that** il n'est pas étonnant que +*sub*

wonderful [ˈwʌndəful] *adj* merveilleux(-euse)

wonderfully [ˈwʌndəfəlɪ] *adv* (+*adj*) merveilleusement; (+*vb*) à merveille

wonky [ˈwɔŋkɪ] *adj* (*Brit inf*) qui ne va or ne marche pas très bien

wont [wəunt] *n*: **as is his/her ~** comme de coutume

won't [wəunt] = **will not**

woo [wuː] *vt* (*woman*) faire la cour à

wood [wud] *n* (*timber, forest*) bois *m* ▷ *cpd* de bois, en bois

wood carving *n* sculpture *f* en or sur bois

wooded [ˈwudɪd] *adj* boisé(e)

wooden [ˈwudn] *adj* en bois; (*fig: actor*) raide; (: *performance*) qui manque de naturel

woodland [ˈwudlənd] *n* forêt *f*, région boisée

woodpecker [ˈwudpɛkəʳ] *n* pic *m* (*oiseau*)

wood pigeon *n* ramier *m*

woodwind [ˈwudwɪnd] *n* (*Mus*) bois *m*; **the ~** les bois *mpl*

woodwork [ˈwudwəːk] *n* menuiserie *f*

woodworm [ˈwudwəːm] *n* ver *m* du bois; **the table has got ~** la table est piquée des vers

woof [wuf] *n* (*of dog*) aboiement *m* ▷ *vi* aboyer; **~, ~!** oua, oua!

wool [wul] *n* laine *f*; **to pull the ~ over sb's eyes** (*fig*) en faire accroire à qn

woollen, (*US*) **woolen** [ˈwulən] *adj* de or en laine; (*industry*) lainier(-ière) ▷ *n*: **~s** lainages *mpl*

woolly, (*US*) **wooly** [ˈwulɪ] *adj* laineux(-euse); (*fig: ideas*) confus(e)

woozy [ˈwuːzɪ] *adj* (*inf*) dans les vapes

word [wəːd] *n* mot *m*; (*spoken*) mot, parole *f*; (*promise*) parole; (*news*) nouvelles *fpl* ▷ *vt* rédiger, formuler; **~ for ~** (*repeat*) mot pour mot; (*translate*) mot à mot; **what's the ~ for "pen" in French?** comment dit-on "pen" en français?; **to put sth into ~s** exprimer qch; **in other ~s** en d'autres termes; **to have a ~ with sb**

toucher un mot à qn; **to have ~s with sb** (*quarrel with*) avoir des mots avec qn; **to break/keep one's ~** manquer à sa parole/tenir (sa) parole; **I'll take your ~ for it** je vous crois sur parole; **to send ~ of** prévenir de; **to leave ~ (with sb/for sb) that ...** laisser un mot (à qn/pour qn) disant que ...

wording ['wə:dɪŋ] *n* termes *mpl*, langage *m*; (*of document*) libellé *m*

word of mouth *n*: **by** *or* **through ~** de bouche à oreille

word-perfect ['wə:d'pə:fɪkt] *adj*: **he was ~ (in his speech** *etc*), **his speech** *etc* **was ~** il savait son discours *etc* sur le bout du doigt

word processing *n* traitement *m* de texte

word processor [-prəusɛsəʳ] *n* machine *f* de traitement de texte

wordwrap ['wə:dræp] *n* (*Comput*) retour *m* (automatique) à la ligne

wordy ['wə:dɪ] *adj* verbeux(-euse)

wore [wɔ:ʳ] *pt of* **wear**

work [wə:k] *n* travail *m*; (*Art, Literature*) œuvre *f* ▷ *vi* travailler; (*mechanism*) marcher, fonctionner; (*plan etc*) marcher; (*medicine*) agir ▷ *vt* (*clay, wood etc*) travailler; (*mine etc*) exploiter; (*machine*) faire marcher *or* fonctionner; (*miracles etc*) faire; **works** (*Brit: factory*) usine *f* ▷ *npl* (*of clock, machine*) mécanisme *m*; **how does this ~?** comment est-ce que ça marche?; **the TV isn't ~ing** la télévision est en panne *or* ne marche pas; **to go to ~** aller travailler; **to set to ~, to start ~** se mettre à l'œuvre; **to be at ~ (on sth)** travailler (sur qch); **to be out of ~** être au chômage *or* sans emploi; **to ~ hard** travailler dur; **to ~ loose** se défaire, se desserrer; **road ~s** travaux *mpl* (d'entretien des routes)

▶ **work on** *vt fus* travailler à; (*principle*) se baser sur

▶ **work out** *vi* (*plans etc*) marcher; (*Sport*) s'entraîner ▷ *vt* (*problem*) résoudre; (*plan*) élaborer; **it ~s out at £100** ça fait 100 livres

▶ **work up** *vt*: **to get ~ed up** se mettre dans tous ses états

workable ['wə:kəbl] *adj* (*solution*) réalisable

workaholic [wə:kə'hɔlɪk] *n* bourreau *m* de travail

workbench ['wə:kbɛntʃ] *n* établi *m*

worked up [wə:kt-] *adj*: **to get ~** se mettre dans tous ses états

worker ['wə:kəʳ] *n* travailleur(-euse), ouvrier(-ière); **office ~** employé(e) de bureau

work experience *n* stage *m*

workforce ['wə:kfɔ:s] *n* main-d'œuvre *f*

work-in ['wə:kɪn] *n* (*Brit*) occupation *f* d'usine *etc* (*sans arrêt de la production*)

working ['wə:kɪŋ] *adj* (*day, tools etc, conditions*) de travail; (*wife*) qui travaille; (*partner, population*) actif(-ive); **in ~ order** en état de marche; **a ~ knowledge of English** une connaissance toute pratique de l'anglais

working capital *n* (*Comm*) fonds *mpl* de roulement

working class *n* classe ouvrière ▷ *adj*: **working-class** ouvrier(-ière), de la classe ouvrière

working man (*irreg*) *n* travailleur *m*

working party *n* (*Brit*) groupe *m* de travail

working week *n* semaine *f* de travail

work-in-progress ['wə:kɪn'prəugrɛs] *n* (*Comm*) en-cours *m inv*; (: *value*) valeur *f* des en-cours

workload ['wə:kləud] *n* charge *f* de travail

workman ['wə:kmən] (*irreg*) *n* ouvrier *m*

workmanship ['wə:kmənʃɪp] *n* métier *m*, habileté *f*; facture *f*

workmate ['wə:kmeɪt] *n* collègue *m/f*

work of art *n* œuvre *f* d'art

workout ['wə:kaut] *n* (*Sport*) séance *f* d'entraînement

work permit *n* permis *m* de travail

workplace ['wə:kpleɪs] *n* lieu *m* de travail

works council *n* comité *m* d'entreprise

worksheet ['wə:kʃi:t] *n* (*Scol*) feuille *f* d'exercices; (*Comput*) feuille *f* de programmation

workshop ['wə:kʃɔp] *n* atelier *m*

work station *n* poste *m* de travail

work study *n* étude *f* du travail

work surface *n* plan *m* de travail

worktop ['wə:ktɔp] *n* plan *m* de travail

work-to-rule ['wə:ktə'ru:l] *n* (*Brit*) grève *f* du zèle

world [wə:ld] *n* monde *m* ▷ *cpd* (*champion*) du monde; (*power, war*) mondial(e); **all over the ~** dans le monde entier, partout dans le monde; **to think the ~ of sb** (*fig*) ne jurer que par qn; **what in the ~ is he doing?** qu'est-ce qu'il peut bien être en train de faire?; **to do sb a ~ of good** faire le plus grand bien à qn; **W~ War One/Two, the First/Second W~ War** la Première/Deuxième Guerre mondiale; **out of this ~** *adj* extraordinaire

World Cup *n*: **the ~** (*Football*) la Coupe du monde

world-famous [wə:ld'feɪməs] *adj* de renommée mondiale

worldly ['wə:ldlɪ] *adj* de ce monde

world music *n* world music *f*

World Series *n*: **the ~** (*US: Baseball*) le championnat national de baseball

world-wide ['wə:ld'waɪd] *adj* universel(le) ▷ *adv* dans le monde entier

World-Wide Web *n*: **the ~** le Web

worm [wə:m] *n* (*also*: **earthworm**) ver *m*

worn [wɔ:n] *pp of* **wear** ▷ *adj* usé(e)

worn-out ['wɔ:naut] *adj* (*object*) complètement usé(e); (*person*) épuisé(e)

worried ['wʌrɪd] *adj* inquiet(-ète); **to be ~ about sth** être inquiet au sujet de qch

worrier ['wʌrɪəʳ] *n* inquiet(-ète)

worrisome ['wʌrɪsəm] *adj* inquiétant(e)

worry ['wʌrɪ] *n* souci *m* ▷ *vt* inquiéter ▷ *vi* s'inquiéter, se faire du souci; **to ~ about** *or* **over sth/sb** se faire du souci pour *or* à propos de qch/qn

worrying ['wʌrɪɪŋ] *adj* inquiétant(e)

worse [wə:s] *adj* pire, plus mauvais(e) ▷ *adv*

plus mal ▷ *n* pire *m*; **to get ~** (*condition, situation*) empirer, se dégrader; **a change for the ~** une détérioration; **he is none the ~ for it** il ne s'en porte pas plus mal; **so much the ~ for you!** tant pis pour vous!

worsen ['wəːsn] *vt, vi* empirer

worse off *adj* moins à l'aise financièrement; (*fig*): **you'll be ~ this way** ça ira moins bien de cette façon; **he is now ~ than before** il se retrouve dans une situation pire qu'auparavant

worship ['wəːʃɪp] *n* culte *m* ▷ *vt* (*God*) rendre un culte à; (*person*) adorer; **Your W~** (*Brit: to mayor*) Monsieur le Maire; (: *to judge*) Monsieur le Juge

worshipper ['wəːʃɪpəʳ] *n* adorateur(-trice); (*in church*) fidèle *m/f*

worst [wəːst] *adj* le (la) pire, le (la) plus mauvais(e) ▷ *adv* le plus mal ▷ *n* pire *m*; **at ~** au pis aller; **if the ~ comes to the ~** si le pire doit arriver

worst-case ['wəːstkeɪs] *adj*: **the ~ scenario** le pire scénario *or* cas de figure

worsted ['wustɪd] *n*: (**wool**) **~** laine peignée

worth [wəːθ] *n* valeur *f* ▷ *adj*: **to be ~** valoir; **how much is it ~?** ça vaut combien?; **it's ~ it** cela en vaut la peine, ça vaut la peine; **it is ~ one's while (to do)** ça vaut le coup (*inf*) (de faire); **50 pence ~ of apples** (pour) 50 pence de pommes

worthless ['wəːθlɪs] *adj* qui ne vaut rien

worthwhile ['wəːθ'waɪl] *adj* (*activity*) qui en vaut la peine; (*cause*) louable; **a ~ book** un livre qui vaut la peine d'être lu

worthy ['wəːðɪ] *adj* (*person*) digne; (*motive*) louable; **~ of** digne de

---

⊙ **KEYWORD**

would [wud] *aux vb* **1** (*conditional tense*): **if you asked him he would do it** si vous le lui demandiez, il le ferait; **if you had asked him he would have done it** si vous le lui aviez demandé, il l'aurait fait

2 (*in offers, invitations, requests*): **would you like a biscuit?** voulez-vous un biscuit?; **would you close the door please?** voulez-vous fermer la porte, s'il vous plaît?

3 (*in indirect speech*): **I said I would do it** j'ai dit que je le ferais

4 (*emphatic*): **it WOULD have to snow today!** naturellement il neige aujourd'hui! *or* il fallait qu'il neige aujourd'hui!

5 (*insistence*): **she wouldn't do it** elle n'a pas voulu *or* elle a refusé de le faire

6 (*conjecture*): **it would have been midnight** il devait être minuit; **it would seem so** on dirait bien

7 (*indicating habit*): **he would go there on Mondays** il y allait le lundi

would-be ['wudbiː] *adj* (*pej*) soi-disant

wouldn't ['wudnt] = **would not**

wound¹ [wuːnd] *n* blessure *f* ▷ *vt* blesser; **~ed in**

the leg blessé à la jambe

wound² [waund] *pt, pp of* **wind²**

wove [wəuv] *pt of* **weave**

woven ['wəuvn] *pp of* **weave**

WP *n abbr* = **word processing**; **word processor** ▷ *abbr* (*Brit inf*) = **weather permitting**

WPC *n abbr* (*Brit*) = **woman police constable**

wpm *abbr* (= *words per minute*) mots/minute

WRAC *n abbr* (*Brit*: = *Women's Royal Army Corps*) auxiliaires féminines de l'armée de terre

WRAF *n abbr* (*Brit*: = *Women's Royal Air Force*) auxiliaires féminines de l'armée de l'air

wrangle ['ræŋgl] *n* dispute *f* ▷ *vi* se disputer

wrap [ræp] *n* (*stole*) écharpe *f*; (*cape*) pèlerine *f* ▷ *vt* (*also*: **wrap up**) envelopper; (*parcel*) emballer; (*wind*) enrouler; **under ~s** (*fig: plan, scheme*) secret(-ète)

wrapper ['ræpəʳ] *n* (*on chocolate etc*) papier *m*; (*Brit: of book*) couverture *f*

wrapping ['ræpɪŋ] *n* (*of sweet, chocolate*) papier *m*; (*of parcel*) emballage *m*

wrapping paper *n* papier *m* d'emballage; (*for gift*) papier cadeau

wrath [rɔθ] *n* courroux *m*

wreak [riːk] *vt* (*destruction*) entraîner; **to ~ havoc** faire des ravages; **to ~ vengeance on** se venger de, exercer sa vengeance sur

wreath [riːθ, *pl* riːðz] *n* couronne *f*

wreck [rɛk] *n* (*sea disaster*) naufrage *m*; (*ship*) épave *f*; (*vehicle*) véhicule accidentée; (*pej: person*) loque (humaine) ▷ *vt* démolir; (*ship*) provoquer le naufrage de; (*fig*) briser, ruiner

wreckage ['rɛkɪdʒ] *n* débris *mpl*; (*of building*) décombres *mpl*; (*of ship*) naufrage *m*

wrecker ['rɛkəʳ] *n* (*US: breakdown van*) dépanneuse *f*

WREN [rɛn] *n abbr* (*Brit*) membre du WRNS

wren [rɛn] *n* (*Zool*) troglodyte *m*

wrench [rɛntʃ] *n* (*Tech*) clé *f* (à écrous); (*tug*) violent mouvement de torsion; (*fig*) déchirement *m* ▷ *vt* tirer violemment sur, tordre; **to ~ sth from** arracher qch (violemment) à *or* de

wrest [rɛst] *vt*: **to ~ sth from sb** arracher *or* ravir qch à qn

wrestle ['rɛsl] *vi*: **to ~ (with sb)** lutter (avec qn); **to ~ with** (*fig*) se débattre avec, lutter contre

wrestler ['rɛsləʳ] *n* lutteur(-euse)

wrestling ['rɛslɪŋ] *n* lutte *f*; (*also*: **all-in wrestling**: *Brit*) catch *m*

wrestling match *n* rencontre *f* de lutte (*or* de catch)

wretch [rɛtʃ] *n* pauvre malheureux(-euse); **little ~!** (*often humorous*) petit(e) misérable!

wretched ['rɛtʃɪd] *adj* misérable; (*inf*) maudit(e)

wriggle ['rɪgl] *n* tortillement *m* ▷ *vi* (*also*: **wriggle about**) se tortiller

wring (*pt, pp* **wrung**) [rɪŋ, rʌŋ] *vt* tordre; (*wet clothes*) essorer; (*fig*): **to ~ sth out of** arracher qch à

wringer ['rɪŋəʳ] *n* essoreuse *f*

wringing ['rɪŋɪŋ] *adj* (*also*: **wringing wet**) tout

W

mouillé(e), trempé(e)

wrinkle ['rɪŋkl] n (on skin) ride f; (on paper etc) pli m ▷ vt rider, plisser ▷ vi se plisser

wrinkled ['rɪŋkld], **wrinkly** ['rɪŋklɪ] adj (fabric, paper) froissé(e), plissé(e); (surface) plissé; (skin) ridé(e), plissé

wrist [rɪst] n poignet m

wristband ['rɪstbænd] n (Brit: of shirt) poignet m; (: of watch) bracelet m

wrist watch ['rɪstwɔtʃ] n montre-bracelet f

writ [rɪt] n acte m judiciaire; **to issue a ~ against sb, to serve a ~ on sb** assigner qn en justice

writable ['raɪtəbl] adj (CD, DVD) inscriptible

write (pt wrote, pp written) [raɪt, rəut, 'rɪtn] vt, vi écrire; (prescription) rédiger; **to ~ sb a letter** écrire une lettre à qn

▸ **write away** vi: **to ~ away for** (information) (écrire pour) demander; (goods) (écrire pour) commander

▸ **write down** vt noter; (put in writing) mettre par écrit

▸ **write off** vt (debt) passer aux profits et pertes; (project) mettre une croix sur; (depreciate) amortir; (smash up: car etc) démolir complètement

▸ **write out** vt écrire; (copy) recopier

▸ **write up** vt rédiger

write-off ['raɪtɔf] n perte totale; **the car is a ~** la voiture est bonne pour la casse

write-protect ['raɪtprə'tɛkt] vt (Comput) protéger contre l'écriture

writer ['raɪtər] n auteur m, écrivain m

write-up ['raɪtʌp] n (review) critique f

writhe [raɪð] vi se tordre

writing ['raɪtɪŋ] n écriture f; (of author) œuvres fpl; **in ~** par écrit; **in my own ~** écrit(e) de ma main

writing case n nécessaire m de correspondance

writing desk n secrétaire m

writing paper n papier m à lettres

written ['rɪtn] pp of **write**

WRNS n abbr (Brit: = Women's Royal Naval Service) auxiliaires féminines de la marine

wrong [rɔŋ] adj (incorrect) faux (fausse); (incorrectly chosen: number, road etc) mauvais(e); (not suitable) qui ne convient pas; (wicked) mal; (unfair) injuste ▷ adv mal ▷ n tort m ▷ vt faire du tort à, léser; **to be ~** (answer) être faux (fausse); (in doing/saying) avoir tort (de dire/faire); **you are ~ to do it** tu as tort de le faire; **it's ~ to steal, stealing is ~** c'est mal de voler; **you are ~ about that, you've got it ~** tu te trompes; **to be in the ~** avoir tort; **what's ~?** qu'est-ce qui ne va pas?; **there's nothing ~** tout va bien; **what's ~ with the car?** qu'est-ce qu'elle a, la voiture?; **to go ~** (person) se tromper; (plan) mal tourner; (machine) se détraquer; **I took a ~ turning** je me suis trompé de route

wrongdoer ['rɔŋduːər] n malfaiteur m

wrong-foot [rɔŋ'fut] vt (Sport) prendre à contre-pied; (fig) prendre au dépourvu

wrongful ['rɔŋful] adj injustifié(e); **~ dismissal** (Industry) licenciement abusif

wrongly ['rɔŋlɪ] adv à tort; (answer, do, count) mal, incorrectement; (treat) injustement

wrong number n (Tel): **you have the ~** vous êtes trompé de numéro

wrong side n (of cloth) envers m

wrote [rəut] pt of **write**

wrought [rɔːt] adj: **~ iron** fer forgé

wrung [rʌŋ] pt, pp of **wring**

WRVS n abbr (Brit: = Women's Royal Voluntary Service) auxiliaires féminines bénévoles au service de la collectivité

wry [raɪ] adj désabusé(e)

wt. abbr (= weight) pds.

WV, W.Va. abbr (US) = **West Virginia**

WWW n abbr = **World-Wide Web**

WY, Wyo. abbr (US) = **Wyoming**

WYSIWYG ['wɪzɪwɪg] abbr (Comput: = what you see is what you get) ce que vous voyez est ce que vous aurez

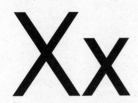

Xx

X, x [ɛks] *n* (*letter*) X, x *m*; (*Brit Cine: formerly*) film interdit aux moins de 18 ans; **X for Xmas** X comme Xavier

Xerox® ['zɪərɔks] *n* (*also:* **Xerox machine**) photocopieuse *f*; (*photocopy*) photocopie *f* ▷ *vt* photocopier

XL *abbr* (= *extra large*) XL

Xmas ['ɛksməs] *n abbr* = **Christmas**

X-rated ['ɛks'reɪtɪd] *adj* (*US: film*) interdit(e) aux moins de 18 ans

X-ray ['ɛksreɪ] *n* (*ray*) rayon *m* X; (*photograph*) radio(graphie) *f* ▷ *vt* radiographier

xylophone ['zaɪləfəun] *n* xylophone *m*

Yy

Y, y [waɪ] *n* (*letter*) Y, y *m*; **Y for Yellow**, (*US*) **Y for Yoke** Y comme Yvonne

yacht [jɔt] *n* voilier *m*; (*motor, luxury yacht*) yacht *m*

yachting ['jɔtɪŋ] *n* yachting *m*, navigation *f* de plaisance

yachtsman ['jɔtsmən] (*irreg*) *n* yacht(s)man *m*

yam [jæm] *n* igname *f*

Yank [jæŋk], **Yankee** ['jæŋkɪ] *n* (*pej*) Amerloque *m/f*, Ricain(e)

yank [jæŋk] *vt* tirer d'un coup sec

yap [jæp] *vi* (*dog*) japper

yard [jɑːd] *n* (*of house etc*) cour *f*; (*US: garden*) jardin *m*; (*measure*) yard *m* (= 914 mm; 3 feet); **builder's ~** chantier *m*

yard sale *n* (*US*) brocante *f* (dans son propre jardin)

yardstick ['jɑːdstɪk] *n* (*fig*) mesure *f*, critère *m*

yarn [jɑːn] *n* fil *m*; (*tale*) longue histoire

yawn [jɔːn] *n* bâillement *m* ▷ *vi* bâiller

yawning ['jɔːnɪŋ] *adj* (*gap*) béant(e)

yd. *abbr* = **yard**; **yards**

yeah [jɛə] *adv* (*inf*) ouais

year [jɪəʳ] *n* an *m*, année *f*; (*Scol etc*) année; **every ~** tous les ans, chaque année; **this ~** cette année; **a** *or* **per ~** par an; **~ in, ~ out** année après année; **to be 8 ~s old** avoir 8 ans; **an eight-~-old child** un enfant de huit ans

yearbook ['jɪəbuk] *n* annuaire *m*

yearly ['jɪəlɪ] *adj* annuel(le) ▷ *adv* annuellement; **twice ~** deux fois par an

yearn [jəːn] *vi*: **to ~ for sth/to do** aspirer à qch/à faire

yearning ['jəːnɪŋ] *n* désir ardent, envie *f*

yeast [jiːst] *n* levure *f*

yell [jɛl] *n* hurlement *m*, cri *m* ▷ *vi* hurler

yellow ['jɛləu] *adj*, *n* jaune (*m*)

yellow fever *n* fièvre *f* jaune

yellowish ['jɛləuɪʃ] *adj* qui tire sur le jaune, jaunâtre (*pej*)

Yellow Pages® *npl* (*Tel*) pages *fpl* jaunes

Yellow Sea *n*: **the ~** la mer Jaune

yelp [jɛlp] *n* jappement *m*; glapissement *m* ▷ *vi* japper; glapir

Yemen ['jɛmən] *N* Yémen *m*

yen [jɛn] *n* (*currency*) yen *m*; (*craving*): **~ for/to do** grande envie de/de faire

yeoman ['jəumən] (*irreg*) *n*: **Y~ of the Guard** hallebardier *m* de la garde royale

yes [jɛs] *adv* oui; (*answering negative question*) si ▷ *n* oui *m*; **to say ~ (to)** dire oui (à)

yesterday ['jɛstədɪ] *adv*, *n* hier (*m*); **~ morning/evening** hier matin/soir; **the day before ~** avant-hier; **all day ~** toute la journée d'hier

yet [jɛt] *adv* encore; (*in questions*) déjà ▷ *conj* pourtant, néanmoins; **it is not finished ~** ce n'est pas encore fini *or* toujours pas fini; **must you go just ~?** dois-tu déjà partir?; **have you eaten ~?** vous avez déjà mangé?; **the best ~** le meilleur jusqu'ici; **as ~** jusqu'ici, encore; **a few days ~** encore quelques jours; **~ again** une fois de plus

yew [juː] *n* if *m*

Y-fronts® ['waɪfrʌnts] *npl* (*Brit*) slip *m* kangourou

YHA *n abbr* (*Brit*) = **Youth Hostels Association**

Yiddish ['jɪdɪʃ] *n* yiddish *m*

yield [jiːld] *n* production *f*, rendement *m*; (*Finance*) rapport *m* ▷ *vt* produire, rendre, rapporter; (*surrender*) céder ▷ *vi* céder; (*US Aut*) céder la priorité; **a ~ of 5%** un rendement de 5%

YMCA *n abbr* (= *Young Men's Christian Association*) ≈ union chrétienne de jeunes gens (UCJG)

yob ['jɔb], **yobbo** ['jɔbəu] *n* (*Brit inf*) loubar(d) *m*

yodel ['jəudl] *vi* faire des tyroliennes, jodler

yoga ['jəugə] *n* yoga *m*

yoghurt, yogurt ['jɔgət] *n* yaourt *m*

yoke [jəuk] *n* joug *m* ▷ *vt* (*also*: **yoke together**: *oxen*) accoupler

yolk [jəuk] *n* jaune *m* (d'œuf)

yonder ['jɔndəʳ] *adv* là(-bas)

yonks [jɔŋks] *npl* (*inf*): **for ~** très longtemps; **we've been here for ~** ça fait une éternité qu'on est ici; **we were there for ~** on est resté là pendant des lustres

Yorks [jɔːks] *abbr* (*Brit*) = **Yorkshire**

 KEYWORD

you [juː] *pron* **1** (*subject*) tu; (*polite form*) vous; (*plural*) vous; **you are very kind** vous êtes très gentil; **you French enjoy your food** vous autres Français, vous aimez bien manger; **you and I will go** toi et moi *or* vous et moi, nous irons; **there you are!** vous voilà!

2 (*object: direct, indirect*) te, t' + *vowel*; vous; **I know you** je te *or* vous connais; **I gave it to you** je te l'ai donné, je vous l'ai donné

3 (*stressed*) toi; vous; **I told you to do it** c'est à toi *or* vous que j'ai dit de le faire

4 (*after prep, in comparisons*) toi; vous; **it's for you** c'est pour toi *or* vous; **she's younger than you** elle est plus jeune que toi *or* vous

5 (*impersonal: one*) on; **fresh air does you good** l'air frais fait du bien; **you never know** on ne sait jamais; **you can't do that!** ça ne se fait pas!

you'd [juːd] = **you had**; **you would**

you'll [juːl] = **you will**; **you shall**

young [jʌŋ] *adj* jeune ▷ *npl* (*of animal*) petits *mpl*; (*people*): **the ~** les jeunes, la jeunesse; **a ~ man** un jeune homme; **a ~ lady** (*unmarried*) une jeune fille, une demoiselle; (*married*) une jeune femme *or* dame; **my ~er brother** mon frère cadet; **the ~er generation** la jeune génération

younger [ˈjʌŋɡəʳ] *adj* (*brother etc*) cadet(te)

youngish [ˈjʌŋɪʃ] *adj* assez jeune

youngster [ˈjʌŋstəʳ] *n* jeune *m/f*; (*child*) enfant *m/f*

your [jɔːʳ] *adj* ton (ta), tes *pl*; (*polite form, pl*) votre, vos *pl*; *see also* **my**

you're [juəʳ] = **you are**

yours [jɔːz] *pron* le (la) tien(ne), les tiens (tiennes); (*polite form, pl*) le (la) vôtre, les vôtres;

is it ~? c'est à toi (*or* à vous)?; **a friend of ~** un(e) de tes (*or* de vos) amis; *see also* **faithfully**; **sincerely**

yourself [jɔːˈsɛlf] *pron* (*reflexive*) te; (: *polite form*) vous; (*after prep*) toi; vous; (*emphatic*) toi-même; vous-même; **you ~ told me** c'est vous qui me l'avez dit, vous me l'avez dit vous-même; *see also* **oneself**

yourselves [jɔːˈsɛlvz] *pl pron* vous; (*emphatic*) vous-mêmes; *see also* **oneself**

youth [juːθ] *n* jeunesse *f*; (*young man*) (*pl* **-s**) [juːðz] jeune homme *m*; **in my ~** dans ma jeunesse, quand j'étais jeune

youth club *n* centre *m* de jeunes

youthful [ˈjuːθful] *adj* jeune; (*enthusiasm etc*) juvénile; (*misdemeanour*) de jeunesse

youthfulness [ˈjuːθfəlnɪs] *n* jeunesse *f*

youth hostel *n* auberge *f* de jeunesse

youth movement *n* mouvement *m* de jeunes

you've [juːv] = **you have**

yowl [jaul] *n* hurlement *m*; miaulement *m* ▷ *vi* hurler; miauler

YT *abbr* (*Canada*) = **Yukon Territory.**

Yugoslav [ˈjuːɡəuslɑːv] *adj* (*Hist*) yougoslave ▷ *n* Yougoslave *m/f*

Yugoslavia [juːɡəuˈslɑːvɪə] *n* (*Hist*) Yougoslavie *f*

Yugoslavian [juːɡəuˈslɑːvɪən] *adj* (*Hist*) yougoslave

yuppie [ˈjʌpɪ] *n* yuppie *m/f*

YWCA *n abbr* (= *Young Women's Christian Association*) union chrétienne féminine

y

Zz

Z, z [zɛd, (US) zi:] n (letter) Z, z m; **Z for Zebra** Z comme Zoé
Zambia ['zæmbɪə] n Zambie f
Zambian ['zæmbɪən] adj zambien(ne) ▷ n Zambien(ne)
zany ['zeɪnɪ] adj farfelu(e), loufoque
zap [zæp] vt (Comput) effacer
zeal [zi:l] n (revolutionary etc) ferveur f; (keenness) ardeur f, zèle m
zealot ['zɛlət] n fanatique m/f
zealous ['zɛləs] adj fervent(e); ardent(e), zélé(e)
zebra ['zi:brə] n zèbre m
zebra crossing n (Brit) passage clouté or pour piétons
zenith ['zɛnɪθ] n (Astronomy) zénith m; (fig) zénith, apogée m
zero ['zɪərəu] n zéro m ▷ vi: **to ~ in on** (target) se diriger droit sur; **5° below ~** 5 degrés au-dessous de zéro
zero hour n l'heure f H
zero option n (Pol): **the ~** l'option f zéro
zero-rated ['zi:rəureɪtɪd] adj (Brit) exonéré(e) de TVA
zest [zɛst] n entrain m, élan m; (of lemon etc) zeste m
zigzag ['zɪgzæg] n zigzag m ▷ vi zigzaguer, faire des zigzags
Zimbabwe [zɪm'bɑ:bwɪ] n Zimbabwe m
Zimbabwean [zɪm'bɑ:bwɪən] adj zimbabwéen(ne) ▷ n Zimbabwéen(ne)
Zimmer® ['zɪmər] n (also: **Zimmer frame**) déambulateur m
zinc [zɪŋk] n zinc m
Zionism ['zaɪənɪzəm] n sionisme m
Zionist ['zaɪənɪst] adj sioniste ▷ n Sioniste m/f
zip [zɪp] n (also: **zip fastener**) fermeture f éclair® or à glissière; (energy) entrain m ▷ vt (file) zipper; (also: **zip up**) fermer (avec une fermeture éclair®)
zip code n (US) code postal
zip file n (Comput) fichier m zip inv
zipper ['zɪpər] n (US) = **zip**
zit [zɪt] (inf) n bouton m
zither ['zɪðər] n cithare f
zodiac ['zəudɪæk] n zodiaque m
zombie ['zɔmbɪ] n (fig): **like a ~** avec l'air d'un zombie, comme un automate
zone [zəun] n zone f
zoo [zu:] n zoo m
zoological [zuə'lɔdʒɪkl] adj zoologique
zoologist [zu'ɔlədʒɪst] n zoologiste m/f
zoology [zu:'ɔlədʒɪ] n zoologie f
zoom [zu:m] vi: **to ~ past** passer en trombe; **to ~ in (on sb/sth)** (Phot, Cine) zoomer (sur qn/qch)
zoom lens n zoom m, objectif m à focale variable
zucchini [zu:'ki:nɪ] n (US) courgette f
Zulu ['zu:lu:] adj zoulou ▷ n Zoulou m/f
Zürich ['zjuərɪk] n Zurich

Grammar
Grammaire

Using the grammar

The Grammar section deals systematically and comprehensively with all the information you will need in order to communicate accurately in French. The user-friendly layout explains the grammar point on a left-hand page, leaving the facing page free for illustrative examples. The numbers, → ❶ etc, direct you to the relevant example in every case.

The Grammar section also provides invaluable guidance on the danger of translating English structures by identical structures in French. Use of Numbers and Punctuation are important areas covered towards the end of the section. Finally, the index lists the main words and grammatical terms in both English and French.

Abbreviations

fem.	*feminine*
infin.	*infinitive*
masc.	*masculine*
perf.	*perfect*
plur.	*plural*
qch	quelque chose
qn	quelqu'un
sb	somebody
sing.	*singular*
sth	something

Contents

Examples

Simple Tenses: formation

In French the simple tenses are:

Present → ❶
Imperfect → ❷
Future → ❸
Conditional → ❹
Past Historic → ❺
Present Subjunctive → ❻
Imperfect Subjunctive → ❼

They are formed by adding endings to a verb stem. The endings show the number and person of the subject of the verb → ❽

The stem and endings of regular verbs are totally predictable. The following sections show all the patterns for regular verbs. For irregular verbs see page 74 onwards.

Regular Verbs

There are three regular verb patterns (called conjugations), each identifiable by the ending of the infinitive:

First conjugation verbs end in **-er** e.g. **donner** to give

Second conjugation verbs end in **-ir** e.g. **finir** to finish

Third conjugation verbs end in **-re** e.g. **vendre** to sell

These three conjugations are treated in order on the following pages.

Examples

1 je donne

I give
I am giving
I do give

2 je donnais

I gave
I was giving
I used to give

3 je donnerai

I shall give
I shall be giving

4 je donnerais

I should/would give
I should/would be giving

5 je donnai

I gave

6 (que) je donne

(that) I give/gave

7 (que) je donnasse

(that) I gave

8 je donne
nous donnons
je donnerais
nous donnerions

I give
we give
I would give
we would give

Verbs

Simple Tenses: First Conjugation

The stem is formed as follows:

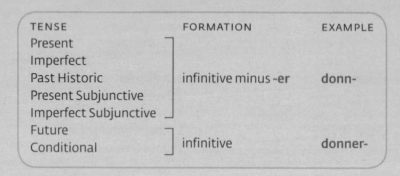

TENSE	FORMATION	EXAMPLE
Present		
Imperfect		
Past Historic	infinitive minus -er	donn-
Present Subjunctive		
Imperfect Subjunctive		
Future	infinitive	donner-
Conditional		

To the appropriate stem add the following endings:

		① PRESENT	**② IMPERFECT**	**③ PAST HISTORIC**
sing.	1st person	-e	-ais	-ai
	2nd person	-es	-ais	-as
	3rd person	-e	-ait	-a
plur.	1st person	-ons	-ions	-âmes
	2nd person	-ez	-iez	-âtes
	3rd person	-ent	-aient	-èrent

		④ PRESENT SUBJUNCTIVE	**⑤ IMPERFECT SUBJUNCTIVE**
sing.	1st person	-e	-asse
	2nd person	-es	-asses
	3rd person	-e	-ât
plur.	1st person	-ions	-assions
	2nd person	-iez	-assiez
	3rd person	-ent	-assent

		⑥ FUTURE	**⑦ CONDITIONAL**
sing.	1st person	-ai	-ais
	2nd person	-as	-ais
	3rd person	-a	-ait
plur.	1st person	-ons	-ions
	2nd person	-ez	-iez
	3rd person	-ont	-aient

Examples

1 PRESENT

je donne
tu donnes
il donne
elle donne
nous donnons
vous donnez
ils donnent
elles donnent

2 IMPERFECT

je donnais
tu donnais
il donnait
elle donnait
nous donnions
vous donniez
ils donnaient
elles donnaient

3 PAST HISTORIC

je donnai
tu donnas
il donna
elle donna
nous donnâmes
vous donnâtes
ils donnèrent
elles donnèrent

4 PRESENT SUBJUNCTIVE

je donne
tu donnes
il donne
elle donne
nous donnions
vous donniez
ils donnent
elles donnent

5 IMPERFECT SUBJUNCTIVE

je donnasse
tu donnasses
il donnât
elle donnât
nous donnassions
vous donnassiez
ils donnassent
elles donnassent

6 FUTURE

je donnerai
tu donneras
il donnera
elle donnera
nous donnerons
vous donnerez
ils donneront
elles donneront

7 CONDITIONAL

je donnerais
tu donnerais
il donnerait
elle donnerait
nous donnerions
vous donneriez
ils donneraient
elles donneraient

Simple Tenses: Second Conjugation

The stem is formed as follows:

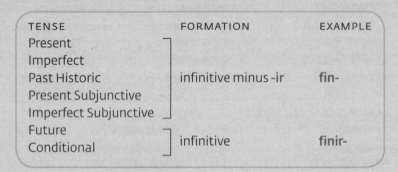

TENSE	FORMATION	EXAMPLE
Present		
Imperfect		
Past Historic	infinitive minus -ir	fin-
Present Subjunctive		
Imperfect Subjunctive		
Future	infinitive	finir-
Conditional		

To the appropriate stem add the following endings:

		① PRESENT	**② IMPERFECT**	**③ PAST HISTORIC**
	1st person	-is	-issais	-is
sing.	2nd person	-is	-issais	-is
	3rd person	-it	-issait	-it
	1st person	-issons	-issions	-îmes
plur.	2nd person	-issez	-issiez	-îtes
	3rd person	-issent	-issaient	-irent

		④ PRESENT SUBJUNCTIVE	**⑤ IMPERFECT SUBJUNCTIVE**
	1st person	-isse	-isse
sing.	2nd person	-isses	-isses
	3rd person	-isse	-ît
	1st person	-issions	-issions
plur.	2nd person	-issiez	-issiez
	3rd person	-issent	-issent

		⑥ FUTURE	**⑦ CONDITIONAL**
	1st person	-ai	-ais
sing.	2nd person	-as	-ais
	3rd person	-a	-ait
	1st person	-ons	-ions
plur.	2nd person	-ez	-iez
	3rd person	-ont	-aient

Examples

1 PRESENT

je finis
tu finis
il finit
elle finit
nous finissons
vous finissez
ils finissent
elles finissent

2 IMPERFECT

je finissais
tu finissais
il finissait
elle finissait
nous finissions
vous finissiez
ils finissaient
elles finissaient

3 PAST HISTORIC

je finis
tu finis
il finit
elle finit
nous finîmes
vous finîtes
ils finirent
elles finirent

4 PRESENT SUBJUNCTIVE

je finisse
tu finisses
il finisse
elle finisse
nous finissions
vous finissiez
ils finissent
elles finissent

5 IMPERFECT SUBJUNCTIVE

je finisse
tu finisses
il finît
elle finît
nous finissions
vous finissiez
ils finissent
elles finissent

6 FUTURE

je finirai
tu finiras
il finira
elle finira
nous finirons
vous finirez
ils finiront
elles finiront

7 CONDITIONAL

je finirais
tu finirais
il finirait
elle finirait
nous finirions
vous finiriez
ils finiraient
elles finiraient

Simple Tenses: Third Conjugation

The stem is formed as follows:

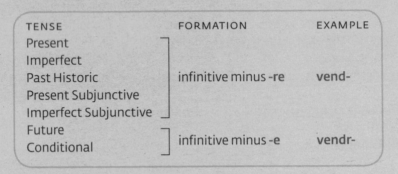

TENSE	FORMATION	EXAMPLE
Present		
Imperfect		
Past Historic	infinitive minus -re	vend-
Present Subjunctive		
Imperfect Subjunctive		
Future	infinitive minus -e	vendr-
Conditional		

To the appropriate stem add the following endings:

		① PRESENT	② IMPERFECT	③ PAST HISTORIC
sing.	1st person	-s	-ais	-is
	2nd person	-s	-ais	-is
	3rd person	–	-ait	-it
plur.	1st person	-ons	-ions	-îmes
	2nd person	-ez	-iez	-îtes
	3rd person	-ent	-aient	-irent

		④ PRESENT SUBJUNCTIVE	⑤ IMPERFECT SUBJUNCTIVE
sing.	1st person	-e	-isse
	2nd person	-es	-isses
	3rd person	-e	-ît
plur.	1st person	-ions	-issions
	2nd person	-iez	-issiez
	3rd person	-ent	-issent

		⑥ FUTURE	⑦ CONDITIONAL
sing.	1st person	-ai	-ais
	2nd person	-as	-ais
	3rd person	-a	-ait
plur.	1st person	-ons	-ions
	2nd person	-ez	-iez
	3rd person	-ont	-aient

Examples

① PRESENT

je vend**s**
tu vend**s**
il vend
elle vend
nous vend**ons**
vous vend**ez**
ils vend**ent**
elles vend**ent**

② IMPERFECT

je vend**ais**
tu vend**ais**
il vend**ait**
elle vend**ait**
nous vend**ions**
vous vend**iez**
ils vend**aient**
elles vend**aient**

③ PAST HISTORIC

je vend**is**
tu vend**is**
il vend**it**
elle vend**it**
nous vend**îmes**
vous vend**îtes**
ils vend**irent**
elles vend**irent**

④ PRESENT SUBJUNCTIVE

je vend**e**
tu vend**es**
il vend**e**
elle vend**e**
nous vend**ions**
vous vend**iez**
ils vend**ent**
elles vend**ent**

⑤ IMPERFECT SUBJUNCTIVE

je vend**isse**
tu vend**isses**
il vend**ît**
elle vend**ît**
nous vend**issions**
vous vend**issiez**
ils vend**issent**
elles vend**issent**

⑥ FUTURE

je vend**rai**
tu vend**ras**
il vend**ra**
elle vend**ra**
nous vend**rons**
vous vend**rez**
ils vend**ront**
elles vend**ront**

⑦ CONDITIONAL

je vend**rais**
tu vend**rais**
il vend**rait**
elle vend**rait**
nous vend**rions**
vous vend**riez**
ils vend**raient**
elles vend**raient**

First Conjugation Spelling Irregularities

Before certain endings, the stems of some '-er' verbs may change slightly.

Below, and on subsequent pages, the verb types are identified, and the changes described are illustrated by means of a representative verb.

Verbs ending:	**-cer**
Change:	c becomes ç before a or o
Tenses affected:	Present, Imperfect, Past Historic, Imperfect Subjunctive, Present Participle
Model:	**lancer** to throw → ❶

Why the change occurs: A cedilla is added to the c to retain its soft [s] pronunciation before the vowels a and o.

Verbs ending:	**-ger**
Change:	g becomes ge before a or o
Tenses affected:	Present, Imperfect, Past Historic, Imperfect Subjunctive, Present Participle
Model:	**manger** to eat → ❷

Why the change occurs: An e is added after the g to retain its soft [ʒ] pronunciation before the vowels a and o.

Examples

1 INFINITIVE
lancer

PRESENT PARTICIPLE
lançant

PRESENT
je lance
tu lances
il/elle lance
nous **lançons**
vous lancez
ils/elles lancent

IMPERFECT
je **lançais**
tu **lançais**
il/elle **lançait**
nous lancions
vous lanciez
ils/elles **lançaient**

PAST HISTORIC
je **lançai**
tu **lanças**
il/elle **lança**
nous **lançâmes**
vous **lançâtes**
ils/elles lancèrent

IMPERFECT SUBJUNCTIVE
je **lançasse**
tu **lançasses**
il/elle **lançât**
nous **lançassions**
vous **lançassiez**
ils/elles **lançassent**

2 INFINITIVE
manger

PRESENT PARTICIPLE
mangeant

PRESENT
je mange
tu manges
il/elle mange
nous **mangeons**
vous mangez
ils/elles mangent

IMPERFECT
je **mangeais**
tu **mangeais**
il/elle **mangeait**
nous mangions
vous mangiez
ils/elles **mangeaient**

PAST HISTORIC
je **mangeai**
tu **mangeas**
il/elle **mangea**
nous **mangeâmes**
vous **mangeâtes**
ils/elles mangèrent

IMPERFECT SUBJUNCTIVE
je **mangeasse**
tu **mangeasses**
il/elle **mangeât**
nous **mangeassions**
vous **mangeassiez**
ils/elles **mangeassent**

First Conjugation Spelling Irregularities *continued*

Verbs ending   **-eler**
Change: -l doubles before -e, -es, -ent and throughout the
    Future and Conditional tenses
Tenses affected: Present, Present Subjunctive, Future, Conditional
Model: **appeler** to call → ❶
EXCEPTIONS: **geler** to freeze; **peler** to peel → like **mener** (page 18)

Verbs ending   **-eter**
Change: -t doubles before -e, -es, -ent and throughout the
    Future and Conditional tenses
Tenses affected: Present, Present Subjunctive, Future, Conditional
Model: **jeter** to throw → ❷
EXCEPTIONS: **acheter** to buy; **haleter** to pant → like **mener** (page 18)

Verbs ending   **-yer**
Change: y changes to i before -e, -es, -ent and throughout
    the Future and Conditional tenses
Tenses affected: Present, Present Subjunctive, Future, Conditional
Model: **essuyer** to wipe → ❸

The change described is optional for verbs ending in **-ayer**
e.g. **payer** to pay; **essayer** to try.

Examples

① PRESENT (+ SUBJUNCTIVE)

j'**appelle**
tu **appelles**
il/elle **appelle**
nous appelons
(appelions)
vous appelez
(appeliez)
ils/elles **appellent**

FUTURE

j'**appellerai**
tu **appelleras**
il **appellera** *etc*

CONDITIONAL

j'**appellerais**
tu **appellerais**
il **appellerait** *etc*

② PRESENT (+ SUBJUNCTIVE)

je **jette**
tu **jettes**
il/elle **jette**
nous jetons
(jetions)
vous jetez
(jetiez)
ils/elles **jettent**

FUTURE

je **jetterai**
tu **jetteras**
il **jettera** *etc*

CONDITIONAL

je **jetterais**
tu **jetterais**
il **jetterait** *etc*

③ PRESENT (+ SUBJUNCTIVE)

j'**essuie**
tu **essuies**
il/elle **essuie**
nous essuyons
(essuyions)
vous essuyez
(essuyiez)
ils/elles **essuient**

FUTURE

j'**essuierai**
tu **essuieras**
il **essuiera** *etc*

CONDITIONAL

j'**essuierais**
tu **essuierais**
il **essuierait** *etc*

First Conjugation Spelling Irregularities *continued*

Verbs ending	**mener**, **peser**, **lever** *etc*
Change:	e changes to è, before -e, -es, -ent and throughout the Future and Conditional tenses
Tenses affected:	Present, Present Subjunctive, Future, Conditional
Model:	**mener** to lead → ❶

Verbs like:	**céder**, **régler**, **espérer** *etc*
Change:	é changes to è before -e, -es, -ent
Tenses affected:	Present, Present Subjunctive
Model:	**céder** to yield → ❷

Examples

1 PRESENT (+SUBJUNCTIVE)
je **mène**
tu **mènes**
il/elle **mène**
nous menons
    (menions)
vous menez
    (meniez)
ils/elles **mènent**

FUTURE
je **mènerai**
tu **mèneras**
il **mènera** *etc*

CONDITIONAL
je **mènerais**
tu **mènerais**
il **mènerait** *etc*

2 PRESENT (+SUBJUNCTIVE)
je **cède**
tu **cèdes**
il/elle **cède**
nous cédons
    (cédions)
vous cédez
    (cédiez)
ils/elles **cèdent**

Verbs

The Imperative

The imperative is the form of the verb used to give commands or orders. It can be used politely, as in English 'Shut the door, please'.

The imperative is the same as the present tense **tu**, **nous** and **vous** forms without the subject pronouns:

donne* give   **finis** finish   **vends** sell
   * The final 's' of the present tense of first conjugation verbs is dropped, except before **y** and **en** → **1**

donnons let's give   **finissons** let's finish   **vendons** let's sell

donnez give   **finissez** finish   **vendez** sell

The imperative of irregular verbs is given in the verb tables, page 74 onwards.

Position of object pronouns with the imperative:
- in *positive* commands: they follow the verb and are attached to it by hyphens → **2**
- in *negative* commands: they precede the verb and are not attached to it → **3**

For the order of object pronouns, see page 170.

For reflexive verbs – e.g. **se lever** to get up – the object pronoun is the reflexive pronoun → **4**

Examples

① Compare:

Tu donnes de l'argent à Paul	You give (some) money to Paul
and:	
Donne de l'argent à Paul	Give (some) money to Paul

②

Excusez-moi	Excuse me
Envoyons-les-leur	Let's send them to them
Crois-nous	Believe us
Expliquez-le-moi	Explain it to me
Attendons-la	Let's wait for her/it
Rends-la-lui	Give it back to him/her

③

Ne me dérange pas	Don't disturb me
Ne leur en parlons pas	Let's not speak to them about it
Ne les appelons pas	Let's not call them
N'y pense plus	Don't think about it any more
Ne leur répondez pas	Don't answer them
Ne la lui rends pas	Don't give it back to him/her

④

Lève-toi	Get up
Ne te lève pas	Don't get up
Dépêchons-nous	Let's hurry
Ne nous affolons pas	Let's not panic
Levez-vous	Get up
Ne vous levez pas	Don't get up

Compound Tenses: formation

In French the compound tenses are:

Perfect → ❶
Pluperfect → ❷
Future Perfect → ❸
Conditional Perfect → ❹
Past Anterior → ❺
Perfect Subjunctive → ❻
Pluperfect Subjunctive → ❼

They consist of the past participle of the verb together with an auxiliary verb. Most verbs take the auxiliary **avoir**, but some take **être** (see page 28).

Compound tenses are formed in exactly the same way for both regular and irregular verbs, the only difference being that irregular verbs may have an irregular past participle.

The Past Participle

For all compound tenses you need to know how to form the past participle of the verb. For regular verbs this is as follows:

First conjugation: replace the **-er** of the infinitive by **-é** → ❽

Second conjugation: replace the **-ir** of the infinitive by **-i** → ❾

Third conjugation: replace the **-re** of the infinitive by **-u** → ❿

See page 50 for agreement of past participles.

Examples

with **avoir**	with **être**
➊ j'ai donné I gave, have given	je suis tombé I fell, have fallen
➋ j'avais donné I had given	j'étais tombé I had fallen
➌ j'aurai donné I shall have given	je serai tombé I shall have fallen
➍ j'aurais donné I should/would have given	je serais tombé I should/would have fallen
➎ j'eus donné I had given	je fus tombé I had fallen
➏ (que) j'aie donné (that) I gave, have given	(que) je sois tombé (that) I fell, have fallen
➐ (que) j'eusse donné (that) I had given	(que) je fusse tombé (that) I had fallen

➑ **donner** to give → **donné** given

➒ **finir** to finish → **fini** finished

➓ **vendre** to sell → **vendu** sold

Compound Tenses: formation *continued*

Verbs taking the auxiliary avoir

PERFECT TENSE
The present tense of **avoir** plus the past participle → ❶

PLUPERFECT TENSE
The imperfect tense of **avoir** plus the past participle → ❷

FUTURE PERFECT
The future tense of **avoir** plus the past participle → ❸

CONDITIONAL PERFECT
The conditional of **avoir** plus the past participle → ❹

PAST ANTERIOR
The past historic of **avoir** plus the past participle → ❺

PERFECT SUBJUNCTIVE
The present subjunctive of **avoir** plus the past participle → ❻

PLUPERFECT SUBJUNCTIVE
The imperfect subjunctive of **avoir** plus the past participle → ❼

For how to form the past participle of regular verbs see page 22. The past participle of irregular verbs is given for each verb in the verb tables, page 74 onwards.

The past participle must agree in number and in gender with any preceding direct object (see page 50).

Examples

1 PERFECT

j'ai donné	nous avons donné
tu as donné	vous avez donné
il/elle a donné	ils/elles ont donné

2 PLUPERFECT

j'avais donné	nous avions donné
tu avais donné	vous aviez donné
il/elle avait donné	ils/elles avaient donné

3 FUTURE PERFECT

j'aurai donné	nous aurons donné
tu auras donné	vous aurez donné
il/elle aura donné	ils/elles auront donné

4 CONDITIONAL PERFECT

j'aurais donné	nous aurions donné
tu aurais donné	vous auriez donné
il/elle aurait donné	ils/elles auraient donné

5 PAST ANTERIOR

j'eus donné	nous eûmes donné
tu eus donné	vous eûtes donné
il/elle eut donné	ils/elles eurent donné

6 PERFECT SUBJUNCTIVE

j'aie donné	nous ayons donné
tu aies donné	vous ayez donné
il/elle ait donné	ils/elles aient donné

7 PLUPERFECT SUBJUNCTIVE

j'eusse donné	nous eussions donné
tu eusses donné	vous eussiez donné
il/elle eût donné	ils/elles eussent donné

Compound Tenses: formation *continued*

Verbs taking the auxiliary être

PERFECT TENSE
The present tense of **être** plus the past participle → ❶

PLUPERFECT TENSE
The imperfect tense of **être** plus the past participle → ❷

FUTURE PERFECT
The future tense of **être** plus the past participle → ❸

CONDITIONAL PERFECT
The conditional of **être** plus the past participle → ❹

PAST ANTERIOR
The past historic of **être** plus the past participle → ❺

PERFECT SUBJUNCTIVE
The present subjunctive of **être** plus the past participle → ❻

PLUPERFECT SUBJUNCTIVE
The imperfect subjunctive of **être** plus the past participle → ❼

For how to form the past participle of regular verbs see page 22. The past participle of irregular verbs is given for each verb in the verb tables, page 74 onwards.

For agreement of past participles, see page 50.

For a list of verbs and verb types that take the auxiliary **être**, see page 28.

Examples

1 PERFECT

je suis tombé(e)	nous sommes tombé(e)s
tu es tombé(e)	vous êtes tombé(e)(s)
il est tombé	ils sont tombés
elle est tombée	elles sont tombées

2 PLUPERFECT

j'étais tombé(e)	nous étions tombé(e)s
tu étais tombé(e)	vous étiez tombé(e)(s)
il était tombé	ils étaient tombés
elle était tombée	elles étaient tombées

3 FUTURE PERFECT

je serai tombé(e)	nous serons tombé(e)s
tu seras tombé(e)	vous serez tombé(e)(s)
il sera tombé	ils seront tombés
elle sera tombée	elles seront tombées

4 CONDITIONAL PERFECT

je serais tombé(e)	nous serions tombé(e)s
tu serais tombé(e)	vous seriez tombé(e)(s)
il serait tombé	ils seraient tombés
elle serait tombée	elles seraient tombées

5 PAST ANTERIOR

je fus tombé(e)	nous fûmes tombé(e)s
tu fus tombé(e)	vous fûtes tombé(e)(s)
il fut tombé	ils furent tombés
elle fut tombée	elles furent tombées

6 PERFECT SUBJUNCTIVE

je sois tombé(e)	nous soyons tombé(e)s
tu sois tombé(e)	vous soyez tombé(e)(s)
il soit tombé	ils soient tombés
elle soit tombée	elles soient tombées

7 PLUPERFECT SUBJUNCTIVE

je fusse tombé(e)	nous fussions tombé(e)s
tu fusses tombé(e)	vous fussiez tombé(e)(s)
il fût tombé	ils fussent tombés
elle fût tombée	elles fussent tombées

Verbs

Compound Tenses *continued*

The following verbs take the auxiliary être

Reflexive verbs (see page 30) → ❶

The following intransitive verbs (i.e. verbs which cannot take a direct object), largely expressing motion or a change of state:

aller to go → ❷	**passer** to pass
arriver to arrive; to happen	**rentrer** to go back/in
descendre to go/come down	**rester** to stay → ❺
devenir to become	**retourner** to go back
entrer to go/come in	**revenir** to come back
monter to go/come up	**sortir** to go/come out
mourir to die → ❸	**tomber** to fall
naître to be born	**venir** to come → ❻
partir to leave → ❹	

Of these, the following are conjugated with **avoir** when used transitively (i.e. with a direct object):

descendre to bring/take down
entrer to bring/take in
monter to bring/take up → ❼
passer to pass; to spend → ❽
rentrer to bring/take in
retourner to turn over
sortir to bring/take out → ❾

ⓘ Note that the past participle must show an agreement in number and gender whenever the auxiliary is **être** except for reflexive verbs where the reflexive pronoun is the indirect object (see page 50).

Examples

1.   je me suis arrêté(e)   I stopped
   elle s'est trompée   she made a mistake
   tu t'es levé(e)   you got up
   ils s'étaient battus   they had fought (one another)

2.   elle est allée   she went

3.   ils sont morts   they died

4.   vous êtes partie   you left (*addressing a female person*)

   vous êtes parties   you left (*addressing more than one female person*)

5.   nous sommes resté(e)s   we stayed

6.   elles étaient venues   they (*female*) had come

7.   Il a monté les valises   He's taken up the cases

8.   Nous avons passé trois semaines chez elle   We spent three weeks at her place

9.   Avez-vous sorti la voiture?   Have you taken the car out?

Verbs

Reflexive Verbs

A reflexive verb is one accompanied by a reflexive pronoun,
e.g. **se lever** to get up; **se laver** to wash (oneself).
The reflexive pronouns are:

	SINGULAR	PLURAL
1st person	me (m')	nous
2nd person	te (t')	vous
3rd person	se (s')	se (s')

The forms shown in brackets are used before a vowel, an **h** 'mute', or the
pronoun **y** → ❶

In positive commands, **te** changes to **toi** → ❷

The reflexive pronoun 'reflects back' to the subject, but it is not
always translated in English → ❸

The plural pronouns are sometimes translated as 'one another',
'each other' (the *reciprocal* meaning) → ❹

The reciprocal meaning may be emphasized by **l'un(e) l'autre (les
un(e)s les autres)** → ❺

Simple tenses of reflexive verbs are conjugated in exactly the same way
as those of non-reflexive verbs except that the reflexive pronoun is always
used. Compound tenses are formed with the auxiliary **être**. A sample
reflexive verb is conjugated in full on pages 34 and 35.

For agreement of past participles, see page 32.

Position of Reflexive Pronouns

In constructions other than the imperative affirmative the pronoun
comes before the verb → ❻

In the imperative affirmative, the pronoun follows the verb and is
attached to it by a hyphen → ❼

Examples

1. Je m'ennuie — I'm bored
   Elle s'habille — She's getting dressed
   Ils s'y intéressent — They are interested in it

2. Assieds-toi — Sit down
   Tais-toi — Be quiet

3. Je me prépare — I'm getting (myself) ready
   Nous nous lavons — We're washing (ourselves)
   Elle se lève — She gets up

4. Nous nous parlons — We speak to each other
   Ils se ressemblent — They resemble one another

5. Ils se regardent l'un l'autre — They are looking at each other

6. Je me couche tôt — I go to bed early
   Comment vous appelez-vous? — What is your name?
   Il ne s'est pas rasé — He hasn't shaved
   Ne te dérange pas pour nous — Don't put yourself out on our account

7. Dépêche-toi — Hurry (up)
   Renseignons-nous — Let's find out
   Asseyez-vous — Sit down

Reflexive Verbs *continued*

Past Participle Agreement

In most reflexive verbs the reflexive pronoun is a *direct* object pronoun → ①

When a direct object accompanies the reflexive verb the pronoun is then the *indirect* object → ②

The past participle of a reflexive verb agrees in number and gender with a direct object which *precedes* the verb (usually, but not always, the reflexive pronoun) → ③

The past participle does not change if the direct object follows the verb → ④

Here are some common reflexive verbs:

s'en aller to go away	se hâter to hurry
s'amuser to enjoy oneself	se laver to wash (oneself)
s'appeler to be called	se lever to get up
s'arrêter to stop	se passer to happen
s'asseoir to sit (down)	se promener to go for a walk
se baigner to go swimming	se rappeler to remember
se blesser to hurt oneself	se ressembler to resemble each other
se coucher to go to bed	se retourner to turn round
se demander to wonder	se réveiller to wake up
se dépêcher to hurry	se sauver to run away
se diriger to make one's way	se souvenir de to remember
s'endormir to fall asleep	se taire to be quiet
s'ennuyer to be/get bored	se tromper to be mistaken
se fâcher to get angry	se trouver to be (situated)
s'habiller to dress (oneself)	

Examples

❶
Je m'appelle	I'm called (*literally*: I call myself)
Asseyez-vous	Sit down (*literally*: Seat yourself)
Ils se lavent	They wash (themselves)

❷
Elle se lave les mains	She's washing her hands (*literally*: She's washing to herself the hands)
Je me brosse les dents	I brush my teeth
Nous nous envoyons des cadeaux à Noël	We send presents to each other at Christmas

❸
'Je me suis endormi' s'est-il excusé	'I fell asleep', he apologized
Pauline s'est dirigée vers la sortie	Pauline made her way towards the exit
Ils se sont levés vers dix heures	They got up around ten o'clock
Elles se sont excusées de leur erreur	They apologized for their mistake
Est-ce que tu t'es blessée, Cécile?	Have you hurt yourself, Cécile?

❹
Elle s'est lavé les cheveux	She (has) washed her hair
Nous nous sommes serré la main	We shook hands
Christine s'est cassé la jambe	Christine has broken her leg

Reflexive Verbs *continued*

Conjugation of: **se laver** to wash (oneself)

1 SIMPLE TENSES

PRESENT

je me lave	nous nous lavons
tu te laves	vous vous lavez
il/elle se lave	ils/elles se lavent

IMPERFECT

je me lavais	nous nous lavions
tu te lavais	vous vous laviez
il/elle se lavait	ils/elles se lavaient

FUTURE

je me laverai	nous nous laverons
tu te laveras	vous vous laverez
il/elle se lavera	ils/elles se laveront

CONDITIONAL

je me laverais	nous nous laverions
tu te laverais	vous vous laveriez
il/elle se laverait	ils/elles se laveraient

PAST HISTORIC

je me lavai	nous nous lavâmes
tu te lavas	vous vous lavâtes
il/elle se lava	ils/elles se lavèrent

PRESENT SUBJUNCTIVE

je me lave	nous nous lavions
tu te laves	vous vous laviez
il/elle se lave	ils/elles se lavent

IMPERFECT SUBJUNCTIVE

je me lavasse	nous nous lavassions
tu te lavasses	vous vous lavassiez
il/elle se lavât	ils/elles se lavassent

Reflexive Verbs *continued*

Conjugation of: **se laver** to wash (oneself)

2 COMPOUND TENSES

PERFECT

je me suis lavé(e)	nous nous sommes lavé(e)s
tu t'es lavé(e)	vous vous êtes lavé(e)(s)
il/elle s'est lavé(e)	ils/elles se sont lavé(e)s

PLUPERFECT

je m'étais lavé(e)	nous nous étions lavé(e)s
tu t'étais lavé(e)	vous vous étiez lavé(e)(s)
il/elle s'était lavé(e)	ils/elles s'étaient lavé(e)s

FUTURE PERFECT

je me serai lavé(e)	nous nous serons lavé(e)s
tu te seras lavé(e)	vous vous serez lavé(e)(s)
il/elle se sera lavé(e)	ils/elles se seront lavé(e)s

CONDITIONAL PERFECT

je me serais lavé(e)	nous nous serions lavé(e)s
tu te serais lavé(e)	vous vous seriez lavé(e)(s)
il/elle se serait lavé(e)	ils/elles se seraient lavé(e)s

PAST ANTERIOR

je me fus lavé(e)	nous nous fûmes lavé(e)s
tu te fus lavé(e)	vous vous fûtes lavé(e)(s)
il/elle se fut lavé(e)	ils/elles se furent lavé(e)s

PERFECT SUBJUNCTIVE

je me sois lavé(e)	nous nous soyons lavé(e)s
tu te sois lavé(e)	vous vous soyez lavé(e)(s)
il/elle se soit lavé(e)	ils/elles se soient lavé(e)s

PLUPERFECT SUBJUNCTIVE

je me fusse lavé(e)	nous nous fussions lavé(e)s
tu te fusses lavé(e)	vous vous fussiez lavé(e)(s)
il/elle se fût lavé(e)	ils/elles se fussent lavé(e)s

The Passive

In the passive, the subject *receives* the action (e.g. I was hit) as opposed to *performing* it (e.g. I hit him). In English the verb 'to be' is used with the past participle. In French the passive is formed in exactly the same way, i.e.:

a tense of **être** + *past participle*.

The past participle agrees in number and gender with the subject → ➊

A sample verb is conjugated in the passive voice on pages 38 and 39.

The indirect object in French cannot become the subject in the passive:

in quelqu'un m'a donné un livre the indirect object **m'** cannot become the subject of a passive verb (unlike English: someone gave me a book → I was given a book).

The passive meaning is often expressed in French by:

- **on** plus a verb in the active voice → ➋
- a reflexive verb (see page 30) → ➌

Examples

1   Philippe a été récompensé — Philippe has been rewarded
Son travail est très admiré — His work is greatly admired
Ils le feront pourvu qu'ils soient payés — They'll do it provided they're paid
Les enfants seront punis — The children will be punished
Cette mesure aurait été critiquée si ... — This measure would have been criticized if ...
Les portes avaient été fermées — The doors had been closed

2   On leur a envoyé une lettre — They were sent a letter
On nous a montré le jardin — We were shown the garden
On m'a dit que ... — I was told that ...

3   Ils se vendent 3 euros (la) pièce — They are sold for 3 euros each
Ce mot ne s'emploie plus — This word is no longer used

The Passive *continued*

Conjugation of: **être aimé** to be liked

PRESENT
je suis aimé(e)
tu es aimé(e)
il/elle est aimé(e)

nous sommes aimé(e)s
vous êtes aimé(e)(s)
ils/elles sont aimé(e)s

IMPERFECT
j'étais aimé(e)
tu étais aimé(e)
il/elle était aimé(e)

nous étions aimé(e)s
vous étiez aimé(e)(s)
ils/elles étaient aimé(e)s

FUTURE
je serai aimé(e)
tu seras aimé(e)
il/elle sera aimé(e)

nous serons aimé(e)s
vous serez aimé(e)(s)
ils/elles seront aimé(e)s

CONDITIONAL
je serais aimé(e)
tu serais aimé(e)
il/elle serait aimé(e)

nous serions aimé(e)s
vous seriez aimé(e)(s)
ils/elles seraient aimé(e)s

PAST HISTORIC
je fus aimé(e)
tu fus aimé(e)
il/elle fut aimé(e)

nous fûmes aimé(e)s
vous fûtes aimé(e)(s)
ils/elles furent aimé(e)s

PRESENT SUBJUNCTIVE
je sois aimé(e)
tu sois aimé(e)
il/elle soit aimé(e)

nous soyons aimé(e)s
vous soyez aimé(e)(s)
ils/elles soient aimé(e)s

IMPERFECT SUBJUNCTIVE
je fusse aimé(e)
tu fusses aimé(e)
il/elle fût aimé(e)

nous fussions aimé(e)s
vous fussiez aimé(e)(s)
ils/elles fussent aimé(e)s

The Passive *continued*

Conjugation of: **être aimé** to be liked

PERFECT

j'ai été aimé(e)	nous avons été aimé(e)s
tu as été aimé(e)	vous avez été aimé(e)(s)
il/elle a été aimé(e)	ils/elles ont été aimé(e)s

PLUPERFECT

j'avais été aimé(e)	nous avions été aimé(e)s
tu avais été aimé(e)	vous aviez été aimé(e)(s)
il/elle avait été aimé(e)	ils/elles avaient été aimé(e)s

FUTURE PERFECT

j'aurai été aimé(e)	nous aurons été aimé(e)s
tu auras été aimé(e)	vous aurez été aimé(e)(s)
il/elle aura été aimé(e)	ils/elles auront été aimé(e)s

CONDITIONAL PERFECT

j'aurais été aimé(e)	nous aurions été aimé(e)s
tu aurais été aimé(e)	vous auriez été aimé(e)(s)
il/elle aurait été aimé(e)	ils/elles auraient été aimé(e)s

PAST ANTERIOR

j'eus été aimé(e)	nous eûmes été aimé(e)s
tu eus été aimé(e)	vous eûtes été aimé(e)(s)
il/elle eut été aimé(e)	ils/elles eurent été aimé(e)s

PERFECT SUBJUNCTIVE

j'aie été aimé(e)	nous ayons été aimé(e)s
tu aies été aimé(e)	vous ayez été aimé(e)(s)
il/elle ait été aimé(e)	ils/elles aient été aimé(e)s

PLUPERFECT SUBJUNCTIVE

j'eusse été aimé(e)	nous eussions été aimé(e)s
tu eusses été aimé(e)	vous eussiez été aimé(e)(s)
il/elle eût été aimé(e)	ils/elles eussent été aimé(e)s

Impersonal Verbs

Impersonal verbs are used only in the infinitive and in the third person singular with the subject pronoun **il**, generally translated as 'it'.

e.g. il pleut it's raining
      il est facile de dire que ... it's easy to say that ...

The most common impersonal verbs are:

INFINITIVE	CONSTRUCTIONS
s'agir	il s'agit de + *noun* → ❶
	it's a question/matter of something, it's about something
	il s'agit de + *infinitive* → ❷
	it's a question/matter of doing; somebody must do
falloir	il faut + *noun object* (+ *indirect object*) → ❸
	(somebody) needs something, something is necessary (to somebody)
	il faut + *infinitive* (+ *indirect object*) → ❹
	it is necessary to do
	il faut que + *subjunctive* → ❺
	it is necessary to do, somebody must do
grêler	il grêle it's hailing
neiger	il neige it's snowing
pleuvoir	il pleut it's raining → ❻
tonner	il tonne it's thundering
valoir mieux	il vaut mieux + *infinitive* → ❼
	it's better to do
	il vaut mieux que + *subjunctive* → ❽
	it's better to do/that somebody does

Examples

① Il ne s'agit pas d'argent — It isn't a question/matter of money

De quoi s'agit-il? — What is it about?

Il s'agit de la vie d'une famille au début du siècle — It's about the life of a family at the turn of the century

② Il s'agit de faire vite — We must act quickly

③ Il faut du courage pour faire ça — One needs courage to do that

Il me faut une chaise de plus — I need an extra chair

④ Il faut partir — It is necessary to leave

We/I/You must leave*

Il me fallait prendre une décision — I had to make a decision

⑤ Il faut que vous partiez — You must leave

Il faudrait que je fasse mes valises — I ought to pack my cases

⑥ Il pleuvait à verse — It was pouring with rain

⑦ Il vaut mieux refuser — It's better to refuse

You/He/I had better refuse*

Il vaudrait mieux rester — You/We/She had better stay*

⑧ Il vaudrait mieux que nous ne venions pas — It would be better if we didn't come

We'd better not come

* The translation here obviously depends on context

Impersonal Verbs

The following verbs are also commonly used in impersonal constructions:

INFINITIVE	CONSTRUCTIONS
avoir	**il y a** + *noun* → **1**
	there is/are
être	**il est** + *noun* → **2**
	it is, there are (*very literary style*)
	il est + *adjective* + **de** + *infinitive* → **3**
	it is
faire	**il fait** + *adjective of weather* → **4**
	it is
	il fait + *noun depicting weather/dark/light etc* → **5**
	it is
manquer	**il manque** + *noun* (+ *indirect object*) → **6**
	there is/are … missing, something is missing
paraître	**il paraît que** + *subjunctive* → **7**
	it seems/appears that
	il paraît + *indirect object* + **que** + *indicative* → **8**
	it seems/appears to somebody that
rester	**il reste** + *noun* (+ *indirect object*) → **9**
	there is/are … left, (somebody) has something left
sembler	**il semble que** + *subjunctive* → **10**
	it seems/appears that
	il semble + *indirect object* + **que** + *indicative* → **11**
	it seems/appears to somebody that
suffire	**il suffit de** + *infinitive* → **12**
	it is enough to do
	il suffit de + *noun* → **13**
	something is enough, it only takes something

Examples

1. Il y a du pain (qui reste)
   There is some bread (left)
   Il n'y avait pas de lettres ce matin
   There were no letters this morning

2. Il est dix heures
   It's ten o'clock
   Il est des gens qui …
   There are (some) people who …

3. Il était inutile de protester
   It was useless to protest
   Il est facile de critiquer
   Criticizing is easy

4. Il fait beau/mauvais
   It's lovely/horrible weather

5. Il faisait du soleil/du vent
   It was sunny/windy
   Il fait jour/nuit
   It's light/dark

6. Il manque deux tasses
   There are two cups missing
   Two cups are missing
   Il manquait un bouton à sa chemise
   His shirt had a button missing

7. Il paraît qu'ils partent demain
   It appears they are leaving tomorrow

8. Il nous paraît certain qu'il aura du succès
   It seems certain to us that he'll be successful

9. Il reste deux miches de pain
   There are two loaves left
   Il lui restait cinquante euros
   He/She had fifty euros left

10. Il semble que vous ayez raison
    It seems that you are right

11. Il me semblait qu'il conduisait trop vite
    It seemed to me (that) he was driving too fast

12. Il suffit de téléphoner pour réserver une place
    It is enough to reserve a seat by phone

13. Il suffit d'une seule erreur pour tout gâcher
    One single error is enough to ruin everything

43

The Infinitive

The infinitive is the form of the verb found in dictionary entries meaning 'to ...', e.g. **donner** to give; **vivre** to live.

There are three main types of verbal construction involving the infinitive:
- with no linking preposition → **①**
- with the linking preposition **à** (see also page 64) → **②**
- with the linking preposition **de** (see also page 64) → **③**

Verbs followed by an infinitive with no linking preposition

devoir, **pouvoir**, **savoir**, **vouloir** and **falloir** (i.e. modal auxiliary verbs: page 52 → **①**).

valoir mieux: see Impersonal Verbs, page 40.

verbs of seeing or hearing e.g. **voir** to see; **entendre** to hear → **④**

intransitive verbs of motion e.g. **aller** to go; **descendre** to come/go down → **⑤**

envoyer to send → **⑥**

faillir → **⑦**

faire → **⑧**

laisser to let, allow → **⑨**

The following common verbs:

adorer to love
aimer to like, love → **⑩**
aimer mieux to prefer → **⑪**
compter to expect
désirer to wish, want → **⑫**
détester to hate → **⑬**

espérer to hope → **⑭**
oser to dare → **⑮**
préférer to prefer
sembler to seem → **⑯**
souhaiter to wish

Examples

①	Voulez-vous attendre?	Would you like to wait?
②	J'apprends à nager	I'm learning to swim
③	Essayez de venir	Try to come
④	Il nous a vus arriver	He saw us arriving
	On les entend chanter	You can hear them singing
⑤	Allez voir Nicolas	Go and see Nicholas
	Descends leur demander	Go down and ask them
⑥	Je l'ai envoyé les voir	I sent him to see them
⑦	J'ai failli tomber	I almost fell
⑧	Ne me faites pas rire!	Don't make me laugh!
	J'ai fait réparer ma voiture	I've had my car repaired
⑨	Laissez-moi passer	Let me pass
⑩	Il aime nous accompagner	He likes to come with us
⑪	J'aimerais mieux le choisir moi-même	I'd rather choose it myself
⑫	Elle ne désire pas venir	She doesn't wish to come
⑬	Je déteste me lever le matin	I hate getting up in the morning
⑭	Espérez-vous aller en vacances?	Are you hoping to go on holiday?
⑮	Nous n'avons pas osé y retourner	We haven't dared go back
⑯	Vous semblez être inquiet	You seem to be worried

The Infinitive: Set Expressions

The following are set in French with the meaning shown:

aller chercher to go for, to go and get → ❶
envoyer chercher to send for → ❷
entendre dire que to hear it said that → ❸
entendre parler de to hear of/about → ❹
faire entrer to show in → ❺
faire sortir to let out → ❻
faire venir to send for → ❼
laisser tomber to drop → ❽
vouloir dire to mean → ❾

The Perfect Infinitive

The perfect infinitive is formed using the auxiliary verb **avoir** or **être** as appropriate with the past participle of the verb → ❿

The perfect infinitive is found:
- following the preposition **après** after → ⑪
- following certain verbal constructions → ⑫

Examples

1. Va chercher tes photos — Go and get your photos
   Il est allé chercher Alexandre — He's gone to get Alexander

2. J'ai envoyé chercher un médecin — I've sent for a doctor

3. J'ai entendu dire qu'il est malade — I've heard it said that he's ill

4. Je n'ai plus entendu parler de lui — I didn't hear anything more (said) of him

5. Fais entrer nos invités — Show our guests in

6. J'ai fait sortir le chat — I've let the cat out

7. Je vous ai fait venir parce que … — I sent for you because …

8. Il a laissé tomber le vase — He dropped the vase

9. Qu'est-ce que cela veut dire? — What does that mean?

10. avoir fini — to have finished
    être allé — to have gone
    s'être levé — to have got up

11. Après avoir pris cette décision, il nous a appelé — After making/having made that decision, he called us
    Après être sorties, elles se sont dirigées vers le parking — After leaving/having left, they headed for the car park
    Après nous être levé(e)s, nous avons lu les journaux — After getting up/having got up, we read the papers

12. pardonner à qn d'avoir fait — to forgive sb for doing/having done
    remercier qn d'avoir fait — to thank sb for doing/having done
    regretter d'avoir fait — to be sorry for doing/having done

The Present Participle

Formation

First conjugation:
Replace the **-er** of the infinitive by **-ant** → ❶
- Verbs ending in **-cer**: **c** changes to **ç** → ❷
- Verbs ending in **-ger**: **g** changes to **ge** → ❸

Second conjugation:
Replace the **-ir** of the infinitive by **-issant** → ❹

Third conjugation:
Replace the **-re** of the infinitive by **-ant** → ❺

For irregular present participles, see irregular verbs, page 74 onwards.

Uses

The present participle has a more restricted use in French than in English.

Used as a verbal form, the present participle is invariable. It is found:
- on its own, where it corresponds to the English present participle → ❻
- following the preposition **en** → ❼
- ⓘ Note, in particular, the construction:
  verb + en + present participle
  which is often translated by an English phrasal verb, i.e. one followed by a preposition like 'to run down', 'to bring up' → ❽

Used as an adjective, the present participle agrees in number and gender with the noun or pronoun → ❾
- ⓘ Note, in particular, the use of **ayant** and **étant** – the present participles of the auxiliary verbs **avoir** and **être** – with a past participle → ❿

Examples

1 donner to give → donnant giving

2 lancer to throw → lançant throwing

3 manger to eat → mangeant eating

4 finir to finish → finissant finishing

5 vendre to sell → vendant selling

6

David, habitant près de Paris, a la possibilité de ...	David, living near Paris, has the opportunity of ...
Elle, pensant que je serais fâché, a dit ...	She, thinking that I would be angry, said ...
Ils m'ont suivi, criant à tue-tête	They followed me, shouting at the top of their voices

7

En attendant sa sœur, Richard s'est endormi	While waiting for his sister, Richard fell asleep
Téléphone-nous en arrivant chez toi	Phone us when you get home
En appuyant sur ce bouton, on peut ...	By pressing this button, you can ...
Il s'est blessé en essayant de sauver un chat	He hurt himself trying to rescue a cat

8

sortir en courant	to run out (*literally*: to go out running)
avancer en boîtant	to limp along (*literally*: to go forward limping)

9

le soleil couchant	the setting sun
une lumière éblouissante	a dazzling light
ils sont dégoûtants	they are disgusting
elles étaient étonnantes	they were surprising

10

Ayant mangé plus tôt, il a pu ...	Having eaten earlier, he was able to ...
Étant arrivée en retard, elle a dû ...	Having arrived late, she had to ...

Verbs

Past Participle Agreement

Like adjectives, a past participle must sometimes agree in number and gender with a noun or pronoun. For the rules of agreement, see below.
Example: **donné**

	MASCULINE	FEMININE
SING.	donné	donnée
PLUR.	donnés	données

When the masculine singular form already ends in **-s**, no further **s** is added in the masculine plural, e.g. **pris** taken.

Rules of Agreement in Compound Tenses

When the auxiliary verb is **avoir**:

> The past participle remains in the masculine singular form, unless a direct object precedes the verb. The past participle then agrees in number and gender with the preceding direct object → ❶

When the auxiliary verb is **être**:

> The past participle of a non-reflexive verb agrees in number and gender with the subject → ❷
> The past participle of a reflexive verb agrees in number and gender with the reflexive pronoun, if the pronoun is a direct object → ❸
> No agreement is made if the reflexive pronoun is an indirect object → ❹

The Past Participle as an adjective

The past participle agrees in number and gender with the noun or pronoun → ❺

Examples

1 Voici le livre que vous avez demandé

Here's the book you asked for

Laquelle avaient-elles choisie?

Which one had they chosen?

Ces amis? Je les ai rencontrés à Édimbourg

Those friends? I met them in Edinburgh

Il a gardé toutes les lettres qu'elle a écrites

He has kept all the letters she wrote

2 Est-ce que ton frère est allé à l'étranger?

Did your brother go abroad?

Elle était restée chez elle

She had stayed at home

Ils sont partis dans la matinée

They left in the morning

Mes cousines sont revenues hier

My cousins came back yesterday

3 Tu t'es rappelé d'acheter du pain, Georges?

Did you remember to buy bread, Georges?

Martine s'est demandée pourquoi il l'appelait

Martine wondered why he was calling her

'Lui at moi nous nous sommes cachés' a-t-elle dit

'He and I hid,' she said

Les vendeuses se sont mises en grève

The shop assistants have gone on strike

Vous vous êtes brouillés?

Have you fallen out with each other?

Les enfants s'étaient entraidés

The children had helped one another

4 Elle s'est lavé les mains

She washed her hands

Ils se sont parlé pendant des heures

They talked to each other for hours

5 à un moment donné

at a given time

la porte ouverte

the open door

ils sont bien connus

they are well-known

elles semblent fatiguées

they seem tired

Modal Auxiliary Verbs

In French, the modal auxiliary verbs are: **devoir**, **pouvoir**, **savoir**, **vouloir** and **falloir**.

They are followed by a verb in the infinitive and have the following meanings:

devoir to have to, must → ❶
to be due to → ❷
in the conditional/conditional perfect:
should/should have, ought/ought to have → ❸

pouvoir to be able to, can → ❹
to be allowed to, can, may → ❺
indicating possibility: may/might/could → ❻

savoir to know how to, can → ❼

vouloir to want/wish to → ❽
to be willing to, will → ❾
in polite phrases → ❿

falloir to be necessary: see Impersonal Verbs, page 40.

Examples

1. Je dois leur rendre visite — I must visit them
   Elle a dû partir — She (has) had to leave
   Il a dû regretter d'avoir parlé — He must have been sorry he spoke

2. Vous devez revenir demain — You're due (to come) back tomorrow
   Je devais attraper le train de neuf heures mais ... — I was (supposed) to catch the nine o'clock train but ...

3. Je devrais le faire — I ought to do it
   J'aurais dû m'excuser — I ought to have apologized

4. Il ne peut pas lever le bras — He can't raise his arm
   Pouvez-vous réparer cette montre? — Can you mend this watch?

5. Puis-je les accompagner? — May I go with them?

6. Il peut encore changer d'avis — He may change his mind yet
   Cela pourrait être vrai — It could/might be true

7. Savez-vous conduire? — Can you drive?
   Je ne sais pas faire une omelette — I don't know how to make an omelette

8. Elle veut rester encore un jour — She wants to stay another day

9. Ils ne voulaient pas le faire — They wouldn't do it / They weren't willing to do it
   Ma voiture ne veut pas démarrer — My car won't start

10. Voulez-vous boire quelque chose? — Would you like something to drink?

Use of Tenses

The Present

Unlike English, French does not distinguish between the simple present (e.g. I smoke, he reads, we live) and the continuous present (e.g. I am smoking, he is reading, we are living) → ❶

To emphasize continuity, the following constructions may be used:
être en train de faire, être à faire to be doing → ❷

French uses the present tense where English uses the perfect in the following cases:
- with certain prepositions of time – notably **depuis** for/since – when an action begun in the past is continued in the present → ❸ Note, however, that the perfect is used as in English when the verb is negative or the action has been completed → ❹
- in the construction **venir de faire** to have just done → ❺

The Future

The future is generally used as in English, but note the following:

Immediate future time is often expressed by means of the present tense of **aller** plus an infinitive → ❻

In time clauses expressing future action, French uses the future where English uses the present → ❼

The Future Perfect

Used as in English to mean 'shall/will have done' → ❽

In time clauses expressing future action, where English uses the perfect tense → ❾

Examples

1. Je fume — I smoke *or* I am smoking
    Il lit — He reads *or* He is reading
    Nous habitons — We live *or* We are living

2. Il est en train de travailler — He's (busy) working

3. Paul apprend à nager depuis six mois — Paul's been learning to swim for six months (and still is)
    Je suis debout depuis sept heures — I've been up since seven
    Il y a longtemps que vous attendez? — Have you been waiting long?
    Voilà deux semaines que nous sommes ici — That's two weeks we've been here (now)

4. Ils ne se sont pas vus depuis des mois — They haven't seen each other for months
    Elle est revenue il y a un an — She came back a year ago

5. Elisabeth vient de partir — Elizabeth has just left

6. Tu vas tomber si tu ne fais pas attention — You'll fall if you're not careful
    Il va manquer le train — He's going to miss the train
    Ça va prendre une demi-heure — It'll take half an hour

7. Quand il viendra vous serez en vacances — When he comes you'll be on holiday
    Faites-nous savoir aussitôt qu'elle arrivera — Let us know as soon as she arrives

8. J'aurai fini dans une heure — I shall have finished in an hour

9. Quand tu auras lu ce roman, rends-le-moi — When you've read the novel, give it back to me
    Je partirai dès que j'aurai fini — I'll leave as soon as I've finished

Verbs

Use of Tenses *continued*

The Imperfect

The imperfect describes:
- an action (or state) in the past without definite limits in time → ①
- habitual action(s) in the past (often translated by means of 'would' or 'used to') → ②

French uses the imperfect tense where English uses the pluperfect in the following cases:
- with certain prepositions of time – notably **depuis** for/since – when an action begun in the remoter past was continued in the more recent past → ③

  Note, however, that the pluperfect is used as in English, when the verb is negative or the action has been completed → ④
    - in the construction **venir de faire** to have just done → ⑤

The Perfect

The perfect is used to recount a completed action or event in the past. Note that this corresponds to a perfect tense or a simple past tense in English → ⑥

The Past Historic

Only ever used in *written*, *literary* French, the past historic recounts a completed action in the past, corresponding to a simple past tense in English → ⑦

The Past Anterior

This tense is used instead of the pluperfect when a verb in another part of the sentence is in the past historic. That is:
- in time clauses, after conjunctions like: **quand, lorsque** when; **dès que, aussitôt que** as soon as; **après que** after → ⑧
- after **à peine** hardly, scarcely → ⑨

The Subjunctive

In spoken French, the present subjunctive generally replaces the imperfect subjunctive. See also page 58 onwards.

Examples

1. Elle regardait par la fenêtre — She was looking out of the window

   Il pleuvait quand je suis sorti de chez moi — It was raining when I left the house

   Nos chambres donnaient sur la plage — Our rooms overlooked the beach

2. Quand il était étudiant, il se levait à l'aube — When he was a student he got up at dawn

   Nous causions des heures entières — We would talk for hours on end

   Elle te taquinait, n'est-ce pas? — She used to tease you, didn't she?

3. Nous habitions à Londres depuis deux ans — We had been living in London for two years (and still were)

   Il était malade depuis 2004 — He had been ill since 2004

   Il y avait assez longtemps qu'il le faisait — He had been doing it for quite a long time

4. Voilà un an que je ne l'avais pas vu — I hadn't seen him for a year

   Il y avait une heure qu'elle était arrivée — She had arrived one hour before

5. Je venais de les rencontrer — I had just met them

6. Nous sommes allés au bord de la mer — We went/have been to the seaside

   Il a refusé de nous aider — He (has) refused to help us

   La voiture ne s'est pas arrêtée — The car didn't stop/hasn't stopped

7. Le roi mourut en 1592 — The king died in 1592

8. Quand il eut fini, il se leva — When he had finished, he got up

9. À peine eut-il fini de parler qu'on frappa à la porte — He had scarcely finished speaking when there was a knock at the door

The Subjunctive: when to use it

For how to form the subjunctive see page 6 onwards.

The subjunctive is used :

After certain conjunctions:

quoique ⎤	
bien que ⎦	although → ①
pour que ⎤	
afin que ⎦	so that → ②
pourvu que	provided that → ③
jusqu'à ce que	until → ④
avant que (... ne)	before → ⑤
à moins que (... ne)	unless → ⑥
de peur que (... ne) ⎤	
de crainte que (... ne) ⎦	for fear that, lest → ⑦

ⓘ Note that the ne following the conjunctions in examples ⑤ to ⑦ has no translation value. It is often omitted in spoken informal French.

After the conjunctions:

de sorte que ⎤	
de façon que	so that (*indicating a purpose*) → ⑧
de manière que ⎦	

When these conjunctions introduce a result and not a purpose, the subjunctive is not used → ⑨

After impersonal constructions which express necessity, possibility etc:

il faut que ⎤	
il est nécessaire que ⎦	it is necessary that → ⑩
il est possible que	it is possible that → ⑪
il semble que	it seems that, it appears that → ⑫
il vaut mieux que	it is better that → ⑬
il est dommage que	it's a pity that, it's a shame that → ⑭

Examples

1. Bien qu'il fasse beaucoup d'efforts, il est peu récompensé — Although he makes a lot of effort, he isn't rewarded for it

2. Demandez un reçu afin que vous puissiez être remboursé — Ask for a receipt so that you can get a refund

3. Nous partirons ensemble pourvu que Sylvie soit d'accord — We'll leave together provided Sylvie agrees

4. Reste ici jusqu'à ce que nous revenions — Stay here until we come back

5. Je le ferai avant que tu ne partes — I'll do it before you leave

6. Ce doit être Paul, à moins que je ne me trompe — That must be Paul, unless I'm mistaken

7. Parlez bas de peur qu'on ne vous entende — Speak softly for fear that someone hears you

8. Retournez-vous de sorte que je vous voie — Turn round so that I can see you

9. Il refuse de le faire de sorte que je dois le faire moi-même — He refuses to do it so that I have to do it myself

10. Il faut que je vous parle immédiatement — I must speak to you right away / It is necessary that I speak to you right away

11. Il est possible qu'ils aient raison — They may be right / It's possible that they are right

12. Il semble qu'elle ne soit pas venue — It appears that she hasn't come

13. Il vaut mieux que vous restiez chez vous — It's better that you stay at home

14. Il est dommage qu'elle ait perdu cette adresse — It's a shame/a pity that she's lost the address

The Subjunctive: when to use it *continued*

After verbs of:
- wishing
  vouloir que
  désirer que ⎤ to wish that, want → ①
  souhaiter que ⎦

- fearing
  craindre que ⎤ to be afraid that → ②
  avoir peur que ⎦

ⓘ Note that **ne** in the first phrase of example ② has no translation value. It is often omitted in spoken informal French.

- ordering, forbidding, allowing
  ordonner que   to order that → ③
  défendre que   to forbid that → ④
  permettre que   to allow that → ⑤

- opinion, expressing uncertainty
  croire que ⎤
  penser que ⎦ to think that → ⑥
  douter que   to doubt that → ⑦

- emotion (e.g. regret, shame, pleasure)
  regretter que   to be sorry that → ⑧
  être content/surpris *etc* **que** to be pleased/surprised *etc* that → ⑨

After a superlative → ⑩

After certain adjectives expressing some sort of 'uniqueness' → ⑪
  dernier ... qui/que   last ... who/that
  premier ... qui/que   first ... who/that
  meilleur ... qui/que   best ... who/that
  seul ... qui/que ⎤
  unique ... qui/que ⎦ only ... who/that

Examples

① Nous voulons qu'elle soit contente

We want her to be happy (*literally*: We want that she is happy)

Désirez-vous que je le fasse?

Do you want me to do it?

② Il craint qu'il ne soit trop tard

He's afraid it may be too late

Avez-vous peur qu'il ne revienne pas?

Are you afraid that he won't come back?

③ Il a ordonné qu'ils soient désormais à l'heure

He has ordered that they be on time from now on

④ Elle défend que vous disiez cela

She forbids you to say that

⑤ Permettez que nous vous aidions

Allow us to help you

⑥ Je ne pense pas qu'ils soient venus

I don't think they came

⑦ Nous doutons qu'il ait dit la vérité

We doubt that he told the truth

⑧ Je regrette que vous ne puissiez pas venir

I'm sorry that you cannot come

⑨ Je suis content que vous les aimiez

I'm pleased that you like them

⑩ la personne la plus sympathique que je connaisse

the nicest person I know

l'article le moins cher que j'aie jamais acheté

the cheapest item I have ever bought

⑪ Voici la dernière lettre qu'elle m'ait écrite

This is the last letter she wrote to me

David est la seule personne qui puisse me conseiller

David is the only person who can advise me

The Subjunctive: when to use it *continued*

After:
  si (…) que however → ❶
  qui que whoever → ❷
  quoi que whatever → ❸

After **que** in the following:
  • to form the 3rd person imperative or to express a wish → ❹
  • when **que** has the meaning 'if', replacing **si** in a clause → ❺
  • when **que** has the meaning 'whether' → ❻

In relative clauses following certain types of indefinite and negative construction → ❼/❽

In set expressions → ❾

Examples

1 si courageux qu'il soit   however brave he may be
    si peu que ce soit   however little it is

2 Qui que vous soyez,   Whoever you are, go away!
    allez-vous-en!

3 Quoi que nous fassions, ...   Whatever we do, ...

4 Qu'il entre!   Let him come in!
    Que cela vous serve de leçon!   Let that be a lesson to you!

5 S'il fait beau et que tu te sentes   If it's nice and you're feeling
    mieux, nous irons ...   better, we'll go ...

6 Que tu viennes ou non, je ...   Whether you come or not, I ...

7 Il cherche une maison qui ait   He's looking for a house which
    une piscine   has a swimming pool
                        (subjunctive used since such a
                        house may or may not exist)

    J'ai besoin d'un livre qui décrive   I need a book which describes
    l'art du mime   the art of mime
                        (subjunctive used since such a
                        book may or may not exist)

8 Je n'ai rencontré personne qui   I haven't met anyone who
    la connaisse   knows her
    Il n'y a rien qui puisse vous   There's nothing that can
    empêcher de ...   prevent you from ...

9 Vive le roi!   Long live the king!
    Que Dieu vous bénisse!   God bless you!

Verbs governing à and de

The following lists (pages 64 to 72) contain common verbal constructions using the prepositions à and de

Note the following abbreviations:

infin.	*infinitive*
perf. infin.	*perfect infinitive**
qch	quelque chose
qn	quelqu'un
sb	somebody
sth	something

accuser qn de qch/de + *perf. infin.*	to accuse sb of sth/of doing, having done → ①
accoutumer qn à qch/à + *infin.*	to accustom sb to sth/to doing
acheter qch à qn	to buy sth from sb/for sb → ②
achever de + *infin.*	to end up doing
aider qn à + *infin.*	to help sb to do → ③
s'amuser à + *infin.*	to have fun doing
s'apercevoir de qch	to notice sth → ④
apprendre qch à qn	to teach sb sth
apprendre à + *infin.*	to learn to do → ⑤
apprendre à qn à + *infin.*	to teach sb to do → ⑥
s'approcher de qn/qch	to approach sb/sth → ⑦
arracher qch à qn	to snatch sth from sb → ⑧
(s')arrêter de + *infin.*	to stop doing → ⑨
arriver à + *infin.*	to manage to do → ⑩
assister à qch	to attend sth, be at sth
s'attendre à + *infin.*	to expect to do → ⑪
blâmer qn de qch/de + *perf. infin.*	to blame sb for sth/for having done → ⑫
cacher qch à qn	to hide sth from sb → ⑬
cesser de + *infin.*	to stop doing → ⑭

* For formation see page 46

Examples

① Il m'a accusé d'avoir menti — He accused me of lying

② Marie-Christine leur a acheté deux billets — Marie-Christine bought two tickets from/for them

③ Aidez-moi à porter ces valises — Help me to carry these cases

④ Il ne s'est pas aperçu de son erreur — He didn't notice his mistake

⑤ Elle apprend à lire — She's learning to read

⑥ Je lui apprends à nager — I'm teaching him/her to swim

⑦ Elle s'est approchée de moi, en disant ... — She approached me, saying ...

⑧ Le voleur lui a arraché l'argent — The thief snatched the money from him/her

⑨ Arrêtez de faire du bruit! — Stop making so much noise!

⑩ Le professeur n'arrive pas à se faire obéir de sa classe — The teacher couldn't manage to control the class

⑪ Est-ce qu'elle s'attendait à le voir? — Was she expecting to see him?

⑫ Je ne la blâme pas de l'avoir fait — I don't blame her for doing it

⑬ Cache-les-leur! — Hide them from them!

⑭ Est-ce qu'il a cessé de pleuvoir? — Has it stopped raining?

Verbs governing à and de *continued*

changer de qch	to change sth → ①
se charger de qch/de + *infin.*	to see to sth/undertake to do
chercher à + *infin.*	to try to do
commander à qn de + *infin.*	to order sb to do → ②
commencer à/de + *infin.*	to begin to do, to start to do → ③
conseiller à qn de + *infin.*	to advise sb to do → ④
consentir à qch/à + *infin.*	to agree to sth/to do → ⑤
continuer à/de + *infin.*	to continue to do
craindre de + *infin.*	to be afraid to do/of doing
décider de + *infin.*	to decide to → ⑥
se décider à + *infin.*	to make up one's mind to do
défendre à qn de + *infin.*	to forbid sb to do → ⑦
demander qch à qn	to ask sb sth/for sth → ⑧
demander à qn de + *infin.*	to ask sb to do → ⑨
se dépêcher de + *infin.*	to hurry to do
dépendre de qn/qch	to depend on sb/sth
déplaire à qn	to displease sb → ⑩
désobéir à qn	to disobey sb → ⑪
dire à qn de + *infin.*	to tell sb to do → ⑫
dissuader qn de + *infin.*	to dissuade sb from doing
douter de qch	to doubt sth
se douter de qch	to suspect sth
s'efforcer de + *infin.*	to strive to do
empêcher qn de + *infin.*	to prevent sb from doing → ⑬
emprunter qch à qn	to borrow sth from sb → ⑭
encourager qn à + *infin.*	to encourage sb to do → ⑮
enlever qch à qn	to take sth away from sb
enseigner qch à qn	to teach sb sth
enseigner à qn à + *infin.*	to teach sb to do
entreprendre de + *infin.*	to undertake to do
essayer de + *infin.*	to try to do → ⑯
eviter de + *infin.*	to avoid doing → ⑰

Examples

①	J'ai changé d'avis/de robe	I changed my mind/my dress
	Il faut changer de train à Toulouse	You have to change trains at Toulouse
②	Il leur a commandé de tirer	He ordered them to shoot
③	Il commence à neiger	It's starting to snow
④	Il leur a conseillé d'attendre	He advised them to wait
⑤	Je n'ai pas consenti à l'aider	I haven't agreed to help him/her
⑥	Qu'est-ce que vous avez décidé de faire?	What have you decided to do?
⑦	Je leur ai défendu de sortir	I've forbidden them to go out
⑧	Je lui ai demandé l'heure	I asked him/her the time
	Il lui a demandé un livre	He asked him/her for a book
⑨	Demande à Alain de le faire	Ask Alan to do it
⑩	Leur attitude lui déplaît	He/She doesn't like their attitude
⑪	Ils lui désobéissent souvent	They often disobey him/her
⑫	Dites-leur de se taire	Tell them to be quiet
⑬	Le bruit m'empêche de travailler	The noise is preventing me from working
⑭	Puis-je vous emprunter ce stylo?	May I borrow this pen from you?
⑮	Elle encourage ses enfants à être indépendants	She encourages her children to be independent
⑯	Essayez d'arriver à l'heure	Try to arrive on time
⑰	Il évite de lui parler	He avoids speaking to him/her

Verbs governing à and de *continued*

s'excuser de qch/de + *(perf.) infin.*	to apologize for sth/for doing, having done → ❶
exceller à + *infin.*	to excel at doing
se fâcher de qch	to be annoyed at sth
feindre de + *infin.*	to pretend to do → ❷
féliciter qn de qch/de + *(perf.) infin.*	to congratulate sb on sth/on doing, having done → ❸
se fier à qn	to trust sb → ❹
finir de + *infin.*	to finish doing → ❺
forcer qn à + *infin.*	to force sb to do
habituer qn à + *infin.*	to accustom sb to doing
s'habituer à + *infin.*	to get/be used to doing → ❻
se hâter de + *infin.*	to hurry to do
hésiter à + *infin.*	to hesitate to do
interdire à qn de + *infin.*	to forbid sb to do → ❼
s'intéresser à qn/qch/à + *infin.*	to be interested in sb/sth/in doing → ❽
inviter qn à + *infin.*	to invite sb to do → ❾
jouer à (+ *sports, games*)	to play → ❿
jouer de (+ *musical instruments*)	to play → ⓫
jouir de qch	to enjoy sth → ⓬
jurer de + *infin.*	to swear to do
louer qn de qch	to praise sb for sth
manquer à qn	to be missed by sb → ⓭
manquer de qch	to lack sth
manquer de + *infin.*	to fail to do → ⓮
se marier à qn	to marry sb
se méfier de qn	to distrust sb
menacer de + *infin.*	to threaten to do → ⓯
mériter de + *infin.*	to deserve to do → ⓰
se mettre à + *infin.*	to begin to do
se moquer de qn/qch	to make fun of sb/sth
négliger de + *infin.*	to fail to do

Examples

1. Je m'excuse d'être (arrivé) en retard — I apologize for being/arriving late

2. Elle feint de dormir — She's pretending to be asleep

3. Je l'ai félicitée d'avoir gagné — I congratulated her on winning

4. Je ne me fie pas à ces gens-là — I don't trust those people

5. Avez-vous fini de lire ce journal? — Have you finished reading this newspaper?

6. Il s'est habitué à boire moins de café — He got used to drinking less coffee

7. Il a interdit aux enfants de jouer avec des allumettes — He's forbidden the children to play with matches

8. Elle s'intéresse beaucoup au sport — She's very interested in sport

9. Il m'a invitée à dîner — He invited me for dinner

10. Elle joue au tennis et au hockey — She plays tennis and hockey

11. Il joue du piano et de la guitare — He plays the piano and the guitar

12. Il jouit d'une santé solide — He enjoys good health

13. Tu manques à tes parents — Your parents miss you

14. Je ne manquerai pas de le lui dire — I'll be sure to tell him/her about it

15. Elle a menacé de démissionner tout de suite — She threatened to resign straight away

16. Ils méritent d'être promus — They deserve to be promoted

Verbs governing à and de *continued*

nuire à qch	to harm sth, to do damage to sth → ❶
obéir à qn	to obey sb
obliger qn à + *infin.*	to oblige/force sb to do → ❷
s'occuper de qch/qn	to look after sth/sb → ❸
offrir de + *infin.*	to offer to do → ❹
omettre de + *infin.*	to fail to do
ordonner à qn de + *infin.*	to order sb to do → ❺
ôter qch à qn	to take sth away from sb
oublier de + *infin.*	to forget to do
pardonner qch à qn	to forgive sb for sth
pardonner à qn de + *perf. infin.*	to forgive sb for having done → ❻
parvenir à + *infin.*	to manage to do
se passer de qch	to do/go without sth → ❼
penser à qn/qch	to think about sb/sth → ❽
permettre qch à qn	to allow sb sth
permettre à qn de + *infin.*	to allow sb to do → ❾
persister à + *infin.*	to persist in doing
persuader qn de + *infin.*	to persuade sb to do → ❿
se plaindre de qch	to complain about sth
plaire à qn	to please sb → ⓫
pousser qn à + *infin.*	to urge sb to do
prendre qch à qn	to take sth from sb → ⓬
préparer qn à + *infin.*	to prepare sb to do
se préparer à + *infin.*	to get ready to do
prier qn de + *infin.*	to beg sb to do
profiter de qch/de + *infin.*	to take advantage of sth/of doing
promettre à qn de + *infin.*	to promise sb to do → ⓭
proposer de + *infin.*	to suggest doing → ⓮
punir qn de qch	to punish sb for sth → ⓯
récompenser qn de qch	to reward sb for sth
réfléchir à qch	to think about sth
refuser de + *infin.*	to refuse to do → ⓰

Examples

1. Ce mode de vie va nuire à sa santé — This lifestyle will damage her health

2. Il les a obligés à faire la vaisselle — He forced them to do the washing-up

3. Je m'occupe de ma nièce — I'm looking after my niece

4. Stuart a offert de nous accompagner — Stuart has offered to go with us

5. Les soldats leur ont ordonné de se rendre — The soldiers ordered them to give themselves up

6. Est-ce que tu as pardonné à Charles de t'avoir menti? — Have you forgiven Charles for lying to you?

7. Je me suis passé d'électricité pendant plusieurs jours — I did without electricity for several days

8. Je pense souvent à toi — I often think about you

9. Permettez-moi de continuer, s'il vous plaît — Allow me to go on, please

10. Elle nous a persuadés de rester — She persuaded us to stay

11. Ce genre de film lui plaît — He/she likes this kind of film

12. Je lui ai pris son mobile — I took his mobile phone from him

13. Ils ont promis à Pascale de venir — They promised Pascale that they would come

14. J'ai proposé de les inviter — I suggested inviting them

15. Il a été puni de sa malhonnêteté — He has been punished for his dishonesty

16. Il a refusé de coopérer — He has refused to cooperate

Verbs governing à and de *continued*

regretter de + *perf. infin.*	to regret doing, having done → ❶
remercier qn de qch/de + *perf. infin.*	to thank sb for sth/for doing, having done → ❷
renoncer à qch/à + *infin.*	to give sth up/give up doing
reprocher qch à qn	to reproach sb with/for sth → ❸
résister à qch	to resist sth → ❹
résoudre de + *infin.*	to resolve to do
ressembler à qn/qch	to look/be like sb/sth → ❺
réussir à + *infin.*	to manage to do → ❻
rire de qn/qch	to laugh at sb/sth
risquer de + *infin.*	to risk doing → ❼
servir à qch/à + *infin.*	to be used for sth/for doing → ❽
se servir de qch	to use sth; to help oneself to sth → ❾
songer à + *infin.*	to think of doing
se souvenir de qn/qch/de + *perf. infin.*	to remember sb/sth/doing, having done → ❿
succéder à qn	to succeed sb
survivre à qn	to outlive sb → ⓫
tâcher de + *infin.*	to try to do → ⓬
tarder à + *infin.*	to delay doing → ⓭
tendre à + *infin.*	to tend to do
tenir à + *infin.*	to be keen to do → ⓮
tenter de + *infin.*	to try to do → ⓯
se tromper de qch	to be wrong about sth → ⓰
venir de* + *infin.*	to have just done → ⓱
vivre de qch	to live on sth
voler qch à qn	to steal sth from sb

* See also Use of Tenses, pages 54 and 56

Examples

1. Je regrette de ne pas l'avoir vue plus souvent quand elle était ici — I regret not having seen her more while she was here

2. Nous les avons remerciés de leur gentillesse — We thanked them for their kindness

3. On lui reproche son manque d'enthousiasme — They're reproaching him for his lack of enthusiasm

4. Comment résistez-vous à la tentation? — How do you resist temptation?

5. Elles ressemblent beaucoup à leur mère — They look very like their mother

6. Vous avez réussi à me convaincre — You've managed to convince me

7. Vous risquez de tomber en faisant cela — You risk falling doing that

8. Ce bouton sert à régler le volume — This knob is (used) for adjusting the volume

9. Il s'est servi d'un tournevis pour l'ouvrir — He used a screwdriver to open it

10. Vous vous souvenez de Lucienne? Il ne se souvient pas de l'avoir perdu — Do you remember Lucienne? He doesn't remember losing it

11. Elle a survécu à son mari — She outlived her husband

12. Tâchez de ne pas être en retard! — Try not to be late!

13. Il n'a pas tardé à prendre une décision — He was not long in taking a decision

14. Elle tient à le faire elle-même — She's keen to do it herself

15. J'ai tenté de la comprendre — I've tried to understand her

16. Je me suis trompé de route — I took the wrong road

17. Mon père vient de téléphoner. Nous venions d'arriver — My father's just phoned. We had just arrived

Irregular Verbs

The verbs listed opposite and conjugated on pages 76 to 131 provide the main patterns for irregular verbs. The verbs are grouped opposite according to their infinitive ending (except **avoir** and **être**), and are shown in the following tables in alphabetical order.

In the tables, the most important irregular verbs are given in their most common simple tenses, together with the imperative and the present participle.

The auxiliary (**avoir** or **être**) is also shown for each verb, together with the past participle, to enable you to form all the compound tenses, as on pages 24 and 26.

For a fuller list of irregular verbs, the reader is referred to Collins Easy Learning French Verbs, which shows you how to conjugate some 2000 French verbs.

Irregular Verbs

avoir
être

'-er':	aller	'-re':	battre
	envoyer		boire
			connaître
'-ir':	acquérir		coudre
	bouillir		craindre
	courir		croire
	cueillir		croître
	dormir		cuire
	fuir		dire
	haïr		écrire
	mourir		faire
	ouvrir		lire
	partir		mettre
	sentir		moudre
	servir		naître
	sortir		paraître
	tenir		plaire
	venir		prendre
	vêtir		résoudre
			rire
'-oir':	s'asseoir		rompre
	devoir		suffire
	falloir		suivre
	pleuvoir		se taire
	pouvoir		vaincre
	recevoir		vivre
	savoir		
	valoir		
	voir		
	vouloir		

acquérir (to acquire)

	PRESENT		IMPERFECT
	j'acquiers		j'acquérais
tu	acquiers	tu	acquérais
il	acquiert	il	acquérait
nous	acquérons	nous	acquérions
vous	acquérez	vous	acquériez
ils	acquièrent	ils	acquéraient

	FUTURE		CONDITIONAL
	j'acquerrai		j'acquerrais
tu	acquerras	tu	acquerrais
il	acquerra	il	acquerrait
nous	acquerrons	nous	acquerrions
vous	acquerrez	vous	acquerriez
ils	acquerront	ils	acquerraient

	PRESENT SUBJUNCTIVE		PAST HISTORIC
	j'acquière		j'acquis
tu	acquières	tu	acquis
il	acquière	il	acquit
nous	acquérions	nous	acquîmes
vous	acquériez	vous	acquîtes
ils	acquièrent	ils	acquirent

PAST PARTICIPLE	IMPERATIVE
acquis	acquiers
	acquérons
	acquérez

PRESENT PARTICIPLE	AUXILIARY
acquérant	avoir

aller (to go)

	PRESENT		IMPERFECT
je	**vais**		j'allais
tu	**vas**	tu	allais
il	**va**	il	allait
nous	allons	nous	allions
vous	allez	vous	alliez
ils	**vont**	ils	allaient

	FUTURE		CONDITIONAL
	j'irai		**j'irais**
tu	**iras**	tu	**irais**
il	**ira**	il	**irait**
nous	**irons**	nous	**irions**
vous	**irez**	vous	**iriez**
ils	**iront**	ils	**iraient**

	PRESENT SUBJUNCTIVE		PAST HISTORIC
	j'aille		j'allai
tu	**ailles**	tu	allas
il	**aille**	il	alla
nous	allions	nous	allâmes
vous	alliez	vous	allâtes
ils	**aillent**	ils	allèrent

PAST PARTICIPLE	IMPERATIVE
allé	**va**
	allons
	allez

PRESENT PARTICIPLE	AUXILIARY
allant	**être**

s'asseoir (to sit down)

	PRESENT		IMPERFECT
je	m'assieds *or* assois	je	m'asseyais
tu	t'assieds *or* assois	tu	t'asseyais
il	s'assied *or* assoit	il	s'asseyait
nous	nous asseyons *or* assoyons	nous	nous asseyions
vous	vous asseyez *or* assoyez	vous	vous asseyiez
ils	s'asseyent *or* assoient	ils	s'asseyaient

	FUTURE		CONDITIONAL
je	m'assiérai	je	m'assiérais
tu	t'assiéras	tu	t'assiérais
il	s'assiéra	il	s'assiérait
nous	nous assiérons	nous	nous assiérions
vous	vous assiérez	vous	vous assiériez
ils	s'assiéront	ils	s'assiéraient

	PRESENT SUBJUNCTIVE		PAST HISTORIC
je	m'asseye	je	m'assis
tu	t'asseyes	tu	t'assis
il	s'asseye	il	s'assit
nous	nous asseyions	nous	nous assîmes
vous	vous asseyiez	vous	vous assîtes
ils	s'asseyent	ils	s'assirent

PAST PARTICIPLE
assis

IMPERATIVE
assieds-toi
asseyons-nous
asseyez-vous

PRESENT PARTICIPLE
s'asseyant

AUXILIARY
être

avoir (to have)

	PRESENT		IMPERFECT
	j'ai		j'avais
tu	as	tu	avais
il	a	il	avait
nous	avons	nous	avions
vous	avez	vous	aviez
ils	ont	ils	avaient

	FUTURE		CONDITIONAL
	j'aurai		j'aurais
tu	auras	tu	aurais
il	aura	il	aurait
nous	aurons	nous	aurions
vous	aurez	vous	auriez
ils	auront	ils	auraient

	PRESENT SUBJUNCTIVE		PAST HISTORIC
	j'aie		j'eus
tu	aies	tu	eus
il	ait	il	eut
nous	ayons	nous	eûmes
vous	ayez	vous	eûtes
ils	aient	ils	eurent

PAST PARTICIPLE
eu

IMPERATIVE
aie
ayons
ayez

PRESENT PARTICIPLE
ayant

AUXILIARY
avoir

battre (to beat)

	PRESENT			IMPERFECT
je	**bats**		je	battais
tu	**bats**		tu	battais
il	**bat**		il	battait
nous	battons		nous	battions
vous	battez		vous	battiez
ils	battent		ils	battaient

	FUTURE			CONDITIONAL
je	battrai		je	battrais
tu	battras		tu	battrais
il	battra		il	battrait
nous	battrons		nous	battrions
vous	battrez		vous	battriez
ils	battront		ils	battraient

	PRESENT SUBJUNCTIVE			PAST HISTORIC
je	batte		je	battis
tu	battes		tu	battis
il	batte		il	battit
nous	battions		nous	battîmes
vous	battiez		vous	battîtes
ils	battent		ils	battirent

PAST PARTICIPLE

battu

PRESENT PARTICIPLE

battant

IMPERATIVE

bats
battons
battez

AUXILIARY

avoir

boire (to drink)

	PRESENT		IMPERFECT
je	bois	je	buvais
tu	bois	tu	buvais
il	boit	il	buvait
nous	buvons	nous	buvions
vous	buvez	vous	buviez
ils	boivent	ils	buvaient

	FUTURE		CONDITIONAL
je	boirai	je	boirais
tu	boiras	tu	boirais
il	boira	il	boirait
nous	boirons	nous	boirions
vous	boirez	vous	boiriez
ils	boiront	ils	boiraient

	PRESENT SUBJUNCTIVE		PAST HISTORIC
je	boive	je	bus
tu	boives	tu	bus
il	boive	il	but
nous	buvions	nous	bûmes
vous	buviez	vous	bûtes
ils	boivent	ils	burent

PAST PARTICIPLE
bu

IMPERATIVE
bois
buvons
buvez

PRESENT PARTICIPLE
buvant

AUXILIARY
avoir

bouillir (to boil)

	PRESENT			IMPERFECT
je	bous		je	bouillais
tu	bous		tu	bouillais
il	bout		il	bouillait
nous	bouillons		nous	bouillions
vous	bouillez		vous	bouilliez
ils	bouillent		ils	bouillaient

	FUTURE			CONDITIONAL
je	bouillirai		je	bouillirais
tu	bouilliras		tu	bouillirais
il	bouillira		il	bouillirait
nous	bouillirons		nous	bouillirions
vous	bouillirez		vous	bouilliriez
ils	bouilliront		ils	bouilliraient

	PRESENT SUBJUNCTIVE			PAST HISTORIC
je	bouille		je	bouillis
tu	bouilles		tu	bouillis
il	bouille		il	bouillit
nous	bouillions		nous	bouillîmes
vous	bouilliez		vous	bouillîtes
ils	bouillent		ils	bouillirent

PAST PARTICIPLE
bouilli

IMPERATIVE
bous
bouillons
bouillez

PRESENT PARTICIPLE
bouillant

AUXILIARY
avoir

connaître (to know)

	PRESENT		IMPERFECT
je	connais	je	connaissais
tu	connais	tu	connaissais
il	connaît	il	connaissait
nous	connaissons	nous	connaissions
vous	connaissez	vous	connaissiez
ils	connaissent	ils	connaissaient

	FUTURE		CONDITIONAL
je	connaîtrai	je	connaîtrais
tu	connaîtras	tu	connaîtrais
il	connaîtra	il	connaîtrait
nous	connaîtrons	nous	connaîtrions
vous	connaîtrez	vous	connaîtriez
ils	connaîtront	ils	connaîtraient

	PRESENT SUBJUNCTIVE		PAST HISTORIC
je	connaisse	je	connus
tu	connaisses	tu	connus
il	connaisse	il	connut
nous	connaissions	nous	connûmes
vous	connaissiez	vous	connûtes
ils	connaissent	ils	connurent

PAST PARTICIPLE	IMPERATIVE
connu	connais
	connaissons
	connaissez

PRESENT PARTICIPLE	AUXILIARY
connaissant	avoir

coudre (to sew)

	PRESENT		IMPERFECT
je	couds	je	cousais
tu	couds	tu	cousais
il	coud	il	cousait
nous	cousons	nous	cousions
vous	cousez	vous	cousiez
ils	cousent	ils	cousaient

	FUTURE		CONDITIONAL
je	coudrai	je	coudrais
tu	coudras	tu	coudrais
il	coudra	il	coudrait
nous	coudrons	nous	coudrions
vous	coudrez	vous	coudriez
ils	coudront	ils	coudraient

	PRESENT SUBJUNCTIVE		PAST HISTORIC
je	couse	je	cousis
tu	couses	tu	cousis
il	couse	il	cousit
nous	cousions	nous	cousîmes
vous	cousiez	vous	cousîtes
ils	cousent	ils	cousirent

PAST PARTICIPLE	IMPERATIVE
cousu	couds
	cousons
	cousez

PRESENT PARTICIPLE	AUXILIARY
cousant	avoir

courir (to run)

	PRESENT		IMPERFECT
je	cours	je	courais
tu	cours	tu	courais
il	court	il	courait
nous	courons	nous	courions
vous	courez	vous	couriez
ils	courent	ils	couraient

	FUTURE		CONDITIONAL
je	courrai	je	courrais
tu	courras	tu	courrais
il	courra	il	courrait
nous	courrons	nous	courrions
vous	courrez	vous	courriez
ils	courront	ils	courraient

	PRESENT SUBJUNCTIVE		PAST HISTORIC
je	coure	je	courus
tu	coures	tu	courus
il	coure	il	courut
nous	courions	nous	courûmes
vous	couriez	vous	courûtes
ils	courent	ils	coururent

PAST PARTICIPLE	IMPERATIVE
couru	cours
	courons
	courez

PRESENT PARTICIPLE	AUXILIARY
courant	avoir

craindre (to fear)

	PRESENT		IMPERFECT
je	crains	je	craignais
tu	crains	tu	craignais
il	craint	il	craignait
nous	craignons	nous	craignions
vous	craignez	vous	craigniez
ils	craignent	ils	craignaient

	FUTURE		CONDITIONAL
je	craindrai	je	craindrais
tu	craindras	tu	craindrais
il	craindra	il	craindrait
nous	craindrons	nous	craindrions
vous	craindrez	vous	craindriez
ils	craindront	ils	craindraient

	PRESENT SUBJUNCTIVE		PAST HISTORIC
je	craigne	je	craignis
tu	craignes	tu	craignis
il	craigne	il	craignit
nous	craignions	nous	craignîmes
vous	craigniez	vous	craignîtes
ils	craignent	ils	craignirent

PAST PARTICIPLE
craint

IMPERATIVE
crains
craignons
craignez

PRESENT PARTICIPLE
craignant

AUXILIARY
avoir

Note that verbs ending in **-eindre** and **-oindre** are conjugated similarly

croire (to believe)

	PRESENT			IMPERFECT
je	crois		je	**croyais**
tu	crois		tu	**croyais**
il	**croit**		il	**croyait**
nous	**croyons**		nous	**croyions**
vous	**croyez**		vous	**croyiez**
ils	croient		ils	**croyaient**

	FUTURE			CONDITIONAL
je	croirai		je	croirais
tu	croiras		tu	croirais
il	croira		il	croirait
nous	croirons		nous	croirions
vous	croirez		vous	croiriez
ils	croiront		ils	croiraient

	PRESENT SUBJUNCTIVE			PAST HISTORIC
je	croie		je	**crus**
tu	croies		tu	**crus**
il	croie		il	**crut**
nous	**croyions**		nous	**crûmes**
vous	**croyiez**		vous	**crûtes**
ils	croient		ils	**crurent**

PAST PARTICIPLE	IMPERATIVE
cru	crois
	croyons
	croyez

PRESENT PARTICIPLE	AUXILIARY
croyant	**avoir**

croître (to grow)

	PRESENT			IMPERFECT
je	croîs		je	croissais
tu	croîs		tu	croissais
il	croît		il	croissait
nous	**croissons**		nous	**croissions**
vous	**croissez**		vous	**croissiez**
ils	**croissent**		ils	**croissaient**

	FUTURE			CONDITIONAL
je	croîtrai		je	croîtrais
tu	croîtras		tu	croîtrais
il	croîtra		il	croîtrait
nous	croîtrons		nous	croîtrions
vous	croîtrez		vous	croîtriez
ils	croîtront		ils	croîtraient

	PRESENT SUBJUNCTIVE			PAST HISTORIC
je	**croisse**		je	**crûs**
tu	**croisses**		tu	**crûs**
il	**croisse**		il	**crût**
nous	**croissions**		nous	**crûmes**
vous	**croissiez**		vous	**crûtes**
ils	**croissent**		ils	**crûrent**

PAST PARTICIPLE
crû

IMPERATIVE
croîs
croissons
croissez

PRESENT PARTICIPLE
croissant

AUXILIARY
avoir

cueillir (to pick)

	PRESENT		IMPERFECT
je	cueille	je	cueillais
tu	cueilles	tu	cueillais
il	cueille	il	cueillait
nous	cueillons	nous	cueillions
vous	cueillez	vous	cueilliez
ils	cueillent	ils	cueillaient

	FUTURE		CONDITIONAL
je	cueillerai	je	cueillerais
tu	cueilleras	tu	cueillerais
il	cueillera	il	cueillerait
nous	cueillerons	nous	cueillerions
vous	cueillerez	vous	cueilleriez
ils	cueilleront	ils	cueilleraient

	PRESENT SUBJUNCTIVE		PAST HISTORIC
je	cueille	je	cueillis
tu	cueilles	tu	cueillis
il	cueille	il	cueillit
nous	cueillions	nous	cueillîmes
vous	cueilliez	vous	cueillîtes
ils	cueillent	ils	cueillirent

PAST PARTICIPLE
cueilli

IMPERATIVE
cueille
cueillons
cueillez

PRESENT PARTICIPLE
cueillant

AUXILIARY
avoir

cuire (to cook)

	PRESENT			IMPERFECT
je	cuis		je	cuisais
tu	cuis		tu	cuisais
il	cuit		il	cuisait
nous	cuisons		nous	cuisions
vous	cuisez		vous	cuisiez
ils	cuisent		ils	cuisaient

	FUTURE			CONDITIONAL
je	cuirai		je	cuirais
tu	cuiras		tu	cuirais
il	cuira		il	cuirait
nous	cuirons		nous	cuirions
vous	cuirez		vous	cuiriez
ils	cuiront		ils	cuiraient

	PRESENT SUBJUNCTIVE			PAST HISTORIC
je	cuise		je	cuisis
tu	cuises		tu	cuisis
il	cuise		il	cuisit
nous	cuisions		nous	cuisîmes
vous	cuisiez		vous	cuisîtes
ils	cuisent		ils	cuisirent

PAST PARTICIPLE
cuit

IMPERATIVE
cuis
cuisons
cuisez

PRESENT PARTICIPLE
cuisant

AUXILIARY
avoir

Note that **nuire** (to harm) is conjugated similarly, but past participle is **nui**

devoir (to have to, to owe)

	PRESENT		IMPERFECT
je	dois	je	devais
tu	dois	tu	devais
il	doit	il	devait
nous	devons	nous	devions
vous	devez	vous	deviez
ils	doivent	ils	devaient

	FUTURE		CONDITIONAL
je	devrai	je	devrais
tu	devras	tu	devrais
il	devra	il	devrait
nous	devrons	nous	devrions
vous	devrez	vous	devriez
ils	devront	ils	devraient

	PRESENT SUBJUNCTIVE		PAST HISTORIC
je	doive	je	dus
tu	doives	tu	dus
il	doive	il	dut
nous	devions	nous	dûmes
vous	deviez	vous	dûtes
ils	doivent	ils	durent

PAST PARTICIPLE
dû

IMPERATIVE
dois
devons
devez

PRESENT PARTICIPLE
devant

AUXILIARY
avoir

dire (to say, to tell)

	PRESENT			IMPERFECT
je	dis		je	**disais**
tu	dis		tu	**disais**
il	**dit**		il	**disait**
nous	**disons**		nous	**disions**
vous	**dites**		vous	**disiez**
ils	**disent**		ils	**disaient**

	FUTURE			CONDITIONAL
je	dirai		je	dirais
tu	diras		tu	dirais
il	dira		il	dirait
nous	dirons		nous	dirions
vous	direz		vous	diriez
ils	diront		ils	diraient

	PRESENT SUBJUNCTIVE			PAST HISTORIC
je	**dise**		je	**dis**
tu	**dises**		tu	**dis**
il	**dise**		il	**dit**
nous	**disions**		nous	**dîmes**
vous	**disiez**		vous	**dîtes**
ils	**disent**		ils	**dirent**

PAST PARTICIPLE	IMPERATIVE
dit	**dis**
	disons
	dites

PRESENT PARTICIPLE	AUXILIARY
disant	**avoir**

Note that **interdire** (to forbid) is conjugated similarly, but the second person plural of the present tense is **vous interdisez**

dormir (to sleep)

	PRESENT		IMPERFECT
je	dors	je	dormais
tu	dors	tu	dormais
il	dort	il	dormait
nous	dormons	nous	dormions
vous	dormez	vous	dormiez
ils	dorment	ils	dormaient

	FUTURE		CONDITIONAL
je	dormirai	je	dormirais
tu	dormiras	tu	dormirais
il	dormira	il	dormirait
nous	dormirons	nous	dormirions
vous	dormirez	vous	dormiriez
ils	dormiront	ils	dormiraient

	PRESENT SUBJUNCTIVE		PAST HISTORIC
je	dorme	je	dormis
tu	dormes	tu	dormis
il	dorme	il	dormit
nous	dormions	nous	dormîmes
vous	dormiez	vous	dormîtes
ils	dorment	ils	dormirent

PAST PARTICIPLE
dormi

IMPERATIVE
dors
dormons
dormez

PRESENT PARTICIPLE
dormant

AUXILIARY
avoir

écrire (to write)

	PRESENT		**IMPERFECT**
	j'écris		j'écrivais
tu	écris	tu	écrivais
il	écrit	il	écrivait
nous	écrivons	nous	écrivions
vous	écrivez	vous	écriviez
ils	écrivent	ils	écrivaient

	FUTURE		**CONDITIONAL**
	j'écrirai		j'écrirais
tu	écriras	tu	écrirais
il	écrira	il	écrirait
nous	écrirons	nous	écririons
vous	écrirez	vous	écririez
ils	écriront	ils	écriraient

	PRESENT SUBJUNCTIVE		**PAST HISTORIC**
	j'écrive		j'écrivis
tu	écrives	tu	écrivis
il	écrive	il	écrivit
nous	écrivions	nous	écrivîmes
vous	écriviez	vous	écrivîtes
ils	écrivent	ils	écrivirent

PAST PARTICIPLE	**IMPERATIVE**
écrit	écris
	écrivons
	écrivez

PRESENT PARTICIPLE	**AUXILIARY**
écrivant	avoir

envoyer (to send)

	PRESENT		IMPERFECT
	j'envoie		j'envoyais
tu	envoies	tu	envoyais
il	envoie	il	envoyait
nous	envoyons	nous	envoyions
vous	envoyez	vous	envoyiez
ils	envoient	ils	envoyaient

	FUTURE		CONDITIONAL
	j'**enverrai**		j'**enverrais**
tu	**enverras**	tu	**enverrais**
il	**enverra**	il	**enverrait**
nous	**enverrons**	nous	**enverrions**
vous	**enverrez**	vous	**enverriez**
ils	**enverront**	ils	**enverraient**

	PRESENT SUBJUNCTIVE		PAST HISTORIC
	j'envoie		j'envoyai
tu	envoies	tu	envoyas
il	envoie	il	envoya
nous	envoyions	nous	envoyâmes
vous	envoyiez	vous	envoyâtes
ils	envoient	ils	envoyèrent

PAST PARTICIPLE	IMPERATIVE
envoyé	envoie
	envoyons
	envoyez

PRESENT PARTICIPLE	AUXILIARY
envoyant	**avoir**

être (to be)

	PRESENT		IMPERFECT
je	suis		j'étais
tu	es	tu	étais
il	est	il	était
nous	sommes	nous	étions
vous	êtes	vous	étiez
ils	sont	ils	étaient

	FUTURE		CONDITIONAL
je	serai	je	serais
tu	seras	tu	serais
il	sera	il	serait
nous	serons	nous	serions
vous	serez	vous	seriez
ils	seront	ils	seraient

	PRESENT SUBJUNCTIVE		PAST HISTORIC
je	sois	je	fus
tu	sois	tu	fus
il	soit	il	fut
nous	soyons	nous	fûmes
vous	soyez	vous	fûtes
ils	soient	ils	furent

PAST PARTICIPLE
été

IMPERATIVE
sois
soyons
soyez

PRESENT PARTICIPLE
étant

AUXILIARY
avoir

faire (to do, to make)

	PRESENT		IMPERFECT
je	fais	je	faisais
tu	fais	tu	faisais
il	fait	il	faisait
nous	faisons	nous	faisions
vous	faites	vous	faisiez
ils	font	ils	faisaient

	FUTURE		CONDITIONAL
je	ferai	je	ferais
tu	feras	tu	ferais
il	fera	il	ferait
nous	ferons	nous	ferions
vous	ferez	vous	feriez
ils	feront	ils	feraient

	PRESENT SUBJUNCTIVE		PAST HISTORIC
je	fasse	je	fis
tu	fasses	tu	fis
il	fasse	il	fit
nous	fassions	nous	fîmes
vous	fassiez	vous	fîtes
ils	fassent	ils	firent

PAST PARTICIPLE
fait

IMPERATIVE
fais
faisons
faites

PRESENT PARTICIPLE
faisant

AUXILIARY
avoir

falloir (to be necessary)

PRESENT
il **faut**

IMPERFECT
il **fallait**

FUTURE
il **faudra**

CONDITIONAL
il **faudrait**

PRESENT SUBJUNCTIVE
il **faille**

PAST HISTORIC
il **fallut**

PAST PARTICIPLE
fallu

IMPERATIVE
not used

PRESENT PARTICIPLE
not used

AUXILIARY
avoir

fuir (to flee)

	PRESENT		IMPERFECT
je	fuis	je	**fuyais**
tu	fuis	tu	**fuyais**
il	fuit	il	**fuyait**
nous	**fuyons**	nous	**fuyions**
vous	**fuyez**	vous	**fuyiez**
ils	**fuient**	ils	**fuyaient**

	FUTURE		CONDITIONAL
je	fuirai	je	fuirais
tu	fuiras	tu	fuirais
il	fuira	il	fuirait
nous	fuirons	nous	fuirions
vous	fuirez	vous	fuiriez
ils	fuiront	ils	fuiraient

	PRESENT SUBJUNCTIVE		PAST HISTORIC
je	**fuie**	je	fuis
tu	**fuies**	tu	fuis
il	**fuie**	il	fuit
nous	**fuyions**	nous	fuîmes
vous	**fuyiez**	vous	fuîtes
ils	**fuient**	ils	fuirent

PAST PARTICIPLE	IMPERATIVE
fui	fuis
	fuyons
	fuyez

PRESENT PARTICIPLE	AUXILIARY
fuyant	**avoir**

haïr (to hate)

	PRESENT			IMPERFECT
je	hais		je	haïssais
tu	hais		tu	haïssais
il	hait		il	haïssait
nous	haïssons		nous	haïssions
vous	haïssez		vous	haïssiez
ils	haïssent		ils	haïssaient

	FUTURE			CONDITIONAL
je	haïrai		je	haïrais
tu	haïras		tu	haïrais
il	haïra		il	haïrait
nous	haïrons		nous	haïrions
vous	haïrez		vous	haïriez
ils	haïront		ils	haïraient

	PRESENT SUBJUNCTIVE			PAST HISTORIC
je	haïsse		je	haïs
tu	haïsses		tu	haïs
il	haïsse		il	haït
nous	haïssions		nous	haïmes
vous	haïssiez		vous	haïtes
ils	haïssent		ils	haïrent

PAST PARTICIPLE
haï

IMPERATIVE
hais
haïssons
haïssez

PRESENT PARTICIPLE
haïssant

AUXILIARY
avoir

lire (to read)

	PRESENT		IMPERFECT
je	lis	je	lisais
tu	lis	tu	lisais
il	**lit**	il	lisait
nous	**lisons**	nous	lisions
vous	**lisez**	vous	lisiez
ils	**lisent**	ils	lisaient

	FUTURE		CONDITIONAL
je	lirai	je	lirais
tu	liras	tu	lirais
il	lira	il	lirait
nous	lirons	nous	lirions
vous	lirez	vous	liriez
ils	liront	ils	liraient

	PRESENT SUBJUNCTIVE		PAST HISTORIC
je	**lise**	je	**lus**
tu	**lises**	tu	**lus**
il	**lise**	il	**lut**
nous	**lisions**	nous	**lûmes**
vous	**lisiez**	vous	**lûtes**
ils	**lisent**	ils	**lurent**

PAST PARTICIPLE
lu

IMPERATIVE
lis
lisons
lisez

PRESENT PARTICIPLE
lisant

AUXILIARY
avoir

mettre (to put)

	PRESENT		IMPERFECT
je	**mets**	je	mettais
tu	**mets**	tu	mettais
il	**met**	il	mettait
nous	mettons	nous	mettions
vous	mettez	vous	mettiez
ils	mettent	ils	mettaient

	FUTURE		CONDITIONAL
je	mettrai	je	mettrais
tu	mettras	tu	mettrais
il	mettra	il	mettrait
nous	mettrons	nous	mettrions
vous	mettrez	vous	mettriez
ils	mettront	ils	mettraient

	PRESENT SUBJUNCTIVE		PAST HISTORIC
je	mette	je	**mis**
tu	mettes	tu	**mis**
il	mette	il	**mit**
nous	mettions	nous	**mîmes**
vous	mettiez	vous	**mîtes**
ils	mettent	ils	**mirent**

PAST PARTICIPLE
mis

PRESENT PARTICIPLE
mettant

IMPERATIVE
mets
mettons
mettez

AUXILIARY
avoir

moudre (to grind)

	PRESENT		IMPERFECT
je	mouds	je	moulais
tu	mouds	tu	moulais
il	moud	il	moulait
nous	moulons	nous	moulions
vous	moulez	vous	mouliez
ils	moulent	ils	moulaient

	FUTURE		CONDITIONAL
je	moudrai	je	moudrais
tu	moudras	tu	moudrais
il	moudra	il	moudrait
nous	moudrons	nous	moudrions
vous	moudrez	vous	moudriez
ils	moudront	ils	moudraient

	PRESENT SUBJUNCTIVE		PAST HISTORIC
je	moule	je	moulus
tu	moules	tu	moulus
il	moule	il	moulut
nous	moulions	nous	moulûmes
vous	mouliez	vous	moulûtes
ils	moulent	ils	moulurent

PAST PARTICIPLE
moulu

IMPERATIVE
mouds
moulons
moulez

PRESENT PARTICIPLE
moulant

AUXILIARY
avoir

mourir (to die)

	PRESENT		IMPERFECT
je	meurs	je	mourais
tu	meurs	tu	mourais
il	meurt	il	mourait
nous	mourons	nous	mourions
vous	mourez	vous	mouriez
ils	meurent	ils	mouraient

	FUTURE		CONDITIONAL
je	mourrai	je	mourrais
tu	mourras	tu	mourrais
il	mourra	il	mourrait
nous	mourrons	nous	mourrions
vous	mourrez	vous	mourriez
ils	mourront	ils	mourraient

	PRESENT SUBJUNCTIVE		PAST HISTORIC
je	meure	je	mourus
tu	meures	tu	mourus
il	meure	il	mourut
nous	mourions	nous	mourûmes
vous	mouriez	vous	mourûtes
ils	meurent	ils	moururent

PAST PARTICIPLE
mort

IMPERATIVE
meurs
mourons
mourez

PRESENT PARTICIPLE
mourant

AUXILIARY
être

naître (to be born)

	PRESENT		IMPERFECT
je	nais	je	naissais
tu	nais	tu	naissais
il	naît	il	naissait
nous	naissons	nous	naissions
vous	naissez	vous	naissiez
ils	naissent	ils	naissaient

	FUTURE		CONDITIONAL
je	naîtrai	je	naîtrais
tu	naîtras	tu	naîtrais
il	naîtra	il	naîtrait
nous	naîtrons	nous	naîtrions
vous	naîtrez	vous	naîtriez
ils	naîtront	ils	naîtraient

	PRESENT SUBJUNCTIVE		PAST HISTORIC
je	naisse	je	naquis
tu	naisses	tu	naquis
il	naisse	il	naquit
nous	naissions	nous	naquîmes
vous	naissiez	vous	naquîtes
ils	naissent	ils	naquirent

PAST PARTICIPLE
né

IMPERATIVE
nais
naissons
naissez

PRESENT PARTICIPLE
naissant

AUXILIARY
être

ouvrir (to open)

	PRESENT		IMPERFECT
	j'ouvre		j'ouvrais
tu	ouvres	tu	ouvrais
il	ouvre	il	ouvrait
nous	ouvrons	nous	ouvrions
vous	ouvrez	vous	ouvriez
ils	ouvrent	ils	ouvraient

	FUTURE		CONDITIONAL
	j'ouvrirai		j'ouvrirais
tu	ouvriras	tu	ouvrirais
il	ouvrira	il	ouvrirait
nous	ouvrirons	nous	ouvririons
vous	ouvrirez	vous	ouvririez
ils	ouvriront	ils	ouvriraient

	PRESENT SUBJUNCTIVE		PAST HISTORIC
	j'ouvre		j'ouvris
tu	ouvres	tu	ouvris
il	ouvre	il	ouvrit
nous	ouvrions	nous	ouvrîmes
vous	ouvriez	vous	ouvrîtes
ils	ouvrent	ils	ouvrirent

PAST PARTICIPLE
ouvert

PRESENT PARTICIPLE
ouvrant

IMPERATIVE
ouvre
ouvrons
ouvrez

AUXILIARY
avoir

Note that **offrir** (to offer) and **souffrir** (to suffer) are conjugated similarly

paraître (to appear)

	PRESENT		IMPERFECT
je	parais	je	paraissais
tu	parais	tu	paraissais
il	paraît	il	paraissait
nous	paraissons	nous	paraissions
vous	paraissez	vous	paraissiez
ils	paraissent	ils	paraissaient

	FUTURE		CONDITIONAL
je	paraîtrai	je	paraîtrais
tu	paraîtras	tu	paraîtrais
il	paraîtra	il	paraîtrait
nous	paraîtrons	nous	paraîtrions
vous	paraîtrez	vous	paraîtriez
ils	paraîtront	ils	paraîtraient

	PRESENT SUBJUNCTIVE		PAST HISTORIC
je	paraisse	je	parus
tu	paraisses	tu	parus
il	paraisse	il	parut
nous	paraissions	nous	parûmes
vous	paraissiez	vous	parûtes
ils	paraissent	ils	parurent

PAST PARTICIPLE	IMPERATIVE
paru	parais
	paraissons
	paraissez

PRESENT PARTICIPLE	AUXILIARY
paraissant	avoir

partir (to leave)

	PRESENT			IMPERFECT
je	pars		je	partais
tu	pars		tu	partais
il	part		il	partait
nous	partons		nous	partions
vous	partez		vous	partiez
ils	partent		ils	partaient

	FUTURE			CONDITIONAL
je	partirai		je	partirais
tu	partiras		tu	partirais
il	partira		il	partirait
nous	partirons		nous	partirions
vous	partirez		vous	partiriez
ils	partiront		ils	partiraient

	PRESENT SUBJUNCTIVE			PAST HISTORIC
je	parte		je	partis
tu	partes		tu	partis
il	parte		il	partit
nous	partions		nous	partîmes
vous	partiez		vous	partîtes
ils	partent		ils	partirent

PAST PARTICIPLE	IMPERATIVE
parti	pars
	partons
	partez

PRESENT PARTICIPLE	AUXILIARY
partant	être

plaire (to please)

	PRESENT		IMPERFECT
je	plais	je	**plaisais**
tu	plais	tu	**plaisais**
il	**plaît**	il	**plaisait**
nous	**plaisons**	nous	**plaisions**
vous	**plaisez**	vous	**plaisiez**
ils	**plaisent**	ils	**plaisaient**

	FUTURE		CONDITIONAL
je	plairai	je	plairais
tu	plairas	tu	plairais
il	plaira	il	plairait
nous	plairons	nous	plairions
vous	plairez	vous	plairiez
ils	plairont	ils	plairaient

	PRESENT SUBJUNCTIVE		PAST HISTORIC
je	**plaise**	je	**plus**
tu	**plaises**	tu	**plus**
il	**plaise**	il	**plut**
nous	**plaisions**	nous	**plûmes**
vous	**plaisiez**	vous	**plûtes**
ils	**plaisent**	ils	**plurent**

PAST PARTICIPLE	IMPERATIVE
plu	plais
	plaisons
	plaisez

PRESENT PARTICIPLE	AUXILIARY
plaisant	**avoir**

pleuvoir (to rain)

PRESENT		**IMPERFECT**	
il	pleut	il	pleuvait

FUTURE		**CONDITIONAL**	
il	pleuvra	il	pleuvrait

PRESENT SUBJUNCTIVE		**PAST HISTORIC**	
il	pleuve	il	plut

PAST PARTICIPLE	**IMPERATIVE**
plu	*not used*

PRESENT PARTICIPLE	**AUXILIARY**
pleuvant	avoir

pouvoir (to be able to)

	PRESENT		IMPERFECT
je	peux*	je	pouvais
tu	peux	tu	pouvais
il	peut	il	pouvait
nous	pouvons	nous	pouvions
vous	pouvez	vous	pouviez
ils	peuvent	ils	pouvaient

	FUTURE		CONDITIONAL
je	pourrai	je	pourrais
tu	pourras	tu	pourrais
il	pourra	il	pourrait
nous	pourrons	nous	pourrions
vous	pourrez	vous	pourriez
ils	pourront	ils	pourraient

	PRESENT SUBJUNCTIVE		PAST HISTORIC
je	puisse	je	pus
tu	puisses	tu	pus
il	puisse	il	put
nous	puissions	nous	pûmes
vous	puissiez	vous	pûtes
ils	puissent	ils	purent

PAST PARTICIPLE	IMPERATIVE
pu	*not used*

PRESENT PARTICIPLE	AUXILIARY
pouvant	avoir

* In questions **puis-je?** is used

prendre (to take)

	PRESENT		IMPERFECT
je	prends	je	prenais
tu	prends	tu	prenais
il	prend	il	prenait
nous	prenons	nous	prenions
vous	prenez	vous	preniez
ils	prennent	ils	prenaient

	FUTURE		CONDITIONAL
je	prendrai	je	prendrais
tu	prendras	tu	prendrais
il	prendra	il	prendrait
nous	prendrons	nous	prendrions
vous	prendrez	vous	prendriez
ils	prendront	ils	prendraient

	PRESENT SUBJUNCTIVE		PAST HISTORIC
je	prenne	je	pris
tu	prennes	tu	pris
il	prenne	il	prit
nous	prenions	nous	prîmes
vous	preniez	vous	prîtes
ils	prennent	ils	prirent

PAST PARTICIPLE
pris

IMPERATIVE
prends
prenons
prenez

PRESENT PARTICIPLE
prenant

AUXILIARY
avoir

recevoir (to receive)

	PRESENT		IMPERFECT
je	reçois	je	recevais
tu	reçois	tu	recevais
il	reçoit	il	recevait
nous	recevons	nous	recevions
vous	recevez	vous	receviez
ils	reçoivent	ils	recevaient

	FUTURE		CONDITIONAL
je	recevrai	je	recevrais
tu	recevras	tu	recevrais
il	recevra	il	recevrait
nous	recevrons	nous	recevrions
vous	recevrez	vous	recevriez
ils	recevront	ils	recevraient

	PRESENT SUBJUNCTIVE		PAST HISTORIC
je	reçoive	je	reçus
tu	reçoives	tu	reçus
il	reçoive	il	reçut
nous	recevions	nous	reçûmes
vous	receviez	vous	reçûtes
ils	reçoivent	ils	reçurent

PAST PARTICIPLE
reçu

IMPERATIVE
reçois
recevons
recevez

PRESENT PARTICIPLE
recevant

AUXILIARY
avoir

résoudre (to solve)

	PRESENT			IMPERFECT
je	résous		je	résolvais
tu	résous		tu	résolvais
il	résout		il	résolvait
nous	résolvons		nous	résolvions
vous	résolvez		vous	résolviez
ils	résolvent		ils	résolvaient

	FUTURE			CONDITIONAL
je	résoudrai		je	résoudrais
tu	résoudras		tu	résoudrais
il	résoudra		il	résoudrait
nous	résoudrons		nous	résoudrions
vous	résoudrez		vous	résoudriez
ils	résoudront		ils	résoudraient

	PRESENT SUBJUNCTIVE			PAST HISTORIC
je	résolve		je	résolus
tu	résolves		tu	résolus
il	résolve		il	résolut
nous	résolvions		nous	résolûmes
vous	résolviez		vous	résolûtes
ils	résolvent		ils	résolurent

PAST PARTICIPLE
résolu

IMPERATIVE
résous
résolvons
résolvez

PRESENT PARTICIPLE
résolvant

AUXILIARY
avoir

rire (to laugh)

	PRESENT		IMPERFECT
je	ris	je	riais
tu	ris	tu	riais
il	**rit**	il	riait
nous	rions	nous	riions
vous	riez	vous	riiez
ils	rient	ils	riaient

	FUTURE		CONDITIONAL
je	rirai	je	rirais
tu	riras	tu	rirais
il	rira	il	rirait
nous	rirons	nous	ririons
vous	rirez	vous	ririez
ils	riront	ils	riraient

	PRESENT SUBJUNCTIVE		PAST HISTORIC
je	rie	je	**ris**
tu	ries	tu	**ris**
il	rie	il	**rit**
nous	riions	nous	**rîmes**
vous	riiez	vous	**rîtes**
ils	rient	ils	**rirent**

PAST PARTICIPLE	IMPERATIVE
ri	ris
	rions
	riez

PRESENT PARTICIPLE	AUXILIARY
riant	**avoir**

rompre (to break)

	PRESENT		IMPERFECT
je	romps	je	rompais
tu	romps	tu	rompais
il	**rompt**	il	rompait
nous	rompons	nous	rompions
vous	rompez	vous	rompiez
ils	rompent	ils	rompaient

	FUTURE		CONDITIONAL
je	romprai	je	romprais
tu	rompras	tu	romprais
il	rompra	il	romprait
nous	romprons	nous	romprions
vous	romprez	vous	rompriez
ils	rompront	ils	rompraient

	PRESENT SUBJUNCTIVE		PAST HISTORIC
je	rompe	je	rompis
tu	rompes	tu	rompis
il	rompe	il	rompit
nous	rompions	nous	rompîmes
vous	rompiez	vous	rompîtes
ils	rompent	ils	rompirent

PAST PARTICIPLE
rompu

IMPERATIVE
romps
rompons
rompez

PRESENT PARTICIPLE
rompant

AUXILIARY
avoir

savoir (to know)

	PRESENT			IMPERFECT
je	sais		je	savais
tu	sais		tu	savais
il	sait		il	savait
nous	savons		nous	savions
vous	savez		vous	saviez
ils	savent		ils	savaient

	FUTURE			CONDITIONAL
je	saurai		je	saurais
tu	sauras		tu	saurais
il	saura		il	saurait
nous	saurons		nous	saurions
vous	saurez		vous	sauriez
ils	sauront		ils	sauraient

	PRESENT SUBJUNCTIVE			PAST HISTORIC
je	sache		je	sus
tu	saches		tu	sus
il	sache		il	sut
nous	sachions		nous	sûmes
vous	sachiez		vous	sûtes
ils	sachent		ils	surent

PAST PARTICIPLE
su

IMPERATIVE
sache
sachons
sachez

PRESENT PARTICIPLE
sachant

AUXILIARY
avoir

sentir (to feel, to smell)

	PRESENT			IMPERFECT
je	sens		je	sentais
tu	sens		tu	sentais
il	sent		il	sentait
nous	sentons		nous	sentions
vous	sentez		vous	sentiez
ils	sentent		ils	sentaient

	FUTURE			CONDITIONAL
je	sentirai		je	sentirais
tu	sentiras		tu	sentirais
il	sentira		il	sentirait
nous	sentirons		nous	sentirions
vous	sentirez		vous	sentiriez
ils	sentiront		ils	sentiraient

	PRESENT SUBJUNCTIVE			PAST HISTORIC
je	sente		je	sentis
tu	sentes		tu	sentis
il	sente		il	sentit
nous	sentions		nous	sentîmes
vous	sentiez		vous	sentîtes
ils	sentent		ils	sentirent

PAST PARTICIPLE	IMPERATIVE
senti	sens
	sentons
	sentez

PRESENT PARTICIPLE	AUXILIARY
sentant	avoir

servir (to serve)

	PRESENT			IMPERFECT
je	**sers**		je	**servais**
tu	**sers**		tu	**servais**
il	**sert**		il	**servait**
nous	**servons**		nous	**servions**
vous	**servez**		vous	**serviez**
ils	**servent**		ils	**servaient**

	FUTURE			CONDITIONAL
je	servirai		je	servirais
tu	serviras		tu	servirais
il	servira		il	servirait
nous	servirons		nous	servirions
vous	servirez		vous	serviriez
ils	serviront		ils	serviraient

	PRESENT SUBJUNCTIVE			PAST HISTORIC
je	**serve**		je	servis
tu	**serves**		tu	servis
il	**serve**		il	servit
nous	**servions**		nous	servîmes
vous	**serviez**		vous	servîtes
ils	**servent**		ils	servirent

PAST PARTICIPLE	IMPERATIVE
servi	**sers**
	servons
	servez

PRESENT PARTICIPLE	AUXILIARY
servant	**avoir**

sortir (to go, to come out)

	PRESENT			IMPERFECT
je	sors		je	sortais
tu	sors		tu	sortais
il	sort		il	sortait
nous	sortons		nous	sortions
vous	sortez		vous	sortiez
ils	sortent		ils	sortaient

	FUTURE			CONDITIONAL
je	sortirai		je	sortirais
tu	sortiras		tu	sortirais
il	sortira		il	sortirait
nous	sortirons		nous	sortirions
vous	sortirez		vous	sortiriez
ils	sortiront		ils	sortiraient

	PRESENT SUBJUNCTIVE			PAST HISTORIC
je	sorte		je	sortis
tu	sortes		tu	sortis
il	sorte		il	sortit
nous	sortions		nous	sortîmes
vous	sortiez		vous	sortîtes
ils	sortent		ils	sortirent

PAST PARTICIPLE
sorti

IMPERATIVE
sors
sortons
sortez

PRESENT PARTICIPLE
sortant

AUXILIARY
être

suffire (to be enough)

	PRESENT		IMPERFECT
je	suffis	je	**suffisais**
tu	suffis	tu	**suffisais**
il	suffit	il	**suffisait**
nous	**suffisons**	nous	**suffisions**
vous	**suffisez**	vous	**suffisiez**
ils	**suffisent**	ils	**suffisaient**

	FUTURE		CONDITIONAL
je	suffirai	je	suffirais
tu	suffiras	tu	suffirais
il	suffira	il	suffirait
nous	suffirons	nous	suffirions
vous	suffirez	vous	suffiriez
ils	suffiront	ils	suffiraient

	PRESENT SUBJUNCTIVE		PAST HISTORIC
je	**suffise**	je	**suffis**
tu	**suffises**	tu	**suffis**
il	**suffise**	il	**suffit**
nous	**suffisions**	nous	**suffîmes**
vous	**suffisiez**	vous	**suffîtes**
ils	**suffisent**	ils	**suffirent**

PAST PARTICIPLE	IMPERATIVE
suffi	suffis
	suffisons
	suffisez

PRESENT PARTICIPLE	AUXILIARY
suffisant	**avoir**

suivre (to follow)

	PRESENT		IMPERFECT
je	**suis**	je	suivais
tu	**suis**	tu	suivais
il	**suit**	il	suivait
nous	suivons	nous	suivions
vous	suivez	vous	suiviez
ils	suivent	ils	suivaient

	FUTURE		CONDITIONAL
je	suivrai	je	suivrais
tu	suivras	tu	suivrais
il	suivra	il	suivrait
nous	suivrons	nous	suivrions
vous	suivrez	vous	suivriez
ils	suivront	ils	suivraient

	PRESENT SUBJUNCTIVE		PAST HISTORIC
je	suive	je	suivis
tu	suives	tu	suivis
il	suive	il	suivit
nous	suivions	nous	suivîmes
vous	suiviez	vous	suivîtes
ils	suivent	ils	suivirent

PAST PARTICIPLE	IMPERATIVE
suivi	**suis**
	suivons
	suivez

PRESENT PARTICIPLE	AUXILIARY
suivant	**avoir**

se taire (to stop talking)

	PRESENT		IMPERFECT
je	me tais	je	me taisais
tu	te tais	tu	te taisais
il	se tait	il	se taisait
nous	**nous taisons**	nous	**nous taisions**
vous	**vous taisez**	vous	**vous taisiez**
ils	**se taisent**	ils	**se taisaient**

	FUTURE		CONDITIONAL
je	me tairai	je	me tairais
tu	te tairas	tu	te tairais
il	se taira	il	se tairait
nous	nous tairons	nous	nous tairions
vous	vous tairez	vous	vous tairiez
ils	se tairont	ils	se tairaient

	PRESENT SUBJUNCTIVE		PAST HISTORIC
je	**me taise**	je	**me tus**
tu	**te taises**	tu	**te tus**
il	**se taise**	il	**se tut**
nous	**nous taisions**	nous	**nous tûmes**
vous	**vous taisiez**	vous	**vous tûtes**
ils	**se taisent**	ils	**se turent**

PAST PARTICIPLE
tu

IMPERATIVE
tais-toi
taisons-nous
taisez-vous

PRESENT PARTICIPLE
se taisant

AUXILIARY
être

tenir (to hold)

	PRESENT		IMPERFECT
je	tiens	je	tenais
tu	tiens	tu	tenais
il	tient	il	tenait
nous	tenons	nous	tenions
vous	tenez	vous	teniez
ils	tiennent	ils	tenaient

	FUTURE		CONDITIONAL
je	tiendrai	je	tiendrais
tu	tiendras	tu	tiendrais
il	tiendra	il	tiendrait
nous	tiendrons	nous	tiendrions
vous	tiendrez	vous	tiendriez
ils	tiendront	ils	tiendraient

	PRESENT SUBJUNCTIVE		PAST HISTORIC
je	tienne	je	tins
tu	tiennes	tu	tins
il	tienne	il	tint
nous	tenions	nous	tînmes
vous	teniez	vous	tîntes
ils	tiennent	ils	tinrent

PAST PARTICIPLE	IMPERATIVE
tenu	tiens
	tenons
	tenez

PRESENT PARTICIPLE	AUXILIARY
tenant	avoir

vaincre (to defeat)

	PRESENT		IMPERFECT
je	vaincs	je	vainquais
tu	vaincs	tu	vainquais
il	vainc	il	vainquait
nous	vainquons	nous	vainquions
vous	vainquez	vous	vainquiez
ils	vainquent	ils	vainquaient

	FUTURE		CONDITIONAL
je	vaincrai	je	vaincrais
tu	vaincras	tu	vaincrais
il	vaincra	il	vaincrait
nous	vaincrons	nous	vaincrions
vous	vaincrez	vous	vaincriez
ils	vaincront	ils	vaincraient

	PRESENT SUBJUNCTIVE		PAST HISTORIC
je	vainque	je	vainquis
tu	vainques	tu	vainquis
il	vainque	il	vainquit
nous	vainquions	nous	vainquîmes
vous	vainquiez	vous	vainquîtes
ils	vainquent	ils	vainquirent

PAST PARTICIPLE	IMPERATIVE
vaincu	vaincs
	vainquons
	vainquez

PRESENT PARTICIPLE	AUXILIARY
vainquant	avoir

valoir (to be worth)

	PRESENT		IMPERFECT
je	vaux	je	valais
tu	vaux	tu	valais
il	vaut	il	valait
nous	valons	nous	valions
vous	valez	vous	valiez
ils	valent	ils	valaient

	FUTURE		CONDITIONAL
je	vaudrai	je	vaudrais
tu	vaudras	tu	vaudrais
il	vaudra	il	vaudrait
nous	vaudrons	nous	vaudrions
vous	vaudrez	vous	vaudriez
ils	vaudront	ils	vaudraient

	PRESENT SUBJUNCTIVE		PAST HISTORIC
je	vaille	je	valus
tu	vailles	tu	valus
il	vaille	il	valut
nous	valions	nous	valûmes
vous	valiez	vous	valûtes
ils	vaillent	ils	valurent

PAST PARTICIPLE	IMPERATIVE
valu	vaux
	valons
	valez

PRESENT PARTICIPLE	AUXILIARY
valant	avoir

venir (to come)

	PRESENT		IMPERFECT
je	viens	je	venais
tu	viens	tu	venais
il	vient	il	venait
nous	venons	nous	venions
vous	venez	vous	veniez
ils	viennent	ils	venaient

	FUTURE		CONDITIONAL
je	viendrai	je	viendrais
tu	viendras	tu	viendrais
il	viendra	il	viendrait
nous	viendrons	nous	viendrions
vous	viendrez	vous	viendriez
ils	viendront	ils	viendraient

	PRESENT SUBJUNCTIVE		PAST HISTORIC
je	vienne	je	vins
tu	viennes	tu	vins
il	vienne	il	vint
nous	venions	nous	vînmes
vous	veniez	vous	vîntes
ils	viennent	ils	vinrent

PAST PARTICIPLE	IMPERATIVE
venu	viens
	venons
	venez

PRESENT PARTICIPLE	AUXILIARY
venant	être

vêtir (to dress)

	PRESENT			IMPERFECT
je	**vêts**		je	**vêtais**
tu	**vêts**		tu	**vêtais**
il	**vêt**		il	**vêtait**
nous	**vêtons**		nous	**vêtions**
vous	**vêtez**		vous	**vêtiez**
ils	**vêtent**		ils	**vêtaient**

	FUTURE			CONDITIONAL
je	vêtirai		je	vêtirais
tu	vêtiras		tu	vêtirais
il	vêtira		il	vêtirait
nous	vêtirons		nous	vêtirions
vous	vêtirez		vous	vêtiriez
ils	vêtiront		ils	vêtiraient

	PRESENT SUBJUNCTIVE			PAST HISTORIC
je	**vête**		je	vêtis
tu	**vêtes**		tu	vêtis
il	**vête**		il	vêtit
nous	**vêtions**		nous	vêtîmes
vous	**vêtiez**		vous	vêtîtes
ils	**vêtent**		ils	vêtirent

PAST PARTICIPLE
vêtu

IMPERATIVE
vêts
vêtons
vêtez

PRESENT PARTICIPLE
vêtant

AUXILIARY
avoir

vivre (to live)

	PRESENT		IMPERFECT
je	**vis**	je	vivais
tu	**vis**	tu	vivais
il	**vit**	il	vivait
nous	vivons	nous	vivions
vous	vivez	vous	viviez
ils	vivent	ils	vivaient

	FUTURE		CONDITIONAL
je	vivrai	je	vivrais
tu	vivras	tu	vivrais
il	vivra	il	vivrait
nous	vivrons	nous	vivrions
vous	vivrez	vous	vivriez
ils	vivront	ils	vivraient

	PRESENT SUBJUNCTIVE		PAST HISTORIC
je	vive	je	**vécus**
tu	vives	tu	**vécus**
il	vive	il	**vécut**
nous	vivions	nous	**vécûmes**
vous	viviez	vous	**vécûtes**
ils	vivent	ils	**vécurent**

PAST PARTICIPLE
vêcu

IMPERATIVE
vis
vivons
vivez

PRESENT PARTICIPLE
vivant

AUXILIARY
avoir

voir (to see)

	PRESENT			IMPERFECT
je	vois		je	voyais
tu	vois		tu	voyais
il	voit		il	voyait
nous	voyons		nous	voyions
vous	voyez		vous	voyiez
ils	voient		ils	voyaient

	FUTURE			CONDITIONAL
je	verrai		je	verrais
tu	verras		tu	verrais
il	verra		il	verrait
nous	verrons		nous	verrions
vous	verrez		vous	verriez
ils	verront		ils	verraient

	PRESENT SUBJUNCTIVE			PAST HISTORIC
je	voie		je	vis
tu	voies		tu	vis
il	voie		il	vit
nous	voyions		nous	vîmes
vous	voyiez		vous	vîtes
ils	voient		ils	virent

PAST PARTICIPLE
vu

IMPERATIVE
vois
voyons
voyez

PRESENT PARTICIPLE
voyant

AUXILIARY
avoir

vouloir (to wish, to want)

	PRESENT		IMPERFECT
je	veux	je	voulais
tu	veux	tu	voulais
il	veut	il	voulait
nous	voulons	nous	voulions
vous	voulez	vous	vouliez
ils	veulent	ils	voulaient

	FUTURE		CONDITIONAL
je	voudrai	je	voudrais
tu	voudras	tu	voudrais
il	voudra	il	voudrait
nous	voudrons	nous	voudrions
vous	voudrez	vous	voudriez
ils	voudront	ils	voudraient

	PRESENT SUBJUNCTIVE		PAST HISTORIC
je	veuille	je	voulus
tu	veuilles	tu	voulus
il	veuille	il	voulut
nous	voulions	nous	voulûmes
vous	vouliez	vous	voulûtes
ils	veuillent	ils	voulurent

PAST PARTICIPLE	IMPERATIVE
voulu	veuille
	veuillons
	veuillez

PRESENT PARTICIPLE	AUXILIARY
voulant	avoir

The Gender of Nouns

In French, all nouns are either masculine or feminine, whether denoting people, animals or things. Unlike English, there is no neuter gender for inanimate objects and abstract nouns.

Gender is largely unpredictable and has to be learnt for each noun. However, the following guidelines will help you determine the gender for certain types of nouns:

> Nouns denoting male people and animals are usually – but not always – masculine, e.g.
>> **un homme** a man
>> **un taureau** a bull
>> **un infirmier** a (*male*) nurse
>> **un cheval** a horse

> Nouns denoting female people and animals are usually – but not always – feminine, e.g.
>> **une fille** a girl
>> **une vache** a cow
>> **une infirmière** a nurse
>> **une brebis** a ewe

> Some nouns are masculine *or* feminine depending on the sex of the person to whom they refer, e.g.
>> **un camarade** a (*male*) friend
>> **une camarade** a (*female*) friend
>> **un Belge** a Belgian (*man*)
>> **une Belge** a Belgian (*woman*)

> Other nouns referring to either men or women have only one gender which applies to both, e.g.
>> **un professeur** a teacher
>> **une personne** a person
>> **une sentinelle** a sentry
>> **un témoin** a witness
>> **une victime** a victim
>> **une recrue** a recruit

Nouns

Sometimes the ending of the noun indicates its gender. Shown below are some of the most important to guide you:

Masculine endings

-age	**le courage** courage; **le rinçage** rinsing EXCEPTIONS: **une cage** a cage; **une image** a picture; **la nage** swimming; **une page** a page; **une plage** a beach; **une rage** a rage
-ment	**le commencement** the beginning EXCEPTION: **une jument** a mare
-oir	**un couloir** a corridor; **un miroir** a mirror
-sme	**le pessimisme** pessimism; **l'enthousiasme** enthusiasm

Feminine endings

-ance, -anse	**la confiance** confidence; **la danse** dancing
-ence, -ense	**la prudence** caution; **la défense** defence EXCEPTION: **le silence** silence
-ion	**une région** a region; **une addition** a bill EXCEPTIONS: **un pion** a pawn; **un espion** a spy
-oire	**une baignoire** a bath(tub)
-té, -tié	**la beauté** beauty; **la moitié** half

Suffixes which differentiate between male and female are shown on pages 134 and 136.

The following words have different meanings depending on gender:

le crêpe crêpe	**la crêpe** pancake
le livre book	**la livre** pound
le manche handle	**la manche** sleeve
le mode method	**la mode** fashion
le moule mould	**la moule** mussel
le page page(boy)	**la page** page (*in book*)
le physique physique	**la physique** physics
le poêle stove	**la poêle** frying pan
le somme nap	**la somme** sum
le tour turn	**la tour** tower
le voile veil	**la voile** sail

Gender: the Formation of Feminines

As in English, male and female are sometimes differentiated by the use of two quite separate words, e.g.

      mon oncle my uncle
      ma tante my aunt
      un taureau a bull
      une vache a cow

There are, however, some words in French which show this distinction by the form of their ending:

Some nouns add an **e** to the masculine singular form to form the feminine → **1**

If the masculine singular form already ends in **-e**, no further **e** is added in the feminine → **2**

Some nouns undergo a further change when **e** is added. These changes occur regularly and are shown on page 136.

Feminine forms to note

MASCULINE	FEMININE	
un âne	une ânesse	donkey
le comte	la comtesse	count/countess
le duc	la duchesse	duke/duchess
un Esquimau	une Esquimaude	Eskimo
le fou	la folle	madman/madwoman
le Grec	la Grecque	Greek
un hôte	une hôtesse	host/hostess
le jumeau	la jumelle	twin
le maître	la maîtresse	master/mistress
le prince	la princesse	prince/princess
le tigre	la tigresse	tiger/tigress
le traître	la traîtresse	traitor
le Turc	la Turque	Turk
le vieux	la vieille	old man/old woman

Examples

① un ami   a (*male*) friend
une amie   a (*female*) friend
un employé   a (*male*) employee
une employée   a (*female*) employee
un Français   a Frenchman
une Française   a Frenchwoman

② un élève   a (*male*) pupil
une élève   a (*female*) pupil
un collègue   a (*male*) colleague
une collègue   a (*female*) colleague
un camarade   a (*male*) friend
une camarade   a (*female*) friend

Regular feminine endings

The following are regular feminine endings:

MASC. SING.	FEM. SING.
-f	-ve → ①
-x	-se → ②
-eur	-euse → ③
-teur	-teuse → ④
	-trice → ⑤

Some nouns double the final consonant before adding **e**:

MASC. SING.	FEM. SING.
-an	-anne → ⑥
-en	-enne → ⑦
-on	-onne → ⑧
-et	-ette → ⑨
-el	-elle → ⑩

Some nouns add an accent to the final syllable before adding **e**:

MASC. SING.	FEM. SING.
-er	-ère → ⑪

Pronunciation and feminine endings

This is dealt with on page 244.

Examples

1. un sportif a sportsman
   un veuf a widower
   une sportive a sportswoman
   une veuve a widow

2. un époux a husband
   un amoureux a man in love
   une épouse a wife
   une amoureuse a woman in love

3. un danseur a dancer
   un voleur a thief
   une danseuse a dancer
   une voleuse a thief

4. un menteur a liar
   un chanteur a singer
   une menteuse a liar
   une chanteuse a singer

5. un acteur an actor
   un conducteur a driver
   une actrice an actress
   une conductrice a driver

6. un paysan a countryman
   une paysanne a countrywoman

7. un Parisien a Parisian (*man*)
   une Parisienne a Parisian (*woman*)

8. un baron a baron
   une baronne a baroness

9. le cadet the youngest (child)
   la cadette the youngest (child)

10. un intellectuel an intellectual
    une intellectuelle an intellectual

11. un étranger a foreigner
    le dernier the last (one)
    une étrangère a foreigner
    la dernière the last (one)

The Formation of Plurals

Most nouns add **s** to the singular form → **1**

When the singular form already ends in **-s**, **-x** or **-z**, no further **s** is added → **2**

For nouns ending in **-au**, **-eau** or **-eu**, the plural ends in **-aux**, **-eaux** or **-eux** → **3**
EXCEPTIONS: **pneu** tyre   (*plural*: **pneus**)
　　　　　　bleu bruise   (*plural*: **bleus**)

For nouns ending in **-al** or **-ail**, the plural ends in **-aux** → **4**
EXCEPTIONS: **bal** ball   (*plural*: **bals**)
　　　　　　festival festival   (*plural*: **festivals**)
　　　　　　chandail sweater   (*plural*: **chandails**)
　　　　　　détail detail   (*plural*: **détails**)

Forming the plural of compound nouns is complicated and you are advised to check each one individually in a dictionary.

Irregular plural forms

Some masculine nouns ending in **-ou** add **x** in the plural. These are:

bijou jewel	**genou** knee	**joujou** toy
caillou pebble	**hibou** owl	**pou** louse
chou cabbage		

Some other nouns are totally unpredictable. The most important of these are:

SINGULAR		PLURAL
œil	eye	**yeux**
ciel	sky	**cieux**
Monsieur	Mr	**Messieurs**
Madame	Mrs	**Mesdames**
Mademoiselle	Miss	**Mesdemoiselles**

Pronunciation of plural forms

This is dealt with on page 244.

Examples

1 le jardin   the garden
    les jardins   the gardens
    une voiture   a car
    des voitures   (some) cars
    l'hôtel   the hotel
    les hôtels   the hotels

2 un bois   a wood
    des bois   (some) woods
    une voix   a voice
    des voix   (some) voices
    le gaz   the gas
    les gaz   the gases

3 un tuyau   a pipe
    des tuyaux   (some) pipes
    le chapeau   the hat
    les chapeaux   the hats
    le feu   the fire
    les feux   the fires

4 le journal   the newspaper
    les journaux   the newspapers
    un travail   a job
    des travaux   (some) jobs

The Definite Article

le (l')/la (l'), les

	WITH MASC. NOUN	WITH FEM. NOUN	
SING.	le (l')	la (l')	the
PLUR.	les	les	the

The gender and number of the noun determines the form of the article → **1**

le and la change to l' before a vowel or an h 'mute' → **2**

For uses of the definite article see page 142.

à + le/la (l'), à + les

	WITH MASC. NOUN	WITH FEM. NOUN
SING.	au (à l')	à la (à l')
PLUR.	aux	aux

The definite article combines with the preposition à, as shown above. You should pay particular attention to the masculine singular form **au**, and both plural forms **aux**, since these are not visually the sum of their parts → **3**

de + le/la (l'), de + les

	WITH MASC. NOUN	WITH FEM. NOUN
SING.	du (de l')	de la (de l')
PLUR.	des	des

The definite article combines with the preposition **de**, as shown above. You should pay particular attention to the masculine singular form **du**, and both plural forms **des**, since these are not visually the sum of their parts → **4**

Examples

MASCULINE	FEMININE
1 le train the train	la gare the station
le garçon the boy	la fille the girl
les hôtels the hotels	les écoles the schools
les professeurs the teachers	les femmes the women
2 l'acteur the actor	l'actrice the actress
l'effet the effect	l'eau the water
l'ingrédient the ingredient	l'idée the idea
l'objet the object	l'ombre the shadow
l'univers the universe	l'usine the factory
l'hôpital the hospital	l'heure the time
3 au cinéma at/to the cinema	à la bibliothèque at/to the library
à l'employé to the employee	à l'infirmière to the nurse
à l'hôpital at/to the hospital	à l'hôtesse to the hostess
aux étudiants to the students	aux maisons to the houses
4 du bureau from/of the office	de la réunion from/of the meeting
de l'auteur from/of the author	de l'Italienne from/of the Italian woman
de l'hôte from/of the host	de l'horloge of the clock
des États-Unis from/of the United States	des vendeuses from/of the saleswomen

Uses of the Definite Article

While the definite article is used in much the same way in French as it is in English, its use is more widespread in French. Unlike English the definite article is also used:

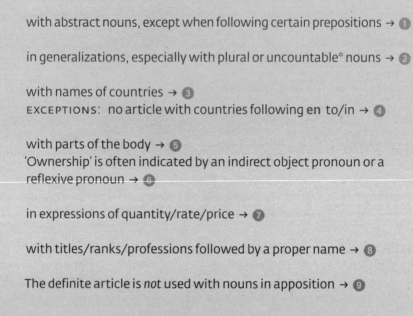

with abstract nouns, except when following certain prepositions → ❶

in generalizations, especially with plural or uncountable* nouns → ❷

with names of countries → ❸
EXCEPTIONS: no article with countries following **en** to/in → ❹

with parts of the body → ❺
'Ownership' is often indicated by an indirect object pronoun or a reflexive pronoun → ❻

in expressions of quantity/rate/price → ❼

with titles/ranks/professions followed by a proper name → ❽

The definite article is *not* used with nouns in apposition → ❾

---

* An uncountable noun is one which cannot be used in the plural or with an indefinite article, e.g. **l'acier** steel; **le lait** milk.

Examples

1 Les prix montent
    L'amour rayonne dans ses yeux
    BUT:
    avec plaisir
    sans espoir

Prices are rising
Love shines in his eyes

with pleasure
without hope

2 Je n'aime pas le café
    Les enfants ont besoin d'être
      aimés

I don't like coffee
Children need to be loved

3 le Japon
    la France
    l'Italie
    les Pays-Bas

Japan
France
Italy
The Netherlands

4 aller en Écosse
    Il travaille en Allemagne

to go to Scotland
He works in Germany

5 Tournez la tête à gauche
    J'ai mal à la gorge

Turn your head to the left
My throat is sore, I have a sore
  throat

6 La tête me tourne
    Elle s'est brossé les dents

My head is spinning
She brushed her teeth

7 4 euros le mètre/le kilo/
      la douzaine/la pièce
    rouler à 80 km à l'heure
    payé à l'heure/au jour/au mois

4 euros a metre/a kilo/a dozen/
  each
to go at 50 mph
paid by the hour/by the day/
  by the month

8 le roi Georges III
    le capitaine Darbeau
    le docteur Rousseau
    Monsieur le président

King George III
Captain Darbeau
Dr Rousseau
Mr Chairman/President

9 Victor Hugo, grand écrivain du
      dix-neuvième siècle
    Joseph Leblanc, inventeur et
      entrepreneur, a été le premier ...

Victor Hugo, a great author of
  the nineteenth century
Joseph Leblanc, an inventor and
  entrepreneur, was the first ...

The Partitive Article

The partitive article has the sense of 'some' or 'any', although the French is not always translated in English.

Forms of the partitive

du (de l')/de la (de l'), des

	WITH MASC. NOUN	WITH FEM. NOUN	
SING.	du (de l')	de la (de l')	some, any
PLUR.	des	des	some, any

The gender and number of the noun determines the form of the partitive → ❶

The forms shown in brackets (**de l'**) are used before a vowel or an h 'mute' → ❷

des becomes **de** (**d'** + *vowel*) before an adjective → ❸
EXCEPTION: if the adjective and noun are seen as forming one unit → ❹

In negative sentences **de** (**d'** + *vowel*) is used for both genders, singular and plural → ❺
EXCEPTION: after **ne ... que** 'only', the positive forms above are used → ❻

Examples

1 Avez-vous du sucre? — Have you any sugar?
J'ai acheté de la farine et de la margarine — I bought (some) flour and margarine
Il a mangé des gâteaux — He ate some cakes
Est-ce qu'il y a des lettres pour moi? — Are there (any) letters for me?

2 Il me doit de l'argent — He owes me (some) money
C'est de l'histoire ancienne — That's ancient history

3 Il a fait de gros efforts pour nous aider — He made a great effort to help us
Cette région a de belles églises — This region has some beautiful churches

4 des grandes vacances — summer holidays
des jeunes gens — young people

5 Je n'ai pas de nourriture/d'argent — I don't have any food/money
Vous n'avez pas de timbres/d'œufs? — Have you no stamps/eggs?
Je ne mange jamais de viande/d'omelettes — I never eat meat/omelettes
Il ne veut plus de visiteurs/d'eau — He doesn't want any more visitors/water

6 Il ne boit que du thé/de la bière/de l'eau — He only drinks tea/beer/water
Je n'ai que des problèmes avec cette machine — I have nothing but trouble with this machine

The Indefinite Article

un/une, des

	WITH MASC. NOUN	WITH FEM. NOUN	
SING.	un	une	a
PLUR.	des	des	some

des is also the plural of the partitive article (see page 144).

In negative sentences, **de** (**d'** + *vowel*) is used for both singular and plural → ❶

The indefinite article is used in French largely as it is in English *except*:

there is no article when a person's profession is being stated → ❷
EXCEPTION: the article *is* present following **ce** (**c'** + *vowel*) → ❸

the English article is not translated by **un/une** in constructions like 'what a surprise', 'what an idiot' → ❹

in structures of the type given in example ❺ the article **un/une** is used in French and not translated in English → ❺

Examples

① Je n'ai pas de livre/d'enfants

I don't have a book/(any) children

② Il est professeur
Ma mère est infirmière

He's a teacher
My mother's a nurse

③ C'est un médecin
Ce sont des acteurs

He's/She's a doctor
They're actors

④ Quelle surprise!
Quel dommage!

What a surprise!
What a shame!

⑤ avec une grande sagesse/un courage admirable
Il a fait preuve d'un sang-froid incroyable
un produit d'une qualité incomparable

with great wisdom /admirable courage
He showed incredible calmness
a product of incomparable quality

Adjectives

Most adjectives agree in number and in gender with the noun or pronoun.

The formation of feminines

Most adjectives add an **e** to the masculine singular form → ❶

If the masculine singular form already ends in **-e**, no further **e** is added → ❷

Some adjectives undergo a further change when **e** is added. These changes occur regularly and are shown on page 150.

Irregular feminine forms are shown on page 152.

The formation of plurals

The plural of both regular and irregular adjectives is formed by adding an **s** to the masculine or feminine singular form, as appropriate → ❸

When the masculine singular form already ends in **-s** or **-x**, no further **s** is added → ❹

For masculine singulars ending in **-au** and **-eau**, the masculine plural is **-aux** and **-eaux** → ❺

For masculine singulars ending in **-al**, the masculine plural is **-aux** → ❻
EXCEPTIONS: **final** (*masculine plural* **finals**)
  fatal (*masculine plural* **fatals**)
  naval (*masculine plural* **navals**)

Pronunciation of feminine and plural adjectives

This is dealt with on page 244.

Examples

1. mon frère aîné   my elder brother
   ma sœur aînée   my elder sister
   le petit garçon   the little boy
   la petite fille   the little girl
   un sac gris   a grey bag
   une chemise grise   a grey shirt
   un bruit fort   a loud noise
   une voix forte   a loud voice

2. un jeune homme   a young man
   une jeune femme   a young woman
   l'autre verre   the other glass
   l'autre assiette   the other plate

3. le dernier train   the last train
   les derniers trains   the last trains
   une vieille maison   an old house
   de vieilles maisons   old houses
   un long voyage   a long journey
   de longs voyages   long journeys
   la rue étroite   the narrow street
   les rues étroites   the narrow streets

4. un diplomate français   a French diplomat
   des diplomates français   French diplomats
   un homme dangereux   a dangerous man
   des hommes dangereux   dangerous men

5. le nouveau professeur   the new teacher
   les nouveaux professeurs   the new teachers
   un chien esquimau   a husky (*literally*: an Eskimo dog)
   des chiens esquimaux   huskies (*literally*: Eskimo dogs)

6. un ami loyal   a loyal friend
   des amis loyaux   loyal friends
   un geste amical   a friendly gesture
   des gestes amicaux   friendly gestures

Regular feminine endings

MASC SING.	FEM. SING.	EXAMPLES
-f	-ve	neuf, vif → ❶
-x	-se	heureux, jaloux → ❷
-eur	-euse	travailleur, flâneur → ❸
-teur	-teuse	flatteur, menteur → ❹
	-trice	destructeur, séducteur → ❺

EXCEPTIONS: **bref**: see page 152

doux, **faux**, **roux**, **vieux**: see page 152

extérieur, **inférieur**, **intérieur**, **meilleur**, **supérieur**: all add **e** to the masculine

enchanteur: *fem.* = **enchanteresse**

MASC SING.	FEM. SING.	EXAMPLES
-an	-anne	paysan → ❻
-en	-enne	ancien, parisien → ❼
-on	-onne	bon, breton → ❽
-as	-asse	bas, las → ❾
-et*	-ette	muet, violet → ❿
-el	-elle	annuel, mortel → ⓫
-eil	-eille	pareil, vermeil → ⓬

EXCEPTION: **ras**: *fem.* = **rase**

MASC SING.	FEM. SING.	EXAMPLES
-et*	-ète	secret, complet → ⓭
-er	-ète	étranger, fier → ⓮

* Note that there are two feminine endings for masculine adjectives ending in -**et**.

Examples

1. un résultat positif — a positive result
   une attitude positive — a positive attitude

2. d'un ton sérieux — in a serious tone (of voice)
   une voix sérieuse — a serious voice

3. un enfant trompeur — a deceitful child
   une déclaration trompeuse — a misleading statement

4. un tableau flatteur — a flattering picture
   une comparaison flatteuse — a flattering comparison

5. un geste protecteur — a protective gesture
   une couche protectrice — a protective layer

6. un problème paysan — a farming problem
   la vie paysanne — country life

7. un avion égyptien — an Egyptian plane
   une statue égyptienne — an Egyptian statue

8. un bon repas — a good meal
   de bonne humeur — in a good mood

9. un plafond bas — a low ceiling
   à voix basse — in a low voice

10. un travail net — a clean piece of work
    une explication nette — a clear explanation

11. un homme cruel — a cruel man
    une remarque cruelle — a cruel remark

12. un livre pareil — such a book
    en pareille occasion — on such an occasion

13. un regard inquiet — an anxious look
    une attente inquiète — an anxious wait

14. un goût amer — a bitter taste
    une amère déception — a bitter disappointment

Adjectives with irregular feminine forms

MASC SING.	FEM. SING.	
aigu	aiguë	sharp; high-pitched → ①
ambigu	ambiguë	ambiguous
beau (bel*)	belle	beautiful
bénin	bénigne	benign
blanc	blanche	white
bref	brève	brief, short → ②
doux	douce	soft; sweet
épais	épaisse	thick
esquimau	esquimaude	Eskimo
faux	fausse	wrong
favori	favorite	favourite → ③
fou (fol*)	folle	mad
frais	fraîche	fresh → ④
franc	franche	frank
gentil	gentille	kind
grec	grecque	Greek
gros	grosse	big
jumeau	jumelle	twin → ⑤
long	longue	long
malin	maligne	malignant
mou (mol*)	molle	soft
nouveau (nouvel*)	nouvelle	new
nul	nulle	no
public	publique	public → ⑥
roux	rousse	red-haired
sec	sèche	dry
sot	sotte	foolish
turc	turque	Turkish
vieux (vieil*)	vieille	old

* This form is used when the following word begins with a vowel or an **h** 'mute' → ⑦

Examples

1. un son aigu — a high-pitched sound
   une douleur aiguë — a sharp pain

2. un bref discours — a short speech
   une brève rencontre — a short meeting

3. mon sport favori — my favourite sport
   ma chanson favorite — my favourite song

4. du pain frais — fresh bread
   de la crème fraîche — fresh cream

5. mon frère jumeau — my twin brother
   ma sœur jumelle — my twin sister

6. un jardin public — a (public) park
   l'opinion publique — public opinion

7. un bel appartement — a beautiful flat
   le nouvel ordinateur — the new computer
   un vieil arbre — an old tree
   un bel habit — a beautiful outfit
   un nouvel harmonica — a new harmonica
   un vieil hôtel — an old hotel

Comparatives and Superlatives

Comparatives

These are formed using the following constructions:

plus ... (que) more ... (than) → ①
moins ... (que) less ... (than) → ②
aussi ... que as ... as → ③
si ... que* as ... as → ④

* used mainly after a negative

Superlatives

These are formed using the following constructions:

le/la/les plus ... (que) the most ... (that) → ⑤
le/la/les moins ... (que) the least ... (that) → ⑥

When the possessive adjective is present, two constructions are possible → ⑦

After a superlative the preposition **de** is often translated as 'in' → ⑧

If a clause follows a superlative, the verb is in the subjunctive → ⑨

Adjectives with irregular comparatives/superlatives

ADJECTIVE	COMPARATIVE	SUPERLATIVE
bon	**meilleur**	**le meilleur**
good	better	the best
mauvais	**pire** *or* **plus mauvais**	**le pire** *or* **le plus mauvais**
bad	worse	the worst
petit	**moindre*** *or* **plus petit**	**le moindre*** *or* **le plus petit**
small	smaller; lesser	the smallest; the least

* used only with abstract nouns

Comparative and superlative adjectives agree in number and in gender with the noun, just like any other adjective → ⑩

Examples

1. une raison plus grave — a more serious reason
   Elle est plus petite que moi — She is smaller than me

2. un film moins connu — a less well-known film
   C'est moins cher qu'il ne pense — It's cheaper than he thinks

3. Robert était aussi inquiet que moi — Robert was as worried as I was
   Cette ville n'est pas aussi grande que Bordeaux — This town isn't as big as Bordeaux

4. Ils ne sont pas si contents que ça — They aren't as happy as all that

5. le guide le plus utile — the most useful guidebook
   la voiture la plus petite — the smallest car
   les plus grandes maisons — the biggest houses

6. le mois le moins agréable — the least pleasant month
   la fille la moins forte — the weakest girl
   les peintures les moins chères — the least expensive paintings

7. Mon désir le plus cher est de voyager — My dearest wish is to travel
   Mon plus cher désir est de voyager

8. la plus grande gare de Londres — the biggest station in London
   l'habitant le plus âgé du village/de la région — the oldest inhabitant in the village/in the area

9. la personne la plus gentille que je connaisse — the nicest person I know

10. les moindres difficultés — the least difficulties
    la meilleure qualité — the best quality

Demonstrative Adjectives

ce (cet)/cette, ces

	MASCULINE	FEMININE	
SING.	ce (cet)	cette	this; that
PLUR.	ces	ces	these; those

Demonstrative adjectives agree in number and gender with the noun → ①

cet is used when the following word begins with a vowel or an **h** 'mute' → ②

For emphasis or in order to distinguish between people or objects, **-ci** or **-là** is added to the noun: **-ci** indicates proximity (usually translated 'this') and **là** distance 'that' → ③

Examples

1 Ce stylo ne marche pas

This/That pen isn't working

Comment s'appelle cette
entreprise?

What's this/that company
called?

Ces livres sont les miens

These/Those books are mine

Ces couleurs sont plus jolies

These/Those colours are nicer

2 cet oiseau

this/that bird

cet article

this/that article

cet homme

this/that man

3 Combien coûte ce manteau-ci?

How much is this coat?

Je voudrais cinq de ces pommes-là

I'd like five of those apples

Est-ce que tu reconnais cette
personne-là?

Do you recognize that person?

Mettez ces vêtements-ci dans
cette valise-là

Put these clothes in that case

Ce garçon-là appartient à ce
groupe-ci

That boy belongs to this group

Adjectives

Interrogative Adjectives

quel/quelle, quels/quelles?

	MASCULINE	FEMININE	
SING.	quel?	quelle?	what?; which?
PLUR.	quels?	quelles?	what?; which?

Interrogative adjectives agree in number and gender with the noun → ❶

The forms shown above are also used in indirect questions → ❷

Exclamatory Adjectives

quel/quelle, quels/quelles!

	MASCULINE	FEMININE	
SING.	quel!	quelle!	what (a)!
PLUR.	quels!	quelles!	what!

Exclamatory adjectives agree in number and gender with the noun → ❸

For other exclamations, see page 214.

Examples

1 Quel genre d'homme est-ce? — What type of man is he?
Quelle est leur décision? — What is their decision?
Vous jouez de quels instruments? — What instruments do you play?
Quelles offres avez-vous reçues? — What offers have you received?
Quel vin recommandez-vous? — Which wine do you recommend?
Quelles couleurs préférez-vous? — Which colours do you prefer?

2 Je ne sais pas à quelle heure il est arrivé — I don't know what time he arrived
Dites-moi quels sont les livres les plus chers — Tell me which books are the most expensive

3 Quel dommage! — What a pity!
Quelle idée! — What an idea!
Quels livres intéressants vous avez! — What interesting books you have!
Quelles jolies fleurs! — What nice flowers!

Possessive Adjectives

WITH SING. NOUN		WITH PLUR. NOUN	
MASC.	FEM.	MASC./FEM.	
mon	ma (mon)	mes	my
ton	ta (ton)	tes	your
son	sa (son)	ses	his; her; its
notre	notre	nos	our
votre	votre	vos	your
leur	leur	leurs	their

Possessive adjectives agree in number and gender with the noun, not with the owner → ❶

The forms shown in brackets are used when the following word begins with a vowel or an h 'mute' → ❷

son, sa, ses have the additional meaning of 'one's' → ❸

Examples

1. Catherine a oublié son parapluie — Catherine has left her umbrella
   Paul cherche sa montre — Paul's looking for his watch
   Mon frère et ma sœur habitent à Glasgow — My brother and sister live in Glasgow
   Est-ce que tes voisins ont vendu leur voiture? — Did your neighbours sell their car?
   Rangez vos affaires — Put your things away

2. mon appareil-photo — my camera
   ton histoire — your story
   son erreur — his/her mistake
   mon autre sœur — my other sister

3. perdre son équilibre — to lose one's balance
   présenter ses excuses — to offer one's apologies

Position of Adjectives

French adjectives usually follow the noun → ❶

Adjectives of colour or nationality *always* follow the noun → ❷

As in English, demonstrative, possessive, numerical and interrogative adjectives precede the noun → ❸

The adjectives **autre** (other) and **chaque** (each, every) precede the noun → ❹

The following common adjectives can precede the noun:

beau beautiful	**jeune** young
bon good	**joli** pretty
court short	**long** long
dernier last	**mauvais** bad
grand great	**petit** small
gros big	**tel** such (a)
haut high	**vieux** old

The meaning of the following adjectives varies according to their position:

	BEFORE NOUN	AFTER NOUN
ancien	former	old, ancient → ❺
brave	good	brave → ❻
cher	dear (*beloved*)	expensive → ❼
grand	great	tall → ❽
même	same	very → ❾
pauvre	poor (*wretched*)	poor (*not rich*) → ❿
propre	own	clean → ⓫
seul	single, sole	on one's own → ⓬
simple	mere, simple	simple, easy → ⓭
vrai	real	true → ⓮

Adjectives following the noun are linked by **et** → ⓯

Examples

1 le chapitre suivant — the following chapter
l'heure exacte — the right time

2 une cravate rouge — a red tie
un mot français — a French word

3 ce dictionnaire — this dictionary
mon père — my father
le premier étage — the first floor
deux exemples — two examples
quel homme? — which man?

4 une autre fois — another time
chaque jour — every day

5 un ancien collègue — a former colleague
l'histoire ancienne — ancient history

6 un brave homme — a good man
un homme brave — a brave man

7 mes chers amis — my dear friends
une robe chère — an expensive dress

8 un grand peintre — a great painter
un homme grand — a tall man

9 la même réponse — the same answer
vos paroles mêmes — your very words

10 cette pauvre femme — that poor woman
une nation pauvre — a poor nation

11 ma propre vie — my own life
une chemise propre — a clean shirt

12 une seule réponse — a single reply
une femme seule — a woman on her own

13 un simple regard — a mere look
un problème simple — a simple problem

14 la vraie raison — the real reason
les faits vrais — the true facts

15 un acte lâche et trompeur — a cowardly, deceitful act
un acte lâche, trompeur et ignoble — a cowardly, deceitful and ignoble act

Personal Pronouns

	SUBJECT PRONOUNS	
	SINGULAR	PLURAL
1ˢᵗ person	je (j') I	nous we
2ⁿᵈ person	tu you	vous you
3ʳᵈ person (*masc.*)	il he; it	ils they
(*fem.*)	elle she; it	elles they

je changes to **j'** before a vowel, an **h** 'mute', or the pronoun **y** → ➊

tu/vous
Vous, as well as being the second person plural, is also used when addressing one person. As a general rule, use **tu** only when addressing a friend, a child, a relative, someone you know very well, or when invited to do so. In all other cases use **vous**. For singular and plural uses of **vous**, see example ➋

il/elle; ils/elles
The form of the 3ʳᵈ person pronouns reflects the number and gender of the noun(s) they replace, referring to animals and things as well as to people. **Ils** also replaces a combination of masculine and feminine nouns → ➌

Sometimes stressed pronouns replace the subject pronouns, see page 172.

Examples

1 J'arrive!   I'm just coming!

J'arrive!	I'm just coming!
J'en ai trois	I've got three of them
J'hésite à le déranger	I hesitate to disturb him
J'y pense souvent	I often think about it

2 Compare:

Vous êtes certain, Monsieur Leclerc?	Are you sure, Mr Leclerc?

and:

Vous êtes certains, les enfants?	Are you sure, children?

Compare:

Vous êtes partie quand, Estelle?	When did you leave, Estelle?

and:

Estelle et Sophie – vous êtes parties quand?	Estelle and Sophie – when did you leave?

3

Où logent ton père et ta mère quand ils vont à Rome?	Where do your father and mother stay when they go to Rome?
Donne-moi le journal et les lettres quand ils arriveront	Give me the newspaper and the letters when they arrive

Personal Pronouns *continued*

	DIRECT OBJECT PRONOUNS	
	SINGULAR	PLURAL
1st person	me (m') me	nous us
2nd person	te (t') you	vous you
3rd person (*masc.*)	le (l') him; it	ils them
(*fem.*)	la (l') her; it	elles them

The forms shown in brackets are used before a vowel, an **h** 'mute', or the pronoun **y** → ❶

In positive commands **me** and **te** change to **moi** and **toi** except before **en** or **y** → ❷

le sometimes functions as a 'neuter' pronoun, referring to an idea or information contained in a previous statement or question. It is often not translated → ❸

Position of direct object pronouns

In constructions other than the imperative affirmative, the pronoun comes before the verb → ❹

The same applies when the verb is in the infinitive → ❺

In the imperative affirmative, the pronoun follows the verb and is attached to it by a hyphen → ❻

For further information, see Order of Object Pronouns, page 170.

Reflexive Pronouns

These are dealt with under reflexive verbs, page 30.

Examples

1. Il m'a vu — He saw me
   Je ne t'oublierai jamais — I'll never forget you
   Ça l'habitue à travailler seul — That gets him/her used to working on his/her own

   Je veux l'y accoutumer — I want to accustom him/her to it

2. Avertis-moi de ta décision — Inform me of your decision
   Avertis-m'en — Inform me of it

3. Il n'est pas là. — Je le sais bien. — He isn't there. — I know that.
   Aidez-moi si vous le pouvez — Help me if you can
   Elle viendra demain. — Je l'espère bien. — She'll come tomorrow. — I hope so.

4. Je t'aime — I love you
   Les voyez-vous? — Can you see them?
   Elle ne nous connaît pas — She doesn't know us
   Est-ce que tu ne les aimes pas? — Don't you like them?
   Ne me faites pas rire — Don't make me laugh

5. Puis-je vous aider? — May I help you?

6. Aidez-moi — Help me
   Suivez-nous — Follow us

Personal Pronouns *continued*

	INDIRECT OBJECT PRONOUNS	
	SINGULAR	PLURAL
1st person	me (m')	nous
2nd person	te (t')	vous
3rd person (*masc.*)	lui	leur
(*fem.*)	lui	leur

me and **te** change to **m'** and **t'** before a vowel or an h 'mute' → ❶

In positive commands, **me** and **te** change to **moi** and **toi** except before **en** → ❷

The pronouns shown in the above table replace the preposition à + *noun*, where the noun is a person or an animal → ❸

The verbal construction affects the translation of the pronoun → ❹

Position of indirect object pronouns

In constructions other than the imperative affirmative, the pronoun comes before the verb → ❺

The same applies when the verb is in the infinitive → ❻

In the imperative affirmative, the pronoun follows the verb and is attached to it by a hyphen → ❼

For further information, see Order of Object Pronouns, page 170.

Reflexive Pronouns

These are dealt with under reflexive verbs, page 30.

Examples

① Tu m'as donné ce livre — You gave me this book
Ils t'ont caché les faits — They hid the facts from you

② Donnez-moi du sucre — Give me some sugar
Donnez-m'en — Give me some
Garde-toi assez d'argent — Keep enough money for yourself
Garde-t'en assez — Keep enough for yourself

③ J'écris à Suzanne — I'm writing to Suzanne
Je lui écris — I'm writing to her
Donne du lait au chat — Give the cat some milk
Donne-lui du lait — Give it some milk

④ arracher qch à qn: — to snatch sth from sb:
  Un voleur m'a arraché mon — A thief snatched my purse from
    porte-monnaie — me
promettre qch à qn: — to promise sb sth:
  Il leur a promis un cadeau — He promised them a present
demander à qn de faire: — to ask sb to do:
  Elle nous avait demandé de — She had asked us to come back
    revenir

⑤ Elle vous a écrit — She's written to you
Vous a-t-elle écrit? — Has she written to you?
Il ne nous parle pas — He doesn't speak to us
Est-ce que cela ne vous intéresse — Doesn't it interest you?
  pas?
Ne leur répondez pas — Don't answer them

⑥ Voulez-vous leur envoyer — Do you want to send them the
  l'adresse? — address?

⑦ Répondez-moi — Answer me
Donnez-nous la réponse — Tell us the answer

Personal Pronouns *continued*

Order of object pronouns

When two object pronouns of different persons come before the verb, the order is: indirect before direct, i.e.

me			
te		le	
nous	before	la	→ ❶
vous		les	

When two 3rd person object pronouns come before the verb, the order is: direct before indirect, i.e.

le			
la	before	lui	→ ❷
les		leur	

When two object pronouns come after the verb (i.e. in the imperative affirmative), the order is: direct before indirect, i.e.

		moi	
		toi	
le		lui	
la	before	nous	→ ❸
les		vous	
		leur	

The pronouns **y** and **en** (see pages 176 and 174) always come last → ❹

Examples

1 Dominique vous l'envoie demain — Dominique's sending it to you tomorrow

Est-ce qu'il te les a montrés? — Has he shown them to you?

Ne me le dis pas — Don't tell me (it)

Il ne veut pas nous la prêter — He won't lend it to us

2 Elle le leur a emprunté — She borrowed it from them

Je les lui ai lus — I read them to him/her

Ne la leur donne pas — Don't give it to them

Je voudrais les lui rendre — I'd like to give them back to him/her

3 Rends-les-moi — Give them back to me

Donnez-le-nous — Give it to us

Apportons-les-leur — Let's take them to them

4 Donnez-leur-en — Give them some

Je l'y ai déposé — I dropped him there

Ne nous en parlez plus — Don't speak to us about it any more

Personal Pronouns *continued*

	STRESSED OR DISJUNCTIVE PRONOUNS	
	SINGULAR	PLURAL
1st person	**moi** me	**nous** us
2nd person	**toi** you	**vous** you
3rd person (*masc.*)	**lui** him; it	**eux** them
(*fem.*)	**elle** her; it	**elles** them
(*reflexive*)	**soi** oneself	

These pronouns are used:
- after prepositions → ❶
- on their own → ❷
- following **c'est, ce sont** it is → ❸
- for emphasis, especially where contrast is involved → ❹
- when the subject consists of two or more pronouns → ❺
- when the subject consists of a pronoun and a noun → ❻
- in comparisons → ❼
- before relative pronouns → ❽

For particular emphasis **-même** (*singular*) or **-mêmes** (*plural*) is added to the pronoun → ❾

moi-même myself	**nous-mêmes** ourselves
toi-même yourself	**vous-même** yourself
lui-même himself; itself	**vous-mêmes** yourselves
elle-même herself; itself	**eux-mêmes** themselves
soi-même oneself	**elles-mêmes** themselves

Examples

1 Je pense à toi — I think about you
Partez sans eux — Leave without them
C'est pour elle — This is for her
Assieds-toi à côté de lui — Sit beside him
Venez avec moi — Come with me
Il a besoin de nous — He needs us

2 Qui a fait cela? — Lui. — Who did that? — He did.
Qui est-ce qui gagne? — Moi. — Who's winning? — Me.

3 C'est toi, Simon? — Non, c'est moi, David. — Is that you, Simon? — No, it's me, David.
Qui est-ce? — Ce sont eux. — Who is it? — It's them.

4 Ils voyagent séparément: lui par le train, elle en autobus — They travel separately: he by train and she by bus
Toi, tu ressembles à ton père, eux pas — You look like your father, they don't
Il n'a pas l'air de s'ennuyer, lui! — He doesn't look bored!

5 Lui et moi partons demain — He and I are leaving tomorrow
Ni vous ni elles ne pouvez rester — Neither you nor they can stay

6 Mon père et elle ne s'entendent pas — My father and she don't get on

7 plus jeune que moi — younger than me
Il est moins grand que toi — He's smaller than you (are)

8 Moi, qui étais malade, je n'ai pas pu les accompagner — I, who was ill, couldn't go with them
Ce sont eux qui font du bruit, pas nous — They're the ones making the noise, not us

9 Je l'ai fait moi-même — I did it myself

The pronoun en

en replaces the preposition **de** + *noun* → ❶

The verbal construction can affect the translation → ❷

en also replaces the partitive article (English = some, any) + *noun* → ❸

In expressions of quantity en represents the noun → ❹

Position: **en** comes before the verb, except in positive commands when it follows and is attached to the verb by a hyphen → ❺

en follows other object pronouns → ❻

Examples

① | Il est fier de son succès | He's proud of his success
| Il en est fier | He's proud of it
| Elle est sortie du cinéma | She came out of the cinema
| Elle en est sortie | She came out (of it)
| Je suis couvert de peinture | I'm covered in paint
| J'en suis couvert | I'm covered in it
| Il a beaucoup d'amis | He has lots of friends
| Il en a beaucoup | He has lots (of them)

② | avoir besoin de qch: | to need sth:
| J'en ai besoin | I need it/them
| avoir peur de qch: | to be afraid of sth:
| J'en ai peur | I'm afraid of it/them

③ | Avez-vous de l'argent? | Do you have any money?
| En avez-vous? | Do you have any?
| Je veux acheter des timbres | I want to buy some stamps
| Je veux en acheter | I want to buy some

④ | J'ai deux crayons | I've two pencils
| J'en ai deux | I've two (of them)
| Combien de sœurs as-tu? — J'en ai trois. | How many sisters do you have? — I have three.

⑤ | Elle en a discuté avec moi | She discussed it with me
| En êtes-vous content? | Are you pleased with it/them?
| Je veux an garder trois | I want to keep three of them
| N'en parlez plus | Don't talk about it any more
| Prenez-en | Take some
| Soyez-en fier | Be proud of it/them

⑥ | Donnez-leur-en | Give them some
| Il m'en a parlé | He spoke to me about it

The pronoun y

y replaces the preposition à + *noun* → **1**

The verbal construction can affect the translation → **2**

y also replaces the prepositions **dans** and **sur** + *noun* → **3**

y can also mean 'there' → **4**

Position: **y** comes before the verb, except in positive commands when it follows and is attached to the verb by a hyphen → **5**

y follows other object pronouns → **6**

Examples

1 Ne touchez pas à ce bouton — Don't touch this switch
N'y touchez pas — Don't touch it
Il participe aux concerts — He takes part in the concerts
Il y participe — He takes part (in them)

2 penser à qch: — to think about sth:
  J'y pense souvent — I often think about it
consentir à qch: — to agree to sth:
  Tu y as consenti? — Have you agreed to it?

3 Mettez-les dans la boîte — Put them in the box
Mettez-les-y — Put them in it
Il les a mis sur les étagères — He put them on the shelves
Il les y a mis — He put them on them
J'ai placé de l'argent sur ce compte — I've put money into this account
J'y ai placé de l'argent — I've put money into it

4 Elle y passe tout l'été — She spends the whole summer there

5 Il y a ajouté du sucre — He added sugar to it
Elle n'y a pas écrit son nom — She hasn't written her name on it
Comment fait-on pour y aller? — How do you get there?
N'y pense plus! — Don't give it another thought!
Restez-y — Stay there
Réfléchissez-y — Think it over

6 Elle m'y a conduit — She drove me there
Menez-nous-y — Take us there

Indefinite Pronouns

The following are indefinite pronouns:
- **aucun(e)** none, not any → ❶
- **certain(e)s** some, certain → ❷
- **chacun(e)** each (one); everybody → ❸
- **on** one, you; somebody; they, people; we (*informal use*) → ❹
- **personne** nobody → ❺
- **plusieurs** several → ❻
- **quelque chose** something; anything → ❼
- **quelques-un(e)s** some, a few → ❽
- **quelqu'un** somebody; anybody → ❾
- **rien** nothing → ❿
- **tout** all; everything → ⓫
- **tous (toutes)** all → ⓬
- **l'un(e) ... l'autre** (the) one ... the other
- **les un(e)s ... les autres** some ... others → ⓭

aucun(e), personne, rien
When used as subject or object of the verb, these require the word **ne** placed immediately before the verb. Note that **aucun** further needs the pronoun **en** when used as an object → ⓮

quelque chose, rien
When qualified by an adjective, these pronouns require the preposition **de** before the adjective → ⓯

Examples

1 Combien en avez-vous? — Aucun.   How many have you got? — None.

2 Certains pensent que ...   Some (people) think that ...

3 Chacune de ces boîtes est pleine   Each of these boxes is full
Chacun son tour!   Everybody in turn!

4 On voit l'église de cette fenêtre   You can see the church from this window

En semaine on se couche tôt   During the week they/we go to bed early

Est-ce qu'on lui a permis de rester?   Was he/she allowed to stay?

5 Qui voyez-vous? — Personne.   Who can you see? — Nobody.

6 Ils sont plusieurs   There are several of them

7 Mange donc quelque chose!   Eat something!
Tu as vu quelque chose?   Did you see anything?

8 Je connais quelques-uns de ses amis   I know some of his/her friends

9 Quelqu'un a appelé   Somebody called (out)
Tu as vu quelqu'un?   Did you see anybody?

10 Qu'est-ce que tu as dans la main? — Rien.   What have you got in your hand? — Nothing.

11 Il a tout gâché   He has spoiled everything
Tout va bien   All's well

12 Tu les as tous?   Do you have all of them?
Elles sont toutes venues   They all came

13 Les uns sont satisfaits, les autres pas   Some are satisfied, (the) others aren't

14 Je ne vois personne   I can't see anyone
Rien ne lui plaît   Nothing pleases him/her
Aucune des entreprises ne veut ...   None of the companies wants ...
Il n'en a aucun   He hasn't any (of them)

15 quelque chose de grand   something big
rien d'intéressant   nothing interesting

Pronouns

Relative Pronouns

qui who; which
que who(m); which
These are subject and direct object pronouns that introduce a clause and refer to people or things.

	PEOPLE	THINGS
SUBJECT	**qui** who, that → ❶	**qui** which, that → ❸
DIRECT OBJECT	**que (qu')** who(m), that → ❷	**que (qu')** which, that → ❹

> **que** changes to **qu'** before a vowel → ❷/❹

> You cannot omit the object relative pronoun in French as you can in English → ❷/❹

After a preposition:
> When referring to people, use **qui** → ❺
> EXCEPTIONS: after **parmi** 'among' and **entre** 'between' use **lesquels/ lesquelles**; see below → ❻

> When referring to things, use forms of **lequel**:

	MASCULINE	FEMININE	
SING.	**lequel**	**laquelle**	which
PLUR.	**lesquels**	**lesquelles**	which

The pronoun agrees in number and gender with the noun → ❼

> After the prepositions **à** and **de**, **lequel** and **lesquel(le)s** contract as follows:
> à + lequel → auquel
> à + lesquels → auxquels   → ❽
> à + lesquelles → auxquelles
>
> de + lequel → duquel
> de + lesquels → desquels   → ❾
> de + lesquelles → desquelles

Examples

1 Mon frère, qui a vingt ans, est à l'université

My brother, who's twenty, is at university

2 Les amis que je vois le plus sont ...
Lucienne, qu'il connaît depuis longtemps, est ...

The friends (that) I see most are ...
Lucienne, whom he has known for a long time, is ...

3 Il y a un escalier qui mène au toit

There's a staircase which leads to the roof

4 La maison que nous avons achetée a ...
Voici le cadeau qu'elle m'a envoyé

The house (which) we've bought has ...
This is the present (that) she sent me

5 la personne à qui il parle
la personne avec qui je voyage
les enfants pour qui je l'ai acheté

the person he's talking to
the person with whom I travel
the children for whom I bought it

6 Il y avait des jeunes, parmi lesquels Robert
les filles entre lesquelles j'étais assis

There were some young people, Robert among them
the girls between whom I was sitting

7 le torchon avec lequel il l'essuie
la table sur laquelle je l'ai mis
les moyens par lesquels il l'accomplit
les pièces pour lesquelles elle est connue

the cloth with which he's wiping it
the table on which I put it
the means by which he achieves it
the plays for which she is famous

8 le magasin auquel il livre ces marchandises

the shop to which he delivers these goods

9 les injustices desquelles il se plaint

the injustices about which he's complaining

Relative Pronouns *continued*

quoi which, what

> When the relative pronoun does not refer to a specific noun, **quoi** is used after a preposition → ❶

dont whose, of whom, of which

> **dont** often (but not always) replaces **de qui**, **duquel**, **de laquelle**, and **desquel(le)s** → ❷

> It cannot replace **de qui**, **duquel** *etc* in the construction *preposition +* *noun +* **de qui/duquel** → ❸

Examples

1 C'est en quoi vous vous trompez
   À quoi, j'ai répondu ...

That's where you're wrong
To which I replied, ...

2 la femme dont (= *de qui*) la
   voiture est garée en face

the woman whose car is parked
   opposite

un prix dont (= *de qui*) je suis fier

an award I am proud of

un ami dont (= *de qui*) je connais
   le frère

a friend whose brother I know

les enfants dont (= *de qui*) vous
   vous occupez

the children you look after

le film dont (= *duquel*) il a parlé

the film of which he spoke

la fenêtre dont (= *de laquelle*) les
   rideaux sont tirés

the window the curtains of
   which are drawn

des garçons dont (= *desquels*) j'ai
   oublié les noms

boys whose names I've
   forgotten

les maladies dont (= *desquelles*)
   il souffre

the illnesses he suffers from

3 une personne sur l'aide de qui on
   peut compter

a person whose help one can
   rely on

les enfants aux parents de qui
   j'écris

the children to whose parents
   I'm writing

la maison dans le jardin
   de laquelle il y a ...

the house in whose garden
   there is ...

Relative Pronouns *continued*

ce qui, ce que that which, what

These are used when the relative pronoun does not refer to a specific noun, and they are often translated as 'what' (*literally*: that which):

ce qui is used as the subject → **1**

ce que* is used as the direct object → **2**

* **que** changes to **qu'** before a vowel → **2**

Note the construction:
tout ce qui
tout ce que everything/all that → **3**

de + ce que → **ce dont** → **4**

preposition + **ce que** → **ce** + *preposition* + **quoi** → **5**

When **ce qui**, **ce que** etc, refers to a previous clause the translation is 'which' → **6**

Examples

1 Ce qui m'intéresse ne l'intéresse pas forcément — What interests me doesn't necessarily interest him

Je n'ai pas vu ce qui s'est passé — I didn't see what happened

2 Ce que j'aime c'est la musique classique — What I like is classical music

Montrez-moi ce qu'il vous a donné — Show me what he gave you

3 Tout ce qui reste c'est ... — All that's left is ...

Donnez-moi tout ce que vous avez — Give me everything you have

4 Il risque de perdre ce dont il est si fier — He risks losing what he's so proud of

Voilà ce dont il s'agit — That's what it's about

5 Ce n'est pas ce à quoi je m'attendais — It's not what I was expecting

Ce à quoi je m'intéresse particulièrement c'est ... — What I'm particularly interested in is ...

6 Il est d'accord, ce qui m'étonne — He agrees, which surprises me

Il a dit qu'elle ne venait pas, ce que nous savions déjà — He said she wasn't coming, which we already knew

Interrogative Pronouns

These pronouns are used in direct questions:

qui? who; whom?
que? what?
quoi? what?

The form of the pronoun depends on:

- whether it refers to people or to things
- whether it is the subject or object of the verb, or if it comes after a preposition

Qui and **que** have longer forms, as shown in the tables below.

Referring to people:

SUBJECT	**qui?**	who? → **1**
	qui est-ce qui?	
OBJECT	**qui?**	who(m)? → **2**
	qui est-ce que*?	
AFTER PREPOSITIONS	**qui?**	who(m)? → **3**

Referring to things:

SUBJECT	**qu'est-ce qui?**	what? → **4**
OBJECT	**que*?**	what? → **5**
	qu'est-ce que*?	
AFTER PREPOSITIONS	**quoi?**	what? → **6**

* **que** changes to **qu'** before a vowel → **2**/**5**

Examples

1   Qui vient?   Who's coming?
      Qui est-ce qui vient?

2   Qui vois-tu?   Who(m) can you see?
      Qui est-ce que tu vois?
      Qui a-t-elle rencontré?   Who(m) did she meet?
      Qui est-ce qu'elle a rencontré?

3   De qui parle-t-il?   Who's he talking about?
      Pour qui est ce livre?   Who's this book for?
      À qui avez-vous écrit?   To whom did you write?

4   Qu'est-ce qui se passe?   What's happening?
      Qu'est-ce qui a vexé Paul?   What upset Paul?

5   Que faites-vous?   What are you doing?
      Qu'est-ce que vous faites?
      Qu'a-t-il dit?   What did he say?
      Qu'est-ce qu'il a dit?

6   À quoi cela sert-il?   What's that used for?
      De quoi a-t-on parlé?   What was the discussion about?
      Sur quoi vous basez-vous?   What do you base it on?

Interrogative Pronouns *continued*

These pronouns are used in indirect questions:

qui who; whom
ce qui what
ce que what
quoi what

The form of the pronoun depends on:

- whether it refers to people or to things
- whether it is the subject or object of the verb, or if it comes after a preposition

Referring to people: use **qui** in all instances → ❶

Referring to things:

SUBJECT	**ce qui**	what → ❷
OBJECT	**ce que***	what → ❸
AFTER PREPOSITIONS	**quoi?**	what → ❹

* **que** changes to **qu'** before a vowel → ❸

Examples

① Demande-lui qui est venu
    Je me demande qui ils ont vu
    Dites-moi qui vous préférez
    Elle ne sait pas à qui s'adresser
    Demandez-leur pour qui elles
      travaillent

Ask him who came
I wonder who they saw
Tell me who you prefer
She doesn't know who to apply to
Ask them who they work for

② Il se demande ce qui se passe

Je ne sais pas ce qui vous fait
    croire que ...

He's wondering what's
    happening
I don't know what makes you
    think that ...

③ Raconte-nous ce que tu as fait
    Je me demande ce qu'elle pense

Tell us what you did
I wonder what she's thinking

④ On ne sait pas de quoi vivent ces
    animaux
    Je vais lui demander à quoi il fait
    allusion

We don't know what these
    animals live on
I'm going to ask him what he's
    hinting at

Interrogative Pronouns *continued*

lequel/laquelle, lesquels/lesquelles?

	MASCULINE	FEMININE	
SING.	lequel?	laquelle?	which (one)?
PLUR.	lesquels?	lesquelles?	which (ones)?

The pronoun agrees in number and gender with the noun it refers to → **1**

The same forms are used in indirect questions → **2**

After the prepositions à and **de**, **lequel** and **lesquel(le)s** contract as follows:

à + lequel? → auquel?
à + lesquels? → auxquels?
à + lesquelles? → auxquelles?

de + lequel? → duquel?
de + lesquels? → desquels?
de + lesquelles? → desquelles?

Examples

1 J'ai choisi un livre. — Lequel?
Laquelle de ces valises est la vôtre?
Amenez quelques amis. — Lesquels?
Lesquelles de vos sœurs sont mariées?

I've chosen a book. — Which one?
Which of these cases is yours?
Bring some friends. — Which ones?
Which of your sisters are married?

2 Je me demande laquelle des maisons est la leur
Dites-moi lesquels d'entre eux étaient là

I wonder which is their house
Tell me which of them were there

Possessive Pronouns

Singular:

MASCULINE	FEMININE	
le mien	la mienne	mine
le tien	la tienne	yours
le sien	la sienne	his; hers; its
le nôtre	la nôtre	ours
le vôtre	la vôtre	yours
le leur	la leur	theirs

Plural:

MASCULINE	FEMININE	
le miens	la miennes	mine
le tiens	la tiennes	yours
le siens	la siennes	his; hers; its
le nôtres	la nôtres	ours
le vôtres	la vôtres	yours
le leurs	la leurs	theirs

The pronoun agrees in number and gender with the noun it replaces, not with the owner → ❶

Alternative translations are 'my own', 'your own' etc; **le sien**, **la sienne** *etc* may also mean 'one's own' → ❷

After the prepositions **à** and **de** the articles **le** and **les** are contracted in the normal way (see page 140):

      à + le mien → au mien
      à + les miens → aux miens   → ❸
      à + les miennes → aux miennes

      de + le mien → du mien
      de + les miens → des miens   → ❹
      de + les miennes → des miennes

Examples

① Demandez à Carole si ce stylo est le sien

Ask Carole if this pen is hers

Quelle équipe a gagné – la leur ou la nôtre?

Which team won – theirs or ours?

Mon portable est plus rapide que le tien

My laptop is faster than yours

Richard a pris mes affaires pour les siennes

Richard mistook my belongings for his

Si tu n'as pas de DVDs, emprunte les miens

If you don't have any DVDs, borrow mine

Nos maisons sont moins grandes que les vôtres

Our houses are smaller than yours

② Est-ce que leur entreprise est aussi grande que la vôtre?

Is their company as big as your own?

Leurs prix sont moins élevés que les nôtres

Their prices are lower than our own

Le bonheur des autres importe plus que le sien

Other people's happiness matters more than one's own

③ Pourquoi préfères-tu ce manteau au mien?

Why do you prefer this coat to mine?

Quelles maisons ressemblent aux leurs?

Which houses resemble theirs?

④ Leur voiture est garée à côté de la tienne

Their car is parked next to yours

Vos livres sont au-dessus des miens

Your books are on top of mine

Demonstrative Pronouns

celui/celle, ceux/celles

	MASCULINE	FEMININE	
SING.	celui	celle	the one
PLUR.	ceux	celles	the ones

The pronoun agrees in number and gender with the noun it replaces → **1**

Uses:
- preceding a relative pronoun, meaning 'the one(s) who/which' → **1**
- preceding the preposition **de**, meaning 'the one(s) belonging to', 'the one(s) of' → **2**
- with **-ci** and **-là**, for emphasis or to distinguish between two things:

	MASCULINE	FEMININE		
SING.	celui-ci	celle-ci	this (one)	→ **3**
PLUR.	ceux-ci	celles-ci	these (ones)	

	MASCULINE	FEMININE		
SING.	celui-là	celle-là	that (one)	→ **3**
PLUR.	ceux-là	celles-là	those (ones)	

- an additional meaning of **celui-ci/celui-là** *etc* is 'the former/the latter'.

Examples

1 Lequel? — Celui qui parle à Anne.

Which man? — The one who's talking to Anne.

Quelle robe désirez-vous? — Celle qui est en vitrine.

Which dress do you want? — The one which is in the window.

Est-ce que ces livres sont ceux qu'il t'a donnés?

Are these the books that he gave you?

Quelles filles? — Celles que nous avons vues hier.

Which girls? — The ones we saw yesterday.

Cet article n'est pas celui dont vous m'avez parlé

This article isn't the one you spoke to me about

2 Ce jardin est plus grand que celui de mes parents

This garden is bigger than my parents' (garden)

Est-ce que ta fille est plus âgée que celle de Gabrielle?

Is your daughter older than Gabrielle's (daughter)?

Je préfère les chiens de Paul à ceux de Roger

I prefer Paul's dogs to Roger's (dogs)

Comparez vos réponses à celles de votre voisin

Compare your answers with your neighbour's (answers)

les montagnes d'Écosse et celles du pays de Galles

the mountains of Scotland and those of Wales

3 Quel tailleur préférez-vous: celui-ci ou celui-là?

Which suit do you prefer: this one or that one?

Cette chemise a deux poches mais celle-la n'en a pas

This shirt has two pockets but that one has none

Quels œufs choisirais-tu: ceux-ci ou ceux-là?

Which eggs would you choose: these (ones) or those (ones)?

De toutes mes jupes, celle-ci me va le mieux

Of all my skirts, this one fits me best

Demonstrative Pronouns *continued*

ce (c') it, that

> Usually used with **être**, in the expressions **c'est, c'était, ce sont** *etc* → ❶

> Note the spelling **ç**, when followed by the letter **a** → ❷

> Uses:
> * to identify a person or object → ❸
> * for emphasis → ❹
> * as a neuter pronoun, referring to a statement, idea *etc* → ❺

ce qui, ce que, ce dont *etc*: see Relative Pronouns (page 184), and
Interrogative Pronouns (page 188).

cela, ça it, that

> **cela** and **ça** are used as 'neuter' pronouns, referring to a statement, an idea, an object → ❻

> In everyday spoken language **ça** is used in preference to **cela**.

ceci this → ❼

> **ceci** is not used as often as 'this' in English; **cela, ça** are often used where we use 'this'.

Examples

① C'est ...

It's/That's ...

    C'était moi

It was me

② Ça a été la cause de ...

It has been cause of ...

③ Qui est-ce?

Who is it?; Who's this/that?; Who's he/she?

    C'est lui/mon frère/nous

It's/That's him/my brother/us

    Ce sont eux

It's them

    C'est une infirmière*

She's a nurse

    Ce sont des professeurs*

They're teachers

    Qu'est-ce que c'est?

What's this/that?

    Qu'est-ce que c'est que ça?

What's that?

    C'est une agrafeuse

It's a stapler

    Ce sont des trombones

They're paper clips

④ C'est moi qui ai téléphoné

It was me who phoned

    Ce sont les enfants qui importent le plus

It's the children who matter most

⑤ C'est très intéressant

That's/It's very interesting

    Ce serait dangereux

That/It would be dangerous

⑥ Ça ne fait rien

It doesn't matter

    À quoi bon faire ça?

What's the use of doing that?

    Cela ne compte pas

That doesn't count

    Cela demande du temps

It/That takes time

⑦ À qui est ceci?

Whose is this?

    Ouvrez-le comme ceci

Open it like this

---

* See pages 146 and 147 for the use of the article when stating a person's profession

Adverbs

Formation

Most adverbs are formed by adding **-ment** to the feminine form of the adjective → ❶

-ment is added to the *masculine* form when the masculine form ends in **-é**, **-i** or **-u** → ❷
EXCEPTION: **gai** → ❸

Occasionally the **u** changes to **û** before **-ment** is added → ❹

If the adjective ends in **-ant** or **-ent**, the adverb ends in **-amment** or **-emment** → ❺
EXCEPTIONS: **lent, présent** → ❻

Irregular Adverbs

ADJECTIVE	ADVERB
aveugle blind	**aveuglément** blindly
bon good	**bien** well → ❼
bref brief	**brièvement** briefly
énorme enormous	**énormément** enormously
exprès express	**expressément** expressly → ❽
gentil kind	**gentiment** kindly
mauvais bad	**mal** badly → ❾
meilleur better	**mieux** better
pire worse	**pis** worse
précis precise	**précisément** precisely
profond deep	**profondément** deeply → ❿
traître treacherous	**traîtreusement** treacherously

Adjectives used as adverbs

Certain adjectives are used adverbially. These include: **bas, bon, cher, clair, court, doux, droit, dur, faux, ferme, fort, haut, mauvais** and **net** → ⓫

Examples

1 MASC./FEM. ADJECTIVE   ADVERB

heureux/heureuse fortunate	heureusement fortunately
franc/franche frank	franchement frankly
extrême/extrême extreme	extrêmement extremely

2 MASC. ADJECTIVE   ADVERB

désespéré desperate	désespérément desperately
vrai true	vraiment truly
résolu resolute	résolument resolutely

3 gai cheerful   gaiement *or* gaîment cheerfully

4 continu continuous   continûment continuously

5

constant constant	constamment constantly
courant fluent	couramment fluently
évident obvious	évidemment obviously
fréquent frequent	fréquemment frequently

6

lent slow	lentement slowly
présent present	présentement presently

7 Elle travaille bien   She works well

8 Il a expressément défendu qu'on parte   He has expressly forbidden us to leave

9 un emploi mal payé   a badly paid job

10 J'ai été profondément ému   I was deeply moved

11

parler bas/haut	to speak softly/loudly
coûter cher	to be expensive
voir clair	to see clearly
travailler dur	to work hard
chanter faux	to sing off key
sentir bon/mauvais	to smell nice/horrible

Position of Adverbs

When the adverb accompanies a verb in a simple tense, it generally follows the verb → ①

When the adverb accompanies a verb in a compound tense, it generally comes between the auxiliary verb and the past participle → ②

Some adverbs, however, follow the past participle → ③

When the adverb accompanies an adjective or another adverb it generally precedes the adjective/adverb → ④

Comparatives of Adverbs

These are formed using the following constructions:

plus ... (que) more ... (than) → ⑤
moins ... (que) less ... (than) → ⑥
aussi ... que as ... as → ⑦
si ... que＊ as ... as → ⑧

＊ used mainly after a negative

Superlatives of Adverbs

These are formed using the following constructions:

le plus ... (que) the most ... (that) → ⑨
le moins ... (que) the least ... (that) → ⑩

Adverbs with irregular comparatives/superlatives

ADVERB	COMPARATIVE	SUPERLATIVE
beaucoup a lot	**plus** more	**le plus** (the) most
bien well	**mieux** better	**le mieux** (the) best
mal badly	**pis/plus mal** worse	**le pis/plus mal** (the) worst
peu little	**moins** less	**le moins** (the) least

Examples

1. Il dort encore — He's still asleep
   Je pense souvent à toi — I often think about you

2. Ils sont déjà partis — They've already gone
   J'ai toujours cru que … — I've always thought that …
   J'ai presque fini — I'm almost finished
   Il a trop mangé — He's eaten too much

3. On les a vus partout — We saw them everywhere
   Elle est revenue hier — She came back yesterday

4. un très beau chemisier — a very nice blouse
   une femme bien habillée — a well-dressed woman
   beaucoup plus vite — much faster
   peu souvent — not very often

5. plus vite — more quickly
   plus régulièrement — more regularly
   Elle chante plus fort que moi — She sings louder than I do

6. moins facilement — less easily
   moins souvent — less often
   Nous nous voyons moins fréquemment qu'auparavant — We see each other less frequently than before

7. Faites-le aussi vite que possible — Do it as quickly as possible
   Il en sait aussi long que nous — He knows as much about it as we do

8. Ce n'est pas si loin que je pensais — It's not as far as I thought

9. Marianne court le plus vite — Marianne runs fastest

10. Le plus tôt que je puisse venir c'est samedi — The earliest that I can come is Saturday

11. C'est l'auteur que je connais le moins bien — He's the writer I'm least familiar with

Common adverbs and their usage

Some common adverbs:

assez enough; quite → ❶ *See also below*
aussi also, too; as → ❷
autant as much → ❸ *See also below*
beaucoup a lot; much → ❹ *See also below*
bien well; very; very much; 'indeed' → ❺ *See also below*
combien how much; how many → ❻ *See also below*
comme how; what → ❼
déjà already; before → ❽
encore still; yet; more; even → ❾
moins less → ❿ *See also below*
peu little, not much; not very → ⓫ *See also below*
plus more → ⓬ *See also below*
si so; such → ⓭
tant so much → ⓮ *See also below*
toujours always; still → ⓯
trop too much; too → ⓰ *See also below*

assez, autant, beaucoup, combien *etc* are used in the construction *adverb + de + noun* with the following meanings:

assez de enough → ⓱
autant de as much; as many; so much; so many
beaucoup de a lot of
combien de how much; how many
moins de less; fewer → ⓱
peu de little, not much; few, not many
plus de more
tant de so much; so many
trop de too much; too many

bien can be followed by a partitive article (see page 144) plus a noun to mean *a lot of*; *a good many* → ⓲

Examples

① Avez-vous assez chaud?   Are you warm enough?
   Il est assez tard   It's quite late

② Je préfère ça aussi   I prefer it too
   Elle est aussi grande que moi   She is as tall as I am

③ Je voyage autant que lui   I travel as much as him

④ Tu lis beaucoup?   Do you read a lot?
   C'est beaucoup plus loin?   Is it much further?

⑤ Bien joué!   Well played!
   Je suis bien content que …   I'm very pleased that …
   Il s'est bien amusé   He enjoyed himself very much
   Je l'ai bien fait   I DID do it

⑥ Combien coûte ce livre?   How much is this book?
   Vous êtes combien?   How many of you are there?

⑦ Comme tu es jolie!   How pretty you look!
   Comme il fait beau!   What lovely weather!

⑧ Je l'ai déjà fait   I've already done it
   Êtes-vous déjà allé en France?   Have you been to France before?

⑨ J'en ai encore deux   I've still got two
   Elle n'est pas encore là   She isn't there yet
   Encore du café, Alain?   More coffee, Alan?
   Encore mieux!   Even better!

⑩ Travaillez moins!   Work less!
   Je suis moins étonné que toi   I'm less surprised than you are

⑪ Elle mange peu   She doesn't eat very much
   C'est peu important   It's not very important

⑫ Il se détend plus   He relaxes more
   Elle est plus timide que Sophie   She is shyer than Sophie

⑬ Simon est si charmant   Simon is so charming
   une si belle vue   such a lovely view

⑭ Elle l'aime tant   She loves him so much

⑮ Il dit toujours ça!   He always says that!
   Tu le vois toujours?   Do you still see him?

⑯ J'ai trop mangé   I've eaten too much
   C'est trop cher   It's too expensive

⑰ assez d'argent/de livres   enough money/books
   moins de temps/d'amis   less time/fewer friends

⑱ bien du mal/des gens   a lot of harm/a good many people

Prepositions

On the following pages you will find some of the most frequent uses of prepositions in French. Particular attention is paid to cases where usage differs markedly from English. It is often difficult to give an English equivalent for French prepositions, since usage does vary so much between the two languages.

In the list below, the broad meaning of the preposition is given on the left, with examples of usage following.

Prepositions are dealt with in alphabetical order, except **à**, **de** and **en** which are shown first.

à

at	**lancer qch à qn** to throw sth at sb
	il habite à St Pierre he lives at St Pierre
	à 2 euros (la) pièce (at) 2 euros each
	à 100 km à l'heure at 100 km per hour
in	**à la campagne** in the country
	à Londres in London
	au lit in bed (*also* to bed)
	un livre à la main with a book in his/her hand
on	**un tableau au mur** a picture on the wall
to	**aller au cinéma** to go to the cinema
	donner qch à qn to give sth to sb
	le premier/dernier à faire the first/last to do
	demander qch à qn to ask sb sth
from	**arracher qch à qn** to snatch sth from sb
	acheter qch à qn to buy sth from sb
	cacher qch à qn to hide sth from sb
	emprunter qch à qn to borrow sth from sb
	prendre qch à qn to take sth from sb
	voler qch à qn to steal sth from sb

Prepositions

descriptive	**la femme au chapeau vert** the woman with the green hat
	un garçon aux yeux bleus a boy with blue eyes
manner, means	**à l'ancienne** in the old-fashioned way
	fait à la main handmade
	à bicyclette/cheval by bicycle/on horseback
	(*but note other forms of transport used with* **en** *and* **par**)
	à pied on foot
	chauffer au gaz to heat with/by gas
	à pas lents with slow steps
	cuisiner au beurre to cook with butter
time, date: at, in	**à minuit** at midnight
	à trois heures cinq at five past three
	au 20ème siècle in the 20th century
	à Noël/Pâques at Christmas/Easter
distance	**à 6 km d'ici** (at a distance of) 6 km from here
	à deux pas de chez moi just a step from my place
destined for	**une tasse à thé** a teacup
	(*compare* **une tasse de thé**)
	un service à café a coffee service
after certain adjectives	**son écriture est difficile à lire** his writing is difficult to read
	(*compare the usage with* **de**, *page* 206)
	prêt à tout ready for anything
after certain verbs	see page 64

Prepositions

de

from	**venir de Londres** to come from London **du matin au soir** from morning till night **du 21 juin au 5 juillet** from 21st June till 5th July **de 10 à 15** from 10 to 15
belonging to, of	**un ami de la famille** a friend of the family **les vents d'automne** the autumn winds
contents, composition, material	**une boîte d'allumettes** a box of matches **une tasse de thé** a cup of tea (*compare* **une tasse à thé**) **une robe de soie** a silk dress
manner	**d'une façon irrégulière** in an irregular way **d'un seul coup** at one go
quality	**la société de consommation** the consumer society **des objets de valeur** valuable items
comparative + a number	**Il y avait plus/moins de cent personnes** There were more/fewer than a hundred people
in (*after superlatives*)	**la plus/moins belle ville du monde** the most/least beautiful city in the world
after certain adjectives	**surpris de voir** surprised to see **Il est difficile d'y accéder** Access is difficult (*compare the usage with* **à**, *page 205*)
after certain verbs	see page 64

Prepositions

en

to, in, on *(place)*	**en ville** in/to town
	en pleine mer on the open sea
	en France in/to France
	(note that masculine countries use **à***)*
in *(dates, months)*	**en 2007** in 2007
	en janvier in January
transport	**en voiture** by car
	en avion by plane
	(but note usage of **à** *and* **par** *in other expressions)*
language	**en français** in French
duration	**Je le ferai en trois jours** I'll do it in three days
	(i.e. I'll take 3 days to do it: compare **dans trois**
	jours*)*
material	**un bracelet en or** a bracelet made of gold
	(note that the use of **en** *stresses the material more*
	than the use of **de***)*
	consister en to consist of
in the manner of, like a	**parler en vrai connaisseur** to speak like a real
	connoisseur
	déguisé en cowboy dressed up as a cowboy
+ *present participle*	**il l'a vu en passant devant la porte**
	he saw it as he came past the door

Prepositions

avant

before	**Il est arrivé avant toi** He arrived before you
+ infinitive (add **de***)*	**Je vais finir ça avant de manger** I'm going to finish this before eating
preference	**la santé avant tout** health above everything

chez

at the home of	**chez lui/moi** at his/my house **être chez soi** to be at home **venez chez nous** come round to our place
at/to *(a shop)*	**chez le boucher** at/to the butcher's
in *(a person, among a group of people or animals)*	**Ce que je n'aime pas chez lui c'est son ...** What I don't like in him is his ... **chez les fourmis** among ants

dans

position	**dans une boîte** in(to) a box
circumstance	**dans son enfance** in his childhood
future time	**dans trois jours** in three days' time (*compare* **en trois jours***, page 207*)

depuis

since *(time/place)*	**depuis mardi** since Tuesday **Il pleut depuis Paris** It's been raining since Paris
for	**Il habite cette maison depuis 3 ans** He's been living in this house for 3 years (*note tense*)

Prepositions

dès

past time	**dès mon enfance** since my childhood
future time	**Je le ferai dès mon retour** I'll do it as soon as I get back

entre

between	**entre 8 et 10** between 8 and 10
among	**Jean et Pierre, entre autres** Jean and Pierre, among others
reciprocal	**s'aider entre eux** to help each other (out)

d'entre

of, among	**trois d'entre eux** three of them

par

by (*agent of passive*)	**renversé par une voiture** knocked down by a car **tué par la foudre** killed by lightning
weather conditions	**par un beau jour d'été** on a lovely summer's day
by (*means of*)	**par un couloir/sentier** by a corridor/path **par le train** by train (*but see also* **à** *and* **en**) **par l'intermédiaire de M. Duval** through Mr Duval
distribution	**deux par deux** two by two **par groupes de dix** in groups of ten **deux fois par jour** twice a day

Prepositions

pour

for

C'est pour vous It's for you
C'est pour demain It's for tomorrow
une chambre pour 2 nuits a room for 2 nights
Pour un enfant, il se débrouille bien
  For a child he manages very well
Il part pour l'Espagne He's leaving for Spain
Il l'a fait pour vous He did it for you
Il lui a donné 5 euros pour ce livre
  He gave him 5 euros for this book
Je ne suis pas pour cette idée I'm not for that idea
Pour qui me prends-tu? Who do you take me for?
Il passe pour un idiot He's taken for a fool

+ infinitive: (in order) to Elle se pencha pour le ramasser
  She bent down to pick it up
C'est trop fragile pour servir de siège
  It's too fragile to be used as a seat

to(wards) être bon/gentil pour qn to be kind to sb

with prices, time pour 30 euros d'essence 30 euros' worth of petrol
J'en ai encore pour une heure
  I'll be another hour (at it) yet

sans

without sans eau without water
sans ma femme without my wife

+ infinitive sans compter les autres without counting the
others

Prepositions

sauf

except (for)	**tous sauf lui** all except him **sauf quand il pleut** except when it's raining
barring	**sauf imprévu** barring the unexpected **sauf avis contraire** unless you hear to the contrary

sur

on	**sur le siège** on the seat **sur l'armoire** on top of the wardrobe **sur le mur** on (top of) the wall (*if the meaning is* 'hanging on the wall' *use* à, *page* 204) **sur votre gauche** on your left **être sur le point de faire** to be on the point of doing
on (to)	**mettez-le sur la table** put it on the table
out of, by (*proportion*)	**8 sur 10** 8 out of 10 **un automobiliste sur 5** one motorist in 5 **la pièce fait 2 mètres sur 3** the room measures 2 metres by 3

Conjunctions

There are conjunctions which introduce a main clause, such as **et** (and), **mais** (but), **si** (if), **ou** (or) and so on, and those which introduce subordinate clauses like **parce que** (because), **pendant que** (while), **après que** (after) and so on. They are all used in much the same way as in English, but the following points are of note:

Some conjunctions in French require a following subjunctive, see page 58

Some conjunctions are 'split' in French like 'both ... and', 'either ... or' in English:

et ... et both ... and → ①
ni ... ni ... ne neither ... nor → ②
ou (bien) ... ou (bien) either ... or (else) → ③
soit ... soit either ... or → ④

si + il(s) → **s'il(s)** → ⑤

que
- meaning *that* → ⑥
- replacing another conjunction → ⑦
- replacing **si**, see page 62
- in comparisons, meaning 'as', 'than' → ⑧
- followed by the subjunctive, see page 62

aussi (so, therefore): the subject and verb are inverted if the subject is a pronoun → ⑨

Examples

1. Ces fleurs poussent et en été et en hiver — These flowers grow in both summer and winter

2. Ni lui ni elle ne sont venus — Neither he nor she came
   Ils n'ont ni argent ni nourriture — They have neither money nor food

3. Elle doit être ou naïve ou stupide — She must be either naïve or stupid

   Ou bien il m'évite ou bien il ne me reconnaît pas — Either he's avoiding me or else he doesn't recognize me

4. Il faut choisir soit l'un soit l'autre — You have to choose either one or the other

5. Je ne sais pas s'il vient/s'ils viennent — I don't know if he's coming/if they're coming
   Dis-moi s'il y a des erreurs — Tell me if there are any mistakes
   Votre passeport, s'il vous plaît — Your passport, please

6. Il dit qu'il t'a vu — He says (that) he saw you
   Est-ce qu'elle sait que vous êtes là? — Does she know that you're here?

7. Quand tu seras plus grand et que tu auras une maison à toi, ... — When you're older and you have a house of your own, ...
   Comme il pleuvait et que je n'avais pas de parapluie, ... — As it was raining and I didn't have an umbrella, ...

8. Ils n'y vont pas aussi souvent que nous — They don't go there as often as we do
   Il les aime plus que jamais — He likes them more than ever
   L'argent est moins lourd que le plomb — Silver is lighter than lead

9. Ceux-ci sont plus rares, aussi coûtent-ils cher — These ones are rarer, so they're expensive

Sentence structure

Word Order

Word order in French is largely the same as in English, except for the following points. Most of these have already been dealt with under the appropriate part of speech, but are summarized here along with other instances not covered elsewhere.

Object pronouns nearly always come before the verb → ❶
For details, see pages 166 to 170

Certain adjectives come after the noun → ❷
For details, see page 162

Adverbs accompanying a verb in a simple tense usually follow the verb → ❸
For details, see page 200

After **aussi** (so, therefore), **à peine** (hardly), **peut-être** (perhaps), the verb and subject are inverted → ❹

After the relative pronoun **dont** (whose), word order can affect the meaning → ❺
For details, see page 182

In exclamations, **que** and **comme** do not affect the normal word order → ❻

Following direct speech:
- the *verb + subject* order is inverted to become *subject + verb* → ❼
- with a pronoun subject, the verb and pronoun are linked by a hyphen → ❽
- when the verb ends in a vowel in the 3rd person singular, **-t-** is inserted between the pronoun and the verb → ❾

For word order in negative sentences, see page 216.

For word order in interrogative sentences, see pages 220 and 222.

Examples

① Je les vois!   I can see them!
Il me l'a donné   He gave it to me

② une ville française   a French town
du vin rouge   some red wine

③ Il pleut encore   It's still raining
Elle m'aide quelquefois   She sometimes helps me

④ Il vit tout seul, aussi fait-il ce qu'il veut   He lives alone, so he does what he likes
À peine la pendule avait-elle sonné trois heures que ...   Hardly had the clock struck three when ...
Peut-être avez-vous raison   Perhaps you're right

⑤ Compare:
un homme dont je connais la fille   a man whose daughter I know
and:
un homme dont la fille me connaît   a man whose daughter knows me

If the person (or object) 'owned' is the object of the verb, the order is:
dont + *verb* + *noun* (*first sentence*)
If the person (or object) 'owned' is the subject of the verb, the order is:
dont + *noun* + *verb* (*second sentence*)
Note also:
l'homme dont elle est la fille   the man whose daughter she is

⑥ Qu'il fait chaud!   How warm it is!
Que je suis content de vous voir!   How pleased I am to see you!
Comme c'est cher   How expensive it is!
Que tes voisins sont gentils!   How kind your neighbours are!

⑦ «Je pense que oui» a dit Luc   ' I think so,' said Luke
«Ça ne fait rien» répondit Julie   'It doesn't matter,' Julie replied

⑧ «Quelle horreur!» me suis-je exclamé   'How awful!' I exclaimed

⑨ «Pourquoi pas?» a-t-elle demandé   'Why not?' she asked
«Si c'est vrai», continua-t-il ...   'If it's true', he went on ...

Sentence structure

Negatives

The following are the most common negative pairs:

ne ... pas not
ne ... point (*literary*) not
ne ... rien nothing
ne ... personne nobody
ne ... plus no longer, no more
ne ... jamais never
ne ... que only
ne ... aucun(e) no
ne ... nul(le) no
ne ... nulle part nowhere
ne ... ni neither ... nor
ne ... ni ... ni neither ... nor

Word order

In simple tenses and the imperative:
- **ne** precedes the verb (and any object pronouns) and the second element follows the verb → ❶

In compound tenses:
- **ne ... pas, ne ... point, ne ... rien, ne ... plus, ne ... jamais, ne ... guère** follow the pattern:
  ne + *auxiliary verb* + **pas** + *past participle* → ❷
- **ne ... personne, ne ... que, ne ... aucun(e), ne ... nul(le), ne ... nulle part, ne ... ni (... ni)** follow the pattern:
  ne + *auxiliary verb* + *past participle* + **personne** → ❸

With a verb in the infinitive:
- **ne ... pas, ne ... point** (*etc*, see above) come together → ❹

For use of **rien, personne** and **aucun** as pronouns, see page 178.

Examples

① Je ne fume pas — I don't smoke
Ne changez rien — Don't change anything
Je ne vois personne — I can't see anybody
Nous ne nous verrons plus — We won't see each other any more

Il n'arrive jamais à l'heure — He never arrives on time
Il n'avait qu'une valise — He only had one suitcase
Je n'ai reçu aucune réponse — I have received no reply
Il ne boit ni ne fume — He neither drinks nor smokes
Ni mon fils ni ma fille ne les connaissaient — Neither my son nor my daughter knew them

② Elle n'a pas fait ses devoirs — She hasn't done her homework
Ne vous a-t-il rien dit? — Didn't he say anything to you?
Ils n'avaient jamais vu une si belle maison — They had never seen such a beautiful house

③ Tu n'as guère changé — You've hardly changed

Je n'ai parlé à personne — I haven't spoken to anybody
Il n'avait mangé que la moitié du repas — He had only eaten half the meal
Elle ne les a trouvés nulle part — She couldn't find them anywhere
Il ne l'avait ni vu ni entendu — He had neither seen nor heard him

④ Il essayait de ne pas rire — He was trying not to laugh

Negatives *continued*

These are the most common combinations of negative particles:

ne ... plus jamais → ①
ne ... plus personne → ②
ne ... plus rien → ③
ne ... plus ni ... ni ... → ④
ne ... jamais personne → ⑤
ne ... jamais rien → ⑥
ne ... jamais que → ⑦
ne ... jamais ni ... ni ... → ⑧
(ne ... pas) non plus → ⑨

non and pas

non (no) is the usual negative response to a question → ⑩
It is often translated as 'not' → ⑪

pas is generally used when a distinction is being made, or for emphasis → ⑫
It is often translated as 'not' → ⑬

Examples

1	Je ne le ferai plus jamais	I'll never do it again
2	Je ne connais plus personne à Rouen	I don't know anybody in Rouen any more
3	Ces marchandises ne valaient plus rien	Those goods were no longer worth anything
4	Ils n'ont plus ni chats ni chiens	They no longer have either cats or dogs
5	On n'y voit jamais personne	You never see anybody there
6	Ils ne font jamais rien d'intéressant	They never do anything interesting
7	Je n'ai jamais parlé qu'à sa femme	I've only ever spoken to his wife
8	Il ne m'a jamais ni écrit ni téléphoné	He has never either written to me or phoned me
9	Ils n'ont pas d'enfants et nous non plus	They don't have any children and neither do we
	Je ne les aime pas. — Moi non plus.	I don't like them. — Neither do I / I don't either.
10	Vous voulez nous accompagner? — Non.	Do you want to come with us? — No (I don't).
11	Tu viens ou non?	Are you coming or not?
	J'espère que non	I hope not
12	Ma sœur aime le ski, moi pas	My sister likes skiing, I don't
13	Qui a fait ça? — Pas moi!	Who did that? — Not me!
	Est-il de retour? — Pas encore.	Is he back? — Not yet.
	Tu as froid? — Pas du tout.	Are you cold? — Not at all.

Question forms: direct

There are four ways of forming direct questions in French:

by inverting the normal word order so that *pronoun subject + verb* becomes *verb + pronoun subject*. A hyphen links the verb and pronoun → ❶

- When the subject is a noun, a pronoun is inserted after the verb and linked to it by a hyphen → ❷
- When the verb ends in a vowel in the third person singular, -**t**-is inserted before the pronoun → ❸

by maintaining the word order *subject + verb*, but by using a rising intonation at the end of the sentence → ❹

by inserting **est-ce que** before the construction *subject + verb* → ❺

by using an interrogative word at the beginning of the sentence, together with inversion or the **est-ce que** form above → ❻

Examples

① Aimez-vous la France?   Do you like France?
Avez-vous fini?   Have you finished?
Est-ce possible?   Is it possible?
Est-elle restée?   Did she stay?
Part-on tout de suite?   Are we leaving right away?

② Tes parents sont-ils en vacances?   Are your parents on holiday?
Jean-Benoît est-il parti?   Has Jean-Benoît left?

③ A-t-elle de l'argent?   Has she any money?
La pièce dure-t-elle longtemps?   Does the play last long?
Mon père a-t-il téléphoné?   Has my father phoned?

④ Il l'a fini   He's finished it
Il l'a fini?   Has he finished it?
Robert va venir   Robert's coming
Robert va venir?   Is Robert coming?

⑤ Est-ce que tu la connais?   Do you know her?
Est-ce que tes parents sont   Have your parents come back
  revenus d'Italie?   from Italy?

⑥ Quel train prends-tu?   ] What train are you getting?
Quel train est-ce que tu prends? ⎦

Lequel est-ce que ta sœur préfère? ⎤ Which one does your sister prefer?
Lequel ta sœur préfère-t-elle? ⎦

Quand êtes-vous arrivé? ⎤
Quand est-ce que vous êtes   When did you arrive?
  arrivé? ⎦

Pourquoi ne sont-ils pas venus? ⎤
Pourquoi est-ce qu'ils ne sont pas ⎟ Why haven't they come?
  venus? ⎦

Question forms: indirect

An indirect question is one that is 'reported', e.g. 'he asked me what the time was'; 'tell me which way to go'. Word order in indirect questions is as follows:

> *interrogative word + subject + verb* → **①**

> when the subject is a noun, and not a pronoun, the subject and verb are often inverted → **②**

n'est-ce pas

This is used wherever English would use 'isn't it?', 'don't they?', 'weren't we?', 'is it?' and so on tagged on to the end of a sentence → **③**

oui **and** si

Oui is the word for 'yes' in answer to a question put in the affirmative → **④**

Si is the word for 'yes' in answer to a question put in the negative or to contradict a negative statement → **⑤**

Examples

1 Je me demande s'il viendra — I wonder if he'll come
Je ne sais pas à quoi ça sert — I don't know what it's for
Dites-moi quel autobus va à la gare — Tell me which bus goes to the station
Il m'a demandé combien d'argent j'avais — He asked me how much money I had

2 Elle ne sait pas à quelle heure commence le film — She doesn't know what time the film starts
Je me demande où sont mes clés — I wonder where my keys are
Elle nous a demandé comment allait notre père — She asked us how our father was
Je ne sais pas ce que veulent dire ces mots — I don't know what these words mean

3 Il fait chaud, n'est-ce pas? — It's warm, isn't it?
Vous n'oublierez pas, n'est-ce pas? — You won't forget, will you?

4 Tu l'as fait? — Oui. — Have you done it? — Yes (I have).

5 Tu ne l'as pas fait? — Si. — Haven't you done it? — Yes (I have).

Numbers

Cardinal (one, two etc)		Ordinal (first, second etc)	
zéro	0		
un (une)	1	premier (première)	1er, 1ère
deux	2	deuxième, second(e)	2ème
trois	3	troisième	3ème
quatre	4	quatrième	4ème
cinq	5	cinquième	5ème
six	6	sixième	6ème
sept	7	septième	7ème
huit	8	huitième	8ème
neuf	9	neuvième	9ème
dix	10	dixième	10ème
onze	11	onzième	11ème
douze	12	douzième	12ème
treize	13	treizième	13ème
quatorze	14	quatorzième	14ème
quinze	15	quinzième	15ème
seize	16	seizième	16ème
dix-sept	17	dix-septième	17ème
dix-huit	18	dix-huitième	18ème
dix-neuf	19	dix-neuvième	19ème
vingt	20	vingtième	20ème
vingt et un (une)	21	vingt et unième	21ème
vingt-deux	22	vingt-deuxième	22ème
vingt-trois	23	vingt-troisième	23ème
trente	30	trentième	30ème
quarante	40	quarantième	40ème
cinquante	50	cinquantième	50ème
soixante	60	soixantième	60ème
soixante-dix	70	soixante-dixième	70ème
soixante et onze	71	soixante et onzième	71ème
soixante-douze	72	soixante-douzième	72ème
quatre-vingts	80	quatre-vingtième	80ème
quatre-vingt-un (une)	81	quatre-vingt-unième	81ème
quatre-vingt-dix	90	quatre-vingt-dixième	90ème
quatre-vingt-onze	91	quatre-vingt-onzième	91ème

Numbers

Cardinal

cent	100
cent un (une)	101
cent deux	102
cent dix	110
cent quarante-deux	142
deux cents	200
deux cent un (une)	201
deux cent deux	202
trois cents	300
quatre cents	400
cinq cents	500
six cents	600
sept cents	700
huit cents	800
neuf cents	900
mille	1000
mille un (une)	1001
mille deux	1002
deux mille	2000
cent mille	100.000
un million	1.000.000
deux millions	2.000.000

Ordinal

centième	$100^{\text{ème}}$
cent unième	$101^{\text{ème}}$
cent deuxième	$102^{\text{ème}}$
cent dixième	$110^{\text{ème}}$
cent quarante-deuxième	$142^{\text{ème}}$
deux centième	$200^{\text{ème}}$
deux cent unième	$201^{\text{ème}}$
deux cent deuxième	$202^{\text{ème}}$
trois centième	$300^{\text{ème}}$
quatre centième	$400^{\text{ème}}$
cinq centième	$500^{\text{ème}}$
six centième	$600^{\text{ème}}$
sept centième	$700^{\text{ème}}$
huit centième	$800^{\text{ème}}$
neuf centième	$900^{\text{ème}}$
millième	$1000^{\text{ème}}$
mille unième	$1001^{\text{ème}}$
mille deuxième	$1002^{\text{ème}}$
deux millième	$2000^{\text{ème}}$
cent millième	$100.000^{\text{ème}}$
millionième	$1.000.000^{\text{ème}}$
deux millionième	$2.000.000^{\text{ème}}$

Fractions

un demi, une demie	a half
un tiers	a third
deux tiers	two thirds
un quart	a quarter
trois quarts	three quarters
un cinquième	one fifth
cinq et trois quarts	
	five and three quarters

Others

zéro virgule cinq (0,5)	0.5
un virgule trois (1,3)	1.3
dix pour cent	10%
deux plus deux	2 + 2
deux moins deux	2 − 2
deux fois deux	2 × 2
deux divisé par deux	2 ÷ 2

ⓘ Note the use of points with large numbers and commas with fractions, i.e. the opposite of English usage.

Other Uses

-aine denoting approximate numbers:

> une douzaine (de pommes) about a dozen (apples)
> une quinzaine (d'hommes) about fifteen (men)
> des centaines de personnes hundreds of people
> BUT: un millier (de voitures) about a thousand (cars)

measurements:

> vingt mètres carrés 20 square metres
> vingt mètres cubes 20 cubic metres
> un pont long de quarante mètres a bridge 40 metres long
> avoir trois mètres de large/de haut to be 3 metres wide/ high

miscellaneous:

> Il habite au dix He lives at number 10
> C'est au chapitre sept It's in chapter 7
> (C'est) à la page 17 (It's) on page 17
> (Il habite) au septième étage (He lives) on the 7th floor
> Il est arrivé le septième He came in 7th
> échelle au vingt-cinq millième scale 1:25,000

Telephone numbers

Je voudrais Édimbourg trois cent trente, vingt-deux, dix
  I would like Edinburgh 330 22 10
Je voudrais le soixante-cinq, treize, vingt-deux, zéro deux
  Could you get me 65 13 22 02
Poste trois cent trente-cinq Extension number 335
Poste vingt-deux, trente-trois Extension number 22 33

ⓘ In French, telephone numbers are broken down into groups of two
  or three numbers (never four), and are not spoken separately as in
  English. They are also written in groups of two or three numbers.

Calendar

Dates

Quelle est la date d'aujourd'hui? Quel jour sommes-nous?	What's the date today?

C'est ... Nous sommes ...	It's the ...
... le premier février	... 1st of February
... le deux février	... 2nd of February
... le vingt-huit février	... 28th of February

Il vient le sept mars	He's coming on the 7th of March

ⓘ Use cardinal numbers except for the first of the month.

Years

Elle est née en 1930	She was born in 1930
le douze février mille neuf cent trente le douze février mil neuf cent trente	(on) 12th February 1930

ⓘ There are two ways of expressing the year (see last example). Note the spelling of **mil** (one thousand) in dates.

Other expressions

dans les années cinquante	during the fifties
au vingtième siècle	in the twentieth century
en mai	in May
lundi (quinze)	on Monday (the 15th)
le lundi	on Mondays
dans dix jours	in 10 days' time
il y a dix jours	10 days ago

Time

Quelle heure est-il?	What time is it?
Il est ...	It's ...

00.00	minuit **midnight, twelve o'clock**
00.10	minuit dix, zéro heure dix
00.15	minuit et quart, zéro heure quinze
00.30	minuit et demi, zéro heure trente
00.45	une heure moins (le) quart, zéro heure quarante-cinq
01.00	une heure du matin **one a.m., one o'clock in the morning**
01.10	une heure dix (du matin)
01.15	une heure et quart, une heure quinze
01.30	une heure et demie, une heure trente
01.45	deux heures moins (le) quart, une heure quarante cinq
01.50	deux heures moins dix, une heure cinquante
01.59	deux heures moins une, une heure cinquante-neuf
12.00	midi, douze heures **noon, twelve o'clock**
12.30	midi et demi, douze heures trente
13.00	une heure de l'après-midi, treize heures **one p.m., one o'clock in the afternoon**
01.30	une heure et demie (de l'après-midi), treize heures trente
19.00	sept heures du soir, dix-neuf heures **seven p.m., seven o'clock in the evening**
19.30	sept heures et demie (du soir), dix-neuf heures trente

Examples

À quelle heure venez-vous? — À sept heures.	What time are you coming? — At seven o'clock.
Les bureaux sont fermés de midi à quatorze heures	The offices are closed from twelve until two
à deux heures du matin/de l'après-midi	at two o'clock in the morning/ afternoon; at two a.m./p.m.
à sept heures du soir	at seven o'clock in the evening; at seven p.m.
à cinq heures précises *or* pile	at five o'clock sharp
vers neuf heures	about nine o'clock
peu avant/après midi	shortly before/after noon
entre huit et neuf heures	between eight and nine o'clock
Il est plus de trois heures et demie	It's after half past three
Il faut y être à dix heures au plus tard/au plus tôt	You have to be there by ten o'clock at the latest/earliest
Ne venez pas plus tard que onze heures moins le quart	Come no later than a quarter to eleven
Il en a pour une demi-heure	He'll be half an hour (at it)
Elle est restée sans connaissance pendant un quart d'heure	She was unconscious for (a) quarter of an hour
Je les attends depuis une heure	I've been waiting for them for an hour/since one o'clock
Ils sont partis il y a quelques minutes	They left a few minutes ago
Je l'ai fait en vingt minutes	I did it in twenty minutes
Le train arrive dans une heure	The train arrives in an hour('s time)
Combien de temps dure ce film?	How long does this film last?

Translation problems

Beware of translating word for word. While on occasion this is quite possible, quite often it is not. The need for caution is illustrated by the following:

> English phrasal verbs (i.e. verbs followed by a preposition) e.g. 'to run away', 'to fall down' are often translated by one word in French → **①**

> English verbal constructions often contain a preposition where none exists in French, or vice versa → **②**

> Two or more prepositions in English may have a single rendering in French → **③**

> A word which is singular in English may be plural in French, or vice versa → **④**

> French has no equivalent of the possessive construction denoted by -'s/-s' → **⑤**

See also at/in/to, page 234.

The following pages look at some specific problems.

-ing

This is translated in a variety of ways in French:

> 'to be ...-ing' is translated by a simple verb → **⑥**
> EXCEPTION: when a physical position is denoted, a past participle is used → **⑦**

> in the construction 'to see/hear sb ...-ing', use an infinitive or **qui** + *verb* → **⑧**

'-ing' can also be translated by:
- an infinitive, see page 44 → **⑨**
- a perfect infinitive, see page 46 → **⑩**
- a present participle, see page 48 → **⑪**
- a noun → **⑫**

Examples

1 s'enfuir — to run away
tomber — to fall down
céder — to give in

2 payer — to pay for
regarder — to look at
écouter — to listen to
obéir à — to obey
nuire à — to harm
manquer de — to lack

3 s'étonner de — to be surprised at
satisfait de — satisfied with
voler qch à — to steal sth from
apte à — capable of; fit for

4 les bagages — the luggage
ses cheveux — his/her hair
le bétail — the cattle
mon pantalon — my trousers

5 la voiture de mon frère — my brother's car (*literally*: ... of my brother)

la chambre des enfants — the children's bedroom (*literally*: ... of the children)

6 Il part demain — He's leaving tomorrow
Je lisais un roman — I was reading a novel

7 Elle est assise là-bas — She's sitting over there
Il était couché par terre — He was lying on the ground

8 Je les vois venir — I can see them coming
Je les vois qui viennent
Je l'ai entendue chanter — I heard her singing
Je l'ai entendue qui chantait

9 J'aime aller au cinéma — I like going to the cinema
Arrêtez de parler! — Stop talking!
Au lieu de répondre — Instead of answering
Avant de partir — Before leaving

10 Après avoir ouvert la boîte, il ... — After opening the box, he ...

11 Étant plus timide que moi, elle ... — Being shyer than me, she ...

12 Le ski me maintient en forme — Skiing keeps me fit

Translation problems

to be

'to be' is generally translated by **être** → ❶

When physical location is implied, **se trouver** may be used → ❷

In set expressions, describing physical and emotional conditions, **avoir** is used:
    avoir chaud/froid to be warm/cold
    avoir faim/soif to be hungry/thirsty
    avoir peur/honte to be afraid/ashamed
    avoir tort/raison to be wrong/right

Describing the weather, e.g. what's the weather like?, it's windy/sunny, use **faire** → ❸

For ages, e.g. he is 6, use **avoir** → ❹

For state of health, e.g. he's unwell, how are you?, use **aller** → ❺

it is, it's

'It is' and 'it's' are usually translated by **il/elle est**, when referring to a noun → ❻

For expressions of time, also use **il est** → ❼

To describe the weather, e.g. it's windy, see above.

In the construction: it is difficult/easy to do sth, use **il est** → ❽

In all other constructions, use **c'est** → ❾

can, be able

Physical ability is expressed by **pouvoir** → ❿

If the meaning is 'to know how to', use **savoir** → ⓫

'can' + a 'verb of hearing or seeing etc' in English is not translated in French → ⓬

Examples

1	Il est tard	It's late
	C'est peu probable	It's not very likely
2	Où se trouve la gare?	Where's the station?
	Quel temps fait-il?	What's the weather like?
3	Il fait beau/mauvais/du vent	It's lovely/miserable/windy
4	Quel âge avez-vous?	How old are you?
	J'ai quinze ans	I'm fifteen
5	Comment allez-vous?	How are you?
	Je vais très bien	I'm very well
	Où est mon parapluie? — Il est là, dans le coin.	Where's my umbrella? — It's there, in the corner.
6	Descends la valise si elle n'est pas trop lourde	Bring down the case if it isn't too heavy
7	Quelle heure est-il? — Il est sept heures et demie.	What's the time? — It's half past seven.
8	Il est difficile de répondre à cette question	It's difficult to reply to this question
9	C'est moi qui ne l'aime pas	It's me who doesn't like him
	C'est Charles/ma mère qui l'a dit	It's Charles/my mother who said so
	C'est ici que je les ai achetés	It's here that I bought them
	C'est parce que la poste est fermée que ...	It's because the post office is closed that ...
10	Pouvez-vous atteindre cette étagère?	Can you reach up to that shelf?
11	Elle ne sait pas nager	She can't swim
	Je ne vois rien	I can't see anything
12	Il les entendait	He could hear them

Translation problems

to (*see also below*)

'to' is generally translated by **à**, see page 204 → **①**

In time expressions, e.g. 10 to 6, use **moins** → **②**

When the meaning is 'in order to', use **pour** → **③**

Following a verb, as in 'to try to do', 'to like to do', see pages 44 and 64

'easy/difficult/impossible' etc to do: the preposition used depends on whether a specific noun is referred to → **④** or not → **⑤**

at/in/to

With feminine countries, use **en** → **⑥**

With masculine countries, use **au** (**aux** with plural countries) → **⑦**

With towns, use **à** → **⑧**

'at/to the butcher's/grocer's' etc: use **à** + *noun* designating the shop, or **chez** + *noun* designating the shopkeeper → **⑨**

'at/to the dentist's/doctor's' etc: use **chez** → **⑩**

'at/to -'s/-s' house': use **chez** → **⑪**

there is/there are

Both are translated by **il y a** → **⑫**

Examples

1. Donne le livre à Patrick — Give the book to Patrick

2. dix heures moins cinq — five to ten
   à sept heures moins le quart — at a quarter to seven

3. Je l'ai fait pour vous aider — I did it to help you
   Il se pencha pour nouer son lacet — He bent down to tie his shoelace

4. Ce livre est difficile à lire — This book is difficult to read

5. Il est difficile de comprendre leurs raisons — It's difficult to understand their reasons

6. Il est allé en France/en Suisse — He has gone to France/to Switzerland
   un village en Norvège/en Belgique — a village in Norway/in Belgium

7. Êtes-vous allé au Canada/au Danemark/aux États-Unis? — Have you been to Canada/to Denmark/to the United States?
   une ville au Japon/au Brésil — a town in Japan/in Brazil

8. Il est allé à Vienne/à Bruxelles — He has gone to Vienna/to Brussels
   Il habite à Londres/à Genève — He lives in London/in Geneva
   Ils logent dans un hôtel à St Pierre — They're staying in a hotel at St Pierre

9. Je l'ai acheté à l'épicérie — I bought it at the grocer's
   Je l'ai acheté chez l'épicier
   Elle est allée à la boulangerie — She's gone to the baker's
   Elle est allée chez le boulanger

10. J'ai un rendez-vous chez le dentiste — I've an appointment at the dentist's
    Il est allé chez le médecin — He has gone to the doctor's

11. chez Christian — at/to Christian's house
    chez les Pagot — at/to the Pagots' house

12. Il y a quelqu'un à la porte — There's somebody at the door
    Il y a cinq livres sur la table — There are five books on the table

General Points

Activity of the lips

The lips play a very important part in French. When a vowel is described as having 'rounded' lips, the lips are slightly drawn together and pursed, as when an English speaker expresses exaggerated surprise with the vowel 'ooh!' Equally, if the lips are said to be 'spread', the corners are pulled firmly back towards the cheeks, tending to reveal the front teeth.

In English, lip position is not important, and vowel sounds tend to merge because of this. In French, the activity of the lips means that every vowel sound is clearly distinct from every other.

No diphthongs

A diphthong is a glide between two vowel sounds in the same syllable. In English, there are few 'pure' vowel sounds, but largely diphthongs instead. Although speakers of English may think they produce one vowel sound in the word 'day', in fact they use a diphthong, which in this instance is a glide between the vowels [e] and [ɪ]: [deɪ]. In French the tension maintained in the lips, tongue and the mouth in general prevents diphthongs occurring, as the vowel sound is kept constant throughout. Hence the French word corresponding to the above example, 'dé', is pronounced with no final [ɪ] sound, but is phonetically represented thus: [de].

Consonants

In English, consonants are often pronounced with a degree of laxness that can result in their practically disappearing altogether although not strictly 'silent'. In a relaxed pronunciation of a word such as 'hat', the 't' is often scarcely heard, or is replaced by a 'glottal stop' (a sort of jerk in the throat). This never occurs in French, where consonants are always given their full value.

Pronunciation of Consonants

Some consonants are pronounced almost exactly as in English:
[b, p, f, v, g, k, m, w].

Most others are similar to English, but slight differences should be noted.

EXAMPLES	HINTS ON PRONUNCIATION
[d] dinde	The tip of the tongue touches the upper
[t] tente	front teeth and not the roof of the mouth
[n] nonne	as in English
[l] Lille	
[s] tous ça	The tip of the tongue is down behind the
[z] zéro rose	bottom front teeth, lower than in English
[ʃ] chose tache	Like the 'sh' of English 'shout'
[ʒ] je gilet beige	Like the 's' of English 'measure'
[j] yeux paille	Like the 'y' of English 'yes'

Three consonants are not heard in English:

[ʀ] rare venir	'r' is often silent in English, e.g. farm. In French the [ʀ] is never silent, unless it follows an e at the end of a word e.g. chercher. To pronounce it, try to make a short sound like gargling. Similar, too, to the Scottish pronunciation of 'loch'
[ɲ] vigne agneau	Similar to the 'ni' of the English word 'Spaniard'
[ɥ] huile lueur	Like a very rapid [y] (see page 239) followed immediately by the next vowel of the word

Pronunciation of Vowels

	EXAMPLES	HINTS ON PRONUNCIATION
[a]	patte plat amour	Similar to the vowel in English 'pat'
[ɑ]	bas pâte	Longer than the sound above, it resembles the English exclamation of surprise 'ah!' Similar, too, to the English vowel in 'car' without the final 'r' sound
[ɛ]	lait jouet merci	Similar to the English vowel in 'pet'. Beware of using the English diphthong [eɪ] as in 'pay'
[e]	été jouer	A pure vowel, again quite different from the diphthong in English 'pay'
[ə]	le premier	Similar to the English sound in 'butter' when the 'r' is not pronounced
[i]	ici vie lycée	The lips are well spread towards the cheeks while uttering this sound. Shorter than the English vowel in 'see'
[ɔ]	mort homme	The lips are well rounded while producing a sound similar to the 'o' of English 'cot'
[o]	mot dôme eau	A pure vowel with strongly rounded lips quite different from the diphthong in the English words 'bone', 'low'

Pronunciation

EXAMPLES	HINTS ON PRONUNCIATION
[u] gen**ou** r**oue**	A pure vowel with strongly rounded lips. Similar to the English 'ooh!' of surprise
[y] r**ue** vêt**u**	Often the most difficult for English speakers to produce: round your lips and try to pronounce [i] (see page 238). There is no [j] sound (see page 237) as there is in English 'pure'
[œ] s**œur** b**eu**rre	Similar to the vowel in English 'fir' or 'murmur', but without the 'r' sound and with the lips more strongly rounded
[ø] p**eu** d**eux**	To pronounce this, try to say [e] (see page 238) with the lips strongly rounded

Nasal Vowels

These are spelt with a vowel followed by a 'nasal' consonant – **n** or **m**. The production of nasal vowels really requires the help of a teacher or a recording of the sound. However, to help you, the vowel is pronounced by allowing the air from the lungs to come partly down the nose and partly through the mouth, and the **n** or **m** is not pronounced at all.

[ã] l**ent** s**ang** d**ans**	In each case, the vowel shown in the
[ɛ̃] mat**in** pl**ein**	phonetic symbol is pronounced as
[ɔ̃] n**on** p**ont**	described above, but air is allowed to come
[œ̃] br**un** **un** parf**um**	through the nose as well as the mouth

Pronunciation

From Spelling to Sounds

Although it may not seem so at first sight, there are some fairly precise 'rules' which can help you to know how to pronounce French words from their spelling.

Vowels

SPELLING	PRONOUNCED	EXAMPLES
a, à	[a]	chatte table à
a, â	[ɑ]	pâte pas
er, é	[e]	été marcher
e, è, ê	[ɛ]	fenêtre fermer chère
e	[ə]	double fenêtre
i, î, y	[i]	lit abîmer lycée
o, ô	[o]	pot trop dôme
o	[ɔ]	sotte orange
u, û	[y]	battu fût pur

Vowel Groups

There are several groups of vowels in French spelling which are regularly pronounced in the same way:

SPELLING	PRONOUNCED	EXAMPLES
ai	[ɛ] or [e]	maison marchai faire
ail	[aj]	portail
ain, aim, (e)in, im	[ɛ̃]	pain faim frein impair
au	[o]	auberge landau
an, am, en, em	[ɑ̃]	plan ample entrer temps
eau	[o]	bateau eau
eu	[œ] or [ø]	feu peur
euil(le), ueil	[œj]	feuille recueil
oi, oy	[wa]	voir voyage
on, om	[ɔ̃]	ton compter
ou	[u]	hibou outil
œu	[œ]	sœur cœur
ue	[y]	rue
un, um	[œ̃]	brun parfum

Pronunciation

Added to these are the many groups of letters occurring at the end of words, where their pronunciation is predictable, bearing in mind the tendency (see page 242) of final consonants to remain silent.

TYPICAL WORDS	PRONUNCIATION OF FINAL SYLLABLE
pas, mât, chat	[ɑ] or [a]
marcher, marchez, marchais, marchait, baie, valet, mes, fumée	[e] or [ɛ]
nid	[i]
chaud, vaut, faux, sot, tôt, Pernod, dos, croc	[o]
bout, bijoux, sous, boue	[u]
fut, fût, crus, crûs	[y]
queue, heureux, bleus	[ø]
en, vend, vent, an, sang, grand, dans	[ɑ̃]
fin, feint, frein, vain	[ɛ̃]
on, pont, fond, avons	[ɔ̃]
brun, parfum	[œ̃]

From Spelling to Sounds *continued*

Consonants

Final consonants are usually silent → ①

n or m at the end of a syllable or word are silent, but they have the effect of 'nasalizing' the preceding vowel(s) (see page 239 on Nasal Vowels).

The letter h is either 'silent' ('mute') or 'aspirate' when it begins a word. When silent, the word behaves as though it started with a vowel and takes a liaison with the preceding word where appropriate.

When the h is aspirate, no liaison is made → ②

There is no way of predicting which words start with which sort of h – this simply has to be learnt with each word

The following consonants in spelling have predictable pronunciations: b, d, f, k, l, p, r, t, v, w, x, y, z.

Others vary:

SPELLING	PRONOUNCED	ENGLISH EXAMPLES
c + a, o, u	[k]	can cot cut → ③
+ l, r		class cram
c + e, i, y	[s]	ceiling ice → ④
ç + a, o, u	[s]	ceiling ice → ⑤
ch	[ʃ]	shop lash → ⑥
g + a, o, u	[g]	gate got gun → ⑦
+ l, r		glass gramme
g + e, i, y	[3]	leisure → ⑧
gn	[ɲ]	companion onion → ⑨
j	[3]	measure → ⑩
q, qu	[k]	quay kit → ⑪
s (*between vowels*)	[z]	rose → ⑫
s (*elsewhere*)	[s]	sit
th	[t]	Thomas → ⑬
t in -tion	[s]	sit → ⑭

Examples

1. éclat [ekla]
chaud [ʃo]

   nez [ne]
aider [ɛde]

2. silent h:
des hôtels [de zotɛl]

   aspirate h:
des haricots [de aʀiko]

3. café [kafe]
classe [klas]

   côte [kot]
croûte [kʀut]

   culture [kyltyʀ]

4. ceci [səsi]

   cil [sil]

   cycliste [siklist]

5. ça [sa]

   garçon [gaʀsɔ̃]

   déçu [desy]

6. chat [ʃa]

   riche [ʀiʃ]

7. gare [gaʀ]
glaise [glɛz]

   gourde [guʀd]
gramme [gʀam]

   aigu [ɛgy]

8. gemme [ʒem]

   gilet [ʒilɛ]

   gymnaste [ʒimnast]

9. vigne [viɲ]

   oignon [ɔɲɔ̃]

10. joli [ʒɔli]

    Jules [ʒyl]

11. quiche [kiʃ]

    quitter [kite]

12. sable [sablə]

    maison [mɛzɔ̃]

13. théâtre [teɑtʀ]

    Thomas [tɔma]

14. nation [nasjɔ̃]

    action [aksjɔ̃]

Pronunciation

Feminine Forms and Pronunciation

For adjectives and nouns ending in a vowel in the masculine, the addition of an e to form the feminine does not alter the pronunciation → ❶

If the masculine ends with a silent consonant, generally -d, -s, -r or -t, the consonant is sounded in the feminine → ❷
This also applies when the final consonant is doubled before the addition of the feminine e → ❸

If the masculine ends in a nasal vowel and a silent n, e.g. -an, -on, -in, the vowel is no longer nasalized and the -n is pronounced in the feminine → ❹
This also applies when the final -n is doubled before the addition of the feminine e → ❺

Where the masculine and feminine forms have totally different endings (see pages 136 and 150), the pronunciation of course varies accordingly → ❻

Plural Forms and Pronunciation

The addition of s or x to form regular plurals generally does not affect pronunciation → ❼

Where liaison has to be made, the final -s or -x of the plural form is pronounced → ❽

Where the masculine singular and plural forms have totally different endings (see pages 138 and 148), the pronunciation of course varies accordingly → ❾

Note the change in pronunciation in the following nouns:

SINGULAR	PLURAL
bœuf [bœf] ox	bœufs [bø] oxen
œuf [œf] egg	œufs [ø] eggs
os [ɔs] bone	os [o] bones

Examples

NOUNS

1. joli [ʒɔli] → jolie [ʒɔli]
   déçu [desy] → déçue [desy]

   un ami [ami] → une amie [ami]
   un employé [ɑ̃plwaje] →
      une employée [ɑ̃plwaje]

2. chaud [ʃo] → chaude [ʃod]

   français [fʀɑ̃sɛ] →
      française [fʀɑ̃sɛz]
   inquiet [ɛ̃kjɛ] →
      inquiète [ɛ̃kjɛt]

   un étudiant [etydjɑ̃] →
      une étudiante [etydjɑ̃t]
   un Anglais [ɑ̃glɛ] →
      une Anglaise [ɑ̃glɛz]
   un étranger [etʀɑ̃ʒe] →
      une étrangère [etʀɑ̃ʒeʀ]

3. violet [vjɔlɛ] → violette [vjɔlɛt]

   gras [gʀɑ] → grasse [gʀɑs]

   le cadet [kadɛ] →
      la cadette [kadɛt]

4. plein [plɛ̃] → pleine [plɛn]

   fin [fɛ̃] → fine [fin]

   brun [bʀœ̃] → brune [bʀyn]

   le souverain [suvʀɛ̃] →
      la souveraine [suvʀɛn]
   Le Persan [pɛʀsɑ̃] →
      la Persane [pɛʀsan]
   le voisin [vwazɛ̃] →
      la voisine [vwazin]

5. canadien [kanadjɛ̃] →
      canadienne [kanadjɛn]
   breton [bʀətɔ̃] →
      bretonne [bʀətɔn]

   le paysan [peizɑ̃] →
      la paysanne [peizan]
   le baron [baʀɔ̃] →
      la baronne [baʀɔn]

6. vif [vif] → vive [viv]
   traître [tʀɛtʀə] →
      traîtresse [tʀɛtʀɛs]

   le veuf [vœf] → la veuve [vœv]
   le maître [mɛtʀə] →
      la maîtresse [mɛtʀɛs]

7. beau [bo] → beaux [bo]

   la maison [mɛzɔ̃] →
      les maisons [mɛzɔ̃]

8. des anciens élèves
      [de zɑ̃sjɛ̃ zelɛv]

   de beaux arbres
      [də bo zaʀbʀ(ə)]

9. amical [amikal] →
      amicaux [amiko]

   un journal [ʒuʀnal] →
      des journaux [ʒuʀno]

245

The Alphabet

A, a [ɑ]	J, j [ʒi]	S, s [ɛs]
B, b [be]	K, k [ka]	T, t [te]
C, c [se]	L, l [ɛl]	U, u [y]
D, d [de]	M, m [ɛm]	V, v [ve]
E, e [ə]	N, n [ɛn]	W, w [dubləve]
F, f [ɛf]	O, o [o]	X, x [iks]
G, g [ʒe]	P, p [pe]	Y, y [igʀɛk]
H, h [aʃ]	Q, q [ky]	Z, z [zɛd]
I, i [i]	R, r [ɛʀ]	

Capital letters are used as in English except for the following:

adjectives of nationality
e.g. une ville espagnole a Spanish town
un auteur français a French author

languages
e.g. Parlez-vous anglais? Do you speak English?
Il parle français et allemand He speaks French and German

days of the week:
lundi Monday
mardi Tuesday
mercredi Wednesday
jeudi Thursday
vendredi Friday
samedi Saturday
dimanche Sunday

months of the year:
janvier January
février February
mars March
avril April
mai May
juin June

juillet July
août August
septembre September
octobre October
novembre November
décembre December

Index

The following index lists comprehensively both grammatical terms and key words in French and English contained in this book.

Index

Index

Index

Index

Index

Index

Index

L'anglais en situation

French in action

Collaborateurs/Contributors

Rose Rociola Daphne Day

Coordination/Coordination

Isobel Gordon

Introduction

The aim of **French in action** is to help you express yourself simply but correctly in fluent, natural French.

The **Sentence builder** section provides hundreds of phrases in which the key elements have been translated, providing an invaluable point of reference when you then construct your own sentences.

The section on correspondence provides practical models of personal and business letters, job applications and CVs, together with examples of standard opening and closing formulae and information on how to address an envelope. This section also offers guidance notes to help the user adapt these models to his/her needs.

A separate section covers fax and e-mail correspondence as well as all the expressions you might need to make different types of phone calls.

We hope you will find **French in action** both relevant and useful and that, used in conjunction with the dictionary, it will improve your understanding and enjoyment of French.

Contents

Introduction

L'anglais en situation a pour objectif de vous aider à vous exprimer en anglais, dans un style simple et naturel.

Dans le **Mémo des tournures essentielles**, vous trouverez des centaines d'expressions anglaises de base, qui vous permettront de construire vos propres phrases dans toutes sortes de contextes.

La partie correspondance contient des modèles de lettres de tous genres, dont vous pourrez vous inspirer pour rédiger à votre tour vos lettres, que ce soit dans un contexte privé ou professionnel. Si vous êtes à la recherche d'un travail, vous y trouverez également des exemples de curriculum vitæ et de lettres de candidature. Pour vous permettre d'adapter ces modèles à vos besoins, nous vous donnons en outre une liste des formules de politesse employées en début et en fin de lettre.

La dernière partie est consacrée à la communication par télécopie, par courrier électronique et par téléphone, et comprend une liste des expressions de base les plus couramment utilisées au téléphone.

L'anglais en situation, complément indispensable de votre dictionnaire, vous permettra de vous exprimer avec aisance dans toutes les situations.

Table des matières

Likes, dislikes and preferences

Saying what you like

J'aime les gâteaux.	I like ...
J'aime que les choses soient à leur place.	I like ...
J'ai bien aimé le film.	I liked ...
J'adore sortir en boîte.	I love ...
Ce que je préfère chez Laurent, c'est son enthousiasme.	What I like most ...
Ce que j'aime par-dessus tout, c'est son sourire.	What I like most of all is ...
La visite des vignobles **m'a beaucoup plu.**	I very much enjoyed ...
J'ai un faible pour le chocolat.	I've got a weakness for ...
Rien ne vaut un bon café.	You can't beat ...
Rien de tel qu'un bon bain chaud !	There's nothing better than ...
Le couscous est **mon** plat **favori.**	My favourite ...
La lecture est **une de mes** activités **préférées.**	... one of my favourite ...
Cela ne me déplaît pas de sortir seule.	I don't mind ...

Saying what you dislike

Je n'aime pas le poisson.	I don't like ...
Je n'aime pas beaucoup parler en public.	I'm not very keen on ...
Je ne l'**aime pas du tout.**	I don't like ... at all.
Cette idée **ne m'emballe pas.**	I'm not particularly keen on ...
Je déteste la chimie.	I hate ...
J'ai horreur du sport.	I loathe ...
Je ne supporte pas qu'on me mente.	I can't stand ...
Sa façon d'agir **ne me plaît pas du tout.**	I don't like ... at all.
Ce que je déteste le plus, c'est le repassage.	What I hate most is ...

Saying what you prefer

Je préfère le rock **à** la musique classique.	I prefer ... to ...
Je préférerais vivre à Paris.	I would rather ...
J'aimerais mieux mourir de faim **que de** lui demander un service.	I'd sooner ... than ...

Expressing indifference

Ça m'est égal.   It's all the same to me.

Je n'ai pas de préférence.   I have no preference either way.

C'est comme vous voudrez.   As you wish.

Cela n'a aucune importance.   It doesn't matter in the least.

Peu importe.   I don't mind.

Asking what someone likes

Est-ce que vous aimez les frites ?   Do you like …

Est-ce que vous aimez faire la cuisine ?   Do you like …

Est-ce que cela vous plaît de vivre en ville ?   Do you like …

Qu'est-ce que vous préférez : la mer ou la montagne ?   Which do you like better …

Vous préférez lequel, le rouge ou le noir ?   Which do you prefer …

Est-ce que vous préférez vivre à la campagne ou en ville ?   Do you prefer …

Qu'est-ce que vous aimez le plus à la télévision ?   What do you like best …

Opinions

Asking for opinions

Qu'en pensez-vous ?   What do you think about it?

Que pensez-vous de sa façon d'agir ?   What do you think of …

Je voudrais savoir ce que vous pensez de son travail.   I'd like to know what you think of …

J'aimerais connaître votre avis sur ce problème.   I would like to know your views on …

Est-ce que vous pourriez me donner votre opinion sur cette émission ?   What do you think of …

Quelle est votre opinion sur la peine de mort ?   What is your opinion on …

À votre avis, hommes et femmes sont-ils égaux ?   In your opinion …

Selon vous, faut-il donner plus de liberté aux jeunes ?   In your opinion …

Expressing opinions

Vous avez raison.	You are right.
Il a tort.	He is wrong.
Il a eu tort de démissionner.	He was wrong to …
Je pense que ce sera possible.	I think …
Je crois que c'est un peu prématuré.	I think …
Je trouve que c'est normal.	I think …
Personnellement, je pense que c'est trop cher.	Personally, I think that …
Il me semble que vous vous trompez.	I think …
J'ai l'impression que ses parents ne la comprennent pas.	I get the impression that …
Je suis certain qu'il est tout à fait sincère.	I'm sure …
Je suis sûr que Marc va gagner.	I'm sure …
Je suis persuadé qu'il y a d'autres solutions.	I am convinced that …
À mon avis, il n'a pas changé.	In my opinion …
D'après moi, il a fait une erreur.	In my view …
Selon moi, c'est impossible.	In my view …

Being noncommittal

Ça dépend.	It depends.
Tout dépend de ce que vous entendez par là.	It all depends what you mean by …
Je ne peux pas me prononcer.	I'd rather not express an opinion.
Je n'ai pas d'opinion bien précise à ce sujet.	I have no definite opinion on this.
Je ne me suis jamais posé la question.	I have never thought about it.

Approval and agreement

Je trouve que c'est une excellente idée.	I think it's an excellent idea.
Quelle bonne idée !	What a good idea!
J'ai beaucoup apprécié son article.	I was very impressed by …
C'est une très bonne chose.	It's a very good thing.
Je trouve que vous avez raison de vous méfier.	I think you're right to …
Les journaux ont raison de publier ces informations.	… are right to …

Vous avez bien fait de laisser vos bagages à la consigne.	You were right to …
Vous n'avez pas tort de critiquer le gouvernement.	You're quite justified in …
Je partage cette opinion.	I share this view.
Je partage votre inquiétude.	I fully share your …
Nous sommes favorables à la création d'emplois.	We are in favour of …
Nous sommes en faveur d'une Europe unie.	We are in favour of …
Il est exact que c'est un risque à prendre.	It is true that …
Il est vrai que cette erreur aurait pu être évitée.	It is true that …
Je suis d'accord avec vous.	I agree with you.
Je suis entièrement d'accord avec toi.	I entirely agree with you.

Disapproval and disagreement

Je trouve qu'il a eu tort d'emprunter autant d'argent.	I think he was wrong to …
Il est dommage qu'il ait réagi ainsi.	It's a pity that …
Il est regrettable qu'ils ne nous aient pas prévenus.	It is regrettable that …
Cette idée **me déplaît profondément.**	I dislike … intensely.
Je ne supporte pas le mensonge.	I can't stand …
Nous sommes contre la chasse.	We are against …
Je refuse cette solution.	I reject …
Je suis opposé à toute forme de censure.	I am opposed to …
Je ne partage pas ce point de vue.	I don't share this point of view.
Je suis déçu par son attitude.	I am disappointed by …
Je suis profondément déçu.	I am deeply disappointed.
Tu n'aurais pas dû lui parler sur ce ton.	You shouldn't have …
Nous ne pouvons accepter de voir la situation se dégrader.	We can't stand by and …
De quel droit agit-**il** de la sorte ?	What gives him the right to …
Je ne suis pas d'accord.	I disagree.
Nous ne sommes pas d'accord avec eux.	We don't agree with …
Je ne suis absolument pas d'accord avec ce qu'il a dit.	I totally disagree with …
C'est faux de dire que cette erreur était inévitable.	It is wrong to say that …
Vous vous trompez !	You're wrong!

Apologies

How to say sorry

Excusez-moi.	Sorry.
Excusez-moi de vous déranger.	Sorry to bother you.
Oh, pardon ! J'ai dû faire un faux numéro.	Oh, sorry!
Je suis désolé de vous avoir réveillé.	I am sorry I ...
Je suis désolé pour tout ce qui s'est passé.	I am sorry about ...
Je vous prie de m'excuser.	I do apologize.
Nous prions nos lecteurs **de bien vouloir excuser** cette omission.	We hope ... will excuse ...

Admitting responsibility

C'est (de) ma faute : j'aurais dû partir plus tôt.	It's my fault, I should have ...
Je n'aurais pas dû me moquer d'elle.	I shouldn't have ...
Nous avons eu tort de ne pas vérifier cette information.	We were wrong not to ...
J'assume seul l'entière responsabilité de cette erreur.	I take full responsibility for ...
Si seulement j'avais préparé ma leçon !	If only I had ...

Disclaiming responsibility

Ce n'est pas (de) ma faute.	It's not my fault.
Ce n'est pas (de) ma faute si nous sommes en retard.	It isn't my fault if ...
Je ne l'ai pas fait exprès.	I didn't do it on purpose.
Je ne pouvais pas faire autrement.	I had no other option.
J'avais pourtant cru comprendre que je pouvais me garer là.	But I thought that ...
J'avais cru bien faire en le prévenant.	I thought I was doing the right thing in ...

Apologizing for being unable to do something

Je regrette, mais ce n'est pas possible.	I'm sorry, but ...
Je suis désolé, mais je ne peux pas vous aider.	I'm sorry, but ...
Il nous est malheureusement impossible d'accéder à votre demande.	Unfortunately, it's impossible for us to ...

Explanations

Causes

Je n'ai rien acheté **parce que** je n'ai pas d'argent.	... because ...
Je suis arrivé en retard **à cause des** embouteillages.	... because of ...
Puisque tu insistes, je rentre dans une semaine.	Since ...
Comme j'habitais près de la bibliothèque, j'y allais souvent.	As ...
J'ai réussi à m'en sortir **grâce au** soutien de . mes amis	... thanks to ...
Je ne pourrai pas venir **car** je n'ai pas fini.	... as ...
Vu la situation actuelle, nous ne pouvons pas nous prononcer.	Given ...
Étant donné la crise, il est difficile de trouver du travail.	Given ...
C'est une rupture d'essieu **qui a provoqué** le déraillement.	It was ... that caused ...
Le théâtre va fermer **faute de** moyens.	... due to lack of ...
Il a donné sa démission **pour des raisons de** santé.	... for ... reasons.
Le projet a été abandonné **en raison de** problèmes juridiques.	... owing to ...
Le malaise des enseignants **est lié à** la difficulté de leur métier.	... is linked to ...
Le problème vient de ce que les gens ont peur des ordinateurs.	The problem is that ...
Le ralentissement des exportations **provient de** la chute de la demande européenne.	... is the result of ...
La haine **résulte de** l'incompréhension.	... results from ...

Consequences

Je dois partir ce soir. Je ne pourrai **donc** pas venir avec vous.	... so ...
La distribution a été améliorée, **de telle sorte que** les lecteurs trouveront leur journal plus tôt.	... so that ...
Le cidre nouveau est très peu fermenté et **par conséquent** très peu alcoolisé.	... consequently ...
Ce manque de concertation **a eu pour conséquence** une duplication inutile de nos efforts.	... has resulted in ...
Voilà pourquoi on s'en souvient.	That's why ...

Comparisons

On peut comparer la télévision **à** une drogue.	... can be compared to ...
C'est une très belle performance **que l'on peut comparer à** celle des meilleurs athlètes.	... which can be compared to ...
Le Centre Pompidou **est souvent comparé à** un paquebot.	... is often compared to ...
Le bruit **était comparable à** celui d'une moto dépourvue de silencieux.	... was comparable to ...
L'Afrique reste un continent sous-peuplé **comparé à** l'Asie.	... compared with ...
Par comparaison avec l'Islande, l'Irlande a un climat tropical.	Compared to ...
Les investissements publicitaires ont connu une légère progression **par rapport à** l'année dernière.	... compared to ...
Cette histoire **ressemble à** un conte de fées.	... is like ...
Il adorait cette campagne qui **lui rappelait** l'Irlande.	... reminded him of ...
Des taux de chômage effrayants, **rappelant ceux** des années 30.	... reminiscent of those ...
Il me fait penser à mon frère.	He reminds me of ...
Le surf des neiges **est l'équivalent** sur neige **de** la planche à roulettes.	... is the equivalent ... of ...
Cette somme **correspond à** six mois de salaire.	... corresponds to ...
C'est la même chose.	It's the same thing.
Cela revient au même.	It comes to the same thing.
Ce disque **n'est ni meilleur ni moins bon que** les autres.	... is no better and no worse than ...

Stressing differences

Aucune catastrophe **ne peut être comparée au** tsunami de 2004.	No ... can compare with ...
On ne peut pas comparer les usines modernes **à** celles où travaillaient nos grands-parents.	... cannot be compared with ...
Les actions de ce groupe **n'ont rien de comparable avec** les agissements des terroristes.	... are in no way comparable to ...
Sa démarche le **différencie de** son frère.	... distinguishes ... from ...
L'histoire des États-Unis **ne ressemble en rien à** la nôtre.	... in no way resembles ...
Il y a des événements bien plus tragiques que de perdre une finale de Coupe d'Europe.	There are worse things than ...
Le gruyère **est meilleur que** le comté.	... is better than ...

Son deuxième film **est moins** réussi **que** le premier.   ... is less ... than ...

L'espérance de vie des femmes est de 81 ans,   ... while ...
   tandis que celle des hommes est de 72 ans.

Alors que la consommation de vin et de bière   While ...
   diminue, l'eau minérale est un marché en
   expansion.

Requests and offers

Requests

Je voudrais trois tartelettes.   I'd like ...

Je voudrais connaître les horaires des trains pour Lille.   I'd like to ...

Pourriez-vous nous donner un coup de main ?   Could you ...

Est-ce que vous pouvez annoncer la bonne nouvelle   Can you ...
   à Éliane ?

Est-ce que vous pourriez venir me chercher ?   Could you ...

Sois gentille, fais un saut chez le boulanger.   Be an angel ...

Auriez-vous l'amabilité de m'indiquer la sortie ?   Could you please ...

Auriez-vous la gentillesse de nous donner   Would you be so kind as
   la recette ?   to ...

Auriez-vous l'obligeance de me garder ma place ?   Would you be very kind
        and ...

Puis-je vous demander de m'accorder un instant ?   Could you ...

Merci de bien vouloir patienter.   If you wouldn't mind ...

Est-ce que cela vous dérangerait d'ouvrir la fenêtre ?   Would you mind ...

Je vous serais reconnaissant de me prévenir dès   I would be grateful if
   que possible.   you would ...

Je vous serais reconnaissant de bien vouloir me   I would be grateful if
   communiquer votre décision d'ici vendredi.   you would ...

Offers

Je peux passer vous prendre, **si** vous voulez.   I can ... if ...

Je pourrais vous accompagner.   I could ...

Ça te dirait, une glace ?   Do you fancy ...

Ça vous dirait d'aller faire un tour ?   Would you like to ...

Que diriez-vous d'une balade en forêt ?   How do you fancy ...

Est-ce que vous voulez que j'aille chercher votre   Do you want me to ...
   voiture ?

Est-ce que vous voulez dîner avec nous un soir ?   Would you like to ...

Advice and suggestions

Asking for advice or suggestions

À ma place, que feriez-vous ?	What would you do, if you were me?
Quel est votre avis sur la question ?	What's your opinion on the matter?
Qu'est-ce que vous me conseillez, les Baléares ou les Canaries ?	Which would you recommend ...
Que me conseillez-vous de faire ?	What would you advise me to do?
Parmi les excursions à faire, laquelle nous conseilleriez-vous ?	... which would you recommend?
Quelle stratégie proposez-vous ?	What ... do you suggest?
Que proposez-vous pour réduire la pollution ?	What, in your opinion, should be done to ...
Qu'est-ce que vous proposez contre le chômage ?	How would you deal with ...

Offering advice or suggestions

À votre place, je me méfierais.	If I were you ...
Si j'étais toi, je ne dirais rien.	If I were you ...
Je peux vous donner un conseil : achetez votre billet à l'avance.	If I may give you a bit of advice ...
Un conseil : lisez le mode d'emploi.	A word of advice ...
Un bon conseil : n'attendez pas le dernier moment pour faire votre réservation.	A useful tip ...
Vous devriez voir un spécialiste.	You should ...
Vous feriez bien de consulter un avocat.	You would do well to ...
Vous feriez mieux d'acheter une nouvelle voiture.	You would do better to ...
Vous pourriez peut-être demander à quelqu'un de vous le traduire.	You could perhaps ...
Vous pourriez montrer un peu plus de compréhension.	You could ...
Pourquoi ne pas lui téléphoner ?	Why don't you ...
Il faudrait peut-être essayer autre chose.	Perhaps we ought to ...
Et si on allait au cinéma ?	How about ...
Je vous propose le 3 mars à 10 h 30.	How about ...
Il vaudrait mieux lui offrir de l'argent qu'un bijou.	It might be better to ...
Il serait préférable d'attendre le résultat.	It would be better to ...

Warnings

Je vous préviens, je ne me laisserai pas faire.
Je te préviens que ça ne sera pas facile.
N'oubliez pas de conserver le double de votre déclaration d'impôts.
Méfiez-vous des apparences.

Surtout, n'y allez **jamais** le samedi.
Si tu ne viens pas, **tu risques de** le regretter.

I warn you ...
I'd better warn you that ...
Don't forget to ...

Remember: appearances can be deceptive.
Whatever you do, don't ...
... you risk ...

Intentions and desires

Asking what someone intends to do

Qu'est-ce que vous allez faire ?
Qu'est-ce que tu vas faire si tu rates ton examen ?
Qu'allez-vous faire en rentrant? **Avez-vous des projets ?**

Quels sont vos projets ?
Est-ce que tu comptes passer tes vacances ici ?
Vous comptez rester longtemps ?
Que comptez-vous faire de votre collection ?

Comment comptez-vous faire ?

Tu as l'intention de passer des concours ?
Songez-vous à refaire un film en Europe ?

What are you going to do?
What will you do if ...
What are you going to do ... ? Do you have anything planned?

What are your plans?
Are you planning to ...
Are you planning on ...
What are you planning to do with ...

What are you thinking of doing?

Do you intend to ...
Are you thinking of ...

Talking about intentions

Je comptais m'envoler pour Ajaccio le 8 juillet.
Elle prévoit de voyager pendant un an.
Il est prévu de construire un nouveau stade.
Ils envisagent d'avoir plusieurs enfants.
Cette banque **a l'intention de** fermer un grand nombre de succursales.
Je songe à abandonner la politique.
J'ai décidé de changer de carrière.
Je suis décidée à arrêter de fumer.

I was planning to ...
She plans to ...
There are plans to ...
They are thinking of ...
... intends to ...

I am thinking of ...
I have decided to ...
I have made up my mind to ...

Je me suis décidée à y aller. — I have decided to …
C'est décidé, nous partons à la campagne. — That's settled …
Il n'a jamais été dans nos intentions de lui cacher la vérité. — We never had any intention of …
Il n'est pas question pour moi de renoncer à ce projet. — There is no question of …

Wishes

Je veux faire du cinéma. — I want to …
Je voudrais savoir jouer aussi bien que lui. — I'd like to …
J'aimerais faire du deltaplane. — I'd like to …
J'aimerais que mes photos soient publiées dans la presse. — I would like …
J'aurais aimé avoir un frère. — I would have liked to …
Lionel voulait à tout prix partir le soir-même. — … wanted at all costs …
Nous souhaitons préserver notre indépendance. — We wish to …
J'espère avoir des enfants. — I hope to …
Nous espérons que les enfants regarderont cette émission avec leurs parents. — We hope that …
Vous rêvez de faire le tour du monde ? — Do you dream of …
Mon rêve serait d'avoir une grande maison. — My dream would be to …

Obligation

Il faut que je me trouve un logement. — I must …
Il faut absolument qu'on se revoie avant le 23 ! — We really must …
Si vous allez en Pologne, vous devez venir nous voir. — … you must …
Les auteurs du détournement ont exigé que l'avion reparte vers New York. — … demanded that …
Ça me force à faire de l'exercice. — … makes me …
Une violente crise d'asthme m'a obligé à consulter un médecin. — … forced me to …
Je suis obligé de partir. — I have to …
Il est obligé de travailler, il n'a pas le choix. — He has to … he has no other option.

On ne peut pas faire autrement que d'accepter. — You have no choice but to …
L'école est obligatoire jusqu'à seize ans. — … is compulsory …
Il est indispensable de voyager pour comprendre les autres. — It is essential to …

Permission

Asking for permission

Je peux téléphoner ?	Can I ...
Je peux vous demander quelque chose ?	Can I ...
Est-ce que je peux passer vous dire un petit bonjour tout à l'heure ?	Can I ...
Ça ne vous dérange pas si j'arrive en avance ?	Is it alright if ...
Ça ne vous dérange pas que je fume ?	Do you mind if ...
Est-ce que ça vous dérange si j'ouvre la fenêtre ?	Do you mind if ...
Vous permettez, Madame, **que** je regarde ce qu'il y a dans votre sac ?	Would you mind if ...

Giving permission

(Vous) faites comme vous voulez.	Do as you please.
Allez-y !	Go ahead!
Je n'y vois pas d'inconvénient.	I have nothing against it.
Vous avez le droit de porter plainte.	You have the right to ...

Saying something is not allowed

Je te défends de sortir !	I forbid you to ...
C'est défendu.	It's forbidden.
Il est interdit de fumer dans les toilettes.	... is forbidden.
Le travail des enfants **est formellement interdit par** une convention de l'ONU.	... is strictly forbidden by ...
Défense d'entrer.	No entry.
Stationnement interdit.	No parking.
Interdiction de stationner.	No parking.
C'est interdit.	It's not allowed.
Elle interdit à ses enfants **d'**ouvrir la porte.	She forbids ... to ...
Tu n'as pas le droit.	You're not allowed.
On n'avait pas le droit de manger ni de boire pendant le service.	We weren't allowed to ...
Il n'en est pas question.	That's out of the question.

Certainty, probability and possibility

Certainty

Il est certain qu'il y aura des problèmes.	Undoubtedly ...
Il ne fait aucun doute que ce produit connaîtra un réel succès.	There is no doubt that ...
Il est évident qu'il traverse une période difficile.	Clearly ...
C'est **de toute évidence** la seule chose à faire.	Quite obviously ...
Il est indéniable qu'il a eu tort d'agir ainsi.	It is undeniable that ...
Je suis sûre que mon frère te plaira.	I am sure that ...
Je suis sûr de gagner.	I am sure that I ...
Je suis certain que nous sommes sur la bonne voie.	I am certain that ...
J'ai la certitude qu'en travaillant avec lui, je ne m'ennuierai pas.	I am sure that ...
Je suis persuadé qu'il y a d'autres solutions.	I am convinced that ...

Probability

Il est probable que le prix du pétrole va continuer d'augmenter.	... probably ...
Le taux d'inflation dépassera **très probablement** les 10 %.	... very probably ...
80 % des problèmes de peau sont **sans doute** d'origine psychique.	... undoubtedly ...
Ils avaient **sans doute** raison.	... no doubt ...
Les travaux **devraient** débuter au mois d'avril.	... should ...
Il se pourrait bien qu'ils cherchent à tester nos réactions.	It is quite possible that ...
On dirait que tout lui est égal.	It's as if ...
Il a dû oublier d'ouvrir les fenêtres.	He must have ...

Possibility

C'est possible.	It is possible.
Il est possible que cela coûte plus cher.	That might ...
Il n'est pas impossible qu'il soit parti à Paris.	It is not impossible that ...
Il se pourrait que l'Amérique ait été découverte par des Chinois.	It is possible that ...
Il se peut que ce virus soit particulièrement virulent.	... may ...
En quelques mois tout **peut** changer.	... could ...
Il a **peut-être** mal compris.	Maybe ...
Peut-être que je me trompe.	Perhaps ...

Doubt, improbability and impossibility

Doubt

Je ne suis pas sûr que ce soit utile.	I'm not sure …
Je ne suis pas sûre d'y arriver.	I'm not sure I'll …
Je ne suis pas certain d'avoir raison.	I'm not sure I'm …
Il n'est pas certain que cela soit une bonne idée.	I'm not sure that …
Il n'est pas certain qu'un vaccin puisse être mis au point.	I'm not sure that …
Je me demande si nous avons fait beaucoup de progrès dans ce domaine.	I wonder if …
Est-ce sage ? **J'en doute.**	I doubt it.
Il se mit à **douter de** la compétence de son médecin.	… to have doubts about …
Je doute fort qu'il accepte de rester inactif.	I very much doubt …
On ne sait pas exactement ce qui s'est passé.	Nobody knows exactly …

Improbability

Il **ne** changera **probablement pas** d'avis.	… probably won't …
Il est peu probable qu'il reste encore des places.	It is unlikely that …
Ça m'étonnerait qu'ils aient ta pointure.	I'd be surprised if …
Il serait étonnant que tout se passe conformément aux prévisions.	It would be amazing if …
Nous ne risquons pas de nous ennuyer.	There's no danger of …
Elles ne risquent pas d'avoir le prix Nobel d'économie.	They are not likely to …
Il y a peu de chances que le taux de croissance dépasse 1,5 %.	There is not much chance of …

Impossibility

C'est impossible.	It's impossible.
Il n'est pas possible qu'il n'y ait rien à faire.	It is not possible that …
Il est impossible que ces renseignements soient faux.	… cannot …
Il n'y a aucune chance qu'ils viennent à notre secours.	There is no chance of …

Greetings

Bonjour !	Hello!
Bonsoir !	Good evening!
Salut !	Hi!
Comment allez-vous ?	How are you?
Comment ça va ?	How's things?

What to say in reply

Très bien, merci, et vous ?	Fine thanks, and you?
Ça va, et toi ?	Fine thanks, and you?
Super bien !	Great!
On fait aller.	So-so.
Couci-couça.	So-so.

Introductions

Je vous présente Charles.	This is ...
Je vous présente mon amie.	May I introduce ...
Marc ; Laurent	Marc, this is Laurent; Laurent, Marc.
Je ne crois pas que vous vous connaissiez.	I don't believe you know one another.

Replying to an introduction

Enchanté.	Pleased to meet you.
Enchanté or Ravi de faire votre connaissance.	Pleased to meet you.
Salut, moi c'est Dominique.	Hi, I'm ...

Leavetaking

Au revoir !	Goodbye!
Bonne nuit !	Good night!
Salut !	Bye!
Ciao !	See you!
À bientôt !	See you later!
À demain !	See you tomorrow!
À la semaine prochaine !	See you next week!
À jeudi !	See you Thursday!

Best wishes

Bon anniversaire !	Happy Birthday!
Joyeux Noël !	Merry Christmas!
Bonne année !	Happy New Year!
Félicitations !	Congratulations!
Bon voyage !	Safe journey!
Bonne chance !	Good luck!
Bienvenue !	Welcome!
Amusez-vous bien !	Have fun!
Bon appétit !	Enjoy your meal!
(À votre) santé !	Cheers!
Tchin-tchin !	Cheers!

Correspondence

How to address an envelope

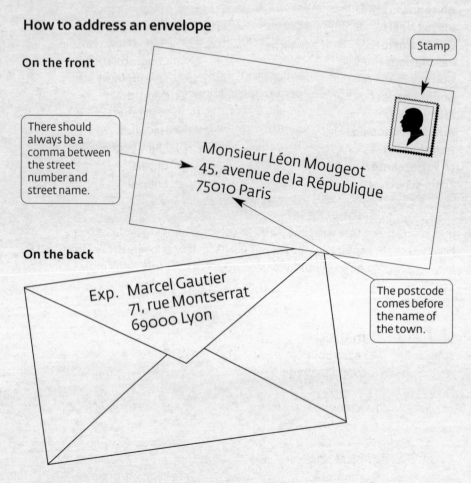

On the front

Stamp

There should always be a comma between the street number and street name.

Monsieur Léon Mougeot
45, avenue de la République
75010 Paris

On the back

Exp. Marcel Gautier
71, rue Montserrat
69000 Lyon

The postcode comes before the name of the town.

Common abbreviations used in addresses

av. = avenue	bd = boulevard	Exp. = expéditeur
fg = faubourg	pas. = passage	pl. = place

Standard opening and closing formulae
In personal correspondence

Cher Monsieur	Je vous envoie mes bien amicales pensées *(fairly formal)*
Chers Jean et Sylvie	Bien amicalement
Chère tante Laure	Je t'embrasse bien affectueusement
Mon cher Laurent	Grosses bises *(very informal)*

In formal correspondence

Monsieur le Directeur (or le Maire etc) Madame le Directeur	Je vous prie d'agréer, [...], l'assurance de ma considération distinguée
Messieurs Monsieur Madame	Je vous prie d'agréer, [...], l'assurance de mes sentiments distingués or Veuillez accepter, [...], l'expression de mes sentiments distingués
Cher Monsieur Chère Madame	Croyez, [...], à l'expression de mes sentiments les meilleurs

Starting a personal letter

Je te remercie de ta lettre ...
Thanks for your letter ...

J'ai été très content d'avoir de tes nouvelles.
It was lovely to hear from you.

Je suis désolé de ne pas vous avoir répondu plus vite.
I'm sorry I didn't reply sooner.

Starting a formal letter

Suite à ... je vous écris pour ...
Further to ... I am writing to ...

Je vous serais reconnaissant de ...
I would be grateful if you would ...

Je vous prie de ...
Please ...

Nous vous remercions de votre lettre ...
Thank you for your letter ...

Ending a personal letter

Transmettez mes amitiés à ...
Give my regards to ...

Dis bonjour à ... de ma part.
Say hello to ... for me.

... t'embrasse ...
... sends you his love ...

Embrasse ... pour moi.
Give my love to ...

Ending a formal letter

Dans l'attente de votre réponse ...
I look forward to hearing from you ...

Je demeure à votre entière disposition pour toute information complémentaire.
I will be happy to supply any further information you may require.

Je vous remercie dès à présent de ...
Thank you in advance for ...

Thank you letter

Name and address of sender.

The town or city from which the letter is being sent should be included along with the date. The article **le** should be included in the date.

Anne et Cyrille Legendre
25, rue des Grillons
69000 LYON

Lyon, le 24 octobre 2007

Chers oncle et tante,

Le grand jour, c'était il y a presqu'un mois déjà …
Ce fut une merveilleuse fête et nous étions très heureux
de vous avoir parmi nous.

Nous tenons à vous remercier chaleureusement de votre
gentil cadeau et nous vous inviterons bientôt pour
inaugurer ce superbe service à raclette comme
il se doit.

Vous trouverez aussi ci-joint une photo-souvenir.

Nous vous embrassons tous les deux,

Anne et Cyrille

For alternatives see p20.

Hotel booking

Name and address of letter's recipient.

Jeanne Judon
89, bd des Tertres
75008 PARIS

Hôtel Renoir
15, rue de Beaumanoir
59000 LILLE

Paris, le 3 novembre 2007

Madame ou Monsieur,

For alternatives see p21.

Me rendant à Lille le mois prochain à l'occasion du Salon de l'esthétique, j'aimerais réserver une chambre avec salle de bains pour deux nuits le mercredi 5 et le jeudi 6 décembre 2007.

Je vous saurais gré de me communiquer vos tarifs et de me confirmer que vous avez bien une chambre libre à cette époque.

Je vous prie de croire, Madame, Monsieur, à l'assurance de mes sentiments distingués.

Jeanne Judon

Letter of complaint

M et Mme DAUNAY
La Longue Haie
35135 CHANTEPIE

Hôtel "Au Bon Accueil"
17, rue Nationale
86000 POITIERS

Chantepie, le 29 décembre 2007

Madame, Monsieur,

Mon mari et moi avons passé la nuit du 23 décembre dans votre hôtel, où nous avions préalablement réservé une chambre. Nous tenons à vous faire savoir que nous avons été très déçus par vos services, en particulier par le bruit – nous avons pourtant demandé une chambre calme – et l'impossibilité de se faire servir un petit déjeuner avant notre départ à 6 h 30.

Cet arrêt dans votre hôtel qui devait nous permettre de nous reposer au cours d'un long voyage en voiture n'a fait que nous fatiguer davantage. Sachez que nous prendrons bien soin de déconseiller votre établissement à nos amis.

Je vous prie d'agréer, Madame, Monsieur, mes salutations distinguées.

[signature]

For alternatives see p21.

Curriculum Vitæ

The words **courriel** or **mél** can also be used.

CURRICULUM VITÆ

LEGUEN Maxime
29, rue de Vannes
35000 RENNES
Tél : 56 02 71 28

29 ans
célibataire
nationalité française

Adresse électronique : mleguen@agriventes.com.fr

EXPÉRIENCE PROFESSIONNELLE

Du 10.3.05 à ce jour :   Adjointe du directeur à l'exportation,
Agriventes, Rennes

Du 8.10.03 au 30.1.05 :   Secrétaire de direction,
France-Exportations, Cognac

DIPLÔMES

2003 :   Diplôme de secrétaire bilingue, délivré par l'École de commerce de Poitiers

2002 :   Licence de langues étrangères appliquées (anglais et russe), Université de Poitiers – plusieurs mentions

1998 :   Baccalauréat (langues) – mention assez bien

AUTRES RENSEIGNEMENTS

Langues étrangères : anglais et russe (courant), allemand (bonnes connaissances)

Stage d'information dans le cadre de la formation continue, 2005

Permis de conduire

Nombreux voyages en Europe et aux États-Unis

If you have British or American etc qualifications you should use wording such as "**équivalence baccalauréat (3 A-levels), équivalence licence de lettres (BA Hons)**" etc.

Job application

This is appropriate if you are writing to a company. However, if you are writing to the holder of a particular post use the following:
Monsieur (or **Madame**) **le Directeur des ressources humaines**
Société GERBAULT etc and begin the letter:
Monsieur le Directeur des ressources humaines,
If you know the name of the person you should use the following:
Monsieur Alain Dupont
Directeur des ressources humaines
Société GERBAULT etc and begin the letter:
Monsieur,

Maxime LEGUEN
29, rue de Vannes
35000 RENNES

Service du Personnel
Société GERBAULT
85, bd de la Liberté
35000 RENNES

Rennes, le 12 juillet 2007

Madame, Monsieur,

Votre annonce parue dans le Monde du 8 juillet concernant un poste d'assistante de direction dans votre service Import-Export m'a particulièrement intéressée.

Mon expérience de quatre ans en tant qu'assistante de direction dans le service d'exportation d'une petite entreprise m'a permis d'acquérir un sens des responsabilités ainsi qu'une grande capacité d'adaptation. Le poste que vous proposez m'intéresse tout particulièrement car j'aimerais beaucoup pouvoir utiliser ma connaissance de la langue et de la culture russe dans le cadre de mon travail.

Je me tiens à votre disposition pour vous apporter de plus amples renseignements sur ma formation et mon expérience.

Je vous prie, Madame, Monsieur, de bien vouloir agréer mes salutations distinguées.

Maxime Leguen

Maxime Leguen
P.J. : CV

= **pièces jointes.** You should add this if you are enclosing any other information with your letter eg a CV.

Invitation to interview

SOCIÉTÉ GERBAULT

85, bd de la Liberté
35000 RENNES
TÉLÉPHONE : 02 99 45 32 88 • TÉLÉCOPIE : 02 99 45 32 90

> Maxime LEGUEN
> 29, rue de Vannes
> 35000 RENNES

Rennes, le 19 juillet

Madame,

Votre candidature au poste d'assistante de direction au sein de notre Compagnie a retenu notre attention.

Nous vous proposons, dans le but de faire plus ample connaissance de part et d'autre, de rencontrer :

Monsieur LAURENT

notre Directeur Régional, le 26 juillet prochain, à 9 h, à l'adresse suivante :

2, bd de Lattre de Tassigny
35000 RENNES

Si cette date ne vous convenait pas, vous seriez aimable d'avertir notre secrétariat (Tél : 02 99 45 32 88) afin de convenir d'un autre rendez-vous.

Nous vous prions de croire, Madame, à l'expression de nos sentiments distingués.

Jean Minet
Jean Minet

For alternatives see p21.

Fax

France-Sanitaires S.A.

55, rue de Strasbourg
75012 Paris
Téléphone : 01 63 13 84 20
Télécopie : 01 63 13 84 32

TÉLÉCOPIE

À : Mme Robin

Date : le 7 janvier 2007

De : M. Edmond
Service clientèle

Nombre de pages à suivre : 1

Réf. : Devis pour installation salle de bains.

Madame,

Suite à notre visite d'avant-hier, veuillez trouver ci-joint notre devis pour l'installation d'une salle de bains dans votre appartement. Les prix comprennent la fourniture du matériel ainsi que la main d'oeuvre.

Dans l'attente de votre réponse, je vous prie, Madame, d'agréer l'expression de mes meilleurs sentiments,

Y. Edmond

E-Mail

Sending messages

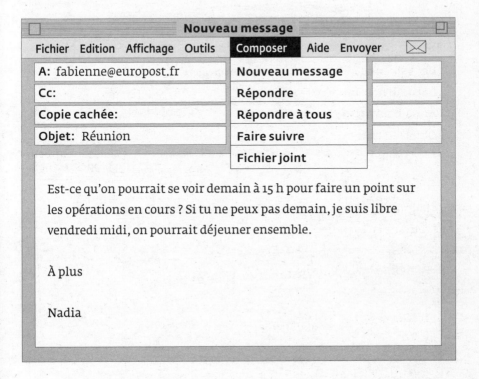

Fichier	File
Édition	Edit
Affichage	View
Outils	Tools
Composer	Compose
Aide	Help
Envoyer	Send
Nouveau message	New
Répondre	Reply to Sender

E-Mail

Receiving messages

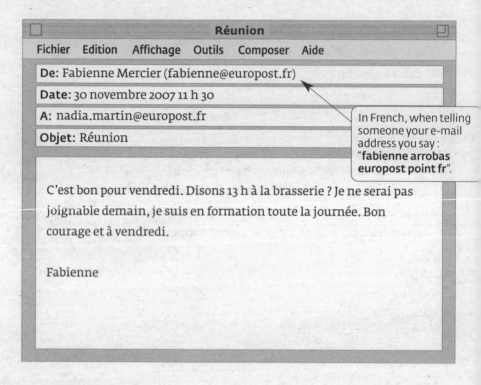

Répondre à tous	Reply to All
Faire suivre	Forward
Fichier joint	Attachment
À	To
Cc	Cc (carbon copy)
Copie cachée	Bcc (blind carbon copy)
Objet	Subject
De	From
Date	Sent

TELEPHONE

Different types of call

Communication locale/interurbaine.	Local/national call.
Je voudrais appeler l'étranger.	I want to make an international call.
Je voudrais appeler Londres **en PCV**.	I want to make a reverse charge call (*Brit*) to a ... number *or* I want to call a ... number collect (*US*).
Comment est-ce que je peux téléphoner à l'extérieur ?	How do I get an outside line?

Asking for information

Quel est le numéro des renseignements ?	What is the number for directory enquiries (*Brit*) *or* directory assistance (*US*)?
Je voudrais le numéro de la société Europost, 20, rue de la Marelle, à Pierrefitte.	Can you give me the number of ...
Quel est l'**indicatif de** la Martinique ?	What is the code for ...
Quel est le numéro de l'**horloge parlante** ?	What is the number for the speaking clock?

Receiving information

Le numéro que vous avez demandé est le 01 40 32 37 12. (zéro-un quarante trente-deux trente-sept douze)	The number you require is ...
Je regrette, mais il n'y a pas d'abonné à ce nom.	I'm sorry, there's no listing under that name.
Le numéro que vous avez demandé est sur liste rouge.	The number you require is ex-directory (*Brit*) *or* unlisted (*US*).

When your number answers

Je voudrais parler à *or* **Pourrais-je parler à** M. Wolff, s'il vous plaît ?	Could I speak to ...
Pourriez-vous me passer le docteur Henderson, s'il vous plaît ?	Could you put me through to ...
Pourriez-vous me passer le poste 52 64, s'il vous plaît ?	Can I have extension ...
Je rappellerai dans une demi-heure.	I'll call back in ...
Pourriez-vous lui demander de me rappeler à son retour ?	Would you ask him to ring me when he gets back?

The switchboard operator speaks

C'est de la part de qui ?	Who shall I say is calling?
Je vous le passe.	I'm putting you through.
J'ai un appel de Tokyo **pour** Mme Thomson.	I have a call from ... for ...
J'ai Mlle Martin **en ligne.**	I've got ... on the line.
Le docteur Roberts **est en ligne, vous patientez ?**	... is on another line. Do you want to wait?
Ne quittez pas.	Please hold.
Ça ne répond pas.	There's no reply.
Voulez-vous laisser un message ?	Would you like to leave a message?

Recorded messages

Le numéro de votre correspondant n'est plus attribué. Veuillez consulter l'annuaire ou votre centre de renseignements.	The number you have dialled has not been recognized. Please consult the directory or directory enquiries.
Le numéro de votre correspondant a changé. Veuillez composer désormais le 33 42 21 70.	The number you have dialled has been changed to ...
Par suite de l'encombrement des lignes, votre appel ne peut aboutir. Veuillez rappeler ultérieurement.	All the lines are busy right now. Please try again later.
Bonjour, vous êtes en communication avec le service des ventes. **Veuillez patienter, nous allons donner suite à votre appel dans quelques instants.**	Hello, you have reached ... Please wait, your call will be answered shortly.
Bonjour, vous êtes bien chez M. et Mme Martin. **Laissez un message après le bip sonore et nous vous rappellerons dès notre retour.** Merci.	Hello, you are through to ... Leave a message after the tone and we'll get back to you.

Answering the telephone

Allô, c'est Anne à l'appareil.	Hello, it's ... speaking.
C'est moi or lui-même (or elle-même).	Speaking.
Qui est à l'appareil ?	Who's speaking?

When in trouble

Je n'arrive pas à avoir le numéro.	I can't get through.
Leur téléphone est en dérangement.	Their phone is out of order.
Nous avons été coupés.	We have been cut off.
J'ai dû faire un faux numéro.	I must have dialled the wrong number.
La ligne est très mauvaise.	This is a very bad line.

Goûts et préférences

Pour dire ce que l'on aime

I **like** cakes.	J'aime ...
I **like** things to be in their proper place.	J'aime que ...
I **really liked** the film.	J'ai bien aimé ...
I **love** going to clubs.	J'adore ...
What I like best about Matthew are his eyes.	Ce que je préfère ...
What I enjoy most is an evening with friends.	Ce que j'aime par-dessus tout, c'est ...
I **very much enjoyed** the trip to the vineyards.	... m'a beaucoup plu.
I've never tasted **anything better than** this chicken.	... rien ... de meilleur que ...
I've got a **weakness for** chocolate cakes.	J'ai un faible pour ...
You can't beat a good cup of tea.	Rien ne vaut ...
There's nothing quite like a nice hot bath!	Rien de tel que ...
My **favourite** dish is lasagne.	... mon ... favori.
Reading is **one of my favourite** pastimes.	... une de mes ... préférées.
I **don't mind** being alone.	Cela ne me déplaît pas de ...

Pour dire ce que l'on n'aime pas

I **don't like** fish.	Je n'aime pas ...
I **don't like** him **at all.**	Je ne ... aime pas du tout.
I'm **not very keen on** speaking in public.	Je n'aime pas beaucoup ...
I'm **not particularly keen on** the idea.	... ne m'emballe pas.
I **hate** chemistry.	Je déteste ...
I **loathe** sport.	J'ai horreur du ...
I **can't stand** being lied to.	Je ne supporte pas que ...
If there's one thing I hate it's ironing.	Ce que je déteste le plus, c'est de ...

Préférences

I **prefer** pop **to** classical music.	Je préfère ... à ...
I **would rather** live in Paris.	Je préférerais ...
I'**d rather** starve **than** ask him a favour.	J'aimerais mieux ... que de ...

Indifférence

It's all the same to me.	Ça m'est égal.
I have no particular preference.	Je n'ai pas de préférence.
As you like.	C'est comme vous voudrez.

It doesn't matter in the least.	Cela n'a aucune importance.
I don't mind.	Peu importe.

Comment demander à quelqu'un ce qu'il aime

Do you like chocolate?	Est-ce que vous aimez ...
Do you like cooking?	Est-ce que vous aimez ...
Which do you like better: football or cricket?	Qu'est-ce que vous préférez : ...
Which would you rather have: the red one or the black one?	Lequel préférez-vous : ...
Do you prefer living in the town or in the country?	Est-ce que vous préférez ...
What do you like best on television?	Qu'est-ce que vous aimez le plus ...

Opinions

Comment demander l'avis de quelqu'un

What do you think about it?	Qu'en pensez-vous ?
What do you think about divorce?	Que pensez-vous du ...
What do you think of his behaviour?	Que pensez-vous de ...
I'd like to know what you think of his work.	Je voudrais savoir ce que vous pensez de ...
I would like to know your views on this.	J'aimerais connaître votre avis sur ...
What is your opinion on the team's chances of success?	Quelle est votre opinion sur ...
Could you give me your opinion on this proposal?	Est-ce que vous pourriez me donner votre avis sur ...
In your opinion, are men and women equal?	À votre avis ...
In your view, is this the best solution?	Selon vous ...

Comment donner son avis

You are right.	Vous avez raison.
He is wrong.	Il a tort.
He was wrong to resign.	Il a eu tort de ...
I think it ought to be possible.	Je pense que ...

I **think** it's a bit premature.	Je crois que …
I **think** it's quite natural.	Je trouve que …
Personally, I think that it's a waste of money.	Personnellement, je pense que …
I **have the impression that** her parents don't understand her.	J'ai l'impression que …
I'm **sure** he is completely sincere.	Je suis certain que …
I'm **convinced that** there are other possibilities.	Je suis persuadé que …
In my opinion, he hasn't changed.	À mon avis …
In my view, he's their best player.	Selon moi …

Comment éviter de donner son avis

It **depends**.	Ça dépend.
It all depends on what you mean by patriotism.	Tout dépend de ce que vous entendez par …
I'd rather not express an opinion.	Je préfère ne pas me prononcer.
Actually, I've never thought about it.	À vrai dire, je ne me suis jamais posé la question.

Approbation et accord

I **think** it's an excellent idea.	Je trouve que c'est une excellente idée.
What a good idea!	Quelle bonne idée !
I **was very impressed by** his speech.	J'ai beaucoup apprécié …
It's a very good thing.	C'est une très bonne chose.
I **think you're right to** be wary.	Je trouve que vous avez raison de …
Newspapers **are right to** publish these stories.	… ont raison de …
You were right to leave your bags in left-luggage.	Vous avez bien fait de …
Third World countries **rightly believe that** most pollution comes from developed countries.	… estiment à juste titre que …
You're quite justified in complaining.	Vous avez bien raison de …
I **share this view.**	Je partage cette opinion.
I **fully share** your concern.	Je partage …
We support the creation of jobs.	Nous sommes favorables à …
We are in favour of a united Europe.	Nous sommes en faveur de …

It is true that mistakes were made.	Il est vrai que ...
I agree with you.	Je suis d'accord avec vous.
I entirely agree with you.	Je suis entièrement d'accord avec toi.

Désapprobation et désaccord

I think he was wrong to borrow so much money.	Je trouve qu'il a eu tort de ...
It's a pity that you didn't tell me.	Il est dommage que ...
It is regrettable that they allowed this to happen.	Il est regrettable que ...
I dislike the idea intensely.	... me déplaît profondément.
I can't stand lies.	Je ne supporte pas ...
We are against hunting.	Nous sommes contre ...
We do not condone violence.	Nous ne tolérons pas ...
I am opposed to compulsory screening.	Je suis opposé au ...
I don't share this point of view.	Je ne partage pas ce point de vue.
I am disappointed by his attitude.	Je suis déçu par ...
I am deeply disappointed.	Je suis profondément déçu.
You shouldn't have said that.	Tu n'aurais pas dû ...
What gives him the right to act like this?	De quel droit ...
I disagree.	Je ne suis pas d'accord.
We don't agree with them.	Nous ne sommes pas d'accord avec ...
I totally disagree with what he said.	Je ne suis absolument pas d'accord avec ...
It is not true to say that the disaster was inevitable.	C'est faux de dire que ...
You are wrong!	Vous vous trompez !

Excuses

Pour s'excuser

Sorry.	Excusez-moi.
Oh, sorry! I've got the wrong number.	Oh, pardon !
Sorry to bother you.	Excusez-moi de vous déranger.

I'm sorry I woke you.
I'm terribly sorry about the misunderstanding.
I do apologize.
We hope our readers will excuse this oversight.

Je suis désolé de ...
Je suis navré de ...
Je vous prie de m'excuser.
Nous prions ... de bien vouloir excuser ...

En assumant la responsabilité de ce qui s'est passé

It's my fault; I should have left earlier.

C'est (de) ma faute : j'aurais dû ...

I shouldn't have laughed at her.
We were wrong not to check this information.

Je n'aurais pas dû ...
Nous avons eu tort de ne pas ...

I take full responsibility for what I did.

J'assume seul l'entière responsabilité de ...

If only I had done my homework!

Si seulement j'avais ...

En niant toute responsabilité

It's not my fault.
It isn't my fault if we're late.

Ce n'est pas (de) ma faute.
Ce n'est pas (de) ma faute si ...

I didn't do it on purpose.
I had no option.

Je ne l'ai pas fait exprès.
Je ne pouvais pas faire autrement.

But I thought that it was okay to park here.

J'avais pourtant cru comprendre que ...

I thought I was doing the right thing in warning him.

J'avais cru bien faire en ...

En exprimant ses regrets

I'm sorry, but it's impossible.
I'm afraid we're fully booked.
Unfortunately we are unable to meet your request.

Je regrette, mais ...
Je regrette, mais ...
Il nous est malheureusement impossible de ...

Explications

Causes

I didn't buy anything **because** I had no money.	... parce que ...
I arrived late **because of** the traffic.	... à cause de ...
Since you insist, I'll come again tomorrow.	Puisque ...
As I lived near the library, I used it a lot.	Comme ...
I got through it **thanks to** the support of my friends.	... grâce à ...
Given the present situation, finding a job will be difficult.	Vu ...
Given that there is an economic crisis, it is difficult to find work.	Étant donné ...
Considering how many problems we had, we did well.	Étant donné ...
It was a broken axle **that caused** the derailment.	C'est ... qui a provoqué ...
He resigned **for** health **reasons.**	... pour des raisons de ...
The theatre is closing, **due to lack of** funds.	... faute de ...
The project was abandoned **owing to** legal problems.	... en raison de ...
Many cancers **are linked to** smoking.	... sont dus à ...
The problem is that people are afraid of computers.	Le problème vient de ce que ...
The drop in sales **is the result of** high interest rates.	... est due à ...
The quarrel **resulted from** a misunderstanding.	... a pour origine ...

Conséquences

I have to leave tonight; **so** I can't come with you.	... donc ...
Distribution has been improved **so that** readers now get their newspaper earlier.	... de telle sorte que ...
This cider is fermented for a very short time and is **consequently** low in alcohol.	... par conséquent ...
Our lack of consultation **has resulted in** a duplication of effort.	... a eu pour conséquence ...
That's why they are easy to remember.	Voilà pourquoi ...

Comparaisons

Gambling **can be compared to** a drug.	On peut comparer ... à ...
The gas has a smell **that can be compared to** rotten eggs.	... que l'on peut comparer à ...

The shape of Italy **is often compared to** a boot.	... est souvent comparé à ...
The noise **was comparable to** that of a large motorbike.	... était comparable à ...
Africa is still underpopulated **compared with** Asia.	... comparé à ...
In the UK, the rate of inflation increased slightly **compared to** the previous year.	... par rapport à ...
What is so special about a holiday in Florida **as compared to** one in Spain?	... par rapport à ...
This story **is like** a fairy tale.	... ressemble à ...
He loved this countryside, which **reminded him of** Ireland.	... lui rappelait ...
Frightening levels of unemployment, **reminiscent of those** of the 30s.	... rappelant ceux ...
The snowboard **is the equivalent** on snow **of** the skateboard.	... est l'équivalent ... de ...
This sum **corresponds to** six months' salary.	... correspond à ...
A 'bap'? **It's the same thing as** a bread roll.	C'est la même chose que ...
It comes to the same thing in terms of calories.	Ça revient au même ...
This record **is no better and no worse than** the others.	... n'est ni meilleur ni moins bon que ...

Pour souligner une différence

No catastrophe **can compare with** the tsunami of 2004.	Aucune ... ne peut être comparée à ...
Modern factories **cannot be compared with** those our grandparents worked in.	On ne peut pas comparer ... à ...
The actions of this group **are in no way comparable to** those of terrorists.	... n'ont rien de comparable avec ...
The newspaper reports **differ** on this point.	... divergent ...
The history of the United States **in no way resembles** our own.	... ne ressemble en rien à ...
There are worse things than losing a European cup final.	Il y a des événements bien plus tragiques que ...
This film **is less** interesting **than** his first one.	... est moins ... que ...
Women's life expectancy is 81 years, **while** men's is 72.	... tandis que ...
While the consumption of wine and beer is decreasing, the consumption of bottled water is increasing.	Alors que ...

Demandes et propositions

Demandes

I'd like another beer.	Je voudrais ...
I'd like to know the times of trains to Lille.	Je voudrais ...
Could you give us a hand?	Pourriez-vous ...
Can you tell Eleanor the good news?	Est-ce que vous pouvez ...
Could you please show me the way out?	Auriez-vous l'obligeance de ...
Could I ask you for a few minutes of your time?	Puis-je vous demander de ...
Be an angel, pop to the baker's for me.	Sois gentille ...
If you wouldn't mind waiting for a moment.	Merci de bien vouloir ...
Would you mind opening the window?	Est-ce que cela vous dérangerait de ...
Would you be very kind and save my seat for me?	Auriez-vous l'obligeance de ...
I would be grateful if you could reply as soon as possible.	Je vous serais reconnaissant de ...

Propositions

I can come and pick you up **if** you like.	Je peux ... si ...
I could go with you.	Je pourrais ...
Do you fancy a bit of Stilton?	Ça te dit ...
How about a pear tart?	Que diriez-vous de ...
Would you like to see my photos?	Ça vous dirait de ...
Would you like to have dinner with me one evening?	Est-ce que vous voulez ...
Do you want me to go and get your car?	Est-ce que vous voulez que ...

Conseils et suggestions

Comment demander conseil

What would you do, if you were me?	À ma place, que feriez-vous ?
Would you accept, **if you were me?**	À ma place ...
What's your opinion on this?	Quel est votre avis sur la question ?
What, in your opinion, should be done to reduce pollution?	Que proposez-vous pour ...
What would you advise?	Que me conseillez-vous ?

What would you advise me to do?	Que me conseillez-vous de faire ?
Which would you recommend, Majorca or Ibiza?	Qu'est-ce que vous me conseillez ...
If we were to sponsor a player, **who would you recommend?**	... lequel nous conseilleriez-vous ?
What strategy **do you suggest?**	Quelle ... proposez-vous ?
How would you deal with unemployment?	Qu'est-ce que vous proposez contre ...

Comment donner un conseil

If I were you, I'd be a bit wary.	À votre place ...
If I were you I wouldn't say anything.	À ta place ...
Take my advice, buy your tickets in advance.	Je vous conseille de ...
A word of advice: read the instructions.	Un conseil ...
A useful tip: always have some pasta in your cupboard.	Un bon conseil ...
As you like languages, **you ought to** study as a translator.	... vous devriez ...
You should see a specialist.	Vous devriez ...
You would do well to see a solicitor.	Vous feriez bien de ...
You would do better to spend the money on a new car.	Vous feriez mieux de ...
You could perhaps ask someone to go with you.	Vous pourriez peut-être ...
You could try being a little more understanding.	Vous pourriez ...
Perhaps you should speak to a plumber about it.	Il faudrait peut-être que ...
Perhaps we ought to try a different approach.	Il faudrait peut-être ...
Why don't you phone him?	Pourquoi ne pas ...
How about renting a video?	Et si on ...
How about 3 March at 10.30am?	... ça vous va ?
It might be better to give her money rather than jewellery.	Il vaudrait peut-être mieux ...
It would be better to wait a bit.	Il serait préférable de ...

Mises en garde

I warn you, I intend to get my own back.	Je vous préviens ...
I'd better warn you that he knows you did it.	Mieux vaut que je te prévienne ...
Don't forget to keep a copy of your income tax return.	N'oubliez pas de ...

Remember: appearances can be deceptive.	Méfiez-vous des apparences.
Beware of buying tickets from touts.	Attention ...
Whatever you do, don't leave your camera in the car.	Surtout, ne ... jamais ...
If you don't book early you risk being disappointed.	... tu risques de ...

Intentions et souhaits

Pour demander à quelqu'un ce qu'il compte faire

What are you going to do?	Qu'est-ce que vous allez faire ?
What will you do if you fail your exams?	Qu'est-ce que tu vas faire si ...
What are you going to do when you get back?	Qu'allez-vous faire ...
Do you have anything planned?	Avez-vous des projets ?
Can we expect you next Sunday?	On compte sur vous ...
Are you planning to spend all of the holiday here?	Est-ce que tu comptes ...
Are you planning on staying long?	Vous comptez ...
What are you planning to do with your collection?	Que comptez-vous faire de ...
What are you thinking of doing?	Que comptez-vous faire ?
Do you intend to go into teaching?	Est-ce que tu as l'intention de ...
Are you thinking of making another film in Europe?	Songez-vous à ...

Pour dire ce qu'on a l'intention de faire

I was planning to go to Ajaccio on 8 July.	Je comptais ...
She plans to go to India for a year.	Elle prévoit de ...
There are plans to build a new stadium.	Il est prévu de ...
The bank intends to close a hundred branches.	... a l'intention de ...
I am thinking of giving up politics.	Je songe à ...
I have decided to get a divorce.	J'ai décidé de ...
I have made up my mind to stop smoking.	Je suis décidé à ...
We never had any intention of talking to the press.	Il n'a jamais été dans nos intentions de ...
That's settled, we'll go to Florida in May.	C'est décidé ...
For me, living abroad is out of the question.	Il n'est pas question ... de ...

Souhaits

I'd like to be able to play as well as him.	Je voudrais ...
I'd like to go hang-gliding.	J'aimerais ...
I would like my photos to be published.	J'aimerais que ...
I would like to have had a brother.	J'aurais aimé ...
I want to act in films.	Je veux ...
Ian **wanted at all costs** to prevent his boss finding out.	... voulait à tout prix ...
We wish to preserve our independence.	Nous souhaitons ...
I hope to have children.	J'espère ...
We hope that children will watch this programme with their parents.	Nous espérons que ...
Do you dream of winning the lottery?	Vous rêvez de ...
I dream of having a big house.	Mon rêve serait de ...

Obligation

I must find somewhere to live.	Il faut que je ...
We really must see each other more often!	Il faut absolument qu'on ...
If you're going to Poland, **you must** learn Polish.	... vous devez ...
He **made** his secretary answer all his calls.	... exigeait que ...
My mother **makes me** eat spinach.	... me force à ...
The hijackers **demanded that** the plane fly to New York.	... ont exigé que ...
A serious illness **forced me to** cancel my holiday.	... m'a obligé à ...
He **was obliged to** borrow more and more money.	... a été obligé de ...
Mary **had no choice but to** invite him.	... n'avait pas pu faire autrement que de ...
The only thing you can do is say no.	Tu ne peux pas faire autrement que de ...
Many mothers **have to** work; **they have no other option.**	... sont obligées de ... elles n'ont pas le choix.
She had the baby adopted because **she had no other option.**	... elle ne pouvait pas faire autrement.
School **is compulsory** until the age of sixteen.	... est obligatoire ...
It is essential to know some history, if we are to understand the situation.	Il est indispensable de ...

Permission

Comment demander la permission de faire quelque chose

Can I use the phone?	Je peux ...
Can I ask you something?	Je peux ...
Is it okay if I come now, or is it too early?	Ça ne vous dérange pas si ...
Do you mind if I smoke?	Ça ne vous dérange pas que ...
Do you mind if I open the window?	Est-ce que ça vous dérange si ...
Would you mind if I had a look in your briefcase, madam?	Vous permettez que ...
Could I have permission to leave early?	Est-ce que je peux vous demander la permission de ...

Autorisation

Do as you please.	(Vous) faites comme vous voulez.
Go ahead!	Allez-y !
No, of course I don't mind.	Bien sûr que non.
I have nothing against it.	Je n'y vois pas d'inconvénient.
Pupils **are allowed to** wear what they like.	... ont le droit de ...

Défense

I forbid you to go out!	Je te défends de ...
It's forbidden.	C'est défendu.
Smoking in the toilet **is forbidden.**	Il est interdit de ...
Child labour is **strictly forbidden by** a UN convention.	... formellement interdit par ...
No entry!	Défense d'entrer !
No parking.	Stationnement interdit.
It's not allowed.	C'est interdit.
You are not allowed to swim in the lake.	Il est interdit de ...
We weren't allowed to eat or drink while on duty.	On n'avait pas le droit de ...
That's out of the question.	Il n'en est pas question.

Certitude, probabilité et possibilité

Certitude

Undoubtedly, there will be problems.	Il est certain que ...
There is no doubt that the country's image has suffered.	Il ne fait aucun doute que ...
It's bound to cause trouble.	Cela va sûrement ...
Clearly the company is in difficulties.	Il est évident que ...
A foreign tourist is **quite obviously** a rare sight here.	... de toute évidence ...
It is undeniable that she was partly to blame.	Il est indéniable que ...
I am sure you will like my brother.	Je suis sûre que ...
I am sure that I will win.	Je suis sûr de ...
I'm sure that I won't get bored working with him.	J'ai la certitude que ...
I am certain that we are on the right track.	Je suis certain que ...
I am convinced that there are other solutions.	Je suis persuadé que ...

Probabilité

The price of petrol will **probably** rise.	Il est probable que ...
Inflation will **very probably** exceed 10%.	... très probablement ...
It is highly probable that they will abandon the project.	Il est fort probable que ...
The trend **is likely** to continue.	Il est probable que ...
80% of skin problems **undoubtedly** have psychological origins.	... sans doute ...
They were **no doubt** right.	... sans doute ...
The construction work **should** start in April.	... devrait ...
He must have forgotten to open the windows.	Il a dû ...

Possibilité

It's possible.	C'est possible.
It is possible that they got your name from the electoral register.	Il est possible que ...
It is not impossible that he has gone to Paris.	Il n'est pas impossible que ...
That might be more expensive.	Il se peut que ...
He may have misunderstood.	Il a peut-être ...
This virus **may** be extremely infectious.	Il se peut que ...
It may be that it will take time to achieve peace.	Il se peut que ...
In a few months everything **could** change.	... peut ...
Perhaps I am mistaken.	Peut-être que ...

Incertitude, improbabilité et impossibilité

Incertitude

I'm not sure it's useful.	Je ne suis pas sûr que ...
I'm not sure I'll manage.	Je ne suis pas certain de ...
I'm not sure that it's a good idea.	Je ne suis pas sûr que ...
We cannot be sure that the problem will be solved.	Il n'est pas sûr que ...
I very much doubt he'll adapt to not working.	Je doute fort que ...
Is it wise? **I doubt it.**	J'en doute.
He began to **have doubts about** his doctor's competence.	... douter de ...
I wonder if we've made much progress in this area.	Je me demande si ...
There is no guarantee that a vaccine can be developed.	Il n'est pas certain que ...
Nobody knows exactly what happened.	Personne ne sait exactement ...

Improbabilité

He **probably won't** change his mind.	... ne ... probablement pas ...
It is unlikely that there'll be any tickets left.	Il est peu probable que ...
I'd be surprised if they had your size.	Ça m'étonnerait que ...
They are not likely to get the Nobel prize for Economics!	Ils ne risquent pas de ...
There is not much chance the growth rate will exceed 1.5%.	Il y a peu de chances que ...
There's no danger we'll get bored.	Nous ne risquons pas de ...
It would be amazing if everything went according to plan.	Il serait étonnant que ...

Impossibilité

It's impossible.	C'est impossible.
It is not possible for the government to introduce this Bill before the recess.	Il n'est pas possible que ...
This information **cannot be** wrong.	Il est impossible que ...
There is no chance of their helping us.	Il n'y a aucune chance que ...

Salutations

Hello!	Bonjour !
Hi!	Salut !
Good morning!	Bonjour !
Good afternoon!	Bonjour !
Good evening!	Bonsoir !
How's it going?	Comment ça va ?
How's things?	Comment (ça) va ?
How's life?	Comment (ça) va ?
How are you?	Comment allez-vous ?

Réponses

Very well, and you?	Très bien, merci, et vous ?
Fine, thanks.	Bien, merci.
Great!	Super bien !
So-so.	Comme ci comme ça.
Could be worse.	On fait aller.

Présentations

This is Charles.	Je te présente ...
Let me introduce you to my girlfriend.	Je vous présente ...
I'd like you to meet my husband.	Je vous présente ...
I don't believe you know one another.	Je ne crois pas que vous vous connaissiez.

Une fois qu'on a été présenté

Pleased to meet you.	Enchanté.
Hello, how do you do?	Enchanté de faire votre connaissance.
Hi, I'm Jane.	Salut, moi c'est ...

Pour prendre congé

Bye!	Au revoir !
Goodbye!	Au revoir !
Good night!	Bonne nuit !
See you!	Ciao !
See you later!	À tout à l'heure !

See you soon!	À bientôt !
See you tomorrow!	À demain !
See you next week!	À la semaine prochaine !
See you Thursday!	À jeudi !

Vœux et félicitations

Happy Birthday!	Bon anniversaire !
Many happy returns!	Bon anniversaire !
Merry Christmas!	Joyeux Noël !
Happy New Year!	Bonne année !
Happy Anniversary!	Bon anniversaire de mariage !
Congratulations!	Félicitations !
Welcome!	Soyez les bienvenus !
Good luck!	Bonne chance !
Safe journey!	Bon voyage !
Have fun!	Amusez-vous bien !
Get well soon!	Bon rétablissement !
Take care!	Fais bien attention à toi !
Cheers!	(À votre) santé !
Enjoy your meal!	Bon appétit !

Correspondance

La rédaction de l'adresse en Grande-Bretagne

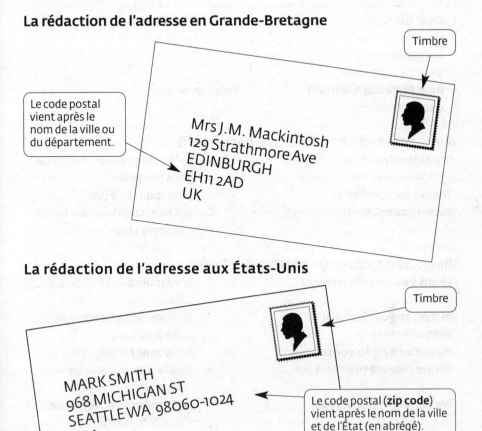

Timbre

Le code postal vient après le nom de la ville ou du département.

Mrs J.M. Mackintosh
129 Strathmore Ave
EDINBURGH
EH11 2AD
UK

La rédaction de l'adresse aux États-Unis

Timbre

MARK SMITH
968 MICHIGAN ST
SEATTLE WA 98060-1024
USA

Le code postal (**zip code**) vient après le nom de la ville et de l'État (en abrégé).

Abréviations couramment employées dans les adresses

Ave = avenue	Dr = drive	Pl = place	Sq = square
Cres = crescent	Gdns = gardens	Rd = road	St = street

Les formes d'adresse et les formules de politesse
Dans les lettres personnelles

Dear Mr and Mrs Roberts	Yours (*assez soutenu*)
Dear Kate and Jeremy	With best wishes
Dear Aunt Jane and Uncle Alan	Love from
Dear Granny	Lots of love from (*familier*)

Dans les lettres d'affaires

Dear Sirs	Yours faithfully
Dear Sir	
Dear Madam	
Dear Sir or Madam	
Dear Professor Meldrum	Yours sincerely
Dear Ms Gilmour	

Pour commencer une lettre personnelle

It was lovely to hear from you.	Cela m'a fait plaisir d'avoir de vos nouvelles.
Thanks for your letter ...	Merci pour ta lettre ...
Sorry I haven't written sooner.	Je suis désolé de ne pas t'avoir écrit plus tôt.

Pour commencer une lettre d'affaires

Thank you for your letter of ...	Je vous remercie de votre lettre du ...
In reply to your letter of ...	En réponse à votre lettre du ...
With reference to ...	Suite à ...
We are writing to you to ...	Nous vous écrivons pour ...
We are pleased to inform you ...	Nous avons le plaisir de vous informer ...
We regret to inform you ...	Nous sommes au regret de vous informer ...

Pour terminer une lettre personnelle

Write soon.	Écris-moi vite.
Give my regards to ...	Transmettez mes amitiés à ...
... sends his/her best wishes.	... me charge de transmettre ses amitiés.
Give my love to ...	Embrasse ... de ma part.

Pour terminer une lettre d'affaires

I look forward to hearing from you.	Dans l'attente de votre réponse.
Thanking you in advance for your help.	En vous remerciant à l'avance pour votre aide.
If you require any further information please do not hesitate to contact me.	N'hésitez pas à me contacter pour toute information complémentaire.

Lettre de remerciement

Adresse de l'expéditeur.

18 Slateford Ave
Leeds
LS24 3PR

25th May 2007

Date

Dear Gran and Grandpa,

Thank you both very much for the CDs which you sent me for my birthday. They are two of my favourite groups and I'll really enjoy listening to them.

There's not much news here. I seem to be spending most of my time studying for my exams which start in two weeks. I'm hoping to pass all of them but I'm not looking forward to the Maths exam as that's my worst subject.

Mum says that you're off to Crete on holiday next week, so I hope that you have a great time and come back with a good tan.

Tony sends his love.
With love from

Jen

Voir également les formules p.49.

Pour réserver une chambre d'hôtel

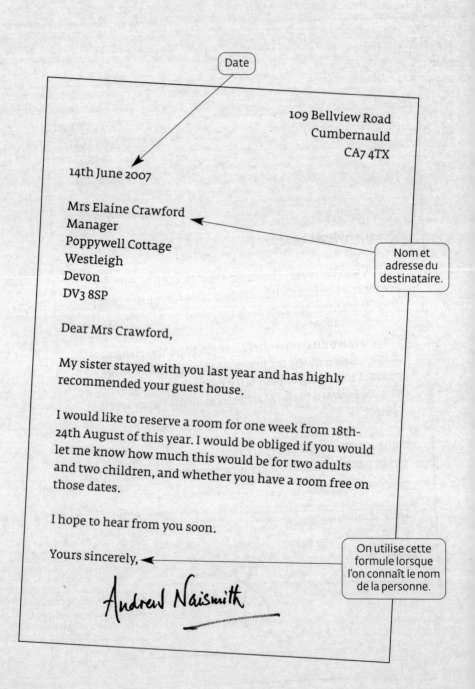

Date

109 Bellview Road
Cumbernauld
CA7 4TX

14th June 2007

Mrs Elaine Crawford
Manager
Poppywell Cottage
Westleigh
Devon
DV3 8SP

Nom et adresse du destinataire.

Dear Mrs Crawford,

My sister stayed with you last year and has highly recommended your guest house.

I would like to reserve a room for one week from 18th-24th August of this year. I would be obliged if you would let me know how much this would be for two adults and two children, and whether you have a room free on those dates.

I hope to hear from you soon.

Yours sincerely,

Andrew Naismith

On utilise cette formule lorsque l'on connaît le nom de la personne.

Lettre de réclamation

Voir également les formules p.50.

85 Rush Lane
Triptown
Lancs
LC4 2DT

20th February 2007

Woodpecker Restaurant
145 Main Street
Triptown
Lancs
LC4 3EF

Dear Sir/Madam

I was to have dined in your restaurant last Thursday by way of celebrating my wedding anniversary with my wife and young son but am writing to let you know of our great dissatisfaction.

I had reserved a corner table for two with a view of the lake. However, when we arrived we had to wait for more than 20 minutes for a table and even then, not in the area which I had chosen. There was no highchair for my son as was promised and your staff made no effort whatsoever to accommodate our needs. In fact, they were downright discourteous. Naturally we went elsewhere, and not only have you lost any future custom from me, but I will be sure to advise my friends and colleagues against your establishment.

Yours faithfully

T. Greengage

On utilise cette formule lorsque l'on commence la lettre par **Dear Sir** etc.

Curriculum Vitæ

CURRICULUM VITÆ

Name:	Rosalind A. Williamson
Address:	11 North Street, Barnton NE6 2BT
Telephone:	01294 476230
E-mail:	rosalind@metalcomp.co.uk
Date of Birth:	18/4/1981
Nationality:	British
Marital Status:	Single

CAREER

2/05 to date: Sales and Marketing Executive, Metal Company plc, Barnton

11/03-1/05: Marketing Assistant, Metal Company plc

> Pour les diplômes obtenus en France, mettre le nom du diplôme suivi d'une brève description en anglais entre parenthèses.

QUALIFICATIONS

1999-2003: University of Newby BA (Hons) Italian with French – 2:1

1992-1999: Barnton Comprehensive School
A-levels: English Literature (D), French (B), Italian (A)
GCSEs: Art, Chemistry, English Language, English Literature, French, German, Italian, Maths

OTHER SKILLS

Computer literate (Word for Windows, Excel, QuarkXPress), good keyboarding skills, full, clean driving licence.

INTERESTS

Travel (have travelled extensively throughout Europe and North Amercia), riding and sailing.

REFEREES

Ms Alice Bluegown
Sales and Marketing Manager
Metal Company plc
Barnton
NE4 3KL

Dr I.O. Sono
Department of Italian
University of Newby
Newby
S13 2RR

> Il est d'usage d'indiquer sur son C.V. les noms de deux personnes prêtes à fournir une recommandation à l'employeur potentiel. L'une d'entre elles doit normalement être un ancien employeur, ou, pour les étudiants, un professeur.

Lettre de candidature

11 North Street
Barnton
NE6 2BY

18 August 2007

The Personnel Director
Clifton Manufacturing Ltd
Firebrick House
Clifton
MK45 6RB

Dear Sir or Madam

> Lorsqu'on ignore si le destinataire est un homme ou une femme, il convient d'utiliser la formule ci–contre. Toutefois, si l'on connaît le nom de la personne, on utilise la présentation suivante :
> **Mrs Lynn Kerr**
> **Personnel Director**
> **Clifton Manufacturing Ltd** etc.
> Pour commencer votre lettre, la formule à employer est la suivante :
> **Dear Mrs Kerr**

With reference to your advertisement in the Guardian of 15 August, I wish to apply for the position of Marketing Manager in your company.

I am currently employed as a Sales and Marketing Executive for the Metal Company in Barnton where my main role is maintaining and developing links with our customers within the UK and producing material for marketing purposes.

I am interested in this position as it offers an opportunity to apply my sales and marketing skills in a new and challenging direction. I enclose my Curriculum Vitae for your consideration. Please do not hesitate to contact me if you require any further details.

Yours faithfully

Rosalind Williamson

Enc.

> On utilise cette formule lorsque l'on commence la lettre par **Dear Sir or Madam** etc.

> = **enclosures.** On ajoute ceci lorsque l'on joint d'autres pièces à la lettre, un C.V. par exemple.

Pour proposer un entretien

Les coordonnées de l'expéditeur sont souvent mentionnées pour faciliter le classement de la correspondance.

Clifton Manufacturing Ltd.

Firebrick House • Clifton MK45 6RB
Tel: (01367) 345 900 • Fax: (01367) 345 901
E-mail: personnel@cliftman.co.uk

Ref: RW/LK

27 August 2007

Ms Rosalind Williamson
11 North Street
Barnton
NE6 2BT

Dear Ms Williamson

Following your recent application for the position of Marketing Manager, I would like to invite you to attend an interview at the above office on Friday 3 September at 11am.

The interview will be conducted by the Sales and Marketing Director and myself and should last approximately one hour.

If this date does not suit please notify Jane Simpson on extension 3287 to arrange an alternative date.

We look forward to meeting you.

Yours sincerely

Lynn Kerr

Lynn Kerr (Mrs)
Personnel Director

On utilise cette formule lorsque l'on commence la lettre par **Dear Ms Williamson** etc.

Télécopie

Brown & Sons

Northport Enterprise Park
Birmingham B45 6JH
Tel: 0121 346 3287
Fax: 0121 346 3288
E-mail: orders@brownandsons.co.uk

FAX

To: Emma Scott, Westcott Hotel

Date: 6 November 2007

From: Malcolm Marshall

No. of pages to follow: 1

Re your order of 23 October for 100 tablecloths (Catalogue number 435789), I regret to inform you that these items are currently out of stock.

The next delivery will be in approximately four weeks' time. However, if this delay is unacceptable to you, please can you let me know so that I can cancel the order.

I am sorry for any inconvenience this may cause.

Regards

Malcolm Marshall

Courrier électronique

Envoyer des messages

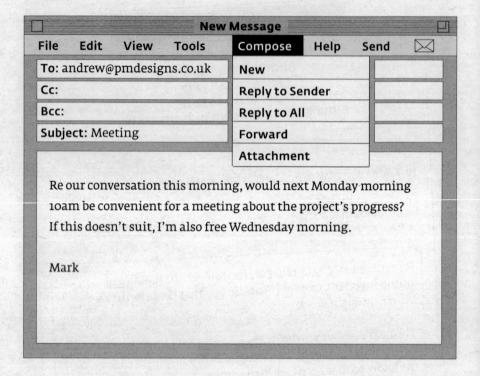

New Message	Nouveau message
File	Fichier
Edit	Édition
View	Affichage
Tools	Outils
Compose	Composer
Help	Aide
Send	Envoyer
New	Nouveau message
Reply to Sender	Répondre

Courrier électronique

Recevoir des messages

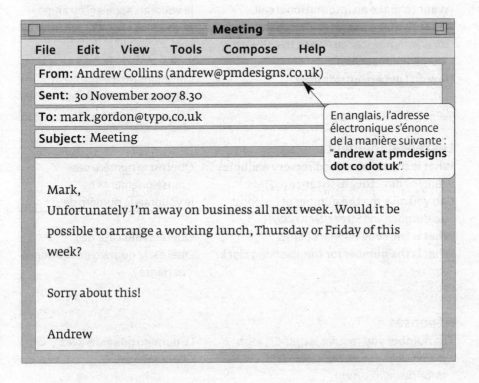

Reply to All	Répondre à tous
Forward	Faire suivre
Attachment	Fichier joint
To	À
Cc (carbon copy)	Cc
Bcc (blind carbon copy)	Copie cachée
Subject	Objet
From	De
Sent	Date

Téléphone

Les différents types de communication

Local/national call.

Communication locale/ interurbaine.

I want to make an international call.

Je voudrais appeler l'étranger.

I want to make a reverse charge call (*Brit*) to a Paris number *ou* I want to call a Paris number collect (*US*).

Je voudrais appeler ... en PCV.

How do I get an outside line?

Comment est-ce que je peux téléphoner à l'extérieur ?

Les renseignements

What is the number for directory enquiries (*Brit*) *ou* directory assistance (*US*)?

Quel est le numéro des renseignements ?

Can you give me the number of Europost, 20 Cumberland Street, Newquay?

Je voudrais le numéro de ...

What is the code for Martinique?

Quel est l'indicatif de ...

What is the number for the speaking clock?

Quel est le numéro de l'horloge parlante ?

Réponses

The number you require is 0181-613 3297. (*o-one-eight-one six-one-three three-two-nine-seven*)

Le numéro que vous avez demandé est le ...

I'm sorry, there's no listing under that name.

Je regrette, mais il n'y a pas d'abonné à ce nom.

The number you require is ex-directory (*Brit*) *ou* unlisted (*US*).

Le numéro que vous avez demandé est sur liste rouge.

Lorsque l'abonné répond

Could I speak to Mr Sanderson, please?

Pourrais-je parler à ...

Could you put me through to Dr Evans, please?

Pourriez-vous me passer ...

Can I have extension 6578, please?

Pourriez-vous me passer le poste ...

I'll call back in half an hour.

Je rappellerai dans ...

Would you ask him to ring me when he gets back?

Pourriez-vous lui demander de me rappeler à son retour ?

Au standard

Who shall I say is calling?	C'est de la part de qui ?
I'm putting you through.	Je vous le passe.
I have a call from Tokyo for Mrs Thomson.	J'ai un appel de ... pour ...
I've got Miss Martin on the line.	J'ai ... en ligne.
Dr Roberts is on another line. Do you want to wait?	... est en ligne, vous patientez ?
Please hold.	Ne quittez pas.
There's no reply.	Ça ne répond pas.
Would you like to leave a message?	Voulez-vous laisser un message ?

Messages enregistrés

The number you have dialled has not been recognized. Please hang up.	Le numéro de votre correspondant n'est plus attribué. Veuillez raccrocher.
The number you have dialled has been changed to 020-7789 0044.	Le numéro de votre correspondant a changé. Veuillez composer désormais le ...
All the lines are busy right now. Please try again later.	Par suite de l'encombrement des lignes, votre appel ne peut aboutir. Veuillez rappeler ultérieurement.
Hello, you have reached Sunspot Insurance. Please wait, your call will be answered shortly.	Bonjour, vous êtes en communication avec ... Veuillez patienter, nous allons donner suite à votre appel dans quelques instants.
Hello, you are through to Emma and Matthew Hargreaves. Please leave a message after the tone and we'll get back to you. Thanks.	Bonjour, vous êtes bien chez ... Laissez un message après le bip sonore et nous vous rappellerons dès notre retour.

Pour répondre au téléphone

Hello, it's Anne speaking.	Allô, c'est ... à l'appareil.
Speaking.	C'est moi.
Who's speaking?	Qui est à l'appareil ?

En cas de difficulté

I can't get through.	Je n'arrive pas à avoir le numéro.
Their phone is out of order.	Leur téléphone est en dérangement.
We have been cut off.	Nous avons été coupés.
I must have dialled the wrong number.	J'ai dû faire un faux numéro.
We've got a crossed line.	Il y a quelqu'un d'autre sur la ligne.
This is a very bad line.	La ligne est très mauvaise.

French
Idioms

Introduction

What is it?

This supplement of French Idioms is an invaluable resource for learners of French who want to be able to communicate more naturally. It will enable you to start to include colourful idiomatic phrases and expressions in both your writing and conversation, increasing your confidence and effectiveness. It can be used to develop your language skills, whether you are studying French at school or university, at home or at an evening class.

Why do you need it?

Developing expertise in writing, speaking and understanding a foreign language means being able to pull together and build on a number of different aspects – vocabulary, grammar, pronunciation, and so on. An important element of increased proficiency in communication is the use of idioms and figurative expressions which will add colour and variety to your writing and conversation as well as enabling you to sound more natural and confident. Idioms are phrases whose meaning may not be obvious from the words they contain. For example, a common English idiom is 'Add fuel to the fire'. If somebody adds fuel to the fire, they make a bad situation worse.

How is it structured?

For maximum clarity, each French idiom is followed by a word-for-word English translation as well as the equivalent idiomatic expression(s) that you would use in English. In many cases, a short background note is included if some explanation or additional information about French language or culture is required. Then, in order to illustrate the use of the idiom in a natural context, a sentence or two of French is provided.

The idioms are listed alphabetically by their keyword. For example, **balle** is the keyword in the French idiom **se renvoyer la balle**.

filer à l'anglaise

> *"to run away in the English way"*
> = to make a getaway
> = to take French leave

It seems that the French and the English feel the same about each other's manners!

avoir une araignée au plafond (informal)

> *"to have a spider on the ceiling"*
> = to have bats in the belfry
> = to have a screw loose

The idea here is that spiders thrive in neglected places, untroubled by human attention.

Quand il a commencé à parler tout seul, on a compris qu'il avait une araignée au plafond.
When he began to talk to himself, we realized he had a screw loose.

se renvoyer la balle

> *"to send back the ball to each other"*
> = to try to pass the buck

The idea here comes from sports where a ball is passed between players.

Comme d'habitude personne ne veut être tenu responsable du déficit et les deux partis se renvoient la balle.
As usual nobody wants to be held responsible for the deficit and the two parties try to pass the buck.

bien mener sa barque

"to steer one's boat well"
= to do alright for yourself

But be careful: **charger sa barque** means *to overdo it.*

Personne ne s'attendait à ce qu'elle réussisse, mais elle a bien mené sa barque et occupe maintenant un poste prestigieux.
Nobody expected her to succeed but she did alright for herself and now holds a prestigious post.

être à l'aise dans ses baskets *(informal)*

"to be fine in your trainers"
= to be comfortable with yourself
= to be at ease with yourself

Also **être bien dans ses baskets.**

Yohann, vingt ans, à l'aise dans ses baskets avec son sourire irrésistible et une brillante carrière d'architecte devant lui.
Yohann is a 20-year-old who's very much at ease with himself. He has an irresistible smile and a glittering career as an architect ahead of him.

être pendu aux basques de quelqu'un *(informal)*

"to be hanging onto somebody's clothes"
= to stick to somebody like glue

The French term, **les basques,** referred to lengths of material which in times past hung down from the waist like a kind of skirt.

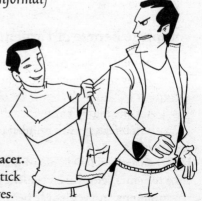

J'avais six ans de moins que ma sœur et j'étais toujours pendu à ses basques, ce qui a fini par l'agacer.
I was six years younger than my sister and I used to stick to her like glue, which ended up getting on her nerves.

mener en bateau

"to take away by boat"
= to take for a ride
= to lead up the garden path

Quand ils arrivent enfin à destination, les voyageurs se rendent compte qu'on les a menés en bateau : l'hôtel est sale et délabré, le guide ne parle pas un mot de français et le programme des visites n'est pas respecté.
When they finally arrive at their destination, the travellers realize that they have been taken for a ride: the hotel is dirty and dilapidated, the guide speaks not a word of French and the tour programme is ignored.

être bête comme ses pieds (informal)

"to be as stupid as your feet"
= to be too stupid for words
= to be thick as a brick

Feet don't always get a very good press: **faire quelque chose comme un pied** means *to be useless at doing something.*

Il est bête comme ses pieds : ça fait quinze fois qu'on lui explique, il n'a toujours pas compris.
He is too stupid for words: that's fifteen times he's had it explained, but he still doesn't understand.

vouloir le beurre et l'argent du beurre

"to want the butter and the money for the butter"
= to want to have your cake and eat it

A staple ingredient in French cooking, butter features in a number of expressions.

Dans l'ensemble, les clients sont corrects, mais il y a toujours ceux qui en veulent plus en payant moins, qui veulent le beurre et l'argent du beurre, quoi !
On the whole customers are ok but there are always those who want more for less, who want to have their cake and eat it.

mettre du beurre dans les épinards

> *"to put butter in the spinach"*
> = to help make ends meet

A staple ingredient in French cooking, butter features in a number of expressions.

Le samedi, je distribue des prospectus : ça ne rapporte pas beaucoup, mais ça met du beurre dans les épinards.
On Saturday I distribute leaflets; it doesn't pay much but it helps to make ends meet.

mettre quelqu'un en boîte *(informal)*

> *"to put somebody in a box"*
> = to pull somebody's leg

You can also say **se payer la tête de quelqu'un**, literally *to buy yourself somebody's head.*

Comme elle vient de Marseille, il s'est mis à imiter l'accent du sud pour lui parler ; ça n'avait rien de méchant, c'était juste pour la mettre en boîte.
Since she comes from Marseilles, he began to put on a southern accent when talking to her; he wasn't being nasty, he was just pulling her leg.

c'est simple comme bonjour

> *"it's as simple as good morning"*
> = it's as easy as ABC

A more informal way of saying this in French would be **bête comme chou**.

Aujourd'hui, la recette du gratin dauphinois – vous allez voir, c'est simple comme bonjour.
Today, the recipe for dauphinoise potatoes – you'll see, it's as easy as ABC.

avoir le cafard *(informal)*

> *"to have the cockroach"*
> = to have the blues
> = to be feeling down

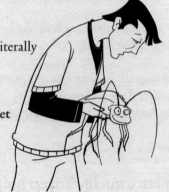

Another expression for this is **avoir le bourdon**, literally *to have the bumblebee.*

Si vous avez le cafard, ne restez pas seul : rien de tel qu'une sortie entre amis pour vous changer les idées et oublier vos problèmes.
If you're feeling down, don't stay on your own: there is nothing like going out with your friends to take your mind off things and help you forget your problems.

pas très catholique *(informal)*

> *"not very catholic"*
> = a bit dodgy

Expressions connected with Roman Catholicism are common in countries like France with a strong religious history. Interestingly, an equivalent expression in English would be *not kosher.*

Ma compagne a été malade toute la nuit. Il faut dire que le restaurant où l'on a mangé n'était pas très catholique.
My partner has been ill all night. To be honest, the restaurant we ate at was a bit dodgy.

avoir la chair de poule

> *"to have chicken flesh"*
> = to have goose pimples/gooseflesh

You can also say **donner la chair de poule**, meaning *to give goose pimples.*

Depuis que j'ai vu ce film, j'ai la chair de poule quand j'entends les chouettes hululer dans les bois la nuit.
Since I saw this film I get goose pimples every time I hear owls hooting in the woods at night.

mettre la charrue avant les bœufs

"to put the plough in front of the oxen"
= to put the cart before the horse

Ton projet de restaurant est intéressant mais tu mets la charrue avant les bœufs : avant de penser au menu, va voir ton banquier !
Your restaurant project is interesting but you are putting the cart before the horse: before thinking about the menu, go and see your bank manager!

il n'y a pas de quoi fouetter un chat

"there is nothing to whip a cat about"
= it is only a trifle
= it's nothing to make a fuss about

As in English, the French language has many expressions to do with cats.

Il a juste volé un paquet de bonbons, il n'y a pas de quoi fouetter un chat.
He's only stolen a bag of sweets: it's not worth making a fuss about.

il n'y a pas un chat *(informal)*

"there isn't a cat"
= there is no one at all
= there is not a soul to be seen

Where there are people, there are bound to be cats somewhere about. So no cats, no people.

Un dimanche soir de novembre dans une petite ville de province : il n'y a pas un chat.
A Sunday evening in November in a small provincial town: there is not a soul to be seen.

avoir un chat dans la gorge

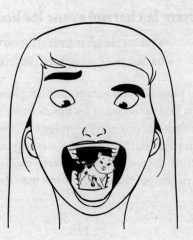

"to have a cat in your throat"
= to have a frog in your throat

The French appear to be almost alone on this one; most other European languages opt for the frog or toad.

Le prof avait du mal à parler, il avait un chat dans la gorge.
The teacher had trouble speaking, he had a frog in his throat.

avoir d'autres chats à fouetter

"to have other cats to whip"
= to have other fish to fry

Le représentant en cuisines est encore passé ; comme d'habitude, je lui ai dit que j'avais d'autres chats à fouetter.
The rep for the kitchen company came by again; as usual I told him that I had other fish to fry.

ça ne me fait ni chaud ni froid

"that makes me neither hot nor cold"
= I couldn't care less
= it doesn't bother me

Sébastien s'évanouit quand il voit du sang. Moi, ça ne me fait ni chaud ni froid.
Sébastien faints when he sees blood. It doesn't bother me.

tiré par les cheveux

> *"pulled by the hair"*
> = far-fetched

The idea here is of something forced or improbable.

Les acteurs jouent bien, mais le scénario est vraiment tiré par les cheveux : on n'y croit à aucun moment !
The acting is good but the script is really far-fetched: you don't believe it for a minute!

ne pas arriver à la cheville de quelqu'un

> *"not to reach somebody's ankle"*
> = not to be a patch on somebody

Note also the idiom **être en cheville avec quelqu'un**, meaning *to be in cahoots with somebody*.

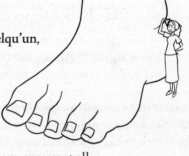

Le guitariste a été remplacé par un autre qui ne lui arrive pas à la cheville ; depuis, le groupe n'a plus aucun succès.
The guitarist was replaced by someone who is not a patch on him; since then the band hasn't had any success at all.

avoir un cœur d'artichaut

> *"to have an artichoke heart"*
> = to fall in love with everyone you meet

The idea here is that by the time you have reached the centre of the vegetable you have pulled off enough leaves to give one to everybody.

Celles et ceux qui ont un cœur d'artichaut ont une vie sentimentale souvent tumultueuse : à peine le coup de foudre passé, c'est la déception... puis très vite le besoin de faire une nouvelle rencontre.
Those who fall in love with everyone they meet often have a tumultuous love life: no sooner have they fallen in love than they're disappointed... then very soon they feel the need to meet someone new.

sauter du coq à l'âne

"to jump from the cockerel to the donkey"
= to jump from one subject to another

You can also say **passer du coq à l'âne**, literally *to go from the cockerel to the donkey*.

C'est un professeur brillant, mais il n'arrête pas de passer du coq à l'âne et ses cours sont difficiles à suivre.
He's an outstanding teacher but he's forever jumping from one subject to another and his lessons are difficult to follow.

avoir le couteau sous la gorge

"to have the knife under the throat"
= to have a gun to the head

If you are the aggressor, the expression is **mettre le couteau sous la gorge à quelqu'un** (*to put a gun to somebody's head*).

L'entreprise a le couteau sous la gorge : elle est très endettée, ses produits se vendent mal, elle doit accepter le partenariat pour ne pas faire faillite.
The company has a gun to its head: it is heavily in debt, its products are not selling: it must accept the partnership if it is not to go bankrupt.

faire une croix sur quelque chose (informal)

"to make a cross on something"
= to say goodbye to something
= to kiss something goodbye

This is similar to the idea in English of crossing something off a list.

J'ai reçu la facture du plombier : je peux faire une croix sur mon voyage au Pérou.
I've received the plumber's bill: I can kiss my trip to Peru goodbye.

avoir une dent contre quelqu'un

"*to have a tooth against somebody*"
= to have a grudge against somebody

Also **garder une dent contre quelqu'un**. The Italians go one step further and talk about the tooth being poisoned.

Avec les efforts qu'elle fait pour ne pas me dire bonjour, elle doit forcément avoir une dent contre moi ; ce que je ne sais pas, c'est pourquoi.
From the efforts she makes to avoid saying hello to me, she really must have a grudge against me; what I don't know is why.

au diable

"*with the devil*"
= miles from anywhere
= at the back of beyond

Les scientifiques vivent dans un poste d'observation situé au diable, accessible par hélicoptère seulement.
The scientists live in an observation post miles from anywhere, which is only accessible by helicopter.

se mettre le doigt dans l'œil

"*to put your finger in your eye*"
= to be kidding yourself

A more informal way of saying this in French would be **se fourrer le doigt dans l'œil**, literally *to stuff your finger in your eye*.

Ceux qui croient aux promesses de la direction se mettent le doigt dans l'œil : il n'y aura pas d'augmentation !
People who believe the promises made by management are kidding themselves: there won't be a pay rise!

être unis comme les doigts de la main

> *"to be joined like the fingers of the hand"*
> = to be joined at the hip
> = to be very close

C'est l'histoire de trois frères unis comme les doigts de la main et que le destin allait séparer.
This is the story of three brothers who were once very close, but were destined to go their separate ways.

faire quelque chose les doigts dans le nez *(informal)*

> *"to do something with the fingers in your nose"*
> = to be able to do something standing on your head
> = to be able to do something with your eyes closed

A graphic way of showing that your hands are otherwise occupied!

Un prodige du piano, qui à l'âge de huit ans jouait Chopin les doigts dans le nez.
A piano prodigy who at the age of eight could play Chopin standing on his head.

avoir bon dos *(informal)*

> *"to have a good back"*
> = to take the blame

This expression can be used both of a person and of an enterprise or undertaking.

Les jeunes ont bon dos : à chaque fois qu'il y a du bruit dans le quartier on les accuse, mais dimanche dernier la musique venait du club du troisième âge !
Young people always get the blame: whenever there's noise in the neighbourhood it's assumed to be their fault, but last Sunday the music was coming from the senior citizens' club!

faire l'école buissonnière

"to make school in the bush"
= to play truant

The idea here seems to be that hiding in the bushes is as good a way as any of avoiding school.

Beaucoup d'élèves font l'école buissonnière et passent leurs journées dans les centres commerciaux alors que leurs parents les croient en classe.
Many pupils play truant and spend their days in shopping centres when their parents think they are at school.

se faire rouler dans la farine *(informal)*

"to be rolled in the flour"
= to be had

The French **rouler quelqu'un dans la farine** means *to dupe somebody*.

Pour acheter sur internet sans se faire rouler dans la farine, il faut prendre un certain nombre de précautions.
To buy online without being had, you need to take a number of precautions.

il n'y a pas le feu *(informal)*

"there is no fire"
= there's no panic

To make the point even more strongly you can also say **il n'y a pas le feu au lac**, literally *the lake is not on fire*.

Ce n'est pas la peine de courir, il n'y a pas le feu. Le film commence dans une heure.
There's no need to run, there's no panic. The film doesn't start for an hour.

donner du fil à retordre à quelqu'un

> *"to give thread to twist again to somebody"*
> = to make life difficult for somebody

Les dialogues qui mélangent plusieurs dialectes italiens **ont donné beaucoup de fil à retordre au traducteur.**
Dialogue which mixes together several Italian dialects made life difficult for the translator.

la goutte d'eau qui fait déborder le vase

> *"the drop of water that makes the vase overflow"*
> = the last straw
> = the straw that broke the camel's back

This expression also exists in Spanish and Italian.

Pour les habitants du quartier excédés par les incivilités quotidiennes, cette agression est **la goutte d'eau qui a fait déborder le vase :** ils ont organisé une manifestation devant la mairie.
For the people living in the neighbourhood, who are infuriated by daily incidents of anti-social behaviour, this attack is the last straw: they have organised a demonstration in front of the town hall.

mettre son grain de sel *(informal)*

> *"to put in your grain of salt"*
> = to stick your oar in
> = to put in your two cents

Greek people put in their tail and the Germans put in mustard.

À la fin de la réunion, tout le monde a voulu **mettre son grain de sel** et on ne comprenait plus rien à la discussion.
At the end of the meeting everyone wanted to stick their oar in, and it was impossible to make out the line of the argument.

avoir la gueule de bois *(informal)*

> *"to have a wooden mouth"*
> = to have a hangover

Quand on a la gueule de bois, la meilleure chose à faire est de boire beaucoup d'eau.
When you have a hangover, the best thing to do is to drink lots of water.

c'est la fin des haricots *(informal)*

> *"it's the end of the beans"*
> = that's the last straw

> Being relatively cheap, beans and pulses were an important part of the diet of poorer people. When you ran out of them, it was a disaster!

On était perdus, la nuit tombait et il pleuvait ; quand j'ai vu qu'on n'avait plus d'essence, je me suis dit : c'est la fin des haricots.
We were lost, it was getting dark and it was raining; when I realized that we had run out of petrol I thought to myself: that's the last straw.

couper l'herbe sous le pied de quelqu'un

> *"to cut the grass under somebody's feet"*
> = to cut the ground from under somebody's feet
> = to pull the rug out from under somebody's feet

En sortant son modèle de voiture électrique deux mois avant ses concurrents, la marque espère leur couper l'herbe sous le pied.
By bringing out its electric car two months ahead of its competitors, the company hopes to cut the ground from under their feet.

une histoire à dormir debout

"a story to make you sleep standing up"
= a cock-and-bull story

Some animals may be able to do it, but humans don't generally sleep standing up. Hence this expression.

Il m'a raconté comment il est arrivé en France à l'âge de quatorze ans dans le coffre d'une voiture : c'est une histoire à dormir debout !
He told me how he arrived in France at the age of 14 in the boot of a car: a cock-and-bull story!

tenir la jambe à quelqu'un *(informal)*

"to hold somebody's leg"
= to pin somebody down

If you hold on to somebody's leg and don't let go, they can't get very far.

Désolé d'être en retard ; je suis tombé sur un représentant qui m'a tenu la jambe, je n'arrivais pas à m'en débarrasser.
Sorry I'm late; I got pinned down by a rep and I couldn't get away.

avoir les jetons *(informal)*

"to have the chips"
= to be petrified
= to have the jitters

If you placed your chips (**jetons**) at the roulette table, you would probably also be scared of losing them.

Pour rentrer à la maison il fallait passer devant le cimetière. La nuit, on avait les jetons, alors on se mettait à courir.
To get home we had to go past the cemetery. At night, we were petrified so we used to run all the way.

donner sa langue au chat

"*to give your tongue to the cat*"
= to give up

This expression means *to give your tongue to the cat* because it's of no use to you, since you don't have the answers.

Ses devinettes sont trop difficiles : nous finissons toujours par donner notre langue au chat.
His riddles are too difficult: we always give up in the end.

poser un lapin à quelqu'un (*informal*)

"*to set down a rabbit for somebody*"
= to stand somebody up

The French term **lapin** has long had an association with doing something without paying, or not fulfilling one's obligations.

J'avais rendez-vous avec Édith mais elle m'a posé un lapin. Je rentre chez moi.
I had a date with Édith but she has stood me up. I'm going home.

être dans la lune

"*to be in the moon*"
= to have one's head in the clouds
= to be in a dream

The moon is traditionally associated with dreams and otherworldliness.

C'était un élève discret en classe qui dessinait, écrivait des poèmes ou était tout simplement dans la lune.
He was an unobtrusive pupil at school who drew, wrote poems or was quite simply in a dream.

mettre la main à la pâte

> *"to put your hand to the dough"*
> = to lend a hand
> = to muck in

Pour la fête de fin d'année, tout le monde met la main à la pâte : les professeurs décorent la salle, les enfants préparent une pièce de théâtre et les parents font des gâteaux.
For the end-of-year celebrations, everybody mucks in: the teachers decorate the hall, the children prepare a play and the parents make cakes.

en mettre sa main au feu

> *"to put your hand into the fire over something"*
> = to stake your life on something
>
> Also en mettre sa main à couper, literally *to put your hand in to be cut off.*

Je la reconnais, je sais que c'est elle, j'en mettrais ma main au feu !
I recognize her, I know it's her, I'd stake my life on it!

se faire la malle *(informal)*

> *"to pack your trunk"*
> = to make yourself scarce
> = to scarper

Quand il est rentré chez lui, il y avait juste une lettre sur la table : c'était sa femme, elle s'était fait la malle avec son meilleur copain.
When he got home, there was just a letter on the table: it was his wife, she had scarpered with his best mate.

faire la grasse matinée

> *"to make a fat morning"*
> = to have a lie-in

Pendant la semaine on se lève à 6h00 tous les jours, donc en général on profite du dimanche pour **faire la grasse matinée.**
During the week we get up at 6am every day so we generally make sure we have a lie-in on Sundays.

vendre la mèche

> *"to sell the fuse"*
> = to give the game away
> = to let the cat out of the bag

If the fuse of a bomb is discovered in time, the bomb can be defused. So the fuse represents something which shouldn't be revealed.

La veille du jour où le braquage était prévu, la police vient frapper à sa porte pour l'arrêter : l'un de ses complices, pris de panique, **a vendu la mèche.**
The day before the robbery was to take place, the police came to his door to arrest him: one of his accomplices panicked and gave the game away.

ce n'est pas la mer à boire *(informal)*

> *"it's not as if you're having to drink the sea"*
> = it's no big deal

Pour le test d'entrée, il y a un QCM et un entretien d'un quart d'heure. **Ce n'est pas la mer à boire.**
For the entry test, there is a multiple-choice paper and a 15-minute interview. It's no big deal.

chercher midi à quatorze heures

> *"to look for midday at two o'clock"*
> = to complicate the issue

Inutile de chercher midi à quatorze heures, vous grillez le feu rouge, vous avez une amende !
No need to complicate the issue: if you go through a red light, you get a fine.

promettre monts et merveilles

> *"to promise mountains and marvels"*
> = to promise the earth

Pendant la campagne électorale, les candidats promettent monts et merveilles, mais une fois élus, ils reviennent vite à la réalité.
During the election campaign the candidates promise the earth but once elected, they quickly return to reality.

prendre la mouche

> *"to take the fly"*
> = to go into a huff
> = to get huffy

The image here seems to be of an animal being bitten by a fly and sent mad by it.

Quand je lui ai fait remarquer que son bureau était en désordre, elle a pris la mouche et elle est sortie en claquant la porte.
When I pointed out to her that her desk was in a mess, she went into a huff and left the room, slamming the door behind her.

la moutarde lui montait au nez

> *"the mustard got up his nose"*
> = he flared up
> = he saw red

La moutarde me monte au nez quand je vois des personnes valides garer leur voiture sur les places pour handicapés.
I see red when I come across able-bodied people parking their cars in disabled spaces.

revenons à nos moutons!

> *"let's come back to our sheep!"*
> = let's get back to the subject

> Instead of **revenons** you can say **retournons** (*let's return*).

Après cette petite anecdote, revenons à nos moutons.
After this little anecdote, let's get back to the subject.

tirer les vers du nez à quelqu'un *(informal)*

> *"to pull the worms from somebody's nose"*
> = to worm information out of somebody

Certains enfants parlent peu de ce qu'ils font à l'école ; leurs parents doivent leur tirer les vers du nez.
Some children don't talk much about what they do at school; their parents have to worm information out of them.

se prendre pour le nombril du monde *(informal)*

> *"to consider yourself the navel of the world"*
> = to think you are the centre of the universe

> But *se regarder le nombril* means *to contemplate your navel.*

Avec les personnes qui se prennent pour le nombril du monde, la communication est impossible : ils ne parlent que de leur travail, leur famille, leurs hobbies et n'écoutent pas ce qu'on leur dit.
It's impossible to communicate with people who think they are the centre of the universe: they talk about nothing but their work, their family and their hobbies, and aren't interested in what you have to say.

avoir un œil au beurre noir *(informal)*

> *"to have an eye in brown butter sauce"*
> = to have a black eye

Stéphanie ne s'est pas rendu compte que son fils était brutalisé à l'école jusqu'au jour où il est revenu à la maison avec un œil au beurre noir.
Stephanie did not realize that her son was being bullied at school until the day he came home with a black eye.

dormir sur ses deux oreilles

> *"to sleep on both your ears"*
> = to sleep soundly

Avec deux chiens de garde, une alarme et des caméras de vidéosurveillance partout dans son magasin, Michel peut dormir sur ses deux oreilles.
With two guard dogs, an alarm and CCTV cameras throughout his shop, Michel can sleep soundly.

avoir du pain sur la planche *(informal)*

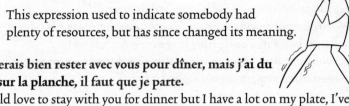

> *"to have bread on the board"*
> = to have a lot to do
> = to have a lot on your plate
> = to have your work cut out

This expression used to indicate somebody had
plenty of resources, but has since changed its meaning.

**J'aimerais bien rester avec vous pour dîner, mais j'ai du
pain sur la planche, il faut que je parte.**
I would love to stay with you for dinner but I have a lot on my plate, I've got to go.

c'est une autre paire de manches *(informal)*

> *"it's another pair of sleeves"*
> = it's another kettle of fish
> = it's another story

**L'équipe de France a réussi à se qualifier contre les îles Féroé, mais cette fois-ci, c'est
une autre paire de manches : elle rencontre le Brésil.**
The French team managed to qualify against the Faroe Islands but it's another story this
time: they are playing Brazil.

montrer patte blanche

> *"to show a white paw"*
> = to show your credentials

This expression was made popular by the fable about a wolf, a goat and its kid.
Left at home alone, the kid was told only to open the door to an animal
that could show a white paw. The wolf, having grey paws, was thus
kept at bay.

**Pour entrer dans le bâtiment, il faut montrer patte blanche :
chaque employé doit présenter sa carte à l'entrée et
connaître le code de son service.**
To gain entrance to the building you have to show your
credentials: each employee has to present their card at the
entrance and know their department code.

vendre la peau de l'ours avant de l'avoir tué

"to sell the bear's skin before you have killed it"
= to count your chickens before they are hatched

This idiom is often shortened to **vendre la peau de l'ours** which matches the English phrase *to count your chickens*.

Nous pensons avoir de bonnes chances de remporter le marché, mais il ne faut pas vendre la peau de l'ours avant de l'avoir tué : la concurrence est rude.
We think we have a good chance of getting the deal but we mustn't count our chickens before they are hatched: the competition is tough.

remettre les pendules à l'heure *(informal)*

"to reset the clocks to the right time"
= to set the record straight

Pour mettre fin aux tensions, la directrice a remis les pendules à l'heure lors d'une réunion avec les chefs de service.
To put an end to the tensions, the director set the record straight at a meeting with department heads.

se lever du pied gauche

"to get out of bed with the left foot"
= to get out of bed on the wrong side

Annick s'était encore levée du pied gauche et ne m'a pas adressé la parole de la matinée.
Annick got out of bed on the wrong side again and hasn't said a word to me all morning.

casser les pieds à quelqu'un (informal)

> "to break somebody's feet"
> = to get on somebody's nerves

La voisine me casse les pieds tous les soirs
depuis deux ans avec son violon. J'ai décidé de
déménager.
My neighbour has been getting on my nerves
with her violin-playing every night for two
years. I've decided to move house.

faire d'une pierre deux coups

> "to make two hits with one stone"
> = to kill two birds with one stone

En augmentant le prix des cigarettes, le gouvernement fait d'une pierre deux coups :
il renforce sa lutte anti-tabac et augmente ses recettes.
By increasing the price of cigarettes, the government is killing two birds with one stone:
it strengthens its anti-smoking campaign and increases its revenue.

ne pas être tombé de la dernière pluie

> "not to have fallen in the last rain"
> = not to be born yesterday

Ce n'est pas la peine de s'inquiéter : Thomas n'est pas tombé de la dernière pluie, il
peut très bien se débrouiller tout seul.
There is no need to worry: Thomas was not born yesterday, he can fend for himself
perfectly well.

deux poids deux mesures

"two weights two measures"
= double standards

Après le verdict, les avocats ont déclaré que la peine très sévère prononcée contre leur client prouve qu'il y a **deux poids deux mesures**.
After the verdict, the lawyers declared that the very harsh penalty handed down to their client is proof of double standards.

reprendre du poil de la bête *(informal)*

"to have more of the hair of the beast"
= to be on the mend again

The meaning of the English expression *hair of the dog* only relates to alcohol: the French is a more positive expression; it comes from the belief that if you apply the hair of the beast that bit you to your wound, you will feel better.

Hélène est sortie de l'hôpital il y a quelques jours seulement, mais à la grande surprise de tous les médecins, elle a déjà **repris du poil de la bête**.
Hélène only came out of hospital a few days ago but to the great surprise of all the doctors she is already on the mend again.

tomber dans les pommes *(informal)*

"to fall in the apples"
= to faint
= to pass out

Au dernier réveillon, Sébastien s'est coupé en ouvrant les huîtres ; il est immédiatement **tombé dans les pommes** car il ne supporte pas la vue du sang.
Last New Year's Eve, Sébastien cut himself opening oysters; he immediately passed out because he can't stand the sight of blood.

enforcer une porte ouverte

"to break down an open door"
= to state the obvious

Also **enforcer des portes ouvertes**.

Pour un ministre de l'Environnement, dire qu'il faut protéger la nature, c'est enfoncer une porte ouverte.
For an Environment Minister, saying that we must protect nature is stating the obvious.

jeter de la poudre aux yeux de quelqu'un

"to throw powder in the eyes of somebody"
= to try and impress somebody

Also note the expression **c'est de la poudre aux yeux**, meaning *it's all just for show*.

Pour les défenseurs de la nature, le ministre jette de la poudre aux yeux en proposant ces mesures démagogiques.
According to conservationists, the minister is trying to impress people by proposing these populist measures.

pour des prunes *(informal)*

"for plums"
= for nothing

Tu veux dire que tous ces efforts n'ont servi à rien, qu'on a fait tout ça pour des prunes ?
You mean to say that all this effort was pointless, and we did all that for nothing?

être fait comme un rat *(informal)*

> *"to be done for like a rat"*
> = to be in for it
> = to have no way out

L'ennemi nous encerclait et il n'y avait aucun espoir de recevoir de l'aide : nous étions faits comme des rats.
We were surrounded and there was no hope of getting help: we had no way out.

en connaître un rayon *(informal)*

> *"to know your shop counter"*
> = to be really clued up

Si tu veux des conseils pour ton nouvel appareil photo, tu devrais demander à Raphaëlle : elle en connaît un rayon sur le sujet.
If you want some advice about your new camera, you ought to ask Raphaëlle: she is really clued up on the subject.

raconter des salades *(informal)*

> *"to tell salads"*
> = to spin yarns
> = to tell stories

> Just as salads are mixtures of different types of leaf, so the stories we tell can be mixtures of truth and fabrication.

Arrête de raconter des salades ! On t'a vu avec cette femme, on a même des photos de vous deux ensemble !
Stop telling stories! You've been seen with that woman, there are even photos of the two of you together!

se faire un sang d'encre

> *"to turn your blood to ink"*
> = to be worried sick

> Also **se faire des cheveux blancs**, literally *to make your hair white*.

L'adolescente était injoignable sur son portable, il était maintenant une heure du matin, personne ne savait où elle se trouvait et sa famille se faisait un sang d'encre.
The teenager couldn't be contacted on her mobile, it was now one o'clock in the morning, no one knew where she was and her family was worried sick.

sentir le sapin *(informal)*

> *"to smell of fir tree"*
> = to have one foot in the grave

> An old French expression alluding to the wood from which coffins were habitually made: if your days are numbered, you'll be starting to notice that pine-fresh smell.

Il tremble de plus en plus : ça sent le sapin.
He's shaking more and more: he's got one foot in the grave.

passer un savon à quelqu'un *(informal)*

> *"to scrub somebody with a bar of soap"*
> = to give somebody a telling-off

Quand elle a vu le dessin sur le mur à côté d'Olivier, la prof lui a passé un savon.
The teacher gave Olivier a telling-off when she saw the drawing on the wall next to him.

être soupe au lait

"to be milk soup"
= to have a short fuse

Watch how milk suddenly rises up when it comes to the boil and you have the graphic image behind this expression.

Notre professeur de français était très soupe au lait : au moindre bruit, il devenait tout rouge et entrait dans des colères terrifiantes.
Our French teacher had a very short fuse: at the slightest sound he would go bright red and fly into a terrifying rage.

une tempête dans un verre d'eau

"a storm in a glass of water"
= a storm in a teacup
= a lot of fuss about nothing

Cette découverte que le scientifique qualifie de révolution pourrait n'être qu'une tempête dans un verre d'eau.
This discovery, which the scientist describes as revolutionary, could just be a lot of fuss about nothing.

être au creux de la vague

"to be in the trough of the wave"
= to have hit rock bottom
= to be at the lowest ebb

Pour un secteur du tourisme qui est déjà au creux de la vague, cet été pluvieux est une catastrophe.
For a tourist industry which has already hit rock bottom, this wet summer is a disaster.